fifth edition

An introduction to

Positive Economics

Richard G. Lipsey

Sir Edward Peacock Professor
of Economics, Queen's University,
Kingston, Ontario

Weidenfeld and Nicolson London

First printed October 1963

Second edition October 1966
Reprinted August 1967
Reprinted May 1968
Reprinted March 1969
Reprinted September 1970
Reprinted November 1970

Third edition August 1971
Reprinted March 1972

PAPERBACK EDITION
first published 1972
Reprinted September 1973
Reprinted May 1974

Fourth edition July 1975
Reprinted 1976

Fifth edition 1979

Part of this fifth edition appeared in the United States in *Economics* by Richard G. Lipsey and Peter O. Steiner, © 1978, published by Harper and Row.

Weidenfeld and Nicolson
91 Clapham High St, London SW4

ISBN 0 297 77597 9 cased
ISBN 0 297 77598 7 paperback

Printed in Great Britain by
Butler & Tanner Ltd
Frome and London

To Diana

Contents

Part 3 The intermediate theory of demand

Part 4 The intermediate theory of supply

Part 5 The theory of distribution

Part 6 The economy as a whole

Part 7 The circular flow of income

Part 8 The importance of money in the circular flow

Part 9 The international economy

Part 10 Growth and development

Part 11 Macroeconomic policy

Fact and theory in economics

'... Einstein started from facts – the Morley Michelson measurements of light, the movements of the planet Mercury, the unexplained aberrancies of the moon from its predicted place. Einstein went back to facts or told others where they should go, to confirm or to reject his theory – by observation of stellar positions during a total eclipse.

'... It is not necessary, of course, for the verification of a new theory to be done personally by its propounder. Theoretical reasoning from facts is as essential a part of economic science as of other sciences, and in a wise division of labour there is room, in economics, as elsewhere, for the theoretician pure and simple, for one who leaves the technical business of verification to those who have acquired a special technique of observation. No one demanded of Einstein that he should visit the South Seas in person, and look through a telescope; but he told others what he expected them to see, if they looked, and he was prepared to stand or fall by the result. It is the duty of the propounder of every new theory, if he has not himself the equipment for observation, to indicate where verification of his theory is to be sought in facts – what may be expected to happen or to have happened if his theory is true, what will not happen if it is false.

'[Now consider by way of contrast the behaviour of the participants in a current controversy in economics.] ... None of them takes the point that the truth or falsehood of ... [a] ... theory cannot be established except by an appeal to the facts; none of them tests it by facts himself. The distinguishing mark of economic science as illustrated by this debate is that it is a science in which verification of generalizations by reference to facts is neglected as irrelevant. ... I do not see how ... [members of the public who survey the controversy] ... can avoid the conclusion that economics is not a science concerned with phenomena, but a survival of medieval logic, and that economists are persons who earn their livings by taking in one another's definitions for mangling.

'... I know that in speaking thus I make enemies. I challenge a tradition of a hundred years of political economy, in which facts have been treated not as controls of theory, but as illustrations. I shall be told that in the Social Sciences verification can never be clean enough to be decisive. I may be told that, in these sciences, observation has been tried and has failed, has led to shapeless accumulations of facts which themselves lead nowhere. I do not believe for a moment that this charge of barrenness of past enquiries can be sustained; to make it is to ignore many achievements of the past and to decry much solid work that is being done at this School and elsewhere. But if the charge of barrenness of realistic economics in the past were justified completely, that would not be a reason for giving up observation and verification. It would only be a reason for making our observations more exact and more numerous. If, in the Social Sciences, we cannot yet run or fly, we ought to be content to walk, or to creep on all fours as infants. . . . For economic and political theorizing not based on facts and not controlled by facts assuredly does lead nowhere.

'There can be no science of society till the facts about society are available. Till 130 years ago we had no census, no knowledge even of the numbers and growth of the people; till fifteen years ago we had no comprehensive records about unemployment even in this country, and other countries are still where we were a generation or more ago; social statistics of every kind – about trade, wages, consumption – are everywhere in their infancy.

'. . . From Copernicus to Newton is 150 years. Today, 150 years from the *Wealth of Nations*, we have not found, and should not expect to find, the Newton of economics. If we have travelled as far as Tycho Brahe we may be content. Tycho was both a theorist and an observer. As a theorist, he believed to his last day in the year 1601 that the planets went round the sun and that the sun and the stars went round the earth as the fixed centre of the universe. As an observer, he made with infinite patience and integrity thousands of records of the stars and planets; upon these records Kepler, in due course, based his laws and brought the truth to light. If we will take Tycho Brahe for our example, we may find encouragement also. It matters little how wrong we are with our existing theories, if we are honest and careful with our observations.'

Extracts from Lord Beveridge's farewell address as Director of the London School of Economics, 24 June 1937. Published in *Politica*, September 1937.

The use of this book

This is an introductory textbook in economics, starting at an elementary stage and progressing, in some places, to an intermediate level. It is designed to be read as a first book in economics. I hope, on the other hand, that the book will not be without interest for someone who has already studied one of the many existing basic textbooks written at a first year university standard.

The book had its beginnings when I was asked to give the basic economic theory lectures for the revised B.Sc.(Econ.) degree introduced at the London School of Economics in October 1961. I started to write my first few lectures and, almost before I knew it, a book was well under way. Had I appreciated at the outset what was involved in carrying such a project through to completion, I would never have begun it, but that is probably true of a great many enterprises in all fields.

There are three major themes of this textbook which should be mentioned here: first, an attempt to explain what economic theory is about and how one can go about criticizing it effectively and hence improving it; second, an attempt to elaborate, in so far as is possible within the confines of an introduction to economic theory, the relation between theory and real-world observations; and third, a consideration of the relation between economic theory and economic policy.

The first major theme of this book is how one can go about being intelligently and constructively critical of the existing body of economic theory. I have tried to address myself throughout to the intelligent student of honours-school quality. I have assumed that the student was interested in the subject and that he or she wished to know, at every stage, what was going on and why. There is a tradition of trying to sneak quite complex bits of analysis past students without telling them what is happening. This may be the best thing to do if the object is to get through an examination a large mass of people who have neither interest nor ability in economics, and who are hostile to the basic idea of a Social Science. I am not interested in reaching such a public. I have assumed that I am addressing an intelligent set of students, who may or may not be honours students and intending specialists, but who want to learn and who do not have closed minds. One of the troubles with the traditional approach of sneaking analysis past the student is that, when the intelligent reader feels that there is something wrong with what has been taught, he or she does not know how to go about being critical of it in an effective way. I have made a point of telling the student what is going on, to say 'now we are doing comparative static equilibrium analysis' or whatever it might be, and I have devoted considerable space to an analysis of both sensible and silly criticisms of the theories described. I do not accept the idea that the possibility of criticizing what has been learned should not be mentioned because if it is the student will be led to make hasty and confused criticisms. A good student will always attempt criticisms and evaluations of what he or she has been taught. It seems to me that criticisms are much more likely to be informed and relevant ones if students are given both practice and instruction in how to set about effectively challenging what they have been taught than if they meet a conspiracy of silence on this topic.

The second major theme is the relation between economic theory and observation. One of the most unfortunate tendencies in the teaching of economics, particularly in Britain, is that of making a clear split between economic theory and applied economics. All too often economic theory is taught merely as logical analysis, and is, at best, only vaguely related to the world, while applied economics becomes description unenlightened by any theoretical framework. Economic theory is meant to be about the real world. We seek, by the use of theory, to explain, understand and predict phenomena in the real world, and our theory must therefore be related to, and tested by, empirical observations. The student of economic theory needs to ask at every stage what are the relevant empirical magnitudes and quantities. This is the theme set by the quotation from Beveridge that opens this book.[1]

The third major theme is the relation between economic theory and economic policy. The distinction between positive and normative statements is well known to professional economists, but all too often we fail to communicate its significance to our students. Even the best American text books often manage to convey the idea that economic theory justifies the private-enterprise, market economies, found in most Western countries. The experience of interviewing, for admission to the London School of Economics and later to the University of Essex, students who had done A-level economics at school made it painfully obvious that from somewhere – I am never sure from where – students get such ideas as the ones that the 'Law' of Comparative Advantage proves that nations *ought* to specialize in the production of certain goods, that economics has proved that rent and price controls are wicked and ought not to be used. The student who can think of good reasons why, under some circumstances, price and rent controls and tariffs might be desirable, reacts by dismissing economics as Medieval Scholasticism, or as a fraud perpetrated by whichever political party he happens not to support; and so he should do if economics did purport to prove such propositions. Economic theory cannot, of course, ever show us what we ought to do, but only what will happen if we do do certain things. The uses and the limitations of economic theory in dealing with matters of public policy is a theme which recurs throughout the book.

The study of economics can be both interesting and rewarding. To students not intending to specialize in economics it can give some understanding of the functioning of the economy, and some appreciation of the issues involved in current controversies over economic policy. It may also give him some idea of the methods which have been applied with some modest success in one Social Science. To would-be economics specialists the study of an introductory book, such as this one, can be

1 I take it that in the last sentence quoted, Beveridge is saying that it does not matter how wrong present theories may be as long as we make careful observations of the facts on which these theories stand or fall, and then discard or amend theories when they are found to be inconsistent with the facts. See also the further discussion of the Beveridge quote on pages xx–xxi and 789–91.

the beginning of a real adventure. The scope of your chosen science opens up before you. At first you encounter theories which add to your understanding of the world, but very soon you begin to encounter problems: observations for which there are no satisfactory explanations, and theories which are generally agreed to be unsatisfactory, but which have not been adequately tested. Both of these constitute a challenge, in the first case for the development of new theories and in the second for the making of a careful set of observations to test an existing theory. One of the interesting things about economics today is that the frontiers of knowledge in terms of unsolved problems can be reached very quickly, even though, as the reader of this book will soon learn, it may take a very long time to reach the frontiers of knowledge in terms of techniques available for the handling of problems.

Economics is a subject quite unlike some other subjects studied at school. Economic theory has a logical structure; it tends to build on itself from stage to stage. Thus the student who only imperfectly understands some concept or theory will run into increasing difficulty when, in subsequent developments, this concept or theory is taken for granted and built upon. Because of its logical structure, quite long chains of reasoning are encountered: if *A* then *B*, if *B* then *C*, if *C* then *D*, and if *D* then *E*. Each step in the argument may seem simple enough, but the cumulative effect of several steps, one on top of the other, may be bewildering on first encounter. Thus when, having followed the argument step by step, the reader encounters the statement 'now obviously if *A* then *E*', it may not seem obvious at all. This is a problem which almost everyone encounters with chains of reasoning. The only way to deal with it is to follow the argument through several times. Eventually, as one becomes familiar with the argument, it will become obvious that, *if A then E*.

Another problem is posed by the fact that economics has a large technical language or jargon. At first students feel that all they are being asked to do is to put complicated names to common-sense ideas. To some extent this is true. At the beginning, economics consists largely of making explicit ideas which appeal strongly to common sense and which one has already held in a vague sort of way. This is an absolutely necessary step, because loose thinking about vaguely formed ideas is one of the quickest routes to error in economics. Furthermore, the jargon, the single word or phrase given to the common-sense idea, becomes necessary in the interests of brevity of expression as the subject is built up. You should try the exercise of removing every technical term from the argument of one of the later chapters in this book and replacing these terms with the full verbal description of the ideas expressed. The argument would then become too cumbersome. If we are going to put several ideas together to see what follows from them, then the single clearly defined word or phrase to refer to these ideas becomes a necessary part of our equipment.

It follows from all of this that you should use this book in quite a different way than you would use a book on many other subjects. A book on economics is to be worked at, and understood step by step, and not to be read like a novel. It is usually a good idea to read a chapter quickly in order to see the general run of the argument and then to re-read it carefully, making sure that the argument is understood step by step. You should be prepared at this stage to spend a very long time on difficult sections. You should not be discouraged if, occasionally, you find yourself spending an hour on only two or three pages. A paper and pencil is a necessary piece of equipment in your reading. Difficult arguments should be followed by building up one's own diagram while the argument unfolds, rather than by relying on the printed diagram which is, perforce, complete from the beginning. Numerical examples should be invented to illustrate general propositions. At various stages you are asked to put the book down and think out the answer to some problem for yourself before you read on: *you should never read on without attempting to do what is asked.* You should also make your own glossary of technical terms, committing the definitions to memory. The first time a technical term is introduced, it is printed in capital letters so that it may easily be recognized as such.

After the book has been read in this detailed manner, it should be re-read fairly quickly from cover to cover; it is often difficult to understand why certain things are done until one knows the end product, and, on a second reading, much that seemed strange and incomprehensible, will be seen to have an obvious place in the analysis.

In short, one must seek to understand economics, not to memorize it (the technical vocabulary must, of course, be committed to memory). Memorization is the royal road to disaster in economics; theories, principles and concepts are always turning up in slightly unfamiliar guises. To one who has understood his or her economics this poses no problem; to one who has merely memorized it, this spells disaster. *The required approach is not more difficult than, but it is different from, that encountered in many other subjects.*

One major aid that is available to you in working through this book is the *Workbook* prepared by Rosemary Clarke, John Stilwell and myself. It is very easy to think you understand a verbal presentation, only to discover that you do not when you come to use what you have tried to learn. The workbook is designed to test your comprehension at every stage and to send you back to the relevant part of the text where your comprehension is faulty. Without using a workbook or doing its equivalent in class exercises, most readers will get much less than they could out of this book.

Students who would like to see a more formal treatment of some of the theories expounded in this book and those who would like an introduction to the mathematics needed to handle the theories formally may consult *An Introduction to a Mathematical Treatment of Economics* (3rd edition, Weidenfeld and Nicolson, 1977) by G. C. Archibald and myself.

The first chapter of this book is a general essay on scientific method, particularly as it applies to the Social Sciences. None of the ideas is unduly difficult but each may seem rather abstract and 'up in the air' to someone unable to relate it to a detailed knowledge of some social science. The ideas are, however, of critical importance. You should read the chapter carefully to get the general drift of the argument. You should refer back to it at times when the issues raised turn up in the contexts of particular bits of economics and, finally, when you have finished the whole book, you should re-read Chapter 1, making sure that you follow the argument fully. This last piece of advice is so important that, were it not for the costs of printing, I should be inclined to print Chapter 1 as both the first and the last chapter of the book. In the notes on the fifth edition I allude briefly to some of the criticisms that have been made of Lord Beveridge's discussion of Einstein. (See pages xx and xxi.)

Chapter 2 deals with the economists' tools of analysis. It is not necessary to be a mathematician to learn economics, but it is necessary to have a mastery of the equivalent of O-Level mathematics. There is not room in an economics textbook to teach the elementary mathematics that is assumed in economics. The Appendix to Chapter 2 does, however, outline some of the most important bits of elementary mathematics commonly used. Readers who are unsure of any of the points briefly outlined must go back to an elementary textbook and review these bits of necessary technique.

You should seek to master completely one textbook, but, generally you should not confine yourself exclusively to this one book; you should read sections in other texts, particularly those sections dealing with ideas that you find difficult. There are many first-class books to which you can refer, and unfortunately there is an even larger number of not-very-good books and you should seek expert advice before adopting a book for major study.

This is a book about economic theory. Although I have tried at all points to relate the theory to the world around us, I have not tried to fill in the institutional detail about any particular economy. Three of the many excellent books that are available are C.D. Harbury, *Descriptive Economics* (Pitman, 5th edition, 1976); NIESR, *The United Kingdom Economy* (Heinemann, 3rd edition, 1977); and A.R. Prest and D.J. Coppock (eds), *The UK Economy: A Manual of Applied Economics* (Weidenfeld and Nicolson, 7th edition, 1978). All of these books are revised frequently and so may be in later editions by the time this passage is being read. The NIESR's book is the briefest and provides an excellent simple overview. The book edited by Prest and Coppock is the most detailed and is suitable for those who wish to follow an in-depth discussion of the UK economy. Harbury's book lies between the other two in comprehensiveness and is an excellent source for those who wish to obtain a good working knowledge of the economy without being bothered by too much detail.

Finally I should like to say a word of thanks to all those people who have made this book possible. In so far as the ideas and viewpoints expressed here are novel, they are the common property of all my colleagues who in the late 1950s and early 1960s were members of the L.S.E. *Staff Seminar on Methodology, Measurement and Testing in Economics*. All that I did in the 1st edition was to give a slightly personal expression to this general viewpoint. Mr K. Klappholz read the manuscript of the 1st edition, removing countless blemishes, and contributed greatly to some of the novel ideas expressed therein. Mr R. Cassen read the proofs and contributed many last-minute improvements. Professor G. C. Archibald and John Black gave detailed scrutiny of the proofs of the second and third editions respectively and their penetrating criticisms led to many improvements. Ms Claire Rubin has contributed greatly to what I hope is the increased readability, clarity and consistency of the 5th edition. The largest single debt of all I owe to Professor P. O. Steiner, who co-authored with me the American textbook *Economics*. To Professor Steiner, who was everywhere my severe critic and often my teacher, I and the substance of the present book owe a very great debt.

The executor of Lord Beveridge's estate has kindly granted permission to quote extracts from Beveridge's farewell address at the London School of Economics. Thanks are also due to Macmillan and McGraw-Hill for permission to quote from Lord Robbins' *Essay on the Nature and Significance of Economic Science* and *The British Economy* respectively. Harper and Row has also been generous in giving their permission to quote at length from material first prepared for the American textbook *Economics*, written by Professor P.O. Steiner and myself.

I am also extremely grateful to the many users, students and teachers, who have taken the trouble to write to me pointing out errors, making comments and suggestions. Economics is a subject in which one never stops learning and it is always gratifying to realize that one can still learn from one's students. I hope that the readers of this book will continue to teach me with as many further comments and criticisms as they have in the past. At one time or another valuable research assistance has been provided by M. V. Blandon, June Wickins, P. Geary, J. Stilwell, A. Popoff, D. Gilchrist, and T. Whitehead. Mrs S. Craig, Mrs Evelyn Dean, Miss Tina Brown, Mrs Joanne Marlieb, and Mrs Marlene Rego have shown unlimited patience in dealing with manuscripts. Thing I, George, Chekov, Pushkin, and Tiger Lilly have sat on my manuscript, chewed my pen and otherwise offered invaluable feline assistance through successive editions. The usual disclaimer of course holds here: for all shortcomings and mistakes remaining I am solely to blame.

R. G. LIPSEY
Sir Edward Peacock Professor of Economics
at Queen's University, Ontario

Notes on the fifth edition

The text of almost every Chapter has been rewritten in some detail to eliminate many passages teaching experience has shown to be rough or unclear in meaning. The micro half of the book remains unchanged in general approach and coverage except for some significant additions and updatings.

Chapter 1 has had a long-overdue re-write. This eliminates the error of equating positive propositions with testable propositions. It also allows me to deal with some mistaken objections to positive economics including the one of equating it with logical positivism. Chapter 3 has a new appendix, providing some material on graphs that has proved useful for beginners. The introductory material on the problems of economics and the general nature of the price system has been reworked and expanded and some new definitions added. All of this material is now included in Part 1.

The details of Part 2 have been heavily revised to increase the tightness and the consistency of the argument. The chapter on applications has been reworked and the section on price control expanded.

To save space I have (reluctantly) dropped the treatment of revealed preference from Part 3. The profession insists that students be trained in indifference-preference theory and there is just not room in an introductory treatment to teach all three theories of demand.

The long chapter on costs in Part 4 has been heavily rewritten. It remains one of the most difficult chapters of the book but I hope that I have made it as accessible as is possible to beginning students. I have added a short but important section on the general notion of administered prices at the beginning of the chapter on oligopoly. The last chapter of Part 4 has been reworked and the section on Galbraith has been both tightened and expanded.

Part 5 on distribution has been shortened and simplified significantly.

Part 6 on microeconomic policy is almost fifty per cent new material. The sections on revenues and expenditures as tools of policy contain much that is new. I have expanded the case for the price system so as to give it equal treatment with the case for intervention. I have also raised the important question of the motivation of government that is usually ignored in textbook treatments of policy issues.

The form of Part 7 is much the same as it was in the fourth edition. Chapter 32 has, however, been rewritten to make the treatment conform much more closely to concepts used in actual national accounts. Also, although the approach to the determination of equilibrium national income remains the same as it was in the fourth edition, I have managed to simplify it somewhat and, I hope, increase its teachability. The concluding chapter on fiscal policy has been heavily revised.

In Part 8 I hope that the completely rewritten chapter on the Importance of Money at last gets the integration of money into national income theory into a form that is both correct and teachable. Previous editions, by taking an historical approach, have been hampered by a failure to distinguish clearly the issue of the effect of money on aggregate demand from that of the effect of money (through aggregate demand) on the price level. In the course of clarifying this distinction I have relegated the treatment of the classical quantity theory of money to an appendix. The integration uses a function relating aggregate expenditure to national income in which the interest rate is a shift parameter. This means that the *IS-LM* integration is done verbally but not formally. Anyone who wishes to go on to *IS-LM* will find the ground well prepared for an immediate application of the Hicksian seeds.

In Part 9 I have totally rewritten the chapter on the gains from trade in response to those who found my previous treatment (unchanged since the first edition) difficult. I have also greatly simplified the chapter on exchange rates by using in the text only a simple demand and supply theory. The formal treatments of both the elasticities and the Scandinavian models are relegated to a new appendix. The chapter on the international payments system has perforce been revised to take account of the final demise of the Bretton Woods system.

Part 10, which has had some minor polishing, is the one part that has not undergone a serious revision.

Part 11 on macro-policy has had the most extensive changes of any of the macro parts. It now contains three chapters. The first, Chapter 48, deals with the four main macro-policy variables, and is an expanded version of the first half of the old Chapter 51. Chapter 49 is a wholly new chapter dealing with the problem of closure. The continuing debate between monetarists and Keynesians is now switching to the really key issue of how the effects of changes in aggregate demand are divided between changes in prices and changes in quantities. Chapter 49 deals with this issue. Chapter 50 is also largely new, although it does incorporate some material from the old Chapter 50. It deals first with those policy debates on inflation and unemployment that turn on the issue of closure and second with the debate over monetarism. I hope that the new Part 11 does come to grips with the crisis of macroeconomic theory and policy that has followed from the new economic disease of 'stagflation' that has beset so many economies in the 1970s. The 'closure' in Part 11 is made to the 'integrated' model of Part 8. Anyone who wishes to work with *IS-LM* curves can use them to determine real national income and then proceed with no further amendments to my discussion of closure. In other words (i) of figures 49.1 and 49.2 on pages 749 and 754 are merely replaced with an *IS-LM* diagram.[1]

I have not provided the postscript on scientific method that I promised for the fifth edition. In its absence I must say a few words on the continuing debate over this subject.

[1] Anyone who wishes to see this integration done graphically using *IS-LM* curves should consult R. G. Lipsey, 'The Place of the Phillips Curve in Macroeconomic Models', in A. R. Bergstrom *et al.* (eds), *Stability and Inflation* (Wiley, 1978).

When I first wrote *Positive Economics* I was concerned to criticize the methodological position associated with the Austrian School and persuasively advocated by Professor (now Lord) Robbins in his *Essay on the Nature and Significance of Economic Science*. This methodology is, as Imré Lakatos has pointed out, basically Euclidean[1]: all knowledge is deduced from self-evident propositions that nevertheless have empirical content. In the first edition I criticized the Euclidean methodology in economics from the point of view of a naive falsificationist. Later I came to accept that evidence is too inconclusive, and theories too full of tolerated anomalies, for dramatic falsification or Popperian critical experiments ever to occur. I now accept, more or less, the methodological view advocated by Lakatos in the works just cited.

Lakatos is rightly critical of Beveridge's naive view of empirical testing and he chides me for keeping the Beveridge quotation after abandoning my naive falsificationist position. One or two points in response seem to be in order[2].

(1) Although accepting Lakatos' basic methodological position, I have retained the Beveridge quotation for at least three reasons. First, it suggests a continuity of views on the general importance of empirical work among L.S.E. staff including Beveridge, Popper, myself and many others. Second, his criticisms of the completely non-empirical approach to evaluating Keynes' *General Theory* still seem to me to be well taken (although I no longer hold that empirical testing is the only valid approach). Third, references to Einstein still seem apposite: the discovery of such bizzare objects as neutron stars and black holes, that were suggested by the equations of general relativity theory, provide excellent examples of the interrelation of factual observation and theoretical reasoning in science.

(2) I reject completely the notion of the critical experiment that forces the abandonment of one theory and the (provisional) acceptance of another[3]. Existing theories always contain logical contradictions and face conflicting facts. When and why the weight of theoretical and empirical contradictions accumulate to cause a rejection of one theory and the acceptance of another is difficult to predict and to understand.

(3) We may never know the answers to fundamental problems of epistemology. That we do learn *something* is, however, attested to by our ability to predict and change the world around us. It is clear that, in any case, we know a lot more about physics and chemistry, and a little more about psychology and economics, than did the ancient Greeks. We may be appalled by what we do not know, but we cannot help but be impressed by what we have learned since the dawn of history and, more particularly, since the consistant application of the scientific method in the modern era.

Whatever I once thought[4], I now understand the message of *Positive Economics* to be the importance of an inter-relation between theory and observation. Our views

---

[1] Imré Lakatos, *Philosophical Papers*, Vols 1 and 2 (Cambridge University Press, 1978). See, in particular, Vol. 2, Chapter 1.

[2] Perhaps I should also record that I stand by the two paragraphs that I wrote in the fourth edition on this subject (see page xx) with the exception that I am now persuaded that logical anomalies counted more for Einstein in his *development* of relativity theory than did such 'crucial' empirical experiments as those made by Michelson and Morley.

[3] See in particular, Lakatos, op. cit., Vol. 2, Chapters 9 and 10.

[4] I do not have to rely solely on a selective and fallible memory here, since I did commit myself in print at the time. See *Economics*, 1964, vol. 5, p. 365.

on the nature of this inter-relation will evolve as philosophers' views on scientific method evolve. But surely into the forseeable future both fact and theory will be needed for a developing science, and they will need to be systematically not just casually related to each other.

Some people have worried that the acceptance of the message of *Positive Economics* may lead us to abandon correct theories because they come into conflict with incorrect observations[1]. Of course either factual observations or theories may be wrong and of course we may make mistaken judgements on the validity of each. This is one of the many reasons why theories are abandoned only under the weight of numerous theoretical and empirical conflicts. Since there can be no absolute certainty in any knowledge, such abandonments are always judgemental and tentative.

Economics is meant to be about the world around us. Economic theory is meant to explain, interpret and predict economic observations. Observations and theory must therefore go hand in hand. If we so mistrust our observations that we will never use them to reject our theories, then our theories have nothing to explain. After all theories are meant to explain what we see, and if we think we can see things then we can see things that are in conflict with our theories, while if we think we can see nothing that is in conflict with our theories, then we can see nothing that requires explanation. Theory and observation can, and do, go hand in hand: our theories led us to make new observations and our new observations lead us to theorize. Accepting this inter-relation does not require accepting any rigid methodology. If there is one valid methodological injunction, it is (probably) *be critical*, subject everything, theories and evidence, to severe criticism and be prepared to change your mind in the light of such critical appraisals

[1]See e.g., J. R. Hicks' review of *Positive Economics, Economica*, N.S. vol. 32, p. 229.
[2]See e.g., Klappholz and Agassi, 'Methodological Prescriptions in Economics', *Economica*, 1959.

Part one

Scope and method

1

Introduction

Why has the history of most capitalist countries been one of several years of boom and plenty followed by several years of depression and unemployment with consequent poverty for a great many citizens? Why, during the 1930s in most capitalist countries, was up to one person in four unemployed while factories lay idle and raw materials went unused; why, in short, was everything available to produce urgently needed goods and yet nothing happened? Are Marxists correct in arguing that only vast expenditure on arms saves the capitalist countries from a return of mass unemployment? Or have we now learned, thanks to the theories propounded by many British and Continental scholars and then synthesized and further developed by an English academic economist writing over forty years ago from King's College, Cambridge, how to avoid forever such devastating situations? Why, then, in the late 1970s, did unemployment in Britain, the United States and several other countries reach the highest levels ever attained since the Great Depression of the 1930s?

What determines exchange rates and why do they change? Why was one British pound sterling worth 4·86 US dollars in 1910, 4·86 in 1930, 2·80 in 1950, 2·39 in 1970, 1·75 in 1977 and 2·00 in 1979? What is the point of international trade and would Britain be better off if it reduced its dependence on trade? Are tariffs needed to protect home industries from unfair competition, particularly from low-wage countries?

Why do the prices of some commodities fluctuate widely while the prices of others are relatively stable? Why, with many agricultural products, do price fluctuations give rise to large variations in the incomes of their producers, while, with some other products, price fluctuations leave producers' incomes unaffected?

What determines the level of wages and what influences do unions have on the share of national income going to labour? What functions do unions fulfil in today's world? Is it possible that having fully achieved the purpose of putting labour on an equal footing with management they have outlived their usefulness?

Must all modern economies make use of money? Could money be eliminated in a truly socialist state? How is it that new money can be created by ordinary commercial banks within broad limits, and by governments without limits? If money is valuable, why do economists insist that countries with large supplies of it are no richer than countries with small supplies?

Why did inflation accelerate so dramatically in most countries in the mid-1970s?

Why did the rate of inflation peak at over 25 per cent in Britain and only 11 per cent in the United States? Are the group of economists called monetarists right in arguing that the primary cause of British inflation is the mismanagement of the British monetary system by that famous and venerable old institution, the Bank of England?

What influence does government have on people's welfare? What are the effects of a government's taxation policies? What are the effects of public expenditure? How important to our welfare is the size of our national debt?

These are the types of questions with which economists concern themselves, and on which the theories of economics are designed to shed some light. Such a list may give you a better idea of the scope of economics than could be obtained at this stage from an enumeration of the common textbook definitions.

When you begin this book you are setting out on a study of positive economics or, to use a slightly more accurate phrase, POSITIVE ECONOMIC SCIENCE. From the questions listed above you now have some idea of the scope of *economics*. Next we must consider in some detail what is meant by the terms *positive* and *science*. After that we will ask whether or not it is really possible to conduct a scientific study of anything that is basically concerned with human behaviour. Economics is generally regarded as a social science, but can any study of human behaviour ever hope to be 'scientific'? Economists claim to be able to understand and to predict certain aspects of human behaviour. To anyone who wishes to be able to evaluate these claims this introductory discussion is critical, because the questions 'What can we hope to learn?' and 'How can we go about it?' are basic to the whole subject. These are also questions over which there is some disagreement among professionals and a vast amount of misunderstanding and even superstition among the general public.

Positive and normative statements

The success of modern science rests partly on the ability of scientists to separate their views on *what does happen* from their views on *what they would like to happen.* For example, until the nineteenth century virtually all Christians and Jews believed that the earth was only a few thousand years old. Then, about two hundred years ago, evidence began to accumulate that some existing rocks were millions of years old, possibly even thousands of millions. Most people found this hard to accept. They did not like it; it would force them to rethink their religious beliefs and abandon those that were based on a literal reading of the Bible. Many would have preferred the evidence to be wrong; they wanted rocks to be only a few thousand years old. Nevertheless, the evidence continued to accumulate until today virtually everyone accepts that the earth is neither thousands, nor millions, but four or five thousand million years old. This advance in our knowledge came because the question 'How old are observable rocks?' could be separated from the feelings of scientists (many of them devoutly religious) about the age they would have liked the rocks to be.

Definitions and illustrations

The ability to distinguish what is from what we would like, or what we feel ought, to be,[1] is based partly on knowing the difference between *positive* and *normative* statements.

> **Positive statements are about what is, was or will be; they assert alleged facts about the universe in which we live. Normative statements are about what ought to be. They depend on our judgements about what is good or bad, and they are thus inextricably bound up with our philosophical, cultural and religious positions.**

We say that normative statements depend on our VALUE JUDGEMENTS.

Let us consider some assertions, questions and hypotheses that can be classified as positive or normative. The statement 'It is impossible to break up atoms' is a positive one that can quite definitely be (and of course has been) refuted by empirical observations, while the statement 'Scientists ought not to break up atoms' is a normative statement that involves ethical judgements, and cannot be proved right or wrong by any amount of evidence. In economics the questions 'What policies will reduce unemployment?' and 'What policies will prevent inflation?' are positive ones, while the question 'Ought we to be more concerned about unemployment than about inflation?' is a normative one. The statement 'A government deficit will reduce unemployment and cause an inflation' is a positive hypothesis. The statement 'Unemployment is a worse evil than inflation' is normative.

As an example of the importance of this distinction in the social sciences, consider the question 'Has the payment of generous unemployment benefits increased the amount of unemployment?' This positive question can be turned into a testable hypothesis by asserting something like: 'The higher are the benefits paid to the unemployed, the higher will be the total amount of unemployment.' If we are not careful, however, our attitudes and value judgements may get in the way of our study of this hypothesis. Some people are opposed to the welfare state and believe in an individualist, self-help ethic. They may hope that the hypothesis will be found correct because its truth could then be used as an argument against welfare measures in general. Others feel that the welfare state is a good thing, reducing misery and contributing to human dignity. They may hope that the hypothesis is wrong because they do not want welfare measures to produce results of which people disapprove. In spite of different value judgements and social attitudes, however, evidence is accumulating on this particular hypothesis. As a result, we have much more knowledge than we had ten years ago of why, where and by how much (if at all) unemployment benefits increase unemployment. This evidence could never have been accumulated or accepted if investigators had not been able to distinguish their feelings on how they wanted the answer to turn out from their assessment of evidence on how people actually behaved.

Positive statements such as the one just considered assert things about the world. If it is possible for a statement to be proved wrong by empirical evidence, we call it a TESTABLE STATEMENT. Many positive statements are testable, and disagreements over them are appropriately handled by an appeal to the facts.

In contrast to positive statements, which are often testable, normative statements are never testable. Disagreements over such normative statements as 'It is wrong to

[1] This word 'ought' has two distinct meanings: the 'logical ought' and the 'ethical ought'. The logical ought refers to the consequences of certain things: e.g., 'you ought to leave now if you don't want to be late'. The ethical ought refers to the desirability of certain things: e.g., 'you ought to leave now because it is impolite to stay too long'. The text obviously refers to the ethical ought.

steal' or 'It is immoral to have sexual relations out of wedlock', cannot be settled by an appeal to empirical observations. Thus, for a rational consideration of normative questions, different techniques are needed to those used for a rational consideration of positive questions. Because of this, it is convenient to separate normative and positive enquiries. We do this not because we think the former are less important than the latter, but merely because they must be handled in different ways.

Some points of possible confusion

Having made this distinction between positive and normative, a number of related points require mention. Although we deal with them only briefly, any one of them could be the subject of extended discussion.

The classification is not exhaustive The classifications 'positive' and 'normative' do not cover all statements that can be made. For example, there is an important class, called *analytic statements*, whose truth or falsehood depends only on the rules of logic. Consider the single sentence: 'If every *X* has the characteristic *Y*, and if this item *Z* is in fact an *X*, then it has the characteristic *Y*.' This sentence is true by the rules of logic, and its truth is independent of what particular items we substitute for *X*, *Y*, and *Z*. Thus the sentence '*If* all men are immortal *and if* you are a man, *then* you are immortal' is a true analytic statement. It tells us that *if* two things are true *then* a third thing must be true. The truth of this *statement* is not dependent on whether or not its individual parts are in fact true. Indeed the sentence 'All men are immortal' is a positive statement which has been amply refuted by myriad deaths. Yet no amount of empirical evidence on the mortality of men can upset the truth of the sentence '*If* all men are immortal *and if* you are a man, *then* you are immortal.'

Not all positive statements are testable A positive statement asserts something about the universe. It may be empirically true or false in the sense that what it asserts may or may not be true of the universe. If it is true, it adds to our knowledge of what can and cannot happen. Many positive statements are refutable: if they are wrong this can be ascertained (within a margin for error of observation) by checking them against data. For example, the positive statement that the earth is less than five thousand years old was tested and refuted by a mass of evidence which had been accumulated in the nineteenth century. The statement 'Angels exist and frequently visit the earth in visible form' is, however, also a positive statement. It asserts something about the universe. But we could never refute this statement with evidence because, no matter how hard we searched, believers could argue that we did not look in the right places or in the right way, or that angels won't reveal themselves to non-believers, or any one of a host of other alibis. Thus statements that could conceivably be refuted by evidence if they are wrong are a subclass of positive statements; other positive statements are irrefutable.

The distinction is not unerringly applied Because the positive-normative distinction helps the advancement of knowledge, it does not follow that all scientists automatically and unerringly apply it. Scientists are human beings. Many have strongly held values and they may let their value judgements get in the way of their assessment of evidence. For example, many scientists are not even prepared to consider evidence that there may be differences in intelligence among races because as good liberals they feel that all races ought to be equal. Nonetheless, the desire to separate *what is* from *what we would like to be* is a guiding light, an ideal, of science. The ability to do so, albeit imperfectly, is attested to by the acceptance, first by scientists and then by the general public, of many ideas that were initially extremely unpalatable – ideas such as the extreme age of the earth and the evolution of man from other animal species.

Ideals can be important even though they are not universally applied. Consider an analogy. (1) Many people try to be good (according to their own lights). (2) Most people do not live up to their own standards of goodness all of the time. (3) Ideas of goodness are an important force in motivating human behaviour. All three of these statements are probably true: the truth of (1) does not preclude the truth of (2) and the truth of (2) does not preclude the truth of (3). In an analogous way all three of the following statements might be true. (1) Positive and normative statements can be distinguished. (2) Not all scientists do, or even could, maintain the distinction all of the time. (3) The distinction has been a potent force in the advancement of knowledge and in the separation of knowledge from prejudice. Statement (1) does not preclude (2) and (2) does not preclude (3).[1]

The nature of positive economics

Positive economics is concerned with the development of knowledge about the behaviour of people and things in the world. This means that its practicioners are concerned with developing propositions that fall into the positive, testable class. This does not mean, however, that every single statement and hypothesis to be found in positive economics will actually be positive and testable. Some time ago a philosophy of knowledge called *logical positivism* was popular. It held that every single statement in the theory had to be positive and testable. This proved to be a harmful and unnecessary strait-jacket.

> **All that the positive economist asks is that something that is positive and testable should emerge from his theories somewhere – for if it does not, his theories will have no relation to the world around him.** [2]

The positive economist seeks ways of answering positive testable questions such as those listed at the outset of this chapter. His approach to these questions can, in a general way, be described as scientific. We must now consider in more detail just what the scientific approach is, and how scientific theories are developed and used.

The scientific approach

Very roughly speaking, the scientific approach consists in relating questions to

[1] Many critics of the idea of positive science have argued otherwise. They feel that because no person can ever be perfectly objective about other people, the idea of an objective, fact-guided science of human behaviour is a contradiction. Fortunately, science based on the testing of positive hypotheses is possible even though no one individual can be relied on completely and always to separate his judgement of facts from his desires on what he would like the facts to be.

[2] Some critics have mistakenly assumed that the positive economist tries to deal only in statements that are positive and testable. In fact the positive economist must spend time worrying about the correctness of analytic statements: 'Is a certain prediction actually implied by a certain set of assumptions?' He must also be prepared to have any number of non-testable assumptions in his theory as long as some testable predictions can be deduced from it.

evidence. When presented with a controversial issue, the scientist will ask what is the evidence on both sides. He may then take a stand on the issue with more or less conviction depending on the weight of the evidence. If there is little or no evidence, the scientist will say that, at present, it is impossible to take a stand. He will then set about searching for relevant evidence. If he finds that the issue is framed in terms of questions about which it is impossible to gather evidence, he will try to recast the questions so that they can be answered by an appeal to evidence.[1] This approach to a problem is what sets scientific inquiries off from other kinds of inquiries.[2]

Experimental and non-experimental sciences

In some fields, the scientist is able to generate observations that will provide evidence for or against any hypothesis that he wishes to test. Experimental sciences, such as chemistry and some branches of psychology, have an advantage because it is possible to produce relevant evidence through controlled laboratory experiments. Other sciences, such as astronomy and economics, cannot do this. They must wait for time to throw up observations that may be used to test hypotheses.

The ease or difficulty with which one can collect evidence does not determine whether a subject is scientific or non-scientific, although many people have thought that it did.[3] The way in which scientific inquiry proceeds does differ radically, however, between fields in which laboratory experiment is possible and those in which it is not. In this chapter we consider general problems more or less common to all sciences. In Chapter 3 we shall deal with problems peculiar to the non-experimental sciences, which must accept such observations as the world of actual experience provides.

The non-scientific attitude in everyday life

It is often said that we live in a scientific age. Over the last several hundred years the citizens of most Western countries have enjoyed the fruits of innumerable scientific discoveries. But the scientific advances that have so profoundly affected the average citizen have been made by an extremely small minority of the population. Most people have accepted these advances without the slightest idea either of the technical nature of the discoveries involved, or of the attitude of mind that made them possible. If we take as a measure of the influence of science the degree of dissemination of the fruits of science, then we live in a profoundly scientific age; but if we take as our measure the degree to which the general public understands and practises the scientific approach, then we are definitely in a pre-scientific era. Indeed, the scientific method of answering questions by appealing to a carefully collected and co-ordinated body of facts is a method that is seldom adopted by the public.

[1] One of the really challenging problems to the scientist is to find out how to pose a question in the general spirit of the problem in which people are interested but in a form capable of being answered by reference to evidence. There is no formula for this; it is a really difficult art.

[2] Other approaches might be to appeal to authority, for example, to Aristotle or the Scriptures, to appeal by introspection to some inner experience (to start off 'all reasonable men will surely agree'), or to proceed by way of definitions to the 'true' nature of the problem or concepts under consideration.

[3] It is often thought that scientific procedure consists of grinding out answers by following blind rules of calculation, and that only in the arts is exercise of real imagination required. This view is misguided. What the scientific method gives is an impersonal set of criteria for answering some questions. What questions to ask, exactly how to ask them and how to obtain the evidence are difficult problems for which there are no rules. They require, upon occasion, great feats of imagination and ingenuity.

Consider, for example, the argument about capital punishment that continues even in many of the countries that have abolished the death penalty. It is possible to advocate capital punishment as an act of pure vengeance, or because we believe that morally a person who kills *ought* himself to be killed. If we argue about capital punishment on these grounds, we are involved in normative questions depending upon value judgements. The great majority of arguments for capital punishment, however, are not of this type. Instead, they depend on predictions about observable behaviour, and thus belong to the field of science. These are usually variants of the general argument that capital punishment is a deterrent to murder. In this general form it is probably very difficult to test the hypothesis; and it will be necessary to state a number of more specific propositions which fall under it. Consider one such example:

> If there is capital punishment for murder involving robbery, then the robber will be less inclined to take a lethal weapon with him on his mission. If he does not take a lethal weapon with him, he will in fact commit fewer murders when surprised in the course of his robbery.

It is truly amazing how people can become committed to agreeing or disagreeing with such propositions without considering the available evidence. A survey of the press, whenever the issue arises, will show that most of the debates that take place are profoundly unscientific. How many of the participants know, for example, what proportion of murders in the course of robbery are done with lethal weapons brought by the criminal to the scene of the crime and what proportion are done with anything found at hand after the criminal has been discovered? Yet it would seem to be impossible to have an informed discussion on the issue without this elementary piece of factual knowledge. More generally, how many people involved in these debates know anything of the mass of evidence on murder rates before and after the abolition of capital punishment in the large number of jurisdictions where it has been abolished?

Indeed most of the arguments for and against capital punishment involve a maximum of empirical questions and a minimum of empirical evidence used to arrive at the answers given. If we really believed in a scientific inquiry into human behaviour, we would try to state the arguments about capital punishment in terms of a specific set of propositions, and then set out systematically to gather evidence relating to each one.

We may conclude that many hotly debated issues of public policy involve positive, not normative, questions, but that the scientific approach to them is very often avoided.

A science of human behaviour?

The preceding discussion raises the question of whether or not it is possible to have a scientific study in the field of human behaviour.

Behaviour in various kinds of sciences

It is often argued that natural sciences deal with inanimate matter that is subject to natural 'laws', whilethe social sciences deal with man, who has free will and cannot, therefore, be made the subject of such (inexorable) laws. Such an argument, however, concentrates on the physical sciences; it omits biology and the other life sciences which deal successfully with animate matter. When this point is granted, it may then be argued that the life sciences deal with simple living material, while only the social sciences deal with human beings who are the ultimate in complexity and who alone possess free will. Today, when we are increasingly aware of our common heritage with apes in particular, and primates in general, an argument that man's behaviour is totally different from the behaviour of other animals finds few adherents among informed students of animal behaviour.

Human behaviour

Nonetheless, many social observers, while accepting the success of the natural and the life sciences, hold that there cannot be a successful social science. Stated carefully, this view implies that inanimate and non-human animate matter will show stable responses to certain stimuli, while humans will not. For example, if you put a match to a dry piece of paper the paper will burn, while if you try to extract vital information from unwilling human beings by torture, some will yield it and others will not, and, more confusingly, the same individual reacts differently at different times. Whether human behaviour does or does not show sufficiently stable responses to factors influencing it as to be predictable within an acceptable margin of error is a positive question that can only be settled by an appeal to evidence and not by *a priori* speculation.[1]

In fact, it is a matter of simple observation that when we consider a group of individuals they do not behave in a totally capricious way, but do display stable responses to various stimuli. The warmer the weather, for example, the higher the number of people visiting the beaches and the higher the sales of ice-cream. It may be hard to say when or why one individual will buy an ice-cream, but we can observe a stable response pattern from a large group of individuals: the higher the temperature the greater the sales of ice-cream.

Many other examples will come to mind where, because we can say what the individual will probably do – without being certain of what he will do – we can say with quite remarkable accuracy what a large group of individuals will do. No social scientist could predict, for example, when an apparently healthy individual is going to die, but death rates for large groups are stable enough to make life insurance a profitable business. It could not be so if group behaviour were capricious. Also, no social scientist can predict what particular individuals will be killed in car accidents next holiday, but we can come very close to knowing how many in total will die, and the more objectively measurable data we have concerning, for example, the state of the weather on the day, and the increase in car sales over the last year, the closer we will be able to predict the total of deaths.

If group human behaviour were in fact random and capricious, existence would be impossible. Neither law, nor justice, nor airline timetables would be more reliable than a roulette wheel; a kind remark could as easily provoke fury as sympathy; one's landlady might put one out tomorrow or forgive one the rent. There is not, and could not be, anything in science fiction to match it. One cannot really imagine a society of human beings that could possibly work like this. Indeed a major part of brainwashing techniques is to mix up rewards and punishments until the victim genuinely does not know 'where he is': unpredictable pressures drive human beings

[1] *A priori* is a phrase commonly used by economists. It may be defined as that which is prior to actual experience, or as that which is innate or based on innate ideas.

mad. In fact, we live in a world which is some sort of mixture of the predictable, or average, or 'most of the people most of the time,' and of the haphazard, contrary, and random.

When we try to analyse our world, and apply our orderly models to it, we need help from specialists in probability – statisticians – but we have not yet found that we need the advice of experts in the behaviour of systems in states of total chaos.

The 'law' of large numbers

We may now ask how it is that we can predict group behaviour when we are never certain what a single individual will do. As a first step, we must distinguish between *deterministic* and *statistical* hypotheses. Deterministic hypotheses admit of no exceptions. An example would be the statement: 'If you torture any man over this period of time with these methods he will *always* break down.' Statistical hypotheses, however, admit of exceptions and purport to predict the probability of certain occurrences. An example would be: 'If you torture a man over this period of time with these methods he will *very probably* break down; in fact if you torture a large number of men under the stated circumstances about 95 per cent of them will break down.' Such an hypothesis does not predict what an individual will certainly do, but only what he will probably do. This does allow us, however, to predict within a determinable margin of error what a large group of individuals will do.

Successful predictions about the behaviour of large groups are made possible by the statistical 'law' of large numbers. Very roughly, this 'law' asserts that random movements of a large number of individual items tend to offset one another. The law is based on one of the most beautiful constants of behaviour in the whole of science, natural and social, and yet the law can be derived from the fact that human beings make errors! This constant is the *normal curve of error* which you will encounter in elementary statistics.

Let us consider what is implied by the law of large numbers. Ask one person to measure the length of a room and it will be almost impossible to predict in advance what sort of error of measurement he will make. Thousands of things will affect the accuracy of his measurements. Furthermore, he may make one error today and quite a different one tomorrow. But ask one thousand people to measure the length of the same room and we can predict with a high degree of accuracy how this *group* will make its errors! We can assert with confidence that more people will make small errors than will make large errors, that the larger the error the fewer will be the number of people making it, that the same number of people will overestimate as will underestimate the distance, and that the average error of all the individuals will be zero.[1] Here then is a truly remarkable constant pattern of human behaviour; a constant on which much of the theory of statistical inference is based.

[1] For purposes of measuring the error we define the 'true' distance to be that measured by the most precise instruments of scientific measurement (whose range of error will be very small relative to the range of error of our one thousand laymen all wielding tape measures). Those familiar with statistical theory will realize that the predictions in the text assume that all the necessary conditions, such as the existence of a large number of independent factors causing individuals to make errors, are fulfilled. The purpose of the discussion in the text is not to give readers a full appreciation of the subtleties of statistical theory, but to persuade them that anyone is misguided who holds the common view that free will and the absence of deterministic certainty about human behaviour makes a scientific study of such behaviour impossible.

If a common cause should act on all members of the group we can successfully predict their average behaviour, even though any one member of the group may act in a surprising fashion. If, for example, we give all our thousand individuals a tape measure which understates 'actual' distances, we can predict that, on the average, the group will now understate the length of the room. It is, of course, quite possible that one member who had in the past been consistently undermeasuring distance because he was depressed will now overestimate the distance because the state of his health has changed; but something else may happen to some other individual that will turn him from an overmeasurer into an undermeasurer. Individuals may do peculiar things which, as far as we can see, are inexplicable, but the group's behaviour, when the inaccurate tape measure is substituted for the accurate one, will nonetheless be predictable, *precisely because the odd things that one individual does will tend to cancel out the odd things some other individual does.*

The nature of scientific theories

So far we have seen that there is real evidence that human behaviour does show stable response patterns. Theories grow up in answer to the question 'Why?'. Some sequence of events, some regularity between two or more things is observed in the real world and someone asks why this should be so. A theory attempts to explain why. One of the main practical consequences of a theory is that it enables us to predict as yet unobserved events. For example, national income theory predicts that a cut in tax rates will reduce the amount of unemployment. The simple theory of market behaviour predicts that, under certain specified conditions, the introduction of a sales tax will raise the price of the commodity concerned and the price increase will be less than the amount of the tax. It also allows us to predict that, if there is a partial failure of the potato crop, the total income earned by potato farmers will increase!

The construction of theories

A theory consists of a set of definitions, stating clearly what is meant by various terms, and a set of assumptions about the way in which the world behaves. Students often worry about what appears to them to be the unrealistic assumptions that they encounter in economics. *It is important to remember, however, that all theory is an abstraction from reality.* If we did not abstract we would merely duplicate the world camera-style, and would add nothing to our understanding of it.

> **A good theory abstracts from full reality in a useful way; a bad theory does not.**

But how do we know if the abstractions of a particular theory are useful or not? To do this we must take the next step in the construction of theories: we follow a process of logical deduction to discover what is implied by the assumptions of the theory. For example, if we assume that businessmen always try to make as much profit as is possible, and if we make assumptions about how taxes affect their profits, we can derive implications about how they will behave when taxes change. These implications are the predictions of our theory. If the theory is useful, its predictions will pass empirical tests. For example, when taxes are next changed, businessmen will react in the way predicted by the theory.[1]

Scientific predictions

We have seen above that a successful theory enables us to predict events. We must now consider with a little more care just what is the nature of a scientific prediction, and in particular whether it is the same thing as a prophecy about the future course of events.

> **A scientific prediction is a conditional statement having the form '*if* you do this *then* such and such will follow.'**

If you mix hydrogen and oxygen under specified conditions, *then* water will be the result. *If* the government has a large budget deficit, *then* unemployment will be reduced. It is most important to notice that this prediction is very different from the statement: 'I prophesy that in two years' time there will be a large increase in employment because I believe the government will decide to have a large budget deficit.' The government's decision to have a budget deficit or surplus in two years' time will be the outcome of many complex factors, emotions, objective circumstances and chance occurrences, most of which cannot be predicted. If the economist's prophecy about the level of employment turns out to be wrong, because in two years' time the government does not have a large deficit, then all we have learned is that the economist is not a good guesser about the behaviour of the government; we will not have found evidence that conflicts with any economic theory. However, *if* the government does have a large deficit (in two years' time or at any other time) and *then* unemployment does not fall, we have found evidence conflicting with a (conditional) scientific prediction in the field of economics.[2]

---

[1] One confusing aspect of assumptions is that they are used in different ways. Consider, for example, a theory that starts out: 'Assume that there is no government.' 'Surely,' says the reader, 'this assumption is totally unrealistic and I cannot take seriously anything that comes out of the theory.' But this assumption may merely be the economist's way of saying that, whatever the government does, even whether or not it exists, *is irrelevant for the purposes of his particular theory*. Now, put this way, the statement becomes an empirical assertion, and the only way to test it is to see if the predictions which follow from the theory do or do not fit the facts that the theory is trying to explain. If they do, then the theorist was correct in his assumption that the government could be ignored; the criticism that the theory is unrealistic is completely beside the point. Assumptions, however, are used in economics for other purposes, particularly to outline the set of conditions under which a theory is meant to hold. Consider a theory that assumes that the government has a balanced budget. This may mean that the theorist intends his theory to apply only when there is a balanced budget; it may *not* mean that the size of the government's budget surplus or deficit is irrelevant to the theory. You may find it confusing that an assumption may mean many different things in economics. When you encounter an assumption in economic theory you should, therefore, do two things: ask what information the assumption is intended to convey, and remember that it is not always appropriate to criticize the simplifying assumptions of a theory on the grounds that they are unrealistic. If one economist believes that a theory assumes away something that is important for the problem at hand, then he must believe, and try to show, that the predictions of the theory are contradicted by the facts.

[2] It is very important not to treat economic forecasting as synonymous with economic prediction. Forecasting is a type of conditional prediction which attempts to predict the future by discovering relations between economic variables of the sort that the value of Y at some future date depends on the value of X today, in which case future Y can be predicted by observing present X. Many conditional predictions are not of this form; those which relate the Y today to the value of X today provide significant and useful relations that allow us to predict 'if you do this to X you will do that to Y', without allowing us to forecast the future. The analogy often drawn between economics and weather forecasting suggests forecasting rather than the wider class of scientific predictions.

The testing of scientific predictions

If we wish to test any theory we confront its predictions with evidence. We seek to discover if certain events have the consequences predicted by the theory. Some of the difficult problems involved in this task are the subject of Chapter 3. In the meantime we should notice that as with most other sciences it is never possible to prove or to refute any theory in economics with 100 per cent certainty.

Proof and refutation Consider the simple economic theory that predicts: 'If a sales tax is levied on the product of a competitive industry, *then* the price of the product will rise but by less than the amount of the tax.' It is not claimed that this prediction holds only for the years 1960–85, or only in odd-numbered years, nor is it supposed to hold in the USA and Germany but not in France and Paraguay. The theory simply says that this result will hold *whenever a sales tax is levied in an industry that is competitive.* We may say that the theory is unbounded both in time and in space. But since we can make only a limited number of observations we can never prove conclusively that the theory is true. Even if we have made a thousand observations which agree with the prediction, it is always possible that in the future we will make observations which conflict with the theory. Since this possibility can never be ruled out completely (no matter how unlikely we might think it to be), we can never regard any theory as conclusively proved.

It is also impossible to refute any theory conclusively. This matter is considered in some detail in Chapter 3. Suffice it to say now that, since human beings make the tests, and since human beings are fallible, it is always possible that a piece of apparently conflicting evidence arose because we made a mistake in our observations. One conflicting observation does not worry us very much, but as a mass of them accumulate we become more and more worried about our theory and will regard it as less and less likely to be true. Eventually we shall abandon it, even though we can never be 100 per cent certain we are not making an error in doing so.

When is a theory abandoned? As a generalization we can say that our theories tend to be abandoned when they are no longer useful, and that they cease to be useful when they cannot predict the consequences of actions in which we are interested better than the next best alternative. When this happens the theory is abandoned and replaced by the superior alternative. In the process of upsetting existing theories we learn new, surprising facts.

Any developing science will continually be having some of its theories rejected; it will also be cataloguing observations that cannot be fitted into (explained by) any existing theory. These observations indicate the direction required for the development of new theories or for the extension of existing ones.[1] On the other hand, there will be many implications of existing theories that have not yet been tested, either because no one has yet figured out how to test them, or merely because

[1] The development of a new theory to account for existing observations is often the result of real creative genius of an almost inspired nature. This step in the development of science is the exact opposite of the popular conception of the scientist as an automatic rule-follower. One could argue for a long time whether there was more original creative genius embodied in a first-class symphony or a new theory of astronomy. Fascinating studies of the creative process may be found in A. Koestler, *The Sleep Walkers* (Hutchinson, 1959), especially the section on Kepler, and J.D. Watson, *The Double Helix* (Weidenfeld and Nicolson, 1968).

no one has got around to testing them. These untested hypotheses provide agenda for new empirical studies.

The state of economics

Economics provides no exception to the comments made in the previous paragraph. On the one hand, there are many observations for which no fully satisfactory theoretical explanation exists. On the other hand, there are many predictions which no one has yet satisfactorily tested. Thus serious students of economics must not expect to find a set of answers to all possible questions as they progress in their study. They must expect very often to encounter nothing more than a set of problems for further theoretical or empirical research. Even when they do find answers to problems, they should accept these answers as tentative and ask, even of the most time-honoured theory: 'What observations might we make that would be in conflict with this theory?' Economics is still a very young science and many problems in it are almost untouched. Those of you who venture further in this book may well, only a few years from now, publish a theory to account for some of the problems mentioned herein, or else you may make a set of observations which will upset some time-honoured theory described within these pages.

Having counselled disrespect for the authority of accepted theory, it is necessary to warn against adopting an approach that is too cavalier. No respect attaches to the person who merely says: 'This theory is for the birds; it is *obviously* wrong.' This is too cheap. To criticize a theory on logical grounds (economists sometimes say 'on theoretical grounds'), one must show that its alleged predictions do not follow from its assumptions. To criticize a theory effectively on empirical grounds, one must demonstrate by a carefully made set of observations that some aspect of the theory is contradicted by the facts. These tasks are seldom easily or lightly accomplished.

Figure 1.1 provides a summary of the discussion of theories. It shows a closed circuit, because theory and observation are in continuous interaction with each other. Starting at the top left (because we must start somewhere), we find the definitions of terms and assumptions of a theory. The theorist then deduces by logical analysis everything that is implied by the assumptions. These implications are the predictions of the theory. The theory is then tested by confronting its predictions with evidence. Tests may be made for the direct purpose of testing a theory, but they are also made incidentally whenever an applied economist uses the theory in a real-world context. If the theory is in conflict with facts, it will most likely be amended to make it consistent with the new facts (and thus make it a better theory); in extreme cases it will be discarded in place of a superior alternative. The process then begins again as the new or amended theory is subjected first to logical analysis and then to empirical testing.

Scientific crises

Sciences often appear to evolve through a series of stages. At first, an existing theory seems to be working well and the main scientific tasks are to extend it in various directions. Then, gradually, observations begin to accumulate that conflict with the theory. For a long time these exceptions are ignored or explained away on an ad hoc basis, but sooner or later the weight of conflicting evidence builds up to a crisis for the theory. Finally a breakthrough occurs, and some genius develops a new theory

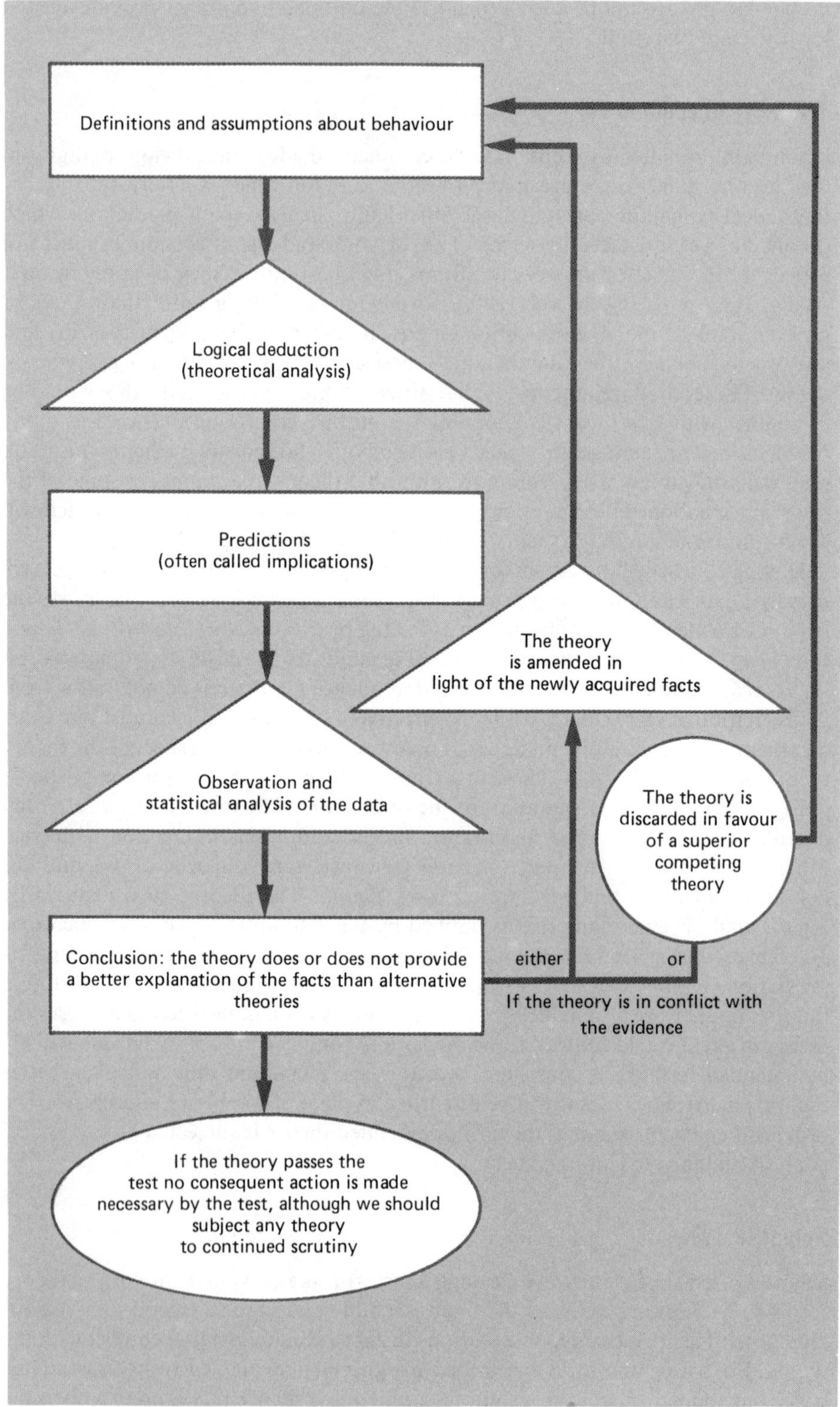

Fig. 1.1 The interaction of deduction and measurement in theorizing

that comprehends both what still seems right in the older theory *and* the observations that were not accounted for. Once the new theory is accepted, often after an interlude of uncertainty and heated controversy, another period of consolidation and extension occurs until new conflicts between theory and observation emerge.

Economics appears to be currently in one of these times of crisis. After a long period of consolidation and development of the theories of 'macroeconomics' (see Part 7), evidence is rapidly accumulating that is not easily explained within the framework of existing theories. As is usual in such times, there is substantial confusion and controversy. Some economists hold that only minor amendments are needed to make existing theories consistent with the new observations; others believe that major theoretical upheavals are necessary. In the heat of these controversies, economists tend to reveal what most scientists reveal in such situations: that they are not dispassionate calculating machines, but human beings with strong emotional commitments to their established positions.

Periods of scientific crisis can be profoundly disturbing for the scientists who become involved in them, to say nothing of those who depend on the scientists for answers to practical questions. Many economists are so committed to particular theories that they will never be convinced by new evidence. It is important, however, that one of the rules of debate should continue to be 'Try to show that your theory fits the evidence better than do competing theories'. Although the most committed protagonists may never change their minds, a new generation of economists, not so committed to old and outdated positions, may be able to judge the issues more dispassionately and be better able to tell which of various competing theories conforms more closely with the evidence.

Science has been successful in spite of the fact that individual scientists have not always been totally objective. Individuals may passionately resist the apparent implications of evidence. But the rule of the game, that facts cannot be ignored and must somehow be fitted into the accepted theoretical structure, tends to produce scientific advance in spite of what might be thought of as unscientific, emotional attitudes on the part of many scientists, particularly at times of scientific crisis.

But if existing protagonists ever succeed in changing the rules of the game by encouraging economists to ignore inconvenient facts or define them out of existence, this would be a major blow to scientific enquiry in economics.

2

The tools of theoretical analysis

If you look at the left-hand side of Figure 1.1 on page 16, you will see two triangles. The first stands for the movement from the assumptions to the implications, or predictions, of theories. To make this move the economist uses the tools of logic, which allow him to deduce the implications of his assumptions. The second triangle stands for the testing of implications against empirical evidence. To do this the economist uses the tools of statistical analysis. This chapter is devoted to the tools of logical deduction or, as they are often called, the tools of theoretical analysis. The tools of statistical analysis are considered in Chapter 3.

Expressing hypotheses

We have already noted that an economic theory consists of definitions and assumptions about the behaviour of people and things. The assumptions of economic theory may be described in words, formulated mathematically or illustrated graphically. Once they are expressed in a precise way, their implications may also be derived by verbal, mathematical or geometrical analysis.[1] To a great extent all of these methods are interchangeable; any piece of logical reasoning that can be done verbally or geometrically can also be done mathematically. Some things that are done in mathematics, however, cannot be done rigorously in verbal or in geometrical analysis. Where various methods can be used, the choice among them will be dictated by considerations of convenience, economy, the techniques at the command of the practitioner and the audience at which he is aiming.

The concept of a functional relationship

The idea that one thing depends on another is one of the basic notions behind all science. The gravitational attraction of two bodies depends on their total mass and on the distance separating them; this attraction increases with size and diminishes with distance. The number of murders in a country is thought to depend on, among other things, the severity of the penalties for murder; the amount of a commodity

[1] Geometry is, of course, a branch of mathematics, but it is convenient to distinguish between 'geometrical' and 'mathematical' methods – meaning by the latter term, mathematical other than the geometrical.

that people will buy is observed to depend on, among other things, the price of the commodity. When mathematicians wish to say that one thing depends on another, they say that one is a *function* of the other. Thus gravitational attraction is a function of the mass of the two bodies concerned and the distance between them; the incidence of murder is a function of the severity of the punishment for it; and the quantity of a product demanded is a function of the price of the product.

There are two steps in giving compact symbolic expressions to the relations we have just described. First, we give each concept a symbol; second, we designate a symbol to express the idea of one factor's dependence on another. Thus, if we let g stand for gravitational attraction, M stand for the mass of two bodies, and d stand for the distance between two bodies, we may write

$$g = \mathrm{f}(M, d),$$

where f is read 'is a function of' and means 'depends upon'. The whole equation defines an hypothesis and is read 'Gravitational attraction is a function of the mass of the two bodies and the distance between them.' This is the same as the verbal statement with which we began.

The second hypothesis, that the number of murders depends on the severity of punishment for murder, may be expressed as

$$K = \mathrm{f}(S),$$

where K is a measure of the frequency of murders and S is a measure of the severity of punishment for being convicted of murder. The final hypothesis, that the quantity demanded depends on the price of the product, is written

$$q^d = \mathrm{f}(p),$$

where q^d is the quantity demanded of some commodity, and p is the price of the commodity.

The expression

$$Y = \mathrm{f}(X)$$

says that Y is a function of X. It means that Y depends upon or varies with X, whatever Y and X may be. The quantities X and Y in this functional relation are called *variables*. The notation often looks frightening to students, especially those who did not get on well with their school mathematics. However, once one becomes familiar with it, this notation is extremely helpful, and since the functional concept is basic to all science, the notation is well worth mastering.

The expression $Y = \mathrm{f}(X)$ merely states that Y is related to X; it says nothing about the form that this relation takes. Does Y increase as X increases? Does Y decrease as X increases? Or is the relation more complicated? Take a very simple example where Y is the length of a board in feet, and X is the length of the same board in yards. Quite clearly, $Y = \mathrm{f}(X)$. Further, in this case we know the exact form of the function, for length in feet (Y) is merely 3 times the length in yards (X); so we may write $Y = 3X$.

This example is not typical of all functional relationships because it is true by definition. It merely states in functional form the relation between the definitions of a foot and a yard. It is nonetheless useful to have a way of writing down relationships that are definitionally true.

Now consider a second example. Let C equal the total spending of a household on all consumption goods in one year, and Y equal the household's income. Now state the hypothesis

$$C = \mathrm{f}(Y), \tag{1}$$

and, more specifically,

$$C = 0{\cdot}8Y. \tag{2}$$

Equation (1) expresses the general hypothesis that a household's consumption depends upon its income. Equation (2) expresses the more specific hypothesis that expenditure on consumption will be four-fifths as large as the household's income. There is no reason why either of these hypotheses *must* be true; indeed, neither may be consistent with the facts. But those are matters for testing. What we do have in each equation is a concise statement of a particular hypothesis.

Thus the existence of some relation between two variables, Y and X, is denoted by $Y = \mathrm{f}(X)$, whereas any precise relation may be expressed by a particular equation such as $Y = 2X$, $Y = 4X^2$, or $Y = X + 2X^2 + 0{\cdot}5X^3$.

If Y increases as X increases (e.g., $Y = 10 + 2X$), we say that Y is an INCREASING FUNCTION of X or that Y and X VARY DIRECTLY with each other. If Y decreases as X increases (e.g., $Y = 10 - 2X$), we say that Y is a DECREASING FUNCTION of X or that Y and X VARY INVERSELY with each other.

Economic theory is based on relations between various magnitudes (e.g., the quantity demanded of some commodity is related to the price of that commodity; the amount spent on consumption is related to income). All such relations can be expressed mathematically. It is this fact that gives mathematical analysis importance in economics. Once our hypotheses are written down in terms of algebraic expressions we can use mathematical manipulation to discover what implications they have about behaviour.

The error term

The examples of functional relations considered above were all *deterministic* ones in the sense that they were expressed as if they held exactly: given the value of X, we knew the value of Y exactly. The relations considered in economic theory are seldom of this sort, except where definitions are being expressed. When an economist says that the world behaves so that $Y = \mathrm{f}(X)$, he does not expect that knowing X will tell him *exactly* what Y will be, but only that it will tell him what Y will be *within some margin of error*.

The error in predicting Y from a knowledge of X arises for two quite distinct reasons. First, there may be other variables that also affect Y. Although we may say that the demand for butter is a function of the price of butter, $D_b = \mathrm{f}(p_b)$, we know that other factors will also influence this demand. A change in the price of margarine will certainly affect the demand for butter, even though the price of butter does not change. Thus we do not expect to find a perfect relation between D_b and p_b that will allow us to predict D_b exactly, from a knowledge of p_b. Second, we can never measure our variables exactly, so that, even if X is the only cause of Y, our measurements will give various Ys corresponding to the same X. In the case of the demand for butter, our errors of measurement might not be large. In other cases, errors might be substantial. In the case of a relation between total spending on consumption goods and total income earned in the nation ($C = f(Y)$), our measurements of both C and Y may be subject to quite wide margins of error. We may thus observe various values of C associated with the same measured value of Y, not because C is varying independently of Y, but because our error of measurement is itself varying from period to period.

If all the factors other than X that affect the measured value of Y are summarized into an error term, ε, we write

$$Y = f(X, \varepsilon).$$

This says that the observed value of Y is related to the observed value of X as well as to a lot of other things, both observational errors and other causal factors, all of which will be lumped together and called ε (the Greek letter epsilon). In economic theory this error term is almost always suppressed, and we proceed as if our functional relations were deterministic. (When we come to test our theories, however, some very serious problems arise precisely because we do not expect our functional relations to hold exactly.)

It is extremely important to remember, both when interpreting a theory in terms of the real world and when testing a theory formally against empirical observations, that the deterministic formulation is a simplification. The error term is really present in all the functional relations with which we deal in economics.

Alternative methods of representing functional relations

A functional relation can be expressed in words, in graphs or in mathematical equations. As a simple example let us consider a hypothetical relation between the annual expenditure of a household on all the goods and services that it consumes (C) and its annual disposable income (Y). The assumed relation may be expressed in three ways.

(1) VERBAL STATEMENT: When income is zero the household will spend £800 a year (either by borrowing the money or by consuming past savings), and for every pound of income that the household obtains net of taxes (called *disposable income*) it will increase its expenditure by £0·80.

(2) GEOMETRICAL (GRAPHICAL) STATEMENT:

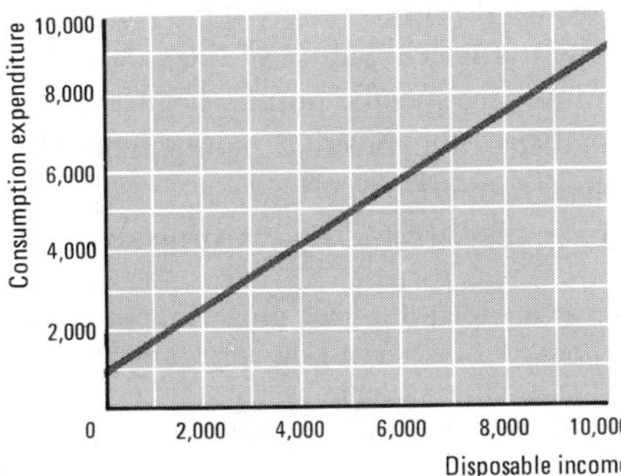

Fig. 2.1 A relation between a household's expenditure and its income

(3) MATHEMATICAL (ALGEBRAIC) STATEMENT: $C = 800 + 0{\cdot}8Y$.

The graphical representation of functional relations

Since we shall make much use of the graphical representation of functional relations, it may be helpful to consider graphical techniques in a little more detail. In the previous section we considered a relation between annual expenditure and annual disposable income for a single hypothetical household:

$$C = 800 + 0{\cdot}8Y. \tag{3}$$

We may refer to this as the household's *consumption function*. For any specified value of Y, we can use the consumption function in (3) to determine the corresponding value of C. Let us start by taking five different levels of income, £0, £2,500, £5,000, £7,500 and £10,000, and calculating the level of consumption expenditure that would be associated with each. Table 2.1 shows these values and for further reference assigns a letter to each pair of values.

Table 2.1 Selected values of the function $C = 800 + 0{\cdot}8Y$

Y(£s)	C(£s)	Reference letter
0	800	A
2,500	2,800	B
5,000	4,800	C
7,500	6,800	D
10,000	8,800	E

We can, if we wish, show the data of Table 2.1 on a graph. To do this, we take each pair of values, i.e. a value of Y and the corresponding value of C, and plot them as a point on a co-ordinate grid, which we do in Figure 2.2(i). In part (ii) of the figure we have plotted not only these five points but a line relating C to every value of Y in the range covered by the graph. You should take the equation $C = 800 + 0{\cdot}8Y$ and plot as many points as necessary to satisfy yourself that they all lie on the straight line that we have drawn in Figure 2.2(ii).

Once we have plotted this line, which *is* the function $C = 800 + 0{\cdot}8Y$ in the interval from $Y = 0$ to $Y = 10{,}000$, we have no further need for the co-ordinate grid, and the figure will be less cluttered if we suppress it, as in Figure 2.2(iii). For some purposes we do not really care about the specific numerical values of the function; we are content merely to represent it as an upward-sloping straight line. This is done in Figure 2.2(iv). We have replaced the specific numerical values of the variables C and Y with the letters C_1, C_2, Y_1 and Y_2 to indicate specific points. Figure 2.2(iv) tells us, for example, that if we increase the quantity of disposable income from OY_1 to OY_2, consumption expenditure will increase from OC_1 to OC_2.[1]

The beginning student may feel that we have lost ground by omitting so much,

[1] In speaking of the quantity of Y as OY_1 or OY_2 we are following good geometric practice and recognizing that a *value* of Y is a *distance* on the Y axis. For brevity, we will usually use a shorter notation and speak of the quantity of Y as Y_1 or Y_2. This is somewhat less cumbrous, but it is important to remember that *any point on the axis represents the distance from the origin to that point* (e.g., Y_1 stands for the distance from O to Y_1).

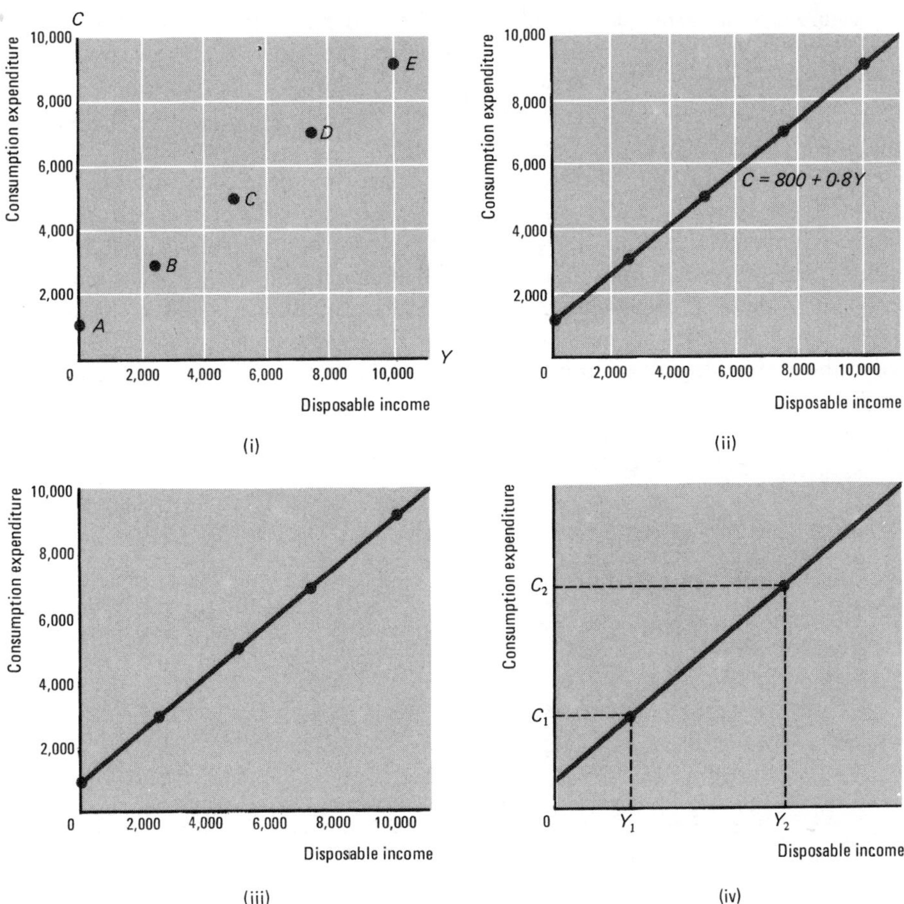

Fig. 2.2 Four different representations of the function $C = 800 + 0{\cdot}8Y$

but it is in the form of (iv) that most diagrams appear in economics texts. The great advantage of illustrating functional relations graphically is that we can easily compare different relations without specifying them in precise numerical form.

Suppose, for example, that we wish to compare and contrast three households, *R*, *S*, and *T*, whose behaviour is described by the following general assumptions. (1) All three have the same amount of consumption expenditure when their disposable income is zero. The amount is greater than zero, which implies that they must be either consuming past savings or going into debt. (2) In response to an increase in disposable income of £1, household *R* increases its consumption expenditure by more than does household *S*, and household *S* increases its consumption by more than does household *T*. (3) The response of each household's consumption expenditure to a change of £1 in its own disposable income is the same whatever its existing level of disposable income. These assumptions are cumbersome to state in words, but they are easily illustrated graphically.

Figure 2.3 shows the postulated relations for the three households. The fact that the consumption lines all intersect the vertical axis at the same point expresses the assumption that all three households spend the same amount, *Oa* (or simply *a*), when their disposable income is zero. The third assumption is shown by the fact that for each household the relationship between C and Y is a straight line. This means that the change in C for a unit change in Y will be the same wherever we measure it on any one of the lines. The second assumption is shown by the fact that R's line is steeper than S's line, which in turn is steeper than T's line. The steeper the line, the larger the change in C for a given change in Y.[1]

When we are dealing with hypotheses that are not specified quantitatively, we normally suppress most of the co-ordinate grid to prevent the figures from being cluttered up with irrelevant details. The grid is always understood to be there, of course, and, when required, we draw in the necessary grid lines. For instance, the coordinates of point p in Figure 2.3 are Ob and Oc, and the grid lines bp and cp are drawn in because they are needed. If you find this at all difficult, you should redraw all of the graphs studied so far on graph paper until you feel at home with graphical analysis.

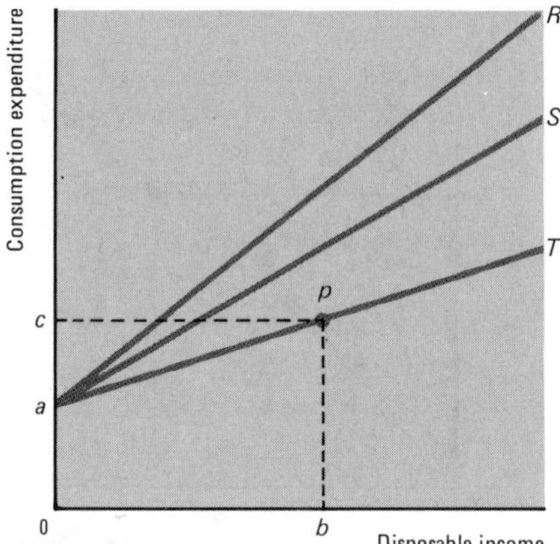

Fig. 2.3 Consumption functions for three hypothetical households

Deriving implications from functional relationships

When the economist has laid out the functional relations that describe the assumptions of his theory, his next task is to discover what they imply. In the process of making logical deductions from his theories, he may again employ verbal, geometrical or mathematical forms of reasoning. His main concerns will be to ensure that his reasoning processes are correct, so that the things he discovers are actually implied by his theory, and are efficient, so that he discovers everything that is implied by his theory.

The use of mathematics in theoretical reasoning

Many people – not just beginning students – are disturbed by the use of mathematics

[1] The same general relations can also be specified algebraically. We have

$$C_r = a + bY_r$$
$$C_s = c + dY_s$$
$$C_t = e + fY_t$$

where the subscripts r, s and t tell us whose income and consumption we are referring to. Assumption (1) means that $a = c = e$. Assumption (2) means that $b > d > f$. Assumption (3) means that the equations are all linear.

in economic reasoning. 'Surely,' they argue, 'human behaviour is too subtle and complex to be reduced to mathematical formulae.' At least four issues can be distinguished here.

First, we might wonder if we can ever understand enough about human behaviour to be able to build useful theories about it. This has to do with our ability to understand, not with the language we should use to express what we do (or think we do) understand. To construct any economic theory, whatever the language it is ultimately to be expressed in, we must begin by assuming that coherent assumptions about relevant human behaviour can be stated. (That we can make coherent assumptions about human behaviour is beyond question, since economic theory is full of them; whether or not they are relevant to the real world is an empirical question that will come up frequently in this book.)

Second, we might wonder if it is possible to express assumptions about human behaviour in mathematical terms. If such assumptions can be stated at all, they can be stated mathematically, since mathematics is just another language like English or Polish – albeit more precise than any of the languages of common speech. Any hypothesis about how two (or more) things are related can be expressed mathematically.

Third, we might wonder if the subtlety and complexity of human behaviour make mathematics *less appropriate* than a verbal language such as English for expressing our assumptions. Verbally, it is always possible to mask fuzziness in our concepts and assumptions. Verbal expression may sometimes be so vague as to *hide* our ignorance, but verbal expression can never *overcome* our ignorance. Mathematical expression is more precise than verbal expression. Not only can a relation between two or more things be stated mathematically, but any qualification to that relation can also be stated mathematically, *if it is clearly understood.* The language of mathematics turns out to be amazingly subtle; anything that we do understand clearly can be expressed most precisely by its terminology. It is an advantage, not a disability, of mathematical formulation that it exposes what is being said and what is left unsaid, and that it makes it hard to employ imprecise qualifications.

Fourth, we might worry about the application of long chains of mechanical mathematical deductions to our theories. This worry is the source of some very serious confusions. Once the assumptions of a theory have been fully stated, all that remains for the theorist is to discover their implications. This stage simply requires logical deduction. It is not a criticism to say that a technique is mechanical if by mechanical we mean that it allows us to discover efficiently and accurately what is or is not implied by our assumptions. It is never an advantage to use a technique that leaves us in doubt on this. If we accept the view that, somehow, verbal analysis (or 'judgement') can solve problems, even though we are unable to state clearly how we have reached the solutions, then we are involved not in a science but in a medieval mystery, in which the main problem is to be able to distinguish between the true and the false prophet.

Mathematics is neither the maker nor the destroyer of good economic theory. It is merely a precise and compact means of expression and an efficient tool for deriving implications from assumptions. Irrelevant or factually incorrect assumptions will yield irrelevant or factually incorrect implications, whatever logical tools are used to derive them.

Examples of theoretical reasoning

In later chapters you will encounter many interesting examples of the process of logical deduction in economics. In the meantime we can illustrate the procedure with some very simple manipulation of the household's consumption function $C = 800 + 0{\cdot}8\ Y$, first introduced on page 22. What can we discover about the behaviour of a household which has such a consumption function? First, it is clear that when its income is zero, the household is using up past savings or going into debt at the rate of £800 per year. Second, it is clear that an increase in income of £1 leads to an increase in consumption of 80p. Third, there will be a level of income at which the household is neither running into debt nor saving any of its income. This is called the *break-even level* of income, and it is easily discovered by finding the level of Y such that C and Y are equal.

To discover the break-even level algebraically, we need to solve the two simultaneous equations $C = 800 + 0{\cdot}8Y$ and $C = Y$. The first tells us how the household's consumption expenditure varies with its income, and the second imposes the condition that consumption expenditure should equal disposable income. If you solve these two equations, you will discover that the break-even level of income for this household is £4,000. A little further experimentation will show that at any level of income less than £4,000, expenditure exceeds income, while at any income level over £4,000, expenditure is less than income. The graphical determination of the break-even level of income is shown in Figure 2.4.

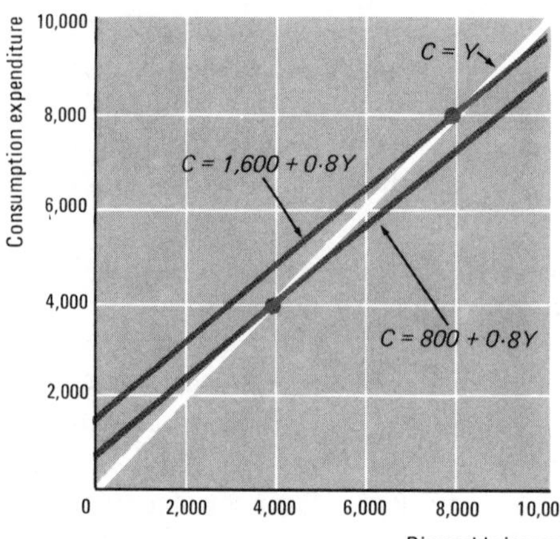

Fig. 2.4 The determination of the break-even level of income

As a final example of elementary theoretical reasoning, let us ask by how much the break-even level of income will increase if the household's behaviour changes so that, at each level of income, consumption expenditure is £800 higher than before. The changed behaviour is described by the new equation: $C = 1{,}600 + 0{\cdot}8\,Y$. To find the new break-even level of income, we solve this simultaneously with $C = Y$ and find the solution to be £8,000. Thus, when consumption is increased by £800 at each level of income, the break-even level of income rises by £4,000. This result, which is illustrated in Figure 2.4, is perhaps a little less obvious than the previous ones.

Is this an accident depending upon the numbers chosen or is there some more general relation being illustrated by this particular example? A bit of experimentation with the algebra or geometry of this case should allow you to prove that, with the consumption function $C = a + b$, any change in the constant a by an amount Δa

will change the break-even level of income by $\Delta a/(1-b)$. This is a general result that holds for all straight-line consumption functions.[1]

Notice how far we have come. We began with a very simple economic hypothesis relating two variables, consumption expenditure and disposable income. We took a numerical example and expressed it algebraically and geometrically. We then made certain simple logical deductions about what was implied by the hypothesis. At first these deductions were obvious, but the last one – that if £800 more is spent at each level of income, break-even Y rises by £4,000 – was not quite so obvious. We then wondered if this not-quite-so-obvious result was an accident depending on the particular numbers we chose. Experimentation showed that there was a single general result for all linear consumption functions: break-even Y rises by $1/(1-b)$ times the rise in the constant a.

All of this illustrates how the tools of logical analysis do allow us to discover what is implied by our assumptions. It also shows how theorizing tends to become cumulative: we obtain one result, possibly quite an obvious one, and this suggests another possible result to us; we check this and find that it is true and this suggests something else. Then we wonder if what we have discovered applies to cases other than the one we are analysing, and before we know it we are led off on a long chase that ends only when we think we have found all of the interesting implications of the theory and have also found out how generally they apply outside the specific case we began by analysing. Of course, when we say the chase ends, we mean it ends for the particular investigator, for he is usually wrong when he thinks he has found all the implications of a complex theory. Some new and ingenious investigator is very likely to come up with new implications or generalizations, and so the chase begins again.

The quantitative relation between variables

The *magnitude* of the change that occurs in one variable in response to changes in another variable is extremely important in economics. We expect the quantity of any commodity that people wish to purchase (which we call 'quantity demanded' and symbolize by q^d) to vary with its own price, $q^d = D(p)$, and we are interested in *how much* q^d changes for a given change in price. We expect the amount of a commodity produced and offered for sale (called 'quantity supplied' and symbolized by q^s) to vary with its own price, $q^s = S(p)$, and again it is important to know *by how much* q^s will change for a given change in price.[1] We expect the volume

[1] This last result can be proved with simple algebra using the delta notation for changes explained in more detail in the Appendix to this chapter on page 32. We have two equations; the first expresses the consumption function, and the second expresses the condition for the break-even level, that consumption should equal income: $C = a+bY$; and $C = Y$. Solving these simultaneously yields:

$$Y = \frac{a}{1-b}.$$

Now let a increase by Δa, and denote the resulting increase in Y by ΔY. We can then write

$$Y+\Delta Y = \frac{a+\Delta a}{1-b} = \frac{a}{1-b}+\frac{\Delta a}{1-b}$$

Subtracting the equation for Y from that for $Y+\Delta Y$ yields

$$\Delta Y = \Delta a/(1-b).$$

of unemployment (U) to vary with the difference between government revenue (R) and expenditure (E), $U = f(R-E)$, and we want to know *by how much* unemployment will change for a given change in the budget.

There is a precise mathematical method of handling problems arising from the question of how one variable changes as another variable on which it depends changes. The branch of mathematics which deals with these problems is called *differential calculus*. A knowledge of the calculus is not necessary in order to read this book. In fact one can usually obtain a first degree in economics without such knowledge, but those who do have some idea of the calculus will find it a great help.[2] The number of people obtaining a first degree in economics while remaining ignorant of mathematics is diminishing rapidly with the passage of time, and the serious student of economics is well advised to learn some mathematics.

[1] Here we have two variables both related to price. To distinguish the two we use two letters, D and S, in the place of the f already used, to indicate the functional relationships. This is discussed further on page 29.

[2] An introduction to the ideas of the differential calculus plus a review of very elementary arithmetic, algebra and geometry can be found in W.W. Sawyer's excellent little book *Mathematician's Delight* (Penguin, 1943); a somewhat more advanced treatment may be found in J. Parry Lewis, *An Introduction to Mathematics for Students of Economics* (Macmillan 2nd edn., 1969). A more rigorous treatment can be found in R.G.D. Allen's classic *Mathematical Analysis for Economists* (Macmillan, 1938). All these books are devoted mainly to mathematics with only passing references to economic applications. An introduction to mathematics with detailed applications to economics at each step can be found in G.C. Archibald and R.G. Lipsey, *An Introduction to a Mathematical Treatment of Economics* (Weidenfeld and Nicolson, 3rd edn., 1977).

Appendix to chapter 2

Some common techniques for theoretical analysis

Certain graphical and mathematical concepts are frequently encountered in economic analysis. In this appendix we deal briefly with the ones most frequently used in this book. Only the barest outlines are possible, and the student who wants a fuller treatment of the ideas expressed here should read the appropriate references listed in footnote 2, page 28.

Every student needs to master the elementary techniques described in this appendix before completing his or her study of introductory economics. Those who find they can manage it at this stage should study the appendix carefully now. Those who had difficulty with simple mathematics at school should read carefully as far as the beginning of the section entitled *Straight Lines, Slopes and Tangents.* Up to that point there is no algebraic manipulation. They should then skim through the rest of the material, making a list of the concepts discussed. When these concepts are encountered later in the text they should be reviewed again carefully here.

(1) The function as a rule

If X and Y are related to each other, we say they are functions of each other.[1] We write this, $Y = f(X)$, and we read it, 'Y is a function of X'. The letter 'f' stands for a rule which we use to go from a value of X to a value of Y. The rule tells us how to operate on X to get Y.

[1] Modern mathematicians distinguish between a correspondence and a function. There is a *correspondence* between Y and X if each value of X is associated with one or more values of Y. Y is a *function* of X if there is *one and only one* value of Y associated with each value of X. Mathematicians of an older generation described both relations as functions and then distinguished between single-valued functions (in modern language, functional relations) and multi-valued functions (in modern language, relations of correspondence). In the text we adopt the older, more embracing usage of the term *functional relation.*

Consider for example, the specific function

$$Y = 5X - 3.$$

The rule here is 'take X, multiply it by 5 and subtract 3'; this then yields the value of Y. In another case we may have

$$Y = X^2/2 + 6.$$

This rule says 'take X, square it, divide the result by 2, then add 6'; again, the result is the value of Y. If, for example, X has a value of 2, then the first rule yields $Y = 7$, while the second rule yields $Y = 8$.

The equations displayed above describe two different rules. We may confuse these if we denote both by the same letter. To keep them separate we can write

$$Y = f(X)$$

for the first and

$$Y = g(X)$$

for the second.

Since the choice of symbols to designate different rules *is* arbitrary, we can use any symbols that are convenient. In the above examples we had $Y = 5X - 3$ and $Y = X^2/2 + 6$ and we chose to indicate these rules by 'f' and 'g'. If we wanted to indicate that these were rules for yielding Y we could use that letter, and then use subscripts to indicate that there were two different rules. Thus we would write

$$Y = \mathrm{Y}_1(X)$$

and $$Y = \mathrm{Y}_2(X),$$

where Y_1 and Y_2 stand for two different rules for deriving Y from any given value of X.

Suppose now that we have two different variables Y and Z both related to X. A specific example would be

$$Y = 3 + 10X$$

and $$Z = 28 - 2X.$$

Again we have two different rules for operating on X; the first rule yields Y and the second rule yields Z. We could denote these rules $\mathrm{f}(X)$ and $\mathrm{g}(X)$ but, since the choice of a letter to denote each rule is arbitrary, we could also write

$$Y = \mathrm{Y}(X)$$

and $$Z = \mathrm{Z}(X).$$

In this case the choice of letters is a memory device which reminds us that the first rule, $3+10X$, yields Y, while the second rule, $28-2X$, yields Z.

(2) Some conventions in functional notation

Assume we are talking about some sequence of numbers, say, 1, 2, 3, 4, 5, ... If we wished to talk about one particular term in this series without indicating which one, we could talk about the ith term, which might be the 5th or the 50th. If we now want to indicate terms adjacent to the ith term, whatever it might be, we talk about the $(i-1)$th and the $(i+1)$th terms.

By the same token we can talk about a series of time periods, say, the years 1900, 1901 and 1902. If we wish to refer to three adjacent years in any series without indicating which three years, we can talk about the years $(t-1)$, t and $(t+1)$.

Consider a functional relation, between the quantity produced by a factory and the number of workers employed. In general, we can write $Q = \mathrm{Q}(W)$, where Q is the amount of production and W is the number of workers. If we wished to refer to the quantity of output where ten workers were employed, we could write $Q_{10} = \mathrm{Q}(W_{10})$, whereas, if we wished to refer to output when some particular, but unspecified, number were employed, we would write $Q_i = \mathrm{Q}(W_i)$. Finally, if we wished to refer to output when the number of workers was increased by one above the previous level, we could write $Q_{i+1} = \mathrm{Q}(W_{i+1})$. This use of subscripts to refer to particular values of the variables is a useful notion, and one that we shall use at various points in this book.

We may use time subscripts to date variables. If, for example, the value of X depends on the value of Y three months ago, we write this as $X_t = \mathrm{f}(Y_{t-3})$. Another convention is the use of... to save space in functions of many variables. For example, $\mathrm{f}(X_1, \ldots, X_n)$ indicates a function containing n (some unspecified number of) variables.

(3) Exogenous and endogenous variables

In economic theories it is convenient to distinguish between EXOGENOUS and ENDOGENOUS VARIABLES. Endogenous variables are ones that are explained *within* a theory; exogenous variables are ones that influence the variables but are themselves determined by factors outside the theory. Assume, for example, that we have a theory of what determines the price of apples from day to day in London. The price of apples in this case is an endogenous variable – something determined within the framework of the theory. The state of the weather, on the other hand, is an exogenous variable. It will influence apple prices but will be uninfluenced by these prices. The state of the weather will not be explained by our theory; it is something that happens from without, so to speak, but it nonetheless influences our endogenous variable, apple prices, because it affects the demand for apples. Exogenous variables are sometimes referred to as AUTONOMOUS VARIABLES.

(4) Identities and equations

A DEFINITIONAL IDENTITY is true for all values of the variables; no values can be found that would contradict it. An example of such an identity is

$$1 \text{ Yard} \equiv 3 \text{ Feet}.$$

It should be noted that identities are often written with a three-bar sign and that the expression $y \equiv x$ is read 'y is identical to x'.

EQUATIONS are relations that are true only for some values of the variables but that can be contradicted by other values. Thus the expression $y = 10+2x$ is an equation. It is written with a two-bar or equals sign and is read y is equal to ten plus two x. This expression is true, for example, for $x = 2$ and $y = 14$, but not for $x = 2$ and $y = 2$. Definitional identities can be used to state definitions in economic theories, but they do not state behavioural hypotheses. Thus a theory that consisted only of definitional identities would tell us nothing about the real world. Equations can be used to state testable hypotheses, since they make statements that are true for some states of the universe but false for others. A theory that has empirical content will usually contain some definitional identities, but it must also contain some equations that express behavioural assumptions and that are not true merely by the way we use words.[1]

(5) Stocks and flows

Some of the most serious confusions in economics have arisen from a failure to distinguish between STOCKS and FLOWS. Imagine a bathtub half full of water with the tap turned on and the plug removed; you have in mind a model similar to many simple economic theories. The level of water in the bath is a stock – an amount that is just there. We could express it as so many gallons of water. The amount of water entering through the tap and the amount leaving through the drain are both flows. We could express them as so many gallons *per minute* or *per hour*. A flow necessarily has a time dimension – there is so much flow *per period of time*. A stock does not have a time dimension – it is just so many tons or gallons or heads.

The amount of wheat produced is a flow, so much per month or per year. The amount of wheat sold is also a flow. The amount of wheat stored (produced but unsold) in the granaries of the world is a stock; it is just so many millions of tons of wheat. The distinction between stocks and flows will arise many times throughout this book.

(6) Necessary conditions and sufficient conditions

It is common in popular discussion to confuse necessary and sufficient conditions. Many futile arguments have been caused by one person arguing that a condition was sufficient for a result and another arguing that it was not necessary, each thinking he was contradicting the other when, in fact, both were correct. Consider, for example, a club that normally admits only males who are graduates of Oxford, but that is also willing to admit all male MPs, whatever their background. Being a male MP is thus sufficient to admit you to the club, but it is not necessary to be one. Being a male is a necessary condition for admission (since no females are admitted on any terms), but it is not a sufficient condition. Being a graduate of Oxford is by itself neither necessary (since non-Oxford graduates who are MPs can be admitted) nor sufficient (since female graduates of Oxford are not admitted). We may summarize the conditions for admission as follows:

To be male is necessary but not sufficient.
To be a male MP is sufficient but not necessary.
To be both a male and an Oxford graduate is sufficient but not necessary.
To be an Oxford graduate is neither necessary nor sufficient.
To be an MP is neither necessary nor sufficient.
To be *either* a male graduate of Oxford *or* a male MP is necessary and sufficient.

In general, a NECESSARY CONDITION is something that must be present but by itself may not guarantee the result. A SUFFICIENT CONDITION is something that, if present, does guarantee the result but that need not be there for the result to occur. A condition (or set of conditions) that is necessary *and* sufficient must be there and, if there, is enough to guarantee the result.

In this club, the necessary and sufficient condition for entry is a compound either-or condition: to be either a male graduate of Oxford or a male MP. If, however, another club were set up that was open to all former members of the House of Commons and to no one else, then a simple condition – to have been an MP – would be both necessary and sufficient for admission.

(7) Graphing functions

A co-ordinate graph divides space into four quadrants, as shown in Figure 2.5. The upper right-hand quadrant, which is the one in which both X and Y are positive, is usually called the *positive quadrant*. Very often in economics we are concerned only with the positive values of our variables, and in such cases we confine our graph to the positive quadrant. Whenever we want one or both of our variables to be allowed to take on negative values we must include some or all of the other quadrants. For example, one of the functions in Figure 2.6(ii) is extended

[1] Confusion between equations and definitional identities is a source of error in economics. One of the most perplexing habits of economists is to warn students about the nature of identities and then to introduce national-income theory with several pages of definitional identities claimed to be the foundation of the theory. A criticism of this practice, and reference to places where it is used, is given in K. Klappholz and E.J. Mishan, 'Identities in Economic Models', *Economica*, May 1962, and R.G. Lipsey in *Essays in Honour of Lord Robbins*, ed. M. Peston and B. Corry (Weidenfeld & Nicolson, 1971).

into the quadrant in which X is positive and Y is negative, while the remaining two functions are not extended beyond the positive quadrant.

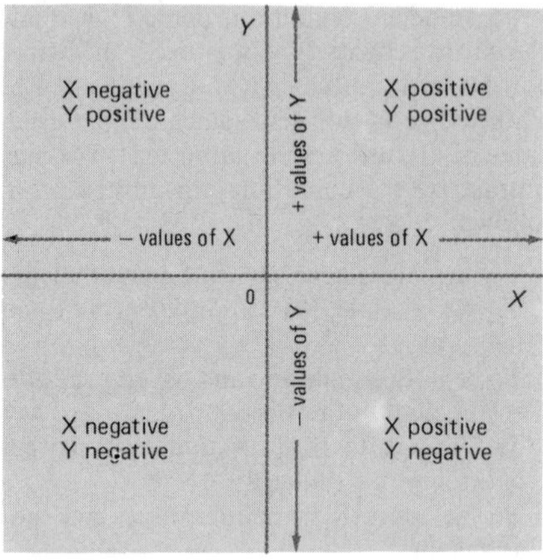

Fig. 2.5 A coordinate graph divides space into quadrants

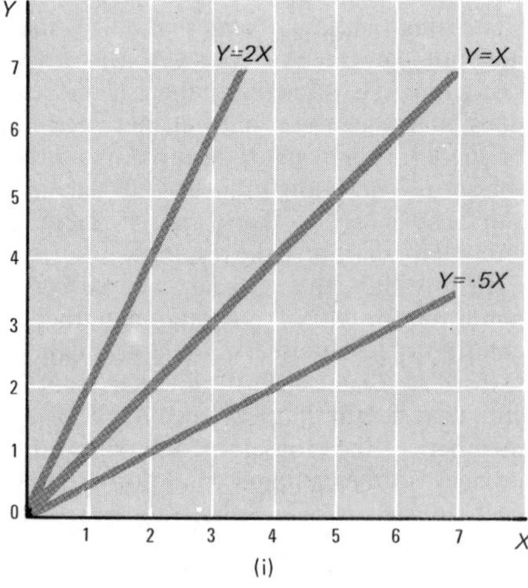

Fig. 2.6 Some linear functions

(8) Straight lines and slopes

Consider the following functional relations:

$$Y = \cdot 5X,$$

$$Y = X,$$

$$Y = 2X.$$

These are graphed in Figure 2.6(i). You will see that they are all lines passing through the origin. This is also obvious from the fact that if we let $X = 0$ in each of the above relations, Y also becomes 0. In the first equation, Y goes up half a unit every time X goes up by one unit; in the second equation, Y goes up one unit every time X goes up one unit; and in the third equation, Y goes up two units every time X goes up one unit.

We now introduce the symbol Δ to indicate a change in a variable. Thus ΔX means the value of the change in X and ΔY means the value of the change in Y. In the first equation if $X = 10$ then Y is 5 and if X goes up to 16, Y goes up to 8. Thus, in this exercise, $\Delta X = 6$ and $\Delta Y = 3$.

Next consider the ratio $\Delta Y/\Delta X$. In the above example it is equal to ·5. In general, it will be noted that, for any change we make in X in the first equation, $\Delta Y/\Delta X$ is always ·5. In the second $\Delta Y/\Delta X$ is unity and in the third the ratio is always 2. In general, if we write $Y = bX$, then, as is proved below, the ratio $\Delta Y/\Delta X$ is always equal to b.

We now define the slope, or gradient, of a straight line to be the ratio of the distance moved up the Y axis to the distance moved along the X axis. We start at the point (X_1, Y_1) and then move to the point (X_2, Y_2). The change in X is $X_2 - X_1$ or ΔX. The change in Y is $Y_2 - Y_1$ or ΔY. Thus the ratio $\Delta Y/\Delta X$ is the slope of the straight line. This

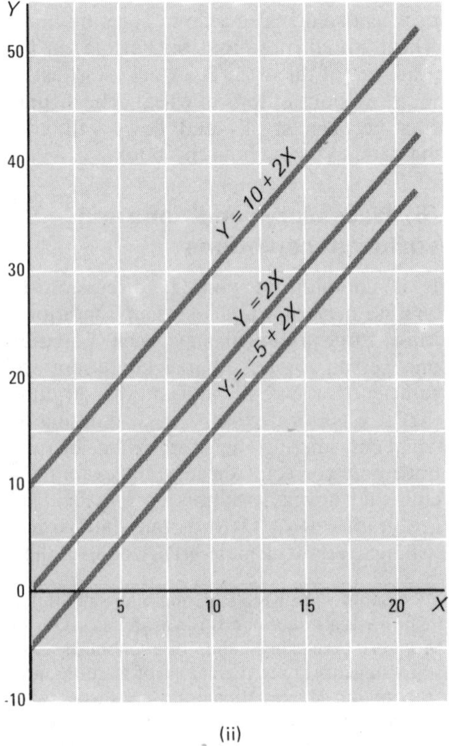

slope tells us the ratio of a change in Y to a change in X.

In trigonometry the tangent of an angle is defined as $\Delta Y/\Delta X$; thus the slope of the line is equal to the tangent of the angle between the line and any line parallel to the X axis. In general, the larger the ratio $\Delta Y/\Delta X$, the steeper the graph of the relation. Figure 2.6(i) shows three lines corresponding to $\Delta Y/\Delta X = 0{\cdot}5$, 1 and 2. Clearly, the steeper the line the larger the change in Y for any given change in X.

Now consider the following equations,

$$Y = 2X$$

$$Y = 10+2X$$

$$Y = -5+2X,$$

which are graphed in Figure 2.6(ii). All three lines are parallel. In other words, they have the same slope. In all three $\Delta Y/\Delta X$ is equal to 2. Clearly, the addition of a (positive or negative) constant does not affect the slope of the line. This slope is influenced only by the number attached to X.

In general, we may write the equation of a straight line as

$$Y = a+bX.$$

By inserting two values of X, say X_1 and X_2, and finding the corresponding Ys, we get

$$Y_1 = a+bX_1$$

and

$$Y_2 = a+bX_2,$$

and, by subtracting the first equation from the second,

$$Y_2 - Y_1 = b(X_2 - X_1)$$

or

$$\Delta Y = b\Delta X$$

$$\Delta Y/\Delta X = b.$$

The constant a disappears when we subtract and so does not influence the slope of the line. What the constant does is to shift the line upward or downward parallel to itself.

(9) Nonlinear functions

All of the examples used so far in this appendix and most of the examples in the text of Chapter 2 concern *linear relations* between two variables. A linear relation is described graphically by a straight line, and algebraically by the equation $Y = a+bX$. It is characteristic of a linear relation that the effect on Y of a given change in X is the same everywhere on the relation.

Many of the relations encountered in economics are *nonlinear*. In these cases the relation will be expressed graphically by a curved line and algebraically by some expression more complex than the one for a straight line. Two common examples are:

$$Y = a+bX+cX^2$$

and

$$Y = a/X^b$$

The first example is a *parabola*. It takes up various positions and shapes depending on the signs and magnitudes of a, b and c. Two examples of parabolas are given in Figures 2.7 and 2.8. The second example becomes a

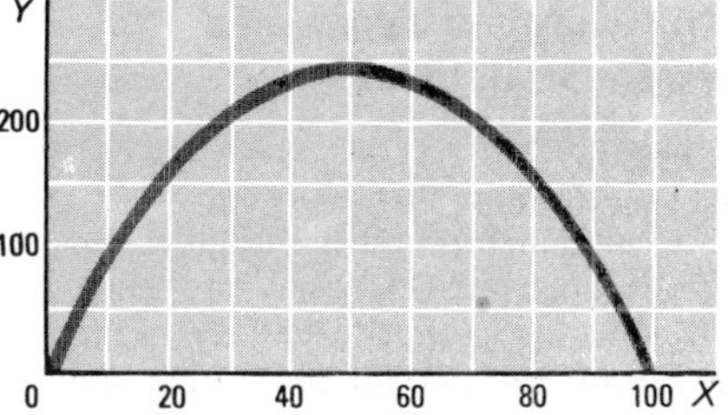

Fig. 2.7 A parabola with a maximum value of Y

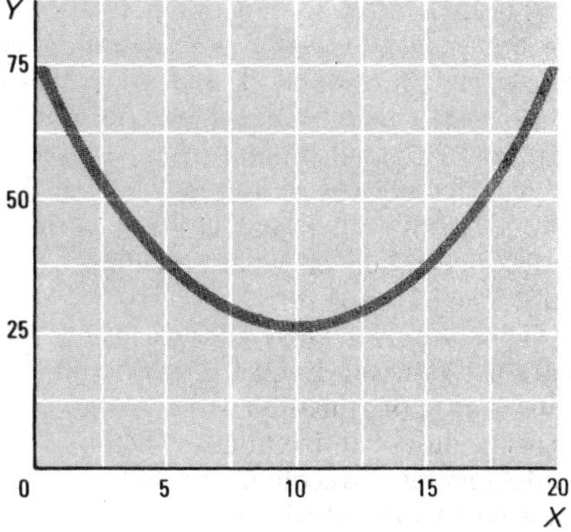

Fig. 2.8 A parabola with minimum value of Y

rectangular hyperbola if we let $b = 1$, and then the position is determined by the value of a. Three examples where $a = 0{\cdot}5$, $2{\cdot}5$ and 5 are shown in Figure 2.9.

There are, of course, many other examples of nonlinear relations between variables. In general, whatever the relation between X and Y, as long as it can be expressed on a graph it can also be expressed by means of an algebraic equation.

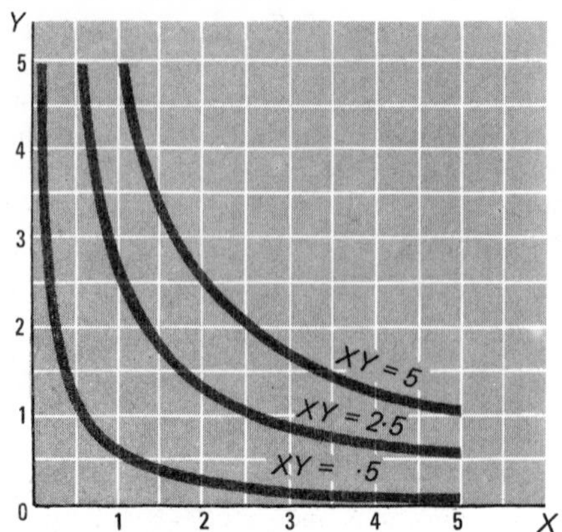

Fig. 2.9 Three rectangular hyperbolae

(10) Marginal values and incremental ratios

Economic theory makes much use of what are called 'marginal' concepts. Marginal cost, marginal revenue, marginal rate of substitution and marginal propensity to consume are a few examples. Marginal means on the margin or border and the concept refers to what would happen if there were a small change from the present position.

Marginals refer to functional relations: the independent variable X is determining the dependent variable Y and we wish to know what would be the change in Y if X changed by a small amount from its present value. The answer is referred to as the marginal value of Y and is given various names depending on what economic variables X and Y stand for.

There are two ways of measuring the marginal value of Y. One is exact and the other is an approximation. Because the exact measure uses differential calculus, introductory texts in economics usually use the approximation which depends only on simple algebra. Students are often justifiably confused because the language of economic theory refers to the exact measure while introductory examples use the approximation. For this reason it is worth explaining each at this time.

Consider the example shown in Figure 2.10 in which a firm's output, Q, is measured on the X axis and the total revenue earned by selling this output, R, is measured on the Y axis. Thus we have the function $R = \mathrm{R}(Q)$. (We shall see later that the graph corresponds to the shape of a monopolist's revenue function, but right now we may take its shape as given.)

The marginal concept that corresponds to this function is *marginal revenue*. It refers to the change in the firm's revenue when sales are altered slightly from their present level. But what do we mean by 'altered slightly'? There are two answers depending on which marginal concept we use.

The approximation to marginal revenue is called the INCREMENTAL RATIO. Let sales in Figure 2.10 be 6, with a corresponding revenue of £70. Now increase sales to 8, so that revenue rises to £100. The increase in sales is 2 and the increase in revenue is £30. Using the Δ notation for changes, we can write this as

$$\Delta R/\Delta Q = £30/2 = £15.$$

Thus incremental revenue is £15 when sales change from 6 to 8. This means that sales are increasing at an average rate of £15 *per unit of commodity sold* over the range from 6 to 8 units. We may call this the marginal revenue

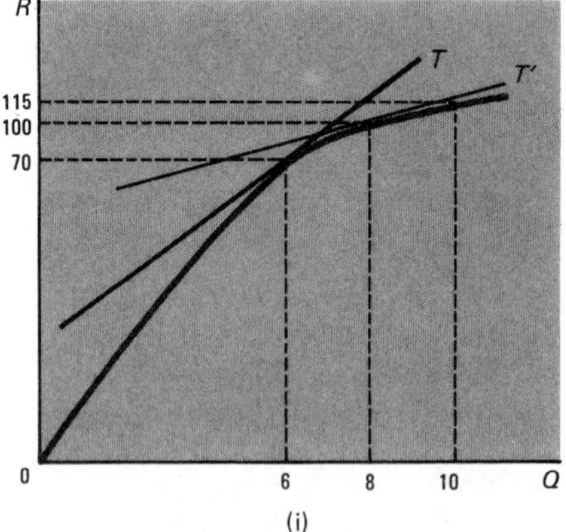

Fig. 2.10(i) The revenue function of a firm

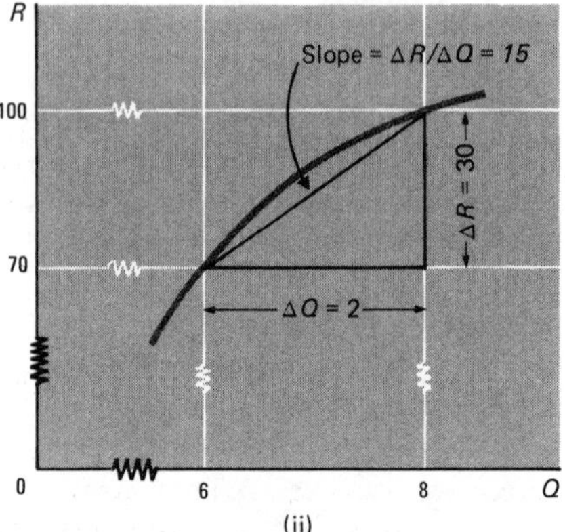

Fig. 2.10(ii) An enlargement of a section of the firm's revenue function

at 6 units of output but, as we shall see, it is only an approximation to the true marginal revenue at that output.

Graphically, incremental revenue is the slope of the line joining the two points in question. In this case they are the two points on the revenue function corresponding to outputs of 6 and 8. This is shown in Figure 2.10(ii), which is an enlargement of the relevant section of the function graphed in 2.10(i). Look at the small triangle created by these points. Its base is 2 units long and its vertical side is 30 units in height. The slope of the hypotenuse of the triangle is $30/2 = 15$, which is the incremental revenue. Visually it is clear that this slope tells us the gradient or steepness of the revenue function over the range from $Q = 6$ to $Q = 8$. It thus tells us how fast revenue is changing as output changes over that range of Q.

Incremental revenue will be different at different points on the function. For example, when output goes from 8 to 10, revenue goes from 100 to 115 and this gives us an incremental revenue of

$$\Delta R/\Delta Q = £15/2 = £7{\cdot}50.$$

This calculation confirms what visual inspection of the figure suggests: the larger is output (at least over the ranges graphed in the figure), the lower is the response of revenue to further increases in output.

The incremental ratio is an approximation to the true marginal concept which is based on the derivative of differential calculus. The derivative is symbolized in general by $\mathrm{d}Y/\mathrm{d}X$, and in the case of the function $R = R(Q)$, by $\mathrm{d}R/\mathrm{d}Q$. It measures the tendency for R to change as Q changes *at a precise point on the curve.* (Whereas the incremental ratio measures the average tendency *over a range of the curve.*) The value of the derivative is given by the slope of the tangent to the point on the function in which we are interested. Thus 'true' marginal revenue at 6 units of output is given by the slope of the tangent, T, to the curve at that point. This slope measures the tendency for R to change *per unit change in* Q at the precise value at which it is evaluated (i.e., the point on the function at which the tangent is drawn).[1]

We saw that the incremental ratio declined as we measured it from larger and larger values of Q. It should be visually obvious that this is also true for marginal revenue: the slope of the tangent to the function will be smaller the larger is the value of Q at which the tangent is taken. Two examples are shown in Figure 2.10(i); one, T, for $Q = 6$ and the other, T', for $Q = 8$.

Now try measuring the incremental ratio starting at 6 units of output but for smaller and smaller changes in output. Instead of going from 6 to 8, go, for example, from 6 to 7. This brings the two points in question closer together and, in the present case, it steepens the slope of the line joining them. It is visually clear in the present example that as ΔQ is made smaller and smaller, the slope of the line corresponding to the incremental ratio starting from $Q = 6$ gets closer and closer to the slope of the tangent corresponding to the true marginal value evaluated at $Q = 6$.

Let us now state our conclusions in general for the function $Y = Y(X)$.

(1) The marginal value of Y at some initial value of X is the rate of change of Y per unit change in X as X changes from its initial value.

(2) The marginal value is given by the slope of the tangent to the curve graphing the function at the point corresponding to the initial value of X.

(3) The incremental ratio $\Delta Y/\Delta X$ measures the average change in Y per unit change in X over a range of the function starting from the initial value of X.

(4) As the range of measurement of the incremental ratio is reduced (i.e., as ΔX gets smaller and smaller), the value of the incremental ratio eventually approaches the true marginal value of Y. Thus the incremental ratio may be regarded as an approximation to the true marginal value, the degree of approximation improving as ΔX gets very small.[2]

[1] The text discussion refers to functions of a single variable. Where Y is a function of more than one variable, $X_1, \ldots, X_n$, then the marginal concept refers to a *partial* derivative: $\partial Y/\partial X_1$ etc. There is then a marginal value of Y with respect to variations in *each* of the independent variables, $X_1, \ldots, X_n$.

[2] This footnote need only concern those who already know some calculus. We must be careful how we state conclusion (4) since on a wavy function the degree of approximation may alternately improve and worsen as ΔX gets smaller, but, providing the conditions for a derivative to exist are met, there *must* be a small neighbourhood around the point in question within which the degree of approximation improves as ΔX gets smaller, with the 'error' going to zero as ΔX goes to zero.

(11) Maximum and minimum values

Consider the function

$$Y = 10X - 0{\cdot}1X^2,$$

which is plotted in Figure 2.7. Y at first increases as X increases, but after a while Y begins to fall as X goes on rising. We say that Y rises to a *maximum*, which is reached in this case when $X = 50$. Until $X = 50$, Y is rising as X rises, but after $X = 50$, Y is falling as X rises. Thus Y reaches a maximum value of 250 when X is 50.

A great deal of economic theory is based on the idea of finding a maximum (or a minimum) value. Since Y is a function of X, we speak of *maximizing the value of the function*, and by this we mean that we wish to find the value of X (50 in this case) for which the value of Y is at a maximum (250 in this case).

Now consider the function

$$Y = 75 - 10X + 0{\cdot}5X^2,$$

which is graphed in Figure 2.8. In this case, the value of Y falls at first while X increases, reaches a *minimum*, and then rises as X goes on increasing. In this case, Y reaches a minimum value of 25 when X is 10. Here we speak of *minimizing the value of the function*, by which we mean finding the value of X for which the value of Y is at a minimum.

(12) Functions of more than one variable

In most of the examples used so far Y has been a function of only one variable, X. In many cases, however, the dependent variable is a function of more than one independent variable. The demand for a good might depend, for example, on the price of that good, on the prices of a number of competing products, on the prices of products used in conjunction with the product with which we are concerned, and on consumers' incomes.

When we wish to denote the dependence of Y on several variables, say, V, W and X, we write $Y = Y(V, W, X)$, which is read Y is a function of V, W and X.

In mathematics and in economics we often wish to discover what happens to Y as X varies, assuming meanwhile that the other factors that influence X are held constant at some stated level. The result is often phrased 'Y varies in such and such a way with X *other things being equal*' or 'Y varies with X in such and such a way *ceteris paribus*'.

Students who do not know mathematics are often disturbed by the frequent use in economics of arguments that depend on the qualification 'other things being equal' (for which we often use the Latin phrase *ceteris paribus*). Such arguments are not peculiar to economics. They are used successfully in all branches of science and there is an elaborate set of mathematical techniques available to handle them.

When mathematicians wish to know how Y is changing as X changes when other factors that influence Y are held constant, they calculate what is called the *partial derivative of Y with respect to X*. This is written symbolically as $\partial Y/\partial X$. We cannot enter here into a discussion of how this expression is calculated. We only wish to note that finding $\partial Y/\partial X$ is a well-recognized and very common mathematical operation, and the answer tells us approximately how Y is affected by small variations in X *when all other relevant factors are held constant*.

3

The tools of statistical analysis

If you look once again at Figure 1.1 on page 16 you will see that the second of the two triangles represents the process of statistical analysis. This is used in economics for two related purposes: first, to test the predictions of our theories against evidence, and, second, to estimate the magnitude of relations among variables. For example, statistical analysis has been used repeatedly to test the prediction that when the price of any product falls people will wish to buy more of it. Statistical analysis has also been used to measure the quantitative relations between the prices of particular products and the amounts bought. This allows economists to reach such conclusions as 'A 1 per cent fall in the price of wheat will lead to an increase in purchases of $\frac{1}{4}$ of 1 per cent, while a 1 per cent fall in the price of dairy cream will lead to a 2 per cent increase in purchases.' In the first case we see statistical analysis being used to test a general prediction of theory; in the second case we see statistics being used to give us precise numerical estimates of *how much* one variable changes in response to changes in a related variable.

An understanding of the intricacies of statistical analysis when used for either of these purposes can be gained only from a detailed study of statistical theory. In this chapter we take a brief look at how statistical analysis is used in economics. Because this is a book about economic theory, we concentrate on the use of statistics in testing theories. Many times throughout the book, however, we shall refer to quantitative statistical estimates of the relations among economic variables.

Kinds of sciences

In order to determine whether or not they do give us predictions that are correct within some acceptable margin of error, we must test our theories against the evidence of what actually happens in the economy. Testing theories against observations is not a task that is easily accomplished (or briefly described). As a first step in discussing the testing of theories, we must distinguish between laboratory and non-laboratory methods.

Laboratory sciences

In some sciences, it is possible to obtain all necessary observations from controlled experiments made under laboratory conditions. In such experiments, we hold constant all the factors that are thought to affect the outcome of the process being studied. Then we vary these factors one by one while we observe the influence that each variation appears to have on the outcome of the experiment.

Suppose, for example, we have a theory that predicts that the rate at which a substance burns is a function of the chemical properties of that substance and the rate at which oxygen is made available during the process of combustion. To test this theory, we can take a number of identical pieces of some substance and burn them, varying the amount of oxygen made available in each case. This allows us to see how combustion varies with the quantity of oxygen used. We can then take a number of substances with different chemical compositions and burn them, using identical amounts of oxygen. This allows us to see how combustion varies with chemical composition.

In such an experiment, we never have to use data that are generated when both chemical composition and the quantity of oxygen are varying simultaneously. Laboratory conditions are used to hold other things constant and to produce data for situations in which factors are varied one at a time.

Non-laboratory sciences

In some sciences we cannot isolate factors one at a time in laboratory experiments. In these sciences observations are still used to establish relationships and to test theories, but such observations appear in a relatively complex form, because several things are usually varying at the same time.

Consider, for example, the hypothesis that one's health as an adult depends upon one's diet as a child. Clearly, all sorts of other factors affect the health of adults: heredity, conditions of childhood other than nutrition, and various aspects of adult environment. There is no possible way to examine this hypothesis in the manner of a controlled experiment, for we are unlikely to be able to find a group of adults whose diet as children varied but for whom all other influences affecting health were the same. Should we conclude that the hypothesis cannot be tested because other facts cannot be held constant? If we did, we would be denying the possibility of many advances in medicine, biology and other sciences concerned with humans that have actually been made during the last hundred years. Testing is harder when one cannot use laboratory methods, but, fortunately, it is still possible.

In a situation in which many things are varying at once, we must be careful in our use of data. If we study only two people and find that the one with the better nutritional standards during his youth has the poorer adult health record, this would not disprove the hypothesis that a good diet is a factor leading to better health. It might well be that some other factor exerted an overwhelming influence on these two individuals. The less healthy man may have lived most of his adult life in a disease-ridden area of the tropics, whereas the more healthy may have lived in a relatively congenial northern climate. Clearly, a single exception does not disprove the hypothesis of a relation between two things as long as we admit that other factors can also influence the outcome.[1]

[1] Note how often in ordinary conversation a person advances a possible relation (e.g., between education and some facet of character), while someone else will 'refute' this theory by citing a single counter-example (e.g., 'my friend went to that school and did not turn out like that'). It is a commonplace in everyday conversation to dismiss an hypothesis with some such remark as 'Oh, that's just a generalization.' All interesting hypotheses are generalizations and it will always be possible to notice some real or apparent exceptions. What we need to know is whether or not the mass of evidence supports the hypothesis as a statement of a general tendency for two or more things to be related to each other. This issue can never be settled one way or the other by the casual quoting of a few bits of evidence that just happen to be readily available.

It is rarely, if ever, possible to conduct controlled experiments with the economy. Thus economics must be a non-laboratory science. A mass of data is, however, being generated continually by the economy. Every day, for example, consumers are comparing prices and deciding what to buy; firms are comparing prices and deciding what to produce and offer for sale; and governments are intervening with taxes, subsidies and direct controls. All of these acts can be observed and recorded. These data then provide the empirical observations against which economic theories can be tested. Given the complexity of data generated under non-experimental conditions, casual observation is not likely to be sufficient for testing economic hypotheses. Modern statistical analysis was developed to test hypotheses rigorously in situations in which many things were varying at once. Its early development was mainly concerned with experiments in biology and agriculture. Later, however, ECONOMETRICS grew up as a special branch of statistics, concerned to develop techniques that would allow rigorous testing of hypotheses against data generated in the circumstances in which economic events typically occur.

Although economics must be a non-laboratory science, the masses of data produced by the economy under continually changing circumstances does provide evidence against which economic theories may be tested.

An example of the statistical testing of economic theories

Consider the hypothesis that one of the important factors influencing the purchase of each commodity is the incomes of consumers. We shall examine one test of this hypothesis made some years ago in the United States – relating incomes and the demand for beef. To conduct the test the US department of Agriculture gathered data for households, rather than for individual consumers. A household is a group of individuals who live under the same roof and make joint consumption decisions.

Let us imagine ourselves in the place of the investigators setting out to make this test. We realize that we need to know each household's income and the amount of beef that it purchased. In this case it is obvious that it would be prohibitively expensive to enumerate all the individual households in the American population, so we must take a smaller number of observations (called a *sample*) and hope that it is typical of all US households.[1]

Table 3.1 Beef consumption and income for three US households

Household	Annual household income (dollars)	Average weekly beef consumption (pounds)
1	4,500	5·10
2	5,500	5·05
3	6,500	4·93

The sample

We start by observing the three households whose data are recorded in Table 3.1. These data may lead us to wonder if the hypothesis is wrong, but, before we jump to

[1] The data for this example are adapted from Daniel B. Suits, *Statistics: An Introduction to Quantitative Economic Research* (Rand McNally, 1963), p. 169.

that conclusion, we should consider the possibility that we may have selected three households that are not typical of all the households in the country. The expenditure on food is undoubtedly influenced by factors other than income and possibly these other factors just happen to be dominant in the three cases selected.

To avoid this possibility, we select a large number of households in order to reduce the chances of consistently picking up untypical ones. Suppose someone does this by taking 100 households from friends and acquaintances. A statistician points out, however, that our new group is a very *biased sample*, for it contains households from only a limited geographical area, probably with only a limited occupational range, and possibly with very similar incomes. It is unlikely that this sample of households will be representative of all households in the United States, which is the group being investigated.

The statistician suggests taking a *random sample* of households. A random sample is one chosen according to a rigidly defined set of conditions that guarantees, among other things, that every household in which we are interested has an equal chance of being selected. Choosing our sample in a random fashion has two important consequences. First, it makes it likely that our sample will be fairly representative of all households, and, second, it allows us to calculate just how likely it is that our sample is unrepresentative in any given aspect by any stated amount. The reason for this second result is that our sample was chosen by chance, and chance events are predictable.

That chance events are predictable may sound surprising. But if you pick a card from a deck of ordinary playing cards, how likely is it that you will pick a heart? an ace? an ace of hearts? You play a game in which you pick a card and win if it is a heart and lose if it is anything else; a friend offers you £5 if you win against £1 if you lose. Who will make money if the game is played a large number of times? The same game is played again, but you get £3 if you win and pay £1 if you lose. Now who will make money over a large number of draws? If you know the answers to these questions, you know that chance events are in some sense predictable.

How does this measurability of chance events apply to our present problem? If we select our households by pure chance we can know the probability of selecting an unrepresentative sample. If, for example, the average income of all American households is $15,000, the most likely single result is that the average income of our random sample will also be $15,000, but we should not be very surprised if it were $14,950 or even $16,000. The further away is the average income of our sample from the true value for all households, the more unrepresentative is our sample.

The predictability of chance events allows us to calculate the probability that the average value of a variable in a random sample will differ by any stated amount from the true average value of the same variable in the whole population. In general, the bigger the deviation the less likely it is to occur in a truly random sample.

The analysis of the data

Once we have chosen our random sample – in the present case it consists of 4,827 households – we collect information from each household on its income and its beef purchases.

The next step is to plot the data in such a way that we can inspect it visually. To do this we use a SCATTER DIAGRAM.[1] We measure household income along the horizontal axis and expenditure on beef along the vertical one. For each household we place a dot on the graph indicating its annual income and the amount of beef it purchases per week. A scatter diagram with 4,827 dots would, however, be unintelligible when reduced to the size of a printed page. We have, therefore, drawn the diagram in Figure 3.1 by taking a 5 per cent random sample of the 4,827 households. Each of these 241 dots is to be thought of as representing 20 of the households in our original sample.

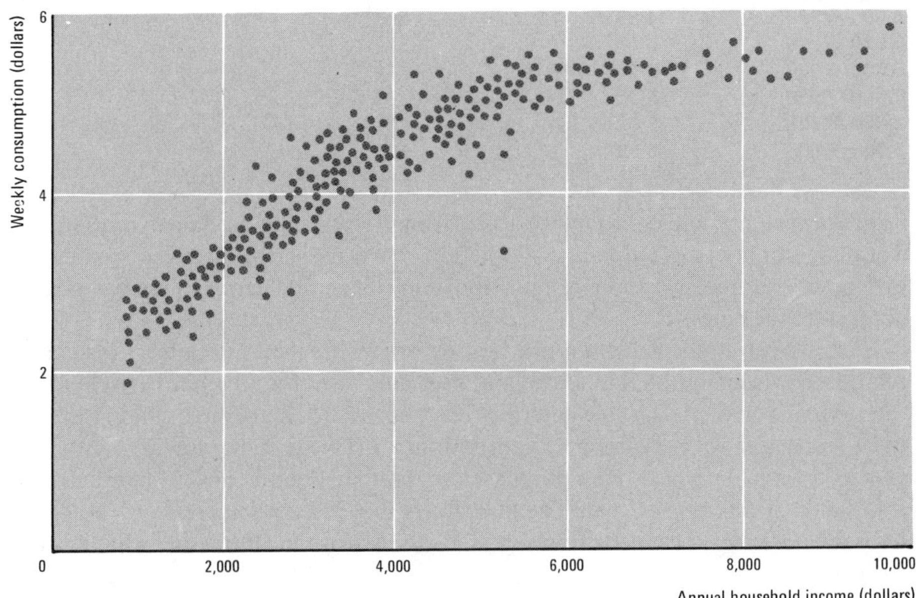

Fig. 3.1 A scatter diagram showing income and expenditure on beef of a random sample of American households.

The scatter diagram suggests a strong tendency that the higher a household's income, the greater its purchases of beef. To use the language introduced in Chapter 2 (page 20), it suggests that beef purchases are an increasing function of household income. The relationship is not deterministic, however, for there is considerable variation in beef purchases that cannot be associated with variations in incomes. These 'unexplained variations' in beef purchases occur for two main reasons: first, there are factors other than income that influence beef purchases; second, there will inevitably be some errors in our measurements (e.g., a household might have incorrectly recorded its beef purchases).

In order to make the data somewhat more manageable, we may gather them into groups. To obtain Table 3.2, the households are divided into 10 groups according to income and the average beef consumption for each income group is calculated. This reduces a mass of 4,827 observations to a mere 10 observations. At the loss of some considerable amount of detail, the table makes clearer the general tendency for beef purchases to rise with income.

[1] The two major techniques for graphing economic data, scatter diagrams and time series charts, are further discussed in the Appendix to this chapter.

Table 3.2 Beef consumption and income for a sample of US households

Average household income ($)	Average weekly beef consumption (pounds)	Number of families
0–999	2·13	532
1,000–1,999	2·82	647
2,000–2,999	3·70	692
3,000–3,999	4·25	867
4,000–4,999	4·86	865
5,000–5,999	5·16	513
6,000–6,999	5·20	371
7,000–7,999	5·30	159
8,000–8,999	5·52	121
9,000–9,999	5·90	60

The next step would be to apply statistical analysis to all of the data in our sample. The details of how this is done must be left to courses in statistics and econometrics, but we can outline here three of the important things that can be done by such an analysis of the data.

First, we can fit to the data a line that represents the best estimate of the actual relation between household income and beef purchases for all 4,827 households in our original sample.[1] This line describes the tendency for higher household incomes to be associated with greater beef consumption. (The equation of a line so fitted is $B = 2{\cdot}35 + 0{\cdot}47Y$, where B is purchases of beef in pounds and Y is income in thousands of dollars per year. The line shows that for every increase of $1,000 in household income, beef consumption tends to increase by about half a pound per week.)

Second, we can obtain a measure of the percentage of the variations in household expenditure on beef that can be accounted for by variations in household income. This is the commonly encountered r^2, which is called the *coefficient of determination.* r^2 can take on any value between zero and unity. If the relationship were deterministic, r^2 would be unity. This would indicate that all of the variations in beef purchases were associated with variations in income. If there were no relationship, r^2 would be zero. If there were some less-than-perfect relationship, r^2 would be greater than zero but less than unity. The larger r^2, the larger the proportion of the variations in beef purchases that are associated with variations in income. Loosely speaking, r^2 is a measure of the degree of scatter of the individual observations around the line that describes the average relation between beef purchases and income: if all points lie on the line, r^2 is unity, while the more diffuse the scatter of points around the line, the weaker the relation and the closer to zero the value of r^2.

Third, we can apply a 'significance test'. This allows us to discover the chances that the relation we have discovered has arisen only because our sample is not representative of all households in the United States. In the present case, there is less than one chance in one million that we could have made the observations that we did if, in fact, there were no positive relation between income and beef purchases for all

[1] Before we fit the line, we must decide if the relation is best described by a straight line or a curve. Fortunately there are tests that allow us to tell if we made an error in thinking that the relation was linear when it really was curvilinear. In the example considered here, the correct relation is slightly curvilinear, but a straight line is a reasonable approximation to the correct relation over the range of most of the data.

US households. Thus we can have a great deal of confidence in the hypothesis that these two variables, beef purchases and household income, are in fact positively related in the United States.

The influence of additional variables

It is clear from the scatter diagram that we cannot account for *all* of the variation in households' purchases of beef by observed variations in household income. We may wish to look for some other factor that might also exert a systematic influence on beef expenditure. What could make one household with an income of $6,000 buy 20 per cent more beef than another household with the same income? One possible factor is that households in different parts of the country faced different prices of beef. Of course, there will be many other factors, such as size of family and religion, but we shall select price as our second factor for the purpose of illustration. Assume that the survey also collected data on the prices of various cuts of beef in each city or town from which a household in the sample bought its meat. These data were then used to calculate the average price of beef facing households in each area.

We now have three observations for each one of our 4,827 households – their annual income, their weekly purchases of beef, and the average price of the beef that they purchase. How should we handle these data? Unfortunately, our scatter-diagram technique has now let us down, since we cannot easily show the relation among three things on a two-dimensional graph. We can, however, group the data in a fashion similar to the way they were grouped in Table 3.2. This time we have two variables that are thought to influence beef consumption, and we have to *cross-classify* the data. To do this we first classify households into five income groups, each with a spread of $2,000.[1] We then subdivide the households in each income group according to the price they paid for their beef. This gives us twenty groups of households. For each we calculate the average purchases of beef and enter it in the appropriate cell of Table 3.3. For example, households that had an income between

Table 3.3 Average household purchases of beef in pounds per week, classified by household income and the average purchase price of beef

Annual household income ($)	Average price of beef per pound			
	$0·80–0·99	$1·00–1·19	$1·20–1·39	$1·40–1·59
0–1,999	2·65	2·59	2·51	2·43
2,000–3,999	4·14	4·05	3·94	3·88
4,000–5,999	5·11	5·00	4·97	4·84
6,000–7,999	5·35	5·29	5·19	5·07
8,000–9,999	5·79	5·77	5·60	5·53

$6,000 and $7,999 and who faced a price of beef between $0·80 and $0·99 a pound bought an average of 5·35 pounds of beef a week, while those households in the same income group who faced a price between $1·40 and $1·59 bought an average of only 5·07 pounds per week.

[1] To prevent the table from becoming too large, we have grouped households into income groups of $2,000 rather than $1,000, as was done in Table 3.2; but this is only a matter of convenience, and the classification can be made as detailed as is required for any particular purpose.

Each row of this table exhibits the effect of *price* on the purchases of beef for a given level of income. Reading across the second row, for example, we see that households with incomes between \$2,000 and \$3,999 bought an average of 4·14 pounds of beef when the price was between 80 and 99¢ per pound, 4·05 pounds when the price was between \$1 and \$1·19, and so on. Each column of the table shows the effect of *income* on purchases of beef in a given price range. For instance, the last column shows how beef purchases varied with income for those households that were subject to a very high average price of beef. When these prices were faced, purchases ranged from 2·43 pounds for the group with the lowest income to 5·53 for the one with the highest income.

It should be clear that this device of cross-classification manages to catch observationally much of the idea of *holding other things constant* that is sometimes thought to be possible only in laboratory sciences.[1] Reading across any row, we are holding income constant within a specified range, which can be made smaller by making the classification finer, and varying price; reading down any column, we are holding price constant within a specified range and varying income.

If we wish to go further than this, we need to apply once again the rigorous tools of statistical analysis. When, as in the present case, we have more than one explanatory variable, we use a technique called *multiple regression analysis*. Just as in the case of one explanatory variable, we can do three important things with this tool. First, we can estimate the numerical relation between weekly beef purchases, on the one hand, and price and income, on the other. Second, it allows us to measure the proportion of the total variation in beef purchases that can be explained by associating it with variations both in income and in price. Finally, it permits us to estimate how likely it is that the relations we have found in our sample are the result of chance rather than an underlying relationship for all US households. Chance enters because we might by bad luck have chosen an unrepresentative sample of households.

Testing and measurement

Statistical techniques help us to judge the probability that any particular theory is false. This is an extremely valuable thing to be able to do. What statistical techniques cannot do is *prove* with certainty that an hypothesis is either true or false. We have already discussed this matter in Chapter 1. We now summarize the earlier discussion and then take it a step further.

Can we prove that an hypothesis is true?

Most hypotheses in economics are what may be called universal hypotheses. They say that, whenever certain specified conditions are fulfilled, cause *X* will always produce effect *Y*. We have already pointed out that universal hypotheses cannot be proved to be correct because we can make only a finite number of actual observations and we can never rule out the possibility that we shall in the future make a large number of observations that conflict with the theory. (See pp. 14–15.)

[1] See the discussions on page 36, 'Functions of More than One Variable'.

Can we prove that an hypothesis is false?

By the same token, we cannot get a categorical disproof of an hypothesis. Consider the hypothesis '*Most* crows are black'. We observe 50 crows; 49 are grey and only one is black. Have we disproved the hypothesis? The answer is, no, for it is *possible* that this was just bad luck, and if we could observe all the crows in the world it would indeed prove to be the case that most are black.

What, then, is required if we are to be able to refute any hypothesis? First, the hypothesis must admit of no exceptions: it must say, for example, '*All* crows are black.' Using the language introduced in Chapter 1, it must be a deterministic, not a statistical hypothesis. (Recall that a deterministic hypothesis admits of no exceptions while a statistical hypothesis deals in general tendencies.) Second, we must be certain that any apparently refuting observations are not mistaken. The observation of 49 black crows and one grey refutes the hypothesis that *all* crows are black only if we are sure that we genuinely saw a grey crow. But are we sure that the odd bird really was a crow? Are we sure that what looked like a grey crow was not a dusty black crow?[1] Errors in observation may always be present. For this reason, an hypothesis cannot be refuted on the basis of a single conflicting observation, and indeed it can never be categorically refuted, no matter how many conflicting observations we make. If we observe 49 grey crows and only one black one, our faith in the hypothesis that all crows are black may well be shaken and as a practical measure we may choose to abandon the hypothesis (see below). We can never be certain, however, that all 49 cases were not due to errors of observation[2] and had we persisted we might have ended up with 999,951 black crows and 49 grey ones. (This would make the hypothesis look pretty good, since a measurement error on 0·005 per cent of our cases might not seem at all improbable.)

Rules for decision-taking

We have seen that in general we can neither prove nor refute an hypothesis conclusively, no matter how many observations we make.[3] Nonetheless, we have to make decisions and act as if some hypotheses were refuted (i.e., we have to reject them) and we have to act as if some hypotheses were proved (i.e., we have to accept

[1] Even if we satisfy ourselves fully that we saw a grey crow, future generations may not accept our evidence unless they go on observing the occasional grey crow. After all we no longer accept the mass of well-documented evidence accumulated several centuries ago on the existence and power of witches, even though it fully satisfied most contemporary observers. Clearly the existence of observational errors on a vast scale has been shown to be possible even though it may not be frequent.

[2] It has been said that there is hardly an accepted theory of physics that is not 'refuted' daily by some schoolboy operating in a school laboratory somewhere in the country. Such isolated 'refutations' do not worry physicists, although they would be worried if some day almost every schoolboy in the country should begin to make observations that appeared to refute some accepted theory.

[3] Advanced students may notice that the above differs from the view expressed by Professor Popper in *The Logic of Scientific Discovery* (Hutchinson, 1959). The difference arises from the fact that I take all hypotheses about observable events to be statistical ones because of the universal existence of errors of observation. We do of course make arbitrary decisions to reject statistical hypotheses but so also do we make arbitrary decisions to accept them. These rules of thumb for practical decision-taking have nothing to do with the methodological questions of whether any hypothesis can be conclusively refuted and whether any hypothesis can be conclusively proved. My answer to both questions is no. Those who are not convinced by my arguments may proceed with the text as long as they are prepared to accept that most hypotheses in economics are statistical hypotheses.

them). Such decisions are always subject to error, but by using statistical analysis we can control the possibility of making errors even if we cannot eliminate it. This is an extremely valuable thing to be able to do. The method of control is to choose the risk we are willing to take of rejecting an hypothesis if it is in fact correct. Conventionally, we use a cut-off point of 5 per cent or 1 per cent. If we use the 5 per cent cut-off point, we say that we will regard an hypothesis as rejected if there exists less than one chance in twenty that we could have made the set of observations we actually made if the hypothesis were correct. Using the 1 per cent decision rule we give the hypothesis a greater measure of reasonable doubt: we reject hypotheses only if there is less than one chance in one hundred that the observations we made could have occurred if the hypothesis were true.

Consider an example. When studying expenditure on beef our hypothesis might have been that the expenditure on beef of US households *falls* as their income rises. We would then ask what the chances were of making the observations shown in Figure 3.1 if the hypothesis were correct. There is always some chance that our sample was untypical of all US households or that the relationship appears as it is because of measurement errors. If we calculate (using the tools taught in courses on statistics) that there is *less* than one chance in 100 of making the observations in Figure 3.1, if the hypothesized relation that beef purchases fall as income rises actually holds for all US households, then we would abandon the hypothesis and for practical purposes regard it as refuted.

When action must be taken, some such rule of thumb is necessary. But it is important to understand, first, that we can never be certain that we are right in rejecting a statistical hypothesis and, second, that there is nothing magical about our arbitrary cut-off points. The cut-off point is a device used because some decision has to be made. Notice also that decisions can always be reversed should new evidence come to light.

Judging among hypotheses

Older statistical methodology tended to emphasize the testing of theories one at a time. As it has become clearer that theories in economics could be neither confirmed nor refuted with finality, the newer methodology has tended to emphasize the use of statistical analysis to choose among two or more competing theories. Although we can never be absolutely sure that one is right and the other is wrong, we can hope to show that the data favours one over the other in the sense that there is a greater chance that we would have observed what we did observe if the causal forces were those described by theory A rather than those described by theory B. To make such tests we must first find out where theories A and B make predictions that conflict with each other. Theory A might for example predict a close relation between variables X and Y because, according to it, X causes Y; theory B might predict no strong relation between the two variables because, according to it, X has no effect on Y one way or the other. The empirical relation between X and Y can then be studied and conclusions reached about the probability that what we saw could have happened if theory A were correct or if theory B were correct.

Quantitative measurement of economic relations

So far we have considered whether certain observations support certain general hypotheses. The actual data do, for example, support the hypothesis that households' expenditures on beef increase as their incomes increase. This, however, is not enough. It is important to quantify such qualitative statements. In this case, we should like to be able to say that American household expenditure on beef increases by some definite amount for every $1·00 that household income increases.[1]

Economic theories are seldom of much use until we are able to give quantitative magnitudes to our relations. For estimating such magnitudes, our common sense and intuitions do not get us very far. Common sense might well have suggested that expenditure on beef would rise rather than fall as income rose, but only careful observation is going to help us to decide *by how much* it typically rises.

One of the major uses of statistical analysis is to help us to quantify our relations. In practice, we can use actual observations both to test the hypothesis that two things are related and to estimate the numerical values of the function describing those relations that do exist.

One of the major uses of statistical analysis is to help us to quantify the general relations suggested by theory. In practice, we can use actual observations both to test the hypothesis that two things are related and to estimate the numerical values of the function describing those relations that do exist.

Sometimes a statistical test of an hypothesis suggests a new hypothesis that 'fits the facts' better than the previous one. You should look back to Figure 1.1 on page 16 once again, this time to see where such new hypotheses enter the picture.[2]

Although there can never be absolute finality in the testing of economic hypotheses, statistical analysis can be used first to establish the probability that we would have seen what we did see if one theory of the operative causal forces was correct; secondly to establish the balance of probabilities between two competing theories; and thirdly to measure the quantitative relations between variables that theory suggests are related.

Words of warning

In the first three chapters of this book I have made a case that economics can be a scientific enquiry. Some words of caution are now in order.

There are major differences among the various sciences. Because of these, methods that work well in one science may not be suitable in another. In particular, what works in physics, the queen of sciences, may not work well in a social science such as economics. What unites all sciences, however, is the explanation and prediction of observed phenomena. The successes and failures of all sciences are judged by their abilities to further these objectives.

Because this is not a text-book in economic statistics, the problems involved in collecting reliable observations, or 'facts', against which to judge our theories, are not stressed.[3] Such problems can be formidable, and there is always the danger of

[1] The actual quantitative relation is somewhat more complex; this simple one is used solely for purposes of illustration.

[2] Hypotheses that originate from data are sometimes called *inductive* hypotheses in contrast to *deductive* ones. But in any science, the sequence of theory and testing is continuous. The question of which came first, theory or observation, is analogous to the debate over the chicken and the egg.

[3] Although I have not stressed it, the question of the reliability of observation is either explicit or implicit in the discussion on pages 11, 14, 20 and 44–5.

rejecting a theory on the basis of mistaken observations. Unreliable observations are all too frequently encountered. It is important to note, however, that if, on the one hand, we think all our observations are totally unreliable, then we have nothing to explain and, hence, no need for any economic theory. If, on the other hand, we believe that we do have observations reliable enough to require explanation, then we must also believe that we have observations reliable enough to provide tests for the predictive powers of our theories.

I have been concerned in this chapter to dispel the common view that economists cannot be scientific in their use of data because they cannot make controlled experiments. The reader should not be left with the view that the statistical tasks described in this chapter are easily accomplished. In fact they are often very difficult, and the pitfalls ready to trap the unwary user of inappropriate statistical procedures are too numerous to mention. Indeed a whole new subject, econometrics, has grown up to amend statistical techniques that were developed for the natural sciences and to develop new ones able to handle the special data problems that occur in economics and other social sciences. To launch into a career in economic or social research without a full knowledge of the field of statistical analysis is to take a severe risk that one's work will be useless or even downright misleading.

Appendix to chapter 3

Graphing economic observations

The popular saying 'The facts speak for themselves' is almost always wrong when there is a large number of facts. Theories are needed to explain how facts are linked together, and summary measures are needed to assist in sorting out what it is that facts do show in relation to theories. The simplest means of providing compact summaries of a large number of observations is through the use of tables and graphs. Graphs play important roles in economics by representing geometrically both observed data and economic theories.

The scatter diagram

The SCATTER DIAGRAM provides a method of graphing any number of observations made on two variables; one variable is measured on each axis and any point on the diagram refers simultaneously to a particular value of each of the variables.

In Chapter 3 data for income and meat purchases for a large number of American households were studied. To show these data on a scatter diagram, income was measured on the horizontal axis and meat purchases on the vertical axis. Any point in the diagram represents a particular income combined with a particular quantity of meat purchased. Thus each household for which there are observations can be represented on the diagram by a dot, the co-ordinates of which indicate the household's income and the amount of beef it purchases.

The scatter diagram is useful because if there is a simple relation between the two variables, it will be apparent to the eye once the data are plotted. Thus in Figure 3.1 (see page 41) meat purchases clearly tend to rise as income rises. It is also apparent that this relation is only approximately linear since, as income rises above \$5,000 a year, beef purchases seem to rise less and less with further equal increases in income. The diagram also gives some idea of the strength of the relation: if income were the only determinant of beef purchases, all of the dots would lie on a single line; as it is, the points are somewhat scattered and particular incomes are often represented by several households, each with different quantities of beef purchased.

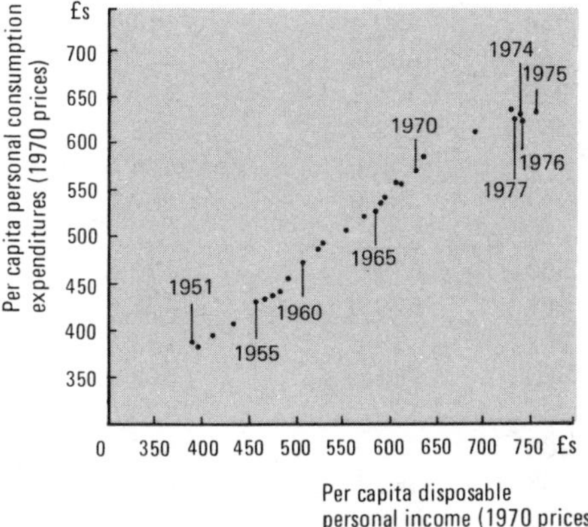

Fig. 3.2 A scatter diagram relating consumption and disposable income

The data used in this example are CROSS-SECTIONAL DATA. The incomes and beef purchases of different households are compared over a single period of time. Scatter diagrams may also be drawn of a number of observations taken on two variables at successive periods of time. Thus, if one wanted to know if there had been any simple relation between personal income and personal consumption in the UK between 1950 and 1977, data would be collected for the levels of personal income and expenditure per capita in each year from 1950–77, as is done in Table 3.4. This information could be plotted on a scatter diagram with income on the *X* axis and consumption on the *Y* axis to discover any systematic relation between the two variables. The data are plotted in Figure 3.2 and do indeed suggest a systematic linear relation. In this exercise a scatter diagram of observations taken over successive periods

Table 3.4 Per capita income and consumption in the UK 1951–77 (1970 prices)

	Disposable personal income (£s)	Personal consumption expenditures (£s)
1951	394·0	387·6
1952	398·8	384·8
1953	416·8	398·4
1954	430·4	414·4
1955	452·8	431·6
1956	461·6	432·8
1957	465·2	438·0
1958	469·6	445·6
1959	490·0	457·2
1960	517·2	472·0
1961	528·0	471·6
1962	529·6	488·8
1963	552·0	508·8
1964	569·2	523·6
1965	579·6	529·2
1966	589·2	536·4
1967	595·6	544·4
1968	604·4	557·6
1969	606·4	555·6
1970	627·6	568·0
1971	642·0	582·4
1972	692·4	614·8
1973	728·8	642·4
1974	745·2	636·4
1975	758·0	639·2
1976	744·8	634·9
1977	734·8	628·0

Source: NIESR

of time has been used. Such data are called TIME-SERIES DATA and plotting them on a scatter diagram involves no new technique: when cross-sectional data are plotted, each point gives the values of two variables for a particular unit (say a household); when time-series data are plotted, each point tells the values of two variables for a particular year.

Time-series graphs

Instead of studying the relation between income and consumption suggested in the previous paragraph, a study of the pattern of the changes in either one of these variables over time could be made. In Figure 3.3 this information is shown for consumption. In the figure, time is one variable, consumption expenditure the other. But time is a very special variable: the order in which successive events happen is important. The year 1965 followed 1964; but they were not two independent and unrelated years. (By way of contrast, two randomly selected households are independent and unrelated.) For this reason it is customary (although this has not been done in Figure 3.3) to draw in the line segments connecting the successive points. A chart such as this figure is called a TIME-SERIES DIAGRAM or, more simply, a time-series: it plots the values of a single variable at successive periods of time. This kind of graph makes it easy to see if the variable being considered has varied in a systematic way over the years or if its behaviour has been more or less erratic.

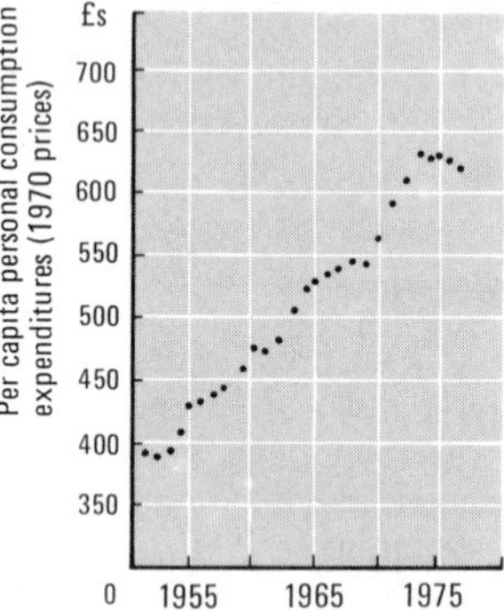

Fig. 3.3 A time-series of consumption expenditures 1950–77

Ratio (logarithmic) scales

Often *proportionate* rather than absolute changes in variables are important. In such cases it is more revealing to use a ratio scale rather than a natural scale. On a NATURAL SCALE the distance between numbers is proportionate to the absolute difference between those numbers. Thus 200 is placed halfway between 100 and 300. On a RATIO SCALE the distance between numbers is proportionate to the absolute difference between their logarithms. Equal distances anywhere on a ratio scale represent equal percentage changes rather than equal absolute changes. On a ratio scale the distance between 100 and 200 is the same as the distance between 200 and 400, between 1,000 and 2,000, and between any two numbers that stand in the ratio 1:2 to each other. For obvious reasons a ratio scale is also called a LOGARITHMIC SCALE.

Table 3.5 Two series

Time period	Series A	Series B
0	£10	£10
1	18	20
2	26	40
3	34	80
4	42	160

Table 3.5 shows two series, one growing at a constant absolute amount of 8 units per period and the other growing at a constant rate of 100 per cent per period. In Figure 3.4 the series are plotted first on a natural scale and then on a ratio scale. Series A, which grows at a constant absolute amount, is a straight line on a natural scale but a curve of ever-decreasing slope on a ratio scale, because the same absolute growth is decreasing percentage growth. Series B, which grows at a rising absolute but a constant percentage rate, is upward-bending on a natural scale but is a straight line on a ratio scale. The natural scale makes it easy for the eye to judge absolute variations, and the logarithmic scale makes it easy for the eye to judge proportionate variations.[1]

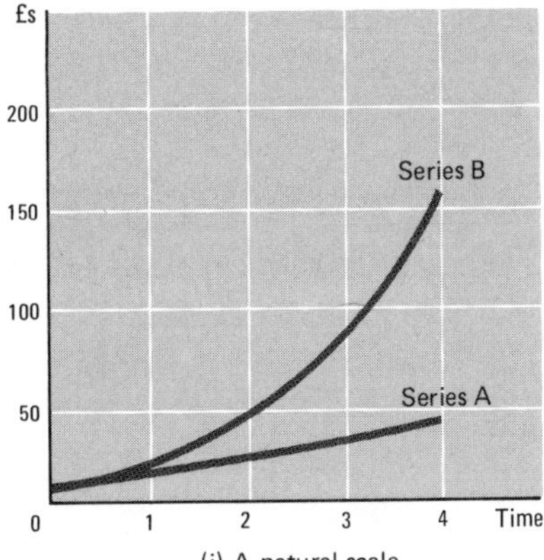

(i) A natural scale

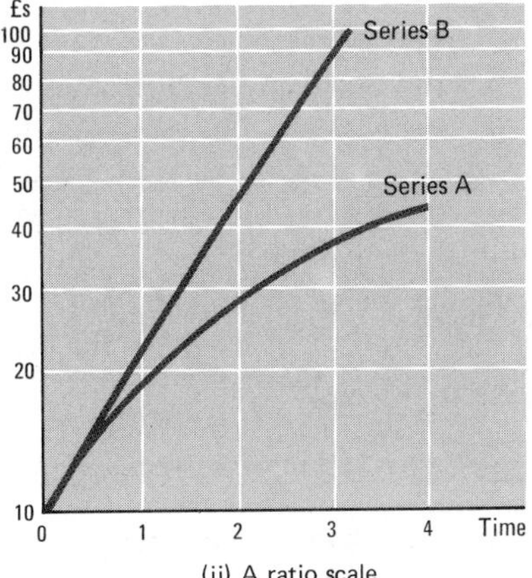

(ii) A ratio scale

Fig. 3.4 The difference between natural and ratio scales

[1] Graphs with a ratio scale on one axis and a natural scale on the other are frequently encountered in economics. In the cases just illustrated there is a ratio scale on the vertical axis and a natural scale on the horizontal (or time) axis. Such graphs are often called *semi-log* graphs. In scientific work graphs with ratio scales on both axes are frequently encountered. Such graphs are often referred to as *double-log* graphs.

4

The problems of economic theory

We are now ready to begin our study of economics. This chapter is intended to convey an idea of the main divisions of the subject which we shall study in subsequent chapters. Theory is meant to relate to problems. If you cannot think of a set of problems to which the theory you are studying might help to provide answers, then either you or the theory has failed. You are advised to refer back to this chapter during the course of your study of the remainder of the book, particularly when you feel that you have lost sight of the problems to which a particular part of economic theory is directed.

The source of economic problems

Resources and scarcity

The resources of a society consist not only of the free gifts of nature, such as land, forests and minerals, but also of human capacity, both mental and physical, and of all sorts of man-made aids to further production, such as tools, machinery and buildings. It is sometimes useful to divide those resources into three main groups: (1) all those free gifts of nature, such as land, forests, minerals, etc., commonly called *natural resources* and known to the economist as LAND; (2) all human resources, mental and physical, both inherited and acquired, called by the economist LABOUR; and (3) all those man-made aids to further production, such as tools, machinery, plant and equipment, including everything man-made which is not consumed for its own sake but is used in the process of making other goods and services, called by the economist CAPITAL. Economists call these resources FACTORS OF PRODUCTION because they are used in the process of production. Often a fourth factor, ENTREPRENEURSHIP (from the French word *entrepreneur*, meaning the one who undertakes tasks), is distinguished. The entrepreneur is the one who takes risks by introducing both new products and new ways of making old products. Thus he is the one who organizes the other factors of production and directs them along new lines. (When it is not distinguished as a fourth factor, entrepreneurship is included under labour.)

The things that are produced by the factors of production are called COMMODITIES. Commodities may be divided into goods and services: GOODS are tangible, as are cars or shoes; SERVICES are intangible, as are haircuts or education. This distinction, however, should not be exaggerated: goods are valued because of the services they confer on their owners. An automobile, for example, is valued because of the transportation that it provides – and possibly also for the flow of satisfaction the owner gets from displaying it as a status symbol.[1] The total output of all commodities in one country over some period, usually taken as a year, is called GROSS NATIONAL PRODUCT, or often just NATIONAL PRODUCT.

In most societies goods and services are not regarded as desirable in themselves; no great virtue is attached to piling them up endlessly in warehouses, never to be consumed.[2] Usually the end or goal that is desired is that individuals should have at least some of their wants satisfied. Goods and services are thus regarded as *means* by which the *goal* of the satisfaction of wants may be reached. The act of making goods and services is called by the economist PRODUCTION, and the act of using these goods and services to satisfy wants is called CONSUMPTION. Anyone who helps to produce goods or services is called a PRODUCER, and anyone who consumes them to satisfy his or her wants is called a CONSUMER.

The wants that can be satisfied by consuming goods and services may be regarded, for all practical purposes in today's world, as insatiable.[3] In relation to the known desires of individuals for such commodities as better food, clothing, housing, schooling, vacations, hospital care and entertainment, the existing supply of resources is woefully inadequate. It is sufficient to produce only a small fraction of the goods and services that people desire. This gives rise to one of the basic problems encountered in most aspects of economics, the problem of SCARCITY.

The nation's resources are insufficient to produce the quantities of goods and services that would be required to satisfy all of its citizens' wants.

Most of the problems of economics arise out of the necessity of using scarce resources to satisfy human wants.

Choice and opportunity cost

Choices are necessary because resources are scarce. Because we cannot produce everything we would like to consume, there must exist some mechanism by which it is decided what will be done and what left undone; what goods will be produced and

[1] The division of resources into land, labour and capital, and the division of consumption commodities into goods and services, are matters of definition. Definitions are to be judged not as matters of fact but on the grounds of usefulness and convenience. The question: 'Is this division likely to be a useful one?' can be discussed fruitfully. Useless arguments about which of many definitions is the correct one are so common that they have been given a name, *essentialist arguments*. An essentialist argument takes place whenever we have no disagreement about the facts of the case but we argue about what name to use to indicate the agreed facts. We might, for example, be in complete agreement on what goes on in the Soviet Union and Communist China, but get into an argument over which system should be referred to as true Socialism. Essentialist arguments are usually a waste of our time. It would be better to call what goes on in the Soviet Union *X* and in China *Y* and see if we can get on with establishing some arguments of substance (e.g., does *X* provide more freedom for the expression of dissent than *Y*?).

[2] This is a positive statement about what is, not a normative statement about what ought to be.

[3] Whether or not it would ever be possible to produce enough goods and services to saisfy all human wants is a question we need not consider here. It would take a vast increase in production, a percentage increase in the thousands to raise all citizens of any country to the standard at present enjoyed by its richer citizens. It is doubtful that, even if this could be done, all them would find their wants fully satisfied so that there would then be no one who would desire more commodities.

what left unproduced; what quantity of each good will be produced; and whose wants will be satisfied and whose left unsatisfied. All societies face these problems and somehow decisions on them must be reached. In most societies many different people and organizations either make or influence these choices. Individual consumers, business organizations, labour unions and government officials all exert some influence. One of the differences among various economies such as those of the United States, the United Kingdom, India and the Soviet Union is the amount of influence that different groups have upon these choices.

If you choose to have more of one thing, then, where there is an effective choice, it will be necessary for you to have less of something else. Think of a man with a certain income answering the question: 'What shall I buy?' If he elects to buy more bread, we could say that the cost of this extra bread is so many pence per loaf. A more revealing way of looking at the cost, however, is in terms of what other consumption he must forgo in order to obtain it. Say that in this case he decides to give up some cinema attendances. If the price of a loaf of bread is one third of the price of a cinema seat, then the cost of three more loaves of bread is one cinema attendance forgone or, put the other way around, the cost of one more cinema attendance is three loaves of bread forgone.

Now consider the same problem at the level of a whole society. If the government elects to build more roads, and finds the required money by cutting down on its school construction programme, then the cost of the new roads can be expressed as so many schools per mile of road. If the government decides that more resources must be devoted to arms production, then less will be available to produce civilian goods and a choice will have to be made between 'guns and butter'. The cost of one will be expressible in terms of the amount of the other forgone. The economist's term for expressing costs in terms of forgone alternatives is OPPORTUNITY COST.

Our discussion may now be summarized briefly. Most of the problems of economics arise out of the use of scarce resources – land, labour and capital – to satisfy human wants. Resources are employed to produce goods and services, which are then used by consumers to satisfy their wants. The problem of choice arises because resources are scarce in relation to the virtually unlimited wants they could be used to satisfy.

The concept of opportunity cost emphasizes the problem of choice by measuring the cost of obtaining a quantity of one commodity in terms of the quantity of other commodities that could have been obtained instead.

Basic economic problems

Most of the specific questions posed at the beginning of Chapter 1 (and many other questions as well) may be regarded as aspects of six more general questions that must be faced in all economies, whether they be capitalist, socialist or communist.

Six questions faced by all economies

(1) Are the country's resources being fully utilized, or are some of them lying idle? We have already noted that the existing resources of any country are not sufficient to satisfy even the most pressing needs of all the individual consumers. It may seem strange, therefore, that we must ask this question at all. Surely if resources are so scarce that there are not enough of them to produce all of those commodities which are urgently required, there can be no question of leaving idle any of the resources that are available. Yet one of the most disturbing characteristics of free-market economies is that such waste sometimes occurs. When this happens the resources are said to be involuntarily unemployed (or, more simply, unemployed). Unemployed workers would like to have jobs, the factories in which they could work are available, the managers and owners would like to be able to operate their factories, raw materials are available in abundance, and the goods that could be produced by these resources are urgently required by individuals in the community. Yet, for some reason, nothing happens: the workers stay unemployed, the factories lie idle and the raw materials remain unused. The cost of such periods of unemployment is felt both in terms of the goods and services that could have been produced by the idle resources, and in terms of the terrible effects on human beings who are unable to find work for prolonged periods of time.

It is one of the most important problems of economics to discover why free-market societies experience such periods of involuntary unemployment *which are unwanted by virtually everyone in the society*. Once it is discovered why this is so, the next problem is to investigate how such unemployment can be prevented from occurring in the future.

These problems have long concerned economists, and have been studied under the heading TRADE CYCLE THEORY. Their study was given renewed significance by the Great Depression of the 1930s. For more than ten years almost all Western countries experienced heavy unemployment. In the USA and the United Kingdom, for example, this unemployment was never less than one worker in ten, and it rose to a maximum of approximately one worker in four. This meant that, during the worst part of the depression, one quarter of these countries' resources were lying involuntarily idle, while many millions of people remained without employment for a period of more than ten years. A great advance was made in the study of these phenomena with the publication in 1936 of the *General Theory of Employment, Interest and Money*, by J.M. Keynes. This book, and the whole branch of economic theory that grew out of it, has greatly widened the scope of economic theory and greatly added to our knowledge of the problems of unemployed resources. This branch of economics is called MACROECONOMICS.

In the mid 1970s high unemployment once again beset Western economies. Unemployment rates, although not nearly as high as in the 1930s, have reached the highest levels since that time. In the UK, for example, the unemployment rate fluctuated between 1·0 and 3·0 per cent of the labour force between 1945 and 1970 but reached 7·6 per cent in 1977.

(2) What commodities are being produced and in what quantities? This question arises directly out of the scarcity of resources. It concerns *the allocation of scarce resources among alternative uses* (a shorter phrase, *resource allocation*, will often be used). The questions 'What determines the allocation of resources in various societies?' and 'What are the consequences of conscious attempts to change resource allocation?' have occupied economists since the earliest days of the subject. In free-market economies, most decisions concerning the allocation of resources are made through the price system. The study of how this system works is the major topic in the THEORY OF PRICE.

(3) By what methods are these commodities produced? This question arises because there is almost always more than one technically possible way in which goods and services can be produced. Agricultural goods, for example, can be produced by farming a small quantity of land very intensively, using large quantities of fertilizer, labour and machinery, or by farming a large quantity of land extensively, using only small quantities of fertilizer, labour and machinery. Both methods can be used to produce the same quantity of some good; one method is frugal with land but uses larger quantities of other resources, whereas the other method uses large quantities of land but is frugal in its use of other resources. The same is true of manufactured goods; it is usually possible to produce the same output by several different techniques, ranging from ones using a large quantity of labour and only a few simple machines to ones using a large quantity of highly automated machines and only a very small number of workers. Questions about why one method of production is used rather than another, and the consequences of these choices about production methods, are topics in the THEORY OF PRODUCTION.

(4) How is society's output of goods and services divided among its members? Why can some individuals and groups consume a large share of the national output while other individuals and groups can consume only a small share? The superficial answer is because the former earn large incomes while the latter earn small incomes. But this only pushes the question one stage back. Why do some individuals and groups earn large incomes while others earn only small incomes? The basic question concerns the division of the total national product among individuals and groups. Economists wish to know why any particular division occurs in a free market society and what forces, including government intervention, can cause it to change.

Such questions have been of great concern to economists since the beginning of the subject, and interest in them is as active today as it was almost two centuries ago when Adam Smith and David Ricardo made their path-breaking attempts to solve them. These questions are the subject of the THEORY OF DISTRIBUTION. When they speak of the division of the national product among any set of groups in the society, economists speak of THE DISTRIBUTION OF INCOME.[1]

(5) How efficient is the society's production and distribution? These questions quite naturally arise out of questions 2, 3 and 4. Having asked what quantities of goods are produced, how they are produced and to whom they are distributed, it is natural to go on to ask whether the production and distribution decisions are efficient.

The concept of efficiency is quite distinct from the concept of justice. The latter is a normative concept, and a just distribution of the national product would be one that our value judgements told us was a good or a desirable distribution. Efficiency and inefficiency are positive concepts. Production is said to be inefficient if it would be possible to produce more of at least one commodity – without simultaneously producing less of any other – by merely reallocating resources. The commodities that are produced are said to be inefficiently distributed if it would be possible to

[1] In the eighteenth century, when the theory of distribution was first developed, the three great social classes were workers, capitalists and landowners, and the problem of distribution was to explain how the national product was split up among these classes. (This was why early economists split up factors of production into three groups, labour, capital and land.) Modern economists do not confine their interest to these three groups, but seek rather to study distribution among numerous different groups in the society.

redistribute them among the individuals in the society, and make at least one person better off without simultaneously making anyone worse off.

Questions about the efficiency of production and allocation belong to the branch of economic theory called WELFARE ECONOMICS. A detailed study of this very difficult branch of economics is beyond the scope of this book.

Questions 2 to 5 are related to the allocation of resources and the distribution of income and are intimately connected, in a market economy, to the way in which the price system works. They are sometimes grouped under the general heading of MICROECONOMICS.

(6) Is the economy's capacity to produce goods and services growing from year to year or is it remaining static? The misery and poverty described in the England of a century and a half ago by Charles Dickens is no longer with us as a mass phenomenon; and this is largely due to the fact that the capacity to produce goods and services has grown about 2 per cent per year faster than population since Dickens' time. Why the capacity to produce grows rapidly in some economies, slowly in others, and not at all in yet others is a critical problem which has exercised the minds of some of the best economists since the time of Adam Smith. Although a certain amount is now known in this field, a great deal remains to be discovered. Problems of this type are topics in the THEORY OF ECONOMIC GROWTH.

There are, of course, other questions that arise, but these six are the major ones common to all types of market economies. Most of the rest of this book is devoted to a detailed study of these questions. We shall study among other things how decisions on these questions are made in free-market societies, the (often unexpected) consequences of settling these questions through the price system, and why and how governments sometimes intervene in an attempt to alter the decisions.

The questions distinguished diagrammatically

Four of the above questions that are most easily confused can be distinguished by introducing a simple diagram. Consider the choice that faces all economies today, between producing armaments and producing goods for civilian use. This is a problem in the allocation of resources: how many resources to devote to producing 'guns for defence' and how many to devote to producing goods for all other purposes. We illustrate this choice in Figure 4.1. On one axis we measure the quantity of military goods produced and on the other axis the quantity of all other goods, which we call *civilian goods*. Next we plot all those combinations of military and civilian goods that can be produced if all resources are fully employed. We join up these points and call the resulting line a PRODUCTION-POSSIBILITY BOUNDARY. Points inside the boundary such as *c* show the combinations of military and civilian goods that can be obtained given the society's present supplies of resources. Points outside the boundary such as *d* show combinations that cannot be obtained because there are not enough resources to produce them. Points on the boundary such as *a* and *b* are just obtainable; they are the combinations that can just be produced using all the available supplies of resources.

The downward slope of the boundary indicates that there is an opportunity cost of producing more of one type of commodity, cost being measured in terms of the quantity foregone of the other type of commodity. Thus if we move from point *a* to point *b* we are reallocating resources out of civilian production and into military

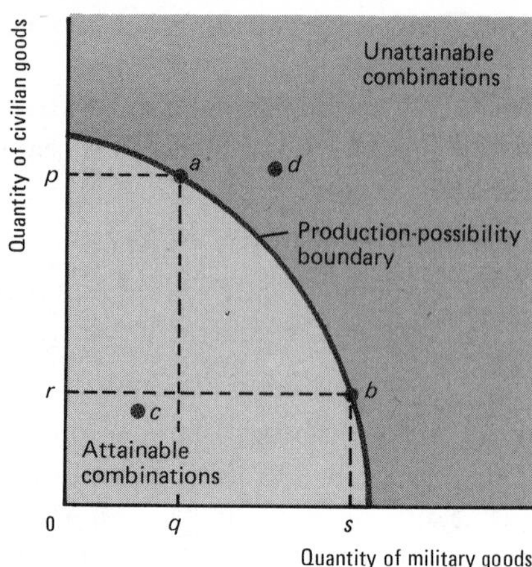

Fig. 4.1 The choice between military and civilian goods

production. The amount of military goods produced increases from *q* to *s*, while the quantity of civilian production falls from *p* to *r*. Thus the opportunity cost of getting $s-q$ more arms produced is $p-r$ civilian goods sacrificed. When we talk about moving between points *a* and *b* we are talking of the allocation of resources discussed in question 2.

If the economy could be at point *b*, then it could also be at point *c*, producing less of both military and civilian goods than at *b*, or indeed at any point inside the boundary. The reader can easily check that, when the economy is located at a point inside the boundary, production of both types of commodity is less than it would be if some points on the boundary were attained. An economy can be producing at some point, such as *c*, inside its production-possibility boundary, either because some of its resources are lying idle (question 1), or because its resources are being used inefficiently in production (question 5).

Let us now ask: 'How can an economy produce more military goods?' Clearly we must know whether the present position is on the boundary or inside it. If the economy is on the boundary, then, assuming for the moment that the boundary cannot be shifted, the answer is: more arms can be obtained only at the cost of producing less civilian goods (e.g., by moving from point *a* to point *b*). If, however, the economy is at some point, such as *c*, inside the boundary, then more of both goods can be produced simultaneously. If the economy is inside the boundary because there is heavy unemployment, then the measures which succeed in reducing unemployment will allow the economy to have more of both goods. If, on the other hand, the economy is inside the boundary because, although existing resources are fully employed, they are being used inefficiently, then measures which increase the efficiency of resource utilization will allow the economy to produce more of both goods.

Finally we come to the question of economic growth (question 6). If the economy's capacity to produce goods is increasing through time, then the production-possibility boundary is being pushed outwards over time as illustrated in Figure 4.2. In this case, if the economy remains on the possibility boundary, it will be possible to increase the production of all goods over time, moving for example from point *a* to point *d*.

Thus we see that in order to increase the production of *all* goods simultaneously, it is necessary to do one of two things. If production is at a point inside the production-possibility boundary, then it may be moved to a point closer to, or actually on, the boundary, from *c* to *b* in Figure 4.1, for example. If the economy is already on the boundary, then it is necessary to take steps which will move the boundary outwards so that production can expand, for example from *a* to *d* in Figure 4.2. It is very important to distinguish between two sorts of movements: (i) a movement from a point within, to a point on, the boundary, and (ii) a movement of the actual boundary. A policy that would succeed in increasing total output if the object were to move from a point within the boundary to a point on the boundary would be a failure if what was necessary was to increase output by moving the actual boundary.

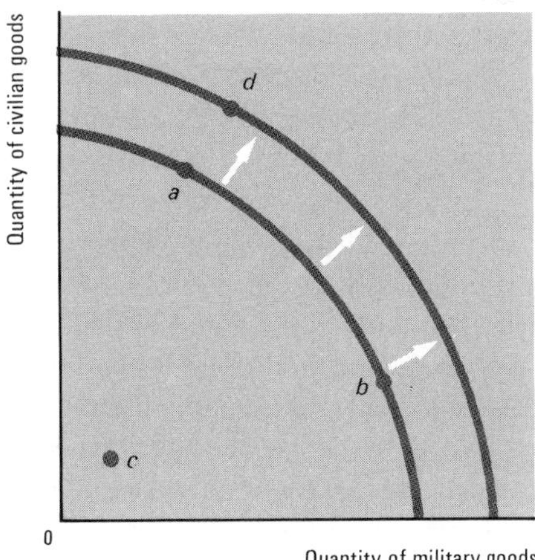

Fig. 4.2 The outward shifting of the production-possibility boundary by economic growth

Economics: a working definition

Our purpose in listing the problem areas of economics is to outline its scope more fully than can be done with short definitions. Economics today is regarded much more broadly than it was even half a century ago. Earlier definitions stressed only the alternative and competing uses of resources, and focused on choices between alternative points on a stationary production-possibility boundary. Other important problems concern failure to achieve the boundary (problems of inefficiency or underemployment of resources) and the outward movement of the boundary over time (problems of growth and development).

Broadly defined, modern economics concerns:
(1) The allocation of a society's resources among alternative uses and the distribution of the society's output among individuals and groups;
(2) The ways in which production and distribution change over time; and
(3) The efficiencies and inefficiencies of economic systems.

5

A general view of the price system

The evolution of market economies

The economic problem as we know it today has existed for a mere eight or nine thousand years – little more than an instant compared to the millions of years humanoid creatures have been on earth. It began with the original agricultural revolution, dated between 6000 and 8000 BC, when people first found it possible to stay in one place and survive. Gradually abandoning the old nomadic life of food gathering, people settled down to tend crops that they themselves had learned to plant and animals that they had learned to domesticate. All societies since that time have faced an all-pervading problem of choice under conditions of scarcity.

Surplus, specialization and trade

Along with permanent settlement, the agricultural revolution brought surplus production: farmers could produce substantially more than they required to satisfy their own needs for survival. The agricultural surplus led to the appearance of new classes of people such as artisans, soldiers, priests, and government officials. Freed from the necessity of growing their own food, these people turned their efforts and their talents to performing other services and producing other goods. They too produced more than they needed themselves, and they traded the excess to obtain whatever else they required.

Economists call this allocation of different jobs to different people SPECIALIZATION OF LABOUR. Specialization has proven extraordinarily efficient compared to universal self-sufficiency, for at least two reasons. First, individual talents and abilities differ, and specialization allows each person to do the thing he or she can do relatively best, while leaving everything else to be done by others. People not only do their own thing; they do their own best thing. Second, a person who concentrates on one activity becomes better at it than could a jack-of-all-trades.

Probably the exchange of goods and services in early societies took place most commonly simply by mutual agreement among neighbours. In the course of time, trading became centred in particular gathering places. These places were called markets, and even today we use the term MARKET ECONOMY to refer to a society in which people specialize in productive activities and meet most of their material wants through exchanges voluntarily agreed upon by the contracting parties.

> **Specialization must be accompanied by trade. People who produce only one thing must trade most of it to obtain all of the other things they require.**

The earliest free-market economies depended on BARTER, the trading of goods directly for other goods. But barter can be very costly in terms of time spent searching out satisfactory exchanges. *Money* evolved to facilitate trade. It eliminates the cumbrousness of barter by allowing the two sides of the barter transaction to be separated. If a farmer has wheat and wants a hammer, he does not have to search for an individual who has a hammer and wants wheat. He merely has to find someone who wants wheat. The farmer takes money in exchange, then finds another person who wishes to trade a hammer, and gives up the money for the hammer.

> **By eliminating the cumbrousness of barter, money greatly facilitates trade and specialization.**

Factor services and the division of labour

Market transactions in early economies involved mostly goods and services for consumption. Producers specialized in making some commodity and then traded it for the other products they needed. The labour services required to make the product would usually be provided by the makers themselves, by apprentices who were learning to become craftsmen or by slaves. Over the last several hundred years many technical advances in methods of production have made it efficient to organize agriculture and industry on a very large scale. These technical developments have made use of what is called the DIVISION OF LABOUR. This term refers to specialization within the production process of a particular commodity. The labour involved is divided into a series of repetitive tasks and each individual does one task that may be a minute fraction of those necessary to produce the commodity. Indeed, it is possible today for an individual to spend years doing a production-line job without ever knowing what commodity emerges at the end of the line!

The division of labour made it necessary to organize production in large and expensive factories. With this development workers lost their status as craftsmen (or peasants) and became members of the proletariat, wholly dependent on their ability to sell their labour to factory (or farm) owners and without any plot of land to fall back on for subsistence in times of need.

> **The day of small craftsmen who made and sold commodities themselves is over. Today's typical workers do not earn their incomes by selling commodities they themselves have produced; rather they sell their labour services to firms and receive money wages in return.**

The allocation of resources

The term ALLOCATION OF RESOURCES, refers to the way in which the available factors of production are allocated among the various uses to which they might be put. For example, the amount of land, labour and capital allocated to producing food, to producing defence, to education, and so on through all commodities. The allocation of resources helps to determine how much of the various kinds of goods and services will actually be produced. In a market economy, millions of consumers decide what commodities to buy and in what quantities; a vast number of firms produce those commodities and buy the factor services that are needed to make them; and millions of factor owners decide to whom they will sell these services. These individual decisions collectively determine the economy's allocation of resources.

In a market economy, the allocation of resources is the outcome of millions of independent decisions made by consumers and producers, all acting through the medium of markets.

How market economies work

Early economists observed the market economy with wonder. They saw that most commodities were made by a large number of independent producers and yet they were made in approximately the quantities that people wanted to purchase. Natural disasters aside, there were neither vast surpluses nor severe shortages of products. These economists also saw that most labourers were able to sell their services to employers most of the time, in spite of the fact that the kinds of products made, the techniques used to make them, and the places in which they were made changed over time.

How does the market produce this order without conscious direction by some central co-ordinating body? It is one thing to have the same commodities produced year in and year out when people's wants and incomes do not change; it is quite another to have production adjusting continually to changing wants, incomes and techniques of production. Yet this *relatively* smooth adjustment is accomplished by the market – albeit with occasional, and sometimes serious, interruptions. It happens because individuals take their private decisions in response to publically known prices, while these prices respond to the collective actions entailed by the sum of all individual decisions. Because of the importance of prices in market economies, we say that they employ a PRICE SYSTEM. This term refers to the role that prices play in determining the allocation of resources and the distribution of national product.

The great discovery of the eighteenth-century economists was that the price system is a social-control mechanism.

In 1776 Adam Smith published his classic *The Wealth of Nations*, the culmination of the early attempts to understand the workings of market economies. Smith spoke of the price system as 'the invisible hand' because it co-ordinated decision-taking that was decentralized among millions of individual producers and consumers.

We may now study two illustrations designed to give some intuitive understanding of how the price system works in market economies.

A change in demand

First consider how the market reacts to a change in the tastes of individual consumers. Let us say, for example, that consumers experience a greatly increased desire for Brussels sprouts and a diminished desire for carrots. It might be the result of some new discovery about the nutritive powers of two vegetables, or it might be a change of fashion caused by a successful advertising campaign by the Association of Brussels Sprout Producers: 'Carrots may be good for you, but Brussels sprouts *taste* good.' The cause, however, is unimportant; all that matters is that consumers desire more sprouts and fewer carrots.

What will be the effects of this change? First, consumers will buy more Brussels sprouts and fewer carrots. With production unchanged, a shortage of Brussels sprouts and a glut of carrots will develop. In order to unload their surplus stocks of carrots, merchants will reduce carrot prices on the principle that it is better to sell them at a reduced price than not to sell them at all. On the other hand, merchants will find that they cannot keep Brussels sprouts on their shelves. Sprouts will become a scarce commodity and the merchants will raise their price. As the price rises, fewer sprouts will be bought. Thus the consumers' demand will be limited to the available supply by the means of making the commodity more expensive.

Farmers will now observe that the price of sprouts is rising while the price of carrots is falling. Brussels sprout production will be more profitable than in the past, for the costs of producing them will be unchanged, while their market price will have risen. Carrot production will be less profitable than it was because costs will be unchanged but prices will have fallen. Thus the change in consumers' tastes, working through the price system, causes the allocation of resources to change in such a way that less resources are devoted to carrot production and more to sprout production. Economists use the term REALLOCATION OF RESOURCES to refer to a change in the use of the economy's resources.

As the production of carrots declines, the glut on the market will diminish, and carrot prices will begin to rise. On the other hand, the expansion in Brussels sprout production will reduce the shortage and the price will fall. These price movements will continue until it no longer pays farmers to reduce carrot production and to increase the production of sprouts.

Let us review this last point. When the price of carrots was very low and the price of sprouts very high, carrot production was unprofitable and sprout production was very profitable. Therefore more sprouts and fewer carrots were produced. These production changes caused sprout prices to fall, and carrot prices to rise. Once the prices of these goods became such that it no longer paid farmers to transfer out of carrots into sprouts, production settled down and price movements ceased.

We can now see how the reallocation of resources takes place. Carrot producers will be reducing their production, and they will therefore be laying off workers, and generally demanding fewer factors of production. On the other hand, Brussels sprout producers will be expanding production by hiring workers and generally increasing their demands for factors of production. Labour can probably switch from carrot to sprout production without much difficulty. If, however, there are certain resources, in this case say certain areas of land, which are much better suited for sprout-growing than for carrot-growing, and other resources, say other areas of land, which are much better suited for carrot-growing than sprout-growing, then their prices will be affected. Since farmers are trying to increase sprout production, they will be increasing their demand for factors which are especially suited for this activity. This will create a shortage and cause the prices of these factors to rise. On the other hand, carrot production will be falling, and hence the demand for resources especially suited for carrot-growing will be reduced. There will thus be a surplus of these resources and their prices will be forced down.

The changes in factor prices in turn influence the distribution of income. Factors particularly suited to sprout production will be earning more than previously, and they will obtain a higher share of total national income than before. Factors particularly suited for carrot production, on the other hand, will be earning less than before and so will obtain a smaller share of the total national product than before.

These changes may now be summarized.

(1) A change in consumers' tastes causes a change in purchases, which causes a shortage or a surplus to appear. This in turn causes market prices to rise in the case of a shortage and to fall in the case of a surplus.

(2) The variations in market price affect the profitability of producing goods, profitability varying directly with price. Producers will shift their production out of less profitable lines and into more profitable ones.

(3) The attempt to change the pattern of production will cause variations in the demand for factors of production. Factors especially suited for the production of commodities for which the demand is increasing will themselves be heavily demanded so that their own prices will rise. Changes in factor prices cause changes in the incomes earned by factors, and this changes the distribution of the national product.

(4) Thus the change of consumers' tastes sets off a series of market changes which causes a reallocation of resources in the required direction and in the process causes changes in the distribution of total national income among the various factors of production.

We shall study changes of this kind more fully later. For now the important thing to notice is how a change initiated in consumers' tastes causes a reallocation of resources in the direction required to cater to the new set of tastes.

A change in supply

For a second example, consider a change originating with producers. Begin as before, by imagining a situation in which farmers find it equally profitable to produce sprouts and carrots, and consumers are willing to buy, at prevailing market prices, the quantities of these two commodities that are being produced. Now imagine that, with no change in prices, farmers become more willing to produce sprouts than in the past and less willing to produce carrots. This shift might be caused by a change in the cost of producing the two goods; for example, a rise in carrot costs and a fall in sprout costs would raise the profitability of sprout production and lower that of carrot production.

What will happen now? For a short time, nothing at all; the existing supplies of sprouts and carrots are the results of decisions taken by farmers some time in the past. But farmers will now plant fewer carrots and more sprouts, and soon the quantities coming on to the market will change. The amounts available for sale will rise in the case of sprouts and fall in the case of carrots. A shortage of carrots and a glut of sprouts will result. The price of carrots will rise and the price of sprouts will fall. As carrots become more expensive and sprouts become cheaper, fewer carrots and more sprouts will be bought by consumers. On the other hand, the rise in carrot prices and the fall in sprout prices will act as an incentive for farmers to move back into carrot production and out of sprout production. We started from a position in which there was a shortage of carrots which caused carrot prices to rise. The rise in carrot prices removed the shortage in two ways: first by reducing the demand for the increasingly expensive carrots, and second by increasing the output of carrots which became increasingly profitable. We also started from a position in which there was a surplus of Brussels sprouts, which caused their price to fall. The fall in price removed the surplus in two ways: first by encouraging the consumers to buy more of this commodity as it became less and less expensive, and second by discouraging the production of this commodity, as it became less and less profitable.

Who controls the free market?

These examples illustrate many important features of the price system. The first thing to notice is that the market responds to the collective decisions of either consumers or producers, even though the decision of any one of them would go unnoticed. There are millions of purchasers of carrots and Brussels sprouts, and a change in the tastes of a single purchaser will have a negligible effect on market prices and resource allocation. But if many consumers change their tastes, the effect will be significant. The situation is similar for producers. There are thousands of farmers and the effect on market prices and resource allocation of the change in the behaviour of a single one of them is negligible. But if many farmers alter their behaviour, the effect on prices will be significant and there will be changes in the allocation of resources.

The second point to notice is that systematic adaptations to changes in demand and supply take place without being consciously co-ordinated by anyone. When shortages develop, prices rise and profit-seeking farmers are led to produce more of the good in short supply. When surpluses occur, prices fall and production is voluntarily contracted. The price system provides a series of automatic signals so that a large number of independent decision-taking units do react in a co-ordinated way.

We have seen that although no single individual may be able to exert any significant control over a free market, the decisions of two groups, producers and consumers, do determine what is produced and sold. Thus the decisions of both groups influence the allocation of resources. A change in either consumers' demand or producers' supply will affect the allocation of resources and thus also the pattern of production and consumption.

It is often remarked that in a free-market society the consumer is king. Such a maxim reveals only half the truth. Prices are determined by supply as well as demand. A free-market society gives sovereignty to two groups, producers and consumers, and the decisions of both groups affect the allocation of resources.

Under certain very special conditions, known as PERFECT COMPETITION, the producer loses his sovereignty and becomes a mere automaton responding to the will of the consumer. These very special conditions are described in Chapter 19. Aside from this special case, however, the producer has at his command, and actually does exercise, considerable power in the allocation of the economy's resources.

This general picture of the working of the price system has left untouched many problems. Before we can handle these, we must formulate the ideas given in this chapter into a more precise theory of price. This will be done in the following chapters.

Variations in actual prices

Figure 5.1 shows that the prices of some commodities do change frequently. Of course, this does not prove that they change in response to the factors described in this chapter. The figure does show, however, that the price changes that we have described as signals do occur frequently, at least for a number of commodities. Indeed there is a great deal of empirical evidence showing that, for many agricultural commodities and industrial raw materials, the price system works very much as described in this chapter. In any retail or wholesale produce market, prices can be observed to react to the state of demand and supply, rising when there is a shortage and falling when there is a surplus. Even the most casual observation of agriculture will show farmers varying their production of different crops as market prices vary.

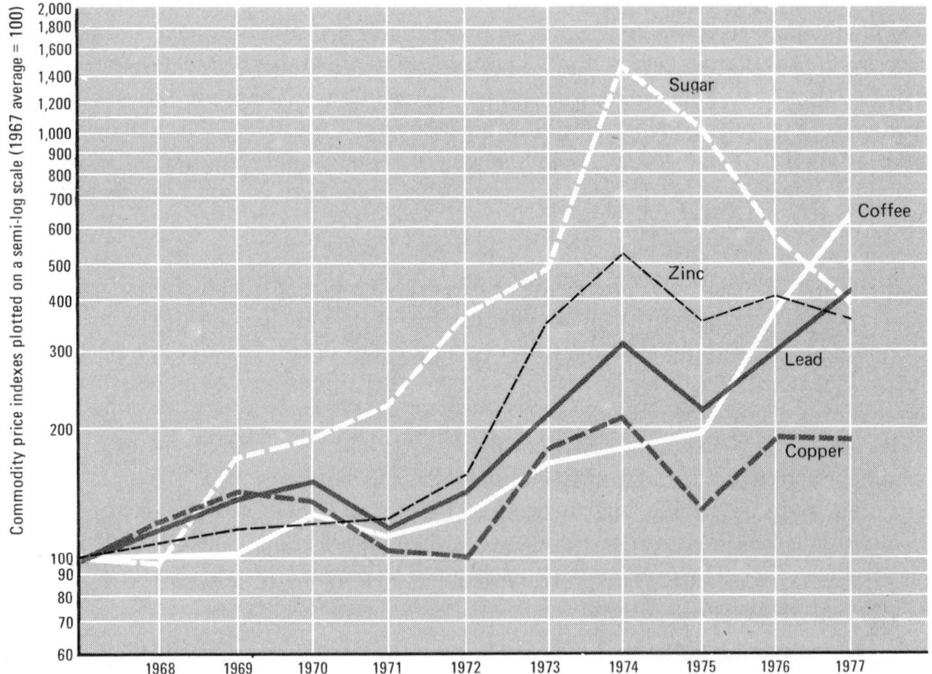

Fig. 5.1 A time-series showing changes in the prices of five commodities.
Source: Calculated from price data in *National Institute Economic Review*

Is it valid, however, to extend this view of the price system to cover all commodities including agricultural goods, manufactured goods and services? This is a much more difficult question and it must be postponed until after the theory of price has been developed more fully.

Part two

The elementary theory of price

6

Basic concepts of price theory [1]

In Part 2 we are going to construct a formal theory of the price system whose behaviour was intuitively sketched in Chapter 5. We begin in this chapter by outlining some basic theoretical concepts. In Chapter 7 we develop the theory of demand, which concerns the behaviour of consumers, and the theory of supply, which concerns the behaviour of producers. After that we combine these two theories to develop in Chapter 8 a theory of how individual markets work. This is called the THEORY OF PRICE or, sometimes, the THEORY OF MARKET BEHAVIOUR. Finally, in Chapter 10, we are able to use this theory to predict the behaviour of actual markets under a variety of interesting circumstances.

The decision-takers

We first introduce some of the concepts and assumptions that form the basis of a theory of market behaviour. Many of these have already been used in Chapter 5. There we could be satisfied with rather rough and ready notions. To build a formal theory, however, we now need more precise concepts.

Economics is about the behaviour of people. Much that we observe in the world, and that we assume in our theories, can be traced back to decisions taken by individuals. There are millions of individuals in most economies. To make our systematic study of their behaviour more manageable, we consolidate them into three important groups: households, firms and central authorities. These are the *dramatis personae* of economic theory, and the stage on which their play is enacted is the market.

Households

In previous chapters we used the term consumer to mean any individual who consumes commodities to satisfy his or her wants. To develop a theory that we can apply to empirical observations, it is better to replace the concept of the consumer with that of the household. A HOUSEHOLD is defined as all the people who live under one roof and who take, or are subject to others taking for them, joint financial decisions. In our theory we give households a number of attributes.

First we assume that each household takes consistent decisions as if it were

[1] No one should begin Part Two without having already studied Chapters 4 and 5, which contain material that is basic to everything that follows.

composed of a single individual. Thus we ignore many interesting problems of how the household reaches its decisions. It may be by paternal dictatorship or democratic voting – that does not matter to us. Intra-family conflicts and the moral and legal problems concerning parental control over minors are dealt with by other social sciences.[1] These problems are avoided in economics by the assumption that the household is the basic decision-taking atom of consumption behaviour.

Second, we assume that each household acts consistently with some goal in mind when it makes its choices. In demand theory we assume that the goal of the household is the maximization of its *satisfaction* or *well-being* or *utility*, as it is variously called. This it tries to do within the limitations of the resources available to it. The concept of satisfaction or utility maximization can be tricky, and it is considered in some detail in Part 3.

Third, we assume that households are the principal owners of factors of production. They sell the services of these factors to producers and receive their incomes in return. It is obvious that labour is 'owned' by those individuals who sell their labour and receive wages and salaries in return. Most capital equipment is owned by firms; but firms are in turn owned by households. Joint stock companies, for example, are owned by the households that hold those companies' stocks. These households provide the firms with the money needed to purchase capital goods and they received the firm's profits as their income. Land is owned by households and firms – which are in turn owned by households. A household may use its land itself or it may make it available to some other user in return for rent which becomes the household's income.[2] In making all these decisions on how much to sell and to whom to sell it, we again assume that households seek to maximize their utility.

Firms

In Chapter 5 we used the term producer to mean someone who made commodities. The terms *producer* and *firm* are used interchangeably in economics, but when one is being precise and formal it is more common to speak of the firm. We define the FIRM as the unit that employs factors of production to produce commodities that it sells to other firms, to households or to the central authorities (defined below). In our theory we give firms a number of attributes.

First, we assume that each firm takes consistent decisions as if it were composed of a single individual. Thus we ignore the internal problems of who reaches particular decisions and how they are reached. In doing this, we assume that the firm's internal organization is irrelevant to its decisions. This allows us to treat the firm as our atom of behaviour on the production or supply side of commodity

[1] In academic work, as well as elsewhere, a division of labour is useful. It is important to remember, however, that when economists speak of *the* consumer or *the* individual they are in fact referring to the group of individuals composing the household. Thus, for example, the commonly-heard phrase *consumer sovereignty* really means *household sovereignty*. These two concepts are, however, quite distinct: it is one thing to say that individuals should be free to decide their own fate, and quite another thing to say that the head of the household should be free to decide the fate of all the members of the household.

[2] The only organization which owns capital and land without itself being a household, or being owned by a household, is the government. Thus all factors of production are owned either by households or by the government.

markets, just as the household is treated as the atom of behaviour on the consumption or demand side.

Second, we assume that the firm takes its decisions with respect to a single goal: to make as much *profit* as it possibly can. This goal of profit maximization is analogous to the household's goal of utility maximization. There is a difference, however: although household satisfaction cannot be directly measured, a firm's profits can be. The assumption of profit maximization has, as we shall see later, come under serious criticism recently, and there are several competing theories of the motivation of firms. We shall consider some of these in Chapter 24, but for now, we can go quite a long way using the simple assumption of profit maximization.

Third, we assume that firms in their role as producers are the principal users of the services of factors of production. In markets where factor services are bought and sold, the roles of firms and households are thus reversed from what they are in commodity markets: in factor markets firms do the buying and households do the selling.

Central authorities

The comprehensive term CENTRAL AUTHORITIES includes all public agencies, government bodies and other organizations belonging to or under the direct control of the government. It includes such institutions as the central bank, the civil service, commissions and regulatory agencies, the cabinet, the police force and all other authorities that can exercise control over the behaviour of firms and households. It is not important to draw up a comprehensive list of all central authorities, but only to have in mind the general idea of a group of organizations that exist at the centre of legal and political power and exert some control over individuals and over markets. Economists often use the simpler, though less accurate, term *government* to refer to the central authorities.

It is *not* a basic assumption of economics that the central authorities always act in a consistent fashion as if they were a single individual. Indeed, conflict among different central-authority agencies is often an important component in theories that explain government intervention in the economy.

> **The decision-taking units in economic theory are households for demand, firms for supply, and central authorities for government regulation and control. Given the resources at their command, each household is assumed to act consistently to maximize its satisfaction, and each firm is assumed to act consistently to maximize its profit.**

The concept of markets

Markets are basic concepts in economics and we must consider them in some detail.

An individual market

Originally the word *market* designated a place where certain things were bought and sold. Once developed, however, theories of market behaviour were easily extended to cover commodities such as wheat, which can be purchased anywhere in the world and the price of which tends to be uniform the world over. Clearly when we talk about 'the wheat market', we have extended our concept of a market well beyond the idea of a single place to which the householder goes to buy something. For our present purposes, we define a MARKET as an area over which buyers and sellers negotiate the exchange of a well-defined commodity. For a single market to exist, it must be possible for buyers and sellers to communicate with each other and to make meaningful deals over the whole market.

The separation of individual markets

Markets are separated from each other by the commodity sold, by natural economic barriers, and by barriers created by the central authorities. To illustrate, consider one example of each type of separation. First, the market for men's shirts is different from the market for refrigerators because they are different commodities. Second, the market for cement in Britain is distinct from the market for cement in the Eastern United States, since transport costs are so high that British purchasers would not buy US cement even if its US price were very much lower than the British price of cement. Third, the market for textiles is separated among many countries since textiles are often the subject of heavy tariffs and restrictive quotas that make it difficult or impossible for firms in one country to sell to households in another.

The interlinking of individual markets

Although all markets are to some extent separated, most are also interrelated. Consider again the three causes of market separation: different commodities, spatial separation and government intervention. First, the markets for different kinds of commodities are interrelated because all commodities compete for consumers' income. Thus if more is spent in one market, less will be available to spend in other markets. Second, the geographical separation of markets for similar commodities depends on transport costs. Commodities with high transport costs per ton relative to their production cost per ton tend to be produced and sold in geographically distinct markets, while commodities with low transport costs are sold in what amounts to a single market. But whatever the transport costs, there will be some price differential at which it will pay someone to buy in the low-priced market and ship to the high-priced one. Thus, there is some potential link between geographically distinct markets, even when shipping costs are high. Third, markets are often separated by policy-induced barriers, such as tariffs. Although high tariffs tend to separate markets, they do leave some link because, if price differences become large enough, it will pay buyers in the high-priced market to switch to the low-priced one and sellers in the low-priced one to switch to the high-priced one, even though they have to pay the tariff as well as the market price.

> **Individual markets are separated from each other either because different commodities are sold in each, or because barriers to the movement of commodities among markets such as transport costs (a natural barrier) and tariffs (a policy-induced barrier) exist. In spite of a substantial degree of separation, most individual markets are more or less interlinked.**

Differences among markets

Competitiveness Individual markets may differ from each other according to the degree of competition among the various buyers and sellers in each market. Throughout Part 2 we shall confine ourselves to markets in which the number of buyers and sellers is large enough so that no one of them has any appreciable influence on price. This is a very rough definition of what economists call COMPETITIVE MARKETS. In Part 4 we shall consider the behaviour of markets that do not meet this competitive requirement.

Goods and factor markets It is often convenient to distinguish two different types of individual markets. GOODS MARKETS are those where goods and services are traded.[1] The sellers in such markets are usually firms; the buyers may be households, other firms or the central authorities. FACTOR MARKETS are markets where factor services are bought and sold. The sellers in such markets are the owners of factors of production (usually households); the buyers are usually firms and the central authorities.

Free and controlled markets A FREE MARKET is one over which the central authorities exert no direct control. Buyers and sellers are free to arrive at any agreements with respect to quantities to be traded and the prices at which trade will occur. A CONTROLLED MARKET is one over which the central authorities exert some substantial, direct control. This can be done in many ways: by requiring that people have licences to buy or sell in the market; by setting legal minimum or maximum (or both) prices at which trade can take place; or by setting a quota of minimum or maximum amounts that individual buyers and sellers may trade in the market.

The national product

In Chapter 4 we noted that the total output of goods and services in any country is called its national product. Some, but not all, of the nation's production passes through markets and some, but not all, is produced by private firms. It is useful at this point to subdivide the total of a country's productive activity in a number of ways.

Market and non-market sectors

Producers make goods and services, and consumers use them. There are two basic ways in which commodities may pass from one group to the other. First, they may be sold by producers and bought by consumers in markets. When this happens the

[1] Since these markets include both goods and services, it might seem better to refer to them as *commodity markets*. Unfortunately, this term is in common use in the business world to refer to markets where basic commodities, such as rubber, tin and jute, are sold. To avoid any possible confusion, economists speak of *goods markets* where, in their own terminology, commodity markets would be better.

producers must cover their costs by the revenues they obtain from the sale of the product. We call this production *marketed production* and we refer to this part of the country's activity as belonging to the MARKET SECTOR. Second, the product may be given away. In this case the costs of production must be covered by some means other than sales revenues. We call this production *non-marketed production*, and we refer to this part of the country's activity as belonging to the NON-MARKET SECTOR. In the case of private charities, the money required to pay for factor services may be raised from the public by voluntary subscriptions. In the case of production by the state – which accounts for the great bulk of non-marketed production – the money is provided from government revenue, which in turn comes mainly from taxes levied on firms and households.

Whenever a state enterprise *sells* its output, its production is in the market sector. Much state output is, however, in the non-market sector by the very nature of the product provided. One could not imagine, for example, the criminal paying the judge for providing him with the service of criminal justice. Other products are in the non-market sector because in some countries the state has decided that there are advantages to removing them from the market sector. In some countries, for example, firms producing medical and hospital services are in the market sector and their products are sold to consumers for a price that must cover their costs. In Britain, however, the production of these services has been taken into the non-market sector; they are provided at little or no cost to users, and costs are covered by the state.

Production falls clearly into one sector or the other when either all, or none, of its costs are covered by selling the products to users. In some cases, however, production falls partly into one sector and partly into the other. If 10 per cent of costs are covered by small charges made to users and 90 per cent by the government, then the production is 10 per cent in the market sector and 90 per cent in the non-market sector. If private firms get a subsidy from the government to cover 10 per cent of their costs, but meet the rest out of sales revenue, then they are 10 per cent in the non-market sector and only 90 per cent in the market sector.

All of the country's national product is produced in either the market or the non-market sector of the economy.

The public and private sectors

The productive activity of a country is often subdivided in a different way to obtain the private and the public sectors. The PRIVATE SECTOR refers to all production that is in private hands; the PUBLIC SECTOR refers to all production that is in public hands. The distinction between the two sectors depends on the legal distinction of ownership. In the private sector, the organization that does the producing is owned by households or other firms; in the public sector, it is owned by the state. The public sector includes all production of goods and services by central authorities plus all production by nationalized industries that is sold to consumers through ordinary markets.

The distinction between the marketed and non-marketed sectors is an economic one: it depends on whether or not the costs of producing commodities are recovered by selling them to their users. The distinction

between the private and the public sectors is a legal one: it depends on whether the organizations that do the producing are owned privately or publicly.

The concept of an economy

An ECONOMY is a rather loosely defined term for any specified collection of interrelated marketed and non-marketed productive activity. It may refer to productive activity in a region of one country, such as *the economy of Western Canada*; it may refer to one country, such as *the UK economy*, or it may refer to a group of countries, such as *the economy of Western Europe*.

The economies of all countries contain market and non-market sectors. A FREE-MARKET ECONOMY is one in which most production is in the market sector and these markets are relatively free from control by the central authorities. In such an economy the allocation of resources is determined by production, sales and purchase decisions taken mainly by firms and households. How these decisions influence the allocation of resources was discussed in Chapter 5.

At the opposite extreme from a free-market economy is a CENTRALLY-CONTROLLED ECONOMY or, as it is sometimes called, a COMMAND ECONOMY. In such an economy all the decisions about the allocation of resources are taken by the central authorities, so that firms and households produce and consume only as they are ordered. In such an economy most production is likely to be in the non-market sector.

Neither the completely free-market economy nor the completely controlled economy has ever existed, at least not in recent history. In practice, all economies are MIXED ECONOMIES in the sense that some decisions are taken by firms and households, and some by central authorities. The emphasis varies, however. In some economies, the influence of the central authorities is substantially less than in others. Not only may the average amount of central control vary among economies, it may also vary among markets within one economy. Thus, in Britain, the day-to-day behaviour of the stock market is relatively free from central control, while the market for rented housing is heavily regulated and controlled by the central authorities.

The economic theory that we are developing applies specifically to the behaviour of free markets, but it can also deal with many types of central control commonly found in Western economies. We shall use the phrase 'free-market economy' to indicate economies in which the decisions of individual households and firms exert a substantial amount of influence over the allocation of resources. The dividing line is an arbitrary one. We must always remember that every possible mixture of centralized and decentralized control exists, and that the economies of Poland and the Soviet Union differ from those of France and the UK only in the average degree to which the central authorities exert an influence over the markets of each economy.

Free-market economies are sometimes called capitalist economies and we shall occasionally use 'capitalist' as a synonym for 'free-market'. The latter term is, however, the more descriptive, since free-market and centrally-controlled economies are differentiated not by the extent of their use of capital (indeed there is more capital per head in the Soviet Union than in many Western countries), but by the extent to which individual markets are controlled by the central authorities.

> **An economy refers to an interrelated set of marketed and non-marketed productive activity. The market behaviour of free-market economies is primarily determined by individual firms and households; the market behaviour of command economies is primarily determined by the central authorities.**

7

The elementary theory of demand and supply

The elementary theory of demand

We saw in Chapter 5 that households' purchases of carrots and Brussels sprouts exerted an important influence on the markets for these commodities. As the next step in building our theory of market behaviour, we will outline a simple theory of the determinants of such purchases. It is called the theory of demand. In this part we develop only the minimum that we need to study market behaviour. In Part 3 we shall study demand in more detail.

The nature of demand

The amount of a commodity that households wish to purchase is called the QUANTITY DEMANDED of that commodity. At the outset we must notice two important things about the quantity demanded. First, it is a *desired* quantity. It is how much households *wish* to purchase, not necessarily how much they actually succeed in purchasing. For example, if a sufficient quantity is not available, the amount households wish to purchase may exceed the amount that they do purchase. We use phrases such as QUANTITY ACTUALLY PURCHASED or QUANTITY ACTUALLY BOUGHT AND SOLD to distinguish actual purchases from quantity demanded. The second thing to note is that quantity demanded is a *flow*. (See page 31.) We are concerned not with a single isolated purchase, but with a continuous flow of purchases, and we must therefore express demand as so much per period of time – one million oranges *per day*, say, or seven million oranges *per week*, or 365 million *per year*.

The concept of demand as a flow appears to raise difficulties when we deal with the purchases of durable consumer goods that are bought only occasionally. It makes obvious sense to talk about consuming oranges at the rate of thirty per month, but what can we say of someone who buys a new television set every five years or a new car every two? This apparent difficulty disappears if we measure the demand for the *services* of the consumer durable. Thus, at the rate of a new set every five years, the television purchaser is using the services of television sets at the rate of $\frac{1}{60}$ of a set per month. If a fall in the price of television sets makes him discard his old set every four years instead of every five, we say that his consumption of the services of television sets has gone up from $\frac{1}{60}$ to the rate of $\frac{1}{48}$ of a set per month.

The determinants of quantity demanded: the demand function

We now introduce four hypotheses about what determines the quantity of a commodity demanded by an individual household.

(1) Quantity demanded is influenced by the price of the commodity.
(2) Quantity demanded is influenced by the prices of other commodities.
(3) Quantity demanded is influenced by the size of the household's income.
(4) Quantity demanded is influenced by the household's tastes.

This list of factors influencing the household's demand may conveniently be summarized using the notation developed in Chapter 2. What we have said is that the amount of a commodity a household is prepared to purchase is a function of (i.e., depends upon) the price of the good in question, the prices of all other goods, the household's income and its tastes. This statement may be expressed in symbols by writing down what is called a DEMAND FUNCTION:

$$q_n^d = D(p_n, p_1, \ldots, p_{n-1}, Y, T),$$

where q_n^d is the quantity that the household demands of some commodity, labelled 'commodity n', where p_n is the price of this commodity, where $p_1, \ldots, p_{n-1}$ is a shorthand notation for the prices of all other commodities, where Y is the household's income and T the tastes of the members of the household.[1]

This is quite a complicated functional relationship, and we shall not succeed in developing a simple theory if we consider what happens to the quantity demanded when these things – prices, income and tastes – all change at once. To avoid doing this, we use a device that is very frequently employed in economic theory. We assume that all except one of the terms in the right-hand side of the above expression are held constant; we then allow this one factor, say p_n, to vary, and consider how the quantity demanded (q_n^d) varies with it, *assuming that all other things remain unchanged*, or, as the economist is fond of putting it, *ceteris paribus*. We then allow some other term, say income (Y), to vary, and consider how, *ceteris paribus*, quantity demanded varies as income varies. We can now consider the relation between quantity demanded and each of the variables on the right-hand side of the demand function, taking them one at a time.[2]

The price of the commodity In the case of almost all commodities, the quantity demanded increases as the price of the commodity falls, income, tastes and all other prices remaining constant. As its price falls, a commodity becomes cheaper relative to its substitutes, and it is therefore easier for it to compete against these substitutes for the household's attention. If, for example, carrots become very cheap, the household will be induced, up to a point, to buy more carrots and less of other vegetables whose prices are now high relative to the price of carrots.

To illustrate the relation between the quantity of a commodity demanded and its price, we shall take imaginary data for the prices and quantities of carrots. Table 7.1 is an example of what is called a DEMAND SCHEDULE. It shows the quantity of carrots that a household would demand at six selected prices. For example, at a price of £40 per ton, the quantity demanded is 10·25 lbs per month. Each of the price-quantity combinations in the table is given a letter for easy reference.

We can now plot the data from Table 7.1 on a graph, with price on the vertical

[1] This functional notation is merely a shorthand notation; it is not of itself mathematics. If you still find this troublesome you should read pages 18–20 and 29–30 of Chapter 2 and its Appendix now.

[2] This technique is duscussed further on page 36, section 12.

axis and quantity on the horizontal one.[1] In Figure 7.1 we have plotted the six points corresponding to the price-quantity combinations shown in Table 7.1. Point *n* on the graph shows the same information as the first row of the table: at £20 a ton, 14 lbs of carrots will be demanded by the household each month. Point *t* shows the same information as the last row of the table: when the price is £120 a ton, the quantity demanded will be only 2·5 lbs per month.

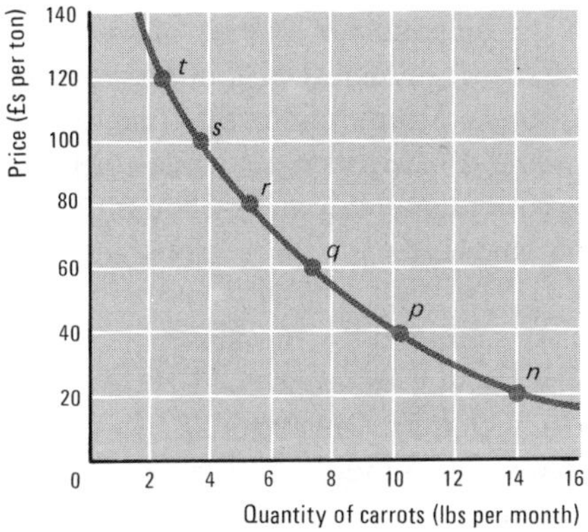

Fig. 7.1 A household's demand curve for carrots

Table 7.1 A household's demand schedule of carrots

	Price (£s per ton)	Quantity demanded (lbs per month)
n	20	14·0
p	40	10·25
q	60	7·5
r	80	5·25
s	100	3·5
t	120	2·5

We now draw a smooth curve through these points. This curve is called the DEMAND CURVE for carrots. It shows the quantity of carrots that the household would like to buy at every possible price; its downward slope indicates that the quantity demanded increases as the price falls.

A single point on the demand curve indicates a single price–quantity relation. *The whole demand curve shows the complete functional relation between quantity demanded and price.* Economists often speak of the conditions of demand in a particular market as given or as known. When they do so they are not referring just to the particular quantity that is being demanded at the moment (i.e., not just to a particular point on the demand curve). They are referring rather to the whole demand curve, to the complete functional relation whereby desired purchases are related to all possible alternative prices of the commodity.

The demand curve for a commodity shows the relation between its price and the quantity a household wishes to purchase per period of time. It is drawn on the assumption that income, tastes and all other prices remain constant, and its downward slope indicates that the lower the price of the commodity, the more the household will desire to purchase.

[1] Readers trained in other disciplines often wonder why economists plot demand curves with price on the vertical axis. The normal convention is to put the independent variable (the variable that does the explaining) on the *X* axis and the dependent variable (the variable that is explained) on the *Y* axis. This would lead us to plot price on the horizontal axis and quantity on the vertical axis. The axis reversal – now enshrined by more than half a century of usage – arose as follows. The analysis of the competitive market that we use today stems from Leon Walras, in whose theory quantity was the dependent variable. Graphical analysis in economics, however, was popularized by Alfred Marshall, in whose theory price was the dependent variable. Economists continue to use Walras' theory and Marshall's graphical representation and thus draw the diagram with the independent and dependent variable in reversed positions on the axes – to the everlasting confusion of readers trained in other disciplines. In virtually every other graph in economics the axes are labelled conventionally, with the dependent variable on the *Y* axis. (See, for example, Figure 7.3.)

The prices of other commodities There are three possible relations between the demand for one commodity and the prices of other commodities: a fall in the price of one commodity may lower the household's demand for another, it may raise it, or it may leave it unchanged.

If a fall in the price of one commodity, *Y*, causes a fall in the demand for another commodity, *X*, the two commodities, *X* and *Y*, are said to be SUBSTITUTES. When the price of one commodity falls, the household buys more of it and less of commodities that are substitutes for it: thus the demand for a commodity varies directly with the price of its substitutes. This relation is illustrated for our imaginary carrot example in Figure 7.2(i). The curve slopes upwards, indicating that as the price of a substitute rises, the household's demand for carrots rises, while when the price of a substitute falls, the demand for carrots falls. Examples of commodities which are substitutes are butter and margarine, carrots and cabbage, cinema tickets and theatre tickets, bus rides and taxi rides.

If a fall in the price of one commodity raises the demand for another commodity, the two are said to be COMPLEMENTS. When the price of one commodity falls, more of it is consumed and more of those commodities that are complementary to it are consumed also. This relation will occur between commodities that tend to be consumed together: motorcars and petrol, cups and saucers, bread and butter, trips to Austria and skis. This is illustrated for our carrot example in Figure 7.2(ii). The curve slopes downwards, indicating that when the price of a complement falls there is a rise in the quantity of carrots demanded.[1]

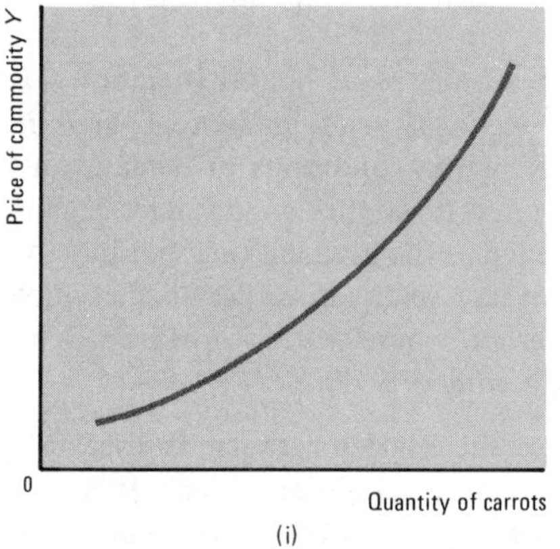

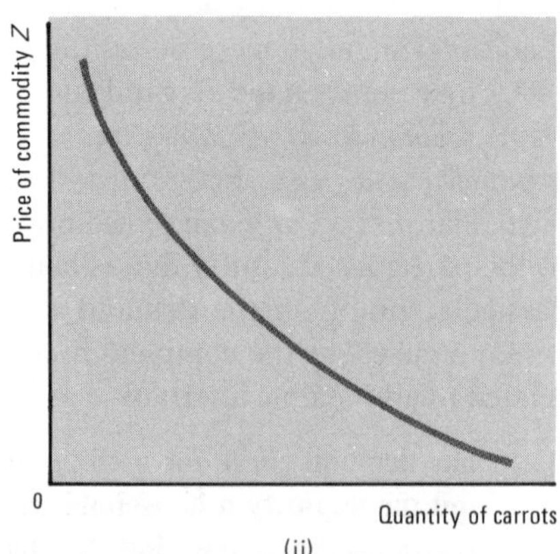

Fig. 7.2 (i) The relations between the quantity of carrots demanded and the price of a substitute (*Y*)
(ii) The relation between the quantity of carrots demanded and the price of a complement (*Z*)

If two commodities are unrelated, then a change in the price of one will have no effect one way or the other on the quantity demanded of the other.

The size of the household's income Ordinarily we would expect a rise in income to be associated with a rise in the quantity of a good demanded. Commodities that obey this rule are called NORMAL GOODS.

[1] Readers familiar with more advanced texts will realize that the definitions used here are those of *gross substitutes* and *gross complements*, rather than those of net substitutes and net complements which are more commonly used in advanced theoretical work.

Two possible exceptions need to be noted. In some cases, a change in income might leave the quantity demanded completely unaffected. This will be the case with goods for which the desire is completely satisfied after a certain level of income is obtained. Beyond this level, variations in income will have no effect on the quantity demanded. This is possibly the case with many of the more inexpensive foodstuffs. It is unlikely, for example, that the demand for salt would be affected by either an increase in a household's income from £5,000 to £5,100 per annum, or by a decrease in its income from £5,000 to £4,900 (although salt purchases might be influenced by income changes if income were as low as, say, £500 per annum). In the case of other commodities, it is possible for a rise in income beyond a certain level to lead to a fall in the quantity that the household demands. Such a relation is likely to occur when one commodity is a cheap but inferior substitute for some other commodity. In many countries beer, potatoes, margarine and black bread provide examples. If the demand for a commodity falls as income rises, it is called an INFERIOR GOOD.

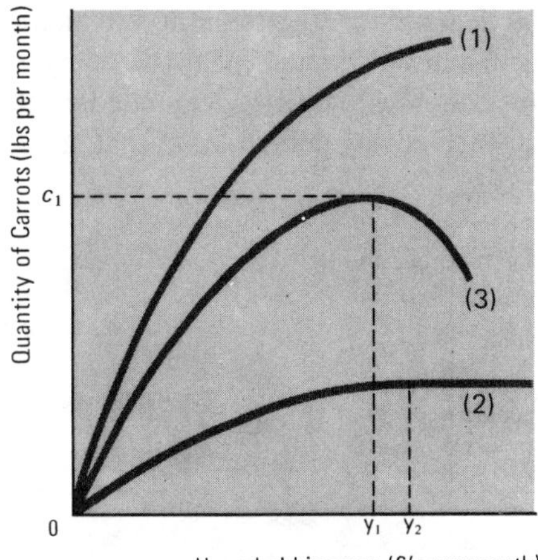

Fig. 7.3 The relation between the quantity of carrots demanded and household income

The three curves in Figure 7.3 indicate the three possible relations between income and the demand for a good under the assumption that all factors other than income remain constant. Curve (1) illustrates the case in which a rise in income brings about a rise in purchases at all levels of income. Such a commodity is a normal good at all levels of income. Curve (2) illustrates the case in which the commodity is normal up to some level of income (y_2 in the figure), while for higher levels of income quantity demanded does not respond to changes in income. Curve (3) illustrates the case in which the commodity is a normal good up to some level of income but then becomes an inferior good at higher levels. In this case quantity demanded rises with income up to y_1 and then falls as income rises beyond y_1. Every actual commodity has its own characteristic curve: many will have a curve similar to (1), with quantity demanded continuing to rise indefinitely with income; some will have curves similar to (2), with a saturation point being reached after which increases in income leave demand unaffected; a few will have curves similar to (3), with demand increasing with income over one range of income variation, and then falling as income rises over a higher range of income variation. (By now you should have no trouble explaining why a commodity cannot be inferior over the entire range of income variation starting from zero.)

The household's tastes If it becomes fashionable among middle-class households to have a second car, the flow of expenditure on cars will increase. This does not mean that everybody will buy a second car, but that some people will, and quantity demanded will rise. When there is change in tastes in favour of a commodity, more of that commodity will be demanded even though its price, the prices of all other commodities and household income have not changed. When there is a change in tastes away from a commodity, less of it will be demanded even though all of the other factors that influence quantity demanded are unchanged.

Some changes in tastes are passing fads, like punk rock and skateboards. Others are permanent, or at least long lasting, such as the switch to filter cigarettes and ball-point pens.

The market demand curve

So far we have discussed how the quantity of a commodity demanded by one household depends on such things as prices and income. To explain market behaviour, however, we need to know the total demand for some commodity on the part of all households. To obtain a market demand schedule from the demand schedules for individual households, we merely sum the quantities demanded by all households at a particular price to obtain the total quantity demanded at that price;

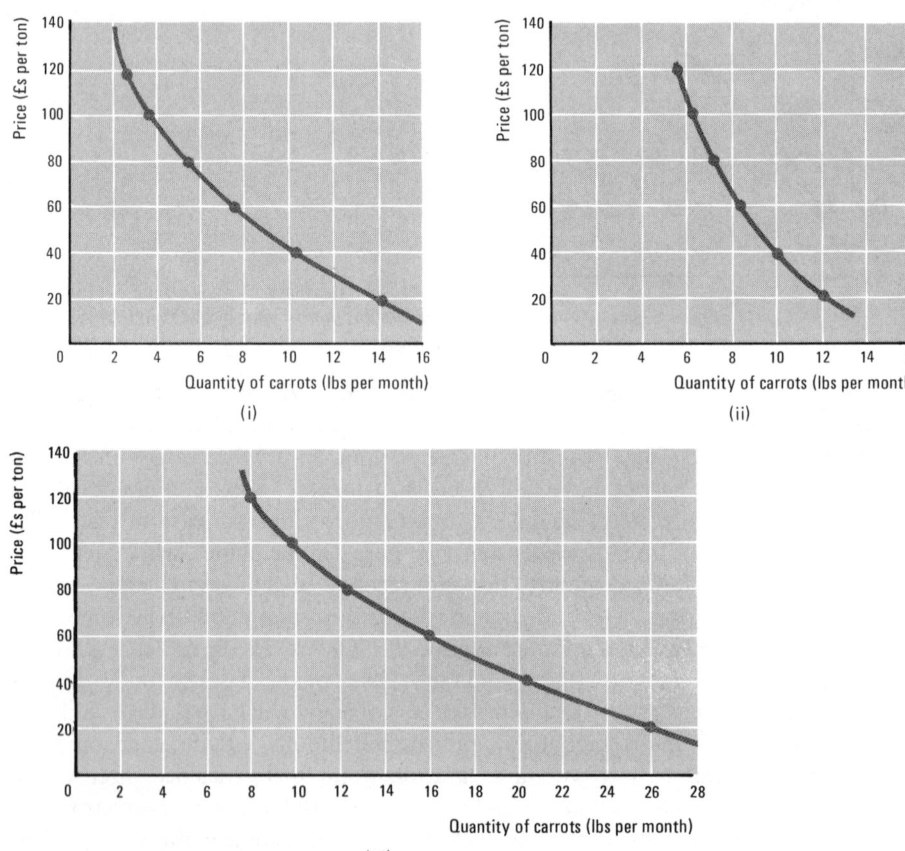

Fig. 7.4 Aggregation of individual demand curves to obtain a market demand curve: (i) First household's demand curve (ii) Second household's demand curve (iii) Total demand curve for the two households

we repeat the process for each price to obtain a schedule of a total or market demand at all possible prices. A graph of this schedule is called the MARKET DEMAND CURVE.

The relation between the individual demand curves of households and the market demand curve is illustrated in Figure 7.4, where, for simplicity, we deal with a market containing only two households. We assume that we know the complete demand curve for each household and we show these in Figures 7.4(i) and (ii). From these individual demand curves we have derived the market demand curve (iii), which merely shows how much will be demanded at each price by both households. Geometrically, the market demand curve in (iii) is derived by a horizontal summation of the two individual curves in (i) and (ii). At a price of £40, for example, household (i) demands 10·25 lbs of carrots and household (ii) demands 10 lbs; the total demand is 20·25 lbs, which quantity is plotted in Figure 7.4(iii) against the price of £40. At a price of £100 household (i) demands 3·5 lbs while household (ii) demands 6·25 lbs, and total demand is 9·75 lbs. Thus the market demand curve is the horizontal sum of the demand curves of all the households in the market.[1]

We have illustrated the market demand curve by summing the demands for only two households. An actual market demand curve will represent the demands of all the households located in the area that makes up the market for a commodity. We shall now assume that we have gathered data for the total market demand for carrots in a particular market. These data are given in Table 7.2 and are shown by the curve D_1 in Figure 7.5.

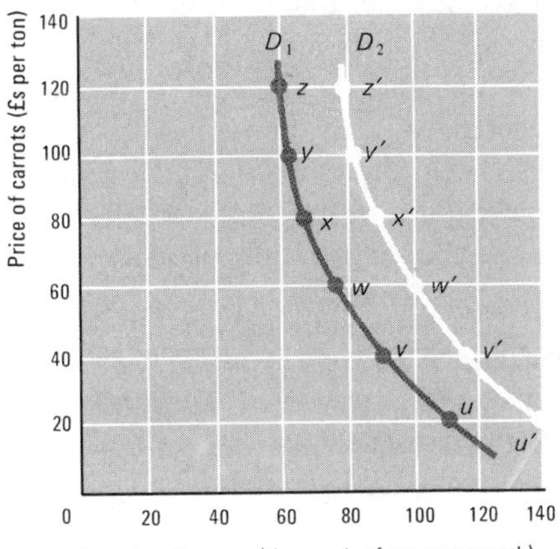

Fig. 7.5 Two market demand curves for carrots

Table 7.2 A market demand schedule for carrots

	Price £s per ton	Quantity demanded (thousands of tons per month)
u	20	110·0
v	40	90·0
w	60	77·5
x	80	67·5
y	100	62·5
z	120	60·0

[1] When summing curves, students sometimes become confused between vertical and horizontal summation. Such a confusion can only result from the application of memory rather than common sense to one's economics. *Consider what would be meant by vertical summation*: measure off equal quantities, say 7·5 lbs in Figure 7.4(i) and (ii). Now add the price to which this quantity corresponds on each household's demand curve. This gives £60 + £82 = £142. If we now plot the point corresponding to £142 and 7·5 lbs in Figure (iii) we have related a given quantity of the commodity to the sum of the prices which households (i) and (ii) are separately prepared to pay for this commodity. Clearly, this information is of no interest to us in the present context. *Every graphical operation can be translated into words.* The advantage of graphs is that they make proofs easier; the disadvantage is that they make it possible to make silly errors. To avoid these, you should always translate into words any graphical operation you have performed and ask yourself: 'Does this make sense and is this what I meant to do?' For example, a market demand curve is meant to tell us total purchases at each price, and hence it is obtained from individual curves by adding up the *quantities* demanded by each consumer at given prices, not by adding the *prices* which each consumer would pay for some given quantity.

In practice, we seldom obtain market demand curves by summing the demand curves of individual households. Our knowledge of market curves is usually derived by observing total quantities directly. The derivation of market demand curves by summing individual curves is a theoretical operation. We do it here because we wish to understand the relation between curves for individual households and market curves.

When we go from the individual household's demand curve to the market demand curve, we must reconsider item (3) in our list of the determinants of demand. 'Household income' now refers to *the total income of all households*. If, for example, the population increases due to immigration and each new immigrant has an income, the demands for most commodities will rise even though existing households have no changes either in their incomes or in the prices that they face.

Once we make our income – the total income of all households – variably we must recognize that demand for many products will also depend on how much of this total income is earned by each of the households in the economy. This means that we must add another factor to the major determinants of demand.

A fifth determinant: income distribution among households Consider two societies with the same total income. In one society the income is distributed very unequally; there are quite a few very rich households and a lot of very poor ones, but hardly anyone is in the middle-income range. In the second society, income is distributed much more equally; most of the households have incomes that do not differ much from the average income for all households. Even if all other variables that influence demand are the same, the two societies will have quite different patterns of demand. In the first there will be a large demand for Mercedes-Benz and Rolls-Royce cars and also for black bread and potatoes. In the second, there will be a small demand for these products, but a large demand for television sets, medium-sized cars and other middle-class consumption goods. Clearly, the distribution of income is a major determinant of market demand.

The total quantity demanded in any market depends on the price of the commodity being sold in that market, on the prices of all other commodities, on the total income of all the households buying in that market, on the distribution of that income among the households, and on tastes.

If we wish to obtain the market demand curve, it is necessary to hold constant all the factors that influence demand, including total income and its distribution among households.

The market demand curve relates the total quantity demanded of a commodity to its own price on the assumption that all other prices, total household income, its distribution among households, and tastes are held constant.

Causes of shifts in the market demand curve

We must now consider the effect on the market demand curve of a change in each of the other factors that were held constant when we drew the curve. These effects are, of course, implicit in what has already been said about the relation between the quantity demanded of any commodity and each of these other factors.

Changes in income It has already been argued that, in the case of most commodities, a rise in income will, *ceteris paribus*, cause an increase in demand. Therefore, if household income rises, we shall find that whatever the price we consider, there will be an increase in the quantity demanded at that price.

Table 7.3 Two alternative demand schedules for carrots

	Price of carrots (£s per ton)	Quantity of carrots demanded at the original level of household income (thousands of tons per month)	Quantity of carrots demanded when household income rises to a new level. (thousands of tons per month)	
u	20	110·0	140·0	*u'*
v	40	90·0	116·0	*v'*
w	60	77·5	100·8	*w'*
x	80	67·5	87·5	*x'*
y	100	62·5	81·3	*y'*
z	120	60·0	78·0	*z'*

Table 7.3 shows, for our hypothetical example of carrots, the possible effect of an increase in the income of each household that purchases carrots. These new data are shown by the white curve, D_2, in Figure 7.5.[1] The original demand curve is also shown and is labelled D_1. We say that the demand curve has *shifted* (in this case it has shifted to the right). The shift from D_1 to D_2 indicates an increase in the desire to purchase carrots at each possible price. At the price of £40 a ton, for example, 116,000 tons are demanded, whereas only 90,000 were demanded at the lower income.[2] A rise in income thus shifts the demand curve to the right, whereas a fall will have the opposite effect, of shifting the curve to the left. In the case of an inferior good, a rise in income will cause a reduction in the quantity demanded at each market price and the whole demand curve will shift to the left.

Changes in the price of other goods Here the effect depends on whether the good whose price changes is a complement or a substitute. Consider, for example, the effect on the demand curve for electric cookers of a rise in the price of electricity. Electricity and electric cookers are complementary commodities and the rise in the price of electricity makes cooking with electricity more expensive than previously.

[1]. The convention used throughout this book for shifts in curves is as follows. The initial position of the curve is indicated by the subscript 1, the position after the first shift by 2, after the second shift by 3, and so on. The equilibrium price and quantity associated with the initial curve are indicated by p_1 and q_1, those associated with the curve after one shift by p_2 and q_2 and so on. When there is no curve shift, and hence no room for ambiguity, the subscripts are often dropped. Thus, for example, there are no subscripts on Figures 7.1 to 7.4, but on Figure 7.5, the initial curve is labelled D_1 and the shifted curve D_2.

Where we wish to indicate two alternative curves rather than a shift of a curve, we use prime (′) marks. Thus, for example, D_1 and D_2 refer to the curve that starts at D_1 and shifts to D_2 while D' and D'' refer to two alternative curves, only one of which will actually exist.

[2] Thus a rightward shift in the demand curve indicates an increase in demand in the sense that more is demanded at a given price, and that a higher price would be paid for the original quantity. It is, of course, true that the amount demanded at Point *y* on D_2 is less than the amount demanded at Point *u* on D_1. This comparison merely shows that, in spite of the increased desire to purchase the good, a sufficiently large rise in price can reduce the quantity actually demanded to an amount lower than it was originally.

Some households will switch to gas when they come to replace their existing cookers and some newly formed households will buy a gas, rather than an electric, cooker when they are setting up their household. Thus the rise in the price of electricity leads to a fall in the demand for electric cookers. Now consider the effect of a rise in the price of gas cookers. Gas and electric cookers are substitutes for each other and when gas cookers rise in price some households will buy electric rather than gas cookers, and the demand for electric cookers will thus rise.

For a general statement we may refer to commodity *X* rather than to electric cookers. A rise in the price of a commodity complementary to *X* will shift the demand curve for *X* to the left, indicating that less *X* will be demanded at each price. A rise in the price of a commodity that is a substitute for *X* will shift the demand curve for *X* to the right, indicating that more *X* will be demanded at each price.

Changes in tastes A change in tastes in favour of a commodity will simply mean that at each price more will be demanded than previously, so that the whole demand curve will shift to the right. On the other hand, a change in tastes away from a commodity will mean that at each price less will be demanded than previously, so that the whole demand curve will shift to the left.

Figure 7.6 summarizes the discussion of the effects on the demand curve of changes in the other things which are assumed constant when the curve is drawn. It is, of course, possible to do the same thing for the curves illustrated in Figures 7.2 and 7.3, and you should check that you understand the analysis by showing what shifts in these curves would be caused by variations in the factors that were assumed to be constant when the particular curve was constructed. (For example, what will happen to the curves in Figure 7.3 if there is a fall in the price of carrots?)

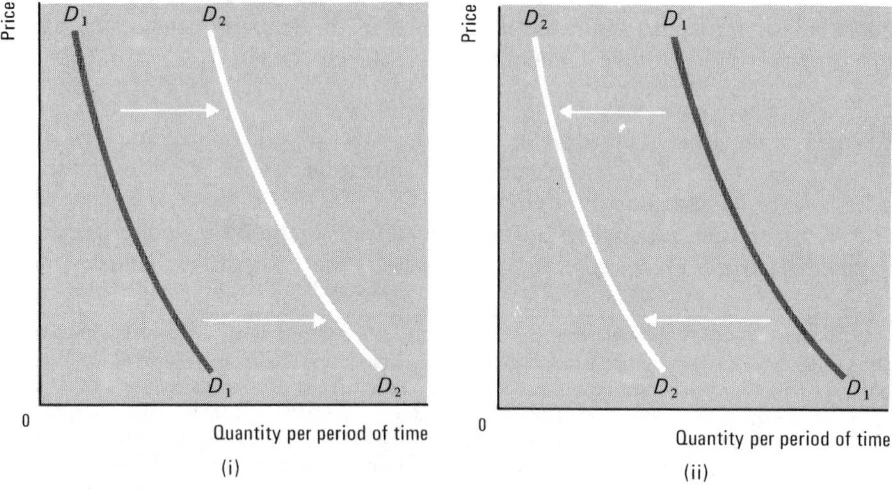

Fig. 7.6 Shifts in demand curves
(i) A rise in demand – the demand curve shifts to the right, indicating a larger quantity is demanded at each price. This can be caused by (1) a rise in income, (2) a rise in the price of a substitute, (3) a fall in the price of a complement, (4) a change in tastes in favour of this commodity
(ii) A fall in demand – the demand curve shifts to the left, indicating a smaller quantity is demanded at each price. This can be caused by (1) a fall in income, (2) a fall in the price of a substitute, (3) a rise in the price of a complement, (4) a change in tastes away from this commodity

Movements along demand curves versus shifts

It is most important to distinguish between a *movement along* a demand curve and a *shift* of the whole curve. A movement along a demand curve indicates that a different quantity is being demanded *because* the price of that commodity has changed. A shift of a demand curve indicates that a different quantity will be demanded at each possible price because something else, either incomes, tastes, or the price of some other commodity, has changed. There is no generally accepted terminology to distinguish between these two quite different occurrences – a movement along one curve and a shift of the whole curve. When economists speak of an increase or a decrease of demand, however, they are usually referring to a shift of the whole curve, because they are more concerned with the whole functional relation between demand and price than with the particular quantity that happens to be demanded at any one moment. We shall follow this usage, and when we speak of *an increase or a decrease in demand* we shall be referring to a *shift* in the whole curve – to a change in the quantity that will be demanded at each possible price. When we refer to a movement along a curve, we shall call it a change in the *quantity demanded*; specifically, an increase in the quantity demanded will indicate a movement down the curve because of a fall in price, a decrease in the quantity demanded will indicate a movement up the curve because of a rise in price.

> **A movement along a demand curve occurs when the quantity demanded changes in response to a change in the commodity's own price. It is referred to as a change in the quantity demanded. A shift in the whole demand curve occurs when a change in any of the other factors that influence demand causes a different quantity to be demanded at every price. It is referred to as a change or a shift in demand.**

The demand for petrol: an example

The preceding discussion of the factors influencing demand may be reviewed by considering petrol as an example. The quantity demanded will vary inversely with its price: as the price falls, more petrol will be consumed. This will occur because existing car owners will use more petrol, because new purchasers of cars will worry less about obtaining cars with low petrol consumption, and because some non-car owners will now feel they are able to afford to run a car. The quantity of petrol demanded may also be expected to vary inversely with the price of cars. As the price of cars falls, more households will purchase them and there will be increased purchases of petrol (the price of petrol remaining unchanged). Petrol and cars are thus complementary goods. On the other hand, the demand for petrol can be expected to vary directly with the price of public transport – a fall in the price of public transport leading to a fall in the demand for petrol, and a rise in the price of public transport leading to a rise in the demand for petrol. If the price of public transport rises, car owners can be expected to use their own vehicles more frequently, and public transport less frequently, and it is possible that some non-car owners will be induced to buy cars because public transport is now more expensive. Public transport and petrol are thus substitutes for one another. The demand for petrol will vary directly with household incomes, a rise in total income leading to a rise in petrol consumption. This will occur because car owners will use their existing cars more frequently, because some households will switch to more expensive cars, which generally use more petrol per mile than do the less expensive ones, and because some non-car owners will now purchase cars as their incomes rise. Finally, the demand for petrol will vary with the distribution of income. If income is redistributed from those who are well enough off to be car owners to those who are not and remain too poor to own cars, then the demand for petrol will fall. If, however, income is redistributed from the very rich to those who are thereby made well enough off to buy cars, then the demand for petrol will rise.

The elementary theory of supply

We saw in Chapter 5 that the amount of carrots and Brussels sprouts that farmers produced and offered for sale had an important influence on the markets for these commodities. Our next task is to outline a simple theory of the determinants of this behaviour. It is called the theory of supply.

The nature of supply

The amount of a commodity that firms are able and willing to offer for sale is called the QUANTITY SUPPLIED of a commodity. Like demand, supply is a desired flow: it measures how much firms would like to sell, not how much they actually sell, and it measures it as so much per period of time.

We shall make a very superficial study of supply in this chapter, establishing only what is necessary for a simple theory of price. In Part 4 we shall devote considerable attention to the theory of production, which is the branch of economics concerned with determination of supply. In Part 4 we will start with the behaviour of individual firms and then aggregate to obtain the behaviour of market supply. For our elementary theory it is sufficient to go directly to market supply, the collective behaviour of all the firms in a particular market.

The determinants of quantity supplied: the supply function

We now introduce five hypotheses about what determines the quantity of a commodity that will be supplied by all the firms in a particular market.

(1) Quantity supplied is influenced by the price of the commodity.
(2) Quantity supplied is influenced by the prices of other commodities.
(3) Quantity supplied is influenced by the prices of factors of production.
(4) Quantity supplied is influenced by the goals of producing firms.
(5) Quantity supplied is influenced by the state of technology.

This list of factors influencing supply may be conveniently summarized using functional notation by writing out what is called a SUPPLY FUNCTION.

$$q_n^s = S(p_n, p_1, \ldots, p_{n-1}, F_1, \ldots, F_m, G, T)$$

where q_n^s is the supply of commodity n, p_n is the price of that commodity, $p_1, \ldots, p_{n-1}$ is shorthand for the prices of all other commodities, $F_1, \ldots, F_m$ is shorthand for the prices of all factors of production, G the goals of producers and T is the state of technology.

Let us now briefly consider the nature of each of the influences summarized in the supply function.

The price of the commodity *Ceteris paribus*, the higher the price of any commodity, the more profitable will it be to make it. We expect, therefore, that the higher the price, the greater will be the quantity supplied.

The prices of all other commodities Generally, an increase in the prices of other commodities will make production of the commodity whose price does not rise relatively less attractive than it was previously. We thus expect that, *ceteris paribus*, the supply of one commodity will fall as the prices of other commodities rise.

The prices of factors of production A rise in the price of one factor of production will cause a larger increase in the costs of making those commodities that use a great deal of that factor, and only a small increase in the costs of producing those commodities that use a small amount of the factor. For example, a rise in the price of land will have a large effect on the costs of producing wheat and only a very small effect on the costs of producing motor vehicles. Thus a change in the price of one factor of production will cause changes in the relative profitability of different lines of production. This will cause producers to shift from one line to another, and so cause changes in the quantities of the various commodities that are supplied.

The goals of firms If producers of some commodity want to sell as much as possible, even if it costs them some profits to do so, more will be offered for sale than if they wanted to make maximum profits. If producers are reluctant to take risks, we would expect smaller production of any good whose production was risky.

In elementary economic theory we assume that the goal of the firm is to make as much profit as possible. The full implications of this hypothesis, the implications of alternative hypotheses and the consequences of rejecting the 'profit-maximizing hypothesis' are considered in detail in Part 4.

The state of technology The enormous increase in production per worker that has been going on in industrial societies for about two hundred years is very largely due to improved methods of production. These in turn have been heavily influenced by the advance of science. Discoveries in chemistry have led to lower costs of production of well-established products, such as paints, and to a large variety of new products made of plastics and synthetic fibres. The new electronics industry rests upon transistors and other tiny devices that are revolutionizing production in television, high-fidelity equipment, computers and guidance-control systems. Atomic energy may one day be used to build canals and to extract fresh water from the sea. At any time, what is produced, and how it is produced, depend upon what is known. Over time, knowledge changes, and so do the supplies of individual commodities.

Market supply

For a simple theory of price we need only to know how the quantity supplied of a commodity varies with its own price, all other things being held constant. We are only concerned, therefore, with the *ceteris paribus* relation, $q^s = S(p)$, where p is the commodity's own price. There is much to be said about the relation between quantity supplied and price. For the moment we shall content ourselves with the intuitively plausible hypothesis that, *ceteris paribus*, the quantity of any commodity that an individual firm will produce and offer for sale will vary directly with the commodity's price, rising when price rises and falling when price falls. This hypothesis has a strong commonsense appeal, since the higher the price of the commodity, the greater the profits that can be earned, and thus the greater the incentive to produce the commodity and offer it for sale.

The hypothesis is known to be correct in a large number of cases, and for the next few chapters we shall proceed assuming it to be generally correct. The exceptions to the hypothesis and their implications will be studied when we come to the theory of production.

As with demand, we can imagine discovering the supply of each individual firm in the market at any given price and then aggregating over all firms to discover the market supply at that price. Repeating this procedure for each price would yield a relation between price and market supply – i.e., the total quantity supplied by all firms in the market. Since the procedure is the same as that already discussed for the demand curve, we shall go directly to market supply.

To illustrate the hypothesis about the relation between quantity supplied and price, we extend the numerical example of the carrot market to include the quantity of carrots supplied. The SUPPLY SCHEDULE given in Table 7.4 is analogous to the demand schedule in Table 7.2, but it records the quantities producers wish to sell at a number of alternative prices rather than the quantities consumers wish to buy. At a price of £80 per ton, for example, 100,000 tons of carrots would come onto the market each month; at a price of £40 per ton, only 46,000 would be forthcoming.

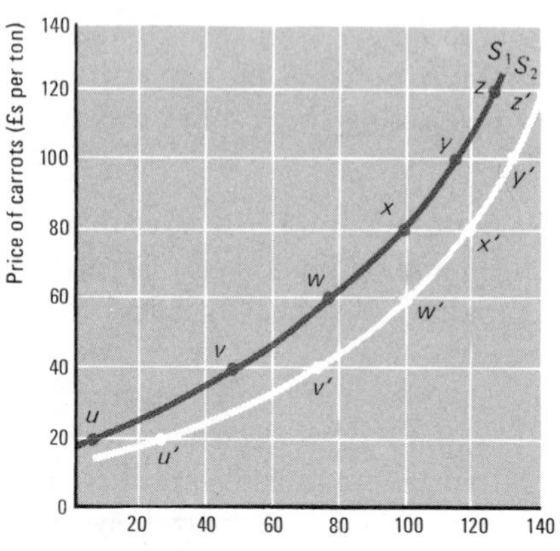

Fig. 7.7 Two supply curves for carrots

Table 7.4 A market supply schedule for carrots

	Price of carrots (£s per ton)	Quantity supplied (thousands of tons per month)
u	20	5·0
v	40	46·0
w	60	77·5
x	80	100·0
y	100	115·0
z	120	122·5

We can now plot the data from Table 7.4 onto a graph similar to the one we used to show the demand curve. In Figure 7.7 price is plotted against the vertical axis and quantity against the horizontal one, and the six points corresponding to each price–quantity combination shown in the table are plotted. The point labelled *u*, for example, gives the same information that is on the first row of the table: when the price of carrots is £20 a ton, 5,000 tons will be produced and offered for sale each month.

Now we draw a smooth curve through the six points. This is the SUPPLY CURVE for carrots. It shows the quantity produced and offered for sale at each price.

> **The supply curve for a commodity shows the relation between its price and the quantity producers wish to sell per period of time. It is drawn on the assumption that all other factors that influence quantity supplied remain**

constant, and its upward slope indicates that the higher the price, the more producers will wish to sell.

Shifts in the supply curve

A shift in the supply curve means that, at each price, a different quantity will be supplied than previously. An increase in the quantity supplied at each price is illustrated in Table 7.5 and plotted as the white curve, S_2, in Figure 7.7. This change appears as a rightward shift in the supply curve for carrots, for example from S_1 to S_2. A decrease in the quantity supplied at each price would appear as a leftward shift, for example, from S_2 to S_1.

Table 7.5 Two alternative supply schedules for carrots

	Price of carrots (£s per ton)	Original quantity supplied (tons per month)	New quantity supplied (tons per month)	
u	20	5	28	u′
v	40	46	76	v′
w	60	77·5	102	w′
x	80	100	120	x′
y	100	115	132	y′
z	120	122·5	140	z′

A bodily shift in the supply curve, such as the one shown in Figure 7.7 must be the result of a change in one of the factors that influence the quantity supplied other than the commodity's own price. The major possible causes of such shifts are summarized under Figure 7.8.

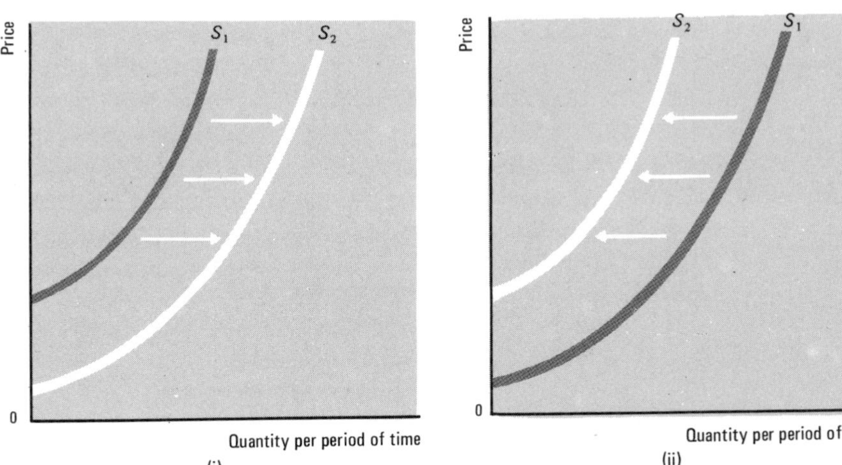

Fig. 7.8 Shifts in supply curves
(i) A rise in supply – the supply curve shifts to the right, indicating that producers wish to make and sell more at each price. This can be caused by (1) improvements in technology, (2) decreases in the prices of other commodities, (3) decreases in the prices of factors of production used in making this commodity, (4) some kinds of changes in the goals of producers
(ii) A fall in the supply – the supply curve shifts to the left, indicating that producers wish to make and sell less at each price. This can be caused by (1) loss of technical knowledge (unlikely), (2) increases in the prices of other commodities, (3) increases in the prices of factors of production used in making this commodity, (4) some kinds of changes in the goals of producers

Movements along supply curves versus shifts

As with demand, it is essential not to become confused between a movement along the supply curve (caused by a change in the commodity's own price) and a bodily shift in the curve (caused by a change in something other than the commodity's own price). To avoid confusion, we adopt the same terminology as with demand: SUPPLY refers to the whole relation between price and quantity supplied, and QUANTITY SUPPLIED refers to a particular quantity actually supplied at a particular price of the commodity. Thus, when we speak of *an increase or a decrease in supply*, we are referring to shifts in the supply curve such as the ones illustrated in Figures 7.7 and 7.8. When we speak of *a change in the quantity supplied*, we shall mean a movement from one particular point on the supply curve to another point on the same curve. An example of such a movement is the one from *w* to *y* in Figure 7.7, where quantity changes from 77,500 to 115,000 tons per year in response to a rise in price from £60 to £100 per ton.

Now that we have studied the basic concepts of demand and supply, we can go on, in the next chapter, to study the theory of the determination of market prices by the interaction of these two forces.

8

The theory of the behaviour of individual competitive markets

We are now ready to get some pay-off for the work we did in the previous chapter. In this chapter we combine our theories of demand and supply into a theory of the behaviour of an individual competitive market. This allows us to derive the famous 'laws' of supply and demand.

The determination of the equilibrium price

It is convenient to continue with the example of carrots. Table 8.1, given below, brings together the market demand and supply schedules for carrots from Tables 7.2 and 7.4. The table defines twelve points. Figure 8.1 shows both the demand and the supply curves on a single graph and the six points on the demand curve are labelled with upper-case letters, while the six points on the supply curve are labelled with lower-case letters, a given letter referring to a common price on both curves.

Table 8.1 Demand, supply and excess demand schedules for carrots (thousands of tons per month)

Price per ton (£s)	Quantity demanded	Quantity supplied	Excess demand (quantity demanded minus quantity supplied)
20	110·0	5·0	+105·0
40	90·0	46·0	44·0
60	77·5	77·5	0·0
80	67·5	100·0	– 32·5
100	62·5	115·0	– 52·5
120	60·0	122·5	– 62·5

The relation between quantity supplied and quantity demanded at various prices

Consider first the point at which the two curves in Figure 8.1 intersect. This point corresponds to a market price of £60; the quantity demanded is 77·5 thousand tons and the quantity supplied is the same. Thus at the price of £60, consumers wish to buy exactly the same amount as producers wish to sell. Provided that the demand curve slopes downwards and the supply curve slopes upwards throughout their entire ranges, there will be no other price at which the quantity demanded is equal to the quantity supplied.

Now consider any price higher than £60, say £100. At this price consumers wish to buy 62·5 thousand tons, while producers wish to sell 115 thousand tons; thus quantity supplied exceeds quantity demanded by 52·5 thousand tons. It is easily seen, and you should check a few examples, that for any price above £60, quantity supplied exceeds quantity demanded. Furthermore, the higher the price, the larger the excess of the one over the other. The amount by which the quantity firms wish to sell exceeds the quantity households wish to buy is called the EXCESS SUPPLY.

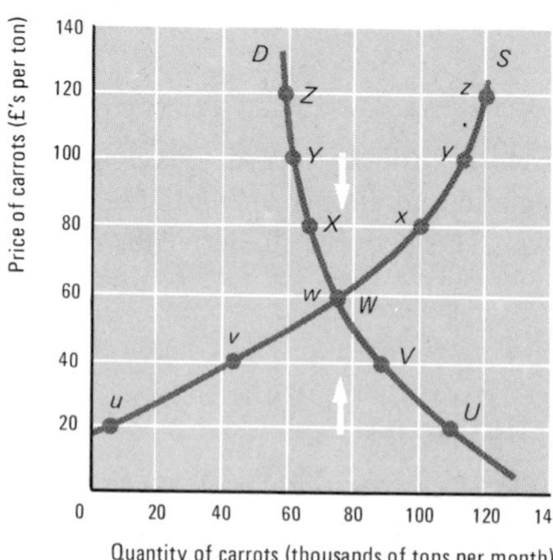

Fig. 8.1 The determination of the equilibrium price of carrots

Finally, consider prices below £60, say £40. At this price, consumers' desired purchases of 90 thousand tons far exceed the producers' desired sales of 46 thousand tons. There is an excess demand of 44 thousand tons. It is easily seen, and you should again check one or two examples, that at all prices below £60 the quantity demanded exceeds the quantity supplied. Furthermore, the lower the price, the larger the excess of the one over the other. The amount by which the quantity households wish to buy exceeds the quantity firms wish to sell is called the EXCESS DEMAND.

Changes in price when there is either excess demand or excess supply

When there is excess demand, households will be unable to buy all they wish to buy; when there is excess supply, firms will be unable to sell all they wish to sell. In both cases some people will not be able to do what they would like to do, and we might expect some action to be taken as a result.

To develop a theory about how the market does behave in the face of excess demand or excess supply, we now make two further assumptions. First we assume that when there is excess supply, the market price will fall. Producers, unable to sell some of their goods, may begin to ask lower prices for them; purchasers, observing the glut of unsold output, may begin to offer lower prices. For either or both of these reasons, the price will fall. This hypothesis is illustrated in Figure 8.1 by the arrow indicating a downward pressure on price at all prices above £60.

Second, we assume that when there is excess demand, market price will rise. Individual households, unable to buy as much as they would like to buy at present prices, may offer higher prices in an effort to get more of the available goods for themselves; suppliers, who could sell more than their total production, may begin to ask higher prices for the quantities that they have produced. For either or both of these reasons, prices will rise when there is excess demand. This hypothesis is illustrated in Figure 8.1 by the arrow indicating an upward pressure on price for all prices below £60.

The equilibrium price

For any price above £60, according to our theory, the price tends to fall; for any price below £60, the price tends to rise. At a price of £60, there is neither excess demand creating a shortage, nor excess supply creating a glut; quantity supplied is equal to quantity demanded and there is no tendency for the price to change. The price of £60, where the supply and demand curves intersect, is the price towards which the actual market price will tend. It is called the EQUILIBRIUM PRICE, which is a general term referring to the price at which quantity demanded equals quantity supplied. The amount that is bought and sold at the equilibrium price is called the EQUILIBRIUM QUANTITY. The term *equilibrium* means a state of balance; it occurs when those who demand desire to buy the same amount that those who supply desire to sell.

When quantity demanded equals quantity supplied we say that the market is in a state of EQUILIBRIUM. When quantity demanded does not equal quantity supplied we say that the market is in a state of DISEQUILIBRIUM. We may now summarize our simple theory.

Hypotheses concerning a competitive market:
(1) Demand curves slope downward continuously;
(2) Supply curves slope upward continuously;
(3) An excess of quantity demanded over quantity supplied causes price to rise;
(4) An excess of quantity supplied over quantity demanded causes price to fall.
Implications:
(1) There is no more than one price at which quantity demanded equals quantity supplied – in the language of economic theory equilibrium is unique;
(2) Only when the equilibrium price rules will the market price be unchanging;
(3) If either the demand or the supply curve shifts, the equilibrium price and quantity will change.

The actual changes are considered below.[1]

[1] For a long time it was thought that the following inference could be drawn from these hypotheses: the market will be *stable* in the sense that, if the price is moved away from its equilibrium level, it will move back towards it and will eventually return to it. This inference cannot be drawn from the theory as presently formulated. This is discussed further in Chapter 11.

Shifts in demand and supply

In Chapter 7 we studied shifts in demand and supply curves. Recall that a rightward shift in the relevant curve means that more is demanded or supplied *at each market price*, while a leftward shift means that less is demanded or supplied *at each market price*. How does a shift in either the demand or the supply curve affect price and quantity?

We start by considering an increase in demand. In Figure 8.2 the original demand curve is D_1 and the supply curve is S. The original equilibrium price and quantity are p_1 and q_1. Now assume that the demand curve shifts to D_2. This shift means that a larger quantity is demanded *at each possible market price*. As a result, excess demand develops because at the original price of p_1, the quantity demanded is now q_3, whereas the quantity supplied remains at q_1. Because of the excess demand, $q_3 - q_1$, price rises towards the new equilibrium price of p_2. When this price is attained, the quantity demanded once again equals the quantity supplied. The new equilibrium quantity bought and sold is q_2: the rise in price from p_1 to p_2 reduces the quantity demanded from q_3 to q_2, whereas it increases the quantity supplied from q_1 to q_2. This analysis establishes our first implication concerning the effects of shifts in demand and supply curves.

> **(1) A rise in the demand for a commodity (a rightward shift of the demand curve) causes an increase in both the equilibrium price and the equilibrium quantity bought and sold.**

The effect of a decrease in demand can also be seen in Figure 8.2 by letting the demand curve shift from D_2 to D_1. The initial equilibrium price and quantity are p_2 and q_2. When the demand curve shifts to D_1, excess supply develops at price p_2 and price falls. The new equilibrium price and quantity are p_1 and q_1. This gives us our second implication.

> **(2) A fall in the demand for a commodity (a leftward shift of the demand curve) causes a decrease in both the equilibrium price and the equilibrium quantity bought and sold.**

The effect of a rise in supply is shown in Figure 8.3. The shift in the supply curve to the right, from S_1 to S_2, indicates an increase in supply: at each price more is now offered for sale than was previously offered. This time, however, the shift of the

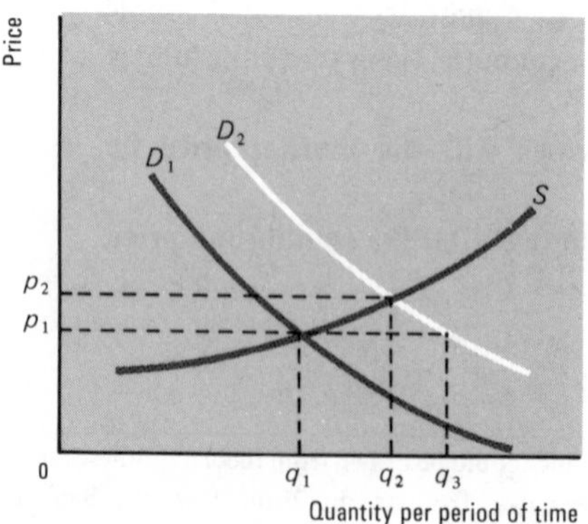

Fig. 8.2 The effects of shifts in the demand curve

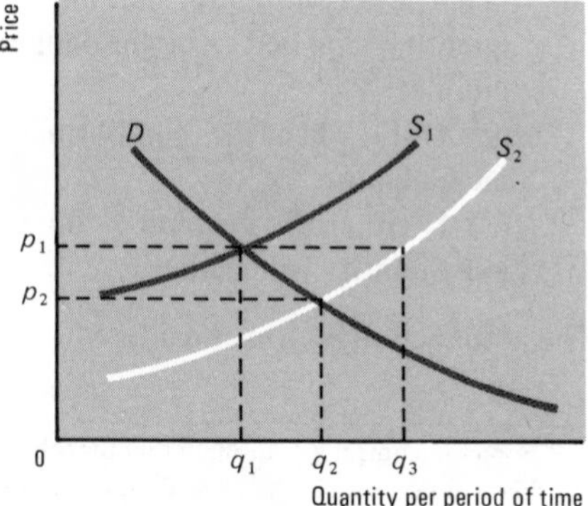

Fig. 8.3 The effects of shifts in the supply curve

curve causes a glut to develop at the old equilibrium price. When the curve shifts, the quantity offered for sale increases from q_1 to q_3 but the quantity demanded remains unchanged at q_1. The excess supply causes price to fall. As the price comes down, the quantity supplied diminishes and the quantity demanded increases. The new equilibrium price is p_2, where the quantity supplied and the quantity demanded equal q_2. This gives us our third implication.

(3) A rise in the supply of a commodity (a rightward shift of the supply curve) causes a decrease in the equilibrium price and an increase in the equilibrium quantity bought and sold.

The effect of a decrease in supply can also be seen in Figure 8.3 by assuming a shift in the supply curve from S_2 to S_1. The leftward shift in the supply curve causes excess demand to develop at the original equilibrium price, p_2. Price rises and, as a result, quantity demanded diminishes, while quantity supplied increases. The new equilibrium price, at which quantity demanded again equals quantity supplied, is p_1. As a result of the fall in supply, equilibrium price increases from p_2 to p_1, and the equilibrium quantity bought and sold decreases from q_2 to q_1.

(4) A fall in the supply of a commodity (a leftward shift in the supply curve) causes an increase in the equilibrium price and a decrease in the equilibrium quantity bought and sold.

In Chapter 7 we studied the many factors that can cause demand or supply curves to shift. These were summarized in Figures 7.6 and 7.8. If we combine this analysis with the four implications just worked out, we can take the many events that cause demand or supply curves to shift and link them to consequent changes in market prices and quantities bought and sold. To take one example, a rise in the price of butter will lead to an increase in both the price and the quantity bought and sold of margerine (because a rise in the price of one commodity causes a rightward shift in the demand curves for its substitutes).

The theory of the determination of price by demand and supply is beautiful in its simplicity and yet, as we shall see, powerful in its wide range of applications.

The 'laws' of supply and demand

It is very common to refer to the four implications just developed as the 'laws' of supply and demand. At this point it may be helpful to say something about the idea of scientific *laws*. The notion of a natural law, as something which is proven to be true once and for all, is an eighteenth- and early-nineteenth-century concept. It has long been discarded from the natural sciences, although traces of it still linger on elsewhere. Even the great 'laws' of Newton were upset after two hundred years, and scientific theories are now accepted not as laws, but as hypotheses which may sooner or later be discovered to be in conflict with facts and be replaced by superior hypotheses.

As with all theories, the implications of the theory of demand and supply may be looked at in two quite distinct ways. First, they are logical deductions from a set of assumptions about behaviour. When we consider the truth of the implications looking at them in this way, we are concerned with whether or not they are logically correct deductions. If we discover that we made mistakes in our reasoning process, then we would conclude that the alleged implications are false in the sense that they do not follow from the assumptions of the theory. Second, the implications are predictions about real-world events. When we consider the truth of the implications looking at them in this way, we are concerned with whether or not they are empirically correct. If one or more of our assumptions do not correctly describe what happens in the real world, then it is possible that the implications of those assumptions will also *not* correctly describe the real-world behaviour. In this case we would conclude that the implications are false in the sense that they are empirically incorrect, i.e. they are contradicted by certain real-world observations.

Consider an example. The sentence '*If* the demand curve for motor-cars slopes downwards and *if* the supply curve slopes upwards, *then* an increase in demand for cars will raise their equilibrium price,' is logically correct in the sense that the 'then' statement follows logically from the two 'if' statements. The sentence 'A rise in the demand for motorcars will increase the price of motorcars,' is one that may or may not be empirically true. If any one of the assumptions of our theory of the determination of price is not empirically correct for the case of motorcars, the statement may be empirically false even though it is a correct logical implication of the theory of market behaviour. If, for example, the market for motorcars does not respond to excess demand with a rise in price, the statement may be empirically false: even though a rise in demand for motorcars does create excess demand, market price will not rise.

Economists are concerned with developing implications that are correct in both senses – that they follow logically from the assumptions of theories, and that they are not contradicted by the evidence of the real world.

The use of the term 'laws' in the popular phrase 'the laws of supply and demand' implies that the four implications have been shown to be true in the empirical sense. We must remember, however, that these 'laws' are nothing more than predictions that follow from price theory and that, as such, they are always open to testing. There is considerable evidence that the predictions are consistent with the facts in many markets. In other markets, especially those for durable consumers' goods such as cars and TV sets, it is not so clear that they are completely consistent with empirical observations. In general, however, we should not speak of 'laws'; we should speak rather of predictions that appear to be empirically at least somewhere near the mark in a considerable number of cases.

An example: sprouts and carrots again

In Chapter 5 we discussed in a preliminary and intuitive way the effects of various changes in the demand for and supply of Brussels sprouts and carrots. To conclude this chapter we can now formalize part of that discussion in terms of our newly developed theory. We do this to gain practice by using our new tools of demand and supply curves in the context of an already familiar problem.

A rise in the demand for sprouts and a fall in the demand for carrots The market for sprouts is illustrated in Figure 8.4(i). The original demand and supply curves are D_1 and S, so that the original equilibrium price is p_1 and quantity is q_1. The demand curve then shifts to D_2. At the original price of p_1, there is an excess of quantity demanded over quantity supplied of $q_3 - q_1$. If, for the time being, the supply of sprouts is fixed at q_1, then the price will rise to p_4, which equates the original quantity supplied with the increased demand. Equilibrium is obtained at first solely by choking off demand through price increases. The supply curve of sprouts is, however, S. At the price p_4 producers would like to grow and sell the quantity q_4. Production will begin to increase and, as the increased flow comes on to the market, the price will fall, for no more than q_1 can be sold at the price p_4. The new equilibrium price is p_2, where the quantities demanded and supplied are both q_2.

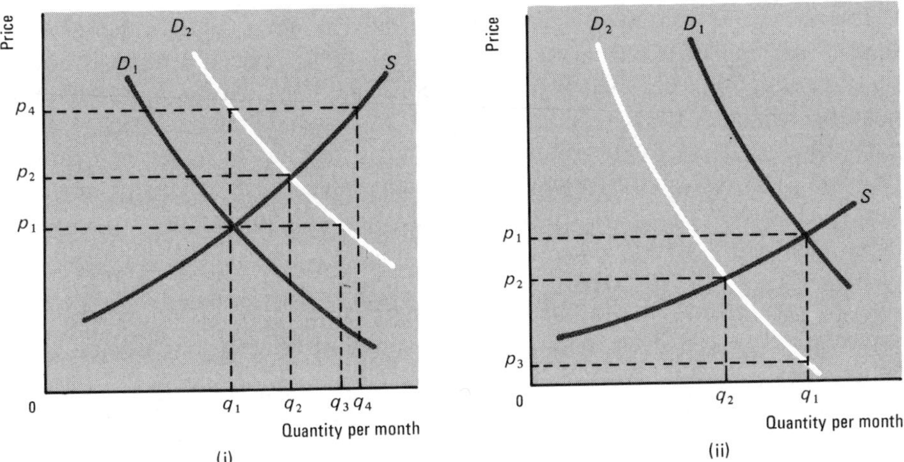

Fig. 8.4 The effects of shifts in the demand curves for carrots and Brussels sprouts: (i) A rise in the demand for sprouts (ii) A fall in the demand for carrots

The effects on carrots, which are shown in Figure 8.4(ii), are the reverse of the effects on sprouts. The leftward shift in demand causes price to fall to p_3 as long as the quantity supplied remains at its original level of q_1. The fall in price, however, causes a contraction in output and then a rise in price to its new equilibrium level of p_2. The fall in demand thus causes both the new equilibrium price and quantity to be lower than their original levels.

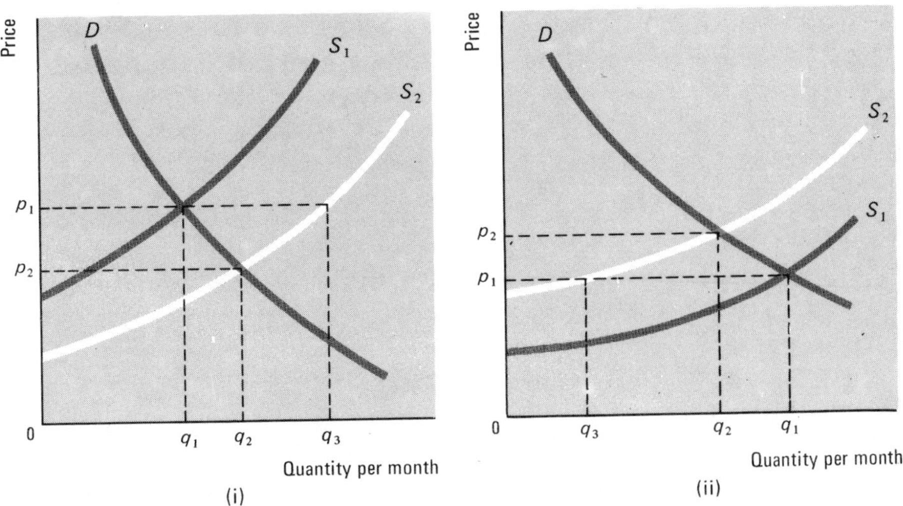

Fig. 8.5 The effects of shifts in the supply curves for carrots and Brussels sprouts: (i) An increase in the supply of Brussels sprouts (ii) A decrease in the supply of carrots

An increase in the supply of sprouts and a decrease in the supply of carrots Figure 8.5 shows that the increase in the supply of sprouts from S_1 to S_2 causes a surplus to appear. In Figure 8.5(i) the surplus is equal to $q_3 - q_1$ at the original equilibrium price of p_1. The surplus causes the price to fall; as it falls, the quantity supplied decreases and the quantity demanded increases. The new equilibrium price of p_2 is lower than the original price, while the new equilibrium quantity of q_2 is higher than the original quantity.

The decrease in the supply of carrots is illustrated in Figure 8.5(ii) by the leftward shift in the supply curve from S_1 to S_2. At the original price of p_1 there is now a shortage of $q_1 - q_3$, because the quantity supplied has fallen from q_1 to q_3, while the quantity demanded has remained unchanged. As a result of the shortage, the price rises. This rise in price reduces the quantity demanded and increases the quantity supplied. The new equilibrium price is p_2, which is higher than the original price by $p_2 - p_1$. The new equilibrium quantity is q_2, which is lower than the original equilibrium quantity by $q_1 - q_2$.

There is one further point of theory which needs to be covered and which is the subject of Chapter 9. Then in Chapter 10 we apply our theory to a wide range of actual cases.

9

Elasticity of demand and supply

When flood damage recently led to a major destruction of the onion crop, onion prices rose across the country. In Hertford they rose 42 per cent in a week. Not surprisingly, onion consumption fell. Very often it is not enough to know merely that quantity rises or falls in response to a change in price; it is also important to know by how much. In this case, the press reported that many consumers stopped using onions altogether, substituting onion salt, leeks, cabbage, and other food products. Others still bought onions, but in reduced quantities. Overall consumption was sharply reduced. Was the aggregate value of onion sales (price *times* quantity) higher or lower? The data above do not tell, but the answer may matter a good deal. A government concerned with the effect of a partial crop failure on farm income will not be satisfied with being told that food prices will rise and, as a result, quantities consumed will fall; to assess the effect on farmers it will need to know approximately by how much they will rise and fall.

Price elasticity of demand

Policy relevance

Recall from our analysis in Chapter 8 that an increase in the supply of carrots led to an increase in the quantity bought and sold and a decrease in their equilibrium price. But how much will price and quantity change in response to a change in supply? This question is analysed in Figure 9.1. In part (i) of the figure, the demand curve is very flat and the increase in supply from S_1 to S_2 causes a large increase in the quantity bought and sold, from q_1 to q_2, while price falls only a bit, from p_1 to p_2. In part (ii) the demand curve is much steeper, and the same shift in supply from S_1 to S_2 causes only a small increase in quantity bought and sold but a large decrease in price. Why are the two cases so different? In both the rightward shift in the supply curve causes excess supply to develop at the initial equilibrium price of p_1. This causes price to fall. In case (i) demand is very responsive to price and only a small fall in price is sufficient to increase the quantity demanded to the point where it is equal to quantity supplied. In case (ii) demand is not very responsive to price and the fall in price mainly reduces the quantity supplied while it only slightly increases the quantity demanded. Price falls a great deal, and at the new equilibrium most of the

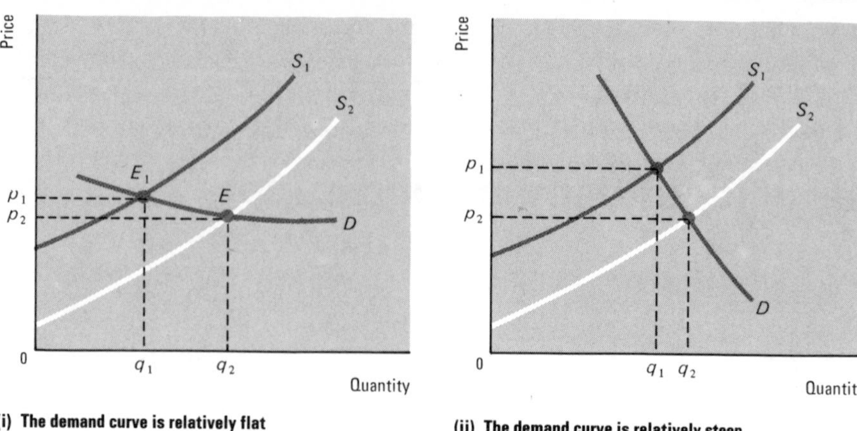

Fig. 9.1 The effect of the shape of the demand curve on a change in supply

extra quantity that was supplied at the old price of p_1 has been choked off by the fall in price. Thus quantity supplied ends up only a little higher than it was before the supply curve shifted.

The difference between these two cases may be significant for policy. Consider what will happen, for example, if the government pays a subsidy for each bushel of carrots grown. This will shift the supply curve of carrots to the right, indicating that more will be produced at each market price. If the demand for carrots is as shown in part (i) of the figure, the effect of the government's policy will be to reduce carrot prices slightly while greatly increasing the quantity grown and consumed. If, however, the demand is as shown in (ii), the effect of the policy will be to reduce carrot prices greatly but to increase carrot production and consumption by only a small amount.

In comparing the two parts of Figure 9.1, it can be seen that in both cases the government's policy has exactly the same effectiveness as far as farmers' willingness to supply the commodity is concerned (the supply curve shifts are identical). But the effects on the equilibrium price and quantity are very different because of the different degrees to which quantity demanded by consumers responds to price changes. If the purpose of the policy is to increase the quantity that is produced and consumed, then the policy will be a great success when the demand curve is similar to the one shown in Figure 9.1 (i), but a failure when the demand curve is similar to that shown in Figure 9.1 (ii). If, however, the main purpose of the policy is to achieve a large reduction in the price of carrots, the policy will be a failure when demand is as shown in (i) but a great success when demand is as shown in (ii).

Measuring the responsiveness of demand to price

Sometimes we wish to know how the responsiveness of demand for one product changes over time, or to compare this responsiveness for several products. We may wish to make statements such as the following: 'The demand for carrots was more responsive to price changes ten years ago than it is today', or 'The demand for meat responds more to price changes than does the demand for green vegetables.' In Figure 9.1 we were able to compare the responsiveness of quantity demanded along the two demand curves because they were drawn on the same scale. But you should not try to compare two curves without making sure that the scales are the same. Also, you must not leap to conclusions about responsiveness of quantity demanded on the basis of the apparent steepness of a single curve. To illustrate the hazards, look at the demand curve in Figure 9.2 (i). Five points on this curve are singled out and labelled *a* to *e* for purposes of comparison. The curve appears rather flat, but by a mere change in scale in Figure 9.2 (ii) we can draw a rather steep demand curve *showing the identical information.*

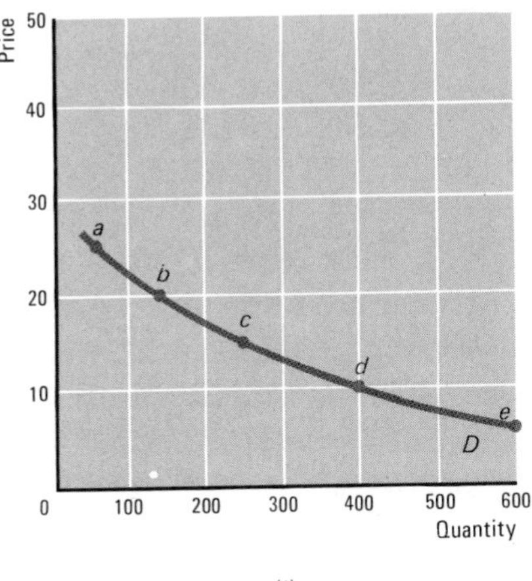

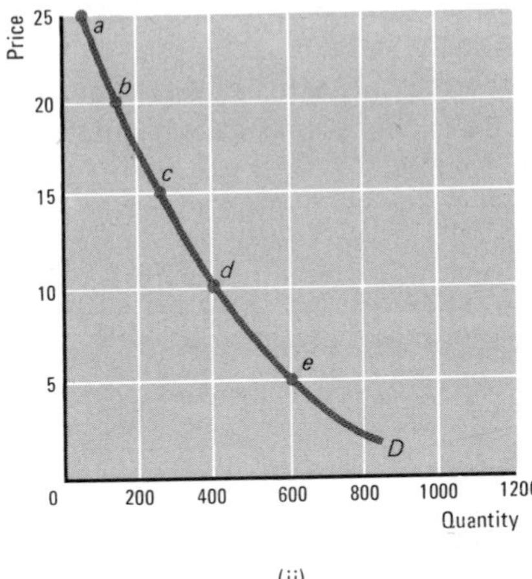

Fig. 9.2 A single demand curve drawn on two different scales

Rather than look at geometrical shape as we just did, we might concentrate on actual quantities. Assume, for illustration, that we have the information shown in Table 9.1. Does this tell us enough to make meaningful comparisons of how quantities demanded respond to price changes? Can we conclude, for example, that the demand for radios is less responsive to price changes than the demand for beefsteak because a 10 pence cut in price gives a large increase in demand for beefsteak, while an equal price cut has very little effect on the demand for radios?

Table 9.1 Changes in prices and quantities for three commodities

Commodity	Reduction in price	Increase in quantity demanded
Beefsteak	£0·10 per pound	7,500 lbs
Men's cotton shirts	£0·5 per shirt	4,500 shirts
Radios	£0·05 per radio	20 radios

There are two problems here. First, a reduction of 10 pence will be a large price cut for a low-priced commodity, but an insignificant price cut for a high-priced commodity. The price reductions listed in Table 9.1 probably represent something in the order of a 15 per cent fall in the price of beefsteak, a 3 per cent fall in the price of cotton shirts, and less than a 1 per cent fall in the price of radios. It is more revealing for purposes of comparison to know the percentage change in the price of the various commodities. Second, by an analogous argument, the quantity by which demand changes is not very revealing, unless we also know the level of demand. An increase of 10,000 tons is quite a significant reaction of demand if the quantity formerly bought was, say 15,000 tons, while it is but a drop in a very large bucket if the quantity formerly demanded was 10,000,000 tons.

Table 9.2 records the original levels of price and quantity as well as the changes in them. From it we can derive what we really need to know: how large is the decrease in price, expressed as a percentage of the original price, and how large is the increase in quantity, expressed as a percentage of the quantity originally being sold? This information is recorded in Table 9.3.

Table 9.2 Changes in prices and quantities demanded related to original prices and quantities for three commodities

Commodity	Original price	Change in price	Original quantity	Change in quantity
Beefsteak (lbs)	£0·80	−£0·10	108,750	7,500
Men's shirts	£4·98	−£0·15	144,750	4,500
Radios	£50·00	−£0·05	10,000	20

Table 9.3 Percentage changes in prices and quantities demanded for three commodities

Commodity	% Change in price	% Change in quantity
Beefsteak	−12·50	6·90
Men's shirts	− 3·01	3·11
Radios	− 0·10	0·20

It is now seen that quite a large percentage change in the price of beefsteak brought about a much smaller percentage change in quantity purchased. On the other hand, although the increase in the number of radios purchased was only twenty, this is seen to be quite a large percentage change in the quantity *in comparison to the percentage change in price that brought it about.*

A formal definition of elasticity

In the above example we compared for each commodity the percentage change in quantity demanded with the percentage change in price that brought it about. This leads us to the concept of the PRICE ELASTICITY OF DEMAND, which is defined as the percentage change in quantity demanded *divided by* the percentage change in price that brought it about, the result being expressed as a positive number. This elasticity is usually symbolized by the Greek letter eta, η, and it can be defined in equation form as

$$\eta = (-1)\frac{\text{percentage change in quantity demanded}}{\text{percentage change in price}}.$$

We shall soon see that many different elasticities are used in economics. To distinguish η from the others, the full term *price elasticity of demand* can be used. Since η is by far the most commonly used elasticity, economists often drop the adjective *price* and refer to it merely as *elasticity of demand*, or sometimes just as *elasticity*. This shorthand can do no harm where there is no room for ambiguity, but where more than one kind of elasticity might be meant, η should be given its full title.

When the above formula is used to calculate η, two problems commonly arise. First, when we deal with a percentage change, we must define the change as a percentage of something. Should it be the original amount? This is simple but has the disadvantage of making the percentage change, and hence the elasticity, depend on the direction of the movement. Thus if we define the percentage change in price as the change from the original price, a movement from £1·00 to £1·20 is a 20 per cent change (price increased by $\frac{1}{5}$), while a movement from £1·20 to £1·00 is only a $16\frac{2}{3}$ per cent change (price decreased by $\frac{1}{6}$). If, however, we take the percentage change to be the change in price divided by the average price (£1·10), both the change from £1·00 to £1·20 and the change from £1·20 to £1·00 give a percentage change of 18·18 per cent. Since we want the elasticity between two points on a demand curve to be a single value, independent of the direction of movement between the two points, we shall take all percentage changes to be the change in price or quantity divided by the average of the original and the new prices or quantities.

The second problem in calculating elasticity arises from the fact that every change has a sign attached to it; it is either an increase (+) or a decrease (−). Since demand curves almost always slope downwards, the change in quantity will usually have the opposite sign to the change in price, which means that the number expressing elasticity will almost always be negative. The minus sign in the formula for elasticity is there simply to make elasticity of demand a positive number. This is a matter of convenience; it has no more profound justification than that. The convenience lies in being able to equate 'more elastic' with 'more responsive'.

Consider an example in which commodities X and Y have elasticities of $+10$ and $+0{\cdot}5$ (calculated according to the above formula). The demand for commodity X is more responsive to price changes than is the demand for commodity Y, and X has the larger measured elasticity ($+10 > +0{\cdot}5$). But if we did not multiply by (-1) the two elasticities would be -10 and $-0{\cdot}5$ so that the commodity with the more responsive demand, X, would have a smaller elasticity than $Y(-10 < -0{\cdot}5)$.

Having dealt with these two problems we can now proceed to calculate the elasticities for the three examples given in Table 9.2. These calculations are shown in detail in Table 9.4.

We now have a precise measure of elasticity. According to this measure, the demand for radios in the above example is more responsive to a price change than the demand for beefsteak and men's shirts. The percentage change in the quantity of radios demanded was twice as large as the percentage change in price that brought it about ($\eta = 2$); the percentage change in the quantity of men's shirts demanded was the same as the price change that brought it about ($\eta = 1$); but the percentage change in the quantity of beefsteak demanded was only half as large as the price change that brought it about ($\eta = 0{\cdot}5$).[1]

[1] The measure of elasticity defined in the text is called *arc elasticity*. In theoretical work the elasticity is defined not between two points on a curve but at each point. This measure is called *point elasticity* and it makes use of derivatives. The relation between arc and point elasticity is further considered in the appendix to this chapter.

Table 9.4 Calculation of elasticities of demand for beefsteak, men's shirts and radios from the data given in Table 9.2

	Old amount	New amount	Change in amount	Average amount	Percentage change	Elasticity
Beefsteak						
price (£s)	0·80	0·70	−0·10	0·750	$\frac{-0{\cdot}10}{0\ 750}$ 100 = −13·33	$\eta = -\frac{+6{\cdot}67}{-13{\cdot}33} = +0{\cdot}5$
quantity (lbs)	108,750	116,250	7,500	112,500	$\frac{7{,}500}{112{,}550}$ 100 = +6·67	
Men's shirts						
price (£s)	4·98	4·83	−0·15	4·905	$\frac{-0{\cdot}15}{4{\cdot}905}$ 100 = −3·06	$\eta = -\frac{+3{\cdot}06}{-3{\cdot}06} = +1{\cdot}0$
quantity	144,750	149,250	4,500	147,000	$\frac{4{,}500}{147{,}000}$ 100 = +3·06	
Radios						
price (£s)	50·00	49·95	−0·05	49·975	$\frac{-0{\cdot}05}{49{\cdot}975}$ 100 = −0·10	$\eta = -\frac{+0{\cdot}20}{-0{\cdot}10} = +2{\cdot}0$
quantity	9,980	10,000	20	9,990	$\frac{20}{9{,}990}$ 100 = +0·20	

Interpreting demand elasticity

The numerical value of elasticity of demand can vary from zero to infinity. Elasticity is zero if there is no change at all in quantity demanded when price changes, i.e. when quantity demanded does not respond to a price change. A demand curve of zero elasticity is shown in Figure 9.3(i). Such a demand curve is said to be *perfectly* or *completely inelastic*.

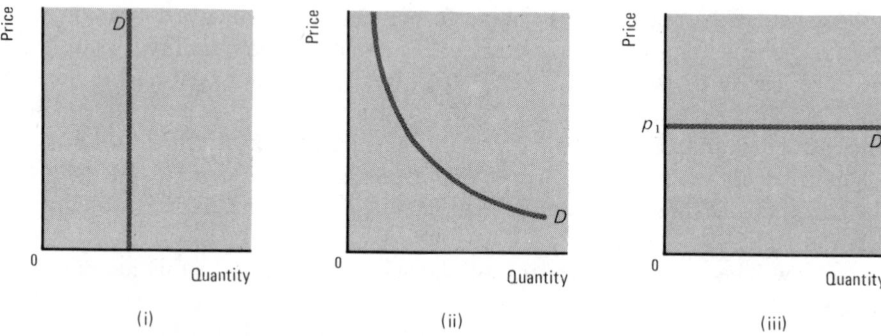

Fig. 9.3 (i) A demand curve of zero elasticity (ii) A demand curve of unit elasticity (iii) A demand curve of infinite elasticity

As long as there is some positive response of quantity demanded to a fall in price, elasticity will exceed zero. The larger the elasticity, the larger the percentage change in quantity demanded for a given percentage change in price. As long as the elasticity of demand has a value of less than one, however, the percentage change in quantity is less than the percentage change in price.

When elasticity is equal to one, the two percentage changes are then equal to each other. This is the important boundary case of unit elasticity. A demand curve having this elasticity over its whole range is shown in Figure 9.3(ii).[1]

When the percentage change in quantity demanded exceeds the percentage change in price, then the elasticity of demand is greater than one. The more responsive the quantity demanded becomes to a given change in price, the higher the elasticity of demand. In the limiting case, quantity becomes infinitely responsive. This means that there exists some small price reduction that will raise demand from zero to infinity. Above the critical price, consumers will buy nothing. At the critical price, they will buy all that they can obtain (an infinite amount, if it were available). The graph of a demand curve having infinite price elasticity is shown in Figure 9.3(iii). Quantity demanded (and hence elasticity) is zero at all prices above p_1, but at price p_1 quantity demanded is infinite. Elasticity is infinite because a small reduction in price to p_1 raises quantity demanded from zero to infinity. Such a demand curve is said to be *perfectly* or *completely elastic*. (This very unlikely-looking case will turn out to be very important later when we study the demand for the output of a single firm with many competitors.)

When the percentage change in quantity is less than the percentage change in price (elasticity less than one), the demand is said to be INELASTIC. When the percentage change in quantity is greater than the percentage change in price (elasticity greater than one), the demand is said to be ELASTIC. Table 9.5 on page 108 summarizes the discussion. The terminology in the table is important, and you should become familiar with it.

Demand elasticity and total expenditure

Money spent by purchasers of a commodity is received by the sellers of the commodity. The total amount spent by purchasers is thus the gross revenue of the sellers. Often in economics we are interested in how total expenditure by purchasers of a commodity, or total gross receipts of sellers of the commodity, reacts when the price is changed.

If the price of a product falls, there will be an increase in quantity sold; what happens to total revenue depends on the amount by which sales rise in response to a given price cut. The simplest example is sufficient to convince us that total revenue may either rise or fall in response. One hundred units of a commodity are being sold at a price of £1·00; the price is then cut to 90 pence. If the quantity sold rises to 101, the total revenue of the sellers falls (from £100 to £90·90), but if quantity sold rises to 120, total revenue rises (from £100 to £108).

[1] The curve is a rectangular hyperbola having the formula: price *times* quantity equals a constant ($pq = C$). Beginners are often confused by the fact that any demand curve having a constant elasticity other than zero or infinity is a curve and *not* a straight line. In Figure 9.3(ii), as we move down on the price axis, equal *absolute* changes in price (say continuous price cuts of 10p) represent larger and larger *percentage* changes. But as we move outwards on the quantity axis, equal *absolute changes* represent smaller and smaller *percentage changes* in quantity, because the quantity from which we start is becoming larger and larger. If the ratio $\frac{\text{percentage change in quantity}}{\text{percentage change in price}}$ is to be kept constant, equal absolute price cuts must be met with larger and larger absolute increases in quantity. Thus, geometrically, the curve must get flatter and flatter as price becomes lower and lower. This increasing flatness of the demand curve, of course, indicates an increasing responsiveness of the absolute quantity demanded to any given changes in price.

Table 9.5 The terminology of elasticity

Terminology	Numerical measure of elasticity	Verbal description
Price elasticity of demand (supply)		
Perfectly, or completely inelastic	Zero	Quantity demanded (supplied) does not change as price changes
Inelastic	Greater than zero, but less than one	Quantity demanded (supplied) changes by a smaller percentage than does price
Unit elasticity	One	Quantity demanded (supplied) changes by exactly the same percentage as does price
Elastic	Greater than one, but less than infinity	Quantity demanded (supplied) changes by a larger percentage than does price
Perfectly, or completely or infinitely, elastic	Infinity	Purchasers (sellers) are prepared to buy (sell) all they can at some price and none at all at an even slightly higher (lower) price
Income elasticity of demand		
Inferior Good	Negative	Quantity demanded decreases as income increases
Normal Good	Positive	Quantity demanded increases as income increases:
Income inelastic	Greater than zero, less than one	less than in proportion to income increase
Income elastic	Greater than one	more than in proportion to income increase
Cross-elasticity of demand		
Substitute	Positive	Price increase of a substitute leads to an increase in quantity demanded of this good (and also less of substitute)
Complement	Negative	Price increase of a complement leads to a decrease in quantity demanded of this good (and also less of the complement)

You should now take the earlier example of radios, shirts and beefsteak, and calculate what happened to total revenue when price fell in each case. When you have done this, you will see that in the case of beefsteak, where the demand was inelastic, a cut in price lowered the revenue of sellers; in the case of the radios, where the demand was elastic, a cut in price raised the revenue earned by sellers. The borderline case is provided by men's shirts; here the demand elasticity was unity, and the cut in price left total revenue unchanged. These relations are no accident. Total consumer expenditure is related to elasticity in the following way: if the demand is inelastic, a change in price causes a less than proportionate change in the quantity demanded, so that total revenue falls when price falls and rises when prices rises. If the demand is elastic, a change in price causes a more than proportionate change in quantity demanded, so that total revenue rises when price falls and falls when price rises. When the elasticity of demand is unity, a change in price is met by an exactly proportionate (and therefore exactly offsetting) change in quantity demanded, and hence total revenue remains constant when price changes.[1] These results are summarized below.

(1) If elasticity of demand exceeds unity (demand elastic), a fall in price increases total consumer expenditure and a rise in price reduces it.
(2) If elasticity is less than unity (demand inelastic), a fall in price reduces total expenditure and a rise in price increases it.
(3) If elasticity of demand is unity, a rise or a fall in price leaves total expenditure unaffected.

What determines demand elasticity?

The importance of substitutes One of the most important determinants of elasticity is undoubtedly the degree of availability of close substitutes. Some commodities, like margarine, cabbage, pork and Ford cars, have quite close substitutes – butter, spinach, beef and British Leyland cars. A change in the price of these commodities, *the prices of the substitutes remaining constant*, can be expected to cause quite substantial substitution – a fall in price leading consumers to buy more of the commodity in question and a rise in price leading consumers to buy more of the substitute. Other commodities, such as salt, housing and all vegetables taken together, have few, if any, satisfactory substitutes. A rise in their price can be expected to cause a smaller fall in quantity demanded than if close substitutes were available.

The false dichotomy between necessities and luxuries The following hypothesis about elasticity of demand is commonly found in popular writing: commodities can be divided into two sets; commodities in the first set are called necessities and have highly inelastic demands; commodities in the second set are called luxuries and have highly elastic demands. The argument for necessities is that they are, as their name implies, necessary to life and that when their prices rise, consumers have no choice but to cut back expenditures on other products and to go on buying the necessities. The argument for luxuries is that they are dispensible and when their prices rise, people will in fact dispense with them; thus they have highly elastic demands.

There is nothing logically wrong with this hypothesis; it is quite easy to imagine a world that behaves like this. The only problem is that the hypothesis does not describe *our* world; it is contradicted by the facts. In all the demand studies that have been made, there is no observable tendency for commodities to fall into two groups, one with very low elasticities and one with very high elasticities. There seem to be goods with all possible elasticities. A few are very low, a few are very high and the remainder are spread out in between. It is true, of course, that food is a necessity in the sense that life cannot go on without some minimum quantity of it, and it is

[1] Algebraically, total revenue is price *times* quantity. If, for example, the equilibrium price and quantity are p_1 and q_1, then total revenue is p_1q_1. On a demand curve diagram, price is given by a vertical distance and quantity by a horizontal distance. It follows that on such a diagram total revenue is given by the *area* of a rectangle, the length of whose sides represent price and quantity.

probably true that food as a whole has an inelastic demand. It does not follow from this, however, that any one food, for example white bread or cornflakes, is a necessity in the same sense, since individual foods have many close substitutes. Thus the quantities demanded of many individual food products fall greatly as a result of rises in their own prices.

> **To a great extent demand elasticity depends on how widely or narrowly a commodity is defined.**

Other demand elasticities

So far we have considered the degree to which quantity demanded responds to a change in the commodity's own price. But the concept of demand elasticity can be broadened to measure the response of quantity demanded to changes in *any* of the factors that influence demand. Besides the commodity's own price, it is important to know how changes in income and the prices of other commodities can affect quantity demanded.

Income elasticity

The reaction of demand to changes in income is extremely important. In many economies, economic growth is doubling real national income every 20 or 30 years. This rise in income is shared more or less equally by all the households in the economy. As they find their incomes increasing, households increase their demands for many commodities. In the richer countries the demand for food and basic clothing does not increase with income nearly so much as does the demand for many other commodities. In all but the richest of the developed countries it is the demand for such durable goods as cars, refrigerators and washing machines that is currently increasing most rapidly as household incomes rise. In the very richest of the Western countries it is the demand for services that is rising most rapidly.

Income elasticity measures this response of quantity demanded to changes in income. The variability of the response is one of the major causes of resource reallocation in all Western economies, and one of the major reasons why we always have with us contracting and depressed industries as well as expanding and buoyant ones. Industries with low income elasticities will find the demands for their products expanding only slowly, while industries with high income elasticities find the demands for their products expanding rapidly. This relation is an extremely important one and we shall study in many times later in this book. Now we must develop a precise measure of income elasticity.

The responsiveness of demand for a commodity to changes in income is termed INCOME ELASTICITY OF DEMAND, and is defined as

$$\eta_Y = \frac{\text{percentage change in quantity demanded}}{\text{percentage change in income}}.$$

For most commodities, increases in income lead to increases in demand, and income elasticity is therefore positive. For these we have the same subdivisions of income elasticity as for price elasticity. Consider a given percentage change in income. If the resulting percentage change in quantity demanded is larger, η_Y will exceed unity and the commodity is said to be INCOME ELASTIC. If the percentage change in quantity demanded is smaller than the change in income, η_Y will be less than unity and the commodity is said to be INCOME INELASTIC. In the boundary case, the percentage changes in income and quantity demanded are equal; η_Y is unity and the commodity is said to have a *unit income elasticity of demand.*

Virtually all commodities have positive price elasticities. Both positive and negative income elasticities, however, are commonly found.

Goods with positive income elasticities are called normal goods (see page 80). Goods with negative income elasticities are called inferior goods; for them, a rise in income is accompanied by a fall in quantity demanded. Normal goods are much more common than inferior goods. The boundary case between normal and inferior goods occurs when a rise in income leaves quantity demanded unchanged so that income elasticity is zero.

If you look back now to Figure 7.3 on page 81, you will see several curves relating demand to income. Whenever such a curve is rising, income elasticity is positive. When demand is unaffected by the level of income, as in the right-hand portion of the curve labelled (2), income elasticity is zero. When the curve declines, as in the right-hand portion of (3), income elasticity is negative.

The important terminology of income elasticity is summarized in Figure 9.4 and Table 9.5 on pages 108 and 111. You should spend time studying the terminology and committing it to memory. Also note, what is clear from the figure, that the same good can be normal at some levels of income and inferior at other levels of income.

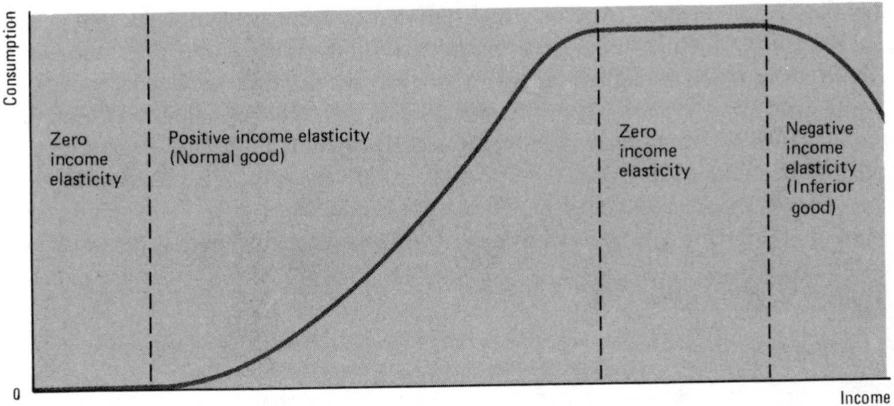

Fig. 9.4 A relation between expenditure on a single commodity and household income

Cross-elasticity

The responsiveness of quantity demanded of one commodity to changes in the prices of other commodities is often of considerable interest. Producers of beans and other meat substitutes find the demands for their products rising when cattle shortages force the price of beef up. Sellers of large cars find their custom falling off when OPEC[1] forces up the price of petrol by raising the selling price of crude oil.

The responsiveness of demand for one commodity to changes in the price of

[1] OPEC stands for the Organization of Petroleum Exporting Countries.

another commodity is called CROSS-ELASTICITY OF DEMAND. It is defined as

$$\eta_C = \frac{\text{percentage change in quantity demanded of commodity } X}{\text{percentage change in price of commodity } Y}.$$

Cross-elasticity can vary from minus infinity to plus infinity. Complementary goods have negative cross-elasticities and substitute goods have positive cross-elasticities.

Bread and butter, for example, are complements: a fall in the price of butter causes an increase in the consumption of both commodities. Changes in the price of butter and the quantity of bread demanded as a result will therefore have opposite signs. Butter and margarine, on the other hand, are substitutes: a fall in the price of butter increases the quantity of butter demanded but reduces the quantity of margarine demanded. Changes in the price of butter and in the quantity of margarine demanded will, therefore, have the same sign.

The closer the relation of substitutability or complementarity, the larger the quantitative reaction to any given price change and thus the larger the absolute value of the cross-elasticity. If the two goods bear little relation to each other, we may expect their cross-elasticities to be close to zero. The terminology of cross-elasticity is also summarized in Table 9.5.

Elasticity of supply

The concept of elasticity may now be expanded to cover the supply as well as the demand side of the market. Just as elasticity of demand measures the response of quantity demanded to changes in any of the factors that influence it, so elasticity of supply measures the response of quantity supplied to changes in any of the factors that influence it. Our discussion will focus mainly on the commodity's own price as a factor influencing supply. For this reason we shall be concerned mainly with *price elasticity of supply*. We shall follow the usual practice of dropping the adjective 'price' and referring simply to 'elasticity of supply' whenever there is no ambiguity in this usage.

A formal definition

The ELASTICITY OF SUPPLY is defined as the percentage change in quantity supplied divided by the percentage change in price that brought it about. Letting the Greek letter epsilon, ε, stand for this measure its formula is

$$\varepsilon = \frac{\text{percentage change in quantity supplied}}{\text{percentage change in price}}.$$

Supply elasticity is a measure of the degree of responsiveness of quantity supplied to changes in the commodity's own price.

Since supply curves normally slope upwards, indicating that an increase in price calls forth an increase in the quantity supplied, supply elasticity, as defined by the above formula, will normally be positive. As with demand elasticity, it is best to calculate percentage changes on the average of the new and old prices and the new and the old quantities when applying the above formula.

Interpreting supply elasticity

Figure 9.5 illustrates three cases of supply elasticity. The case of zero elasticity is one in which the quantity supplied does not change as price changes. This would be the case, for example, if suppliers persisted in producing a given quantity, q_1 in Figure 9.5 (i), and dumping it on the market for whatever it would bring. Infinite elasticity is illustrated in Figure 9.5 (ii). The supply elasticity is infinite at the price p_1, because nothing at all is supplied at lower prices, but a small increase in price to p_1 causes supply to rise from zero to an infinitely large amount, indicating that producers would supply any amount demanded at that price. The case of unit elasticity of supply is illustrated in Figure 9.5(iii). Any straight-line supply curve drawn through the origin has, in fact, an elasticity of unity. For a proof of this, see proposition (4) on page 115 of the Appendix to this chapter.

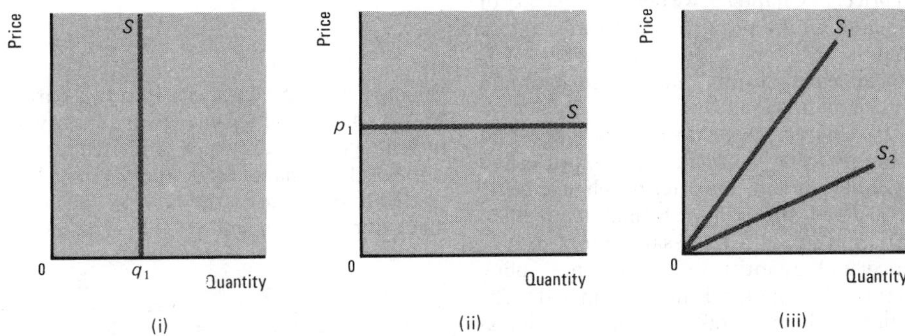

Fig. 9.5 Supply curves of (i) zero, (ii) infinite and (iii) unit elasticity

The case of unit supply elasticity illustrates that the warning given earlier for demand applies equally to supply: do not confuse geometric steepness of supply curves with elasticity. Since *any* straight line supply curve that passes through the origin has an elasticity of unity, it follows that there is no direct simple correspondence between geometrical steepness and supply elasticity. The reason is that varying steepnesses (when the scales are constant) refers to varying *absolute* reactions, while elasticity refers to *proportionate* reactions. The terminology of supply elasticity is also summarized in Table 9.5.

What determines supply elasticity?

Supply elasticities are very important in economics. The brevity of our treatment here reflects two main facts: first, that much of the technique of demand elasticity carries over to the case of supply and does not need repeating, and, second, that we will have more to say about the determinants of supply elasticity in Part 4. In the meantime, we may note that supply elasticity depends to a great extent on how costs behave as output is varied. If unit costs rise rapidly as output rises, then the stimulus to expand production in response to a price rise will quickly be choked off by those increases in production costs that occur as output increases. In this case, supply will tend to be rather inelastic. If, on the other hand, unit costs rise only slowly (or not at all) as production increases, a rise in price that raises profits will call forth a large increase in quantity supplied before the rise in costs puts a halt to the expansion in output. In this case, supply will tend to be rather elastic.

Appendix to chapter 9

A formal analysis of elasticity

Arc elasticity of demand is defined as the ratio of the percentage change in the quantity demanded to the percentage change in price. In Chapter 9, we defined elasticity of demand as the negative of this amount so that it would be a positive number. It is convenient in formal analysis to maintain this simplification.

In Chapter 9 we also took price and quantity to be the average of the prices and quantities before and after the change being considered; for the more formal treatment in this appendix it is more satisfactory to take price and quantity to be the ones ruling before the change being considered. The difference between taking p and q as original or as average amounts diminishes as the magnitude of the change being considered diminishes.

The elasticity measure commonly used in theoretical treatments is called POINT ELASTICITY. Arc elasticity, described in Chapter 9, may be regarded as an approximation to it.

We shall consider arc and then point elasticity, but first we must define some symbols:

$\eta \equiv$ elasticity of demand;
$\varepsilon \equiv$ elasticity of supply;
$q \equiv$ the original quantity;
$\Delta q \equiv$ the change in quantity;
$p \equiv$ the original price;
$\Delta p \equiv$ the change in price.

We can now express the definition of arc elasticity in symbols:

$$\eta \equiv -\frac{\Delta q/q}{\Delta p/p}.$$

By inverting the denominator and multiplying, we get

$$\eta \equiv -\frac{\Delta q}{q}.\frac{p}{\Delta p}.$$

Since it does not matter in which order we do our multiplication (i.e., $q.\Delta p \equiv \Delta p.q$), we may reverse the order of the two terms in the denominator and write

$$\eta - \frac{\Delta q}{\Delta p}.\frac{p}{q}. \qquad (1)$$

We have now split elasticity into two parts: $\Delta q/\Delta p$, the ratio of the change in quantity to the change in price, which is related to the slope of the demand curve, and p/q, which is related to the place on the curve at which we made our measurement.

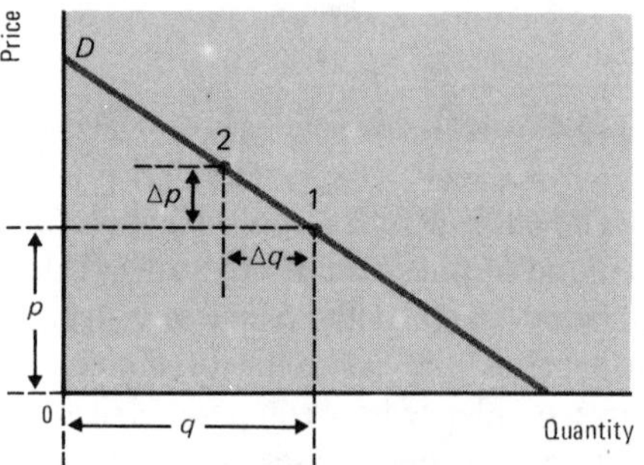

Fig. 9.6 A straight-line demand curve

Figure 9.6 shows a straight-line demand curve by way of illustration. If we wish to measure the elasticity at point 1, we take our p and q at that point and consider a price change, taking us, say, to point 2, and measure our Δp and Δq as indicated. The slope of the straight line joining points 1 and 2 is $\Delta p/\Delta q$ (if you have forgotten this, refer to the appendix to Chapter 2, pp. 32–3), and the term in equation (1) is $\Delta q/\Delta p$, which is the reciprocal of $\Delta p/\Delta q$. We conclude, therefore, that the first term in our elasticity formula is the reciprocal of the slope of the straight line joining the two price-quantity positions under consideration.

We may now develop a number of theorems relating to the elasticity of demand and supply.

(1) *The elasticity of a downward-sloping straight-line demand curve varies from infinity* (∞) *at the price axis to zero at the quantity axis.* We first notice that a straight line has a constant slope so that the ratio $\Delta p/\Delta q$ is the same anywhere on the line. Therefore, its reciprocal, $\Delta q/\Delta p$, must also be constant. We can now infer the changes in η by inspecting the ratio p/q. At the price axis $q = 0$ and p/q is undefined, but as we let q *approach* zero, without ever quite reaching it, the ratio p/q increases without limit. Thus $\eta \to \infty$ as $q \to 0$. As we move down the line, p falls and q rises steadily; thus p/q is falling steadily so that η is also falling. At the q axis the price is zero, so the ratio p/q is zero. Thus $\eta = 0$.

(2) *Comparing two straight-line demand curves of the same slope, the one farther from the origin is less elastic at each price than the one closer to the origin.* Figure 9.7 shows two parallel straight-line demand functions. Pick any price, say p, and compare the elasticities of the two curves at that price. Since the curves are parallel, the ratio $\Delta q/\Delta p$ is the same on both curves. Since we are comparing elasticities at the same price on both curves, p is the same, and the only factor left to vary is q. On the curve farther from the origin, quantity is larger (i.e., $q_2 > q_1$), and hence p/q is smaller; thus η is smaller.

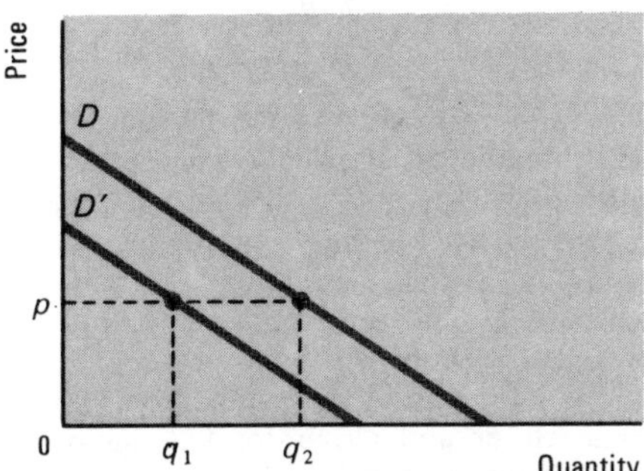

Fig. 9.7 Two parallel straight-line demand curves have unequal price elasticities at p

It follows from Theorem 2 that a parallel shift of a straight-line demand curve lowers elasticity (at each price) if the line shifts outward, and raises elasticity if the line shifts inward.

(3) *The elasticities of two intersecting straight-line demand curves can be compared at the point of intersection merely by comparing slopes, the steeper curve being the less elastic.* In Figure 9.8 we have two intersecting curves. At the point of intersection p and q are common to both curves, and hence the

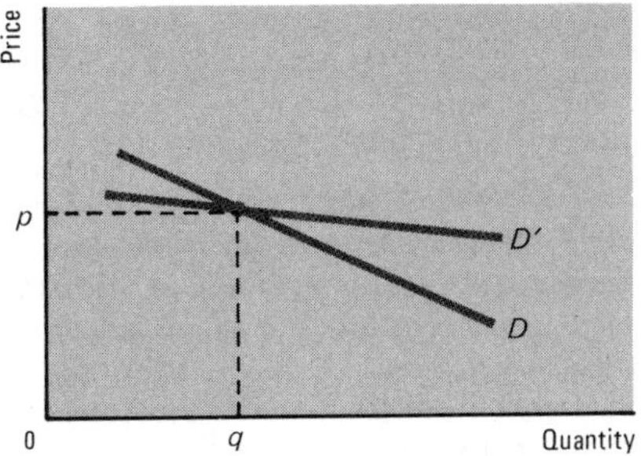

Fig. 9.8 Two intersecting straight-line demand curves have different elasticities at the point where they cross

ratio p/q is the same. Therefore η varies only with $\Delta q/\Delta p$. On the steeper curve $-\Delta p/\Delta q$ is larger than on the flatter curve; thus the ratio $-\Delta q/\Delta p$ is smaller on the steeper curve than on the flatter curve, so that elasticity is lower.

(4) *Any straight-line supply curve through the origin has an elasticity of one.* Such a supply curve is shown in Figure 9.9. Consider the

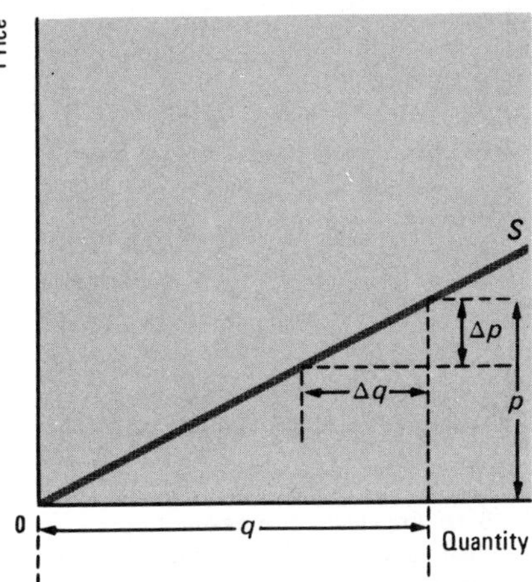

Fig. 9.9 A straight-line supply curve through the origin has an elasticity of one

two triangles with the sides p, q, and the S curve, and Δp, Δq, and the S curve. Clearly these are similar triangles. Therefore the ratios of their sides are equal, i.e.,

$$\frac{p}{q} = \frac{\Delta p}{\Delta q}. \tag{2}$$

Elasticity of supply is defined as

$$\varepsilon = \frac{\Delta q}{\Delta p} \cdot \frac{p}{q}, \tag{3}$$

which, by substitution from (2), gives

$$\varepsilon = \frac{q}{p} \cdot \frac{p}{q} \equiv 1. \qquad (4)$$

(5) *With a straight-line demand curve, the elasticity measured from any point (p, q), according to equation* (1) *above, is independent of the direction and magnitude of the change in price and quantity.* This follows immediately from the fact that the slope of a straight line is a constant. If we start from some point (p, q) and then change price, the ratio $\Delta q/\Delta p$ will be the same whatever the direction or the size of the change in p.

(6) *The elasticity measured from any point* (p, q), *according to equation* (1) *above, is in general dependent on the direction and magnitude of the change in price and quantity.* Except for a straight-line demand curve (for which the slope does not change) the ratio $\Delta q/\Delta p$ will not be the same at different points on a demand curve. Figure 9.10 shows a demand curve that is not a straight line. We desire to measure the elasticity from point 1. The figure makes it apparent that the ratio $\Delta q/\Delta p$, and hence the elasticity, will vary according to the size and the direction of the price change. This result is very inconvenient. It happens because we are averaging the reaction of Δq to Δp over a section of the demand curve, and, depending on the range that we take, the *average reaction* will be different.

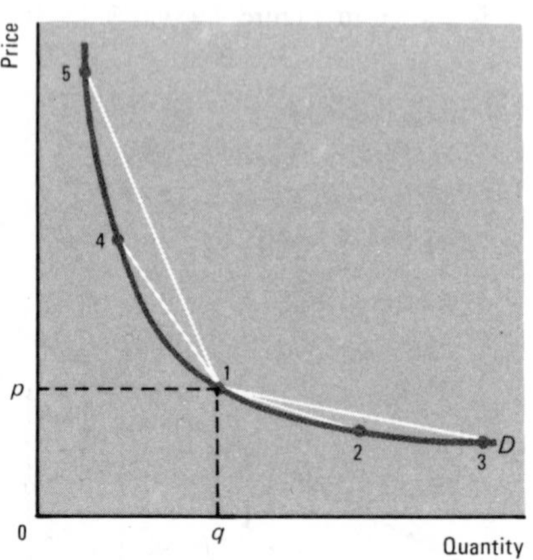

Fig. 9.10 Arc elasticity measured from a particular point (1) on a demand curve that is not a straight line

If we wish to measure the elasticity at a point, we need to know the reaction of quantity to a change in price at that point, not over a whole range. We call the reaction of quantity to price change at a point dq/dp, and we define this to be the reciprocal of the slope of the straight line (i.e., $\Delta q/\Delta p$) tangent to the demand curve at the point in question. In Figure 9.11 the point elasticity of demand at a is the ratio p/q (as it has been in all previous measures) now multiplied by the ratio of $\Delta q/\ \Delta p$ measured along the straight-line tangent to the curve at a. This definition may now be written as

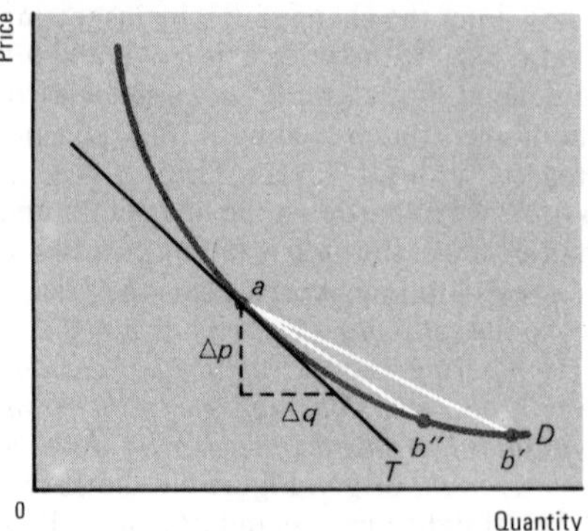

Fig. 9.11 Point elasticity of demand measured from a particular point (a) on the demand curve

$$\eta = -\frac{dq}{dp} \cdot \frac{p}{q}. \qquad (5)$$

The ratio dq/dp, as we have defined it, is in fact the differential-calculus concept of the derivative of quantity with respect to price.

This elasticity is the one normally used in economic theory. Equation (1) may be regarded as an approximation to this expression. It is obvious by inspecting Figure 9.11 that the elasticity measured from (1) will come closer and closer to that measured from (5) the smaller the price change used to calculate the value of (1). From (1), change the price so that we move from a to some point b'; the ratio $\Delta q\ \Delta p$ is the reciprocal of the slope of the straight line joining a and b'. The smaller the price change that we make, the closer the point comes to point a and the closer the slope of the line joining the points comes to the slope of the line tangential to the curve at a. If the slopes of these two lines get closer together, so also do the reciprocals of the slopes and, thus, so do the elasticities as measured by equations (1) and (5). Thus, if we consider (1) as an approximation to (5), the error will diminish as the size of Δp diminishes.

10

Some predictions of the theory of price

The theory of the determination of price by supply and demand is an extremely powerful tool, allowing us to explain and to predict behaviour in competitive markets[1] that are relatively free of government intervention. The theory is also useful in analysing the behaviour of the increasingly large number of markets that are subject to some form of government intervention. In such markets it provides predictions of what would have happened in the absence of intervention which provide useful benchmarks for assessing the effects of the intervention. It is also possible to use the theory to predict the consequences of certain forms of intervention directly.

Before applying our theory to particular markets, a few words should be said about the method of analysis used. When we developed our theory, we concentrated first on the determination of the equilibrium price and quantity, and second on the effects of various shifts in the demand and supply curves. These 'effects' are the implications or predictions of our theory. As mentioned in Chapter 8, we are interested in their correctness in two senses. First, are they logically correct in the sense that they follow from our assumptions? Second, are they empirically correct in the sense that they are not contradicted by observations of the facts? In order to use our theory to develop predictions about real-world markets, we advance three hypotheses: (1) that the assumptions of our theory (e.g., about the shapes of demand and supply curves) adequately describe relations that exist in the particular market being studied; (2) that once the actual price is equal to the equilibrium price, the actual price will not change unless the equilibrium price changes; and (3) that if there is a change in the equilibrium price, the actual price will move fairly quickly towards the new equilibrium price. *If* these hypotheses are correct, *then* the propositions of our theory will provide useful predictions about how prices and quantities will actually behave; if not, the predictions of our theory will frequently be contradicted by the evidence.

The cases studied in this chapter are examples chosen both to illustrate the use of price theory and to give you practice in using it. It is a mistake to try to commit particular examples to memory. Working through these examples should develop your own facility with the tools of price theory, so that you will be able to use the theory yourself to analyse new problems that you encounter.

---

[1] 'Competitive' in the sense discussed on page 74.

Price control and rationing

Maximum-price legislation

Since the dawn of history, governments have passed laws regulating the prices at which some commodities have been sold. In this section we shall concentrate on laws setting *maximum* permissible prices, which are often called 'price ceilings'. Such laws have had many purposes. Often they were an attempt to hold down the prices of foodstuffs during severe temporary shortages caused by crop failures. Medieval city governments often sought to protect their citizens from the consequences of local wheat crop failures by regulating the maximum price of bread. Modern governments in several countries, including the UK, have employed rent controls in an attempt to make housing available at a price that could be afforded by lower-income groups. In both the First and the Second World Wars (1914–18 and 1939–45) many governments attempted to control the overall rate of inflation by imposing price controls on a wide range of individual markets. The same policy has often been used in the last decade in an attempt to control British inflation.

Whatever the motivation of the policy, the theory of the determination of price by demand and supply makes some quite general predictions about the consequences of price controls. Before reading on, it would be a good exercise to ask yourself what you would expect to be the consequences of fixing some prices by law rather than allowing them to be determined by demand and supply.

The effects on price and quantity Figure 10.1 shows the demand and supply curves for some commodity. The equilibrium price is p_1 and the equilibrium quantity is q_1. What would happen if the central authorities were able to enforce a maximum price at which this commodity was to be sold? If the maximum price were set above the equilibrium price, the intervention would have no effect. The equilibrium price would still be attainable and the market equilibrium would not be inconsistent with the maximum-price law. On the other hand, suppose the maximum price is set at a level below equilibrium, say at p_2. The equilibrium price is no longer legally obtainable. Prices must be reduced from p_1 to p_2, and as a result, the quantity demanded will expand from q_1 to q_2; the quantity supplied, on the other hand, will fall from q_1 to q_3. Thus a shortage of the commodity will develop, the quantity demanded exceeding the quantity supplied. (In Figure 10.1 the excess demand is equal to $q_2 - q_3$.)

We now have our first prediction about the effect of price control in a competitive market.

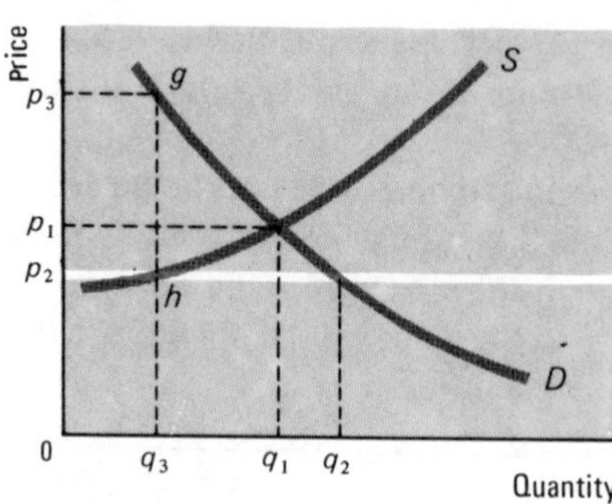

Fig. 10.1 Maximum price controls

The setting of maximum prices either will have no effect (maximum price set at or above the equilibrium) or will cause a shortage of the commodity (maximum price set below the equilibrium), reducing the quantity actually bought and sold below its equilibrium value.

Allocation of available supply In the case of an effective price ceiling, production will not be sufficient to satisfy everyone who wishes to buy the commodity, and price will not be allowed to change so as to allocate the available supply among the would-be purchasers. It follows, then, that some other method of allocation will have to be adopted. Our theory does not predict what this other method will be, but experience has shown a number of alternatives that may arise.

If shops sell their available supplies to the first customers who arrive, then people are likely to rush to those stores that are rumoured to have any stocks of the scarce commodity. Long queues will develop, and allocation will be on the basis of luck, or to those knowing enough to gain from the principle of 'first-come-first-served'.[1] Another system may develop if shopkeepers themselves decide who will get the scarce commodities and who will not. They might keep commodities under the counter and sell them only to regular customers, or only to people of a certain colour or religion. When commodities are allocated according to such criteria we refer to it in general as ALLOCATION BY SELLERS' PREFERENCES.[2]

If the central authorities dislike the somewhat arbitrary system of allocation that grows up as the result of price ceilings, they can ration the goods, giving out ration coupons sufficient to purchase the quantity q_3 in Figure 10.1. The authorities can then determine, as a conscious act of policy, how the available supply is to be allocated. The coupons might be distributed equally, or on the basis of age, sex, marital status, number of dependents or any other criterion. Thus we are led to make another prediction.

Where there is a feeling against allocation on the basis of first-come-first-served or sellers' preferences, effective price ceilings will give rise to strong pressure for a centrally administered system of rationing.

Black markets Under certain circumstances, price control with or without rationing is likely to give rise to a BLACK MARKET, a market in which goods are sold illegally at prices that violate the legal restrictions. For many products, there are only a few manufacturers but many retailers. Although it is easy to police the producers, it is difficult even to locate all those who are, or could be, retailing the product, much less police them. Although the central authorities may be able to control the price that producers get, they may not be able to control the price at which retailers sell to the public. If this were the case with the commodity represented in Figure 10.1, what would you predict would happen?

First, the amount produced will remain unchanged at q_3, because producers will continue to receive the controlled price for their product. At the retail level,

[1] In Europe during both World Wars, the rumour that a shop was selling supplies of some very scarce commodity was sufficient to cause a local stampede. Housewives often spent days tracking down such rumours and then hours standing in line to gain entrance to a shop. Usually the supplies were exhausted while many housewives remained unserved.

[2] In wartime Britain, to move from one town to another meant losing one's status as a 'regular' in many shops. Unless one was a long-term regular at some shop it was difficult to obtain cigarettes or beer, both of which were subject to price control while being unrationed.

however, a black market will arise, because purchasers will be willing to pay more than the controlled price for the limited amounts of the commodity available. If the whole quantity were sold on the black market, it would fetch a price of p_3 per unit. The total amount paid by consumers would be p_3 *times* q_3 which in the figure is the rectangle bounded by $0p_3gq_3$. The total amount of the illegal receipts of black marketeers would be the rectangle bounded by p_2hgp_3.

The theory predicts that the potential for a profitable black market will exist whenever effective price ceilings are imposed. The actual growth of such a market depends on there being a few people willing to risk heavy penalties by running a black-market supply organization and a reasonably large number of persons prepared to purchase goods illegally on such a market. It is an interesting comment on the strengths of various human motives that there has never been a case documented where effective price ceilings were not accompanied by the growth of a black market.

It is unlikely that all goods will be sold on the black market – both because there are some honest people in every society and because the central authorities always have some power to enforce their price laws. Thus we would normally expect not the extreme result given above, but rather that some of the limited supplies would be sold at the controlled price and some would be sold at the black-market price.

An economist's evaluation of a black-market situation can be made only when it is known what objectives the central authorities were hoping to achieve with their price-control policy. If they are mainly concerned with an equitable distribution of a scarce product, it is very likely that effective price control on manufacturers plus a largely uncontrolled black market at the retail level produces the worst possible results. If, however, they are mainly interested in restricting production in order to release resources for other more urgent needs, such as war production, the policy works effectively, if somewhat unfairly. Where the purpose is to keep prices down, the policy is a failure to the extent that black marketeers succeed in raising prices, and a success to the extent that transactions at controlled prices actually take place.

Empirical evidence There is much evidence confirming predictions which we have shown to follow from our simple theory of price. Practically all belligerent countries in both the First and Second World Wars set ceilings on many prices well below free-market, equilibrium levels. The legislation of maximum prices was always followed by shortages, then by either the introduction of rationing or the growth of some private method of allocation such as sellers' preferences, and finally by the rise of some sort of black market. The ceilings were more effective in limiting consumption than in controlling prices, although they did restrain price increases to some extent.

Rent control, an illustration The most common form of peacetime price control is control over rents of private accommodation. In the UK, the rents of cheaper unfurnished flats and houses have been controlled since the First World War. The coverage of rent control legislation has varied over the years, but the drift has been towards subjecting a wider range of accommodations to controls. In 1974 controls were extended to cover furnished accommodations which, to a great extent, serves the market for casual and transient tenants such as students, foreign visitors and workers looking for more permanent accommodation.

The major consequences of such legislation, as predicted by theory and confirmed by many empirical studies, may now be laid briefly with the help of Figure 10.2. The free-market rent is r_1 and the quantity of rented accommodation is q_1. Control legislation is then passed placing a ceiling of r_2 on rents. Over a few years the supply of unfurnished flats and houses is fairly inelastic, since once rental housing is built, little else can be done but to rent out for whatever it will fetch. This is shown by the supply curve S_1 which shows the supply of rental accommodation over the next year or two as being the same as existed before the institution of controls. The effect of rent control legislation that reduces the price from r_1 to r_2 is to create a shortage only as far as the quantity demanded increases as the price comes down. The quantity bought and sold remains the same because of the inelastic supply.

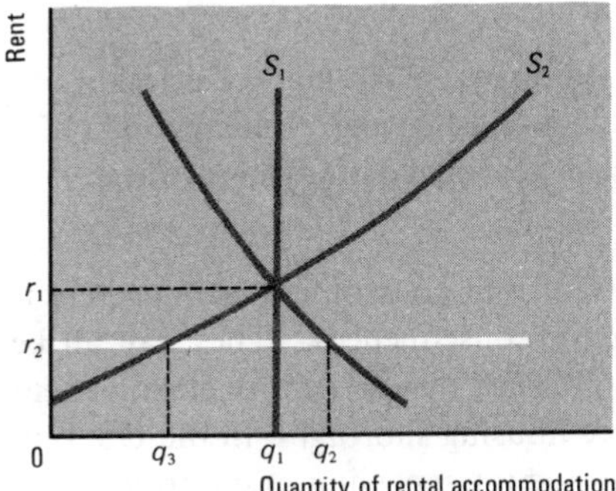

Fig. 10.2 The creation of excess demand

After a few years, however, the lowered return on rental housing will cause the quantity supplied to shrink: new housing will not be built, since the return on the investment is reduced by the legislation; old housing will not be kept up as much as if the equilibrium rent could be earned. Indeed, if rents are held below the cost of upkeep, landlords may simply abandon their buildings so that they literally collapse with rot and decay. As a result, the supply curve showing the quantity that will be supplied after sufficient time has elapsed for the stock of housing to adjust fully to any given price, will be rather elastic. Such a supply curve is S_2 in the figure. It follows that the housing shortage caused by rent control will grow over time as a result of a steady fall in the quantity of housing available. The legislation reducing rents from r_1 to r_2, therefore, causes an immediate shortage of $q_2 - q_1$, which grows to $q_2 - q_3$ as the effects of the controls on supply make themselves felt.

Once the housing shortage becomes significant, landlords will discover that they can rent the available accommodations at prices very much in excess of the controlled price. Since this is illegal, they may resort to charging a fixed 'entrance fee' to new tenants in return for allowing them to have the accommodations. This fee is the lump-sum equivalent of the difference between the fixed price and the free-market price, and constitutes a black-market price for the rent-controlled accommodations. Landlords would then have an incentive to evict existing tenants in order to charge the entrance fee to new tenants. The state might then intervene by passing *security of tenure laws* making it difficult or impossible to evict sitting tenants without satisfying the court that there is 'just cause' for eviction. These laws are necessary if the rent controls are to be effective, but it is difficult for them to discriminate between eviction of a sitting tenant solely to charge a premium to an incoming tenant and eviction for such legitimate reasons as excessive noise, damage to the flat or non-payment of rent. Thus the laws have the effect of further restricting the supply of rental housing by making it even less attractive to invest money in building houses and flats for letting.[1]

The growing housing shortage then puts pressure on the state to relieve the shortage by building the accommodation that private investors will not supply at controlled prices. The shortage will also make people who do have rent-controlled housing reluctant to move, since they would have to search for new accommodations under conditions of severe shortage. This means, for example, that people will be reluctant to move from areas of high unemployment to areas where there is a better chance of obtaining jobs, and that people will be reluctant to move out of accommodations that are no longer suitable because families have grown up and moved away.

Effective rent control leads to housing shortages, black-market prices, security-of-tenure laws, pressure for public housing and reluctance of sitting tenants to move from their present accommodations even when these are no longer suitable.

Although there is debate on the desirability of rent-control legislation, there is little doubt that the above are among its major consequences.[2] They can all be observed in the UK. Furthermore, it is well established that areas with effective rent control legislation tend to have the most severe housing shortages. In the US, rent control is in the hands of individual cities and the interspersing of controlled and uncontrolled markets for housing makes testing predictions about the effects of rent control relatively easy. For example, rent control in the Bronx borough of New York is accompanied by severe housing shortages; whole blocks of buildings have been abandoned, although they would probably have lasted several more centuries with care. Uncontrolled markets in the Southwest, on the other hand, have seen supplies increase rapidly to meet the growing demands for housing as population moved there. Rent control was introduced in Rome in 1978 and almost immediately increased the shortage of accommodation.

Minimum-price legislation

Governments sometimes pass laws stating that certain goods and services cannot be sold below some stated minimum price. In many Western countries today there are minimum-wage laws specifying 'floors' for the wages to be paid to different kinds of labour. Resale price maintenance, which exists in many countries, gives the

[1] The Rent Act of 1974 extended rent control to cover furnished accommodation. This produced a more immediate shortage of furnished accommodation than the above analysis suggests. Unfurnished accommodation is mainly in blocks of flats that have zero opportunity cost and hence the short-run supply *is* inelastic. Furnished accommodation is often in private homes whose owners are temporarily absent. Security of tenure laws led to an immediate withdrawal of much unfurnished accommodation from the rental market as private owners did not wish to risk becoming saddled with an unevictable sitting tenant when they wished to reoccupy their house.

[2] For two views on this desirability see *Eclipse of the Private Landlord* (Conservative Political Centre, 1974) and *The End of the Private Landlord*, Fabian Research Series No. 312 (1973). The authors of the Fabian pamphlet accept most of the consequences outlined in the text but welcome rent control as a means of eliminating private landlords, thus making way for the complete state provision of all rented accommodation.

manufacturer power to prevent the retailer from selling below prices set by the manufacturer. Before reading on, see if you can work out for yourself what our theory predicts about the effects of minimum-price laws.

The effects on price and quantity The case of a commodity subject to minimum-price legislation is illustrated in Figure 10.3. The free-market equilibrium price is p_1, and

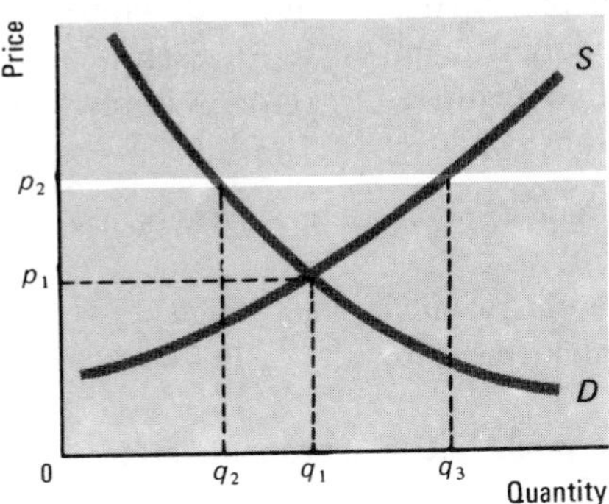

Fig. 10.3 Minimum price controls

the equilibrium quantity traded is q_1. If the minimum price is set below the equilibrium price, it has no effect on the market. The attainment of the free-market equilibrium and the fulfilment of the minimum-price law are perfectly compatible. On the other hand, if the minimum price is set above the equilibrium, say at p_2, the free-market equilibrium will be legally unobtainable. At price p_2 there will be an excess of quantity supplied over quantity demanded. Suppliers would like to sell q_3, but purchasers are only willing to buy q_2. The actual amount bought and sold will thus be q_2 and there will be excess supply of $q_3 - q_2$. This leads to our first prediction about minimum prices:

> **The setting of minimum prices either will have no effect (minimum prices set at or below the equilibrium) or will cause a surplus of the commodity (minimum price set above the equilibrium), reducing the quantity actually bought and sold below its equilibrium value.**

No alternative allocation systems and no black markets In this case there is, at the legally inforced price, no scarcity of the controlled commodity. Therefore we do not predict that alternate allocative systems will grow up. There will, however, be a shortage of purchasers, and potential suppliers may compete in various ways for the available customers. Methods of price cutting will be searched for; some will find loopholes in the law and some will merely flout it. For example, travel clubs and other organizations grew up rapidly in the early 1970s in order to take advantage of cheap group rates which the scheduled airlines are not legally allowed to offer individual passengers.

There will be no opportunity for black-market operators to take over the distribution of the product, since they would lose money by buying at the controlled price and selling at the free-market price. There will, however, be an incentive for an individual producer to sell his product at less than the controlled price as long as his only alternative is not to sell it at all. Thus we predict:

Effective minimum-price laws will not give rise to alternative allocation systems or to organized black markets, but will be accompanied by some clandestine selling by individual producers at prices below the legal minimum.

Minimum-wage laws, an illustration As an example of minimum price policies, consider the case of minimum-wage laws. Applying our theory to the labour market is a bit of a jump in the dark, but we can note in passing that the theory developed in Part 5 does allow us to use a downward-sloping demand curve for each type of labour. If we hypothesize that our theory of competitive markets will apply to a labour market, we have the following predictions.

When an effective minimum-wage law is applied in only a few markets of the economy:
(1) It will raise the wages of some of those who remain in employment;
(2) It will lower the actual amount of employment (by $q_1 - q_2$ in Figure 10.3);
(3) It will create a surplus of labour which would like to but cannot obtain jobs in the occupation affected;
(4) It will create an incentive for some workers to try to evade the law by offering to work for less than the legal wage.

Empirical evidence There is ample evidence confirming most of these predictions. The illegal offering of their services for part-time and evening work is a well-established reaction of many workers to union regulation of minimum allowable wages. A great deal of empirical work in the US has established that federal minimum-wage laws have created quite substantial unemployment among the least skilled members of the labour force, particularly blacks, who would have obtained employment at wages below the legal minimum. In Canada, minimum wage laws are passed by each of the ten provinces; the substantial differences among provinces makes empirical assessment of their effects relatively easy. High minimum-wage laws appear to be associated with high unemployment among youths and unskilled workers of all ages.

It is remarkable how many predictions our simple theory yields about the effects of minimum and maximum price controls, and how, how often these predictions have been confirmed by the evidence. It is also interesting, and not a little depressing, to see how often governments are prepared to pass price-control laws without appearing to foresee their likely effects.

Tax incidence

What is the effect of taxes on the sale and purchase of commodities, such as customs and excise duty, on petrol, tobacco or whisky? Do such taxes leave prices unchanged or do they cause prices to rise? Does the producer pay the tax or is he able to pass it on to the consumer through higher prices? Many such age-old controversies are to be found in the field of tax theory.

The effect of tax on the supply curve

As a first step in discovering what our theory predicts about the results of taxes, we shall consider the effect of a tax on the supply of a commodity. Look at Table 10.1, which repeats in columns 1 and 2 the supply schedule for carrots from Table 7.4, page 90. The schedule shows the relation between the price that farmers get for their carrots and the total amount that all farmers are willing to produce and sell. If no tax is levied, sellers receive the whole market price for which the commodity is sold. If a tax is levied, however, sellers will receive on each unit sold the market price of the commodity *minus* the amount of the tax. *If producers are to receive the same amount per unit that they were receiving prior to the tax, the market price will have to rise by the full amount of the tax*, as shown by column 3 of the table.

Table 10.1 Derivation of a supply schedule when a per-unit tax is levied

Pre-tax supply schedule If the seller receives the price listed in column 1, he will offer for sale the quantity listed in column 2		If a tax of £30 per ton is placed on the sale of carrots, they must be *sold* for the price listed in column 3 (col.1 +£30) if the seller is to *receive* the amount listed in column 1
Column 1 £ per ton received by the seller	Column 2 Thousands of tons supplied per month	Column 3 Market price in £s per ton after a tax of £30 per ton is levied
20	5·0	50
40	46·0	70
60	77·5	90
80	100·0	110
100	115·0	130
120	122·5	150

To illustrate this, we assume that a tax of £30 per ton is placed on the sale of carrots. Every time a producer sells a ton of carrots, he must pay £30 to the government and can keep for himself only what is left after that. The table shows that producers were prepared to supply 5,000 tons of carrots a month when they

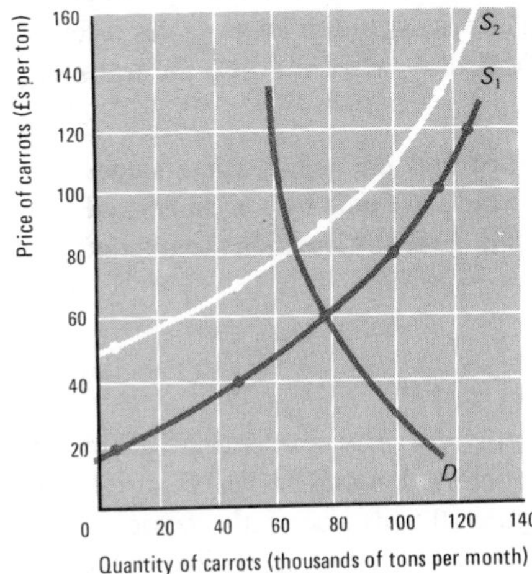

Fig. 10.4 The effect of a tax of £30 per ton on the equilibrium price and quantity of carrots

received £20 a ton for themselves. Thus 5,000 tons per month will be supplied at a market price of £20 a ton when there is no tax, but at a market price of £50 per ton when there is a tax. Taking another example from the table, we see that producers are prepared to grow and to sell 115,000 untaxed tons a month at a market price of £100 per ton, but they will grow and offer for sale this amount only at a market price of £130 per ton when a £30 per ton tax is levied.

We may summarize this change in more general terms as follows. Assuming that the willingness of sellers to supply the commodity is unchanged after a tax has been levied, every quantity supplied will be associated with a market price higher by the amount of the tax than the one previously required.

In Figure 10.4 the no-tax relation between the quantity of carrots supplied and their market price is shown by the supply curve labelled S_1 and the after-tax relation is shown by the supply curve S_2.

The effect of a tax on a commodity is to shift every point on its supply curve vertically upward by the amount of the tax.

The effect of a tax on price

So far, we have only shown what would have to happen to market price if the quantity supplied were to remain the same. But what actually happens to price depends on demand as well as on supply. Before we can say anything about the price, we must add a demand curve. Figure 10.4 shows the demand curve for carrots as well as the pre- and post-tax supply curves. The original equilibrium price is £60 and the quantity traded is 77,500 tons per month. If, following the imposition of the tax, the price were to rise by the full amount of the tax, from £60 to £90, the quantity demanded would fall, and there would be an excess of quantity supplied over quantity demanded. This would causė the price to fall until it reached the equilibrium point where the new supply curve cuts the demand curve. In the example illustrated in Figure 10.4, the new equilibrium price is £82 a ton. This is the price that will be paid by consumers. When the tax of £30 per ton is deducted, the producers will receive £52. Thus, in this example, the tax has the effect or raising the price paid by consumers by £22 and lowering the price received by producers by £8. The incidence of the tax falls by just under three-quarters on the consumers and just over one-quarter on the producers. The term *incidence* is used to describe where the burden of a tax actually falls, in terms of higher prices paid or lower prices received.

If we drop the specific numerical example of the carrot market, the following, more general, prediction may be made:

When the demand curve slopes downward and the supply curve slopes upward, the imposition of a tax will raise the price paid by consumers and lower the price received by producers, in both cases by less than the amount of the tax.

The influence of elasticity

Figure 10.5, like Figure 10.4, shows two supply curves, representing before- and after-tax situations. It combines them with different demand curves. Figure 10.5 (i) shows a perfectly inelastic demand curve, Figure 10.5 (ii) a perfectly elastic one and Figure 10.5 (iii) two intermediate cases. In the case of the perfectly inelastic curve,

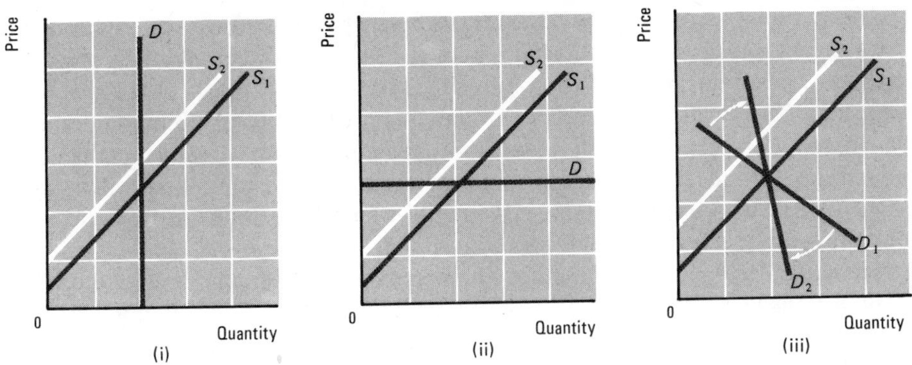

Fig. 10.5 The effect of a tax on price and quantity, given demand curves of various elasticities

the equilibrium price increases by the full amount of the tax; in the case of the perfectly elastic curve, the equilibrium price is unchanged in spite of the shift in the supply curve. This suggests the following general prediction:

> **The more inelastic the demand for a commodity, the greater the rise in the price paid by consumers and the less the fall in the price received by producers as a result of the imposition of any given tax.**

The derivation of this prediction is illustrated in Figure 10.5 (iii). Look at demand curve D_1, which intersects the original supply curve, S_1, to determine the equilibrium price. Note the post-tax equilibrium price given by the intersection of the original demand curve with the new supply curve S_2. Now consider *pivoting* the demand curve through the original equilibrium point, as shown in the figure. Clearly, the steeper, and thus also the more inelastic, the demand curve at the equilibrium point, the greater the rise in price paid by consumers and the smaller the fall in the price received by producers.[1]

These tax predictions are quite general ones which are applicable to all more-or-less competitive markets. As an illustration of their wide range of applicability, we shall consider some of the major effects of real-estate taxes.

Real-estate taxes, an example

Property taxes, which are a percentage of the assessed market value of land and buildings, are levied by local governments throughout the world. In the UK they are called *local rates*. Property owners often protest that the crushing burden of these taxes makes property investment unprofitable, while many tenants believe that the taxes are borne fully by them in the form of higher rents. Both groups cannot be right in alleging that they bear the whole burden of the tax! The theory of competitive markets suggests that the truth lies somewhere between the two extremes – that part of the tax is borne by landlords and part is passed on to tenants.

---

[1] We have earlier warned against confusing the slope of a demand curve with its elasticity. When two or more demand curves intersect, however, their relative elasticities at the point of intersection can be inferred from their slopes: the steeper the curve, the more inelastic it is. (See page 115 of the Appendix to Chapter 9 for a proof.)

To see what is involved, start with a situation in which there are no rates, and then assume that one is imposed. If each one of the thousands of landlords in the city decides to raise rents by the full amount of the tax, what does the theory predict will happen? There will be a decline in the quantity of rental accommodations demanded. Higher rents will induce some people to move outside the city boundaries, where rents for equivalent accommodations are lower, and will induce some of those who stay to economize by renting a smaller or not-so-attractive place, or by moving to a less expensive neighbourhood. The same two effects will also be observed with shopkeepers and other commercial users of the city's real estate. The decline in the quantity demanded, without any change in the quantity supplied, will cause a surplus of rental accommodations. Landlords will find it difficult to replace tenants who move out, and the typical rental unit will remain empty between tenancies longer than previously. Prospective tenants will find many alternative sites from which to choose and will become very particular in what they expect from eager landlords.

This situation will lead some prospective tenants to offer to pay rents below the going ones and will lead some landlords to accept these offers, rather than earn nothing from vacant premises. Once some landlords cut their rentals, others will have to follow suit or else leave their properties unrented for long periods of time. As the rents received by landlords fall, there will be a gradual contraction in the quantity of rental accommodations supplied. Home-owners will be less willing to rent out parts of their homes, and when blocks of flats are replaced, as they are continuously, it will not pay to build them quite so high as previously. This reduction in the quantity will prevent rents from coming down to their original pre-tax level.

Eventually, rentals will reach a new equilibrium at which the quantity demanded equals the quantity supplied. This equilibrium will be higher than the original pre-tax rent but lower than the rent that passes the whole tax on to tenants. Thus the burden of the tax will be shared by landlords and tenants, the proportion in which it is shared depending on elasticities of demand.

Notice that this result can emerge even though neither the landlords nor the tenants realise what is happening. Both sides may think, for example, that the landlord is fully passing the tax on, even though this is not the case. In fact, in Britain and parts of Europe, it is common for the tenant to be sent the tax account and to pay it directly to the local authority that levies it. Even so, the landlord bears part of the burden of the tax, for as long as the existence of the tax reduces the quantity demanded below what it otherwise would be, the amount received by landlords will be depressed. The reason why this can occur without landlords and tenants being aware of it is that neither is likely to have much idea of what equilibrium rentals would be in the absence of the tax. It doesn't do much good to look at what happens immediately after tax rates are changed, since, as we have already seen, the full effect takes time. Landlords may begin by raising rents by the full amount of the tax, creating a disequilibrium, but in the final position, prices will have risen by less than the tax. Furthermore, prices of rentals are changing for many reasons, including general inflationary pressures, local changes in costs, and shifts in demand resulting from changes in living habits. Where many things are changing at once, only careful statistical analysis can sort out the influence of one particular variable, such as changes in tax rates.

The problems of agriculture

To the casual observer, the agricultural sector of almost any advanced Western economy presents a series of paradoxes. Food is one of the truly basic necessities of life. Yet, over the last century, agricultural sectors have been declining in relative importance, and many of those persons who have remained on the land have been receiving incomes well below national averages.

Governments have felt it necessary to intervene. As a result, a bewildering array of controls, supports and subsidies has been built into agricultural markets. Subsidies and price floors have led to the accumulation of vast government surpluses which have sometimes rotted in their storage bins and sometimes been sold abroad at prices well below their costs of production. All of this has gone on against a backdrop of endemic malnutrition and occasional outbursts of famine in the 'Third World'. Today, as the world's population increases and the spectre of undernourishment and starvation is growing more frightening, it begins to look as though the problem of surplus agricultural production may give way to the problem of deficient agricultural production.

Why has agriculture so often been a problem industry in the past? Is it possible that it may cease to be one in the near future?

Short-term fluctuations in prices and incomes

The production of many agricultural goods is subject to quite large variations due to factors completely beyond human control: lack of rainfall, invasion of pests, floods and other natural events are all capable of reducing output to a level well below that planned by farmers, while exceptionally favourable conditions can cause production to be well above the planned level. We may now ask what our theory of prices predicts about the effect of these unplanned fluctuations on the price of agricultural commodities and on the revenues earned by farmers for the sale of their crops.

A supply curve is meant to show desired output and sales at each market price. If there are unplanned variations in output, then actual output and sales will diverge from their planned level. The supply curve drawn in Figure 10.6 shows the total

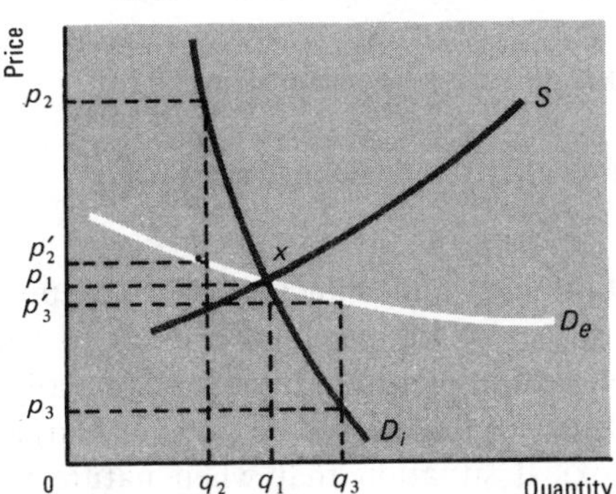

Fig. 10.6 Fluctuations in price caused by unplanned fluctuations in supply operating on elastic and inelastic demand curves

quantity farmers desire to produce and offer for sale at various prices. If the price were p_1, then planned production would be q_1, but actual production would vary around this planned amount, owing to causes beyond the farmers' control. Two demand curves are drawn in Figure 10.6, one is relatively elastic (D_e) and the other is relatively inelastic (D_i) over the quantity range from q_2 to q_3. In a world in which plans were always fulfilled, price would settle at the equilibrium level of p_1 with output q_1. But unplanned fluctuations in output will cause the actual price to fluctuate. If, for example, the crop is poor so that the actual production is q_2, then a shortage will develop; prices will rise to p_2 in the case of demand curve D_i, and p'_2 in the case of curve D_e. In each case the quantity demanded will be reduced to a point at which it is equal to the available supply. If, on the other hand, growing conditions are particularly favourable, actual production will exceed planned production, a surplus will occur and price will fall. For example, when production is q_3, price will fall to p_3 in the case of curve D_i and to p'_3 in the case of curve D_e. In each case the fall in price will increase the quantity demanded sufficiently to absorb the extra unplanned supply, but the fall in price will be larger when the demand curve is D_i than when it is D_e.

We have now derived the following prediction:

Unplanned fluctuations in output will cause price variations in the opposite direction (the higher the output, the lower the price); for given output fluctuations, the smaller the elasticity of demand for the product, the larger the price variations.

Now consider the effects on the revenues received by farmers from the sale of their crops.[1] Here the relations are a bit more complex, but they all follow immediately from the results established on page 109. If the good in question has an elasticity of demand greater than unity, then unplanned increases in supply raise farmers' revenues while unplanned decreases lower them. If, on the other hand, the good has an inelastic demand, consumers' total expenditure on the product, and thus farmers' revenues, will rise when price rises and fall when price falls. Thus, good harvests will bring reductions in total farm revenues, while bad harvests will bring increases in farm revenues![2] If the elasticity happens to be unity, then farmers' revenues will not vary as output and prices vary because every change in output will be met by an exactly compensating change in price so that total expenditure remains constant.

Unplanned variations in output will cause producers' sales revenue:
(1) To vary in the same direction as output varies whenever demand for the product is elastic,
(2) To vary in the opposite direction as output varies whenever demand for the product is inelastic,
(3) To fluctuate more the further does the elasticity of demand diverge from unity in either direction.

Evidence for these predictions is fairly abundant. Unplanned fluctuations in output occur frequently in agriculture. Where the prices of the products are left to be determined by the free market, large price fluctuations do result. In the case of many agricultural goods, the demand is quite inelastic. In these cases we find very large price fluctuations together with the paradoxical situation that when nature is

[1] While we can only make predictions in this section about the revenues, such receipts are closely related to the incomes of farmers. We can, therefore, without risk of serious error, extend these predictions to incomes.

[2] It does not follow that every individual farmer's income must rise (after all, some farmers may have nothing to harvest); it follows only that the aggregate revenue earned by *all* farmers must rise.

unexpectedly kind and produces a bumper crop, farmers see their incomes dwindling, while when nature is moderately unkind so that supplies fall unexpectedly, farmers' incomes rise. The interests of the farmer and those of the consumer then appear to be exactly opposed.

Cyclical fluctuations in prices and incomes

Agricultural markets are subject not only to short-run instabilities due to uncontrollable changes in output, but also, like most raw materials markets, to cyclical instability due to shifts in demand. In periods of prosperity, full employment prevails, incomes are high and demand for all commodities is high. In periods of depressed business activity, there is substantial unemployment, incomes fall and demand for most commodities falls as a result. As the pulse of business prosperity ebbs and flows, we thus find demand curves for all commodities rising and falling. What effect will this have on commodity prices? Industrial products typically have rather elastic supply curves, so that demand shifts cause fairly large changes in outputs but only small changes in prices. Agricultural commodities tend to have rather inelastic supplies. Thus, when demand falls due to a recession in general business activity, prices tend to fall drastically in agriculture but to remain fairly stable in the manufacturing sector.

Since we do not have cost figures, we cannot reach a final conclusion about incomes. But from the point of view of fluctuations in total receipts caused by cyclical fluctuations in demand, it is just as much a curse to have a very elastic supply as it is to have a very inelastic one! When demand falls and the supply is very inelastic, revenue falls because *price* falls a great deal; when demand falls and the supply is very elastic, revenue falls because *quantity* falls a great deal.

Agricultural stabilization programmes

In free-market economies, agricultural incomes often tend to fluctuate around a low *average* level. Agricultural stabilization programmes have two goals: to reduce the fluctuations and to raise the average level of farm incomes. Many countries have schemes designed to reduce agricultural fluctuations. The two goals, stable incomes and reasonably high incomes, as we shall see, often conflict. We shall illustrate the working of stabilization schemes to lessen the effects of unplanned fluctuations in supply. A similar analysis could be carried out for policies to lessen the effects of cyclical fluctuations in demand.[1]

Market fluctuations due to unplanned fluctuations in output Figure 10.7 shows the demand and supply curves for some agricultural product. According to its definition, the supply curve shows the amount firms are willing to produce and offer for sale at each price. Thus it shows the total *planned production* of all farmers. If there were no uncertainties in the agricultural world, actual production would be equal to planned production and price and quantity would settle at p_1 and q_1 respectively. We know, however, that many uncertain events affect agricultural

[1] We are concerned here only with action to stabilize prices. After we have studied the theory of perfect competition in Chapter 19, we shall return to the topic of producers' organizations and study their attempts to raise the average level of their members' incomes. At that time we shall develop a theory of the inherent instability of producers' co-operatives.

production. Thus when planned production is p_1, actual production will fluctuate, say between p_1 and p_3. If the price fluctuates so as to equate demand and actual production, the market price will fluctuate between p_2 and p_3 as a result.

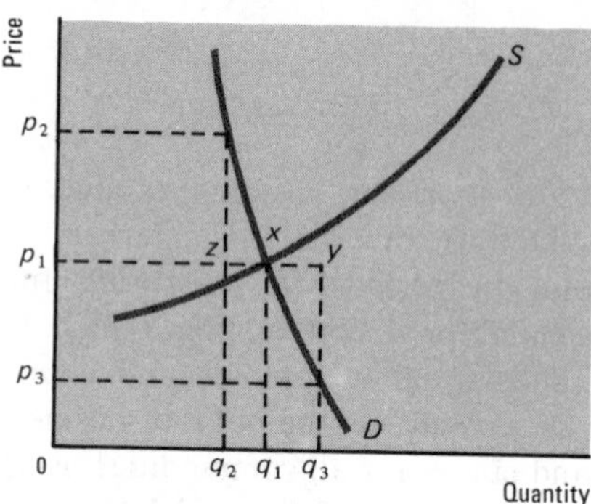

Fig. 10.7 Policies designed to stabilize price in the face of unplanned fluctuations in supply

In this analysis we shall make the simplifying assumption that planned production remains at q_1 and actual output varies only because of unplanned fluctuations. In Chapter 11 we shall reconsider this example, allowing planned production to change in response to changes in market price.

Market stabilization by a producers' association One method of preventing fluctuations in prices and incomes is for the individual farmers to form a producers' association which tries to even out the supply actually coming on to the market, in spite of variations in production. Since one firm's output is a very insignificant part of total production, it would be futile for an individual firm to hold some of its production off the market in an effort to force up the price. This behaviour would only reduce the firm's own income without having any appreciable effect on price. But if many firms get together and agree to vary the supply coming on to the market, then collectively they can have a major effect on price.

Under the conditions illustrated by Figure 10.7, a producers' association might be quite successful in keeping the price at p_1 and incomes at the level indicated by the area of the rectangle Op_1xq_1. What would the association's policy have to be? Any excess of production over q_1 would have to be stored away unsold. If, for example, production for one year were q_3, then $q_3 - q_1$ would have to be added to the association's stocks while q_1 was sold at price p_1. Any deficiency of production below q_1, on the other hand, would have to be made good by sales out of the association's stocks. If production were q_2, for example, then $q_1 - q_2$ would be sold out of stocks, making total sales again equal to q_1 at a price of p_1. In this way the producers' association could keep sales, price and incomes stabilized, in spite of fluctuations in production.

Provided that the level of sales to be maintained (q_1 in Figure 10.7) was equal to average production, the policy could be carried on indefinitely. If, however, the producers attempted to keep the price too high, so that sales were less than the average amount produced, then, taken over a number of years, additions to stocks would exceed sales from stocks, and the stocks held by the association would tend to increase. The successful policy is one that keeps sales constant at q_1 (by adding to or subtracting from stocks). Since income accrues to the producers when the goods are actually sold, total producer income will be stabilized at p_1 *times* q_1, which in Figure 10.7 is the area of the rectangle Op_1xq_1.

Market stabilization by government sales and purchases What will happen if a producers' association is not formed but the government attempts to stabilize the incomes of farmers by entering the market itself, buying and adding to its own stocks when there is a surplus, and selling goods from its stocks when there is a shortage? If the government wishes to stabilize farmers' incomes, what policy should it adopt? Should it aim, like the producers' association, at keeping prices constant at all times?

Before reading further, attempt to work out for yourself the consequences of a government policy designed to keep price fixed at level p_1 in Figure 10.7 by buying goods when production is in excess of q_1 and selling goods when production falls short of q_1. The government is assumed not to consume any of the commodity but only to hold stocks, adding to them when it buys and subtracting from them when it sells.

If the average level of production around which the year-to-year figure fluctuates is q_1, then there is no reason why the government should not successfully stabilize the price at p_1 indefinitely. This policy will not, however, have the result of stabilizing farmers' incomes. Farmers will now be faced with an infinitely elastic demand at price p_1: whatever the total quantity produced, they will be able to sell it at price p_1; if the public will not buy all the production, then the government will purchase what is left over. If total production is q_3, then q_1 will be bought by the public and q_3-q_1 by the government. Total farm income in this case will be the amount indicated by the area of the rectangle Op_1yq_3 (the quantity q_3 multiplied by the price p_1). If total production in another year is only q_2, then this quantity will be sold by farmers and the government also will sell q_1-q_2 out of its stocks so that price will remain at p_1. Total farm income will then be the amount indicated by the rectangle Op_1zq_2 (quantity q_2 multiplied by the price p_1). It is obvious that if prices are held constant and farmers sell their whole production each year, farmers' incomes will fluctuate in proportion to fluctuations in production. This government policy, therefore, will not eliminate income fluctuations but will simply reverse their direction. Now bumper crops will be associated with high incomes, while small crops will be associated with low incomes.

What, then, must a government's policy be if it wishes to stabilize farmers' revenues through its own purchases and sales in the open market? Too much price stability causes revenues to vary directly with production, as in the case just considered, while too little price stability causes them to vary inversely with production, as in the free-market case originally considered. It appears that the government should aim at some intermediate degree of price stability. In fact, if it allows prices to vary exactly in proportion to variations in production, revenues will be stabilized. A 10 per cent rise in production should be met by a 10 per cent fall in price, and a 10 per cent fall in production by a 10 per cent rise in price.

The government policy necessary to achieve the requisite price fluctuations is shown in Figure 10.8. The analysis becomes a bit difficult at this stage. The best way to follow it is to draw your own graph, building it up step by step as the argument proceeds, using Figure 10.8 as a guide. The curves D and S should first be copied. As before, planned production is p_1. Actual production, however, fluctuates between q_2 and q_3, and these fluctuations, given the very inelastic demand curve D, would cause price to fluctuate between p_2 and p_3. Now construct through the point x (the equilibrium point when actual production is equal to planned production) a curve of unit elasticity throughout its whole range. This constructed curve is the white rectangular hyperbola in the figure labelled $\eta = 1$. If q_1 is produced and sold at price p_1, total income is that indicated by the rectangle Op_1xq_1. The white curve now shows the market price that must rule if production and sales are allowed to vary but income is held constant.

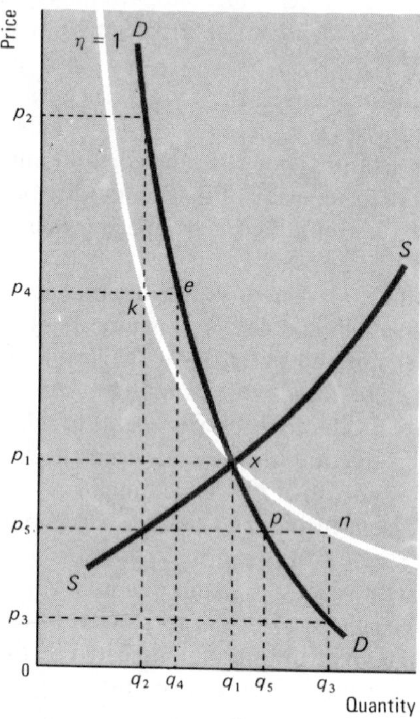

Fig. 10.8 Government policies designed to stabilize income in the face of unplanned fluctuations in supply

Consider first what happens if production is q_3. Market price must be held at p_5 if income is to be unchanged. But, at market price p_5, the public only wishes to purchase q_5 and it is therefore necessary for the government to buy up the remaining production, $q_3 - q_5$, and add it to its stocks. Farmers' total sales are q_3 at price q_5, and since the white curve is a rectangular hyperbola, it follows that income p_5 *times* q_3 is equal to income p_1 *times* q_1.

Now consider what must happen if production is equal to q_2. If farm income is to be unchanged, then the price must be allowed to rise to p_4 (by construction the area of rectangle Op_4kq_2 is equal to the area of rectangle Op_1xq_1). But at price p_4, the public will wish to buy q_4 so that the government must sell $q_4 - q_2$ out of its stocks.

If this policy is successful, it will have the following results. First, there will be smaller fluctuations in the price of this product than if price were determined on a completely free market. Second, total revenues of the producers will be stabilized in the face of fluctuations in production. Finally, the government scheme should be self-financing. In fact, if we ignore costs of storage, the scheme will show a profit, for the government will be buying at low prices (below p_1) – the lower the price the more it buys – and selling at high prices (above p_1) – the higher the price, the more it sells. The actual existence of a profit will depend on the costs of storing the stocks from the periods of glut when they are purchased until the periods of shortage when they are sold. In any case, this scheme has a financial advantage over the previous one in which the government completely stabilized prices. In that case there would necessarily be a loss, for all purchases and sales would be made at the same price, p_1, and there would be no trading profit to set against the costs of storage.

Problems with stabilization policies

The above analysis is meant merely to illustrate some of the many types of stabilization schemes and to show how the theory of price can be used to predict their consequences. If such schemes have all of the advantages outlined above, why is it that there is so much trouble with most stabilization programmes that are actually operated?

Choosing the proper price level One of the major problems with stabilization schemes arises from uncertainty, combined with political pressure applied by farmers. Demand and supply curves are never known exactly, so the central authorities do not know what the average production will be over a number of years at each possible price. They do not know, therefore, exactly what level of income they can try to achieve while also keeping sales from stocks equal to purchases for stocks on average over a large number of years. Since farmers have votes, there is strong pressure on any government to err in the direction of fixing the income to be stabilized at too high a level. If the level of income, and hence price, is fixed too high, then the central authorities will find it necessary to buy unsold crops most years. Thus, stocks will build up more or less continuously and, sooner or later, they will have to be destroyed, given away, or dumped on the market for what they will bring, thus forcing the market price down, defeating the purpose for which the crops were originally purchased.

The authorities' plan will now show a deficit, for goods will have been purchased which cannot be sold at all. This deficit will have to be covered by taxation, which means that people in cities will be paying farmers for producing goods which are never consumed. The next step is often to try to limit the production of each farmer. Quotas may be assigned to individual farmers and penalties imposed for exceeding them, or bonuses may be paid for leaving land idle. Such measures attempt to get around the problem that too many resources are allocated to the agricultural sector by preventing these resources from producing all that they could.

> **Government policies that stabilize prices at too high a level will cause excess supply, a rising level of unsold stocks, and pressure for further government intervention to restrict output.**

The long-term problem of resource reallocation Even if the temptation to set too high a price is avoided, there is still a formidable problem facing the managers of agricultural-stabilization programmes. It results from the fact that the productive capacity of almost all economies is growing over time. Owing to better health, better working conditions, and more and better capital equipment, each worker can produce more than he or she previously did. In the United Kingdom, the increase in *per capita* production has averaged almost 2 per cent a year over the last hundred years. If the allocation of resources were to remain unchanged, there would be an increase in the output of each commodity in proportion to the increase in productivity in that industry.

The real incomes of the population will also increase, on average at a rate equal to the production increase. How will the people wish to consume their extra income?

The relevant measure in this case is the income elasticity of demand, which measures the effect of increases in income on the demands for various commodities. Only in the unrealistic case in which all commodities have unit income elasticities of demand would the proportions in which commodities are demanded not change as income changed: in this special case an x per cent rise in income would lead to an x per cent rise in the demand for every commodity.

Assume that productivity expands more or less uniformly in all industries. The demand for commodities with low income elasticities will be expanding slower than the supplies; excess supplies will develop, prices and profits will be depressed, and it will be necessary for resources to move out of these industries. Exactly the reverse will happen for commodities with high income elasticities: demand will expand faster than supply, prices and profits will tend to rise, and resources will move into those industries. Table 10.2 illustrates this. It gives a simple numerical example of an economy divided into an agricultural and a manufacturing sector. Originally, resources are divided equally between the two. Productivity then doubles in both sectors. The incomes of all consumers double and the income elasticity of demand for manufactured goods is higher than the income elasticity of demand for agricultural goods. The rise in productivity causes a surplus equal to one-quarter of the agricultural production, and a shortage equal to one-quarter of the manufactured-goods production. If the productivity increases are going on continuously, there will be a *continual tendency* toward excess supply of agricultural goods and excess demand for manufactured goods. Thus it will be necessary to have a continuous movement of resources out of agriculture and into the manufacturing industries.

Table 10.2 Surpluses and shortages resulting from uniform increases in productivity and differing income elasticities of demand

	Agriculture	Manufacturing
Production originally was	50·0	50·0
Production after productivity change, if there were no reallocation of resources, would be	100·0	100·0
Income elasticity of demand is	0·50	1·5
Therefore quantity demanded after rise in income is	75·0	125·0
Therefore surplus or shortage is	25·0 (surplus)	25·0 (shortage)

In a free-market economy, this reallocation will take place under the incentives of low prices, wages and incomes in the declining sector, and high prices, wages and incomes in the expanding sector. Look at Table 10.2 again. Because there is excess supply in the agricultural sector, prices will fall and incomes of producers will fall. There will be a decline in the demand for farm labour and the other factors of production used in agriculture, and the earnings of these factors will decline. At the same time, exactly the opposite tendencies will be observed in manufacturing. Here demand is expanding faster than supply; prices will rise; incomes and profits of producers will be rising. There will be a large demand for the factors of production used in manufacturing industries, so that the price of these factors, and consequently the incomes that they earn, will be bid upward. In short, manufacturing will be a buoyant, expanding industry and agriculture will be a depressed, contracting industry.

In a free-market society, the mechanism for a continued reallocation of resources out of low-income-elasticity industries and into high-income-elasticity ones is a continued depressing tendency of prices and incomes in contracting industries, and a continued buoyant tendency of prices and incomes in expanding industries.

Frequently, in a wealthy society where real incomes are expanding year by year, people feel that the agricultural sector *ought* to share in this prosperity. Stabilization programmes often aim at providing farmers with incomes comparable to urban incomes. Positive economics has nothing to say about the ethics of such a policy; it merely tries to discover its consequences. The main problem is that a programme that succeeds in giving the rural sector a high level of income may frustrate the reallocation mechanism. If incomes are guaranteed, there will be no monetary incentives for resources to transfer out of the agricultural sector. Unless some other means is found to persuade resources to transfer, a larger and larger proportion of the resources in agriculture will become redundant since productivity growth will be raising quantity supplied faster than income growth is raising quantity demanded. If, however, the government does not intervene at all, leaving the price mechanism to accomplish the resource reallocation, it will be faced with the problem of a more or less permanently depressed sector of the community.

Economics cannot prove that governments ought or ought not to interfere with the price mechanism. Such a conclusion cannot be *proved*; it is a *judgement*, which depends on a valuation of the risks of such intervention. Positive economics, by providing some insight into the workings of the price mechanism, can be used to predict some of the gains and losses, and to point out problems that must be solved if intervention is to be successful.

If the problem of reallocating resources out of the rural sector is not solved, intervention to secure high and stable levels of farm incomes will be unsuccessful over any long period of time. It will give rise to a characteristic, and predictable, set of problems that will eventually defeat the original purposes of the schemes.

A better future for agriculture?

Throughout the 1950s and 1960s the agricultural sectors of Western European and North American economies showed ample behaviour confirming the predictions developed above. Subsidies and price supports led to over-production and ever-growing surpluses that strained government warehouses everywhere to overflowing. Then, however, came a very significant change. Throughout the 1970s, the demands for many of the agricultural products produced by advanced Western countries have been soaring. A few of the most important reasons may be mentioned.

First, the world population explosion has reached dramatic proportions, adding in a matter of decades thousands of millions of new mouths to feed. Of course, more people do not automatically mean more demand for foodstuffs. They must be able to pay for the agricultural output at a price that will cover its costs of production. But more people, even in poor countries, usually means more output and hence more income to spend, so that demands for imported foodstuffs have risen.

Second, agricultural production, particularly of grains, has been disappointingly low in the USSR and other countries of the Eastern Bloc. Rising population and some spectacular crop failures have contributed to local shortages in the Eastern countries, but a major cause has been a failure of their system of collectivized agriculture to produce anything like the rate of growth that farmers of Western countries have experienced. As a result, the 1970s have seen massive sales of Western output to Eastern countries. At first, these sales eliminated the embarrassingly large stocks of surplus output that had built up in government storehouses for the reasons analysed earlier in this chapter. Within a few years, stocks that had built up over decades and that seemed destined for decay and destruction were sold off. In the years since the stocks were run down, large sales of current output have been made to Eastern countries in years when their own outputs fell short of their targets.

Third, although the income elasticities of demand for many foodstuffs are low in advanced Western countries, they remain quite high for meat in general, and for beef in particular. Meat is a technically inefficient way of turning grain into calories for human consumption. Grain may be used as food directly, by making it into such commodities as bread and breakfast cereal, or it may be used indirectly by feeding it to cattle that are then consumed as meat. The indirect method requires several times as much grain as the direct method to produce a calorie consumed by a human being. This means that even if the total calories consumed per person does not rise with income, the switch from farinaceous products to meat that commonly accompanies a rise in income produces a very large rise in the demand for grains.

At the same time as demand has risen, production has become more difficult for many countries. As nitrogen fertilizers are a petroleum product, a worldwide shortage followed the dramatic rise in oil prices in the 1970s. Moreover, the cost of pumping irrigation water by power pumps is now prohibitive in some poorer countries. For them the rise in oil prices, an inconvenience to advanced Western countries, was disastrous.

For these and other reasons, the chronic excess supply and rising stocks of unsold output that characterized Western agriculture in the 1950s and 1960s are much abated. The United States, a leading supplier of food exports for the rest of the world, has reduced its payments to farmers for keeping land out of production, and has brought nearly all of its idle crop land back into production. For that nation, then, three decades of agricultural surpluses, which grew to seemingly unmanageable proportions, have given way to several years of excess demand. It is possible that rising world demand will push agricultural prices to such levels that European agriculture will no longer need its present complex structure of supports and that it too will face excess demand rather than mounting surpluses.

Whatever the future has in store for agriculture, many of the problems it faces, and many of the complications caused by government intervention, will continue to be rendered understandable and predictable by relatively simple price theory.

11

The elementary dynamic theory of price

Statics and dynamics

All the theories developed in previous chapters have one characteristic in common. For example, refer back to Figure 10.4 on page 125, which illustrates the theory of tax. A tax on a commodity shifts its supply curve vertically upwards by the amount of the tax. The new equilibrium price is above the old one, but not by the full amount of the tax. This theory thus predicts that the effect of a tax will be to raise the price paid by consumers by less than the full amount of the tax, and to lower the price received by producers, again by less than the full amount of the tax.

Notice that the predictions are derived by comparing the new equilibrium position with the original equilibrium position. A moment's reflection will show that this has been the method of analysis used throughout all of the previous chapters. To form a hypothesis about the effect of some change in the data – for example, the introduction of a tax or a change in the conditions of demand – we start from a position of equilibrium and then introduce the change to be studied. The new equilibrium position is determined and compared with the original one; we therefore know that the differences between the two are due to the change that was introduced. This kind of analysis, based on a comparison of two positions of equilibrium, is called COMPARATIVE STATIC EQUILIBRIUM ANALYSIS – a rather cumbersome expression usually abbreviated to COMPARATIVE STATICS.

Theories based on comparative statics are useful for many purposes. The technique, however, cannot be used to handle two important classes of problems. It cannot be used to predict the path a market follows when moving from one equilibrium to another, and it cannot predict whether or not a given equilibrium position will ever be attained. In many cases we are not interested so much in the position of equilibrium as in how the market behaves when it is out of equilibrium. For these purposes we require DYNAMIC ANALYSIS, which may be defined as the study of the behaviour of systems (single markets or whole economies) in disequilibrium situations.

Agricultural price fluctuations

In the previous chapter, we applied comparative static analysis to a very simple case of agricultural price fluctuations. In that example planned production was constant and price fluctuations were caused by unplanned, exogenous changes in supply. After each change there was time for the price to settle at its new equilibrium level, equating demand with the current supply well before supply was subject to another unplanned change. The price fluctuations in the market could thus be viewed as a series of movements between successive equilibrium positions, each one equating the current supply with demand.

Many agricultural markets exhibit regular oscillations in price which cannot be accounted for by unplanned shifts in supply. In such markets there is definite evidence that the fluctuations in price result from *planned* fluctuations in farmers' output that follow a definite cyclical pattern. The classic example is the corn–hog cycle in the United States, which was first documented in the 1930s by Professor M. Ezekiel. Here we have a different phenomenon from that studied in Chapter 10. In this case farmers' output plans are fulfilled, yet these very plans give rise not to a movement towards a stable price-output configuration, but to a set of continuing oscillations. This phenomenon requires explanation, and the explanation lies, as we shall see, in the observation that all decisions take some time to implement, and some decisions take a very long time.

Supply lags

The fact that decisions take time to implement has an important effect on supply responses:

> **Output coming onto the market at any one time is the result of production decisions taken in the past, while decisions taken about production in the present will not have their effect on quantity supplied until some time in the future.**

The supply curve relates the price of the commodity to the quantity producers wish to sell. If price changes, they will want to sell a different quantity. But a change in price will at first lead to a *desired* change in quantity supplied. Only after sufficient time has elapsed to give full effect to decisions to change supply, will there be a change in actual quantity supplied. The delay between the decision to do something and its actually being done is generally called a TIME LAG. The delay between the decision to change quantity supplied and its actually being changed is usually called a SUPPLY LAG.

Time lags in general, and supply lags in particular, may be of two sorts. In one, the full adjustment occurs instantaneously but only after a lapse of time. For instance, the decision to double output may take a year to implement, but at the end of the year production may suddenly be doubled. In such a case we refer to a DISCRETE LAG. In the other kind of time lag the adjustment is spread over time. For instance, the decision to double output may give rise to a 10 per cent increase in output for each subsequent month until the rate is finally doubled ten months later. In this case we refer to a DISTRIBUTED LAG.

Every commodity has its own characteristic supply lag, and many are quite complex. Consider two examples. If the owner of a rubber plantation wishes to produce more rubber in response, say, to a rise in the market price of rubber, he will be able to increase actual production fairly rapidly if there exist stocks of mature rubber trees not now being tapped. But once such stocks of unused capacity are utilized (assuming that they exist at all), it will take at least five years for newly planted trees to reach maturity and begin to yield latex. As another example, an increase in the demand for raw milk can be met to some extent almost immediately by diverting milk from other uses; to a greater extent within 27 months by not slaughtering calves at birth but allowing them to reach maturity; and to an ever-increasing extent over the long term by allowing the larger population of adult cows to give birth to a larger number of calves. In both of these cases we have rather complex distributed lags.

Often in agriculture the time interval between successive crops is the major factor determining the supply lag. The simplest possible lag occurs when this year's price has no effect whatsoever on this year's supply. Farmers look to the existing market price when deciding what crops to plant, and thus *next year's* supply depends on *this year's* price, while this year's supply depends on last year's price. Thus we have a discrete time lag equal to one year in the adjustment of quantity supplied to a change in price.[1]

In many cases supply lags are important and comparative statics will successfully predict the market behaviour in which we are interested. In other cases supply lags exert an important influence and many, even if not all, aspects of market behaviour require dynamics for their analysis.

Agricultural markets tend to have rather long supply lags. Comparative statics is nonetheless useful in analysing the long-term behaviour of such markets. For example, the secular upward trend in the amount of beef production and in the amount of land devoted to growing grain for cattle feed can be understood in comparative static terms. Each decade income is higher than in the previous decade. Given the high income elasticity of demand of beef, the demand curves for beef and for feed-grain can be seen as shifting rightwards decade by decade. Thus we would expect the quantities of beef and grain and their prices (relative to other prices) to be rising decade by decade. This is what has in fact been happening.

Large cyclical ups and downs in cattle prices and production have, however, been superimposed on this upward secular trend. These cyclical movements, particularly when they take prices temporarily to unusually high levels, loom large in newspaper reports and popular discussion. To understand them, we need to take account of supply lags and use at least some elementary dynamic theory.

The cobweb theory

We shall now introduce an elementary dynamic theory that accounts for some of the aspects of behaviour discussed above. In this theory, we assume that producers' output plans are fulfilled, but with a time lag, and we show how *planned* changes in supply can give rise to oscillations in market behaviour. We shall consider only the simplest possible time lag, but even this will be quite sufficient sometimes to complicate the working of the market adjustment mechanism. This simple time lag is the one already discussed, in which this year's price has no effect whatsoever on this year's supply, the full adjustment to this year's price being made all at once next

[1] In the terminology of the Appendix to Chapter 3 (page 30) we may write

$$S_t = S(p_{t-1}),$$

which reads: supply at time period t depends on (i.e., is a function of) the price ruling in the previous time period, $t-1$, where time periods are measured in years.

year. We have already seen that such lags are typical of many agricultural products, such as wheat, oats and barley, that give one crop annually.

Markets subject to simple one-year time lags are illustrated in Figures 11.1 and 11.2. Look first at Figure 11.1. The demand curve shows the relation between the price ruling in any year and the quantity that will be demanded in the same year; the supply curve shows the relation between the price ruling in any year and the quantity that will be supplied to the market in the following year. The price that equates demand and supply is p_1. At this price q_1 units will be produced and sold.

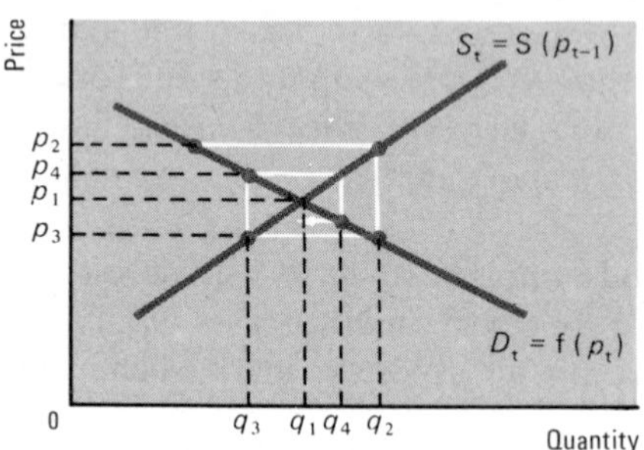

Fig. 11.1 A stable cobweb

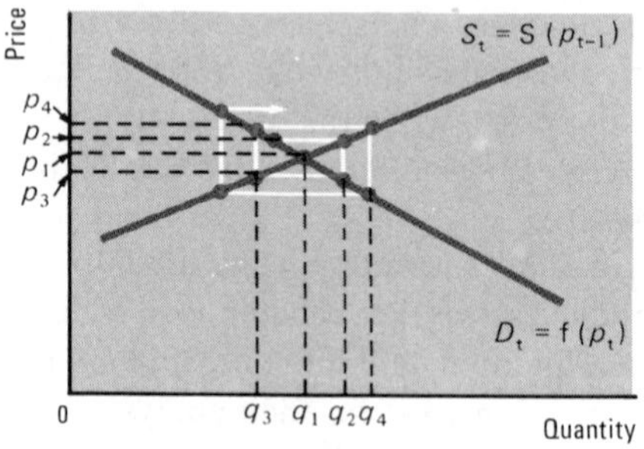

Fig. 11.2 An unstable cobweb

What will happen if this equilibrium is disturbed by, for example, a temporary fluctuation in either of the curves? If in one year, year t, the price is p_2, farmers will plan to produce q_2 in the following year. In that year, 'year $t + 1$', q_2 will come on the market, and, in order that q_2 may be sold, the price will have to fall to p_3. The price of p_3 will induce farmers to produce the quantity q_3. When this quantity comes on the market in the following year, 'year $t+2$', the price will rise to p_4. This price will call forth a supply of q_4 the next year 'year $t+3$', and this will depress the price below p_4. It is clear from this that, in the market described in Figure 11.1, the price and quantity will oscillate around their equilibrium values in a series of diminishing fluctuations, so that, if nothing further disturbs the market, price and quantity will eventually approach their equilibrium values, p_1 and q_1.

Now consider the case illustrated in Figure 11.2. Exactly the same argument as in the previous paragraph applies here, and the text of that paragraph should be re-read to describe the process in this market. Notice that here, however, the last sentence of the previous paragraph does *not* apply: this time the oscilliations get larger so that the equilibrium is never restored.

The market in Figure 11.1 has an adjustment mechanism which is *stable*, while Figure 11.2 has one which is *unstable*. A STABLE ADJUSTMENT MECHANISM is one which will take the market to its equilibrium; the actual price and quantity will tend towards their equilibrium values. An UNSTABLE ADJUSTMENT MECHANISM is one which will not take the market to its equilibrium; the actual price and quantity will tend away from equilibrium values. What makes one of these markets stable and the other unstable? It would be a very good exercise to try to answer this question for yourself before reading further.

Given the simple supply lag that we are considering, the difference between the stable and unstable markets is in the relative slopes of the demand and supply curves. In Figure 11.1 the demand curve is flatter than the supply curve. As price changes, the absolute quantity demanded changes more than the absolute quantity supplied. Excess demand or supply can be eliminated with only a small price change, and the price change in turn causes only a very small change in supply in the following year. Hence the supply change has only a small effect on next year's price. In Figure 11.2 the supply curve is flatter than the demand curve; the quantity supplied responds more to price changes than the quantity demanded. When there is excess supply, a large price fall is necessary to call forth the required demand. This price fall causes a large reduction in the next year's supply (because supply is very responsive to price). Next year there is a large shortage and a very big price increase is necessary to reduce quantity demanded to the level of the available supply. This price rise causes a very large increase in quantity supplied the following year, and so it goes, in a series of alternating periods of ever-increasing surplus and shortage.

In the case of the unstable equilibrium the oscillations get bigger and bigger. There is nothing in our theory so far to say that these oscillations will not become infinitely large. In practice, however, this will not happen; the oscillations will tend to reach limits. A full theory of such a market would require an analysis of these limits, which is beyond the scope of this book. We have, however, established the following:

> **Although the price system does allocate resources, it does not always cause adjustments to occur in a smooth fashion. Where supply lags are long and delayed reactions are large, fluctuations around equilibrium are possible with alternatively too much and too little being produced.**

The cobweb model is a very simple theory and more complicated lags on demand and supply are easy to imagine. Most such complications cannot, however, be handled without the help of mathematical analysis.[1] The study of the simplest cobweb model does, however, serve to introduce dynamic theory, and to illustrate its value by providing a reasonably satisfactory explanation of an interesting real-world phenomenon: the tendency toward oscillations in many agricultural markets with periods of shortages and high prices alternating with periods of surpluses and low prices for reasons that cannot be blamed on such uncontrollable factors as the weather. It also shows in a fairly dramatic way that even very simple competitive markets can show oscillatory behaviour,[2] and may therefore require dynamic analysis rather than simply comparative statics.

[1] The interested student should consult Chapter 1 of R. D. G. Allen, *Mathematical Economics* (Macmillan. 1966).

[2] It was thought for a very long time that the static theory of Chapter 8, summarized on page 95, permitted the inference that the market would always be stable in the sense that equilibrium would always be reached. (See note 1, page 95) The present analysis shows why this inference cannot be drawn. That excess demand should cause price to rise and excess supply should cause price to fall is not sufficient to ensure stability. Such models as the one illustrated in Figure 11.2 contain all the assumptions listed in Chapter 8, yet they are unstable. In these models excess demand pushes the price up towards equilibrium *but it pushes it too far*; excess supply pushes price down towards equilibrium *but also pushes it too far*. Thus an endless series of oscillations around the equilibrium is possible.

12

A postscript and a preview

The interrelationships of markets: a postscript

In Part 2 we have developed a theory of the behaviour of individual, competitive markets. The economy, however, does not consist of a series of self-contained markets functioning in isolation. It is, rather, an interlocking system in which anything happening in one market has profound effects on many others and could, potentially, influence all of them. Thus our study of the behaviour of individual markets is only the first step towards understanding the behaviour of a whole economy. We also need a theory of how the individual markets are linked together and of how they act and react on each other. We shall consider this, albeit very briefly, in Part 6. In the meantime let us try to assemble an intuitive picture of the interaction within a market economy.

The motorcar industry: an example

Consider, for example, the effects of a rise in the demand for motorcars. Fairly soon it will be met by a rise in car production. If the rise in demand is considerable, and judged to be permanent, there will also be a planned increase in productive capacity in the car industry. Employment will rise and producers may try to attract labour from other industries by offering higher wages. Thus, one of the first impacts on other markets will be a loss of labour and possibly a need to raise wages in order to compete effectively with the car industry for that labour. This will cause profits to fall in these other industries.

The increased employment in the car industry may occasion some geographical movement of labour. In this case there will be a rise in the demand for housing in the car-production centres and a corresponding fall in demand elsewhere. New housing construction in the car-producing areas will lead to a rise in the demand for construction workers and materials. Quarries and brickworks may have to take on additional labour and expand output.

Further, there will be a rise in the demand for raw materials used in car construction. Such diverse spots as the glass-making areas of the Midlands, the steel-manufacturing sections of Wales and the rubber plantations of Malaya may feel the effects. If new investment in plant and equipment takes place in the car industry, there will be a rise in the demand for many captial goods; shortages and bottlenecks may develop, and other industries which use these capital goods may find that their costs go up and they have trouble meeting delivery dates. There will also be a change in consumers' expenditure because some people's earnings will be increased and other people's reduced. Thus the effects of a change in one market will spread through the economy rather like the ripples which spread out over the smooth surface of a pond after a pebble has been dropped into it.

The price system: a control mechanism

The example considered above illustrates two very important points. First, the various markets of the economy are interrelated: a single initial change in demand has numerous repercussions throughout the economy. Second, adaptations to the initial shift take place without anyone's conscious co-ordination. When shortages develop, prices rise and profit-seeking entrepreneurs want to produce more of the commodities in short supply. When surpluses occur, prices fall and producers voluntarily contract the supply. It was the great discovery of the eighteenth-century economists that a competitive price system produces a co-ordination of effort in which – by seeking their own private gains and responding to such public signals as prices, costs and profit rates – individuals automatically react in orderly combination to changes in demand and supply.

> **The price system was not consciously created. It does not require that anyone consciously foresee and co-ordinate the necessary changes; adjustments occur automatically as a result of the separate decisions taken by a large number of individuals, all seeking their own best interests, but all responding to the same changes in demands and prices.**

Efficient and inefficient control mechanisms

Having grasped the idea that the price system is an automatic control mechanism, beware of jumping to the conclusion that it has been shown to be the *best* system of regulating the economy. The word 'automatic', which we have used, is not equivalent to the phrase 'perfectly functioning', which we have not used. It is easy enough to control the heat in your house by means of an automatic thermostatic control, but it is equally easy to have such a badly designed or imperfectly functioning system that you actually achieve worse temperature control than you would have done by 'stoking up' and 'damping down' by hand. To say that the price system functions automatically, i.e., without conscious centralized co-ordination, is not to say how *well* it functions. We have seen, for example in the case of the 'cobweb' in Chapter 11, that the automatic working of the price system can produce oscillations in price and output.

The reader who believes that behaviour in a free-market economy is unplanned and unco-ordinated must abandon this notion. The existence of a co-ordinating mechanism – the price system – is beyond dispute. The question of how well it works in comparison with practical alternative co-ordinating systems has been a matter of dispute for two hundred years and is still a great unsettled social question.

Demand and supply: a preview

In developing a theory of the behaviour of competitive markets – markets in which no single buyer or seller is important enough to exert any significant influence on prices, we first introduced a theory of households' demands and a theory of firms' supply (Chapter 7). We must now consider in much more detail the theory of demand (Part 3) and the theory of supply (Part 4). The theory of demand will occupy us for only three chapters because we never need to depart from our competitive assumption that each household is a price-taker, totally unable to influence by any action of its own the market prices of the commodities it purchases.

The theory of supply will require much more space. This is because a large proportion of production is carried on by firms in non-competitive situations – in the sense that each *is* able to exert a significant influence on market price. Serious complications arise as a result. Therefore, although we do not need to alter any of the hypotheses about demand introduced in Chapter 7, it becomes necessary, as a result of the existence of these non-competitive situations, to abandon the hypothesis that there *always* exists a simple relation between market price and firms' supply. Moreover, many interesting issues of economic policy are encountered in the theory of supply. But first we must turn our attention to the theory of demand.

Part three

The intermediate theory of demand

13

Effects of changes in prices and incomes

Is a household's consumption affected differently if its money income falls than if the prices of commodities rise? Does an increase in the level of all prices hurt everybody? Does it hurt anybody? Can we predict the effect of price changes on a household's behaviour? To answer these and similar questions, we must look in more detail at the behaviour of the millions of independent decision units whose aggregate behaviour is summarized in the market demand curve.

In this chapter we shall study the effects on a household's consumption of changes in relative prices, absolute prices and incomes. In the following chapter we shall show some alternative methods of deriving from assumptions about household behaviour the basic prediction that the demand curve for a commodity slopes downwards. We have already discussed in Chapter 6 the general assumptions made about the household, which is the basic decision unit on the side of demand, and you should now review pages 70–1 of that chapter.

Choices facing the household

We shall study a single household allocating the whole of its money income between only two goods, food and clothing. We assume that the household spends all of its income on the purchase of food and clothing for current consumption; it neither spends more than its income nor saves any of it.[1] We start with numerical examples, but later go on to state the argument in general terms.

In Figure 13.1 the quantity of food is measured on the horizontal axis and the quantity of clothing on the vertical one. Any point on the graph represents a combination of the two goods. Point *m*, for example, represents 40 units of food and 60 units of clothing.

The budget line

We now construct the household's BUDGET LINE, which shows all those

[1] These assumptions are not as restrictive as they at first seem. Two goods are used so that the analysis can be handled geometrically; the argument can easily be generalized to any number of commodities with the use of mathematics. Savings are ignored because we are interested in the allocation of expenditure between commodities for current consumption. The possibilities of saving or borrowing (or using up past savings) can be allowed for, but they affect none of the results in which we are interested here.

combinations of the goods that are just obtainable, given the household's income and the prices of the two commodities.[1] Assume, for example, that the household's income is £120 per month, that the price of clothing is £2 per unit, and the price of food is £4 per unit. What combinations of the two are open to the household? First, it could spend all its money on clothing, obtaining each month 60 units of clothing and no food (this combination is indicated by point *a* on Figure 13.1). It could also buy 30 units of food and no clothing (point *b*). Other combinations open to it are 58 units of clothing and 1 unit of food, 56 units of clothing and 2 units of food, 54 units of clothing and 3 units of food, and so on.

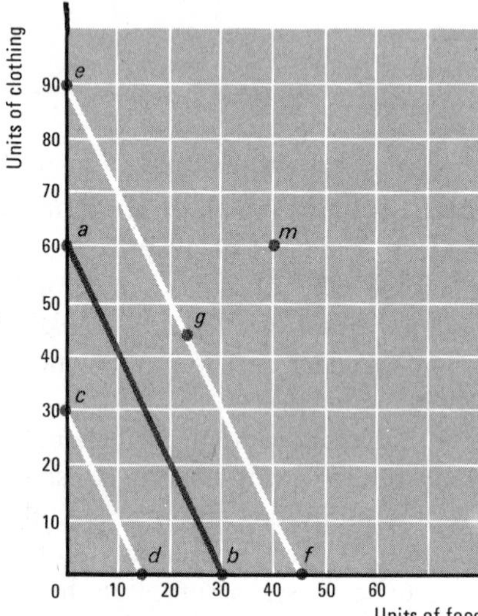

Fig. 13.1 Shifts in the budget line caused by changes in household income

All the possible combinations of food and clothing obtainable by the household are shown by the straight line *ab* in Figure 13.1. Points between *ab* and the origin do not use all the household's income, and points above *ab* require more than the household's income. Points on *ab* are just attainable in the sense that they require all the household's income and no more.

Changes in income

What happens to the budget line when the household's income changes? If, for example, income is halved from £120 to £60 per month, prices being unchanged, then the amount of goods the household can buy will also be halved. If the household spends all of its income on clothing, it will now get only 30 units of clothing and no food (point *c*); if it spends all of its income on food, it will get just 15 units of food and no clothing (point *d*). All combinations now open to the household appear on budget line *cd*. Note that this line is parallel to budget line *ab*, but closer to the origin.

If the household's income rises to £180, it will be able to buy more of both

[1] This budget line is analogous to the production-possibility boundary shown in Figure 4.1 on page 57. The budget line shows the combinations of commodities available to one household given its income and prices, while the production-possibility curve shows the combinations of commodities available to the whole society given its techniques of production and supplies of resources.

commodities than it could previously. If it buys only clothing, it can now have 90 units (point *e*); if it buys only food, it can have 45 units (point *f*); if it divides its income equally between the two, it can have 45 units of clothing and $22\frac{1}{2}$ units of food (point *g*). All the combinations available to the household appear on budget line *ef*.

We conclude that variations in the household's income, with prices constant, shift the budget line to a position parallel to its original one, inward towards the origin when income falls, and outward away from the origin when income rises. For practice you should now try drawing your own budget lines for incomes of £100 and £40 per month, with the same prices for food and clothing that were used in the above example.

Proportional changes in all prices

Let us start with the budget line *ab* in Figure 13.1, which corresponds to an income of £120 and prices of £2 and £4 respectively for clothing and food. If we now double both prices, we will halve the amount of both goods that the household can purchase. The budget line becomes *cd*, because the income of £120 will now buy 30 units of clothing and no food, 15 units of food and no clothing, or any combination of food and clothing on the straight line joining these two points.

Now let us go back to line *ab* and halve both prices, so that clothing costs £1 while food costs £2. The household can now have twice as much of both goods as previously, and the budget line moves outward to *ef*. Notice that changing both prices in the same proportion shifts the budget line parallel to itself in the same way that a change in income shifted it.

Offsetting changes in prices and income

The results obtained in the last two sections suggest that we can have offsetting changes in money prices and money income. Consider the budget line *ab* in Figure 13.1. This budget line was originally obtained from an income of £120, with prices of £4 and £2 for food and clothing respectively. What will happen if the household's income doubles to £240? The budget line will shift outward, since the household can buy twice as many units of both goods as it could previously. But what if both prices double as well? This cuts the household's consumption possibilities in half, and the budget line is back to *ab*. A rise in money income and a proportionate rise in the money prices of both goods leave the position of the budget line unchanged.

Opportunity cost, relative prices and the slope of the budget line

Why does changing either income or both prices in the same proportion shift the budget line to a parallel position? The reason is that the slope of the budget line indicates the opportunity cost of one commodity in terms of the other, and either a change in income with prices unchanged or a proportionate change in both prices leaves this opportunity cost unaffected.[1]

Consider an example. If clothing costs £2 and food costs £4, then 2 units of clothing must be forgone in order to be able to purchase 1 unit of food; if clothing

---

1 See Chapter 4, pp. 53–4, for a general discussion of the concept of opportunity cost.

costs £4 and food costs £8 it is still necessary to forgo 2 units of clothing to be able to purchase one more unit of food. In fact, as long as the price of food is twice the price of clothing, it will be necessary to forgo two units of clothing in order to be able to purchase one more unit of food. More generally, the amount of clothing that must be given up to obtain another unit of food depends only on *the relation between the price of clothing and the price of food.* If we take the money price of food and divide it by the money price of clothing, we have the opportunity cost of food in terms of clothing (the quantity of clothing that must be forgone in order to be able to purchase one more unit of food). This may be written:

$$\frac{p_f}{p_c} = \text{opportunity cost of food in terms of clothing,}$$

where p_f and p_c are the money prices of food and clothing. It is apparent that changing income and/or changing both prices in the same proportion leaves the ratio p_f/p_c unchanged. [1]

In economics, any price expressed as a ratio of another price is called a RELATIVE PRICE. The relative price must be distinguished from the MONEY PRICE of a single commodity, which is also called its ABSOLUTE PRICE. These concepts can prove tricky and the reader is urged to invent and experiment with some numerical examples.[2]

Changes in relative prices

A change in the relative price p_f/p_c may be accomplished either by changing both money prices but in a different proportion or by holding one money price constant and changing the other. It is useful for illustrative purposes to do the latter.

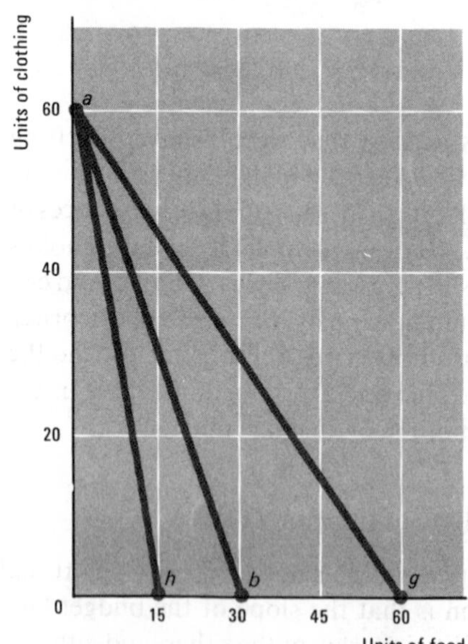

Fig. 13.2 Shifts in the budget line caused by changes in the price of food

[1] Those who prefer an algebraic derivation may refer now to the proof of this proposition on page 156 of the Appendix to this chapter.

[2] For example, if the prices of food and clothing are £2 and £6 respectively, what are the values of: (i) the relative price of food, (ii) the relative price of clothing, (iii) the opportunity cost of food measured in units of clothing, (iv) the opportunity cost of clothing measured in units of food and (v) the slope of the buget line drawn with food on the horizontal and clothing on the vertical axis?

Figure 13.2 repeats the budget line *ab* from Figure 13.1, which corresponds to an income of £120 and prices of £2 and £4 respectively for clothing and food. On the one hand, a fall in the price of food to £2 doubles the quantity of it that can be purchased along with any given quantity of clothing. This has the effect of pivoting the budget line to the position *ag*. On the other hand, a rise in the price of food from £4 to £8 halves the quantity of food that can be purchased along with any given quantity of clothing. This pivots the budget line to *ah*.

We conclude that a change in the relative price changes the slope of the budget line; the higher the price of food relative to the price of clothing, the steeper the budget line.

Implications and predictions

We have now derived a number of implications about the effects on the budget line in prices and incomes. These are summarized below.

> **(1) A change in money income, with money prices (and thus, necessarily, relative prices) constant, shifts the budget line parallel to itself, inward towards the origin when income falls, and outward away from the origin when income rises.**
> **(2) An equal percentage change in all absolute prices leaves relative prices unchanged. If money income remains unchanged the budget line shifts parallel to itself, inward towards the origin when prices rise, and outward away from the origin when prices fall.**
> **(3) Multiplying all money prices by the same constant, λ, while holding money income constant, has exactly the same effect on the budget line as multiplying money income by $1/\lambda$ while holding money prices constant. For example, doubling all money prices has the same effect on the budget line as halving money income.**
> **(4) A change in relative prices causes the budget line to change its slope.**
> **(5) An equal percentage change in all absolute prices combined with a percentage change in income, of the same magnitude and in the same direction as the price change, leaves the budget line exactly where it was before the changes occurred.**

The five implications listed above are matters of logic. The effects on the budget line of changes in prices and incomes are incontrovertible. In order to translate these implications into predictions about household behaviour, we advance the hypothesis that a household's market behaviour depends solely on the tastes of the members of the household and the location of the household's budget line. This behavioural hypothesis, along with the five propositions above, will allow us to make testable predictions about the behaviour of households. The following are two important examples.[1]

The change in a household's market behaviour will be the same if either its income changes by λ or all money prices change by $1/\lambda$.

[1] Strickly speaking, these predictions apply only to households that do not have any significant quantities of bonds, cash or other assets whose value is fixed in money units and whose real value thus changes when money prices change. (For example, the real value of a cash hoard would be halved by a doubling of the price level.) The predictions apply to those households for whom income is the main determinant of current expenditure.

A household's market behaviour will be unaffected if its money income and all money prices change simultaneously by λ.

Further predictions will be derived in Chapter 14 after we have developed a theory of the household's tastes.

Real and money income

We must now make an important distinction between two concepts of income. MONEY INCOME measures a household's income in terms of some monetary unit; for example, so many pounds sterling or so many dollars. REAL INCOME measures a household's income in terms of the command over commodities that the money income confers. A rise in money income of x per cent combined with an x per cent rise in all money prices leaves a household's ability to buy commodities, and hence its real income, unchanged. When we speak of the real value of a certain amount of money, we are referring to the goods and services that can be bought with the money; that is, to the PURCHASING POWER of the money.

Allocation of resources: The importance of relative prices

Price theory predicts that the allocation of resources depends on the structure of relative prices. If the money value of all prices, incomes, debts and credits were doubled, there would, according to our theory, be little noticeable effect. The economy would function as before. The same set of relative prices and real incomes would exist, and there would be no incentive for any reallocation of resources.

This prediction is an implication of the theories of the behaviour of households and firms. We have already seen that doubling all money prices and money income leaves the household's budget line unchanged and so, according to the theory of household behaviour, gives it no incentive to vary the quantity of each commodity that it purchases. As far as producers are concerned, if all prices, both of final goods and of factors of production, double, then the relative profitability of different lines of production will be unaffected, as indeed will the real level of profits in all lines of production.[1] Thus producers will have no incentive to alter production rates so as to produce more of some things and less of others.

If *relative* prices changes, however, then our theory predicts that resources will be reallocated. Households will buy more of the cheaper commodities and less of the expensive ones, and producers will expand production of those commodities whose prices have risen relatively and contract production of those whose prices have fallen relatively (since the latter will be relatively less profitable lines of production).

The theory of price and resource allocation is a theory of relative, not absolute, prices.

Inflation and deflation: The importance of absolute prices

The average level of all money prices is called the PRICE LEVEL. If all money prices double, we say that the price level has doubled. An increase in the price level is called

[1] Since all prices will have doubled, money profits will have doubled, but since all costs will also have doubled, the purchasing power of these profits will be just what it was before.

an INFLATION, a decrease is called a DEFLATION. If a rise in all money prices and incomes has little or no effect on the allocation of resources, it may seem surprising that so much concern is expressed over inflation. Clearly, a person who spends all of his income, and whose money income goes up at the same rate as money prices, loses nothing from inflation. His real income is unaffected.

Inflation, while having no effect on a household whose income rises at the same rate as prices, does nonetheless have serious consequences. These are studied in detail in Part 8, along with theories of the causes of and possible cures for inflation.[1]

Until we reach Part 8 *we shall assume that the price level is constant*. A change in one money price is then necessarily a change in that price *relative* to the average of all other prices in the economy. The theory can easily be extended to situations in which the price level is changing. Then every time shifts in demand or supply required a change in a commodity's relative price, its price would change *faster* (its relative price rising) or *slower* (its relative price falling) than the general price level. Explaining this each time can be cumbersome. It is, therefore, simpler to deal with relative prices in a theoretical setting in which the price level is constant. It is important to realize, however, that even though we develop the theory in this way, it is not limited to such situations. The propositions we develop can be applied to changing price levels merely by making explicit what is always implicit: that in the theory of relative prices 'rise' or 'fall' *always* means rise or fall *relative to the average of all other prices*.

[1] Anyone who wishes to understand why inflation is important in spite of the propositions demonstrated in this chapter, can read pages 573–8.

Appendix to chapter 13

A formal analysis of the budget line

In this appendix we shall use simple algebra to prove the five propositions given on page 153.

Let the household's money income be M. Let p_x and p_y be the prices of food and clothing, and let X and Y be the quantities of food and clothing purchased by the household. Total expenditure is thus $p_xX + p_yY$. If we assume, as we did in the text, that the household spends all of its income on these two goods, we have the following equation:

$$p_xX + p_yY = M. \tag{1}$$

Rearrangement of terms yields the equation of the budget line as it is plotted in Figures 13.1 and 13.2. To do this, we subtract p_xX from both sides, and then divide through by p_y to obtain:

$$Y = \frac{M}{p_y} - \frac{p_x}{p_y}X. \tag{2}$$

Equation (1) is a linear equation of the form

$$Y = a - bX, \tag{3}$$

where $a = M/p_y$ and $b = p_x/p_y$. The intercept a is the number of units of Y that can be purchased by spending all of M on Y, i.e., money income divided by the price of Y. The slope depends on the relation between p_x and p_y.

We first prove that the opportunity cost, the slope of the budget line and the relative price are identical. If we take first-differences representing changes in quantities, with prices constant, we get from (1):

$$p_x\Delta X + p_y\Delta Y = \Delta M.$$

This says that the sum of any changes in the value of purchases of X and the value of purchases of Y must be equal to the change in income (since income determines the total value of purchases).

Along a budget line expenditure is constant, so we can write

$$p_x\Delta X + p_y\Delta Y = 0,$$

which says that if income does not change, the change in the total value of purchases must be zero. Simple manipulation of the above equation yields:

$$p_x/p_y = -\Delta Y/\Delta X. \tag{4}$$

Now $-\Delta Y/\Delta X$ is the change in Y per unit change in X. It is thus the opportunity cost of X measured in units of Y: the amount of Y sacrificed (gained) per unit of X gained (sacrificed). From (4) this is equal to the relative price of X, which, from (2), is the slope of the budget line.

We may now prove the five propositions on page 153 of the text.

PROPOSITION (1): A change in money income, with money prices (and thus, necessarily, relative prices) constant, shifts the budget line parallel to itself, inward towards the origin when income falls, and outward away from the origin when income rises.

PROOF: If we change the value of M in (2), we change the value of a in (3) in the same direction: $\Delta a = \Delta M/p_y$, but b is unaffected since M does not appear in that term; thus changing M shifts the budget line inwards ($\Delta M < 0$) or outwards ($\Delta M > 0$) but leaves the slope unaffected.

PROPOSITION (2): An equal percentage change in all absolute prices leaves relative prices unchanged. If money income remains unchanged, it will shift the budget line parallel to itself, inward towards the origin when prices rise, and outward away from the origin when prices fall.

PROOF: Multiplying both prices in equation (2) by the same constant λ gives

$$Y = \frac{M}{\lambda p_y} - \frac{\lambda p_x}{\lambda p_y}X.$$

Since the λs cancel out of the slope term, b is unaffected; the a term however is changed. If $\lambda > 1$, then a is diminished, while if $\lambda < 1$ then a is increased.

PROPOSITION (3): Multiplying all money prices by the same constant, λ, while holding money income constant, has exactly the same effect on the budget line as multiplying money income by $1/\lambda$ while holding money prices constant.

PROOF: Multiply both money prices in (2) by λ:

$$Y=\frac{M}{\lambda p_y}-\frac{\lambda p_x}{\lambda p_y}X.$$

Cancelling the λs from the slope term gives:

$$Y=\frac{M}{\lambda p_y}-\frac{p_x}{p_y}X.$$

Finally bringing the λ from the denominator to the numerator of the constant term gives:

$$Y=\frac{(1/\lambda)M}{p_y}-\frac{p_x}{p_y}X.$$

PROPOSITION (4): A change in relative prices causes the budget line to change its slope.

PROOF: The relative price p_x/p_y in (2) is the slope term, b, in (3). Thus changing the relative price is necessary and sufficient for changing the slope of the budget line.

Note that to pivot the budget line, keeping its Y intercept (and money income) constant as in Figure 13.2, it is necessary to change the relative price by changing p_x only. This can be seen algebraically by inspection of (2), since p_x does not appear in the constant term. If the relative price change is accomplished solely, or partly, by changing p_y, then both the slope and the Y intercept change. This is because in (2) p_y appears in both the a and the b term. The common sense of these results is that the Y intercept measures the quantity of Y that can be consumed by buying only Y and this obviously depends on money income and the price of Y.

We conclude that any change in the relative price necessarily changes the slope of the budget line; while with money income constant, a change in p_y changes the Y intercept and (by analogous reasoning) a change in p_x changes the X intercept of the budget line.

PROPOSITION (5): An equal percentage change in all absolute prices combined with a percentage change in income of the same magnitude and in the same direction as the price change, leaves the budget line exactly where it was before the changes occurred.

PROOF: Multiply M and both prices in equation (2) by λ:

$$Y=\frac{\lambda M}{\lambda p_y}-\frac{\lambda p_x}{\lambda p_y}X.$$

Cancel out the λs from the intercept and the slope terms to obtain:

$$Y=\frac{M}{p_y}-\frac{p_x}{p_y}X.$$

which is equation (2) once again.

14

Theories of household demand

The early economists, struggling with the problem of what determines the relative prices of commodities, encountered what they came to call the PARADOX OF VALUE: necessary commodities, such as water, were observed to have prices that were low compared to the prices of many luxury commodities, such as diamonds. Writing some two hundred years ago, these early economists argued in the following manner. Water is necessary to our very existence, whereas diamonds are a frivolous luxury that could disappear tomorrow from the face of the earth without causing any real upset. Does it not seem odd, therefore, that water is so cheap and diamonds so expensive? It took a long time for economists to resolve this apparent paradox. Thus it is not surprising that even today the confusion persists and clouds many policy discussions.

We have already encountered one key to the paradox of value: it is supply and demand, not 'necessity' or 'luxury', that determines price in any competitive market, and the equilibrium price that equates supply and demand is relatively low for water and relatively high for diamonds. But why is the demand for a necessity not enough to assure that its price is high? After all, it is necessary to life itself. To address this more fundamental question we must go behind the market demand curve, which is the aggregate of all households' desired purchases at each possible price, and look at the behaviour and motivation of individual households. In this chapter two theories of household behaviour are studied. They provide alternative rather than competing explanations, since they lead to almost the same set of basic predictions about household demand.

The utility theory of household behaviour

The first half of the chapter covers utility theory. This is the oldest of these theories, but it is still worth studying because the distinction it makes between marginal and total utility has widespread significance for practical policy.

Marginal and total utility

The satisfaction a household receives from consuming commodities is called *utility*. The total utility obtained from consuming some commodity can be distinguished from the marginal utility of consuming one unit more or one unit less of it.

The concepts defined TOTAL UTILITY refers to the total satisfaction gained from consuming some commodity. MARGINAL UTILITY refers to the change in satisfaction resulting from consuming a little more or a little less of that commodity. Thus, for example, the total utility of consuming ten units of some commodity is the total satisfaction that those ten units provide. The marginal utility of the tenth unit consumed is the satisfaction gained by consuming that unit – or, in other words, the difference in total utility between consuming nine units and consuming ten units.[1]

The nature of this distinction can be seen by asking two questions. (1) If you had to give up the consumption of one of the following commodities completely, which would you choose: water or the cinema? (2) If you could have only one of the following, which would you choose: 35 more gallons of water a month (the amount required for an average bath) or attending one more cinema performance each month?

In the first choice you are comparing the value you place on your total consumption of water with the value you place on your total attendances at the cinema. You are comparing the *total utility* of your water consumption with the *total utility* of your cinema consumption. Of course everyone would answer question (1) in the same way, revealing that the total utility derived from consuming water exceeds the total utility derived from attending the cinema.

In making the second choice you are comparing the value you place on a small addition to your water consumption with the value you place on a small addition to your cinema attendances. You are comparing your *marginal utility* of water with your *marginal utility* of cinema performances. The response to question (2) is far less predictable than the response to choice (1). Some people might select the extra cinema performance; others might say that they have already seen all the films they wanted to see (marginal utility of another visit to the cinema, *zero*) and select the extra water. Furthermore, their choice would depend on whether water was plentiful at the time, so that they had more or less all they wanted (marginal utility of a little more water, *low*), or whether water was scarce, so that a little more of it would be very desirable (marginal utility of a little more water, *high*).

Choices of type (1) are encountered much less commonly than choices of type (2). If our income rises a little, we have to decide to have some more of one thing or another. If our income falls, or if we find that we are overspending, we have to decide what to cut down on.

Real choices are often influenced by marginal utilities since they are relevant to choices concerning a little more or a little less.

The hypothesis of diminishing marginal utility The following is the basic hypothesis of utility theory. It is sometimes called the 'law of diminishing marginal utility'.

---

[1] In elementary economics it is common to use interchangeably two concepts that mathematicians distinguish. Technically, *incremental* utility is measured over a discrete interval, such as from nine to ten, whereas marginal utility is a rate of change measured over an infinitesimal interval. But in economists' common usage the word *marginal* is used when the last unit is involved, even if a one-unit change is not *infinitesimal*. The difference between incremental and marginal values is discussed further in Section 10, p.34, of the Appendix to Chapter 2. This is an important discussion and it should be read, or reread, at this time.

Readers who are familiar with elementary calculus may imagine a utility function in which utility depends on the quantity of goods X, Y,... consumed: $U = U(X, Y, \ldots)$. Incremental utility of X is then $\Delta U/\Delta X$, while marginal utility of X is $\partial U/\partial X$.

The utility that any household derives from successive units of a particular commodity will diminish as total consumption of that commodity increases, the consumption of all other commodities being held constant.

Consider further the case of water. Some minimum quantity of drinking water is absolutely necessary to sustain life, and a person would, if necessary, give up all of his or her income and wealth to obtain that quantity. The marginal utility of that quantity is extremely high. Much more than this bare minimum can be drunk, but the marginal utility of successive glasses of water drunk over some time period will decline steadily. Evidence for this hypothesis will be considered later, but you can convince yourself that it is at least reasonable by asking yourself a number of questions. How much money would induce you to cut your consumption of water by one glass per week? The amount would not be large. How much would induce you to cut it by a second glass? By a third glass? Back to only seven glasses per week? The fewer glasses you are consuming already, the higher the marginal utility to you of one more glass.

But water has many uses other than for drinking. A fairly high marginal utility will be attached to some minimum quantity for bathing, but much more than this minimum will be used for more frequent baths and for having a water level in the bath higher than is absolutely necessary. The last weekly gallon used for bathing is likely to have quite a low marginal utility. Again, some small quantity of water is necessary for brushing one's teeth, but many people leave the water running while brushing, and they can hardly pretend that the water so consumed between wetting and rinsing the brush has a high utility. When all the extravagant uses of water by the modern consumer are considered, it is certain that the marginal utility of the last, say, 30 per cent of all units consumed is very low, even though the total utility of *all* the units consumed is extremely high.

Utility schedules and graphs Let us assume for purposes of illustration that utility can be measured. The schedule in Table 14.1 is hypothetical and is intended only to illustrate the assumptions that have been made about utility. It shows total utility rising as the number of films seen per month rises. Everything else being equal, the household gets more satisfaction, the more films it sees—at least over the range

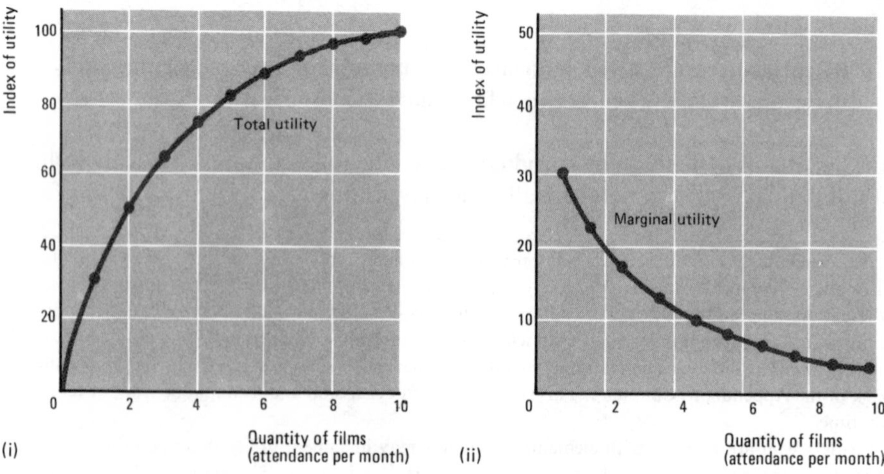

Fig. 14.1 Total and marginal utility curves

shown in the table. But the marginal utility of each additional film attended per month is less than that of the previous one (even though each adds something to the household's satisfaction); thus the marginal utility schedule shows a declining value as quantity consumed rises. These same data are shown graphically in Figure 14.1.

Table 14.1 Total and marginal utility schedules

Number of cinema performances attended per month	Total utility	Marginal* utility
0	0	
1	30	30
2	50	20
3	65	15
4	75	10
5	83	8
6	89	6
7	93	4
8	96	3
9	98	2
10	99	1

* The marginal utility of 20, shown as the second entry in the last column, arises because total utility increased from 30 to 50 – a difference of 20 – with attendance at the second cinema performance. Technically, this is 'incremental utility' over the interval from 1 to 2 units. When plotting marginal utility on a graph, this value is plotted at the mid-point of the interval over which it is computed.

Can marginal utility ever reach zero? With many commodities there is some maximum consumption after which additional units would confer no additional utility. If a person were forced to consume more, the additional units would actually reduce his or her total utility. Cigarettes provide an obvious example. There is some maximum number of cigarettes that most people would smoke per day, even if they did not have to worry about the cost. For non-smokers that number is zero. Few smokers would want to go to the point of chain smoking from the second they awoke until the second they fell asleep. Long before consumption reached this point, additional cigarettes smoked would cease to add to utility and would in fact begin to subtract from it; that is, additional cigarettes would have a negative marginal utility or, as it is sometimes called, a marginal *disutility*. The same is undoubtedly true of many other commodities such as food, alcoholic beverages and most games. (Although we know one economist who would be happy to play golf from sunrise to sunset seven days a week for the rest of his life, most people would not.)

Maximizing utility

A basic assumption of the utility theory of household behaviour is that

The members of a household seek to maximize their total utility.

This is just another way of saying that they try to make themselves as well off as they possibly can in the circumstances in which they find themselves. This assumption is sometimes taken to mean that households are assumed to be narrowly selfish and devoid of any altruistic motives. On the contrary, if a household derives satisfaction from giving its money away to others, this can be incorporated into the analysis, and the marginal utility that it gets from £1 given away can be compared with the marginal utility that it gets from £1 spent on itself.

The equilibrium of a household How can a household adjust its expenditure so as to maximize the total utility of its members? Should it go to the point at which the marginal utility of each commodity is the same—i.e., the point at which it values equally the last unit of each commodity consumed? This would make sense only if all commodities had the same price per unit. But if a household must spend £3 to buy an additional unit of one commodity and only £1 for a unit of another, the first commodity would represent a poor use of its money if the marginal utilities of both were equal: the household would be spending £3 to get satisfaction that it could have acquired for only £1.

The household is concerned to get the maximum satisfaction from spending its income on commodities. Therefore what it needs to consider is not the utility of the last unit of each commodity consumed, but the utility of the last penny spent on each commodity. To illustrate, imagine a household whose utility from the last penny it spent on carrots is three times the utility it gets fron the last penny it spent on Brussels sprouts. The household's total utility could clearly be increased by switching a penny of expenditure from sprouts to carrots and gaining the difference between the utility obtained from a penny spent on each.

The utility-maximizing household will continue to switch its expenditure from sprouts to carrots as long as a penny spent on carrots yields more utility than a penny spent on sprouts. But this switching reduces the quantity of sprouts being consumed and, given the law of diminishing marginal utility, raises the marginal utility of sprouts: at the same time, it increases the quantity of carrots consumed, and thereby lowers the marginal utility of carrots. Eventually the marginal utilities will have changed enough so that the utility yielded by a penny spent on carrots is just equal to the utility yielded by a penny spent on sprouts. At this point, there is nothing to be gained by a further switch of expenditure from sprouts to carrots. If the household did persist in reallocating its expenditure, it would further reduce the marginal utility of carrots (by consuming more of them) and raise the marginal utility of sprouts (by consuming less of them). Further reallocation would then lower total utility, because the utility of a penny spent on sprouts would now exceed the utility of a penny spent on carrots.

The household maximizing its utility will allocate its expenditure among commodities so that the utility of the last penny spent on each is equal.

Let us now leave carrots and sprouts and deal with commodities in general. Denote the marginal utility of the last unit of one commodity, X, by M_x and its price by p_x. Let M_y and p_y refer to the marginal utility and the price of a second commodity, Y. The marginal utility per penny spent on X will be M_x/p_x. For example, if the last unit of X adds 30 units to utility and costs 2p, then its marginal utility per penny is $30/2 = 15$.

The condition required for a household to maximize its utility is, for *any* pair of commodities, X and Y,

$$\frac{M_x}{p_x} = \frac{M_y}{p_y}. \qquad (1)$$

This is just another way of writing the condition that the household will allocate its expenditure so that the utilities gained from the last penny spent on all commodities are equal.

This is the fundamental equation of the utility theory of demand. Each household demands each commodity (for example, cinema attendances) up to the point at which the marginal utility per penny spent on it is the same as the marginal utility per penny spent on every other commodity (for example, water). When this condition is met, the household cannot increase its total utility by shifting a penny of expenditure from one commodity to another.

An alternative interpretation of household equilibrium A slight rearrangement of equation (1) produces the following:

$$\frac{M_x}{M_y} = \frac{p_x}{p_y}. \qquad (2)$$

The right-hand side of this equation is given to the household by the market; it states the *relative* price of the two commodities. It is outside the control of the individual household, which reacts to market prices but is powerless to change them. The left-hand side concerns the ability of the commodities to add to the household's satisfaction and is within the control of the household. By determining the quantities of different commodities it buys, the household also determines their marginal utilities.

If the two sides of equation (2) are not equal, the household can increase its total satisfaction by rearranging its purchases. Assume, for example, that the price of a unit of X is twice the price of a unit of Y, ($p_x/p_y = 2$), while the marginal utility of a unit of X is three times that of a unit of Y, ($M_x/M_y = 3$). It will now pay the household to buy more X and less Y. If, for example, it reduces its purchases of Y by two units, it will free enough purchasing power to buy a unit of X. Since one new unit of X bought yields 1.5 times the satisfaction of two units of Y forgone, this switch is worth making. What about a further switch of X for Y? As the household buys more X and less Y, the marginal utility of X will fall and the marginal utility of Y will rise. The household will carry on rearranging its purchases—reducing Y consumption and increasing X consumption—until, in this example, the marginal utility of X, like its price, is only twice that of Y. At this point total utility cannot be increased further by rearranging purchases between the two commodities.

Now consider what the household is doing. It is faced with a set of prices that it cannot change. It responds to these prices, and maximizes its satisfaction, by adjusting the things it can change, the quantities of the various goods it purchases, until equation (2) is satisfied for all pairs of commodities.

This sort of equation occurs frequently in economics. One side represents the choices the outside world presents to decision-takers and the other side represents the effect of their decisions on their utility. Such an equation expresses the equilibrium position reached when decision-takers have made the best adjustment they can to the external conditions that limit their choices.

When all households are fully adjusted to a given set of market prices, all households will have identical ratios of their marginal utilities for each pair of goods. This is because each household faces the same set of market prices. Of course, a rich household may consume more of each commodity than a poor household. The rich and the poor households (and every other household) will, however, adjust their *relative* purchases of each commodity so that the relative marginal utilities are the same for all households. Thus, if the price of X is twice the price of Y, each household will purchase X and Y to the point at which the household's marginal utility of X is twice its marginal utility of Y.

The derivation of the household's demand curve

To derive the household's demand curve for a commodity, it is necessary only to ask what happens when there is a change in the price of that commodity. To do this for carrots, take equation (2) and let X stand for carrots and Y for all other commodities.

Now assume that carrots involve such a small proportion of the household's total expenditure that the marginal utilities of all *other goods* are unaffected when it spends a little more or a little less on carrots. Consider an example. If total expenditure on carrots rises from £1 to £2 a month in response to a 10 per cent fall in the price of carrots, this represents a large increase in carrot consumption and the marginal utility of carrots must fall. But the extra pound spent on carrots may mean only 1p less spent on each of a hundred different commodities. This reduction in the consumption of each of them is so small that it will have a negligible effect on their marginal utilities.

The slope of the demand curve What will happen if, with all other prices constant, the price of carrots rises? The household that started from a position of equilibrium will now find itself in a situation in which[1]

$$\frac{MU\ of\ carrots}{MU\ of\ Y} < \frac{price\ of\ carrots}{price\ of\ Y}. \tag{3}$$

To restore equilibrium, it must buy less carrots, thereby raising their marginal utility until once again equation (2) is satisfied (where X is carrots). The common sense of this is that the marginal utility of carrots *per penny* falls when its price rises. If the household began with the utility of the last penny spent on carrots equal to the utility of the last penny spent on all other goods, the rise in carrot prices makes this no longer true. The household must buy fewer carrots (and more of other goods) until the marginal utility of carrots has risen enough that the utility of a penny spent on carrots is the same as it was before. Thus, if carrot prices have doubled the quantity purchased must be reduced until the marginal utility of carrots has doubled.

This analysis leads to the basic prediction of demand theory.

> **A rise in the price of a commodity (with income and the prices of all other commodities held constant) will lead to a decrease in the quantity of the commodity demanded by each household.**

[1] The inequality sign (<) always points to the smaller of two magnitudes. Since the price of carrots rose, the right-hand side of equation (2) increased and the left-hand side stayed the same. Thus equation (2) was replaced by the inequality shown in (3).

If this prediction is valid for each household, it is also valid for all households taken together. Thus the theory predicts a downward-sloping market demand curve.

Elasticity of demand We often want to know not only the direction in which quantity demanded will change when price changes, but also the amount by which it will change. When the price of carrots rises, will the household cut its purchases a lot or a little? If the price doubles, we have already predicted that the household will reduce its purchases until the marginal utility has doubled, but we do not yet know if this will be accomplished by a large or a small reduction in purchases. Figure 14.2 shows two possibilities. If carrots have a marginal utility curve such as X', which is flat over the relevant range, consumption is cut from q_1 to q_3 before the marginal utility is doubled from u_1 to u_2. Up to that point there is a clear gain in transferring expenditure from carrots to other goods. If carrots have a steep marginal utility curve over the relevant range, such as X'', only a slight reduction in purchases from q_1 to q_2 suffices to double their marginal utility. In both cases the household reaches an equilibrium that satisfies equation (2), but in one case purchases fall by a large amount, whereas in the other case they fall only a little.

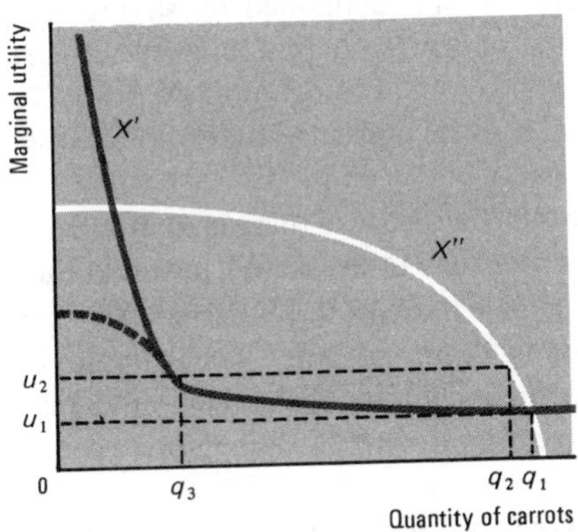

Fig. 14.2 Two alternative marginal utility schedules for carrots

Curve X' is shown in two forms in Figure 14.2. The solid version has a higher total utility than X'' because the utility of the first units consumed is very high. The dashed version has a much lower total utility than X''. Notice that the reactions to the rise in price are independent of the shape of the curve outside the relevant range. Curve X' could be as shown by the solid line or it could be shown by the broken line, and the result would be the same when the household cuts consumption to raise marginal utility from u_1 to u_2.

This leads to the following important conclusion.

> **The magnitude of the response of quantity demanded to a change in price (i.e., the elasticity of demand) depends on the marginal utility over the relevant range and has no necessary relation to total utility.**

Confusion between total and marginal utilities: some examples

The 'paradox of value' discussed at the beginning of this chapter arises because an intuitively appealing hypothesis is obviously refuted by any number of day-to-day observations. Early economists believed that commodities with high total utilities should be expensive because people valued them highly, while commodities with low total utilities should be cheap because people did not value them highly. They were thus arguing that market values should be related to total utilities. These economists referred to market values as *exchange values* and to total utilities as *use values*. They posed their problem by saying that use values should be, but were observed not to be, related to exchange values.

The hypothesis compares the total market value of two commodities with their total utilities.[1] A precise statement of it would be:

$$\frac{p \times q \text{ of diamonds}}{p \times q \text{ of water}} = \frac{\text{total utility of diamonds}}{\text{total utility of water}}. \tag{4}$$

This relation does not hold in the real world since the total utility of diamonds is always less than the total utility of water, while at many times and places the total market value of diamonds traded exceeds the total market value of water.

We have seen already that we should not expect market behaviour to have any relation to total utility. When the price of carrots doubles in Figure 14.2, for example, the reaction of quantity demanded is the same with the broken marginal utility curve X' as with the solid curve X'. Yet these two curves imply very different total utilities of carrots. The paradox of value is thus explained by saying that relation (4) is not a valid deduction from the assumption that households are utility-maximizers. Utility maximization depends on relating market prices to marginal utilities (equation 2), not on relating the total market values of purchases to total utilities (equation 4).

To see this intuitively, remember that water is cheap because there is so much of it that people consume it to the point at which its *marginal* utility is very low, and they are not prepared to pay a high price to obtain a little more of it. Diamonds are very expensive because they are scarce (the owners of diamond mines keep diamonds scarce by limiting output), and people have to stop consuming them at a point where marginal utility is still high. Thus consumers are prepared to pay a high price for an additional diamond.

Necessities, luxuries and total utility On page 109 we discussed the common tendency to divide commodities into two groups: necessities, having very low price elasticities of demand, and luxuries, having very high elasticities. The reasoning behind this division can be re-stated using the language of utility theory. There are certain commodities, called luxuries, that have low total utilities. Since they can easily be dispensed with, they have highly elastic demands because when their prices rise, consumers can stop purchasing them. There are other commodities, called necessities, that are essential to life and have high total utilities. These commodities have almost completely inelastic demands because when their prices rise, the consumer has no choice but to continue to buy them. Many goods fall into one or the other of these classes, entertainment being an example of a luxury and food an example of a necessity.

In the earlier discussion we pointed out that the facts do not support this hypothesis. We can now see *why* this is so. The trouble with the hypothesis is that it tries to predict elasticity, which is the reaction of the quantity demanded to a small change in price, from a knowledge of total utilities. But as we saw above, elasticity is

[1] We cannot relate the total utilities of two commodities simply to their relative market *prices*, since we can make the latter be anything we want by choosing our units appropriately. For example, a bushel of diamonds is expensive relative to a gallon of water, but a small industrial diamond is cheap relative to a million gallons of water.

related to marginal, not total, utility. Those who predict relative demand elasticities on the basis solely of relative total utilities can thus expect to be wrong as often as they are right, since we do not expect elasticities and total utilities to be related one way or the other.

Pricing policies related to total utilities There is very little doubt that the emotional reaction of people to goods is in response to their total rather than to their marginal utilities. We often hear an argument such as the following: 'Water is a necessity of life, and it would be wrong to make people pay for it.' Such views often produce curious results. If, for example, water is provided free instead of at a modest price, the additional consumption that will occur will be on account of the many uses that yield a relatively low utility (such as letting the water run while cleaning one's teeth). The relevant question when deciding between a zero and a modest price for water is not 'Is water so necessary that we would not want to deprive anyone of *all* of it?' but rather 'Are the marginal uses of water which our policy will encourage so necessary that we want to encourage them in spite of the fact that it is costly to provide the water for these uses?' Clearly, these two questions can be given different answers.

Evidence about the consumption of water at various prices suggests that the marginal utility curve for water is shaped somewhat like the curve labelled X' in Figure 14.2, so that much more water is consumed at a zero price than at a modest positive price. This additional water has an opportunity cost, since its provision requires resources. If the utility of the commodities foregone is higher than the utility of the extra water consumed, then people are worse off as a result of receiving water free. A charge for water would release resources from water production to produce goods that yield a higher utility. (Against this, of course, would have to be set the cost of metering water consumption and collecting accounts.)

The observation that some minimum quantity of water is so important that no one should be deprived of it is quite irrelevant to the policy decision about whether to provide water free or at a modest price. One may, indeed, wish to provide some minimum of water free to the very poor, but this is not the primary effect of making water generally free.

> **Extreme caution should be used in basing policies on a consideration of total utilities. Usually, if not always, it is marginal utilities that are relevant.**

The measurement of total utilities by attitude surveys Consider the type of attitude surveys that are so popular these days in sociology and political science. They seek answers to such questions as:

'Do you prefer blondes or brunettes?'

'Do you like the Conservatives more than the Socialists?'

'In deciding to live in High Whimper, rather than Nether Whimper, what factors influenced your choice? List the following in order of importance: neighbours, schools, closeness to swimming area, price, quality of house, amount of free land, play areas for children, general amenities.'

Notice that *all of the above surveys, and most of the others you will encounter, attempt to measure total rather than marginal utilities.*[1] There is, of course, nothing

[1] I am indebted to Professor G. C. Archibald for making this penetrating point when we were discussing the practical value of a particular attitude survey.

wrong with this in itself. Anyone is free to measure anything that interests him or her, and in some cases knowledge of total utilities may be useful. But in many cases it will be marginal utilities that influence actual behaviour. If one attempts to predict behaviour in these cases from a knowledge of total utilities, even if the information is correct, one will be hopelessly in error.

Where the behaviour being predicted involves an either-or decision, such as to vote for the Socialist or the Conservative candidate, the total utility that is attached to each party or candidate will indeed be what matters, because the voter must choose one and reject the other. Where the decision is a marginal one regarding a little more or a little less, however, total utility is not what will determine behaviour.

Let us consider an example of how such surveys can be misleading. A political party made a survey to determine what types of public expenditure people thought most valuable. Unemployment benefits rated very high. The party was subsequently astonished when it aroused great voter hostility by increasing unemployment benefits. Although the party was surprised, there was nothing inconsistent or irrational in the voters' feeling that protection of the unemployed was a very good thing, providing a high total utility, while increased payments were unnecessary and therefore had a low or even negative marginal utility.

Indifference theory

The utility theory of household behaviour came first historically and is still valued because of the great insights provided by the concept of marginal utility. With the publication in 1939 of Sir John R. Hicks's classic *Value and Capital,* an alternative approach, called *indifference-preference analysis*, or just *indifference theory* for short, became popular in English-language economics. This is not a competing theory, but a slightly different way of looking at choices made by households. Its major innovation was that it did not invoke the notion of a *measurable* concept of utility.

In utility theory, we start by asking what happens to the household's satisfactions if it consumes more or less of one commodity. In indifference theory, we start by asking a different, but closely related, question: 'If the household is consuming two commodities, how much more of one must it be given to compensate for reducing its consumption of the other by some small amount?' To parallel the questions with which we opened our discussion of utility theory, we now ask: 'How many extra films would you need to see per month to compensate you for reducing your consumption of water by 35 gallons per month?' We can interpret the word *compensate* to mean 'leave your total utility unchanged by the change in commodities consumed'.

An indifference curve

We start by taking an imaginary household and giving it some quantity of each of two commodities, say 18 units of clothing and 10 units of food. (A consumption pattern for a household that contains quantities of two or more distinct commodities is called a BUNDLE or a COMBINATION OF COMMODITIES.) Now offer the household an alternative bundle, say 13 units of clothing and 15 units of food. This alternative has 5 units fewer of clothing and 5 units more of food than the first one. Whether the household prefers this bundle depends on the relative value that it places on 5 units more of food and 5 units less of clothing; if it values the extra food more than the forgone clothing, it will prefer the new bundle to the original one. If it values the food less than the clothing, it will prefer the original bundle. There is a third alternative: if the household values the extra food the same as it values the forgone clothing, it would gain equal satisfaction from the two alternative bundles. In this case the household is said to be *indifferent* between the two bundles.

Assume that after much trial and error several bundles have been identified, each of which gives equal satisfaction. These are shown in Table 14.2. There will, of

Table 14.2 Alternative bundles of food and clothing giving equal satisfaction to a household

Bundle	Clothing	Food
a	30	5
b	18	10
c	13	15
d	10	20
e	8	25
f	7	30

course, be combinations of the two commodities other than those enumerated in the table that will give the same level of satisfaction to the household. All of these combinations are shown in Figure 14.3 by the smooth curve that passes through the points plotted from the table. This curve is an indifference curve. In general, an INDIFFERENCE CURVE shows all combinations of commodities that yield the same satisfaction to the household. A household is *indifferent* between the combinations indicated by any two points on one indifference curve.

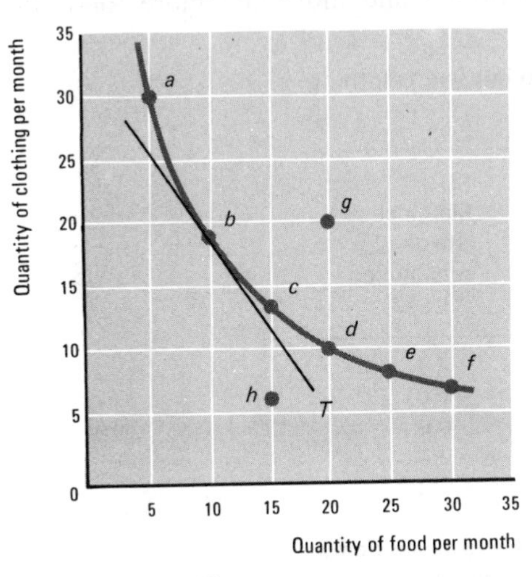

Fig. 14.3 An indifference curve

Quantity of clothing per month

0

Quantity of food per month

I_1 I_2 I_3 I_4 I_5

Fig. 14.4 An indifference map for a household

Any points above and to the right of the curve show combinations of food and clothing that the household would prefer to combinations indicated by points on the curve. Consider, for example, the combination of 20 food and 20 clothing, which is represented by point *g* in the figure. Although it might not be obvious that this bundle must be preferred to bundle *a* (which has more clothing but less food), it is obvious that it will be preferred to bundle *c*, because there is both less clothing and less food represented at *c* than at *g*. Inspection of the graph shows that *any* point above the curve will be obviously superior to *some* points on the curve in the sense that it will contain both more food and more clothing than those points on the curve. But since all points on the curve are equal in the household's eyes, the point above the curve must thus be superior to *all* points on the curve. By a similar argument, points such as *h*, which are below and to the left of the curve, represent bundles of goods that are inferior to bundles represented by points on the curve.

The hypothesis of a diminishing marginal rate of substitution

The basic postulate in utility theory is that of diminishing marginal utility: the more of a commodity already consumed by the household, the lower the utility of a bit more of it. The analogous assumption in indifference theory is that of DIMINISHING MARGINAL RATE OF SUBSTITUTION.

> **The hypothesis of diminishing marginal rate of substitution states that the less of one commodity presently being consumed by a household, the more unwilling will it be to give up a unit of that commodity to obtain an additional unit of a second commodity.**

This hypothesis is illustrated in Table 14.3 which is based on the example of food and clothing shown in Table 14.2. When, for example, the household moves from consumption bundle *a* to bundle *b*, it is sacrificing 12 units of clothing while gaining 5 units of food, making a rate of substitution of −2.4. This means that the household is prepared to give up 2.4 units of clothing for every extra unit of food obtained. As we move down the table through points *b* to *f*, the household is consuming bundles with less and less clothing and more and more food. In

Table 14.3 The marginal rate of substitution between clothing and food*

Movement	(1) Change in clothing	(2) Change in food	(3) Marginal rate of substitution (1) ÷ (2)
From *a* to *b*	−12	5	−2·4
From *b* to *c*	− 5	5	−1·0
From *c* to *d*	− 3	5	−0.6
From *d* to *e*	− 2	5	−0·4
From *e* to *f*	− 1	5	−0·2

* This table is based on Table 14.2. When the household moves from *a* to *b*, it gives up 12 units of clothing and gains 5 units of food; it remains at the same level of overall satisfaction. The household at point *a* was prepared to sacrifice 12 clothing for 5 food (i.e., 12/5 = 2·4 units of clothing per unit of food obtained). When the household moves from *b* to *c*, it sacrifices 5 clothing for 5 food (a rate of substitution of 1 unit of clothing for each unit of food).

accordance with the hypothesis of diminishing marginal rate of substitution, the rate at which the household is willing to give up further clothing to get more food diminishes. When the household moves from *c* to *d*, for example, it is only prepared to give up 6/10 of a unit of clothing to get a further unit of food, while when it moves from *e* to *f*, it will only give up 2/10 of a unit. These calculations illustrate the hypothesis: the less clothing and the more food does the household already consume, the smaller the further marginal sacrifice in clothing the household will be willing to make to get a further unit of food.

The geometrical expression of this hypothesis is found in the shape of the indifference curve. Look closely, for example, at the slope of the curve in Figure 14.3. Its downward slope indicates that, if the household is to have less of one commodity, it must have more of the other to compensate. Diminishing marginal rate of substitution is shown by the fact that the curve is convex viewed from the origin: moving down the curve to the right, its slope gets flatter and flatter. The slope of the curve is the marginal rate of substitution, the rate at which one commodity must be substituted for the other in order to keep total utility constant. Geometrically the slope of the indifference curve at any point is indicated by the slope of the tangent to the curve at that point. The slope of tangent *T* drawn to the curve at point *b* shows the marginal rate of substitution at that point. It is visually obvious that moving down the curve to the right, the slope of the tangent, and hence the marginal rate of substitution at that point, gets flatter and flatter.[1]

The indifference map

So far we have constructed only a single indifference curve. There must, however, be a similar curve through other points in Figure 14.3. Starting at any point, such as *g*, there will be other combinations that will yield equal satisfaction to the household and, if the points indicating all of *these* combinations are connected, they will form another indifference curve. This exercise can be repeated as many times as we wish, generating a new indifference curve each time.

In the previous section points *g* and *h* were compared to the indifference curve in Figure 14.3. It follows from this discussion that the farther away any indifference curve is from the origin, the higher is the level of satisfction given by the combinations of goods indicated by it.

A set of indifference curves is called an INDIFFERENCE MAP. An example is shown in Figure 14.4. It specifies the household's tastes by showing its rate of substitution between the two commodities for every level of current consumption of these commodities. When economists say that a household's tastes are *given*, they do not mean merely that the household's current consumption pattern is given; rather, they mean that the household's entire indifference map is given.

---

[1] Table 14.3 calculates the rate of substitution between distinct points on the indifference curve. Strictly speaking these rates are the incremental rate of substitution between the two points. Geometrically this incremental rate is given by the slope of the chord joining the two points. The marginal rate refers to the slope of the curve at a single point and is given by the slope of the tangent to the curve at the point. It should be visually obvious, and it is a fundamental proposition in the differential calculus, that the slope of the chord approaches the slope of the tangent as the distance separating the two distinct points is diminished towards zero. Thus the average rate *between* two points may be taken as an approximation to the marginal rate at either of the two points, with the degree of approximation improving as the two points get closer and closer together.

The equilibrium of the household

The indifference map describes the preferences or tastes of a household. In a sense, it tells us what the household would like to do: move to higher and higher indifference curves. To find out what the household will actually do, we must know what it can do. This information is supplied by the budget line which we first derived in Chapter 13.

Figure 14.5 brings together the household's tastes, as shown by its indifference curves, and the possibilities actually open to it, as shown by its budget line. The particular budget line shown is drawn on the assumption that the household has an income of £75 a month and faces prices of £2·50 per unit of clothing and £3·00 per unit of food. Any point on the budget line can be attained. Which one will the satisfaction-maximizing household actually choose?

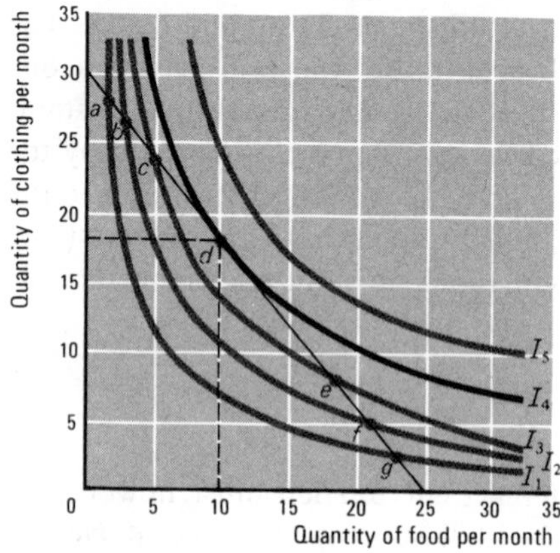

Fig. 14.5 The equilibrium of a household

Suppose that it starts at point *a* in Figure 14.5, where it is on indifference curve I_1. If it moves to point *b*, it is still just on its budget line, but it has moved to a preferred position, i.e., to a combination of goods on a higher indifference curve. The household can continue this process, moving down the budget line through point *c* and attaining higher curves, until it reaches point *d*. If it moves further, however, to points *e*, *f*, and *g*, it will begin to move to lower indifference curves.

If we start the household at a point to the right of *d*, say at *g*, the same argument will apply: the household can attain higher curves by moving up its budget line to the left. As it moves, it attains higher curves until it reaches *d*, but if it persists beyond *d*, it moves to lower curves. This leads to the following conclusion.

Satisfaction is maximized at the point where an indifference curve is tangent to a budget line. At that point the slope of the indifference curve (the marginal rate of substitution of the goods in the household's preferences) is equal to the slope of the budget line (the opportunity cost of one good in terms of the other as determined by market prices).[1]

The common sense of this result is that, if the household values commodities at a different rate than does the market, there is room for profitable exchange. The household can give up the commodity it values less than the market does and take in return the commodity it values more than the market does. When the household is

[1] See the discussion of relative prices, opportunity costs and the slope of the budget line on page 151.

prepared to swap commodities at the same rate as they can be traded on the market, there is no further opportunity for it to raise its utility by substituting one commodity for the other.

Notice that this conclusion is very similar to the one we reached with marginal utility theory. The household is presented with market information (prices) that it cannot change. It adjusts to these prices by choosing a bundle of goods such that, at the margin, its own subjective relative evaluation of the two commodities conforms with the objective relative evaluations given by market prices.

When the household has chosen the consumption bundle that maximizes its satisfactions, it will go on consuming the goods in the proportions indicated unless something changes. The household is thus in equilibrium.

What happens if something disturbs the household's equilibrium?

A change in income Changes in income lead to parallel shifts of the budget line—inwards towards the origin when income falls, and outwards away from the origin when income rises (see page 150). For each level of income there will, of course, be an equilibrium position at which an indifference curve is tangent to the relevant budget line. Each such equilibrium position means that the household is doing as well as it possibly can for that level of income.

An example is shown in Figure 14.6. As the household's income is twice increased, the budget line moves outwards from a tangency with indifference curve I_1 to I_2 to I_3. If we move the budget line through all possible levels of income, and join up all the points of equilibrium, we will trace what is called an INCOME-CONSUMPTION LINE. This line shows how consumption bundles change as income changes, with relative prices held constant.[1]

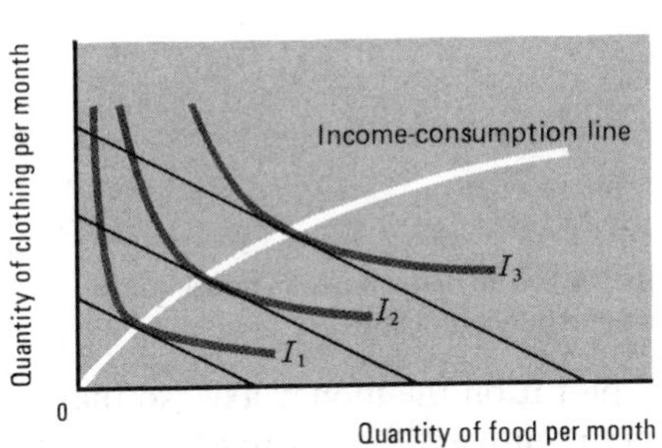

Fig. 14.6 The income-consumption line showing the reaction of the household to changes in its money income with money prices constant

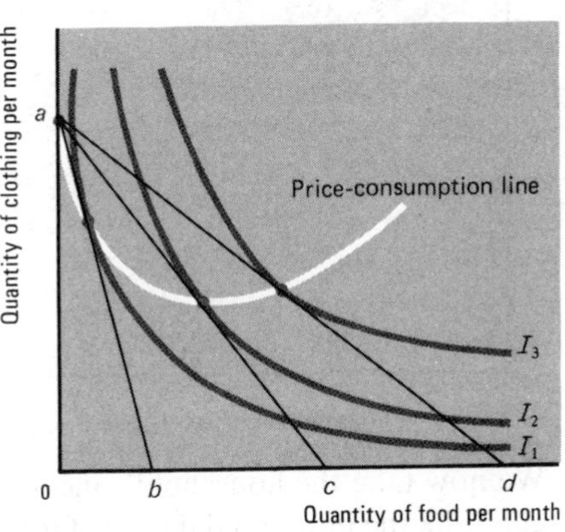

Fig. 14.7 The price-consumption line showing the reaction of the household to changes in the price of food with the price of clothing and money income held constant

A change in price We saw in Chapter 13 that a change in the relative prices of the two commodities changed the slope of the budget line. Assume now that the money price

[1] We can use this income-consumption line to derive the curve relating consumption ofone commodity to income that we first introduced on pp. 80–1. To do this, we merely take the quantity of either good consumed at the equilibrium position on a given budget line and plot it against the level of money income that determined the position of the particular budget line. By repeating this for each level of income, we produce the required curve.

of food falls, the money price of clothing being held constant. This is illustrated in Figure 14.7 in which the fall in the price of food pivots the budget line from *ab* to *ac* to *ad*. Equilibrium points of tangency are successively with indifference curves I_1, I_2 and I_3.

If we now vary the price of food continuously, we will find an equilibrium position for each price, and by connecting these, we can trace out what is called a PRICE-CONSUMPTION LINE. This line shows how consumption of the two commodities varies as the price of one changes, the price of the other and the household's money income being held constant. An illustration is shown by the white line in Figure 14.7.

The household's demand curve

To derive the household's demand curve for any commodity, we need to depart from our world of two commodities. We are now interested in what happens to the household's demand for some commodity, say carrots, as the price of that commodity changes, *all other prices being held constant* (see page 78). We plot a new indifference map in Figure 14.8 in which we represent the quantity of carrots on the horizontal axis and the value of all other commodities consumed on the vertical axis. The indifference curves tell us the rate at which the household is prepared to swap carrots for money (which allows it to buy all other goods) at each level of consumption of carrots and of other goods.

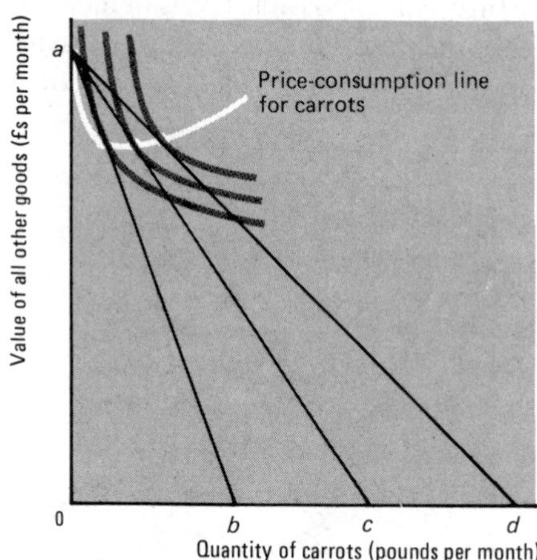

Fig. 14.8 The derivation of a household's demand curve for carrots

We now take the household's income and plot it on the money axis, so that in Figure 14.8 the household has £*a* of income per month and is thus able to consume £*a* worth of all other goods, if it keeps its carrot consumption at zero. Given the money price of carrots and the household income, we obtain a budget line showing all those combinations of carrots and other goods that the household can consume. We now change the money price of carrots (thus changing the slope of the budget line through *a*). By joining the points of equilibrium, we trace out a price-consumption line between carrots and all other commodities in just the same way as we traced out such a line for food and clothing in Figure 14.7.

Note that Figure 14.8 is very similar to Figure 14.7. The axes are labelled differently and the price-consumption line in Figure 14.8 is crowded into the upper part of the diagram, indicating that whatever the price of carrots, the household does not spend a large part of its income on them.

Every point on the price-consumption line corresponds to one money price of carrots and one quantity of carrots demanded. If we plot these pairs of values on a new figure with price on one axis and quantity on the other, we have the household's demand curve for carrots. In Figure 14.8 the quantity of carrots consumed increases as the price of carrots falls, so that when we plot it, the demand curve will have a downward slope.

Can the household's demand curve ever slope upward? The income and substitution effect[1] The demand curve that we derived above has a downward slope. a fall in the price of carrots increases the quantity demanded. Is this a necessary result or merely a consequence of the way in which we happened to draw the graph? To answer this question we must distinguish between the income and substitution effects.

A fall in the price of carrots has something of the effect of a rise in income since it makes it possible for the household to have more of all goods. To see this, look again at Figure 14.8. A fall in the price of carrots takes the budget line, for example, from *ac* to *ad*. Wherever the household was located on *ac*, it clearly can, if it wishes, move to *ad* by going upwards to the right thus consuming more carrots *and* more of everything else.

We can imagine removing this INCOME EFFECT of a price change by insisting that the household remain on its original indifference curve in spite of any change in price. A change in relative prices changes the slope of the budget line, but, if the household is to remain on its original indifference curve, money income must be changed just enough—so that the budget line slides around the same curve, always remaining tangent to it.

Assume for example, that the price of carrots is cut in half, so that the slope of the budget line becomes only half as steep, the actual line pivoting from *ab* to *ac* in Figure 14.9. The household was initially in equilibrium at point e_1 on Figure 14.9. If

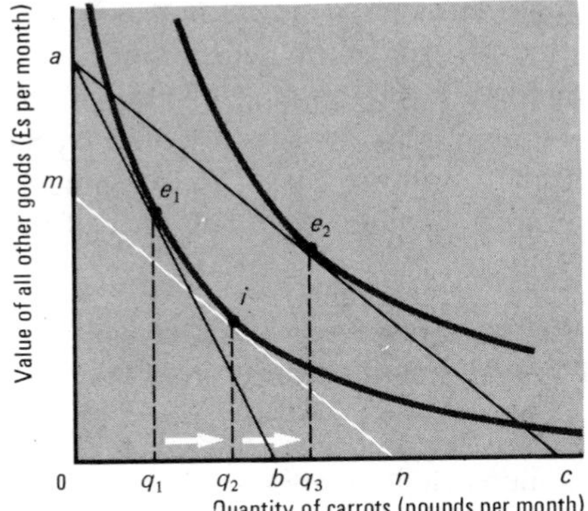

Fig. 14.9 The income and substitution effects of a fall in the price of carrots

we adjust the position of the budget line after the price fall so as to keep the household on its initial indifference curve, the new position of equilibrium is at *i*. (The line *mn* is parallel to *ac*, and thus its slope conforms to the new set of relative prices.) The increase in the consumption of carrots from q_1 to q_2 can be termed the

[1] This section deals with a topic that is often left for intermediate courses and it may be omitted without loss of continuity.

SUBSTITUTION EFFECT, the effect on carrot consumption of a fall in the price of carrots, household *utility* held constant. Because the indifference curve slopes downward to the right, it follows that a fall in the price of carrots necessarily raises the quantity bought, if the level of utility is held constant. The substitution effect is thus a negative one: a change in price leads quantity demanded to change in the opposite direction.

We have said that halving the price of carrots will cause the household to move from e_1 to i on the *same* indifference curve. But this, of course, is not what happens when the price of carrots falls in the real world. No economic dictator reduces everyone's money income to remove any increases in utility they might otherwise get from the change. We have seen that the budget line actually pivots through a, indicating that the household could obtain more of all goods if it wished. In Figure 14.9 the new budget line is ac and the new equilibrium position is e_2. Thus, when the price falls, carrot consumption rises from q_1 to q_3. This movement can, however, be broken up conceptually into a substitution effect from q_1 to q_2, between the points e_1 and i, which is the result of a change in relative prices, and the increase from q_2 to q_3, between points i and e_2, which is called the *income effect*. This income effect is equivalent to the increase in consumption that would have occurred owing to an outward shift in the budget line, relative prices being held constant at their new level.

In indifference theory the substitution effect is the change in consumption that would occur if relative prices changed but the household was held on its original indifference curve. The income effect is the change in consumption as a result of the movement between the original indifference curve and the new indifference curve when the relative prices are held constant at their new level.

This distinction permits a concise statement of the conditions under which the demand curve slopes downward. The change in demand for one commodity in response to a change in its price can be thought of as a composite of the income and the substitution effects. The theory predicts that the substitution effect is negative. Thus a fall in the relative price of a commodity, with the level of utility held constant, leads to a rise in the demand for that commodity. Unless we would expect an increase in income to lead to a *reduction* in consumption, because the commodity is an inferior good, the theory gives the unambiguous prediction that more of the commodity will be demanded when its price falls.

A normal good must have a downward-sloping demand curve. A decrease in its price will lead to an increase in quantity demanded owing to both the substitution and income effects.

In the case of an inferior good, we cannot obtain a definite prediction about what will happen. The income effect of a fall in price leads to a tendency for a decrease in the consumption of the good. But the substitution effect still works for an increase in the quantity demanded. Thus the final result depends on the relative strengths of the two effects. Two cases of a negative income effect are shown in Figure 14.10. The original equilibrium is at e_1, with q_1 pounds of carrots consumed per month. The price of carrots falls, and the pure substitution effect would move the household to i (with $q_2 - q_1$ *more* carrots consumed each month). The income effect is negative, but if it moves the household only to e_2, the net effect is for household consumption to rise from q_1 to q_3. In the second case, the negative income effect is stronger, and the final equilibrium is at e_2'' with the consumption of carrots falling by q_1–q_4 per month as a result of the fall in their price.

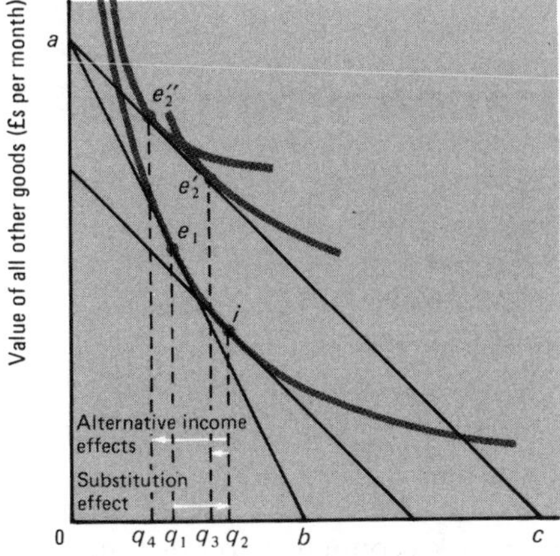

Fig. 14.10 Two alternative negative income effects

A commodity whose price and quantity vary in the same direction is called a GIFFEN GOOD, after the Victorian economist first alleged to have observed such a case. It must be an inferior commodity whose income effect outweighs its normal substitution effect. Such a commodity appears to be a rarely observed, but theoretically possible, exception to the 'law' of demand that all demand curves slope downwards.[1]

We conclude from this analysis than an upward-sloping demand curve for a product is a theoretical possibility. It would require that the commodity be an inferior good and the change in price have a large enough negative income effect to offset the substitution effect. We do not expect such a combination of circumstances to occur often, therefore we must expect an upward-sloping market demand curve to be a rare exception to the general prediction that demand curves slope downward. We shall examine this exception further in Chapter 15.

[1] Indeed there now seems to be some doubt if Giffen actually made and documented the famous alleged observations that upset the apparent universal applicability of the law of demand.

15

The theory of demand: measurements and tests

Much of what economists do to earn a living involves the use of demand measurements. The British electricity producers ask economists to draw up long-term investment plans based upon estimated demand for electric power over the next decade; the United States National Parks Service asks economists to review its procedures for selling grazing rights and timber stands to private firms. Will a fare increase help to ease the deficit of the London Transport underground and bus system or of the Panama Canal? These are questions that cannot be answered reliably without knowledge of price elasticity of demand. When the United Nations Food and Agricultural Organization (FAO), or a producers' co-op, projects quantities of food demanded by crop and area, it needs to know income and price elasticities of demand. Today many industries need to know their products' cross-elasticities of demand with petroleum in order to estimate the effects of sharply rising petroleum prices. To deal effectively with many applied problems, knowledge of relevant demand conditions is indispensible. Fortunately, as we shall see in the first part of this chapter, a great deal of this demand information is available. Where it is not available it can be obtained without great cost or difficulty. The methods for doing so have been carefully worked out. Solutions to two of the most troubling problems concerning demand measurement are discussed in the second part of this chapter.

Critics of demand theory do not quarrel with the *need* for demand information, or even with the usefulness of applied economics. Some, however, have argued that the theory of demand is wrong, in the sense that its predictions are in conflict with empirical evidence; others have argued that it is empty, in the sense that all it tells us is that 'anything can happen'. In the final part of this chapter we shall consider these criticisms.

Demand measures

The solution of the stastical problems associated with demand measurement has led to a large accumulation of data on demand elasticities. The value of these data to the applied economist is the ultimate proof of the usefulness of demand theory.

Price elasticities

Much of the early work on demand measurement concentrated on the agricultural sector. Large fluctuations in agricultural prices provided both the incentive to study this sector and the empirical observations on which to base estimates of price elasticities of demand. Professors Richard Stone, in the UK, and Henry Schultz, in the US, did much of the pioneering work. Many agricultural research centres extended their work, and even today make new estimates of the price elasticities of foodstuffs. The resulting data, which is illustrated in Table 15.1, mostly confirm the general belief in low price elasticities for food products as a whole as well as for many individual products.

Table 15.1 Estimated price elasticities of demand in the UK (selected commodities)

Inelastic demand (less than unity)	
Potatoes	0·3
Sugar	0·3
Public transportation	0·4
All foods	0·4
Cigarettes	0·5
Gasoline	0·6
All clothing	0·6
Consumer durables	0·8
Demand of approximately unit elasticity*	
Beef (US)	
Beer	
Marijuana (US)	
Elastic demand (greater than unity)	
Furniture	1.2
Electricity	1·3
UK lamb and mutton	1·5
Automobiles	2·1
Millinery	3·0

*Greater than 0·9 and less than 1·1.

The policy payoff of this knowledge in terms of understanding agricultural problems has been enormous; it represents an early triumph of empirical work in economics. (See the discussion in Chapter 10.)

Although agricultural commodities often have inelastic demands, notice in Table 15.1 that the demand for some commodities, such as beef in the United States and domestically produced lamb and mutton in the United Kingdom, are elastic. The reason for this is that these products have close substitutes. For example, British households can choose between locally produced lamb and mutton and imported varieties (which typically have a somewhat lower quality and price). Similarly, American households can choose among beef, pork and chicken on the basis of price. The data also support the generalization that the broader the category of related products, the lower the observed price elasticity of demand.

Although the importance of the agricultural problem led early investigators to concentrate on the demand for foodstuffs, modern studies have expanded to include virtually the whole range of commodities on which the household spends its income. Particular interest has been attached to the demand for consumers' durables such as cars, radios, refrigerators, television sets and houses. Demands for these types of goods are particularly interesting because they constitute a large fraction of total demand and because they can vary markedly from one year to the next. A durable commodity can always be made to last for another year; thus purchases can be postponed with greater ease than can purchases of non-durables such as food and services. If enough households decide simultaneously to postpone purchases of durables for even six months, the effect on the economy can be enormous.

Durables as a whole have an inelastic demand (0·8 according to Table 15.1) while many individual durables, including those listed in the table have elastic demands. This is another example of the general proposition that the broader the category, the lower the elasticity because the fewer the close substitutes. Indeed, whether durable or non-durable, most specific manufactured goods have close substitutes, and studies show that they tend to have price-elastic demands. Millinery, for example, has been estimated to have a demand elasticity of 3·0. In contrast, the demand for all clothing tends to be inelastic. The accumulated data on price elasticity confirm this generalization.

Any one of a group of close substitutes will tend to have an elastic demand, even though the demand for the group as a whole may be inelastic.

Income elasticities

Table 15.2 provides a sample of the vast amount of data that are available on income elasticities. Because changes in income exert a major effect on quantities

Table 15.2 Estimated UK income elasticities of demand (selected commodities)

Inferior goods (negative income elasticities)	
Whole milk	−0·5
Pig products (US)	−0·2
Starchy roots (US)	−0·2
Inelastic normal goods (0·0 to 1·0)	
Coffee	0·0
Wine (France)	0·1
All food	0·2
Poultry	0·3
Cheese	0·4
Beef	0·5
Housing	0·6
Cigarettes	0·8
Elastic normal goods (greater than 1·0)	
Gasoline	1·1
Wine	1·4
Cream	1·7
Wine (Canada)	1·8
Consumer durables	1·8
Poultry	2·0
Restaurant meals	2·4

demanded over time, the FAO has found it useful to estimate income elasticities for dozens of agricultural products, country by country. The data tend to show that the more basic, or staple, a commodity, the lower its income elasticity: food as a whole has an income elasticity of 0·2 in the UK, while in the US pork and such starchy roots as potatoes are inferior goods so that their quantity consumed falls as income rises.

The data confirm that the lower income elasticities of many foodstuffs hold true particularly in high-income countries. It may seem odd at first sight, therefore, that restaurant meals should have such a high income elasticity. The explanation is, however, fairly straightforward. Restaurant meals are almost always more expensive, calorie for calorie, than meals prepared at home. It would thus be expected that restaurant meals would be regarded as an expensive luxury at lower ranges of income, and that the demand for them would expand substantially as households became better off. This is, in fact, what happens. Does this mean that the market demand for the foodstuffs that appear on restaurant menus will also have high income elasticities? Generally the answer is No. When a household eats out rather than at home, the main difference is not in what is eaten but in who prepares it. The additional expenditure on food goes mainly to pay the wages of cooks and waiters and to yield a return on the restaurateur's capital. Thus, when a household expands its expenditure on restaurant food by 2·4 per cent in response to a 1 per cent rise in its income, most of this represents an increased demand for a service to replace the housewife's unpaid work, rather than an increased demand for food. Most of the extra expenditure on restaurant meals goes to persons in the service industry; little, if any, finds its way into the pockets of farmers. We have here a striking example of the general tendency for households to spend a higher proportion of their income on services as their income rises.

The interesting relationship shown in Table 15.2 between whole milk, cheese and cream suggests that as incomes rise, people tend to change the form of the milk products they consume: less whole milk, more cheese and more cream. (Ice-cream, not included in the FAO data, had a high income elasticity for German, French and American consumers in measurements of two decades ago. Today the income elasticity is much lower. To an earlier generation ice-cream was a special treat; at current income levels and prices, ice-cream has become a staple.)

Empirical studies tend to confirm that, as income rises, household expenditures follow broadly similar paths in different countries. Summarizing recent studies, Robert Ferber wrote that they tend to bear out earlier findings on income elasticity yielding low elasticities for food and housing, elasticities close to unity for clothing and education and higher elasticities for various types of recreation, personal care, home operation and other services. Of course there are exceptions to country-wide uniformity, as Table 15.2 shows. If a commodity plays a very different role in the consumption patterns of different groups, it may be expected to have different demand characteristics, even at comparable levels of income. Wine is a basic part of the French consumption bundle, and its consumption in France is little affected by changes in level of income. Wine in Canada and the United States is evidently a luxury good rather than a necessity at lower levels of income. The difference in income elasticity of demand for poultry between the United Kingdom and Ceylon is a matter of the level of average income as well as of differences in taste.

The accumulated data on income elasticity confirm this generalization.

The more basic an item is in the consumption pattern of households, the lower its income elasticity will be.

Cross-elasticities of demand

In many countries monopoly is illegal. Economic analysis has proved its great practical applicability in court cases to decide on the allegation that a monopoly exists. Many of the most interesting studies of cross-elasticity have been made as part of anti-combine inquiries in the United States, in the course of attempts to determine whether specific products are substitutes. Whether yeast extract and marmite, or aluminium cable and copper cable, are or are not substitutes may determine the question of the existence of monopoly under the law. As we have seen, the size and the positive or negative sign of cross-elasticities shed light on the extent to which commodities are substitutes.

To illustrate, assume that the US government brings suit against a company for buying up all of the firms making aluminium cable, claiming the company has created a monopoly of the product. The company replies that it needs to own all of the firms in order to compete efficiently against the several firms producing copper cable. It argues that these two products are such close substitutes that the firms producing each are in intense competition, so that the only producer of aluminium cable cannot be said to have an effective monopoly over the whole market for cable. Measurement of cross-elasticity can be decisive in such a case. A cross-elasticity of 10, for example, would support the company by showing that the two products were such close substitutes that a monopoly of either was not an effective monopoly of the cable market. A cross-elasticity of 0·5, on the other hand, would support the government's contention that the monopoly of aluminium cable was a monopoly over a complete market.

Other variables

Modern studies show that demand is often influenced by a wide variety of socio-economic factors—family size, age, geographical location, type of employment, wealth and income expectations—not included in the traditional theory of demand. Although significant, the total contribution of all of these factors to changes in demand tends to be small. Typically, less than 30 per cent of the variations in demand are accounted for by these 'novel' factors and a much higher proportion is explained by the traditional variables of prices and current incomes.

Problems of demand measurement

We have observed here just the tip of the iceberg of accumulated knowledge about the determinants and the specific demand elasticities. The data are so plentiful that any economist who wishes to make an applied study of a particular market is likely to have some established evidence on which to draw.

This relatively recent explosion of knowledge came about when econometricians overcame major problems in measuring demand relationships. A full discussion of these problems must be left to a course in econometrics, but some aspects of such measurements are sufficiently troubling to most students to make them worth mentioning.

Everything is changing at once

Since in a market economy all kinds of things are happening at once, how can they be sorted out into the neat theoretical categories we have created? When market demand changes over time, it is usually because *all* of the influences that affect demand have been changing.

What, for example, is to be made of the observation that the quantity of butter consumed per capita rose by 10 per cent over a period in which average household income rose by 5 per cent, the price of butter fell by 3 per cent and the price of margarine rose by 4 per cent? How much of the change is due to income elasticity of demand, how much to price elasticity and how much to the cross-elasticity between butter and margarine? If there is only this one observation, the question cannot be answered. If, however, there is a large number of observations showing, say, quantity demanded, income, price of butter and price of margarine every month for four or five years, it is possible, as we saw in Chapter 3, to discover the separate influence of each of the variables. The most frequently used technique for estimating the separate effect of each of these variables on demand is called *multiple-regression analysis*, which can be used directly to estimate each of the elasticities mentioned.[1]

Separating the influences of demand and supply

A second set of problems concerns using data on price and quantity actually bought and sold to estimate demand and supply curves. We do not see what people want to buy and what producers want to sell. Rather, we see what they do buy and what they do sell. The problem of how to estimate both demand and supply curves from observed market data on prices and quantities actually traded is called the IDENTIFICATION PROBLEM.

The nature of the problem can be illustrated simply. We start by assuming that all situations observed in the real world are equilibrium ones, in the sense that they are produced by the intersection of demand and supply curves. If, as in Figure 15.1 (i), the demand curve stays put while the supply curve moves up and down, possibly because of crop variations in some agricultural commodity, then the price-quantity observations illustrated in Figure 15.1 (ii) will be generated. If we draw a line through these observed points, we will trace out the demand curve of Figure 15.1 (i).

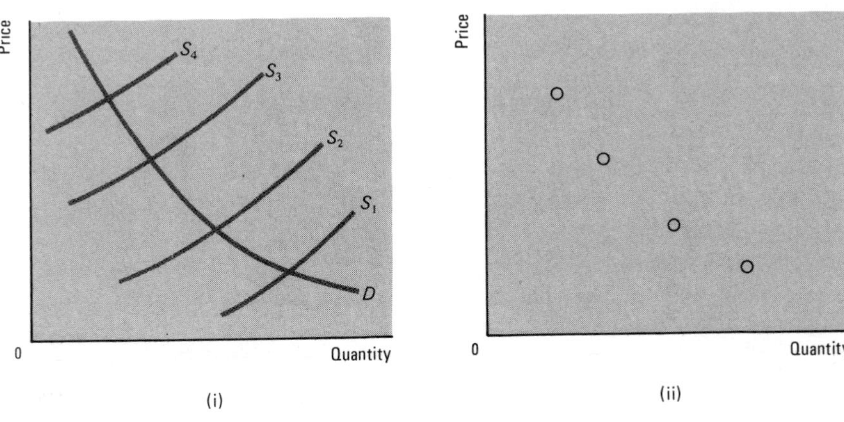

Fig. 15.1 (i) A shifting supply curve and a fixed demand curve
(ii) Observations generated by (i)

Now assume, as illustrated in Figure 15.2 (i), that the supply curve stays put while the demand curve moves about, owing perhaps to changes in the number of consumers or in their incomes. Now the price-quantity relations that will be

[1] Regression analysis was discussed briefly in Chapter 3.

observed are those given in Figure 15.2 (ii). If we draw a curve through these points, it will trace out the supply curve in Figure 15.2 (i).

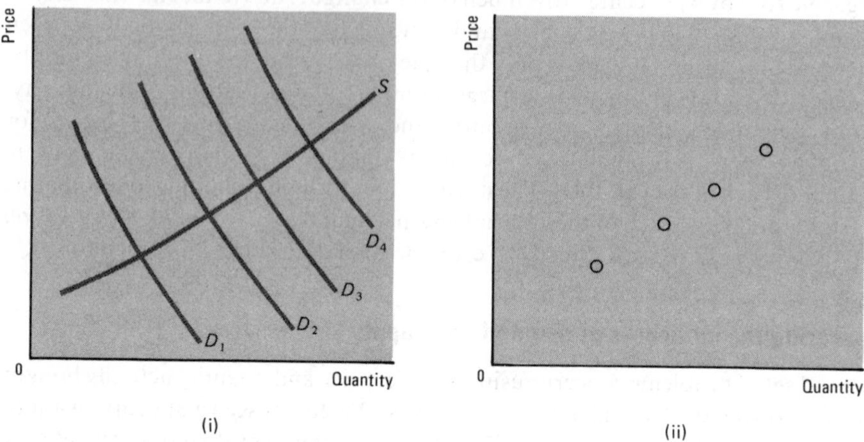

Fig. 15.2 (i) A shifting demand curve and a fixed supply curve
(ii) Observations generated by (i)

So far so good. But what if both curves shift. Assume for example that the demand and supply curves in Figure 15.3 (i) shift randomly among the three positions shown by each curve. At any one time there is only one demand and one supply curve, but over time every one of the nine possible combinations of one of the demand curves and one of the supply curves shown will exist. As this happens, the series of market observations shown in Figure 15.3 (ii) will be obtained. These trace out neither the demand nor the supply curves that generated them.

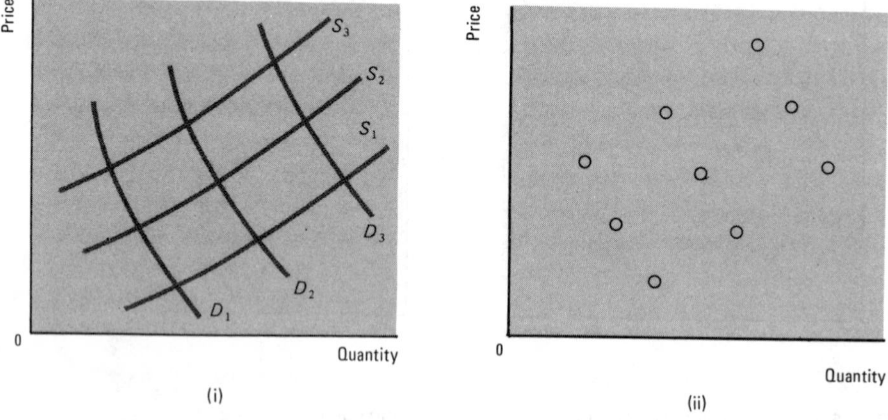

Fig. 15.3 (i) Shifting demand and supply curve
(ii) Observations generated by (i)

The identification problem is surmountable. The key to identifying the demand and supply curves separately is to bring in variables other than price, and then to relate demand to one set and supply to *some other* set. For example, supply of the commodity might be related not only to the price of the commodity but also to its cost of production, and demand might be related not only to the price of the commodity but also to consumers' incomes. Provided that both of these other variables, cost of production and income, vary sufficiently, it is possible to determine the relation between quantity supplied and price as well as the relation between quantity demanded and price. The details of how this is done will be found in a course on econometrics.

In serious applied work, concern is usually given to the identification problem. Sometimes, however, the problem is ignored. Whenever you see an argument such as the following: 'Last year the price of whisky rose by 10 per cent and whisky exports hardly fell at all, so we know that the foreign elasticity of demand must be very low', you should ask if the author has really identified the demand curve. If the rise in price was due to a rise in foreign demand for whisky, we may actually have discovered that the short-run *supply curve* of whisky is very inelastic (since whisky takes several years to manufacture). The general proposition to keep in mind is:

> **Unless we have some additional information telling us that one curve has shifted while the other has not, price and quantity data alone are insufficient to reveal anything about the shape of either the demand or the supply curve.**

Why the measurement of demand is important

The work on demand elasticity that we have just surveyed is of great value because it provides our theory of price with empirical content. If we knew *nothing* about demand elasticities, then all of the exercises we have gone through in previous chapters would have very little application to the real world. Some economists hold a different view of the importance of empirical measures of demand. A classical statement of this alternative view was made many years ago by Lord Robbins:[1]

> Our deductions do not provide any justification for saying that caviare is an economic good and carrion a disutility. Still less do they inform us concerning the intensity of the demand for caviare or the demand to be rid of carrion.... But is it not desirable to transcend such limitations? Ought we not to be in a position to give numerical values to the scales of valuation, to establish quantitive laws of demand and supply?... No doubt such knowledge would be useful. But a moment's reflection should make it plain that we are here entering into a field of investigation *where there is no reason to suppose that uniformities are to be discovered*....
>
> A simple illustration should make this clear. Suppose we are confronted with an order fixing the price of herrings at a point below the price hitherto ruling in the market. Suppose we are in a position to say, 'According to the researches of Blank (1907–8) the elasticity of demand for common herring (*Clupea haregus*) is 1·3; the present price-fixing order therefore may be expected to leave an excess of demand over supply of two million barrels.'

---

[1] L. Robbins, *An Essay on the Nature and Significance of Economic Science* (Macmillan, 1932), pages 98–101. Every economics specialist should read this provocative work. It contains the classic statements of many views still held by economists. It also states a view on the nature of economic theory and its relation to empirical observations that is contradictory to the one presented in this book. Many other economists of Lord Robbins' time shared this view. We quote from him because his is such a clear statement. For a similar one see L. von Mises, *Human Action* (Hodge, 1949), Chapter 2. For a view much closer to the one presented in the earlier parts of this chapter, however, see L. Robbins, 'The Present Position of Economics' *Rivista Di Economica*, September 1959.

> But can we hope to obtain such an enviable position? Let us assume that in 1907–8 Blank had succeeded in ascertaining that, with a given price change in that year, the elasticity of demand was 1·3.... But what reason is there to suppose that he was unearthing a constant law? Is it possible reasonably to suppose that coefficients derived from the observation of a particular herring market at a particular time and place have any *permanent* significance – save as Economic History?

The above argument runs somewhat as follows: 'I can think of no reasons why the relationship in question (e.g., the relation between demand and price) should be a stable one; I can in fact think of several reasons why it should not be stable; I conclude, therefore, that in the real world the relationship will not be stable, and attempts to *observe* whether or not it is stable can be ruled out on *a priori* grounds as a waste of time.'

Several criticisms can be made of Robbins' argument. First, *a priori* arguments, although they may strongly suggest the hypothesis that certain relationships will not be stable ones, can never establish this. Even if the *a priori* arguments turn out to be correct most of the time, there always exists the possibility that in a few cases they will be wrong. Only empirical observation is capable of discovering the cases in which the *a priori* argument is wrong.

The second major criticism is that it is extremely important to *economic theory* to know just how variable any given relationship is. If, for example, tastes are so variable that demand curves shift about violently from day to day, then all of the comparative static equilibrium analysis of the previous chapters would be useless, for only by accident would any market be near its equilibrium, and this would occur only momentarily. If, on the other hand, tastes and other factors change extremely slowly, then we might do very well to regard the relation between demand and price as constant for purposes of all predictions of, say, up to twenty years. Even if we could show, on *a priori* grounds, that every relation between two or more variables used in economic theory was necessarily not a stable one, it would be critical for purposes of theory to know the quantitative amount of the lack of stability. Only empirical observations can show this, and such observations are thus important for economic theory as well as for economic history.

Let us consider an example of this point. Say that the relation between the demand for herrings and their price was so variable that the elasticity of demand was 1·37 in 1903, 0·01 in 1905, 8·73 in 1907 and 41·2 in 1908. If demand for all goods varied in such a capricious way, price theory would be of very little use, for we would be unable to predict the effects of the sort of shifts in costs, taxes, etc., that we have been considering. If, on the other hand, all the measures of the elasticity of demand for herrings over a period of twenty years lay between 1·2 and 1·45, then we could predict the effects of various changes in the herring market with a close degree of accuracy and with a high degree of confidence. We would be astounded, and indeed we would suspect a fraud, if a large number of measures of the elasticity of herring demand, made in several places and over a large number of years, all produced the value of, say, 1·347. What we want to know, however, is *how much* spatial and temporal variation there is in the demand for herrings. Only empirical observations can settle this question.

The third criticism is that even if we find substantial variations in our relations, we want to know if these variations appear capricious or if they display a systematic pattern that might lead us to suspect that herring demand is related to other factors. We might, for example, find a strong but sometimes interrupted tendency for the elasticity of demand for herrings to fall over time. We might then find that this systematic variation in price elasticity could be accounted for by income variations (as the population gets richer its demand for herrings is less and less affected by price variations and so the demand becomes more and more inelastic). We might now find that a high proportion of the changes in herring demand could be accounted for by assuming a *stable relation* between demand on the one hand, and price *and* income on the other. In general, what looked like a very unstable relation between two variables might turn out to be only part of a more stable relation between three or more variables. All of this leads us to the following conclusion.

Empirical measurements are critical to economics. Without some quantitative evidence of the magnitude and the stability or instability of particular relations (e.g., the relation between price and quantity), we cannot use economic theory to make useful predictions about the real world.

Since the time when Lord Robbins made his criticism, modern research has gone a long way in establishing quantitative demand relations. As time goes by, further evidence accumulates at a rapid rate, and we find ourselves far beyond merely wondering if demand curves slope downward. Many methodological problems have been resolved and techniques sharpened. Not only do we now know the approximate shape of many demand curves, we also have information about how demand curves shift. Our knowledge of demand relations increases significantly every year.

Criticisms of demand theory

Students often find demand theory excessively abstract and feel that it is unrealistic. Some very senior critics have often felt more or less the same way. Here we shall take up the question of whether demand theory is obviously unrealistic.

Is demand theory in conflict with everyday experience?

It is easy to prove that people do not always behave in the rational manner assumed by demand theory. Does that mean that the theory does not really apply to real life? The answer depends on what we want demand theory to accomplish. Three uses may be distinguished. First, we may be interested in the aggregate behaviour of all households as shown by the market demand curve for a product. Second, we may want to make probabilistic statements about an individual household's actions under certain circumstances. Third, we may want to make statements about what *all* households *always* do.

The aggregate use of the theory of demand is the most common one in economics. All of the predictions developed in Chapter 10, you will recall, depend on having some knowledge of the shape of the relevant market demand curves, yet they did not require that we be able to predict the behaviour of each individual household. The second use, though much less common than the first, is important; we do sometimes want to be able to say what a single household will probably do. The third use of demand theory is by far the least important of the three. Rarely do we wish to make categorical statements about what all households will always do.

Fortunately, the criticism cited at the beginning of this section applies only to this third use of demand theory. The observation that households sometimes behaved in ways not predicted by demand theory would, if carefully documented, refute the assertion that the theory's predictions *always* applied to *all* households.

Neither the existence of a relatively stable downward-sloping market demand curve, nor our ability to predict what a single household will probably do requires that all households invariably behave in the manner assumed by the theory. Such fully consistent behaviour on the part of everyone at all times is sufficient but not necessary for a stable market demand curve. Consider two other possibilities. First, some households may always behave in a manner not predicted by the theory. Households whose members are mental defectives or have serious emotional disturbances are obvious possibilities. The inconsistent or erratic behaviour of such households will not cause market demand curves for normal goods to depart from their downward slope, provided that these households account for a minority of purchases of any product. Their erratic behaviour will be swamped by the normal behaviour of the majority of households. Second, an occasional irrationality or inconsistency on the part of every household will not upset the downward slope of the market demand curve for a normal good. As long as these isolated inconsistencies are unrelated across households, occurring now in one and now in another, their effect will be swamped by the normal behaviour of most households most of the time.[1]

> **The downward slope of the demand curve requires only that at any moment of time most households are behaving as is predicted by the theory. This is quite compatible with behaviour contrary to the predictions of the theory by some households all of the time and by all households some of the time. Thus we cannot test the theory about the behaviour of market demand by observing the behaviour of only a few individual households, and we must consider what can be learned by observing such things as market demand for a product, the price of the product, other prices, and the total income of all consumers, which are the variables that appear in our theory of market demand. This is best done by considering in turn the relationship between demand and each of the influencing variables.**

Is demand theory just an elaborate way of saying that anything can happen?

Many serious critics of demand theory have argued that the theory has very little substantive content. They argue that, with respect to the commodity's own price, the theory says nothing more than that most demand curves slope downwards most of the time. They also argue that, with respect to such other variables as income and the prices of other commodities, the theory says nothing more than that when each influencing variable changes, quantity demanded may go up, go down or stay the same. If all we can say is that anything can happen, we hardly need to base this agnostic position on an elaborate theory. According to these critics, demand theory is a lot of sound and fury signifying (almost) nothing. To weigh their claims, we must consider the relation between quantity demanded and the various factors that influence it, taken one at a time.

---

[1] See the discussion of the 'law of large numbers' on page 11 of Chapter 1.

Demand and tastes The proposition that demand and tastes are related is not really testable unless we have some way of measuring a change in tastes. Since we do not have an independent measure of taste changes, what we usually do is infer them from the data for demand. We make such statements as: 'In spite of the rise in price, quantity purchased increased, so there must have been a change in tastes in favour of this commodity.' More generally, we are likely to account for all of the changes in demand that we can in terms of prices and incomes, and then assert that the rest must be due to changes in tastes (and to errors of measurement). This does not concern us unduly because we are not particularly interested in establishing precise relations between tastes and demand; we are prepared to take it as obvious from even the most casual observation that tastes do influence demand.

The fact that we cannot identify those changes in demand that are due to changes in tastes does, however, cause trouble when we come to consider the relation between demand and other factors. Whenever we see something happening that does not agree with our theory it is always possible that a change in tastes accounts for it. Say, for example, *incomes and other prices were known to be constant*, while the price of some commodity rose and, at the same time, more of it was observed to be bought. This gives us observations such as the two illustrated in Figure 15.4(i).

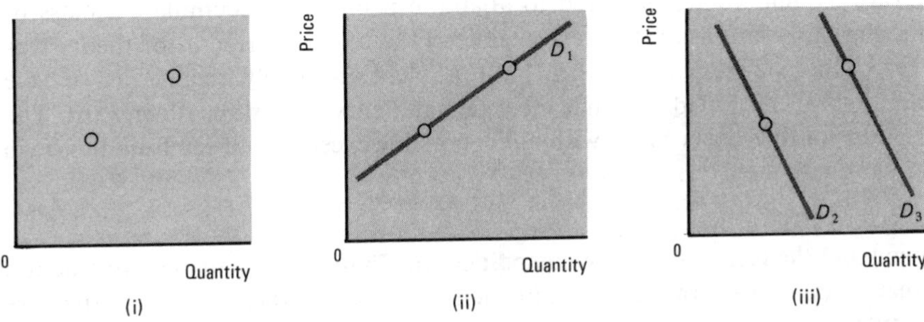

Fig. 15.4 Alternative interpretations of two price-quantity observations: either the demand curve slopes upwards or it has shifted

It may be that the demand curve for the product has a shape similar to that shown by the line D_1 in Figure 15.4(ii), but it may also be that the rise in price coincided with a change in tastes, so that the demand curve shifted from D_2 to D_3 in Figure 15.4(iii). If we have only two observations, we will not be able to distinguish between these two possibilities since we have no independent way of telling whether or not tastes changed. If, however, we have many observations, we can get some idea of where the balance of probabilities lies between two explanations. If *after removing the effects estimated to be due to changes in income and other prices*[1] we have the 26 observations (say the commodity's own price changed each week over a period of six months) illustrated in Figure 15.5, we will have to stretch the point a great deal to avoid the conclusion that the evidence conflicts with the hypothesis of a downward-sloping demand curve.

Of course, we can always explain away these observations by saying that tastes must have changed in favour of this commodity each time its price rose and against the commodity each time its price fell. This 'alibi' can certainly be used with effect to

[1] This can be done through multiple regression analysis or other more sophisticated statistical techniques in the manner alluded to in Chapter 3.

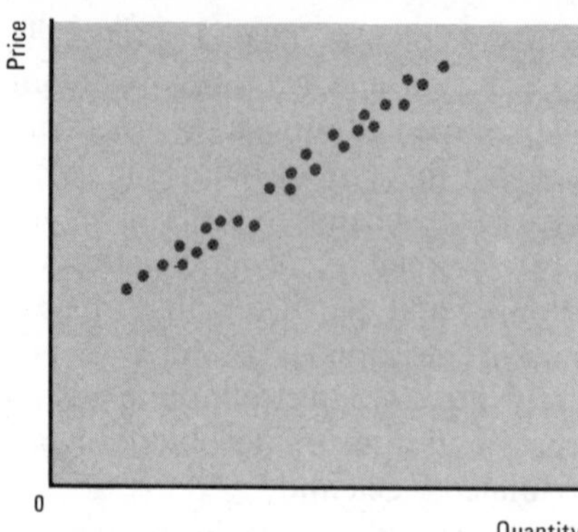

Fig. 15.5 Twenty-six price quantity observations

explain away a single conflicting observation, but we would be uncomfortable using the same alibi 26 times in six months. Indeed we should begin to suspect a fault in the hypothesis that demand and price vary inversely with each other.

We now have a problem in statistical testing of the sort described in Chapter 3. We are not prepared to throw away a theory after only one or two conflicting observations, but we are prepared to abandon it once we accumulate a mass of conflicting observations that were very unlikely to have occurred if the theory was correct[1]. Thus, statistically, the theory is testable. Fortunately, there is, as we have seen, a great deal of evidence that most demand curves do slope downward. The predictions of the theory have, with a few possible exceptions, been found to be in agreement with the facts.

Demand and the prices of other commodities In Chapter 7, we made a distinction between commodities that are complements to one another and those that are substitutes. Consider the demand for commodity X. This demand will *vary inversely* with the price of a complement (when the price of a complement falls, demand for X will rise), and will *vary directly* with the price of a substitute (when the price of a substitute falls, demand for X will fall). There may also be a group of commodities for which price variations leave demand for X unchanged. These commodities lie on the boundary dividing substitutes for X from complements to X.

These three reactions—demand for X rises, falls or remains unchanged when the price of some other good varies—cover all conceivable possibilities. There is nothing else that could possibly happen. So far we merely have a set of labels to attach to all possibilities. We do not have a useful theory unless we have a way of *deciding in advance* which goods are substitutable for and which are complementary to X.

Fortunately, we can sometimes decide this from technical knowledge alone. To do so is particularly easy when we are considering the demands for inputs in production. Steel plates, electric welders and welder operators are complementary.

[1] If changes in tastes are not related to changes in price, we can easily calculate the odds that the observations in Figure 15.5 are consistent with a downward-sloping but continually-shifting demand curve. If tastes changed randomly each week, there is a 50-50 chance that tastes changed in a direction to offset the first week's price change. In the second week there is also a 50-50 chance. The chances that they changed the 'right' way in both weeks are $(1/2)(1/2) = 1/4$ and the chance that they changed the right way for 26 successive weeks is $(1/2)^{25} = 1/33{,}554{,}432$!

Thus, we can predict that a fall in the price of any one will lead to an increase in the demand for all three. Cranes and crane operators, steam shovels and lorries, trains and rails, roads and fences, any piece of equipment and its human operator are all examples of pairs of commodities that are complements to each other. You will be able to expand this list more or less indefinitely. A similar list can be drawn up for inputs that are substitutes. It would include such things as wood, bricks and concrete in construction; manure and artificial fertilizers; and a building full of statistical clerks with desk calculators and a computer.

There are also many consumer goods for which we can predict complimentarity or substitutability. Complementarity exists, for example, between electric razors and pre-shave lotion; ordinary razors, razor blades and shaving cream; golf clubs and golf balls; grass seed and lawn mowers; electric stoves and electricity; and marriage and services of obstetricians, marriage guidance counsellors and divorce court judges.[1] The list of substitute goods includes such obvious examples as various green vegetables, beef and pork, private automobiles and public transport, open fireplaces and central heating, gas and electric cookers, holidays in Spain and on the Italian Riviera, skiing in Switzerland and Austria—such a list could be extended to cover many pages.

Whenever the technical data tell us which goods are substitutes and which are complements, we can predict in advance the effect of a change in the price of one good on the demand for another.

Demand and income Just as with the prices of other commodities, our theory says it is possible for a change in income to have any conceivable effect on demand: a rise in income may cause the demand for a product to rise, to fall or to remain unchanged. Since we cannot rule out any possibility, the theory is of no use to us unless we have a way of knowing in advance what the reaction will be to a change of income in the case of a particular commodity – otherwise we can predict nothing and can only classify changes after they have occurred.

In this situation there are two facts that help to give content to the theory. *First, we observe that income elasticities are fairly stable over time.* If, over the last 20 years, the income elasticity of demand for some agricultural product has been observed to fall from 0·70 to 0·40, we are pretty safe in predicting that a rise in income next year will be met by a less than proportionate rise in the demand for that product. If, on the other hand, the income elasticity of demand for cars and electricity are both observed to have been above unity for several years and also to be rising, it is fairly safe to predict that rises in income in the next few years will be met by more than proportionate rises in the demand for cars and electricity. The fact that these elasticities are observed not to change rapidly or capriciously allows us to predict into the near future from a knowledge of the level and direction of change of existing income elasticities.

The second observation that helps give empirical content to the theory is that *all households throughout the Western world tend to behave in a broadly similar*

[1] A somewhat high-minded reader once objected to this passage. Her objection illustrates the difference between positive and normative economics. Whatever we may think of the ethics of divorce, if we know that a stable or rising fraction of marriages end in divorce, we can predict with some confidence that an increase in marriages now will lead in the future to an increase in the demands for the factors of production that produce the commodity divorce.

fashion. (Indeed it is not even clear that the qualification Western is necessary.) At low levels of income food tends to have a fairly high income elasticity of demand, but as the level of income rises, the income elasticity of demand for food tends to fall well below unity, so that very little of any additional amount of income is spent on food. This phenomenon has been observed in every growing country that has approached the levels of income currently enjoyed by the countries of Western Europe. Thus we can confidently predict (1) that as long as productivity growth continues in agriculture the long-run drift from the land will continue in Western countries (unless they have a large export market for their agricultural goods), and (2) that when other countries of the world achieve sustained positive rates of growth they will soon encounter the problem of a declining agricultural sector.

> **Incomes in Western countries are doubling every thirty years or so. Over such periods of time, changes in income exert a major influence on changes in demand. Knowledge of what income elasticities are, and what they are likely to be, is one of the economist's most potent tools for predicting the future behaviour of the economy.**

Demand for the commodity and the commodity's own price The marginal utility theory of demand predicts that all demand curves will always slope downward (see p. 164). This prediction has long been known as the law of demand: the price of a product and the amount demanded vary inversely with each other.

Giffen Goods: Great interest was attached to a refutation of the law of demand, supposedly made by the Victorian economist Sir Robert Giffen. Giffen was reputed to have observed that an increase in the price of wheat led to an increase in the consumption of bread by nineteenth-century English peasants. If this observation is correct, it does refute the hypothesis that all demand curves always slope downwards. Does it refute the modern theory of demand? The answer is 'No', because this is just the type of rare exception to the normal case that is envisaged by the modern indifference-preference theory.[1]

Thus the modern theory of demand makes an unequivocal prediction only when we have extraneous information about income elasticities of demand. Since incomes change continuously as a result of economic growth, we are fortunate enough to have such information about most commodities. When we know that the income effect is positive (income elasticity of demand exceeds zero), as it is for most commodities, we can predict in advance that the quantity demanded will vary inversely with its price. When we know the income effect is negative (i.e., the good is inferior), we cannot be sure of the result. The only thing we can then say is that the smaller the proportion of total expenditure accounted for by this commodity, the less important the income effect and the more likely we are to get the normal result of price and quantity varying inversely with each other. Finally, if we have no

[1] Students who have read the optional section on page 175 will understand the following explanations. The rest must take the text statement on trust. The possible explanation is in terms of a negative income effect swamping a normal substitution effect. Wheat accounted for a very large fraction of the total expenditure of the households affected by the price change. If wheat is an inferior good, so that the income effect is negative, it is possible that the large negative income effect overcame the normal substitution effect when the price of wheat rose.

knowledge about the income effect we can still hazard a probabilistic statement. The great weight of existing evidence suggests that if we had to guess with no prior knowledge whether the demand curve for some commodity X was downward or upward sloping, the former choice would be the odds-on favourite.

Alternative theories of the source of household utility: Some very different exceptions to the 'law of demand' are suggested by some of the theories of demand developed in the last thirty years. The several possibilities all depend on the assumption that household satisfaction is a function of variables in addition to the quantities of commodities consumed.

Assume, for example, that a household's satisfaction also depends on the price it has to pay for some of the commodities. The household may, for example, buy diamonds not because its members particularly like diamonds *per se*, but because they wish to show off their wealth in an ostentatious but socially acceptable way. In the words of Thorstein Veblen, 'they indulge in *conspicuous consumption*, and when their neighbours copy them they are indulging in *pecuniary emulation*.'[1] The household values diamonds precisely because they are expensive; thus, a fall in their price might lead it to stop buying them and switch to a more satisfactory object of ostentatious display. Such households will have upward-sloping demand curves for diamonds: the lower the price, the fewer they will buy. If enough households act similarly, the market demand curve for diamonds could slope upwards as well.

But an upward-sloping market demand curve for diamonds and other similar products has never been observed. Why? A moment's thought about the industrial uses of diamonds, and the masses of lower-income consumers who could buy diamonds only if they were sufficiently inexpensive, suggests the upward-sloping demand curves for some individual households are much more likely than an upward-sloping market demand curve for the same commodity. Recall the discussion on page 188 about the ability of the theory of the downward sloping demand curve to accommodate odd behaviour on the part of a small group of households (this time the 'odd' group is the rich, rather than the mentally defective or the emotionally disturbed).

Conclusion

Today we not only do believe that most demand curves slope downward, we also have a good idea of the elasticity in many cases. Reasonably precise knowledge about demand curves is a necessity if we are to make real-world applications of the demand and supply theory developed in this book. If we knew nothing at all empirically about these curves, the theory would be devoid of any real-world application. Since we do have this knowledge, we can predict in advance the effects of changes in many factors such as taxes, costs, the amount of competition in a particular market, and so forth. The more accurate our knowledge of the shape of demand curves, the smaller will be the margin of error in such predictions. Fortunately, as we have seen in this chapter, economists have accumulated a great store of the requisite empirical knowledge.

---

[1] These phrases are drawn from a book which is worth browsing in because of its many insights which are still relevant to today's world. Thorstein Veblen, *The Theory of the Leisure Class* (1899, published in paperback by Allen & Unwin, 1971).

Part four

The intermediate theory of supply

16

Background to the theory of supply

In Part 2 we simply assumed the existence of a supply curve relating the price of a commodity to the quantity firms would be willing to produce and offer for sale. In this part we shall go behind this supply curve and explain it in terms of the decisions of individual producers. Thus Part 4 does for the supply curve what Part 3 did for the demand curve.

There is an apparently bewildering series of theories built on other theories relating to supply. For the moment we shall distinguish between the THEORY OF THE FIRM, which deals with the behaviour of individual firms, and the THEORY OF THE INDUSTRY or the THEORY OF SUPPLY, which deals with collective behaviour of all the firms producing a single product.

The theory that we shall develop here is important because we always wish to trace aggregate behaviour back to the decisions taken by the individual units that comprise the aggregate. The theory is also a first step towards dealing with a host of interesting policy questions, of which the following are a few examples. What is the effect of various forms of competition or monopoly on the efficiency and level of production in an industry? What are some of the causes and consequences of advertising? Why do firms combine? Is there a tendency for monopoly to replace competition as the dominant form of production? What are the causes and consequences of take-over bids? Will taxing the domestic consumption of a good encourage its export?

In an introductory textbook we can do little more than outline the basic theory and show a few applications. This chapter presents some background material. A formal theory is constructed in subsequent chapters.

The nature of the firm

In Chapter 6 we assumed that all firms, whatever their internal structure, maximize their profits. This means that the behaviour of the firm is unaffected by its internal structure. Thus the standard theory of firm behaviour assumes away, or abstracts from, the structure of the firm.

The assumption that a firm's behaviour can be understood and predicted independently of its structure has come under frequent and sustained attack. We shall consider these attacks after we have outlined the standard theory of the firm.

First, however, we shall say something about the structure of modern firms. This will show what organizational features are being abstracted from and set the stage for subsequent consideration of the argument that a successful theory cannot be built on such abstractions.

Forms of business organization

There are three major forms of private business organization: the single proprietorship, the partnership and the joint-stock company (which in North America is called the corporation). In the SINGLE PROPRIETORSHIP there is one owner who is personally responsible for everything done by the firm. In the PARTNERSHIP there are two or more joint owners, each of whom is personally responsible. A JOINT-STOCK COMPANY is a firm regarded in law as having an identity of its own; its owners are not personally responsible for anything that is done in the name of the firm.

In most Western countries it is necessary to add two other forms of organizing production: nationalized industries and the provision of goods and services by the state without direct charge to consumers. Nationalized industries are owned by the state and are usually under the direction of a more or less independent, state-appointed board. Although their ownership differs, the organization and legal status of these firms is very similar to that of the joint-stock company and they are usually very large firms. Their activity is also similar, in the sense that they gain their revenue by selling the product that they produce. In the United Kingdom about 10 per cent of the national product is accounted for by these firms, the most important of which in 1978 were airlines, coal, electric power, gas, postal and telephonic communication, railways, ship-building, steel and some of the car industry. The fifth method of organizing production differs from all the others in that the output is provided to consumers free (or at a nominal price), while costs of production are paid from the government's general tax revenue. Important examples found in all countries are agencies providing defence, roads and education. In the UK we must also add the National Health Service, which provides medical and hospital services free (or at very small charges) to the general public. In countries without nationalized medical services, hospitals and doctors behave just as other firms do: they purchase factors of production on the open market and gain revenue by selling their services to those people who wish to, and can afford to, purchase them.

Proprietorships and partnerships, advantages and disadvantages The major advantages of the single proprietorship are that it is easy to set up and that the owner can readily maintain full control over the firm. The disadvantages are first, that the size of the firm is limited by the capital the owner can raise for himself, and second, that the owner is personally responsible in law for all debts of the firm.

The partnership overcomes to some extent the first disadvantage of the proprietorship, but not the second. Ten partners may be able to finance a much bigger enterprise than one owner could, but they are still subject to what is called UNLIMITED LIABILITY: each partner is fully liable for all of the debts of the firm. As a direct consequence of unlimited liability, it is difficult to raise money from many persons through a partnership. An investor may be willing to risk £1,000, but not to jeopardize his entire fortune; if, however, he joins a partnership in order to do the former, he cannot avoid doing the latter.

A further disadvantage of an ordinary partnership is that any time a partner dies or resigns, the partnership agreement must be redrawn. This makes it difficult to have as a partner someone who is not genuinely interested and involved in the business but wishes merely to invest in it, for such a partner may wish, at any time, to liquidate his interest by selling it to someone else. While this is possible under partnership law, it is not easy.

The LIMITED PARTNERSHIP is designed to avoid some of these difficulties. General partners continue to have unlimited authority and unlimited liability, but it is possible to have a second type of partner, whose liability is limited to the amount that he or she has invested in the firm. The limited partner may neither participate in the management of the firm, nor engage in agreements on its behalf. In effect, the limited partnership permits some division of the functions of decision-making, on the one hand, and provision of capital and risk-taking on the other.

In most respects this division of responsibility is more effectively managed through the joint-stock company. But there are certain professions in which the partnership form is traditional and in which its survival is made feasible by use of limited partnership permits some division of the functions of decision-making, on the one hand, and provision of capital and risk-taking, on the other.

The joint-stock company, advantages and disadvantages The joint-stock company is regarded in law as an entity separate from the individuals who own it. It can enter into contracts, it can sue and be sued, it can own property, it can contract debts, and its obligations are not those of its owners. This means that the company can enter into contracts in its own right, and that its liability to adhere to such contracts can be enforced only by suing the company, not by suing owners. The right to be sued may not seem to be an advantage, but it is this right that makes it possible for others to enter into enforceable contracts with the company.

Some joint-stock companies are very small, or have their stock owned by a very small group that also manages the firm; the form of the joint-stock company that we are chiefly interested in is one that issues shares that are purchased by the general public. The company obtains the money paid for the shares, and the shareholders become the owners of the company. They are entitled to share in the profits of the company, which, when they are paid out, are called DIVIDENDS. They are also entitled to split up the assets of the company, should it be liquidated, after all debts are paid off.

This method of finance usually means that the owners of the firm cannot all be the managers. The line of control is as follows. The shareholders (and there may be tens of thousands of them) elect a board of directors. The board of directors is supposed to act as a cabinet. It sets broad lines of policy and appoints senior managers. The managers are supposed to carry out the wishes of the directors, translating the broad lines of policy laid down by them into a series of detailed decisions.

The most important aspect of a joint-stock company from the point of view of its owners is that they have limited liability. Should the company be forced into liquidation,[1] the personal liability of any shareholder is limited to whatever he or she has actually paid to purchase the firm's shares. The great advantage of the joint-stock company is that it can raise capital from a very large number of individuals, all

[1] Although in popular discussion the terms are often used interchangeably, individuals go *bankrupt*, but firms go into *liquidation*.

of whom get shares in the firm's profits but have no liabilities beyond risking the loss of the amount they actually invest. Thus each investor may sit back and collect dividends without knowing anything about the firm that he or she, along with many others, owns. Corporate stocks are readily transferable among individuals (a form of exchange that stock markets are organized to facilitate). Thus a joint-stock company can have a continuity of life that is unaffected by frequent changes in the identity of its owners.

One disadvantage of the joint-stock company from the point of view of investors is that they may have little say in the management of the firm. (For example, if the directors decide that the company should not pay dividends, an individual investor cannot compel them to pay him his share of the earnings.) In some countries this form of organization is currently spreading to the service industries and agriculture, as firms in these industries grow to the point where they need large quantities of capital to function effectively.

The financing of the modern firm

So far our discussion has emphasized the raising of money from the owners of the firm. It should not be thought, however, that all the money needed by the firm to carry on its business is subscribed by the owners. The most important sources of funds for modern firms are (1) selling *equities* either by private or public sale; (2) borrowing by the sale of *bonds*; (3) borrowing from banks and other financial institutions; and (4) reinvesting the firm's profits.

Owners' capital The first source of funds is from the firm's owners. In individual proprietorships and partnerships one or more owners will put up some or all of the funds required by the firm. A joint-stock company acquires funds from its owners by selling STOCKS, SHARES or EQUITIES (as they are variously called) to them. These are basically ownership certificates. The money goes to the company and the purchasers become owners of the firm, risking the loss of their money and gaining the right to share in the firm's profits.

Stocks in a firm often proliferate into a bewildering number of types. Basically, however, there is common stock and preferred stock. COMMON STOCK usually carries voting rights and has a residual claim on profits. After all other claims have been met, including those of holders of preferred shares, the remaining profits, if any, belong to the common-stock holders. Firms are not obliged by law to pay out any fixed portion of their profits as dividends, and indeed the practice among companies as to the *payout ratio* varies greatly.

There are many varieties of PREFERRED STOCKS, but basically they are distinguished from common stocks by their prior claim to any profits that may be available after other obligations have been met. If profits are earned, the company is obliged to pay a dividend to preferred-stock holders, but there is a stated maximum to the rate of dividends that will be paid per pound originally invested.

Bonds and bondholders The bondholders are creditors, not owners, of the firm. They have loaned it money in return for a BOND, which is a promise both to pay a stated sum each year, and to repay the loan at some stated time in the future (say, five, ten or twenty years hence). The amount that is paid to the bondholder each year is called the INTEREST, while the amount that will be repaid at the stated date in the future is called the PRINCIPAL. The time at which the principal is repaid is called the REDEMPTION DATE of the bond. It is the firm's legal obligation to make periodic interest payments and to repay the principal on the redemption date. If the payments cannot be made, the bondholders can force the firm into liquidation. Should this happen, they have a claim on the firm's assets prior to that of any of the shareholders. (Only if the bondholders, and all other creditors, have been repaid in full can the shareholders recover anything for themselves.)

The disadvantage of raising capital through the sale of bonds is that the company must meet interest payments whether or not there are any profits. Many a firm that would have survived a temporary crisis had all its capital been share capital has been forced into liquidation because it could not meet its contractual obligation to pay interest to its bondholders.

Other borrowing Many short-term needs and some long-term ones are met by borrowing from banks and other financial institutions. This is true of giant companies and small businesses. Indeed, making commercial and industrial loans is one of the major activities of the banking system. Little needs to be said about such loans at this stage, except to note that 'term' (i.e., short-term) borrowing tends to be expensive for firms, so they usually prefer other methods of raising money for long-term purposes. Banks often limit their lending to specified fractions of a company's total financial needs. Some companies are forced to seek funds from other financial institutions, at yet higher rates of interest. Many small businesses which are not well-established cannot sell stocks to the public and must borrow from banks and other financial institutions to finance their activities.

Reinvested profits For the established firm, as distinct from the new one, an additional and very important means of obtaining funds is by reinvesting, or ploughing back, its own profits. One of the easiest ways for the controllers of the firm to raise money is to retain some current profits rather than paying them out as dividends to shareholders. Financing investment from *undistributed profits* has become an extremely important source of funds in modern times.

> **The modern firm finances itself by obtaining money from its owners, by borrowing from the public and from financial institutions and by reinvesting its own undistributed profits.**

The firm in economic theory

In Chapter 6 we defined the firm as the unit that takes decisions with respect to the production and sale of commodities. This single concept of the firm covers a variety of business organizations, from the single proprietorship to the joint-stock company, and a variety of business sizes, from the single inventor operating in his garage and financed by whatever he can extract from a reluctant bank manager, to vast undertakings with many thousands of shareholders and creditors. We know that in large firms decisions are actually taken by many different individuals. We can, nonetheless, regard the firm as a single consistent decision-taking unit because of the assumption that all decisions are taken in order to achieve the common goal of maximizing profits. This assumption is critical to the whole traditional theory of the firm and we may state it formally as follows:

We assume that the same principles underlie each decision taken within a firm and that the decision is uninfluenced by who takes it. Thus the theory abstracts from the peculiarities of the persons taking the decisions and from the organizational structure in which they work.

Whether a decision is taken by a small independent proprietor, a plant, a manager, or a board of directors, as far as the theory is concerned that person or group *is* the firm for the purposes of that decision. This is a truly heroic assumption. It amounts to saying that for purposes of predicting their behaviour, at least in those aspects that interest us, we can treat the farm, the corner grocery, the large department store, the small engineering firm, the giant chemical combine, the vast oil firm and that largest of all business organizations, the Exxon Corporation, all under the umbrella of a single theory of the behaviour of the firm. Even if this turns out to be only partially correct it will represent an enormously valuable simplification which will show the power of theory in revealing some unity of behaviour where to the casual observer there is only a bewildering diversity.[1]

Criticisms of the theory for ignoring the importance both of decision-takers and of the institutional structure within which decisions are taken, are discussed in Chapter 24. Some competing hypotheses about actual business behaviour will also be discussed at that time. The final test of whether or not such factors can be legitimately ignored is an empirical one: if the theory that we develop by ignoring these factors is successful in predicting the outcome of the kind of events in which we are interested, then we can conclude that we were correct in assuming that these factors could be safely ignored.

The motivation of the firm

The assumption of profit maximization enables us to predict the behaviour of the firm with regard to the various choices open to it. We do this by studying the effect that each of the choices would have on the firm's profits. We then predict that the firm will select alternatives that produces the largest profits.

We assume that the firm takes decisions in such a way that its profits will be as large as possible; we say that it maximizes its profits.

At this point you might wonder if we are justified in building an elaborate theory based on such a crude assumption about the firm's motives. It is well known that some businessmen are inspired some of the time by motives other than an overwhelming desire to make as much money as possible. Cases in which they have gone after political influence, and others in which decisions have been influenced by philanthropic motives, are not difficult to document. Should we not, therefore, say that the assumption that firms seek to maximize profits is refuted by empirical evidence?

The real world is complex. A theory picks on certain factors, and deals with them

[1] Do not be surprised if at first encounter the theory seems rather abstract and out of touch with reality. Because it does generalize over such a wide variety of behaviour, it must ignore those features with which we are most familiar and which in our eyes distinguish the farmer and the grocer from Royal Dutch Shell. Any theory that generalizes over a wide variety of apparently diverse behaviour necessarily has this characteristic, because it ignores those factors that are most obvious to us and which create in our minds the appearance of diversity.

on the assumption that they are the important ones, and that the ones ignored are relatively less important. If it is true that the key factors have been included, then the theory will be successful in predicting what will happen under specified circumstances. If follows that it is not an important criticism to point out that a theory ignores some factors known to be present in the world; this tells us nothing more than that the theory is a theory and not just a photographic reproduction of reality in its full complexity. If the theory has ignored some important factors, then its predictions will be contradicted by the evidence, at least in those situations where the factor ignored is quantitatively important.

How does this discussion relate to the theory of the firm's behaviour that is based on the assumption of profit maximization? First, the theory does not require that profit is the only factor that ever influences the firm. It is believed only that profits are an important consideration, important enough that a theory assuming profit maximization to be the sole motive will produce predictions that are substantially correct. It follows from this that to point out that businessmen are sometimes motivated by considerations other than profits does not constitute a relevant criticism of the theory. It may well be that the theory is substantially wrong, but if so, the way to demonstrate this is to show that its predictions are in conflict with the facts. We cannot, of course, even consider such a possibility until we know what the theory does and does not predict. Accordingly, we shall press on to develop the theory. When we have completed this task we shall ask how the theory might be tested against empirical evidence. Finally, in Chapter 24, we shall consider several alternative theories of the firm's motivation.

Nationalized industries

Earlier in this chapter we noted that a significant amount of total British production is in the hands of industries that are owned by the state. Do we need a separate theory of the behaviour of nationalized industries? Usually they are run by boards that are appointed by the state but given considerable autonomy within the framework of broad directives on what goals to pursue. If the nationalized industries seek to maximize their profits, then their behaviour will be indistinguishable from that of private firms. If, however, they are given other goals, such as just to cover all their costs so as to make neither profits nor losses, then their behaviour may differ from that of the private sector. Once we know the objectives of these industries we shall be able to predict their response to changes in market signals. In the next few chapters we shall confine ourselves to the behaviour of privately owned firms, but in Chapter 31 we shall return to the question of nationally owned ones.

A preview of the theory of supply

We are interested in the behaviour of profits because firms seek to maximize their profits.[1] Profits (π) are the difference between revenues derived from the sale of commodities (R) and the cost of producing these commodities (C):

$$\pi = R - C.$$

[1] Economists often speak of the 'behaviour' of such inanimate things as profits. The term *behaviour of profits* refers to how profits vary as the factors that influence them vary.

Thus, the behaviour of profits may be broken down into the behaviour of revenues and of costs.

In developing the theory of supply, we first explain the special meaning that economists give to the concept of costs and then develop a theory of how costs vary with output. This theory is common to all firms. We then consider how revenues vary with output and find that it is necessary to deal separately with firms in competitive and in monopolistic situations. Once this has been done, costs and revenues are combined to determine the profit-maximizing behaviour for firms in various competitive and monopolistic situations. When the firm has maximized its profits it is said to be in a position of equilibrium.

Once the theory of the equilibrium of the firm (and groups of firms that compose industries) has been developed, it can be used to predict the outcome of changes in such things as demand, costs, taxes and subsidies. These predictions can then be tested against observations. It is the steps of deriving predictions and testing them in which we are really interested, and towards which all previous steps are directed. We must be prepared, however, for some quite hard work before these last steps can be taken. The necessary theory is built up over the next few chapters.

17

The theory of costs

Profit, we have seen, is the difference between revenue and cost. We must now find out how to calculate the cost associated with a given level of output produced with given techniques. Any rate of output will have a set of inputs associated with it. In order to arrive at the cost of producing this output we need to be able to put a value on each of the separate inputs used. The assignment of monetary values to physical quantities of inputs is easy in some cases and difficult in others. Furthermore, different people or different groups may assign different values to the same input.

Economists study the production behaviour of firms for a variety of reasons:

(1) to predict how the behaviour of firms will respond to specified changes in the conditions they face;

(2) to help firms make the best decisions they can in achieving their goals; and

(3) to evaluate from society's point of view how well firms use scarce resources.

The same measure of cost need not be correct for all of these purposes. For example, if the firm happens to be misinformed about the value of resource, it will behave according to that misinformation. In predicting the firm's behaviour, economists should use the same information the firm does, even if they know it to be incorrect. But in *guiding* firm behaviour, in helping firms to achieve their goals, economists should substitute the correct information.

Economists know exactly how to define costs for purposes (2) and (3) above. If we assume that businessmen use the same concept, the economist's definition will also be appropriate for purpose (1). We shall assume for this moment that it is; the consequences of being in error are discussed in Chapter 24.

The measurement of the firm's opportunity cost

Although the details of economic costing vary, costing is governed by a common principle that is sometimes called user cost but is more commonly called opportunity cost, since it is an application of the concept that we first studied on pages 53–4.

> **The cost of using something in a particular venture is the benefit forgone by (or opportunity cost of) not using it in its best alternative use.**

In principle, measuring opportunity cost is easy. The firm must assign to each factor of production it uses a monetary value equal to what it sacrifices in order to have the use of that factor. Applying this principle to specific cases, however, reveals some tough problems. Assigning costs is most straightforward when the firm buys a factor on a competitive market and uses up the entire quantity purchased during the period of production. Materials purchased by the firm fall into this category. If the firm pays £50 per ton for coal delivered to its factory, it has sacrificed its claims to whatever else £50 can buy, and thus the purchase price is a reasonable measure of the opportunity cost of using one ton of coal.

For hired factors of production, where the rental price is the full price, the situation is the same as for purchased factors. Most labour services are hired, but typically the cost is more than the wages paid because employers usually have to contribute to national insurance, to pension funds, to various kinds of unemployment and disability insurance, and other fringe benefits. The cost of these must be added to the direct wage in determining the opportunity cost of labour services used.

Imputed costs

A cost must also be assigned to factors of production that the firm neither purchases nor hires because it already owns them. The costs of using such factors are called IMPUTED COSTS. They are reckoned at values reflecting what the firm could earn if it shifted these factors to their next best use. Important imputed costs arise from the use of owners' money, the depreciation of capital equipment, the need to compensate risk-taking, and the need to value any special advantages (such as franchises or patents) that the firm may posses. Correct cost imputation is needed if the firm is to discover the most profitable lines of production.

The cost of money Consider a firm that uses £100,000 of its own money that could have been loaned out to someone else at 7 per cent interest per year. Thus £7,000 (at least) should be deducted from the firm's revenue as the cost of funds used in production. If the firm makes only £6,000 over all other costs, then it should not calculate that it made a profit of £6,000 by producing, but rather that it lost £1,000. This is because if the firm closed down completely and merely loaned its money to someone else, it could earn £7,000.[1]

[1] The cost of money may be higher than this if the best alternative use of the firm's own money could yield more than the market interest rate. Many firms cannot borrow nearly as much money as they would wish. If a firm is rationed in the amount of funds it can borrow, it will place a high value on the funds that it does have. In these circumstances, the firm must look at the other ventures it might have undertaken in order to assign opportunity cost because its inability to raise all the money it wants means that it will be unable to do all the things it wants. Many business firms operate with 'cut-off rates of return' that approximate the opportunity cost of money to the firm. They are chosen to approximate the return on projects that the firm cannot undertake because it lacks sufficient funds. The return on projects that the firm is just able to undertake is called the firm's internal rate of return. Empirical studies of manufacturing industries suggest that the opportunity cost of money is often substantially in excess of the rate of interest on bonds. An accurate figure may well be as high as 25 per cent. The fact that it is so high helps explain why many firms are anxious to retain a major portion of their profits and why many stockholders (who do not have similar personal investment opportunities) are willing to have corporations pay dividends that are substantially less than earnings and reinvest the remainder to earn their internal rate of return.

Special advantages Suppose a firm owns a valuable patent or a highly desirable location, or produces a product with a popular brand-name such as Coca Cola, Triumph or Player's. Each of these involves an opportunity cost to the firm in production (even if it was acquired free) because if the firm did not choose to use the special advantage itself, *it could sell or lease it to others*. Typically, the value of these things will differ from the cost at which the firm originally acquired them. This last cost is called the HISTORICAL (or HISTORIC) COST and must be sharply distinguished from the current opportunity cost.

Depreciation of existing equipment The cost of using capital equipment the firm owns, such as buildings and machinery, consists of the loss in the value of the asset, called DEPRECIATION, caused by its use in production. Accountants use various conventional methods of calculating depreciation based on the price originally paid for the asset. While such historical costs are often useful approximations, they may, in some cases, seriously differ from the depreciation required by the opportunity-cost principle. Two examples of the possible error involved follow.

Example 1. The owner of a firm buys a £4,000 automobile that she intends to use for six years for business purposes and then discard. She may think this will cost her £667 per year. But if after one year the value of her car on the used-car market is £3,000, it has cost her £1,000 to use the car during the first year. Why should she charge herself £1,000 depreciation during the first year? After all, she does not intend to sell the car for six years. The answer is that one of the purchaser's alternatives was to buy a one-year-old car and operate it for five years. Indeed, that is the very position she is in after the first year. Whether she likes it or not, she has paid £1,000 for the use of the car during the first year of its life. If the market had valued her car at £3,900 after one year (instead of £3,000), the correct depreciation charge would have been only £100.

Example 2. A firm has just purchased a set of machines for £100,000. They have an expected lifetime of 10 years and the firm's accountant calculates the 'depreciation cost' of these machines at £10,000 per year. The machines can be used to make only one product and since they are installed in the firm's factory, they can be leased to no one else and have a negligible secondhand or scrap value. Assume that if the machines are used to produce the firm's product, the cost of all other factors utilized will amount to £25,000 per year. Immediately after purchasing the machines the firm finds that the price of the commodity in question has unexpectedly fallen, so that the output can now only be sold for £29,000 per year instead of the £35,000 that had originally been expected. What should the firm do?

If in calculating its costs the firm adds in the historically determined 'depreciation costs' of £10,000 a year, the total cost of operation comes to £35,000; with the revenue at £29,000 this makes a loss of £6,000 per year. It appears that the commodity should not be made! But this is not correct. Since the machines have no alternative use whatsoever, their imputed opportunity cost to the firm (which is determined by what else the firm could do with them) is zero. The total cost of producing the output is thus only £25,000 per year, and the whole current operation shows a return over cost of £4,000 per year rather than a loss of £6,000. (If the firm did not produce the goods, in order to avoid expected losses, it would be worse off by £4,000 per year than if it carried on with production.)

Of course, the firm would not have bought the machines had it known that the price of the product was going to fall, but once it has bought them, the cost of using them is zero, and it is profitable to use them as long as they yield any net revenue whatsoever over all other costs.

The principle illustrated by both of these examples may be stated in terms of an important general maxim:

> **Bygones are bygones and should have no influence in deciding what is currently the most profitable thing to do.**[1]

New capital equipment Once capital equipment is installed it may, as Example 2 showed, have little or no opportunity cost. In this case, it will be operated as long as it lasts, provided only that all other costs of production can be covered. But capital equipment wears out over time and has to be replaced. Money will not be spent to replace capital equipment unless the expected return from that investment is at least equal to what could be earned by investing the same amount in capital equipment in other industries. Thus, over an extended period of time, the firm's activities must yield a return to its capital equal to what an equivalent investment could earn in other industries. If it does not, the owners will be able to do better by transferring their capital elsewhere, which they can do by not replacing old machinery as it wears out and by investing in other industries the funds that could have been used for replacement.

It is helpful to divide the return to capital into a pure return, a risk premium and pure profit. The PURE RETURN is what the capital could earn in a riskless investment. The RISK PREMIUM is what capital must earn to compensate the owners for the risk of losing it which accompanies *any* business venture in a world of less than perfect certainty. The riskier a particular use of capital, the higher the risk premium. Both of these elements are costs when viewed over a period of time long enough for capital equipment to be replaced. If the firm does not produce a return on its capital sufficient to cover the return on a riskless investment *and* sufficient to compensate for the riskiness involved, the owners of the capital are not covering their opportunity costs.

Using cost to calculate profit

Profit, as the term is used in economics, refers to PURE PROFIT, an excess of revenue over all opportunity costs including those of capital. To discover whether such profit exists, take the revenue of the firm and deduct the costs of all factors of production other than capital. Then deduct the pure return on capital and any risk

[1] This is a very important principle that extends well beyond economics and is often ignored in these other areas as well. In many poker games, for example, the cards are dealt a round at a time and betting proceeds after each player's hand has been augmented by one card. Players who bet heavily on early rounds because their hands looked promising often stay in through later rounds on indifferent hands because they 'already have such a stake in the pot'. The professional player knows that, after each round of cards, his bet should be made on the probabilities that the hand he currently holds will turn into a winner when all the cards have been dealt. If the probabilities look poor after the fourth card has been dealt (five usually constitutes a complete hand), he should abandon the hand and refuse to bet further whether he has put 5p or £5 into the pot already. The amateur who bases his current decisions on what he has put into the pot in earlier rounds of betting will be a long-term loser if he plays in rational company. In poker, war and economics bygones *are* bygones, and to take account of them in current decisions is to court disaster!

premium necessary to compensate the owners of capital for the risks associated with its use in this firm and industry. Anything that remains is pure profit. It belongs to the owners of the firm and therefore may be regarded as an additional return on their capital. (Since the firm owns its capital, the owners of the firm are the owners of its capital.)

Profit in the sense just defined is variously called pure profit, economic profit or sometimes just profit, where there is no room for ambiguity.

The production function

We have now seen how to calculate the cost and profit associated with any particular output. But the firm can elect to produce at different rates of output. Which should it choose? The profit-maximizing firm will choose the rate of output that yields the largest profits. To discover the most profitable output level we need to see how costs and revenues vary with output. This will tell us, by subtraction, how profit varies with output. It will then be a simple matter to select the profit-maximizing output. In this chapter we shall confine our attention to costs; in subsequent chapters we shall study revenues.

To discover how costs (the value of inputs used) vary with output we first study how output varies with inputs of factors of production. We then place a value on the inputs used according to the principles already established and this tells us how costs (the value of inputs used) vary with output.

Generally the more factors of production used by the firm the higher we would expect its output to be. The PRODUCTION FUNCTION describes the purely technological relation between what is fed into the productive apparatus by way of inputs of factor services and what is turned out by way of product. In stating this relation it must not be forgotten that production is a flow: it is not just so many units; it is so many units *per period of time*. If we speak of raising the level of monthly production from, say, 100 to 101 units, we do not mean producing 100 units this month and one unit next month, but going from a rate of production of 100 units each month to a rate of 101 units each month.

The production function is written simply as:

$$q = \mathrm{q}(f_1, \ldots, f_m), \qquad (1)$$

where q is the quantity of output and $f_1, \ldots, f_m$ are the quantities of m different factors used in production, all expressed as rates per period of time.

For the rest of this chapter we shall consider a very simple example of some industrial product. We ignore land as being relatively unimportant and divide all the other inputs into the two categories – labour, L, and capital, K. We then have the simple production function:

$$q = \mathrm{q}(L, K), \qquad (2)$$

where q is tons of output per day, L is labour days employed, and K is units of capital services (e.g., machine days) used. This will make our task easier while still getting at the essential aspects of our problem.

Suppose now that the firm wishes to increase its rate of output. To do so it must increase the inputs of one or both factors of production. But the firm cannot vary all of its factors with the same degree of ease. It can take on or lay off labour on fairly short notice (a week or a month), but a long time is needed to install more capital.

To capture the fact that different kinds of inputs can be varied with different speeds we think of the firm as making three distinct types of decisions: (1) how best to employ its existing plant and equipment; (2) what new plant and equipment and production processes to select, within the framework of existing technology; and (3) what to do about encouraging the development of new techniques. These decisions are logically distinct although they abstract from the more complicated nature of real decisions. The first set of decisions is said to be made over the short run; the second, over the long run; the third, over the very long run.

The short run

The SHORT RUN is defined as the period of time over which the inputs of some factors, called FIXED FACTORS, cannot be varied. The factor that is fixed in the short run is usually an element of capital (such as plant and equipment), but it might be land, or the services of management, or even the supply of skilled, salaried labour. What matters is that at least one significant factor is fixed. Let us say that in our simplified case, described by the production function in (2) above, it is capital that is fixed in the short run.

In the short run, production must be varied by changing the quantities used of those inputs that can be varied; these are called VARIABLE FACTORS. In our simple example the variable factor is labour services. Thus, in the short run, q is varied by varying L, with K held fixed.

It is worth noting that the short run does not correspond to a fixed time period. In some industries the short run may extend over many years; in others it may be only a matter of weeks or months. In the electric-power industry, for example, where it takes three or more years to acquire and install a steam-turbine generator, an unforeseen increase in demand will involve a long period during which the extra demand must be met as well as possible with the existing capital equipment. At the other end of the scale, a machine shop can acquire new equipment (or sell existing equipment) in a few weeks, and thus the short run is correspondingly short. The length of the short run is influenced by technological considerations such as how quickly equipment can be manufactured and installed. But these things may be influenced to some extent by the price the firm is willing to pay.

The long run

The LONG RUN is defined as the period long enough for the inputs of all factors of production to be varied, but not so long that the basic technology of production changes. In our simple two-factor example, the firm varies q in the long run by varying L *and* K, using a given production function. Again, the long run is not a specific period of time, but varies among industries.

The special importance of the long run in production theory is that it corresponds to the situation facing the firm when it is *planning* to go into business, or to expand or contract the scale of its operations.

The planning decisions of the firm are characteristically made with fixed technical possibilities but with freedom to choose whatever factor inputs seem most desirable. Once these planning decisions are carried out – once a plant is built, equipment purchased and installed, and so on – the firm has fixed factors and makes operating decisions in the short run.

The very long run

Unlike the short and the long run, the VERY LONG RUN is concerned with situations in which the technological possibilities open to the firm are subject to change, leading to new and improved products and new methods of production.

> **In the very long run production function itself changes: technological advances mean that the same quantity of inputs will yield a higher rate of output.**

The firm may bring about some of these changes itself, particularly through its programmes of research and development. For the moment we shall ignore the possibility that the firm may incur costs in an effort to change its own technology, and consider only its choice of techniques of production under a given technology.

We shall now make an extended study of the firm's production possibilities and its costs under each of these 'runs'.

The short run

In the theory of the short run we are concerned with what happens to output and costs as more or less of the variable factor is applied to given quantities of the fixed factors. For simplicity in developing our theory we confine ourselves to the simplified production function of (2) above, and assume that capital is fixed and labour is variable in the short run.

Short-run variations in output

Assume that a firm starts with a fixed amount of capital (say 10 units) and contemplates applying various amounts of labour to it. Table 17.1 shows three different ways of looking at how output varies with the quantity of the variable factor. As a preliminary step, some terms must be defined.

(1) TOTAL PRODUCT (*TP*) means just what it says: the total amount produced during some period of time by all the factors of production employed. If the inputs of all but one factor are held constant, total product will change as more or less of the variable factor is used. This variation is shown in column (2) of Table 17.1, which gives a total product schedule. Figure 17.1 (i) shows such a schedule graphically. (The shape of the curve will be discussed shortly.)

(2) AVERAGE PRODUCT (*AP*) is merely the total product per unit of the variable factor, which is labour in the present illustration:

$$AP = TP/L.$$

Average product is shown in column (3) of Table 17.1. Notice that as more of the variable factor is used, average product first rises and then falls. The point where average product reaches a maximum is called the POINT OF DIMINISHING AVERAGE PRODUCTIVITY. In the table, average product reaches a maximum when 7 units of labour are employed.

(3) MARGINAL PRODUCT (*MP*), sometimes called *incremental product*, is the change in total product resulting from the use of one more (or one less) unit of the variable factor:[1]

$$MP = \Delta TP/\Delta L,$$

where ΔTP stands for the change in the total product and ΔL stands for the change in labour input that caused *TP* to change.

Table 17.1 Variation of output (one fixed, one variable factor), with capital fixed at 10 units

(1) Quantity of labour *L*	(2) Total product *TP*	(3) Average product *AP*	(4) Marginal product* *MP*
1	43	43	43
2	160	80	117
3	351	117	191
4	600	150	249
5	875	175	275
6	1,152	192	277
7	1,372	196	220
8	1,536	192	164
9	1,656	184	120
10	1,750	175	94
11	1,815	165	65
12	1,860	155	45

* Marginal product shows what happens when the variable input changes from one value to another. It should thus be viewed as occurring in the interval *between* these two values of the variable input. In the table the marginal values occur *between* the units in question, and on a graph they should also be plotted between these units. Thus, for example, the marginal product of 117 refers to the interval $L = 1$ and $L = 2$, and should be plotted graphically £L = 1·5.

Computed values of the marginal product appear in column (4) of Table 17.1. For example, the *MP* corresponding to 4 units of labour is given as 249 bushels. This reflects the fact that the increase in labour from 3 to 4 units ($\Delta L = 1$) increases output from 351 to 600 ($\Delta TP = 249$). *MP* in the example reaches a maximum between $L = 5$ and $L = 6$ and thereafter declines. The level of output where marginal product reaches a maximum is called the POINT OF DIMINISHING MARGINAL RETURNS.

Figure 17.1 (ii) shows the average and marginal product curves plotted from the data in Table 17.1. Notice (1) that *MP* reaches its maximum at a lower level of *L* than does *AP*, and (2) that $MP = AP$ when *AP* is a maximum. These relations are discussed below.

[1] The marginal product thus measures the rate at which total product is changing as one factor is varied. Students familiar with elementary calculus will recognize the marginal product as the partial derivative of the total product with respect to the variable factor. In symbols: $MP = \partial TP/\partial L$. In the text we refer only to finite changes, but the phrase 'a change of one unit' should read 'a very small change'. At this time it would be helpful to read, or reread, the discussion of the marginal concept given in section 10 of the Appendix to Chapter 2 (p.34).

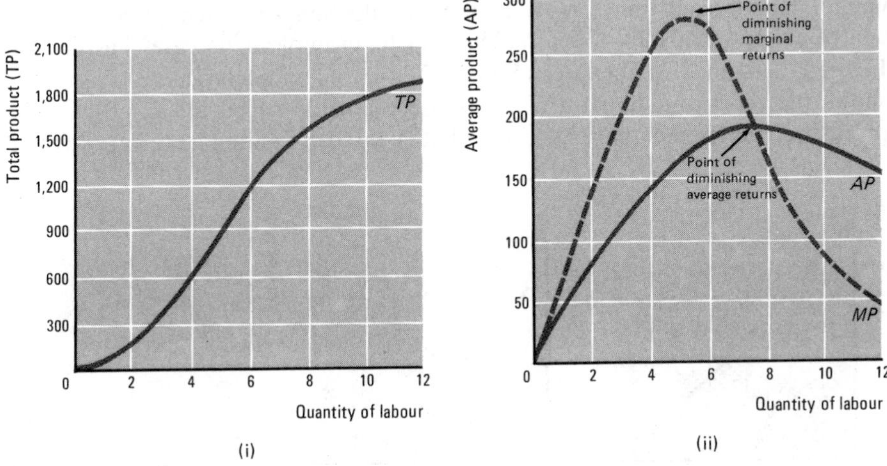

Fig. 17.1 (i) Total product from Table 17.1 ($K = 10$)
(ii) Average and marginal product curves plotted from data in Table 17.1

Finally, bear in mind that the schedules of Table 17.1 and the curves of Figure 17.1 all assume a specified quantity of the fixed factor. If the quantity of capital had been, say, 6 or 14 instead of the 10 units that were assumed, there could be a different set of total, average, and marginal product curves. The reason for this is that if any specified amount of labour has more capital to work with, it can produce more output: its total product will be greater.

The hypothesis of diminishing returns The variations in output that result from applying more or less of a variable factor to a given quantity of a fixed factor are the subject of a famous economic hypothesis called the LAW OF DIMINISHING RETURNS.

> **The Law of Diminishing Returns states that if increasing quantities of a variable factor are applied to given quantities of fixed factors, the marginal product and the average product of the variable factor will eventually decrease.**

Empirical evidence in favour of the hypothesis of diminishing returns is strong in many fields. Indeed, were the hypothesis incorrect, there would be no need to fear that the present population explosion will cause a food crisis. If the marginal product of additional workers applied to a fixed quantity of land were constant, then world food production could be expanded in proportion to the increase in population merely by keeping the same proportion of the population on farms. As it is, diminishing returns means an inexorable decline in the marginal product of each additional labourer as an expanding population is applied, with static techniques, to a fixed world supply of agricultural land. Thus, unless there is a continual and rapidly accelerating improvement in the techniques of production, the population explosion must bring with it declining living standards over much of the world, and eventual widespread famine.

The law of diminishing returns is illustrated in Figure 17.2. It is consistent with the law that marginal and average returns diminish from the outset, so that the first unit of labour contributes most to total production and each successive unit contributes less than the one before. This is so, for example, in the cases illustrated in Figure 17.2 (i) and (ii). The case in Figure 17.2 (ii) is of particular interest, because it shows the short-run shape of a widely used function called the Cobb-Douglas production function. Situations such as that pictured in Figure 17.2 (iii) are possible

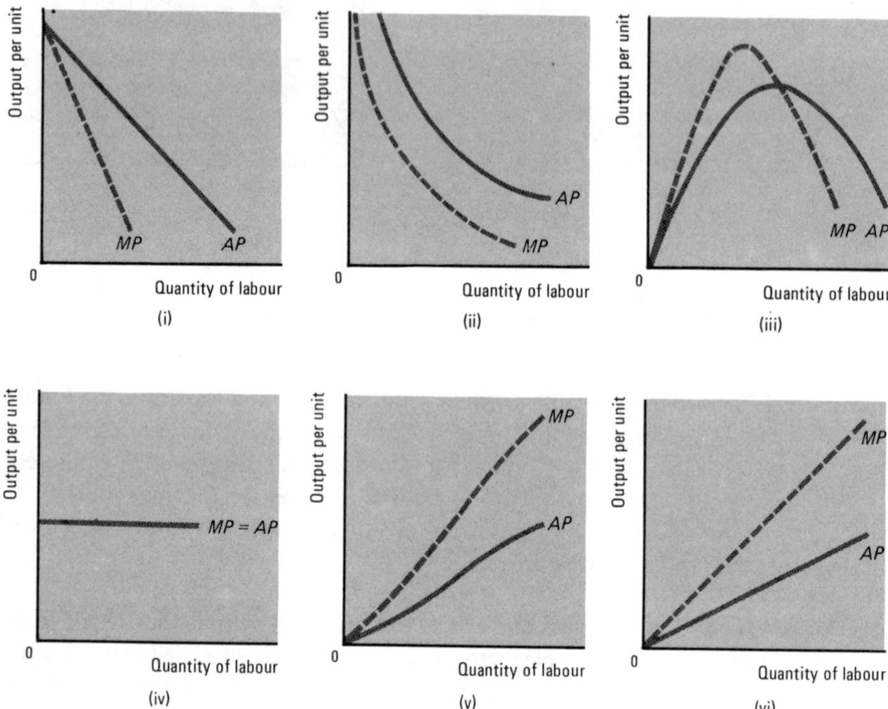

Fig. 17.2 The hypotheses of eventually diminishing productivity admit the possibility of (i) (ii) and (iii) but not, indefinitely, (iv) (v) and (vi)

and have been extensively studied. In such cases, both marginal and average returns increase for a while and only later diminish. This would happen if it were impossible to use the fixed factor efficiently with only a small quantity of the variable factor (if, say, one man were trying to farm 1,000 acres). In this case increasing the quantity of the variable factor makes possible a better organization and a more efficient division of labour, so that the addition of another unit of the variable factor would make all units more productive than they were previously. According to the hypothesis of diminishing returns, the scope for such economies must eventually disappear, and sooner or later the marginal and average product of additional workers must decline.

The relation between marginal and average product curves Notice that in Figure 17.1 (iii) the *MP* curve cuts the *AP* curve at the latter's maximum point. Although the relation between marginal and average curves is a mathematical one and not a matter of economics, it is nonetheless very important to understand it.

The average product curve slopes upward as long as the marginal product curve is above it; it makes no difference whether the marginal curve is itself sloping upward or downward. The common sense of this relation is that if an additional worker is to raise the average product of all workers, it is necessary and sufficient that a worker's output be greater than the average output of all other workers. It is immaterial whether his contribution to output is greater or less than the contribution of the worker hired immediately before him; all that matters is that his contribution to output exceeds the average output of *all* the workers hired before him.[1]

Short-run variations in cost

We now know how, according to economic theory, output varies with factor inputs in the short run and we know how to value the firm's inputs. By combining these two things, we can discover how a firm's output is related to the costs of producing it.

For the time being we consider firms that are not in a position to influence the prices of the factors of production they employ. These firms must pay the going market price for factors. Given the prices paid for factors and the physical returns summarized by the product curves, the costs of different levels of output can quickly be computed.

Cost concepts defined The following brief definitions of several cost concepts are closely related to the product concepts defined earlier in this chapter.

(1) TOTAL COST (*TC*) means just what it says: the total cost of producing any given rate of output. Total cost is divided into two parts, total fixed costs (*TFC*) and total variable costs (*TVC*). FIXED COSTS are those costs that do not vary with output; they will be the same if output is 1 unit or 1 million units. These costs are also often referred to as 'overhead costs' or 'unavoidable costs'. All of those costs that vary directly with output, rising as more is produced and falling as less is produced, are called VARIABLE COSTS. In the previous example, since labour was the variable factor of production, the wage bill would be a variable cost. Variable costs are often referred to as 'direct costs' or 'avoidable costs'.[2]

(2) AVERAGE TOTAL COST (*ATC*) is the total cost of producing any given output divided by the number of units produced, or the cost per unit. *ATC* may be divided into AVERAGE FIXED COSTS (*AFC*) and AVERAGE VARIABLE COSTS (*AVC*) in just the same way as total costs were divided.

---

[1] To check your understanding, try an example in which five workers produce 50 units of output. In the first case a sixth worker adds 16 and a seventh worker adds 14 to total output. In the second case, the sixth worker adds 14 and the seventh worker adds 16 to total output. When you do the calculations you will find that *AP* is rising in both cases, although *MP* is declining in the first case and rising in the second.

[2] In symbols we may write

$$TC = TFC + TVC$$
$$TFC = K$$
$$TVC = wL$$

where K is some constant amount, L is the quantity of the variable factor used, and w is the price per unit of this factor. Since fixed costs are constant and since variable costs necessarily rise as output rises, total costs rise with output or, to put the point more formally, TC is a function of total product and varies directly with it: $TC = f(q)$.

Although average *variable* costs may rise or fall as production is increased (depending on whether output rises more rapidly or more slowly than total variable costs), it is clear that average fixed costs decline continuously as output increases. A doubling of output always leads to a halving of fixed costs per unit of output. This is a process popularly known as 'spreading one's overheads'.

(3) MARGINAL COST (MC), sometimes called incremental cost, is the increase in total cost resulting from raising the rate of production by one unit.[1] Because fixed costs do not vary with output, marginal fixed costs are always zero. Therefore marginal costs are necessarily marginal variable costs, and a change in fixed costs will leave marginal costs unaffected. For example, the marginal cost of producing a few more potatoes by farming a given amount of land more intensively is the same whatever the rent paid for the fixed amount of land.[2]

These three measures of cost are merely different ways of looking at a single phenomenon, and they are mathematically interrelated. Sometimes it is convenient to use one, and sometimes another.

Short-run cost curves Let us take the production relationships in Table 17.1 and assume that the price of labour is £20 per unit and the price of capital is £10 per unit. In Table 17.2, we present the cost schedules computed for these values. (It is important that you see where the numbers come from; if you do not, review Table 17.1 and the definitions of cost just given.) Figure 17.3 (i) shows the total cost curves; Figure 17.3 (ii) plots the marginal and average cost curves.

Notice that the marginal cost curve cuts the ATC and AVC curves at their lowest points. This is another example of the relation (discussed above) between a marginal and an average curve. The ATC curve, for example, slopes downward as long as the marginal cost curve is below it; it makes no difference whether the marginal cost curve is itself sloping upward or downward.

In Figure 17.3 the average variable cost curve reaches a minimum and then rises. With fixed factor prices, when average product per worker is at a maximum, average

---

[1] In symbols:

$$MC = \frac{\Delta TC}{\Delta q}.$$

For a one-unit change, $MC_n = TC_n - TC_{n-1}$, i.e., the marginal cost of the nth unit of output is the total cost of producing n units minus the total cost of producing $n-1$ (i.e., one less) units of output. If we are producing a number of identical units of output, we cannot, of course, ascribe a separate (and different) cost to each unit. When we speak, therefore, of the marginal cost of the nth unit we mean nothing more than the change in total costs when the rate of production is increased from $n-1$ units to n units per period of time.

[2] Only the simplest bit of algebra is necessary to prove this important proposition:

$$\begin{aligned} MC_n &= TC_n - TC_{n-1} \\ &= (TVC_n + TFC_n) - (TVC_{n-1} + TFC_{n-1}), \end{aligned}$$

but

$$TFC_n = TFC_{n-1} = K;$$

therefore,

$$\begin{aligned} MC_n &= (TVC_n + K) - (TVC_{n-1} + K) \\ &= TVC_n - TVC_{n-1} \end{aligned}$$

Hence marginal costs are independent of the size of fixed costs.

Table 17.2 Cost schedules for data in Table 17.1 (price of labour, £20 per unit; price of capital, £10 per unit)

		Total cost			Average cost			Marginal cost*
(1) Labour	(2) Output	(3) Fixed	(4) Variable	(5) Total	(6) Fixed	(7) Variable	(8) Total	
L	*q*	*TFC*	*TVC*	*TC*	*AFC*	*AVC*	*ATC*	*MC*
1	43	£100	£ 20	£120	£2·326	£·465	£2·791	£·465
2	160	100	40	140	·625	·250	·875	·171
3	351	100	60	160	·285	·171	·456	·105
4	600	100	80	180	·167	·133	·300	·080
5	875	100	100	200	·114	·114	·229	·073
6	1,152	100	120	220	·087	·104	·191	·072
7	1,372	100	140	240	·073	·102	·175	·091
8	1,536	100	160	260	·065	·104	·169	·122
9	1,656	100	180	280	·060	·109	·169	·167
10	1,750	100	200	300	·057	·114	·171	·213
11	1,815	100	220	320	·055	·121	·176	·308
12	1,860	100	240	340	·054	·129	·183	·444

* 'Marginal' cost is really 'incremental' cost, $MC = \frac{\Delta TC}{\Delta q}$, for intervals indicated in the table. Thus the *MC* of ·171 in line 2 is $\frac{£140-£120}{160-43} = ·171$. For graphical purposes this should be plotted at the level of output halfway between 43 and 160.

variable cost is at a minimum.[1] The common sense of this proposition is that each additional worker adds the same amount to cost but a different amount to output, and when output per worker is rising the cost per unit of output must be falling, and vice versa.

> **The law of diminishing returns implies increasing marginal cost and increasing average variable cost.**

[1] This point is easily seen if a little algebra is used:

$$AVC = \frac{TVC}{q}$$

but

$$TVC = L{\cdot}w$$

and

$$q = AP{\cdot}L,$$

where L is the quantity of the variable factor used and where w is its cost per unit.

Therefore

$$AVC = \frac{L{\cdot}w}{AP{\cdot}L} = \frac{w}{AP}.$$

In other words, average variable cost equals the price of the variable factor divided by the average product of the variable factor. Since w is constant, it follows that AVC and AP vary inversely with each other, and when AP is at its maximum value AVC must be at its minimum value.

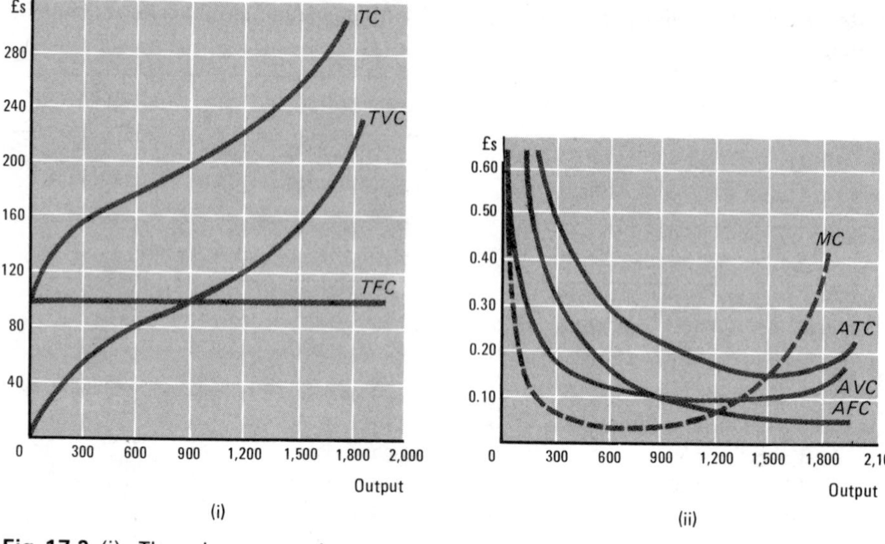

Fig. 17.3 (i) Three short-run total cost curves
(ii) Marginal and average cost curves

Short-run *ATC* curves are often drawn U-shaped. This reflects the assumptions that (i) average productivity is increasing when output is low, but (ii) at some level of output average productivity begins to fall fast enough to cause average total cost to increase.[1]

The definition of capacity The output that corresponds to the minimum short-run total cost is often called *optimal capacity, plant capacity*, or just CAPACITY. Capacity in this sense is not an upper limit on what can be produced, as you can see by looking again at Table 17.2. In the example, capacity output is between 1,536 and 1,656 units, but higher outputs can be achieved. A firm producing *with excess capacity* is producing at a rate of output below the point of minimum average total cost. A firm producing *above capacity* is producing above this point, and is thus incurring costs higher than the minimum achievable.

A family of short-run cost curves A short-run cost curve shows how costs vary with output for a given quantity of the fixed factor – say a given size of plant.

> **There is a different short-run cost curve for each given quantity of the fixed factor.**

A small plant for manufacturing nuts and bolts will have its own short-run cost curve. A medium-size and a very large-size plant will each have its own short-run cost curve. If a firm expands by replacing its small plant with a medium-size plant, it will move from one short-run cost curve to another. This change from one size of plant to another is a long-run change. The study of how short-run cost curves of

[1] The law of diminishing returns implies only that average costs will *eventually* rise. 'Eventually' may not mean whenever output is increased. The empirical evidence does show rising costs, but often the shape of the curve is very flat – more like a saucer than a cup – in the relevant range of outputs.

different size plants are related to each other is the subject of the next section of this chapter.

The long run

In what way does the long run differ from the short run? In the short run, with only one factor variable, there is only one way to produce a given output: by adjusting the input of the variable factor until the desired level of output is achieved. Thus, in the short run, the firm must make a decision about its output, but once it has decided on a rate of output there is only one technically possible way of achieving it. In the long run, all factors are variable. If a firm decides on some rate of output, it has an additional decision to make: by which of the many technically possible methods will the output be produced? Should the firm adopt a technique that uses a great deal of capital and only a small amount of labour, or should it adopt one that uses less capital but more labour?

Since there are almost always many ways of achieving the same total output, the firm needs some method of choosing among them. The hypothesis of profit maximization provides a simple rule for this choice: any firm that is trying to maximize its profits will select the method of producing a given output that incurs the lowest possible cost. We call this the implication of cost minimization. Cost minimisation is not a separate hypothesis from profit maximization. It is an implication of profit maximization, since a firm that is not minimizing its costs is not maximizing its profits. Indeed cost minimization follows from other assumptions as well. As long as the firm is trying to maximize anything that uses economic resources it will wish to minimize the costs it incurs to produce any given level of output. This can be stated formally as follows:

> **For any specific output, the firm chooses the least costly method of production from the alternatives open to it.**

If there is a known stable required rate of output, and if the costs of factors are known, this is all there is to it.

Long-run planning decisions are important because today's variable factors are tomorrow's fixed ones. A firm deciding on a new, fully equipped plant will have many alternatives to choose from, but once installed, the new equipment is fixed for a long time. If the firm errs now, its very survival may be threatened; if it estimates shrewdly and its rivals don't, it may reward its owners and its far-sighted managers with large profits and bonuses.[1]

Conditions for cost minimization

The firm wishes to choose the least costly alternative for producing its desired output. If it could substitute one factor for another in such a way as to keep its

[1] Long-run decisions are among the most difficult and most important the firm makes. They are difficult because the firm must anticipate what methods of production will be efficient not only today but in the years ahead when costs of labour and raw materials may have changed. They are difficult because the firm must estimate its desired future output. Is the industry growing or declining? Is the firm's share of the market going to increase or decrease? Will new products emerge to render its own products less useful than an extrapolation of past sales might suggest?

output constant while reducing its total cost, it has not succeeded. This can be stated more formally as follows:

> **The profit-maximizing firm will substitute one factor for another factor as long as the marginal product of the one factor per penny expended on it is greater than the marginal product of the other factor per penny expended on it.**

The firm cannot have minimized its costs as long as these two magnitudes are unequal. This leads to the following important condition of cost minimization (using K to represent capital, L labour, and p the price to the firm of a unit of the factor).[1]

$$\frac{MP_K}{p_K} = \frac{MP_L}{p_L} \tag{3}$$

To see why this condition needs to be fulfilled if costs of production are to be minimized, suppose the left-hand side was equal to 10, showing that the last penny spent on capital produced 10 units of output, while the right-hand side was equal to 4, showing that the last penny spent on labour added only 4 units to output. In such a case, the firm by using £2·50 less of labour would reduce output by approximately 10 units. But it could regain that lost output by spending approximately £1 more on capital.[2] Making such a substitution of capital for labour would leave output unchanged and reduce cost by £1·50. Thus the original position was not cost-minimizing. Whenever the two sides of (3) are not equal, there are factor substitutions that will reduce costs.

By rearranging the terms in (3) we can look at the cost-minimizing condition in a slightly different way;

$$\frac{MP_K}{MP_L} = \frac{p_K}{p_L} \tag{4}$$

The ratio of the marginal products on the left-hand side compares the contribution to output of the last unit of capital and the last unit of labour. If the ratio is 4, this means 1 unit more of capital will add 4 times as much to output as 1 unit more of labour. The right-hand side shows how the cost of 1 unit more of capital compares to the cost of 1 unit more of labour. If it is also 4, it does not pay the firm to substitute capital for labour or vice versa. But suppose the right-hand side is 2. Capital, although twice as expensive, is 4 times as productive, and it will pay the firm to switch to a method of production that uses more capital and less labour. If, however, the right-hand side is 6 (or *any* number more than 4), it will pay to substitute labour for capital.

This formulation shows how the firm can adjust the things over which it has control (the quantities of factors used, and thus the marginal products of the

---

[1] This condition is directly analogous to the condition for the utility-maximizing household, given on page 163, in which the household equated the marginal utility per penny spent on each of the two goods. Later in this chapter the condition is given a graphic analysis similar to that given for household behaviour in the second half of Chapter 14.

[2] The argument in the previous two sentences assumes that the marginal products do not change very much when expenditure is changed by a few pounds. If they did not change at all the 'approximatelys' could be eliminated.

factors) to the things that are typically given to it by the market (the prices or opportunity costs of the factors). A precisely analogous adjustment process was involved (see page 162) in households' adjusting their consumption of goods to the market prices of those goods.

The principle of substitution

Suppose that a firm is producing where the cost-minimizing conditions shown in (3) or (4) are met, but that the cost of labour increases while the cost of capital remains unchanged. As we have just seen, the least-cost method of producing any output will now use less labour and more capital than was required to produce that same output before the factor prices changed. This prediction, called the PRINCIPLE OF SUBSTITUTION, follows from the assumption that firms try to minimize their costs.

> **Methods of production will change if the relative prices of factors change; relatively more of the cheaper factor and relatively less of the more expensive one will be used.**

This proposition plays a central role in the theory of the allocation of resources because it shows how individual firms will respond to changes in relative factor prices. Such changes are caused by the changing relative scarcities of factors in the whole economy. Individual firms are thus motivated to use less of factors that have become scarcer in overall supply.

Cost curves in the long run

There is a best (least-cost) method of producing each rate of output when all factors are free to be varied. In general this method will not be the same for different levels of output. If factor prices are given, a minimum cost can be found for each possible level of output and, if this minimum achievable cost is expressed as an amount per unit of output, we can obtain the long-run average cost of producing each level of output. When this information is plotted on a graph, the result is called a LONG-RUN AVERAGE TOTAL COST (*LRATC*) CURVE. Figure 17.4 shows such a curve.

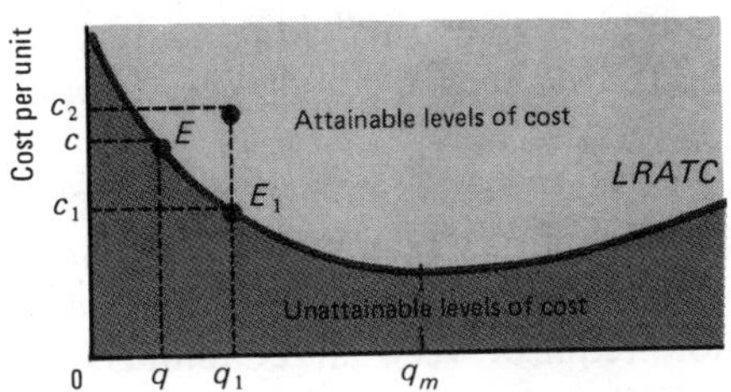

Fig. 17.4 A long-run average total cost curve

The long-run average total cost curve provides a boundary between attainable and unattainable levels of cost. If the firm wishes to produce output q in Figure 17.4, the lowest attainable cost is c per unit. Thus point E is on the $LRATC$ curve. E_1 represents the least-cost method of producing q_1. Suppose, however, that a firm is producing at E and desires to increase output to q_1. In the short run the firm will not be able to vary all factors, and thus costs above c_1, say c_2, must be accepted. In the long run, a plant optimal for output q_1 can be built and a cost of c_1 can be attained. Output q_m is the output at which the firm attains its lowest possible unit cost of production for the given technology and factor prices.

This *LRATC* curve is determined by the technology of the industry (which is assumed to be fixed) and by the prices of the factors of production. It is a 'boundary' in the sense that points below the curve are unattainable, points on the curve are attainable if sufficient time elapses for all factors to be adjusted, and points above the curve are also attainable. Indeed, points above the *LRATC* curve may represent the best that can be done in the short run when all factors are not freely variable.

> **The *LRATC* curve divides the cost levels that are attainable with known technology and given factor prices from those that are unattainable.**

The shape of the long-run average total cost curve

The long-run average cost curve in Figure 17.4 is shown as falling at first and then rising. This curve is often described as being U-shaped.

Decreasing costs Over the range of output from zero to q_m the firm has falling long-run average total costs. An expansion of output results in a reduction of costs per unit of output once enough time has elapsed to allow adjustments in the techniques of production. Since the prices of factors are assumed to be constant, the reason for the decline in costs per unit must be that output increases faster than inputs as the scale of the firm's production expands. Over this range of output the firm is often said to enjoy long-run INCREASING RETURNS.[1] Increasing returns may arise as a result of increased opportunities for specialization of tasks made possible by the division of labour even with no substitution of one factor of production for another. Or they may arise because of factor substitution. Even the most casual observation of the differences in production technique used in large-size and small-size plants shows the existence of the differences in factor proportions. These differences arise because large, specialized machinery and equipment are useful only when the volume of output that the firm can sell justifies its employment.

For example, the use of the assembly line technique, body-stamping machinery, and multiple-boring engine-block machines in car production is economically efficient only if individual operations are to be repeated thousands of times. The use of elaborate harvesting equipment (which combines many individual tasks that could be done by hand and by tractor) provides the least-cost method of production on a big farm but not on a few acres.

Typically, the substitution involved is of capital for labour and of complex machines for simpler ones. Automation is a contemporary example of this kind of substitution. Electronic devices can handle a very large volume of operations very quickly, but unless the level of production requires very large numbers of operations, it does not make sense to use these techniques.

Increasing costs Over the range of outputs greater than q_m in Figure 17.4 the firm encounters rising costs. An expansion in production, even after sufficient time has elapsed for all adjustments to be made, will be accompanied by a rise in average costs per unit of output. If the prices of factors of production are constant, this rise

---

[1] Economists often shift back and forth between speaking in physical output terms and cost terms. Thus a firm with increasing (physical) returns to scale (output rises more than in proportion to input in the long run) is also spoken of as a firm with decreasing long run costs (costs rise less than in proportion to output in the long run).

in costs must be the result of an expansion in output which is proportionately less than the expansion in inputs. Such a firm is said to suffer long-run DECREASING RETURNS.[1] Decreasing returns imply that the firm suffers diseconomies of scale. As its scale of operations increases, diseconomies – of management or otherwise – are encountered that increase the quantity of factors that must be used per unit of output produced.

Minimum costs At the output q_m in Figure 17.4 the firm has reached its lowest possible long-run costs per unit of output. If the firm were to produce at that output it could be said to be producing efficiently in the sense that the costs of producing a unit of output would be as low as they possibly could be (for given technology and factor prices). We shall see in Chapter 19 that under certain conditions (called those of perfect competition) each firm will, in equilibrium, produce at the minimum point on its *LRATC* curve.

Constant costs The firm's long-run average costs are shown in Figure 17.4 as falling to output q_m and rising thereafter. Another possibility should be noted: the firm's *LRATC* curve might be flat over some range of output around q_m. If such a flat portion existed, the firm would be said to be encountering constant costs over the relevant range of output. This would mean that the firm's average cost per unit of output was not changing as its output changed. If factor prices are assumed to be fixed, this must mean that the firm's output is increasing exactly as fast as its inputs are increasing. Such a firm would be said to be encountering CONSTANT RETURNS.

The relation between long-run and short-run costs

The various short-run cost curves derived earlier in this chapter and the long-run cost curve just studied are all derived from the same production function, and each assumes given prices for all factor inputs. In the long run, all factors can be varied; in the short run, some must remain fixed. The long-run average total cost (*LRATC*) curve shows the lowest cost of producing any output when all factors are variable. The short-run average total cost (*SRATC*) curve shows the lowest cost of producing any output when one or more factors is not free to vary.

The short-run cost curve cannot fall below the long-run curve because the latter curve represents the *lowest* attainable costs for every output. It might be the same

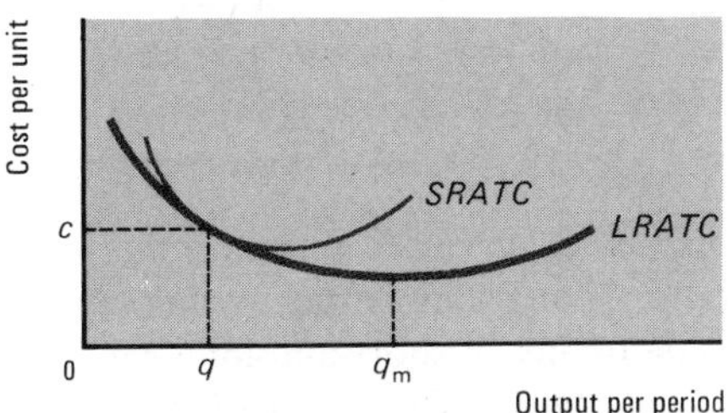

Fig. 17.5 Long-run and short-run average total cost curves

[1] Long-run decreasing returns differ from the short-run diminishing returns that we encountered earlier. In the short run at least one factor is fixed and the law of diminishing returns ensures that returns to the variable factor will eventually diminish. In the long run all factors are variable and it is possible that physically diminishing returns would never be encountered – at least as long as it was genuinely possible to increase inputs of all factors.

curve, but the law of variable proportions predicts that as output is changed, a different-sized plant would be required to achieve the lowest attainable cost. This is illustrated in Figure 17.5. Note that the short-run cost curve is tangent to (touches) the long-run curve at the level of output for which the quantity of the fixed factor is optimal and lies above it for all other levels of output. If output varies around q units, with plant and equipment fixed at the optimal level for producing q, costs will follow the short-run cost curve. If some output other than q is to be sustained, costs can be reduced to the level of the long-run curve when sufficient time has elapsed to adjust all factor inputs. While *SRATC* and *LRATC* are at the same level for output q – since the fixed plant is optimal for that output – for all other outputs there is either too little or too much of the fixed factor and *SRATC* lies above *LRATC*.

We saw earlier in this chapter that an *SRATC* curve, such as the one shown in Figure 17.5, is but one of many such short-run curves. Each one shows how costs vary as output is varied from a base output, holding some factors fixed at the quantities most appropriate to the base output. This is illustrated in Figure 17.6.

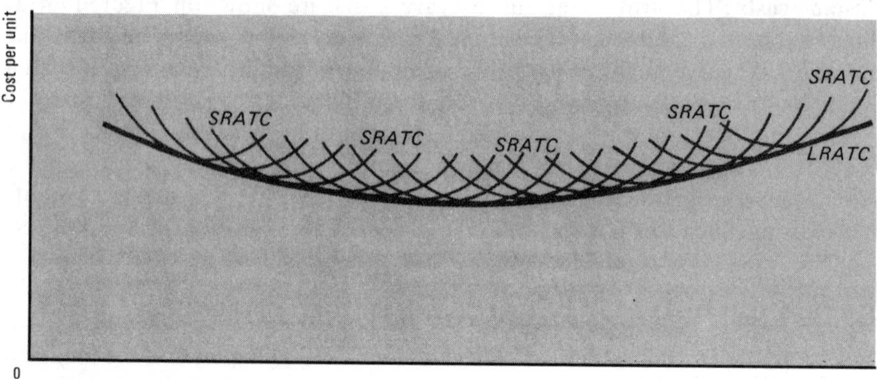

Fig. 17.6 The envelope relation between the long-run average total cost curve and all the short-run average total cost curves

There is an associated short-run cost curve tangent to every point on the long-run cost curve. Each short-run curve shows how costs vary if output varies, with the fixed factor held constant at the level that is optimal for the output at the point of tangency. The long-run curve is sometimes called an ENVELOPE CURVE that encloses the whole family of short-run curves. [1]

Shifts in cost curves

The cost curves we have derived so far show how cost varies with output, given constant factor prices and fixed technology. Changes in either technological knowledge or factor prices will cause the whole family of short-and long-run cost curves to shift. Loss of existing technological knowledge is a rare thing, so technological change normally works in one direction only, to shift cost curves

1 Each short-run curve touches the long-run curve at one point and lies above it everywhere else. This leads to an important, though subtle, consequence. Two curves that are tangent at a point have the same slope at that point. If *LRATC* is decreasing where it is tangent to *SRATC*, then *SRATC* must also be decreasing.

downward. Improved ways of making existing commodities mean that lower cost methods of production become available. Factor prices can, however, exert an influence in either direction. If a firm has to pay more for any factor that it uses, the cost of producing each level of output will rise; if the firm has to pay less, costs fall.

A rise in factor prices shifts the whole family of short- and long-run cost curves upwards. A fall in factor prices or a technological advance shifts the whole family of cost curves downwards.

Isoquants: an alternative analysis of the firm's long-run input decisions [1]

The production function gives the relation between the factor inputs that the firm uses and the output that it obtains. In the long run the firm can choose among many different combinations of inputs that will yield it the same output. The production function and the choices open to the firm can be given a graphical representation using the concept of an isoquant.

A single isoquant

Table 17.3 gives a hypothetical illustration of those combinations of two inputs (labour and capital) that will each serve to produce a given quantity of output. The table lists some of the methods indicated by a production function as being available to produce 6 units of output. The first combination uses a great deal of capital (K) and very little labour (L). Moving down the table, labour is substituted for capital in such a way as to keep output constant. Finally, at the bottom of the table, most of the capital has been replaced by labour. The rate of substitution between the two factors is calculated in the last three columns of the table. Note that as we move down the table, the absolute value of the rate of substitution declines.

Table 17.3 Alternative ways of producing 6 units of output

K	L	ΔK	ΔL	Rate of substitution $\Delta K/\Delta L$
18	2			
		−6	1	−6·0
12	3			
		−3	1	−3·0
9	4			
		−3	2	1·5
6	6			
		−2	3	−0·67
4	9			
		−1	3	−0·33
3	12			
		−1	6	−0·17
2	18			

[1] The material from here to the middle of page 230 can be omitted without loss of continuity.

The data from Table 17.3 are plotted in Figure 17.7. Points *a* to *d* refer to the first four points in the table. A smooth curve is drawn through the points to indicate that there are additional ways, not listed in the table, of producing 6 units.

This curve is called an ISOQUANT, and it shows the whole set of technologically efficient possibilities for producing a given level of output – 6 units in this example. It is analogous to an indifference curve that shows all combinations of commodities that yield an equal utility.

The convex shape of the isoquant reflects a diminishing marginal rate of substitution. Starting from point *a*, which uses relatively little labour and much capital, and moving to point *b*, 1 additional unit of labour can substitute for 6 units of capital (while holding production constant). But from *b* to *c*, 1 unit of labour substitutes for only 3 units of capital. To replace the next 3 units of capital (to move from *c* to *d*) requires adding 2 units of labour. Capital is becoming scarcer. In order to keep production constant, moving from *a* to *b* to *c* to *d*, larger and larger quantities of labour must be added to compensate for equal reductions in the quantity of capital. The geometrical expression of this is that moving along the isoquant to the right, the slope of the isoquant becomes flatter.

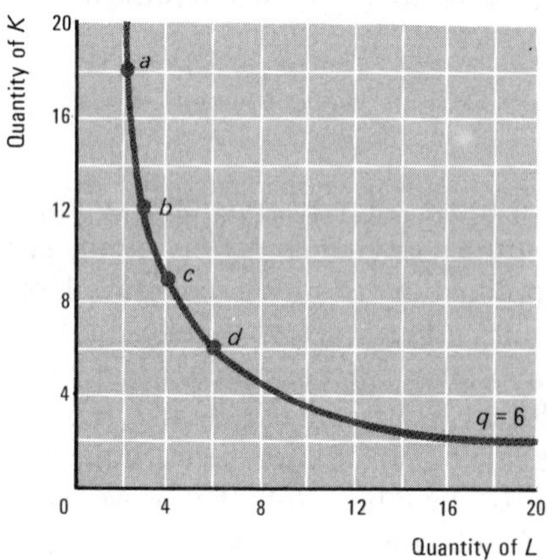

Fig. 17.7 An isoquant for output of six units

As we move from one point on an isoquant to another we are *substituting one factor for another* while holding output constant. If we move from point *b* to point *c*, we are substituting 2 units of capital for 3 units of labour. The MARGINAL RATE OF SUBSTITUTION measures the rate at which one factor is substituted for another with output held constant. Graphically the marginal rate of substitution is measured by the slope of the isoquant at a particular point. Table 17.3 shows the calculation of some rates of substitution between various points of the isoquant.[1]

The marginal rate of substitution is related to the marginal products of the factors of production. To see how, consider an example. Assume that at the present level of inputs of labour and capital the marginal product of a unit of labour is 2 units of output while the marginal product of capital is 1 unit of output. If the firm reduces its use of capital and increases its use of labour so as to keep output constant, it needs to add only one half unit of labour for one unit of capital given up. If, at another point on the isoquant with more labour and less capital, the marginal

[1] The table calculates the rate of substitution between distinct points on an isoquant. The marginal rate of substitution refers to substitutability at a particular point on the isoquant. Again the discussion of section 10 of the Appendix to Chapter 2 is relevant.

products are 2 for capital and 1 for labour, then the firm will have to add two units of labour for every unit of capital it gives up. The general proposition that this example illustrates is:

> **The marginal rate of substitution between two factors of production is equal to the ratios of their marginal products.**

Isoquants satisfy two important conditions: they are downward-sloping and they are convex viewed from the origin. What is the economic meaning of each of these conditions?

The downward slope indicates that each of the factor inputs has a positive marginal product. If the input of one factor is reduced and that of the other is held constant, output will be reduced. Thus, if one input is decreased, production can only be held constant if the other factor input is increased. Thus the marginal rate of substitution has a negative value: increases in one factor must be balanced by decreases in the other factor if output is to be held constant.

Now consider what happens as the firm moves along the isoquant of Figure 17.7 downward and to the right. This movement means that labour is being added and capital reduced so as to keep output constant. If labour is added in successive increments of exactly one unit, how much capital may be dispensed with each time? The key to the answer is that both factors are assumed to be subject to the law of diminishing returns. Thus the gain in output associated with each additional unit of labour added is *diminishing*, while the loss of output associated with each additional unit of capital forgone is *increasing*. It therefore takes ever-smaller reductions in capital to offset equal increases in labour in order to hold production constant. This implies that the isoquant is convex viewed from the origin.

An isoquant map

The isoquant drawn in Figure 17.7 referred to 6 units of output. There is another isoquant for 7 units, another for 7,000 units, and another for every other rate of output. Each isoquant refers to a specific output and connects alternative combinations of factors that are technologically efficient methods of achieving that output. If we plot a representative set of these isoquants on a single graph, we obtain an ISOQUANT MAP. Such a map is shown in Figure 17.8. The higher the level of output along a particular isoquant, the further away from the origin it will be.

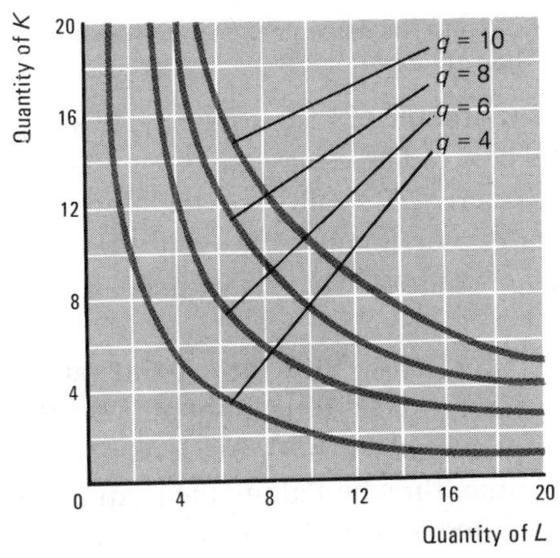

Fig. 17.8 An isoquant map

Isoquants and the conditions for cost minimization

Finding the efficient way of producing any output requires finding the least-cost factor combination. To find this combination when both factors are variable, factor prices need to be known. Suppose, to continue the example, that capital is priced at £4 per unit and labour at £1. In Chapter 13, a budget line was used to show the alternative combinations of goods a household could buy; now an ISOCOST LINE is used to show alternative combinations of factors a firm can buy for a given outlay. Four different isocost lines are shown in Figure 17.9. The graph shows the four

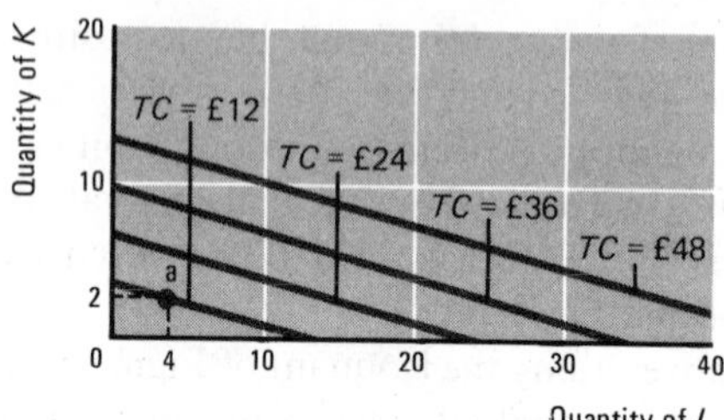

Fig. 17.9 Isocost lines

isocost lines that result when labour costs £1 a unit and capital £4 a unit and expenditure is held constant at rates of £12, £24, £36 and £48, respectively. The line labelled TC = £12 represents all combinations of the two factors that the firm could buy for £12. Point *a* represents 2 units of K and 4 units of L. The slope of the isocost line depends upon *relative* commodity prices. For given factor prices, a series of parallel isocost lines reflects alternative levels of expenditure on factors. The higher the expenditure, the farther from the origin is the isocost line.

In Figure 17.10 the isoquant and isocost maps are brought together. Consider

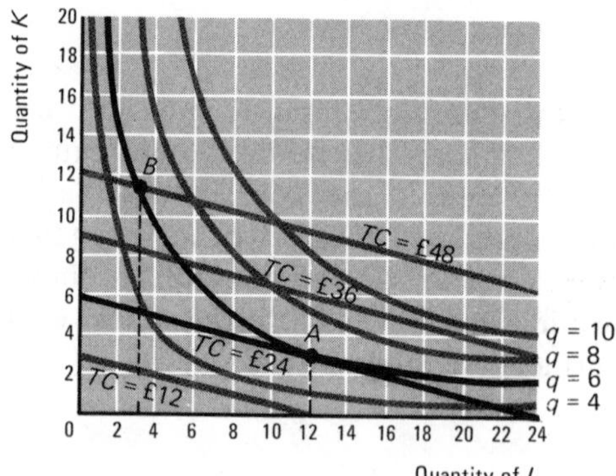

Fig. 17.10 The determination of the least-cost method of output

point A in the figure. It is on the 6-unit isoquant and the £24 isocost line. Thus it is possible to achieve the output $q = 6$ for a total cost of £24. There are other ways to achieve this output, for example, at point B, where TC = £48. Moving along the isoquant from point A in either direction increases cost. Similarly, moving along the isocost line from point A in either direction lowers output. Thus either move would raise cost per unit.

The economically most efficient method of production must be a point on an isoquant that just touches (i.e., is tangent to) an isocost line. If the isoquant cuts the isocost line, it is possible to move along the isoquant and reach a lower level of cost. Only at a point of tangency is a movement in either direction along the isoquant a movement to a higher cost level. The lowest attainable cost of producing 6 units is

£24, and this cost level can be achieved only by operating at the point where the £24 isocost line is tangent to the 6-unit isoquant. The lowest average cost of producing 6 units is thus £24/6 = £4 per unit of output.

The least-cost position is given graphically by the point of tangency between the isoquant and the isocost lines.

Notice that point A in Figure 17.10 indicates not only the lowest level of cost for 6 units of output but also the highest level of output for £24 of cost.[1]

The slope of the isocost line is given by the ratio of the prices of the two factors of production. The slope of the isoquant is given by the ratio of their marginal products. When the firm reaches its least-cost position, it has equated the price ratio (which is given to it by the market prices) with the ratio of marginal products (which it can adjust by varying the proportions in which it hires the factors). In symbols,

$$\frac{MP_K}{MP_L} = \frac{p_K}{p_L}$$

This is equation (4) on page 220. We have now derived this result by use of the isoquant analysis of the firm's decisions.

Isoquants and the principle of substitution

Suppose now that with technology unchanged – that is, with the isoquant map fixed – the price of one factor changes. Suppose that with the price of capital unchanged at £4 per unit, the price of labour rises from £1 to £4 per unit. Originally, the efficient factor combination of producing 6 units was 12 units of labour and 3 units of capital. It cost £24. To produce that same output in the same way would cost £60 at the new factor prices. Figure 17.11 shows why that is not efficient.

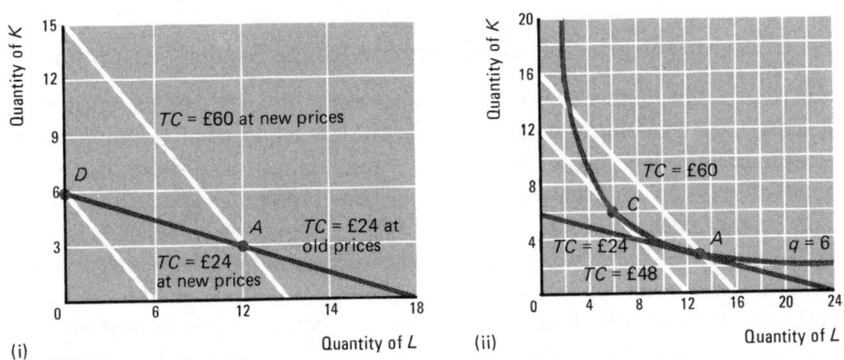

Fig. 17.11 The effects of a change in factor prices on costs and factor proportions: (i) the effect on the isocost line of an increase in the price of labour; (ii) substitution of capital for labour due to an increase in the price of labour

An increase in the price of labour pivots the isocost line inward and thus increases the cost of producing any output. It also changes the slope of the isocost line and thus changes the least-cost method of production. The steeper isocost line is tangent to the isoquant at C, not A in Figure 17.11 (ii). Costs at C are higher than they were

[1] Thus we find the same solution if we set out *either* to minimize the cost of producing 6 units of output *or* to maximize the output that can be obtained for £24. One problem is said to be the 'dual' of the other.

before the price increase, but not as high as if the factor substitution had not occurred. The slope of the isocost line has changed making it efficient to substitute the now relatively cheaper capital for the relatively more expensive labour.

This result illustrates the principle of substitution.

> **Changes in relative factor prices will cause a partial replacement of factors that have become relatively more expensive by factors that have become relatively cheaper.**

Of course, substitution of capital for labour cannot fully offset the effects of a rise in the cost of labour, as Figure 17.11 (i) shows. Consider the output attainable for £24. In the figure there are two isocost lines representing £24 of outlay – at the old and new price of labour. The new isocost line for £24 lies everywhere inside the old one (except where no labour is used). The isocost line must therefore be tangent to a lower isoquant. This means that if production is to be held constant, higher costs must be accepted – but because of substitution it is not necessary to accept costs as high as would accompany an unchanged factor proportion. In the example 6 units can be produced for £48 rather than the £60 that would have been required if no change in factor proportions had been made (i.e., if inputs were held at A rather than changed to B).

This leads to the prediction that:

> **A rise in the price of one factor with all other factor prices constant will (1) shift upward the cost curves of commodities that use that factor and (2) lead to a substitution of factors that are now relatively cheaper for the factor whose price has risen.**

Both of these predictions were stated in the first part of this chapter; they have now been derived formally using the isoquant technique.

The significance of the principle of substitution for the economy as a whole

The relative prices of factors of production in an economy will tend to reflect their relative scarcities. In a country with a great deal of land and a small population, for example, the price of land will be low while, because labour is in short supply, the wage rate will be high. In such circumstances firms producing agricultural goods will tend to make lavish use of (cheap) land and to economize on (expensive) labour; a production process will be adopted that is labour extensive and land intensive. On the other hand, in a small country with a large population, the demand for land will be high relative to its supply. Thus, land will be very expensive and firms producing agricultural goods will tend to economize on it by using a great deal of labour per unit of land. In this case a productive process will tend to grow up that is labour intensive and land extensive.

Thus we see that relative factor prices will reflect the relative scarcities (in relation to demand) of different factors of production: abundant factors will have prices that are low relative to the prices of factors that are scarce. Firms seeking their own private profit will be led to use much of the factors with which the whole country is plentifully endowed, and to economize on the factors that are in scarce supply in the whole country.

This discussion provides an example of what we mean when we say that the price system is an automatic control system. No single firm need be aware of national factor surpluses and scarcities. Prices determined on the competitive market tend to reflect these, and individual firms that never look beyond their own private profit are nonetheless led to economize on factors that are scarce in the nation as a whole. We should not be surprised therefore, to discover that methods of producing the same commodity differ in different countries. In the United States, where labour is highly skilled and very expensive, a steel company may use very elaborate machinery to economize on labour. In China, where labour is abundant and capital very scarce, a much less mechanized method of production may be appropriate. The Western engineer who feels that the Chinese are way behind because they are using methods abandoned in the West as inefficient long ago may be missing the truth about economic efficiency in use of resources. The suggestion, often made, that to aid underdeveloped countries we need merely to export Western 'know-how' may be misguided.

In spite of the tendency of the price system to induce profit-maximizing firms to take account of the nation's relative factor scarcities when deciding which of the possible methods of production to adopt, one must avoid jumping to the conclusion that whatever productive processes are adopted are the best possible ones and should never be interfered with. There is, however, a strong common-sense appeal in the idea that:

> **Any society interested in getting the most out of its resources should take account of their relative scarcities in deciding what productive processes to adopt, which is what the price system leads individual firms to do.**

The very long run

In the long run, when technology and hence the production function are given, a certain quantity of inputs produces a certain output. In the very long run, technology may change: the same quantities of inputs may then produce a larger quantity of output than before.

Changes in supply over the very long run are strongly influenced by changes in the techniques of production, by changes in the goods being produced, and by changes in the quality of factor inputs. Most economic theory focuses attention on short- and long-run decisions taken within the context of given factor supplies, given products, and known techniques of production. These decisions are important but, if we are interested in the performance of the economic system over long time periods, questions concerning the causes and consequences of very-long-run changes cannot be ignored. In this section we shall confine ourselves to the question of how the economic system will respond in the very long run to changes in demands, prices and costs such as we considered in the short and long run. In doing this we shall concentrate on changes in *productivity*. Many of the wider aspects of very-long-run changes must be postponed until Chapter 46, which deals with the whole problem of long-term economic growth.

Productivity

There is no doubt whatever that over the last years the material standard of living of the typical family has increased enormously in all of the world's industrialized countries. Much of this increase has been due to the invention of new, improved ways of making products. This causes an increase in PRODUCTIVITY, which is output per unit of input employed.

The magnitude of increases in productivity deserves some attention.

> **The apparently modest rate of increase of output per man-hour of labour of 2·0 per cent per year leads to a doubling of output per man-hour every 36 years.**

Productivity in the United Kingdom has increased at approximately this rate over the last 100 years.

Between 1945 and 1970 productivity growth in the UK was closer to 3 per cent per year (which doubles output every $23\frac{1}{2}$ years), while in other countries it has been much higher. In Japan, for example, it has been increasing at about 10 per cent per year, a rate which doubles output per man-hour approximately every seven years.

Productivity changes and the theory of supply There is no doubt that productivity changes affect the supplies of commodities. What is in doubt is the extent to which productivity changes themselves are an endogenous response to economic signals and incentives, and the extent to which they are an exogenous consequence of the spontaneous creative activity of scientists, inventors and many other researchers. The answer to the question will greatly influence our judgement of the ability of the economy to adjust to various disturbances that impinge on it.[1]

Sources of increases in productivity Long-run increases in efficiency are due to, and can be divided into, scale effects, increases in the quality of the inputs, changes in the known techniques of production and improvements in products. Mere population growth, other things equal, will permit higher productivity if most products are subject to increasing returns to scale. Substitution of more and more capital for labour as the level of production expands is likely to lead to greater productivity. Better raw materials, better trained or educated labour, or better machines will increase productivity even if no changes in factor quantities or proportions take place. Better organization of production alone can account for increases in productivity. New ideas can raise efficiency by being applied to new products: imagination can design a better mousetrap, with no change in the quantity, quality or proportions of factors.

Inventions and innovations

An INVENTION is defined as the discovery of something new, such as a new production technique or a new product. An INNOVATION is defined as the introduction of an invention into use.

> **It is generally accepted that innovation responds to economic incentives. New products and methods will not be introduced unless it appears profitable to do so, and a change in economic incentives can change the apparent profitabilities of various possible innovations.**

But innovation can occur only when there has already been an invention. If there is a dramatic rise in labour costs, firms may now decide to take up some labour-

[1] See page 30 for a discussion of the distinction between exogenous and endogenous variables.

saving process that hitherto has been ignored since its invention, but they cannot do so if the invention has not yet been made. If we are concerned with the response of the economy to such economic signals as changes in the relative prices both of consumer goods and of inputs, then we need to know the extent to which invention responds to such incentives. A number of hypotheses about the sources of invention have been put forward.

(1) Invention is a random process Some people are by nature both curious and clever. Thousands of attempts will be made to invent better ways of doing things. Many will fail, and they remain nameless, but a few succeed. These are the Hardwicks, Stephensons, Whitleys, Edisons and Fords. The successful inventions become a pool of potential innovations, and, when the climate is right, they are introduced into production.

(2) Invention is a response to the institutional framework Things like the patent laws, the tax structure, or the organization of business enterprise stimulate or retard the process of invention. Invention, in this view, is not exogenous to society, but it does not respond primarily to economic variables, and it certainly is exogenous to the individual *firm.*

(3) Invention and innovation are the product of the inherent logic and momentum of science Science has a logic and momentum of its own. There was a time for the discovery of the steam-engine, the aeroplane, hybrid corn, the electron tube and the rocket. Particular men are the instruments, not the causes, of scientific discovery. Had Edison never been born we would still have had, at about the same time, both the light bulb and the gramophone. According to this view, the present is the electronic age, and automation is its industrial application.

(4) Necessity is the mother of invention Ignorance is only skin deep. With enough expenditure of funds, people can do anything – split the atom, conquer cancer, fly to Mars or cultivate the desert. The pace and rate of invention depend upon how many resources are devoted to solving problems, and resources are devoted according to needs. A firm for which a certain factor is becoming scarce will discover ways to economize on it, or will develop a more plentiful substitute for it. (For example, the scarcity of high-grade iron ore led to the development of ways of using low-grade ores.) In this view, automation is a response to expensive labour. The impetus for invention may thus come from within the firm. But it may also come from without: governments may set priorities and do the research that leads to major discoveries and innovations. Atomic energy, for example, is the result of the United Kingdom's, and later the United States', desire to develop superweapons during the Second World War.

(5) Profits are the spur The profit motive not only leads individuals and firms to seize the best methods known, but to develop new ways to meet both old and new needs and wants.

Which of these hypotheses are correct? Possibly all of them are. They are not self-contradictory and the evidence for one cannot be regarded as disproving the others. The fact that some firms spend millions of pounds on research and development to overcome specific problems or invent new products does not change the fact that many discoveries are made in university laboratories by men who have little knowledge of, or interest in, current prices and scarcities. The fact that many patentable discoveries are given to the world does not prove that others are not motivated by the prospect of huge personal gain. And so on.

We have asked whether the direction of invention responds to economic incentives. We are also critically interested in the pure volume of invention. Even if its direction does not exactly respond to current market signals, it is still a potent source of increases in living standards. Inventions that reduce the quantities of all inputs required to gain a given output are absolutely efficient and will raise living standards even if they save just as much on plentiful as on scarce factors of production.

Invention and economic incentives

Does it matter how invention is determined? Consider a single example to illustrate why it does.

Hypothesis 1: This hypothesis accepts the third view of invention listed above. This is the age of electronics and automation, and scientists just go on inventing methods that replace unskilled labour with capital, thereby creating unemployment among the unskilled. The normal corrective of the price system is for the relative price of unskilled labour to fall, thus inducing a substitution in favour of unskilled labour until the unemployment is eliminated. But, according to this hypothesis, scientists are uninfluenced by the incentives of relative factor prices. Now assume that each new technique invented is *absolutely* more efficient than its predecessors in the sense that it uses less of *all* factors than its predecessors – but at the same time it uses less unskilled labour *relative* to other inputs. Firms will now be motivated to adopt the absolutely more efficient new techniques, but in so doing they will adopt a factor combination that increases the unemployment amongst the unskilled.

Hypothesis 2: This hypothesis accepts the fifth view of invention given above. When unemployment amongst the unskilled drives down their relative wage, firms will be led to select from amongst existing techniques those that are more intensive in the use of unskilled labour. If there is still unemployment amongst the unskilled, their factor services will remain cheap and there will be a profit incentive to develop *new* techniques that substitute cheap unskilled labour for the more expensive factors of production.

Thus, in hypothesis 1, the long-term effects of invention and innovation are to increase the problem of 'structural unemployment' of the unskilled, while in hypothesis 2 the effect of the same inventive activity is to reduce this unemployment. Clearly it matters whether in the long run invention proceeds more or less autonomously or under the influence of such economic incentives as relative factor prices.

Summary of the basic theory of costs

This concludes our study of the theory of costs. A number of the subjects covered, although important, are digressions from the point of view of developing a theory of the behaviour of the firm. We shall now summarize the basic points that you should know before proceeding to the next few chapters on the theory of supply. Anyone who is not clear about the following points should review his or her understanding of them by re-reading the relevant parts of the preceding two chapters.

(1) We hypothesize that firms strive to maximize their profits, and, since profits are the difference between the costs and revenues of the firm, it is necessary to consider what we mean by costs and how these vary as output varies.

(2) The cost to the firm of any input that it uses is given by what the firm must give up to have the use of the input.

(3) In the case of any factor service that the firm hires from outside, the cost to the firm is adequately measured by the price paid, since that sum of money cannot be used for other purposes.

(4) In the case of factors owned by the firm, the cost is measured by what the factor could be leased out (or sold) for on the open market. This cost may bear little relation to the cost originally paid to purchase these factors.

(5) Points (2)–(4) summarize an opportunity-cost principle of input valuation: the cost of using an input is the cost of the alternatives that are forgone by so doing.

(6) So far we have seen how to value inputs. To see how costs vary as production varies we need to see how inputs vary as production varies. This relation is described by the production function. When we have costed the inputs we can derive a cost function showing how costs vary as production varies.

(7) In the short run, some factors are fixed and some are variable. The variations in output that accompany variations in the input are described by the hypothesis of diminishing returns. Given the price of the variable factor, we can move directly from returns curves to cost curves. The short-run marginal and average cost curves are assumed to be U-shaped with the *MC* curve cutting the *AC* curve at its lowest point.

(8) In the long run, all factors are variable and the long-run average cost curve shows the lowest attainable average cost for each level of output, on the assumption that the proportion in which inputs are used is so adjusted as to make costs as low as possible

(9) Each short-run cost curve touches the long-run cost curve at one point and elsewhere lies above it.

(10) The principle of substitution says that the long-run effect of a change in factor prices is to cause a substitution of the relatively less expensive factors for the relatively more expensive ones. Thus a change in price induces an economizing of factors whose prices rise and a more lavish use of factors whose prices fall.

(11) In the very long run, technological knowledge changes, and the question of how costs change as output changes depends on the question of how changes in technological knowledge respond to changes in economic incentives.

18

The equilibrium of a profit-maximizing firm

In Chapter 16 we hypothesized that firms seek to maximize their profits, which are the difference between the total revenue derived from selling their product and the total cost of making it. In Chapter 17 we developed a theory of *the variation of cost with output*. This theory is meant to apply to all firms. In the present chapter we shall develop the rules for profit-maximizing behaviour as they apply to all firms. When we come to apply these rules, however, we find that we cannot develop a single theory of *the variation of revenue with output* that is applicable to all firms. In subsequent chapters we shall develop separate theories of revenue for firms in different market situations. In the meantime, we shall confine ourselves to what can be said for all firms.

Various revenue concepts

The revenues of a firm are the receipts that it obtains from selling its products. We can look at these revenues as totals, averages or marginal quantities, exactly as we looked at costs in the previous chapter.

(1) TOTAL REVENUE (TR) refers to gross revenue, the total amount of money that the firm receives from the sale of its products. This will vary with a firm's sales, so we may write:

$$TR = \mathrm{R}(q),$$

where TR is total revenue and, as in the last chapter, q is total production over some period of time.[1] Total revenue is obviously equal to the quantity sold multiplied by the selling price of the commodity, i.e.,

$$TR = pq,$$

where p is the price per unit. The unqualified term *revenue* is often used to refer to total revenue and whenever we speak of revenue or use the symbol R we shall mean total revenue.

[1] Since we are not concerned with the holding of stocks of commodities, we can equate production with sales.

(2) AVERAGE REVENUE (AR) is total revenue divided by the number of units sold (pq/q). Quite obviously, average revenue is the price of the commodity:

$$AR = p.$$

It follows from this that the curve which relates average revenue to output is the same thing as the demand curve that relates price to output.

(3) MARGINAL REVENUE (MR) is the change in total revenue resulting from an increase of one unit in the rate of sales per period of time (say per annum). The marginal revenue resulting from the sale of the nth unit of a commodity is thus the total revenue resulting from the sale of n units per annum minus the total revenue that would have been earned if only $n-1$ (i.e., one less) units had been sold per annum. Do not think that $n-1$ units are sold at some time and an extra unit at some later time. Marginal revenue refers to alternative sales policies *at the same period of time*. Thus, to find the marginal revenue of the 100th unit we compare the total revenue resulting when 100 units are sold over some period of time, with the total revenue that would have resulted if 99 units had been sold over the same period of time. In general we may write[1]:

$$MR_n = TR_n - TR_{n-1}.$$

Behavioural rules for profit maximizing

We now translate the assumption of profit maximization into several formal rules for a firm's behaviour. We do not suppose that the firm consciously follows these rules, but as long as it succeeds somehow in maximizing its profits the rules will allow us to predict its behaviour.

A rule to decide whether or not to produce

A firm always has the option of producing nothing. If it produces nothing, it will have an operating loss equal to its fixed costs. Unless production adds at least as much to revenue as it adds to costs, production will increase the loss suffered by the firm.

> **Rule 1. A firm should produce only if total revenue is equal to or greater than total variable cost.**

Another way of stating this rule is that the firm should produce output only if average revenue (price) is equal to or greater than average variable cost.

A rule to ensure that profits are either at a maximum or at a minimum[2]

If the firm is going to produce at all according to Rule 1, it will have to decide how

---

[1] This definition invokes finite changes. Students familiar with the calculus will recognize marginal revenue as the *derivative* of total revenue with respect to quantity sold: $MR = dTR/dq$. See section 10 of the Appendix to Chapter 2 for important additional discussion of the marginal concept.

[2] Advanced students will realize that the possibility of a stationary point of inflexion in the profit function is ignored in this treatment.

much it should produce. If, on the one hand, the firm finds that at its present level of production the cost of making another unit (marginal cost) is less than the revenue that would be gained by selling that unit (marginal revenue), total profit could clearly be increased by producing another unit of output. Thus whenever a firm finds that at the current level of output marginal revenue exceeds marginal cost, it can increase its profit by producing more. If, on the other hand, the firm finds that at the present level of production the cost of making the last unit exceeds the revenue gained by selling it, total profit could clearly be increased by not producing the last unit. Thus, whenever the firm finds that marginal cost exceeds marginal revenue it can increase its total profit by reducing its output.

Now we have the result that the firm should change its output whenever marginal cost does not equal marginal revenue, raising output if $MR > MC$ and lowering output if $MC > MR$. Rule 2 follows from this.

Rule 2. If a firm is to be in a position where it does not pay it to alter its output – i.e., in a profit-maximizing position – it is necessary that marginal revenue equal marginal cost.

At the profit-maximizing output the last unit produced should add just as much to revenue as it adds to cost.

A rule to ensure that profits are maximized rather than minimized

It is possible to fulfil Rule 2 and have profits at a minimum rather than a maximum. Figure 18.1 illustrates. The firm has a short-run marginal cost curve similar to the ones derived in Chapter 17 and it is assumed to be able to sell all its output at the going market price, so that the market price is the firm's marginal revenue. (If all units can be sold at the prevailing market price then each unit adds that price to the firm's total revenue.)

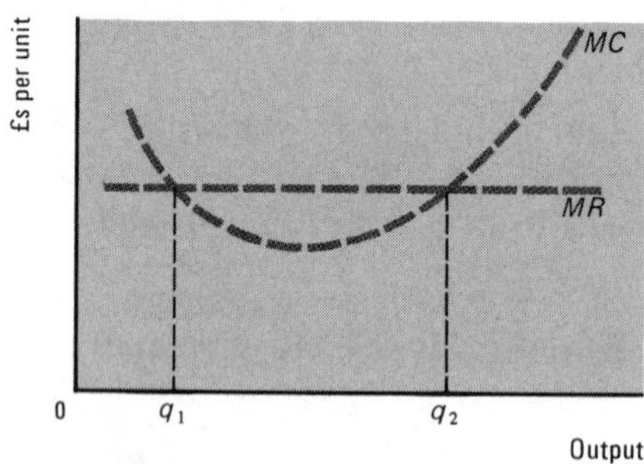

Fig. 18.1 Marginal cost = marginal revenue is a necessary but not a sufficient condition for a profit maximum

In the figure there are two outputs, q_1 and q_2, where marginal cost equals marginal revenue. Output q_1, however, is a minimum-profit position because a change of output in either direction would increase profit: for outputs below q_1 marginal cost exceeds marginal revenue and profits can be increased by *reducing* output, while for outputs above q_1 marginal revenue exceeds marginal cost and profits can be increased by *increasing* output.

Output q_2, however, is a maximum-profit position since at outputs just below it marginal revenue exceeds marginal cost and profit can be increased by *increasing* output towards q_2, while at outputs just above it marginal cost exceeds marginal revenue and profit can be increased by *reducing* output towards q_2.

Rule 3 is needed to distinguish minimum-profit positions such as q_1 from maximum-profit positions such as q_2.

> **Rule 3. For an output where marginal cost equals marginal revenue to be profit-maximizing rather than profit-minimizing, it is sufficient that marginal cost be less than marginal revenue at slightly lower outputs and that marginal cost exceed marginal revenue at slightly higher outputs.**

The geometric statement of this condition is that, at the profit-maximizing output, the marginal cost curve should intersect the marginal revenue curve from below. This ensures that $MC < MR$ to the left of, and $MC > MR$ to the right of, the profit-maximizing output.[1]

The profit-maximizing output

The above three rules determine the output that will be chosen by any firm that maximizes its profits: (i) if the output is positive, total revenue is equal to or exceeds total variable cost; (ii) marginal cost equals marginal revenue; and (iii) if output were reduced slightly, marginal cost would be less than marginal revenue, while if output were increased slightly, marginal cost would exceed marginal revenue.

When the firm has chosen the output that maximizes its profits, we say that the firm is in equilibrium. In this position there are no forces acting on the firm to cause it to change its output. Output will thus remain constant unless either the revenues or the costs associated with various levels of output change.

The meaning and significance of profits

We have talked of the firm maximizing its profit, which is the difference between its revenue and its cost, but the special meaning that we have given to the concept of cost also implies a special meaning for the concept of profit. (This was first discussed on pp. 208–9). Positive profit means an excess of revenues derived from the sale of output over the full opportunity costs of all the factors used to produce the output; negative profit, more commonly called losses, means that revenues fall short of opportunity cost.

This use of the words *profit* and *loss* gives specialized definitions to words that are in everyday use. They are, therefore, a potential source of confusion.

Other definitions of profits

The businessman defines profits as the excess of revenues over the costs with which his accountant provides him. The major differences are that, since the accountant does not include charges for risk-taking and use of the owner's own capital as costs, these items are recorded by the businessman as part of his profits. When the businessman says he *needs* profits of such and such an amount in order to stay in business, he is making sense within his definition, for his 'profits' must be large

[1] Those students who are familiar with elementary calculus can follow the formal derivations of these three rules given in the Appendix to this chapter.

enough to pay for those factors of production that he uses but does not account for as costs.

The economist would express the same notion by saying that the businessman needs to cover *all* of his costs, including those not included by accounting conventions. If the firm is covering all its costs (in the sense that we have defined costs), then it follows that it could not do better by using its resources in any other line of activity than the one currently being followed. Indeed, it would probably do worse in most other lines of activity; it certainly would do no better. Thus a situation in which revenues equal costs (profits of zero) is a satisfactory one – because all factors, hidden as well as visible, are being rewarded at least as well as in their *best* alternative uses[1].

The income-tax authorities have yet another definition of profits, which is implicit in the thousands of rules about what may be (and what may not be) included as a deduction from revenue in arriving at taxable income. In some cases, the taxing authorities allow more for cost than the accountant recommends; in other cases they allow less.

It is important to be clear about different meanings of the term *profits* not only to avoid fruitless semantic arguments but also because a theory that predicts that certain behaviour is a function of profits defined in one way will not necessarily predict behaviour accurately given some other definition. For example, if the economist predicts that new firms will enter an industry whenever there are profits, his prediction will frequently be wrong if he is working from the businessman's definition of profits. The economist's definition of profits is for many purposes the most useful, but if we wish to apply it to business behaviour or to tax policy, we must be prepared to make the appropriate adjustments. Also if we wish to use accounting or tax data to test particular economic theories, we must be prepared to rectify the data.

Profits and resource allocation

When resources are valued by the opportunity-cost principle, we have seen that the amounts assigned show how much these resources might earn if used in their best alternative uses. If there is some industry in which revenues typically exceed opportunity costs, the firms in that industry will be earning profits. This will mean that profit-maximizing firms will want to move resources into this industry, because the earnings potentially available there are greater than in alternative uses of the resources. If, in some other industry, firms are incurring losses, some or all of this industry's resources are more highly valued in other uses, and profit-maximizing firms will want to reallocate some of the resources at their command.

---

[1] In some economics texts of an earlier generation the pure return to capital and the risk premium are not called costs. These returns are included in profits, and profits are divided between normal profits and super-normal profits. Normal profits are what must be earned to induce a firm to remain in an industry and they are thus the same thing as the returns to capital and risk-taking. Super-normal profits are anything in excess of normal profits and are thus the same thing as our profits. The difference is purely semantic. To say that an industry is in equilibrium when its firms are just earning normal profits, where such profits include returns to capital and risk-taking, is the same thing as saying that an industry is in equilibrium when its firms are earning neither profits nor losses when costs include returns to capital and risk-taking.

Profits in some activity are the signal that resources can profitably be moved into that activity. Losses are the signal that they can profitably be moved elsewhere. Profits and losses thus play a crucial role in the workings of a free-market system. Only if they are zero (revenues equal to opportunity costs) is there no incentive for resources to move into or out of an industry.

The next step

When we derived total average and marginal revenue we assumed that revenue was a function of (i.e., varied with) the firm's output. The firm was then in equilibrium when it chose the profit-maximizing output – the output for which marginal revenue equals marginal cost. In Chapter 17 we saw how cost varied with output. In subsequent chapters we shall study how revenue varies with output for firms in various situations. The key to the behaviour of revenue is the competitive situation in which the firm finds itself.

Appendix to chapter 18

A mathematical derivation of the rules of profit maximization

In this brief appendix we provide formal derivations of the three rules for profit maximization. The first derivation uses only algebra and can be read by anyone. The second and third use elementary calculus and should not be attempted by those who are unfamiliar with simple derivatives.

Condition 1: Profits, π, are defined as follows:

$$\pi = R-(F+V),$$

where R is total revenue, F is total fixed cost and V is total variable cost. Now let subscript n stand for a state where there is no production and p for one where there is production. It pays the firm to produce if there is at least one level of production for which

$$\pi_p \geq \pi_n.$$

When the firm does not produce, R and V are zero, so the above condition becomes

$$R-F-V \geq -F$$

or

$$R \geq V.$$

Dividing both sides by output, Q, we get: price $\geq AVC$.

Condition 2:

$$\pi = R-C,$$

where C is total cost $(R+V)$.

Both revenues and costs vary with output, i.e., $R = \mathrm{R}(Q)$ and $C = \mathrm{C}(Q)$. Thus we may write

$$\pi = \mathrm{R}(Q)-\mathrm{C}(Q).$$

A necessary condition for the maximization of profits is[1]

$$\frac{d\pi}{dQ} = \mathrm{R}'(Q)-\mathrm{C}'(Q) = 0$$

or

$$\mathrm{R}'(Q) = \mathrm{C}'(Q).$$

But these derivatives define marginal revenue and marginal cost, so we have

$$MR = MC.$$

Condition 3: To ensure that we have a maximum and not a minimum for profits, we require

$$\frac{d^2\pi}{dQ^2} = \mathrm{R}''(Q)-\mathrm{C}''(Q) = \frac{dMR}{dQ}-\frac{dMC}{dQ} < 0$$

or

$$\frac{dMR}{dQ} < \frac{dMC}{dQ},$$

which means that the algebraic value of the slope of the marginal cost curve must exceed, at the point of intersection, the algebraic value of the slope of the marginal revenue curve. This translates into the geometric statement that the marginal cost curve should cut the marginal revenue curve from below.

[1] Note the convenient use of a prime for a derivative. Thus for the function $\mathrm{F}(X)$, the two notations d/dX and $\mathrm{F}'(X)$ mean the same thing and d^2/dX^2 and $\mathrm{F}''(X)$ mean the same thing.

19

The theory of perfect competition

Is Saxone in competition with Dolcis? Does Selfridge's compete with Marks & Spencer's? Is a Yorkshire farmer in competition with a Somerset farmer? In the ordinary sense of competition the answer to the first two of these questions are plainly yes, and the answer to the third question is probably no. Saxone and Dolcis both advertise extensively to persuade the same group of buyers to buy *their* products. Everyone knows that many shoppers check the respective prices and qualities offered by two nearby department stores such as Selfridge's and Marks & Spencer's. But there is nothing that the Yorkshire farmer can do that will affect the sales or the profits of the Somerset farmer. Indeed, they are unlikely even to know each other and will probably never meet.

Firm behaviour and market structure

To sort out the questions of who is competing with whom and in what sense they compete, it is necessary to distinguish between the behaviour of individual firms and the type of market in which the firms operate. Economists use the term *market structure* to refer to the latter concept. The concept of competitive behaviour is quite distinct from the concept of competitive market structure. The degree of *competitive* behaviour refers to the degree to which individual firms indulge in active competition with one another. The degree of *competitiveness of the market structure* refers to the degree to which individual firms have power over that market – power to influence the price or other terms on which their product is sold. In everyday use the term 'competition' usually refers only to competitive behaviour. Economists, however, are interested both in the behaviour of individual firms and in market structures.

Saxone and Dolcis certainly engage in competitive (i.e., rivalrous) behaviour. It is also true that both individually and together they have some power over the market. Either firm could raise its prices and still continue to sell its product, each has the power to decide – within limits set by buyers' tastes and the prices of competing products – what price consumers will pay for its own product.

The Yorkshire and the Somerset farmers do not engage in active competitive behaviour with each other. They operate, however, in a market over which they have no power. Neither one has significant power to change the market price for its product by altering its own behaviour.

To get to one extreme of competitive market structures, economists use a model in which no one firm has any market power. There are so many firms that each must accept the price set by the forces of market demand and supply. In this theory of the perfectly competitive market structure there is no need for individual firms to behave competitively with respect to one another since none has any power over the market and one firm's ability to sell its product is uninfluenced by the behaviour of any other single firm. The apparent paradox that inter-firm competition does not occur in perfectly competitive markets is resolved when we recognize the distinction between inter-firm competitive behaviour and the competitive *structure* of the market in which the firm operates.

The theory of the perfectly competitive market structure applies directly to a number of real-world markets, particularly agricultural goods and industrial raw materials. It also provides a benchmark for comparison with other market structures in which there are few enough firms that each one has some significant market power.

From the point of view of a household, the MARKET consists of those firms from which it can buy a well-defined product; from the point of view of a firm, the market consists of those buyers to whom it can sell a well-defined product. A group of firms that sells a well-defined product, or a closely related set of products, is said to constitute an INDUSTRY. The market demand curve is the demand curve for an industry's product.

Consider a firm that produces a specific product for sale in a particular market and competes for customers with other firms in the same industry. If a profit-maximizing firm knows precisely the demand curve it faces, it knows the price it could charge for each rate of sales, and thus it knows its potential revenues. If it also knows its costs, it can readily discover the profits that would be associated with any rate of output, and it can choose the rate that maximizes its profits. But what if the firm knows its costs and only the *market* demand curve for its product? It does not know what its own sales would be. In other words, it does not know its *own* demand curve. In order to determine what fraction of the total market demand will be met by sellers other than itself, it needs to know how other firms will respond if it changes its price. If it reduces its price by 10 per cent, will other sellers leave their prices unchanged or will they also reduce them? If they reduce their prices, will they do so by less than 10 per cent, by exactly 10 per cent, or by more than 10 per cent? Obviously, each of the possible outcomes will have a different effect on the firm's sales and thus on its revenues and profits.

The answers to questions about the relation of a firm's demand curve to the market demand curve depend on such things as the number of sellers in the market and the similarity of their products. These are aspects of MARKET STRUCTURE, which is defined as the characteristics of market organization that are likely to affect a firm's behaviour and performance.

For example, if there are only two large firms in an industry, each may be expected to meet most of the other's price cuts but if there are 500 small firms, a price cut by one may go unmatched. For another example, if two firms are producing identical products, they may be expected to behave differently with respect to each other than if they are producing similar but not identical products. These two aspects of market structure (number of sellers and similarity of product) suggest the central hypothesis of the branch of economics called industrial organization: firm behaviour will be affected by market structure.

There are many other aspects of market structure that may affect firm behaviour. These include the ease of entering the industry, the nature and size of the purchasers of the firm's products, and the firm's ability to influence demand by advertising. To reduce these aspects to manageable proportions, economists have focused on a few theoretical market structures that are thought to represent a high proportion of the cases actually encountered in market societies. In this chapter and the next two, we shall look at four of these; perfect competition, monopoly, monopolistic competition, and oligopoly.

In this chapter we shall study the theory of perfect competition. First we introduce the critical assumptions, then we derive the firm's demand curve and examine the equilibrium, and finally we examine the equilibrium of the competitive *industry* in both the short run and the long run.

The assumptions of perfect competition

The theory of PERFECT COMPETITION is built on two critical assumptions, one about the behaviour of the individual firm and one about the nature of the industry in which it operates.

The *firm* is assumed to be a PRICE TAKER. This means that the firm is assumed to act as if it can alter its rate of production and sales within any feasible range without its actions having any significant effect on the price of the product it sells. Thus the firm must passively accept whatever price happens to be ruling on the market.

The *industry* is characterized by FREEDOM OF ENTRY AND EXIT. This means that any new firm is free to set up production if it so wishes and that any existing firm is free to cease production and leave the industry if it so wishes. Existing firms cannot bar the entry of new firms and there are no legal prohibitions on entry or exit.

The ultimate test of the theory based on these assumptions will be the usefulness of its predictions, but because students are often bothered by the first assumption, it is worth examining whether it is in any way reasonable. To see what is involved in the assumption of price taking, contrast the demands for the products of a car manufacturer and a wheat farmer.

A car manufacturer

British Leyland is aware of the fact that it has some market power. If it substantially increases its prices, sales will fall off; if it lowers prices substantially, it will be able to sell more of its products. If Leyland contemplates a large increase in production that is not a response to some known or anticipated rise in demand, it knows that it will have to reduce prices in order to sell the extra output. The car manufacturing firm is *not* a price taker. The quantity that it is able to sell will depend on the price it charges, but it does not have to accept passively whatever price is set by the market. In other words, the firm manufacturing cars is faced with a downward-sloping demand curve for its product. It may select any price-quantity combination consistent with that demand curve.

A wheat farmer

In contrast, an individual firm producing wheat will be one of a very large number of firms all growing the same product; one firm's contribution to the total production of wheat will be a very small drop in an extremely large bucket. Ordinarily the firm will assume that it has no effect on price and will think of its own demand curve as being horizontal. Of course the firm can have *some* effect on price, but a straightforward calculation will demonstrate that the effect is small enough that the firm can justifiably neglect it.

The market elasticity of demand for wheat is approximately 0·25. This means that if the quantity of wheat supplied in the world increased by 1 per cent, the price would have to fall by 4 per cent to induce the world's wheat buyers to purchase the whole crop. Even a very large farmer produces a very small fraction of the total crop. In a recent year an extremely large Canadian wheat farm produced about 50,000 tons, only about 1/4,000 of the world production of 200 million tons. Suppose that a large wheat farm increased its production by 20,000 tons, say from 40,000 to 60,000 tons, a very large percentage increase in its own production but an increase of only 1/100 of 1 per cent in world production. Table 19.1 shows that this increase would lead to a

Table 19.1 The calculation of a firm's elasticity of demand (η_E) from market elasticity of demand (η_M)

Given $\eta_M = 0{\cdot}25$

World output = 200 million tons

Firm's output increases from 40,000 to 60,000 tons, a 40% increase over the average quantity of 50,000 tons

Step 1. Find the percentage change in world price

$$\eta_M = -\frac{\text{percentage change in world output}}{\text{percentage change in world price}}$$

$$\text{Percentage change in world price} = -\frac{\text{percentage change in world output}}{\eta_M} = -\frac{1/100 \text{ of } 1\%}{0{\cdot}25} = -4/100 \text{ of } 1\%$$

Step 2. Compute the firm's elasticity of demand:

$$\eta_F = -\frac{\text{percentage change in firm's output}}{\text{percentage change in world price}} = -\frac{+40\%}{-4/100 \text{ of } 1\%} = +1000$$

decrease in the world price of 4/100 of 1 per cent (4p in £100) and give the firm an elasticity of demand of 1,000! This is a very high elasticity of demand; the farm would have to increase its output 1,000 per cent to bring about a 1 per cent decrease in the price of wheat. Because the farm's output cannot be varied this much, it is not surprising that the firm regards the price of wheat as being unaffected by any changes in output that it could conceivably make.[1]

It is only a slight simplification of reality to say that the firm is unable to influence the world price of wheat and that it is able to sell all that it can produce at the going world price. In other words, the firm is faced with a perfectly elastic demand curve for its product – it is a price taker.

[1] This table relies on the concept of elasticity of demand developed on page 105. Step 1 shows that a 40 per cent increase in the firm's output leads to only a tiny decrease in the world's price. Thus, as step 2 shows, the firm's elasticity of demand is very high: 1,000. The arithmetic is not important, but understanding why the firm will be a price taker in these circumstances is vital.

The difference between firms producing wheat and firms producing cars is one of degree of market power. The wheat firm, as an insignificant part of the whole market, has no power to influence the world price of wheat. But the car firm does have power to influence the price of cars because its own production represents a significant part of the total supply of cars.

Demand and revenue curves for the perfectly competitive firm

In perfect competition the individual firm faces a perfectly elastic demand curve for its product. Since the market price is unaffected by variations in the firm's output, it follows that the marginal revenue resulting from an increase in the volume of sales by one unit is constant and is equal to the price of the product. If, for example, a farmer faces a perfectly elastic demand for wheat at a market price of £2 a bushel, it follows that each additional unit sold will bring in that amount, i.e., the marginal revenue is £2, and the average revenue (equals total revenue/number of units sold) is also £2. The demand curve facing the firm is thus identical with both the average and the marginal revenue curve. All three of these curves coincide in the same straight line, showing that $p = AR = MR$; all remain constant as output varies. Total revenue does, of course, vary with output; since price is constant, it follows that total revenue rises steadily as output rises.

Calculations of these revenue concepts for a price-taking firm are illustrated in Table 19.2. The table shows that as long as the firm's output does not affect the price

Table 19.2 Revenue concepts for a price-taking firm*

Quantity sold (units) q	Price p	$TR = p \cdot q$	$AR = TR/q$	$MR = \Delta TR/\Delta q$
10	£3.00	£30.00	£3.00	
				£3.00
11	£3.00	33.00	3.00	
				3.00
12	3.00	36.00	3.00	
				3.00
13	3.00	39.00	3.00	

* Marginal revenue is shown between the lines because it represents the change in total revenue (e.g., from £33 to £36) in response to a change in quantity (from 11 to 12 units),

$$MR = \frac{36-33}{12-11} = £3 \text{ per unit.}$$

of the product it sells, both average and marginal revenue will be equal to price at all levels of output. Thus, graphically (as shown in Figure 19.1), average revenue and marginal revenue are both horizontal lines at the level of market price. Since the firm can sell any quantity it wishes at this price, the same horizontal line is also the *firm's* demand curve.

> **If the market price is unaffected by variations in the firm's output, the firm's demand curve, the average revenue curve and the marginal revenue curve coincide in the same horizontal line.**

Total revenue, of course, does vary with output. Since price is constant, it follows that total revenue rises in direct proportion to output.

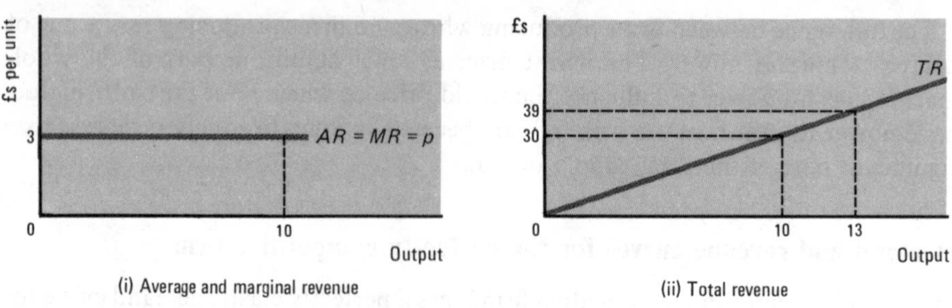

Fig. 19.1 Revenue curves for a price-taking firm (numerical values correspond to those shown in Table 19.2, but the shapes of the curves are general to all firms in perfect competition)

Short-run equilibrium: firm and industry

Equilibrium output of a firm in perfect competition

The firm in perfect competition (being a price taker) can adjust to differing market conditions only by changing the quantity it produces. In the short run it has fixed factors, and the only way it can vary its output is by using more or less of those factors that it can vary. Thus the firm's short-run cost curves are relevant to its output decisions.

We saw earlier that any profit-maximizing firm will seek to produce at a level of output where marginal cost equals marginal revenue. We saw in the immediately preceding section that a perfectly competitive firm's demand and marginal revenue curves coincide in the same horizontal line whose height represents the price of the product. Thus price equals marginal revenue, and it follows immediately that a perfectly competitive firm will equate its marginal cost of production to the market price of its product (as long as price exceeds average variable cost).

The market determines the price at which the firm can sell its product. The firm then picks the quantity of output that maximizes its profits. This is the output for which $p = MC$. When the firm is maximizing profits, it has no incentive to change its output. Therefore, unless prices or costs change, the firm will continue producing this output because it is doing as well as it can do, given the situation it faces. The firm is thus said to be in SHORT-RUN EQUILIBRIUM. The short-run equilibrium of a firm in perfect competition is illustrated in Figure 19.2. When $p = MC$, as at q_E, the

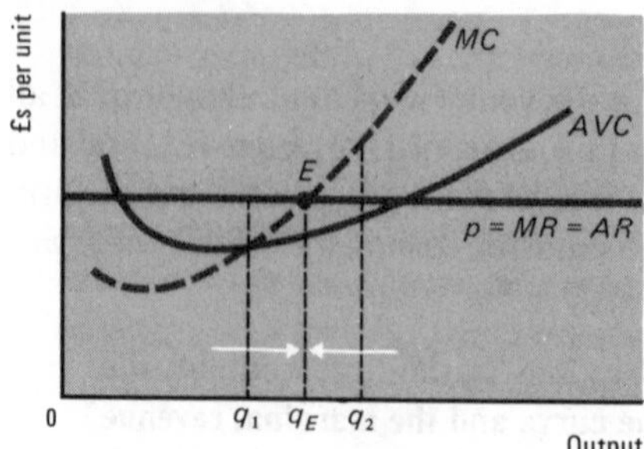

Fig. 19.2 The equilibrium of a competitive firm

firm would decrease its profits if it either increased or decreased its output. At any point left of q_E, say q_1, price is greater than the marginal cost, and it pays to increase output. At any point to the right of q_E, say q_2, price is less than the marginal cost, and it pays to reduce output. The equilibrium output for the firm is q_E.

> **The competitive firm is a mere quantity adjuster. It pursues its goal of profit maximization by increasing or decreasing quantity until it equates its short-run marginal cost with the prevailing price of its product – a price that is given to it by the market.**

The market price to which the perfectly competitive firm responds is itself set by the forces of demand and supply. The individual firm, by adjusting its quantity produced to whatever price is ruling on the market, helps to determine market supply. The link between the behaviour of the firm and the behaviour of the competitive market is provided by the market supply curve.

Short-run supply curves

The supply curve shows the relation between quantity supplied and price. For any given price we need to ask what quantity will be supplied. This question may be answered by supposing that a price is specified and then determining how much each firm will choose to supply. Next a different price is supposed and quantity supplied is again determined – and so on, until all possible prices have been considered.

The supply curve of one firm

Figure 19.3 (i) shows a firm's marginal cost curve with four alternative demand curves. The firm's marginal cost curve gives the marginal cost corresponding to each

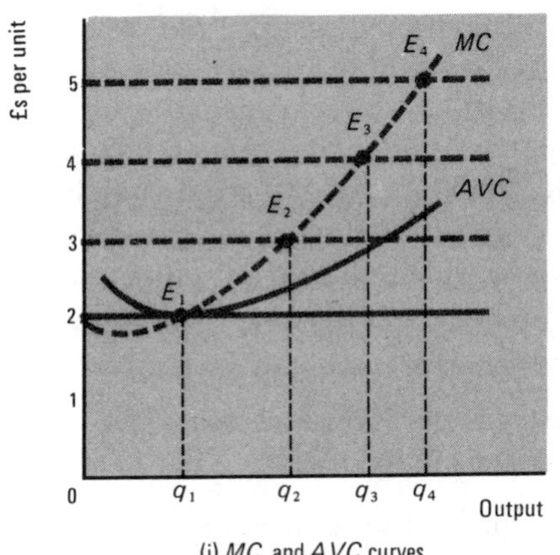

(i) *MC* and *AVC* curves

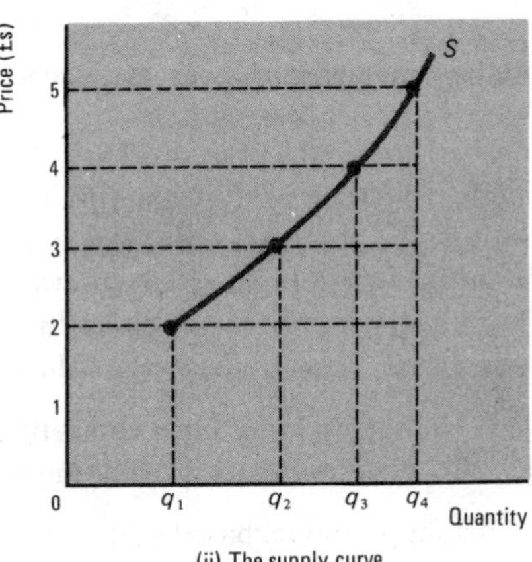

(ii) The supply curve

Fig. 19.3 Deriving the supply curve for a price-taking firm

level of output. From this we wish to derive a supply curve that gives the quantity the firm will supply at every price. For prices below *AVC*, the firm will supply zero units (Rule 1 in Chapter 18). For prices above *AVC*, the firm will equate price and marginal cost (Rule 2, modified by the proposition that $MR = p$ in perfect competition). As price rises in the figure from 2 to 3 to 4 to 5, the firm wishes to increase its production from q_1 to q_2 to q_3 to q_4. For prices below £2, output would be zero because the firm is better off if it shuts down. The point E_1, where price equals

AVC, is called the shutdown point. The firm's supply curve is shown in (ii).
From this it follows that:

In perfect competition the segment of the firm's marginal cost curve that is above the AVC curve has the same shape as the firm's supply curve.

This proposition is so obvious that it sometimes causes difficulty to the student who is looking for something difficult and profound. If you are not absolutely certain that you understand the proposition, construct the firm's supply curve for yourself. Given perfect competition, profit maximization, and the cost curves of Figure 19.3 (i), you can discover the output of the firm corresponding to any given market price. You can then plot the firm's supply curve on a graph of your own by relating market price to quantity produced by the firm. Once you have done this, you will see that the supply curve you have constructed is identical in shape to the marginal cost curve above *AVC* (see Figure 19.3).

The supply curve of an industry

Figure 19.4 illustrates the derivation of an industry supply curve for an example of

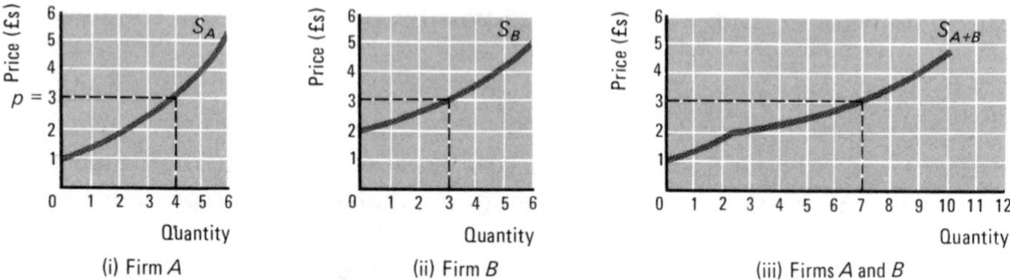

Fig. 19.4 The derivation of an industry supply curve

only two firms. At a price of £3 firm A would supply 4 units and firm B would supply 3 units. Together, as shown in (iii), they would supply 7 units. If there are hundreds of firms, the process is the same: each firm's supply curve (which is derived in the manner shown in Figure 19.3) shows what the firm will produce at any given price *p*. The industry supply curve relates the price *p* to the sum of the quantities produced by all firms. Thus we have the following result:

The supply curve for a competitive industry is the horizontal sum of the marginal cost curves of all the individual firms in the industry.

This supply curve, based as it is on the short-run marginal cost curves of the firms in the industry, is the industry's SHORT-RUN SUPPLY CURVE. In Part 2 we used short-run industry supply curves as part of our theory of price. We have now derived these curves for a competitive industry, and we have seen how they are related to the behaviour of individual, profit-maximizing firms.

The determination of short-run equilibrium price

The short-run supply curve and the demand curve for the industry's product together determine the market price. (This happens in the manner analyzed in Chapter 8.) Although no one firm can influence market price significantly, the collective actions of all firms in the industry (as shown by the industry supply curve) and the collective actions of households (as shown by the industry's demand curve) together determine market price at the point where the demand and supply curves intersect.

At the equilibrium market price each firm is producing and selling a quantity for which its marginal cost equals the market price and no firm is motivated to change its output in the short run. Since total quantity demanded equals total quantity supplied, there is no reason for market price to change in the short run; the market and all the firms in the industry are in short-run equilibrium.

Short-run profitability of the firm

Although we know that when the industry is in short-run equilibrium the competitive firm is maximizing its profits, we do not know *how large* these profits are. It is one thing to know that a firm is doing as well as it can in particular circumstances; it is another thing to know how well it is doing.

Figure 19.5 shows three possible positions for a firm in short-run equilibrium. The diagrams show a firm with given costs faced with three alternative prices p_1, p_2, p_3. In each part of the diagram, E is the point at which $MC = MR =$ price. Since in all three cases price exceeds AVC, the firm is in short-run equilibrium at E. In (i) price is p_1 and the firm suffers losses since price is below average total cost. Since price exceeds average variable cost, it pays the firm to keep producing, but it does *not* pay it to replace its capital equipment as its capital wears out. In (ii) price is p_2 and the firm is just covering its total costs. It does pay the firm to replace its capital as it wears out, since it is covering the full opportunity cost of its capital. In (iii) price is p_3 and the firm is earning profits in excess of all its costs.

In all three cases, the firm is maximizing its profits by producing where $p = MC$, but in (i) the firm is making losses, in (ii) it is just covering all costs, and in (iii) it is making profits in excess of all costs. In (i) it might be better to say that the firm is minimizing its losses rather than maximizing its profits, but both statements mean the same thing. The firm is doing as well as it can do, given its costs and prices.

All three of these are possible short-run equilibrium positions for the profit-maximizing firm in perfect competition. But not all of them are possible equilibrium positions in the long run.

Long-run equilibrium

The long run in outline

The key to long-run equilibrium under perfect competition is entry and exit. We have seen that when firms are in *short-run* equilibrium they may be making profits or losses or they may be just breaking even. Since costs include the opportunity cost of capital, firms that are just breaking even are doing as well as they could if they invested their capital elsewhere. Thus there will be no incentive for existing firms to leave the industry; neither will there be an incentive for new firms to enter the industry, because capital can earn the same return elsewhere in the economy. If, however, existing firms are earning profits over all costs, including the opportunity cost of capital, new capital will enter the industry to share in these profits. If existing firms are making losses, capital will leave the industry because a better return can be obtained elsewhere in the economy. Let us consider the process in a little more detail.

If all firms in the competitive industry are in the position of the firm in Figure 19.5 (iii), new firms will enter the industry, attracted by the profits being earned by

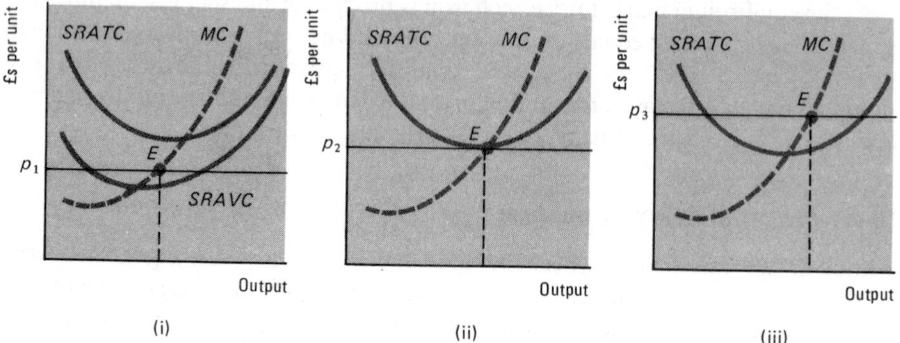

Fig. 19.5 Alternative short-run equilibrium positions of a competitive firm

existing firms. Suppose that in response to high profits for 100 existing firms, 20 new firms enter. The market supply curve that formerly added up the outputs of 100 firms now must add up the outputs of 120 firms. At any price, more will be supplied because there are more suppliers. This shift in the short-run supply curve, with an unchanged market demand curve, means that the previous equilibrium price will no longer prevail. The shift in supply will cause the equilibrium price to fall, and both new and old firms will have to adjust their outputs to this new price. This is illustrated in Figure 19.6. The initial equilibrium is at the intersection of D and S_1. If the supply curve shifts to S_2 by virtue of new entry, the equilibrium price must fall to

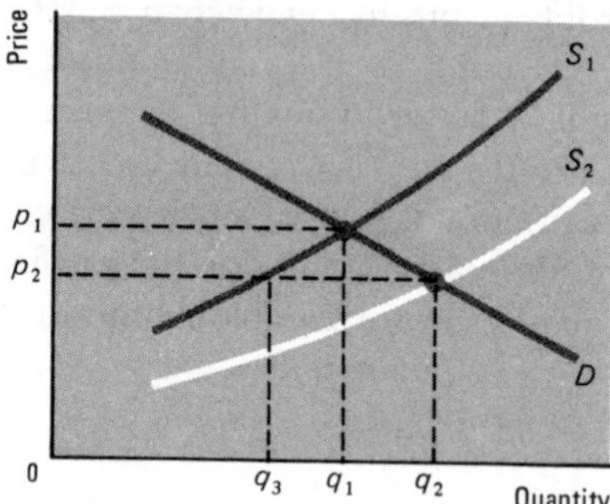

Fig. 19.6 The effect of new entrants on the supply curve

p_2 while output rises to q_2. At this price before entry, only q_3 would have been produced. The extra output is supplied by the new productive capacity.

Entry will proceed and price will continue to fall until all firms in the industry are just covering their total costs. Firms will then be in the position of the firm in Figure 19.5 (ii), which is called a *zero-profit equilibrium.*

> **Profits in a competitive industry are a signal for the entry of new capital; the industry will expand, forcing price down until the profits earned by firms, old and new, fall to zero.**

If the firms in the industry are in the position of the firm in Figure 19.5(i), they are suffering losses. They are covering their variable costs, but the return on their capital is less than the opportunity cost of this capital; the firms are not covering their total costs. This is a signal for exit of capital. As plant and equipment wears out it will not be replaced. As a result, the industry's short-run supply curve shifts left and market price rises. Capital continues to exit and price continues to rise until the remaining firms can cover their total costs – that is, until they are all in the zero-profit equilibrium illustrated in Figure 19.5(ii). Exit then ceases.

Losses in a competitive industry are a signal for the exit of capital; the industry will contract, driving price up until the remaining firms are covering their total costs.

In all of this we see profits fulfilling their function of allocating resources among the industries of the economy. For many purposes this is as far as we need to go with the analysis of the long run.

A more detailed analysis of the long run[1]

For some purposes it is important to understand some complications omitted from the foregoing broad treatment. The rest of this chapter will be devoted to a more detailed examination of the long-run behaviour of a perfectly competitive industry.

Consider the position of the firm and the industry when full long-run equilibrium obtains. There must be no change that the firm could make over the short or the long run that would increase its profits. This requirement can be stated as three distinct conditions.

1. *No firm will want to vary the output of its existing plants: short-run marginal cost (SRMC) must equal price.*

2. *Profits earned by existing plants must be zero.* (If they were positive there would be entry; if they were negative there would be exit; in neither case would the industry be in long-run equilibrium.) This implies that short-run *ATC* must equal price – that is, firms must be in the position of the firms in Figure 19.5(ii).

3. *No firm can earn profits by building a plant of a different size.* This implies that each existing firm must be producing at the lowest point on its long-run average cost curve.

Taken together, these conditions mean that all firms in the industry should be in the position illustrated in Figure 19.7.[2] The firm is seen to be operating at the

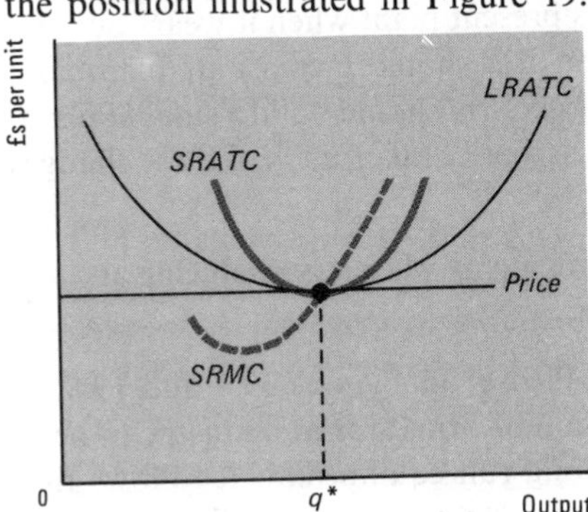

Fig. 19.7 The equilibrium of a firm when the industry is in long-run equilibrium

[1] The remainder of this chapter may be omitted without loss of continuity.

[2] The text discussion implies that all existing firms and all new entrants face identical *LRATC* curves. This merely means that all firms face the same set of factor prices and have the same technology available to them. Do not forget that we are in the long run where technological knowledge is given and constant.

minimum point of its long-run cost curve and thus also at the minimum point on the short-run plant cost curve associated with its present plant.

We have already seen why the first two conditions must hold. Now let us look at the third condition. Figure 19.8 shows two firms that have identical *LRATC* curves,

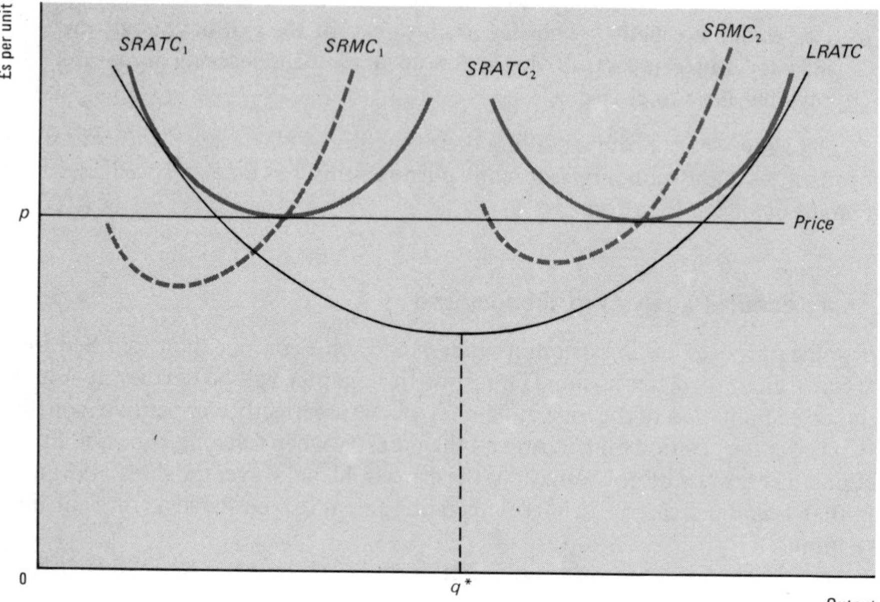

Fig. 19.8 Short-run versus long-run equilibrium of a competitive firm

but one firm has too small a plant, with costs of $SRATC_1$, while the other firm has too large a plant, with costs of $SRATC_2$. Both firms are in short-run equilibrium at price $p = MC = ATC$ but neither is in long-run equilibrium. Firm 1 can increase its profits by building a larger plant (thereby moving downward to the right along its *LRATC* curve). Firm 2 can increase its profits by building a smaller plant (thereby moving downward to the left along its *LRATC* curve). Each of these firms can, therefore, increase its profits by discarding its present plant when it wears out and building a plant of different size. The smaller firm should increase its plant size, thereby lowering its average total costs. The larger firm should build a smaller plant, thereby also lowering its *ATC*. Since each firm is a price taker, each of these changes will increase the firm's profits.

> **A price-taking firm is in long-run equilibrium only when it is producing at the minimum point on its LRATC curve.**

The firm must be producing at the point labelled q^* in Figures 19.7 and 19.8.

An industry is nothing more than a collection of firms; for an industry to be in long-run equilibrium, each firm must be in long-run equilibrium. It follows that when a perfectly competitive industry is in long-run equilibrium, all firms in the industry will be selling at a price equal to minimum *SRATC* – that is, they must be in zero-profit equilibrium, as in Figure 19.5 (ii). It follows that the short-run industry supply curve – which tells us how much all existing firms will supply at each market price – must intersect the market demand curve at that particular price.

The long-run response of a perfectly competitive industry to a change in demand

Now suppose that the demand for the product increases. Price will rise to equate demand with the industry's short-run supply. Each firm will expand output until its short-run marginal cost once again equals price. Each firm will earn profits as a result of the rise in price, and the profits will induce new firms to enter the industry. This will shift the short-run supply curve to the right and force down the price. Entry will continue until all firms are once again just covering average total costs. To recapitulate: the short-run effects of the rise in demand will be a rise in price and output; the long-run effects will be a further rise in output and a fall in price.

Now consider a fall in demand. The industry starts with firms in long-run equilibrium as shown in Figure 19.7 and the market demand curve shifts left and price falls. There are two possible consequences.

First, the decline in demand forces price below *ATC* but leaves it above *AVC*. Firms are then in the position shown in Figure 19.5 (i). They can cover their variable costs and earn some return on their capital, so they remain in production for as long as their existing plant and equipment lasts. But it is not worth replacing capital as it wears out. Exit will occur as old capital wears out and is not replaced. As firms exit, the short-run supply curve shifts left and market price rises. This continues until the remaining firms in the industry can cover their total costs. At this point it will pay to replace capital as it wears out, and the decline in the size of the industry will be brought to a halt. In this case the adjustment may take a very long time, for the industry shrinks in size only as existing plant and equipment wear out.

The second possibility occurs if the decline in demand is so large that price is forced below the level of *AVC*. In this case firms cannot even cover their variable costs and some will shut down immediately. Thus the reduction in capital devoted to production in the industry occurs rapidly because some existing capacity is scrapped or sold for other uses. Once sufficient capital has been withdrawn so that price rises to a level that allows the remaining firms to cover their *AVC*s, the rapid withdrawal of capital will cease. Further exit occurs more slowly, as described above.

> **Entry of new capital into a profitable industry occurs at the speed at which new plants can be built and new equipment installed. Exit of existing capital from an industry with losses may occur very quickly if price is less than average variable cost but only at the rate at which old plant and equipment wear out if price exceeds average variable cost.**[1]

This adjustment process is examined in greater detail in the following section.

The long-run industry supply curve

Possible adjustments of the industry to the kinds of changes in demand just discussed are shown by the LONG-RUN INDUSTRY SUPPLY (LRS) CURVE. This curve shows the relation between equilibrium price and the output firms will be willing to supply after all desired entry or exit has occurred.

[1] If the capital has no alternative use it may not be scrapped; instead it may be 'mothballed' in case of future need. As far as its influence on current production and price is concerned, however, it has withdrawn from the industry.

The long-run supply curve connects positions of long-run equilibrium after all demand-induced changes have occurred.

When induced changes in factor prices are considered, it is possible for *LRS* to rise, fall, or remain constant. The various cases are illustrated in Figures 19.9 to 19.11.

In Figure 19.9 the shift in demand from D_1 to D_2 first raises the price to p_2 as industry output expands along the short-run supply curve. Firms will be earning profits and entry will thus occur. This induces a shift in the short-run supply curve from S_1 to S_2. In the case illustrated the increase in supply is just sufficient to keep the price at p_1. Thus output has been increased along *LRS* at constant cost in the long run.

The long-run supply curve in Figure 19.9 is horizontal. This indicates that the industry will, given time, adjust its size to provide whatever quantity may be demanded at a constant price. Such conditions obtain if factor prices do not change as the output of the whole industry expands or contracts. An industry with a horizontal long-run supply curve is said to be a CONSTANT-COST INDUSTRY. While conditions of constant *LRS* may exist, such conditions are not necessary. Other possibilities are considered below.

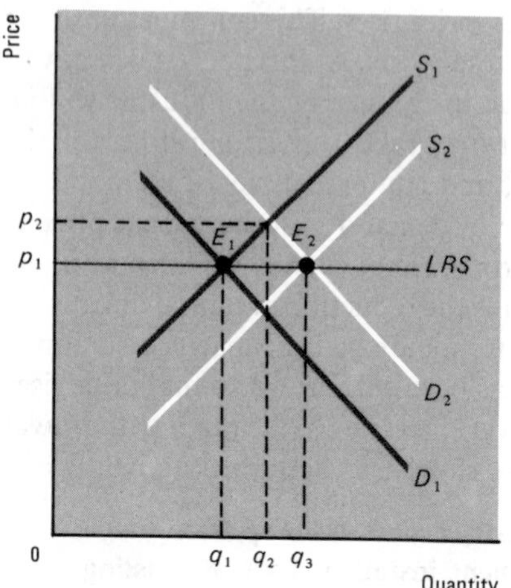

Fig. 19.9 A long-run supply curve under conditions of constant cost

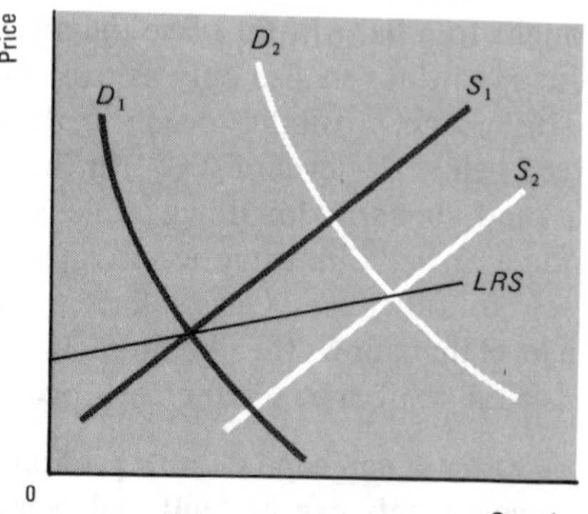

Fig. 19.10 A rising long-run supply curve

Changing factor prices and rising long-run supply curves When an industry expands its output, it needs more inputs. The increase in demand for these inputs may bid up their prices. If costs rise with increasing levels of industry output, so too must the price at which the producers are able to cover their costs. As the industry expands, the short-run supply curve shifts outwards but the firms' *ATC* curves shift upwards because of rising factor prices. The expansion of the industry comes to a halt when price is equal to minimum *LRATC* for existing firms. This must occur at a higher price than ruled before the expansion began, as illustrated in Figure 19.10.

Rising *LRS* – RISING SUPPLY PRICE, as it is sometimes called – is often a characteristic of sharp and rapid growth. A competitive industry with rising long-run supply prices is often called a RISING-COST INDUSTRY.

Can the long-run supply curve decline? So far we have suggested that the long-run supply curve may be constant or rising. Could it ever decline, thereby indicating that higher outputs were associated with lower prices in long-run equilibrium?

It is tempting to answer yes, because of the opportunities of more efficient scales of operation using greater mechanization and more effective specialization of labour. But this answer would not be correct for perfectly competitive industries, because each firm in long-run equilibrium must already be at the lowest point on its *LRATC* curve. If a firm could lower its costs by building a larger, more mechanized plant, it would be profitable to do so without waiting for an increase in demand. Since any single firm can sell all it wishes at the going market price, it will be profitable to expand the scale of its operations as long as its *LRATC* is falling.

There is a reason, however, why the long-run supply curve might slope downward: the expansion of an industry might lead to a fall in the prices of some of its inputs. If this occurs, the firms will find their cost curves shifting downward as they expand their outputs.

As an illustration of how the expansion of one industry could cause the prices of some of its inputs to fall, consider the early stages of the growth of the car industry. As the output of cars increased, the industry's demand for tyres grew greatly. This, as suggested earlier, would have increased the demand for rubber and tended to raise its price, but it also provided the opportunity for tyre manufacturers to build large modern plants and reap the benefits of increasing returns in tyre production. At first these economies were large enough to offset any factor price increases and tyre prices charged to car manufacturers fell. Thus car costs fell, because of lower prices of an important input.

To see the effect of a fall in input prices caused by the expansion of an industry, suppose that the demand for the industry's product increases. Price and profits will rise and new entry will occur as a result. But when expansion of the industry has gone far enough to bring price back to its initial level, cost curves will be lower than they were initially because of the fall in input prices. Firms will thus still be earning profits. A further expansion will then occur until price falls to the level of the minimum points on each firm's new, lower *LRATC* curve.

This case is illustrated in Figure 19.11. From an original equilibrium at E_1, an

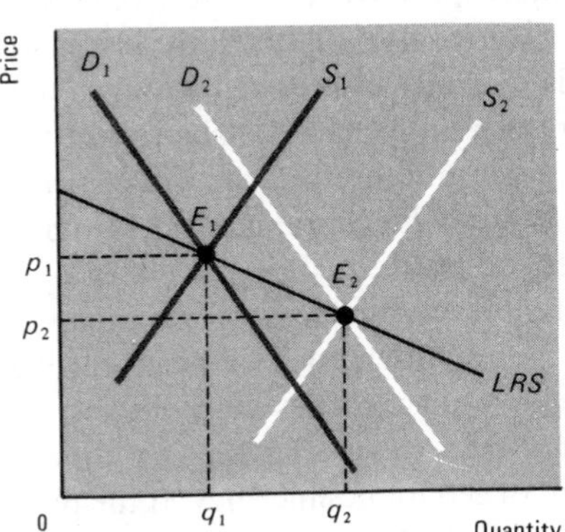

Fig. 19.11 A declining long-run supply curve

increase in demand to D_2 leads to an increase in supply to S_2 and a new equilibrium at E_2. Price p_2 is below the original price p_1 because lower factor prices allow firms to cover their total costs at the lower price. An industry that has a declining long-run supply curve is often called a FALLING-COST INDUSTRY.

The response of a perfectly competitive industry to a change in technology

Consider an industry in long-run equilibrium. Since the industry is in equilibrium, each firm must be in zero-profit equilibrium. Now assume that some technological development lowers the cost curves of newly built plants. Since price is just equal to the average total cost for the old plants, new plants will now be able to earn profits and they will be built immediately. But this expansion in capacity shifts the short-run supply curve to the right and drives price down. The expansion in capacity and the fall in price will continue until price is equal to the *ATC* of the *new* plants. At this price old plants will not be covering their long-run costs. As long as price exceeds their average variable cost, however, such plants will continue in production. As the outmoded plants wear out they will gradually disappear. Eventually a new long-run equilibrium will be established in which all plants use the new technology.

What happens in a competitive industry in which technological change occurs not as a single isolated event but more or less continuously? Plants built in any one year will tend to have lower costs than plants built in any previous year. Figure 19.12

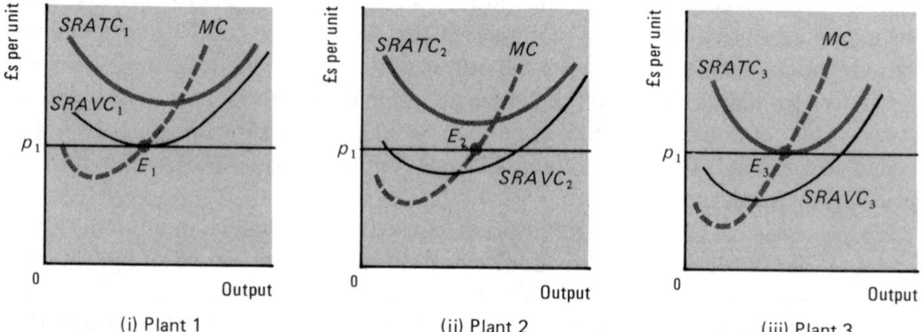

Fig. 19.12 Plants of different ages in an industry with continuing technical progress

illustrates such an industry. Plant 3 is the newest plant, with the lowest costs. Price will be determined by the average total costs of plants of this type, since entry will continue as long as the owners of the newest plants expect to earn profits from them. Plant 1 is the oldest plant in operation; it is just covering its *AVC* and if the price falls any further it will be closed down. Plant 2 is a plant of intermediate age. It is covering its variable costs and earning some return on its capital. The return will shrink over time as entry of new plants with lower and lower costs drives prices lower and lower. Real-world industries like this, with continual technological changes, have a number of interesting characteristics.

One is that plants of different ages and different levels of efficiency will exist side by side. This is dramatically illustrated by the variety of vintages of steam turbine generators found in any long-established electric utility. Critics who observe the continued use of older, less efficient plants and urge that 'something be done to eliminate these wasteful practices' miss the point of economic efficiency. If the plant is already there, the plant can be profitably operated as long as it can do anything more than cover its variable costs. As long as a plant can produce goods that are valued by consumers at an amount above the value of the resources currently used up for their production (variable costs), the value of society's total output is increased by producing these goods.

A second characteristic of such an industry is that price will be governed by the minimum *ATC* of the most efficient plants. Entry will continue until plants of the latest vintage are just expected to earn normal profits over their lifetimes. The benefits of the new technology are passed on to consumers because all units of the commodity, whether produced by new or old plants, are sold at a price that is related solely to the *ATC*s of the new plants. Owners of older plants find their returns over variable costs falling steadily as more and more efficient plants drive the price of the product down.

A third characteristic is that old plants will be discarded when the price falls below their *AVC*. This may occur well before the plants are physically worn out. In industries with continuous technical progress, capital is usually discarded because it is economically obsolete, not because it has physically worn out. This illustrates the economic meaning of obsolete: old capital is obsolete when its average variable cost exceeds the average total cost of new capital.

Does a long-run competitive equilibrium exist?[1]

A necessary condition for a long-run competitive equilibrium is that any economies of scale that are available to a firm should be exhausted at a level of output that is small relative to the whole industry's output. We have seen that a competitive firm will never be in equilibrium on the falling part of its *LRATC* – if price is given and costs can be reduced by expanding scale, profits can also be increased by doing so. Thus firms will grow in size at least until all scale economies are exhausted. Provided that the output that yields the minimum *LRATC* for each firm is small relative to the industry's total output, there will be a large number of firms in the industry and the industry will remain competitive. If, however, reaching the minimum *LRATC* makes firms so large that each one has significant market power, they will cease to be price takers and perfect competition will cease to exist. Indeed if scale economies exist over such a large range that one firm's *LRATC* would still be falling if it served the entire market, a single firm may come to monopolize the market. This is what the classical economists called the case of *natural* monopoly; it is considered further in Chapter 31.

Only if the firm's *LRATC* curve is U-shaped will there be a determinate size of the firm in a competitive industry. To see why, assume instead that *LRATC* falls to a minimum at some level of output and then remains constant for all larger outputs. All firms will have to be at least the minimum size, but they can be just that size or much larger, since price will equal *LRATC* for any output above the minimum efficient size. In other words, there will then be no unique size for the firm.

There are very good reasons why the *LRATC* curve for a single-plant firm may be expected to be U-shaped. There is a great deal in modern technology that results in lower average costs for large, automated factories compared with smaller factories in which a few workers use relatively unsophisticated capital equipment. As a single plant becomes too large, however, costs may rise because of the sheer difficulty of planning for, and controlling the behaviour of, a vast integrated operation. Thus we have no problem accounting for a U-shaped cost curve for the *plant*.

What of the U-shaped cost curve for the *firm*? A declining portion will occur for the same reason that the *LRATC* for one plant declines when the firm is so small that

[1] This section deals with a difficult point that is often postponed until intermediate or even advanced courses. It may be omitted without loss of continuity.

it operates only one plant. Now, however, let the firm be operating one plant at the output where its *LRATC* is a minimum. (Call that output q^*.) What if the firm decides to double its output to $2q^*$? If it tries to build a vast plant with twice the output of the optimal size plant, the firm's average total cost of production may rise (because the vast plant has higher costs than a plant of the optimal size). But the firm has the option of *replicating* its first plant in a physically separate location. If the firm obtains a second parcel of land, builds an identical second plant, staffs it identically, and allows its production to be managed independently, there seems no reason why the second plant's minimum *LRATC* should be different from that of the first plant. *Because the firm can replicate plants and have them managed independently, there seems no reason why any firm faced with constant factor prices should not face constant LRATCs at least for intiger multiples of the output for which one plant achieves the lowest plant LRATC.*

In the modern theory of perfect competition, a U-shaped *firm* cost curve is merely assumed. Without it – although a competitive equilibrium may exist for an arbitrary number of firms – there is nothing to determine the equilibrium size of the firm and hence the number of firms in the industry when price equals each firm's *LRATC* (and when, therefore, there is incentive for neither entry nor exit). The basic point is that for perfect competition to persist there must be something that stops firms, not just plants, from increasing in size indefinitely.

20

The theory of monopoly

The market form of MONOPOLY is at the opposite extreme from that of perfect competition. It exists whenever an industry is in the hands of a single producer. In the case of perfect competition there are so many individual producers that no one of them has any power whatsoever over the market; any one firm can increase or diminish its production without affecting the market price significantly. A monopoly, on the other hand, has power to influence the market price. By reducing its output it can force the price up, and by increasing its output it can force the price down. In the first half of this chapter we shall confine ourselves to the case of monopolies that must charge a single price for the goods that they sell; in the second half we shall consider cases in which the monopoly can sell its goods at different prices either to different classes of customers or in different geographical markets.

The monopoly that sells its product at a single market price

You should now review the section on total, average and marginal revenue on pages 236–7. Since the monopoly firm is the only producer of its product, the demand curve that it faces *is* the market demand curve. Also, since a 10 per cent variation in the firm's output *is* a 10 per cent variation in the industry's output, it follows that the firm's elasticity of demand is the same as the market elasticity of demand.

In perfect competition the price is unaffected by variations in the firm's output, and it follows that the addition to revenue resulting from increasing the level of sales by one more unit is the market price of that unit. Thus the marginal and average revenue curves coincide in the same horizontal straight line. With a monopoly, however, the average revenue curve, which is the same as the market demand curve, is *downward* sloping. Furthermore, the marginal revenue curve does not coincide with the demand curve: since the sale of an extra unit forces down the price at which *all* units can be sold, the sale of an extra unit results in a net addition to revenue of an amount less than its own selling price.

The relation between a monopolist's average and marginal revenue

To inquire in more detail into the relation between average and marginal revenues, we consider the simple example illustrated in Table 20.1. We assume that the

Table 20.1 Alternative price and sales combinations for a monopolist, together with the corresponding marginal revenues

	Price	Rate of sales per year	Total revenue	Marginal revenue
Situation 1.	£2·00	100	£200	
				£0·99
Situation 2.	£1·99	101	£200·99	
				−£0·05
Situation 3.	£1·97	102	£200·94	

monopoly is selling 100 units each year of some commodity, at a price of £2. This yields a total revenue of £200. The firm then steps up its rate of sales to 101 units per year, but, as a consequence of the downward-sloping demand curve this drives the price down to, say, £1·99. The firm's total revenue is now £200·99. Thus, the increase in revenue resulting from the sale of an additional unit per year is only £0·99, even though the extra unit sells for £1·99. A moment's thought will show that there is no mystery about the fact that the marginal revenue (£0·99) is less than the price (£1·99) at which the extra unit is sold. One hundred units per year could have been sold for £2, but in order to sell the extra unit, the firm reduces the price *on all units* by 1p. Thus, there is a loss of 1p per unit on each of the 100 units. This makes a total loss of £1·00, which must be deducted from the extra revenue of £1·99 obtained from the sale of the 101st unit. Thus, the net increase in revenue associated with the sale of the 101st unit is only £0·99. This numerical example illustrates the proposition that:

> **Whenever the demand curve slopes downward, the marginal revenue associated with an increase in the rate of sales by one unit per period will be less than the price at which that unit is sold.**[1]

This proposition may also be illustrated graphically. In Figure 20.1, sales are assumed to increase from the rate of q_1 units per year to q_2 units. The extra revenue gained from the sale of the extra unit is equal to the area of the rectangle marked 'Gain in revenue'. This, however, does not represent pure gain, for q_1 units that could have been sold at price p_1 must now be sold at price p_2, because the extra unit is to be sold as well. This makes a loss of $p_1 - p_2$ per unit on all q_1 units, which is indicated by the area of the rectangle 'Loss in revenue'. Marginal revenue of selling the additional amount $q_1 - q_2$ is equal to the difference between these two areas.

Since the monopolist's demand curve is the market demand curve, the monopoly faces the same relation between elasticity of the market demand curve and total revenue as we discussed on page 107.

[1] It is easy to prove algebraically that, if the demand curve slopes downwards, marginal revenue is always less than price. Let subscripts n and $n+1$ indicate the revenue associated with the sale of n and $(n+1)$ units, so that, e.g., TR_n is the total revenue associated with the sale of n units per period.

$$\begin{aligned} MR_{n+1} &= TR_{n+1} - TR_n \\ &= (n+1)P_{n+1} - nP_n \\ &= nP_{n+1} + P_{n+1} - nP_n \\ &= n(P_{n+1} - P_n) + P_{n+1}. \end{aligned}$$

Since the demand curve slopes downwards P_{n+1} (the price ruling when $n+1$ units are sold) will be less than P_n (the price ruling when n units are sold). Thus the MR of the $n+1$th unit is less than P_{n+1}.

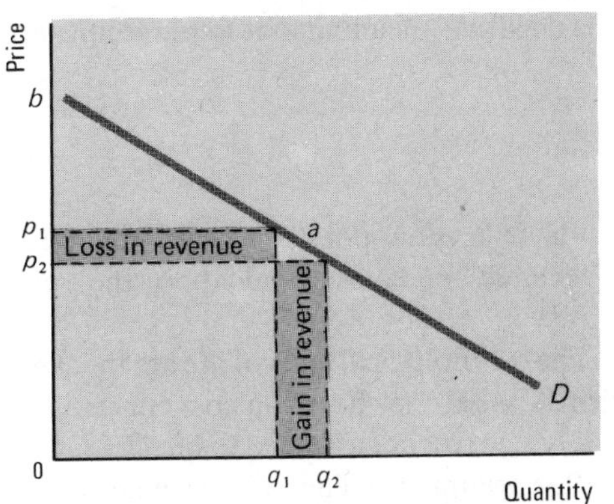

Fig. 20.1 The change in a monopolist's revenue resulting from a small increase in the amount sold

If the market demand curve is elastic, a cut in price and a rise in sales will cause the monopolist's total revenue to increase; if the market demand curve is inelastic, a cut in price and a rise in sales will cause the monopolist's total revenue to decrease.

If total revenue falls when price is cut, marginal revenue is negative. This is illustrated by the move from Situation 2 to 3 in Table 20.1.

Figure 20.2 shows a numerical example of a demand curve for a monopoly and its corresponding marginal and total revenue curves. The demand curve shows the price corresponding to any given rate of sales, and the *MR* curve shows the change in total revenue that is brought about by increasing the rate of sales by one unit per period. For example, for $q = 25$ units the price is £7·50, but the *MR* is £5, which means that the 25th unit adds £5 to total revenue. When $q = 50$, price is £5, but *MR* is zero. To sell the last unit costs as much in lost revenue (because of the price reduction necessary to persuade the extra buyer to buy) as the price it commands.

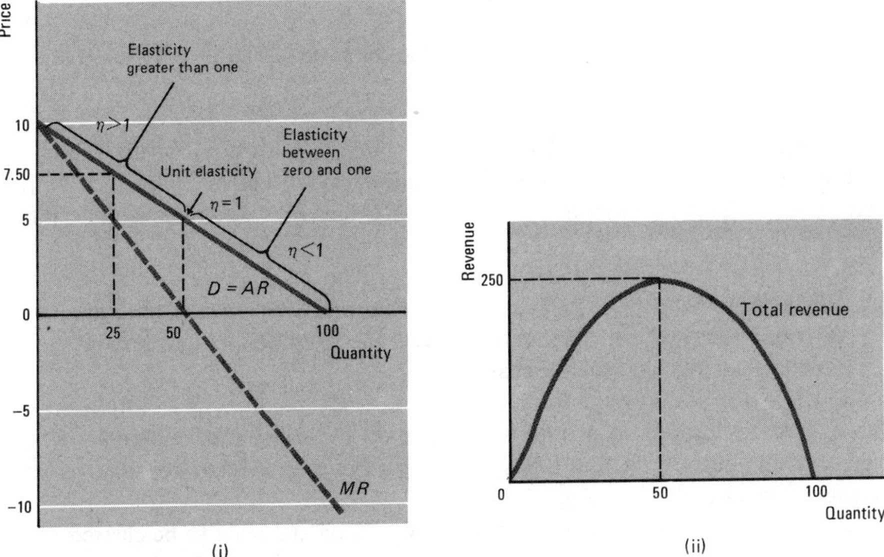

Fig. 20.2 The relation of total, average and marginal revenue to elasticity of demand (η)

For quantities greater than 50 units *MR* is negative, meaning that total receipts are decreased by additional sales.

The equilibrium of a monopolist

To describe the profit-maximizing position of a monopoly, we need only bring together information about the firm's revenues and costs and apply the rules developed in Chapter 18.

This is done graphically in Figure 20.3. The technological facts of life are the same for the monopoly as for a competitive firm, so that the short-run cost curves have the same shape in both cases. (The monopoly's curves are assumed to be *AVC*, *ATC* and *MC* – the curve *ATC′* relates to a latter argument.) The difference lies in the demand conditions. The perfectly competitive firm (of Figure 19.1) is faced with a perfectly elastic demand for its product, while the monopoly of Figure 20.3 is faced with a downward-sloping demand curve.

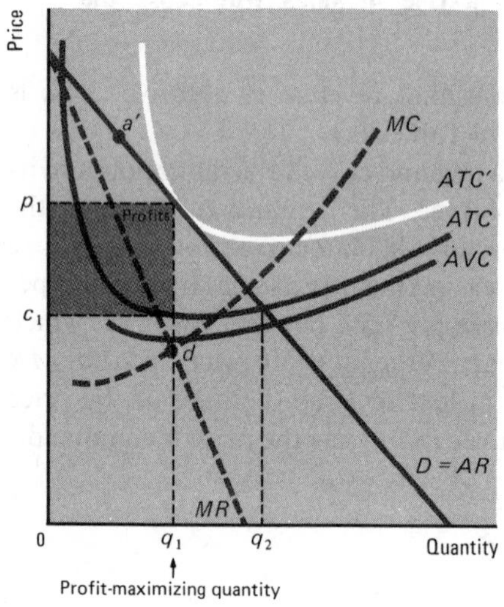

Fig. 20.3 The equilibrium of a monopolist

The equilibrium output and price are q_1 and p_1. This equilibrium meets the several conditions for profit-maximizing behaviour described in Chapter 18. Notice that ouput is determined from the *MR* and *MC* curves, while price is determined from the *D* curve.

When the monopoly is in equilibrium, marginal cost equals marginal revenue; marginal cost cuts marginal revenue from below; and price is greater than average variable cost.

The aggregate amount of profits is represented by the shaded rectangle, which represents the output, q_1, multiplied by the gap between average revenue, p_1, and average total cost, c_1.

Two common misconceptions about monopoly profits need to be cleared up at this point. First, nothing guarantees that a monopoly will make profits in the short run. If you shift the *ATC* curve upward but leave all other curves unchanged, you will see that profits shrink as the curve moves up. When the curve gets as high as ATC', so that it is tangent to the demand curve, the monopoly earns zero profits at output q_1 (and losses anywhere else). All that the condition $MC = MR$ tells us is that the monopoly does better at that output than at other levels of output. It is possible for the firm to continue producing in the short run even if its ATC curve lies everywhere above D, as long as its AVC curve lies somewhere below D. In these circumstances the firm can set a price in excess of its AVC and lose less by producing than by letting its fixed factors stand idle.

The second common misconception about monopoly profits is that a monopoly that is not maximizing its profits must be making losses. This is, of course, not correct. At output q_1, where $MC = MR$, total profits are as large as possible. If output is increased beyond q_1, $MC > MR$, so that any additional units sold are *reducing* total profits, but *total* profits are still positive. In fact total profits remain positive until output reaches q_2 units. At that level, average total cost equals average revenue so that total cost equals total revenue. Should output be increased beyond q_2, total profits would finally become negative.

Firm and industry, short run and long run

A monopoly, as defined here, is the only producer in an industry. There is, thus, no need to have a separate theory of the firm and the industry. The monopoly firm *is* the industry.

In a monopolized industry, as in a perfectly competitive one, profits provide an incentive for new firms to enter. If a profitable monopoly is to persist in the long run, other firms must be discouraged from entering the industry. Circumstances that protect the monopolist by discouraging entry of other firms even when the monopolist is earning profits are called BARRIERS TO ENTRY. These barriers may take several forms: patent laws may create and perpetuate monopolies by conferring on the patent holder the sole right to produce a particular commodity. The government may grant a firm a charter or a franchise that prohibits competition by law. Monopolies may also arise because of economies of scale. The established firm may retain a monopoly through a cost advantage because it can produce at a lower cost than could any new, and necessarily smaller competitor. A monopoly may also be perpetuated by force: potential competitors can be intimidated by threats ranging from sabotage to a price war which the established monopoly has sufficient financial resources to win.

Because there is no entry into a monopolistic industry, any profits that the firm does make may persist over time. In perfect competition, the long run differs from the short run because the process of entry forces profits down to zero in the long run. There is no such tendency under monopoly, and the long run differs from the short run only in terms of the cost curve on which the monopolist is operating. Consider a monopoly fully adjusted to a given demand curve: the appropriate sized plant has been constructed and *long-run marginal cost* has been equated to marginal revenue. Now assume that there is a permanent rise in demand. The best the firm can do in the short run is to work its existing plant more intensively, expanding output until the short-run marginal cost curve associated with the fixed plant intersects the marginal revenue curve. In the long run, however, a larger plant could be built, and any other relevant adjustments made to 'fixed' factors until the monopoly is again in a position at which long-run marginal cost equals marginal revenue.

Absence of a supply curve under monopoly

The next stage in our study is to consider the relation between the price of the product and the quantity supplied under monopoly. In the case of perfect competition we were able to discover a unique relation between price and quantity supplied. This gave rise to a supply curve for each firm and, by aggregation, to a supply curve for the industry.

> **In monopoly, there is no unique relation between market price and quantity supplied.**

As with all profit-maximizing firms, the monopolist equates marginal cost to marginal revenue. Unlike the situation of firms in perfect competition, however, marginal revenue does not equal price. Hence the monopoly does *not* equate marginal cost to price. Under these circumstances it is possible for different demand conditions to give rise to the same output but to differing prices. In order to know the amount produced at any given price, we need to know the demand curve as well as the marginal cost curve.

The proposition that when a firm faces a downward-sloping demand curve there is no unique relation between price and output is illustrated in Figures 20.4 and 20.5. In Figure 20.4 two different demand curves both result in the same output, q_2, but in two different prices. When demand is D_1 marginal revenue equals marginal cost at output q_2 and price is p_1. When demand is D_2 marginal cost again equals marginal revenue at output q_2 but price is at p_2.

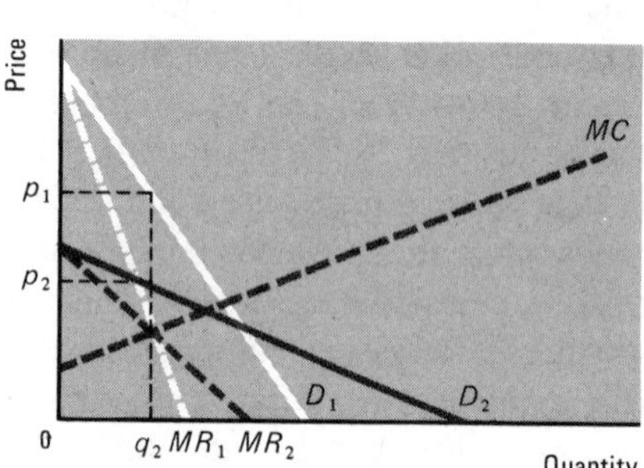

Fig. 20.4 Two different prices associated with the same output

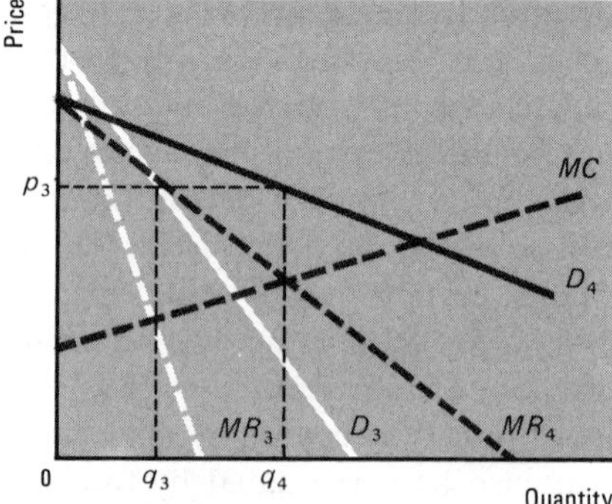

Fig. 20.5 Two different outputs associated with the same price

In Figure 20.5 we illustrate the same general point by showing a case in which the same price is associated with two different quantities. When demand is D_3 marginal revenue equals marginal cost at output q_3 and the resulting price is p_3. When demand is D_4 marginal revenue equals marginal cost at output q_4 but price is again p_3.

A monopoly that can price discriminate

So far in this chapter we have assumed that the monopolist charges the same price for every unit of his product no matter to whom, or where, he sells it. But other situations are possible. Milk is often sold at one price if it is for drinking, but at a lower price if it is to be used to make ice-cream or cheese. Doctors, lawyers and business consultants sometimes vary their fees according to the incomes of their clients. Cinemas charge lower admission prices for children. American railways charge different rates per ton mile for different kinds of loads. Firms often sell their products cheaper abroad than at home. Electrical companies in many countries sell electricity more cheaply for industrial use than for home use. All of these are examples of PRICE DISCRIMINATION. In general we may say that price discrimination occurs when a producer sells a commodity to different buyers at different prices *for reasons not associated with differences in costs.*

Why price discrimination pays

A formal analysis of price discrimination is given in the Appendix to this chapter. Here we shall discuss the common sense of price discrimination only intuitively.

Price discrimination occurs because different units of a commodity can be sold at different prices, and it will be profitable for the seller to take advantage of this if he can. Some of the issues involved in discriminatory pricing can be seen looking at the demand curve in Figure 20.1 on page 263 and thinking of it as describing a market containing a large number of individual buyers, each of whom wishes to buy one unit, and each of whom has indicated the maximum price he is prepared to pay for it. Suppose a single price, p_1, is charged. The quantity q_1 will be sold because the buyers of each of the p_1 units are willing to pay at least q_1 per unit. Although one buyer was willing to pay only p_1, all of the other buyers were willing to pay more. They have benefited because the price was limited to p_1. If the seller could negotiate with each buyer individually, he might be able to charge some buyers more than p_1. In fact, by charging each person the maximum that he is prepared to pay, the seller could greatly increase his profits.[1] If he must charge a single price, and if he wishes to raise his rate of sales from q_1 to q_2, he will have to lower the market price from p_1 to p_2. Marginal revenue is less than the new price charged because of the effect that the reduction in price has on the revenues from the first q_1 units (the reduction was not necessary to sell *them*, since *they* were already being sold at the higher price). If the seller had been able to sell the extra amount $q_2 - q_1$ at p_2 without reducing the price on the first q_1 units (if, in other words, he had been able to discriminate), he would have profited by doing so.

When is price discrimination possible?

> **The conditions under which a firm can succeed in charging discriminatory prices are, first, that it can control what is offered to a particular buyer, and, second, that it can prevent the resale of the commodity by one buyer to another.**

However much the local butcher would like to charge the banker's wife twice as much for a lamb chop as he charges the street sweeper, he cannot succeed in doing so. The banker's wife can always go into a supermarket where her husband's

---

[1] The area under the demand curve above the line at p_1 in Figure 20.1 (= the area p_1ba) is sometimes called *consumers' surplus*. It represents the amount consumers would have been willing to pay, unit by unit, for the quantity q_1, *above the amount they actually paid* when the price was set at p_1.

occupation is not known. Even if the butcher and the supermarket agreed to charge her twice as much, she could hire the street sweeper to do her shopping for her. The surgeon, on the other hand, may succeed in discriminating (if all reputable surgeons will do the same) because it will not do the banker much good to hire the street sweeper to have his operations for him.

The first of the two conditions – control over supply – is the feature that makes price discrimination an aspect of the theory of monopoly. Monopoly power in some form is necessary (but not sufficient) for price discrimination.

The second of the two conditions – ability to prevent resale – tends to be associated with the character of the product, or the ability to classify buyers into readily identifiable groups. Services are less easily resold than goods, and those goods requiring installation by the manufacturer (like heavy equipment) are less easily resold than are movable commodities (like household appliances).[1] Transportation costs, tariff barriers or import quotas serve to separate classes of buyers geographically and may make discrimination possible.

To summarize, price discrimination will be both profitable and possible where the supplier(s) can control the amount and distribution of supply, where the buyers can be separated into classes among which resale is either impossible or very costly,[2] and where there are significant differences in willingness to pay among the distinct classes of buyers.[3]

The positive effects of price discrimination

The positive consequences of price discrimination are summarized in the following two propositions, which we state and try to make intuitively plausible, but do not prove:

> **(1) For any given level of output, the best system of discriminatory prices will provide higher total revenue to the firm (and thus also higher average revenue) than the best single price.**

If this is not obvious you should review the first pages of this chapter.

> **(2) Output under monopolistic discrimination will generally be larger than under single-price monopoly.**

It may be a help at this stage to review the discussion on pages 262–3. Marginal revenue will tend to be higher, given the possibility of price discrimination, because the lower price the producer must charge in order to sell an additional unit will not

[1] An interesting example of non-resalability occurs in the case of plate glass. Small pieces sell much more cheaply per square foot than bigger pieces, but the person who needs a 6′ × 10′ plate window cannot use four pieces, each of which is 3′ × 5′.

[2] The discussion of this paragraph relates directly to discrimination among *classes of buyers*. Discrimination among *units of output* follows similar rules. Thus the tenth unit purchased by a given buyer in a given month can be sold at a different (higher or lower) price than the fifth unit *only* if the seller can keep track of who buys what. This can be done by the seller of electricity through his meter readings, or by the magazine publisher, who can distinguish between renewals and new subscriptions. The owner of a car-wash establishment and the manufacturer of aspirin find it more difficult, although by such devices as coupons or 'one-penny' sales, they too can determine which unit is being purchased.

[3] 'Willingness to pay' is reflected in the demand curves. The fact that demand curves slope downward shows that some units could always be sold at a higher price if sellers were permitted to deviate from a single price.

apply to all previous units sold. The common sense of this is as follows: the monopolist who must charge a single price produces less than the perfectly competitive industry, because he is aware that by producing and selling more he drives down the price against himself. Price discrimination allows him to avoid this disincentive. To the extent that he can sell his output in separate blocks, he can sell another block without spoiling the market for the block already being sold. In the case of *perfect* price discrimination, where every unit of output is sold at a different price, his output would be the same as the output of a perfectly competitive industry. This is easily seen as follows. If each unit can be sold at a separate price, the seller does nothing to spoil the market for previous units by selling an additional unit. The marginal revenue of selling an additional unit is the price of that unit. Thus the demand curve becomes the marginal revenue curve, and the monopolist reaches equilibrium at a point where the price (in this case, marginal revenue) equals marginal cost. This is also the point of competitive equilibrium.

The normative aspects of price discrimination

Price discrimination often has a bad reputation. The very word *discrimination* has undesirable connotations. In the United Kingdom railways were for many years prevented by law from charging discriminatory prices. In the United States the Robinson–Patman Act makes many kinds of price discrimination illegal. Much of the impetus for US railroad regulation came from the outraged cries of farmers that they were being discriminated against and forced into bankruptcy by the railways, who were at first not legally prohibited from charging discriminatory prices.

Whether an individual judges price discrimination to be good or bad is likely to depend upon the details of the case, as well as upon his own personal value judgements. Certainly there is nothing in economic theory to suggest that price discrimination is always in some sense worse than non-discrimination under conditions of monopoly or oligopoly. The following examples should serve to illustrate the varying aspects of price discrimination.

Example 1 A very large oil refiner agrees to ship his product to a market on a given railway, but only if the railway gives his company a secret rebate on the transportation cost and does not give a similar concession to rival refiners. The railway agrees, and is thus charging discriminatory prices. This rebate gives the oil company a cost advantage that it uses to drive its rivals out of business or to force them into a merger on dictated terms. (John D. Rockefeller is alleged to have used such tactics in forming the original Standard Oil Trust in the US in the late nineteenth century.)

Example 2 Some years ago British Rail was not allowed to discriminate between passengers in different regions. To prevent discrimination, a fixed fare per passenger mile was laid down and had to be charged on all lines whatever the density of their passenger traffic and whatever the elasticity of demand for their services. In the interests of economy, branch lines which could not cover costs were often closed down. This meant that some lines closed even though the users preferred rail transport to any of the available alternatives and the strength of their preference was such that they would voluntarily have paid a price sufficient for the line to have covered its costs. The lines were nonetheless closed because it was thought inequitable to charge the passengers on their line more than the passengers on other lines. More recently, British Rail has been allowed to charge prices that take some account of market conditions. This seems to have increased profits.

Example 3 Doctors in private practice very often charge discriminatory prices for their services. When they are accused of behaving unfairly they point out that if they had to charge a uniform fee for all patients, it would have to be so high – if the doctor were to obtain a reasonable income – as to price their services out of the reach of the lower-income groups. The discriminatory price system, they argue, is what allows them to make their services available to all income groups while still securing a high enough income to ensure a continued supply of doctors.

Example 4 A product that a number of people want has cost and demand curves such that there is no single price at which costs can be covered (i.e., the average cost curve lies everywhere above the demand curve). However, if a monopolist is allowed to charge discriminatory prices, it will make a profit. (Public utility companies are often thought to operate under these conditions.)

Example 5 The government decides to offer primary school education to all children. The cost is estimated at £600 per child per year. Instead of charging tuition to each child's parents, the government chooses to make the school free and to raise the money by a school tax that is proportional to the value of the houses of the people who live in the community, whether or not they have children.

Each of these examples, as well as those at the beginning of this chapter, involves price discrimination. Few readers would regard them all as equally good or bad situations. There are two points to be stressed. First, the consequences of price discrimination can differ in many ways from case to case; second, no matter what an individual's values are, he is almost bound to evaluate the individual cases differently.

The nature and extent of monopoly power

There are certain conceptual difficulties with the theoretical concept of monopoly. No firm has complete monopoly power. Some firms which have fairly close competitors will face quite elastic demand curves; other firms with fewer close competitors will face less elastic demand curves.

A perfect monopoly?

In order to clarify the concept of monopoly, economists of an earlier generation sometimes tried to define a *perfect monopoly* that would be at the opposite end of the spectrum from perfect competition. Two ideas were put forward; both proved unsatisfactory. Since it took economists some time to see the problem, it is worthwhile studying them here to warn against repeating these mistakes. The first idea was that a perfect monopolist would be selling a good for which the demand was *perfectly inelastic* (this seemed the opposite of a perfect competitor, who faces a *perfectly elastic* demand). You should be able to see the contradiction in the idea of a profit-maximizing monopolist facing a perfectly inelastic demand curve.

Such a case would never come about. No profit-maximizing monopolist would ever sell at a price at which the demand for his product was perfectly inelastic. Clearly he would go on raising price while not losing sales, and would thus go on increasing profits. In fact, he would continue to raise his price, not only until the demand ceased to be perfectly inelastic, but until the demand ceased to be inelastic at all (for marginal revenue is negative as long as elasticity of demand is less than one; see page 263).

The second idea was that a perfect monopolist is a firm that has a monopoly of all goods, and hence a firm that takes in the consumer's entire income (ignoring saving). The monopolist would thus be faced with a demand curve of unit elasticity: any increase in price would be met by a proportional fall in quantity bought, so that total expenditure (= total consumers' income) would remain constant.

The problems here are more subtle than in the case of the completely inelastic demand. Let us first consider what a profit-maximizing monopolist would do if faced with a demand curve of unit elasticity. The marginal revenue corresponding to such a demand curve is, of course, zero. A 1 per cent increase in sales is always accompanied by a 1 per cent fall in price, while a 1 per cent reduction in sales causes a 1 per cent rise in price, so that total revenue remains unchanged. Clearly the monopolist will cut down output, thus reducing costs but leaving total revenue unaffected, and hence increasing profits. If the demand curve were truly of unit elasticity throughout its whole range, the monopolist's output would approach zero, while his price would approach infinity until finally he sold virtually nothing at all and sold it at an infinitely high price, absorbing the whole of income as his profits! Now all of income becomes the monopolist's profits and, since nothing is produced, no money will be paid out to factors of production. Thus next period the only purchaser left for the monopolist to exploit would be the monopolist himself!

What is the reason for these absurdities? The theories of the firm and of individual markets are based on *ceteris paribus* assumptions. When we draw a market and a firm's demand curve we assume that other things – prices, incomes, etc. – remain constant and are not affected by any change in the industry under consideration. The assumption that the total income of purchasers is constant depends upon the industry being small. If the industry is very large, then a change in the level of production will affect factor earnings, and thus incomes, significantly and so cause a *shift in the demand curve*. Clearly, we could not use the theory of the last few chapters if the demand curve for a firm's product shifted every time the firm's output changed.[1]

Attempting to consider a perfect monopolist as one who takes all income founders on the rock that it is no longer a situation in which the *ceteris paribus* assumptions hold. The attempt to apply our tools of analysis to such a situation can only produce absurd results. The theory of the firm that we have outlined here is concerned with productive units which are *small* in relation to the total economy. We conclude that the two ideas of a perfect monopoly considered here are self-contradictory.

Monopoly power as a variable

We have seen that the attempt to define a perfect monopolist runs into impossible complications.

[1] The applicability of partial and general equilibrium theory is further discussed in Chapter 30.

It is impossible for a firm to be without any significant competition. It may have a complete monopoly of a particular product, but every product has some substitutes that can provide more or less the same services.

Some products have fairly close substitutes, and even a single seller producing such a product will have close rivals for his customers' expenditure. Not only will his demand be relatively elastic, but new entrants into closely allied fields may shift his demand curve. Even if there is no very close substitute for his product at the moment, high profits may induce rivals to develop substitutes to cut into his market.

If other firms in other industries influence the monopolist's behaviour, they must do so by shifting his demand curve. The less the influence of other firms on the monopolist, the less their actions will cause shifts in his demand curve and the more insulated, (i.e., the more monopolistic) he will be. Thus, it may be useful to think of monopoly as a variable rather than as an absolute. In general, the extent of monopoly power will be greater, the smaller the shifts in demand caused by the reactions of sellers of other products, and the smaller the shifts in demand caused by the entry of new sellers. How large these shifts will be depends upon a great variety of other variables, which will be considered in Chapter 21.

Measuring monopoly power Our theory predicts that behaviour in monopolistic markets will differ from behaviour in perfectly competitive markets. We have also seen that it is more reasonable to regard monopoly power as a variable than as an absolute. Thus if we are to apply the theory of monopoly we must be able to measure the extent of monopoly power in various markets. Also, it is often felt by government agencies (acting on behalf of the people) that uncontrolled monopoly power is undesirable. These governmental agencies must know where monopoly power exists if they are to control or eliminate it. For both of these reasons, and for others as well, it becomes important to measure the extent of monopoly power in various markets.

Ideally, one would like to compare the prices, outputs and profits of firms in any industry with what prices, outputs and profits would be if all firms were under unified (monopoly) control and were fully insulated from entry. But this hypothetical comparison does not lend itself to measurement.

Concentration ratios In practice, two alternative measures are widely used. The first of these is the CONCENTRATION RATIO. A concentration ratio shows the fraction of total market sales controlled by the largest group of sellers. Common types of concentration ratios cite the share of total industry sales of the largest four or eight firms. The inclusion in concentration ratios of the market shares of several firms rests upon the possibility that large firms will adopt a common price-output policy that is no different from the one they would adopt if they were in fact under unified management. But of course they may not. Thus high concentration ratios may be necessary for the exercise of monopoly power, but they are not sufficient. It is nevertheless interesting to know where potential monopoly power exists.

Profits as a measure of monopoly power Many economists, following the lead of Professor Joe S. Bain, use profit rates as a measure of monopoly power. By 'high' profits the economist means returns sufficiently in excess of all opportunity costs to motivate potential new entrants into the industry. If profits are *and remain* high, so goes the logic of this measure, it is indirect evidence that neither rivalry among sellers nor entry of new firms prevents existing firms from pricing as if they were monopolists.

Using profits in this way requires care, because, as we have seen (page 239), the profits reported in firms' income statements are not pure profits over opportunity cost. In particular, allowance must be made for differences in risk and in required payments for the use of the owners' capital.

While neither concentration ratios nor profit rates are ideal measures of the degree of market power that a firm, or group of firms, actually exercises, both are of some value and both are widely used. In fact, concentration ratios and high profit rates are themselves correlated. Because of this, alternative classifications of industries according to their degree of monopoly power, measured in these two ways, do not differ very much from one another.

Appendix to chapter 20

A formal analysis of price discrimination

Consider a monopoly firm that sells a single product in two distinct markets, *A* and *B*. Customers in one market cannot buy in the other, either directly or by having a customer in the other market resell the product to them; the two markets are completely insulated from each other. The demands and marginal revenue curves are shown in Figure 20.6.

Since the firm can discriminate, it is under no necessity to charge the same in market *A* that it charges in market *B*. How then will it

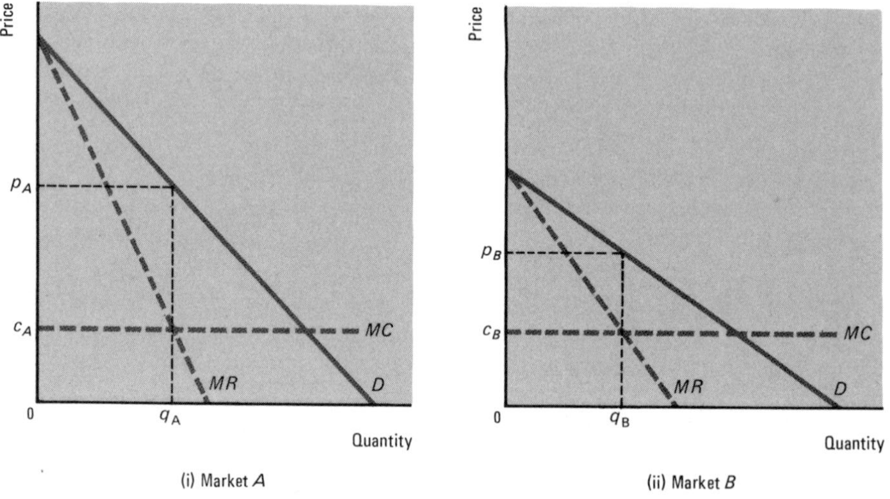

Fig. 20.6 Equilibrium of a price-discriminating monopolist with constant marginal costs

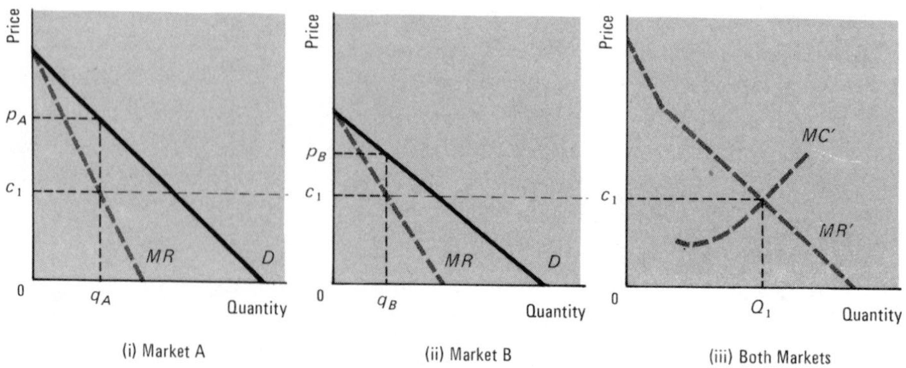

Fig. 20.7 Equilibrium of a price-discriminating monopolist with variable marginal costs

behave in each market? The simplest way to discover what it should do is to imagine it deciding how best to allocate any given output, Q^*, between the two markets. Since output is fixed arbitrarily at Q^*, there is nothing the monopolist can do about costs. The best thing it can do, therefore, is to maximize the revenue that it gets by selling Q^* in the two markets. *To do this it will allocate its sales between the markets until the marginal revenues of the last unit sold in each are the same.* Consider what would happen if it did not. If the marginal revenue of the last unit sold in market A exceeded the marginal revenue of the last unit sold in market B, the firm would keep its overall output constant at Q^* but reallocate a unit of sales from B to A, gaining a net addition in revenue equal to the difference between the marginal revenues in the two markets. Thus it will always pay a monopoly firm to reallocate a given total quantity between its markets as long as marginal revenues are not equal in the two markets.

If we assume that marginal cost is constant, we can determine the profit-maximizing course of action from Figure 20.6. The MC curve in both figures shows the constant marginal cost. The firm's total profits are maximized by equating MR in each market to its constant MC, thus selling q_A at p_A in market A and q_B at p_B in market B. Marginal revenue is the same in each market ($c_A = c_B$) so that the firm has its total output correctly allocated between the two markets and marginal costs equals marginal revenue, showing that the firm would lose profits if it produced more or less total output.

Now assume that marginal cost varies with output, being given by MC' in Figure 20.7 (iii). Now we cannot just put the MC curve onto the diagram for each market, since the marginal cost of producing another unit for sale in market A will depend on how much is being produced for sale in market B and vice versa. To determine what overall production should be, we need to know overall marginal revenue. To find this we merely sum the separate quantities in each market that correspond to each particular marginal revenue. If, for example, the 10th unit sold in market A and the 15th unit sold in market B each have a marginal revenue of £1 in their separate markets, then the marginal revenue of £1 corresponds to overall sales of 25 units (divided 10 units in A and 15 in B). Consider a second example. Let the marginal revenue of the 17th unit sold in market A be 57p and let the 24th unit sold in market B have a marginal revenue of 57p. Thus when the monopolist sells a total of 41 units, divided optimally between the two markets (17 in A and 24 in B), the overall marginal revenue is 57p, since a little more or a little less sold in the two markets will change revenue by 57p per unit change in sales. The examples illustrate the general principle: the overall marginal revenue curve to a discriminating monopolist is the horizontal sum of the marginal revenue curves in all markets. This overall curve shows the marginal revenue associated with an increment to production on the assumption that sales are divided between the two markets so as to keep the two marginal revenues equal.

This overall MR curve is shown in Figure 20.7 (iii) and is labelled MR'. The firm's total profit-maximizing output is at Q_1 where MR' and MC' intersect (at a value of c_1). By construction, marginal revenue is c_1 in each market although price is different. To find the equilibrium price and quantity in each market, find the quantities, q_A and q_B, that correspond to this marginal cost; then find the prices in each market that correspond to q_A and q_B. All of this is illustrated in parts (i) and (ii) of the figure.

An application

In some industries firms sell competitively on international markets while enjoying a home market that is protected from foreign competition by tariffs or import quotas. To illustrate the issues involved consider the following extreme case. A firm is the only producer of product X in country A. There are thousands of producers of X in other countries so that X is sold abroad under conditions of perfect competition. The government of country A grants the firm a monopoly in the home market by prohibiting imports of X. The firm now can be a discriminating monopolist. It is faced with a downward-sloping demand curve at home and a perfectly elastic demand curve abroad at the prevailing world price of X.

What will it do? To maximize profits the firm will divide its sales between the foreign and the home market so as to equate marginal revenues in the two. On the world market its average and marginal revenues are equal to the world price. Thus the firm will equate marginal revenue in the home market with the world price, and since price exceeds marginal revenue at home (because the demand curve slopes downward), price at home must exceed price abroad.

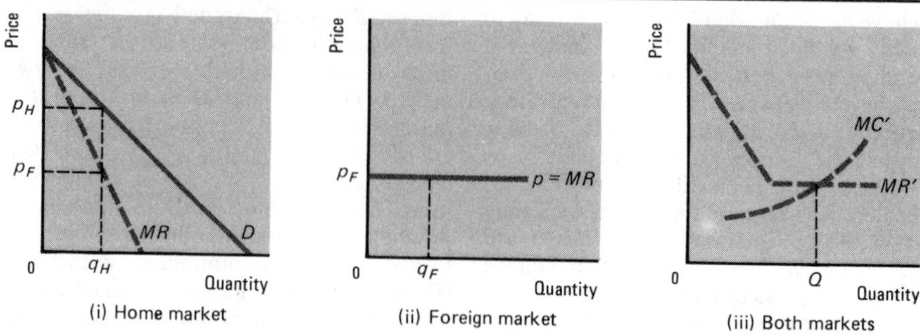

Fig. 20.8 Equilibrium of a firm with a monopoly in the home market but selling under perfectly competitive conditions abroad

The argument is illustrated in Figure 20.8. The home market is shown in (i), the foreign market in (ii) and the sum of the two marginal revenue curves in (iii). Provided that the marginal cost curve cuts the marginal revenue curve to the right of the kink (i.e., *MC* does not exceed the world price when only the home market is served), both markets will be served at prices of p_H at home and p_F abroad. The total quantity sold will be Q, of which q_H is allocated to the home market and the rest ($q_F = Q - q_H$) is sold abroad.[1]

[1] It is an interesting exercise to consider the effect on the firm's exports of a tax on the sale of *X* in the home market.

21

Theories of imperfect competition

Shell, BP and Exxon are three of the 'major' oil companies. They are not, singly or collectively, monopolists, nor are they firms in perfect competition. Yet they are typical of many real firms in our economy. Similar comments apply to Coca Cola and Pepsi Cola. Do the two basic theories of pricing behaviour we have studied – perfect competition and monopoly – have any relevance to their behaviour? The essential features of perfect competition are price taking and free entry; the essential features of monopoly are effective entry barriers and a demand curve that is substantially the same for the firm and for the industry. Do the theories of perfect competition and monopoly provide a sufficient basis for predictions about price and market behaviour in the real economy? Forty years ago most economists would have said 'Yes'; today most would say 'No', although the matter is still subject to debate.

Up to now we have dealt with the two extreme market forms of perfect competition and monopoly. A detailed consideration of the whole range of market forms that lie between these two extremes is beyond the scope of this book. In this chapter we shall, however, introduce the two major intermediate categories: monopolistic competition and oligopoly. Before we do this, however, we shall make one key distinction between perfect competition and all other market forms.

Administered prices

In perfect competition firms are price takers. They face a market price that they are quite unable to affect and they adjust their quantities to that price. When market conditions change, the signal that the firm sees is a change in the market prices of the commodity it sells.

> **In perfect competition firms are price takers and quantity adjusters. Changes in market conditions are signalled to firms by changes in the market prices that they face.**

In all other market forms, firms have some control over their price. Firms can if they wish set their price and then sell what they can at that price. (They can also decide on a quantity and sell it for what it will fetch on the market.) If they are unsatisfied with their price-output position they can change the price that they quote. In such circumstances we say that the firm administers its price. The term ADMINISTERED PRICES refers to prices that are set by the decisions of individual firms rather than by impersonal market forces.

When a firm sets its price, the amount that it sells is determined by its demand curve. Changes in market conditions will be signalled to the firm by changes in demand – by changes, that is, in the amount that can be sold at its administered price. The changed conditions may or may not lead the firm to change the price that it charges.

> **With market forms other than perfect competition, firms can administer their prices and then let demand determine their sales. Changes in market conditions are signalled to the firm by changes in the quantity the firm can sell at its administered price.**

The market system still works as a general signalling and co-ordinating system when prices are administered. There is some reason to think it may not work as smoothly or as efficiently in the face of administered prices than it would if all markets were perfectly competitive, but it does work. A rise in the demand for some commodity will cause a rise in the demand curves for the firms that produce that commodity. These firms will see their sales rising and they will usually be led to produce more to meet the extra demand. Although the signalling system works differently, it is there and it works. The allocation of resources may be different under perfect competition than under administered prices. Resources will, however, be reallocated in the face of major shifts in demand and costs, just, as they would under perfect competition.

We have already considered one market form that leads to administered prices – monopoly. In this chapter we consider two further market forms that also lead to administered prices – monopolistic competition and oligopoly.

Imperfect competition among the many: monopolistic competition

Consider an industry in which there is a large number of producers with free entry and exit, but in which *each producer sells a product that is somewhat different from that sold by his competitors*. We say that the product is DIFFERENTIATED. There might, for example, be a large number of competing firms selling different brands of soap, all similar but by no means identical products. Each soap would differ in physical composition from competing soaps; it would also have different packaging, and, as the advertisers say, a different 'brand image' from its competitors. Industries of this kind are referred to as being monopolistically competitive. The term MONOPOLISTIC COMPETITION describes a situation similar to perfect competition, with the single important difference that each producer sells a product that is somewhat differentiated from the products sold by his competitors.

Product differentiation implies that each firm does not face a perfectly elastic demand curve. We may now construct the demand curve of such a firm *on the assumption that competing firms hold their prices constant*. On the one hand, if the firm raises its price it will lose business to its competitors, but it will not lose all of its customers just because its prices rise slightly. (The fact that its product is differentiated from competing products means that some people will prefer it even though it is somewhat more expensive. As its price is raised higher and higher above those of similar products, the firm can expect that fewer and fewer customers will remain loyal.) On the other hand, if the firm lowers its price below that charged by competitors, it can expect to attract customers, but not everyone will be attracted by a small price differential.

The firm is faced with a downward-sloping demand curve. Generally the less differentiated the product, the more elastic the firm's demand curve will be. (If there is no differentiation, the demand curve will be perfectly elastic because the smallest decrease in price above those of competitors will attract *all* of the competitors' customers.)

Picture, as in Figure 21.1, a monopolistically competitive firm faced with a downward-sloping, but rather flat, demand curve. The firm will, of course, have the usual U-shaped short-run cost curve. The short-run equilibrium of the firm is exactly the same as that of a monopolist. The firm is not a passive price taker; it may juggle price and quantity until profits are maximized. This occurs at output q_1 and price p_1 in the figure. [1]

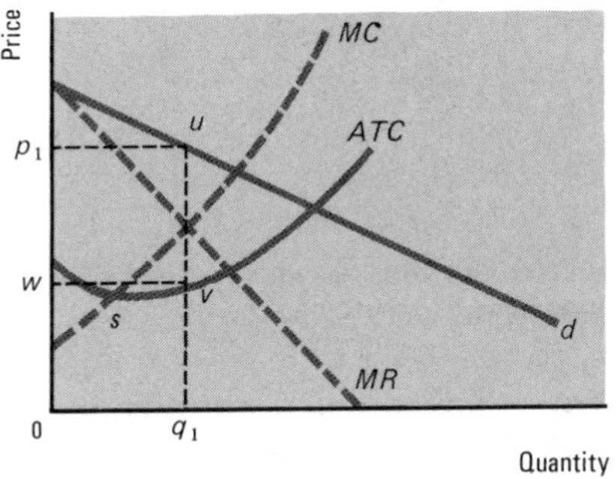

Fig. 21.1 The short-run equilibrium of a firm in monopolistic competition

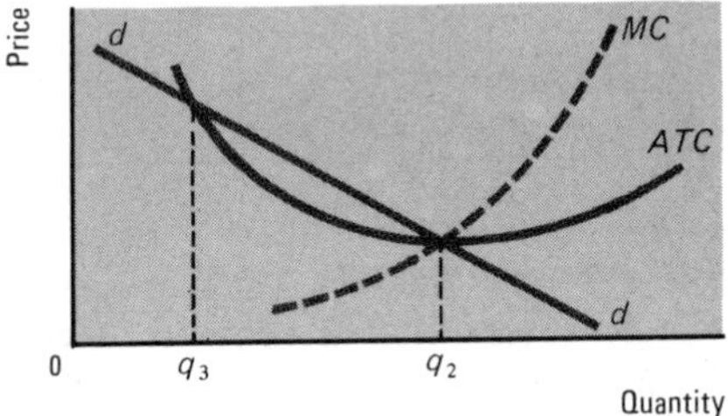

Fig. 21.2 The firm can make profits for any output between q_3 and q_2

We may now ask about the long-run equilibrium of the industry. The firm shown in Figure 21.1 is earning profits ($= p_1uvw$), and, if it is typical of the other firms in the industry, new entrants will be attracted. As more firms enter, the market demand for the product must be shared out among a larger number of firms, so that each can expect to have a smaller share of the market. Thus, at any given price, each firm can expect to sell less than it did before the influx of new firms: each firm's demand curve shifts left. This must continue until no profits are being earned; as long as profits exist, there is an attraction for new firms to enter and the industry will continue to expand.

Before reading further you should make a genuine effort to see if you can discover the final equilibrium position for yourself. Start from Figure 21.1 and observe that as new firms enter the industry the demand curve *dd* facing our one firm will shift to

[1] The complete theory of monopolistic competition also deals with a type of price cutting that leads to a short-run equilibrium of the *industry*. We jump straight from the short-run equilibrium of the firm to the long-run equilibrium of the industry because we only wish to develop those predictions of the theory that follow the long-run equilibrium positions. Readers already familiar with the theory may assume that the point *u* in Figure 21.1 is at the intersection of the *dd* and the *DD* curves, so that there is no further tendency for short-run price competition.

the left. Also observe that this will continue until there are no further profits. What will be the position of final equilibrium?

Assume, to begin with, that the demand curve shifts to the position indicated in Figure 21.2 where it intersects the average total cost curve at the point of lowest average cost. Will this do? Surely if the firm produces output at q_2, it will just be covering its costs. But if it restricts output below q_2, it will increase average revenue more than average costs and move into a range of output at which profits can be earned. In Figure 21.2 costs are just covered at outputs q_2 and q_3, while profits are earned at any output between these levels.

The final position must be that indicated in Figure 21.3. The demand curve touches the average total cost curve at only one point, x, corresponding to quantity q_4 and price p_4: the demand curve is *tangential* to the average cost curve at point x. When output is at q_4 costs are just being covered, since average revenue equals average total costs. Losses occur at any other level of output, since average revenue is less than average total costs.

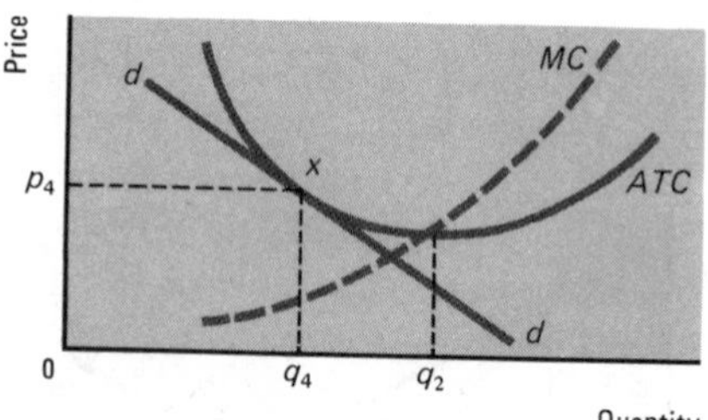

Fig. 21.3 The long-run equilibrium of a firm in monopolistic competition

Thus we see that a zero-profit equilibrium is possible under conditions of monopolistic competition, in spite of the fact that the individual firm is faced with a downward-sloping demand curve. Each firm is forced into a position in which it has EXCESS or UNUSED CAPACITY. (Recall the definition of capacity given on page 218.) The firm in Figure 21.3 could expand its output from q_4 to q_2 and reduce average costs, but it does not make use of this productive capacity because doing so would reduce price by even more than it would reduce average costs. If the demand curve *cuts* the average total cost curve, as in Figure 21.2, it is always possible to make profits by producing in the range over which the demand curve lies above the cost curve. A monopolistically competitive equilibrium in which profits cannot be earned but total costs can be covered requires that the demand curve should be tangential to the average total cost curve; this in turn implies that in equilibrium the firm will have some unused capacity (equal to $q_2 - q_4$ in Figure 21.3).

Predictions of the theory

What are the major propositions of the theory of monopolistic competition that differ from those of perfect competition? The first is the one we have just derived.

> **(1) The equilibrium output of the monopolistically competitive firm is less than the output where average total cost is at a minimum. (This is known as the excess capacity theorem.)**

This is one of the more important insights in the whole theory of the firm. It tells us that a long-run, zero-profit equilibrium can occur even though each firm is like a monopolist in the sense of having a downward-sloping demand curve. It will occur because so many firms will enter the industry that each individual firm will be unable to utilize all of the capacity at its command. The theory predicts that industries in monopolistic competition will exhibit a continual tendency towards excess capacity.

The next two propositions can be established by inspecting Figure 21.3 and recollecting that in a long-run, perfectly competitive equilibrium, price is equal to minimum average cost.

(2) Under monopolistic competition equilibrium price is higher and output is lower, ceteris paribus, than under perfect competition.
(3) Under monopolistic competition equilibrium price is greater than marginal cost.

The fourth proposition is related to product differentiation.

(4) Monopolistically competitive firms will offer a wider variety of brands, styles and possibly qualities than firms in perfect competition.

Monopolistic competition is predicted to produce more products, but less cheaply, than perfect competition. Whether the added cost of differentiated output (and production at less than capacity) is 'worth it' to buyers is a question involving empirical estimates of costs and value judgements about various benefits.

A fifth proposition of the theory is as follows.

(5) Monopolistically competitive firms will engage in non-price competition, whereas perfectly competitive firms will not.

To see that this is an implication, recall that a firm in perfect competition can sell as much as it wishes at the going price and that it regards itself as a price taker. Therefore, it does not need to spend money to increase the amount it can sell. But in monopolistic competition, expenditures on product differentiation, product quality or advertising can change the position of the firm's demand curve and thereby increase short-run profits.

The applicability of the theory

The motivation for the development of the theory of monopolistic competition was the inability of the perfectly competitive model to deal with cases where firms competed to sell products which they advertised and whose price they set. It seemed clear to many observers that the two polar cases of monopoly and perfect competition did not explain much of what we see. Detractors of the theory of monopolistic competition argue, however, that it also fails to explain much of what we see.

One of the problems is that many industries which seem, on casual observation, to be monopolistically competitive turn out not to be. Consider for example, the market for soaps and detergents. Among the well-known brands on sale in the United States are Ivory, Dash, Joy, Comet, Cascade, Camay, Lava, Duz, Tide, Cheer, Dreft, Oxydol, Spic 'n' Span and Zest. Surely this is an impressive array of differentiated products! On first glance, this might appear to be a perfect example of monopolistic competition. But all of the products named above are manufactured by a single company, Procter and Gamble, which alone accounts for more than half of the US sales of soaps, cleansers and detergents.[1] Will Procter and Gamble really believe that if it lowers its prices its largest rival, Lever Brothers, will not lower theirs? Does the soap industry exhibit revenues that do not exceed costs and does it have free entry? The answer to each question is no. Clearly this is not a case of monopolistic competition.

Many examples of intense competition among a multitude of only slightly differentiated manufactured products turn out to be similar to the soap case: many brands produced but by a few firms. Such cases cannot be handled by the theory of monopolistic competition, but we shall say more about them later under theories of oligopoly.

Many branches of retailing, however, are much closer to the concept of a monopolistically competitive industry. Every shop selling a particular line of goods, whether groceries, men's clothing or drugs is differentiated from every other shop selling the same line of goods, both by the location of the shop and the personality of the staff. Each is a monopolist to some extent, yet there is freedom of entry and a consequent long-run tendency for profits to be pushed to zero. Profits are forced to zero because in long-run equilibrium there are more outlets than are necessary to handle the custom, so that each shop and its staff operate for most of the time at substantially less than full capacity. Whatever the detractors of the theory may say, it seems that the model of a downward-sloping demand curve resulting from product differentiation, with the additional condition of freedom of entry, is a very useful one for the economist to have in his tool kit, because we do sometimes encounter industries that come close to fulfilling these two conditions.

The theory of monopolistic competition was first developed at a time when perfect competition was under severe attack for its unrealistic assumptions. The new theory studied the implications of product differentiation such as the ability of firms to influence prices, and their need to advertise. The new theory also encouraged economists to consider the general effects of product differentiation on the operation of the price system. Furthermore, it rekindled economists' interest in such important issues as how and when firms took each other's reactions into account, what made for easy or restricted entry, and the significance to competition of different but roughly similar products.

Imperfect competition among the few: theories of oligopoly

We now need to consider the behaviour of firms that have only a few close competitors. An industry containing only a few firms is called an OLIGOPOLY. A special case of this market form is DUOPOLY, an industry with only two producers. A high proportion of manufacturing industries in all Western countries are oligopolistic. In the British car industry, for example, 90 per cent of the production is in the hands of five large firms. Oligopoly also exists in the motor-tyre, chemical, synthetic fibre, electric wire and cable, and match industries.

When we move from competition among the many to competition among the few, the whole price-output problem of the firm takes on a new dimension, that of

---

[1] The three-firm concentration ratio exceeds 80 per cent. This illustration is from J. W. Markham's article in the *American Economic Review*, May 1964, p. 54. His point is that the multi-product firm is not the multi-product industry of monopolistic competition, and that we require a different theory to explain its behaviour.

the possible reaction of the firm's few competitors. A firm's policy now depends on how it *thinks* its competitors will react to its moves, and the outcome of its policy depends on how they *do* in fact react. There is no simple set of rules for the equilibrium either of the firm or of the small group of firms that constitutes the industry. Neither is there a set of simple predictions about how the firms will react, either individually or collectively, to changes in such things as taxes, costs and market demand.[1]

Because the problem of oligopoly behaviour is complex, it is not surprising that there is no single well-developed theory of the functioning of oligopolistic markets. Indeed, the problem has been attacked in two quite different ways.

Developing theoretical models by assuming how firms react

One attempt has been to develop a series of models by assuming that individual firms will react in particular ways, and then seeing what follows from these assumptions. A. A. Cournot developed the first known theory of duopoly in 1838. He had each firm choose its profit-maximizing output on the assumption that the other firm would hold its own output constant. He then showed that if each firm in turn adjusted to the last move made by its competitor, a stable equilibrium would be reached in which the market was divided between the two in a definite way. The assumption that each firm expects no reaction from its competitors, although the competitor always does react, seems rather naive. In the 135 years since Cournot, economists have advanced many models of oligopolistic behaviour, and have sought to make them more seemingly relevant than Cournot's rather special, though path-breaking, one.

The German economist H. von Stackelberg developed a theory in the 1930s that included Cournot's model as a special case. In Stackelberg's theory it was possible to handle the question of whether it would pay the firm to be a price leader or a price follower. A follower is a firm who lets the leader set any price and then passively adjusts to it, while a leader sets its own price, confident that the follower will accept it.

Also in the 1930s, the American economist Harold Hotelling approached the oligopoly problem from a novel direction. He developed a series of models in which there was a tendency for competition among a few oligopolists to produce a result that was less socially desirable than the result produced by a single monopolist. We shall return to Hotelling's basic model in Chapter 23.

The theory of games, which is a study of rational strategies in small-group situations, has done a great deal to increase our knowledge of how to behave rationally – i.e., how to choose actions that maximize the chances of obtaining stated objectives – in such diverse fields as cold war military strategy and card games. Some economists feel that the theory can be fruitfully applied to oligopoly problems.[2] *But an analytical technique is only as useful as the real-world information*

[1] It is often said that, under these circumstances, price and output are *indeterminate*. Such a statement is misleading (the price and output do, of course, get determined somehow), and what is meant is that, under oligopoly, price and output are not determined by the same factors as in large-group cases. In small-group cases an additional set of factors – competitors' real and imagined reactions to each other's behaviour – contributes to the determination of price and output.

[2] For an entertaining general introduction to the theory in its many established applications, see J. D. Williams, *The Compleat Strategyst* (McGraw-Hill, 1954).

that it is used to analyse. Even the most powerful new techniques will be empty without empirical knowledge of how firms actually behave in typical small-group situations.

So far the attack on oligopolistic behaviour through the development of general models has produced disappointingly few results. There are few clear predictions that are capable of being tested against evidence.

Generalizing from hypotheses about observed behaviour

The second major attack on the problem of understanding oligopolistic behaviour has been an attempt to build up a theory piecemeal by developing testable hypotheses to explain actual observed behaviour. The hope is that these piecemeal explanations will eventually produce the necessary elements for a general theory of oligopoly. Although we cannot enter into a detailed discussion of these elements in this book, we can (1) describe a general hypothesis that serves as a framework for integrating many subsidiary hypotheses, (2) give examples of some of the subsidiary hypotheses in order to illustrate their general nature, and (3) discuss two or three hypotheses at greater length (those related to barriers to entry).

The hypothesis of qualified joint profit maximization The hypothesis of qualified joint profit maximization is the key general hypothesis. If all the firms in an industry maximize their joint profits, their combined profits are the same as those that would be earned by a single profit-maximizing monopolist running the industry. Thus an industry in which all firms practise unqualified joint profit maximization behaves exactly as if it were controlled by a single monopolist. Competing firms cannot, however, usually attain the unqualified joint profit-maximizing position, although they may approach it. We may now state the hypothesis of *qualified* joint profit maximization as follows:

> **Firms that recognize that they are in rivalry with one another will be motivated by two opposing forces. One moves them towards policies that maximize the combined profits of the existing group of sellers; the other moves them away from the joint profit-maximizing position. Both forces are associated with observable characteristics of firms, markets and products; thus we can make predictions about market behaviour on the basis of these characteristics.**

To make the hypothesis testable, we need to identify the forces that lead the firm towards joint profit maximizing and the forces that lead it away.

Hypotheses about oligopoly behaviour Below are eight hypotheses about behaviour in oligopolistic markets. The first five concern relationships of a firm with its present rivals; the last three concern the effect on a firm's behaviour of potential entrants into the industry.

1. The tendency toward joint profit maximization is greater for small numbers of sellers than for larger numbers. The argument offered in support of this hypothesis concerns both ability and motivation. When there are a few firms, they are sure to be in direct rivalry with one another and will soon discover this fact of life. Thus there is no chance that any one can gain sales without inducing retaliation by its rivals. At the same time, a smaller number of firms can co-ordinate their policies with less difficulty than a larger number.

2. *The tendency toward joint profit maximization is greater for producers of very similar products than for producers of clearly differentiated products.* The argument here is that the more nearly identical the products of sellers are, the closer will be the direct rivalry for customers and the less the ability of one firm to gain a decisive advantage over its rivals. Thus, other things being equal, such sellers will prefer joint efforts to achieve a larger industry market over individual attempts to take customers away from each other.

3. *Stable joint profit-maximizing behaviour tends to be easier in a growing than in a contracting industry.* The argument here is that under expansionary circumstances firms tend to be able to utilize their capacity fully without resorting to attempts to 'steal' their rivals' customers. In contrast, when firms have excess capacity, their marginal costs are very low and they are tempted to give discounts or secret price concessions in order to pick up customers. Eventually their rivals retaliate and large price cuts may become general.

4. *Prices will tend to be more inflexible the more uncertain the firm is about what its rivals' responses will be.* Uncertainty can take many forms and have many consequences. One of these concerns willingness to jeopardize a moderately satisfactory situation in pursuit of something that *might* be much worse. In periods of industry-wide excess capacity, firms that are covering costs may be unwilling to risk causing a price war by making price change in either direction.

5. *Prices will tend to be more inflexible, the more effective tacit agreement is.* Because price changes are costly, owing to the need to print new price books, advertise anew and so on, a monopolist might well change prices infrequently. When this is the case, a group of tacitly agreeing oligopolists would do the same. In contrast, oligopolists striving to increase their own shares might make more frequent price changes than a monopolist. This hypothesis is an alternative to hypothesis 4: it argues that price stability may be itself an object and a consequence of tacit agreement, not a result of uncertainty about how rivals will react.

6. *Non-price competition will tend to be more vigorous, the greater the limitation on price competition.* Suppose firms agree tacitly to avoid price cutting in order to avoid expensive and potentially explosive price wars. This hypothesis says that the basic rivalry of the sellers for customers will find other outlets, as firms seek to maintain or improve their market positions.

7. *Industry price will tend to be closer to the joint profit-maximizing price, the greater the barriers to the entry of new firms.* This hypothesis rests on the possibility that the threat of new firms' entering an industry leads existing firms to adopt lower prices in order to discourage entry. The greater the barriers to entry, the less the need for such price reductions.

8. *Non-price competition will tend to be greater, the weaker the other barriers to the entry of new firms.* The argument here is that advertising or product differentiation may give an established firm an advantage over potential entrants that is very possibly a crucial deterrent to entry. This motive for advertising is greater, the greater the threat of entry. The operation of non-price competition when natural barriers to entry are weak is examined below.

Barriers to entry

As with so much in the field of industrial organization and oligopoly, the topic of entry barriers was first given systematic, detailed study by Professor Joe S. Bain. We shall consider two of the many ways analysed by Bain in which existing firms may have advantages over potential entrants.

Absolute cost advantages An absolute cost advantage means that existing sellers have average cost curves that are significantly lower over their entire range than those of potential new entrants. Possible sources of such an advantage include 'going-concern value', control of crucial patents or resources, and knowledge that comes only from 'learning by doing' in the industry. Each of these may be regarded as a source of only temporary disadvantages for new firms, which, given time, might catch up.

Scale advantages of existing sellers Suppose existing firms have no absolute cost advantage, but that they are large in size and that the technology of the industry is such that there are economies of large-scale production.

Such economies imply that new firms, which inevitably begin with only a small share of the market, will have high costs. They will thus find it hard to compete with large established firms that are large enough to exploit existing economies of scale. This important point is illustrated in Figure 21.4. The *ATC* curves show the long-run average costs of a single firm subject to decreasing costs.

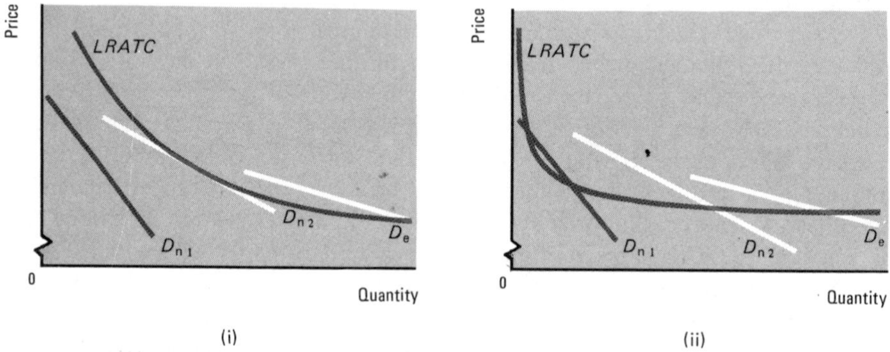

Fig. 21.4 Two alternative long-run average total cost curves compared with given demand curves

The established firm has a demand curve D_e, and it is able to earn profits above all its opportunity costs. For the situation pictured in Figure 21.4 (i), if a new firm enters the industry with a demand curve D_{n1}, there is no output at which it can cover its costs. If it takes time for the firm to establish itself in the market and to have the demand for its product build up to a higher level, it must accept temporary losses. These losses will continue until its demand has shifted to D_{n2}, at which time it can cover all its costs by producing at the output corresponding to the point of tangency between D_{n2} and *ATC*. Figure 21.4 (ii) differs from Figure 21.4 (i) in that quite a small level of output is sufficient to exploit all the significant economies of scale. The curve D_{n1} for the new entrant is shown in exactly the same position as in Figure 21.4 (i), but this time the firm can make profits even though it has a very small share of the market. Clearly, entry is much easier in an industry whose costs are like those in (ii) than in an industry where costs are like those in (i).

The nature of this kind of barrier to entry depends on the shape of the cost curve and particularly on the size of what is called the MINIMUM EFFICIENT SCALE (*MES*). This term refers to the smallest size of plant that can reap all of the available economies of scale. Figure 21.4 (i) illustrates a large *MES* and a large entry barrier; Figure 21.4 (ii) shows a small *MES* and a correspondingly smaller entry barrier.

Barriers to entry in the absence of scale advantages in cost curves Is there any way in which firms with small minimum efficient scales may be able to forestall entry? We may examine two possibilities. First, if consumers switch brands frequently, then increasing the number of brands sold by existing firms will reduce the expected sales of a new entrant (thus keeping D_{n1} as far over to the left as possible). Say, for example, that an industry contains three large firms, each selling one brand of cigarettes, and suppose that each year 30 per cent of all smokers abandon their existing brand allegiance and choose new brands in a random fashion. If a new firm enters the industry, it can expect to pick up 25 per cent of these smokers (it has one brand out of a total of four available brands). This gives it $7\frac{1}{2}$ per cent (25 per cent of 30 per cent) of the total market as a result merely of picking up its share of the random switchers. If, however, the existing three firms had five brands each, there would be fifteen already available, and a new small firm selling one new brand could expect to pick up only one-sixteenth of the brand switchers, giving it less than 2 per cent of the total market on this account.

A second defensive policy that may be adopted by an industry that faces potential entrants owing to a low *MES*, is to attempt to shift the cost curves (of itself *and* of potential entrants) upward and to the right by advertising. If there is much brand-image advertising, then a new firm will have to spend a great deal on advertising its product in order to bring it to the public's attention. If the firm's sales are small, advertising costs *per unit sold* will be very large. Thus, heavy advertising expenditures in an industry without economies of scale in production have the effect of changing total cost curves from the general shape illustrated in Figure 21.4 (ii) to that illustrated in Figure 21.4 (i).

This proposition is illustrated in Figure 21.5. The curve labelled *ATC* (*production*) is copied from Figure 21.4 (ii) and it shows a case in which economies of scale are all exhausted at a quite modest level of output, with constant long-run average costs beyond that level. Such an industry is easy to enter. We now add a fixed level of

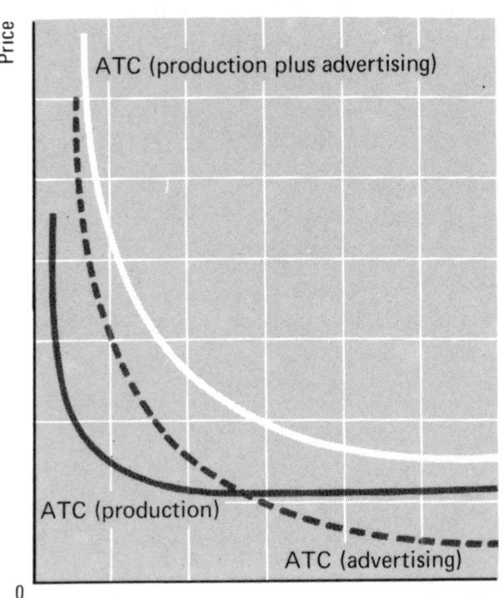

Fig. 21.5 Average total cost curves allowing for both production and advertising costs

advertising costs necessary to establish a new brand against the heavy advertising of existing brands. When we divide this fixed cost by the number of units produced, we obtain the curve *ATC* (*advertising*), which shows how advertising cost per unit sold declines as output is raised, thus spreading the fixed cost over more and more units. If we add these two curves, we obtain the curve *ATC* (*production plus advertising*), which shows how *all* long-run costs vary as output varies. The curves are drawn to scale, and it is clear from inspection that there are substantial scale economies up to a much higher level of output than when advertising was not a component of costs. A small new entrant will now be at a substantial cost disadvantage when competing against a large, established firm.

These hypotheses about non-price competition creating barriers to entry help clarify two apparently paradoxical aspects of everyday experience: one firm often sells many different brands of the same product in direct competition with each other, and each firm often spends considerable sums on advertising, competing not only against the products of rival firms but also against other products of its own. The soap and cigarette industries provide classic examples of this behaviour. In both of these industries there is only a small number of firms, but a very large number of only slightly differentiated but heavily advertised products. The explanation is that technological barriers to entry are weak in these industries – a small plant can produce at an *ATC* just about as low as can a large plant. Product differentiation and brand-image advertising create substantial barriers where technological ones are weak, and they thus allow existing firms to move in the direction of joint profit maximization without fear of a flood of new entrants attracted by the high profits.

A final word

Many hypotheses about oligopolistic behaviour have been mentioned. Some of them have been tested; others have not. But all are subject to empirical testing. When testing has proceeded to a point where we can be reasonably sure which hypotheses are confirmed and which are rejected, it will be much easier to use those that survive as the building blocks for a more comprehensive theory. There can be no doubt, however, that even in our introductory treatment of this subject we have come very close to one of the frontiers of modern economics.

22

Some predictions of the theories of competition and monopoly

In this chapter we shall use comparative-static analysis to derive some implications of the theories of competition and monopoly. These can be viewed in two different ways. First, they are logical implications. When we derive them, we are engaged in a purely logical process of finding out what propositions are implied by the theory's assumptions. From this point of view the truth of a certain proposition is a simple matter of right or wrong: a certain proposition either is or is not implied by our theory. This is a matter on which we can come to a perfectly definite conclusion, and the probability that errors in logic still remain in this well-worked field is extremely small.

Second, these implications may be regarded as empirical hypotheses. Whether or not these hypotheses are consistent with the facts is a matter for testing and, in the absence of strong empirical evidence, it is not necessary to accept the propositions as true in the empirical sense.

Whether or not a given proposition is implied by, or follows from, some theory, is a purely logical question that can be settled definitely without reference to facts; but whether or not a given proposition (which follows from a theory) fits the facts or is inconsistent with them can be settled only by an appeal to real-world observations.

In the present chapter we shall be concerned with the logical problem of deriving propositions from our theories. In subsequent chapters we shall consider some problems of empirical testing. We shall begin by re-examining those problems of perfectly competitive industries that we first illustrated in Chapter 10. In that chapter we considered producers' co-operatives that were designed to iron out year-to-year fluctuations in incomes. Most producers' co-operatives have a second objective, to raise as well as to stabilize producers' incomes.

The drive to monopolize perfectly competitive industries

Cocoa producers in West Africa, wheat producers in the United States and Canada, coffee growers in Brazil, oil producers in the Arab countries, taxi drivers in many cities and labour unions throughout the world have all sought to obtain, through collective action, some of the benefits of departing from perfectly competitive situations.

The motivation behind this drive for monopoly power is not hard to understand. The equilibrium position of a perfectly competitive industry is *invariably* one in which a restriction of output and a consequent increase in price would raise the profits of all producers. This is particularly obvious when, as is often the case with agricultural goods, the demand for the product is inelastic at the equilibrium price. In this case marginal revenue for a variation in the industry's output is negative and marginal cost positive. Thus a reduction in output will not only raise the total revenues of all producers but will also reduce total costs, and if costs fall and revenues rise, total profits must rise. It is equally true, although not so obvious, that total profits can be increased if demand is elastic at the competitive equilibrium price. At any competitive equilibrium, each firm is producing where marginal cost equals price (see page 294). But as long as the demand curve slopes downward, marginal revenue for the industry is less than price and thus also less than marginal cost. Thus, in competitive equilibrium the last unit sold necessarily contributes less to the industry's revenue that to its costs. From this we derive the basic prediction:

> **It would always pay the producers in a perfectly competitive industry to enter into an output-restricting agreement.**

We shall call an association formed for such a purpose a producer's co-operative, or a co-op for short.

Once an output-restricting agreement has been concluded, there is a force tending to break down the producers' co-operative behaviour. Clearly, any one firm can raise its output without affecting the market price. Since this firm's actions would not affect the price, its income would rise because it could sell its pre-co-op output at the post-co-op prices. Thus, unless the co-op is very carefully policed and has the power to enforce its quota restrictions on everyone's output, there will be a tendency for member firms to violate quotas once prices have been raised. Furthermore, the co-op must have power over all producers, not merely over its members; otherwise a firm could avoid the quota restrictions on its output merely by leaving the co-op.

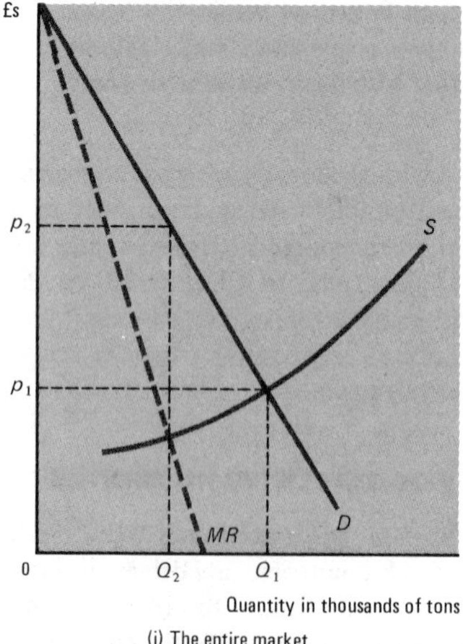

(i) The entire market

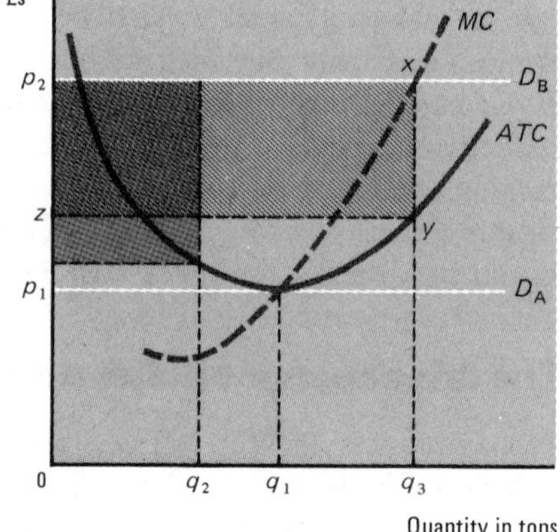

(ii) An individual farmer

Fig. 22.1 The effect of crop restriction schemes

These two tendencies are illustrated graphically in Figure 22.1. Figure 22.1 (i) represents the market conditions of supply and demand; Figure 22.1 (ii) represents the conditions of demand and cost for an individual firm. Suppose that before the co-op is formed the market is in competitive equilibrium at price p_1 and output Q_1 (where the demand curve intersects the supply curve); the individual firm is producing output q_1 and just covering costs. The co-op is formed in order to allow producers to exert a monopolistic influence on the market. By persuading each firm to reduce its output, market output is reduced to Q_2 (where the marginal revenue curve intersects the supply curve, which is also the industry's marginal cost curve) and the price p_2 is achieved. The firm in Figure 22.1 (ii) has a quota of q_2, but even though it has reduced its output it has improved its position. It is now earning profits of the amount shown by the darker section of the shaded area. This leads to our first prediction, that every firm will be better off if a co-op is formed and succeeds in raising price to p_2, than if no co-op is formed and price remains at p_1.

Once price is raised to p_2, the individual firm will want to increase its output because price is greater than its marginal cost. At q_2, price (and thus any firm's marginal revenue) exceeds marginal cost, and it follows that, left to itself, the firm will want to increase its output. It will want to move to output q_3 where marginal cost equals its marginal revenue and where it will earn the profits shown by the shaded area p_2xyz in Figure 22.1 (ii). But if everyone produces q_3 then output in Figure 22.1 (i) exceeds Q_1, price falls below p_1 and everyone makes losses. This leads to our second prediction, that each co-op member can increase its profits by violating its output quota, provided that the other members do not violate theirs.

These two predictions highlight the dilemma of the producer's co-op. Each firm is better off if the co-op is formed and is effective. But each is even better off if everyone else co-operates and it does not. Yet if everyone cheats (or stays out of the co-op), all will be worse off.

Producers' co-ops formed to raise prices by restricting output in competitive industries will be able to raise producers' incomes, provided that they are able to enforce quotas on the outputs of all firms. Such co-ops will, however, exhibit unstable tendencies, for it will always be in the interest of any single member firm to raise its output. If many firms do so, the co-op will collapse and all firms will lose.

The history of schemes to raise farm incomes by limiting crops bears ample testimony to the empirical applicability of these predictions. Very often crop restriction breaks down, and prices fall as individuals exceed their quotas. The great bitterness and occasional violence that is sometimes exhibited by members of output-restriction schemes against cheaters and non-members is readily understandable.

Changes in demand and costs

We must now spend some time studying the response of both competitive and monopolistic industries to changes in their demand and cost functions. Although the analysis may seem formal and abstract at the outset, it is important because it sets the stage for a study of the effects of taxes, subsidies, innovations and a host of other things, all of which affect either the revenues or the costs of firms.

Changes in demand

A rise in demand under competition Figure 22.2 shows the cost and demand conditions for a single firm (i) and for a whole industry (ii) under perfect competition. When the demand curve is D_1, both the individual firm and the industry are in equilibrium at price p_1. (If you have any doubts about this, you should review Chapter 19 now.) There is no incentive for any firm to change its output, nor is there incentive for entry or exit of firms.

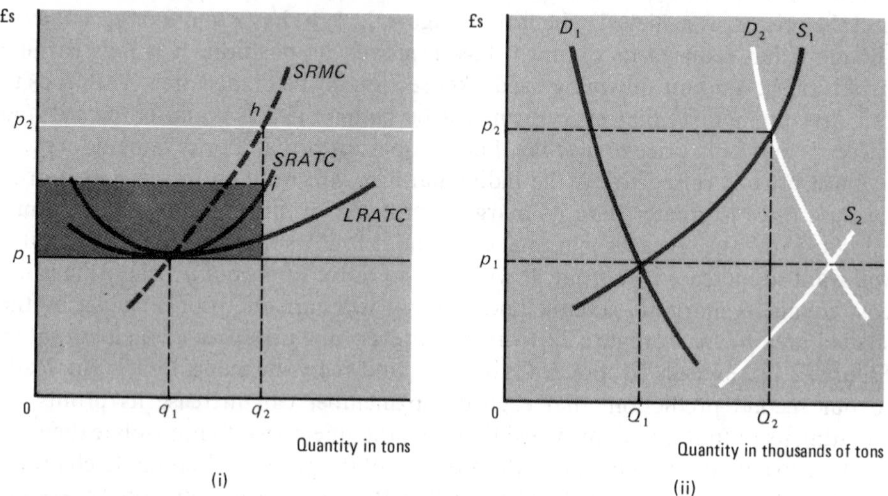

Fig. 22.2 The effects of an increase in demand under perfect competition: (i) equilibrium of a single firm (ii) equilibrium of the industry

Now assume that the market demand curve in Figure 22.2 (ii) shifts from D_1 to D_2. This causes a shortage to develop. The shortage causes a rise in price, which in turn causes firms to increase their output. In the short run, the market price rises to p_2, total industry production rises to Q_2, and the individual firm that we are considering produces q_2. The firm will be making profits on each unit equal to the difference between the price per unit and its short-run average total cost ($q_2h - q_2i = hi$). Thus the firm's total profit is equal to the area of the shaded rectangle in Figure 22.2 (i).

In the short run, a rise in demand in a competitive industry will cause:
(1) Price to rise;
(2) An increase in the quantity supplied by each firm and hence by the industry;
(3) Each firm to earn profits.

The long-run effects follow from the third prediction. Since firms are now making profits, this industry will attract new investment. The entry of new firms will cause an increase in supply that will force the price below the previously established short-run equilibrium price p_2. Since in perfect competition all firms have access to the same technology, all firms have the same costs. Thus each new firm that enters the industry will have costs identical to those of the firm shown in Figure 22.2 (i). Thus new firms as well as old ones will be able to earn profits as long as price exceeds p_1.

The process of entry will stop when price is driven back to p_1 and each original firm is producing its original quantity q_1, but the whole industry's output has expanded because there are more firms in the industry. When the expansion has come to a halt the new short-run supply curve in Figure 22.2 (ii) will be S_2, which is the sum of the marginal cost curves of the new larger number of firms in the industry. The total industry output is Q_2, which is divided between Q_1 produced by old firms and $Q_2 - Q_1$ produced by the new ones.

This leads in the long run to an expansion of output at a constant price. The argument is simple: if p_1 is the price equal to the minimum point on the long-run average total cost curve of all existing and potential firms, then p_1 is the only price consistent with long-run equilibrium (all firms just covering total costs).

Are other results possible? The main reason for answering 'Yes' is that the industry's expansion may bid up the prices of factors of production heavily used in that industry.[1] If this happens, then each firm's *LRATC* curve will shift upwards (see page 224) and the expansion of the industry will come to a halt before price is driven down to p_1. Such an industry will have an increase in demand associated with an increase in price as well as output in the long run.

It is also conceivable, although rather unlikely, that the expansion of the industry could cause factor prices to fall.[2] This would cause the firm's *LRATC* curves to shift downwards, and expansion would continue until prices were driven below p_1 (to the minimum points on the new *LRATC* curves).

> **In the long run, a rise in demand in a competitive industry will cause:**
> **(1) The scale of industry to expand;**
> **(2) Profits to return to zero eventually;**
> **(3) The new equilibrium price to be above, below or equal to the original price; but (i) constant factor prices and (ii) identical cost curves for new and old firms are sufficient to ensure that price returns to its original level.**

A fall in demand under competition Next consider a fall in demand. Figure 22.3 shows the firm and industry in their initial long-run equilibrium with price at p_1. When demand falls to D_2, a glut of the commodity is created; supply exceeds demand at the original price p_1; price then falls to p_3. At price p_1, the individual firm was just covering all opportunity costs. At the new price, p_3, the firm will produce q_3, the output for which marginal cost equals marginal revenue.

Individual firms will now be suffering losses. Average total cost is q_3a, and average revenue is q_3b ($= p_3$); losses per unit are ab. Would it not be worth while to close down its operations altogether, instead of running at a loss? The answer to this is 'No'. We have already seen, on page 237, that the profit-maximizing firm should continue producing in the short run as long as price exceeds average variable costs.

We conclude, therefore, that if price falls below average total cost but exceeds

[1] It is also possible that costs could rise if there were real diseconomies of scale external to the firm so that with *factor prices constant* the expansion of the industry caused existing firms' *LRATC* curves to shift upwards. This possible, but rather unlikely, case can be left for more advanced treatments that need to cover all logical possibilities.

[2] It is a well-known result in more advanced theory that if all industries have constant returns to scale (the location of minimum point on a firm's *LRATC* curve is independent of the size of the industry) and if different industries use factors of production in different proportions, the production-possibility surface will be concave to the origin, which means that all industries will find their costs and long-run equilibrium prices rising as they expand.

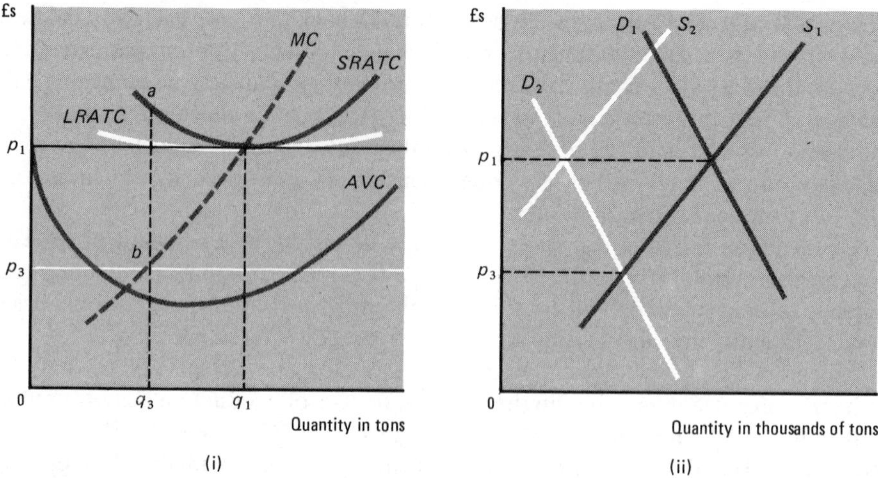

Fig. 22.3 The short-run effects of a fall in demand under competition: (i) short-run equilibrium of a firm in perfect competition (ii) short-run equilibrium of a perfectly competitive industry

average variable cost, the firm will make losses, but will stay in production at least in the short run. Only if price falls below average variable cost will the firm exit.

> **In the short run, a fall in demand in a competitive industry will cause:**
> **(1) Price to fall;**
> **(2) A decrease in the quantity supplied by each firm and hence by the industry;**
> **(3) Each firm to make losses;**
> **(4) Firms to cease production immediately if they are unable to cover their variable costs of production.**

The long-run effects follow from the third prediction. Since firms in the industry are not covering all costs, the industry is not an attractive place in which to invest. No new capital will enter the industry; as old plant and equipment wear out, they will not be replaced. Thus the scale of the industry will contract. The short-run supply curve, showing how production varies with price, capital equipment being held constant, shifts to the left. But as the supply diminishes, the price of the product begins to rise. This price rise will continue until the firms remaining in the industry can cover their total costs.

The analysis for a rise in demand applies in this case with only minor changes. If factor prices remain constant, then price must return to p_1 before the remaining firms can reach the minimum points on their *LRATC* curves. If, however, the contraction of the industry causes a fall in the prices of factors of production used especially heavily by the industry, the cost curves of the remaining firms will shift down and price need not rise as far as p_1 before costs can be covered, thus stopping further contraction. In the unlikely event that the contraction causes the industry's heavily used factors to rise in price, cost curves rise and price must rise above p_1 before the remaining firms can cover their costs.

> **In the long run, a fall in demand in a competitive industry will cause:**
> **(1) The scale of the industry to contract;**
> **(2) Losses to eventually return to zero;**

(3) Price to be above, below or equal to its original level; but (i) constant factor prices and (ii) identical cost curves for all firms are sufficient to ensure that price returns to its original level.

A change in demand in monopoly On page 266, in the section on the absence of a supply curve under monopoly, we saw that we cannot predict that a rise in demand will always cause an increase in both the price and output of a monopolist, even in the short run. It is possible, provided that the elasticity of demand changes sufficiently, for a rise in demand to cause a fall either in price or in output.

At this level of generality, we are left with the implication that a rise in demand for a monopoly can cause both its price and its output to rise, but that either price or output might fall. This may seem a disappointingly vague conclusion, but it is all that the theory implies. In order to get a more specific prediction we need to know more about the demand curve than that it merely slopes downwards. If, for example, we know the slopes of the demand curves before and after the shift, we can make a definite prediction.

There are some interesting cases in which such predictions are possible: (1) every point on the demand curve shifts upwards or downwards by the same amount and (2) the demand curve pivots through its point of intersection on the price axis. In both of these cases price and quantity rise when demand rises, and fall when demand falls. These cases are important because they can be adapted to study the effects of a per-unit and an *ad valorem* tax or subsidy on the monopolist's output. The second case also arises if the market expands because of the addition of new customers with the same tastes as those initially in the market. They are illustrated in Figure 22.4 (i) and (ii).

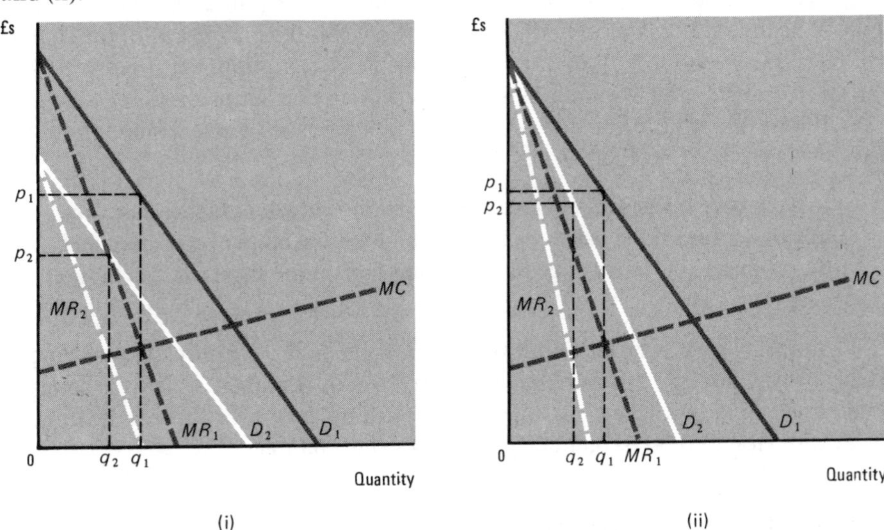

Fig. 22.4 (i) A parallel shift in the monopolist's demand curve changes the price and quantity in the same direction as the change in demand (ii) A pivoting of the monopolist's demand curve through the price intercept changes the price and quantity in the same direction as the changes in demand

Changes in costs

Competition Consider a case in which marginal costs are reduced by a given amount at all levels of output for all firms. This is shown by a downward shift in the marginal cost curves. In a competitive industry the short-run supply curve will shift downwards by the amount of the downward shift in the firm's marginal cost curves, and this will lead to a greater output at a lower price. But the price will fall by less than the vertical downward shift in the marginal cost curve, while profits will now be earned because of the lower costs of production.

> **In the short run under perfect competition, a fall in variable cost causes price to fall but by less than the reduction in marginal cost. The benefit of the reduction in cost is thus shared between the consumers, in terms of lower prices, and the producers, in terms of higher profits.**

In the long run, however, profits cannot persist in an industry having freedom of entry. New firms will enter the industry, and this influx will increase output and drive price down until all profits are eliminated.

> **In the long run under perfect competition, all of the benefits of lower costs are passed on to consumers in terms of higher output and lower prices.**

The case of a rise in costs is just the reverse, and in the short run the effects will be shared between consumers, in terms of higher prices, and producers, in terms of losses. In the long run, however, firms will leave the industry until those remaining can cover all their costs. Therefore, the effects of higher costs are borne fully by consumers in terms of lower output and higher prices in the long run.

Monopoly In a monopoly, a fall in marginal costs will cause a reduction in price and an increase in output. (You should draw a graph to illustrate this for yourself.) Thus, the direction of the change in price and output in response to a change in cost is the same in monopoly as in perfect competition. But the magnitude of the change will be less in monopoly than in competition. Since a monopolist necessarily has barriers to entry (or he wouldn't be a monopolist), the higher profit that he earns as a result of a fall in his costs does *not* attract new entrants whose competition will drive profits to their original level.

> **In monopoly the benefits of lower costs and the burden of higher costs are shared between the consumers, in terms of price and output variations, and the producers, in terms of profit variations both in the short run and in the long run.**

We now have a powerful tool at our command: once we can relate anything in which we are interested to a change in either costs or revenues, we have a series of predictions already worked out. We shall see examples of how this can be done in the next section of this chapter and in the following chapter.

The effect of taxes on price and output

There are many kinds of taxes which affect the costs of a firm. We shall consider only three of them here; a tax that is a fixed amount per unit produced; a tax that is a fixed amount; and a tax that is a fixed percentage of profits. The first is called a per-unit tax, the second a lump-sum tax and the third a profits tax.

Per-unit tax A per-unit tax increases the cost of producing each unit by the amount of the tax. The marginal cost curve of every firm shifts vertically upwards by the amount of the tax. In perfect competition, this means that the industry supply curve shifts upward by the amount of the tax. Now all we need is to refer to the results of the previous section in order to derive the required predictions.

The effects of a per-unit tax on the output of a competitive industry are as follows:
(1) In the short run, the price will rise but by less than the amount of the tax, so that the burden will be shared by consumers and producers;
(2) In the long run, the industry will contract, profits will return to normal and the whole burden will fall on consumers;
(3) If cost curves of firms remaining in the industry are unaffected by the contraction in the size of the industry, price will rise in the long run by the full amount of the tax.

The second of the above predictions is an example of a most important general prediction that recurs constantly: in an industry with freedom of entry or exit, profits (as the term is defined in economics) must be forced to zero in the long run. Thus, any temporary advantage or disadvantage given to the industry by government policy, by private conniving or by anything else, must be dissipated in the long run, since free entry and exit will ensure that surviving firms earn zero profits.

Government intervention in an industry with freedom of entry and exit can influence the size of the industry, the total volume of its sales, and the price at which its goods are sold; but intervention cannot influence the long-run profitability of the firms that remain in the industry.

Many a government policy has started out to raise the profitability of a particular industry and only ended up increasing the number of firms operating at an unchanged level of profits.

Although the monopolist has no supply curve, the tax does shift his marginal cost curve. The analysis given in the chapter allows us to state the following:

In the short run and in the long run, the burden of a tax per unit on a monopoly will be shared between consumers, in terms of lower output and higher prices, and the producer, in terms of lower profits.

Lump-sum tax Consider now the effect of a lump-sum tax. Such taxes increase the fixed costs of the firm but do not increase marginal costs. The short-run effects on price and output of a change in fixed costs is zero, both in perfect competition and in monopoly. Since both marginal costs and marginal revenues remain unchanged, the profit-maximizing level of output cannot be affected. Hence we deduce the implication:

A lump-sum tax leaves price and output unchanged in the short run unless the tax is so high that it causes firms simply to abandon production at once.

The long-run effects of a lump-sum tax differ between monopolistic and competitive industries. Consider monopoly first. Assuming that the firm was previously making profits, the tax merely reduces the level of these profits. But, since the monopolist was making as much money as he possibly could before the tax, there is nothing that he can do to shift any of the tax burden onto his customers.

In the long run, the lump-sum tax has no effect on a monopolist's price and output.

(Of course, if the lump-sum tax is so large that, even at the profit-maximizing level of output, profits become negative, the monopolist will cease production in the long run.)

In perfect competition, the lump-sum tax will have a long-run effect on price and output. If the industry was in equilibrium with zero profits before the tax was instituted, then the tax will cause losses. Although nothing will happen in the short run to price and output, equipment will not be replaced as it wears out. Thus, in the long run, the industry will contract, and price will rise until the whole tax has been passed on to consumers and the firms remaining in the industry are again covering total costs.

A lump-sum tax will have no effect on a competitive industry in the short run, but in the long run it will cause the exit of firms, lower output and higher price until the whole of the tax is borne by consumers.

Profits tax A famous prediction is that a tax on profits (in the economist's sense) will have no effect on price and output. Let us first see how the prediction is derived and then consider its application to real-world situations.

In perfect competition there are no profits in long-run equilibrium. Since profits taxes would not be paid by a perfectly competitive firm when it was in long-run equilibrium, it follows that the existence of the tax would not affect the firm's long-run behaviour. A monopoly firm usually earns profits in the long run and therefore would pay the profits tax. The tax would reduce its profits but would not cause the firm to alter its quantity produced nor (hence) its price. This is illustrated in Figure 22.5, in which profits are shown as varying with the quantity the monopolist sells.

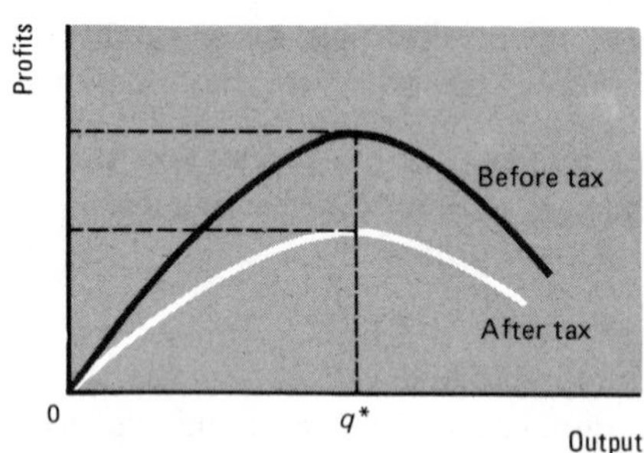

Fig. 22.5 A tax on pure profits will affect neither price nor output

(Since the firm faces a downward-sloping demand curve, every quantity implies a particular price.) Before the profits tax, the firm maximized profits by selling the quantity q^*. Now assume that a 20 per cent profits tax is imposed. Since every level of output is associated with 20 per cent less profit than before, the level of output, q^*, that produced the highest profits before the tax would still do so after the tax was imposed. Since q^* would remain the profit-maximizing output, the monopolist's price would not change.

A tax on profit, as it is defined in economics, affects neither price nor output in perfect competition and in monopoly. Hence it has no effect on the allocation of resources.

Does this prediction apply to 'profits taxes' as they are levied in the real world? The answer is an emphatic 'No' because profits as they are defined in tax law are very different from profits as defined in economics. In particular the tax-law definition includes earnings of the factor of production, capital, and the reward for risk-taking. To economists these are a part of costs but for tax purposes they are a part of profits.

We may notice one or two of the many consequences of such 'profits' taxes. First, perfectly competitive firms will pay 'profits' taxes even in long-run equilibrium, since they use capital and must earn enough money to pay a return on it. Second, the tax will affect costs differently in different industries. Assume that one industry is very labour-intensive, so that 90 per cent of its costs of production go to wages and only 10 per cent to capital and other factors, while another industry is very capital-intensive, so that fully 50 per cent of its costs (in the economist's sense) are a return to capital. The 'profits' tax will take a very small bite of the total earnings of the first industry and a large bit of those of the second industry. If the industries were equally profitable (in the economist's sense) before the 'profits' tax, they would not be afterwards, and there would be a tendency for producers to be attracted into the first industry and out of the second one. This would cause prices to change until both industries became equally profitable, after which no further movement would occur.

A tax on profit as it is defined in tax law does not leave the allocation of resources unaffected.

Many further ways in which real-world taxes on profits influence the allocation of resources could be mentioned, but enough has been said to suggest that those who fail to make the distinction between taxes levied on what the economist means by profits and taxes levied on what the tax inspector means by profits will make predictions about the real world that do not in fact follow from their own theory. The theory predicts that a tax on 'pure profits' will have no effect on the price and output policy of firms, but that a tax on 'profits' as they are defined by the taxing authorities will have a definite effect on these decisions. Clearly, great care must be taken when the same term is given one meaning by economists and another meaning by the general public or by government officials.

A competitive industry that becomes monopolistic

As well as yielding certain testable predictions based on the minimal amount of knowledge normally assumed, the theory of the firm and industry provides a framework into which more detailed knowledge can be fitted. Further testable predictions can then be developed. If, for example, we know the elasticity of demand, and how the demand curve is shifting through time, and if we have detailed information about costs, the theory will yield some very precise predictions. In this section we shall consider one example of the use of the theory in a specific context. This example, although hypothetical, is not unlike many actual situations, particularly those in the retail trades.

Assume that in a particular city the barbers all belong to a single trade association. There is freedom of entry into the industry in the sense that anyone who has obtained a stated set of qualifications can set up as a barber. All barbers, however, must join the association and must abide by its rules. The association sets the price of haircuts and strictly enforces this single price. Thus there is no price competition among barbers.

Periodically the association raises the fixed price of haircuts in an attempt to raise the incomes of its members. The association is strong enough to prevent any illicit price-cutting and to resist all attempts to secede. The question is: will the barbers succeed in raising their incomes by raising the price of haircuts? If you were a consulting economist called in to advise the barbers' association, what would you predict to be the consequences of this price rise? Try to develop these predictions for yourself before you read on.

Clearly we need to distinguish between the short- and the long-run effects of this increase in the price of haircuts. In the short run the number of barbers is fixed. Thus in the short run the answer is simple enough: it all depends on the elasticity of the demand for haircuts. If the demand elasticity is less than one, total expenditure on haircuts will rise and so, therefore, will the income of barbers; if demand elasticity exceeds one, the barbers' incomes will fall. The problem in the short run amounts to that of getting some empirical knowledge about the elasticity of demand for haircuts. If you were actually advising the barbers' organization you might be lucky enough to be able to refer to a full-scale econometric study of demand. In the case of haircuts this is unlikely and you would probably have to try to gain some idea of demand elasticity by studying the effects of changes in haircut prices either at other times or in other places. We cannot go into this matter except to mention that you should not fall into the trap of reasoning as follows: 'Haircuts are a necessity, for no one goes without one. Therefore the demand for haircuts will be almost perfectly inelastic.' The reader should easily spot the fallacy in this argument. There are many reasons why the demand for haircuts is not perfectly inelastic. For example, the time between haircuts is by no means a constant. An increase in the average period between haircuts from three to four weeks would cause a 28·5 per cent decline in demand; if this change in habits were occasioned by a 15 per cent rise in price, then the demand elasticity over this price range would be 1·9! Furthermore, habits can change drastically, as the change in fashion in the 1960s in favour of long hair shows. Sometimes such changes may be caused by non-economic factors, but they can also occur in response to a price change.

Let us say, however, that, on the basis of the best available evidence, you estimate the elasticity of demand *over the relevant price range* to be substantially less than one, say 0·3. You then predict that the barbers will be successful in raising incomes in the short run; a 20 per cent rise in price will be met by a 6 per cent fall in custom, so that total revenue of the typical barber would rise by about 15 per cent. In predicting the consequences you would also need to estimate the length of the short run for this industry (a couple of years?).

Now what about the long run? If barbers were just covering all costs before the price change, they will now be earning profits. Barbering will become an attractive trade relative to others requiring equal skill and training, and there will be an inflow of barbers into the industry. As the number of barbers rises, the same amount of business must be shared among more firms, so that a typical barber will find a steady decrease in the amount of trade that he does. His profits will thus decrease. Profits may also be squeezed from another direction. Faced with increasing excess capacity – a typical barber could handle much more business than does in fact come his way – barbers may compete against each other for the limited number of customers. Since they are unable to compete through price cuts, they can only compete in service. They may redecorate their shops and buy expensive magazines. In these ways competition will raise costs. Thus, the profits of the individual barber will be attacked from two directions: falling revenues and rising costs. This movement will continue until barbers are once again just covering all costs. After which there will be no further attraction to new entrants. The industry will settle down in a new position of long-run equilibrium in which individual barbers are just covering all of their opportunity costs. There will be more barbers than in the original situation, but each barber will be working a lower fraction of the day and will be idle for a larger fraction (i.e., there will be excess capacity); the total number of haircuts given by each will be diminished, and possibly the level of costs and service will have increased. Thus your report would say 'You may succeed in the short run (if demand is sufficiently inelastic) but the policy is bound to be self-defeating in the long run'.

The general moral of the story is now familiar:

> **If you cannot control entry, you cannot succeed in earning profits in the long run. If price competition is ruled out, then profits will be driven down by the creation of excess capacity. Producers' associations that maintain positive profits must succeed in restricting entry.**

Is oligopoly theory necessary?

So far in this chapter we have managed to analyse a number of cases using only the theories of perfect competition and monopoly – plus some of the concepts of monopolistic competition, in the barber example. Some economists argue that these two polar theories are all that are necessary to predict the outcome of any situation in which we might be interested. These economists recognize the existence of small-group industries, but they believe that such industries will behave either like perfectly competitive ones or like monopolies; thus no other theories will be needed to understand and predict their behaviour. Probably the majority of economists do not accept this view and believe that much behaviour, particularly in the manufacturing industries, cannot be understood without an explicit theory of oligopoly. These economists would point to such cases as the two that follow.

Cigarettes The American cigarette industry is one of the most highly concentrated of manufacturing industries. It has three dominant firms: the American Tobacco Company, R. J. Reynolds and Liggett & Myers. If we were to analyse it using the theory of monopoly, we would predict that the cigarette companies would avoid competing with one another either in buying tobacco or in setting the price of cigarettes. We would also predict that substantial profits would persist for many years. These things *have* happened. In an anti-trust suit against these three companies, it was shown that they conspired to purchase tobacco in auctions without bidding against one another, and that all kept their prices of cigarettes high relative to the costs of production. A dramatic (and monopolistic) episode occurred in June 1931, when, in the depths of the Depression and in the face of the lowest tobacco-leaf prices in a quarter of a century, the three big cigarette companies (which then controlled 90 per cent of the market among them) all raised their prices.

But here the monopoly analogy breaks down, since the policy proved spectacularly unsuccessful. Smokers shifted in large numbers to cheaper brands made by other companies, and ultimately prices fell well below the May 1931 level as the big three tried to regain their market shares. (They have never regained as large a share as they held in May 1931.)

The profits of these cigarette companies were, and remain, well above the average for all manufacturing industries. In this respect, the theory of monopoly predicts well. It is also successful in predicting the lack of competition in the leaf market and the absence of serious price competition in the last 45 years.

But there are other characteristics of the cigarette industry that are not predicted by the theory of monopoly. The most notable is the enormous expenditure on advertising by each of the companies. Advertising expenditure raises costs and lowers profits. Some kinds of advertising are consistent with monopoly theory. If a monopolist, through advertising, can change consumers' preference towards his product in such a way as to shift the demand curve to the right, or make it more inelastic, he may increase revenues by more than the cost of the advertising. But such advertising is product-oriented advertising ('smoke!'), not brand-name advertising ('smoke Player's'). It certainly would not pay a monopolist to advertise two of his brands in competition with each other.

Advertising by cigarette companies has two aspects. First, it represents intense non-price competition among the existing firms, who recognize that it does not pay to compete by price cutting; second, it represents an attempt to raise barriers against potential new entrants. The high cost of establishing a new brand name represents a really substantial barrier to entry, and the theory of oligopoly predicts that advertising will occur for these reasons. Neither the kind nor the amount of cigarette advertising that actually goes on is of the sort that could be explained by the theory of monopoly.

Steam-turbine generators Three electrical manufacturers, General Electric, Westinghouse and Allis-Chalmers, produce more than 95 per cent of all the steam-turbine generators in the United States. In 1960, these three firms were charged with having held a series of meetings beginning at least as early as June 1957, for the purpose of agreeing on prices and sharing the market among themselves. Subsequently each of the firms pleaded guilty. Do we need a theory of oligopoly to explain this behaviour, or is the theory of monopoly sufficient? Certainly, the behaviour as charged in the indictments is fully consistent with the theory of monopoly. For the period from July 1957 to May 1958, the conspiracy apparently succeeded in producing something very close to joint profit-maximizing behaviour, including extensive price discrimination.

Midway in 1958, however, the co-operative behaviour broke down: prices fell very drastically, and the three sellers became involved in vigorous price competition among themselves. Among the reasons for this change was the threat by the Tennessee Valley Authority to ask for foreign bids on a turbine generator it required, a slackening of demand, and rumours of anti-trust prosecution. All attempts to stop the price cutting were in vain. Behaviour had ceased to be monopolistic.

In analysing the market behaviour in this industry, the monopoly model would have led to accurate predictions for one period and to very poor predictions for another. Simple models that predict with accuracy under some circumstances but not under others are useful if we know, or can define, the situations in which they will work and those in which they will not work. *But defining these situations is precisely the purpose of more complex or elaborate theories.* For example, if the theory of oligopoly were to tell us that the monopoly model will work well for steam-turbine generators in periods of strong demand, but will not work when firms develop excess capacity, it would be useful in itself and would also increase the usefulness of monopoly theory.

The predictions of the theory of the firm and industry

In this chapter we have developed a number of quite general predictions of the theory of the firm and industry, and we have also illustrated the use of the theory in yielding predictions after certain specific information has been added to its general assumptions. It is fashionable these days amongst professional economists to emphasize the inadequacies and the failures of the traditional theory of the firm. Such shortcomings, real though they are, should not be allowed to obscure the fact that this theory is an outstanding intellectual achievement. The theory of perfect competition shows in a quite general way how a large number of separate profit-maximizing firms can, with no conscious co-ordination, produce an equilibrium which depends only on the 'technical data' of demand and costs. Individual attitudes and eccentricities of producers and a host of other factors are successfully ignored, and it is shown how an equilibrium follows solely from the conditions of costs and demand. The analysis extends *mutatis mutandis* to the cases of monopolistic competition and monopoly. It does not extend, however, to oligopoly. In the case of competition among the few, it is no longer true that the solution depends only on the 'objective' factors of costs and market demand. The attitudes of each competitor to the stratagems of his few opponents becomes important, and, for the same costs and market demand, the equilibrium of the industry will vary considerably as the psychology of the competitors varies. It is here that the traditional theory has had the least success, and it may be true that an entirely different framework will have to be worked out in order to deal successfully with some aspects of oligopoly.

The consumer goods with which the ordinary citizen is most familiar – motor cars, radios, TV sets, washing machines, cookers etc. – are mostly produced by oligopolistic industries. For this reason we must beware of reaching the false conclusion that the perfectly competitive model is not applicable to any significant number of markets. This is emphatically not so. Markets where buyers and sellers adjust quantities to a given price that they cannot change by their own individual efforts abound in the economy. Foreign-exchange markets, markets for raw materials, markets for many agricultural commodities, most futures markets, the markets for gold and other precious metals and stock and bond markets are but a few whose behaviour is comprehensible with, but makes no sense without, the basic model of perfect competition (possibly augmented by one or two specific additional assumptions to catch the key institutional details of each case).

Manufactured consumer goods are, as already mentioned, dominated by oligopolistic industries. Retail trades and many service industries come close to the conditions of monopolistic competition in that there is free entry, a large number of competing firms and product differentiation (the person who provides the service matters, and each person is different).

Clearly, the whole armoury of market forms is relevant to our economy. Happily, as illustrated in this chapter, existing theories do make many important predictions about how our economy behaves. Unhappily, however, there are all too many situations for which current theory does not provide clear predictions.

23

Monopoly versus competition: predictions about performance

Monopoly has been regarded with suspicion for a very long time. Even today in some quarters it is given a major portion of the blame for inflation, for the energy shortage, for discrimination in employment and for inequalities in income. It is widely believed that modern economic theory has *proved* that monopoly is a system whereby the powerful producer exploits the consumer, whereas the competitive system always works to the consumer's advantage. In *The Wealth of Nations* (1776), Adam Smith developed a ringing attack on monopolies and monopolists. Since that time, most economists have criticized monopoly and advocated freer competition.

Is the hostility towards monopoly justified? In this chapter we shall first consider the case for choosing between the two polar forms of monopoly and perfect competition. We shall then go on to consider policy problems that relate the market forms in between these two extremes.

The case for preferring perfect competition to monopoly

The classical anti-monopoly case is based first on establishing the differences in behaviour between a competitive and a monopolized industry, and second on the argument that there are clear reasons for preferring the results of perfect competition to those of monopoly. This case is based on the static theory of resource allocation *within the context of a given technology*. It is based, in other words, on comparative static analysis of long-run situations. We shall see in the second part of this chapter that serious doubts about the validity of the case arise when it is transferred to the very long run.

Price and output under monopoly and perfect competition

The comparison that we need here was first made in the first section of Chapter 22, so that only a brief rehearsal is given now.

Equilibrium under perfect competition occurs where supply equals demand. Since the supply curve is the sum of the marginal cost curves, it follows that in equilibrium, marginal cost equals price. This is illustrated in Figure 23.1. The competitive supply curve is labelled *MC* to remind us that it is the sum of the marginal cost curves of the individual firms; the competitive output is q_c and the competitive price is p_c.

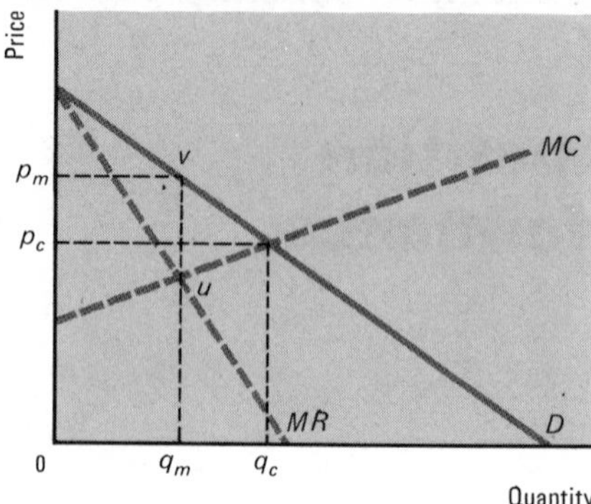

Fig. 23.1 The effect on price and output of the monopolization of a perfectly competitive industry

Now assume that this industry is monopolized as a result of a single firm buying out all the individual producers. Further assume that each plant's cost curve is unaffected by this change. In other words, assume that there are neither economies nor diseconomies resulting from the co-ordinated planning of production by a single unit. This means that the marginal cost will be the same to the monopolist as to the competitive industry: the competitive industry's supply curve will be the marginal cost curve to the monopolist. But the monopolist who seeks to maximize profits will equate marginal cost to marginal revenue, not to price. The output of the industry falls from q_c to q_m, while the price rises from p_c to p_m.

> **A monopolist facing the same costs and market demand as a competitive industry will have a lower output and a higher price than the competitive industry.**

Why the perfectly competitive result is thought superior

Are we justified in saying that a lower-price, higher-output situation is in any sense better, or more nearly optimal, than the reverse? We cannot go into this inquiry in any detail here, and we shall have to satisfy ourselves with a rather intuitive statement of why the allocation of resources resulting from perfect competition can be regarded as superior to that resulting from monopoly. The argument is based mainly on two predictions about production under conditions of perfect competition: at equilibrium, the level of cost is the lowest level attainable, given the existing technology; and marginal cost equals price.

The advantage of having output produced at the lowest average total cost

The first prediction follows from the proposition that perfectly competitive firms must, in long-run equilibrium, be producing at the minimum point on their long-run average total cost curves. (See page 254.) The significance of producing output at the lowest possible cost is obvious: the fewer the resources devoted to producing a given quantity of any one commodity, the greater the total output of all other commodities that can be obtained from any given national supply of resources.

The advantage of having marginal cost equated to price

We saw on page 251 that in a perfectly competitive equilibrium marginal cost equals price. We also saw on page 264 that in a monopolistic equilibrium, marginal cost is less than price (since it equals marginal revenue). What is the advantage of the former situation over the latter?

The price of the commodity indicates the money value that consumers place on the last unit of the commodity that they purchase. Consider the individual household's demand curve, shown in Figure 23.2. As the price rises, the household

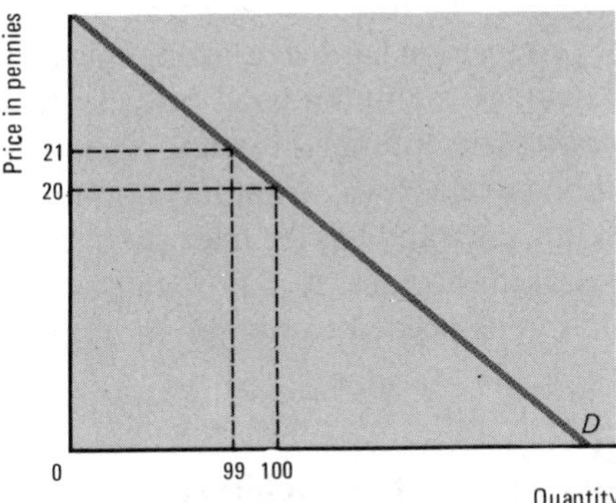

Fig. 23.2 An individual demand curve: the household is prepared to pay more than the market price for all but the last unit bought

buys fewer units. If the market price settles at 20p, it will buy 100 units; thus it gets all but the last unit at a price *less* than it would be prepared to pay for them. (It is prepared, for example, to pay 21p each to get 99 units.) Thus, assuming that the household's demand curve is downward sloping, the price measures what it is prepared to pay for the last unit it purchases, but it would be prepared to pay more than the current price in order to obtain all but the last unit (which is why it would continue to buy them at higher prices). To obtain additional units, the household is prepared to pay only an amount less than the market price (which is why it does not at present buy these additional units).

Since marginal cost equals price in perfectly competitive equilibrium, it follows that households are prepared to pay, for the last unit they actually purchase, an amount exactly equal to the cost of producing that last unit. In monopoly, however, price exceeds marginal cost and it follows that households pay, for the last unit they actually purchase, an amount greater than the cost of producing it. Furthermore, households would be prepared to buy further units for an amount greater than the cost of producing these units; they are, however, not allowed to purchase these extra units because the monopoly firm is restricting output in order to maximize its profits. In Figure 23.1, for example, the marginal cost at the monopolist's equilibrium is $q_m u$ and price is $q_m v$ so that households are prepared to pay uv more for another unit than the actual cost of producing that unit. They would also be willing to buy at a price in excess of the marginal cost of production a total of $q_c - q_m$ units more than they are permitted to buy.

There is a strong intuitive appeal to the idea that consumers will in some sense be 'better off' when marginal cost equals price than when it is less than price. It can in fact be shown, and it is a well-known proposition in welfare economics, that, given a number of conditions, the equating of marginal cost to price in all lines of production will yield an optimal allocation of resources *in the sense that it will be impossible to produce more of one commodity without simultaneously producing less of at least one other commodity*; while when marginal costs do not equal prices in some industries, this will result in a non-optimal allocation *in the sense that it will be possible to produce more of one commodity without simultaneously having to produce less of any other commodity, simply by reallocating resources among the economy's industries.* The potential advantage of an optimal over a non-optimal allocation of resources is obvious: if more of something can be produced without producing less of anything else, it would be *possible* to distribute this extra output so as to make all of the society's households better off.

The demonstration of the above proposition can be found in any textbook of welfare economics. There is no doubt that the proposition has had a strong effect on attitudes towards the value of the price system. If the unhindered price system operating through perfect competition produces an optimal situation, then any interference by the central authorities can only move us away from this optimum. Because the proposition has exerted so much influence and has led many to oppose all forms of market intervention by the central authorities, it is probably worth pointing out just how restrictive are the conditions needed to obtain an optimal allocation of resources.

Requirements for an optimum allocation of resources to be achieved

The proposition that perfect competition leads to an optimal allocation of resources requires, among other things, that the following conditions be met.

(1) *For an optimal allocation of resources under perfect competition, there should be no divergence between private and social cost anywhere in the economy* (see Chapter 30). From society's point of view it pays to produce a good up to the point at which the revenue gained from the last unit equals the opportunity cost of making it, only if the firms' private costs reflect the opportunity costs to society of using the resources elsewhere, and if the firms' private revenues reflect the gains to society of having an extra unit of this good produced. We shall see in Chapter 30 that social and private costs often diverge. This critical condition is therefore by no means always fulfilled.

(2) *For an optimal allocation of resources, there should be perfect competition in all sectors of the economy, ensuring that marginal cost equals marginal revenue everywhere.* It this is not so, we have no idea what the effect will be of making marginal cost equal marginal revenue somewhere in the economy. Specifically, if in a world of mixed market structures, we break up one monopoly and make it into a competitive industry, we have no general presumption even in a theoretical model that this will move us closer to an optimum position.[1]

(3) *For an optimal allocation of resources under perfect competition, there should be no external economies or diseconomies of scale.* An external economy or diseconomy is beyond the influence of a single firm and thus does not enter into the firm's calculations, even though it may be important for society.

[1] This important proposition upsets much of the basis of piecemeal welfare economics. We know how to identify the best of all possible worlds (from the limited point of view of the optimum we are discussing), but we have little clear idea how to order two states of the very imperfect world in which we live. If this were not so economists could not disagree as much as they do about specific policy measures. More advanced students may wish to consult one of the early demonstrations of this proposition given in R. G. Lipsey and K. J. Lancaster, 'The General Theory of Second Best', *The Review of Economic Studies*, Vol. XXIV, No. 63, 1956–7.

It is clear that these conditions for an optimal allocation of resources are not fulfilled in any modern economy. In particular, perfect competition does not prevail everywhere, since many firms face downward sloping demand curves. These firms will not take production to the point where marginal cost equals price.

The theory of the optimal allocation of resources under perfect competition provides very little firm guidance to practical policy concerning market intervention by the central authorities. Economic theory does *not* predict that in our societies of mixed market structures any increase in the degree of competitiveness will necessarily increase the efficiency of resource allocation. To evaluate current policy we need to know the effect on the efficiency of resource allocation of intervention to produce a little more or a little less competition in a few sectors of the economy. Unfortunately this is just what we cannot do in general, and every case must be studied and evaluated in terms of its own specific circumstances.

The political appeal of perfect competition

To someone who believes in the individual and fears all power groups,[1] the perfectly competitive model is almost too good to be true. In the perfectly competitive world, no single firm and no single consumer has any power over the market whatsoever. Both individual consumers and individual producers are members of a group of many similar consumers and producers, and no single one of them can affect the market. Individually they are passive quantity adjustors. If we add to this the assumption that firms are profit maximizers, all firms become passive responders to market signals, always doing what is most desirable from the society's point of view. The great impersonal force of the market produces an appropriate response to every important change. If, for example, tastes change, prices will change and the allocation of resources will move in the appropriate direction. But throughout the whole process, no one will have any power over anyone else. Millions of firms are reacting to the same price changes. If one refuses to react, there will be countless other profit-maximizing firms eager to make the appropriate changes. If one firm refuses to take coloured employees or takes any other decision based on prejudice, there will be millions of other firms that will recognize that profit-maximization is not consistent with discrimination on the basis of race, colour or creed or anything other than how hard a man is prepared to work.

It is a noble model: no one has power over anyone, and yet the system behaves in a systematic and purposeful way. Many will feel that it is a pity that it corresponds so imperfectly to economic reality as we know it today. Not surprisingly, some people still cling tenaciously to the belief that the perfectly competitive model describes the world in which we live; so many problems would disappear if only it did.

Unsettled questions of monopoly versus competition

The classical condemnation of non-competitive forms of behaviour was based on the belief that the alternative to monopoly was perfect competition. Today we

[1] As Lord Acton put it a long time ago, 'power tends to corrupt and absolute power corrupts absolutely.'

realize that very often the effective choice is not between monopoly and perfect competition, but between more or less oligopoly, so that we are not sure what effects a specific intervention will have on price and output. Thus, even if we accept the perfectly competitive result as being more desirable than a completely monopolistic one, this does not in itself tell us much about the real decisions that face us. In the remainder of this chapter we shall talk about competitive and monopolistic situations in general terms. We do this because we wish to study and evaluate the effects of encouraging a little more or less competition than we now have.

The importance of the given-cost assumption

The classical predictions about monopoly depend critically on the assumption that costs are unaffected when an industry is monopolized. If any savings are effected by combining numerous competing groups into a single integrated operation, then the costs of producing any given level of output will be lower than they were previously. If this cost reduction does occur, then it is possible for output to be raised and price to be lowered as a result of the monopolization of a perfectly competitive industry.

Such a situation is illustrated in Figure 23.3. The competitive equilibrium price is

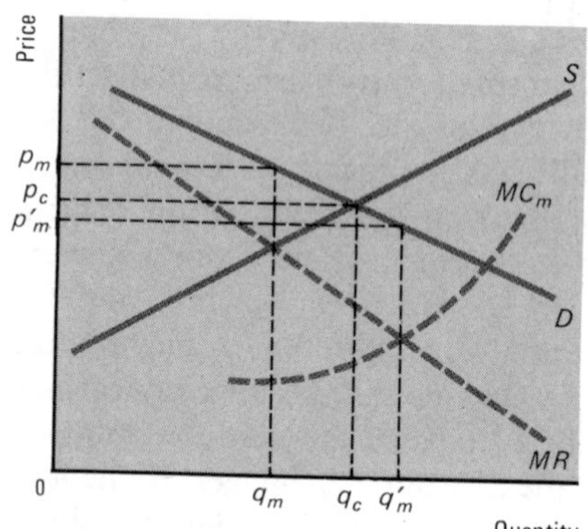

Fig. 23.3 Possible effects on price and output of a monopoly that is more efficient than a large number of competing firms

p_c and quantity is q_c. If the industry were monopolized and costs were unaffected, production would fall to q_m and price would rise to p_m. If, however, the integration of the industry into a single unit causes some increase in the efficiency of organization and thereby reduces costs, then the marginal cost curve will shift downward. If it shifts to MC_m, then production will rise to q'_m and price will fall to p'_m.

The monopolization of an industry, combined with a sufficiently large consequent increase in efficiency, can result in a fall in price and a rise in quantity produced, as compared to the competitive industry.[1]

Of course, it is also possible that the monopolization of an industry will reduce the efficiency of production and so shift the marginal cost curve upward. In this case, monopolization will, *a fortiori*, raise price and lower output as compared to the

[1] You should be able to show for yourself that if the elasticity of demand were less than one at the competitive price, the monopolist would reduce output and raise price, no matter how large the reduction in his costs.

competitive industry. You should draw your own diagram, showing the effects on price and output of a monopolization that caused costs to rise above those ruling under competition.

On the one hand, it is sometimes argued that monopolization will lower costs because wasteful duplication will be eliminated, and because economies of scale will result from, for example, establishing one co-ordinated management body for the industry. On the other hand, it is sometimes argued that competition forces the individual firm to be efficient because it will not survive unless it keeps its costs as low as its competitors', whereas although monopolistic inefficiency reduces profits, it need not drive the monopolistic firm out of business. What is clear is that we cannot predict the effects on price and output of monopolizing a competitive industry unless we know the effect of this change on the industry's costs. This is as far as our theory can take us. It can predict what empirical magnitudes are important, but until we have some evidence of the effects of monopolization on an industry's cost structure, we cannot predict the effect that it will have on price and output.

The effect of market structure on innovation: the very long run

The classical case against monopoly concerns the allocation of resources within the context of a fixed technology. We are now going to consider the very long run, where the production function is changing due to the discovery of lower-cost methods of producing old products and the introduction of new and improved products. We shall ask if market organization affects the rate of innovation. Before reading on it would be helpful to refresh your memory of the discussion of invention and innovation by re-reading pages 232-4.

The incentive to introduce cost-saving innovations Both the monopolist and the perfect competitor have a profit incentive to introduce cost-reducing innovations. A monopoly can always increase its profits if it can reduce its costs. We saw in Chapter 22 (page 296) that a cost reduction will cause the monopoly to produce more, to sell at a lower price, and thus to increase its profits. Furthermore, since it is able to prevent the entry of new firms into the industry, these additional profits will persist into the long run. Thus, from the standpoint of maximizing profits, a monopoly has both a short- and a long-run incentive to reduce its costs.

The firm in perfect competition or in monopolistic competition has the same incentive in the short run, but not in the long run. In the short run, a reduction in costs will allow a firm that was just covering costs to earn profits. In the long run, other firms will be attracted into the industry by these profits. Existing firms will copy the cost-saving innovation, and new firms will enter the industry using the new techniques. This will go on until the profits of the innovator have been eliminated.

The effectiveness of profits as an incentive to reduce costs for a firm in competition will thus depend on the magnitude of the extra profits and on how long they persist. If, for example, it only takes a few months for existing firms and new entrants to copy and install the new invention, then the original innovating firm will earn profits for only a few months. These may not be sufficient to compensate for the risks and the costs of developing the innovation. In such cases, the incentive to innovate will be absent from a competitive industry. On the other hand, if it takes several years for other firms to copy and install the cost-saving innovation, then the profits earned over these years by the innovating firm may be more than sufficient to compensate for all costs and risks. In this case, the incentive to innovate is present in a competitive industry.

> **Monopolies have both a short and a long-run incentive to innovate; competitive firms have only a short-run incentive.**

Funds for research and development So far we have considered the profit incentive to introduce new innovations. Another consideration is the availability of the resources needed to finance research to invent new methods and new products. It is often held that the large profits available to monopolistic firms provide a ready fund out of which research and development will be financed. The typical, perfectly competitive firm, according to this argument, is only earning enough money to cover all its costs, and it will have few funds to spare for research and development. Supporters of this view can point to much illustrative evidence. They note, for example, that few of the innovations that have vastly raised agricultural productivity over the last century were developed by the typical competitive farming unit; they were developed, rather, by a few oligopolistic or monopolistic manufacturers of farm equipment and by researchers in universities and in government-financed research institutions.

Penalties for not innovating A further argument is that competitive firms *must* innovate or they will lose out to their competitors, while, although monopolists have an incentive to innovate, they do not need to do so because they are insulated from potential competitors by their barriers to entry. There is lack of agreement on the importance of this argument. Opponents of it would argue, first, that it is wrong to think a monopolist or oligopolist is shielded from all competition. It is always possible that some new firm will be able to break into the market by developing some new, similar, but superior product that evades existing patents and other barriers to entry. Furthermore, the larger the monopoly profits of the existing firm(s), the larger the incentive for new firms to break into the market. Thus, it is argued, all monopoly and oligopoly firms are in potential competition with possible new entrants, and the firm that sits back and does not innovate will not long remain profitable. The second argument that opponents would advance is that the penalty for not innovating is not always high in perfect competition. If innovations are hard to copy, then there *is* a strong incentive for a competitive firm to innovate and a big penalty for firms who do not innovate because a long time will be needed before other firms can copy and catch up with the innovator. On the other hand, if innovations are easy to copy, there is a smaller incentive for the competitive firm to innovate and a smaller penalty for the firm that fails to innovate, since it is easy for it to copy and catch up with the innovator. The above discussion may be summarized as follows:

> **All firms have an incentive to innovate since they can increase their profits with a successful innovation. The greater the barriers to entry and the harder it is for other firms already in the industry to copy the innovation, the longer will the profits of innovating persist and, thus, the larger will be the incentive to innovate. In competitive industries without barriers to entry, there will be little incentive to make innovations that are very easily copied, since both the profits of innovating and the losses from not innovating ahead of other firms will be very short-lived.**

Schumpeter's defence of oligopoly and monopoly The greatest opponent of the classical position on monopoly was the distinguished Austrian (and later American) economist, Joseph A. Schumpeter.[1] Schumpeter's theory relies on many of the forces just discussed. His basic argument has two main parts. The first is that innovations that lower costs of production – by increasing output per head and creating economic growth – have a much larger effect on living standards than any 'misallocation' of resources causing too much production of one kind of commodity and too little of another at any one time. The second part is based on his theory that innovation is functionally related to market forms in such a way that there is likely to be much more innovation under monopoly and oligopoly than under monopolistic and perfect competition. Let us look at each of these points in turn.

According to the classical case, monopoly results in a misallocation of resources with too few resources devoted to producing goods in the monopolistic sector and too many in the competitive sector. Schumpeter believed that the losses due to this misallocation were small relative to the gains and losses due to variations in the rate of economic growth. Modern measures made since Schumpeter wrote have tended to support him in this contention. It appears very unlikely that the losses due to monopolistic and oligopolistic misallocations can amount to more than 2 or 3 per cent of a country's national income.[2] But the national income of most countries is growing at that rate each year, and a growth rate of 3 per cent per year doubles material living standards in under 25 years.

The second part of Schumpeter's argument is that monopolistic and oligopolistic market forms are more conducive to growth than perfect competition. He claimed that only the incentive of profits leads people to take the great risks of innovation, and that monopoly power is much more important than competition in providing the climate under which innovation occurs. The large short-run profits of the monopolist provide the incentive for others to try to usurp some of these for themselves. If a frontal attack on the monopolist's barriers to entry is not possible, then the barriers will be circumvented by such dodges as the development of similar products against which the monopolist will not have entry protection. Schumpeter called the replacing of one monopoly by another through the invention of new products or new production techniques the *process of creative destruction.*

Since, in Schumpeter's theory, monopoly and oligopoly are more conducive to growth-creating innovations than perfect or monopolistic competition, it follows that the 'worse' the allocation of resources at any moment of time, i.e. the greater the amount of monopolization, the more rapid the rate of innovation and the resulting long-run rise in living standards. This very important hypothesis cannot be handled with normal long-run theory, because long-run theory *assumes* constant technology.

Schumpeter put part of his argument in the following words:

> What we have got to accept is that it [monopoly and oligopoly] has come to be the most powerful engine of progress and in particular of the long-run expansion of total output not only in spite of, but to a considerable extent through, this strategy [of creating monopolies] which looks so restrictive when viewed in the individual case and from the individual point

[1] His most famous book is *The Theory of Economic Development* (English edn.; Harvard University Press, 1934). The beginning student is referred to the lucid but less technical *Capitalism, Socialism and Democracy* (5th edn.: Allen & Unwin, 1977). Both works are available in paperback.

[2] In one of the most famous of these studies Professor Harberger of the University of Chicago puts the figure at about $\frac{1}{10}$ of 1 per cent of the US national income!

of time. In this respect, perfect competition is not only impossible but inferior, and has no title to being set up as a model of ideal efficiency. It is hence a mistake to base the theory of government regulation of industry on the principle that big business should be made to work as the respective industry would work in perfect competition.[1]

Schumpeter's theory leads to the policy conclusion that attempting to break up monpolies and oligopolies and trying to make the economy behave as if it were perfectly competitive is undesirable, since it will reduce rather than raise the rate of growth of living standards.

Consider an illustrative example. Let there be two countries, each with a national income of 100 that is growing at 3 per cent per annum. Country *A* breaks up its monopolies and thereby achieves an immediate rise of national income to 105 but a fall in its growth rate to 2 per cent. Country *B* lives with its monopolies and continues to have a 3 per cent growth rate. Country *B* will catch up to country *A* in five years' time, and in 50 years' time country *B* will have an income of just over 1·5 times that of country *A*. Clearly, given these figures, the long-term losses caused by breaking up *A*'s monopolies are very large indeed.

The effect of alternative market forms on the process of innovation and economic growth is an extremely important question. Unfortunately it is one on which existing theory and empirical studies shed all too little light.

Ballpoint pens: an example of Schumpeterian creative destruction Much of the previous discussion can be illustrated by the rather spectacular case of the behaviour of the economy in response to the introduction of a revolutionary new technique for writing, the ballpoint pen. In 1945, Milton Reynolds acquired a patent on a new type of pen that used a ball bearing in place of a conventional point. He formed the Reynolds International Pen Company, capitalized at $26,000 and began production on 6 October 1945.

The Reynolds pen was first introduced with a good deal of fanfare by the New York department store, Gimbels, which guaranteed that the pen would write for two years without refilling. The price was set at $12·50 (the maximum price allowed by the wartime Office of Price Administration, which was the body with which the American central authorities sought to control prices during and after World War II). Gimbels sold 10,000 pens on 29 October 1945, the first day they were on sale. In the early stages of production, the cost of production was estimated to be around 80 cents per pen.

The Reynolds International Pen Company quickly expanded production. By early 1946, it employed more than 800 people in its factory and was producing 30,000 pens per day. By March 1946 it had $3 million in the bank. Demand was intense. Macy's, Gimbels' traditional department-store rival, introduced an imported ballpoint pen from South America. Its price was $19·98 (production costs unknown).

The heavy sales quickly elicited a response from other pen manufacturers. Eversharp introduced its first model in April, at $15·00. In July 1946, the business magazine, *Fortune*, reported that Schaeffer was planning to put out a pen at $15·00, and Eversharp announced its plans to produce a 'retractable' model priced at $25·00. Reynolds introduced a new model, but kept the price at $12·50. Costs were estimated at 60 cents per pen.

[1] *Capitalism, Socialism and Democracy* (3rd edn: Harper & Row, 1950), p. 106.

The first signs of trouble emerged. The Ball-point Pen Company of Hollywood (disregarding a patent infringement suit) put a $9·95 model on the market, and a manufacturer named David Kahn announced plans to introduce a pen selling for less than $3·00. *Fortune* reported fear of an impending price war in view of the growing number of manufacturers and the low cost of production. In October, Reynolds introduced a new model, priced at $3·85, that cost about 30 cents to produce.

By Christmas, 1946, approximately 100 manufacturers were in production, some of them selling pens for as little as $2·98. By February 1947, Gimbels was selling a ballpoint pen made by the Continental Pen Company for 98 cents. Reynolds introduced a new model priced to sell at $1·69, but Gimbels sold it for 88 cents in a price war with Macy's. Reynolds felt betrayed by Gimbels and introduced a new model listed at 98 cents. By this time ballpoint pens had become economy items rather than luxury items, but were still highly profitable.

In mid-1948, ballpoint pens were selling for as little as 39 cents, and costing about 10 cents to produce. In 1951, prices of 25 cents were common. Today there is a wide variety of models and prices, ranging from 25 cents to $25·00, and the market appears stable, orderly and only moderately profitable. Ballpoint pens were no passing fad, as every reader of this book knows. Their introduction has fundamentally changed the writing-implement industry in America and in the world.

The ballpoint pen example has interested observers in many fields.

From the point of view of economic theory, the ballpoint pen case illustrates several things:
(1) That a monopoly (in this case a patent monopoly) can in the short-run charge prices not remotely related to costs and earn enormous profits.
(2) That entry of new firms (even in the face of obstacles) will often occur in response to high profits.
(3) That where it does occur, entry will in time drive prices down to a level more nearly equal to the costs of production and distribution.
(4) That the lag between an original monopoly and its subsequent erosion by entry may nevertheless be long enough that the profits to the innovator, as well as to some of the early imitators, may be very large indeed.

(It is estimated that Reynolds earned profits as high as $500,000 *in a single month* – or about 20 times its original investment.)

Pocket calculators Although a spectacular case, the ballpoint pen is not an isolated illustration of the process of innovation in a market economy. Pocket calculators provide one of many more recent examples. When they were first introduced in the early 1970s their capacities were limited: prices were high and so were the profits on each calculator sold. Customer acceptance was, however, immediate. As a result, many firms producing other products, and many new firms, rushed into production. Technological advance was rapid. While the capacities of the machines expanded, competition forced their prices down. Today consumers can choose from a vast array of calculators ranging from the simple to the sophisticated, and the prices paid are closely related to costs so that producing firms find these lines only moderately profitable.

Policy issues

Anti-monopoly laws The belief that competition produced an optimal allocation of resources led at once to the notion of legally prohibiting the practice of monopoly. Anti-monopoly laws, or *anti-combine laws,* as they are called in the UK, were perhaps the first manifestation of the classical down-with-monopolies policy. They gave the courts the power to dissolve an existing monopoly into a number of independent companies.

A second policy – *public-utility regulation* – grew out of the belief that, in some sectors (for example, in transportation and public utilities), competition was impossible. We saw in Chapter 19 that unexploited economies of scale are incompatible with perfect competition (see pages 253–4). Perfect competition can exist only in industries in which the output at which the *LRATC* curve reaches its minimum is small in relation to the total market demand. In this case the total necessary output can be produced by many competing firms, all producing at minimum average total costs. If, on the other hand, the output at which the *LRATC* curve reaches a minimum is large in relation to the market demand, then perfect competition is impossible and firms will expand under the incentive of falling long-run costs until the market is dominated by a few large producers, or possibly by only one. Such industries were regarded as NATURAL MONOPOLIES since competition among many firms would quickly give way to oligopoly or monopoly. The advantage of having one or a few large firms producing at a lower cost than could be achieved by many small firms is evident. In order to prevent monopolistic exploitation in terms of higher price and lower output than was necessary to cover opportunity cost, however, the intervention was needed. The central authorities were advised to regulate prices in such a way that the industry would earn only the competitive rate of return on its capital. Thus costs would be lowered by the monopolization, but the price would be held to its competitive level by the state's intervention.

In practice, there are many difficulties in deciding on what is a 'reasonable' or 'normal' rate of return for a natural monopoly to earn on its capital. Nonetheless, the regulation of naturally monopolistic industries is common throughout the world, particularly in the case of public utilities such as gas, electricity, transportation and communications.

A strong case has been made, particularly by American economists who have studied them, that regulatory bodies often work to the benefit of the firms they are supposed to control and to the detriment of consumers, whose interests they are supposed to protect. One of the major reasons set forth is that regulatory bodies must be staffed by experts in the relevant industry. The most obvious choices as experts are persons with management experience in that industry. These people are often sympathetic to the industry, and work to protect its profits rather than to force price down to the level of costs.

The evidence from many studies suggests that regulatory bodies often succeed both in supervising the establishment of joint-profit-maximizing prices among firms that might otherwise compete with each other and in providing effective barriers to the entry of new firms who would otherwise be attracted into the industry by existing profit levels. For example, when President Carter directed the US Civil Aeronautics Board to stop regulating US airline prices, substantial price competition broke out and effective air fares fell drastically. In 1979 US passengers faced internal fares per mile that are less than half of those charged in Europe by the more highly regulated local airlines.

Patents Economists who believe that competitive market structures best serve consumers by assuring them low prices, but who worry about the possible lack of incentives to innovate under competition, believe that other institutions, such as the patent laws, can provide the necessary incentives. Patent laws confer a temporary monopoly on the use of an invention. They represent an attempt to lengthen the short-run period during which whoever controls the invention can earn pure profits as a reward for inventing it. Once the patent expires, and sometimes even before, as we saw in the case of ballpoint pens, other firms can copy the innovation. If there are no other barriers to entry, production will expand until profits fall to normal. There is little doubt that were there no patent laws, many inventions would be copied sooner and the original innovators would not earn as much extra revenue to compensate them for the costs and risks of development.

Because patented items *can* be imitated, the real advantage of patents to the competitive firm should not be exaggerated. Some have argued that patents may be of even greater advantage to a monopolistic than to a competitive firm. A monopolist, so goes the argument, has the resources to develop, patent, and 'keep on the shelf' processes that might enable a potential competitor to challenge its position.

Reduction of entry barriers Those who accept Schumpeter's theory hold that anti-monopoly and public utility regulation policies are really unnecessary. They feel that the state may intervene positively to reduce existing entry barriers but they worry more that state intervention may inadvertently create entry barriers that will help to protect the profits of existing firms. They hold, therefore, that the state's main task is to avoid erecting barriers to entry that protect existing firms from the process of creative destruction. Otherwise they feel that the state should not attempt to control or regulate monopolies.

Nationalization Those who reject Schumpeter's argument often support anti-monopoly and public utility regulation policies. Some also support nationalization as the strongest and most direct way in which the central authorities can prevent monopolies and oligopolies from exploiting the public by selling 'too little' for 'too much'.

Supporters of Schumpeter's theory argue that nationalization, like public regulation, will defeat its own purpose. They argue that even if the nationalized industry works to the short-term advantage of consumers by forcing prices down to the level of the industry's costs, it will work to their long-term disadvantage by frustrating the process of creative destruction. A government monopoly is the ultimate in barriers to entry. To the extent that progress in new products, and new ways of producing old products, comes through new firms entering to attack the entrenched position of existing, sometimes sleepy and over-confident firms, this progress may be inhibited by the legal and fully enforceable monopoly created by the nationalisation of an industry. Supporters of this view point to the USSR's evident desire to buy technology from the US and argue that the rapid development of new products and processes in the oligopolistic and monopolistic US industries gives strong support to Schumpeter's view.

The effect of market structure on consumer's range of choice

It is sometimes argued that one of the virtues of competition among several producers is that it presents the consumer with a wide range of differentiated commodities, while complete monopoly with only one producer tends towards uniformity of product. We shall not ask here to what extent a variety of products is desirable, but we shall ask if we would in fact expect competition to produce more diversity of product than monopoly.

An example from radio and television A very interesting case, in which competition tends to produce a nearly uniform product while monopoly tends to produce widely differentiated ones, has been studied in detail.[1] This is the case of radio and television. Consider a case in which there are two potential radio audiences: one group, comprising 80 per cent of the total audience, wishes to hear pop music; the other group, comprising 20 per cent, wishes to listen to a concert of chamber music. Each individual radio station seeks to maximize its own listening audience.

If there is only the one station, it will produce pop music. If a second competing station is now opened up, its most profitable policy will be to produce a similar pop-music programme on the grounds that half of the large audience is still better than all of the small one. A third station would also prefer a third of the large audience to all of the small one. In fact, five stations would be needed before it would be profitable for any one station to produce a programme of chamber music. Thus competition between two or three stations would tend to produce two or three almost identical pop-music programmes, each competing for its share of the large audience.

A monopoly controlling two stations would not, however, pursue this policy. To maximize its total listening audience it would produce pop music on one station and chamber music on the other. The monopoly might spend more money on preparing the programme for the larger audience, but it would not spend money to produce a similar programme on its second station – the optimal policy for its second station would be to go after the other 20 per cent of potential listeners so that, between the two channels, the monopoly would have the largest possible audience.

In both cases, of monopoly and competition, each individual firm tries to maximize its own listening audience, but two competing stations will both go after the same large audience, ignoring the minority group, while two stations owned by one monopoly will go after both audiences, one for each station. Under these circumstances, competition produces a uniformity of product which ignores the desires of the minority, while monopoly produces a varied product catering to the desires of both the majority and the minority group.

---

[1] P. O. Steiner, 'Monopoly and competition in TV: some policy issues', *The Manchester School* (1961); 'Program Patterns and Preferences and the Workability of Competition in Radio Broadcasting', *Quarterly Journal of Economics*, May 1952.

At the time the case was studied, British radio was a three-station monopoly, and British television was based on competition between two stations, each taking as its criterion of success its own listening audience. It was found that the three stations of the monopolized radio produced very little similarity between the products offered at any one time, while the two competing stations of British television produced almost identical products a great deal of the time. Thus at a randomly selected time of the day the radio listener was likely to have two or three varied possibilities, while the television viewer was often forced to choose between two quite similar programmes.

The principle of minimum differentiation In some ways this radio example is a special case. We may now consider the problem in somewhat more general and abstract terms, as it was first laid out by Harold Hotelling.

Consider a product with only one independent characteristic which we can measure on a scale from – 10 to + 10. This is illustrated in Figure 23.4. The product

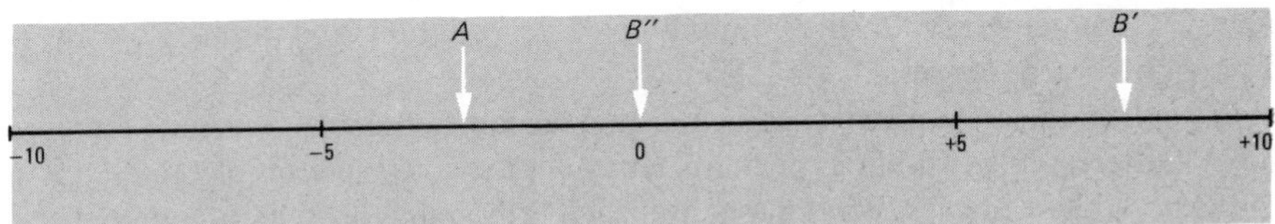

Fig. 23.4 The differentiation of a product with one independent characteristic

might, for example, be soap powder in which harshness was associated with cleansing power and mildness with lack of it. A rating of +10 might indicate a soap which had great cleansing power but removed the skin from the unfortunate user's hands, and −10 a soap which was positively beneficial to the hands but would not remove the merest speck of grease.[1] Let us assume that firm *A* has settled its product on the scale at −2. If firm *B* now wishes to produce a competing product, what will be its optimal policy? It might go to an extreme, producing a soap which had strong cleansing power but was also rather harsh on the hands, going out as far as, say, +8 on the scale (indicated by *B′* in the figure). Consumers whose tastes lead them to prefer something *between* the two products would, presumably, choose the product which came closest to satisfying their tastes. Firm *A* would get all customers who preferred a product ranging from −10 to +3, while *B* would get all those who preferred a product in the range +3 to +10. Now let us assume that, having decided to make a product with more cleansing power and more harshness than the competitor's product, firm *B* goes only a little way in this direction, just enough to make the difference noticeable but not enough to cause a major difference between the two products. Let us say it goes to zero on our scale (see *B″* in the figure). Now firm *B* should get all customers who would like a product rating between −1 and +10. Clearly firm *B* does better placing its product at *B″* rather than at *B′*, and equally clearly the best policy is to locate the product just enough to the right of *A* on the scale for the difference to be noticeable. That the optimal policy is often to make your product different enough from your competitor's product for the difference to

[1] This product has two characteristics, cleansing power and effect on skin, but they are not independent of each other; we have assumed that they vary directly with each other.

be noticeable but no more so, is sometimes referred to as the PRINCIPLE OF MINIMUM DIFFERENTIATION.[1]

An example of oligopolistic complexity If we now add a third competing firm, any simple competitive strategy will lead to an unstable process. If, for example, A is at -1 and B is at zero, then the optimal strategy for the new firm C is to produce a product rated at $+1$. But now, assuming that the customers are distributed evenly along the scale according to their tastes, firm B will have only 5 per cent of the market (i.e., those customers preferring a product between $-1/2$ and $+1/2$) and it will pay it to move outside either A or C. Say B goes to $+2$. Now C has only a small part of the market and it will pay it to go to -2, putting A in the position of being bracketed by the other two so that it goes to $+3$ (or to -3). You can prove for yourself that if each firm moves in sequence, and makes the move which will give it the biggest share of the market without worrying about what its competitors might do, an unstable situation will develop so that the process of move and counter-move will not lead to an equilibrium position. In this example the addition of a third firm removes the tendency towards minimum differentiation and replaces it by a tendency towards perpetual oscillation.

If we drop the assumption that each firm does not look beyond its next move, a host of interesting possibilities open up. Consider the consequences of at least a few of the possible strategies. What happens if each firm looks ahead to its competitors' next move? What happens if two firms collude? It is interesting to note that in this last case the two colluding firms can take the lion's share of the market by locating at $+5$ and -5, thus leaving the third firm unable to retaliate; but the third firm can, by locating anywhere between -4 and $+4$, determine how this share is split up between the two colluding partners.

All of this is a simple illustration of the general point made in Chapter 21 that the outcome of an oligopolistic situation is influenced by the strategies adopted by the competing firms.

A conclusion

We have been concerned in this chapter with what could be said about monopoly and competition on the basis of positive economic theory. On many crucial points, theory has not been adequately tested. It is obviously necessary to keep an open

[1] The principle of minimum differentiation has applicability well beyond the scope of economics. It goes a long way, for example, in explaining why in a two-party political system, both parties tend to gravitate towards a middle-of-the-road position that minimizes the real choice given to voters. The principle does not, however, generalize to more than two firms. The observed clustering of many firms must be explained by forces not covered by this principle. One other force is clearly that for many durable goods, customers engage in comparison shopping: they visit several shops to compare prices and qualities before making their purchase. The clustering of two firms in Hotelling's model *is not* in consumers' interest, it denies them a range of choices they would like to have available; the clustering of two or more firms in response to comparison shopping *is* in consumers' interests since it facilitates the making of desired comparisons. (Intermediate and advanced students who wish to see these issues considered further might like to consult B. C. Eaton and R. G. Lipsey, 'The Introduction of Space into a Neo-Classical Model of Value Theory', in M. J. Artis and A. R. Nobay (eds.) *Studies in Modern Economic Analysis*, The Proceedings of the Association of University Teachers of Economics, Edinburgh (Basil Blackwell, 1976.)

mind on the subject and to admit that, on the basis of existing theory, it is impossible to make out an overwhelming case either for or against monopoly and oligopoly as compared with competition. Everyone will have his or her own guess, hunch or prejudice on the subject, often based on bits of personal experience. But from the point of view of economic science we are interested in carefully documented, objective evidence, and on these grounds much still remains to be discovered about the comparison of the effects of monopoly and oligopoly with those of monopolistic and pure competition.

24

Criticisms and tests of the theory of supply

In previous chapters we have derived a number of testable implications from the theory of supply. The theory itself is tested every time one of these implications is confronted with facts in such a way that a conflict between theory and observation is possible. In many cases, if a particular implication is in conflict with the facts, this necessitates only a minor change in the basic theory. In other cases, however, empirical observations have been alleged that strike at the very core of the theory. If these conflicting observations were substantiated, it would be necessary either to make very drastic amendments to existing theory or to abandon it completely.

In this chapter we shall first discuss some general approaches to testing the theory and then consider a number of criticisms that have been raised against it. The final criticism relates to the work of Professor J. K. Galbraith, who has attacked some of the most fundamental aspects of the theory and suggested that its apparent policy implications are profoundly misleading.

Approaches to testing the theory

Over the last several chapters we have developed an elaborate theory of the behaviour of firms and industries. Although it does not cover all questions in which we might be interested, it does, as we have seen, provide predictions about a large number of interesting situations. But is the theory right? Are we not being misled by accepting its predictions as telling us about behaviour in the real world? How can we assess such worries? The answer to this question is fundamental to an assessment of the practical value of economics. Several approaches to providing the answer have been used from time to time, and we shall now consider three of them.

Formulate an alternative (and competing) theory that makes different predictions

Given alternative theories, one can enumerate their conflicting predictions and choose to accept the one that comes closer to predicting what actually is observed to happen. We might hypothesize, for example, that firms choose to maximize their sales rather than their profits, and we would then have two competing theories. We could then derive their predictions. Next we would select those that conflict with each other, and confront them with the evidence. This is a satisfactory way of choosing between two theories.

See if decision-takers behave as the theory predicts

We might observe, for example, how a certain executive takes a decision: what records he consults, what questions he asks, and so on. Or we might create a laboratory situation and give 'subjects' a chance to take decisions, then record and analyse their decisions.

This approach does not by itself provide a test of an existing theory, since it does not tell us whether the procedure actually employed by the decision-taker really makes any difference in his decision. If, for example, an executive systematically discusses proposed price changes with his sales manager and his lawyer, but rarely with his cost accountant, it may suggest the hypothesis that demand and anti-monopoly considerations loom larger in his mind than cost conditions, but it does not demonstrate that these things play a more important role than cost in pricing decisions. Other explanations are possible. For example, the executive might be an expert on cost conditions, or he might need less time to acquaint himself with cost data than with demand data, or his cost accountant may provide him with lucid memos, whereas his sales manager can only communicate orally.

The approach may, however, suggest fruitful new theories. If we find that firms habitually follow certain procedures that seem to lead them away from profit maximization, we can formulate a new theory in which these procedures play a prominent role. We would then have two conflicting theories, and we could proceed to test between them in the manner discussed in the previous section.

Ask decision-takers how they take decisions

Another approach to testing the theory of profit maximization is merely to ask businessmen: 'Do you seek to maximize profits?'. This approach has from time to time been tried and it will not surprise you to learn that, when asked if their sole motive were to make as much money as possible, businessmen replied that it was not, and that they sought to charge a 'fair price', to make only a reasonable profit and generally to conduct their affairs in a manner conducive to the social good. Asking people what they do and why they do it may well provide some interesting hunches and suggest hypotheses about behaviour for further testing. If you have always taken it for granted that people do a certain thing and inquiry shows that everyone denies it, then this may make you suspicious and lead you to check your theories further. But consider what the denials might mean: (i) the people were lying; (ii) the people told what they thought was the truth, but they were not aware of their own motives and actions; (iii) the denials were true.

How are we to judge which of these possibilities is correct? One needs only a nodding acquaintance with elementary psychology to realize that we are not likely to discover very much about human motivation by asking a person what motivates him. Generally he or she will have either no idea at all, or else only a pleasantly acceptable rationalization.

Direct questioning at best (assuming the subject tries to be scrupulously honest) tells us what the person questioned thinks he is doing. Such information can never refute an hypothesis about what the person actually is doing. To challenge such an hypothesis, we must observe what he does, not ask him what he thinks he does.

We shall now consider five separate criticisms of the theory. Some attack only parts of the theory; others strike at its very core.

The allegation that firms do not have adequate information for profit maximization

One group of critics say that profit-maximizing theory is inadequate because firms, however hard they may try, cannot reach decisions in the way the theory predicts. This criticism has a number of aspects, some of them very crude and some quite sophisticated.

Businessmen do not understand marginal concepts

One of the crudest criticisms is based on the observation that businessmen do not calculate in the manner assumed by the theory. Sometimes businessmen are interviewed and it is discovered (apparently to the surprise of the interviewer) that they have never heard of the concepts of marginal cost and marginal revenue. It is then argued that: (i) the theory assumes businessmen equate marginal cost to marginal revenue; (ii) empirical observations show that businessmen have not heard of marginal cost and marginal revenue; (iii) therefore the theory is refuted, because businessmen cannot be employing concepts of which they are unaware.

This observation, assuming it to be correct, does refute the theory that firms take decisions by calculating marginal values and consciously equating them. But it does not refute the theory that firms maximize profits. The mathematical concepts of marginal cost and marginal revenue (these are just the *first derivatives* of the total cost and total revenue functions by another name) are used by the economic theorist to discover what will happen as long as, by one means or another – be it guess, hunch, clairvoyance, luck or good judgement – the firms do approximately succeed in maximizing their profits. The constructs of the theory of the firm are purely logical tools employed by the economist to discover the consequences of certain behaviour patterns. They are not meant to be a description of *how* firms reach their decisions. If firms are maximizing their profits, then the tools of economic theory allow us to predict how they will react to certain changes – e.g., the introduction of a tax – and this prediction is independent of the thought process by which firms actually reach their decisions.

Business calculations are much cruder than is assumed by profit-maximizing theory

A similar argument stems from the observation that firms do not calculate down to single units with such a nice degree of accuracy as is assumed in profit-maximizing theory. In the verbal presentation of the theory of the firm, it is usually stated that firms will increase production until the cost of producing the very last unit is just equal to the revenue gained from its sale. This is merely a verbal statement of the mathematical conditions for the maximization of the profit function. The observation that firms do not calculate down to single units is not of itself relevant as a test of the theory. The marginal analysis allows us to predict how firms will respond to certain changes in the data; if they are maximizing their profits they will be observed to respond in this way even though they calculate in a much cruder fashion than mathematicians do.

Firms have inadequate information

More sophisticated critics point out that the information available to decision-takers is simply not adequate to permit them to reach the decisions that economists predict they will reach. This argument generally takes one of three forms: that firms are the victim of their accountants, and base their decisions on accounting concepts, which differ from economic ones; that the natural lag between accumulating and processing data is such that important decisions must be made on fragmentary and partially out-of-date information; or, that firms cannot afford to acquire as much information as economists assume them to have.

The hypothesis of full-cost pricing

Out of these lines of criticisms has come the hypothesis of FULL-COST PRICING, which was originally suggested by firms' answers to questions on how they set prices.

> **The full-cost pricing hypothesis explicitly denies that firms will charge the profit-maximizing price. According to it, firms use available data to compute full costs per unit (variable costs plus overhead) and add to this a conventional mark-up; price is set at this figure and sales are determined by what the market will absorb at that price.**

Thus firms are conceived of as having perfectly elastic supply curves set at the level of 'full costs'.

This theory leads to some predictions that differ from those of profit-maximizing theory. For instance, prices will be stable in the face of large fluctuations in demand. On the other hand, it leads to some similar predictions, such as those that output will fluctuate directly with demand and that rises in input prices will lead to increases in commodity prices.

Although full-cost pricing has occasioned considerable heated argument, no generally accepted authoritative test of it exists. Many of the tests that have been made have been rather equivocal in suggesting more price stability than profit-maximizing would suggest, but less than would result from complete full-cost pricing.

The allegation that decisions made by the firm are strongly influenced by the institutions within the firm

A major attack on profit-maximizing theory comes from a group of economists who reject the critical assumption made on pages 201–2, that the firm's decisions are independent of its particular organizational set-up. These economists advocate ORGANIZATIONAL THEORY.

Organizational theory holds that in big organizations decisions are made after much discussion by groups and committees, and that the structure of the process affects the substance of the decisions, so that different decisions will result from different kinds of organization, even if all else is unchanged.

Thus the firm cannot be regarded as an entity taking consistent decisions in respect of definite and unchanging goals. The firm will take different decisions faced with identical situations but using different decision-taking institutions.

Although it has proved easier for organizational theorists to express their central point of view than to formulate specific testable hypotheses, they have formulated a number of the latter. One is that a large and diffuse organization finds it necessary to develop standard operating procedures to help it in making decisions. These decision rules arise as a compromise among competing points of view and, once adopted, are changed only reluctantly. One prediction following from this hypothesis is that the procedures used may be non-optimal and will persist for long periods of time, despite changes in conditions affecting the firm. For either reason, profits will not be maximized. Another prediction is that this procedure will lead large firms to adopt conservative policies and avoid large risks. Smaller firms will take bigger risks.

Imprecise hypotheses like these are difficult to test. Proponents of organization theory feel that the evidence supports them; critics feel that the hypotheses are undemonstrated. It is hard to avoid the view that at the present time the evidence is inconclusive as far as firm behaviour is concerned.

Although organizational theory has not won complete approval among economists studying the behaviour of firms,[1] it has made a major impact in other fields of study. For example, the economist's assumption that the decision-taking unit can be treated as if it were a single consistent individual is often transferred to the field of political decision-taking. We constantly talk of 'the USSR' doing this, 'the US' reacting by doing that, and 'the UK' trying to intervene as honest broker to advocate 'this *and* that'. Such modes of expression assume a model in which decision-taking by national units can be treated *as if* individuals took the decisions. On the political level, the evidence is fairly strong that this is often a very bad assumption. It would appear that when 'the USSR' takes a decision and when 'the US' retaliates, this behaviour is better understood by a model that recognizes competing organizations within each country having conflicting motives and varying powers, than by a model that treats the USSR and the US each as a single, consistent decision-taking entity. This a matter of critical importance because, for example, the appropriate 'US' reaction to a move by the USSR may depend critically on whether the move was taken by a single Soviet actor concerned only about his effect on the US or by one among many who was as much concerned about the effect of what he did on other competing Soviet bureaucrats as on Americans.[2]

[1] One of its major exponents, Professor Herbert Simon, was awarded the 1978 Nobel Prize in economics for his work on firm behaviour.

[2] The issues briefly discussed here are critical for our very survival. Students of the social sciences should give them serious consideration. An excellent beginning is to read the fascinating book by G. T. Allison, *Essence of Decision: Explaining the Cuban Missile Crisis* (Little Brown, 1971).

The allegation that firms do not seek to maximize short-run profits

A major class of criticisms strikes directly at the assumption of profit maximization. 'Firms', it is argued, 'do not seek to maximize profits at all. Of course they must make some profits or they will go out of business, but after that they pursue some totally different goal; the actions necessary to achieve this goal are substantially different from those necessary to achieve profit maximization.' This is stronger than saying that firms are prevented from achieving maximum profits by the lack of available information or by the organization's structure. This hypothesis states that the firm does not even *try* to maximize profits.

The first set of criticisms under this general heading centre around the question of who actually controls the firm. The owners of the firm are its shareholders, and they are the ones who, presumably, have most to gain from a policy of profit maximization. Perhaps the great bulk of ordinary shareholders are not able to exercise any significant control over the firm's behaviour. Many investigators have forcefully advocated the view that groups other than the majority of ordinary shareholders exert the determining influence on firm's behaviour. For this to matter to positive economics, the controlling group must wish to pursue goals other than profit maximization so that their behaviour will be different from that desired by the majority of ordinary shareholders.

We shall now consider three hypotheses about the control, as opposed to the ownership, of the modern firm.

The hypothesis of minority control

This hypothesis runs as follows: *Because of the widespread distribution of shares, the owners of a minority of the stock are usually able to control a majority of the voting shares and thus to exercise effective control over the decisions of the company.*

Let us see how these results might occur. Votes in a company are proportional to shares owned. Any individual or group controlling 51 per cent of the stock clearly controls the majority of the votes. Shareholders vote at the annual meeting; they may vote in person or they may assign a 'proxy' to someone who will be attending. But suppose one group owns 30 per cent of the shares, with the remaining 70 per cent distributed so widely that few of the dispersed group even bother to vote. In this event 30 per cent may be the overwhelming majority of the shares *actually voted.* How large a percentage is actually required to control the majority depends on the pattern of ownership and on whether there has been a major effort to collect proxies. A colourful, but rare phenomenon in business history is the 'proxy fight' in which competing factions of shareholders (or management) attempt to collect the voting rights of the dispersed and generally disinterested stockholders. In general, a very small fraction of shares, sometimes as small as 5 per cent, actively voted may exercise a dominant influence at meetings of shareholders.

Another aspect of minority control is made possible through the *holding company*. Suppose, in a certain company, call it *A*, ownership of 20 per cent of the stock would give dominant control. Now a new company, which we shall call *B*, is formed. *B* purchases 20 per cent of the shares in *A*. Company *B* can now control *A*. But no more than 51 per cent of the shares of *B* is required to control the shares in *A*. Indeed, if 20 per cent ownership of *B* is sufficient to control *B*'s affairs, an amount of money equal to only 4 per cent of the value of A's shares (20 per cent of 20 per cent) is required for a group to gain control of B and thus of A. Now suppose a new company, C, is formed to purchase 20 per cent of company B! This pyramiding of control via holding companies has no limits in logic, but it is limited both in law and in practicality. (It should also be mentioned that holding companies serve many purposes other than the rather suspect one described here.)

Dispersed ownership and minority control are well established in the corporate sector of most advanced free-market economies. Does it matter? As far as the behaviour of the firm is concerned, the hypothesis of minority control is important only if the controlling shareholders have interests and motives different from those of the majority of the firm's shareholders. If all shareholders are mainly interested in having the firm maximize its profits, then it does not matter, as far as market behaviour is concerned, which set of shareholders actually influences the firm's policy. There is no accepted evidence to show that controlling groups of shareholders habitually seek objectives different from those sought by the majority.

The hypothesis of intercorporate control groups

The hypothesis runs as follows: *Whole sectors of the economy are effectively controlled by small groups of people through the mechanism of interlocking directorships.*

If each member of a small group holds directorships in several companies, the group can control the boards of directors of many different companies without being so obvious as to have the identical set of persons on each and every board. By controlling the boards of directors, this group can exert effective and relatively unostentatious control over the companies themselves.

The factual basis of this hypothesis is that many individuals are directors of many companies. These 'interlocking directorships' have been widely studied.

There is no law against a particular individual being a director of many companies. Some individuals are wanted by many companies for the prestige that their names convey. Certain bank officers appear on many different boards of directors. They represent their banks' interest in companies to which they have loaned money. The hypothesis of inter-corporate control groups is important to positive economics only if boards of directors are able to control the policies of companies in ways that would not be approved by managers or shareholders. Indeed, there does not seem to be any evidence that the common directors exert any significant influence altering the firms' behaviour from what it would be if no such interlocking existed.

The hypothesis of the separation of ownership from control

Because of diversified ownership and the difficulty of assembling shareholders or gathering proxies, the managers rather than the shareholders exercise effective control over the decisions of the company.

The argument offered in support of this hypothesis is as follows. Shareholders elect directors who appoint managers. Directors are supposed to represent shareholders' interests and to determine broad policies that the managers merely carry out. In order to conduct the complicated business of running a large firm, however, a full-time professional management group *must* be given broad powers of decision. Although managerial decisions can be reviewed from time to time, they cannot be supervised in detail. In fact, the links are typically weak enough so that top management often does truly control the destiny of the company over long periods of time. As long as directors have confidence in the managerial group, they accept and ratify their proposals, and shareholders characteristically elect and re-elect directors who are proposed to them. If the managerial group behaves badly, it may later be removed and replaced, but this is a drastic action and a disruptive one, and it is infrequently employed. Within very wide limits, then, effective control of the company's activities does reside with the managers, who need not even be shareholders. Although the managers are legally the employees of the shareholders, they are able to remain largely unaffected by them. Indeed, the management group characteristically asks for, and typically gets, the proxies of a very large number of shareholders and thus perpetuates itself in office.

This hypothesis was put forcibly about forty years ago by the American professors A. A. Berle and G. C. Means in a pioneering study of the large company. The study showed that in nearly 60 per cent of the largest companies no dominant ownership group could be identified with as much as 10 per cent of the shareholdings. Professor Robert Larner has recently shown that this percentage is much higher today in the US – above 80 per cent – than it was in the 1930s. But again, what is the significance of the fact?

For the hypothesis of the separation of ownership and control to be important, it is necessary not only that the managers should be able to exert effective control over business decisions, but also that they should wish to act differently from the way the shareholders and directors wish to act. If the managers are motivated by a desire to maximize the firm's profits – either because it is in their own interests to do so or because they voluntarily choose to reflect the shareholders' interests – then it does not matter that they have effective control over decisions. If the managers wish to pursue goals different from those of the owners, the behaviour of the firm will be different according to whether the managers or the owners exercise effective control.

This is a genuinely competing hypothesis to that of profit maximization, but before we go on to consider it in detail we should notice that it is also in conflict with the two hypotheses outlined previously. Clearly one cannot hold simultaneously that managers take the effective decisions, ignoring the interests of shareholders and directors, and that directors take the effective decisions, ignoring the interests of managers and shareholders, and that a minority of shareholders take effective decisions, ignoring the interests of the other groups.

The satisficing hypothesis

Organization theorists have criticized the profit-maximizing model and suggested an alternative that they call SATISFICING. Professor Herbert Simon says, 'We must expect the firm's goals to be not maximizing profits but attaining a certain level or rate of profit, holding a certain share of the market or a certain level of sales.'

> **According to the satisficing hypothesis, firms will strive hard to achieve certain target levels of profits, but having achieved them they will not strive to improve their profit position further.**

This means that the firm could produce any one of a range of outputs that yield at least the target level of output rather than the unique output that maximizes profits. This lack of uniqueness is illustrated in Figure 24.1 which is discussed below.

The sales-maximization hypothesis

Another theory, first offered by Professor William Baumol, is that firms seek to maximize not their profits but their sales revenue. Firms, it is assumed, wish to be as large as possible and, faced with a choice between profits and sales, would choose to increase their sales rather than their profits.

This hypothesis starts from the separation of management and ownership. In the giant corporation, the managers need to make some minimum level of profits to keep the shareholders satisfied; after that they are free to seek growth unhampered by profit considerations. This is a sensible policy on the part of mangement, so the argument runs, because salary, power and prestige all vary with the size of a firm as well as with its profits; generally, the manager of a large, normally profitable corporation will earn a salary considerably higher than that earned by the manager of a small but highly profitable corporation.

The sales-maximization hypothesis says that managers of firms seek to maximize their sales revenue, subject to a profit constraint.

Sales maximization subject to a profit constraint leads to the prediction that a sales-maximizing firm will sacrifice some profits by setting price below, and output above, their profit-maximizing levels. This is demonstrated in Figure 24.1, which shows the level of profits associated with each level of output. A profit-maximizing firm produces output q_m. A satisficing firm, with a target level of profits of π_c, is willing to produce any output between q and q_1. A sales-maximizing firm, with a minimum profit constraint of π_C, produces the output q_1. Thus satisficing allows a range of outputs on either side of the profit-maximizing level, while sales maximization predicts a higher output than does profit maximizing.

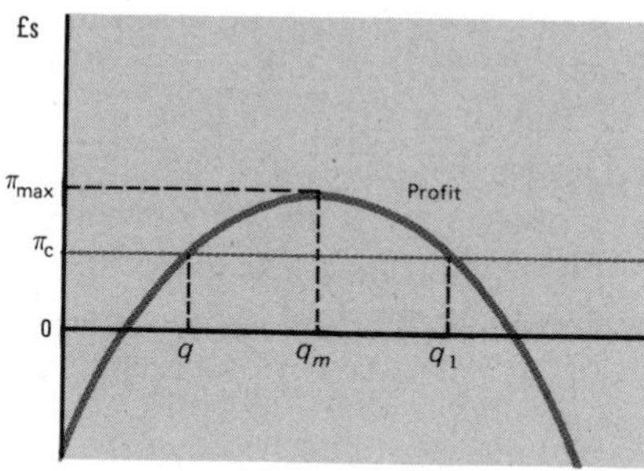

Fig. 24.1 Output of the firm under satisficing, profit maximizing and sales maximizing

Both sales-maximizing and satisficing behaviour are constrained by outside forces. If the present management departs too far from profit-maximizing behaviour, it leaves its firm vulnerable to a take-over bid by a new owner who does intend to maximize profits. This is discussed further below.

The long-run profit-maximination hypothesis

In order to take account of various criticisms of the assumption of profit maximization, some economists modify profit maximization to mean long-run profit maximization. For example, sales maximization is interpreted as long-run profit maximization because sales are the key to growth and growth is the key to future profits. This eliminates any conflict between sales and profit maximization. In much the same way, the 'long-run' approach can be used to account for other facts that appear to contradict predictions based on short-run profit maximization. For one example, consumer goodwill gained by not taking advantage of temporary shortages may be worthwhile in terms of long-run profits. For another example, a firm may be right to avoid risky ventures, even if they promise large short-run profits, because the surest way to long-run profits is to survive in the short run. Long-run profitability requires survival and survival may require caution.

It is, however, exceptionally difficult to give such a long-run theory any testable content. If we are not careful, we may find ourselves rationalizing, whenever we find a firm not maximizing profits, by saying merely that it was maximizing over *some time period other than* the one we were considering. Unless we include in our theory a means of identifying the long-run period over which profits are supposed to be maximized, our theory becomes consistent with absolutely any business behaviour and as a result becomes totally uninteresting.

It is not unreasonable, however, to regard profit maximizing as occurring over a realistic time horizon, such as one or two years, rather than day by day. Nor is it unreasonable to construct a testable theory of a firm attempting to maximize the 'present value' of future profits.[1] In either of these ways long-run maximization can be brought into a profit-maximizing model.

How far can corporations depart from profit-maximizing behaviour?

Many of the criticisms that we have just considered assume that firms seek to do things other than maximize their profits. If the present management elects not to maximize its profits, this implies that some other management could make more money by operating the firm. A major restraint on existing managements is the threat of a shareholder revolt or a take-over bid. As we shall see in some detail in Chapter 28, the maximum amount one can afford to pay for any asset depends on how much it is expected to earn. If I can make an asset produce more than you, I can rationally outbid you for it.

A management that fails to come close to achieving the profit potential of the assets it controls becomes a natural target for acquisition by a firm that specializes in taking over inefficiently run firms. The management of the acquiring firm makes a TENDER OFFER (or TAKE-OVER BID as it is sometimes called) to the shareholders of the target firm, offering them what amounts to a premium for their shares, a premium it can pay because it expects to increase the firm's profits. Managers who wish to avoid take-over bids cannot let the profits of their firm slip far from the profit-maximizing level – because their unrealized profits provide the incentives for take-overs. Some, though by no means all, of the so-called conglomerate firms have specialized in this kind of take-over. In the last decade the example par excellence of this has been International Telegraph and Telephone, which acquired (among other companies) Avis Car Rental, Continental Baking, Sheraton Hotels, Canteen Food Service and Hertford Life Insurance. In each case it substantially increased the operating profits of the acquired company after the take-over. The pressure of the threat of take-overs must be regarded as limiting the discretion of corporate management to pursue goals other than profit maximization.

[1] The concept of present value is developed in Chapter 28. It is sufficient here to understand that the value to you *now* of £100 to be given to you five years from now is greater than zero but less than £100.

The allegation that the observed shape of the short-run cost curve is not what is assumed in the theory

In Chapter 17, we argued that the marginal-cost curve would be U-shaped, falling at first, as a more efficient combination of the fixed and variable factors became possible, and then rising as diminishing returns set in. Empirical evidence has several times suggested that many marginal cost curves were flat up to the capacity level of output, so that each extra unit would cost as much to produce as did the previous unit, until the plant was operated at capacity, after which costs would begin to rise.

The economic theorist should ask three questions when faced with such evidence about the shape of the marginal cost curves: (i) Is the evidence reliable? (ii) What part of my theory does it refute? and (iii) Does this upset any important predictions that I have previously relied on? There does seem to be enough persistent evidence to answer 'yes' to question (i), at least for firms in some industries. What of question (ii)? The argument for a declining portion of the *MC* curve (see pages 213–14) rests on having too low a ratio of the variable factor to the fixed factor. As production is increased, more of the variable factor is used and a more efficient combination with the fixed factor achieved. This clearly implies that all of the fixed factor must be used all of the time; in other words, that the fixed factor be *indivisible*. If the fixed factor is *divisible* so that part of it may go unemployed, then there is no need, as production is decreased, to depart from the optimum ratio of the actual employed quantities of the fixed to the variable factor. Thus, costs will be constant up to the point at which all the fixed factor is used. Beyond this point, production can only be increased by combining more of the variable factor with the constant (total) amount of the fixed factor. Under these circumstances costs would be rising. Consider as a simple example a 'factory' that consists of 10 sewing machines in a shed, each with a productive capacity of 20 units per day when operated for 8 hours by one girl. If 200 units per day are required, then all 10 machines are operated on a normal shift. If demand falls to 180, then one girl is laid off. But there is no need to combine the 9 girls with 10 machines. Clearly one machine can be 'laid off' as well, and the ratio of labour/machines used in production is not varied. Clearly, production can go from 1 to 200 without any change in factor proportions. In this case we would expect the factory to have constant marginal costs up to 200 units, and only then to encounter rising costs, as production was expanded, by means of overtime and other methods of combining more labour with the 10 machines.

Thus, the answer to question (ii) is that constant marginal costs do not refute any part of the theory of costs, provided the fixed factor is divisible. Constant marginal costs with an indivisible fixed factor would, however, refute the theory of costs *which predicts that marginal and average costs must vary when factor proportions vary.*

To deal with the final question, the economist places the new cost curve (flat up to capacity and then rising) in his theoretical models in place of the former U-shaped one. The main result of making this change is that under competitive conditions the short-run industry supply curve may have a perfectly elastic portion, while if oligopolistic firms have flat *MC* curves, their prices may stay constant as their demand curves rise and fall. Thus there may be more short-run stability in prices in the face of cyclical changes in demand than we would otherwise suspect. Such short-run price stability over the business cycle (see Part 7) has in fact been observed, and the amended theory just considered is consistent with these observations.

The allegation that firms have a degree of political and economic power over the market that is not recognized in conventional economic theory

A very different hypothesis from the ones considered so far is advocated by John Kenneth Galbraith of Harvard University. In Galbraith's theory it is *not* consumers' basic wants that create the market signals that in turn provide the profit opportunities that motivate business behaviour. Instead large corporations create and manipulate demand.[1]

Firms must plan, and invest, for an uncertain future, and the profitability of the enormous investments that they make is threatened by the unpredictability of events. In Galbraith's theory, firms render the future less unpredictable, in order to protect their investments, by actively manipulating market demand and by co-opting government agencies that are supposed to control their activities. We shall now examine this hypothesis in some detail.

Manipulation of demand

The most important source of unpredictable events that may jeopardize corporate investments is unexpected shifts in market demand curves. To guard against the effects of unexpected declines in demand, corporations spend vast amounts on advertising that allows them to sell what they want to produce rather than what consumers want to buy. At the same time, corporations hold off the market products that consumers would like to buy. One way to do this is by buying up patents on new goods and then doing nothing with them. This reduces the risks inherent in investing in wholly new and untried products and avoids the possibility that those new products that are successful might spoil the market for existing products.

According to this hypothesis, consumers are the victims of the corporations; they are pushed around at whim, persuaded to buy things they do not really want, and denied products they would like. In short, they are brainwashed ciphers with artificially created wants, exercising little real autonomy with respect to their own consumption.

Corruption of public authorities

A second threat to the long-range plans and investments of corporations comes from uncontrollable and often unpredictable changes in the nature of government interference. This political threat is met by co-opting or corrupting legislators, who pass laws affecting corporations and the government agencies that are supposed to be regulating them. Corporation managers, according to the theory, indirectly subvert public institutions (from universities to regulatory agencies). Government, instead of regulating business and protecting the public interest, has become the

[1] Although this theory was commonly advanced in the UK over the 1950s and 1960s, it became incredible in the 1970s to ascribe the required degree of power and influence to UK firms who were clearly being forced by governments and by unions into behaviour they thought profoundly undesirable. The hypothesis that firms exert significant arbitrary control over the economy is, however, still advanced in the US. Because it is superficially more plausible in the US than in the UK, it has been subject to more empirical testing there. For this reason, we shall discuss it in the light of US rather than UK experience.

servant of the corporation. It supplies the corporate sector with such essential inputs into its productive process as educated, trained, healthy and socially secure workers. Government also serves the giant corporation through policies concerning tariffs, import quotas, tax rules, subsidies and research and development. These policies protect and insulate the industrial establishment from competitive pressures and reinforce its dominance and its profitability.

Corruption of social values

These tasks, and the requirements of production, create a class of managers – a techno-structure – that exerts the dominant influence in the corporation. The managers have great power. The corporations they manage earn large profits that can be reinvested to further the achievement of the values of the ruling techno-structure – values that emphasize industrial production, rapid growth, and highly materialistic aspirations at the expense of the better things of life (such as cultural and aesthetic values) and the quality of the environment.

More importantly, the industrial managerial group joins with the military in a military-industrial complex that utilizes, trains and elevates the technicians to positions of power and prestige not only in industry but in the army, the defense establishment and the highest positions of government. In so doing, the corporations and their managers threaten to dominate if not subvert foreign as well as domestic policies.

The new industrial state

The foregoing is an outline of what Galbraith calls the New Industrial State.[1] If Galbraith's theories of the behaviour of modern corporations were substantially correct, we would have to make major revisions in our ideas of how free-market economies work.

> **According to the concept of the New Industrial State, the largest corporations (i) tend to dominate the economy; (ii) largely control market demand rather than being controlled by it; (iii) co-opt government processes instead of being constrained by them; and (iv) utilize their substantial discretionary power in ways that go against the interests of society.**

The evidence for the hypothesis

Superficially at least, many of the facts of Western economies in general and the American economy in particular lend support to Galbraith's hypothesis. Corporations do account for approximately two-thirds of all business done in the United States today, and large corporations dominate the corporate sector. Of nearly 200,000 manufacturing corporations, roughly 1 per cent of them have $10 million or more in assets. These large corporations hold approximately 85 per cent

[1] These views did not, however, originate with the publication in 1967 of Galbraith's book by that title or with the formation of 'Nader's Raiders'. Much earlier, James Burnham wrote *The Managerial Revolution* and Robert Brady sounded an alarm in *Business as a System of Power*. Thorstein Veblen had predicted the techno-cratic take-over of society in *The Engineers and the Price System* in 1921, and Karl Marx predicted the subversion of the government bureaucrat by the businessman over a century ago.

of manufacturing assets. The 200 to 250 largest corporations – $\frac{1}{10}$ of 1 per cent of all manufacturing corporations – control approximately 50 per cent of the total assets of manufacturing.

Many of the giant corporations are highly profitable, and most are so widely owned that management, rather than shareholders, exercises effective control. If power comes with size, a 'few' people – several thousand strategically placed executives of a few hundred leading corporations – have great power over economic affairs. Moreover, these people are primarily white, male, wealthy, and politically conservative. As for political influence, individual corporations and trade associations have lobbyists and exercise whatever persuasion they can. Executives of many of these corporations serve on public commissions and frequently take important government positions. Executives often make large contributions to political compaigns. Political influence is exercised at all levels of government; indeed there have been cases where entire city governments have been effectively in the pockets of local corporations.

The political activities of corporations are not confined to the home markets. The Lockheed Aircraft Corporation was recently implicated in scandals involving million-dollar bribes to secure foreign orders. The list of persons involved included (among many others) a former Japanese prime minister, the husband of the ruling Queen of the Netherlands, and several former Italian Christian Democrat cabinet ministers. There is no longer any doubt that corporations have succeeded in corrupting governments at the highest levels (or at least in harnessing the corruption that was already there) and through political channels have achieved results that they might never have achieved in the marketplace.

The great corporations, along with many smaller firms, spend vast amounts on advertising – as the hypothesis predicts. In 1975 the total advertising expenditure of US corporations was $28 billion. This sum was 2·4 per cent of the value of the contribution of the private sector to the American GNP. These expenditures are obviously designed to influence consumers' demand, and there is little doubt that if firms such as Lever Brothers (soap), Gulf Oil (petroleum products), Schlitz (beer) and General Motors (cars), cut their advertising, they would lose sales to their competitors.

It is also true that much of the pollution of the environment is associated with industries that consist of well-known large firms. If automobiles, electric power, steel, oil, industrial chemicals, detergents and paper are the primary sources of pollution, surely Ford, Consolidated Edison, Bethlehem Steel, Texaco, Monsanto, Proctor & Gamble, and International Paper are significantly to blame. Each of these is among the 100 largest industrial corporations in the US.

Doubts about the hypothesis

Sensitivity to the market pressures Even the largest and most powerful industries are not immune to market pressures. The failure of the Edsel, a car once produced by the Ford Motor Company in the US and marketed with a vast advertising campaign, was a classic example of market rejection of a product. The penetration of small foreign cars into the American market forced the US automobile industry first into producing the compact car and then the still cheaper small cars. The decline of railroading as a mode of passenger travel is manifest in many ways, as the financial history of once great railroading corporations shows. The failure of the Penn Central Railroad Company is one example. Another is the fact that the Pullman Company, maker of railway sleeping cars, was America's tenth largest firm in 1909; today it is not even in the top 300. The rise of air and motor travel and the decline of railroading were accompanied by a rise in the use of oil and a decline in the use of coal. More recently, the surge in demand for electric power and the shortage of oil have revitalized the coal industry.

Changes in demands and in tastes are sometimes sudden and dramatic, but in the main they are gradual and continuous and less noticeable month by month than decade by decade. On average about two new firms enter the top 100 every year, and, as a consequence, two others leave. This means a significant change over a decade.

Turnover in the list of leading American companies is continuous and revealing. Only two, US Steel and Exxon (Standard Oil of New Jersey), were in the top 10 both in 1909 and a half-century later. Consider these giants of 1909, none of them among the largest 250 today: International Mercantile Marine (today United States Lines), United States Cotton Oil, American Hide and Leather. American Ice, Baldwin Locomotive, Cudahy, International Salt and United Shoe Machinery. They have slipped or disappeared largely because of the relative decline in the demand for their products. Today's giants include automobile, oil and airline companies and electric power producers – for the obvious reason that demand for these products is very strong.

Are these shifts in demand explained by corporate manipulation of consumers' tastes through advertising or by more basic changes? Advertising has two major aspects: it seeks to inform consumers of the characteristics of the available products and it seeks to influence consumers by altering their demands. The first aspect, informative advertising, plays an important part in the efficient operation of any free-market system; the second aspect is one through which firms seek to control the market rather than being controlled by it.

Clearly, advertising does influence consumers' demand. We have observed that if General Motors stopped advertising, it would surely lose sales to Ford and Chrysler, but it is hard to believe that the automotive society was conjured up by the advertising industry or that when an American is persuaded to 'fly the friendly skies of United (Airlines)' his real alternative is to use a covered wagon, a bicycle or even a Greyhound bus – more likely he is forgoing American, Eastern or Northwest Airlines. Careful promotion can influence the success of one rock group over another, but could it sell the waltz to today's youth? Advertising – taste making – unquestionably plays a role in shaping demand, but so too do more basic human attitudes, psychological needs, technological opportunities and many fads and fashions stemming from sources other than advertising.

Certainly advertising shifts demands among very similar products. It is hard to believe, however, that the American economy, or the average American's system of values, would be fundamentally changed if there were available one more or one less make of automobile or TV set or brand of shoes. A look at those products that have brought basic changes to the economy – and perhaps to value systems – suggests that these products succeeded *because consumers wanted them*, not because the advertising industry brainwashed people into buying them. Consider a few of the major examples.

The automobile transformed society and is now in demand everywhere in the world, even in Communist countries where only informative advertising exists. The Hollywood movie had an enormous influence in shaping society and in changing values; it was – and still is – eagerly attended everywhere in the world, whether or not it is accompanied by a bally-hoo of advertising. The aeroplane – and the jet in particular – has shrunk the size of the world: it has allowed major league sports to expand beyond the confines of the Northeastern and Midwestern United States (i.e., those cities which could be reached by an overnight bus or rail journey); it has made the international conference a commonplace among professionals; it has made European, Hawaiian and Caribbean vacations a reality for the many rather than a luxury for the very few. For better or worse, the revolution in behaviour caused by the birth control pill is still being worked out. TV has changed the activities of children (and adults) in fundamental ways and has brought to viewers a sense of immediacy about distant events that newspapers could never achieve. It also provided news coverage that both caused and partially compensated for the decline in the number of newspapers in many American cities.

Many factors, including advertising and salesmanship, affect consumers' purchasing patterns. However, the new products that have really influenced the allocation of resources and the pattern of society – such as those mentioned in the previous paragraph – have succeeded because consumers wanted them; most of those that failed did so because they were not wanted – at least not at prices that would cover their costs of production.

The evidence suggests that the allocation of resources in any market economy owes more to the tastes and values of consumers than it does to corporate advertising and related activities.

Thus the Galbraithian view that corporations are able to create the demand for their products seems less consistent with the evidence than the conventional view that consumers are a major force in determining the economy's allocation of resources.

Who controls the government? Is the American government subservient to big business? Lobbying is a legal, large-scale activity employed by many groups. Big business has its influence, but so too do farmers, labour unions and small business groups. Some American corporations have certainly exercised illegal and improper influence on both domestic and foreign governments. Cases of corrupt behaviour have been documented at all levels of government; it does not follow from this, however, that government is subservient to the corporations and that decisions taken by the former are *dominated* by the wishes of the latter. It is easy to assert that 'everyone knows that the oil lobby dominates the US Congress', but such assertions do not resolve empirical questions. Lobbying and influence may well help to explain why for years the United States imposed quotas on foreign oil imports, but lobbying by the oil companies did not prevent a delay of the Alaska pipeline for many years, the reduction in special tax reliefs or restrictions imposed on offshore oil drilling. Relaxation of many anti-pollution restrictions came because of the oil shortages of the 1970s, not political pressure. Government contracts bolster the aerospace industry, but Boeing and Lockheed have been in deep financial trouble, partly as a result of government decisions. Tobacco companies have seen government agencies first publicize the hazards of their principal product and then restrict their advertising.

Thus, while business often succeeds in its attempts to protect its commercial interests through political activity, it does so within limits. Where the truth lies between the extremes of 'no influence' and 'no limits' is a matter now being subjected to substantial research. It is a matter that will be clarified by further research, not by mere assertion. In the meantime we can safely say, first, 'corporations have a lot of political influence' and, second, 'there are some serious constraints on the ability of corporations to exert political influence over all levels of American government'.

Neglect of the public interest?

A receptive public has acclaimed one aspect of the Galbraithian critique: the apparent disregard by large corporations for the adverse effects of productive activities on the environment. The problems of pollution arise from activities of both small and large corporations, and from activities of government units and citizens as well. Do such polluting activities represent in a significant degree irresponsible behaviour by corporations that can be countered by such things as Campaign GM – 'a campaign to make General Motors responsible'?

What has come to be known as the 'consumerist' view, or 'consumerism', is that corporations ought on their own volition to serve the general public's interest, not merely the interests of their shareholders. Thus, for example, General Motor's directors must be made to recognize that automobiles both pollute and cause accidents, and General Motor's abundant resources should be invested in developing and installing both safety and anti-pollution devices. This, consumerists argue, is proper use of General Motor's profits, even if General Motor's shareholders do not see it that way and even if automobile purchasers do not want to pay the cost of the extra safety and anti-pollution devices.

The main arguments *for* this view are that only the company can know the potentially adverse effect of its action and that by virtue of holding a corporate charter, the corporation assumes the responsibility to protect the general welfare while pursuing private profits.

The main argument *against* the consumerist view is that managers of companies have neither the knowledge nor the ability to represent the general public interest; they are largely selected, judged and promoted according to their ability to run a profit-oriented enterprise, and the assumption that they are especially competent to decide broader *public* questions is unjustified. Moral (as distinct from economic) decisions – such as whether to make or use nerve gas, to make or use internal combustion engines, to manufacture or smoke cigarettes and to manufacture or utilize DDT or aerosol sprays – cannot properly be delegated to individual corporations or their executives. Some of them are individual decisions; others require either the expertise or the authority of a public regulatory agency. Whoever makes decisions on behalf of the public must be politically responsible to the public.

Those who oppose the consumerist view hold that most required changes in corporate behaviour should be accomplished not by exhorting business leaders to behave responsibly, nor by placing consumer representatives on the corporation's board of directors, but by regulations or incentives that force or induce the desired corporate behaviour. Let corporations pursue their profits – subject to public laws. For example, Congress can require all cars to have seat belts or require auto manufacturers to install anti-pollution valves or to meet specific standards of emission levels. Another alternative is to open the way for law-suits against corporations that either enjoin certain behaviour or force corporations to pay for the damages their products cause.

The controversy over policy alternatives is important, and much of the credit for its existence is due to Galbraith. It is essential to recognize that the policy issues at stake – whether and how to change the behaviour of corporations – can arise whether corporations are primarily responding to market signals or whether they are impervious to them. If citizens do not approve of the results of corporate behaviour, they will want to control the behaviour, whatever the cause, provided that the costs – including undesirable side effects – do not exceed the benefits.

The general demand and supply theory of a market economy

In Chapter 5 we noted that there was evidence that markets for agricultural goods and other primary products did function as assumed in the theory of demand and supply. We also stated that the generalization of this demand-and-supply theory to a theory of the whole economy was a rather speculative leap in the dark. We have now studied the theory of production sufficiently to realize that we cannot in fact apply our simple demand-and-supply theory to the whole economy. This theory is a theory of *competitive* markets, markets in which there is a large number of buyers and sellers. Most manufactured goods, however, are produced under conditions of oligopoly in which there are a very few firms. These firms may or may not compete actively with each other, and in cases in which they do compete they are quite likely to change their prices only occasionally and to compete from day to day by adjusting such things as service, delivery dates, quality and special features of the product.

How important is it that the manufacturing sector is primarily oligopolistic? Does this fact undermine our ability to use economic theory as a successful predictive device? At least two things seem fairly clear.

First, we do have difficulty predicting the detailed effects on the manufacturing industries of such things as changes in tax rates, changes in the number of firms in an industry, and small changes in demands, costs and government regulations. In administered-price situations there is considerable non-price competition. Since we do not have a single well-tested theory of non-price competition, it is often, although by no means always, unclear what will be the effects of changes such as those just listed.

Second, if we wish to predict general long-term trends our theory is more helpful. There is substantial empirical evidence to support each of the following statements. The prices of most primary products are set on competitive markets and these prices do fluctuate in response to shifts in demands and supplies. Large changes in the relative prices of inputs do cause firms to change the proportions in which they use factors, since *whatever* the firm's objectives, they can usually be better served by minimizing costs rather than by wasting money unnecessarily. Continual changes in the prices of inputs sooner or later lead firms to change the prices of their outputs. (Even a non-profit-maximizing monopoly cannot afford to let its profits become significantly negative.) This means that over the long term relative prices of manufactured commodities do change to reflect major changes in the relative costs of producing these commodities. When relative commodity prices change, consumers react, and many long-term changes in consumption patterns that are often casually ascribed to changes in tastes, fashions and habits, are actually responses to changes in relative prices. Observers who predict the broad reactions to such major changes as the recent increases in the price of oil from OPEC countries make disastrous errors when they ignore this general long-term adaptability of the economy which makes it behave in broad outline as would a perfectly competitive economy. (An example of one such blunder is considered in the concluding section of Chapter 46.)

This assessment would probably command general, although by no means universal, acceptance among economists. But just *how* bad is our ability to predict in detail (especially in the oligopolistic part of the economy), and just *how* good is our ability to predict long-term trend reactions to major events? (Do not forget that we are not trying to foretell the future, but to make conditional predictions about the reactions of the economy to given events. See pages 12–13.) Because it is hard to assemble the mass of available evidence so as to focus it on this issue, economists are left to their personal assessments of the balance between success and failure, and debate goes on among those who assess it differently. About all that it seems safe to say is that, when judged by its ability to predict the outcome of events in which we are interested, the theory of the allocation of resources reveals many substantial successes and some major failures.

Part five

The theory of distribution

25

The demand for and supply of factors of production

Are the poor getting poorer and the rich richer, as Karl Marx thought they would? Are the rich getting relatively poorer and the poor relatively richer, as Alfred Marshall hoped they would? Is the inequality of income a social constant, determined by forces possibly beyond man's understanding and probably beyond his control, as Vilfredo Pareto thought they were? These questions concern what is called *the size distribution of income.*

The founders of classical economics, Adam Smith and David Ricardo, were concerned with the *functional distribution of income*: how income was shared among the three great social classes of their day–workers, capitalists and landowners. They defined three basic factors of production: labour, capital and land, according to the functions that they fulfilled in production. The return to each of these factors was the income of each of the three classes. Smith and Ricardo were interested in two questions: 'What determines the income of each group in relation to the total income?' and 'How will the economic growth of society affect the distribution of income?' Their theories predict that landlords would become relatively better off and that capitalists would become relatively worse off as society progressed, while labourers would be constantly pushed to the subsistence level. Karl Marx accepted this classical pair of questions but provided different answers. He concluded that captialists would become relatively better off and workers and landlords relatively worse off as society developed.

The factual background

Income takes many forms: wages and salaries, rental income from property, interest and profits, to name the major ones. Table 25.1 shows the income received by each of the major factors of production in the UK in 1972. The Table shows the amounts of income paid to the various factors of production rather than the amounts paid to various individuals or households. A single individual may receive income from several different factors of production. A man may get income for his own labour services, from renting property that he owns, and from his holdings of shares in various joint-stock companies. When we classify income according to the factor of production that is its source, we are dealing with the FUNCTIONAL DISTRIBUTION OF INCOME.

Table 25.1 Functional distribution of income in the UK, 1976

	£s million	Percentage of total
Income from employment	78,639	69·2
Income from self-employment	10,208	9·0
Gross trading profits of companies	12,445	11·0
Gross trading surplus of public corporations	4,460	3·9
Gross trading surplus of other public enterprises	120	0·1
Rent	7,771	6·8
Total domestic income before providing for depreciation and stock appreciation	113,643	100·0

Source: CSO, *Annual Abstract of Statistics*, 1977

Most of the theory of distribution that we shall discuss in Part 5 is concerned with the functional distribution of income. But economists are also interested in the distribution of income among individuals and families. When we classify income according to the size of income received by each earner irrespective of the sources of that income, we are dealing with the SIZE DISTRIBUTION of income. Many economic policies are designed to modify the size distribution of income.

The basic facts about the size distribution of income are given in Tables 25.2 and 25.3. Table 25.2 shows the distribution of incomes in the UK by income level. Table 25.3 focuses on the inequality in the size distribution of income; the 20 per cent of the population at the bottom of the income scale receive only 7 per cent of the nation's income; the 20 per cent at the top receive 35 per cent of it.

It is tempting to give superficial explanations of differences in income: 'People are

Table 25.2 The size distribution of income for income earners in the UK*

	Percentage of Earning Persons with incomes above £400 (in 1969–70 £s)	
1969–70 £s	1969–70 Quinquennial Survey	1974–5 Annual Survey
400–749	21·84	18·19
750–999	15·71	12·88
1,000–1,499	29·60	26·46
1,500–1,999	20·12	18·79
2,000–2,999	8·90	17·82
3,000–4,999	2·62	4·49
5,000–9,999	0·98	1·10
10,000–19,999	0·20	0·16
20,000–49,999	0·03	0·08
50,000 and over	0·004	0·006

Source: CSO, *Annual Abstract of Statistics*, 1977

* The data relate only to those with taxable income. Because the basic exemption has changed between 1969–70 and 1974–5, the data are not fully comparable over the two years.

Table 25.3 Inequality in income distribution

1969–70 Quinquennial Survey			1974–5 Annual Survey		
Percentage of: earning persons	before-tax income	after-tax income	Percentage of: earning persons	before-tax income	after-tax income
9·02	2·78	3·25	9·54	2·93	3·50
24·48	9·92	11·18	24·65	10·04	11·38
39·65	19·72	21·68	40·29	20·35	22·27
54·61	32·15	34·76	55·60	33·25	35·70
68·26	45·99	49·18	68·78	46·83	49·70
79·73	59·73	63·30	86·32	69·43	72·66
93·95	80·94	84·48	93·74	81·76	84·83
96·68	85·00	88·93	96·59	87·59	90·41
99·22	94·17	96·39	99·11	94·55	96·63
99·96	99·10	99·73	99·99	99·58	99·90

Source: CSO, *Annual Abstract of Statistics*, 1977

paid what they are worth.' But the economist must ask: 'Worth what to whom? What gives them value?' Sometimes it is said that people earn according to their ability. But note that incomes are distributed in a very much more unequal fashion than any measured index of ability such as IQ or physical strength. In what sense is Cleo Laine 20 times as able as the promising new pop singer? She earns 20 times as much. In what sense is a lorry driver more able than a schoolteacher? In what sense is a football player more able than a wrestler?

If answers couched in terms of worth and ability seem superficial, so are answers like 'It's all a matter of luck', or 'It's just the system'. We are concerned now with discovering whether or not the theories of economics provide explanations of the distribution of income that are more satisfactory than the ones mentioned above.

Factor prices and factor incomes

The traditional theory states that distribution is simply a special case of price theory. The income of any factor of production (and hence the amount of the national product that it is able to command) depends on the price that is paid for the factor and the amount that is used. If we wish to build a theory of distribution, we need a theory of factor prices. Such a theory involves little that is not already familiar.

The free-market price of any commodity is determined by demand and supply. In Figure 25.1 the original curves for some factor of production are D_1 and S. The

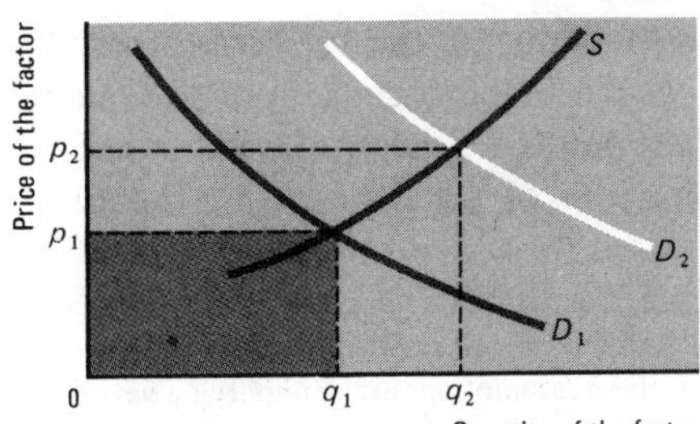

Fig. 25.1 The determination of the price, quantity and income of a factor of production

equilibrium price and quantity are p_1 and q_1. The total income earned by the factor is the shaded area.

We assume that the price of all other factors of production, the prices of all goods, and the level of national income are given and constant.[1] Fluctuations in the equilibrium price and quantity will now cause fluctuations in the money earnings of the factor, in its relative earnings (compared to other factors) and in the share of national income going to the factor. Assume, for example, that the demand curve for the factor in question rises from D_1 to D_2. Now the money price of the factor rises from p_1 to p_2, and the relative price rises from p_1/F to p_2/F where F is the average price of *all* other factors. The total earnings rise from p_1q_1 to p_2q_2 and, if the total income in the whole economy remains constant at γ, then the share of income going to this factor rises from p_1q_1/γ to p_2q_2/γ. This gives us the free-market determination of a factor's price and its share of national income. Onto this theory we can then, if necessary, superimpose the effects of any government interventions (as we did in Chapter 10) or any monopolistic elements (as we did in Chapter 20). According to standard theory:

> **The problem of distribution in a free-market society can be reduced to the question of the determinants of the demand and supply of factors of production, plus the problem of determining the effect of the departures from a free market caused by such forces as monopolistic organizations, government action, and unions.**

The demand for factors

Firms require land, labour, raw materials, machines and other inputs to produce the goods and services that they sell. The demand for any input therefore depends on the existence of a demand for the goods that it helps to make. We say that the demand is a DERIVED DEMAND.

Obvious examples of derived demand abound. The demand for computer programmers is growing as industry turns increasingly to electronic computers. The demand for university teachers varies directly with the number of students going to university. The demand for coal miners and coal-digging equipment declines as the demand for coal declines. Indeed, anything that increases the demand for a commodity – such as population changes and changes in tastes – will increase the demand for the factors required to make it. Typically, of course, one factor will be used in making many goods, not just one. Steel is used in dozens of industries, as are the services of carpenters. The total demand for a factor will be the sum of the derived demands for it in all productive activities.

In this section we are mainly concerned with deducing the prediction that the demand curve for a factor is downward sloping. We do this because derived demand provides a link between the pricing of factors and the pricing of products. This allows us to connect our theory of the behaviour of the firm to our theory of distribution.

---

[1] We make these assumptions because we are concerned with a factor's relative share of total national income. As we observed in the last paragraph of page 155, these assumptions are a simplifying device for our analysis, but they do not seriously restrict its applicability.

The quantity of a factor demanded in equilibrium

We first derive a famous relation that will hold in equilibrium for every factor employed by a wide class of firms. Recall that in Part 4 we established a set of conditions necessary for the maximization of profits in the short run. Some factor was fixed (usually capital) and some other factor was allowed to vary, and we saw that the profit-maximizing firm would increase its output to the level at which the last unit produced added just as much to cost as it did to revenue or, in technical language, until marginal cost equalled marginal revenue. Another way of stating exactly the same thing is to say that *the profit-maximizing firm will increase production up to the point at which the last unit of the variable factor employed adds just as much to revenue as it does to cost.*

Just as it is true that all profit-maximizing firms, whether they are selling under conditions of perfect competition, monopolistic competition or monopoly, produce to the point at which marginal cost equals marginal revenue, so it is true that all profit-maximizing firms will hire units of the variable factor up to the point at which the marginal cost of the factor (i.e., the addition to the total cost resulting from the employment of one more unit) equals the marginal revenue produced by the factor. Since we have already used the term *marginal revenue* to refer to the change in revenue resulting from the sale of an additional unit of product, we shall use another term, MARGINAL REVENUE PRODUCT, to mean the addition to revenue resulting from the sale of the product contributed by an additional unit of the variable factor. It is true, therefore, of *all* profit-maximizing firms that are in equilibrium:

Marginal cost of the variable factor =
marginal revenue product of that factor (1)

This must be true for every factor that the firm can vary, and thus *in the long run* it must hold for all factors. If there were a single factor for which (1) did not hold, the firm could increase its profits by varying the employment of that factor. Thus (1) is a relation that must hold in equilibrium for *all* profit-maximizing firms with respect to all variable factors of production.

Now let us consider all those firms that are unable to influence the prices of the factors that they purchase (i.e., firms that buy their factors in perfectly competitive markets). In this case the marginal cost of a factor is merely its price. The cost, for example, of obtaining an extra person on the payroll is the wage that must be paid to that person. For firms that take factor prices as given, we may state condition (1) in the following form:

Price of the factor = marginal revenue product of the factor. (2)

The firm's demand curve for a factor[1]

Conditions (1) and(2) describe relations that hold in equilibrium. We now wish to derive the demand curve for a factor of production. We shall do this assuming that the firm is unable to influence the price of the factor. (We shall drop this assumption in Chapter 27.) For the moment we shall also assume that there is only a single variable factor of production. This allows us to use condition (2) to derive the firm's demand for a factor as soon as we have its marginal revenue product curve.

[1] The following sections are difficult and may be omitted without loss of continuity by skipping directly to the summary that begins on the bottom of page 155.

The derivation of the demand curve from the marginal revenue product curve Figure 25.2 shows a marginal revenue product for some factor.[1] This shows how much would be added to revenue by employing one more unit of the factor for each level of total employment of the factor. Condition (2) states that the profit-maximizing firm will employ additional units of the factor up to the point at which the marginal revenue product equals the price of the factor. If, for example, the price were £1,200 per year, then it would be most profitable to employ 50 workers. (There is no point in employing a fifty-first, since that would add just less than £1,200 to revenue but £1,200 to costs, and hence would *reduce* total profits.)

The curve in Figure 25.3 shows the quantity of labour employed at each price of labour. Such a curve can be derived from Figure 25.2 by picking various prices of the variable factor, and reading off the amount used from the marginal revenue product curve in just the way described above for the price of £1,200.

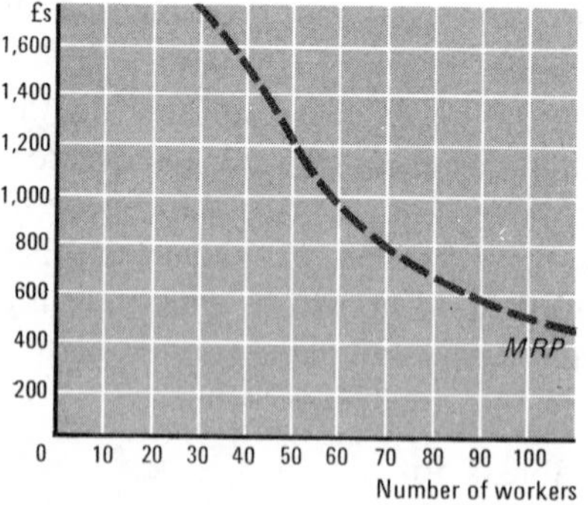

Fig. 25.2 A marginal revenue product curve for a factor

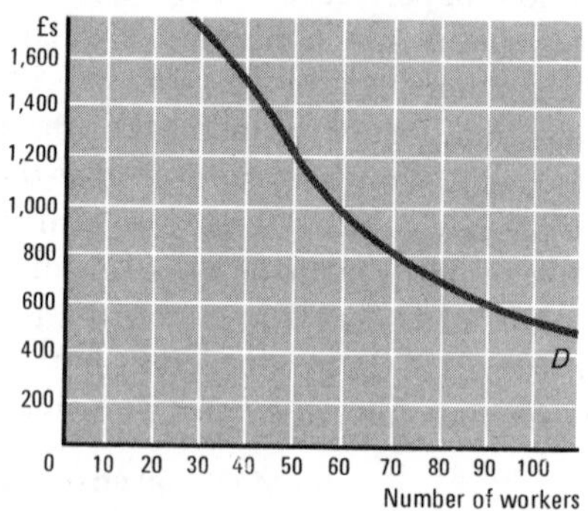

Fig. 25.3 A firm's demand curve for a factor of production when only one factor can be varied is the marginal revenue product curve of that factor

Note that the curve in Figure 25.3 is identical with the marginal revenue product curve in Figure 25.2. The curve in Figure 25.3 relates the price of the variable factor to the quantity employed. Hence, it is the demand curve for the variable factor.

> **The marginal revenue product curve of a factor has the same shape as the firm's demand curve for that factor.**

The derivation of the marginal revenue product curve We have related the firm's demand for a single variable factor to the marginal revenue product curve. Next we shall inquire into the derivation of this curve. The marginal revenue product of the factor is defined as the addition to total revenue resulting from the employment of an additional unit. This may be broken up into a physical and a value component, and we must now consider how each of these varies as the quantity of the factor varies.

The physical component: We have assumed that we have only one variable factor of

[1] We avoid a long chain of reasoning without any immediate payoff by first showing how to derive a demand curve *given* a marginal revenue product curve and then showing how to derive the marginal revenue curve itself. A more straightforward but less immediately motivated development of the argument would be to derive the *MRP* curve first and then the demand curve.

production. As we vary the quantity of this factor, output will vary. The hypothesis of diminishing returns that we developed in Chapter 17 predicts that, as we go on adding more and more units of the variable factor to the given quantity of the fixed factor, the extra output produced by successive increments of the variable factor will decline. This extra output is called the marginal physical product (*MPP*) of the variable factor and its behaviour is shown in Figure 25.4.

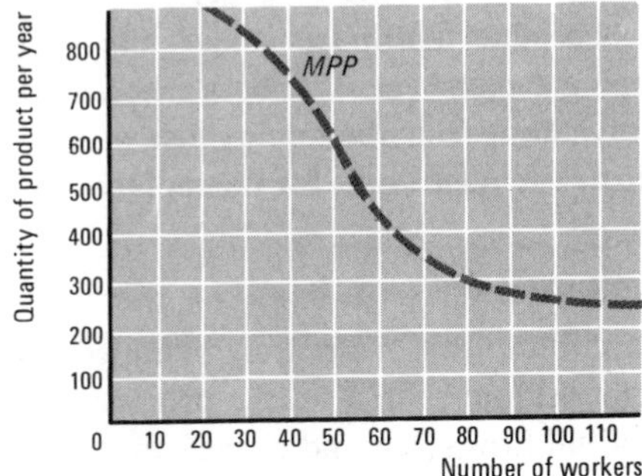

Fig. 25.4 The marginal physical product curve

The value component: Now to convert the marginal physical product curve of Figure 25.4 into a marginal revenue product curve, we need to know the value of the extra physical product. The marginal physical product depends solely on the technical conditions of production, but the value to the firm of this extra product depends on the price of the product. There are two cases to consider. If the firm sells its product in a perfectly competitive market, the price is given, and it accurately measures the value to the firm of an additional unit. Thus, in the case of perfect competition, the marginal revenue product is given by:

marginal physical product multiplied by price of the product. (3)

If, on the other hand, the firm faces a downward-sloping demand curve for its product, the value to the firm of an extra unit of output will be less than its price, because to sell the extra unit it will have to reduce the price on all other units to be sold (see page 262). In this case the marginal revenue due to an extra unit of output is less than its price. Thus, where any firm faces a downward-sloping demand curve for its product, the marginal revenue product is given by:

marginal physical product multiplied by marginal revenue associated with the sale of the extra unit. (4)

In both cases the firm is interested in the gain in revenue. The only difference is that in (3) the marginal revenue is the price, while in (4) it is less than price (because the firm faces a downward-sloping demand curve for its product). We have avoided unnecessary terminology by referring to both (3) and (4) as marginal revenue product. Sometimes, however, when it is desirable to distinguish between the two, (3) is called *the value of the marginal product*, while the term *marginal revenue product* is reserved for (4).

Summary All of this no doubt sounds very forbidding at first reading. It is an example of a chain of reasoning, referred to in the Introduction (see page xv), where each step is simple enough, but the cumulative effects of several steps can seem complex. And there are more steps to come! Perhaps it would be a good idea, before going on, to summarize the argument so far:

> **Any profit-maximizing firm will hire a variable factor up to the point at which the last unit adds as much to revenue as to costs. The addition to costs is the price of the factor (if the firm buys factors in a competitive market). The addition to revenue is the marginal physical product multiplied by the price of the product if the firm sells in a perfectly competitive market, and marginal physical product multiplied by marginal revenue if the firm faces a downward-sloping demand curve. In both cases, the curve showing the addition to revenue resulting from the employment of each additional unit of the factor is the firm's demand curve for the factor.**

The industry's demand for the factor

When we derived the market demand for a commodity, we merely summed the demands of individual households. We cannot rely on such a simple procedure in the case of a factor of production. The individual firm's demand curve shows how the quantity of the factor demanded varies with the factor's price, *assuming that the price of the firm's output remains constant*. This assumption is valid only if all other firms keep their outputs fixed. If the price of the variable factor changes, however, we should expect all firms to vary their production. If, for example, the price of the factor falls, then all firms will hire more of the variable factor and the resulting rise in output will cause a fall in the market price of the commodity. This fall in price will cause the marginal revenue product of the factor – the amount added to total revenue by the employment of one more unit of the factor – to be less than if the price of the product had remained unchanged. We may now derive a demand curve on the assumption that when factor prices change, all firms in the industry will vary their outputs in order to maximize their profits. We assume that we know the marginal physical product curves for all firms in the industry, and also the demand curve for the product produced by the industry, and we proceed in the following manner. (1) Assume some particular price of the factor and find the equilibrium price for the product. This is done in the manner described in Chapter 19: once the factor price is known, the marginal physical product curves can be translated into marginal cost curves; these cost curves are then summed, giving an industry supply curve which, together with the demand curve, determines the equilibrium price of the product. (2) Next, take the marginal physical product curve of the firm in which we are interested, and multiply each quantity by the market price determined in (1) above.

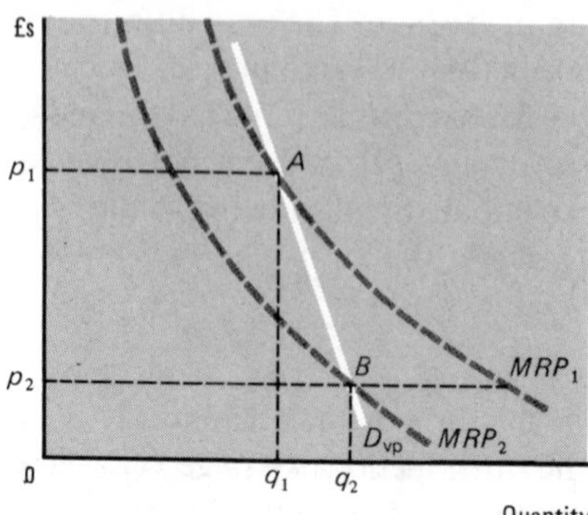

Fig. 25.5 Derivation of the firm's demand curve for a factor on the assumption that all firms change their output so that the price of a product changes when the price of the factor changes

This gives a marginal revenue product curve on the assumption that market price remains constant as output is varied. This is the curve MRP_1 shown in Figure 25.5. Locate the point A in Figure 25.5, corresponding to the existing price of the factor and the quantity actually being employed. *This curve, MRP_1, is the firm's demand curve for the variable factor, on the assumption that the price of the commodity is fixed; its slope depends solely on the technical conditions of production i.e., on the slope of the marginal physical product curve.*

(3) Now consider a lower price of the factor, say p_2, instead of p_1. Our firm, in an effort to maximize profits, will hire more labour and increase its output. But so will all other firms and, as a result, the price of the product will fall. This causes the curve showing marginal physical product (MPP) multiplied by existing market price to *shift inwards towards the origin* – to MRP_2 in the Figure. Thus the firm moves towards equilibrium in two ways: by hiring more labour and by having its curve showing marginal physical product *times* market price shift inwards. A possible equilibrium is illustrated by point B. The lower price of the product gives rise to a new curve showing MPP *times* market price and the new quantity of labour hired is q_2 instead of q_1. We repeat the procedure for each possible price of labour and generate a set of points such as A and B. We then join up these points and obtain a demand curve for labour allowing for the price changes in the final product. This curve, which is shown by the white line in Figure 25.5, is steeper than any of the fixed price demand curves. How much steeper depends upon how much the price of the product falls as all firms expand output, i.e., on the elasticity of the market demand for the product. In order to derive the industry's demand curve for the factor, we merely aggregate the demand curves we have developed.

An alternative derivation of the industry's demand curve

Alternatively, we can derive the industry demand curve for a factor in the following way. Take the MPP curve for each firm. Assume some specific price of the variable factor. Derive a marginal cost curve for each firm by the means used in Chapter 17. Sum these to obtain an industry supply curve. Now repeat the process for each possible price of the variable factor. This gives rise to a whole family of short-run industry supply curves, each corresponding to a particular price of the variable factor. Such a family of curves is illustrated in Figure 25.6 (S_{10} corresponding to a factor price of £10 a day, S_8 to a factor price of £8, etc.). Assume a particular factor price, say £6. By using the market demand curve and the supply curve S_6, the equilibrium price and quantity can be derived. Now draw a horizontal line, RQ, through the point of intersection of S_6 and D. The points of intersection of RQ and the various supply curves tell how production would vary as factor prices varied, *if*

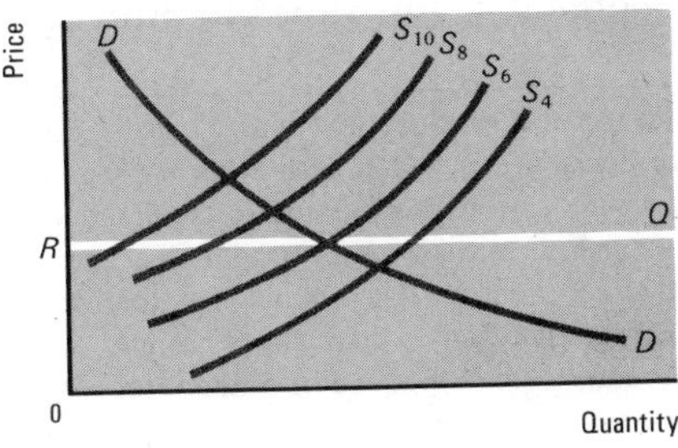

Fig. 25.6 Derivation of the demand curve for a factor by perfectly competitive industry

the market price did not change. The points of intersection of the actual demand curve, *D*, and the various supply curves show how production would vary if market prices varied. Since we now know the amount of production corresponding to each particular price of the variable factor, we know the amount of the variable factor that must be employed. Plotting this amount against its price gives the industry demand curve for the factor. Clearly, for given changes in factor prices, the variations in production, and hence the elasticity of demand for the variable factor, are less when the commodity's price varies than when it is assumed to be constant. Now draw for yourself a diagram similar to Figure 25.6, but with a much steeper demand curve than the one in the printed figure. You will then be able to show yourself that *the lower the elasticity of demand for the product, the lower the elasticity of demand for a factor.*

One other important relation can be derived from this analysis. Consider two factors of production: expenditure on factor *A* accounts for two per cent of the total costs of production; expenditure on factor *B* accounts for fifty percent of total costs. Consider a one per cent change in the price of each factor. Clearly, the supply curves in Figure 25.6 will shift less in response to the change in factor *A*'s price than in response to the change in *B*'s. The smaller the shift in the marginal cost curve, the smaller the change in equilibrium output. The smaller the change in output, the smaller the change in the quantity of the variable factor required as an input. This leads to the conclusion that *the smaller the proportion of total cost accounted for by a given factor of production, the more inelastic its demand.*[1]

Demand for a factor when more than one factor is variable

If there is more than one variable factor, the marginal revenue product curve is no longer the firm's demand curve for the factor. This curve shows what happens to revenues as the quality of the factor employed is varied *while all other factors are held constant.* If there is more than one variable factor, a change in the price of one factor will lead to a substitution between the variable factors; more of the now cheaper factor will be bought *even if the firm's output is unchanged.* Thus, the firm's demand curve for a factor will be more elastic than the marginal revenue product curve of the factor, the amount of additional elasticity depending on the ease with which one factor can be substituted for another.

How easy it is to substitute one factor for another depends on the technical conditions of production. It is very easy to underestimate the degree of substitutability. It is fairly obvious that a bushel of wheat can be produced by combining land either with a lot of labour and a little capital or with a little labour and a lot of capital. It is common, however, to think in terms of using inputs in fixed proportions in manufacturing. A bit of casual observation of any manufacturing industry over time will show that factor proportions can be varied to produce a

[1] This is necessarily true when we have only one variable factor of production, but care must be taken when there are many variable factors. The elasticity of demand depends in such cases both on the proportion of costs accounted for by the factor, and on the ease with which other factors can be substituted for it. Thus, we would not expect there to be an inelastic demand on British building sites for Irish labourers from the city of Cork because, although they account for a low proportion of total costs, other labourers are perfect substitutes for them. On the other hand, we would expect there to be an inelastic demand for door handles because, not only are they a small proportion of the total cost of building a house, it is very hard to build a satisfactory house without them.

given product. There is, for example, the case in which glass and steel turn out to be very good substitutes for each other. One would never guess this by considering their physical qualities in general, but in the case of car manufacture one can be substituted for the other over a wide range merely by varying the dimensions of the windows.

We have looked at some alternative ways of deriving the demand curve for a factor. However we do this, or whether we do it at all, the following will always hold:

Any profit-maximizing firm in equilibrium will always be equating the marginal cost of each of its variable factors with the marginal revenue product of that factor.

Summary of the theory of the demand for a factor

Our discussion of the demand for a factor of production leads to the conclusion that the elasticity of the demand for a factor depends on both the technical conditions of production and the market demand for the commodity that the factor produces. The main influences may be summarized as follows:

An industry's demand for a factor will be more elastic:
(1) The more elastic is the demand for the commodity produced by the industry;
(2) The larger is the proportion of total cost accounted for by payments to the factor;
(3) The easier it is to substitute other factors for the one in question.

As well as predicting the forces that influence elasticity of demand, the theory shows certain relations that must hold in equilibrium for any firm that is unable to influence the prices of the factors that it purchases:

(1) If the firm sells its product in a perfect market, the price paid to a factor will be equal to the value of that factor's marginal product, i.e., marginal physical product multiplied by the price of the product.
(2) If the firm faces a downward-sloping demand curve for its product, the price of a factor will be equated in equilibrium with the marginal revenue product of the factor, i.e., marginal physical product multiplied by the marginal revenue resulting from the sale of the extra product. This amount is necessarily less than the value of the marginal physical product multiplied by the price of the product.

Finally, we note that although the above relations hold in all equilibrium situations, it does *not* follow from our theory that the sum of the firms' marginal revenue product curves is the industry's demand curve for the factor.

The supply factors

We first make a distinction between the total supply of a factor to the whole economy and the supply to some small part of the economy, say to one industry or to one firm. We shall deal first with the total supply of factors to the economy.

The total supply of factors

At first glance it may seem plausible to assume that the total supply of most factors is fixed. After all, there is only so much land in the world, or in England, or in London. There is an upper limit to the number of workers. There is only so much coal, oil, copper and iron ore in the earth. These considerations do indeed put absolute maxima upon the supplies of factors. But in virtually every case we are not near these upper limits, and the determinants of changes in the total *effective* supply of land, labour, natural resources or capital need to be considered.

Labour The number of people willing to work is called the LABOUR FORCE; the total number of hours they are willing to work is called the SUPPLY OF EFFORT or, more simply, THE SUPPLY OF LABOUR.

> **The supply of effort is a function of three things: the size of the population, the proportion of the population willing to work and the number of hours worked by each individual.**

Population: Populations vary in size, and these variations are influenced to some extent by economic factors. There is some evidence that the birth rate is higher in good times than in bad. Much of the variation in population is, however, explained by factors outside of economics.

The Labour force: The labour force varies considerably in response to variations in the demand for labour. Generally, a rise in the demand for labour, and an accompanying rise in earnings, will lead to an increase in the proportion of the population willing to work. More married women and elderly people enter the labour force when the demand for labour is high. The dramatic increase in the proportions of married women and persons over 65 who were employed during World War II is a case in point.

Hours worked: Variations in the number of hours people are willing to work have resulted in a substantial reduction in the supply of labour over a long period of time. Generally, a rise in real wages, such as has occurred in most Western countries over the last two centuries, leads households to consume more commodities *and also to consume more leisure*. This means that they will be willing to work fewer hours per week, a fact that, unless offset by a rise either in total population or in the proportion of the population in the labour force, will lead to a decline in the supply of labour.

Workers are in the position of trading their leisure for goods; by giving up leisure (by working), they obtain money and, hence, goods. A rise in the wage rate means that there is a change in the relative price of goods and leisure. Goods become cheaper relative to leisure, since each hour worked results in more goods than before, and each hour of leisure consumed is at the cost of more goods forgone. This is illustrated in Figure 25.7. Leisure is measured on the vertical axis and the money value of goods consumed on the horizontal axis. Each individual starts with 24 hours of his own time. If the wage rate is 50 pence per hour, he can have 24 hours of leisure and no goods, or £12 worth of goods and no leisure (much less any sleep), or any combination of goods and leisure indicated by points on budget line A. Assume, first, that he chooses the position indicated by point x, so that he consumes 14 hours of leisure and trades the other 10 (at 50 pence per hour) for £5 worth of goods. Now

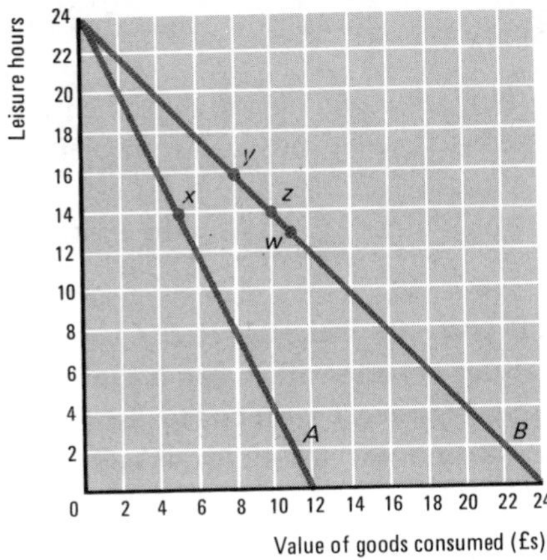

Fig. 25.7 The choice between income and leisure

assume that the wage rate rises to, say, £1 per hour. He can now have any combination of goods and leisure indicated by points on budget line *B*. If he continues to work for 10 hours per day, he moves to point *z* and now gets £10 worth of goods, but there is nothing to stop him from moving to a point above and to the right of *x*, in which case he can have more goods *and* more leisure. If, for example, he moves to the position indicated by *y*, he will have an extra two hours of leisure and an extra £3 worth of goods. On the other hand, the extra income that can be obtained *per unit of leisure sacrificed* might make him more willing to give up leisure to get goods. He might, for example, move to point *w* and work one more hour, getting £11 worth of goods.[1]

The above analysis leads to the following conclusion:

> **Standard theory makes no prediction about the effect of an increase in wage rates on the overall supply of effort, which may rise, fall or remain unchanged.**

Much of the long-run evidence tends to show that as real earnings per hour rise, people wish to reduce the number of hours they work. This evidence is, of course, concerned with the supply of effort to the whole economy; there is also evidence to suggest that a rise in earnings in one industry will increase the supply of effort to that industry by attracting workers from other industries.

Land If by 'land' we mean the total area of dry land, then its supply is pretty well fixed. A rise in the earnings of land cannot result in much of an increase in supply, unless land under water can be drained. The traditional assumption in economics is that the supply of land is absolutely inelastic. However, if by 'land' we understand all the fertile land available for cultivation, then the supply of land is subject to large fluctuations. Considerable care and effort is required to sustain the productive power of land, and if the return to land is low, its fertility may be allowed to be exhausted within a short period of time. On the other hand, a high return to land

[1] The movement from his original position on *A* to his new position on *B* is due to an income effect and a substitution effect. When the wage rate rises, the substitution effect works to increase the supply of labour, because giving up leisure to get goods is now a more profitable occupation than before. The income effect works to decrease the supply of labour (increase the consumption of leisure), because the person can consume more of everything including leisure. Whether the rise in wages causes a rise or a fall in the number of hours people will wish to work depends on the relative strengths of these two effects.

may provide incentives for irrigation, drainage and fertilization schemes that can greatly increase the supply of arable land.[1]

There is no value in debating which is 'real' land, the total land area or the total supply of arable land. The magnitude we are interested in depends on the problem at hand. For most problems in agricultural economics – for example, in the effect of land taxes on the prices of agricultural goods – what we need to know is the elasticity of the total supply of cultivable land.

> **The total supply of cultivable land is not perfectly inelastic. It can be expanded greatly by irrigation and other forms of reclamation, and it can be contracted drastically and rapidly – as many farmers have found to their sorrow – through neglect and failure to observe the principles of soil conservation.**

Land is usually defined to include the natural resources found in or on it. The quantity of a given natural resource existing in the world is of course limited. But the problem of actual exhaustion does not arise as often as one might think. Often a large undiscovered or unexploited quantity exists, and a shortage of the resource that raises its price encourages exploration and the development of previously unprofitable sources. The world's proven and exploitable supply of any natural resource thus usually varies considerably with the price of the resource. This is certainly true today of both petroleum and natural gas, the worry about the 'energy crisis' not withstanding. Of course there is an upper limit, and resources can be totally exhausted. Worse, they can be polluted or otherwise despoiled so that they are rendered useless long before they have been consumed.

Capital Capital is a man-made factor of production. The supply of capital in a country consists of the existing machines, plant, equipment, etc. and it is called the CAPITAL STOCK. This capital is used up in the course of production, and the supply is thus diminished by the amount that wears out or is otherwise destroyed each year. On the other hand, new capital goods are produced each year. New machines and new buildings replace ones that wear out (although they will rarely be identical with the capital they are 'replacing'). The total amount of capital goods produced is called GROSS INVESTMENT. Capital goods that are not replacing worn-out equipment, and therefore represent net additions to the capital stock, are called NET INVESTMENT. Expenditure on capital goods is called INVESTMENT EXPENDITURE. To distinguish the two types of capital goods we talk of GROSS and NET INVESTMENT EXPENDITURE.

The supply of capital has been observed to increase considerably over time in all modern countries. The volume of net investment determines the rate of increase of the capital stock. There is considerable evidence that net additions to the stock of capital vary considerably over the trade cycle, being low in periods of slump and high in periods of boom.

> **Taking the long view and ignoring cyclical fluctuations, there has been a fairly steady tendency for the stock of capital to increase over a very long period of time.**

[1] It used to be common practice, following David Ricardo, a British economist of the early nineteenth century, to define land as the *original and inexhaustible powers of the soil.* Ricardo wrote before the phenomenon of dust bowls, which turn large tracts of land into barren deserts, was widely known, and before we were aware that the deserts of North Africa had once been fertile areas.

The theory of investment, which we shall develop in subsequent sections of this book, is thus a theory of changes in the stock of capital.

The supply of factors to particular uses

The question of what determines the allocation of factors of production among various possible uses is a very general one. Even if all factors had only one use, it would still be necessary to allocate them among competing firms in the same industry. As it is, factors have many uses. A given piece of land can, for example, be used to grow a variety of crops, and it can also be subdivided for a housing development. A machinist from Coventry can work in a variety of automobile plants, or in a dozen other industries, or even in the physics laboratories at Cambridge. Factors must be allocated among different industries and among different firms in the same industry.

If the owners of factors are mainly concerned with making as much money as they can, they will move their factors to that use in which they earn the most. This movement of factors out of the one use into another will continue until the earnings of any one factor in all of its various possible uses are the same. Owners of factors, in fact, take other things besides money into account, including, for example, risk, convenience and a good climate. Factors will, therefore, be moved among uses until there is no net advantage in further movement, allowing for both the monetary and non-monetary advantages. We may now restate this discussion as the HYPOTHESIS OF EQUAL NET ADVANTAGE:

> **Owners will choose that use of their factors that provides them with the greatest net advantage. Net advantage includes both monetary and non-monetary elements.**

This hypothesis plays the same role in the theory of distribution that the profit-maximization hypothesis plays in the theory of production. It leads to the prediction that factors of production will be allocated among various uses in such a way that they receive the same net return in each use. This hypothesis is, however, unsatisfactory as it stands.

The influence of non-monetary advantages Difficulties arise unless we can measure non-monetary advantages. Suppose we observe that a mechanic is working in London for £500 a year less than he could make in Newcastle. Is this evidence against the hypothesis, or does it merely mean that the non-monetary benefits of living in London (or of *not* living in Newcastle) are £500? A moment's thought will make it clear that any conceivable observation could be rationalized to fit the hypothesis as long as we do not have an independent measure of non-monetary advantages. To make the hypothesis useful we must do one of two things: either we must define in a measureable way the non-monetary benefits that we believe are important to choices, or we must make an assumption about the relative stability of monetary and non-monetary advantages. The first alternative is generally regarded as impossible unless we assume that the hypothesis is correct, in which case whatever monetary difference occurs between the earnings of a factor in two uses is assumed to measure the extent of the difference in non-monetary advantages. The second alternative, to make an assumption about the relative stability of monetary and non-monetary advantages, is more promising. If, for example, we assume that the difference in non-monetary advantages between two uses of a factor remains constant over time, we can predict that variations in monetary advantages will cause variations in net advantage, and that some resources will flow in response to the change.

It is not necessary, however, to make the very strong assumption that non-monetary advantages are constant. We can assume instead that they change, but more slowly than monetary ones. In this case, we can still extract predictions about behaviour. This weaker assumption leads us to the following important prediction:

> **Any change in the relative price paid to a factor in two uses will lead owners of the factor to increase the quantity they supply to the use in which the relative price has increased, and decrease the quantity they supply to the use in which it has decreased.**

This prediction implies a rising supply curve for a factor in any particular use. Such a supply curve (like all supply curves) can shift in response to changes in other variables. One of these is the size of the non-monetary benefits.

Factor mobility How fast will factors move among uses when net advantages vary? FACTOR MOBILITY refers to the readiness of factors to respond to signals that indicate where factors are wanted. If a factor is highly mobile in the sense that owners will quickly shift from use *A* to use *B* in response to a small change in the relative factor price, then supply will be highly elastic. If, on the other hand, factor owners are 'locked in' to some use and will not, or cannot, respond quickly, the supply will tend to be inelastic. In Part 4 we discussed factor mobility with respect to capital and also the barriers that impede that mobility. We will now generalize that discussion to include all factors.

Mobility of land: Consider agricultural land. Many crops can be harvested within a year and a totally different crop planted. A farm on the outskirts of a growing city can be sold for subdivision and development on very short notice. Once land is built upon, as urban land usually is, its mobility is much reduced. One can convert a hotel site into an office-building site, but it takes a very large differential in the value of land use to make tearing down the hotel worthwhile.

> **Land, which is physically the least mobile of all factors, is paradoxically one of the most mobile in an economic sense.**

Although the land is highly mobile among alternative uses, it is completely immobile as far as location is concerned. There is only so much land within the borders of any given city, and no increase in the price offered can induce more land to relocate within the city. This locational immobility has, as we shall see, important consequences.

Mobility of capital: Most capital equipment, once constructed, is immobile. A great deal of machinery is specific: it must either be used for the purpose for which it was designed, or not be used at all. This is, of course, not true of all pieces of capital equipment – a shed, for example, may be used for a large number of purposes. It is the immobility of most capital equipment that makes exit of firms from declining industries a slow and difficult process.

During the life of a piece of capital, the firm may make allowances for depreciation so that capital goods can be replaced when they wear out. If conditions of demand and cost have not changed, the firm may spend money to replace the worn-out piece of equipment with an identical one. It may also do other things with its funds: buy a newly designed machine to produce the same goods, buy machines to produce totally different goods, or even lend money to some other firm. In this way, the long-run allocation of a country's stock of capital among various uses changes.

> **Physical capital is often immobile in the short run, but in the long run the processes of depreciation and replacement mean that the capital stock can change greatly in its composition and allocation among users.**

In popular discussion, money is often referred to as 'capital'. Money provides a claim on resources. A firm or a household that has saved money can spend it on anything that it desires. For example it can choose to buy beer or machines; by doing so, it will direct the nation's resources to the production of beer or machinery. Also, the firm or household can lend its money to other firms or households and thereby allow the borrowers to determine what the nation's resources will be used to produce.

Mobility of labour: Labour is unique as a factor of production in that the supply of the service implies the physical presence of the owner of the source of the service. Landlords may live in the place of their choice while obtaining income from renting out land located in remote parts of the world. Investors can shift their capital from one firm to another so that their income is earned from activities throughout the world while they themselves never leave New York or Tokyo or London. But if a worker employed by a firm in Coventry decides to offer his labour services to a firm in South London, he must physically travel to South London to do so. If a capitalist decides to invest in steel mills, he need never visit one; if a labourer decides to work in a steel mill, he must be on the premises. This is, of course, all quite obvious, but it has one important consequence: non-monetary factors are much more important in the allocation of labour than in the allocation of other factors of production. If the rate of return is even slightly higher in steel mills than elsewhere, other things being equal, capital will move into steel. But the wage paid in steel mills can be substantially above that in other industries without inducing an analogous flow of labour, if people find working in steel mills unpleasant.

An important variable affecting labour mobility is *time*. In the short term, it is difficult for people to change occupations. It is not difficult for a file clerk to move from one company to another, or to take a job in London instead of in Colchester, but it will be difficult for her to become an editor or an advertising executive in a short period of time. There are two considerations here: ability and training. Lack of either will stratify some people and make certain kinds of mobility difficult.

Over long periods, labour mobility among occupations is very great indeed. In assessing this mobility, it is important to remember that the labour force is not static. At one end, young people enter from school, and, at the other end, older persons exit through retirement or death. The turn-over due to these causes would make it possible to reallocate three or four per cent of the labour force annually merely by directing new entrants to jobs other than the ones left vacant by persons leaving the labour force. Over a period of twenty years, a totally different occupational distribution could appear without a single individual ever changing his or her job.

Studies have been made to determine the amount of mobility displayed by labour in moving from job to job and from place to place. In general, that mobility is low in the UK. During depressions, geographical mobility is also low. There appears to be some evidence that in periods of more or less full employment, differentials in wages among areas and occupations do reflect relative scarcities, and that to some extent, labour does tend to move from low-wage sectors of the economy to high-wage ones. There seems to be even stronger evidence, however, that labour is attracted more by the chance of obtaining a job than by the wage rate actually paid for that job. By way of contrast, studies of labour mobility over the generations, or *social stratification*, as the sociologists call it, indicate impressive mobility. The data show very substantial movement, both up and down the scales of education, skill, training and social status, over the course of two or three generations.

> **Labour is much more mobile in the long run than in the short run. Over a given time period, it is more mobile among jobs in the same location and occupation than among locations (where movements of the family is a deterrent) or among occupations (where lack of skills is a deterrent).**

Man-made barriers to labour mobility: Many organizations, private and public, adopt policies that influence labour mobility. When labour unions negotiate seniority rights for their members, not only do they protect old employees from being laid off in a cutback of production, but they also make them very reluctant to change jobs. Likewise, if a firm provides employees with a non-transferable pension plan, they may not want to forfeit this benefit by changing jobs. When the government of an individual state in the US provides compensation to unemployed residents, these residents may be reluctant to leave the state, even to find work.

There are other barriers as well. Licensing is required in dozens of trades and professions. Barbers, electricians, doctors and, in some places, even pedlars must have licences. There is, of course, a generally acceptable reason for requiring licences when the public must be protected against incompetents, quacks or nuisances. But licensing can also have the effect of limiting supply. The fact that, in countries without national health services, medicine is often one of the highest paid occupations, while doctors are still in short supply, is a result of the difficulty of getting into medical schools, the long internship and residency requirements, the rules concerning certification, and so forth. It is possible that in these countries doctors' earnings are high because the barriers to entry into the profession prevent even long-run increases in the proportion of the population being admitted to medical practice. Whether such barriers as exist are designed to protect the standards of the profession or to keep the supply limited (and the earnings high) is often debated.

Trade unions often impose similar barriers to mobility. The 'closed shop', for example, which requires all employees of a plant or a trade to be members of a particular union, also gives unions the power to limit the supply of labour that they represent. They can, therefore, raise the earnings of their members while being protected against the flood of new entrants their policy would generate in the absence of entry barriers. Racial prejudice, discrimination against women and other similar attitudes also limit the mobility of labour.

26

The pricing of factors in competitive markets

We have now developed theories of both the demand for and the supply of factors of production. This is all we need for a theory of the pricing of factors in a competitive market:

> **Given that factor prices are free to vary, they will move to a level at which quantity demanded equals quantity supplied.**

Furthermore, shifts in either the demand for or the supply of factors will have the effects on prices, quantities and factor incomes predicted by normal price theory.

The theory of factor prices is quite general. If one is concerned with labour, one should interpret factor prices to mean wages; if one is thinking about land, factor prices should be interpreted to mean rent, and so on. In this chapter we assume that factors are bought and sold on competitive markets by a large number of buyers and sellers. In Chapter 27, we shall introduce monopolistic elements into factor markets.[1]

Relative factor prices under competitive conditions

Conditions for every unit of one factor to be paid the same price If there were only one factor of production, if all units were identical, and if non-monetary advantages were the same in all uses, then the prices of all units would tend towards the same level. Units of the factor would tend to move from low-price to high-price occupations. The supply of the factor would thus diminish in occupations in which prices were low, and the resulting shortage would tend to force the price up; the supply of the factor would increase in occupations in which prices were high, and the resulting surplus would force the price down. The movement would continue until there was no further incentive to transfer, i.e., until the price paid to the factor was the same in all its uses.

Conditions for different units of the same factor to be paid different prices We observe in the world that units of one factor are paid different prices in different uses. Why is

[1] We continue to make the simplifying assumption (first introduced on p. 346) that total income and all other prices remain constant so that a variation in the money price of a factor causes a simultaneous variation both in its relative price and in the share of the national income going to the factor.

this so? Causes of differences in the prices paid to different units of one particular factor are of two sorts, dynamic or disequilibrium, and static or equilibrium causes. The differences that exist for these causes may themselves be called dynamic and static differences. DYNAMIC DIFFERENCES are associated with changing circumstances, such as the rise of one industry and the decline of another. Such differentials set up movements in factors that will themselves act to remove the variations. The differences in prices may persist for a long time, but there is a tendency for them to be reduced, and in equilibrium they will be eliminated. STATIC or EQUILIBRIUM DIFFERENCES, on the other hand, are differences that persist in a state of equilibrium: there is no tendency for them to be removed by the competitive forces of the market. They are associated with such things as differences among various units of one factor and differences among the non-monetary compensations available in the various uses to which that factor may be put.

Dynamic differentials and factor mobility First consider dynamic differentials. If there were a rise in the demand for product *A* and a fall in the demand for product *B*, there would be an increase in the (derived) demand for factors in industry *A* and a decrease in the (derived) demand for factors in industry *B*. Factor prices would go up in *A* and down in *B*. This is an example of a dynamic change in relative prices, for the changes themselves will cause factors to move from industry *B* to industry *A*, and this movement will cause the price differentials to lessen and eventually to disappear. How long this process takes depends on factor mobility. Labour may in particular circumstances be relatively immobile in the short run so that dynamic differentials often last for a long time in the labour market. The factors that affect labour mobility and thus determine the duration of dynamic differentials were discussed in Chapter 25.

Equilibrium differentials One cause of equilibrium differentials in factor prices is different non-monetary advantages of different factor employments. *Ceteris paribus*, a job with high non-monetary rewards will have a lower equilibrium wage rate than a job with low non-monetary rewards. For example, people in academic and research jobs are often willing to accept less than they would be able to earn in the world of commerce and industry, because there are substantial non-monetary advantages associated with university employment. If labour were paid the same in both jobs, then it would move out of industry and into academic employment. Excess demand for labour in industry and excess supply in universities would then cause industrial wages to rise relative to academic ones until the movement of labour ceased.

A second cause of equilibrium differentials is differences among different units of one factor. Thus the high pay of skilled workers relative to unskilled workers reflects the fact that there is a shortage of skilled workers relative to the demand for them. No movement from unskilled to skilled jobs eliminates this differential, because it is difficult for most adult unskilled workers to become skilled ones. It is important to realize that the high pay of the skilled person relative to the unskilled one merely reflects demand and supply conditions for these two types of labour. There is nothing in the nature of competitive markets that ensures that skilled workers always get higher pay just because they are skilled. If, on the one hand, the demand for skilled workers fell off so much that, even though the supply was small, there was a glut of such workers, their wages would come down. If on the other hand, there was a change in education so that unskilled workers could acquire skills more easily, the wages of skilled workers would fall relative to those of unskilled workers.

History is replete with examples of particular groups of skilled workers who have lost their privileged positions when there was a change in the demand for their services. Many middle-class people feel that it is both unjust and incomprehensible that, since the Second World War, lorry drivers and coal miners have been earning much more money than many relatively highly educated office workers. Whatever the justice of the matter, it is certainly not incomprehensible. A rise in the supply of office workers relative to the demand for their services and a decline in the supply of lorry drivers and coal miners relative to the demand for their services will, according to the normal workings of the market, raise the earnings of lorry drivers and coal miners relative to those of office workers. If there are substantial non-monetary benefits to being an office worker rather than a coal miner or a lorry driver, then the earnings differentials will not set up a flow of labour out of the latter occupations into the former and the differential will persist (i.e., it will be an equilibrium differential).

> **Dynamic differentials are disequilibrium phenomena which set up forces leading to their elimination. Equilibrium differentials can persist indefinitely, and are associated with differences among various units of one factor and among non-monetary rewards in various uses to which one factor can be put.**

Transfer earnings and economic rent

We now wish to study equilibrium differentials in factor prices further. To do this we divide a factor's equilibrium earnings into two components. TRANSFER EARNINGS are the amount that any unit of a factor must earn in order to prevent it from transfering to another use. Thus transfer earnings are the minimum that must be paid to a unit of any factor to hold it in its present use. ECONOMIC RENT is any excess over transfer earnings that a unit of the factor actually earns: economic rent equals the factor's actual earnings *minus* its transfer earnings.

The development of the distinction

The term just defined uses 'rent' very differently from its ordinary usage as a payment for the hire of land and buildings. To understand this technical usage of 'rent' it may help to see how it arose.

The history of the concept of economic rent In the early part of the nineteenth century, when British economics was in its infancy, there was a controversy about the high price of 'corn' (the generic term for all grains). One group held that corn had a high price because the landlords were charging very high rents to the farmers, and in order to meet these high rents, farmers had to charge a very high price for their product. Thus, it was argued, the price of corn was high because the rents of agricultural land were high. The second group, which included David Ricardo, one of the great figures of British classical economics, held that exactly the reverse was true. The price of corn was high because there was a shortage caused by the

Napoleonic Wars. Because corn had a high price there was keen competition among farmers to obtain land, and this competition bid up the rents of corn land. If the price of corn were to fall so that corn growing became less profitable, then the demand for land would fall, and the rent paid for the use of land would fall as well. Thus, this group held that the rent of corn land was high because the price of corn was high and not vice versa.

The modern student of economics will recognize in the Ricardian argument the idea of *derived demand.* Landlords, Ricardo was saying, cannot just charge any price they want for land; the prices they get will depend on demand and supply. The supply of land is pretty well fixed, and the demand depends on the price of corn. The higher the price of corn, the more profitable corn growing will be, the higher the demand for corn land will be, and the higher the price that will be paid for its use.

The argument was elaborated by making the assumption that land had only one use, the growing of corn. The supply of land was given and virtually unchangeable, i.e., land was in perfectly inelastic supply and landowners would prefer to rent out their land for some return rather than leave it idle. Nothing had to be paid to prevent land from transferring to uses other than growing corn, because it had none. Therefore, went the argument, all of the payment to land was a surplus over and above what was necessary to keep it in its present use. *Given the fixed supply of land,* the price depended on the demand for land, which was itself a function of the price of corn.

Rent, which originally referred to the payment for the use of land, thus became the term for a surplus payment to a factor over and above what was necessary to keep it in its present use. Subsequently two facts emerged. First, it was realized that factors of production other than land often earn a surplus over and above what is necessary to keep them in their present use. Film stars, for example, are in very short and pretty well fixed supply, and their possible earnings in other occupations are probably quite moderate. Because there is a huge demand for their services in the film industry, they may receive payments greatly in excess of what is needed to keep them from transferring to other occupations. Second, it was realized that land itself often has many alternative uses, so that *from the point of view of any one use*, part of the payment made to land would be a *necessary* inducement to keep the land in its present employment. Thus it appeared that all factors of production were pretty much the same in these respects: part of the payment made to them is necessary to keep them from transferring to other uses, and part is a surplus over and above that amount. This surplus came to be called economic rent, whatever the factor of production that earned it.

Two meanings of the term 'rent' The term 'economic rent' is a most unfortunate one. The adjective 'economic' is often dropped and the economist often speaks of rent when he means economic rent, causing a confusion between the concept described above and the payment made to landlords for the hiring of land and buildings. When a tenant speaks of his 'rent', he is referring to what he pays his landlord, much of which is a transfer earning. When the economist speaks of the same tenant's 'rent', he may be referring to what the tenant pays in excess of transfer earnings. It is important to guard against confusing the two uses of 'rent'.

The modern distinction between transfer earnings and economic rent In most cases the actual earnings of a factor of production will be a composite of transfer earnings and economic rent. It is possible, however, to imagine limiting cases in which all earnings are either one or the other. Consider some individual firm or some industry faced with a perfectly elastic supply curve of a factor of production; it will be able to obtain all that it wants at the going price but, if it does not pay this price, it will be unable to obtain any of the factor. In such a case, which is illustrated in Figure 26.1, the whole price paid to the factor represents transfer earnings.

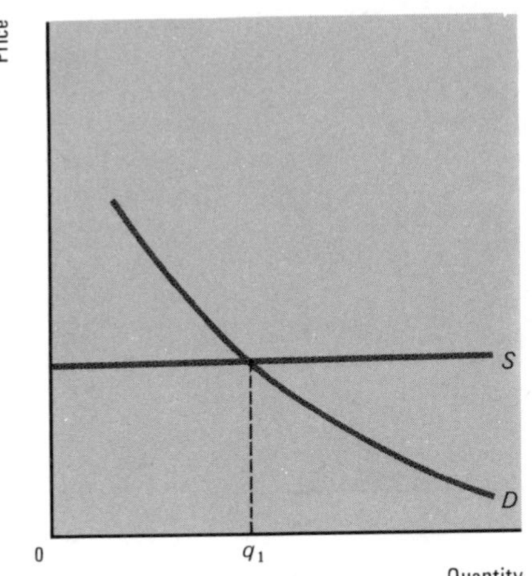

Fig. 26.1 All of the income earned by the factor is transfer earnings

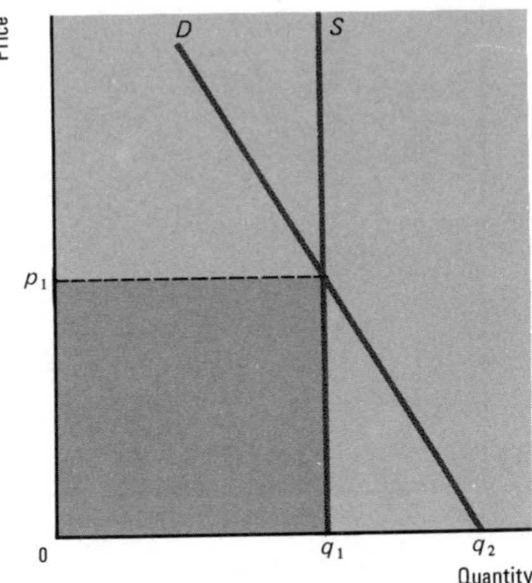

Fig. 26.2 All of the income earned by the factor is an economic rent

Now consider the case of a factor that is fixed in supply and has only one use. Assume that this factor is put on the market by its owners and sold for whatever it will fetch, on the grounds that some income is better than none. The whole supply is owned by thousands of different owners, so there is no point in any one of them withholding his own (small) supply from the market in an effort to raise the price. Such a factor will be in perfectly inelastic supply: the amount offered for sale will be the same whatever the price. This case is illustrated in Figure 26.2. The whole of the price that is paid to the factor is economic rent because even if a lower price were paid, the factor would not transfer to an alternative use. It might be thought that in such a case the factor would not command any price, but this is not so. The price, is determined by demand and supply. The fixed quantity available is the amount q_1 in Figure 25.2; if the price were zero, the amount demanded would be q_2. Thus at a price of zero there would be excess demand for the factor. Competition among buyers would force the price upwards until it reached p_1, at which price there is no excess demand. The income the factor would then earn is indicated by the area of the shaded rectangle.

Finally, consider a factor with an upward-sloping curve such as the one shown in Figure 26.3. Given the demand curve, D, the equilibrium price would be p_5 and the employment q_5; total factor income would be p_5 *times* q_5. If q_5 units of the factor are to be attracted into the industry, and if a single price must be paid, then it is necessary to pay the price p_5. However, all but the last unit would be prepared to remain in the industry for a price less than p_5. In fact, q_1 of these units would be prepared to remain if the price were as low as p_1. If the price rose from p_1 to p_2, an additional q_2 *minus* q_1 units would be attracted into the industry; if the price rose to p_3, an additional q_3 *minus* q_2 units would enter the industry. Clearly, for any unit that we care to choose, the point on the supply curve corresponding to it shows the minimum price that must be paid in order to keep that unit in the industry (i.e., its transfer earnings). Equally clearly, if the supply curve slopes upward, all units to the

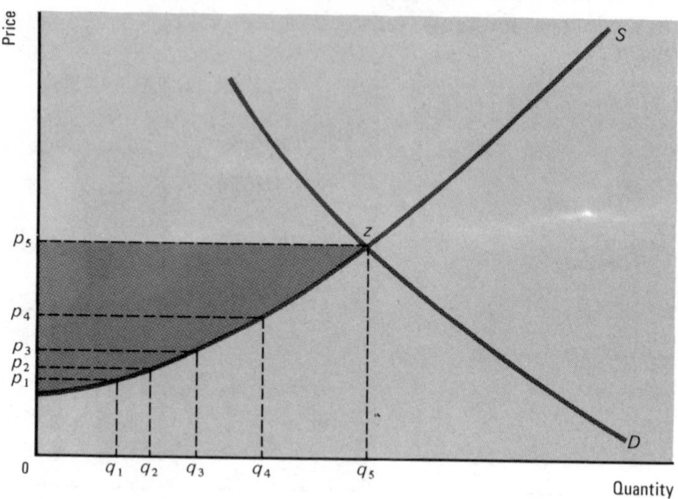

Fig. 26.3 Some of the income earned by the factor is a transfer earning and the remainder is economic rent

left of the one being considered have lower transfer earnings. Thus the total transfer earnings of the q_5 units is the unshaded area *below* the supply curve. Since the total payment made is the rectangle Op_5zq_5, it follows that the economic rent earned by the factor is the shaded area *above* the supply curve and below the line p_5z.

> **Transfer earnings are shown by the area below a factor's supply curve. Economic rent is shown by the area above the supply curve and below the factor's market price.**

The following example illustrates why a rising supply curve involves rents: if universities increase the salaries paid to professors of economics in order to attract additional economists away from industry and government and into university teaching, those economists who are persuaded to make the switch will be receiving only transfer earnings. But those economists who were already content to be university professors will find that their salaries have increased as well, and for them this increase will be economic rent.

Figures 26.1, 26.2 and 26.3 suggest the following important conclusion:

> **The more elastic the supply curve, the less the amount of the payment to factors is rent and the more is transfer earnings.**

Kinds of transfers

How much of a given payment to a factor is economic rent and how much is transfer earnings depends on what sort of transfer we are considering.

Consider first the transfer of a factor from one firm to another within a single industry. The supply of the factor to one firm will be highly elastic since factors can easily move among firms in the same industry. Thus almost all of the factor's earnings will be transfer earnings. If the firm in question did not pay the factor the going price, then the factor would transfer to another firm in the same industry. Secondly consider the transfer of a factor from one industry to another. Mobility among industries will be less than mobility among firms in one industry. Thus the supply curve of a factor to one industry will be less elastic than the supply curve to one firm. Thus from the point of view of the industry, part of the payment will be transfer earnings and part economic rent. The moral to this story is that we cannot point to a given factor – a labourer, say – and assert that of his income of £1,000, £800 is transfer earnings and £200 rent, for it all depends on what transfer we are considering.

Economic rent and transfer earnings in the payment to labour Some labour is always able to move from job to job, and something must be paid to keep a given unit of labour in its present use. This amount is transfer earnings. How much has to be paid to keep labour in its present use depends upon what the use is.

Consider first the movement among firms in one industry. Assume, for example, that carpenters receive £16 for working a normal eight-hour day. Then a single small construction firm will have to pay £16 per day or it will not obtain the services of any carpenter. To that one firm the whole £16 is a transfer payment; if it were not paid, carpenters would not remain with that firm.

Secondly, consider movement among industries. Consider, for example, what would happen if the construction industry encountered difficulties so that all construction firms were forced to reduce the wages offered to carpenters. In this case carpenters could not move to other construction firms to get more money. If they did not like the wages offered, they would have to move to another industry. If the best they could do elsewhere was £12 per day, then they would not begin to leave the construction industry until wages in that industry fell below £12. In this case the transfer earnings of carpenters in construction would be £12. When they were receiving £16 (presumably because there was a heavy demand for their services), the additional £4 was an economic rent from the point of view of the construction industry.

Thirdly, consider movement among occupations. Assume that there is a decline in the demand for carpenters in all industries. The only thing left to do, if one does not like the wages, is to move to another occupation. If no one was induced to do this until the wage fell to £10, then £10 would be the transfer earnings for carpenters in general. The wage of £10 would have to be paid to persuade people to be carpenters at all.

Some very highly specialized types of labour are in inelastic supply. Some singers and actors, for example, have a special style and talent which cannot be duplicated, whatever the training. The earnings that such persons receive are mostly in the nature of economic rent: they enjoy their occupations and would pursue them for very much less than the high remuneration they actually receive. Their high rewards occur because they are in *very scarce supply relative to the demand for their services*. When the demand for their services rises, their earnings rise permanently; when the demand falls, their earnings fall permanently.

Rent and transfer earnings in the return to capital If a piece of capital equipment has several uses, then the analysis of the last section can be repeated for the case of the machine. Many machines, however, have only one use. In this case, any income that is made from the operation of the machine is in the nature of rent. Assume, for example, that when a machine was installed it was expected to earn £5,000 per annum in excess of all its operating costs. If the demand for the product now falls off so that the machine can earn only £2,000, it will still pay to keep it in operation rather than scrap it. Indeed it will pay to do so as long as it yields any return at all over its operating costs.[1] Thus, if the machine does yield a return of exactly £5,000 per annum in any one year, we can say that all of the return is economic rent because the machine would still have been allocated to its present use – it has no other – as long as it yielded even £1 above its operating costs. Thus, *once the machine has been installed*, any net income that it earns is rent (i.e., a payment not necessary to keep it in its present use). However, the machine will wear out eventually, and it will not be replaced unless it is expected to earn a return over its lifetime sufficient to make it a good investment for its owner. Thus, over the long run, some of the revenue earned by the machine is transfer earnings; if the revenue is not earned, a machine will not continue to be allocated to that use in the long run.

In the case just considered, whether a payment made to a factor is economic rent or a transfer earning depends on the time span under consideration. In the short run all of the income of a machine with a specific use is in the nature of rent, while in the long run some (possibly all) of it is in the nature of transfer earnings. Factor payments which are economic rent in the short run and transfer earnings in the long run are called QUASI-RENTS.

Economic rent and transfer earnings in the payment to land The formal analysis for land is identical to that given in the case of labour. How much of the payment made to a given piece of land is a transfer payment depends upon the nature of the transfer.

Consider, first, the case of an individual wheat farmer. He must pay the going price of land in order to prevent the land from being transferred to the use of other wheat farmers. From his point of view, therefore, the whole of the payment that he makes is transfer earnings to land.

Second, consider a particular agricultural industry that uses land. In order to secure land for, say, wheat production, it will be necessary to offer at least as much as the land could earn when put to other uses. From the point of view of the wheat industry, that part of the payment made for land which is equal to what it could earn in its next most remunerative use is transfer earnings. If that much is not paid, then the land will in fact be transferred to the alternative use. If, however, land particularly suitable for wheat growing is scarce relative to the demand for it, then the actual payment for the use of this land may be above the transfer earnings; any additional payment is an economic rent.

Next consider movement between agricultural and urban uses. Land is very mobile between agricultural uses because its location is usually of little importance. In the case of urban uses, however, location of the land is critical and, from this point of view, land is of course completely immobile. If there is a shortage of land in central London, such land as is available will command a high price, but no matter what the price paid, the land in rural areas will not move into central London. The

[1] This is just another way of stating the proposition given in Chapter 22, page 294, that it pays a firm to continue in operation in the short run as long as it can cover its variable costs of production.

very high payments made to urban land are economic rents. The land is scarce relative to demand for it, and it commands a price very much above what it could earn in agricultural uses. The payment that it receives is thus well in excess of what is necessary to prevent it from transferring from urban back to agricultural uses.

From the point of view of one particular type of urban use, however, high rents are transfer earnings. Cinemas, for example, account for but a small portion of the total demand for land in central London; if there were no cinemas at all, rentals of land would be about what they are now. Thus the cinema industry faces a perfectly elastic supply of land in central London, and the whole of the price that it pays for its land is a transfer payment which must be paid to keep the land from transferring to other urban uses.[1]

Some implications of the distinction between transfer earnings and economic rent

Increasing the supply of a factor An important policy implication of the distinction between economic rent and transfer earnings concerns the effect of wage increases on the quantity of labour supplied. For example, if the central authorities want more physicists, should they subsidize physicists' salaries? As we have seen, such a policy may well have an effect on supply. It may influence schoolchildren uncertain about whether to become engineers or physicists to become physicists. But it will also mean that a great deal of money will have to be spent on extra payments to people who are already physicists. These payments will be economic rents, since existing physicists have demonstrated that they are prèpared to be physicists at their old salaries. Although some may have been considering transferring to another occupation, such movements are not common. An alternative policy, which may produce more physicists per pound spent, is to subsidize scholarships and fellowships for students who will train to become physicists. This policy tends to operate at the margin on persons just deciding whether or not to enter the occupation. It avoids the payment of additional rents to persons already in the occupation. Graphically, it is shown by a rightward shift in the supply curve because there will now be *more* persons in the occupation at each price of the factor.

> **If the supply curve is quite inelastic, an increase in the quantity supplied may be achieved more easily and at less cost by shifting the supply curve to the right rather than by moving along it.**

Urban land values and land taxes The high payments made to urban land are largely economic rents. The land is scarce relative to the demand for it, and it commands a price very much above what it could earn in agricultural uses. The payment it

[1] Thus the old examination question 'Is it correct to say that the price of cinema seats is high in central London because the price of land is high?' should be answered in the affirmative, not in the negative, as examiners often seemed to expect. The view that the prices of *all* goods and services in central London are high because rents are high can, however, be denied.

[2] International mobility, it is clear, is another matter. One of the reasons for the considerable migration of trained professionals of all ages from Britain to the United States is the very much higher monetary rewards to be earned in the United States compared with the United Kingdom. Clearly, many British professionals are being paid less than their international transfer earnings, and the result is a steady 'brain drain' from Britain to America.

receives is thus well in excess of what is necessary to prevent it from transferring from urban back to agricultural uses. A society with rising population and rising per capita real income tends also to have steadily rising urban land prices. This fact has created a special interest in taxes on land values.

Who ultimately pays taxes on the value of land? If the same tax rate is applied to land in all uses, the relative profitability of different uses will be unaffected, and thus a landlord will not be tempted to change the allocation of his land. Land will not be forced out of use, because land that is very unprofitable will command little rent and so pay little tax. Thus there will be no change in the supply of goods that are produced with the aid of land, and, since there is no change in supply, there can be no change in prices. *The tax cannot be passed to the consumers.*[1] Farmers will be willing to pay exactly as much as they would have offered previously for the use of land. The prices of agricultural goods and the prices paid by tenants for land will be unchanged, and the whole of the tax will be borne by the landlord. The incomes earned by landlords will fall by the full amount of the tax, and land values will fall correspondingly (because land is now a less attractive investment relative to, say, bonds than it was previously).

The single-tax movement Taxation of land values has had enormous appeal in the past. The peak of its appeal occurred nearly 100 years ago, when the 'single-tax movement' led by the American economist Henry George commanded great popularity. George's book *Progress and Poverty* is – as books on economic issues go – an all-time best seller. It pointed out that the fixed supply of land, combined with a rapidly rising demand for it, allowed the owners of land to gain from the natural progress of society without contributing anything. Along with many others, George was incensed at this 'unearned increment' from which huge fortunes accrued to landlords. He calculated that most of government expenditure could be financed by a single tax that did nothing more than remove the landlords' unearned increment.

When George died he left the huge royalties from his book to finance schools of 'economic science' which were to propogate his theories and policy recommendations. These schools are maintained throughout the world even today.

A further appeal of taxes on land values arises from the fact that economic rent can be taxed away without affecting the allocation of resources. Thus, for someone who does not wish to interfere with the allocation resulting from the free play of the market, the taxation of economic rent is attractive. Two problems arise, however, in any attempt to tax this economic rent. First, the theoretical statement refers to *economic rent*, not to the payment actually made by tenants to landlords. What is called rent in the world is, as we have seen, partly an economic rent and partly a return on capital invested by the landowner. The policy implications of taxing rent depends on being able in practice to identify *economic rent*. At best, this is difficult; at worst, it is impossible.

The second problem is a normative one. If, in the interests of justice, we want to treat all recipients of economic rent similarly, we will encounter insurmountable difficulties because economic rent also accrues to factors other than land. It accrues to the owners of any factor that is in fixed supply and faces a rising demand. If there is, for example, a fixed supply of opera singers in the country, they gain economic rent as the society becomes richer and the demand for opera increases, without there

[1] See the discussion on pp. 124–7 on how taxes do get passed to consumers.

being any corresponding increase in the supply of singers. No one has yet devised a scheme that will tax the economic rent but not the transfer earnings of such divergent factors as land, patents, football players and High Court judges.

The appeal of a single tax has now receded, both because of the difficulties mentioned above and because, with the great increase in the size of the government, even an effective tax on economic rent would finance only a tiny portion of government expenditures. But the movement has left behind one curious anachronism in the tax policies of those American cities that levy their real-estate taxes at a higher rate on the assessed value of the land than on the assessed value of the buildings erected on the land.

27

Wages and collective bargaining

The last chapter referred to the pricing of all types of factors in competitive markets. In this and the next chapter we shall discuss the specific cases of labour and capital. The analysis of the previous chapter requires substantial amendment when it is applied to labour, because labour is often sold in non-competitive markets. In this chapter we shall extend the theory to cover cases in which labour markets are dominated by monopolistic buyers and/or sellers.

The determination of wages without unions

In considering the determination of wages in the absence of unions, there are two important cases to study: first, where there are many purchasers of labour, and second, where they are only a few purchasers (possibly only one). In both cases labour is assumed to be supplied competitively, in the sense that there are many individual workers, each of whom must take the existing wage rate as being beyond his control and needs to decide only how much of his labour services to provide at that wage.

When labour is supplied and demanded competitively

When there are many purchasers of labour services, no one of them can influence the wage rate. In other words, the labour market is perfectly competitive. As we saw in Chapter 26, the wage rate and the volume of employment in such a market will be determined at the intersection of the demand and supply curves. Although the demand curve is *not* the marginal revenue product curve, it is true that in equilibrium the wage rate will be *equal to* the value of the marginal product of labour. This is illustrated in Figure 27.1, where the equilibrium wage and the marginal value product are w_c, and quantity of employment is q_c.

When labour is supplied competitively but demanded monopsonistically

When there are few firms purchasing some type of labour, each one realizes that it can influence the wage rate by varying the amount that it purchases: the purchasers of labour are *not* price-takers in the labour market. For simplicity, we shall deal with a case in which the few purchasers form an employers' association and act as a single decision-taking unit in the labour market.

The sole purchaser in any market is called a MONOPSONIST. In this situation we speak of labour being purchased monopsonistically. The monopsonist purchasing labour can offer any wage rate it chooses, and workers must either work for that wage or move to other markets (i.e., change occupation or location). For any given quantity that is purchased, the labour supply curve shows the price per unit that

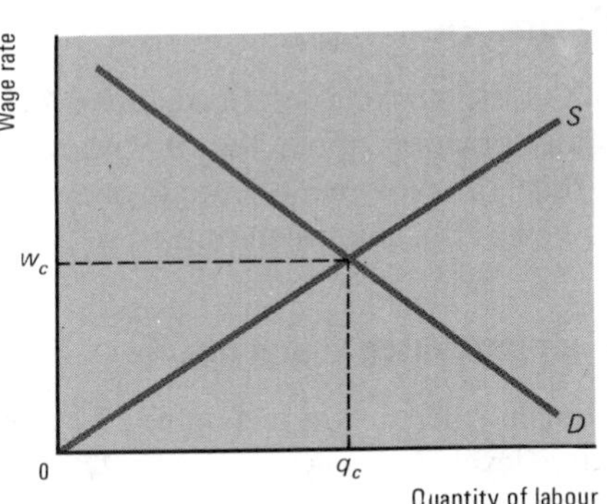

Fig. 27.1 The determination of wages in a competitive market

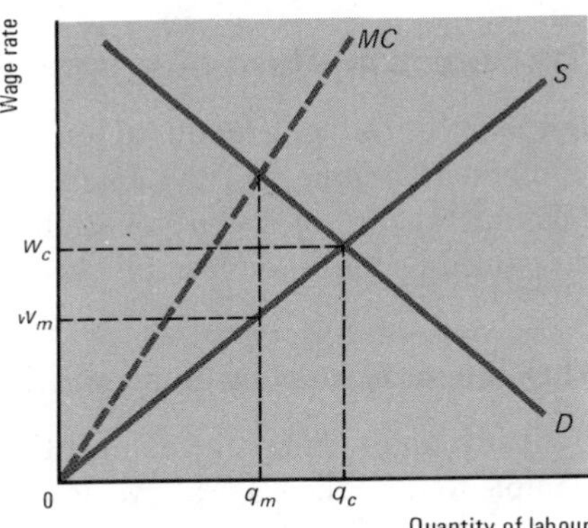

Fig. 27.2 The determination of wages when labour is sold competitively but bought monopsonistically

must be paid; to the monopsonist, this is the average cost curve. For example, if 100 units are employed at 50p per hour, then total cost is £50 and average cost per unit is 50p. If 101 units are employed and the factor price is driven up to 52p, then total cost becomes £52·52; the average cost per labourer is 52p, but the total cost has increased by £2·52 as a result of hiring one more labourer.

> **Whenever the labour supply curve is upward sloping, the marginal cost to a monopsonist of obtaining an extra labourer will exceed the wage paid, because the increased wage rate necessary to attract the labourer must also be paid to all those already employed.**

Thus, in Figure 27.2 we can draw a marginal cost curve for labour that will lie above the average cost curve. The profit-maximizing monopsonist will equate the marginal cost of labour with its marginal revenue product. In other words, it will go on hiring labour until the last unit hired increases total cost by as much as it increases total revenue.

Thus, in equilibrium, marginal cost, and not the wage rate, will be equated with the marginal revenue product of labour. Since marginal cost exceeds the wage rate, it follows that the wage rate will be less than the marginal revenue product. Also, since the supply curve of labour is upward sloping, the volume of employment must be less than it would be if the market were perfectly competitive.

This analysis is illustrated in Figure 27.2, in which w_c and q_c are the competitive wage and the volume of employment, while w_m and q_m are the corresponding values under monopsony. Since the monopsonist wishes to employ a quantity of labour equal only to q_m, it need pay a wage of only w_m to call forth that quantity.

Monopsony results in a lower level of employment and a lower wage rate than when labour is purchased competitively.

The reason is that the monopsonistic purchaser is aware that, by trying to purchase more of the factor, it is driving up the price against itself. It will, therefore, stop short of the point that is reached when the factor is purchased by many different firms, none of which can exert an influence on its price.

The determination of wages with unions

Now let us introduce a labour union into each of the markets described above. For the moment assume that the union can fix any price of labour that it wishes by unilateral action or by negotiation, but that the volume of employment is determined by the amount employers wish to hire at the union-determined wage.

When labour is supplied monopolistically but purchased competitively

Say that a union enters the competitive labour market shown in Figure 27.1 and attempts to raise the wage above its competitive level. As shown in Figure 27.3 for

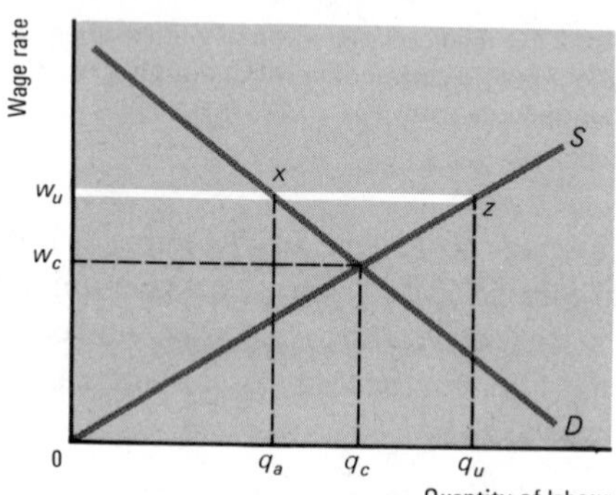

Fig. 27.3 The effect on wages and employment of the entry of a union into a competitive labour market

example, the union raises the wage from w_c to w_u. This creates a perfectly elastic supply of labour up to the quantity q_u (since this is the quantity of labour supplied at the union wage). The supply curve now becomes $w_u zS$ and equilibrium is at x, where the demand curve cuts the new supply curve. The union has succeeded in raising the wage rate above its competitive level, but at the cost of reducing employment from q_c to q_a.

Notice also that there are would-be workers who cannot find employment (excess supply equals $q_u - q_a$ or $z - x$). They would even be prepared to work for a wage *less than* w_u. It is clearly to the employers' advantage to hire some of these workers at less than the going wage and, given the chance, they will do so. This implies that only if it can strictly enforce the wage it sets, resisting wage-cutting pressure from unemployed workers, can a union succeed in raising the wage rate against a perfectly competitive set of demanders of labour.

A union entering a perfectly competitive labour market can raise the wage above the free-market level, but only at the cost of lowering the amount of employment. The new wage will create an excess supply of labour at the

going rate and consequent pressure for wage-cutting, which the union must be powerful enough to resist if it is to be successful in holding wages up.

When labour is supplied monopolistically and demanded monopsonistically

We now consider the effects of introducing a union into the monopsonistic labour market illustrated in Figure 27.2. We shall arrive at the surprising prediction that in this market the union can raise wages by a substantial margin and at the same time raise the volume of employment! We start in Figure 27.4 with the same labour supply curve, *S*, and marginal cost curve, *MC*, as shown in Figure 27.2. The analysis now becomes a little tricky and we shall take it in two steps.

First, consider the effect on the supply curve (i.e., the average cost curve) and on the marginal cost curve of labour when the union enforces some given wage on the market. This creates a perfectly elastic supply curve up to the point at which the union wage cuts the supply curve. If the union wage is w_1, the supply curve for labour in Figure 27.4 now becomes w_1xS.[1] Up to an employment level of q_1, the marginal cost curve is also w_1x (since the wage rate is constant, the marginal cost of the extra worker is only the wage that must be paid to him). If the employer wants more than q_1 of labour, however, he can obtain it by paying everyone more than the union wage – to which the union will have no objection. The marginal cost of labour then jumps from x to y (i.e., it has a discontinuity at q_1) and thereafter becomes

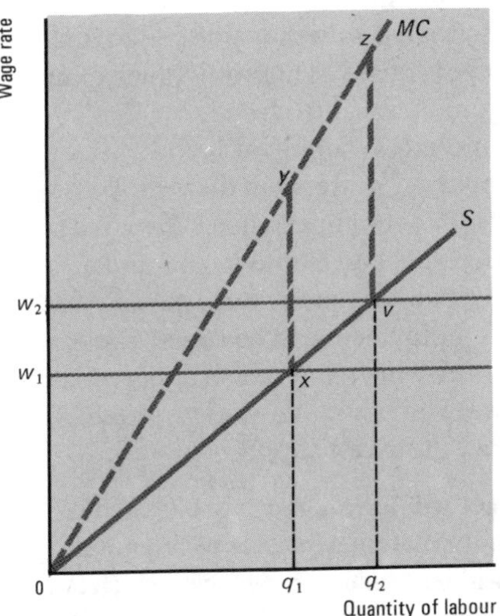

Fig. 27.4 The effect of a union-determined wage on the average and marginal cost curves of labour

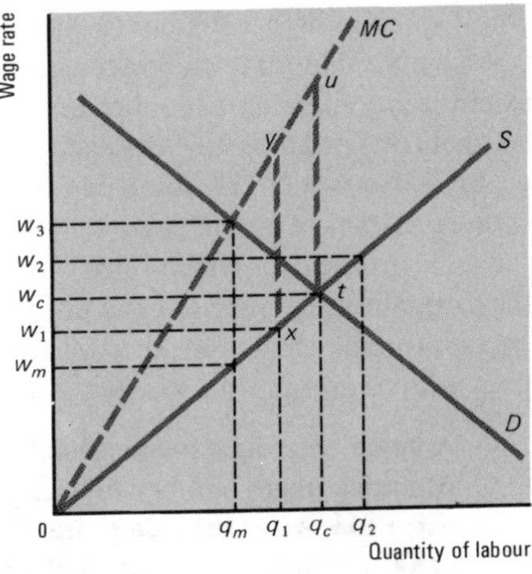

Fig. 27.5 The effect on wages and employment of the entry of a union into a monopsonistic labour market

yMC. This is easily seen by the fact that once the employer is operating on the segment xS of the supply curve, the existence of the union minimum wage w_1 is irrelevant to him (because he is already paying more than that), and so his situation is exactly the same as if no union existed: *S* is the supply curve of labour that he now

[1] Note that this form of expression identifies a line to which the points or labels are attached. It is *not* a product of separate numbers.

faces, and MC is its marginal cost curve. If, to take one more example, the union negotiates a new minimum wage of w_2, the supply curve becomes w_2vS and the marginal cost curve becomes w_2vzMC, with a discontinuous jump at an employment level of q_2.[1]

The second step in the analysis is to study the effects on employment when the union sets various alternative wage rates. In Figure 27.5 the curves S, MC and D are reproduced from Figure 27.2. The wage and employment levels without a union are w_m and q_m. Now assume that the union negotiates a wage of w_1. This creates the kinked supply curve w_1xS and a marginal cost curve w_1xyMC. The monopsonistic purchaser of labour will now be in equilibrium at employment q_1, since up to that level of employment the marginal cost of labour is less than the marginal revenue product, while for levels above q_1 the reverse is true. The union has raised both wages and employment! The reason for this result is that before the entry of the union, the monopsonistic purchaser kept employment down because it was aware of the fact that as it increased employment it forced up the wage that must be paid to those already employed. The introduction of the union wage now faces the purchaser with a perfectly elastic supply curve, so that there is no point in keeping employment low for fear of driving up the wage.

The maximum level of employment, q_c, is reached at a negotiated wage of w_c, which duplicates the perfectly competitive result. Here the supply curve is w_ctS and the MC curve is w_ctuMC. Above this wage a conflict emerges between wages and employment, further wage increases being obtained at the cost of lowered employment. The wage w_2, for example, is associated with the same employment as the wage w_1. Note, however, that until the wage is raised as high as w_3 the volume of employment is higher than it was before the union was introduced.

Also note that up to the wage w_c, there is no excess supply of labour. At w_1, for example, q_1 of labour is supplied and q_1 is employed. Only when the wage passes the competitive level of w_c does an excess supply of labour appear. Thus there is a range w_m to w_c over which the union can raise both wages and employment, and also not create a surplus of labour eager to work at less than the union rate. There is a further range, w_c to w_3, over which both wages and employment can be raised above what they were in the absence of the union, but over which an excess supply of labour occurs, forcing the union to resist a downward pressure on wages exerted by the unemployed group. For example, at a wage w_2 the excess supply is $q_2 - q_1$.

A union entering a monopsonistic market will have a range over which it can raise wages and employment without creating a surplus of labourers eager to work at the going rate. There will be a further range over which it can raise both wages and employment above their pre-union levels but at the cost of creating an excess supply of labour.

So far we have dealt with the simple case of a union that fixes a wage and allows employment to be determined by demand. Other methods of raising wages are available, and unions also have goals in addition to raising wages. Before we consider these, we shall embark on a slight digression to fill in a few institutional and historical details. We shall be able to use the theory already developed to understand

[1] Students trained in the calculus will realize that the kink in the average cost curve (i.e., the supply curve) at v means a similar kink in the total cost curve, which is thus non-differentiable at the associated quantity. This means that MC is not uniquely defined at that point.

some of the events that have occurred in the past and some of the institutions that have emerged.

Labour market institutions

Potential monopsonists

Any large firm has some degree of monopsony power by virtue of its size and the number of employees that it hires. It recognizes that its actions affect the wage rate, especially for those kinds of labour that are somehow limited to the industry. EMPLOYERS' ASSOCIATIONS are groups of employers who band together for the purpose of adopting a common policy in labour negotiations. This allows them to achieve the same result as could be obtained by a single monopsonistic buyer of labour.

Potential monopolists

A union is many things: a social club, an educational instrument, a political club, a bargaining agent for an individual worker, and, to some people, a way of life. For the purposes of our discussion, a UNION is an association of individual workers that represents them as a unit in negotiations with their employers.

Unions today have two principles of organization. In trade (or craft) unions, workers with a common set of skills are joined in a common association, no matter where or for whom they work. In industrial unions, all workers in a given plant or a given industry are collected into a single union, whatever their skills.

Industrial unions became common in the United States with the rise in the 1930s of the Congress of Industrial Organizations (CIO). Among the prominent industrial unions in the US are the United Auto Workers and the Steel Workers Union. The existence of these unions means that the great automobile companies deal with one union, and so do the steel companies. A single agreement over wages, working conditions or union practices is sufficient to change the situation throughout the entire industry.

A single union covering an entire industry is less common in the UK, and in many other countries. When an employer has to deal with many unions, – and twenty or more within a single firm is not uncommon in the UK, as, for example, in Times Newspapers – agreement between labour and management can be hard to reach. DEMARCATION DISPUTES often break out over which union is to be responsible for which jobs. An experienced observer of the British industrial scene has said: 'On occasion, new capital instruments have been inadequately used, and production has been held up by disputes among rival unions about the types of workers to be employed on new operations or new materials. The shipbuilding, printing and building industries have provided examples of this obstruction.'[1]

Of course, such demarcation disputes may merely reflect power struggles between the managements of various unions. They do, however, have at least one substantial economic cause, and this lies in forces that we have already studied. In situations in which unions are holding the wage above its competitive level, we have seen that there will be an excess supply of labour at the going wage rate. Since more people

[1] G. C. Allen, *The Structure of Industry in Britain* (Longmans, 2nd edition, 1966), page 170.

would like to work in the occupation than can do so, both the union leaders and the rank and file will be acutely aware of the trade-off between wages and unemployment, and of the possibility that some workers who are currently employed may find themselves without work. (This does not mean, of course, that they must become permanently unemployed but only that they must move to less remunerative occupations.) In terms of Figure 27.3, if the union loses a demarcation dispute, the demand curve for its members shifts to the left and the excess supply rises, while, if the union wins the dispute, the demand curve shifts to the right and the excess supply diminishes. Such problems could not arise if the wage were set so that quantity demanded equalled quantity supplied, but:

> **Whenever the wage is such that excess supply develops, then the outcome of jurisdictional disputes genuinely affects employment opportunities and the amount of downward pressure on the wage rate exerted by unsatisfied suppliers of labour in a particular occupation.**

Clearly, however undesirable the consequences of such disputes might be, the caricature of them as squabbles about trivia is wide of the mark.

Kinds of bargaining arrangements

Many different kinds of bargaining arrangements exist even today. In an OPEN SHOP a union represents its members, but does not have exclusive negotiating rights for all the workers of one kind. Membership in the union is not a condition of getting or keeping a job. Unions usually oppose such an arrangement and it is easy to see why. Consider an open-shop negotiating situation. If, on the one hand, employers accede to union demands, the non-members achieve the benefits of the union without paying dues or sharing the risks. If, on the other hand, employers choose to fight the union, they can run their plants with the non-union members, thus weakening the power of the union in the fight.

Now consider what will happen if the union does succeed in obtaining a wage above the competitive level in an open-shop industry. We have already seen that when wages exceed the competitive level, there arises an excess supply of labour *willing to work at less than the union wage.* With an open shop there is nothing to prevent these workers from accepting work below the union wage, undermining the union's power to maintain high wages. If, however, all workers must join the union, then it can prevent its members from accepting lower wages, and can thus maintain high wages in spite of the existence of excess supply. The desire to avoid the open shop leads to other union arrangements. In a CLOSED SHOP, only union members may be employed and the union controls its membership however it sees fit. Employers sometimes regard this as an unwarranted limitation on their right to choose their employees. This sometimes leads to the compromise solution of the union shop. In a UNION SHOP employers may hire anyone they choose, but everyone hired must join the union within a specified period. This leaves employers free to hire whomever they wish, but gives the union power to prevent anyone from accepting employment below the union wage.

Weapons of conflict

The STRIKE is the union's ultimate weapon. It consists in the concerted refusal of the members of the union to work. It is the strike, or the threat of a strike, that backs up the union's demands in the bargaining process. PICKET LINES are made up of striking workers who parade before the entrance to their plant or firm. Members of other unions will often not 'cross' a picket line. This means, for example, that if bricklayers strike against a construction firm, carpenters may not work on the project even though they themselves have no grievance against the firm and lorry drivers may not deliver supplies to a picketed site. Pickets represent an enormous increase in the negotiating power of a small union. (Much of the very strong feeling expressed by employers against demarcation disputes arises from the fact that an employer may be unable to settle with *either* union without the other union setting up a picket line that may bring the entire plant to a stop.) The LOCK-OUT is the employer's equivalent of a strike. By closing the plant, a firm locks out the workers until such time as the dispute is settled. STRIKE BREAKERS are workers who are used by management to operate the plant while union members are on strike. A BLACK LIST is an employers' list of workers who have been discharged for union activities, and who are not supposed to be given jobs by other employers. All of these employers' weapons are used much less commonly today than they were in the past. The modern firm relies mainly on its skill at the negotiating table, and its resources to withstand strikes, as its weapons in resisting union demands.

Collective bargaining

The term COLLECTIVE BARGAINING refers to the whole process by which unions and employers (or their representatives) arrive at and enforce agreements. It usually describes a situation of monopoly *versus* monopsony in which there is one seller, the union, and one buyer, either a single firm or an employers' association.

The basic difference between collective bargaining and the theoretical analysis with which we began this chapter is that in collective bargaining both sides must agree to the wage, while in our analysis we assumed that the union set a wage and the employer decided how much labour to buy at that wage. In collective bargaining there is always a substantial range for compromise. In particular cases the actual range will depend on the goals of the two negotiating parties. Thus, economic theory does not predict a precise outcome to the collective bargaining process. By analysing the effects on unions and management it can, however, isolate some of the economic factors that will influence the final bargain. Just as in oligopolistic competition between firms, the outcome will be significantly influenced by such political and psychological factors as skill in bargaining, ability to bluff and one side's assessment of the other side's reactions to its own moves. (For example, the employers will ask, 'How much can we resist without provoking the unions into calling a costly strike?' and the union will ask, 'Will the employers force us to strike only for a token period so they can tell their shareholders they *tried* to resist, or do they think this is a really serious matter so that they intend to hold out to the bitter end against any strike that we might call?'.) It is because monopoly *versus* monopsony allows more than one acceptable economic solution that these non-economic factors become so important.

The evolution of the modern institutions

Unionism today is both stable and fairly widely accepted. It was not always so. Less than a hundred years ago unions were fighting for their lives, and union organizers and members were risking theirs.

Trade unionism had its origins in the pitifully low standard of living of the average nineteenth-century worker and his family. The explanation of the low standard of living throughout the world lay in the small size of the total national output relative to the population. In 1800, even in the wealthiest of countries, an equal division of national income among all families would have left everyone in poverty by our present standards.

Poverty had existed for centuries. It was accentuated, however, by the twin processes of urbanization and industrialization. The man who was moderately content working his land usually became restive and discontented when he moved into a grimy, smoky, nineteenth-century city, took employment in a sweatshop or a factory, and settled with his family in a crowded, insanitary slum.[1] Stories of the suffering during the industrial revolution could fill many volumes. One example will at least illustrate some of the conditions that lay behind the drive for change and reform.

> In the cotton-spinning work, these creatures [the workers] are kept, fourteen hours in each day, locked up, summer and winter, in a heat of from *eighty to eighty-four degrees*. The rules which they are subject to are such as no negroes [i.e., slaves] were ever subjected to. . . . The door of the place wherein they work, is *locked, except half an hour*, at tea-time, the work-people are not allowed to send for water to drink, in the hot factory; even *the rain water is locked up*, by the master's order. . . . If any spinner be found with his *window open*, he is to pay a fine of a shilling! . . . for a large part of the time, there is the abominable and pernicious stink of the *gas* to assist in the murderous effects of the heat. . . . the notorious fact is, that well constitutioned men are rendered old and past labour at forty years of age, and that children are rendered decrepit and deformed, and thousands upon thousands of them slaughtered by consumption [tuberculosis], before they arrive at the age of sixteen. . . . [2]

Out of these conditions came the full range of radical political movements from revolutionary socialism, which today we call Marxism or communism, to Fabian socialism, which tried to effect change gradually through existing political systems. Out of them also came the union, which was to some extent a club providing protection for unemployed, disabled or retired workers, and to some extent a negotiating agent. For a long time unions were resisted by the full power of both employers and the central authorities.

The union organizers perceived that ten or a hundred men acting together had more influence than one acting alone. The union was the organization that would provide a basis for confronting the monopsony power of employers with the collective (i.e., monopoly) power of the workers. But it was easier to see the solution than to achieve it. Employers did not accept organizations of workers passively. Agitators who tried to organize other workers were often dismissed and black-listed; in some cases they were physically assaulted or even killed. In order to realize the ambition of creating some effective power over the labour market, it was necessary to gain control of the supply of labour and to have the financial resources

[1] Of course, many moved because they had no choice, having been driven off their land by the enclosure movements. Thus we cannot assume that they made a free choice in the belief that the urban life was preferable to their rural one. Their rural life had been destroyed; the urban life was simply preferable to starvation.

[2] William Cobbett, *Political Register*, vol. LII, 20 November 1824, as quoted by E. Royston Pike, *Human Documents of the Industrial Revolution in Britain* (Allen & Unwin, 1966), p. 60–1. This fascinating book chronicles some of the most common horrors of the nineteenth-century industrial revolution. Every student of society should spend at least one evening browsing through its pages.

necessary to outlast employers. There was no 'right to organize', and the union usually had to force a hostile employer to negotiate with it. Since early unions did not have large resources, the employer had to be attacked where he was weakest.

All of these considerations explain why it was the unions of the highly skilled and the specialist types of labour that first met with success. The previous discussion provides two main reasons for this. First, it was easier to control the supply of skilled workers than that of unskilled workers. Organize the unskilled or the semi-skilled and the employer could find replacements for them. But the skilled workers – the coopers, the bootmakers, the shipwrights – were another matter. There were few of them, and they controlled the access to their trade by controlling the conditions of apprenticeship. The original unions were in effect closed shops: one had to belong to the union to hold a job, and the union set the rules of admission. The second main reason was that a union of a small number of highly skilled specialists could attack the employer where he was most likely to give in, and thus would need fewer resources to withstand employer resistance than would be needed by unions of the unskilled. In Chapter 25 (page 353) we discussed the determinants of the elasticity of demand for a factor. A particular skilled occupation is very difficult to dispense with in an industrial process, so that other factors cannot easily be substituted for it. Also, labour in a particular skilled occupation is likely to account for a relatively low proportion of total costs, so that the relative cost to the employers of giving in to a demand for, say, a twenty per cent wage increase, would be much less than the cost of giving in to an equivalent demand from the very numerous unskilled workers. Thus a low ability to substitute other factors plus a small contribution to total costs combined to give the unions of skilled workers an advantage in fighting the employer.

Even in such cases unions had their ups and downs. When employment was full and business booming, the cost of being fired by joining a union was not so great, for there were other jobs. During periods of depression and unemployment, however, the risks were greater. Workers knew that other unemployed members of their trade would be there to take their jobs if they caused trouble. Slowly but not steadily during the course of the nineteenth century, unions grew in size and power. A clear cyclical swing in membership is observable, with gains in periods of prosperity and setbacks in periods of business depression. By the inter-war period the union had established itself as an integral part of the industrial scene.

Unions have been important forces in most countries since the end of World War II. In Britain unions have continued to grow in both political and industrial power. Today over 50 per cent of the UK labour force is unionized. Also the Employment Protection Act of 1978 gives workers the right to set up closed shops in any industry or firm where a majority of employees request it.

In some other countries union power has stabilized or even fallen off in recent periods. In the US, for example, the high-water mark of unionization was reached around 1950 when about thirty-five per cent of the labour force was unionized. By 1975 the percentage had shrunk to twenty-five per cent. Union power has also been restricted by the *right-to-work legislation* passed by a number of state governments. The laws permit the open shop – the right to work without belonging to unions. A further limiting force has been the migration of many firms from the old industrial centres of the Northeast with its long-established and well-entrenched unions to the newly emerging areas of the South and Southwest where right-to-work legislation is common and unions are less well entrenched.

The methods and the objectives of the modern union

Wages

At the beginning of this chapter we considered a union that could set the wage rate but had to take the supply of labour as given, and let the employer fix demand. In fact, unions can also attempt to influence both of these variables.

In this section we shall consider the supply of labour to a particular occupation or industry. An alternative to setting the wage and letting that determine the quantity of labour provided is to try to determine the quantity of labour supplied and then let the wage be that which equates demand and supply. This is illustrated in Figure 27.6, which shows a labour market that would be perfectly competitive in the absence of the union. The union can raise its wage above the perfectly competitive level, w_c, by two alternative policies. First, as already analysed, it can negotiate a wage of w_u, let the volume of employment fall from q_c to q_a and allow an excess supply of labour of $q_u - q_a$ to develop. The second policy is to restrict entry into the occupation by methods such as lengthening apprenticeship periods and rationing places for trainees. Such tactics will make it more expensive, or otherwise more difficult, to enter the occupation. Thus, at any given wage rate, the quantity supplied will be reduced; the supply curve shifts to the left. If it shifts to S_2, the wage w_u is set in the competitive market without the union having to intervene in the process of wage setting. Furthermore, there is no excess supply at w_u since the supply curve has been shifted. Thus, there is no wage-reducing pressure from unemployed job seekers.

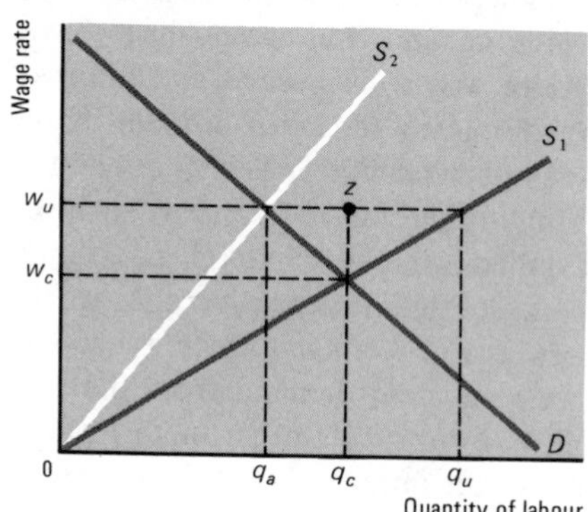

Fig. 27.6 An increase in wages caused by an entry restriction into a particular labour market

Which of the two tactics will appeal to a particular union will depend on many factors, such as the ease with which supply can be restricted, the ease with which union wages can be negotiated and enforced, and the public's reaction to these two tactics in particular situations. As an example of the force of the last point, consider doctors in countries such as the United States, where medical services are not nationalized. It is unlikely that either the public or the central authorities would accept a situation in which doctors raised the price of their services above the competitive level by collective agreement and then allowed an unemployed surplus of doctors to develop. So many people could clearly use more medical services than they receive that the existence of any substantial amount of unemployed medical talent would not be tolerated. Thus, doctors are forced back on the second alternative, which produces the same result but by more socially acceptable methods. They raise training periods and training costs and restrict entry into medical schools. By these and other tactics they shift the supply curve of qualified doctors to the left. If they shift it to S_2 in Figure 27.6, they give themselves the same wage as if they had left the supply curve at S_1 and regulated the wage at w_u, but they avoid what would be a very embarrassing surplus of unemployed doctors. In both cases the actual supply of doctors to the public is less (by $q_c - q_a$) than it would have been under competitive conditions.[1]

Wages versus employment

We have already seen that in many situations the union faces a trade-off between wages and employment: an increase in wages can be obtained only at the cost of lowered employment. But in some cases it is possible to avoid this conflict by bargaining with the employer about *both* wages and employment. This can be accomplished by manning agreements forcing employers to use more labour than they need for a given level of output; such agreements are very common in the UK.

The result is illustrated by point z in Figure 27.6. The demand curve shows for each wage rate the amount of labour the firm would like to hire. But it may prefer to hire some other amount rather than to go without labour altogether. When wages are w_c and employment is q_c the union might offer firms the alternative of employing q_c at a wage of w_u or of facing a strike. If the firm accepts the former alternative, it will move to point z, which is off its demand curve. The union thus raises the wage rate and the total real income of its members without causing any reduction in employment. The union's success in pursuing such a policy will probably depend on the size of the profits in the industry (i.e., on the extent to which the industry departs from the perfectly competitive equilibrium), and also on the state of the market, which will determine the relation between the losses resulting from hiring more than the desired quantity of labour at the agreed wage rate, and the expected losses resulting from a strike. If there are no pure profits, the union may succeed in the short run but lose in the long run when firms exit from the industry because their total costs now exceed their total revenues.

Wages versus job security

Unions vary greatly in the extent to which they adopt a defensive or an offensive attitude to the labour market. Until recently the leaderships of unions, management and government were dominated by people who were in their twenties during the Great Depression of the 1930s. Not surprisingly, the labouring members of this age group have been strongly conditioned to a defensive attitude towards jobs. They lived through a period when unemployment never fell below twenty per cent of the labour force as a national average, and when it was over fifty per cent in many of the hardest-hit areas. They saw people grow up, marry and raise children on the dole. They saw young men, who were eager to work but were unable to find any form of employment, slowly have their spirits broken as they had to confess their failure to

[1] Of course, some of the high standards for entry into the medical profession are needed to protect the public from incompetent doctors. Most investigations have concluded, however, that restrictions on entry are much greater than they need to be and partly serve the function analysed in the text.

wives and children. They suffered the humiliation of being read lessons on hard work, thrift, and patience by a London-based, middle-class bureaucracy that had not directly experienced unemployment itself. When occasionally the unemployed rose up, as in the General Strike or the Hunger March, the troops were called out against them.

In those days of mass unemployment, the installation of a new machine in a factory condemned the worker it replaced to an indefinite future on the dole. It is little wonder that labour-saving machines were opposed bitterly, and that job-saving restrictive practices were adhered to with tenacity. The defensive attitude which was so understandable in the 1930s survived in the UK into the post-war period, when circumstances were very different. This was a time of full employment. New jobs were available to replace old ones that had been destroyed by technological change. In such a world the determination to preserve existing jobs at all costs made much less sense than in the 1930s.

Sustained economic growth means change, and change means that old jobs will be destroyed and new jobs created. The defensive attitude to old jobs persisted more in the UK than either in Europe, where the old order had been more disrupted by World War II, or in the US, where unions were never as strong as in the UK. The net effect was that the process of changing the structure of employment, which must accompany growth, was slowed. Studies of comparable factories in Britain, France and Germany show often up to twice as many workers used to produce the same output in Britain as on the continent. Thus UK growth and hence the rise in living standards of the average person were slower than in Europe and in North America. Although particular jobs were saved in the UK, there is no evidence that the overall level of unemployment has been lower in the UK over the decades than in those countries where unions have been less defensive about preserving existing jobs.

Protecting existing jobs may be a successful way to protect the living standards of the average worker in the short term, but over the longer term it lowers living standards below what they would be if the structure of jobs were allowed to change according to the requirements of a growing, changing economy.

Unions and the structure of relative wages

So far we have considered the influence of one particular union, operating in a small section of the total labour market, on the wages of its members. Our theory predicts that a powerful union can in such circumstances raise the wages earned by its members, possibly at the expense of lowering the volume of employment. This prediction seems to be supported by substantial empirical evidence that all unions do influence the structure of relative wages by raising wages in some industries and occupations where they are particularly strong, without a corresponding rise in wages elsewhere. For example, the American economist Albert Rees, one of the leading students of the influence of unionism on wages, concluded, 'I would say that perhaps a third of the trade unions have raised the wages of their members by 15 to 20 per cent above what they might be in a non-union situation, another third by 5 per cent to 10 per cent, and the remaining third, not at all.'[1]

[1] Albert Rees, *Wage Inflation* (National Industrial Conference Board, 1957).

Unions and the functional distribution of income

A question in which trade unionists and many other observers have been interested for a very long time is: 'Are unions able to influence the share of total national income going to labour in general?'. This question does not concern the power of one small union to raise the wages of its members, possibly at the expense of workers in less powerful situations. It concerns, rather, the ability of unions to raise the earnings of labour in general at the expense of the earnings of land and capital. Many of the efforts of the early classical economists were directed towards developing theories that would explain the functional distribution of income. A great deal of the concern of early trade unionists was over increasing the share of total national income going to labour – helping one group of labourers at the expense of other groups would not have had nearly the general appeal as helping all the workers at the expense of the capitalists and the landowners. It may seem surprising that in spite of all this early, and continued, interest, we cannot say very much about this question even now.

We have seen that we do have a well-developed micro-market theory that allows us to predict the effect on relative wages of a particular intervention of a union, an employers' organization, or the central authorities in any one market. We do not, however, have an accepted theory of the overall distribution of national income that allows us to predict the consequences of a particular intervention, such as the growth of trade unions, for the functional distribution of income.

To illustrate this problem, let us consider what effect trade union intervention may have in raising wages above their competitive level in all industries. The predictions for one industry are illustrated in Figure 27.3: the wage rate rises but employment falls. But if this occurs simultaneously in *all* industries we cannot apply the same analysis. The analysis of Figure 27.3 was based on demand curves, which are in turn based on assumptions of other things being equal. If unions raise the wage rate of even a significant part of the labour force, they will cause incomes to change significantly; this will cause demand curves for consumers' goods to *shift*; this will cause outputs to vary; and this, in turn, will cause shifts in the derived demand curves for labour. Unless we have a theory of how each of these changes is related to the other, we cannot attempt to answer this question. In fact, there is no generally accepted, well-worked-out theory which would allow us to deal with it. Here, then, is a real challenge to the advanced student interested in questions of labour and income: to develop and test a theory which will shed light on this important question.[1]

There is no doubt that unions are extremely powerful organizations, particularly in the UK, and that they have important effects on the economy. Just how much they succeed in changing the functional distribution in labour's favour, however, remains an unsettled question.

---

[1] The discussion on pages 409–13 is also relevant to this point.

28

Interest and the return on capital

To many Marxists the capitalist is a villain. To many socialists he is at best a dispensable drone. To many liberals he is an important part of the productive process, as necessary as the providers of land and labour. To many conservatives he is a heroic figure captaining the economy along the risky channels leading to ever-higher living standards.

A capitalist is someone who owns capital, which we have defined as all man-made aids to further production. In this chapter we shall study the determinants of capital's share in the functional distribution of income. Capital theory, however, is one of the most difficult branches of economics and we can do little more than examine its outer surface in an introductory book.

At the outset let us clear up three possible misconceptions. *First, is capital itself either a villain or a dispensable drone in the productive process*? None but the most extreme and unrealistic members of the back-to-nature school would say 'Yes'. A primitive society in which there are no capital goods – not a spear, a lever, a washing tub nor a stone axe – is almost impossible to imagine, and has never occurred in recorded history.

Second, is a payment for the use of capital necessary? Early communist societies thought not. Such payments were officially barred during the early years after the Russian revolution of 1917. The trouble with doing this, however, is that capital is scarce; all producers would like to have more of it than they now have. If there is no price, how is the available supply to be allocated among the virtually limitless demands for it? Of course the state could allocate it. But how? Any state that is interested in maximizing production will want to allocate its scarce capital to its most productive uses. For this reason, virtually all communist states today assign a price to capital, and allow firms to use more of it only if the capital will earn enough to cover its cost. Furthermore, the planners in these societies worry about setting the right price of capital. The answer to the second question is therefore 'Yes'.

Third, does capital need to be in private hands so that the price of capital becomes an income for its private owners? This time the answer is clearly 'No'. In many communist countries capital is owned by the state and the payments made for its use go to the state rather than to private 'capitalists'. The advantages of private versus public ownership of the 'means of production' (the term often used in socialist and communist literature to describe capital) is still hotly debated.

Capital is indispensable in any modern economy, and its efficient use requires that it be priced. When capital is privately owned, its price becomes the income of its owners; when it is publicly owned its price goes to the state.

The productivity or efficiency of capital

Capital is productive, but in what sense? Rarely, if ever, do we make any consumers' good[1] directly with the aid of such simple tools as nature provides. Productive effort goes first into the manufacture of capital – tools, machines and other goods that are desired not in themselves but only as aids to making other commodities. The capital goods are then used to make the consumers' goods. The use of capital renders production processes *roundabout*. Instead of making what we want directly, we engage in the indirect process of first making the goods that we use in making what we finally want.

In many cases, production is very roundabout indeed. For example, a worker may be employed in a factory making machines that are used in mining coal; the coal may be burned by a power plant to make electricity; the electricity may provide power for a factory that makes machine tools; the tools may be used to make a tractor; the tractor may be used by a potato farmer to help in the production of potatoes; and the potatoes may be eaten by a consumer. This kind of indirect production is worthwhile *if* the farmer, using his tractor, can produce more potatoes than could be produced by applying all the factors of production involved in the chain directly to the production of potatoes (using only such tools as were provided by nature). In fact, the capital-using, roundabout method of production is very often more efficient than the direct method. The difference between the flows of output that would result from the two methods is called either the PRODUCTIVITY OF CAPITAL or the EFFICIENCY OF CAPITAL. Unfortunately, the extra output is not achieved without cost.

Generally speaking, a decision to increase the amount of capital available entails a present sacrifice and a future gain. The present sacrifice occurs because resources are diverted from producing consumption goods to producing capital goods. The future gain occurs because production is higher with the new capital than without it (even after allowing for maintenance and replacement of the capital goods).

The rate of return on capital

Because capital is productive its use yields a return over all other costs of production. How is this return determined? Take the receipts from the sale of the goods produced by a firm and subtract the appropriate costs for purchased goods and materials, for labour, for land and for the manager's own contributed talents. Subtract from this an allowance for the taxes the firm will have to pay, and what is left may be called the GROSS RETURN ON CAPITAL. We saw in Chapter 17 (page 208) that it is convenient to divide this gross return into:

[1] In capital theory the term 'consumers' goods' refers to all goods and services consumed because of the direct utility they yield to households; the term 'producers' goods' is a synonym for capital goods. In modern terminology 'commodity' would be better, but 'good' is enshrined by over a century of usage.

(i) the pure return on capital, which is the amount that capital could earn in riskless investment in equilibrium;
(ii) a risk premium, which compensates the owners for the actual risks of the enterprise; and
(iii) the economic profits.

In a competitive society profits are a signal that resources should be reallocated because earnings exceed opportunity costs in some lines of production. Profits are thus a phenomenon of disequilibrium. In order to study the return to capital in its purest form, we consider a competitive economy that is in equilibrium with respect to the allocation of existing factors of production among all their possible uses. Profits will be zero. (Note: This does not mean that the owners of capital get nothing; it only means that the gross return to capital does not now include a profit element that signals the need to reallocate resources.)

To further simplify things at the outset, let us deal with a world of perfect certainty: everyone knows for sure what the productivity of an existing new unit of capital will be in any of its possible uses. We shall return to uncertainty later. If there is no risk, then the gross return to capital does not include a risk premium. We have now simplified things to the point where the gross return to capital is all pure return. This is the income earned by the owners of capital when a competitive and riskless economy is in equilibrium with respect to the allocation of its current resources.

What determines the pure return on capital? Why is it high in some time periods and low in others? What causes it to change?

The present value of future income

The productivity of a particular piece of capital, say a machine tool, takes the form of a flow of gross returns over its life time. If we wish to measure the productivity of a particular machine per pound invested in it, we need to put a single money value on the future flow of returns and compare this to the cost of the machine. How do we put a money value on the flow of future returns?

The value of a single future payment For purposes of illustration, let us assume that the rate of interest on a perfectly safe loan is 5 per cent and then ask three separate questions.

(1) *How much money would you have to invest today if you wished to have £100 in one year's time?* Letting X stand for the answer, we have: $X(1{\cdot}05) = £100$. Or $X = £100/1{\cdot}05 = £95{\cdot}24$. What this tells us is that, if you lend out £95·24 today at 5 per cent interest, you will receive £100 a year from now (£95·24 as repayment of the principal of the loan and £4·76 as interest).

(2) *What is the maximum amount you would be prepared to pay now to acquire the right to £100 in cash in one year's time?* Surely this is £95·24. If you paid more you would be losing money, since you can loan out £95·24 at 5 per cent and receive £100 in a year's time. If you could buy the right to £100 cash for anything less than £95.24 it would be profitable to do so, since you could borrow £95·24 now in return for your promise to repay £100 one year from now.[1]

[1] Suppose, for example, you were offered the right to £100 a year from now for £90 now. If the market rate of interest is 5 per cent, you could borrow £95·24 now, buy the right to £100 next year for £90 and pocket £5·24 as your profit. Next year you claim the £100, which is just enough to repay the loan of £95·24 plus interest (at 5 per cent) of £4·76.

(3) *What is the most you could borrow today in return for your promise to repay £100 a year from now?* If lenders were perfectly certain you would meet your promise, they would lend you £95·24. No one would lend you any more since the lender has the option of lending his or her money elsewhere at 5 per cent. If you offered to take less (say £90) then everyone would rush to lend you money since lending to you would yield more than the going rate of return on safe loans of 5 per cent.

The present value of a single future payment These three questions can be reduced to one question: 'How much money now is equivalent to £100 payable for certain a year from now when the interest rate on perfectly safe loans is 5 per cent?' This sum is called the present value of £100 a year from now at a 5 per cent interest rate. In general, PRESENT VALUE (PV) refers to the value now of payments to be received in the future. The present value clearly depends on the rate of interest that is used in the calculation. When a future sum is turned into its equivalent present value, we say that sum is DISCOUNTED. Discounting always takes place at some particular rate of interest.

Of course the numerical example given above depended on the 5 per cent interest rate that was chosen to illustrate the calculations. If the interest rate is 7 per cent, the present value of the £100 receivable next year is £100/1·07 = £93·45. In general, the present value of £X one year hence, at an interest rate of i per cent per year,[1] is

$$PV = \frac{X}{(1+i)}.$$

Now consider what would happen if the payment date is further away than one year. If we lend £X at 5 per cent for one year we will be paid £(1·05) X. But if we immediately relend that whole amount, we would get back at the end of the second year an amount equal to 1·05 *times* the amount lent out, i.e. £(1·05) (1·05)X. Thus £100 payable two years hence has a present value (at 5 per cent) of

$$\frac{£100{\cdot}00}{(1{\cdot}05)\,(1{\cdot}05)} = £90{\cdot}70.$$

The amount of £90·70 lent out now, with the interest that is paid at the end of the first year lent out for the second year, would yield £100 in two years.[2] In general, the present value of £X after t years at i per cent is

$$PV = \frac{X}{(1+i)^t}.$$

Inspection of the above expression shows that as either i or t is increased the denominator increases and hence PV decreases. This leads to the following conclusion:

> **The farther away the payment date and the higher the rate of interest, the smaller the present value of a given sum payable in the future.**

[1] In all these calculations the interest rate is expressed as a ratio of interest divided by principal, so that a rate of 100 per cent is written 1, 10 per cent as 0·1 and so on.

[2] Readers familiar with this type of calculation will realize that the argument in the text is based on an annual compounding of interest.

The present value of an infinite stream of payments So much for a single sum payable in the future; now consider the present value of a stream of income that continues indefinitely. While at first glance that might seem very high, since as time passes the total received grows without reaching any limit, considerations of the previous section suggest that one will not value highly the far distant payments. To find the present value of £100 a year, payable forever, we need only ask how much money would have to be invested now at an interest rate of i per cent per year to obtain £100 each year. This is simply $i \times X = £100$, where i is the interest rate and X the sum required. This tells us that the present value of the stream of £100 a year forever is

$$PV = \frac{£100}{i}.$$

If the interest rate were 10 per cent, the present value would be £1,000, which merely says that £1,000 invested at 10 per cent would yield £100 per year, forever. Notice that here, as above, PV is *inversely* related to the rate of interest: the higher the interest rate, the less the (present) value of distant payments.

The present value of a finite stream of income It is also possible to obtain the present value of some finite stream of income and then convert it into an equivalent infinite stream. This is of considerable theoretical value, since it allows us always to deal with the equivalent infinite stream, even if the problem we are considering concerns a finite and irregular stream. Consider, for example a machine that yields the following stream of gross returns: £100 now, £275 in one year, £242 in 2 years, £133·10 in 3 years, £87·84 in four years, and nothing thereafter. The present value of this flow of income, when the market rate of interest is 10 per cent (and hence $1+i = 1{\cdot}1$) is

$$\begin{aligned} PV &= £100 + \frac{£275}{1{\cdot}1} + \frac{£242}{(1{\cdot}1)^2} + \frac{£133{\cdot}10}{(1{\cdot}1)^3} + \frac{£87{\cdot}84}{(1{\cdot}1)^4} \\ &= £100 + £250 + £200 + £100 + £60 \\ &= £710. \end{aligned}$$

But £710 invested at 10 per cent interest will yield a flow of £71 per annum in perpetuity. Thus the irregular finite flow listed above is equivalent to (i.e., has the same present value as) the smooth flow of £71 forever. Thus, in any practical problem concerning an irregular flow we can substitute the equivalent regular flow, which can be handled with much greater ease.

Calculating the productivity or efficiency of capital

So far we have seen how to calculate the present value of a piece of capital that yields a flow of gross returns in the future. We do this by discounting the flow at the current rate of interest.

> **We can obtain a measure of the productivity or efficiency of capital by finding the rate of discount, *e*, that will just make the present value of the flow of receipts equal to the purchase price of the capital.**

If we take the case of a constant flow that goes on forever, we can show this easily.

We wish to find e such that

$$P = X/e.$$

where P is the purchase price of the piece of capital, X is its constant flow of gross returns and e is the unknown value of the productivity or efficiency of capital. In this simple case we can solve for e as:

$$e = X/P.$$

When the flow is irregular, or does not continue indefinitely, the procedure is the same, although the calculations are more tedious. We must find e such that

$$P = \frac{X_1}{1+e} + \frac{X_2}{(1+e)^2} + \ldots + \frac{X_n}{(1+e)^n}$$

where $X_1, \ldots, X_n$ is the gross return produced for each of n years and P is again the purchase price of the piece of capital. If we think of a firm having an array of capital equipment and making a marginal decision to install one more bit of capital, we may call the e associated with this marginal increment the MARGINAL EFFICIENCY OF CAPITAL (*mec*). Thus e is the efficiency of *any* unit of capital and *mec* is the efficiency of the *marginal* unit.

The demand for capital

We can now use this analysis of the efficiency of capital to determine the demand for capital goods. We first consider a single firm and then the whole economy.

The firm's demand for capital

What is the significance of calculating e such that the prevent value of the flow of gross receipts is equal to the purchase price of the capital? The answer is that the value to the firm now of the flow of its gross receipts is its present value, while the purchase price is the cost to the firm now of the capital. The former value is the addition to revenue of a unit of capital; the latter value is its addition to cost. We know from previous chapters that the profit-maximizing firm will go on adding units of any factor of production as long as its marginal revenue product exceeds its marginal cost. Thus the profit-maximizing firm will go on adding capital as long as the present value of the flow of gross receipts from the marginal unit exceeds its purchase price.

The value of e is the rate of discount at which these two are just equal. But present value is calculated from the market rate of interest, i. Thus when *mec* equals i, the present value of the returns to the marginal unit of capital equal its price. Thus the firm's capital would be of equilibrium size; it would not pay the firm to add more.

This is an extremely important and subtle point. It may thus be worth going over it again using a slightly different argument. How does the firm decide whether or not to buy a piece of capital? One way is to use the market rate of interest to calculate the present value of the gross return and then compare it with the purchase price. Suppose, for example, that for £8,000 a firm can purchase a machine that yields £1,000 a year net of all non-capital costs *into the indefinite future*. Also suppose that the firm can borrow (and lend) money at an interest rate of 10 per cent. The present value of the stream of income produced by the machine (the capitalized value of the machine) is £1,000/0.10 = £10,000; the present value of £8,000 now is (of course) £8,000. Clearly, the firm can increase its value if it purchases for £8,000 something that is worth £10,000 to itself. Another way to see this is to suppose that the only uses a firm has for its money are to buy the machine or to lend out its £8,000 at 10 per cent interest. Buying the machine is the superior alternative since this yields £1,000 per annum while lending out the £8,000 purchase price yields only £800 per annum.

In general, a capital good should be purchased if

$$\frac{X}{i} > P$$

where X is the flow of gross returns expressed as an infinite stream of payments. The term X/i is the present value of the stream of gross returns produced by the capital good or, in other words, the capitalized value of the asset.

It pays to purchase a capital good whenever the present value of its future stream of gross returns exceeds the purchase price of the capital good.

This same relationship can be looked at in another way, by rearranging the terms in the algebraic inequality above:

$$\frac{X}{P} > i.$$

But X/P is the marginal efficiency of capital. Thus we have the rule:

It pays to purchase a further unit of capital whenever its marginal efficiency exceeds the rate of interest.

Looked at in this way, *mec* is a measure of the return on a marginal unit of capital to the firm, while i is a measure of the opportunity cost of capital (always assuming that the firm can borrow and lend at the going rate of interest).

We now assume that capital is subject to the law of diminishing marginal returns within the firm. Every further investment in capital equipment that the firm makes yields a lower return than previous investments. The rule outlined above now implies the following equilibrium condition:

A profit-maximizing firm will be in equilibrium with respect to the size of its capital stock when its marginal efficiency of capital is equal to the interest rate (*mec* = *i*).

The market demand for capital

Consider increasing the quantity of capital throughout the entire economy. It is convenient now to think of society as having a total quantity of capital, called the CAPITAL STOCK, and measured by a single number.[1] When more capital is

[1] The idea of a stock of capital being measured by a single number is a simplification. Society's stock of capital goods is made up of a diverse bundle of factories, machines, bridges, roads and other man-made aids to further production. For expository purposes, it is useful to make the heroic assumption that all of these can be reduced to some common unit and summed to obtain a measure of the society's *physical* stock of capital.

accumulated under conditions of fixed technology and constant supplies of land and labour, diminishing returns implies that the marginal efficiency of capital will fall. The economy's marginal efficiency of capital (*MEC*) schedule relates the size of the capital stock to the return on the marginal unit of capital. (*mec* refers to one firm; *MEC* refers to the economy as a whole.) It is downward-sloping and an illustration is shown in Figure 28.1.

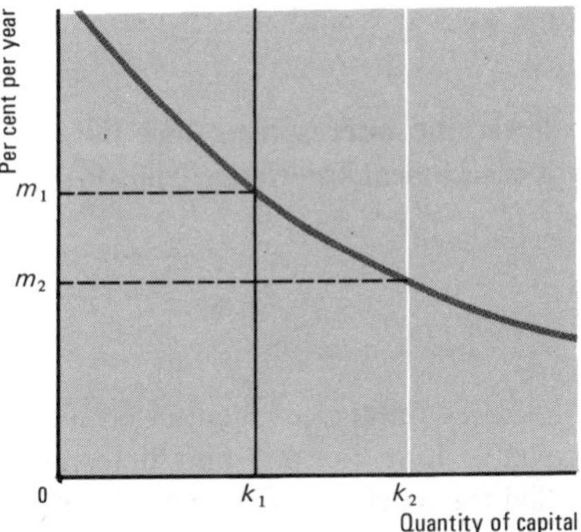

Fig. 28.1 In equilibrium the rate of interest is equal to the marginal efficiency of capital

A simple theory of the determination of the interest rate

Since each firm in the economy is in equilibrium with respect to its capital stock when its *mec* is equated with *i*, this will also be true of the economy. It follows that:

> **The *MEC* schedule is the economy's demand schedule for capital with respect to the rate of interest.**

A fixed stock of capital

The existing stock of capital can be changed only very slowly. Thus we may take the stock of capital as fixed over shortish time periods. If we assume that the present capital stock is k_1 in Figure 28.1, then the equilibrium rate of interest will be m_1.

How is this rate established? To answer this question assume that some other rate rules temporarily. First, assume that the rate is m_2. With the stock of capital k_1, the MEC of m_1 exceeds the interest rate of m_2. Investment will now look profitable to all firms and there will be a rush to borrow funds to invest in new capital equipment. The shortage of investment funds will bid up the rate of interest until it approaches m_1. Second, assume that the rate exceeds m_1. Now no firms will wish to borrow money for investment purposes and the glut of funds will bring the interest rate down.

> **Over short periods of time the capital stock, and hence the *MEC*, is given so that the interest rate moves towards the *MEC*.**

A growing stock of capital

Over time, firms and households save and invest in new capital equipment, causing the capital stock to grow. This is shown by a slow rightward shifting of the line indicating the given capital stock. This has the effect of reducing the marginal efficiency of capital and the equilibrium interest rate. For example, if the stock grows from k_1 to k_2 in Figure 28.1, the *MEC* and *i* will both fall from m_1 to m_2. Thus in an economy with static technology and fixed supplies of land and labour, capital accumulation will tend to lower the marginal efficiency of capital and the rate of interest.

The growth of technical knowledge, however, provides new productive uses for capital. This tends to push the *MEC* schedule outwards and *ceteris paribus* will raise *MEC* and *i*.

> **The accumulation of capital tends to lower the interest rate and the marginal efficiency of capital. The growth of technical knowledge tends to raise both of these rates.**

Some complications

The simple theory outlined above takes the stock of capital as exogenous (constant over a short period and growing slowly over a long period) and determines simultaneously the pure return on capital, called the marginal efficiency of capital, and the rate of interest. The rate of interest so determined is called the pure rate because it is the rate on a riskless loan to purchase capital (see the assumptions on page 388). According to this theory the marginal efficiency of capital must in equilibrium be equal to the pure rate of interest.

To obtain a theory of the actual rate of interest that rules in the market, which is called the MARKET RATE OF INTEREST (or sometimes simply 'the' rate of interest), we must allow for a number of complications. These will cause the market rate of interest to diverge somewhat from the pure rate.

Uncertainty

So far we have discussed the present value of a *certain* future stream of gross returns. In reality, uncertainty will be attached to (i) the physical stream of goods the capital will produce; (ii) the value of the stream of goods (i.e., the gross monetary returns) the capital will produce; and (iii) the ability of a person who borrows money to repay the loan.

The physical output of capital Generally one can be fairly clear on the flow of goods one expects to gain from a piece of capital equipment. In these days of shortages of many raw materials and the possible outright exhaustion of others, however, some uncertainty must inevitably be attached to the flow of goods that capital will produce.

The value of the gross return to capital Even if everyone were perfectly certain about the physical productivity of capital, great uncertainty would inevitably attach to the expected value of the stream of gross returns associated with the capital goods. Even in the world of full employment, the prices of outputs and inputs fluctuate greatly. A favourable combination of changes—output prices up and input prices down—can greatly increase the value of the return to capital produced by the capital goods. An unfavourable combination can reduce this value or even eliminate it completely. In times of major depressions, demand for consumers' goods declines drastically as unemployment rises. Even if capital is physically productive, it will produce a zero stream of gross value returns if the goods that it produces cannot be sold.

All of these uncertainties vary among firms and among industries. People investing their own money (e.g., by buying equities) in firms that are in high-risk industries will only do so if they expect a high yield from the capital their money will be used to purchase. People lending their money (e.g., by purchasing bonds) to firms in high-risk industries will only do so if they are offered a high rate of interest in return. For these reasons the return on capital and the rate of interest paid on borrowed money will differ among firms and industries.

The rate of interest will also differ systematically with the TERM(i.e. the duration) of the loan, for reasons that are ultimately related to uncertainty. Borrowers are usually willing to pay more for long-term loans than for short-term loans because they are certain of having use of the money for a longer period. Lenders usually require a higher rate of interest the longer the term of the loan, because the risk element is greater. (Will the borrower be able to repay? What will happen to the price level?) Thus, other things being equal, the shorter the term of a loan, the lower the interest rate.

All of these considerations affect the risk premium which is a part of the gross return to capital in addition to its pure return.

Inflationary expectations

So far we have implicitly assumed a constant price level. In a world in which the purchasing power of money is constantly changing, it is necessary to distinguish between the real rate and the money rate of interest. The MONEY RATE OF INTEREST is measured simply in money paid. If you pay me £8 interest for a £100 loan for one year, the money rate is 8 per cent. The REAL RATE OF INTEREST concerns the ratio of the *purchasing power* of the money returned to the *purchasing power* of the money borrowed, and it may be different from the money rate.

Consider further my £100 loan to you at 8 per cent. The real rate that I earn depends on what happens to the overall level of prices in the economy. If the price level remains constant over the year, then the real rate that I earn is also 8 per cent. This is because I can buy 8 per cent more real goods and services with the £108 that you repay me than with the £100 I lent you. If, however, the price level were to rise by 8 per cent, the real rate would be nil because the £108 you repay me will buy the same quantity of real goods as the £100 I gave up. If I were unlucky enough to have lent money at 8 per cent in a year in which prices rose by 10 per cent, the real rate would be minus 2 per cent. This example illustrates the general proposition that the real rate of interest is the difference between the money rate of interest and the rate of change of the general price level.

In discussing the relation between the real and the money rates of interest, it is important to distinguish between an inflation that is fully anticipated by everyone (as might be the case when say a steady 5 per cent inflation has been going on for a long time) and an inflation that is unanticipated (as might be the case when the rate of inflation suddenly accelerates). Consider first the case of a fully anticipated inflation. The relation between real and money rates of interest often leads to much misunderstanding during times of anticipated inflation. Say, for example, that the equilibrium value of the real rate of interest is a modest 3 per cent and that the rate of inflation is now, and is expected to continue, at 5 per cent. The money rate should then be 8 per cent. Now assume that the rate of inflation accelerates to 15 per cent per year and is expected to remain at that figure. The money rate should now rise to 18 per cent. The 18 per cent money rate combined with a 15 per cent inflation rate represents the same real burden on borrowers as did the 8 per cent money rate combined with a 5 per cent rate of inflation. Yet when such changes occur it is common for the public to become very concerned at the 'crushing' burden of the rising interest rates on those with mortgages and other debts. But consider what would happen if in response to this worry the government legislated maximum interest rates of say 12 per cent in the face of the 15 per cent inflation. Now the real rate of interest would be negative: in real terms *lenders* would be paying for the privilege of being able to lend their money to the *borrowers*! This seems counter-intuitive to many people, but consider the example of a person who borrows £100 and repays £112 one year hence in the face of a 15 per cent inflation. The purchasing power of the £112 returned is less than the purchasing power of the £100 borrowed so that the real rate of interest has in fact proved negative in spite of the seemingly high money rate paid on the loan.

The real rate of interest is the money rate minus the rate of change of the general price level. A constant real rate of interest requires that the money rate increase by the same amount as any increase that occurs in the inflation rate.

If an inflation is fully expected, the money rate can be set to give any desired real rate of interest. Problems arise, however, when the inflation rate changes unexpectedly. Consider, for example, a loan contract that the parties wish to carry a 3 per cent real rate of interest. If a 7 per cent inflation rate is expected, the money rate will be set at 10 per cent. But what if the inflationary expectations turn out to be wrong? If the inflation rate is only 4 per cent, the real rate of interest will be 6 per cent. If, on the other hand, the inflation rate is 12 per cent, the real rate of interest will be −2 per cent; the lender, even after paying the interest on the loan, will give back less purchasing power at the end of the period than he or she borrowed at the beginning.

Unexpected changes in the rate of inflation cause the real rate of interest on contracts already drawn up to vary in unexpected ways. An unexpected fall in the inflation rate is beneficial to lenders; an unexpected rise is beneficial to borrowers.

Uncertainty about the rate of inflation is an added complication, because people are uncertain about what the real rate of interest will be. If the rate of inflation accelerates unexpectedly borrowers gain; if it decelerates unexpectedly lenders gain. The effect on the current money rate of interest depends on how both borrowers and lenders react to uncertainty about the real rate of interest.

Other demands to borrow money

So far we have considered only the purchase of new capital as a reason to borrow money. While capital equipment is a major source of the demand for funds, it is not the only source. Households borrow money to buy goods. The central authorities at all levels are major borrowers. Shifts in the demand to borrow money on the part of households or central authorities can cause the market rate of interest to change with no immediate change in the marginal efficiency of capital.

The influence of the central bank

Central banks often have active policies about what interest rates should be. The bank will intervene in the market for bonds in an attempt to influence the yield of these bonds. The central bank is a large enough potential buyer and seller of bonds to be able to do just this, and the exact way in which it is accomplished is analysed in Chapter 40.

Bank administration of interest rates

The rate of interest does not fluctuate in response to every minor fluctuation in the demand to borrow money. Banks, for example, consider many factors when they fix the rate of interest that they charge on loans. They are reluctant to change these rates every time changes occur in the demand to borrow money. If there is an excess demand for loanable funds (because the *MEC* is greater than *i*), rather than raising the rate of interest, banks often ration the available supply of funds among their customers according to such criteria as the borrower's credit rating, how long the banker has known him and the amount of business he does. Credit rationing is commonly found in lending institutions in most Western countries. When the market rate of interest is below the pure return on capital, money will appear 'tight' – difficult to borrow – to the typical businessman.

Differences in the cost of administering credit

So far we have not considered what it costs the lender to earn his money. There is, in fact, great variation in the costs of different kinds of credit transactions. It is almost as cheap (in actual numbers of pounds) for a bank to lend £1 million to an industrial firm that agrees to pay the money back with interest after one year as it is for the same bank to lend you £1,200 to buy a new car on a loan that you agree to pay back over two years in 24 equal instalments. The difference in the cost *per pound* of each loan is considerable. The bank may very well make less profit per pound on a £1,200 loan at 18 per cent per year than on a £1 million loan at 8 per cent per year. In general, the bigger the loan and the fewer payments, the less the cost per pound of servicing the loan. Why, then, do banks and loan companies usually insist that you repay the loan in frequent instalments? They worry that, if you do not pay regularly, you will not have the money when the loan comes due.

Many rates of interest

In the real world there are many different rates of interest, not just a single one. Speaking in terms of the rate can, however, be a valid simplification for many purposes because the whole set of rates does *tend* to move upward or downward together. Concentrating on one 'typical' rate as 'the' rate of interest in such cases is quite acceptable. For some purposes, however, it is important to take into account the multiplicity of interest rates.

At any moment in time, there are many different market rates of interest. At the time that you receive an interest rate of 6 or 7 per cent on deposits at a building society, you may have to pay 10 or 11 per cent on a loan from the same building society to buy a house. Interest rates on hire-purchase credit of 16 per cent and 20 per cent are common. A small firm pays a higher interest rate than a giant corporation on funds it borrows from banks. Different government bonds pay different rates of interest, depending on the length of the period for which the bond runs. Corporation bonds tend to pay interest at a higher rate than government bonds, and there is much variation among bonds of different companies. Considering the extreme mobility of money, why do such great differences exist? Why do funds not flow between different uses to diminish these differences? The answer is that quoted interest rates are composites of many things such as differences in risk, term and cost of administration among different loans.

Recapitulation

(1) Capital is productive in that it provides a flow of gross returns over and above all non-capital costs of production.
(2) It will pay a firm to buy any piece of capital as long as the present value of its flow of gross returns exceeds its purchase price.
(3) The efficiency of capital is measured by the rate of discount that makes the present value of the flow of gross returns equal to its purchase price. It pays a firm to buy any piece of capital where efficiency exceeds the rate of interest.
(4) Capital is assumed to be subject to diminishing marginal returns so that the marginal efficiency of capital to each firm and to the economy as a whole declines as the capital stock rises.
(5) If the *MEC* exceeds the pure rate of interest, everyone will wish to borrow money and buy capital equipment. If the *MEC* is less than the pure rate of interest, no one will wish to borrow money to buy capital equipment. Thus in equilibrium the pure rate of interest tends to equal the marginal efficiency of capital.
(6) The income earned by an owner of capital, whether he uses it himself and gains the marginal efficiency of capital or lends it to someone and earns the pure rate of interest, is thus determined by the marginal efficiency of capital.
(7) The total return to capital includes, in addition to the pure return on capital, a risk premium and pure profits. If there are no barriers to entry, pure profits are a disequilibrium phenomenon which exists only until new capital enters the industry, expanding output and reducing prices so that the pure profits disappear (if there are barriers to entry the pure profits may persist in the long run).
(8) Actual interest rates differ from the pure rate of interest for a number of identifiable reasons such as risk and term of the loan.

The price of an income-producing asset

What determines the market price of any existing asset that will produce a stream of income over time? The asset might be a piece of land, a machine, a slave or a block of flats. It will produce a stream of output and the market conditions of demand and supply will determine the price of this output. This allows us to convert the stream of output into a stream of money. Now that we know how to calculate the present value of a stream of money, it only remains to make the obvious point that the equilibrium market price of the asset will be equal to the present value of the stream of money associated with it.

Thus the present value of a productive asset that produces the equivalent of £100 a year *net* income indefinitely is £2,000 if the appropriate rate of interest is 5 per cent, because £2,000 invested at 5 per cent per year would yield £100 a year. It would pay an investor to buy the equipment for any price up to and including £2,000. (Of course, the equipment will not produce income indefinitely, but we are making use of the result that for any finite, and possibly irregular, stream of income actually produced by the machine there will be an equivalent constant, infinite stream.) If the price were less than £2,000 everyone would be eager to buy the equipment and its price would rise. If the price were more than £2,000 it would not pay anyone to buy it. If, for example, the price were £2,500 and the equipment was bought with borrowed money, the purchaser would have to pay £125 a year to borrow the money necessary to purchase an asset that would yield only £100. If it were bought with the purchaser's own money, the purchaser could have lent the £2,500 out at the going rate of interest and earned £125 a year rather than buying the equipment and getting only £100. Thus no one would be willing to buy it and its price would fall. The only price at which people would be prepared to both buy and sell the piece of equipment is £2,000.

In general, if the market price of any asset is greater than the present value of the income stream it produces, no one will want to buy it, while if the market price is below its present value, everyone will want to buy it.

In a competitive market the equilibrium price of any asset will be the present value of the income stream it produces.

We have already noted that when we obtain the present value of any asset that yields a stream of future income, we speak of *discounting the future income stream* to get the CAPITALIZED VALUE of the asset. This is nothing other than the present value of the stream of income that the asset is expected to yield.[1]

A most important application of these general considerations concerns the relationship between the rate of interest and the price of bonds.

Consols A CONSOL, or *perpetuity*, is a bond that pays a fixed sum of money each year forever. It has no redemption date. The price of a consol promising to pay for example, £100 per year, is £2,000 when the interest rate is 5 per cent and £1,000 when the rate is10 per cent. *The price of a consol varies inversely with the rate of interest.*

Now consider a world in which consols are the only interest-earning asset, and assume that many people have excess money balances that they wish to invest. If everyone tries to buy consols their price will be bid up. If the price of consols paying

---

[1] A major problem in arriving at the present value of a future stream of money income is deciding on the appropriate interest rate to use in discounting the future stream. If the firm can borrow as much money as it wants at *i* per cent per year, it should discount at *i* per cent per year. If the firm cannot borrow all that it wishes, its internal rate of return on an extra pound invested may be substantially above the market rate of interest. In this case the firm should discount at its own opportunity cost of capital. The general principle is that the rate of discount should reflect the genuine opportunity cost of capital to the firm.

£100 a year rises from say, £5,000 to £10,000, this means that the interest rate that lenders are prepared to accept has fallen from 10 per cent to 5 per cent. (If existing consols sell at £10,000 any new borrower can also sell a newly issued consol for £10,000.)

Any action of investors that causes the price of consols to change also causes the rate of interest to change in the opposite direction: a rise in the price of consols is the same thing as a fall in the rate of interest.

Redeemable bonds Most bonds are not consols. Instead they pay a fixed sum of money in interest each year but also have a redemption date on which the principle of the loan will be repaid. A bond with a redemption value of £1,000 payable ten years hence and yielding £100 a year in the interim, would be worth the present value of a ten-year stream of £100 per year *plus* the present value of £1,000 payable in ten years. It is obvious that the same principles apply to redeemable bonds as to consols:

(i) The price of bonds and the rate of interest vary inversely with each other; (ii) Any action of investors that bids up the market price of existing bonds means that the rate of interest lenders are prepared to accept has fallen.

A redeemable bond also differs from a consol in that the present value of the former becomes increasingly dominated by the fixed redemption value as the redemption date approaches. Taking an extreme case, if a bond is to be redeemed for £1,000 in a week's time its present value will be very close to £1,000 and will hardly change if the rate of interest goes from 5 to 10 per cent.

The closer to the present the redemption date of a bond, the less its value changes with a change in the rate of interest.

29

Criticisms and tests of the theory of distribution

In Part 5 we have developed the traditional theory of distribution in several contexts. Repeating what is basically the same analysis in a number of different guises helps to develop a 'feel' for the workings of the price system that is very important to the economist. It has the disadvantage, however, of making the theory appear to have much more content than it actually has. In fact, the whole of distribution theory depends on a very few basic hypotheses about the behaviour of factor owners and firms. Before going on to consider various criticisms and tests of the theory, it may be useful to lay out its underlying structure.

The theory re-stated

The traditional theory of distribution maintains that factor prices can be explained by demand and supply. The theory of factor supply is based on the assumption that factors will move among occupations, industries and places in search of the highest net advantage, taking both monetary and non-monetary rewards into account. Factors will move in such a way as to equalize the net advantages their owners could gain from using those factors in any of their possible uses. Because there are impediments to the mobility of factors, there may be lags in their response to changes in prices. The elasticity of supply will depend on what factor is being discussed and what time horizon is being considered.

The demand for a factor is a derived demand, depending for its existence on the demand for the commodity produced by the factor. The elasticity of an industry's demand curve for a factor will vary directly with (i) the elasticity of demand for the product produced by the industry; (ii) the proportion of total production costs accounted for by the factor; and (iii) the extent to which it is technically possible to substitute other factors for the one in question.

In equilibrium *all* profit-making firms will employ *all* variable factors up to the point at which the marginal unit of each type of factor adds as much to revenue as to costs. All profit-maximizing firms that are price-takers in the factor market will employ factors up to the point at which the price paid for the last unit equals the increase in revenue caused by its employment. For firms selling goods in competitive markets, the increase in revenue is the marginal physical product *times* the price; for firms facing downward-sloping demand curves for their products, the increase in revenue is marginal physical product *times* marginal revenue.

These equilibrium relations necessarily apply to all firms that are successfully maximizing their profits. On the one hand, the firm that is not equating the marginal revenue product of each of its factors with that factor's price is not maximizing its profits. On the other hand, a firm that is maximizing its profits is necessarily equating each factor's price to its marginal revenue product. The theory thus stands or falls with the theory of profit maximization. It is merely an implication of profit maximization, and the only reason for spelling it out in detail is that this helps us to develop interesting and useful hypotheses about the effects of various changes in the economy on the markets for factors of production.

When one thinks of all the heated arguments over the traditional theory of distribution, and of all the passionate denunciations and defences that it has occasioned, it is surprising to observe how few predictions it makes, and how uncontroversial most of them are. For example, the theory predicts that demand for a factor depends on, and varies with, the demand for the products made by the factor. This was undoubtedly a great discovery when it was first put forward; now, however, it is almost a platitude. The theory also predicts that (assuming the supply curve does not shift) changes in the factor price must reflect changes in the demand for the commodities made by the factor. On the supply side, the theory predicts that movement of resources will occur in response to changes in factor prices. It is very hard to quarrel with any of these predictions, which are supported by voluminous evidence. They are important since they frequently apply to practical issues of policy.

Criticisms of the theory

We have seen that marginal productivity theory relates to the demand for factors of production. It constitutes half of the traditional theory of distribution; the other half is the theory of supply, the theory of factor movement in search of the highest net advantage. It is the marginal productivity half of the theory that has been subject to most criticism and about which so many misconceptions exist. We shall first discuss four common misconceptions, all of which have been drawn from real sources.

(1) *The theory assumes perfect competition in all markets.* This is just not correct. The relationship between the marginal physical product and the marginal value product will be altered if the degree of competition alters, but the marginal value product will be equated with the price of the factor in perfect competition, imperfect competition, oligopoly and monopoly, provided only that firms are price-takers in the factor market.

(2) *The theory assumes that the amount and value of the marginal product of a factor are known to the firm.* The theory assumes no such thing! Critics argue that the firm will not pay any factor the value of its marginal product because the firm will generally have no idea what that marginal product is and would be unable to calculate this magnitude even if it tried. What firms do or do not know about marginal products is irrelevant. It has already been pointed out that payment according to marginal revenue product occurs *automatically* whenever the firm is maximizing its profits. It does not matter *how* the firm succeeds in doing this – by

guess, luck, skill or by calculating marginal quantities. As long as profits are maximized, factors will be getting the values of their marginal products. The theory does not purport to describe how firms calculate; it merely predicts how they will react to various situations on the assumption that they are maximizing profits.

(3) *The theory is inhuman because it treats labour in the same way as it treats an acre of land or a wagon load of fertilizer.* One must be careful to distinguish one's emotional reaction to a procedure that treats human and non-human factors alike from one's evaluation of it in terms of positive economics. Those who accept this criticism must explain carefully why separate theories of the pricing of human and non-human factors are needed. They must also show that their 'human' theory makes predictions that differ from those made by marginal productivity theory. Marginal productivity theory is only a theory of the *demand* for a factor. It predicts that firms' desired purchases of labour (and all other factors) depend on the price of the factor in question, the technical conditions of production and the demand for the product made by labour. No evidence has yet been gathered to indicate that it is necessary to have separate theories of the *demand* for human and non-human factors or production. *Supply* conditions will differ between human and non-human factors, but these differences are accommodated within the theory. Indeed, one of the important insights from the theory of net advantage is that non-monetary considerations are more important in allocating labour than other factors because the owner of labour must be physically present to supply his factor's services, while the owner of land and capital need not be.

(4) *When all factors are paid according to their marginal products, the resulting distribution of income will be a just distribution.* Some supporters of the theory of marginal productivity have held not only that the theory was correct, but that it described a functional distribution of income that was a *just* one because factors were rewarded according to the value of their contributions to the national product. Many critics of the low level of wages prevailing in the nineteenth century reacted with passion against a theory that was claimed to justify these rates of pay.

It is beyond the scope of a book on positive economics to enter into normative questions of what constitutes a just distribution of income. It is, however, worth getting the facts straight. According to marginal productivity theory, each labourer (or each unit of any other factor) does *not* receive the value of what he or she personally contributes to production. Each labourer, instead, receives the value of what the last labourer employed would add to production *if all other factors of production were held constant*. If one million identical labourers are employed, then each of the one million receives as a wage an amount equal to the extra product that would have been contributed by the millionth labourer if he had been hired while capital, etc., had remained unchanged. Whatever the justice of the matter, it is not correct to say that each factor receives the value of *its own* contribution to production. Indeed, where many factors co-operate in production, it is generally impossible to divide up the *total production* into amounts contributed by each.

So much for crude misinterpretations. We must now consider more basic criticisms. It is often alleged that the theory does not explain factor allocation – and thus will not, for example, be able to predict the effect on factor allocation of the vast number of specific government interventions into factor markets. To make this general case, one of two things must be established: *either* the theory does not explain relative factor earnings, *or* factors do not move in response to relative earnings. Conversely, if the theory is to stand up to these criticisms, *both* of these allegations must be shown to be wrong. We shall consider them in turn.

Do market conditions determine factor earnings?

Factors other than labour

Most non-human factors are sold on competitive markets. The theory predicts that changes in the earnings of these factors will be associated with changes in market conditions. The overwhelming preponderance of evidence supports this. Consider some examples:

Raw materials A dramatic example was provided during the Korean conflict when a rapid increase in the demand for many strategic materials sent their prices soaring, to the extent that the incomes earned by their owners soared as well. The prices of copper, tin, rubber and hundreds of other materials fluctuate daily in response to changes in the demand and supply of these products. Current shortages of certain key raw materials are almost always signalled by price increases. Materials prices also show a strong cyclical component. They rise on the upswing of the trade cycle when their (derived) demand rises, and fall on the downswing when their (derived) demand falls.

> **There is little question that the theory of factor pricing in competitive markets provides a good explanation of raw material prices and of the incomes earned by their producers.**

Land values Values of land in the hearts of growing cities rise steadily in response to increasing demand. Often it is even worthwhile to destroy durable buildings and convert land to more productive uses. The New York and London skylines are monuments to the high value of urban land. The increase in the price of land on the periphery of every growing city is another visible example of the workings of the market.

Agricultural land appears at first glance to provide counter-evidence. The classical economists predicted 150 years ago that, as population and the demand for agricultural products grew, the price of the fixed supply of land would rise enormously. The price of agricultural land, however, has *not* skyrocketed. Although the demand for agricultural produce did expand in the predicted fashion because of the rise in population, the productivity of agricultural land has increased in quite unexpected ways with the invention of the vast range of machines and techniques that characterize modern agriculture. The prediction was falsified, not because the price of agricultural land is not determined by market forces, but because some of the market forces were incorrectly foreseen.

Taxis: an example Very different systems are used to regulate taxis in London and New York. The theory successfully predicts the consequences of these schemes.[1]

The supply of New York taxis is rigidly controlled by a licensing system, which

[1] Taxis are a factor of production to the taxi industry, which provides the services of door-to-door transportation in urban areas.

keeps the number of cabs well below what it would be in a free-market situation. The medallion, which confers the right to operate a cab, acquires a scarcity value (presently over $36,000). As the demand for taxi rides rises due to increases in population and average incomes, the price of medallions rises correspondingly, so that new entrants earn only the opportunity cost of capital on the money they invest in the medallion. If fares are increased and the demand proves to be inelastic so that gross income from operating a cab rises, the price of the medallion also rises correspondingly. The fare increase thus amounts to a free gift to the current holders of medallions; it does nothing to raise the net incomes of cab operators newly entering the industry.

Many North American cities other than New York use the medallion system, and observers are often surprised to discover that the relative price of medallions is not related to the size of cities. The theory of demand and supply correctly predicts that the price of a medallion in city A will be the present discounted value of the flow of profits that is created by the restrictions on the supply of taxi cabs. Thus the relative price of medallions among cities depends on the extent of supply restriction imposed. City size will influence demand, but the price of the medallion depends on the amount by which quantity supplied is reduced below quantity demanded at the going price of taxi rides.

In London, fares are rigidly regulated but entry is free to anyone who can pass a set of tests. Periodically fares are raised in an effort to raise incomes. If demand is inelastic incomes rise in the short run, but this attracts new entrants, who continue to come in until each existing cab is carrying just enough fares to cover its full opportunity cost, at which price profits have been reduced to zero. This case is in fact analytically identical to that of the barbers discussed on pages 299–301.

Labour

When we apply our theory to labour, we encounter two important sets of complications: first, labour markets are a mixture of competitive and non-competitive elements, the proportions of the mixture differing from market to market; second, labour being the human factor of production, non-monetary considerations loom large in its incentive patterns. These complications help to make labour economics one of the most difficult – and interesting – fields of economics. Monopolistic elements and non-monetary rewards, both of which are difficult to measure, require careful specification if the theory that labour earnings respond to market prices is to be made testable. Nevertheless, we do have a mass of evidence to go on. We do have cases in which a strong union – one able to bargain effectively and to restrict entry of labour into the field – has caused wages to rise well above the competitive level. Unions can and do succeed in raising wages and incomes when they operate in small sections of the whole economy; the high earnings do attract others to enter the occupation or industry; and the privileged position can be maintained only if entry can be effectively restricted. Closed-shop laws are the most obvious way of doing this.

Not only can monopoly elements raise incomes above their competitive levels, they can also prevent incomes from falling and reflecting decreases in demand. Of course, if demand disappears more or less overnight (as it did for silent-movie stars and carriage makers), there is nothing any union can do to maintain incomes. But the story may be different if, as is more usual, demand shrinks steadily over a few decades. In this case, unions *that are powerful enough virtually to prohibit new entry of labour into the industry* can often hold wages up in the face of declining demand. The industry's labour force thus declines, through death and retirement, in spite of the relatively high wage being paid to the employees who remain. This has occurred in US railways and coal mines.

Wages also respond to fluctuations in competitive conditions of demand and supply. Consider some examples. Competitive theory predicts that a decline in the demand for some product will cause a decline in the derived demand for the factors that make the product, a decline in their income, and the exit of factors to other uses. With the advent of the motor car, many skilled carriage makers found the demand for their services declining rapidly. Earnings fell, and many craftsmen who were forced to leave the industry found that they had been earning substantial rents for their scarce, but highly specific, skills. These men were forced to suffer large income cuts when they moved to other industries. Many silent-screen actors whose voices were unsuitable for the talkies suffered disastrous cuts in income and fell into oblivion when the demand for silent films disappeared. Much earlier, the same fate had met those music-hall stars whose talents did not project onto the flat, flickering screen of the early silent films. A similar but less dramatic fate hit many radio personalities who were unable to make the transition to television and had to compete in a greatly reduced market for radio talent. How soon will television entertainers, who have enormous incomes due to the high demand for their services, go the same way when a yet newer mass entertainment medium sweeps away the present one? When in a competitive, changing society you hear the bell toll for some once-wealthy and powerful group, always remember that someday it could easily be tolling for you!

These variations in factor earnings are caused by changes in market conditions, not by changes in our notions of the intrinsic merit of various activities. To illustrate, ask yourself why, if you have the talent, you can make a lot of money writing copy for a London advertising agency, whereas even if you have great talent you are unlikely to make a lot of money writing books of poetry. Not because any economic dictator or group of philosophers has decided that advertising is more valuable than poetry, but because in the British economy there is a large demand for advertising and only a tiny demand for poetry. A full citing of all such evidence would cover many pages, and it would point to the conclusion that:

> **Earnings of labour do respond to changes in market forces. Some factor markets are competitive and some are monopolistic, and the evidence seems to suggest that the theory of competitive and monopolistic market behaviour helps to explain factor incomes.**

Do factors move in response to changes in earnings?

In the previous section we saw that earnings do tend to change in response to the conditions of demand and supply. Changes in earnings are signals that attract resources into those lines of production in which more are needed and out of lines in which less are needed. But do changes in factor prices produce the supply responses predicted by the theory?

Land

In the case of land, there is strong evidence that the theory is able to predict the actual course of events quite accurately. Land is transferred from one crop to another in response to changes in the relative profitabilities of the crops. Recently in the US, for example, the price of meat was held down as part of an unsuccessful attempt to control inflation by a system of direct price controls. A shortage of meat quickly developed as farmers switched their land to more profitable lines of production. When the controls were removed prices rose in response to the shortage, and in response to the rise in prices output expanded as land was brought back into meat production. Countless similar examples of the effects of controlling some but not all prices (and hence of changing relative prices) have been documented.

Land on the edge of town is transferred from rural to urban uses as soon as it can earn substantially more as a building site than as a corn field. Although physically immobile, land is constantly transferred among its possible uses as the relative profitabilities of these uses change. Little more needs to be said here; the most casual observation will show the allocative system working with respect to land much as described by the theory.

Capital

The location of, and of products produced by, the nation's factories have changed greatly over the last two centuries. Over a period of, say, fifty years the change is dramatic; from one year to the next, it is small. Most plant and machinery is relatively specific. Once installed, it will be used to produce the commodity for whose output it was primarily designed, as long as the variable costs of production can be covered. But if full, long-run opportunity costs are not covered, the capital will not be replaced as it wears out. Investment will take place in other industries instead.

Long-run movements in the allocation of capital clearly occur in response to market signals.

The mechanism will work easily as long as there is freedom of entry and exit. Exit is difficult to prevent (other than by government legislation and subsidy), but monopolies and oligopolies, government regulations, and nationalized industries do erect barriers to entry. Profits in a monopolized industry where by definition entry is blocked do not induce flows of new investment, and they therefore serve no apparent long-run allocative function.

Although monopoly profits appear to play no role in long-run allocation, we are not certain that they have no function in the *very long run*. In Chapter 23 we saw that one eminent economist, Joseph Schumpeter, felt that they were the mainspring of capitalist economic growth in the very long run. He believed that monopolistic, and oligopolistic, profits help to cause the technological changes that have made living standards in market economies double every twenty or thirty years. Schumpeter saw monopoly profits as an inducement to people to innovate, and to run large risks knowing that the few who succeed will earn large profits. Furthermore, he saw innovation, the rise of new products and industries, and the accompanying destruction of apparently well-entrenched monopolies as a very-long-run process that makes the economy much more competitive and amenable to change than it appears to be when viewed at any particular moment in time. He felt that an unregulated free-market economy would protect its citizens through the process of creative destruction; he worried that nationalization of industries ostensibly to protect citizens would in the end hurt them by putting the whole enormous power of the state in the service of protecting established monopolies. This is an issue on which economists have insufficient evidence to give a final answer. It should serve, however, as yet another warning about the dangers of ignoring the very long run in which the main cause of changes in per capita output is changing technology.

Labour

Countless studies of labour mobility have been made, but they do not point to a simple answer to the question of how much labour moves in response to monetary incentives. On the one hand, it is clear that the great migration of Americans to the West Coast during World War II was induced by expanding employment opportunities and soaring wages in the shipyards and aircraft factories of California. On the other hand, why were the depressed areas of Wales not depopulated ten years ago when the coalmines began to shut down?

High relative wages do attract and hold labour in such unattractive parts of the world as the Canadian North, Siberia and the Amazon jungles, while occupations with much leisure and pleasant working conditions tend to pay much lower wages. There is a supply as well as a demand element at work here. Unpleasant but unskilled jobs are often poorly paid because anyone can do them, but even so, dustmen in the frozen Canadian North are paid more than dustmen in Montreal because otherwise they would not stay in the unattractive climate.

At the risk of grossly oversimplifying a complex situation, it may be said that the following hypotheses are consistent with the evidence.

(1) There exists a fairly mobile component of labour in any group. It tends to consist of the youngest, the most adaptable and often the most intelligent members of the group.

(2) This mobile group can be attracted from one area, occupation, or industry to another by relatively small changes in economic incentives.

(3) Provided that the pattern of demand for resources does not shift too fast, most of the necessary reallocation can be accomplished by movements of this mobile group. Of course, the same individual need not move over and over again. The group is constantly replaced by new entrants into the labour force.

(4) As we go beyond these very mobile persons, we get into ranges of lower and lower mobility until, at the very bottom, we find those who are completely immobile. The most immobile are the very old, those with capital sunk in nonmarketable assets, the timid, the weak and those who receive high rents in their present occupation or location. It is difficult for them to move; in extreme cases, even the threat of starvation may not be enough since some people believe, rightly or wrongly, that they will starve even if they do move.

Thus, shifts in earnings may create substantial inflows of workers into an expanding occupation, industry or area and an outflow of workers from a depressed occupation, industry or area. Over long periods of time, outflows have been observed from depressed areas such as Appalachia and parts of New England in the US, the Maritime Provinces of Canada, Sicily and Southern Italy, the Highlands of Scotland, declining areas of northeastern England and rural parts of central France. Although *some* out-migration occurs readily, it is difficult for large transfers to take place in short periods of time. When demand falls rapidly, pockets of poverty tend to develop. Labour has been leaving each of the geographical areas mentioned above, but poverty has increased too. The reason is that the rate of exit has been slower than the rate of decline of the economic opportunities in the area. Indeed, the exit itself causes further decline, for when a family migrates all the locally provided goods and services that it once consumed suffer a reduction in demand, leading to a further decline in the demand for labour.

Marginal productivity theory and the Macro-distribution of income

The theory of distribution discussed above concentrates on the pricing of factors in each of the many markets of the economy. The previous discussion has repeatedly shown that the theory does successfully predict the consequences for particular prices and quantities of changes that impinge on particular markets. (e.g., what will be the effects of holding down the salaries of headmasters of state schools at a time when all other wages and salaries are increasing?)

The concept of macro-distribution

We have referred several times to the functional distribution of income among such broad classes of factors as land, labour and capital. Can we say anything about what determines the distribution of income at this level of aggregation? What, for example, determines the share of total income going to labour as a class? What influences do unions and government policy have on this share? Questions of distribution at this level of aggregation are often referred to as questions about *macro-distribution* (as opposed to *micro-distribution*, which refers to such questions as what determines the share of total income going to headmasters of state schools). Table 25.1 on page 344, for example, shows some data for the macro-distribution of income: the share of national income going to all wage and salary earners (i.e., to labour as a factor of production).

Marginal analysis and macro-distribution

Questions of the macro-distribution of income between the great social classes of the society, labourers, landlords and capitalists, were of great concern to classical economists such as Ricardo, Malthus and Marx. With the development of marginal analysis in the last half of the nineteenth century emphasis shifted to the determination of factor prices and quantities in millions of individual markets. The theory that grew out of this development (often called marginal productivity theory after its demand half) offers few general predictions about the macro-distribution of income. It holds that to discover the effect of some change, say a tax or a new trade union, on the macro-distribution between wages, profits and rent, we would need to be able to discover what would happen in each individual market of the economy and then aggregate to find the macro-result. To do this we would need to know the degree of monopoly and monopsony in each market, we would need to be able to predict the effect on oligopolists' prices and outputs of changes in their costs, and we would need to have a theory of the outcome of collective bargaining in situations of bilateral monopoly (see page 375). We would also need to know how much factor substitution would occur in response to any resulting change in relative factor prices. Finally, we would need a general equilibrium theory linking all of these markets together (see Chapter 30). Clearly we are a long way from being able to do all this: with our present state of knowledge, marginal productivity theory provides few if any predictions about the effects on macro-distribution of such changes as shifts in total factor supplies, taxes on one factor, and the rise of trade unions.

This conclusion is not necessarily a criticism of the theory. It may well be that relative shares are determined by all the detailed interactions of all the markets in the economy, and that general predictions about the effects of various events on macro-distribution can be obtained only after we have enough knowledge to solve the general equilibrium problem outlined in the previous paragraph.

Many economists argue that we should not expect to get further than this. They hold that the great macro-questions on the scale of *labour versus capital* are largely unanswerable, and that, pedestrian though it may seem, the ability of the traditional theory to deal with micro-questions is a remarkable triumph. One reason advanced for the view that the great macro-distribution questions are unanswerable is that it only makes sense to talk about laws governing macro-distribution if labour, capital and land are each relatively homogeneous and each subject to a common set of influences not operating on the other two factors whereas, in fact, (so goes the view), there is likely to be as much difference between, say, two different types of labour as between one kind of labour and, one kind of machine. On the one hand, the micro-distribution of income can be thought of as subject to understandable influences because it deals with innumerable relatively homogeneous factors. On the other hand, macro-distribution is nothing more than the aggregate of the micro-distributions, and there is no more reason to expect that there should be simple laws governing the macro-distribution of income among land, labour and capital than to expect that there should be simple laws governing the macro-distribution between blondes and brunettes.[1]

Alternative theories of distribution

Many economists have been dissatisfied with the answer that there is no answer to the great question of macro-distribution. This dissatisfaction has lead to alternative theories which deal explicitly with macro-distribution problems.

Macro-marginal productivity theories An attempt that is in the tradition of marginal productivity theory is based on the postulated existence of a *macro-production*

[1] In case it is not obvious to the reader trying to guard against the author's biases, I am in general agreement with this view (although, like most other economists who believe that their subject can explain some of what we see in society, I should be overjoyed if someone did succeed in getting a workable theory of macro-distribution that stood up to some serious empirical tests).

function for the whole economy. Assume that total national output can be treated as a simple composite commodity that varies in amount according to the inputs of three homogeneous factors: labour, land and capital. This allows us to write a single production function for the economy as a whole:

$$Y = Y(L, N, K),$$

where Y stands for output and L, N and K for inputs of land, labour and capital respectively. If the total supply of each factor is fixed at any one time, and if the economy is usually at, or near, full employment of all factors, then the inputs of L, N and K are determined and so, through the production function, is Y.

Each factor of production will have a marginal product – the change in output that would occur if the quantity of the factor were varied slightly, the quantity of the other factors being held constant – and this will determine the price of the factor. The total payment going to the factor measured in real terms will be the quantity of the factor multiplied by its marginal product. The macro-distribution of income is thus determined by the nature of the production function (which determines marginal products) and the supplies of the three factors that are available in the economy.

Although aggregate production functions of this sort are commonly used in theoretical models, there is little evidence that they are good descriptions of the behaviour of total output over long periods of time or that they isolate important forces that determine the macro-distribution of income.[1]

The degree-of-monopoly and Keynesian theories A more radical departure from traditional theory was expounded by Michael Kalecki, who sought to explain labour's share in terms of the overall degree of monopoly in the economy. Mention should also be made of the many 'macro-theories' that followed from Keynes's general theory. Theories of this sort make use of the Keynesian aggregates that we shall not study until Part 7, so we will say no more about them here. We can observe, however, that, in spite of the obvious appeal of being able to relate distribution to only a few measurable variables, such theories have received no significant empirical support.

[1] The Cobb-Douglas production function was an early attempt to explain labour's share. In the two-factor version, real national output (Y) is determined in inputs of labour (N) and capital (K), according to the single macro-production function applying to the whole economy:

$$Y = AN^{\alpha}C^{1-\alpha},$$

where A and α are positive constants and α is also less than unity. The real wage of labour (w) is its real marginal product which those who know calculus will recognise as the partial derivative of Y with respect to N:

$$w = \frac{\partial Y}{\partial N} = \alpha A N^{\alpha-1}K^{1-\alpha}.$$

The total wage bill is

$$wN = \frac{\partial Y}{\partial N}.\ N = \alpha A N^{1-\alpha},$$

and the share of wages in the national product is

$$\frac{wN}{Y} = \frac{\alpha A N^{\alpha}C^{1-\alpha}}{AN^{\alpha}K^{1-\alpha}} = \alpha.$$

Thus the Cobb-Douglas national production function leads to the prediction that labour's share of the national product will be a constant, α, and will be independent of the size of the labour force.

The Cambridge School Finally, and perhaps most important in the list of dissenters from orthodox distribution theory, we should mention a group of radical dissenters at Cambridge University which includes such famous economists as Professors Joan Robinson, Pierro Sraffa and Nicholas Kaldor. The most outspoken member of the group has been Professor Robinson, who has written numerous influential attacks on orthodox distribution theory. She has for many years propounded the view that distribution theory went off on the wrong track with the late nineteenth-century development of marginal productivity theory. In her view we need to go back to the classical theories of Ricardo and Marx and develop them into satisfactory theories of macro-distribution. It is impossible to do justice to Professor Robinson's view, to say nothing of criticizing it in depth, within the confines of this book. Rather than present a capsule summary that would inevitably be a caricature, it is probably fairer to refer interested readers to Professor Robinson's own writings in which she attacks the traditional theory of distribution and propounds her own 'classical' alternative.[1] Two specific criticisms of capital theory that are made by the Cambridge School should be at least mentioned. These concern the concept of the quantity of capital and the so-called reswitching problem.

The Quantity of Capital: In the simple development of the theory of capital and interest in Chapter 28 we talked of changes in 'the' quantity of capital and invoked the 'law' of diminishing returns to predict that the marginal efficiency of capital would decline as the stock of capital grew.

But society's stock of capital is in fact a very heterogeneous collection of tools, factories, equipment, etc. How can we speak of 'the' stock of capital? How can we reduce this heterogeneous collection of capital goods to a single number so that we can say that the capital stock is increasing or decreasing?

The obvious way is to use a price. If we take the price of capital we can value all these diverse physical things and obtain the total value of the economy's capital stock. But if we then use this quantity of capital in combination with the *MEC* schedule to determine the price of capital (i.e., the pure return on capital which in equilibrium is equal to the pure rate of interest) we may be involved in circular reasoning: if we wish to use 'the' quantity of capital in conjunction with 'the' production function *to determine the price of capital* (and hence the share of total income going to the owners of capital) we cannot use the price of capital to determine the quantity of capital.

For over a decade a debate has raged over the possibility of calculating a single measure of the quantity of capital that could, without circularity, be placed into a macro-production function to determine the price of capital. The outcome of the

[1] See, in particular, Joan Robinson and John Eatwell, *An Introduction to Modern Economics* (McGraw-Hill, 1973). Cambridge critics are often unwilling to give any points at all to the 'marginal productivity theory'. It seems to me, however, that when new theories replace old ones they should save what is valid in the old theories as well as discard what is invalid. Traditional theory is very successful in explaining micro-distribution problems. If it were to be supplanted by new theories, it would be a serious blunder to throw away the baby of successful micro-applications along with the admittedly dirty bath water of unsuccessful macro-applications. Furthermore, it is not clear to me how Cambridge-style classical distribution theories can even be brought to bear on the sort of micro-distribution problems outlined earlier in this chapter. It seems only fair to add that I think Professor Robinson's 'classical alternative' says very little of a positive nature about the economy. Thus I do not so much think it is wrong but rather nearly empty of positive content.

debate appears to be that this cannot be done.[1] For the economist who wishes to combine marginal productivity theory with a macro-production function in order to deal with the macro-distribution of income, this is a serious matter. To the economist who accepts only the traditional micro-theory of distribution it is not so upsetting. Such an economist believes that there are thousands of distinct factors, which it may sometimes be convenient to group into such broad classes as land, labour and capital, but which get separately priced and which are more or less substitutable for each other. In this view there is no particular reason to believe that labour as a whole will be subject to one set of influences, land as a whole to another distinct set and capital as a whole to yet a third distinct set. Thus the inability to measure *the* quantity of capital (and *the* quantities of labour and land) is not a particularly serious matter.

Reswitching: A second controversy concerning capital theory revolves around the 'reswitching debate' that arose out of Professor Sraffa's famous book *Production of Commodities by Means of Commodities*[2]. This debate is too technical to be discussed here, but its burden is the view by the Cambridge School that a smoothly declining *MEC* schedule cannot necessarily be derived. Once again this appears to be correct. The possibility of other situations has been established by numerical illustrations. The empirical relevance of the possibilities raised by the Cambridge School remains to be demonstrated.[3]

Conclusion

For the traditional theorist there are at least two distinct issues: 'Does a demand-and-supply model of factor pricing shed any light on micro-distribution problems? and 'Does marginal productivity theory adequately explain the demand for factors of production, particularly the demand for capital?' Some traditional theorists would answer 'yes' to both questions. Other economists would say that the answer to the second question may be 'no', particularly in respect to capital, but that the answer to the first question is surely 'yes'. They would hold that the questions of macro-distribution theory are not really interesting, whereas questions of micro-distribution concerning both functional shares among many factors and the size distribution among households are important and relevant to most government policies that attempt to change the distribution of income.

[1] It is worth noting at this point that the same problems exist with land and labour. The society's stock of land is a heterogeneous collection of good, bad and indifferent land, some suited for some crops and some for others. The society's stock of labour is a heterogeneous collection of human beings no two of whom are the same: if identical quantities of other factors are combined first with individual *A* and then with individual *B*, very different quantities of output may result. To talk about 'the' quantity of labour and 'the' quantity of land is just as heroic an oversimplification as to talk about 'the' quantity of capital. Furthermore, just as with capital, to obtain 'the' quantities of labour and land by aggregating their values (i.e., multiplying each kind of labour by its price and then aggregating, and similarly for land), and then to use these aggregate quantities to determine the prices of land and labour is to engage in circular reasoning.

[2] (Cambridge University Press, 1975).

[3] An excellent summary and critique of the Cambridge School from the standpoint of orthodox theory is given by M. Blaug. *The Cambridge Revolution: Success or Failure?*, Hobart Paperback No. 6 (Institute of Economic Affairs, 1975).

Part six

The economy as a whole

30

Successes and failures of the price system

An unkind critic of economics once said that economists have two great insights: *markets work* and *markets fail*. An unkind critic of politics once added that economics was thus a step ahead of both the political left and the political right, each of which accepts only one of these insights. Indeed economists try to take the critical step of showing when each of the insights applies and why. In this chapter we shall consider the questions of when and why markets do and do not work. Then in Chapter 31 we shall go on to consider government intervention in the working of the economy.

The interrelationship of markets

The nation's economy consists of thousands upon thousands of individual markets. There are markets for agricultural goods, for manufactured goods and for all types of consumers' services; there are markets for semi-manufactured goods, such as steel and pig iron, which are outputs of some industries and inputs of others; there are markets for raw materials such as iron ore, trees, bauxite and copper; there are markets for land, and for thousands of different types of labour; there are markets for the lending of new capital and for the transfer of existing loans. So far we have studied these markets more or less in isolation. Only in the case of factors of production have we stressed the interrelation of markets through the idea of the *derived demand for a factor*. In reality, the interrelation of markets is the rule.

> **An economy should not be viewed as a series of markets functioning in isolation, but as an interlocking system in which anything happening in one market will greatly affect many others. What goes on in the markets of an economy is co-ordinated by the price system. Changes in surpluses and scarcities are reflected in price and quantity changes that signal to decision takers what is happening throughout the economy.**

As an example of the way in which markets affect each other, consider the motorcar industry. Assume that there is a rise in demand for cars. This will be met fairly soon with a rise in output, which will be achieved by working existing plant and equipment harder through overtime and other expedients. If the rise in demand is considerable, and judged to be permanent, there will also be a planned increase in capacity in the car industry. Employment will rise and labour may be lured from other industries by the offer of higher wages. Thus one of the first impacts on other industries will be a need for them to raise wages in order to compete with the car industry for labour. This may cause profits to fall in these other industries. The increased employment opportunities in the car industry may cause some workers to move to Dagenham, and that may occasion a rise in the demand for housing there, and a corresponding fall in demand elsewhere. The new housing construction will lead to a rise in the demand for construction workers and materials. Quarries and brickworks will have to take on additional labour and expand output. There will also be a rise in the demand for banking services, cinemas, haircuts and the thousands of other goods and services that households want to consume. Furthermore, there will be a rise in the demand for raw materials used in car construction, and the effects of this may be felt in such diverse places as the glass-making areas of the Midlands, the steel-manufacturing sections of Wales and the rubber plantations of Malaysia. New investment in plant and equipment in the car industry will bring about a rise in the demand for many capital goods; shortages and bottlenecks may develop; other industries that use these materials may experience increases in their costs and trouble in meeting delivery dates. There will also be a change in consumers' expenditures because some people's earnings will be increased and other people's reduced. Thus the effect of one change, a rise in the demand for cars, will be felt throughout the entire economy.

The price system allows the adaptations to the initial shift to take place without being consciously co-ordinated by anyone. When shortages develop, prices rise and/or inventories fall so that profit-seeking entrepreneurs are led to produce more of the commodity that is in short supply. When surpluses occur, prices fall and/or inventories build up so that supply is voluntarily contracted.

> **The price system produces a series of signals which cause a large number of different decision-making units (firms) automatically to co-ordinate their efforts. How well they co-ordinate them depends on how well prices reflect current and future scarcities and surpluses, and on how fast and effectively firms respond to the changing price signals.**

Feedback

Not only will a change in one market affect many other markets of the economy, but the changes in these other markets may in turn affect (we say 'feedback' onto) the original market.

The example above showed that a decision to expand capacity in the car industry would have repercussions throughout the economy. To predict the precise effects of the feedback onto the car industry is very difficult. There is no doubt that the regional pattern of car sales would be affected. Sales would rise in the car-producing areas as workers migrated there, and would fall in areas from which they came. It is also possible that an overall national increase in car sales could occur if the increase in employment in the car industry brought more workers into the income range at which they would be able to buy a new car rather than a second-hand one.

Where feedback is significant, it is difficult to use the sort of economic analysis that we have relied on completely up to this point, and which is called *partial equilibrium analysis*. We have already distinguished in Chapter 11 between equilibrium (static) analysis and disequilibrium (dynamic) analysis; we must now distinguish between partial and general equilibrium analysis.

Partial equilibrium analysis

The distinguishing features of partial and general equilibrium are illustrated in Figure 30.1. We start by considering some *sector* of the economy called A in the figure – the market for cabbages, for carpenters or for cars. If there is some change

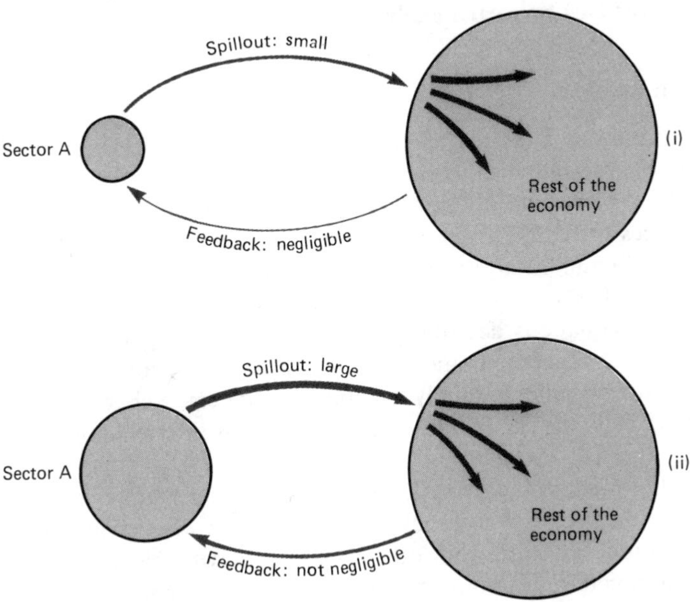

Fig. 30.1 (i) Partial equilibrium analysis is possible (ii) General equilibrium analysis is necessary

in, say, the cabbage market, it will cause changes in the rest of the economy. These effects may be called the 'spillout' from the initiating market onto the rest of the economy. The induced changes in the rest of the economy will, in turn, reflect back on the cabbage market, causing further changes there. Let us assume, for example, that the initial change is a fall in the supply of cabbages. This will cause an increase in their price and a fall in the quantity bought. The rise in the price of cabbages will cause other demands to change; in general, we would expect to find increases in the demands for goods that are close substitutes for cabbages and decreases in the demands for goods that are complementary with cabbages. As a result, the prices of these other goods will change. The original demand curve for cabbages that we used to derive our prediction was based on the assumption that all other prices were given. Now that the prices of substitutes for cabbages have risen because of increased demand, there will be a *shift* in the original demand curve for cabbages. This is the reflection onto the original sector of the induced changes in the rest of the economy. *It is a basic assumption of partial equilibrium analysis that such effects are small enough to be ignored.*

Partial equilibrium analysis is based on the *ceteris paribus* assumption that all other things in the economy are unaffected by any changes in the sector under consideration. This assumption is always violated to some extent, because anything that happens in one sector will cause changes in some others. That does not matter, as long as those changes are sufficiently small and diffuse that the feedback effect they have on sector *A* can safely be ignored.

There is no simple rule telling us when partial analysis can safely be employed. The final test is whether or not its predictions are refuted by the facts. As a first approximation, it is probably safe to say that the smaller the sector under consideration, the more likely its behaviour can successfully be predicted by partial analysis.

General equilibrium analysis

General equilibrium analysis attempts to deal explicitly with interrelationships between sectors. The microeconomic theories of Parts 1 to 5 are all partial theories (interrelations are dealt with, but only in an impressionistic, intuitive way). The macroeconomic theories of Parts 7 and 8 are of the general equilibrium type.

The father of general equilibrium analysis was the nineteenth-century French economist Leon Walras. It was his great insight to conceive of the economy as a system of simultaneous equations describing the demands and supplies of each commodity. The prices of all commodities occurred in each equation so that a change in any one of the demand or supply equations would cause changes in all prices and quantities. Thus the model illustrated the general interrelation of all markets.

Today a great deal of modern theory makes use of general equilibrium models. Pure theorists concern themselves with problems such as under what conditions a unique general equilibrium can exist, while others, concerned with a wide range of problems from international trade to monetary theory, find it necessary to analyse their problems within general equilibrium models. The actual practice of general equilibrium theory requires mathematical tools, so we must confine ourselves in this text to the intuitive discussion above.

Market successes

We have already observed that markets co-ordinate independent decisions by providing public signals to which producers react. Markets also give signals to consumers that allow them to respond to relative scarcities in the economy.

The housing market: an example

Say, for example, that every family in the Greater London area decides that it wants its own house with garden. This would be physically impossible because there is not nearly enough land in all of the Home Counties surrounding London to house its population at the low density consistent with single-family dwellings. If the entire populace tried to move to such dwellings, they would, on the one hand, vastly bid up the price of land and the price of existing housing, while, on the other hand, causing the rent of flats to plummet. Reacting to these signals, many people would decide that, although they preferred to live in single-family dwellings at the original prices, they preferred to live in multi-family units at the now relatively cheap rents. With a price system, no central administrator has to calculate scarcities and decide what proportion of the population must live in multi-family dwellings. Furthermore, no one has to have the unenviable task of saying who is allowed to live in each type of dwelling. If there is excess demand for one type and excess supply of the other, their relative prices will change. As this happens, some people will switch from demanding the type that is becoming more expensive to demanding the type that is now relatively cheaper. Once the excess demand and supply are eliminated, the relative prices of the two will be in equilibrium. If there is a change in tastes with respect to the two types of accommodation, their relative prices will change once again, and this will lead to an adjustment on both the demand and the supply sides of the market.

The significance of having prices related to costs

The advantage in allowing consumers to respond to relative prices is greatest if relative prices reflect relative costs of production. This is not always the case. In many Western countries, for example, various government policies hold the price of fuel oil for central heating well below its real cost. People building new houses and blocks of flats then calculate that it is cheaper to save on the high costs of insulation and accept burning more low-price oil as a result.[1] If the price of oil were not subsidized, these same decision-takers would find it financially advantageous to spend more on insulation and save on oil. If maintaining a given house temperature through more insulation requires fewer of the nation's resources than maintaining that temperature by burning more oil, then it is a waste of resources to encourage consumers to do otherwise.

> **Having relative prices reflect relative costs is efficient in that it encourages consumers to choose the alternative that uses fewer of the nation's resources. Producing any output with the fewest possible of a nation's scarce resources clearly raises average living standards because it allows the most output to be produced.**

The price of energy: a second example

The price system provides adjustments to myriad small and gradual changes that go on all of the time. It also can provide dramatic adjustments to large and abrupt changes that impinge on the economy. For example, in 1974 OPEC (the Organization of Petroleum Exporting Countries) took action that caused the real price of oil paid by oil importing countries to rise by nearly 30 per cent. If their domestic market prices of petroleum products had risen to reflect fully the cost increase without any further government intervention, some dramatic changes would have occurred. On the demand side, consumers would have made some drastic readjustments in their consumption pattern: firms would have switched to alternative sources of power, and households would have cut down on oil consumption by a series of measures ranging from insulating homes to buying cars with lower fuel-consumption ratings. On the supply side, as prices rose with unchanged

[1] This particular decision to provide heat through more oil burned or more insulation provided is, as we shall see, complicated in the UK by further forms of government intervention.

costs oil companies would have made massive profits from oil produced in such non-OPEC areas as the North Sea, Alaska and Alberta. These profits would have provided incentives to search for further conventional petroleum supplies, and to develop technologies to tap such alternative sources as the Alberta tar sands in Canada. The profits would also have set up a process of Schumpeterian creative destruction (see pp. 311–15) as everyone from large international corporations to back-yard inventors scrambled to collect a share of the profits. Alternative sources of energy would have been rapidly developed. Solar heating, which, for example, is being perfected slowly at today's low domestic oil prices, would have been developed with greater speed in many competing forms. (Dozens of technologies for solar heating have already been invented by individuals working in garden sheds and small firms.) Devices to economize on petrol and oil would have been invented and marketed in profusion. On all sides, the signals of the price system would have been effectively urging: 'Cut down on your use of petroleum products in equipment that now uses it, switch to alternative energy sources that are now available, find more petroleum, invent new petroleum-economizing devices, and invent new technologies that use alternative energy sources.'

As it was, this market adjustment mechanism was at least partially frustrated when most Western governments were unwilling to allow the giant oil firms the windfall profits they would have earned if prices had risen to the world level. Instead, they used complicated systems of taxes, subsidies and exchange-rate interventions. These ensured that while the OPEC countries were paid the full price of oil, prices in their domestic market did not rise to the full extent of the increase in world prices and the profits that would have resulted from the price rises that did occur were taxed away. Thus in a typical country domestic prices might have risen by only 50 per cent of the world price rise and 80 per cent of the profits resulting from the price rise that did occur might have been taxed away.

Thus although the real resource cost of the petroleum rose, consumers were not presented with domestic prices that fully reflected this. They paid the full extra cost, but in terms of taxes used to subsidize the price of oil for domestic use. Being unaware of this extra cost, consumers did not have the full incentive to economize on oil. Because profits in domestic markets were low, firms in the non-OPEC countries had no added incentive to discover new oil or to invent oil-substitutes. In the short term, governments then tried to do the job of the price system through such means as the UK legislation granting either £50 or the cost of materials for insulating a roof (whichever was lower), the US legislation that cars must have much higher miles-per-gallon ratings in the 1980s than they did in the 1970s and by subsidizing research into alternative energy sources. In the meantime, however, firms and households were making decisions on new capital and new housing that used oil in ways that made sense at the subsidized market prices of oil but were wasteful at the real world price. Slowly most Western countries allowed their domestic market prices to rise towards the world price. On present plans these two prices may be equated by sometime in the mid-1980s. This will allow the price mechanism eventually to operate in the ways described. In the meantime there is a chronic energy crisis in most of these countries – one which, for example, has caused the oil-importing countries much trouble, since petroleum imports continued unabated as long as consumers faced prices substantially below world prices.

The reasons why many governments adopted this policy with respect to oil rested on alleged undesirable side effects, and will be discussed in the next chapter. Here our concern is only to show that the adjustment could have been much more rapid and effective had the price system been allowed to do the job.

The impersonality of the market mechanism This example also illustrates the impersonality of the market in a rather dramatic way. When the government elected to hold prices down, but to subsidize research, they had to decide whom to subsidize. Government funds are scarce, and inevitably they will go to known persons and firms, not to unknown people operating – as did so many great inventors in their early work – out of their converted garden sheds. Government subsidization forces a decision by bureaucrats from among competing claimants, and tends to support existing large companies at the expense of unknown upstarts. If the price system had been used, the high price and profits would have provided a public signal and incentive. Anyone with an idea and a source of funds could 'have a go'. Furthermore, people would have risked their own money, not that of the taxpayers'. Inevitably, most of the upstarts would have lost their money, but a few would have succeeded and provided new products that reduced real energy costs. The successful few would have earned large profits, allowing their firms to grow and challenge existing firms. Copiers would then have arrived, and eventually profits in energy industries would have been forced down.

Self-fulfilling prophecies of market failure Here we have an example of the self-fulfilling nature of prophecies that the price system cannot work. Many governments, including that of the US, said in effect that the economy is dominated by large firms that must be prevented from earning large short-term profits. Those governments then took steps that effectively prevented a fluid situation out of which would have flowed new small, but growing, firms to challenge existing large firms in countless fields from heating to fertilizer to automobile engines.

The general case for the market

Leaving aside the particular example above, let us turn to the general case for the free market. The major argument is that it provides a reasonably efficient and impersonal method of regulating the ever-changing pattern of the allocation of resources. The great value of the market is in providing automatic signals *as a situation develops*, so that all of the changes consequent on, say, building a new car plant do not have to be anticipated and allowed for by a body of central planners. Millions of adaptations to millions of changes in tens of thousands of markets are required every year; and it would be a Herculean task to anticipate these and plan for them all. Should we produce yellow hats or green hats or both, and if both, in what proportion? Such matters, so goes the argument, do not need to be decided centrally; they are best left to the market. The experience of planned economies such as those in the Soviet block is that it is very difficult and very expensive (in terms of scarce manpower) to try to plan centrally *everything* about the economy. This becomes particularly so as per capita output rises and an increasing variety of consumers' goods is produced. The observable trend in these centrally planned countries is to keep the most important decisions, such as those about the division of resources between the production of capital goods and consumers' goods, in the hands of the central authorities, but to try to decentralize such decisions as how many resources should be devoted to the production of yellow and green hats respectively.

> **If decisions regarding resource allocation are to be decentralized, then (i) some form of market signals must exist, and (ii) there must be some incentive for firms and the owners of factors of production to react appropriately to these signals.**

The effects of alternative allocation schemes We have seen that allocation by the market tends to be more impersonal than allocation by many other methods. We have also observed earlier that the control of prices at non-equilibrium values without rationing tends to create allocation by sellers' preferences (see pages 119–20). If the market is determining prices, the tobacconist will sell cigarettes to anyone who enters his shop. If the price of cigarettes is well below the equilibrium value, the tobacconist will be unable to satisfy everyone who comes into his shop, and will be forced to decide whom he is going to satisfy. He might work on the first-come-first-served principle, or he might serve people whose colour, manner, dress or sex he liked and refuse others.

Furthermore, the incentive for bribery and corruption is clearly present in situations of excess demand. If, for example, state housing is available at prices well below the market price, there will be a queue to get into the flats that do become available. The official who controls the allocations from the waiting list will be in a position of power and might take a bribe for moving someone's name up in the queue. Even if he doesn't take bribes, he can allocate by his own preference, pushing one family up in the queue and holding another back for whatever reasons he may have. If the state charged the market price for its housing, this opportunity for allocation by administrator's preferences, or by downright corruption, would be removed because, temporary and unforeseen fluctuations aside, everyone who was prepared to pay the price could obtain accommodation.

> **In all cases in which the government holds price below equilibrium, creating excess demand, alternative allocation systems *must* be found. The queue is the one most commonly used, but the incentive for corruption is always present and there can be no doubt that people often succumb to it.**

Allegations that bribes can be effective in getting to the top of the queue for such diverse things as medical services in Italy, telephones in Britain and licences to import in India are as commonly heard as they are difficult to substantiate and quantify.

The advantage of having prices reflect costs Finally, as long as relative prices approximately reflect relative costs, market choices are made in the light of social opportunity costs. The resulting choices will tend to maximize the total output of the society, and hence the average standard of living of its citizens. Firms will not choose methods that use more resources over methods that use less, and households will not choose commodities that use more resources to produce over commodities that use less, unless they value them correspondingly more at the margin.

Market failures

We may now consider a number of major reasons for government intervention into the working of free markets. No list can be exhaustive, of course, but many of the major considerations are discussed below.

Divergencies between private and social costs

When a firm is calculating the profitability of alternative production plans, it must estimate its cost and revenue. The opportunity cost of producing a given output will normally be determined by the market prices of the factor services it uses. If these market prices adequately reflect the factor's alternative uses from the whole society's point of view, then the firm's decisions will be based on a consideration of the social value of the alternative uses of these resources. There are many reasons why this is not always so, and this leads us to distinguish the concepts of private cost and social cost.

PRIVATE COST measures the opportunity cost to the firm of the resources that it uses. This opportunity cost is based on the alternatives that are available to the firm. If a firm uses a resource for which it has no alternative use, then the private cost is zero. Private cost is usually based on the market value of the factors currently purchased by the firm and the price that could be obtained by selling to outsiders the services of factors owned by the firm.

SOCIAL COST measures the opportunity cost to the whole society of the resources that the firm uses. This opportunity cost is based on the alternatives that are available to the whole society. If a firm uses resources for which the society has alternative uses, then the social cost of these resources is their value in their best alternative use.

> **The social value of resources in alternative uses is measured by social costs; the value to the firm is measured by private costs. If the two diverge, the firm's choices will not reflect the interests of the society as a whole. Divergences between private and social cost are one of the most important reasons for intervening in free markets.**

Some examples We shall now study a number of illustrative examples of the divergence between private and social cost, and shall consider the social consequences of having decisions based on private costs as seen by producing firms. Note that many of these examples come under the general heading of *pollution.*

(1) A factory discharges its waste into a river. The resulting pollution destroys fish living downstream, and forces several communities to install costly water-purification plants. The private cost to the firm of using the river as a waste disposal unit is zero, since the firm has no alternative use for the river, and it pays no price for the convenience. The social cost consists of the fish that are destroyed and the resources used in the purification plants. The social cost of using the river to dispose of waste may well be greatly in excess of the social cost of having the factory's waste disposed of in a chemical treatment plant. Yet there will be no incentive for the private firm to adopt what is socially the least costly method, since the private costs of the two alternative methods do not reflect the social costs.

(2) An industrial complex discharges smoke into the atmosphere. Although the private cost is zero, the social cost when this is done on a large scale is prodigious.

Over the last hundred and fifty years very large amounts of industrial waste have been disposed of into the atmosphere. The cost shows up in a great many ways: higher laundry and cleaning bills, the periodic sandblasting of grime-encrusted buildings, smog blankets which often slow and sometimes even halt all of a city's business, chronic diseases caused by air pollution, and a general shortening of life expectancy.

(3) An off-shore oil well disposes of its waste oil by dumping it into the sea. The private cost is virtually zero. The social cost is very high, and is measured in such terms as ruined beaches, fish and birds destroyed, and tourist industries damaged.

(4) An oil company proposes to send tankers through the waters of the Arctic Ocean. Assume that the risks are such that approximately one voyage every ten years will end in disaster. The private cost of taking this risk is the small insurance premium necessary to insure against it. The oil firm will be led to use this route if all costs including the insurance premium are less than the value of the oil shipped. The social cost is measured in terms of both the possibly irreversible damage to the fragile Arctic environment and all of the (government financed) resources that will be used to cope, in so far as one can cope, with the resulting pollution.

(5) A private timber firm cuts a forest and thereby destroys a natural watershed bringing drought and destruction on neighbouring farms. The social cost exceeds the private cost by all the forgone agricultural output plus the resources subsequently used to provide a stable water supply to the farms.

(6) The choice among alternative transport systems is usually made after comparisons of private costs. For instance, in deciding whether to ship its goods by rail or by road, a firm will consider, among other things, the price of each. These prices will in turn be related to the private costs to the railroad and the road haulage firm of moving the goods. It is sometimes argued that the social costs of transporting freight by road greatly exceed the private costs. People who hold this view argue that the cost of building and maintaining roads would be greatly reduced if they did not have to be strong enough to sustain the pounding of heavy lorries and that road congestion, which is aggravated by lorry traffic, imposes heavy costs on other users, particularly where a route goes through a town. It is then argued that the taxes paid by transport firms do not come close to covering these extra costs that road transport imposes on society. A classic case of the failure of the unhindered price system would occur *if* the cost situation for freight transport were as follows:

ROAD HAULAGE	RAIL HAULAGE
private cost $<$ revenue	private cost $>$ revenue
social cost $>$ revenue	social cost $<$ revenue

If this were the case, the free market would divert traffic onto the roads, although from society's point of view the margin of advantage lies with rail traffic.

Market imperfections

A second major source of market failure is market imperfections. If actual markets always behave as do markets in the theory of perfect competition, the economic system would behave perfectly. Unfortunately, actual behaviour is often far from what would occur under perfect competition.

Imperfections affecting factor behaviour If factors are relatively immobile, the supply will tend to be inelastic in the short run, and even large increases in the price offered may induce only small factor movements. Unions can also put up substantial barriers to the movement of labour. For example, they can limit membership and simultaneously insist on closed shops.

Markets may also be poor allocators of labour among possible uses if labour is ignorant of the signals being provided by the market. Signals do not work if they are not received. Before dismissing this imperfection as trivial, ask yourself if you have any clear idea of the expected lifetime income of a person following the subject of study you have chosen and that of persons following the subject your friends have chosen. Also, do you know enough to be able to compare the lifetime earnings of the few people who are unusually successful with the earnings of those who have only average success in each of the occupations?

Imperfections affecting firm behaviour Profit maximization in a world of perfect competition makes firms into passive adjusters who follow market signals without exerting any personal pressure on the outcome. When we depart from perfect competition and/or profit-maximizing behaviour, firms achieve the power to interfere with the behaviour of the market. Profit-maximizing monopoly presents one pure case. Monopoly power prevents resources from moving in response to market signals. A rise in demand for a monopolist's product will cause a rise in the monopolist's profits. In a perfectly competitive industry this would lead to an increase in resources allocated to the production of this good until profits fell to zero, but if the monopolist can restrict entry into his industry, no such resource reallocation will occur except as the monopolist finds it profitable to increase his own output.

If the firm is not concerned with profit maximization, the market mechanism may not work as well as described by our theory. A rise in demand will not even necessarily be met by a rise in output of the existing monopolist if he is not a profit maximizer.

Imperfections affecting consumer behaviour Economists usually do not pass judgement on the tastes of consumers. A market system is said to work if it responds to consumers' tastes whatever the nature of the tastes. But the market will not work effectively if consumers are misinformed about the products they buy. Lack of correct information can be an important cause of market failure.

Collective consumption goods

Certain goods or services, if they provide benefits to anyone, necessarily provide them to a large group of people. Such goods are called COLLECTIVE CONSUMPTION GOODS OR PUBLIC GOODS. National defence is a prime example. If we have an adequate defence establishment, it protects us all. It protects you, even if you do not care to 'buy' any of it. The quantity of national defence to be provided must be decided collectively, and there is no market where you can buy more or less of it than your neighbour.

There are many other examples. The beautification of a city provides a service to all residents and visitors. A barrage that protects a city from a flood is also a collective consumption good, as is a storm-warning system. Another important example is police protection. If a police force reduces the number of crimes, everyone gains. In a market system, even if you did not pay to have the police watch your house, you would gain from the fact that your neighbour did.

In general, market systems cannot compel payment for a public good, since there is no way to prevent a person from receiving the services of the good if he refuses to pay for it. Only governments, through their power to tax, can compel payments by all. Indeed, it is the existence of collective consumption goods that necessitates putting some of our production into government hands and prevents the government from selling everything it produces on the free market just as any other firm does (and as the government does with postal services but does not, and cannot, do with military and police services).

The costs of collecting revenue

A good that is not a collective consumption good will still not be produced privately if the cost of collecting revenue from individual consumers is prohibitive. Here it is not the nature of the good but the absence of a low-cost, private mechanism to collect revenue that leads to market failure.

Consider an example. Suppose motorists in a metropolitan area are willing to pay to have a high-speed urban motorway system leading into and out of town. Suppose that there are enough people willing to pay 6 pence a mile to cover the costs of building such a road system, but that different groups of them want to use different sections of the system. A private company would find it profitable to build and operate the road if it could collect 6 pence a mile from everybody willing to pay that much. But if it must build a toll house at every entrance and exit to the road in order to collect this money, the costs of the system would be increased and the venture might seem an unprofitable one. Intra-urban motorways with many access points and many short-journey travellers are often unsuitable for private ventures, because the cost of collecting tolls is too high. It is no accident that in countries where privately built toll roads are common, virtually all toll roads are *inter-urban* roads which require relatively few access points and where the average journey is a long one.

The neglect of non-market goals

Exclusive reliance on markets, even if they perform efficiently with respect to allocation of resources among competing uses, may lead to the neglect of other goals that seem important to members of society. Individuals who value these other goals will consider their neglect by the market system as a case of market failure. Consider four examples.

The protection of the individual from the actions of others In economics the household is assumed to be the basic decision-taking unit. We must not forget that most households contain several persons and that the process of making a choice within the household is a political one. Whose desires are to be favoured and by how much in taking the purchasing decisions for the household? One example should suffice to show how important this point is. In an unhindered free market the adult members of the household will take decisions about how much education to buy, and thereby exert a profound effect on the lives of their children. A selfish parent may buy no education, while an egalitarian one may buy the same quantity for all his children. The central authorities may interfere in this choice both to protect the child and to ensure that some of the scarce educational resources are unequally distributed according to intelligence rather than wealth. Most governments force all households to educate their children and we provide strong inducements, through student grants, for the more able to consume much more education than either they or their parents might have voluntarily selected if they had to pay the whole cost themselves. The latter is done probably because of a divergence between social and private costs, but the former is done in the belief that the head of the household should not have perfect freedom to take decisions that affect the welfare of other members of the household, particularly when they are minors.

The protection of the individual from his or her own actions In the case of education, society interferes to protect children from possibly deleterious decisions taken on their behalf by others. In other cases the state seeks to protect individuals against themselves. Laws prohibiting opium and other hard drugs and laws prescribing the wearing of seat belts in motor cars protect individuals against their own ignorance or shortsightedness. Arguments for and against such policies go well beyond economics. Advocates of such laws say, for example, that this is one way of educating people about what is in their own best interests. Opponents often argue that it is a basic tenet of a free society that the individual must be assumed to be the best judge of his or her own interests and that the individual's right to do what he or she thinks best, even to take what may seem to others to be reckless risks of life and limb, should be interfered with only if the behaviour has serious adverse effects on others.[1]

Intervention by the government to protect the individual from himself or herself is called PATERNALISM. There is no question that much actual intervention into the market has paternalistic motives: the central authorities feel they know better than the individual citizen what is in that citizen's own best interest. There is great debate about the pros and cons of paternalistic intervention and the debate will be considered further in the next chapter.

The existence of social obligations In a market system, if you can pay for something, you can have it. If you have to clean your house and if you can persuade someone else to do the job for you in return for £5, presumably both parties to the transaction are better off: you would prefer to part with £5 rather than clean the house yourself and your cleaner prefers £5 to not cleaning your house. Normally we do not interfere with people's ability to negotiate such mutually advantageous contracts.

Most people do not feel this way, however, about activities which are regarded as social obligations. A prime example is military service. At times and places in which military service is compulsory, contracts similar to the one between the housewife and her cleaner could also be struck. Some persons faced with the obligation to do military service could no doubt pay enough to persuade others to do their turn of service for them. By exactly the same argument as we used above, we can presume that both parties will be better off if they are allowed to negotiate such a trade. But

[1] There are many other arguments. Advocates of seat belts and other compulsory road safety regulations claim that disabled survivors of 'unnecessary' accidents may become public charges and that this gives the state a right to prevent such injuries from occurring. Opponents reply that this slim possibility is not enough to justify governmental interference with individual freedom.

such contracts are usually prohibited. Why? Because there are values other than those that can be expressed in a market. In times when it is necessary, military service by all healthy males is usually held to be an obligation independent of their tastes, wealth, influence or social position. It is felt that everyone *ought* to do this service, and trades between willing traders are prohibited.

Compassion A free-market system rewards certain groups and penalizes others. The workings of the market may be stern, even cruel; consequently, it may seem humane to intervene. Should unproductive farmers be starved off the farm? Should men be forced to bear the full burden of their misfortune if, through no fault of their own, they lose their jobs? Indeed, even if they lose their jobs through their own fault, should they and their families have to bear the whole burden, which may include starvation? Should the ill and aged be thrown on the mercy of their families? What if they have no families? Should small businessmen have to compete with chain stores and discount houses? A great many government policies are concerned with modifying the distribution of income that results from such things as where one starts, how able one is, how lucky one is and how one fares in the free-market world.

The optimal correction of market failure

In the discussion above, we noted some of the reasons why people acting through their government may wish to achieve a different quantity, quality and distribution of goods than the free market provides. This is the case against *complete laissez-faire*. But members of a society may have other goals as well. One of these may be a belief in the individual's freedom to act on his own and to make his own choices. Multiple goals often involve conflicts, and conflicts require choices. The decision on when and where and to what extent to interfere with the free-market system must require value judgements about the relative values to be placed on alternative policy goals whenever they come into conflict. The decisions are likely to be better by almost any criterion if they are informed by a knowledge of their economic consequences.

The spirit of our times has led many to treat all problems of market failure, such as pollution, as a national scandal and perhaps even as an imminent crisis of survival. The problems in fact, run the whole range from threats to human survival down to minor nuisances. Virtually all activity leaves some waste product behind it. To say that all pollution must be removed, whatever the cost, is certainly to try for the impossible and probably to get a vast commitment of society's scarce resources to some projects which will yield a low utility. If by emitting smoke a factory is appreciably lowering the life expectancy of those in surrounding communities, it is clearly worthwhile investing a great deal in purifying the effluent. But suppose that the smoke from another factory is not a health hazard, but does smell bad. Further assume that the 10,000 local residents affected by this pollution would be willing to pay on average no more than £10 a year to be rid of the smell. The social cost of the present smoke emission is thus £100,000 a year. Say that the firm was forced to adopt an alternative disposal method at a cost of £500,000 a year. This means that £500,000 worth of society's scarce resources will be used to create a result that society values at only £100,000. Because these resources could have produced other goods valued at £500,000, there is an overall loss of £400,000.

This example points to an important problem: control of pollution and other externalities is costly; it makes sense where the benefits have a higher value than the cost. Pollution control, as with other services, may have great benefits at first and then run into diminishing returns. Instances of the need for external control where social costs are great (e.g., control of nuclear wastes) are obvious and dramatic; in other cases social costs are more nearly equal to private costs.

Which activities to prohibit and which to modify, which to clean up after and which to tolerate, are important choices. The economist can help those who have to make these choices by carefully designating costs and benefits. It is important to note that the choices made may vary among communities and over time. As a society grows wealthier, the value placed on improvements in the quality of life relative to material gains may rise. Poor communities may welcome new industries for the employment and tax revenues they bring, while richer communities may seek to remove these same industries in order to avoid the unpleasant social costs they bring.

31

Microeconomic policy

The central authorities play a major role in all of the world's economies. The nature and amount of intervention differ greatly from country to country. Britain is somewhere in the middle between the extremes to be found in such command economies as the USSR and China and in such relatively free-market economies as the US and Brazil. Even in the latter countries, however, the economic activities of the central authorities are widespread, and many individual markets are largely controlled. In this chapter we shall take a brief look at government microeconomic policy, a topic that requires a whole book for adequate coverage. We shall look first at the major tools available to the central authorities and then at the goals of policy, relating the tools to the goals.

The tools of policy

The central authorities have three main tools with which to implement their economic policies: rules and regulations, taxation and expenditure. We shall consider each of these in turn.

Regulation

Rules pervade economic activities. Shop hours and working conditions are regulated. Employees of British firms have the right under the 1978 Employment Protection Act to have a closed shop set up on their request. Discrimination between labour services provided by males and by females is illegal in the UK and in a large number of other countries. There is growing pressure in the US to make termination of employment solely on account of age illegal. Children cannot be served alcoholic drinks. They must attend school in most countries and be innoculated against certain communicable diseases in many. Laws prohibit people from selling or using certain drugs. Prostitution is prohibited in many societies, although it usually takes place between a willing buyer and a willing seller. In many countries you are forced to purchase insurance for the damage you might do to others with your private motorcar, even if you don't want to carry insurance. In some countries a person who offers goods for sale cannot refuse to sell them to someone just because he does not like the customer's colour or dress. There are rules against fraudulent advertising and the sale of sub-standard, adulterated or poisonous foods. In some countries, such as the United States, anyone who wants to can purchase a wide variety of firearms ranging from pistols to machine guns. In other countries, such as the United Kingdom, it is extremely difficult for a private citizen to obtain a gun.

Most business practices are controlled by rules and prohibitions. In many countries agreements among oligopolistic firms to fix prices or divide up markets are illegal. The mere existence of monopoly is also often outlawed; monopoly firms are then broken up into independent competing firms. When the cost advantages of monopoly resulting from scale economies are considerable, the prices a monopolistic firm can charge and the return it can earn on its capital investment are often regulated. The reality of such control is beyond question; its advisability and its effectiveness are subject to substantial debate.

Taxation

Taxes are of major importance in the pursuit of many government policies. They provide the funds to finance expenditure, but they are also used as tools in their own right for a wide range of purposes including altering the distribution of income.

Direct and indirect taxes Taxes are divided into two broad groups depending on whether persons or things are taxed. DIRECT TAXES are levied directly on persons and vary with the status of the taxpayer. The most important direct tax is the income tax. The personal income tax falls sometimes on the income of households and sometimes separately on each member of the household. It varies with the size and source of the taxpayer's income and various other characteristics laid down by law, such as marital status and number of dependents. Joint stock companies also pay taxes on their income. This is a direct tax both in the legal sense that the company is an individual in the eyes of the law and in the economic sense that the company is owned by its shareholders so that a tax on the company is a tax on them. An expenditure tax (as advocated for Great Britain by a recent royal commission headed by Nobel-prize-winning economist James Meade) is also a direct tax. It is based on what a person spends, rather than on what he or she earns, and has exemptions that are specific to the individual taxpayer. A poll tax, which is simply a lump-sum tax levied on each voter, is also a direct tax. Inheritance taxes, based on the amount of money an individual inherits from someone else's estate, are also direct taxes.

The rate of tax is the tax expressed as a percentage of the thing on which it is levied. The rate of income tax, for example, is a percentage of the income on which it is levied. It is important to distinguish between average and marginal rates. The AVERAGE RATE OF TAX paid by a person is that person's total tax divided by his or her income. The MARGINAL RATE OF TAX is the rate he or she would pay on another unit of income. To take an example, a single man in Britain with a taxable income of £10,000 per year would pay just over £4,000 in tax, making an average rate of just over 40 per cent. If his taxable income rose to £10,001 he would pay an extra 60 pence in tax on the extra pound of income, making a marginal rate of 60 per cent.

An INDIRECT TAX is levied on a thing, and is paid by an individual by virtue of association with that thing. Local rates on property are indirect taxes. They vary with the value of the real estate and are paid by either the owner or the occupier of the real estate, independent of his or her circumstances. Taxes and stamp duties on the transfer of assets from one owner to another are also indirect taxes since they depend on the circumstances of the transaction, not on those of the person making it. Estate duties, which depend on the size of the estate and not on the circumstances of the beneficiaries, are an indirect tax. By far the most pervasive and important of the indirect taxes are taxes on the sale of currently produced commodities. These taxes are called excise taxes when they are levied on manufacturers, and sales taxes when they are levied on the sale of goods from retailer to consumer. The EEC countries levy a comprehensive tax of this sort on all transactions whether at the retail, wholesale or manufacturer's level. This tax is called the VALUE ADDED TAX (VAT).[1] It is an indirect tax because it depends on the value of what is made and sold, not on the wealth or income of the maker. Thus two self-employed fabric designers, each with a 'value added' of £4,000 in terms of designs produced and sold, would pay the same VAT even if one had no other source of income while the other was independently wealthy.

Indirect taxes may be levied in two basic ways. An AD VALOREM tax is a percentage of the value of the transaction on which it is levied. An 8 per cent retail sales tax would mean, for example, that the retail firm had to charge a tax of 8 per cent of the value of everything it sold. A SPECIFIC or PER UNIT TAX is a tax expressed as so much per unit, independently of its price. Taxes on cinema and theatre tickets, and on each gallon of petrol and alcohol independent of the price at which they are produced or sold, are specific taxes.

Shifting and incidence The INCIDENCE of a tax refers to who bears it. The SHIFTING of a tax refers to the passing of its incidence from the person who initially pays it to someone else. Consider an example in which a tax is placed on every new painting sold by its painter. If painters raise the prices of their paintings by the full amount of the tax and (miraculously) continue to sell as many paintings as before, the incidence of the tax shifts entirely from the painters to the collectors. More commonly, as we saw in Chapter 10, the final incidence of a tax falls partly on the person who initially pays it and partly on others.

Progressivity How does the amount of a tax vary with the taxpayers' incomes? The general term for the relation between income and the percentage of income paid by a tax is PROGRESSIVITY. A REGRESSIVE TAX takes a smaller percentage of people's incomes the larger is their income. A PROGRESSIVE TAX takes a larger percentage of people's incomes the larger is their income. A PROPORTIONAL TAX is the boundary case between the two: it takes the same percentage of income from everyone. Taxes on food, for example, tend to be regressive because the proportion of income spent on food tends to fall as income rises. Taxes on alcoholic spirits tend to be progressive since the proportion of income spent on spirits tends to rise with income. Taxes on beer, on the other hand, are regressive.

Progressivity can be defined for any one tax or for the tax system as a whole. Different taxes have different characteristics. Inevitably some will be progressive and some regressive. The impact of a tax system as a whole on high, middle and low-

[1] Value added is the difference between the value of factor services and materials that the firm purchases as inputs and the value of its output. It therefore represents the value that a firm adds by virtue of its own activities. See pages 459–60 for a more extended discussion of the concept.

income groups is best judged by looking at the progressivity of the whole set of taxes taken together. For example, income taxes are progressive in all countries and steeply progressive in the UK and Sweden. The whole tax system is also progressive in these two countries, but much less so than one would guess from studying only the income tax rates. This is because much revenue is raised by indirect taxes, all of which are less progressive than income taxes and some of which are even regressive.

Expenditure

The value of total government expenditure on goods and services in the UK was 26 per cent of the country's national income in 1977. In the same year it was 21 per cent in Germany and 19 per cent in the US. If we include transfer payments, the figures were 48 per cent for the UK and 42 and 43 per cent for Germany and the US respectively. In assessing the impact of government expenditure, this distinction is extremely important. Some government expenditures are in return for goods and services that count as part of current output – i.e., as part of the national product. They create a claim by the central authorities on the economy's factors of production. When the government purchases more factors of production to produce goods and services in the public sector of the economy, there are fewer factors available to produce output in the private sector.

The remainder of government expenditure goes for TRANSFER PAYMENTS, which are payments *not* made in return for any contribution to current output. Old-age pensions, unemployment insurance benefits, welfare payments, disability payments and a host of other expenditures made by the modern welfare state are all transfer payments. They do not add to current marketable output; they merely transfer the power to purchase output from those who provide the money (usually taxpayers) to those who receive it. Transfer payments do not represent a claim by the government on real productive resources.[1] Revenue must nonetheless be raised to pay them.

Goals of policy

Governments use the tools of economic policy to intervene in the markets of the economy for many reasons. The economist's traditional view of economic policy treats the government as a passive agent that intervenes only to correct clearly identified shortcomings of the market. More recently economists have become increasingly aware that this view of government leaves much observed behaviour unexplained. Theories are now being developed that allow governments their own objectives, analogous to those of firms and households. In a simple example of such a theory we might assume that households seek to maximize their utility, that firms seek to maximize their profits and governments seek to maximize the votes they get in the next election. In this theory, the government would favour a scheme that would reduce economic efficiency and lower standards of living in ten years' time but was popular with voters now.

This is no doubt a rather simplistic view, but it may be less so than the old view

[1] It does, of course, take resources to make the transfers, but the salaries of civil servants who do this are counted as an expenditure on current output. Thus *providing* transfer payments is a part of current national product, while the transfers themselves are not.

that the central authorities have no utility function of their own but merely do whatever has been shown to be good for the economic well-being of the populace. Many economists now feel that the analysis of government behaviour will not be fully successful until a politician's utility[1] function is specified and tested.

We shall, in the rest of this chapter, ask what economic rationale exists for government economic activity. This is as far as economics can take us now, but we must guard against the belief that in so doing we are explaining the real motives behind *all* government interventions in the economy.

Efficiency

Many of the economic reasons for government intervention come under the heading of increasing the efficiency of the market system. All of the 'market failures' discussed in the previous chapter provide such reasons.

The provision of collective consumption goods is one obvious way to improve the efficiency of the system since, if the government does not provide them, few will be provided.[2] Defence, police and fire protection, street lighting, the judicial system, regulatory bodies of all sorts, public parks and monuments, clean air and rivers, weather forecasting, and navigational aids are all goods and services which, once provided, are freely available to everyone and therefore would not be produced in a completely free-market economy. Commodities which are not strictly collective consumption goods but are hard to market privately because of the high cost of raising revenue present in practice a very similar case to genuine collective consumption goods. Urban roads and various kinds of information services are examples. Divergencies between private and social cost provide a major reason for intervention. EXTERNALITIES are social costs that are not taken into account by the firm because they are not internal to the firm. The central authorities can levy taxes equal to the excess of social costs over private costs and thus force the firm to take account of these costs. When the state does this, it is said to be INTERNALIZING AN EXTERNALITY. Taxes, regulations and prohibitions are all used in these cases. Firms that pollute are sometimes taxed an amount equal to the social costs of their pollution; firms are often forced by regulation to adopt alternative, more privately costly technologies that are less polluting. Households are also regulated in their polluting activities by such controls as restrictions on the kinds of fuel that can be used in urban areas and emission standards for private cars.

The alleviation of market imperfections is another major goal of interventions. Where cost conditions make it possible, monopolies are broken up. Where cost conditions create natural monopolies, these are regulated as to the price they can charge and the profits they can earn (or else they are nationalized, as we shall see below). Labour mobility can be enhanced by providing information, by subsidizing relocation and by retraining. (This type of labour market policy is prevalent in

---

[1] Household utility depends on the quantities of goods the household consumes; similarly, a government's utility might depend on several things including its position in the popularity polls and its chances of winning the next election, as well as more 'altruistic' motives such as the good it can do for its citizens.

[2] It would not be correct to say 'none', since private clubs can be formed to provide some such goods. For this to be practical, either the collective consumption must extend over a small range so that all the potential consumers can be included in the club or there must be a way to exclude non-club members from consuming the good.

Sweden, less so in the UK.) Many other policies, such as legislation of closed shops and the provision of council housing below cost but with long waiting lists may inhibit labour mobility.

All kinds of intervention to set minimum standards of quality, ensure correct information and to prevent fraud come under the general classification of compensating for market imperfections. The economic system is clearly not working efficiently if someone is poisoned by a tin of beans she thought was edible, or if someone else wants to know the calorie count on some particular product but cannot find out. Myriad government rules and regulations seek to protect consumers from forces beyond their control and provide them with reliable information on which to base their own utility-maximizing choices.

Paternalism

The above reasons for intervention are based on improving the efficiency with which the market responds to household demand. Accepting this as a policy goal depends on believing that the household is the best judge of its own interests. This is called INDIVIDUALISM. An alternative view that often leads to quite similar-looking behaviour is paternalism, as we saw in the previous chapter. It holds that the central authorities are a better judge of the household's self-interest than the household itself. Paternalistic intervention may take the form of downright prohibitions on the consumption of commodities such as certain drugs and gambling. In many countries, for example, off-track betting is illegal – as it was until the 1960s in the UK – on the grounds that the punter must be protected against him or herself. In Canada, for another example, pubs used to close for an hour from 5.30 to 6.30 on the grounds that this would force the man of the house to go home, where his wife could get her hands on some of his pay before he had spent it all on beer. Paternalism often takes more subtle forms of subsidizing certain commodities such as milk and housing on the grounds that it is in households' own interests to consume more of these commodities than they would consume voluntarily if they were merely given an income transfer equal in value to the subsidy. (The individualistic view of such a policy is that if households are thought to be too poor they should be given a simple income supplement and left to spend it as they wish.)

The issue of individualism versus paternalism raises many fascinating issues concerning human freedom and social justice. Suffice it to say here that much existing economic policy is paternalistic in the sense that it is predicated on the grounds that the central authorities understand the household's best interests better than does the household itself.[1]

The distribution of income and wealth

The central authorities attempt to change the distribution of income in countless ways. Some attempts are general in their effects, but some are quite specific and localized.

[1] The distinction between individualism and paternalism would be much clearer than it actually is if all households contained only one member. Because households typically have many members, including minors, some apparently paternalistic interventions can be understood as protecting some members from the paternalism of others. This really replaces one form of paternalism with another. Difficult cases aside, however, influencing actions that primarily affect the person taking the action is clearly paternalistic.

The functional distribution of income Governments have many policies with respect to the functional distribution of income. For example, in the UK income arising from the provision of labour services (called *earned income*) is taxed at lower effective income tax rates than income over £1,700 that arises from the sale of the services of capital (called *unearned income*). This is done by levying a tax on investment income of over £1,700 per annum on a progressive scale that rises to 98 per cent! Few other Western industrial countries discriminate in this way among functional shares in their tax policies. This UK policy tends to redistribute income among the owners of factors away from those who provide capital and in favour of those who provide labour. Also, by reducing the return to invested capital, it may provide a disincentive to saving and investing, although this has not been conclusively demonstrated.

Governments also have policies affecting the distribution of income within the broad functional class of labour income. Labour governments may try to redistribute income from professional-managerial and other middle-class groups to skilled and unskilled workers who are members of the working class. Conservative governments may try to resist, or reverse, this redistribution.

Governments also change the distribution of income in favour of all sorts of relatively small special-interest groups. Special tax treatment, subsidies, legislation that restricts competition, and a host of other measures operate in many countries to turn the distribution of income in favour of various groups – small businessmen, farmers in general and poultry and milk producers in particular, households with large numbers of children, certain professional groups, some groups of skilled workers and unmarried mothers, for example.

The treatment afforded to many of these special-interest groups is often hard to explain on grounds of correcting inefficiencies or of changing the distribution of income according to any generally agreed-upon canons of justice. Many economists believe that these kinds of redistribution can be understood only in terms of the theory of the vote-maximizing government. Such a government would adopt policies that greatly help each member of a small identifiable group and slightly hurt each member of a large, diffuse, unorganized group.

In case this notion sounds scandalous, remember that the basic idea of democracy is that politicians are supposed to respond to the wishes of the people. The proof that they are doing so is their ability to get re-elected.

> **Economists have actually come late to the vote-maximizing view of government. They have done so only after repeated failures to explain and predict much government behaviour using a model in which the government sought solely to make the economy work efficiently and to alter the distribution of income in ways that satisfied generally accepted ideas of social justice.**

The size distribution of income Governments try to alter the size distribution of income in some ways that are widely accepted as socially desirable. In looking at the size distribution of income government is concerned with large and small incomes, irrespective of the source of income. Most governments seek to narrow the range of the distribution, reducing the incomes of those at the upper end and raising the incomes of those at the lower end. The more egalitarian the government, the more it seeks to do this, but all governments recognize a trade-off between equality and efficiency. Some jobs are more skilled, more difficult, more unpleasant or more risky than others and, unless the former are more highly paid than the latter, people will not be persuaded to do them. Even communist governments allow major inequalities in the size distribution of income in order to provide the incentives needed to make the economic system function relatively efficiently.

The major tax tool for changing the size distribution of income is the progressive income tax, whose rates are shown in Table 31.1. The marginal rate of tax is constant at 35 per cent over the very wide range of taxable income from £50 to

Table 31.1 UK Income Tax, Single Persons, No Dependants, 1975–76[1]

	All earned		All investment	
Income	Income tax	Average tax rate	Income tax	Average tax rate
£s	£s	%	£s	%
600	—	—	—	—
700	8·75	1·3	8·75	1·3
800	43·75	5·5	43·75	5·5
900	78·75	8·8	78·75	8·8
1,000	113·75	11·4	113·75	11·4
1,500	288·75	19·3	338·75	22·6
2,000	463·75	23·2	563·75	28·2
3,000	813·75	27·1	1,063·75	35·5
4,000	1,163·75	29·1	1,563·75	39·1
5,000	1,513·75	30·3	2,063·75	41·3
6,000	1,921·25	32·0	2,621·25	43·7
7,000	2,387·50	34·1	3,237·50	46·3
8,000	2,903·75	36·3	3,903·75	48·8
9,000	3,470·00	38·6	4,620·00	51·3
10,000	4,070·00	40·7	5,370·00	53·7
15,000	7,402·50	49·4	9,452·50	63·0
20,000	11,118·75	55·6	13,918·75	69·6
30,000	19,364·75	64·5	23,664·75	78·9
50,000	35,964·75	71·9	43,264·75	86·5
100,000	77,464·75	77·5	92,264·75	92·3

[1] The table shows the tax payable by single persons after deduction of the personal allowance. Any further reliefs to which the tax payer might be entitled would reduce the tax payable below the amount shown in the table.

Source: The British System of Taxation, C.O.I., London, R5271/75.

£8,000. Since the first £985 of income is not taxed, however, the average rate of tax is mildly progressive over the range up to £8,985. Above that figure, however, the marginal rate becomes steeply progressive, rising to a maximum of 83 per cent for taxable incomes in excess of £24,000. This is one of the highest income tax rates in Western countries.

The disincentive of these very high marginal rates of tax is still a subject of debate. If we consider a 'closed economy' where there is no possibility of emigration, then there seems little evidence that rates of up to 50 per cent are a strong disincentive. Some people work less hard but others work harder in order to restore their after-tax income to what it would have been if tax rates were lower. Above 50 per cent there seems to be more disincentive effect, and clearly, as rates approach 100 per cent, the disincentive effect becomes absolute. Indeed, very high rates have other effects that reduce efficiency. People whose income is high for a few years and low thereafter pay very high taxes, and therefore suffer disincentives relative to others with the same lifetime income that is spread more evenly over the years. People with high incomes spend much time and expense on lawyers and accountants to shield their incomes from taxes. Such activities produce no other net output for the society as a whole. When taxes get high enough, downright evasion becomes common and tax yields are lower than they would have been if rates were lower but the taxes were actually paid.

In an open society where emigration is possible, it is clear that very high marginal rates of tax can have major effects. Authors, artists, pop groups and others who 'strike it rich' are strongly tempted to emigrate to other countries that will allow them to keep a higher proportion of their incomes. The temptation is particularly strong when there are countries with common linguistic and cultural environments and substantially lower tax rates. Emigration of successful people of this type from the UK to the US and various even lower-tax countries has been significant. From the point of view of maximizing tax revenues and reducing tax burdens on middle- and lower-income groups, it would be better to have these successful people still in the country paying tax rates of 40–50 per cent than out of the country, totally avoiding tax rates of 83 per cent.

It is possible to imagine for each income tax bracket a tax rate that would maximize the tax yields. Zero yields nothing. So does 100 per cent, since people would not continue to earn income if it were all to be paid in tax. Somewhere in between is the rate that maximizes the total tax yield.

If the tax rate is set too high the yield will fall. Among other things, it will pay people to spend much money and effort on ways to avoid paying tax legally; some people will cheat under the incentive of very high tax rates; and some – particularly the very successful – will leave the country.

Although no definitive study has been made, it seems to many observers that the upper ranges of UK income tax rates are above their yield-maximizing levels. If this is the case, the justification of these high rates must lie somewhere *other than* in trying to maximize the taxes actually paid by those at the upper end of the income scale and correspondingly reducing taxes paid by those at the lower end of the scale. The theory of the vote-maximizing government may provide an explanation.

The first prong of any government's attempt to change the size distribution of income is its tax policy. The idea is to have a tax system that is progressive when viewed as a whole. The second prong is its expenditure policy. If, to take an extreme case, government expenditure benefited people in proportion to the taxes they paid, the overall effect of the government would not at all be to redistribute income. What it took away with one hand it would give back with the other. An effective redistribution scheme requires a progressive tax system and a proportional or regressive expenditure system (a constant or higher proportion of benefits from expenditure the lower is income). Transfer payments tend to fulfill this criterion since many of them are welfare payments to various classes of needy such as the aged, the incapacitated, the unemployed, the unemployable and the very young. For government payments for goods and services that are part of national income, and that are provided at a zero or a subsidized price, the case is not so clear. Education, for example, tends to be consumed more by higher than lower income groups, since the higher a household's income, the more likely it is that its children will stay on beyond the minimum age. This kind of relation, which exists for other commodities as well, means that much of the non-transfer part of the expenditure system is progressive, with larger benefits being received the larger the household's income at least up to some middle range of income.

The combined net effect of the tax and expenditure system on the size distribution of income is shown in Table 31.2.

Table 31.2 Redistribution of income through taxes and expenditure, 1975

Original income	Income after all taxes and benefits	% change as a result of government intervention
1032	1259	+22%
1276	1531	+20%
1540	1606	+ 4%
1766	1765	+ 0%
2023	1887	− 7%
2546	2270	−11%
3376	2789	−17%
4706	3619	−23%
6636	4819	−27%
10,694	7024	−34%

Source: Social Trends, No. 8, 1977, Table 6.22.

The distribution of wealth It is sometimes argued that egalitarian economic policy should concern itself more with the distribution of wealth and less with income than it now does. Certainly wealth does confer economic power and equally certainly wealth is more unequally distributed than is income. Heavy estate duties in the UK

Table 31.3 Share of personal wealth owned by wealthiest sectors of adult population

	Top 1% of population	Top 10% of population
1911–13	69	92
1924–30	62	91
1936–8	56	88
1954	43	79
1960	38	77
1966	32	72
1972	30	72
1975	23	62

Source: Royal Commission on the Distribution of Income and Wealth (HMSO, 1975).

have, however, caused a substantial reduction in the inequality of wealth distribution over this century. This is shown in Table 31.3.

There are two main ways in which the distribution of wealth can be made less unequal. The first is to levy taxes on wealth at the time that wealth is transferred, either by gift during the lifetime of the owner or by bequest after death, from one owner to another. In the UK such transfers are subject to a CAPITAL TRANSFER TAX. The rate of tax is progressive and rises to 75 per cent on taxable transfers in excess of £2 million. The second method is an annual tax on wealth held in the hands of its owners. A wealth tax of this sort has been under consideration since 1975 in the UK. It has aroused much controversy, and as yet there has been no agreement as to its provisions or its basic desirability. Certainly it poses some formidable difficulties and may cause some serious disincentive effects. People holding wealth that is not easily marketable, or that is not earning current income, may be put into very difficult circumstances by an annual levy on their wealth.

Distribution versus efficiency

A number of conflicts between advice given by economists and policy decisions taken by governments can be understood in terms of a difference in emphasis: efficiency considerations for economists and distribution considerations for the central authorities. There is little doubt that from a pure efficiency point of view the correct policy was to let domestic oil prices in all oil-importing countries rise along with the world price. Instead, many governments held the price down – being concerned, among other things, with the effect of rising prices on the profits earned by large oil companies and on the welfare of poorer citizens. 'We just can't let the poor find their heating bills rise so much and so fast' was a typical consideration.

Here is a genuine conflict for which economics cannot provide a solution, for in the end the consumer must rest on value judgements. Economics can, however, make the consequences of various choices apparent, and suggest policy alternatives. The consequences of holding down the price of oil because of concern about the effect on the poor was to lead, in the manner discussed in Chapter 31, to an inefficient use of the countries' resources. This meant that total production was reduced and some new investment was misdirected into high- rather than low-cost methods of production. Thus in the long run average standards of living were reduced. Whether the reduction in the average was a reasonable price to pay for shielding the poor is an open question, but it is unlikely that the question was ever really posed or the calculations ever made.

Changes in prices and quantities always hurt someone. If the price system is not allowed to do its job because of effects on particular groups, then the society is effectively opting for some more centrally controlled form of resource allocation. An alternative is to let the price system do its job of signalling relative scarcities and costs, thus ensuring some efficiency in the allocation of resources, and then use the tax-expenditure system to ensure that the poor have some minimum living standard. This method does not seek to help the poor, or other under-privileged groups, by subsidizing oil or any other prices and thus presenting everyone with prices that do not reflect opportunity costs. It seeks rather to provide these groups with sufficient income by direct income transfers, and then leaves producers and consumers to respond to relative prices that approximately reflect relative opportunity costs. Advocates of this method argue that it is surer, more direct and less costly in its side effects than the method of subsidizing the prices of particular goods. The price-subsidy method surely produces a somewhat haphazard method of distribution, since some who *are not* in the under-privileged group gain as well, and some who *are* in the under-privileged group – those who don't want or can't get the subsidized commodity – do not gain at all.

Opponents claim that certain commodities such as food, heat, medical care and housing are basic to a civilized life and should be provided to households cheaply whatever their real opportunity cost. They feel that the inefficiencies resulting from presenting people with prices that do not reflect opportunity costs are a small price to pay for ensuring that everyone can afford these basics. They reject the view that a minimum living standard can be provided simply by allowing a minimum income and letting the recipients spend it at market-determined prices. They feel, possibly paternalistically, that some commodities should be provided cheaply to everyone.

As with all such issues, it is impossible to do justice to both sides of this one in a few pages. The purpose of this discussion is to make the reader aware of the question, in the hope that further discussion will bring to light many of the considerations omitted from this necessarily brief account.

A further consideration of government expenditure

So far we have considered government activity intended to increase the efficiency of the economic system and to change the distribution of income. Some government production of goods and services is hard to classify this way, although there may be an element of each type in them. It is convenient, therefore, to complete our discussion of government policy by considering the production of goods and services by the public sector as a topic in its own right.

Collective consumption goods

Much government production is of collective consumption goods. These are clearly meant to raise the efficiency of the economy in satisfying consumers' demands, and have thus been discussed already under earlier headings. The resource costs of this production must be met from general taxation since the very nature of the products imply that they cannot be sold to individual users.

The provision of commodities free or at a price below their cost of production

Collective consumption goods must, by their very nature, be paid for out of general tax revenue. Many other commodities that could be sold at a price that would cover costs, are in fact provided at a lower price (zero in the limit) with the shortfall between price and costs being made up out of tax revenue.

The opportunity cost of 'free' goods Voters sometimes opt to have the government subsidize a product, or even provide it free, because it seems a good idea to avoid cost wherever this is possible. Such policies do not, however, remove the cost; they merely transfer it from one set of persons, the consumers, to another set, the taxpayers. The opportunity cost of using resources to produce one commodity is the other commodities that could have been produced with the resources instead of that commodity. The money equivalent of this is the market value of the resources being used. Whenever a commodity is provided free by the government, the costs are met by taxes.[1] The taxpayers thus forgo what they would have consumed by spending their tax money, and the free commodity is consumed by its users instead. Insofar as they are the same people, then the consumers merely pay in a different form: taxes rather than purchase prices. Insofar as they are different people, there is a transfer of income from taxpayers to the consumers of the free commodity.

Providing a commodity free does not remove the opportunity cost, it merely transfers it from consumers of the product to taxpayers.

The case against free commodities If a commodity is provided free and all demand is met, then households will go on consuming it until the last unit consumed has a zero marginal utility. As long as extra units consumed have a positive marginal utility (no matter how small) and a zero marginal private cost, households can raise their total utility by raising their consumption of the commodity. Thus, resources will have to be used up in producing units of the commodity which have zero marginal utility to each and every household. Since resources are scarce, they must be taken from the production of other goods that have positive marginal utilities for all households (i.e., households would like to have more of them). To use scarce resources to produce commodities with zero or even very low marginal utilities when the same resources could produce commodities with higher marginal utilities ensures that all households will have lower total utilities than they could have. If a price were charged for the commodity, its consumption would decline and resources would be freed to move to uses where their product would have a higher marginal utility.[2]

The quantitative extent of this problem depends on the shape of the marginal utility schedule. Commodity I in Figure 31.1 (i) has a very flat schedule and there is a great

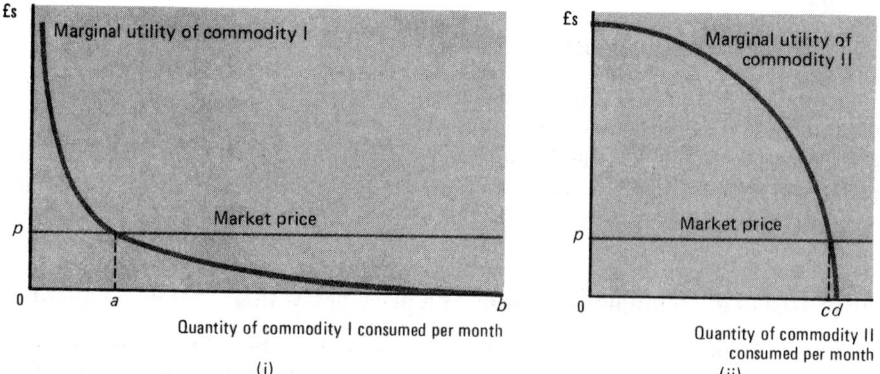

Fig. 31.1 (i) Providing the commodity free greatly increases the amount of resources allocated to producing it
(ii) Providing the commodity free increases only slightly the amount of resources allocated to producing it

difference between the consumption of *a* when the market price is charged and the consumption of *b* when the commodity is free. Commodity II in part (ii) of the figure has a steep schedule, and the consumption of *d* at zero price is not much higher than

[1] This assumes that government expenditure is financed by taxes. We shall see in Chapter 38 that there are other methods of finance. These do not, of course, avoid the cost; they merely shift it to other groups.

[2] This case against free goods can be maintained *without* having to admit any practical policy relevance of the proposition that perfect competition provides an optimal allocation of resources.

the consumption of c when the market price is changed. The case against providing commodity I free is that this will absorb some of the nation's scarce resources in providing units of the commodity which have a very low marginal utility. The case against providing commodity II free is the same, but quantitatively it is much less serious.

We have already discussed the case of water (see pages 166–7). This is an example of a very weak case. Water undoubtedly has a flat marginal utility schedule of the sort illustrated in Figure 31.1 (i) thus the no-price policy means that a great deal of the economy's scarce resources must be committed to producing units of water which have a very low marginal utility. Furthermore, water does not provide a case where there are obvious social gains from encouraging consumption beyond what the individual would voluntarily choose. Indeed, if a commercially profitable market price were charged, there is little reason to believe there would be serious divergencies between social and private costs. Here is a case in which it is hard to see a rationale behind existing policy.

The case for free commodities The case for providing some commodities such as medical services and education at a price below cost (zero in the limit) rests partly on a divergence between social and private costs, partly on compassion, and partly on more subtle welfare arguments.

Water may provide a weak case for a free good. The case for hospitals and schools, however, is somewhat different. First, there is some doubt that many people waste free hospital care in the way they are observed to waste free water. Studies suggest a low incidence of unnecessary hospitalization in a free-hospital system. In the case of education up to the statutory age, consumption is compulsory in any case.[1] Secondly, whereas the annual cost of necessary medical and hospital care can easily be in excess of a household's annual income, it is not a great burden for a household to pay a commercial rate for all the water that is necessary for a moderately civilized life. Charging a price that covers costs of production would deny medical and educational services to many. Thirdly, in both cases social and private costs and benefits are thought to diverge substantially: if I choose not to, or cannot afford to, buy a cure for an infectious disease, the effects are not felt by me alone. If all children are better educated, not only do they and their parents gain, but everyone gains from any rise in output that results from an increase in their labour productivity. Thus, there are arguments for reducing the private cost of these services below the market rate by means of a subsidy. There is debate, however, on whether the cost should merely be lowered or should actually be reduced to zero. Part of this argument concerns the positive question of the elasticity of demand for these services in the range between a moderate and a zero price. If this elasticity is high, then the difference between a modest and a zero price will be a large quantity of society's scarce resources producing services that provide households with only low marginal utilities.

The alternative scheme is to make full hospital and medical insurance compulsory. The compulsion can be justified either on grounds of paternalism; on

[1] Indeed, there is some evidence that the consumption of 'free' education paid for by all taxpayers whether or not they are parents of school-age children leads to a lower consumption of education than would result from education paid for solely by the households that were consuming, and obviously benefiting from, it.

grounds of externalities – that others are affected adversely when some people do not get adequate care; or on the grounds of social obligation – that society must not stand by and let uninsured people suffer from inadequate treatment.

Goods sold on the open market

Finally we come to public expenditure used to produce commodities that are then sold on the open market at prices that are intended to cover their full opportunity cost, just as by any private firm. Public firms may not, however, seek to maximize profits; often they seek just to cover costs. Various reasons for nationalizing industries have been put forward and we can only give very brief mention to some of them.

(1) *To confiscate the return on capital for the welfare of the general public instead of the private capitalist.* This is the standard reason – stemming from both Marxian and Fabian Socialist policies – for the production and sale of goods by government on the open market: the state should own the means of production (capital) and the return on it should go to the people rather than to a capitalist class privately owning the capital. (The discussion on page 386 is relevant here.) After the experience of running planned economies communists came to realize that capital had to be priced if it were to be allocated efficiently among its alternative uses. They continued to believe, however, that this price should not produce an income for a group of households in the economy. In this view the state – in the person of taxpayers – must provide the capital and receive the return on capital. This means that taxpayers are forced to save and invest in the nation's industries and then receive the return – in the sense that profits will be available to be spent by the state. This compares with private ownership, where those who wish to save and invest do so and then receive the return on capital as a reward.

There are two problems with this view as far as UK nationalized industries are concerned. First, as nationalized industries raise capital by reinvesting their own profits, by selling stock to the public, or by borrowing from the government money that was originally raised by selling stock to the public, their behaviour is indistinguishable from that of private firms. When money is raised by selling stock to the public, the return on capital is paid to the stockholders, not to the state. Second, very few of the nationalized industries in the UK have ever produced a surplus which they paid to the state as the return on capital going to the people rather than to private capitalists.

(2) *To get more co-ordination where private costs do not reflect social costs.* Nationalization of all forms of transport, for example, might be used to produce a single transport policy wherein decisions made by railways took into account the costs imposed on the road haulage industry and vice versa. Whatever the facts of such interrelationship, the British nationalized industries have up to now made little attempt to look beyond their own parochial boundaries when taking decisions.

(3) *To obtain a radically different pattern of production than would have been obtained under private enterprise.* If this were a goal, the nationalized industries would require a clear directive as to how their output and prices were to be determined. In fact they have usually been given the major task of trying to avoid losses, which requires that they make average revenue equal to average costs. In industries presently making losses, the attempt to cut losses is profit-maximizing behaviour. Thus behaviour in these industries is indistinguishable from what the

private firm's behaviour would be. In the case of a profitable industry, on the other hand, the directive 'cover costs' ($AR = ATC$) will lead to higher output and a lower price than the directive 'maximize profits' ($MR = MC$) and you should not read on until you have drawn a graph to demonstrate this. But if more of something is produced there will be less of something else, and the extra production of nationalized industries pricing at average costs represents a gain only if this production is valued higher than the production forgone elsewhere. In fact, no one has ever suggested principles to be followed by nationalized industries that would lead to a different and clearly superior allocation of resources.

(4) *To control a natural monopoly*. Industries such as the postal, telegraph, telephone, gas and electricity industries are natural monopolies. The alternatives here are public regulation of privately-owned industry or public ownership. One of the main purposes set forth for nationalization is to secure effective control over such natural monopolies. All countries seem to accept this argument in the case of the post office, and many countries also accept it for the great public utility industries such as gas and electricity. Those who believe that privately-owned industries cannot be controlled effectively through regulation favour nationalization. It is difficult to believe that the price-output decisions of such public utility firms are very different when they are nationalized from when they are privately owned but under effective public regulation. The major difference is once again in the ownership of their capital. When they are privately owned, the capital is raised by people who voluntarily contribute it and who receive its return as their income. When such firms are publicly owned, they have a call on the taxpayer for capital, although in practice they often raise capital from private savers by selling stocks on the open market, or by borrowing money that the government has raised by selling stocks (which comes to the same thing since the return on capital is paid out as interest to stockholders). They also have a call on the taxpayer to meet operating deficits where current expenditures exceed current revenues.

(5) *To get greater efficiency and a more dynamic growth policy than under private industry*. The relative efficiency of private versus public production is still the subject of heated debate. Although universal agreement is not forthcoming, I would hazard the personal guess that the experience of nationalized industries in the United Kingdom suggests that they have been neither vastly better nor vastly worse than their private predecessors in running their day-to-day affairs. There are, however, longer-term considerations. Are private industries unimaginative and unenterprising, ignoring existing possibilities to modernize and become profitable? Can public firms encourage innovation and very-long-run change as easily as private firms?

Coal mining – an example The view that public control was needed to save an industry from the dead hand of third-rate, unenterprising, private owners was very commonly held about the British coal industry in the inter-war period, and was undoubtedly a factor leading to its nationalization in 1946. This view was clearly held by the Commission which reported in 1926 on the state of the coal industry.

> It would be possible to say without exaggeration of the miners' leaders that they were the stupidest men in England, if we had not had frequent occasion to meet the owners.[1]

[1] Quoted in David Thomson, *England in the Twentieth Century* (Pelican Books, 1965), p. 110. But see also L. S. Amery's reply that the Commission had ignored the very strong claim of the government to be so considered. Some of the policies that gave the government that claim are discussed on pages 500–1.

On the other hand, Sir Roy Harrod argued that the run-down state of the coal industry in South Wales and Yorkshire and the advanced state of the pits in Nottinghamshire and Derbyshire represented the correct response of the owners to the signals of the market. He writes:

> The mines of Derbyshire and Nottinghamshire were rich, and it was worth sinking capital in them. If similar amounts of capital were not sunk in other parts of the country, this may not have been because the managements were inefficient, but simply because it was known that they were not worth these expenditures. Economic efficiency does not consist in always introducing the most up-to-date equipment that an engineer can think of but rather in the correct adaptation of the amount of new capital sunk to the earning capacity of the old asset. In not introducing new equipment, the managements may have been wise, not only from the point of view of their own interest, but from that of national interest, which requires the most profitable application of available capital ... it is right that as much should be extracted from the inferior mines as can be done by old-fashioned methods (i.e., with equipment already installed), and that they should gradually go out of action.[1]

Declining industries always present a sorry sight to the observer. Revenues have fallen below long-run total costs, and as a result new equipment is not brought in to replace old equipment as it wears out. The average age of equipment in use thus rises steadily. A declining industry will *always* display an old age-structure of capital and thus 'antiquated' methods. The superficial observer, seeing the industry's very real plight, is likely to blame the antiquated equipment, which is actually the effect, not the cause, of the industry's decline.

To modernize at high capital costs merely makes the plight worse, since output and costs will rise in the face of declining demand and prices. To nationalize a declining industry in order to install new plant and equipment which privately owned firms are unwilling to install is to use the nation's scarce resources where they will not lead to large increases in the value of output. Capital resources are scarce: if investment occurs in mines, there is less for engineering, schools, roads, computer research and a host of other things. To re-equip a declining industry which cannot cover its capital costs is to use scarce resources where by the criterion of the market their product is much less valuable than what it would be in other industries. The correct response to a steadily declining demand is indeed not to replace old equipment, but to continue to operate what exists as long as it can cover its variable costs of production.

Innovation under private and public control One of the major issues concerning public versus private ownership concerns the relative incentive to innovate under each. Innovation of new products and techniques has been the source of the phenomenal economic growth that has transformed living standards throughout much of the world over the last two centuries. Innovation not only raises living standards under given environmental conditions, but it is the main hope for allowing the world to cope with such changing circumstances as the eventual exhaustion of fossil fuels.

The pro-public ownership argument is as follows. First, private firms, particularly very large ones, are conservative and unwilling to take risks. Indeed, there does seem to be some evidence that larger firms are more risk-adverse than small firms. Second, the state has the willingness and the capital to take risks and

[1] Roy Harrod, *The British Economy* (McGraw-Hill, 1963), p. 54.

innovate where private firms either will not or cannot. Third, the state is in a better position than private firms to assess the direction that research and innovation should take. Uncoordinated private activity will lead to much waste in 'going off in all directions at once' and a centrally co-ordinated effort will be much more effective. Fourth, the profits from innovation should go to the people, not to a private class of innovators.

The pro-private ownership view argues as follows. First, the incentive structure of public bueaucracies is even more unfavourable to risk taking than that of large private firms. It is largeness, not 'privateness', that leads to risk aversion. Second, the state's record in ventures like the Concorde aircraft is disastrous (for understandable reasons, because political calculations becloud economic ones). In the private sector, even if existing firms are slow to innovate, the Schumpeterian process of creative destruction will cause new firms to arise whenever conditions are ripe for successful innovations. Nationalization, its critics argue, places the full coercive power of the state behind the preservation of the existing state monopoly and tends to frustrate the Schumpeterian process, which is the ultimate free-market protection against the inefficiencies of established monopolies. Third, it is argued, there is protection in diversity. Co-ordinated state action can throw all of the economy's resources down what subsequently turns out to be a blind alley. Private enterprise will cause every promising direction to be explored. Those who go down blind alleys lose their money; those who find successful routes prosper. Fourth, in such an inherently risky business as innovation it is better to risk the money voluntarily subscribed by private savers than the money forcibly extracted from taxpayers.

Conclusion

The tools available for government economic policy, and the major economic objectives that can be pursued, are fairly uncontroversial. To what extent the government pursues selfish, vote-maximizing objectives described by its own utility function is a matter of current controversy. There seems little doubt, however, that the model that gives the government no selfish objectives and makes it a mere selfless public servant, has been refuted by evidence and is correctly rejected. Correct determination of the balance between selfishness and altruism awaits the formulation and testing of more elaborate models.

Another subject of current controversy is the cost of meeting various social objectives such as a more equal income distribution. There seems little doubt that this particular objective is pursued at a cost of more inefficiency in the economic system (which reduces the total output available for everyone). 'How much is lost?' and 'Is it worth it?' remain questions on which disagreement is rampant.

A major debate concerns the long-run and very-long-run behaviour of free-market and centralized economies. Since great flexibility will be needed to meet forthcoming crises such as the exhaustion of certain raw materials, increasing scarcity of fossil fuels, climate changes and population explosions, the long-run flexibility of various alternative systems is a matter of great significance today as well as for the generations to come. Here again, although there is evidence from the workings of various types of economies now and in the past, there is still room for vast differences in honestly held opinions.

Part seven

The circular flow of income

32

The circular flow of income and the concept of national income

On pages 54–7 of Chapter 4 we briefly noted that economics is divided into two main branches called microeconomics and macroeconomics. So far we have been studying microeconomics; for most of the rest of the book we shall study macroeconomics.

From micro to macro economics

Our first task is to distinguish between the two branches a little more fully than was necessary earlier.

The microeconomic view of the circular flow of income

In microeconomics, we start with households whose members have needs and desires for goods and services. They have, in varying amounts, resources – incomes, assets, time and energy – with which to attempt to satisfy their wants. But the limitations on their resources force them to make choices, and this they do through markets where they are offered many ways to spend their money, their energy and their time. The signals to which the households respond are market prices; given a set of prices, each household will make a given set of choices. In so doing, they also, in the aggregate, affect those prices. The prices signal to firms what goods they may profitably provide. Given technology and the cost of factors, firms must choose (i) among the products they might produce, (ii) among the ways of producing them, and (iii) among the various quantities (and qualities) they can supply. In so doing, they affect prices. Firms demand factors of production, in quantities depending on their output decisions, which in turn depend upon consumers' demands. These derived demands for factors will affect the prices of labour, managerial skill, raw materials, buildings, machinery, land and all other factors. The owners of factors, and the possessors of the skills that provide factor services, respond to factor prices by deciding how much of their services to offer and where to offer them. These choices determine factor supplies. Payments by firms to factor owners provide the owners of the factors with income. The recipients of these incomes are members of households who have needs and desires for goods and services, and we now come full circle.

The process described above is often referred to as the *circular flow of income*: money passes from households to firms in return for goods and services produced by firms, and money passes from firms to households in return for factor services provided by households. In microeconomics we study individual parts of this flow in microscopic detail.

The macroeconomic view of the circular flow of income

We now wish to study the circular flow in a broad macro-scopic view. We surpress its details and ask such questions as: 'What determines the total amount of the flow?' and 'Why does this total flow vary over time?' Macroeconomics is a study of the characteristics and determinants of the circular flow looked at in the large context with most of its interesting, but bewildering, detail surpressed.

Another useful way of putting the same distinction is to say that microeconomics deals with detailed or *disaggregated* data, while macroecoomics deals with *aggregated* data expressed in terms of large totals or averages. In microeconomics we are concerned, for example, with prices and quantities in thousands of individual markets for consumers' goods and services. In macroeconomics, however, we aggregate all of these markets and study both the single total flow of expenditure on all consumers' goods produced and sold in the economy and the single average price at which all sales of consumers' goods take place.[1]

The distinction illustrated

There is no clear-cut dividing line between macro and microeconomics. Perhaps the best way of showing the scope of each is to list the most important sets of problems with which we shall be concerned in the remainder of this book, contrasting them with the related problems dealt with in micro-theory.

(1) Macroeconomics studies the total amount of employment of each of the major factors of production, with special attention to the total amount of labour employed. Microeconomics takes the total volume of employment of resources as given and studies how the employed resources are allocated among their alternative uses.

(2) Macroeconomics studies the total volume of output produced, and income earned, in the whole economy. Microeconomics studies the details of this output as determined in thousands of individual product markets and the details of the distribution of this income as determined in thousands of individual factor markets.

(3) Macroeconomics studies the average level of prices in all product markets (called 'the' price level) and the average level of money wage rates in all labour markets (called 'the' level of money wages). Microeconomics takes these levels as given and studies the structure of *relative* product prices as determined in all of the economy's individual markets for commodities and the structure of *relative* wages as determined in all of the economy's individual factor markets. In short, microeconomics is concerned with the structure of *relative* wages and prices, while macroeconomics is concerned with the average level of *absolute*, or money, wages and prices.

[1] The averages used in macroeconomics are often index numbers. These show the percentage increase over a base year which is arbitrarily assigned a value of 100.

tell us, we must study it in some detail. We start with the national income of a very simple economy and then introduce, one by one, the complications needed to make the concept applicable to real-world economies.[1]

The Spendthrift economy

In the simple Spendthrift economy, there are only two groups of decision takers, households and firms. Each group earns all of its income by selling goods and services to the other group, and each group spends all of its income by buying goods and services from the other group. Households earn their income by selling the services of factors of production – land, labour and capital – to firms, and they spend all of their incomes on purchasing goods and services produced by firms. Firms sell all of their outputs to households and receive money in return. All of the money received by firms is in turn paid out to households. Part goes as payments for factor services, and the rest is profit paid out as DIVIDENDS to the households that own the firms. In short, neither households nor firms save anything in the Spendthrift economy; everything that one group receives is paid out to buy goods and services from the other group. Expenditure is the order of the day!

The Spendthrift economy is illustrated in Figure 32.2. Payments are shown

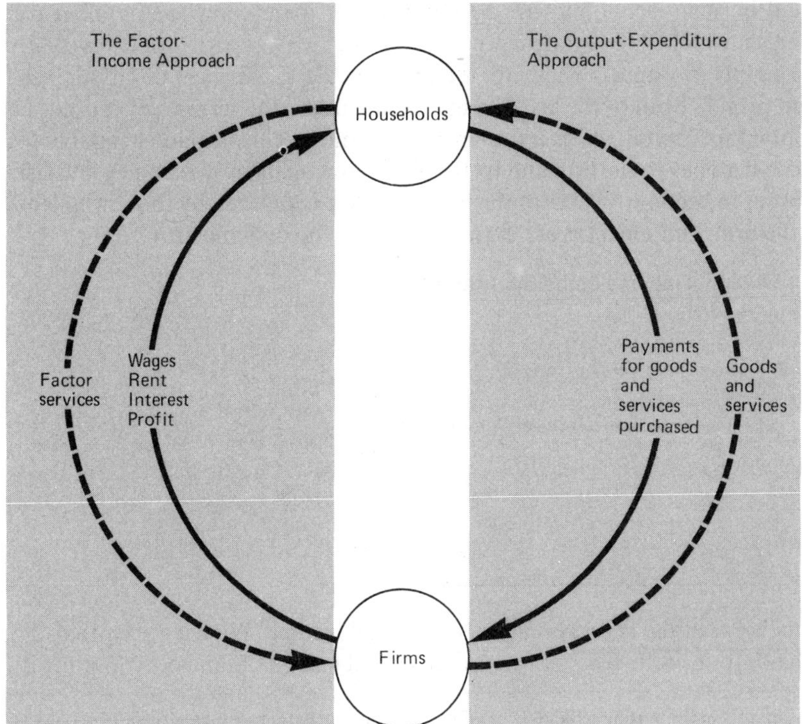

Fig. 32.2 Real and money flows between firms and households

[1] This method of argument is common in economics. It is based on the idea that it is easier to study things one at a time than all at once. Indeed, early economists made this explicit when they spoke of abstractions from reality followed by a build-up to realism through a series of 'successive approximations'.

flowing from households to firms in return for goods and services, and from firms to households in return for factor services.

Two approaches to measuring national income

Now suppose we wish to calculate the total value of the Spendthrift economy's annual output. We can do this by making calculations based on either side of the circular-flow diagram shown in Figure 32.2.

The output-expenditure approach The output-expenditure approach uses calculations based on the flows on the right-hand side of the figure. When we use this approach we calculate the total expenditure needed to purchase the nation's output. In the simple Spendthrift economy all output is sold to households, and we can get the total we require by measuring the actual expenditure of households on currently produced goods and services.

The factor-income approach The second method of calculation is based on the flows in the left-hand side of Figure 32.2. It calculates national income by measuring the value of factor inputs or, what is the same thing, the factor incomes generated by the process of production.

It is usual in macroeconomics to distinguish four main components of factor incomes: RENT, which is all rental income to persons,[1] WAGES AND SALARIES (often referred to simply as wages), which are the payment for the services of labour, and interest and profits. Both of the last two are payments for the services of capital. In order to obtain its capital goods a firm requires money. This is made available by those who lend money to the firm and by those who put up their own money and risk its loss in order to become owners of the firm. INTEREST is earned by those who lend money to the firm, and PROFITS are earned by those who own the firm.[2]

Table 32.1 National income in the Spendthrift economy (millions of pounds)

Factor income		Value of output
Rent	£ 100	Consumption Commodities (C)
Wages	650	£1,000
Interest	160	
Profits	90	
	£1,000	£1,000

The relation between the two approaches to national income We have seen that the value of the output produced over a specific period can be obtained by looking at

[1] This may arise from the renting of land or buildings, and also includes royalties earned from patents and copyrights.

[2] The concepts of rent, wages, interest, and profits used in macroeconomics do not correspond exactly to the microeconomic concepts that go under the same names. In macroeconomics they correspond to the incomes of land, labour and capital, the income of capital being split between borrowed and equity capital. Thus profits in macroeconomics correspond to what is called the 'gross return to capital' in microeconomics. Profits in microeconomics refer to a return over and above all opportunity costs including those of capital.

either the output-expenditure *or* the factor-income side of the economy. Can the two approaches yield different answers? The answer is 'no' because of the definition of profits. The profits on a firm's output are defined by the national income accountant as the value of that output minus all claims for rent, wages, and interest that arise out of its production. This definition ensures that the sum of rent, wages, interest and profit is equal to the value of output.[1]

Because the value of output produced is equal to the value of income earned (by virtue of the definition of profits), we can talk about either *national income* or *national product*. National income emphasizes the input, or factor-income, aspects of production, while national product emphasizes the output aspect. Since both terms refer to the same total, they are used interchangeably.

An example of the calculation of national income in the Spendthrift economy is given in Table 32.1. In the Spendthrift economy goods and services produced and sold for consumption account for the total value of all production. Factor incomes earned by the households who supply the services of land, labour and loan capital account for most of the total value of goods produced, while the remainder is profits. Both sides of the table add up to the same total by virtue of the definition of profits.

Intermediate products and inter-firm sales

We must now alter our model of the Spendthrift economy to deal with one very important complication. So far all firms have sold their outputs to households; this implies that all firms produce commodities in a form ready for consumption by households. In this case, the value of output is the sum of the values of all sales made by firms. In reality, however, production of commodities is divided into stages; firms and industries often specialize in only one stage of production. For example, one set of firms may mine iron ore; they may sell it to another set for manufacture into steel, the steel may be sold to another set of firms for use in making household tools, the manufacturer of the tools may sell them to a wholesaler, who sells them to a retailer, who in turn finally sells them to households.

We now alter our Spendthrift economy to allow for stages of production and the consequent inter-firm sales. This raises a new problem when applying the output-expenditure approach to measuring national income. If we merely added up the market values of the outputs of all firms, we would obtain a total greatly in excess of the value of output actually available to be consumed by the households in the Spendthrift economy. Suppose we took the value of all farmers' outputs of wheat

[1] The definitional identity of factor earnings and the value of output is easily shown for those who prefer algebraic demonstrations. Let P, R, W and I stand for profits, rent, wages and interest respectively and let O stand for the value of output. Using the three bar identity sign to indicate that all this is a matter of how we define terms (not a matter of how the world does and does not behave) we write the *definition* of profits as:

$$P \equiv O-(R+W+I),$$

rearranging terms:

$$P+R+W+I \equiv O,$$

i.e., factor earnings $\equiv$ value of output.

and added to it the value of all flour mills' outputs of flour, plus the value of the outputs of bakeries, plus the value of the sales of bread by all retail shops. The resulting total would be much larger than the value of the final product – bread – produced by the economy. We would have counted the value of the wheat four times, of the flour three times, of the bread produced by the bakery twice, and of the services of the retail shop once.

This is called the problem of DOUBLE COUNTING. *Multiple counting* would be a better term, since if we add up the values of all sales, the same output is counted *every time* it is sold from one firm to another. To avoid this problem, national income accountants use the important concept of the value added. Each firm's VALUE ADDED is the value of its output *minus* the value of the inputs that it purchases from other firms. Thus a flour mill's value added is the value of its output of flour *minus* the value of the grain it buys from the farmer and the values of any other inputs such as electricity and fuel oil that it buys from other firms. The relation between value added and total value of sales is illustrated in Exhibit 1.

In macroeconomics a firm's OUTPUT is defined as its value added; the sum of all values added must be the value of all goods and services produced by the economy.

The idea of value added suggests an important distinction between intermediate and final products. INTERMEDIATE PRODUCTS are all goods and services used as inputs into a further stage of production. FINAL PRODUCTS are the outputs of the economy after eliminating all double counting. In the previous example, grain, flour, electricity, and fuel oil were all intermediate products used at various stages in the process leading to the final product, bread. In the first version of the Spendthrift economy there were no intermediate products. In the second version, all final products are produced by firms and sold to households for consumption, while all intermediate products are sold from one firm to another.

Exhibit 2 shows an example of the identity between the factor-income and output-expenditure approaches when the value of one firm's sales includes the values of outputs it has bought from other firms and used as inputs. Output is then defined as value added.

The Frugal economy

The Spendthrift economy is an economy of the here and now; all income is spent on goods and services for current consumption and all current output is consumed. In the Frugal economy households and firms look to the future, and as a result both saving and investment occur.

Saving

SAVING is income not spent on goods and services for current consumption. Both households and firms can save. Households save when they elect not to spend part of their current income on goods and services for consumption. Firms save when they elect not to pay out to their owners some of the profits that they have earned. All profits belong legally to the owners, but only some are actually paid out, while the rest are withheld by firms for their own uses. DISTRIBUTED PROFITS are profits actually paid out to the owners of firms, and UNDISTRIBUTED PROFITS are profits

Exhibit 1

Value added through stages of production: an example

Because the output of one firm often becomes the input of other firms, the total value of goods sold by all firms greatly exceeds the value of the output of final goods. This general principle is illustrated by a simple example in which firm R starts from scratch and produces goods (raw materials) valued at £100; the firm's value added is £100. Firm I purchases raw materials valued at £100 and produces semi-manufactured goods that it sells for £130. Its value added is £30 because the value of the goods is increased by £30 as a result of the firm's activities. Firm F purchases the semi-manufactured goods for £130 and works them into a finished state, selling them for £180. Firm F's value added is £50. The value of final goods, £180, is found either by counting the sales of firm F or by taking the sum of the values added by each firm. This value is less than the £410 that we obtain by adding up the market value of the commodities sold by each firm. The following table summarizes the example.

Transactions between firms at three different stages of production

	Firm R	Firm I	Firm F		All firms
A. Purchases from other firms	£ 0	£100	£130		£230 = Total inter-firm sales
B. Purchase of factors of production (wages, rent, interest, profits)	100	30	50		180 = Value added
Total A+B = value of product	£100	£130	£180 = Value of final goods and services		£410 = Total value of all sales

Exhibit 2

Value added, value of output and factor incomes: an example

Last year in the Spendthrift economy a tenant farmer produced £25,000 worth of wheat. His wage bill was £10,000 (including a payment for his own labour services); his rent was £3,500; and he paid interest of £1,250 on a bank loan. He also spent £7,000 on seeds, electricity, fertilizer, and a host of other inputs that were produced by other firms. This left him an income of £3,250 in return for supplying and risking his own capital in his farming enterprise. His transactions are summarized in the table which shows that his contribution to total national income is £18,000. This figure can be obtained by calculating the farmer's value added or by calculating the factor income generated by his productive activities.

Take	Total value of sales	£25,000		
Subtract	Cost of materials purchased	7,000		
To obtain	Value added (output)			£18,000
Take	Rent	3,500		
Plus	Wages	10,000		
Plus	Interest	1,250		
Subtract them from value added			−£14,750	
To obtain	Profits		3,250	
Add back profits to rent, wages, and interest				
To obtain	Factor income			£18,000

held back. Undistributed profits constitute savings made by firms on behalf of their owners, since they are incomes earned but not spent on current consumption.

Investment

The terms *investment* and *investment goods* are used in the same way in macro as in microeconomics. INVESTMENT is defined as the act of producing goods that are not for immediate consumption; the goods themselves are called INVESTMENT GOODS.[1] They are produced by firms and they may be bought either by firms or by households. Three major components of investment are inventories, capital goods such as plant and equipment and residential housing.

Investment in inventories Virtually all firms hold inventories of their inputs and of their outputs. Inventories of inputs allow production to continue at the desired pace in spite of short-term fluctuations in the deliveries of inputs bought from other firms. Inventories of outputs allow firms to meet orders in spite of temporary, unexpected fluctuations in the rate of output or sales.

Inventories are an inevitable part of the productive process, and they require an investment of the firm's money since the firm has paid for them but has not yet sold them. An accumulation of inventories counts as current investment because it represents goods produced but not used for current consumption, while a drawing down – often called a decumulation – counts as *dis*investment because it is a reduction in the stock of goods produced in the past.

Intended and unintended inventory investment Inventory investment may be either intentional or unintentional. If the firm produces and holds goods that it planned to use to build up its inventories, then its investment is intentional, or planned. If the firm produces goods that it plans to sell but does not sell because expected orders do not materialize, then its inventory investment is unintentional, or unplanned. Similarly, inventory disinvestment may be intentional or unintentional. If the firm plans to produce less than it sells its inventory disinvestment is intentional, while if sales are unexpectedly greater than output, then the resulting inventory disinvestment is unintentional.

Investment in capital goods Capital was discussed in detail in Chapter 28. The production of new capital goods is part of total investment. Such goods may either replace capital that has been used up in the process of production (or otherwise consumed) or make net additions to the stock of capital.

Investment in housing A house is a very durable asset that yields its utility slowly over a long life. For this reason housing construction is counted as investment expenditure rather than as consumption expenditure. The national income accountant assumes that the investment is made by the firm that builds the housing, and that when it is sold to consumers, this is a mere transfer of ownership that is not a part of national income. Behaviourally, however, investment in housing is

[1] In common speech an individual speaks of 'investing' his money when he or she buys an equity or a bond. From the national income point of view this is a transfer of ownership of an existing asset; investment expenditure must be expenditure on currently produced goods.

different from investment in capital goods in that housing is built to be sold to households, while other capital goods are built to be sold to firms.

Total investment The total investment that occurs in the economy is called GROSS INVESTMENT. The amount necessary for replacement is called the CAPITAL CONSUMPTION ALLOWANCE and is often referred to as DEPRECIATION; the remainder is called NET INVESTMENT. It is net investment that increases the economy's total stock of capital, while the replacement investment keeps the existing stock intact by replacing what has been worn out or otherwise used up.

Income and output in the Frugal economy

There are two sorts of current production of final commodities in the Frugal economy. First, there are consumption goods and services actually sold to households. Second, there are investment goods that consist of capital goods plus inventories of semi-finished and finished goods still in the hands of firms. The symbols C and I stand for currently produced consumption goods and currently produced investment goods, respectively.

In an economy that uses capital goods, as does the Frugal economy, it is helpful to distinguish between two concepts of national income (or national product). GROSS NATIONAL INCOME (or GROSS NATIONAL PRODUCT, GNP) is the sum of all values added in the economy. Since it is the sum of the values of all final goods produced for consumption and investment, it is also the sum of all factor incomes earned in the process of producing the nation's output. NET NATIONAL INCOME (or NET NATIONAL PRODUCT, NNP) is GNP minus the capital consumption allowance. NNP is thus a measure of the net output of the economy after deducing from gross output an amount necessary to maintain the existing stock of capital intact.

Output and expenditure in the Frugal economy

In the Spendthrift economy all currently produced goods and services are sold to households, so obviously the value of final output is equal to the value of expenditure on that output. In the Frugal economy some final output is sold to households, some – such as plant and equipment – is sold to other firms, and some – newly produced inventories of a firm's own output – is not sold at all. The national income accountant includes production of goods for inventories as part of total expenditure. Thus, by expenditure we mean *what would have to be spent* to buy total output, not *what is actually spent* to buy that part which is actually sold. Thus the accountant calculates total expenditure as the actual expenditure on final goods and services sold, plus the market value of final commodities currently produced and added to inventories. This definition makes total expenditure the same thing as the value of all final commodities produced, thus ensuring that the measured value of expenditure is identical with the measured value of output in any economy.

Calculating GNP in the Frugal economy

Table 32.2 gives an illustration of the calculation of GNP for the Frugal economy. The GNP measures the value of output at market prices. The income claims it generates are equal to the total value of output. The profit figure generated is,

Table 32.2 National income in the Frugal economy (millions of pounds)

Factor Income		Value of Output	
Rent	120	Consumption commodities (*C*)	1000
Income	780	Investment goods (*I*)	
Interest	190	Capital goods	280
Gross profit	215	Inventory accumulation	25
GNP at market price	1305	GNP at market prices	1305
less Capital consumption allowance	105	*less* Capital consumption allowance	105
NNP	1200	NNP	1200

however, gross in that it includes depreciation. To keep its capital intact the firm must deduct depreciation before arriving at net profits that can be either paid out to the firm's owners or saved on their behalf by the firm and then reinvested in the firm. The deduction of the capital consumption allowance yields NNP.

The governed economy

We now give our economy a government. The Governed economy contains central authorities, often simply called 'the government', who levy taxes on firms and households, and who engage in activities that we studied in detail in Chapter 31, such as defending the country, making and enforcing the laws, building roads, running schools and predicting the weather.

The treatment of government expenditure in the GNP

Payments for currently produced goods and services When the government produces goods and services that households desire, such as roads and air traffic control, it is obviously engaged in useful activity and is adding to the sum total of valuable output. With other government activities the case may not seem quite so clear. Everyone knows people who feel that many of the activities of government are wasteful or even downright harmful. The national income accountant does not enter into such speculation. Instead he counts as part of the GNP every government expenditure on goods and services, whether it is to build the Concorde, to provide police protection, or to pay a civil servant to file and re-file papers from a now-defunct ministry. He does so not only because no two people could ever agree on precisely which government expenditures were productive and which wasteful, but also, and more fundamentally, because GNP is meant to measure total output and total use of factors of production, regardless of individual opinions about the value of the things produced. Thus GNP includes all government expenditures along with the outputs of such goods as gin, Bibles and contraceptives.

Total national income of the Governed economy includes all factor incomes generated by the activities of firms and governments. Just as wheat production uses factors and generates factor incomes, so do the activities of any branch of government such as the Department of the Environment.

Transfer payments There is one exception to the rule that all government expenditure is included in the GNP. If the government taxes a wage-earner and uses the money to make payments to a mother of five children whose husband has deserted her, income is transferred from the taxpayer to the recipient. The government does not receive any marketable productive services from the deserted mother in return for the payments. The expenditure itself adds neither to employment of factors nor to total output. Indeed, this is true whether the government raises this money by taxes, by borrowing, or by printing brand new money (which, as we shall see in a later Chapter, is something that it can do). The term GOVERNMENT TRANSFER PAYMENTS refers to any payments made to households by the government that are not in return for the services of factors of production. Such payments do not lead directly to any increase in marketable output and for this reason they are not included in the nation's GNP.[1]

> **The government expenditure that is included in GNP is net of any transfer payments.**

Disposable income

One magnitude that national income statisticians are concerned with measuring is the amount of income that households actually have available to spend or to save. This is called DISPOSABLE INCOME. To calculate disposable income, which is indicated by Y_d, the statistician must make several adjustments to GNP. First he deducts all those elements of the value of output that are not paid out to households: business savings represent receipts by firms from the sale of output that are withheld by firms for their own uses, and corporation taxes are receipts that are paid over to the government. Second, personal income taxes must be deducted from the income paid to households in order to obtain the amount households actually have available to spend or save. Finally, it is necessary to add government transfer payments made to households. Although these are not themselves a part of GNP, they are made available to households to spend and save and are thus a part of disposable income. To sum up, disposable income is GNP *minus* any part of it that is not actually paid over to households, *minus* the personal income taxes paid by households, *plus* transfer payments received by households.

Calculating GNP in the Governed economy

Government expenditure net of transfer payments is usually given the symbol G, and the GNP in the Governed economy can then be expressed as GNP $= C+I+G$. For the Governed economy the value of output is made up of consumption, investment and government goods and services.

Table 32.3 gives an illustration of GNP in the Governed economy. The introduction of government requires that we distinguish between GNP at market prices and GNP at factor cost. This is because the market value of GNP includes all indirect taxes on output. To get at the incomes earned by the factors producing the goods, we must deduct the part of the market value that is collected by the

[1] This point often provokes strong emotional responses: 'My bringing up the kids is just as productive as his slinging cow dung.' The point is that, whatever their 'true values' the farmer's output is a part of marketable total output while the housewife's output is not.

Table 32.3 National income in the Governed economy (millions of pounds)

Factor Income		Value of Output		
Rent	140	Consumption commodities (*C*)		1180
Wages	920	Investment (*I*)		
Interest	225	Capital goods		250
Gross profits	260	Inventory accumulation		65
GNP at factor cost	1545	Government		
		Total expenditure	325	
		less Transfer payments	150	
Indirect taxes (less subsidies)	125	Government contribution to GNP (G)		175
GNP at market prices	1670	GNP at market prices		1670
Capital consumption allowance	135	Capital consumption allowance		135
NNP	1535	NNP		1535

government through taxes on production. When this deduction is made, we obtain *GNP valued at factor cost.*[1] If it helps, you can think of indirect taxes as the government's share of the value of total output and what is left as the share belonging to the households whose factor services produced the GNP.

The open economy

None of the three economies considered so far engaged in foreign trade. They are called CLOSED ECONOMIES. In contrast, OPEN ECONOMIES engage in significant amounts of foreign trade, so that some of the commodities produced at home are sold abroad while some of the commodities sold at home are produced abroad.

Calculating GNP in the Open economy

The GNP of any economy, open or closed, is the total value of final goods and services produced in that economy. Some care is required, however, when the expenditure approach is used to measure the GNP of any open economy. It is necessary to allow for the facts that part of the expenditure on the domestic economy's GNP comes from foreign firms, households and governments (the domestic economy's exports) and that part of the expenditure of domestic firms, households and governments goes to the GNP of foreign countries (the domestic economy's imports).

To allow for these facts, the GNP of an Open economy may be thought of as being calculated in three steps. First, the total expenditure by domestic firms, governments and households on all final commodities, whether produced at home

[1] A subsidy lowers the market value of output below its factor cost. Thus subsidies must be *added* to GNP at market prices to get GNP at factor cost.

or imported, is calculated. This is $C+I+G$. Second, the value of all exports, X, is added to total expenditure. This accounts for domestic production sold abroad. The total $C+I+G+X$ is called TOTAL FINAL EXPENDITURE (TFE), and it gives the value of all expenditure required to purchase these four categories of output when they are valued at their market prices. Third, the value of all imported commodities, M, is deducted. This remainder is the total purchases of domestic and foreign spending units on all domestically produced goods and services. The resulting figure is the nation's GNP valued at market prices.

In symbols, the GNP for the Open economy is:

$$\text{GNP} = C+I+G+(X-M). \tag{1}$$

The value $X-M$ is called NET EXPORTS. This value is usually small in relation to the total value of either X or M. Thus, the correction to GNP when we move from a closed economy, where $\text{GNP} = C+I+G$, to an open economy, where $\text{GNP} = C+I+G+(X-M)$, will not usually be large. However, a change in either X or M, not matched by a change in the other, will cause the GNP to change in the same way as would a change in C, I, or G.

An alternative method

There is an alternative method of allowing for imports and exports in national income. This method is closer to the concepts required in a theoretical model of the behaviour of national income, but it is very difficult to apply when making actual measurements. To use this method, we calculate national income as the amount of expenditure on consumption, investment and exported goods and services that falls on commodities actually produced domestically. The rest we call the *import content* of consumption, investment, government expenditure and exports. Thus we can define four new concepts:

$$\begin{aligned} C^* &= C-C_M \\ I^* &= I-I_M \\ G^* &= G-G_M \\ X^* &= X-X_M, \end{aligned}$$

where C_M, I_M, G_M and X_M are the import contents of C, I, G and X respectively. You should not be surprised to hear that exports can have an import content. An exported car, for example, may have imported steel and rubber in it.

With these new definitions, GNP is defined by the following relation:

$$\text{GNP} = C^*+I^*+G^*+X^*. \tag{2}$$

The four terms give us the values of *domestic outputs* of consumption, investment, government commodities and exports.

It is easy to show that the two approaches come to the same thing by substituting the definitions of each of the starred terms into expression (2) for GNP. The substitution yields

$$\text{GNP} = C-C_M+I-I_M+G-G_M+X-X_M.$$

Gathering up all the import terms gives

$$\text{GNP} = C+I+G+X-(C_M+I_M+G_M+X_M),$$

and using M to stand for the sum of all imports yields

$$\text{GNP} = C+I+G+(X-M),$$

which is the first expression for GNP, numbered (1) in the previous subsection.

Thus the two ways of allowing for imports and exports come to the same thing. That of equation (1) is usually used in applied work since it is much easier to measure C, I, G and X than C^*, I^*, G^* and X^*. If we wish, however, to get the demands for domestic production under each of these categories, it is the starred terms that we require.

Measuring the GNP: a summary

Because the GNP can be looked at in various ways, students do not always find it immediately apparent that there is one, and only one, value of GNP for any one year. Basically, GNP measures the total value of the economy's output of final goods. We may look at this output either in terms of expenditure required to purchase it, E, or in terms of factor incomes that it generates, Y.

First, consider the expenditure required to purchase the economy's total output. When currently produced final commodities are sold, the market value of the output is equal to the amount actually spent to purchase the output. When currently-produced final commodities are added to the inventories of their producers, and not sold, the market value of the output is equal to the amount that would have to be spent if this output were purchased. The national income accountant defines expenditure not as what is actually spent, but as what would have to be spent to purchase all of the nation's output of final goods and services. By including the value of goods and services produced, but not sold, (as well as those that are produced and sold) in the definition of 'actual expenditure', the statistician ensures that[1]

$$\text{GNP} \equiv E.$$

Second, consider the factor incomes generated by the production of the GNP. This is the income of households who sell their factor services to producers. Factor incomes are divided into rent, wages and salaries, interest and profits. The national income accountant defines rent, wages and salaries, and interest as the value of land, labour and borrowed capital used in the course of production, whether or not payments were actually made to the owners of these factors of production during the year; and he defines profits as the total value of output minus rent, wages and salaries, and interest. This definition ensures that

$$\text{GNP} \equiv Y,$$

where Y stands for total factor incomes.

The definitions are such that output can be measured by expenditure or by factor incomes. It follows that the national income accountant uses terms in such a way that total expenditure and total factor incomes are identical with each other.

> **The definitions used by the national income accountant are such that $Y \equiv \text{GNP} \equiv E$, all three of which are alternative ways of looking at the nation's total output.**

[1] The three-bar identity sign emphasizes that these two values are equal by definition.

Real and nominal GNP

GNP measures the total *money* value of final goods produced during a year. Thus, it has a price and a quantity component, and a particular change in GNP can be caused by many different combinations of price and quantity changes. A 10 per cent rise might, for example, have been caused by a 10 per cent rise in prices, all quantities remaining unchanged; by a 10 per cent rise in quantities, all prices remaining unchanged; or by smaller increases in both prices and quantities. For some purposes the money value of national income is just the measure required. This is not always the case, however. Sometimes we wish to know what is happening to the actual quantity of output, and then we need to separate changes in the GNP that were caused by variations in market prices from changes that were caused by variations in the quantities of output.

To estimate the physical change in GNP, output is valued in constant prices. Each year the total quantities of output are determined. Instead of being valued at current prices, however, they are valued at a set of prices that ruled at some time in the past, called the *base year*. When the current GNP is valued in constant 1970 prices, we measure what the total value of output would have been if prices had not changed since 1970. The change in the GNP valued at constant prices is a measure of the pure quantity change. Thus if GNP at constant prices is up 30 per cent over what it was in 1970, this means that physical output has increased by 30 per cent since 1970 in the sense that price changes have not been allowed to affect these figures.

The GNP of a real economy

It remains only to relate our general discussion to the actual statistics for a real economy. Tables 32.4 and 32.5 show the major categories of the GNP for the UK.

Table 32.4 shows the GNP of the UK from the expenditure side. The terminology changes slightly from the general terms used in economic theory and employed in the previous tables. This table and the one that follows use the terms employed in the actual UK national income accounts. The first four terms are the same as those found in the earlier tables for our hypothetical economies. They correspond to *C*, *G* and *I*, with the last broken up between inventory and non-inventory investment. The fifth item allows for exports, which is that part of the output of an open economy that is sold abroad. The sum of these five items is total final expenditure (TFE) at market prices. It tells us, as we have already seen, the total amount needed to purchase all the final goods produced in the UK economy when they are valued at their market prices. But this expenditure includes the import contents of each of the items listed, and it also includes indirect taxes. To get to what is called Gross Domestic Product (GDP) at factor cost, it is necessary to deduct the value of imports and indirect taxes (less subsidies). This later deduction is called 'adjustment to factor cost' in UK accounts. The GDP tells us the value of all output produced in the UK valued at the costs of the factor services that went to produce them. One final adjustment is needed to get from GDP to GNP. This is net property income from abroad. This is another complication caused by the open economy. It represents the value of incomes earned by selling UK factor services abroad, mainly the services of capital invested overseas. This is income earned by UK households as a result of a contribution to current output. But it arises from foreign rather than

UK output, so although it is a part of income earned, it is not a part of output produced domestically. The adjustment is small and we ignore it in the theory that follows, thus treating GDP and GNP as equal.

Table 32.4 GNP at current prices, UK 1976: the output-expenditure approach

	£m
Consumers' expenditure	73,656
General government final consumption	26,562
Gross domestic fixed investment	23,427
Investment in stocks	359
Exports of goods and services	34,837
Total final expenditure at market prices	158,841
Less imports of goods and services	−36,564
Less adjustment to factor cost	−13,197
Gross domestic product at factor cost	109,080
Net property income from abroad	1,179
Gross national product at factor cost	110,259

Table 32.5 GNP at current prices, UK 1976: the factor-income approach

	£m
Income from employment	78,639
Income from self-employment	10,208
Income from rent	7,771
Gross trading profits of companies	12,445
Gross trading surplus of public corporations and other public enterprises	4,580
Imputed charge for consumption of non-traded capital	1,012
Total domestic income (before providing for stock appreciation)	114,655
Less stock appreciation	−6,557
Residual error	982
Gross domestic product at factor cost	109,080
Net property income from abroad	1,179
Gross national product at factor cost	110,259

Table 32.5 shows the GDP and GNP from the factor-income side. The categories are a little different from those used in our theoretical discussion, but most are self-explanatory. Income from employment is what we have called wages and salaries. In our theoretical models we count the self-employed as firms just like any other producing unit. Thus this income would in our theoretical categories be partly wages and partly profits. The profits figure in the actual accounts is sub-divided into private and public-sector profits. The imputed charge for consumption of non-traded capital is the capital consumption allowance. The final deduction concerns changes in the value of inventories due solely to price changes. The way the data are collected, a rise in the value of inventories that was due solely to a rise in their prices would show up as a part of GDP. Since this rise in value does not represent any new physical output, an adjustment is made to remove it from the total.

33

The determination of national income

The most obvious pattern in the historical statistics for the GNP for most Western industrial countries, and many agricultural ones as well, is a strong upward trend. Much of this is due to inflation, a rise in the prices at which each nation's output is valued. Even when the GNP data are calculated in constant prices to obtain series for real GNP, the upward trend remains strong in almost all countries and is present whatever income series we use, GNP, NNP or Y_d measured in total or in per capita figures.

If a long-term rising trend is the major theme of the twentieth-century GNP saga, a strong secondary theme is short-term fluctuations. These short-term fluctuations cause some serious problems. Rapid rises in real GNP often cause labour shortages, balance-of-payments problems and severe inflations. Declining real GNP often causes bouts of heavy unemployment, static or falling living standards and pockets of severe poverty.

Why does national income behave the way it does? Can governments do anything to influence the course of national income, employment and prices? In particular, can they do anything to prevent lapses from full employment and to restrain the inflations that appear to accompany periods of relatively full employment?

To deal with these and many related questions, we need to develop a theory of national income. We begin with preliminary definitions and assumptions; then, because it is easier to study complex things one at a time rather than all at once, we shall proceed in a series of small steps. In this chapter we shall build a theory of what determines the level of national income. In Chapter 34 we shall use this theory to explain why it changes. After that we shall investigate what the central authorities can do to influence either the short-term fluctuations or the long-term growth of GNP.

Preliminary definitions

National income In measuring national income, distinctions are made among such concepts as GNP, GDP and NNP. In their theories, economists usually use the generic concept of national income (indicated by the symbol Y) rather than such specific concepts as the GNP or the NNP. Usually Y may be thought of as interchangeable with GNP.

Equilibrium income Equilibrium is a state of rest, usually brought about by a balance between opposing forces. National income is said to be in equilibrium when there is no tendency for it either to increase or to decrease. The actual national income achieved at that point is referred to as the EQUILIBRIUM NATIONAL INCOME. In this chapter we study the forces that determine the size of equilibrium national income, which is often described as the problem of the *determination of national income*.

Autonomous and induced expenditure Any expenditure that is taken as a constant, unaffected by any economic variables within our theory, is called AUTONOMOUS EXPENDITURE. Any expenditure that is determined by, and thus varies with, economic variables within our theory is called INDUCED EXPENDITURE. For example, in the simple theory of the determination of national income, investment expenditure is assumed to be autonomous and consumption is assumed to be induced expenditure. (Note that, using the terminology introduced on page 30, autonomous and induced are the same, respectively, as exogenous and endogenous.)

Labour definitions The labour force is the number of persons willing to work (n), which number is made up of those actually working (l) and those willing to work but unable to find jobs, i.e., unemployed, (u). Thus $n = l+u$. If the labour force remains constant, then the number of employed and the number of unemployed vary inversely with each other (i.e., $u = n-l$).

The percentage of the labour force unemployed (U) is

$$U = \frac{u}{l+u} \times 100,$$

and the percentage of the labour force employed (L) is

$$L = \frac{l}{l+u} \times 100 = 100 - U.$$

(Notice that lower-case letters refer to absolute numbers and capitals refer to percentages.)

Actual income and full-employment income We have already noted that national income data show a long-term upward trend and short-term fluctuations. To separate these, a concept called FULL-EMPLOYMENT NATIONAL INCOME or POTENTIAL NATIONAL INCOME is used. This is the national income that could be produced if the country's factors of production were fully employed.[1] This concept is given the symbol Y_F. Actual national income, symbolized by Y, can be below Y_F if there is more unemployment than the frictional minimum. By working resources overtime and otherwise harder than normal, Y can occasionally rise above Y_F. The

[1] Because there are always people changing jobs, entering and leaving the labour force, etc., there will always be some unemployment. This unavoidable minimum amount of unemployment is called 'frictional unemployment'. 'Full employment' is defined to occur when there is no more than this minimum amount of frictional unemployment. In Britain it was defined in 1944 as occurring at 3 per cent unemployment, but postwar experience suggested a figure closer to 2 per cent. Recent experience has led, however, to some suggestion that the figure should now be revised upwards. In America full employment is currently said to occur when 5 per cent of the labour force is unemployed.

concept of Y_F is extremely important, and the terms potential and full-employment national income will occur throughout the analysis.

The circular flow We have already referred several times to the concept of the circular flow. We may now give it a precise definition. The CIRCULAR FLOW OF INCOME is the flow of payments and receipts for factor services and currently produced output passing between domestic (as opposed to foreign) firms and households.

Basic assumptions

In constructing our theory of the determination of national income we start by making some simplifying assumptions. These assumptions are designed to isolate the main forces that determine national income. The consequences of dropping them are considered later in this book.

(1) Potential national income is constant This assumption allows us to isolate the forces that strongly influence national income over short periods of time. When Y_F is constant, real (constant-price) national income changes only because of changes in the amount of employment of factors of production.

Because an economy's productive capacity changes only slowly from year to year, potential national income also changes slowly. Thus, although the cumulative effects of small annual changes in Y_F can be dramatic over several decades, the effects are relatively minor over a period of a year or two. As a result, assuming Y_F to be constant is not greatly unrealistic for short periods of time.[1]

(2) There are unemployed supplies of all factors of production This assumption implies that output can be increased by employing land, labour and capital that is currently unemployed. In subsequent chapters we shall study the behaviour of national income when unemployment has reached such a low level that it is difficult, if not impossible, to increase output by putting to work factors of production that are currently unemployed.

(3) The level of prices is constant The reason for making this assumption now is that it allows us to isolate the causes of changes in *real national income*. When prices are fixed, any change in national income must reflect a change in real quantities produced, whereas if prices increase, a change in national income will reflect a mixture of price and quantity changes. Later, when we come to study inflation, we shall drop this assumption.

Armed with the three assumptions just stated, we can focus on the problem of what determines the equilibrium level of real national income. The procedure is to take a

[1] The constancy of Y_F follows from two more basic assumptions. The total supply of inputs, and the output produced per unit of input used (productivity) are both assumed constant. Given these assumptions, full employment of all inputs, including labour, implies a particular quantity of employment, and this quantity of employment in turn implies a particular quantity of real output. Later, when we study the long-term behaviour of national income, we will be concerned with the changes in productivity and in factor supplies that cause Y_F itself to change.

model of an economy and discover what determines its equilibrium national income. (We shall begin with the simplest of the hypothetical economies met in the last chapter.) How the behaviour of national income in the model relates to the behaviour of national income in the real world, and the insight that the one gives us into the other, are discussed in subsequent chapters.

Equilibrium national income in the Spendthrift economy

Recall the three essential features of the Spendthrift economy. First, there are only two groups of decision takers, firms and households. Second, households spend all of their incomes buying consumption goods and services produced by firms. Third, firms pay all of their earnings out to households in the form of rent, wages, interest and distributed profits; there are no deductions for taxes (since there is no government), for depreciation (since if capital exists it lasts forever) or for business saving (since there is no investment in new capital). For the Spendthrift economy the circular flow, shown in Figure 33.1, is a genuinely closed circuit: whatever is

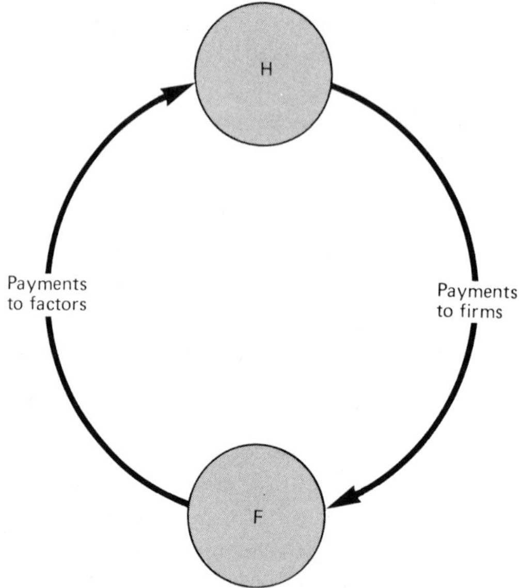

Fig. 33.1 The circular flow of income in the Spendthrift economy

received by households is passed on the firms and whatever is received by firms is passed on to households. No existing expenditure is ever withdrawn from the flow and no new expenditure is ever injected into it from outside.

If we start national income at any level in this economy, that level will persist indefinitely. If, for example, firms produce £1,000 worth of goods per week they will pay out £1,000 in factor incomes, and households will spend £1,000 on buying the output of firms. Households will just be able to spend all their income at current market prices and firms will be just able to sell all of their output at these same prices. Thus neither households nor firms have any reason to alter their behaviour. This would also be true if we started production at £10,000 per week, at £1 million per week or at any other figure (as long as resources were available to produce the output). Any level of national income once set going, will persist forever, since there is no reason for it to change. Since Y can be in equilibrium at any level there is nothing – except accident – to explain why it is at one level rather than another.

Unreal though this economy is, using it as a model allows us to isolate the forces that do determine the level of national income in more complicated economies such as the Frugal economy, to which we now turn.

Equilibrium national income in the Frugal economy

The Frugal economy differs from the Spendthrift economy in two essentials. First, households spend only part of their incomes on consumption, and they save the rest. Second, firms devote only part of their efforts to producing consumption goods for sale to households, and the remainder goes to producing investment goods. To simplify matters at the outset, we assume that all saving is done by households and all investing is done by firms. Thus investment and savings decisions are taken by different groups. This separation has one obvious, but very important, implication:

> **There is no reason why a change in the desire of households to save or in the desire of firms to invest should automatically be matched by a similar change on the part of the other group.**

Investment decisions

Firms make plans about how much to invest in new capital equipment. For this chapter it is convenient to study how the level of national income adjusts to a fixed level of investment. Thus we assume that firms plan to make a constant amount of investment in plant and equipment each year and that they plan to hold their inventories constant. In Chapters 36 and 37 we shall drop these assumptions and study the important effects on national income of changes in the level of investment.

Consumption-saving decisions

Each household makes plans about how much to spend on consumption, C, and how much to save, S. These are not, however, independent decisions. Since saving is income not spent on consumption, it follows that households have to decide on a single division of their income between saving and consumption.

How do households in the aggregate actually divide their income between C and S? This question is studied in detail in Chapter 35. In the meantime we shall make the simple assumption that consumption and saving are constant fractions of income. If, for example, every household spends 80 per cent of its income and saves the remaining 20 per cent, then in the Frugal economy consumption will be 80 per cent of national income and saving will be 20 per cent. The assumption of constancy is an acceptable 'first approximation' that we shall amend in later chapters.

Withdrawals and injections

Saving and investment are examples of two more general categories of expenditure called withdrawals and injections. A WITHDRAWAL is any income that is not passed on in circular flow. Thus if households earn income and do not spend it on domestically produced goods and services, this is a withdrawal from the circular flow. Similarly, if firms receive money from the sale of goods and do not distribute it as payments to factors, this is a withdrawal from the circular flow. An INJECTION is an addition to the income of domestic firms that does not arise from the expenditure of domestic households or an addition to the income of domestic households that does not arise from the spending of domestic firms. If, for example, firms gain income by producing investment goods which they sell to other firms, this is an injection, because the income of firms rises without households having increased their expenditure.

Now consider the effect of withdrawals on national income. If, for example, households decide to increase their saving and correspondingly reduce the amount they spend buying consumption goods, this reduces the income of firms and reduces the payments they will make to factors of production. Thus national income falls.

Withdrawals, by reducing expenditure, exert a contractionary force on national income.

Next consider the effect of injections on national income. If, for example, firms increase their sales of machines to other firms, their incomes and their payments to households for factor services will rise without there having been an increase in household expenditure. Thus national income rises.

Injections, by raising expenditure, exert an expansionary force on national income.

In the Frugal economy saving is the only withdrawal. It is income that households receive but do not spend buying goods and services from firms. Also investment is the only injection. It is the income of firms that does not arise from the spending of households. The circular flow in this economy is shown in Figure 33.2. The black

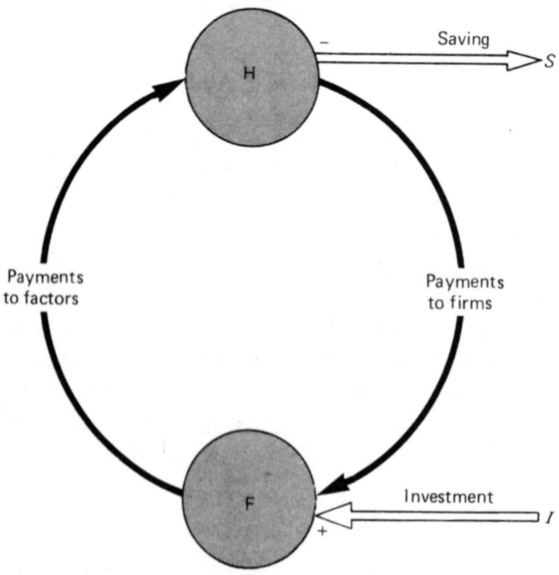

Fig. 33.2 The circular flow of income in the Frugal economy

arrows show the circular flow from domestic firms to domestic households and back again; the white arrows show the flow of saving as a withdrawal and the flow of investment as an injection.

The behaviour of the circular flow in the Frugal economy

We now consider how equilibrium income is determined in this model. To do this we first study what forces operate on income when it is not in equilibrium. This then allows us to discover the conditions for income to be in equilibrium – i.e., to be unchanging over time.

If we are ever to observe income out of equilibrium, there must be lags in the flow around the circuit pictured in Figure 33.2, because if all adjustments were instantaneous, the economy could never be out of equilibrium. The way the flow behaves out of equilibrium will depend critically on these lags. Since we are mainly interested in discovering the equilibrium income, we can employ very simple assumptions concerning lags as long as they are sufficient to reveal the forces determining the equilibrium. Here are the five assumptions we shall use.

(1) *Time is divided into discrete periods called weeks.*

(2) *Production adjusts to demand with no time lag.* Thus, whatever is demanded this week is produced and sold this week without any need for inventories of goods produced in the past to change. This amounts to assuming that firms correctly foresee any changes in demand that are going to occur.

(3) *Income is paid to households one week in arrears.* Thus if production rises this week, more factors are employed, but household disposable income does not rise until pay day which is at the end of the week. The income received on pay day is not therefore available for spending until the following week.

(4) *Households save a constant proportion of their disposable income each week and spend the remainder purchasing currently produced goods and services.*

(5) *Investment expenditure is an exogenous constant.*

A numerical illustration Table 33.1 illustrates the behaviour of the Frugal economy with the added specific assumptions that households save 20 per cent of their disposable incomes and consume the remaining 80 per cent, while investment expenditure is constant at 20 per week.[1] The example is not difficult, but it is critical to everything that follows so it will repay very careful study.

We assume that national income has been in equilibrium for some time in the past. The table shows these equilibrium values persisting over weeks 1 and 2 and then being disturbed in week 3.

Look first at the equilibrium. Households start week 1 with a disposable income of 100 which was earned producing a total output of 100 the previous week. They save 20 of this and spend the remaining 80 on consumption. Firms spend 20 on newly produced investment goods. The total value of output produced in week 1 is thus 100. The wages, rent, interest and profits generated by this production are paid out to households at the end of the week. Households thus start week 2, just as they started week 1, with a disposable income of 100. It is clear that national income is in equilibrium because, unless it is disturbed, the situation will repeat itself week after

[1] All quantities are measured in monetary units, and since prices are constant, values change only when real quantities change. The unit is left undefined, since it could just as well be an index number as a sterling or a dollar value.

Table 33.1 The behaviour of the circular flow of income in the Frugal economy: an example of a rise in investment

Col. 1	Col. 2	Col. 3	Col. 4	Col. 5	Col. 6
Week	Disposable income, Y_d (= the value of last week's national income)	Saving, S (= $0{\cdot}2Y_d$)	Consumption, C (= $0{\cdot}8\ Y_d$)	Investment, I (= an exogenous constant)	National income, Y (= value of this week's production, $C+I$)
1	100	20	80	20	100
2	100	20	80	20	100
3	100	20	80	40	120
4	120	24	96	40	136
5	136	27·2	108·8	40	148·8
.	.	.	.	.	.
.	.	.	.	.	.
.	.	.	.	.	.
n	200	40	160	40	200
$n+1$	200	40	160	40	200

week with output of 100, disposable income of 100, induced consumption expenditure of 80, and autonomous investment expenditure of 20. Notice that the amount households save is exactly equal to the amount firms invest (so that all investment could be financed by selling bonds and equities to households).

A rise in investment Now let us disturb the equilibrium with a sudden investment boom. At the beginning of week 3 firms become more optimistic about the future and decide to double their investment expenditure. (They cannot borrow this new amount from households and will have to borrow from financial institutions or else use their own accumulated reserves.)

Look carefully at what happens in weeks 3 and 4. Households start week 3 with a disposable income which they earned from producing output in week 2. Because they have the same Y_d as in previous weeks, their saving remains at 20 and their consumption expenditure remains at 80. Firms, however, now demand 40 of investment goods and output expands immediately to meet this demand (assumption 2 above). Thus national income rises to 120 in week 3. Why did national income rise? The reason is that investment made by firms (column 5) exceeds saving made by households (column 3) and this discrepancy exerts a net expansionary force on the circular flow of income.

In week 4 household disposable income rises to 120 because households are paid for the extra work done in week 3. Their saving now rises to 24, and their consumption expenditure rises to 96. The output of consumption goods rises immediately to 96 to meet this extra demand (assumption 2 once again). The value of total output rises to 136 ($C+I=96+40$).

This 136 is paid out to households at the end of the week and becomes their disposable income in week 5. Expenditure rises once again, and this causes disposable income to rise again in week 6. Where will this stop? To understand where, add another two rows in the table yourself, allowing households to start the first week with a disposable income (= value of last week's output) of any number greater than 148.8 but less than 200. Pick this entry for column 2 yourself, then work out the entries for the remaining columns. The last entry you make in column 6 becomes the entry in column 2 for the second of the two weeks you study. If you do this now, you will greatly help your understanding of the process we are discussing.

If you now check the figures you have just calculated, you will see two important features: (i) whatever the disposable income you chose for the first week (provided only that it was less than 200), national income in that week, and hence disposable income in the following week, will be higher and (ii) saving as recorded in column 3 will be less than investment as recorded in column 5.[1]

Now consider the income of 200, which is recorded in the table under weeks n and $n+1$. When households have a disposable income of 200 they save 40 and spend 160 on consumption. Firms also spend 40 on investment, so that the total value of output is 200. This 200 becomes the disposable income of households in the following week, and the whole process repeats itself. Clearly, unless something changes to disturb these flows, national income and all of the other flows in the table will repeat themselves week by week. The expansionary forces that raised income above its initial equilibrium value of 100 are now spent. Why? The reason is that the withdrawal from the circular flow caused by saving just matches the injection caused by investment. The circular flow is now in an equilibrium in which the contractionary and expansionary forces of saving and investment just balance each other.

Table 33.2 The behaviour of the circular flow of income in the Frugal economy: an example of a fall in investment

Col. 1	Col. 2	Col. 3	Col. 4	Col. 5	Col. 6
Week	Disposable income, Y_d (= the value of last week's national income)	Saving, S (= 0·2 Y_d)	Consumption, C (= 0·8 Y_d)	Investment, I (= an exogenous constant)	National income, Y (= value of this week's production, $C+I$)
1	100	20	80	20	100
2	100	20	80	20	100
3	100	20	80	10	90
4	90	18	72	10	82
5	82	16·4	65·6	10	75·6
.	.	.	.	.	.
.	.	.	.	.	.
.	.	.	.	.	.
n	50	10	40	10	50
$n+1$	50	10	40	10	50

A fall in investment Now consider a disturbance that lowers national income. The argument exactly parallels the one already given for a rise in investment.

Table 33.2 repeats the original situation for weeks 1 and 2 but then assumes that

[1] For example, if income is 180 at period x, Y_d will be 180 in the next period, S will be 36, C will be 144, and with an I of 40, income will rise to 184. Also the S of 36 is less than the I of 40.

in week 3 there is a sudden rush of pessimism, rather than of optimism, and a halving of investment rather than a doubling. In week 3 investment expenditure falls from 20 to 10 and, since this was foreseen by producers, total output falls from 100 to 90. In the following week disposable income falls to 90, and as a result saving falls to 18 and consumption to 72. Because output adjusts immediately to this fall in consumption expenditure, national income falls to 82 in week 4 ($C+I = 72+10$). Notice that in weeks 3 and 4 investment as defined by column 4 is less than saving as defined by column 2. This excess of saving over investment exerts a net contractionary force on the circular flow and causes national income to fall.

A check of any intermediate value for household disposable income less than 76.5 but greater than 50 will show: (i) that national income that week, and hence disposable income generated for the following week, is lower and (ii) that household saving exceeds investment.[1]

Once national income reaches 50, however, the contractionary forces are spent. The table shows this for the two periods labelled n and $n+1$. With a disposable income of 50, households save 10 and spend 40 on consumption. Investment is 10, making a total output of 50, which generates a disposable income of 50 to be spent in the following period. At this level of income, the withdrawal from the circular flow caused by saving just matches the injection caused by investment. The flow is in an equilibrium in which contractionary and expansionary forces just balance each other.

In the Frugal economy equilibrium national income occurs where saving equals investment. When saving exceeds investment, income falls; when investment exceeds saving, income rises.

Saving and investment are here defined by columns 3 and 5 of Tables 33.1 and 33.2.

The measurement of saving and investment in the model of the circular flow

We have used definitions of saving and investment that correspond to the actual flows in a circular flow model. The definitions are illustrated in Figure 33.3. Part (i) shows the model in equilibrium as shown in weeks 1 and 2 in Tables 33.1 and 33.2. Part (ii) shows week 3 from Table 33.1. The left-hand flow shows the factor payments actually available to households for spending during the week. The right-hand flows show money actually laid aside by households for saving, money actually spent on consumption during the week and actual expenditure on investment goods.[2] National income is clearly not in equilibrium, and since investment exceeds saving, income will rise in subsequent weeks, which is what Table 33.1 shows happens.

Part (iii) shows week 3 in Table 33.2. Investment has just fallen from 20 to 10, but disposable income will not fall until next week. As a result the amount actually

[1] For example, if income were 60 last week, Y_d will be 60 this week, saving will be 12, consumption will be 48 and national income will be 58 ($C+I = 48+10$). Also saving of 12 is greater than the investment of 10.

[2] If, for example, households lend all of their savings to firms by purchasing newly issued bonds, the amount of bonds sold by firms to households will be 20 in week 3 (as it is in weeks 1 and 2).

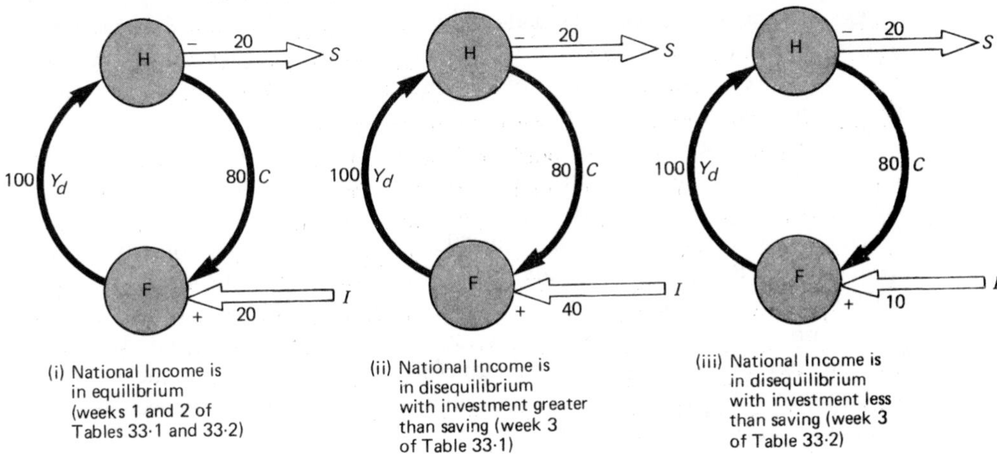

Fig. 33.3 Flows in the Frugal economy in situations of equilibrium and disequilibrium

withdrawn by household saving exceeds the amount actually injected by firms' investment[1] and we must expect national income to fall in the subsequent week.

The measurement of saving and investment by the national income statistician[2]

The national income statistician approaches the Frugal economy as follows. He defines GNP as the value of total output (O), which is made up of consumption and investment goods. Thus

$$\text{GNP} \equiv O \equiv C+I,$$

where the three bar signs remind us that we are dealing with relations that hold by definition. The statistician also allocates all the value of output to factor incomes generated in the process of producing the GNP. He then allocates this income between two categories of expenditure: what is spent, C, and what is saved, S. Thus

$$\text{GNP} \equiv Y \equiv C+S.$$

This use of terms makes saving identical with investment:

$$C+I \equiv O \equiv Y \equiv C+S;$$
$$\therefore \quad I \equiv S.$$

The trick here is that the national income statistician is not making measurements at various points in the circular flow – as we did when we described its disequilibrium behaviour in Tables 33.1 and 33.2 and Figure 33.3. He is measuring the circular flow at one point: the point F in Figure 33.3. He is, in fact, measuring the value of total output. When he speaks of factor incomes generated in a particular

[1] For example, if firms finance all of their new investment by selling bonds to households, there will be 10 units of bonds sold and households will find themselves with an additional 10 of saving that they are unable to invest by lending it to firms.

[2] This section can be omitted on first reading. It deals with a confusion between saving and investment in the national income accounts and saving and investment in the circular flow model. If you have not already encountered the confusion, it might be better to omit the discussion until you have mastered the circular flow model.

'week' (or year) he does not mean the value of incomes actually paid out to households during that 'week' – or year (not even in the Frugal economy, where all income is eventually paid out to households). Instead he means a notional allocation of the value of current output into the income claims that can be put on it – the amount that is owed to land, to labour and to borrowed capital, plus the amount that is left for the residual claim of profits. Thus in Figure 33.1 (ii), the statistician would say that national income in week 3 was 120. He would also say that factor incomes were 120. Since only 80 was spent on consumption, savings must have been 40. But households only laid aside 20 out of their disposable income in week 3, so where is the other 20 of what the statistician calls saving? The answer is simple enough: during week 3 firms produced and sold 120 worth of goods, but only paid out 100 in actual payments to factors (because payments are made in arrears). So firms are saving the extra 20 (which will be paid out to factors to become part of their disposable income for next week).

The national income statistician measures the value of output during the week. He also measures the claims on the value of that output on the part of factors (and he measures them in such a way that they add up to exactly the value of the output). Thus in part (ii) of Figure 33.3, the statistician measures the flow of output at point F; he takes this, subtracts C and calls the remainder S. Since output is $C+I$, it follows that S and I are two terms for the same thing. All of these measurements are made at the same point in the circular flow. (In fact, he may take measurements at many points, but they are all then adjusted to be consistent with one point, the value of output.)

The statistician's measurements are extremely useful in telling us the size of the circular flow and whether or not it is changing over time. They are not to be confused, however, with what is happening at various points in the circular flow as, for example, in the various parts of Figure 33.3. They do not help us to explain why the circular flow is changing. That explanation lies in comparing, as we did in the tables, the amount actually saved in any one week with the amount actually invested in that week. Clearly we cannot do this if we work with definitions in which these two magnitudes are necessarily the same.[1]

When we speak of saving exceeding or falling short of investment, we are using the terms as defined in Tables 33.1 and 33.2. There is no conflict between our use of savings and investment as unequal in the tables and the statisticians' use in which savings are always equal to investment, since the statisticians define the terms differently than we do in our theory of the circular flow.[2]

A graphical approach to determining equilibrium national income in the Frugal economy

Dynamic analysis of the circular flow out of equilibrium, such as we did above,

[1] Another way of putting this point is that the behaviour of expenditure, output and income around the circuit will depend critically on the lags when the flows are changing, but the statisticians' concepts which make $E \equiv O \equiv Y$ are unlagged. This is because they take the current value of output and divide it into the income claims on it and the expenditure needed to purchase it, which is not the same thing as the income actually paid out or the expenditure actually made during the period.

[2] The problem in reconciling the use of the terms as being equal and unequal together with a detailed critique of the illegitimate attempt in many text books to deduce empirical statements from definitional identities can be found in R. G. Lipsey, 'The Foundations of the Theory of National Income: An Analysis of Some Fundamental Errors,' *Essays in Honour of Lord Robbins* (Weidenfeld: London), 1972.

rapidly becomes very difficult and requires some advanced mathematics. We can, however, get a long way by confining ourselves to positions of equilibrium and using the method of comparative statics to see how a shift in any of the forces that influence national income changes its equilibrium value.

To do this we need to introduce two new and very useful graphs which show two alternative approaches to determining equilibrium national income.

The saving-investment approach Figures 33.4 and 33.5 introduce a type of graphical representation that we shall use frequently. Look first at Figure 33.4. On the horizontal axis we measure national income, on the vertical axis expenditure. The graph thus allows us to relate national income to various kinds of expenditure.

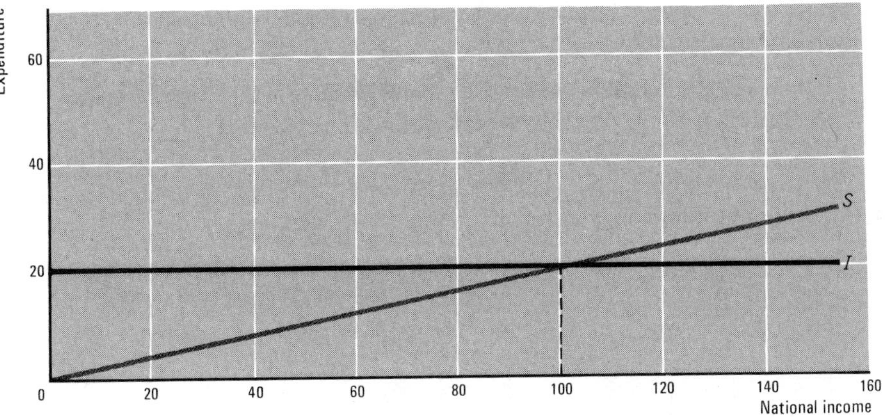

Fig. 33.4 Determination of equilibrium national income in the Frugal economy by the saving-investment approach

The lines in the figure are drawn to correspond with the behaviour assumed for the initial equilibrium shown in Tables 33.1 and 33.2. Investment is exogenous and is constant at the level of 20. The investment line, *I*, in Figure 33.4 is thus shown as a horizontal straight line at a value of 20. This shows that *I* is the same whatever the level of national income.

The saving line, *S*, relates saving to national income. In the case studied in Tables 33.1 and 33.2 there are lags in the relation between saving and national income. Saving in any week is 20 per cent of that week's disposable income, but that week's disposable income is equal to the previous week's national income (i.e., output). This lag between national income (= output produced) and the disposable income available to be spent means that saving this week depends on national income last week. (You can easily check that the entry in column 3 for any week is 20 per cent of the entry in column 6 for the previous week.) But this is only one very simple lag and many others are possible. Since we are interested only in equilibrium positions, we can avoid the complication of lags as follows. We plot the relation between saving and current national income that would exist if income were repeated for enough weeks that the effects of any lags were removed. Thus, for example, if national income were constant at a value of 140 in the Frugal economy, current disposable income would also be 140 and saving would be 20, which is 28 per cent of current national income. This procedure allows us to relate current *S* to current *Y* by simple relation $S = 0{\cdot}2Y$.[1] Thus the savings line in Figure 33.4 is shown by the upward-sloping straight line: whatever level of Y we choose, the line tells us that S will be 20 per cent of that value. Any point on the S line tells us that *if* Y were held constant at the value indicated on the income axis, S would be the value indicated on the expenditure axis. Because it tells us what households would like to save if their income were constant at each indicated value, it is called the *desired saving function.*

We can now use the diagram to determine the equilibrium level of national income. Equilibrium is where the savings and investment functions intersect. This is at a value of 100 in the present example. If national income were to be held constant at any value *less than* 100, households would save less than firms wished to invest, and national income would rise under the expansionary pressure of an excess of investment over saving. If national income were to be constant at an amount in excess of 100, households would save more than firms would wish to invest and national income would fall.

Graphically the equilibrium level of national income in the Frugal economy occurs where the saving and investment functions intersect.

The income-expenditure approach The second method of determining equilibrium national income graphically is shown in Figure 33.5, which is also drawn to conform

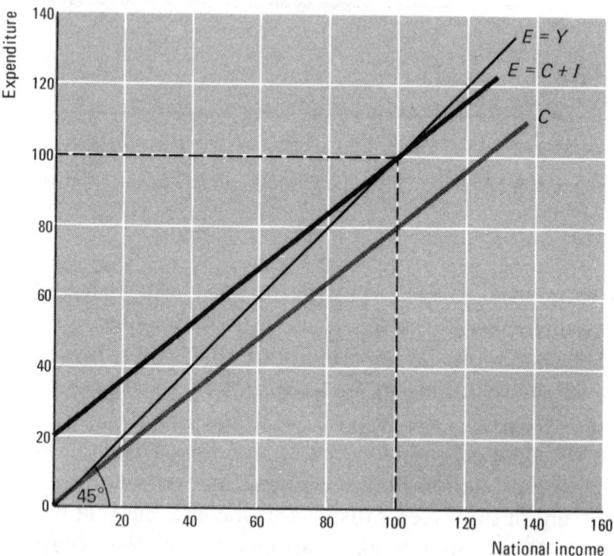

Fig. 33.5 Determination of national income in the Frugal economy by the income-expenditure approach

with the example of weeks 1 and 2 of Tables 33.1 and 33.2. Income and expenditure are again plotted on the two axes. Three lines are shown on the figure. We must introduce these one at a time.

[1] Algebraically this is done as follows. For purposes of this one footnote denote disposable income by Y^d and let the t subscript refer to time periods. Table 33.1 tells us $C_t = 0{\cdot}8Y_t^d$ and $Y_t^d = Y_{t-1}$ so that $C_t = 0{\cdot}8Y_{t-1}$ which is a one-period lag. But if we let income repeat itself for two periods, we have $Y_t = Y_{t-1}$, so that $C_t = 0{\cdot}8Y_t$. This tells us that if Y were held constant for 2 periods, then C would be 80 per cent of this current, constant value of Y. Thus *saving* would be 20 per cent of Y: $S = 0{\cdot}2Y$.

The 45° line: If we locate all the points showing annual expenditure exactly equal to annual income and join them up, we shall trace out the line labelled $E = Y$ in the figure. This line makes an angle of 45° with the Y-axis and is often referred to as the 45° LINE. Points above or to the left of the 45° line show combinations for which expenditure exceeds income; points below or to the right of the 45° line show combinations for which expenditure is less than income.[1]

Consumption: The line labelled C is the CONSUMPTION FUNCTION. It relates household consumption expenditure to national income. In drawing this line we encounter the same problem we encountered with the S function in Figure 33.4: lags mean that current consumption may be related to previous income. We use the same solution, graphing the relation of current C to current Y that will occur when Y has been constant long enough to remove the effects of any lags. The consumption line thus tells us what the associated level of consumption would be if national income were held constant at any indicated level. Since in the example of Tables 33.1 and 33.2 consumption is 80 per cent of income, this line slopes upwards with a slope of 0·8.[2] The gap between the C line and the 45° line shows household saving. (Since in the Frugal economy all income must be saved or consumed, consumption plus saving must add up to total income, so when Y is plotted against $C+S$, it must yield the 45° line.)

Aggregate expenditure: The third line is labelled $E = C+I$. It is variously called the AGGREGATE EXPENDITURE FUNCTION and the AGGREGATE DEMAND FUNCTION and we shall use both terms interchangeably. It relates national income to the total demand for all forms of production. Since in the Frugal economy there is only consumption and investment, E is the sum of C *plus* I. Since I is assumed constant, the E line is parallel to the C line.[3] Since the aggregate expenditure function is the sum of $C+I$, any point on it tells us how much spending units would like to spend to purchase the economy's output if income were held constant at the level of Y indicated by that point.

Equilibrium income: In this approach the equilibrium level of national income is determined where the aggregate expenditure function cuts the 45° line. If national income is held at that point, aggregate demand will be just sufficient to buy up the total of all goods produced. If national income is held above that point, aggregate expenditure will be less than the value of output. *If*, for example, national income were held at 200, aggregate demand would be only 180 ($C+I = 160+20$). If firms persisted in producing an output of 200 (an assumption *not* made earlier when we assumed that output adjusted instantaneously to demand), inventories of unsold goods would pile up and sooner or later output would have to be cut.

If national income were held week after week at a value below its equilibrium in Figure 33.5, then aggregate expenditure would exceed the value of output. If, for example, output were held at 50, total demand would be 60 ($C+I = 40+20$). If firms did not raise output, either inventories would fall as sales exceeded current output or queues of unsatisfied customers would develop. In either case there would

[1] The equation of the 45° line is $E = Y$.

[2] The equation of the C line in the present example is $C = 0{\cdot}8\,Y$.

[3] In this example we have $I = 20$ and $C = 0{\cdot}8\,Y$, and since $E = C+I$, this yields an equation for the E line of $E = 20+0{\cdot}8\,Y$.

be a clear signal that firms can increase their sales by increasing their output. Sooner or later output and national income would rise. Only where E cuts the 45° line does aggregate expenditure remain just sufficient, no more and no less, to buy the value of output if that level of output persists week after week.[1]

Graphically, the equilibrium level of national income occurs where the aggregate expenditure function cuts the 45° line.

Desired and actual expenditure

In the examples illustrated in Tables 33.1 and 33.2 we made assumptions that implied that firms and households always met their savings and investment plans. Thus firms always suceeded in investing the constant amount that they wished to invest, and households always succeeded in spending 80 per cent of their disposable income. The discussion of equilibrium income in the income-expenditure approach suggested that this might not always be the case. If firms have unintended changes in inventories, their actual investment expenditure will diverge from their planned or desired expenditure. Assume, for example, that firms purchase their planned 20 units of new capital goods but also make 10 more units of consumers' goods that they expect to sell but do not. Total investment is then 30 which is made up of 20 of intended or desired investment and 10 of unintended or undesired inventory investment. If, to take a second example, households desire to spend 80 of disposable income on consumption goods but cannot because only 70 of such goods are available for purchase, they will have undesired or inintended saving of 10 as a result of the shortfall of actual from desired consumption expenditure.

For this reason the E function in Figure 33.5 and the I and S functions in 33.4 are called *desired* expenditure, investment and saving functions. They show what spending units would like to spend (and save) at each level of national income. In equilibrium everyone must succeed in buying what they wish to buy, but in disequilibrium they may not. Thus in disequilibrium there may be discrepancies between desired and actual expenditure flows. An example is shown in the Appendix to this chapter.

A link between saving and investment

Earlier in this chapter we stressed that saving and investment decisions were made

[1] The equivalence of the savings-investment and the aggregate expenditure approaches in the Frugal economy can be shown algebraically as follows: total expenditure on currently produced output, E, is divided between the two categories of consumption and investment goods. Total income, Y, is either consumed or saved. Thus we have

$$E = C + I$$
$$Y = C + S$$

The equilibrium condition in the income-expenditure approach is

$$E = Y.$$

Substituting in from the above gives

$$C + I = C + S$$
$$I = S,$$

which is the equilibrium condition in the savings-investment approach.

by different groups, and that there was no necessary reason why households should decide to save the same amount that firms decide to invest. We have just concluded, however, that in the simple Frugal economy, national income is in equilibrium when saving is equal to investment. Does this not mean that we have found a mechanism that ensures that households end up desiring to save an amount equal to what firms desire to invest? The answer is 'yes'. Is there not, then, a conflict between what we said at first and what we have now concluded? The answer is 'no'.

The explanation of the apparent conflict provides the key to the theory of the determination of national income in the simple Frugal economy. There is no reason why the amount that households wish to save at a randomly selected level of national income should be equal to the amount that firms wish to invest at that same level of income. This is the meaning of the statement made at the outset. But when saving is not equal to investment, there are forces at work in the economy that cause national income to change until the two do become equal. This is the meaning of the latter statement.

The graphical expression of this is that the saving function does not everywhere coincide with the investment function. Where it does not, desired saving does not equal desired investment at the indicated level of income. But the two functions do intersect somewhere, and the equilibrium level of income, in the simple Frugal economy, occurs at the intersection point. To recapitulate:

> **There is no reason why saving should equal investment at any randomly chosen level of income, but when they are not equal in the Frugal economy, national income will change until they are brought into equality.**

A generalization of the theory of equilibrium national income

The necessary condition for national income to be in equilibrium in the model of the Frugal economy can be stated in either of two ways.

(1) *Aggregate desired expenditure equals national income.* When this happens, desired expenditure is just sufficient to purchase the whole of the nation's output, and there is thus no tendency for output to change.

(2) *Saving equals investment.* When this happens, the contractionary force of income earned by households but not spent (saving) is just balanced by the expansionary force of income earned by firms that does not arise from household spending (investment). When these two forces are in balance, there will be no tendency for total output either to rise or to fall.

These results generalize with surprising ease to all circular flow models. To see this, consider the two alternative equilibrium conditions one at a time.

The first holds, without amendment, for any circular flow model.

> **When aggregate desired expenditure is less than total income, national income will fall; when aggregate desired expenditure exceeds total income, national income will rise. Equilibrium national income occurs where aggregate desired expenditure is equal to total national income.**

In moving from one circular flow model to another, all we need to do is identify any new components of aggregate expenditure, and make assumptions about how each new component is related to national income.

The second equilibrium condition, saving equals investment, requires a slight but important reinterpretation before it can be extended to all circular flow models. We have already noted that saving is an example of what is called a withdrawal from the circular flow of income. Recall that a withdrawal is any income received by households and not passed on through spending to firms, and any income received by firms not passed on as income payments to households. Withdrawals exert a contractionary force on the circular flow. Investment is an example of what is called an injection into the circular flow. Recall that an injection is income received by either firms or households that does not arise out of spending of the other group. Injections exert an expansionary force on the circular flow of income.

In the Frugal economy, saving is the only withdrawal and investment is the only injection. Thus it makes no difference if we say that national income is in equilibrium when saving equals investment or when withdrawals equal injections. In more complex models, however, there are many withdrawals and many injections. In such economies, national income will be in equilibrium when the aggregate contractionary force of all withdrawals is equal to the aggregate expansionary force of all injections.

When withdrawals exceed injections, national income will fall; when injections exceed withdrawals, national income will rise. Equilibrium national income occurs where withdrawals equal injections.

All that is required to apply this theory to any particular model is to identify the withdrawals and injections in the model and to make assumptions about how each is related to national income.

We are now ready to extend the theory of the determination of equilibrium national income to the Governed and the Open economies.

Equilibrium national income in the Governed economy

The Frugal economy contains only households and firms. The Governed economy allows for the third major spending unit in the economy, the government. We may study the determination of national income in this economy through either of the two equilibrium conditions.

The withdrawals-injections approach in the Governed economy

The elements of withdrawals and injections In the Frugal economy saving is the only withdrawal from the circular flow. In the Governed economy, taxes levied by the government are a second withdrawal. If the government taxes firms, some of what firms earn is not available to be passed on to households. If the government taxes households, some of what households earn is not available to be passed on to firms. Of course, some of the tax revenue will find its way back into the circular flow if the government subsequently spends it on commodities purchased from firms or factor services purchased from households. If the government does not spend the money, however, but merely lets it accumulate as a reserve against some future expected expenditure, it will remain outside of the flow.

Whatever subsequently happens to the money raised, taxes withdraw expenditure from the circular flow.

In the Frugal economy investment is the only injection. In the Governed economy, however, government expenditure on currently produced goods and services is a second injection. Such expenditure creates income for firms that does not arise from the spending of households, and it creates income for households that does not arise from the spending of firms. If, for example, the government spends money to buy aircraft from private firms, the incomes of these firms will rise, as will the incomes of those households who supply factor services to the firms.

Whatever the source of the funds, government spending injects expenditure into the circular flow.

Letting G stand for government expenditure, T for total taxes, J for injections and W for withdrawals, we can summarize our definitions for the Governed economy in symbols as follows:

$$W = S + T \quad \text{and} \quad J = G + I.$$

Figure 33.6 shows the model of the circular flow of income in the Governed economy, with saving and taxes as withdrawals and investment and government expenditure as injections.

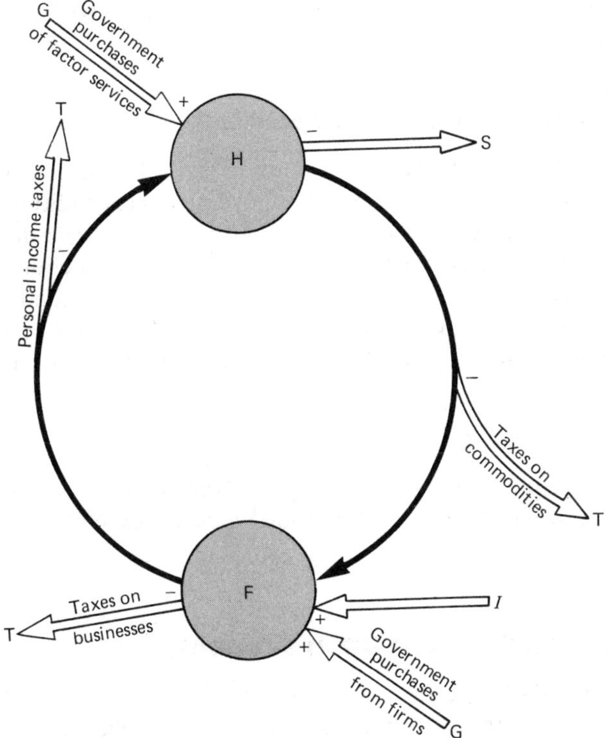

Fig. 33.6 The circular flow of income in the Governed economy

Equilibrium in terms of withdrawals and injections It is convenient to start by assuming that both injections, I and G, are constant. This allows us to study how national income adjusts to a fixed level of investment and government expenditure.

Later we shall study the response of national income to changes in G. We will also see how G is sometimes changed by the government for the express purpose of influencing the level of national income.

Withdrawals, however, cannot be assumed to be constant. We have already assumed that saving will rise as national income rises. The government's tax revenue can also be expected to rise with national income: if all tax rates are held constant, tax yields must rise with income. Sales and excise taxes, and income taxes will all produce more revenue as the value of total output produced and total incomes earned increases. Thus we expect the withdrawals of both savings and taxes to rise as income rises.

National income will be in equilibrium when total withdrawals, saving plus taxes, are equal to total injections, investment plus government expenditure. The equilibrium condition for national income can thus be written as

$$W = J, \text{ or } S+T = G+I.$$

If withdrawals are less than injections there will be a net expansionary force in the economy. Income will rise. Tax receipts and saving will rise along with income, and the expansion will come to a halt when total withdrawals have risen to the level of total injections. If withdrawals exceed injections there will be a net contractionary force in the economy. Income will fall. Tax receipts and saving will fall along with income, and the contraction will come to a halt when total withdrawals have fallen to the level of total injections.

The income-expenditure approach in the Governed economy

In the Governed economy, total expenditure is consumption expenditure, C, and investment expenditure, I, as in the Frugal economy, plus government expenditure, G. Government expenditure is reckoned net of transfer payments, since transfer payments do not of themselves create demand for the nation's output. Of course when households spend their government transfer payments this creates demand – but is shown up as a consumption expenditure; the transfer payment itself does not create demand and thus is not counted as part of aggregate expenditure. Aggregate expenditure, E, may be expressed as

$$E = C+I+G.$$

National income will be in equilibrium when aggregate desired expenditure is equal to national income because in that case desired purchases will exactly equal total production.

Equilibrium national income in the Open economy

The Open economy allows for the influence of foreign trade. The effects of such trade need to be introduced into both the withdrawals-injections and the income-expenditure approaches.

The withdrawals-injections approach in the Open economy

The elements of withdrawals and injections In addition to the withdrawal of saving and taxes already allowed for, there is now a third withdrawal, imports. When households spend their incomes on imported goods instead of domestic ones, incomes are created for foreign firms and foreign households, instead of for domestic firms and domestic households. If British households decide to buy fewer Cortinas and more Volkswagens, a smaller proportion of the income received by British households will be passed back to the British car producer and a larger proportion will be withdrawn from the circular flow of the British economy. The British car firm will now earn less income and will hire fewer factors of production, so that incomes of British households will fall.

Whatever subsequently happens to the money spent, imports withdraw expenditure from the circular flow.

One country's imports are another country's exports. In the Open economy, the list of injections that already includes I and G must be augmented to include exports. In the previous example, there was an increase of imports of Volkswagens into Britain, but there was simultaneously an increase in exports of Volkswagen from Germany. This increase in exports means that the German car company gains an increase in its income and, because more factors of production will be needed to produce more, there will also be an increase in the incomes of German households. This increase in the circular flow in Germany did not arise because of any change in the expenditures of German households (it was the expenditure patterns of British households that changed), and so it constitutes an injection into the German circular flow of income.

Whatever the source of the money spent, exports inject expenditure into the circular flow.

Letting M stand for imports and X for exports, we can summarize our definitions of withdrawals and injections as follows:

$$W = S+T+M \quad \text{and} \quad J = I+G+X.$$

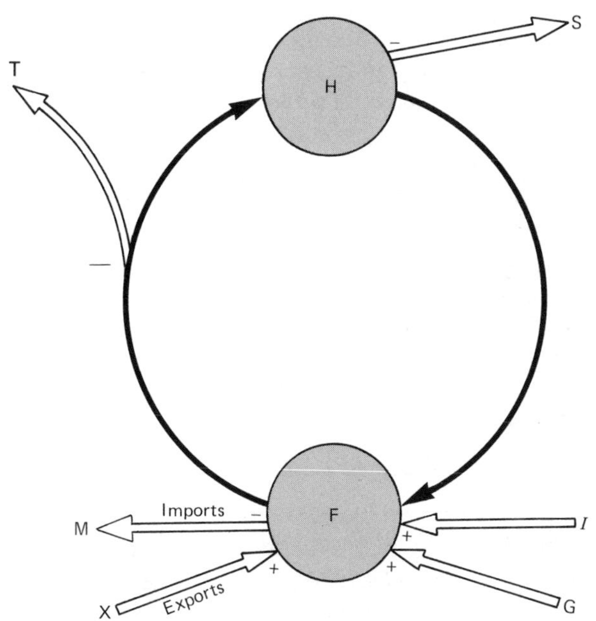

Fig. 33.7 The circular flow of income in the Open economy

Figure 33.7 shows the model of the circular flow of income in the Open economy with saving, taxes and imports shown as withdrawals and investment, government expenditure and exports shown as injections. To prevent the figure from becoming unduly complex, all of government taxes are compressed into a single flow and so are government expenditures. Exports are shown as creating income for firms in the first instance. Imports are shown as a leakage arising from the expenditure of firms. Some firms import raw materials and semi-finished goods which are then used to manufacture final goods subsequently sold to households (C), other firms import finished consumer's goods and capital goods which they sell in unchanged form to households and firms. The costs of operating the firm that does the importing are, however, part of domestic value added. Thus these imports can be thought of as intermediate products to which domestic firms add value in just the same way as they do to imported raw materials or semi-finished goods.

Equilibrium in terms of withdrawals and injections We have already assumed G and I to be fixed. What about the new injection of exports? The amount of our exports depends upon the domestic prices of the goods we sell, on our exchange rate (which determines the foreign prices of these goods), on the prices of competing goods from other countries, and on foreign incomes. As with I and G, it is convenient to see how national income adjusts to a fixed level of exports before seeing how it reacts when exports change. Thus exports are assumed constant fòr the remainder of this chapter.

The withdrawals already allowed for, S and T, are both assumed to rise with income. Imports are expected to exhibit similar behaviour. They will tend to rise as national income rises, both because domestic households spend a fraction of their consumption expenditure on foreign rather than on domestically produced commodities, and because almost all domestic output has some import content of raw materials and semi-manufactured goods. Iron ore, oil, paper and lumber are but a few of the many examples. Thus we expect all withdrawals, S, T and M, to rise as income rises.

If withdrawals are less than injections there will be a net expansionary force in the economy. Income will rise. Tax receipts, saving and imports will all rise along with income. The expansion will come to a halt when total withdrawals have risen to the level of total injections. If withdrawals exceed injections, there will be a net contractionary force in the economy. Income will fall. Tax receipts, saving and imports will all fall along with income, and the contraction will come to a halt when total withdrawals have fallen to the level of total injections.

National income will be in equilibrium when total desired withdrawals equal total desired injections. Thus the equilibrium condition is, once again, $W = J$. Allowing for all withdrawals and injections, this becomes

$$S+T+M = I+G+X.$$

The income-expenditure approach in the Open economy

In the Open economy, aggregate expenditure includes expenditure by foreign firms, households and governments on domestically produced goods and services. Aggregate expenditure thus includes the total of all exports. On the other side of the account, however, some consumption expenditure made by domestic households, some investment expenditure made by domestic firms, and some government expenditure may go to purchase goods and services produced in foreign countries. To arrive at aggregate expenditure on domestically produced commodities, which is domestic national income, we must, as we saw on page 447 of Chapter 32, subtract imports to arrive at a total for aggregate expenditure on domestically produced final goods of

$$E = C+I+G+(X-M).$$

The total is consumption plus investment plus government expenditure plus net exports.

Once again, national income will be in equilibrium when aggregate desired expenditure is equal to national income. When this is true, total desired purchases will be just equal to total production.

Equilibrium national income: a general graphical approach

Figure 33.8 shows the equilibrium level of national income in terms of both the

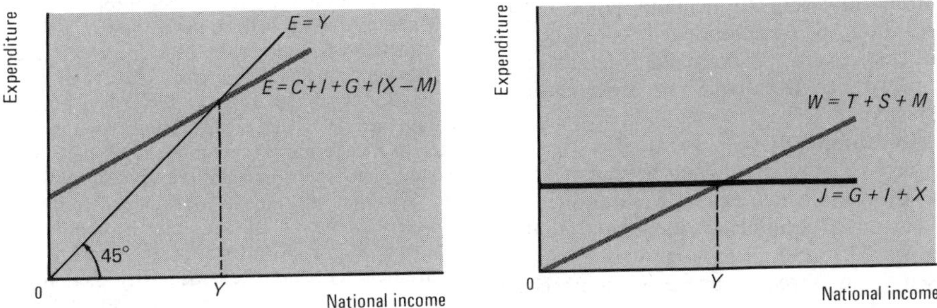

Fig. 33.8 The general graphical expression of equilibrium national income through the income-expenditure and withdrawals-injections approaches

income-expenditure and withdrawals-injections approaches. The analysis is essentially the same whether aggregate expenditure is merely $C+I$, as in the Frugal economy, $C+I+G$, as in the Governed economy, or $C+I+G+(X-M)$, as in the Open economy. Similarly, it is incidental whether there is one injection and one withdrawal, as in the simple Frugal economy, or two of each as in the Governed economy, or three of each, as in the Open economy.

> **Equilibrium income always occurs where aggregate desired expenditure equals national income and where withdrawals equal injections.**

Appendix to chapter 33

The effect of lags on the path of national income

The path taken by national income when it is not in equilibrium depends critically on the kinds of lags that are assumed to exist in the circular flow. The text used a simple example in which disposable income lagged one 'week' behind actual output, but output adjusted instantaneously to changes in demand. This has the effect of leaving inventories constant. An alternative model, which is often described verbally in elementary texts, has output adjusting to demand with a one period lag, while assuming the existence of sufficient inventories so that any demand can be met out of inventories until production is adjusted.

An example of such a model is given in Table 33.3 in which the lag between output and disposable income is still maintained.

The initial equilibrium, identical to that in Tables 33.1 and 33.2, is shown repeating itself through weeks 1 and 2. Then in week 3 there is an investment boom. Sales of capital goods rise from 20 to 40. Output of machines does not rise and the whole of the additional demand is met by running down inventories. Thus overall investment, which is the sum of columns 5 and 6, remains constant. Current output remains unchanged at 100 and disposable income available in week 4 does not rise.[1] In week 4 sales are 80 of consumption goods and 40 of machines but production is adjusted to meet the expanded

[1] Since in this case there is a lag between purchases and output, it is possible for expenditure and output, as defined in the flow model, to diverge from each other. In week 3, for example, total expenditure on the purchase of consumption goods and machines rises to 120, while output remains at 100. Thus, using definitions appropriate to measuring the magnitudes of the flows around the circuit, expenditure exceeds output. The national income statistician, in contrast, measures the flow at the output point and measures $E \equiv Y = 100$ in week 3. There is no contradiction because the statistician is measuring the expenditure that *would be needed* to purchase the output of 100 produced in week 3, while in the theoretical model it is the actual expenditure made during week 3 that is referred to.

Table 33.3 The behaviour of the circular flow of income in the Frugal economy with lags between Y_d and Y and between output and expenditure

Col. 1	Col. 2	Col. 3	Col. 4	Col. 5	Col. 6	Col. 7
Week	Disposable income, Y_d (= the value of last week's national income)	Saving, S ($= 0{\cdot}2\,Y_d$)	Consumption, C ($= 0{\cdot}8Y_d$)	Purchases of investment goods (= an exogenous constant)	Inventory changes, ΔV (= last week's Y *minus* this week's $C+I$)	National income, Y (= value of this week's production, i.e. $C+I+\Delta V$)
1	100	20	80	20	0	100
2	100	20	80	20	0	100
3	100	20	80	40	−20	100
4	100	20	80	40	0	120
5	120	24	96	40	−16	120
6	120	24	96	40	0	136
7	136	27·2	108·8	40	−12·8	136
8	136	27·2	108·8	40	0	148·8
n	200	40	160	40	0	200

demand for machines. National income thus rises to 120 in week 4 and this amount is available to households for their spending in week 5. Thus in week 5 consumption expenditure rises to 96 (80 per cent of 120) but the rise in demand is unanticipated, so inventories of consumers' goods fall by 16. National income does not rise, so neither does disposable income rise in week 6. But in that week production of consumers goods rises to meet the extra demand. The course of national income proceeds in the uneven increases shown in the table until eventually it reaches its equilibrium level of 200.

In these theories the equilibrium level of national income is independent of the lags that are assumed to exist in the circular flow, but the path of adjustment towards equilibrium is not.[1]

An algebraic treatment

The model of the Frugal economy is easily handled using only simple algebra. The text version runs as follows (see the assumptions on page 477).

$$Y_t = C_t + I_t \quad (1)$$

$$Y^d_{t+1} = Y_t \quad (2)$$

$$Y^d_{t+1} \equiv C_{t+1} + S_{t+1}, \quad (3)$$

where t is time measured in weeks.

[1] It is worth noting that if there is a desired ratio of inventories to sales, national income will not remain at 200 the first time it reaches it. There will have been a cumulative reduction in inventories during the adjustment process and when firms try to replace these, they will push national income temporarily above 200 thus setting up the type of inventory cycle discussed in Chapter 37.

Equation (1) states that output adjusts to consumption and investment expenditure without lag. Equation (2) states that household disposable income lags behind output by one week. Equation (3) states that disposable income must be allocated between consumption and saving. Substitution of (3) into (2) yields

$$C_{t+1} + S_{t+1} = Y_t$$

and substitution of this expression into (1) gives

$$C_{t+1} + S_{t+1} = C_t + I_t.$$

Rearranging and writing I for I_t, since I is assumed constant, gives

$$C_{t+1} - C_t = I - S_{t+1},$$

or

$$C_t - C_{t-1} = I - S_t.$$

In other words, if consumption is rising $I > S$; if consumption is falling, $I < S$; and if consumption is constant, $I = S$. Since $C_t = aY^d_t$ (where $0 < a < 1$), and since $Y^d_t = Y_{t-1}$, the same remarks apply substituting Y^d and Y for C.

The equilibrium condition is that expenditure flows should remain stable:

$$C_t = C_{t-1}$$

from which it follows that in equilibrium

$$S_t = I.$$

Of course the flows are defined in the ways appropriate to the model, not in the way they are defined by the national income accountant.

34

Some predictions of the simple theory of national income

In the last two chapters we developed the basic model of the circular flow of income, and determined the conditions for the equilibrium of this flow. In this chapter we shall use comparative static analysis to derive some important predictions concerning the effects on national income of changes in the behaviour of households, firms and the central authorities. We shall first consider the directions, and then the magnitudes of the changes. (Recall from the previous chapter that the equilibrium conditions for national income can be stated using either the aggregate expenditure function and the 45° line, or the withdrawals and injections functions. We shall use these approaches interchangeably.)

Movements along curves versus shifts of curves

As a preliminary to this study, recall the important distinction between movements along curves and shifts of curves. We first made this distinction with respect to demand and supply curves. We now apply it to the curves used in macroeconomics.

If desired consumption expenditure rises, it makes a great deal of difference whether the rise is in response to a change in national income or to an increased desire to consume *at each level of national income* including the present one. The former change is represented by a movement along the aggregate consumption curve; it is the response of consumption to a change in income. The latter change is represented by a shift in the consumption curve that occurs in response to a change in the proportion of income that households desire to consume. It is the type of change that can itself disturb an existing equilibrium.

Figure 34.1 illustrates this important distinction. The lines in the figure conform to our assumptions about how consumption, injections, and withdrawals are related to national income. The components of injections – I, G and X – have all been assumed constant. Thus the sum of the three is shown as a constant amount that does not vary with national income. Consumption expenditure, however, is assumed to rise as income rises, and the consumption line thus slopes upward. The three withdrawals – S, T and M – are all assumed to rise as national income rises. Their sum – total withdrawals – is thus also assumed to rise as income rises, as shown by the upward-sloping W curve in the figure.

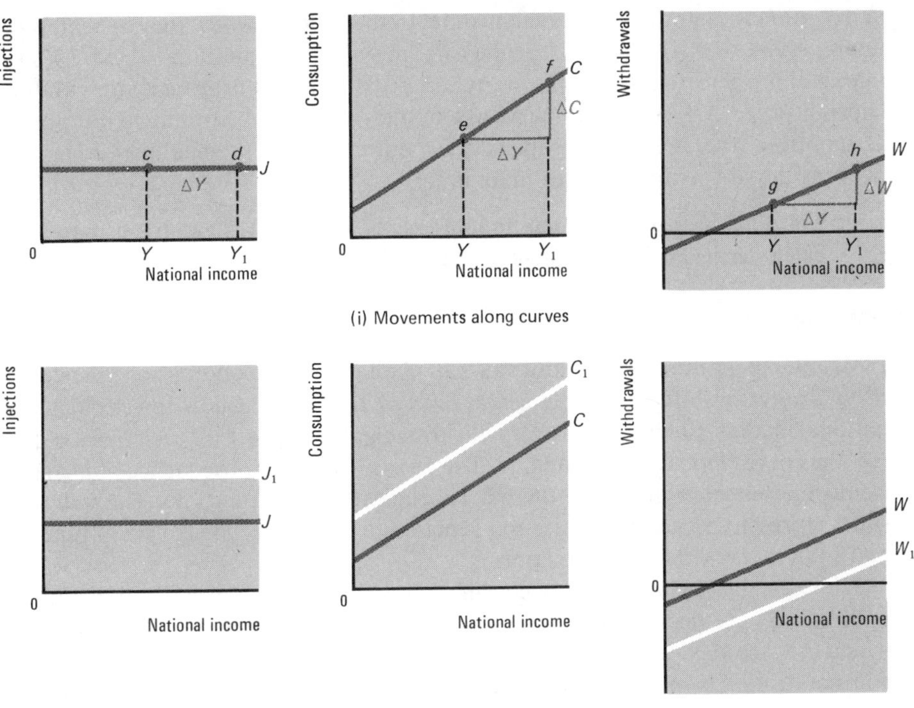

Fig. 34.1 Movements along and shifts of curves

Movements along curves

In part (i) of Figure 34.1, in response to an increase in income from Y to Y_1, we must *move along* the J, C and W curves to determine the new flows of injections consumption and withdrawals, respectively. The change in income of ΔY leads to an increase in withdrawals of ΔW and in consumption of ΔC. Injections do not change – i.e., ΔJ equals zero and is not therefore shown. The slopes of the curves show the ratios of the changes in the variables to the changes in income (i.e., the *responses* of those variables to changes in income). They are known as MARGINAL PROPENSITIES.

> **The response of injections, consumption, and withdrawals to a change in income is indicated by a movement along the injection, consumption, and withdrawal curves and is shown graphically by the slope of the relevant curve.**

There is a marginal propensity for any of the flows of expenditure included in a national income model. For example, the MARGINAL PROPENSITY TO CONSUME (MPC) is the ratio of the change in consumption to the change in income that brought it about, $\Delta C/\Delta Y$; the MARGINAL PROPENSITY TO SAVE (MPS) is the ratio of the change in saving to the change in income that brought it about, $\Delta S/\Delta Y$. The marginal propensities that relate to the curves in Figure 34.1 (i) are the marginal propensities to consume and the two aggregate marginal propensities that relate changes in total injections $(I+G+X)$ and changes in total withdrawals

$(S+T+M)$ to changes in national income. In the order in which they appear in the figure, these are (i) marginal propensity to inject expenditure $= \Delta J/\Delta Y$; (ii) marginal propensity to consume $= \Delta C/\Delta Y$; (iii) marginal propensity to withdraw expenditure $= \Delta W/\Delta Y$, to which we assign the symbol w. According to our present assumption, the marginal propensity to inject is zero, while the other two propensities are positive, but less than unity.

Marginal propensities relate to movements along curves and tell us how much particular flows respond to changes in income.

Shifts of curves

Flows of expenditures or withdrawals can change for a second reason: the curves *themselves* may shift, indicating a new level of the relevant flow for *each* level of national income. Such shifts are also illustrated in Figure 34.1. In each panel of part (ii), the curve *shifts* to the white line. The change is not a consequence of a change in income but of a change in the whole relationship with income. The indicated shifts represent a rise in the injection function, a rise in the consumption function and a fall in the withdrawal function.

While the figure shows three such shifts, the shift in consumption and the shift in withdrawals are necessarily interrelated. Consider again the Frugal economy in which households save whatever part of their income that is not spent on consumption. An upward shift in the consumption curve, for example, indicates an increase in the desired consumption expenditure that is associated with each level of income. In this case, desired household saving must fall at each level of income, since S is all disposable income not spent on consumption. Therefore, since saving is one component of aggregate withdrawals, a rise in the consumption curve implies a fall in the withdrawal curve.

Why national income changes

We may now begin our study of the major forces that can cause equilibrium national income to change.

A shift in the injections function

What will happen to national income if investment, government expenditure or exports change? Fortunately, the same analysis applies to all three changes. In Figure 34.2 an increase in any of these is shown by an upward shift in the injections function from J_1 to J_2. At the original level of income, Y_1, injections now exceed withdrawals so that income must rise. As this happens, withdrawals, which are a function of income, also rise, as shown by the upward slope of the withdrawals function W. The rise in income continues until, at income Y_2, withdrawals are again equal to the (now higher level of) injections. *A shift in the injections function creates a disequilibrium which is removed as withdrawals rise due to a movement along the W function.*[1]

[1] It is important to remember that we are dealing with continuous flows measured as so much per period of time. At the original equilibrium level, withdrawals and injections were both steady at E_1 *per year*. Injections then rose autonomously to E_2 *per year* and, as a result, income rose until withdrawals had risen to the rate E_2 *per year* as well.

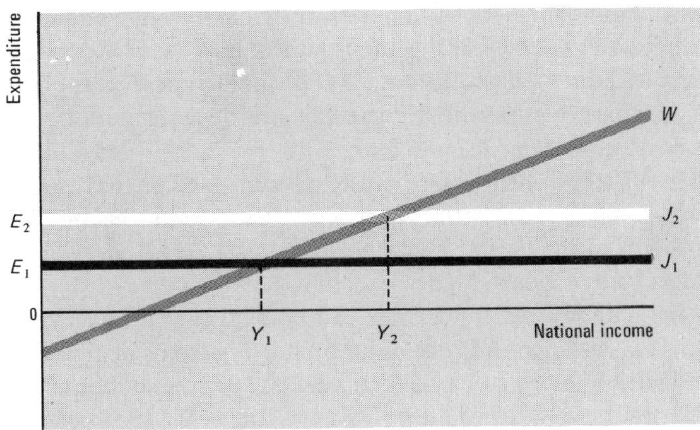

Fig. 34.2 The effect on the equilibrium level of national income of a change in the level of injections

We can analyse a fall in investment, exports, or government spending by assuming that income starts at Y_2, and that injections then fall from J_2 to J_1. This reduces equilibrium income to Y_1.

We have now derived two predictions from our theory:

> **(1) A rise in investment expenditure, exports or government expenditure raises equilibrium national income.**
> **(2) A fall in investment expenditure, exports or government expenditure lowers equilibrium national income.**

A shift in the withdrawals function

How will a change in saving, imports or taxes affect national income? A downward shift in the saving, import or tax function will shift the withdrawals function so that, at each level of income, the flow of withdrawals will be lower than it was previously. Such a shift is shown in Figure 34.3. The original level of income is Y_1, with the annual flows of withdrawals and injections both equal to E_1. The withdrawals

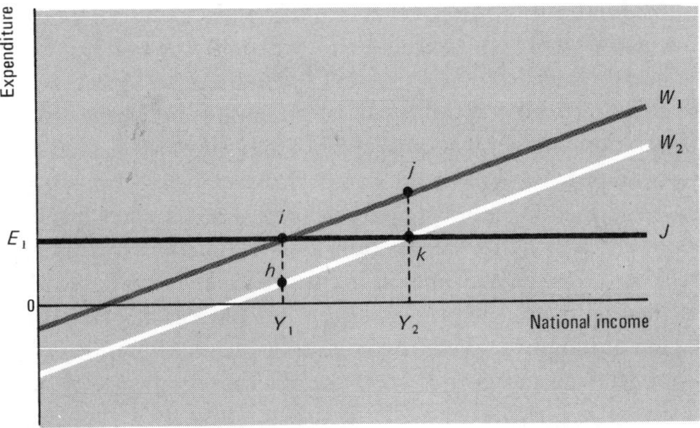

Fig. 34.3 The effect on the equilibrium level of national income of a change in the withdrawals function

function shifts downwards from W_1 to W_2 so that at the original level of income the new annual flow of withdrawals (Y_1h) is *hi* less than the annual flow of injections. The fact that less is being withdrawn from the circular flow of income than is being injected into it causes income to rise until withdrawals are once again equal to injections. This occurs once income has risen to Y_2.

The downward shift in the withdrawals curve causes national income to rise until the resulting movement along the new withdrawals curve exactly cancels out the effect of the downward shift in the curve. Thus the actual flow of withdrawals is restored to its original level but at a new, higher level of national income.

An upward shift in the withdrawals function is caused by a rise in the saving, import or tax function. This is shown in Figure 34.3 by starting from the function W_2 with income Y_2 and letting the withdrawals function rise to W_1, so that at the original level of income withdrawals exceed injections (by *kj* per year). Income must fall as a result. As income falls, the volume of actual withdrawals falls as well. This continues until income has fallen to Y_1 and withdrawals are once again equal to injections at the rate E_1 per year.

We have now derived two further predictions:

(3) A fall in the taxation, saving or import function lowers the aggregate withdrawals function and raises equilibrium national income.
(4) A rise in the taxation, saving or import functions raises the aggregate withdrawals function and lowers equilibrium national income.

The paradox of thrift

Predictions (3) and (4) above have one interesting and counter-intuitive application. It is normally assumed, by analogy with an individual household, that on a national scale thrift is a good thing and prodigality is a bad thing, the former leading to increased wealth and prosperity and the latter to eventual bankruptcy.

Household saving What happens if, *ceteris paribus*, all households try to increase the amount they save at each level of income? This increase in thriftiness shifts the withdrawals function upwards, say from W_2 to W_1 in Figure 34.3. As long as income remains at its original equilibrium level Y_2, the volume of savings is increased by *kj*. But now income will begin to fall, and it will continue to do so until total withdrawals have been reduced to their original level so that they are again equal to injections. The effect on actual withdrawals of the shift of the withdrawals function from W_2 to W_1 is totally offset by a movement along the new *W* schedule from *j* to *i*.

Now consider an increase in households' desire to consume at each level of income. This means that less will be saved at each level of income so that the withdrawals function will be shifted downwards in Figure 34.3, say from W_1 to W_2. But this will mean that income is no longer in equilibrium. Income will rise until withdrawals are once again equal to the unchanged level of injections. In this case the downward shift in the withdrawals curve from W_1 to W_2 raises national income from Y_1 to Y_2. It also leads to no change in the actual amount of withdrawals because the effect of the shift is offset by the movement along the new curve. We have now derived the prediction of the so-called *paradox of thrift*.

(5) Other things being equal, the more frugal and thrifty households are, the lower will be the level of national income and total employment. The more prodigal and spendthrift households are, the higher the level of national income and employment will be.

This is not actually a paradox. It is in fact a straightforward corollary of prediction (4) above, which in turn follows logically from the theory of the determination of national income. It is called a paradox because it seems paradoxical to those people who expect good advice to a single household, which wishes to raise its wealth and its future income ('save, save and save some more'), to apply also to the economy as a whole.

Government taxing and spending The paradox of thrift applies to governments as well as to households. If governments decide to save more, they must raise taxes or cut expenditure. The first alternative shifts the withdrawals function upwards and the second shifts the injections function downwards. Either policy causes national income to fall until withdrawals are once again equal to injections. If governments decide to save less (i.e., to become more spendthrift) they lower taxes and/or raise spending. This shifts the withdrawals function downwards and/or the injections function upwards. Either policy raises national income.

The paradox of thrift leads to the prediction that substantial unemployment is corrected by encouraging governments, firms and households to spend rather than to save. In times of unemployment and depression, frugality will only make things worse. This prediction goes directly against our inclination to tighten our belts when times are tough. The idea that it is possible to spend one's way out of a depression offends the consciences of people who were reared in the belief that success is based on hard work and frugality and not on prodigality. As a result, the suggestion very often provokes great hostility.

The paradox of thrift was not generally understood during the Great Depression of the 1930s. At that time, many mistaken policies were followed. One such is suggested in a message delivered by King George V to the House of Commons on 8 September 1931, on the occasion of the formation of a new national government after the collapse of the Labour administration.

> The present condition of the National finances, in the opinion of His Majesty's Ministers, calls for the imposition of additional taxation, and for the effecting of economies in public expenditure.[1]

At the time, the unemployment rate stood at 21 per cent of the labour force!

In the US, President Roosevelt, though he achieved the reputation of grappling vigorously with the problems of the decade while others shilly-shallied, showed no more appreciation of the real nature of the basic situation than did the British leaders. In his very first inaugural address in 1933 he stated:

> Our greatest primary task is to put people to work. ... [This task] can be helped by insistence that the Federal, State and local governments act forthwith on the demand that their cost be drastically reduced. ... There must be a strict supervision of all banking and credits and investments.

At the time, the American unemployment rate was 23 per cent.

---

[1] Quoted in David Thomson, *England in the Twentieth Century* (Pelican, 1965), p. 136.

National income theory predicts that the correct response to the Great Depression of the 1930s was to encourage firms, households and governments to spend and not to save. Attempts to save or to cut government expenditure would only serve to lower national income and raise unemployment even further. The suffering and misery of that unhappy decade would have been greatly reduced had those in authority known even as much economics as is contained in this chapter.

Conditions necessary for the paradox to operate The striking prediction of the paradox of thrift depends critically on two of the basic assumptions of the elementary theory of national income.

(1) There is a significant amount of unemployment of all resources, capital equipment as well as labour, so that the level of output depends upon total spending, and anything that reduces spending reduces output and employment.

(2) Injections are assumed to be completely independent of withdrawals; in particular, the volume of investment is independent of the volume of saving. There is no reason, according to the theory, why the amount that firms wish to spend on investment at any level of income should bear any particular relation to the amount that households wish to save.

If the economy is at, or near, full employment of any important factor of production, then the first assumption will not be correct. Where full employment already obtains, an increase in household saving and an increase in consumption expenditure will not cause an increase in real output and employment. In such circumstances the effect of an increase in spending will probably be to cause the price level to rise. An increase in saving, however, with its accompanying decrease in spending, will tend to reduce output and employment.

If the second assumption is not correct, the paradox of thrift will not apply. If, for example, the withdrawals and injections functions are linked together because changes in household saving cause changes in investment, there will be offsetting shifts in *both* the withdrawals and injections functions whenever the desire to save changes. An increase in the desire to save, for example, will shift the withdrawals function upwards but, by permitting more investment, it may also shift up the injections function and there may be no downward pressure on national income.

> **The predictions of the paradox of thrift, and most of the other predictions of the elementary theory of national income, depend critically on the assumption that saving and investment decisions are taken to a great extent by different groups in society and that there is no mechanism whereby a change in the amount that is desired to be saved at a particular level of income will cause a change in the amount that is desired to be invested at the same level of income.**

We will return to discuss this assumption later.

An alternative method of deriving the basic predictions

We saw in Chapter 33 that the equilibrium level of national income can be determined using either the withdrawals-injections approach or the income-expenditure approach. You should not be surprised to learn, therefore, that the predictions derived so far in this chapter using the withdrawals-injections approach can also be derived using the income-expenditure approach. Without repeating the whole analysis in detail, the essence of the argument can be illustrated by referring to Figure 34.7 on page 511.

If the aggregate expenditure schedule is E in the top half of part (i) of the figure, equilibrium national income is at Y_E, where E cuts the 45° line, indicating that total demand is just sufficient to purchase total output.

Investment expenditure, exports and government expenditure are all components of aggregate expenditure. An increase in any of these components shifts the aggregate expenditure function upwards; a decrease shifts it downwards. The effects can be seen by shifting the expenditure function upwards from that shown in the first panel to that shown in the second, thus increasing equilibrium income (Y_E), and by shifting it downwards from that shown in the second panel to that shown in the first, thus lowering equilibrium income. This gives predictions (1) and (2) on page 499.

The aggregate expenditure function is also affected by shifts in the saving, import or taxes function. A rise in saving or taxes lowers consumption expenditure and so lowers aggregate expenditure. A rise in imports has the same effect on aggregate expenditure. (Recall that aggregate expenditure is equal to $C+I+G+(X-M)$.) A fall in saving, taxes or imports raises aggregate expenditure. Thus a rise in any withdrawal lowers aggregate expenditure from, say, that shown in the second panel of Figure 34.7 to that shown in the first panel, thus lowering Y_E, while a fall in any withdrawal raises aggregate expenditure and raises Y_E. This gives predictions (3) and (4) on page 500.

The magnitude of the changes in national income: the multiplier

The direction of the effect on national income of various shifts in injections has been considered, but what about the magnitude of these effects? If the annual flow of government expenditures changes by some amount, ΔG, *by how much* will income change? For example, in a severe depression the government might be urged to spend money in order to create employment. The analysis of the previous section suggests that a given increase in government expenditure will in fact increase income and employment. Now we wish to know *by how much*. Likewise, if there is a fall in private investment of some stated amount, we wish to know how much national income and employment will be reduced.

The definition of the multiplier

A central prediction of national income theory is that a change in expenditure, whatever its source, will cause a change in national income that is greater than the initial change in expenditure. The MULTIPLIER is defined as the ratio of the change in national income to the change in expenditure that brought it about. The change in expenditure might come, for example, from an increase in private investment, from new government spending, from a rise in exports or from additional household consumption expenditure accompanied by a decline in household saving. All of these are shifts in functions.

The importance of the multiplier in national income theory makes it worthwhile to use more than one approach to developing it, and to show why its value exceeds unity.

An intuitive statement

What would you expect to happen to national income if there were a rise in government expenditure on road building of £1 million per year with no corresponding rise in taxes? Will national income rise by only £1 million? Anyone who has mastered the theory developed so far should not have too much trouble in replying, 'no, national income will rise by more than £1 million'. This could be argued in either of two ways, remembering that we are dealing with flows and that a rise of £1 million means that much extra spent on roads *each year*. First, we could say that a permanent increase in government expenditure of £1 million per annum will cause further induced increases in consumption expenditure. The impact of the initial rise will be felt by the construction industry and by all those industries that supply it. Income and the employment of factors will rise by £1 million as a result. But these newly employed factors will spend much of their income buying food, clothing, shelter, holidays, cars, refrigerators and a host of other products. This is the induced rise in consumption expenditure, and when output expands to meet this extra demand, employment will rise in all of the affected industries. When the owners of factors that are newly employed spend their incomes, output and employment will rise further; more income will then be created and more expenditure induced. Indeed, at this stage we might begin to wonder if the increase in income will ever come to an end. This question is easier to answer if we look at the second way of describing the process of income expansion.

The initial rise in government expenditure is a rise in injections. This will increase income, but, as income rises, the volume of withdrawals (tax receipts, imports and saving) will rise. Income will continue to rise until additional withdrawals of £1 million have been generated. At this point, withdrawals will have risen by as much as the original (permanent) rise in injections and, assuming we began from a position of equilibrium, we will be back in equilibrium. For example, if 40 per cent of all income is withdrawn through taxes, saving and imports, then the rise in income will come to a halt when income has risen £2·5 million. At this higher level of income, an extra £1 million in withdrawals will have been generated, and since the rise in withdrawals equals the initial rise in injections, income will no longer be rising.

Thus the increase in income does come to a halt. In this example, the multiplier is 2·5, since a rise in government expenditure of £1 million causes a rise in national income of £2·5 million.

This is as far as intuitive arguments can take us. Now we must look for a more formal demonstration of these propositions.

A numerical statement

Suppose that spending in a closed economy behaves in this simple way: every time people receive some additional income they spend 60 per cent of it on domestically produced goods and services and withdraw 40 per cent for taxes and saving. This economy's marginal propensity to spend is 0·60 and its marginal propensity to withdraw is 0·40.

Now suppose that injections increase in the form of the government's spending £1 billion a year on new roads. National income rises by £1 billion. But that is not the end of it; there is a second round of spending. The factors involved directly and indirectly in road building withdraw £400 million for saving and taxes, but they spend an extra £600 million each year on domestically produced goods and services. The recipients of this £600 million in turn spend an extra £360 million a year (60 per cent of £600 million), which is a third round of additions to aggregate expenditure. And so it continues, with each successive recipient of new income spending 60 per cent of it on domestically produced goods. Each additional round of expenditure creates new income and yet an additional round of expenditure.

Table 34.1 below carries the process through ten rounds. You may compute as many rounds in the process as you wish and notice that the sum of the rounds of

Table 34.1 A numerical example of the multiplier process

	Increases in expenditures (£s million)	Increases in withdrawals (£s million)
Assumed new government expenditure *per year*	1,000·00	
2nd round (increase in expenditures and withdrawals)	600·00	400·00
3rd round " " " "	360·00	240·00
4th round " " " " "	216·00	144·00
5th round " " " " "	129·60	86·40
6th round " " " " "	77·76	51·84
7th round " " " " "	46·66	31·10
8th round " " " " "	28·00	18·66
9th round " " " " "	16·80	11·20
10th round " " " " "	10·08	6·72
Sum of 1st 10 rounds	2,484·90	989·92
All subsequent rounds	15·10	10·08
Total	2,500·00	1,000·00

expenditures approaches £2·5 billion, which is two and a half times the initial injection of £1 billion.[1] This argument then leads to the same result as did the intuitive argument in the text. The multiplier is 2·5, given these numerical assumptions about spending and withdrawals.

A graphical statement

The withdrawals and injections functions are depicted in Figure 34.4. When the equilibrium level of income is Y_1, withdrawals and injections are in equilibrium at the amount E_1 $(= Y_1e)$. When the injections function shifts to J_2, income rises to Y_2 where withdrawals and injections are again in equilibrium, this time at the amount of E_2 $(= Y_2g)$. The change in income is the distance bracketed as ΔY, while the changes in withdrawals and injections are indicated by the distances bracketed as $\Delta J = \Delta W$. The slope of the withdrawals line, W, is given by $\Delta W/\Delta Y$. This slope shows the marginal propensity to withdraw expenditure from the circular flow, i.e., w. The multiplier, K, is the ratio $\Delta Y/\Delta J$, the change in income divided by the change

[1] We sum the rounds because each additional round represents new expenditure *in addition to* that generated in all previous rounds. Thus, for example, the first round of £1,000 million is earned by those factors directly employed by the road programme and they continue to get this income as long as the programme continues (which we have assumed to be indefinitely).

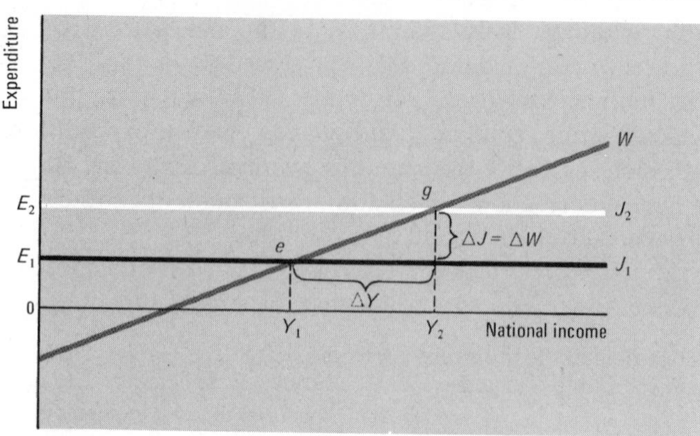

Fig. 34.4 Determining the size of the multiplier

in injections. This is the reciprocal of $\Delta J/\Delta Y$ and, since $\Delta J = \Delta W$, it is also the reciprocal of the slope of the withdrawals function. Thus the value of the multiplier, K, is equal to $1/w$.

To see the influence of the slope of the withdrawals function on the multiplier graphically, look at Figure 34.5. The withdrawals line marked W' has a steep slope;

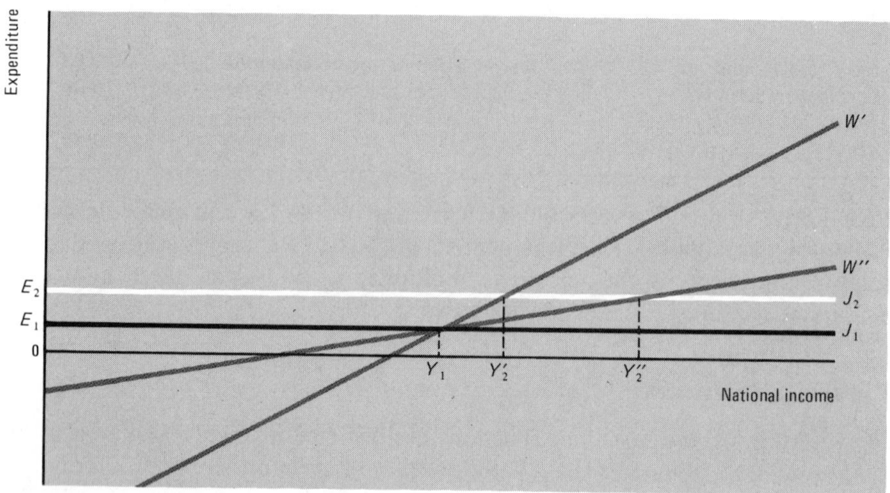

Fig. 34.5 The relation between the value of the multiplier and the slope of the withdrawals schedule

the one marked W'' has a very flat slope. In each case, suppose the injection function is J_1, and the equilibrium income level is Y_1. Now, *in each case*, suppose injections increase to J_2. The new income level is Y'_2 in the case of W' and Y''_2 in the case of W''. The multiplier is much greater for the flatter curve than for the steeper one. The common sense of this is that the flatter the curve, the greater the increase in income necessary to bring forth an addition to withdrawals equal to the increase in injections.

An algebraic statement[1]

The multiplier is the ratio of the change in income to the permanent change in the flow of expenditure that brought it about. It is symbolized by K and defined thus:

$$K = \frac{\Delta Y}{\Delta J}. \qquad (1)$$

When national income is in equilibrium it is necessary that:

$$W = J, \qquad (2)$$

which says that the volume of withdrawals must equal the volume of injections.

Now let us disturb the equilibrium by a change in injections. If J increases by ΔJ, then W must increase by the same amount in order to re-establish equality (2). Thus we have

$$\Delta W = \Delta J. \qquad (3)$$

This says nothing more than that, if withdrawals equal injections originally, and if injections rise by ΔJ (say by £1 million per year), then withdrawals must rise by the same amount in order to restore the equality of W and J.

Withdrawals depend on income. In the simple theory, withdrawals are a constant fraction, w, of income. We write this $W = wY$. From this it follows that the change in withdrawals must be w *times* the change in income

$$\Delta W = w\Delta Y. \qquad (4)$$

If, as in our previous example, 40 per cent of extra income is not passed on as new spending, then $w = 0{\cdot}4$, and the change in withdrawals is 40 per cent of the change in income.

If we substitute (4) into (3), we obtain

$$w\Delta Y = \Delta J,$$

dividing both sides by w,

$$\Delta Y = \frac{1}{w}\Delta J. \qquad (5)$$

But from (1) we have:

$$\Delta Y = K\Delta J. \qquad (6)$$

Substituting (6) into (5) and cancelling ΔJ yields

$$K = \frac{1}{w}. \qquad (7)$$

This demonstrates that the value of the multiplier, K, is equal to the reciprocal of the fraction of income withdrawn from the circular flow, i.e., the reciprocal of the marginal propensity to withdraw. With a w of 0·4, the multiplier is 2·5; if it were 0·2, then the multiplier would be 5, and so on.

[1] This section can be omitted without loss of continuity.

Conclusions

We have now derived two further important predictions of national income theory:

> **(6) For any given shift in aggregate expenditure, the larger the proportion of income spent and the smaller the proportion withdrawn (the smaller is *w*), the greater the change in income.**
> **(7) The value of the multiplier is equal to the reciprocal of the fraction of income withdrawn from the circular flow (*w*).**

How large is the multiplier?

Following Keynes' lead, many early national income theories used a model in which saving was the only withdrawal and investment the only injection. In such a model, the multiplier is the reciprocal of the marginal propensity to save. In most countries this fraction is quite low, say between 0·2 and 0·1, and for a long time it was widely believed that the value of the multiplier was between 5 and 10. Subsequently, both the experience of post-war fluctuations and some careful empirical calculations, made mainly in the US, led to the conclusion that the multiplier was substantially smaller than this, most probably in the range of 1·5 to 2·5. The two withdrawals of imports of both raw materials and finished goods and of taxes cause the marginal propensity to withdraw, w, to be much larger than the marginal propensity to save. They also cause the multiplier to be smaller in a relatively open economy such as Britain than in a relatively closed economy such as the US.

Inflationary and deflationary gaps

So far we have stuck to the assumptions that there are some unemployed resources and that prices are constant. In these circumstances, every change in aggregate expenditure causes a change in real national income, output and employment. What would happen if a rise in desired aggregate expenditure brought the economy into the range of full employment of all resources? Once this occurred, further sharp rises in aggregate expenditure could not be met by increases in real output. Prices would rise instead.

Situations of unemployment are referred to as deflationary, and situations in which there is full employment and excess aggregate demand are referred to as inflationary. In *deflationary situations* prices often tend to be fairly steady and real output tends to vary as aggregate expenditure varies.[1] In *inflationary situations* output tends to be fairly steady at its full-employment level but prices tend to rise.

So far our macro-models have all been applied to deflationary situations. We will shortly need to extend them to inflationary situations, and we may now see one way in which this can be done.

---

[1] This is unfortunate terminology because the word 'deflation' commonly refers to decreases in the price level, and thus in this context it suggests that prices will be falling. The assumption in the present theory is that prices are constant at less than full employment. A better term might be 'contractionary'. But, for better or worse, the term 'deflationary' has come to be attached to situations of less than full employment.

The kinked relation between national income and inflation

While we are beginning our study of national income theory, it is convenient to draw a sharp distinction between two situations. The first is characterized by unemployed supplies of all factors of production, and in this situation all changes in aggregate demand are met by changes in output and employment while prices remain unchanged.[1] This is the situation that we have dealt with until now. The second situation is characterized by full employment of all factors of production; all increases in aggregate demand are then met by increases in prices – that is, by an inflation.

The assumptions just described are embodied in the kinked function shown in Figure 34.6. Note that this is an altogether new type of figure. On the horizontal axis

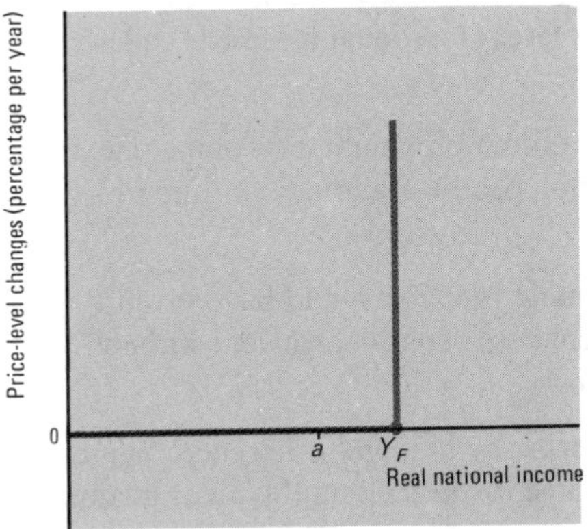

Fig. 34.6 The kinked relation between national income and changes in the price level

we have national income which we have plotted many times before. On the vertical axis, however, we have the rate of change of the price level (i.e., the rate of inflation) which we have not plotted before. The graph shows that when Y is less than full-employment or potential national income, Y_F (i.e., the economy is on the horizontal portion of the kinked function), the rate of inflation will be zero (i.e., the price level will be constant). It also shows that when national income is equal to Y_F, the price level can be constant or can be rising at any rate (i.e., the economy is on the vertical portion of the kinked function). How fast the price level will be rising will depend on factors not yet studied. All that the relation in the figure shows is that inflation *cannot* occur unless Y is equal to Y_F, but when Y does equal Y_F, any amount of inflation *may* occur.

In an economy to which the kinked relation applies, real national income and employment vary with the level of aggregate expenditure as long as national income is below the full-employment point. Once national income reaches full employment, however, further increases in real output and employment are impossible. To see the effect of further increases in aggregate expenditure in such situations, suppose that the economy has been at equilibrium at the full-employment level of national income and that the aggregate expenditure schedule

[1] It is a matter of common observation that the price level tends to be very sticky in a downward direction. There has not been a year since World War II in which the British price level has declined significantly. Even in the 1930s, in the face of massive unemployment, only very modest reductions in the price level were observed and then only in a very few years. Thus the assumption that the price level does not fall in times of unemployment is very close to the mark.

then shifts upward. Real output cannot increase no matter how great expenditure may be. If total desired expenditure exceeds the value of full-employment output, all that will happen is that prices will rise. Instead of national income rising because more output is produced at constant prices, national income will rise because the full-employment level of real output will be sold at higher and higher money prices.

The 'gaps' defined

If national income is in equilibrium at less than full employment, a sufficiently large upward shift in the aggregate demand function would raise national income to its full-employment level.

> **The extent to which the aggregate demand function would have to shift upward to produce the full-employment level of national income is called the** DEFLATIONARY GAP**.**

If aggregate demand exceeds output at the full-employment level of income, there is inflationary pressure; the economy cannot produce enough output to satisfy demand at current prices.

> **The extent to which the aggregate demand function would have to shift downward to produce the full-employment level of national income without inflation is called the** INFLATIONARY GAP**.**

In fact both gaps can be expressed in terms of a single difference: aggregate desired expenditure at full-employment income *minus* full-employment income. If this difference is negative, we speak of a deflationary gap; if it is positive, we speak of an inflationary gap.

The gaps are illustrated in Figure 34.7. The top half of each panel uses the aggregate expenditure function, *E*, and the 45° line, while the bottom half shows the same situation using the withdrawals and injections functions. In each case the equilibrium level of national income is designated Y_E and the level of income that would produce full employment of resources at the present price level is designated Y_F.

The first panel shows the deflationary gap as the bracketed amount *D*. In the upper diagram equilibrium income is Y_E. If full employment income, Y_F, were to prevail, expenditure would fall short of income by *D*. The lower diagram illustrates the identical situation. The equilibrium level of income, where withdrawals equal injections, is Y_E and this is less than the full-employment level of Y_F. If Y_F were to be temporarily achieved, injections would fall short of withdrawals by the amount *D*, and this is the magnitude of the deflationary gap. Of course, in such a situation, income will fall to its equilibrium level of Y_E.

The third panel differs from the first only by the fact that the injections function, and thus the expenditure function as well, has been raised. This panel illustrates an inflationary gap. The equilibrium level of income is Y_E, but there are only sufficient resources available to produce national income of Y_F at the existing price level. The inflationary gap is shown by the bracketed distance *F*. At full employment there is a situation of excess demand: households, firms and the government are trying to spend an amount greater than the value of total national output. Thus, unless something is done, an inflation will ensue. The figure in the lower half of the panel shows the identical situation. Equilibrium national income exceeds full-employment

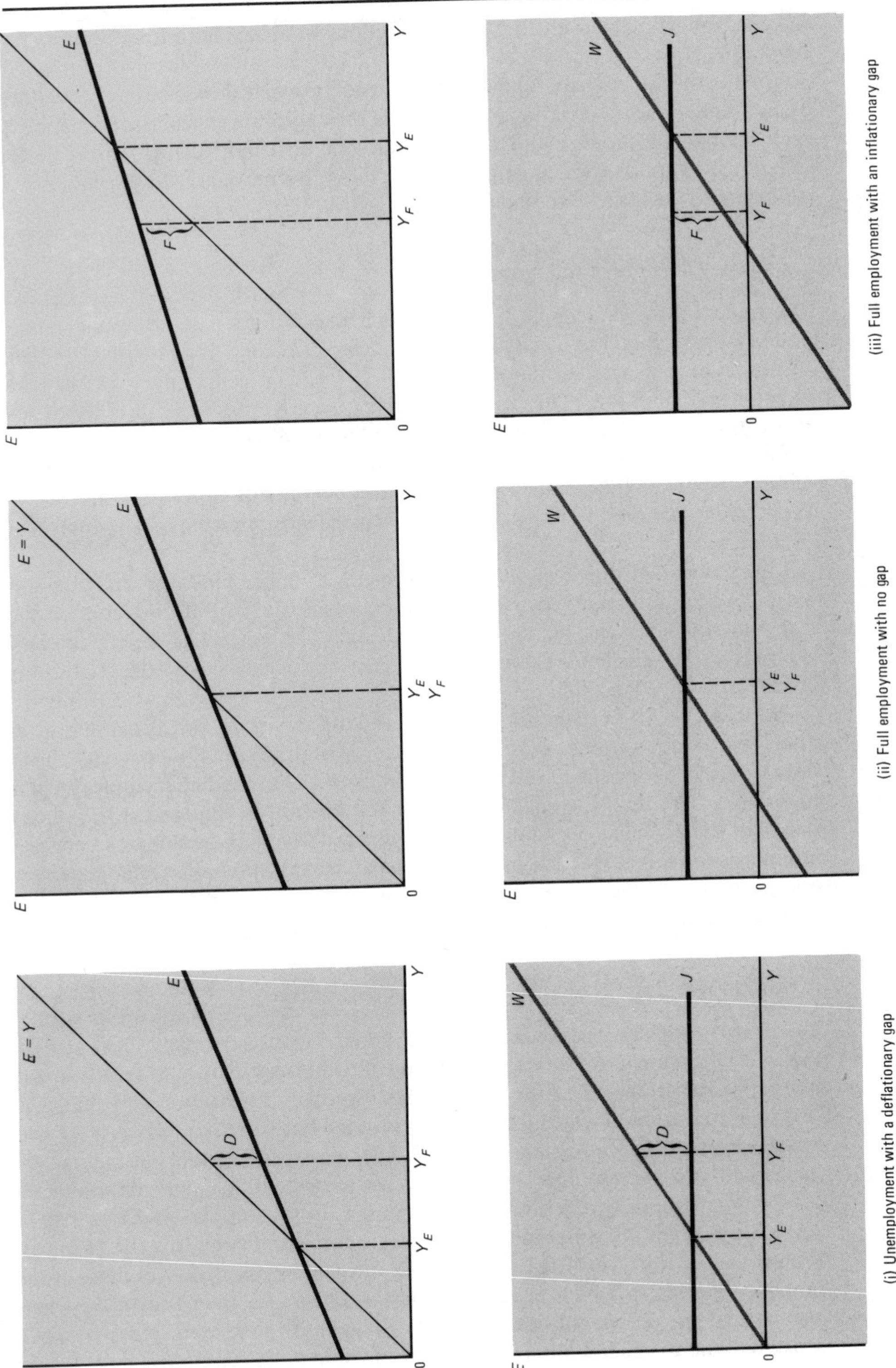

Fig. 34.7 Inflationary and deflationary gaps

income, and if income were at Y_F, then injections would exceed withdrawals by the amount F.

Finally, the middle panel shows the intermediate situation where there is neither an inflationary nor a deflationary gap. Here the aggregate expenditure function is high enough to produce full employment, but not high enough to create an inflationary gap. At the full-employment level of income aggregate expenditure is just equal to the value of total output.

Using the concepts of the 'gaps'

The modern theory of income determination is an elaboration of the original model put forward by John Maynard Keynes in his *General Theory*, first published in 1936. In the original Keynesian model, the emphasis was on deflationary, rather than inflationary, conditions. This was not surprising since Keynes was concerned to find cures for the Great Depression, which had had disastrous consequences for the tens of millions of workers who made up the massive armies of unemployed in Western industrial nations. Indeed, the Depression was undermining the very social fabric of Western democracies. Finding a cure for it was the most pressing social problem of the time.

The extension of the theory to cover problems of full employment and inflation did not come until the Second World War, when those problems replaced the nightmare of persistent, massive unemployment. The concept of the inflationary gap proved the vehicle for extending the theory beyond the conditions that it was originally designed to explain.

The concepts of both inflationary and deflationary gaps will prove useful in discussing policy questions of how to achieve stability in the economy. That discussion can be foreshadowed by noting that one way to combat unemployment is to estimate the size of the deflationary gap and attempt to eliminate it by policies that shift the aggregate expenditure curve upward. Similarly, one way to combat inflation is to estimate the size of the inflationary gap and attempt to eliminate it by policies that shift the aggregate expenditure curve downwards. Such policies are discussed in detail in subsequent chapters.

A word of warning

The sharp distinction between deflationary and inflationary gaps illustrated in Figure 34.7 represents a severe simplification of reality that can aid us greatly in our study of some problems. Later on we shall drop this simplification and study the very important case in which the economy is in the border region between the two situations. In this region there is enough unemployment so that output can be increased but some resources are close enough to being fully employed so there is also some inflationary pressure in the economy. In such circumstances a rise in aggregate expenditure will lead both to a rise in real output and to a rise in prices. Such situations are dealt with in Part 11. Meanwhile, we can make good use of the simplified model, in which national income is *either* less than full-employment income and prices are constant *or* at its full-employment level and prices are constant if there is no inflationary gap, or rising if there is one.

35

The consumption function

Consumption is by far the largest component of aggregate expenditure of all countries. In the UK it represents nearly half of total final expenditure. This makes the consumption function one of the most important functions in macroeconomics. If we are to predict the effects of shifts in government taxation and spending policies on the other elements of private expenditure, we need to know the shape of the consumption function. For as we saw in the discussion of the multiplier, when one function shifts the magnitude of the effects on income depends on the slope of the other function.

Not only is the shape of the consumption function important in determining the reaction of the economy to shifts in other functions, the consumption function itself can shift. If at the same level of income households elect to cut their consumption expenditures by the modest amount of 6 per cent, this represents nearly a 3 per cent fall in total final expenditure. Combined with a multiplier of 2 this would reduce national income by 6 per cent. This may not sound like a lot, but if employment changed in proportion to the change in income, then this could turn a situation of 3 per cent unemployment into 9 per cent, which is an enormous shift by the standards of fluctuations in unemployment over the last few decades.

In this chapter we go beyond the crude assumption used so far that households always consume a constant fraction of their income, and thus also save a constant fraction. First we shall look in more detail at the Keynesian theory of the consumption function, then we shall outline some modern theories that go beyond the basic Keynesian hypothesis that current consumption depends on current income.

The Keynesian theory of the consumption function

The basic hypothesis of the Keynesian theory of the consumption function is that current consumption is related to current income. To describe this relation Keynes coined the twin concepts of the average and the marginal propensities to consume. AVERAGE PROPENSITY TO CONSUME (APC) is the proportion of income spent on consumption. To calculate this value, take total consumption expenditure, C, and divide it by Y, total income, $APC = C/Y$. We can obtain an average propensity to consume by using either total income, Y, or disposable income, Y_d, as the divisor. Which of these concepts is being used is almost always obvious from the context.

We defined the concept of marginal propensities on page 497. Recall that the *MPC* measures the relation between changes in consumption, ΔC, and changes in income, ΔY. By dividing ΔY into ΔC, we measure how much of the last pound's worth of income is consumed; in symbols, $MPC = \Delta C/\Delta Y$. Table 35.1 illustrates these definitions by showing the details of the calculations for the *APC* and the *MPC* for two assumed levels of disposable income and consumption.

Table 35.1 Calculation of the average and marginal propensities to consume

Disposable income, Y_d	Consumption expenditure, C	Average propensity to consume (*APC*)	Marginal propensity to consume (*MPC*)
£300	£270	$\frac{270}{300} = 0{\cdot}90$	
			$\frac{50}{100} = 0{\cdot}5$
£400	£320	$\frac{320}{400} = 0{\cdot}80$	

In the previous chapter we used the simple assumption that households always consume a constant proportion of their incomes. In the example it was 80 per cent. This made the *APC* and the *MPC* both equal to 0·8. We shall soon have to introduce a more complex hypothesis to deal with short-term data.

Consumption and disposable income

Empirical studies suggest that many factors influence consumption. We begin by concentrating on income, assuming that other factors capable of influencing consumption remain constant. Changes in these other factors can then be allowed for by studying how they shift the function relating consumption to income.

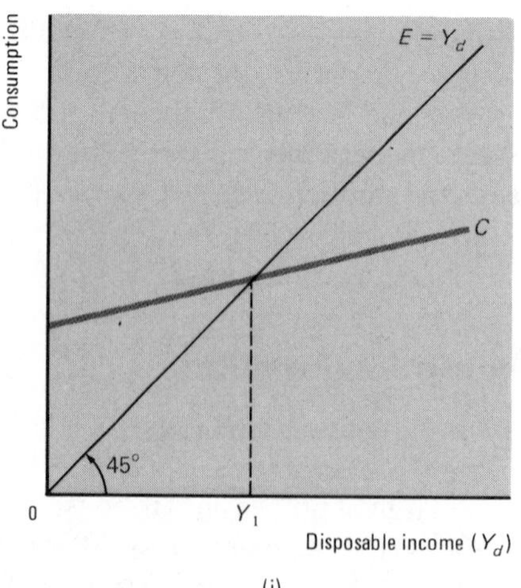

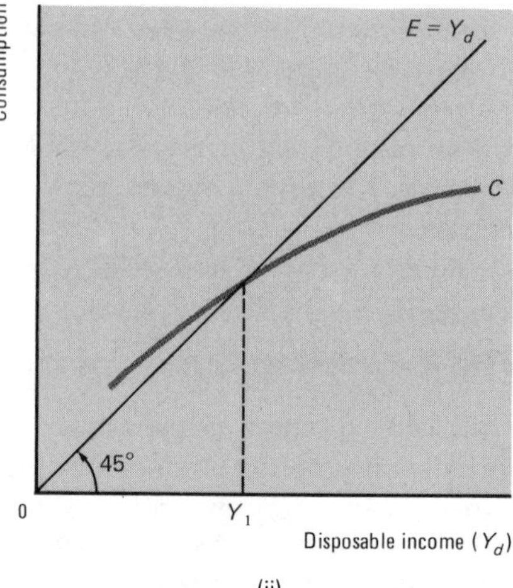

Fig. 35.1 Two possible shapes for a consumption function: (i) the *MPC* is constant but the *APC* declines as income rises; (ii) both the *APC* and the *MPC* decline as income rises

Two basic hypotheses provide the core of the Keynesian theory of the consumption function:

(1) There is a break-even level of income at which *APC* = 1. Below this level, *APC* is greater than unity and above it *APC* is less than unity.
(2) The *MPC* is greater than zero but less than unity for all levels of income.

Figure 35.1 shows two consumption functions that are consistent with these two hypotheses. While the hypotheses greatly restrict the nature of the relationship between consumption and income, it is well to notice that they only predict an *MPC* between 0 and 1, and are thus consistent with an *MPC* very near to unity (say, 0·99) or very near to zero (say, 0·01). They are also consistent with an *MPC* that remains constant as income rises, as shown in the first part of Figure 35.1, or with an *MPC* that declines as income rises, as shown in the second part of the same Figure.

Aggregation problems

An aggregate consumption function shows how the society's total consumption expenditure varies as its total disposable income varies. Conceptually, the society's function is aggregated from all the functions of the individual households that compose it. But aggregation is not without problems. On the one hand, it was noted earlier (see pp. 10–11) that aggregate behaviour is less capricious than individual behaviour because the odd things done by individual households tend to cancel each other out. On the other hand, a stable aggregate consumption function may not exist even if all households have perfectly stable individual consumption functions. If, for example, households have different *MPC*s, then the same total income will lead to different levels of consumption depending on how that income is distributed among households.

What are the conditions under which stable individual consumption functions will give rise to a stable aggregate consumption function? Two conditions, either of which is sufficient, are worth noticing here. The first condition is that all households have the same *MPC*. In this case, changes in the distribution of income between households will have no effect on the level of total consumption expenditure. If, for example, all households have an *MPC* of 0·8, then redistributing a given national income among households will leave the aggregate level of consumption unchanged, because any household that loses £1 of income lowers its expenditure by 80 pence while any household that gains an extra pound of income raises expenditure by 80 pence. Thus, in this situation, the level of total consumption depends only on the level of total income; it is independent of the distribution of this income among households.

If *MPC*s differ among households, a second sufficient condition for a stable aggregate consumption function is that the distribution of income among households does not change. Thus, if national income rises or falls by 10 per cent, each household's income will rise or fall by 10 per cent, and total consumption expenditure will be uniquely related to total income. But this is a very strong assumption, and a weaker one is sufficient. If for each level of income there is only one associated distribution of income, then there will be only one associated level of total household consumption. This assumption permits the distribution of income to change over the trade cycle.

As long as there is a unique distribution associated with each phase of the trade cycle, there will be a unique level of total consumption expenditure associated with each level of national income.

Thus, the use of a stable aggregate consumption function that relates total disposable income to total consumption expenditures, in a world in which *MPC*s are known to vary among households, requires that most changes that do occur in the distribution of income are themselves associated with changes in the level of income.

There is considerable empirical evidence that the distribution of income changes only slowly, and also that much of the short-period change that does occur is systematically related to phases of the trade cycle. This appears to be why it has been possible to estimate reasonably stable aggregate consumption functions.

From disposable income to national income

An individual household's consumption is related to its disposable income, and aggregate consumption is thus related to aggregate disposable income. In developing theories of national income, we normally relate aggregate expenditure, of which consumption is an important part, to national income. The transition from a relation between *consumption and disposable income* to one between *consumption and national income* is easily accomplished if disposable income and national income are themselves related to each other. To illustrate, assume that disposable income is always 60 per cent of national income. Then whatever the relation between consumption, C, and disposable income, Y_d, we can always substitute $0{\cdot}6Y$ for Y_d. Thus if consumption were always 90 per cent of Y_d, then C would always be 54 per cent (60 per cent of 90 per cent) of Y. If, to take another example, consumption were £1,000 + $\sqrt{Y_d}$ then consumption would be £1,000 + $\sqrt{0{\cdot}6Y}$. From now on we will assume that we can write consumption as a function either of disposable income or of national income.[1]

Causes of shifts in the consumption function

An important consequence of the relationships just described is that the function relating consumption to national income can shift for either of two quite distinct reasons:

(1) the relation between national income and disposable income may change;
(2) the relation between consumption and disposable income that describes household spending behaviour may change.

In the first case, there is no change in the propensity to consume out of disposable income. In the second case, there is a change in the propensity to consume out of disposable income which reflects a change in the basic expenditure decisions of households.

Consider an example of each of these changes. Start by recalling that in the

[1] If consumption is any linear function of Y_d and Y_d is a constant fraction of Y, we can write $C = a + bY_d$ and $Y_d = eY$. Substitution then gives C as a linear function of Y: $C = a + beY$. More generally, if $C = f(Y_d)$ and $Y_d = g(Y)$, then $C = f[g(Y)]$.

previous numerical example the propensity to consume out of disposable income was 0·9, while disposable income was linked to national income by the relation $Y_d = 0{\cdot}6Y$. This implied a relation between consumption and national income of $C = 0{\cdot}54Y$. As an example of (1) above, assume that the propensity to consume out of disposable income falls to $C = 0{\cdot}75Y_d$ with an unchanged relation between Y_d and Y. This implies a relation between consumption and national income of $C = 0{\cdot}45Y$. As an example of (2), assume that the propensity to consume out of disposable income remains at 0·9, but disposable income falls from $0{\cdot}6Y$ to $0{\cdot}5Y$. This shifts the relation between consumption and national income to $C = 0{\cdot}45Y$. The changes in both of these examples cause the same shift in the observed relation between consumption and national income (since 0·75 *times* 0·6 = 0·9 *times* 0·5 = 0·45).

Shifts in the relation between national income and disposable income Government policy-makers can very easily change the relation between national income and disposable income by altering tax rates. An increase in income tax rates will, for example, reduce the amount of disposable income that reaches the hands of households out of any given level of national income. A reduction in tax rates will have the opposite effect. Thus, according to the theory that consumption depends upon disposable income, government policy-makers can shift the aggregate consumption function (and hence the aggregate expenditure function) downwards or upwards by increasing or decreasing tax rates, even though they may be unable to affect the propensity to consume out of disposable income.

> **An increase in tax rates lowers the aggregate expenditure function by lowering the ratio of disposable income to national income. A decrease in tax rates has the opposite effect.**

Shifts in the relation between consumption and disposable income The second reason why the function relating consumption to national income can shift is because the function relating consumption to disposable income shifts. What factors would cause such a shift?

Changes in income distribution: If households have different *MPC*s, aggregate consumption depends not only on aggregate income but also on the distribution of this income among households. In this case, which was discussed in detail on page 515, a change in the *distribution* of income will cause a change in the aggregate level of consumption expenditure associated with any given *level* of national income.

Since the distribution of income tends to change fairly slowly, such changes do not destroy stable consumption-income relationships. Nevertheless, such changes can occur, and they cause the consumption function to shift.

Changes in the terms of credit: Many durable consumer goods are purchased on credit, whose terms may range from a few months to pay for a radio, to two or three years to pay for a car. If credit becomes more difficult or more costly to obtain, many households may postpone their planned, credit-financed purchases. If the typical initial payment required for goods purchased on hire purchase was increased from 10 per cent to 20 per cent, households that had just saved up 10 per cent of the purchase price of the goods they wished to consume would now find this sum inadequate, and would have to postpone their planned purchases until they saved 20 per cent of the purchase price. There would then be a temporary reduction in current consumption expenditures until these extra savings had been accumulated.

Monetary authorities can, by controlling the cost and availability of credit, shift the consumption function and thus affect aggregate demand.

Changes in existing stocks of durable goods: It is now recognized that any period in which durables are difficult or impossible to purchase and monetary savings are accumulated is likely to be followed by a sudden outburst of expenditure on durables. Such a flurry of spending will also follow a period of unemployment, during which many families may have refrained from buying durables.

The emphasis here is on durable goods (e.g., cars and refrigerators) because purchases of non-durable consumer goods (e.g., food and clothing) and of services (e.g., car repairs) cannot be long postponed. While expenditures on non-durables are relatively steady, purchases of durables are volatile and can lead to sharp shifts in the consumption function.

Changes in price expectations: If households expect an inflation to occur, they may be willing to purchase durable goods they would otherwise not have bought for another one or two years. In such circumstances, purchases made now yield a saving over purchases made in the future. By the same argument, an expected deflation may lead to postponing purchases of durables in hopes of purchasing them later at a lower price.

The permanent-income and life-cycle hypotheses

In the Keynesian theory of the consumption function, current consumption expenditure is related to current income – either current disposable income or current national income. In recent years empirical observations have several times seemed to conflict with this Keynesian hypothesis. The attempt to reconcile the basic theory of the consumption function with existing evidence has led to a series of modified theories that relate consumption to some longer-term concept of income than the income that the household is currently earning.

The two most influential theories of this type are the PERMANENT-INCOME HYPOTHESIS (PIH), developed by Professor Milton Friedman, and the LIFE-CYCLE HYPOTHESIS (LCH), developed by Professor Franco Modigliani and Albert Ando and the late Professor Aldo Brumberg. For our purposes the similarities between these theories are more important than their differences, and they may be looked at together when studying their major characteristics. In doing this it is important to ask: What variables do these theories seek to explain? What assumptions do the theories make? What are the major implications of these assumptions? How do the theories reconcile the apparently conflicting empirical evidence? And what implications do they have for the overall behaviour of the economy?

Variables

The three important variables used in these theories are consumption, saving and income. These need to be considered carefully since they are defined somewhat differently than in Keynesian theory.

Consumption Keynesian type theories seek to explain the amounts that households spend on purchasing goods and services for consumption. This concept is called *consumption expenditure*. Permanent-income theories seek to explain the actual flows of consumption of the services that are provided by the commodities that households buy. This concept is called *actual consumption*.[1] With services and nondurable goods, expenditure and actual consumption occur more or less at the same time and the distinction between these two concepts is not important. The consumption of a haircut, for example, occurs at the time it is purchased, and an orange or a package of corn flakes is consumed soon after it is purchased. Thus, if we knew purchases of such goods and services at some time, say last year, we would also know last year's consumption of these goods and services. But this is not the case with durable consumer goods. A screwdriver is purchased at one point in time, but it yields up its services over a long time, possibly as long as the purchaser's lifetime. The same is true of a house and a watch and, over a shorter period of time, of a car and a dress. For such products, if we know purchases last year, we do not necessarily know last year's consumption of the services that the products yielded.

Thus one important characteristic of durable goods is that *expenditure* to purchase them is not necessarily synchronized with consumption of the stream of services that the goods provide. If in 1975 Mr Smith buys a car for £2,000, runs it for six years, and then discards it as worn out, his expenditure on automobiles is £2,000 in 1975 and zero for the next five years. His consumption of the services of automobiles, however, is spread out at an average annual rate of £333 for six years. If everyone followed Mr Smith's example by buying a new car in 1975 and replacing it in 1981, the automobile industry would undergo wild booms in 1975 and 1981 with five intervening years of slump even though the actual consumption of automobiles would be spread more or less evenly over time. This example is extreme, but it illustrates the possibilities, where consumers' durables are concerned, of quite different time paths of *consumption expenditure*, which is the subject of Keynesian theories of the consumption function, and *actual consumption*, which is the subject of permanent-income type theories.

Saving Now consider saving. The change in emphasis from consumption expenditure to actual consumption implies a change in the definition of saving. Saving is no longer income minus consumption expenditure; it is now income minus the value of actual consumption. When Mr Smith spent £2,000 on his car in 1975 but used only £333 worth of its services in that year he was actually consuming £333 and saving £1,667. The purchase of a consumers' durable is thus counted as saving, and only the value of its services actually consumed is counted as consumption.

Income The third important variable in this type of theory is the income variable. Instead of using current income the theories use a concept of long-term income. The precise definition varies from one theory to another, but basically it is related to the household's expected income stream over a fairly long planning period. In the *LCH*

[1] Because Keynes's followers did not always distinguish carefully between the concepts of consumption expenditure and actual consumption, the word 'consumption' is often used in both contexts. We follow this normal practice, but where there is any possible ambiguity in the term we will refer to 'consumption expenditure' and to 'actual consumption'.

it is the income that the household expects to earn over its lifetime.[1]

Every household is assumed to have a view of its expected lifetime earnings. This is not as unreasonable as it might seem. Students training to be doctors have a very different view of expected lifetime income than those training to become primary school teachers. Both of these expected income streams – for a doctor and for a primary school teacher – will be very different from that expected by an assembly-line worker or a professional athlete.

One such possible lifetime income stream is illustrated in Figure 35.2. The graph shows a hypothetical expected income stream from work for a household that expects to live 40 years from 1975. The current actual income rises to a peak, then falls slowly for a while, and then suddenly falls to zero on retirement.

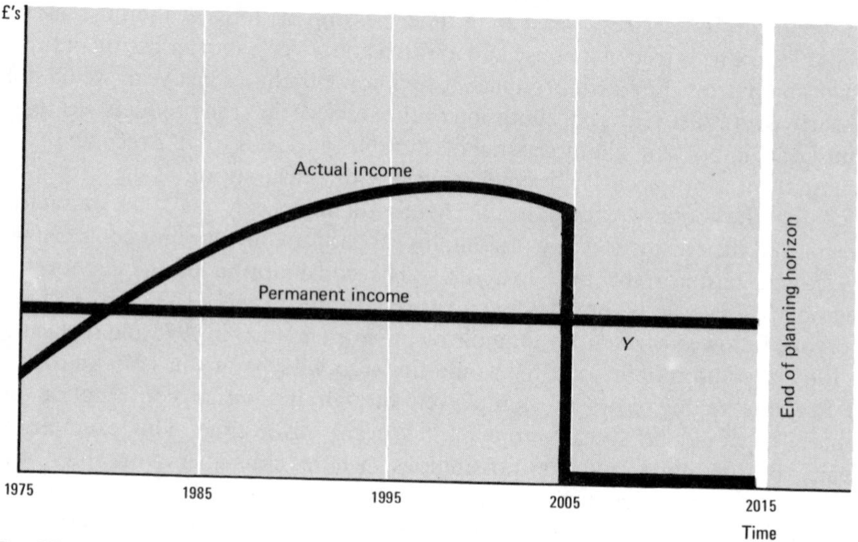

Fig. 35.2 Actual current income and permanent income

The household's expected lifetime income can be converted into a single figure for *annual* PERMANENT INCOME. In the life-cycle hypothesis this permanent income is the maximum amount the household could spend on consumption each year without accumulating debts *that are passed on to future generations*. If a household were to consume a constant amount equal to its permanent income each year, it would add to its debt in years when current income was less than permanent income and reduce its debt or increase its assets in years when its current income exceeded its permanent income; however, over its whole lifetime it would just break even, leaving neither accumulated assets nor debts to its heirs. If the interest rate were zero, permanent income would be just the sum of all expected incomes divided by the number of expected years of life. With a positive interest rate, permanent income will diverge somewhat from this amount because of the costs of borrowing and the extra income that can be earned by investing savings.

[1] In the *PIH* the household has an infinite time horizon and the relevant permanent-income concept is the amount the household could consume forever without increasing or decreasing its present stock of wealth.

Assumptions

The basic assumption of this type of theory, whether *PIH* or *LCH*, is that the household's actual consumption is related to its permanent rather than to its current income. Two households that have the same permanent income (and are similar in other relevant characteristics) will have the same consumption patterns even though their current incomes behave very differently.

Implications

The effect on consumption of changes in income The major implication of these theories is that changes in a household's current income will affect its actual consumption only so far as they affect its permanent income. Consider two income changes that could occur to a household with a permanent income of £5,000 per year and an expected lifetime of 30 more years. In the first, suppose the household receives an unexpected extra income of £1,000 *for this year only*. The increase in the household's permanent income is thus very small. If the rate of interest were zero, the household could consume an extra £33·33 per year for the rest of its expected lifespan; with a positive rate of interest the extra annual consumption would be more because money not spent this year could be invested and would earn interest.[1] In the second case, the household gets a totally unforeseen increase of £1,000 a year for the rest of its life. In this event the household's permanent income has risen by £1,000 because the household can actually consume £1,000 more every year without accumulating any new debts. Although in both cases current income rises £1,000, the effects on permanent income are very different in the two cases.

Keynesian theory assumes that *consumption expenditure* is related to current income and therefore predicts the same change in this year's consumption expenditure in each of the above cases. Permanent-income theories relate *actual consumption* to permanent income and therefore predict very different changes in actual consumption in each of these cases. In the first case there would be only a small increase in actual annual consumption, while in the second case there would be a large increase.

> **In permanent-income theories, any change in current income that is thought to be temporary will have only a small effect on permanent income and hence on actual consumption.**

Implications for the behaviour of the economy According to the permanent-income and the life-cycle hypotheses, actual consumption is not much affected by temporary changes in income. Does this mean that aggregate expenditure, $C+I+G+(X-M)$, is not much affected? *Not necessarily*. Consider what happens when the household in the previous example gets a temporary increase in its income of £1,000 for one year. If actual consumption is not greatly affected by this, then households must save most of the temporary increase in their incomes. But from the point of view of these theories, households save when they buy a durable good just as much as when they buy a financial asset such as a bond. In both cases actual current consumption is not changed. The household in this example could have bought a 30-year

---

[1] If the rate of interest were 7 per cent the household could invest the £1,000, consume an extra £80·50 per year, and just have nothing left at the end of 30 years.

annuity worth its £1,000 and spent the £80·50 it would receive each year. It could also, however, have bought some durable consumer good for £1,000 and consumed it over the next 30 years.

Thus spending a temporary increase in income either on financial assets or on a new car is consistent with both the *PIH* and the *LCH*. But it makes a great deal of difference to the short-run behaviour of the economy which is done. If households buy financial assets, aggregate expenditure on currently produced final goods does not rise when income rises temporarily;[1] if households buy automobiles or any other durable consumer good, aggregate expenditure on currently produced final goods does rise when income rises temporarily. Thus the *PIH* and the *LCH* leave unsettled the question that is critical for the measurement of the size of the multiplier: What is the reaction of household *expenditures* on currently produced goods and services, particularly durables, to short-term, temporary changes in income?

The permanent-income and life-cycle theories leave unsettled the critical question of the ability of short-term changes in fiscal policy to remove inflationary and deflationary gaps by affecting consumption expenditure.

Assume, for example, that a serious deflationary gap emerges and that the government attempts to stimulate a recovery by giving tax rebates and by cutting tax rates – both on an announced temporary basis. This will raise households' current disposable incomes by the amount of the tax cuts, but it will raise their permanent incomes by only a small amount. According to the *PIH*, the flow of actual current consumption should not rise much. But it is quite consistent with the *PIH* that households should spend their tax savings on durable consumer goods, the consumption of which can be spread over many years. In this case, even though actual consumption this year would not respond much to the tax cuts, expenditure would respond a great deal. Since current output and employment depend on expenditure rather than real consumption, the tax cut *would be* effective in stimulating the economy. It is, however, also consistent with the *PIH* that households spend only a small part of their tax savings on consumption goods and seek to invest the rest in bonds and other financial assets. In this case the tax cuts may have only a small stimulating effect on the economy. It is important to note that the *PIH* and the *LCH* do *not* predict unambiguously that changes in taxes that are announced to be only short-lived will be ineffective in removing inflationary or deflationary gaps. They do, however, open up this possibility, which was not allowed for by Keynesian theory of the consumption function.

[1] Except for any indirect effect through changes in interest rates.

36

Investment

Keynes spoke of the 'animal spirits' of capitalists. He saw alternating periods of optimism and pessimism causing investment expenditure to vary dramatically from year to year. These changes would be caused by nothing more substantial than states of mind and yet they were a major source of instability in national income. We have already seen how this instability can come about: if the injection of investment expenditure varies greatly from year to year, national income will vary in the same direction and by amounts magnified by the multiplier relation. Even today, some followers of Keynes refer to Keynesian models incorporating investment as a stable function of a number of economic variables as 'bastard Keynesianism'. Everyone agrees that the investment can, and does, vary. The issue, however, is between movement along and shifts of the investment function. Many economists feel that much of the variation in investment can be explained as a stable response to changes in variables that determine investment, such as the rate of interest. Others feel, as Keynes did, that any investment function will shift unpredictably since many, perhaps most, changes in investment will be determined by such non-economic and unquantifiable forces as business confidence.

The determinants of investment

To study variations in investment, and other problems concerning investment in the circular flow of income, we shall have to drop our assumption that investment is an exogenous constant. In this section we discuss some of the major forces that can cause investment to vary.

The rate of interest

Much investment is made with borrowed money. As we saw in Chapter 28, it pays a firm to borrow money to finance its investment projects as long as the marginal efficiency of its capital exceeds the rate of interest (see page 392). Because the lower the rate of interest, the lower the cost of borrowing money for investment purposes, it might seem natural to expect that the lower the rate of interest, the higher the amount of new investment in plant and equipment. And yet this possible relation between investment and the rate of interest has been, and still is, the subject of much controversy. We must now look at it more closely.

We saw in Chapter 28 that firms would always like to add to their existing capital as long as the marginal efficiency of that capital exceeded the interest rate. If we assume that capital is subject to diminishing returns, then the *MEC* will fall as the stock of capital increases, as illustrated by the curve in Figure 36.1. The capital stock

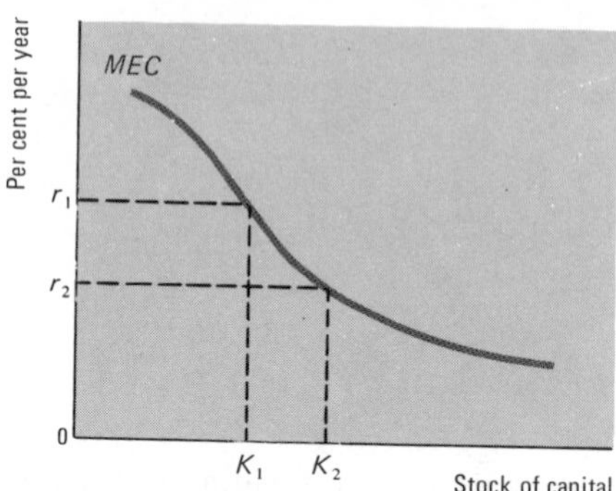

Fig. 36.1 The marginal efficiency of capital schedule

will thus be of equilibrium size when *MEC* equals the rate of interest. From this it follows that the equilibrium size of the capital stock varies inversely with the rate of interest. In particular, a fall in the rate of interest will lead to a rise in the desired capital stock; firms will all wish to add to their capital, which is to say they will wish to engage in positive net investment. In Figure 36.1, for example, a fall in the rate of interest from r_1 to r_2 causes an increase in the desired capital stock from K_1 to K_2. This requires that $K_2 - K_1$ of new investment take place.

The rate of interest and investment in capital equipment A desired increase in the capital stock generates investment only while the increase is under way. Suppose, for example, that in response to a fall in interest rates there is an increase of £10 billion in the desired capital stock. If the capital stock is raised by £10 billion within a year, net investment will rise for a year and then fall to zero. In this case a fall in the interest rate will lead to an increase in the amount of investment for only one year.

But the timing of investment may be more complicated than this; it may depend on how fast the stock of capital can be built up to its new desired level. The actual volume of investment in plant and equipment that takes place each year is limited by the capacities of the capital-goods and the construction industries. Assume that all the firms in the economy decide that they want a total of 3,000 newly built and equipped factories in operation next year, but that factories can only be built and equipped at the rate of 1,000 a year. Also assume that this situation has just been generated by a fall in the rate of interest. It will take three years before the desired addition to the capital stock is achieved. If, at the end of the first year, a rise in the rate of interest decreases the desired overall addition to the capital stock to 2,000 factories instead of 3,000, this new change will have no effect on investment in 'year two' because the capital-goods industries would still have to work to capacity to create the desired addition. Alternatively, if a fall in interest rates at the end of the first year raised the desired overall addition from 3,000 to 5,000 this, too, would not affect the rate of *current* investment, which is already at its maximum. The upper limit to annual investment in plant and equipment is set by the capacity of the capital-goods producing industries. Whenever the desired increase in the capital stock is more than can be produced in a year, there will be a backlog of orders. Thus substantial variations in the interest rate affect the length of the backlog rather than a level of investment in a particular year. If so, these variations will affect the *duration* of an investment boom generated by changes in desired capital stock, but will have only a minor (or even a zero) effect on the *amount of investment* occurring in one year during that boom.

Of course this picture is over-simplified, since it is always possible to produce more capital to some extent by working overtime, or extra shifts. This extra capital will usually be produced at higher cost and so will not be profitable unless there is a particularly urgent demand for new capital. The urgency will depend on the expected profitability of new investment, which will tend to be higher the lower the rate of interest.

For the reasons outlined above, major changes in interest rates are often associated with changes in investment. If they lead to large changes in the relation between the present and the desired capital stock, they may lead to changes in the rate at which the capital stock is growing. But there is no reason in theory to expect a permanent, stable relation between the rate of interest and the amount of investment. The permanent relation, *ceteris paribus*, is between the rate of interest and the stock of capital.

A fall in the rate of interest may lead to temporary spurts of investment in plant and equipment.

One important implication of this point is that an unstable relation between investment and the rate of interest does not require unstable 'animal spirits' for its explanation. It would occur even in a world where firms were perfectly certain about the *MEC* of every piece of capital in which they might invest.

The rate of interest and inventory investment The opportunity cost of holding inventories is what the firm could earn by selling the inventories and investing their value in something else. A measure of this is the interest rate, since the firm could certainly lend out its funds and earn the market rate of interest. A rise in the rate of interest raises the cost of holding inventories, and should cause firms to reduce their inventories until the advantage of the marginal unit of inventories is just equal to the rate of interest. Thus the desired stock of inventories should vary inversely with the rate of interest. But as with the stock of physical capital, inventory investment occurs only when inventories are being changed. Thus:

A fall (rise) in the rate of interest may lead to temporary spurts of inventory investment (disinvestment).

The rate of interest and investment in housing Interest payments are a large part of total mortgage payments. Typically, around half of the money paid on a twenty-year mortgage is interest, while only half is for repayment of principal. Changes in interest rates can therefore have large effects on the cost of buying a house and thus on the purchase of new housing.

A fall in the rate of interest will lead to temporary spurts of investment in new housing.

The rate of interest and total investment expenditure Although, for the reasons outlined above, investment does not necessarily bear a stable permanent relation to the rate of interest, most econometric studies show some relation. It is not fully stable, and it is also rather weak in the sense that changes in the rate of interest cause relatively small changes in the amount of investment – at least over the shortest time periods studied (usually measured in years rather than decades). Nonetheless, sufficient relation does seem to exist so that policy makers can rely on the fact that, at least in normal times, large changes in the rate of interest will change investment expenditure.

National income

The level of income Empirical evidence tends to indicate that investment may be more responsive to the level of demand for goods than to interest rates. There are two reasons for this. First, the higher the level of demand and income, the more *willing* businessmen will be to invest in new risky enterprises because they will have favourable expectations about the future. Second, the higher the level of demand, output and hence profits, the more businessmen will *be able* to invest. This aspect of the theory assumes that most businessmen are not able to borrow all the funds they require at the current rate of interest; in fact, so goes the hypothesis, they are severely limited in the quantity of funds they can borrow at any moment of time. As a result of this, the businessman is forced to look within his own firm for funds to finance many of his desired investment projects. These funds can be obtained by not distributing profits to shareholders. If we now add to this the hypothesis that profits will tend to be high when demand and income are high, we obtain the hypothesis that investment will depend on the level of income.[1]

The theory that investment is influenced by the level of profits has been subjected to considerable testing and has occasioned much controversy. The discussion is complex, and much of it concerns the statistical difficulties in determining whether the observations conform to the predictions of the theory. One of the main problems is that the observation that investment is high when profits are high is not necessarily evidence supporting the theory. The causal connection could be in the opposite direction: high investment causes a high level of income (by the multiplier process), which causes high profits. The argument has not yet been settled, and all that we can say at this stage is that there is no really compelling evidence to date that would lead one to reject the theory.

> **There is some evidence that investment varies directly with the level of national income both because when income is high demand for the output of capital goods is high and because profits, which are a major source of investment funds, also tend to be high.**

Changes in income According to the accelerator theory (usually called the ACCELERATOR) investment is related to the rate of change of national income.[2] When income is increasing, it is necessary to invest in order to increase the capacity to produce consumption goods; when income is falling, it may not even be necessary to replace old capital as it wears out, let alone to invest in new capital.

---

[1] In symbols, $I = \mathrm{I}(R)$, where R stands for profits; if we add the hypothesis that profits vary with income, $R = \mathrm{R}(Y)$, we obtain $\mathrm{I}[\mathrm{R}(Y)]$.

[2] In symbols, $I = \mathrm{I}(\Delta Y)$.

The main insight which the accelerator theory provides is the emphasis on the role of net investment as a *disequilibrium* phenomenon – something that occurs when the stock of capital goods differs from what firms and households would like it to be. Net investment would not occur when the desired quantities of inventories, buildings, and equipment had been achieved. Anything that changes those desired quantities can generate investment. The accelerator focuses on one such source of change, changing national income. This gives the accelerator its particular importance in connection with *fluctuations* in national income. As we shall see, it can itself contribute to those fluctuations.

How the accelerator works: To see how the theory works, assume that there is a particular capital stock needed to produce a given level of an industry's output. (The ratio of the value of capital to the annual value of output is called the CAPITAL-OUTPUT RATIO.) Given this assumption, suppose that the industry is producing at capacity and the demand for its product increases. If the industry is to produce the higher level of output, its capital stock must increase. This necessitates new investment.

Table 36.1 An illustration of the accelerator theory of investment

(1) Year	(2) Annual sales	(3) Change in sales	(4) Required stock of capital, assuming a capital-output ratio of 5/1	(5) Net investment: increase in required capital stock
1	£10	£0	£ 50	£ 0
2	10	0	50	0
3	11	1	55	5
4	13	2	65	10
5	16	3	80	15
6	19	3	95	15
7	22	3	110	15
8	24	2	120	10
9	25	1	125	5
10	25	0	125	0

Table 36.1 provides a simple numerical example of the accelerator. Assume that it takes £5 of capital to produce £1 of output per year. In years 1 and 2, there is no need for investment. In year 3, a rise in sales of £1 requires investment of £5 to provide the needed capital stock. In year 4, a further rise of £2 in sales requires an additional investment of £10 to provide the needed capital stock. As columns (3) and (5) show, the amount of net investment is proportional to the *change* in sales. When the increase in sales tapers off in years 7 to 9, investment declines. When, in year 10, sales no longer increase, net investment falls to zero because the capital stock of year 9 is adequate to provide output for year 10's sales.

Three general predictions of the accelerator are:
1. Rising rather than high levels of sales are needed to call forth net investment;
2. For net investment to remain constant, sales must rise by a constant amount per year;

3. The amount of net investment will be a multiple of the increase in sales because the capital-output ratio is greater than one.[1]

The data in Table 36.1 are for a single industry, but if many industries behave in this way, one would expect aggregate net investment to bear a similar relation to changes in national income. This is what the accelerator theory predicts.

The accelerator theory says nothing directly about replacement investment, but it does have implications for such investment. When sales are constant (no net investment required), replacement investment will be required to maintain the capital stock at the desired level. When sales are increasing from a position of full capacity both net investment and replacement investment will be acquired. When sales are falling so that the desired capital stock is below the actual capital stock, not only will net investment be zero but there will be a tendency to postpone replacement investment as well until the capital stock falls to the desired level.

Limitations of the accelerator: Taken literally, the accelerator posits a mechanical and rigid response of investment to changes in sales (and thus, aggregatively, to changes in national income). It does this by assuming a proportional relationship between changes in income and the size of the desired capital stock, and by assuming a fixed capital-output ratio. Each assumption is invalid to some degree.

Changes in sales that are thought to be temporary in their effect on demand will not necessarily lead to new investment. It is usually possible to increase the level of output for a given capital stock by working overtime or extra shifts. While this would be more expensive per unit of output in the long run, it will usually be preferable to making investments in new plant and equipment that would lie idle after a temporary spurt of demand had subsided. Thus expectations about what is the required capital stock may lead to a much less mechanistic response of investment to income than the accelerator suggests.

A further limitation of the accelerator theory is that it takes a very limited view of what constitutes investment. The fixed capital-output ratio emphasizes investment in what economists call CAPITAL WIDENING, the investment in additional capacity that uses the same ratio of capital to labour as existing capacity. It does not explain CAPITAL DEEPENING, which is the kind of increase in the amount of capital per unit of labour expected in response to a fall in the rate of interest. Neither does the theory say anything about investments brought about as a result of new processes or new products. Furthermore, it does not allow for the fact that investment in any period is likely to be limited by the capacity of the capital-goods industry.

For these and other reasons, the accelerator does not by itself give anything like a complete explanation of variations in investment in plant and equipment, and it should not be surprising that a simple accelerator theory provides a relatively poor overall explanation of changes in investment. Sophisticated tests have found evidence of an accelerator-like relationship, but it is one complicated by other factors.

What the accelerator theory does do is provide yet another reason why investment expenditure may vary from year to year as a result of perfectly

[1] In the example in the table the capital-output ratio is 5. Why should anyone spend £5 on capital stock to get £1 of output? It is not unreasonable to spend £5 to purchase a machine that produces only £1 of output *per year*, provided that the machine will last enough years to repay the £5 plus a reasonable return on this investment.

sensible decisions taken by firms that have nothing to do with swings between excessive optimism and pessimism.

Expectations

Investment takes time. A firm that decides to expand capacity may not see the fruits of its investment for several years. The decision to invest now is thus to a great extent an act of faith concerning the future. The penalties for a wrong guess can be great. If the firm decides not to expand capacity and the market for its product expands, it can fall irrevocably behind its more farsighted competitors. If, on the other hand, it decides to expand capacity and its market does not expand, it can be saddled with unused plant and equipment, the fixed costs of which may be ruinous. The firm does its best to predict its future demand, but many things that are unpredictable can influence sales. A new government may adopt different taxing and spending policies; the apparent success, or failure, of a disarmament conference may cause some lines of production to look more profitable and others less profitable. The rise of a new method of transportation, or a revolution in South America, may cause a decline in future sales. Occasionally, mob psychology may become the major determinant of investment decisions, and a feeling of pessimism about the future can snowball into a general cut in investment expenditure, or a feeling of optimism can snowball into an investment boom.

The effects of investment

The theory of income determination that we are studying in Part 7 takes the economy's technology and its supply of factors of production – land, labour *and* capital – as given. This means that potential national income, Y_F, is given. The theory then looks to fluctuations in aggregate demand to determine the degree to which resources are utilized and hence also the size of national income. This is basically a short-run theory of national income. In the long run investment increases the capital stock and thus causes changes in potential national income.

In the long run, the decisive effect of investment on national income is through its effects on the capital stock and hence on full-employment national income. In the short run, the important effect of investment is on aggregate demand, hence on the degree to which existing resources are employed, and through that on national income.

The effect of investment on growth of full-employment national income will be discussed in Chapter 46. In the meantime, we continue to study investment expenditure as a force influencing aggregate demand.

If we assume investment to be an unexplained part of aggregate expenditure then it causes national income to change when it changes autonomously. These effects have already been studied, and are summarized in predictions 1 and 2 on page 499.

If we allow for the possible dependence of investment on the rate of interest, we can no longer take investment as an autonomous constant. We must, then, consider the possibility that investment may be partially endogenous, being determined from within our theory. To see this we first consider how investment is financed.

The financing of investment

Generally, in speaking of the circular flow we speak of withdrawals and injections in pairs: imports and exports, government expenditure and government revenue, and saving and investment. This pairing is no accident and, in the case of saving and investment, it reflects the fact that the savings of firms and households are the major source of finance for investment. When households and firms save funds, the money must go somewhere; when firms spend on investment, the money must come from somewhere. Much of the money spent on current investment projects comes from the current saving of firms and housholds. (The various ways in which firms raise money by attaining funds that have been saved were discussed in detail on pages 200–1.)

If the volume of investment expenditure exceeds the volume of funds currently saved, where does the money come from? Basically there are two main sources: the money may come from funds accumulated in the past by firms or households, or it may be money *newly created* by the banking system. In Chapter 40, we shall study in detail how the banking system can create and destroy money within very wide limits. In the meantime, we must note that if banks can create money, they can lend this money to firms for investment expenditure without there being any corresponding saving of funds on the part of households and firms.

There is one more possibility: investment may fall short of saving. In this case all form of idle funds owned by either households or firms and held either by them or by financial institutions on their behalf.

Saving, investment and the rate of interest

How might the rate of interest respond to a situation in which the flow of current saving was less than the amount that firms wished to spend on current investment? There could be a shortage of investment funds and competition among would-be borrowers to obtain the available funds might bid up the rate of interest. It is also possible that when desired investment is substantially less than current saving, the rate of interest will fall because some savers will be unable to invest their money at all and so will be prepared to accept lower rates of interest rather than leave savings idle.

A rise in investment will tend to cause a shortage of funds to borrow and will hence force up the rate of interest. A fall in investment will tend to cause a surplus of funds to borrow and hence will force down the rate of interest.

Now assume that national income is in equilibrium with savings equal to investment. In Chapter 34, we saw that an autonomous rise in investment would raise income until new withdrawals sufficient to restore equilibrium had been created. The magnitude of the rise in income depends on the value of the multiplier.

If a rise in investment raises the rate of interest, as we have just hypothesized, then this will help to restore equilibrium by choking off some of the extra investment expenditure.

This is shown in Figure 36.2. Suppose the aggregate expenditure function is the one labelled E_1. The equilibrium income is Y_1. Now investment increases by ΔI, shifting the aggregate demand function to E_2. If all of the adjustment were thrown

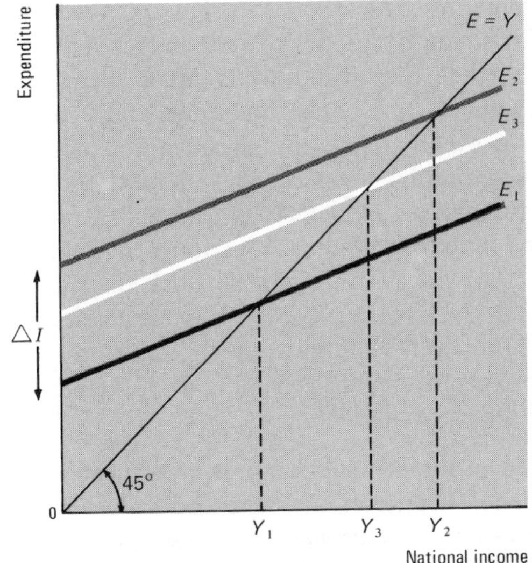

Fig. 36.2 The effect of shifts in investment on the aggregate expenditure function and on the equilibrium level of income

onto income changes, as we have assumed up until now, income would have to rise to Y_2. But if interest rates rise and investment falls, as a result, the aggregate demand function will shift downward to, say, E_3, and the new equilibrium will be reached at the lower level of income Y_3. If, when investment increases, the rate of interest rises quickly, and this greatly reduces investment, then income need not change much to generate the extra withdrawals to match the (small) increase in investment. On the other hand, if the rate changes only a little or very slowly, and if the change in interest does not affect investment much, then most of the burden of adjustment is placed on changes in income.

We can arrive at this result in another way. In Figure 36.3 the curve relating

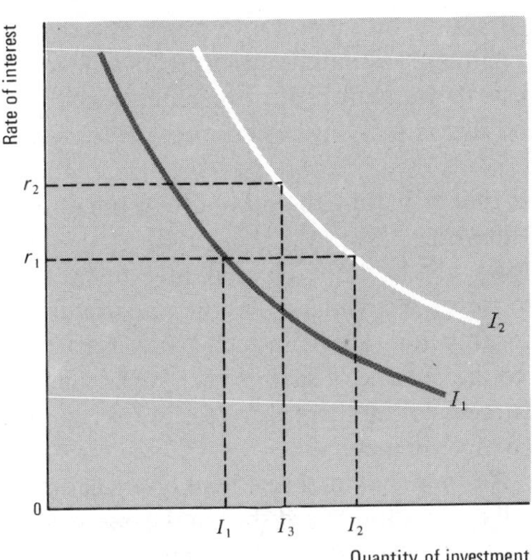

Fig. 36.3 The effect on investment of changes in the rate of interest

investment to the rate of interest is I_1, the current rate of interest is r_1 per cent per year, and the current quantity of investment is I_1 per year.

Now assume that the investment function shifts to I_2. If the rate of interest remains unchanged at r_1, investment rises by the amount $I_2 - I_1$. This amount is the autonomous ΔI of Figure 36.2. If the interest rate remains unchanged, then the whole of the burden of adjustment is thrown onto national income, and income will rise by the multiplier process to Y_2, where new withdrawals equal to ΔI are generated. If, however, the interest rate rises to r_2, then investment falls to I_3. Investment is now only above its original level by $I_3 - I_1$, and the change in income necessary to restore equilibrium is correspondingly reduced. The amount $I_3 - I_1$ is the vertical shift between the expenditure curves E_1 and E_3 in Figure 36.2. As a result of the rise in the rate of interest and the corresponding reduction in investment expenditure, income only rises to Y_3. It is obvious from Figure 36.3 that the fall-off of investment from I_2 to I_3 will be greater, the larger the rise in the interest rate and the more elastic the investment demand function. The greater the fall-off from I_2 to I_3, the larger will be the reduction in the expenditure function in Figure 36.2 from E_2 to E_3 and hence the closer E_3 will be to the original function E_1.

The change in income in response to an autonomous change in investment will be smaller, the greater is the change in interest rates in response to the change in investment, and the more sensitive is the quantity of investment expenditure to changes in the rate of interest.

Two limiting cases of the relation between investment and the rate of interest

The classical theory The prevailing view about the working of the economy (at least among English-speaking economists) prior to the publication of Keynes's *General Theory* has come to be called 'classical'. Historians are quick to point out that there are many disagreements among economists of the time, and that to talk of '*the* classical theory' is to caricature a complex situation. Nonetheless, there was a more or less common view on many points and, for better or worse, the term 'classical theory' or 'classical model' has come to be used to express one consistent version of the views prevalent before Keynes. This book is not a treatise on the history of economics, and we would not bother to describe this view of investment and saving were it not for the fact that it has recently gained substantial support from a group of economists who believe that the profession was altogether too uncritical in its acceptance of the Keynesian theory and accompanying rejection of the classical theory.

The basic proposition of the classical theory is that changes in investment and saving cause changes only in the rate of interest.

The theory can be summarized as follows: (1) the desired level of investment falls as the rate of interest rises; (2) the desired level of saving rises as the rate of interest rises; (3) the rate of interest changes smoothly and rapidly in such a way as to keep the volume of investment always equal to the volume of saving. As long as the rate of interest always keeps saving and investment equal, there is no reason for changes in either saving or investment to cause changes in income.

Consider one case by way of example. Assume that an investment boom causes a greatly increased desire to invest. This will cause a rightward shift in the investment function, say from I_1 to I_2 in Figure 36.3. With the increase in the desire to invest, firms will be trying to increase their borrowings, and they will quickly bid up the rate of interest. As the rate of interest rises, the quantity of money firms wish to borrow and spend on investment falls (since the cost of borrowing rises), and the quantity households are prepared to save and lend to firms increases. The rate of interest continues to rise until the diminished investment is exactly equal to the augmented quantity of saving. The whole process happens quickly enough that there is no significant rise in income generated during the time in which investment exceeded saving. (You should not read on before you have worked out for yourself the effects of the other three shifts: a fall in the desire to invest, and a rise and a fall in the desire to save.)

The clasical theory of saving, investment and interest is built on two important assumptions: (1) the investment schedule is sufficiently interest-elastic that suitable variations in the rate of interest can bring about investment sufficient to match any volume of saving that may be forthcoming; and (2) the rate of interest is perfectly free to vary, so that saving and investment are quickly brought into equality.

Notice that this theory provides an automatic link between the most important withdrawal and the most important injection: it ensures that, except for temporary fluctuations, the volume of saving will be equal to the volume of investment. Thus as long as the central authorities pursue a balanced-budget policy ($G = T$), the volume of withdrawals can differ from the volume of injections only by the difference between imports and exports, which will generally be a trivial amount compared to the whole volume of national income.[1]

The Keynesian theory The theory that the interest rate will fluctuate so as to equate saving and investment was challenged by Keynes's theory of interest rates. The extreme version of the Keynesian theory was that the interest rate was completely stabilized by the speculative actions of bondholders: bondholders have an idea of the normal rate of interest, and whenever fluctuations in current savings and investment cause even small changes in the price of bonds, they will buy or sell from their existing stocks of bonds, thus preventing the actual rate of interest from diverging far from what they believe to be the normal rate.[2]

If the interest rate is not free to vary, what will restore equilibrium when there is a large shift in either savings or investment? The equilibrium-restoring mechanism in the Keynesian theory is income fluctuations of the kind we have already analysed.

A major difference between the Keynesian and the classical theory is that in the former, income fluctuates in order to bring injections and withdrawals into equality, while in the latter the rate of interest does the same job.

---

[1] In the classical theory, the equilibrium level of national income was that which, with only temporary aberrations, produced full employment. It was believed that, if there was unemployed labour, wage rates would fall, and the demand for labour increase until full employment prevailed. This labour-market mechanism kept income at the full-employment level; it then did not matter how much people wished to save at this equilibrium level of income, because the interest rate would fluctuate until firms wished to invest exactly what households wished to save. This model of the economy is very close to that espoused by the modern group of economists called monetarists.

[2] See pages 398–400 for a discussion of the important relation between the price of bonds and the rate of interest.

An eclectic theory Although the theory that all adjustments take the form of changes in the level of income is now generally regarded as too extreme. Keynes' theory did focus attention on what has come to be understood as one of the important mechanisms for adjusting saving and investment: fluctuations in the level of income and employment are *observed to occur*, and it is believed that this is often in response to shifts in the saving and investment schedules.

The balance of empirical evidence seems to many economists to support an eclectic theory that combines both the Classical and the Keynesian adjustment mechanism. In that theory fluctuations in saving or investment cause fluctuations *both* in interest rates and in income. Although, as a general rule, more of the burden of equilibriating the system in the short run probably falls on changes in income rather than on changes in interest rates, the relative importance of these two mechanisms varies among times and places. The relative importance of the two will depend upon the extent that the interest rate is free to change in response to changes in saving and investment, and to the extent that the volume of saving and investment reacts to changes in interest rates. This modified model, in which both national income and the rate of interest change in order to equilibrate the system, will be considered further in Chapter 41.

According to the eclectic theory, an imbalance between withdrawals and injections will cause both national income and the rate of interest to change until withdrawals and injections are again equal. The less of the job of equating withdrawals and injections is done by the rate of interest, the larger will be the change in national income.

37

Fluctuations in national income

Output, employment and living standards have all shown an upward trend in advanced countries over the last two centuries. If you compare any year in this decade with any year in the first decade of this century, your overwhelming impression will be one of growth, even if you choose a recent year of low activity and compare it with a boom year from the 1900s.

If, however, you take each year of the 1960s and 1970s and compare it with the year following, you will find that economic activity proceeds in an irregular path, with forward spurts followed by pauses and even relapses. These short-term fluctuations are commonly known as *trade cycles* or *business cycles*, the word 'cycle' suggesting a regular oscillation of good times and bad. At some times and places, the patterns have been remarkably regular, at other times less so.

Figure 37.1 shows a time series of the percentage of the labour force unemployed

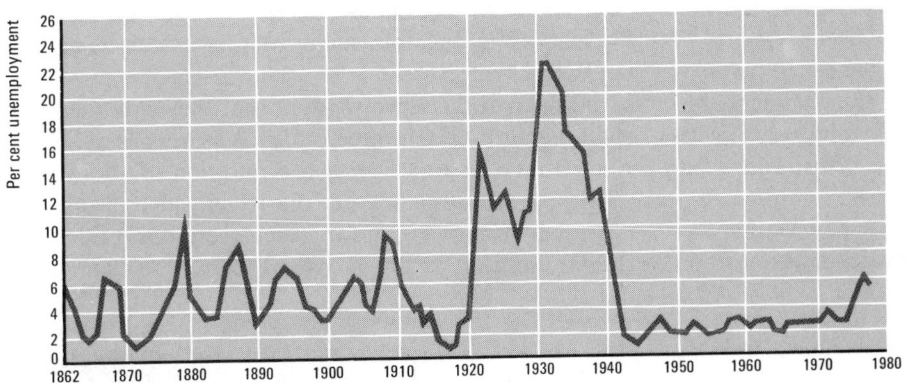

Fig. 37.1 Unemployment in Great Britain, 1861–1978 (Figures for 1862–1939 relate to the unionized labour force. The subsequent figures relate to the total registered working population)

in the United Kingdom from 1861 to 1978.[1] In the nineteenth century there was a reasonably regular cycle of varying amplitude, with a duration of between eight and ten years. The level of unemployment varied continously; there were no *prolonged*

[1] The data for the nineteenth century refer only to trade unions, which probably covered the more volatile parts of the economy. Thus the actual variations for the whole labour force may have been somewhat less than those recorded for the unionized sector.

periods either of full employment or of heavy unemployment. Here, then, is a regularity in the data that requires explanation.

The period between the two world wars presents a dismal picture of heavy unemployment. The unemployment of the late 1920s was an isolated British phenomenon associated with the return to the gold standard and with the long-term decline in some of Britain's staple export industries. The high British unemployment rate was not matched elsewhere in the world in that decade; in the United States, for example, the mid-1920s was a period of boom. The 1930s however, saw heavy unemployment throughout the world. At the worst point in the depression almost one person in four was unemployed in the United Kingdom. A similar situation ruled in America and in many other industrialized countries. The data displayed in Figure 37.1 show that no other depression in the last 100 years has been as severe or as long as the Great Depression of the 1930s. Note, however, that unemployment did not remain at a constant level throughout the period; there was considerable variation from one year to the next.

During the Second World War unemployment fell to an extremely low level indeed. After the war unemployment still fluctuated. But from 1945 until the early 1970s the fluctuations were over a much narrower range than in any comparable period. Even with all possible allowances for changes in the definitions of the unemployment figures, the period following 1945 experienced a substantial reduction in the average level of unemployment. Was it by accident or design?

In 1974 the world entered the worst recession since the Great Depression. Unemployment in the UK began a steady upward climb that took it from 2·6 per cent in 1974 to 4·1 per cent in 1975, 5·6 per cent in 1976, peaking at 6·1 per cent in 1977 and falling off slightly to 5·7 per cent in 1978.

Figure 37.2 shows the percentage of the labour force unemployed in the United States and the United Kingdom for each year since the Second World War. Fluctuations are clearly present in both economies. It is clear, however, that since the Second World War, fluctuations in unemployment rates have been much less regular than before the First World War.

Some students of industrial fluctuations have thought that they could discern several types of cycles in economic activity. One type, which is clearly observable in the British nineteenth-century employment series, had a duration of about nine years from peak to peak. This nine-year cycle was the one usually identified in the past as *the* trade cycle. A second type of cycle, for which there is considerable evidence, is one of much shorter duration, lasting anywhere from 18 to 40 months.

Fig. 37.2 The percentage of the total labour force unemployed in the US and the UK 1945–78

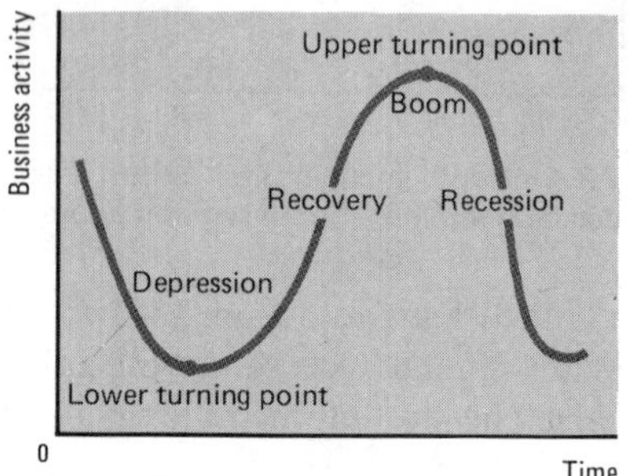

Fig. 37.3 Phases of the trade cycle

This cycle is sometimes associated with variations in inventories: when inventories are being built up, purchases by firms will exceed their sales; when inventories are being reduced, purchases will be less than sales. We shall see that the building up and running down of inventories can give rise to cyclical oscillations in the economy. Finally, some economists have thought that they could perceive a very long cycle, of about 50 years' duration, that was associated with, among other things, major fluctuations of investment activity following some fundamental innovation. Each burst of invention was thought to be followed by exploitation of all the obvious new lines, then by a long pause in investment. Of all the 'cycles', this long-wave one is the most conjectural, and we shall say nothing further about it in this book.

Over the years, many different theories have been put forward to explain these fluctuations. In this chapter we can do little more than provide a very general introduction to this interesting and difficult subject.

Phases of the trade cycle

Figure 37.3 shows a stylized cycle and divides it into four periods. We shall first briefly describe the general characteristics of each phase of the cycle, and then consider some theories that may explain it.

Depression A depression is characterized by heavy unemployment, a low level of consumers' demand and a substantial amount of unused industrial capacity. Some prices may be falling while others will be unchanged, but few, if any, will be rising. The average level of prices will tend to be constant or to drift slowly downward. Business profits will be low or even negative. Confidence in the future will be lacking, and as a result firms will be unwilling to take risks in making new investments. Banks and other financial institutions will have surplus funds that no one whom they consider a reasonable credit risk wishes to borrow.

Recovery The point at which a recession turns into a recovery is often called the *lower turning point*. Once begun, the pace of recovery quickens. Old and obsolete machinery is replaced. Employment, income and consumers' spending all begin to rise. Expectations become more favourable as a result of increases in production, sales and profits. Investments that once seemed risky may now be undertaken as the climate of business opinion begins to change from one of pessimism to one of optimism. As demand expands, production can be expanded with relative ease merely by employing the existing unused capacity and unemployed labour. Prices tend either to stay constant or to rise slowly.

Boom As the recovery proceeds, bottlenecks begin to occur in various industries: existing capacity will be fully utilized first in some industries, then in others; labour shortages will begin to occur, particularly in certain skilled categories; and shortages of certain key raw materials will develop. It now becomes difficult to increase output merely by putting unused resources to work, since the supply of unused resources is rapidly disappearing. Output can be raised further only by means of investment, which raises the productivity of already-employed labour. Further rises in demand are now met more by increases in prices than by increases in production. A situation of general excess demand for labour develops. Costs and prices rise, and business remains generally very profitable. Losses are infrequent, since a money profit can be earned merely by holding onto those goods whose prices are rising over time. Investment expenditure is high, investment funds are in short supply, and interest rates rise in the face of an excess demand for loanable funds. Investment may be made that requires further rises in prices and sales to render it profitable.

Recession The point at which the boom turns into recession is often called the *upper turning point*. Once a recession sets in, it tends to gather its own momentum. Consumption demand falls off. Investments that looked profitable when sales and prices were expected to go on rising suddenly becomes unprofitable. High interest payments, which seemed easily bearable when sales and prices were rising steadily, now become a heavy burden. Business failures, which were relatively infrequent in the boom period, now become more common. Production falls, employment falls, and, as a result, income and expenditure fall. More and more firms get into difficulties as prices and profits fall, and new investment is reduced to a very low level. It is very often not even worth replacing capital goods as they wear out, since unused capacity is increasing steadily. When the decline is spent, a period of full depression may set in, and we are back at the beginning of the cycle.

No two cycles are exactly the same. In some, the recession phase is short and the resulting depression is not severe; in others, a full-scale period of stagnation sets in. In some cycles the boom phase develops into a severe inflation; in others, the pressure of excess demand is hardly felt.

The multiplier-accelerator theory of the cycle

We may now ask: Why is it that free-market economies do not settle down into some position of equilibrium, maintaining more or less full employment at all times? We shall develop a theory of the cyclical behaviour of the economy, a theory which attempts to account for the fact that such economies tend to progress cyclically rather than smoothly. This elementary theory brings together a number of ideas and theories developed throughout Part 7. It is divided into three steps: first, a theory of cumulative upswings and downswings explaining why, once started, booms and slumps tend to carry on; second, a theory of floors and ceilings, explaining why upward and downward movement are eventually brought to a halt; and third, a theory of instability which explains how, once a process of upward or downward movement is brought to a halt, it tends to reverse itself.

Cumulative movements

Why does a period of expansion or contraction, once begun, tend to develop its own momentum? First, the multiplier process tends to cause cumulative movements. As soon as a revival begins, some unemployed labourers find work again. These people, with their newly acquired income, can afford to make much-needed consumption expenditures. This new demand causes an increase in production and creates new jobs for other unemployed workers. As incomes rise, demand rises; as demand rises, incomes rise. Just the reverse happens in a downswing. Unemployment in one sector causes a fall in demand for the products of other sectors, which leads to a further fall in employment and a further fall in demand.

A second major factor is to be found in the accelerator theory of investment demand, discussed in Chapter 36. New investment is needed to expand existing productive capacity and to introduce new methods of production. When consumer demand is low and there is excess capacity, investment is likely to fall to a very low level; once income starts to rise and entrepreneurs come to expect further rises, investment expenditure may rise very rapidly. Further, when full employment of existing capacity is reached, new investment becomes the only way available for entrepreneurs to increase their output. Since a capital good lasts many years, the value of a machine will generally be much greater than the annual value of consumption goods that it produces. If a machine costing £4,000 produces £1,000 worth of goods every year, it will be necessary to spend £4 on investment for every desired increase of £1 in the annual production of consumers' goods. For these reasons, investment demand may rise by very much more than consumer demand, and even a moderate fall-off in consumer demand may reduce desired new investment almost to zero.

A third major explanation for cumulative movements may be found in the nature and importance of expectations. All production plans take time to fulfil. Current decisions to produce consumers' goods and investment goods are very strongly influenced by business expectations. Such expectations can sometimes be volatile, and can sometimes be self-fulfilling. If enough people think, for example, that stock-market prices are going to rise, they will all buy stocks in anticipation of a price rise, and these purchases will themselves cause prices to rise. If, on the other hand, enough people think stock-market prices are going to fall, they will sell now at what they regard as a high price and thereby actually cause prices to fall. This is the phenomenon of *self-realizing expectations*. If enough businessmen think the future looks rosy and begin to invest in increasing capacity, this will create new employment and income in the capital-goods industries, and the resulting increase in demand will help to create the rosy conditions, whose vision started the whole process. One cannot lay down simple rules about so complicated a psychological phenomenon as the formation of expectations, but they do occasionally show a sort of band-wagon effect. Once things begin to improve, people expect further improvements, and their actions, based on this expectation, help to cause yet further improvements. On the other hand, once things begin to worsen, people often expect further worsening, and their actions, based on this expectation, help to make things worse.

The multiplier-accelerator process combined with changes in expectations that cause expenditure functions to shift is sufficient to explain the cumulative tendencies of economic upswings and downswings.

Floors and ceilings

The next question that arises is: Why do these upward and downward processes ever come to an end? Why do we not carry on exploding upwards or downwards once we get started off in one direction or the other? Consider first the revival from a recession. While there is unused capacity, income can continue to rise at a very fast rate. However, once full employment has been achieved, real national income can rise only as fast as productivity can be increased through new investment. Thus an automatic check is placed on the rapid expansion of real income once full employment is reached. Now consider the recession phase. The worst that can happen to gross investment is that it falls to zero. This would happen if no new investment were occurring, and if existing machinery were not being replaced as it wore out. This is a very extreme situation, but even in this 'worst of all possible worlds' income would not sink to zero. As income falls, fewer and fewer people save and such saving as does occur is matched by the dissaving of others. Once the society in the aggregate is no longer saving, consumption will equal income, and income will no longer decrease. This is the lowest conceivable floor to equilibrium income. (Graphically, it occurs at the point where the consumption function cuts the 45° line.) Although gross investment may sink to zero in some sectors of the economy, it is unlikely to do so in the whole economy. Between 1930 and 1932, gross investment fell drastically, but at the depth of the depression it was still well above zero in all Western countries. As long as gross investment exceeds zero in some sectors, it will exceed zero for the whole economy. In some sectors – for example, in the industries providing food, basic clothing and shelter – demand may remain fairly high in spite of quite large reductions in national income. These industries will certainly be carrying out some gross investment to replace equipment as it wears out, and they may even undertake some net investment. The floor to income occurs where withdrawals are equal to the minimum level of injections. Thus:

> **Although cumulative movements may continue at very rapid rates in either direction for considerable periods of time, floors and ceilings are eventually encountered. The floor stops the contraction; the ceiling slows down the rate of expansion to that made possible by increases in productivity.**

Turning points

Next we introduce a theory that predicts that it is difficult to stabilize the level of national income and that once income is prevented from either expanding or contracting at a rapid rate, a turning point will occur. When we have developed this theory, we shall have completed our larger theory, which says (1) that things, once started, tend to go on cumulatively in the same direction, (2) that there are limits, floors and ceilings that slow or stop upward and downward processes, and (3) that, once such a process is stopped or slowed down, it will reverse its direction.

We saw in the previous section that the accelerator theory of investment helps to explain the cumulative nature of upswings and downswings. It is also the best known of the theories accounting for the reversal of direction of expansions and contractions. We have seen that the accelerator makes the desired level of *new* (not replacement) investment depend upon the rate of change of income. If income is rising at a constant rate, then investment will be at a constant *level*. If the speed at which income is rising slackens, then the level of investment will decline. This means that a *levelling off* in income at the top of a cycle will lead to a *decline* in the level of investment. The accelerator thus provides a theory of the upper turning point. The decline in investment at the upper turning point will cause a decline in the level of income that will be intensified through the multiplier process. If the fall in income continues, the floor will eventually be reached. What, then, accounts for the lower turning point? After a while, investment may rise exogenously. If it does not, once existing capacity falls to the level suitable to current output, there will be a revival of replacement investment and new machines will be bought as old ones wear out. This rise in the level of activity in the capital-goods industries causes, by way of the multiplier, a further rise in income in response to which new investment will take place, leading to yet further rises in income.

A multiplier and an accelerator combined with 'ceilings' and 'floors' may be sufficient to set up an endless cyclical process in the economy.

Such multiplier-accelerator models have been worked out in detail. They provide some real insight into cyclical processes, but it is doubtful if, by themselves, they provide complete explanations of the cyclical fluctuations in any real economy.

The theory of the inventory cycle

All firms hold inventories of materials and finished goods, and these inventories fluctuate widely. Such sharp fluctuations are a major cause of the short-term variations in the level of activity. The theory of inventory cycles is very similar to the accelerator mechanism, only now we emphasize investment in *inventories* of goods, rather than in plant and equipment.

Start by assuming that national income is in equilibrium, with withdrawals equal to injections at full employment. Now, in order to get the process started, assume that there is an autonomous rise in the propensity to save (a fall in the propensity to consume). The first result of the fall in demand will be a piling up of unsold goods on dealers' shelves. After some time, dealers will reduce their orders so as to prevent inventories from increasing indefinitely; retailers will reduce purchases from wholesalers; after wholesalers' stocks have risen, they in turn will reduce their purchases from manufacturers. Manufacturers may maintain production for a while, adding the unsold goods to inventories, in the hope that the fall in demand is only temporary. If this proves not to be the case, manufacturers will cut back on production, laying off some workers and reducing the hours worked by the remainder. Thus income and output will begin to fall; at this stage inventories will have risen to an abnormally high level. Once production falls to a level equal to the new (lower) level of consumer demand, there will be no further rise in the level of stocks.

Unfortunately, however, matters will not remain at this point. Stocks will now be too high on two counts: first, because sales will be at a lower level than they were originally, and second, because stocks will have increased during the transitional process. In order to work off excess inventories, retailers will buy less from wholesalers than they are selling to consumers, wholesalers will buy less from manufacturers than they are selling to retailers, and manufacturers will produce less than they are selling to wholesalers. Thus the current level of output, and hence of income earned by households selling factor services to firms, will fall below the current level of sales. This fall in income will reduce the level of demand still further. As long as production can be held below the level of current sales, inventories will be falling even though the level of sales is itself falling.

Once inventories are reduced to the desired level, the retailers and wholesalers will increase their orders, so that their purchases are equal to their current sales. Their inventories will thus be held constant. Manufacturers will also increase the levels of their outputs until output is equal to the (increased) level of sales, thus keeping their own stocks at a constant level. But this means that production, and hence income earned by households, is increased. As this happens, the demand for goods will rise. The initial impact here will be on inventories, which will be run down as sales rise unexpectedly. Now the whole process is set into reverse. For a while, everyone's inventories will be run down, but then orders will increase, first from retailers, then from wholesalers. Finally, the output of manufacturers will increase. This means that income, and with it the level of demand, will rise even further. Once production is increased to the level of current sales, inventories will no longer be decreasing.

But now the level of inventories is too low for two reasons: first, because the level of sales is higher than it was when inventories were at the correct level, and second, because inventories have been run down during the transitional phase. In order now to build up their inventories, retailers will order more from wholesalers than they sell to consumers, wholesalers will buy more from manufacturers than they sell to retailers, and manufacturers will produce more than they sell to wholesalers. This rise in production will raise incomes, and thus the level of demand, still further. As long as production is kept above the level of sales, however, inventories will be rising in spite of the fact that sales are also rising. Once the inventories are brought up to the desired level, orders will fall off. Retailers and wholesalers will reduce orders to the level of current sales, and manufacturers will reduce output to that level as well. But this fall in output will reduce incomes and, with them, demand. For a while, inventories will pile up, but orders and output will be cut back, thus reducing the level of income and demand. Now the whole downward process is set in motion again. If you go back to the beginning of this section and start to read there, you will continue the process.

Verbal analysis of the sort just given can provide some general ideas of such a cyclical process. But if we should wish to carry our analysis much further, verbal and geometrical reasoning becomes inadequate and mathematical tools become essential. In some branches of economics one can get a long way by means of careful verbal and geometrical analysis. In the field of dynamic fluctuations one can get only a short distance. We might want to ask such questions as: What are the effects of varying the time lags with which firms react to changes in their sales? What if the reaction does not occur suddenly but is *distributed* through time? Under what circumstances will such a cycle die out rapidly so that income *converges* on its equilibrium level? In what circumstances will the self-exciting process continue indefinitely so that the cycle will go on indefinitely unless stopped by conscious government policy? What will be the effect of government controls built into the system to damp down these fluctuations? What difference will it make if the government's control mechanism itself acts with a time lag? To analyse such questions, mathematical tools are indispensable, particularly the sort of mathematics electrical engineers use to analyse self-exciting (*closed loop*) control systems.[1]

A theory relying on random events and long lags

The two theories outlined so far cover investment cycles both in capital equipment and in inventories. Their main driving forces are the multiplier and the accelerator.

[1] One of the best surveys of the formal economic theory of fluctuations and the mathematics used therein is to be found in the first half of R.G.D. Allen, *Mathematical Economics* (Macmillan, 1956).

Such theories are often called Keynesian, because they represent early attempts to extend the Keynesian model of national income determination to cover dynamic fluctuations. This theory looks to cyclical oscillations in the behaviour of households and firms to explain cyclical oscillations in the economy's major macro-variables.

An alternative and quite different theory does not require cyclical behaviour from firms and households in order to generate cycles. This theory begins with lags. Most macro-models that are designed to fit the data have quite long lags in their behavioural relations. For example, if a fall in the rate of interest makes a new investment programme profitable, it may take six months to plan it, three months to let contracts, six more months before spending builds up to its top rate and another twenty-four to complete the project. This means that investment expenditure will be subject to a distributed time lag (see page 140): changes in the rate of interest will cause a reaction in investment expenditure that is distributed over quite a long period of time. Generally, whatever expenditure flow is being explained, empirical macro-models find it necessary to use distributed lags to relate any expenditure flow to the variables that influence it.

A pioneering study by two American economists, Irma and M.A. Adelman, established that, if occasional random shifts in exogenous expenditure disturb a system of expenditure-determining equations all of which contain long lags, a cycle is generated. Here the disturbing influences are random or erratic, but the consequences are a cyclical path to the major endogenous macro-variables such as national income and unemployment. Major candidates for the erratic shifts that may have done the job from time to time are investment, government expenditure, consumption and exports. Thus:

> **Each of the major components of aggregate expenditure have sometimes undergone shifts large enough to disturb the economic system significantly. The long lags in the expenditure function can then convert these shifts into cyclical oscillations in national income.**

A policy-induced cycle?

Cycles of the sort just described can sometimes be unwittingly exaggerated by poorly conceived government policies. The government can in principle damp down such cyclical fluctuations by its fiscal and monetary policy. Unless the government is very sophisticated, however, its timing may accentuate rather than dampen cyclical fluctuations. This can be true whether the basic cause is the one described just above or the multiplier-accelerator mechanism discussed earlier. Government stabilization policy is further discussed in Chapter 38.

UK experience

We have already observed that fluctuations in the UK economy were relatively mild in the 30 years from the end of the Second World War to the mid-1970s, when a really major recession developed. These fluctuations certainly seemed much milder than those experienced, for example, by the countries of North America.

It is in line with this British experience that the major components of aggregate demand in Britain have shown relatively small fluctuations over the post-war years, but that investment in plant and equipment has declined more often then it has risen in the 1970s. The relevant variations are shown in Table 37.1. It may also be noted in passing that the volatile 'animal spirits' that Keynes saw as a source of short-run disturbances through variations in investment expenditure have not been much in evidence over this period. There have been only two years in the period covered by the table when the annual change in investment expenditure was in excess of one and a half per cent of TFE. Changes in consumption and exports have been larger than changes in investment in most of the years under consideration.

> **Severe short-term disturbances in year-to-year national income, emanating from extreme variability of investment, do not seem to have been the rule over the past 30 years.**[1]

An exogenous theory of the cycle

All of the theories considered so far look to forces within the economy as the cause of cycles. Of course the world as a whole is a closed economy, and cyclical movements in world national income and employment must have endogenous causes (although once upon a time a plausible theory was advanced linking trade cycles to cyclical activity in sun spots!). Small parts of the world, such as Britain or any one of the other EEC countries, are open economies. For these economies, cyclical fluctuations may have exogenous causes. To see how this can happen, assume that the countries of North America enter a recession. Their national incomes fall, and as a result all of their elements of aggregate expenditure, including their imports, will fall. But North America's imports are the rest of the world's exports. The impact on the other countries of the world will thus be an exogenous fall in their exports. This will cause a reduction in their national incomes, just as a fall in their own investment expenditure would. (See prediction 2, page 499.)

Because of international trade, the various economies of the world are interlinked. A fall in the national income of a major importing country means a fall in the exports of other countries. This causes their national incomes to fall and in turn they cut their imports. This then cuts other countries' exports, their national incomes fall and so do their imports, and so the process goes on. This process whereby recessions (or booms) in one major trading country are transferred to other trading countries through changes in imports and exports is called the INTERNATIONAL TRADE MULTIPLIER. Formally, this multiplier measures the change in one country's national income in response to a fall in its exports by £1.

The more open an economy, the more vulnerable it is to 'imported' cyclical fluctuations in its national income. Since exports are a larger part of the UK's total final expenditure than is investment expenditure, it is clear that the UK is open to such international effects. A glance at Table 37.1 will show that UK exports have risen in most years since 1962. The economy was given strong upward shocks by unusually large increases in exports in the years 1968, 1969, 1971, 1973, and 1974. In 1975, however, the economy was subject to the reverse shock when not only did

[1] Recall also that the 'animal spirits' refer to *shifts* of the investment function, i.e., only to that fraction of the change in investment that cannot be explained as a stable response to changes in the values of the variables in the investment function.

Table 37.1 Annual changes in major components of aggregate demand, expressed as a percentage of Total Final Expenditure

	Consumer's expenditure	General government final consumption	Exports of goods and services	Gross Domestic Capital Formation (Excluding dwellings)	(dwellings)	Value of physical changes in inventories	Total investment
1962–3	2·4	0·3	0·6	0·1	0·1	0·4	0·6
1963–4	1·7	0·3	0·7	1·6	0·6	1·5	3·7
1964–5	0·9	0·4	0·8	0·6	0·1	−0·6	0·1
1965–6	1·0	0·4	0·6	0·3	0·1	−0·4	0·0
1966–7	1·1	0·9	0·3	0·9	0·3	−0·1	1·2
1967–8	1·3	0·1	1·8	0·6	0·1	0·2	0·5
1968–9	−0·7	−0·3	1·6	0·2	−0·1	0·0	0·1
1969–70	2·3	0·2	1·0	0·6	−0·2	−0·1	0·3
1970–1	1·6	0·4	1·4	0·1	0·2	−0·5	−0·2
1971–2	2·9	0·6	0·3	−0·1	0·1	−0·1	−0·1
1972–3	2·4	0·6	2·2	1·0	−0·1	2·0	2·9
1973–4	−0·6	0·3	1·2	−0·1	−0·2	1·1	0·8
1974–5	−0·6	0·8	−0·6	0·6	0·1	−2·0	−1·3
1975–6	0·2	0·4	1·5	−0·3	0·0	1·4	1·1
1976–7	−0·4	0·0	1·3	−0·2	−0·3	0·5	0·1

Source: Table A-1 of the Appendix, Prest and Coppock (eds), *The UK Economy*.

exports fail to rise at their trend rate of increase, they actually fell.

There is a second mechanism by which cycles have been transmitted internationally. Today there are large international flows of capital. A recession in a capital-exporting country that makes its firms and households less willing to invest abroad as well as at home, will show up to the capital-importing countries as exogenous falls in their investment expenditure.

There is no doubt that trade cycles are to some extent linked throughout the world. The latest illustration is the world-wide recession that set in during 1974. This, to most trading countries, was a deeper trough than any they had experienced since the Great Depression of the 1930s. Furthermore, the fact that the same pattern of only slow and halting recovery has been observed from 1975 to 1979 in all trading countries is no doubt due at least partly to international linkages.

There is some evidence that UK fluctuations since 1945 were partly domestic in origin. There can be no doubt, however, that they were also in some measure exogenous to the UK economy, having been 'imported' through the links of international trade and capital flows.

38

Government and the circular flow of income

There is no doubt that government can exert a major influence on the circular flow of income. During major wars, when governments throw fiscal caution to the winds and engage in massive military spending, both GNP and employment tend to rise to unprecedented heights. UK government expenditure rose dramatically in real terms and as a percentage of GNP from 1938 to 1944 as the UK converted from a peacetime to a wartime economy. At the same time the unemployment rate fell from 13 to less than 1 per cent. Economists agree that it was the increase in the government's aggregate expenditure that caused the rise in the GNP and the fall in unemployment. Most European countries had similar experiences during rearmament in the late 1930s or early 1940s.

The use of government policies for the express purpose of influencing employment and national income is called FISCAL POLICY. Since such policy attempts to influence the economy by altering aggregate demand, it is often referred to as DEMAND MANAGEMENT, particularly in Britain. When appropriately used, fiscal policy can certainly be an important tool for influencing the economy. In its heyday – the 1940s, 1950s, and 1960s – many economists believed that it was all that was necessary to regulate the economy. That day is past, although a few 'pure fiscalists' are still to be found. Today most economists are aware of the limitations of fiscal policy, and there is much discussion of other tools that can supplement it.

In this chapter we shall ask what can be expected from fiscal policy under the most favourable circumstances. The limitations of fiscal policy and the alternatives to it will be studied in later chapters.

The theory of fiscal policy

Not so many years ago it was generally accepted, and indeed many people still fervently believe, that a prudent government should always balance its budget. The argument is based on an analogy with what seems prudent for an individual: it is a foolish person whose current expenditure consistently exceeds his current revenue so that he gets steadily further into debt, and – so went the argument – what is good for the individual must be good for the nation.[1]

[1] The first part of this chapter takes what may be called the Keynesian view of budget deficits. Opposing views which have recently been much in evidence are discussed briefly at the end of the chapter.

The paradox of thrift, discussed in Chapter 34 suggests that the analogy between government and household may be misleading. When a government follows a balanced-budget policy, as most governments tried to do even during the Great Depression of the 1930s, it must restrict its expenditure during a recession because its tax revenue will necessarily be falling. During a recovery, when its revenue is high and rising, it increases its spending. In other words, government rolls with the economy, raising and lowering its expenditure in step with everyone else.

By the end of the 1930s, many economists had come to the conclusion that the government, by going along with the crowd, was not making the most of its potential to control the economy in a beneficial manner. Why, they asked, should the government not try to stabilize the economy by doing just the opposite of what everyone else was doing – by increasing its demand when private demand was falling and lowering its demand when private demand was rising? 'After all,' they might have added, 'even a prudent household will go into debt when it knows its income is unusually low and save to repay its debt when its income is unusually high.'

When the American Nobel Prize-winning economist Milton Friedman, generally known as a critic of Keynesian economics, said 'We are all Keynesians now', he was referring to (among other things) the general acceptance of the view that a government's budget is much more than just the revenue and expenditure statement of a very large organization. Whether we like it or not, the very size of that budget inevitably gives it a powerful influence on the size of the GNP and the total amount of employment.

Precisely how do the government's fiscal actions influence national income?

Balanced and unbalanced budgets

Just as a household earns income over the year from the sale of the factor services that it controls, and spends its income on purchasing goods and services, governments raise current revenue by levying taxes and spend it on all the projects they undertake. If current revenue is exactly equal to current expenditure, the government has a BALANCED BUDGET. If revenue exceeds expenditure, there is a BUDGET SURPLUS; if revenue falls short of expenditure, there is a BUDGET DEFICIT. When there are deficits and surpluses the budget is said to be UNBALANCED.

If the government spends more without raising its taxes, its extra expenditure is said to be *deficit-financed.* If the extra spending is accompanied by an equal increase in tax revenue, we speak of a *balanced-budget change in spending.*

If the government spends more than it raises, where does the money come from? If the government raises more than it spends, where does the money go? The difference between expenditure and tax revenue is reflected in changes in the level of the government's debt. If expenditures exceed revenues, the balance, which is called the government's borrowing requirement, must be borrowed from someone; if revenues exceed expenditures, the balance pays off some of the loans that were made in the past.

A deficit requires an increase in borrowing, for which there are two main sources: the central bank and the private sector of the economy – banks and other financial institutions, firms and households. The government borrows money from these sources by selling them treasury bills or bonds. A TREASURY BILL is a promise to repay a stated amount in the near future (in the UK, 90 days from its date of issue), and it is sold in return for a smaller amount paid to the government now. The difference between the two sums represents the interest on the loan.[1] A government bond is also a promise to pay a stated sum of money in the future, but in the more distant future, possibly as long as 25 years from now. It carries fixed interest payments in the meantime.

A surplus allows the government to reduce its outstanding debt by redeeming treasury bills and bonds from tax revenue when they fall due, rather than from money raised by selling new bills and bonds.

When the government makes new loans from, or repays old loans to, the private sector, this action merely shifts funds between the two sectors. When the government 'borrows' from the central bank, however, the central bank creates new money, as we shall see in Chapter 40. Since, unlike the private sector, the central bank can create as much money as it wishes, there is no limit to what the government can 'borrow' from the central bank, while there is a limit to what it can borrow from the private sector.

The effect of government expenditure on aggregate demand

An increase in government expenditure on currently produced goods and services that is not matched by any change in tax rates may provide a net addition to aggregate demand. In this case it will have a major impact on GNP and total employment. Alternatively, it may merely be an expenditure that would have been made in any event, but by other spending units (firms and households) and for other purposes. In this case the government spending will serve to reallocate expenditure among the sectors of the economy, but it will have little effect on the overall level of aggregate demand, GNP and total employment; the increase in government expenditure will have been matched by an equivalent decrease in private expenditure. Any reduction of private expenditure by firms and households that occurs as a result of an increase in government expenditure is called the CROWDING-OUT EFFECT.[2]

In this chapter we shall discuss the important extreme case in which all government expenditure represents a net addition to aggregate demand: the crowding-out effect is zero. This may be called the Keynesian case since it was the case mainly assumed in the textbooks written in the wake of Keynes's *General Theory*. The opposite extreme case would occur if all government expenditure merely replaced an equivalent amount of private expenditure; the crowding-out effect would then be 100 per cent. Intermediate cases are also possible. If every extra £1 of government expenditure crowded out 60p worth of private expenditure, the crowding-out effect would be 60 per cent and net additions to injections would be only 40p. In this case, to get a desired net increase of £1 in new injections, the government would have to spend £2.50.

Probably the great majority of economists believe that intermediate cases, in which the crowding-out effect exceeds zero but is less than 100 per cent, are more

---

[1] For example, if a Treasury bill promising to pay £100 in 90 days sells on its day of issue for £98, this represents an interest rate of (2/98) (100)=2.0408 per cent for 90 days. This is a rate of 8·277 per cent over 365 days. The bill is said to be *discounted* when it sells for a current price less than its redemption value – which, of course it must do if it is to yield a positive rate of interest to its purchaser.

[2] The crowding-out mechanism is closely related to the discussion on pages 530–2. An increase in any expenditure (government or private) increases income, but this tends to drive up the interest rate and cause a reduction in interest-sensitive private expenditure.

common than either extreme. The analysis of this chapter will nevertheless help to clarify the general consequences of fiscal policy. The results obtained carry over in general terms (even if not in every specific detail) to all cases in which an increase in government expenditure causes some net increase in injections – that is, to all cases in which the crowding-out effect is less than 100 per cent.

The effect of taxes and government expenditure on national income

The key proposition in the theory of fiscal policy is that taxes and government expenditures can be used to remove inflationary and deflationary gaps. The basic analysis needed to establish this proposition was developed in Chapter 34. We shall briefly summarize here the relevant aspects of that analysis.

Figure 38.1 uses the income-expenditure approach to analyse the removal of a deflationary gap. The appropriate policy is for the government to either raise expenditure or lower taxes until aggregate demand shifts upwards enough to remove the gap. It must shift from AD_1 to AD_2 in the figure. (Recall that aggregate demand and aggregate expenditure mean the same thing.)

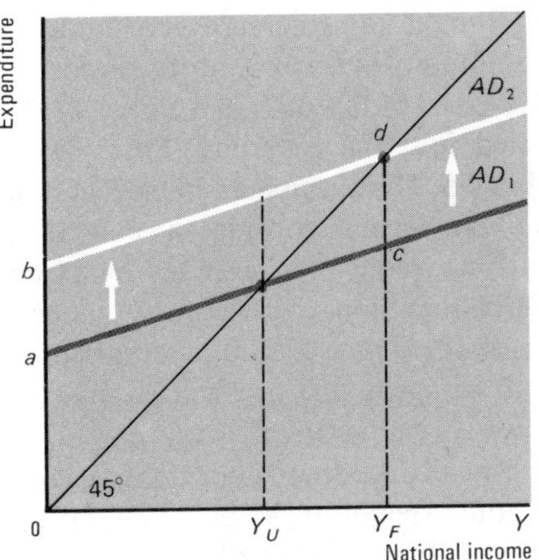

Fig. 38.1 Using a deficit to eliminate a deflationary gap

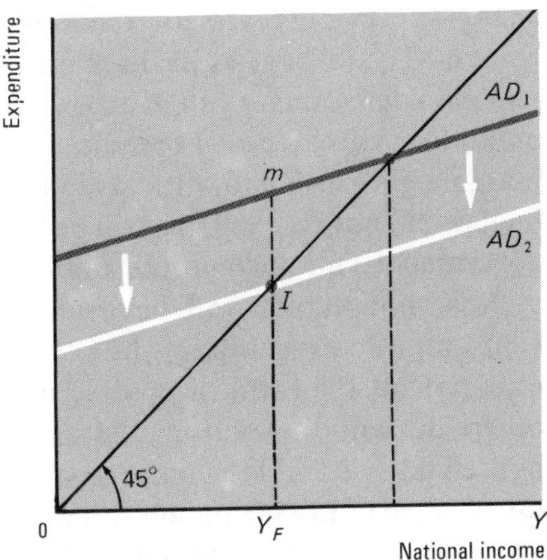

Fig. 38.2 Using a surplus to eliminate an inflationary gap

There is one complication we need to consider. An increase in government expenditure will shift the aggregate demand function upwards, parallel to itself, as shown in the figure. This is because it adds the same amount to total expenditure whatever the level of income. A change in tax rates, however, will change the *slope* of the function, since tax revenues will vary with national income. A cut in tax rates will shift the aggregate demand function upwards and change its slope. The appropriate cut would be one that made the new function pass through the point *d*, thus bringing equilibrium income to Y_F.[1]

[1] Consider an example in which the personal income tax rate is $0{\cdot}2Y$ and $C = 0{\cdot}8Y_d$, so that $C = 0{\cdot}64Y$. Now let taxes be cut to $0{\cdot}1Y$, so that $Y_d = 0{\cdot}9Y$. Now with no change in households' propensity to consume out of disposable income, the consumption function shifts to $C = 0{\cdot}72Y$. The slope of the function gets steeper, indicating an increase in the marginal propensity to spend out of national income. This example relies on the analysis of page 516.

Figure 38.2 uses the same approach to analyse the policy required for removing an inflationary gap. The appropriate policy is for the government to lower expenditure or to raise taxes until the aggregate demand function shifts downwards enough to remove the gap. Again the figure shows the shift appropriate to a change in government expenditure: the *AD* function must be made to pass through point *m*.

The same analysis can also be made using the withdrawals and injections approach. When there is a deflationary gap, a rise in government expenditure raises injections, and a fall in tax rates lowers the withdrawals associated with each level of income. Each of the changes increases equilibrium national income. When there is an inflationary gap, a cut in government expenditure lowers injections, and a rise in tax rates raises withdrawals. Each of these changes reduces the inflationary gap, and a large enough change will remove it.

A deflationary gap may be removed by an appropriate increase in expenditure or decrease in tax rates. An inflationary gap may be removed by an appropriate decrease in expenditure or increase in tax rates.

Comparative effects of expenditure and tax changes If the same job can be done by changing either tax rates or expenditure, does it make any difference which policy is chosen? To see that it does, look first at the amount of extra expenditure needed to remove a deflationary gap. If expenditure is raised by £1,000 million per year, £1,000 million worth of new expenditure is injected into the economy. Suppose the marginal propensity to withdraw out of GNP is 0·5. The multiplier is then 2, and the final rise in national income will be £2,000 million. Second, consider tax cuts. If the government cuts income tax rates sufficiently to reduce its revenues by £1,000 million, households will have an extra £1,000 million of disposable income. Consumption expenditures, however, will rise *by less than* £1,000 million because only part of the extra disposable income will be spent (the rest will be saved or otherwise withdrawn from the circular flow). If only 75p of every new £1 of household disposable income is spent on domestically produced goods, then a cut in tax revenue of £1,000 million will raise household expenditure by only £750 million and, combined with a multiplier of 2, will raise GNP by £1,500 million.

What must the government do if it wishes to generate £2,000 million of extra GNP by a tax cut? Given a multiplier of 2, it will have to generate initial new expenditure of £1,000 million. This will require (in this example) an initial cut in *tax revenue* of approximately £1,333 million. With a marginal propensity to spend out of disposable income of 0·75, this will cause an initial increase in expenditure of £1,000 million, which is the same as was obtained when the government raised its expenditure by £1,000 million. It follows that a given increase in aggregate expenditure will require a larger budget deficit if taxes are cut rather than expenditure increased.

The increase in government expenditure necessary to remove a given deflationary gap is less than the decrease in tax revenue necessary to do the same job.

The common sense of this result is that government expenditure of £1 generates £1 of new expenditure, while a cut in income tax revenue of £1 generates an additional £1 of disposable income, but less than £1 of new consumption expenditure because some of the new disposable income will be saved.

The same analysis can be applied to an inflationary gap to arrive at a corresponding conclusion:

> **The decrease in government expenditure necessary to remove a given inflationary gap is less than the increase in tax revenue necessary to do the same job.**

This second conclusion follows from the fact that the initial effect of a decrease in government expenditure of £1 is a decrease in aggregate expenditure of £1, while the initial effect of an increase in tax revenue of £1 is a decrease in consumption expenditure (and hence in aggregate expenditure) of less than £1 because part of the £1 of tax revenue would have been withdrawn from the domestic circular flow and only the remainder would have been spent on consumption.

The initial and the final size of the budget deficit With tax rates held constant, total tax revenue rises and falls with national income. Thus, if government expenditure is held constant, deficits will decrease (or surpluses will increase) when national income rises, and deficits will increase (or surpluses decrease) when national income falls. This proposition has a number of important applications. We shall consider one of these now and others later.

We have seen that the government can eliminate a deflationary gap by increasing its spending by the amount of the gap while holding tax rates constant. The initial deficit is thus equal to the extra government expenditure. But income will now rise and so will tax receipts.

Can we say anything about the relative size of the deficit for which the government must initially budget and the deficit that will remain once the full-employment level of GNP has been established? Suppose, for example, that the deflationary gap is £10,000 million and the government raises expenditure by £10,000 million, creating an initial government deficit of that amount. National income now begins to rise under the impact of the extra injection of government expenditure and, with constant tax rates, the government's tax revenue rises. When national income reaches its new equilibrium level, the budget deficit will have been decreased substantially. If, for example, the multiplier is 2 and taxes account for 30 per cent of all national income,[1] then in response to the new government expenditure of £10,000 million, national income will rise by £20,000 million and tax revenue will rise by £6,000 million. Thus the initial budget deficit of £10,000 million will, in this example, shrink to £4,000 million when national income reaches its new equilibrium.

Could the rise in income ever be large enough to eliminate the deficit completely? The answer is 'No'. The extra government expenditure is a new injection and income will rise until a matching flow of withdrawals has been generated. Since taxes are only one of several withdrawals, it follows that the rise in taxes must be less than the rise in government expenditure.[2]

---

[1] All of the important points in this chapter can be demonstrated using the simple assumption that taxes always take a constant proportion of national income. This makes the marginal and average propensities to tax the same (they are 0.3 in the present example).

[2] This is the answer from the present theory of equilibrium national income. In a dynamic model the rise in income could itself cause an accelerator-style rise in investment that would take income high enough to remove the deficit altogether. In the equilibrium model we have $G+X+I=T+M+S$ and

(note continued)

The full-employment deficit or surplus It is now clear that we can talk not only about the *actual* (or 'current') budget deficit or surplus at the present level of national income, but also about the *potential* budget deficit or surplus at any other level of national income, given current rates of taxes and expenditure. The potential deficit or surplus that would occur if the economy were at full employment is called the FULL-EMPLOYMENT BALANCE.[1] The actual deficit or surplus in any one year is referred to as the CURRENT BALANCE.

The full-employment balance is illustrated in Figure 38.3. For given tax rates, total tax payments vary with the level of income, as shown by the line T. Government expenditure is assumed not to vary with income and is shown by the horizontal line G. The distance between the T and G lines shows the deficit or surplus corresponding to each level of income. The level of income for which the budget is balanced is Y_b. If full-employment income is less than Y_b, say Y_1, there is a full-employment deficit; if full-employment income is greater than Y_b, say Y_2, there is a full-employment surplus. Only if the full-employment level of income is Y_b will there be a balanced budget at full employment.

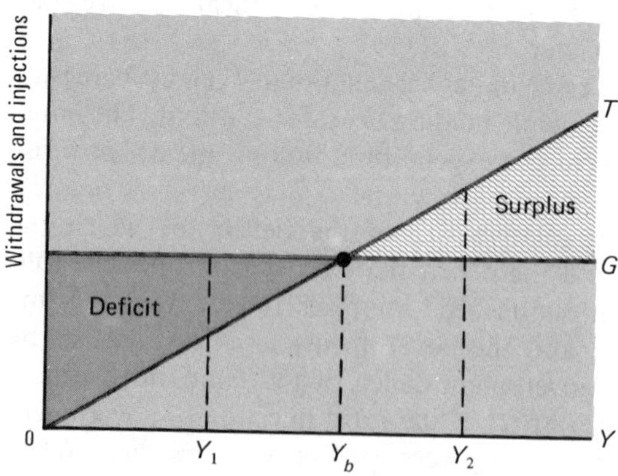

Fig. 38.3 Full-employment balance

The figure reveals the following important relation:

> **For any economy whose current income is less than its full-employment income, the current deficit will be larger than the full-employment deficit.**

The reason for this relation is that as income rises the yield from a given set of tax rates rises and hence the deficit falls.

The importance of this point is that the deficit or surplus can change for two quite different reasons. First, it can change because national income changes. A fall in income should lower the surplus or raise the deficit. A rise should have the opposite

---

since the only injection to change is G, we must have $\Delta G = \Delta T + \Delta M + \Delta S$ when we move to the new equilibrium. The elimination of the budget deficit requires $\Delta G = \Delta T$, which could only occur if $\Delta M = \Delta S = 0$, which contradicts our basic assumption that each of these is an increasing function of income.

[1] The standard terminology can be confusing. The budget balance is the difference between revenue and expenditure. The balance may be positive (a surplus), a negative (a deficit), or zero. If revenues are equal to expenditures so that the budget balance is zero, it is common to speak of a balanced budget. Thus the *budget balance* is $T - G - Q$, while a *balanced budget* means that $T = G + Q$, where Q is transfer payments.

effect. Second, the deficit can change because the government changes its revenue or expenditure policy, shifting the G or the T function in Figure 38.3. If one wishes to judge the policy stance of the government, one does not wish to confuse these two types of changes. One way to keep them separate is to judge changes in fiscal policy by changes in the full-employment surplus. This tells us what the budget balance would be if full employment were achieved; changes in it from one year to the next will reflect changes in the government's tax or expenditure policy.

The balanced-budget multiplier

So far the effects of changing either revenues or expenditures have been considered. What would happen if, during a time of unemployment, the government raised *both* its expenditure and its taxes, seeking to keep the budget balanced at all times? It is sometimes thought that such action would produce no net effect on the level of income, but this is not so. We have already seen that £1,000 million of extra G will have a different effect than a £1,000 million reduction of T. If the government raises an extra £1,000 million a year in new tax revenue at the same time that it spends an extra £1,000 million a year, the circular flow will be unaffected *only* if the whole of the £1,000 million of tax revenue would have been spent by taxpayers in any case. The effect of the government policy will then be to reduce private expenditure by £1,000 million and to raise its own expenditure by £1,000 million; total expenditure, and hence national income and employment, will be unchanged. Usually, however, a rise in taxes causes not only a fall in consumption but a fall in saving. Thus, taking an extra £1,000 million away from households in taxes will reduce spending on domestically produced goods by less than £1,000 million. It might, for example, reduce domestic consumption expenditure by only £750 million. If the government spends the entire £1,000 million on currently produced goods, there will be an increase of £250 million in total final expenditure. In this case the balanced-budget increase in public expenditure will have an expansionary effect.

> **A balanced-budget increase in government expenditure will have an expansionary effect on national income and a balanced-budget decrease will have a contractionary effect.**

The BALANCED-BUDGET MULTIPLIER measures these changes. It is defined as the change in income divided by the balanced-budget change in government expenditure that brought it about. Thus, if an extra £2,000 million of government spending, financed by an extra £2,000 million of taxes, causes national income to rise by £1,000 million, then the balanced-budget multiplier is 0·5; if income rises by £2,000 million, it is 1.

The common sense behind the balanced-budget multiplier is that when the government makes a balanced increase in G and T, it is transferring income from the private sector, whose marginal propensity to spend out of disposable income is less than unity, to the public sector, whose marginal propensity to spend is unity. The initial impact on expenditure per pound transferred is the difference between these two marginal propensities. Of course, when the government makes a balanced decrease in G and T, it is transferring income to the private sector, whose propensity to spend is less than the government's. This has a contractionary effect on aggregate expenditure.

The use of fiscal policy: fine tuning versus large adjustments

Now that we have seen that fiscal policy can be used to remove inflationary and deflationary gaps, the second principal question of this chapter is this: What can the government reasonably expect to achieve by using fiscal policy?

We can distinguish two objectives that differ in the scope of required policy intervention. The first objective is the more ambitious of the two. In this case, the authorities try to keep national income at exactly its full employment level by trying to offset every fluctuation in private investment, consumption or export expenditure that occurs. The second objective is much less ambitious. In this case the authorities accept fluctuations as inevitable. They recognize that from time to time large and persistent inflationary or deflationary gaps will develop. The task of demand management is then seen as offsetting these major gaps so as to prevent both deep and persistent depressions and long and rapid inflations from occurring. Views on which objective was feasible have changed substantially over the years since fiscal policy became an acceptable tool of macro-management of the economy.

Fine tuning

In the 1950s and 1960s many economists throughout the world advocated the use of fiscal policy to remove even minor fluctuations in national income around the full-employment level. These economists felt that G and T could be changed frequently and by relatively small amounts to hold national income almost exactly at its full-employment level. When this is attempted, fiscal policy is said to be used to FINE TUNE the economy.

Fiscal fine tuning was popular in many countries during this period. British Chancellors of the Exchequer introduced budgets each year, sometimes more often, that varied taxes and expenditure in an attempt to influence the economy's aggregate expenditure function. Careful assessment of the results, where such policies were followed, shows that their successes fell short of expectations.

The basic policy recommendations for fine tuning were based on comparative static analysis of the national income model. This is also the analysis we have mainly relied on in this book. We have taken a *given* inflationary or deflationary gap and have asked how to eliminate it. In fact, the economy is continually fluctuating. (Some of the reasons for this were analysed in Chapter 37.) The problems of stabilization in a continually changing economy can be very much more difficult than those in a static economy with a given inflationary or deflationary gap. Let us briefly consider why.

All of the fiscal policies that seek to stabilize the economy create NEGATIVE FEEDBACK. Negative feedback is a technical term meaning that, when any system deviates from its target level, forces are set in motion that push the system back *towards* its target level.[1] Thus, when demand is too high, so that inflationary conditions prevail, demand is reduced; when demand is too low, so that unemployment prevails, demand is increased. Negative feedback is a necessary but not a sufficient condition for stability. If any control system operates with delay, or

[1] The *system* may be anything from an economy to an aeroplane using an automatic pilot; the *target level* may be anything from full employment national income, to a compass course.

lags, that are large relative to the period of fluctuations it is seeking to control, it can do the very opposite of stabilizing: the controls actually accentuate rather than check fluctuations.[1]

The importance of time lags

Controls operate with lags for two main reasons. The first is called the DECISION LAG: it takes time to assess a situation and decide what corrective action should be taken. Our knowledge of what is happening is always somewhat out of date. At a minimum it takes a month or so, and often very much longer, to gather data about current happenings. Our current information thus tells us not what is happening today, but what was happening anywhere from a month to six months ago. Once we have our data on what has happened, this data must be interpreted. Questions such as: 'Is the downturn the beginning of a large potential slide or just a temporary aberration?' will need to be answered. After the situation is assessed, alternative corrective actions need to be considered and finally a decision taken on what action is appropriate.

The second main source of lag is called the EXECUTION LAG: the time it takes to initiate corrective policies and for their corrective influence to be felt. For example, if the corrective action *is* a large increase in G in the form of a new road-building programme, it may take months to make surveys, hear objections from persons affected by chosen routes and sign contracts. And once the government has done its work it may take time before the effects on the private sector are felt. A strike in the cement industry may delay still further the flow of wage payments to construction workers that will raise disposable income and finally lead to an induced rise in consumption expenditure throughout the economy.

Given that lags exist, what influence do they have on the outcome of fiscal policy? A simple explanation of their effect can be developed along the following lines.[2] Consider a system that is oscillating around a full-employment level of output as illustrated in Figure 38.4(i). Time is measured along the horizontal axis, and on the

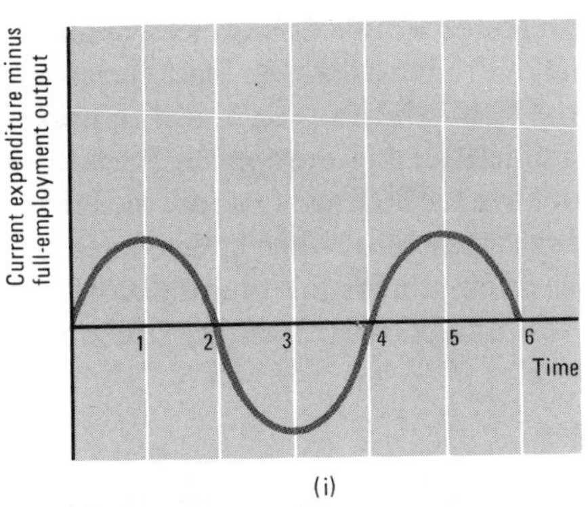

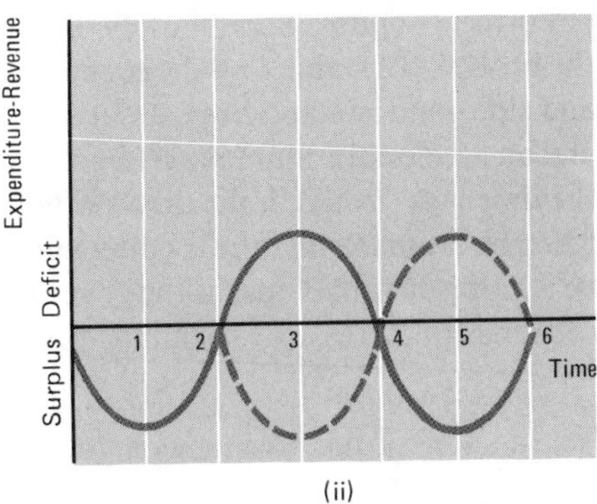

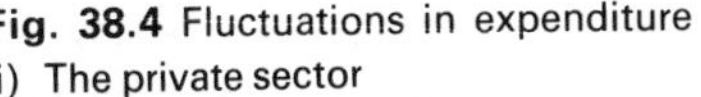
Fig. 38.4 Fluctuations in expenditure
(i) The private sector

(ii) The government sector

[1] We illustrated this point in the case of a single competitive market. See the discussion of the cobweb theory in Chapter 11.

[2] This particular formulation of the problem is taken from A. W. Phillips, 'Employment, Inflation and Growth', *Economica*, February 1962.

vertical axis we measure the difference between full-employment output and current desired expenditure. The fluctuations are such that a boom in which aggregate expenditure exceeds full-employment output is followed by a slump in which aggregate expenditure falls short of full-employment output. Assume that the government plans to vary its own expenditure so as to offset these fluctuations exactly. The government wants its plan to have the impact shown by the solid line in Figure 38.4(ii). At first, it plans a surplus that will reduce total expenditure; later, in period 3, it plans a deficit that will raise aggregate expenditure. If there are no decisions and execution lags, then the addition of the solid lines in Figure 38.4(i) and 38.4(ii) will produce aggregate expenditure for the private plus the public sector, which is always equal to full-employment output. The government's deficit or surplus exactly counterbalances the difference between aggregate expenditure and full-employment output in the private sector, so that its stabilization policy is completely successful.

Now assume that there are decision and execution lags. Further assume, to make the point as clear as possible, that the overall effect of these lags is equal to half the period of the cycle. Now the balanced budget planned at period zero will not actually occur until period 2; the maximum surplus planned for period 1 will not occur until period 3, when the economy is already in a slump; and the maximum deficit planned for period 3 will not occur until period 5, when the economy is already in a period of boom. Although planned government expenditure still follows the solid line in Figure 38.4(ii), actual government expenditure now follows the dotted line. Instead of stabilizing the economy as intended, the policy will actually destabilize it. The combination of public and private demand will give rise to larger fluctuations than would have occurred if the government had done nothing!

This simple example is sufficient to show that the problem of controlling the economy is not so simple as comparative static analysis can make it seem. In general, policies designed to stabilize the economy will have differing effects, depending on the time lags both in the actual working of the economy and in the functioning of the stabilization scheme.

Former London School of Economics' professor Frank Paish once compared the problem of stabilizing the economy to that of driving a car with blackened front and side windows and only a rear-view mirror from which to see, and with brakes and an accelerator that take effect only a long time after they are applied. Because of the time lags involved, the driver often has to have the courage to apply the brakes when he estimates that he is going uphill and the accelerator when he estimates that he is going downhill, just as the government, in attempting to fine tune the economy, often has to increase its spending during a boom and decrease it during a slump.

The decline of fine tuning as a goal of policy

Theoretical reasoning of the sort just described made an increasing number of economists suspicious of fine tuning throughout the 1950s.[1] Then in the 1960s a series of applied studies were made suggesting that stabilization policy had sometimes succeeded in destabilizing the economy, making fluctuations in income

[1] Some of the basic theoretical work showing the difficulties of fine tuning was done in the 1950s by the late Professor A.W. Phillips, the inventor of the famous Phillips curve that we shall study in Part 11.

and employment larger than they would have been in the absence of any 'stabilizing' policy. As a result of this work, most economists and government policy-makers set much less ambitious objectives for fiscal policy in the 1970s and 1980s than they did in the 1950s and 1960s.

The economy occasionally develops fairly severe and persistent inflationary or deflationary gaps. Such gaps last long enough for their major causes to be studied and for possible fiscal remedies to be carefully planned and executed without worrying too much about short-term time lags.

Many economists who do not believe in the viability of fine tuning believe that fiscal policy can be used to aid in removing persistent gaps.

Tools of fiscal policy

What are the major tools that governments can use to effect their fiscal policies? These tools can be classified in many ways; one is based on the division between automatic and discretionary measures.

Automatic tools of fiscal policy: built-in stabilizers

As a result of factors discussed in Chapter 37, the level of aggregate demand is continually fluctuating. A stabilization policy for fine tuning the economy thus requires a policy that is itself ever-changing. If such a conscious fine-tuning policy is impossible, because of time lags, is there no room for fiscal policy to correct short-term fluctuations in the economy?

Fortunately, much of the job of adjusting fiscal policy to an ever-changing economic environment is done automatically by what are called built-in-stabilizers. A BUILT-IN STABILIZER is anything that tends to cause injections to increase or withdrawals to decrease as national income falls, and injections to decrease or withdrawals to increase as national income rises, without the government's having to make policy decisions to bring about these changes.

Taxes The higher national income, the more most taxes tend to yield. Sales and excise tax yields rise as total purchases and sales rise (and this happens as income rises). The same is true of taxes on wage payments such as national insurance payments. Thus, with rates constant, the total tax yield and hence the total of withdrawals from the circular flow of income rises and falls as national income rises and falls.

The effect is even more marked with taxes that are progressive rather than proportional. Steeply progressive tax rates ensure that as income rises, tax receipts rise more than in proportion. These extra withdrawals exert a contractionary force on the economy. Conversely, if income falls, tax receipts fall sharply, withdrawals are reduced, and the contractionary pressures on the economy are to some extent alleviated.

Figure 38.5 illustrates the stabilizing effect of taxes that rise as national income rises. The subscripts 1 and 2 refer to different economies. Both have the same government expenditure function, but different tax functions. Economy 2 has a higher degree of built-in stability than economy 1. As income rises above Y_b, the budget surplus rises faster in 2 than in 1. And as income falls below Y_b, the budget

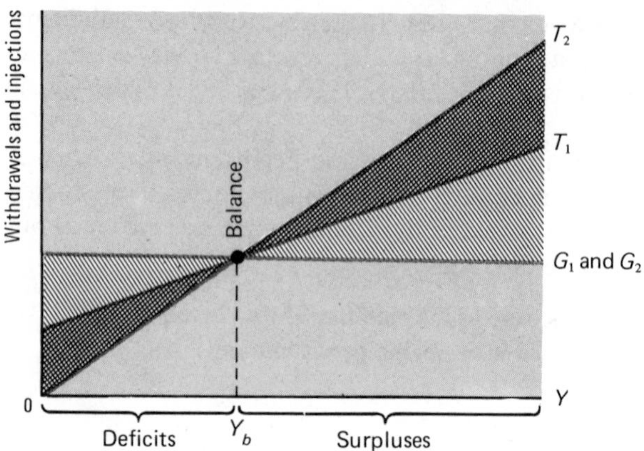

Fig. 38.5 Automatic stabilizing effects of taxes on national income

deficit increases faster in 2 than in 1. Thus variations in the government deficit or surplus tend to mitigate both booms and slumps more in 2 than in 1.

> **The greater the tendency of tax receipts to vary as income varies, the greater the degree of built-in stability.**

So far in this book we have taken government expenditures to be a constant. In fact, many government expenditures tend to vary in a systematic way with national income. Government expenditures are automatically stabilizing to the extent that they rise during periods of recession and depression, and decline during periods of prosperity and boom. This follows directly from the facts that a rise in G has a stimulating effect on the economy similar to a fall in T, while a fall in G has a contractionary effect similar to a rise in T.

The built-in-stabilizing effect of government expenditures is shown in Figure 38.6. The three economies have the same tax function, T. Government expenditure varys inversely with national income in Economy 1, directly in Economy 3 and is constant in Economy 2. It is clear that Economy 1 has the most built-in stability. As income rises above Y_b, a large budget surplus develops in Economy 1, and the fall in

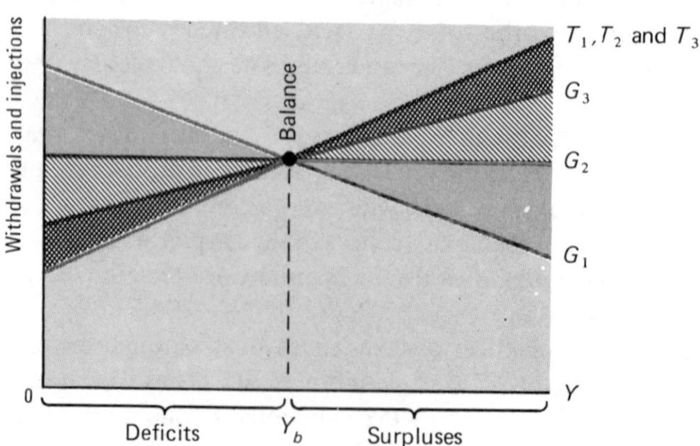

Fig. 38.6 Automatic stabilizing effect of government expenditures on national income

G exerts a downward pressure on aggregate expenditure. When income falls below Y_b, a deficit develops in Economy 1, and the rise in government expenditure raises aggregate expenditure above what it would otherwise be. In Economy 2 government expenditure is constant and the only stabilizing effect comes from the tax system. In Economy 3 government expenditure actually helps to accentuate swings since it rises when income is high and falls when it is low.

National insurance and welfare services All unemployment benefits and welfare payments tend to rise in times of falling national income with its accompanying unemployment and hardship. Many welfare schemes are financed by taxes based on national insurance payments which tend to yield less when income is low. Thus welfare schemes tend to be net injectors into the circular flow in times of slumps. They also tend to be net withdrawers in times of boom and full employment, when payments are low and revenues high. These net deficits and surpluses on unemployment benefits and welfare expenditures tend to stabilize the economy just as if the money were used to build dams or bridges.

Welfare and unemployment payments of all types are transfer payments. Thus they do not inject expenditure directly into the economy. Their payment, however, raises household disposable income and when households spend their receipts consumption expenditure rises. Thus the net effect of these transfer payments is to raise expenditure.[1] In so far as they vary inversely with national income they act as an important built-in stabilizer.

Agricultural-support policies When there is a slump in the economy there is a general decline in the demand for all goods, including agricultural produce. The free-market price of agricultural goods tends to fall, and government agricultural supports come into play. This ensures that government expenditure on this form of activity will rise as the level of national income falls. This is as true of EEC agricultural-support policies as it is of most support policies in developed countries throughout the world.

The origin of built-in stabilizers Most of these built-in stabilizers are fairly new phenomena. Fifty years ago agricultural-stabilization policies, steeply progressive income taxes and large unemployment and other national income payments were unknown in the UK. Each of these built-in stabilizers is the unforeseen by-product of policies originally adopted for other reasons. The progressive income tax arose out of a concern to make the distribution of income less unequal. The growth of the government sector has been the result of many factors other than a desire for cyclical stability. Social insurance and agricultural support programmes were adopted more because of a concern with the welfare of the individuals and groups involved than to preserve the health of the economy. But, unforeseen or not, they work as effective stabilizers.

Stability around what level of income? A large degree of built-in stability is a good thing if the economy is tending to oscillate around a high level of income and employment. The same degree of built-in stability can, however, be very undesirable if the

[1] They raise the relation between disposable income and national income in just the way that a tax cut does.

economy is in a serious slump. Consider an economy that is reviving from a severe depression under the impetus of new private investment or new government expenditure. The more rapidly tax yields rise as national income rises, the more rapidly withdrawals will rise. Thus the large rise in taxes will tend to bring an expansion quickly to a halt by re-establishing the equality between injections and withdrawals after only a small rise in income. The larger the marginal propensity to tax, the smaller will be the multiplier – and thus the smaller the expansion in income resulting from a given rise in injections.

Undesirable built-in stability that inhibits recovery from a period of low demand and high unemployment can be a very serious matter indeed.

> **Built-in stability is desirable when the level of income and employment being stabilized is close to full employment, but it is undesirable when the level being stabilized is well below full employment.**

How much stability? How important are built-in stabilizers? In the US, the President's Council of Economic Advisors has estimated that with the present tax system and schedules of unemployment compensation benefits, a decline in GNP automatically produces a reduction in government receipts and an increase in transfer payments that limits a decline in after-tax income to about 65 cents for each $1 of reduction of GNP. Thus, about a third of any decline is automatically offset.

No matter how lucky governments have been in finding built-in stabilizers, however, these cannot reduce fluctuations to zero. Stabilizers work by influencing income in such a way as to produce stabilizing reactions to changes in income. But until the change in income occurs, the stabilizer is not even brought into play.

The evidence of the behaviour of the UK economy reviewed in the previous chapter suggests two important conclusions. First, fluctuations have been less extreme since 1945 than they were in earlier periods. This is due in part to the operation of powerful built-in stabilizers that were not on the scene before the Second World War. Second, the magnitude of the post-1945 fluctuations has nonetheless been sufficient to cause policy makers serious concern.

Discretionary fiscal policy: the choice between changes in tax rates and government expenditure

Short-term, minor fluctuations that are not removed by automatic built-in stabilizers cannot, with present knowledge and techniques, be removed by consciously fine tuning the economy. We have already noted, however, that larger and more persistent gaps sometimes appear. In these cases there is time for the government to operate a DISCRETIONARY FISCAL POLICY, which means to institute changes in taxes and expenditures designed to offset gaps. To do this effectively the government needs to make periodic conscious decisions to change fiscal policy. Its advisers must study current economic trends and forecast the probable course of the economy. If it looks unsatisfactory, the cabinet may introduce, and Parliament may pass, the necessary legislation to alter it.

There is often sharp debate on whether taxes or expenditures or both should be used to achieve those stabilizing changes that are generally agreed to be desirable. What issues are involved in these debates? What factors affect the choice between changes in G and changes in T?

Location of effects The multiplier effects of an increase in aggregate demand tend to spread over the whole economy, causing a rising demand for virtually every commodity. If a slump is a general one with widespread unemployment, this will be an advantage. If, however, a slump has severely localized characteristics, with a major depression in a particular industry (such as automobiles) or area (such as South Wales), then it may be desirable to achieve a disproportionate effect in the seriously depressed industry or area. In this case, raising expenditure has a distinct advantage over cutting taxes. The tax cut will have its initial impact on the entire economy, but by careful choice of projects much of the initial effect of extra expenditure can be channelled into the depressed industry or area. Thus, if specific impact effects are important, *G* has an advantage over *T*.

The duration of the time lag Long time lags in fiscal policy are undesirable both because they delay the desired effects and because they introduce the possibility of destabilizing the economy since the situation the policy was designed to ameliorate may have altered substantially by the time the policy comes into effect. Tax cuts have a substantial advantage over expenditure increases in respect to the execution lag. We have already noted, for example, that the execution lag can be extremely long for a new road-building programme. The lag can, however, be very short for changes in taxes and transfer payments. Once legislation for tax reduction has been passed by Parliament, taxes withheld from pay envelopes can be reduced quickly. Thus, only a matter of weeks after the tax cut is legislated, wage earners may find themselves with more take-home pay because their employers are withholding tax payments at a lower rate than before. Similarly transfer payments can be changed within days of the enactment of the necessary legislation.

The reversibility of the policy One of the most important principles of anti-cyclical fiscal policy is that the policy must be reversible. Excessive concentration on comparative static analysis can make one think in terms of policies to remove what would otherwise be permanent inflationary or deflationary gaps. In fact, as we saw in Chapter 37, the private sector of the economy undergoes continual oscillations in its expenditure. Thus the aggregate expenditure function of the private sector is changing. Even when a persistent gap develops the one thing that is clear, at least if past experience is any guide, is that the gap will sooner or later change as a result of changes in private expenditure.

> **One of the most important principles of anti-cyclical fiscal policy is that the policy should be reversible.**

A government stimulus to remove a deflationary gap should be easily altered to become a government restraint when private expenditure alters to produce an inflationary gap.

On this count, tax policy seems superior to government expenditure on goods and services or to transfer payments. Transfer payments are usually part of social policy, and it would seem callous to change the rates on such payments every time inflationary or deflationary gaps developed. Government expenditures can be increased, but experience shows they are not easy to cut. A very high proportion of *G* is committed through statutory programmes. Although *G* could no doubt be reduced over a decade by a really determined effort, the degree of discretion that any government has to reduce it over the period of one year is surprisingly small.

Furthermore a new line of expenditure following from a decision to increase G usually requires a new set of civil servants to administer it. These people become a vested interest who will resist any cuts in the expenditure flows that support them. This behaviour is quite understandable but it helps to explain why expenditure changes are not easy vehicles for anti-cyclical policies. Tax rates, on the other hand, do not suffer from this inertia. The same civil service apparatus is required to administer one set of income-tax rates as another set. Of course there may be voter resistance, but experience suggests that in practice tax rates are easier to vary in both directions as an anti-cyclical device than are expenditures. Income and many other tax rates can only be varied with parliamentary approval and hence only annually, or occasionally more frequently when subsidiary budgets are introduced. Rates on certain indirect taxes can, however, be varied quickly and substantially, since power to do so for regulatory purposes has been granted by blanket parliamentary agreement. In the US attempts to get similar blanket approval for the administration to vary indirect tax rates on its own initiative have not been successful. The Congress has not been willing to give up its hold on the details of the purse strings and, as a result, tax changes are used much less frequently as a stabilizing device in the US than in the UK.

The public's reaction to short-term changes An economist advising on how to stabilize a fluctuating economy through tax policy might advocate temporary tax increases to remove an inflationary gap and temporary tax reductions to remove a deflationary gap. These tax changes would cause changes in household disposable income, and, according to the Keynesian theory of the consumption function, the resulting changes in consumption would tend to stabilize the economy. Consumption expenditure would increase as taxes were cut in times of deflationary gaps and decrease as taxes were raised in times of inflationary gaps.

This theory of the stabilizing effects of short-term tax changes relies on the assumption that household consumption depends on current disposable income. Many of the recent theories of the consumption function have emphasized households' expected *lifetime income* or *permanent income* as the major determinant of consumption. According to such theories, which we studied in Chapter 35, households have expectations about their lifetime incomes and adjust their consumption to these expectations. When temporary fluctuations in income occur, households maintain their long-term consumption plans and use their stocks of wealth as a buffer to absorb income fluctuations. Thus, when there is a purely temporary rise in income, households will save all the extra, and when there is a purely temporary fall in income, households maintain their long-term consumption plans by using up part of their wealth (accumulated through past savings).

To the extent that this kind of influence is at work, it has serious consequences for short-run fiscal stabilization policies. A temporary tax reduction raises household disposable income, but households, recognizing this as temporary, might not revise their expenditure plans but save the money instead. Thus the hoped-for increase in aggregate expenditure would not materialize. Seen from the withdrawals and injections approach, the effect is that the decline in one withdrawal, government taxes, is balanced by an equal increase in another withdrawal, household saving. Overall withdrawals are unchanged and so is national income. Similarly, a temporary rise in taxes reduces disposable income, but it may merely cause a fall in saving. Thus, total expenditure and total withdrawals are again unchanged, and a temporary surcharge fails to reduce the inflationary gap.

If households' consumption is more closely related to lifetime than to current income, then the efficacy of fiscal measures that are known to be of short duration is uncertain.

According to these theories, if a tax reduction is thought to be temporary, households will use most of it to add to their stock of wealth rather than to engage in a temporary burst of present consumption. There remains, however, the important questions of what kind of assets households acquire when they add to their wealth. According to these theories, households save and add to their wealth just as much when they buy consumer durables such as washing machines and TV sets (which are consumed slowly over long periods of time) as when they buy financial assets such as local authority bonds or shares in ICI. But the effect on the economy is very different in the two cases. If households spend their temporary increase in income on financial assets such as shares and bonds, this will not add directly to aggregate demand for currently produced goods and services. (There may, however, be an indirect effect if the rate of interest is affected by the increased household demand for financial assets.) If, however, households spend their temporary increase in income on consumer durables (which add to their present stock of wealth and are consumed slowly over many years), this does add to aggregate demand for current output. Such spending will tend to raise both the GNP and total employment. What matters for the efficacy of short-term tax changes is whether households allow short-term fluctuations in income to affect their expenditures on current output of either durables (including investment goods such as new housing) or non-durables, or whether such fluctuations affect only their expenditures on financial assets such as shares and bonds, building society deposits and life insurance.

Changes in tax rates will have a weak effect on the economy if both of the following are true: Households feel that the government-induced changes in their disposable income are transitory, and households allow transitory fluctuations in income to affect the rate at which they are accumulating financial assets rather than the rate at which they are spending to purchase currently produced output. Changes in tax rates will have a strong effect if either or both of the following are true: Households regard the government-induced changes in disposable income as permanent, and households allow their fluctuations in income, whether regarded as permanent or temporary, to affect the rate at which they are prepared to spend on currently produced output.

Doubts about the possible efficacy of short-term variations in tax rates give a reason favouring government expenditure. Since government expenditure is itself a direct injection into the circular flow, its effect on income and expenditure is more reliable. It does not rely on giving money to others and then having the effect depend on what they elect to do with it.

Fiscal policy in practice

Keynesian economics in general, and fiscal policy in particular, has come under very severe criticism in the 1970s. It is not uncommon to hear it said that the Keynesian model is totally 'wrong' and its policy recommendations totally misguided. The British economist David Laidler, now at the University of Western Ontario, describes British demand management as 'intellectually false'.[1] We cannot go into these extreme views here. Suffice it to say that the view that *basic* Keynesian theory is misguided is difficult to sustain. The concept of the circular flow of income long predates Keynes.[2] Every econometric model in existence today uses it. Of course certain behavioural relations used in particular models and certain policy recommendations based on these models may be open to criticism; but the view that the model itself, and all of the aggregates based on it, are useless just does not seem to stand up to careful analysis.

What can fiscal policy accomplish? In the United States, where fiscal policy was not seriously used until the 1960s, there is a school of extreme monetarists who argue that fiscal policy has no effect on the economy because the crowding-out effect is 100 per cent: every change of $1 in government expenditure causes a change in the opposite direction of $1 in private expenditure. The experience of Britain and other countries where fiscal policy has been used over the past 30 years makes it very hard to take this view seriously (indeed it does not command majority support among US economists).

The empirical evidence seems to provide overwhelming support for the theory that the central authorities can influence aggregate demand by making sufficiently large changes in expenditures or taxes.

The open issue today, as we shall see later, is the impact of these changes in aggregate demand on prices and on quantities: if aggregate demand is changed, how much of its effect will be on prices and how much on such important quantities as real national income, employment and unemployment? This is the great unanswered question of macroeconomic policy. Part 11 is devoted to it, so we shall put it aside until then. In the meantime, we are interested in the use of fiscal policy to influence aggregate demand and must record that the overwhelming preponderance of empirical evidence and the majority of economic theories, suggest that such an influence does exist.[3]

The costs of government activity

We have seen that the operation of fiscal policy may well entail government expenditure in excess of tax receipts. This implies increases in the public debt. In recent decades, increases have far outweighed decreases in most Western countries,

[1] David Laidler, 'The End of Demand Management', in Milton Friedman, 'Unemployment versus Inflation?', Institute of Economic Affairs Occasional Paper 44, London, 1975.

[2] A very clear statement is to be found in Chapter 1 of Schumpeter's great book, *The Theory of Economic Development: An Inquiry into Profits, Capital, Credit, Interest and the Business Cycle*, English Translation, Harvard University Press, Cambridge, Mass., 1934. (First published in German, 1912).

[3] Fiscal policy has gone through some extraordinary variations in the UK over the last few decades. There is substantial debate about the wisdom of some of these budgetary changes. Indeed, one well-known authority writing about the period referred to '... this extraordinary combination of self-inflicted errors and externally imposed misfortunes ... '. M.V. Posner writing in M. Posner (ed.), *Demand Management* (Heinemann, London, 1978). This is an excellent book for those who wish to get the flavour of current controversies over macro policy in the UK. The summaries of these policies in Prest, *op. cit.*, are also valuable to the student of the UK economy.

so that the trend of the debt has been upward. Does an increasing debt matter? Would an ever-increasing debt lead to an ultimate collapse of market economies? Does the debt represent a burden we are passing on to our heirs? It is to these and related questions that we now turn.

To the extent that it is held within the country, the national debt represents money that the government has borrowed, via the sale of its bonds to domestic households, firms, and financial institutions. In this sense the national debt is owed by all of us to some of us.

All government debt arises because the government has chosen to finance certain of its expenditures not by taxes but by borrowing. In discussing the significance of the debt, it is important to keep the costs of the *actual expenditure* distinct from the costs of the *method of financing* the expenditure. Both are important, but only the second is a 'cost of the debt'. Before discussing the particular consequences of debt financing, let us note certain benefits and costs of government expenditures that exist no matter how the expenditures are financed. This turns out to have a bearing on the questions of financing.

The benefits and costs of government activity

Governments provide a variety of goods and services. Some are clearly current services such as running hospitals, controlling air lanes, providing police and military protection and providing education. Others are clearly capital goods, such as dams, roads and schools, that will yield a flow of services to some users over many years. Other governmental services are harder to classify, but they are no less important: expenditures on military equipment, and expenditures primarily designed to prevent unemployment, for example, may be providing protection from the onset of a depression. Expenditures on satellite programmes or on foreign aid are beneficial in other senses. We often debate whether or not the benefits of some particular governmental activity justify the costs, but, except in rare cases, there are always some benefits.

We saw in Chapter 4 that the cost of doing something can be measured in terms of the things that might have been done instead. The opportunity cost of a particular government expenditure depends on what resources the government project will use and from where they are drawn. In times of heavy unemployment, most of the resources used in government activity might otherwise have remained unemployed. In this case there is no opportunity cost in employing them in the government activity because there is no alternative current production sacrificed by so doing. In contrast, if, in a fully employed economy, the government builds dams, roads, schools and nuclear submarines, the opportunity cost of these are the consumer goods and capital goods that would have been produced instead.

To the extent that the resources for the government activity were drawn away from the production of consumer goods and services, the opportunity cost is necessarily borne by the present generation in terms of a reduced consumption of goods produced by the private sector of the economy. To the extent that the resources are drawn away from the production of capital goods, the opportunity cost will be spread out over the future, because the current generation is giving up not consumption, but capital goods. This leads to a smaller stock of capital, and to a lower capacity to produce goods and services for consumption in the future than there would have been had the government activity not taken place.

The difference between these capital-good and current-consumption opportunity costs requires further study. In the case in which all the resources for government expenditure are drawn from production of consumption commodities, the sacrifice of consumers could cease the minute the government stopped using these resources, and thus the opportunity cost is all borne by the current generation. However, if the resources used by the government had been drawn entirely from the production of capital goods, once the government activity ceased the production of capital goods could be resumed. In the interim, however, a large supply of capital goods will have gone unproduced, and the consequences of this will be felt in the future. The stock of capital will for a long time be smaller than it would have been had the government activity not occurred. Because it is the stock of capital that provides the means of producing consumption goods, if follows that the output of such goods will be less than it otherwise would have been for as long as the *stock* of capital (*not* the current output of capital goods) is smaller than it would otherwise have been. Thus, the opportunity cost in terms of a reduced output of goods for current consumption will be spread over a long period of time after the government activity ceases.

The opportunity cost of government activity is in terms of the commodities that would have been produced instead. This cost can approach zero in times of unemployment but it is always significant in times of full employment of any factor of production. To the extent that the commodities forgone are consumer's goods the cost is all borne currently, to the extent that the commodities forgone are capital goods, the cost is spread out over the future.

Alternative means of financing government activity

There are essentially three different ways in which a government can finance an expenditure: (1) it can raise the money by increasing taxes, thus transferring purchasing power from taxpayers to itself; (2) it can borrow the money from willing lenders, thus transferring current purchasing power from them to itself in return for the promise of future purchasing power; (3) it can (actually, or in effect) print enough money to permit itself to bid the resources it needs away from other potential users.

The primary effect of the method of financing concerns who in the community bears the cost of forgone production. In other words, it is concerned with the question of how the cost is distributed among people. This can, as we shall see, have some effect on the division between current production and capital production forgone, and the method of financing can also create some additional costs to society. But the major effect of the method of financing government expenditures is on *who* bears the costs, not on how much they are.

Suppose the economy is at a full-employment level, so that the government must incur real opportunity costs in order to produce its commodities. If the cost of a new government programme is met by increases in taxes, then the current taxpayers bear the cost by having their purchasing power reduced. Their purchases of goods and services will be decreased, and resources will be transferred to production in the public sector.

If the government expenditure is financed by borrowing from households and firms, the reduction in purchasing power for current consumption is suffered by those who lend their money to the government instead of spending it on currently produced goods and services. People who do not buy government stocks do not postpone current consumption and thus do not bear any of the real current cost of the government activity.

The third possibility is that the activity is financed by creating new money. (As we shall see later, the way this is done in the modern world is for the government to sell bonds to the central bank. In return, the central bank credits the government with a deposit on which the government can draw cheques to pay for its purchases.) Because the economy is already in a state of full employment, this method of finance must create an inflationary gap and thus cause a rise in the price level. Aggregate demand, already high enough to purchase all the output the economy is producing, becomes excessive as the government enters the market with its own new demand. The rise in prices will mean that households and firms will be able to buy less than they would otherwise have bought, and the government will be able to obtain resources for its own activities. Thus fewer resources will be available for private consumption and private capital formation. The result in the aggregate is the same as if the government had reduced private expenditure by taxation.

As far as distributing the opportunity cost is concerned, inflationary finance is similar to financing by taxes, although the identity of the groups forced to cut back on their own purchases is likely to be different in the two cases. By choosing which taxes to increase, the government using tax finance can exert a considerable influence on the distribution of the burden (although we must never forget that taxes may be shifted from the groups on which they are levied to other groups in surprising ways – see pages 124–8). Under inflationary finance, the government bids up prices and leaves it to the market to determine those groups that are to reduce their consumption and thus to pay the current cost. Retired persons and others on fixed incomes will bear much of the cost. Those whose incomes respond only slowly to changes in price levels will bear more of the cost than those whose incomes rise nearly as fast as prices. Some, indeed, will not pay any of the cost. Inflationary finance is usually regarded as a less just method of taxation than income and corporate taxes, because it places much of the burden on the economically weak, the unfortunate, and the uneducated, and taxes least those who can adjust to rising prices, often the richest and most powerful groups.

The opportunity cost of government activity in terms of forgone alternatives is incurred whether the money to pay for the projects is raised by taxes, by borrowing from the public, or by creating new money. Methods of finance determine who bears the costs but do not affect the total cost.

Now consider what happens once the government project is finished. To the extent that it was financed by current taxes (or by inflationary creation of new money) the matter is finished once the government expenditure has been made. Resources can then be transferred back to the production of goods and services, and households' real disposable income can be allowed to rise by reducing taxes. But to the extent that the government activity was financed by borrowing from the private sector, the debt remains after the activity has been completed. It is necessary to pay interest each year to the bondholders and eventually to repay the bonds as they reach maturity. To the extent that interest payments and eventual redemption of the bonds are made from tax revenue, taxpayers now suffer a reduction in their consumption below what it would otherwise have been. The transfer is thus reversed. In return for bearing the original reduction in consumption, bondholders (or their heirs) now enjoy a rise in consumption and taxpayers who are not bondholders suffer a reduction. For a community, the cost in terms of forgone output was borne during the original activity. Once the activity is finished, total production goes back to normal. The opportunity cost could not be postponed, but individuals who did not buy bonds must now pay for their share of the cost of the activity by transferring some claims on current production to other individuals.

Is there any economic limit to the size of the debt?

There has been a general trend for national debts to rise in most Western countries, and we must wonder if it matters. Are most countries approaching a limit beyond which undesirable or even disastrous consequences will ensue?

To the extent that the money raised by borrowing is spent on capital goods that increase future national income, the borrowing creates the extra income out of which extra taxes can be raised to pay the interest. To the extent that the money is spent on consumption goods it will become necessary to increase existing tax-rates in order to provide funds to meet the future interest payments. Up to a point, this will not cause any serious problems, since the process of paying interest on the debt involves only a transfer from some citizens (taxpayers) to other citizens (holders of government bonds). That there is a limit beyond which it is not safe to go can be seen by the following example. Suppose the government borrows a sum equal to 5 per cent of the national income each year in order to enhance the beauty of the countryside, and suppose that national income is growing at 2.5 per cent per year. If this policy went on forever, and if no old debt were ever paid off, then eventually the national debt would become so large that current interest payments would exceed current national income. In order to raise enough money to meet its interest bill, the government would have to tax all incomes at a rate exceeding 100 per cent!

Clearly, then, there is a grain of truth in the worry over the size of the interest payments on the national debt. But this worry applies only to those expenditures that do not themselves generate the extra income out of which interest payments can be met. And the worry becomes significant only if such non-income-creating debt is increasing *very much faster* than the national income. Such a situation existed in most Western countries during the crisis periods of the First and Second World Wars. Both of these periods were, by historical standards, very short, and at no other time has this class of debt been increasing at a rate anything like the rate of increase of national income.

A very good measure of whether the size of the debt is approaching dangerous levels is the willingness of borrowers to buy government bonds at various rates of interest. Well before a government reached an absolute debt limit (in terms of its ability to raise the money to pay the interest on its bonds), experienced investors would lose confidence in government bonds. Their prices would fall, and interest rates would rise as borrowers demanded a premium for risk. The fact that in virtually all Western industrial countries government bonds are regarded as the least risky of investments provides compelling evidence that the financial community is not concerned about the size of the debt.[1] (opposite)

A non-Keynesian view of the national debt

The view of the national debt that we have just discussed may be called the Keynesian view. Its basic points are: (1) the size of the debt is of no great practical importance and (2) the debt should be increased or decreased according to the needs of full-employment policy.

An alternative view, which may be called *fiscal conservatism*, uses the theory of government behaviour first discussed on pp. 435–6. Its first premise is that governments are not passive agents doing what is necessary to create full employment and otherwise to maximize social welfare; instead they seek to maximize their own utility functions. This they do by spending as much as they can and by levying as few taxes as they can get away with. Spending is desirable to the central authorities because some of it, such as civil service salaries, expense accounts and pensions, is for the authorities' own consumption and because much of the rest benefits the public and thus helps gain votes and keep the present party (whichever it is) in power. Taxation is undesirable because heavy taxes tend to loose votes for the party in power and may also cause pressure for reductions in spending which may reduce the consumption of the central authorities themselves. In this view any government is a body that is rather irresponsible by economists' standards: it seeks to increase its own welfare by making its budget deficit as large as possible. The theory of national income predicts that whenever the economy is at or near full-employment income, this policy is undesirable because it will create an inflationary gap.

The non-Keynesian view takes a broad historical perspective. It says that in the eighteenth century spendthrift rulers habitually spent more than their tax revenues and created inflationary gaps. The resulting inflations were harmful to the economy because they reduced the purchasing power of everyone's savings and disrupted trade. All through that century a battle was fought between Parliament – advocating fiscal responsibility, and the rulers – practising fiscal irresponsibility. When Parliament won the battle, it did so by imposing on the rulers the obligation to balance the nation's budget.

Thus the balanced-budget doctrine was not the silly irrational doctrine that Keynes made it out to be. It was, instead, the symbol of the peoples' victory in a century of struggle to control the spendthrift proclivities of the nation's rulers. The doctrine that had been well established by the end of the nineteenth century was that a balanced budget is the citizens' only protection against profligate spending and wild inflation. The Keynesian revolution swept that view away. Budget deficits became, according to Keynesians, the tool by which a benign, enlightened set of central authorities sought to ensure full employment. But, say the anti-Keynesians, this let the tiger out of the cage: it took 100 years to get him in and the Keynesians let him out in a decade. Released from the nearly century-old constraint of balancing the budget, the central authorities went on a series of wild spending sprees. Inflationary gaps, deflationary gaps, or full employment notwithstanding, governments spent

[1] Lack of confidence in the government's ability to pay interest on the debt and to repay the principal on time should not be confused with an unwillingness to take up new debt at too low a money rate of interest in the face of inflationary expectations. Few investors would be willing, for example, to buy new government bonds yielding an 8 per cent nominal interest rate if they expected a 16 per cent annual rate of inflation. The inability to sell bonds on these terms has nothing to do with investors' confidence in the government's ability to meet its contractual obligations. The problem is rather that investors would not wish to make a perfectly safe loan to anyone on such unfavourable terms.

and spent and spent. Deficits accumulated, the national debt rose, and inflation became the rule of the day. Inflation robbed the people of the real value of their savings by lowering the purchasing power of money saved. In the end the inflations even defeated the full-employment goal: when governments were finally forced to accept the need to reduce inflation, they imposed massive deflationary gaps in order to reduce the inflations that had developed an inertia of their own.[1] Today we see the legacy of these disastrous policies: the simultaneous occurrence of high inflation, high unemployment rates and large budget deficits.

> **According to fiscal conservatism the long, hard struggle to enforce a balanced-budget policy on the state was a victory for the common people against the forces of central-authority prodigality. Then, when Keynes swept the balanced-budget doctrine away, he released the selfish forces that would lead the central authorities back into a position of chronic deficit. This caused a chronic inflationary gap which inflicted suffering and misery on all those who could not protect themselves against the ensuing inflation.**

Here is an issue in political economy that is very important for our views on the functioning of the modern state. The interested student will want to pursue this matter further.[2]

---

[1] The nature of the inertia to which this view appeals is the expectations theory of inflation that is outlined in Part 11.

[2] The pro-Keynesian view can be found in almost any modern textbook on macroeconomics. The view of the fiscal conservatives is well expounded in J.M. Buchanan, J. Burton, and R.E. Wayne, *The Consequences of Mr. Keynes* (Institute of Economic Affairs, London, 1978).

Part eight

The importance of money in the circular flow

39

The nature and history of money

Just about everyone understands the importance of money to his or her own welfare. Many of us believe that money is one of the most important things in life and that we can never have enough of it. But all that money provides is a command over goods, and increasing the world's money supply would not change the quantity of goods available. What, then, is the significance of money to the economy as a whole, and why are economists concerned about it? Indeed, what is money, and how did it come to play its present role?

The importance of money

The real and money parts of the economy

In eighteenth- and nineteenth-century economic theories the economy was thought of as conceptually divisible into a 'real part' and a 'monetary part'. The allocation of resources was determined in the real part of the economy by the forces of demand and supply. This allocation depended on the structure of *relative* prices. Whether or not much beef was produced relative to pork depended on the relation between the prices of the two commodities. If the price of beef was higher than the price of pork and both commodities cost about the same to produce, the incentive would be to produce beef rather than pork. This argument depends on the relationship between the real prices of the two commodities, not on the money price of each. At 50p a pound for pork and £1·50 for beef, the *relative* incentive will be the same as it would be at £1 for pork and £3 for beef.

According to the early economists, the price *level* was determined in the monetary part of the economy. An increase in the money supply led to an increase in the money prices of all transactions. In the example above, an increase in the total money available might raise the price of pork from 50p to £1 a pound and the price of beef from £1·50 to £3, but in equilibrium it would leave relative prices unchanged and hence would have no effect on the real part of the economy, that is, on the amount of resources allocated to beef and to pork production. If the quantity of money were doubled, the prices of everything bought would double, but money income would also double, and everyone earning income would be made no better or worse off by the change. Thus, in equilibrium, the real and monetary parts of the economy have no effect on each other.

Because early economists believed that the most important questions – How much does the economy produce? What share of it does each group in the society get? – were answered in the real sector, they spoke of money as a 'veil' behind which occurred the real events that affected material well-being. The doctrine that the quantity of money influences the level of money prices but has no effect on the real part of the economy is referred to as the doctrine of the NEUTRALITY OF MONEY.

Modern economists still accept the insights of the early economists that relative prices are a major determinant of the real allocation of resources and that the quantity of money has a lot to do with determining the absolute level of prices. Our next task in this chapter is to look at the experience of price level changes – one aspect of the importance of money. Following that, we look at the nature of money itself.

The experience of price level changes

Figure 39.1 shows a remarkable price-level series calculated some time ago by Professor Henry Phelps-Brown of the London School of Economics. It is an index of prices of the basic items in a worker's budget of food, clothing and fuel. It pertains to southern England and extends from 1275 to 1959! The trend line shows that the average change in prices over the whole period was 0·5 per cent per year. The shaded areas indicate periods of major, unreversed inflation. The series also shows that the perspective of one century can be misleading in the broader view because long periods of stable or greatly falling prices tended to alternate with long periods of rising prices. Figure 39.2 shows the experience of the twentieth century in more detail. The inflation rate here is measured by the retail price index, which is more broadly based than Professor Phelps-Brown's index, reflecting the prices of the main items on which a typical worker spends his income today.

Table 39.1 shows some international comparisons of inflation rates. The UK ranked in the middle, with the tenth highest rate of inflation of the twenty-one countries in the 1960s, but had the sixth highest rate in the period 1970–7.

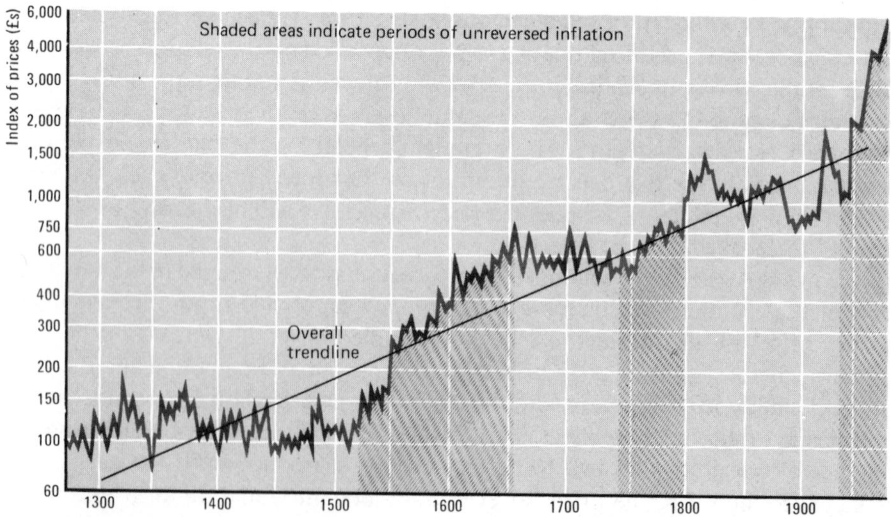

Fig. 39.1 Price index of consumables in southern England 1275–1970 (1451 – 75 = 100). The cost-of-living index has been used to extend the series beyond 1959. Source: *Lloyds Bank Review*, No. 58, October 1960

Table 39.1 Inflation rates of selected countries 1960–70 and 1970–7

	Average annual rate of increase of consumer prices			
	1960–70	Rank	1970–7	Rank
Argentina	19·2	2	139·9	2
Canada	2·7	16	7.5	19
Chile	24·1	1	233·4	1
China (Nationalist)	3·3	14	11·8	10
Denmark	5·7	6	9·6	15
Ecuador	4·2	9	13·1	7
France	4·0	10	9·0	16
India	6·2	5	8·6	17
Iran	1·7	21	12·3	9
Italy	3·9	13	13·0	8
Japan	5·7	6	11·0	12
Mexico	2·7	16	14·8	4
Netherlands	4·0	10	8·4	18
Norway	4·4	8	10·1	13
South Korea	12·3	3	14·8	4
Switzerland	3·3	14	10·1	13
Syria	1·9	20	11·5	11
United Kingdom	4·0	10	14·1	6
United States	2·7	16	6·6	20
West Germany	2·6	19	5·6	21
Yugoslavia	11·7	4	17·7	3

Source: Calculated from IMF *International Financial Statistics*, various issues.

Why inflations and deflations matter

Economists have devoted much effort in recent times to identifying and measuring the consequences of inflation. Even the early economists, with their strict division between the real and monetary sectors, were strongly opposed to rapid inflations or deflations because of the harm that could be done during the transition from one price level to another. Indeed, it may take years to move from one equilibrium price level to another, and in the course of the movement many people may be hurt. The consequences of an inflation depend significantly on whether or not it is anticipated.

The effects of unanticipated inflations Unanticipated inflations cause more upset

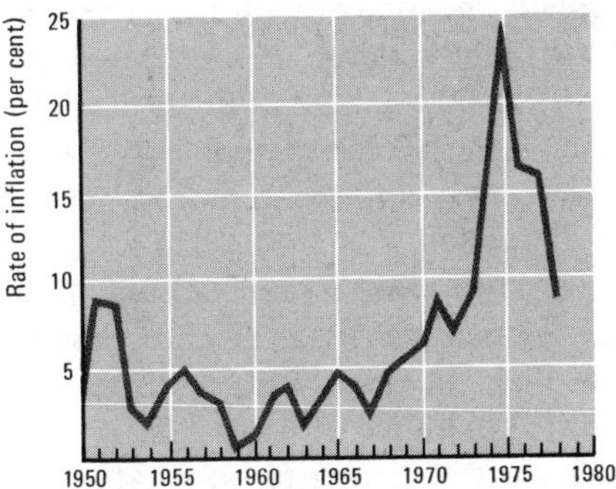

Fig. 39.2 The annual rate of UK retail price inflation, 1950–78. Sources: CSO, *Economic Trends*, annual supplement, 1977; IMF, *International Financial Statistics*, October 1978.

than do anticipated inflations. Contracts freely entered into when the price level was expected to remain constant yield hardships for some and unexpected gains for others when an unanticipated inflation occurs.

A continuing inflation will influence the allocation of resources by changing *relative* prices (including *relative* wages), often in haphazard fashion. In a market economy, changes in relative prices are supposed to signal resource shifts in response to changing patterns of demand and supply. In an inflationary period other influences may also play a major (and potentially distorting) role. For example, members of strong unions will be able to keep their wages rising as fast as prices; they may even be able to do better than they would have done if prices had never risen. In other occupations, wages and salaries may adjust very slowly and people in these occupations may lose substantially because of the inflation. Schoolteachers often find themselves in this group. Not only do such individuals suffer, but the changes in relative wages will affect the allocation of resources. Suppose, for example, that the fall in the real income of teachers relative to that of plumbers reduces the supply of new entrants into the teaching profession below what it would have been in the absence of inflation. This is a real effect, and an adverse one, unless there is a surplus of teachers and a shortage of plumbers.

A second effect of unanticipated inflations is to redistribute wealth from lenders to borrowers, whereas unanticipated deflations do the opposite. To see why this is true, suppose that Mr Jones lends Mr Smith £100 at 5 per cent interest for one year. If the price level rises by 10 per cent over the year, Jones has actually earned a negative rate of interest on the loan. The £105 Jones gets back from Smith can buy fewer goods than the £100 Jones originally parted with. As well as doing without the money for a year, Jones is worse off in terms of puchasing power at the end of the year than at the beginning. Jones's loss, however, is Smith's gain. Smith did not even have to use the £100 in any productive business enterprise to show a gain. All he needed to do was to buy and hold goods while their prices rose merely by the average rate of inflation. At the end of the year, Smith can sell these for £110, pay back the £100 he borrowed plus £5 interest, and show a gain of £5. This sort of redistribution occurs not just on borrowing and lending contracts, but on all contracts that are stated in terms of monetary units.

A third effect of inflation, whether anticipated or unanticipated, is to reduce the living standards of those on fixed incomes. Consider the case of Mr and Mrs McLaughlan who have invested their personal savings in an annuity designed to provide them with a fixed annual income after retirement. The McLaughlans saved enough throughout their working lives to provide themselves with an income of £3,000 a year on retirement; they figured that with the children no longer at home and with their durable goods already purchased, £3,000 would provide them with a good standard of living for their retirement years. If the price level doubles just after the McLaughlans retire, however, the purchasing power of their money income will be halved. They will still get £3,000 a year, but it will now buy only half as many goods as they have expected it to buy. Furthermore, if after the McLaughlan's retirement the price level continues to rise at 6 per cent per year, which is slow by recent British standards, they will have to cut their real purchases of goods and services by a steady 6 per cent each year. If they should live for twelve years after retirement, their living standard will have been cut to one quarter of what it was when they retired. By that time they will be able to buy only as many goods per year as if the price level had never changed and they had saved only enough to provide themselves with an income of £750 a year. Instead of realizing their expectations of a modest but satisfactory living standard, the McLaughlan's will have been made progressively worse off, until finally they are reduced to poverty.

This may sound extreme, but it has been the experience of those British who saved during the 1920s and 1930s and found themselves living on fixed money incomes through the rapid inflation of the 1940s and the creeping inflations of the 1950s and 1960s. Similar reductions hit those unlucky enough to be living on fixed money incomes during the rapid inflation of the 1970s. The fall in the purchasing power of money savings is one of the most dramatic and most obvious effects of an inflation, and it helps to explain the hostility to inflation felt by anyone who has suffered seriously from it.

The effects of anticipated inflations To the extent that inflations are anticipated, some of their haphazard effects can be avoided by drawing up contracts in real terms or with 'indexed features' that build changes in average price levels into specific wage and price contracts. Such contracts are common in labour agreements, in long-term raw material contracts and in many government purchasing agreements. Even without a formal contract in real terms it is possible to allow for the effects of an inflation if the inflation is foreseen. Wage and price contracts are major examples: if, say, a 10 per cent inflation is expected over the next year, a money wage that rises by 10 per cent over that period may represent the minimum demand of a union intent on at least preserving the purchasing power of its members. A bank will demand 13 per cent interest for the use of money if 3 per cent is the real rate of interest and 10 per cent is the anticipated rate of inflation. While some people, such as old-age pensioners, may not be able to avoid the effects of inflation even if they see it coming, most people usually can.

Even a fully foreseen inflation has some real effects. This is because many practices – such as business accounting conventions, definitions of allowable expenses given in tax laws and many private pension schemes – make use of money definitions that cannot be altered. In addition, not everyone can adjust to an anticipated inflation without incurring substantial transactions costs – for example, paying commissions for buying and selling the property that is to be held as a hedge against inflation. These transactions costs may be prohibitive for those with relatively small amounts to protect.

Does everyone lose by inflations? Contrary to popular opinion, inflation does not generally make everyone, or even the vast majority of people, worse off. This is because inflation does not normally have major effects on the economy's total output. The popular concept of the average person becoming slowly impoverished as money prices rise steadily faster than his or her money income is mistaken. The effects of inflation are in sharp contrast to those of a serious recession, which will typically lower average living standards because many of the country's resources – its labour, its factories and its raw materials – lie idle.

> **The main effects of inflation, whether foreseen or unforeseen, are to redistribute income: contracts stated in money terms do not have the effects in terms of real purchasing power that were expected of them. Since contracts are two-sided, one person's losses are another's gains.**

Thus, *typical* households and firms are wrong when they say that inflation is pricing everything out of their reach.[1] When income-earning households and firms say that inflation is ruining them, what they are probably thinking is how much better off they would be if they had this year's money income to spend at the prices ruling several years ago. But this is impossible, since there is not that much output available. Few would prefer the prices of, say, ten years ago *and* their money incomes of ten years ago, because real income has been rising, inflation notwithstanding. Of course, some groups are seriously hurt by inflation, but the *average* household and the *average* firm are not, since in most years money incomes rise faster than money prices.

This is an example of what the classical economist meant by the 'veil' of money. It is real output that determines average living standards. The price at which that output is valued and sold has no effect on the average living standard of the population.

In recognizing that the main effects of inflation are redistributional, there is a danger of thinking that inflation is unimportant. This would be a gross error. After all, what causes the distribution of income among the various social classes was *the* major problem faced by the classical economists, and the call for a major redistribution from capitalists to workers was, and still is, an important part of Marxian economics. Rapid inflations often cause major, arbitrary, and socially destructive redistributions. The continual erosion of the purchasing power of fixed money incomes is little short of tragic to those who suffer it, and such erosion is only one of the many serious redistributive effects of inflation.

Inflation has other effects that may also be serious. For example, social and personal tensions arise from the race to keep up with the rise in prices and from the knowledge that some people gain from inflation at the expense of others who lose.

The nature of money

In the previous section we discussed the effects of inflation. Inflation is a monetary phenomenon in the sense that a rise in the general level of prices is the same as a decrease in the purchasing power of money. But what exactly *is* money? There is probably more folklore and general nonsense believed about money than about any other aspect of the economy. In the remainder of this chapter the functions of money will be described and the history of money will be outlined. One purpose of this account is to remove some of these misconceptions.

Traditionally in economics MONEY has been defined as any generally accepted medium of exchange – anything that will be accepted by virtually everyone in exchange for goods and services. In fact money has several different functions: to act as a medium of exchange, as a store of value, and as a unit of account. Different kinds of money vary in the degree of efficiency with which they fulfil these functions, and we shall consider the functions one at a time.

[1] Some things may go nearly out of reach if their *relative* prices rise. For example, the rise in the relative price of prime cuts of beef over the last twenty years (because of rapidly rising demand as real income has risen) certainly has been dramatic. This, however, has not been due, as is often alleged, to inflation, but rather to a change in relative prices. Even if the overall price level had remained constant, prime cuts of beef would have risen in price, and households would have found it just as expensive to buy a steak *relative to their overall budget* as they do in today's inflationary world. The general point that is illustrated here is that inflation may go on at the same time as, and have its effects combined with, other changes that do reduce living standards, such as increases in the real cost of producing food stuffs and unfavourable movements in the international terms of trade (defined on page 635).

A medium of exchange

Without money, our complicated economic system based on specialization and the division of labour would be impossible and we would have to return to a very primitive form of production and exchange. It is not without justification that money has been called one of the great inventions contributing to human freedom.

If there were no money, goods would have to be exchanged by *barter*, one thing being swapped directly for another. This is a cumbersome system in which every transaction requires a *double coincidence of wants*. If I have a donkey to trade, for example, I must search not only for someone who wants a donkey, but for someone who wants a donkey *and* has something that I would like to acquire. Furthermore, there is no way to give change on the transaction. If I find someone to trade with and we decide that a donkey is worth nine chickens, then we are in trouble if he has only six chickens: I can hardly give him two-thirds of my donkey. Thus, goods that are not readily divisible make poor subjects for barter transactions.

If we were restricted to barter, therefore, we would have to spend a great deal of time searching for satisfactory transactions. We would also have to be prepared to produce most of the things we need ourselves Otherwise we could not be certain of obtaining all of our necessities. The use of money as a medium of exchange removes these problems, as long as the money is readily accepted by everyone. If I wish to trade my donkey, then all I need to do is to find someone who wants a donkey. I hand over my animal and take money in return; it matters not that the individual who takes my donkey has no goods that I require. I now take my money and search for someone who has chickens that he wishes to trade. When I find him, I hand over my money and take his chickens; it does not matter that he had no use for a donkey.

The difficulties of barter restrict the degree to which people can specialize in the production of a single commodity. The use of money as a medium of exchange permits specialization. With specialization in the direction of each person's natural talents and abilities, there comes a great increase in the production of all commodities. To serve as an efficient medium of exchange, money must have a number of characteristics: it must be readily acceptable; it must have a high value for its weight, for it would otherwise be a nuisance to carry around; it must be divisible, for money that comes only in large denominations is useless for transactions having only a small value; and it must not be readily counterfeitable, for if money can be easily duplicated by individuals, it will lose its value.

A store of value

Money is a handy way to store purchasing power. In barter, you must take some other good in exchange immediately; with money, you can sell goods today and store the money until you need it. This means that you have a claim on someone else's goods that you can exercise at some further date. Separating the two sides of the barter transaction confers an obvious increase in freedom. To be a satisfactory store of purchasing power, however, money must have a stable value. If prices are stable, one knows how much command over real goods and services has been stored up when a certain sum of money has been accumulated. If prices change rapidly, then one has little idea how many goods an accumulated sum of money will be able to command. Clearly, rapid fluctuation of the general level of prices reduces the usefulness of money as a store of value.

Money can serve as a perfectly satisfactory store of accumulated purchasing power for individuals, but not for the society as a whole. If a single individual stores up money, he will, when he comes to spend it, be able to command the current output of some other individual. The whole society cannot do this. If everyone saved their money and all simultaneously retired to live on their savings, there would be no current production to purchase and consume. The society's ability to satisfy wants depends on goods and services being available; if want-satisfying capacity is to be stored up for the *whole society*, then goods that are currently produced must be left unconsumed and carried over to future periods.

A unit of account

Money may also be used purely for accounting purposes, without having any real physical existence of its own. For instance, a government store in a Communist society might say that everyone had so many 'dollars' at his or her disposal each month. Goods could then be given prices and each consumer's purchases recorded, the consumer being allowed to buy all he or she wanted until the supply of 'dollars' was exhausted. The money would have no existence other than as entries in the store's books, but it would be serving as a perfectly satisfactory unit of account (although it could serve as a medium of exchange between individuals only if the store agreed to transfer credits from one customer to another at the customers' request).[1]

The origins of money

The origins of money are lost in antiquity. Most primitive tribes known today make use of some form of it; and its ability to free people from the cumbersome necessity of barter is a powerful incentive to do so.

Metallic money

All sorts of things have been used as money at one time or another, but precious metals must have gained ascendancy early as the most satisfactory media. They were in heavy and permanent demand for ornament and decoration, and they were in continous supply (since they do not easily wear out). Thus they tended to have a high and stable value. They were easily recognized and generally known to be commodities which, because of their stable price, would be accepted by most people. They were also divisible into extremely small units (gold, to a single grain, for example).

Precious metals thus came to circulate as money and to be used in many transactions. But it was still awkward carrying them about in bulk. When a purchase was to be made, the requisite quantity would have to be weighed out carefully on a scale. A sack of gold and a highly sensitive set of scales were thus the common equipment of the merchant and trader. This system, although workable and better than barter, was still rather cumbersome. 'Princes', to use Machiavelli's

[1] A fourth function of money is sometimes distinguished: that of a standard of deferred payments. Payments that are to be made in the future, on account of debts etc., are reckoned in money terms. Money is then being used as a unit of account with an added dimension in time, for the account is not settled until some time in the future.

term for rulers, perceiving the inconvenience suffered by traders and merchants, decided to do the weighing for once and for all. They took a fixed quantity of precious metal for value, mixed it with some base metal for durability, and minted the mixture into a coin. An imprint of the Prince's own seal was affixed, guaranteeing the coin's content of precious metal. Thus, for example, if a certain coin was stated to contain exactly $\frac{1}{16}$ of an ounce of gold and a commodity was priced at $\frac{1}{8}$ of an ounce of gold, two coins could simply be handed over as payment. This was clearly a great convenience, as long as traders knew that they could accept a coin at its 'face value'.

Abuse of metallic money The prince's subjects, however, could not let a good opportunity pass, and soon someone had the idea of clipping a thin slice off the edge of the coin. If the subject collected a coin stamped as containing half an ounce of gold, he could clip a slice off the edge and pass the coin off as still containing half an ounce. ('Doesn't the stamp prove it?' he would argue.) If he were successful, he would have made a profit equal to the market value of the clipped metal. If this practice became common, even the most myopic of traders would notice that things weren't what they used to be in the coinage world. Mistrust would grow, and it would once again be necessary to weigh each coin. Back would come the scales and most of the usefulness of the coins would be lost. To get around this problem, the prince began to mint his coins with a rough edge, which made it obvious if a coin had been clipped. The rough edge still survives on some coins today as an interesting anachronism reminding us of times when the market value of the metal in a coin was equal to its face value, the coin itself being nothing more than a guaranteed amount of precious metal.

The subjects, when presented with an opportunity of getting something for nothing, were ingenious enough to surmount even the obstacle of the rough edge. They invented the practice of *sweating* which meant placing a large number of coins in a bag and shaking it vigorously. The dust that flaked off the coins was their reward. This practice seems never to have been as disruptive to the money system as clipping was, possibly because it was difficult to remove very much metal without defacing the coin, but possibly also because the disruption was eclipsed by the effects of the Prince's own periodic debasement of the coinage.

Debasement of metallic money Not to be outdone by the cunning of his subjects, the Prince himself was quick to seize the chance of getting something for nothing. As the maker of the coins, he was in a very good position to work a *really* profitable fraud. When he found himself with accounts that he could neither settle nor repudiate, he used a suitable occasion – a marriage, an anniversary, an alliance – as an excuse to re-mint the coinage. The subjects would bring their coins to the mint, where they would be melted down and coined afresh with a new stamp. The subjects could then go away the proud possessors of one new coin for every old coin that they had brought in. Between the melting down and the re-coining, however, the prince had only to toss some inexpensive base metal into the works to earn himself a handsome profit. If the coinage was debased by adding, say, one part base metal to every four parts of melted down coins, then five new coins could be made for every four turned in. The prince could return one new coin for every old coin brought in by a subject but for every four coins brought in, the prince could have one left over for himself as profit. With these coins, he could pay his bills.

The result would be an inflation. The subjects would have the same number of coins as before and hence could demand the same number of goods. Once the prince paid his bills, however, his creditors could be expected to spend some or all of the extra coins. The extra demand would bid up prices. Debasing of coinage thus led pretty certainly to a rise in prices. (Early economists, observing these processes in action, propounded the *quantity theory of money*. They argued that there was a relation between the average level of prices and the quantity of money in circulation, such that a change in the quantity of money would lead to a change in the price level in the same direction. We shall have more to say about this theory in Chapter 41.)

Gresham's law The early experience of currency debasement leads to a famous economic 'law' that still has many applications even today. The hypothesis that has come to be known as GRESHAM'S LAW, after the financial expert who first explained its workings to Queen Elizabeth the First, is that 'bad money drives out good'.

Assume that the currency has been seriously debased so that there are gold soverigns in circulation containing only half their alleged gold content. Assume that the ruler, wanting to make trade more secure, decides to improve the coinage by minting new sovereigns with the correct gold content and feeding them into circulation hoping eventually to replace the entire stock of debased sovereigns. What will happen is that the new sovereigns will disappear as fast as they are minted and the debased sovereigns will remain the only coinage in circulation. The bad money will have driven out the good. Why? The answer lies in the fact that the two kinds of sovereigns have the same face values but one has twice the precious metal content as the other. Anyone who has both kinds will pay his bills with the debased coins and melt down the new ones, gaining enough metal to make two debased sovereigns.

Gresham's law is as valid today as it was when it was first propounded nearly four hundred years ago. A modern example concerns metallic coins in high-inflation countries over the last few decades. Ten or twenty years ago coins were typically made of copper, nickel and even silver, which had a significant market value but one that was less than the face value of the coins. There might, for example, have been 2 pesetas worth of metal in a 10 peseta coin. Governments then printed vast amounts of paper money, and prices of everything, including the metal in the coins, rose. In the example just given, anything over a fivefold rise in prices would make the value of the metal in a coin worth more than the face value of the coin. As soon as this happened paper money became 'bad money' and coins 'good money' in Gresham's sense of the terms. The coins were melted down and the metal sold, yielding more than the face value of the coins. In country after country where inflation rates were really high, the traditional metal coins disappeared when they became 'good money' The coinage then had to be replaced using metals that were very much cheaper and hence worth much less than the face value of the coins that contained them. This is why in most high-inflation countries the coins are made of very light, low-cost alloys rather than the tradition metals of silver, nickel and copper.

As a specific, more selective example of the same phenomenon you will never find a Canadian 10 cent piece of an earlier date than 1967. Coins minted before that date had a silver content that long ago rose in value to over 10c. As soon as that happened the 'good' coins disappeared from circulation almost overnight.

Paper money

The next important step in the history of money was the evolution of paper currency. Goldsmiths – craftsmen who worked with gold – naturally kept very secure safes in which to store their supplies.[1] The practice grew up among the public of storing their gold with a goldsmith for safe keeping. The goldsmith would give a depositor a receipt for the gold, promising to hand it over on demand. If the depositor wished to make a large purchase, he could go to the goldsmith, reclaim his gold, and hand it over to the seller of the goods. Chances were that the seller would not require the gold, but would carry it back to the goldsmith for safe keeping. Clearly, if people knew the goldsmith to be reliable, there was no need to go through the cumbersome and risky business of physically transferring the gold. The buyer need only transfer the goldsmith's receipt to the seller, who could accept it secure in the knowledge that the goldsmith would pay over the gold whenever it was needed. If the seller wished to buy a good from a third party who also knew the goldsmith to be reliable, this transaction too could be effected by passing along the goldsmith's receipt. The convenience of using these bits of paper instead of gold is obvious. Thus, the first paper money represented a promise to pay on demand so much gold.

Eventually the goldsmiths were replaced by bankers. As long as these institutions were known to be reliable, such pieces of paper would be 'as good as gold'. The paper money was *backed* by precious metal and was *convertible* on demand into this metal.

In the nineteenth century, paper money was commonly issued by banks; in Britain the commercial banks issued their own notes, backed by their own reserves. Also, the Bank of England issued notes backed by the country's gold reserves, for, although it was nominally a private institution until 1947, the Bank always had close links with the government. Since these notes were convertible on demand into gold, the country was said to be on a *gold standard.*

Fractionally backed notes For most transactions, individuals were content to use paper currency. This made it unnecessary, therefore, to keep an ounce of gold in the vaults for every claim to an ounce circulating as paper money. It *was* necessary to keep *some* gold on hand, because for some transations paper would not do. If an individual wished to make a purchase from a distant place where his local bank was not known, he might have to convert his paper into gold and ship the gold. Further, if he was going to save up money for use in the distant future, he might not have perfect confidence in the bank's ability to honour its pledge to redeem the notes in gold at that time. His alternative was to exchange his notes for gold and store the gold himself until he needed it. For these and other reasons, some holders of notes would be demanding gold. On the other hand, some of the bank's customers would be receiving gold in various transactions and wanting to store it in the bank. They would accept promises to pay (i.e. bank notes) in return. At any one time, therefore, some of the bank's customers would be withdrawing gold, others would be depositing it, and the great majority would be carrying out their transactions using only the bank's paper notes. Thus the bank would be able to issue more money redeemable in gold than it actually had gold in its vaults. This was a profitable thing

[1] All the basic ideas about paper money can be displayed by concentrating on the goldsmiths, although there were earlier sources of paper money in various negotiable evidences of debt.

to do, because the bank could use the money either to purchase securities that yield a return, or to make interest-earning loans to households and firms.

This discovery was made early on by the goldsmiths and down to the present day, banks have had many more claims outstanding against them than they actually had gold available. In such a situation, we say that the currency is *fractionally backed* by gold. A rough rule of thumb is that a 10 per cent backing for these claims is more than sufficient: if a bank holds £10,000 worth of gold and has issued £100,000 in notes, it will be perfectly safe in normal times and will be able to convert into gold all of its notes that are presented for conversion.

The major problem of a fractionally backed currency is maintaining its *convertibility* into the precious metal with which it is backed. In the past, the imprudent bank that issued too much paper money found itself unable to redeem its currency in gold when the demand for gold was even slightly higher than usual. This bank would then have to suspend payments, and all holders of its notes would suddenly find them worthless. The prudent bank, which kept a reasonable relation between its note issue and its gold reserve, found that it could meet the normal everyday demand for gold without any trouble. It was always the case with fractionally backed currency, however, that, if all note-holders demanded gold at once, they could not be satisfied. Thus, if ever the public lost confidence and, *en masse*, demanded redemption of their currency, the banks would be unable to honour their pledges, and the holders of their notes would lose everything. The history of nineteenth- and early twentieth-century banking on both sides of the Atlantic is replete with examples of banks ruined by momentary runs on their reserves. Future social historians may wonder how, in the face of such a system, early economists could have believed that free-market capitalism showed the work of the hidden hand of perfection guiding the economic affairs of mankind.

The development of flat currencies As time went on, note issue by commercial banks became less common, and central banks took over a steadily increasing share of this responsibility. The paper currency was, as it always had been, freely convertible into gold. It was also only fractionally backed by gold. The commercial banks retained the power to create money, but this was no longer done by printing paper money; instead, deposit money was created.

During the period between the two World Wars, virtually all the countries of the world abandoned the gold standard. (The reasons for this cannot be gone into in detail here, but will be mentioned briefly in Chapter 45.) The result of abandoning the gold standard was that currency was no longer convertible into gold.

Central banks The central bank was itself a natural outcome of the whole system. Where were the private banks to keep their cash reserves? Their own vaults, although safer than those of their customers, were not safe against a really determined attempt at robbery. Where were the commercial banks to turn if they had made good loans and investments that would mature in the future, but were in temporary need of reserves to meet an exceptional demand to withdraw gold by their depositors? If banks provided loans to the public against reasonable security, why should not some other institution provide loans to *them* against the same sort of security? CENTRAL BANKS evolved in response to these and other needs. At first they were private profit-making institutions, providing services to ordinary banks, but their potential to influence the behaviour of commercial banks and through them that of the whole economy led them to develop close ties with central governments. In Europe, these ties eventually became formalized as central banks were taken over by governments. The Bank of England was nationalized in 1947.

Modern money

What is money today is a result of the evolution that we have just discussed. Some countries (including the United States, until 1965) preserve the fiction that their currency is backed by gold, but none allows it to be converted into gold as a right. The past is recalled by the following statement on the British pound note, 'I promise to pay the bearer on demand the sum of One Pound (signed) Chief Cashier, Bank of England'. If anyone takes this seriously today and demands his 'One Pound', he can hand over his one pound note and receive in return a new one pound note! In the days of the gold standard, paper money was valuable because everyone knew it could be converted into gold on demand. Today, paper money is valuable because it is generally accepted. Because, by habit, everyone accepts it as valuable, it *is* valuable; the fact that it can no longer be converted into anything has no effect on its functioning as a medium of exchange.

This fact, that present-day paper money is not convertible into anything – that it is nothing but paper whose value derives from common acceptance through habit – often disturbs students. They feel that money should be more substantial than that; after all, what of the 'prestige of the pound', 'dollar diplomacy' and 'the bed-rock value of the Swiss franc'?.

Once it is accepted that the value of money is based on nothing more than custom, habit and the need for some medium of exchange, the next question that comes to mind is: does it matter? Gold derived its value because it was scarce relative to the heavy demand for it (the demand being derived from its monetary and its non-monetary uses). Tying a currency to gold meant that the quantity of money in a country was left to such chance occurrences as the discovery of new gold supplies. In early times this was not without advantage, the most important being that it provided a check on the prince's ability to cause inflation. Gold cannot be manufactured at will; paper currency can. There is little doubt that, if the money supply had been purely paper, many governments would have succumbed to the temptation to pay their bills by printing new money rather than by raising taxes. Such increases in the money supply would have led to inflation in just the same way as did the debasement of metallic currency. Thus, the gold standard provided some check on inflation by making it difficult for the government to change the money supply. Periods of major gold discoveries, however, brought about inflations of their own. In the sixteenth century, Spanish gold and silver flowed into Europe from the New World, bringing inflation in their wake. On the other hand, it is usually desirable to increase the money supply in a period of rising trade and income. On a gold standard, this cannot be done – unless, by pure chance, gold is discovered at the same time. The gold standard took discretionary powers about the money supply out of the hands of the central authorities. Whether or not one thought that this was a good thing depended on how one thought the central authorities would use this discretion. In general, a gold standard is probably better than having the currency managed by an ignorant or irresponsible government, but worse than having the currency supply adjusted by a well-informed, intelligent one. Better and worse in this context are judged by the criterion of having a money supply that varies adequately with the needs of the economy, but does not vary so as to cause violent inflations or deflations.

Deposit money

In most countries today, the money supply consists of notes and coins issued by the government and the central bank, and deposit money. The inconvertible monies that we have already discussed are notes and coins. DEPOSIT MONEY is money that is *created* by the commercial banking system. *When the individual banks lost the right to issue notes of their own, the form of money creation changed but the substance did not.* Today, banks have money in their vaults (or on deposit with the central banks) just as they always did, only the money is no longer gold; it is the legal tender of the times, paper money. Banks' customers sometimes deposit paper money with the banks for safe keeping just as, in former times, they deposited gold. The bank takes the money and gives the customer a promise to pay it back on demand. Instead of taking the form of a printed bank note, as in the past, this promise to pay is recorded as an entry on the customer's account. If the customer wishes to pay a bill, he may come to the bank and claim his money in pound notes; he may then pay the money over to another person, and this person may redeposit the money in a bank. Just as with the gold transfers, this is a cumbersome procedure, particularly for large payments, and it would be much more convenient if the bank's promise to pay cash could merely be transferred from one person to another. This is done by means of a *cheque*. If individual *A* deposits £100 in a bank, the entry of a £100 credit in his account is the bank's promise to pay £100 cash on demand. If *A* pays *B* £100 by giving him a cheque that *B* then deposits in the same bank, the bank merely reduces *A*'s deposit by £100 and increases *B*'s by the same amount. Thus the bank still promises to pay out on demand the £100 originally deposited, but it now promises to pay it to *B* rather than to *A*. If *B* now pays *C* £100 by cheque and *C* deposits the cheque, then the promise to pay (i.e., the credit entry in someone's account at the bank) will be transferred from *B* to *C*.

Banks can create money by issuing more promises to pay than they actually have cash to pay out. Banks can grant loans by crediting customers' accounts with the amounts of the loans. If borrowers use their loans to pay accounts by cheque, then deposits are transferred from person to person. In most circumstances, any one bank can have liabilities greatly in excess of the amount of cash that it has in reserve. These deposits can be used to buy goods and services through the medium of cheques. Since they are generally accepted means of exchange, that can be transferred among persons by the medium of cheques, bank deposits are money. The great majority of transactions (by value) take place by cheque; only a small proportion involve notes and coins. Thus, in the modern world the greater proportion of the money supply is the deposit money that is created by commercial banks. The banks can, if they wish, contract the money supply by not creating deposits, or they can expand it by creating deposits up to the limit of prudence or law (so that there is just enough cash to meet either the normal demands of customers who do not wish to pay by cheque or the requirements set by law). It is, of course, in the banks' interest to expand deposits up to the limit of safety, because every pound created can be used to grant a loan, to purchase a bond, or to acquire some other asset that pays a return to the bank.

Today, just as in the past, banks can create money by issuing more promises to pay (deposits) than they have money available to pay out.

Sight deposits and time deposits If a customer has a deposit in a bank, he can keep it in one of two forms: as a sight or demand deposit (current account), or in a time deposit (savings or deposit account). The distinction between the two is commonly made through much of the world, although the terms applied to them vary.

The two main characteristics of a SIGHT DEPOSIT or a DEMAND DEPOSIT, as it is variously called, are that the owner can withdraw his or her money on demand, and that the bank agrees to transfer demand deposits from one person to another when ordered to do so by the writing of a cheque. The first characteristic makes the demand deposit a satisfactory store of value, since the holder of a demand deposit can withdraw cash from the account without having to give any prior notice. The second characteristic helps to make the demand deposit a medium of exchange.

TIME DEPOSITS or DEPOSIT ACCOUNTS differ in both of these essential features. The owner of a time deposit must legally give notice (possibly as much as 30 or 60 days) of his intention to withdraw his or her money. Although banks often do not enforce this law, they could do so at any time if they wished. Furthermore, holders of deposit accounts cannot pay their bills by writing cheques ordering their banks to pay their creditors out of their deposits. Banks always pay a higher rate of interest on time deposits than on sight deposits. (Sight deposits frequently, although not invariably, carry a zero interest rate.)

Over the last 10 years banks have created a number of new deposit instruments. The most important of these is the CERTIFICATE OF DEPOSIT (CD). With a CD money is genuinely tied up for a period of time ranging from a month to several years and it earns a higher rate of interest than when deposited into a saving account where in effect the money can be withdrawn at any time. Some CDs are negotiable, others are not.

Evolution of monetary instruments

Over the past two centuries what has been accepted by the public as money has expanded from gold and silver coins to include, first, bank notes and then bank deposits subject to transfer by cheque. Until recently, most economists would have agreed that money stopped at that point. No such agreement exists today, and an important debate centres around a definition of money appropriate to the present world.

If we concentrate only on the medium-of-exchange function of money, there is little doubt about what is money in most countries today. It consists of notes, coins, and deposits subject to transfer by cheque or cheque-like instruments such as standing orders to transfer funds from one account to another. No other asset constitutes a generally accepted medium of exchange. The problem of deciding what is money stems from the fact that anything that can fulfil the medium-of-exchange function can also fulfil the store-of-value function, but many things that can fulfil the second do not fulfil the first.

Near money Assets which adequately fulfil the store-of-value function and are readily converted into a medium of exchange but are not themselves a medium of exchange are sometimes called NEAR MONEY.

As long as all sales and purchases do not occur at the same moment, everyone needs a temporary store of value between the act of selling and the act of buying. Whatever serves the function of a medium of exchange can be held and thus can also serve the function of a temporary store of value. But other assets can also be used for this store-of-value function. If, for example, you have a time deposit at a bank or a building society, you know exactly how much purchasing power you hold (at today's prices) and, given modern banking practices, you can turn your deposit into cash or a current account deposit at short notice. Additionally, your time deposit will earn some interest during the period that you hold it. Why then does not everybody keep their money in time deposits instead of in demand deposits or currency? The answer is that the inconvenience of continually shifting money back and forth may outweigh the interest that can be earned. One week's interest on £100 (at 5 per cent per year) is only about 10 pence, not enough to cover bus fare to the bank or the cost of posting a letter. For money that will be needed soon, it would hardly pay to shift it to a time deposit.

In general, whether it pays to convert cash or demand deposits into interest-earning time deposits for a given period depends on the inconvenience and other transaction costs of shifting funds in and out and on the amount of interest that can be earned.

There is a wide spectrum of assets in the economy that yield an interest return and also serve as reasonably satisfactory temporary stores of value. The difference between these other assets and time deposits is that their capital values are not quite as certain as are those of time deposits. If I elect to store my purchasing power in the form of some financial asset that matures in 30 days, its price on the market may change between the time I buy it and the time I want to sell it – say 10 days later. If the price changes, I will suffer or enjoy a change in the purchasing power available to me. But because of the short horizon to maturity, the price will not change very much. (After all, the government will pay its face value in a few weeks.) Such a security is, thus, a reasonably satisfactory short-run store of purchasing power. Indeed, any readily saleable capital asset whose value does not fluctuate significantly with the rate of interest will satisfactorily fulfil this short-term, store-of-value function.

There are many near monies in the economy, assets which because of their secure capital value adequately fulfil the store-of-value function but which also yield an interest income. Households and firms will hold money only if the cost and inconvenience of buying near monies outweighs the interest income over the period that purchasing power is to be stored.

Money substitutes Things that serve as a temporary medium of exchange but are not a store of value are sometimes called MONEY SUBSTITUTES. Credit cards are a prime example. With a credit card many transactions can be made without either cash or a cheque. But the evidence of credit, in terms of the credit slip you sign and hand over to the store, is not money because it cannot be used to effect further transactions. Furthermore, when your credit card company sends you a bill you have to use money in (delayed) payment for the original transaction. The credit card serves the short-run function of a medium of exchange by allowing you to make purchases even though you have no cash or bank deposit currently in your possession. But this is only temporary; money remains the final medium of exchange for these transactions when the credit account is settled.

Definitions of money

What is an acceptable medium of exchange has changed and will continue to change over time. Furthermore, new monetary assets are continously being developed to serve some, if not all, of the functions of money, and these are more or less readily covertible into money.

Economists now distinguish at least two concepts of money[1]:

> **M_1, the narrow definition of money, defines money as currency plus sight deposits held by the private sector. M_3, the broader definition of money, defines money as M_1 plus private-sector time deposits with banks and public-sector deposits whether time or sight.**

The first definition concentrates on the medium-of-exchange function. The second definition adds in time deposits with banks, which serve the temporary-store-of-value function and are in practice instantly convertible into a medium of exchange at a known and completely secure price that does not fluctuate with the rate of interest (£1 on deposit in a time account is always convertible into a £1 sight deposit or £1 in cash).

Economists use the terms SUPPLY OF MONEY and MONEY SUPPLY to refer to the total amount of money (defined as either M_1 or M_3), in the economy. It is a relatively easy matter to collect statistics on the total amount of currency in circulation (since the currency is issued by the central bank) and the total of bank deposits (since banks must publish their balance sheets). Thus, we can know with a high degree of accuracy what the money supply is at any moment of time.

The Bank of England has the ultimate legal control over the supply of money in the UK. The supply can also be influenced, as we shall see, by the decisions of the ordinary commercial banks.

It is also very useful to distinguish the nominal from the real money supply. The NOMINAL MONEY SUPPLY is measured in monetary units. The REAL MONEY SUPPLY is measured in purchasing power units and expressed in constant prices ruling in some base year. To obtain the real money supply the nominal money supply is deflated by a price index. For example, the nominal money supply (M_1) was £9,635 million in 1970 and £23,660 million in 1977. The real money supply, measured in 1970 prices, was £9,635 million in 1970 and £9,502 million in 1977. The latter figure is found by dividing the nominal money supply of £23,660 by the index of retail prices for 1977 of 249 (1970 = 100). Thus, although the nominal money supply increased by nearly two-and-a-half fold, the real money supply – the purchasing power of the existing money stock – actually fell slightly over the period in question.

---

[1] The wider definition of money is called M_2 in America and M_3 in Britain. The magnitude referred to as M_2 in Britain is now seldom used.

40

The banking system and the supply of money

Our primary concern in this chapter will be with the determinants of the supply of money. In order to study these, we must look at the nature of the banking system, at the way in which banks create deposit money, and at the way in which attempts are made to regulate the money supply through public policy. The principles involved are the same in all Western countries, although the institutional arrangements through which they operate differ significantly from one country to another.

The most visible units in the banking system are the privately-owned banks that deal with the ordinary public. These banks are variously called COMMERCIAL BANKS, LISTED BANKS or CLEARING BANKS. (The latter term covers most, but not all, of the commercial banks.)

These banks are profit-seeking firms. They accept sight and time deposits (defined on page 587), they transfer sight deposits among their customers and banks when ordered to do so by cheque, they make loans to customers, called ADVANCES, charging them interest in return, and they invest in interest-earning financial assets.

In the United Kingdom commercial banks are called LISTED BANKS. The most important of these are the London clearing banks, which manage payments in England and Wales, and the clearing banks of Scotland and Northern Ireland. The four largest London clearing banks dominate the system in terms of value of deposits held. They have numerous branches throughout the country. For this reason the UK system is called a 'branch banking' system, as opposed to the US system, which is a 'unit' system. In the US, banks are not allowed to have branches in more than one state and in some states there is a limit to the number of branches allowed. This means that the group of American commercial banks is composed of a large number of individual banks (over 15,000 in 1978), each with at most only a few branches.

The second main element of the UK banking system is the DISCOUNT HOUSES. These specialized institutions, which are peculiar to the UK, borrow money at call (i.e., repayable on demand) or at very short notice from banks and other lending institutions. They then use this money to purchase such short-dated financial assets as treasury bills and local authority bills. Since they borrow money that is repayable on demand and lend it out for terms of up to a month or more (as they do when, for example, they buy a treasury bill that has 30 days to run to maturity), they are in the classic exposed position of borrowing short and lending (relatively) long.[1] The advantage to the regular banks of this arrangement is that they can earn interest on their cash reserves. (Loans to the discount houses are repayable at call and hence are as good as cash.)

The third main element of the banking system is the CENTRAL BANK. Almost all advanced countries have central banks, and their functions are similar: to be banker to the government and the commercial banking system, to manage the public debt, to control the money supply and to regulate the country's monetary and credit system. The central bank is always an instrument of the central authorities, whether or not it is owned publicly. The Bank of England is one of the oldest and most famous of the central banks. It began to operate as the central bank of England in the seventeenth century, but was not officially nationalized until 1947. It operates in two self-contained sections, the issue department and the banking department, each of which publishes its own balance sheet. In the US the central bank is the Federal Reserve System, which was organized in 1913.

Most banking systems also have a variety of other specialized institutions. Some of these accept time deposits from the public and lend money out on a longer-term basis. Two British examples are finance houses and building societies. Finance houses make loans to finance hire-purchase acquisitions of durable goods, while building societies grant mortgates for the purchase of real estate. These institutions are often called FINANCIAL INTERMEDIARIES, since they stand between those who save money and those who ultimately borrow it.

How commercial banks create and destroy deposit money

One part of the money supply, deposit money, is under the control of the privately owned commercial banks. We have already seen that the ability of banks to create deposit money depends on the fact that bank deposits need to be only fractionally backed by notes and coin. If all deposits had to be backed 100 per cent, banks would be nothing more than safety deposit vaults for their customers' money. If a customer deposited £100 in a bank, that bank would credit the customer's account with £100 and the £100 cash would go into the bank's vault to 'back' the deposit. Nothing further would happen. Because the bank does not need to keep 100 per cent reserves, however, it can use some of the £100 to purchase income-yielding investments.

To see how banks do create deposit money we shall study a number of hypothetical cases. We start with the simplest case of a system with only one commercial bank and then introduce the complications caused by the existence of many independent banks.

A single monopoly bank

Consider first a country with only one bank (with as many physical branches as is necessary) and assume that someone makes a new deposit of £100 in cash. Table

[1] The discount houses provide a good example of the division of labour. They are specialists in the short-term money market. Institutions that specialize in other forms of loans do not find it worth their while to acquire detailed knowledge of the short-term market. They lend those funds that they can commit only for short terms to the discount houses who, guided by their specialist knowledge, can lend them profitably.

40.1 shows how this transaction will be recorded on the books of the bank. The balance sheet will show new assets of £100 in the form of cash, and new liabilities of £100 in the form of the customer's deposit. This deposit, and all others like it, is a liability of the bank, since the bank owes the money to the customer and must pay it to him whenever he demands it. Since there is only one bank in the country, the bank

Table 40.1 A new deposit of £100 is made

Liabilities		Assets	
Deposit	£100	Cash	£100

can immediately create new deposits by some multiple of £100, depending on the reserve requirements. Let us say that all deposits need to be backed by a 10 per cent cash reserve. The monopoly bank could immediately create further deposits of £900. Assume, by way of example, that the bank loans £500 to a customer and buys £400 worth of bonds in the open market. The bank does this by permitting the borrower to write cheques on his account to the amount of £500, and by writing £400 to the credit of the account of the person who sold bonds to the bank. Table 40.2 shows how these transactions will appear on the bank's books once the

Table 40.2 £900 is invested in loans and bonds with no cash drain

Liabilities		Assets	
Deposits	£1,000	Cash	£100
		Loans	£500
		Bonds	£400

borrower has written cheques to the allowable amount. The bank's assets include the £100 cash of the original deposit, the loan of £500 (it is an asset of the bank, since the borrower owes this money to the bank and must repay it at some stated date), and the £400 of bonds (these are an asset, since they can be sold again for cash). The bank's liabilities are now £1,000 in deposits: £100 to the account of the original depositor, £500 to the account of the persons who have received payment from the customer who borrowed from the bank, and £400 to the account of the person who sold the bonds to the bank. Note that by a few strokes of the pen the bank has created £900 in deposit money. The customers of the bank are now able to spend £900 more than they could yesterday, and no one else is forced to spend any less.

The persons who borrowed the money and sold the bonds can be expected to spend their money. In most cases, they will do so by writing cheques. If all the bank's customers are content to hold their money in deposit accounts and to make their payments by cheque, no cash ever leaves the bank, and the bank can effect payments from one person to another merely by debiting and crediting the accounts of individual customers. The total of the bank's deposit liabilities need not change in the process.

Many banks, a single new deposit

The whole system is somewhat more complicated when there are many banks. If a depositor in Bank *A* writes a cheque to someone whose account is with Bank *B*, then a mere book transfer will not do, because Bank *A* now owes money to Bank *B*. By writing the cheque, the depositor in Bank *A* is saying, 'I claim the money owed me and ask that it be passed over to the person indicated on the cheque'. When the recipient of the cheque deposits it in Bank *B*, he is saying, 'I want my money held for me by Bank *B*'; thus Bank *A* must pay the money over to Bank *B*. It is exactly the same as if one individual withdrew cash from Bank *A* and gave it to the second individual, who deposited it in Bank *B*. When the transaction is done by cheque, however, the banks, rather than the individuals, transfer the money.

There are, of course, many such transactions in the course of a day. If the banks are staying the same size in relation to each other, these transactions between banks will tend to cancel each other out. If, for example, Mr Brown who banks with *A* gives a cheque for £100 to Mr Harris who banks with *B*, and if, at the same time, Mrs Jones who banks with *B* gives a cheque for £100 to Miss Fitch who banks with *A*, then these two transactions cancel each other out. Bank *A* loses £100 to *B* on account of the first transaction, but gains a like sum from *B* on account of the second. No money need move from bank to bank; all that needs to happen is for *A* to reduce Mr Brown's account by £100 and increase Miss Fitch's by the same amount, and for *B* to reduce Mrs Jones's account by £100 and raise Mr Harris's by the same amount.

Multibank systems make use of a CLEARING HOUSE where interbank debts are cancelled out. At the end of the day, all of the cheques drawn by Bank *A*'s customers and deposited in Bank *B* are totalled, and set against the total of all of the cheques drawn by Bank *B*'s customers and deposited in Bank *A*. It is only necessary to settle the difference between these two sums. This is done for every pair of banks. The actual cheques are passed through the clearing house back to the bank on which they are drawn. The bank is then able to adjust each individual's account by a set of book entries; a flow of cash between banks is necessary only if there is a net transfer of deposits from the customers of one bank to those of another.

What would happen if, in a multibank system, one bank received a new deposit of £100 in cash? In this case, the bank could *not* immediately create another £900 in additional deposits because, when cheques were written on these deposits, the majority would be deposited in other banks. Thus, the bank must expect much of its £100 in cash to be drained away to other banks as soon as it creates new deposits for its own customers.

Table 40.3 Bank *A* expands deposits as far as possible while other banks do not

Bank *A*				All other banks in the system			
Liabilities		Assets		Liabilities		Assets	
Deposits	£109·89	Cash	£10·98	New deposits	£89·02	New cash	£89·02
		Loans	£54·95				
		Bonds	£43·96				
	£109·89		£109·89				

If, for example, the bank that obtains the new deposit has only 10 per cent of the total deposits held by the community, then on average 90 per cent of any new deposits it creates will end up in other banks. If other banks are not simultaneously creating new deposits, then this one bank will be severely restricted in its ability to expand deposits. The reason for the restriction is that the bank will suffer a major cash drain as cheques are written payable to individuals who deal with other banks.

If the bank illustrated in Table 40.1 were only one bank in a multibank system (say with one-tenth of the total deposits in the system), and if the other banks refused to expand deposits, then the final situation would be as illustrated in Table 42.3.

What has happened between Tables 40.1 and 40.3 is that the bank has created £98·91 in new deposits by granting loans and buying bonds. But 90 per cent of these have ended up in other banks, so that the original bank ends up with only £9·89 of the new deposits held by its own customers. The remainder is distributed among the other banks. The total increase in deposits is only 98·91 per cent of the original cash deposit, as opposed to 900 per cent in the monopoly-bank case illustrated in Table 40.2. This leads us to the following conclusion:

> **One bank in a multibank system cannot produce a large multiple expansion of deposits based on an original accretion of cash, unless other banks also expand deposits.**

If all other banks are willing to expand deposits whenever they gain extra cash, the situation shown in Table 40.3 will not represent an equilibrium position. All other banks in the system will have excess cash: the £89·02 in new cash and new deposits will be distributed among them. All these banks will have their new deposits backed 100 per cent by cash. This should lead all banks to expand deposits simultaneously and produce a different situation from the one shown in Table 40.3, since there will no longer be a cash drain from one bank to another. The final outcome will become obvious after the next case has been studied.

Many banks, many new deposits

Assume that, in a system with many banks, each bank obtains new deposits in cash (possibly because of a general increase in the money supply due to a change in government policy).[1] Say, for example, that the community contains ten banks of equal size and that each receives a new deposit of £100 in cash. Now each bank is in the position shown in Table 40.1 and each can begin to expand deposits based on the £100 of reserves. On the one hand, since each bank does one-tenth of the total banking business, on average 90 per cent of the value of any newly created deposit will find its way into other banks as customers make payments by cheque to others in the community. This represents a cash drain to these other banks. On the other hand, 10 per cent of the new deposits created by each other bank should find its way into this bank. Thus, if all banks receive new cash and all start creating deposits simultaneously, no bank should suffer a significant cash drain to any other bank. All banks can go on expanding deposits without losing cash to each other; they need only worry about keeping enough cash to satisfy those depositors who occasionally require cash. Thus the expansion can go on, with each bank watching its own ratio

[1] The ways in which such changes in the money supply can be effected are discussed later in this chapter.

of cash reserves to deposits, expanding deposits as long as the ratio exceeds 1:10 and ceasing when it reaches that figure. The process will come to a halt when each bank has created £900 in additional deposits, so that, for each initial £100 cash deposit, there is now £1,000 in deposits backed by £100 in cash. Now *each* of the banks will have entries in its books similar to those shown in Table 40.2.

We can think of this process as taking place in steps. During the first day, each bank gets £100 in new deposits and the books of each bank show entries similar to those shown in Table 40.1. During the second day, each bank makes loans, expecting that it will suffer a cash drain on account of these loans. Indeed, 90 per cent of the new loans made by Bank *A* do find their way into other banks, but 10 per cent of the new loans made by each other bank finds its way into Bank *A*. Thus, there is no net movement of cash between banks. Instead of finding itself in a position such as that shown in Table 40.3, each bank's books at the end of the day contain the entries shown in Table 40.4.

Table 40.4 Expansion of credit in expectation of a 90 per cent cash drain to other banks when no cash drain actually occurs

Liabilities		Assets	
Deposits	£198·91	Cash	£100·00
		Loans and bonds	£98·91
	£198·91		£198·91

Cash is now just over 50 per cent of deposits, instead of only 10 per cent as desired. Thus each bank can continue to expand deposits in order to grant loans and to purchase income-earning assets. As long as all banks do this simultaneously, no bank will suffer any significant cash drain to any other bank, and the process can continue until each bank has created £900 worth of new deposits and then finds itself in the position shown in Table 40.2.[1]

> **Since a fractional reserve requirement is the essential ingredient of deposit creation, a multibank system creates deposit money just as a single monopoly bank would.**

A complication: cash drain to the public

So far we have ignored the fact that the public actually divides its money holdings in a fairly stable proportion between cash and deposits. This means that when the banking system as a whole creates significant amounts of new deposit money, the whole system will suffer a cash drain as the public withdraws enough cash from the banks to maintain its desired ratio of cash to deposits.

[1] Textbooks often take a case in which one bank creates a deposit on the basis of an accretion of cash, and all of this ends up in a second bank, and the second bank then creates deposits, all of which end up in a third bank, and so on. Two objections can be raised against such a case. First, the situation in which all banks get extra cash is much more common in the real world than the situation in which one bank gets a significant amount of extra cash. Second, even if only one bank did get extra cash, the deposits it creates should end up distributed among all other banks. Thus, after round one, we are immediately in the case of many banks and many new deposits, rather than in a case in which a second bank is the sole holder of a new deposit.

An example Assume, for example, that the public wishes to hold 10 per cent of its money in cash and 90 per cent in the form of deposits. Now when the commercial banks create new deposits, 90 per cent of the value will circulate in the form of cheques and so will stay with the banking system. The other 10 per cent, however, will be withdrawn as cash. This means that if banks receive new deposits of £100, the system cannot create as much as £900 of new deposits (assuming a 10 per cent reserve requirement). Banks will begin to expand deposits, but as they do, they will suffer a cash drain. When their reserve ratio falls to 10 per cent of their deposits, their deposit expansion must cease. Given the figures in the example, the final figures will be those shown in Table 40.5. The cash drain to the public is £52·63. This yields a ratio of cash held by the public to total money held (cash plus deposits) of $52{\cdot}63/(473{\cdot}68+52{\cdot}63) = 0{\cdot}10$. The banks are left with £47·37 of reserves which provide the legal 10 per cent backing for deposits of £473·68.

A significant cash drain to the public greatly reduces the expansion of deposit money that can be supported by any new deposits accruing to the banking system.

Table 40.5 Equilibrium deposit expansion with a cash drain

Liabilities		Assets	
Deposits	£473·68	Cash reserves	£47·37
		Loans and bonds	£426·31
	£473·68		£473·68

The general case[1] This argument is easily generalized using simple algebra. Let there be new deposits of £N reaching the banking system. Banks find themselves with reserves and deposits in this amount. When they expand deposits, some of their reserves will be lost as a cash drain, C, to the public and the rest will remain as reserves, R. Thus

$$C+R=N. \tag{1}$$

Now assume that there is a required reserve ratio of α. This allows us to write

$$\alpha D=R, \tag{2}$$

where D is the total deposits that will be created as a result of the new deposit of £N. Finally, assume that the public wishes to hold a fraction, β, of all its money in cash:

$$C=\beta(C+D). \tag{3}$$

Substituting the second and third equations into the first and solving for D yields:

$$D=\frac{1-\beta}{\beta+\alpha-\alpha\beta}N. \tag{4}$$

If, for example, you put into equation (4) a bank's required reserve ratio of 0·10 and a public's desired cash to money ratio of 0·10, and then substitute back through equations (1) to (3), you will be able to verify the numerical results given in Table 40.5.

[1] This section can be omitted without loss of continuity.

Equation (4) shows if the public's desired cash ratio is zero, deposits rise by the reciprocal of the cash reserve ratio. A positive β, however, means that the resulting cash drain lowers the increase in deposits since it reduces the value of the numerator and raises that of the denominator in equation (4).

The role of the central banks

The central bank is the agent of MONETARY POLICY, which can be defined as the attempt to regulate the economy by regulating the supply of money and the terms and availability of credit. Banking institutions, and the instruments that central banks use to achieve their goals, vary substantially from country to country. These institutional details can have major effects on the workings of central bank policy. In this introductory treatment we shall concentrate mainly on what can be said about central banks in general.[1] First we shall discuss the major functions of central banks; then we shall consider how they affect monetary policy.

The central bank is many things to many people. To the economist it is the arm by which the central authorities apply their monetary policy. To a financial institution it is another part of the country's financial system, a part that is prepared to play big brother both in helping and disciplining all other institutions. What then are its major functions?

Banker to the government Governments too need to hold their funds in an account into which they can make deposits and against which they can draw cheques. Such government deposits are usually held by the central bank, although some governments attempt to spread their surplus deposits through the commercial banks while keeping only a working balance at the central bank.

Manager of the public debt The central bank helps the government with its debt requirements. It does its best to smooth over the effects that might otherwise ensue from uneven borrowing and lending requirements. The Bank of England generally purchases any part of new issues of public debt that is not taken up by other lenders on the day of issue, at what seems like a reasonable interest rate. If the Bank has judged the market correctly, it will be able to sell the remaining part of the new debt over the next week or so. If it has guessed incorrectly, it may end up holding some of the new debt indefinitely. (We shall see that in this case the money supply will have been increased.) The Bank also enters the market if there is a large issue of government debt due for early redemption. The central bank buys this issue up over a period of time, thus preventing a sudden large accretion of cash to the public on redemption date.

In its capacity as manager of the public debt, the central bank is motivated to keep interest rates, and thus the government's interest payments, as low as possible. If the public will not take up all of the government debt being offered at the going rate of interest, either interest rates can rise until all of the debt is taken up, or the bank can buy up whatever the public will not take at the present rate of interest. If banks

[1] It is more important here than almost anywhere else in the book that the text material be supplemented by further reading. One source for the UK economy is Chapter 2.III of A. Prest and D. Coppock, *The UK Economy: A Manual of Applied Economics*, Seventh edition (Weidenfeld: London) 1978.

choose the latter course they are holding down interest rates. As we shall soon see, this leads to an expansion of the money supply.

Banker to commercial banks Commercial banks also need a banker: they need a place to deposit their funds, they need someone to transfer their funds among themselves, and they need someone to lend them money when they are short of cash. The central bank accepts deposits from commercial banks and will on order transfer these deposits among them. In this way the central bank provides the commercial banks with the equivalent of a cheque account, and with a means of settling debts among themselves. Commercial banks hold their required cash reserves against outstanding deposit liabilities in the form of their own deposits at the central bank.

Lender of last resort Commercial banks often have sudden needs for cash and one way of getting it is to borrow from the central bank. Historically, the central bank has been the lender of last resort: if all other sources failed, the central bank would lend money to commercial banks with good investments but in temporary need of cash. In many countries the commercial banks borrow directly from the central bank. (They can, of course, only borrow against approved assets.) In the UK the discount houses stand between the commercial banks and the central bank. If the commercial banks find themselves in need of cash, they recall some of their demand loans made to the discount houses. But the discount houses will have used their borrowed money to buy short-term financial assets. Thus they are not in a position to repay the deposit banks out of their own cash reserves. If they cannot borrow money from private sources they can always obtain the money by borrowing from the Bank of England. They must put up approved financial assets (mainly short-term government securities) as security. They pay interest on the loan at a rate that used to be called the *bank rate* but is now called the MINIMUM LENDING RATE.

There are two ways in which the central bank can provide assistance when the banking system is short of cash. First, it can lend money to the discount houses as described above. Second, it can buy bills and bonds directly. If clearing banks tried to sell bills and bonds in large quantities this would force down the price of these assets. But if the central bank enters the market and buys everything offered at the present prices, this allows any holder who is in need of cash to sell those financial assets and to obtain cash in return.

Supporter of money markets What is often referred to as the support function of the central bank arose from its operation as a lender of last resort to the commercial banks. Today the support function relates to the whole of the financial system. Many financial institutions borrow short and lend long. If their lending rates can only be raised slowly while their borrowing rates rise quickly (because their borrowing contracts are short-term ones while their lending contracts are long-term ones), then a rapid rise in interest rates may put them in danger of insolvency. Rather than let this happen, the central bank may try to slow down the rise in interest rates. To do this it enters the open market and buys bonds, thus preventing their prices from falling as much as they otherwise would. In its efforts to control the level and speed of change of interest rates in general support of the financial system, the central bank necessarily varies the money supply. The changes in the money supply required if the central bank is to pursue its support function may be very different from the changes in the money supply needed if it seeks to control aggregate demand with a view to removing inflationary and deflationary gaps.

Regulator of the money supply The central bank has great power to influence the money supply. The fact that central banks sometimes do not choose to use this power directly does not change the fact that the power is there.

Currency control: In most countries the central bank has the sole power to issue paper money. In Britain this is done by the Issue Department of the Bank of England. No attempt is made, however, to control the overall money supply by controlling the quantity of bank notes in circulation. Suppose that the public wishes to increase the fraction of the total money supply it holds as notes and coin (as it does, for example, each Christmas season). Faced with a cash drain to the public, the commercial banks will withdraw deposits from the Bank of England and the Bank will print the necessary bank notes.[1]

The reserve base: Much more important than currency control is the central bank's control over the reserves available to the banking system. The central bank requires banks to hold reserves against their deposit liabilities. These reserves are called the RESERVE BASE of the money supply. In Britain the things that qualify as reserves are called RESERVE ASSETS. The liabilities against which reserves must be held are called ELIGIBLE LIABILITIES. The ratio of required reserve assets to eligible liabilities is called the REQUIRED RESERVE RATIO.

In most countries today, as in the UK before 1971, central banks enforce a reserve base in terms of cash. Where such reserves are required, the cash held as reserves is called the CASH BASE of the money supply. This cash is held on deposit at the central bank. Thus a 10 per cent cash reserve ratio means that 10 per cent of the value of deposit liabilities of the banking system must be backed by deposits to the credit of the banking system recorded on the books of the central bank. We saw earlier in the chapter that the commercial banks' ability to create deposit money is limited by the amount of reserves available to them. If the central bank can control the size of these reserves it can control the quantity of deposit money created by the commercial banks.

In the UK since 1971 the reserve base includes more than cash reserves held on deposit with the central bank. The consequences of this difference in practice from that followed in most other countries will be discussed later in the chapter.

Monetary policy

The central bank is responsible for the operation of monetary policy, which, as we have observed, attempts to influence the economy by control of monetary magnitudes. We now need to study both the objectives and tools of monetary policy in much more detail.

[1] The accounting would be kept straight by the banking department transferring financial assets to the currency department who would issue currency against these. Thus if the commercial banks withdraw £*X* cash, the banking department, reduces its deposit liabilities to commercial banks by £*X* and its holdings of interest earning assets by the same amount. The currency department increases its holdings of interest earning assets and increases its note issue (which is a liability) by £*X*.

One major objective of monetary policy is to influence aggregate demand and through that national income, employment and prices. Another is to protect or 'support' the country's financial system from the kinds of panics and crashes that have caused occasional havoc.

The major tools of monetary policy have changed over the years. In the past, most central banks sought to influence the economy by influencing the terms and availability of credit. They sought, therefore, to affect interest rates and to make credit more or less available at going rates of interest. Easy terms and availability of credit were thought to raise aggregate expenditure by making it easier and cheaper to borrow money to spend on such things as investment. High interest rates and tight supplies of credit were thought to lower aggregate expenditure by making it harder and more expensive to borrow in order to spend.

More recently, central banks throughout the world have shifted the emphasis to controlling the supply of money directly and expecting this to have a definite effect on interest rates and the amount of loan-financed expenditure. There are several ways in which the central bank may attempt to control the supply of money. The major ones work through the reserve base. We shall study these first where the reserve base is a cash base and later where the base is broader, as it now is in the UK.

Regulation of the money supply with a required cash base

Most central banks enforce a reserve ratio between the deposit liabilities of commercial banks and their cash reserves. Central banks then have two tools of control: they can alter the cash reserves available to the commercial banks or they can alter the required ratio of deposits to cash reserves.

Changing the cash base The central bank can change the cash reserves available to the banking system by what are called its OPEN-MARKET OPERATIONS, which are, quite simply, the purchase and sale by the central bank of financial assets traded in

Table 40.6 Changes resulting from the purchase of a £100 bond by the central bank from a private household

Central Bank

Liabilities	Assets
Deposits of commercial banks + £100	Bond + £100

Commercial Banks

Liabilities	Assets
Deposit of households + £100	Deposits with central bank + £100

Private Households

Liabilities	Assets
No change	Bonds − £100 Deposits with commercial banks + £100

the open market. Assume first that the central bank enters the open market and buys bonds.

To see the effect of such purchases let us follow through the transactions that they cause. The bank buys a bond from some holder in the private sector. The bank pays for the bond by making out a cheque drawn on it, payable to the seller. The seller deposits this cheque in his own bank. The commercial bank presents the cheque to the central bank for payment. The central bank makes a book entry increasing the deposit of the commercial bank at the central bank. At the end of these transactions, the central bank will have acquired a new asset in the form of a bond and a new liability in the form of a deposit by the commercial bank. The individual will have reduced his bond holdings and will have raised his cash holdings. The commercial bank will have a new deposit equal to the amount paid for the bond by the central bank. Thus the commercial bank will find its cash assets and its deposit liabilities increased by the same amount. The balance sheets of the three parties concerned will show the changes indicated in Table 40.6 after £100 worth of open-market purchases have been completed.

The commercial banks are now in the position that was originally illustrated in Table 40.1. They have received a new deposit of £100 against which they hold £100 of reserves on deposit with the central bank. Now they can engage in a multiple expansion of deposits of the kind already studied in the earlier parts of this chapter. Notice that everything has been accomplished by a set of book transactions. The commercial banks have extra cash *to their credit on the books of the central bank*. No new notes or coins have been created. If the subsequent credit expansion causes some cash drain to the public, only then will the commercial banks withdraw some of their deposits from the central bank, and only then will new notes and coins have to be created by the central bank.

A central bank purchase of any financial asset has the effect of increasing the cash reserves of the banking system.

Table 40.7 Changes resulting from the sale of a £100 bond by the central bank to a private household

Central Bank

Liabilities	Assets
Deposits of commercial banks −£100	Bond −£100

Commercial Banks

Liabilities	Assets
Deposits of households −£100	Deposits with central bank −£100

Private Households

Liabilities	Assets
No change	Bonds +£100 Deposits with commercial banks −£100

Second, let the central bank enter the open market and sell bonds to the public. Now follow through the set of transactions caused by this sale. The central bank sells a bond to someone in the private sector. It hands over the bond and receives in payment the buyer's cheque, drawn on his deposit at his own bank. The central bank presents the cheque to the commercial bank for payment. The payment is made merely by a book entry reducing the commercial bank's deposit at the central bank.

Now the central bank has reduced its assets by the value of the bond it sold, and reduced its liabilities in the form of cash owed to commercial banks. The individual has increased his holding of bonds and reduced his cash on deposit with his own bank. The commercial bank has reduced its deposit liability to the individual and reduced its cash assets (on deposit with the central bank) by the same amount. Each of the asset changes is balanced by a liability change.

The balance sheets of the three parties concerned will initially show the changes indicated in Table 40.7 after £100 worth of open-market sales have been accomplished. This is not the end of the story, for the clearing banks find that as a result of suffering an equal change in their cash assets and their deposit liabilities, their ratio of cash to deposits falls. If this ratio was previously at the legal minimum, it will now have fallen below the minimum and the commercial banks will have to take rapid steps to restore their cash ratio. The necessary reduction in deposits can be effected by not making new investments when old ones are redeemed (e.g., by not granting a new loan when old ones are repaid) or by selling existing investments (e.g., by selling bonds to the public and receiving payment in cheques, which reduces the deposits held by the public).

A central bank sale of any financial asset has the effect of decreasing the cash reserves of the banking system.

Any open-market purchase or sale by the central bank has the effects just analysed. If the Bank buys bills and bonds directly from the government, this also increases the cash base and allows a multiple expansion of deposit money. In the first instance it is the government's account with the central bank that gains the new credit balance. But as soon as the government spends the money, writing cheques to households and firms, the money finds its way into the commercial banks, which are once again in the position of securing new deposits that simultaneously increase both their cash assets and their deposit liabilities by an equal amount. This permits a multiple expansion of deposit money.

Furthermore, it does not matter *why* the central bank engages in open-market operations; the effect is the same whatever the purpose of the purchase or sale. The open-market operations might have been engaged in for the express purpose of changing the cash base, or for the purpose of assisting the government to float new loans, or to prevent an anticipated rise in short-term interest rates. Whatever the reason for a particular open-market operation, the effect on the cash base is unavoidable.

Varying the required cash-reserve ratio The other technique that the central bank can use, still working with the cash base, is to change the required cash-reserve ratio. A fall in this ratio can permit a multiple expansion of deposits. The effect is similar to open-market purchases by the central bank because both policies present the banking system with excess reserves – in one case because reserves rise, and in the other case because reserve requirements fall. To see this effect in its simplest form return to Tables 40.1 and 40.2 and work out for yourself what would happen if the single monopoly bank were required to have a cash-reserve ratio of 0·05 rather than the 0·10 assumed on the example. The result, you will find, is that the deposits sustainable by a given amount of cash reserves are doubled. Thus if the central bank lowers the cash-reserve ratio, it enables a multiple expansion of deposit money by the banks. Conversely, if the required cash-reserve ratio is raised, banks find themselves with inadequate reserves. They are then forced to initiate a multiple contraction of deposits in order to achieve the newly required ratio.

Open-market purchases by the central bank and/or reductions in the cash-reserve ratio permit a multiple expansion of deposit money by presenting the banking system with excess reserves. Open-market sales and/or increases in the cash-reserve ratio force a multiple contraction of deposit money by making the banking system's existing reserves inadequate.

Regulation of the money supply with a required reserve-asset base

In principle, the control of the money supply works in the same way whatever items are included in the reserve base. The degree of control over the money supply varies, however, with the degree of control the central bank can exercise over the reserve base held by the commercial banks. If the total supply of reserve assets cannot be controlled by the central bank, then there is no equivalent of open-market operations which change the cash base. Even if the total supply of reserve assets can be controlled by the central bank, this will not be an effective method of control if commercial banks can respond by obtaining more reserves rather than being forced to respond by changing their deposit liabilities.

Control of the reserve-asset base In Britain since 1971, operating under the *Competition and Credit Control Document*, the Bank of England has enforced a required reserve-asset ratio on all commercial banks. This ratio is between what are called *reserve assets* and *eligible liabilities*. *Eligible liabilities* are most deposit liabilities with the exception of certificates of deposit of over a two-year original term. British *reserve assets*, however, are more than just cash. They include, as their major elements, 'normal' deposits of the banking system with the Bank of England (cash reserves), Treasury bills, money loaned out at call to the discount houses and other similar institutions, UK local authority bills, British government stocks, and bonds of nationalized industries that are guaranteed by the government and have less than one year to run to maturity. This list makes it obvious that the total supply of assets that banks can use for their reserve base cannot be controlled by the Bank of England. This contrasts with the situation when a cash-reserve base is used. There is one and only one source of cash reserves plus cash in the hands of the public, and that is the central bank. When the central bank buys financial assets, it creates money which can only end up in two places: as bank reserves held on deposit with the central bank or as cash in the hands of the public. (Look again at Table 42.6 and the discussion that surrounds it.)

Now assume that the commercial banks are short of reserves. If they are to get more reserves, then either the total supply must change or they must persuade the public to hold less of the given total supply so that the banks can hold more. With the UK reserve-asset base, it is not impossible to persuade the public to hold fewer of these assets. They are similar to, and hence highly substitutable for, other assets that are not in the reserve base. Hence slight changes in prices of the assets will make it possible for the banks to acquire more of these as people switch to other assets. This is difficult to do, however, with a cash-reserve base. If the commercial banks are short of cash reserves, the only way they can get more is to persuade the public to hold a lower proportion of their money in cash and a higher proportion in deposits. (If this did occur, the public would deposit the cash they did not want and hold deposits instead; this would present the banks with new cash in the form of deposits and would raise their cash/deposit ratio.) But the public's demand for cash is highly stable and in practice the banks cannot replenish cash reserves by attracting cash from the public. Thus when they are short of reserves they must reduce deposit liabilities.

Central bank control of the money supply depends on the central bank's ability to control the total supply of reserve assets and on the commercial banks' inability to obtain more of these assets from the public by offering to buy them at a slight increase over their present market price.

When these conditions obtain, two things result. First, the central bank can control the *total supply* of the reserve asset. Second, since the public's demand for this asset is stable, the *proportion available to banks* as their reserves will vary only with the total supply.

A cash-reserve base satisfies the above requirements. The reserve assets used in the UK do not, however, meet these requirements. The central bank cannot tightly control their total supply, which is under the separate controls of the various bodies that issue them. Furthermore, since these assets are merely part of a spectrum of interest-earning assets held by the public, they are very close substitutes for other assets not included in the reserve base. The public can therefore be induced, by relatively small changes in prices and interest rates, to alter their holdings of reserve assets, holding more or less of other assets instead. Thus the commercial banks are in a position to alter their holdings of UK reserve assets in a way that they cannot alter their cash reserves.

The total supplies of the assets included as UK bank reserves cannot easily be controlled by the central bank and the fraction held by the non-bank public can be influenced easily by actions of the banks themselves.

Changes in the reserve-asset ratio In the US, the Federal Reserve System does change the required cash-reserve ratio from time to time as a means of influencing the volume of deposit liabilities of the banking system. The Bank of England has tried to do this by requiring banks to hold what are called *Special Deposits* at the Bank. The amount required is altered from time to time.

The Special Deposit scheme was introduced in the early 1960s as a method of altering reserve requirements for British banks. From time to time the Bank of England could require that the commercial banks make special deposits with it. This had the effect of increasing the required reserve ratio. Whether or not it could be effective in controlling the money supply would depend on whether or not the Bank of England took steps to make it easy for banks to make special deposits when required to do so. At the end of 1973 a new variant of the scheme was introduced. The Bank of England announces a target for the expansion of deposit money, and if this target is exceeded, banks must place amounts of money (determined on a sliding scale) in special non-interest-earning deposits with the Bank. This is intended to provide a disincentive against exceeding the target for growth in the money supply.

Other tools of monetary policy

So far we have studied the Bank's monetary policy that attempts to control the supply of money by working through the reserves required to be held against deposit liabilities. A central bank can change the supply of money and credit through a variety of other devices that operate through interest rates and through so-called 'selective credit controls'. Although these devices are much less important than open-market operations or reserve requirements, they are used from time to time.

Open-market operations affect interest rates as well as the quantity of money. Buying large quantities of bonds tends to force up their price. This, as we saw on page 400, is equivalent to forcing down the rate of interest. Selling large quantities of bonds, however, tends to force down their price and force up the rate of interest. Thus, an open-market policy designed to expand the money supply also tends to lower interest rates, and a policy designed to contract the money supply tends to raise them.

There is a variety of selective credit controls designed not to regulate the over-all volume of money or credit, but rather to limit (or encourage) particular forms of it. Stock-market fluctuations can be controlled to some extent through margin requirements. Consumer credit, which can be highly volatile, can be controlled in several ways. Minimum necessary initial payments and maximum terms for hire-purchase contracts can be set. The final tool is direct order or suggestion. If the banking system is prepared to cooperate, the central bank can operate a tight money policy merely by asking banks to be conservative in granting loans. When the restrictive policy is removed, the commercial banks can then be told that it is all right to go ahead granting loans and extending deposits up to the legal maximum.

Theories of the determination of the money supply

Two extreme situations concerning the determination of the money supply are imaginable. In the first, the money supply is exactly the amount determined by the central bank. It neither expands nor contracts with the ebb and flow of business activity unless the central bank decides to allow it to do so. In such a case, economists speak of an EXOGENOUS MONEY SUPPLY.

In the other extreme situation, the money supply is completely determined by forces such as the level of business activity and rates of interest, and is wholly out of the control of the central bank. In such a case, economists would say that there was an ENDOGENOUS MONEY SUPPLY, which means that the size of the money supply is not imposed from outside by the decisions of the central bank, but is determined by what is happening within the economy (just as is the production of steel plates or motor cars).

Exogenous theories

The traditional theory of the determination of the money supply related the total quantity of money to the cash base by means of the so-called DEPOSIT

MULTIPLIER, which relates deposits to reserves according to equation (6) below. The assumptions of the theory are (i) that the central bank fixes a minimum cash-reserve ratio and (ii) that the profit incentive of commercial banks leads them to avoid holding excess reserves if at all possible. Idle cash reserves earn nothing for a bank, while loans and other investments always yield some interest income. Therefore banks will always try to be fully loaned up (i.e., have no excess reserves).

We can write assumption (i) as

$$\frac{R}{D} \geqslant \alpha, \tag{5}$$

where R is cash reserves, D is deposit liabilities, α is the minimum required cash-reserve ratio and the sign '$\geqslant$' is read greater than or equal to. Assumption (ii) above allows us to replace the '$\geqslant$' sign with an '$=$' sign since banks are assumed never to carry significant amounts of excess reserves. Now re-write the equation as follows:

$$D = \frac{R}{\alpha}. \tag{6}$$

This gives us the quantity of deposit money expressed as a function of the cash base and the required cash-reserve ratio. If we allow for a cash drain to the public, the deposit multiplier becomes a little more complex. It is then given by equation (4) on page 596. (The difference between (6) and (4) occurs because with a cash drain all money newly created by the central bank's open-market operations, N, does not end up as reserves of the banking system since some is withdrawn and held as cash by the public.)

With or without a cash drain this is a theory of an exogenous money supply, because the cash base is assumed to be under the complete control of the central bank through its open-market operations. Thus the total supply of deposit money can be set by the central bank. Assume, for example, that the central bank wishes to reduce the money supply.

(1) The bank sells bonds on the open market.

(2) The bank receives cheques from the public in payment for the bonds. When it presents these cheques for payment, commercial banks suffer a loss in their cash reserves.

(3) In order to restore their required reserve ratio, banks must engage in a multiple contraction of deposit money.

Endogenous theories

There are many theories of how the money supply may become an endogenous variable. First, the central bank may be concerned with the rate of interest rather than the quantity of money. If the bank is to engage in whatever open-market operations are needed to stabilize the price of bonds and other financial assets, then the change in the money supply will be determined by the necessary amount of open-market operations. If the price of bonds would be falling on the open market, the bank must buy bonds in order to hold their price up. (This, as we have seen, tends to expand the money supply.) If the price of bonds would be rising on the open market, the bank must sell bonds in order to hold their price down. (This, as we have seen, tends to contract the money supply.)

If the bank behaves in this way the money supply becomes endogenous and fluctuates with the demand and supply for financial assets, since the bank must make up the difference between demand and supply at the fixed price of these assets.

If the object of the central bank's open-market policy is to fix interest rates, the cash base becomes endogenous and cannot be fixed by the central bank at any particular predetermined level.

A second way in which the money supply can become endogenous is if the bank sets a reserve base which the commercial banks themselves can control. This, as we have seen, appears to be true to some extent of the reserve base used in the UK since 1971. Large quantities of these reserve assets are held by the non-banking private sector, and the banks can obtain more or less of these by purchasing them at a price favourable enough to persuade the public to sell them and hold other closely substitutable assets instead. In Chapter 50 we shall study yet another important way in which the money supply can become endogenous.

Mixed theories

In practice, the money supply is partly endogenous, because commercial banks are able to change it in response to economic incentives, and partly exogenous, because the central bank is able to set limits beyond which the commercial banks are unable to increase the money supply.

In the next chapter we shall assume an exogenous money supply, which means that the central bank can make it whatever it wants it to be. This allows us to study the importance of money. Once we have seen how changes in the supply of money can influence the economy, we shall be ready to appreciate the full significance of debates over the extent to which the money supply is determined exogenously and endogenously. Some of the most important controversies in economics today, those concerning the cause and control of the rapid inflation of the 1970s, turn on the question of the degree to which the money supply is exogenous or endogenous. It is difficult to mention a more important current issue in macroeconomics.

41

The importance of money

Now that we know what money is and how its supply is influenced by the behaviour of the banking system, we can proceed to pose and to answer a series of questions. The following summary may help you to follow the structure of the argument.

Question: What determines the demand for money?

Answer: The demand for money depends on national income and the rate of interest.

Question: What happens if the supply of money exceeds its demand or *vice versa*?

Answer: An excess supply of money will cause aggregate expenditure to rise; excess demand for money will cause aggregate expenditure to fall. The link from money to expenditure is called the *transmission mechanism*.

Question: We already know the effects of variations in aggregate expenditure under the assumptions listed on page 473. What happens when there are no unemployed resources, so that actual income equals potential income?

Answer: A rise in aggregate expenditure when actual income already equals potential income will open up an inflationary gap and so cause the price level to rise.

Question: What will be the effect of this rise in the price level back onto the aggregate expenditure function?

Answer: The rise in the price level will operate through a *monetary adjustment mechanism* to reduce the aggregate expenditure function, removing the inflationary gap and bringing the inflation to a halt.

Question: Can this adjustment mechanism be frustrated so that the inflationary gap, and thus the inflation, persists indefinitely?

Answer: The *only* way this can be done is to increase the money supply at a percentage rate that at least matches the rate at which the inflation is raising the price level.

The last answer explains why, as we saw in Chapter 39, changes in the quantity of money and changes in the price level have been associated with each other since the very beginnings of economics:

> **An inflation that is not accompanied by a corresponding increase in the money supply must cause a fall in aggregate demand, which, sooner or later, will eliminate the inflationary gap. The gap can be maintained indefinitely in the face of an inflation only if the money supply increases at (at least) the same rate as the price level.**

As we shall see, this is a proposition that follows from virtually all macroeconomic theories used today. The debate – and here there is almost total disagreement – is over its relevance to government anti-inflationary policy.

Note that in Part 8 we are confining ourselves to inflations that occur as a result of an inflationary gap as defined on page 510. Such inflations are called DEMAND-PULL INFLATIONS or sometimes just DEMAND INFLATIONS. Economists are in agreement that demand inflations have often occurred, but they disagree on the importance of other causes of inflation. Alternative theories of inflation will be studied in Part 11.

We must now proceed to pose, one at a time, the questions listed above. In each case we shall outline the economic theories on which the answers already given are based.

The determinants of the demand for money

There is a cost of holding any money balance because the money held could have been used to purchase income earning assets instead and would then have earned interest as a return. It could, for example, be deposited with a building society, or used to buy a certificate of deposit or a government bond.

> **The opportunity cost of holding each unit of money balances is the rate of interest that could have been earned if the money had been used to purchase income earning assets such as bonds.**

Clearly, then, money will be held only if it provides services to the holders that are at least as valuable as the opportunity cost of holding it.

The total amount of money balances that everyone wishes to hold for all purposes is called the DEMAND FOR MONEY. Notice that the quantity of money is a *stock* and that the demand for it is a demand for a stock: people wish to hold so much money in cash or deposits. This makes the demand for money different from the demand for commodities, which is a flow demand. When we say, for example, that the demand for carrots is 7 million tons, we must say over what time period this is measured. If we specify 'per month', then the demand is to purchase a flow of carrots of 7 million tons each month. When we say, however, that the demand for money is £30,000 million, we mean that the total of all money balances that people wish to hold is £30,000 million. This is a stock and thus does not have a time dimension.

The transactions demand for money

Virtually all transactions in our economy require money. Money is passed from households to firms to pay for the goods and services produced by firms, and money is passed from firms to households to pay for the factor services supplied by households. Money balances that are held because of these flows are called TRANSACTIONS BALANCES, and the desire to hold balances to finance these flows is called the TRANSACTIONS MOTIVE. The quantity of transactions balances people want to hold is called the TRANSACTIONS DEMAND FOR MONEY.

In an unreal world where the receipts and disbursements of households and firms were perfectly synchronized, it would be unnecessary to hold transactions balances. If every time a household wished to spend £10 it received £10 as part payment of its income, no transactions balances would be needed. In the real world, however, receipts and disbursements are not perfectly synchronized.

Consider, for example, the balances held in order to make wage payments. The level of balances that must be held depends on the pay period and on the size of the wage bill. Assume, for purposes of illustration, that firms pay wages every Friday, that households spend all their wages on the purchase of goods and services, and that expenditure is spread out evenly over the week. Thus, on Friday morning, firms must hold balances equal to the weekly wage bill, while on Friday afternoon, households will hold these balances. Over the week, households' balances will run down as a result of purchasing goods and services. By the same token, the balances held by firms will build up as a result of selling goods and services until, on the following Friday morning, firms will again have amassed balances equal to the wage bill that must be met on that day. On the average over the week, firms will hold balances equal to half the wage bill and so will households. Total balances held between them will equal the weekly wage bill. Notice that although the balances circulate so that each group holds a varying balance over the week, the total demand for balances summed over both groups is constant.

It follows that total transactions balances held will vary with the value of the total wage bill. The wage bill will in turn vary with national income. To understand the link between the wage bill and national income, notice first that if output rises, employment of labour will rise, and second that if the price level rises, the price of labour will rise with everything else. In both cases the value of the weekly wage bill will rise.

The amount of transactions balances held will also vary with the degree to which payments and receipts are desynchronized. This in turn depends on institutional arrangements. To illustrate these effects, assume that the pay period changes from weekly to monthly. Now payments and receipts are less well synchronized and transactions balances will have to be equal to the month's wage bill. Immediately after pay day, households will have money balances equal to a month's wages. As they spend their incomes over the month their balances will run down, but firms will be accumulating the money spent on their balances. Just before the next pay day, households' transactions balances will have been run down to zero, while firms' balances will be equal to the monthly wage bill that they are just about to pay. The average monthly transactions balances held by households will be equal to half a month's wages, and the same will be true for firms. Thus total transactions balances will be equal to a month's wages. The length of the pay period, and the other considerations that determine the degree of desynchronization of payments and receipts, are part of the society's institutional arrangements. In the short term these may be taken as given, although in the long term they can change significantly.

We have conducted this discussion in terms of the wage bill, but a similar analysis holds for payments for all factor services. The critical conclusion is that, for given institutional arrangements, the demand for transactions balances depends on the value of transactions (i.e., all of the payments and receipts of firms and households).

Next we must ask how the total value of transactions is related to national income. Because of the 'double counting' problem first discussed on page 459, the value of all transactions exceeds the value of the economy's final output. When the flour mill buys wheat from the farmer and when the baker buys flour from the mill, both are transactions against which money balances must be held, although only the value added at each stage is part of national income. Typically, the total value of transactions tends to be five to ten times as large as the total value of final output which is national income.

We now make an added assumption that there is a stable relation between transactions and national income. If, for example, a 10 per cent rise in aggregate demand leads to a 10 per cent rise in national income, this will lead to a 10 per cent rise in the total value of all transactions and hence to an associated rise in transactions balances held by firms. This allows us to relate transactions balances to national income.

Transactions balances are held because of the non-synchronization of payments and receipts. Transactions balances held will be larger (i) the larger the value of national income measured at current prices and (ii) the less the degree of synchronization of payments and receipts.

If we assume that the transactions demand for money is a constant proportion of transactions, and that transactions are a constant proportion of national income, then the transactions demand for money becomes a constant proportion of national income.[1] In symbols we may write this $M_D^T = kY$, where M_D^T is the demand for transactions balances, Y is national income and k is some constant. To illustrate the relations involved here assume that $\frac{1}{12}$ of the value of annual transactions is held in transaction balances (i.e., $M_D^T = T/12$). Further assume that the value of transactions is five times the value of national income (i.e., $T = 5Y$). This gives $M_D^T = \frac{5}{12}Y$.

The precautionary demand for money

Uncertainty plays no role in the need for transactions balances. If there is uncertainty about the exact timing of receipts and payments, households and firms will tend to hold additional balances called PRECAUTIONARY BALANCES in response to the PRECAUTIONARY MOTIVE for holding money. Let us see how this demand arises.

Many goods and services are sold on credit, and the seller can never be quite certain when these goods will be paid for, whereas the buyer can never be quite certain of the day of delivery and thus of the day on which payment will fall due; nor can he be certain of the degree to which his suppliers will be pressing for prompt payment. In order to be able to continue in business during times in which receipts are abnormally low and/or disbursements are abnormally high, firms carry money balances. The larger such balances, the greater the degree of insurance against being unable to pay bills because of some temporary fluctuation in either receipts or disbursements. If the firm is pressed for cash or has other very profitable uses for its funds, it may run down these balances and take the risk of being caught by some temporary fluctuations in receipts and disbursements. How serious this risk is depends on the penalties of being caught without sufficient reserves. A firm is unlikely to be pushed into insolvency, but it may have to incur considerable costs if it is forced to borrow money at high interest rates for short periods in order to meet such temporary crises. The cost depends on the lines of short-term credit open to the firm.

[1] This rather crude assumption is not too far away from the empirical evidence, which suggests that the demand for transactions balances often varies roughly in proportion to variations in national income. All that really matters for the theory we are developing, however, is that the demand varies directly with income and the evidence for this general relation is overwhelming.

Whereas the transactions demand arises from the certainty of non-synchronization of payments and receipts, the precautionary demand arises from uncertainty about the degree of non-synchronization.

The precautionary motive arises, therefore, out of stochastic disturbances in the flows of payments and receipts.

The protection provided by precautionary balances depends on the degree to which payments and receipts are subject to haphazard fluctuations and on the volume of payments and receipts. If the volume rises, then a given amount of money held will provide less protection. To provide the same degree of protection as the volume of business rises, more money is necessary. Thus, the firm's demand for money can be expected to rise as its own sales rise. Aggregating over all firms and households, the total demand for money will rise as national income rises.

Firms can also be expected to hold more funds for precautionary purposes the lower the opportunity cost of holding such funds. If the market rate of interest provides a measure of how expensive it is to hold funds, then the precautionary demand for money can be expected to vary inversely with the rate of interest as well as directly with the level of income.[1]

The precautionary demand for money will vary directly with the value of national income and inversely with the interest rate.

The speculative demand for money

A third major reason for holding money arises from uncertainty about the future. Because the future is never certain, any transaction that takes place over time is necessarily somewhat speculative. If one thinks prices are now very low and will soon rise, the tendency is to buy now and to put off selling until prices rise. If one thinks prices are high now and will soon fall, the tendency is to sell now and to postpone buying until prices fall. This applies to anything that is bought and sold.

To develop the argument in its simplest form, assume that each person has in his or her mind an idea of a *normal* price of bonds.

If the price of bonds[2] is very high in relation to what people think is the normal price (i.e., the rate of interest is thought to be low), people will tend to sell bonds now and postpone intended purchases until prices have come down. In such a situation, large quantities of money may be held in anticipation of a more favourable chance to purchase bonds in the future. If, however, the price of bonds is very low in relation to what is thought to be the normal price (the rate of interest is high), the tendency will be to buy bonds now and to postpone sales until a more favourable price can be obtained. In this case, the tendency will be to hold as little money as possible and hold bonds instead. This argument makes the demand to hold money very inversely with the interest rate.

Whereas the transactions and precautionary motives emphasize money's role as a medium of exchange, the speculative motive emphasizes its role as a store of wealth. A household or firm can hold its wealth in money or in such interest-earning assets

[1] Institutional arrangements affect the precautionary demand just as they affect the transactions demand. In the past, for example, a traveller would have to carry a substantial precautionary balance in cash, but today his credit card covers him against almost any unforeseen expense that may arise in his travels.

[2] This argument applies to any financial asset whose price can vary, but for simplicity we concentrate on bonds.

as bonds. If there was perfect certainty that the price of bonds would never change, there would be no reason to hold any wealth in the form of money, since bonds yield an interest payment while money does not. If people believe that the price of bonds may change in the future, there may be a reason to hold money rather than bonds. If, on the one hand, the price of bonds is expected to fall, there will be capital losses for people holding bonds. It will then pay to hold money rather than bonds as long as the expected capital loss from the fall in price exceeds the interest that can be earned by holding the bond. If, on the other hand, the price of bonds is expected to rise, it will pay to hold bonds rather than money, since there will be a capital gain when their price rises. People who are certain about the direction in which they expect the price of bonds to move will tend to hold all their wealth in bonds (price of bonds expected to rise) or all their wealth in money (price of bonds expected to fall). It is easy to show, however, that when investors are uncertain about what will happen to bond prices in the future many of them will want to hedge their bets by holding both bonds and money. SPECULATIVE BALANCES are wealth held in the form of money rather than interest-earning assets because of expectations that the prices of those assets may change. The motive for holding such balances is called the SPECULATIVE MOTIVE.[1]

> **The speculative demand for money has its source in uncertainty about future bond prices. It will vary inversely with the rate of interest.**

The total demand for money: recapitulation

The demand for money is defined as the total amount of money balances that everyone in the economy wishes to hold. The previous discussion about the motives for holding money can be summarized by listing two hypotheses about the demand for money.

The demand for money varies directly with the national income valued in current prices. The higher the level of income, the larger the amount of money held for transactions purposes. The higher the value of income, the larger also is the amount needed to provide a given level of security against unforeseen fluctuations in receipts and payments. Both transactions and precautionary motives lead to this hypothesis.

The demand for money varies inversely with the rate of interest. The market rate of interest reflects the opportunity cost of money holdings (the money could be lent out and earn the market rate). Thus, the higher the rate of interest, the higher the cost of holding money and the less money will be held for precautionary purposes. The rate of interest also influences decisions as to whether to hold money for speculative purposes. Given some expectations about a normal rate of interest, the lower the current rate, the less attractive bonds will seem to be and so the higher the demand will be to hold money instead of bonds. Both the precautionary and speculative motives lead to this hypothesis.

When households and firms decide how much of their monetary assets they will

[1] The development of the speculative demand for money given by Keynes emphasized differences between the current price of bonds and the expected or 'normal' price of bonds. The modern theory following the work of Professor James Tobin of Yale University emphasizes uncertainty about future bond prices. It shows that even if each person expects the future price to be the same as the present price, he will be led to hold his wealth partly in bonds and partly in money as long as there is some uncertainty about future bond prices. Thus the speculative motive arises primarily out of uncertainty and does not require Keynes' construct of a normal or expected price of bonds that may differ from the current price.

hold as money rather than as bonds (and other interest-earning assets), they are said to be exercising their preference for liquidity. LIQUIDITY PREFERENCE thus refers to the demand to hold assets as money rather than as interest-earning bonds (or stocks). This demand is assumed to vary inversely with the rate of interest. The schedule relating the demand for money to the rate of interest is called the LIQUIDITY-PREFERENCE SCHEDULE.

We have now answered the first question listed at the outset of the chapter.

> **The demand for money is a function of national income and the rate of interest. It varies directly with the former and inversely with the latter.**

The consequences of an excess supply of, or an excess demand for, money: the transmission mechanism

For the time being we shall assume an exogenous money supply: the money supply is a given amount set by the central bank through its open-market operations. We shall then ask what happens if the demand for money does not equal its supply.

Ever since the original quantity theory was formulated in the eighteenth century, theories of money have been in agreement that when an excess demand for or supply of money develops, this will cause a change in the aggregate expenditure function. The mechanism by which excess demand for or supply of money makes its effects felt on the aggregate demand expenditure function is called the TRANSMISSION MECHANISM. Views on the transmission mechanism have changed greatly over the years. The classical quantity theory emphasized a very direct link: if households had larger money balances than they required, they spent the excess on currently produced goods and services; if they had less than they required, they cut their expenditures below their incomes and used the resulting savings to add to their money balances.

Modern theories use a less direct link that emphasizes money as just one method of holding wealth. There is a whole series of assets – from currency and sight deposits, through time deposits, to treasury bills and short-term bonds, to very long-term bonds and equities – that are alternative ways of holding wealth. With the exception of currency and demand deposits, each of these assets yields a return of interest or dividends and each carries uncertainty as to its future price. The longer the term of the bond, the larger the fluctuations in the bond's price for a given fluctuation in the rate of interest (see page 400).

Thus financial assets can be thought of as a chain stretching from the ones with the least uncertainty attached to their money prices to the ones with the most uncertainty. Money itself has the least uncertainty as to its money price (zero uncertainty); long-term bonds have the most. Wealth holders will typically hold a portfolio that includes some money and quantities of some or all of these other assets. If households find themselves with larger money balances than they require, they will transfer some money into short-term bonds, and the extra demand will cause the prices of those bonds to rise. The rise in the price of short-term bonds will make longer-term bonds seem more attractive and households will move into them, making their price rise in turn. Eventually a whole chain of substitutions will occur, with short- and long-term interest rates changing as households try to hold less money and more of other interest-earning assets. The change in interest rates will in turn affect interest-sensitive expenditures.

From excess demand to the rate of interest

We can derive the results of the modern theory of the transmission mechanism that concerns us here by working with the very simplified version used by Keynes. In this version there are only two financial assets which can be used as a store of wealth: money, which earns no interest but has a perfectly secure money value, and bonds, which earn interest but have a money value that varies inversely with the rate of interest. With only two assets, wealth holders face a single decision: how to divide their wealth between bonds and money. The decision, for example, to hold 80 per cent of wealth in bonds *implies* a decision to hold the other 20 per cent in money.

An excess demand for money If a single firm or household is short of money balances, it can sell some of its bonds and immediately replenish its stocks of money. On the other hand, if the firm or household has excess stocks of money, it can invest these forthwith by buying bonds on the open market. If everyone tries to do this simultaneously, however, it will not be possible unless there are changes in the stocks of money or of bonds. If the stocks of money and bonds are fixed in size, then general attempts to add to or subtract from bond holdings will only succeed in altering their price. Assume, for example, that the money supply is reduced so that all firms and households are short of money. They try to sell bonds to replenish their money holdings. This causes the price of bonds to fall which means, of course, a rise in the interest rate. As the interest rate rises, people will try to economize on cash holdings; they will also tend to reduce speculative balances of cash, since bonds now seem like very good investments. Eventually, the rate will rise high enough so that people will no longer be trying to add to their cash balances by selling bonds. The demand for money will again equal supply. There will no longer be an excess supply of bonds, so the interest rate will stop rising. The net effect of the original excess demand for money will have been an increase in the rate of interest.

> **An excess demand for money causes firms and households to try to sell bonds. This raises interest rates until the quantity of money demanded equals its unchanged supply.**

An excess supply of money Now consider a case in which firms and households hold larger money balances than they wish to hold. A single household would purchase bonds with its excess balances. It would thus reach the desired holdings of money by adjusting quantities of money and bonds at given prices. But what one household or firm can do, all cannot do. When all households enter the bond market and try to purchase bonds with unwanted stocks of money, all they do is to bid up the price of existing bonds (i.e., bid down the rate of interest). As the rate of interest falls, households and firms are willing to hold a larger quantity of money (i.e., they move along their demand-for-money functions in response to a fall in the rate of interest). This rise in the price of bonds continues until firms and households stop trying to convert bonds into money. It continues, that is, until everyone is content to hold the existing supplies of money and bonds. Thus the whole society arrives at equilibrium because the price of bonds changes until the quantities demanded of money and bonds equal their fixed supplies: whereas a single individual reaches equilibrium holdings of money and bonds by adjusting quantities at fixed prices, the whole society reaches equilibrium by having prices adjust so that people are willing to hold the existing fixed quantities of money and bonds.

An excess supply of money causes firms and households to try to buy bonds. This lowers interest rates until the quantity of money demanded equals its unchanged supply.

From the interest rate to aggregate expenditure

The second link in the transmission mechanism from money to aggregate expenditure is the one we have already discussed linking interest rates to expenditure. We saw in Chapter 36 that expenditures on consumer durables, on inventory accumulation, on residential construction, and on plant and equipment are all expected to respond to changes in the rate of interest. Other things being equal, a decrease in the rate of interest makes borrowing cheaper and also makes it less costly to have funds tied up in such non-interest-yielding assets as machines, houses, and consumer durables. Thus a decrease in interest rates is predicted to touch off bouts of new expenditure.

Modern economists hypothesize that overall there will be an inverse relation between the rate of interest and the quantity of investment and other interest-sensitive expenditure.[1] This leads to a function relating such expenditure inversely to the rate of interest: the lower the rate of interest, the higher is interest-sensitive expenditure.

The transmission mechanism works from excess demand or supply of money, to changes in the demand or supply of bonds, to changes in bond prices and interest rates, to changes in interest-sensitive expenditure.

It remains for us to ask how excess demand for or supply of money arises in the first place. Excess demand for or supply of money can be caused by shifts in either the money demand function or the supply of money. We shall assume a stable demand for money function and concentrate on disturbances caused by changes in the supply of money. These disturbances can be induced by the central bank through such channels as its open-market operations. Thus the central bank can change the money supply, and the effects of this will operate through the transmission mechanism of bond prices and interest rates onto aggregate expenditure. *This will cause expenditure to vary directly with the money supply.*

Effects on national income and the price level of a rise in aggregate expenditure

We have seen that a rise in the money supply can cause an increase in aggregate expenditure. What are the consequences of this? The answer depends on whether the increase occurs at a time of unemployment or of full employment of resources.

Unemployed resources This is the case that we have studied at length in Part 7. The conclusions should be familiar by now: a rise in aggregate expenditure raises national income while a fall lowers it. Since throughout Part 7 the price level was assumed constant, there was no need to distinguish between real national income measured in constant prices and nominal national income measured in current prices. The changes in both statistics would be the same. When resources are

[1] As we saw on pages 524–6 (Chapter 36) the timing of investment in response to changes in interest rates may be complex; low interest rates may induce a temporary bout of new investment rather than a permanent increase. But at least for some time, even if not forever, a fall in interest rates should lead to a rise in expenditure.

unemployed the price level is assumed to be constant, so our earlier conclusions apply directly.

All we have added in this chapter is a new cause of changes in expenditure. Changes in the money supply, by creating excess demand for or supply of money, can change expenditure. Combining this new conclusion with the results arrived at earlier leads to the following composite result:

> **When actual national income is below its full-employment level, an increase in the money supply will increase national income while a reduction in the money supply will reduce national income. Monetary policy is thus an alternative to fiscal policy for influencing aggregate expenditure and hence national income.**

Full employment Let us go to the opposite extreme from what we have so far assumed in all of our macro-analysis. Assume now that national income is in equilibrium at full employment, so that actual and potential income are the same. A fall in aggregate expenditure would take us back to the situation already studied with unemployment of all resources, but what of a rise in expenditure? This will open up an inflationary gap. Equilibrium income exceeds potential income, but it is impossible to produce more than potential income, so prices rise instead.

> **An inflationary gap means excess demand at full-employment income and, since real output cannot rise in response, prices will rise instead. National income measured in current prices rises, while national income measured in constant prices remains unchanged.**

This tells us that the effect of aggregate demand exceeding full-employment output is a rise in prices. What, then, is the effect of the rise in prices?

The effect on the aggregate expenditure function of a rise in the price level

We now come to the critical relation that is the reason why money and the price level have been linked since the early days of economics: rises in the price level operate, through a *monetary adjustment mechanism*, to lower aggregate expenditure and thus remove the inflationary gap that causes the price level to rise. To see how this works, note that on the one hand the supply of money, M_S, is given in nominal terms while the demand for money, M_D, is given in real terms.

The money supply is so many thousand million pounds sterling, marks, rupees, or whatever units the country's currency is expressed in. The central bank can determine the nominal money supply, M_S, by its open-market operations but it cannot determine the real money suppy, M_S/P. (See page 589 for definitions of these terms.) The size of the real money supply depends partly on the price level, which cannot be directly fixed by the central bank.

The demand for money is given in real terms: for any given level of real national income and any given relative attractiveness of bonds and money, which depends on the rate of interest, firms and households will wish to hold so much purchasing power as money balances. In our earlier example of transactions balances, this was an amount sufficient to purchase one week's total labour supply or one week's purchases of commodities by suppliers of labour.

The effects of a rise in the price level on the demand for and supply of money Now consider the effects of a rise in the price level on the demand for and supply of money with real national income and the rate of interest unchanged. On the one hand, the nominal supply of money, M_S, will be unchanged but the real money supply, M_S/P, will be lowered. The purchasing power of the given nominal supply of money will fall in proportion to the rise in the price level. On the other hand, the real demand for money measured in purchasing power units, M_D, will be unchanged but the nominal demand, PM_D, must rise in proportion to the rise in the price level. Assume, for example, that households wish to keep real balances equal to 10 per cent of annual national income. If the price level doubles, thus doubling the nominal value of full-employment national income, they will then have to double the nominal balances that they hold. If we express the demand for money in *nominal* terms, it is clear that, say, a doubling of the price level must double the nominal demand for money if households and firms are to hold transactions balances sufficient to finance the same real level of sales and receipts.

> **A rise in the price level leaves the real demand for money and the nominal supply of money unchanged, but raises the nominal demand for money and lowers the real supply of money in proportion to the price level change.**

Disequilibrium caused by a change in the price level The condition that the demand for money should equal the supply of money can be expressed as either:
(i) the real demand should equal the real supply ($M_D = M_S/P$) or
(ii) nominal demand equals nominal supply ($PM_D = M_D$),
where M^D is the amount of purchasing-power units people wish to hold as money balances and M^S is the nominal supply of money measured in pounds, dollars, marks, or whatever units the country's currency is expressed in. Looking at the first way of expressing this demand-supply equilibrium condition, we can say that a rise in the price level creates excess demand for money because it reduces the real supply, leaving real demand unchanged. Looking at the second way, we can say again that a rise in the price level creates excess demand for money, this time because it leaves the nominal supply unchanged but raises the nominal demand. These are two ways of saying the same thing.

The common-sense of this disequilibrium can be seen by going back to the wage example on page 610. Looking at the disequilibrium in the first way mentioned above, we see that, for example, a doubling of the price level halves the real value of money balances. Thus firms and households who hold a given nominal supply of money will find it no longer sufficient to finance a week's transactions. They will need to build up their nominal balances to twice their original level. Until they do, there will be excess demand for money. Looking at the disequilibrium in the second way mentioned above, we see that a doubling of the price level doubles the nominal demand for money. In order to finance a week's transactions, firms and households need to hold twice as much nominal money as previously. With a constant nominal money supply there will thus be an excess demand for money.

> **A rise in the price level, with the nominal supply of money and real national income constant at its full-employment level, creates an excess demand for money.**

The effect of excess demand for money To see what happens next, we merely recall our earlier consideration of the consequences of an excess demand for money (see page 615). An excess demand for money will lead to a fall in bond prices as households and firms seek to sell bonds in order to increase their money holdings. The fall in the price of bonds means a rise in the rate of interest, and this will reduce aggregate expenditure by reducing all forms of interest-sensitive expenditure, such as investment in plant and equipment, new housing construction and new hire-purchase contracts.

If the nominal money supply is held constant, a rise in the price level causes an excess demand for money, which causes a rise in the rate of interest which in turn causes a decline in aggregate expenditure.

A summary The operation of the monetary adjustment mechanism may now be summarized. Assume that an inflationary gap opens up in an economy initially operating at full-employment income. Output cannot be increased, so the excess demand causes prices to rise. The rise in the price level increases the demand for money expressed in nominal units. If the nominal money supply is constant, an excess demand for money develops. This leads to an attempt to trade bonds for money to replenish money balances. But given a fixed stock of money, not everyone can do this, so the price of bonds falls until everyone is content to hold the existing stocks of bonds and money. This means that interest rates rise. As a result, aggregate expenditure falls. The process continues until the inflationary gap is removed.[1]

A common error in relating changes in the price level to changes in aggregate expenditure Before leaving this section we should clear up one potential source of serious confusion. Students sometimes put forward an argument that seems quite plausible, to the effect that inflation will obviously lower the aggregate expenditure function since people will be able to buy less with their incomes as prices rise. This argument is incorrect because it confuses real and nominal values. The aggregate expenditure function is expressed in real units. It shows how real expenditure (measured in constant prices) is related to real national income (measured in constant prices). An inflation that raises the nominal value of all prices and all incomes will leave the aggregate expenditure function unchanged. Of course the inflation may have redistributive effects, but for any given level of real national income anyone's loss *must be* someone else's gain. Thus inflation will only shift the aggregate expenditure function downwards through its effects on money incomes, if it redistributes income systematically from people with high marginal propensities to consume to people with lower propensities. (We ignore this redistributive effect here since there is no evidence that it exerts a systematic and continuous force to shift the expenditure function in one direction or the other.) Thus inflation does not shift the aggregate expenditure function through its effects on the purchasing power of people's incomes.

There are two ways to see the common sense of this result. First inflation raises factor prices as well as commodity prices. Thus money incomes rise along with prices of consumers' goods, leaving the purchasing power of the average income

[1] Anyone familiar with the Hicksian *IS-LM* analysis will recognize that the monetary adjustment mechanism takes the form in that model of a leftward shift in the *LM* curve whenever the price level rises. This leads to a rise in the rate of interest and a fall in total expenditure – i.e., a movement up the *IS* curve. The present text gives a verbal analysis of the same process. In the form in which it is presented here, the mechanism shifts downwards the function relating aggregate expenditure to national income *ceteris paribus* because the interest rate rises.

unchanged. Second, at any given level of real national income it is impossible that everyone should be worse off. Since total income is given, any person's loss must be someone else's gain. Thus, whatever the price level we may assume that, distributed effects aside, a given level of real national income will be associated with a given level of real desired expenditure.

Can the monetary adjustment mechanism be frustrated?

The theory just outlined shows that inflationary gaps tend to be self-correcting. They do cause inflations, but these very inflations set up a chain of events in asset markets that eventually remove the inflationary gap. (If this were not so, any demand inflation, once started, would necessarily go on forever.)

This is the reason why price levels and the money supply have for so long been linked in economics. There are many reasons why the price level may rise temporarily; some of them are still subject to current debate. Whatever the reason for the rise, unless the money supply is continually expanded, the price-level increase will itself set up forces that continually reduce the aggregate expenditure function. This will sooner or later remove any initial inflationary gap, and hence bring any demand inflation to a halt. Inflations that have causes other than excess demand may continue after the inflationary gap is removed. If so, the monetary adjustment mechanism will continue to produce falling aggregate expenditure, falling national income and rising unemployment.

Virtually all theories of the circular flow contain this monetary adjustment mechanism in one form or another. There is some debate about its exact transmission mechanism, the speed with which it works, and by how much the price level must rise to eliminate a given inflationary gap. But its existence is fairly generally accepted.

The only way in which this self-correcting mechanism can be frustrated indefinitely is to have the nominal money supply increase at the same rate as prices are rising. Say, for example, that the price level is going up 10 per cent each year under the pressure of a large inflationary gap. Nominal demand for money will be rising at about 10 per cent per year. Now say that the central bank (or any other force that can do the job) increases the nominal money supply at 10 per cent per year. No excess demand for money will develop, since the extra money needed to meet the rising demand for nominal money balances will be forthcoming; the real interest rate will not rise; and the inflationary gap will not be reduced.[1]

If the nominal money supply increases at the same rate that the price level rises, the real money supply is held constant, no excess demand for money emerges, and the monetary adjustment mechanism that automatically removes an inflationary gap is frustrated.

There is great debate on the policy relevance of this mechanism. A group of economists called monetarists make it the centrepiece of their policy recommendations. They maintain that central banks can and should hold the nominal

[1] With a continuing inflation we need to distinguish the real and the nominal rate of interest (see pages 395–6). The real rate (on which expenditure depends) will be unchanged, but the nominal rate will rise by the rate of inflation. Thus if the equilibrium real rate of interest is 3 per cent, the nominal rate will be 3, 5 and 10 per cent when the inflation is expected to continue at a rate of 0, 2 and 7 per cent respectively.

money supply constant in the face of increases in the price level, and that this behaviour is both necessary and sufficient to control inflation. Opponents are divided into several groups. Some say that it is not within the power of central banks to control the nominal supply of money. Others say that, given the political and economic objectives of governments, it is quite unrealistic to expect them to attempt to hold the money supply constant in the face of an inflation, even if they can do so. Still others say that although an inflation might be stopped by the monetary adjustment mechanism, the economic and social costs of doing so would be too great. Therefore, say this last group, the central bank *should* frustrate the monetary adjustment mechanism, and the government should seek other ways of bringing the inflation under control. We shall return to these very important debates in Part 11.

Conclusion

Excess demand for or supply of nominal money balances may be brought about in two basic ways (assuming a stable demand function for money). Either the central authorities can change the nominal supply of money, or the price level may change thus causing a change in the nominal demand for money.

The first possibility provides the basis for monetary policy. If the central bank raises or lowers the money supply, it will exert respectively an expansionary or a contractionary effect on aggregate demand and thence on national income. This effect works through the transmission mechanism analysed on pages 614–16. The effect of monetary policy will be larger the greater the change in the rate of interest brought about by a given change in the quantity of money, and the greater the change in interest-sensitive expenditure brought about by a given change in interest rates. The effect of monetary policy will be weak if either or both of the following are true: interest rates are not very responsive to changes in the quantity of money and expenditure is not very sensitive to interest rates. This analysis means that monetary policy may be used as an alternative, or as a supplement to, expansionary or contractionary fiscal policy.

The second possibility provides the basis for the monetary adjustment mechanism which may play a key role in the control of inflation. An inflation combined with a constant nominal money supply must cause the aggregate expenditure function to shift downwards (through its effects on interest rates). If the inflation is of the demand-pull variety, this monetary adjustment mechanism will remove the excess demand and bring the inflation to a halt. If the inflation has other causes and continues even when there is no excess demand, then the monetary adjustment mechanism will cause the inflation to be combined with an ever-decreasing level of real national income.

In part 11 we shall return to the matters discussed in the present part. In the meantime, however, two important matters need to be discussed. First, we must allow for the fact that all economies are open, engaging in substantial amounts of international trade. Second, we must analyse one further major goal of macroeconomic policy, the rate of economic growth. Part 9 deals with problems of international trade and payments, while Part 10 deals with growth and development. Then in Part 11 all of the analyses of parts 7 to 10 are brought together in a discussion of some of today's major problems of macroeconomic policy.

Appendix to Chapter 41

The classical quantity theory of money

The classical quantity theory of money arrived at results very similar to those outlined in Chapter 41 for the modern theory. The classical theory, however, used a simpler transmission mechanism that went straight from an excess demand for or supply of money to the aggregate expenditure function. As a result the classical theory could use a simpler demand function for money balances.

The demand for and supply of money

In the classical theory the demand for money depends solely on the transactions motive. This demand, expressed in *nominal* money units, is written

$$M_d = kPY, \qquad (1)$$

where P is the price level and Y is real national income.[1] The value of k is the fraction of the annual value of national income that firms and households wish to hold as transactions balances – which is the only reason for holding money.

Next we express the assumption that the supply of money is a constant determined by the central authorities:

$$M_s = M, \qquad (2)$$

where M_s is the supply of money and M is some constant amount (measured in pounds sterling). Equation (2) merely says that the supply of money does not depend on any other factors in the economy; it is simply what the central authorities want it to be.

Finally we write a condition for equilibrium between the demand for money and the supply of it. This is written as

$$M_d = M_s. \qquad (3)$$

[1] Dividing through by P yields the money demand in real terms, M_d/P, that was used in the text and symbolized M_D.

When (3) holds, households and firms will have, in the aggregate, just the amount of money balances they require. When (3) does not hold, they will have too much or too little money. The effect that this will have on the economy depends on the transmission mechanism.

The transmission mechanism

The transmission mechanism in the classical theory was a very direct one. If, on the one hand, firms and households hold more money than they wish to hold, there is excess supply of money. According to the classical theory, excess money balances are spent to purchase currently produced goods and services. If, on the other hand, firms and households hold smaller money balances than they would like to hold, then there is excess demand for money and they cut their expenditures below their incomes in an effort to build up their balances.

Comparing the classical theory and the modern theories, the transmission mechanism differs but the final result is the same: excess demand for money reduces aggregate expenditure and excess supply increases it.

The quantity theory with full employment

To see how the quantity theory works, let us first assume that real national income is constant at its full-employment level, so that excess aggregate demand must cause the price level to rise. The questions of the quantity theory are summarized in Table 41.1. Substitution of (1) and (2) into the equilibrium condition (3) produces the basic relation between P and M as shown in the fourth equation, which merely states that the

Table 41.1 The equations of the quantity theory

(1) Demand for money	$M_d = kPY$
(2) Supply of money	$M_s = M$
(3) Equilibrium condition	$M_d = M_s$
(4) Equations (1), (2), and (3) give	$kPY = M$
or	$P = \frac{1}{kY} \cdot M$

If k and Y are constant, P varies proportionately with M.

demand for money (kPY) should equal its supply (M).

> **If we are dealing with inflationary-gap situations so that income is constant at its full-employment level and if k is constant, then the price level must rise in proportion to any increase in the quantity of money.**

To see how this result comes about we must consider disequilibrium behaviour. Assume that the economy begins in a situation of full-employment equilibrium with the demand for money equal to its supply. Now assume that the central bank increases the supply of money in the hands of households and firms by 10 per cent. According to the behavioural hypothesis of the quantity theory, the firms and households try to convert this extra cash into goods and services but, since the economy is already at full employment, their efforts can only open up an inflationary gap. Indeed, the price level must rise until the demand for money is again equal to its supply. Since the demand for money is kPY, and since k is fixed by assumption, and since Y cannot change because the economy remains at the same level of full-employment output, the demand for money will increase by exactly 10 per cent when P increases by 10 per cent. Until that time the demand for money will be less than its supply, and the attempt to convert the excess money into currently-produced goods and services will generate excess demand that will cause further inflation. Thus, equilibrium can be restored only when the price level rises by the same percentage as did the supply of money.

Often the quantity theory is presented and discussed using V (VELOCITY OF CIRCULATION) instead of k. V stands for the average number of times a unit of money turns over in the transactions that create GNP. It is defined as the reciprocal of k. Table 41.2 shows the effect of substituting symbols. Of course it makes no difference whether we work with k or V, as long as we are careful about the way we interpret these two variables.

The stock of money people wish to hold might, for example, be one-tenth of the annual value of national income. If k is 0·1, then V must be 10. This indicates that if the money supply is to be one-tenth of the value of national income, the average unit of money must change hands ten times in order to bring about an aggregate value of income ten times as large as the stock of money.

Table 41.2 From k to V

If the demand for money, kPY, equals the supply, M, we have, from Table 41.1,

(4) $kPY = M$

(5) Rewriting (4) gives $PY = M\frac{1}{k}$

(6) Letting V stand for $\frac{1}{k}$ gives $PY = MV$

The quantity theory with unemployment

The quantity theory became a part of the Classical Model in which the *equilibrium* level of national income was always at full employment. Thus Y remained fixed at its full-employment value, and not only did P rise in proportion to a rise in the money supply, but P also *fell* in proportion to a *reduction* in the money supply. Thus Y was determined by its full-employment level and P was determined by the quantity of money. To adapt the classical quantity theory to situations in which actual income is less than potential income, we merely use our assumption that in this situation the price level is constant while national income varies with aggregate demand. This makes P a constant and Y a variable but preserves the link provided by the quantity theory between the excess demand for money and changes in aggregate demand.

To see what is implied we take the theory in the form:

$$kPY = M,$$

which is equation (4) in Table 41.1 and divide through by kP to obtain:

$$Y = \frac{1}{kP}M.$$

This tells us that:

> **If P is constant during periods of unemployment, national income (and hence output and employment) will vary in proportion to the money supply.**

The reason for this is analogous to the reasons given in the discussion of disequilibrium under inflationary conditions. If firms and households have too much money, they spend it and the resulting increase in aggregate demand raises output and employment. If firms and households have too little money, they lower their expenditures in an attempt to increase their money balances, and the resulting fall in aggregate demand lowers the equilibrium level of output.

> **The basic prediction of the quantity theory is that there will be a change in the *money value* of national income, in proportion to any change in the quantity of money. In some cases the change will be mainly a price change (a change in P); in others it will be a change in output and employment (a change in Y). In either case, control over the money supply becomes a potent method of controlling national income.**

Part nine

The international economy

42

The gains from international trade

The British buy Volkswagens, Germans take holidays in Italy, Italians buy spice from Tanzania, Africans import oil from Kuwait, Arabs buy Japanese cameras, the Japanese depend heavily on American soyabeans and Americans buy British sportscars. *International trade* refers to all such exchanges of goods and services that take place across international boundaries. This trade gives rise to a number of characteristic problems.

Chapter 34 studied the effects of changes in imports and exports on the circular flow of income. At that time we emphasized the effect on aggregate expenditure, and we regarded imports as a withdrawal from total domestic expenditure and exports as an injection. We now wish to enquire into the problems of international trade in a more fundamental way. In this chapter we shall ask if there are gains from international trade and if so, what their source is. In Chapter 43 we shall inquire into exchange rates, asking what they are, what they do and why they vary. In Chapter 44 we shall study reasons that have been advanced for interfering with the free flow of trade that would result from the operation of the unhindered price system. Finally in Chapter 45 we shall study the international payments systems of the present and the recent past.

A word of warning

In what follows we shall often speak of nations, e.g., the United Kingdom and the United States, trading various commodities. This convenient anthropomorphism should not mislead you into thinking that all, or even the majority of, decisions about trade are actually taken by governments. In most countries governments do play some more or less important role in foreign trade. It must never be forgotten, however, that in market economies most of the decisions determining the size, content and direction of foreign trade are taken by households and firms. Firms may see an opportunity of selling goods abroad and arrange to have these goods exported; other firms may see an opportunity of selling foreign goods in the home market and arrange to have these goods imported. If households either at home or abroad find such goods attractive and purchase them, the ventures will be successful; if they do not, the goods will remain unsold and will no longer be imported or exported. Governments may, of course, try to influence this process:

they may put subsidies on exports, seeking to encourage foreign sales of domestically produced goods by making their prices more attractive; they may put tariffs on imports, seeking to discourage domestic sales of foreign-produced goods, by making their prices less attractive. None of this should obscure the basic fact that in free-market economies foreign trade, just like domestic trade, is determined mainly by thousands of independent decisions taken by firms and households and co-ordinated – more or less effectively – by the price system.

The major difference between foreign trade and domestic trade results from the fact that the domestic trade of different countries makes use of different monies. The rupee, for example, while generally accepted in India, will not be acceptable to firms and households in Britain. If an importer in India wishes to purchase British goods, he cannot pay for them in rupees; he will have to obtain pounds sterling first.

> **In general, trade between nations can occur only if it is possible to exchange the currency of one nation for that of another.**

For the moment we shall ignore this problem of different currencies and ask the following question: assuming that trade between different economies takes place, is there any gain from it? If so, what is the source of this gain?

Interpersonal, interregional and international trade

Economists have long recognized that the principles governing the gains from trade apply equally well to both foreign and domestic trade. Governments tend to regard the two aspects of trade in very different lights, but economists were prominent in the fight for recognition that the causes and consequences of international trade were merely an extension of the principles governing domestic trade. Some of these principles were developed quite early, but it was not until the mid-nineteenth century that the British economist John Stuart Mill advanced a theory showing satisfactorily how international trade could be explained by exactly the same principles as those explaining domestic trade.

> **Economists now recognize that they are asking the same question whether they ask what is the advantage of trade between two individuals, between two groups, between two regions or between two countries.**

The source of such gains is easiest to study by considering the differences between a world with trade and one without it.

First, consider trade among individuals. If there were none, each person would have to be self-sufficient, producing all the food, clothing, shelter, medical services, entertainment, and luxuries of life that were required. Although the idea of universal self-sufficiency is wildly unreal, it does not take much imagination to realize that living standards would be very low in such a world. Trade between individuals allows people to specialize in things they can do well and to buy from others the things they cannot easily produce. Someone who is a bad carpenter but a good doctor can specialize in medicine, providing a physician's services not only for his or her own family but also for a person who is an excellent carpenter yet has neither the training nor the ability to practise medicine. Thus trade and specialization are intimately connected. With trade everyone can specialize in what he does well.

The same principles apply to regions. Without interregional trade, each region would have to be self-sufficient. With such trade, plains regions can specialize in growing grain, mountain regions in mining and lumbering, and regions with abundant power sources in manufacturing. Cool regions can produce wheat and other crops that thrive in such conditions, and tropical regions can produce bananas and coconuts. One would suspect – and soon we shall demonstrate – that living standards in all regions will be higher if the inhabitants of each specialize in those lines of production in which they have some natural or acquired advantage, obtaining other products by trade, than if each region is self-sufficient.

Identical remarks apply to nations. Whatever the divisions represented by national boundaries, they tend to be arbitrary with respect to the advantages of regional specialization and trade. There is no reason to expect that a national boundary will define an area that could be fully self-sufficient at little cost to itself. Thus nations, like regions or persons, can gain from specialization and the international trade that must accompany it.

Sources of the gains from trade

This preliminary discussion suggests one important possible gain from trade:

> **With trade, each individual, region or nation is able to concentrate on producing things in which it has an advantage while trading to obtain things that it could not produce efficiently itself.**

In order to concentrate on the sources of gains from trade one at a time, we begin by ruling out any gains in *productivity* that result from specialization. Assume that each region can produce goods at certain levels of productivity and that these levels are independent of the degree to which it specializes in the production of any good. What, in these circumstances, is the gain from regional specialization?

A special case: reciprocal absolute advantage

The gains from specialization are clear if there is a simple situation involving reciprocal absolute advantage. ABSOLUTE ADVANTAGE relates to the quantities of a single product that can be produced with the same quantity of resources in two different regions. One region is said to have an absolute advantage over another in the production of commodity *X* if an equal quantity of resources can produce more *X* in the first region than in the second.

Suppose region *A* has an absolute advantage over region *B* in one commodity, while *B* has an absolute advantage over *A* in another. We refer to this as a case of *reciprocal absolute advantage*: each region has an absolute advantage in some commodity. In such a situation, total production of both can be increased (relative to a situation of self-sufficiency) if each region specializes in the commodity in which it has the absolute advantage. Table 42.1 provides a simple example on the assumption that, with a given quantity of resources, America can produce 10 bushels of wheat or 6 yards of cloth, while England (with the same quantity of resources) can produce 5 bushels of wheat or 10 yards of cloth. The top half of the table shows the production of wheat and cloth that can be achieved in each country by using one unit of resources. Suppose at first that America and England are both self-sufficient, each producing wheat and cloth for its home markets. Now assume that trade is opened between the two countries and America moves resources out of cloth into wheat, while England moves resources out of wheat into cloth. The gains and losses in each country are summarized in the table. There is an increase in world

Table 42.1 Gains from specialization with reciprocal absolute advantage

	One unit of resources can produce	
	Wheat (bushels)	*Cloth* (yards)
America	10	6
England	5	10

Changes resulting from the transfer of 1 unit of American resources into wheat production and 1 unit of English resources into cloth production

	Wheat (bushels)	*Cloth* (yards)
America	+10	− 6
England	− 5	+10
World	+ 5	+ 4

production of 5 bushels of wheat and 4 yards of cloth: worldwide there are gains from specialization. The total world production of both wheat and cloth increases when this reallocation of production takes place – as is shown by the fact that there is both more wheat and more cloth for the same use of resources.

> **When there is reciprocal absolute advantage, specialization makes it possible to produce more of both commodities.**

These potential gains from *specialization* make possible gains from *trade*. England is producing more cloth and America more wheat than when they were self-sufficient. America is thus producing more wheat and less cloth than American consumers wish to buy, and England is producing more cloth and less wheat than English consumers wish to buy. If consumers in both countries are to get cloth and wheat in the proportions in which they desire them, it will be necessary for America to export wheat to England and to import cloth from that country.

> **International trade is necessary to achieve the gains that international specialization makes possible.**

Because specialization and trade go hand in hand – no one would be motivated to achieve the gains from specialization without being able to trade the goods produced for goods desired – it is usual to use the term *gains from trade* to embrace them both.

A first general statement: comparative advantage

When each country has an absolute advantage over the other in one commodity, the gains from trade are obvious: if each produces the commodity in the production of which it is more efficient than the other, world production will be higher than if each tries to be self-sufficient. But what if America can produce both wheat and cloth more efficiently than England? In essence, this was the question David Ricardo posed over 150 years ago, and his answer forms the basis of the theory of comparative advantage that is still accepted by economists as a valid statement of the potential gains from trade.

Assume that American efficiency increases above the levels recorded in the previous example, so that a unit of American resources can produce either 100 bushels of wheat or 60 yards of cloth, while English efficiency remains unchanged, so that a unit of English resources can produce either 5 bushels of wheat or 10 yards of cloth. Now surely America, which is better at producing both wheat and cloth than England, has nothing to gain by trading with this inefficient island country! It *does* have something to gain, however, and it is important to see how this comes about.

Table 42.2 Gains from specialization with comparative advantage

	One unit of resources can produce	
	Wheat (bushels)	*Cloth* (yards)
America	100	60
England	5	10

Changes resulting from the transfer of $\frac{1}{10}$ of 1 unit of American resources into wheat production and 1 unit of English resources into cloth production

	Wheat (bushels)	*Cloth* (yards)
America	+10	− 6
England	− 5	+10
World	+ 5	+ 4

Table 42.3 Absence of gains from specialization where there is no comparative advantage

	One unit of resources can produce	
	Wheat (bushels)	*Cloth* (yards)
America	100	60
England	10	6

Changes resulting from the transfer of 1 unit of American resources into wheat production and 10 units of English resources into cloth production

	Wheat (bushels)	*Cloth* (yards)
America	+100	−60
England	−100	+60
World	0	0

The gain from specialization in this case is illustrated in Table 42.2. The new figures make America 10 times as efficient as she was in the situation of Table 42.1. England no longer has an absolute advantage in producing either commodity. Total production of both commodities can nonetheless be increased by specialization. The movement of one-tenth of one unit of American resources out of cloth and into wheat and the opposite movement in England of one unit of resources causes world production of wheat to rise by 5 bushels and cloth by 4 yards. This shows that it is still possible to increase world production of both wheat and cloth by having America produce more wheat and less cloth and England produce more cloth and less wheat. Thus reciprocal absolute advantage is not necessary for gains from trade.

There is a gain from specialization because although America has an absolute advantage over England in the production of both wheat and cloth, its margin of advantage differs in the two commodities. America can produce 20 times as much wheat as can England using the same quantity of resources, but only 6 times as much cloth. America is said to have a COMPARATIVE ADVANTAGE in the production of wheat and a comparative disadvantage in the production of cloth. England has a comparative disadvantage in the production of wheat and a comparative advantage in the production of cloth.

The most important proposition in the theory of international trade is:

> **The gains from specialization and trade depend on the pattern of comparative, not absolute, advantage.**

A comparison of Tables 42.1 and 42.2 shows that the absolute *levels* of efficiency of two areas do not affect the gains from specialization. What matters is that the margin of advantage that one area has over the other must differ between commodities. As long as this is true, total world production can be increased if each area specializes in the production of the commodity in which it has a comparative advantage.

Comparative advantage is not only sufficient for gains from trade, it is also necessary. This is illustrated by the example in Table 42.3, in which America has an absolute advantage in both commodities but neither country enjoys a comparative advantage over the other in the production of either commodity. America is 10 times as efficient as England in the production of wheat and also in the production of cloth. Now, try as you may, there is no way to increase the production of both wheat and cloth by reallocating resources within America and within England. The lower half of the table provides one example of this. You should try others. It is possible to reallocate resources so as to get more of one commodity and less of the other, but this is also possible within either country. Absolute advantage without comparative advantage does not lead to gains from trade.

> **Where there is no comparative advantage, there is no reallocation of resources within each country that will increase the production of both commodities.**

A second general statement: opportunity costs

Much of the previous argument has made use of the concept of a unit of resources and has also assumed that units of resources can be equated across countries, so that such statements as 'America can produce 10 times as much wheat with the same quantity of resources as England' are meaningful. Measurement of the real-resource cost of producing commodities poses many difficulties. If, for example, England uses land, labour, and capital in proportions different from those used in America, it may not be clear which country gets more output 'per unit of resource input'. Fortunately, the proposition about the gains from trade can be restated without any reference to absolute efficiencies and in a way that should make even clearer the sources of gain in the previous examples.

To do this, return to the examples of Tables 42.1 and 42.2 and calculate the opportunity cost of wheat and cloth in the two countries. If resources are assumed to be fully employed, the only way to produce more of one commodity is to reallocate resources and thus produce less of the other commodity. Table 42.1 shows that a unit of resources in America can produce 10 bushels of wheat *or* 6 yards of cloth, from which it follows that the opportunity cost of producing a unit of wheat is 0·6 units of cloth, while the opportunity cost of producing a unit of cloth is 1·67 units of wheat. These data are summarized in Table 42.4. The table also shows that in England the opportunity cost of 1 unit of wheat is 2 units of cloth forgone, whereas the opportunity cost of a unit of cloth is 0·50 units of wheat. These

Table 42.4 The opportunity cost of 1 unit of wheat and 1 unit of cloth in America and England

	Wheat	*Cloth*
America	0·6 yards cloth	1·67 bushels wheat
England	2·0 yards cloth	0·50 bushels wheat

opportunity costs can be obtained either from Table 42.1 or from Table 42.2. The English opportunity cost of one unit of wheat is obtained by dividing the cloth output of one unit of English resources by the wheat output. The resulting figure of 2 shows that 2 yards of cloth must be sacrificed for every extra unit of wheat produced by transferring English resources out of cloth production into wheat. The other three cost figures are obtained in a similar manner.

Comparative advantages can always be expressed in terms of opportunity costs that differ between countries.

The sacrifice of cloth involved in producing wheat is much lower in America than in England, and world production can be increased if America rather than England produces wheat. Looking at cloth rather than wheat production, one can see that the loss of wheat involved in producing one unit of cloth is lower in England than in

Table 42.5 Gains from specialization when opportunity costs differ

Changes resulting from each country's producing one more unit of commodity in which it has the lower opportunity cost

	Wheat (bushels)	*Cloth* (yards)
America	+1·0	−0·6
England	−0·5	+1·0
World	+0·5	+0·4

America. England is a lower (opportunity) cost producer of cloth than is America, and world production can be increased if England rather than America produces cloth. This situation is shown in Table 42.5.

The gains from trade arise from differing opportunity costs in the two countries.

The conclusions about the gains from trade in the hypothetical example of two countries and two commodities may be generalized as follows.

1. One country has a comparative advantage over a second country in producing a commodity if the opportunity cost (in terms of some other commodity) of

production in the first country is lower. This implies, however, that it has a comparative disadvantage in the other commodity.

2. Opportunity costs depend on relative costs of producing two commodities, not on absolute costs. (To check this, notice that the data in both Tables 42.1 and 42.2 give rise to the opportunity cost in Table 42.4.)

3. If opportunity costs are the same in all countries, there is no comparative advantage and no possibility of gains from specialization and trade. (You can illustrate this for yourself by calculating the opportunity costs implied by the data in Table 42.3.)

4. If opportunity costs differ in any two countries, and both countries are producing both commodities, it is always possible to increase production of both commodities by a suitable reallocation of resources within each country.

This proposition is illustrated in Table 42.5. The calculations in the table show that there are gains from specialization given the opportunity costs of Table 42.4. To produce one more bushel of wheat, America must sacrifice 0·6 yards of cloth. To produce one more yard of cloth, England must sacrifice 0·5 bushels of wheat. Making both changes raises world production of both wheat and cloth.[1]

Although we derived Table 42.4 from the data in Table 42.1 and 42.2, the determination of opportunity cost does not require that we are able to compare output per unit of resources in various countries. The gains from trade require only that the sacrifice of one commodity needed to get one unit of a second commodity is different in the various countries. It does not matter how this difference comes about, nor do we have to be able to measure output per unit of resources; all that is needed is that, for any reason, opportunity costs do differ.

Nonetheless, the statement of the gains from trade in terms of comparative advantage is a great insight. It is commonly believed by the general public that absolute efficiences can be measured and that inefficient countries cannot gainfully trade with efficient ones. The statement in terms of comparative advantage effectively refutes this belief. It shows that *if* the concept of absolute efficiency can be given any meaning, then there is potential for mutual gains from trade when absolutely efficient countries trade with absolutely inefficient ones – provided only that the *comparative* advantages exist.

If, but only if, opportunity costs differ among countries, specialization of each country in producing those commodities in which it has comparative advantages will make it possible to achieve gains from trade.

Additional sources of the gains from trade: learning by doing and economies of scale

So far it has been assumed that costs are constant. It has been shown that even then there are gains from specialization and trade as long as there are interregional differences in opportunity costs. If costs are not constant, additional sources of gain are possible. Classical economists placed great importance on a factor that is now called *learning by doing*. They felt that as regions specialized in particular tasks, the workers and managers would become more efficient in performing them. As people acquire expertise, or know-how, costs tend to fall. A substantial body of modern

[1] In practice the gains from specialization must be large enough to cover the real resource costs involved in transporting the goods between two countries. In this elementary treatment this minor complication is ignored.

empirical work suggests that this really does happen. If this is the case, then output of cloth per worker may rise in England as England becomes more specialized in that commodity, while the same may happen to output of wheat per worker in America. This is, of course, an additional gain to that which occurs if costs are constant.

A further reason why costs might fall as regions specialize concerns economies of larger-scale production. If costs fall as output increases, world output can be greater when there is one large cloth industry in England and one large wheat industry in America, rather than two half-size cloth industries and two half-size wheat industries, one in each country.

The terms of trade

So far it has been shown that world production can be increased if America and England specialize in the production of the commodity in which they have a comparative advantage and that specialization requires trade. How will these gains from specialization and trade be shared between the two countries? The division of the gain depends on the terms at which trade takes place. The TERMS OF TRADE are defined as the quantity of domestic goods that must be given up to get a unit of imported goods. Thus the terms of trade are nothing more than the opportunity cost of obtaining goods through international trade rather than producing them directly.

In the example of Table 42.4, the American domestic opportunity cost of one unit of cloth is 1·67 bushels of wheat. If Americans can obtain cloth by international trade at terms of trade more favourable to them than 1·67 bushels of wheat, they will gain by doing so. Suppose that international prices are such that one yard of cloth exchanges for (i.e., is equal in value to) one bushel of wheat. At those prices, Americans can obtain cloth at a lower wheat opportunity cost by trade than by domestic production. Therefore the terms of trade favour selling wheat and buying cloth on international markets.

By a similar argument, English consumers in the example of Table 42.4 gain if they can obtain wheat abroad at any terms of trade more favourable than 2 yards of cloth per bushel of wheat, which is the English domestic opportunity cost. If the terms of trade are 1 bushel of wheat for 1 yard of cloth, the terms of trade favour English traders' buying wheat and selling cloth on international markets. Both England and America in this example gain from trade: each can obtain the commodity in which it has a comparative disadvantage at a lower opportunity cost through international trade than through domestic production.

Indeed both countries will gain from trade as long as the terms of trade lie between the domestic opportunity cost ratios of the two countries. Although we do not go into it here, it is possible to show that if the terms of trade lie in the range where one of the countries would lose from trade, the price system would cause that country not to trade.

In practice, changes in the terms of trade are usually measured by changes in the ratio

$$\frac{\text{an index of export prices}}{\text{an index of import prices}}.$$

If this measure rises, say, from 1 to 2 it means that a given amount of exports will purchase twice as many imports as before. Rises and falls in the measure are referred to as favourable and unfavourable changes in the terms of trade.

43

The theory of exchange rates

In the previous chapter we saw that individuals, regions and nations all benefit from trade in the same ways. There is, however, one basic complication that distinguishes international trade from other kinds of trade: although everyone within the same country uses the same money, different nations do not. The currency of one country will not usually be accepted by households and firms in another country. When a British producer sells his products he requires payment in sterling. He must meet his wage bill, pay for his raw materials, and reinvest or distribute his profits. If he sells his goods to British purchasers there is no problem, since they will pay in sterling. If, however, he sells his goods to an Indian importer, either he must accept rupees or the Indian must exchange his rupees for pounds to pay for the goods. The British producer will accept rupees only if he knows that he can exchange them for the sterling that he requires. The same is true for producers in all countries; each must eventually receive payment for the goods that he sells in the currency of his own country.

Foreign-exchange transactions

Suppose that a US dealer wishes to purchase a British sportscar to sell in the United States. The British manufacturer requires payments in sterling. If the car is priced at, say, £2,000, the American importer can go to his bank, purchase a cheque for £2,000 and send it to the British seller. The price that he pays for this cheque is called the *exchange rate*. We shall assume an exchange rate of $2.00 to £1. Given this exchange rate, the US importer would write a cheque on his own account for $4,000 in payment of his £2,000 sterling cheque or 'draft'. The British producer would deposit the cheque in his own bank. When all this was done, the banking system would have exchanged obligations to Americans for obligations to residents of the UK. The deposits of the American purchaser, which are liabilities of his bank, would be reduced by $4,000 and the deposits of the British seller, which are liabilities of the British bank, would be increased by £2,000. The banking system, as a whole, makes a profit by charging a small commission for effecting such transactions.

Now let us consider a second transaction. Assume that a British wholesaler wishes to purchase ten American refrigerators for sale in Britain. If the refrigerators are priced at $400 each, the American seller will require a total payment of $4,000. To pay it, the British importer goes to his bank, writes a cheque on his account for

£2,000 and receives a cheque drawn on a US bank for $4,000. This reduces the deposit liabilities of the British bank by £2,000. When the American seller deposits this cheque, his deposits, which are liabilities of the US banking system, are increased by $4,000. Thus the banking system as a whole has merely switched liabilities, this time from the UK to the US.

These two transactions cancel each other out, and there is no net change in international liabilities. The balance sheets of the British and the American banks will show the changes in Table 43.1. No money need flow between the banks; each merely increases the deposits of one domestic customer and lowers those of another. Indeed, as long as the flows of payments between the two countries are equal, so that Americans are paying as much to UK residents as UK residents are paying to Americans, all payments can be managed as in this example and there is no need for a net payment in either direction.

Table 43.1 Changes in the balance sheets of two banks

UK Bank			US Bank		
Liabilities		Assets	Liabilities		Assets
Deposits of car exporter	+£2,000	No change	Deposits of car importer	−$4,000	No change
Deposits of refrigerator importer	−£2,000		Deposits of refrigerator exporter	+$4,000	

The EXCHANGE RATE is the price at which purchases and sales of foreign currency (or claims on it, such as cheques and promises to pay) take place; it is the price of one currency in terms of another. The term FOREIGN EXCHANGE refers to what is traded, actual foreign currency or various claims on it. When the exchange rate between British pounds sterling and American dollars is £1 = $2·06, one pound exchanges for two dollars and six cents, and one dollar exchanges for £0·48½. There are similar exchange rates between sterling and every other nation's currency. In 1978, one pound was worth approximately 1,690 Italian lire, 3·7 German Marks, or 143 Spanish pesetas.

Every transaction in the foreign-exchange market is two-sided. Every time a holder of sterling *demands* some foreign money he must *supply* sterling in exchange. Every time a holder of foreign currency *demands* sterling he must *supply* foreign currency in exchange.

> **On the foreign-exchange market, a demand for foreign money implies a supply of an equivalent value of domestic money, while a supply of foreign money implies a demand for an equivalent value of domestic money.**

The balance of payments

The balance of actual payments

In order to know what is happening to the course of international payments, governments keep track of the actual transactions among countries. The record of such transactions is called the BALANCE OF PAYMENTS. Each transaction, such as a shipment of exports or the arrival of imported goods, is recorded and classified according to the payments or receipts that would typically arise from it.

Any item that typically gives rise to a purchase of foreign currency is recorded as a debit item on the balance-of-payments accounts, and any item that typically gives rise to a sale of foreign currency is recorded as a credit item.

If, for example, a British importer buys an American washing machine to sell in the United Kingdom, this appears as a debit in the UK balance of payments because when the machine is paid for, sterling will be sold and dollars purchased. On the other hand, if a US shipping firm insures with Lloyd's of London a cargo destined for Egypt, this represents a credit in the UK balance of payments, because when the insurance premium is paid, the shipping firm will have to buy sterling in order to pay Lloyd's. Of course, what is a credit item to one country is a debit item to the other, and vice versa. Thus the washing machine transaction is a credit and the insurance transaction is a debit item in the US balance of payments.

In order to study the behaviour of the foreign-exchange market we would really like to be able to measure purchases and sales of foreign exchange, but we are able to measure only the movement of goods and services. In order to relate what we can measure to what we want to measure, we have to make a number of assumptions, some of them quite arbitrary. How, for example, should we record gifts of goods to foreigners? If the goods had been sold, they would have given rise to purchases of domestic currency, but when they are given away they do not. What should we do with an export to a foreign firm that buys a good on credit and subsequently defaults on the debt? Such problems are important both to the statistician who is attempting to measure the balance of payments and to the careful observer who is attempting to account for very detailed movements in the flows of trade and payments. For our more general purposes, however, we can assume that the balance of payments measures what we would like it to measure: the actual flow of payments among nations.[1]

The first thing that we need to notice about the record of international transactions is that *the balance of payments always balances*. Although it is possible for holders of sterling to want to purchase more dollars in exchange for pounds than holders of dollars want to sell in exchange for pounds, it is not possible for sterling holders actually to buy more dollars than dollar holders sell. Every dollar that is bought must be sold by someone, and every dollar that is sold must be bought by someone. Since the dollars actually bought must be equal to the dollars actually sold, the payments made between countries must balance, even though desired payments may not.

In the *balance-of-payments accounts*, an attempt is made to record the reasons for which payments are made. Thus, we hope to be able to tell what volume of payments is (or will be) made by foreigners to UK citizens for such purposes as the purchase of British goods, the use of British services (shipping, insurance, etc.), the lending of

---

[1] The procedure adopted for handling the two problems cited in this paragraph are as follows. The export of a gift is recorded as a credit item just as if the good had been sold, but a compensating debit item is recorded under 'unilateral capital transfers'. Thus we assume that we *give away* the money and that the money is then used to *buy* our goods. The export that is not paid for because the buyer defaults will appear as a normal credit item, and an offsetting debit will probably be recorded under 'residual errors'.

money to British households, firms, or governments, or the investment of money in Britain. The accounts should also tell us what volume of payments is (or will be) made by UK residents to foreigners for similar reasons.

Although the total number of pounds bought on the foreign-exchange market must equal the total number sold, the value of purchases and sales for a particular purpose may not be equal. It is quite possible, for example, that more pounds were sold for the purpose of obtaining foreign currency to import foreign cars than were bought for the purpose of buying British cars for export to other countries. In such a case, we would say that the UK had a balance-of-payments deficit on the 'car account', meaning that the value of UK imports of cars exceeded the value of its exports of cars. For most general purposes, we are not interested in the balance of payments for single commodities but only for larger classes of transactions.

The major divisions of the balance of payments are illustrated in Table 43.2, which shows the UK data for the years 1973, 1975 and 1977.

Table 43.2 UK summary balance of payments, 1973–7 (£m)

	1973	1975	1977
Current account (credit + /debit −)			
Exports (fob) (+)	12,115	19,462	32,176
Imports (fob) (−)	14,469	22,667	33,788
Visible trade balance	−2,354	−3,205	−1,612
Government services and transfers (net)	−768	−999	−1,901
Other invisibles and transfers (net)	+2,239	+2,590	+3,478
Invisible trade balance	+1,471	+1,591	+1,577
Current balance	−883	−1,614	−35
Capital transfers	−59	—	—
Investment	−275	+91	+3,068
Overseas currency borrowing (net) by UK banks:	+665	+245	+592
Exchange reserves in sterling:	−201	−133	+1,182
Total investment and other capital flows	+49	+203	+4,802
Balancing item	+122	−54	+2,596
Total currency flow	−771	−1,465	+7,363
Official financing			
Net transactions with IMF	—	—	+1,113
Net transactions with overseas monetary authorities plus foreign currency borrowing by H.M. government	+999	+810	+1,112
Drawings on (+)/additions to (−) official reserves	−228	+655	−9,588
Total official financing	+771	+1,465	−7,363

Source: Bank of England Quarterly Bulletin, March 1978.

The current account The CURRENT ACCOUNT records all transactions in goods and services. VISIBLES are goods, i.e., things such as cars, pulpwood, aluminium, coffee, and iron ore, that we can see when they cross international borders.

INVISIBLES are services, i.e., those things that we cannot see, such as insurance and freight haulage and tourist expenditures. Another main invisible item on the current account is the receipt of interest and dividends on loans and investments in foreign countries. If, for example, British residents hold shares in the International Telephone and Telegraph Company (IT & T), they will receive dividend payments in US dollars. If they wish to spend these at home, they will have to exchange the dollars for pounds. Interest and dividends on foreign loans and investments thus provide foreign exchange and are entered as a credit item.

The capital account The CAPITAL ACCOUNT records transactions related to movements of long- and short-term capital. Consider, for example, holders of sterling who wish to invest abroad by lending money to American industry. We say that they are exporting capital from the UK to the US. Suppose they wish to buy bonds being sold in New York by expanding American firms. In order to do this, they need to obtain dollars. They are demanders of foreign exchange and suppliers of sterling. Their transactions are, therefore, debit items in the UK balance-of-payments account.

Capital movements may be divided in several ways. One important division is between direct and portfolio investment. DIRECT FOREIGN INVESTMENT occurs when firms themselves transfer funds in order to create new capital in foreign countries. If a UK firm decides, for example, to invest some of its sterling profits in building a new plant abroad, this is direct foreign investment. It is a debit item on the balance of payments because the UK firm will have to enter the foreign-exchange market selling sterling and buying foreign money in order to obtain the funds to build its factory. PORTFOLIO INVESTMENT occurs when equities or bonds are purchased. If, for example, a UK saver buys a share issued by the American company IBM, this is a portfolio investment and it represents a debit item on the UK balance of payments.

Capital movements may also be classified according to their term. If a UK citizen buys a Brazilian tin mining company's bond that will mature in 2005, this is a long-term capital outflow from the UK. If a British firm elects to transfer some of its working balances from London to its New York bank, this is an outflow of short-term capital, since the New York bank has the obligation to pay the deposit on demand.

Short-term capital holdings arise in many ways. The mere fact of international trade forces traders to hold money balances. Traders' receipts and expenditures are not perfectly synchronized, and they necessarily hold transactions and precautionary balances because they must be able to pay their bills when these fall due. It usually does not matter where such funds are held. The funds can easily be moved from one currency to another in response to small changes in incentives or because of real or imaginary fears of all sorts. When short-term capital is transferred from one country to another, purchases and sales of foreign exchange must occur.

It is sometimes confusing to beginners that the export of capital is a debit item and the export of a good is a credit item. The situation is, however, really very simple. The export of a good earns foreign exchange, and the export of capital uses foreign exchange. Therefore they have opposite effects on international payments. Another way of looking at it is that the capital transaction involves the purchase, and hence the *import* of a foreign bond or share; this has the same effect on the balance of payments as the purchase, and hence the import, of a foreign good. Both transactions use foreign exchange and are thus debit items in the UK balance of payments.

Official financing The OFFICIAL FINANCING item represents transactions involving the central bank of the country whose balance of payments is being recorded; in this case, the Bank of England. There are three ways in which credit items may occur on the official financing account. First, the Bank of England may borrow from the IMF. This represents a capital inflow and is thus a credit item on the balance of payments. (Repayment of old IMF loans is a debit item.) Second, the Bank may borrow from other central banks through a network of arrangements built up in the 1960s to defend fixed exchange rates against speculative attacks. Such foreign borrowing by the Bank of England is a credit item on the balance of payments. Third, the Bank may run down its official reserves of gold and foreign exchange. This is a credit item because it gives rise to a sale of foreign exchange and a purchase of sterling. The running down of reserves occurs when the Bank of England is supporting the value of sterling on the foreign-exchange market. The Bank then enters the free market selling foreign exchange and buying sterling.

The relation among the three main divisions The discussion above should have made it obvious that there is nothing necessarily good about credit items or bad about debit items on the balance of payments. For example, investment by UK firms in foreign countries that will yield future profits for UK owners is a debit item; the running down of Bank of England reserves of foreign currencies is a credit item, as is the transfer of ownership of UK firms to foreigners.

The relation among the three divisions of accounts follows simply from the fact that their sum must be zero:

$$C + K + F \equiv 0$$

where C, K and F are, respectively, the *balance* on current, capital and official settlement accounts.

> **A deficit on current account must be matched by a net surplus on capital plus official settlement accounts, which means borrowing abroad or running down exchange reserves. A surplus on current account implies a deficit on the sum of the other two accounts.**

To illustrate this relation, assume that in a given year, the value of UK imports exceeds the value of UK exports, considering all current-account transactions. The foreign currency necessary to finance the imports that were in excess of exports had to come from somewhere. It must have been lent by someone or else provided out of the government's reserves of gold and foreign exchange. If foreigners are investing funds in the UK, they will be selling foreign currency and buying sterling in order to be able to buy equities and bonds issued by UK firms. Such foreign lending can provide the foreign exchange necessary to allow the UK to have an excess of imports over exports. The other possibility is that the Bank of England financed the current-account deficit either by selling some of its reserves of foreign exchange or by borrowing from the IMF or other central banks.

Now consider a situation in which the value of exports is in excess of the value of imports. This means that foreigners will not have been able to obtain all the sterling they need in order to buy UK goods from the UK sources who wish to supply sterling in return for foreign currency in order to buy foreign goods. The excess of exports over imports could only have been paid for if foreigners obtained sterling from other sources. There are several possibilities. First, sterling may be provided by UK investors wishing to obtain foreign currency so that they can buy foreign stocks and bonds. In this case, the excess of exports over imports is balanced by UK loans and investments abroad. Second, the UK Government, rather than its firms or citizens, may have lent money to foreign governments to finance their purchases of British-produced goods or services. Third, the UK Government may have given money away as aid, particularly to underdeveloped countries. Such gifts allow these countries to purchase more from the UK than they sell to it. The fourth main possibility is that the Bank of England has added to its reserves of foreign exchange by selling sterling on the foreign-exchange market.[1]

We have already noted that when we add up all the uses of foreign currency, and all the sources from which it came, these two amounts are necessarily equal, and thus the overall accounts of all international payments necessarily balance. What, then, do we mean when we say that payments are not in balance, that there is a deficit or a surplus on the balance of payments?

When we speak of a balance-of-payments deficit or surplus, we refer to the balance on some part of the accounts. Usually, we are referring to the balance on current plus capital account. A balance-of-payments deficit thus means that the reserves of the central bank are being run down or its foreign indebtedness is rising, while a surplus means the opposite.

The balance of desired payments

We have seen that *actual* payments must always be in balance, because foreign exchange bought must equal foreign exchange sold. At a given exchange rate, however, *desired* payments need not be in balance: people may wish to buy more foreign exchange than others wish to sell. If, at the curent rate of exchange, the demand for US dollars exceeds the supply, it follows that holders of sterling are trying to make more payments in dollars than holders of dollars wish to make in sterling. If, on the other hand, the supply of US dollars exceeds the demand, holders of dollars are trying to make more payments in sterling than holders of sterling wish to make in dollars.

We must now develop a theory of how exchange rates are determined on free markets by the balance of desired payments.

The determination of exchange rates

In today's world, exchange rates are detemined in highly competitive free markets where the rates change as often as necessary to equate desired payments among countries. The theory of the market determination of exchange rates is thus nothing more than an application of the theory of market behaviour that we developed in Part 2.

The theories and descriptions of this chapter apply to international payments

[1] This is an open-market operation in which the Bank buys foreign exchange rather than domestic bonds. The effect on the domestic money supply is the same in both cases: the Bank creates new money by its open-market purchases.

among all countries and to all exchange rates, but for the sake of simplicity we shall refer to two countries, the UK and the US, and to the rate between their two currencies, pounds sterling and dollars. Since one currency is traded for another on the foreign-exchange market, it follows that a demand for dollars implies a supply of pounds while an offer (supply) of dollars implies a need (demand) for pounds. If, at an exchange rate of £1 = $3, a British importer demands $6 he must be offering £2, and if an American importer offers $6 he must be demanding £2. For this reason we can deal either with the demand for and the supply of dollars, or with the demand for and the supply of pounds sterling; we do not need to consider both. We shall conduct the argument in terms of dollars.

When we refer to payments between Britain and the US we are concerned with the sterling-dollar exchange rate. This can be expressed in either of two ways: the amount of sterling needed to buy one dollar or the amount of dollars needed to buy one pound. Since we are conducting the argument in terms of dollars, we shall use the former measure. This is nothing more than a matter of convenience because there is only one rate but there are two ways of expressing it. Thus, for example, the statements that $3 exchanges for £1 and that £0·33 exchanges for $1 mean the same thing.

The determination of exchange rates by demand and supply

In our two-country model of the foreign-exchange market there are only two groups of private traders: people who have sterling and want dollars trade with people who have dollars and want sterling. We shall concentrate for the moment on current and capital account dealings by assuming that the Bank of England does not intervene in the market.

The demand for dollars The demand for dollars arises because holders of sterling wish to make payments in dollars; it thus arises from imports of American goods and services into the UK and from capital movement from the UK to the US.[1]

The supply of dollars Dollars are offered in exchange for sterling because holders of dollars wish to make payments in sterling. The supply of dollars on the foreign-exchange market arises, therefore, because of British exports of goods and services to the United States and because of capital movements from the US to the UK.

Exchange rate changes When the free-market price of one currency rises in terms of another currency, we say that the exchange rate has APPRECIATED and that the value of the first currency has appreciated on the foreign-exchange market. When the free-market price of a currency falls in terms of foreign currencies we say that the exchange rate has DEPRECIATED. Since there is only one exchange rate between any two currencies, an appreciation of sterling against the dollar is the same thing as a depreciation of the dollar against sterling.

[1] Beware of a possible source of confusion. Up to Part 9 capital has always meant real capital: plant and equipment, inventories and the housing stock. In Part 9, where we are concentrating on payments, capital refers to financial capital: sums of money that are available to put in bank accounts, to buy financial assets or to *buy* real capital goods. Thus, a capital transfer in exchange rate literature refers to the movement of funds that may or may not be the financial counterpart of a movement of real capital goods.

Price changes caused by exchange-rate changes Consider an American good whose price delivered to a shipping point in New York is \$10 (in commercial language this is called its price FOB New York). When the exchange rate is £1 = \$3 (\$1 = £0·33) it will cost a UK purchaser £3·33 to obtain the foreign exchange needed to buy that commodity. When the exchange rate is £1 = \$2 (\$1 = £0·50), however, it will cost the UK purchaser £5·00. The same would be true of a US stock or bond selling for \$10 on the US market.

> **A depreciation of sterling makes it more expensive for holders of sterling to purchase a commodity or a financial asset whose price is quoted in dollars.**

Now consider a British good whose price FOB Liverpool is £5. When the exchange rate is £1 = \$3, it will cost a US purchaser \$15 to obtain the foreign exchange needed to buy that commodity. When the exchange rate is £1 = \$2, however, the transaction will cost the holder of dollars only \$10. Identical remarks apply to a British stock or bond selling in London for £5.

> **A depreciation of sterling makes it less expensive for holders of dollars to purchase a commodity or a financial asset whose price is quoted in sterling.**

The graphical representation of the determination of the exchange rate

In Figure 43.1 we measure the sterling price of a dollar on the vertical axis. (You may be more familiar with the exchange rate expressed the other way round, as the dollar price of one pound sterling. For practice, convert a few of the prices in Figure 43.1 into the more familiar mode of expression. What, for example, is the dollar price of one pound if the sterling price of one dollar is 30p?)

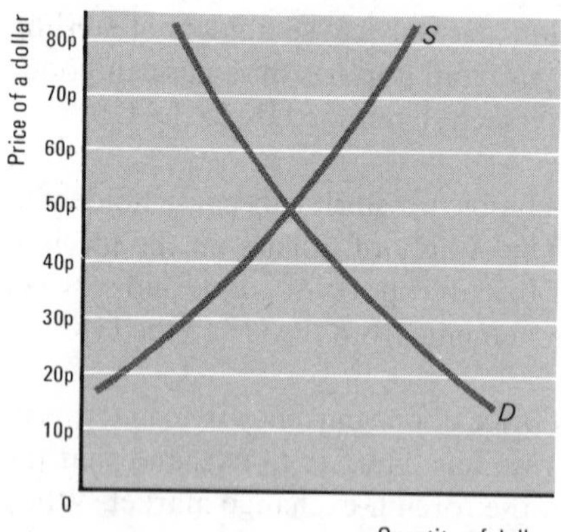

Fig. 43.1 The determination of the equilibrium exchange rate under competitive conditions

The demand curve for dollars is downward sloping. This indicates that as the dollar becomes cheaper, holders of sterling will demand more dollars in order to buy American goods and to invest funds in America. American goods and American financial assets become better and better bargains to sterling holders, the less it costs in sterling to buy a dollar. (When considering the demand curve, remember that the figures on the vertical axis tell us the number of pence that a holder of sterling must spend in order to obtain the foreign exchange needed to buy an American good priced at \$1.)

The supply curve for dollars is upward sloping. This indicates that as sterling becomes cheaper, holders of dollars will offer more dollars in order to buy pounds with which to purchase British commodities and British financial assets. (A rise in the sterling price of dollars, which is what is measured on the vertical axis of the figure, means a fall in the dollar price of sterling. For example, if $1 goes from 33p to 50p, this means that £1 has gone from $3 to $2.) Thus as we move to a higher and higher sterling price of dollars (lower dollar prices of sterling), British commodities and British financial assets become better and better bargains to holders of dollars.

The determination of the equilibrium exchange rate Assume that the current price of dollars is too low, say 33p to the dollar. At this exchange rate the demand for dollars exceeds the supply. In other words, desired payments are not in balance, for desired payments to the US exceed desired payments from the US to Britain. Some people who require dollars to make payments to America will be unable to obtain them, and the price of dollars will be bid up. The value of the dollar *vis-a-vis* the pound will appreciate or, what is the same thing, the value of the pound *vis-a-vis* the dollar will depreciate. This rise in the price of the dollar reduces the quantity demanded and increases the quantity supplied. Where the two curves intersect, demand equals supply and the exchange rate is in equilibrium. In Figure 43.1 the equilibrium exchange rate is at $1 = 50p, which is £1 = $2.

Now let us see what will happen if the price of dollars is too high. In this case the demand for dollars will fall short of the supply; the dollar will be in excess supply, so that some people who wish to convert dollars into pounds will be unable to do so. The price of dollars will fall, fewer dollars will be supplied, more will be demanded and an equilibrium will be re-established.

Some comparative static results

We may now use the theory just developed to generate predictions about changes in which we may be interested. Five important changes are studied here.

A rise in the price of imports First, consider the effects of a large rise in the price at which some important import is supplied. Assume that the dollar price of an American export rises. Assume also that the UK has an inelastic demand for that export, so that UK purchasers end up spending more dollars on it. This shifts the demand curve for dollars in Figure 43.2 to the right from D_1 to D_2. The price of

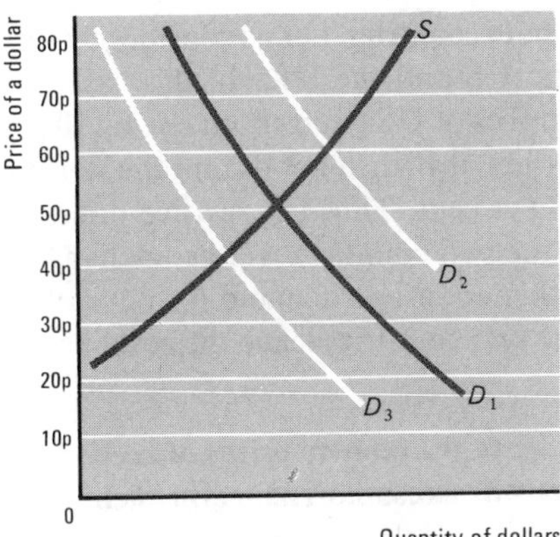

Fig. 43.2 The effects of shifts in demand for dollars on the equilibrium exchange rate

dollars thus appreciates from 50p to 60p, which is the same thing as a depreciation of sterling from \$2 to \$1·67.

A good example of this effect is the 1970s experience of oil-importing countries with the OPEC cartel. The large rise in the price of oil following the formation of OPEC caused depreciations in the exchange rates of major oil-importing countries including the US and the UK. The US is a major oil importer whose demand for imported oil is growing year by year. This is one of the major forces that led to the enormous depreciation of the exchange value of the dollar in the late 1970s.

The development of an import-substituting domestic industry Now assume that, sometime after the rise in price of an import from the US, Britain develops a low-cost domestic industry that captures the domestic market formerly served by the high-priced import from the US. Imports from the US will fall off drastically, so that at every exchange rate fewer dollars will be demanded (because fewer US imports will be demanded). The demand curve will now shift to the left. It will not only go as far as D_1, where it was when the commodity was imported from the US, at its original price; it will go to D_3 because now the commodity will not be imported at all. This lowers the sterling value of the dollar in Figure 43.2 to £0·43, which means an appreciation of the dollar value of sterling to \$2·33. Sterling underwent such an appreciation when North Sea oil came into production, largely replacing imported oil in the UK market. (In this case, of course, the imports came from the OPEC countries rather than from the US.)

A change in the price level of one country Consider, for example, the case of an inflation in the UK. This means that the sterling price of British goods will rise, British goods will become more expensive in the US and the supply of dollars will diminish. The sterling price of American exports to Britain will remain unchanged, while the price of British goods sold at home will have increased. Thus US goods will be more attractive compared to British goods (because they have become *relatively* cheaper) and more of them will be bought in Britain, so that at any given exchange rate the demand for dollars will be increased. The demand curve for dollars will shift to the right while the supply curve shifts to the left, so that the equilibrium price of dollars must rise.

A local British inflation will lead to a depreciation of the equilibrium value of the pound (an appreciation of the value of the dollar).

An equal percentage change in the price level in both countries Let us consider by way of example a 10 per cent inflation in both the US and the UK. In this case, the sterling prices of British goods and the dollar prices of US goods both rise by 10 per cent. At any given exchange rate, the dollar prices of British goods and the sterling prices of American goods will also rise by 10 per cent. Thus the relative prices of imports and domestically produced goods in the two countries will be unchanged. There is no reason to expect any change in either country's demand for imports at the original exchange rate; the inflations in the two countries leave the equilibrium exchange rate unchanged.

Offsetting inflations in two countries will leave the relative prices of their imports and exports unchanged and thus will cause no change in their exchange rates.

Consideration of the last two cases, of changes in price levels, shows that what matters is the relative rates of inflation between two trading countries. Differences in the inflation rates will cause differences in the relative prices of imports and exports. This will cause changes in quantities demanded and supplied on the foreign-exchange market and hence changes in the exchange rate between the two currencies. The general conclusion that follows from a simple extension of the two cases just studied is:

> **If the price level of one country is rising faster (falling slower) than that of another country, the equilibrium value of the first country's currency will be falling relative to that of the second country.**

Capital movements What will happen if American investors wish to make long-term loans in Britain, possibly to British firms? What will happen if firms holding working balances in dollars decide to transfer them to London in response to a rise in short-term interest rates in London? From the American point of view these are capital exports; from the British point of view they are capital imports. The British firm will require pounds, and the Americans will, therefore, have to purchase pounds on the foreign-exchange market. Such a transaction entails a rise in the demand for pounds, which, in a free market, will bid up their price.

> **Movements of either short- or long-term capital tend to appreciate the value of the capital-importing country's currency and depreciate the value of the capital-exporting country's currency.**

What causes the exchange rate to change?

It follows from our theory that the simple answer to the question posed above is: 'changes in demand or supply in the foreign-exchange market'. The question then needs to be rephrased as: 'What causes these changes in demand and supply?' We shall concentrate on causes of major changes that will have large and long-lived effects on the exchange rate.

Differing rates of inflation

There can be no doubt that, *ceteris paribus*, the exchange rates of countries that inflate fastest will be depreciating, while the exchange rates of countries that inflate slowest will be appreciating.[1] Changes in relative price levels and exchange rates can exactly offset each other, leaving relative international competitive positions unchanged. To illustrate, consider an example in which the British price level doubles relative to the US price level while sterling depreciates by half on the foreign-exchange market – which is roughly what happened in the twenty-five years from 1945 to 1970. The depreciation of sterling will double the sterling price of imports from the US, but since the sterling price of British-produced goods has also doubled, due to the British inflation, the relative prices of US and British goods in the British market are unchanged. The inflation doubles the sterling price of British

[1] The text discusses the case in which changes in relative price levels cause changes in the exchange rate. The Appendix to this chapter discusses the opposite possibility, that changes in the exchange rates can cause price levels to change.

exports and, at an unchanged exchange rate, doubles their dollar price too. But the depreciation of sterling on the foreign-exchange market *halves* the dollar price of British exports. The net effect is that their dollar price does not change relative to the dollar price of US goods in the US market.

As a first approximation we would expect sterling to depreciate in terms of a second currency in the same proportion as the British price level rose relative to the second country's price level. This is a weak version of what is called the PURCHASING POWER PARITY THEORY of exchange rates, which says that a change in the relative price levels of two countries will cause a corresponding percentage change in the exchange rate between their two currencies. There can be little doubt that this theory describes one of the major forces operating on exchange rates.

Capital movements

Major capital flows can exert major influences on exchange rates, appreciating the currencies of capital-importing countries and depreciating the currencies of capital-exporting countries. Assume, for example, that British savers wish to invest much of their savings in the US (as they did up until the First World War). An increased desire to invest in the US will lead to an increased demand for US dollars. The demand will rise, say, from D_1 to D_2 in Figure 43.2. As a result, the dollar will appreciate in value and sterling will depreciate.

The appreciation of the dollar will make US exports expensive, while imports will fall in price. This will open up a US current-account deficit equal to the capital-account surplus. Britain, on the other hand, will find that the depreciation of sterling on the foreign-exchange market encourages British exports and discourages imports. This will open up a current-account surplus which matches its capital-account deficit. Ignoring any central bank intervention (which would be relatively minor, in any case) we have the following important conclusions:

(1) Net capital exports are a deficit on capital account and they must depreciate a country's exchange rate until a current-account surplus of the same magnitude as the capital-account deficit is opened up.
(2) Net capital imports are a surplus on capital account and they must appreciate a country's exchange rate until a current-account deficit of the same magnitude as the capital-account surplus is opened up.

These conclusions can be seen mechanically from the simple balancing equation on page 641. The exchange-market mechanism is that if more people are buying dollars than are selling them to effect capital transactions (a UK deficit on capital account), fewer people must be buying dollars than are selling them to effect current-account transactions (a UK surplus on current account).

Structural changes

At the existing price levels, an economy can undergo structural changes that affect the exchange rate. 'Structural change' is an omnibus term for changes in cost structures, the invention of new products or anything else that affects the pattern of comparative advantage. For example, a country might be less dynamic than its competitors, so that at the initial set of prices consumers' demand shifts slowly away from the home country products towards those of foreign countries. This would cause a slow trend depreciation in the home country's exchange rate.

Dramatic changes such as the formation of OPEC will have similar effects, except that they will occur suddenly over a space of months rather than gradually over a space of years. Big events such as the production of North Sea oil will also cause major changes in equilibrium exchange rates.

Long-term changes in exchange rates can be accounted for mainly by the purchasing power parity theory and structural changes, both of which influence the current account, plus any persistent capital flows.

Central bank management of the exchange rate

So far we have considered exchange rates that are left free to be determined by the market forces of demand and supply. Such exchange rates are called FREE, or FLEXIBLE, or FLUCTUATING EXCHANGE RATES. In practice, however, exchange rates are seldom left free from any influence by the central authorities.

Fixed exchange rates

Under the Bretton Woods System that lasted from 1944 until the early 1970s, governments did not allow their currencies to fluctuate freely on foreign-exchange markets. The rates were fixed within very narrow margins. Each government stated an official price for its currency (usually in terms of US dollars), which was called the currency's PAR VALUE. The central bank then entered the market, buying and selling foreign exchange in whatever quantities were necessary to prevent the exchange rate from deviating more than a stated amount in either direction from its par value. (Originally, fluctuations were held within 1 per cent of the par value.) Such an exchange rate is called a FIXED or PEGGED EXCHANGE RATE. When it is changed, the country's currency is said to be DEVALUED or REVALUED in the cases, respectively, of a fall or a rise in its par value. The details of the Bretton Woods system are outlined in Chapter 45.

In the case of fixed exchange rates our theory does not predict the actual rate, since this is set by government decree. The theory does, however, make predictions about the extent of the deficit or the surplus on the balance of payments at the fixed rate of exchange. Let us consider this further.

Assume, for example, that the exchange rate in Figure 43.2 is fixed at 50p per dollar (i.e., £1 = \$2·00) at a time when the demand curve for dollars is D_2. At this rate of exchange the quantity of dollars demanded clearly exceeds the quantity supplied. There is thus an excess demand for dollars. To stop the exchange rate from changing the Bank of England will have to enter the exchange market and sell sufficient dollars to make demand equal supply at 50p. Now assume that the demand curve for dollars shifts to D_3. On the free market the dollar would depreciate (sterling appreciate). To stabilize the rate the Bank would have to enter the market and buy dollars (sell sterling) once again to make demand equal supply at 50p. Thus fixing the exchange rate requires that the central bank enter the market and buy or sell foreign exchange so as to stabilize its price. To sell foreign exchange (dollars in this case) the Bank must first have it. One of the problems with fixed exchange rates is to provide sufficient reserves of foreign exchange so that central banks can stabilize the rate when demand and supply curves fluctuate. Of course the Bank cannot try to stabilize a rate at which there is *always* excess demand for dollars because it will then always have to sell dollars and sooner or later it will exhaust its dollar reserves.

Managing flexible exchange rates

In current systems exchange rates are not stabilized at any announced par value but central banks do nonetheless intervene from time to time to influence the exchange rate. What tools does the Bank have for this task?

First, the bank can attempt to influence the long-term equilibrium exchange rate by various forms of payments restrictions. If holders of domestic currency are prevented from purchasing all the foreign exchange they would like to purchase to effect current and capital account transactions, the demand for foreign exchange is held permanently below what it would be on a completely free market.

Second, the Bank can attempt to iron out short- and medium-term fluctuations in the exchange rate by open-market purchases and sales of foreign exchange. If the Bank enters the market selling sterling and buying foreign exchange, this will cause sterling to depreciate. If the Bank does the opposite, buying sterling and selling foreign exchange, this will cause sterling to appreciate. The exchange rate can be held above its equilibrium value only for as long as the Bank's reserves of foreign exchange last. For this reason the policy cannot be a permanent alteration of the rate from its free-market level. But the Bank can hold the rate away from its level for quite some time – for as long, indeed, as its own reserves last and until its lines of credit with the IMF and foreign central banks are exhausted. The main difference between the Bank's behaviour in this instance and under fixed rates is that today it is *not* committed to defending a publicly announced rate. It can resist changes it thinks are transitory, and yield to changes it feels are the result of long-term forces.

Another method open to the bank for short-run control is through the interest rates. If the Bank of England uses monetary policy to raise interest rates in the UK, it can induce an inflow of short-term capital from other financial centres which will come into London in search of higher yields. For as long as the inflow persists, the demand for sterling on the foreign-exchange market will be high and so the value of sterling will be held high.

Exchange rates and national pride

It is interesting that the value of the exchange rate often becomes an important symbol of national pride. As economists we do not seek to explain this phenomenon, but we can wonder at it. Certainly there are circumstances when a rise in the value of a country's currency may be taken as a good sign. But such a change can also be symptomatic of a domestic situation about which it would be unusual to be proud. A major local depression and deflation, for example, could easily lead to a rise in the external value of a country's currency. On the other hand, major technical innovations which reduced domestic costs and prices – hardly a cause for shame – will often lead to a fall in the exchange rate. A large inflow of foreign capital will cause an appreciation of the exchange rate, but what if the capital inflow leads to the transfer abroad of control over a domestic industry?

A similar situation occurs when, as a result of fixed exchange rates, national pride and self-confidence become related to fairly trivial changes in the balance of payments, and to the size of foreign-exchange reserves held by the central authorities. Throughout the late 1950s and 1960s the UK was commonly thought of as the sick man of Europe, beset by crises and unable to hold its own in the modern world. To a great extent this view was based on the recurrent problems brought on by an effort to keep sterling priced at a value well above its equilibrium rate. When devaluation was finally forced on an unwilling government in 1967, the balance of payments improved and the image suddenly changed: Britain was thought to be healthier than any of its continental rivals because it had a stronger balance-of-payments position than any of them. People in Britain spoke at the time of the British miracle. Yet nothing basic was changed overnight by changing the price of sterling. UK managers remained as good or as bad as they were the year before; the school system and the political-decision mechanism were unchanged. Any basic evaluation would have shown the society to have been the same in 1970 as it was in 1967. The image it presented at home and abroad changed dramatically for what economic theory tells us is a trivial reason. Any country can have a 'favourable' balance of payments (at least for a while) if it sets its exchange rate below its equilibrium level. To judge a society by the state of its balance of payments, then, must be misguided, and yet a study of the current or past press will show that this is done over and over again.

By 1974 the UK balance of payments was once again in what was judged by many to be a poor state, and sterling was weak on foreign-exchange markets. In the press and on the political platform the 'British miracle' of 1970 had given way to the 'British disease' of 1974. By 1977 North Sea oil was coming into production. As British oil imports were reduced, sterling appreciated on foreign-exchange markets. The British 'disease' of a falling external value of sterling ceased to occupy popular discussion. Yet the underlying condition of the British economy was unchanged. Per capita income continued to grow more slowly than in the countries of Western Europe, and export industries continued to have difficulty competing in foreign markets.

Exchange rates can appreciate or depreciate for many different reasons. To take the price of one's currency *per se* as a symbol of national pride is to commit oneself in advance to being proud of a great rag bag of varied events.

Appendix to chapter 43

More on exchange rates

A number of important and fairly fundamental issues were not pursued in the brief treatment of exchange rates in Chapter 43. This appendix is designed for those who wish to study these issues further. We first raise the very basic question of the relation between the exchange rate and the terms of trade. We study this question in two rather extreme cases that are embodied in the so-called *elasticities* and *Scandinavian* models. We then ask whether the exchange rate really does fluctuate so as to equilibrate international payments. We consider doubts on this issue based first on elasticity pessimism and second on the possibility that the effects of exchange-rate changes are cancelled out quickly by offsetting price-level changes.

Does the exchange rate influence the terms of trade?

What fundamentally happens when the exchange rate changes? Basically, some relative prices change and expenditure is reallocated (switched) in response. Thus a change of the exchange rate is called an EXPENDITURE SWITCHING POLICY.

There are two basic theories of how this effect works. The first is called the ELASTICITIES THEORY. It takes the price levels of trading countries as given by their domestic circumstances and assumes that the exchange rate determines the terms of trade – i.e., the relative prices of imports and exports. This theory is most applicable to trade between large countries that are specialized in non-overlapping ranges of products.

The second theory is based on the so-called SCANDINAVIAN MODEL. It assumes that internationally traded commodities have their prices set on international markets, and that these prices are not affected by a country's exchange rate. International terms of trade are thus given. The effect of a change in the exchange rate is to change the relative price of internationally traded commodities on the one hand and domestically produced, non-traded commodities on the other hand, thus switching expenditures between these two classes. This model is most applicable when a small country exports products identical to those exported by many other countries.

The elasticities model

The simplest and most applicable case of the elasticities theory occurs when two countries trade with each other and each is specialized in a single commodity (or bundle of commodities), some of which it consumes at home and the rest of which it exports. This is similar to the model used in Chapter 42, in which England specializes in producing cloth and America in wheat. In the elasticities theory we assume that the sterling price of British goods and the dollar prices of American goods are set by domestic forces and are independent of the exchange rate.

Price changes caused by exchange-rate changes Given the British price level, a British manufacturer wishes to receive a certain payment for his goods in pounds sterling. It follows that the dollar price at which these goods must be sold in America depends upon the exchange rate between pounds and dollars. If a British manufacturer wishes to sell his good for one pound per unit, then they must sell in America (ignoring the cost of transport) for three dollars per unit when the exchange rate is £1 = \$3, or for two dollars when the rate is £1 = \$2. Given the American price level, an American manufacturer wishes, when he sells his goods, to be paid a certain number of dollars. It follows that the sterling price for which these goods must be sold in Britain also depends on the rate of exchange between sterling and dollars. If the manufacturer wishes to obtain \$1 for each unit of his goods, then they must sell in the UK for £0·33 when the exchange rate is £1 = \$3, or for £0·50 when the rate is £1 = \$2.

In general, a rise in the value of the pound *vis-à-vis* the dollar raises the dollar price of British exports to America, and lowers the sterling price of British imports from America. A fall in the value of the pound has the reverse effect.

The relation between the elasticities of demand for imports and exports and the elasticities of supply and demand for dollars

The amount of dollars offered in exchange for sterling depends on the amount of money American importers need to pay for the purchases they wish to make from Britain. What can we say about how this amount of money will vary if the dollar price of British exports varies? The Americans can be expected to have a downward-sloping demand curve for British goods (as they will have for all goods). We can therefore say, in general, that the *quantity* of British exports to America will vary inversely with their price. What happens to the *value* of exports, however, depends on the elasticity of the American demand. If the Americans have an elastic demand for British goods, then a fall in the dollar price of British goods will make them spend more dollars on them, while a rise will make them spend less. If, on the other hand, the Americans have an inelastic demand for British goods, then a fall in the dollar price of these goods will cause the Americans to reduce their total expenditure on British goods, while a rise in price will cause them to spend more. We thus reach a most important conclusion:

The supply of dollars – i.e., the amount of dollars Americans wish to exchange for pounds in order to purchase British goods – will increase or decrease as the dollar price of British exports falls, according as the American demand for British goods is elastic or inelastic.

We have already seen that a fall in the exchange value of the pound *vis-à-vis* the dollar will lower the dollar price of British exports. We can therefore restate this conclusion in the following manner:

A depreciation of the pound will increase or decrease the dollar value of British exports, and hence the supply of dollars on the foreign-exchange market, according as the American demand for these exports is elastic or inelastic.

Now let us consider the demand for dollars. The demand for dollars in exchange for pounds arises on account of the need to obtain dollars to pay for American goods imported into Britain. What can we say about what happens to the volume of this demand for dollars as the pound price of American goods varies? Let us assume that the dollar price of these American goods remains unchanged, but their sterling price changes in consequence of a change in the exchange rate. (For example, an American good with a constant price of \$1 will have a sterling price of 33⅓p when the exchange rate is \$3 = £1, a price of 50p if the exchange rate falls to \$2 = £1, and a price of 25p if the exchange rate rises to \$4 = £1.) If the sterling prices of American goods fall because of a depreciation in the value of the dollar, British purchasers will buy more goods and will spend more or less sterling on them according as their elasticity of demand is greater or less than unity. Since the quantity of goods bought rises and their dollar price is unchanged, however, *they will necessarily spend more dollars on them.* On the other hand, if the sterling price of American goods rises as a consequence of a fall in the value of the pound, fewer goods will be bought and, although the sterling expenditure on them will go up or down depending on the elasticity of demand, the dollar expenditure on these goods will necessarily fall since we are assuming that dollar prices are unaffected by the devaluation. We have now reached the following important conclusion:

A depreciation of the pound will necessarily decrease the dollar value of British imports and hence decrease the demand for dollars on the foreign-exchange market. The more elastic is the British demand for American goods, the more the demand for dollars will fall with any given depreciation.

The argument leading up to the last three conclusions is not an easy one. You should now go back and re-read this section. When you reach this point a second time, put the book down and make sure that you can work out the argument for yourself.

This analysis has important implications for the slopes of the demand and supply curves for dollars. The demand for dollars is necessarily downward sloping, as shown, for example, in Figure 43.1. The supply curve may be upward sloping as shown in that figure, but this requires that the American demand curve for British exports be elastic. If this demand is inelastic, a depreciation of sterling that lowers the dollar price of British goods in the American market will reduce the dollar expenditure on their goods. In this case the supply curve for dollars will slope upwards to the left. The conditions under which this occurrence would cause the exchange market to behave perversely will be studied in a later section of this appendix.

The exchange rate and the terms of trade Assume that one unit of British exports costs £1, while one unit of US exports costs $1. When the exchange rate is £1 = $2, the real terms of trade are that 1 unit of British exports exchanges for 2 units of US exports. First let sterling depreciate, say, to £1 = $1·50. Now the British terms of trade have deteriorated so that 1 unit of British exports exchanges for only 1·5 units of US exports.[1] Second, let sterling appreciate from its original rate to, say, £1 = $3. Now the British terms of trade have appreciated because 1 unit of British exports exchanges for 3 units of US exports.

In the elasticities model a country's terms of trade worsen when its exchange rate depreciates and improve when its rate appreciates.

Maintaining a payments balance Except in the case of extreme elasticity pessimism (considered further below), the free-market exchange rate will fluctuate to maintain a balance in international payments. To illustrate, assume that there are no significant capital flows and at the current exchange rates desired imports into the UK exceed desired imports into the US. In this case the demand for dollars (to buy US goods for import to Britain) will exceed the supply of dollars (to buy sterling to buy UK goods for import to the US). The dollar will appreciate and sterling will depreciate. American goods become more expensive in the UK and fewer dollars are demanded to buy them; British goods become cheaper in the US and more dollars are supplied to buy them. This movement continues until the quantity of dollars demanded on the foreign-exchange market equals the quantity of dollars demanded. When this occurs the exchange rate will be at its equilibrium value. International payments will also be in balance, since the values of imports and exports will be equal (we have already assumed a zero balance on capital account).

In the elasticities model domestic prices are given and the exchange rate determines the price of a country's imports measured in its domestic currency and the price of its exports measured in the other country's currency. Relative prices change to equilibrate international payments by switching expenditure away from imports in depreciating countries and towards imports in appreciating countries.

The Scandinavian model

In the Scandinavian model a country's real terms of trade are set in competitive markets in which all internationally traded goods are bought and sold. The terms of trade are thus totally unaffected by a country's exchange rate. The model is meant to be consistent with the following observations that seem to conflict with the elasticities model. (1) There are many commodities that are produced simultaneously by many different countries; these commodities have a single world price and there is little that one producer, acting on its own, can do to affect that price. (2) Many commodities are highly substitutable for each other, and as a result their relative prices cannot change very much; a large rise in the relative price of French cars would, for example, throw most of its market to its close competitors. (3) The domestic price level appears to be quite closely linked to the exchange rate, with devaluations of currencies under fixed exchange rates usually being followed by domestic inflations that remove some, but not all, of the competitive advantage conferred on the country's exports by the devaluation.

[1] When the prices of imports rise relative to the prices of exports, the common terminology is that the terms of trade have 'worsened', or 'deteriorated' or 'changed unfavourably'. Note, however, that these words are misleading. It is possible to have prices that are too high as well as too low. An inflation that raised the prices of exports would (if the exchange rate were fixed) cause a 'favourable' change in the terms of trade but if exports were priced out of international markets the final outcome would be unfavourable to the country in spite of the 'favourable' change in the terms of trade.

Assumptions of the model The extreme version of the Scandinavian model is based on the following assumptions. All commodities can be separated into two categories: internationally tradeable and non-tradeable commodities. Tradeables are sold on world markets at a single world price; they are, or could be, produced by many countries no one of whom can affect the price significantly by its own actions. Non-tradeables do not enter directly into *international* trade, either because they cannot be transported (e.g., services such as haircuts, road transport, and restaurant meals) or because the cost of transport is prohibitively high (e.g., cement).

The effect of changes in the exchange rate A change in any country's exchange rate does not affect relative prices among different tradeable commodities, since these relative prices are all set in world markets. The main effect of an exchange-rate change in one country is on the relative prices of tradeables and non-tradeables in that country.

Consider an example. A small country specializes in the export of a commodity, *X*, which has a given international price that can be expressed in US dollars (some *X* is also consumed at home). It imports a second commodity, *Y*, which is produced in many countries, and it also produces a third commodity, *Z*, which is a non-tradeable commodity. (In a real application there would be three groups of commodities each with its own price index.) The international prices of *X* and *Y* are $2 and $4, the price of *Z* is £1, the current exchange rate is pegged at £1 = $3, and *X* and *Y* thus sell domestically for £0·66⅔ and £1·33⅓.

Now assume that a deficit opens up on the balance of payments as a result of, say, a growth of real income combined with a high income elasticity of demand for tradeables and a low income elasticity for non-tradeables. On the free market the exchange rate depreciates, say to £1 = $2. In the elasticities model the price of *X* falls in the international market. Given the assumptions of the Scandinavian model, the prices of *X* and *Y* remain at $2 and $4 respectively, so their domestic prices both rise. The domestic price of *X* becomes £1 and that of *Y* becomes £2. Thus the relative price of imported and exported goods does not change in the devaluing country's home market. Thus its terms of trade do not change. But both prices rise relative to the price of the non-tradeable, *Z*, which remains at £1. (This means that the domestic price level will rise, since the prices of all tradeable goods rise in terms of domestic currency by the full amount of the devaluation.) Domestic demand will now shift away from both the imported and the exported good. This helps to improve the balance of payments by reducing imports and by freeing more goods for export. Demand increases for domestically produced non-tradeables. If there is excess capacity at home, the extra demand can be met. If there is already full employment, the government must take steps to stop the extra demand from causing a domestic inflation that will raise the price of *Z* to £1·50. This would restore relative prices to what they were before the devaluation and remove any effect of the devaluation. (In terms of the analysis of Chapter 34, the devaluation shifts up the aggregate expenditure function by reducing imports and raising domestic consumption. If full employment exists already, the government must use fiscal and/or monetary measures to shift the expenditure function down again, thus preventing the emergence of an inflationary gap.)

Both the elasticities model and the Scandinavian model predict that exchange rate changes will equilibrate international payments by causing expenditure switching in response to changes in relative prices. In the elasticities model it is the relative prices of imports and exports that change with the exchange rate. In the Scandinavian model the relative prices of imports and exports do not change when a country's exchange rate changes; instead the expenditure switching is between all tradeables (imports and exports), on the one hand, and domestically produced non-tradeables, on the other.

Does the exchange rate equilibrate international payments?

It may seem surprising that the question above should be asked at all. After all, exchange rates have been free since the early 1970s, and they have fluctuated so as to equilibrate international payments. There has been substantial central bank intervention from time to time, but this has been to iron out short-term fluctuations. Sometimes banks have bought, sometimes they have sold, but taken over several years, their net purchases or sales have not been large. Thus in the long term, exchange rates have equilibrated payments flows without substantial interference by central banks. In doing this job, exchange rates have fluctuated quite widely from time to time. Probably it is safe to say that rates have fluctuated more than those who advocated flexible exchange rates thought they would. Although the fluctuations have occasionally been quite wide, rates have shown no tendency to instability. If they had been unstable, a payments deficit would cause the exchange rate to depreciate, and this would *widen* the payments deficit. This would depreciate the rate further, widening the deficit even more, and so on, with exchange rates exploding continually downwards for deficit countries and upwards continually for surplus countries.

Instead, payments have responded in the stabilizing direction when rates have changed: depreciations have reduced deficits while appreciations have reduced surpluses.

> **The evidence since the freeing of exchange rates in the early 1970s is that rates do fluctuate in such a way as to keep international payments in balance, although the range of fluctuations has been somewhat wider than many economists had anticipated.**

In spite of this evidence, two major worries have often been expressed. The first concerns the magnitude of elasticities of demand for internationally traded goods; the second concerns the relation between the exchange rate and the domestic price level.

Elasticity pessimism

This problem arises in the context of the elasticities theory. We shall discuss it in our two-country example. If the American demand for British goods and the British demand for American goods are both sufficiently inelastic, a perverse case is possible in which a depreciation of the exchange rate can increase rather than reduce the balance-of-payments deficit of the depreciating country. To see that this is a possibility, consider the most extreme case in which the US and the UK each have perfectly inelastic demands for the goods produced by the other (note that this implies that they have very dissimilar tastes). Now assume that the UK is in balance-of-payments deficit and the US in surplus. If sterling depreciates by, say, 10 per cent, this will in fact worsen the balance of payments. This is because the UK has a completely inelastic demand for imports from the US and will thus buy the same quantity of these goods as before. It requires the same quantity of dollars to effect these purchases. Thus the demand for dollars on the foreign-exchange market will be unchanged. UK export prices, however, will fall by 10 per cent in dollars, but no more will be sold, since the US has zero elasticity of demand for UK goods. Thus the supply of dollars on the foreign-exchange market will fall by 10 per cent (export prices fall by 10 per cent but quantities sold remain unchanged). In these extreme circumstances, a 10 per cent UK depreciation will *worsen* the UK's balance of payments by approximately 10 per cent.

In the case just considered the demand curve for dollars in Figure 43.1 would be vertical, while the supply curve would slope upwards to the left (with an elasticity of minus unity). If the value of the dollar were above its equilibrium there would be excess demand for dollars. The price of dollars would rise and the gap between the demand and supply curves would *increase*.

It is a well-known proposition in the theory of international trade that, if domestic prices are unaffected by variations in foreign demand, the perverse case can occur only if the sum of the elasticities of demand for imported goods in the two countries is less than *one*.[1] In other words, quite highly inelastic demands are required to produce this case. Nonetheless, *if* this situation were commonly encountered, the case for freely fluctuating rates would be dealt a crippling blow. Far from improving matters, exchange depreciations in the face of balance-of-payments deficits, and exchange appreciation in the face of surpluses, would make matters worse. In this case exchange markets would be unstable: deficits would cause depreciations and depreciations would cause increased deficits.

Shortly after the Second World War, a number of studies of price elasticities in international trade were made. They uniformly produced alarmingly low elasticities.

[1] In terms of Figure 43.1 it is not sufficient that the supply curve for dollars should slope upwards to the left (which occurs if the US elasticity of demand for British goods is less than unity). It is necessary that the supply curve should be flatter than the demand curve (which occurs if the sum of the elasticities of demand for each other's good is less than unity).

Indeed, so low were the estimated elasticities that the efficacy of freely fluctuating rates as an automatic adjustment mechanism was called into serious question. Later, however, both economic and statistical theorists discovered a number of general reasons why the measured figures were likely to have been serious underestimates of the real elasticities. The statistical reasons for a 'downward bias' in the estimated elasticities are beyond the scope of an introductory treatment, but if you proceed in economics, later in your studies you will want to consult the classic treatment of this problem by Guy Orcutt.[1]

Some of the theoretical problems can, however, be mentioned even at this stage. The possibility of very low trade elasticities is made to seem more plausible than it probably is, by the usual assumption of a two-country, two-commodity model. Consider a world of many countries and many commodities. Typically, one commodity will be produced in many countries. Thus if *one* deficit country devalues its exchange rate, it will find a large increase in the demand for any one of its own products, even though the world elasticity of demand for that product is very low. This is because devaluation and the consequent fall in export prices allows the country to increase its share of the world market for the commodities that it exports. This effect is analogous to the proposition in the theory of perfect competition that the elasticity of demand for the product of one perfectly competitive producer can approach infinity, even though the elasticity of the market demand curve is very low. The Scandinavian model is an extreme version of this situation. A devaluation does not change the international price of a country's exports at all. The beneficial effects are concentrated on substitutions by domestic consumers between tradeable and non-tradeable goods. The second theoretical consideration concerns the range of commodities in trade. Even though the elasticities of demand for a country's existing exports are very low, a sufficiently large devaluation will allow the country to sell new products abroad, and the foreign elasticities of demand for its traditional exports will cease to be the only factors determining the change in the balance of payments when the exchange rate is changed.

For these and many other reasons, most economists today dismiss the perverse case as a theoretical curiosity of little practical importance – except in the very rare case of a country that accounts for almost the whole of the world's supply of a product that is in highly inelastic demand, and that has few alternative lines of production to which it might turn when its exchange rate falls.

It is perhaps worth noting that if international elasticities were so low as to produce the perverse case, inflation would improve a country's balance of payments. A depreciation lowers the prices of exports relative to imports. An inflation in one country does the opposite and is thus the equivalent of an appreciation of the exchange rate.

If depreciation worsens the balance of payments, an inflation must improve it.

Until the early 1970s, when countries were on fixed exchange rates, it was generally acknowledged that rapid inflations worsened the balance of payments of the inflating country. This suggests that elasticities were high enough to rule out the perverse case.

Does the price level determine the exchange rate or vice versa?

There is little doubt that the countries with rapidly rising price levels have been the ones with depreciating exchange rates, while countries with low rates of inflation have had appreciating exchange rates. The elasticities approach sees the causal sequence running from domestically caused inflations to exchange rates.

Some economists accept the correlation between inflation and exchange depreciations but hold that the sequence runs the other way. They argue that a 10 per cent depreciation will cause a 10 per cent inflation that will eliminate all of the effects of the depreciation on the terms of trade. The extreme version just stated seems hard to take seriously. If it were true, countries that developed balance of payments deficits for any reason, such as a shift in demands or supplies for imports or exports, would fall into an unstable, never-ending spiral of depreciation and inflation. Exchange rates do change and by changing do bring payments into balance. Thus the view that their effects are quickly cancelled by changes in domestic price levels cannot be wholly correct.

[1] Guy Orcutt, 'Measurement of Price Elasticities in International Trade', *Review of Economics and Statistics*, May, 1950.

Strong evidence is provided by the period 1945–72 when exchange rates were fixed. During this time span, there were only two major rounds of adjustments of rates, the first in 1949 and the second in 1967. The first round set exchange rates that persisted for nearly 20 years until differences in inflation rates finally called for a realignment. If inflations did cancel out the effects of the 1949 devaluation, the process took decades rather than months as the pessimistic view often implies. Indeed, it seems rather far fetched to argue that the British inflation of the 1960s was caused by the devaluation of 1949 rather than by domestic demand and cost forces operating during the 1960s. In 1967, 17 trading countries devalued their exchanges relative to the US dollar by amounts ranging from 5 per cent for Macao to 24·8 per cent for Nepal. The extreme deficits and surpluses that characterized the payments positions of many countries immediately before the adjustments were greatly reduced afterwards. Although inflations continued after the adjustments, there is no evidence that the favourable effects on payments were quickly removed by ensuing inflations.

During the period of flexible rates of the 1970s, it is clear that depreciations have often occurred in response to inflation-caused payments deficits and that the depreciations have not had their full effects removed by ensuing depreciation-caused inflations. From 1972 to 1978, for example, Canada inflated faster than the US, but its exchange rate was held up by large inflows of US capital coming into Canada. When the capital flows fell off, the current-account deficit caused the Canadian dollar to depreciate nearly 20 per cent relative to the US dollar. This major depreciation improved the Canadian current-account-payments position and caused only a slight interruption in the trend for the Canadian inflation rate to fall back to the US rate.

What are the causal links between exchange rates and domestic price levels? The truth seems to lie somewhere between the two extremes – the elasticities model (where exchange depreciations have no effect on the prices of domestically produced goods) and the pessimistic view (where exchange depreciations cause fully offsetting inflations). The grain of truth in the pessimistic view seems to be that exchange depreciations do cause some rise in domestic prices. The main reasons why depreciations cause domestic inflations are associated with what may be called *import cost push*. A depreciation raises the domestic prices of all imports. In an open economy such as the UK, this means that the prices of innumerable imported raw and semi-finished goods rise. Inevitably these cost increases are passed on as increases in the prices of the final commodities that embody these imports. Also, since a rise in the prices of imports consequent on a depreciation of the exchange rate raises the price level (for the reason just mentioned and also because many final goods are imported), there will be an upward pressure on wages as workers seek to protect their real incomes in the face of a rising consumer price index.

The rise in domestic prices consequent on the depreciation of the exchange rate partly reverses the favourable effects of the devaluation on the trade balance. This may be one of the reasons why the fluctuations in exchange rates needed to equilibrate international payments have been larger than were originally anticipated.

44

Tariffs and the gains from trade

In the classical theory, specialization according to comparative advantage is the main source of the gains from trade. In this chapter we shall first consider this theory of the gains from trade as a positive hypothesis about the real world, and then go on to consider the case for interfering with free trade through tariffs.

We have demonstrated that where opportunity costs differ among countries some degree of specialization, with some consequent amount of trade, will raise world standards of living. There is abundant evidence that such cost differences do occur, so that potential gains from trade do exist. No one seriously advocates complete self-sufficiency today, but some people do advocate increasing or diminishing the present quantity of trade. This, as we shall see, is a more difficult issue to settle than whether we should have any trade at all.

A theory of the gains from trade commonly held in the past, and still occasionally encountered today, is called the *exploitation theory of trade*. According to this theory, it is impossible for trade between any two parties to be to their mutual advantage, because one trading partner must always reap its gain at the expense of the other. The principle of comparative costs, which shows that it is possible for both parties to gain from trade, even if one of them is more efficient than the other in all lines of production, completely refutes this theory. Seen in this light, comparative costs is to be viewed as a *possibility theorem*. It shows that, if opportunity-cost ratios differ in two countries, specialization and the accompanying trade make it possible to produce more of all commodities, and thus make it possible for both parties to get more goods as a result of trade than they could get in its absence. Thus the answer to the question: 'Is it *possible* for trade to be mutually advantageous?' is an emphatic 'Yes'. The answer to the question: 'Is trade *in fact* mutually advantageous?' is quite another matter.

The nature and purpose of tariffs

A TARIFF is a tax applied on imports, often on an *ad valorem* (percentage of value) basis. Such a tax has the effect of raising the price of the taxed commodity. Tariffs can be used for two different and opposite purposes: for revenue and for protection. The latter use is more common, to raise the price of imported goods in order to discourage imports by offsetting (to some extent, at least) a cost advantage that foreign producers have over domestic producers of a particular product. The protective function of a tariff is opposed to the revenue function because the tariff will not yield much revenue if it is effective in cutting imports. This chapter concentrates on the protective feature of tariffs.

What determines the amount people are willing to pay for an imported good? Their tastes for the product naturally play a role, but beyond this the important limit is provided by the cost of purchasing the good domestically. Considered generally, there is a potential demand for those imports that can be delivered to a country at a cost lower than that at which they can be produced at home. At any time there is a whole array of potentially importable commodities, some with large cost savings, some with moderate ones, and some with no cost advantage at all.

A world of FREE TRADE would be one with no tariffs and no restrictions of any kind on importing or exporting. In such a world, a country would import all those commodities that it could buy from abroad at a delivered price lower than the cost of producing them at home.

Now suppose that a country imposes a 20 per cent tariff on all imports. This does not prohibit trade, but by making all imported goods more expensive, it affects what it is profitable to import. Any foreign good that enjoys a cost advantage of less than 20 per cent is now effectively prohibited. A 20 per cent tariff thus provides protection to domestic industries that produce at a cost disadvantage of up to 20 per cent. Imported goods that enjoy cost advantages in excess of 20 per cent will still be in demand, but they will not be as big a bargain as before. Because their price will be higher, a smaller quantity will be demanded than if there were no tariff.

If a country desires to prohibit trade in any specific commodity, it might do so by setting a tariff that is larger than the cost advantage of the lowest-cost foreign producer. If a country desires to prohibit all trade, it might do so by setting very high tariffs 'across the board' or by setting a tariff on each item high enough to price that import completely out of the market.

In today's world two facts about international trade stand out. First, there is a great deal of it. Second, virtually every government interferes to some extent with free trade.

The reasons behind these facts need to be examined.

The case for free trade

In Chapter 42 it was demonstrated that, where opportunity costs differ among countries, some degree of specialization with some consequent amount of trade will raise world standards of living. Free trade allows all countries to specialize in the production of commodities in which they have comparative advantages and thereby to produce (and thus to consume) more of all commodities than would be available if this kind of specialization had not taken place. In brief, free trade makes it possible to maximize world production and makes it *possible* for every household in the world to consume more goods than it could if free trade did not exist. There is abundant evidence to show that real differences in comparative costs do exist and that there are potential gains from trade because of these differences. There is, of course, also ample evidence that trade does occur, that no nation tries to be self-sufficient or refuses to sell to foreigners the things it produces cheaply and well.

This case for free trade is a powerful one that can be briefly stated. What needs to be explained is the fact that trade is not wholly free, that tariffs and quotas exist 200 years after Adam Smith stated the case for free trade. Do these interferences exist merely because policy makers are ignorant of the principles of comparative advantage, or are there reasons not included in the case for free trade that make it sensible for a nation to levy some tariffs? Is there any valid case for interfering with trade? If so, how does one find the balance between the advantages of more, and those of less, trade?

The case for protectionism

PROTECTIONISM refers to the protection of domestic industries from foreign competition. Such protection may be achieved either by tariffs that raise the price of foreign goods or by such non-tariff barriers as quotas which make importing difficult or impossible. Two kinds of arguments for protection are common. The first concerns objectives other than maximizing output, and the second concerns the difference between the welfare of a single nation and that of the world.

Objectives other than raising living standards

It is quite possible for someone to accept the prediction that production is higher with free trade and yet rationally oppose free trade because of a concern with policy objectives other than production and consumption. There are, after all, policy goals other than maximizing national income.

For example, comparative costs might dictate that a country should specialize in the production of a single commodity, say bananas. The government might decide, however, that there are distinct social advantages to having a more diverse economy – one that would give citizens a wider range of occupations in which to develop their talents. The authorities might decide that the social and psychological gains from having a diverse economy more than compensate for a reduction in living standards by, say, 5 per cent below what they could be with complete specialization of production.

Specializing in the production of one or two commodities, although dictated by comparative advantage, may involve risks that a country will wish to avoid. One such risk is a technological advance that renders its basic product obsolete. A different sort of risk is cyclical fluctuations in the prices of basic commodities, which may face depressed prices for years at a time, then periods of very high prices. For a country specializing in the production of such commodities, this means that the incomes of the producers will be subject to wide fluctuations. Even though the average level of income over a long period might be higher by specializing in production of such commodities, the serious social problems associated with a widely fluctuating national income may lead the government to decide to sacrifice some income in order to reduce fluctuations. Such a government policy might encourage the expansion of several stable industries that are protected by tariffs.

Yet another reason for protectionism may be the desire to maintain national traditions. For example, many Canadians are passionately concerned with maintaining a separate nation with traditions that differ from those of the United States. Many of these Canadians believe that the tariff helps them to do this, and they are prepared to accept a 5 or 10 per cent cut in living standards in order to maintain this independence.

The most frequently cited non-economic defence of tariffs concerns national defence. It has traditionally been argued, for example, that the United States requires an experienced merchant marine in case of war and that this industry should be fostered by protectionist policies, even though it is less efficient than the foreign competition.

There is nothing irrational in a country's decision-makers being willing to accept substantial costs in order to attain objectives other than the maximizing of living standards. Although most people would agree that, *ceteris paribus*, they prefer more income to less, economists cannot pronounce as unreasonable a nation that chooses to sacrifice some income in order to achieve other goals.

Tariffs as a means of raising national living standards

If a country produces a significant portion of the world output of some commodity, it may be able to exploit its monopoly position by interfering with the free flow of trade. By selling less of its commodity abroad and, of course, by buying less of other commodities, it can affect world prices and may be able to appropriate for itself a larger share of total world production than it would obtain if all prices were set on competitive markets. If other countries follow a fairly passive policy, one country may be able to reap quite substantial monopoly gains. If, however, several countries all try to do the same thing, a battle of move and countermove will ensue until, at the end, everyone may be worse off than they were under free trade.

A second, and probably the most important, argument under this heading is the one relating to economies of scale: the INFANT-INDUSTRY ARGUMENT FOR TARIFFS. If an industry has large economies of scale, costs and prices must be high when the industry is small, but they will fall as the industry grows. In such an industry, the country first in the field has a tremendous advantage over latecomers. A newly developing country may find that its industries are unable to compete in the early stages of their development with established foreign rivals. A tariff may protect these industries from foreign competition while they grow up. Once they are large enough they will be able to produce as cheaply as foreign rivals and will thus be able to stand on their own feet without tariff support.

A similar argument in favour of tariffs concerns 'learning by doing': if giving a domestic industry protection from foreign competition enables it to learn to be efficient, it may pay the government to protect the industry while it learns.

Trade versus tariffs

It appears from what has already been said that while there is a very strong case for allowing trade, in order to realize the gains from it, there may also be reasons for departing from completely free trade.

It is not necessary to choose between free trade on the one hand and complete protectionism on the other; a country can have some trade and some protectionism too.

Free trade versus no trade

It would undoubtedly be possible, by using greenhouses, to grow oranges, cotton, and other now-imported raw materials and foodstuffs in Norway and to grow coffee in the United Kingdom. But the cost in terms of other commodities forgone would be prodigious because these artificial means of production require lavish inputs of factors of production. It would likewise be possible for a tropical country currently producing foodstuffs to set up industries to produce all the types of manufactured products that it consumes. The cost in terms of resources used, for a small country without natural advantages in industrial production, would be very large. It thus appears that there is a large gain to all countries in having specialization and trade. The real output and consumption of all countries would be very much lower if each had to produce domestically all the goods that it consumed.

> **If it were necessary to make an all-or-nothing choice, decision-takers in virtually all countries would choose free trade over no trade.**

Some trade versus no trade

Table 44.1 shows the level of tariffs on selected commodities in the mid 1970s. It is clear that these tariffs are not sufficient to offset widely differing cost conditions in certain countries, the most dramatic being those associated with climate. Even the most casual observation reveals such major cost differences among countries that no one could doubt that there are significant gains from trading for commodities in which a country has a large comparative disadvantage. Careful empirical measurement might put an actual numerical value on the amount of gains, but it is inconceivable that it could refute the general hypothesis that production and consumption in the world, and in each major trading country, are higher with trade than they would be with no trade.

A little more trade versus a little less trade

At the level of tariffs existing today we have trade between nations, but it is not

Table 44.1 Tariffs on selected commodity groups (*ad valorem* rates)[1]

Commodity	United States	EEC	Japan
Weighted average of all dutiable manufactures	9·0	9·6	10·7
Paper and paperboard	0·9	9·5	9·2
Plastics	8·6	10·0	12·1
Clothing and clothing accessories	25·5	16·5	18·1
Iron and steel, manufactured goods	7·9	8·0	8·7
Coal, petroleum, natural gas (crude)	3·2	0·4	10·6
Coffee	0·0	21·0	35·0
Rubber, manufactured articles	5·0	8·6	10·1

Source: GATT, Basic Documentation for Tariff Study, 1973, Summary Table No. 3 and *Commerce America*, 12 April 1976.

[1] The figures are based on rates that came into existence during 1972 after the completion of all tariff reduction in the Kennedy Round.

perfectly free. Would we be better off if all of today's tariffs were reduced or increased a little bit? It is quite a jump from the proposition that 'Some trade is better than no trade' to the proposition that 'A little more trade than we have at present is better than a little less trade.' Yet most arguments about commercial policy involve the latter sort of proposition, not the former. Most actual policy disagreements concern the relative merits of free trade versus controlled trade with tariffs of the order of, say, 5, 10, or 15 per cent. Such tariffs would not cut out imports of bananas, coffee, diamonds, bauxite, or any of the commodities in whose production the UK would be really inefficient. (Yet these are just the commodities that defenders of free trade sometimes use as examples when the hypothesis of the gains from trade is challenged.) If one accepts the hypothesis that some trade is better than no trade, one is not necessarily committed to accepting the hypothesis that free trade is better than controlled trade with, say, 15 per cent tariffs; nor is one committed to saying that 9 per cent tariffs would be better than 10 per cent tariffs.

As a rule, tariffs are seldom advocated to protect industries that are extremely inefficient compared to foreign industries; they are usually advocated to protect industries that can very nearly compete, but not quite. As a simplified version of the sort of argument that really does take place over commercial policy, compare the effects of a 20 per cent uniform *ad valorem* tariff with those of free trade. How much would be gained by removing 20 per cent tariffs or how much lost by imposing 20 per cent tariffs in a situation of free trade? Tariffs of 20 per cent will protect industries up to 20 per cent less efficient than foreign competitors. If the costs of the different tariff-protected industries were spread out evenly, some would be 20 per cent less efficient than their foreign competitors, but others would be only 1 per cent less efficient, and their average inefficiency would be about half the tariff rate. In other words, they would be on average about 10 per cent less efficient than their foreign competitors. Suppose that as a result of tariffs, approximately 10 per cent of a country's resources are allocated to industries different from the ones to which they would be allocated to if there were no tariffs. This means that about 10 per cent of a country's resources would be working in certain industries only because of a tariff protection. If the average protected industry is 10 per cent less efficient than its foreign rival, we have a situation in which approximately 10 per cent of a country's resources are producing about 10 per cent less efficiently than they would be if there were no tariffs. This causes a reduction in national income of something on the order of 1 per cent as a result of tariff protection.

This rather rough-and-ready calculation is meant to do no more than illustrate why the gains from removing modest tariffs may be small. The conclusion has been established by three careful studies of the effect of tariffs in Great Britain and Europe. Professor P. J. Verdoorn estimated that the gain to the six European Common Market countries from eliminating tariffs on trade among themselves to be about 0·05 per cent of their national incomes. Professor Harry Johnson estimated that the maximum cost to Britain of staying out of the Common Market would have been equal to approximately 1 per cent of her national income. And Professor W. Welmesfelder estimated that the gain to Germany from major tariff reductions in 1956 and 1957 would have been less than 1 per cent of German national income.

The net gains from somewhat freer trade than there is today are not so large as to make it certain that the removal of all remaining tariffs is desirable.

Even moderate costs associated with removing tariffs could offset the small predicted advantage. Whether this is in fact so is properly an empirical matter, not a logical one.

The main concern in this section has been not to argue for or against free trade but to investigate what can be said about trade and tariffs on the basis of economic analysis. There are benefits to be achieved by international trade, and there are benefits of a different sort to be achieved by imposing certain tariffs. Whether free trade is better than a policy of moderate tariffs depends on the policy goals that one is trying to attain and the magnitude of the benefits and costs of the actions. There is thus a highly important area for study and debate about trade and tariffs. There is also, however, a lot of assertion that does not advance the debate; fallacious arguments are heard on both sides. Because these arguments have been around so long, it is worthwhile discussing them.

Fallacious anti-tariff arguments

Free trade always benefits all countries It is not necessarily so. The potential gains from trade may be offset by the costs of trade, such as unemployment or economic instability, or the interference with policy objectives other than maximizing income, and these may render some tariff interference desirable.[1]

Infant industries never grow up It is often argued that to grant tariffs on an infant-industry basis is a mistake in practice because infant industries seldom admit to having grown up and will cling to their tariff protection even when they are adults. Even if this alleged fact were true, it would not be a sufficient reason for avoiding such tariffs. If the economies of scale are realized, the real costs of production are reduced and resources are freed for other uses. Whether or not the tariff remains, a cost saving has been effected by the scale economies.

Fallacious pro-tariff arguments

Keep the money at home This argument runs somewhat as follows: 'If I buy a foreign good, I have the good and the foreigner has the money, whereas if I buy the same good locally, I have the good and our country has the money too'. The argument assumes that domestic money actually goes abroad physically when imports are purchased and that trade flows in only one direction. When British importers purchase Italian-made goods, they do not send sterling abroad. They (or some financial agents activated by their decision) buy Italian lire (or claims on them) and use these to pay the Italian manufacturer. They purchase the lire on the foreign exchange market by giving up sterling *to someone who wishes to use it for expenditure in the UK*. Even if the money did go abroad physically – that is, if an Italian firm accepted a shipload of pound notes – it would be because the firm (or someone to whom it could sell the sterling) wanted them to spend in the only country where they are legal tender, the United Kingdom. Currency ultimately does no one any good except as purchasing power. It would be miraculous indeed if pieces of paper could

[1] To see how sensitive the gains from trade are to other considerations, suppose that totally free trade led to an allocation of resources that was 1 per cent more efficient than one resulting from 20 per cent tariffs, but led simultaneously to an average level of unemployment 1·2 per cent higher. In this case, free trade would bring losses rather than gains.

be exported in return for a quantity of real goods. After all, the central bank has the power to create as much new money as it wishes. It is only because the paper money can buy things in Britain that others want it.

Protection against low-wage foreign labour 'Surely,' the argument goes, 'the products of Oriental sweatshops will drive our products from the market, and the high UK standard of living will be dragged down to that of the impoverished Orient.' Arguments of this sort have, through the years, swayed many voters. As a prelude to considering them, stop and think what the argument would imply if taken out of the international level and put into a local one, where the same principles govern the gains from trade. Is it really impossible for a rich person to gain from trading with a poor one? Would the local millionaire be better off if he did all his own typing, gardening, and cooking? No one believes that a rich person cannot gain from trading with those who are less rich. Why then must a rich group of people lose from trading with a poor group? 'Well,' you say, 'the poor group will price their goods too cheaply.' Does anyone believe that consumers lose from buying in a cut-price shop or a supermarket, just because they sell at a lower price than the old-fashioned corner shop? Consumers gain if they can buy the same goods at a lower price. If the Koreans pay low wages and sell their goods cheaply, then *their labour may suffer*, but we gain because we obtain their goods at a low cost in terms of the goods that we must export in return. The cheaper our imports are, the better off we are in terms of the goods and services available for domestic consumption.

Stated in more formal terms, the gains from trade depend on comparative, not absolute, advantages. World production is higher when any two areas, say the United Kingdom and Japan, specialize in the production of the goods for which they have a comparative advantage than when they both try to be self-sufficient.

Might it not be possible, however, that Japan will undersell the UK in all lines of production and thus appropriate all, or more than all, of the gains for herself, leaving the UK no better off, or even worse off, than if it had remained self-sufficient? The answer is 'No', and the clue to why this is not so is found in Chapter 42.

Assume that trade exists between the UK and Japan and that, at the present rate of exchange between pounds and yen, the Japanese can undersell the UK in all commodities. Everyone will want to buy Japanese goods, and thus everyone will need yen. No one will want to buy UK goods, and thus no one will need sterling. On the foreign exchange market there will be a big demand for yen and no demand for sterling. In a free market, sterling will depreciate in value and the yen will appreciate. As this happens, the price of UK exports will fall, whereas the prices of Japanese exports will rise. This will continue until some UK goods become cheaper than their Japanese equivalents. Then the United Kingdom will begin to buy fewer goods from Japan and the Japanese will buy some goods from the UK. Sterling will continue to depreciate until demand and supply for sterling are equated, that is, until – ignoring capital movements – the value of the demand for exports equals the value of the demand for imports. Equality of demand and supply on the foreign exchange market ensures that trade flows in both directions.

Imports can be obtained only by spending the currency of the country that makes the imports. Claims to this currency can be obtained only by exporting goods and services or by borrowing. Thus, lending and borrowing aside, imports must equal exports. All trade must be in two directions. We can buy only if we can also sell. In the long run, trade cannot hurt a country by causing it to import without exporting. Trade, then, always provides scope for international specialization, with each country producing and exporting those goods in which it has a comparative advantage.

Exports raise national income; imports lower it We saw in Chapter 33 that exports are injections that, *ceteris paribus*, raise national income, and imports are withdrawals that, *ceteris paribus*, lower national income. 'Surely', this argument goes, 'it is desirable to encourage exports and discourage imports.'

Saying that exports raise national income means that they add to the value of output, but they do not add to the value of domestic consumption. In fact, exports are goods produced at home and consumed abroad, while imports are goods produced abroad and consumed at home. The standard of living in a country depends on the goods and services available for *consumption*, not on what is produced.

If exports were really good and imports really bad, then a fully employed economy that managed to increase its exports without any corresponding increase in its imports ought to be made better off thereby. Such a change, however, would result in a reduction in current standards of living because when more goods are sent abroad and no more are brought in from abroad, the total goods available for domestic consumption must fall.

What happens if a country does achieve a surplus of exports over imports for a considerable period of time? It will be accumulating claims to foreign exchange for which there are three possible uses: (1) to add to foreign exchange reserves, (2) to buy foreign goods, and (3) to make investments abroad. Consider each of these.

Foreign exchange reserves are required for the smooth functioning of a system of fixed exchange rates. Accumulation of reserves over and above those required to cope with fluctuations in private payments serves no purpose. Permanent excess reserves represent claims on foreign output that are never made effective.

American dollars or Indian rupees cannot be eaten, smoked, drunk, or worn. But they can be spent to buy American and Indian goods that can be eaten, smoked, drunk, or worn. When such goods are imported and consumed, they add to UK living standards. Indeed, the main purpose of foreign trade is to take advantage of international specialization; trade allows more consumption than would be possible if all goods were produced at home. From this point of view, the purpose of exporting is to allow the importation of goods that can be produced more cheaply abroad than at home.

An excess of exports over imports may be used to acquire foreign exchange needed to purchase foreign assets, but such foreign investments add to living standards only when the interest and profits earned on them are used to buy imports that do not have to be matched by currently produced exports – that is, when, in the future, they produce an excess of imports over exports. From this point of view, the purpose of exporting more than one is importing in order to make foreign investments is eventually to be able to import more than one is exporting.

In summary:

> **The living standards of a country depend on the goods and services consumed in that country. The importance of exports is that they permit imports to be made. This two-way international exchange is valuable**

because more goods can be imported than could be obtained if the same goods were produced at home.

Can tariffs reduce domestic unemployment? It is sometimes thought that an economy with substantial amounts of unemployment, such as the UK in the 1930s or the late 1970s, provides an exception to the case for freer trade. Assume that the central authorities can engineer a rise in exports without a corresponding rise in imports, perhaps because of a subsidy on exports and increased rates of tariffs on imports. According to the theory of the multiplier, this rise in exports will increase income and employment. Surely, in a time of unemployment, this is to be regarded as a 'good thing'.

Two points need to be made about such a policy. In the first place, the goods being produced by the newly employed workers in the export sector are not available for domestic consumption and so do not directly raise domestic standards of living. Would it not be better if, instead of subsidizing exports, the central authorities subsidized the production of goods for the home market so that all the goods produced – instead of only those produced in response to the increased incomes – would contribute to a rise in domestic living standards? Or, if one objects to the government subsidization of private firms, the government could create new employment by building more roads, schools, and research laboratories. As a result, income and employment would go up but there would be something more tangible to show for it in the first instance than the smoke of ships disappearing over the horizon bearing the subsidized exports to foreign markets.

The second point to be made concerns the foreign effects of such a policy of fostering exports and discouraging imports in a situation of general world unemployment. Although the policy raises domestic employment, it will have the reverse effect abroad where it creates unemployment. Such a policy is referred to as 'exporting one's unemployment'. Other countries will suffer a rise in their unemployment because their exports will fall and their imports rise. This will set up a multiplier process that reduces their levels of income and employment. They will soon be forced to take steps to remove these effects. If they do this by restricting imports, the original country will lose the stimulus that it originally obtained by encouraging exports. If all countries adopt a policy of expanding exports and discouraging imports, the net effect is likely to be a large fall in the volume of international trade without much change in the level of employment in any country.

Although one can think of many cases in which a tariff policy has been pursued after a rational assessment of the approximate cost, it is hard to avoid the conclusion that, more often than not, high tariff policies are pursued for rather flimsy objectives of national prestige with very little idea of the actual costs involved or because the central authorities believe one or another of the fallacious pro-tariff arguments.

International agreements concerning trade and tariffs

In the past any one country could impose any desired set of tariffs on its imports. But when one country increases its tariffs, the action may trigger retaliatory changes by its trading partners. Just as an arms race can escalate, so can a tariff war; precisely this happened in the world during the 1920s and early 1930s.

The Great Depression of the early 1930s produced a high-water mark on tariffs, with every nation trying to reduce its unemployment by encouraging exports and discouraging imports. The net effect of these tariff wars was less trade all around and no more employment. International attempts to roll back tariffs from these high levels began in the mid 1930s but did not produce substantial results until the period following the Second World War.

The general agreement on tariffs and trade (GATT)

One of the most notable achievements of the post-Second World War world in moving back from the high level of protectionism achieved in the 1930s was the General Agreement on Tariffs and Trade (GATT). Under this agreement, member countries meet periodically to negotiate bilaterally on mutually advantageous cuts in tariffs. They agree in advance that any negotiated cuts will be extended to all member countries. Some significant tariff reductions have occurred but to some extent, however, the tariffs were merely replaced by NON-TARIFF BARRIERS TO TRADE. These are defined as things other than tariffs that impede the free flow of international trade; they include import quotas, production and export subsidies, standards purporting to maintain the quality of imports, and complex administrative procedures. For this reason, it is hard to assess the overall quantitative effect of the GATT, but there can be little doubt that even when all qualifications are allowed, it has represented a significant force in the direction of freer international trade.

The European Economic Community (EEC)

In 1957, the Treaty of Rome joined France, Germany, Italy, Holland, Belgium, and Luxembourg into the European Economic Community (EEC). The original six were joined in 1973 by the UK, the Republic of Ireland and Denmark.

The EEC is dedicated to bringing about free trade, complete mobility of factors of production, and eventual harmonization of fiscal and monetary policies among the member countries. Tariff reductions were made according to a time schedule that eliminated all tariffs on manufactured goods among the original six before 1970. If the development continues, western Europe will be, before the end of the century, a single economic community with a free movement of goods, labour and capital among the member countries.

The overall effects on Britain of EEC membership are very difficult to assess. Supporters of British entry put much stress on alleged dynamic aspects. The British growth rate was supposed to be given a boost both by the expansion of decreasing-cost industries and by an increase in productivity of UK management and labour in response to the 'chill winds of foreign competition'. These dynamic factors, by their very nature, tend to defy measurement. It seems, however, that cases of the exploitation of significant scale economies are hard to find. It is also apparent that in some cases, at least, the pessimists were right in holding that foreign competition would destroy rather than improve the performance of British industries. For the car industry, for example, the loss of tariff protection against European cars proved a disaster; it is doubtful how much of even the drastically shrunken industry of today would have survived without major infusions of public money that show little chance of ever yielding a significant rate of return for the taxpayers who provided them. The whole issue of the pros and cons of British entry into the EEC remains moot. In the absence of clear evidence, opinions are spread over every extreme, from 'a disaster' through 'little effect one way or the other' to 'a major boost to the economy in general (even if not in every particular part)'.

45

Twentieth-century international monetary systems

The gold standard, the dollar problem, the Bretton Woods system, the International Monetary Fund, the Smithsonian agreements, the European snake – all of these terms are part of the history of the international monetary system. As periods of crisis and upsets to world trade alternated with periods of stability, the world's monetary system has changed several times in this century.

The century began with a system of fixed exchange rates under the gold standard. A ten-year period of recurring crises began with the First World War and ended with the onset of the Great Depression of the 1930s. During this time the gold standard broke down and was abandoned by one country after another. The 1930s saw a period of experimentation with flexible, market-determined exchange rates, which ended with the Second World War, when governments fixed exchange rates and managed international payments with the successful waging of war as their main policy objective. In 1944 an era of fixed exchange rates in peacetime was once again instituted. This lasted for over a quarter of a century, until its shortcomings and periods of crises seemed to prevail over its advantages and periods of stability. After several attempts to patch it up, the system finally broke down and was abandoned as countries one by one went over to the system of market-determined flexible exchange rates under which we now operate.

Do the issues involved in the workings and possible reform of the monetary system affect the welfare of ordinary citizens, or only the interests of a small group of international traders, bankers, and financiers? Can any of the problems and issues be solved, or must we merely learn to live with them as best we can? Do economists agree on solutions or on possible accommodations? To answer these questions we shall consider the development of international institutions from the time of the gold standard to the present.

Before the Second World War

The twentieth century before the Second World War saw a period of fixed exchange rates followed by a period of fluctuating rates. First, consider the case of the fixed rate under the gold standard.

The gold standard

Although the detailed workings of the gold standard are now mainly of historical interest, a few of its features provide important insights into the present system.[1] The gold standard was not *designed*. Like the price system, it just happened. It arose out of the general acceptance of gold as the commodity to be used as money. In most countries, paper currency was freely convertible into gold at a fixed rate.

The gold standard is an example of a fixed-exchange-rate system. Rates of exchange between the standard units of currency of various countries were fixed by their values in terms of the standard unit, gold. In 1914, the US dollar was convertible into 0·053 standard ounces of gold, while the British pound sterling was convertible into 0·257 standard ounces. This meant that the pound was worth 4·86 times as much as the dollar in terms of gold, thus making one pound worth US $4·86.[2]

As long as all countries were on the gold standard, a person in any one country could be sure of being able to make payments to a person in any other country. If one were unable to buy or sell claims to the foreign currencies on the foreign exchange market, one could always convert one's currency into gold and then ship the gold.

The gold flow, price level mechanism How was the gold standard supposed to work to maintain a balance of international payments? Consider a country that was in payments deficit because the value of what its citizens were importing (i.e., buying) from other countries exceeded the value of what they were exporting (i.e., selling) to other countries. The demand for foreign exchange would exceed its supply on this country's foreign exchange market. Some people who wished to make foreign payments would be unable to obtain foreign exchange. No matter – they would merely convert their domestic currency into gold and ship the gold. Therefore, some people in a surplus country would secure gold in payment for exports. They would deposit this to their credit and accept claims on gold – in terms of convertible paper money or bank deposits – in return. Thus deficit countries would be losing gold while surplus countries would be gaining it.

Under the gold standard, the whole money supply was linked to the supply of gold (see pp. 583–5). The international movements of gold would therefore lead to a fall in the money supply in the deficit country and a rise in the surplus one.[3] According to the quantity theory of money, changes in the domestic money supply cause changes in domestic price levels. Deficit countries would thus have falling price levels, while surplus countries would have rising price levels. The exports of deficit countries would become relatively cheaper, while those of surplus countries would become relatively more expensive. The resulting changes in quantities bought and sold would move the balance of payments toward an equilibrium position.

Actual experience of the gold standard The half-century before the First World War was the heyday of the gold standard; during this relatively trouble-free period, the

---

[1] The gold standard is in fact of more than mere historical interest since a few countries – most notably France – and a few famous economists – most notably Robert A. Mundell of Columbia University – have seriously advocated returning to it.

[2] In practice, the exchange rate did fluctuate within narrow limits set by the cost of shipping gold.

[3] When the person who received gold deposited it in a bank, this would put the bank in the position of the bank in Table 40.1, page 592, and a multiple expansion of deposit money would ensue.

automatic mechanism seemed to work well. Subsequent research has suggested, however, that the gold standard succeeded during the period mainly because it was not called on to do much work. Trade flowed between nations in large and rapidly expanding volume, and it is probable that existing price levels were never far from the equilibrium ones. No major trading country found itself with a serious and persistent balance-of-payments deficit, and so no major country was called upon to restore equilibrium through a large change in its domestic price level.

Inevitably there were short-run fluctuations, but these were ironed out, either by movements of short-run capital in response to changes in interest rates, or by changes in national income and employment.

In the 1920s the gold standard was called on to do a major job. It failed utterly, and it was abandoned. How did this come about? During the First World War, most belligerent countries had suspended convertibility of currency: they went off the gold standard. Most countries suffered major inflations, but the degree of inflation varied from country to country. After the war, nations returned to the gold standard by restoring convertibility of their currencies into gold. For reasons of prestige, some insisted on returning at the prewar rates. This meant that some countries' goods were overpriced and others' were underpriced. Large deficits and surpluses in the balances of payments inevitably appeared, and the adjustment mechanism required that price levels change in each of the countries in order to restore equilibrium. Price levels changed very slowly and, by the onset of the Great Depression, equilibrium price levels had not yet been attained. By this time, it was too late to achieve equilibrium, and the financial chaos brought on by the Depression destroyed the existing payments system.

The 1930s: a period of experimentation

After the abandonment of the gold standard, various experiments were tried with both fixed and fluctuating rates. Often a rate would be allowed to fluctuate on the free market until it had reached what looked like equilibrium, and it would then be fixed at that level. Sometimes, as with the British pound, the rate was left to be determined by a free market throughout the whole period. Sometimes rates would be changed in an attempt to secure domestic full employment without any consideration of the state of the balance of payments.

The period of experimentation coincided with the Great Depression of the 1930s. Trade everywhere was being reduced, both because of rising unemployment and increasing uncertainty about the future of international markets. This was a terrible period of mass unemployment, and governments began to cast around for any measure, no matter how extreme, that might alleviate their domestic unemployment problem. One superficially plausible way of doing this was to cut back on imports and produce those goods domestically. If one country managed to reduce its imports, then its unemployment might be reduced because people would be put to work producing replacement goods at home. Other countries would, however, find their exports falling and unemployment rising as a consequence. Because such policies attempt to solve one country's problems by inflicting them on others, they are called BEGGAR-MY-NEIGHBOUR POLICIES.

If the policies worked, there would at least be selfish arguments in their favour. But they work only as long as other countries do not try to protect themselves. Once they find their exports falling and unemployment rising, these other countries may retaliate by reducing their own imports and producing the goods at home, and the first country will find its exports falling and unemployment rising as a result. The simultaneous attempts of all countries to cut imports without suffering a comparable cut in exports is bound to be self-defeating. The net effect of such measures is to decrease the volume of trade, thereby sacrificing the gains from trade without raising worldwide employment.

When unemployment is due to insufficient world aggregate demand, it cannot be cured by measures designed to redistribute, among nations, the fixed and inadequate total of demand.

In the 1930s the policy of discouraging imports and encouraging exports was attempted, using such instruments of commercial policy as import duties, export subsidies, quotas, prohibitions, and, particularly, exchange-rate depreciation. If a country with a large portion of its labour force unemployed devalues its exchange rate, two effects can be expected: exports will rise, and domestic consumers will buy fewer imports and more domestically produced goods. Both of these changes will have the effect of lowering the amount of unemployment in the country. If other countries do nothing, the policy succeeds. But again, the volume of unemployment in other countries will have increased because exports to the devaluing country will have been reduced. If other countries try to restore their positions, they may devalue their currencies as well. If all countries devalue their currencies in the same proportion, they will all be right back where they started, with no change in the relative prices of goods from any country and, hence, no change in relative prices from the original situation. A situation in which all countries devalue their currencies in an attempt to gain a competitive advantage over one another is called a situation of COMPETITIVE DEVALUATIONS.[1]

The rise and fall of the Bretton Woods system, 1944–72

The one lesson that everyone thought had been learned from the 1930s was that either a system of freely fluctuating exchange rates or a system of fixed rates with easily accomplished devaluations was the road to disaster in international affairs. In order to achieve a system of orderly exchange rates that would be conducive to the free flow of trade following the Second World War, representatives of most countries that had participated in the alliance against Germany, Italy, and Japan met at Bretton Woods, New Hampshire, in 1944. The international monetary system that developed out of the agreements reached at Bretton Woods consisted of a large body of rules and understandings for the regulation of international transactions and payments imbalances.

It was the first and so far the only international payments system that was consciously designed and then implemented through international governmental cooperation. In the words of Charles Kindleberger of MIT, the Bretton Woods meeting was 'the biggest constitution-writing exercise ever to occur in international

[1] Under a paper-currency system, a simultaneous devaluation of all currencies would have no effect, beneficial or harmful. In a gold standard world, however, each country devalues by lowering the gold content of its currency. Thus a full round of competitive devaluations of *X* per cent leaves relative exchange rates unchanged, but it raises the price of gold (measured in all currencies) by *X* per cent. The effect of this is to enrich those producing gold and those holding stocks of it and thus to increase their claims on the world's output.

monetary relations'. The system lasted until the early 1970s, when it broke down and was replaced by the piecemeal adoption of a system of flexible, free-market exchange rates.[1]

The object of the Bretton Woods system was to create a set of rules that would maintain fixed exchange rates in the face of short-term fluctuations; to guarantee that changes in exchange rates would occur only in the face of long-term, persistent deficits or surpluses in the balance of payments; and to ensure that when such changes did occur they would not spark a series of competitive devaluations.

The basic characteristic of the Bretton Woods system was that US dollars held by foreign monetary authorities were made directly convertible into gold at a fixed price (of approximately $35 an ounce) by the US government, while foreign governments fixed the prices at which their currencies were convertible into US dollars. It was this characteristic that made the system a GOLD EXCHANGE STANDARD: gold was the ultimate reserve, but the currencies were held as reserves because directly or indirectly they could be *exchanged* for gold.

The rate at which each country's currency was convertible into dollars was fixed, or pegged. The pegged rate could be changed from time to time in the face of a 'fundamental disequilibrium' in the balance of payments. A system with these two characteristics, a rate that is pegged against short-term fluctuations but that can be adjusted from time to time, is referred to as an ADJUSTABLE PEG SYSTEM.

In order to maintain convertibility of their currencies at fixed exchange rates, the monetary authorities of each country had to be ready to buy and sell their currency in the foreign exchange markets.[2] In order to be able to support the exchange market by buying domestic currency, the monetary authorities had to have stocks of acceptable foreign exchange to offer in return. In the Bretton Woods system, the authorities held reserves of gold and claims on key currencies – mainly the American dollar and the British pound. When a country's currency was in excess supply, their authorities would sell dollars, sterling, or gold. When a country's currency was in excess demand, their authorities would buy dollars or sterling. If they then wished to increase their gold reserves they would use the dollars to purchase gold from the Federal Reserve System (the US central bank, hereinafter called the 'Fed'), thus depleting the US gold stock. The problem for the United States was to have enough gold to maintain fixed-price convertibility of the dollar into gold as demanded by foreign monetary authorities. The problem for all other countries was to maintain convertibility (on a restricted or unrestricted basis, depending on the country in question) between their currency and the US dollar at a fixed rate of exchange.

The Bretton Woods international payments system was an adjustable peg, gold exchange standard where the ultimate international money was gold. Countries held much of their exchange reserves in the form of US dollars, which they could convert into gold, and British pounds, which they could convert into US dollars.

---

[1] Like the gold standard, the Bretton Woods system is of more than historical interest. Many people would like to return to a system of fixed exchange rates, but any such system would face problems similar to those that beset the Bretton Woods system. The design of any new system of fixed rates would inevitably be heavily influenced by the experience of the last thirty-five years.

[2] The exchange rates were not quite fixed. They were permitted to vary by one per cent on either side of their par values. The central bank had to intervene to prevent the rate from going outside of the narrow bands of permitted fluctuations. Later the bands of permitted fluctuation were widened to 2·25 per cent on either side of par.

The International Monetary Fund

The most important institution created by the Bretton Woods system was the International Monetary Fund (also called the IMF or the Fund). The Fund had several tasks. First, it tried to ensure that countries held their exchange rates pegged in the short run. Second, it made loans – out of funds subscribed by member nations – to governments that needed them to support their exchange rates in the face of temporary payments deficits. Third, the Fund was supposed to consult with countries wishing to alter their exchange rates to ensure that the rate was really being changed to remove a persistent payments disequilibrium and that one devaluation did not set off a self-cancelling round of competitive devaluations. The importance of the Fund is attested by the fact that it has outlived the system that created it and is as active an instrument of international monetary co-operation today as it was under the Bretton Woods system.

Problems of an adjustable peg system

Three major problems of the Bretton Woods system were (1) providing sufficient reserves to iron out short-term fluctuations in international receipts and payments while keeping exchange rates fixed; (2) making adjustments to long-term trends in receipts and payments, and (3) handling speculative crises. Since these problems would be present in any adjustable peg system that might be designed in the future, they are worth studying in detail in the forms in which they plagued the Bretton Woods system.

Reserves to accommodate short-term fluctuations Reserves are needed to accommodate short-term balance-of-payments fluctuations arising from both the current and the capital accounts. On current account, normal trade is subject to many short-term variations, some systematic and some random. This means that even if the value of imports does equal the value of exports, taken on average over several years, there may be considerable imbalances in these over shorter periods of time.

On a free market, fluctuations in current and capital account payments would cause the exchange rate to fluctuate. To prevent such fluctuations when rates are fixed, the monetary authorities buy and sell foreign exchange as required, to keep the exchange rate pegged. These operations require that the authorities hold reserves of foreign exchange.

The amount of reserves that the authorities need to hold depends on their estimate of the maximum amount of foreign exchange they might have to sell to stabilize the exchange rate in the face of a particularly unfavourable period of excess demand. If the authorities run out of reserves, they cannot maintain the pegged rate, so they will want to hold some safety margin over the maximum they expect to use. It is generally felt that the absolute size of any gap they may have to fill with their own foreign exchange sales increases as the volume of international payments increases.

> **Since there was a strong upward trend in the volume of overall international payments, there was also a strong upward trend in the demand for foreign exchange reserves.**

The ultimate reserve in the Bretton Woods gold exchange standard was gold, which entailed two serious problems. First, the world's supply of monetary gold did not grow fast enough to provide adequate total reserves for an expanding volume of trade. The gold backing needed to maintain convertibility of currencies became increasingly inadequate throughout the 1960s. Second, the country whose currency is convertible into gold must maintain sufficient reserves to ensure convertibility. During the 1960s the United States lost substantial gold reserves to other countries that had acquired dollar claims through their balance-of-payments surpluses with the United States. By the late 1960s the loss of US reserves had been sufficiently large to undermine confidence in America's continued ability to maintain dollar convertibility.

By 1970 there was an inadequate world supply of gold for monetary uses, and the United States had too small a proportion of the supply that did exist.

Under the Bretton Woods system the supply of gold was augmented by reserves of key currencies, the US dollar and the British pound. Because the need for reserves expanded much more rapidly than the gold stock in the period since the Second World War, the system required nations to hold an increasing fraction of their reserves in dollars and sterling. Of course they would do this only as long as they had confidence in the convertibility of these currencies, and maintaining confidence was made difficult by a continually declining percentage of gold backing for the dollar.

A major disadvantage of using a national currency as a supplementary reserve is the potential inability to maintain convertibility of that currency into gold. Another major disadvantage occurs if the country whose currency is used for reserves wishes to devalue because of severe balance-of-payments problems. If it does devalue, all countries holding that currency find the value of these reserves slashed. If it tries to avoid devaluation, fear that it may be unable to do so impairs the usefulness of the currency as a reserve because other countries become reluctant to hold it. Furthermore, the domestic policy of the country in question becomes subservient to the overriding need to maintain the existing exchange rate. This was the case in Britain during the Bretton Woods era. A debate raged all through that period as to whether the advantages to Britain of having sterling used as a reserve currency outweighed the disadvantages of the serious constraints that were put on domestic fiscal and monetary policy by the need to avoid devaluations of the pound.

The desire to provide a supplementary reserve not tied to the currency of a particular country led to the development in 1969 of SPECIAL DRAWING RIGHTS (SDRS) at the IMF. SDRs were designed to provide a supplement to existing reserve assets by setting up a Special Drawing Account kept separate from all other operations of the Fund. Each member country of the Fund was assigned an SDR quota that was guaranteed in terms of a fixed gold value and that it could use to acquire an equivalent amount of convertible currencies from other participants. SDRs could be used without prior consultation with the Fund, but only to cope with balance-of-payments difficulties.

SDRs might have gone a long way toward alleviating the system's difficulties if the system had not been overwhelmed by much more fundamental problems in the early 1970s. In any case SDRs outlasted the Bretton Woods system that they were first designed to assist.

Adjusting to long-term disequilibria With fixed exchange rates, long-term disequilibria (what the IMF used to call *fundamental disequilibria*) can be expected to develop because of secular shifts in the demands for and supplies of foreign exchange. There are three important reasons for these long-term shifts in demands and supplies in the foreign exchange market. First, different trading countries have different rates of inflation. Chapter 43 discussed how these cause changes in the equilibrium rates of exchange and, if the rate is fixed, cause excess supply or excess demand to develop in each country's foreign exchange market. Second, changes in the demands for and supplies of imports and exports are associated with long-term economic growth. Because different countries grow at different rates, their demands for imports and their supplies of exports would be expected to be shifting at different rates. Third, structural changes, such as major new innovations or the rise in the price of oil, cause major changes in imports and exports.

The associated shifts in demand and supply on the foreign exchange market imply that, even starting from a current account equilibrium with imports equal to exports at a given rate of exchange, there is no reason to believe that equilibrium will exist at the same rate of exchange 10 or 20 years later (any more than equilibrium relative prices would be expected to remain unchanged over 20 years within any one country).

The rate of exchange that will lead to a balance-of-payments equilibrium will tend to change over time; over a decade the change can be substantial.

Governments may react to long-term disequilibria in at least three ways.

1. The exchange rate can be changed whenever it is clear that a balance-of-payments deficit or surplus is a result of a long-term shift in the demands and supplies in the foreign exchange market, rather than the result of some transient factor. This was the solution envisaged by the framers of the IMF when they allowed member countries, after consultation with the IMF, to change their exchange rates in the face of a 'fundamental disequilibrium'. During the period of the Bretton Woods system, there were three major rounds of exchange rate adjustments. The first two were led by a devaluation of sterling, the second of the world's two reserve currencies. The third round was led by the devaluation of the US dollar in December 1971.

2. Domestic price levels can be allowed to change in an attempt to establish an equilibrium set of international prices. Changes in domestic price levels have all sorts of domestic repercussions (e.g., reductions in aggregate demand intended to lower the price level are more likely to raise unemployment than to lower prices), and one might have expected governments to be more willing to change exchange rates – which can be done by a stroke of a pen – than to try to change their price levels. A deflation is difficult to accomplish, while an inflation is thought to be accompanied by undesirable side effects.

3. Restrictions can be imposed on trade and foreign payments. Imports and foreign spending by tourists and governments can be restricted, and the export of capital can be slowed or even stopped. Surplus countries were often quick to criticize such restrictions on international trade and payments. As long as exchange rates were fixed and price levels proved difficult to manipulate, the deficit countries had little option but to restrict the quantity of foreign exchange their residents were permitted to obtain so as to equate it to the quantity available.

Handling speculative crises When enough people begin to doubt the ability of the central authorities to maintain the current rate, speculative crises develop. The most important reason for such crises is that over time equilibrium exchange rates get further and further away from any given set of fixed rates. When the disequilibrium becomes obvious to everyone, traders and speculators come to believe that a realignment of rates cannot long be delayed. At such a time, there is a rush to buy currencies expected to be revalued and a rush to sell currencies expected to be devalued. Even if the authorities take drastic steps to remove the payments deficit, there may be doubt as to whether these measures will work before the exchange reserves are exhausted. Speculative flows of funds can reach very large proportions, and it may be impossible to avoid changing the exchange rate under such pressure.

Speculative crises were, and will always be, one of the most intractible problems of any adjustable peg system. The impact of such crises might be reduced if governments had more adequate reserves. If a speculative crisis precedes an exchange rate adjustment, however, more adequate reserves may just mean that speculators will make larger profits since more of them will be able to sell the currency about to be devalued and to buy the currency about to be revalued before the monetary authorities are forced to act.

During the Bretton Woods period governments tended to resist changing their exchange rates until they had no alternative. This made the situation so obvious that speculators could hardly lose, and their actions set off the final crises that forced exchange rate readjustments. More frequent and expected changes made before they had become inevitable might have diminished the occurrence of speculative crises. These would, however, have removed the day-to-day certainty associated with the system of fixed exchange rates that was its chief advantage. Moreover, surprise changes might lead to suspicion that a devaluation was made to gain a competitive advantage for their exports rather than to remove a fundamental disequilibrium. After all, governments were not supposed to devalue until it was clear that they were faced with a fundamental disequilibrium, and if this was clear to them it was also clear to ordinary traders and speculators.

Collapse of the Bretton Woods system

The Bretton Woods system worked reasonably well for nearly twenty years. Then it was beset by a series of crises of ever-increasing severity that reflected the system's underlying weaknesses.

Speculation against the British pound Throughout the 1950s and 1960s the British economy was more inflation-prone than the US economy and the British balance of payments was generally in a less satisfactory state. Holders of sterling thus had reason to worry that the British government might not be able to maintain its pledge to keep sterling convertible into dollars at a fixed rate. When these fears grew strong there would be speculative rushes to sell sterling before it was devalued. The various crises of the 1960s were of this kind. By the mid 1960s it was clear to everyone that the pound was seriously overvalued. Finally in 1967 it was devalued, in the midst of a serious speculative crisis. Many other countries with balance-of-payments deficits followed, bringing about the first major round of adjustments in the pegged rates since 1949.

Speculation against the American dollar The US dollar was not devalued in 1967. The lower prices of those currencies that were devalued in 1967, plus increasing Vietnam War expenditures by the United States, combined to produce a growing deficit in the American balance of payments. This deficit led to the belief that the dollar itself was becoming seriously overvalued. People rushed to buy gold because a devaluation of the dollar would take the form of raising its gold price.

The first break in the Bretton Woods system came when the major trading countries were forced to stop pegging the free-market price of gold. Speculative pressure to buy gold could not be resisted, and the market price was allowed to go free in 1968. From that point there were two prices of gold: one was the official price at which monetary authorities could settle their debts with each other by transferring gold; the other was the free-market price, determined by the forces of private demand and supply independent of any intervention by central banks. The free-market price quickly rose far above the official US price of $35 an ounce.

Once the free-market price of gold was allowed to be determined independently of the official price, speculation against the dollar shifted to those currencies that were clearly undervalued relative to the dollar.[1] The German mark and the Japanese yen were particularly popular targets, and billions and billions of dollars flowed into speculative holdings of these currencies. The ability of central banks to maintain pegged exchange rates in the face of such vast flights of funds was in question; on several occasions all exchange markets had to be closed for periods of up to a week.

Devaluation of the dollar

By 1971 the American authorities had come to the conclusion that the dollar would have to be devalued. This uncovered a problem, inherent in the Bretton Woods system, that had so far gone virtually unnoted. Because the system required that each foreign country fix its exchange rate against the dollar, the American authorities could not independently fix their exchange rate against other currencies.[2] This system worked reasonably well while the American price level was relatively stable. Countries that were inflating a bit too fast could occasionally devalue their exchange rates, and countries that were inflating even more slowly than the United States could occasionally revalue their exchange rates in an upward direction. Occasional upward and downward readjustments relative to the dollar served to keep the system near equilibrium.

But if the United States began to inflate rapidly (or to do anything else that put it in a serious payments deficit with most other countries), it became necessary to devalue the US dollar relative to most other currencies. Any other country in this situation would merely unilaterally devalue its currency relative to the US dollar.

[1] Under a Bretton Woods type of system the dollar is devalued by raising the official price at which the Fed will allow foreign central banks to convert dollars into gold. When the free-market price was held the same as the official price, a devaluation of the dollar entailed a rise in the free-market price – and hence profit for all holders of gold. Once the free-market price was left to be determined by the forces of private demand and supply independent of any central bank intervention, there was no reason to believe that a rise in the official price of gold would affect the (much higher) free-market price. Speculators against the dollar then had to hold other currencies whose price was sure to rise against the dollar in the event of the dollar's being devalued.

[2] If, for example, the British authorities pegged the pound at $2·40 as they did in 1967, then the dollar was pegged at £0·417 and the American authorities could not independently decide on another rate. Similar considerations applied to all other currencies.

But the only way that the required US devaluation could be brought about was for all other countries to agree to revalue their currencies upward relative to the dollar.

Under the Bretton Woods system any country other than the United States could devalue its currency by a unilateral decision; a US devaluation, however, required the co-operation of all other countries against whose currency the dollar was to be devalued.

Prompted by continuing speculation against the dollar, President Nixon announced the suspension of the gold convertibility of the dollar in August 1971. He also made known the intention of the United States to achieve a de facto devaluation of the dollar by persuading those nations whose balance of payments were in surplus to allow their rates to float upward against the dollar.

By ending the gold convertibility of the dollar the US government brought the gold exchange standard aspect of the Bretton Woods system officially to an end.

The fixed exchange rate aspect of the system lasted a little longer.

The immediate response to the announced intention of devaluing the dollar was completely predictable: a speculative run against that currency. The crisis was so severe that for the second time in the year foreign exchange markets were closed throughout Europe. When the markets reopened after a week, several countries allowed their rates to float. The Japanese, however, announced their intention of retaining their existing rate. In spite of severe Japanese controls, $4 billion of speculative funds managed to find their way into yen in the last two weeks of August, and the Japanese were forced to abandon their fixed-rate policy by allowing the yen to float upward.

After some very hard bargaining, an agreement between the major trading nations was signed at the Smithsonian Institution in Washington DC in December 1971. The main element of the agreement was that all countries consented to a 7·9 per cent devaluation of the dollar against their currencies. Thus the third major realignment of exchange rates since the Second World War was accomplished.

The de facto dollar standard

Since the Smithsonian agreements, the world has been on a de facto DOLLAR STANDARD. Foreign monetary authorities hold their reserves in the form of dollars and settle their international debts with dollars. But the dollar is not convertible into gold or anything else. The ultimate value of the dollar is given not by gold but by the American goods and services that dollars can be used to purchase. One major problem with a dollar system is that the kind of American inflation that upset the Bretton Woods system is no less upsetting to a dollar standard because the real, purchasing-power value of the world's dollar reserves is eroded by such an inflation.

Breakdown of the system of fixed exchange rates

The US inflation continued unchecked and the US balance of payments never returned to the relatively satisfactory position that had been maintained all through the 1960s. Within a year of the agreements, speculators began to believe that a further realignment of rates was necessary.

In January 1973 heavy speculative movements of capital once again began to occur. Then in February the United States proposed a further 10 per cent devaluation of the dollar, to be accomplished by raising the official price of gold to \$42·22 an ounce. Needless to say, intense speculative activity followed this extraordinary announcement. Five of the member countries of the EEC then decided to stabilize their currencies against each other but to let them float against the dollar. This joint EEC float was called the SNAKE. Norway and Sweden later became associated with this arrangement. The other EEC countries (Ireland, Italy, and the UK) and Japan announced their intention to allow their currencies to float in value. In June 1972 the Bank of England had announced that it had 'temporarily' abandoned its commitment to support sterling at a fixed par against the US dollar. The events of 1973 led to 'temporarily' becoming 'indefinitely'.

Fluctuations in exchange rates were severe. By early July the currencies of the five EEC countries involved in the joint float had appreciated about 30 per cent against the dollar, but by the end of the year they had returned nearly to their February values.

The dollar devaluation was formally put into effect in October. Most industrialized countries maintained the nominal values of their currencies in terms of gold and SDRs, thereby appreciating in terms of the US dollar by 11 per cent. The devaluation quickly became redundant, since in spite of attempts to restore fixed rates the drift to flexible rates had become irresistible.

The present system

By 1974, many industrial countries – Austria, Canada, Italy, Japan, Switzerland, the United Kingdom and the United States – were not maintaining rates for exchange transactions within announced margins, while other industrial countries – Belgium, Denmark, France, Germany, Luxembourg, the Netherlands, Norway, and Sweden – maintained fixed bands for exchange transactions among their currencies but not against the dollar. A large proportion of the remaining countries maintained stable rates of exchange for their currencies in terms of one of the three major currencies – the US dollar, pound sterling, or the French franc. This implied that such a country's rate fluctuated against the major currencies to which its national currency was not tied.

Although exchange rates are determined on the free market, there is nevertheless substantial intervention in these markets by central banks. Central banks try to reduce short-term fluctuations in rates and sometimes try to resist longer-term trends. The difference between the present system and Bretton Woods is that central banks no longer have announced values for exchange rates (values that they are committed in advance to defend even at heavy cost). Central banks do not need to say what their targets are; they are completely free to change them as circumstances change. Sometimes they leave the rate completely free to fluctuate, and at other times they interfere actively to alter the exchange rate from its free-market value. Such a system is called a MANAGED FLOAT or a DIRTY FLOAT. The rate floats because it is not pegged at any publicly announced par value. The floating rate, however, is managed (or dirty) because the central bank does influence it from time to time by intervening in the foreign exchange market.

To manage exchange rates, central banks still hold reserves in the form of gold, foreign exchange and SDRs. Since the dollar is no longer convertible into gold, the world remains on a de facto dollar standard. The growing importance of SDRs suggests that in the future they may become the ultimate reserve. If this happens the system will have adopted an 'international paper money standard', since the SDR is a genuine international paper money.

The present international monetary system is a dollar standard with managed exchange rate flexibility.

The experiences of the period of managed flexibility have been mixed. On the one hand, short-term movements in exchange rates have been more volatile than advocates of flexible rates would perhaps have hoped; on the other, exchange rates have been managed without any overt clashes of national interest and have been allowed to change to compensate for substantial national differences in inflation rates.

Sterling has seen some large fluctuations since it was turned loose on the free market. For policy purposes the external value of sterling is now judged by the 'effective exchange rate', which is a weighted average of the price of sterling in terms of the currencies of the UK's most important trading partners. The general trend of sterling was towards depreciation from 1972 to 1976. Since the beginning of 1977 sterling has been on a gradually rising trend. By the end of 1978, however, sterling had still been depreciated by over 30 per cent on the exchange markets of the world relative to its value in June 1972.

One of the most remarkable events in this period has been the enormous downward slide of the exchange value of the US dollar over a very few years in the late 1970s. From mid 1976 to mid 1978 the US dollar depreciated 20 per cent against the German mark and 35 per cent against the Japanese yen. The major forces operating here were the continued high rate of inflation in the US and the inability of the American Congress to pass an effective set of legislative measures to reduce American dependence on imported oil. (These measures were made necessary because the American government elected to use a legislated rather than a market solution to the 'energy problem' – see the discussion on pages 421–3.)

Current and future problems

Management of exchange rates The managed aspect of managed floating rates poses several potential problems for the international monetary system. These include the possibilities of mutually inconsistent exchange rate stabilization policies, competitive exchange rate depreciation, and instability of exchange rates in the face of speculative pressures. To help avoid these problems the IMF issued guidelines for exchange rate management in June 1974. The guidelines emphasized the point that exchange rate policy is a matter for international consultation and surveillance by the IMF and that intervention practices by individual central banks should be based on three principles: (1) exchange authorities should prevent sudden and disproportionate short-term movements in exchange rates and ensure an orderly adjustment of exchange rates to longer-term pressures; (2) in consultation with the IMF, countries should establish a target zone for the medium-term values of their exchange rates and keep the actual rate within that target zone; (3) countries should recognize that exchange rate management involves joint responsibilities.

The experiences of 1972 and 1973 underlined one of the most important problems faced by any exchange rate system in current circumstances: coping with the massive volume of short-term funds which can be switched very rapidly between financial centres. Short-term capital flows forced the abandonment of exchange rates that were agreed on in 1971 and have caused fluctuations in floating rates. Various attempts have been made to limit such flows. Italy has adopted a 'two-tier' foreign exchange market where there is one price for foreign exchange to finance current account transactions and another price (and another set of controls) for foreign exchange to finance capital movements. Germany has used direct controls on overseas borrowing. There has also been considerable extension of arrangements under which central banks in surplus countries lend the funds they are accumulating back to central banks in deficit countries, thereby greatly enhancing the ability of banks to maintain stable exchange rates in the face of short-term speculative flights of capital.

The Bank of England has engaged in substantial exchange rate management since 1972. Generally its purpose is to remove short- (and sometimes medium-) term fluctuations while not resisting longer-term movements. Evidence of times when the Bank has tried to resist major trends in the rate suggest that the lessons learned under the Bretton Woods system are relevant today: central banks cannot hold exchange rates far away from equilibrium rates set by the influences of purchasing-power parity and non-speculative capital movements. If it does try to do so, the flood of speculative capital flows will force it to abandon its attempt.

Experience suggests that exchange rate management can smooth out temporary fluctuations but cannot resist underlying trends in equilibrium rates as set by relative inflation rates, structural changes and persistent, non-speculative capital flows.

The rise in the price of oil The most serious event affecting the future of the payments system – and indeed the whole of international economic relations – was the raising of the price of oil following the formation of the OPEC cartel. The price rises have generated an unprecedented imbalance in the international economic system in the form of a massive payments surplus for the oil producers and a corresponding deficit for the oil-importing countries. The producing countries cannot spend their oil revenues on goods and services fast enough,[1] nor can the consuming countries produce these goods and services at the necessary rate for all the oil revenues to be spent without creating enormous inflationary pressures.[2] As a result, the OPEC countries are piling up massive capital balances, some in the form of very short-term loans.

It is estimated that by 1980 the cumulative payments surplus of the OPEC countries might reach as much as $300 billion (measured in 1974 US dollars)! This vast sum is more than twice the value of all the world's total reserves of gold, foreign exchange, and SDRs.

It is generally agreed that the OPEC countries have no serious alternative to investing their surplus revenues in the advanced industrialized nations, thereby

[1] There is a limit to the speed with which any country can absorb foreign goods, and many oil-producing countries are at that limit. Ships wait months to unload for want of dock capacity, unloaded goods sit in dockside stockpiles for months – even years – for want of transportation capacity, and so on.

[2] Production of the goods would produce factor incomes and thus add to domestic demand, but their export removes them from domestic markets and thus reduces domestic supplies.

returning on capital account the purchasing power extracted from the current accounts of the oil-importing nations. This situation raises many serious problems. One of the most important is the havoc which would result in foreign exchange markets if surplus oil funds were invested in liquid assets and switched between currencies in response to changes in interest rates and expected capital gains arising from possible exchange rate alterations. Clearly, some means must be found of placing the funds in less liquid investments and/or creating sufficient central bank co-operation to allow the funds to be moved without upsetting foreign exchange markets completely. Since 1974 the IMF has been administering medium-term loans from the oil-exporting countries and those industrialized countries in a relatively strong payments position, the proceeds to be lent to the countries most severely affected by rising oil prices. Although a welcome short-term relief, these loans meant that countries were mortgaging their futures to pay for oil for current consumption.

Although the industrial countries have managed to arrange balance-of-payments finance without too much difficulty, major problems still face the less developed countries despite a rising total of OPEC disbursements to the Third World.

New international reserves Governments operating dirty floats need reserves, just as do governments operating adjustable pegs. The search for an adequate supply of reserves has gone on unabated since the demise of the Bretton Woods system. In January 1976, agreement was reached for a 30 per cent average increase in the quotas of funds that member countries must provide to the IMF and from which the IMF can make loans to countries wishing to support their exchange rates.

At the same time, several longer-term measures relating to the role of gold and the permissible types of future exchange rate regimes were agreed upon. Countries need no longer supply 25 per cent of their IMF quotas in gold, nor are they obliged to use gold in other transactions they may undertake with the IMF. The IMF has also been selling off some of its gold stock on the free market and using the proceeds to establish a trust fund to provide balance-of-payments assistance on concessionary terms to the poorer countries. A further one-sixth of the IMF gold stock has been transferred to IMF members at the official price.

> **Recent developments have helped to eliminate gold from the international monetary system and to establish the SDR as the principal reserve asset in place of the dollar.**

These changes may, however, take a long time to come into full effect. At the beginning of 1978, SDRs constituted only 3·6 per cent of total world reserves, while gold and the US dollar accounted for 16 and 69 per cent respectively.

Survival of the IMF in a world of floating exchange rates

The IMF has proved to be a very resilient institution. Although it bitterly resisted the drift toward floating exchange rates, it has now accommodated itself to them and promises to be as effective a means of securing international financial co-operation under a system of managed floating rates as it was under fixed rates.

The changing position of the IMF is illustrated by the amendments to Article 4 of its charter that were agreed to in 1976 after an international conference in Jamaica. These amendments while allowing for the return to fixed rates at some possible future date, have legalized floating rates within the framework of the IMF system.

1. With the concurrence of the IMF, any country may abandon its par value and adopt a floating exchange rate.
2. The exchange rate management of a floating currency must be subject to IMF surveillance and must not be conducted so as to disadvantage other countries.
3. The agreed practices with respect to floating rates will operate until such time as a general return to par values is attained. If new par values are ever fixed they will be set in terms of SDRs rather than gold or US dollars.

A final word

One of the most impressive aspects of international payments history in the last thirty years has been the steady rise of effective international co-operation. When the gold standard broke down and the Great Depression overwhelmed the countries of the world, 'every man for himself' was the rule of the day. Rising tariffs, competitive exchange rate devaluations, and all forms of beggar-my-neighbour policies abounded.

After the Second World War the countries of the world co-operated in bringing the Bretton Woods system and the IMF into being. The system itself was far from perfect, and it finally broke down as a result of its own internal contradictions. But the international co-operation that was necessary to set the system up survived the collapse of the system itself. For example, the joint co-operative actions of central banks allowed them to weather in the 1970s speculative crises that would have forced them to devalue their currencies in the 1950s.

The collapse of Bretton Woods therefore did not plunge the world into the same chaos that followed the breakdown of the gold standard. The world was also able to cope better than it could have earlier with the terrible strains caused by the sharp rise in oil prices in the 1970s. There are still enormous oil-related problems. How can the real price of imported oil be covered without massive foreign borrowing? What will be the implications of large long-term foreign investments by OPEC countries? How can the payments system be stabilized against flows of short-term funds held by OPEC countries?

Whatever the problems of the future may be, it seems clear that the world has a better chance of coping with them – or even of just learning to live with them – when its countries co-operate through the IMF and other international organizations than when every country seeks its own selfish solution without concern for the interests of others.

Part ten

Growth and development

46

Economic growth

In Chapters 34 and 37 we saw that investment expenditure can play a role in causing fluctuations. The theory developed in those chapters is a short-run theory. It takes potential income as constant and concentrates on the effect of investment expenditure on aggregate demand. From this short-term viewpoint an increase in investment expenditure raises national income and puts pressure on the economy's existing productive capacity.

The Keynesian theory of the determination of national income is a short-run theory that concentrates on the effects of investment on aggregate demand and thus on variations of actual national income around a given potential income.

In the long run, investment is responsible for the creation of more and better capital equipment. By adding to the economy's capital stock, investment raises potential national income. In the long run, investment has been a major cause of the rapid growth of living standards over the last two centuries. An eightfold or more increase in material living standards over the span of a single lifetime has been a common experience.

The theory of economic growth is a long-run theory. It ignores short-run fluctuations of actual national income around potential income and concentrates on the effects of investment on raising potential income.

Since the average gap between actual and potential national income shows no long-term tendency to change, increases in actual income and living standards over the decades will be due mainly to long-term increases studied in the theory of growth, rather than to the short-term fluctuations studied in the Keynesian theory of national income.

The nature of economic growth

Economic growth has been one of the dominant forces in industrial nations over the last 200 years. It has been the source of some of industrialization's greatest triumphs: it has raised living standards to levels where leisure, travel and luxury goods are within the reach of ordinary people for the first time in human history. In industrial nations it has produced standards of living that are the envy of the peoples of the rest of the world, many of whom have striven – with varying degrees of success – to imitate that performance. Economic growth has also been the source of spectacular failures – including pollution of the air, water and land by chemicals, heat and noise.

Members of developed societies have come to accept growth. Even when they worry about such things as pollution, they ask 'How can we remove this or that side-effect of growth?' Only a few people ask 'How can we stop growth?' and even fewer take those few seriously. But growth, which seems inevitable to most of us. has not always been present, nor is it present everywhere today. There have been historical periods of increases in living standards followed by long periods of no change. One of the latter was documented by Professor Phelps-Brown, of the London School of Economics, who showed that there was no significant trend increase in the real incomes of English building-trade workers between 1215 and 1798, a period of almost six centuries. Peasants in many poor countries today enjoy a living standard little different from that of their ancestors 1,000 or more years ago.

Rapid growth, when it occurs, is impressive. Recent data show that total world output has doubled in the last 15 years. Despite dramatic population growth, output per person for the world as a whole has increased sharply also. It was twice as high in 1975 as in 1950! These figures provide evidence of man's mastery of aspects of the environment, but they are misleading in one respect: most of the growth in *output* has occurred in countries that comprise only about one-fifth of the world's population, while much of the *population* growth has occurred in countries that have not experienced output growth. In this chapter and again in Chapter 47, we shall ask why, for many countries, the phenomenon of growth is absent.

The definition of economic growth

In a typical Western industrial country, where GNP has increased at least tenfold in half a century and personal-consumption expenditures per capita have doubled in real terms in less than 30 years, growth is easy to recognize. It is not so easy to measure, because of a series of potential confusions. Because each of these confusions is found in some contemporary discussions, it is worth bearing them in mind as you read of some country's spectacular achievements.

Capacity versus utilization The growth in an economy's national income over three or four years reflects changes in either its productive capacity or its percentage utilization of that capacity, or both. Productive capacity can be measured by the concept of potential national income, Y_F. Percentage utilization can be measured by expressing actual income, Y, as a percentage of potential income: $(Y/Y_F) \times 100$.

If there have been large changes in percentage utilization, very high rates of increase in actual national income will be observed, but such increases will not be sustainable once capacity is fully utilized. A great deal of confusion would be avoided if the term 'growth rate' were used to refer only to the growth of potential national income, and if comparisons of national income figures for one country over several years were divided into two parts: changes due to the growth rate (i.e., growth in productive capacity) and changes due to variations in the employment of existing productive capacity.

Money versus real output Part of any increase in the money value of full-employment output may be due to a rise in prices rather than in output. Use of constant-price measures is essential in measuring growth. This is now the common practice of all major statistical agencies in reporting growth rates.

Total versus per capita measures The economy's growth in real potential output is measured by its growth of constant-price potential output. This measure is relevant to such things as the nation's capacity to wage war and to influence other nations by giving foreign aid.

Growth in per capita output is growth in potential income per person. This is a measure of the economy's ability to produce output for each person in the society. Where population growth is rapid, countries often find their total output burgeoning while their output per person is static or growing only slowly. In these cases, growth in total output has been matched by growth in the number of mouths to feed, leaving the amount per person constant. Improvement in living standards is clearly more closely related to growth in per capita than in total output.

In theoretical discussions of growth, it is often desirable to measure the ability of an economy to convert its resources into goods and services. A widely used measure of growth in productive capacity is average output per man-hour, often called more simply PRODUCTIVITY.

The cumulative nature of growth

A growth rate of 2 per cent per year may seem rather insignificant, but if it is continued for a century it will lead to more than a sevenfold increase in real national income! To see the cumulative effect of what seem like very small differences in growth rates, notice that if one country grows faster than another, the gap in their living standards will widen progressively. If two countries start from the same level of income and country *A* grows at 3 per cent while *B* grows at 2 per cent per year, *A*'s income per capita will be twice *B*'s in 69 years. You may not think it matters much

Table 46.1 Growth of GDP per capita in the EEC countries 1960–76

	1960		1976	
	per capita GDP[1]	Rank	per capita GDP	Rank
Luxembourg	1568	1	4938	2
UK	1374	2	2824	6
France	1337	3	4474	5
Germany	1298	4	5412	1
Belgium	1253	5	4648	3
Netherlands	979	6	4602	4
Italy	696	7	2449	7
EEC (the Six)[2]	1110		4160	
EEC (the Nine)[3]	1168		3950	

[1] Based on International Units of account which may be roughly equated with 1970 US dollars.
[2] All countries in the table excluding the UK.
[3] All countries in the table plus Denmark and the Irish Republic.

whether your economy grows at 2 per cent or 3 per cent, but your children and grandchildren will!

> **Small differences in growth rates make enormous differences in levels of potential national income over a few decades.**

The dramatic cumulative effects of small differences in growth rates are illustrated in Table 46.1. In 1960 UK per capita income was second only to that of Luxembourg among the original six EEC countries. It was also well above the average for those six and for the nine present EEC countries (those shown in the table plus the UK, the Irish Republic and Denmark). But the UK's growth rate at the time was one of the slowest in Europe. By 1976 its per capita income had fallen below the average of both 'the six' and 'the nine'. Indeed, it was higher only than Italy's, and even here the UK's per capita income, which was twice Italy's in 1960, was only 15 per cent higher in 1976. Furthermore, by the 1970s the UK began to be overtaken in per capita GNP by the more prosperous of the Eastern European countries.

Benefits of growth

There is no doubt that growth confers many benefits. A few of the most important are discussed here.

Improved living standards

A primary reason for desiring growth is to raise the general living standards of the population as measured by per capita national income. A country whose per capita GNP is growing at 3 per cent per year is doubling its living standards approximately every 24 years. (A helpful approximation device is the 'rule of 68'. Divide any growth rate into 68 and the resulting number approximates the number of years it will take for income to double.)

The extreme importance of economic growth in raising income can be illustrated by comparing the real income of a father with the real income of the son who follows in his footsteps. If the son neither rises nor falls in the relative income scale compared with his father, his share of the country's national income will be the same as his father's. If the son is 30 years younger than his father, he can expect to have a real income nearly twice as large as his father's at the same age. These figures assume that the father and son live in a country such as the UK, where the growth rate is about 2 per cent per year. If they lived in Japan, where the growth rate was about 8 per cent over the 1950s and 1960s, the son's income would be about 10 times as large as his father's.

For those who share in it, growth is a powerful weapon against poverty. A family earning £3,000 today can expect to earn £3,800 within eight years (plus a further increase due to any inflation) if it just shares in a 3 per cent growth rate (compounded annually). The transformation of the lifestyle of the ordinary industrial worker over the present century is a notable example of the escape from poverty made possible by growth. Unfortunately, not everyone benefits equally from growth. Many of those who are poorest are not even in the labour force, and so will not enjoy the higher wages through which the gains from growth are generally distributed to the population.

Growth and income redistribution

Economic growth makes many kinds of income redistribution easier to achieve. For example, a rapid rate of growth makes it much more feasible politically to alleviate poverty. If existing income is to be redistributed, someone's standard of living will actually have to be lowered. If, however, there is economic growth and the increment in income is redistributed (through government intervention), then it is possible to reduce income inequalities without actually having to lower anyone's income. It is much easier for a rapidly growing economy than for a static one to be generous toward its less fortunate citizens, or its neighbours.

Growth and lifestyle

A family often finds that a big increase in its income leads to a major change in the pattern of its consumption – that extra money buys important amenities of life. In the same way, the members of society as a whole may find that some goods are increasingly attainable as income rises. For example, the households in a rapidly growing country find it desirable not only to demand more cars and highways but also more parks and recreational areas. Furthermore, once the basic needs of food, etc. have been met for a substantial majority of the population, the society may even begin to worry about the litter, etc. that comes with growth itself.

National defence and prestige

If one country is competing with another for power or prestige, then rates of growth are important. If our national income is growing at 2 per cent, for instance, while the other country's is growing at three per cent, all the other country has to do is wait for our relative strength to dwindle. Also, the faster a nation's productivity is growing, the easier the expense of an arms or a space race will be to bear.

More subtly, but similarly, growth itself has become part of the currency of international prestige. Countries that are engaged in persuading other countries of the might or right of their economic and political systems frequently point to their rapid rates of growth as evidence of their achievements.

> **Growth is an enormous long-term force in raising living standards and it dwarfs anything that can be done by redistributive policies to raise the ordinary employed person's standard of living.**

Costs of growth

The benefits discussed above suggest that growth is a great blessing. It is surely true that, other things being equal, most people would regard a fast rate of growth as preferable to a slow one. But other things are seldom equal.

Social and personal costs of growth

Industrialization, unless very carefully managed, causes deterioration of the environment. Unspoiled landscapes give way to highways and factories and billboards; air and water become polluted; unique and priceless relics of earlier ages

– from flora and fauna to ancient ruins and works of art – disappear. With urbanization people move out of the simpler life of farming and small towns into the crowded, unhealthy life of an urban slum. Further growth may turn the urban area into a pleasant place in which to live a few generations later, but by that time many people will have lived and died there. The growth was 'worth it' for their descendants, but was it so for those who originally moved? When the original movement to cities occurs those who remain behind find that rural life, too, has changed because of large-scale farming, the decline of population and the migration of young people from the farm to the city. The faster tempo of life brings joy to some, but tragedy to others. Accidents, ulcers, crime rates, suicides, divorces and murder all tend to be higher in periods of rapid change and in more developed societies.

A growing economy is a changing economy. Innovation leaves obsolete machines in its wake, and also partially obsolete people. Rapid growth requires rapid adjustments, and these can cause upset and misery to the individuals affected. The decline in the number of unskilled jobs means that when an untrained worker loses his job, he may not find another, particularly if he is over 50. It is not only the unskilled who may suffer. No matter how well-equipped you are at 25, in another 25 years you are likely to be partially obsolete. This can happen to a doctor or an engineer as well as to a mechanic.

It is often argued that the costs of growth are a small price to pay for its great benefits. But some of these costs are not so small. Moreover, they are very unevenly borne; many of those for whom growth is most costly (in terms of jobs) share least in the fruits of growth.[1] At the other extreme, it is foolish to see only the costs – to yearn for the good old days – while thriving on higher living standards that growth alone has made possible.

The opportunity cost of growth

In a world of scarcity, almost nothing is free. Growth usually requires an investment of resources in capital goods, in education and in health. Such investments do not yield any *immediate* return in terms of goods and services for consumption. Growth, which promises more goods tomorrow, is achieved by consuming fewer goods today because resources must be diverted to producing capital. For the economy as a whole, this is a primary cost of growth.

A hypothetical example will illustrate the basic choice involved: a more rapid rate of growth may be purchased at the expense of a lower rate of current consumption. Suppose a particular economy has full employment and is experiencing growth at the rate of 2 per cent per year. Its citizens are consuming 85 per cent of the GNP and investing 15 per cent. Suppose that if consumption were reduced to 77 per cent of GNP immediately, the country would produce more capital and that this would shift them at once to a 3 per cent growth rate, which could be maintained as long as saving and investment were held at 23 per cent of national income. Should this be done?

Table 46.2 illustrates the choice open to the society by showing two alternative growth paths of real consumption, C and C'. Path C is what will happen if resources

[1] One aspect of this problem, 'structural unemployment, is discussed in Chapter 48.

Table 46.2 The opportunity costs of growth

In year	The level of consumption: 2% growth rate of consumption (C)	3% growth rate of consumption (C')
0	85·0	77·0
1	86·7	79·3
2	88·5	81·8
3	90·3	84·2
4	92·1	86·8
5	93·9	89·5
6	95·8	92·9
7	97·8	95·0
8	99·7	97·9
9	101·8	100·9
10	103·8	103·9
15	114·7	120·8
20	126·8	140·3
30	154·9	189·4
40	189·2	255·6

are not reallocated. In year zero total income is 100, of which 15 is allocated to investment and 85 to consumption. This percentage division of resources is maintained so the output of investment and consumption goods continues to grow at 2 per cent per year. The alternative growth path of consumption is shown in the C' column. In year zero national income is 100, but now the resources are reallocated so that output of investment goods is 23, while output of consumption goods falls to 77·0. Everything now starts to grow, however, at 3 per cent per annum. The economy holds this new percentage distribution of its resources between consumption and investment output. Consumption now grows at 3 per cent per annum and follows the path shown by the column C'.

On the assumed figures, it takes 10 years for the actual level of consumption to catch up to what it would have been had no re-allocation been made. But the cumulative losses in consumption must be made up before society can really be said to have broken even. It takes an additional 9 years before total consumption over the whole period is as large as it would have been if the economy had remained on the 2 per cent path. This comparison looks only at actual amounts of consumption. If future income is discounted at a positive rate of interest, so that a quantity of goods now is preferred to the same quantity in the future, it will take longer than 9 years to compensate consumers for the loss of goods during the first 10 years. But at some point after 20 years, the initial sacrifice yields bigger and bigger dividends.

Policies to raise growth rates by increasing investment always have this characteristic: present consumption is to be reduced so that future consumption can be raised. Many people will be unattracted by sacrifice whose payoff is 10 or 20 years away. The question of how much of our present living standards should be sacrificed to raise the living standards of our heirs, who are going to be richer in any case, is troublesome. As one sceptic put it: 'Why should we sacrifice for them? What have they ever done for us?'

Theories of economic growth

Economists have done a great deal of theorising about economic growth over the last thirty years. Although many elegant models have been built and many conceptual issues clarified, it is probably safe to say that such meagre advice as we can give to policy makers in market economies as yet owes little to these modern theories. In what follows we shall discuss growth from the view of the relation between the stock of capital and opportunities for investment in new capital.

Growth in a world without learning

Suppose that there is a known and fixed stock of projects that might be undertaken. Whenever the opportunity is ripe, some of them are undertaken, thus increasing the stock of capital goods and depleting the reservoir of unutilized investment opportunities. Of course, the most productive investments will be made first. Such a view of investment opportunities can be represented by a fixed marginal efficiency of capital function, of the kind met in Chapter 28. A function relating the stock of capital to the productivity of an additional unit of capital is drawn in Figure 46.1.

The downward slope of the *MEC* function indicates that, with knowledge, constant increases in the stock of capital are assumed to bring smaller and smaller increases in output per dollar. In other words, the rate of return on successive units of capital declines. This shape is a prediction based on the 'law' of diminishing returns. If, with land, labour and knowledge constant, more and more capital is used, the net amount added by successive increments is predicted to diminish and possibly eventually to reach zero. Given this schedule, as capital is accumulated in a state of constant knowledge the society will move down its *MEC* function. Thus when the capital stock increases from K_1 to K_2 to K_3 the marginal return on capital falls from r_1 to r_2 to r_3. Eventually, when the capital stock is K_4, the marginal return reaches zero.

In such a 'non-learning' world, where new investment opportunities do not appear, growth occurs only as long as there are unutilized opportunities to use capital effectively to increase output. Growth is a transitory phenomenon that occurs because the society has a backlog of unutilized investment opportunities.[1]

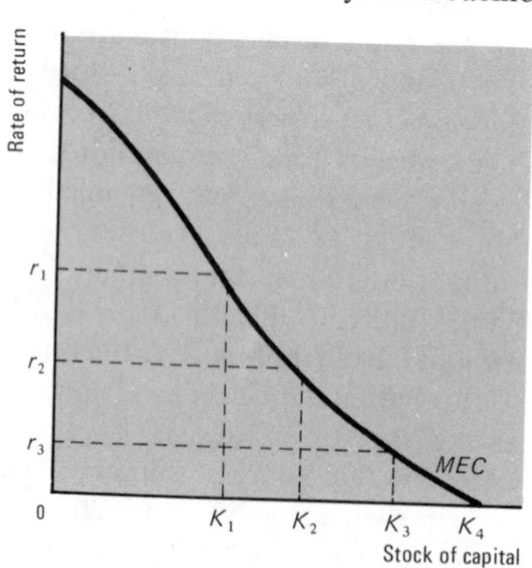

Fig. 46.1 The marginal efficiency of capital function

[1] The argument has been conducted using concepts such as 'the' quality of capital, and 'the' productivity of capital. All that it requires is that there be a finite number of investment opportunities which can be arranged in descending order of the yield that they provide.

So far we have discussed the marginal efficiency of capital. The average efficiency of capital refers to the average amount produced in the whole economy per unit of capital employed. It is measured by the ratio of total output to total capital; this is the OUTPUT/CAPITAL RATIO. Its inverse, the amount of capital divided by the amount of output, is the CAPITAL/OUTPUT RATIO.[1]

Suppose, as is commonly believed, that both the average and the marginal efficiencies of capital are declining. In such an economy the output/capital ratio will be falling and the capital/output ratio will be rising as the capital stock grows.

Two important implications of this theory of growth through capital accumulation with constant knowledge are the following:
(1) successive increases in capital accumulation will be less and less productive, and the capital/output ratio will be increasing; and
(2) the marginal efficiency of new capital will be decreasing and will eventually be pushed to zero as the back-log of investment opportunities is used up.

Growth with learning

The steady depletion of the country's growth opportunities in the previous model resulted from the fact that new investment opportunities were never discovered or created. If, however, investment opportunities are created as well as used up by the passage of time, then the *MEC* function will shift outward period after period, and the effects of increasing the capital stock may be different. This is illustrated in Figure 46.2. Such outward shifts can be regarded as the consequences of 'learning' either about investment opportunities or about the techniques that create such opportunities. If learning occurs, it is next necessary to know how rapidly the *MEC* function will shift relative to the amount of capital investment being undertaken.

Three possibilities are shown in Figure 46.2. In each case, the economy at period 1 has the *MEC* curve, a capital stock of K_1, and a rate of return of r_1. In period 2, the curve shifts to MEC_1 and there is investment to increase the stock of capital to K_2. In period 3 the curve shifts to MEC_2 and there is new investment that increases the

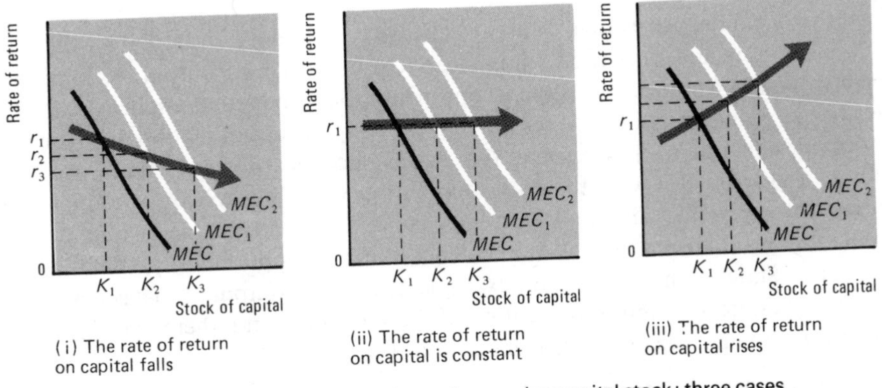

Fig. 46.2 Shifting investment opportunities and a growing capital stock: three cases

[1] Of course, the two ratios measure the same thing. If, for example, the average efficiency of capital is declining, the output/capital ratio will be declining, indicating less output on average per unit of capital used, and the capital/output ratio will be rising, indicating more capital used per unit of output produced.

capital stock from K_2 to K_3. It is the relative size of the shift of the *MEC* curve and the additions to the capital stock that are important. In part (i), investment occurs more rapidly than increases in investment opportunities and r must fall along the grey arrow. In (ii), investment occurs at exactly the same rate as investment opportunities and r is constant. In (iii), investment occurs less rapidly than increases in investment opportunities and r will rise.

Gradual reduction in investment opportunities: the classical view If, as in Figure 46.2(i), investment opportunities are created but at a slower rate than they are used up, there will be a tendency for a falling rate of return and an increasing ratio of capital to output. The predictions in this case are the same as those given above for the 'non-learning state', although the cause is not lack of learning, but too slow a discovery of new investment opportunities.

This figure illustrates one version of the theory of growth held by the Classical economists. They saw the economic problem as one of fixed land, a rising population and a gradual exhaustion of investment opportunities. These things, they said, would ultimately force the economy into a static condition with no growth, very high capital/output ratios, and the marginal return on additional units of capital forced down to zero.

Constant or rising investment opportunities: one contemporary view The classical economists were pessimistic because they failed to appreciate the possibility of really rapid innovation – of technological progress that could push investment opportunities outward as rapidly as, or more rapidly than, they were used up. These two cases are shown in parts (ii) and (iii) of Figure 46.2.

Because the facts (as will be seen in a moment) suggest that the economy generates new investment opportunities at least as rapidly as it uses up old ones, a general rethinking of the causes of growth has occurred. More attention is now devoted to understanding the *shifts* in the *MEC* curve over time than to its *shape*. The record shows that it is the shifts over time that have led to sustained growth.

Factors affecting growth

Quantity of capital per worker Man has always been a tool user, and it is still true today that more and more tools tend to lead to more and more output. As long as a society has unexploited investment opportunities, productive capacity can be increased by increasing the stock of capital. Capital accumulation has such a noticeable effect on output per man that it was once regarded as virtually the sole source of growth. If it were the only source of growth, however, it would lead to movement down the marginal efficiency curve, as in Figure 46.1, and to the predictions printed on page 697. The evidence does not support these predictions. In the United States in this century, for example, the capital/output ratio has remained constant despite enormous quantities of new capital, and there has been no downward trend in the rate of return on capital.

This evidence[1] suggests that investment opportunities have expanded at least as rapidly as investment in capital goods, so that the marginal

[1] This 'evidence' depends on being able to measure the quantity of capital. It is thus open to Cambridge criticisms of the concept of 'the' quantity of capital.

efficiency of capital has not declined in spite of a great increase in the capital stock. Thus although capital accumulation has accounted for much observed growth, it cannot have been the only source of growth.

Innovation New knowledge and inventions can contribute markedly to the growth of potential national income. In order to see this, assume that a society devotes just enough of its resources to the production of capital goods to replace capital as it wears out. If the old capital is merely replaced in the same form, the capital stock will be constant and there will be no increase in the capacity to produce. Now assume that there is new knowledge, so that as old equipment wears out it is replaced by a different, more productive kind. National income will now be growing because of the increase in knowledge rather than because of the accumulation of more and more capital. This sort of increase in productive capacity is called EMBODIED TECHNICAL CHANGE because it inheres in the *form* of capital goods in use. Its historical importance is clearly visible.

The prevalence of the surnames Black and Smith in English-speaking countries (and their equivalents elsewhere) attests to the enormous proportion of human resources once devoted to the upkeep of horses, the main source of power a mere century ago. Nor was only labour involved. Over half of the world's arable land was devoted to growing feed for horses and other work animals. Vast investment opportunities were created when the horse was replaced by fossil fuels as a source of power. The freeing of resources to make other products also led to great improvements in living standards. The assembly line, and then automation, transformed the means of production. The aeroplane revolutionized transportation, and electronic devices have come to dominate communications. The silicone chip, which compresses thousands of electronic circuits in the space taken by one circuit 10 years ago, will make fundamental changes by computerizing many business and household activities. These innovations, plus less well-known but no less profound ones such as improvements in the strength of metals, the productivity of seeds and the techniques for recovering materials from the earth, have all tended to create new investment opportunities.

Less visible but nonetheless important changes occur through DISEMBODIED TECHNICAL CHANGE. These concern innovations that are not embodied in the form of the capital goods or raw materials used. One example is improved techniques of managerial control. Another follows from a better educated and healthier labour force.

The quality of human capital 'Labour' is often talked about as if it were a uniform, well-understood input into production. But, clearly, a 'man-hour' is very different for a skilled mechanic, a scientist or a ditch-digger, because what each of them produces in an hour is valued differently by the market.

The 'quality' of human capital has several aspects. One of these involves the health and longevity of the population. Improvements in these things are, of course, desired as ends in themselves, but they have consequences for production and productivity as well. There is no doubt that productivity per man-hour has been increased by cutting down on illness, accidents and absenteeism. At the same time the extension of the normal lifespan, with no comparable increase in the working lifespan, has created a larger group of retired persons that exercises a claim on total output. Thus whether health improvements alone have increased output per capita is not clear.

A second aspect of the quality of human capital concerns technical training, from learning to operate a machine to learning how to be a scientist. More subtly, there are often believed to be general social advantages to an educated population. It has been shown that productivity improves with literacy and that, in general, the better educated a person is the more adaptable he is to new challenges, and thus, in the long run, the more productive.

The quantity of labour The size of a country's population and the extent of participation in the labour force are important in and of themselves, not merely because they affect the quantity of a factor of production. For this reason, it is less common to speak of the quantity of people available for work as affecting growth than it is to speak of the quantity of capital or iron ore in this way. But, clearly, for any given state of knowledge and supplies of other factors of production, the size of the population can affect the level of output per capita. Every child born has both a mouth and a pair of hands, and, on average, it is perfectly possible to speak of overpopulated or underpopulated economies, depending on whether the contribution to production of additional people would raise or lower the level of per capita income.

Figure 46.3 relates population to per capita income and illustrates a case in which there is an optimal population for which living standards are at a maximum. The curve is drawn in the shape illustrated because resources and knowledge are assumed constant at any moment in time, and alternative populations are assumed to be exploiting them. After a certain size, the pressure of more and more population applying given techniques to a given quantity of resources will force diminishing returns into operation. Once output does not grow in proportion to additional population, output per person must fall.

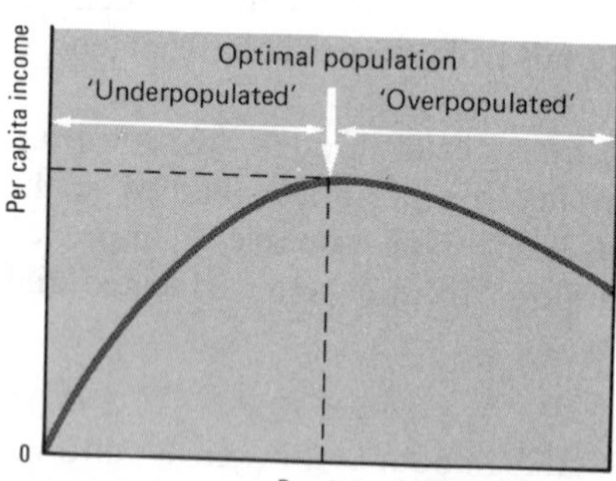

Fig. 46.3 One concept of the optimal population

Many countries have had conscious policies aimed at changing the size of their populations. America in the nineteenth century sought immigrants, as did Australia in the 1950s and 1960s. Germany under Hitler paid people bonuses to have additional children and offered other incentives to create more Germans. Greece today is trying to stem emigration to Western Europe. All of these activities bespeak fear of insufficient population, although the motives are not purely economic in every case. In contrast, many of the less developed countries of South America and Asia are trying to limit population growth. One of the most dramatic and controversial of the recent programmes of this sort has been the mass sterilization of many males in India. The problem of 'excessive' population will be discussed further in Chapter 47.

Social and legal institutions Social and religious habits can affect economic growth. In a society in which children are expected to stay in their fathers' occupations, it is more difficult for the labour force to change its characteristics and thus adapt to the requirements of growth than where upward mobility is itself a goal. Max Weber argued that the 'Protestant ethic' encourages the acquisition of wealth and is thus more likely to encourage growth than an ethic that directs activity away from the economic sphere.

Legal institutions may also affect growth. The pattern of ownership of land and natural resources, in affecting the way such resources are used, may affect their productivity. To take one example, if agricultural land is divided into very small parcels, one per family, it may be much more difficult to achieve the advantages of modern agriculture than if the land were available for large-scale farming. Many economists are thus concerned with patterns of land tenure.

Economists are interested in such relationships for positive reasons, not for normative ones. If it is true that social, religious or legal patterns make growth more difficult, this does not mean that they are undesirable; instead, it means that the benefits of these institutions must now be weighed against the costs, of which their effect on growth is one. If people derive satisfaction from a religion whose beliefs inhibit growth, if they value a society in which everyone owns his own land and is more nearly self-sufficient than in another society, they may be quite willing to pay a price in terms of growth opportunities forgone.

Of course, some institutions inhibit growth without having wide appeal to the people. For example, the concentration of land ownership in the hands of a few absentee landlords who are not concerned with maximizing their profits can be detrimental to growth. If a landlord's holdings are so vast that he can obtain all the income he desires without using his land effectively, he may have no motivation to introduce advanced techniques. In many societies with this system of land ownership, land reform, which usually implies the confiscation of land, becomes a necessary condition for growth. Not surprisingly, such reforms are resisted by existing governments, which tend to support the interests of the economically powerful. Land reform can often be accomplished only in the wake of political revolution.

Policies to influence growth

Centrally controlled economies, in which growth is the overriding goal of policy, have often shown substantial initial successes in altering the growth rate. The main policy required is to engineer a massive and fairly abrupt shift of resources from current consumption to investment. There is usually such a backlog of obviously useful investment projects that, whether or not they are exploited wastefully, and whatever system of free enterprise or central control is used, the large-scale, new investment pays off in a more rapid growth rate for some considerable time.

Sustaining a high growth rate, even in an economy in which growth remains the overriding objective, may require things other than a high proportion of resources devoted to investment. Research and development of new ideas is important, and so are the entrepreneurial activities of innovating. Here there is much debate and little hard knowledge. Economists and historians will no doubt continue to debate the experience of Soviet Russia, India, China and other centrally planned economies for a long time to come. When they do, one of the basic questions will be: 'Is it possible for the bureaucracy of a centrally planned economy to sustain the risk-taking activities that are one of the basic components of the growth process in the same way that they are sustained by many private profit-seeking entrepreneurs in a free-market system?' Past experience with the conservative tendencies of bureaucratic systems must suggest that here is one of the most vulnerable points in the position taken by advocates of central planning. Conservatism is not something that just happens inexplicably in bureaucracies; it happens for the quite comprehensible reason that the incentive system often discourages individuals from taking risks: punishment for failure is focused on a few individuals, while reward for success is diffused throughout the system.

In the mixed economies of Western Europe, North America, and other industrially developed regions, growth is but one of a half a dozen or more of the key objectives of the central authorities. In such economies the problem is much more difficult than in the 'growth-dominated' economies referred to above. The policy-makers in these relatively advanced economies want more growth, but only if it does not conflict too much with other goals of policy. They may ask what tools are available to encourage a little more growth without fundamentally changing the present nature of the economy. They may attempt to influence each of the factors listed earlier as affecting growth. The problem, however, is that although we have some qualitative knowledge, we have little quantitative knowledge. If, for example, we spend £10 million more on education each year, what will be the quantitative effect on our growth rate and on other goals? (There will be £10 million less to spend on other projects.) Nonetheless, central authorities do have growth policies, and they do try to influence the factors thought to affect growth.

The first major policy is to try to increase the overall level of investment. There are two ways in which this can be attempted. First, investment may be encouraged by policies to keep interest rates low and to make borrowing otherwise easy. An easy money policy is thus thought to be a growth policy. Even this, however, is not certain, and Professor Frank Paish has long been an advocate of the view that periods of mild unemployment are more conducive to growth than periods of very high demand, with consequent inflationary pressures.

The second method of encouraging investment recommends itself to those who are uncertain about the desirability of increasing investment by increasing all of aggregate demand. They wish to encourage investment only by a series of special measures running from direct subsidies on investment expenditures to various types of tax relief. Such measures are largely concerned with the quantity of capital. As noted earlier, recent empirical studies suggest that accumulation of capital is less important and that such factors as innovation and education are more important than had previously been thought. The best guess based on current knowledge is that substantially less than half of the increase in productive capacity in all Western countries is due to capital accumulation, while over half is due to other things.

Invention and innovation clearly play an important role in growth, but it is not so easy to turn them on and off. There is substantial faith that increases in research and development (R and D) do pay off in more rapid innovation. The government itself engages in a good deal of R and D, provides research grants to others, and in certain areas participates in joint projects with business firms. We are still uncertain about the quantitative importance of R and D in the growth process. Much current research is being devoted to estimating its importance.

Furthermore, a great deal of government-fostered R and D goes into industries that produce rockets, aeroplanes and other defence or highly technically oriented products. Currently there is substantial uncertainty about the genuine growth effects of this expenditure. Some people feel that the spillover onto the rest of the economy is small and that the government investment merely subsidizes a privileged group of technologists who would otherwise not exist, and who contribute little to the growth of the economy. Others feel that in these activities the government is encouraging research and development that will be generally useful, and thus is contributing significantly to the long-run growth rate. Here is a very important positive question on which we have too little knowledge now, but about which we will undoubtedly learn much more over the next decade.

Public expenditures on education at all levels, but particularly on higher education and training of scientific personnel, have been high and are growing. It is often thought that these expenditures foster growth, both in the sense of positively promoting it by increasing the likelihood of discovering new and better techniques, and by avoiding barriers to it that arise if there are not enough competent people to operate the new machines that are invented.

Education too requires careful evaluation. Serious empirical studies indicate that, at the present levels of education, further expenditures on education 'pay' in the sense of providing benefits in excess of all costs, including the output forgone during the educational period. Obviously for a society, as for an individual, a point can be reached beyond which further education is not wise, but the present evidence indicates that we have not yet reached that point.

Growth requires change. Labour and other factors of production must be reallocated from industries that are declining in terms of total employment and into industries that are expanding. If restrictive practices and union-enforced manning agreements prevent much of this reallocation from occurring, growth will be greatly slowed. Some potentially cost-saving innovations will not be introduced because their benefits cannot be reaped. Others will be adopted but their full effect on growth will not be felt because labour will be allocated to 'overmanning' the new machines rather than being reallocated to other industries where it could increase output. Thus measures to enhance labour mobility and to allow the potential cost reductions of new innovations actually to be achieved can greatly affect the growth rate.

This brief discussion must make it clear that we are not able to control the growth rate with the nice degree of precision with which we can control the level of total demand or even the balance of payments. Indeed, central authorities in Western countries do not have the ability to raise or to lower the growth rate at all by changing their policies, let alone to alter it by x per cent. We must conclude that, although we do know something about the growth process, we do not know nearly enough to give policy-makers in market economies the ability to exert *measurable* control over the rate of economic growth, at least over small ranges of variation.

Current controversies over economic growth

Current controversies over economic growth concern whether or not further sustained growth is either desirable or possible. The question of desirability can be reviewed by examining the cases that might be made by advocates and opponents of further economic growth.

An open letter to the ordinary citizen from a supporter of the Growth-Is-Good School

Dear Ordinary Citizen:

You live in the world's first civilization that is devoted principally to satisfying *your* needs rather than those of a privileged minority. Past civilizations have, without exception, been based on leisure and high consumption for a tiny upper class, a reasonable living standard for a numerically small middle class, and hard work with little more than subsistence consumption for the great mass of people. In the past, the average person (who may or may not have been allowed the title 'citizen') saw little of the civilized and civilizing products of the economy, except when he or she was toiling to produce them.

What is unique about the continuing Industrial Revolution is that it is based on mass-produced goods for consumption by the ordinary citizen. It also ushered in a period of sustained economic growth that has raised the consumption standards of ordinary citizens to levels previously reserved throughout the entire history of civilization for a tiny privileged minority. Reflect on a few examples: travel, live and recorded music, art, good food, inexpensive books, universal literacy and a genuine chance to be educated if you want to be. Most important of all, there is enough leisure to provide time and energy to enjoy these and myriad other products of the modern industrial economy.

Would any ordinary citizen seriously doubt the benefits of growth and wish to be back in the world of 150 or 500 years ago, in the same relative social and economic position? Most surely the answer is no. But we cannot say the same for persons with incomes in the top 1 to 2 per cent of the income distribution. Economic growth has destroyed much of their privileged consumption position: They must now vie with the masses when visiting the world's beauty spots and be annoyed, while lounging on the terrace of a palatial mansion, by the sound of chartered jets carrying ordinary people to holidays in far places. Many of the rich resent their loss of exclusive rights to luxury consumption, and it is not surprising that they find their intellectual apologists.

Whether they know it or not, the anti-growth economists – such as John Kenneth Galbraith of Harvard, Joan Robinson of Cambridge, and E.J. Mishan of the London School of Economics – are not the social revolutionaries they assume themselves to be. They are the counter-revolutionaries who would set back the clock of material progress for the ordinary person. They say that growth has produced pollution and wasteful consumption of trivia that contribute nothing to human happiness. But the democratic solution to pollution is not to reduce output to such a low level that pollution is trivial; it is to accept pollution as a transitional phase connected with the ushering in of mass consumption, to keep the mass consumption, and to learn to control the pollution.

It is only through further growth that the average citizen can enjoy consumption standards (of travel, culture, medical and health care, etc.) now available to people in the top 25 per cent of the income distribution – which includes the intellectuals who earn large royalties from the books they write denouncing growth. If you think that extra income confers little or no real benefit, ask that top 25 per cent of the income distribution to trade incomes with the average citizen.

Ordinary citizens, do not be deceived by disguised elitist doctrines. Remember that the very rich and the elite have much to gain by stopping growth – and even more by rolling it back – but you have everything to gain by letting it go forward.

Onward!

I. Growthman

An open letter to the ordinary citizen from a supporter of the Growth-Is-Bad School

Dear Ordinary Citizen:

You live in a world that is being despoiled by a mindless search for ever higher levels of material consumption at the cost of all other values. Once upon a time, men and women knew how to enjoy creative work and to derive satisfaction from simple activities undertaken in scarce, and hence highly valued, leisure time. Today the ordinary worker is a mindless cog in an assembly-line process that turns out ever more goods that advertisers must work overtime to persuade the worker to consume.

Statisticians and politicians count the increasing flow of material output as a triumph of modern civilization. Consider not the flow of output in general, but the individual products that it contains. You arise from your electric-blanketed bed, clean your teeth with an electric toothbrush, open with an electric tin-opener a tin of the sad remains of a once-proud orange, you eat your bread baked from super-refined and chemically refortified flour, and you climb into your car to sit in vast traffic jams on exhaust-polluted motorways. And so the day goes, with endless consumption of high-technology products that give you no more real satisfaction than the simple, cheaply produced products consumed by your grandfathers: soft woolly blankets, natural bristle toothbrushes, real oranges, old-fashioned and coarse but healthy bread, and public transport that moved on uncongested roads and gave its passengers time to chat with their neighbours, to read, or just to daydream.

The slick magazines of today tell you that by consuming more you are happier. But happiness lies not in increasing consumption but in increasing the ratio of *satisfaction of wants* to *total wants*. Since the more you consume the more the advertisers persuade you that you want to consume, you are almost certainly less happy than the average citizen in a small town in 1900, whom we can visualize sitting on the family porch, sipping a cool beer or a lemonade, and enjoying the antics of the children as they play with discarded barrel staves and skipping ropes.

Today the landscape is dotted with countless factories producing the plastic trivia of the modern industrial society and drowning you in a cloud of noise, air, and water pollution. The countryside is despoiled by slag heaps and dangerous nuclear power stations that produce the energy that is devoured insatiably by modern factories and motor vehicles.

Worse still, our precious heritage of natural resources is fast being used up. Spaceship earth flies, captainless, in its senseless orgy of self-consuming consumption.

Now is the time to stop this madness. We must stabilize production, reduce pollution, conserve our natural resources, and seek justice through a more equitable distribution of existing total income.

A long time ago Malthus taught us that if we do not limit population voluntarily, nature will do it for us in a cruel and savage manner. Today the same is true of output: If we do not halt its growth voluntarily, the halt will be imposed on us by a disastrous increase in pollution and a rapid exhaustion of natural resources.

Citizens, awake! Shake off the shackles of growth worship, learn to enjoy the bounty that is yours already, and eschew the endless, self-defeating search for increased happiness through ever-increasing consumption.

Upward!

A. Non-growthman

Both of these cases have real merit. Possibly a balanced judgement lies somewhere in between, but both extremes have their sincere supporters. It may be interesting to ask yourself where you stand on these issues.

Are there limits to growth?

Those opposed to growth argue that sustained growth for another century is undesirable; some even argue that it is impossible. Of course all terrestrial things have an ultimate limit. Astronomers predict that the solar system itself will die as the sun burns out in another 6,000 million or so years. To be of practical concern, however, a limit must be within some reasonable planning horizon. Recent books by Jay Forrester and D.H. Meadows *et al.* predict the imminence of a growth-induced doomsday.[1] They predict that living standards will reach a peak about the turn of the century and then, in the words of Professor Nordhaus, a leading critic of these models, will 'descend inexorably to the level of Neanderthal man'.

Not surprisingly, this debate has received widespread attention in the popular press. Whatever the final verdict, there can be no doubt that the debate that has raged about these so-called doomsday models has helped to give needed awareness of, and attention to, problems of population growth, pollution, and exhaustion of the supplies of specific natural resources. While there is debate, on many matters there is also substantial consensus.

The increasing pressure on natural resources The years since the Second World War have seen a rapid acceleration in the utilization of the world's resources, particularly the fossil fuels and the basic minerals. The world's population has increased from under 2·5 billion to over 4 billion in that period, which alone increases the demand for all of the world's resources. But the fact of population growth greatly understates the pressure on resources. Calculations by Professor Nathan Keyfitz and others focus on the resource use by the so-called middle class, defined roughly as those who can claim a lifestyle of the level enjoyed by 90 per cent of American families. This middle class, which today includes about one-sixth of the world's population, consumes 15 to 30 times as much oil per capita and, overall, at least five times as much of the earth's scarce resources per capita as do the other 'poor' five-sixths of the population.

[1] Jay Forrester, *World Dynamics* (Wright Allen Press, 1972) and D.H. Meadows *et al.*, *Limits to Growth.*

The world's poor are not, however, content to remain poor for ever. Whether they live in the USSR, Brazil, Korea or Kenya, they have evidently let their governments know that they expect policies leading to enough growth to give *them* the higher consumption levels that people in developed nations take for granted. This aspiration is being fulfilled to a degree. The world's middle class has grown by nearly 4 per cent per year – twice the rate of population growth – over the post-war period. The resulting increases in demand in the last two decades have outstripped discovery of new supplies and caused crises in energy and mineral supplies as well as food shortages. Yet the 4 per cent growth rate of this middle class is too slow for the billions who live in underdeveloped countries and see the fruits of development all around them. Even if population growth is reduced, therefore, the pressure on our resources of energy, minerals, and food is likely to accelerate.

Another way to look at the problem of resource pressure is to note that present technology and resources could not possibly support the present population of the world at the standard of living of today's average West German, French or American middle-class family. Such a shift in level of living, if made overnight, would more than quadruple the world's demand for resources. The demand for oil would increase tenfold. Since these calculations (most unrealistically) assume no population growth anywhere in the world and no growth in living standards for the richest sixth of the world's population, the fact of insufficient resources is manifest. On all of this there is no serious disagreement among informed people.

Doomsday predictions Some people forsee imminent doom. The doomsday advocates combine the undoubted acceleration of resource utilization referred to above with a series of more questionable assumptions: first, that there is no technical progress; second, that no new resources are discovered or rendered usable by new techniques; and third, that there is no substitution of more plentiful resources for those that become scarce. Under these circumstances, exhaustion of one or more key resources is predictable. If, in addition, population growth continues at historical rates, this exhaustion will occur relatively quickly – certainly within the next century. And if the increasing production continues to pollute the atmosphere faster than the pollutants can be absorbed, the capacity to produce will be diminished and the quality of life further diminished.

These are the basic assumptions of the doomsday models. Doom can come in several ways (or in any combination of them): natural resources depletion, famine due to overpopulation, or an increasing and ultimately fatal pollution of the land, sea or air.

The many possible routes to disaster forseen by doomsday advocates mean that no single restraint will suffice to prevent it. If both natural resource usage and pollution are controlled, doom results from overpopulation. Population control will prove self-defeating because it leads to an increase in the per capita food supply and in the standard of living – which in turn generates forces to trigger a resurgence in population growth. The only way to prevent disaster is to stop economic growth at once through a comprehensive plan, drastically curtailing natural resource use (by 75 per cent), pollution generation (by 50 per cent), investment (by 40 per cent), and the birth rate (by 30 per cent). Since the countries of the world are not likely, within the next forty years, to agree on the stern measures needed to meet these targets, a descent down the slippery slope of declining living standards during our own lifetimes is inevitable – and disaster looms for our grandchildren.

A reply to doomsday Critics reply that predictions of imminent doom are as old as human life itself and about as reliable as predictions of the arrival of universal peace and goodwill on earth. They recognize the pressures on the world's resources, and they concede that at present rates of utilization we would clearly run out of specific resources – particularly oil, gas, and certain minerals – in the foreseeable future. They argue, however, that the doomsday models can be faulted in several critical ways.

(1) The assumption of constant technology (the case of growth without learning is analysed on page 696) is nonsense in the light of past human history. Constant technology and a declining marginal efficiency of capital is sufficient by itself to reduce first the marginal and then the average product of capital to zero. The attempt to sustain growth in such a world must eventually produce zero per capita output! But, they argue, all of our economic history shows this key assumption of the doomsday models to be invalid. Nothing could be clearer than that technology is not constant and that people are ingenious in finding ways not only to economize on the use of scarce resources but also to substitute materials that are common for those that become scarce. Just as ample taconite replaced scarce iron ore in making steel, just as ample coal replaced scarce charcoal in smelting steel, and just as synthetic rubber replaced natural rubber in making tyres, so it is reasonable to expect new energy sources to replace fossil fuels. The potential supplies of nuclear and solar energy are inexhaustible.

(2) The assumption of a fixed and relatively small supply of resources that are consumed by production of goods and services is nonsense. It defies the law of conservation of mass energy and denies the fact that in the earth's crust beneath the sea and further in towards the core there are vast supplies of mineral resources, some located and charted and others known to exist in a general way. As with assumption (1), this assumption is sufficient to produce disaster by itself. A finite supply of limited resources that is destroyed in the course of production must soon be exhausted if output increases exponentially.

(3) The model has no place for the coordinating effects of the price system. As a particular resource becomes scarce its price rises and this has many effects: people are induced to try harder to discover new supplies, it becomes profitable to produce from known sources that were previously too costly, producers are induced to substitute other resources within already known technologies and a search for new substitutes and new technologies is encouraged. Such trends are observable in the pattern of use of most resources over the past centuries, yet the model makes no allowance for them.

The list has been extended to a score or more of similar points, all of which, say the critics, show the pitfalls ready to trap the person who approaches the economy without using the insights provided by a century of theory and observation of the operation of the price system. Thus, say the critics, the model only proves the consistency of logic: from silly assumptions one can only derive silly conclusions. Can it be doubted, ask the critics of doomsday models, that a society that has developed birth-control pills and explored Mars can solve the problems of over-population and pollution.

A tentative verdict Most economists agree that conjuring up absolute limits to growth based on the assumptions of constant technology and fixed exhaustible resources is not warranted. But this does not mean there is no cause for concern.

Any barrier can perhaps be overcome by technological advances – but not in an instant, and not automatically. Clearly there is a problem of timing: how soon can we discover and put into practice the knowledge required to solve the problems that are made ever more imminent by growth in population, growth in affluence, and the desire for growth of many who now live at very low incomes. There is no guarantee at all that a whole generation will not be caught in transition, with enormous, if not cataclysmic, social and political consequences. The nightmare conjured up by the doomsday models may have served its purpose if it helps to focus our attention on these problems.

A postscript on kinds of investment

From the Keynesian point of view, any activity that puts income into people's hands will raise aggregate demand. Thus the short-run effect on national income is the same if a firm 'invests' in digging holes and refilling them or in building a new factory. From the growth point of view, however, we are concerned only with that part of investment that adds to a nation's productive capacity. The point is important because much of what is classified as investment in the national income accounts, and that does add to aggregate demand, is really consumption expenditure. Assume, for example, that a firm discards an adequate but dingy office building and 'invests' in a lavish new head-office block with superior facilities for its staff. This will count as investment in the national income data and the expenditure will add to aggregate demand. From the growth point of view, however, it is really disguised consumption for the firm's staff.

Similar remarks apply to public-sector expenditure. Any expenditure will add to aggregate demand and raise national income if there are unemployed resources. Only some expenditure adds to the growth of full-employment income. Indeed some investment expenditure that shores up an industry that would otherwise be declining, in order to create employment, may have an anti-growth effect. It may prevent the reallocation of resources in response to shifts both in the pattern of world demand and in the country's comparative advantage. Thus in the long run the country's capacity to produce commodities that are demanded on open markets may be diminished.

47

Growth and underdeveloped economies

The problems of economic growth that we considered in Chapter 46 are of particular concern to the poorer countries of the world. In the civilized and comfortable urban life of the highly developed countries, most people lost sight of the fact that a very short time ago, *very* short in terms of the lifespan of the earth, man lived like any other animal, catching an existence as best he could from what nature threw his way. It has been less than 10,000 years since the agricultural revolution, when people changed from food gathering to food producing, and it has been only within the last century or two that a large proportion of the population of even the richest countries could look forward to anything but an endless struggle to wrest an existence from a reluctant nature. Most earlier civilizations were based on a civilized life for a privileged minority and unremitting toil for the vast majority.

The uneven pattern of development

There are over 4,000 million people alive today. The wealthy parts of the world, where people work no more than forty or fifty hours per week and enjoy substantial amounts of leisure and a consumption similar to that of Western Europe, contain only about 20 per cent of the world's population. Many of the rest struggle for subsistence. About 2,000 million people exist at a level at or below that enjoyed by peasants in the more advanced civilizations of 5,000 years ago.

If one were studying the effect of variations in rainfall from year to year in Great Britain or Holland, one would find that they were reflected in agricultural output and income: for each inch that rainfall fell below some critical amount, output and income would vary in a regular way. By stark contrast, in poorer countries such as China, India and Ethiopia, variations in rainfall are often reflected in the death rate. Many people in such countries have so few alternatives to living off their own current production that even slight fluctuations in their food supply bring death by starvation.

The fact that effects measured in money units in rich countries are often measured in lives in poor ones makes the problem of economic growth very much more urgent in poor countries. Reformers in poor countries, therefore, often feel a sense of urgency not felt by their counterparts in the developed world.

Table 47.1 shows how few countries have made the transition from poverty to

Table 47.1 Income and population differences among groups of countries, 1974

Classification (based on GNP per capita in 1974, US dollars)	Number of countries (1)	GNP (billions) (2)	Population (millions) (3)	GNP per capita (4)	Percentage of the world's GNP (5)	Percentage of the world's Population (6)	Growth rate[1] (7)
I Less than $175	26	$ 147	1,099	$ 134	2·7	28·6	1·2
II $175–349	20	320	1,075	298	5·9	28·0	3·5
III $350–699	27	95	191	497	1·7	5·0	3·1
IV $700–1399	20	384	378	1,016	7·0	9·8	3·8
V $1400–2799	16	910	406	2,241	16·6	10·6	3·9
VI $2800–5599	15	1,445	361	4,003	26·4	9·4	4·7
VII $5600 or more	11	2,172	331	6,562	39·7	8·6	3·0
Totals	135	$5,473	3,841	$1,425	100·0	100·0	

Source: International Bank for Reconstruction and Development, Economics and Social Data Division, *World Atlas 1977*, and unpublished data.

[1] Average annual percentage rate of growth of GNP per capita, 1960–1974.

relative comfort. The unequal distribution of the world's income is shown in columns 5 and 6. Groups I–III, with over 60 per cent of the world's population, earn only 10 per cent of world income. Groups VI–VII, with 18 per cent of the world's population, earn 66 per cent of world income. Column 7 shows that the gap in income between rich and poor countries is not being closed.

Over half of the world's population live in poverty: many of the poorest people are in countries with the lowest growth rates, and thus fall ever farther behind.

The meaning of underdevelopment

We must now see what light economics can shed on the problem of raising living standards in poor countries. It is often thought that an important first step is to find the 'true' definition of underdevelopment. Books on the subject often start by raising this conceptual problem. The only purpose here in making clear the meaning we attach to the term is to delimit our area of concern – to say 'We are concerned with these countries and these problems, and not with those countries and those problems.' Of course, different investigators may concern themselves with different groups of countries and different problems. One, for example, defines an underdeveloped country as one with a per capita national income of less than $700. Another confines his study to countries with substantial quantities of under-developed resources. Each of these groups of countries can be studied, and it is completely futile to argue which group is properly defined as 'underdeveloped'.

Underdevelopment has many aspects. We may measure development in dozens of different ways, among them: income per head; the percentage of resources unexploited; capital per head; savings per head; conduciveness to growth of the social system; conduciveness to growth of local religion; amount of 'social capital' (i.e., roads, railroads, schools, etc.); degree of education of the working classes, and so on.

Countries that are 'underdeveloped' in one of these ways may not be underdeveloped in another. For example, one country may have a lower income per head than others, but have a higher percentage utilization of existing natural resources. For this reason we cannot have a unique ranking of the various countries in terms of degree of development. We cannot say that one country is more underdeveloped than another as long as all of these characteristics affect our view of underdevelopment. Furthermore, the problem of raising the income of a country that has low capital per head, much unemployed labour, but few unexploited natural resources is likely to be very different from that of raising the income of a country which is underpopulated and has many unexploited natural resources. In either case, the problems will be more difficult if the country has a religious system that places a low value on economic activity and savings. Instead of trying to define *the* problem of underdevelopment, we should look for some common problems in various groups of countries, remaining prepared to find major differences in both the problems and the solutions in whatever group of countries we study.

Many terms have been used to describe the countries that are our concern in this chapter. They have variously been referred to as *underdeveloped, developing, emerging* and *less well developed.* Fads and fashions grow up around particular terms, but none of them will be descriptive of all of the economies in question, for the very reason that their present characteristics and the problems they face differ. We shall mainly use one of the older terms, underdeveloped, and use this with no connotations of disapproval and in full realization that it covers a great variety of countries with a great variety of levels and rates of growth of real national income.

Barriers to economic development

If income per head is taken as a crude index of the level of economic development, a country may develop by any set of devices that causes its aggregate income to grow faster than its population. A growing population, a shortage of natural resources or inefficiency in the way resources are used can each be an important barrier to development.

Population growth

Population growth is a central problem of economic development. If population expands rapidly, a country may make a great effort to raise the quantity of capital only to find that a corresponding rise in population has occurred, so that the net effect of its 'growth policy' is a larger population now maintained at the original low standard of living. They have made appreciable gains in income, but much of it has been eaten up (literally) by the increasing population.

This is illustrated in Table 47.2. The very poorest countries have *both* a relatively low growth rate of national income and a relatively high growth rate of population. The middle group shows rising living standards despite large population growth, by virtue of a high growth rate of national income. The wealthiest countries owe much of their growth in living standards to a low rate of population increase.

> **Growth in per capita real income depends upon the difference between growth rates of real national income and of population.**

If population control in the poor countries is left to nature, nature often solves it in a cruel way. Population increases until many are forced to live at a subsistence level; further population growth is halted by famine, pestilence and plague. This grim situation was perceived early in the history of economics by Thomas Malthus. In some ways, the population problem is more severe today than it was even a generation ago because advances in medicine and in public health have brought sharp and sudden decreases in death rates. It is ironic that much of the compassion for the poor and underprivileged people of the world has traditionally taken the form of improving their health, thereby doing little to avert their poverty. Men laud the medical missionaries who brought modern medicine to the regions where it was previously unobtainable, but the elimination of malaria has doubled the rate of population growth in Ceylon. Cholera, once a killer, is now largely under control. No one would argue against controlling disease, but other things must also be done if the child who survives the infectious illnesses of infancy is not to die of starvation in early adulthood.

Figure 47.1 illustrates actual and projected population growth in the world today. It took about 40 to 50 thousand years after the emergence of modern Cro-Magnon Man for the world's population to reach 1,000 million. It took 100 years to add a

Table 47.2 The relation of population growth in per capita GNP, 1960–1974 (percentages)

Classification of countries (GNP per capita, 1974 US dollars)			Average annual rate of growth of:			Population growth as percentage of real GNP growth
Group[1]	Income level	Percentage of population	Real GNP	Population	Real GNP per capita	
I	less than $175	28·6	3·6	2·4	1·2	66
II–IV	$175–1399	42·8	5·9	2·1	3·8	36
V–VII	over $1400	28·6	4·7	1·1	3·6	24

Source: International Bank for Reconstruction and Development, Economics and Social Data Division, *World Atlas 1976*, and unpublished data.

[1] The groups are defined in Table 47.1.

second thousand million and 30 years to add the third thousand million. If present trends continue, the 1980 population of 4,000 million will be doubled in 30 years.

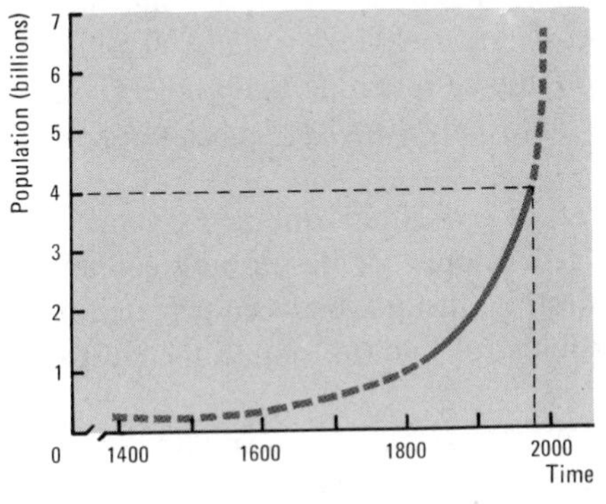

Fig. 47.1 World population growth. (The broken line gives projections of the population from 1975 to 2000.)

The growth of world population has been so explosive over the last two centuries that scientists can, with some realism, speak of the human animai as having reached the swarming stage.

Economists sometimes speak of a 'critical minimum effort', by which they mean an increase in GNP sufficiently large to provide an appreciable increase in per capita living standards in spite of the rise in population. Experience suggests that when people become used to higher living standards they will seek to protect these by voluntarily limiting the sizes of their families. When and if this happens, the population 'problem' solves itself through voluntary individual decisions.

Resource limitations

Kuwait has the world's highest income per capita because of its good fortune in sitting on top of the world's largest known oil field. Lack of oil proved a devastating blow to many of the least developed countries when the OPEC cartel quadrupled oil prices during the early 1970s. Without oil their development efforts would be crippled; but to buy oil took too much of their scarce foreign exchange. Unlike many developed countries, which also bought oil, the least-developed countries were not markets in which the oil producers spent their new wealth.

It might seem obvious that development would be easier in a country lavishly endowed with natural resources than in a country poorly endowed. But as so often happens in development economics, propositions that seem obvious turn out to be suspect on closer attention. Kuwait and the United States are examples of countries that have developed on a base of plentiful natural resources – a single resource in one case and a multiplicity in the other. That natural resources are not sufficient is shown by the fact that the North American Indians lived with the American resources for centuries. Although they were well above the subsistence level and had civilizations of their own, there is no evidence that the Indians living in what is now the US or Canada had anything other than static living standards for many centuries. That natural resources are not necessary is shown by the long list of diverse economies that have developed without indigenous resources and sometimes in such hostile environments as malaria-ridden swamps. Consider, for example, Holland, Hong Kong, Japan, Singapore, Switzerland, Taiwan and Venice.

Financial capital Investment plays a vital role in economic growth, as was seen in Chapter 46. It may take as much as £10 of capital to increase national income by £1 per year. If this is so, it will take £58,000 million of capital to raise average income per year by £100 in a country of 58 million people such as Mexico. £58,000 million is a lot of money in any country, but it is roughly as much as the whole GNP of Mexico. The shortage of investment funds is almost always a bottleneck on the road to development.

One source of financial capital is the savings of households and firms. Banks and banking are particularly important in underdeveloped or developing economies because if they do not function well and smoothly, the link between private saving and investment may be broken and the problem of finding funds for investment greatly intensified.

Reliance on deposit money and faith in bankers is limited to a small fraction of the world's economies. Many people in undeveloped economies do not trust banks, and they will therefore either not maintain deposits, or periodically panic, withdraw their money, and seek security in mattresses, in gold or in real estate. When this happens, increases in savings do not become available for investment in productive capacity. If banks cannot count on their deposits being left in the banking system, they cannot engage in the multiple expansion of credit. Thus, distrust of banks, and of deposit money, may impede economic development even if private individuals are willing to refrain from current consumption.

Social-overhead capital The progress of economic development is reflected in the increasing flow of goods and services from a nation's farms and factories to its households. But the ability to sustain and expand these flows depends on many supporting services, particularly transportation and communications, which are sometimes called the 'infrastructure' of the economy. In the early stages of the development of western industrial nations much of the infrastructure grew up slowly due to private enterprise. Today people usually look to the government to provide the infrastructure, but there is debate over the extent to which this is necessary. The absence, whatever the reason, of a dependable infrastructure can impose severe barriers to economic development.

Human capital A well-developed entrepreneurial class of persons motivated and trained to organize resources for efficient production is often lacking in underdeveloped countries. This lack may be a heritage of a colonial system that gave the local population no opportunity to develop[1]; it may result from the fact that managerial positions are awarded on the basis of family status or political patronage; it may reflect the presence of economic or cultural attitudes that do not favour the acquisition of wealth by organizing productive activities; or it may simply be due to a lack of the required education or training.

Poor health is another source of inadequate human resources. Less time is lost and more effective effort is expended when the labour force is in good health. The economic analysis of medical advances is a very young field, however, and there is a great deal to be learned about the quantitative importance of such gains.

[1] Some did; some did not. For example, the British colonial system, whatever else can be said against it, was remarkable in encouraging education and skill development among many of the populations that it controlled.

Inefficiency in the use of resources

Low levels of income and slower than necessary growth rates may result from inefficient use of resources as well as from scarcity of key resources.

Allocative inefficiency and X-inefficiency It is useful to distinguish between two kinds of inefficiency. A man-hour of labour would be used inefficiently, for example, even though the labourer was working at top efficiency, if he was engaged in making a product that no one wanted. Using society's resources to make the wrong products is an example of ALLOCATIVE INEFFICIENCY. In terms of the production-possibility boundary encountered in Chapter 4, allocative inefficiency represents operation at the wrong place on the boundary. If 2 tons of coal and 50 man-hours of labour are being used to make steel in the most efficient way, this may, nevertheless, be inefficient if this coal and labour could be more productive making electric power to be used to make aluminium. Allocative inefficiency will arise if the signals to which people respond do not reflect opportunity costs – both monopoly and tariffs are commonly cited sources of distortions – or if market imperfections prevent resources' moving to their best uses.

A second kind of inefficiency has come to be called X-inefficiency, following Professor Harvey Leibenstein. X-INEFFICIENCY arises whenever resources are used in such a way that even if they are making the right product, they are doing so less productively than is possible. If a labourer, for example, is debilitated by disease, unmotivated, or inhibited by taboos, an hour of his labour may be less productive than it could be, even in its best use. Similarly, land or coal may be poorly used because of ignorance, indifference or poor technology.

While the two kinds of inefficiency can occur simultaneously, X-inefficiency is now believed to be far more important than allocative inefficiency in accounting for both the low levels of income and the difficulties in development of the less developed countries.

Sources of X-inefficiency Both inadequate education and poor health, discussed above, may be important sources of X-inefficiency. For example, as modern techniques are introduced, a large rise in the educational standards of the work force is necessary. A man who cannot read or write or do simple calculations will be much less efficient in many jobs than one who can. A manager who is trained in modern methods of bookkeeping, inventory control and personnel management is likely to be much more effective in getting the most output from a given input than one who is ignorant of these techniques.

Traditions, institutions and habitual ways of doing business vary among societies, and not all are equally conducive to productivity. Often personal considerations of family, of past favours, or of traditional friendship or enmity are more important than market signals in explaining behaviour. One may find a too-small firm struggling to survive against a larger rival and learn that the owner prefers to stay small rather than expand because expansion would require use of nonfamily capital or leadership. To avoid paying too harsh a competitive price for his built-in inefficiency, the firm's owner may then spend half his energies attempting to influence the government to prevent larger firms from being formed or trying to secure restrictions on the sale of output, and he may well succeed. Such behaviour is very likely to inhibit economic growth.

Do a society's customs reflect cherished values or only such things as the residual influences of a passing social system or a former oligarchical political structure? This is an important question to the policy-makers who must decide whether or not the cost in terms of inefficiency should be paid to maintain the customs. In any case, cultural attitudes are not easily changed. If people believe that your father's background is more important than your present abilities, it may take a generation to persuade employers to change their attitudes and another generation to persuade workers that things have changed. Structuring incentives is a widely used form of policy action in market-oriented economies, but this may be harder to do in a traditional society than in a market economy. If people habitually bribe the tax collector instead of paying taxes, they will not be likely to respond to policies that are supposed to work by changing marginal tax incentives. All that will change is the size of the bribe.

Several empirical studies have shown large differences in productivity from country to country in particular industries using the same technologies of production. In some cases, great increases in productivity have been achieved simply by changing incentive systems. These facts suggest a large quantitative importance to X-inefficiency and a large payoff to overcoming it.

X-inefficiency, which refers to a lower level of productivity than could be achieved due to social attitudes and structures, seems to be a major cause of low levels and rates of growth of national income in many underdeveloped countries.

Fostering economic development

Economic development policy involves identifying the particular barriers to the level and kind of development desired and then devising policies to overcome them. Governments can seek funds for investment, and they can attempt to identify cultural, legal, social and psychological barriers to growth. They can undertake the programmes of education, legal reform, resource development, negotiation of trade treaties or actual investment that smooth the way to more rapid growth. All of this is more easily said than done. Further, as the dozens of 'development missions' sent out by the World Bank and other international, national and private agencies have discovered, the problems and strategies vary greatly from country to country. Economic development as a field of economic expertise is in its infancy. A few choices, however, seem to be pervasive and therefore worth mentioning here.

Planning or *laissez-faire*?

How much government control over the economy is necessary and desirable? Practically every shade of opinion has been seriously advocated, from 'The only way to grow is to get the government's dead hand out of everything' to 'The only way to grow is to get a fully-planned, centrally controlled economy'. Such extreme views are easily refuted by factual evidence. Many economies have grown with very little government assistance. Great Britain, the United States and Holland are important examples. Others, such as the Soviet Union and Poland, have sustained growth with a high degree of centralized control. In still other countries, there is almost every conceivable mix of government and private initiative in the growth process.

What sense can be made of these apparently conflicting historical precedents? Probably the most satisfactory answer is that the appropriate action depends on the circumstances presently ruling in the country. In some cases, ineffective governments may have been interfering with the economy to the point of discouraging private initiative, in which case growth may well be enhanced by a reduction in government control over the economy. In other cases, where major quantities of social capital are needed or where existing institutional arrangements, such as land tenure, are harmful to growth, active intervention by the central authorities – 'planning', as it is called – may be essential. On the question of which is the best mix between state and private initiative at a particular time and in a particular place, there is likely to be much disagreement.

The case for planning The active intervention of the central authorities in the management of a country's economy rests upon the real or alleged failure of market forces to produce satisfactory results. The two major appeals of planning are that it can accelerate the pace of economic development and that it can significantly influence its direction.

Any one of the barriers to development may be lowered by actions of the central authorities. Consider, for example, the way that central authorities might seek to mitigate a shortage of investment funds. In a fully employed free-market economy, investment is influenced by the quantity of savings households and firms make, and thus the division of resources between consumption and saving is one determinant of the rate of growth.

When living standards are low, people have urgent uses for their current income. Left to individual determination, saving may be low, and this is an impediment to investment and growth. In a variety of ways, central authorities can intervene and force people to save more than they otherwise would. Such compulsory saving has been one of the main aims of most of the 'plans' of communist governments. The justification offered for this compulsory sacrifice of present living standards for future benefits is that without it growth would be slow or non-existent, inflicting a low living standard on all future generations.

The goal of the five-year plans of Russia, Poland and China is to raise savings and thus to lower current consumption below what it would be, given complete freedom of choice. Extra savings may be the subject of planning even in less centrally controlled societies, through tax incentives and monetary policies. The object is the same: to increase investment in order to increase growth, and thus to make future generations better off.

Central governments of an authoritarian sort can be particularly effective in overcoming some of the sources of X-inefficiency. A dictatorship may supress social and even religious institutions that are barriers to growth, and hold on to power until a new generation grows up that did not know and does not value the old institutions. It is much more difficult for democratic government, which must command popular support at each election, to do currently unpopular things in the interests of long-term growth.

> **One of the reasons why authoritarian governments often have a large initial success in raising growth rates is their willingness and ability to sweep away some of the sources of X-inefficiency, often against the wishes of a large part of the society. The value judgement as to whether the growth gains are worth the social sacrifices is, of course, outside economics.**

The case for *laissez-faire* Most people would agree that government must play an important part in any development programme. The sectors of the economy that are reserved for public enterprise in most developed economies – education, transportation, and communication – are very important to development. But what of the sectors usually left to private enterprise in advanced capitalist countries?

The advocates of *laissez-faire* in these sectors place great emphasis on human drive, initiative and inventiveness. Once the infrastructure is established, an army of entrepreneurs will do vastly more to develop the economy than will an army of civil servants. The market will provide opportunities and direct their efforts and individuals will act energetically within it once they are given a self-interest in doing so. People who seem irretrievably lethargic and unenterprising when held down by lack of incentives will show amazing bursts of energy when given sufficient self-interest in economic activity.

Furthermore, goes the argument, individual capitalists are far less wasteful than civil servants of the country's capital. An individual entrepreneur who risks his own capital will push investment in really productive directions. If he fails to do so, he loses his investment and thus his role in deciding on the allocation of the country's capital. A bureaucrat, however, investing capital that is not his own – possibly raised from the peasants by a state marketing board that buys cheap and sells dear – will behave very differently. His first thought may be to enhance his own prestige by spending too much money on cars, offices and secretaries, and too little on really productive activities. Even if he is genuinely interested in the country's well-being the incentive structure of a bureaucracy does not encourage creative risk-taking. If his ventures fail his own head is likely to roll; if they succeed he will not receive the profits anyway, and his superior may get the medal.

This is a brief suggestion of the case that is often argued for leaving much of the main thrust of development in the hands of private producers. It is a very emotive subject and readers are likely to have had strong reactions to it. Those with 'leftish' leanings are likely to have reacted to this case in a hostile fashion, and those with 'rightish' leanings in a favourable fashion. Clearly people have strong, divergent and often doctrinaire views on these matters; equally clearly, these are matters of life and death to millions in underdeveloped countries who will suffer or die if their governments adopt an inappropriate road to development. Human welfare would be well served if these issues could be removed from the realm of emotion into that of precise statement and careful testing.

Educational policy

Most studies of underdeveloped countries suggest that undereducation of various kinds is a serious barrier to development and urge increased expenditures on education. This poses the choice of how to spend educational funds. Should they go to erasing illiteracy and increasing the level of mass education, or to training a small cadre of scientifically and technically trained specialists? The problem is serious, because education of any kind is very expensive and does not pay off quickly. Basic education requires a large investment in school buildings, in teacher training and in curriculum revision that will result in little visible change in the level of education after 5 or 10 years, and even less payoff to the economy in terms of greater productivity in that time span. Thus, with many urgent demands, the opportunity cost of such expenditures always seems high. Yet it is essential to make them sometime because the gains will be critical to economic development a generation later.

Many, perhaps most, developing countries have put a large fraction of their educational resources into training a small number of highly educated people because the tangible results of a few hundred doctors or engineers or PhDs are relatively more visible than the results from raising the school-leaving age by a year or two, say, from age 10 to age 12. It is not yet clear whether this policy pays off, but it is clear that there are some drawbacks to it. Many of this educated elite are recruited from the privileged classes on the basis of family position, not merit; many regard their education as the passport to a new aristocracy, rather than as a mandate to serve their fellow citizens; and, in addition, an appreciable fraction emigrate to countries where their newly acquired skills bring higher pay than at home. Of those who stay home, many seek the security of a government job and become part of the new establishment.

Although the risks of waste may be large, so also are the gains from a successful specialist educational policy. Engineers, agronomists, economists and a host of other experts can be very productive when their talents are used successfully.

Population control

The race between population and income has been a dominant feature of many underdeveloped countries. There are two possible ways for a country to win this race. One is to create conditions that produce a growth rate well in excess of the rate of population growth. The second is to control population growth. The problem *can* be solved by restricting population growth. This is not a matter of serious debate, although the means of restricting population growth are, for considerations of religion, custom and education, are involved.

Positive economics cannot decide whether population control is morally good or bad, but it can describe the consequences of any choice made. Both Sweden and Venezuela have death rates of about 10 per 1,000 population per year. The birth rate in Sweden is 14; in Venezuela it is 42. While the causes of variations in birth rates are complex, they have inescapable economic consequences. Thus, in Venezuela the net increase of population per year is 32 per 1,000 (3·2 per cent), but it is only 4 per 1,000 (0·4 per cent) in Sweden. If each country achieved an overall rate of growth of production of 3 per cent per year, Sweden would be increasing her living standards by 2·6 per cent per year, while Venezuela would be lowering hers by 0·2 per cent per year. In 1977 Sweden's income per capita ($7,700) was three and a half times as high as Venezuela's ($2,200), and Venezuela was the wealthiest country in South and Central America. The gap will widen rapidly, if present population trends continue.

Acquiring capital

A country can acquire funds for investment in three distinct ways: from the savings (voluntary or forced) of its domestic households and firms, by loans or investment from abroad, or by contributions from foreigners.

Capital from domestic saving If capital is to be created at home by the country's own efforts, it is necessary to divert resources from the production of goods for current consumption. This requires a cut in present living standards. If living standards are already low, such a diversion will be difficult. At best, it will be possible to re-allocate only a small proportion of resources to the production of capital goods. Such a situation is often described as the *vicious circle of poverty*: because a country has little capital per head, it is poor; because it is poor, it can devote only a few resources to creating new capital rather than producing goods for immediate consumption; because little new capital can be produced, capital per head remains low; because capital per head remains low, the country remains poor.

The vicious circle can be made to seem an absolute constraint on growth rates. Of course it isn't, since if it were we would all be back at the level of Neanderthal man. Also, it should not be forgotten that many countries that count as underdeveloped now already have per capita GNPs that must be larger than were those of many early free-market economies when they began on a path of sustained economic growth. The grain of truth in the vicious circle argument is probably that some surplus must be available somewhere in the society to promote saving and investment. In a poor society with an even distribution of income, so that nearly everyone is on the subsistence level, saving may be very difficult. But this is not the common experience. Usually there will be at least a small middle class that can save and invest if opportunities for profitable uses of funds arise. Also, even in poor societies the average household is usually above the physical subsistence level. Even the poorest households will find that they can sacrifice some present living standards for a future gain. After all, presented with a profitable opportunity, Ghanaians planted cocoa plants at the turn of the century even though there was a seven-year growing period before any return could be expected!

This last example points to an important fact. Often in underdeveloped countries one resource that is *not* scarce is labour hours. Profitable home or village investment that requires mainly labour inputs may be made with relatively little sacrifice in current living standards. This is not the kind of investment, however, that may appeal to central authorities who are mesmerised by such large, spectacular, symbolic investments as dams, nuclear power stations and steel mills.

Imported capital Another way of accumulating the capital needed for growth is to borrow it from abroad. If a poor country, A, borrows from a rich country, B, it can use the borrowed funds to purchase capital goods produced in B. Country A thus accumulates capital and needs to cut its current output of consumption goods only to pay interest on its loans. As the new capital begins to add to current production, it becomes easier to pay the interest on the loan and also to begin to repay the principal out of the increase in output. Thus, income can be raised immediately, and the major sacrifice postponed until later, when part of the increased income that might have been used to raise domestic consumption is used to pay off the loan. This method has the great advantage of allowing a poor country to have an initial increase in capital goods far greater than it could possibly have created by diverting its own resources from consumption industries.

Many countries, developed or undeveloped, are suspicious of foreign capital, lest the foreign investor gain control over their industries or their government. The extent of foreign control depends on the form that foreign capital takes. If the foreigners buy bonds in domestic companies, they do not own or control anything; if they buy common stocks, they own part or all of the company; if they subsidize a government, they may feel justified in exacting political commitments. Whether foreign ownership of one's industries carries political disadvantages is a subject of debate. In Canada, for example, there has been significant political opposition to having so much of Canadian industry owned by US nationals who are presumably more open to pressure from US central authorities than from Canadian authorities. Nonetheless, the advantages seem to outweigh the disadvantages in the people's eyes, since there has been no action to restrict the inflow of US capital.

Contributed capital From the point of view of the receiving country, contributed capital in the form of foreign aid expenditures of individual countries and international institutions would seem to be ideal. It has the advantage of enabling the country to shift to more rapid growth without either sacrificing consumption now or having to repay later. There is significant resistance to accepting aid in some countries. The explanation lies in the country's suspicions of the motives of the givers and fear that hidden strings may be attached to the offer. Independent countries prize their independence and want to avoid either the fact or the appearance of being satellites. Pride – a desire to be beholden to no one – is also a factor. The economist cannot say that these fears and aspirations are either foolish or unworthy. He can only note that they do have a cost, for there is no doubt that economically it is better to receive than to give.

Patterns of development

To what extent should a developing country pursue a policy of BALANCED GROWTH, pushing expansion in all sectors of the economy, rather than one of UNBALANCED GROWTH, pushing specialization in certain sectors? How should it decide how much effort to devote to increasing agricultural production, needed to feed its masses, and how much to the industrialization that might change its role in the world economy? If it is to push industrialization, what commodities should it manufacture – those for which there is a large export market, or those which will free it from the need to import?

Comparative advantage: the case for unbalanced growth

The principle of comparative advantage provides the traditional case for the desirability of unbalanced growth. By specializing in those sectors in which it has the greatest comparative advantage, a country can achieve the most rapid growth in the short run. Its potential for growth is certainly not equal in all sectors of the economy. Balanced growth pursued to the extreme of equal growth in all sectors would be virtually sure to result in a lower living standard than would result from some degree of specialization accompanied by increased international trade.

These are cogent reasons in favour of *some* specialization. But specialization involves risks that may be worth avoiding even at the loss of some income. Specialization involves concentrating one's production in one or a few products. This makes the economy highly vulnerable to cyclical fluctuations in world demand and supply. Even more seriously, if technological or taste changes render a product partially or wholly obsolete, the country can face a major calamity for generations. Just as individual firms and regions may become overspecialized, so may countries.

Unplanned growth will usually tend to exploit the country's *present* comparative advantages. A planned economy, through the planners, may well choose a pattern of growth that involves changing the country's *future* comparative advantage.

A country need not passively accept its current comparative advantages.

Many skills can be acquired, and the fostering of an apparently uneconomic domestic industry may, by changing the characteristics of the labour force, develop a comparative advantage in that line of production. The Japanese were in a feudal state and showed no visible comparative advantage in any industrial skill when their country was opened to Western influence in 1854, yet they became a major industrial power by the end of the century. Soviet planners in the 1920s and 1930s chose to create an industrial economy out of a predominantly agricultural one and succeeded in vastly changing the mix between agriculture and industry in a single generation. These illustrations should serve as cogent reminders that an excessive reliance on current comparative advantage may lead to an excessive defence of the status quo in the pattern of international specialization.

Agricultural development versus industrialization

India, Pakistan and Taiwan, along with other Asian countries, have achieved dramatic results by the application of new technology – and particularly new seed – to agricultural production. Increases of up to 50 per cent in grain production have been achieved, and it has been estimated that with adequate supplies of water, pesticides, fertilizers and modern equipment, production could be doubled or even trebled. This has been labelled the 'green revolution'. When the Nobel Prize Committee gave the 1970 Peace Prize to Norman Borlaug, it recognized the potential importance of these developments in alleviating, for at least a generation, the shortage of food that the population explosion was expected to bring.

The possibilities of achieving such dramatic gains in agricultural output may seem almost irresistible at first glance, but many economists think they should be resisted and point to a series of problems.[1] One is that a vast amount of resources are required to irrigate land and mechanize production, and these resources alternatively could provide industrial development and industrial employment opportunities. Thus there is a clear opportunity cost. Critics of the agricultural strategy argue that the search for a generation free from starvation will provide at best only a temporary solution, because population will surely expand to meet the food supply. Instead, they argue, underdeveloped countries should start at once to reduce their dependence on agriculture. Let someone else grow the food; industrialization should not be delayed.

A second problem with the agricultural strategy is that the great increases in world production of wheat, rice and other agricultural commodities that the 'green revolution' makes possible could depress their prices and not lead to increased earnings from exports. What one agricultural country can do, so can others, and there may well be a glut on world markets.

A third problem with the agricultural development strategy has arisen where increasing agricultural output has been accompanied by decreasing labour requirements in agricultural production without any compensating increase in employment opportunities elsewhere in the economy. Requirements of labour per

[1] An excellent account of the issues barely touched in the text is C.R. Wharton, Jr., 'The Green Revolution: Cornucopia or Pandora's Box?' *Foreign Affairs*, April 1969.

acre have dropped by one half. Millions of tenant farmers – and their bullocks – have been evicted from their tenant holdings by owners who are buying tractors to replace them. Many are wandering around the country vainly seeking other work. In other areas, unemployment is disguised rather than visible, but it is no less real. If 10 people work full time on a farm because they are all being supported by it and have nothing better to do, even though the same output could be achieved by only 6 people, then the marginal productivity of the last 4 workers is zero. It is as if 6 were gainfully employed and 4 were unemployed. Where there is visible or disguised unemployment, devoting resources to labour-saving innovations makes little sense, unless at the same time there is development of new jobs for the displaced labour. Without such jobs, the potential increases in output that labour-saving techniques make possible will not be achieved.

Import substitution

In the period since the Second World War, industrialization of underdeveloped countries has largely taken the form of producing domestically goods that were previously imported, largely for sale in the home market. Because these countries characteristically suffered from a significant comparative disadvantage in such production, it proved necessary both to subsidize the home industry and to restrict imports. A study of such policies in seven countries – Argentina, Brazil, Mexico, India, Pakistan, the Philippines and Taiwan – concludes that

> **although there are arguments for giving special encouragement to industry, this encouragement could be provided in forms which would not discourage exports, including agricultural exports, as present policies often do; which would promote greater efficiency in the use of resources; and which would create a less unequal distribution of income and higher levels of employment in both industry and agriculture.**[1]

These conclusions are controversial, and critics point to the fact that Taiwan, for example, represents one of the great successes of economic development. Its income per capita has averaged a rate of increase of over 6 per cent during the whole of the last two decades.

Implementing an import substitution policy is relatively easy because it can be done by imposing import quotas and by raising tariffs. Such tariffs and other restrictions on imports provide incentives for the development of domestic industry by carving out a ready-made market and by providing a substantial price umbrella that promises high profits to successful local manufacturers and to foreign investors who might enter with both capital and know-how. Subsidies, governmental loans and other forms of encouragement have also been used in many cases.

Little, Scitovsky and Scott concluded that policies of industrialization accomplished by effective rates of protection that varied from 25 per cent for Mexico to over 200 per cent for Pakistan aggravated inequalities in the distribution of income by raising the prices of manufactured goods relative to agricultural goods and by favouring profits over wages. Moreover, they found that productivity

[1] Little, Scitovsky and Scott, *Industry and Trade in Some Developing Countries* (Oxford University Press, 1970), p. 1.

increased more than employment opportunities, and that unemployment has grown because of the discouraging of such labour-using industries as textiles and the encouraging of the use of capital-intensive, labour-saving processes.

In brief, the argument against these industrialization policies is that they have given too much attention to the advantages of self-sufficiency and too little to comparative advantage. Moreover, the opportunities for import substitution are limited: Once the country runs out of imports to substitute for, what then? Industrialization, these critics argue, ought to be encouraged, but along the lines where infant industry arguments are truly valid: where, once the development period is past, the country will have a reliable industry that can compete in world markets.

Industrialization

Obviously, if Chad or Burma could quickly develop steel, shipbuilding and manufacturing industries that operated as efficiently as those of Japan or West Germany, they, too, might share in the rapid economic growth that has been enjoyed by these industrial countries. Indeed, if a decade or two or even three of protection and subsidization could give infant industries time to mature and to become efficient, the price might be worth paying. After all, both Japan and Russia were recently underdeveloped countries.

The greatest problem with such a strategy is that there is no guarantee that it will succeed. Even if the country has the required basic natural resources, it may be backward enough that it is unlikely to have the labour or managerial talent to achieve success within a reasonable time. India may create a steel industry and have its productivity increase year by year, but it must do more. It must catch up to the steel industries of other countries if it is to compete in world markets.

The catch-up problem is a race against a moving target. Suppose one is committed to having a given industry competitive in 10 years. In such a situation, it is not sufficient to be making gains in productivity; they must be made at a fast enough rate to overcome a present disadvantage against an improving opponent. Suppose you must improve by 50 per cent to achieve the present level of a competitor who is improving at r per cent per year. If you want to catch him in 10 years you must improve at $r+4$ per cent per year. If r is 6 per cent, you must achieve 10 per cent. To achieve 6 per cent or 7 per cent may be admirable, but you will lose the race just the same.

Thus, while the industrialization route to development is available, it depends both on having required resources and on overcoming the things that contribute to X-inefficiency. This often means devoting resources for a long period to education, training, development of an infrastructure, and overcoming the various cultural and social barriers to efficient production.

All of this is difficult, although not impossible. Countries sometimes seek a short cut, and pursue certain lines of production on a subsidized basis either for prestige purposes or because of a confusion between cause and effect. Because most wealthy nations have a steel industry, the leaders of some underdeveloped nations regard their countries as primitive until a domestic steel industry has been developed. If a country has a serious comparative disadvantage in steel, however, then having a steel industry will make that country poor. It is doubtful if a nation really gains international prestige by having an uneconomical steel industry, an unprofitable national airline or a sleek aeroplane that no airline can afford to operate even if it were given to them free. In the long run, prestige probably goes to the country that grows rich, rather than to the one that stays poor but produces, at high cost, a few prestigious commodities that its government regards as signs of wealth.

Some awkward issues

The speed of development Reformers in underdeveloped countries often think in terms of transforming their economies within a generation or two. The sense of urgency is quite understandable but unless it is tempered by some sense of historical perspective, totally unreasonable aspirations may develop – only to be dashed all too predictably. Many underdeveloped countries are probably in a stage of development analogous to that of medieval England – they have not yet developed anything like the commercial sophistication of the Elizabethan era. It took 600 years for England to develop from that stage to its present one. To do the same elsewhere in half the time of 300 years would be a tremendous achievement; to aspire to do it in 50 or 100 years may be to court disaster.

Some controversies The view presented in this chapter is neo-Malthusian and constitutes what is the probably current conventional wisdom on underdevelopment. There are, however, opposing views.

The neo-Malthusian view gives no place for the value of children in parents' utility functions. Critics point out that the psychic value of children should be included as part of the living standards of their parents. They also point out that in rural societies even quite young children are a productive resource because of the work they can do; while fully grown children provide old-age security for their parents in societies where state help for the aged is negligible.

The neo-Malthusian theory is also criticized for asserting that people breed blindly like animals. Critics point out that traditional methods of limiting family size have been known and practised since the dawn of history. Thus they argue that large families in rural societies are a matter of choice. The population explosion came not through any change in 'breeding habits' but by medical advances that greatly extended life expectancy (which surely must be counted as a direct welfare gain for those affected). The critics argue that once an urban society develops, family size will be reduced voluntarily. This was certainly the experience of Western industrial countries and why, ask the critics, should it not be the experience of the now-developing countries?

A second criticism of the conventional wisdom concerns the alleged heavy opportunity cost of creating domestic capital. Production of consumption and capital goods are substitutes only if factor supplies are constant. But, say the critics, the development of a market economy will lead people to substitute work for leisure. For example, the arrival of Europeans with new goods to trade led the North American Indians to collect furs and other commodities needed for exchange. Until they were decimated by later generations of land-hungry settlers, the standard of living of the Indians rose steadily with no immediate sacrifice. They created the capital needed for their production – weapons and means of transport – in their abundant leisure time so that their consumption began to rise immediately. This too, the argument runs, could happen in underdeveloped countries if market transactions were allowed to evolve naturally. The spread of a market economy would lead locals to give up leisure in order to produce goods needed to buy the goods that private traders were introducing from the outside world.

Other controversies exist but this discussion should be sufficient to suggest that in development economics, as in all other branches of the subject, established views should always be regarded as open to challenge from conflicting theories and awkward facts.

Part eleven

Macroeconomic policy

48

Goals and instruments of macro-policy

Today macroeconomics is in a period of crisis. A decade ago there was a strong consensus that the macro-behaviour of the economy was fairly well understood and that policy goals could be achieved by the available instruments. Policy conflicts might be imposed by the nature of the economy that would make it impossible to achieve all goals simultaneously. Thus hard choices among alternative goals might be necessary, but, once made, we had sufficient knowledge to enforce them through macro-policy.

Today the consensus no longer exists. There is debate over the causes of the severe inflations that have beset Western countries in the 1970s. Ten years ago economists spoke confidently about the choice between unemployment and inflation. Today high unemployment *and* high rates of inflation often exist simultaneously, and this has given rise to a new economic term – STAGFLATION – which refers to the coexistence of high unemployment and rapid inflation.[1]

In this chapter we shall discuss the main goals of macro-policy and the instruments that are available for its operation. The discussion will review and add to topics already introduced in widely separated parts of this book. In the next chapter we shall study some unresolved theoretical issues on which many current policy conflicts turn. In the final chapter, we shall discuss some of the most important current policy debates – debates whose outcome will determine the degree of success of macro-policy and will affect the welfare of all citizens over the next decade.

Macro-policy variables

The four major goals of macro-policy are: (1) to maintain a low and stable level of unemployment; (2) to maintain a relatively stable price level; (3) to maintain a satisfactory balance of payments and (4) to sustain a high rate of growth.

At the outset we need to distinguish three kinds of variables. First, there are

[1] These disagreements among economists are serious ones, and their outcome will profoundly affect the average citizen. Many of them are over issues that go well beyond introductory economics. Thus although some of the issues can be outlined here, there is no way in which the full nature of what is involved in many of the debates can be appreciated without at least an intermediate, and possibly also an advanced, course in macroeconomics and monetary theory.

POLICY VARIABLES, those variables in which the policy-maker is ultimately interested. In the present context there are four key policy variables; unemployment (U), the price level (P), the balance of payments (B) and the growth rate (G). Policy variables are the ultimate goals of economic policy. Second, there are INSTRUMENTAL VARIABLES. These are the variables on which our policies can act directly. They include such things as the rates of taxes and the level of government expenditure, the cash reserves of the commercial banks and laws of all sorts. Between these two there may be a link created by many variables, which we call INTERMEDIATE VARIABLES. These are variables that our policies cannot affect directly, and in whose behaviour policy-makers are not directly interested except in so far as they in turn affect the behaviour of policy variables. The great value of economic theory to the policy-maker is the link that it provides, through intermediate variables, between the instrumental variables whose behaviour central authorities can change, and the policy variables whose behaviour they wish to change. In a simple example, a change in the instrumental variable of government spending affects an intermediate variable, aggregate demand, which in turn affects the policy variable of unemployment. The above discussion is summarized in Tables 48.1 and 48.2, using arrows to indicate these causal links. We now pass on to a consideration of each of the four main policy variables.

Table 48.1 The link between governmental action and the ultimate goals of policy

Government policy	→	An instrumental variable	→	Any number of intermediate variables	→	The policy variable

Table 48.2 The link between governmental action and unemployment

Government fiscal policy	→	The level of government expenditure	→	The level of aggregate expenditure	→	GNP	→	The rate of unemployment

Growth

Why policy-makers are concerned

By and large, economic growth is accepted as desirable. It is the major cause of changes in living standards. With growth, each generation can expect, on the average, to be substantially better off than all preceding generations. The horrors of the early industrial revolution are no longer with us to a great extent because economic growth has removed the necessity of 14-hour days worked in extremely harsh conditions.

Differential growth rates also cause enormous gaps among living standards of various countries within little more than a decade. As we saw in Chapter 46, slow British growth rates have moved Britain down the list of present EEC countries from the second highest per capita GNP in 1960 to the second lowest in 1978. If present growth rates persist to the end of this century, West Germany's per capita GNP will be 6 times Britain's. This is the same relative discrepancy as now exists between Britain and Guatamala.

We have seen, however, that growth is not without its costs. Most people would probably agree that the gains from growth were worth the economic costs incurred by those who lose by it, *even if they were forced to pay sufficient taxes to fully compensate the losers*. Since growth doubles average living standards over 20 to 30 years, it is clearly *possible* by suitable redistributive policies to make *everyone* better off as a result of growth. But growth has other more basic effects on our environment, and, today, people are not so sure that unrestricted growth is worth all of its costs, particularly since the price in terms of the deterioration, or even the destruction, of the environment is not yet fully known. What does seem clear, however, is that although growth may now be slowed, it is not going to be halted because of environmental problems.

Causes of growth

Economic growth is the policy variable about which we know least. In spite of a great deal of study, and the accumulation of isolated bits of knowledge, we do not really understand the complex causes of growth sufficiently well to be able to alter the growth rate as easily as we can alter the unemployment rate. No case in which a government has intervened in a free-market society with the purpose of varying the growth rate by 1 or 2 percentage points from year to year is generally agreed to have been a success. Growth, therefore, has always been the enigma of macro-policy; we agree that it is one of the most important of all the variables, and we also agree that it is the one we know least how to control.

Important policy issues are involved. Consider, for example, the experiences of Britain and West Germany over the past 35 years. Both countries came out of the Second World War in an impoverished state. The destruction in Germany had certainly been worse than that in Britain, and in 1946–47 the UK economy was capable of producing very much more per capita than the West Germany economy. In the first few years after the war, each economy made a fundamental decision. The UK elected a socialist government in 1945 and decided to deal with post-war economic problems by using the apparatus of central economic planning: rationing, quotas, exchange controls and physical allocation of resources to industries according to the priorities set by the planners. There is still debate and uncertainty about this decision. Some think it was correct. Others agree with Professor John Jewkes, who spoke of Britain's having been subjected to a counter-productive 'Ordeal by Planning'. The West Germans chose another path. In 1947 physical controls were swept away and the German leaders placed their faith in the innovative abilities of individual entrepreneurs operating in a basically free-market environment.

The superficial evidence (see page 691) favours the German route. It must be remembered, however, that Germany had a growth rate higher than the UK's for much of the period prior to 1914. It is possible that factors other than the institutional set-ups adopted after 1945 accounted for the different performances of these two economies, but we really do not know. A government that would like to copy the German and avoid the British performance desperately needs to know to what extent these institutional choices influenced growth paths.[1]

The balance of payments and exchange rates

Concern about the balance of payments has been important in the recent past. It arises as a result of a prior policy decision to support a fixed exchange rate rather than to allow the rate to be determined on the free market. Under the Bretton Woods system any country whose balance of payments was in deficit had to make the achievement of a satisfactory payments position a major goal of policy – sometimes the overriding goal. Since 1972–3 most major industrial countries have allowed their exchange rates to fluctuate on the free market. As a result, obtaining a satisfactory balance of payments in order to defend the existing exchange rate has ceased to be the dominant policy consideration. The adoption of floating exchange rates has allowed macroeconomic policy-makers to turn their attentions to domestic rates of inflation, unemployment, and growth, while leaving the balance of payments more or less to take care of itself. The free-market exchange rate fluctuates (in the manner analyzed in Chapter 43), ensuring that international payments are in balance.

Governments, through their central banks, still intervene in foreign exchange markets, but they do so only with a view to smoothing out short-term fluctuations in exchange rates. This intervention can be important in some circumstances, but it is trivial compared with the overriding attention that must be given to the balance of payments when exchange rates are fixed.

The adoption of a floating exchange rate was an enormous policy change for the UK. From 1945 to 1972 the overriding goal of economic policy had been to preserve the existing sterling exchange rate, whatever it then happened to be. Sometimes this was not a major problem, since the free-market equilibrium exchange rate was not far from the pegged rate. At other times, however, all other policy goals had to be subservient to maintaining the rate, since the equilibrium rate was diverging further and further from the pegged rate.

Unemployment

Keynes distinguished between voluntary and involuntary unemployment. Voluntary unemployment occurs when there is a job available but the unemployed person is not willing to accept it at the going wage rate. Involuntary unemployment occurs when a person is willing to accept a job at the going wage rate but no such job can be found. Clearly when we are concerned about the undesirable social effects of

[1] Readers with pronounced political leaning to the left or the right will tend to have pre-judged answers to these problems. But in so far as one's politics are the choice of means judged to be best for achieving such ends as higher living standards, one must try to keep an open mind. There are many facts that can easily be unearthed in a comparative study of the performance of the economies of the UK and West Germany that are disturbing to the dogmatic positions of either the left or the right. Anyone who wishes to study history to gather evidence on some basic questions rather than to collect only those facts that agree with some preconceived opinions, should study the performances of these two economies with great care.

unemployment in terms of lost output and human suffering, it is involuntary unemployment that concerns us. When we use the word *unemployment*, hereafter, we mean involuntary unemployment.

Why policy-makers are concerned

The social and political importance of the figure that expresses the unemployment rate is enormous. It is widely reported in newspapers; the government is blamed when it is high and takes credit when it is low; it is often a major issue in elections; and few macroeconomic policies are formed without some consideration of their effect on it. No other summary statistic, with the possible exception of the retail price index, carries as much weight as both a formal and an informal objective of policy as does the percentage of the labour force unemployed.

There are two main reasons for worrying about unemployment: it produces economic waste and it causes human suffering. The economic waste is fairly obvious. Factor services are the least durable of economic commodities. If a fully employed economy with a constant labour force has 30 million labour years available to it in 1978, these must either be used in 1978 or wasted. If only 27 million are used because 10 per cent of the labour force is unemployed, the potential output of three million labour years is lost forever. In an economy characterized by scarcity, where there is not nearly enough output to meet everyone's needs, this waste of potential output seems undesirable to most people.

In addition to economic waste there is the human cost of unemployment. The severe hardship and misery that can be caused by prolonged periods of unemployment were discussed earlier; there is little doubt that these are heavy costs. But it is wrong to think that if the number of unemployed rises by, say, 100,000, this means that 100,000 workers join the ranks of the permanently unemployed. Modern research has shown that short-term variations in the unemployment rate at or near the full-employment level are caused to a great extent by changes in the duration of short-term unemployment. Moreover, many people stay unemployed rather than accept a lower-level job than the one they lost because they feel the margin of difference between what they would earn and their unemployment benefits is too small. For such people unemployment is an alternative they choose.

When, however, a deep recession is followed by a long trough and only a slow recovery, as was the case in the mid 1970s, long-term unemployment increases. This can have more serious effects on the morale and the social outlook of the unemployed than short-term bouts of unemployment. When a region develops heavy long-term unemployment, possibly due to the decline of a large industry, the economic and social effects are felt by everyone including those who remain employed or are in business for themselves. Furthermore, heavy and prolonged unemployment among members of some groups, such as youths, can cause major social upheavals.

Before a value judgement can be made about the human costs of a rise in unemployment, we need to know how that increase is distributed between long-term and short-term unemployment, and between those for whom there is no work alternative and those for whom there is a non-preferred employment alternative.

> **The costs in terms of human suffering will usually be much higher for long-term, or involuntary, than for short-term, or voluntary, unemployment.**

Causes of unemployment

In discussing the causes of involuntary unemployment it is helpful to distinguish among a number of kinds of unemployment.

Frictional unemployment The amount of unemployment that is associated with normal turnover of labour is called FRICTIONAL UNEMPLOYMENT. People leave jobs for all sorts of reasons, and they take time to find new jobs; old persons leave the labour force and young persons enter it, but often new workers do not fill the jobs vacated by those who leave. Inevitably all of this movement takes time and gives rise to a pool of persons who are 'frictionally' unemployed while in the course of finding new jobs.

Frictional unemployment is inevitable in any free society.

National income theory seeks to explain the causes of, and cures for, unemployment in excess of unavoidable frictional unemployment.

Structural unemployment Structural changes in the economy can be a cause of unemployment. As economic growth proceeds, the mix of required inputs changes, as do the proportions in which final goods are demanded. These changes require considerable readjustment in the economy. STRUCTURAL UNEMPLOYMENT occurs when the adjustments do not occur fast enough, so that severe pockets of unemployment occur in areas, industries, and occupations in which the demand for factors of production is falling faster than is the supply. In Britain today, for example, structural unemployment exists in Wales and in the shipbuilding industry.

Structural unemployment can increase because either the pace of change accelerates or the pace of adjustment to change slows down. Policies that discourage movement among regions, industries and occupations can raise structural unemployment. Policies that prevent firms from replacing some labour with new machines may protect employment in the short term. If, however, they lead to the decline of an industry because it cannot compete with more innovative foreign competitors, such policies can end up causing severe pockets of structural unemployment.

Structural unemployment may be said to exist when there is a mismatching between the unemployed and the available jobs in terms of regional location, required skills, or any other relevant dimension.

As with many distinctions, the one between structural and frictional unemployment becomes blurred at the margin. In a sense structural unemployment is really long-term frictional unemployment. For illustration, consider a change that requires a reallocation of labour. If the reallocation occurs quickly we call the unemployment frictional while it lasts; if the reallocation occurs slowly – possibly only after the person who has lost a job dies or retires from the labour force and has been replaced by a new person with different and more marketable skills – we call the unemployment structural.

One useful measure of the total of frictional *plus* structural unemployment is the percentage of the labour force unemployed when the number of unfilled job vacancies is equal to the number of persons seeking jobs. When these two magnitudes are equal, there is some kind of job opening to match every person seeking a job and the unemployment that occurs must be either frictional or structural.

On this measure structural plus frictional unemployment has risen significantly in the UK over the last 10–15 years. The percentage of the labour force unemployed when aggregate unemployed equalled aggregate vacancies remained fairly constant up until 1966 and then began to rise for adult males. Now there is substantially more unemployment than there used to be at times when, in the aggregate, the supply of new jobs equals the demand for them. Similar shifts have been observed in many other developed economies. Although the reasons are still subject to debate, the change is certainly consistent with a rise in structural unemployment among adult male workers.

Deficient-demand unemployment Unemployment that occurs because there is insufficient aggregate demand to purchase full-employment output is called DEFICIENT-DEMAND UNEMPLOYMENT. One useful measure of this kind of unemployment is the difference between the number of persons seeking jobs and the number of unfilled job vacancies (i.e., total unemployment *minus* frictional and structural unemployment) expressed as a percentage of the labour force. This statistic shows the excess of the supply of workers looking for jobs over the number of jobs available. It will be positive when there is deficient aggregate demand and negative when there is excess aggregate demand.

> **Deficient-demand unemployment may be measured by the number of unemployed who are not matched by any vacant job, whether suitable or unsuitable.**

At times of heavy unemployment, frictional, structural, and deficient-demand causes may all be operative. It will not usually be possible to say that one particular worker is unemployed because of deficient demand and another for structural reasons. Nonetheless, all three causes can operate and can contribute to the total volume of unemployment.

Search unemployment We have already seen that national income theory is concerned with causes and cures for the unemployment that is in excess of unavoidable frictional, plus structural, unemployment. Unfortunately it is not all easy in practice to draw dividing lines among the several types of involuntary unemployment we have discussed or even between those who are unemployed involuntarily and those who are voluntarily not working. What do we say, for example, about an unemployed woman who refuses to accept a job at a lower skill category than the one for which she feels she is qualified? And what if she turns down a job for which she is trained because she feels that she may get a higher wage offer for the same job from another firm? People who could find work of the type for which they are fitted but who remain unemployed in order to search for a better offer than they have so far received are said to be in SEARCH UNEMPLOYMENT. In one sense they can be said to be voluntarily unemployed because they could find some job; in another sense they can be said to be involuntarily unemployed because they have not yet succeeded in finding a job for which they are suited at a rate of pay that they believe exists somewhere in the economy. Those in search unemployment can be said to have been frictionally unemployed if they find an acceptable job in a reasonable period of time; they may be judged to be in structural unemployment if a long search reveals that there are no longer enough jobs to employ everyone with their particular training and experience.

> **Search unemployment is in a grey area between voluntary and involuntary, and between frictional and structural, unemployment. It exists when workers who could find jobs remain unemployed to look for something better.**

Workers do not have perfect knowledge of all available jobs and rates of pay, and they may be able to find information only by searching the market. In the face of this uncertainty it may be quite sensible to refuse the first job offer that one comes across since it may well prove to be a very poor offer when further market information has been collected. How long it pays to remain in search unemployment depends on the economic costs of being unemployed.

Two recent developments are believed to have increased the amount of search unemployment in many Western economies. First, there has been a large increase in the number of households with more than one income earner. If both husband and wife work, it is possible for one to support them both while the other looks for 'a really good job' rather than accepting the first job offered. Second, unemployment benefits and income-related supplementary benefits reduce the income loss caused by being unemployed and enable a person to prolong the search for 'the right job'.

Sufficient search unemployment to allow people time to find the job that best uses their talents and training is socially desirable. Too much search – for example, holding off while being supported by others, in the hope of stumbling into a job better than the one for which one is really suited – would appear to be an economic waste. Here again search unemployment is a grey area: some of it is useful and some of it is wasteful.

Measured and non-measured unemployment The number of persons unemployed in the UK is estimated from a monthly count of those who have registered at an Employment Office during the month and who are on the day of the count classified as 'capable of and available for' full-time work. The two main reasons for registering are to obtain unemployment benefits and to receive help in finding a job.[1] The total number estimated to be unemployed is then expressed as a percentage of the civilian labour force (employed plus unemployed).

There are reasons why this measured figure for unemployment may not reflect the number of people who are truly unemployed *in the sense that they would accept the offer of a job for which they were qualified.* On the one hand, the measured figure may overstate unemployment by including people who are not truly unemployed in the sense we have just defined. Some people defraud the system by registering as unemployed (and collecting unemployment benefits) when they are employed. Some people do not really wish to work because the difference between their unemployment benefits and what they can earn in work is not sufficient to compensate them for the disutility of work. These people have voluntarily withdrawn from the work force, but they register as unemployed in order to collect their benefits. Others, for reasons of age or disability, are unemployable but register

[1] In other countries such as the US and Canada, the number unemployed is estimated from a monthly sample survey to locate people who are without a job but say they have actively searched for one during the sample period. The two methods, a sample survey of job searches and a tally of those registered as unemployed, each have their own biases and will give different estimates of 'total unemployment'.

in order to receive benefits. On the other hand, the measured figure may understate involuntary unemployment. For example, some people who have worked in the past are not or do not think themselves eligible for unemployment benefits and therefore do not bother to register. Also, those who have not worked before are not eligible for benefits. School leavers and housewives who would work if a booming economy offered them jobs may never show up on the statistics as unemployed.

In the UK, estimates are available of the size of most of the important groups that contribute to under- and over-measurement of true employment. In the early 1970s, for example, it was estimated that 11 per cent of males and 18 per cent of females who were registered as unemployed were not in fact involuntarily unemployed. On the other hand, it has been estimated that between 10 and 20 per cent of male unemployment and as much as 50 per cent of female unemployment goes unregistered. The ratio of unregistered to registered unemployment seems to have a marked cyclical pattern, rising in the boom and falling in the slump in the UK. (The reverse cyclical pattern is evident in the US, for well-understood reasons connected with the institutional arrangement for unemployment benefits. This suggests that international comparisons of unemployment performance must be made with caution and only in the light of detailed knowledge of what the figures show.)

The coexistence of some sharp labour shortages and heavy general unemployment in the late 1970s have led some observers to suggest that a higher proportion of registered unemployment may be voluntary than in the past. Very careful study is needed, however, to distinguish structural from voluntary unemployment, since both will give rise to the observation just mentioned.

Control of unemployment

Frictional unemployment is inevitable in any changing economy, and thus a certain minimum amount of unemployment must be accepted as being 'in the nature of things'. Any policy measure that makes moving between jobs easier or quicker can, however, reduce the volume of frictional unemployment somewhat.

Structural unemployment may be attacked by policies for retraining and relocating labour as part of a general effort to facilitate the adjustment of labour supplies to the changing pattern of demands. It may also be attacked by trying to persuade labour to accept changes that, although removing some specific jobs, maintain the competitive position of an industry and thus protect the remaining jobs in that industry. This reduces the need for reallocation of labour over the long run.

Unemployment that is due to deficient aggregate demand can be attacked by increasing aggregate demand. This may be done by any of the expansionary fiscal and monetary policies discussed in Parts 7 and 8 of this book.

Genuine search unemployment may be reduced, first, by making it easier for individuals to locate job vacancies and, second, by increasing the chance that individuals will accept an offer received early in their search period. The first can be done, for example, by the provision of market information on job availability; the second requires increasing the cost of search to the unemployed individual. A reduction in unemployment benefits or a tightening of the conditions for eligibility, for example, increases the income loss associated with continued search and makes it more likely that individuals will keep their searches as short as possible. This may not always be desirable; as we have observed, a certain amount of search unemployment is useful in ensuring that people find jobs for which they are well suited. Phony (no intention of accepting a job) and unreasonable (looking for a job beyond one's capabilities) search unemployment might be reduced by screening applicants more carefully before they are allowed to collect unemployment benefits.

Experience of unemployment

Figure 37.2 on page 536 shows the behaviour of the UK unemployment rate since 1945. The postwar period has been and still is significantly better in its unemployment performance than the interwar period during which unemployment was rarely less than 10 per cent. Throughout the first quarter-century after the Second World War, unemployment was usually less than 3 per cent, and in the mid-1970s it exceeded 4 per cent for the first time since the 1930s. It rose steadily in the mid 1970s, reaching 7 per cent early in 1978. Over the entire postwar period unemployment has drifted up slowly but perceptibly, each peak in the trade cycle having more unemployment than the previous peak, and each trough having more than the previous trough.

There is marked inequality of unemployment rates among regions and among types of labour. Northern Ireland, Scotland and north-eastern England have tended to have rates three to four times as high as those in south-eastern England. Much of this is structural unemployment connected with the decline of the old staple industries concentrated in the north and the rise of new technologically based industries in the south-east. In recent years unemployment rates among youths and among males have been higher than female rates. The male-female relation in the UK is in striking contrast to that in the US and Canada, where unemployment among males from 25 to 65 years of age has typically been much lower than unemployment among females.

Inflation

An INFLATION is a rise in the price level.[1] This means a rise in all prices including commodities and factors of production. Thus in an inflation, money incomes rise on average as fast as the money prices of commodities. A DEFLATION is a fall in the price level.

Why policy-makers are concerned[2]

By and large, governments do not have policies about the price level *per se*. No one feels that the price level ruling in Britain in 1770 was intrinsically better or worse than the one ruling in 1970. The *level* of prices of commodities and factors of production at which the economy's transactions occur is irrelevant to living standards. If, for example, all prices (and incomes which depend on factor prices)

[1] Monetarists like to reserve the term inflation for a *sustained* rise in the price level so they can say inflations require increases in the money supply. In this usage there are *changes in the price level* (non-sustained) and *inflations* (sustained changes in the price level). There is no point arguing about terms but it should be pointed out that 'sustained' is a non-operational concept. Defining inflation as any rise in the price level and then referring to inflations of various durations avoids the necessity of an arbitrary answer to the question: 'For how long and how fast must the price level rise for an inflation to be said to occur?'

[2] This matter is discussed at greater length in Chapter 39, pages 574–8.

were doubled overnight, standards of living of income earners would be unchanged.

Although the price level itself does not matter, *changes* in the price level do. Changes in the price level, inflations and deflations, do have serious effects. What are these? Contrary to popular belief, there is no strong evidence that inflation lowers real national income. Inflation does not seem permanently to increase the gap between actual and full-employment national income,[1] nor does it seem to lower the growth rate of full-employment income. It follows, therefore, that inflation does not reduce *average* living standards. The main consequence of inflation is to *redistribute* income among people, benefiting some and hurting others. These redistributions often are large and haphazard and produce serious social tensions. This itself is one reason for trying to avoid inflations.

The proposition that inflation does not affect total real income but does redistribute that income refers to the effect of inflation *ceteris paribus*. Of course, inflation may accompany a fall in living standards, as, for example, when the price level rises during a recession. Here, though, the cause of the fall in living standards is the fall in real output associated with the downturn in the trade cycle, not the rise in the price level. A rise in prices may also be the mechanism by which a fall in living standards due to some other cause is accomplished. When, for example, OPEC quadrupled oil prices, the living standards of major oil importers had to fall. The mechanism by which this was brought about in most countries was a rise in prices relative to earnings. But other mechanisms are possible, and the cause of the fall in living standards was actually the adverse change in the terms of trade of oil-importing countries. The main point is that if the force that causes the inflation also lowers living standards (e.g., a rise in oil prices) then inflation will be accompanied by a fall in living standards, while if the force that causes the inflation does not itself lower living standards (e.g., a rise in the money supply) then the inflation itself will not do so.

Causes of inflation

Most economists today agree that there are at least two senses in which inflation is a monetary phenomenon. First, very rapid inflations, such as those in South America, have been caused by rapid expansions of the money supply. Such expansions have often been due to large and persistent government budget deficits incurred to finance development projects that governments could not, or would not, pay for out of tax receipts. Second, whatever its causes, inflation cannot continue for a sustained period without increases in the money supply.

In spite of this agreement, there is serious controversy over the proximate causes of the mild inflations experienced by North American and Western European countries in the 1950s and 1960s and of the more rapid inflations of the 1970s. Several competing diagnoses – demand-pull, wage-cost-push, import-cost-push, price-push, structural rigidity, and expectational – have been advanced as explanations.

Demand-pull inflation The DEMAND-PULL theory of inflation links price level changes to inflationary and deflationary gaps. In essence, it says that changes in price levels are to be accounted for by changes in aggregate demand. A rise in

[1] But it can do so temporarily, as we shall see in some detail in Chapter 50.

aggregate demand in a situation of more or less full employment will create excess demand in many individual markets, and prices will be bid upward. The rise in demand for goods and services will cause a rise in demand for factors, and their prices will be bid upward as well. Thus inflation in the prices of both consumer goods and factors of production is caused by a rise in aggregate demand.

> **Virtually all economists agree that excess aggregate demand can be, and often has been, a major cause of inflation.**

Wage-cost-push inflation The COST-PUSH theory of inflation says that rises in costs not themselves associated with excess demand – particularly wage costs – are the initiating cause of inflation. Powerful unions are seen as demanding increases in wages even when there is no excess demand for labour. Employers, the theory says, generally accede to these demands and pass the increased wage costs on to the consumer through higher prices. Thus the root cause of the inflation is union power, the original upward push to prices being generated from the cost side rather than from the demand side. This theory commands strong support from a significant body of British economists, but is much less favoured by North American economists.

Import-cost-push inflation The IMPORT-COST-PUSH theory relies on linkages among countries arising from international trade. A demand-pull inflation in country A raises all of its prices including those of its exports. If country B uses country A's exports as inputs, and as final goods, A's demand-pull inflation becomes B's import-cost-push inflation. A's export prices may also rise for reasons other than a general inflation in A. For example, when OPEC increased the prices of petroleum products, this caused significant import-cost-push inflations in the oil-importing countries. An import-cost-push inflation thus refers to a rise in a country's price level due to a rise in the prices of imports.

Except for rare disturbances such as that created by OPEC, this theory can account for inflation in only a small group of countries. Basically, all it does is to place the initiating cause of an inflation in some other country. Country B can import country A's inflation through a rise in its import prices. But why did A have an inflation in the first place? Thus the import-price-push theory is a theory of the transmission of inflation from the initiating countries to receiving countries, but it is not a theory of the cause of inflation in the initiating countries.

Importation of inflation is easiest in a regime of fixed exchange rates. Then a rise in the domestic prices of country A's exports is immediately transmitted into a rise in the prices in country B's currency of imports from A. With flexible exchange rates, A's exchange rate may depreciate in response to a rise in A's export prices. If, for example, A's prices rise by 20 per cent in its own currency and the exchange rate is determined solely by current account transactions, A's exchange rate will depreciate by 20 per cent, leaving A's export prices unchanged when expressed in B's currency. Imported inflation is, however, still possible under flexible exchange rates if private capital movements or central bank intervention stabilizes the exchange rate so that it does not move to offset fully changes in import prices.

Price-push inflation The PRICE-PUSH, or administered-price, theory of inflation is similar to the wage-cost-push theory. The price-push theory predicts the same sequence of events as the cost-push theory, with firms rather than unions as the main culprits. The theory says that sellers have monopoly power and would like to raise prices but are restrained from doing so by fear of anti-monopoly laws, adverse public opinion, or regulatory review of their prices. Under these circumstances cost increases can provide the necessary excuse for price increases. During wage negotiations, for example, sellers grant wage increases and then use them as an excuse to raise prices by more than is required to offset the rise in wage costs. This theory is more popular in North America than in Britain, but even in North America relatively few economists espouse it.

Structural rigidity inflation The STRUCTURAL RIGIDITY theory of inflation assumes that resources do not move quickly from one use to another and that it is easy to increase wages and prices but difficult to decrease them. Given these conditions, when patterns of demand and costs change, real adjustments occur only very slowly. Shortages appear in potentially expanding sectors, and prices rise because the slow movement of resources prevents those sectors from expanding rapidly enough. Contracting sectors keep factors of production on part-time employment or even in full unemployment because mobility is low in the economy. Because their prices are rigid, there is no deflation in these potentially contracting sectors. Thus the mere process of adjustment in an economy with structural rigidities causes inflation to occur. Prices in expanding sectors rise, and prices in contracting sectors stay the same. On average, therefore, prices rise. This theory is not thought to explain much of the rapid inflations of the 1970s, but many economists feel that it does explain the apparent positive floor on the inflation rate of 2 or 3 per cent. Earlier, during the times when there appeared to be no inflationary gaps (particularly in the late 1950s), the inflation rates in most countries remained stubbornly at 1–3 per cent per annum instead of falling to zero as the demand-pull theory said they should.

Expectational inflation The EXPECTATIONAL theory of inflation depends on a general set of expectations of price and wage increases. Suppose, for example, that both unions and firms expect that a 10 per cent inflation will occur next year. Unions will tend to start negotiations from a *base* of a 10 per cent increase in money wages (which would merely hold their real wages constant). They will argue that firms will be able to meet the extra 10 per cent on the wage bill out of the extra revenues that will arise because product prices will go up by 10 per cent. Starting from this base, unions will then negotiate over how much of an increase in real wages they can obtain. Firms will also be inclined to begin bargaining by conceding at least a 10 per cent increase in money wages, since they expect that the prices at which they sell their own products will rise by 10 per cent. The real substance of the debate between unions and employers will thus centre around how much money wages can rise in excess of 10 per cent, and here such factors as profits, productivity, and bargaining power will be important.

Thus if both firms and unions expect an inflation of 10 per cent (or any other figure), their behaviour in wage and price setting will tend to bring that rate of inflation about, whatever the state of monetary and fiscal policy. This is yet another example of the common phenomenon of self-realizing expectations that we have met at several points in this book.

It is unlikely that an expectational inflation will break out all by itself, because expectations of continuing inflation do not arise out of thin air. They are more likely to be a projection from actual rates of inflation in the recent past. If the economy has been experiencing inflation rates on the order of 6 or 8 per cent in the recent past, it is unlikely that a spontaneous change in inflationary expectations will suddenly produce a 20 per cent inflation.

What *is* likely, however, is that an expectational inflation may take over from a demand-pull inflation once the excess demand is reduced or eliminated. Say, for example, that the government has been generating a demand-pull inflation of 15 per cent per year for two or three years as a result of spending well in excess of its tax revenue and creating new money to finance its budget deficit. Firms and unions may now expect this rate to continue; if so, they will grant 15 per cent wage and price increases at a minimum. Next suppose that the government eliminates its budget deficit and stabilizes the money supply but that the expectations of 15 per cent inflation persist. Wage and price increases of at least 15 per cent will occur in the *expectation* of continuing inflation. At this point what was a demand-pull inflation becomes an expectational inflation.

The danger of expectational inflation is that it may cause a demand-pull (or any other kind of) inflation that has gone on for several years to persist long after its original causes have been removed.

Once inflationary expectations become established it may not be an easy matter to force decision-takers to revise them downward, changed governmental fiscal and monetary policies notwithstanding.

Everyone agrees that expectational inflations are possible. Most economists agree that they have occurred from time to time. Monetarists rely heavily on this theory to explain observations of high unemployment combined with high inflation that would otherwise be inconsistent with their beliefs.

A dominant cause? Today few economists would rule out all structural influences, but almost none believe structural rigidity to be the major cause of inflations. Many believe that all significant inflations have their initiating causes in excess aggregate demand. Others believe that some of the mild inflations of the 1950s, 1960s, and early 1970s were initiated on the cost side. Most economists would agree that demand-pull inflations have occurred in the past and would accept that mild cost-push or price-push inflations are at least possible. They also believe that OPEC caused significant import-cost-push inflation, and that similar inflations have beset some major importing economies at other times. Moreover, they believe that inflations, once started, often generate inflationary expectations that can cause the inflation to persist for some time after the initiating causes have been removed.

Debate continues on the balance between demand-pull and cost-push as forces causing inflation in the contemporary inflationary climate. Until the causes of inflation are fully understood, there will be debate about appropriate anti-inflationary policies. By the same token, however, the success or failure of particular policies may shed additional light on causes. Of course there does not have to be only one cause of inflation, and certainly the weight of different causes can vary from time to time and place to place. For this reason people who look for a single dominant cause of inflations may be obscuring the real issue of the balance between various causes at different times and places.

The control of inflation: validated and unvalidated inflation

When an inflation is allowed to persist because the government permits the money supply to expand at the same rate as the inflation, economists speak of the inflation as being *validated* by increases in the money supply. When an inflation occurs that is not accompanied by an increase in the money supply it is *unvalidated.* The consequences of validated and unvalidated inflations were analysed on pages 617–19 and this very important section should be reviewed at this time. What we established in that earlier section was that any inflation that is not validated by an increase in the money supply will cause the interest rate to rise and aggregate demand to fall. The reduction in aggregate demand will first eliminate any inflationary gap and will then cause real income to fall and unemployment to rise.

> **A continuing inflation that is not validated by increases in the money supply continually shifts the aggregate expenditure function downward, thus eventually producing ever-falling levels of output and ever-rising levels of unemployment.**

This result leads to an important distinction. Demand-pull inflations caused by increases in the money supply (e.g., the government's financing a budget deficit by creating new money) can go on indefinitely because they bring their own monetary validation with them; all other kinds of inflation will, however, be brought to a halt sooner or later by falling output and rising unemployment if the money supply is held constant. But the consequences of bringing a cost-push, price-push or expectational inflation to a halt by refusing to increase the money supply will be at least a temporary fall in output and rise in unemployment. If the push or expectational factors prove stubborn, the inflation may persist for some time in the face of falling output and rising unemployment.

When this occurs policy-makers are faced with a serious dilemma. Should they let the recession persist, knowing that if it is deep and long-lasting enough it will break the inflationary spiral, or should they validate the inflation by increasing the money supply thereby removing the disincentives (provided by the recession) to further increases in wages and prices? The control of inflation will be discussed further in Chapter 50.

The UK experience of inflation

Figure 39.2 on page 575 shows the inflation rate for each year since the Second World War. Throughout the 1950s and 1960s the UK inflation rate was high enough in most years to worry policy-makers and voters. Although the rate was never as high as 5 per cent, it was high enough seriously to erode the purchasing power of money and other assets with fixed money values. Indeed, the purchasing power of the pound was approximately cut in half over these two decades. Then in the late 1960s the United Kingdom followed the rest of the developed world into a period of accelerating inflation that is commonly thought to have been initiated in the United States. From 1967 to 1971 the inflation rate rose steadily, from 2·5 to 4·7 to 5·4 to 6·4 to 9·4 per cent. The path of inflation over the late 1960s and early 1970s was similar to that of most developed countries, although the level was somewhat higher than many other countries. Then, after a slight deceleration in 1972, the rate of inflation accelerated to rates never before seen in the UK during peace time. By

1975 the annual rate of inflation was approximately 25 per cent! This rate halves the purchasing power of money in just over three years. Had it persisted, it would have reduced a fixed money income to one-tenth of its original purchasing power within 10 years. The inflation rate did not, however, remain at this very high level. It came down to 16·5 per cent in 1976, 15·8 per cent in 1977 and 8·5 per cent in 1978. This was an improvement, but still a disastrously high rate for anyone with income or assets that were fixed in monetary terms. The inflation rate over this extraordinary decade was such that a household retiring with a comfortable fixed income of £2,500 per annum in 1967 could buy only £850 worth of commodities (valued at 1967 prices) ten years later.

49

The closure of the circular flow model

We saw in Chapter 38 how the central authorities use fiscal policy as an instrument of demand management. We also saw in Chapter 41 that the money supply can exert an influence on the aggregate expenditure function. Thus both fiscal and monetary policy can be used to shift the aggregate demand function.

If we combine our theory of the short-run determination of national income by aggregate demand with the kinked function (see page 509), we may wonder why the government has so much trouble with its macroeconomic policy. According to this function all the government must do to prevent the emergence of inflationary or deflationary gaps is manage aggregate demand so as to achieve 'full employment without inflation'. Indeed, this was the goal that most governments set for themselves at the end of the Second World War and continued to pursue into the 1950s. Then, towards the end of that decade, the goal of really stable prices began to look more and more difficult to attain. Throughout the 1960s governments accepted that they might not be able to achieve full employment and zero inflation, and they came to think in terms of a trade-off between these two goals. In the 1970s inflation rates exploded to levels unprecedented in the peacetime experiences of advanced industrial countries. As a result, governments came to wonder whether the inflation-unemployment trade-off might be illusory. The ensuing debate divided governments and economists into several groups whose divergent views constitute the current great debates on macro-policy. One group says that there is no trade-off and, furthermore, that there is one and only one level of national income that is compatible with long-run equilibrium. Another group rejects all existing theories of the price level that have been worked out over two centuries. Members of this group argue that the rise of the modern union has created a mechanism whereby the price level is determined by the unions. Yet another group holds that a modified version of the demand-pull theory of inflation explains the modern experience.

The problem of closure

There is little doubt that governments can manipulate the aggregate expenditure function through fiscal and monetary tools. Why, then, does demand management cause such great policy problems? The difficulty is not in manipulating demand. This we know how to do, at least within a reasonable margin of error. Where there is grave uncertainty is in how the impact of a change in aggregate demand will be divided between real quantity changes and nominal price changes. Say, for example, that the government engineers a 10 per cent increase in aggregate expenditure. At one time this might lead to a 10 per cent increase in real output with prices constant. At another time it might lead to a 10 per cent increase in prices with output constant. At still other times it might lead to any number of different combinations of price and quantity changes that combine to make up a 10 per cent increase in national income valued at current prices.

The great problem of macroeconomics in the late 1970s and 1980s arises from the fact that although governments can cause changes in aggregate expenditure they are uncertain about how the effects of such changes will be divided between quantities and prices.

What is needed, then, is a theory of the determination of the price level which will explain why the level is what it is, and why it changes. The problem of completing a model of income determination so that the price level as well as real income is determined is called the problem of CLOSURE. A closed model[1] determines both real and nominal national income, and hence determines how much of the effects of a change in aggregate demand will be on real GNP and how much will be on the price level. To understand modern controversies and the modern crisis in both macroeconomic theory and macro-policy, we must consider the problem of closing our model of national income. This is the purpose of the present chapter. The policy debates that turn on alternative methods of closure will be discussed in Chapter 50.

Closure with a kinked aggregate supply curve

The earliest method of closing a Keynesian model made a sharp dichotomy between the behaviour of the economy at less than full employment and its behaviour at full employment. This is the method we have used so far in this book (See pages 508–12.) With the kinked relation, the price level is inflexible downwards: it can rise but it cannot fall. Thus when national income is less than full-employment income, the price level is constant and variations in aggregate expenditure cause variations in real income, output and employment. When national income reaches its full-employment level, however, it cannot rise further in real terms because full employment is an absolute constraint: no more can be produced. Further increases in aggregate expenditure can only cause prices to rise.

This theory is illustrated in Figure 49.1, which is important and which will repay substantial study. Part (i) of the figure is the familiar diagram determining equilibrium national income through the aggregate expenditure function and the equilibrium condition that expenditure should equal output. The full-employment level of income is indicated by Y_F. Part (ii) is a new diagram, plotting national income against the *price level*. The dark curve shown is called an AGGREGATE SUPPLY FUNCTION; it relates real national income to the price level. The current price level is P_1 and, since the price level is assumed never to fall, the aggregate supply function is shown as perfectly elastic at the present price level. Thus firms will

[1] Do not confuse this term with open and closed ecomomies: i.e. those that do and do not engage in foreign trade. *Closure* and *a closed model*, in the present context, refer to having a model which, when laid out formally, has enough equations to determine both real national income and the price level.

produce whatever they can sell at the going prices right up until all resources are fully employed. This means that in the range of Y less than Y_F, national income is *demand determined.*

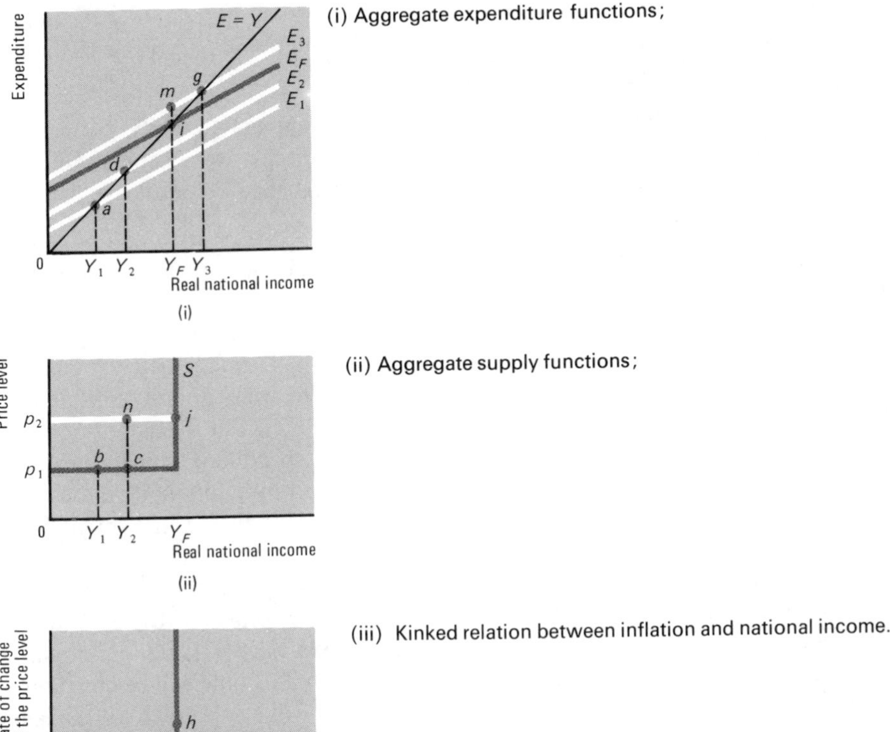

(i) Aggregate expenditure functions;

(ii) Aggregate supply functions;

(iii) Kinked relation between inflation and national income.

Fig. 49.1 Closure with a kinked aggregate supply function.

For example, if the aggregate expenditure function is E_1 in part (i) of the figure, the economy is at point *a* with equilibrium national income of Y_1. This income, which is determined by forces shown in part (i), can then be transferred to the other parts of the figure. In part (ii), the economy is at point *b* with the price level P_1 and national income Y_1. Part (iii) of the figure repeats Figure 34.6 from page 509. It relates the level of real national income to the *rate of change* of the price level, i.e.,the rate of inflation. When income is Y_1 the economy is at point *c* in part (iii), indicating a level of income Y_1 and a zero rate of inflation. The three points *a, b* and *c* are alternative ways of showing a single equilibrium position for the economy. Point *a* in part (i) shows that expenditure and income are equal at Y_1. Part (ii) shows that income Y_1 is associated with the price level P_1. Part (iii) shows that income Y_1 is associated with the zero rate of inflation.[1]

[1] In a more advanced treatment of the theory just described, real national income would be determined by the *IS* and *LM* curves that are described in any intermediate macro text. This would not, however, change the nature of the 'closure' of the model since parts (ii) and (iii) of the figure would be unchanged. In the *IS-LM* model the monetary adjustment mechanism is the shift in the *LM* curve consequent on a *ceteris puribus* change in the price level.

Behaviour of the closed model

If aggregate expenditure now changes, say to E_2, national income changes to Y_2 and since there are still unemployed resources, the price level stays constant. Thus the economy moves to *d* in part (i) with income equal to expenditure at Y_2, to *e* in part (ii) with income of Y_2 combined with price level P_1 and to *f* in part (iii) with income of Y_2 combined with a zero rate of inflation.

> **When the model is closed with the kinked aggregate supply curve, fluctuations in the aggregate expenditure function that leave equilibrium income at or below Y_F will cause real output to change but will leave the price level constant.**

This analysis merely makes explicit the model we have been using throughout most of this book.

Now consider what happens if the expenditure function shifts upwards enough to take equilibrium national income in part (i) above Y_F. The aggregate expenditure function might rise, say, to E_3 in part (i). If there were no full-employment constraint, equilibrium national income would rise to Y_3. But this is not possible. Once real output reaches Y_F nothing further can be produced, since all existing resources are fully employed. But, given the expenditure function, there is an inflationary gap at Y_F. Desired expenditure exceeds output by the amount *im*. Since nothing more can be produced, prices rise.

The economy will not actually go to point *g*, since income Y_3 cannot be produced. Instead, real income will remain at Y_F and prices will rise. Thus the economy will be observed at some point such as *h* in part (iii): full-employment income combined with an inflation. In part (ii) national income will be constant at Y_F but the price level will be *rising*; thus the economy will be observed to be *moving* up the vertical part of the aggregate supply function with a constant output combined with a rising price level.

The rise in the price level now brings into play the monetary adjustment mechanism first described on pages 617–19. Recall how it works. The rise in the price level means that the real value of money held by firms and households will be reduced. If the nominal money supply remains constant, the real money supply (measured in terms of what money will buy) must fall. Firms and households will not have enough money to meet their transactions demand, and they will seek to add to their money holdings by trying to sell bonds. But since the total supply of bonds is fixed at any moment in time, all they will succeed in doing is bidding down the price of bonds, which means that the rate of interest will rise. As the rate of interest rises, people will economize on their cash holdings. Sooner or later the rate of interest will be high enough that people will no longer be trying to sell bonds to obtain cash. At this point the price of bonds will stop falling and the rate of interest will stop rising. But much of aggregate expenditure – such as investment in plant, equipment, inventories and housing, credit-financed consumer purchases (hire purchases) – is interest-sensitive. The rise in the interest rate will lower all of this expenditure and hence will lower the aggregate expenditure function.

> **The monetary adjustment mechanism implies that as a demand inflation progresses the rate of interest will be driven up as a result of the decline in the real money supply, until the aggregate expenditure function intersects the 45° line at full-employment income.**

Thus the monetary adjustment mechanism ensures that a rise in the price level will shift the aggregate expenditure function downwards, because it ensures that an inflation will cause the interest rate to rise. Equilibrium will finally be established once the price level has risen far enough to shift the aggregate expenditure function down to E_F in part (i) of the Figure 49.1.

Once the inflation is removed, the economy will come to rest at point i in part (i) with income equal to expenditure at Y_F. There will be some new higher equilibrium price level, say P_2, so that in part (ii) the economy is at rest at point j with income Y_F and price level P_2. In part (iii) the economy has now moved to point k with income Y_F and a zero rate of inflation. Since the price level is inflexible downwards, *the new aggregate supply function in part (ii) becomes $P_2 j S$.* This means that if aggregate expenditure falls to, say, E_2, national income will fall but the price level will remain constant at its new higher level of P_2. Thus the economy will go to n rather than returning to e.

The kinked aggregate supply curve is kinked at Y_F and is subject to a ratchet effect, since an inflationary gap raises the price level and this raises the perfectly elastic portion of the supply function, while a deflationary gap lowers income but leaves the price level unchanged.[1]

Policy implications

Closing the model with the kinked aggregate supply curve has a number of implications. First, full employment with stable prices is an achievable objective. The central authorities merely strive through fiscal and monetary policy to offset any shifts in the private sector's expenditure function, thus holding the aggregate expenditure function at E_F. This holds the economy at point j in part (ii) of Figure 49.1 (assuming that the current price level is P_2) and at point k in part (iii). Second, if the central authorities hold the nominal money supply constant, any inflationary gap that does develop because of an upward shift in the expenditure function will be automatically removed when the price level rises sufficiently to force the function down again to E_F. Third, if the authorities do not wish to allow an inflationary gap to cause an inflation, they can hold the price level constant at its present value merely by using fiscal policy to shift the aggregate expenditure function down sufficiently to remove the inflationary gap at the present price level. Finally, inflation occurs if and only if desired aggregate expenditure exceeds income when income is at its full-employment level.

This is the theory that lay behind the policy for full employment and stable prices that most governments attempted in the 1950s.

Empirical relevance

The kinked aggregate supply curve was meant to capture in its horizontal section the observed fact that even very large deflationary gaps did not seem, in the twentieth century at least, to lower the price level. By and large, the price level seems

[1] The kinked aggregate supply function has a horizontal portion starting at the P axis at the current price level and running out as far as Y_F. It then has a vertical portion starting at Y_F and the current price level. When the current price level rises, the horizontal portion rises and the vertical portion between the old and the new price level no longer applies.

remarkably inflexible in a downward direction. It can be forced down by long and persistent depressions, but the rate of decline is so slow that for all practical purposes of economic policies that are concerned with what happens over the next half dozen years, the price level may be assumed to be totally inflexible downwards. Although some modern theories often drop this assumption of downward inflexibility of the price level, persuasive evidence that the price level is in fact flexible downward with a speed of decline that is relevant to policy has yet to be produced.[1]

Whatever the outcome of current theoretical debates, the observed facts in virtually all developed countries during the twentieth century support the view that the price level is relatively inflexible downwards.

The second characteristic of the kinked aggregate supply function is the sharp dichotomy it makes between situations of unemployment, when variations in aggregate expenditure cause only quantities to change, and situations of full employment, when increases in aggregate expenditure cause only prices to change. Assume the economy starts out, say, at Y_2 in Figure 49.1, and that the aggregate expenditure function shifts upwards. Real income rises and the price level remains constant until Y_F is reached. Then suddenly, when the full-employment constraint is reached, real income stops rising and further increases in expenditure have their effects only on prices. This either/or type of behaviour – only quantity changes below Y_F and only prices change at Y_F – seems to contradict our obvious experience: as national income approaches full employment, inflationary forces build up gradually. Further increases in aggregate expenditure seem always to have some additional effect on real output although they have more and more of an influence on prices as full-employment output is approached. But even full-employment output is not an absolute constraint. Wartime, and extreme boom conditions in peacetime, show that it is almost always possible to squeeze a little more output from the economy. Overtime can be worked, extra shifts can be added, more women, youths and elderly people can be drawn into the labour force. Thus, the normal full employment of resources does not indicate that the last possible unit of output is being squeezed from the economy.

Why do we observe these results that seem to contradict the simple kink in the aggregate supply curve? The problem is easily understood if we consider the behaviour in individual markets that is implied by the kink in the curve. Consider the possibility of the economy really being at the point where full employment is combined with a stable price level. Full employment implies that there is no excess supply in any market; a constant price level implies that there is no excess demand in any market. Thus each and every market in the economy must be in equilibrium when the economy is at the point of full employment without inflation (indicated by the corner of the kinked aggregate supply curve).

In fact, all of the markets of the economy cannot be expected to be in complete

---

[1] Modern theory tries to give microeconomic underpinnings to macroeconomic relations by explaining macro relations in terms of the decisions of individual firms and households whose aggregate behaviour creates the macro relation. It is certainly difficult and probably impossible to explain the horizontal portion of the kinked aggregate supply curve in terms of a micro theory of perfectly competitive markets. The micro underpinnings are rather (i) flat short-run cost curves (see page 332), (ii) oligopolies with administered prices (see page 277) which led to short-run downward price rigidity and (iii) implicit contract theory with seniority rules (beyond the scope of this book) which leads to downward rigidity in wages.

equilibrium relative to each other, displaying neither excess demands nor excess supplies. This is because the economy is continually being subjected to the disturbances that necessarily accompany economic growth. As productivity grows, the supplies of some commodities expand faster than others; and as real incomes grow, the demands for some commodities expand faster than others. A reallocation of resources is necessary to adjust to such changes. Such reallocations do not, however, happen instantaneously. Thus at any moment of time, some markets will exhibit excess demands while others exhibit excess supplies.

To see what follows from this situation, consider the economy during a major slump with heavy unemployment in all areas. Now let aggregate demand be increased; output will rise and unemployment will fall. Sooner or later, however, bottlenecks will develop in some markets while there are still substantial excess supplies in other markets. Thus inflationary pressures will develop at first only in isolated parts of the economy. As aggregate demand rises it will always be possible to squeeze a bit more output out of the economy, and thus output will rise as demand rises. But the higher the current level of output rises, the harder it is to produce still more, since an increasing number of industries are already producing at, or in excess of, full capacity. Thus further rises in demand will increasingly exert their primary effect on the price level rather than on output.

This argument suggests that the higher the level of aggregate demand, the greater is the short-term effect on price and the smaller the short-term effects on output and employment of yet further increases in demand.

Closure with the Phillips curve

By breaking the empirically unjustified 'either/or' characteristic of the kinked aggregate supply curve, the late Professor A.W. Phillips sought to make assumptions that would capture the mixture of price and quantity reactions to changes in aggregate expenditure in the neighbourhood of full employment. The relation he described is based on two assumptions that are different from those explicit in the kinked aggregate supply curve: (1) at least some prices fall when there is excess supply and (2) all markets do not reach equilibrium simultaneously when aggregate demand is expanded toward its full-employment level. These assumptions give rise to a relation between the rate of change of prices and national income shown by the curve in part (ii) of Figure 49.2 and called the PHILLIPS CURVE.[1]

The relation between the level of national income and changes in the price level illustrated in part (ii) of Figure 49.2 shows prices falling slowly for low levels of real national income; at the full-employment level of national income, labeled Y_F, the price level remains steady; and the price level rises when national income exceeds Y_F. The higher the level of national income, the more rapid is the rise in prices, but it

[1] Professor Phillips, of the London School of Economics, studied the relationship between price changes and national income by drawing graphs of British data from 1862 to 1958, showing the rate of change of *money wages* and the percentage of *unemployment*. Figure 49.2 shows the rate of change of prices and the level of national income. This has the effect of making the curve slope upward to the right instead of upward to the left as did Phillips's original curve. The basic behaviour being described by the two curves is, however, identical. (Unemployment and national income are inversely related, while the rate of increase of money wages and money prices are directly related to each other.)

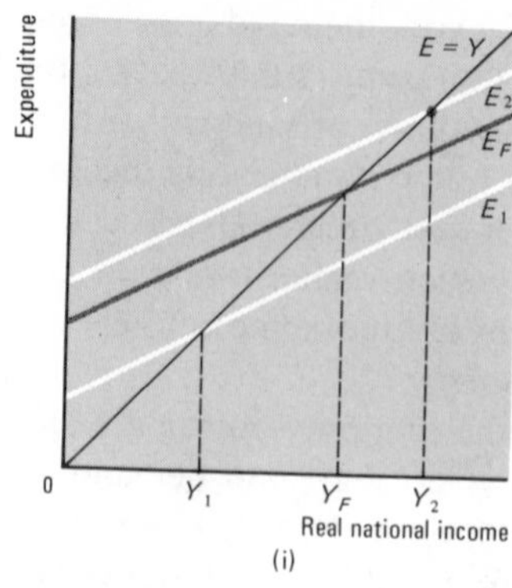

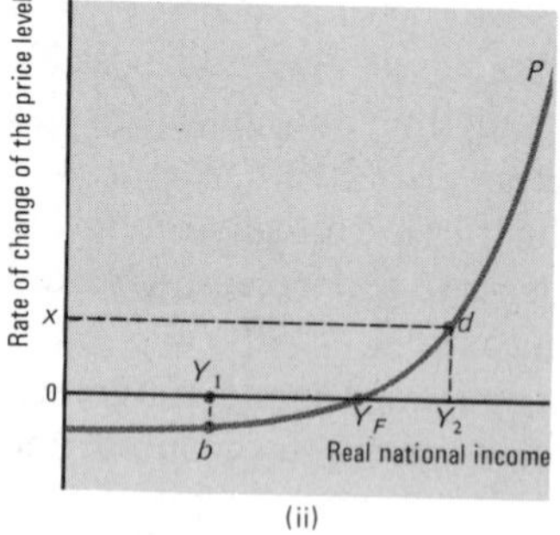

Fig. 49.2 Closure with a stable Phillips curve.
(i) Aggregate expenditure functions;
(ii) A Phillips curve.

is always possible to obtain a further increase in national income (and hence a fall in unemployment) at the cost of a more rapid rise in prices.

> **With the Phillips curve, the economy does not move abruptly from a situation of underemployment of resources and constant prices to a situation of full employment with rising prices; instead, it moves by degrees from one situation to the other.**

Behaviour of the closed model

To see how the model behaves when closed by a Phillips curve, assume that the aggregate expenditure function is initially E_1. National income is in equilibrium at Y_1. In part (ii) of Figure 49.2 the economy is in equilibrium at point b with income Y_1 combined with a very slow deflation; possibly the price level will be falling at 1 per cent per year.[1] Now if aggregate expenditure rises, national income rises as before. When the expenditure function is E_F, full employment and stable prices

[1] The fall in the price level will bring into play a monetary adjustment mechanism that would eventually restore full employment. As the price level falls, the real-purchasing-power value of money holdings rises. Firms and households find themselves with more money than they need, and they will seek to buy bonds with the excess. This forces up the price of bonds or, what is the same thing, forces down the rate of interest. The fall in the rate of interest encourages interest-sensitive expenditure. This shifts upwards the aggregate expenditure function in part (i). Sooner or later this process will raise national income to Y_F. But if the fall in the price level is very slow – about 1 per cent per year seems to be all we can expect in modern times – this process will take decades rather than years to operate and will be of no practical interest for the operation of full-employment policy with time horizons that are of interest to policy-makers.

exist. But if aggregate expenditure rises further, national income will rise *and* inflation will develop. For example, if the expenditure function is E_2, income will be Y_2 and inflation will be at the rate of x per cent per annum.

If the nominal money supply is held constant, the monetary adjustment mechanism will come into play. This raises the rate of interest and reduces interest-sensitive expenditure, thus shifting the aggregate expenditure function downwards. The economy will then move downwards to the left along its Phillips curve in part (ii), with declining output and a falling inflation rate. When the aggregate expenditure function has fallen to E_F national income will be Y_F and the economy will be in equilibrium with income Y_F and a zero rate of inflation.

In full equilibrium, the Phillips curve behaves like the kinked aggregate supply curve model: income can come to rest at less than full employment,[1] but it cannot come to rest at more than full employment provided that the nominal money supply is held constant. The inflation will lower aggregate expenditure until the inflationary gap is removed and the economy comes to rest at a stable price level.

But this is what happens in equilibrium. Out of equilibrium, the Phillips curve allows shifts in aggregate expenditure to have effects both on real output and on prices. Assume, for example, that the economy begins in equilibrium with stable prices and income of Y_F. This means that the aggregate expenditure function is E_F. Now let the function shift upwards to E_2. This raises equilibrium income to Y_2. Since there is no absolute full-employment constraint on output, actual income rises to Y_2 but the strain on the economy causes prices to rise. The economy moves temporarily to point d on its Phillips curve, with national income of Y_2 and an inflation of x per cent per year. Eventually the monetary adjustment mechanism will restore full-employment income, but in the interim extra output has been obtained at the cost of some inflation.

The Phillips curve allows an inflationary gap to cause both an increase in output and an increase in prices in the short term.

Cyclical analysis The main purpose of the Phillips curve as seen by its creator was to make more realistic the analysis of the trade cycle and of government stabilization policy designed to dampen the cycle. Assume that cyclical fluctuations in aggregate expenditure, due, say, to a multiplier-accelerator process, are causing the aggregate expenditure function in Figure 49.2(i) to move upwards and downwards between E_1 and E_2. This would make national income fluctuate between Y_1 and Y_2. On part (ii) of the figure the economy would move up and down its Phillips curve between points b and d. As national income rose on the upswing, inflationary pressures would develop and at the boom stage further increases in expenditure would mainly, but not exclusively, have their effects on prices rather than output. On the downswing, as the economy went to the left of Y_F, variations in aggregate demand would have their effects mainly in variations in real output.

---

[1] Provided that we ignore the very weak monetary adjustment mechanism that will shift the aggregate expenditure function slowly upwards as a result of the slow fall in the price level. Notice that we have not drawn an aggregate supply curve for the Phillips curve model. Strictly speaking it would be vertical through Y_F, since this is the only level of national income at which the price level would remain constant. The downward drift when Y is less than Y_F is, however, too slow to be relevant for policy.

For an analysis of short-term cyclical fluctuations the main purpose of the Phillips curve was to soften the strict dichotomy made by the kinked aggregate supply curve between the behaviour of the economy at less than full employment and at full employment. The Phillips curve made the economy change by degrees between situations in which variations in aggregate expenditure had their main effect on output and situations in which these variations had their main effect on prices.

Policy implications

Shortly after the Phillips curve was put forward, an important application to economic policy was made by two American economists, P.A. Samuelson and R.M. Solow (since that time Professor Samuelson has been awarded the Nobel Prize in economics). They asked what would happen if the government took steps to *hold* the aggregate expenditure function at E_2 and hence income at Y_2 and inflation at x per cent per year. To do this the government must frustrate the monetary adjustment mechanism which would otherwise shift the expenditure function back to E_F. The adjustment mechanism works because the inflation lowers the real purchasing power of the country's money stock, and induces firms and households to try to sell bonds to restore their money holdings to their original real values. This mechanism is easily frustrated if the central bank creates new money at the same rate as prices are rising. Then the real purchasing power of the money stock will not fall and the monetary constraint is removed from the economy. Thus the expenditure function will not shift left from its initial function at E_2 and the government will have achieved a permanent increase in real output above Y_F at the cost of some permanent positive rate of inflation.

If the government increases the nominal money supply at the same rate as inflation, it holds the real money supply constant and thus prevents the monetary adjustment mechanism from shifting the aggregate expenditure function downwards as the price level rises.

Once this implication was established, governments were faced with a policy choice between inflation and unemployment. The INFLATION-UNEMPLOYMENT TRADE-OFF referred to the choice among alternative positions on the Phillips curve as long-term goals of policy. One government might choose point *a*, opting for income Y_F and stable prices; another might choose point *d*, opting for higher output but a positive rate of inflation validated by a positive rate of monetary expansion.

The acceptance of a stable Phillips curve presented governments with a policy conflict between output and inflation: real national income could always be increased but only at the cost of a higher rate of inflation.

Measuring the shape of the Phillips curve became a vast industry employing many academic and government economists in the 1960s. If the curve were steep, the trade-off would be a poor one, with a little more output 'costing' a lot more inflation. If the curve were flat, the trade-off would be a good one, with quite a bit more output 'costing' only a little more inflation.

The Phillips curve dominated inflation-unemployment policy in the 1960s, as governments debated their choice of a position on the trade-off curve. Then, towards the end of the 1960s, a disturbing phenomenon began to appear all over the world. More and more observations were above existing Phillips curves. The Phillips curve seemed to be shifting upwards everywhere, with ever higher rates of inflation being associated with any given ratio of current national income to full-employment income. In some countries any resemblance of a stable relation seemed to disappear fairly quickly; in other countries a relation seemed to remain, but one that had shifted upwards substantially.

By the early 1970s it seemed clear to most observers that a full explanation of current inflation rates could not be found in a stable relation between inflation and current excess demand as indicated by the relation between current Y and Y_F (i.e., the economy's present position on a stable Phillips curve). Explanations went in two, not necessarily mutually exclusive, directions: cost-push explanations of inflation and expectations-augmented versions of demand-pull theories of inflation. Our consideration of these alternatives takes us into the controversies that began in the early 1970s and continue unabated today.

Closure with an expectations-augmented Phillips curve

In the late 1960s Professors Milton Friedman of the University of Chicago and Edmund Phelps of Columbia University mounted an attack on the theoretical underpinnings of the theory of a stable Phillips curve. By the mid 1970s their view that there was no unique stable Phillips curve had been widely accepted, while the theory they put in its place had gained substantial acceptance and empirical support in some countries but little or none in others. Phelps and Friedman argued that the Phillips curve describes a transitory relationship that cannot exist over the long term. Its biggest weakness was that it gave no place to people's expectations of inflation in determining actual inflationary experience. According to the Phillips curve, if the economy were to be held in some position such as *d* in Figure 49.2 the rate of inflation would remain constant. According to Phelps and Friedman, however, people would soon come to realize that the inflation was permanent. Unions would then demand even larger wage increases, and others would also change their behaviour to adjust to their expectations of continued inflation. This new behaviour would accelerate the inflation to a higher rate. Once people came to accept this new higher rate as permanent, they would again revise their behaviour, and this would accelerate the inflation still further. Extensive empirical research over the first half of the 1970s has given support to the view that the Phillips curve would not remain stable if the economy were to operate at a low level of unemployment and a high rate of inflation for a sustained period.

This theory is a mixture of demand-pull and expectational inflation, and it has a number of important aspects which we must study in detail.

The short-term Phillips curve for zero expected inflation

In the Phelps-Friedman theory, a critical role is played by inflationary expectations. We shall use the symbol $\dot{P}_e$ to refer to the rate of inflation that decision-makers *expect* will rule over their planning period – say, the next year.[1]

[1] A dot over a symbol is commonly used to refer to its rate of change. Here we use dots to refer to *proportionate* rates of change. Thus P is the price level and $\dot{P}$ is the percentage rate of change of the price level, i.e., the percentage rate of inflation or deflation. P_e is the expected price level and $\dot{P}_e$ is the expected rate of inflation or deflation. Those familiar with the calculus will recognize $\dot{P}$ as $(dP/dt)/P$.

The pure demand-pull element of the Phelps-Friedman theory is illustrated in Figure 49.3 by the Phillips curve labelled $P(\dot{P}_e = 0)$. *This particular Phillips curve is drawn on the assumption that people expect a zero rate of inflation.* (This is indicated by the notation $\dot{P}_e = 0$.) The curve shows that the higher the level of national income (i.e., the higher the level of aggregate demand), the higher will be the associated rate of inflation. The point where the P curve for zero expected inflation cuts the axis, labeled Y_F, indicates the level of national income at which there is no significant demand-pull inflation. The percentage of the labour force unemployed at Y_F is called NATURAL RATE OF UNEMPLOYMENT. Because of frictional unemployment the natural rate of unemployment will certainly be positive.

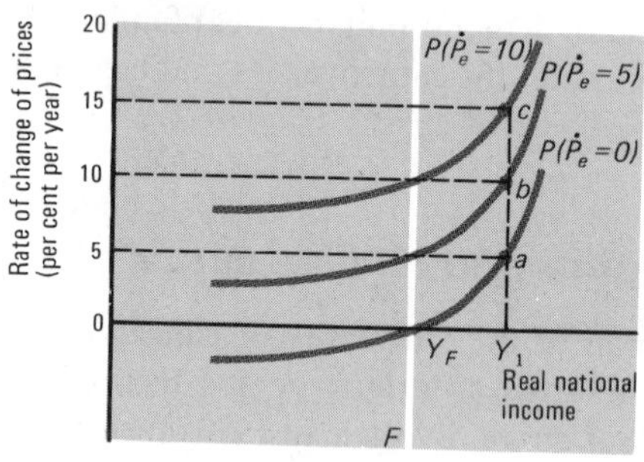

Fig. 49.3 The Phelps-Friedman theory of the Phillips curve.

Why does the Phillips curve for zero expected inflation cut the axis at Y_F? When national income is at its full-employment level, the Phelps-Friedman theory envisages all markets in the economy being in equilibrium, with demands equal to supplies. Thus, there is no market pressure on any price either to rise or to fall. In these circumstances all prices, and hence the price level, will remain stable.

Why does the Phillips curve for zero expected inflation show prices rising when national income exceeds its full-employment level and falling when national income is less than its full-employment level? Let the economy begin at full-employment income. Consider, first, the effects of a rise in aggregate demand. All individual demand curves shift outward, creating excess demands in all markets. Decision-takers will respond in two ways: (1) they will increase their outputs (working overtime, extra shifts, etc.), and (2) they will raise their money prices, seeking thereby to raise their relative prices. Since this will happen in all markets, there will be an increase in national income combined with a rise in the price level. Next, consider what happens when there is a fall in aggregate demand with national income initially at its full-employment level. Decision-takers will respond by reducing output and by cutting money prices, seeking thereby to lower their relative prices. Since this will happen in all markets, there will be a fall in national income combined with some downward movement in the price level.

Why does the price level continue to change as long as national income remains unequal to its full-employment level? When there is excess demand in all markets, we have seen that all decision-takers raise their money prices, seeking thereby to raise their relative prices. But by definition *all* relative prices cannot rise. (It is impossible, for example, for whisky to become more expensive relative to gin while at the same time gin becomes more expensive relative to whisky.) Thus, at least some decision-takers will be frustrated in their attempts to raise their *relative* prices. Consider a very simple example. If they all raise their money prices by 5 per cent, seeking thereby to raise their relative prices by 5 per cent, a 5 per cent inflation will be generated; but they will not have succeeded in raising their own prices relative to other prices. As long as the excess demand persists, people will go on raising their money prices, thereby trying unsuccessfully to raise their relative prices. (Some may succeed, but everyone cannot.) Thus, general excess demand will be associated with a level of national income above its full-employment level and a *continuing* rise in prices.

An exactly parallel argument shows that when there is general excess supply, decreases in money prices by all decision-takers, in an attempt to cut relative prices, will lead to a fall in the general price level, but many *relative* prices will not be decreased. Decision-takers, therefore, will cut prices further. Because of these vain attempts to cut relative prices, any level of national income that is below its full-employment level associated with *continuing* downward pressure on prices.[1]

In summary, the Phelps-Friedman theory holds, first, that general excess demand in the economy will be associated with national income above its full-employment level ($Y > Y_F$) and with continuing inflation and, second, that general excess supply will be associated with national income below its full-employment level ($Y < Y_F$) and with a continuing downward pressure on prices. In other words, the Phillips curve for zero expected inflation is upward sloping, and it cuts the axis at Y_F. This curve which relates P to $Y - Y_F$ may be written $P = F(Y - Y_F)$.

The actual inflation rate

The foregoing discussion of upward and downward pressure on the price level relied on the desire to raise relative prices when national income exceeded Y_F and to lower them when national income fell short of Y_F. Since any decision-taker's relative price is the relation between his or her own price and the general price level,[2] it follows that any decision to change relative prices means changing one's money price *relative* to what one *expects* the price level to be (over the time for which one's own price is being set). If a decision-taker wishes to raise his or her relative price by 5 per cent, this requires a 5 per cent increase in the money price if no inflation is expected, a 10 per cent increase in the money price if a 5 per cent inflation is expected, and so on. If, on the other hand, the decision-taker wishes to reduce his or her relative price by 2 per cent, this requires a 2 per cent reduction in the money price if no inflation is expected but a 3 per cent *increase* in the money price if a 5 per cent inflation is expected, and so on. In general, a decision to change a relative price by x per cent requires a change in the money price by an amount equal to x per cent *plus* the expected rate of inflation.

[1] Note that this theory assumes price adjustment when there is a deflationary gap. It is different, therefore, from the kinked aggregate supply function, which assumes stable prices and quantity adjustments when there is a deflationary gap. The micro underpinnings of the Phelps-Friedman theory are perfectly competitive producers. The micro underpinnings of the kinked aggregate supply function are oligopolistic producers who hold prices rigid but reduce outputs when demand takes them below capacity output.

[2] That is, a relative price is p/P where p is the individual price in question and P is the general price level (which is an average of the economy's prices).

The above discussion explains what determines the actual rate of inflation:

> **According to the Phelps-Friedman theory, the actual rate of inflation is given by the demand-pull element *plus* the expected rate of inflation.** [1]

Thus, for example, if everyone expects a 5 per cent inflation, prices and wages will be raised by 5 per cent, *plus* the amount due to the pull of excess demand, which is shown by the Phillips curve for $\dot{P}_e = 0$.

Another way of making the same point is to say that there is a separate Phillips curve relating actual inflation to national income for each expected rate of inflation. Each curve is defined for a particular expected rate of inflation, and each is called a short-run Phillips curve. (Each curve is short-run in the sense that the Phillips curve on which the economy is located will be given at any moment of time but will change whenever $\dot{P}_e$ changes.) This point is illustrated for three levels of expected rates of inflation in Figure 49.3.[2]

The relation between actual and expected inflation

Actual inflation is equal to expected inflation *plus* an allowance for demand pressure. It follows that actual inflation will exceed expected inflation when national income exceeds Y_F, because demand pressures are then positive. When national income equals Y_F, demand pressures are zero, and actual inflation will equal expected inflation. Whan actual national income is less than Y_F, demand pressures are negative, and actual inflation will be less than the expected rate.[3]

Summary

The discussion so far may be summarized by referring to Figure 49.3. There is a separate Phillips curve for each expected rate of inflation. The Phillips curve, shown here as $P(\dot{P}_e = 0)$, relates national income to inflation on the assumption that the price level is expected to remain stable. It thus shows the 'pure' effects of inflationary and deflationary gaps on inflation. The actual rate of inflation depends upon the relation between Y and Y_F *and* on the expected rate of inflation. Thus for each expected rate of inflation the associated short-run Phillips curve lies above the $\dot{P}_e = 0$ curve by the amount of the expected rate of inflation. Consider for example an inflationary gap with national income at Y_1. The actual rate of inflation will be 5 per cent when the expected rate is zero (point *a*), 10 per cent when the expected rate is 5 per cent (point *b*), and 15 per cent when the expected rate is 10 per cent (point *c*).

The expected rate of inflation determined

Next we must consider how the expected rate of inflation, $\dot{P}_e$, is determined. There

---

[1] In symbols: $\dot{P} = F(Y - Y_F) + \dot{P}_e$ where $\dot{P}$ is the actual rate of inflation, $Y - Y_F$ is negative for deflationary gaps and positive for inflationary gaps, $F(Y - Y_F)$ is the inflation rate caused by demand pressure, and $\dot{P}_e$ is the expected rate of inflation.

[2] Each short-run Phillips curve plots the relation between $\dot{P}$ and $F(Y - Y_F)$ for a *given* $\dot{P}_e$:

$$P = F(Y - F_F) + \bar{P}_e.$$

Thus changing $\bar{P}_e$ shifts the Phillips curve vertically by the amount of the change.

[3] Manipulation of the equation in footnote 1 above shows $P - P_e = F(Y - Y_F)$.

are a number of theories of how expectations are formed. We shall confine ourselves to the simple theory called *adaptive expectations*: people are assumed to base their expectations about the inflation rate in the immediate future on the actual rates that have occurred over the recent past. Thus whenever actual rates of inflation exceed expected rates, expectations will catch up – but with a lag. For example, if people are expecting a 5 per cent inflation but continue to experience a 7 per cent inflation, they will sooner or later revise their expectations upward and come to expect a 7 per cent inflation. Conversely, if people are expecting a 7 per cent inflation but are only experiencing a 5 per cent inflation they will sooner or later revise their expectations downward and come to expect only a 5 per cent inflation.

The behaviour of the closed model

Accelerating inflation An important implication of the Phelps-Friedman theory is that if national income is *kept* above Y_F, the rate of inflation will accelerate continuously. Say that the economy starts in full-employment equilibrium at stable prices – that is, at the point where the Phillips curve for $\dot{P}_e = 0$ cuts the axis. Now let aggregate demand increase. Excess demand is created; national income increases; and the economy moves up its short-run Phillips curve to a higher level of national income and, say, a 5 per cent inflation. This is shown by point *a* in Figure 49.3. This inflation occurs because people are trying to adjust their *relative* wages and prices upward in response to excess demand. No one expects an inflation. If the inflation persists, however, it will eventually come to be expected. People will then add a catch-up factor of 5 per cent to any wage and price change they plan to make. When they do this the rate of inflation will then accelerate to 10 per cent (point *b*). Sooner or later this will come to be expected, and the rate of inflation will then accelerate to 15 per cent (point *c*), of which 10 per cent is to keep ahead of expected inflation and 5 per cent is a response to excess demand.

> **According to the Phelps-Friedman theory, whenever the economy has a level of national income above full-employment income (or, what is the same thing, a level of unemployment below the natural rate of unemployment), the actual rate of inflation will eventually accelerate. How fast it accelerates depends on how fast current inflationary expectations adjust to past actual rates.**

It follows that if the government tries to maintain excess aggregate demand in the mistaken view that it can increase real national income above Y_F (i.e., lower unemployment below its natural rate) at the cost of a stable rate of inflation, it is in for a nasty shock. For a while people may not expect the inflation to continue; as a result it will proceed at a stable pace. Sooner or later, however, people will come to expect the inflation to continue; they will revise their inflationary expectations upward, and this will cause the inflation to accelerate. Later the new higher rate will come to be accepted; expectations of future inflation will be revised upward and the actual rate of inflation will once again accelerate.[1]

[1] Of course, as we saw in Chapter 41, the government will have to induce ever more rapid rates of monetary expansion to validate an ever-accelerating inflation rate. But if the government does try to hold national income above Y_F, it will induce, according to this theory, an ever-accelerating rate of inflation that will *have to be validated* by ever-increasing rates of monetary expansion.

The long-run Phillips curve is vertical When national income equals Y_F in the Phelps-Friedman theory there is no excess demand pressure on inflation. *Thus the only inflation that can occur when $Y = Y_F$ is expectational inflation.* If everyone expects 5 per cent inflation, then all prices will be raised by 5 per cent and an actual inflation rate of 5 per cent will occur. If the money supply is increased by 5 per cent to validate this inflation, then full-employment income and the natural rate of unemployment can be maintained indefinitely with a 5 per cent expected and 5 per cent actual inflation. But the same argument could be repeated for 10 per cent or for any other rate of inflation (or deflation).

In general, since at the natural rate of unemployment there is neither upward nor downward pressure on prices due to excess demand, the only cause of inflation arises from attempts to try to keep up with whatever rate of inflation is expected. Thus full-employment national income and its associated natural rate of unemployment are compatible with *any* actual rate of inflation, provided that, first, the inflation is expected and second, that it is validated by monetary expansion.

> **The long-run Phillips curve that relates national income to a stable rate of inflation is vertical at full-employment income.**

The long-run curve is shown by the vertical white line labelled *F* in Figure 49.3. It shows that according to the Phelps-Friedman theory a stable rate of inflation is compatible only with Y_F and that Y_F is compatible with *any* stable rate of inflation, including a zero rate (provided, of course, that any positive rate is validated by suitable increases in the money supply).

Policy implications

The Phelps-Friedman theory has a number of implications for economic policy. If the theory turns out to be substantially correct, these policy implications will be extremely important. A first implication has already been discussed.

> **Attempts to reduce unemployment below its natural rate or, what is the same thing, to raise Y above Y_F, will eventually cause the rate of inflation to accelerate.**

A second implication concerns the natural rate of unemployment.

> **It is essential to discover the natural rate of unemployment because it is the only acceptable target for long-run stabilization policy.**

To see why knowing the natural rate of unemployment is so important, assume that the economy has functioned satisfactorily for some time at an average unemployment rate of 3 per cent and that the inflation rate has shown no tendency to accelerate. Policy-makers will conclude that 3 per cent is the natural rate of unemployment. Now assume, however, that unbeknown to the policy-makers the natural rate of unemployment rises to 6 per cent. If they go on trying to stabilize the economy around a 3 per cent unemployment rate, the first indication they will have that something has gone wrong is that the inflation rate will begin to accelerate. It may take some time before policy-makers conclude that the acceleration is not due to some transient cause but represents a genuine tendency for continual acceleration. By the time they reach that conclusion and decide to stabilize the economy around a higher level of unemployment, a very rapid inflation may already exist and may have been built into people's expectations. Thus, if the Phelps-Friedman theory is correct, quick and accurate determination of the natural rate of unemployment must be an important part of any effective anti-inflationary policy.

Once an expectational inflation is under way, policy-makers may have to take account of a third important policy implication.

A period of excess demand and accelerating inflation will lead to accelerating inflationary expectations. A prolonged period with unemployment above the natural rate may be required before inflationary expectations are revised downward sufficiently to permit the actual inflation rate to fall.

If the expected rate of inflation is rising, a fall in national income can easily be associated with a rise in the actual rate of inflation. This implication is illustrated in Figure 49.4. The economy is at point *g* with a level of national income of Y_1, an expected rate of inflation of 2 per cent, and an actual rate of 6 per cent. Since the actual rate exceeds the expected rate, expectations will be revised upward. Suppose people come to expect a 6 per cent inflation in the next period. If national income is held constant at Y_1, the economy will move to point *h* and the actual rate of inflation will accelerate to 10 per cent. In order to offset this increase in inflationary expectations and hold inflation to 6 per cent, national income must be reduced all the way to Y_2 (point *i*). If national income *falls* to any amount less than Y_1 but greater than Y_2, the economy will move to some point such as *j* and *falling* real national income will be associated with *rising* inflation.

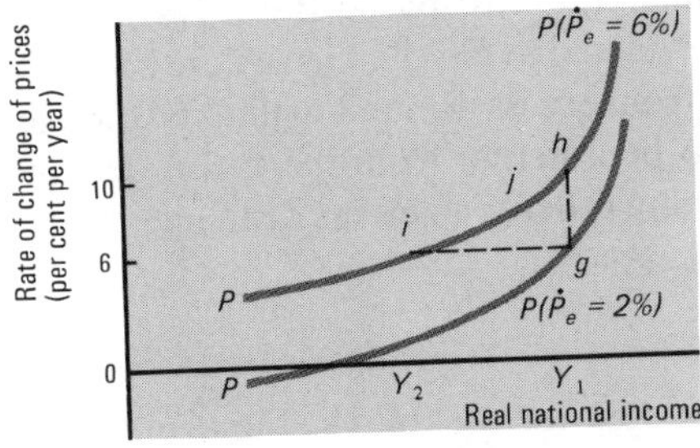

Fig. 49.4 Falling real national income and rising inflation (stagflation)

In the early stage of a contraction in national income that is designed to bring an *accelerating* inflation under control, the effect of accelerating expectations may dominate the effect of declining demand and output. As a result, falling national income and rising unemployment may be associated with constant or even rising rates of inflation. When this occurs the economy is suffering a 'stagflation'.

Thus the Phelps-Friedman theory make stagflation the result of a expectational inflation which is itself the lagged result of an excess-demand inflation.

Closure with cost-push theories

The second strand of reaction to the accelerating rates of inflation in the late 1960s was the much wider acceptance of cost-push theories. These may be complementary to the demand-pull theories discussed above, or they may be complete substitutes for them. Let us look at them first as substitute methods of closure and then consider the possibility of an eclectic theory that includes both.

Wage-cost push

Consider first domestic wage-cost push. If unions have the power to set wages independently of the state of demand in the economy, and if they exercise it, the price level becomes union-determined. If unions raise wages by 20 per cent this year, firms will have no option but to raise prices by something like 20 per cent. There is a little slack, in that profit margins can be varied, but by and large an increase in costs must in the long run be passed on as an increase in prices. Profit margins do vary a bit over the trade cycle, but any theory that explains what happens to costs will explain most of what happens to prices.

> **Closure by a complete wage-cost-push theory yields a union-determined theory of the price level.**

Since inflation rates are observed to vary greatly from year to year, a wage-cost-push theory needs to explain why the cost-push varies from year to year. There are two possible routes here. The behaviour can either change arbitrarily from year to year or be related systematically to some other variable. In the former case we have a theory that the price level is determined arbitrarily. This is unsatisfactory because it provides no explanation of systematic variations in the rate of inflation over time and across countries. In the latter case we have a theory that the price level is determined by whatever variables determine the cost-push. If the variable is aggregate demand, so that wage increases are related to $Y - Y_F$, then we are back to a demand-pull theory with just an added link from excess demand to unions to wages to prices. Thus for the wage-cost theory to be different from the excess demand theory, the cost-push must vary with something other than excess demand.

Policy implications

Several important implications of the wage-cost theory follow. First, inflations cannot be controlled by demand management, since unions determine wages, and hence prices, in response to urges not related to demand. Second, if the nominal money supply is held constant, a wage-cost push will lead to an ever falling level of national income with its accompanying ever-rising level of unemployment. This is because an unvalidated inflation must shift the aggregate expenditure function downwards by the operation of the monetary adjustment mechanism. If sooner or later unions moderate their wage push in the face of high enough unemployment rates, then a cost-push inflation with a constant money supply is self-correcting, but only at the level of unemployment at which unions are induced to stop their wage-cost push. Third, if the government seeks to prevent the cost-push inflation from raising unemployment, it can do so by validating the inflation. This frustrates the monetary adjustment mechanism and stops the aggregate expenditure function from shifting downwards. The inflation may then continue indefinitely. Fourth, if the government wishes to control inflation without having the rise in unemployment required by the operation of the monetary adjustment mechanism, its only remaining policy is to operate on the strength of the cost-push itself. It may seek to restrain the consequences of cost push by employing the legal prohibitions of wage and price controls. It may also seek to change the unions' wage-cost-push behaviour by various forms of income policies or social contracts. These have the characteristic that they offer unions other things that they desire in return for a moderation of wage claims.

Import-cost push

If exchange rates are fixed, as they were until the early 1970s, the operation of import-cost push is obvious. If prices of exports from the rest of the world rise because of an inflation in the rest of the world, then the prices of imports into a non-inflationary country must rise. This will cause a rise in the importing country's price level. The magnitude of the rise will depend on the importance of imports in the domestic economy.

The operation of the import-cost push is a little less certain when exchange rates are flexible, as they have been since the early 1970s. If prices double in the rest of the world there is no reason, in principle, why one non-inflating country cannot let its exchange rate change so as to offset this completely. This requires, among other things, a perfectly flexible exchange rate influenced only by the current balance of trade. In practice, exchange rates have a substantial stickiness to them, primarily because of capital movements but also because of central bank intervention. Thus, in practice, a rise in export prices in the rest of the world almost always means a rise in the prices of imports in any one country's domestic market measured in terms of its domestic currency. This means a rise in the country's price level, the extent of which depends on the degree of openness of the economy. Thus inflations are imported to some extent, but it also seems likely that, except for the smallest most open economies, import-cost push is not the complete explanation of inflation.

An eclectic theory

So far we have treated the cost-push and demand-pull theories as competing explantions of inflation. It is, of course, possible that all of the forces analysed contribute to inflation with weights that may vary from time to time and from place to place. An eclectic theory of inflation can be symbolized as follows:

$$\dot{P} = a_1(Y - Y_F) + a_2\dot{P}_e + a_3C + a_4\dot{M} - \varepsilon.$$

Here the actual rate of inflation is indicated by P. The term $Y - Y_F$ stands for the pressure of demand working on commodity prices and on factor costs. The term $\dot{P}_e$ stands for the expected rate of inflation; the term C stands for a wage-cost push by unions that is independent of the state of aggregate demand; and $\dot{M}$ stands for the inflation caused by rising import prices. Finally, ε stands for everything else, including the peculiarities of particular index numbers that can influence the recorded rate of inflation. The coefficients a_1 to a_4 gives weights to each of these possible forces. Pure demand-pull theories assign zero to a_3 and a_4. Pure cost-push theories assign a zero to a_1 and may or may not assign a zero to a_2.[1]

[1] The point here is that expectations on their own are not a theory of inflation until we know how expectations are formed. If they depend on past actual rates, then it all depends what caused the past actual rates. For a demand-pull theorist, a_3 and a_4 are zero and P_e becomes the lagged effect of past excess demands. For a cost-push theorist, a_1 is zero and P_e becomes the lagged effect of past wage and import-cost pushes.

Eclectic theorists believe that all coefficients are positive but that the magnitude of each may vary from time to time and from place to place. This, they believe, is why UK and US economists differ so much on their view on inflation. Most US economists (as well as some UK economists) give a_3 a low or even a zero value. An influential body of UK economists, however, give a_3 a large positive value, possibly even making it the most important of the four coefficients. It is possible that these differences arise not because different economists assess the same evidence differently but because each group is looking primarily at its own economy and that the relative strengths of the cost-push and demand-pull forces differ between the two economies. (By any criterion, British unions are certainly much more powerful than American unions.) It should be added, however, that there are also major differences among British economists over the relative weights to be assigned to each of these four coefficients. Some follow American economists in giving a low value to a_3 while giving the major weight to a_1. We shall pursue such debates in the next chapter.

50

Policy issues and debates

Can the government control inflation and simultaneously produce something close to full employment? Can it alter the growth rate at the same time? What can be done about the exchange rate and the balance of payments? The debates on these issues have evolved over a long time.

Two extreme views

Two extreme views on government policy to manage the economy have been mentioned in this book. The first view, which is surprisingly common, is that the entire Keynesian model of income determination is in some sense conceptually wrong or misconceived. It seems very hard, however, to sustain this charge. The concept of the circular flow of income long predates Keynes[1] and it is the conceptual basis for almost every macroeconomic model used in government and academic circles today. Of course, there is room for different assumptions about how various elements in the flow behave. Indeed, there is much active debate about the behavioural assumptions used in alternative models. For example, the Keynesian assumption about the independance of saving and investment decisions might be wrong. But a revised behavioural assumption in which, say, investment was a function of saving would still be fitted into the structure of the circular flow of income. It is also quite possible to argue that certain *policy implications* that have been drawn from the Keynesian model are misguided or wrong. There is general agreement, among those who try to apply economic models to real-world data, however, that circular-flow models provide the required structure.

> **In spite of frequently occurring statements that Keynesian economics is wrong or totally discredited, the model of the circular flow of income remains the only conceptual model with which to study flows of income and expenditure in the economy.**

The second extreme view is that fiscal policy cannot shift the aggregate demand function. The basic argument here is that the crowding-out effect (see page 548) is 100 per cent. If the government raises aggregate demand, the interest rate rises,

[1] For example, a very clear statement can be found in Schumpeter's great book *The Theory of Economic Development* (full citation on page 564).

which reduces interest-sensitive private expenditure and the rate of interest continues to rise until every pound of new government expenditure is matched by a one-pound reduction in private expenditure. This view can be based on various rather subtle theories. It is very difficult, however, to take it seriously in the light of the experience of countries such as the UK, where demand management has been used consistently over the past 35 years. The view has survived mainly in the US, where over the same period there have been no more than two or three experiments with demand management.[1]

> **The evidence from the UK and several other countries that have pursued active fiscal policies is that fiscal policy can be effective in shifting the aggregate expenditure function.**

Goals and instruments

It is an important proposition in the theory of economic policy that to achieve a given number of independent objectives the central authorities should have at least as many instruments of policy as they have objectives. To try to achieve, say, two objectives with only one instrument is to court failure. What should policy-makers do, for example, if they are on target for objective one but not for objective two? (If the one instrument is used to get closer to the target for objective two, it will take them away from the target for objective one.)

We have identified four main objectives of policy that have been influential at one time or another since the Second World War: stable prices, low unemployment, rapid growth, and a satisfactory balance of payments. What are the instruments that can be used to achieve these objectives?

Growth

Growth refers to a rise in full-employment income, that is, to a rightward movement in the point Y_F in Figures 49.1 to 49.3. With growth, the national income of a fully employed society rises continually. Growth first became an important objective of UK policy sometime in the 1950s. At that time national income data became available, covering a long-enough period of time to suggest a significantly lower growth rate in the UK than in France, West Germany and several other countries.

Since that time, two views have been evident in British policy. The first is that policies to change the growth rate require instruments other than demand management. This is the view that is supported by economic theory. Theory predicts that the growth rate of potential national income is a function of many influences – not, however, including aggregate expenditure. According to the theory of national income, aggregate expenditure determines the current level of national

[1] The fact that a significant number of American economists can believe that fiscal policy cannot shift the aggregate expenditure function is a potent warning against adopting overly parochial views, which often happens in both the US and the UK. Often, when the evidence from one's own country is too scanty to rule out a wide range of competing hypotheses, a close study of a few other countries will be sufficient to do so. As a result of recent debate summarized in such advanced volumes as *Monetarism*, edited by G. Stein (North Holland Publishing Co., 1976), even US monetarists seem to be retreating from their extreme position that fiscal policy cannot shift the *E* function significantly.

income, Y, and hence the difference between actual and potential national income, $Y - Y_F$, but it does not in itself influence Y_F.

Indicative planning The search for effective instruments to determine the growth rate has been hampered by the fact that there is no well-tested theory of the variables that the government can control in order to affect the growth rate. Probably the most serious attempt to find appropriate policy instruments took place in the early 1960s under the National Economic Development Council (NEDC). The basic idea behind the NEDC was that, 'if a sufficient number of major industrialists could be persuaded that a faster growth rate was indeed likely, then they would untertake the investment programmes which would make this more rapid growth rate possible.'[1] This was called *indicative planning*. It consisted of publishing the desired growth rate, 4 per cent in this case, and arguing that there were no *insuperable* barriers to prevent its achievement. (It is inconceivable that a study could demonstrate that there were *insuperable* barriers to a 4 per cent growth rate in *any* industrial economy.) The whole NEDC exercise can be thought of as a piece of propaganda based on the naive view that the underlying reactions governing economic processes can be manipulated by the mere statement that the government would like them to be other than they are.

Demand management The (all too predictable) failure of indicative planning left the central authorities with no obvious instrument to influence growth rates. More or less by default, they fell back on the view, quite unsupported by any substantial economic theory or evidence, that the growth rate of potential income could also be affected by aggregate demand.

The most dramatic attempt to influence growth rates through demand management came in the early 1970s under the Conservative Government led by Prime Minister Edward Heath. The 'dash for growth' policy of 1972–3 consisted of raising the aggregate expenditure function to produce a rapid rise in national income, which was at the time significantly below its full-employment level (unemployment of labour was at a post-war high at the time), while simultaneously trying to hold down wage costs by an incomes policy. The policy failed: when Y reached Y_F, Y_F did not shift; instead a major inflation ensued. Attempts to control the inflation through an incomes policy failed dismally. The failure illustrated two propositions that should have been well known but apparently were not. First, there is no reason to think that the rate of growth of potential income, Y_F, will be affected by the speed with which actual income hits the full-employment constraint. The view that it will be so affected can only be explained by the wishful thinking borne of desperation: only one instrument, aggregate demand, could be manipulated, so why not hit the target we are trying to move, Y_F, very hard and hope it moves! The second lesson to be learned from the policy is that it is difficult to restrain wage costs when there is substantial excess demand in the system. Once the dash for growth produced an inflationary gap there was upward pressure on all prices and factor costs due to excess demand in goods and factor markets. In such circumstances it is difficult for government restraints to hold down factor prices.

So much for growth. The growth performance of the UK economy is poor by international standards (see pages 691–2). The central authorities would like to

[1] NIESR, *The United Kingdom Economy*, 3rd edn. (Heinemann, 1977), p. 116.

improve it; but in common with the authorities in all free market economies they have no ready instruments with which to do so.

Balance of payments and exchange rates

The dismissal of growth leaves three main macro goals. In the period since the Second World War balance-of-payments problems have been of frequent concern to policy-makers. We must study them briefly here. We shall first consider the problems as they have occurred throughout most of the period since the Second World War, in the context, that is, of *fixed exchange rates*.

Causes of balance-of-payments problems Causes of balance-of-payments problems may be divided into changes abroad and changes at home. The central authorities have little or no control over the former, so we shall concentrate on the latter.

Two main causes of balance-of-payments problems may be distinguished. The first is domestic inflation. Inflation creates no problems for the balance of payments if all one's competitors are also inflating at the same rate, since it is relative prices that matter in international trade, as in domestic trade. If, however, one country's price level is rising faster than the price levels of competitor countries, imports will rise, exports will fall and balance-of-payments problems will ensue.

The second cause is changes in consumption patterns that occur in the course of economic growth. A dramatic example occurred after the First World War, when a technological innovation allowed oil to replace coal as the fuel for ships' boilers. This change greatly reduced Britain's export market for coal, and also increased her import bill since the change over was made by British as well as foreign ships. Less dramatic shifts occur due to differing income elasticities of demand for imports and exports. Consider two countries with identical rates of economic growth. The first country has a comparative advantage in commodities with low income elasticities, while the second has comparative advantage in commodities with high income elasticities. The first country will be in persistent balance-of-payments problems at a fixed exchange rate.[1]

Capital account problems can be caused both on long-term account, if domestic savers wish to invest heavily abroad, and on short-term account when short-term capital flows out because of such factors as higher interest rates abroad and fears of devaluation at home.

Control Broadly speaking, two main sets of policies can be adopted to solve a balance-of-payments problem. First, national income may be reduced by raising taxes or by lowering government expenditure. The fall in income will reduce the expenditure of households on all goods, including imports. This policy is called an EXPENDITURE-DAMPENING POLICY; it relies on a general reduction in aggregate expenditure to accomplish its goal of a reduction in expenditure on imports. How successful the policy will be depends on the proportion of income that is spent on imports. Where this proportion is small, as in the US, a large reduction in income will be needed to accomplish a given change in imports. Where the proportion of

[1] This does not mean that the country will lose if it allows its exchange rate to depreciate steadily. This may well be the policy that maximizes the growth in its standard of living.

income spent on imports is large, as in Britain, a smaller change in income will be needed to produce any given change in imports.

The second major policy is an EXPENDITURE-SWITCHING POLICY. The expenditure of domestic households can be switched from foreign to domestic goods to reduce imports, and the expenditures of foreign households can be switched from goods produced abroad to goods produced at home to increase exports. Expenditure switching is accomplished by changing the prices of foreign goods relative to domestic goods. This can be done by taxing imports and subsidizing exports, or by devaluing the exchange rate. Expenditure-switching policies were analysed in detail in the Appendix to Chaper 43.

Expenditure-switching and expenditure-dampening policies can both affect the balance of payments in the desired direction. Both, however, have certain side-effects.

A policy of expenditure dampening to reduce imports is somewhat like shooting at a close target with a shotgun. The bull's eye will usually be hit, but so will a lot of other things. Specifically, a reduction in aggregate expenditure will reduce expenditures on all domestically produced commodities. This means that output and standards of living will fall and that unemployment will rise. These are side-effects that are not usually regarded as desirable, especially by those affected.

An expenditure-switching policy will also have an effect on the level of domestic income, output and employment. If a devaluation of the British pound lowers the prices of British goods relative to the prices of foreign ones, both foreign and UK households will buy more UK-produced goods and fewer foreign-produced goods. This will raise incomes in those British industries that produced the newly demanded good, and, when the extra incomes are spent, a multiplier process will be set up that will raise all incomes in the UK. On the other hand, if the pound is appreciated, then foreign and British households will buy fewer goods. This will lower the income of those sectors of the UK economy that produce those goods for which demand has now fallen. Once the incomes of households in these sectors have fallen, their expenditures will be reduced, and incomes throughout the UK will fall. One important side effect of such a policy will be a redistribution of income among sectors of the UK economy.

Expenditure-switching policies tend to raise demand and national income by increasing expenditure on domestic output. Such policies will tend to appeal to policy makers in situations in which income and employment are below the desired level. A successful expenditure-switching policy in these circumstances will simultaneously improve both the balance of payments and the unemployment situation. If an expenditure-switching policy is to be successful in a period of full employment, however, it must be accompanied by a policy of reducing domestic expenditure. There is no point in switching foreign demand onto your products if you are in a situation in which full employment of resources already exists, because it will not be possible to produce more output to meet the extra demand. The appropriate policy in such a situation is to accompany an expenditure-switching policy with an expenditure-dampening one that reduces domestic expenditure by exactly the same amount as the increase in foreign expenditure on domestically-produced goods. This keeps national income and employment unchanged, but directs a larger share of total output to exports, thus improving the balance-of-payments situation.

On capital account, there are two main tools of control. First, direct controls on movement of capital can be employed as they have been by several countries. Second, the domestic rate of interest can be manipulated. If the central bank raises domestic short-term rates, this will induce an inflow of short-term capital to take advantage of the higher rates. A lowering of domestic interest rates will have the opposite effect as capital moves elsewhere to take advantage of the relatively higher foreign rates.

The stop-go cycle Throughout the 1950s and 1960s the maintenance of a fixed rate of exchange for sterling was an overriding goal of the central authorities in the UK and in most other countries. The fixing of the exchange rate left the authorities with one instrument, demand management,[1] to achieve three goals: low unemployment, low inflation and a stable exchange rate. This set up a classic situation for policy conflicts. The limitations of economic policy implied by having more targets than instruments was alleged at the time to lead to what was referred to as a *stop-go cycle*. There is some debate about the extent and even the existence of this cycle, but one authoritative view of it is provided by the following quotation:

> ... begin at the end of a period of stagnation, say, 1958. ... The government becomes disturbed about rising unemployment; [and] stimulates[s] demand. ... [Because of] time lags it appears[s] that the first 'injection' of purchasing power is not working. As a result further stimulus is applied perhaps [by encouraging] nationalized industries to accelerate their spending plans. Eventually the stimulus will take hold; output will begin to rise and ... unemployment will begin to fall.
>
> Within a year the first signs will begin to appear of a worsening in the balance of payments. ... Then at some point along the road ... there is a speculative run against sterling. This, in the fixed exchange rate period, forced the government to take severe deflationary action, which it normally did in the form of a 'package' of measures ... a hasty collection ... [to] restore confidence among foreign bankers. So the boom would be brought to an end. There were normally other factors, as well as the imposition of government restraints, which served to slow down the rise in output. ... So it happened on more than one occasion that government restraints were imposed on an economy where the rise in output was already slowing down.
>
> At this point in the policy cycle the period of relative stagnation in output begins; after a time lag unemployment begins to rise. With the very slow rise in output, there is also a slowing down in the rise in the volume of imports. Again after a time lag, the increase in private investment is checked and reversed. The balance of payments gradually moves back into surplus, and the stage is set for the next episode of policy-induced expansion.[2]

The removal of the fixed-exchange-rate goal In the early 1970s, as we saw in Chapter 45, the Bretton Woods system was abandoned and the world moved to a system of flexible exchange rates. The world has since then proceeded with (to say the least) no more upsets than were caused by the periodic crises under fixed rates. As a result, maintaining the existing exchange rate has ceased to be an overriding policy goal for the central authorities of the UK and of most other countries. Central banks still intervene in the exchange market for all sorts of reasons, including the smoothing out of short-term fluctuations. But even when it is intervening, any central bank can let the rate slide whenever it feels it cannot, or does not wish to, resist the forces of demand and supply. This removes the exchange rate as a target of policy and returns

[1] There was some experimentation with a second instrument, incomes policies, but this proved ineffectual, at least at the time. See the later discussion on incomes policies in the text.

[2] *The UK Economy*, op. cit., pp. 115–16.

it to its traditional role: as an instrument that fluctuates to equate international payments

Full employment and stable prices

In the 1970s two macro goals remained that economic policy-makers could reasonably hope to influence: securing low rates of unemployment and controlling inflation. Do we require one instrument or two to deal with these two targets? The answer depends on whether or not inflation and unemployment are independant variables in the economy. If they are independant, we need two instruments. If they are dependant on each other, then one instrument that controls one of them will automatically control the other. The relation between inflation and unemployment in our theories depends on the method used to close the model of the circular flow of national income. Thus, the theoretical discussion in Chapter 49 is relevant to the policy discussion in this chapter. We shall first consider theories that require only one instrument and then go on to theories requiring two.

Pure demand-pull theories The amount of employment in the economy varies inversely with real national income: greater production requires greater labour inputs. If the labour force is constant, unemployment will vary inversely with national income. Therefore control of aggregate expenditure is the instrument for controlling deficient-demand unemployment (although other instruments are needed to control structural and unwanted search unemployment). If inflation is also a function of aggregate expenditure, the same instrument will also control inflation. Whether or not there is a conflict between these two objectives depends on how they are related.

The kinked aggregate supply curve yields no conflict. The central authorities try to hold the aggregate expenditure function at E_F in Figure 49.1, page 749, and thus hold the economy at the point of full-employment without inflation in parts (ii) and (iii) of the figure. Furthermore, since there is no trade-off, full employment without inflation is fully achievable. The central authorities may not, however, be able to offset *all* fluctuations in private expenditure. If E falls below E_F there will be deficient-demand unemployment, and if E rises above E_F the price level will rise. But errors apart, the goal of policy is clear and is attainable with the single instrument of demand management.[1]

This theory was rejected because it did not seem to be a good description of the behaviour of the economy. In the 1960s it was replaced by the theory of the Phillips curve. Once again, however, inflation and unemployment were not independent variables. The single instrument of demand management is sufficient to hold the economy on some point on its Phillips curve giving any desired position on the trade-off between unemployment and inflation.[2] Now, however, there is a policy conflict: unemployment can always be lowered by raising aggregate expenditure and thus raising national income, but only at the cost of a higher inflation rate.

[1] The unemployment that occurs at Y_F is due to all causes other than deficient aggregate demand. To lower this non-deficient-demand unemployment requires other instruments that can attack such causes as structural imbalances between demands for supplies of labour. These instruments are briefly discussed towards the end of this chapter.

[2] Note that demand management now must include a monetary policy that validates the inflation occurring at the chosen point on the trade-off curve.

The demand-pull, Phillips-curve model (buttressed by import-cost pushes in open economies) performed moderately well until the end of the 1960s. As indicated in Figures 50.1 and 50.2, there seemed to be a definite relation between the pressure of demand in the economy and the rate of inflation.[1] The job of demand management was to keep the economy as close as possible to the chosen point on the trade-off curve. Wage-cost-push theorists provided an alternative explanation of inflation in the 1950s and 1960s. At the time this was a minority view among economists and we shall consider it in the next section.

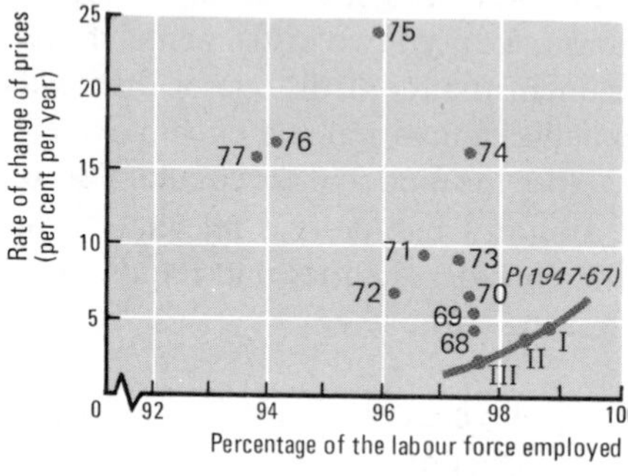

Fig. 50.1 UK stagflation in the 1970s

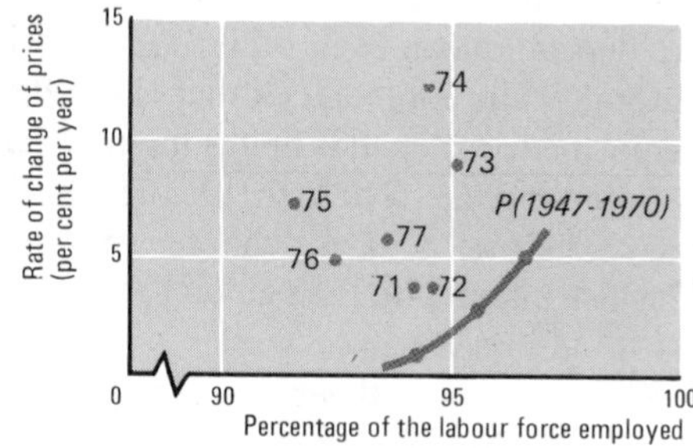

Fig. 50.2 US stagflation in the 1970s

During the late 1960s and early 1970s many economies experienced accelerating rates of inflation at any given level of resource use. This led many demand-pull theorists to accept the theory of the expectations-augmented Phillips curve. Indeed, it led many others as well to accept the potential importance of expectations of inflation in influencing actual inflation.

The American experience shown in Figure 50.2 seems to be consistent with a model closed by an expectations-augmented Phillips curve. The British experience shown in Figure 50.1 seems harder to fit into a pure demand-plus expectational theory of inflation. For this reason we discuss the American experience in this section and the British experience in a later section. The explanation of the American experience as given by demand-pull theorists runs as follows. The economy started from a trough in 1972 and then a boom developed that took the rate of inflation from 3·3 per cent in 1972 to well over 10 per cent in 1974. This was a conventional demand-pull inflation. Since the late 1960s the natural rate of unemployment had been drifting slowly upward, thereby raising the amount of unemployment that existed when excess demand inflation set in. This explains why the boom of 1973–4 that led to an inflation rate of over 10 per cent only barely reduced the unemployment rate below 5 per cent. By 1974 inflationary expectations had become firmly entrenched: both labour and management expected inflation to continue and, if anything, to accelerate. Wage and price contracts were thus drawn up on the assumption that a nominal 10 per cent increase would be needed just to keep any price or wage in line with the average of all wages and prices. Added to this was a temporary import-cost-push inflation due to rising prices of oil, other energy sources, and some other basic commodities.

Then in the latter half of 1974 aggregate demand fell off; when it did, demand-pull pressures were removed. At this point the inflation became an expectational inflation with some added cost-push elements (due to such things as the continuing rise in energy prices). The economy then entered the stagflation phase: wages and prices continued to rise in the face of a really severe slump. Inflationary expectations were finally moderated, however, and as this happened, the actual rate of inflation began to fall as well.

As the slump persisted, inflationary expectations fell from their peak of 10–11 per cent but seemed to become fixed in the range of 5–6 per cent. In the face of the most serious recession since the 1930s and of a very slow recovery stretching from 1976 to 1979, the US inflation rate held stubbornly at around 6 per cent. To many observers this seemed to be a pure expectational inflation: because everyone expected a 6 per cent inflation their wage and price formation behaviour produced a steady inflation. An ever-growing group of American economists began to seek new ways of breaking expectational inflation.

A second instrument for control of expectations: Modern demand-pull theorists explain inflation by the equation $\dot{P} = F(Y - Y_F) + \dot{P}_e$. Their main instrument for control is demand management, which influences $Y - Y_F$. We have seen, however, that curing an inflation that has been going on long enough to have well-established inflationary expectations may require a period of stagflation. (See page 763.) As long as expectations of inflations are high, actual inflations are high. If aggregate demand is then reduced, low output will be combined with high inflation. It may take a very long time for inflationary expectations to fall in response to the slump in the economy. Until $\dot{P}_e$ does fall, the recession *with* high inflation will continue.

Many demand-pull theorists have seen a new place for wage-price controls or weaker forms of incomes policies to reduce these inflationary expectations faster than they would be revised downwards in the normal course of events. INCOMES POLICIES are any form of government intervention into wage and price formation in an attempt to control the price level. Such policies fall into three main types. First, GUIDELINE POLICIES are published maximum rates of wage and price increases that the government would like to see observed voluntarily by the private sector. Second, WAGE-PRICE CONTROLS are legal wage-price ceilings usually expressed in the form of maximum permitted annual rates of increase of wage rates and prices. Third, *social contracts* are agreements gaining labour's voluntary co-operation in reducing the rate of wage increases in return for other concessions. Examples of such concessions are measures designed to shift the functional distribution of income in labour's favour and laws encouraging the spread of closed shops.

To illustrate the place of incomes policies as an instrument for controlling the expectational component of inflation, assume that the economy has been experiencing excess demand, $Y > Y_F$, and an accelerating inflation that has now reached 16 per cent. The government could induce a recession with $Y < Y_F$ and wait for a downward revision of the expected inflation rate to bring the actual rate downwards. It could, however, also follow a second policy. It could remove the excess demand pressure without inducing a serious slump setting, $Y = Y_F$. At this point any inflation is an expectational inflation. The government then puts on wage-price controls, forcing inflation down to 12, 8 and 4 per cent in three successive years. The rate of monetary expansion is also cut to 12, 8 and 4 per cent, thus keeping the real money supply constant. After three years the controls are removed. If expectations have followed the actual inflation rate downwards, the inflation rate

[1] The two figures show Phillips curves as they appeared to exist to policy makers in the late 1960s. The curves are drawn by averaging data for three intervals of unemployment and plotting the index of utilization as 1-U against the average rate of inflation in years when 1-U was in that interval; the American curve is calculated up to 1971, the British curve up to 1967.

will stay low. The advantage of this policy is that it avoids the temporary period of slump with $Y < Y_F$, needed in the normal course of events to cause people to revise their inflationary expectations downwards.

Many American demand-pull theorists have swung around to advocating temporary bouts of incomes policies, an approach they had previously opposed. In the past, demand-pull theorists thought that inflation depended solely on excess demand, $\dot{P} = \mathrm{F}(Y - Y_F)$ and that the only cure for inflation was removing the excess demand. In these circumstances it was believed that price controls were only an attack on the symptom, not the cause (which was $Y > Y_F$), and that the inflation would break out again as soon as the controls were removed. Once the $\dot{P}_e$ term was added, however, there was room for a second instrument to control $\dot{P}_e$ directly.

Pure cost-push theories Although there has been substantial disagreement on the *weight* to be given to import-cost push as a cause of British inflation, no one has argued that import-cost push *cannot* be a contributing cause. Few economists have argued that it is the only cause, except in very small, very open economies. Thus in our general discussion of policy controversies we shall not say much more about the import-cost push.

The main domestic force identified by cost-push theorists is wage costs. Pure cost-push theorists assume that a_1 in the equation on page 765 is zero. They may or may not give importance to expectational inflation, but in what follows we shall ignore it. Thus their inflation theory is $P = a_3\dot{W} + a_4\dot{m}$. This makes inflation and unemployment *independent* of each other. Inflation depends on the cost-push, while unemployment depends on demand factors (aggregate expenditure and national income). Since the two objectives are independent, two policy instruments are needed to control them. Cost-push theorists usually advocate demand management to control unemployment and various forms of incomes policies to control inflation.

Although cost-push and demand-pull theorists are often of different political complexions, the differences between them do not turn on politics or value judgements but on a straight, positive assessment of the empirically correct way to close the circular-flow model so as to determine the price level as well as real income. If, as demand-pull theorists believe, $P = \mathrm{F}(Y - Y_F)$, price controls are unnecessary and cannot attack the cause of inflation, which is an inflationary gap. If, as cost-push theorists believe, $P = a_3 W + a_4\dot{m}$, controlling aggregate demand will not control inflation. Instead some way must be found of controlling wages, either by the legal constraints of wage controls or by the inducements of incomes policies that persuade labour to reduce their wage demands

Opinions differ on the pure cost-push model. Inflation rates have varied over time in each country and over countries at any moment of time. The challenge to the pure cost-push theorists is to account for the variations in the cost-push that caused the variations in inflation. Demand-pull theorists believe that these variations are largely related to variations in the pressure of demand. They therefore reject the pure wage-push model of post-1945 inflations as providing no alternative explanation of various observed inflation rates. They also maintain that the observed variations in inflation rates can be reasonably, if not perfectly, explained by variations in the pressure of demand.

Cost-push theory has from time to time been accepted as a possible explanation of UK inflation over the quarter century 1945–70. This has led to a number of experiments with incomes policies, varying in severity from mere guidelines to wage-price controls with sanctions for violation. Although there can never be finality in any assessment of empirical evidence, the many studies made have all assigned a very minor anti-inflationary influence to the incomes policies of the 1950s and 1960s. The influence seems to have ranged from an occasional high of 2 percentage points off the inflation rate to zero.

Mixed theories Many economists are attracted to a mixed theory that attributes a possible influence to all of the variables listed in the equation on page 765. There is no doubt statistically that inflation rates have varied with the pressure of demand. The inflation of 1973–4 was no exception; there was a substantial boom associated with a substantial rate of inflation. The boom is understated if one looks at unemployment as an index of pressure of demand, since the amount of unemployment consistent with Y_F has been drifting upwards in most countries since the late 1960s. The pressure of demand, however, cannot account for the 16 per cent UK inflation in 1974, its acceleration to 25 per cent in 1975 and its continuance in the mid-teens in 1976–7. A world recession set in during 1974, and by 1975 demand-pull and expectional inflations had begun to moderate in other countries.

Clearly, a major cause of British inflation in the mid-1970s was import-cost push. As a result of OPEC and a rise in other basic material prices, the index of British import prices, which had risen by just less than 5 per cent in 1971, rose by 27 per cent in 1973, 56 per cent in 1974 and 14 per cent in 1975. When it is imports of final goods that rise in price, the effect on the UK price level is immediate but when it is the prices of raw and semi-finished materials that rise in price, the effect may take up to 18 months to filter through completely onto the British price level.

The British inflation during the period seems to have been exacerbated by some substantial wage-push inflation. The first period in which a really strong case for an independent wage cost-push can be made is 1970. There was at that time a pay explosion that raised money wages by 6 to 8 per cent more than had previously been associated with the same excess-demand pressure. Even here, however, the situation is not entirely clear since the pay explosion followed the end of a period of incomes policy. Part of the explosion may have been a catching up with what had been held back in the past, and only part may have been an independant outburst of wage-cost push.

The period 1974–6 was one of heavy inflation. Many feel that union militancy was involved here. In the early part of this period wage increases were dominated by an agreement reached earlier between the government and the unions in an effort to control wage inflation. Wages were allowed to rise by the full amount of any rise in the cost-of-living index after the latter had passed a threshold rate of increase. The rapid rise in import prices caused the cost-of-living increase to go well beyond the threshold so that wages were then linked fully to the cost of living. This meant that when prices rose because of rapid increases in import prices, wages were automatically dragged up with them which then caused prices to rise even further.

This experience illustrates the hazards involved in indexing contracts to make their real values secure. This is a satisfactory hedge against inflation caused by domestic monetary expansion; in this case the real product available to be distributed is constant, and indexing prevents arbitrary redistributions of that product. When, however, the real terms of trade turn against a country, average living standards must fall. This is because out of a fixed GNP more must be exported to pay for the same amount of imports. The normal mechanism by which this fall in living standards is imposed is for prices to rise faster than wages and other incomes. But if everyone is indexed to prevent this, an explosive 'wage-price spiral' may be set off. This process was clearly operating in Britain, until the wage-price link was removed by the Labour government at the end of 1975.

There is some doubt in Britain about how much the expectational component contributed to inflation. Clearly it did not hold inflation at the disastrous rate of 25 per cent once the causes of that high rate were removed. The US experience is consistent with a large expectational component to inflation. Indeed, the US evidence is not inconsistent with the pure demand explanation that explains $\dot{P}$ fully by $F(Y - Y_F)$ and $\dot{P}_e$. This does not appear to be the case in Britain and the extent to which the various forces of demand pull, expectations and cost push contributed to the British inflation is the subject of substantial research and intense debate.

The monetarist debate

There is a group of economists called monetarists who have a particular diagnosis of inflation and unemployment that applies to all countries at all times. The group is a large one and includes many famous economists in every important country of the world. Their intellectual leader is the Nobel Prize-winning American economist Milton Friedman

Ranged against the monetarists are many groups. The most important anti-monetarist group in the US is composed of economists called neo-Keynesians. Their intellectual leader is James Tobin of Yale University. These neo-Keynesians accept the national income model given in this book, including the monetary restraint mechanism that brings inflations to a halt provided the nominal supply of money is held constant. The differences they have with the monetarists are largely about quantitative magnitudes.

Keynesians in the UK are a wide group, with many views that differ among themselves, but they are by and large *not* the same as neo-Keynesians in the US. Many British Keynesians deny the importance of money more or less completely. In the UK many Keynesians hold a wage-cost-push theory of the price level, while in the US most Keynesians are demand-pull theorists. In both countries the Keynesians tend to be sceptical of the economy's ability to produce full employment most of the time unaided, and they thus advocate active demand management. Many American Keynesians advocate free trade and flexible exchange rates; many British Keynesians advocate protecting local industries with tariffs and pegging the exchange rate by using a battery of exchange controls and trade barriers to maintain the fixed rate.

Our main purpose here is to examine the monetarist view of the economy and the debates that centre around it. We shall do this by studying the monetarist views of fluctuations that take the economy away from full employment and of inflation.

Causes of cyclical fluctuations

Monetarist views Monetarists hold that monetary causes are the major source of serious fluctuations in national income.[1] Monetarist research on the trade cycle has

[1] The view that fluctuations often have monetary causes is not new. The English economist R.G. Hawtrey, the Austrian Nobel laureate F.A. von Hayek, and the Swedish economist Knut Wicksell are prominent among those who earlier gave monetary factors an important role in their explanations of the turning points in cycles and/or the tendency for expansions and contractions, once begun, to become cumulative and self-reinforcing. Modern monetarists carry on this tradition.

been pursued most thoroughly in the United States. The modern interpretation of American trade cycles as having mainly monetary causes relies heavily on the evidence advanced by Milton Friedman and Anna Schwartz in their monumental *A Monetary History of the United States, 1867–1960*. They establish that there is a strong correlation between changes in the money supply and changes in the level of business activity. Major recessions are found to be associated with absolute declines in the money supply, and minor recessions with the slowing down of the rate of increase in the money supply below its long-term trend.

The correlation between changes in the money supply and changes in the level of business activity is now accepted by virtually all economists. But there is controversy over how it is to be interpreted: do changes in the money supply cause changes in the level of business activity, or vice versa?

Friedman and Schwartz argue that changes in the money supply cause changes in business activity – for example, that the severity of the Great Depression of the 1930s was due to a major contraction in the money supply. Their analysis runs along the following lines. The stock market crash of 1929, and other factors associated with a moderate downswing in business activity during the late 1920s, led to a reduction in the public's desire to hold demand deposits and an increase in its desire for cash. The banking system could not meet this increased demand for liquidity without help from the Federal Reserve System[1], which is the central bank of the United States. The Fed had been set up to provide just such emergency assistance to banks that were in a basically sound position but unable to meet sudden demands for cash on the part of their depositors. It refused, however, to extend the necessary help, and successive waves of bank failures followed as a direct result. During each wave, literally hundreds of banks failed, ruining many of their depositors and thereby making the already severe depression even worse. During the last half of 1931, for example, almost 2,000 American banks were forced to suspend operations! One consequence was a sharp drop in the money supply – by 1933 the mony supply was 35 per cent below the level of 1929.

For monetarists, fluctuations in the money supply cause fluctuations in national income; the money supply is exogenous.

Neo-Keynesian views Neo-Keynesians emphasize variations in investment as a cause of business cycles and stress non-monetary causes of these variations. Many pre-Keynesian economists had also taken this view.[2] There was an important difference, however: the theories developed by earlier economists were theories of alternating bouts of prosperity and depression. Economists who accepted such theories might or might not have believed that government policy could significantly shorten a period of depression, but they would almost certainly have believed that in the

[1] As we saw in Chapter 40 banks are never able to meet from their own reserves a sudden demand to withdraw currency on the part of a large fraction of their depositors. Their reserves are always inadequate to meet such a demand.

[2] Like the monetarists, the neo-Keynesians are modern advocates of some views that have a long history. The great Austrian (and later American) economist Joseph Schumpeter stressed such explanations early in the present century. The Swedish economist Wicksell and the German Speithoff both stressed this aspect of economic fluctuations before the emergence of the Keynesian school of thought.

absence of government intervention, the recovery and boom would almost inevitably follow the period of depression.

Underemployment equilibrium: What was new in Keynes's *General Theory* was the concept of UNDEREMPLOYMENT EQUILIBRIUM: the economy could come to rest with substantial unemployment and without any significant forces operating to push the economy back to full employment. This was more than a theory of cyclical alternations of prosperity and depression; it was a theory of the possibility of permanent (or at least very long-lived) depression.

A great deal of controversy did (and still does) go on about the sense in which we can speak of underemployment *equilibrium*. One of the simplest interpretations is given in the three paragraphs that follow.

The short-term equilibrium of the economy is at the level of income where withdrawals equal injections (or, as Keynes would have put it, where saving equals investment, since he worked with a one-withdrawal and one-injection model). In the face of any change in withdrawals or injections, the economy will move fairly quickly to a new equilibrium level of national income. Once there, however, national income will remain constant if withdrawals and injections do not change. This may well be at a level of income below the full-employment level.

If the economy comes to rest in a state of underemployment equilibrium, there will in fact be forces at work tending to move it back to full employment, but in practice these forces will be so weak and so slow-acting that they can be ignored.[1]

Since forces tending to move the economy back to full employment probably do exist, it might be more accurate to describe a state of underemployment as a state of *underemployment disequilibrium* that is slowly moving toward a full-employment equilibrium. But since these forces act very slowly, they are of little interest in the context of coping with a major depression and its accompanying massive unemployment. For all practical purposes we may regard a situation where desired expenditure equals income at less than full-employment income as a short-run equilibrum which can be changed only by a further shift of the expenditure function. Those who, in the 1930s, were content to wait for long-run forces to produce full employment without government intervention could have been confronted with Keynes famous words which he had in fact uttered earlier in another context: 'In the long run we are all dead'. Modern Keynesians might add that the Great Depression of the 1930s came to an abrupt end only after the Second World War forced the adoption of Keynesian remedies in the form of massive, deficit-financed government expenditures. They might well go on to conjecture that without these Keynesian remedies it might have taken another decade for full employment to have been produced by the economy's natural forces. Keynes did not, of course, hold that the economy would always settle in a position of underemployment equilibrium, only that it *could* settle there.

Modern neo-Keynesians use elaborations of the basic model of the circular flow of income developed by Keynes. They also accept the Keynesian views of the importance of such nonmonetary factors as new inventions and business confidence in explaining variations in investment. Although the idea of underemployment

[1] In Keynes's theory these forces would have been set in motion by a fall in the real wage rate, as prices fell more than wages. This would induce employers to hire more labour. Also, if the price level is flexible downwards, the monetary adjustment mechanism will shift the aggregate expenditure function upwards.

equilibrium has been muted somewhat, neo-Keynesians mostly accept the view that government action is called for when the economy shows signs of suffering from a persistent deflationary gap.

The role of money as a cause of fluctuations in national income: Neo-Keynesians reject what they regard as the extreme monetarist view that only money matters in explaining cyclical fluctuations. Many of them believe that both monetary and nonmonetary factors are important in explaining the behaviour of the economy. Although they accept that serious monetary mismanagement is one potential source of economic fluctuations, they do not believe that it is the only, or even the major, source of such fluctuations. Thus they must deny the monetary interpretation of trade cycle history given by Friedman and Schwartz. Let us see how the neo-Keynesians argue to this conclusion.

Neo-Keynesians accept the correlation between changes in the money supply and changes in the level of economic activity, but their explanation reverses the causality suggested by the monetarists. The neo-Keynesians argue that changes in the level of economic activity tend to cause changes in the money supply rather than vice versa. They offer several reasons, but only the most important one needs to be mentioned here.

Neo-Keynesians point out that from 1945 to the early 1970s most central banks tended to stabilize interest rates as the target variable of monetary policy. To do this they had to increase the money supply during upswings in the trade cycle and to decrease it during downswings. This created the positive correlation. The central bank follows this monetary policy when an expansion gets under way because the demand for money will tend to increase and, if there is no increase in the money supply, interest rates will rise. The Bank can prevent this rise in interest rates (by buying bonds offered for sale at current prices), but in so doing it will, as we saw in Chapter 40, increase banks' reserves and thereby inject new money into the economy. Similarly, in a contraction interest rates will tend to fall unless the Bank steps in and sells bonds to keep interest rates up. But this will decrease the money supply (see pages 600–2). Thus the money supply tends to be positively correlated with the cycle, but the direction of causation is the opposite from that given in the monetarist explanation.

For neo-Keynesians, fluctuations in national income cause fluctuations in the money supply; the money supply is endogenous.

This argument applies to relatively mild cyclical swings; many neo-Keynesians accept that major exogenous changes in the money supply can be the cause of changes in national income.

Control of cyclical fluctuations

Monetary versus fiscal policy Monetarists believe that national income can be influenced heavily by monetary policy but only lightly by fiscal policy. Keynsians believe that fiscal policy may be more potent than monetary policy. The disagreement turns on the empirical magnitudes of two relations that both groups accept as existing.

The first relation is the demand for money. Monetarists believe it to be interest-inelastic. Keynesians believe it to be interest-elastic, because money is highly substitutable for a whole range of short-term, interest-earning assets. An expansionary monetary policy creates an excess supply of money. Firms and households seek to buy bonds with their surplus money and this lowers the rate of interest. The rate falls until everyone is prepared to hold the enlarged supply of money. If the monetarists are right, this requires a large fall in the interest rate; if the Keynesians are right, only a small fall is necessary. A contractionary monetary policy creates excess demand by lowering the supply of money. Firms and households seek to restore their money balances by selling bonds and the rate of interest rises until everyone is satisfied to hold only the reduced money supply. If the monetarists are right, this requires a large rise in the interest rate; if the Keynesians are right, only a small rise is necessary.

The second relation is the aggregate expenditure function. A rise in the rate of interest shifts the aggregate expenditure shown in Figures 41.1, 41.2 and 41.3 downwards, while a fall shifts it upwards. Monetarists hold that aggregate expenditure is highly interest-elastic. Keynesians believe that aggregate expenditure is influenced mainly by sales, profits and expectations, but does not respond greatly to the rate of interest.

According to the monetarists, changes in the money supply cause large changes in interest rates which in turn cause large changes in aggregate expenditure. According to the Keynesians, changes in the money supply cause small changes in interest rates which in turn cause small or negligible changes in aggregate expenditure.

The same assumptions about elasticities cause monetarists and Keynesians to disagree over the potency of fiscal policy. An increase in government expenditure raises national income and creates excess demand for money, because of a rise in the quantity of transactions balances required. Firms and households seek to sell bonds in an attempt to augment their transactions balances. The rate of interest rises until everyone is content to hold the existing stock of money. The rise in the interest rate lowers private interest-sensitive expenditure. This is the crowding-out effect of expansionary fiscal policy. An exactly parallel analysis applies to a decline in government expenditure.

According to the monetarists, changes in government expenditure will induce large changes in interest rates which in turn cause large offsetting changes in private interest-sensitive expenditure, leaving a small net effect on aggregate demand. According to the Keynesians, changes in government expenditure cause only small changes in interest rates which in turn cause small or negligible offsetting changes in private expenditure.

Active versus passive stabilization policy Monetarists oppose an active stabilization policy for two reasons. First they hold that the economy is inherently self-regulating. Full employment is the norm and major prolonged departures are caused mainly by misguided government policies. For example, they argue that the depression of the 1930s was greatly prolonged by misguided contractionary monetary policies. They also argue that the severe recession of the last half of the 1970s was brought about by at least two policy errors. First there was the need to curb accelerating inflations that arose from the misguided policy of trying to push unemployment below its natural rate. Second, unemployment has been kept very high by over-generous unemployment benefits that encourages labour to remain voluntarily unemployed.

Their second reason for opposing an active stabilization policy follows from their belief that the money supply exerts its powerful effects on the economy with time lags that are long and that vary for reasons not yet fully understood. Thus, they argue that even the most enlightened attempt to use monetary policy as a short-run stabilizer may do more harm than good. By the time an anti-inflationary, contractionary policy begins to take hold, for example, the economy may already have turned into a downswing that will only be accentuated by the delayed effects of monetary policy. They also believe that central banks tend to over-react to changes in the economy, first indulging in too much monetary restraint and then panicking at the resulting recession and indulging in inordinate monetary expansion that soon causes a severe inflation.

Thus, monetarists feel that our ignorance of the behaviour of the economy, our knowledge of the behaviour of most central-bank decision-makers, and our knowledge of the potency of the money supply all lead to the conclusion that discretionary control over the money supply should be removed from central banks. The best results, they believe, would be obtained if the money supply were expanded at a constant rate year by year. The actual figure is itself subject to debate, but as a first approximation an expansion equal to the rate of growth of real national income is recommended. This would allow the money supply to expand to suit the needs of business as national income rose, but would eliminate the disturbing effects of large short-term variations in the quantity of money. They feel that their rule will put monetary policy in a neutral stance that will allow the economy's own self-regulatory powers to work, producing no more than relatively mild fluctuations around full-employment national income with neither serious inflations nor severe recessions.

In contrast to the monetarists, neo-Keynesians take the view that an active stabilization policy is not only possible but is also desirable. They hold that the economy's self-regulating mechanisms are weak and slow-acting. Thus they believe that in the absence of stabilization policy severe inflationary or deflationary gaps could persist for very long periods of time.

On stabilization policy they take a more eclectic view of monetary and fiscal policy than do the monetarists. They believe that monetary policy can influence national income by its effects on interest rates. They tend to deny, therefore, that there is serious conflict between monetary and fiscal policies; they see the policies rather as complements to each other.

Neo-Keynesians do tend, however, to place heavy emphasis on fiscal policy. They do this because they believe that monetary policy may be particularly weak in major depressions when it is particularly important to have some policy intervention. In addition they are disturbed by the uneven incidence of monetary policy. A restrictive monetary policy, for example, tends to hit particularly heavily at home-owners, small businesses, and rapidly expanding firms specializing in the production of new products. It is worth looking at each of these groups briefly.

When monetary restraints are applied, house building tends to be seriously affected because interest costs are such a major part of the total expense of purchasing a house. Thus, monetary policy hits at the home-owner, particularly at those home-owners with modest means who may find it most difficult to raise a mortgage in any case. Small firms tend to find more trouble in acquiring credit than do large firms. Thus, it might be argued, the continual use of monetary policy reinforces the already strong tendencies for large firms to dominate the economy. New products are often produced by a host of small, new, and rapidly expanding firms. Since costs of production must be met before goods are sold, rapidly expanding firms usually find themselves in constant need of more and more credit to meet the gap between paying their costs and receiving money from the sale of their goods. These new firms are the source of much economic growth, but they are just the firms who are hardest hit, and sometimes driven into insolvency, by restrictive monetary policies that make it impossible for them to obtain the credit that they need.

For all these reasons, neo-Keynesians call for an active stabilization policy with fiscal policy playing a major role and monetary policy playing, at most, a supporting part.

Inflation

The monetarist view of causes The monetarist model of inflation is a pure demand-pull model based on the expectations-augmented Phillips curve. Monetarists do not accept wage-cost push as an independent cause of inflation. The reasons for rejection vary, however, from economist to economist. The extreme version is that rational decision-taking among monopolistic unions and monopolistic employers would not lead to a wage-cost inflation. This theoretical assertion must be judged not proven at the moment.[1] The weaker strand in this argument is that wage-cost push does not in fact occur. On the one hand, monetarists argue that no one has produced persuasive evidence that wage-cost push really does exist and really does cause inflation. On the other hand, they point to the persuasive evidence that demand-pull inflations have often existed. With a few apparent exceptions their case is on strong grounds here. Although the issue is not fully settled, no one has produced persuasive evidence that there is a strong wage-cost push that is a major, let alone the only, influence on inflation all of the time. The frequency, and the extent, to which wage-cost push operates remains, however, a matter of serious debate.

British labour unions are very much stronger, both economically and politically, than American unions. It is quite possible, therefore, that the cost-push is less strong in America than in the UK and that is why a much higher proportion of American economists reject wage-cost push theories of inflation than do British economists.

> **Monetarists hold that all inflations are caused by current excess demand or by expectations of inflation based on past actual demand-pull inflations.**

What causes the aggregate expenditure function to shift upwards, creating an inflationary gap and a demand-pull inflation? Monetarists are inclined to say that 'inflation is everywhere and always a monetary phenomenon'. Some monetarists take this to mean that inflation always has monetary causes. A classic case would occur if the government financed an increase in expenditure by selling bonds to the

[1] The assertion is based on the assumption that a general equilibrium model of the economy that included the various forms of union-wage bargaining we find in the world would have an equilibrium that (i) exists, (ii) is unique and (iii) is stable. (If it were not stable the wage bargaining process could lead the economy away on a divergent path.) Since no one has shown for such a non-competitive economy the existence of an equilibrium having these properties, the assertion that it does exist, and has the required properties, is only conjecture.

central bank, thus causing an increase in the money supply. It is clear, however, that a rise in the price level can occur if the money supply is constant. On page 750 we saw a rise in expenditure causing the price level to rise. On page 764 we saw wage-cost push raising the price level. To preserve their position monetarists have re-defined inflation to be a sustained increase in the price level. On the surface 'sustained' appears undefined. Careful study, however, reveals that *sustained* means 'for so long a time that it could not have continued if the nominal money supply had not been increased'. This, however, makes the proposition 'a necessary and sufficient condition for inflation is an increase in the money supply into a definitional tautology.

It is clear that a temporary inflation or, in monetarist terminology, a rise in the price level, can occur for all sorts of reasons not related to an increase in the money supply. All standard models predict this. It is also clear, however, that unless the money supply is increased, inflations will first eliminate the inflationary gap and, if they persist, will then cause continually falling output and continually rising unemployment.

The neo-Keynesian view of causes Whereas extreme monetarists hold that inflation is *always* a monetary phenomenon, neo-Keynesians hold that non-monetary factors can cause substantial inflations such as those experienced in the 1960s and early 1970s in North American and western European countries. A prime example would be an investment boom caused by the opening up of major new investment opportunities. Neo-Keynesians agree that such inflations cannot go on indefinitely unless 'validated' by monetary expansions, but they are inclined to stress two further points. First, such inflations may go on for quite a long time even if there is no monetary expansion. Second, the necessary monetary expansion may occur for quite a while *as a response* of the banking system to the heavy demand.

The balance between the views On the causes of inflation there is really little more than a difference of emphasis between monetarists and those neo-Keynesians who accept the demand-pull theory of inflation. Both agree that a non-validated rise in the price level will reduce national income. Both agree that a continuing inflation not accompanied by falling real income and rising unemployment requires monetary validation. Both agree that increases in the money supply can be an initiating cause of inflation. Both agree that inflation can be caused by other factors, such as a rise in private expenditure, and can continue if the central bank validates it in an effort to avoid the fall in national income that would otherwise result. Keynesians are more inclined than monetarists to believe that inflations occur for the last reason stated. Monetarists are more inclined than neo-Keynesians to believe that inflations are caused by monetary expansions, but this *is* little more than a difference in judgement over the facts of particular inflations.

Keynesians who accept cost push as an important cause of inflation differ sharply from the monetarists. They believe that wage-cost push by unions can be an important cause of inflation. They accept that if not validated by increases in the money supply, cost-push inflations will lead to declining income and rising unemployment. Some hold, however, that the validation is automatic, since the central bank cannot control the money supply. Others hold that although the validation is a policy decision by the bank, there is no question that the causal sequence runs from union behaviour to the price level to induced increases in the money supply by the Bank. This reverses the causal sequence as seen by the monetarists, which runs from monetary increases to expenditure increases to inflation of prices and wages.

Virtually all economists accept that an unvalidated inflation will cause the aggregate expenditure function to shift downwards. This is the common agreement among all mainstream economic theories and models. The difference between monetarists and the others is in the policy relevance of this proposition.

Extreme Keynesians like Nicholas Kaldor of Cambridge University argue that the central bank cannot control the money supply. They see the supply as being essentially demand-determined. If the central bank did decide to try to control inflation by squeezing the money supply, new money substitutes would be invented. At least in the short-period, this view encounters a number of problems. First, inflations due to excess money have occurred, particularly after the Second World War, and these came to a halt when the real money supply was reduced to its pre-war levels. Apparently the monetary adjustment mechanism did work to halt the inflations then. Secondly, if there is no real constraint on the money supply, why does it not grow without limit and why does it grow fast sometimes and slow at other times? Finally, during the 1970s central banks throughout the world became converted to the view that the money supply was an important determinant of the rate of inflation. Bank after bank announced targets for monetary growth rates, and they have had remarkable success in meeting these.

Controversies over the monetarist view of inflation control Monetarists believe that the operation of the monetary constraint is necessary and sufficient to stop any existing inflation. To monetarists, therefore, the control of inflation is a relatively simple matter. The central bank must hold the nominal money supply constant (or, if Y_F is itself growing, the Bank must let the money supply grow at the same rate as Y_F grows). The monetary constraint will then reduce aggregate expenditure; this will reduce equilibrium income and when Y falls to Y_F any demand-pull causes of inflation will be removed; the remaining expectational inflation, given a persistent mild recession, will sooner or later be eliminated.

> **The critical policy recommendation of the monetarists is that control of the nominal money supply is necessary and sufficient to control inflation.**

The reforms of 1971 (see page 603) make controlling the money supply somewhat harder for the Bank of England than it is for other central banks whose reserve base is a cash base, but even the Bank of England has been moderately successful in meeting its money supply targets. It may be that in the longer run money substitutes will grow up, but at least over a period of a decade control of the money supply seems possible.

Some monetarists argue that the Bank will not control the money supply because of a conflict between its monetary-control and its support functions. In pursuit of the latter it has to prevent rapid changes in interest rates. There are several theoretical links in this reasoning, but we shall not lay them down here since the view does not seem to have stood up. Certainly in pursuit of its support function the Bank of England, along with other central banks, once took as one of its main policy objects either to fix, or at least to slow down the rate of change of the interest rate (see page 598). When banks set monetary targets in the 1970s, however, they seem to have been able to meet them without doing things inconsistent with their support function. (What the support function seems to dictate is that the monetary levers be changed gradually rather than abruptly since very abrupt changes can severely upset money markets.)

Some Keynesians have argued that wage-cost push means that attempts to control inflation by controlling the money supply will lead to recessions and to levels and durations of unemployment that are politically quite unacceptable. This is one of the main battlegrounds between the monetarists and their opponents, so we will devote some time to it.

There is no doubt that the monetarists case is much stronger if all inflations are demand inflations. Everyone agrees that an inflation acting on a fixed nominal money supply will lower the real money supply and thus lower aggregate expenditure, therefore eliminating the excess demand.

But what if the inflation is due to wage-cost push? If the authorities hold the nominal money supply constant in the face of a wage-cost-push inflation, the monetary adjustment mechanism will reduce aggregate real expenditure. National income will fall and unemployment will rise. This will continue as long as the wage-cost-push inflation lasts. At some point, presumably, labour will become more concerned about growing unemployment than about obtaining higher wages for those who are employed. Also, as sales fall and profits turn into losses, firms may become more resistant to the wage push. But this is not guaranteed and it may not come until unemployment reaches 10, 15 or 20 per cent. No government could accept such figures politically; long before they were reached, goes the anti-monetarist argument, the government would have to adopt an expansive monetary policy. It would then validate the inflation and prevent further downward shifts in the expenditure function.

We saw on pages 781–2 that monetarists have three lines of defence against this argument. First, they argue that wage-cost push is irrational. Rational unions out to maximize the incomes of their members will seek to get the best wage they can relative to the price of the product they help to make, but this behaviour will not lead to an explosive wage push. Second, they argue that, according to the empirical evidence, wage push does not in fact happen. Third, they point out that even if wage push occurs, holding the nominal money supply constant must eventually stop the inflation.

Thus the monetarist view is that a viable cure for inflation is to reduce the rate of expansion of the real money supply and let the monetary adjustment mechanism bring the inflation to a halt. But what if the inflation comes to a halt with substantial unemployment such as Y_1 in Figure 49.1 on page 749. Some monetarists then define Y_1 as the natural rate of unemployment and say that union activity causes the natural rate to be higher than it would otherwise be. But we do not wish to define away a real problem. It is clear that wage-cost push, if it exists and if it is combined with a constant nominal money supply may lead to equilibrium but at a much higher level of unemployment than would exist if wage pushes were absent.

Monetarists seek to control inflation solely by controlling the money supply. Neo-Keynesians seek to control inflation by use of monetary and fiscal policy to prevent the emergence of inflationary gaps, by temporary wage-price controls to stop an entrenched expectational inflation and (for those who accept an independant wage-cost push) by incomes policies to reduce cost-push forces. The stress that they put on each policy differs according to the importance that they place on each of the possible causes of inflation.

Further instruments for lowering unemployment

Everyone, including those who hold that recent inflations have all been cost-push, agrees that demand inflations can occur. Thus, everyone agrees that national income cannot be held above Y_F indefinitely without causing inflation. The goal of stable prices thus requires that the maximum target for national income be set at Y_F. The amount of unemployment occurring at Y_F is often referred to as the natural rate of unemployment. This is a misleading term insofar as it implies that this unemployment is unavoidable. There is nothing inevitable about the unemployment that occurs at full-employment income; it occurs for frictional and structural causes. This unemployment can be reduced by measures that speed up the reallocation of labour among geographical regions, skill categories, industries and occupations.

There seems to be some evidence that the natural rate of unemployment has been rising in many countries since the late 1960s. If so, then even pure demand-pull theorists will be led to look for instruments other than demand management to lower the level of unemployment from undesirably high rates.

Causes of structural unemployment

Structural unemployment, as we saw in Chapter 48, is related to growth and change in the economy. These factors can cause dramatic changes in the structure of output over time. But the changes in employment may be even more dramatic. As long as an industry's income elasticity of demand exceeds zero (i.e., as long as the commodity is not an inferior good), output will rise as economic growth proceeds. Employment, however, will not increase unless demand expands *faster than output per manhour*. An industry in which productivity is growing at 3 per cent per year and in which demand is growing at 2 per cent per year will be an expanding industry in terms of output but a declining industry in terms of employment. The displaced worker sees that change (or growth) has destroyed his job, and he is likely to conclude that growth destroys jobs in general and thus creates unemployment in the economy. But this, of course, is not the case if labour let go in one sector of the economy finds employment in another. Few people remain permanently unemployed when they lose a job. Thus the genuine fear should be about the sometimes very heavy short-term costs of moving from one job to another, not about the possibility of there being no jobs at all. Of course, movements of labour may be both slow and costly. How much of the economy's apparent gains in output due to growth would be lost if the costs of transitional unemployment were accounted for is an important empirical question.

Moreover, these costs are borne unequally by members of society. The cost to those with heavy investments in education and experience in particular occupations can be enormous. A man of forty-five or fifty whose skills are special to a declining industry may, should he lose his job, find the market value of his services cut drastically. Just as the machine that was built to produce a product no one now wants is worthless, so the human capital investment in skills no longer required is worthless. Further, if the declining industry is a major part of the economy of a particular geographical area, the whole area may be a declining one, and all of its residents may suffer because of the decline in demand for all goods and services in this area. Because of this, the unemployed man who wishes to move to an area where jobs are plentiful may be unable to sell his house for anything near its replacement cost in a growing area. He thus will not be in a postion to buy anything like a comparable house in a new area. The costs of growth and change are borne by a small section of the society, and although they may seem small in the aggregate, they are very serious to those who bear them.

The long-run evidence about structural unemployment

Every major innovation and every major depression since the Industrial Revolution has rekindled the fear of steadily shrinking employment opportunities. Two pieces of evidence are unmistakable: (1) that in all growing Western economies over the last century, lapses from full employment have been temporary; and (2) that there has been no long-term tendency for average levels of unemployment to rise over the decades in spite of prolonged periods of sustained growth.

One modern argument for rising structural unemployment is based on the view that the quality of technological innovation has changed. In the first Industrial Revolution, technology destroyed the jobs of skilled artisans by inventing machines to do the work and created jobs for unskilled workers who could operate the machines. In other words, formerly skilled jobs were broken up into a series of unskilled ones to be done by men and machines. Although the artisan might suffer a reduction in real income, he was not lacking in employment opportunities since he was always capable of performing one of the unskilled tasks on the machines. The new Industrial Revolution, automation, the argument continues, has reversed the technological trend. Now the production process is being reintegrated. The machine in the automated factory now performs all the unskilled tasks, and only a few highly skilled people are necessary to operate the machine and repair it when trouble develops. Thus it is the unskilled who suffer from modern technological advance, and they cannot step into the new jobs without long preparation. Modern technological advance is thus destroying the jobs of the unskilled and not replacing them with other accessible jobs. At the very best, therefore, we would expect to find a rising number of (mainly unskilled) persons unemployed for long periods of time; at worst, there may be a rising number of persons who can never acquire the skills necessary to fit into the new industrial process.

There is no question that the demand for unskilled labour has been shrinking. The theory of competitive price determination predicts that this should lead to a substantial fall in the wages earned by the unskilled. We know, however, that there is downward rigidity in wage rates, because unions and such things as minimum-wage laws prevent wages from falling nearly as much as they would in a wholly free market. In the face of this wage rigidity, the theory predicts an excess supply of labour – in other words, unemployment.

If the labour supply responds to the probability of getting jobs, as well as to the wage rate earned by those who do get jobs, we would expect a leftward shift in the supply curve for unskilled labour. A sophisticated version of the hypothesis of increasing structural unemployment is, then, that the demand curve for unskilled labour is shifting to the left faster than is the supply curve, so that at more or less constant wages the gap between supply and demand has been increasing. We must now wonder how this hypothesis fits the facts.

The first fact is that, decade by decade, the education and training of the labour force has been increasing.[1] There as yet is no solid evidence of any growing gap between the skills demanded by industry and the training provided by educational institutions and firms. Recent trends of rising unemployment among the young and unskilled are however causing worries that such a gap may be developing. Second, much of the increase in demand for labour is coming in the service sectors that do not require a highly skilled labour force. Thus, although it may be very depressing to contemplate a fully automated manufacturing plant and wonder how to create jobs for the displaced unskilled workers by inducing further increases in demand for the output of the automated plant, it becomes somewhat less depressing if one realizes that a large fraction of any increment in demand will fall on service industries in which there are still many employment opportunities for the unskilled and semi-skilled. Third, the evidence on retraining programmes, both within industry and outside, seems to suggest that many of those displaced can be fitted to new employment.

Another cause of structural unemployment can be the failure of industry to adapt to changing circumstances. Sometimes management may be insufficiently progressive. Sometimes unions may not permit the introduction of cost-saving techniques, because they fear their members will become *redundant* and thus lose their jobs. Many unions seek to protect the jobs of their members by resisting the implementation of new labour-saving machinery or accepting it only if it is manned by more labour than necessary – which is referred to as a *restrictive manning agreement*. If unions in other countries do not do the same, domestic firms will lose out to foreign competitors. When the firms decline or go into liquidation, workers lose their jobs and may join the ranks of the long-term unemployed.

Restrictive policies designed to prevent loss of some jobs through redundancy can end up destroying far more jobs due to structural unemployment.

Paradoxically, in countries where unions accept redundancy and do not resist innovation the level of unemployment may be lower because technologically dynamic, expanding industries create new jobs to replace old ones destroyed by technological advances. Certainly there is no evidence that over the decades the average level of unemployment has been lower in the UK, where unions have been more successful in resisting the redundancy caused by technological change than in France and Germany, where the amount of labour used per unit of output has fallen faster due to rapid rates of innovation.

Demand management and structural unemployment

Demand management provides no cure for structural unemployment. Raising aggregate demand will cure unemployment only if there are unemployed supplies of all resources that only lack demand for their potential outputs to put them to work. If firms and their capital no longer exist, unemployed labour will not be put to work merely because people have more money to spend.

[1] One must wonder if the current breakdown in the schools and the admitted failure of the Victorian programme to make everyone literate and numerate may lead to an *increase* in the supply of unskilled workers over the next decade in the face of a continuing fall in demand.

Demand management can cure deficient demand unemployment, but will not reduce structural unemployment.

Economic theory predicts that to the extent that the rising unemployment in the UK and elsewhere is structural, an attempt to cure it by raising demand will only cause an inflation without reducing the unemployment. Insofar as the unemployment is structural, therefore, the failure of demand management to cure it does not indicate a failure of economic theory. The best that demand management can do is to raise national income to its full capacity level (i.e., make Y equal to Y_F) but it cannot lower the amount of unemployment that is associated with Y_F – i.e., frictional and structural unemployment.

An attempt to arrest rising structural unemployment by increasing aggregate expenditure will only lead to an inflation accompanying the rising level of unemployment.

The composition of macro variables

We have seen that macroeconomic policy is concerned with the behaviour of key averages and aggregates such as the average level of all price and overall level of unemployment. In fact, we care about more than just these averages and aggregates. We also care about their composition. Is the overall level of unemployment made up of very unequal rates of unemployment such as those among industries, occupations or areas, or is it made up of rates that are very similar across all of these classifications? We would assess a 6 per cent overall unemployment rate in the UK very differently if it resulted from 6 per cent unemployment in all industries, occupations and geographical areas than if it resulted from 15 per cent unemployment in some areas and only 1 or 2 per cent in others.

Levels of unemployment of 15 or 20 per cent are very serious matters, indeed. They imply a level of social and personal upheaval that just does not accompany rates of the order of 4 or 5 per cent. The degree of regional and occupational inequality in unemployment rates in both the UK and the US has remained quite high throughout the whole postwar period. Clearly although policy-makers could be satisfied that the overall rate in Britain was held at a very low level from 1945 until the mid 1970s, there was always reason to be disturbed at the high rates that persisted in some places.

Why did these localized high rates occur – why is it that in the midst of the 'fully employed' society we had these persistent pockets of poverty that would not respond to the cure of raising aggregate expenditure? Why does the market not adjust to bring about approximate equality in unemployment rates? Shouldn't regions and occupations with excess supplies of labour find their relative wages declining so that there is an incentive to employers to demand more of the relatively cheap labour and for suppliers to move to higher wage markets? Does this market mechanism work at all? How fast does it work? Does the shifting pattern of economic growth continue to disturb markets so that the adjustment mechanism can never catch up? Would things be better if we interfered more in the market mechanism? What government policies would reduce these labour-market disequilibria? Would things be better if we interfered less with the market mechanism? How much do restrictive practices, union manning agreements and resistance to the introduction of new technologies contribute to structural unemployment?

A similar set of 'disaggregated observations' could be produced for any macro variable, and they would provide a similar set of questions. But to state just one set is enough to show that we have now gone full circle and are back at the *micro*-economics with which we began our study. To tackle these problems, we need to return to market theory, the study of which we began in Part 2.

There is no sharp distinction between micro- and macroeconomics. There are merely higher and lower levels of aggregation and a series of questions appropriate to each level of aggregation, with each series shading one into the other.

The progress of economics

The operation of scientific method is not a simple matter in economics. We lack laboratory conditions. We cannot get the holders of opposing views to agree on critical tests and then repeat them over and over until everyone must agree on the results. The call that economics try to be a science is a plea that economists try to relate their theories to observations. If we hold that the truth of economic theories is totally independent of successful empirical applications, it is difficult to see how economics can claim to be in any way useful in interpreting the world around us.

In economics, general acceptance that theories should be tested by confronting their predictions with the available evidence is fairly new. At this point you should re-read the quotation from Lord Beveridge given at the beginning of this book (see pages xi and xii). The controversy that Beveridge was describing was the one that followed the publication in 1936 of Keynes' *General Theory of Employment, Interest and Money*. Keynes' work gave rise to the macroeconomics that we have developed in Part 7 and on which we have so often relied in subsequent parts. At many points in the present book, we have raised the question of how various parts of macroeconomic theory could be tested; we have also discussed some of the tests that have already been conducted. Reflect on the differences between this approach to the problem of accepting or rejecting theories and the one described by Beveridge.

There is no doubt that since economics first began some progress, albeit irregular and halting, has been made in relating theory to evidence. This progress has been reflected in the superior ability of governments to achieve their policy objectives. The pathetic efforts of successive British governments to deal with the economic catastrophe that overwhelmed the country after the return to the gold standard in the 1920s and even more so during the Great Depression of the 1930s show measures adopted in all sincerity which in most cases actually served to make things worse. Across the Atlantic President Roosevelt's attempts to reduce American unemployment in the same decade were greatly hampered by the failure of most economists to realize the critical importance of budget deficits in increasing aggregate demand and hence national income. The contrast between the unhappy 1930s and the present period is great. When President Kennedy wished to do something about the high levels of unemployment in the 1960s his main problem was to persuade the American Congress to adopt what most economists agreed was an appropriate cure – a tax cut; in 1964, when President Johnson finally persuaded Congress to accept the tax cut, the ensuing rise in output and employment was very close to what the economists had predicted. Several times during the 1950s and 1960s successive British governments have altered the Budget in pursuit of a 'stop' or a 'go' policy. Many economists are critical of the motives behind these policy oscillations, but the fact that each time the economy moved in the direction predicted by economic theory is evidence that we have learned a great deal in the last 40 years.

It is in such important policy areas as the curing of major depressions and the handling of major inflations that the general thrust of our theories is tested, even if all their specific predictions are not. In some general sense, then, economic theories have always been subjected to empirical tests. When they were wildly at variance with the facts, the ensuing disaster could not but be noticed, and the theories were discarded or amended in the light of what was learned.[1]

The debate between monetarists and neo-Keynesians, particularly as it has proceeded in the US, is another illustration of the value of the rule of evidence. Monetarists have several times had to revise their positions in the face of evidence. For example, they no longer hold that the demand for money is completely interest-inelastic, nor that fiscal policy cannot affect aggregate expenditure. Emotionally committed monetarists and neo-Keynesians will never abandon their basic positions, but through the testing of their specific positions those who have open minds really do learn about the behaviour of the economy.

What we do not know covers vast areas, which should give all economists a sense of humility. But those who feel that we know nothing need only involve themselves in a policy-making situation with non-economists to lose some of their feelings of inferiority. First, we really do know positive things about the behaviour of the economy that help us to evaluate policy choices. Second, we have a method of looking at problems that is potentially enlightening to almost any problem whether or not it is conventionally described as economic.

The advance of economics in the last 40 years partly reflects a change in economists' attitudes towards empirical observation. Today, we are much less likely to dismiss theories just because we do not like them and to refuse to abandon theories just because we do like them. Today, we are more likely to try to base our theories as much as possible on empirical observation, and to accept empirical relevance as the ultimate arbiter of the value of those theories. As human beings, we suffer much anguish at the upsetting of a pet theory; as scientists, we should try to train ourselves to take pleasure in it because of the new knowledge we gain thereby. It has been said that one of the great tragedies of science is the continual slaying of beautiful theories by ugly facts. As economists, we are all too often swayed by aesthetic considerations. In the past, we have too often clung to our theories because they were beautiful or because we liked their political implications; as scientists, we must always remember that when theory and fact come into serious conflict, it is theory, not fact, that must eventually give way.

[1] The discussion on pages xx and xxi of Lord Beveridge's quotation is also relevant here.

Index

mini MNE

>>Cultural Habits Spread: In Vino, India?

The next big Indian export may be not computer chips but something a bit stronger. More precisely, wine in Mahaharashtra. In parts of this west Indian state, conditions for grape growing mimic those of other grape-growing regions of the world, so a domestic wine industry has sprung up. Well, conditions aren't exactly right—it is too hot for the best conditions—so the grape-growing season is in the winter. Sula Vineyards, started by a software engineer with Oracle in Silicon Valley, has brought in eight harvests and is producing over a million bottles of wine. Sula wines are already being exported, mainly to Indian restaurants abroad. But so far it and most other Indian wines are mostly for domestic consumption because there is an Indian tariff of 264 percent on foreign wine imports. Thus, foreign winemakers are coming to the area—Seagram started producing wine in the same area in 2005.

Will other cultures be making incursions against French winemakers? Mexico is better known for tequila, but seven states already make wine, and the first official winery in the Western Hemisphere was in Mexico. Mexican wineries tend to take their inspiration more from European than Californian wines. And the Chilean reputation for wine is actually quite solid. Australia is also a large producer. So the answer is yes.

Source: Higo Restall, "Indo Vino Nouveau," *The Wall Street Journal*, May 17, 2006, p. D14: "Vino Mex," http://mexicanwines.homestead.com (June 27, 2006).

Americans, Be Prompt If an appointment is made to see a group of Germans at 12 noon, we can be sure they will be there, but to get the same response from Brazilians, we must say "noon English hour." If not, the Brazilians may show up anytime between noon and 2 o'clock.

Should Americans follow the local custom or be prompt? It depends. In Spain, a general rule is to never be punctual. If you are, you will be considered early. However, in the Middle East, the American penchant for punctuality is well known and lateness by Americans is considered impolite. The Arabian executives, nonetheless, usually will not arrive at the appointed hour; why should they change their lifetime habits for a stranger?

Mañana Some visitors to Latin American are puzzled by the term *mañana*. The literal translation is "tomorrow," but it really means "in the near future." This example illustrates that the ability to speak the local language is only half the task of communicating. A manager of an American subsidiary in Saudi Arabia says, "You can be talking the same language with someone, but are you talking on the same wavelength?" He states that he has met few Japanese or Koreans fluent in Arabic, yet they are able to understand and adapt to local conditions much better than Westerners can because they seem to be more sensitive to the Middle Easterner's mentality.[19]

Adios, Siesta The revered three-hour siesta has disappeared from Mexico. In 1999 the federal government began requiring that most public employees, from clerks to cabinet ministers, begin work at 9 A.M. and leave work at 6 P.M., and instead of three hours for lunch, they now have only one hour. To be sure that people leave at 6 P.M. and not at 8 P.M., the lights and air-conditioning are turned off at 6 P.M. sharp. One result of this change is that people are finding that much work is being done before noon, a rarity under the old schedule. Since people are no longer drowsy in the afternoon as a result of the banquet they used to eat at lunchtime, they now tend to make decisions in the afternoon instead of waiting until the evening.[20]

In Spain the three-hour siesta is less common in the big cities. Spain's growing economy has allowed young people to move to the suburbs, but this has created longer commutes, making it more difficult to dash home for a siesta. A survey taken by a Spanish mattress company found that only 25 percent of all Spaniards surveyed still take a siesta and few people actually get into bed anymore. The company's marketing director claimed, "The siesta is nothing more than a cliché for most working people in Spain. They don't have time for it."[21] But this may not be true for areas outside the larger cities.

Directness American directness and drive are interpreted by many foreigners as brash and rude. Americans want to get to the point in a discussion, and this attitude often irritates others. Formalities help establish amicable relations, which are considered in many countries to be a necessary prerequisite to business discussions. Any attempt to move the negotiations along by ignoring the accepted courtesies invites disaster.

Deadlines Western emphasis on speed and deadlines may also be a liability abroad. In Far Eastern countries such as Japan, an American may be asked how long he or she plans to stay at the first meeting. Then negotiations are purposely not finalized until a few hours before the American's departure, when the Japanese know they can wring extra concessions from the foreigner because of his or her haste to finish and return home on schedule.

Three Americans, none of whom had ever been to Japan, went to sell tractors to Japanese buyers. They thought the discussions had gone well and prepared to wrap up the deal. However, there was no reaction from the Japanese. The silence became disquieting, and so the Americans lowered the price. Because there was still no reaction, they again lowered the price. This went on until their price was far lower than they had planned. What they didn't know was that the Japanese had become silent not to indicate rejection of the proposition but merely to think it over, a customary Japanese negotiating practice.[22]

ATTITUDES TOWARD ACHIEVEMENT AND WORK

"Germans put leisure first and work second," says a German-born woman now living in the United States. "In America, it's the other way around."

Angela Clark was born in Germany but now works for JCPenney as a merchandising manager in Washington, D.C. Andreas Drauschke has a comparable job for comparable pay in Berlin. There is no comparison, however, in the hours each works. Drauschke works a 37-hour week, with a six-week annual vacation. Clark works a minimum of 44 hours a week, including evenings and often Saturdays and Sundays. She brings work home and never takes more than one week's vacation at a time. "If I took any more, I'd feel like I was losing control," she says.[23]

demonstration effect
Result of having seen others with desirable goods

To the consternation of expatriate managers, the promise of overtime may fail to keep workers on the job. In fact, raising employees' salaries can actually result in their working less (economists call this effect the "backward-bending" labor supply curve). But it is important to note that another change has occurred repeatedly in developing countries as more consumer goods have become available. The **demonstration effect** (seeing others with these goods) and improvements in infrastructure (roads to bring the products to consumers and electric power to operate the products) cause workers to realize they can have greater prestige and pleasure by owning more goods. Thus, their attitude toward work changes not because of any alteration of their moral or religious values but because they now want what only money can buy.

A Mexican distributor once complained that many of his salesmen were producing well for the first week or two of the month but were then slacking off. Investigation showed that the commissions plus salary earned during the periods of high production were about the same each time. It was apparent that the salesmen had earned what they required to live, so they could loaf the rest of the month. By instituting contests and informing the salesmen's wives about the prizes to be won, the company obtained considerable improvement.

In the industrialized nations, trends are generally downward. After peaking at 43.3 hours per week in 1994, the U.S. weekly average for production workers had already dropped to 42.6 hours by 1996. The 1996 averages for Germany and France were 39.0 and 38.3 hours, respectively (France and Germany officially have a 35-hour workweek). Even in Japan the weekly average, which reached 43 hours in 1988, fell to 39.5 hours in 1996. In fact, by 2001 Japanese workers were putting in nearly 25 hours less per month than their counterparts in 1988.[24]

Job Prestige Another aspect of the attitude toward work is the prestige associated with certain kinds of employment. The distinction between blue-collar workers and office employees is especially great, as typified by the use of two words in Spanish for the worker—*obrero* (one who labors) signifies a blue-collar worker, whereas an office worker is an *empleado* (employee).[25]

Religion

Religion, an important component of culture, is responsible for many of the attitudes and beliefs affecting human behavior. A knowledge of the basic tenets of some of the more popular religions will contribute to a better understanding of why people's attitudes vary so greatly from country to country. Figure 6.1 presents a map of the major religions of the world.

WORK ETHIC

We have already mentioned differences in attitudes toward work. Europeans and Americans are believed to view work as a moral virtue and look unfavorably on the idle. This view may stem in part from the **Protestant work ethic** as expressed by Luther and Calvin, who believed it was one's duty to glorify God by hard work and the practice of thrift.

Protestant work ethic
Duty to glorify God by hard work and the practice of thrift

In Asian countries where Confucianism is strong, the same attitude toward work is called the **Confucian work ethic**. As mentioned, because of other factors—such as a growing feeling of prosperity and a shift to a five-day workweek (with two days off, workers develop new interests)—Japanese employers are finding that younger workers may not have the same dedication to their jobs as their predecessors had. Workers rarely show up early to warm the oil in their machines before work starts, and some management trainees are actually taking all of their vacation time. A recent college graduate claims, "Students ski in the winter and play tennis in the summer. What the companies sometimes find out is that some new employees like skiing better than working."[26]

Confucian work ethic
Drive toward hard work and thrift; similar to Protestant work ethic

ASIAN RELIGIONS

People from the Western world will encounter some very different notions about God, people, and reality in **Asian religions.** In the Judeo-Christian tradition, this world is real and significant because it was created by God. Human beings are likewise significant; so is time, because it began with God's creation and will end when His will has been fulfilled. Each human being has only one lifetime to heed God's word and achieve everlasting life.

Asian religions
Primary ones: Hinduism, Buddhism, Jainism, and Sikhism (India); Confucianism and Taoism (China); and Shintoism (Japan)

In the religions of India, there is a notion that this world is an illusion because nothing is permanent. Time is cyclical, and so all living things, including humans, are in a constant process of birth, death, and reincarnation. The goal of salvation is to escape from the cycle and move into a state of eternal bliss *(nirvana)*. The notion of *karma* (moral retribution) holds

"The Protestant work ethic isn't cutting it, so we're switching to Shinto."

Source: From *The Wall Street Journal*—Permission, Cartoon Features Syndicate.

FIGURE 6.1 World Religions

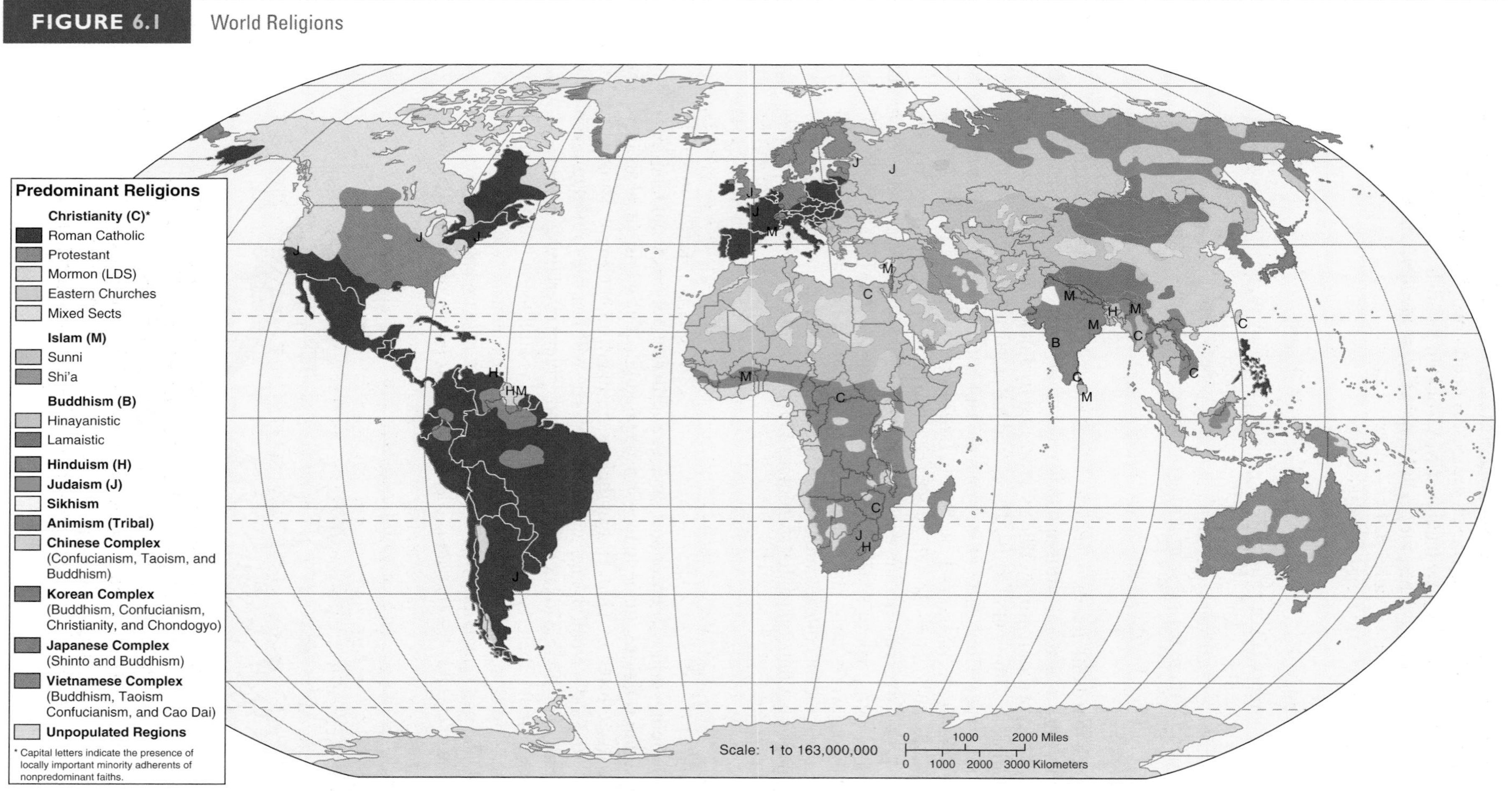

Source: Map 18, "World Religions," *Student Atlas of World Geography,* 3rd ed., by John L. Allen. Copyright 2003: The McGraw-Hill Companies, Inc.

that evil committed in one lifetime will be punished in the next. Thus, *karma* is a powerful impetus to do good so as to achieve a higher spiritual status in the next life. Asians who hold these views cannot imagine that they have not had past lives in which they may have been plants, animals, or human beings. Of the seven best-known religions that originated in Asia, four came from India (Hinduism, Buddhism, Jainism, and Sikhism), two from China (Confucianism and Taoism), and one from Japan (Shintoism).

Hinduism Hinduism does not have a single founder or a central authority but is practiced by more than 80 percent of India's population. Although there is great diversity among regions and social classes, Hinduism has certain characteristic features. Most Hindus believe that everything in the world is subject to an eternal process of death and rebirth *(samsura)* and that individual souls *(atmans)* migrate from one body to another. They believe one can be liberated from the samsura cycle and achieve eternal bliss *(nirvana)* through (1) yoga (purification of mind and body), (2) devout worship of the gods, or (3) good works and obedience to the laws and customs *(dharmas)* of one's caste.

A knowledge of the **caste system** is important to managers because the castes are the basis of the social division of labor. The highest caste, the Brahmins or priesthood, is followed by the warriors (politicians, landowners), the merchants, the peasants, and the *dalits,* a Hindi word meaning "downtrodden" or "oppressed" that has replaced *untouchables.*[27] An individual's position in a caste is inherited, as is that person's job within the caste, and movement to a higher caste can be made only in subsequent lives. Although the government of India has outlawed discrimination based on the caste system and has worked to improve the situation of those in the lower castes, such discrimination still exists. Indian newspapers usually carry a classified section for those seeking marriage partners, and ads are often explicit about the caste of the ad buyer and the caste requirement of the marriage partner.

caste system
An aspect of Hinduism by which the entire society is divided into four groups (plus the outcasts) and each is assigned a certain class of work

In Japan a somewhat similar system exists, as a holdover from the 17th century, when the feudal Tokugawa regime imposed a rigid social pecking order. The warrior-administrator samurai were at the top. Below them were farmers and artisans, then merchants, and, at the bottom, those with occupations considered dirty and distasteful, such as slaughterers, butchers, and tanners. As in India, where discrimination against untouchables is illegal, all natives of Japan who are of Japanese descent are legally equal. However, the descendants of the lowest Japanese class remain trapped in their ghettos, working in small family firms that produce knitted garments, bamboo wares, fur and leather goods, shoes, and sandals. They call themselves *burakumin* ("ghetto people") and claim they number about 3 million people living in some 6,000 ghettos. Their average income is far below that of other Japanese.

Buddhism Buddhism began in India as a reform of Hinduism. At the age of 29, Prince Gautama rejected his wife, son, and wealth and set out to solve the mysteries of misery, old age, and death. After six years of experimenting with yoga, he suddenly understood how to break the laws of *karma* and the cycle of rebirth *(samsura).* Gautama emerged as the Buddha (the Enlightened One). He renounced the austere self-discipline of the Hindus as well as the extremes of self-indulgence, both of which depended on a craving that locked people into the cycle of rebirth. Gautama taught that by extinguishing desire, his followers could attain enlightenment and escape the cycle of existence into nirvana. By opening his teaching to everyone, he opposed the caste system.

Jainism The Jain religion was founded by Mahavira, a contemporary of Buddha. Jain doctrine teaches that there is no creator, no god, and no absolute principle. Through right faith, correct conduct, and knowledge of the soul, Jains can purify themselves, become free of samsura, and achieve nirvana. Although relatively few in number, Jains are influential leaders in commerce and scholarship. Their greatest impact on Indian culture is manifested in the widespread acceptance of their doctrine of nonviolence, which prohibits animal slaughter, war, and even violent thoughts.

Sikhism Sikhism is the religion of an Indian ethnic group, a military brotherhood,* and a political movement that was founded by Nanak, who sought a bridge between Hinduism and Islam. Sikhs believe there is a single god, but they also accept the Hindu concepts of samsura, karma, and spiritual liberation. More than 80 percent of Sikhs live in the state of Punjab.[28]

Confucianism The name of Confucius is inseparable from Chinese culture and civilization, which were already well developed when he set out to transform ancient traditions into a system capable of guiding personal and social behavior. Confucianism may be considered a religion since Confucius built his philosophy on the notion that all reality is subject to an eternal mandate from heaven. Confucius taught that each person bears within himself or herself the principle of unselfish love for others, *jen,* the cultivation of which is its own reward. A second principle, *li,* prescribes a gentle decorum in all actions and may account for the Chinese emphasis on politeness and deference to elders.

Taoism Taoism is a mystical philosophy founded by Lao-tzu, a contemporary of Confucius. It is just as likely that he never existed, and that the *Lao Tzu* is an anthology. Taoism, which means "philosophy of the way," holds that each of us mirrors the male and the female energies (yin and yang) that govern the cosmos. The aim of Taoist meditation and rituals is to free the self from distractions and become empty to allow the cosmic forces to act.[29]

Shintoism Shintoism is the indigenous religion of Japan. Shinto legends define the founding of the Japanese empire as a cosmic act, and the emperor was believed to have divine status. As a part of the World War II settlement, the emperor was forced to renounce such a claim. Shintoism has no elaborate theology or weekly worship. Many homes contain a small Shinto shrine.

ISLAM

About 1.3 billion followers make this faith the second largest after Christianity, which has 2 billion adherents. Islam accepts as God's eternal word the Koran, a collection of Allah's

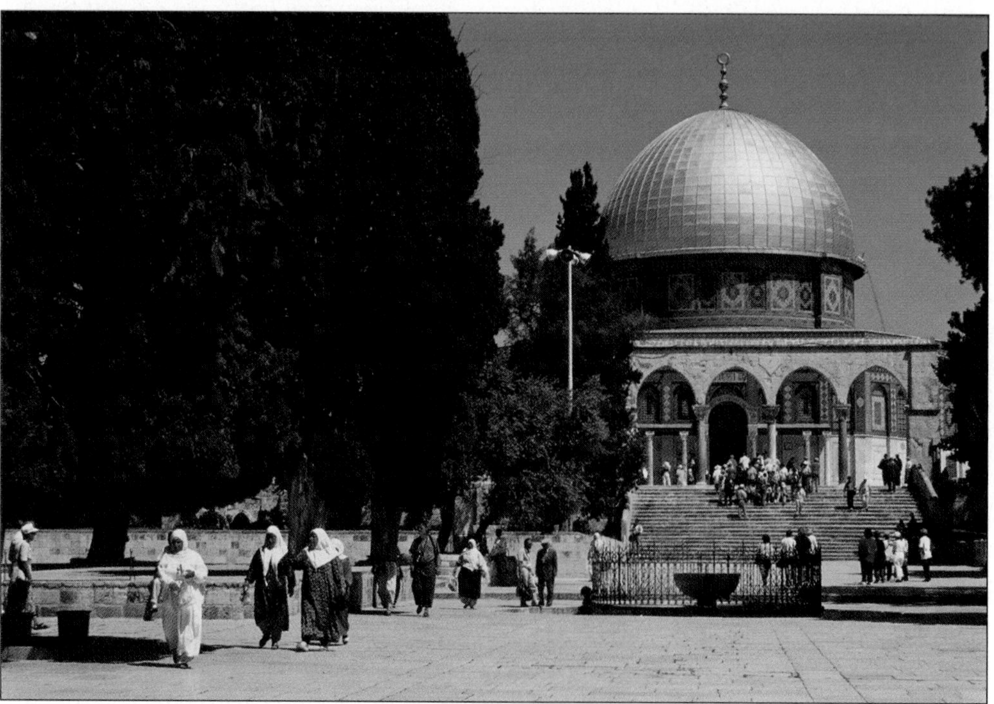

The Dome of the Rock mosque in Jerusalem is a historic center of worship for Muslims, followers of Islam. With 1.3 billion followers, Islam is the second-largest faith after Christianity.

*Baptism into the Sikh brotherhood requires that all members take *Singh* as a second name.

(God's) revelations to Muhammad, who is viewed by Muslims as the messenger of God. Muhammad was not only the prophet of God, but also led the Islamic state.

The basic spiritual duties of all Muslims consist of the five pillars of faith: (1) accepting the confession of faith ("There is no God but God, and Muhammad is the Messenger of God"), (2) making the five daily prayers while facing Mecca (Muhammad's birthplace), (3) giving charity, (4) fasting during the daylight hours of Ramadan, a 29- or 30-day month in Islam's lunar calendar, and (5) making a pilgrimage to Mecca at least once in a person's lifetime. Some Muslims claim there is another duty, *jihad,* which refers to the various forms of striving for the faith, such as the inner struggle for purification. However, this term is often translated as "holy war." We discuss other aspects of jihad in Chapter 9.

A dispute over the succession to leadership after Muhammad died led to the formation of two major divisions, the Sunnis and the Shiites (Shia). The Sunnis may be less authoritarian and more pragmatic than the Shiites. In their view, as long as Muslims accept Allah, they are free to interpret their religion as they like. The Shiites, in contrast, insist that those claiming to be Muslim must put themselves under the authority of a holy man *(ayatollah).*[30] This has created a clergy that wields enormous temporal and spiritual power, with the result that religious leaders affect business as well as religion.

Sunni-Shia Conflict

Businesspeople doing business with Muslim countries should understand the Sunni-Shia conflict. Although most Muslim countries are Sunni-governed, many of them, such as Kuwait, the emirates, Bahrain, and other small states in the Gulf, have substantial Shia populations. Furthermore, small Shia minorities can cause trouble for the government. For example, Saudi Arabia's Shia population is very small—only 250,000—and is concentrated in the eastern oil fields. Iran's Shia government continually broadcasts appeals to the Saudi Shiites to overthrow the regime. The group Hamas is Sunni; Hezbollah is Shiite.

Two of the five pillars of faith can be bothersome to foreign managers. Dawn-to-dusk fasting during the month of Ramadan causes workers' output to drop sharply, and the requirement to pray five times daily also affects output, because when Muslim workers hear the call to prayer they stop whatever they are doing and pray where they are.

ANIMISM

In a number of African and Latin American countries, animism, a kind of spirit worship that includes magic and witchcraft, is a major religion. It is often combined with other religions to present a mixture of mysticism, taboos, and fatalism. According to historians, animism is perhaps one of humanity's oldest beliefs, with its origin probably dating back to the Paleolithic age. The term *animism* derives from the Latin word *anima,* meaning "breath" or "soul." Animism is the belief that everything in nature—including living things like trees and plants and even nonliving rocks or streams—has its own spirit or divinity. Japanese shintoism is equated by some to animism.

Religions have a pervasive influence on business. Religious holidays and rituals can affect employee performance and work scheduling. When members of different religious groups work together, there may even be strife within the work force. Managers must respect the religious beliefs of others and adapt business practices to the religious constraints present in other cultures. Of course, to be able to do this, they must first know what those beliefs and constraints are.

material culture
All human-made objects; concerned with *how* people make things (technology) and *who* makes *what* and *why* (economics)

Material Culture

Material culture refers to all human-made objects and is concerned with *how* people make things (technology) and *who* makes *what* and *why* (economics).

TECHNOLOGY

The *technology* of a society is the mix of the usable knowledge that the society applies and directs toward the attainment of cultural and economic objectives; it exists in some form in every cultural organization. It is significant in the improvement of living standards and a vital factor in the competitive strategies of multinational firms. Technological superiority is the goal of most companies, of course, but it is especially important to international companies for a number of reasons:

1. It enables a firm to be competitive or even attain leadership in world markets.

   The Korean firm Samsung was once known for cheap and unappealing electronics. But its skills in the design of sleek, attractive products have made it a leader in cell phones, and it tops global markets for color televisions, flash memory, and LCD panels. Samsung's elegant Experience showroom in New York City draws 1,500 visitors on a typical Saturday.

2. It can be sold (via licensing or management contract), or it can be embodied in the company's products.

3. It can give a firm confidence to enter a foreign market even when other companies are already established there.

4. It can enable the firm to obtain better-than-usual conditions for a foreign market investment because the host government wants the technology that only the firm has (for example, permission for a wholly owned subsidiary in a country where the government normally insists on joint ventures with a local majority).

   IBM, confident of its superior technology, insisted on and obtained permission from the Mexican government to set up a wholly owned subsidiary when other computer manufacturers were forced to accept local partners.

5. It can enable a company with only a minority equity position to control a joint venture and preserve it as a captive market for semiprocessed inputs that it—but not the joint venture—produces.

6. It can change the international division of labor. Some firms that moved production overseas where labor was cheaper have returned to their home countries because production methods based on new technology have reduced the direct labor content of their products. With labor costs as low as 5 percent of total production costs, going overseas to save 30 to 40 percent in labor costs, for example, produces only about a 2 percent cost saving. This may be more than offset by the transportation costs to bring the finished merchandise to the United States. Fender Musical Instruments Co. makes Fender guitars in both Ensenada, Mexico, and Corona, California, and sales of guitars from both locations are about even.

7. It is causing major firms to form competitive alliances in which each partner shares technology and the high costs of research and development. This is known as *strategic technology leveraging,* which is the concept of using external technology to complement rather than substitute for internal technology.

Cultural Aspects of Technology

Technology's cultural aspects are certainly important to international managers, because new production methods and new products often require that people change their beliefs and ways of living. A self-employed farmer may find that factory work is unappealing. If workers have been accustomed to the conditions of cottage industries in which each individual performs all the operations, they find it difficult to adjust to the monotony of tightening a single bolt. The "throw away instead of repair" philosophy behind the design of many new products necessitates a change in the use habits of people who have been accustomed to repairing something to keep it operating until it is thoroughly worn out. Generally, the greater the difference is between the old and the new method or product, the more difficult it is for the firm to institute a change.

Technological Dualism

Technological dualism is a prominent feature of many developing nations. In the same country, one industry sector may be technologically advanced, with high productivity, while the production techniques of another sector may be old and labor-intensive. This condition may be the result of the host government's insistence that foreign investors import only the most modern machinery rather than used but serviceable equipment that would be less costly and could create more employment.

Sometimes the preferences are reversed. A host government beset by high unemployment may argue for labor-intensive processes, while the foreign firm prefers automated production both because it is the kind the home office is most familiar with and because its use lessens the need for skilled labor. To understand which policy the host government is following, management must study its laws and regulations and talk with host country officials.

technological dualism
The side-by-side presence of technologically advanced and technologically primitive production systems

Appropriate Technology

Rather than choosing between labor-intensive and capital-intensive processes, many experts in economic development recommend **appropriate technology,** which can be labor-intensive, intermediate, or capital-intensive. The idea is to choose the technology that most closely fits the society using it.

Appropriate technology may be embodied in product delivery. For example, the development of single chips that will handle many cell phone functions has vastly expanded the cell phone market in India because the physical phone cost has dropped.

appropriate technology
The technology (advanced, intermediate, or primitive) that most closely fits the society using it

Boomerang Effect

One reason firms sometimes fear to sell their technology abroad is the **boomerang effect.** For example, Japanese firms have been less willing to sell their technology to industrialized economies such as Korea. Interestingly, fear of the boomerang effect caused some American firms to restrict the sale of their technology to the Japanese. However, a study of the flat-panel-display industry suggested that there was no difference between U.S. and Japanese firms' tendency to share, or appropriate, knowledge from the rest of the world.

boomerang effect
Situation in which technology sold to companies in another nation is used to produce goods to compete with those of the seller of the technology

THE INFORMATION TECHNOLOGY ERA

The information technology industry is changing at a pace that is bewildering to many business executives. Managing the flood of data available electronically is a challenge, but capturing information from transaction data, for example, offers profitable opportunities to mine the data for trend spotting. The Internet's worldwide reach has enabled firms to enter global markets with a minimal investment. It also, of course, has brought new competition to these companies in their own home markets. Apparently, the investment in new information technology is worth it. As early as 2000 the Internet economy had already reached $850 billion, exceeding the size of the life insurance and real estate industries.[31]

MATERIAL CULTURE AND CONSUMPTION

One of the unique expressions of Japanese material culture is the wide use of automation—not only in robots for manufacturing but in vending machines for a variety of items, including hot meals and (until recently) alcohol. Until a ban was enacted in 2000, Japan had nearly 170,000 alcohol vending machines. Teenage males were buying beer that they were too young to buy in a store (Japan's official age for alcohol purchase is 20). Of course, it is feared that the vacuum will be filled by convenience stores that won't bother to check the age of patrons.[32]

Language

Probably the most apparent cultural distinction that the newcomer to international business perceives is in the means of communication. Differences in the spoken language are readily discernible, and after a short period in the new culture it becomes apparent that there are variations in the unspoken language (manners and customs) as well.

SPOKEN LANGUAGE

Language is the key to culture, and without it, people find themselves locked out of all but a culture's perimeter. At the same time, in learning a language, people can't understand the nuances, double meanings of words, and slang unless they also learn the other aspects of the culture. Fortunately, the learning of both goes hand in hand; a certain feel for a people and their attitudes naturally develops with a growing mastery of their language.

Languages Delineate Cultures Spoken languages demarcate cultures just as physical barriers do. In fact, nothing equals the spoken language for distinguishing one culture from another. If two languages are spoken in a country, there will be two separate cultures (Belgium); if four languages are spoken, there will be four cultures (Switzerland); and so forth.

The sharp divisions in Canada between the English- and French-speaking regions is ample evidence of the force of languages in delineating cultures. The differences among the Basques, Catalans, and Spaniards and the differences between the French and Flemish in Belgium are other notable examples of the sharp cultural and often political differences between language groups. However, it does not follow from this generalization that cultures are the same wherever the same language is spoken. As a result of Spain's colonization, Spanish is the principal language of 21 Latin American nations, but no one should believe that they are culturally similar. Moreover, generally because of cultural differences, many words in both the written and the spoken languages of these countries are completely different. A Chilean told one of the authors of her surprise at seeing Puerto Rican coffee selling under the "El Pico" brand. In Chile, she said, *el pico* is a reference to the male sex organ.

lingua franca
A foreign language used to communicate among a nation's diverse cultures that have diverse languages

Foreign Language When many spoken languages exist in a single country (India and many African nations), one language usually serves as the principal vehicle for communication across cultures. Nations that were formerly colonies often use the language of their exrulers; thus, French is the **lingua franca,** or "link" language, of the former French and Belgian colonies in Africa; English, in India; and Portuguese, in Angola. These are the only languages many speak in some previously colonized African countries. Thus they may be more, or less, effective than the native tongues for reaching mass markets or for day-to-day conversations between managers and workers. Even in countries with only one principal language, such as Germany and France, problems of communication arise because of the large numbers of "guest workers" who were recruited to ease labor shortages. A German supervisor may have workers from three or four countries and be unable to speak directly with any of them. To ameliorate this situation, some managers try to separate the work force according to origin; for instance, all Turks are placed in the paint shop, all Greeks on the assembly line, and so on. But the preferred solution is to teach managers the language of their workers. Invariably, such training has resulted in an increase in production, fewer product defects, and higher worker morale.

English, the Link Language of Business When a Swedish businessperson talks with a Japanese businessperson, the conversation generally will be in English. English as a business *lingua franca* has spread so rapidly in Europe that well over half of EU adults can speak English. Over 40 percent of people in the EU speak it as a second language. An even larger percentage—69 percent—agree that "everyone should speak English."[33]

At the same time, other languages are not being abandoned. For example, EU headquarters in Brussels estimated that, after the EU was enlarged, interpreters would be needed for all possible combinations of about 22 languages—a total of 462 combinations![34]

Must Speak the Local Language Even though more and more businesspeople are speaking English, when they buy, they often insist on doing business in their own language. The seller who speaks the local language has a competitive edge. Moreover, knowing the language of the area indicates respect for its culture and people. Figure 6.2 shows a map of the major languages of the world. As we have said, usually it is a social blunder to begin a business conversation by talking business. Most foreigners expect to establish a social relationship first, and the casual, exploratory conversation that precedes business talks may require several meetings. Obviously, people can establish a better rapport in a one-on-one conversation than through an interpreter. Consider the trouble this person would have avoided if he had spoken Spanish:

> *A German engineer, in Colombia to work on a pipeline, arrived at a hotel in the interior, where he tried to explain to the desk clerk that he had a suitcase full of cash that he wanted the hotel to keep. Because he knew no Spanish, he was having difficulty making himself understood. During the conversation, the desk clerk opened the suitcase in front of everyone in the lobby. A week later, the engineer was kidnapped by a guerrilla group and held for a month.*[35]

Translation The ability to speak the language well does not eliminate the need for translators. The smallest of markets requires technical manuals, catalogs, and good advertising ideas, and a lack of local talent to do the work does not mean that the organization must do without these valuable sales aids. The solution is to obtain this material from headquarters and have it translated if the costs are not prohibitive and suitable reproduction facilities are available locally. Remember, though, a French or Spanish translation will be up to 25 percent longer than its English equivalent.

Allowing headquarters to translate can be extremely risky because words from the same language frequently vary in meaning from one country to another or even from one region to another, as was mentioned earlier. A famous example that illustrated how only a single word incorrectly translated can ruin an otherwise good translation occurred in Mexico. The American headquarters of a deodorant manufacturer sent a Spanish translation of the manufacturer's international theme, "If you use our deodorant, you won't be embarrassed in public." Unfortunately, the translator used the word *embarazada* for "embarrassed," which in Mexican Spanish means "pregnant." Imagine the time that the Mexican subsidiary had with that one.[36]

Back Translations To avoid translation errors, the experienced marketer will prefer what are really two translations. The first will be made by a bilingual native, whose work will then be translated back by a bilingual foreigner to see how it compares with the original. This work preferably should be done in the market where the material is to be used. No method is foolproof, but the back-translation approach is the safest way devised so far.

Some problems with translations:

- A sign in a Paris hotel that sought to discourage Americans from wearing slacks in the plush dining room: "A sports jacket may be worn to dinner, but no trousers." The menu advised patrons that they could enjoy "tea in a bag just like mother."
- In a Copenhagen airline ticket office: "We take your bags and send them in all directions."
- In a Japanese hotel: "You are invited to take advantage of the chambermaid."
- A Bangkok dry cleaner's boast: "Drop your trousers here for best results."
- An Acapulco hotel that wanted to reassure guests about the drinking water: "The manager has personally passed all the water served here."
- Sign in a Czech tourist office: "Take one of our horse-driven city tours—we guarantee no miscarriages."
- Infoscope, a prototype PDA-type translator, translated a Bank of America sign in Chinese as "Great Wall of Money Bin."

Technical Words Translators have difficulty with technical terms that do not exist in a language and with common words that have a special meaning for a certain industry. Portuguese, for example, is rich in fishing and marine terms, but it is limited with respect to technical terms for the newer industries. The only solution is to employ the English word or fabricate a new word in Portuguese. Unless translators have a special knowledge of the industry, they will go to the dictionary for a literal translation that frequently makes no sense

FIGURE 6.2 Major Languages of the World

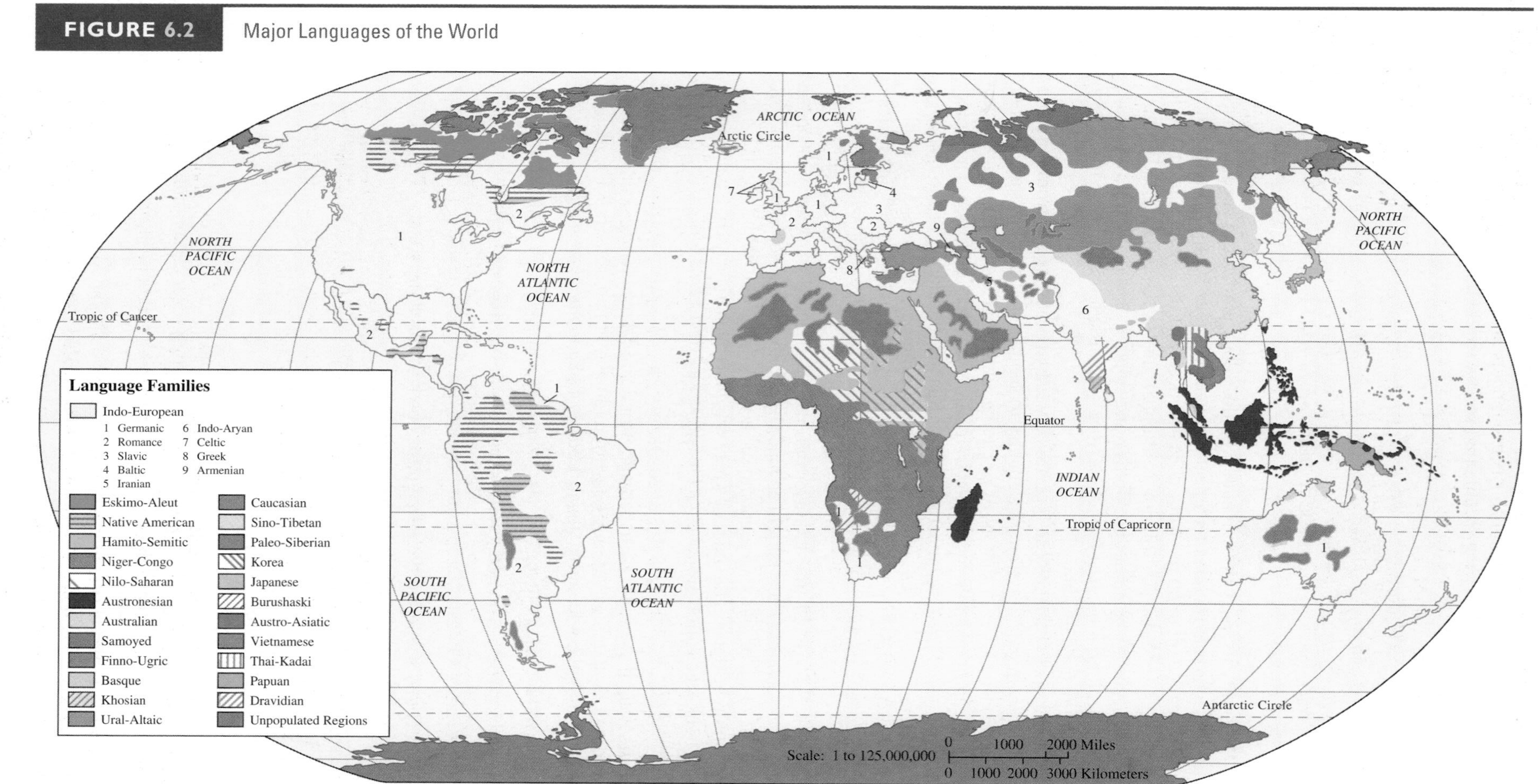
ARCTIC OCEAN
Arctic Circle
NORTH PACIFIC OCEAN
NORTH ATLANTIC OCEAN
NORTH PACIFIC OCEAN
Tropic of Cancer
Equator
INDIAN OCEAN
Tropic of Capricorn
SOUTH PACIFIC OCEAN
SOUTH ATLANTIC OCEAN
Antarctic Circle
Scale: 1 to 125,000,000
0 1000 2000 Miles
0 1000 2000 3000 Kilometers
Language Families
Indo-European
1 Germanic
2 Romance
3 Slavic
4 Baltic
5 Iranian
6 Indo-Aryan
7 Celtic
8 Greek
9 Armenian
Eskimo-Aleut
Native American
Hamito-Semitic
Niger-Congo
Nilo-Saharan
Austronesian
Australian
Samoyed
Finno-Ugric
Basque
Khosian
Ural-Altaic
Caucasian
Sino-Tibetan
Paleo-Siberian
Korea
Japanese
Burushaski
Austro-Asiatic
Vietnamese
Thai-Kadai
Papuan
Dravidian
Unpopulated Regions

or is erroneous. Resolving such problems by using English words may not be a satisfactory solution even if the public understands them, especially in France and Spain, which have national academies to keep the language "pure." The French, in their effort to keep their language free of English words, prohibit the use of foreign words and phrases in all business and government communications and advertising when there are suitable French equivalents. Two out of five songs broadcast on French radio must be in French. In Spain, the Royal Spanish Academy attempts to perform much the same function for Spanish.

French Crackdown on English In a continuing effort to protect the French language against the encroachment of other languages, various French watchdog groups, partially funded by the Culture Ministry, regularly sue those who in their opinion have violated the law. In 1997, they filed suits against the French campus of Georgia Tech for writing its Internet site in English, the Body Shop for selling products in France without French labels, and an electronics chain for selling computer games with English-only instructions.[37]

"First, le coca cola. Now peanut butter. Who will save La Belle Langue Française?"

Source: *Pearson/Knickerbocker News,* NY/Rothco. Reprinted with permission.

Although the French government and other defenders of the French language are struggling to maintain a French presence on the Internet, they are losing. An estimated 75 percent of the world's Internet sites are in English.[38] Adding insult to injury, France is McDonald's most profitable subsidiary in Europe. It adapts to both French language and tastes ("Croque McDo" is a version of the *croque monsieur,* a ham-and-cheese French favorite).[39] More than pride is involved here. One scientific rule of thumb is to "publish in English, or perish in French."

Note the economic reason for keeping the language pure and separate from other languages. Those learning a foreign language not only are potential tourists but are likely to be empathetic toward anything that comes from that country. An Argentine fashion buyer who speaks German and not Bulgarian may feel more comfortable attending fashion shows in Germany than in Budapest.

In Japan, the reverse situation exists, probably because for decades the country coveted foreign products while it struggled to overtake the West. Even now, most Japanese cars sold in the domestic market have almost nothing but English on them. A Nissan official explains that English is thought to be more attractive to the eye. Perhaps this is why people quench their thirst with a best-selling soft drink called "Pocari Sweat" and order from menus announcing "sand witches" and "miss Gorilla" (mixed grill). They also puff away on a cigarette called "Hope."[40]

No Unpleasantness One last aspect of the spoken language worthy of mention is the reluctance in many areas to say anything disagreeable to the listener. The politeness of the Japanese makes *no* a little-used word even when there are disagreements. An American executive, pleased that her Japanese counterpart is nodding and saying yes to all of her proposals, may be shaken later to learn that all the time the listener was saying yes ("I hear you") and not yes ("I agree"). Western managers who ask Brazilians whether something can be done may receive the answer *meio deficil* ("somewhat difficult"). If managers take this answer literally, they will probably ask that it be done anyway. The Brazilians will then elaborate on the difficulties until, they hope, it will dawn on the executives that what they ask is impossible but the Brazilians don't want to give them the bad news.

UNSPOKEN LANGUAGE

Nonverbal communication, or the **unspoken language,** can often tell businesspeople something that the spoken language does not—if they understand it. Unfortunately, the differences in customs among cultures may cause misinterpretations of the communication.

unspoken language Nonverbal communication, such as gestures and body language

Gestures Although gestures are a common form of cross-cultural communication, gestures vary from one region to another. For instance, Americans and most Europeans understand the thumbs-up gesture to mean "all right," but in southern Italy and Greece, it transmits

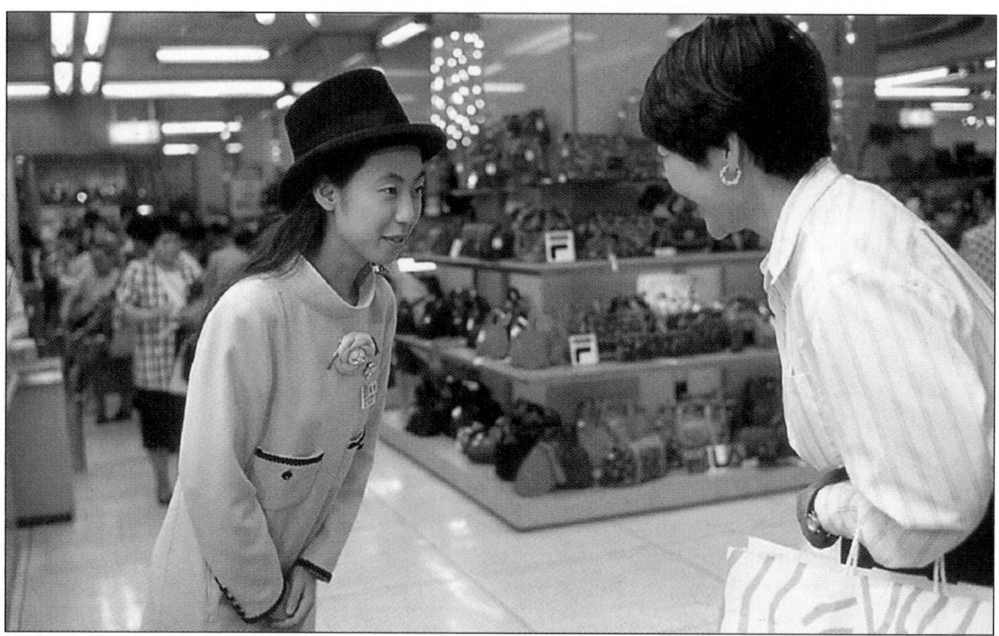

Department store greeter in Tokyo bows politely to a customer.

the message for which we reserve the middle finger. Making a circle with the thumb and the forefinger is friendly in the United States, but it means "you're worth nothing" in France and Belgium and is a vulgar sexual invitation in Greece and Turkey.[41]

Former Japanese prime minister Yoshiro Mori paid his respects to his predecessor, Keizo Obuchi, by bowing *twice* before an urn containing Obuchi's ashes. Unfortunately, Japanese etiquette requires bowing *three* times to show respect for the deceased. Mori's gaffe was obvious to the 6,000 mourners in the hall and to millions watching on TV.[42]

Closed Doors Americans know that one of the perquisites of an important executive is a large office with a door that can be closed. Normally, the door is open as a signal that the occupant is ready to receive others, but when it is closed, something of importance is going on. Contrary to the American open-door policy, Germans regularly keep their doors closed. Hall, the anthropologist mentioned earlier in this chapter, says that the closed door does not mean that the person behind it wants no visitors but only that he or she considers open doors sloppy and disorderly.[43]

Office Size Although office size is an indicator of a person's importance, it means different things in different cultures. In the United States, the higher the status of the executive, the larger and more secluded the office, but in the Arab world, the president may be in a small, crowded office. In Japan, the top floor of a department store is reserved for the "bargain basement" (bargain penthouse?), not for top management. The French prefer to locate important department heads in the center of activities, with their assistants located outward on radii from this center. To be safe, never gauge people's importance by the size and location of their offices.

Conversational Distance Cultural experts report that conversational distances are smaller in the Middle East, and possibly larger in Asia, than the Western average. Conversational distances vary by gender as well as culture, and comfortable distance may also vary by the degree of familiarity of the parties involved: We have an intimate distance for embracing or whispering (6 to 18 inches), a personal distance for conversations among good friends (1.5 to 4 feet), a social distance for conversations among acquaintances (4 to 12 feet), and a public distance for public speaking (12 feet or more).[44]

THE LANGUAGE OF GIFT GIVING

Gift giving is an important aspect of every businessperson's life both here and overseas. Entertainment outside office hours and the exchange of gifts are part of the process of getting better acquainted. However, the etiquette or language of gift giving varies among cultures, just as the spoken language does, and although foreigners will usually be forgiven for not knowing the language, certainly they and their gifts will be better received if they follow local customs.

Acceptable Gifts

In Japan, for example, one never gives an unwrapped gift or visits a Japanese home empty-handed. A gift is presented with the comment that it is only a trifle, which implies that the humble social position of the giver does not permit giving a gift in keeping with the high status of the recipient. The recipient, in turn, will not open the gift in front of the giver because the recipient knows better than to embarrass the giver by exposing the trifle in the giver's presence.

The Japanese use gift giving to convey thoughtfulness and consideration for the receiver, who over time builds up trust and confidence in the giver. White and yellow flowers are not good choices for gifts because in many areas they connote death. In Germany, red roses given to a woman indicate strong feelings for her, and if you give cutlery, always ask for a coin in payment so that the gift will not cut your friendship. Cutlery is a "friendship cutter" for the Russians and French also. Traditions vary greatly throughout the world, but generally safe gifts everywhere are chocolates, red roses, and a good Scotch whiskey (not in the Arab world, however—instead, bring a good book or something useful for the office).[45]

Gifts or Bribes?

Occasional bribery scandals have exposed the practice of giving very expensive gifts and money to well-placed government officials in return for special favors, large orders, and protection. Some payments were **bribes;** that is, payments were made to induce the payee to do something for the payer that is illegal. But others were the result of **extortion,** the demand for payment to keep the payee from harming the payer in some way. Still others were tips to induce government officials to do their jobs.[46]

bribes
Gifts or payments to induce the receiver to do something illegal for the giver

extortion
Demand for payment to keep the receiver from causing harm to the payer

Welcome to the murky world of payments for services Some other examples (from the U.S. perspective): If you tip the head waiter to get a good table, that is a bribe, but if you tip him because you know that without it he'll put you near the kitchen, that's extortion. If you tip him for good service after eating, that is a tip. Gifts or payments are sometimes needed to obtain favorable action from government officials, whether to obtain a large order, avoid having a plant shut down, or receive faster service from customs agents. Their pervasiveness worldwide is illustrated by the variety of names for these payments—*mordida* ("bite"—Latin America), *dash* (West Africa, where it might also mean "tip"), *pot de vin* ("jug of wine"—France), *la bustarella* (envelope left on Italian bureaucrat's desk), and *grease* (United States).

Questionable Payments

These come in all forms and sizes, from the small "expediting" payments necessary to get poorly paid government officials to do their normal duties to huge sums to win large orders.

> *One of the writers was able to reduce by one-half the average age of receivables from a major Mexican governmental customer through the payment of $4 a month to a clerk whose sole job was to arrange suppliers' invoices according to their dates, so that the oldest were on top and would be paid first. The invoices of the writer's company were placed on top regardless of their date and were paid promptly.*

Transparency International (TI) has a mission to "create change toward a world free of corruption."[47] Its Corruption Perception Index (CPI) draws on surveys of businesspeople and political analysts. The CPI is designed so that countries perceived to be the *least corrupt* are given the highest score, 10. TI urges analysts to look at scores, not rankings, to understand how business perceives corruption in individual countries. Frequently, a country will have a higher score from one year to the next but will still fall in the ranking. See Figure 6.3 for 2003 CPI scores and rankings.

FIGURE 6.3 2003 Corruption Perception Index Scores and Ranking

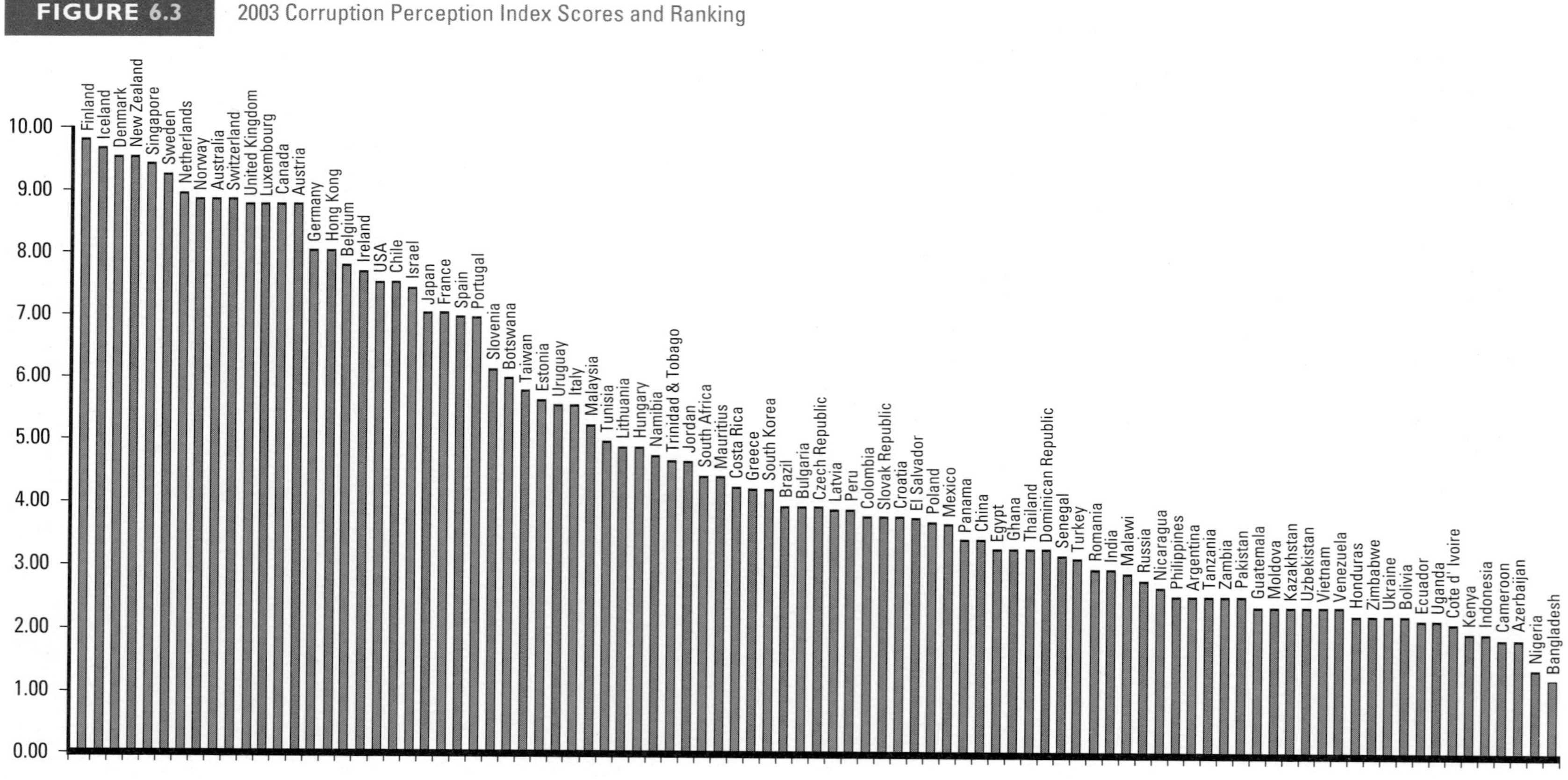

Source: *Global Corruption Report 2003,* Transparency International, http://www.globalcorruptionreport/download/gcr2003.html.

Societal Organization

Every society has a structure or an organization that is the patterned arrangement of relationships defining and regulating the manner by which its members interface with one another. Anthropologists generally study this important aspect of culture by breaking down its parts into two classes of institutions: those based on *kinship* and those based on the *free association* of individuals.

KINSHIP

The family is the basic unit of institutions based on kinship. Unlike the American family, which is generally composed of the parents and their children, families in many nations—especially the developing ones—are extended to include all relatives by blood and by marriage.

Extended Family

For the foreign firm, the **extended family** is a source of employees and business connections. The trust that people place in their relatives, however distant, may motivate them to buy from a supplier owned by their cousin's cousin, even though the price is higher. Local personnel managers are prone to fill the best jobs with family members, regardless of their qualifications.

extended family
Family that includes blood relatives and relatives by marriage

Member's Responsibility

Although the extended family is large, each member's feeling of responsibility to it is strong. An individual's initiative to work is discouraged if he or she is asked to share personal earnings with unemployed extended-family members no matter what the kinship is. Responsibility to the family is frequently a cause of high absenteeism in developing countries, where the worker is often called home to help with the harvest. Managements have spent large sums to provide comfortable housing for workers and their immediate families, only to find them living in crowded conditions after members of their extended families have moved in.

PEDRO DIAZ MARIN

In Latin America, where the extended-family form is common, individuals use the maternal family surname (e.g., Marin) as well as the paternal (e.g., Diaz) to indicate both branches of the family. It is common to see two people, when meeting for the first time, exploring each other's family tree to see whether they have common relatives. If they find any kinship at all, the meeting goes much more smoothly, since they're relatives. By the way, in Korea, China, and Japan, the paternal family name appears first of all.

ASSOCIATIONS

Social units not based on kinship, known as **associations** by anthropologists, may be formed by age, gender, or common interest.[48]

associations
Social units based on age, gender, or common interest, not on kinship

Age

Manufacturers of consumer goods are well aware of the importance of segmenting a market by age groups, which often cut across cultures. This fact has enabled marketers to succeed in selling such products as clothing and records to the youth market in both developed and developing nations. However, international marketers may go too far if they assume that young people everywhere exert the same buying influence on their parents as they do here. Kellogg's attempt to sell cereals in Great Britain through children was not successful because English mothers are less influenced by their children with respect to product choice than are American mothers. Senior citizens form an important segment in the United States, where older people live apart from their children, but where the extended-family concept is prevalent, older people continue to live with and exert a powerful influence on younger members of the family.

Gender

As nations industrialize, more women enter the job market and thus assume greater importance in the economy. This trend is receiving further impetus as the women's movement for equality of the sexes spreads to the traditionally male-dominated societies of less developed countries. Whatever the workplace status of women in a particular market, consumer purchasing in virtually any country is likely to reflect a strong female influence.

While the Chinese husband is sometimes referred to as the "minister of defense," the wife is the "minister of the interior."

Free Association *Free-association groups* are composed of people joined together by a common bond, which can be political, occupational, recreational, or religious. Even before entering a country, management should identify such groups and assess their political and economic power. As we will see in later chapters, consumer organizations have forced firms to change their products, promotion, and prices, and investments have been supported or opposed by labor unions, which are often a powerful political force. The increasing popularity of social networks pioneered by myspace.com and others may have an influence on firms in the future.

ENTREPRENEURIAL SPIRIT

One common interest that may be unexpected by many people is the desire to be an entrepreneur. We may assume that some countries may have a more intrinsically entrepreneurial culture than others, and this turns out to be true, but the countries with more would-be entrepreneurs may be unexpected. In a straightforward study where researchers asked whether citizens would prefer to be an employee or to be self-employed, Blanchflower and Oswald found that the percentage of the would-be self-employed is high. And even in countries at the bottom of their sample, a quarter of the working-age population wanted to be self-employed. Figure 6.4 shows the results of their survey.

Understanding National Cultures

Geert Hofstede, a Dutch social psychologist, analyzed an employee survey database, collected by the IBM World Trade Corporation, that contained over 116,000 questionnaires from 72 countries. He found that the differences in respondents' answers to 32 statements could be based on four value dimensions: (1) individualism versus collectivism, (2) large versus small power distance, (3) strong versus weak uncertainty avoidance, and (4) masculinity versus femininity.[49] (Hofstede later added a fifth dimension, long- versus short-term orientation.)

FIGURE 6.4

Pecent Preferring to Be Self-Employed

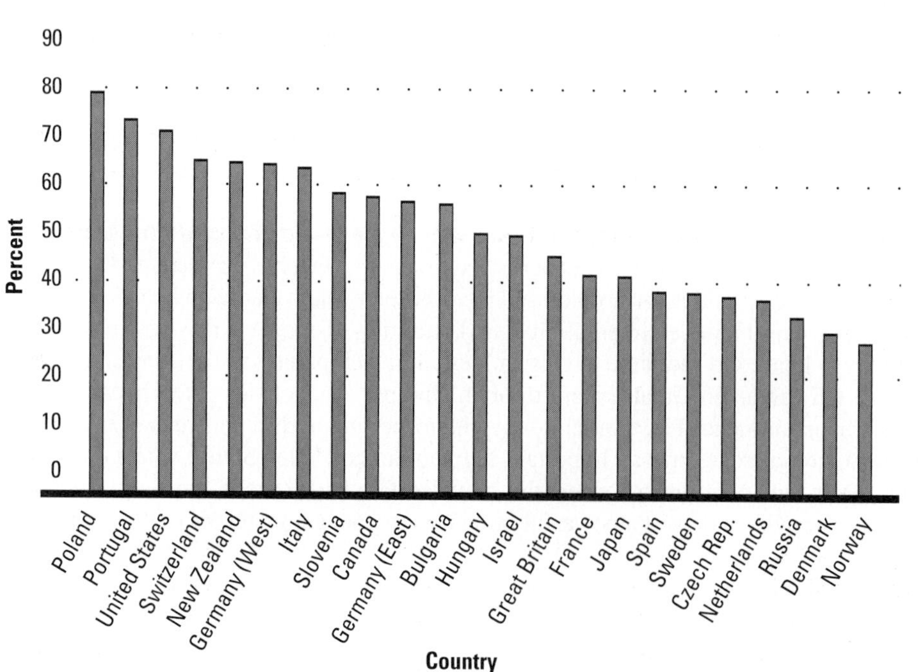

Source: David Blanchflower and Andrew Oswald, "Countries with the Spirit of Enterprise, *The Financial Times,* February 17, 2000, p. 27. Reprinted with permission.

INDIVIDUALISM VERSUS COLLECTIVISM

According to Hofstede, people in *collectivistic* cultures belong to groups that are supposed to look after them in exchange for loyalty, whereas people in *individualistic* cultures are supposed to look after only themselves and the immediate family.[50] Therefore, organizations operating in collectivistic cultures are more likely to rely on group decision making than are those in individualistic cultures, where the emphasis is on individual decision making.

LARGE VERSUS SMALL POWER DISTANCE

Power distance is the extent to which members of a society accept the unequal distribution of power among individuals. In large-power-distance societies, employees believe their supervisors are right even when they are wrong, and thus employees do not take any initiative in making nonroutine decisions. On the other hand, a participative management style of leadership is likely to be productive for an organization in a low-power-distance country.[51]

STRONG VERSUS WEAK UNCERTAINTY AVOIDANCE

Uncertainty avoidance is the degree to which the members of a society feel threatened by ambiguity and are rule-oriented. Employees in high-uncertainty-avoidance cultures, such as Japan, Greece, and Portugal, tend to stay with their organizations for a long time. In contrast, those from low-uncertainty-avoidance nations, such as the United States, Singapore, and Denmark, are much more mobile.

It should be apparent that organizational change in high-uncertainty-avoidance nations is likely to receive strong resistance from employees, which makes the implementation of change difficult to administer.[52]

MASCULINITY VERSUS FEMININITY

The *masculinity-femininity* dimension is the degree to which the dominant values in a society emphasize assertiveness, acquisition of money and status, and achievement of visible and symbolic organizational rewards (masculinity) compared to the degree to which they emphasize relationships, concern for others, and the overall quality of life (femininity).[53]

THE FOUR DIMENSIONS AND MANAGEMENT IMPLICATIONS

Table 6.1 presents the scores for Hofstede's four dimensions for about one-third of the countries in his sample.

TABLE 6.1 Scores for Hofstede's Value Dimensions

Country	Power Distance	Uncertainty Avoidance	Individualism	Masculinity
Mexico	81	82	30	69
Venezuela	81	76	12	73
Colombia	64	80	13	64
Peru	90	87	16	42
Chile	63	86	23	28
Portugal	63	104	27	31
United States	50	46	91	62
Australia	49	51	90	61
South Africa (SAF)	49	49	65	63
New Zealand	45	49	79	58
Canada	39	48	80	52
Great Britain	35	35	89	66
Ireland	28	35	70	68

Source: Geert Hofstede, "Cultural Dimensions in Management and Planning," *Asia Pacific Journal of Management*, January 1984, p. 83.

FIGURE 6.5

Plot of Selected Nations on Power Distance and Uncertainty Avoidance

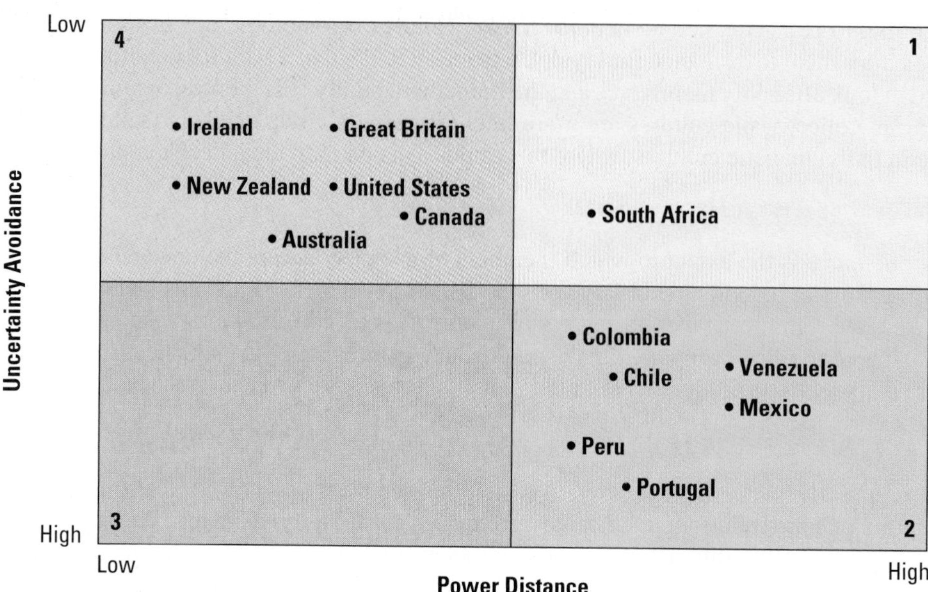

Figure 6.5 plots the scores for selected Anglo and Latin American (Hofstede's terms) nations on the power-distance and uncertainty-avoidance dimensions. The Latin American countries in the second quadrant scored relatively high on power distance and uncertainty avoidance. The lines of communication in organizations in these countries are vertical, and employees know who reports to whom. By clearly defining roles and procedures, the organizations are very predictable. The Anglo nations in the fourth quadrant scored low on both dimensions. Organizations in these countries are characterized by less formal controls and fewer layers of management. More informal communication is used.[54]

The scores for individualism and power distance are plotted in Figure 6.6. The Latin countries (first quadrant) scored relatively high on power distance and low on individualism. Employees tend to expect their organizations to look after them and defend their interests. They expect close supervision and managers who act paternally. On the other hand, people in the Anglo countries (third quadrant), which scored low on power distance and high on individualism, prefer to do things for themselves and do not expect organizations to look after them.

FIGURE 6.6

Plot of Selected Nations on Individualism and Power Distance

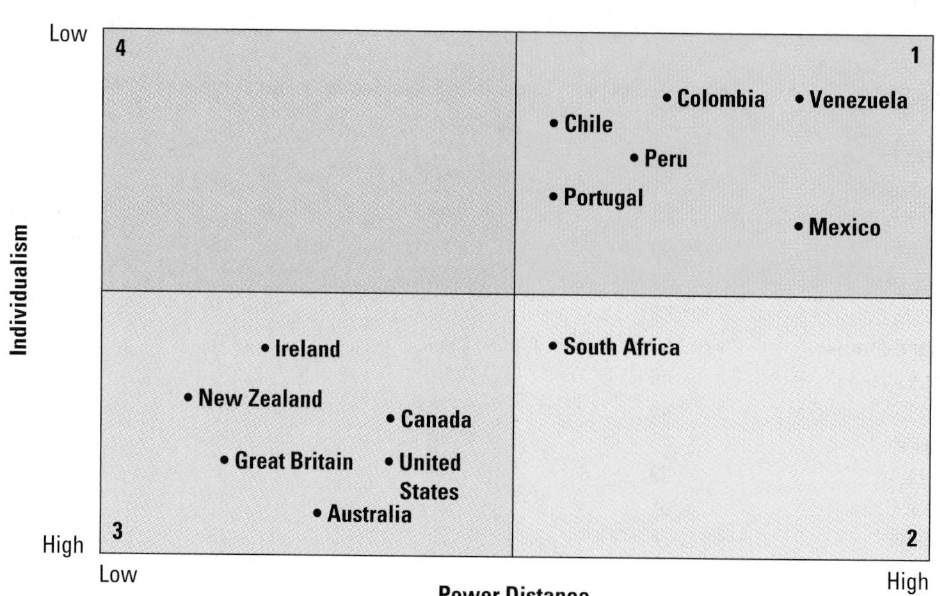

Hofstede's four dimensions have given managers a basis for understanding how cultural differences affect organizations and management methods. They assist in showing that management skills are culturally specific; that is, "a management technique or philosophy that is appropriate in one national culture is not necessarily appropriate in another." Clearly, managing in different Western countries requires different activities, and thus generalizations are not justified. However, other researchers, using other data, have found the same or closely similar dimensions, leading Hofstede to conclude that "there is solid evidence that the four dimensions are, indeed, universal."[55]

Summary

Explain the significance of culture for international business.

To be successful in their relationships overseas, international businesspeople must be students of culture. They must not only have factual knowledge; they must also become culturally sensitive. Culture affects all functional areas of the firm.

Identify the sociocultural components of culture.

Although experts differ about the components of culture, the following are representative of what numerous anthropologists believe exist: (1) aesthetics, (2) attitudes and beliefs, (3) religion, (4) material culture, (5) language, (6) societal organization, (7) education, (8) legal characteristics, and (9) political structures.

Discuss the significance of religion to businesspeople.

Knowing the basic tenets of other religions will contribute to a better understanding of their followers' attitudes. This may be a major factor in a given market.

Explain the cultural aspects of technology.

Material culture, especially technology, is important to managements contemplating overseas investment. Foreign governments have become increasingly involved in the sale and control of technical assistance. Technology may enable a firm to enter a new market successfully even if its competitors are already established there. It often enables the firm to obtain superior conditions for an overseas investment because the host government wants the technology.

Discuss the pervasiveness of the information technology era.

Businesspeople must keep abreast of the changes in information technology to avoid falling behind their competitors. The Internet enables small firms to compete in the global market, a fact that provides new opportunities for some firms and new competition for others. Businesspeople who can capture information from transaction data have a significant advantage over those who cannot. The opinion in the retailing industry is that this capability is the primary reason for Wal-Mart's success, for example.

Explain the importance of the ability to speak the local language.

Language is the key to culture. A feel for a people and their attitudes naturally develops with a growing mastery of their language.

Discuss the importance of unspoken language in international business.

Because unspoken language can often tell businesspeople something that spoken language does not, they should know something about this form of cross-cultural communication.

Discuss the two classes of relationships within a society.

A knowledge of how a society is organized is useful because the arrangement of relationships within it defines and regulates the manner in which its members interface with one another. Anthropologists have broken down societal relationships into two classes: those based on kinship and those based on free association of individuals.

Discuss Hofstede's four cultural value dimensions.

Geert Hofstede analyzed IBM employees in 72 countries and found that the differences in their answers to 32 statements could be based on four value dimensions: (1) individualism versus collectivism, (2) large versus small power distance, (3) strong versus weak uncertainty avoidance, and (4) masculinity versus femininity. These dimensions help managers understand how cultural differences affect organizations and management methods.

Key Words

culture (p. 160)
ethnocentricity (p. 160)
aesthetics (p. 164)
demonstration effect (p. 168)
Protestant work ethic (p. 169)
Confucian work ethic (p. 169)
Asian religions (p. 169)
caste system (p. 171)
material culture (p. 173)
technological dualism (p. 175)
appropriate technology (p. 175)
boomerang effect (p. 175)
lingua franca (p. 176)
unspoken language (p. 179)
bribes (p. 181)
extortion (p. 181)
extended family (p. 183)
associations (p. 183)

Questions

1. Why is it helpful for international businesspeople to know that a national culture has two components?
2. A knowledge of culture has been responsible for Disney's success in Tokyo, and ignorance of culture was responsible for the company's large losses in Paris. Discuss.
3. Why do international businesspersons need to consider aesthetics when making marketing decisions?
4. How can the demonstration effect be used to improve productivity? To improve sales?
5. Some societies view change differently than do Americans. What impact does this have on the way American marketers operate in those markets? The way American production people operate?
6. Why must international businesspeople be acquainted with the beliefs of the major religions in the areas in which they work?
7. What Buddhist belief would cause American marketing and production managers to think carefully before transferring their marketing plans or bonus plans to an area where Buddhists are present in large numbers?
8. Why is technological superiority especially significant for international firms?
9. What is the significance of the extended family for international managers?
10. Use Hofstede's four dimensions to analyze this situation: John Adams, with 20 years of experience as general foreman in the United States, is sent as production superintendent to his firm's new plant in Colombia. He was chosen because of his outstanding success in handling workers. Adams uses the participative management style. Can you foresee his having any problems on this new job?

Research Task

globalEDGE.msu.edu 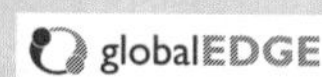

Use the globalEDGE site (http://globalEDGE.msu.edu/) to complete the following exercises:

1. Assume you own an exporting company that specializes in consumer products. You have been selling your products in several different countries but have yet to enter the Asian market. You have chosen South Korea as the first Asian country to enter. Since you have not previously sold your products in any Asian market, you think it would be a good idea to form a strategic alliance with a local firm. You strongly believe that the first impression is important. Therefore, you have decided to collect some information regarding the business culture and local habits of South Korea from the *"Kwintessential"* Web site. Prepare a short report in terms of the most shocking characteristics that may influence business interactions in this country.
2. The cultural distance of countries in which your firm operates is one of the many explanations of significant differences that your U.S.-based employees face when travelling to different affiliates worldwide. Typically, an index of cultural distance can be determined by summing the differences of country-level scores such as those introduced by Hofstede's cultural dimensions. At the present time, your firm has operations in Austria, Guatemala, Iran, Malaysia, and South Africa. Using the *Hofstede Resource Center* based on studies involving cultural dimensions to assess all five countries, determine which affiliates are located in a culture that is least and most similar to the U.S. As there are four main components of each overall cultural distance score, which component(s) can be considered most influential for each country?

Be Attuned to Business Etiquette Minicase 6.1

The proverb "When in Rome, do as the Romans do" applies to business representatives as well as tourists. Being attuned to a country's business etiquette can make or break a sale, particularly in countries where 1,000-year-old traditions can dictate the rules for proper behavior. Anyone interested in being a successful marketer should be aware of the following considerations:

- *Local customer, etiquette, and protocol:* An exporter's behavior in a foreign country can reflect favorably or unfavorably on the exporter, the company, and even the sales potential for the product.
- *Body language and facial expressions:* Often, actions do speak louder than words.
- *Expressions of appreciation:* Giving and receiving gifts can be a touchy subject in many countries. Doing it badly may be worse than not doing it at all.
- *Choices of words:* Knowing when and whether to use slang, tell a joke, or just keep silent is important.

The following informal test will help exporters rate their business etiquette. See how many of the following you can answer correctly. (Answers follow the last question.)

1. You are in a business meeting in an Arabian Gulf country. You are offered a small cup of bitter cardamom coffee. After your cup has been refilled several times, you decide you would rather not have any more. How do you decline the next cup offered to you?
   a. Place your palm over the top of the cup when the coffeepot is passed.
   b. Turn your empty cup upside down on the table.
   c. Hold the cup and twist your wrist from side to side.
2. In which of the following countries are you expected to be punctual for business meetings?
   a. Peru. c. Japan. e. Morocco.
   b. Hong Kong. d. China.
3. Gift giving is prevalent in Japanese society. A business acquaintance presents you with a small wrapped package. Do you:
   a. Open the present immediately and thank the giver?
   b. Thank the giver and open the present later?
   c. Suggest that the giver open the present for you?
4. In which of the following countries is tipping considered an insult?
   a. Great Britain. b. Iceland. c. Canada.
5. What is the normal workweek in Saudi Arabia?
   a. Monday through Friday.
   b. Friday through Tuesday.
   c. Saturday through Wednesday.
6. You are in a business meeting in Seoul. Your Korean business associate hands you his calling card, which states his name in the traditional Korean order: Park Chul Su. How do you address him?
   a. Mr. Park. b. Mr. Chul. c. Mr. Su.
7. In general, which of the following would be good topics of conversation in Latin American countries?
   a. Sports. c. Local politics. e. Travel.
   b. Religion. d. The weather.
8. In many countries, visitors often are entertained in the homes of clients. Taking flowers as a gift to the hostess is usually a safe way to express thanks for the hospitality. However, both the type and the color of the flower can have amorous, negative, or even ominous implications. Match the country where presenting them would be a social faux pas.
   a. Brazil. 1. Red roses.
   b. France. 2. Purple flowers.
   c. Switzerland. 3. Chrysanthemums.
9. In Middle Eastern countries, which hand does one use to accept or pass food?
   a. Right hand. b. Left hand. c. Either hand.
10. Body language is just as important as the spoken word in many countries. For example, in most countries, the thumbs-up sign means "OK." But in which of the following countries is the sign considered a rude gesture?
   a. Germany. b. Italy. c. Australia.

Answers: 1—*c*. It is also appropriate to leave the cup full. 2—*a, b, c, d,* and *e*. Even in countries where local custom does not stress promptness, overseas visitors should be prompt. 3—*b*. 4—*b*. 5—*c*. 6—*a*. The traditional Korean pattern is surname, followed by two given names. 7—*a, d,* and *e*. 8—*a* and 2 (purple flowers are a sign of death in Brazil), *b* and 3 (the same is true of chrysanthemums in France), *c* and 1 (in Switzerland, as well as in many other north European countries, red roses suggest romantic intentions). 9—*a*. Using the left hand would be a social gaffe. 10—*b, c*.

How's Your Business Etiquette?

Add up your correct answers:

8–10: Congratulations, you have obviously done your homework when it comes to doing business overseas.

5–7: Although you have some sensitivity to the nuances of other cultures, you still might make some social errors that could cost you sales abroad.

1–4: Look out, you could be headed for trouble if you leave home without consulting the experts.

Where to Turn for Help

Whether you struck out completely in the business etiquette department or just want to polish your skills, there are several sources you can turn to for help:

- *Books:* Most good bookstores today carry a variety of resource materials to help the traveling business representative.
- *Workshops and seminars:* Many private business organizations and universities sponsor training sessions for the exporter interested in unraveling the mysteries of doing business abroad.
- *State marketing specialists:* In some states, your first contact should be your state commerce or agriculture department, where international specialists can pass on their expertise or put you in touch with someone who can.

Source: *Foreign Agriculture,* U.S. Department of Agriculture, February 1987, pp. 18–19.

7 Natural Resources and Environmental Sustainability

Swiss Mountain Valley

Climate change may prove to be the most important business issue of the 21st century. Managers who wish to be responsible to shareholders and the broader community must be prepared to face the challenges and opportunities presented by our shifting climate. Trillions of dollars, millions of lives, thousands of species-infinite solutions.

—*Stanford University's Graduate School of Business,* The MBA's Climate Change Primer

If an economy is to sustain progress, it must satisfy the basic principles of ecology. If it does not, it will decline and eventually collapse. There is no middle ground.

—*Lester Brown, President, Earth Policy Institute*

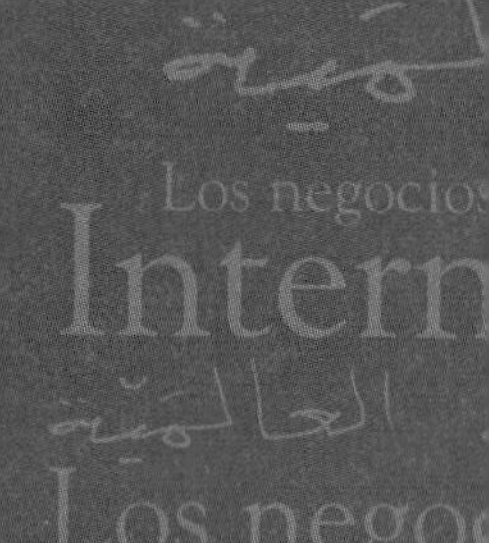

Switzerland, Where Geography Drives Competitive Advantage: Geography, Watches, Chocolate, and Cheese

Watches, lace, carvings, chocolate, cheese, precision machinery, pharmaceuticals—what do they have in common? All are produced in Switzerland; all have a high value per kilo; the Swiss versions are known for their quality; and Switzerland's natural resources, or lack of them, are partially responsible for their being produced in Switzerland.

To appreciate why this is so, consider the following: (1) Switzerland is mostly mountainous, with little level land; (2) it is close to the heavily populated lowlands of Western Europe; (3) transportation across the mountains to these markets is relatively expensive; and (4) Switzerland has practically no mineral resources.

One way to overcome these endowment disadvantages—lack of local sources of raw materials and high transportation costs—is to import small amounts of raw materials, add high value to them, and export a lightweight finished product. The Swiss have done precisely this with the manufacture of watches. They import small volumes of high-quality Swedish steel costing 40 cents per ounce that they then convert to watch movements selling for $60 per ounce. Because of their light weight, the cost of transporting these movements to market is minimal. Precision machinery and pharmaceuticals are other products that minimize the need for importing bulky raw materials. For all of these products, emphasis is placed on the value added by manufacturing, a process that is based on skill, care, and tradition.

Now think about the highly protected Swiss agricultural sector. Although the mountain slopes do not support much agriculture, they are adequate for raising cattle and goats. Production of milk is no problem, but getting it to its major markets outside Switzerland is. Fluid milk is bulky in relation to its value and expensive to transport. The dairymen do to the milk what the watchmakers do to the steel—convert it to a concentrated, high-value product: cheese. Because Swiss cheesemakers have no advantage over their counterparts in the lowland dairying areas nearer to the important markets, they have to compete on the basis of high quality and reputation, which they have carefully promoted.

The plentiful supply of milk is responsible for another product: milk chocolate. The Swiss import the raw chocolate and convert the milk into another high-value-per-kilo product. Certainly the Swiss manufacturer pays higher transportation costs to bring sugar and chocolate in and ship the finished product out than does Hershey in Pennsylvania. Again, the Swiss product must be perceived to be superior so that it will bring a higher price to offset the greater costs.

What about the Swiss lace and carvings? Here, too, is evidence of adjustment to geography—this time, climate. The heavy snowfall and cold temperatures of the Swiss winter leave the farmers with little to do. About the only work necessary is feeding the animals with stored hay. To help pass the time and earn some money, Swiss women make lace and embroidery while the men carve wooden figures. ■

Source: Adapted from Rhoads Murphey, *The Scope of Geography,* 2nd ed. (Skokie, IL: Rand McNally, 1973), pp. 65–67.

CONCEPT PREVIEWS

After reading this chapter, you should be able to:

describe the role of location, topography, climate, and natural resources as factor conditions in Porter's diamond model

explain how surface features contribute to economic, cultural, political, and social differences among nations and among regions of a single country

comprehend the importance of inland waterways and outlets to the sea

recognize that climate exerts a broad influence on business

understand the options available for nonrenewable and renewable energy sources

explain how factor conditions can impact innovation

describe environmental sustainability and its characteristics

draw on the stakeholder theory as a framework for environmental sustainability

Gli Affari Internazionali
ionales
onales Geschäft Παγοσμιο Business
Negócios Internacionais Los Negócios Internacionais
nternacionales Affaires Internationales 國際商務 Παγοσμιο Business

As the Swiss example illustrates, geography—location, topography, climate, and natural resources—can have a profound impact on the way people organize their activities, because the physical environment provides the basic context in which we conduct our economic lives. Other basic factors that influence us include the cultural, political, legal, and economic characteristics of a country. They determine what decisions we make about resource use and the nature of the economy.

We consider the physical elements as largely uncontrollable forces because, much like the foreign environmental forces we discussed in Chapter 1, they are givens around which managers must adjust their strategies to compensate for differences in these forces among markets. Still another way to explain the importance of the environment and natural resources is to examine Michael Porter's diamond, a model he developed to explain differing levels of success among the many national players in world markets.[1] Please see Figure 3.3 on page 79.

Porter's diamond model considers four aspects of a country's economic environment that impact its competitive position: factor conditions, related and supporting industries, demand conditions and firm strategy, and structure and rivalry. His theory suggests that competitively successful countries are the ones that have the most favorable "diamonds." It is the box on the left, **factor conditions,** that we are considering when we examine the natural environment. Porter actually breaks factor conditions into *basic factors,* which are those a country inherits, such as the mountains for the Swiss, and *advanced factors,* those a country readily can mold, such as the labor force and infrastructure.

factor conditions
Attributes that a country inherits, such as climate and natural resources, and those a country can mold, such as the labor force and infrastructure

In this chapter, we address the basic factors, the ones over whose existence we have either no or quite limited control, such as the topography, climate, and natural resources. Earlier economists called these inherited factors "land" (as part of the trio of land, capital, and labor factors of production that Marx refers to as "the holy trinity"). Porter makes the point that local disadvantages in factor conditions can be recognized as advantages and become a force for innovation. Adverse conditions such as local terrain and climate or scarce raw materials, at the basic-factor level, or labor shortages, at the advanced-factor level, force firms to develop new methods, and this innovation often leads to a national comparative advantage. Hence, understanding these attributes is important.

Going back to the Swiss example of high-value-added concentrated goods, the Swiss have developed expertise areas that take into account their geography, in this case, mostly constraints (basic factors), by intentionally developing advanced-factor conditions that recognize and incorporate these basic, inherited conditions. The Swiss have built an educated, skilled, and specialized workforce; they protect agriculture against foreign competition; they pursue neutrality, thus keeping trade relationships open; they have established a reliable transportation system that overcomes their topographical challenges; and they have encouraged high levels of savings, so they can draw on both domestic and foreign savings in Switzerland. Switzerland has taken a strategic approach to developing its resources by drawing on its basic endowments and building its advanced endowments. This approach has led to the Swiss competitive advantage in the areas of watches, chocolate, and cheese, among others.

The scope of the topic *natural resources* by its very nature is quite broad. We begin with a consideration of the basics, location, topography, and climate, and then continue with a focus on the major natural resources of energy and nonfuel minerals. The consideration of natural resources leads directly to concerns about their stewardship. The final section addresses those issues through a focus on environmental sustainability.

Location

Where a country is located, who its neighbors are, and how its capital and major cities are situated are basic-factor conditions (Porter's diamond). These factors, as well as how they contribute to the way a country builds its competitive advantage, should be part of the general knowledge of all international businesspeople. Location helps to explain a number of a country's political and trade relationships, many of which directly affect a company's operations. We look first at the connection between location and political relationships and then at that between location and trade relationships.

POLITICAL RELATIONSHIPS

At the height of the cold war, the location of Austria enabled that country to be a political bridge between the noncommunist nations of the West and the communist nations of the East (see Figure 7.1). It was bounded on the west by Germany and Switzerland, on the northeast by Czechoslovakia, on the east by Hungary, and on the south by Italy and Yugoslavia (Slovenia). In addition, Austria's political neutrality made it a popular location for the offices of international firms servicing Eastern European operations. Furthermore, since Austria had led the Austro-Hungarian Empire until 1918, the Austrians were completely familiar with the cultures and practices of those neighboring countries that they had once been joined to. Finally, Vienna, Austria's capital, is only 40 kilometers (24 miles) from the Czech Republic and 60 kilometers (36 miles) from Hungary.

Because of the political and economic changes in both Western and Eastern Europe, Austria took advantage of its location to (1) increase trade with the East, (2) become the principal financial intermediary between the two regions, and (3) strengthen its role as the regional headquarters for international businesses operating in Eastern Europe.

The collapse of the Soviet bloc (COMECON, consisting of Bulgaria, Czechoslovakia, East Germany, Hungary, Romania, Poland, the Soviet Union, Cuba, Mongolia, and Vietnam) in 1991 forced Eastern European enterprises to reorient their trade toward the West. Because of their location—sharing borders with the Czech Republic, Slovakia, Hungary, and Slovenia—and their location-based relationships, Austrian entrepreneurs have captured an important share of the Western nations' exports to the East. Because of low wage costs in the East and low transport costs due to Austria's proximity to its Eastern neighbors, Austrian producers send textiles, furniture, and machinery components to Eastern countries for further processing and assembly and then bring them back to Austria. Called **passive processing,** this is similar to what foreign firms do in the Mexican maquiladoras. In addition, Austria has been active in bridge building to the east, increasing contacts at all levels with Eastern Europe and the states of the former Soviet Union. Austrians maintain a constant exchange of business representatives, political leaders, students, cultural groups, and tourists with the countries of Central and Eastern Europe. The Austrian government and other organizations provide assistance to former Eastern bloc countries to help them adjust to the changes under way in the region.[2]

passive processing The finishing or refining in Eastern European countries of semifinished goods from the West, which are then returned to the West after finishing; similar to Mexican maquiladora operations

FIGURE 7.1

Austria and Her Neighbors

Finland is another country whose location has contributed to shaping its political relationships. The Finns had been part of the Swedish kingdom from the 12th century until they became part of the Russian Empire in the 19th century. Finland achieved its independence from Russia in 1917, before the Bolshevik Revolution. Then Finland, which shared a 780-mile border with the Soviet Union, thrived on a balancing act it did between that country and Western Europe while maintaining a policy of neutrality. It was the only nation in the world that was at the same time a member of the Soviet trading bloc (COMECON) and the European Free Trade Association (EFTA). However, with the Soviet collapse, Finland lost an important market in the East and turned more fully toward the West. As a result of its active participation in the earlier EC/EFTA negotiations, Finland had already established a high level of integration with the European Union (EU). Finland became a full member of the EU in 1995.

TRADE RELATIONSHIPS

Geographical proximity is often the major reason for trade between nations. As we saw in Chapter 2, the two largest trading partners of the United States—Canada and Mexico—lie on its borders. In 2005, Canada and Mexico represented 27.3 percent of U.S. imports and 36.6 percent of U.S. exports.[3] With proximity, delivery is likely to be faster, freight costs are lower, and service costs for sellers to their clients are likely to be lower, too. Geographic proximity has always been a major factor in the formation of trading groups such as the EU, EFTA, and NAFTA.

Proximity to the market also helps to explain why Japan is one of the Association of Southeast Asian Nations' (ASEAN's) major trading partners, along with the United States, and usually its top source for foreign direct investment. (For membership of ASEAN, see Figure 7.2) Because of Japan's proximity to China, and because Japan needs to maintain good political relationships with its fast-growing neighbor, Japan has also increased its agricultural imports from China, including fresh vegetables. China has been able to take over part of the soybean and wheat imports that were formerly supplied by the United States.

Chile's location in the southern hemisphere accounts, in part, for its exports of grapes, peaches, and raspberries that we eat in North America November through March, when there are few domestically grown supplies. Chile's export of fruit to the United States, which represents more than 20 percent of all Chilean fruit exports and averages over $1 billion in sales annually, is possible because the nation is located where the growing seasons are the opposite of those of the northern hemisphere (Europe and the United States).[4]

FIGURE 7.2

ASEAN Members

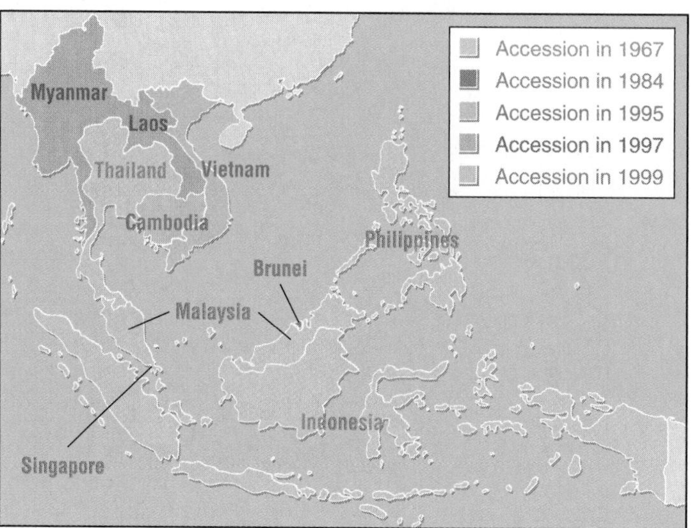

Topography

We now examine some of the principal surface features to establish an idea of which of these physical features may impact business and how. Surface features such as mountains, plains, deserts, and bodies of water contribute to differences in economies, cultures, politics, and social structures both among nations and among regions of a single country. Physical distribution is aided by some features and hindered by others. Differences in **topography,** the features on the surface of the land, may require that products be altered. For example, the effects of altitude on food products begin to be seen at heights above 3,000 feet, so producers of cake mixes must change their baking instructions. Internal combustion engines begin to lose power noticeably at 5,000 feet, which may require the manufacturer of gasoline-powered machinery to use larger engines.

topography
The surface features of a region

MOUNTAINS AND PLAINS

Mountains are barriers that tend to separate and impede exchange and interaction, whereas level areas (plains and plateaus) facilitate them, unless climate makes exchange unlikely, as in the Sahara and Gobi deserts. The extent to which mountains serve as barriers depends on their height, breadth, and length; the ruggedness of the terrain; and whether there are any transecting valleys.

One example of such a barrier is the Himalaya Mountains. Travel across them is so difficult that transportation between India and China is by air or sea rather than overland. The contrast between the cultures of the Indo-Malayan people living to the south of the mountains and those of the Chinese living to the north is evidence of the Himalayas' effectiveness as a barrier. Another example of the influence of mountain barriers is found in Afghanistan, where mountains dominate the landscape, running northeast to southwest through the center of the country, including the Hindukush ("Hindu Killer") area. Over 40 percent of Afghanistan lies above 6,000 feet.[5] For comparison, there are two peaks east of the Mississippi in the United States that hit 6,000 feet, Mt. Mitchell in North Carolina and Mt. Washington in New Hampshire. In Afghanistan, high passes transect the mountains, creating a network for caravans. There are at least 10 major ethnic groups and 33 languages spoken in Afghanistan itself.[6] Figure 7.3. illustrates Afghanistan's topography. In similar fashion, the Alps, Carpathians, Balkans, and Pyrenees have long separated the Mediterranean cultures from those of northern Europe.

FIGURE 7.3

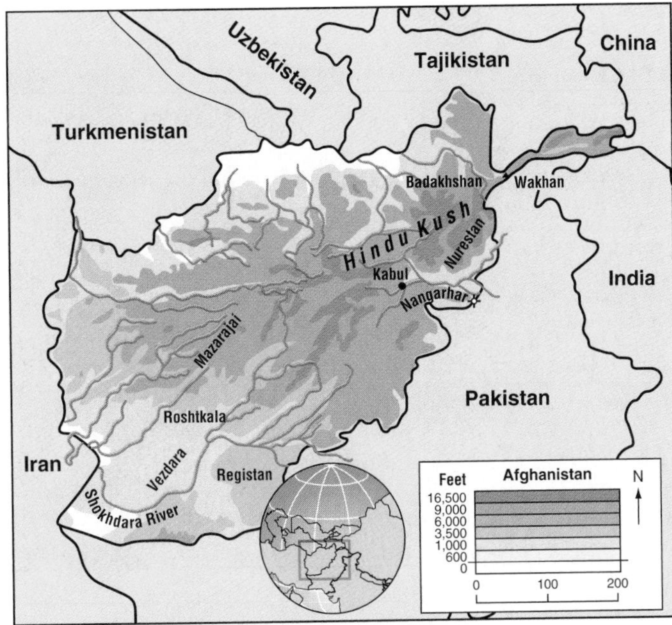

Afghanistan Mountains

Nations whose mountain ranges divide them into smaller regional areas, as in Afghanistan, pose a serious challenge to businesspeople because each regional market will have its own distinctive industries, climate, culture, dialect, and sometimes even language. We now look more closely at four such market examples, Spain, Switzerland, China, and Colombia.

Spain Spain's 17 provinces are often divided into five regions, whose cultural differences are great. Two of them, Catalonia and the Basque country (see Figure 7.4), have separate languages, Catalan and Euskara. Each also has sizable minorities that wish to secede from Spain to form a separate nation. Although the Basques and the Catalans can speak Spanish, when they are among themselves they use their own languages, which are completely unintelligible to other Spaniards. This creates the same kinds of problems as those found wherever there are language differences: Spanish-speaking managers do not attain the empathy with their local employees that they do in other parts of Spain, and sales representatives who speak the local language are more effective. Moreover, the language differences increase promotional costs if, to be more effective, Spanish companies choose to prepare their material in Euskara, Catalan, and Spanish.[7]

You may be aware of the Basques due to the political unrest that is prevalent among them (similar unrest is present, to a lesser extent, among the Catalans). Since 1968 an armed terrorist group called ETA, the Basque-language acronym for Basque Homeland and Liberty (Euskadita Askatasuni), has killed over 800 people, mostly members of the security forces, in its campaign for Basque independence. ETA financed its attacks by charging local businesses

FIGURE 7.4

Spain

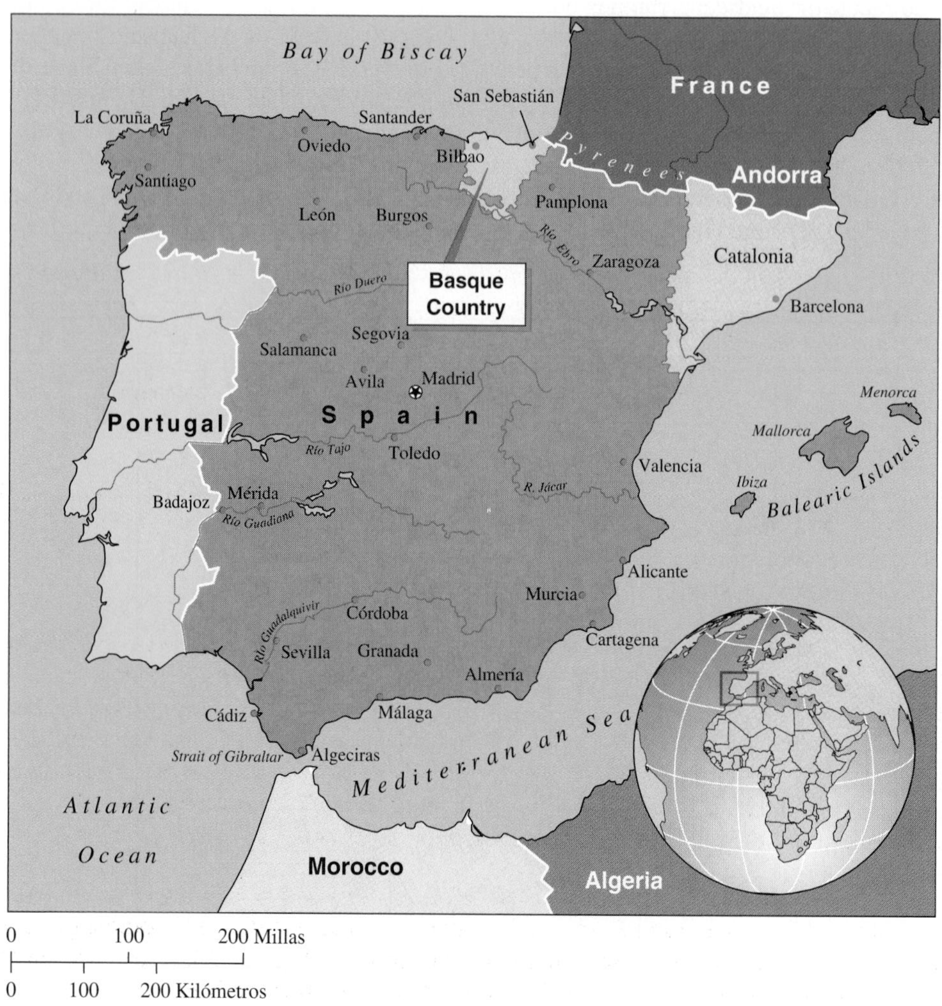

FIGURE 7.5 The Cantons and Major Language Areas of Switzerland

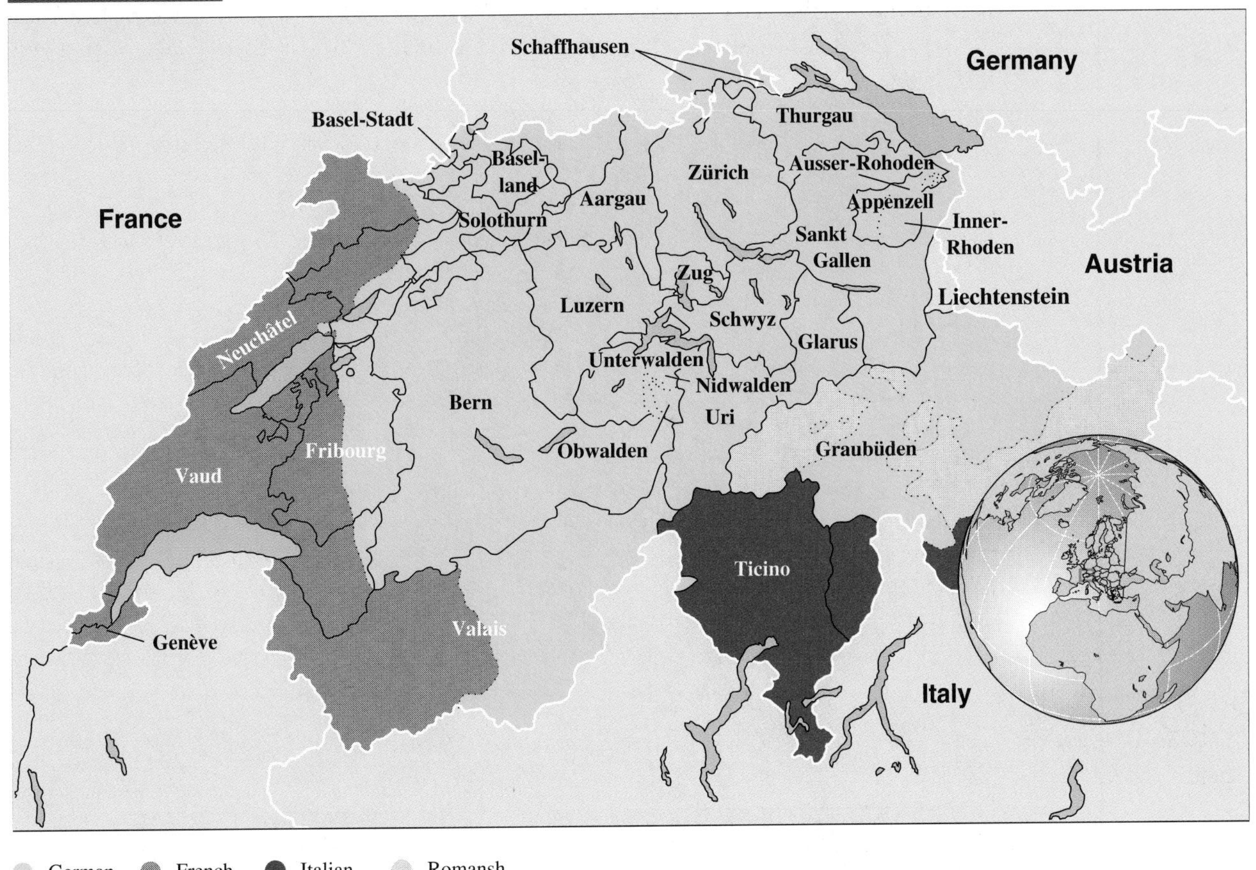

a "revolutionary tax" or by holding wealthy businesspeople for ransom. In March 2006, ETA declared a permanent cease-fire.[8] The Spanish and French governments had arrested many Basque activists, and the Madrid train bombings in March 2004, thought to be the work of Islamic terrorists, has made the public unsympathetic to violence as a political tool.

Switzerland Switzerland is another country separated into distinctive cultural regions by mountains. In a country one-half the size of Maine, four different languages—Italian, French, German, and Romansh (related to Latin)—are spoken, along with over 35 dialect variations among them (see Figure 7.5). To the consternation of advertising managers attempting to reach all the regions of the country, each of the three major language groups—German (75 percent), French (20 percent), and Italian (4 percent)—has its own radio and television network, and the German stations broadcast in Romansh, too.

China In China, dozens of languages, each having many dialects, developed in villages separated by mountains. This caused a communication problem that hindered economic development until the government decreed Mandarin to be the official language, known as *Putonghua*, in 1956. Today, though, many dialects persist. The written language is shared among the many language groups, but spoken language is virtually incomprehensible across language borders. Look at the map on the right in Figure 7.6 and compare it to the topographical map beside it. Note that the language areas correspond to topographical features such as mountains and plains.

Colombia Colombia is similar to Switzerland in that mountains divide its markets. Three ranges of the Andes run like spines from north to south and divide Colombia into four separate markets, each with its own culture and dialects (see Figure 7.7). Depending on the product, marketers may need to create four distinctive promotional mixes.

FIGURE 7.6 Topographical and Language Maps of China

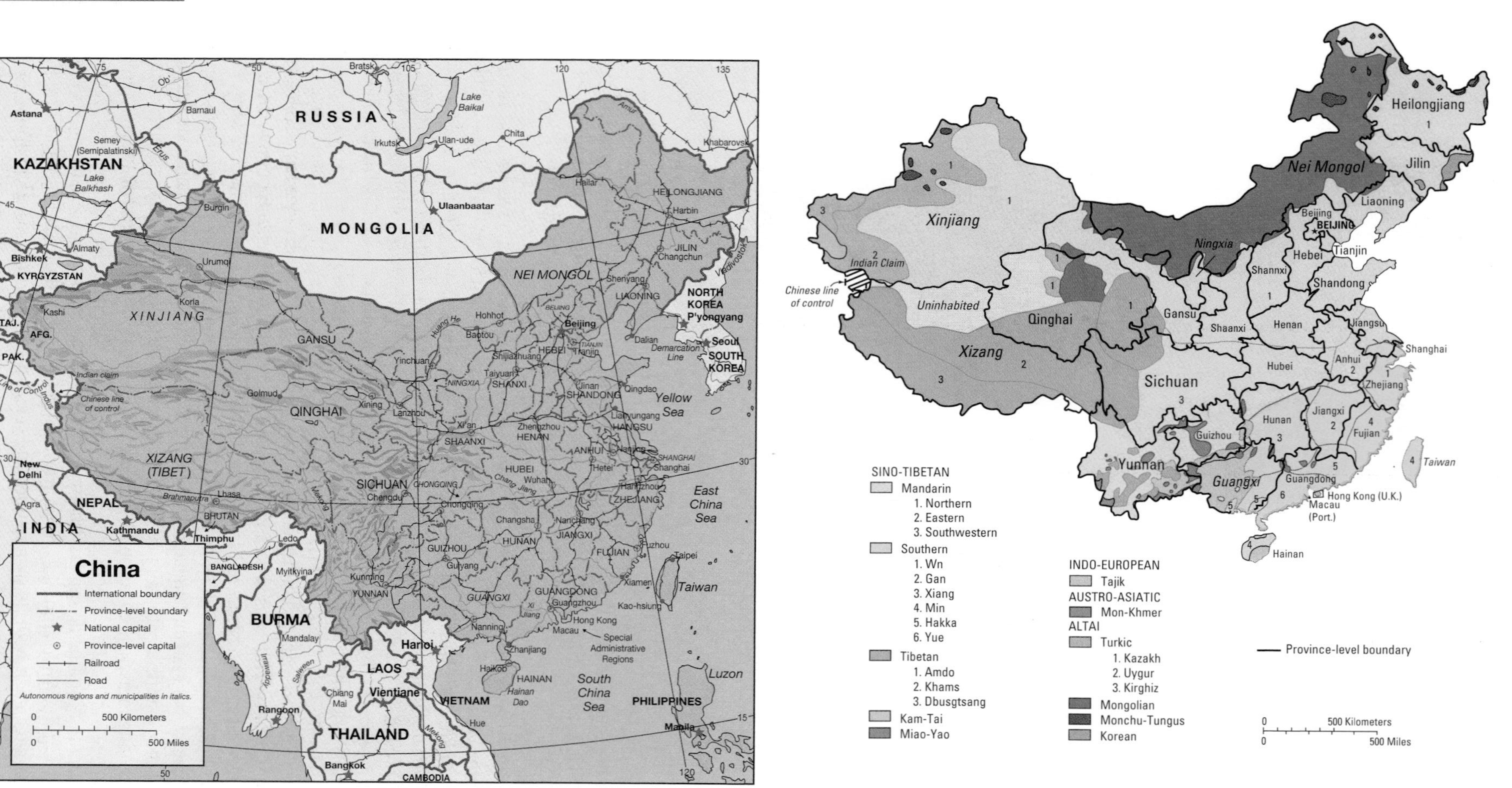

FIGURE 7.7

Colombia

Colombia differs from Switzerland, however, in that besides containing distinct cultures within its borders, it experiences a range of distinct climates. Because of its location near the equator, Colombia has no seasons, but the great differences in altitude throughout habitable parts of the country result in a variety of climates. These range from hot and humid at sea level (mean average temperature of 82 degrees in Barranquilla) to cold and dry in the 10,000-foot-high snowcapped mountains (57 degrees in Bogotá). Such variation creates production and inventory challenges for a manufacturer that must produce a distinct product and package for each zone. A product with adequate cooling and lubrication for the temperate zone would function well in Bogotá but might be woefully deficient in tropical Barranquilla. Similarly, a machine powered with an internal combustion engine might perform well in Barranquilla but be severely underpowered in the 10,000-foot altitude of Bogotá.

Such climatic conditions are not peculiar to Colombia, so international businesspeople should examine topographical maps to see which tropical countries possess this combination of lowlands and mountains. If the firm's products will not function properly in such climate extremes, the firm must either redesign the products or bypass at least part of the market.

We also see in Colombia another effect of mountains. Because they function as barriers and causes of climate variations, they create concentrations of population. These concentrations occur either because the climate is more pleasant at higher altitudes or because the mountains are barriers to population movement. For example, nearly 80 percent of Colombia's population is located in the western highlands (only one-third of the nation's area) because the

FIGURE 7.8

Australia

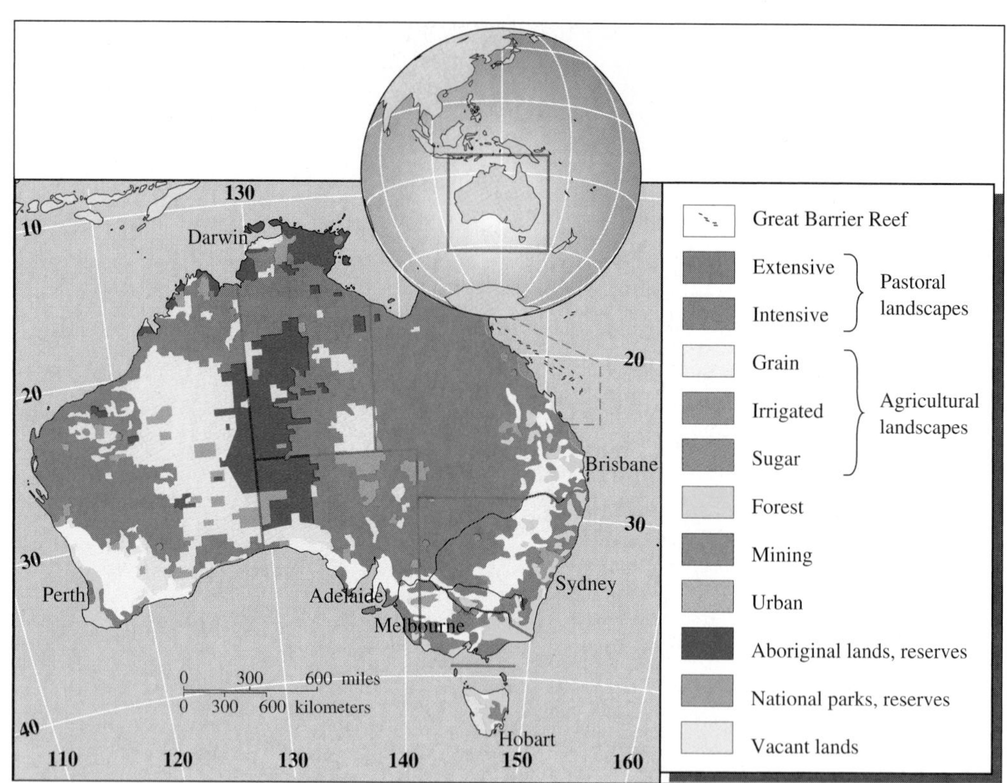

climate there is moderate. Except in the tropics, the population density generally decreases as the elevation increases. If you were to place a population map over a topographical map, the blank areas on the population map would generally coincide with the areas of higher elevation. For example, 90 percent of Switzerland's population is located in a narrow belt at the base of the Alps. The reason for this is that dense population requires commerce, manufacturing, and agriculture, which all depend on the good transportation and ease of communication afforded by the plains.

DESERTS AND TROPICAL FORESTS

Deserts and tropical forests, like mountains, separate markets, increase the cost of transportation, and create concentrations of population.

Deserts Over one-third of the earth's surface consists of arid and semiarid regions located either on the coasts, where the winds blow away from the land, or in the interior, where mountains or long distances cause the winds to lose their moisture before reaching these regions. Every continent has them, and every west coast between 20 and 30 degrees north or south of the equator is dry. Since people, plants, and animals must have water to exist, the climate and vegetation deserts are also human deserts. Only where there is a major source of water, as in Egypt, is there a concentration of population.

Nowhere is the relationship between water supply and population concentration better illustrated than in Australia, a continent the size of the continental United States but with only 20.1 million inhabitants. This compares with a U.S. population of 295.7 million. Australia's surrounding coastline is humid and fertile, whereas the huge center of the country is mainly a desert closely resembling the Sahara. Figure 7.8 illustrates this. Because of its geography, Australia's population has tended to concentrate along the coastal areas in and around the state capitals, which are also major seaports, and in the southeastern fifth of the nation, where more than one-half of the population lives. This gives Australia one of the highest percentages of urban population in the world, 85 percent.

FIGURE 7.9

Canadian Shield

The distances between Australian cities and the fact that they are seaports make coastal shipping preferred over road and rail transportation. However, the long distances between major markets result in transportation accounting for as much as 30 percent of the final cost of the product, compared with the more usual 10 percent in the United States and Europe.

The population distribution in Australia also has a profound impact on the media. Most TV and print media are concentrated in capital city areas and are not national. This requires that advertisers buy space or time on a state-by-state or city-by-city basis. Although most capital city areas have three commercial TV channels, there is little networking.

Even though 70 percent of the country is arid or semiarid, some areas in the northern rim of Australia receive up to 100 inches of rainfall annually, much like the monsoon areas of India. Thus, firms entering the Australian market face the same extreme differences of temperature and humidity as encountered in Colombia.

Australia has little land above 3,000 feet in altitude. Were it not for this uniform topography, the temperature differences there would be great, as they are in countries with large, hot desert areas and irregular surfaces. Iran is such a nation. In the summer, temperatures may reach 130ºF, whereas winter temperatures in high altitudes may drop to –18ºF. From December to March, it is possible to ski just an hour and a half's drive from Teheran, the capital. Like Australia, Iran's population distribution is heavily influenced by climate and topography. More than 70 percent of the country—consisting mostly of mountains and deserts—is uninhabited, and one-half of the population lives in urban areas.

Tropical Forests At the other extreme from deserts, tropical rain forests also are a barrier to economic development and human settlement, especially when they are combined with a harsh climate and poor soil. This occurs in the tropical rain forests located in the Amazon basin, Southeast Asia, and the Congo. Except in parts of West Africa and Java, rain forests are thinly populated and little developed economically. For example, the greatest rain forest of them all—in the Brazilian Amazon basin—has been called one of the world's greatest deserts because of its low population density. Although it covers more than 1 million square miles (one-fourth of the U.S. land area) and occupies one-half of Brazil, the Brazilian rain forest is inhabited by just 4 percent of the country's population. Only true deserts have a population density lower than the Amazon's one person per square mile.

Canadian Shield
A massive area of bedrock covering one-half of Canada's landmass

The Canadian Shield Although the **Canadian Shield** is neither a desert nor a tropical forest, this massive area of bedrock covering one-half of Canada's landmass merits mention because it has most of their characteristics—forbidding topography, poor soil, and harsh climate (see Figure 7.9 on the previous page). The Shield is swept by polar air, which permits a frost-free growing season of only four months. During that time, residents are joined by swarms of black flies and mosquitoes. Like deserts and tropical forests, its population density is very low: Only 10 percent of Canada's population inhabits this region of 3,000,000 square miles.[9]

Managers know that in more densely populated nations, marketing and distributing their products costs less because population centers are closer, communication systems are better, and more people are available for employment. Therefore, when they compare population densities such as Canada's 3 inhabitants per square kilometer, Australia's 2, Brazil's 21, and the United States' 30 with the Netherlands' 395 or Japan's 337, they may draw the wrong conclusions.[10] However, if they are aware that the population in Canada, Australia, or Brazil is highly concentrated in a relatively small area, for the reasons we have been examining, then a very different situation prevails.

The next section explores how bodies of water also are responsible for concentrations of population.

BODIES OF WATER

Bodies of water, unlike mountains, deserts, and tropical forests, attract people and facilitate transportation. A world population map clearly shows that bodies of water have attracted more people than have areas remote from water (see Figure 7.10). Densely populated regions that do not coincide with rivers or lakes are generally close to the sea. As you can see from the population map, people cluster around the Amazon, the Congo, the Mississippi, the St. Lawrence, and the Great Lakes. In Europe, the plains of the Po River in Italy and the Rhine, running from the glaciers in Switzerland, past Liechtenstein, Austria, and France, into

FIGURE 7.10

World Population Map

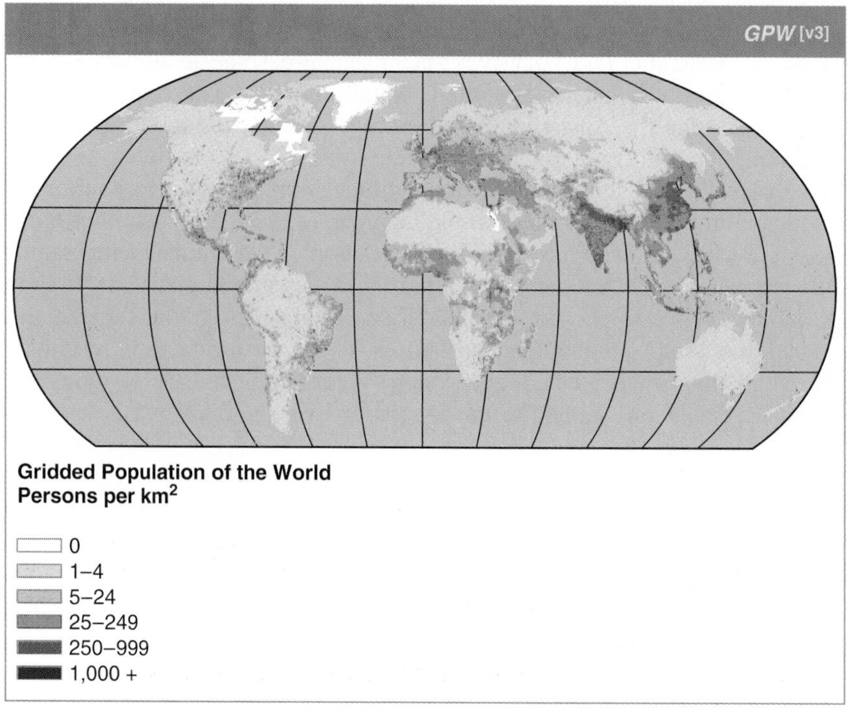

Germany and on to the Netherlands on its way to the North Sea, are easily recognizable. So are rivers that cross deserts, such as the Nile, the Indus (Pakistan), the Tigris-Euphrates (Iraq), and the Amu Darya (central Asia), although these rivers are more important for the irrigation water and fertile soil they bring than for transportation.

Inland Waterways Bodies of water that are significant because they provide inexpensive access to markets in the interior of various nations are called **inland waterways.** Before the construction of railways, water transport was the only economically practical carrier for bulk goods moving over long distances. Water transport increased even after the building of railroads; and today, in every continent except Australia, which has no inland waterways, extensive use is still made of water transportation. The importance of waterways relative to railroads, however, has diminished everywhere with one exception—the Rhine waterway, the world's most important inland waterway system.

inland waterways
Waterways that provide access to interior regions

Europe The **Rhine waterway,** the main transportation artery of Europe, carries a greater volume of goods than do the combined railways that run parallel to it. To illustrate the Rhine's significance, one-half of Switzerland's exports and nearly three-fourths of its imports pass through the city of Basel, the Swiss inland port. This cargo is carried on the country's own 31-vessel oceangoing fleet via the Rhine waterway to Rotterdam, 500 miles to the north. (See Figure 7.11.) From ancient times, shipments have moved between the Netherlands, Belgium, Germany, France, Austria, Liechtenstein, and Switzerland by means of the Rhine and its connecting waterways. The Rhine-Main-Danube Canal, completed in 1992, creates access from the Netherlands and the North Sea through 15 countries to the Black Sea. From there, shipments can continue to Moscow over the interconnected system of the Volga and Don rivers. Not many ships undertake the entire 30-day voyage from Rotterdam to the Black Sea (3,500 kilometers), but this waterway has stimulated shipping over shorter east-west

Rhine waterway
A system of rivers and canals that is the main transportation artery of Europe

FIGURE 7.11 Rhine-Main-Danube Canal

Source: Center for International Earth Science Information Network (CIESIN), Columbia University; and Centro Internacional de Agricultura Tropical (CIAT). Used by permission. http://ciesin.columbia/edu/gpw

WORLD view   

U.S. Inland Ports Offer Global Shippers a New Advantage

Congestion, security, and environmental concerns have continued to play major roles in U.S. coastal ports, both on the East and West coasts. (They have also become increasingly burdensome in other modes of transportation, air, rail, and road, as anyone who has traveled recently can testify.) At the coastal ports, huge cargo ships arrive from Asia, Latin America, and Europe and find themselves beginning the slowest part of their journey, waiting in a queue for dock space, unloading, and reloading. Inland ports offer global shippers to the United States a solution. They can be quick, efficient, and reliable and can cut the costs of reaching the middle of the nation.

At inland ports, large global shipments can be unloaded, warehoused, sorted for further movement in the delivery process (called *break bulk services*), and sent on their ways. The availability of rail, road, and air routes and major trade corridors make intermodal transport attractive, as well.

One example of a new inland port that has been thriving is in Kansas City. *Kansas City SmartPort* was created as a nonprofit entity in 2001 to unify a number of efforts by several area organizations concerned with trade and commerce. The area is on the Missouri River, which connects to the Mississippi, forming the largest inland waterway in the United States. Three major interstate highways connect at its center, as does the second-busiest U.S. rail yard.

International businesspeople see the advantages of operations such as SmartPort. Chris Gutierrez, SmartPort's president, notes that a number of business distribution centers have located in Kansas City. Case New Holland, the agricultural and industrials equipment designer and manufacturer, has built a 500,000-square-foot facility, and Musician's Friend, the largest music equipment company in the nation, has built a 700,000-square-foot facility. Take a look at SmartPort's operations at www.kcsmartport.com.

Roger Morton, "Logistics Today," June 2006, www.logisticstoday.com/showStoryBody.asp?SID={C8B678CB-4698-447F-BC76-DEB2F199AA7E}&nID=7961 (accessed June 6, 2006).

routes, such as Nuremburg to Budapest and Vienna to Rotterdam. Increasingly, firms have been turning to the Rhine waterway as an environmentally friendly alternative to road transportation.

The EU recently announced a new program to shift transportation toward inland waterways. Called Navigation and Inland Waterway Action and Development in Europe (NAIADES),[11] the program will run from 2006 to 2013. Naiads are the mythological nymphs who preside over bodies of fresh water. The NAIADES fleet of 11,000 vessels has a capacity equivalent to 10,000 trains or 440,000 trucks. Inland waterways can make transport in Europe more efficient, reliable, and environmentally friendly. According to the commissioner in charge of transport, inland waterways in the Benelux countries and France have captured significant shares of the transport business, The Netherlands uses inland waterways the most intensively of any European country, with approximately 40 percent of its transport traffic on these important arteries. In comparison, in Central and Eastern Europe, only 7 to 10 percent of the Danube's capacity is being tapped. (Because water transport tends to be inexpensive and create little pollution, recently many governments have developed programs to increase the use of inland waterways. The Worldview box describes such a program in Kansas City, aimed at more fully developing use of the Missouri River.)

South America In South America, the Amazon and its tributaries offer some 57,000 kilometers of navigable waterways during the flood season (see Figure 7.12). Oceangoing vessels can reach Manaus, Brazil (1,600 kilometers upstream), and smaller river steamers can go all the way to Iquitos, Peru (3,600 kilometers from the Atlantic).

Farther south, the Mercosur governments of Argentina, Brazil, Paraguay, and Uruguay are working to develop the Paraná and Paraguay rivers as a trade corridor connecting the vast landlocked interior of South America with seaports at the River Plate estuary near Montevideo (see Figure 7.13 on page 206). Although at present the rivers are only partly navigable, Argentina uses river ports on the Paraná to handle 25 percent of its exports and Paraguay imports most of its fuel on the Paraguay River. The Mercosur governments embarked on a $1 billion project called Hidrovia to dredge the 3,400-kilometer river system to permit reliable barge transport from the heart of South America's farmland in northern Argentina, eastern Bolivia, and western Brazil to the port of Rosario, near Buenos Aires. However, the project was suspended in 2001 due to environmental concerns. The original plans would not have spared the Pantanal, the world's largest tropical wetlands. More environmental studies are under way, and the shape that the Hidrovia project will take is still uncertain.

FIGURE 7.12 Amazon River

Asia In Asia, the major waterways are the Yangtze (China), the Ganges (India), and the Indus (Pakistan). Rivers are especially important in China because water is the least expensive, and often the only, means of moving industrial raw materials to the manufacturing centers.

FIGURE 7.13

Parana-Paraguay Rivers Trade Corridor

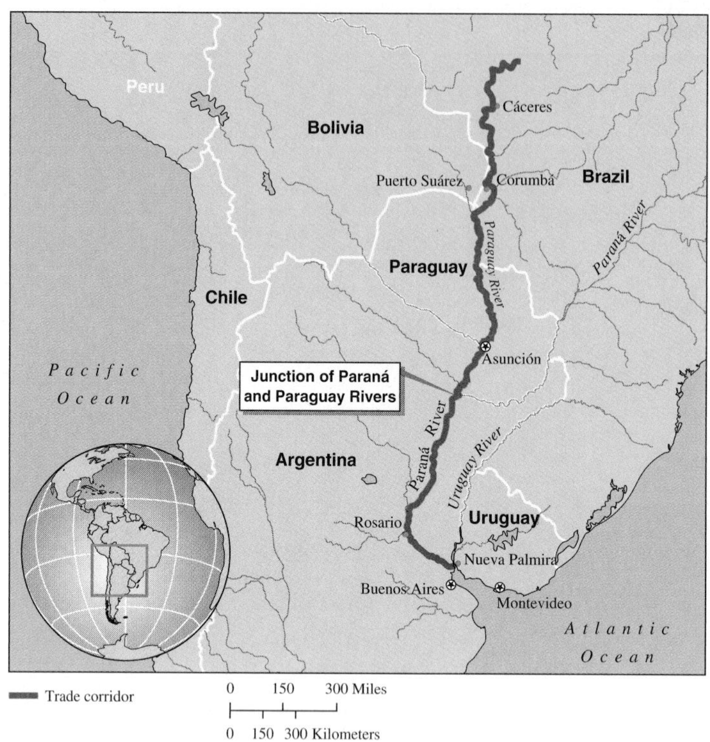

Oceangoing vessels can travel up theYangtze as far as Wuhan, 1,000 kilometers from the sea. When the massive Three Gorges dam hydroelectric project is finished in 2009, oceangoing vessels will be able to continue past Wuhan to Chongquing, which will become an inland seaport 2,400 kilometers from the ocean. The dam itself, the largest concrete dam ever constructed, was completed in May 2006,[12] but the project has other construction to complete before it begins to operate. The reservoir the dam creates is 650 kilometers long. An estimated 1.9 million persons have lost their homes along the river's densely populated shores as a result. Because of environmental issues (the project is flooding an area comparable to the Grand Canyon in the United States, but with three gorges) as well as the human rights issues, the World Bank refused to fund the dam. Multinational construction companies and some commercial banks have participated in the project. The Chinese government estimates that the total cost of the dam will reach $24.5 billion by the time it is finished. At the International Rivers network site,[13] you can view a video of the clearing of a village area connected to the Three Gorges project and travel on a boat on the Yangtze. See www.irn.org/programs/threeg.

United States The United States depends heavily on two waterways. One, the Great Lakes–St. Lawrence, enables ocean freighters to travel 3,700 kilometers inland, thus transforming lake ports into ocean ports. The other waterway, the Mississippi, connects the Great Lakes to the Gulf of Mexico and is especially important for carrying bulky commodities, such as wheat, cotton, coal, timber, and iron ore.

Outlets to the Sea

Outlets to the sea are another notable aspect of waterways. Historically, navigable waterways with connections to the ocean have permitted the low-cost transportation of goods and people from a country's coast to its interior, and even now they are the only means of access from the coasts of numerous developing nations. In Africa, where 14 of the world's 20 landlocked developing countries are located, access to the coast is a major issue. Governments must construct costly, long truck routes and extensive feeder networks for relatively low volumes of traffic. Furthermore, governments in countries with coastlines through which the imports and exports of the landlocked nations must pass are in a position to exert considerable political influence. Struggles for outlets to the sea still exist as important political and economic factors.

Cargo ships passing through Germany on Europe's main transportation artery, the Rhine waterway.
Hans Wolf

Bolivia offers a good example of this struggle. It lost an outlet to the Pacific Ocean in the 1879–83 War of the Pacific with Chile. Many decades of discussions followed with no workable agreement. Bolivia must ship through Arica, the free port in northern Chile, and inland waterways. In 1996, Bolivia opened its first paved road link to the Pacific, a 192-kilometer highway to the Bolivian-Chilean border, the last section of Bolivia's 1,000-kilometer Export Corridor, which has opened Asian markets to Bolivian and Brazilian farmers (see Figure 7.14). Although Bolivia uses a Chilean port as an outlet to the sea, the country still does not maintain full diplomatic relations with Chile, having severed them in 1978 over this very issue. This dispute affects business relations beyond transportation. Neither country is inclined to buy from its neighbor.[14]

FIGURE 7.14

Bolivia's Export Corridor

Climate

climate
Meteorological conditions, including temperature, precipitation, and wind, that prevail in a region

Climate (temperature, precipitation, and wind) is the most important element of the physical forces because it, more than any other factor, sets the limits on what people can do, physically and economically. Where the climate is harsh, there are few human settlements, but where it is permissive, there tends to be population density. However, climate is not deterministic—it allows certain developments to occur, but it does not cause them. Nonclimatic factors, such as mineral deposits, accessibility to an area, economic and political organizations, cultural tradition, availability of capital, and the growth of technology, are more important than climate in the development of trade and manufacturing. That is, in terms of Porter's diamond, although climate is an inherited asset as a factor condition, technology can be applied to modify its impact.

Similar climates occur in similar latitudes and continental positions, and the more water-dominated an area, the more moderate its climate. Thus, the northwest United States and northwest Europe, which are at similar latitudes and are both influenced by the sea, have mild, moist climates. Southeast Australia, New Zealand, and part of South Africa are at the same latitude and close to the sea, and they too have mild, moist climates. At the other extreme, Kansas and Central Asia, which are at the same latitude but far from the sea, are dry and have cold winters and hot summers.

CLIMATE AND DEVELOPMENT

For centuries, writers have used climatic differences to explain differences in human and economic development. They have suggested that the greatest economic and intellectual development has occurred in the temperate climates of northern Europe and the United States because the less temperate climates limit human energy and mental powers.[15] However, businesspeople must not be taken in by this ethnocentric reasoning, which fails to explain the difference in the level of technology employed in the 1600s by the inhabitants of northeastern North America and the inhabitants of northern Europe. Clearly there were other factors involved, such as the Industrial Revolution, population size, and location. The Pulitzer Prize–winning *Guns, Germs, and Steel: The Fates of Human Societies,* by Jared Diamond, explores the basis of these factors.[16] Diamond argues that the gaps in technology among human societies are caused by environmental differences amplified by feedback loops and that these differences do not lead to intellectual or moral superiority.

Climate has had some influence on economic development. Studies by the World Bank have shown that many of the factors responsible for the underdeveloped state of most tropical nations are present because of the tropical climate. Continuous heat and the lack of winter temperatures to constrain the reproduction and growth of weeds, insects, viruses, birds, and parasites result in destroyed crops, dead cattle, and people infected with debilitating diseases.[17] As grim as this may sound, there is hope. The World Bank points out that techniques are becoming available to control pests and parasites. Once this is accomplished, the very characteristics that are now detrimental to tropical Africa will give it sizable advantages over the temperate zones in agriculture. The resulting income would create a market in tropical Africa that could easily surpass that of the Middle East. In a similar way, the huge development shift from the northern to the southern U.S. states was supported by two technological innovations, DDT for malaria and air-conditioning.[18]

CLIMATE IMPLICATIONS

The differences in climate conditions among a firm's manufacturing locations and markets can have a significant impact on its manufacturing and its product mix. For example, internal combustion engines designed for temperate climates generally require extra cooling capacity and special lubrication to withstand the higher temperatures of the tropics. Goods that deteriorate in high humidity require special, more expensive packaging; machinery operating in dusty conditions needs special dust protection; and so forth.

When climatic extremes exist in a single market and the product is temperature- or humidity-sensitive, the company may have to produce and stock two distinct versions to satisfy the entire market. Severe winters, such as those in Canada, or the heavy monsoon rains that fall in northern Australia and India can impede distribution. This may require that the firm carry extraordinarily large inventories in its major markets to compensate for delays in delivery from the factory. All these conditions may have an adverse effect on profitability.

Location, topography, and climate form the basic, inherited context for business ventures; they are some of the givens. Try as the Swiss might to alter things, Switzerland is likely to continue to be a mountainous country with a heavily populated plain at the foot of the Alps. Of course, people may undertake massive modifications: Holland, situated below the North Sea level, has protected itself through a system of dykes. Singapore has greatly increased its landmass by reclaiming land from the surrounding sea, as have the Japanese in their expansion into Tokyo Harbor through extensive landfill. In a sense, these countries have affected their natural resources through human action. Such modification of an inherited factor illustrates Porter's idea of changing a disadvantage to an advantage.

Yet for the most part, location, topography, and climate are permanent facts. Often, attempts to change these natural characteristics can backfire. Right now in central China, the Badain Jaran desert is fast swallowing entire villages and leaving lakebeds near the provincial city of Minqin dry and dusty.[19] As Chia Erlong, an environmentalist who lives in Minqin, explains, "We must find ways to live with nature in some kind of balance. The government mainly wants to control nature, which is what did all the harm in the first place." In contrast, natural resources, our next focus, present businesspeople with sources of raw materials that, unlike location, topography and climate, are extractable and malleable.

Natural Resources

What are **natural resources**? For our purposes, we define them as anything supplied by nature on which people depend. Some of the principal types of natural resources important to business are energy and nonfuel minerals. In this section, we look first at energy sources, both nonrenewable and renewable. These two types of important natural resources are central to productive capacity. Then we direct our attention to nonfuel minerals. The final section of this chapter addresses sustainability.

natural resources
Anything supplied by nature on which people depend

ENERGY

Natural resources related to energy can be categorized as nonrenewable and renewable. The fossil fuels, which are the source of much of our energy, include petroleum, coal, and natural gas and are *nonrenewable*—once we use them, their supplies are depleted. Among renewable energy sources are hydroelectric, wind, solar, geothermal, waves, tides, biomass, and ocean thermal energy conversion. Figure 7.15 illustrates the world's energy supply by fuel. We look first at the major nonrenewable energy sources, and then at the burgeoning area of renewable energy sources.

Nonrenewable Energy Sources The principal nonrenewable energy sources are the fossil fuels and nuclear power.

Petroleum Petroleum has been a cheap source of energy and a raw material for plastics, fertilizers, and other industrial applications. According to some analysts, the world is running out of oil, but according to other sources, there are reserves sufficient to last for 50 years at the present rate of consumption.[20] Estimates of reserves change for a number of reasons:[21]

- New discoveries continue to be made in proven fields with the aid of improved prospecting equipment.
- Governments open up their countries to exploration and production. For example, the countries of the former Soviet Union have allowed commercial exploitation of the reserves under the Caspian Sea.

FIGURE 7.15

Total Primary Energy Supply

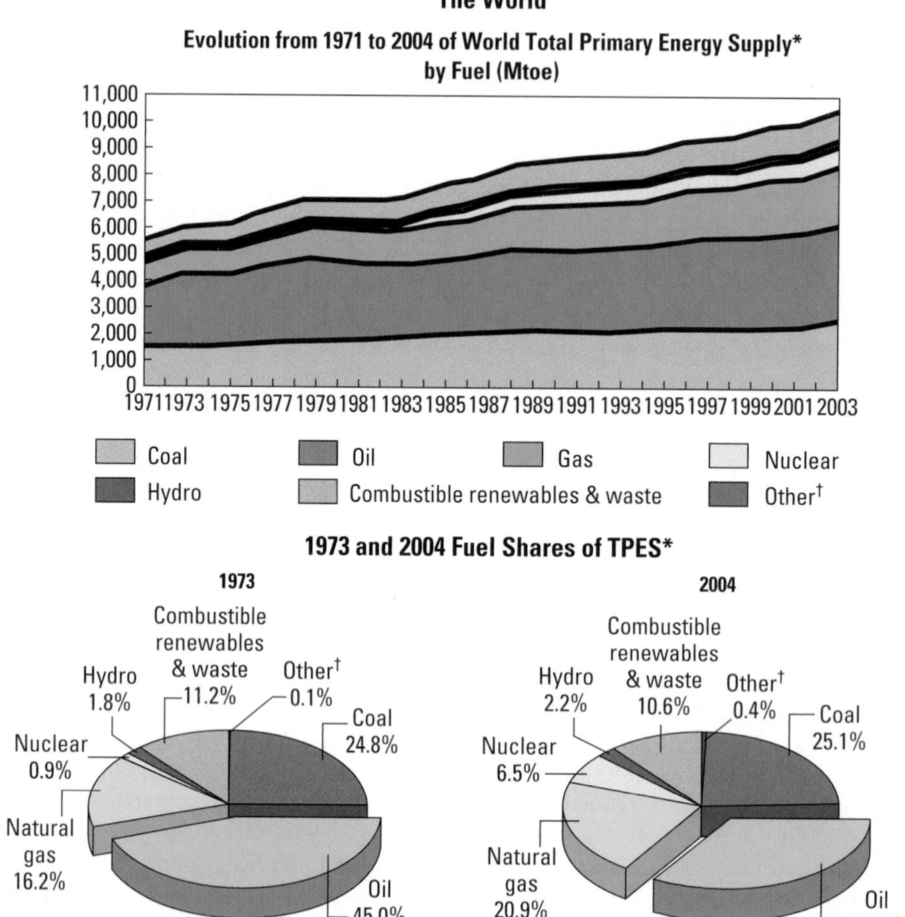

*Excludes international marine bunkers and electricity trade.
†Includes geothertmal, solar, wind heat, etc.

Source: International Energy Agency, Key World Energy Statistics, 2005.

- New techniques, such as steam and hot water injection, enable producers to obtain greater output from wells already in operation, thus increasing the recoverable amount in an oil field.
- Automated, less expensive equipment lowers drilling costs; for instance, wellheads located on the ocean floor can replace expensive offshore platforms. This allows a company to profitably work smaller-sized discoveries that otherwise it would not touch.

Nevertheless, there is no doubt that we face a dependency issue with oil. A group of oil industry professionals, the Association for the Study of Peak Oil and Gas, points out that we are probably in the peak production time period right now.[22] The question is, How long do we have to make adjustments before the price of oil becomes prohibitive? This association of scientists interested in the impact of resource constraints notes that running out of oil is not the issue: rather, it is affording the price of this depleting resource once there are signs that we have reached the production peak.

The U.S. Energy Information Administration projects that world energy consumption will continue to increase through 2025, with dramatic increases in developing countries such as China and India as they industrialize.[23] Oil is projected to remain the world's dominant

TABLE 7.1 Greatest Oil Reserves, by Country

Rank	Country	Proved Reserves (billion barrels)
1	Saudi Arabia	261.9
2	Canada	178.8
3	Iran	125.8
4	Iraq	115.0
5	Kuwait	101.5
6	United Arab Emirates	97.8
7	Venezuela	77.2
8	Russia	60.0
9	Libya	39.0
10	Nigeria	35.3

Source: *Oil & Gas Journal* 102, no. 47 (December 10, 2004). From U.S. Energy Information Administration, www.eia.doe.gov/emeu/international/petroleu.html.

energy source in this period. Present production is around 84 million barrels per day. Conservative analysts suggest that at 90 million barrels per day, the peak may come 30 years out.[24] Whether 30 years or 50 years, we know that such a day is coming. Table 7.1 shows the greatest oil reserves by country.

There are unconventional sources of synthetic petroleum whose usefulness, as conventional sources are depleted, increases. Among them are oil sands, oil-bearing shale, coal, and natural gas. The last two are also used to generate energy on their own.

The *oil sands* are located primarily in Canada (Athabasca, in Alberta) and in Venezuela. The sands, which contain bitumen, a tarlike crude oil, account for about 39 percent (1 million barrels per day) of Canada's crude oil production. However, production capacities are increasing, and the latest estimates are that oil-sands production will reach 2.7 million barrels per day by the year 2012.[25] At the June 2006 rate of US$75 per barrel, the cost of extracting bitumen, the source material for the oil, is competitive with that of conventional crude. The oil that can be recovered economically from the Canadian oil sands with present extraction techniques is estimated to be in the range of 180 billion barrels, exceeding the proven oil reserves of every oil-producing country except Saudi Arabia. At present consumption rates, 180 billion barrels would supply the planet for about five years.[26] A new technology, steam-assisted gravity drainage (SAGD), enables producers to exploit additional resources that are too deep to mine from the surface.

Oil-bearing **shale** is fine-grained sedimentary rocks that yield 25 liters or more of liquid hydrocarbons per ton of rock when heated to 500°C. The largest source of this material is the three-state area of Utah, Colorado, and Wyoming, in the U.S. This source has remained undeveloped because of the availability of less expensive conventional oil, the environmental problems of waste rock disposal, and the great quantities of water needed for processing. Recent technological advances have increased the likelihood that such recovery can be done with minimal environmental impact. A March 2004 Department of Energy report describes the increasing significance of the oil shale resource in the United States and calls for cooperation among federal and state agencies to shepherd oil shale projects through the permitting process, which can present a considerable hurdle.[27] An Australian oil shale project was cancelled after Greenpeace campaigned against it. The major Greenpeace argument was that extracting the oil from shale created four times the greenhouse impact as did extracting conventionally drilled oil. The project also received considerable government funding. The Greenpeace position was that putting money and effort into developing more nonrenewable energy sources, when we know that we will have to switch to renewable energy sources, doesn't make sense. "We face a switch either to clean energy sources or to fuels even dirtier than today's, such as shale oil. It beggars belief that anyone would choose the latter."[28]

shale
A fissile rock (capable of being split) composed of laminated layers of claylike, fine-grained sediment

As conventional sources of oil become depleted, synthetic petroleum sources, such as oil sands, oil-bearing shale, coal, and natural gas, are becoming more useful.

Coal and natural gas can also be converted to oil through a complex chemical process. During the South Africa apartheid boycotts, when oil exporters refused to sell oil to that nation, the South African government commercialized a process developed in Germany, the Fischer-Tropsch process, to obtain oil from coal through a catalyzed chemical reaction. Coal, under pressure and at high temperature, is converted to crude gas. After cooling and purification, the gas passes through a conversion process in which high-value chemical components and synthetic oil are produced.[29] A similar process can be used for natural gas. Oil companies have long had a problem disposing of large, isolated gas reserves that are too far from markets to be profitable. However, converting the gas to a liquid enables it to be produced profitably and moved to world markets less expensively than is possible with the gaseous form. Through this process, the oil companies use gas that otherwise would be burned off and also produce cleaner fuels than are produced with other refining methods. Chevron has a joint venture with Sasol, the innovative South African petrochemical company, for worldwide use of its gas-to-liquid (GTL) technology. One of its successful projects is a GTL plant for the Nigerian National Petroleum Company.

Nuclear Power Nuclear power was predicted to be on its way out, largely because, although the process does not create greenhouse gasses, its waste material's storage is problematic and accidents at the plants themselves can be dangerous far beyond the local surroundings, as we learned from Chernobyl, the 1986 Ukrainian nuclear disaster.[30] Yet because nuclear power plants generate little pollution in their normal operation, because the price of oil has increased, and because new, passive designs are available, nuclear power has not declined. Fewer nuclear plants are being retired, and those in service have a higher-capacity utilization.

Higher nuclear growth is expected in developing countries, where most of the reactors under construction worldwide are being built: India (8 reactors), Russia (6), Japan (3), Ukraine (2), Iran (1), Canada (1), and Romania (1). China has committed to two per year over the next 20 years, which is good for the rest of the world, since China's main source of energy is heavy-polluting coal.[31] In addition, France has made a concerted effort to curb fossil fuel consumption and, in doing so, has turned heavily to nuclear generation. France produces 78 percent of its electricity by nuclear power, and it has one of the lowest rates of greenhouse gas emissions in the industrialized world.[32] If the price of oil stays high, nuclear power is likely to continue to grow from its present 18 percent share of the world's energy grid. It's almost certain that nuclear is back on the horizon.

Coal Coal, much like nuclear power, was predicted to be on its decline as an energy source, largely because it pollutes heavily, but this anticipated reduction is not occurring. However, because other fuel sources are developing at a faster pace than is coal, it will continue to account for a shrinking share of world primary energy consumption. Its share of world energy consumption declined from 27 percent to 22 percent in 2002 and since then has flattened out.[33] It is projected to fall to 20 percent of world primary energy consumption by 2020. This decline in share would be even greater if it were not for the consumption by China and India. Together they account for 97 percent of the expected annual increase in the use of coal of 1.7 percent through 2020.[34] The United States has coal reserves to last 200 years at current consumption rates,[35] which, as Figure 7.16 illustrates, puts the United States at the top of countries with substantial recoverable coal reserves.

Kyoto Protocol
United Nations Framework Convention on Climate Change, which calls for nations to reduce global warming by reducing their emissions of the gasses that contribute to it

Unfortunately, burning coal creates emissions that are directly responsible for global warming. Presently the United States has no regulations on carbon dioxide emission reductions, but the issue has become a political one, with vocal supporters for emissions control from both major parties. The United States has signed the United Nations Framework Convention on Climate Change, known as the **Kyoto Protocol,** which calls for nations to work together to reduce global warming by reducing their emissions of the gasses that contribute

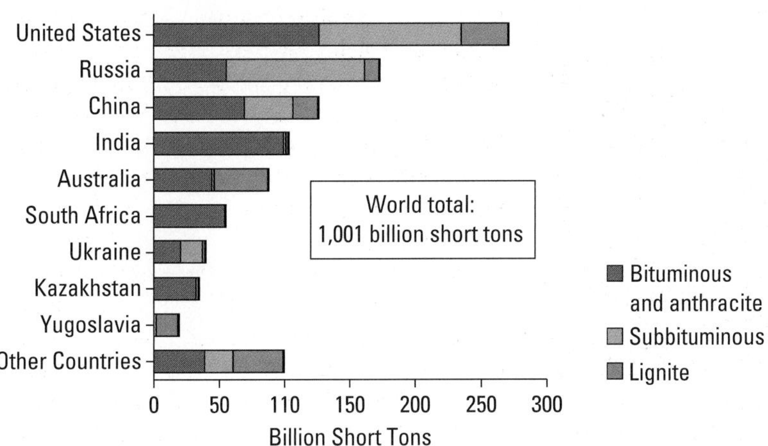

FIGURE 7.16

World Recoverable Coal Reserves

Note: Data for the United States represent recoverable coal estimates as of January 1, 2004. Data for other countries are as of January 1, 1003.

Source: Energy Information Administration, *International energy Annual 2003,* DOE/EIA-0219 (2003) (Washington, DC, June 2005), table 8.2; Web site: www.eia.doe.gov/iea.

to it, carbon dioxide first among them. To date, only the U.S. and Australian governments have declined to ratify the Kyoto Protocol. The United States and China are the two largest producers of coal-generated carbon dioxide, the principal global-warming gas. Together they produce more than half of the world's carbon dioxide emissions.[36]

Under development are several new technologies that promise to reduce emissions from coal-fired plants, one that vents the emissions deep into the ground, another that pulverizes the coal before it is burned, and another that uses the Fischer-Tropsch process to change the coal to a gas before it is burned. Given the coal reserves in the United States and in the developing countries of China and India, the total global use of coal may increase in the 21st century.

Natural Gas Natural gas has been the fastest-growing source of energy, whose use is projected to almost double between 1999 and 2020. As a percentage of total energy consumption, natural gas should rise from 23 percent in 1999 to 28 percent in 2030. Its use surpassed that of coal (BTU basis) for the first time in 1999 and is expected to exceed the use of coal by 38 percent in 2020.[37]

Renewable Energy Sources

Most people in the energy industry believe that one day renewable energy sources will replace fossil fuels, either because the price of nonrenewable energy sources will become too high or the sources themselves will be depleted. There are at least eight alternative energy sources: hydroelectric, solar, wind, geothermal, waves, tides, biomass fuels such as ethanol, and ocean thermal energy conversion. None is available everywhere, but all appear to have applications under appropriate conditions. Of the eight, hydroelectric has had an extensive use—7 percent of the total energy consumed in the world comes from hydroelectric installations. Over 48 countries have programs to support the development and use of renewable energy.

Improved technology has resulted in new support for solar energy and wind power in many parts of the world. The fastest-growing energy technology right now is solar, in the form of grid-connected solar photovoltaic (PV) cells, whose capacity grew by 60 percent per year from 2000 to 2004, notably in Japan, Germany, and the United States. Developing nations such as India, Kenya, and Indonesia are using solar-powered PV cells for rural electrification in isolated communities that are far from power lines and have small electricity requirements. In developed countries, on the other hand, their primary use is for water and space heating.[38] Second is wind power, which grew by 43.4 percent last year.[39] The United States led in the percentage increase in wind power generating capacity, with an increase of 21.1 percent. Figure 7.17 shows wind power capacities by world region.

Ethanol is a **biomass** fuel and, coincidentally, the source of alcohol in alcoholic beverages. *Biomass* means that the energy source is photosynthesis, through which plants

biomass
A category of fuels whose energy source is photosynthesis, through which plants transform the sun's energy into chemical energy; sources include corn, sugarcane, wheat

A wind turbine farm in Palm Springs, California.

transform the sun's energy into chemical energy. Thus the plant sources of this energy are collectively known as "biomass" sources. Ethanol has risen in use since the cost of oil has increased beyond ethanol's production cost, $41 a barrel.[40] The sources of ethanol are diverse, with corn, wheat, and sugarcane among the popular ones. Brazil meets 40 percent of its gasoline demand with ethanol produced from sugarcane. Brazil has also pioneered the concept of flexible-fuel vehicles and has added 25 percent ethanol to fuel sold there. Technology to generate ethanol from agricultural waste such as corncobs is under development.

FIGURE 7.17 Global Installed Wind Power Capacity – Regional Distribution

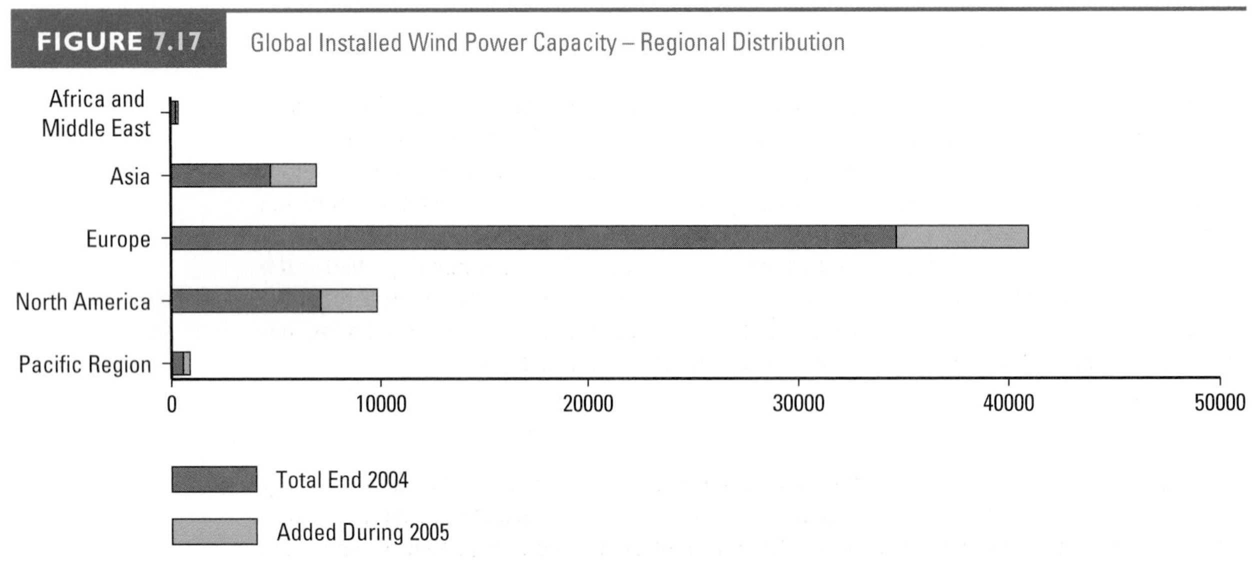

mini MNE

>>Small Business: Ocean Mining and Environmental Impact

Nautilus Minerals, a mining company in Vancouver, Canada, has been scouring the ocean floor for dormant hydrothermal vents and has found them off the coast of Papua New Guinea. [Note that Papua New Guinea has the same place name as Papua (formerly Irian Jaya), Indonesia.] These vents are known to contain metal sulphides, rich sources of gold and copper. Nautilus is now working on environmental studies to allow it to apply for a mining lease from the Papua New Guinea government.

The world's two largest diamond-mining companies, De Beers and Namibian Mining, are mining diamonds off the coast of Namibia by using truck-size remote-controlled crawlers to excavate seabed sediment with a powerful pump and transport the sediment to a surface ship, where the diamonds are sorted and classified. A new daily production record was set on July 23, 2002, when a crawler produced 16,418 carats. The day's production consisted of 54,240 diamonds at an average size of 0.30 carat.[a]

Yet not everyone is thrilled by plans to mine the ocean floor. Craig Cary, a marine biologist at the University of Delaware in Newark, says the prospect is unthinkable because of the potential effects on marine life. "If I was in charge of reviewing permit requests there would be some serious questions to answer. Metal sulphides are nasty substances—how are they going to deal with that?"[b] In addition, what happens to the sand that is brought to the surface? Natural habitats of fish and bottom creatures are destroyed in the process.

There are already major problems in this area. The Chinese-owned Ramu Mine on the other half of the Papua island, in Papua New Guinea, has been the subject of considerable controversy both there and in Australia, in particular due to concerns that its ocean dumping affects the ocean ecology. Local people in Papua New Guinea, depend on the ecological health of the region, and river communities downstream from the mine are worried, too. For these reasons, the New Guinean National Fisheries Authority wrote in a report, "The Ramu Nickel Mine Project is an unsustainable project socially, economically, and environmentally; and cannot be allowed to proceed."[c]

Ocean mining is one of the new frontiers whose environmental regulation is developing while the projects move forward.

[a] "Underwater Gold," www.questacon.edu.au/innovaus/c4s4_004.html (September 21, 2000); "Namibian Minerals Corporation Announces a New Daily Production Record," *MBendi Profile*, July 26, 2002, www.mbendi.co.za/a_sndmsg/news_view.asp?P=O+PG=11+1=38744+M=O (September 3, 2002); "Namibian Minerals Corporation," *MBendi Profile*, www.mbendi.co.za/orgs/cbi7.htm (September 21, 2000); and "NAMCO—Exploiting Profitable Diamond Niche," *Bull and Bear Financial Reporter*, www.thebullandbear.com/bb-reporter/bbfr-archive/nameco-1.html (September 21, 2000).

[b] "The Ocean Floor—Can They Dig It?" NewScientist.com News Service, June 4, 2006, www.newscientist.com/article/dn9266-the-ocean-floor--can-they-dig-it.html (accessed June 9, 2006).

[c] Oceanlink, http://oceanlink.island.net/oceanmatters/undersea%20mining.html (accessed June 9, 2006).

As Figure 7.15 illustrates, renewable energy is still a small portion of the world's energy supply, yet it is a growing part.

NONFUEL MINERALS

Although much of the world's attention to natural resources has centered on the discovery of new energy sources, there are other mineral resources about which governments and industry need to think strategically. Nonfuel minerals are used in all areas of modern living, from house construction to the manufacture of computers and motor vehicles. Nearly all of the world's chrome, manganese, platinum, and vanadium are produced by South Africa and the former Soviet Union. Chrome and manganese are indispensable for hardening steel; platinum is a vital catalytic agent in the oil-refining process and is used in automotive catalytic converters; and vanadium is used in forming aerospace titanium alloys and in producing sulphuric acid. China produces most of the world's tin, barite and tungsten.

INNOVATION AND FACTOR CONDITIONS

Returning to Porter's diamond, we can see that innovation has a large role to play in the way natural resources, both energy resources and nonfuel minerals, contribute to a country's factor conditions. For example, with energy, there are alternative sources, some of which are

WORLD view   

LOST May Not Be Lost

After six years of negotiations over the provisions of the United Nations Law of the Sea Treaty (LOST), representatives of 127 nations agreed on rules governing deep-seabed mining to be administered by the UN's International Seabed Authority (ISA). This is the first time regulations have been made to govern deep-seabed resources beyond national jurisdiction.

The ISA's code regulates the exploration and mining of potato-size polymetallic nodules lying outside the 200-mile economic zone of any country, as well as the metal deposits found in the crust of 100-foot-high chimneylike structures formed when hot water rushes up from volcanic vents in the seafloor. The recovery of hydrocarbons is also regulated. The new regulations empower the ISA to sign exploration contracts with registered pioneer investors (the first firms to make large investments in the survey of nodules). They include five companies, one each from Japan, France, Russia, and China and one jointly owned by Poland, Cuba, Bulgaria, Slovakia, and the Czech Republic.

American firms are not yet involved because the U.S. Senate has yet to approve the treaty, although the government has voiced support for it. Still to be worked out are sticking points for some members of the House of Representatives Committee on Foreign Relations, who play an advisory role in this matter to the Senate. These points are the treaty's stipulations requiring the transfer of mining technology to less developed countries (LDCs); the lack of weighted voting (the United States would be responsible for about 25 percent of the Seabed Authority's budget and have one vote along with each of the other members); and the treaty's attempt to regulate military intelligence gathering, such as submarine activity.

Source: Marjorie Ann Browne, "The Law of the Sea Convention and U.S. Policy," CRS Issue Brief for Congress, June 16, 2000, www.cnei.org/nle/mar-16.html (September 22, 2000); "Mines at Bottom of the Sea Move a Step Closer," *Financial Times*, August 15, 2000, p. 22; and International Seabed Authority, www.isa.org (June 11, 2006).

renewable such as wind and solar. These sources can be developed for broader use when the production of nonrenewable fossil fuels has peaked. In addition, synthetic fuels are being developed, as well as new processes, such as satellite mapping, for the acquisition of traditional fuels and and new methods for their processing. Then there are new technologies, such as fuel cells that use electrochemical processes to release energy. Interest in fuel cell technology has grown rapidly because of its increased fuel economy potential.[41]

Although to many the natural resource situation may appear bleak due to the threat of depletion, remember that innovation combined with sustainability can play a crucial role and also that we are discussing only known reserves. Other energy sources, attainable both through new technology and through traditional approaches, await our development. Alternative, renewable energy sources have great potential. Then, too, only relatively small areas, mostly in the traditional mining countries, have been adequately explored for the traditional fuel sources. Recent new discoveries have been reported in Brazil, Malaysia, and Libya. From a country perspective, energy and nonfuel minerals are factor conditions that can be modified through innovation as well as through import.

Environmental Sustainability

The concept of sustainability has broad scope. *Sustainability* is about maintaining something, and that something might be the environment, society, the economy, people within the economy, or the organization.[42] By its very nature, sustainability is a systems concept. The thing we are trying to sustain (a business, a way of life, the natural world) exists within a larger system, and if that larger system is not sustained, the subsystem is unlikely to survive. For example, the language of the Kamoro and Amungme peoples of Papua—will it be sustained if their communal way of life shifts to a settlement way of life and their children travel to cities in East Asia to become teachers, international bankers and marketing managers? Or let's take an ecological example. The Everglades—is it likely to be sustained if temperature and precipitation change significantly? The point here is that, given a specific, local geography, the likelihood of its being sustained if the larger environment is not sustained is quite slim. All sustainability is actually local and global, or international, in its very nature because it involves systems that are global.[43] The survival and maintenance or possible improvement of our quality

WORLD view   

Why Europe Leads the Way: The Environment and Business

While the United States has been lowering environmental standards and stepping away from cooperation on environmental treaties (Kyoto Protocol, International Seabed Authority), the new Europe, the 25-member European Union, has made a concerted effort to raise environmental standards. Many of the European environmental regulations address the waste and toxic pollution that are by-products of manufacturing. Among EU initiatives are required vehicle recycling, elaborate tracing and checks on genetically modified crops, electronics recycling, bans on the most toxic chemicals used in electronics, chemical testing, and green design.[a] The EU has come to accept an approach to environmentalism known as the *precautionary principle.* This approach suggests regulation at the first sign of a possible danger rather than waiting for research to establish the facts. The precautionary principle puts the onus on the industry to prove that its products are not dangerous. In marked contrast, the U.S. approach tends toward, "If it ain't broke, don't fix it."

In the late 1960s, soon after publication of environmentalist Rachel Carson's book *Silent Spring* (1962), the United States led the world in environmental awareness, legislation, and responsibility. Congress established the Environmental Protection Agency (EPA) and passed the National Environmental Policy Act, the Clean Air Act, the Endangered Species Act, and the Clean Water Act. Yet recently the EU has far outpaced the United States in this area. Why? There is no one simple explanation for such a shift, but commentators point to cultural and demographic differences as a part of it. Most Europeans live in densely populated cities, so that environmental problems such as air and water pollution have a stronger, more directly observed impact on them than they do on the more spread-out rural and suburban American population.

Another reason for the shift may be attributable to culture. The United States was founded to protect individual citizens from a meddlesome, intrusive state. Business practices in the United States are thought of as acts of individual freedom. In Europe, business is thought to have quite a different purpose, one that includes obligations to society and higher levels of social responsibility. Such obligations reflect the demographic and cultural differences between the EU and the United States.

One example of the contrast in approach is the recent EU chemical industry restrictions: Registration, Evaluation and Authorization of Chemicals (REACH). In an address to the EU-U.S. Chemicals Conference, EU environment commissioner Margot Wallström observed that the success of chemicals as a key industrial sector could also be the Achilles' heel of our society: "We have developed a very high dependence on chemicals. Yet this is not matched by sufficient knowledge about their potential risks and long-term effects, for which we are paying a high price." The purpose of the EU regulations, which require that chemical companies show that their materials are not harmful, is to close this knowledge gap.

[a]http://ec.europa.eu/environment/policy_en.htm (accessed June 11, 2006).

Source: Samuel Lowenberg, "Old Europe's New Ideas," *Sierra*, January–February 2004; address by Margot Wallström, April 27, 2004, Charlottesville, VA, www.europa.eu.int/comm/environment/chemicals/reach.htm (accessed August 6, 2004).

of life is local in our experience of it and global in its larger context, from a system's perspective. Figure 7.18 illustrates this "act locally, think globally" truth of sustainability.

environmental sustainability Economic state in which the demands placed upon the environment by people and commerce can be met without reducing the capacity of the environment to provide for future generations

Environmental sustainability rests on the commitment of business to operate without reducing the capacity of the environment to provide for future generations.[44] An approach to the environment that commits to sustainability involves actions that have a positive, long-term social and/or environmental benefit and meet the needs of the present without compromising the ability of future generations to meet their own needs.[45] The challenges of such an approach are great, as the world has seen with the Three Gorges Dam project in China. The purpose of the dam is hydroelectric power generation to fuel China's development with a clean and low-environmental-impact energy source whose day-to-day operations are not costly. The initial project is very costly, both in money and human terms—$25 billion and displacement of 1.9 million people; once the dam is operating, however, the water that is the power source has little cost, unlike the cost of petroleum products for a conventional power plant. At the same time, the decision made by today's Chinese to sacrifice their future children's access to one of the major natural wonders of the world seems a costly one. The developed world moved forward by degrading natural resources, and, as many leaders of developing nations have pointed out, such degradation might be thought of as a given in development. An environmentally sustainable approach searches for alternatives. In doing so, it usually takes into account three areas, ecological, social, and economic, representing the contexts of participating systems—the natural world; the social world; and the world of value-added activities, the economic world. In this section, we look at characteristics of

FIGURE 7.18

Sustainability Is Local and International

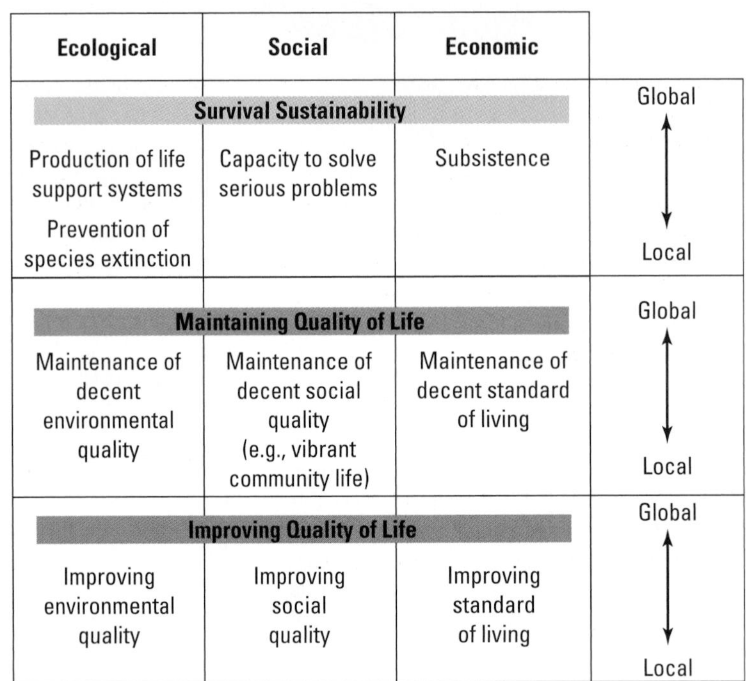

Ecological	Social	Economic	
Survival Sustainability			Global ↕ Local
Production of life support systems Prevention of species extinction	Capacity to solve serious problems	Subsistence	
Maintaining Quality of Life			Global ↕ Local
Maintenance of decent environmental quality	Maintenance of decent social quality (e.g., vibrant community life)	Maintenance of decent standard of living	
Improving Quality of Life			Global ↕ Local
Improving environmental quality	Improving social quality	Improving standard of living	

Source: Philip Sutton, www.green-innovations.asn.au/sustblty.htm#local-global.

sustainable business practices, examine the stakeholder model for sustainability, and review two examples of businesses that promote sustainability.

CHARACTERISTICS OF ENVIRONMENTALLY SUSTAINABLE BUSINESS

There are three characteristics of evolving sustainable business practices that are widely agreed upon: limits, which apply to the ecological system; interdependence, which applies to the social system as well as to the other two; and equity in distribution, which applies to the economic system.[46] *Limits* have to do with the recognition that environmental resources are exhaustible. Water, soil, and air can become toxic, and their use needs to be informed by awareness of that danger. The current focus on greenhouse gasses and their contribution to global warming offers one example of limits. Control of emissions would be an ecologically responsible decision. If such standards are inevitable in order to maintain survival sustainability, given the serious effects of global warming, a business that learns how to operate within the limits of emissions control early on in the adoption process would accrue advantages because they would be ahead of their competition by having learned how to do so.

An aerial view of a giant mine run by the U.S. firm Freeport-McMoran Cooper & Gold Inc. at the Grassberg mining operation. Indonesia will not hesitate to sue U.S. mining giant Freeport-McMoran if it fails to follow through on recommendations to stop pollution from its Papua operations, Environment Minister Rachmat Witoelar said.

Interdependence describes the relationship among ecological, social, and economic systems. Action in one system affects the others. This interdependence can be seen in stark dimensions in the extractive industries. Mining operations in Papua (formerly Irian Jaya), Indonesia, have settled areas that had previously been the hunting grounds of indigenous hunter-gatherer tribes, among them the Kamoro and Amungme, causing considerable social stress in those groups. The mining operations involve some river and stream pollution from tailings, which can be and in many cases have been abated. The mining company, Freeport McMoRan, provides health care and

BUILDING YOUR GLOBAL RÉSUMÉ

Be Geo-Savvy: Know about the World in Which You Live and Will Work

Understanding the world in which you live and will work will set you apart and help to make you a "citizen of the world." But there is more to understanding the world than just reading an international paper, listening to *BBC World Service,* or appreciating world music. Do you really understand your world? What do you know about world geography? Do you understand global population distributions? What do you know about natural resources of the world? Can you answer the questions below?

- Which country produces more than 90 percent of the world's commercial and industrial diamonds?
- Bauxite is the primary mineral in aluminum. Where are the largest deposits of bauxite located?
- What is the longest river in the world?
- Which country has the largest landmass? Which ones are the next four in rank order?
- Which country has approximately 94 percent of its population living within 100 miles of its closest foreign neighbor's border?
- Which country is made up of over 17,000 islands?
- Which country produces the largest amount of natural rubber in the world?

If you are committed to a career in international business, your library, either digital or hardcopy, should have a comprehensive, detailed, up-to-date world atlas, one that contains statistics about natural resources, population, and climatic conditions, as well as topographical maps with the names of cities, mountains, rivers, seas, and oceans.

Aside from being "geo-savvy," you should be aware of many less-than-pleasant but important issues regarding our natural resources. Consider these facts from the Global Policy Forum:

- Illegal diamond sales in Angola, Liberia, Sierra Leone, and the Democratic Republic of Congo have been used to buy weapons, escalating local conflicts.
- Scarce water in some areas has caused conflict between neighboring countries due to perceived ownership rights of common waterways. "Water wars" are real in the Middle East and India and between Israel and the areas of Egypt, Syria and Jordan known as Palestine.
- Massive deforestation by loggers has displaced indigenous populations in Indonesia and Ecuador, to name just a few countries.
- Oil and natural gas extraction has caused military repression and human rights abuse in Sudan, Nigeria, Cameroon, Chad, and Sao Tome.

World Wide Resources:

http://geography.about.com
www.mywonderfulworld.org
www.globalpolicy.org/security/docs/minindx.htm
www.globalpolicy.org/visitctr/about.htm

Career Option: Global resource management or natural resource management are alternative international careers you might consider. Companies whose business involves the geosciences (petroleum, natural gas, coal and mineral mining, marine geology, forestry, environmental cleanup from biohazards, and waste and pollution management) also need professionals with business skills to manage the business side of their enterprise. Governments also take a leading role in resource management and offer many career opportunities for people with diverse skills.

World Wide Resources:

www.earthscienceworld.org/careers/brochure.html
http://edis.ifas.ufl.edu/FR127

education for the indigenous peoples in the area and appears to have made efforts to be a good citizen and a helpful, socially responsible neighbor. Yet the advancement the company brings is threatening the continued existence of the indigenous people, through development and education. Imagine the strains on a social system in which parents, wearing loincloths and using poisoned blow arrows to kill game, are living as traditional hunter-gatherers, while their children are being educated using Internet technologies and eating Western-style food. The interrelatedness of mining operations in a remote area and good corporate citizenship issues go beyond pollution and infringement of hunting grounds to complicated ethical and social issues related to development. The social, economic, and ecological systems are all players whose sustainability is threatened in this situation. In less stark dimensions, examples of interdependence among ecological, social, and economic systems cluster around decisions related to manufacturing and waste disposal. Filmmaker Michael Moore's eulogy to Flint, Michigan, *Roger and Me*, addresses one of those issues, location. It explores the economic, social, and ecological implications of GM's decision to move production out of Flint.

Equity in distribution suggests that for interdependence to work, there cannot be vast differences in the distribution of gains. Especially in a globalizing world, where relationships among populations are increasingly closer, or at least information about them is, vast inequities may lead to unrest and violence. Examples of corporate challenges presented by lack of equity in distribution include Shell Oil's operations in southern Nigeria, which have been forced to shut down after raids by groups claiming to speak for the local Ijaw tribe. The tribe claims they have been "cheated of oil wealth pumped from their land by the central government and oil companies."[47] Political tensions related to equity in distribution have also informed Venezuela's and Bolivia's oil businesses. These issues raise interesting questions about sustainability from a social perspective. Shell Oil has built a positive relationship with the president of Nigeria, whose southern populations, near the oil deposits, are close to insurrection because they see no gain from the oil that is in their territory. Shell needs to make decisions about sustainability that satisfy the president of Nigeria and that also satisfy the local population. It appears Shell has fallen short in the latter.

Increasingly, companies will need to make decisions about setting limits on how their operations affect the environment. They will also encounter increased signs of the interdependence that exists among the social, economic, and ecological systems that form the context for their business. Equity in distribution is one of the ways that such interdependence can work. It requires a business model that allocates gain from the business's value creation to all actors in the context. It's the notion that a rising tide raises all boats. Sam Palisano, CEO of IBM, recently spoke about this new way of understanding business when he said that IBM wanted to end its colonial company model and move on to a truly globally integrated model where high levels of trust persist among all stakeholders.[48]

THE STAKEHOLDER MODEL FOR SUSTAINABLE BUSINESS

The concept of sustainability is a complex one because it impacts all aspects of business decisions. Some of the areas that are most commonly involved are:

Alternative fuels	Office maintenance
Brownfield (contaminated-site) remediation	Pollution prevention
Corporate accountability	Social investing
Ecological development	Sustainable technology
Ecotourism	Transportation alternatives
Energy conservation	Waste reduction
Green building design	Water conservation

stakeholder theory
An understanding of how business operates that takes into account all identifiable interest holders

One model that offers a helpful framework for thinking about environmental sustainability as it relates to business is **stakeholder theory.**[49] Developed by R. Edward Freeman, this approach differs from the traditional input-process-output economic business model because it involves identification and consideration of the network of tensions caused by competing demands that any business exists within. The traditional economic model of business considers a far narrower scope of influences (employees, owners, and suppliers) that are driven by the single goal of creating profits. Stakeholder theory forces a business to address *underlying values and principles*. It "pushes managers to be clear about how they want to do business, specifically, what kind of relationships they want and need to create with their stakeholders to deliver on their purpose."[50] The theory also posits that the tensions among the varying interests in a business environment can be balanced. Business then becomes about relationships in the larger context and the responsibilities that develop from them. In stakeholder theory, profits are a *result* of value creation rather than the primary driver in the process, as in the economic model. Freeman points out that there are many companies whose operations are consistent with stakeholder theory, including J&J, eBay, Google, and Lincoln Electric.

To achieve this balance among competing tensions, the company sees itself in relation to its stakeholders, as illustrated in Figure 7.19. The company then views itself in a social context to identify its purpose, principles, and responsibilities clearly. Figure 7.20 illustrates this important step. It is at this point that limits, interdependence, and equity of distribution are addressed. One way to measure the company's activities in this larger context is the

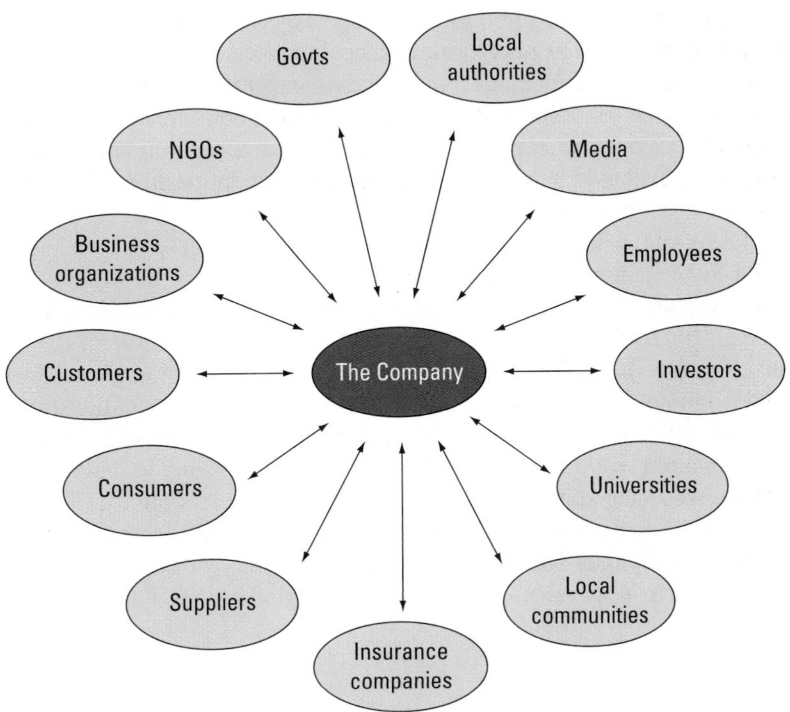

FIGURE 7.19

Stakeholder-Based View

Source: "The Stakeholder Based View, Who Are My Stakeholders?" Courtesy of Novo Nordisk A/S; World Resources Institute.

process of triple-bottom-line accounting. Here the company measures, in addition to its traditional economic performance, its social and environmental performance. For an example of triple-bottom-line reporting, see Freeport McMoRan's accounting of its mining operations in Indonesia (www.fcx.com, especially the Sustainable Development Report and the videos). The company's public materials suggest it is using a stakeholder approach, increasing value and contributing to the quality of life for its constituencies, including locals, while operating low-impact mining.

Culture matters in the process of moving toward environmentally sustainable business. Here are two examples of its potential impact: First, relationships matter more to collectivist

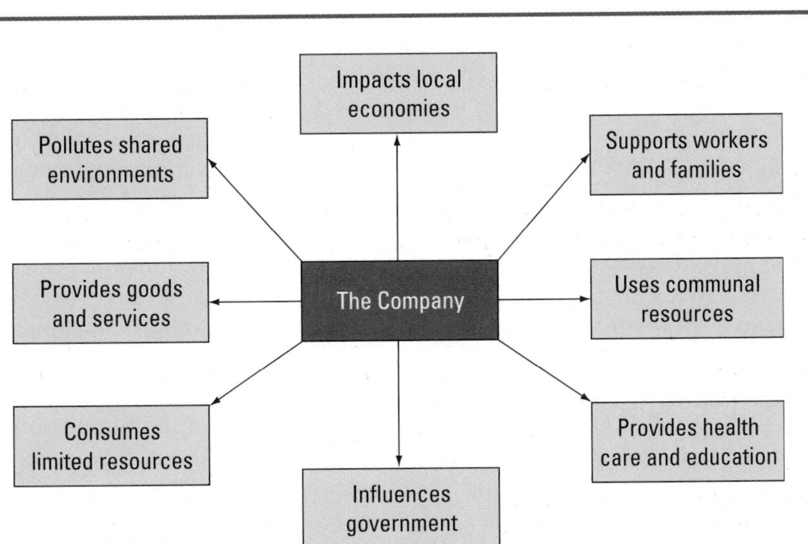

FIGURE 7.20

The Company in a Societal Context

Source: "Your Company in a Societal Context," Slide 7 from Pathways PowerPoint presentation "Sustainability and Business," World Resources Institute, http://pathways.wri.org/index.asp?Topic1/,2004.

cultures than to individualist ones. This concept, explained in Chapter 3, suggests that in relationship-rich cultures, the transition to sustainable ways of operating might be more in line with traditional attitudes. For example, European cultures tend to focus more on relationships than does the U.S. culture, which has a more individualist orientation. That Europe is well on its way in the practice of sustainable business and that green approaches are demanded by European consumers may be explained partially by Europeans' assumptions about what business is and how it should be conducted. Traditionally, relationships and their obligations for Europeans suggest that the underlying purpose of business includes a level of social responsibility far beyond what American assumptions would suggest.

Second, another cultural dimension that may come into play as we move toward sustainability is found in the set of basic values, unarticulated and, unless challenged, usually invisible to their holders, that members of a culture hold about the role of the individual in connection to nature. In their values orientation theory, anthropologists Kluckhohn and Strodtbeck posit three value dimensions to describe an individual's relationship to the natural environment: mastery, submission, and harmony.[51] The mastery value posits an understanding of the natural world as a source of inputs; the relationship to nature is to control it. Submission involves understanding humans as objects of nature's forces. Harmony suggests that nature and humans can coexist without the destruction of one by the other. A strong orientation toward mastery may need to move toward the harmony dimension for sustainability to become a strong business value. That process has begun, as the following examples show.

EXAMPLES OF SUSTAINABILITY IN BUSINESS

Patagonia Patagonia, Inc., the international outdoor gear and apparel company, has awareness of sustainability at the core of its business. In the 1970s, the climber Yvon Chouinard, from French-speaking Maine, founded Patagonia with the goal of providing equipment for "clean climbing," that is, climbing that minimizes environmental impact. Its purpose statement is,"Patagonia exists as a business to inspire and implement solutions to the environmental crisis." Michael Crooke, president and CEO, holds that the traditional approach to doing business, focusing on quarterly earnings and generally accepted accounting principles (GAAP), is not sustainable. He points out that such accounting does not account for negative externalities, such as environmental degradation and social ills, creates an unrealistic view of economic performance, and is bound to lead to an environmental crisis if something does not change. Crooke proposes an alternative "ecosystem model" for sustainability. Just as the elements of an ecosystem must work in harmony, a sustainable business model relies on the synergies between the environmental, social, and financial elements of a business. This synchronization creates a virtuous cycle: The company's environmental and social commitment attracts loyal customers and employees, which improves the financial performance of the firm, which facilitates further commitment, and so on.[52]

Patagonia has a series of social and production-related efforts to move the issues of sustainability forward. On the production side, it uses recycled materials, both in its building construction and in its products. In its fiber use, plastic soda cans are the source of much of the fleece, and organic cotton is used exclusively. Patagonia supports environmental causes, both indirectly through grant programs and directly through its sourcing decisions. Through its commitment to sustainability, Patagonia is developing a model for doing business in a sustainable way that may be of use to other companies as we move forward. As Chouinard observed several years ago, "No business can be done on a dead planet. A company that is taking the long view must accept that it has an obligation to minimize its impact on the natural environment."[53]

Dow Jones Sustainability Index Dow Jones launched the Sustainability Index in 1999 as a global index to track the financial performance of sustainability-driven companies. Dow Jones reviews candidates for the index by conducting a thorough examination of the company's environmental, economic, and social performance. In 2005, 57 companies were added to the index and 54 deleted. Qualifying for the index and being accepted are two separate challenges, since the index members are limited to 20 percent per sector, with nationality not being considered. There are actually two versions of the Sustainability World index, one that excludes companies in the alcohol, armaments, firearms, tobacco, and gambling businesses. As of June 2006, the indexes listed 318 businesses. Among the U.S. businesses are General Electric, CitiGroup, Intel, Johnson & Johnson, Procter and Gamble, and Hewlett-Packard. Such is the demand for sustainable indexes that in January 2006, in addition to the Sustainability World indexes, Dow Jones launched more limited sustainability indexes that focus on specific sectors: European Blue Chip companies, American, North American, and Islamic companies. These can be explored at www.sustainability-indexes.com.

Summary

Describe the role of location, topography, climate, and natural resources as factor conditions in Porter's diamond model.

Location, topography, climate, and natural resources are inherited factors that underlie inputs that companies draw on. Local disadvantages in factor conditions can be recognized as advantages and become a force for innovation. Adverse conditions such as local terrain and climate or scarce raw materials, at the basic-factor level, or labor shortages, at the advanced-factor level, force firms to develop new methods, and this innovation often leads to a national comparative advantage. Hence, understanding these factors is important.

Explain how surface features contribute to economic, cultural, political, and social differences among nations and among regions of a single country.

Mountains divide nations into smaller regional markets that often have distinct cultures, industries, and climates. Sometimes even the languages are different. Deserts and tropical forests act as barriers to people, goods, and ideas.

Comprehend the importance of inland waterways and outlets to the sea.

Bodies of water attract people and facilitate transportation. Water transportation has increased even after the building of railroads and highways. Various European firms are shipping goods in barges on the Rhine waterway instead of using highways.

Recognize that climate exerts a broad influence on business.

The differences in climate conditions among a firm's markets and manufacturing sites can significantly affect its operations. In the case of the marketing mix, a product sold for use in northern Canada may need protection against cold weather, while the same product used in the tropics may require extra cooling to resist the heat. Heavy seasonal rains or long, very cold or dry spells can require that the firm carry large inventories because of the difficulty of replenishing stock in inclement weather. Other distribution challenges related to climate include protection from the cold, heat, and humidity.

Understand the options available for nonrenewable and renewable energy sources.

Nonrenewable energy sources include petroleum, both from conventional sources and nonconventional sources such as shale, oil sands, coal, and natural gas. Other nonrenewable sources are coal, nuclear power, and natural gas. Renewable energy sources include hydroelectric, wind, solar, geothermal, waves, tides, biomass, and ocean thermal energy conversion. Each of these energy sources has a cost that impacts its use. As nonrenewable sources approach depletion, renewable sources will become more widely applied as their relative cost decreases.

Explain how factor conditions can impact innovation.

Porter makes the point that local disadvantages in factor conditions can, if recognized, become a force for innovation. Adverse conditions such as local terrain and climate or scarce raw materials, at the basic-factor level, or labor shortages, at the advanced-factor level, may force firms to develop new approaches. This innovation often may lead to a national comparative advantage. Understanding these attributes is important.

Describe environmental sustainability and its characteristics.

Environmental sustainability rests on the commitment of business to operate without reducing the capacity of the environment to provide for future generations. There are three characteristics of evolving sustainable business practices that are widely agreed upon: limits, which apply to the ecological system; interdependence, which applies to the social system as well as to the other two; and equity in distribution, which applies to the economic system

Draw on the stakeholder theory as a framework for environmental sustainability.

Stakeholder theory forces a business to address its underlying values and principles. Stakeholder theory encourages managers to articulate clearly how they want to do business. What kind of relationships do they want and need to create with their stakeholders to deliver on their purpose? In this way, operating with stakeholder theory leads to a public discussion about responsibility of the business among all stakeholders.

Key Words

factor conditions (p. 192)
passive processing (p. 193)
topography (p. 195)
Canadian Shield (p. 202)
inland waterways (p. 203)
Rhine waterway (p.203)
climate (p. 208)
natural resources (p. 209)
shale (p. 211)
Kyoto Protocol (p. 212)
biomass (p. 213)
environmental sustainability (p. 217)
stakeholder theory (p. 220)

Questions

1. Of the 30 nations listed by the UN as the least developed nations, 16 are landlocked. Is this a coincidence, or might the lack of a seacoast contribute to their slower development?
2. Analyze the potential of oil shale and oil sands as future energy sources.
3. a. Why do you suppose the blank areas on a population map generally coincide with the areas of higher elevation on a topographical map?
   b. Why are the tropics an exception to this rule?
4. "International businesspeople, unless they are in the business of refining minerals or petroleum, have no need to concern themselves with world developments in natural resources." Agree or disagree with this assertion, and explain your reasoning.
5. Mountains, deserts, and tropical rain forests are generally culture barriers. Explain.
6. In 2005, Switzerland, a landlocked country, won the America's Cup sailing competition. How might this be explained using Porter's factor conditions?
7. From a multinational businessperson's point of view, how would you apply what you have learned about factor conditions as you explore locations for manufacturing?
8. Explain how the stakeholder model applies to an example of sustainable business. This example can be from your community.
9. How is the concept of sustainable business practice both local and global?

Research Task

globalEDGE.msu.edu 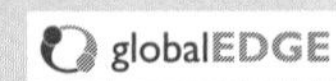

Use the globalEDGE site (http://globalEDGE.msu.edu/) to complete the following exercises:

1. Your small firm is an energy provider to a variety of markets in the United States and Canada. As such, you have been assigned to determine the general climate of the energy industry for the coming decades. By combining population data with energy consumption estimations, one can analyze trends in energy use per capita and differences in per capita energy use between countries. BP, one of the world's largest energy companies, provides an annual report with statistical data on energy trends worldwide. Using the *BP Statistical Review of World Energy* as reference, find which country consumes the most energy per person. How has energy consumption varied with a growing world population? What does this mean for your firm's future as an energy provider?
2. You are working for a pontoon manufacturer that is considering expansion to South America. An important determinant of the firm's market strategy to date, upper management strongly believes that bodies of water are an essential element for a pontoon market to develop. Therefore, by analyzing data on each Latin American country's ecosystem, your firm should invest in the country with abundant bodies of water. On the basis of management's single criterion, use the *EarthTrends* resource published by the World Resources Institute to suggest a South American country that best satisfies top management's ambition. What are other factors that may encourage the expansion of a private boat market?

Sustainability and Collaboration: A New Way of Thinking — Minicase 7.1

United Steelworkers and the Sierra Club: A Case in Point

The largest manufacturing union in the United States, the United Steelworkers (USW), and the largest environmental action group in the nation, the Sierra Club, have joined forces in a collaboration called the "Blue/Green Alliance." This is an unexpected partnership that crosses geography and economic class. The environmentalists have opposed drilling for oil in the Alaskan Arctic National Wildlife Refuge, which the unions supported. The unions have often opposed environmentalism because their belief was that it cost jobs.

Now these two large groups (USW with 850,000 members and Sierra Club with 750,000) have joined forces to push for stronger environmental and worker protections in trade agreements, for ratification of the Kyoto Protocol to limit greenhouse gasses, and for higher fuel efficiency standards. "Good Jobs, a Clean Environment, and a Safer World" is their banner.

David Foster, the executive director of the alliance and the Steelworkers' regional director for the Northwest, explained: "The companies that embrace the soundest environmental principles, that move to alternative and renewable forms of energy, those will be the companies that survive. We're seeing a lot of that played out in the auto industry today."[a]

W. Leo Gerard, international president of USW, agrees: "Good jobs and a clean environment are important to American workers—we cannot have one without the other. . . . . In fact, secure 21st century jobs are those that will help solve the problem of global warming with energy efficiency and renewable energy."[b]

The executive director of the Sierra Club suggests that we are at a point globally where we can use resources for sustainability or "to create an ever more dangerous polarization of wealth and poverty."

[a]Steven Greenhouse, "Steelworkers and Sierra Club Unite," *New York Times*, June 8, 2006, www.nyt.com (accessed June 10, 2006).

[b]"Sierra Club, United Steelworkers Announce Blue/Green Alliance," June 7, 2006, www.uswa.org/uswa/program/content/3035.php (accessed June 12, 2006).

8 Economic and Socioeconomic Forces

There are well over one billion people in seventeen developing nations and three transition nations with enough income to rank as thoroughly middle class. They enjoy a collective spending power, measured in local purchasing capacity, of $6.3 trillion per year. They could well increase their numbers by half as soon as 2010, and their spending power by still more. This is the biggest consumption boom ever known in such a short time.

—*Norman Myers, author of* The New Consumers: The Influence of Affluence on the Environment

Of Zippies and the China-India Development Race

Newspapers in India refer to young people with good jobs as "zippies"—walking with confidence (zip in their step) and with plenty of money in their pockets. And there are plenty of these relative youngsters—by 2006, India's 20- to 34-year-old population was over 281 million. They are the young consumerist edge of a population of 1.11 billion and the fourth-largest economy in the world (based on purchasing power parity). The country's middle-income population in 2006 was estimated at nearly 600 million people.

But is India or China likely to "hit it rich" first? The current assumption is that China will be rich faster. China has a larger population as well as a larger economy. China has a higher savings rate. India attracted only 7 percent as much as the more than $600 billion in foreign direct investment that poured into China from 1990 to 2006. China's manufacturing productivity is higher: One source says that a Chinese worker makes 35 shirts in the time it takes an Indian to make 20.

China also has more high-net-worth individuals, with approximately 250,000 millionaires versus only 83,000 in India as of 2005. China is ranked third in the world in sales of luxury goods, accounting for more than 5 percent of the total world luxury market.

Looking further down the road, however, India has advantages for the long run. Not only do more Indians speak English—one estimate is that 150 million to 200 million Indians are completely fluent in English, and perhaps 20 million speak it as their primary language—but many are watching "Friends" reruns at employer expense to become accentless. And there may be more Indians in college, although the numbers are disputed. India's strength so far has been in services; China is the manufacturing powerhouse.

In fact, many observers feel that both India and China will have larger economies than that of the United States by mid-century. ■

Source: U.S. Census Bureau, *International Data Base,* www.census.gov/ipc/www/idbpyr.html (October 8, 2006); "What's behind the Overseas Forays of U.S. Online Giants?" Knowledge@Wharton, July 14–27, 2004, knowledge.wharton.upenn.edu/article/1013.cfm; Om Malik, "The New Land of Opportunity," *Business 2.0,* July 2004, pp. 74–79; Jeffrey D. Sachs, "Welcome to the Asian Century," *Fortune,* January 2004, pp. 53–54; Anand Krishnamoorthy, "India Eases into the Lap of Luxury," *International Herald Tribune,* July 28, 2004, p. B4; S Rajagopalan, "Millionaires in India Grew by 19.3% in 2005: Survey," *Hindustan Times,* June 21, 2006, www.hindustantimes.com/news/181_1725069,00020008.htm (October 8, 2006); and "Millionaire Boom Favors Banks," *The Standard,* September 20, 2006, www.thestandard.com.hk/news_detail.asp?pp_cat=22&art_id=27647&sid=9992379&con_type=1 (October 8, 2006).

CONCEPT PREVIEWS

After reading this chapter, you should be able to:

state the purpose of economic analyses

identify different categories based on levels of national economic development and the common characteristics of developing nations

recognize the economic and socioeconomic dimensions of the economy and different indicators used to assess them

discuss the importance of a nation's consumption patterns and the significance of purchasing power parity

discuss the new definition of economic development, which includes more than economic growth

explain the degree to which labor costs can vary from country to country

discuss the significance for businesspeople of the large foreign debts of some nations

Gli Affari Internazionali
nales Geschäft Παγοσμιο Business
Negócios Internacionais Los Negócios Internacionais
ernacionales Affaires Internationales 國際商務 Παγοσμιο Business

Economic forces are among the most significant uncontrollable forces for managers. To keep abreast of the latest developments and also to plan for the future, firms for many years have been assessing and forecasting economic conditions at the national and international levels.

To do so, analysts use data published by governments and international organizations such as the World Bank and the International Monetary Fund (IMF). The data published by these organizations may not be as timely or as accurate as business analysts would like, but there is a large amount available.

Analysts do not work solely with government-published data. Private economic consultants—such as Data Resources, Inc., Chase Econometric Associates, Business International, the Economist Intelligence Unit, and Wharton Economic Forecasting Associates—provide economic forecasts (some do industry forecasts as well) to which many multinationals subscribe. Other sources are various industry associations, which generally provide industry-specific forecasts to their members.

In addition, economists and marketers use certain economic indicators that predict trends in their industry. We discuss the use of market indicators further in Chapter 15, "Assessing and Analyzing Markets."

The purpose of economic analyses is first to appraise the overall outlook of the economy and then to assess the impact of economic changes on the firm. An examination of Figure 8.1 will illustrate how a change in just one factor in the economy can affect all the major functions of the company.

A forecast of an increase in employment in a particular market would cause most marketing managers to revise their sales forecasts upward, which in turn would require that production managers augment production. This might be accomplished by adding an additional work shift, but if the plant is already operating 24 hours a day, new machinery will be needed. Either situation may require more workers and raw materials, which will result in an extra workload for the personnel and purchasing managers. Should both the raw materials and labor markets be tight, the firm will probably have to pay higher-than-normal prices and wage rates.

The financial manager may then have to negotiate with the banks for a loan to enable the firm to handle the greater cash outflow until additional revenue is received from increased sales. Note that this cascade of effects occurs because of a change in only one factor. Actually, of course, many economic factors are involved, and their relationships are complex. The object of an economic analysis is to isolate and assess the impact of those factors believed to affect the firm's operations.

FIGURE 8.1 Impact of Economic Forecast on Firm's Functional Areas

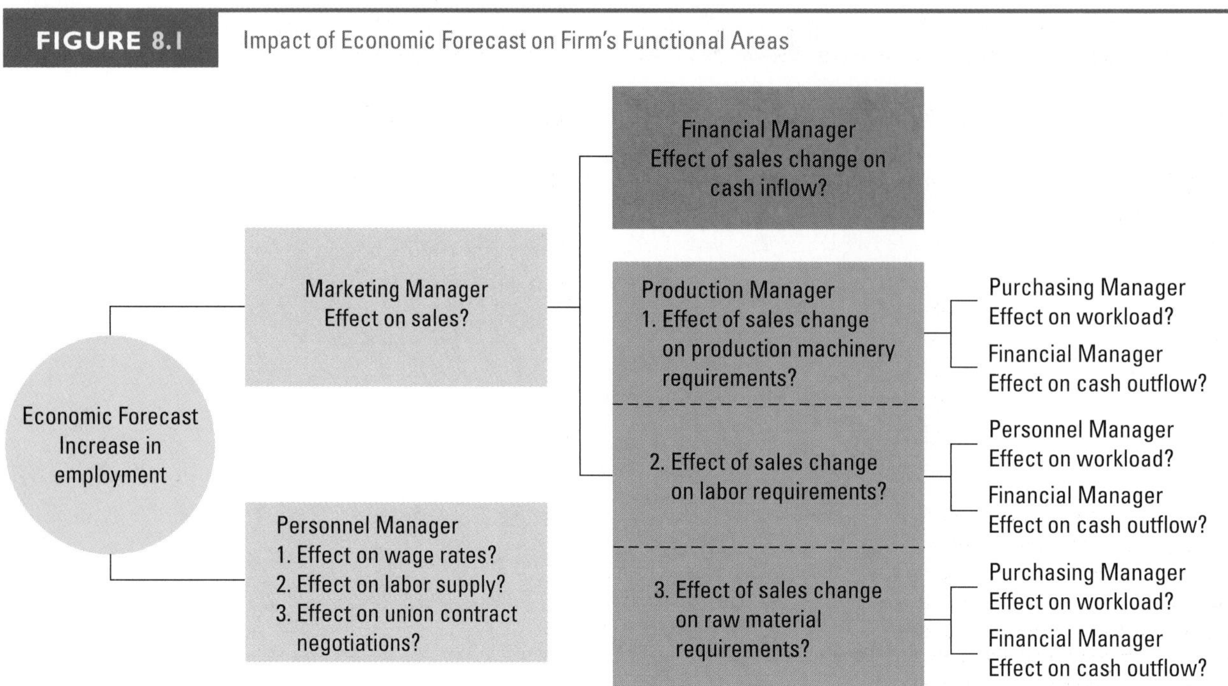

International Economic Analyses

When a firm enters overseas markets, economic analyses become more complex because now managers must operate in two new environments: foreign and international. In the foreign environment, there are many economies instead of one, and they are highly divergent.

Because of these differences, policies designed for economic conditions in one market may be unsuitable for conditions in another market. For example, headquarters may require that its subsidiaries maintain the lowest inventories possible, and the chief financial officer may decree that they make only foreign currency–denominated loans because of more favorable interest rates. For nations whose annual inflation rates are low (0 to 15 percent), these policies usually work well. But what about countries such as Angola, with a 1995 inflation rate of 2,672 percent, and Zimbabwe, with an estimated 1,216 percent in 2006?

The least desirable scenario is for the subsidiaries in these countries to have cash or foreign currency–denominated loans, and so the policy for markets with high inflation rates will be just the reverse of what it is for countries with low inflation rates (see Table 8.1). Besides monitoring the foreign environments, analysts must stay informed of the actions taken by components of the international environment, such as regional groupings [European Union (EU), Central American Free Trade Agreement (CAFTA)] and international organizations [United Nations (UN), International Monetary Fund (IMF), World Trade Organization (WTO)]. American firms are very attentive to the EU's progress in reaching its goals and to the impact this will have on EU-U.S. trade relations. They are also following closely the UN's progress in developing world pollution standards, health standards, and so forth. Any of these actions can seriously affect firms.[1]

International economic analyses should provide economic data on both actual and prospective markets. As part of the competitive forces assessment, many companies monitor the economic conditions of nations in which their major competitors are located, because changing conditions may strengthen or weaken their competitors' ability to compete in world markets. Because of the importance of economic information to the control and planning functions at headquarters, the collection of data and the preparation of reports are usually the responsibility of the home office. However, foreign subsidiaries and field representatives are expected to contribute heavily to studies concerning their markets. Data from areas where the firm has no local representation can usually be somewhat less detailed and are generally available from national and international agencies.[2] The reports from central or international

TABLE 8.1 Annual Rates of Inflation for Selected Countries

Country	1995	2001	2003	2006[e]
Angola	2,672%	325%[a]	106%[b]	13%
Turkmenistan	1,005	35	11[c]	9
Ukraine	376	15	8[c]	9
Russia	197	14	12[c]	10
Georgia	163	8	5[c]	10
Brazil	66	5	9[c]	5
Uruguay	42	5	10[c]	6
Zimbabwe	26	100	700[d]	1,216
Argentina	3	1	4[c]	4

[a] 2000 estimate, from www.cia.gov/cia/publications/factbook/index.html.

[b] 2002 estimate, from www.cia.gov/cia/publications/factbook/geos/ao.html#Econ.

[c] 2003 estimate, from www.odci.gov/cia/publications/factbook/rankorder/2092rank.html.

[d] 2004 estimate, from www.odci.gov/cia/publications/factbook/geos/zi.html#Econ (July 20, 2004).

[e] 2006 estimate, from International Monetary Fund, *World Economic Outlook 2006,* table 11, www.imf.org/external/pubs/ft/weo/2006/02/index.htm (October 7, 2006).

Source: www.imf.org/external/pubs/ft/weo/2000/02/index.htm (October 7, 2006).

BUILDING YOUR GLOBAL RÉSUMÉ — Tips from Your Personal Global Mentor

Tim Taddei (left) on a press check

Tim Taddei is cofounder and director of operations of RTO Group Limited, in Fairfield, Connecticut. RTO Group Limited is an international printing and graphics services company with annual revenues approaching $10 million. International clients include Absolut Vodka, Sara Lee Coffee and Tea, Unilever, Pfizer, Lenox China, and Vineyard Vines, among others. RTO maintains an on-site facility at Pepsi-Cola, providing prepress services for promotions, advertising, and packaging, as well as project and digital asset management. The Printing Division of RTO uses overseas vendors for printing and ships finished products globally for clients. RTO does business in Canada, Mexico, Slovenia, Poland, Korea, and France.

Tim's advice on how to get a job in international business:

- "Study foreign languages, especially Spanish and Chinese as they are spoken in today's most prevalent emerging marketplaces."
- "Intern overseas (or with a domestic company doing business overseas) to find the critical mix of culture and business opportunity that fits your career development."
- "Travel; use your language, sales and personal skills to develop your international business 'niche.'"
- "Be willing to take risks both personally and financially. Entrepreneurship requires hard work and patience — dealing with foreign entities can be time-consuming and frustrating—patience, perseverance and dedication to your cause are not clichés; they work to turn problems into opportunities."

Tim's advice on succeeding in international business:

- "Develop an intimate understanding of the metric system—conversions, measurements, and even transportation rely on the metric system throughout the world. Manufacturing depends on accurate and precise measurements (in metric)."
- "Study current socioeconomic trends in the countries you deal with—understand labor rates, labor laws, emerging trends effecting the eco-climate, culture, economy, and political climate within a given country."
- "Understand exchange rate management—fluctuating currency can dramatically impact your cost/profit ratios."
- "Understand import/export laws—know *exactly* what you can import/export to/from the U.S. and the cost ramifications before embarking on a manufacturing or production project."
- "Understand timing issues related to overseas shipping and Customs clearance."

World Wide Resource:

www.rtogroup.com

banks are especially good sources for economic information on single countries. Other possible sources are the chambers of commerce located in most of the world's capitals, the commercial officers in embassies, the United Nations, the World Bank, the International Monetary Fund, and the Organization for Economic Cooperation and Development.[3]

Levels of Economic Development

When managers move from domestic to international business, they encounter markets with far greater differences in levels of economic development than those in which they have been working. It is important to understand this because a nation's level of economic development affects all aspects of business, including marketing, production, and finance. Although nations vary greatly with respect to economic development levels, we commonly group them into categories based on their level of economic development.

CATEGORIES BASED ON LEVELS OF ECONOMIC DEVELOPMENT

developed
A classification for all industrialized nations, which are the most technically developed

Developed is the name given to the industrialized, or postindustrial, service-based nations that have achieved high income per capita. Countries identified as being economically developed include the Western European nations, Japan, Australia, New Zealand, Canada, Israel, South Korea, and the United States. The term **developing** is a classification for the world's lower-income nations, which are less technically developed. Characteristics of developing countries are included in the nearby Worldview box, "Characteristics of Developing

Nations." At one time, **newly industrializing countries (NICs)** was a category that included only the four Asian tigers (Taiwan, Hong Kong, Singapore, and South Korea). These countries (1) had what the World Bank considers to be fast-growing, middle-income or higher economies, (2) possessed a heavy concentration of foreign investment, and (3) exported large quantities of manufactured goods, including high-tech products. Subsequently, other nations have achieved sufficient progress in their industrialization process to also be classified as NICs by various organizations. Depending on the criteria employed, more recent listings of NICS include some or all of the following countries: Brazil, Mexico, Argentina, Malaysia, Thailand, Chile, Venezuela, Hungary, South Africa, Indonesia, Pakistan, and China.

Because the economies of the four tigers have grown faster than those of other NICs and are approximating the size of developed nations' economies, the IMF and other organizations have begun to use the term **newly industrialized economies (NIEs)** to refer to the tigers.

You will also find that various different classification systems are employed by international agencies such as the United Nations, International Monetary Fund, and World Bank for reporting statistics.* For example, the IMF combines the NIEs with the industrialized nations to form a category termed *advanced economies.*

The rest of the noncommunist nations are in the category *developing countries,* which has a subcategory, *emerging market economies,* that includes Chile, Malaysia, China, Thailand, and Indonesia. The third category, called *transition countries,* includes the former communist countries. The UN uses simply *developed* and *developing economies* and refers to the former communist nations as *Eastern Europe* and the *former USSR.* When speaking of developed and developing nations as a bloc, UN economists frequently use the terms *North* and *South,* respectively.

The World Bank, by contrast, uses a classification based on 2004 gross national income per capita:

1. Low income ($745 or less).
2. Lower middle income ($746–$2,975).
3. Upper middle income ($2,976–$9,205).
4. High income ($9,206 or more).

The World Bank formerly employed a classification system based on gross national product (GNP) per capita, but in 2002 it changed to **gross national income (GNI)** per capita, which follows the current statistical practice of most countries. GNI measures the income generated by a nation's residents from international and domestic activity and is preferred by international organizations to gross domestic product (GDP), which measures income generated from domestic activity by residents of the country as well as nonresidents. Every economy is classified as low income, lower middle income, upper middle income, and high income, classes which are based on the World Bank's operational lending categories. The Bank also employs the term *developing countries* to refer to low- and middle-income countries.[4]

developing
A classification for the world's lower-income nations, which are less technically developed

newly industrializing countries (NICs)
The four Asian tigers and the middle-income economies such as Brazil, Mexico, Malaysia, Chile, and Thailand

newly industrialized economies (NIEs)
The fast-growing upper-middle-income and high-income economies of South Korea, Taiwan, Hong Kong, and Singapore

gross national income (GNI)
The total value of all income generated by a nation's residents from international and domestic activity

Dimensions of the Economy and Their Relevance for International Business

To estimate market potentials as well as to provide input to the other functional areas of the firm, managers require data on the sizes and the rates of change of a number of economic and socioeconomic factors. In order to be a potential market, an area must have sufficient people with the means to buy a firm's products. Socioeconomic data provide information on the number of people, and the economic dimensions tell us if they have purchasing power.

ECONOMIC DIMENSIONS

Among the more important economic indicators are gross domestic product, gross national income, distribution of income, private consumption expenditures, personal ownership of goods, private investment, unit labor costs, exchange rates, inflation rates, and interest rates.

*These agencies are discussed in Chapters 4 and 5.

WORLD view   

Characteristics of Developing Nations

Although there is great diversity among the many developing nations, most share the following common characteristics:

1. GNI/capita of less than $9,206 (World Bank criterion).
2. Unequal distribution of income, with a very small middle class.
3. *Technological dualism*—a mix of firms employing the latest technology and companies using very primitive methods.
4. *Regional dualism*—high productivity and incomes in some regions and little economic development in others.
5. A majority of the population earning its living in a relatively unproductive agricultural sector.
6. Disguised unemployment or underemployment—two people doing a job that one person could do.
7. High population growth (2.5 to 4 percent annually).
8. High rate of illiteracy and insufficient educational facilities.
9. Widespread malnutrition and a wide range of health problems.
10. Political instability.
11. High dependence on a few products for export, generally agricultural products or minerals.
12. Inhospitable topography, such as deserts, mountains, and tropical forests.
13. Low savings rates and inadequate banking facilities.

You can see from these characteristics that a tremendous gap exists between the levels of living of the inhabitants of developing nations and those of developed nations. Although economists have studied and theorized about the various aspects of economic development for over two centuries, their preoccupation with the poorer nations of the world really began only after World War II. Among the developing nations, the United Nations lists the following as the 50 least developed countries in the world:

Afghanistan
Angola
Bangladesh
Benin
Bhutan
Burkina Faso
Burundi
Cambodia
Cape Verde
Central African Republic
Chad
Comoros
Democratic Republic of the Congo
Djibouti
Equatorial Guinea
Eritrea
Ethiopia
Gambia
Guinea
Guinea-Bissau
Haiti
Kiribati
Lao People's Democratic Republic
Lesotho
Liberia
Madagascar
Malawi
Maldives
Mali
Mauritania
Mozambique
Myanmar
Nepal
Niger
Rwanda
Samoa
São Tomé and Principe
Senegal
Sierra Leone
Solomon Islands
Somalia
Sudan
Timor-Lesté
Togo
Tuvalu
Uganda
United Republic of Tanzania
Vanuatu
Yemen
Zambia

Source: "Country Classification," World Bank, http://web.worldbank.org/WBSITE/EXTERNAL/DATASTATISTICS/0,contentMDK:20420458~menuPK:64133156~pagePK:64133150~piPK:64133175~theSitePK:239419,00.html (October 6, 2006); "List of Least Developed Countries," United Nations Office of the High Representative for the Least Developed Countries, Landlocked Developing Countries and Small Island Developing States, www.un.org/special-rep/ohrlls/ldc/list.htm (October 7, 2006); "Glossary," United Nations, www.un.org/cyberschoolbus/infonation3/menu/advanced.asp (October 7, 2006); and "The World's Economies," www.infoplease.com/cig/economics/world-economies.html (October 7, 2006).

Gross National Income As mentioned earlier in this chapter, GNI is a measure of the income generated by a nation's residents from international and domestic activity. Most international organizations prefer GNI to GDP as a measure of economic size, since GDP measures income generated from domestic activity by residents of the country as well as nonresidents. GNIs range from $13.0 trillion for the United States to $0.2 billion for Guinea-Bissau.[5] What is the relevance of GNI for the international businessperson? Is India, with a 2005 GNI of $793 billion, a more attractive market than Denmark, whose $257 billion GNI is less than one-third the size? To compare the purchasing power of nations, managers need to know how many people GNI is divided among.

GNI/Capita Employing GNI per capita from the tables of the World Bank to compare purchasing power reveals that Denmark is far richer than India: GNI/capita is $47,390 in Denmark versus $720 in India. Although India's economic pie is more than three times as big as Denmark's, there are almost 220 times as many people to eat it.

What can we learn from GNI/capita? We can generally assume that the higher its value, the more advanced the economy. Generally, however, the rate of growth is more important to marketers because a high growth rate indicates a fast-growing market—for which they are always searching. Frequently, given the choice between investing in a nation with a higher GNI/capita but a low growth rate and a nation in which the conditions are reversed, management will choose the latter.

Although GNI per capita is widely used to compare countries with respect to the well-being of their citizens and to assess market or investment potential, managers must use it with caution. For example, to arrive at GNI, government economists must impute monetary values to various goods and services not sold in the marketplace, such as food grown for personal consumption. Moreover, many goods and services are bartered in both low-income nations (because people have little cash) and high-income countries (because people wish to reduce reported income and thus pay less income tax). Transactions of this type are said to be part of the *underground economy.*

Underground Economy Much has been written about the part of the national income that is not measured by official statistics because it is either underreported or unreported. Included in this **underground economy** (also referred to as *black, parallel, informal, submerged, or shadow economy)* are undeclared legal production, production of illegal goods and services, and concealed income in kind (barter). As a general rule, the higher the level of taxation and the more oppressive the government red tape, the bigger the underground economy will be. Figure 8.2 shows estimates of some underground economies. The underground economy in the United States increased from 4 percent of GDP in 1970 to nearly 9 percent in 2003. On average for the 1999–2000 time period, it is estimated that the underground economy accounted for 18 percent of GDP in OECD countries, 38 percent of GDP in transition economies, and 41 percent of GDP in developing countries.[6] During the 1999–2000 time period, the underground economy in several nations exceeded 50 percent of GDP, including over 67 percent in Bolivia and Georgia. Estimates of the underground economy vary widely because of the different methodologies used to compile them; also, people who have undeclared income are not likely to admit it and be liable to prosecution for tax evasion. In addition to reducing the total taxes paid to government, the underground economy can result in distortions of economic data, which managers must take into account when using these data for business decisions.

underground economy
The part of a nation's income that, because of unreporting or underreporting, is not measured by official statistics

FIGURE 8.2 Underground Economies in Selected Nations (percentage of GNP, 2002–2003)

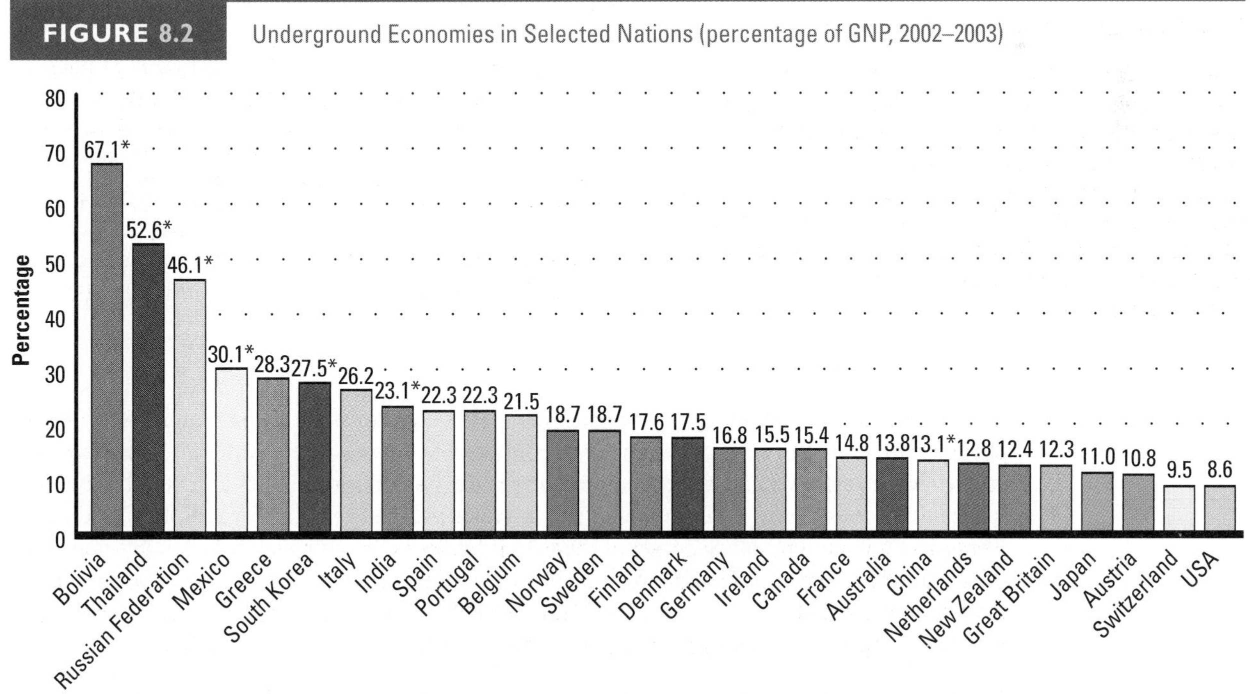

* Refers to Figures for 2002.

Source: Friedrich Schneider and Robert Klinglmair, "Shadow Economies around the World: What Do We Know?" March 2004, http://papers.ssrn.com/so13/papers.cfm?abstract_id=518526 (October 8, 2006).

Currency Conversion Another problem with GNI estimates is that to compare them, the GNIs in local currency must be converted to a common currency—conventionally the dollar—by using an exchange rate. If the relative values of the two currencies accurately reflected consumer purchasing power, this conversion would be acceptable. However, the World Bank recognizes that "the use of official exchange rates to convert national currency figures to U.S. dollars does not reflect domestic purchasing powers of currencies."[7]

purchasing power parity (PPP)
The number of units of a currency required to buy the same amounts of goods and services in the domestic market that one dollar would buy in the United States

To overcome this deficiency, the UN International Comparison Program (ICP) has developed a method of comparing GNIs that is based on **purchasing power parity (PPP)** rather than on the international demand for currency (exchange rates). Here is how purchasing power parity rates are calculated.

Suppose Thailand reports to the World Bank that its GNI/capita for last year is 93,624 baht/capita. The Bank must translate this value to U.S. dollars. If the current exchange rate is 37.6 baht = $1, then using this rate would convert 93,624 baht to $2,490 (93,624 /37.6). How well does this measure Thailand's welfare? What can a Thai citizen consume with the 93,624 baht compared with what an American can consume with the $41,440 per capita income of the United States? Suppose that the following table reflects local prices in both countries of the same basket of goods:

Goods	Thailand (baht)	U.S. ($)
Soap (bar)	40	0.50
Rice (lb.)	25	0.35
Shoes (pair)	495	60.00
Dress	580	450.00
Socks (pair)	95	2.00
Total	1,235	$107.85

In Thailand 1,235 baht buys what $107.85 buys in the United States. Therefore, comparing the purchasing power of the currencies, 1,235 baht/$107.85 = 11.45 baht per $1. Using the exchange rate of 11.45 baht per dollar, Thailand's GNI/capita is now 93,624/11.45 = $8,177. At the official exchange rate of 37.6 baht/$1, Thailand's GNI is $2,490. At the purchasing power parity rate of 11.45 baht/$1, Thailand's GNI is $8,177.

Table 8.2 illustrates that comparisons based on purchasing power parity result in GNI/capita values that are considerably higher than those regularly given for developing nations and lower for many developed nations; that is, in considering purchasing power, the differences between the GNIs of developing and developed nations are smaller than those generally published. You will note how the smaller buying power of the Japanese yen compared to that of the U.S. dollar affects the GNI/capita based on purchasing power parity.

The Atlas Conversion Factor Dissatisfaction with both the PPP and the conversion by using official exchange rates caused the World Bank to adopt the Atlas methodology to derive per capita GNI estimates. The *Atlas conversion factor* is the arithmetic average of the current exchange rate and the exchange rates in the two previous years adjusted by the ratio of domestic inflation to the combined inflation rates of the euro zone, Japan, the United Kingdom, and the United States. Incomes measured by the Atlas conversion factor are generally more stable over time and changes in income rankings are more likely to be due to relative economic performance than fluctuations in the exchange rate.

Although differences in GNI/capita do tell us something about the relative wealth of a nation's inhabitants, the information is somewhat misleading because wealth is usually not evenly spread. This first crude estimate of purchasing power must be refined by incorporating data on how national income is actually distributed.

TABLE 8.2 GNI/Capita Based on UN ICP for Selected Countries, 2004

Country	GNI/Capita in US$ Converted at World Bank–Adjusted Exchange Rates	Adjusted Exchange Rates Ranking	GNI/Capita in US$ Based on Purchasing Power Parity	Purchasing Power Parity Ranking
United States	$41,440	5	$39,820	3
Japan	37,050	9	29,810	18
Sweden	35,840	10	29,880	17
Canada	28,310	21	30,760	16
Mexico	6,790	70	9,640	80
Argentina	3,580	93	12,530	66
Russian Federation	3,400	94	9,680	79
Thailand	2,490	104	7,930	88
China	1,500	129	5,890	108
India	620	159	3,120	144
Nigeria	430	175	970	190

Source: *World Development Indicators 2006* (Washington, DC: World Bank, 2006), table 1.6.

income distribution A measure of how a nation's income is apportioned among its people, commonly reported as the percentage of income received by population quintiles

Income Distribution Data on **income distribution** are gathered by the World Bank from a number of sources and published yearly in the *World Development Indicators* (see Table 8.3). Despite the difficulties associated with income distribution studies, such as inconsistent measuring practices and wide variations in the representativeness of samples, the data provide useful insights for business.

1. They confirm the belief that, generally, income is more evenly distributed in the richer nations, although there are important variations among both developed and developing nations.
2. Comparisons over time demonstrate that income redistribution proceeds very slowly, so that older data are still useful.
3. The same comparisons indicate that income inequality increases in the early stages of development, with a reversal of this tendency in the later stages. For example, even as China's economy skyrockets, the number of truly destitute grew by 800,000 to nearly 85 million in 2004.[8] The fact that the middle quintiles in some nations are growing at the expense of the top and bottom 20 percent signifies an increase in middle-income families, which are especially significant to marketers.

Depending on the type of product and the total population, either situation (relatively even or uneven income distribution) may represent market opportunities. For example, although Costa Rica's GNI was $42 billion in PPP terms in 2005, the fact that just 20 percent of the population receives nearly 55 percent of that income indicates that a sizable group of people are potential customers for low-volume, high-priced luxury products. On the other hand, the market is rather small (4 million population) for low-priced goods requiring a high sales volume. This simple calculation based on GNI, total population, and income distribution may be all that is required to indicate that a particular country is not a good market; however, if the results look promising, the analyst will proceed to gather data on private consumption.

Private Consumption One area of interest to marketers is the manner in which consumers allocate their disposable income (after-tax personal income) between purchases of essential and nonessential goods. Manufacturers of household durables, for instance, will want to know the amounts spent in that category, whereas producers of nonessentials will be interested in the

TABLE 8.3 Percentage Share of Income or Consumption

Country	Lowest 20 Percent	20–40 Percent	40–60 Percent	60–80 Percent	Highest 20 Percent	Highest 10 Percent
Argentina (2003)	3.2%	7.0%	12.1%	20.7%	56.8%	39.6%
Brazil (2003)	2.6	6.2	10.7	18.4	62.1	45.8
Bulgaria (2003)	8.7	13.7	17.2	22.1	38.3	23.9
Canada (2000)	7.2	12.7	17.2	23.0	39.9	24.8
Chile (2000)	3.3	6.6	10.5	17.4	62.2	47.0
China (2001)	4.7	9.0	14.2	22.1	50.0	33.1
Colombia (2003)	2.5	6.2	10.6	18.0	62.7	46.9
Costa Rica (2001)	3.9	8.1	12.8	20.4	54.8	38.4
Czech Rep. (96)	10.3	14.5	17.7	21.7	35.9	22.4
El Salvador (2002)	2.7	7.5	12.8	21.2	55.9	38.8
Finland (2000)	9.6	14.1	17.5	22.1	36.7	22.6
Germany (2000)	8.5	13.7	17.8	23.1	36.9	22.1
Ghana (99)	5.6	10.1	14.9	22.9	46.6	30.0
Hungary (2002)	9.5	13.9	17.6	22.4	36.5	22.2
India (2000)	8.9	12.3	16.0	21.2	43.3	28.5
Indonesia (2002)	8.4	11.9	15.4	21.0	43.3	28.5
Israel (2001)	5.7	10.5	15.9	23.0	44.9	28.8
Italy (2000)	6.5	12.0	16.8	22.8	42.0	26.8
Jamaica (2000)	6.7	10.7	15.0	21.7	46.0	30.3
Japan (1993)	10.6	14.2	17.6	22.0	35.7	21.7
Kazakhstan (2003)	7.4	11.9	16.4	22.8	41.5	25.9
Latvia (2003)	6.6	11.2	15.5	22.0	44.7	29.1
Malaysia (1997)	4.4	8.1	12.9	20.3	54.3	38.4
Mexico (2002)	4.3	8.3	12.6	19.7	55.1	39.4
Nepal (2003–2004)	6.0	9.0	12.4	18.0	54.6	40.6
Netherlands (1999)	7.6	13.2	17.2	23.3	38.7	22.9
Nigeria (2003)	5.0	9.6	14.5	21.7	49.2	33.2
Norway (2000)	9.6	14.0	17.2	22.0	37.2	23.4
Pakistan (2002)	9.3	13.0	16.3	21.1	40.3	26.3
Peru (2002)	3.2	7.1	11.8	19.3	58.7	43.2
Philippines (2000)	5.4	8.8	13.1	20.5	52.3	36.3
Poland (2002)	7.5	11.9	16.1	22.2	42.2	27.0
Russian Fed. (2002)	6.1	10.5	14.9	21.8	46.6	30.6
Senegal (1995)	6.4	10.3	14.5	20.6	48.2	33.5
South Africa (2000)	3.5	6.3	10.0	18.0	62.2	44.7
Sri Lanka (1999–2000)	8.3	12.5	16.0	21.0	42.2	27.8
Sweden (2000)	9.1	14.0	17.6	22.7	36.6	22.2
Thailand (2002)	6.3	9.9	14.0	20.8	49.0	33.4
United Kingdom (1999)	6.1	11.4	16.0	22.5	44.0	28.5
United States (2000)	5.4	10.7	15.7	22.4	45.8	29.9
Venezuela (2000)	4.7	9.4	14.5	22.1	49.3	32.8
Vietnam (2002)	7.5	11.2	14.8	21.1	45.4	29.9
Zambia (2002–2003)	6.1	10.2	14.2	20.7	48.8	33.7

Note: Numbers in parentheses indicate year of study.

Source: From *World Development Indicators 2006* by World Bank. Copyright © 2006 by World Bank. Reproduced with permission of World Bank via Copyright Clearance Center.

magnitude of **discretionary income** (disposable income less essential purchases), for this is the money available to be spent on their products. Fortunately, disposable incomes and the amounts spent on essential purchases are available from the *UN Statistical Yearbook,* and discretionary income may be obtained by subtracting the total of these items from disposable income. More detailed expenditure patterns can be found in the *World Development Indicators* published by the World Bank. Data from that publication are reproduced in Table 8.4, which includes data on private consumption expenditures for 10 high-income and 10 low-income economies, using PPP equivalents.

discretionary income
The amount of income left after paying taxes and making essential purchases

Because PPP-based consumer expenditures eliminate differences in relative prices, marketers use these data to analyze how the composition of consumption changes with the level of development. For example, the percentages of household expenditures spent on food and clothing by residents of developing nations are double the percentages consumers in industrialized nations spend. On the other hand, the percentages spent on (1) transport and communication, (2) consumer durables, (3) health care, and (4) other consumption (beverages, tobacco, and services, including meals eaten in restaurants or taken out) by households of developed nations are twice the percentages of those in developing nations. Note that the percentage differences within a consumption category do not vary with the consumption expenditures per capita. An example is clothing and footwear. Interestingly, in spite of the allure of French haute-couture, the percentage spent on clothing in France is less than half that spent by the residents of Hong Kong and only 78 percent of U.S. expenditures.

TABLE 8.4 Private Consumption Based on Purchasing Power Parity

				Percentage of Household Consumption					
Country	GNI/ Capita Based on Exchange Rates, 2005	GNI/ Capita Based on PPP, 2005	Household Consumption Expenditure % of GDP, 2005	Food	Clothing and Footwear	Education	Health Care	Transportation and Communication	Other Consumption
Austria	36,980	33,140	56	20	10	9	4	9	48
Canada	32,600	32,220	56	14	5	21	4	9	47
Belgium	35,700	32,640	54	17	6	1	3	7	66
Denmark	47,390	33,570	48	16	6	17	3	5	53
France	34,810	30,570	56	22	7	8	3	12	48
Germany	43,580	29,210	59	14	6	10	2	7	61
Hong Kong China	27,670	34,670	59	10	17	8	2	6	57
Japan	38,980	31,410	57	12	7	22	2	13	44
Kenya	530	1,170	70	31	9	8	2	3	47
Madagascar	290	880	84	61	8	2	2	5	22
Malawi	160	650	95	50	13	6	2	9	20
Mali	380	1,000	79	53	15	5	4	2	21
Nigeria	560	1,040	41	51	5	8	2	2	22
Sierra Leone	220	780	90	47	9	13	3	8	20
Switzerland	54,930	37,080	61	19	6	18	3	8	46
Tajikistan	330	1,260	95	48	7	14	0	5	26
Tanzania	340	730	77	67	6	12	4	6	5
United States	43,740	41,950	71	13	9	6	4	8	5
Yemen	600	920	80	25	5	5	3	5	57
Zambia	490	950	70	52	10	11	2	3	22

Source: *World Development Indicators 2004,* www.worldbank.org/data/wdi2004/tables/table1-1.pdf (July 2, 2004); *World Development Report 2003,* pp. 238–39 and pp. 234–35; and *World Development Report 2007,* pp. 288–89.

WORLD view   

Telephones: An Economic Indicator?

Cellular phone vendor Wilfred Perera (right) shows handsets to a customer in Colombo, Sri Lanka, in February 2004. Sri Lanka was the first South Asian nation to introduce cellular phones in the late 1980s and there are now more than a million mobile phone users in a country of 18.6 million people.

Sena Vidanagama/AFP/Getty Images

What is the best gauge for measuring a country's level of development? Is it (1) per capita income, (2) state of the construction industry, (3) density of pollution, or (4) number of telephones? If you selected number 4, you are right, according to the International Telecommunications Union (ITU), a specialized agency of the United Nations. The ITU published an article in which the author claimed that the total number of telephone lines installed in a country is often a better indicator of a nation's level of development than is even per capita income.

Generally, the wealthier a country is, the more telephone lines it has. In 2005, the richest countries already had more than one phone line for every two people. The increase in mobile phone use has also been extremely rapid. China's mobile phone subscribers went from 1.6 million to 300 million between 1995 and 2005, making that country the largest mobile phone market in the world. In Finland the density of mobile phones approaches twice that of fixed phones (it has reached a multiple of three or four in other nations, such as Kuwait and Saudi Arabia). In fact, mobile phone use has increased across countries at all income levels. In Cambodia and Sri Lanka, for example, the number of cell phones per 1,000 people was already greater than that for mainlines by the late 1990s. For poor countries, it is faster and less expensive to add cell phone networks than to put in a mainline infrastructure.

ITU statistics show that about 34 percent of the world's inhabitants have a cell phone subscription and almost 20 percent have a fixed line. Allowing for duplication, that is considerable penetration. Admittedly, in countries such as Chad, there are only about 15 phones per 1,000 persons. However, that represents a tenfold increase for Chad in the last few years. It is evident that developing nations therefore are beginning to get a grip on their communications problem.

Source: *World Development Indicators 2000, 2001, 2006,* www.china-embassy.org/eng/xw/t140234.htm (August 6, 2004); ITU sources from Table 8.5.

International business managers know better than to underestimate the importance of small percentage differences among nations. They are aware that each percentage point is worth a large sum of money. To appreciate its value, try multiplying the total per capita consumption expenditure by 1 percent of the population. French designers might want to note that if American consumers had spent 1 percent more on clothing, for example, this would have amounted to \$43,740 × 0.01 × 296 million inhabitants, or \$129.5 billion in additional sales for the clothing industry.

Other indicators that add to our knowledge of personal consumption are those concerned with (1) the ownership of goods and (2) the consumption of key materials. For example, commercial energy use per capita is related to the size of the modern sectors—*urban areas, industry,* and *motorized transport.* The World Bank has found that the populations living in high-income economies use nearly seven times as much commercial energy per capita as do people in developing economies, and the quantity and mix of energy constitute a rough indicator of a country's level of development. As Table 8.5 illustrates, the more industrialized nations have considerably higher values for these indicators than do the developing nations. See the nearby Worldview box for an Asian Development Bank expert's opinion about the most significant indicator.

unit labor costs
Total direct labor costs divided by units produced

Unit Labor Costs

One factor that contributes to a favorable investment opportunity is the ability to obtain **unit labor costs** (total direct labor costs/units produced) lower than those currently available to the firm. Foreign trends in these costs are closely monitored because each country experiences a different rate of increase.

Countries with slower-rising unit labor costs attract management's attention for two reasons. First, they are investment prospects for companies striving to lower production costs, as discussed in Chapter 2; second, they may become sources of new competition in world markets if other firms in the same industry are already located there.

Changes in wage rates may also cause a multinational firm that obtains products or components from a number of subsidiaries to change its sources of supply.

TABLE 8.5 Per Capita Ownership or Consumption of Key Goods and Services for Selected Countries

Region/Country	Telephone Main Lines per 100 Inhabitants, 2005	Mobile Subscribers per 100 Inhabitants, 2005	Electricity Consumption/ Capita (1,000 kWh), 2003	Internet Users per 100 Inhabitants 2005
Europe				
Switzerland	69	92	8,191	50
Germany	67	96	6,896	45
France	59	79	—	43
Sweden	72	93	15,403	75
United Kingdom	56	102	6,209	63
Italy	43	124	5,620	48
Middle East				
Israel	43	112	6,599	47
Kuwait	19	89	14,808	26
Saudi Arabia	15	54	6,259	7
Egypt	14	18	1,127	7
Africa				
Mauritius	29	57	—	15
South Africa	10	72	4,399	11
Cameroon	1	14	178	1
Ghana	1	13	248	2
Ethiopia	1	1	28	0.2
Asia				
Japan	46	74	7,818	50
South Korea	49	79	7,018	68
China	27	30	1,379	8
India	5	8	435	5
Bangladesh	1	6	128	0.2
South America				
Uruguay	31	19	1,781	21
Chile	22	68	2,880	62
Brazil	23	46	1,883	12
Colombia	17	48	834	10
Bolivia	7	26	422	5
Eastern Europe				
Hungary	33	92	3,637	30
Czech Republic	31	115	6,070	50
Poland	31	76	3,329	26
Russia	28	84	5,480	15
Kazakhstan	17	33	3,510	3
North America and Caribbean				
United States	61	68	13,078	63
Canada	57	51	17,290	62
Trinidad and Tobago	25	61	4,721	12
Mexico	18	44	1,801	17
Haiti	2	5	31	6

Source: Electricity consumption—*World Development Indicators 2006,* table 5.9, http://devdata.worldbank.org/wdi2006/contents/Section5.htm (October 6, 2006); telephone mainlines, mobile phones, and Internet hosts—International Telecommunication Union, www.itu.int/ITU-D/icteye/Indicators/Indicators.aspx# (October 6, 2006).

Nike, which produces none of the shoes it sells in the United States, began using Japanese plants in 1964. When labor costs rose there in the mid-1970s, the company changed to factories in South Korea and Taiwan. Later, Nike added Thailand. But as labor costs rose in those countries, Nike began buying in over 50 Indonesian factories and in China. Alarmed because its $75 to $100 (retail) shoes were costing as much as $10 to produce and ship to the United States, Nike contracted for production in Vietnam and is also the largest seller of athletic shoes in China.[9]

What are the reasons for the relative changes in labor costs? Three factors are responsible: (1) compensation, (2) productivity, and (3) exchange rates. Hourly compensation tends to vary more widely than wages because of the differences in the size of fringe benefits. Unit labor costs will not rise in unison with compensation rates if gains in productivity outstrip increases in hourly compensation. In fact, if productivity increases fast enough, the unit costs of labor will decrease even though the firm is required to pay more to the workers.

Table 8.6 reveals why international firms keep a close watch on labor compensation rates around the world. For example, in 1975 Sweden had the highest hourly rate, with the United States and Germany tied for fifth place. Note that Japan's average hourly rate was less than half the American rate. However, by 1985, the U.S. rate was the world's highest, and American

TABLE 8.6 Labor Compensation Costs, 1975–2004*

	Average Hourly Rate Including Fringe Benefits (US$ and local currencies)							
	2004		1995		1985		1975	
Country	US$	Local	US$	Local	US$	Local	US$	Local
Americas								
Canada	21.42	27.89	16.04	22.02	10.94	14.94	5.96	6.07
United States	23.17	23.17	17.19	17.19	13.01	13.01	6.36	6.36
Mexico	2.50	28.22	1.51	9.66	1.59	409.00	1.47	18.00
Asia and Oceania								
Hong Kong	5.51	42.90	4.82	37.30	1.73	13.46	0.76	3.73
Japan	21.90	2,370.00	23.66	2,223.00	6.34	1,512.00	3.00	889.00
Taiwan	5.97	199.1	5.82	154.26	1.50	59.60	0.40	15.17
Europe								
Austria	28.29	22.75	25.38	255.87	7.58	156.75	4.51	78.46
Belgium	29.98	24.11	26.88	792.10	8.97	532.39	6.41	235.10
Denmark	33.75	202.1	24.26	135.86	8.13	86.18	6.28	36.00
Finland	30.67	24.66	24.83	108.64	8.16	50.56	4.61	16.88
France	23.89	19.21	19.34	96.45	7.52	67.49	4.52	19.34
Germany†	34.05	26.15	31.85	45.61	9.60	28.23	6.35	15.59
Italy	20.48	16.46	16.52	26,911.00	7.63	14,563.00	4.67	3,048.00
Netherlands	30.76	24.73	24.18	38.79	8.75	29.04	6.58	16.59
Norway	34.64	233.5	24.38	154.46	10.37	89.11	6.77	35.29
Spain	17.10	13.75	12.70	1,582.00	4.66	792.00	2.53	145.00
Sweden	28.42	208.8	21.64	154.51	9.66	83.12	7.18	29.73
Switzerland	30.26	37.61	29.30	34.61	9.66	23.71	6.09	15.72
United Kingdom	24.71	13.49	13.73	8.70	6.27	4.84	3.37	1.52

*Dollar conversions are at average annual exchange rates.

†Former West Germany.

Source: Bureau of Labor Statistics, "International Comparisons of Hourly Compensation Costs for Production Workers in Manufacturing, Supplementary Tables," www.bls.gov/fls/hcompsupptabtoc.htm (October 6, 2004).

managers were searching for overseas production sites. Yet just 10 years later, the United States had fallen to 13th place in the hourly compensation cost ranking. Every European nation but the United Kingdom and Spain had higher costs. In 1995, American costs were still in 11th place, but there was one important change in the rankings: Japan's labor compensation rate, which was less than half of the U.S. rate in 1985, had jumped to 138 percent of the U.S. compensation rate. By that point many Japanese firms had moved significant parts of their production to other Asian countries with lower labor costs, such as Thailand, China, and Indonesia. (This movement abroad was also influenced by the retirement of many skilled machinists and other artisans in Japan, which made foreign labor more attractive.) By 2004, 11 European nations had higher labor costs than the United States, led by Norway's premium of 50 percent, while Japan's relative labor costs had declined to only 95 percent of those in the United States.

Other Economic Dimensions We have mentioned only a few of the many economic indicators that analysts study, and you will learn about the importance to businesspeople of interest rates, balances of payments, and inflation rates in Chapter 11, "Financial Forces." The analyst will choose which economic measures to study depending on the industry and the purpose of the study.

The large international debts of a number of middle- and low-income nations are causing multiple problems not only for their governments but also for multinational firms. Just look at the situation of the countries with the highest debts that are listed in Table 8.7.

Is this a problem for international bankers only, or should it concern multinational managements as well? Is it significant to global and multidomestic firms with subsidiaries in these countries that high-indebtedness indicators such as debt to GDI and debt service to exports are a cause for concern? The World Bank claims that an empirical analysis of developing countries' experience shows that "debt service difficulties become increasingly likely when the ratio of the present value of debt to exports reaches 200–250 percent and the debt service ratio exceeds 20–25 percent."[10] If management agrees, then it will expect periodic reports on this situation from its analysts. Let's examine the ramifications of these large foreign debts for an international firm.

If a major part of the foreign exchange a nation earns cannot be used to import components used in local products, then either local industries must manufacture them or the companies that import them must stop production. Either alternative can cause the multinational

TABLE 8.7 Major International Debtors

	Total External Debt ($ billion)			2004 Debt as Percentage of 1980 Debt
Country	**2004**	**1990**	**1980**	**Percent**
Brazil	$222	$120	$72	308%
Mexico	139	104	57	244
Argentina	169	62	27	626
China	249	55	5	4,980
Russia	197	6	—	3,283*
Indonesia	141	70	21	671
Turkey	162	49	19	853
India	123	84	21	586

* Comparison is to 1990 debt

Source: www.oecd.org/dac/debt/htm/data_index.htm, various country files; *World Bank Indicators 1999;* http://siteresources.worldbank.org/GDFINT2004/summary-tables/20179304/reg-external-debt.PDF (July 20, 2004); and *World Development Indicators 2006* (October 7, 2006).

vertically integrated
Descriptive term for a firm that produces inputs for its subsequent manufacturing processes

to lose sales if it has been selling the parts made in one of its home country plants to its subsidiary, a common occurrence because the home plant is usually more **vertically integrated** than its subsidiaries. A scarcity of foreign exchange can also make it difficult for the subsidiary to import raw materials and spare parts for its production equipment. If headquarters wants its affiliate to continue production, it may have to lend the foreign exchange and wait for repayment.

Campbell Soup, Revlon, and Gerber closed their operations in Brazil because of this problem. Other multinationals have resorted to barter or have begun to export their subsidiaries' products even though these actions have reduced exports or even local sales of their domestic plants.

Governments may impose price controls (which make it difficult for a subsidiary to earn a profit), cut government spending (which reduces company sales), and impose wage controls (which limit consumer purchasing power). The economic turmoil that follows can turn into a political crisis, as occurred in Argentina and Peru when rioting resulted after their presidents tried to impose austerity measures. During the Asian financial crisis, South Korea experienced nationwide strikes in response to laws passed to ease that country's economic problems.

Scarcity of foreign exchange can affect even firms that merely export to nations with high foreign debt because the governments will surely impose import restrictions. When Latin American debt increased rapidly from 1981 to 1983, that region's share of U.S. exports dropped by one-third. To protect these export markets, firms had to extend long-term credit. From this you can see that managements will expect to receive information on the status of the foreign debt in nations where it is high in addition to the other economic data we have been examining. This is especially important now that the same American banks that were involved in the developing-country debt crisis in the 1980s are once again lending huge sums to developing nations.

SOCIOECONOMIC DIMENSIONS

A complete definition of market potential must also include detailed information about the population's physical attributes as measured by the socioeconomic dimensions. We shall begin this section with an analysis of total population.

Total Population

Total population, the most general indicator of potential market size, is the first characteristic of the population that analysts examine. Population sizes vary immensely, from more than a billion inhabitants in China and India to 2,701 for Svalbard and the uninhabited Bassas da India. The fact that many developed nations have fewer than 10 million inhabitants makes it apparent that population size alone is a poor indicator of economic strength and market potential. Only for a few low-priced products, such as soft drinks, cigarettes, and soap, might population size alone provide a basis for estimating consumption.

For products not in this category, large populations and populations that are increasing rapidly may not signify an immediate enlargement of the market, but if incomes grow over time, eventually some part of the population will become customers. Insight into the speed at which this is occurring may be obtained by comparing population and economic growth rates. Where GNI increases faster than the population, there is probably an expanding market, whereas the converse situation not only indicates possible market contraction but may even point out a country as a potential area of political unrest. This possibility is strengthened if an analysis of the educational system discloses an accumulation of technical and university graduates. These groups expect to be employed as and receive the wages of professionals, and when enough new jobs are not being created to absorb them, the government can be in serious trouble. Various nations already face this difficulty; Egypt is an example.

human-needs approach
View that defines economic development as a reduction of poverty and unemployment as well as an increase in income

Age Distribution

Because few products are purchased by everyone, marketers must identify the segments of the population that are more apt to buy their goods. For some firms, age is a salient determinant of market size, but the distribution of age groups within populations varies widely. Generally, because of higher birth rates, developing countries have more youthful populations than do industrial countries.

New Approaches to Economic Development

Until the 1970s, economists generally considered *economic growth* to be synonymous with *economic development.* A nation was considered to be developing economically if its real output per capita as measured by GNI/capita was increasing over time. However, the realization that economic growth does not necessarily imply development—because the benefits of this growth so often have applied to only a few—has led to the widespread adoption of a new, more comprehensive definition of economic development.

The **human-needs approach** defines economic development as the reduction of poverty, unemployment, and inequality in the distribution of income. The definition of poverty also has been broadened. Instead of being defined in terms of income, as is common in developed countries, a reduction in poverty has come to mean less illiteracy, less malnutrition, less disease and early death, and a shift from agricultural to industrial production or service-based economic activity.

Because of the increased emphasis on human welfare and the lack of a clear link between income growth and human progress, the United Nations Development Program has devised a Human Development Index (HDI) based on three essential elements of human life: (1) a long and healthy life, (2) the ability to acquire knowledge, and (3) access to resources needed for a decent standard of living. These elements are measured by (1) life expectancy, (2) adult literacy, and (3) GDP/capita, adjusted for differences in purchasing power. In its latest report, as shown in the table below, the program ranked Norway as the most developed with respect to the HDI, followed by Iceland, Australia, Luxembourg, Canada, Sweden, Switzerland, Ireland, Belgium, and the United States. The 24 lowest-ranked countries are all located in Africa, a fact that further highlights the significant development challenges that confront that continent and its residents.

(continued)

HDI Rank	Country	Life Expectancy at Birth (years), 2003	Adult Literacy Rate (% ages 15 and above), 2003	GDP per Capita (PPP, US$), 2003
1	Norway	79.4	99%	$37,670
2	Iceland	80.7	99	31,243
3	Australia	80.3	99	29,632
4	Luxembourg	78.5	99	62,298
5	Canada	80.0	99	30,677
6	Sweden	80.2	99	26,750
7	Switzerland	80.5	99	30,552
8	Ireland	77.7	99	37,738
9	Belgium	78.9	99	28,335
10	United States	77.4	99	37,562
168	Mozambique	41.9	47	1,117
169	Burundi	43.6	59	648
170	Ethiopia	47.6	42	711
171	Central African Republic	39.3	49	1,089
172	Guinea-Bissau	44.7	40	711
173	Chad	43.6	26	1,210
174	Mali	47.9	19	994
175	Burkina Faso	47.5	13	1,174
176	Sierra Leone	40.8	30	548
177	Niger	44.4	14	835
High income		78.8	99	29,898
Middle income		70.3	90	6,104
Low income		58.4	61	2,168
High human development		78.0	99	25,665
Medium human development		67.2	79	4,474
Low human development		46.0	58	1,046
World		67.1	—	8,229

No accepted general theory of development

The inclusion of noneconomic variables has made it impossible to formulate a widely accepted general theory of development. Instead of pursuing a general theory, development economists are concentrating on specific problem areas, such as population growth, income distribution, unemployment, transfer of technology, the role of government in the process, and investment in human versus physical capital.

What is the relevance of a lack of consensus among specialists about development theory? If a particular theory has fallen into disfavor among the experts, can managers neglect it when dealing with government officials? That depends. Perhaps those officials still subscribe to it. In that case, managers should emphasize the parts of their proposals that are germane to the theory, which is generally not too difficult because nearly every proposal will provide not only investment in physical capital but also training of employees, employment, and the transfer of technology. There will even be some redistribution of income through the creation of a middle class composed of managers and highly skilled technicians. As an example, let's look at how managers might emphasize investment in human capital when making a proposal.

Investment in human capital

This development theory recognizes that more than just capital accumulation is needed for growth. There must also be investment in the education of people so that there will be managers to ensure that the capital is productive and skilled workers to operate and maintain the capital equipment. For developed countries, research suggests that investment in human capital has a return estimated at 4 to 12 percent per year of education. If basic labor has an income level of 100, then the return for 12 years of educational investments would yield an increased return ranging from 160 to 390 percent of that generated by basic labor.*

If managers know that this theory has strong acceptance in the country where they have an operation or are seeking permission to establish one, they should emphasize this aspect of their investment. A multinational or global firm that does not have training programs for workers is rare, and nearly all send local managers to the home office to update their skills.

Import substitution versus export promotion

Another strategy followed by some developing nations has been **import substitution.** Although developing nations have long considered the exporting of primary products (agricultural and raw materials) to be an important facet of their development strategy, many of these countries have not aggressively promoted the exporting of manufactured goods. Instead, they have concentrated on substituting these domestically manufactured products for imports as a way to lessen their dependence on developed countries.

Unfortunately, import substitution has not reduced their dependence on developed nations as much as it has changed the composition of imports from finished products to capital and semiprocessed inputs. Often, however, developing nations are unable to obtain these inputs because of a lack of foreign exchange, which can stop entire industries and throw thousands of people out of work, further increasing dependence on developed nations. This situation happened in several Asian nations as a result of the Asian economic crisis that began in 1997 and of subsequent events such as tightening of money supplies in conjunction with IMF assistance.

Another serious problem with the import substitution strategy stems from the protection to local industry that governments grant by levying high import duties on goods that also are made domestically. Under this umbrella, local manufacturers may not feel pressured to either lower their costs or improve their quality. Without such pressure, they rarely become competitive in world markets and thus cannot export. Furthermore, other domestic firms that must buy inputs from these protected industries cannot export either because their costs are excessive or their quality is inadequate.

Problems such as these have caused numerous governments to change from a strategy of import substitution to one of promoting exports of manufactured goods. Spurring them on to this decision has been the rapid export growth of the newly industrializing nations and the general opening of world markets to international trade and investment.

This change in strategy affects international firms in a variety of ways. First, local affiliate managers must be prepared for demands to export by government officials. They may even be given ultimatums, as some foreign manufacturers operating in China have reported: "If you need to import parts for your output, you must earn the foreign exchange to pay for them by exporting part of your production." Foreign companies seeking permission to set up a manufacturing facility are commonly asked by government administrators about plans for exporting. This is a new phenomenon to longtime managers accustomed to restricting an affiliate's sales to its internal market to save the export market for home country production. Second, managers can no longer count on having permanent protection from competing imports, as they once could. In some countries, they are likely to be told that after a certain date they will lose their protection and will be expected to compete internationally. Last, in a situation where two firms are competing for permission to establish a plant, the deciding factor may be that one offers its multinational channels of distribution to the affiliate's exports.

*If basic labor has an income level of 100, and if each year of education yields a return of 4 to 12 percent, then a worker with 12 years of education would produce returns from $100 \times (1.04)^{12} = 160$ to $100 \times (1.12)^{12} = 390$.

Source: *Human Development Report 2005* (New York: United Nations Development Program), pp. 219–22, http://hdr.undp.org/reports/global/2005 (October 6, 2006); Charles Kindleberger and Bruce Herrick, *Economic Development* (New York: McGraw-Hill, 1977), p. 1; George Psacharopoulos, "Returns to Investment in Education: A Global Update," *World Development* 22 (1994), p. 9; and Jean-Philippe Cotis, "Economic Growth and Productivity," www.oecd.org/dataoecd/49/34/37179645.pdf (October 6, 2006).

import substitution
The local production of goods to replace imports

The population of developing countries is over three-quarters of the world's total population. Figure 8.3 shows that of the 10 nations predicted to have the largest populations by the year 2050, only one is a high-income country (the United States); the rest are primarily low-income countries.

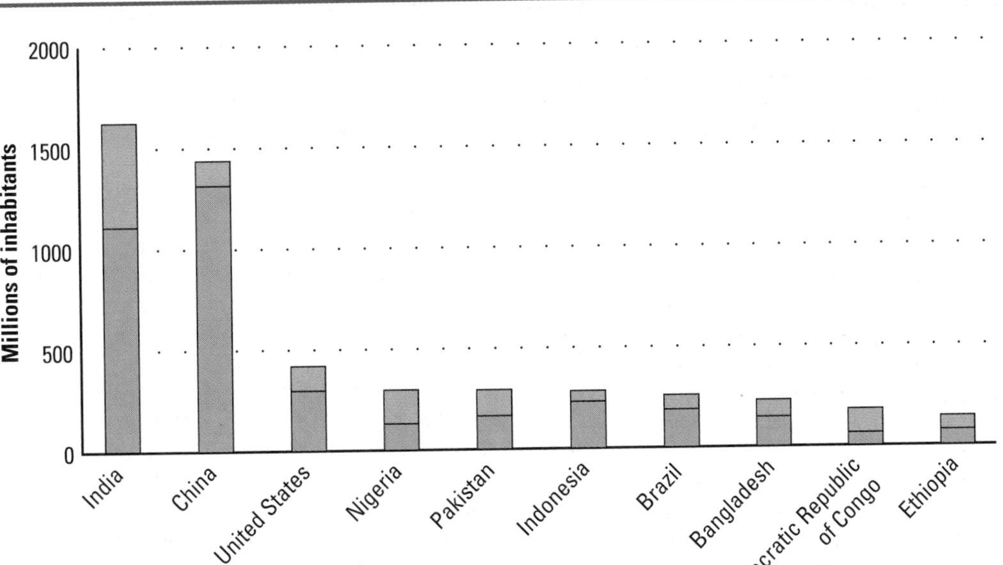

FIGURE 8.3

Population Growth of the World's 10 Most Populated Countries by 2050 (millions of inhabitants)

Source: U.S. Census Bureau, *International Data Base*, www.census.gov/ipc/www/idbpyr.html (October 8, 2006); and Population Reference Bureau, *2006 World Population Data Sheet*, p. 2, www.prb.org/pdf06/06WorldDataSheet.pdf (October 8, 2006).

What does this mean for business managers? For the developed nations, there will be a decrease in the demand for products used in schools and for products bought by and for children, a smaller market for furniture and clothing, but an increased demand for medical care and related products, tourism, and financial services. Firms confronted by a decreasing demand for their products will have to look for sales increases in the developing economies, where the age distribution is reversed.

Many forces are responsible for reductions in birthrates. Governments are supporting family planning programs, to be sure, but there is ample evidence that improved levels of health and education along with an enhanced status for women, a more even distribution of income, and a greater degree of urbanization are all acting to reduce the traditional family size. In fact, experts have been claiming for some time that the combined effect of an effective family planning program and female education beyond the primary level is extremely powerful in reducing family size.

Concern in Developed Nations The decrease in family size is welcomed by some countries in Africa and the Middle East, where fertility rates are as high as seven children per woman. But declining birthrates are causing concern in industrialized nations. The World Bank reports that the fertility rates in these countries are considerably below the *replacement number* of 2.1 children.* India, Mexico, and China have also experienced declines in their birthrates.

An increasing number of young Europeans are not marrying, and those who do marry are doing so later and having fewer children. Italy's population will fall by 15 million by mid-century, and the birthrate in Spain and Russia is even lower. By the year 2025 the present 9 percent unemployment rate in the European Union will be replaced by a shortage of workers. European governments will have to provide medical care and pensions for the 22 percent of their population that will be over 65 years old, and there will be fewer working taxpayers (see Figure 8.4).

*Number of children that will be born to a woman if she lives to the end of her childbearing years and bears children according to present age-specific fertility rates.

FIGURE 8.4 Percentages of Elderly (over 65) in Population, Selected Countries, 2006 and 2025

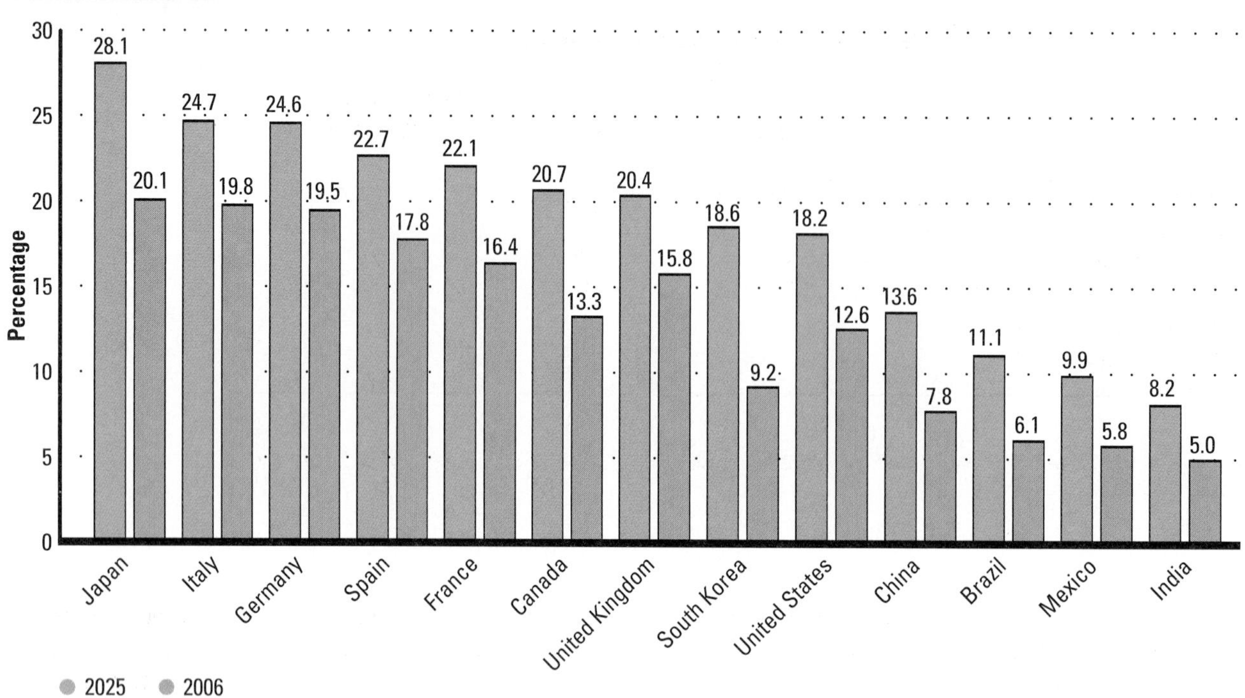

Source: U.S. Census Bureau, *International Data Base,* www.census.gov/ipc/www/idbpyr.html (October 8, 2006).

Japan's situation seems to be even more serious. Its fertility rate is only 1.5 children per woman, well below the 2.1 population replacement value, and in the year 2025 Japan's population age 65 and older will make up 26.8 percent of its total population, whereas the same age group in the United States will amount to only 18.5 percent of the total population. By the year 2025 Japan, which is the fastest-graying nation in the industrial world, will have twice as many old people as it has children. The government's reserve of social security funds will have run dry because retirement and health costs for the elderly are forecast to consume 73 percent of national income.

Early retirements and the fact that retirees are living longer are also straining the social security systems of many other countries. In the industrialized nations, not only are the costs of social security systems rising because of the growing number of retirees, but there are fewer people working and paying into the system to support them. However, in developing nations, just the opposite is occurring. The higher birthrates result in a younger population, and this reduces the dependency ratios and the costs to the workers supporting the system.

population density
A measure of the number of inhabitants per area unit (inhabitants per square kilometer or square mile)

population distribution
A measure of how the inhabitants are distributed over a nation's area

Population Density and Distribution

Other aspects of population that concern business managers are **population density** and **population distribution.** Densely populated areas tend to make product distribution and communications simpler and less costly than they are in areas where population density is low; thus you might expect Pakistan, with 192 inhabitants per square kilometer, to be an easier market to serve than Canada (3 inhabitants/square kilometer) or Brazil (22 inhabitants/square kilometer).[11] The expectation, though, is another of those based on an arithmetic mean. We must know how these populations are distributed. One needs only to compare the urban percentages of total population to learn that Canada and Brazil possess population concentrations that facilitate the marketing process. While only 34 percent of Pakistan's population is urban, the percentages for Brazil and Canada are 83 and 80 percent, respectively.[12] The physical forces, as we saw in Chapter 7, contribute heavily to the formation of these concentrations.

An important phenomenon that is changing the population distribution is the **rural-to-urban shift,** which is occurring everywhere, especially in developing countries, as people move to cities in search of higher wages and more conveniences. An indicator of the extent of this movement is the change in the percentages of urban population. As Table 8.8 indicates,

TABLE 8.8 Rural-to-Urban Shift

	Percentage of Population in Urban Areas					
	1950	1970	1990	2005	2015 (estimated)	Percentage Change, 1950–2015
World	29%	36%	43%	49%	53%	82.8%
More developed regions	52	65	71	74	76	46.2
Less developed regions	18	25	35	43	48	166.7
Least developed countries	7	13	21	27	32	357.1
Less developed regions excluding least developed countries	20	27	37	46	51	155.0

Source: United Nations, *World Urbanization Prospects: The 2005 Revision Population Database,* http://esa.un.org/unup/index.asp?panel=1 (October 7, 2006).

the greatest urban shifts are occurring in the low- and middle-income countries. This shift is significant to marketers because city dwellers, being less self-sufficient than persons living in rural areas, must enter the market economy.

rural-to-urban shift
The movement of a nation's population from rural areas to cities

City governments also become customers for equipment that will expand municipal services to handle the population influx. Figure 8.5 contains some good sales prospects. Note that most of the fast-growing cities projected to be megacities by the year 2015 are in developing nations.

Other Socioeconomic Dimensions

Other socioeconomic dimensions can provide useful information to management. The increase in the number of working women, for example, is highly significant to marketers because it may result in larger family incomes, a greater market for convenience goods, and a need to alter the **promotional mix.** Personnel managers are interested in this increase because it results in a larger labor supply. It also signifies that changes may be required in production processes, employee facilities, and personnel management policies.

promotional mix
A blend of the promotional methods a firm uses to sell its products

Data on a country's divorce rate will alert the marketer to the formation of single-parent families and single-person households, whose product needs and buying habits differ in many respects from those of a two-parent family. In many countries, important ethnic groups require special consideration by both marketing and personnel managers.

Wal-Mart has had language problems on both sides of the border. In a country where labels and communications are made in English and French, the retailer mailed English-only circulars to residents of Quebec, where 83 percent of the population are French speakers. After apologizing for this mistake, Wal-Mart officials had to apologize a week later when the company was criticized severely for ordering Canadian employees to work 12 hours a week extra without pay by means of memos that also were in English only.

One month later, the company had language-law problems on the other border when Mexican trade inspectors temporarily closed its Mexico City superstore, claiming that the firm had violated a 40-year-old law that requires the seller to place Spanish-language labels on all products on display.[13]

INDUSTRY DIMENSIONS

Every firm is concerned about the general economic news because of its impact on consumer purchases, prices of raw materials, and investment decisions, but certain factors are more significant than others to a given industry or to a specific functional area of a firm. The size and growth trend of the automobile industry are of paramount importance to a tire manufacturer,

FIGURE 8.5 25 Megacities 1970–2015 (millions)

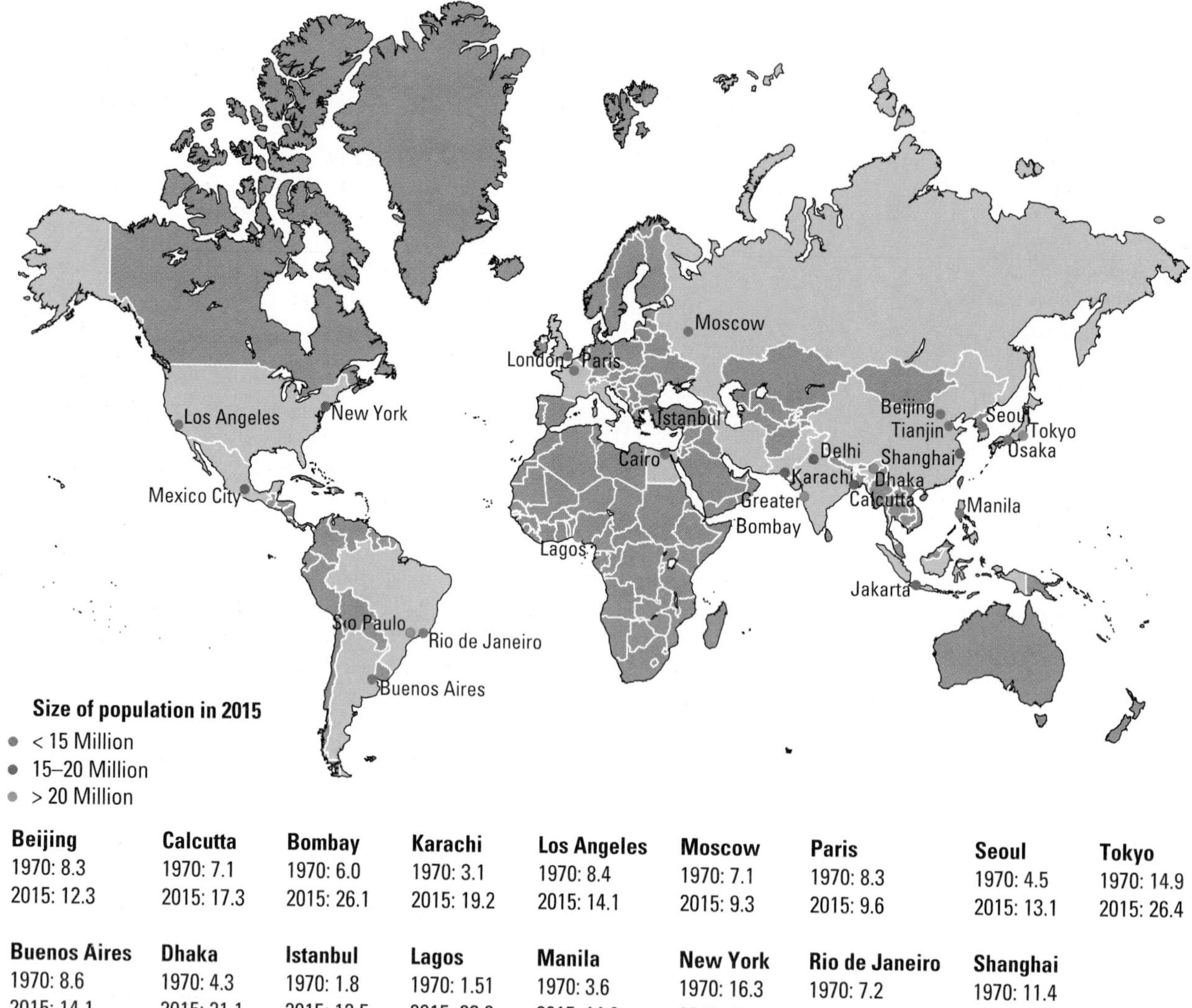

Beijing 1970: 8.3 2015: 12.3	**Calcutta** 1970: 7.1 2015: 17.3	**Bombay** 1970: 6.0 2015: 26.1	**Karachi** 1970: 3.1 2015: 19.2	**Los Angeles** 1970: 8.4 2015: 14.1	**Moscow** 1970: 7.1 2015: 9.3	**Paris** 1970: 8.3 2015: 9.6	**Seoul** 1970: 4.5 2015: 13.1	**Tokyo** 1970: 14.9 2015: 26.4
Buenos Aires 1970: 8.6 2015: 14.1	**Dhaka** 1970: 4.3 2015: 21.1	**Istanbul** 1970: 1.8 2015: 12.5	**Lagos** 1970: 1.51 2015: 23.2	**Manila** 1970: 3.6 2015: 14.8	**New York** 1970: 16.3 2015: 17.4	**Rio de Janeiro** 1970: 7.2 2015: 11.9	**Shanghai** 1970: 11.4 2015: 19.1	
Cairo 1970: 5.7 2015: 13.8	**Delhi** 1970: 3.6 2015: 16.8	**Jakarta** 1970: 4.5 2015: 17.3	**London** 1970: 10.6 2015: 7.1	**Mexico City** 1970: 9.1 2015: 19.2	**Osaka** 1970: 7.6 2015: 11.0	**São Paulo** 1970: 8.2 2015: 20.4	**Tianjin** 1970: 6.9 2015: 10.7	

Source: United Nations, 1995, www.megacities.nl/top 15/topworld/.html; *The Economist,* April 29, 1995, p. 122; *World Development Report 1994,* pp. 222–23; and www.jhuccp.org/pr/urbanpre.stm.

for example, but are of no interest to an appliance manufacturer. Nor would the quantity of machine operators graduated by technical schools be useful to financial officers, although these data are of vital interest to human resources managers of manufacturing plants. Managers want data not only about the firm's industry but also about industries that supply and purchase from the company. Minicase 8.2 at the end of this chapter illustrates the use of both macroeconomic and industry-specific data.

Industry studies are generally made by the firm's economists or its trade association, but they can also be purchased from independent research organizations, such as Fantus (New York) and the Economist Intelligence Unit (London). Government agencies, chambers of commerce, and trade publications such as *Advertising Age* publish them as well. Many international banks publish free newsletters containing useful economic data.

mini MNE

>>Using the Internet for Economic Research

You own a small business, and you don't have the money to hire an economic analyst. Yet you need economic and socioeconomic data to help you plan for market expansion just as the big multinationals do. What can you do? Do you have a personal computer with an Internet connection? Use it to get the information free of charge that the analyst you were going to hire would have gotten and then charged you for.

Suppose that up to now you have confined yourself to the U.S. market, but you are curious about the possibilities of expanding into the Canadian and Mexican markets. They are both nearby and relatively easy to get to. Can you find information about doing business with these countries on the Internet?

A quick search using an Internet search engine should uncover many sources of information for you. For example, you can obtain a free online report on "Doing Business in Canada," including key economic trends, trade regulations, and standards, by visiting the U.S. Department of Commerce's Commercial Services Web site at www.buyusa.gov/canada/en/ccg.html. This site also offers such services as assistance for American exporters in finding agents and distributors, mailing products, and establishing a Canadian office. For trade statistics, geography, and culture, you can go to the Government of Canada's official Web site at http://canada.gc.ca/main_e.html.

To get data on Mexico, go to www.latinworld.com/norte/mexico/index.html for economic forecasts and an extensive Mexican financial commentary.

Michigan State University supports Global-EDGE, an excellent site for information on Mexico, Canada, or other countries. You can access this site at http://globaledge.msu.edu/ibrd/ibrd.asp. Using the Country Guide and typing in "Mexico" will bring you to an extensive list of resources, including the "Mexico: Country Commercial Guide" and "Mexico: Economist Country Briefing." You can also go to the Commercial Section of the U.S. embassy in Mexico City, which offers services to companies that want to do business in Mexico. Go directly from the GlobalEDGE site, or go directly to http://mexico.usembassy.gov/mexico/eeconomic.html. Another site, www.zonalatina.com, will provide even more information.

With the information you obtain from these sites, you should be able to decide whether you want to move into these new international markets.

Summary

State the purpose of economic analyses.

To keep abreast of the latest economic developments and also to plan for the future, firms regularly assess and forecast economic conditions at the local, state, and national levels. When they enter international operations, the economic analysis increases in complexity because managers are operating in two new environments: foreign and international. There are more economies to study, and these economies are frequently highly divergent.

Identify different categories based on levels of national economic development and the common characteristics of developing nations.

Managers involved in international business encounter markets with far greater differences in levels of economic development than those in which they have been working in domestic business settings. A nation's level of economic development affects all aspects of business, and we commonly group them into categories based on their level of economic development, such as developed, developing, newly industrializing, and newly industrialized economies. Developing nations have certain common characteristics, including unequal distribution of income, technological and regional dualism, a large percentage of the population in agriculture, high population growth, high illiteracy rate, insufficient education, and low savings rates.

Recognize the economic and socioeconomic dimensions of the economy and different indicators used to assess them.

The various functional areas of a firm require data on the size and rates of change of a number of economic and socioeconomic factors. Among the more important economic dimensions are GDP, GNI, distribution of income, personal consumption expenditures, private investment, unit labor costs, and financial data, such as exchange rates, inflation rates, interest rates, and the amount of a nation's foreign debt. The principal socioeconomic dimensions are total population, rates of growth, age distribution, population density, and population distribution.

Discuss the importance of a nation's consumption patterns and the significance of purchasing power parity.

Marketers must know how consumers allocate their discretionary incomes, since this is money spent on their products.

They must also use purchasing power parity (PPP) to understand what the true purchasing power of a nation is. Consumers in a nation whose GNI appears to be too low to be a viable market may have some discretionary buying power when the GNI based on market exchange rates is converted to a GNI based on PPP.

Discuss the new definition of economic development, which includes more than economic growth.

The human-needs approach defines economic development as the reduction of poverty, unemployment, and inequality in the distribution of income.

Explain the degree to which labor costs can vary from country to country.

Hourly labor rates, especially when stated in U.S. dollars, change rather rapidly. There are three factors that are responsible: (1) real changes in compensation, (2) changes in productivity, and (3) changes in exchange rates.

Discuss the significance for businesspeople of the large foreign debts of some nations.

Large foreign debts may indicate that the government will impose exchange controls on its country's businesses. If a large part of the country's export earnings go to service its external debt, there will be little remaining for use by firms in the country to pay for imports of raw materials, components used in their products, and production machinery. The government could impose price and wage controls. There is also the possibility that firms can buy some of the discounted debt to obtain local currency at a favorable exchange rate.

Key Words

developed (p. 230)
developing (p. 231)
newly industrializing countries (NICs) (p. 231)
newly industrialized economies (NIEs) (p. 231)
gross national income (GNI) (p. 231)
underground economy (p. 233)
purchasing power parity (PPP) (p. 234)
income distribution (p. 235)
discretionary income (p. 237)
unit labor costs (p. 238)
vertically integrated (p. 242)
human-needs approach (p. 243)
import substitution (p. 244)
population density (p. 246)
population distribution (p. 246)
rural-to-urban shift (p. 246)
promotional mix (p. 247)

Questions

1. Management learns from the economic analysis of Country A that wage rates are expected to increase by 10 percent next year. Which functional areas of the firm will be concerned? Why is management concerned?
2. What are "international dollars"? What is their significance to international businesspeople?
3. What common problem does the use of GNI per capita and population density values present?
4. If the clothing industry association to which your firm's Swiss subsidiary belongs could mount a successful promotional program to cause the Swiss to increase their clothing expenditures by 1 percent annually, what would be the total increase in sales for the clothing industry?
5. In 2004, Italy's average labor compensation costs stated in U.S. dollars were $20.48 compared to $16.52 in 1995, and they were 16.46 euros compared to 26,911 lira.
    a. What was the percentage increase or decrease in dollars?
    b. What accounts for the huge difference in local rates between 1995 and 2004 (hint: euros versus lira)?
6. The staff economist of a large multinational with an Argentine subsidiary has given to the firm's chief financial officer a report on Argentina's foreign debt situation, as shown in Table 8.7. What concerns might the chief financial officer have?
7. What would be the concerns of the chief financial officer in question 6 if he or she were to receive the information on annual inflation rates from Table 8.1?
8. Of what importance to marketers is a nation's level of economic development?
9. What problems with the import substitution strategy have caused some governments to increase their emphasis on export promotion?
10. What problems is the reduction in birthrates causing for European and Japanese governments?
11. Choose a country and a product and estimate the market potential of the product based on the economic and socioeconomic dimensions. What other environmental forces should you investigate?

globalEDGE globalEDGE.msu.edu

Research Task

Use the globalEDGE site (http://globalEDGE.msu.edu) to complete the following exercises:

1. The *Foreign Labor Statistics (FLS)* program provides international comparisons of hourly compensation costs; productivity and unit labor costs; labor force, employment and unemployment rates; and consumer prices. Using this resource, your firm is interested in comparing the real gross national income (GNI) per capita of five countries in which it has facilities: Australia, Belgium, Denmark, Japan, and Norway. From this list, which country has the highest GNI per capita? Which has the lowest?
2. You are working for a company that is planning to invest in Italy. Your company's executives have requested a report from you regarding Italy's current economic situation. One of your colleagues mentioned a useful Web site called *Country Briefings,* published by the *Economist* magazine. This site contains comprehensive information on 60 countries, including country profiles, recent news, political and economic forecasts, statistics, and more. Using this site, prepare a short executive report outlining Italy's current economic situation.

The Impact of Galawi's Development Policy Minicase 8.1

Armando Suarez, CEO of Industrias Globales, and Pedro Garcia, the firm's director of international operations, are discussing a statement made today by the secretary of treasury in Galawi.

Suarez: Pedro, did you listen to the secretary's comments today about the proposed change in development strategy?

Garcia: Yes, I did, and I'm concerned. We have spent considerable time and money planning our entry into the Galawi market, and if the government proceeds with the new economic strategy, we've got to change our plant design, plan to produce different product lines, and completely change our marketing plans.

Suarez: This apparently is more serious than I thought. How can a change in their development strategy from import substitution to export promotion affect us?

Garcia: Hang on to your chair, Chief, and I'll explain each strategy and how the change will affect our entire start-up program in Galawi. Oh, and by the way, our Galawi competitors are going to have to make changes, too.

Imagine you are Pedro Garcia.

1. Describe the two strategies for the CEO.
2. Explain how the change in development strategy will affect the firm in many ways.
3. What changes in its entry plans will the firm have to make?

World Laboratories Minicase 8.2

World Laboratories (WL) is a large multinational pharmaceutical manufacturer specializing in the production of ethical pharmaceuticals (available to the public only by prescription). These products are characterized by a high degree of research, and because of the limited protection offered by patents, they have a relatively short product life. WL does make some over-the-counter products, but these products account for only about 20 percent of total company sales.

The South American division manager must make a sales forecast for ethical drugs, which he will use to set quotas for the six countries in his division that have manufacturing plants. These products produce about 75 percent of the total sales in each market. At present, WL's market share and sales by category of drug (pediatric, general, geriatric) in each country are as shown in the accompanying table.

Total health care has grown faster than world population and world income since 1970. A conservative average of the total amount per capita spent on health care, both private and public, for pharmaceuticals in South America is 20 percent. This is lower than in the United States and Europe, but in government clinics, medicine is generally offered without charge or at a substantial discount from the price charged in pharmacies. According to WL's subsidiaries, the patients at clinics pay, on average, 40 percent of the drugs' listed prices when the drugs given at no charge are included. Obviously, private drugstores that get only 40 percent off list (60 percent of list price is their cost) cannot compete. WL, however, still earns a 12 percent profit based on its selling prices when it sells to governments at list less 50 percent because of the low marketing costs on such large volumes, compared to an average 20 percent of selling price on sales to private pharmacies.

Here are the data that the staff economist has just given to the South American division manager. Help him do the forecast. If you have to make any assumptions, please make a note of them. If marketing costs for government sales average 6 percent of WL's selling price while they average 11.5 percent to private pharmacies, should the division manager try to change the present government–private pharmacy sales ratio that now prevails in any of the six markets? Should he have any other concerns based on these data?

	Market Share (percent)	Pediatric (0–14 years)	General (15–64 years)	Geriatric (65 and older)
Argentina	30%	32.0%	58.0%	10.0%
Brazil	24	29.3	65.7	5.0
Chile	55	32.1	65.8	5.1
Paraguay	65	41.2	55.4	3.4
Peru	45	42.0	56.5	1.5
Uruguay	38	27.0	63.9	9.1

	GDP (billions of dollars)				Foreign Debt (billions of dollars)			
	1989	1992	1999	2003	1989	1992	2000	2004
Argentina	$67.8	$200.3	$283.2	$129.6	$64.7	$49.1	$146.4	$157.7
Brazil	375.1	425.4	751.5	492.3	111.3	99.2	201.3	171.7
Chile	22.9	37.1	67.5	72.4	18.2	14.9	31.0	36.4
Paraguay	4.3	6.0	7.7	6.0	2.5	1.5	1.5	2.8
Peru	23.0	21.3	51.9	60.6	19.9	15.6	30.5	28.7
Uruguay	8.1	10.4	20.8	11.2	3.8	3.4	3.4	7.7

	Total Debt Service as Percentage of Export Receipts				Total Government Expenditures as Percentage of GNP				Percentage of Government Expenditures on Health Care			
	1989	1992	2000	2004	1989	1992	1998	2003	1989	1992	1998	2002
Argentina	36.1%	34.4%	85.5%	28.1%	15.5%	13.1%	20.4%	19.8%	2.0%	3.0%	4.9%	4.5%
Brazil	31.3	23.1	77.7	47.4	30.6	25.6	38.8	36.7	6.1	6.9	2.9	3.6
Chile	27.5	20.9	15.8	24.2	32.5	22.1	25.9	24.5	5.9	11.1	2.7	2.6
Paraguay	11.9	40.3	8.0	13.3	8.9	9.4	9.4	9.2	3.0	4.3	1.7	3.2
Peru	6.8	23.0	44.9	17.1	11.6	12.5	18.0	19.1	5.5	5.6	2.4	2.2
Uruguay	29.4	23.2	30.2	35.4	25.8	28.7	28.7	27.5	4.5	5.0	1.9	2.9

	Population per Physician				Annual Inflation Rate				Population (millions)				Population Distribution, 2003		
	1984	1990	1993	2004	1989	1992	2001	2005	1989	1992	1999	2003	0–14 Years	15–64 Years	65 + Years
Argentina	370	n.a.	373	332	3,081%	25%	1%	9%	31.9	33.1	36.6	38.0	27.1	64.2	8.7
Brazil	1,080	n.a.	746	485	1,431	1,022	1	7	147.8	153.9	168.2	181.4	28.4	66.7	4.9
Chile	1,230	2,150	926	917	17	15	4	7	13.0	13.6	15.0	16.0	26.1	67.3	6.6
Paraguay	1,460	1,250	1,493	854	3,127	15	n.a.	9	4.2	4.5	5.4	5.9	38.4	58.6	3.0
Peru	1,040	960	1,370	855	399	74	4	3	21.2	22.4	25.2	27.2	33.2	62.7	4.1
Uruguay	510	n.a.	324	275	81	68	5	2	3.1	3.1	3.3	3.4	24.5	64.0	11.5

	Percentage of GNP for Private Consumption Expenditure			Percentage of Private Consumption Expenditure for Health Care	
	1989	1992	2004	1998	2002
Argentina	54.8%	73.3%	67.3%	5.4%	4.4%
Brazil	55.3	60.0	59.7	3.7	4.3
Chile	72.7	65.8	68.4	3.1	3.2
Paraguay	75.9	69.3	70.2	3.6	5.2
Peru	84.6	72.6	71.5	3.7	2.2
Uruguay	64.0	65.8	67.3	7.2	7.1

9 Political Forces

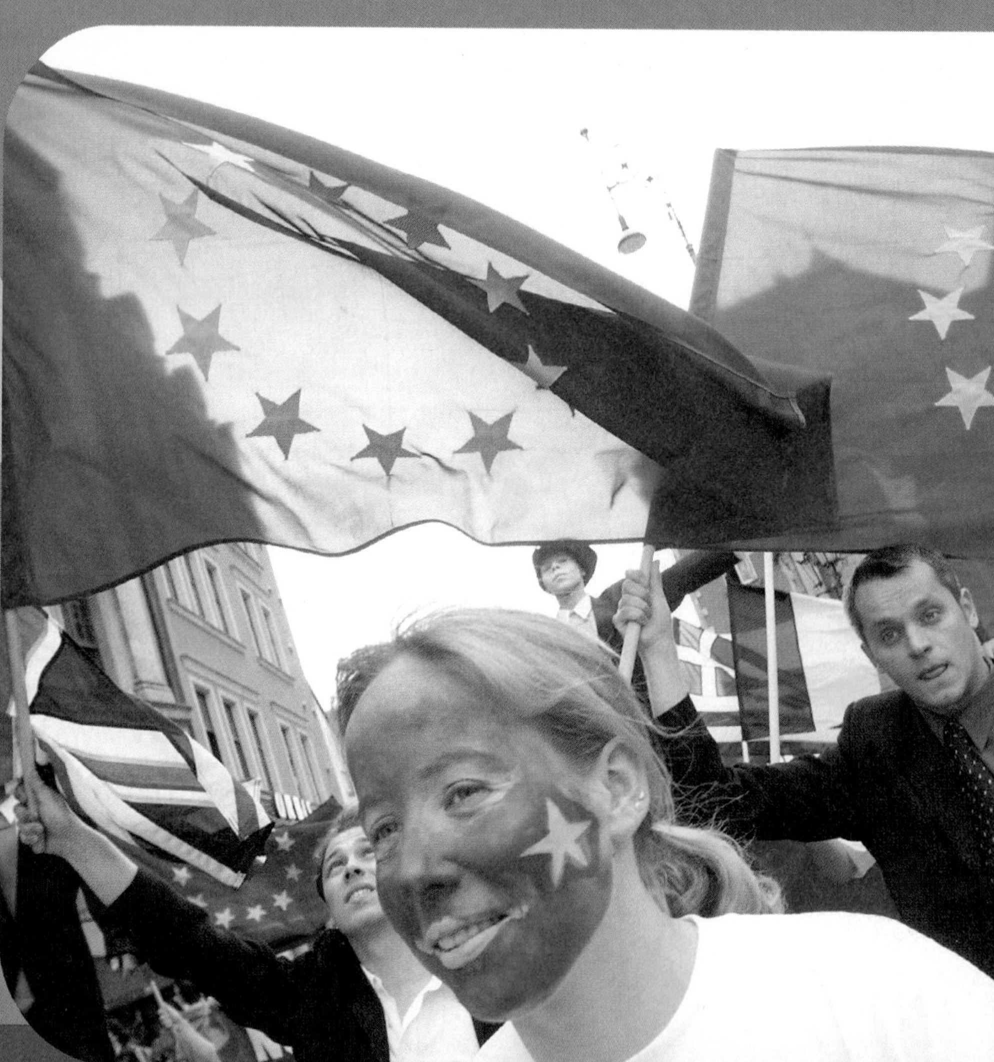

Enthusiastic Poles celebrate their country's admission to the EU.

©Sean Gallup/Getty Images

Politics have no relation to morals.

—*Niccolò Machiavelli*

There Are Two Polands—Which One Joined the EU?

Poles are entrepreneurial. Over 1.5 million small and mid-size companies have been created since 1989. An example is Kross Bicycles, which has become the second-largest bike maker in Europe. Another is Delphia Yachts, which exports more that 90 percent of its output to Europe and elsewhere. Still another is Comarch, a software systems provider. Its 2nd quarter 2006 operating profit was 3 times higher than for the same period in 2005.

Foreign investors are arriving. Among them are Whirlpool Corp., which has been in Poland since 1993 and made significant new investments in 2005. It has been joined by the Spanish appliance maker Fagor and by the white-goods producer Merloni Electrodomestici from Italy.

Poland's GDP growth of some 3.2 percent is faster than the old EU countries' rates. In addition, Poland's productivity increase of over 3.7 percent in 2004 was over twice the EU average. Its labor costs are less than a sixth of the German costs.

Those facts present a picture of one of the Polands. But there is a second one.

This one is a dysfunctional political system sitting astride a communist-era welfare state. The bureaucracy is one of the worst in Europe. For example, the delay in securing permits to begin a business is commonly 8 to 10 months. Many Poles are concerned at the prospect of combining the Polish paper pushers with the substantial bureaucracy already operating on the EU payroll in Brussels.

Bureaucrats in Poland are blamed for the loss by Poland of investments by three of the largest automobile makers in Eastern Europe in the past several years. Another one, MG Rover of Britain, complained that negotiations for an auto plant near Warsaw were frustrated by the glacially slow decision making by Polish bureaucrats. It threatened to take its investment to China (and in fact is now owned by Nanjing Automobile).

Matters are made worse by the requirement to file tax returns every month. Naturally, they are quite complicated.

Two present EU members demonstrate the good and bad possible roads Poland may travel as a member. After joining, Spain boomed. It spent EU funds wisely and productively. It liberated and deregulated the economy and successfully restructured state finances. The bad road was followed by Greece. It squandered billions of EU funds on inefficient, government-owned companies.

The way Poland goes is important. It is far and away the largest of the 10 countries that joined the EU in 2004. It accounts for 41 percent of their total GDP, and more than half their population. ■

Source: David Fairlamb and Bogdan Turek, *BusinessWeek,* May 10, 2004, pp. 54–56. Reprinted by special permission. Copyright © 2004 by the McGraw-Hill Companies, Inc. Other information from corporate Web sites.

CONCEPT PREVIEWS

After reading this chapter, you should be able to:

identify the ideological forces that affect business and understand the terminology used in discussing them

discuss the fact that although most governments own businesses, they are privatizing them in growing numbers

explain the changing sources and reasons for terrorism and the methods and growing power of terrorists

explain steps that traveling international business executives should take to protect themselves from terrorists

evaluate the importance to business of government stability and policy continuity

explain country risk assessment by international business

In a number of ways, the political climate of a country in which a business operates is as important as the country's topography, its natural resources, and its meteorological climate. Indeed, we shall see examples in which a hospitable, stable government can encourage business investment and growth despite geographic or weather obstacles and a scarcity of natural resources. The opposite is equally true. Some areas of the world that are relatively blessed with natural resources and manageable topography and weather have been very little developed because of government instability. Occasionally, a country's government is hostile to investment in its territory by foreign companies even though they might provide capital, technology, and training for development of the country's resources and people.

Many of the political forces with which business must cope have ideological sources, but there are a large number of other sources. These sources include nationalism, terrorism, traditional hostilities, unstable governments, international organizations, and government-owned business.

The international company itself can also be a political force. Some firms have budgets or sales larger than the gross national product (GNP) of some of the countries with which they negotiate. Although budgets and GNPs do not translate directly into power, it should be clear that companies with bigger budgets and countries with bigger GNPs possess more assets and facilities with which to negotiate. Refer back to Table 1.3 in Chapter 1 for some examples.

This chapter will provide an indication of the types of risks political forces pose to private business. As we shall see, some of the risks can stem from more than one political force.

Ideological Forces

Such names as communism, socialism, capitalism, liberal, conservative, left wing, and right wing are used to describe governments, political parties, and people. These names indicate ideological beliefs.

COMMUNISM

It is communist doctrine that the government should own all the major factors of production. With exceptions, all production in communist countries is done by state-owned factories and farms. Labor unions are government-controlled.

communism
Marx's theory of a classless society, developed by his successors into control of society by the Communist Party and the attempted worldwide spread of communism

Communism as conceived by Karl Marx was a theory of social change directed toward the ideal of a classless society. As developed by Lenin and others, communism typically involves the seizure of power by a conspiratorial political party, the maintenance of power by stern suppression of internal opposition, and commitment to the ultimate goal of a worldwide communist state.

Communist Government Takeover of a Previously Noncommunist Country

One of communism's basic tenets is state ownership of all the productive factors. This occurred in Russia after the 1917 Bolshevik Revolution, and it has been repeated after each communist takeover of a country.

Compensation for Expropriated Property To date, none of the communist governments has compensated the foreign former owners directly. A few of the owners have gotten some reimbursement indirectly, from assets of the communist government seized abroad. For example, the U.S. government seized assets of the Soviet Union in the United States after American property in the Soviet Union was confiscated. American firms or individuals whose property had been confiscated in the U.S.S.R. could file claims with a U.S. government agency, and if they could substantiate their loss, a percentage of it was paid.

Expropriation and Confiscation The rules of traditional international law recognize a country's right to expropriate the property of foreigners within its jurisdiction. But those rules require that the country compensate the foreign owners, and *in the absence of compensation,* **expropriation** *becomes* **confiscation.**[1]

expropriation
Government seizure of the property within its borders owned by foreigners, followed by prompt, adequate, and effective compensation paid to the former owners

confiscation
Government seizure of the property within its borders owned by foreigners without payment to them

Communism Collapses

We have insufficient space to detail the reasons for communism's failure as an economic and social system. We shall present a couple of basic reasons and a few anecdotes that illustrate the results. See the endnotes for more.

The U.S.S.R. concentrated its best scientists, engineers, managers, and raw materials in production for the military and neglected production of consumer goods. Gross production was the goal, and managers would go to ridiculous extremes to meet the production targets set by government central planners. For example, central planning allowed only one condom factory and birth control pills were very expensive, so the two products were not easily available. Abortion was the most common form of birth control. The abortions were then counted as part of doctors' gross production and therefore swelled the reported national income.

Factories under construction got a certificate putting them into commission on the scheduled completion date even though they were almost never actually completed on schedule. Because of the certificate, the factory had to report production coming from it even though it had not yet produced anything.

Some enterprises used other deceptions. For instance, a factory reaching only 50 percent of its targeted output could have made a small change in its next shipped machine and doubled the price, say, from $10,000 to $20,000—presto, doubled output.[2]

Tale of Two Cities

A spectacular result of communism's collapse was the reunification of East Germany with West Germany, accompanied by the revival of Berlin as the capital. The capital of West Germany had been Bonn, while East Germany's capital had been in its part of the divided Berlin. As reunited Berlin was renovated in the east and as hundreds of new buildings were constructed throughout the city, it resembled and was called a high-construction site. The picture on this page illustrates a small part of that.

CAPITALISM

The capitalist, free enterprise ideal is that all the factors of production should be privately owned. Under perfect **capitalism,** government is restricted to those functions that the private

capitalism
An economic system in which the means of production and distribution are for the most part privately owned and operated for private profit

Berlin under reconstruction after being restored as the capital of the new Germany in 1990. Formerly, the city and country had been divided, with East Berlin belonging to communist East Germany and West Berlin belonging to democratic West Germany.

sector cannot perform. These include national defense; police, fire, and other public services; and government-to-government international relations.

No such government exists. The reality in so-called capitalist countries is quite complex. The governments of such countries typically regulate privately owned businesses quite closely, and these governments also own businesses.

Regulations and Red Tape

All businesses are subject to countless government laws, regulations, and red tape in their activities in all capitalist countries. Special government approval is required to practice such professions as law and medicine. Tailored sets of laws and regulations govern banking, insurance, transportation, and utilities. States and local governments require business licenses and impose use restrictions on buildings and areas.

Complying with all the laws and regulations and coping with the red tape require expertise, time, and, of course, expense. A business found in noncompliance may incur fines or even the imprisonment of its managers.

SOCIALISM

socialism
Public, collective ownership of the basic means of production and distribution, operating for use rather than profit

Socialism advocates government ownership or control of the basic means of production, distribution, and exchange. Profit is not an aim.

In practice, so-called socialist governments have frequently performed in ways not consistent with the doctrine. One of the most startling examples of this is Singapore, which professes to be a socialist state but in reality is aggressively capitalistic.[3]

European Socialism

In Europe, socialist parties have been in power in several countries, including Great Britain, France, Spain, Greece, and Germany. In Britain, the Labour Party—as the socialists there call their political party—in the past nationalized some basic industries, such as steel, shipbuilding, coal mining, and the railroads, but did not go much further in that direction. A vocal left wing of the Labour Party advocates nationalizing all major British businesses, banks, and insurance companies.

The Germans use the term Social Democrats for their socialist political party. The Social Democrats are currently in a coalition government with the Christian Democrats. The socialist governments of France and Spain have embarked on programs to privatize government-owned businesses; such programs do not conform to socialist doctrine. In fact, since neither capitalism nor socialism seems to fit well, the words "corporatism" or "co-determination" are used to describe this Western European blend of capitalism and socialism.

Socialism in Developing Countries

The developing countries often profess some degree of socialism. The government typically owns and controls many of the factors of production. Shortages of capital, technology, and skilled management and labor are characteristic of developing countries, and developed countries or international organizations often provide aid through a developing country's government. Also, many of the educated citizens of a developing country tend to be in or connected with the government. It follows that the government would own or control major factories and farms.

Whatever a government's political label, most will permit and often seek capital investment. This happens when the developing country perceives advantages that would not be possible without the private capital, such as more jobs for its people, new technology, skilled managers or technicians, and export opportunities.

CONSERVATIVE OR LIBERAL

conservative
A person, group, or party that wishes to minimize government activities and maximize private ownership and business

We should not leave the subject of ideology without mention of the words *conservative* and *liberal* as they are currently used. Politically, in the United States, the word **conservative** connotes a person, group, or party that wishes to minimize government activity and maximize the activities of private businesses and individuals. *Conservative* is used to mean something similar to **right wing,** but in the United States and the United Kingdom, the latter term is more extreme. For instance, the Conservative Party, one of the major political parties in the United Kingdom, is said to have a right-wing minority.

right wing
A more extreme conservative position

Also, connotations of *conservative* can differ depending on the application. For example, as China and the countries of Eastern Europe and the former Soviet Union move from centrally planned economies to market economies and from dictatorships toward democracies, the people and groups trying to impede, stop, or reverse such movements are called *conservatives*. These people, often members of communist (usually renamed) parties or the armed forces, long for "the good old days" when the governments owned and ran everything. That is the opposite of the wishes of conservatives in the United States and the United Kingdom, who want the least possible government involvement.

In the United States the word **liberal** now means the opposite of what it meant in the 19th century. It now connotes a person, group, or party that urges greater government participation in the economy and regulation or ownership of business. Liberal and **left wing** are similar, but the latter may indicate a more extreme position closer to socialism.

liberal
In the contemporary United States, a person, group, or party that urges greater government involvement in business and other aspects of human activities

left wing
A more extreme liberal position

Unique to the United States

This usage has not spread outside the United States. For example,

> *A conversation one of the authors had with an Italian lawyer at lunch in Rome turned to politics. The Italian identified himself as a liberal, and the author understood it in the American sense. As the conversation proceeded, the author learned that he had been wrong. The lawyer was a member of the Liberal Party, a political party near the right end of the Italian political spectrum.*

We do not want to overemphasize the importance of the labels *conservative, liberal, right wing,* and *left wing*. For one thing, individuals and organizations may change over time or as they perceive shifts in the moods of voters. These labels are simplistic or even naive, and reality is more complex. Nevertheless, we wanted to bring them to your attention because they are used in discussions of international events and because different political forces flow from, for example, a right-wing government than from a left-wing one. Businesspeople must do their best to influence those political forces and then forecast and react to them.

Examples of "left" and "right" terminology in current international political reporting are widespread. Excerpts from news articles illustrate this, for example, "Right wing coalition confident of French poll win," and "Mr. Jospin's sudden exit created a vacuum in the leadership of the left."[4] Political advocacy organizations, both left and right, grow in size and power every year. In the United States, one list shows about 60 of these groups beginning with the letter "A" alone. They are equally influential and powerful in the corridors of power of the European Union and other countries. Less well known but just as important, these organizations litigate precedent-setting lawsuits that affect judicial decisions for years to come. These court decisions, as well as the laws that result from such organizations' lobbying, powerfully affect business at every level.[5]

Government Ownership of Business

One might assume that government ownership of the factors of production is found only in communist or socialist countries, but that assumption is not correct. Businesses are owned by the governments of countries that do not consider themselves either communist or socialist. From country to country, there are wide differences in the industries that are government-owned and in the extent of government ownership.

WHY FIRMS ARE NATIONALIZED

A number of reasons, sometimes overlapping, explain why governments put their hands on firms. Some of them are (1) to extract more money from the firms—the government suspects that the firms are concealing profits; (2) profitability—the government believes it could run

WORLD view   

Getting Nationalization Right

Bolivia's president Evo Morales nationalized its oil and gas industry in 2006 by sending in troops. But he has had difficulty in doing more. State energy company YPFB (Yacimientos Petroliferos Fiscales Bolivianos) has asked the central bank for a $180 million credit line to finish the takeover. Fellow South American nations Venezuela and Ecuador have also turned to state intervention, but Bolivia's situation is perhaps the most dire. The current impass in some ways reflects Bolivia's earlier attempts—this is the third nationalization of Bolivia's energy industry in the past 100 years. Nor is the nationalization target "Big Oil" from North America. Rather, Bolivia's single largest client is Brazil, and the Brazilian state oil company is the largest investor in Bolivia's energy. And although Bolivia may be able to increase revenue by charging Brazil higher prices, Brazil is itself developing natural-gas reserves which could allow it to walk away from Bolivian suppliers in a few years. Says one commentator, "[Venezuelan President] Chavez and Morales are both playing a game of chicken with foreign oil companies."

Source: David Luhnow, "Bolivia Renationalization Hits Snag," *The Wall Street Journal,* August 15, 2006, p. A5; and David Luchow and Jose de Cordoba, "Bolivia's President Morales Orders Nationalization of Natural Gas," *The Wall Street Journal,* May 2, 2006, pp. A1, A15.

the firms more efficiently and make more money; (3) ideology—governments sometimes nationalize industries, as has occurred in Britain, France, and Canada; (4) job preservation—to save jobs by putting dying industries on life-support systems; (5) because the government has pumped money into a firm or an industry, and control usually follows money; or (6) happenstance, as with the nationalization after World War II of German-owned firms in Europe.

UNFAIR COMPETITION?

Where government-owned companies compete with privately owned companies, the private companies sometimes complain that the government companies have unfair advantages. Some of the complaints are that (1) government-owned companies can cut prices unfairly because they do not have to make profits, (2) they get cheaper financing, (3) they get government contracts, (4) they get export assistance, and (5) they can hold down wages with government assistance.

Another advantage state-owned companies enjoy over privately owned business comes in the form of direct subsidies: payments by the government to those companies. The EU Commission has been trying to discourage such subsidy payments. For years it has required annual financial reports from state-controlled companies as part of a crackdown on the subsidies that can distort competition.[6]

GOVERNMENT–PRIVATE FIRM COLLABORATION DIFFICULT

The objectives of private firms and those of government agencies and operations usually differ. Figure 9.1 illustrates some of the differences.

Privatization

privatization
The transfer of public sector assets to the private sector, the transfer of management of state activities through contracts and leases, and the contracting out of activities previously conducted by the state

Britain's former prime minister, Margaret Thatcher, was the acknowledged leader of the **privatization** movement. During her 11 years in office, Thatcher decreased state-owned companies from a 10 percent share of Britain's GNP to 3.9 percent. She sold over 30 companies, raising some $65 billion.[7] Thatcher pioneered in what has become a worldwide movement to privatize all sorts of government activities.

AIRPORTS, GARBAGE, POSTAL SERVICES, AND...?

For example, the Lockheed Company began by running Burbank Airport in California for decades and then expanded abroad. As owner or manager, Lockheed has operated or bid to operate airports in Canada, Russia, Turkmenistan, Australia, Turkey, Hungary, Argentina,

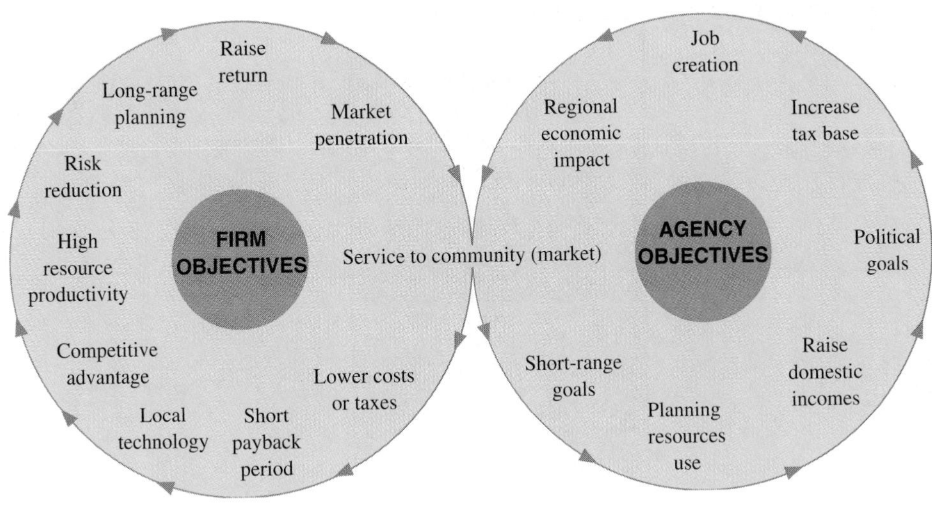

FIGURE 9.1

Planners and Business Investors—Why Can't They Collaborate?

Source: Reprinted from *Long Range Planning*, Vol. 3, No. 1, Vichas et al., "Public Planners and Business Investors," p. 83. Copyright © 1981, with permission of Elsevier Science.

and Venezuela. Hughes Aircraft Company is in that business with Trinidad and Tobago and has completed studies for Ukraine on ways to upgrade that country's airports.[8]

Similarly, the management of Amsterdam's Schiphol Airport found that managing foreign airports was an excellent business. Schiphol Airport Group manages terminals in New York and Brisbane, Australia.[9]

One study found that it cost the New York Department of Sanitation $40, of which $32 was for labor, to deal with a ton of rubbish. It cost private collectors only $17 (of which $10 was for labor).[10]

Several countries are privatizing their postal services. Germany's Deutsche Post was privatized and is often counted as a privatization success story. Japan's postal system is scheduled to be privatized in 2007. Japan Post holds over $3 trillion in private savings accounts and insurance, so it is not just a mail service.

In 1997, the government of Mozambique brought in the British company Crown Agents to run its customs service. Given the low levels of public sector pay, bribery was endemic from top to bottom. Crown Agents set up antismuggling teams, and successes came quickly, stopping the smuggling of cigarettes, alcohol, electrical goods, meat, condensed milk, and even yogurt.[11]

Even the formerly rigid People's Republic of China now encourages state-run enterprises to diversify ownership. Private and even foreign investors may acquire stakes.[12] In 2006, Initial Public Offering (IPO), M&A, and privatization indices were begun to track China's super-hot economy.

Africa is not being left out of the privatization parade. Mozambique we mentioned above, and as illustrated by the advertisement shown in Figure 9.2, Nigeria, the most populous central African country, is cooperating with *Business in Africa International Magazine* to encourage privatization.[13]

The solvency and stability of the banking sector were found to be improved by the privatization of industrial and commercial companies. Privatized companies have improved their profitability more rapidly, which has led to notable improvements in the banks' loan portfolios.[14]

The list of government-owned businesses and activities being sold to private owners or turned over to private companies to manage and operate goes on and on. The space available here is too limited to treat the subject thoroughly; instead, we refer you to the chapter endnotes and to articles on privatization that frequently appear in newspapers and periodicals and on Web sites.

FIGURE 9.2

Privatization in Africa

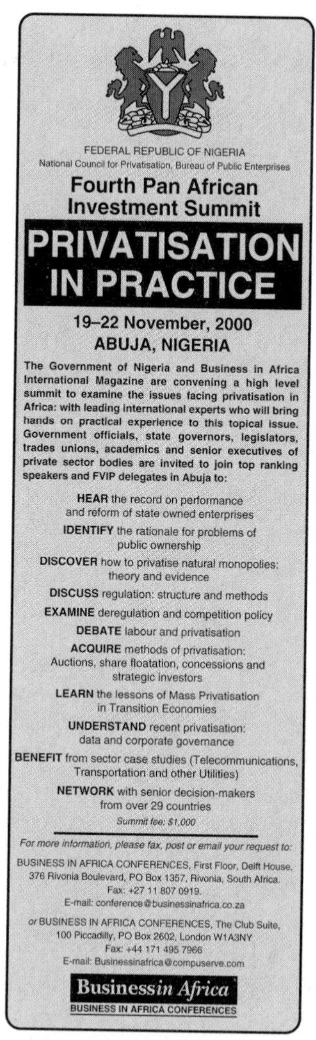

Source: Courtesy of *Business in Africa Magazine.*

PRIVATE BUYERS DO WELL, BUT AN AMERICAN NEEDS A PASSPORT

Although privatization is a sizzling political trend all over the world, the activity is not as great in the United States.

Fortunately, American investors can partake in the trend by buying mutual funds that hold shares of the world's newly privatized companies.[15]

PRIVATIZATION ANYWHERE AND ANY WAY

Privatization does not always involve ownership transfer from government to private entities. Activities previously conducted by the state may be contracted out, as Mozambique has contracted a British firm to run its customs administration and Thailand has private companies operating some of the passenger trains of its state-owned railroad.

Governments may lease state-owned plants to private entities, as Togo has done. They may combine a joint venture with a management contract with a private group to run a previously government-operated business. Rwanda did this with its match factory.

Even unemployment services are being privatized. Australia is a leader in this field, and it has found church groups to be the most successful employment agency operators. Those groups have secured lucrative government contracts, and community-based and charitable agencies have been about 25 percent better than the average in helping the long-term unemployed.[16]

FIGURE 9.3

Privatizations by Region

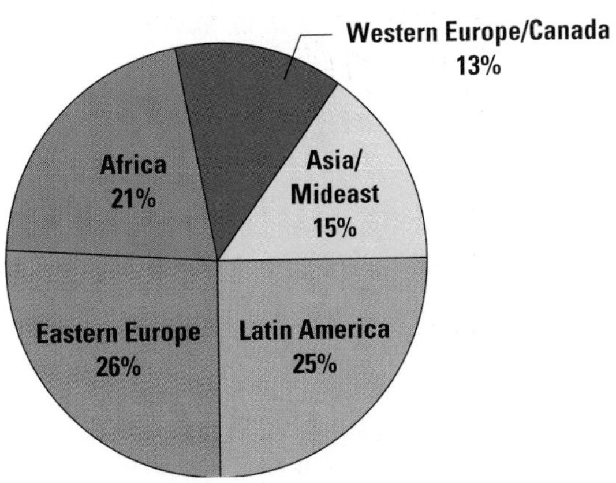

Source: "Privatization Worldwide Summary," prepared for the Transnational Corporations and Management Division of the United Nations. Used here by permission of the author, Michael S. Minor.

Figure 9.3 shows privatization by geographic region. The percentages in the figure total 100 without reference to the United States; this illustrates that neither the U.S. government nor the individual state governments are participating substantially in the privatization trend.

THE SUPER BOWL: GOVERNMENT VERSUS PRIVATE

A direct comparison is available. In England the Conservative government privatized the water industry in 1989. From 1989 to the present, the water industry in England has been in private company hands, while next door in Scotland it has been government-owned and -operated.

Over that period Scottish household water bills have increased 94 percent, while English bills have gone up 22 percent. A medium-size office in Scotland pays 16 times more than its English counterpart. And not only have Scottish water prices soared above those in England, but water quality and service have deteriorated. Scots get poorer drinking water and more pollution from their sewers, and their pipes are more than twice as leaky.

Scotland is now moving toward privatization, but water bills won't start coming down before 2007. Before they come down, Scottish Water must find some £2 billion to upgrade the machinery, pipes, and sewers.[17]

Government Protection

A historical function of government, whatever its ideology, has been the protection of the economic activities—farming, mining, manufacturing, and so forth—within its geographic area of control. These activities must be protected from attacks and destruction or robbery by bandits, revolutionaries, foreign invaders or terrorists. In 1990, the Iraqi armed forces invaded Kuwait, quickly overwhelming the defenders of that much smaller country. Although Kuwait is small, it is oil-rich. If Iraq held Kuwait, the combined petroleum reserves of the two countries would make Iraq a major player in petroleum politics.

An even greater prize was lying next door: Saudi Arabia, with the world's largest proved petroleum reserves. With armed forces no match for those of Iraq, Saudi Arabia might easily have fallen. That would have made Iraq the world's mightiest petroleum power and permitted it to influence the policies and actions of Europe, Japan, North America, and most of the rest of the world.

A UN-sanctioned international coalition mobilized and transported armed forces to the Middle East. A short war, code-named Desert Storm, in early 1991 forced Iraqi forces out of Kuwait, although they set fire to hundreds of Kuwaiti oil wells as they retreated.

The aftermath of this war demonstrates the influence of politics on business. In gratitude for American leadership of Desert Storm, Kuwait and other Gulf Cooperation Council

BUILDING YOUR GLOBAL RÉSUMÉ — Your Understanding of the Impact of Geopolitics on Business

Every international business transaction is impacted by two governments, that of the home country and that of the host country. You must abide by the laws, rules, and regulations of each country. You must also understand the political orientation of each country and geographic region in which you do business because the government and its political structure will determine your ability to do business in that country. Geopolitics goes well beyond government and politics. It includes, but is not limited to, such issues as:

- Country and regional economics.
- Terrorism and its support or condemnation.
- Military alliances.
- Human rights.
- Religion and the degree of separation between "church and state."
- Public policy.
- Natural resources.
- Government stability.
- Attitudes toward dumping and counterfeiting products.
- Arms control, chemical and biological warfare, and nuclear threat.

Political risk assessment is a major component of doing a potential market-entry analysis to determine the feasibility and risks of entering into a specific foreign market. Keeping current with the ever-changing global political scene and doing political risk assessment in market-entry planning are two critical tools of the successful international business professional.

World Fact: The U.S. government maintains comprehensive economic embargoes on the countries of Cuba, Iran, North Korea, and Sudan; arms embargoes on Liberia, Rwanda, Somalia, and the Federal Republic of Yugoslavia (Serbia and Montenegro); and an arms and commodity embargo on UNITA in Angola.

Culture Cue: In dealing with your foreign counterparts, socially or in business settings, it is extremely wise *not* to get into heated discussions or arguments about the importance or correctness of one political system over another. This also applies to any discussions of religion. In many parts of the world, the political and religious systems may be closely aligned or even one and the same.

World Wide Resources:

www.stratfor.com

www.sipri.org/contents/it/db/db3

countries—Saudi Arabia, Qatar, Bahrain, the United Arab Emirates, and Oman—bought some $36 billion of American arms. But in a 1997 competition to sell Kuwait 72 self-propelled howitzers, a Chinese company beat out an American company's widely considered superior versions. In private conversations, Kuwaiti officials said their reasons for buying Chinese had nothing to do with range, price, or accuracy and everything to do with politics. It seems China suggested it would withhold its support at the United Nations for extending trade sanctions against Iraq unless Kuwait gave the estimated $300 million order to the Chinese company. "Sometimes you get to a state when you feel you're being blackmailed," a senior Kuwaiti official said. "We lean toward the U.S. equipment, but we have to find a way to please the Chinese and not upset them in the Security Council."[18]

TERRORISM

terrorism
Unlawful acts of violence committed for a wide variety of reasons, including for ransom, to overthrow a government, to gain release of imprisoned colleagues, to exact revenge for real or imagined wrongs, and to punish nonbelievers of the terrorists' religion

Since the 1970s, the world has been plagued by **terrorism.** Various groups have hijacked airplanes, shot and kidnapped individuals, and bombed people and objects. During the 1970s and 1980s, Italy was particularly hard hit by terrorist violence directed against businesses and politicians. Between 1975 and 1982, terrorist groups almost shattered Italy's ability to govern itself. However, the Italian government struck back successfully by creating a special 25,000-strong antiterrorist squad. Once caught, terrorists were tried, convicted, and sentenced to prison by the Italian courts.

Coinciding with those events, the attraction of terrorist groups lessened for educated, idealistic young Italians, the original source of the groups' recruits. And with their cachet fading, the groups had many defectors. As these young Italians became disenchanted, terrorist leaders turned to more conventional crime. They began cooperating with the Mafia, which is growing and becoming more feared by Italian authorities. The Bank of Italy warned that the Mafia threatened to contaminate Italy's financial system.

September 11, 2001 On September 11, 2001, terrorists struck New York massively and lethally. They hijacked four civilian American airliners just after they took off from airports in Boston, Washington, D.C., and Newark, New Jersey, the planes fully loaded with jet fuel. They flew two of them into the two World Trade Center towers in New York and crashed one into the Pentagon in a Virginia suburb of Washington, D.C. The hijackers of the fourth plane were overwhelmed by the passengers, and the plane crashed in Pennsylvania. All told, thousands of lives were lost.

The United States immediately considered itself at war although there was no formal declaration of war by the U.S. Congress. There was no national government to declare war against as responsible for the attacks, which had been planned and executed by an Islamic fundamentalist organization calling itself al Qaeda, with headquarters and training camps at that time in Afghanistan and cells in many countries.

A main objective of the United States and its allies is to prevent Afghanistan from again becoming a base and hiding place for al Qaeda. Whether the West has the staying power to achieve this remains to be seen. At the same time, the campaign is ongoing to eradicate al Qaeda cells in countries around the world, even in the United States. There is a concern that al Qaeda will establish camps and headquarters in countries such as Somalia or Yemen. This struggle promises to be long, costly, and complex.

In the United States there have been widespread changes in airport and border security, immigration policy, student visas, and security of sensitive areas such as nuclear power plants and government installations. President George W. Bush called for and Congress approved a new cabinet-level government agency, the Homeland Security Department, to combine activities of many agencies protecting in many ways against terrorism. There are about 184,000 employees in the department, and housing them has been a challenge. For an idea of the size of that challenge, consider that the Pentagon, a 3.7-million-square-foot structure that boasts the largest roof in the world, accommodates a mere 23,000 workers.

Terrorism Worldwide Al Qaeda is by no means the only terrorist organization in the world. Among the better-known groups are the Irish Republican Army (IRA), Hamas and other Islamic fundamentalist groups, the Basque separatist movement (ETA), the Japanese Red Army, the German Red Army Faction, and various terrorist organizations in Latin America.

Government-Sponsored Terrorism: An Act of War A number of countries have financed, trained, and protected terrorists. In 1986, a British court convicted a Palestinian of trying to smuggle explosives (concealed in the baggage of his pregnant girlfriend) aboard an Israeli El Al 747 aircraft. The flight from London to Tel Aviv would have been blown up over Austria. It was revealed at the trial that the material for the explosives had been brought into London in Syrian diplomatic pouches aboard the Syrian government airline; the Syrian ambassador had sanctioned or even directed the operation. In international law, government action to damage or kill in another country is an act of war. The U.S. State Department has identified several countries that finance, sponsor, and train terrorists and/or provide sanctuaries for them. The current list includes Cuba, Iran, North Korea, Sudan, and Syria.[19]

Kidnapping for Ransom Kidnapping is another weapon used by terrorists. The victims are held for ransom, frequently very large amounts, which provides an important source of funds for the terrorists. Estimates are that there are 8,000 to 10,000 ransom and kidnapping situations per year and that kidnappers take home up to $500 million. A list of FAQs from one firm engaged in corporate risk consulting notes that large ransoms can be physically daunting—$1 million in mixed $20 and $100 bills weighs about 66 pounds.

Colombia and Peru have become dangerous places for American executives, and a long stay by a high-ranking executive in either country is risky. Brief visits are usually fairly safe because kidnappings take a while to plan, and so top executives practice what is called "commando management." They arrive in Bogotá or Lima as secretly as possible, meet for a few days with local employees, and fly off before kidnappers learn of their presence.

Paying Ransom Becomes Counterproductive The hostage business is booming. A remarkable deal concluded in the Philippines in 2000 explains why.

Libya's Colonel Muammar Qaddafi, trying to shake off that country's pariah status, bought the release of several Western hostages held by a band of Islamist bandits in the Philippines. The price was about $1 million each. The kidnappers evidently have learned two lessons: Holding a few hostages keeps the army away, and grabbing more keeps the money rolling in. Within weeks after receiving the ransom money, the Philippine kidnappers had bought new weapons and a new speedboat with which to capture more people to sell.[20] As an illustration of the global reach of terrorism, the Philippine group is thought to have links with al Qaeda. It calls itself Abu Sayyaf.[21]

A Successful Counterterrorist Operation

A terrorist organization not named above, the Tupac-Amaru Revolutionary Movement (MRTA), seized the residence of the Japanese ambassador to Peru in Lima. It was just before Christmas in 1996, and the ambassador was hosting a large party; 104 hostages were taken, including high-level business, church, diplomatic, and government officials.

The terrorists demanded the release of 400 MRTA members being held in Peruvian prisons, money, and safe passage out of Peru to Cuba. Peru refused their demands, and there was much argument about whether they should be more accommodating to the terrorists to secure the hostages' release without endangering lives or should use troops to storm the building. Those advocating the use of force pointed out that giving in to terrorists' demands encourages more terrorism, and not only in Peru; indeed, the Lima hostage story was being carried by the media worldwide. For example, part of the information presented in these paragraphs comes from an article in a Bangkok, Thailand, newspaper.

The Peruvians carried out spirited negotiations with the terrorists and tunneled under the residence, covering the digging sounds by bombarding it with loud music. The tunnel went under a ground-floor room where several of the terrorists played a game of indoor soccer each afternoon, and during a game one afternoon in April 1997, the government detonated a bomb. It caught 8 to 10 of the terrorists, and about half of them were killed.

The blast was the signal for assault troops to pour in from all sides. It was a short battle with remarkably few casualties. Although all the terrorists were killed, only two Peruvian troopers and one hostage died. Michael Radis, an expert on guerrilla groups at the Foreign Policy Research Institute in Philadelphia, says that "it will go down in the books among the great counterterrorist operations in history."

Countermeasures by Industry

Insurance to cover ransom payments, antiterrorist schools, and companies to handle negotiations with kidnappers have come into being. The insurance is called KRE (kidnap, ransom and extortion), and it can pay for the ransom, the fees of specialist negotiators, the salary of the hostage, and counseling for the victim and the family. Unfortunately, the effects of the terrorist attacks on September 11, 2001, may mean that executives are less likely to be insured because there have been big premium increases for KRE insurance.[22]

As kidnapping and extortion directed against businesses and governments have become common fund-raising and political techniques for terrorists, insurance against such acts has grown into a multimillion-dollar business. The world's largest kidnapping and extortion underwriting firm is located in London. The firm, Cassidy and Davis, underwriter for Lloyd's of London, says that it covers some 9,000 companies. Cassidy and Davis does not sit back and wait for claims to be filed. It runs antiterrorism training courses for executives, with subjects ranging from defensive driving techniques—escape tactics and battering through blockades—to crisis management. Country-by-country risk analyses are instantly available on international computer hookups.

Cassidy and Davis works closely with Control Risk, Ltd., a London-based security service company that advises firms and families in negotiations with kidnappers. Cassidy and Davis encourages its clients to use Control Risk services. Of course, it is vastly preferable to stay out of such situations. Malcolm Nance of Real World Rescue says that while KRE insurance is highly desirable, what employers really should be doing is training employees to avoid being kidnapped in the first place.

FIGURE 9.4 Before Leaving

- Your personal and legal affairs should be in order.
- Except on a need-to-know basis, tell no one about your travel plans. This is not hysterical paranoia; it's good discipline. A business executive on a fishing boat out of Miami who discusses an upcoming business trip to Central America in the presence of Cuban deckhands may find that future stay in Central America considerably longer than planned.
- Sanitize all documents and business identity. All company logos and identification should be removed from briefcases and luggage. A last name, or a fictitious name you've created, is sufficient identification on these items. If you use business cards, acronyms such as CIA for certified internal auditor should be eliminated. Whatever documents you need to conduct your business can be mailed or wired ahead so that they are waiting for you. If the trip comes up very suddenly or there are no company offices to receive the documents, carry them in your luggage. Never carry any business identification or documents on your person. In addition to a passport with visas, a jewelry bracelet or pendant-type ID with name, Social Security number, and blood type is the only identification you would need while in transit.
- Check with your company and other companies to find someone who has conducted business in the country you are going to. Contact that person and ask questions about cultural mores and the political climate in that country. Then look in an encyclopedia or go to the library and read all you can on the subject.
- If your company doesn't already have an individual designated to coordinate and monitor foreign trips, contact the appropriate management and see that someone knows the where, when, and how of your trip. Your family should be given that person's name and phone numbers.
- The company should have an established code for use by all its personnel who are engaged in foreign business. If not, a simple code system should be devised so that communication can be made under extraordinary circumstances (like on a video made by terrorists who have kidnapped you). The code should be provided to the company and your family.
- Have your company acquire a telephone directory for the State Department from the Government Printing Office. It can be used to contact the appropriate departmental sections for pretrip inquiries (operational intelligence). And, in the unfortunate event of a company employee kidnapping, it would be an absolute necessity in crisis management.

Source: Reprinted with permission from the October 1986 issue of *Internal Auditor*, published by the Institute of Internal Auditors, Inc.

Figures 9.4 and 9.5 are checklists for executives traveling to and in countries where they are at risk of being kidnapped. Figure 9.4 indicates what should be done before leaving the home country; Figure 9.5 discusses what to do once in the host country.

In the United States, antiterrorist surveillance detection and evasive driving training are available. They are offered by International Training, Inc. (ITI), which teaches some 5,000 students each year how to frustrate would-be assassins and kidnappers. The students are company executives and high-wealth individuals.

To enhance your chances of success with your ITI training, you can harden your automobile. O'Gara Security Associates' car-armoring business for business executives and government officials is growing rapidly. It now has manufacturing facilities in Cincinnati in the United States and in Brazil, France, Italy, Mexico, and Russia.[23]

Ethnoterrorism In the former Yugoslavia Croats, Muslims, and Serbs perpetrated "ethnic cleansing" against each other. In Africa, the Tutsis and Hutus have done the same. Violence of tribe against tribe, race against race, religion against religion is prevalent in the world, as witnessed in Ireland and the Middle East.

Nuclear Terrorism Failing security standards at former Soviet nuclear installations are permitting uranium to be stolen, which is then smuggled for sale to unauthorized buyers such as terrorists. NATO describes this as the greatest threat to international security since the end of the cold war.

Interpol, the international police agency, has set up a specialized group involving police forces in 24 European nations, but the smuggling continues. Interpol is treating 30 cases as

FIGURE 9.5 After Arriving

- First, slow down. Leave yourself time to think and evaluate. You're not in America. The rush and rat-race pace of hyperactivity typical of American businesspeople will only get you in trouble here.
- Take nothing for granted. Locate where elevators and stairways are so you can find them, even in the dark.
- Learn your rooms. Locate windows and doors and check to see if they are locked or if they can be locked. If you are not satisfied with your room, either change rooms or change hotels. Remember, if you change hotels, let the company and your family know.
- Do not conduct any business in your room or over the phone. The reasons are obvious.
- Whenever possible, you schedule business meetings and the locations. If this is not possible, check with your contacts and determine whether the location of scheduled meetings is safe. Remember, it's not the people you're conducting business with that present the threat (unless you're a major corporate executive and that fact is well known in advance); the danger is in becoming an object of surveillance.
- You are most vulnerable when you're moving, particularly if that movement is predictable. Vary times and methods of movement. Whether you're using a company-provided car and driver or taxis, use different entrances and exits when you enter and leave the hotel. If you are using company or rented transportation, change cars whenever the mood strikes you. Always follow your instincts.
- Always be aware of your surroundings and alert for surveillance. If terrorists are following you and they realize you recognize that fact, you've just made yourself a higher risk for them to consider. Terrorists will not just be lurking in the streets waiting for someone they can attack. They will spend many hours and much effort to observe potential targets. Then they will select the target that's going to cost them the least. Being alert makes you a more difficult target and raises the possibility, from the terrorist's point of view, that you have notified or will notify the authorities.
- Avoid being photographed.
- Do not respond to telephone inquiries or apparent spontaneous interest by people you meet to know more about you, however innocent or sincere either may seem. Handle it diplomatically.
- Avoid night movements, but if you must go, never walk. Not walking anywhere, anytime, is the best rule; but if it can't be avoided, be particularly sensitive to surveillance and try to stay in crowded areas.
- Read newspapers and stay in touch with your in-country contacts on a daily basis to keep informed on political climate indicators.
- Try to fit in with the native people as much as possible regarding dress and manners. This not only ingratiates you with the locals but also makes you more difficult to see.

Source: Reprinted with permission from the October 1986 issue of *Internal Auditor*, published by the Institute of Internal Auditors, Inc.

extremely serious, but this could be just the tip of the iceberg. Some cases involve as much as 250 kilograms of weapons-grade uranium; others may involve more. It takes only 7 kilograms of such uranium to make a nuclear bomb.[24]

Chemical and Biological Terrorism In 1995, the Aum Shin Rikyo cult launched a nerve gas attack in the Tokyo subway that killed 12 people and injured 5,500, many of whom suffered severe nerve damage. A malfunction in the bomb delivery system is believed to have prevented thousands of additional casualties. Sarin was the nerve gas used in the Tokyo subway attack. Chemical information about sarin is available on the Internet, making threats possible from self-taught terrorists anywhere.

stability
Characteristic of a government that maintains itself in power and whose fiscal, monetary, and political policies are predictable and not subject to sudden, radical changes

SECURITY IN THE FUTURE

For a recent global terrorism index, see Figure 9.6. It was prepared by the World Market Research Centre.

Government Stability

Government **stability** can be approached from two directions. One can speak of either a government's simple ability to maintain itself in power, or the stability or permanence of a

FIGURE 9.6

Global Terrorism Index

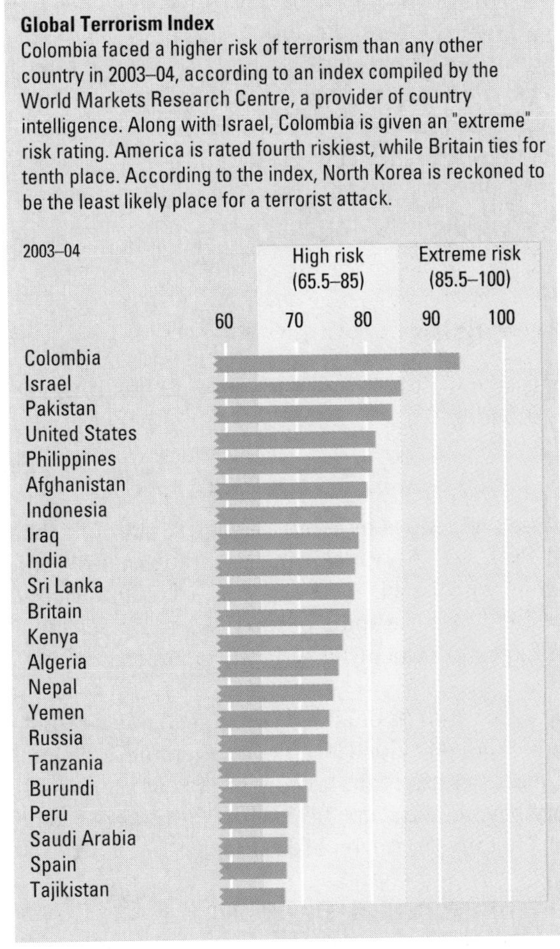

Source: *The Economist,* August 30, 2003, p. 74. © 2003 The Economist Newspaper Group, Inc. Reprinted with permission. Further reproduction prohibited. www.economist.com.

government's policies. It is safe to generalize that business (indeed almost all agricultural, commercial, and financial activities) prospers most when there is a stable government with permanent—or at most gradually changing—policies. Instability can be caused by revolution, invasion from abroad, or racial conflict.

STABILITY AND INSTABILITY: EXAMPLES AND RESULTS

Instability in Lebanon Here is a classic example of the impact of a change from order to chaos—from stability to **instability**—on the business and finances of a prosperous country. Until 1974, Lebanon prospered as the trading, banking, international company regional headquarters, business services (that is, accounting, legal, and financial services), transportation, and tourist center of the Middle East.

instability
Characteristic of a government that cannot maintain itself in power or that makes sudden, unpredictable, or radical policy changes

Then civil war broke out in Lebanon. Offices, banks, stores, transportation, communications, and hospitals were destroyed. The people fled the country or fought and survived as best they could. Almost all of the previous commercial activities ended. The fighting between Israel and Lebanon in 2006 had much the same effect—tourists from other Arab countries fled to Egypt or Europe instead.

Instability in Zimbabwe Zimbabwe was a relatively rich African country that was a net exporter of food. The Zimbabweans elected resistance leader Robert Mugabe as prime minister. In the 1990s he decided to seize much land and equipment from big farms and to redistribute it to small holders. People close to Mugabe were able to get the best of the land, but they have failed to work it and produce food.

As a result, there is severe food shortage, and the country now depends on foreign aid. But the aid-donating countries have grown impatient with corruption in the government, army, courts, and police and are cutting back their aid. It is also generally conceded that Mugabe stole the last presidential election in 2003.

The resulting instability has caused a loss of confidence by potential foreign investors, so money, expertise, and technology are no longer coming in. Poverty and starvation are the lot of many Zimbabweans now.

Traditional Hostilities

traditional hostilities
Long-standing enmities between tribes, races, religions, ideologies, or countries

We need mention only a few of the world's **traditional hostilities** to illustrate their powerful impact on business and trade.

ARAB COUNTRIES AND ISRAEL

Israel is surrounded on three sides by Arab countries, but until the peace efforts initiated by former Egyptian President Anwar Sadat, the Arab countries would not trade or have other peaceful dealings with Israel. Indeed, some Arab countries still boycott companies that trade with Israel, and because some of the Arab countries are extremely rich Organization of Petroleum Exporting Countries (OPEC) members, the boycott can be financially painful.*

Israel then made peace with its neighbor Jordan and made progress in negotiations with the Palestine Liberation Organization (PLO). However, those ongoing and complex negotiations had not been successful as of the writing of the current edition of this book. This is a long and painful story beyond the scope of this text. Several issues remain, but the most difficult seems to be sovereignty over parts of Jerusalem.

HUTUS AND TUTSIS IN BURUNDI AND RWANDA

The majority Hutus and the Tutsis have been at each other's throats for many years. But hostilities were kept at low levels until the 1990s, first in Burundi, where they were quelled, and then in 1993 and 1994 in Rwanda. The Hutus ran the government and army in Rwanda, and at least part of the army embarked on a campaign to exterminate the Tutsis. Some million people were massacred, and a Tutsi-led army coming in from Uganda retaliated. The Tutsi army defeated the Hutus, whose subsequent retreat led to the worst refugee situation in the world's history. Over a million Hutus fled into the Congo, where they were held in camps at the border. Cholera and dysentery took thousands of lives.

Fighting among Hutus, Tutsis, and other tribal groups continued into 2005. At least some of the expense of the fighting, such as buying arms and ammunition, is met by mining and selling diamonds. Some of the part of Central Africa where the fighting is occurring is rich in diamond mines, and whichever tribe controls the mines takes out their riches. Such commandeering of diamond profits for misuse in civil wars has spread to other West African countries, jeopardizing the reputation of the diamond industry itself.

This has led to efforts by the mining company De Beers and by several countries where diamonds are cut and prepared for market to refuse to buy "dirty diamonds" that are being used to finance the fighting. That is proving difficult because rough diamonds are nearly identical and could have come from any mine.

TAMILS AND SINHALESE IN SRI LANKA

The Tamils form a substantial minority of the Sri Lankan population. An armed group calling itself the Tamil Tigers has been fighting with the Sri Lankan army.

*See Chapter 10 for a discussion of U.S. law dealing with this boycott.

mini MNE

>>Businesses—and People—Are Resilient

It's business as usual in Bombay, India, where these commuters are making their way to work.

In mid-July 2006 bomb blasts killed 200 and wounded over 700 in Mumbai, India. Three years earlier, 60 people had died in the same city. In fact, India has suffered a number of terrorist attacks over the past few years.

Has this repeated terrorism slowed India down? The evidence seems to be that any effect is small and temporary. One key indicator is that the Bombay stock market index went up 3 percent the next day after the Mumbai attack. One study found that a sample of Indian firms actually had abnormally high returns for foreign investors who had bought their stock for the period after terrorist attacks. Similarly, Indians themselves quickly returned to "life as normal" after a Sikh separatist movement in the early 1990s resulted in thousands of deaths.

Source: Akash Dania, "Country Risk and ADR Volatility—Diversification in the Indian Subcontinent," working paper, 2005; and Peter Wonacott and Eric Bellman, "India Is Resilient in Wake of Deadly Blasts," *The Wall Street Journal*, July 13, 2006, p. A5.

The Tamils want a separate state, and a large Tamil population in India has given them support. The late Indian president Rajiv Ghandi sent troops to Sri Lanka in an attempt to suppress the Tamil uprising. They failed, and the troops were withdrawn, but Ghandi reaped Tamil hatred for his attempt. His murder—by a bomb hidden in a flower arrangement offered to him by a woman when he was campaigning for election in the Indian Tamil state—was blamed on the Tigers or their allies.

The Sinhalese-Tamil battles continued into 2006. As with other conflicts, business is adversely affected; businesspeople are afraid to enter combat areas even to attempt short-term sales, and companies are even less apt to risk people on longer-term investment bases. These areas are thus deprived not only of qualified people but also of the capital and technology that would come with them.

International Companies

International business is not merely a passive victim of political forces. It can be a powerful force in the world political arena. As noted in Chapter 1, about half of the world's 100 biggest economic units are firms, not nations.

International companies (ICs) repeatedly make decisions about where to invest, where to conduct research and development, and where to manufacture products. The country or area in which an investment is made or a laboratory, research facility, or manufacturing plant is located can benefit as jobs are created, new or improved technology becomes available, or products are produced that can be exported or substituted for imports.

Of course the IC will seek the country and area where it can operate most beneficially and profitably. It will negotiate with the national and local areas in which it is considering an investment or location in efforts to maximize benefits such as tax breaks, infrastructure improvements, and worker training programs.

The financial size of many ICs provides them with a strong negotiating position. And an IC's power need not rest solely on size. It can come from the possession of capital, technology, and management skills, plus the capability to deploy those resources around the world. An IC may have the processing, productive, distributive, and marketing abilities necessary for the successful utilization of raw materials or for the manufacture, distribution, and marketing of certain products. Those abilities are frequently not available in developing countries. Recognition of the desirability of IC investments is growing.[25]

Country Risk Assessment

country risk assessment (CRA)
An evaluation, conducted by a bank or business having an asset in or payable from a foreign country or considering a loan or an investment there, that assesses the country's economic situation and policies and its politics to determine how much risk exists of losing the asset or not being paid

Country risk assessment (CRA) involves many risks other than political risks. So we shall only introduce you to CRA here; if your interest runs deeper, you can find material in the growing literature on the topic.

The political events of recent years have caused firms to concentrate much more on CRA. Firms that had already done CRA updated and strengthened the function, and many other companies began to engage in the practice.

TYPES OF COUNTRY RISKS

Country risks are increasingly political in nature. Among them are wars, revolutions, and coups. Less dramatic, but nevertheless important for businesses, are government changes caused by election of a socialist or nationalist government, which may be hostile to private business and particularly to foreign-owned business.

The risks may be economic or financial. Countries may have persistent balance-of-payments deficits or high inflation rates. Repayment of loans may be questionable. Labor conditions may cause investors to pause. Labor productivity may be low, or labor unions may be militant.

Laws may be changed in regard to such subjects as taxes, currency convertibility, tariffs, quotas, and labor permits. The chances for a fair trial in local courts must be assessed.

Terrorism may be present. If it is, can the company protect its personnel and property?

INFORMATION CONTENT FOR CRA

The types of information a firm will need to judge country risks vary according to the nature of its business and the length of time required for the investment, loan, or other involvement to yield a satisfactory return.

Nature of Business

Consider, for example, the needs of a hotel company compared with those of heavy-equipment manufacturers, manufacturers of personal hygiene products, or mining companies. Banks have their own sets of problems and information needs. Sometimes variations exist between firms in the same industry or on a project-to-project basis. The nationality—home country—of the company may be a factor; does the host country bear a particular animus or friendly attitude toward the home country?

Length of Time Required

Export financing usually involves the shortest period of risk exposure. Typically, payments are made within 180 days—usually less—and exporters can get insurance or bank protection.

Bank loans can be short-, medium-, or long-term. However, when the business includes host country assembly, mixing, manufacture, or extraction of oil or minerals, long-term commitments are necessary.

With long-term investment or loan commitments, risk analysis entails inherent problems that cannot be resolved. Most such investment opportunities require 5, 10, or more years to pay off. But the utility of risk analyses of social, political, and economic factors decreases precipitously over longer time spans.

WHO DOES COUNTRY RISK ASSESSING?

General or specific analyses, macro or micro analyses, and political, social, and economic analyses have been conducted—perhaps under different names—for years. The Conference Board located bits and pieces of CRA being performed in various company

FIGURE 9.7 Assistance in Country Risk Assessment

WARNING: ONE OF THESE COUNTRIES COULD DAMAGE YOUR FINANCIAL HEALTH

You can now limit the risks to your business in 97 emerging and highly-indebted countries by subscribing to just one publication—the **Risk Ratings Review** from the Economist Intelligence Unit.

Every three months you receive ratings of the political, economic and financial risks for 97 emerging markets–providing early warnings of economies in trouble, and a spotlight on countries where conditions for trade, investment and lending are becoming more favourable.

The Risk Ratings Review–a one stop shop for reducing your risks around the world

The **Risk Ratings Review** offers you the highlights of the **Country Risk Service**, the Economist Intelligence Unit's international country credit rating service. It is an ideal introduction to the service and gives you access to all its ratings at a cost effective price.

Every three months the **Country Risk Service** publishes risk assessment reports for each of the 97 countries it covers. These project up to 180 economic and financial variables over a two year forecast horizon and include detailed ratings of political, economic and financial risk around the globe.

Identify deteriorating and improving economies–at a glance

The Risk Ratings Review summarises these findings, helping you to spot global trends and identify countries whose risk profile is changing. Each issue includes:

- **Comparative risk ratings tables–** listings of the current risk ratings scores produced by the Country Risk Service for all 97 countries;
- **Global and regional analysis**–what this quarter's rankings reveal about international and region-wide patterns of risk;
- **Up-to-date ratings focus**–an analytical summary of each country whose risk rating has changed in the previous quarter;
- **Watchlist**–early warnings of countries likely to deteriorate or improve over the next three-to-six months, and the factors that need to be monitored most carefully.

The **Risk Ratings Review**: the first place to turn for country-by-country assessments of financial solvency, political stability and economic health.

Monitor these risks for all 97 countries:

- Overall country risk
- Political risk
- Economic structure risk
- Economic policy risk
- Liquidity risk
- Currency risk
- Sovereign debt risk
- Banking risk

Countries covered in the Risk Ratings Review

Western Europe
Cyprus
Greece
Italy
Portugal
Spain
Turkey

Middle East & North Africa
Algeria
Bahrain
Egypt
Iran
Iraq
Israel
Jordan
Kuwait
Lebanon
Libya
Morocco
Oman
Qatar
Saudi Arabia
Sudan
Syria
Tunisia
UAE
Yemen

Asia
Australia
Bangladesh
China
Hong Kong
India
Indonesia
Malaysia
Myanmar
New Zealand
Pakistan
Papua New Guinea
Philippines
Singapore
South Korea
Sri Lanka
Taiwan
Thailand
Vietnam

Sub-Saharan Africa
Angola
Botswana
Cameroon
CÔte d'Ivoire
Gabon
Ghana
Kenya
Malawi
Nigeria
Namibia
Senegal
South Africa
Tanzania
Zambia
Zimbabwe

Eastern Europe & the former Soviet Union
Azerbaijan
Baltic Republics: Estonia, Latvia, Lithuania
Bulgaria
Croatia
Czech Republic
Hungary
Kazakstan
Poland
Romania
Russia
Slovakia
Slovenia
Ukraine
Uzbekistan
Yugoslavia (Serbia-Montenegro),
Macedonia

Latin America & the Caribbean
Argentina
Bolivia
Brazil
Chile
Colombia
Costa Rica
Cuba
Dominican Republic
Ecuador
El Salvador
Guatemala
Honduras
Jamaica
Mexico
Nicaragua
Panama
Paraguay
Peru
Trinidad & Tobago
Uruguay
Venezuela

Keep alert to worldwide patterns of risk—subscribe to the Risk Ratings Review today

Order form

How to order your **Risk Ratings Review** subscriptions. Complete your personal details, choose your payment method and post to: The Economist Intelligence Unit, NA, Incorporated. The Economist Building, 111 West 57th Street, New York, NY 10019, USA. Alternatively, you can order by telephone on: (1.212) 554 0600, by fax on (1.212) 586 11813 or by E-mail: newyork@eiu.com

Personal details

Name (Mr/Mrs/Ms/Dr) ______________________

Job title ______________________

Company name ______________________

Department ______________________

Address ______________________

City ______________ State ______________

Zip + 4 ______________ Country ______________
Please add zip+4 to ensure fastest possible delivery

Nature of business ______________________

Tel ______________ Fax ______________

E-Mail ______________________

	Quantity	Price	Sub-total
Risk Ratings Review		US $795*	
Postage is included *Add applicable sales tax in Florida and Massachusetts. In Canada add 7% GST #R 132 494 238.		Tax	
		Total	

❒ Please send me details of the full **Country Risk Service.**

Payment details

❒ I enclose a check for US$ __________ payable to **The Economist Intelligence Unit, NA, Incorporated**

❒ Please charge US$__________ to my ❒ Visa ❒ Mastercard ❒ Amex ❒ Diners Club

Account Number ______________________

Signed ______________________ Expiry date ______________

❒ Please proforma invoice me (Report will be sent on receipt of payment)

Billing address if different from above ______________________

❒ I do not wish to receive promotional material from other companies

E•I•U
The Economist Intelligence Unit

1ABLWA

Source: *The Economist,* December 6, 1997; p. 94. Reproduced by permission of the Economist Intelligence Unit.

departments—for example, the international division and the public affairs, finance, legal, economics, planning, and product-producing departments. Sometimes the efforts were duplicative, and the people in one department were unaware that others in the company were similarly involved.

Outside consulting and publishing firms are another source of country risk analysis. As CRA has mushroomed in perceived importance, a number of such firms have been formed or have expanded. Some of the better-known outside consulting and publishing firms for CRA include:

- Business Environment Risk Intelligence (BERI) S.A.
- Control Risks Information Services.
- Economist Intelligence Unit (EIU). Figure 9.7 on the previous page is an EIU advertisement for its *Risk Ratings Review* publication, and Figure 9.8 below is a chart showing EIU's country risk ratings.
- Euromoney.
- StratFor, Inc.
- *Harvard Business Review*'s Global Risk Navigator.
- Standard and Poor's Rating Group.
- Moody's Investor Services.[26]

Instead of or in addition to using outside consultants, a number of firms have supplemented their internal risk analysis staffs by hiring such experts as international business or political science professors or retired State Department, CIA, or military people.

FIGURE 9.8 Country Risk

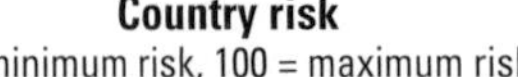

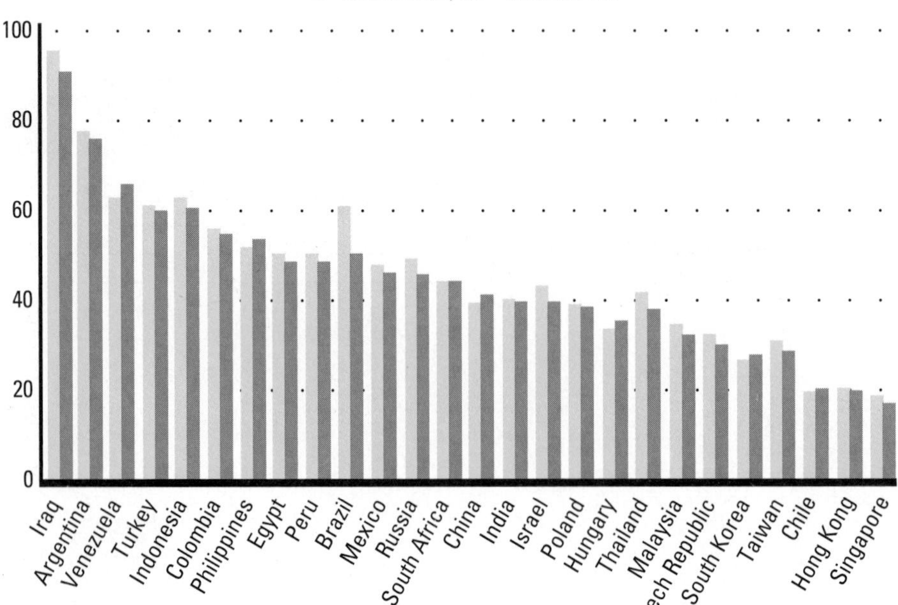

Source: *The Economist,* February 14, 2004, p. 98. www.economist.com.

Summary

Identify the ideological forces that affect business and understand the terminology used in discussing them.

Ideological forces include capitalism, communism, and socialism. The chapter discusses terminology (conservative, liberal, right wing, and left wing) used to describe various political positions.

Discuss the fact that although most governments own businesses, they are privatizing them in growing numbers.

Even governments that consider themselves capitalist and conservative own some businesses. But almost all governments—with the United States lagging behind—are privatizing and getting out of business.

Explain the changing sources and reasons for terrorism and the methods and growing power of terrorists.

The former Soviet Union and Eastern European satellites no longer finance, train, and shelter terrorists, but they have been replaced by countries such as Iran and North Korea. Radical Islamic fundamentalists represent a growing threat. They are infuriated by the peace moves between Israel and its Arab neighbors. Nuclear terrorism is a new fear, as security has failed at nuclear sites in the former Soviet Union and enriched uranium is being stolen and smuggled around the world.

Explain steps that traveling international business executives should take to protect themselves from terrorists.

Figures 9.4 and 9.5 offer several suggestions. For example, Figure 9.4 suggests keeping travel plans confidential. At the same time, it is important to keep the firm aware of where business travelers are. This is true in case of natural disasters as well. One recent problem is that, with the presence of discounted tickets, some travelers stop using a travel management service. When a plot to blow up planes at London's Gatwick Airport was uncovered in August 2006, travel managers put in extra time helping traveling employees to rebook flights or avoid London entirely.

Evaluate the importance to business of government stability and policy continuity.

Business can rarely thrive in a country with an unstable government or rapid, drastic policy changes. The situation in Bolivia illustrates the problems.

Explain country risk assessment by international business.

Country risk assessment is now considered a necessity by most international businesses before they commit people, money, or technology to a foreign country. CRA involves evaluating a country's economic situation and policies as well as its politics.

Key Words

communism (p. 256)
expropriation (p. 257)
confiscation (p. 257)
capitalism (p. 257)
socialism (p. 258)
conservative (p. 258)
right wing (p. 259)
liberal (p. 259)
left wing (p. 259)
privatization (p. 260)
terrorism (p. 264)
stability (p. 268)
instability (p. 269)
traditional hostilities (p. 270)
country risk assessment (CRA) (p. 272)

Questions

1. a. What is ideology?
   b. Why is it important to international business?
2. a. What is the capitalist, free enterprise ideal?
   b. What is the actual situation in capitalist countries?
3. What impact can terrorism have on business?
4. Why does business fear sudden changes in government policies?
5. How can traditional hostilities affect business?
6. How can ICs use their strengths to influence government policies?
7. Is country risk assessment (CRA) an exact science? Explain.
8. a. In terms of exposure to political risk (for example, expropriation), which of the following businesses would you consider the most and least vulnerable? Explain.

banks	cosmetics manufactures
mines	manufactures of personal hygiene products
oil fields	automobile manufactures
oil refineries	
heavy-equipment manufacturers	
hotels	

   b. Are the most vulnerable businesses high-profile or low-profile? What are some ways to change the profile of a company in a foreign country?
9. Discuss the lessons CRA analysts should have learned from the world debt crises.
10. Islamic fundamentalism is a growing terrorist threat. Why?

Research Task

globalEDGE.msu.edu 

Use the globalEDGE site (http://globalEDGE.msu.edu) to complete the following exercises:

1. The *Enterprise Surveys* conducted by the World Bank examine the investment climate in a wide range of countries undergoing social transformation. You have been asked to develop a report that analyzes corruption and black-market practices in different countries. A coworker recently indicated that one proxy for this is the level of informality that firms use in reporting sales amounts for tax purposes. Identify the top three transition economies in which reported sales are most similar to actual sales amounts. Which three countries have the lowest reporting of sales amounts for tax purposes?
2. Financial stability is an important component of economic development. In fact, your colleagues indicate that the amount of capital a country exports can be an indication of its financial stability. As such, you have since discovered a "Global Financial Stability" report to assist in your assessment of international financial markets. Which three countries are the largest exporters of capital? Which three countries import the largest amount of capital?

Company Privatization Minicase 9.1

You are the chief executive officer of a company that the government has just denationalized by selling the company's stock to the company's employees. In the past, any major decision about company policy required approval by a government agency, which was time-consuming. Wages and salaries had been established by reference to civil service "equivalents," and incentive payments were unheard of. Maintenance of the plant and equipment was lax, breakdowns were frequent and expensive, and utility expenses were high.

You want the newly privatized company to be a success. Suggest some programs that you would institute to improve its chances of success.

10 Legal Forces

The Peace Palace in The Hague, the Netherlands, is home to the International Court of Justice.

The role which the Court [International Court of Justice] plays, through the power of justice and international law . . . is widely recognized and evidenced by the number of cases on the Court's docket. . . . It is not uncommon that these cases deal with issues concerning international peace and security. In performing its dispute resolution function, the Court, which embodies the principle of equality of all before the law, acts as a guardian of international law, and assures the maintenance of a coherent international legal order.

—Judge Shi Jiuyong, former president of the International Court of Justice, to the General Assembly of the United Nations, October 31, 2003

When a Local Issue Can Have International Ramifications

The world has become increasingly interrelated, and the law reflects this trend. What may appear to be a local issue may take on national and often worldwide importance. In June 1996, the Commonwealth of Massachusetts decided to take a position against Myanmar (formerly Burma) for repressive actions the Myanmar government had taken. The Massachusetts legislature passed an act barring Massachusetts state entities from buying goods or services from businesses doing business with Myanmar. This included businesses having operations or franchises in Myanmar or providing any goods or services to the government of that country. Massachusetts exempted business entities providing medical supplies or international telecommunication goods or services or reporting the news. Three months after Massachusetts passed that law, the U.S. Congress passed the Foreign Operations, Export Financing, and Related Programs Appropriations Act, which banned aid to the Myanmar government with the exception of funds for certain forms of humanitarian assistance, funds used to fight drugs, and funds used to promote human rights and democracy. Congress also directed the U.S. president to develop a strategy to bring democracy to Myanmar and improve human rights practices there. The president was further empowered to waive any sanction if it was determined that the application of that sanction would be contrary to U.S. national security interests.

The National Foreign Trade Council, a private trade group, brought suit in the federal court in Massachusetts against Massachusetts state officials, seeking to prevent them from administering the state law. The federal district court agreed with the National Foreign Trade Council and blocked enforcement of the Massachusetts law. This decision was upheld by the federal court of appeals. The matter finally reached the U.S. Supreme Court, which agreed that enforcement of the Massachusetts law should be prevented. The Supreme Court found that the Massachusetts law was unconstitutional because Congress had intended to give the president flexibility and effective authority over economic sanctions against Myanmar. The Supreme Court held that it was "simply implausible" that Congress would have gone to such lengths if it had intended to permit state statutes to "blunt the consequences of discretionary Presidential action." On the basis of the Constitution's Supremacy Clause, the Supreme Court struck down the Massachusetts law because it conflicted with federal law. Massachusetts attempted to do something that was under the exclusive province of the federal government. Under the Constitution, the president and Congress have the power to set foreign policy. State laws that violate constitutional mandates will be struck down. ■

Source: U.S. Supreme Court, *Crosby v. National Foreign Trade Council,* No. 99–474, 530 U.S. 363 (2000).

CONCEPT PREVIEWS

After reading this chapter, you should be able to:

discuss the complexity of the legal forces that confront international business

recognize the importance of foreign law

explain contract devices and institutions that assist in interpreting or enforcing international contracts

recognize the need and methods to protect your intellectual property

recognize that many taxes have purposes other than to raise revenue

discuss enforcement of antitrust laws

explain the risk of product liability legal actions, which can result in imprisonment for employees or fines for them and the company

discuss some of the U.S. laws that affect international business operations

It is important for participants in international business to understand the enormous breadth and depth of laws in various jurisdictions worldwide. Unlike some other forces around which businesses must operate, legal forces cannot be ignored. Anyone studying legal forces affecting international business soon realizes that the immensity and variety of these forces complicate the task of understanding the laws. Laws too numerous to count enacted by governments at all levels on virtually every subject affect international business.

While on the one hand businesses must be aware of laws in order to comply, on the other hand businesses also expect that laws will assist them when necessary. An issue of great concern to businesses that operate internationally is the stability of a host government and its legal system. When a business enters a country, the business needs to know whether the country's host government will be able to protect the foreign business with an adequate legal system. The legal system must be able to enforce contracts and protect the basic rights of employees. In examining international legal forces, one must keep in mind that a stable government and an adequate court system are necessary to ensure a welcome environment for foreign businesses.

This chapter examines international law and looks at specific national laws that influence international business.

International Legal Forces

RULE OF LAW

When examining countries around the world, it is important to determine whether the country is governed by the rule of law. It is desirable that a country base its functions on the rule of law, instead of rule by political dictatorship or rule by a powerful elite. Basing a country's legal system on the rule of law makes encouraging foreign investment easier because foreign businesses will know that their interests will be protected. Following the rule of law also makes ensuring protection of human rights of local people easier.

In China, for example, Hong Kong has an advantage over Shanghai in attracting foreign investors because Hong Kong has a tradition of law adopted from British colonial days while Shanghai courts tend to favor Chinese litigants. "It is absolutely impossible for a foreign party to win a case against a Chinese party in a Chinese court," says Cao Siyuan, a Chinese commentator. This disparity in legal systems between the two cities is seen to give Hong Kong an advantage as a location for foreign firms.[1]

public international law
Legal relations between governments

private international law
Laws governing transactions of individuals and companies that cross international borders

treaties
Agreements between countries, which may be bilateral (between two countries) or multilateral (involving more than two countries); also called *conventions, covenants, compacts,* or *protocols*

WHAT IS INTERNATIONAL LAW?

Each sovereign nation is responsible for creating and enforcing laws within its jurisdiction. Once laws cross international borders, the matter of enforcement is complicated by the necessity of agreement between nations. The same concepts that apply to domestic laws do not always apply to international law.

What is called *international law* can be divided into public international law and private international law. **Public international law** includes legal relations between governments, including laws concerning diplomatic relations between nations and all matters involving the rights and obligations of sovereign nations. **Private international law** includes laws governing the transactions of individuals and companies crossing international borders. For example, private international law would cover matters involved in a contract between businesses in two different countries.

SOURCES OF INTERNATIONAL LAW

International law comes from several sources, the most important of which are bilateral and multilateral **treaties** between nations. Treaties are agreements between countries and may also be called *conventions, covenants, compacts,* or *protocols*. International organizations such as the United Nations have provided a forum for creation of many treaties. The UN has sponsored many conferences that have led to agreements among nations on a large range of matters, including postal delivery and use of driver's licenses in other countries. In addition, the International Court of Justice, one of the organs of the UN, creates international law when it decides disputes brought before it by member-nations.

Another source of international law is customary international law, which consists of international rules derived from customs and usage over centuries. An example of customary international law is the prohibition against genocide (there is also a specific international statute against genocide).

EXTRATERRITORIALITY

Many countries, including the United States and member-countries of the European Union, often attempt to enforce their laws outside their borders. This is referred to as **extraterritorial application of laws.** This attempt to enforce laws abroad is done not by force but through traditional legal means. For example, the U.S. government imposes taxes on U.S. citizens and U.S. permanent residents regardless of either the source of income or the residence of the taxpayer. If a U.S. citizen is living in Madrid and receives all of her income from Spanish sources, the United States will still expect the taxpayer to comply with U.S. tax laws. Likewise, when U.S. companies operate in other countries with U.S.-based personnel, the U.S. companies must comply with U.S. laws, including employment laws. Of course, these companies must also comply with the laws of the host country. Extraterritorial application of U.S. laws has been extended in many other areas including antitrust and environmental laws.

extraterritorial application of laws
A country's attempt to apply its laws to foreigners or nonresidents and to acts and activities that take place outside its borders

International Dispute Settlement

LITIGATION

Litigation can be extremely complicated and expensive. In addition to involving the trial itself, most lawsuits entail lengthy pretrial activities, including a process called *discovery.* Discovery is the means of finding facts relevant to the litigation that are known to the other side, including obtaining documents in the other side's possession. Some discovery methods can seem quite intrusive since courts grant parties great latitude in obtaining information in the possession of the opposing side. Discovery is one reason many people outside the United States dislike litigation in the United States.

Litigation involving disputes that cross international lines can arise in both state and federal courts. Special rules exist for obtaining discovery in other countries, and they vary from country to country. Some countries freely allow U.S. litigators to obtain discovery. Others have restrictions. For example, if discovery is to occur in Switzerland even in a case involving only U.S. parties, permission must be obtained from Swiss authorities. Failure to obtain permission may result in penalties, including possible criminal sanctions.

One of the major problems usually involved in cross-border litigation is the question of which jurisdiction's law should apply and in which location the litigation should occur. Each country (and each state in the United States) has elaborate laws for determining which law should apply and where litigation should occur. As with any other disputed matter, the final decision on these issues rests with the court. Occasionally, courts in two countries (or two states) will attempt to resolve the same dispute. Again, this is resolved by reference to the particular choice of law provisions and can be quite complicated. For this reason, it is prudent to include in contracts a choice-of-law clause and a choice-of-forum clause in the event of a dispute. A *choice-of-law clause* is a paragraph in a contract that specifies which law will govern in the event of a dispute. For example, if there is a U.S. seller and an Australian buyer, the parties may agree that U.S. law would govern any dispute. A *choice-of-forum clause* is a paragraph in a contract that specifies where the dispute will be settled. For example, the parties in the above example may agree to have the dispute decided in California state courts in Los Angeles County, California.

PERFORMANCE OF CONTRACTS

Whenever businesses enter into agreements with other businesses, the possibility exists that there may be problems getting the other side to perform its obligations. No worldwide court has the power to enforce its decrees. The worldwide courts that do exist, such as the UN's

International Court of Justice (see Chapter 4), rely on the voluntary compliance of the parties before it. Each nation in the world is a sovereign nation and has its own rules for recognizing decrees and judgments from other nations.

When contracting parties are residents of a single country, the laws of that country govern contract performance and any disputes that arise between the parties. That country's courts have jurisdiction over the parties, and the courts' judgments are enforced in accordance with the country's procedures. When residents of two or more countries contract, those relatively easy solutions to dispute resolution are not available. Enforcing contracts that cross international lines is often quite complicated.

United Nations Solutions When contract disputes arise between parties from two or more countries, which country's law is applicable? Many countries, including the United States, have ratified the UN Convention on Contracts for the International Sale of Goods (CISG) to solve such problems.

The CISG established uniform legal rules to govern the formation of international sales contracts and the rights and obligations of the buyer and seller. The CISG applies automatically to all contracts for the sale of goods between traders from different countries that have ratified the CISG. This automatic application will take place unless the parties to the contract expressly exclude—opt out of—the CISG.[2]

Private Solutions—Arbitration As mentioned before, many people outside the United States dislike the U.S. court system. Likewise, many U.S. businesspeople dislike or at least fear litigation in other countries. For these reasons, international businesspeople often agree that any disputes will be resolved by arbitration, rather than by going to court in any country. **Arbitration** is a dispute resolution mechanism that is an alternative to litigation. Arbitration is usually quicker, less expensive, and more private than litigation, and it is usually binding on all parties. At least 30 organizations now administer international arbitrations, the best known of which is probably the International Court of Arbitration of the International Chamber of Commerce in Paris. In addition, London and New York are centers of arbitration. Some organizations specialize in the type of arbitration cases they will consider. For example, the World Intellectual Property Organization Arbitration and Mediation Center handles technological, entertainment, and intellectual property disputes. The International Centre for the Settlement of Investment Disputes specializes, logically, in investment disputes.

arbitration
A process, agreed to by parties to a dispute in lieu of going to court, by which a neutral person or body makes a binding decision

In summary, people and businesses may prefer arbitration for several reasons. They may be suspicious of foreign courts. Arbitration is generally faster than law courts, where cases are usually backlogged. Arbitration procedures are usually more informal than court procedures. Arbitration may be confidential, avoiding the perhaps unwelcome publicity accompanying an open court case. And generally it may be less expensive.

Enforcement of Foreign Arbitration Awards Courts in countries around the world usually enforce arbitration awards, but occasionally enforcement can pose problems. One solution is the UN Convention on the Recognition and Enforcement of Foreign Arbitral Awards. The United States and many UN member-countries have ratified this convention. It binds ratifying countries to compel arbitration, when the parties have so agreed in their contract, and to enforce the resulting awards.

Other organizations are working toward a worldwide business law. The Incoterms of the International Chamber of Commerce and its Uniform Rules and Practice on Documentary Credits now receive almost universal acceptance. The UN Commission on International Trade Law and the International Institute for the Unification of Private Law are doing much useful work. The Hague-Vishy Rules on Bills of Lading sponsored by the International Law Association have been adopted by a number of countries.[3]

DESPITE LEGAL UNCERTAINTIES, INTERNATIONAL BUSINESS GROWS

Despite legal uncertainties of doing business in other countries, the trend indicates that international business activities will increase in the future. For this reason, international

Earn a Law Degree with Specialization in International Law

Every business transaction involves a contract. Developing, writing, and executing contracts in international business transactions is very complex because there are typically:

- Two sets of expectations as to what the contract represents.
- Two languages.
- Two currencies.
- Two legal systems.
- Two political systems backing the two legal systems.
- At least two legal views and opinions on how each of the issues must be dealt with.

Earning a law degree with a specialization in international law can place you in a high corporate position dealing directly with the legal issues companies face daily in global commerce. You will also be in an extremely small group of legal professionals. The International Legal Committee of the American Bar Association's Section on International Law and Practice determined in a 1997 study that only 37 percent of law school students took any class in foreign law. A review of the current literature indicates that this has not changed to any significant degree. Yet, according to a study presented in the *American Journal of Comparative Law,* well over 10 percent of the revenue generated by the 100 largest American law firms comes from foreign clients. If the study's data are indicative of a trend, there could be a growing need for attorneys with expertise in international law. If you apply the law of supply and demand to the international law profession, you can only imagine what the rewards might be . . . and you'll also see the world on someone else's expense account. A growing area of corporate concern impacting international law is dealing with patent, copyright, and brand infringement that occurs when counterfeit products are sold in global markets.

World Fact: Counterfeiting of products and brands is a major legal problem, and it is growing. The World Trade Organization estimates that 7 percent of annual global trade involves the sale of counterfeit products. This translates to a $456 billion industry worldwide.

Culture Cue: The laws of many countries are steeped in the country's religious heritage. This means that breaking a law in such a country may also be seen as an act of huge disrespect for a population's religious beliefs. World religions such as Islam, Hinduism, and Buddhism clearly define accepted behavior and serve as a basis for the laws in countries where these religions are dominant. Become sensitive to and respectful of the religious influence in the countries with which you trade.

World Wide Resources:

www.eisil.org

www.smu.edu/ilra/til.htm

businesspeople must be aware of the legal environment in which they find themselves. Legal systems vary significantly from country to country, and it is important to understand the differences. The assumptions one makes on the basis of the U.S. legal system may not apply in other countries.

Intellectual Property: Patents, Trademarks, Trade Names, Copyrights, and Trade Secrets

A *patent* is a government grant giving the inventor of a product or process the exclusive right to manufacture, exploit, use, and sell that invention or process. *Trademarks* and *trade names* are designs and names, often officially registered, by which merchants or manufacturers designate and differentiate their products. *Copyrights* are exclusive legal rights of authors, composers, creators of software, playwrights, artists, and publishers to publish and dispose of their works. *Trade secrets* are any information that a business wishes to hold confidential. All are referred to as **intellectual property.**

intellectual property Patents, trademarks, trade names, copyrights, and trade secrets, all of which result from the exercise of someone's intellect

Trade secrets can be of great value, but each country deals with and protects them in its own fashion. The duration of protection differs, as do the products that may or may not be protected. Some countries permit the production process to be protected but not the product. International companies must study and comply with the laws of each country where they may want to manufacture, create, or sell products.

PATENTS

In the field of patents, the International Convention for the Protection of Industrial Property, sometimes referred to as the Paris Union, provides some degree of standardization. Some 168 countries adhere to this convention—even North Korea is a contracting party. Most Latin American nations and the United States are members of the Inter-American Convention, which provides protection similar to that afforded by the Paris Union.

A major step toward the harmonization of patent treatment is the European Patent Organization (EPO). Through EPO, an applicant for a patent need file only one application in English, French, or German to be granted patent protection in all 24 member-countries. Before the EPO, an applicant had to file in each country in the language of that country.

The World Intellectual Property Organization (WIPO) is a UN agency that administers 16 international intellectual property treaties. WIPO advises developing countries on such matters as running patent offices and drafting intellectual property legislation. Interest in intellectual property matters has been growing in developing countries.[4] There is also another organization called TRIPS, "trade-related aspects of intellectual property," that operates under the aegis of the World Trade Organization.

At the UN, representatives of developing nations have been mounting attacks on the exclusivity and length of patent protection. They want to shorten the protection periods from the current 15 to 20 years down to 5 years or even 30 months. But companies in industrialized countries are resisting the changes. They point out that the only incentives they have to spend the huge amounts required to develop new technology are periods of patent protection long enough to recoup their costs and make profits.

An added problem is the growth of so called "patent trolls," who can be likened to modern-day highway robbers cashing in on the problem. These are lawyers and investors who buy patents that were mistakenly granted, mostly to failed companies. In one case a patent troll claimed that a patent bought for about $50,000 was infringed by Intel's microprocessors and threatened to sue Intel for $7 billlion in damages.

TRADEMARKS

Trademark protection varies from country to country, as does its duration, which may be from 10 to 20 years. Such protection is covered by the Madrid Agreement of 1891 for most of the world, though there is also the General American Convention for Trademark and Commercial Protection for the Western Hemisphere. In addition, protection may be provided on a bilateral basis in friendship, commerce, and navigation treaties.

An important step in harmonizing the rules on trademarks was taken in 1988 when regulations for a European Union trademark were drafted. A single European Trademark Office known as the Office of Harmonization in the Internal Market (OHIM) is responsible for the recognition and protection of proprietary marks in all EU countries, including trademarks belonging to companies based in non-EU member-countries.

Many companies such as Coca-Cola market their products throughout the world and understand the importance of protecting trademarks worldwide.

TRADE NAMES

Trade names are protected in all countries that adhere to the International Convention for the Protection of Industrial Property, which was mentioned earlier in connection with patents. Goods bearing illegal trademarks or trade names or false statements about their origin are subject to seizure upon importation into these countries.

COPYRIGHTS

Copyrights are protected under the Berne Convention of 1886, which is adhered to by 77 countries, and the Universal Copyright Convention of 1954, which has been adopted by some 92 countries. The United States did not ratify the Berne Convention until 1988. At that point, it was driven to do so by the need for greater protection against pirating of computer software. We discuss software piracy in Chapter 14.

mini MNE

>>A New Understanding of Patent Theory

Economist Petra Moser's recent work reveals that economic theory might be wrong on the purpose of patents. Until recently, the common wisdom among economists was that patents existed to stimulate innovation. Her historical research uncovered an interesting detail: "Many of the best innovators in what was the high technology of the day [19th century Denmark, the Netherlands, and Switzerland] came from some of the smallest countries in Europe, and these nations did not have patent laws." Further, at that time less than one in five inventors actually relied on patents, rather than secrecy.

Source: Teresa Riordan, "Patents," *New York Times*, September 19, 2003, p. C10. Copyright 2003 The New York Times Co. Reprinted with permission See also web.mit.edu/moser/www/Research.html (June 21, 2006).

TRADE SECRETS

Laws in most nations protect trade secrets. Employers everywhere use employee secrecy agreements, which are rigorously enforced in some countries.

Common Law or Civil Law?

Historically, there has been a clear distinction between the common law, which developed in England and spread to the English colonies, and civil law, which originated on the continent of Europe. Courts made common law as they decided individual cases; kings, princes, or legislatures issuing decrees or passing bills made civil law. Judges in a common law jurisdiction have the power to *interpret* the law, while judges in a civil law jurisdiction have the power only to *apply* the law. The difference can be quite significant. Judges in common law jurisdictions have more power to expand rules to fit particular cases. The civil law, by contrast, is more rigid in its application. A judge in a civil law jurisdiction is bound by the words in the code. This strict adherence to the language of the code, though, makes the civil law system much more predictable than the common law system. As time has passed, legislatures and government agencies in the United States have made more and more laws and regulations. The courts in turn have interpreted these laws and regulations as parties have argued about what they mean.

EUROPEAN PRACTICE

Europe has a history of thousands of years of tyranny, recently evolving to democracy. Such a long history gives people in Europe greater reason to fear their governments, compared with people in the United States. Before a new law is presented to the legislature (which, unlike legislatures in the United States, is always controlled by the same political party that controls the executive branch), consensus is achieved among most of the people, businesses, and government agencies that will be affected. In contrast to U.S. practices, European legislation is rarely amended, and regulations are rarely revised. Courts are not as often asked to give their interpretations, and if they are, the decisions are rarely appealed. Once a consensus has been reached, it is considered very bad form to open the subject again, and those who do may find themselves left out of the consultations the next time around.

The EU is a grouping of sovereign nations. As explained in Chapter 4, even though all EU member-countries have yielded a certain amount of sovereignty to the EU, the EU still has limited power to implement comprehensive legislation throughout the EU. That power is increasing, though. It is important to remember that the EU establishes laws in a manner very different than does the United States. The main policy-setting institution in the EU remains the Council of Ministers, which is controlled by the national governments. The EU may some day resemble the United States in terms of lawmaking, but not yet.

UNITED STATES PRACTICE

In contrast to European custom, people and businesses in the United States have a weaker tradition of obeying governments and have had very little fear of them. U.S. citizens are much more likely than Europeans to challenge laws in the courts, in the streets, or by disobedience. Legislation in the United States is a product of an ongoing adversarial proceeding, not of consensus; law is written by one independent branch of government for execution by a second and interpretation by a third. Different political parties or people with conflicting philosophies frequently control the three different branches of government.

In the United States, laws and regulations are constantly being amended or revised by the legislatures and the agencies. Courts interpret laws in ways that are sometimes surprising; the courts may strike laws down as being unconstitutional. Legislative power is vested by the U.S. Constitution in Congress, which has the authority to write laws for the whole country, subject to veto by the president.

DIFFERENCES BETWEEN THE UNITED STATES AND ENGLAND

As this chapter shows, it is important to be aware of differences between laws in different parts of the world. Even countries such as the United States and the United Kingdom, which share many legal traditions, including the common law, have significant differences in the modern practice of law. Here are five differences between the legal systems in the United States and England:

1. *England has a split legal profession with barristers and solicitors.* In the United States, there is no distinction in the legal profession. Once admitted to practice, a lawyer in the United States can represent clients in court. In England, by contrast, clients hire solicitors to advise them on legal matters. If an appearance is necessary in court, though, in most cases the solicitor must hire a barrister. Thus, in England, each party in a court case usually must retain at least two lawyers: the solicitor and the barrister.

2. *England has no jury for civil court actions.* Pursuant to the Constitution of the United States, parties in civil actions in the United States who are seeking monetary damages generally are entitled to have their cases heard by a jury. This is not the case in England. Parties in civil cases in England can have their cases heard by a jury only in certain specific cases, which are very unusual. Criminal defendants in both countries are entitled to a jury.

3. *Payment to lawyers differs.* It is common in the United States for a lawyer to take a case on a contingency fee basis, which means the lawyer will recover a fee only when the client receives money through settlement or a trial. Usually, the fee is a percentage, such as one-third, of the amount recovered. England also has contingency fees but this arrangement is less common.

4. *Award of costs to the winner in civil litigation differs.* In litigation in the United States, attorneys' fees are awarded only in very limited cases, when a contract or statute provides for an award of those fees. In England, the losing party must pay most (usually 60 to 70 percent) of the costs, including the attorneys' fees of the winning party.

5. *Pretrial discovery differs.* There is a significant difference between the United States and England in pretrial discovery. Pretrial discovery is the opportunity for the parties to learn facts known by or to obtain documents in the possession of the other party. Even though some U.S. courts are limiting discovery, compared to England the United States allows discovery with few restrictions. In the United States, parties are able to examine witnesses before trial at what is called a *deposition.* Discovery in the United States is much more far-reaching than it is in England. In England, parties generally are entitled to receive a list of witnesses with a brief explanation of the expected testimony.

Standardizing Laws around the World

Many attempts have been made to standardize laws among various countries. To international business, the advantage of standardization is that business flows much better when there is a uniform set of rules. Worldwide harmonization is progressing slowly, though, in most areas. For now, businesspeople must confront the reality of differing standards.

In the tax area, there are tax conventions, or treaties, among nations. Each country tries to make each such treaty as similar as possible to the others, and so patterns and common provisions may be found among them.

In antitrust, the EU member-nations operate under Articles 81 and 82 of the Treaty of Rome, which are similar to the antitrust laws in the United States. In an unusual bilateral move, Germany and the United States signed an executive agreement on antitrust cooperation. This was the first attempt by national governments to cooperate on antitrust matters concerning firms operating in both countries. There have been proposals to create worldwide agreements on antitrust.

Some agreement exists in the field of international commercial arbitration, including enforcement of arbitral awards. If the disputed contract involves investment from one country into another, it can be submitted for arbitration by the International Center for Settlement of Investment Disputes at the World Bank. Chapter 4 covered a number of other UN-related organizations and other worldwide associations. Each of them has some harmonizing or standardizing effect on laws in the member-countries. The same can be said of the regional international organizations dealt with in Chapter 4.

The UN Convention on the International Sale of Goods (CISG) provides uniformity in international sales agreements for those parties who elect to use it.

There have been attempts to make accounting and bankruptcy standards uniform worldwide. A Model Law on Cross-Border Insolvencies from UNCITRAL served as the basis for Chapter 15 of the U.S. Bankruptcy Code, for example.

Two standardizing organizations are the International Organization for Standardization (ISO) and the International Electrotechnical Commission (IEC). The IEC promotes standardization of measurement, materials, and equipment in almost every sphere of electrotechnology. The ISO recommends standards in other fields of technology. Most government and private purchasing around the world demands products that meet IEC or ISO specifications. All IEC and ISO measurements are in the metric system, so there is a cost of conversion for U.S. firms exporting products without metric measurements. The number of other nations which haven't gone metric is very small.

Some Specific National Legal Forces

TAXATION

Purposes The primary purpose of certain taxes is not necessarily to raise revenue for the government, which may surprise those who have not studied taxation. Some of the many **nonrevenue tax purposes** are to redistribute income from one group to another in a country, to discourage consumption of such products as alcohol and tobacco, to encourage consumption of domestic rather than imported goods, to discourage investment abroad, to achieve equality of taxes paid by taxpayers earning comparable amounts, and to grant reciprocity to resident foreigners. Even this short list of purposes suggests the economic and political pressures influencing government officials responsible for tax legislation and collection. Powerful groups in every country push for tax policies that favor their interests. These groups and interests differ from country to country and frequently conflict, accounting in part for the complexity of the tax practices that affect multinationals.

nonrevenue tax purposes
Purposes such as redistributing income, discouraging consumption of products such as tobacco and alcohol, and encouraging purchase of domestic rather than imported products

National Differences of Approach Among the many nations of the world, there are numerous differences in tax systems.

Tax Levels Tax levels range from relatively high in some Western European countries to zero in tax havens, where income of defined types incurs no tax liability. Some countries impose capital gains taxes,* and some do not. Those countries that have them tax at different levels. The capital gains tax is controversial. Those favoring a higher capital gains tax argue that the tax rate should remain high because any reduction would reward the rich. Those who oppose a higher capital gains tax argue that the capital gains tax locks in money that would be better invested elsewhere. (A capital gains tax is imposed every time assets are sold. Thus, a high capital gains tax tends to cause money to stay put.) Some maintain that the United States should levy no capital gains tax,[5] following the example of several other countries.

Tax Types Although the United States levies a relatively high capital gains tax, it relies for most of its revenue on the income tax. As indicated by the name, this tax is levied on the income of individuals and businesses. Income taxes are common in industrialized countries. Figure 10.1 shows tax rates on wage income in the member-countries of the Organization for Economic Cooperation and Development (OECD). Among the OECD members, the United States has a fairly low income tax rate. A generality, subject to exceptions, is that the higher the income, the higher the income tax. In the 1970s and 1980s, much discontent developed among Americans over the impact of the income tax and other taxes. Possibly as a result, support for a value-added tax (VAT) has been growing in the U.S. Congress and Treasury.

Many suggest that the United States should use a VAT similar to the VATs in effect in the EU, where they are main sources of revenue. (A VAT is similar to a sales tax in that it is a tax based on the value of goods and services.) A simplified example of how a VAT works on a loaf of bread can be seen in Table 10.1. We will assume a VAT of 10 percent. The wheat farmer sells to the miller for 30 cents the part of the wheat that eventually becomes the loaf. So far, the farmer has added 30 cents of value by planting, growing, and harvesting the wheat. The farmer sets aside 3 cents (10 percent of 30 cents) to pay the VAT. The miller makes loaves of bread out of the wheat and sells them to the wholesaler for 50 cents each. Thus, the miller has added

FIGURE 10.1 Highest Statutory Personal Income Tax Rates in OECD Countries, 2003 (central government)

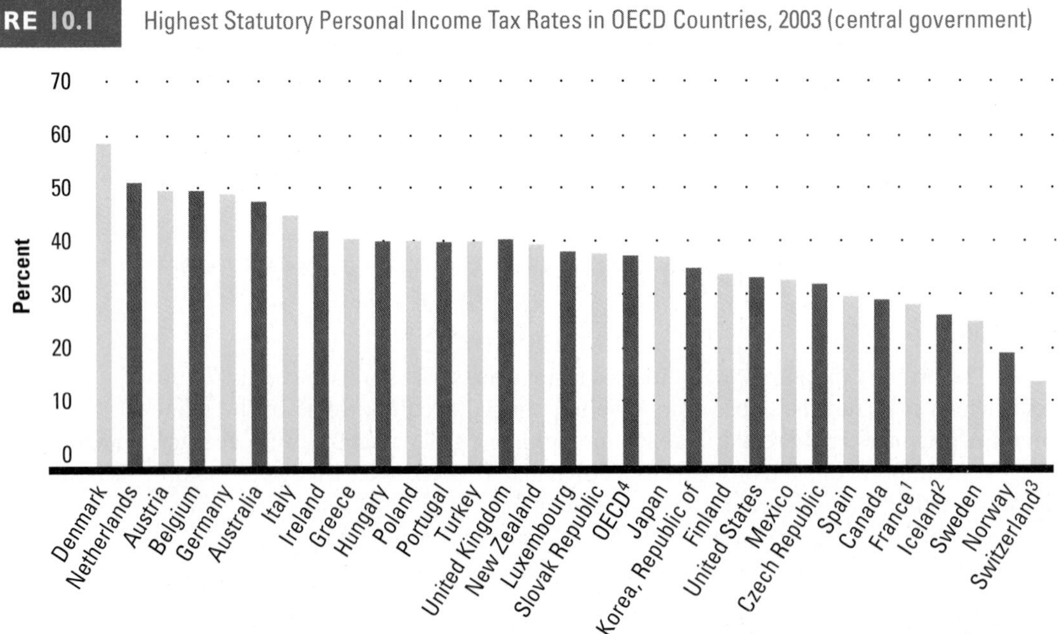

[1] Estimated rate for married taxpayers. Estimated top rate for single taxpayers is 35.7%.

[2] 2001 Rate from OECD Tax Database.

[3] The top marginal rate is 13% for spouses living together and 13.2% for other taxpayers. For incomes over CHF 788,400 and CHF 664,300, respectively, the tax rate is 11.5%.

[4] Midpoint tax rate used for countries with multiple tax rates.

Source: PricewaterhouseCoopers, *Individual Taxes 2003–2004: Worldwide Summaries* (2004).

*A capital gain is realized when an asset is sold for an amount greater than its cost.

TABLE 10.1	Value-Added Tax on a Loaf of Bread			
Stage of Production	**Selling Price**	**Value Added**	**VAT at 10%**	**Cumulative VAT**
Farmer	30¢	30¢	3¢	3¢
Miller	50¢	20¢	2¢	5¢
Wholesaler	70¢	20¢	2¢	7¢
Retailer	$1.10	40¢	4¢	11¢

20 cents of value (50 cents minus 30 cents) and must pay a VAT of 2 cents (10 percent of 20 cents). The wholesaler now advertises and distributes the loaves, selling them to retailers for 70 cents. The wholesaler has added 20 cents of value and owes 2 cents of VAT. Finally, the retailer adds 40 cents through its display, advertising, and sales efforts and owes 4 cents of VAT. The loaf of bread is sold for $1.10 retail and has borne a cumulative VAT of 11 cents, 10 percent of $1.10.

The VAT has proponents and opponents. The proponents say the VAT is relatively simple and can be raised or lowered easily to collect the amount of income desired by the government. The opponents argue that it is a consumption-type tax that bears most heavily on the poor.

In addition, some U.S. VAT proponents argue that the present situation, in which the major European countries rely heavily on the value-added tax while the United States does not, is unfair to the United States because of World Trade Organization (WTO)* regulations, which permit a rebate of VAT when a product is exported from a country but does not permit a rebate of income taxes. The rebates enable exporting countries to offer lower-priced, more competitive goods. VAT proponents want the United States to institute the VAT and lower income taxes to take advantage of these WTO rules.

Another tax on international companies that has been controversial for several decades is the unitary tax imposed by several U.S. states. Most states have since repealed such tax laws under threats of retaliation by foreign governments. International tax treaties are almost universally built on the "arm's length" or "water's edge" principle: Taxable profits for a subsidiary in a country will be assessed as though the subsidiary were conducting its business independently. The unitary tax system, by contrast, calculates the worldwide income of an international company and then assesses the tax due in proportion to the percentage of the group's property, payroll, and sales in the state.

Complexity of Tax Laws and Regulations From country to country, the complexity of tax systems differs. By anyone's standards, the United States has a very complex tax code. The U.S. Department of the Treasury's Internal Revenue Service administrates the tax code. The tax law is part of U.S. federal law and includes thousands of pages. In addition, the Department of the Treasury also writes thousands of pages of tax *regulations* explaining or expanding the tax laws.

Many provisions of the IRC refer to other provisions of the IRC, making interpretation difficult. In addition, Congress frequently changes provisions of the IRC. Congress typically debates major tax legislation in every session. Once Congress approves provisions of the IRC, it often leaves it up to the Department of the Treasury to issue regulations. The Department of the Treasury has large numbers of staff members who write these regulations. As with the IRC, the regulations issued by the Department of the Treasury run thousands of pages. In addition to the IRC and the regulations, there are numerous court decisions interpreting the tax laws.

Who Obeys the Law? Compliance with tax laws and their enforcement vary widely. Some countries, such as Germany and the United States, are strict. Others are relatively lax. Costa Rica estimates a tax evasion rate of 70%. The Italian practice allows a taxpayer to declare a very low taxable income to which the government counters with a very high amount. They then negotiate a compromise figure. It has been said that in Italy 83 percent of the people report an income of less than 4,000 Euros (about $5,110). In addition to paying

*See Chapter 4 for a discussion of the World Trade Organization.

corporate income tax, businesses in Italy may find themselves paying a chamber of commerce tax, a license tax, a trade association tax, a stamp tax, the local tax, a rental-agreement tax, a tax for registering with the office that collects the VAT, a tax for health inspection, a tax for the accounting books, a tax for the welfare system, a tax for water, and even a tax for an awning outside. By one estimate, businesses are expected to pay 300 separate taxes in Italy.[6]

Other Differences There are many other differences in taxation, too numerous to list fully here. They include tax incentives to invest in certain areas, exemptions, costs, depreciation allowances, foreign tax credits, timing, and double corporate taxation (taxation of the profits of a corporation and then of dividends paid to its stockholders). U.S. tax laws give U.S. taxpayers relief from possible double taxation by more than one jurisdiction. For example, if a U.S. taxpayer is living and working in Sweden, that taxpayer is subject to tax laws both of the United States and of Sweden. Without some form of tax relief, that taxpayer could end up paying more than 100 percent of her or his income in taxes. This tax relief comes in the form of **foreign tax credits** and provisions of various tax treaties. U.S. tax laws allow U.S. taxpayers to take a credit against their U.S. taxes for taxes paid to another country. This relief is especially important because U.S. citizens and U.S. permanent residents (green card holders) are taxed on their worldwide income regardless of the source of the income and regardless of the residence of the taxpayer.

foreign tax credits
Allowances by which U.S. taxpayers who reside and pay income taxes in another country can credit those taxes against U.S. income tax

tax treaties
Treaties between countries that bind the governments to share information about taxpayers and cooperate in tax law enforcement; often called *tax conventions*

Tax Treaties or Conventions

Because of the innumerable differences between nations' tax practices, many of them have signed **tax treaties** or tax conventions with each other. Typically, tax treaties define such things as income, source, residency, and what constitutes taxable activities in each country. They address how much each country can tax the income earned by a national of one country living or working in the other. All these treaties contain provisions for the exchange of information between the tax authorities of the two countries. The United States has tax treaties with over 50 countries. Table 10.2 lists the countries with which the United States currently has tax treaties.

TABLE 10.2 U.S. Network of Tax Treaties

The United States Has Tax Treaties with the Following Countries		
Argentina	India	Philippines
Australia	Indonesia	Poland
Austria	Ireland	Portugal
Barbados	Israel	Romania
Belgium	Italy	Russian Federation
Canada	Jamaica	Singapore
Chile	Japan	Slovak Republic
China, People's Republic of	Kazakstan	South Africa
Cyprus	Korea, Republic of	Spain
Czech Republic	Latvia	Sweden
Denmark	Lithuania	Switzerland
Egypt	Luxembourg	Thailand
Estonia	Mexico	Trinidad and Tobago
Finland	Morocco	Tunisia
France	Netherlands	Turkey
Germany	New Zealand	Ukraine
Greece	Norway	United Kingdom
Hungary	Pakistan	Uruguay
Iceland	Panama	Venezuela

Note: Some small states and territories have been omitted for purposes of brevity.
Source: "U.S. Tax Treaties," www.undefed.com/ForTaxProfs/Treaaties (November 9, 2006).

The presence or absence of a tax treaty is often a factor in international business and investment location decisions. Tax treaties make business operations much more predictable because they facilitate international flows of goods, capital, services, and technology. Countries, however, sign treaties for different motives. Most OECD countries regard treaties as providing a standard framework for all countries in allocating taxing jurisdiction. Tax treaties often determine which country will tax which income. In emerging-market countries, tax treaties may be viewed by foreign investors as a key sign of stability.[7]

The Disappearing Taxpayer

Electronic commerce—combined with the growing ease with which firms and people can shift their operations and residences from one country to another—make it easier for people to leave countries where taxes are high or to avoid taxes altogether by doing their business on the Internet, where it is often difficult to trace transactions.

Not all firms, workers, and products are equally mobile. Entrepreneurs, scientists, tennis players, and film stars may be able to uproot themselves in search of lower taxes, but the average worker is still unlikely to become a tax refugee. Thus, governments may have to cut taxes on the most mobile factors of production, notably skilled workers, while taxes on less mobile unskilled workers may rise. Other tax law changes being considered are to shift the tax base from income toward consumption and property.[8]

Taxing Americans Who Work Abroad

Observing a **national tax jurisdiction** rather than a **territorial tax jurisdiction,** the United States is almost alone among countries in taxing citizens according to nationality rather than on the basis of where they live and work. As was mentioned before, U.S. citizens and permanent residents (green card holders) are taxed on their worldwide income regardless of its source and regardless of the residence of the taxpayer. As a result, U.S. citizens and permanent residents living or working in another country must pay taxes to that country and to the United States. In addition to facing higher tax payments, these people are burdened by the time and expense of completing two sets of complicated tax returns. In 1981, the sections of the IRC dealing with this subject were again amended. Although the burden of completing two tax returns was not lifted, the new law gave relief, starting in 1982, in the amount of U.S. taxes to be paid by exempting the first $85,000 of earned income.* This exemption has been changed several times and is currently $82,400, with changes due to inflation after 2007. However, the 2006 version of the law reduces the amount of housing costs that the expat may deduct, so for most the total tax bill will increase.

national tax jurisdiction
A tax system for expatriate citizens of a country whereby the country taxes them on the basis of nationality even though they live and work abroad

territorial tax jurisdiction
A tax system in which expatriate citizens who neither live nor work in the country—and therefore receive none of the services for which taxes pay—are exempt from the country's taxes

Effect of U.S. Taxes

Suppose a U.S.-based multinational wants to open a new factory, store, warehouse, or office building in the United States. That expansion would create new jobs in the United States, along with all the benefits that flow from new jobs. But when the company's executives look at U.S. tax laws, they may hesitate because of the section dealing with allocation of interest expense. When a U.S. company with subsidiaries in many countries borrows money to finance a U.S. business, the interest is treated as if it were paid in part to finance foreign operations. That results in a partial loss of the interest tax deduction and thus a higher after-tax interest cost.

Foreign companies—including foreign-based multinationals—have no such requirement and can deduct 100 percent of interest on borrowings to finance a U.S. operation. Therefore, they have lower after-tax interest costs and, to that extent, can be more competitive in the United States than many U.S. companies.[9] Certainly, the tax code complicates the lives of U.S. businesspeople operating in other countries.

*Earned income includes salaries, bonuses, and commissions. Interest, dividend, and royalty income is called *unearned income.*

ANTITRUST LAWS

Antitrust laws are intended to prevent inappropriately large concentrations of economic power, such as monopolies. Actions brought to enforce antitrust laws usually involve government actions brought against business, but also may involve business actions against other businesses.

U.S. Laws and Attitudes Are Different—but the Differences Are Narrowing

antitrust laws
Laws to prevent price fixing, market sharing, and business monopolies

competition policy
The European Union equivalent of antitrust laws

The U.S. **antitrust laws** are strict and vigorously enforced. The U.S. Department of Justice is charged with enforcing U.S. antitrust laws. Other countries, as well as the European Union, are becoming more active in the antitrust field. In the EU, these laws sometimes are referred to as **competition policy.** The EU Commission is responsible for enforcing EU competition policy. In addition to enforcing competition policy against businesses, the EU Commission also has the power to force EU member-governments to dismantle state monopolies that block progress toward an open, communitywide market.[10]

A number of important differences in antitrust laws, regulations, and practices exist between the United States, other nations, and the EU. One difference is the per se concept of the U.S. law. Under the U.S. laws, certain activities, such as price fixing, are said to be illegal per se. This means that they are illegal even though no injury or damage results from them. The EU Treaty of Rome articles dealing with restrictive trade practices do not contain the per se illegality concept of U.S. antitrust law. For example, a cartel that allows consumers a fair share of the benefits is legally acceptable in the EU. Also, the treaty is not violated by market dominance—only by misuse of that dominance to damage competitors or consumers.

The U.S. focus on antitrust legislation is concerned with the impact of the business deal on the consumer, while the EU is more concerned about the industry's competitive structure and thus pays attention to rivals' objections.[11] In Japan, antitrust legislation was introduced by the United States during its occupation of Japan after World War II. This legislation, the Japanese Anti-Monopoly Law, was modeled on U.S. antitrust law and did not harmonize well with the existing cooperative *zaibatsu* (conglomerates) the Japanese government had established. In fact, the Japanese approach to a rational development of the economy regarded antitrust measures as an impediment. However, with increasing foreign presence, especially in the United States and in Europe, given the EU competition law, Japanese companies have incorporated antitrust thinking into their strategies. Since the Japanese culture so values cooperation, this is a challenge, especially when it comes to cartels.[12]

Worldwide Application of U.S. Antitrust Laws The U.S. government often attempts to enforce its antitrust laws extraterritorially. For example, in 1979, a grand jury in Washington, D.C., indicted three foreign-owned ocean shipping groups on charges of fixing prices without getting approval from the U.S. Federal Maritime Commission. The other governments, European and Japanese, protested bitterly, arguing (1) that shipping is international by definition, so the United States has no right to act unilaterally, and (2) that the alleged offenses were both legal and ethical practices outside the United States.[13] The U.S. Supreme Court on several occasions has permitted overseas application of U.S. antitrust laws.[14]

EU Extraterritorial Application of Its Competition Policy The EU Commission is charged with enforcement of EU competition policy. Like the U.S. Department of Justice, the EU Commission has increasingly sought enforcement of its competition policy abroad when there is an effect on commerce within the EU. For example, the EU Commission had to give its approval before merger talks between America Online and Time Warner could proceed. Before its approval was given to the merger, AOL–Time Warner had to agree to sever all ties with the German media group Bertelsmann. The EU has also viewed Microsoft as anticompetitive and in 2006 fined the firm €280 million ($358.3 million).[15]

Criminal Cases U.S. antitrust laws contain both civil and criminal penalties.* A decision by the U.S. federal court of appeals held that criminal antitrust laws apply to foreign

*Civil liability calls for payment of money damages. Criminal liability may result in fines or imprisonment.

companies even if the conspiracy took place outside the United States. While earlier decisions had permitted U.S. antitrust laws to be used against foreign companies in civil cases, this decision, which was against Nippon Paper Industries, set the precedent that antitrust laws could be used also to get criminal convictions.[16]

Japan's "Toothless Tiger" Japan's Fair Trade Commission (FTC), whose responsibility is to enforce antitrust laws, has been nicknamed the "toothless tiger." It is viewed as one of the weakest bodies in Japanese government, easily bullied by the powerful ministries of finance and international trade and industry (MITI), which have vested interests in ensuring that Japan's traditional, collaborative ways of doing business prevail. Most of the FTC's targets are small, foreign, or weak; when it has investigated powerful industries such as domestic cars, car parts, and construction, it has punished them at worst with "recommendations." The recommendations are usually accepted by the targeted company. If not, hearings follow, and then directives.

A major difference between American and Japanese trust busting is that around 90 percent of U.S. complaints are initiated by private parties, while in Japan a private antitrust action can be brought only if the FTC has investigated the case first. Because of Japan's limited discovery laws, the only way the FTC can obtain information on a firm is to raid it. As a result, the FTC won't make a move unless it is sure the laws are being broken. It is almost impossible to be sure of that without information. Given all this, it is easy to understand why the FTC is considered to be a toothless tiger.[17]

Proposal for Global Antitrust Approval It is often difficult for international businesses to comply with the variety of antitrust laws worldwide. A good example is Microsoft. In the 1990s, the U.S. government and several U.S. states brought antitrust actions against Microsoft. The actions continued well into the early 21st century, with Japan's FTC issuing a recommendation to Microsoft in July 2004. The EU also brought an action against Microsoft. The Microsoft case is a good example of how one company can get bogged down with antitrust laws in multiple jurisdictions. In light of the numerous countries that impose antitrust rules worldwide, many argue that greater worldwide cooperation in antitrust enforcement is needed. Some think that the WTO is the proper avenue for such worldwide cooperation. Others believe an international antitrust authority would be appropriate. Reaching such an agreement would be difficult because of the differing interests involved.[18] The U.S. government has proposed a world organization for the clearance of antitrust issues. If approved, the organization would probably take the form of a clearinghouse for merger filings. Calls for such an entity are increasing because of the multinational nature of most large mergers.[19]

BANKRUPTCY

In a similar vein to proposed antitrust cooperation, the World Bank has also called for a global bankruptcy agreement in light of the large number of multinational companies that have problems with creditors worldwide. It is thought that a worldwide bankruptcy agreement would make it easier for creditors and others involved in bankruptcy proceedings. Now creditors must comply with rules in various countries before receiving relief from companies in bankruptcy.[20]

TARIFFS, QUOTAS, AND OTHER TRADE OBSTACLES

Although we introduced trade obstacles in Chapter 3, they are also legal forces. For that reason, we mention them again here. Every country has laws on these subjects. The stated purpose of a tariff is to raise revenue for the government, but it may serve the additional objective of keeping certain goods out of a country. Quotas limit the number or amount of imports.

There are many other forms of protection or obstacles to trade in national laws. Some are health or packaging requirements. Others deal with language, such as the mandatory use

TABLE 10.3 Worldwide Examples of Tariffs and Other Trade Obstacles

Product	Destination	Barrier
U.S. apples	Japan	Orchard inspection, buffer zones
U.S. beverages and syrups	Mexico	20% duty on non–cane sugar sweeteners
Integrated computer circuits	China	Tax rebates for locally produced circuits give them unfair price advantage against imports
Japanese carbon steel	United States	Charges of dumping
U.S. grains	EU	EU moratorium on biotech products (genetically modified grains)
U.S. computer technology	Brazil	30% tariffs
U.S. poultry	Russia	Import restrictions (quotas)

Source: Office of U.S. Trade Representative, Monitoring and Enforcement Press Releases, www.ustra.gov (August 1, 2004).

of French on labels and in advertising, manuals, warranties, and so forth, for goods sold in France, including Web sites located on servers physically in France. Table 10.3 is a sampling of trade barriers.

In many countries, U.S. and EU exports may encounter weak patent or trademark protection, high tariffs, quarantine periods, and a variety of other obstacles.

The United States has many options in dealing with trade obstacles abroad. It can impose retaliatory barriers on products from countries imposing barriers against U.S. goods. It sometimes uses tariffs and quotas. It also uses a form of quota called by some "voluntary" restraint agreements (VRAs) and by others "voluntary" export restraints (VERs). Voluntary is in quote marks because these barriers are imposed by the U.S. government on the exporting countries. The inevitable result is higher costs to American consumers, as exporters send only the higher-priced top of their lines and importers charge more for scarcer products.[21] The United States is not the only country that imposes VRAs and VERs on its trading partners—far from it. Japan, Canada, the EU countries, and many others require that countries exporting to them "voluntarily" limit the number or value of goods exported.

Other countries have found other ways to deal with trade barriers. The French came up with a novel protectionist device. Japanese videotape recorders were one of the French imports causing a large balance-of-payments deficit with Japan. The recorders normally entered France through the major port of Le Havre, which had a large detachment of customs officers to process imports. Then the French government issued a decree requiring that all the recorders enter France through the inland city of Poitiers, which had a tiny customs post. The result was long delays that reduced the number of recorders entering France. Japan then "voluntarily" agreed to limit the number of recorders it exported to France.

TORTS

Torts are injuries inflicted on other people, either intentionally or negligently. Tort cases in the United States often result in awards of very large sums of money. Other countries have tort laws that restrict the amount of money that can be obtained in tort actions.

product liability
Standard that holds a company and its officers and directors liable and possibly subject to fines or imprisonment when their product causes death, injury, or damage

Product Liability—Civil and Criminal

One important area of torts, especially in the international arena, is **product liability.** Product liability laws hold a company and its officers and directors liable and possibly subject to fines or imprisonment when its product causes death, injury, or damage. Such liability for faulty or dangerous products was a growth area for the U.S. legal profession beginning in the 1960s. Liability insurance premiums soared, and there were concerns that smaller, weaker manufacturing companies could not survive. In the 1980s that boom spread to Europe and elsewhere. In a Conference Board survey of more than 500 chief executives, more than one-fifth believed strict U.S. product liability laws had caused their companies to lose business to foreign competitors.[22] But as foreign firms buy or build U.S. plants, they are being hit by the same liability and insurance problems long faced by U.S. companies.

Manufacturers of products are often held to a standard of **strict liability,** which holds the designer/manufacturer liable for damages caused by a product without the need for a plaintiff to prove negligence in the product's design or manufacture. There are several reasons to believe that the impact of strict liability on product designers and manufacturers in Europe and Japan will not be as heavy or severe as it is in the United States. The EU allows companies to use "state-of-the-art" or "developmental risks" defenses, which allow the designer/manufacturer to show that at the time of design or manufacture, the most modern, latest-known technology was used. They also are permitted to cap damages. By comparison, damages awarded by American juries have been in the hundreds of millions of dollars.

strict liability
Standard that holds the designer/manufacturer liable for damages caused by a product without the need for a plaintiff to prove negligence in the product's design or manufacture

Other differences in legal procedures in the United States compared with those in Europe and Japan will limit or prevent product liability awards by European and Japanese courts. As mentioned, in the United States, but not elsewhere, lawyers take many cases on a contingency fee basis whereby the lawyer charges the plaintiff no fee to begin representation and action in a product liability case. The lawyer is paid only when the defendant settles or loses in a trial, but then the fee is relatively large, running between one-third and one-half of the settlement or award. In addition, outside the United States, when the defendant wins a lawsuit, the plaintiff is often called upon to pay all the defendant's legal fees and other costs caused by the plaintiff's action.[23]

In the United States, product liability cases are heard by juries that can award plaintiffs actual damages plus punitive damages. As the name indicates, punitive damages have the purpose of punishing the defendant, and if the plaintiff has been seriously injured or the jury's sympathy can be otherwise aroused, it may award millions of dollars to "teach the defendant a lesson." Outside the United States, judges, not juries, hear product liability cases. Judges are less prone to emotional reactions than juries are, and even if the judge is sympathetic toward a plaintiff, punitive damages are not awarded by non-U.S. courts.[24]

Punitive Damage Effects on Medicine

Multimillion-dollar punitive damage awards by U.S. courts have caused foreign firms to keep their products out of the United States. For instance, Axminster Electronics, a British firm whose devices help prevent crib death by monitoring a baby's breathing, does not sell in the United States because it cannot secure product liability insurance. Within the United States, every drug company knows that if a person uses a drug and subsequently gets ill, there is a chance that a jury somewhere in the United States may impose liability on the manufacturer and order it to pay damages.[25] Merck's recent judgments in the case of Vioxx is an example.

Buyer Beware in Japan

The Japanese law on product liability requires that the plaintiff prove design or manufacturing negligence, which is difficult with complex, high-tech devices. The plaintiffs' difficulties are exacerbated by the unique Japanese legal procedures to provide discovery, the process by which plaintiffs can seek defendants' documents relevant to their cases. Discovery is available to plaintiffs in U.S. courts but is limited in Japan.[26]

MISCELLANEOUS LAWS

Individuals working abroad must be alert to avoid falling afoul of local laws and police, army, or government officials. Some examples make the point.

A Plessey employee, a British subject, is serving a life sentence in Libya for "jeopardizing the revolution by giving information to a foreign company." Two Australians were executed in Malaysia for possession of 15 grams or more of hard drugs. Saudi Arabia and other Muslim countries strictly enforce sanctions against importing or drinking alcohol and wearing revealing clothing. Foreigners in Japan who walk out of their homes without their alien registration cards *(gaikakujin Toroku)* can be arrested, as happened to one man while he was carrying out the garbage. In Thailand, people can be jailed for mutilating paper money or for

WORLD view   

Americans Accused in Film Piracy in China

In summer 2004, two American men were arrested in China and charged with intellectual piracy of motion picture DVDs. The men, Randolph Hobson Guthrie III (37) and Cody Abram Thrush (34), were taken into custody on July 1. Under Chinese law, a suspect can be held for 30 days without a formal arrest, and their arrests were announced July 29. They were tried and convicted. Both served prison sentences and paid fines. Upon their extradition to the United States, they were arrested and face trials here.

Their arrest was a result of cooperation between American and Chinese investigators and grew out of a federal operation in Gulfport, Mississippi, that spread to Houston, Washington, Beijing, and Shanghai. Chinese and American authorities seized more than 210,000 counterfeit movie DVDs and close to $1,000 in cash. In addition, authorities destroyed three warehouses used to store DVDs. The Chinese news agency Xinhua reported that the Americans had sold 1 million of the DVDs worldwide.

A *New York Times* report described a Web-based profile of Guthrie, which mentioned his MBA from Columbia University and his move to China in 1995. The site also described his claim to $25,000 monthly income from a DVD sales Web site.

The theft of intellectual property is a major problem for American filmmakers, estimated to cost them $3.5 billion a year. The Chinese government says it is committed to eliminating piracy. Vice Premier Wu Yi promised exactly this when she visited Washington. The irony of this public enforcement case involving two American businessmen whose alleged actions contribute to Chinese intellectual piracy is a good example of globalization.

Source: Michael Janofsky, "Two Americans Held in China on Charges of Film Piracy," *New York Times*, July 31, 2004, p. A12; and "The Cornerstone Report: Two Americans Convicted in China for DVD Piracy," www.ice.gov/pi/cornerstone/reports/CornerstoneReports_122805_Web3.htm (September 1, 2006).

damaging coins that bear the picture or image of the royal prince, as was one foreigner who stopped a rolling coin with his foot. Jaywalking, littering, and spitting are taken seriously in Singapore, and caning is permitted for some offenses. In China, unmarried couples—foreigners included—face a possible 10 days in jail if they stay overnight in the same room. In Greece, travelers who exceed their credit card limits may be sentenced to prison for as long as 12 years.

A Philadelphia law firm, International Legal Defense Counsel (ILDC), has made a reputation dealing with countries where American embassies and consulates are of little legal help and where prison conditions are so squalid that survival is the first concern. One of its cases involved a Virginia photographer named Conan Owen, who agreed to transport a package of cocaine from Colombia to Spain, where he was arrested and slapped with a stiff prison sentence. The U.S. attorney general personally interceded with no success, and Owen languished in prison for nearly two years. Then ILDC obtained his freedom through the use of a bilateral prisoner transfer treaty that permits American inmates in foreign jails to do their time in a facility back home. Once in the United States, Owen was quickly freed.

U.S. Laws That Affect the International Business of U.S. Firms

Although every law relating to business arguably has some effect on international activities, some laws warrant special notice. We will look briefly at several U.S. laws. Although many U.S. laws affect activities of international firms, there has not been a successful effort to coordinate them. Some are even at cross-purposes, and some diminish the ability of U.S. businesses to compete with foreign companies.

FEDERAL EMPLOYMENT LAWS

Numerous federal laws attempt in some manner to prevent unwarranted discrimination in employment. Even though there is no single federal law prohibiting illegal discrimination in employment, Title VII of the federal Civil Rights Act of 1964 is largely recognized as the focal point of federal employment discrimination law. Title VII prohibits discrimination in employment based on race, color, religion, sex, or national origin. Other major pieces of federal employment discrimination law include the Age Discrimination in Employment Act of 1967 (ADEA) and the Americans with Disabilities Act of 1990 (ADA).

Congress specifically intended these federal employment laws to apply extraterritorially. Title VII, ADEA, and ADA generally cover U.S. citizens working for U.S. companies abroad. For example, if a woman who is a U.S. citizen is denied a promotion because of her gender while working in Germany for an American company, she may bring an action in the United States under Title VII against her employer for unlawful discrimination in employment. Congress enacted one exception to the extraterritorial application of federal employment laws, though, and that is an exception for local foreign laws. It is not a violation of U.S. law for an employer to engage in conduct that ordinarily would constitute illegal behavior if such behavior is required by local law in the country where the conduct takes place. For example, certain countries prohibit women from engaging in certain activities, such as driving. If a U.S. company is required to discriminate in order to comply with the laws in such a nation, the U.S. company will be protected from suits in the United States for discrimination. Exceptions to Title VII's prohibitions, however, are extremely unusual.

FOREIGN CORRUPT PRACTICES ACT

During the 1970s, revelations of **questionable or dubious payments** by American companies to foreign officials rocked governments in the Netherlands and Japan. Congress considered corporate bribery "bad business" and "unnecessary." As a result, in 1977, Congress passed the **Foreign Corrupt Practices Act (FCPA)** and the president signed it into law.

questionable or dubious payments
Bribes paid to government officials by companies seeking purchase contracts from those governments

Foreign Corrupt Practices Act (FCPA)
U.S. law against making payments to foreign government officials for special treatment

Uncertainties

There are a number of uncertainties about terms used in the FCPA. An interesting one involves "grease." According to the FCPA's drafters, the act does not outlaw *grease,* facilitating payments made solely to expedite nondiscretionary official actions. Such actions as customs clearance and telephone calls have been cited. There is no clear distinction between supposedly legal grease payments and illegal bribes. To confuse matters further, U.S. Justice Department officials have suggested that they may prosecute some grease payments anyway under earlier antibribery laws written to get at corruption in the United States.

Other doubts raised by the FCPA concern the accounting standards it requires for compliance. That matter is connected to questions about how far management must go to learn whether any employees, subsidiaries, or agents may have violated the act; even if management were unaware of an illegal payment, it could be in violation if it "had reason to know" that some portion of a payment abroad might be used as a bribe.* [27]

The FCPA makes it unlawful to bribe foreign government officials to obtain or retain business. Facilitating payments for routine government actions such as visa issuance, import approvals, and the processing of government papers are permissible under the FCPA.

Critics at the time believed that the FCPA would harm American companies' competitiveness abroad because it would demand of American companies a higher standard of behavior than was common in the competitive environment. Congress decided that the potential economic damage to exports would be minimal and that the only companies that would be hurt would be those whose only means of competing was through the payment of bribes. The United States actively lobbied the international community to introduce similar legislation,

*Other words with similar connotations are *dash, squeeze, mordida, piston, cumshaw,* and *baksheesh.*

which it did in 1997, with the OECD Convention on Bribery. Thirty-five countries have signed the convention. There is also a UN Convention against Corruption, whose signing began in December 2003.

You may wonder if because of U.S. laws on bribery, U.S. businesses may be at a disadvantage in international competition. What seems to have happened on the bribery front is interesting. The FCPA, along with the OECD convention and the UN initiative, have brought a discussion of bribery and transparency out into the open. Such discussions were further stimulated by the Asian financial crisis of 1997, one of whose causes was widely attributed to lack of transparency in financial dealings. Having an international reputation for transparency and being perceived as "aboveboard" have become increasingly important for global companies. There appears to be a strong move for company values that support integrity in the belief that integrity is better for business than are corrupt activities.

In addition, the organization Transparency International (www.transparency.org) publishes a bribe payers index. Its data for 2006 are based on a survey of 11,232 respondents from 125 countries. The position of U.S. businesses, 10th on the list, suggests that businesspeople in the 9 nations that rank higher on the index than does the United States have found ways to conduct more transparent international business. These countries, such as Switzerland, Sweden, Canada, the Netherlands, Belgium, the United Kingdom and Germany, are headquarters for many major, competitive international companies (see Table 10.4).

ACCOUNTING LAW

Investor confidence in the integrity of financial reporting and corporate governance has been shaken by U.S. financial scandals including Enron, WorldCom, and Tyco. This crisis of confidence has substantially damaged the economic prospects of numerous companies, employees, retirees, customers, suppliers, and other stakeholders.

In the face of these concerns, the U.S. Congress passed the Sarbanes-Oxley Act in July 2002. It brings major changes to the regulation of corporate governance and financial practice. Sarbanes-Oxley addresses issues of auditor independence and attorney conduct. The act generally applies to any company, including non-U.S. companies, that has securities registered or is

TABLE 10.4 Bribe Payers Index

	Rank				Rank		
Country	2002	1999	2006	Country	2002	1999	2006
Australia	1	2	3	France	12	13	15
Sweden	2	1	2	Japan	13	14	11
Switzerland	2	5	1	United States	13	9	10
Austria	4	4	4	Malaysia	15	15	25
Canada	5	2	5	Hong Kong	15	n.a.	18
Netherlands	6	6	8	Italy	17	16	20
Belgium	6	8	9	South Korea	18	18	21
United Kingdom	8	7	6	Taiwan	19	17	26
Germany	9	9	7	China	20	19	29
Singapore	9	11	12	Russia	21	n.a.	28
Spain	11	12	13				

Source: Transparency International, "Bribe Payers Index 2002," www.transparency.org/cpi/2002/bpi2002.en.html; www. transparency.org/news_room/in_focus/bpi_2006.

required to file reports under the Securities Exchange Act of 1934. The provisions of the act affect the operation of public companies in several dimensions, including corporate governance, financial disclosure, officer and director activities and responsibilities, and auditor independence. The act also creates and regulates the Public Company Accounting Oversight Board to oversee public company audits and establishes conflict-of-interest rules for securities analysts. Most notably, the act bars a company's outside auditors from consulting and advising roles with the company; it requires CEO and CFO sign-off on financial statements; it requires the reporting of any off–balance sheet transactions; and it requires the independence of security analysts.

U.S. accounting practice is guided by the Securities and Exchange Commission (SEC) and the Financial Accounting Standards Board (FASB) and follows standards known as Generally Accepted Accounting Principles (GAAP), while many other countries, including those in the EU, follow standards issued by the International Accounting Standards Board (IAS) and the International Financial Reporting Standards (IFRS) issued by the European Federation of Accountants. These various standards differ in many aspects. The reporting requirements of Sarbanes-Oxley may lead to some harmonization of accounting standards across international markets, yet the trend outside the United States appears to be toward IAS.

Summary

Discuss the complexity of the legal forces that confront international business.

International business is affected by many thousands of laws and regulations issued by states, nations, and international organizations. Some are at cross-purposes, and some diminish the ability of firms to compete with foreign companies.

Recognize the importance of foreign law.

Miscellaneous laws in host countries can trip up foreign businesspeople or tourists. Charges can range from not carrying an alien registration card to narcotics possession.

Explain contract devices and institutions that assist in interpreting or enforcing international contracts.

International contracts should specify which country's law and courts should apply when disputes arise. The UN's CISG and the EU's Rome Convention have established rules for solving contract disputes. Arbitration is an increasingly popular solution.

Recognize the need and methods to protect your intellectual property.

Patents, trademarks, trade names, copyrights, and trade secrets are referred to as intellectual properties. Pirating of those properties is common and is expensive for their owners. The UN's World Intellectual Property Organization (WIPO) was created to administer international property treaties, as was TRIPS, a WTO agency with a similar purpose.

Recognize that many taxes have purposes other than to raise revenue.

Certain taxes have purposes other than to raise revenues. For example, some aim to redistribute income, discourage consumption of certain products, encourage use of domestic goods, or discourage investment abroad. In addition, taxes differ from country to country. Tax treaties, or conventions, between countries can affect decisions on investment and location.

Discuss enforcement of antitrust laws.

The United States and the European Union enforce antitrust laws extraterritorially. This is a concern for companies operating in many countries because of the complexity of dealing with so many laws in different jurisdictions.

Explain the risk of product liability legal actions, which can result in imprisonment for employees or fines for them and the company.

Product liability refers to the civil or criminal liability of the designer or manufacturer of a product for injury or damages it causes. In several ways, product liability is treated differently in the U.S. legal system than it is in other countries. For example, only in the United States does one find lawyers' contingency fees, jury trials of these cases, and punitive damages. Although the principle of strict liability has been adopted in Europe, defendants are permitted to use state-of-the-art defenses and countries can put a cap on damages. Product liability is virtually unknown in Japan.

Discuss some of the U.S. laws that affect international business operations.

Many U.S. laws affect international business operations, both of U.S. and of foreign companies. The United States applies federal employment laws to any U.S. company operating anywhere. This extraterritoriality means that U.S. companies operating in foreign countries are required to follow U.S. employment law as it applies to U.S. nationals. The Foreign Corrupt Practices Act and the Sarbanes-Oxley Act also apply to U.S. businesses in their foreign operations and to foreign businesses that conduct operations in the United States.

Key Words

public international law (p. 280)
private international law (p. 280)
treaties (p. 280)
extraterritorial application of laws (p. 281)
arbitration (p. 282)
intellectual property (p. 283)
nonrevenue tax purposes (p. 287)
foreign tax credits (p. 290)
tax treaties (p. 290)
national tax jurisdiction (p. 291)
territorial tax jurisdiction (p. 291)
antitrust laws (p. 292)
competition policy (p. 292)
product liability (p. 294)
strict liability (p. 295)
questionable or dubious payments (p. 297)
Foreign Corrupt Practices Act (FCPA) (p. 297)

Questions

1. What is the significance of determining whether a country follows the rule of law?
2. How does international law differ from national law? What are the sources of international law?
3. What objections do other countries have to extraterritorial application by the United States of its laws?
4. What are advantages of submitting contract disputes to arbitration instead of to litigation in courts?
5. Why do companies concern themselves with intellectual property issues?
6. Often taxes are used for reasons other than raising revenues. What are the other purposes for which taxes are used?
7. Why do some people feel that a VAT should replace some or all of the U.S. income tax?
8. Are tariffs the only type of obstacle to international trade? If not, name some others.
9. Can product liability be criminal? If so, in what sorts of situations would product liability become criminal behavior?
10. a. What are the differences in practices between the legal systems in the United States and England?
    b. What are the reasons for those differences?

Research Task

globalEDGE.msu.edu 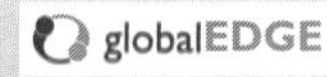

Use the globalEDGE site (http://globalEDGE.msu.edu) to complete the following exercises:

1. Prior to internationalizing your corporate legal representation firm, management is hoping to better understand which countries efficiently enforce legal contracts. The *Doing Business Indicators* follow statistics on many countries and regions of the world to provide users with an indication of the economic and legal conditions worldwide. Locate the three measures used by the resource to measure how different countries are enforcing contracts. Which countries rank as the five most and least efficient legal systems for each measure? Do any countries appear multiple times across these rankings? If so, list the countries that would be most and least appealing for your firm to enter. If not, are there specific regions that are represented in your analysis? From this information, develop a brief report for management that outlines your recommendation for an internationalization strategy.
2. The *Corruption Perceptions Index (CPI)* is a comparative assessment of a country's integrity performance. Provide a description of this index and its ranking. Identify the five countries with the lowest and the five with the highest CPI scores according to this index. Do you see any trends between CPI scores and the level of economic and social development of a country?

Italian Law Minicase 10.1

A California-based company is expanding very well and has just made its first export sale. All of its sales and procurement contracts up to now have contained a clause providing that if any disputes arise under the contract, they will be settled under California law and that any litigation will be in California courts.

The new foreign customer, who is Italian, objects to these all-California solutions. She says she is buying and paying for the products, so the California company should compromise and allow Italian law and courts to govern and handle any disputes.

You are the CEO of the California company, and you very much want this order. You are pleased with the service your law firm has given, but you know it has no international experience.

What are the various forms of dispute resolution available to your California company? What are the advantages and disadvantages of each for your company?

11 Financial Forces

Money makes the world go round
The world go round, the world go round
Money makes the world go round
It makes the world go round
A mark, a yen, a buck or a pound
A buck or a pound, a buck or a pound
Is all that makes the world go round
That clinking, clanking sound
Can make the world go round

—*Kander and Ebb, "Money, Money, Money,"* Cabaret

U.S. Consumers Credited with Saving the World from Recession: Heavy Lifting May Be Over

The U.S. consumers have been like Atlas recently, carrying the world on their shoulders. Larry Summers, former Treasury secretary under President Clinton and former president of Harvard University, likens the world economy to a plane flying on one engine, the U.S. economy.[a] The spending of Americans has been relentless, compared to that of Europeans and Asians, despite serious stock market dips, the Katrina natural disaster, terrorism, and war. A wide range of economists suggests that this spending has been an important factor in averting a deep world recession. This Atlas-like role has come at a cost to the United States: a huge current account deficit in the balance of payments. It looks, though, as if economic growth is evening out at last. Japan, the EU, and many emerging economies seem poised for increased growth.

Although U.S. consumers have been the main engine of their own economy and, Atlas-like, of the whole world's, the global economy may now be less vulnerable. This judgment is based on a view presented at the World Economic Forum in Davos in February 2006 by the chief economist at Goldman Sachs, Jim O'Neill. He argued that any slowdown in the United States would not lead to a global slowdown.

In Japan, industrial output jumped by an annual rate of 11 percent in the fourth quarter of 2005. Japan's labor market is also strengthening. In December the ratio of vacancies to job applicants rose to its highest since 1992. It is easier to find a job now than at any time since the Japanese bubble burst in the early 1990s. Stronger hiring by firms is also pushing up wages after years of decline. Workers are enjoying the biggest rise in bonuses for over a decade. That means that people are shopping again in Japan, 3.2 percent more in December 2005 than a year earlier. Domestic consumption growth in Japan suggests that exports will play a less significant role in Japan's economic health. Retail sales are reported to have risen in 2005 for the first time since 1996.

In Europe, the European Commission's surveys of business sentiment are showing positive results. They indicate that domestic demand has also been the main source of growth in Europe. *The Economist* reports that Germany's domestic demand is expected to contribute more to growth in 2006 than its net exports will. According to Morgan Stanley, since 1999 Germany has been the source of 95 percent of the EU's GDP growth.

In addition to stronger domestic demand in Japan and the EU, emerging economies appear to be building domestic demand. Goldman Sachs' calculations indicate that Brazil, Russia, India and China combined have in recent years contributed more to the world's domestic demand than to its GDP growth.

This growth suggests that a slowdown in the United States need not halt the economies of the rest of the world. Ten years ago it would have. The increase in domestic consumption suggests that the economies will be more stable and resistant to external shocks than they would be if they were export-dependent. Today, Europe and Japan combined account for a larger portion of global GDP than does the United States. Increased growth there will help to keep the global economy flying.

One of the outcomes of huge rates of U.S. consumption is the huge deficit in the U.S. current account. A rebalancing of demand away from the United States to the rest of the world might also shrink this deficit. ■

[a]"The World Economy: Testing All Engines," *The Economist,* February 2, 2006, www.economist.com/displaystory.cfm?story_id=5474963 (accessed June 25, 2006).

Source: Christopher Swann, "Carefree Spenders Take Care of World Economy," *Financial Times,* February 10, 2004, p. 7.

CONCEPT PREVIEWS

After reading this chapter, you should be able to:

explain how money can be made—and lost—in the foreign exchange (FX) markets

understand FX quotations, including cross rates

describe currency exchange controls

explain how financial forces such as tariffs, taxes, inflation, and the balance of payments affect international management

Gli Affari Internazionali
onales
nales Geschäft Παγοσμιο Business
Negócios Internacionais Los Negócios Internacionais
ternacionales Affaires Internationales 国際商務 Παγοσμιο Business

In this chapter, we discuss the uncontrollable financial forces that confront international managers. These forces include currency exchange rate fluctuation and its related exchange risk, as well as other financial forces that are external to the firm but have a great impact on the firm's management, such as currency exchange controls, tariffs, taxation, inflation, and national-level balance-of-payments account balances. *Uncontrollable* means that these financial forces originate outside the business and are beyond its influence. However, financial managers of a company are not helpless in the face of these forces. Possible ways to manage around them are discussed in Chapter 21, where we consider financial management.

In the sections below, we look at exchange rate quotations, the causes of exchange rate fluctuations, and exchange rate forecasting. We also look at currency exchange controls, tariffs, taxation, inflation, and balance-of-payments accounts as the sources of other, external financial forces in whose context international managers need to operate.

Fluctuating Currency Values

In a post–Bretton Woods monetary system, freely floating currencies fluctuate against each other. At times, central banks occasionally intervene in the foreign exchange markets by buying and selling large amounts of a currency, yet, for the most part, the major currencies (the U.S. dollar, the British pound sterling, the Japanese yen, and the European Union euro) are allowed by their central banks to fluctuate freely against each other. As we discussed in Chapter 5, these fluctuations may be quite large. For example, in January 1999, the euro rate was established at US$1.1667. In May 2000, the euro had sunk to US$0.8895, a 23.75 percent drop. Then the trend reversed, as Figure 11.1 indicates, and by June 2006, the euro was trading at US$1.2644, an increase of 42.14 percent over its May 2000 rate. The euro had strengthened considerably against the dollar.

Such fluctuations have considerable impact on financial transactions. Imagine that you are operating with U.S. dollar earnings and that in May 2000 you signed a purchase agreement for the amount of $100,000, payable in euro when you receive your purchase. At that time, the cost of each euro was $0.8895. Now your purchase arrives, but the cost of each euro has risen to $1. So every euro costs you $0.1105 more than it did when you committed to the purchase. Your $100,000 purchase will cost you $11,050 more in U.S. dollars. That's a substantial difference. Why these currency fluctuations occur, that is, what forces determine exchange rates, is our focus below. We begin with an explanation of foreign exchange (FX) quotations and then move on to their causes.

FIGURE 11.1

U.S. Dollar to Euro Exchange Rate

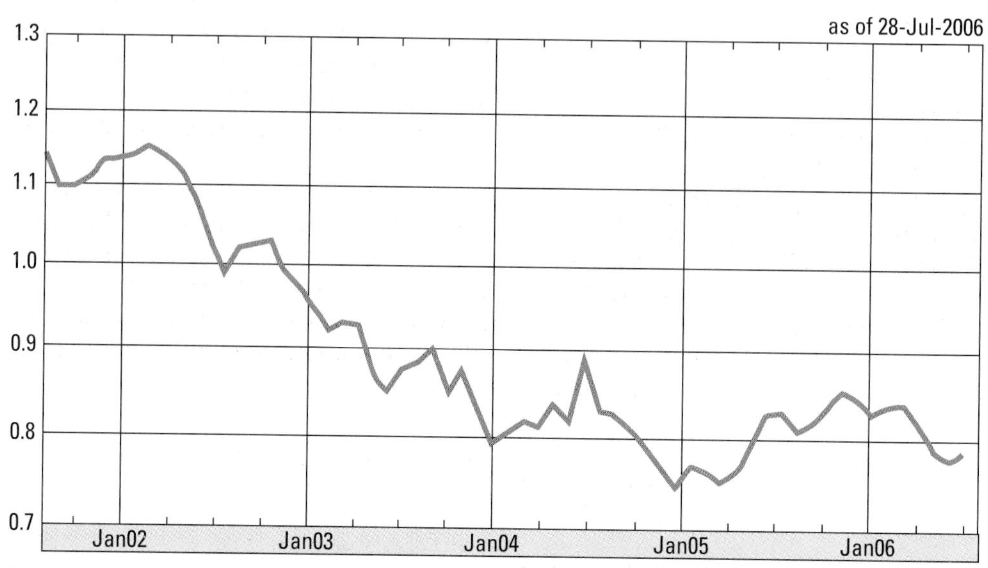

Source: Copyright 2006 Yahoo Inc.

WORLD view

Other Countries Use the $ Symbol Too

In the United States, the symbol "$" generally refers to U.S. dollars. One must be careful, as the $ symbol is also used elsewhere in the world to denote local currencies. For example, Australia, Canada, and New Zealand call the local currency the dollar and use the $ symbol to refer to the local currency, as do Singapore, Taiwan, and Zimbabwe. The same is true in Hong Kong. And Mexico, which calls its currency the peso, uses the $ symbol to denote the Mexican peso. Argentina's peso, Brazil's real, and Chile's peso also use the dollar sign to indicate their currency.

Foreign Exchange

Foreign exchange quotations—the price of one currency expressed in terms of another—usually are reported in the world's currency exchange markets in terms of the U.S. dollar. Recent research shows that from 1998 to 2001, the U.S. dollar was on one side of around 90 percent of the foreign exchange transactions.[1] Even if a holder of Japanese yen wants British pounds, the trade, particularly if it involves a large amount, usually will be to buy U.S. dollars with the yen and then to buy pounds with the U.S. dollars. The reasons for this procedure are both historical and practical. On the historical side, the procedure goes back to Bretton Woods and the fixed rate exchange system with the dollar pegged to gold. The practical reasons for the continuing central position of the US$ in the foreign exchange process involve the functions it performs in the world. It is a main **central reserve asset** of many countries. It is the most used **vehicle currency** and **intervention currency.**

central reserve asset
Asset, usually currency, held by a government's central bank

vehicle currency
A currency used as a vehicle for international trade or investment

intervention currency
A currency used by a country to intervene in the foreign currency exchange markets, often to buy (strengthen) its own currency

EXCHANGE RATE QUOTATIONS

Figure 11.2 is the listing of currency trading from *The Wall Street Journal* for the two business days preceding Tuesday, June 20, 2006. Figure 11.2 is divided into two main sections, "Key Currency Cross Rates" and "Exchange Rates." We will look at exchange rates first.

The Exchange Rates part of Figure 11.2 shows the US$ equivalent rate and the currency per US$ rate. The *US$ equivalent rate* is the cost in U.S. dollars of one unit of another currency. For example, the price (indicated as the US$ equivalent rate) of Switzerland's currency, the franc, on Monday, June 19, 2006, was .8058. This means that 1 Swiss franc cost US$0.8058, or about 80.5 cents. For another example, look at the Japanese yen, which is quoted at .008664. Each yen costs that fraction of a dollar, less than but approaching 1 cent. An example of a currency that costs more than a U.S. dollar is the British pound, listed under "U.K." at $1.8412, meaning 1 pound can be purchased for about $1.84.

We have looked at the cost of foreign currency in U.S. dollars. The *currency per US$ rate,* on the other hand, is the price of 1 U.S. dollar in the other currency, or how much of the foreign currency 1 U.S. dollar will buy. The currency per US$ rate of the Australian dollar for Monday, June 19, 2006, was 1.3574. That means 1 U.S. dollar costs about 1.36 Australian dollars.

Depending on the transaction, you may want to convert from the US$ equivalent rate to the currency per US$ rate. By using the reciprocal of the US$ equivalent rate, you can reach the currency per US$ rate, and vice versa:

$$\frac{1}{\text{US\$ equivalent rate}} = \text{currency per US\$ rate}$$

$$\frac{1}{\text{currency per US\$ rate}} = \text{US\$ equivalent rate}$$

FIGURE 11.2

Exchange Rates for June 19 and June 16, 2006

Key Currency Cross Rates

Late New York Trading Monday, June 19, 2006

	Dollar	Euro	Pound	SFranc	Peso	Yen	CdnDlr
Canada	1.1197	1.4082	2.0616	0.9023	.09753	.00970	...
Japan	115.42	145.16	212.51	93.006	10.053	...	103.082
Mexico	11.4811	14.4397	21.139	9.2514	...	.09947	10.2537
Switzerland	1.241	1.5608	2.2849	...	.10809	.01075	1.1083
U.K.	.54310	.6831	...	.4376	.04731	.00471	.48506
Euro	.79510	...	1.4639	.64069	.06925	.00689	.71011
U.S.	...	1.2577	1.8412	.80580	.08710	.00866	.89310

Source: Reuters

06.20.06 PA-16 WSJ.

Exchange Rates

June 19, 2006

The foreign exchange mid-range rates below apply to trading among banks in amounts of $1 million and more, as quoted at 4 p.m. Eastern time by Reuters and other sources. Retail transactions provide fewer units of foreign currency per dollar.

	U.S. $ EQUIVALENT		CURRENCY PER U.S. $	
Country	**Mon**	**Fri**	**Mon**	**Fri**
Argentina (Peso)-y	.3248	.3248	3.0788	3.0788
Australia (Dollar)	.7367	.7389	1.3574	1.3534
Bahrain (Dinar)	2.6525	2.6524	.3770	.3770
Brazil (Real)	.4440	.4456	2.2523	2.2442
Canada (Dollar)	.8931	.8909	1.1197	1.1225
1-month forward	.8938	.8916	1.1188	1.1216
3-months forward	.8955	.8933	1.1167	1.1194
6-months forward	.8980	.8958	1.1136	1.1163
Chile (Peso)	.001824	.001835	548.25	544.96
China (Renminbi)	.1249	.1250	8.0077	7.9983
Colombia (Peso)	.0003909	.0003909	2558.20	2558.20
Czech. Rep.(Koruna)				
Commercial rate	.04414	.04433	22.655	22.558
Denmark (Krone)	.1687	.1695	5.9277	5.8997
Ecuador (US Dollar)	1.0000	1.0000	1.0000	1.0000
Egypt (Pound)-y	.1738	.1737	5.7551	5.7574
Hong Kong (Dollar)	.1288	.1288	7.7663	7.7639
Hungary (Forint)	.004545	.004621	220.02	216.40
India (Rupee)	.02185	.02188	45.767	45.704
Indonesia (Rupiah)	.0001066	.0001076	9381	9294
Israel (Shekel)	.2248	.2252	4.4484	4.4405
Japan (Yen)	.008664	.008686	115.42	115.13
1-month forward	.008701	.008723	114.93	114.64
3-months forward	.008777	.008800	113.93	113.64
6-months forward	.008890	.008913	112.49	112.20
Jordan (Dinar)	1.4114	1.4112	.7085	.7086
Kuwait (Dinar)	3.4577	3.4583	.2892	.2892
Lebanon (Pound)	.0006634	.0006634	1507.39	1507.39
Malaysia (Ringgit)-b	.2726	.2746	3.6684	3.6417
Malta (Ura)	2.9297	2.9454	.3413	.3395
Mexico (Peso)				
Floating rate	.0871	.0874	11.4811	11.4390
New Zealand (Dollar)	.6166	.6177	1.6218	1.6189
Norway (Krone)	.1601	.1610	6.2461	6.2112
Pakistan (Rupee)	.01655	.01656	60.423	60.387
Peru (new Sol)	.3063	.3064	3.2648	3.2637
Philippines (Peso)	.01878	.01882	53.248	53.135
Poland (Zloty)	.3087	.3116	3.2394	3.2092
Russia (Ruble)-a	.03697	.03715	27.049	26.918
Saudi Arabia (Riyal)	.2666	.2666	3.7509	3.7509
Singapore (Dollar)	.6258	.6272	1.5980	1.5944
Solvak Rep. (Koruna)	.03299	.03327	30.312	30.057
South Africa (Rand)	.1427	.1451	7.0077	6.8918
South Korea (Won)	.0010404	.0010463	961.17	955.75
Sweden (Krona)	.1354	.1362	7.3855	7.3421
Switzerland (Franc)	.8058	.8124	1.2410	1.2309
1-month forward	.8084	.8150	1.2370	1.2270
3-months forward	.8139	.8206	1.2287	1.2186
6-months forward	.8218	.8285	1.2168	1.2070
Taiwan (Dollar)	.03069	.03080	32.584	32.468
Thailand (Baht)	.02599	.02601	38.476	38.447
Turkey (New Lira)-d	.6248	.6307	1.6005	1.5855
U.K. (Pound)	1.8412	1.8498	.5431	.5406
1-month forward	1.8422	1.8508	.5428	.5403
3-months forward	1.8448	1.8534	.5421	.5395
6-months forward	1.8483	1.8571	.5410	.5385
United Arab (Dirham)	.2724	.2724	3.6711	3.6711
Uraguay (Peso)				
Financial	.04200	.04200	23.810	23.810
Venezuela (Bollvar)	.000466	.000466	2145.92	2145.92
SDR	1.4737	1.4734	.6786	.6764
Euro	1.2577	1.2639	.7951	.7912

Special Drawing Rights (SDR) are based on exchange rates for the U.S., British, and Japanese currencies. Source: International Monetary Fund.

a-Russian Central Bank rate. b-Government rate. d-Rebased as of Jan. 1, 2005. y-Floating rate.

Source: *The Wall Street Journal.*

spot rate
The exchange rate between two currencies for delivery within two business days

forward currency market
Trading market for currency contracts deliverable 30, 60, 90, or 180 days in the future

forward rate
The exchange rate between two currencies for delivery in the future, usually 30, 60, 90, or 180 days

There is more to be learned from reading the exchange rate quotes. The Exchange Rates part of Figure 11.2 includes rates for the preceding Friday. Comparing the two prices tells you whether the currency is weakening or strengthening in the short term. For example, on Friday, June 16, 1 dollar would buy 115.13 Japanese yen. After the weekend, on Monday, that dollar would buy 115.42 yen. The dollar can buy more yen, so we describe it as strengthening against the yen; that is, the yen is weakening against the dollar. From Friday to Monday, the yen became cheaper or less expensive in dollar terms. Such rates are called the **spot rate,** the exchange rate for a trade today for delivery within two days. The spot rate for the euro on Friday, June 16, was $0.7912. By the way, the spot rate on Monday, after the weekend, was $0.7951, so the dollar was weakening against the euro. The euro was trading *at a premium* to the dollar.

You'll note, too, that *The Wall Street Journal* quotes a 1-, 3-, and 6-month price for several currencies, the yen, the Canadian dollar, the Swiss franc, and the British pound sterling. Those forward prices in dollar terms (U.S. equivalent) show what the market expects of the currency in these time periods. The **forward currency market** allows managers to lock in purchases of other currencies at known rates. The **forward rate** is the cost today for a commitment to buy or sell an agreed amount of a currency at a fixed, future date. The commitment is a forward contract, and for frequently traded currencies such as those listed in *The Wall Street Journal,* contracts are usually available on a 30-, 60-, 90-, or 180-day basis. You also may be able to negotiate with banks for different time periods or for contracts in other currencies.

In the Exchange Rates part of Figure 11.2, look under "Switzerland" and refer to the Swiss franc (CHF) one-month forward US$ equivalent quotation. For Monday, June 19, 2006, CHF 1 bought US$0.8084. Compare that rate with the spot rate of US$0.8058, and you will see that 1 Swiss franc will buy more dollars for delivery in one month than for delivery today. And the trend continues in the forward market quotes. The Swiss franc is **trading at a premium** in the forward market. If a currency's forward rate quotes are weaker than the spot rate, the currency is said to be **trading at a discount** in the forward market.

trading at a premium
Situation in which a currency's forward rate quotes are stronger than spot

trading at a discount
Situation in which a currency's forward rate quotes are weaker than spot

Whether there is a premium or a discount and what its size is depend on the expectations of the world financial community, businesses, individuals, and governments about what the future will bring. These expectations factor in such considerations as supply and demand forecasts for the two currencies, relative inflation in the two countries, relative productivity and unit labor cost changes, expected election results or other political developments, expected government fiscal, monetary, and currency exchange market actions, balance-of-payments accounts, and a psychological aspect.[2]

Look again, in Figure 11.2, at the "Currency per U.S. $" column for Monday, and you will see that it took not quite 115.5 yen to buy 1 U.S. dollar, whereas in the United Kingdom, a little over half a pound (.5431) was enough for a dollar. Glancing up and down the column, you find that an Indonesian rupiah holder would need over 9381 rupiahs for US$1 and that holders of each of the other currencies quoted require a different number. It might seem that the fewer units of a currency required to buy a dollar, the "harder" or better that currency is compared to the others, but that is not the case. Look at Japan, for example, an expensive market for dollar-based consumers. Note that currency prices alone tell us nothing about the relative purchasing power of the foreign currency.

Now turn to the "Key Currency Cross Rates" section of Figure 11.2. In addition to the U.S. dollar, currencies of other developed countries are also important in world transactions and are becoming more important. This is particularly true of the Japanese yen and the EU euro. Many expect the euro to become as frequently used as the dollar, both for transactions and as a reserve currency. Although most large currency exchanges go through the US$, it is possible to find exchange rates for trading directly between non-U.S. dollar currencies. These rates are called **cross rates.**

cross rates
Currency exchange rates for trading directly between non-US$ currencies

Until now, we have not discussed the way the foreign exchange market actually operates. Most of the transactions in the foreign exchange market are *over the counter (OTC),* meaning that there is no actual trading floor; trades are done electronically. Most of the market is composed of banks and other large financial institutions such as pension funds and mutual funds. Prices consist of a **bid price** and an **ask price,** with the bid lower than the ask. "Buy low, sell high" is the general approach to currency trading. The difference between the two prices, known as the *bid-ask spread,* provides a margin for the bank or agency. The rates listed in financial publications, such as those we are using from *The Wall Street Journal,* are interbank rates, for customers buying large quantities, usually US$1 million or more. The rates charged to small customers are much less favorable to the customer. Banks intend to make a profit in currency transactions.

bid price
Price offered to buy

ask price
Sales price

As you can imagine, the FX markets are large, liquid, and quite competitive, with 24-hour trading through international banks. The Bank for International Settlements reported daily turnover averages in the foreign exchange markets at $1.9 billion for 2004.[3] The FX markets are largely unregulated, as well. A *Wall Street Journal* article described them as "a Wild West of global capitalism where more than $1.2 trillion [2002] changes hands each day. Unlike major stock and commodities markets, the foreign-exchange market, or FX, operates with virtually no government or regulatory oversight."[4] In a world where many would say we are overregulated, this sector stands out.

CAUSES OF EXCHANGE RATE FLUCTUATION

Since 1973, the relative values of floating currencies and the ease of their convertibility have been set by market forces, which are influenced by many factors, including basic supply and demand of the currency, interest rates, inflation rates, and expectations of the future. Monetary

monetary policies Government policies that control the amount of money in circulation and its growth rate

fiscal policies Policies that address the collecting and spending of money by the government

law of one price Concept that in an efficient market, like products will have like prices

arbitrage The process of buying and selling instantaneously to make profit with no risk

Fisher effect The relationship between real and nominal interest rates: The real interest rate will be the nominal interest rate minus the expected rate of inflation

international Fisher effect Concept that the interest rate differentials for any two currencies will reflect the expected change in their exchange rates

purchasing power parity (PPP) Theory that predicts that currency exchange rates between two countries should equal the ratio of the price levels of their commodity baskets

and fiscal policies of the government, such as decisions on taxation, interest rates, and trade policies, and other forces external to the business, such as world events, all may play significant roles in this process. **Monetary policies** of a government control the amount of money in circulation, whether it is growing, and, if so, at what pace. **Fiscal policies** address the collecting and spending of money by the government.

What determines exchange rates is a wide and complex variety of factors, such that economists have not yet developed a widely accepted theory that explains them. However, most economists would agree that inflation, interest rates, and market expectations play central roles in exchange rate determination. Economists have determined several *parity relationships,* that is, relationships of equivalence, among some of the various complex factors involved in exchange rate movements. We look now at two of these relationships, interest rate parity and purchasing power parity, because they are fundamental to our further consideration of exchange rates. They both rest on the **law of one price,** which states that in an efficient market, like products will have like prices. If there are differences, the process of **arbitrage** (buying and selling to make a profit with no risk) will quickly close any gaps and the markets will be at equilibrium.

When the law of one price is applied to interest rates, it suggests that interest rates vary to take account of different anticipated levels of inflation. An investor would want to earn more in a high-inflation environment to compensate for the effect of inflation on the investment. The economic explanation of this relationship, which results in interest rate parity, is the **Fisher effect.** It states that the real interest rate will be the nominal interest rate minus the expected rate of inflation. Where the real rate of interest (r_r) is equal to the nominal interest rate (r_n) minus the expected rate of inflation (I):

$$r_r = (r_n) - I$$

So an increase in the expected inflation rate will lead to an increase in the interest rate. A decrease in the expected inflation rate will lead to a decrease in the interest rate.

The difference between the nominal interest rates in two countries reflects the expected change in exchange rates. For example, if the nominal interest rate in the United States is 5 percent per year and in the EU it is 3 percent, we would expect the dollar to decrease against the euro by 2 percent over the year. This is known as the **international Fisher effect:** The interest rate differentials for any two currencies reflect the expected change in their exchange rates.[5]

A second parity relationship is **purchasing power parity (PPP).** PPP is the result of the law of one price applied to a basket of commodity goods. PPP suggests that for a dollar to buy as much in the United Kingdom as in the United States, the cost of the goods in the UK should equal their U.S. cost times the exchange rate between the dollar and pound. This relationship is expressed in the following equation, where P is the price of a basket of commodity goods,

$$£P(\$/£) = \$P$$

Another way to think about what the PPP theory states is that currency exchange rates between two countries should equal the ratio of the price levels of their commodity baskets. That is, for the British pound sterling (£) and the U.S. dollar, where P is the price of a basket of commodity goods,

$$(\$/£) = \$P/£P$$

For example if a basket of goods costs $1,500 in the United States and £1,000 in the United Kingdom, the PPP exchange rate would be $1.50/£. If, in the trading market, the actual spot exchange rate was $2/£, the pound would be overvalued by 33 percent, or, equivalently, the dollar undervalued by 25 percent.

The Economist, a British weekly focused on, as its name suggests, economic news, presents a playful application of PPP theory twice a year. It compiles a "Big Mac index," using PPP theory and substituting a Big Mac for a basket of goods. This index, whose May 2006 figures are displayed in Table 11.1, suggests that, in the long term, many of the developing countries' currencies are undervalued and the euro and many European currencies are overvalued. The Big Mac PPP is the exchange rate that would have burgers in other countries costing what

TABLE 11.1 The Big Mac Index

	Big Mac Prices				
	In Local Currency	In Dollars	Implied PPP[*] of the Dollar	Actual Dollar Exchange Rate May 22	Under (−)/ Over (+) Valuation Against the Dollar, %
United States[†]	$3.10	3.10	–	–	–
Argentina	Peso 7.00	2.29	2.26	3.06	−26
Australia	A$3.25	2.44	1.05	1.33	−21
Brazil	Real 6.40	2.78	2.06	2.30	−10
Britain	£1.94	3.65	1.60[‡]	1.88[‡]	+18
Canada	C$3.52	3.14	1.14	1.12	+1
Chile	Peso 1,560	2.94	503	530	−5
China	Yuan 10.5	1.31	3.39	8.03	−58
Czech Republic	Koruna 59.05	2.67	19.0	22.1	−14
Denmark	DKr27.75	4.77	8.95	5.82	+54
Egypt	Pound 9.50	1.65	3.06	5.77	−47
Euro area[ß]	€2.94	3.77	1.05[∂]	1.28[∂]	+22
Hong Kong	HK$12	1.55	3.87	7.75	−50
Hungary	Forint 560	2.71	181	206	−12
Indonesia	Rupiah 14,600	1.57	4,710	9,325	−49
Japan	¥250	2.23	80.6	112	−28
Malaysia	Ringgit 5.50	1.52	1.77	3.63	−51
Mexico	Peso 29.00	2.57	9.35	11.3	−17
New Zealand	NZ$4.45	2.75	1.44	1.62	−11
Peru	New Sol 9.50	2.91	3.06	3.26	−6
Philippines	Peso 85.00	1.62	27.4	52.6	−48
Poland	Zloty 6.50	2.10	2.10	3.10	−32
Russia	Rouble 48.00	1.77	15.5	27.1	−43
Singapore	S$3.60	2.27	1.16	1.59	−27
South Africa	Rand 13.95	2.11	4.50	6.60	−32
South Korea	Won 2,500	2.62	806	952	−15
Sweden	SKr33.00	4.53	10.6	7.28	+46
Switzerland	SFr6.30	5.21	2.03	1.21	+63
Taiwan	NT$75.00	2.33	24.2	32.1	−25
Thailand	Baht 60.00	1.56	19.4	38.4	−50
Turkey	Lire 4.20	2.72	1.35	1.54	−12
Venezuela	Bolivar 5,701	2.17	1,839	2,630	−30
Aruba	Florin 4.95	2.77	1.60	1.79	−11
Bulgaria	Lev 2.99	1.94	0.96	1.54	−37
Colombia	Peso 6,500	2.60	2,097	2,504	−16
Costa Rica	Colon 1,130	2.22	365	510	−28
Croatia	Kuna 15.0	2.62	4.84	5.72	−15
Dominican Rep	Peso 60.0	1.84	19.4	32.6	−41
Estonia	Kroon 29.5	2.40	9.52	12.3	−23
Fiji	Fiji $4.65	2.69	1.50	1.73	−13
Georgia	Lari 4.15	2.31	1.34	1.80	−26
Guatemala	Quetzal 17.25	2.27	5.56	7.59	−27
Honduras	Lempira 35.95	1.90	11.6	18.9	−39
Iceland	Kronur 459	6.37	148	72.0	+106
Latvia	Lats 1.35	2.47	0.44	0.55	−20
Lithuania	Litas 6.50	2.41	2.10	2.69	−22
Macau	Pataca 11.1	1.39	3.59	7.99	−55

(continued)

TABLE 11.1 The Big Mac Index *Continued*

	Big Mac Prices				
	In Local Currency	In Dollars	Implied PPP* of the Dollar	Actual Dollar Exchange Rate May 22	Under (-)/ over (+) Valuation Against the Dollar, %
Moldova	Leu 23.0	1.75	7.42	13.2	−44
Morocco	Dirham 24.5	2.82	7.92	8.71	−9
Norway	Kroner 43.0	7.05	13.9	6.10	+127
Pakistan	Rupee 130	2.16	41.9	60.1	−30
Paraguay	Guarani 9,000	1.63	2,903	5,505	−47
Saudi Arabia	Riyal 9.00	2.40	2.90	3.75	−23
Slovakia	Koruna 58.0	1.97	18.7	29.5	−37
Slovenia	Totar 520	2.76	168	189	−11
Sri Lanka	Rupee 190	1.85	61.3	103	−40
Ukraine	Hryvna 8.50	1.68	2.74	5.05	−46
UAE	Dirham 9.00	2.45	2.90	3.67	−21
Uruguay	Peso 42.3	1.77	13.6	23.9	−43

*Purchasing-power parity: local price divided by price in United States.

†Average of New York, Chicago, Atlanta, and San Francisco.

‡Dollars per pound.

§Weighted average of prices in euro area.

∂Dollars per euro.

Source: From *The Economist,* May 26, 2004. www.economist.com.

they do in the United States. So, for example, in China the Big Mac costs 10.5 yuan, whereas in the United States a three-city average price is $3.10. To make the prices equal, the exchange rate would have to be 3.39 yuan for 1 dollar. The market rate is actually 8.03 yuan to the dollar. So the yuan is 56 percent below the implied PPP exchange rate. That's a pretty inexpensive burger. *The Economist* claims that in the long run its Big Mac index performs pretty well, with many of the discounted and premium-fetching currencies correcting. Remember, too, that the price of a Big Mac represents more than a basket of tradable goods, the situation PPP theory describes. The McDonald's service we may receive with our Big Mac can't be traded, nor can the rent McDonald's pays for its building, for example. Nevertheless, the Big Mac index is a helpful and playful way to get a quick sense of relative currency values and where they may be heading.

Now that we have looked at two parity relationships, interest rate parity and purchasing power parity, we can look more closely at exchange rate prediction.

EXCHANGE RATE FORECASTING

Because exchange rate movements are so important to all aspects of international business—production, sourcing, marketing, and finance—many business decisions take the risk of exchange rate movement into consideration. There are several approaches to forecasting, and three of the main ones are the efficient market approach, the fundamental approach, and the technical approach. We briefly examine each of them.

efficient market approach
Assumption that current market prices fully reflect all available relevant information

In the **efficient market approach,** the assumption is that current prices fully reflect all available relevant information. That suggests that we look at the forward exchange rates and assume that they are the best possible predictor of future spot rates because they will have taken into account all the available information. If interest rates are different between two countries, for example, the forward rate will reflect this (international Fisher effect). The efficient market approach does not suggest that the forward rates will be the future spot rates with perfect accuracy. Rather, the divergences will be random. A related approach is called the **random walk hypothesis,** and it holds that the short-term unpredictability of factors suggests that the best predictor of tomorrow's prices is today's prices.[6]

random walk hypothesis
Assumption that the unpredictability of factors suggests that the best predictor of tomorrow's prices is today's prices

The **fundamental approach** to exchange rate prediction looks at the underlying forces that play a role in determining exchange rates and develops various econometric models that attempt to capture the variables and their correct relationships. The variables might include those mentioned above, such as the inflation rate, the interest rate, and the economic growth rate. Fundamental analysis builds on this set of independent variables, to which values or weighting is assigned. So, for a forecaster to predict an exchange rate two years forward, the first step would be to select a model. Then the predictor would estimate the values of the independent variables two years ahead. Already we have two major issues to consider: Is the formula correct? And then, are the variables predicted correctly? Cheol Eun and David Resnick, two noted international finance scholars, have surveyed the research on the various fundamental models and conclude that "the fundamental models failed to more accurately forecast exchange rates than either the forward rate model [what we have termed the efficient market model] or the random walk model."[7] OECD's Web site provides a good source of macroeconomic data used in fundamental analysis (www.oecd.org).

fundamental approach
Exchange rate prediction based on econometric models that attempt to capture the variables and their correct relationships

Technical analysis looks at history and then projects it forward. It analyzes historic data for trends and then, assuming that what was past will be future, projects these trends forward. Technical analysts think in terms of waves and trends. Since there is no theoretical underpinning to the technical approach, scholarly academic studies tend to dismiss it. Yet a review of currency-trading marketing materials suggests that traders often use it.

technical analysis
An approach that analyzes data for trends and then projects these trends forward

As for the performance of these various approaches, recent research by Eun and Sabherwalon the exchange rate forecasts of major commercial banks indicates that the 10 banks in the study could not outperform the random walk model.[8] Their findings also suggest that the forward exchange rate and the spot rate were both about equal in value for predicting future exchange rates. In another study, Richard Levich evaluated the forecasting of 13 professional forecasting services, whose approaches to forecasting varied. In only 24 percent of the cases did forecasters outperform the forward exchange rate as a predictor.[9] The evidence available indicates that neither the technical nor the fundamental approach outperforms the efficient market approach.

Other Financial Forces

We have examined a major financial force that international managers have to address, foreign exchange fluctuations, their causes and their prediction. How managers actually address the risk that such exposure creates is a topic we address in Chapter 21, "Financial Management," in our discussion of swaps and hedging. There are many other financial forces that international managers have to address, and presently we look at some of the more significant ones, beginning with currency exchange controls, tariffs, and taxation and then moving on to inflation and balance-of-payments effects.

CURRENCY EXCHANGE CONTROLS

Controls differ greatly from country to country and even within a country, depending on the type of transaction. In general, the developed countries have few or no currency exchange controls, but these nations are a minority of the world's countries. The majority of countries do impose some form of exchange control. Many developing countries, though, such as Mexico, have reduced or eliminated such controls in order to encourage foreign investment. The international business manager must be aware of whether currency exchange controls exist both before and while doing business in any country, because the situation can change quickly.

Currency exchange controls limit or prohibit the legal use of a country's currency in international transactions. When a currency is not freely convertible, its value is arbitrarily fixed, typically at a rate higher than its value in the free market, and the government decrees that all purchases or sales of other currencies be made through a government agency. The limitations might apply to residents of the country, while the currency is still externally convertible, or the limitations could be for both residents and nonresidents, resulting in a nonconvertible currency.

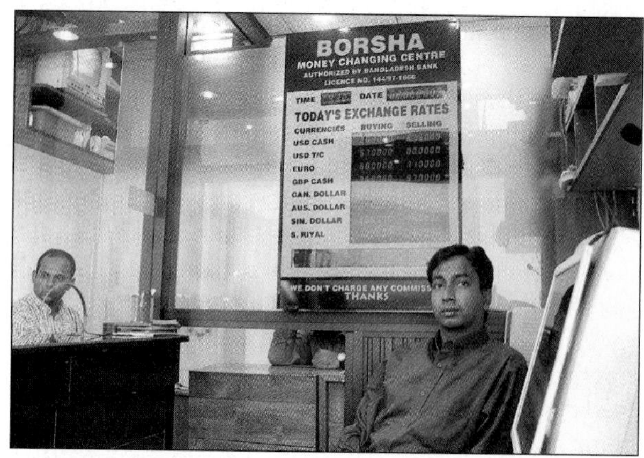

Employees wait for customers at a currency exchange, licensed by the Bank of Bangladesh, in Dhaka. Some countries set " official rates" for currency and decree that all purchases or sales of other currencies be made through a government agency.

Limitations might also restrict the amount of domestic currency transferred into foreign currency. A black market inevitably springs up alongside such restrictions, but it is of little use to the international manager who wants to abide by the laws of a country in which the company is operating. In addition, the black market is rarely able to accommodate transactions of the size involved in international business.

Countries put limitations on the convertibility of their currency when they are concerned that their foreign reserves could be depleted. Foreign reserves are a source of currency for foreign debt service, import purchases, and other demands for foreign currency that domestic banks might encounter. In the banking world, these countries are known as "Article 14 countries," after the International Monetary Fund's provision for exchange controls for transitional economies. An example of a country with exchange controls is China, whose renmimbi (RMB) is convertible in current accounts (accounts for day-to-day banking) but not capital accounts (longer-term accounts). China is in the process of reducing the restrictions on foreign exchange controls of domestic company activities, allowing them to engage in direct foreign investment. Cuba operates with two currencies: One, the national peso, is not convertible and is the domestic currency, having no value outside Cuba. The other, the convertible peso, is the currency of tourism and is pegged to the dollar at $1.08. Neither currency is traded outside Cuba. The Iranian rial had an official exchange rate for imports and another for exports until 2002. The import rate was used for imports of essential goods and for oil exports, and often it was much lower than the export rate, by almost 50 percent. The export rate was used for nonoil exports and luxury imports. The Tunisian dinar is not allowed outside Tunisia; the Algerian dinar is not exportable by foreigners, but Algerian citizens are allowed to export small amounts.

Often when a government requires permission to purchase foreign currency, the international business must pay more than the free-market rate. If permission is not granted or if the cost of foreign currency is uneconomically high, the blocked currency can be used only within the country. Such repatriation limitations usually present the problem of finding suitable products and investments within the country.

People will go to remarkable extremes to get blocked money out of exchange-controlled countries. When faced with blocked currency in the former Soviet Union, Pepsi once bought an oil tanker in Russia and filled it with vodka, all paid for with blocked currency and all for export. Pepsi also bought decommissioned Soviet submarines, paying for them in rubles, and sold them for scrap in the West. In New Delhi, the local manager of a major international airline gave a case of Scotch to a government official. Shortly thereafter, the agency for which that official worked granted the airline permission to use blocked rupees to buy almost US$20 million and transfer them to the airline's home country. This was an extreme method of converting a blocked currency to a convertible currency. It was also illegal. Most financial managers would be hesitant to accept the vulnerability that accompanies such approaches. They can take legal steps to protect their firms from the adverse effects of currency exchange controls, as you will see in Chapter 21.

TARIFFS

In addition to currency exchange rates and restrictions, tariffs or duties (the terms often are used interchangeably) present international managers with challenges because they represent increased costs. Tariffs, as you remember from Chapter 3, are taxes, usually on imported goods. They may be ad valorem, specific, compound, or variable. There are two ways to cover increased costs: to increase price or to decrease profit margins. In a sector where there is price competition, neither of these options seems attractive.

BUILDING YOUR GLOBAL RÉSUMÉ — A Career in International Finance—Where Do You Look for a Job?

The allure and the rewards of a career in international finance—such as being a power broker who deals in stocks and bonds, commodities, or currency on a 24/7 basis across the time zones of the world—can be quite dramatic. So where are the jobs in international finance located? Where are the major financial markets of the world? The top 14 banking centers of the world are:

1. New York
2. London
3. Hong Kong
4. Singapore
5. Tokyo
6. Zurich/Geneva
7. Frankfurt/Hamburg
8. Paris
9. Los Angeles/San Francisco
10. Milan/Rome
11. Brussels
12. Toronto/Montreal
13. Amsterdam
14. Panama

Major commodities exchanges (not in rank order) are located in:

- Chicago
- Kansas City
- Minnesota
- New York
- Hong Kong
- Paris
- Singapore
- Sidney
- Winnipeg
- Montreal
- Tokyo
- London
- Madrid

World Fact and Culture Cue: Considering the monetary rewards that can be earned in a career in international finance, where are the best places to live in order to pursue such a career? In 2006, *WealthBriefing* announced that the two top wealth management centers in the world are Geneva and Zurich. In the same year, Mercer Human Resources Consulting ranked 215 of the world's cities on their quality of living: Zurich and Geneva ranked 1st and 2nd, respectively, with Düsseldorf in 5th place, Frankfurt in 7th, Munich in 8th, and Bern and Sydney, tied, in 9th. London ranked 39th and New York 46th. Baghdad came in at 215.

World Wide Resources:

www.fincareer.com
www.finix.at/fin/selinks.html
www.tdd.lt/slnews/Stock_Exchanges/Stock.Exchanges.htm
www.libraries.rutgers.edu/rul/rr_gateway/research_guides/busi/stocks.shtml
www.xpresstrade.com/more_futures.html
www.unctad.org/infocomm/exchanges/ex_overview.htm

The European Union and other groups of nations that have moved toward economic integration (discussed in Chapter 4) have lowered or abolished tariffs on trade among member-countries. (Lower tariffs are a significant factor that a country would consider when deciding whether to join a group of nations, but they are not the only factor.) Such developments add new dimensions to the decision-making processes of companies located outside the groupings. From a company point of view, an existing tariff in a large market might be a factor in the decision to produce in that foreign market. For example, at Toyota's 11, soon to be 14, foreign production facilities in the United States, the Toyota cars, vans, and trucks produced are not subject to tariffs or any other trade-restrictive agreement such as quotas. Presently the United States levies a 25 percent tariff on imported trucks. This tariff was initially imposed by President Lyndon Johnson in 1963 to object to unfair trade practices by Germany in regard to U.S. frozen-chicken exports, so it is known as the "chicken tax." In 1963, trucks were a good target in Germany because major truck manufacturers were there, including Volkswagen, which were pushed out of the U.S. sector by the tariff. Almost all of the trucks in the United States today are manufactured domestically because an imported \$20,000 truck would have to sell for \$25,000 to recoup the cost of the tariff. In effect, the tariff, gives domestic producers the OK for a \$5,000 price increase, which represents a significant advantage for them.

You can see the present U.S. tariff schedule at the U.S. International Trade Commission Web site (www.usitc.gov/tata/hts/bychapter/index.htm). One interesting aspect of the tariff schedule is how specific it is. For example, in Harmonized Tariff Schedule (HTS) category 0704.10.20, cauliflower, the tariff rate is 2.5 percent between June 5 and October 25, when the U.S. crop is being harvested. If the cauliflower is cut or sliced, the rate is 14 percent at any time. The tariff for HTS 8703.2x.00, motor cars, is 2.5 percent, but for trucks (HTS 8704.22.50), it is 25 percent. The financial force of a tariff can be significant. (Tariffs as a legal force are discussed in Chapter 10.)

TAXATION

In Chapter 10, the legal aspects of taxation were covered. Taxation is also a financial force. Governments around the world widely use three types of taxation to generate revenue: income tax, value-added tax (VAT), and withholding tax.[10] The *income tax* is a direct tax on personal and corporate income. Table 11.2 compares corporate taxation rates in selected countries. The impact of taxes is a significant one, and if a corporation can achieve a lower tax burden than that of its competitors, it can lower prices to its customers or generate higher revenue with which to pay higher wages and dividends.

A *value-added tax (VAT)* is a tax charged on the value added to a good as it moves through production from raw materials to final purchaser. It is really a sales tax whose payment documentation from one stage to another in the production process becomes important for tax credits, since the seller collects the tax for the goods sold and then receives credits for VAT already paid earlier in the production process. Within the EU, VAT rates are still to be harmonized, so the process of moving goods across borders can have a VAT impact. For example, in Cyprus the rate is 15 percent, while in both Sweden and Denmark it is 25 percent. From a VAT perspective, sourcing in Sweden or Denmark would be 10 percent more costly, all else being equal. Countries that levy value-added taxes are permitted by World Trade Organization (WTO) rules to rebate the value-added taxes to exporters, an incentive that makes the exports less expensive and thus more competitive.

The third general tax category is the *withholding tax.* This is an indirect tax levied on passive income (income such as dividends, royalties, interest) that the corporation would pay out to nonresidents, people or companies in another tax jurisdiction. Countries establish bilateral tax treaties to categorize the various passive-income withholding rates. For example,

TABLE 11.2 Corporate Tax Rates

Country	Percent
Ireland	12.50
Singapore	20.00
Switzerland[1]	24.10
Austria	25.00
Finland	26.00
Denmark	28.00
Netherlands	29.60
Australia	30.00
Japan	30.00
United Kingdom	30.00
France	33.33
United States[2]	35.00
Germany[3]	41.60

[1]This rate includes federal and canton taxes, which vary. The rate given is typical and would be for a company in Zurich.

[2]This is the federal tax rate. State and local tax rates range from 0 to 20%.

[3]This includes a professional tax, which is around 18% but varies by city from 12% to 20%.

Source: PricewaterhouseCoopers, "Corporate Taxes Worldwide Summaries, 2006." See www.taxsummaries.pwc.com.

on interest, the United States withholds 30 percent from residents of non-tax treaty countries. From UK residents it withholds nothing, while from residents of Pakistan it withholds 30 percent.

At the international level, taxes become important as a complex financial force about which companies have to be concerned. International companies need to understand tax laws in all countries in which they operate and how those tax laws relate to tax laws in other countries. This additional tax burden can create financial risk, but it can also be an opportunity for savings, given good tax planning. We will look at tax planning in Chapter 21, when we examine financial management.

INFLATION

Inflation is a trend of rising prices. Economists disagree on the underlying cause of inflation. Some hold that it is caused by demand exceeding supply, while others view the cause as an increase in the money supply. All, however, agree that in an inflated economy, prices increase. Figure 11.3 maps the world by inflation levels. Japan, the EU, and the United States have had relatively good records in keeping inflation down in recent years. Many Latin American countries have inflation troubles. From 1970 into the 1990s, the worst inflation in Latin America occurred in Bolivia, where the inflation rate reached 11,750 percent in 1985. That far outstripped Brazil, in second place with 3,118 percent in 1990. In a dramatic turnaround, Bolivia slashed its inflation to only 7.9 percent in 1996 and further pushed it down to 4.9 percent in 2005. Similarly, Brazil decreased its inflation to 5.7 percent in 2005. Chile is another Latin American economic success story, decreasing inflation from 505 percent in 1974 to 7.4 percent in 1996 and 3.2 percent in 2005. Argentina reduced inflation from 3,080 percent in 1989 to 12.3 percent in 2005. Mexico brought down inflation from 132 percent in 1988 to 3.3 percent in 2005. The United States is now in a period of relatively low inflation. In the 1970s and early 1980s, the United States had relatively high inflation, with the rate reaching around 20 percent.

Most inflation is measured by a *consumer price index (CPI),* the price changes in a basket of consumer goods. OECD measures inflation by a broader indicator, the *gross domestic*

FIGURE 11.3 Inflation Map

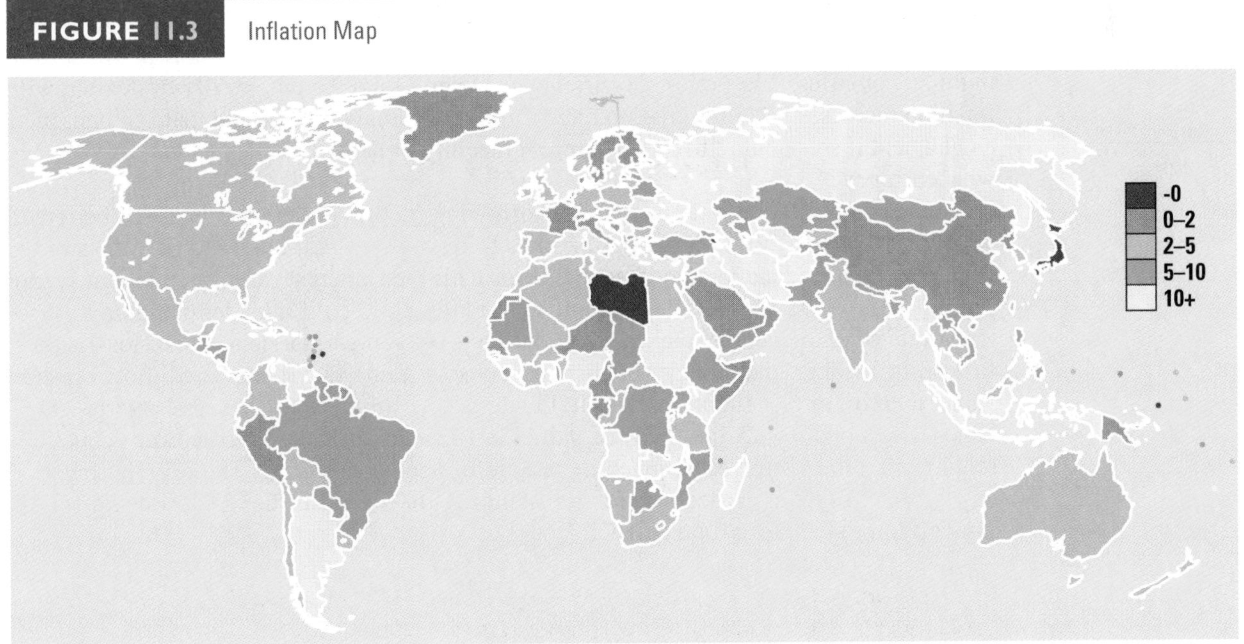

Source: CIA Factbook, 2006. Data reflects 2005 measures.

FIGURE 11.4 GDP Deflator: Average Annual Growth in Percentage, 1991–2004

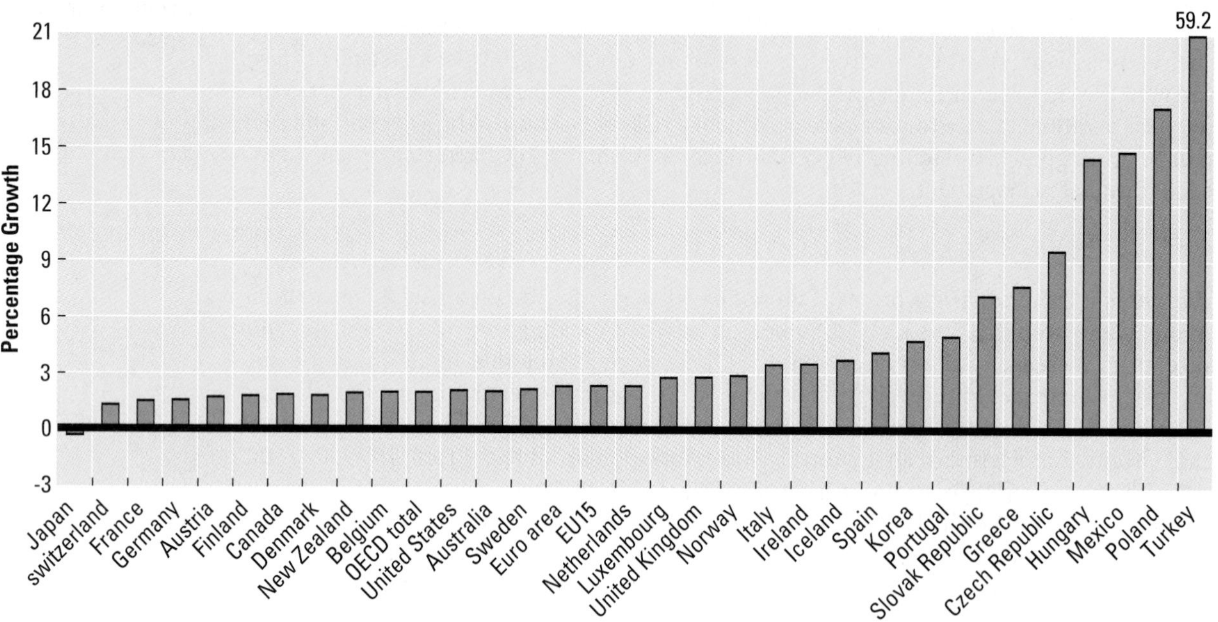

Source: OECD Factbook 2006, http://hermia.sourceoecd.org/vl=9709825/cl=11/nw=1/rpsv/factbook/02-02-04-g01.htm (accessed 22 June 2006).

product (GDP) deflator, which takes into account the prices of intermediate goods and services, not just those in a consumer basket, and the prices of capital assets. Figure 11.4 shows the inflation rates of OECD countries using the GDP deflator measure.

Inflation is a financial force, external to companies, that impacts international business in several major ways. Almost every company must borrow money occasionally, and the inflation rate determines the real cost of borrowing in capital markets.* You'll recall the Fisher effect, in our discussion of exchange rates. Even within a single country, inflation is of concern to management. High inflation rates make capital expenditure planning more risky. For example, management may allocate US$1 million for a plant and be forced to pay much more to complete construction because of the effects of inflation. When a firm operates in multiple countries, it has multiple currency exposures, and the complexity of dealing with inflation increases because inflation rates vary among countries. Should management raise capital, and if so, should this be done through equity or debt? In which capital markets? In what currency?

Increasing inflation rates encourage borrowing (debt) because the loan will be repaid with cheaper money. But high inflation rates bring high interest rates and may discourage lending. Potential lenders may fear that even with high interest rates, the amount repaid plus interest would be worth less than the amount lent. Even if a lender can obtain an interest rate of 25 percent, if the rate of inflation is 30 percent, the lender will lose money. Instead of lending, the money holder may buy something that is expected to increase in value, thereby further fueling inflation. Lenders have begun to use variable interest rates, which rise or fall with inflation, to shift the financial risk to the borrower. This shift requires that the borrower be much more careful about borrowing. The original rate and any future changes are based on a reference interest rate, such as the U.S. prime rate or the London Interbank Offer Rate (LIBOR).

*Real interest rates are found by subtracting inflation from the nominal interest rates.

FIGURE 11.5

Evolution of Long-Term Interest Rates

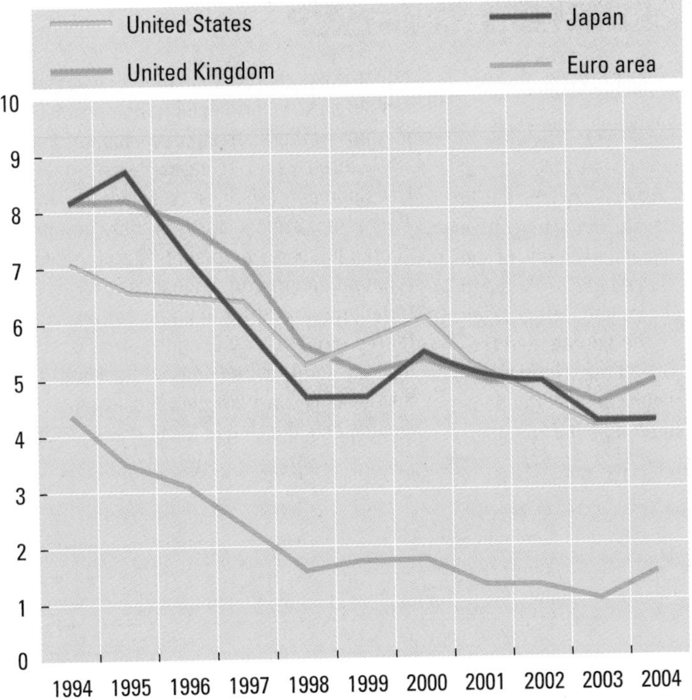

Source: Evolution of long-term interest rates, Main Economic Indicators, © OECD 2005. Used by permission.

As Figure 11.5 suggests, the long-term trend of interest rates has been toward conversion. They averaged 10 percent in 1991 but 4 percent by 2004. This trend may be explained by the globalization of financial markets as they become more integrated.[11]

As we have reviewed in our discussion on exchange rates, comparative inflation rates also will affect the comparative currency values (international Fisher effect), as the currencies of high-inflation countries weaken against the currencies of countries with lower inflation rates. Management usually will try to minimize holdings of the weaker currencies. Thus, relatively higher rates of inflation tend to discourage new investment.

Higher inflation rates cause the cost of the goods and services produced in a country to rise, and thus the goods and services become less competitive globally. The company's affiliate in the high-inflation country finds export sales more difficult, as do all other producers there. Such conditions may lead to balance-of-payments (BOP) deficits in the trade account, so under these conditions management must be alert to government policy changes that attempt to correct these deficits. Such changes could include more restrictive fiscal or monetary policies, currency controls, export incentives, and import obstacles.

BALANCE OF PAYMENTS

The balance-of-payments (BOP) account was discussed in some detail in Chapter 5, but we mention it here as it is a potential financial force. The state of a nation's BOP tells observant management much about the state of that country's economy. If the BOP is slipping into deficit, the government may be considering possible measures to correct or suppress that deficit. Management should be alert for either currency devaluation or restrictive monetary or fiscal policies to induce deflation. Another possibility is that currency or trade controls may be coming.

With foresight, the firm's management can adjust to the changing government policies or at least soften their impact. On the export side, the company may start shopping for export incentives—government incentives to make exporting easier or more profitable.

WORLDview

The Financial Force of Foreign Aid for Developing Countries

Promises aside, which rich countries actually have policies that bring important foreign aid into a developing country in order to help the poor? Such foreign aid is the traditional gauge of a country's commitment to development. The United States is the biggest donor in absolute terms, but it is the stingiest relative to the size of its economy, spending only 0.14 percent of its GDP on foreign aid. Of this aid, 72 percent is tied to the purchase of U.S. exports. Denmark's aid is .92 percent of GDP, while Norway's is .94 percent of GDP. However, aid is not the only, or even the best, measure of help. Trade policy is crucial: Shutting out developing countries' exports is a sure way of condemning the poor to remain poor. Liberal immigration policies can also help, because migrant workers' remittances support their home economies.

A three-year-old index dawn up by the Center for Global Development (CGD), a Washington think tank, with *Foreign Policy* magazine, ranks 21 rich countries by averaging their scores in six development-related policies: aid, trade, the environment, migration, investment, and peacekeeping. In 2005, Denmark scored the highest overall. See the chart below and, for more details, www.cgdev.org. The United States scores well on trade and investment, and private giving by U.S. citizens is also strong, but with plenty of room for improvement on other dimensions, the United States ranked 12th.

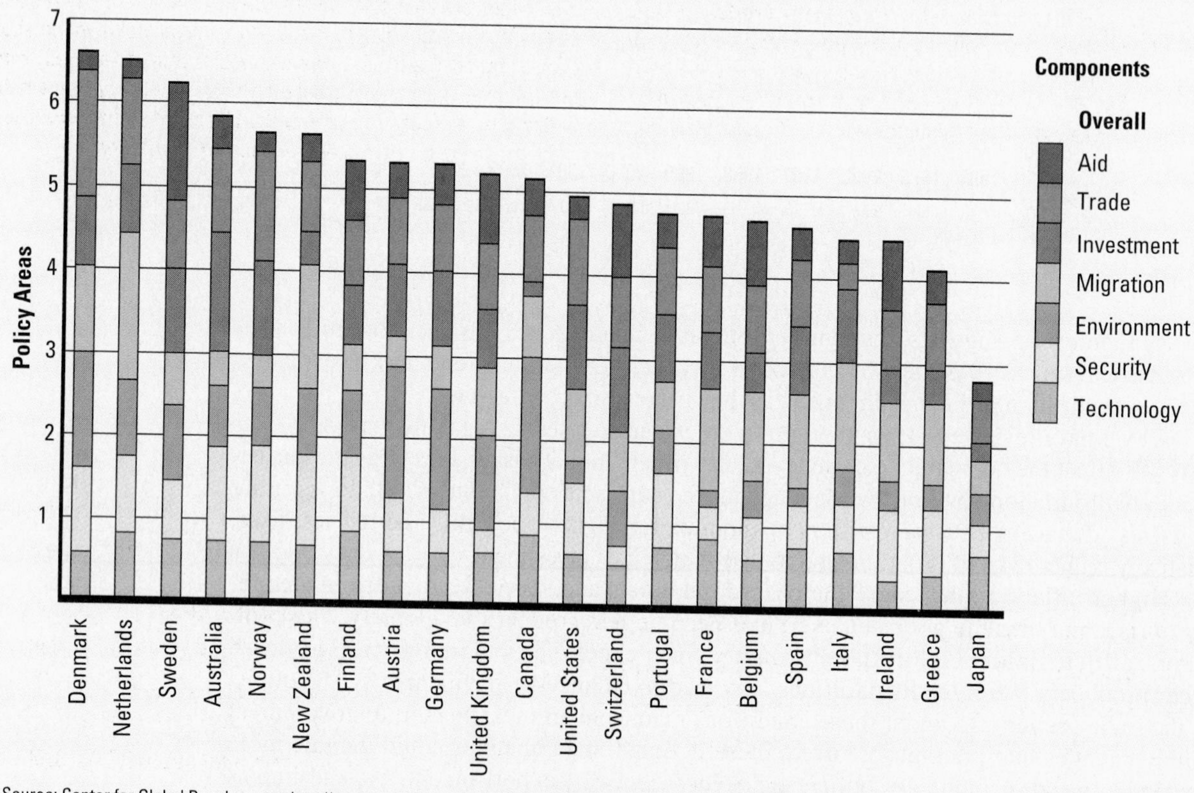

Source: Center for Global Development, http://www.cgdev.org/section/initiatives/_active/cdi (accessed 20 May, 2006).

Lower-cost capital may be available if the company can demonstrate that exports will be increased. Governments worldwide generally encourage exports, as they are viewed as positive for the economy. Therefore, some governments provide lower-cost capital if exports can be increased by doing so. One of the most common export incentives is export financing by a government agency that offers foreign buyers lower interest rates than they could get from other local capital markets. Sometimes the agency's loans are accompanied by aid grants, which need not be repaid.

Summary

Explain how money can be made—and lost—in the foreign exchange (FX) markets.

The foreign exchange (FX) markets are worldwide and collectively involve more money than any other market. On most days, you can trade money 24 hours somewhere in the world. As a result, there are ample opportunities for buying and selling foreign currency. Making or losing money in these markets depends on exchange rate movements.

Understand FX quotations, including cross rates.

FX information can be found in financial publications such as *The Wall Street Journal,* the *Financial Times,* and the financial section of major newspapers. *The Wall Street Journal* lists major currencies in terms of their trades with the US$. The spot rate (for delivery in two business days) is reported for all currencies. For the more heavily traded currencies, 30-, 60-, and 90-day forward rates are reported. Cross rates are exchange rates for trading directly between non-US$ currencies.

Describe currency exchange controls.

Many developing countries have instituted a system of currency exchange controls, which restrict the use of local and foreign currencies. Developing countries often have far less hard (convertible) currency than they need. They therefore ration the hard currency. Anyone wanting hard currency may have to apply to a government agency, specifying how much is wanted and the use to which it will be put.

Explain how financial forces such as tariffs, taxes, inflation, and the balance of payments affect international management.

Business managers must be prepared to react to financial forces that can affect their business. Tariffs are an added cost that, because they are changing, are not always predictable. Taxes also increase costs, but they tend to be more predictable in the short term. Inflation may impact where capital is sourced as well as the cost of doing business. The balance of payments may impact the ability to move funds. In general, the effects of these forces tend to increase costs or constrain the movement of funds.

Key Words

central reserve asset (p. 305)

vehicle currency (p. 305)

intervention currency (p. 305)

spot rate (p. 306)

forward currency market (p. 306)

forward rate (p. 306)

trading at a premium (p. 307)

trading at a discount (p. 307)

cross rates (p. 307)

bid price (p. 307)

ask price (p. 307)

monetary policies (p. 308)

fiscal policies (p. 308)

law of one price (p. 308)

arbitrage (p. 308)

Fisher effect (p. 308)

international Fisher effect (p. 308)

purchasing power parity (PPP) (p. 308)

efficient market approach (p. 310)

random walk hypothesis (p. 311)

fundamental approach (p. 311)

technical analysis (p. 311)

Questions

1. In a U.S. financial paper, you see the quotation: "Norway (krone) U.S.$ equiv. .1601." What does that mean?
2. What is the difference between spot and forward currency rates? Why would someone be interested in buying a currency at the forward currency rate?
3. What is meant by saying that a currency is trading at a premium to the US$ in the forward market?
4. If you agree to pay a certain amount of foreign currency to someone in six months, who bears the currency fluctuation risk—you or the person you will pay? Explain.
5. What are currency exchange controls? Why are they imposed? What effect do they have in the country imposing them and elsewhere?
6. How might tariffs influence international business decisions?
7. How might knowledge of the Fisher effect aid an international manager?
8. How might the Big Mac index be useful for an international manager?
9. What are some ways in which inflation affects business decisions?
10. What is the importance of the balance of payments (BOP) to international managers?

Research Task

globalEDGE.msu.edu 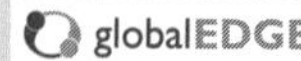

Use the globalEDGE site (http://globalEDGE.msu.edu/) to complete the following exercises:

1. In general, your current position in a company based in the United States requires you to keep updated on trends in the *foreign exchange market*. As such, a recent capital project will require a significant greenfield investment in Japan. Download the most recent forecast that analyzes the U.S. dollar and Japanese yen and prepare a brief report. What particular trends must your company keep in mind while continuing with this investment project? Are there any dangers you should keep aware of in the near future?
2. As an entrepreneur, you are interested in expanding your business to either Sweden or Turkey. As part of your initial analysis, you would like to know how much minimum investment is needed to enter each of these markets. To have an appropriate estimate, you hire a consulting firm to perform an initial investment analysis. The consulting firm provides a short report concerning the level of minimum investment needed for each country. Taken from the report, the minimum investment amounts enclosed are: one hundred million Swedish krona and forty-five million Turkish lira. To make a clear comparison by using current exchange rates, you must convert each currency to U.S. dollars and suggest which country provides the better investment.

Management Faces a BOP Deficit Minicase 11.1

You are the chief executive officer of a multinational's subsidiary in a developing host country. The subsidiary has been in business for about eight years, making electric motors for the host country's domestic market, with mediocre financial results. Before you left the home country a month ago, you were told to make the subsidiary profitable or consider closing it.

After a month in the host country, you have discovered that it is running a worsening balance-of-payments (BOP) deficit and that the government officials are very concerned about the situation. They are considering various measures to stanch or reverse the deficit flow.

What measures might they adopt? Given that you would prefer to keep the subsidiary open, since it employs locals and contributes to the country's economy in other ways also, can you think of some ways your company might profit from or at least minimize the damage of these potential measures?

12 Labor Forces

Oternachi Financial Center, Tokyo, Japan

Globalization is not only striving to grow revenues by selling goods and services in global markets. It also means globalizing every activity of the company. . . . Globalization especially means finding and attracting the unlimited pool of intellectual capital—the very best people—from all around the globe.

—General Electric, "Key Growth Initiatives"

Differences in Labor Conditions: Examples of Japan and China

As is discussed in this chapter, there are many differences across regions and nations of the world regarding such human resource issues as the role of women in the work force, the presence of immigrant, child, or forced labor, and the extent of new labor moving from rural to urban areas. While it is not possible to discuss all of the different variations in labor conditions based on cultural or geographic factors, it will be illustrative to begin the chapter's discussion by considering two specific examples: Japan and China.

JAPAN

Japan's "jobs-for-life" culture is disappearing. The prestigious Toyota Motor Corporation has begun hiring experienced automotive designers on a contract basis. These new employees, who may be of any age or nationality, are being hired on the basis of experience, and they will be offered merit-based rather than seniority-based pay increases. In taking these steps, Toyota has made it easier for other companies to follow suit: Honda and Fujitsu are among the companies that have already done so. But changing practices regarding human resource management is typically a challenge and often is accompanied by a host of associated problems.

In the past decade, Japan has lost more than a million full-time jobs; at the same time, it has been creating part-time and temporary ones. Companies also are outsourcing services they once did in-house, such as accounting, information technology, marketing, personnel management, procurement, and training. Even many manufacturing operations have been moved to other nations where labor is cheaper and more abundant, such as China.

Japan's declining birthrate and growing number of elderly persons are creating what its government calls a "crisis" in the labor force. This could be good news for the people who are losing their jobs due to the end of the jobs-for-life culture; indeed, a labor shortage could result in new job opportunities for them.

However, the government is worried about meeting future pension liabilities. On the basis of current projections, Japan will have only two workers to pay for each pensioner by 2020, about half the number it had in 2005.

CHINA

China's shift toward a market economy has been dramatic. Since 1978, the proportion of the national economy attributable to state-owned enterprises has declined from 80 percent to approximately 15 percent.

China's shift from a rural to an urban economy has been equally dramatic. At least 300 million people have moved from villages to cities since the late 1970s, and up to 500 million more are expected to move by 2020.

In response to these trends, the need for skilled human resources in China has skyrocketed. Correspondingly, the number of students graduating from China's colleges has more than doubled since 2002. Yet, despite this surge in college-educated graduates, multinational companies say that the shortage of talented people is the biggest constraint on growth in China. This problem may largely be the result of an inability of traditional Chinese institutions to adequately adapt to the rapidly changing commercial and industrial context. For example, under the communist system, college "job allocation offices" placed students in lifetime jobs with the state and graduates had few employment options besides these

CONCEPT PREVIEWS

After reading this chapter, you should be able to:

identify forces beyond management control that affect the quantity and quality of labor in a nation

explain the reasons people leave their home countries to work abroad

discuss the reasons that some countries have guest workers

explain factors associated with employment policies, including social roles, gender, race, and minorities

discuss differences in labor unions from country to country

Gli Affari Internazionali
cionales
onales Geschäft Παγοσμιο Business
Negócios Internacionais Los Negócios Internacionais
internacionales Affaires Internationales 國際商務 Παγοσμιο Business

state-determined ones. In the more market-driven economy of contemporary China, the offices for aligning graduates with guaranteed jobs with state enterprises have disappeared, yet few employment agencies have been created to take their place. Currently, newly formed college "student employment centers" are attempting to meet new market needs, but they are understaffed and the learning curve is steep.

Many employers, particularly foreign companies operating in China, claim that Chinese schools—which emphasize memorization and minimize creativity—are not adequately preparing graduates for business careers. In many cases, classes are taught by professors with little real-world experience relevant to a market economy. As a spokesperson for L'Oreal, the multinational cosmetics and beauty supplies company, said, "Because of the characteristics of the China market, the best results are with the people we grow from the beginning. We form them in line with our culture."

In many cases, older workers from the United States are filling China's demand for experienced employees in manufacturing, education, and service industries. Of senior management expatriates working in China, 31.4 percent came from Hong Kong, 23.8 percent moved from the United States, 23.3 percent were European, and 21.4 percent came from other Asian countries. ■

Source: Leslie Chang, "China's Grads Find Jobs Scarce," *The Wall Street Journal*, June 22, 2004, p. A17; "Japan's Worry about Work," *The Economist*, January 26, 1999, pp. 35–36; "Spurring Performance in China's State-Owned Enterprises," www.forbes.com/business/2004/11/04/cx_1104mckinseychina6.html (July 28, 2006); Victor Mallet, "A Vast Human Tide Floods to the Cities," *Financial Times*, December 16, 2003, p. 5; Matt Forney, "Tug-of-War over Trade," *Time*, December 22, 2003, p. 43; James T. Areddy, "Older Workers from U.S. Take Jobs in China," *The Wall Street Journal*, June 2, 2004, p. B6; and Jihann Moreno, "Compensation Trends in Greater China," Hewitt Associates, www.hewittassociates.com/Intl/AP/en-CN/KnowledgeCenter/ArticlesReports/compensation_trends.aspx (July 28, 2006).

The quality, quantity, and composition of the available labor force within a nation are of great importance to an employer, especially since the employer must be efficient, competitive, and profitable.

labor quality
The skills, education, and attitudes of available employees

labor quantity
The number of available employees with the skills required to meet an employer's business needs

Labor quality refers to the attitudes, education, and skills of available employees. **Labor quantity** refers to the number of available employees with the skills required to meet an employer's business needs. Circumstances can arise in which there are too many available workers; this can be good or bad for the business.

If there are more qualified people than a company can economically employ, its bargaining position is strengthened and it can choose the best employees at relatively low wages. On the other hand, high unemployment can cause social and political unrest, which are usually not conducive to profitable business.

Many of the labor conditions in an area are determined by social, cultural, religious, attitudinal, and other forces discussed throughout this text. Other determinants of labor conditions are political and legal forces, and in this chapter we expand on some of those introduced in Chapters 9 and 10. In particular, we will look at labor, the reasons for its availability or scarcity, the types of labor likely to be available or scarce under different circumstances, and employer-employee relationships. We will see how these relationships are affected by government and by employee organizations such as labor unions.

Worldwide Labor Conditions and Trends

The quantity and quality of labor varies across nations and regions of the world and also over time. A brief review of demographic data provides a starting point for examining labor conditions. This section also examines other international labor trends, including the aging of populations, increasing migration from rural to urban areas, unemployment, immigration, participation by children in the labor force, and forced labor.

OVERALL SIZE AND SECTOR OF THE WORK FORCE

Let us begin by looking at the overall situation in the world, in terms of some very macro demographic data. In 2006, the world had 6.5 billion inhabitants, 46 percent of whom were under the age of 25 and 27 percent under the age of 15.[1] Due to high birthrates and a decline in the rate of infant mortality, populations in the developing nations tend to be growing as well as becoming younger. Approximately 43 percent of the world's 15- to 24-year-olds, a key source of new workers during the next decade, live in just two developing countries: India and China.[2]

In contrast, populations in many developed countries are projected to decline in the coming years, due to factors such as low birthrates and low levels of immigration. For example, between 2006 and 2050, Japan's population is projected to decline from 127.5 million to 99.9 million, Russia's from 142.9 million to 110.8 million, and Germany's from 82.4 million to 73.6 million. Countries that have admitted large numbers of immigrants, such as the United States, the United Kingdom, Canada, and Australia, are projected to have continued population growth due to the often-younger age and higher birthrates of the immigrant populations. For example, between 2006 and 2050, the United States is projected to grow from 298.4 million to 420.1 million, and Canada from 33.1 million to 41.4 million.

In which sectors of the economy is the work force working? On a worldwide basis, the proportion of jobs in the service sector has been increasing in recent decades, while the proportion employed in agriculture has been shrinking. Over the past decade, only the regions of the Middle East and North Africa have not seen an increase in the proportion of service sector jobs.[3] As shown in Figure 12.1, services are now the largest sector for labor force employment in most of the nations of the world, exceeding the proportion employed in either agriculture or industry.

AGING OF POPULATIONS

The rapid increase in the proportion of the world's population that is age 65 or older has received much attention in recent years. As shown in Figure 12.2, 7.4 percent of the world's population was 65 or older in 2006, versus 6.6 percent only a decade earlier. The proportion of those 65 or older is projected to increase to 8.4 percent of the world's population in 2015 and 16.4 percent by 2050.[4]

FIGURE 12.1 Primary Occupation of National Labor Force

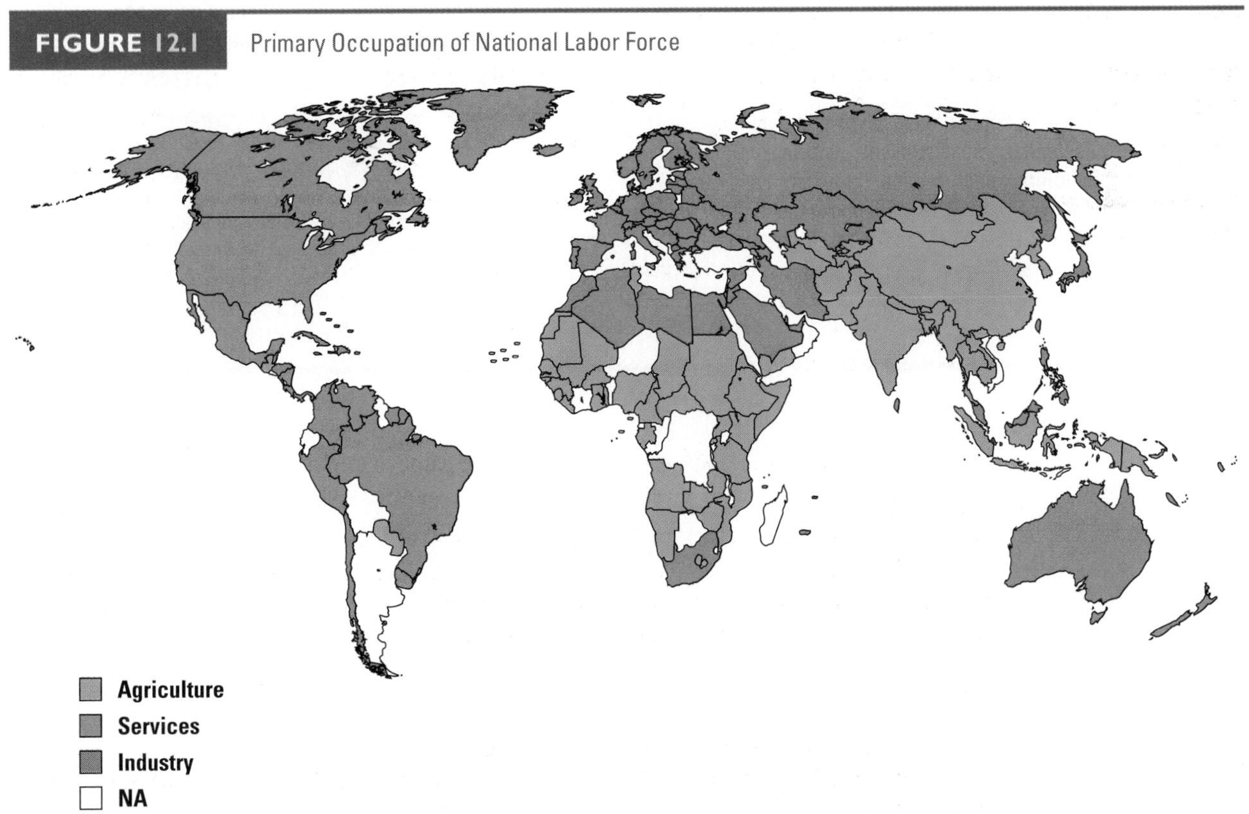

Source: https://www.cia.gov/cia/publications/factbook/fields/2048.html (July 25, 2006).

mini MNE

>>Small Businesses and Jobs

Only 1 percent of the 23 million businesses in the EU have more than 250 employees, and only 7 percent have more than 9. Small businesses are particularly important in such nations as Italy, the Czech Republic, and Hungary, where companies with fewer than 20 employees account for over 90 percent of all employment. As a result, the European Commission has been directed to take several steps to mobilize and assist small businesses in job creation.

One step is the creation of the European Investment Fund to finance or guarantee job-creating projects. Another step is encouraging member-countries to simplify administrative formalities. They are also being encouraged to expand national or regional policies of support to small business. European tax systems have traditionally penalized small businesses, and the European Commission has issued a legally binding recommendation to EU member-countries to end this tax discrimination.

In Latin America, millions of women have turned to self-employment to support themselves and their families. They work as vendors, seamstresses, food makers, microscale manufacturers, and service providers and frequently expand to hire employees, subcontract, and grow to larger businesses. The Inter-American Development Bank's Microenterprise Division gives them access to credit on fair market terms and advice on managing their businesses and marketing their products. Loans can be in small amounts—as little as $50—to serve the needs of even the smallest-scale microentrepreneurs. Similar programs have been launched in sub-Saharan Africa and other less developed regions, generally with impressive results. (See Chapter 11 for more discussion of micro-lending.)

Men are not discriminated against and can get small business loans, but lenders say women are a better investment. For one thing, women are more likely than men to pay back their loans on time and in full. They also have a solid track record of using their loans to expand their businesses, boost profits, and hire new workers.

The United States Peace Corps is seeking people to help countries around the world in small business development. They want people with education or experience in all fields of business, including finance, marketing, accounting, international trade, management, retail operations, credit programs, information systems, hotel management, tourism, agribusiness, and cost analysis.

The Peace Corps has people in Africa, Latin America, Central Europe, and the former Soviet republics. Some of the countries that are hosting Peace Corps workers in small business are in Africa (Togo, Tonga, and Zimbabwe), in Latin America (Chile, Nicaragua, and Uruguay), and in Central or Eastern Europe (Czech Republic, Poland, and Slovak Republic). To discuss Peace Corps jobs, phone 1-800-424-8580 from anywhere in the United States or go to its Web site at www.peacecorps.gov.

Source: "About the Peace Corps," www.peacecorps.gov/index.cfm?shell=learn (July 27, 2006); *OECD Factbook*, http://titania.sourceoecd.org/vl-3065972/cl=20/nw=1/rpsv/factbook/data/02-04-03-t01.xls (July 27, 2006); "For Women: Big Gains from Micro-Business," *IDB Erta*, Inter-American Development Bank, 1994; and "EU Regulations: A Raw Deal for Small Businesses?" *EIU Views Wire*, March 16, 2006.

Not all nations or regions are experiencing the same extent of aging of their populations. This trend is more pronounced for the developed countries, which grew from 10 percent of the population being 65 or older in 1996 to 11.5 percent in 2006 and is projected to rise to 25.4 percent by 2050. An aging population in most of the developed countries will have important implications for labor force size and skill, for policies regarding immigration (for example, as a means of maintaining the size of the work force and population), for economic growth, and for a range of political issues related to pension plans, health care, and other key social, economic, and political factors in those nations. For example, the European Commission predicts that Europe's share of world output could decline from its current 18 percent to 10 percent by 2050, and Japan's from 8 to 4 percent, unless major policy changes are undertaken. In contrast, a more youthful United States could expand its world output share from 23 to 26 percent during the same time.

FIGURE 12.2

Percentage of Population Age 65 or Over

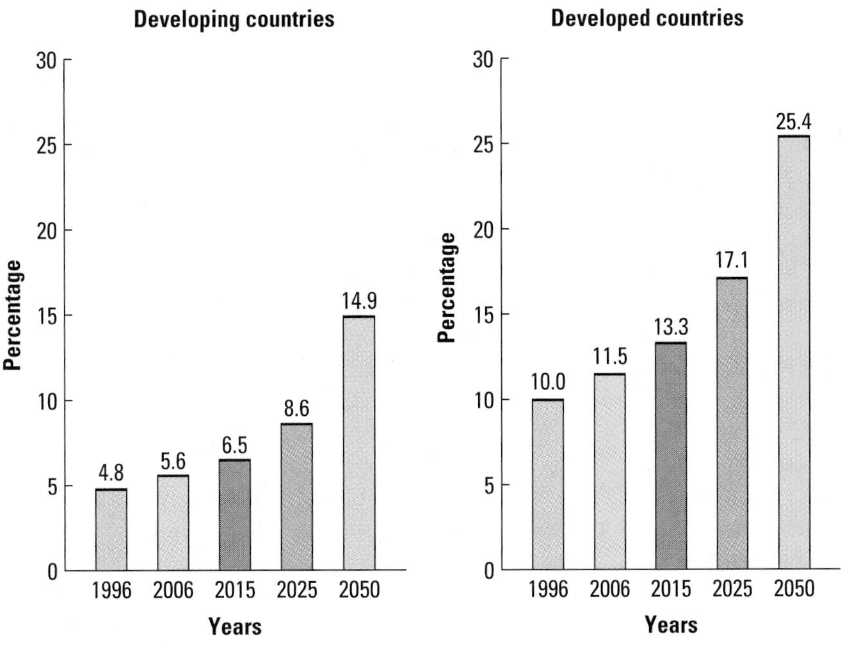

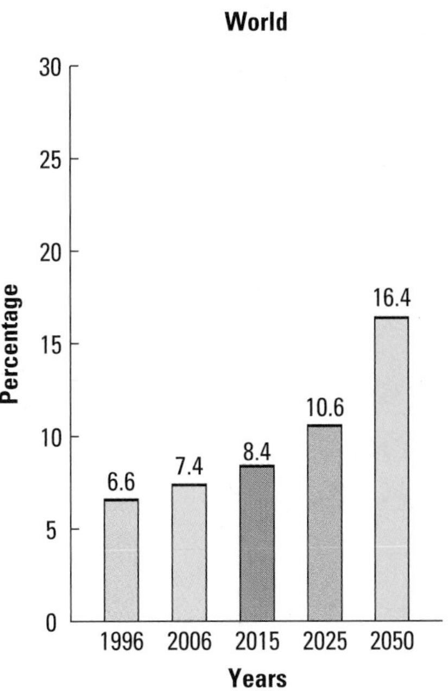

Source: U.S. Census Bureau, International, "Midyear Population, by Age and Sex," www.census.gov/cgi-bin/ipc/idbagg (July 27, 2006).

In comparison with developed countries, the developing countries will have only about one-half the proportion of people age 65 and older, at least through 2025. India, a large developing country that had approximately one-sixth of the world's population of 20- to 64-year-olds in 2006, is projected to experience an even slower aging of its population. Due to India's large proportion of young people, its proportion of people age 65 or older is projected to rise from 4.9 percent of the nation's population in 2006 to 5.9 percent in 2015 and 14.6 percent in 2050. A much larger proportion of Indians will be of traditional working age (20 to 64) than will be the case for most of the rest of the world, especially the developed countries. That may have important implications for international companies (ICs), such as those considering where to locate production as well as those seeking markets for products that target working-age adults.

RURAL TO URBAN SHIFT

The population and labor force worldwide have been shifting dramatically from rural to urban during the past century. As shown in Figure 12.3, less than 29 percent of the world's population lived in urban areas in 1950. By 2007, over half of the population will be urban, and this proportion is projected to increase to 61 percent by the year 2030. Although the level of urbanization is higher in developed countries, the rate of urbanization was four times faster in developing countries from 1975 to 2005 as these nations experienced rapid increases in population as well as increasing economic development.

As populations migrate from rural areas to urban areas, particularly within developing nations, they also move from agriculturally based employment to employment in industry and service sectors. Often, this influx of labor from rural areas creates a pool of low-cost—but low-skilled—workers. While labor trainers for ICs in developing nations have found that the people learn industrial skills rapidly, a more difficult challenge is teaching new workers who come from farms and villages how to adjust socially and psychologically to work life in industry or service sectors. Some of these workers must be taught not only job skills but also the concept of time. They are not accustomed to reporting to work at the same time and place each workday, for example, or to meeting production schedules. They must be introduced to factory teamwork and to an industrial hierarchy. Frequently, the company must compromise and not attempt to change customary farm and village practices too quickly and completely.

A Spanish company opened a factory in Guatemala, hired local people, and tried to operate as if it were in Europe. The Spanish management installed work hours and production routines and schedules that had worked efficiently in Spain. But in Guatemala, in its early stage of economic development, the procedures were nearly disastrous.

The people refused to work and became hostile. Guatemalan troops were needed to protect the factory. Management at last considered local needs and compromised, and mutually satisfactory solutions were found.

The solutions included four-hour breaks between two daily work periods. During the breaks, the male employees took care of their farms and gardens and the female employees attended to household needs and cared for their children. As another part of the solution, the employees were willing to work on Saturdays to make up production lost during the breaks.

FIGURE 12.3

Increasing Urbanization of the World's Population

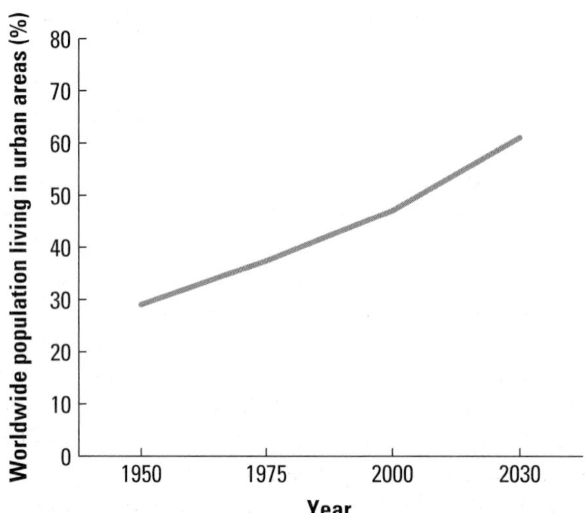

Source: *World Urbanization Prospects: The 2003 Revision* (New York: United Nations, 2003), pp. 3–4.

BUILDING YOUR GLOBAL RÉSUMÉ

Consider International Jobs and Careers Other Than in Business

The first thought that typically comes to mind when you hear "international careers" is jobs in the corporate world, working for a Fortune 500 firm that services international markets and has a global reputation. This is not the only track to an international career. Many outstanding international career opportunities for people with desirable interpersonal and language skills are not in mainstream business but may require basic business expertise. Explore these options to become a part of the global work force:

- Travel, tourism, and hospitality (a major international industry found in virtually every country of the world).
- Engineering (all types).
- Health professions and health care management.
- Information technology and computer science (experiencing major worldwide growth).
- Translation and language teaching abroad.
- Environmental and natural resource management.
- International chambers of commerce.
- Foreign trade divisions of state offices of economic development.
- The U.S. government:

  U.S. Counselor Service

  Foreign Service—U.S. State Department

  Central Intelligence Agency and the National Security Agency

  Agency for International Development (AID)

  Export-Import Bank

  International Trade Commission

  U.S. Information Agency

  Peace Corps
- International education exchange (teaching abroad).
- Volunteer and social service agencies.
- Arts and architecture.

The skills and experiences offered by any of these career options are highly sought after and readily transferable between the public and the private sectors.

World Wide Resources:

www.global.ucsb.edu/students/career_faq.html

www.state.gov/m/dghr/flo/rsrcs/pubs/12545.htm

www.transitionsabroad.com/listings/work/careers/keywebsitesprofessionspecific.shtml

Through compromise and patience, European managers, operating in a preindustrial setting, were able to achieve satisfactory production. They studied, negotiated, and adapted to local needs. The alternatives were low production and perhaps even a destroyed factory.

UNEMPLOYMENT

As we discussed in Chapter 2, trade liberalization is a key driver for development of nations and economies. However, at the same time, trade liberalization often has short- to medium-term implications for labor. This is especially the case in terms of creating "winners" and "losers" from the effects of trade and investment, both within and across nations. The individuals and groups who tend to be most susceptible to negative impacts from internationalization, due to their ability to cope quickly and effectively with trade-related reforms, include the poor, the elderly, women, and workers with low levels of skills. Compounding this issue is the fact that most developing countries lack well-developed programs—such as retraining programs, unemployment benefits, pension programs (especially ones that are portable between employers)—for dealing effectively with such a situation.[5]

Worldwide, there are more than 2.8 billion people classified as working, although 1.4 billion of these do not earn enough to enable themselves and their families to rise above the $2-per-person per-day poverty level. The overall level of unemployment is 192 million people, which is the highest volume ever. The highest level of unemployment is in the Middle East and North Africa, with 13.2 percent, followed by sub-Saharan Africa and Central and Eastern Europe and the Commonwealth of Independent States, both with 9.7 percent. Latin America and the Caribbean have a 7.7 percent rate of unemployment, and the developed economies are at 6.7 percent. Southeast Asia and the Pacific with 6.1 percent, South Asia with 4.7 percent, and East Asia with 3.8 percent had the lowest levels of unemployment.[6]

Over 88 million of the unemployed, 45 percent of the total, were youths between the ages of 15 and 24. Many of the youths who did have jobs were employed in positions that were only temporary or involuntarily part-time, with few benefits and limited potential for advancement. Unemployment also remains higher for women than for men in most countries, although that gap has been narrowing in the past decade. For example, in the OECD nations, the unemployment rate for men declined from 7.1 percent in 1994 to 6.6 percent in 2004. The unemployment rate for women in these countries declined from 8.2 percent to 7.4 percent over the same period of time.[7]

IMMIGRANT LABOR

labor mobility
The movement of people from country to country or area to area to get jobs

Although classical economists assumed that labor was immobile, we now know that **labor mobility** does exist. For example, at least 60 million people left Europe to work and live overseas between 1850 and 1970. During part of that time, between the end of World War II and the mid-1970s, some 30 million workers from southern Europe and North Africa flowed into eight northern European countries where they were needed because of the economic boom there. When possible, people move to secure better economic situations, regardless of their socioeconomic level, and immigration is at least partly the result of the relative supply of and demand for labor as well as regulations influencing those factors.

Figure 12.4 shows immigration into Organization for Economic Cooperation and Development (OECD) countries. This immigration is divided into two categories, *foreign-born* and *foreign.* The foreign-born population comprises those immigrants whose move is permanent and may include taking citizenship. The foreign population consists of those who are guest workers, transient and impermanent in their residence in the country.

The International Labor Organization estimates that there are 86 million migrant workers worldwide, with 34 million of them in developing nations.[8] However, international migrants increasingly are concentrated in developed countries, particularly the United States, Europe, and Australia.[9] Migrant labor ranges from highly skilled jobs such as in information technology or medicine to lower-skilled jobs in agriculture, cleaning, and domestic service. Many migrants are involved in "3-D" jobs—dirty, dangerous, and degrading—that a nation's own workers reject or for which there are not enough available workers.

FIGURE 12.4 Foreign and Foreign-Born Populations in Selected OECD Countries

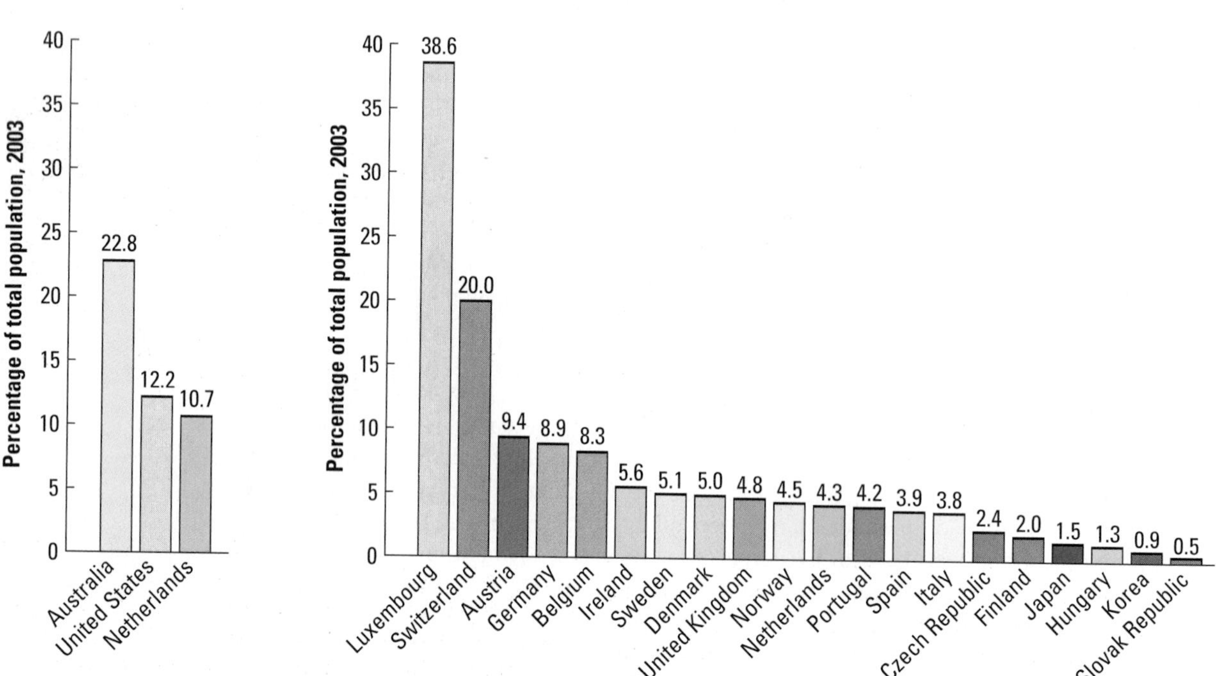

Source: "Immigrant and Foreign Population," *OECD Factbook 2006—Economic, Environmental and Social Statistics,* http://puck.sourceoecd.org/vl=1424480/cl=13/nw=1/rpsv/factbook/data/01-03-01-t01.xls (July 28, 2006). Based on Population and migration-elderly population – ageing societies, *OCED FFactbook 2006: Economic, Environmental and Social Statistics,* ©**OECD** 2006. Used by permission.

The movement of large numbers of immigrants, often unskilled laborers, within and particularly between nations has become an increasingly salient issue in terms of human resource management as well as macro policy setting and political debate. The extent of this problem is illustrated by Malaysia's decision in July 2002 to deport illegal immigrants, an action that resulted in a significantly reduced work force nationally, as only 750,000 of the country's 2 million immigrant workers are legally registered.[10] Significant illegal immigrant populations also exist in other nations.[11] Estimates indicate that 10 to 15 percent of all migration is "irregular"—involving entry or work without authorization from the host countries.[12] High levels of exploitation, forced labor, and human rights abuses are associated with irregular migration.

Even legal immigration is an issue in many nations and regions. For example, several EU countries responded to fears of an unmanageable influx of workers from the EU's most recently admitted Eastern European member-states by erecting various restrictions to employment and social security programs. George Schöpflin, politics professor at London University's School of Slavonic and East European Studies, says: "Restrictions contradict the ideals of unity. But there are deep cultural fears of being overwhelmed by immigrants from the east."[13] In contrast, high levels of immigration have helped to promote economic growth in nations such as Spain, contributing to housing demand, growth in the construction sector, and expansion in other areas of the economy. About one-third of immigrants to the EU go to Spain, where the country's immigrant community has reached 9 percent of the population, a fourfold increase since 2000.[14]

Although the United States has only about 5 percent of the world's population, it has 20 percent of the world's migrants.[15] According to the U.S. Census Bureau, in 2004, 12 percent of the people residing in the United States were foreign-born, up from 5 percent in 1970, and 42 percent of the increase in the U.S. population between 2000 and 2005 came from immigration. Nearly half of the immigrants who have entered the United States since 2000 are in the country illegally.[16] About 58 percent of the new jobs created since 1995 have been filled with foreign-born workers, including over 85 percent of new positions for mechanics and construction workers and over 60 percent of service positions.[17] Overall, over 23 percent of the U.S. population either is foreign-born or has one or both parents who were foreign-born. Immigrants come to the United States from all over the world, with the largest number of foreign-born coming from Latin America (53 percent), Asia (25 percent), and Europe (14 percent).[18]

The International Labour Organization (ILO) estimates that migrant workers send home $250 billion per year.[19] This amount exceeds all official governmental assistance worldwide for development and is a major influence on economic development in many developing nations. Migrant workers also enhance home country development by transferring skills and technology when workers return to their home nations.

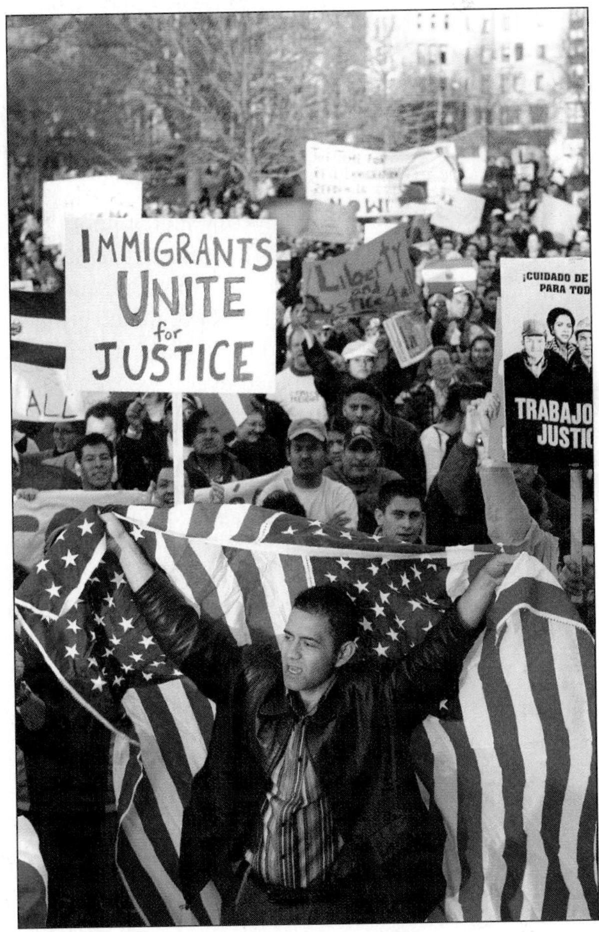

Thousands of immigrants and supporters rallied and marched in downtown Boston in March 2006 to protest restrictive new immigration policies being debated in Congress and to call for fair immigration reform.

CHILD LABOR

According to the ILO, 218 million (one in seven) of the world's children age 5 to 17 work in streets, factories, mines, and rock quarries or as maids in homes.[20] Often they work and live in dangerous or filthy conditions for miserable wages or no compensation at all. Although most working children—122 million—are in Asia, the highest proportion is found in Africa, where 26 percent of

child labor
The labor of children below 16 years of age who are forced to work in production and usually are given little or no formal education

all children work. **Child labor** also exists in developed countries, although the proportion is lower than is frequently found in developing nations. Overall, nearly 70 percent of child labor is in agriculture.

Sumptuous, high-pile, hand-knotted carpets produced in Nepal by children account for a significant portion of that country's export income. Nepal is one of the world's poorest countries, and it, along with other countries where child labor is prevalent, resents criticism from sources such as the ILO, which Nepal feels is dominated by the rich countries. Nepal and similar countries are suspicious of campaigns such as those by the ILO and others to eradicate countries' child labor and improve the lot of their work forces. They consider these to be masked attempts to wipe out one of the few advantages they enjoy in the world economy: low wages. They point out also that in the poorest countries, most children have no other opportunities. School exists for only the wealthy, a tiny portion of the overall population. The owner of a Nepalese carpet factory says, "If a child is not employed, it will beg or lie in the street, or use drugs."

Both the World Bank and UNICEF have made comments that are at least partly supportive of this point of view. The World Bank says that children's work can be in their own interests and that a family's survival may depend on it. UNICEF advocates banning only work that can harm children's development. It goes on to observe that forcing children out of factories and into schools may actually hurt them; unless their families are compensated for the lost income, such a policy can worsen their destitution.

Himnat Yenealem, a 13-year-old Ethiopian girl, works as a maid washing clothes, scrubbing floors, and roasting coffee beans for her employer, in exchange for shelter, food, and clothing. Her parents died of AIDS-related illnesses when she was 9, leaving her homeless. "I was in a bad dilemma, so I said 'yes' to working. I felt too scared. But at least this way, I wouldn't be homeless and I could try to upgrade myself," she explained. The woman she works for has been "moderate with me and never beat me for mistakes. She even let me go to school part time. I feel so happy about that, and now I work for her even harder."[21] In Ethiopia, only 38 percent of children attend school, and only 4 percent attend school without also working or housekeeping.

Governments of poor countries, once reluctant to even admit child labor problems, now are in a few cases trying to solve them. For example, in rural Brazil, families that promise to send their children to school can borrow a goat for breeding and keep the offspring. Police in Thailand have raided brothels holding slave child prostitutes. The Pakistani government is responding to parents' demands for better schools. In many cases, these government efforts are joined by, or even result from, initiatives from international companies.

Ikea, the giant Swedish home furnishings retailer, sources its carpets in the Indian carpet belt in the state of Uttar Pradesh. About 500,000 people work in carpet weaving there, including about 40,000 children. Apologists for child labor have claimed that children were better suited than adults for carpet weaving, due to their dexterity, and that children would be worse off if they were not employed in this business. However, Fida Hussain, who heads Deluxe Carpets in Badohi, India, disagrees with these assertions, saying, "Weaving carpets requires strength and, at every stage of production, adults are better at it." Further, "Children are put to work because their parents are in debt. It has nothing to do with how well they work." Seeking to minimize child labor and the damaging negative publicity that can accompany it, Ikea has begun a child labor initiative to source only from companies that do not use child labor. This effort includes a program to promote financial independence among poorer women in the carpet belt, giving them an opportunity to improve their work performance while simultaneously escaping the viselike grip of loan sharks and the resulting pressure to have their children take up employment. "Now that we are financially independent, we can take our children and put them in school," said one woman in the village of Suiyawan. Over 21,000 children have subsequently become literate, and several thousand women have gained financial independence.[22]

Are these efforts by governments, businesses, and nongovernmental agencies having an effect? The ILO's report *The End of Child Labour—Within Reach* claims that the number of child laborers declined by 11 percent (28 million children) between 2002 and 2006. An even sharper decline has occurred in the employment of children for hazardous work, where there has been a reported 33 percent reduction in the number of children employed.[23] Juan Somavia, the ILO's director-general, said, "We have witnessed a sea change in the awareness of child labor across the world and a broad consensus has emerged on the urgency of eradicating this scourge."[24]

However, the picture may not be as rosy as the ILO maintains. Its report is based on survey data from only 17 countries, including Brazil and India. However, nations such as Indonesia and China, which have large populations and a history of child labor, were not included in the surveys. Nor is Myanmar, a country with a weak record on many aspects of human rights, including child labor. While reducing child labor, particularly in its most hazardous forms, is a worthy goal, the attainment of this goal will require continued effort worldwide by governments, businesses, nongovernmental organizations, consumers, and the general public.

FORCED LABOR

Forced labor, which is most common in South and East Asia, northern and western Africa, and parts of Latin America, may affect as many as 27 million people today. Women, children, and low-income men are typical victims of forced labor. For example, the army in Myanmar (formerly Burma) has been reported to have forcibly recruited farmers, their wives, and children to work as porters, laborers, and human mine detectors.[25] Some forms of prison labor are also considered forced labor.[26]

BRAIN DRAIN

Record numbers of immigrants are moving to many OECD countries in search of jobs. The latest edition of the OECD's annual *Trends in International Migration* notes that even economic downturns in some OECD countries in the first part of the 21st century have not affected the upward trend in international migration that began in the mid-1990s.[27] There has been a significant increase in labor-related migration of both temporary and permanent workers and across all employment categories—skilled workers, seasonal employees, trainees, working holiday makers, staff transfers within multinational companies, and cross-border workers.

When skilled workers migrate from developing economies, a phenomenon known as **brain drain,** they generally do so for professional opportunities and economic reasons. Brain drain has become a serious problem for developing countries, especially when emigration involves the loss of such skilled professionals as scientists, IT specialists, engineers, teachers, and health care professionals. The World Bank says that the countries that are most impacted by brain drain are small, poor nations in Africa, Central America, and the Caribbean. For example, 90 percent of doctors trained in Kenya's public hospitals subsequently emigrate, leaving many areas of the country without adequate medical care.[28] Figure 12.5 shows 10 countries that have from 30 to 84 percent of their college-educated citizens living in other nations, suggesting how much these countries are being damaged by the loss of their most skilled workers.

brain drain
The loss by a country of its most intelligent and best-educated people

Traditionally, a major destination for these skilled workers has been the United States, due to such factors as the existence of top-quality universities, dynamic companies, an open, merit-based economic system, the social environment, and the standard of living. Because of the salary and research opportunities available, the United States continues to attract scientists and engineers from other countries, and these immigrants have become an essential element for the health of the U.S. economy. For example, almost 25 percent of college-educated workers in the United States are foreign-born, as are over 50 percent of workers with doctorates in engineering. Roughly 53 percent of foreign students remain in the United States after receiving doctorates in science. Figure 12.6 shows the country of birth for foreign-born individuals in the United States who have a doctoral degree in science or engineering. Over one-third of these people are from the developing countries of China and India.

FIGURE 12.5

Brain Drain: Countries with the Highest Percentage of Their College-Educated Citizens Living in Other Countries

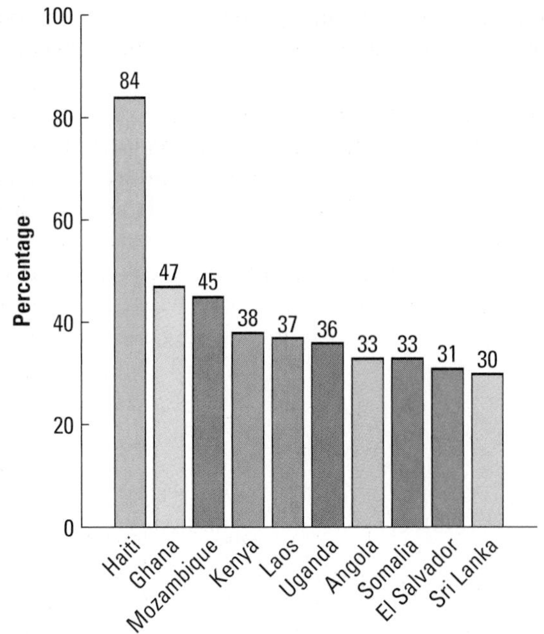

Note: Chart includes only those nations with populations of at least 5 million people.

Source: *International Migration, Remittances and the Brain Drain* (Washington, DC: World Bank, 2005). Reprinted by permission of The World Bank via The Copyright Clearance Center.

FIGURE 12.6

Foreign-Born Individuals with Science or Engineering Doctorate Degree, Living in the U.S., by Nation of Birth, 2003

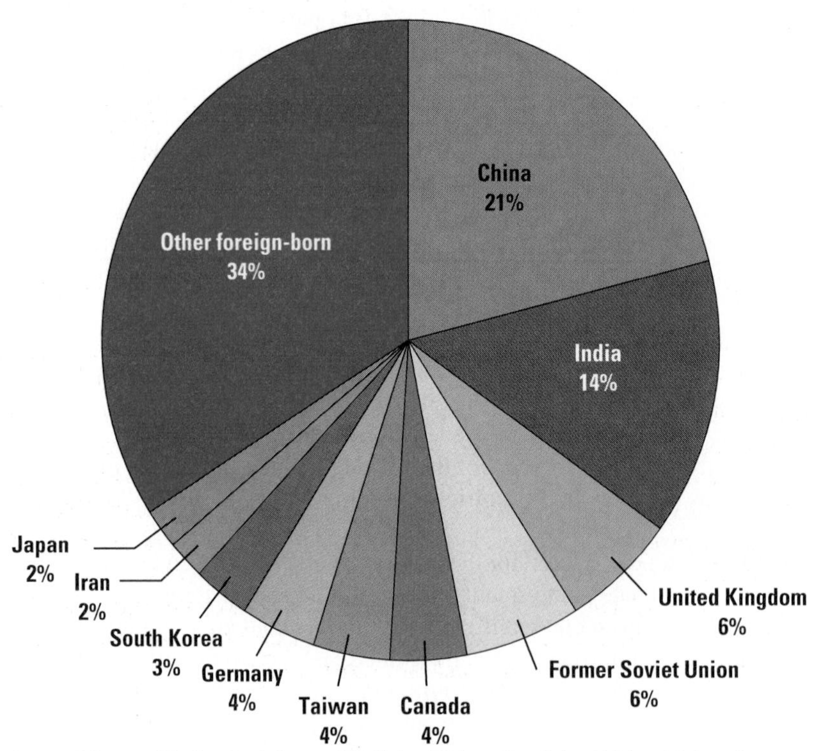

Source: *Science and Engineering Indicators 2006*, National Science Foundation, Division of Science Resources Statistics, www.nsf.gov/statistics/seind06/c3/fig03-39.htm (July 29, 2006).

Seeing the benefits that the United States has received from attracting these skilled foreign workers, countries such as the United Kingdom, Canada, and Australia have reformed their immigration policies to improve their ability to attract the best minds from abroad. The result of this competition is the creation of even more opportunities for skilled workers to migrate, threatening to exacerbate the brain drain problem in developing countries. For example, the UN expected 100,000 high-tech professionals per year to leave India for positions abroad.[29]

Government authorities who are concerned with the loss of skilled workers have come to realize that there must be changes in order to avoid being sucked into a downward cycle of underdevelopment. A high level of emigration of skilled workers is symptomatic of deep economic, political, and social problems in a country. There must be faster creation of new, well-paying jobs, not only to stop the costly loss of human capital but also to avoid serious political repercussions. The pressure of the unemployed educated is also forcing officials in many areas to soften the terms for foreign investment as an option for creating incentives for these skilled people to stay in their home country.

Reverse Brain Drain Recently, American educators and businesspeople have become concerned about a *reverse brain drain,* a trend related to the growth of outsourcing and a willingness of the federal government to allow "controversial" scientists to move to other countries.[30] The growth of outsourcing in developing economies such as India is beginning to pull Indian talent back home. As one recent returnee said, "We give up the swimming pool in favor of a maid." American firms are contributing aggressively to this aspect of reverse brain drain as they outsource knowledge work—engineering, software, product design, and development—to such countries as China, India, and Russia. Intel chairman Craig Barrett has warned that Russia, China, and India already have as many as 250 million to 500 million knowledge workers—the kind of highly educated, technologically skilled employees who can write computer code, design sophisticated products, and manage high-end production processes.

Some of the scientists involved in controversial science, such as stem cell research, which is limited in the United States by the federal government, are moving to environments where such cutting-edge research is supported.

In some developing countries whose scientists and engineers have gone to industrialized nations, organizations sponsored by local industry and occasionally by governments have reverse-brain-drain programs. For example, the National Science and Technology Development Agency of Thailand sponsors a Reverse Brain Drain Association.[31]

GUEST WORKERS

Countries that receive many refugees or have high birthrates may have too many people for the available jobs, but there are also countries that have too few people. France, Germany, the Scandinavian countries, and Switzerland, all of which have low birthrates, fall into the latter category. And to those countries have come the so-called **guest workers** to perform certain types of jobs, usually in service, factory, or construction work. Most of the guest workers in these countries are from such places as Turkey, Eastern Europe, and North Africa. See the Worldview on the next page for a discussion of guest workers in Japan.

guest workers
People who go to a foreign country legally to perform certain types of jobs

Guest workers provide the labor that host countries need, which is desirable as long as the economies are growing. But when the economies slow, fewer workers are needed and problems appear. Unemployment increases among citizens, who then want the jobs held by guest workers. To appease their citizens, some countries refuse to renew guest workers' permits. In other countries, where work is seasonal, guest workers are deported at the end of the season instead of being permitted to stay and take other work.

Considerations in Employment Policies

Companies considering doing business in international markets must consider a range of issues related to the employment policies to use. Some of these issues, such as social status, sexism, racism, the existence of minorities within traditional societies, and overall labor situations commonly encountered in developing nations, are discussed in this section.

WORLD view   

Guest Workers in Japan?

Although Japan is facing a shortage of labor in many sectors, a situation exacerbated by the rapid aging of its population, the country is famous for its resistance to immigration. To help address this problem, Japan established an elaborate system in the 1990s to create more temporary openings for foreigners of Japanese descent. Brazil, with the largest population of people of Japanese descent outside Japan, subsequently has been the source of over 300,000 persons. The highly restrictive Japanese system also allows entry by other qualified persons, including those qualifying under training-with-employment schemes established primarily for people from less developed countries in the region, but work visas are offered in only 17 fields of employment. For example, Vietnam has approximately 3,000 workers legally in Japan under training-employment programs.

Beyond those restricted categories, Japan does not have guest workers in the European sense, where they are legal. Yet there are thousands of other foreign workers in Japan, coming mostly from such nations as Vietnam, the Philippines, Bangladesh, and Pakistan. These workers commonly enter Japan with tourist or entertainment visas, as students, or as trainee-probationers, often on false passports, and then they find jobs and stay. In 2006, then Prime Minister Junichiro Koizumi said there were 250,000 illegal migrant workers in Japan.

The law only prohibits these migrant laborers from working in Japan; it does not prohibit employers from hiring them. So clandestine workers in Japan essentially have no legal rights. They cannot force employers to pay fair wages or appeal to the police for help.

A Japan Labor Ministry survey showed that on average these illegal workers earn less than half the wages of their Japanese coworkers. Firms save even more on labor costs because illegal workers do not receive the insurance or other benefits usually demanded by Japanese employees. These non-Japanese laborers often work 60 to 70 hours a week in small factories, the fast-food industry, or construction.

Japan's contractors and smaller manufacturers have begun to depend on cheap foreign labor to offset rising costs and competition from lower-cost nations such as China. Even at much higher legal wages and benefits, there is a severe shortage of Japanese laborers who are willing to perform the dangerous or dirty work done by the illegal workers.

The situation is particularly dangerous for young women employed in the bars and massage parlors of Japan's ubiquitous "entertainment industry." As frequently happens, young women come to Japan expecting to work as waitresses or hotel clerks, but exploitative business owners take their passports away and force them to work as prostitutes.

Japan historically has relied heavily on foreign workers to fill labor shortages, but it is far from a melting pot. Thousands of Koreans and Chinese were forcibly recruited during World War II to work in factories and mines. Most of the more than 600,000 people of Korean and Chinese ancestry who remain in Japan are virtually indistinguishable from their Japanese neighbors. Over 75 percent were born in Japan and speak Japanese fluently. Nevertheless, they are still classified as "resident aliens," must carry alien registration cards, and are regarded as "other" by many Japanese.

Source: Charles Barneholtz, "Guests, but Not So Welcome," www.westernreview.com/barney3.htm (July 28, 2006); "Migration News: Japan, Korea," http://migration.ucdavis.edu/mn/more.php?id=3191_0_3_0 (July 28, 2006); Wolfgang Herbert, *Foreign Workers and Law Enforcement in Japan* (New York: Columbia University Press, 1997); "Assessment for Koreans in Japan," www.humansecuritygateway.info/data/item819082824/view (July 28, 2006); and "Guest Workers Urged to Learn New Language," www.vneconomy.com.vn/eng/index.php?param=article&catid=09&id=74ff2a118356a5 (July 28, 2006).

SOCIAL STATUS

Chapter 6 discussed the importance of culture to international business. Culture is especially important with respect to the labor force, since culture so dominates human behavior and attitudes. Understanding social status is necessary to understanding cultures because in some cultures, social divisions are more extreme than in others. The Worldview on page 337 provides a brief overview of social status in three nations: the United Kingdom, India, and Japan.

SEXISM

Acceptability of women as full participants in the work force ranges from a trend toward improvement in the United States and Western Europe to almost no acceptability in some other countries. In many countries, laws, customs, and attitudes continue to act as barriers to women in business. Sexism, the denial of equal participation in a society for women, developed as an inherent part of many cultures, based as they are on patriarchal values. Greater awareness of the importance of providing equal opportunity for both genders and changing attitudes toward the roles of women in society in general and business in particular have made it possible for women to succeed in business in many parts of the world. Culture and tradition, though, continue to make full and equal participation difficult for women.

WORLD view

Social Status in the United Kingdom, India, and Japan

United Kingdom

The class system in the United Kingdom may be eroding, but people there are still classified by the accents they acquire at home and school. When Margaret Thatcher was elected prime minister, commentators saw fit to point out that she was "only" the daughter of a small-store owner even though her accent was "upper class," apparently acquired at Oxford University. Although class differences do not cause riots in the United Kingdom, as caste differences have in India, a foreign employer should nevertheless be conscious of the possibilities for friction arising from lack of knowledge of those differences and their potential impacts.

India

There are societies in which people's social status is established by the *caste* into which they are born. India presents an extreme example of the caste system. Intercaste battles that cause fatalities and home burnings still occur occasionally between upper-caste Hindus and the untouchables, whom Mahatma Gandhi called *Harijans*, the children of God. An employer must tread carefully when both upper-caste Hindus and Harijans are in the employee pool.

Caste remains pervasive in India, a populous country of growing importance in the world. Any businessperson venturing to India must understand some facts about caste. At the top is the *Brahmin* (priest, teacher), followed by the *Kshatriya* (variously landholder, warrior, or ruler). At the third level is the *Bania* (businessman), which is a step above the *Shudra* (laborer). The top three are considered upper caste and include 15 percent of India's population and have ruled the country for 3,000 years. Another 50 percent of the population belongs to the laboring, or Shudra, caste. Roughly 20 percent are casteless or untouchables considered beyond the pale of Hindu society. The remaining 15 percent belong to other religions—11 percent are Muslim, and the others are Buddhists, Christians, Parsis, and Sikhs.

Caste rules are rigid, and those who deviate from them are shunned. Caste divides Indian society into groups whose members do not intermarry and usually will not eat with each other.

Change is occurring, though. The young, including the children of the Brahmins and Kshatriya, no longer view civil service as the career of choice. Many want to get an MBA and go into business; money, rather than power, is what motivates many young people. Another change is the conversion of Hindus to other religions to escape their low caste or untouchable status.

Japan

In Japan, there remains a caste holdover from the 17th century, when the feudal Togugawa regime imposed a rigid social pecking order on the country. The warrior-administrator samurai were at the top. Below them were farmers and artisans, then merchants, and, at the very bottom, those with occupations considered dirty and distasteful, such as slaughterers, butchers, and tanners.

As in India, where discrimination against untouchables is illegal, all natives of Japan who are of the Japanese race are legally equal. However, the descendants of the lowest Japanese class remain trapped in their ghettos, working in small family firms that produce knitted garments, bamboo wares, fur and leather goods, shoes, and sandals. They call themselves *burakumin* (ghetto people) and claim they number about 3 million people living in some 6,000 ghettos. Their average income remains below that of other Japanese.

The word *burakumin* is almost never aired in the Japanese media, and foreign books that touch on the problem have all references to it deleted when they are translated into Japanese. One woman, Sue Sumii, although she was not a burakumin, lived near one of their ghettos and recorded and decried its residents' plight in speeches, articles, and a series of stories. Sumii made links between the Japanese imperial family's wealth and burakumin wretchedness and between the shared religious roots of emperor worship and scorn for the burakumin.

Women encounter major problems in making or retaining progress, as sexism is widespread throughout the world. It is often difficult for women to do business in Saudi Arabia and other Middle Eastern countries. For example, the law and customs in Saudi Arabia have prevented the commingling of men and women in the workplace, and women have been prohibited from driving vehicles. Reports of sexism, particularly versus migrant workers, are rampant.[32] Yet, even in Saudi Arabia, the role of women is changing. For example, programs have recently been set up to encourage women to start businesses, the range of sectors in which women can work has been expanded, and women managers can have males as their subordinates.[33]

Worldwide, 59 percent of all businesses include women in senior management positions, although women fill less than 19 percent of all senior management jobs. Women are senior managers in 70 percent of New Zealand businesses, although only one-third of all senior management positions in New Zealand are held by women. Only 22 percent of senior managers in Australia are female. Only 29 percent of companies in Japan have filled senior management slots with women, and women constitute only 8 percent of senior managers. In Russia,

FIGURE 12.7 Female Illiteracy

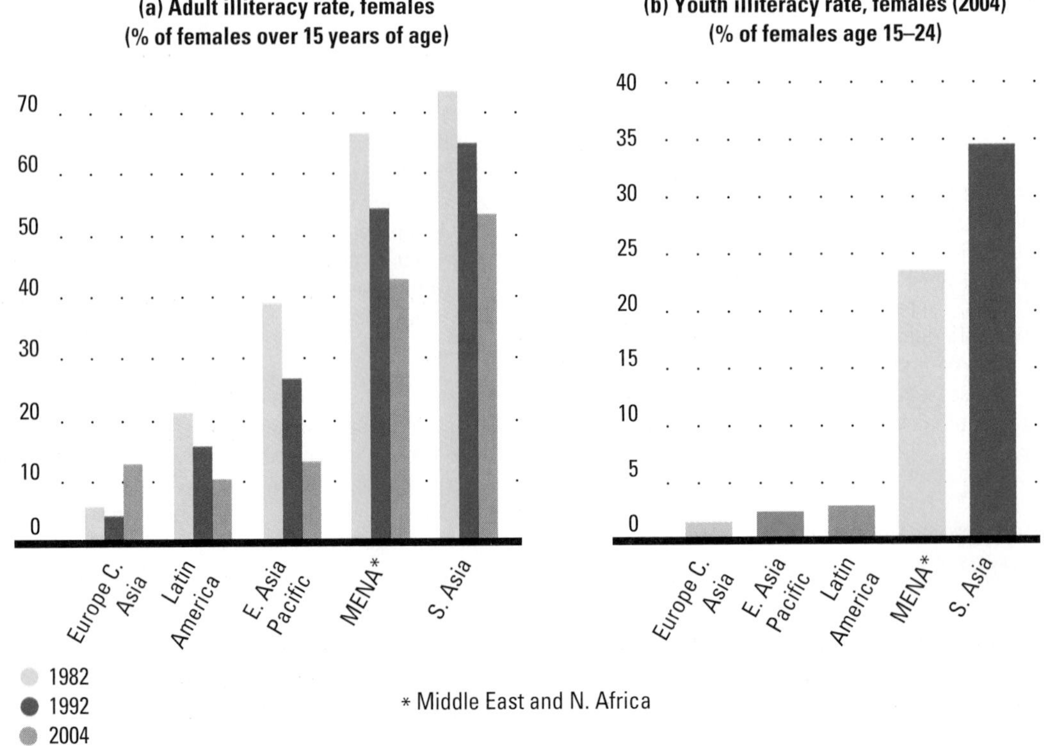

Source: *World Development Indicators,* World Bank (2006). Copyright © 2006 by World Bank. Reproduced with permission of World Bank in the format textbook via Copyright Clearance Center.

89 percent of the companies have staffed senior management positions with women, and 42 percent of their management positions are filled by women.[34]

Women's Education Studies show a persistent correlation between the length of women's schooling and birthrates, child survival, family health, and a nation's overall prosperity. As Figure 12.7 indicates, women's education is making marked improvements, with the rate of illiteracy declining significantly across all regions during the past two decades. An increasing number of countries are realizing the importance of educating females. For example, the Egyptian government is integrating a successful concept of girl-friendly community schools into the formal education system. These schools use female teachers, active learning, and child-centered class management. In one region of China, villages and households that send girls to school are given priority for loans or development funds. A promising initiative in Tanzania aims to find solutions to obstacles to the social and academic development of girls by encouraging girls to speak out about their problems.[35] In the United States, for the first time, the group of women between the ages of 25 and 35 has more formal education than does its male counterpart. About half the students in American business schools are now women.

Problems Persist Even in countries where women have made some strides, their progress is not necessarily secure. When the fundamentalist Islamic government took control from the shah in Iran in 1979, it separated the sexes, ordering women to return to their strict traditional dress and roles. In recent years, women have regained some opportunities. Iran is a society with firm gender roles, as are Afghanistan, Iraq, and many other collectivist societies with high "power distance" (see Chapter 6, "Sociocultural Forces"). Even in the United States today, women have made great advancements yet continue to face discrimination, especially in advancing into the higher levels of business management.

Another measure of the prevalence of women in positions of authority is the proportion of their membership in national parliaments. Figure 12.8 shows the percentages of seats held

FIGURE 12.8 Women in Parliament, Selected Nations, 2006

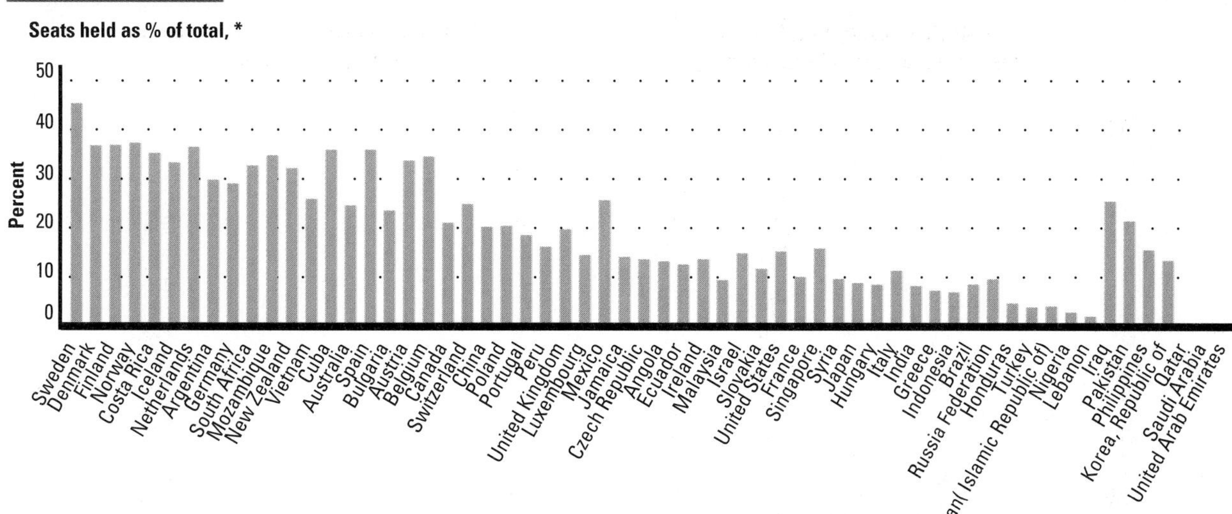

* Lower or single house.

Source: UN Statistics Division, "Seats Held by Women in National Parliament, Percentage," http://mdgs.un.org/unsd/mdg/SeriesDetail.aspx?srid=557 (July 30, 2006).

for various nations, with Sweden having the highest at 45.3 percent and Qatar, Saudi Arabia, and the United Arab Emirates having the lowest, with zero percent. Note that the proportion of women in parliament lags their proportion in the society as a whole for each one of these countries.

Another persistent gender-related problem in the labor markets is the issue of maternity and ensuing family responsibilities. Although in the United States there is much talk of "family-friendly" business practices, as Table 12.1 indicates, the maternity leave arrangements in the United States are not comparable to those of EU countries. The challenges for women who choose to be mothers and have professional careers just begin at childbirth. There is no public day care and only the best employers make such support available. Depending on location, private day care standards vary greatly.

Throughout most of the world, women on average still earn only a fraction of the level of pay that men earn for comparable positions, as shown in Table 12.2 for the OECD nations. However, as this table shows, the gap between women and men has been shrinking in most of the OECD countries.

RACISM

Unfortunately, examples of racial conflicts and discrimination are found worldwide. There are black-versus-white conflicts in the United States, South Africa, Great Britain, and elsewhere, and Arab-, Indian-, or Pakistani-versus-black conflicts in Africa. Racial friction exists related to the guest workers in parts of Europe. There has been bloody conflict in Sri Lanka between Tamils and Sinhalese. The list goes on: Bosnia, Kosovo, Zimbabwe, Rwanda, Burundi, the Sudan.

If we think of racism as a form of extended and institutionalized prejudice, globalization, as it increases individual contacts among quite different people, may work against racism. This hope may not be shared by some, who see the process of globalization as a source of increased racism. The reasoning for hope is that successful international managers develop a global mind-set,[36] made up of cognitive complexity and a cosmopolitan attitude that, in its openness to the world and valuing of difference, leaves no room for racism.

The United Nations–sponsored World Conference on Racial Discrimination, Xenophobia, and Related Intolerance, held in South Africa, has initiated efforts to establish nation-level bodies to address these particular issues: trafficking in women and children, migration

TABLE 12.1 Maternity Leave Legislation

Country	Maternity Leave: Length (weeks)	Payment (% earnings)	Continuation of Payment by Employer	Parental Leave: Length (months)	Maximum Child Age (years)	Payment
Austria	16	100	Low-wage workers	3–24	2	410 euros/month
Netherlands	16	100	No	6	8	Unpaid
Spain	16	100	No	—	3	Unpaid
Luxembourg	16	—	No	6	5	1,487 euros/month
Germany	14	100	No	—	3	306 euros/month
Greece	14	100	No	3.5	3.5	Unpaid
Italy	18	80	No	10	3	30% earnings
France	16–26	84	Yes	—	3	461 euros/month
United Kingdom	14	90	No	3.25	5	Unpaid
Portugal	12.5	100	No	6	3	Unpaid
Denmark	18	67	Yes	2–12	8	920 euros/month
Finland	17.5	66	Yes	6.5	3	10 euros/day
Belgium	15	82 first month, 75 rest	No	3	4	505 euros/month
Ireland	14	70	No	3.5	5	Unpaid
Sweden	12	80	—	18	8	80% earnings
United States	12	Unpaid	No	—	—	—

Source: Ghazala Azmat, Mara Güell, and Alan Manning, "Gender Gaps in OECD Countries," www.oecd.org (2004).

and discrimination, gender and racial discrimination, racism against indigenous peoples, and protection of minority rights. See the United Nations Personal Pledge against Racism in Figure 12.9.

MINORITIES IN TRADITIONAL SOCIETIES

traditional societies Tribal peoples before they turn to organized agriculture or industry; traditional customs may linger after the economy changes

minorities A relatively smaller number of people identified by race, religion, or national origin who live among a larger majority

Traditional societies present opportunities as well as problems for employers. In some societies, merchants, businesspeople, and bankers are looked down on and people prefer political, religious, military, professional, or agricultural careers. In such societies, outsiders may dominate commercial and banking activities. Some examples are the Indians and Pakistanis in East Africa, the Chinese in Southeast Asia, and the Greeks in Turkey.

An advantage for a foreign employer moving into these societies is that such **minorities** may be immediately available, bringing financial and managerial skills to the employer. They speak the local language and usually one or more others, and they are less nationalistic than the majority. A disadvantage is that such people are often unpopular with the majority local population. Foreign employers can easily become too dependent on minority employees, thus becoming isolated and insulated from the world of the majority. Discrimination against such minorities has often occurred. In Uganda, for example, the government seized the property, shops, and land of people of Indian and Pakistani heritage, drove them out, and turned the seized assets over to native Ugandan citizens. In Zimbabwe, the government seized the land and assets of whites and gave these assets to black Zimbabweans, most of whom were supporters of President Mugabe's ruling party.

TABLE 12.2 Ratio of Wages, Women versus Men, Selected OECD Countries

Country	1990–1993	1999–2001
Australia	0.80	0.84
Austria	0.68	0.80
Belgium	0.75	0.88
Canada	0.69	0.74
Denmark	0.83	0.86
Finland	0.75	0.82
France	0.75	0.88
Hungary	0.81	0.79
Iceland	0.87	0.84
Ireland	0.80	0.80
Italy	0.83	0.85
Japan	0.56	0.64
Netherlands	0.72	0.79
Norway	0.85	0.86
Poland	0.82	0.85
Spain	0.72	0.86
Sweden	0.78	0.83
Switzerland	0.69	0.78
United States	0.73	0.78
United Kingdom	0.69	0.75
West Germany	0.74	0.81

Source: Nicole M. Fortin, "Gender Role Attitudes and the Labour Market Outcomes of Women across OECD Countries," www.econ.ubc.ca/nfortin/genderole.ppt (July 30, 2006).

LABOR IN DEVELOPING NATIONS

The labor situation in many developing economies faces several formidable challenges. First are the effects of poverty, which, as we have seen, impact the quality of the labor force. Low education levels, which are found in many developing nations, especially among females, are a critical handicap. In addition, with the growth of globalization, businesses in many developing nations face global-level competition. Increasingly, there is less tolerance in the globalizing marketplace for local inefficiencies. As if these developments were not enough in the way of challenge, the devastations of HIV/AIDS, exacerbated by local poverty, low levels of education, and social unrest, have created labor shortages that many developing nations will face for the foreseeable future. In these economies, up-skilling, or training the local work force to minimally acceptable standards, is a primary employer challenge.

In developing nations where there is a high level of education, outsourcing of production, IT support, and, increasingly, service functions such as customer service help lines and marketing lead follow-ups have been the recent trend. This has become a political issue in the United States, because it represents jobs transferred from the U.S. economy to a developing economy such as India. But from the developing country's point of view, it may be seen as one of the benefits of globalization.

Employer-Employee Relationships

The relationship between employers and employees varies in countries around the world. In some countries, employers must deal with strong labor unions. In others, employers must deal with governments representing employees. In any case, a company seeking to employ people must be aware of the local employment context.

FIGURE 12.9

UN Pledge against Racism

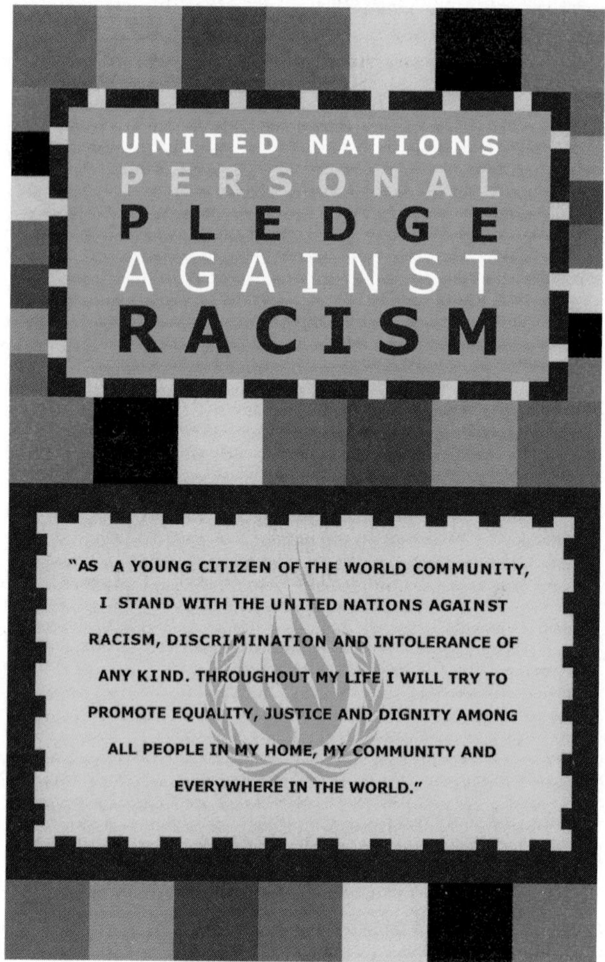

Source: Photo courtesy of UN, www.UN.org/WCAR (2006).

IMPORTANCE OF PROPER PREPARATION WHEN ENTERING A MARKET

labor market
The pool of available potential employees with the necessary skills within commuting distance from an employer

When a foreign company arrives in a **labor market,** it must take what it finds. Of course, a prudent company will study the labor market when considering whether to invest in a country. A company does not even have to travel to a prospective host country to gain information about its labor force. In addition to *Foreign Labor Trends* released by the Bureau of International Labor Affairs of the U.S. Department of Labor, two good information sources are the *Handbook of Labor Statistics* (available from the Bureau of Labor Statistics of the U.S. Department of Labor in Washington, D.C.) and the *Yearbook of Labor Statistics* (published by the United Nations' International Labor Office in Geneva, Switzerland). These sources give information for most countries of the world on several subjects, including the number of labor strikes, or work stoppages, per year. The number of workers who went on strike is indicated, as is the number of working days lost. Last, but perhaps most informative, the days lost per thousand employees in nonagricultural industries for each country is reported. The countries about which those labor figures are reported vary greatly in size, culture, labor laws, and militancy of labor unions. Thus, the days lost per thousand is the only direct comparison among them. Figure 12.10 shows the average number of working days lost through labor disputes per 1,000 employees for selected OECD nations across the most recent decade. These statistics are all raw numbers, and potential employers should investigate more deeply when considering a labor market.

Here are some other questions that employers should look into: (1) Was the period abnormal for any of the countries? (2) Were the strikes peaceful, or were they accompanied by violence, destruction, or death? (3) Were the strikes industrywide, or were they only against

FIGURE 12.10 Country Strike Rates, Selected OECD Nations

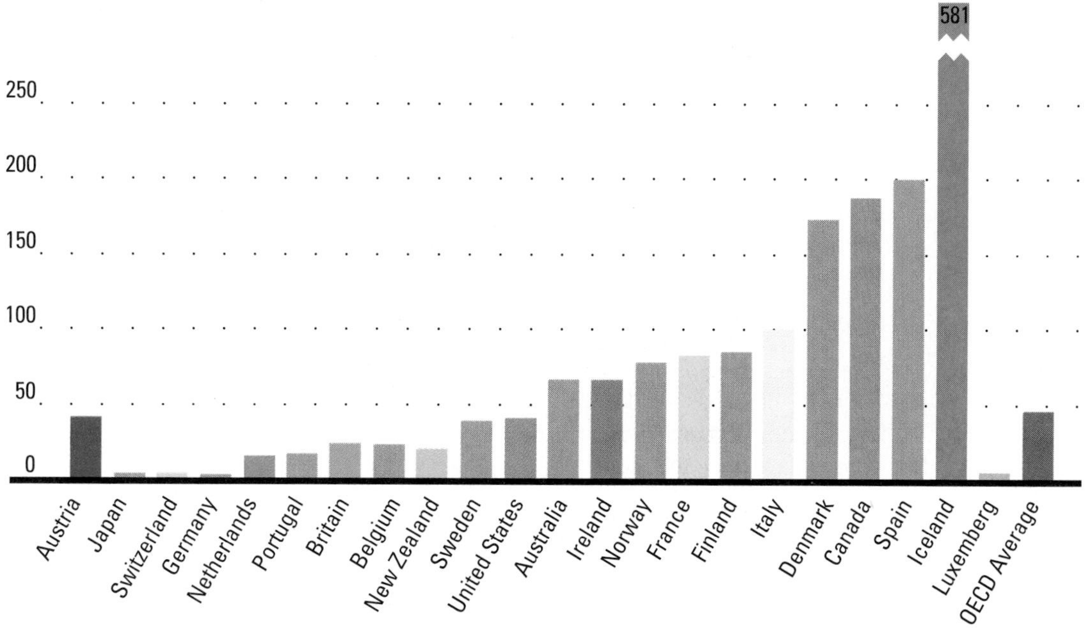

Source: Rachel Beardsmore, "International Comparisons of Labour Disputes in 2004," in Office for National Statistics (U.K.), *Labor Market Trends,* April 2006, p. 119, http://www.statistics.gov.uk/articles/labour_market_trends/Int_labourdisputes.pdf (November 13, 2006). © Crown Copyright. Reproduced under the terms of the Click-Use License.

selected employers? (4) Were the strikes wildcat (unannounced), or was there usually warning that they were coming? and (5) Do the unions and the workers abide by labor agreements, and if not, what can the employer do?

Companies planning to invest in traditional-society developing countries will examine the cultural, religious, tribal, and other factors discussed elsewhere in this text. Of course, religious, racial, and linguistic schisms are not confined to developing countries.

LABOR UNIONS: EUROPE, UNITED STATES, AND JAPAN

Labor unions vary significantly from country to country. Labor unions tend to be more effective in developed countries, but even comparing Europe, the United States, and Japan, it is apparent that labor unions serve different purposes and influence employee matters differently.

labor unions
Organizations of workers

European labor unions are usually identified with political parties and socialist ideology. A sense of worker identity is common in these unions, probably because European labor gained freedom from feudalism as well as various rights and powers through collective action.

In the United States, by contrast, laborers already possessed many civil rights, including the vote, by the time unions became important. As a result, unionism in the United States often has been viewed as more pragmatic than political and more concerned with the immediate needs of workers.

collective bargaining
The process in which a union represents the interests of a bargaining unit (which sometimes includes both union members and nonmembers) in negotiations with management

Labor legislation in the United States has mostly confined itself to the framework of **collective bargaining.** Collective bargaining is the process in which a union represents the interests of everyone in a bargaining unit (which sometimes includes both union members and nonmembers) in negotiations with management. In Europe, government's role is more active, with wages and working conditions frequently legislated. Many Latin American governments are very active in employer-employee relationships, frequently because the unions are weak and the union leaders are inexperienced or uneducated.

In Germany and France, the influences of law and government administrative actions on work conditions are extensive and evident. Labor negotiations are conducted on national or regional levels, and in France, government representatives take part in the negotiations.

Japanese unions are enterprise-based rather than industrywide and, as a result, tend to identify strongly with the interests of the company. For example, if unions are convinced a high wage increase would hurt the company's competitiveness, they tend to not ask for much of a pay raise.

Labor Union Membership Trends

For the past four decades there has been a steady decline in union membership internationally. The reasons for this trend are several:

- Employers have made efforts to keep their businesses union-free, including putting employees on business boards and instituting profit-sharing plans. This co-option approach has had its desired effect in many cases.
- More women and teenagers have joined the work force, and since theirs are usually secondary incomes, they accept lower wages and have little loyalty toward organized labor.
- The unions have been successful. Their results have led to wage increases, which have led to higher costs and lower competitiveness of their employers, which have led to layoffs, downsizing, and movement of jobs to lower-cost locations. So in this sense, unions have been the victims of their own success.
- As developed countries transition to a knowledge economy, the industrial jobs that have formed the core of union membership are declining.

MULTINATIONAL LABOR ACTIVITIES

The internationalization of business has been under way for many years, and international companies have expanded rapidly since the 1950s. National unions have begun to perceive opportunities for companies to escape the organizing reach of unions through the relatively simple step of international outsourcing, transferring production to another country. Unions see such steps as dangerous. To combat those dangers, national unions have begun to (1) collect and disseminate information about companies, (2) consult with unions in other countries, (3) coordinate with those unions' policies and tactics in dealing with some companies, and (4) encourage international companies' codes of conduct. Such multinational labor activity is likely to increase, although unions are divided by ideological differences and are frequently strongly nationalistic. Vastly more effort and money have been spent on lobbying for protection of national industries than on cooperating with unions in other countries.

An important first arena in which successful multinational unionism may develop is the European Union. The EU member-countries are steadily eliminating or harmonizing their tariffs, taxes, monetary systems, laws, and much more. As further progress is made in this harmonization process, the resulting atmosphere may be more hospitable for the cooperation of national unions.

Also working in this area is the European Trade Union Confederation (ETUC), an umbrella organization representing 81 national union federations, representing 60 million members in 36 nations.[37] Some ETUC member-unions are doing very well on their own, cooperating across borders in pursuit of a common goal.

The U.S. union federation, the AFL-CIO, cooperates with labor organizations worldwide, including ETUC, the International Confederation of Free Trade Unions (ICFTU), the Asia Pacific Regional Organization (APROICFTU), and the Latin America Regional Organization (ORIT-ICFTU).

Union Network International was formed in 2000 to promote global union efforts in response to the increasing level of globalization of industries and employers. Based in Switzerland, it includes 900 unions with over 15 million members in over 140 nations.

International Labor Organization

The International Labor Organization (ILO) is a specialized agency of the UN whose purpose is to promote social justice and internationally recognized human and labor rights worldwide. The ILO was founded in 1919 and is the only surviving major creation of the Treaty of Versailles, which founded the League of Nations. It became the first specialized agency of the UN in 1946. Today, the ILO formulates international labor standards in the form of treaties and recommendations setting minimum standards for basic labor rights: freedom of association, the right to organize, collective bargaining, abolition of forced labor, equality of opportunity and treatment, and other standards regulating working conditions. More information can be obtained at the ILO's Web site, www.ilo.org.

Trade Union Advisory Committee to the OECD As discussed in Chapter 4, the Organization for Economic Cooperation and Development (OECD) is an international organization designed to assist with economic development issues in its member-nations. The Trade Union Advisory Committee (TUAC) is an international trade union organization with consultative status with the OECD and its various committees. TUAC's role is to ensure that labor issues are considered in global markets. TUAC represents the views of the trade union movement as it regularly consults with the various OECD committees. More information about TUAC can be found at the organization's Web site, www.tuac.org.

Would Harmonized Labor Standards Boost Trade and Income? Labor unions, human rights activists, and some developed country governments argue that access to their markets should be dependent on improved labor standards in developing countries and that trade sanctions should be imposed for violation of those standards (the so-called social clause). Other governments in both developed and developing countries see the social clause as protectionism. Yet even in trade agreements, governments argue for strict labor standards. NAFTA, which was negotiated among the United States, Canada, and Mexico, includes major sections involving labor matters.

According to the International Monetary Fund (IMF), the economic arguments for harmonizing labor standards are weak. In fact, well-intentioned attempts to impose higher labor standards on developing countries may actually be detrimental to workers, especially if they are enforced through trade sanctions. Low labor standards are not the primary source of developing countries' comparative advantage, while most labor standards—such as minimum wages—are not attainable in many poor countries.

Higher labor standards, the IMF points out, are primarily a consequence rather than a cause of economic growth, and the surest way to improve labor standards in poor countries is through economic growth, which international trade facilitates. Accordingly, pursuing trade and labor market policies conducive to high growth rates will be far more effective in raising labor incomes than will be mandating levels of wages and benefits or imposing trade sanctions for perceived violations.

Summary

Identify forces beyond management control that affect the quantity and quality of labor in a nation.

Labor quality and labor quantity are forces beyond a company's control. A finite number of employees are available in any labor pool with the skills required to meet an employer's needs. Populations are aging and are projected to decline in many developed countries in coming years. Labor is shifting significantly from rural to urban locations, especially in developing nations. Unemployment remains a problem in many regions and particularly among youths between the ages of 15 and 24. Large numbers of immigrant laborers, often unskilled, are moving within and particularly between nations. Although progress is being made, an estimated one in seven children between the ages of 5 and 17 is a laborer and most of these child laborers are in the developing countries.

Explain the reasons people leave their home countries to work abroad.

In many parts of the world, wars, revolutions, racial and ethnic battles, and political repression cause people to flee. Others go to other countries in hopes of better jobs and pay.

Discuss the reasons that some countries have guest workers.

Guest workers move to a host country to perform specific types of jobs, usually in service, factory, or construction work. But when a country's economy slows, its native workers may want the jobs held by guest workers. Racial friction has developed in some countries because of guest workers.

Explain factors associated with employment policies, including social roles, gender, race, and minorities.

ICs typically must adjust their labor practices to succeed in international markets, due to a range of factors influencing employment policies and practices. Even where laws have changed to prohibit the practice, cultural, historical and other factors cause social status to be a relevant consideration regarding employment practices. Although women are making progress toward equality in many nations, sexism remains a problem throughout the world. Women continue to have higher levels of illiteracy and lower levels of wages than their male counterparts in virtually all regions of the world, and they are underrepresented in business and political positions of authority. Racism also remains an issue worldwide.

Discuss differences in labor unions from country to country.

Historically, labor unions have tended to be more political in Europe and more pragmatic in the United States. In response to globalization of businesses, many unions have begun to establish international collaboration in an effort to extend their influence.

Key Words

labor quality (p. 324)
labor quantity (p. 324)
labor mobility (p. 330)
child labor (p. 332)
brain drain (p. 333)
guest workers (p. 335)
traditional societies (p. 340)
minorities (p. 340)
labor market (p. 342)
labor unions (p. 343)
collective bargaining (p. 343)

Questions

1. a. How could an excess of qualified employees be beneficial for an employer?
   b. How could it be detrimental?
2. Why is the average age of the population increasing in some nations, particularly the developed countries? What are some of the implications of this trend, especially for international companies?
3. Classical economists assumed the labor factor of production to be immobile. Is this assumption correct in the modern world? Explain.
4. Analyze arguments made by representatives of Nepal and other poor countries in justifying the child labor they utilize.
5. What is brain drain, and why does it occur? What actions might countries take in order to reduce or even reverse brain drain?
6. What trends are evident in the way women are treated relative to men in terms of education, employment, and positions of authority? How and why do these trends vary across countries and regions of the world?
7. In several Southeast Asian and South Pacific countries, the Chinese minority is prominent in banking, finance, and business. What are the dangers for a foreign employer staffing the local company primarily with such a minority?
8. What is a major difference between unions in Europe, the United States, and Japan?
9. What are the prospects for effective multinational union collaboration? Discuss.

Research Task

globalEDGE.msu.edu 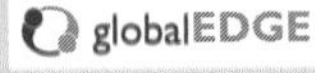

Use the globalEDGE site (http://globalEDGE.msu.edu/) to complete the following exercises:

1. The participation of women in the labor force varies from one country to another. After finding a report on *International Labor Comparisons*, find information concerning labor force participation rates by gender for France, Germany, Japan, Sweden, and the United States. For the last year in which data were available for these five countries, develop a ranking based on the level of participation of women in the workforce. Which country had the highest level? Which had the lowest?
2. According to this textbook, a nation's immigration policy is a good reference point for examining labor mobility. Using CIA's *World Factbook* Web site, identify five countries with the highest net immigration rate in Europe.

Staffing Your Operations Abroad Minicase 12.1

Your company, an international company based in the United States, has decided to expand aggressively in Asia. It plans to outsource many of its raw materials, to subcontract, and to manufacture and market throughout Asia, from Japan in the north through New Zealand in the south.

You were appointed to organize and direct this major new effort and to determine where to locate the regional headquarters for the Asian division. After considerable study, you selected the island nation of Luau.

Luau's advantages are several. It is about equidistant between New Zealand and Japan. It was a British colony, so the main language is English. It has a relatively efficient telecommunications system, good ports, and good air service to all the major Asian destinations in which you are interested and to the United States.

Not least important, the Luau government is delighted to have your company locate and invest there. It has made very attractive tax concessions to the company and to its personnel who will move there.

The company moves in, leases one large building, and puts out invitations to bid on the construction of a larger building, which will be its permanent headquarters. Now, as you begin to work more with the private banking and businesspeople of Luau and less with government officials, you begin to be more aware of a Luau characteristic that you had not thought much about previously. Almost all the middle- and upper-management personnel in the business and finance sector are of Chinese extraction. The native population of Luau, which constitutes the great majority, is Micronesian.

On inquiring why the Chinese are dominant in banking and business while the Micronesians stay in farming, fishing, government work, and manual labor, you are told that this is the way it developed historically. The Chinese enjoy and are good at banking and business, while the native Luauans do not like those activities and have stayed with their traditional occupations. The two groups buy and sell from and to each other, but there are almost no social relations and very little business or professional overlap between the groups. Occasionally, some of the Micronesians study abroad, and some work abroad for periods; when they return, they frequently go to work in a bank or business or take a government position.

You must staff your headquarters with middle- and lower-management people and with clerical help. You find that the only applicants for the jobs are Chinese, and you select the best available. They are quite satisfactory, and the operation gets off to a good start.

Then, as the months pass, you notice a gradual change of attitude toward you and the company among government officials and among the people in general. They have become less friendly, more evasive, and less cooperative. You ask your Chinese staff about it, but they have noticed nothing unusual.

What could be happening? Why might the Chinese staff not notice it? What might you do to improve government and public relations?

Παγοσμιο Business
Negócios Internaciona
Gli Affari Internazional
التجارة العالمية
Los negocios internacionales
Internationales Geschäft
Affaires Internationale
International Business
Los negocios internacionales
國際商
Internationales
Παγοσμιο Busine
國際商務
Gli Affari Internazionali
Negócios Internacionais
Gli Affari Internazionali
التجارة العالمية

section four

The Organizational Environment

In the preceding three sections, the primary focus has been on the broad environmental context in which international businesses compete. Section One introduced you to issues regarding the nature of international business, including international business, trade, and investment. Section Two presented the framework of international organizations and the monetary system in which international business functions. Section Three discussed forces that affect international business and with which management must cope.

In Section Four, our attention shifts away from the external environment and focuses instead on the business itself, including actions that managers can take to help their companies compete more effectively as international businesses. In identifying potential management responses and solutions to problems caused or magnified by the foreign and international environments, this book is intended to be only an introduction to international business. Deeper discussions into specific areas can be found in textbooks specializing in those areas.

Chapter 13 deals with the concept of international competitive strategy and how companies use strategic planning to address international business opportunities and challenges. Chapter 14 looks at organizational design and the different ways in which international companies can be structured. Chapter 15 deals with assessing and analyzing international markets. Chapter 16 explores ways in which a company can enter international markets. Chapter 17 deals with practices and procedures for exporting and importing. Chapter 18 explores international marketing and ways in which it differs from domestic marketing. Chapter 19 deals with operations management in international companies, including management of international supply chains. Chapter 20 presents material on managing human resources in international businesses, particularly nonexecutive, technical, or sales employees. Chapter 21 covers financial management issues that arise in conjunction with international business activities.

13 International Competitive Strategy

What business strategy is all about— what distinguishes it from all other kinds of business planning—is, in a word, competitive advantage. Without competitors there would be no need for strategy, for the sole purpose of strategic planning is to enable the company to gain, as effectively as possible, a sustainable edge over its competitors.

— Kenichi Ohmae, McKinsey & Company consultant

Thinking Strategically about the Future in an Uncertain World

What would happen if the prices of oil or copper were to skyrocket (as they did during much of 2005 and 2006) or suddenly crash? What are the chances of a host government nationalizing an industry, such as Bolivia did in its oil and natural gas sector in May 2006? What are the implications of increasing urbanization and industrialization in emerging markets, such as India, China, or Brazil? These are examples of scenarios—stories about possible futures—that the global energy company Royal Dutch Shell employs in its strategic planning process. The objective of this process is to force executives to question their assumptions about the environments in which the company operates and successfully incorporate the uncertainty and potential changes that might profoundly impact their strategic and operational performance around the world.

Back in the 1970s, Shell used scenario planning as a fundamental tool for thinking strategically about the future, working on how to handle uncertainty in the company's long-range planning. The strategic planning group adapted techniques developed by the Rand Corporation for the U.S. Department of Defense. They developed scenarios in order to improve the quality of decisions that had huge financial implications for Shell, expensive undertakings such as whether to build a new offshore oil rig or begin exploring for oil in new areas.

Recently, companies like Shell have begun modifying their approach to using scenarios in their strategic planning efforts. Formerly, the planners made the scenarios and presented them to the line managers—a kind of "show and tell." There was no involvement of the managers. Now there is an emphasis in the company on getting managers to bring scenarios into their decision processes because Shell's top management is convinced that scenario building is an important management tool.

The objective of scenario planning is to envision possible futures in a more realistic light, plan for uncertainties and discontinuous events, and develop strategies to help a company cope with these potential future states. Scenario planning helps to emphasize that the business environment is uncertain and might evolve in totally different ways, thus helping to challenge traditional perspectives regarding the organization and its environment. This provides a useful context for developing long-term strategic plans, as well as shorter-term contingency plans, which are appropriate for risky and uncertain operating situations. Scenario planning gives close attention to external and internal factors that may normally not be considered relevant but that have influence on the future.

Scenarios are plausible and challenging stories, but they are not forecasts; that is, they do not extrapolate from past data to make predictions. In fact, they are a means to force managers to realize that their assumptions based on past experience no longer apply. Also, if managers have thought out the possible outcomes, they should be quicker to react when one of those outcomes occurs. As Shell's former planning head expresses it, "They can remember the future."[a]

Managers typically work in teams of six to eight people to build scenarios. They first agree about the

CONCEPT PREVIEWS

After reading this chapter, you should be able to:

explain international strategy, competencies, and international competitive advantage

describe the steps in the global strategic planning process

explain the purpose of mission statements, vision statements, values statements, objectives, quantified goals, and strategies

describe the methods of and new directions in strategic planning

explain home replication, multidomestic, regional, global, and transnational strategies and when to use them

describe the sources of competitive information

discuss the importance of industrial espionage

Gli Affari Internazionali

nales

nales Geschäft Παγόσμιο Business

Negócios Internacionais Los Negócios Internacionais

ernacionales Affaires Internationales 國際商務 Παγόσμιο Business decision that must be made and then gather information by reading, observing, and talking with knowledgeable people. Next, the team works to identify the driving (environmental) forces and the "critical uncertainties" (the unpredictables) and prioritizes them. Three or four scenarios are commonly prepared, based on issues critical to the success of the decision. Each should depict a credible future and not be written to show the best-case, worst-case, and most likely situations. The team then identifies the implications of the scenarios and the leading indicators management must follow.

A member of a consulting firm that trains managers to use scenarios writes:

> *Using scenarios is rehearsing the future, and by recognizing the warning signs and the drama unfolding, one can avoid surprises, adapt, and act effectively. Decisions which have been pretested against a range of what fate may offer are more likely to stand the test of time, produce robust and resilient strategies, and create distinct competitive advantage. Ultimately, the end result of scenario planning is not a more accurate picture of tomorrow, but better decisions today.*[b]

The uncertainty of the world seems to have increased rather dramatically in recent years, especially in the aftermath of events such as the "9/11" tragedy in the United States, instability in global oil markets, or the tsunami that struck Asia in 2004. As a result, it is likely that international companies and their managers will demonstrate an increased interest in scenario planning as an essential part of their strategic planning activities. ■

[a]"A Glimpse of Possible Futures," *Financial Times,* August 25, 1997, p. 8.

[b]"Using Scenarios," *GBN Scenario Planning,* www.gbn.org/usingScen.html (March 20, 1998).

Source: A. J. Vogl, "Big Thinking," *Across the Board* 41, no. 1 (January–February 2004), pp. 27–33; Julie Verity, "Scenario Planning as a Strategy Technique," *European Business Journal* 15, no. 4, pp. 185–95; "20:20 Vision," *Global Scenarios,* www.shell.com/b/b2_03.html (March 15, 1998); and Hugh Courtney, "Decision-Driven Scenarios for Assessing Four Levels of Uncertainty," *Strategy and Leadership* 31, no. 1, pp. 14–22.

In the preceding three sections of this book, the primary focus has been on the broad environmental context in which international businesses compete. This discussion has included the theoretical framework for international trade and investment, the international monetary and other organizations that influence international business, and the financial, economic, physical, social, political, legal, and other institutions found in various nations. Our attention now shifts away from the external environment, and we focus instead on the business itself, including the actions managers can take to help their companies compete more effectively as international businesses. In this chapter, we will discuss the concept of international strategy and how companies use strategic planning and the analysis of competitive forces to improve their global competitiveness.

The Competitive Challenge Facing Managers of International Businesses

In Chapter 2, we discussed some of the important reasons that motivate companies to pursue international business opportunities, including the potential to increase profits and sales through access to new markets; to protect existing markets, profits, and sales; and to help satisfy management's overall desire for growth. However, in order to succeed in today's global marketplace, a company must be able to quickly identify and exploit opportunities wherever they occur, domestically or internationally. To do this effectively, managers must fully understand why, how, and where they intend to do business, now and over time. This requires that managers have a clear understanding of the company's mission, a vision for how they intend to achieve that mission, and an understanding of how they plan to compete with other companies. To meet these challenges, managers must understand the company's strengths and weaknesses and be able to compare them accurately to those of their worldwide competitors. Strategic planning provides valuable tools that help managers address these global challenges.

What Is International Strategy, and Why Is It Important?

International strategy is concerned with the way firms make fundamental choices about developing and deploying scarce resources internationally.[1] International strategy involves decisions that deal with all the various functions and activities of a company and the interactions among them, not merely a single area such as marketing or production. To be effective, a company's international strategy needs to be consistent among the various functions, products, and regional units of the company (internal consistency) as well as with the demands of the international competitive environment (external consistency).

international strategy
The way firms make choices about acquiring and using scarce resources in order to achieve their international objectives

The goal of international strategy is to achieve and maintain a unique and valuable competitive position both within a nation and globally, a position that has been termed **competitive advantage.** This suggests that the international company must either perform activities different from those of its competitors or perform the same activities in different ways. To create a competitive advantage that is sustainable over time, the international company should try to develop skills, or competencies, that (1) create value for customers and for which customers are willing to pay, (2) are rare, since competencies shared among many competitors cannot be a basis for competitive advantage, (3) are difficult to imitate or substitute for, and (4) are organized in a way that allows the company to exploit fully the competitive potential of these valuable, rare, and difficult-to-imitate competencies.[2]

competitive advantage
The ability of a company to have higher rates of profits than its competitors

Wal-Mart has become a strong competitor in the international retailing industry because it has been able to develop more effective processes for performing critical activities, such as the logistics of tying point-of-purchase data to the company's inventory management and purchasing activities. Competitors have had continued difficulties matching Wal-Mart's competencies, enabling Wal-Mart to consistently earn a return on sales that is twice the average of its industry. As a result, Wal-Mart has been able to exploit these competencies internationally by entering markets such as Canada, Mexico and other Latin American countries, Europe, and Asia, as we see in the minicase at the end of this chapter.

Managers of international companies that are attempting to develop a competitive advantage face a formidable challenge since resources—time, talent, and money—are always scarce. There are many alternative ways to use these scarce resources (for example, which nations to enter, which technologies to invest in, and which products or services to develop and offer to customers), and these alternatives are not equally attractive. A company's managers are forced to make choices regarding what to do and what *not* to do, now and over time. Different companies make different choices, and those choices have implications for each company's ability to meet the needs of customers and create a defensible competitive position internationally. Without adequate planning, managers are more likely to make decisions that do not make good sense competitively, and the company's international competitiveness may be harmed.

Global Strategic Planning

WHY PLAN GLOBALLY?

Companies are confronting a set of political, economic, social, technological, legal, and environmental forces that are increasingly complex, global, and subject to rapid change. In response, many international firms have found it necessary to institute formal global strategic planning to provide a means for top management to identify opportunities and threats from all over the world, formulate strategies to handle them, and stipulate how to finance and manage the strategies' implementation. Strategic plans help to ensure that decision makers have a common understanding of the business, the strategy, the assumptions behind the strategy, the external business environment pressures, and their own direction, as well as of promoting consistency of action among the firm's managers worldwide. Strategic plans also encourage the participants to consider the ramifications of their actions in the other geographic and functional areas of the firm. These plans provide a thorough, systematic foundation for raising key questions about what a business should become and making decisions regarding what resources and competencies the company should develop, when and how to develop them, and how to use those competencies to achieve competitive advantage. This is intended to help the organization to respond more effectively to challenges than can its competitors. Strategic planning is also intended to help increase the likelihood of strategic innovations, promoting the development, capture, and application of these new ideas in order to promote success in a challenging competitive environment. McKinsey's 2006 Global Survey revealed that 85 percent of respondents perceived their company's business environment to be "more competitive" or "much more competitive" than it was five years earlier, with the intensity of competition increasing for both small and large companies and across all industries.[3] Despite complaints about the challenges of effectively implementing planning efforts, especially within large and international companies, Bain & Company's Management Tools & Trends survey reported that strategic planning continues to be the most commonly used management tool among global executives.[4]

GLOBAL STRATEGIC PLANNING PROCESS

Global strategic planning is a primary function of a company's managers, and the ultimate manager of strategic planning and strategy making is the firm's chief executive officer. The process of strategic planning provides a formal structure in which managers (1) analyze the company's external environments, (2) analyze the company's internal environment, (3) define the company's business and mission, (4) set corporate objectives, (5) quantify goals, (6) formulate strategies, and (7) make tactical plans. For ease of understanding, we present this as a linear process, but in actuality there is considerable flexibility in the order in which firms take up these items. In company planning meetings that one of the authors attended, the procedure was iterative; that is, during the analysis of the environments, committee members could skip to a later step in the planning process to discuss the impact of a new development on a present corporate objective. They then often moved backward in the process to discuss the availability of the firm's assets to take advantage of the environmental change. If they concluded that the company had such a capability, the committee would try to formulate a new strategy. If a viable strategy was developed, the members would then establish the corporate objective that the strategy was designed to attain.

Global and Domestic Planning Processes Similar You will note that the global planning process, illustrated in Figure 13.1, has the same basic format as the planning process for a purely domestic firm. As you know by now, most activities of the two kinds of operations are similar. It is the variations in values of uncontrollable forces that make the activities in a worldwide corporation more complex than they are in a purely domestic firm.

Analyze Domestic, International, and Foreign Environments Because a firm has little opportunity to control these forces, its managers must know not only what the present values of the forces are but also where the forces appear to be headed. An environmental

FIGURE 13.1 The Global Strategic Planning Process

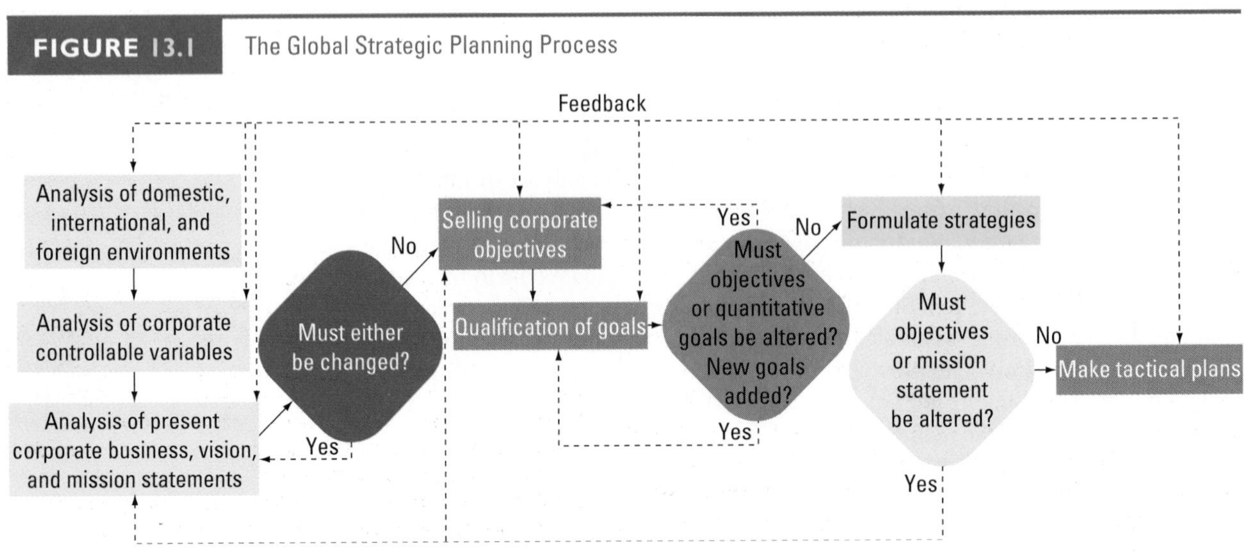

scanning process similar to the market screening process described in Chapter 15 can be used for continuous gathering of information. Yet recognition of the nature and implications of the current and future domestic, international, and foreign environments is an essential input into the global strategic planning process, as indicated by the following assessment by General Electric:

"Future economic growth will be uneven. To succeed, companies must navigate major global trends that will have significant impact on valuation. These include:

- An increasingly interdependent global economy wracked by excess manufacturing capacity and the resulting price pressure. This is why unemployment remains stubborn and margin growth is tough to achieve. Winning companies will invest in innovation and build new revenue streams from their current capabilities.
- A new economic order of global competitiveness and growth. Competition from places like China and India has evolved beyond low-cost manufacturing labor to include highly competitive engineering graduates who earn less than production workers in the developed world. Winning companies must think globally, but understand local consequences. Only competitive companies can serve investors, employees and stakeholders during this dramatic phase of globalization.
- A move to consolidate distribution channels, which creates value for consumers but makes it difficult for manufacturers to maintain margins. Winning companies will have strong direct sales forces, low costs and value propositions that tie their own profitability to their customers'.
- An opportunity to build growth platforms based on unstoppable demographics. Winning companies will sustain long-term growth by betting on high-growth markets to which they can bring unique technical and management capabilities.
- A more volatile and uncertain world. The underlying insecurity created by 9/11 and the stock market bubbles will not end soon. Winning companies will keep the confidence of customers, investors and employees by maintaining financial and cultural strength."[5]

Analyze Corporate Controllable Variables An analysis of the forces controlled by the firm will also include a situational analysis and a forecast. The managers of the various functional areas will either personally submit reports on their units or provide input to the planning staff (if there is one), who will in turn prepare a report for the strategy planning committee.

Often management will analyze the firm's activities from the time raw materials enter the plant until the end product reaches the final user, what is often called a *value chain analysis.* As part of this process, management must address three key questions about the business: (1) Who are the company's target customers? (2) What value does the company want to deliver to these customers? And (3) how will this customer value be created? The value chain analysis itself focuses primarily on the third question, and it refers to the set of value-creating activities that the company is involved with, from sources for basic raw materials or components to the ultimate delivery of the final product or service to the final customer. A simplified value chain is shown in Figure 13.2. The goal of this analysis is to enable management to determine the set of activities that will comprise the company's value chain, including which activities the company will do itself and which will be outsourced. Management must also consider where to locate various value chain activities (for example, should assembly be done in the company's home nation, located in a

Today's clothing sale prices appeal to customers but may pose challenges for businesses. To succeed in today's competitive global environment, companies need to navigate several major global trends, including an increasingly interdependent global economy wracked by excess manufacturing capacity and the resulting price pressure.

FIGURE 13.2

The Value Chain

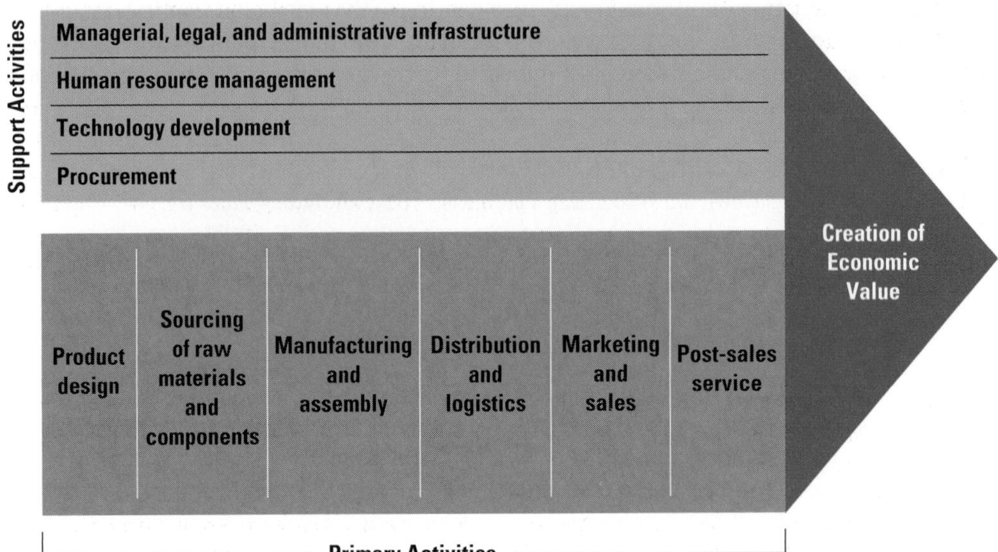

Source: Adapted from M. E. Porter, *Competitive Advantage* (New York: Free Press, 1985).

lower-cost location abroad, or located close to a customer abroad?). It is also necessary for management to examine the linkages among the activities in the value chain (for example, between sales and product development, in order to ensure that customer needs are effectively communicated and incorporated in new products). Linkages must be examined not merely across activities within the company but also in terms of managing relationships with external entities such as suppliers, alliance partners, distributors, or customers within and across nations. The desired outcome of this analysis is the identification and establishment of a superior set of well-integrated value chain activities and linkages, a system that will permit the organization to more effectively and efficiently develop, produce, market, and sell the company's products and services to the target customers, thereby creating the basis for global competitive advantage.

Knowledge as a Controllable Corporate Resource In today's highly competitive, rapidly changing, and knowledge-intensive economy, companies have the potential to achieve competitive advantages through leveraging their organizational knowledge across national boundaries. This organizational knowledge base includes the capabilities of employees (individually and in teams) as well as the knowledge that gets built into the overall organization through its various structures, systems, and organizational routines. As a valuable, scarce, and often unique organizational resource, knowledge is increasingly recognized by management as the basis for competitive advantage. As a result, managers are undertaking efforts to identify and evaluate the pool of knowledge that is contained within their companies on a global basis, including assessments of which knowledge and associated competencies will be the foundation for the company's future success. To help accelerate the acquisition, development, and exploitation of competitively valuable knowledge, managers are developing sets of techniques and practices to facilitate the flow of knowledge into and within their companies, to build knowledge databases, to transfer best practices within and across their international network of operations, and otherwise to create the foundation for a knowledge-based competitive advantage.

To effectively manage knowledge, companies must encourage individuals to work together on projects or somehow share their ideas. Much valuable knowledge is tacit, which means that it is known well by the individual but is difficult to express verbally or to document in text or figures. As a result, systems are needed in order to convey this tacit knowledge to others, possibly by converting it into explicit, codified knowledge and then making this knowledge accessible quickly and effectively to other employees who need it. In addition, to effectively design and deliver products that meet customers' needs, it is often necessary to also gain access to valuable knowledge of suppliers, customers, and other partner organizations. In some cases, it is even necessary to establish company facilities in other locations in order to gain access to this knowledge. For example, both Nokia and Ericsson established offices in the Silicon Valley in order to tap into the latest thinking of suppliers and customers located in that region and then transfer this knowledge back to headquarters in Europe. Companies face an ongoing challenge of creating mechanisms that will systematically and routinely identify opportunities for developing and transferring knowledge and for ensuring that subsidiaries are willing and able both to share what they know and to absorb knowledge from other units of the company. They also must ensure that this proprietary knowledge is managed in a way that will protect it from diffusion to competitors, in order to help the company maintain its competitiveness over time.

Sharp Electronics of Japan announced that it would begin production of system liquid crystal displays (LCDs) and build a plant for end-to-end manufacturing of large LCD televisions. Both production initiatives would be based in Japan, due to the need for close linkages between R&D and manufacturing personnel in order for Sharp to maintain competitiveness in production technology. Moving these operations to lower-cost locations abroad could have constrained the flow of ideas between Sharp's operating units, thereby hindering production improvements and the potential for fresh R&D initiatives. To limit leakage of proprietary production technology to competitors, Sharp patents many of its innovative product and production technologies. While patent applications can ensure rights to the patent holder, they also reveal technological details to the public, and proving patent violations can be expensive and time-consuming. Therefore, Sharp also identifies critical technologies that it strategically decides not to patent, choosing to instead keep these technologies completely in-house, concealed from other companies. In this way, Sharp attempts to create a barrier against competitors who try to lever off of Sharp's innovations.[6]

The importance of knowledge and its management is recognized by international companies such as DuPont, which states, "Knowledge intensity is a DuPont term meaning getting paid for what the company knows rather than simply for what it makes. Knowledge intensity is the opposite of capital intensity. It's creating value from two centuries of experience, know-how and brand equity."[7]

In order to receive a $900 million contract to provide high-tech electricity-generating turbines to China, General Electric was forced to agree to share its sophisticated technology—which GE had spent over $500 million developing—with two Chinese companies that wanted to manufacture the equipment themselves eventually. Wanting to compete in advanced manufacturing sectors in the future, China pushes foreign companies to give access to their crown jewels in technology in exchange for access to the huge Chinese market. In the case of GE's turbine contract, Chinese officials wanted to get not only the drawings for the turbine but also the modeling and mathematics underlying the shape of the blades, how blades were cooled during rotation, and the chemistry associated with the blades and with the thermal protective coating on them. Said Delbert Williamson, who was GE's president of global sales, "It was a difficult negotiation. They're interested in having total access to technology and we're interested in protecting the technology that we made significant financial investment in."[8]

After the analysis of corporate controllable variables, the planning committee must answer questions such as the following: What are our strengths and weaknesses? What are our human and financial resources? Where are we with respect to our present objectives? Have we uncovered any facts that require us to delete goals, alter them, or add new ones? After completing this internal audit, the committee is ready to examine the company's mission, vision, and values statements.

mission statement
A broad statement that defines the organization's purpose and scope

Define the Corporate Mission, Vision, and Values Statements

These broad statements communicate to the corporation's stakeholders (employees, stockholders, governments, partners, suppliers, and customers) what the company is, where it is going, and the values that will guide the behavior of the organization's members. Some firms combine two or all three of these into a single statement, whereas others have separate statements. The **mission statement** defines the purpose for a company's existence, including its business,

vision statement A description of the company's desired future position if it can acquire the necessary competencies and successfully implement its strategy

values statement A clear and concise description of the fundamental values, beliefs, and priorities of the organization's members.

objectives, and approach for reaching those objectives. A **vision statement** is a description of the company's desired future position, of what it hopes to accomplish if it can acquire the necessary competencies and successfully implement its strategy. In contrast, a **values statement** is intended to be a clear, concise description of the fundamental values, beliefs, and priorities of the organization's members, reflecting how they want to behave with each other and with the company's customers, suppliers, and other members of the global community. A Booz Allen Hamilton/Aspen Institute survey of corporations in 30 countries revealed that 89 percent of these organizations had explicit, written statements of corporate values and that greater success in linking a corporation's values to its operations was related to superior financial results.[9] Over time, the planning committee must evaluate these statements against the changing realities uncovered in the external and internal analyses and then alter them when necessary.

Some Examples Johnson & Johnson has a mission statement that says:

> *Our Mission is to pursue the growth of Johnson & Johnson based on providing scientifically sound, high quality products and services that help heal, cure disease, and improve the quality of life for people everywhere.*[10]

Unilever states the following about its mission:

> *Unilever's mission is to add vitality to life. We meet the everyday needs for nutrition, hygiene, and personal care with brands that help people feel good, look good, and get more out of life.*[11]

Amazon.com states the following:

> *We seek to be Earth's most customer-centric company, where customers can find and discover anything they might want to buy online, and endeavor to offer customers the lowest possible prices.*[12]

DuPont states the following in defining the vision of the company and its mission:

> *We, the people of DuPont, dedicate ourselves daily to the work of improving life on our planet. We have the curiosity to go farther . . . the imagination to think bigger . . . the determination to try harder . . . and the conscience to care more. Our solutions will be bold. We will answer the fundamental needs of the people we live with to ensure harmony, health and prosperity in the world. Our methods will be our obsession. Our singular focus will be to serve humanity with the power of all the sciences available to us. Our tools are our minds. We will encourage unconventional ideas, be daring in our thinking, and courageous in our actions. By sharing our knowledge and learning from each other and the markets we serve, we will solve problems in surprising and magnificent ways. Our success will be ensured. We will be demanding of ourselves and work relentlessly to complete our tasks. Our achievements will create superior profit for our shareholders and ourselves. Our principles are sacred. We will respect nature and living things, work safely, be gracious to one another and our partners, and each day we will leave for home with consciences clear and spirits soaring.*[13]

Sumitomo Corporation of Japan states its nine basic values as being:

> *(1) Integrity and sound management: To comply with laws and regulations, while maintaining the highest ethical standards, (2) Integrated Corporate Strength: To create no boundaries within the organization; always to act with a company-wide perspective, (3) Vision: To create a clear vision of the future, and to communicate to share it within the organization, (4) Change and Innovation: To accept and integrate diversity in values and behavior, and to embrace change as an opportunity for action, (5) Commitment: To initiate, own, and achieve organizational objectives, (6) Enthusiasm: To act with enthusiasm and confidence, and to motivate to others through such action, (7) Speed: To make quick decisions and act promptly, (8) Human Development: To fully support the development of others' potential, and (9) Professionalism: To achieve and maintain high levels of expertise and skills.*[14]

After defining any or all of the three statements, management must then set corporate objectives.

BUILDING YOUR GLOBAL RÉSUMÉ — Tips from Your Personal Global Mentor

Katherine McCormick

Katherine McCormick is director of international marketing for TransUnion, working at World Headquarters in Chicago, Illinois, where she leads international marketing projects in Canada, Mexico, Dominican Republic, Guatemala, Honduras, Nicaragua, Costa Rica, Chile, Trinidad and Tobago, Italy, Thailand, India, China (mainland and Hong Kong SAR), and South Africa. Katherine has traveled professionally in over 24 countries. TransUnion is a global intelligence leader, providing technology and analytical tools to help businesses around the world make better business decisions at every stage of the customer life cycle, including acquisition, customer management, and collections, and throughout the entire residential loan process. As director of international marketing, Katherine serves as the marketing generalist for associates leading international marketing projects, providing guidance for marketing efforts as well as strategic direction. In providing this direction, she continually works to enhance brand awareness through positioning, product performance and development, public relations, and promotional activities (e.g., trade shows). Katherine also oversees international communications and brand audits and executes brand architecture decisions within and across markets in the form of joint ventures and cobrand programs to ensure the success of current and future international acquisitions.

Katherine's advice on how to get a job in international business:

- "Don't look for a job in international business right from the get-go; first find a company that has business overseas and try to get a job working with them in your area of expertise. As soon as you can, let them know your interests in international business and try to network internally to introduce yourself to the international leaders. A couple years later, when you have gained experience with the company and have had exposure to the international business unit, you can try to make a move."
- "If international business is your true passion, pursue it wholeheartedly. Don't give up. Network as much as you can and travel internationally as much as you can."

Katherine's advice on succeeding in international business:

- "The ability to develop relationships and relate to people of different backgrounds and cultures is critical. I cannot stress that enough. You must be able to demonstrate a knowledge and understanding of the country you are working with. I find that patience, flexibility and creativity are a must for international business workers. You can't have a U.S. mindset and be successful!"
- "Job-related skills depend on the industry you are in, but what I look for when hiring someone is that they have traveled extensively and have had exposure to different cultures. You need to demonstrate an intimate understanding of the differences that exist in U.S. business vs. business in other countries."

Katherine's most memorable international business experience:

- "TransUnion was a sponsor at a conference two years ago in China. We hosted an event with music, cocktails and food right on the Great Wall of China as the sun was setting. I had one of those 'I get paid to do this!' moments where I was in awe of how truly blessed I am to do what I do."

World Wide Resource:

www.transunion.com/business

Set Corporate Objectives Objectives direct the firm's course of action, maintain it within the boundaries of the stated mission, and ensure its continuing existence. McDonald's states that its vision is "to be the world's best quick service restaurant experience. Being the best means providing outstanding quality, service, cleanliness, and value, so that we make every customer in every restaurant smile." To achieve this vision, the company focuses on three worldwide objectives: (1) to be the best employer for its people in each community around the world, (2) to deliver operational excellence to its customers in each of its restaurants, and (3) to achieve enduring profitable growth by expanding the brand and leveraging the strengths of the McDonald's system through innovation and technology.[15]

Intel's mission is to "delight our customers, employees, and shareholders by relentlessly delivering the platform and technology advancements that become essential to the way we work and live." Its objectives are stated as (1) extend leadership in silicon and platform manufacturing, (2) deliver architectural innovation for market-driving platforms, and (3) drive worldwide growth.[16]

How does Intel know whether it achieves these objectives? How will the company assess whether it has successfully delivered "architectural innovation for market-driving platforms," for example?

Quantify the Objectives In order to enhance a company's ability to develop and implement an effective strategy, one that will enable the company's objectives to be attained, it is important that efforts be made to quantify these objectives.

> *At BP, the U.K.-based energy multinational, strategic objectives are established through a process directed by headquarters. Implementation of these objectives is decentralized to the business units. Performance contracts are set in place for the executive management from each of the company's business units and strategic performance units, holding these managers accountable for that area of the business. The performance contracts include financial and operating performance objectives, as well as nonfinancial elements such as safety and environmental performance. The company states that it attempts to establish objectives that "(1) are challenging but achievable, (2) enable us to be responsive to change, (3) are clear and unambiguous to all, both within and outside the company, (4) provide indicative ranges of performance against which we can measure progress in a balanced way, (5) can be agreed [to] and accepted by all whose performance is measured against them, (6) encompass both clear financial or operational benefits, as well as clear social and environmental objectives, and (7) are intended to deliver value to the company's shareholders but with due care to all our stakeholders' interests."*[17]

Of course, strategic planning for international operations typically involves a range of qualitative as well as quantitative factors, which complicates efforts to quantify objectives. However, when objectives can be quantified in a relevant manner, they should be. For example, the stated objectives of 3M, a $21 billion diversified technology company with worldwide operations, included (1) growth in earnings per share of more than 10 percent a year on average, (2) growth in economic profit exceeding growth in earnings per share and return on invested capital among the highest among industrial companies, (3) at least 30 percent of sales from products introduced during the past four years, and (4) 8 percent productivity improvement per year, measured in terms of sales per employee in local currencies.[18] Similar quantification of objectives is evident for Goodyear Tire and Rubber Co., the world's largest tire company with manufacturing in 29 nations and sales and marketing operations in virtually every nation, which announced the following:

> *Goodyear's objectives for the 2006–2008 time period include:*
>
> 1. *To build on recent performance improvements by further reducing costs by $750 million to $1 billion. About one-third of the cost is expected to come from business process improvements and product reformulations.*
> 2. *Reduce the company's global manufacturing footprint, with anticipated savings of $100 million to $150 million per year. The target is to reduce the company's manufacturing capacity by 15 million to 20 million tires, or approximately 8 percent to 12 percent of its capacity.*
> 3. *Exploit its new purchasing office in China to increase the company's low-cost sourcing of tires, raw materials, indirect materials, and capital equipment, with targeted savings of $150 million to $200 million.*
> 4. *Simplifying the way the company processes transactions and the way it is organized, reducing costs by $150 million to $200 million from reducing selling, administrative, and general expenses.*
> 5. *Reduce working capital requirements, freeing cash to meet financial obligations and invest in improving performance.*[19]

These examples illustrate that despite the strong preference of most top managers for verifiable objectives, they frequently do have nonquantifiable or directional goals. One of PepsiCo's objectives, for example, is to accelerate profitable growth. Although this goal is not quantified, it does set the direction for managers and requires that they formulate more specific strategies to attain it. Incidentally, objectives do tend to be more quantified as they progress down the organization to the operational level, because, for the most part, strategies at one level become the objectives for the succeeding level. Up to this point, only *what, how much,* and *when* have been stipulated. *How* these objectives are to be achieved will be determined in the formulation of strategies.

Formulate the Competitive Strategies Generally, participants in the strategic planning process will formulate alternative **competitive strategies,** and corresponding plans of action, that seem plausible considering the directions the external environmental forces are taking and the company's strengths, weaknesses, opportunities, and threats (something that endangers the business, such as a merger of two competitors, the bankruptcy of a major customer, or a new product that appears to make the company's product obsolete).

competitive strategies
Action plans to enable organizations to reach their objectives

Suppose (1) their analysis of the external environment convinces them that the Japanese government is making it easier for foreign firms to enter the market and (2) the competitor analysis reveals that a Japanese competitor is preparing to enter the United States (or wherever the home market is). Should the firm adopt a defensive strategy of defending the home market by lowering its price there, or should it attack the competitor in its home market by establishing a subsidiary in Japan? Management may decide to pursue either strategy or both, depending on its interpretation of the situation.

When developing and assessing strategic alternatives, it is important to remember that companies competing in international markets confront two opposing forces: reduction of costs and adaptation to local markets. In order to be competitive, firms must do what they can to lower costs per unit so that customers will not perceive their products or services as being too expensive. This often results in pressure for some of the company's facilities to be located in places where costs are low, as well as for developing products that are highly standardized across multiple nations.

However, in addition to responding to pressures to reduce costs, managers also must attempt to respond to local pressures to modify their products to meet the demands of the local markets in which they do business. This modification requires that the company differentiate its strategy and product offerings from nation to nation, reflecting differences in distribution channels, governmental regulations, cultural preferences, and similar factors. However, modifying products and services for the specific requirements of local markets can involve additional expenses, which can cause the company's costs to rise.

As a consequence of these two opposing pressures, companies basically have five different strategies that they can use for competing internationally: home replication, multidomestic, regional, global, and transnational. As suggested in Figure 13.3, the strategy that would be most appropriate for the company, overall and for various activities in the value chain, depends on the amount of pressure the company faces in terms of adapting to local markets and achieving cost reductions. Each of these strategies has its own set of advantages and disadvantages, as summarized below.

Home Replication Strategy* According to this typology, companies pursuing a home replication strategy typically centralize product development functions in their home country. After they develop differentiated products in the home market, these innovations are then transferred to foreign markets in order to capture additional value. To be successful, the company has to possess a valuable distinctive competency that local competitors lack in the foreign markets. The company's home country headquarters usually maintains tight control over marketing and product strategy, and the primary responsibility of local subsidiaries is to leverage home country capabilities. The extent of local customization of product offerings or marketing strategy tends to be limited. However, competitive advantage depends on the effective management of the international product life cycle that was discussed in Chapter 3. As a result, once local demand and circumstances justify such an investment, the company will tend to establish manufacturing and marketing functions in each major country in which it does business. This strategy can be appropriate if the company faces relatively weak pressures for local responsiveness and cost reductions. When there are strong pressures for local responsiveness, however, companies pursuing a home replication strategy will be at a disadvantage compared to competitors that emphasize customization of the product offering and market strategy for local conditions. Companies pursuing a home replication strategy may also face high operating costs, due to duplication of manufacturing facilities across the markets they serve.

*Although a home replication strategy is sometimes called an "international strategy," to avoid the potential for confusion between this specific use of "international strategy" and the more general term *international strategy,* we will use only the term *home replication strategy* for this strategic framework.

FIGURE 13.3

Cost and Adaptation Pressures and Their Implications for International Strategies

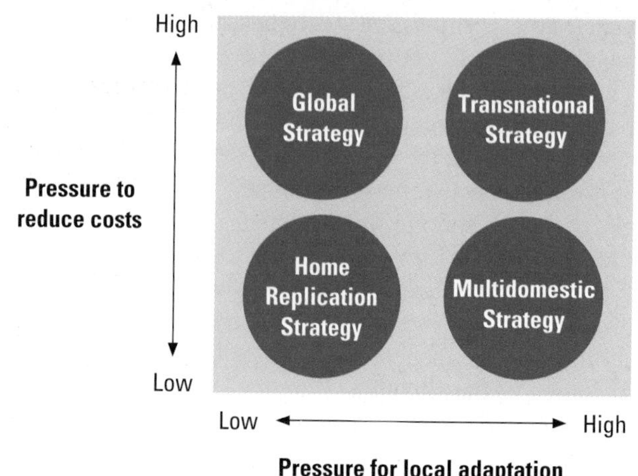

Examples of firms pursuing home replication strategies include Microsoft and McDonald's. For example, Microsoft has traditionally developed the core architecture for the company's computer operating system and application software products at its headquarters in Washington state. Subsidiaries in other nations have engaged in relatively limited product customization, primarily to address such basic differences as alphabet or language.

Multidomestic Strategy A multidomestic strategy tends to be used when there is strong pressure for the company to adapt its products or services for local markets. Under these circumstances, decision making tends to be more decentralized in order to allow the company to modify its products and to respond quickly to changes in local competition and demand. Subsidiaries are expected to develop and exploit local market opportunities, which means that knowledge and competencies are expected to be developed at the subsidiary level. By tailoring its products for specific markets, the company may be able to charge higher prices. However, local adaptation of products usually will increase the company's cost structure. In order to effectively adapt products, the company will have to invest in additional capabilities and knowledge in terms of local culture, language, customer demographics, human resource practices, government regulations, distribution systems, and so forth. Adapting products too much to local tastes may also take away the distinctiveness of a company's products. For example, KFC's chicken outlets in China are highly popular because they are perceived to reflect American values and standards, something that might be lost if the company tried to adapt the stores and products to be more like other Chinese food outlets. The extent of local adaptation may also change over time, as when customer demands start to converge due to the emergence of global telecommunications, media, and travel, as well as reduced differences in income between nations. The cost and complexity of coordinating a range of different strategies and product offerings across national and regional markets can also be substantial.

Schneider Electric, a large French electrical products company with operations in 130 countries, attempts to serve international customers through a strategy that adapts products to the standards and practices of each country. Local operations have a high level of autonomy and are strongly rooted in their host nations. The organizational structure is designed to react quickly and effectively to local market conditions, facilitating customized innovations for local customers' needs. As an example, Schneider is trying to exploit its localization strategy to dominate several sectors of the marketplace in China. Chief Operating Officer Jean-Pascal Tricoire said, "China is a core country for us and is as important as the United States and Europe," likely to become the third-largest market for Schneider after the United States and France. Schneider's business in China is expected to maintain an average annual growth rate of at least 20 percent through 2009, and localization is a primary strategy to achieve this growth rate. Schneider Electric China has about half of the corporation's employees and is expected to expand the Chinese workforce from 4,000 to 7,000 by 2007. The

WORLD view   

Regional Strategies for Competing Globally

Many researchers in the field of international business have argued that the emergence of broad economic liberalization, declining transportation costs, advances in telecommunications and computer technology, and other factors have produced a "borderless" world. In such a world, it has been argued that a global strategy is an appropriate or even necessary approach for multinational companies to adopt in order to achieve success.

Multinationals do represent a major force driving economic globalization, with the 500 largest multinational enterprises being responsible for about half of world trade and over 90 percent of the global stock of foreign direct investment. Yet investigations of large multinationals in manufacturing and service sectors reveal that most of these companies generate the majority of their revenues within a single region rather than having broad and deep penetration of international markets as a whole. For the large majority of these firms, an average of about 80 percent of their worldwide revenues are generated within their home region of the three largest economic regions of North America, the European Union, and Asia. These data suggest that, at least for most companies and industries, the world marketplace is triad-based rather than global in nature.

Some researchers have suggested that this triad-based competitive situation, sometimes termed *semiglobalization,* may merely reflect a stage in the evolution of international companies. From this perspective, increased globalization of sales and other value chain activities may be expected to occur over time as companies accumulate sufficient international experience and are thus able to successfully more fully extend their reach globally. Experimentation and innovation with business models may be necessary in order to accomplish this. There may also be a "threshold of internationalization" beyond which a multinational's performance may decline, at least until the competencies necessary for more globally dispersed operations are able to be developed and managed successfully. In fact, some research which has found that multinationals' revenues tend to be concentrated in a single nation also suggests that broader assessment of value chain activities than merely sales—including sourcing of labor, capital, production, and knowledge—might produce a less region-centric interpretation of multinationals' strategies.

Nevertheless, one result of this recent research on the region-based nature of multinational sales is the potential value to be derived from thinking of international strategy within the context of a region-by-region perspective, rather than merely a nation-by-nation versus a global basis. In part, this argument emphasizes the continued heterogeneity that companies may encounter in the world's marketplaces, such as differences in local cultures, discriminatory treatment from national or regional governments or other governing bodies, and complexities of dealing with multiple institutions in the host markets. To the extent that a multinational's market position varies substantially across regions, strategies may also need to vary by region in order to accommodate the differing competitive circumstances that confront an international company. Yet, even when considering the appropriate strategy to use within each region, it may be useful to consider the relative extent of pressure for local adaptation versus pressure to reduce costs, as discussed in this section, "Formulate the Competitive Strategies."

Source: Alan M. Rugman and Alain Verbeke, "A Perspective on Regional and Global Strategies of Multinational Enterprises," *Journal of International Business Studies* 35, no. 1 (2004), pp. 3–18; J. Michael Geringer, Paul W. Beamish, and Richard C. DaCosta, "Diversification Strategy and Internationalization: Implications for MNE Performance," *Strategic Management Review* 10, no. 2 (1989), pp. 109–19; Lei Li, "Is Regional Strategy More Effective than Global Strategy in the U.S. Service Industries," *Management International Review* 45, special issue (2005), pp. 37–57; Pankaj Ghemawat, "Semiglobalization and International Business Strategy," *Journal of International Business Studies* 34, no. 2 (2003), pp. 138–52; Eden Yin and Chong Ju Choi, "The Globalization Myth: The Case of China," *Management International Review* 45, pp. 103–20; Allen J. Morrison, David A. Ricks, and Kendall Roth, "Globalization versus Regionalization: Which Way for the Multinational?" *Organizational Dynamics* 19, no. 3 (1991), pp. 17–29; and Pankaj Ghemawat, "Regional Strategies for Global Leadership," *Harvard Business Review*, December 2005, pp. 98–108.

company's Chinese research and development center will triple to 300 employees. Already accounting for 70 percent of production in the Asia Pacific region, Schneider will also add more production capability in China and diversify its operations into components and parts.[20]

Global Strategy A global strategy tends to be used when a company faces strong pressures for reducing costs and limited pressure to adapt products for local markets. Strategy and decision making are typically centralized at headquarters, and the company tends to offer standardized products and services. Overseas offices are expected to adopt the most efficient strategies found within the entire corporation. Value chain activities are often located in only one or a few areas, to assist the company in achieving cost reductions due to economies of scale. International subsidiaries are expected to transmit information to headquarters and to submit to centralized controls imposed by headquarters. There tends to be strong emphasis on close coordination and integration of activities across products and markets, as well as the development of efficient logistics and distribution capabilities. These strategies are common in industries such as semiconductors (e.g., Intel) or large commercial aircraft (e.g., Boeing). However, global strategies may also confront challenges such as limited ability to adjust quickly and effectively to changes in customer needs across national or regional markets, increased transportation and tariff costs for exporting products from centralized production sites, and the risks of locating activities in a centralized location (which can, for example, cause the firm to confront risks from political changes or trade conflicts, exchange rate fluctuations, and similar factors).

Vodafone Group PLC of Britain, the world's largest cell phone operator, discovered that too much emphasis on implementing a global strategy could be a problem. In 2002, the company acquired control of the third-largest Japanese cell phone operator, J-Phone Co., a fast-growing company with an image for being on the cutting edge of cellular technology. The company was subsequently rebranded under the Vodafone name, and Vodafone heavily promoted its image as a global brand and company. Said Arun Sarin, Vodafone's CEO, "We acquired a lot of companies to become what we are today. Now we have to make this series of companies work as one operating company." Being a service provider in 28 nations allows Vodafone to specify technical requirements to handset manufacturers and to achieve powerful economies of scale in sourcing. The company is trying to achieve a standard Vodafone "look and feel" for all of its cellular phones, in order to enhance the company's branding and pricing power. Sarin said, "Branding is a very big issue for us. When you think about fast food, you think of McDonald's. When you think about a soft drink, you think of Coke. What we would like is when people think mobile products and services, they go to Vodafone."

Yet, after its acquisition, Vodafone's Japanese operations suffered and the company lost market share to market leaders NTT DoCoMo Inc. and KDDI Corporation. In a nation where consumers love the latest technological gadgets, Vodafone's phones were viewed as dull and unoriginal. New subscriptions were declining, year after year, and annual revenues fell. The problem? How to implement a global strategy while simultaneously meeting the demands of the local market. Vodafone failed to provide Japanese consumers with technologically sophisticated, feature-packed phones, instead offering a narrow, run-of-the-mill product line. "They just discontinued popular phones and popular services. They were looking at the global market instead of looking at what Japanese users wanted," said Hayato Yoshida, a salesperson at a Tokyo mobile phone retailer. Vodafone was also late in introducing the newest cellular services being offered by competitors. For example, Vodafone's emphasis on global services resulted in a delay in its Japanese launch of 3G phones: preferring to offer phones that functioned both within and outside Japan led to longer development times and delayed product introduction by more than a year after DoCoMo introduced its own 3G service. Kazuyo Katsuma, a telecom analyst with J.P. Morgan, said, "The biggest reason they are struggling is a mismatch of their strategy and the Japanese environment." Rather than achieving success through mere global scale and standardization, Sarin commented, "It is . . . becoming increasingly clear that the greatest benefits come from strong local and regional scale." In 2006, Vodafone conceded defeat and sold its Japanese operations, booking an $8.6 billion charge for losses associated with Japanese investment."[21]

Transnational Strategy A transnational strategy tends to be used when a company simultaneously confronts pressures for cost effectiveness and local adaptation and when there is a potential for competitive advantage from simultaneously responding to these two divergent forces. The location of a company's assets and capabilities will be based on where it would be most beneficial for each specific activity, neither highly centralized as with a global strategy nor widely dispersed as with a multidomestic strategy. International subsidiaries are expected to contribute actively to the development of the company's capabilities, as well as developing and sharing knowledge with company operations worldwide. Typically, more "upstream" value chain activities, such as product development, raw materials sourcing, and manufacturing, will be more centralized, while the more "downstream" activities, such as marketing, sales, and service, will be more decentralized, located closer to the customer. Of course, achieving an optimal balance in locating activities is a challenge for management, as is maintaining this balance over time as the company faces changes in competition, customer needs, regulations, and other factors. Management must ensure that the comparative advantages of the locations of the company's various value chain activities are captured and internalized, rather than wasted due to limitations of the organization's people, structures, and coordination and control systems. The complexity associated with the strategic decisions, as well as the supporting structures and systems of the organization, will be much greater with a transnational strategy. Caterpillar, for example, has tried to manufacture many of the standardized components of its products in a few locations worldwide. At the same time, the company has set up assembly operations in each major market, sometimes accompanied by specialized local production capability, thereby promoting its ability to tailor products to local needs.

When considering the four types of strategies discussed above, it is also important to remember that management must consider the corporate culture when choosing among strategic alternatives. If the company decides to put into effect a quality control system that includes quality circles and heretofore has had little employee participation in decision making, the strategy will have to include the cost of and time for training the employees to accept this cultural change.

Standardization and Planning While the preceding discussion addressed basic strategic alternatives at a business or corporate level, it should be remembered that not all activities of an organization confront the same mix of globalization and localization pressures (also see the Worldview box on page 363, "Regional Strategies for Competing Globally"). For example, historically, more aspects of research and development and manufacturing have been standardized and coordinated worldwide by companies than has been the case for other value chain activities such as marketing. Many top executives believe marketing strategies are best determined locally because of differences among the various foreign environments. Yet there remains a desire within many international companies to achieve benefits from standardizing various elements of marketing strategies as well as the total product itself, which leads to their inclusion in the global strategic planning process. Of course, the standardization of elements of a firm's marketing strategy can also be the *result* of strategic planning as the company's managers search for ways to lower costs and present a uniform company image as a global producer of quality products. In making such strategic plans, however, it is essential that companies look beyond what makes sense under current circumstances and also consider how the situation may change in the future and the implications of these changes. This helps to explain companies' increasing use of scenarios in the planning process.

Scenarios As discussed in the introductory example of this chapter, because of the rapidity of changes in the uncontrollable variables, many managers have become dissatisfied with planning for a single set of events and have turned to **scenarios,** which are multiple, plausible stories for probable futures. Scenario analysis allows management to assess the implications for the company of various economic conditions and operating strategies. Managers can brainstorm various "what-if" scenarios, raising and challenging their assumptions and projected outcomes before committing to a specific course of action. Often, the what-if questions reveal weaknesses in present strategies. Some of the common kinds of subjects for scenarios are large and sudden changes in sales (up or down), sudden increases in the prices of raw materials, sudden tax increases, and a change in the political party in power. Frequently, scenarios are used as a learning tool for preparing standby or contingency plans, enhancing the company's ability to perform within uncertain international markets. (See the Worldview box on page 366, "Scenarios: Improving Strategic Planning by Telling Stories.")

scenarios
Multiple, plausible stories about the future

Contingency Plans Many companies prepare **contingency plans** for worst- and best-case scenarios and for critical events as well. Every operator of a nuclear plant has contingency plans, as do most producers of petroleum and hazardous chemicals since such ecological disasters as the *Valdez* oil spill and the tragic Bhopal gas leak occurred. Because of the important impact on profits of changes in the prices of jet fuel, contingency planning is a common strategic activity for domestic and international airlines. The deadly terrorist attack on the World Trade Center in New York on September 11, 2001, an event that also severely impacted operations of numerous companies, reminded many organizations of the importance of developing contingency plans to ensure the effective continuation of their operations in the event that their headquarters or other key locations are attacked or otherwise incapacitated for a period of time.

contingency plans
Plans for the best- or worst-case scenarios or for critical events that could have a severe impact on the firm

WORLD view   

Scenarios: Improving Strategic Planning by Telling Stories

A key role of strategic planning is to describe and effectively communicate a future that is attractive enough to help create, and to capture, the competitive advantages that arise from preparing for this future and helping to make it happen. In essence, a key element in strategic planning is telling stories, creating scenarios regarding the future. A popular and increasingly utilized strategic planning tool, scenarios are carefully developed stories that integrate a variety of ideas about the future, including key certainties and uncertainties, and present these ideas in a useful and comprehensible manner. Scenarios should be developed in a manner that is consistent with and helps to clarify the priorities of the company, and these stories are then tied into strategic and operational decisions that a company must make today and over time.

Although the origins of scenario planning are unclear, the multinational company Royal Dutch/Shell is widely recognized as a pioneer in popularizing the technique. Shell made scenario planning a staple of its strategic planning efforts 30 years ago, when it was confronted with a severe and unexpected global oil shortage. In dealing with such uncertainty and change, traditional strategic planning approaches based on extrapolation of historical conditions are of limited value. Managers find it difficult to break away from their existing view of the world, one that results from a lifetime of training and experience. Through presenting other ways of seeing the world, scenarios allow managers to envision alternatives that might lie outside their traditional frame of reference. Such an approach is particularly useful for international companies that face high levels of change and uncertainty regarding political, technological, competitive, and other forces because it allows management to anticipate and prepare for opportunities and threats that cannot be fully predicted or controlled. Examples of scenarios created by Shell to assist in anticipating and responding to such uncertainty can be viewed at www.shell.com/home/Framework?siteId=royal-en&FC2=&FC3=/royal-en/html/iwgen/our_strategy/scenarios/introduction_to_global_scenarios/intro_jvdv_scenarios_28022005.html.

Because of the problems inherent in the list of objectives that had characterized 3M's strategic planning efforts, the company adopted a scenario-based approach that it termed "planning by narrative." First, the strategic planner sets the stage as any storyteller does. This includes an analysis of the current situation, including uncontrollable environmental forces and corporate controllable variables. Then the narrator discusses the dramatic conflict. What are the obstacles to success? Once the obstacles are presented, the plan must show how the firm can conquer them and triumph. The audience is made aware of the writers' thought processes in arriving at their conclusions, and the assumptions are brought out in the open, enabling executives to evaluate the plan and then ask perceptive, incisive questions and offer valuable advice. One 3M manager stated, "If you just read bullet points, you may not get it, but if you read a narrative plan, you will. If there's a flaw in the logic, it glares out at you. With bullets, you don't know if the insight is really there or if the planner has merely given you a shopping list." 3M management believes that narrative plans can motivate and mobilize an entire organization.

In his classic book, *The Art of the Long View,* Peter Schwartz identifies the following seven steps to successful scenario planning:

1. Determine the area, scope, and timing of the decisions with greatest relevance to or impact on your organization.
2. Research existing conditions and trends in a wide variety of areas (including those areas you might not typically consider).
3. Examine the drivers or key factors that will likely determine the outcome of the stories you are beginning to build.
4. Construct multiple stories of what could happen next.
5. Play out what the impact of each of these possible futures might be for your business or organization.
6. Examine your answers and look for those actions or decisions you'd make that were common to all two or three of the stories you built.
7. Monitor what does develop so as to trigger your early response system.

De Kluyver and Pearce identify four qualities that should be embodied in the final set of scenarios:

1. Relevance to the users (e.g., executives or middle management).
2. Internal consistency.
3. Descriptiveness regarding futures that are generically different, rather than merely being variations on a single theme.
4. Able to be acted upon in an environment that will exist for a period of time, and thus give the organization a chance to benefit from its preparations and resulting actions, rather than for a future that will be very short-lived.

The primary value of scenario planning efforts is not so much the strategic plans that are created but, instead, the transformation in strategic thinking that results from this activity.

Source: "Planning for What's Next," *Growth Strategies,* August 2002, pp. 3–4; Anthony Lavia, "Strategic Planning in Times of Turmoil," *Business Communications Review,* March 2004, pp. 56–59; Ian Wylie, "There Is No Alternative to . . . ," *Fast Company,* July 2002, p. 106, http://pf.fastcompany.com/magazine/60/tina.html (October 16, 2004); Peter Schwartz, *The Art of the Long View—Planning for the Future in an Uncertain World* (New York: Doubleday, 1996); Shell, "Introduction to Shell Global Scenarios to 2025 by Jeroen van der Veer, Chief Executive," www.shell.com/home/Framework?siteId=royal-en&FC2=&FC3=/royal-en/html/iwgen/our_strategy/scenarios/introduction_to_global_scenarios/intro_jvdv_scenarios_28022005.html (June 28, 2006); Don Sull, "Good Things Come to Those Who Actively Wait," *Financial Times,* February 6, 2006, p. 8; Cornelis A. de Kluyver and John A. Pearce II, *Strategy: A View from the Top* (Upper Saddle River, NJ: Pearson Prentice Hall, 2006), p. 39; and Gordon Shaw, Robert Brown, and Philip Bromiley, "Strategic Stories: How 3M Is Rewriting Business Planning," *Harvard Business Review,* May–June 1998, pp. 41–50.

Prepare Tactical Plans Because strategic plans are fairly broad, tactical (also called *operational*) plans are a requisite for spelling out in detail how the objectives will be reached. In other words, very specific, short-term means for achieving the goals are the objective of tactical planning. For instance, if the British subsidiary of an American producer of prepared foods has as a quantitative goal a 20 percent increase in sales, its strategy might be to sell 30 percent more to institutional users. The tactical plan could include such points as hiring three new specialized sales representatives, attending four trade shows, and advertising in two industry periodicals every other month next year. This is the kind of specificity found in the tactical plan.

STRATEGIC PLAN FEATURES AND IMPLEMENTATION FACILITATORS

Sales Forecasts and Budgets Two prominent features of the strategic plan are *sales forecasts* and *budgets*. The sales forecast not only provides management with an estimate of the revenue to be received and the units to be sold but also serves as the basis for planning in the other functional areas. Without this information, management cannot formulate the production, financial, and procurement plans. Budgets, like sales forecasts, are both a planning and a control technique. During planning, they coordinate all the functions within the firm and provide management with a detailed statement of future operating results.

Plan Implementation Facilitators Once the plan has been prepared, it must be implemented. Two of the most important plan implementation facilitators that management employs are policies and procedures.

Policies Policies are broad guidelines issued by upper management for the purpose of assisting lower-level managers in handling recurring problems. Because policies are broad, they permit discretionary action and interpretation. The object of a policy is to economize managerial time and promote consistency among the various operating units. For example, if a company's distribution policy states that sales will be made through wholesalers, marketing managers throughout the world would know that they should normally use wholesalers and avoid selling directly to retailers. Similarly, publicity regarding the widespread occurrence of bribery in various international markets has prompted numerous companies to issue policy statements condemning this practice. Managers have thus been put on notice by these statements that they are not to offer bribes.

Procedures Procedures prescribe how certain activities will be carried out, thereby ensuring uniform action on the part of all corporate members. For instance, most international corporate headquarters issue procedures for their subsidiaries to follow in preparing annual reports and budgets. This assures corporate management that whether the budgets originate in Thailand, Brazil, or the United States, they will be prepared using the same format, which facilitates comparison.

Performance Measures A key part of strategic planning is measuring performance in order to assess whether the strategy and its implementation are proceeding successfully or whether modifications may need to be made. Companies need to consider at least three types of measures when assessing strategic performance: (1) measures of the company's success in obtaining and applying the required resources, such as financial, technological, and human resources; (2) measures of the effectiveness of the company's personnel, within and across the firm's international network of operations, in performing their assigned jobs; and (3) measures of the company's progress toward achieving its mission, vision, and objectives and doing so in a manner consistent with the company's stated values.[22] A range of concepts and tools, including the balanced scorecard and triple-bottom-line accounting, have been promoted as alternatives for helping to measure strategic performance. For example, the balanced scorecard approach is based on an integration of strategic planning with a company's budgeting processes, and short-term results from the balanced scorecard can serve as a means of monitoring progress in achieving strategic objectives.[23]

KINDS OF STRATEGIC PLANS

Time Horizon Although strategic plans may be classified as short-, medium-, or long-term, there is little agreement about the length of these periods. For some businesses, long-range planning may be for a five-year period. For others, this would be the length of a medium-term plan; their long range might cover 15 years or more. Short-range plans are usually for one to three years; however, even long-term plans are subject to review annually or more frequently if a situation requires it. Furthermore, the time horizon will vary according to the age of the firm and the stability of its market. A new venture is extremely difficult to plan for more than three years in advance, but a five- or six-year horizon may be sufficient for a mature company in a steady market.

Level in the Organization Each organizational level of the company will have its level of plan. For example, if there are four organizational levels, as shown in Figure 13.4, there will be four levels of plans, each of which will generally be more specific than the plan that is at the level above. In addition, the functional areas at each level will have their own plans and sometimes will be subject to the same hierarchy, depending mainly on how the company is organized.

METHODS OF PLANNING

top-down planning
Planning process that begins at the highest level in the organization and continues downward

Top-Down Planning In **top-down planning,** corporate headquarters develops and provides guidelines that include the definition of the business, the mission statement, company objectives, financial assumptions, the content of the plan, and special issues. If there is an international division, its management may be told that this division is expected to contribute $75 million in profits, for example. The division, in turn, would break this total down among

FIGURE 13.4

3M Strategic Planning Cycle

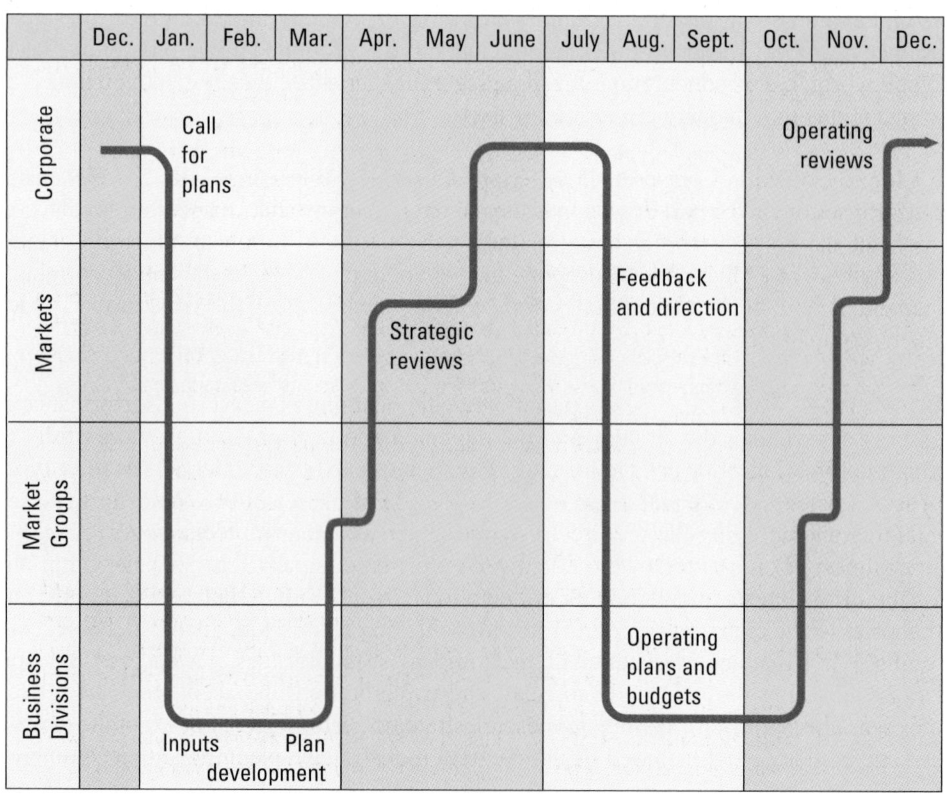

the affiliates under its control. The managing director in Germany would be informed that the German operation is expected to contribute $5 million; Brazil, $800,000; and so on. An advantage of top-down planning is that the home office, with its global perspective, should be able to formulate plans that ensure the optimal corporatewide use of the firm's scarce resources. This approach may also promote creativity, since a corporatewide perspective on market opportunities may yield insights that are not readily observable lower in the organization, such as by managers within individual national markets.

Disadvantages of top-down planning are that it restricts initiative at the lower levels and shows some insensitivity to local conditions, particularly within ethnocentric management teams. Furthermore, especially in an international company, there are so many interrelationships that consultation is necessary. Can top management, for example, decide on rationalization of manufacturing without obtaining the opinions of the local units as to its feasibility?

Bottom-Up Planning **Bottom-up planning** operates in the opposite manner. The lowest operating levels inform top management about what they expect to do, and the total becomes the firm's goals. The advantage of bottom-up planning is that the people responsible for attaining the goals are formulating them. Who knows better than the subsidiaries' directors what and how much the subsidiaries can sell? Because the subsidiaries' directors set the goals with no coercion from top management, they feel obligated to make their word good. Their hands-on perspective may allow them to recognize potentially innovative opportunities to create and leverage value, thus serving as a basis for improved performance or even strategic experimentation. However, bottom-up planning has a disadvantage: Since each affiliate is free to some extent to pursue the goals it wishes to pursue, there is no guarantee that the sum total of all the affiliates' goals will coincide with those of headquarters. When discrepancies occur, extra time must be taken at headquarters to eliminate them. Japanese companies, particularly larger firms, almost invariably use bottom-up planning because they strive for a consensus at every level.

bottom-up planning
Planning process that begins at the lowest level in the organization and continues upward

Iterative Planning It appears that **iterative planning** (see Figure 13.4) is becoming more popular, especially in global companies that seek to have a single global plan while operating in many diverse foreign environments. Iterative planning combines aspects of both top-down and bottom-up planning. An example of iterative planning is the approach used in 3M.

iterative planning
Repetition of the bottom-up or top-down planning process until all differences are reconciled

In 2005, 3M generated over 60 percent of its $21.2 billion in sales from outside the United States, where it has operations in over 60 nations and sales in over 200. Strategic planning plays a key role in the company's resource allocation decisions and global expansion. Figure 13.4 illustrates how 3M's iterative planning process functions. Planning starts with the operating managers of the company's six operating business segments, who analyze strengths and weaknesses and external forces, such as new technology and government regulatory changes; perform a competitor analysis; and determine the company resources they will need to achieve their objectives. Their plans then go to the Market Group, in which from three to five business divisions are typically located. They are reviewed by the Market Group management and consolidated for presentation to the strategic planning committee, consisting of the 12 vice presidents at headquarters who represent the Markets into which the Market Groups are divided. The plans are reviewed, and the results of this review are discussed with the Market Group management. Any differences between Market and Market Group managements are reconciled.

Two months later (July), the corporate headquarters' management committee, to which the strategic planning committee vice presidents belong, reviews the plans and votes on spending priorities. Feedback and direction are given to the business divisions, which then prepare operating plans and budgets by December and submit them to headquarters. They are finalized with corporate worldwide plans.

A few days before the December operating reviews, the management committee holds brainstorming sessions to discuss trends and developments over the coming 15 years. The general manager of each business division presents the best picture possible for that industry for the period. The outcome of this meeting is a broad guide for strategic planning. Although operating managers do the planning, the director and staff of a planning services and development unit provide an analysis of 3M's 20 principal competitors worldwide and any other information the divisions require. They also try to identify opportunities and new products.

As an indication of the vitality of the organization, 3M's chairman and CEO stated, "Our objective is to double the number of qualified new 3M product ideas and triple the value of products that win in the marketplace. We're already seeing good results. . . . Our new product pipeline holds the potential to generate more than $5 billion of annual sales."[24]

NEW DIRECTIONS IN PLANNING

Strategic planning, particularly in its more traditional, bureaucratic form that typified the 1960s and 1970s and still is practiced in too many companies today, has been described as a calendar-driven ritual, not an exploration of the company's potential. This traditional strategic planning approach commonly consisted of a company's CEO and the head of planning getting together to devise a corporate plan, which would then be handed to the operating people for execution. Too frequently, companies' annual strategic planning processes have become ritualistic and devoid of discovery, with the planners working "from today forward, not from the future back, implicitly assuming, whatever the evidence to the contrary, that the future will be more or less like the present."[25] Tending to generate projections based on historical conditions and performance, this traditional planning approach tended to fall victim to collective—and frequently outdated—mind-sets about the competitive environment. Not surprisingly, the resulting strategic planning documents often failed to be implemented successfully.

Increasingly, the old process is being replaced by a *strategic management* approach, which combines strategic thinking, strategic planning, and strategic implementation and which is increasingly recognized as a fundamental task of line management rather than merely specialized planners in staff positions. Although still susceptible to problems such as groupthink, this more contemporary approach attempts to incorporate changes in three areas: (1) who does the planning, (2) how it is done, and (3) the contents of the plan.

Who Does Strategic Planning?

By the mid-1970s, strategic planners had become influential executives, especially in many large U.S. corporations. They were accustomed to writing a blueprint for each subsidiary, which they would then present to the management of each operating unit. The planners' power grew and the operating managers' influence waned, and of course there was hostility between the two groups.

By the 1980s, detailed long-range planning was no longer practical for most international companies, due to world uncertainty, and stronger international competition made a practical knowledge of the company and the industry an essential input to strategic planning. This brought senior operating managers into the planning process, enabling companies to change the role and reduce the size of their planning staffs.

General Electric's widely renowned central planning department was dismantled under former chairman Jack Welch. The company's business unit heads have now been made responsible for planning. As a result, they meet with GE's chairman and CEO, Jeffrey Immelt, and his top management team to tell them what their plans are, the new products they are investigating, and what their competition is doing. These meetings are conducted not merely during the annual strategic planning process but on an ongoing basis at other times of the year, as appropriate. The Corporate Executive Council, a group of top GE executives, also meets four times a year to study each business and where it is headed. No one in the company has the formal title of strategic planner.

Although CEOs report that they would like to spend about one-third of their workday on strategy, strategic planning is no longer something that only the company's most senior executives do.[26] Top management, at the urging of strategy consultants, is assigning strategic planning to teams of line and staff managers from different businesses and functional areas, much as it has done with process-improvement task forces and quality circles. Frequently these teams include a range of ages—from junior staff members who have shown the ability to think creatively to experienced veterans near retirement age who will "tell it like it is." Another difference between the new and the old approaches: Formerly, planning was a company activity done in seclusion. Now, consultants say it should include interaction with such parties as important customers, distributors, suppliers, and alliance partners, in order to gain firsthand experience with the firm's markets. Other important stakeholders such as governments or stakeholder activists are also relevant influences, if not necessarily direct participants, in this strategic planning process. Incorporating these diverse perspectives can help a company to identify creative and effective ways to address the challenge of increasingly uncertain and changing international competitive environments. A.G. Lafley, the CEO of Procter & Gamble, commented, "Like it or not, we are in a global economy and a global political world. Honest to god, the responsibility is huge."[27] As a result, engaging in broad "dialogue among stakeholders" is not a choice, but a requirement, for an international company and its executives.

"We have lots of information technology. We just don't have any information."

Source: © The New Yorker Collection 2002, Sidney Harris from Cartoonbank.com. All Rights Reserved.

How Strategic Planning Is Done By the 1980s, firms were using computer models and sophisticated forecasting methods to help produce the voluminous plans we just mentioned. Those plans were not only huge but also very detailed. As a Texas Instruments executive put it, "The company let its management system, which can track the eye of every sparrow, creep into the planning process, so we were making more and more detailed plans. It became a morale problem because managers knew they couldn't project numbers out five years to two decimal points."[28]

The heavy emphasis on these methods tended to result in a concentration on factors that could be quantified easily. However, the less quantifiable factors relating to sociopolitical developments around the world were becoming increasingly important. Also, the rapid rise in the levels of uncertainty made it clear to top managers that there was no point in using advanced techniques to make detailed five-year forecasts when various international crises were exposing the nonsense of many previous forecasts. Before 1973, for example, there had been great discussion about whether the price of crude oil would ever go above $2 per barrel.

Because of these problems, many firms have moved toward less structured formats and much shorter documents. General Electric's former chairman, Jack Welch, said, "A strategy can be summarized in a page or two."[29]

The top management of companies generally accepts the fact that "a good strategic planning process must allow ideas to surface from anywhere and at any times."[30] As indicated in Figure 13.1, objectives and strategies are intertwined, as are tactics and strategy. If the planning team is unable to come up with suitable tactics to implement a strategy, the strategy must be altered. In a similar fashion, if strategies cannot be formulated to enable the firm to reach the objective, the objective must be changed.[31]

Contents of the Plan The contents of the plan are also different. Many top managers say they are much more concerned now with focusing on issues, strategies, and implementation and with incorporating creative, forward-looking ideas that are essential to competitive success within a changing and uncertain international environment. The planning director of Royal Dutch/Shell, the British-Dutch energy transnational, said:

> *The Shell approach has swung increasingly away from a mechanistic methodology and centrally set forecasts toward a more conceptual or qualitative analysis of the forces and pressures impinging on the industry. What Shell planners try to do is identify the key elements pertaining to a particular area of decision making—the different competitive, political, economic, social, and technical forces that are likely to have the greatest influence on the overall situation. In a global organization, the higher level of management is likely to be the most interested in global scenarios—looking at worldwide developments—while the focus becomes narrower as one proceeds into the more specialized functions, divisions, and business sectors of individual companies.*[32]

In the contemporary global competitive environment, where firms often must place bigger bets on new technologies and other competitive capabilities, companies cannot afford to devote large amounts of money in one direction only to discover years later that this was the wrong direction for investing. "Bets on aircraft engine technology must be made up to 10 years before they result in a sale. Investments in regional jet engine technology that GE began making in the 1980s paid off last year (2002) in the winning bid to supply the engine for China's new regional jet, the ARJ-21."[33] Clearly, as indicated in this comment from Jeffrey Immelt, chairman and CEO of General Electric, competition in today's global competitive environment requires an approach to strategic planning that effectively incorporates a long-term perspective to strategic decision making and resource allocation decisions.

SUMMARY OF THE INTERNATIONAL PLANNING PROCESS

Perhaps a good way to summarize the new direction in planning is to quote Frederick W. Gluck, a principal architect of the strategic management practice in the multinational management consulting firm McKinsey & Co. Gluck said that if major corporations are to develop the flexibility to compete, they must make the following major changes in the way they plan:

1. Top management must assume a more explicit strategic decision-making role, dedicating a large amount of time to deciding how things ought to be instead of listening to analyses of how they are.
2. The nature of planning must undergo a fundamental change from an exercise in forecasting to an exercise in creativity.
3. Planning processes and tools that assume a future much like the past must be replaced by a mind-set that is obsessed with being first to recognize change and turn it into a competitive advantage.
4. The role of the planner must change from being a purveyor of incrementalism to being a crusader for action and an alter ego to line management.
5. Strategic planning must be restored to the core of line management responsibilities.[34]

Analysis of the Competitive Forces

The success of strategic management and the strategic planning process depends in large part upon the quality of information that goes into the process, as well as the interpretation of this information. Decisions are only as good as the information that goes into them, and "the biggest single problem in international planning is the lack of efficient and good competitive information." This is the conclusion of *Business International*'s study of 90 worldwide companies. The study also found that many companies have no organized approach to global competitive assessment; whatever is done is diffused among the various parts of the company. Yet competitor intelligence techniques are increasingly being viewed as a weapon for outmaneuvering competitors and increasing revenues, and there is growing use of organized competitor assessment and competitor intelligence systems, especially for larger companies and those that are competing internationally.

IS COMPETITOR ASSESSMENT NEW?

Sales and marketing managers have always needed information about their competitors' products, prices, channels of distribution, and promotional strategies to plan their own marketing strategies. Sales representatives are expected to submit information on competitors' activities in their territories as part of their regular reports to headquarters. It also has been common practice to talk to competitors' customers and distributors, test competitors' products, and stop at competitors' exhibits at trade shows. Larger firms maintain company libraries whose librarians regularly scan publications and report their findings to the functional area they believe would have an interest in the information. At times, companies have even resorted to **industrial espionage** in order to obtain information about their competitors.

industrial espionage
Act of spying on a competitor to learn secrets about its strategy and operations

Two representatives from a Taiwanese firm that wanted to steal information about an anti-cancer drug from Bristol-Myers Squibb were trapped in an FBI sting operation. The Taiwanese representatives thought they were dealing with a Bristol-Myers scientist who was going to provide the technical data they were seeking, in return for $200,000 cash, a $1,000 monthly retainer, and a share of future profits. When the agreement was reached, the FBI, which had been filming the operation, moved in for the arrest.[35]

Inasmuch as gathering information about the competition has been going on for so long, what is different about present-day **competitor analysis**? Essentially, the difference lies in top management's recognition that (1) increased competition has created a need for a broader and more in-depth knowledge of competitors' activities and (2) the firm should have a **competitor intelligence system (CIS)** (sometimes called a *business intelligence system*) for gathering, analyzing, and disseminating information to everyone in the firm who needs it. A competent competitor intelligence department should be able to obtain at least 80 percent of the information the company wants, using publicly available sources.[36] This is because most corporations fail to identify their most essential information and commonly disclose it willingly to anybody who asks for it. Moreover, many firms hire consultants or firms specializing in competitor analysis to provide information, and others send employees to seminars to learn how to do it themselves. Some even employ former CIA agents or investigators to handle data gathering and analysis.

competitor analysis
Process in which principal competitors are identified and their objectives, strengths, weaknesses, and product lines are assessed

competitor intelligence system (CIS)
Procedure for gathering, analyzing, and disseminating information about a firm's competitors

"Overzealous" subcontractors working for Procter & Gamble phoned the hair care division of P&G's archrival Unilever. Falsely claiming that they were students, these subcontractors asked for sensitive information, which Unilever provided. In addition, Unilever employees frequently threw out sensitive documents, without first shredding them. The P&G subcontractors trespassed onto Unilever's property and retrieved some of these sensitive documents from the dumpster. (If they had waited until the dumpster was moved to the street, their actions would not have been trespassing and removal of the papers would have been legal.) These actions by the subcontractors, which effectively generated competitively valuable information albeit by crossing legal and ethical boundaries, were discovered by P&G's CEO and voluntarily reported to Unilever.[37]

Effective use of competitor intelligence systems can result in the legal and ethical acquisition of competitively valuable information that can provide a company with a range of benefits, such as the ability to (1) improve bidding success by better understanding competitors' costs, markups, and contractual priorities; (2) identify key customers for competitors, in order to better target marketing and sales efforts; (3) identify plant or other facility expansion plans of competitors, or changes in strategic priorities or investments among businesses or product lines; and (4) improve understanding of competitors' product formulations, production volumes, and supply chains.

SOURCES OF INFORMATION

There are five primary sources of information about the strengths, weaknesses, and threats of a firm's competitors: (1) within the firm, (2) published material, including computer databases, (3) suppliers/customers, (4) competitors' employees, and (5) direct observation or analysis of physical evidence of competitors' activities. These sources are all used in the United States and other industrialized countries, but they can be especially helpful in developing nations, which usually have a paucity of published information.

Within the Firm

As was mentioned previously, a firm's sales representatives are the best source of information about competitors. Librarians, when firms have them, can also provide input to the CIS. Another source is the technical and R&D people, who, while attending professional meetings or reading their professional journals, frequently learn of developments before they become general knowledge. Incidentally, government intelligence agencies from all countries subscribe to and analyze other nations' technical journals.

Published Material

In addition to technical journals, other types of published material provide valuable information. Databases such as *ABI Inform, Dialog, Dow Jones News/Retrieval, Lexis-Nexis,* and *NewsNet* enable analysts to obtain basic intelligence about sales, revenues, profits, markets, and other data needed to prepare detailed profiles of competitors. These services also enable users to create clipping folders based on search words such as the names of competitors, major customers, and suppliers, or words describing a product's technology.

The amount of useful information on the Internet, including general and specialist search sites, online versions of journals and other publications, and various monitoring services, continues to grow.* Company Web sites can be an important source of basic information about a company, including information about products, services, pricing, locations, financial performance, strategy, and key executives. Monitoring services can be hired, for a fee, to track a company or industry that you are interested in, notifying you whenever news appears on the Internet or in other locations. England's Economist Intelligence Unit and the United States' Predicast publish useful industry reports, and under the Freedom of Information Act, American firms and their foreign competitors can get information about companies from public documents. Public data sources such as building permits, environmental reports, and SEC reports can contain a wealth of competitively valuable information. Aerial photographs of competitors' facilities are often available from the U.S. Environmental Protection Agency (EPA) or the U.S. Geological Survey if the company is near a waterway or has done an environmental impact study. The photos may reveal an expansion or the layout of the competitor's production facilities. Be careful not to take unauthorized aerial photographs—this is trespassing and is illegal.

Suppliers/Customers Companies frequently tell their customers in advance about new products to keep them from buying elsewhere, but often the customer passes this information on to competitors. A company's purchasing agent can ask its suppliers how much they are producing or what they are planning to produce in the way of new products. Because buyers know how much their company buys, any added capacity or new products may be intended for sale to the firm's competitors. They can also allege that they are considering giving a supplier new business if the sales representative can prove the firm has the capacity to handle it. Salespeople often are so eager for the new business that they divulge the firm's total capacity and the competitor's purchases to prove they can handle the order.

Competitors' Employees Competitors' employees, actual or past, can provide information. Experienced human relations people pay special attention to job applicants, especially recent graduates, who indicate they have worked as interns or in summer jobs with competitors. They sometimes reveal proprietary information unknowingly. Companies also hire people away from competitors, and unscrupulous ones even advertise and hold interviews for jobs they don't have to get information from competitors' employees.

Direct Observation or Analysis of Physical Evidence Companies sometimes have their technical people join a competitor's plant tour to get details of the production processes. A crayon company sent employees to tour a competitor's plants under assumed names. Posing as potential customers, they easily gained access and obtained valuable information about the competitor's processes; admittedly, this was unethical, although standing outside a plant to count employees and learn the number of shifts a competitor is working is not considered unethical.

We have already mentioned the common practice of reverse engineering, which is an example of analyzing physical evidence, but intelligence analysts even buy competitors' garbage. It is illegal to enter a competitor's premises to collect it, but it is permissible to obtain refuse from a trash hauler once the material has left the competitor's premises. Another interesting analysis was done by a Japanese company, which sent employees to measure the thickness of rust on train tracks leaving an American competitor's plant. They used the results to calculate the plant's output.

*Presumably, you have seen the many endnotes in this text citing Internet sources and have looked at the Internet site directory we have provided on the McGraw-Hill/Irwin Web site (www.mhhe.com/ball11e) that is solely for sources of business information.

We have pointed out when an act is legal or illegal, and we have also commented on whether, in our opinion, it was ethical. Certainly, businesspeople have a responsibility to use all ethical means to gather information about their competitors.

USING COMPETITOR ASSESSMENT TO LOOK FORWARD, NOT BACK

Most companies have traditionally focused their competitor assessment activities to compile competitor profiles, newsletters, or other deliverables that are intended to reveal what actions a competitor has recently taken. Yet the strategic advantage of this sort of information can be limited. Instead, executives need to ensure that their competitor assessment efforts are focused on delivering predictive and actionable information, allowing them to anticipate threats and opportunities and to avoid "surprises." The competitor assessment activities should enhance information sharing and strategic decision making across the levels of the organization, and promote the use of competitor intelligence practices within a range of functional areas. Especially when tied into strategic planning techniques such as scenario analysis, the organization can anticipate and prepare for potential competitor moves, as well as develop intelligence indicators that can be scanned in order to quickly alert the company's managers when a significant competitive change is taking place. As a result of such efforts, executives may be able to improve the level of competitive awareness in their companies and enhance prospects for developing strategies for preemptively launching or defending products, or otherwise positioning themselves for advantage over competitors.[38]

BENCHMARKING

This is an increasingly popular way for firms to measure themselves against world leaders. Whereas competitor analysis will help a firm to spot differences between its performance in the market and that of its competitors, it does not provide a deep understanding of the processes that cause these differences. **Benchmarking,** in contrast, improves a company's performance through the identification and application of best practices within and across the company's various operations and sales activities.

benchmarking
A technique for measuring a firm's performance against the performance of others that may be in the same or a completely different industry

Benchmarking involves several stages:

1. Management examines its firm for the aspects of the business—the products, services, or processes—that need improving and the appropriate metrics to use in assessing performance on these aspects.
2. It then looks for companies that are world leaders in performing similar processes.
3. The firm's representatives visit those companies, talk with managers and workers, and determine the best operating practices that enable those companies to perform so well. Because the people who are going to use the newly acquired knowledge are line personnel, they, not staff people, should make these visits.
4. The company then conducts appropriate analyses to identify ways to not merely imitate but also innovatively tailor the best practices and incorporate them into their own activities, and it implements these practices in a manner that can meet the company's performance goals and is acceptable to the organization's members.

The problem, of course, is identifying which company to use as a benchmark. Some firms have been successful in choosing companies in their own industries, but often the ideal benchmark is in a related or perhaps even a completely different industry. Managers have a choice of using one or more of the four basic types of benchmarking:

1. *Internal:* comparing one operation in the firm with another. Because it is in-house, internal benchmarking is relatively easy to implement. It produces about a 10 percent improvement in productivity and can facilitate the creation of a network through which innovative ideas and information can be exchanged.

WORLD view   

Using Industrial Espionage to Assess Competitors

Shekhar Verma, an Indian software engineer who had been fired from Bombay-based Geometric Software Solutions Ltd. (GSSL), claimed that he had the source code for Solidworks Plus' 3-D computer-aided design package. GSSL provides offshore outsourcing services in the area of information technology for clients in the United States and elsewhere, and the company had been debugging this software package for Solidworks. Verma had offered to sell the source code to a number of Solidworks' competitors, and Nenette Day had responded with interest to Verma's offer. She arranged to meet him in the Ashoka hotel in New Delhi. After confirming that he actually possessed Solidworks' source code, Day agreed to pay Verma $200,000 for the information. After she left the room, agents from India's Central Bureau of Intelligence (CBI) rushed in and arrested him. They did not arrest Day, because she was actually an agent from the FBI's Boston Cybercrime Unit, working undercover with the CBI on this case. Verma's arrest resulted in the first prosecutorial filing in India regarding outsourcing-related theft of intellectual property.

The theft of trade secrets, particularly involving competitors, is a chronic concern for businesses of all types. For years, companies have been acquiring information about each other by hiring competitors' employees, talking to competitors' customers, and so forth. Recently, however, intensified competition has motivated firms to become more sophisticated in this endeavor, even to the point of committing illegal acts. Mitsubishi was indicted on charges of stealing industrial secrets from Celanese, and Hitachi pleaded guilty to conspiring to transport stolen IBM technical documents to Japan. In another instance, a Russian spy was able to get samples of vital metal alloys by posing as a visitor and picking up metal shavings on crepe rubber soles on his walk through the plant. Businesspeople traveling abroad routinely report incidents of briefcases and laptop computers being tampered with or of hotel rooms being searched while they are away. Richard Isaacs, senior vice president of a company specializing in protecting intellectual assets, reported, "We had a client trying to do business in France, a country that believes it has an obligation to support local industry. Our client assumed that the way his French competitors always fractionally underbid him was a case of bad luck. Being less trusting, we had him hand-carry his next bid in a locked briefcase that was rigged to detect being opened. His proposal, a bogus one, was purloined and returned while he was at dinner, the detection system revealed. The next morning he went to his office, removed a diskette that was taped to his body, and printed out the real bid, which he then hand-delivered. A competitor later told him, 'I see you're learning.' "

These are not isolated incidents. A survey of Fortune 1000 companies by the American Society for Industrial Security claims that intellectual property losses from foreign and domestic espionage may total more than $300 billion. Major companies reported more than 1,100 documented and 500 suspected incidents of economic espionage. The Computer Security Institute's (CSI's) annual survey revealed that 64 percent of the 538 participating companies and large institutions acknowledged that they had suffered financial losses during the prior year due to breaches of their computer systems, most occurring over the Internet. Key targets for espionage included research and development, customer lists, and financial data. Perhaps not surprisingly, high-tech firms, especially in Silicon Valley, were the most common targets.

Economic espionage, which can damage competitive advantage, erode market share, reduce sales, and damage investor confidence, is expected to intensify as the race to control scarce resources and global markets increases. The rise of the knowledge-based economy has caused information to become a more important and valuable portion of many corporations' assets, and information is portable and increasingly compressible. "Basically, someone can put an entire file cabinet onto something they can slip into their pocket and walk out with" or transmit via e-mail, said Mark Radcliffe, an attorney with the technology-focused law firm Gray Gary. Today's offices have a range of technological options for storing vast amounts of data, including thumb-size USB memory sticks, portable hard drives, external CD burners, personal digital assistants, portable MP3 players, digital memory pens, and digital cameras.

Given this situation, protecting valuable intellectual assets against economic espionage has proved to be an increasing challenge. Companies are becoming more physically distributed, and their management and administration more dispersed. They increasingly rely on distributed, computer-based information systems, which can result in more potential sites from which competitors can collect valuable information. Although few companies have anybody assigned specifically to deal with espionage directed against them, almost all large companies and many smaller ones have competitive intelligence departments, often with substantial levels of funding. A Chinese spy manual noted that 80 percent of the desired military intelligence was available through public sources. A similar figure might be applicable to corporate spying, especially with the growing number of company Web sites holding increasingly detailed information about organizational structures, products, employees, facilities, contact information, and other potentially valuable data.

"Intellectual property has become one of the major targets of the illicit gaining of information," says Michael Marks, a director of Spymaster Communications and Surveillance Systems of the

2. *Competitive:* comparing the firm's operation with that of a direct competitor. Obviously, this is the most difficult kind of benchmarking to do. Productivity improves about 20 percent.
3. *Functional:* comparing the firm's functions with similar functions at firms in one's broadly defined industry—American Airlines' comparing its freight handling procedure

United Kingdom. "The terrible thing today is that if you gain access to a company's computer, you can get access to all of its inner secrets. In the past, you gained information piecemeal from people and departments; now it's centralized on computers and the amount of corporate internal fraud is quite astounding." Perhaps surprisingly, leading-edge technologies are not the only ones being targeted. In less economically developed nations, there is often a preference for older, "off-the-shelf" hardware and software that costs less, is easier to purchase or produce, and can be readily applied within their economic context. It appears that mid-level companies might be targeted even more than large companies for industrial espionage activities, particularly since they have more competitors to engage in espionage and they often have inadequate controls on proprietary information.

Governments and corporations have made attempts to respond to the growing challenges of economic espionage. The U.S. government passed the Economic Espionage Act in 1996, which made it a federal crime to provide American businesses' trade secrets to a foreign entity. The law does not apply to non-U.S. citizens who commit such acts outside American borders, however. In 2001, the Group of Eight leading industrial nations agreed to collaborate more closely to fight international computer-based crime (dubbed "cyber crime") and to possibly develop common law enforcement standards. The European Union proposed a cyber crime framework that would call for mandatory jail sentences for cyber crimes that cause significant damage to a business, but this framework would have limited enforceability if the crime was committed by someone in a country outside the EU. In 2004, Japan enacted legislation that made it a crime to leak corporate trade secrets. Yoshinori Komiya, director of the intellectual property office in the Ministry of Economy, Trade and Industry, said, "The flow of technology out of Japan is leading to a decline in competitiveness and employment. We believe that there is some technology that should be transferred, but what is happening now is that technology that top management does not want transferred is getting passed on." Elsewhere in Asia, notoriously high levels of counterfeiting and piracy indicate the widespread extent of industrial espionage, and the vast proportion of countries lack strong legislative frameworks to deal effectively with the issue. An executive from Sony stated, "We would certainly welcome a comprehensive regulatory system to protect intellectual property in countries such as China and South Korea." Clearly, much opportunity remains for governments to effectively attack the problem.

Corporations have attempted to introduce improved security systems to counter the threat of industrial espionage, causing the worldwide corporate market for monitoring and filtering products to grow to nearly $1 billion. One thing that companies can do is focus their efforts on identifying the aspects of their business that are most critical to protect from espionage. Each industry is unique and the bases for competitive advantage vary across companies. That means each company has to analyze its own strategy, operations, and capabilities and identify what provides it with a competitive advantage, things that it does not want competitors or other organizations to know. In many cases, key activities or knowledge can be isolated, and the company can focus on effectively managing the type and number of employees that might have access to them. In the West, it is common to restrict knowledge of sensitive projects to a small group of people, but in places such as Japan a large group of people usually has access to all of the information, even on very important projects. Some companies refrain from filing patents on manufacturing processes, fearing that difficulties in determining whether such processes are being copied makes it difficult to protect these valuable trade secrets. Sometimes operational security requirements will require the development and management of highly elaborate systems to control information. Yet managing the risk may also include a range of simpler actions. For example, Samsung banned the use of camera phones in some of its facilities in order to keep spies from taking pictures of new product models and transmitting them to competitors or others.

Despite these efforts, the FBI says that foreign spies have increased their attacks on American industry. After the cold war ended, most nations shifted the bulk of their spying to economic espionage. The *Annual Report to Congress on Foreign Economic Collection and Industrial Espionage* estimated that industrial espionage and the loss of proprietary information costs U.S. companies over $300 billion a year, or more than a General Electric or Wal-Mart corporation annually. The FBI told Congress that at least 23 countries were actively involved in industrial espionage against the United States and that FBI agents were involved in 800 separate investigations into economic spying by foreign countries. The major offending nations include China, Japan, Israel, France, Germany, Russia, South Korea, Taiwan, and India. The FBI confirmed that economic spying by countries considered friends as well as by adversaries is increasing. Yet it does not take James Bond–type technologies and procedures for these spies to be effective. The U.S. Office of Counterintelligence reports that the methods most widely used for acquiring sensitive information or technologies include e-mail, phone, and fax.

Source: Jim Joyce, "The Reality of Espionage," *Communications News*, May 2006, p. 38; Jeffrey Benner, "Nailing the Company Spies," *Wired News*, March 1, 2001, www.wired.com/news/print/0,1294,41968,00.html (September 1, 2002); William A. Wallace, "Industrial Espionage Experts," www.newhaven.edu/california/CJ625/p6.html (September 1, 2002); National Counterintelligence Center, *Annual Report to Congress on Foreign Economic Collection and Industrial Espionage 2000* (Washington, DC: National Counterintelligence Center, 2000), www.ncix.gov/nacic/reports/fy00.htm (September 1, 2002); "FBI Warns Companies to Beware of Espionage," *International Herald Tribune*, January 13, 1998, p. 3; Michael Barrier, "Protecting Trade Secrets," *HR Magazine*, May 2004, pp. 52–57; Mei Fong, "The Enemy Within," *Far Eastern Economic Review*, April 22, 2004, pp. 34–36; Richard Isaacs, "A Field Day for Spies: While a Deal Advances," *Mergers and Acquisitions*, January 2004, pp. 30–35; Michiyo Nakamoto, "Japan Goes after Industrial Spies," *Financial Times*, February 9, 2004, p. 8; and Michael Fitzgerald, "At Risk Offshore: U.S. Companies Outsourcing Their Software Development Offshore Can Get Stung by Industrial Espionage and Poor Intellectual Property Safeguards," *CIO*, November 15, 2003, p. 1.

with that of Federal Express, for example. Functional benchmarking is easier to research and implement than competitive benchmarking. It frequently can improve productivity, with improvements of 35 percent or more having been reported by numerous companies and studies.

4. *Generic:* comparing operations in totally unrelated industries. When Xerox decided to improve its order-filling process, it went to L.L.Bean, a mail-order house famous for filling orders quickly and correctly. Although the industries and the kinds of products were very different, Xerox saw that both firms handled a wide variety of shapes and sizes that made it necessary to pack them by hand. By learning from Bean, Xerox reduced its warehousing costs 10 percent.

When Nissan's Infiniti division wanted to change the negative view many people have of service in the car industry, it went to famous service companies for its role models. McDonald's taught the Infiniti team the value of a clean, attractive facility and teamwork. Nordstrom, the department-store chain, taught Infiniti the importance of rewarding employees for providing outstanding service. When China Air wanted to enhance its competitiveness in the international air travel industry, it conducted a benchmark quality comparison relative to key competitors, including British Airways, Singapore Airlines, and Virgin Airlines, across a range of service dimensions in economy, business, and first-class air travel.[39]

Although sometimes a visit to another firm will provide an idea that can be used without change, generally some adaptation will be needed. The basic purpose of benchmarking is to make managers and workers less parochial by exposing them to different ways of doing things so as to encourage creativity, promote organizational learning, enhance cost and performance, and build competitive advantage.

Summary

Explain international strategy, competencies, and international competitive advantage.

International strategy is concerned with the way in which firms make fundamental choices about developing and deploying scarce resources internationally. The goal of international strategy is to create a competitive advantage that is sustainable over time. To do this, the international company should try to develop skills, or competencies, that are valuable, rare, and difficult to imitate and that the organization is able to exploit fully.

Describe the steps in the global strategic planning process.

Global strategic planning provides a formal structure in which managers (1) analyze the company's external environment, (2) analyze the company's internal environment, (3) define the company's business and mission, (4) set corporate objectives, (5) quantify goals, (6) formulate strategies, and (7) make tactical plans.

Explain the purpose of mission statements, vision statements, values statements, objectives, quantified goals, and strategies.

Statements of the corporate mission, vision, and values communicate to the firm's stakeholders what the company is and where it is going, as well as the values to be upheld among the organization's members in their behaviors. A firm's objectives direct its course of action, and its strategies enable management to reach its objectives.

Describe the methods of and new directions in strategic planning.

Strategic planning is traditionally done either in a top-down, bottom-up, or iterative process. Operating managers, rather than dedicated staff planners, now have assumed a primary role in planning. Firms use less structured formats and much shorter documents. Managers are more concerned with issues, strategies, and implementation.

Explain home replication, multidomestic, regional, global, and transnational strategies and when to use them.

When developing and assessing strategic alternatives, companies competing in international markets confront two opposing forces: reduction of costs and adaptation to local markets. As a result, companies basically have five different strategies that they can use for competing internationally: home replication, multidomestic, global, transnational, and regional. (Regional strategies are included because, as some researchers have argued, considering them is of value since few firms are truly global in their scope and operations.) The most appropriate strategy, overall and for various activities in the value chain, depends on the amount of pressure the company faces in terms of adapting to local markets and achieving cost reductions. Each of these five strategies has its own set of advantages and disadvantages.

Describe the sources of competitive information.

Sources of competitive information are within the firm, published material, suppliers/customers, competitors' employees, and direct observation or analysis of physical evidence.

Discuss the importance of industrial espionage.

Industrial espionage is costing domestic and international companies billions of dollars annually in lost sales and may even put a company's long-term competitiveness and survival at risk. The threat of espionage is increasing, particularly as information and knowledge increasingly represent the foundation for companies' competitiveness.

Key Words

international strategy (p. 353)
competitive advantage (p. 353)
mission statement (p. 357)
vision statement (p. 358)
values statement (p. 358)
competitive strategies (p. 361)
scenarios (p. 365)
contingency plans (p. 365)
top-down planning (p. 368)
bottom-up planning (p. 369)
iterative planning (p. 369)
industrial espionage (p. 372)
competitor analysis (p. 373)
competitor intelligence system (CIS) (p. 373)
benchmarking (p. 375)

Questions

1. What is international strategy, and why is it important?
2. What is the difference between strategic planning conducted in domestic companies and that conducted in international companies?
3. Suppose the competitor analysis reveals that the American subsidiary of your firm's German competitor is about to broaden its product mix in the American market by introducing a new line against which your company has not previously had to compete in the home market. The environmental analysis shows that recent weakness in the dollar-euro exchange rate is expected to continue, making American exports relatively less expensive in Germany. Do you recommend a defensive strategy, or do you attack your competitor in its home market? How will you implement your strategy?
4. You are the CEO of the Jones Petrochemical Company and have just finished studying next year's plans of your foreign subsidiaries. You are pleased that the European plan is so optimistic because that subsidiary contributes heavily to your company's income. But OPEC is meeting next month. Should you ask your planning committee, which meets tomorrow, to construct some scenarios? If so, about what?
5. Your firm has used bottom-up planning for years, but the subsidiaries' plans differ with respect to approaches to goals and assumptions—even the time frames are different. How can you, the CEO, get them to agree on these points and still get their individual input?
6. What are the main strengths and weaknesses of each of the competitive strategies: home replication, multidomestic, regional, global, and transnational? Under what circumstances might each strategy be more or less appropriate?
7. What strategic issues arise as a firm considers an international transfer of skills and products resulting from its distinctive competencies in its home country?
8. What is scenario analysis? Why would scenario analysis be of value to an international company? What might limit the usefulness of such an approach?
9. What are some information sources used in competitor analysis? What ethical issues might be involved in using these various sources?

Research Task

globalEDGE globalEDGE.msu.edu

Use the globalEDGE site (http://globalEDGE.msu.edu/) to complete the following exercises:

1. Your company has developed a new product that is expected to achieve high penetration rates in any country where it is introduced regardless of average income. Considering the costs of the product launch, the management team has decided to initially introduce the product only in countries that have a sizable population base. Using the *World Population Data Sheet*, published by the Population Reference Bureau, you are asked to prepare a preliminary assessment of the top ten countries by population. Since growth opportunities are another major concern, the average population growth rate for each country should be listed for management's consideration.

2. You are working for a company that is planning to invest in a foreign country. Management has requested a report regarding the attractiveness of alternative countries based on the potential return of foreign direct investment (FDI). Accordingly, the ranking of the top 25 countries in terms of FDI attractiveness is a crucial ingredient for your report. A colleague mentioned a potentially useful tool called the "FDI Confidence Index" which is updated periodically. Find this index and provide additional information regarding how the index is constructed.

Minicase 13.1 Wal-Mart Takes On the World

Founded in the U.S. state of Arkansas by Sam Walton in 1962, Wal-Mart has developed into the largest retailer in the world and the largest company on the Fortune 500 list, with sales of $312.4 billion in fiscal 2006. Embodying high levels of service, strong inventory management, and purchasing economies, Wal-Mart overpowered competitors and became the dominant firm in the U.S. retail industry. After rapid expansion during the 1980s and 1990s, Wal-Mart faces limits to growth in its home market and has been forced to look internationally for opportunities.

Many skeptics claimed that Wal-Mart's business practices and culture could not be transferred internationally. Yet, in its first decade of operations outside the United States, the company's globalization efforts progressed at a rapid pace. As of 2006, over 40 percent of Wal-Mart's stores were located outside the United States. Its more than 2,700 international retail units employ over 450,000 associates in 13 international markets. In fiscal 2007, Wal-Mart planned to open at least 220 additional international units. Wal-Mart's sales from international operations are expected to reach $78 billion in 2007, a level that is expected to increase substantially over the next decade. If the international business were an independent chain, it would be the fourth-largest retailer in the world, behind Wal-Mart's U.S. operations, Home Depot, and Carrefour.

Globalizing Wal-Mart: Where and How to Begin?

When Wal-Mart began to expand internationally, it had to decide which countries to target. Although the European retail market was large, to succeed there Wal-Mart would have had to take market share from established competitors. Instead, Wal-Mart deliberately selected emerging markets as its starting point for international expansion. In Latin America, it targeted nations with large, growing populations—Mexico, Argentina, and Brazil—and in Asia it aimed at China. Because the company lacked the organizational, managerial, and financial resources to simultaneously pursue all of these markets, Wal-Mart pursued a very deliberate entry strategy for the emerging markets, focusing first on the Americas rather than the more culturally and geographically distant Asian marketplace.

For its first international store, opened in 1991 in Mexico City, the company used a 50-50 joint venture. This entry mode helped Wal-Mart manage the substantial differences in culture and income between the United States and Mexico. Its Mexican partner, the retail conglomerate, Cifra, provided expertise in operating in the Mexican market and a base for learning about retailing in that country. When it entered Brazil in 1996, Wal-Mart was able to leverage its learning from the Mexican experience to take a majority position in a 60-40 venture with a local retailer, Lojas Americana. When the company subsequently entered Argentina, it did so on a wholly owned basis. After gaining experience with partners, in 1997 Wal-Mart expanded further in Mexico by acquiring a controlling interest in Cifra, which it renamed in 2000 to Wal-Mart de México S. A. de C. V. By 2006, Wal-Mart operated 808 units in Mexico in 30 states, achieving annual sales of $15.8 billion and employing over 130,000. It accounts for over half of all supermarket sales in Mexico.

Still, learning the dos and don'ts was a difficult process. "It wasn't such a good idea to stick so closely to the domestic Wal-Mart blueprint in Argentina, or in some of the other international markets we've entered, for that matter," said the president of Wal-Mart International. "In Mexico City we sold tennis balls that wouldn't bounce right in the high altitude. We built large parking lots at some of our Mexican stores, only to realize that many of our customers there rode the bus to the store, then trudged across those large parking lots with bags full of merchandise. We responded by creating bus shuttles to drop customers off at the door. These were all mistakes that were easy to address, but we're now working smarter internationally to avoid cultural and regional problems on the front end."[a] Wal-Mart's initial entry into Brazil used greenfield store sites and emphasized aggressive pricing to build market share, but the French retailer Carrefour and other Brazilian competitors retaliated, launching a costly price war. Wal-Mart's strength in international sourcing was initially of limited assistance in Brazil, since the leading sales category—food—was primarily sourced locally, where Carrefour and others already had strong relationships with local suppliers. Over time, Wal-Mart changed its competitive emphasis to customer service and a broader merchandise mix than smaller local companies could match. The company also pursued acquisitions to supplement internal growth, buying 118 Bompreço stores in 2004 and 140 Sonae stores in 2005. By 2006, Wal-Mart was the third-largest retailer in Brazil, operating 293 stores and employing 50,000 associates.

The Challenge of China

The lure of China, the world's most populous nation, proved too great to ignore. Wal-Mart was one of the first international retailers in China when it set up operations in 1996. Before Wal-Mart's arrival, state-owned retailers typically offered a limited range of products, often of low quality, and most stores were poorly lit, dirty, and disorganized.

Concerned about their potential impact on local firms, Beijing restricted the operations of foreign retailers. These restrictions included requirements for government-backed partners and limitations on the number and location of stores. Initially, Wal-Mart's partner was Charoen Pokphand, a Thai conglomerate with massive investments in China and a strong track record with joint ventures. This venture was terminated after 18 months, due to differences regarding control. A new venture was subsequently formed with two politically connected partners, Shenzhen Economic Development Zone and Shenzhen International Trust and Investment Corporation, and Wal-Mart was able to negotiate a controlling stake in the venture. The first Chinese Wal-Mart store was in Shenzhen, a rapidly growing city bordering Hong Kong. The company chose to concentrate its initial activities in Shenzhen while it learned about Chinese retailing.

Wal-Mart had many well-publicized miscues while learning how to do business in China. For example, some household items found at American Wal-Marts are not found in the Chinese stores. "Their shopping list isn't as extensive as ours. If you ask the majority of people here what a paper towel is, they either don't know or they think it's some kind of luxury item," said the president of Wal-Mart China.[b] The company eliminated matching kitchen towels and window curtains, since the wide variety of Chinese window sizes caused people to make their own curtains. Consumers purchased four times the number of small appliances than projected, but Wal-Mart no longer tries to sell extension ladders or a year's supply of soy sauce or shampoo to Chinese customers, who typically live in cramped apartments with limited storage space. Yet, although "people say the Chinese don't like sweets, we sure sell a lot of M&Ms," said Joe Hatfield, president of Wal-Mart's Asian retailing operations.[c]

Operationally, the scarcity of highly modernized suppliers in China frustrated Wal-Mart's initial attempts to achieve high levels of efficiency. Bar coding was not standardized in China, and retailers had to either recode goods themselves or distribute labels to suppliers, procedures that increased costs and hindered efficiency. Pressured to appease the government's desire for local sourcing of products, while maintaining the aura of being an American shopping experience, Wal-Mart's solution was to source about 85 percent of the Chinese stores' purchases from local manufacturers but heavily weight purchasing toward locally produced American brands (such as products from Procter & Gamble's factories in China). Wal-Mart also mass-markets Chinese products that were previously available only in isolated parts of the country, such as coconut juice from Guangdong province, hams and mushrooms from rural Yunnan, and oats from Fujian province. "What this place is going to look like 10 to 20 years from now—and what the consumer will be ready to buy—is hard to even think about. There are 800 million farmers out there who've probably never even tasted a Coke," said Hatfield.

Wal-Mart also learned the importance of building relationships with agencies from the central and local governments and with local communities. Bureaucratic red tape, graft, and lengthy delays in the approval process proved to be aggravating. The company learned to curry favor through actions such as inviting Chinese officials to visit Wal-Mart's headquarters in the United States, assisting local charities, and even building a school for the local community. Wal-Mart expected its small-town folksiness to be a strong asset in China. "Price has been an issue, but there's always somebody who can undersell you. A young person who's smiling and saying, 'Can I help you?' is a big part of the equation. Most places in this country you don't get that," said the president of Wal-Mart International.[d] "Over the last two years, Wal-Mart has learned a tremendous amount about serving our Chinese customers, and our excitement about expanding in the market and in Asia has never been stronger."[e]

Wal-Mart was only the 20th-largest retailer in China at the end of 2005, with sales less than half those of industry leader Carrefour of France. Wal-Mart's 59 stores in China, employing over 30,000 associates, represented a small fraction of its worldwide retailing operations. Yet, Wal-Mart estimated that its operations in China could be nearly as large as in the U.S. within 20 years and the lessons Wal-Mart has learned have positioned the company to exploit future market-opening initiatives in China. It purchases nearly $20 billion worth of local merchandise annually, making it China's sixth-largest export market if it were a company. Wal-Mart's objective is to use its existing stores and growing supplier network as a basis for the creation of a nationwide chain. Wal-Mart's head of Asian operations stated, "We are not just going to march out all over China." The focus was instead on expanding slowly, trying to make friends and gain respect as it does so. In March 2006, the company announced that it would hire about 150,000 workers in China during the next five years as part of its planned expansion strategy.

A major change in Wal-Mart's China growth strategy occured in October 2006. It was announced that the company had outbid competitors Carrefour, the United Kingdom's Tesco, and Lianhua of China to acquire Trust-Mart, a chain of over 100 supercenters located in 20 cities across China. This acquisition, for approximately $1 billion, would immediately give Wal-Mart the largest network of food and department stores in China, with combined sales of over $3 billion for 2006.

A Different Approach for Entering Canada and Europe

After focusing initial international expansion efforts on large developing nations, Wal-Mart began to pursue the Canadian and European markets. Strong, entrenched competitors in these mature, developed country markets hindered Wal-Mart's prospects for obtaining critical mass solely through internal growth. Rather than first developing its retail operations from scratch, as in Latin America and Asia, Wal-Mart entered via acquisitions.

The company entered Canada by acquiring 122 Woolco stores in 1994. Wal-Mart quickly restructured the money-losing Canadian operations, applying many of the practices that had been successful in the United States. Transition teams were brought in from the United States to help with the transformation, and within two years the Canadian operations were profitable. Its 278 stores, employing 70,000 associates, now account for more than 35 percent of the Canadian discount- and department-store retail market. Wal-Mart's "Buy Canadian" program, launched in 1994, has resulted in more than 80 percent of the company's merchandise being purchased from suppliers that operate in Canada.

In Europe, Wal-Mart entered Germany by acquiring the profitable 21-unit Wertkauf hypermarket chain in 1998 and 74 Interspar stores in 1999. The company entered the United Kingdom in 1999 through the acquisition of the 229-store ASDA Group. These acquisitions allowed Wal-Mart to build market share quickly within the highly advanced and competitive European retail market. From this base, additional growth is anticipated through the opening of new stores, supplemented with further acquisitions. By 2006, the company had 88 Supercenters in Germany. It is the second-largest supermarket chain in the United Kingdom, with 321 stores and 140,000 associates, but has been losing ground to industry leader Tesco Plc.

Although successful in rapidly building European market share, Wal-Mart still encountered difficulties. Acquiring two German companies within a year proved too much for the company to handle with its limited European infrastructure. Efforts to centralize purchasing and leverage Wal-Mart's famous competencies in information systems and inventory management were stymied by problems with suppliers that were not familiar with such practices.

The introduction of Wal-Mart's "always low prices" approach met resistance from competitors and regulators. Indeed, the company was ordered by Germany's Cartel Office to raise prices, charging that Wal-Mart had helped to spark a price war by illegally selling some items below cost. Wal-Mart also challenged existing retail practices regarding hours of operation. Laws required shops to close by 8 P.M. on weekdays and 4 P.M. on Saturdays and to remain closed on Sundays. However, Wal-Mart stores began to open by 7 A.M., two hours earlier than most competitors, and the company has lobbied for additional reforms to allow later closing times. These changes have sparked vehement opposition from smaller competitors and employees' unions.

As it struggled to build a strong competitive base, Wal-Mart Germany lost between $120 million and $200 million in 1999, and the losses continued each year following. Lacking the scale of operations to create competitive advantage, and facing strong competition in a mature marketplace, in July 2006 Wal-Mart announced that it was selling its German operations to a competitor, Metro. Earlier that year, Wal-Mart had also announced that it was selling its Korean operations to competitor Shinsegae after Wal-Mart failed to achieve successful scale and performance in that Asian market.

A Base for Continued Globalization Efforts

Wal-Mart's path to internationalization has been littered with challenges. The company has persevered and seems to have learned from its mistakes, however, and it seems well positioned for continued growth. In 2005, the company acquired one-third of Central American Retail Holding Co. which has 363 stores in Guatemala, Honduras, El Salvador, Nicaragua, and Costa Rico, and it increased its share to 51 percent in 2006 and changed the name to Wal-Mart Central America. There are still many potential markets for a Wal-Mart store, and the company is committed to exploiting these opportunities, whether they are at home or abroad. International is Wal-Mart's fastest-growing division, and the company announced that it was exploring growth opportunities in Russia and India, indicating that these countries might soon be part of the company's international market coverage.

India: Anticipating the Opening Up of a Billion-Person Market

Wal-Mart is currently positioning for entry into India, which has the largest population of any nation the company is not currently in. Although it is the world's eighth-largest retail market at $250 billion, the inefficiency of the Indian retail sector is well known. Over 95 percent of retail sales are made through tea stands, newspaper stalls, and mom-and-pop stores. Strict government barriers have prevented foreign-owned retail businesses, although that situation might change soon. "Many smart people—much smarter than I—believe that India could be the next China," said John Menzer, the former head of Wal-Mart's international operations and current vice chair of the company's U.S. stores. "So, certainly, as a retailer it's a place where we'd like to be."[f]

However, exploiting the potential of India could be a major challenge, particularly given the country's notoriously frustrating bureaucracy and poor infrastructure. Wal-Mart will have to learn to manage highly protectionist and anticapitalist political parties, a bad road system, frequent power outages, and lack of adequate distribution and cold-storage systems, among other concerns. The diversity of the country could also prove problematic, with 18 official languages and widely varying regional consumer cultures. Savvy new Indian chains, such as Provogue and Shoppers' Stop, are starting to emerge, and nationalistic sentiments may produce much consternation for expansion efforts of foreign companies such as Wal-Mart.

In preparation for an eventual opening of the market, Wal-Mart has been building a foundation by establishing relationships with Indian suppliers, distributors, and consumers. The company has been conducting market studies, hiring a team of local managers, and building relationships with Indian politicians and bureaucrats. In 2005, Wal-Mart purchased $1.5 billion in Indian products for export and sale in its stores abroad. "What we found in China as we get stores on the ground and get more mass, we get to know a lot more of the suppliers. And when we know the suppliers, it gives us the opportunity to learn the product of the suppliers and actually export them," said Mr. Menzer.[g] Clearly, Wal-Mart will need to understand the political and market dynamics and exploit the lessons it has learned from entering other emerging markets in order to achieve success when the Indian market finally opens up.

Discussion Questions

1. Why has Wal-Mart viewed international expansion as a critical part of its strategy?

2. What did Wal-Mart do to enable the company to achieve success in Canada and Latin America? Why did Wal-Mart fail to achieve similar success in Europe?

3. What should Wal-Mart do—or not do—to help ensure that the company achieves success in China and India?

[a]"ASDA Purchase Leads Way for Wal-Mart's International Expansion," *Wal-Mart Annual Report 2000,* p. 10.

[b]James Cox, "Great Wal-Mart of China Red-Letter Day as East Meets West in the Aisles," *USA Today,* September 11, 1996, p. B1.

[c]Tyler Marshall, "Selling Eel and Chicken Feet—Plus M&Ms and Sony TVs," *Los Angeles Times,* November 25, 2003, p. A15.

[d]Cox, "Great Wal-Mart of China Red-Letter Day."

[e]"Wal-Mart China Expansion to Accelerate," www.Walmartstores.com/newsstand/archive/prn_980605_chinaexpan.shtml (June 5, 1999).

[f]Eric Bellman and Kris Hudson, "Wal-Mart Stakes India Claim," *The Wall Street Journal,* January 18, 2006, p. A9.

[g]Ibid.

Source: "International Operations," www.walmartfacts.com/newsdesk/wal-mark-fact-sheets.aspx#a1826 (June 28, 2006); Peter Wonacott, "Wal-Mart Finds Market Footing in China," *The Wall Street Journal,* July 17, 2000, p. A31; "Big Chains Set for Post-WTO Scrap," *South China Morning Post,* November 3, 2000, p. 5; Glenn Hall, "Wal-Mart Germany Told to Raise Prices: Choking Small Retailers," *National Post,* September 9, 2000, p. D3; Wal-Mart, "Timeline," http://walmartstores.com/GlobalWMStoresWeb/navigate.do?catg=6 (June 28, 2006); Mike Troy, "In South America, Ahold's Loss Is Wal-Mart's Gain," *DSN Retailing Today,* March 22, 2004, pp. 1–2; and "Wal-Mart to Become Biggest Big-Box in China," http://money.cnn.com/2006/10/16/news/international/walmart_hypermarkets.reut/index.htm?postversion=2006101706 (October 17, 2006).

14 Organizational Design and Control

We are in the midst of a major transition from organization and management practices that began around the turn of the 20th century. Our cloudy crystal ball won't allow us to see which organization structure or model will dominate the 21st century. Since we're no longer in an age of mass production and standardization, there won't likely be just one type. Rather, we'll see our top organizations grow and shed a variety of structures and models to suit their changing circumstances.

—Jim Clemmer, in "High Performance Organization Structures and Characteristics"

Kraft Foods—Reorganizing to Become a "Best of Global and Best of Local" Company

Kraft Foods announced a complex reorganization of its worldwide operations in 2004, with a goal of transforming the company into an integrated, global company. With over $34 billion in sales and 94,000 employees worldwide, Kraft is the largest branded-food and -beverage company headquartered in North America and the second largest in the world, behind Nestlé. Kraft's mission is "to be widely recognized as the undisputed leader of the global food industry." The company's products—including such brands as Kraft cheese, Maxwell House coffee, Nabisco cookies and crackers, Philadephia cream cheese, Jello desserts, Oscar Mayer meats, and Post cereals—are sold in over 155 nations.

Kraft's reorganization was triggered in part by slowing growth in several product categories, especially within developed country markets, which caused a decline in earnings in recent years. Many of the company's performance difficulties were attributed to problems with its prior organizational structure. To address this situation, under its new structure, Kraft is creating a matrix organization that includes:

1. A new global marketing and category development group to accelerate growth and global expansion through developing global category strategies, new product platforms, and marketing excellence.
2. Two geographic-based commercial units, for the regions of North America and International. These units will be responsible for driving strong results, country by country, through local consumer and customer knowledge, local sales and marketing execution, and responsibility for profits and losses.
3. Key functions, including technology and quality, supply chains, finance, human resources, law, information systems, corporate and governmental affairs, and strategy and business development, will be managed on a global basis in order to achieve greater economies of scale, better lever technologies and best practices internationally, and drive brands and ideas around the world faster.
4. The activities of the preceding three groups will be coordinated with the company's five global product sectors—snacks and cereals, cheese and food service, beverages, convenient meals, and grocery.

Kraft's CEO said, "The most important opportunities and pressing challenges that we face today and going forward demand that we become a more unified, global company. But in becoming more global, we must keep and strengthen the local expertise that has built our success. By moving quickly to create Kraft's new global 'One Company' structure, we can immediately begin to capture the 'best of global and best of local' and act with greater focus and speed than ever before." In terms of enhanced organizational effectiveness, Kraft's leadership anticipated that this outcome would be achieved through accelerated innovation, improved application of category/functional expertise, strong local execution, improved management

CONCEPT PREVIEWS

After reading this chapter, you should be able to:

explain why the design of organizational structure is important to international companies

discuss the organizational dimensions that must be considered when selecting organizational structures

discuss the various organizational forms available for structuring international companies

explain the concept of the virtual corporation

explain why decisions are made where they are among parent and subsidiary units of an international company (IC)

discuss how an IC can maintain control of a joint venture or of a company in which the IC owns less than 50 percent of the voting stock

list the types of information an IC needs to have reported to it by its units around the world

Gli Affari Internazionali

ionales

onales Geschäft Παγοσμιο Business

Negócios Internacionais Los Negócios Internacionais

nternacionales Affaires Internationales 國際商務 Παγοσμιο Business development, and faster decision making. Enhanced efficiency would be facilitated by elimination of functional duplication and facility consolidation. The new organizational structure resembles that of other major consumer products companies, such as Gillette and Procter & Gamble.

A particular objective of the reorganization was to produce a more integrated and balanced global business by accelerating Kraft's growth outside its home market of the United States and generating a higher proportion of international sales, consistent with the performance of key rivals such as Nestlé and Unilever. The maturing North American region generated a 1 percent decline in profits in 2005, versus a more than 20 percent profit growth in international markets. Overall, Kraft's international sales grew from less than a quarter of total company revenues in the early 1990s to over 31 percent in 2005. Kraft's executive vice president commented, "This new structure will help us accelerate our growth and move faster as a company in our decision-making process. All of it is designed to help us deliver realistic, sustainable growth for our shareholders."

Within Kraft's international segment, developed country markets accounted for over 60 percent of sales in 2005. Approximately 60 percent of these revenues were concentrated in just four nations: Germany, France, Italy, and the United Kingdom. As with other developed countries, these markets were confronting problems of slowing population growth, increasingly value-conscious consumers, high trade concentration, and the growing role of discount retailers and private-label products. In developed countries, the company anticipated that its reorganization would promote growth by leveraging its leading share positions in core categories, while building superior brand value and accelerating innovation.

Another important objective of Kraft's new organizational structure was to enhance growth prospects within developing country markets. Revenues from developing markets had increased from $1 billion in 1992 to $2 billion in 2000 and $4 billion in 2005. These markets represented only about 12 percent of overall revenues, and the company envisioned substantial future growth from these areas. In the developing markets, Kraft planned to expand its core categories into large countries with the greatest growth potential. The four top developing countries that Kraft planned to focus on—Mexico, Brazil, Russia, and China—had a combined population of nearly 2 billion but represented less than $1.5 billion of Kraft's annual sales in 2005.

Under the new structure, Kraft's strategy for developing country markets is based on four main components: (1) Introduce additional snack, beverage, and cheese categories in developing markets where it already has a presence, (2) introduce additional brands across key price segments within the categories where it already has a presence, (3) enter developing markets where it does not yet have a presence, and (4) pursue tactical fill-in acquisitions, especially in snacks and beverages. Strategic and operational improvements from the new matrix structure were expected to enhance the implementation of these initiatives and Kraft's position in the global food and beverage industry. ■

Source: "Company Structure Encourages Best of Global, Best of Local," www.kraft.com/profile/company_structure.html (June 20, 2006); Neil Buckley, "Kraft Works to Become a More Global Business," *Financial Times*, January 9, 2004, p. 20; "Kraft Foods Announces New Global Organizational Structure," January 8, 2004, www.industrypages.com/artman/publish/Industry News 3702.stm (July 24, 2004); "Strategies for Growth," http://164.109.46.215/investors/strategies.html (July 24, 2004); "Visuals from Presentation by Roger Deromedi, CEO, Kraft Foods, to Investment Community, January 27, 2004," http://media.corporate-ir.net/media_files/nys/kft/presentations/kft_o40127b2326.pdf (July 24, 2004); Business Wire, "Kraft Foods Inc. Reports 2005 Results and Issues 2006 Outlook; Announces Expanded Restructuring Program as Part of Sustainable Growth Plan," January 30, 2006, p. 1.

organizational structure
The way that an organization formally arranges its domestic and international units and activities, and the relationships among these various organizational components

Organizations exist for the purpose of enabling a group of people to effectively coordinate their collective activities and accomplish objectives.[1] **Organizational structure** refers to the way that an organization formally arranges its various domestic and international units and activities and the relationships among these organizational components. A company's structure helps to determine where formal power and authority will be located within the organization, and this structure is what is typically presented in a company's organization chart.

Creating and evolving the structure of an international organization over time are fundamental tasks of senior management. Few executives except those in the senior levels of the organization are capable of establishing or changing the overall structure of an international company, because people at an organization's lower levels lack the broad perspective necessary for making the various trade-offs that will influence the organization as a whole. Nevertheless, all of the company's managers have to perform their job responsibilities within the context created by this structure. Further, most managers need to be able to effectively structure the various activities that are within their area of responsibility and to do so in a manner that is consistent with the company's overall structure. As a result, developing an understanding of the different ways in which international companies can be structured and the relative strengths and weaknesses of each of the various structural alternatives is an essential skill for managers.

In this chapter, we will discuss the different organizational forms an international company can take and key strategic issues that managers must address in choosing among these various organizational designs. Included in the discussion will be the identification of concerns that managers have regarding their ability to control the international activities of their companies.

What Is Organizational Design, and Why Is It Important for International Companies?

Organizational design is a process that deals with how an international business should be organized in order to ensure that its worldwide business activities are able to be integrated in an efficient and effective manner. As suggested in Figure 14.1, in designing an international organization, it is essential that the structures and systems being implemented are not merely consistent with each other but also consistent with the environmental context in which the organization is operating and the strategy the company is using for competing in this international environment. The size of the organization and the complexity of its business operations must also be considered in the design of a company.

The structure of an international company must be able to evolve over time, in order to enable the organization to respond to change and to efficiently and effectively reconfigure the way in which its competencies and resources are integrated within and across various units of the enterprise. This is a major challenge for the management of international companies, especially as these companies' activities are increasingly dispersed across the globe as well as subject to rapid and ongoing environmental and strategic change. Failure to successfully deal with this challenge threatens the organization's performance and, indeed, its long-term survival.

The international company's strategic planning process itself, because it encompasses an analysis of the firm's external environments as well as its strengths and weaknesses within these environments, often discloses a need to alter the organization. Changes in an international company's strategy may require changes in the organization, but the reverse is also true. For instance, a new CEO may join the firm, or the company may acquire a company in another nation or in another area of business activity. Strategic planning and organizing are so closely related that usually the structure of the organization is treated by management as an integral part of the strategic planning process.

ORGANIZATIONAL DESIGN CONCERNS

Two of the concerns that management faces in designing the organizational structure for an IC are (1) finding the most effective way to departmentalize to take advantage of the efficiencies gained from the specialization of labor and (2) coordinating the activities of those

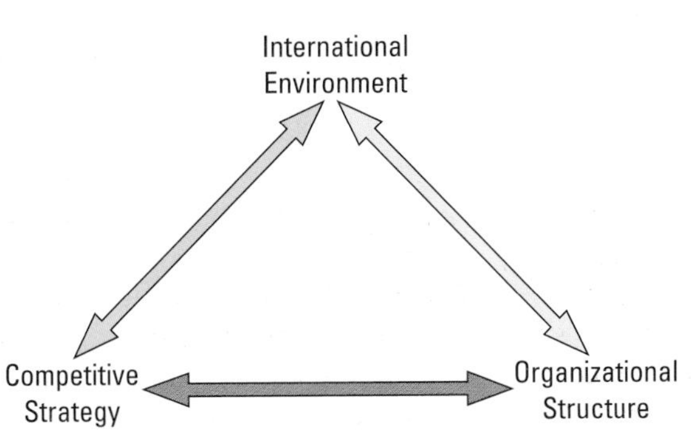

FIGURE 14.1

The Relationship among International Environment, Competitive Strategy, and Organizational Structure departments to enable the firm to meet its overall objectives. As all managers know, these two concerns run counter to each other; that is, the gain from increased specialization of labor may at times be nullified by the increased cost of coordination. It is the search for an optimum balance between them that often leads to a reorganization of the international company's structure.

As suggested in the introductory case on Kraft Foods, there are four primary dimensions that need to be considered when designing the structure of an international company:

1. *Product and technical expertise* regarding the different businesses that the company participates in.
2. *Geographic expertise* regarding the countries and regions in which the company operates.
3. *Customer expertise* regarding the similarity of client groups, industries, market segments, or population groups that transcend the boundaries of individual countries or regions.
4. *Functional expertise* regarding the various value chain activities that the company is involved with.

International companies can and do vary with respect to the way in which these four dimensions are structured and integrated. No single structure is best for all companies and contexts. Rather, managers have to consider the nature of their company's international operating environment and strategy—both currently and how they are expected to change in the future—when deciding when and how to modify the company's organizational structure. In the sections below, we discuss the most common types of organizational designs for international companies. In reality, due to the complex nature of their operating environments and nuances of their historical origins and evolution, the structure of many international companies deviates to some extent from these basic organizational designs. Nevertheless, understanding attributes associated with these basic designs can assist managers of international companies in selecting an organizational structure appropriate for their current and anticipated future circumstances.

EVOLUTION OF THE INTERNATIONAL COMPANY

As discussed in Chapters 2, 3, and 16, companies have often entered foreign markets first by exporting and then, as sales increased, by forming overseas sales companies and eventually setting up manufacturing facilities. As the firm's foreign involvement changed, its organization frequently changed as well. It might first have had *no one* responsible for international business; the firm's marketing department might have filled the export orders. Next, an export department might have been created, possibly in the marketing department; and when the company began to invest in various overseas locations, it could have formed an **international division** to take charge of all overseas involvement. Larger firms, such as Ford, IBM, and Goodyear, commonly organized their international divisions on a regional or geographic basis (Figure 14.2). Today, we still see companies—both those that are relatively modest in size and those that are some of the largest in the world—that are organized into a primary domestic division, supplemented by an international division to serve the rest of the world.

international division
A division in the organization that is at the same level as the domestic division and is responsible for all non-home country activities

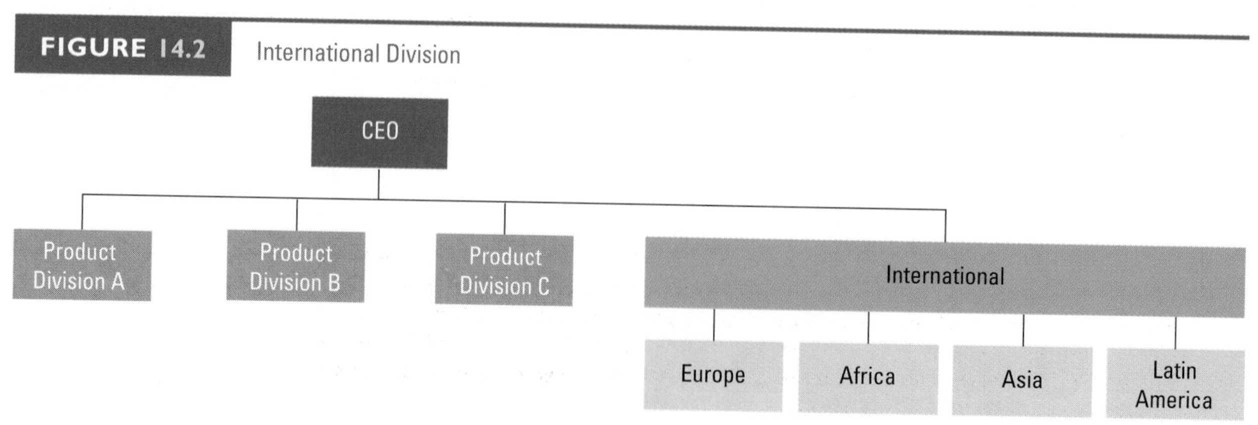

BUILDING YOUR GLOBAL RÉSUMÉ Tips from Your Personal Global Mentor

Michelle Teteak

Michelle Teteak is senior vice president–multinational consultant for the Northern Trust Company and works at corporate headquarters in Chicago, Illinois. Michelle works with multinational organizations on global pension plan management strategies for client companies with employees located worldwide, most notably in the United States, Canada, the United Kingdom, Netherlands, Germany, Ireland, Luxembourg, Switzerland, Belgium, Australia, Sweden, Norway, Japan, and Mexico. With the downturn in the equity markets a few years ago, pension plans worldwide came to be in underfunded positions. Subsidiaries looked to their corporate headquarters to make up the funding shortfalls. Many multinationals were surprised by the funding requirements they faced. Corporate management's desire to avoid future surprises, combined with growth in global pension plans because of an increasingly global workforce and more stringent regulatory reporting on worldwide pension plans, is driving multinational organizations to effect new forms of global pension management. Northern Trust offers three main services to multinationals that enable them to better govern their foreign pension plans: (1) consolidated headquarter reporting, (2) global custody, and (3) cross-border pension pooling. Michelle leads the business development process for each of these services and works to strategize the best solution for each multinational client and its employees on the basis of its profile.

Michelle's advice on how to get a job in international business:

- "Take advantage of networking opportunities offered to you by your parents, teachers, counselors, managers, mentors, etc."
- "Take advantage of foreign semester study programs through your schools."
- "Position yourself with a global company and express your interest in an international assignment."
- "Be patient—often you are most valuable to your company as an international representative after you have earned broad experience at the home office."
- "Show dedication and hard work in everything you do—show you can be trusted."
- "Embrace a mentoring relationship (not necessarily your manager). These informal relationships can prove to be very helpful. Seek a mentor if one is not occurring naturally."
- "Consider the timing of the international portion of your career. Often these are not life-long assignments. Balance the timing so that you have enough experience to be valuable, yet do not find yourself away from home too much during periods that might require more personal commitment, such as trying to start and raise a family or caring for an elder."

Michelle's advice on the skills required to succeed in international business:

- *Solid writing, communication, and presentation skills:* It is especially important to be concise and direct (yet thorough) with your written and spoken words when dealing with multiple countries to avoid any misunderstandings.
- *Solid understanding of your product/service:* Many questions are asked in international business, and people will see right through you if you do not have a firm command of your material.
- *Ability to understand what is important to different cultures* and then adjust your interaction accordingly.
- *Tolerance for different cultures* and different ways of doing things.
- *Responsiveness:* Often very little differs between you and the global competition—the degree of your responsiveness with clients and prospects can truly set you apart.
- *Tenaciousness, patience, and flexibility:* Global projects can take a while to implement—you need to stick with the opportunities to the end. You also need to be available for business interaction well outside of "normal" working hours and often in the middle of the night, if necessary, to accommodate varying time zones.

"International travel sounds glamorous; however, this is not always the case. It is great when you can build in a few extra days to explore new countries. Realistically, business demands are such that more often than not, you are in and out of locations and may not see more than the airport and office buildings. If you are able to handle the logistical challenges, an international career can be very exciting and assisting a company with global growth can be very rewarding."

World Wide Resource:

www.ntrs.com

Met-Pro Corporation, a New York Stock Exchange–listed company involved in the manufacture of a range of pollution control and fluid handling equipment, achieved sales of $85.1 million in the 2006 fiscal year. The company is organized into eight product divisions that provide sales and service for the company's "home market" of the United States and Canada. All sales and service activities involving other nations and regions of the world are handled by a separate International Division.[2]

Wal-Mart Stores, Inc., the world's largest retailer, with over $312 billion in sales in fiscal 2006, is organized into three business segments: Wal-Mart Stores, Sam's Club, and International. These segments account for 67.2, 12.7, and 20.1 percent of the company's overall sales, respectively. The International segment is responsible for operating several different types of retail stores and restaurants, including discount stores, supercenters, and Sam's Clubs, in 13 countries and Puerto Rico.[3]

As their overseas operations increased in importance and scope, most managements, with some exceptions, felt the need to eliminate international divisions and establish worldwide organizations based on *product, region, function,* or *customer classes.* At secondary, tertiary, and still lower levels, these four dimensions—plus (1) process, (2) national subsidiary, and (3) international or domestic—provide the basis for subdivisions. As a result, as they grow over time, most international companies move away from the use of international divisions and instead implement one of the global structures that we present in the following sections of this chapter. The initial choice of organizational structure after discarding the international division is usually one based on either global product or global geographic factors. These alternative paths for the design and evolution of the international company are presented in the international stages model of organizational structures, which was originally developed by John Stopford and Louis Wells and is shown in Figure 14.3.[4]

Managements that changed to these types of organizations felt they would (1) be more capable of developing competitive strategies to confront the increasing global competition, (2) obtain lower production costs by promoting worldwide product standardization and manufacturing rationalization, and (3) enhance technology transfer and the allocation of company resources.

Global Corporate Form—Product Frequently, this structure represents a return to pre-export department times in that the domestic product division has been given responsibility for global line and staff operations. In the present-day global form, product divisions are responsible for the worldwide operations such as marketing and production of products under their control. Each division generally has regional experts, so while this organizational form avoids the duplication of product experts common in a company with an international division, it creates a duplication of area experts. Occasionally, to avoid placing regional specialists in each product division, management will have a group of managerial specialists in an international division who advise the product divisions but have no authority over them (see Figure 14.4). For

FIGURE 14.3

The International Structural Stages Model

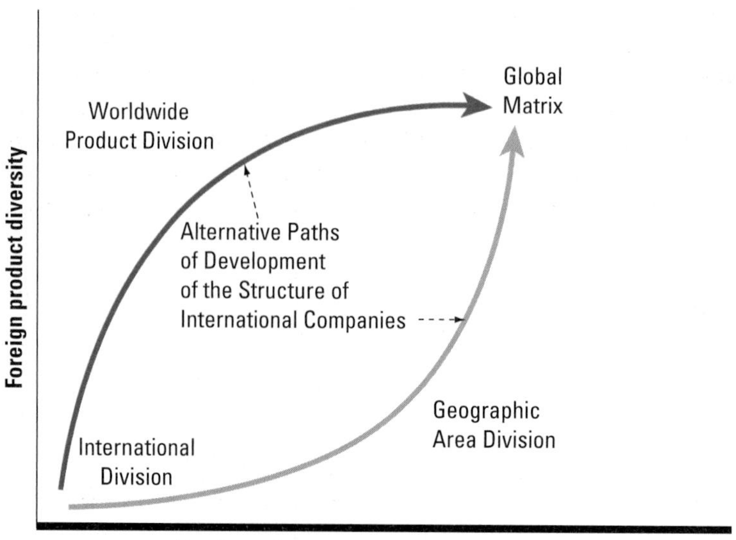

Source: Based on John M. Stopford and Louis T. Wells, *Strategy and Structure of the Multinational Enterprise* (New York: Basic Books, 1970).

FIGURE 14.4 Global Corporate Form—Product

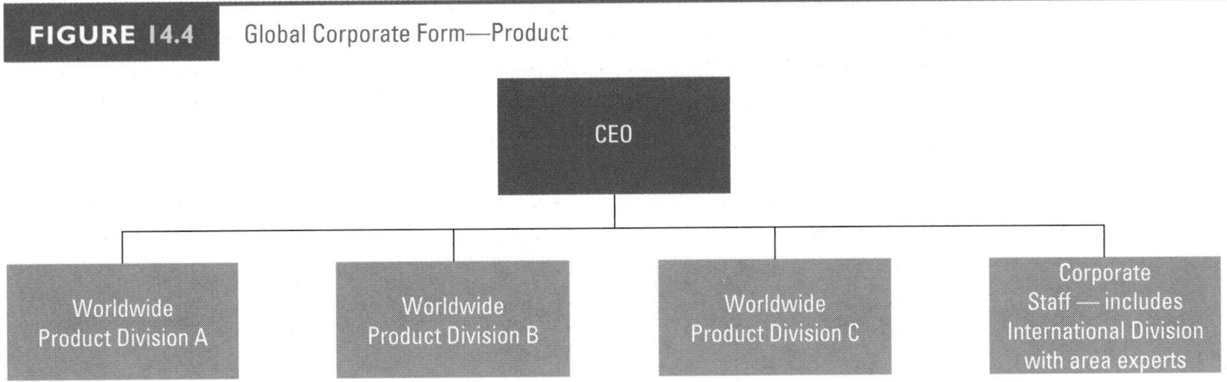

example, all of General Electric's businesses are managed through a global line-of-business structure, and investment opportunities are identified and assessed on a global basis by managers within each of these business areas.

Deutsche Post World Net, a global logistics services provider, has approximately 500,000 employees in over 220 countries and territories and 2005 revenues of over €44.5 billion. Based in Germany, the company is structured into five divisions: Mail (including Deutsche Post), Express (including DHL), Logistics (including the DHL Business division), Financial Services (including Postbank), and Services (established at the beginning of 2006).[5]

After the merger of Exxon and Mobil, the energy company restructured its operations worldwide. To improve the capital productivity of the combined organizations, ExxonMobil moved from a multifunctional, geographically based regional organization to an organization based on global businesses to facilitate identification and sharing of technology and best practices worldwide. Under the new structure, each global business is responsible for running its operations on a worldwide basis.[6]

Global Corporate Form—Geographic Regions Firms in which geographic regions are the primary basis for division put the responsibility for all activities under area managers who report directly to the chief executive officer. This kind of organization simplifies the task of directing worldwide operations, because every country in the world is clearly under the control of someone who is in contact with headquarters (see Figure 14.5).

Of course, this organizational type is used for both multinational (multidomestic) and global companies. Global companies that use it consider the division in which the home country is located as just another division for purposes of resource allocation and a source of management personnel. Some U.S. global companies have created a North American division that includes Canada, Mexico, and Central American countries in addition to the United States, possibly in part to emphasize that the home country is given no preference.

The regionalized organization appears to be popular with companies that manufacture products with a rather low, or at least stable, technological content that require strong marketing ability. It is also favored by firms with diverse products, each having different product

FIGURE 14.5 Global Corporate Form—Geographic Regions

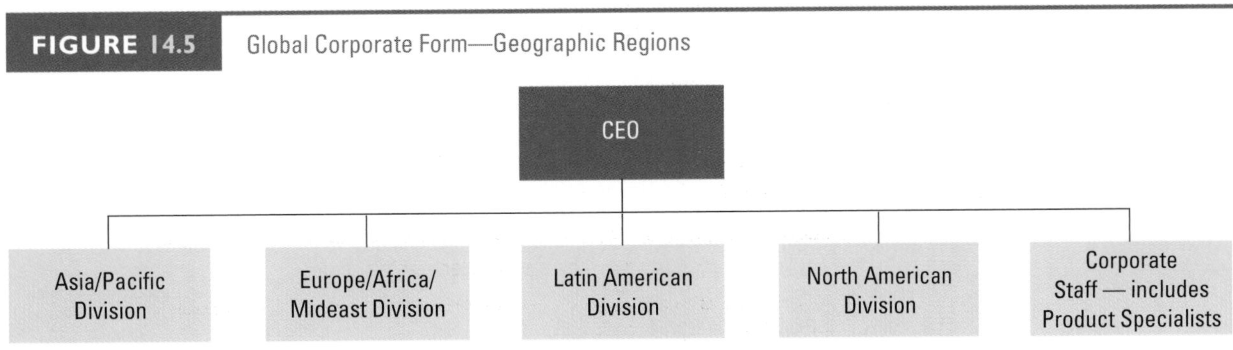

requirements, competitive environments, and political risks. Many producers of consumer products, such as prepared foods, pharmaceuticals, and household products, employ this type of organization. The disadvantage of an organization divided into geographic regions is that each region must have its own product and functional specialists, so although the duplication of area specialists found in product divisions is eliminated, duplication of product and functional specialists is necessary.

Mittal Steel is the world's largest and most global steel company, with 2005 revenues of over $28 billion. The company has 224,000 people, over 30 steel-making operations scattered across 16 nations, and customers in over 150 countries. The company's global operations are organized within three geographic regions: (1) the Americas, (2) Europe, and (3) Asia and Africa.[7]

An interesting organizational structure based on regional factors relating to level of economic development rather than geography was introduced by Kimberly-Clark:

Kimberly-Clark Corporation is one of the world's largest producers of health and hygiene products, with sales in over 150 countries and manufacturing in 37. The company reorganized its main business operations into a developing and emerging markets business unit in addition to a developed market business unit. This change replaces its previous structure based on geographic regions. Three global businesses—Personal Care, Consumer Tissue, and Business-to-Business—continue to exist. The logic for moving to a developed/developing market structure was that countries in regions such as Western Europe and North America face a different set of competitive pressures from those faced by emerging countries in Asia, Latin America, and elsewhere. For example, the company's Kleenex tissues and Huggies disposable diapers are much more extensively used in developed country markets than in the developing countries. "We are facing many of the same issues in developing markets: How do you drive innovation at an affordable cost? Combining the emerging markets into one division will give that part of the company a louder voice," said Thomas J. Falk, Kimberly-Clark's CEO. "These changes will increase our speed in pursuing growth opportunities around the world, improve our execution of global strategies, and enable more consistent brand positioning and deployment of other best practices," Falk said.[8]

Production coordination across regions presents difficult problems, as does global product planning. To alleviate these problems, managements often place specialized product managers on the headquarters staff. Although these managers have no line authority, they do provide input to corporate decisions concerning products.

Global Corporate Form—Function Few firms are organized by function at the top level. Those that are obviously believe worldwide functional expertise is more significant to the firm than is product or area knowledge. In this type of organization, those reporting to the CEO might be the senior executives responsible for each functional area (marketing, production, finance, and so on), as in Figure 14.6. The commonality among the users of the functional form is a narrow and highly integrated product mix, such as that of aircraft manufacturers or oil refining companies.

FIGURE 14.6 Global Corporate Form—Function

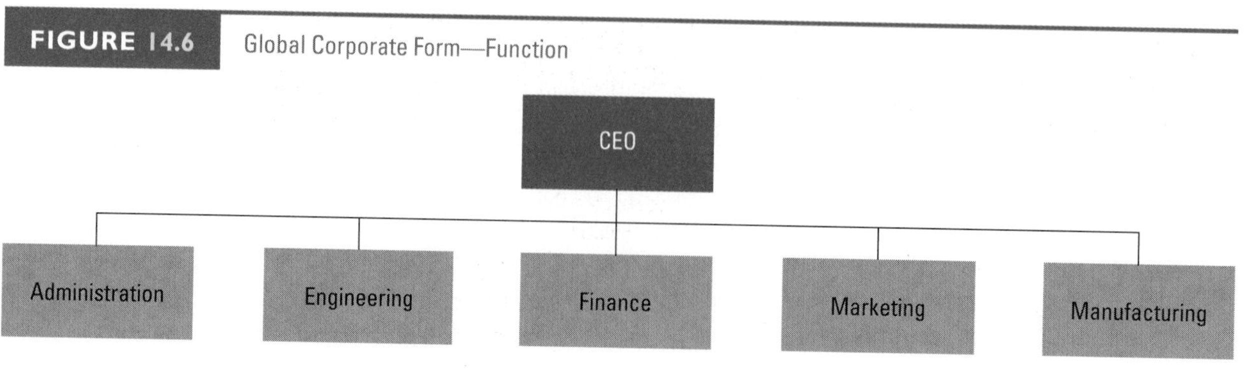

Genentech, the San Francisco, California, company that was the first to bring a biotechnology drug to market, achieved revenues of $6.6 billion in 2005, including over $870 million from foreign markets. The company is organized into four functional areas: research, product development, product operations, and commercial operations.[9]

hybrid organization
Structure organized by more than one dimension at the top level

Hybrid Forms In a **hybrid organization,** a mixture of the organizational forms is used at the top level and may or may not be present at the lower levels. Figure 14.7 illustrates a simple hybrid form. Such combinations are often the result of a regionally organized company having introduced a new and different product line that management believes can best be handled by a worldwide product division. An acquired company with distinct products and a functioning marketing network may be incorporated as a product division even though the rest of the firm is organized on a regional basis. Later, after corporate management becomes familiar with the operation, it may be regionalized.

Unilever, the global consumer products company, had 2005 revenues of almost $47 billion and over 550,000 employees. To speed up decision making and execution within the fast-paced consumer products sector, Unilever has adopted a hybrid structure that includes three regions (Europe, Americas, and Asia Africa), two product segments (Foods and Home and Personal Care), and five functions (finance, human resources, IT, communications, and legal).[10]

A mixed structure may also result from the firm's selling to a sizable, homogeneous class of customers. Special divisions for handling sales to the military or to original equipment manufacturers, for example, are often established at the same level as regional or product divisions.

matrix organization
An organizational structure composed of one or more superimposed organizational structures in an attempt to mesh product, regional, functional, and other expertise

Matrix Organizations The **matrix organization** has evolved from management's attempt to mesh product, regional, and functional expertise while still maintaining clear lines of authority. It is called a matrix because an organization based on one or possibly two dimensions is superimposed on an organization based on another dimension. In an organization of two dimensions, such as area and product, both the area managers and the product managers will be at the same level, and their responsibilities will overlap. An individual manager—say, a marketing manager in Germany—will have a multiple reporting relationship, being responsible to the area manager and in some instances to an international or worldwide marketing manager at headquarters. Figure 14.8 illustrates an extremely simple matrix organization based on two organizational dimensions. Note that the country managers are responsible to both the area managers and the product line managers.

FIGURE 14.7

Hybrid Organizational Form

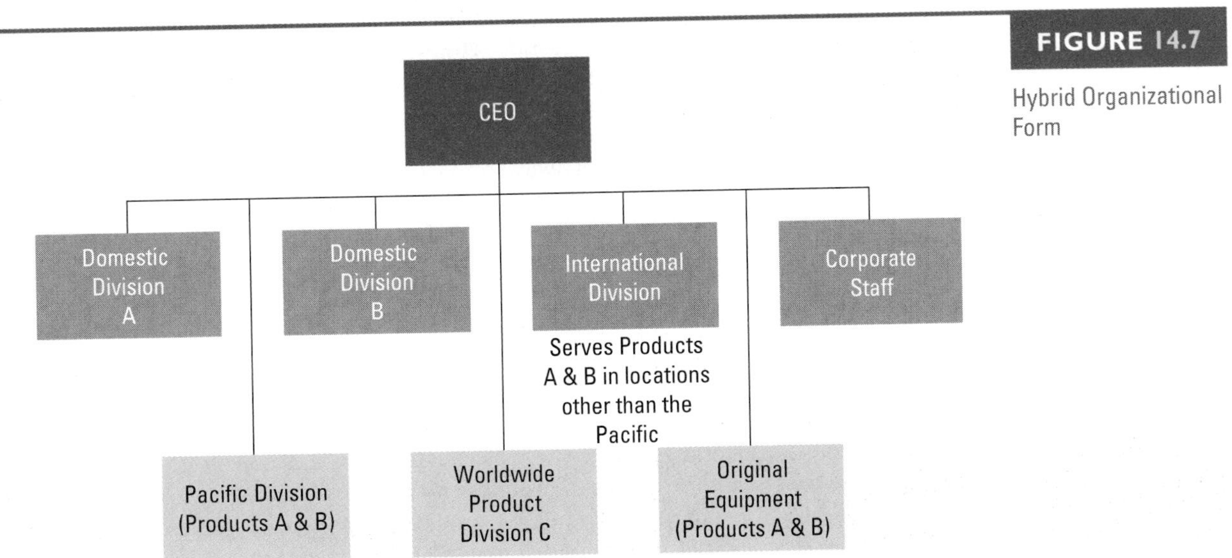

FIGURE 14.8

Regional–Product Matrix

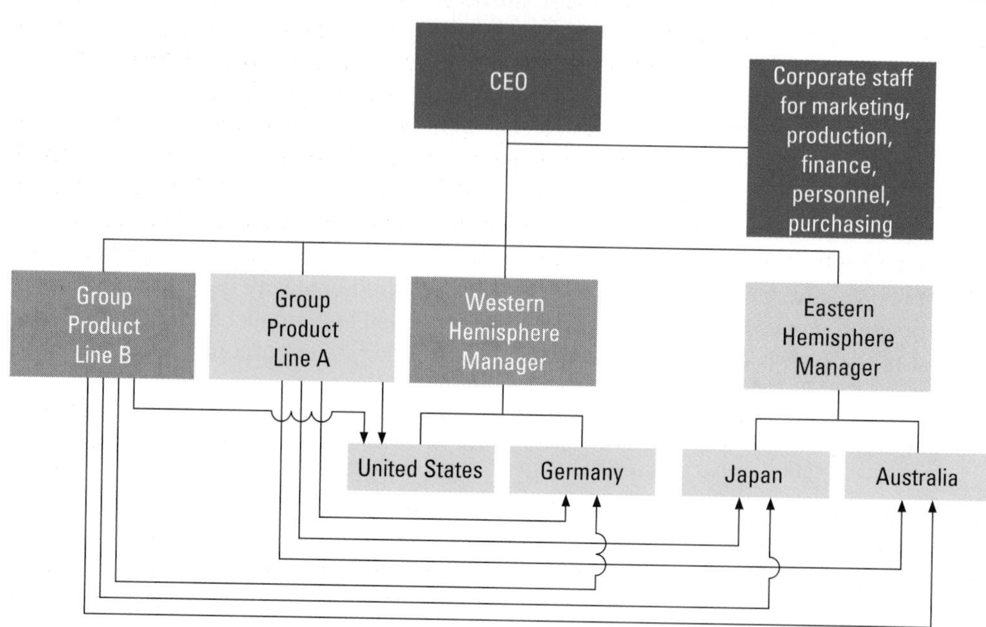

Nokia, the Finnish multinational that is the world's largest maker of cellular phones, established a matrix based on four business groups (mobile phones, multimedia, networks, and enterprise solutions) and two functionally based areas (customer and market operations, and technology platforms).[11]

BP, the British multinational with primary operations in oil, gas, and petrochemicals, is organized in a matrix based on 3 businesses (exploration and production; gas, power and renewables; and refining and marketing), 4 regions (Europe; the Americas; Africa, Middle East, Russia, and the Caspian; and Asia, the Indian Subcontinent, and Australasia), and 10 functions (diversity and inclusion; global property management and services; health, safety, security, and the environment; human resources management; marketing; planning; procurement; technology; finance and tax; and accounts).[12]

Michelin, the French manufacturer of tires, has a complex five-way matrix structure based on 9 product lines, a technology center, 5 geographic zones (Europe, North America, South America, Africa and Middle East, and Asia-Pacific), 10 group services, and distribution networks.[13]

Problems with the Matrix Although at one time it seemed that the matrix organizational form would enable firms to have the advantages of the product, regional, and functional forms, the disadvantages of the matrix form have kept most worldwide companies from adopting it. One problem with the matrix is that the two or three managers (if it is a three-dimensional matrix) must agree on a decision. This can lead to less-than-optimum compromises, delayed responses, and power politics in which more attention is paid to the process than to the problem. When the managers cannot agree, the problem goes higher in the organization and takes top management away from its duties.

Because of these difficulties associated with the matrix structure, many firms have maintained their original organizations based on product, function, region, or international divisions and have built into the structure accountability for the other organizational dimensions; this is called by some a **matrix overlay.**

matrix overlay
An organization in which top-level divisions are required to heed input from a staff composed of experts of another organizational dimension in an attempt to avoid the double-reporting difficulty of a matrix organization but still mesh two or more dimensions

Matrix Overlay The matrix overlay attempts to address the problems of the matrix structure by requiring accountability of all functions in the organization while avoiding the burdensome management stresses of a pure matrix structure. We have already mentioned how a firm organized by product may have regional specialists in a staff function with the requirement that they have input to product decisions. They may even be organized in an international division, as was mentioned previously. Conversely, a regional organization would have product managers on its staff who provide input to regional decisions.

Strategic Business Units

Strategic business units (SBUs), a concept that General Electric is credited with originating, are an organizational form in which product divisions have been defined as though they were distinct, independent businesses. An SBU is defined as a self-contained business entity with a clearly defined market, specific competitors, the ability to carry out its business mission, and a size appropriate for control by a single manager. Most SBUs are based on product lines, such as Caterpillar's 22 autonomous profit center business units.[14] If a product must be modified to suit different markets, a worldwide SBU may be divided into a few product/market SBUs serving various markets or groups of countries. Shell Chemical Company's SBUs, which it calls product business units (PBUs), are global.[15] BP's business units, which it calls strategic performance units (SPUs), are also global.[16]

strategic business unit (SBU)
Business entity with a clearly defined market, specific competitors, the ability to carry out its business mission, and a size appropriate for control by a single manager

CHANGES IN ORGANIZATIONAL FORMS

The rapidly changing business environment caused by increased global competition, customer preference for custom-made rather than mass-produced products, and faster technological change is pressuring companies to step up their search for organizational forms that will enable them to act more quickly, reduce costs, and improve the quality of product offerings. Not only are they mixing older, established forms; they are also changing to different forms, many of which are modified versions of long-established forms with new names.

What is new is the acceptance by many companies of the need for frequent reorganization. Present in these reorganizations, called *reengineering* by many, are a significant reduction in the levels of middle management, restructuring of work processes to reduce the fragmenting of the process across functional departments, improvement in the speed and quality of strategy execution, empowerment of employees, and the use of computers for instant communication and swift transmittal of information. CEOs are striving to make their organizations lean, flat, fast to respond, and innovative.

Vodafone, an international telecommunications services company based in the United Kingdom, reorganized itself in mid-2006 into three business groups: European operations; emerging markets and other affiliates; and new services and technologies. The objective of the structural change was "to focus the business according to different market and customer requirements. There are three key principles to the new structure: (1) to drive operational benefits and cost reduction from local and regional scale in more mature markets, (2) to drive profitable growth from the company's emerging market portfolio, and (3) to position the company to capture new revenue streams by extending its reach into converged and IP (internet protocol) services."[17]

Coca-Cola, the world's largest beverage company, announced the creation of the new position of president, Coca-Cola International, in early 2006. This position includes responsibility for all operations outside North America. Chairman and Chief Executive Officer Neville Isdell said, "As we focus even more intently on execution, it is appropriate that our international operations—which accounted last year for more than 70 percent of our total volume and close to 80 percent of our total operating income—be put under the leadership of a dedicated, full-time executive with extensive operational expertise."[18]

CURRENT ORGANIZATIONAL TRENDS

Two organizational forms are now receiving the attention of many CEOs: the virtual corporation and the horizontal corporation.

Virtual Corporation

A **virtual corporation,** also called a *network corporation,* is an organization that coordinates economic activity to deliver value to customers using resources outside the traditional boundaries of the organization. In other words, it relies to a great extent on third parties to conduct its business. Outsourcing once was used for downsizing and cost reduction, but now companies are using it to obtain specialized expertise that they don't have but need in order to serve new markets or adopt new technology.

virtual corporation
An organization that coordinates economic activity to deliver value to customers using resources outside the traditional boundaries of the organization

The evolution of the technology infrastructure has made possible changes in the work force and working methods, such as teleworking, home offices, and flexible working practices. All these factors have contributed to the increase in virtual corporations. Global networking on the

WORLD view   

Accenture's "Virtual" Global Structure

Accenture Ltd. delivers a range of consulting, outsourcing, and technology services to clients around the world, harnessing its more than 129,000 employees to generate revenues of over $15 billion in 2005. Its clients include 87 of the companies listed on the Fortune Global 100 and almost two-thirds of the Fortune Global 500 largest international companies. Yet, according to the company's senior management, Accenture has neither an operational headquarters facility nor any formal branch facilities. Instead, the company's approach to organizing its global operations might be termed *virtual.*

Prior to 2000, Accenture had been the consulting arm of the now-defunct Arthur Andersen accounting company. During that time, the consulting operations had been managed for decades by the Swiss-based Andersen Worldwide. After consulting was split off from Andersen's accounting operations and subsequently became a separate organization under the name Accenture, the partners could not agree on a location for the new, Bermuda-incorporated company's headquarters. Since they typically spent a major portion of their time on the road, Accenture's executives decided to live where each of them wanted and forgo an organization built around a central headquarters. As a result, the chief financial officer lives in California's Silicon Valley, the chief technology officer lives in Germany, and many of the company's globally diverse work force of consultants are traveling nearly nonstop to client sites worldwide. Even the company's Boston-based CEO, Bill Green, doesn't have a permanent desk or office location.

Coordinating this geographically dispersed work force is facilitated by technology. Employees log on to Accenture's intranet daily, either from home, from a hotel or airport, or from a temporary cubicle in one of the company's 110 leased locations around the world. Employees identify where they are working that day, access files and e-mails, download or share documents, and conduct a myriad of other tasks. Phone calls are patched through to wherever the employee is located, and clients often do not realize that they are speaking to a consultant or executive who might be nations or continents away. Team meetings are often conducted by teleconference, although scheduling such meetings can be problematic due to the different time zones of the participants. A "magic hour" for scheduling global teleconferences is 1 p.m. London time, which is midnight in Australia, 9 p.m. in Beijing, and 5 a.m. in California. This time "isn't too grim" for anyone, comments Adrian Lajtha, who as the head of Accenture's financial services group spends about 85 percent of his time traveling.

Every six weeks or so, the 23 members of the company's executive leadership team meet face-to-face for several days, with the location for the meetings rotating among different cities worldwide. Says Mr. Green, "We land somewhere, meet clients in the area, meet employees, then get together as a team to make decisions—and head out again." Says Mr. Lajtha, "Anyone who says managing this way is easy is lying."

Source: "Have Advice, Will Travel," *The Wall Street Journal*, June 5, 2006, pp. B1, B3; Accenture, Ltd., "Company Description," www.accenture.com/Global/About_Accenture/Company_Overview/CompanyDescription.htm (June 20, 2006); Yongsun Paik and David Y. Choi, "The Shortcomings of a Standardized Global Knowledge Management System: The Case Study of Accenture," *Academy of Management Executive* 19, no. 2 (2005), pp. 81–84; and Glenn Simpson, "The Economy: Consultants Accenture, Monday Take Steps That May Reduce Taxes," *The Wall Street Journal*, eastern ed., July 3, 2002, p. A2.

Internet has made worldwide outsourcing possible for firms of all sizes. Dell Computer is a well-known example of a company that has used tight integration with its global network of suppliers in order to assemble and deliver semicustomized computers to its international customers within days of receiving an order, and without carrying large volumes of expensive inventory that is prone to losing value through technological obsolescence. The nearby Worldview box, "Accenture's 'Virtual' Global Structure," discusses one company that has developed a virtual alternative to more traditional organizational structures.

Although the name is new, the virtual corporation concept has existed for decades. It has been extremely common for a group of construction firms, each with a special area of expertise, to form a consortium to bid on a contract for constructing a road or an airfield, for example. After finishing the job, the consortium would disband. Other examples of network organizations are the various clothing and athletic shoe marketers such as DKNY, Nike, and Reebok. The latter firms are also called *modular corporations.*

The virtual corporation concept has several potential benefits. In particular, it permits greater flexibility than is associated with more typical corporate structures, and rather than building competence from the ground up and incurring high start-up costs that could limit future production decisions, virtual corporations form a network of dynamic relationships that allow them to take advantage of the competencies of other organizations and respond rapidly to changing circumstances. However, this form of organization can have disadvantages, including the potential to reduce management's control over the corporation's activities (it is vulnerable to the opportunistic actions of partners, including cost increases, unintended "borrowing" of technical and other knowledge, and potential departure from the relationship at inappropriate times). From the standpoint of employees, this form of organization may replace the security of long-term employment and the promise of ever-increasing salaries with the insecurity of the market—a global market.

Horizontal Corporation

Another organizational form, the **horizontal corporation,** has been adopted by some large technology-oriented global firms in highly competitive industries such as electronics and computers. Firms such as 3M, General Electric, and DuPont have chosen this organizational form to give themselves the flexibility to respond quickly to advances in technology and be product innovators. In many companies *teams* are drawn from different departments to solve a problem or deliver a product.

horizontal corporation
A form of organization characterized by lateral decision processes, horizontal networks, and a strong corporatewide business philosophy

This organization has been characterized as "antiorganization" because its designers are seeking to remove the constraints imposed by the conventional organizational structures. In a horizontal corporation, employees worldwide create, build, and market the company's products through a carefully cultivated system of interrelationships. Marketers in Great Britain speak directly to production people in Brazil without having to go through the home office in Germany, for example.

Proponents of the horizontal organization claim lateral relationships incite innovation and new product development. They also state that this approach to organizing helps to place more decision-making responsibility in the hands of middle managers and other skilled professionals, who do not have to clear each detail and event with higher-ups. The objective is to substitute cooperation and coordination, which are in the interest of everyone, for strict control and supervision. Pursued effectively, this approach can help to develop international communities of skilled workers that create and exploit valuable intangible assets.[19]

CORPORATE SURVIVAL IN THE 21ST CENTURY

Managers in many international companies can expect to make greater use of the *dynamic network structure* that breaks down the major functions of the firm into smaller companies coordinated by a small-size headquarters organization. Business functions such as marketing and accounting may be provided by separate organizations—some of them owned partially or fully by the international company, some of them not—that are connected by computers to a central office. To attain the optimum level of vertical integration, a firm must focus on its core business. Anything not essential to the business can often be done cheaper, faster, and better by outside suppliers.[20]

As companies engage in the global battles of the 21st century, we must remember that organizations, like people, have life cycles. In their youth, they're small and fast-growing, but as they age, they often become big, complex, and out of touch with their markets. The firms of tomorrow must learn how to be both large and entrepreneurial. As one CEO put it, "Small is not better; focused is better."

Control

Every successful company uses controls to put its plans into effect, evaluate their effectiveness, make desirable corrections, and evaluate and reward or correct executive performance. The challenges associated with achieving effective control are more complicated for an international company than for a one-country operation. In earlier chapters, we discussed several of the complicating causes. They include different languages, cultures, and attitudes; different taxes and accounting methods; different currencies, labor costs, and market sizes; different degrees of political stability and security for personnel and

WORLD view

How to Become More Globally Competitive

A recent survey suggests that over 75 percent of new research and development sites planned for the 2006–2009 period will be established in China and India.

A recent survey of senior executives revealed that the primary strategy adopted by respondents to become more competitive globally was to concentrate on core businesses. Other structural changes adopted by about 70 percent of the companies included flattening the organization by removing layers of management, merging with other companies to form new structures, decentralizing business units, and forming new global business units.

Dow Chemical Company, which has operations in over 175 countries, is an example of a firm that has made changes to become more globally competitive. Dow changed its organizational structure from a geographic matrix to one of global business processes and 16 global business units that have individual global profit-and-loss responsibility. Management layers in the organization were reduced from 10 to 12 down to 4 to 6. Said Dow's CEO, "Dow is now making two to three times the earnings it used to make at an equivalent position in the global chemical market cycle, and we are earning the cost of capital at the trough of the cycle, something we have never done before."

Ninety percent of the executives responding to one survey stated that the strategies that have been effective in increasing their firms' global competitiveness are (1) placing profit-and-loss responsibility at lower levels in the firm, (2) reducing operating expenses, and (3) forming strategic alliances with customers, suppliers, and competitors.

Another noteworthy result was that those respondents who had adopted value chain strategies judged the following strategies to be most effective in increasing a firm's global competitiveness:

1. Planning jointly with suppliers and customers.
2. Maintaining less inventory.
3. Managing production on a global basis.

Another survey revealed that innovation is becoming increasingly global, and over 75 percent of new research and development sites planned for the 2006–2009 period will be established in China and India. Yet most executives reported that their companies were struggling to establish the organization structures and systems that were required in order to manage and integrate global innovation activities. Respondents projected that they could achieve a 37 percent improvement in time to market and a 24 percent reduction in costs if they had an innovation network that was efficiently organized and integrated with their worldwide operations. Achieving that would be enhanced if companies would (1) centralize decision making on research and development project portfolios to take advantage of the power of the company's international network, (2) standardize organizational structure, systems, and processes throughout the global innovation network, so that time was not lost in trying to understand how other sites operated, and (3) develop a diverse set of global managers and then allow them to make necessary adjustments for national and cultural circumstances that might affect the efficiency of operations.

Other surveys suggest widespread dissatisfaction among executives regarding their companies' ability to respond to change, especially with regard to information technology structures and systems. Concerns included the adequacy of access to relevant, real-time business information; difficulty in adapting and modifying key business processes and more rapidly delivering applications for competitive advantage; and the overall ability of the company's information technology infrastructure to keep up with the increasing pace of change and be able to promote the creation of business value.

Source: Booz Allen Hamilton, "The Growth of Global Innovation Networks Creates New Management Challenges," www.boozallen.com/home/services/services_article/3220998?tid=934306&lpid=660624 (June 21, 2006); Tim Stevens, "Winning the World Over," *Industry Week Online*, November 15, 1999, www.industryweek.com/CurrentArticles/asp/articles.asp?ArticleI0=~656 (November 28, 1999); "New Study Finds Executives Dissatisfied with Their Companies' Ability to Sense and Respond to Business Change; Despite Current Challenges in Keeping Pace, IT Viewed as More Important Than Ever," www.webmethods.com/meta/default/folder/0000005139?pressReleaseDetails%5Fparam0=6879 (June 21, 2006); and "IP Adoption Is Key Competitive Advantage to Global Survey of Senior Executives," www.att.com/news/2005/10/17-1 (June 21, 2006).

property; and many more. For these reasons, international companies need controls even more than do domestic ones.

subsidiaries
Companies controlled by other companies through ownership of enough voting stock to elect board-of-directors majorities

SUBSIDIARIES

The words **subsidiaries** and **affiliates** sometimes are used interchangeably, and we shall examine first the control of those in which the parent has 100 percent ownership. This avoids for now the additional complications of joint ventures or subsidiaries in which the parent has less than 100 percent ownership. We shall deal with those later in the chapter.

SUBSIDIARIES 100 PERCENT OWNED: WHERE ARE DECISIONS MADE?

affiliates
A term sometimes used interchangeably with *subsidiaries*, but more forms exist than just stock ownership

There are three possibilities. Theoretically, all decisions could be made either at the international company (IC) headquarters or at the subsidiary level. As common sense would indicate, they are not; instead, some decisions are made at headquarters, some are made at subsidiaries, and—the third possibility—some are made cooperatively. Many variables determine which decision is made where. Some of the more significant variables are (1) product and equipment, (2) the competence of subsidiary management and reliance on that management by the IC headquarters, (3) the size of the IC and how long it has been one, (4) the detriment of a subsidiary for the benefit of the enterprise, and (5) subsidiary frustration. We discuss each of these variables in the sections that follow.

Product and Equipment

As to decision location, questions of standardization of product and equipment and second markets can be important for international companies. In Chapter 18, we will discuss how large global manufacturers of consumer products, such as Procter & Gamble (P&G) and Colgate, are developing standardized products from the outset for global or at least regional markets. In these situations, the affiliates have to follow company policy. Of course, in the case of P&G, representatives of the affiliates have an opportunity to take part in the product design, contrary to the way new products were typically introduced before the globalization strategy became so popular. Then, as we discussed in Chapter 3 on the international product life cycle, new products often have been introduced first in the home market. After the production process has been stabilized, the specifications are sent to the affiliates (second markets) for local production, where adaptations can be made if the local managements deem them necessary for their markets.

In a firm without a global product policy, the preference of the operations management people in the home office has always been to standardize the product or at least the production process in as many overseas plants as possible, as we will explain in Chapter 19. If, however, any subsidiary can demonstrate that the profit potential is greater for a product tailored for its own market than what the company would realize from global standardization, the subsidiary ordinarily is allowed to proceed. Of course, the decision in such a case is cooperative in that the parent has the power to veto or override its subsidiary's decision.

Competence of Subsidiary Management and Headquarters' Reliance on It

Reliance on subsidiary management can depend on how well the executives know one another and how well they know company policies, on whether headquarters management feels that it understands host country conditions, on the distances between the home country and the host countries, and on how big and old the parent company is.

Moving Executives Around

Many ICs have a policy of transferring promising management personnel between parent headquarters and subsidiaries and among subsidiaries. Thus, the manager learns firsthand the policies of headquarters and the problems of putting those policies into effect at subsidiary levels.

A result of such transfers, which is difficult to measure but nevertheless important, is a network of intra-IC personal relationships. This tends to increase the confidence of executives in one another and to make communication among executives easier and less subject to error. Another development is that some ICs have moved their regional executives into headquarters to improve communications and reduce cost.

Understanding Host Country Conditions

One element in the degree of headquarters' reliance on subsidiary management is the familiarity of headquarters with conditions in the subsidiary's host country. The less familiar or the more different conditions in the host country are perceived to be, the more likely headquarters is to rely on subsidiary management.

How Far Away Is the Host Country?

Another element in the degree of headquarters' reliance on subsidiary management is the distance of the host country from home headquarters. Thus, an American parent is likely to place more reliance on the management of an

Indonesian subsidiary than on the management of a Canadian subsidiary. This occurs for two reasons: American management typically perceives management conditions in Canada to be more easily understood than conditions in Indonesia, and Indonesia is much farther from the United States than Canada is, not merely geographically but also in terms of culture, politics, and other variables.

Size and Age of the IC As a rule, a large company can afford to hire more specialists, experts, and experienced executives than can a smaller one. The longer a company has been an IC, the more likely it is to have a number of experienced executives who know company policies and have worked at headquarters and in the field. Successful experience builds confidence. In most ICs, the top positions are at headquarters, and the ablest and most persistent executives will typically get positions there eventually. Thus, over time, the headquarters of a successful company is run by experienced executives who are confident of their knowledge of the business in the home and host countries and in combinations thereof.

It follows that in larger, older organizations, more decisions are made at headquarters and fewer are delegated to subsidiaries. Smaller companies, in business for shorter periods of time, tend to be able to afford fewer internationally experienced executives and will not have had time to develop them internally. Smaller, newer companies often have no choice but to delegate decisions to subsidiary managements. However, with the increasing pace of change and intensity of competition in many markets of the world, as well as continued differences across many markets, even large and experienced companies are finding the need to delegate at least some decision making authority to subsidiary managements in order to effectively sense pressures for adaptation, to serve as tools for developing and communicating innovation, and to promote effective execution of strategy.

Benefiting the Enterprise to the Detriment of a Subsidiary An IC has opportunities to source raw materials and components, locate factories, allocate orders, and govern intrafirm pricing that are not available to a non-IC. Such activities may be beneficial to the enterprise yet may result in **subsidiary detriment.**

subsidiary detriment
Situation in which a small loss for a subsidiary results in a greater gain for the total IC

Moving Production Factors For any number of reasons, an IC may decide to move factors of production from one country to another or to expand in one country in preference to another. In addition to the cost, availability, or skill levels of labor, other possible reasons include such factors as taxation, market, currency, and political stability issues.

The subsidiary from which factors are being taken would be unenthusiastic about giving up control over existing activities. Its management would be slow, at best, to cut the company's capacity or to downsize or eliminate local operations. Headquarters would typically have to make such decisions.

Which Subsidiary Gets the Order? Similarly, if an order—say, from an Argentine customer—could be filled from a subsidiary in France or another in South Africa or a third in Brazil, parent headquarters might decide which subsidiary gets the business. Among the considerations in the decision would be transportation costs, production costs, comparative tariff rates, customers' currency restrictions, comparative order backlogs, governmental pressures, and taxes. Having such a decision made by IC headquarters avoids price competition among members of the same IC group.

Multicountry Production Frequently, the size of the market in a single country is too small to permit economies of scale in manufacturing an entire industrial product or offering a full range of services for that one market. An example is Ford's production of a light vehicle for the Asian market. In that situation, Ford negotiated with several countries to the end that one country would make one component of the vehicle for all the countries involved. Thus, one country makes the engine, a second country has the body-stamping plant, a third makes the transmission, and so forth. In this fashion, each operation achieves the efficiency and cost savings of economies of scale. Of course, this kind of multinational production demands a high degree of IC headquarters' control and coordination.

Which Subsidiary Books the Profit? In certain circumstances, an IC may have a choice of two or more countries in which to declare profits. Such circumstances may arise where two or more units of the IC cooperate in supplying components or services under a contract with a customer unrelated to any part of the IC. Under these conditions, there may be opportunities to allocate higher prices to one unit or subsidiary and lower prices to another within the global price to the customer.

If the host country of one of the subsidiaries has lower taxes than the other host countries, it would be natural to try to maximize profits in the lower-tax country and minimize them in the higher-tax country. Other differences between host countries could dictate the allocation of profit to or from the subsidiaries located there. Such differences could include currency controls, labor relations, political climate, and social unrest. It is sensible to direct or allocate as much profit as reasonably possible to subsidiaries in countries with the fewest currency controls, the best labor relations and political climate, and the least social unrest, for example.

The intrafirm transaction may also give a company choices regarding profit location. Pricing between members of the same enterprise is referred to as *transfer pricing,* and while IC headquarters could permit undirected, arm's-length negotiations between itself and its subsidiaries, this might not yield the most advantageous results for the enterprise as a whole.

Price and profit allocation decisions like these are usually best made at parent company headquarters, which is supposed to maintain the overall view, looking out for the best interests of the enterprise. Naturally, subsidiary management does not gladly make decisions to accept lower profits, largely because its evaluation may suffer as a result of the apparent reduction in performance at the subsidiary level.

The following two tables illustrate how the total IC enterprise may profit even though one subsidiary makes less. Assume a cooperative contract by which two subsidiaries are selling products and services to an outside customer for a price of $100 million. The host country of IC Alpha levies company income taxes at the rate of 50 percent, whereas IC Beta's host country taxes its income at 20 percent. The customer is in a third country, has agreed to pay $100 million, and is indifferent to how Alpha and Beta share the money. The first table below shows the enterprise's after-tax income if Alpha is paid $60 million and Beta is paid $40 million. Thus, after tax, the enterprise realizes $62 million.

	Receives ($ millions)	Tax ($ millions)	After Tax ($ millions)
Alpha	$60	$30	$30
Beta	40	8	32
			$62

The second table shows the after-tax income if Alpha is paid $40 million and Beta is paid $60 million. Thus, after taxes, the enterprise realizes $68 million.

	Receives ($ millions)	Tax ($ millions)	After Tax ($ millions)
Alpha	$40	$20	$20
Beta	60	12	48
			$68

These simple examples illustrate that the IC would be $6 million better off if it could shift $20 million of the payment from Alpha to Beta, while the customer is no worse off, as it pays $100 million in either case. Alpha, having received $20 million less in payment, is $10 million worse off after taxes, but Beta is $16 million better off and the enterprise is $6 million ahead on the same contract. Given the number of countries and tax laws in the world, there are countless combinations for how such savings can be accomplished. Financial management awareness and control are the keys.

We do not mean to leave the impression that the host and home governments are unaware of or indifferent to transfer pricing and profit allocating by ICs operating within their borders. The companies must expect questioning by host and home governments and must be prepared to demonstrate that prices or allocations are reasonable. This may be done by showing that other companies charge comparable prices for the same or similar items or, if there are no similar items, by showing that costs plus profit have been used reasonably to arrive at the price. As to allocation of profits, the IC in our example would try to prove that the volume or importance of the work done by Beta or the responsibilities assumed by Beta, such as financing, after-sales service, or warranty obligations, justify the higher amount being paid to Beta. Of course, the questioning in this instance would come from the host government of Alpha if it got wind of the possibility of more taxable income for Beta and less for itself.[21]

Several large U.S. companies are being investigated by the U.S. Treasury Department and the Internal Revenue Service because of the approaches that they have used for allocating intellectual property and other assets to their subsidiaries in low-tax Ireland. It has been suggested that the approaches used by these companies to value assets across subsidiaries and to allocate revenues and profits has cost the American government billions of dollars in taxes and other fees. Microsoft's Round Island One (RIO) subsidiary in Ireland, for example, controls over $16 billion in assets. Most of RIO's assets are associated with copyrighted software code. This code is asserted to have originated in Microsoft's U.S. operations but subsequently been transferred to RIO at submarket rates. As a result, RIO controls the rights for licensing Microsoft software in Europe, the Middle East, and Africa, and the earnings from this licensing activity are credited to the Irish operations. RIO is the most profitable company in Ireland, and it pays no U.S. taxes. Through earning its income in foreign countries that tax at lower rates, such as Ireland, Microsoft's effective worldwide tax rate declined in one year from 33 percent to only 26 percent.[22]

Subsidiary Frustration An extremely important consideration for parent company management is that the management of its subsidiaries be motivated and loyal. If all the big decisions are made, or are perceived to be made, at the IC headquarters, the managers of subsidiaries can lose incentive and prestige or face with their employees and the community. They may grow hostile and disloyal.

Therefore, even though there may be reasons for headquarters to make decisions, it should delegate as many as is reasonably possible. Management of each subsidiary should be kept thoroughly informed and be consulted seriously about decisions, negotiations, and developments in its geographic area. The trend for many ICs of shifting power away from subsidiaries toward the parent has caused predictable frustration to subsidiary management, sometimes followed by resignations. Some companies reporting this development were IBM, Nestlé, European International, and CS First Boston.

JOINT VENTURES AND SUBSIDIARIES LESS THAN 100 PERCENT OWNED

A *joint venture* may be, as defined in Chapter 16, a corporate entity between an IC and local owners or a corporate entity between two or more companies that are foreign to the area where the joint venture is located, or it may involve one company working on a project of limited duration (constructing a dam, for example) in cooperation with one or more other companies. The other companies may be subsidiaries or affiliates, but they may also be entirely independent entities.

All the reasons for making decisions at IC headquarters, at subsidiary headquarters, or cooperatively apply equally in joint venture situations. However, headquarters will almost never have as much freedom of action and flexibility in a joint venture as it has with subsidiaries that are 100 percent owned.

Loss of Freedom and Flexibility The reasons for that loss of freedom and flexibility are easy to see. If shareholders outside the IC own control of the affiliate, they can block efforts of IC headquarters to move production factors away, fill an export order from another affiliate or subsidiary, and so forth. Even if outside shareholders are a minority and cannot directly control the affiliate, they can bring legal or political pressures on the IC to prevent it from diminishing the affiliate's profitability for the enterprise's benefit. Likewise, the local partner in a joint venture is highly unlikely to agree with measures that penalize the joint venture for the IC's benefit.

Control Can Be Had

With less than 50 percent of the voting stock and even with no voting stock, an IC can have control. Some methods of maintaining control are:

- A management contract.
- Control of the finances.
- Control of the technology.
- Putting people from the IC in important executive positions.

As might be expected, ICs have encountered resistance to putting IC personnel in the important executive positions from their joint venture partners or from host governments. The natural desire of these partners and governments is that their own nationals have at least equality in the important positions and that they get training and experience in the technology and management.

REPORTING

For controls to be effective, all operating units of an IC must provide headquarters with timely, accurate, and complete reports. There are many uses for the information reported. Among the types of reporting required are (1) financial, (2) technological, (3) market opportunity, and (4) political and economic.

Financial

A surplus of funds in one subsidiary should perhaps be retained there for investment or contingencies. On the other hand, such a surplus might be more useful at the parent company, in which case payment of a dividend is indicated. Or perhaps another subsidiary or affiliate needs capital, and the surplus could be lent or invested there. Obviously, parent headquarters must know the existence and size of a surplus to determine its best use.

Technological

New technology should be reported. New technology is constantly being developed in different countries, and the subsidiary or affiliated company operating in such a country is likely to learn about it before IC headquarters hundreds or thousands of miles away does. If headquarters finds the new technology potentially valuable, it can gain competitive advantage by being the first to contact the developer for a license to use it.

Market Opportunities

The affiliates in various countries may spot new or growing markets for some product of the enterprise. This could be profitable all around, as the IC sells more of the product while the affiliate earns sales commissions. Of course, if the new market is sufficiently large, the affiliate may begin to assemble or produce the product under license from the parent company or from another affiliate.

Other market-related information that should be reported to IC headquarters includes competitors' activities, price developments, and new products of potential interest to the IC group. Also of importance is information on the subsidiary's market share and whether it is growing or shrinking, together with explanations.

Political and Economic

Not surprisingly, reports on political and economic conditions have multiplied mightily in number and importance over the past 20 or so years as revolutions—some bloody—have toppled and changed governments. Democracies have replaced dictatorships, one dictator has replaced another, countries have broken apart or reunited—changes have been occurring on almost every continent.

"DE-JOBBING"

The conditions that created jobs 200 years ago—mass production and large organizations—are disappearing. Technology enables companies to automate production lines where many job holders used to do repetitive tasks. Instead of long production runs where the same thing has to be done again and again, firms are increasingly customizing production. Big firms, where most of the good jobs used to be, are unbundling activities and farming them out to little firms. New computer and communication technologies are **de-jobbing** the workplace, changing from the traditional, fixed-jobs approach to one in which teams perform tasks. And the composition of these teams changes as the tasks evolve.

de-jobbing
Replacing fixed jobs with tasks performed by evolving teams

Today's organization is rapidly being transformed from a structure built out of jobs into a field of work needing to be done. A fast-moving organization, such as Intel, will hire a person to be part of a specific project. As the project changes over time, the person's responsibilities and tasks change with it. Then the person is assigned to another project, probably before the first is finished, and then maybe to a third. As projects evolve and change, the person will work with several team leaders, keeping different schedules, being in various places, and performing a number of different tasks.

hierarchy
A body of persons organized or classified according to rank or authority

Hierarchy Implodes

Under these conditions, **hierarchy** cannot be maintained; people no longer take their cues from a job description or a supervisor's instructions. Signals come from the changing demands of the project. Workers focus their efforts and collective resources on work that needs doing, changing as that changes.

Traits of Companies with De-Jobbed Workers

Companies with de-jobbed workers share four traits:

- They encourage employees to make the kinds of operating decisions that used to be reserved for managers.
- They give employees the information they need to make such decisions.
- They give employees lots of training to create the kind of understanding of business and financial issues that used to concern only an owner or executive.
- They give employees a stake in the fruits of their labor—a share of the profits.[23]

MANAGING IN A WORLD OUT OF CONTROL

The Internet may be the closest thing to a working anarchy the world has ever seen. Nobody owns it, nobody runs it, and most of its half-billion or so citizens get along by dint of online etiquette, not rules and regulations. The Internet was built up without any central control because the U.S. Defense Department wanted to ensure that the Net could survive a nuclear attack. The Net has proved to be a paragon of hothouse expansion and constant evolution. Though it may be messier and less efficient than a similar system designed and run by an agency or company, this organically grown network is also more adaptable and less susceptible to a systemwide crash.

The consequence for management in a world out of control, such as the Internet, is a recipe developed at MIT for devising a system of distributed control: (1) Do simple things first, (2) learn to do them flawlessly, (3) add new layers of activity over the results of the simple task, (4) don't change the simple things, (5) make the new layer work as flawlessly as the simple one, and (6) repeat ad infinitum. Many organizations would benefit by adopting organizing principles as deceptively simple as these.

Increasingly, the most successful companies, like the machines and programs so many of them now make, and the networks on which they all will rely will advance only by evolving and adapting in this organic, bottom-up way. Successful leaders will have to relinquish control. They will have to honor error because a breakthrough may at first be indistinguishable from a mistake. They must constantly seek disequilibrium.

Control: Yes and No

We have spoken of control within the IC family of parent, subsidiaries, affiliates, and joint ventures. This deals with where decisions are made on a variety of subjects under different circumstances.

Timely and accurate reporting to the parent is necessary for success of the IC family. The trend in this area of control is toward centralized decision making, with more being done by the parent.

The other control of which we have spoken involves the design, production, and order-filling functions of companies. Here, the explosion of software, computer networks, and information technology, including the Internet, has tended to decentralize and de-job organizations. More and more, workers do evolving tasks with changing teams of other workers. Hierarchies dissolve and successful leaders relinquish control as workers are trained and encouraged to cope with evolving tasks and rewarded for coping well.

Summary

Explain why the design of organizational structure is important to international companies.

The structure of an international organization involves how its domestic and international units and activities are arranged and where formal power and authority will be located inside the company. It helps determine how efficiently and effectively the organization will be able to integrate and leverage its competencies and resources within and across various units of the enterprise, and thus contribute to successful implementation of the company's strategy.

Discuss the organizational dimensions that must be considered when selecting organizational structures.

The organizational structure selected for a company must be consistent with the organization's capabilities and resources, as well as with the environmental context in which the organization operates and with its strategy. In selecting an organizational structure, managers of an international company must consider the requirements for expertise in terms of product and technology, geography, customer, and function.

Discuss the various organizational forms available for structuring international companies.

Companies may (1) have an international division, (2) be organized by product, function, or region, or (3) have a mixture of them (hybrid form). To attain a balance between product and regional expertise, some managements have tried a matrix form of organization. Its disadvantages, however, have caused many managements to put a matrix overlay over a traditional product, regional, or functional form instead of using the matrix.

Explain the concept of the virtual corporation.

A virtual corporation enables companies to come together quickly to take advantage of a specific marketing opportunity. Because each member concentrates on what it does best, a virtual corporation can have capabilities superior to those of any member. Once the opportunity ends, the virtual corporation normally will disband.

Explain why decisions are made where they are among parent and subsidiary units of an international company (IC).

Several considerations govern where decisions are made in an IC family of organizations. They include the desirability of standardizing products as opposed to differentiating them for different markets, the competence of organization managements, the size and age of the IC, the benefit of one part of the family to the detriment of another, and building confidence or avoiding frustration of management.

Discuss how an IC can maintain control of a joint venture or of a company in which the IC owns less than 50 percent of the voting stock.

Control can be maintained over a joint venture or a company in which the IC owns less than 50 percent of the voting stock by several devices, including a management contract, control of the finances, control of the technology, and putting people from the IC in key executive positions.

List the types of information an IC needs to have reported to it by its units around the world.

Subsidiaries should report to the IC information about financial conditions, technological developments, market opportunities and developments, and economic and political conditions.

Key Words

organizational structure (p. 386)
international division (p. 388)
hybrid organization (p. 393)
matrix organization (p. 393)
matrix overlay (p. 394)
strategic business unit (SBU) (p. 395)
virtual corporation (p. 395)
horizontal corporation (p. 397)
subsidiaries (p. 398)
affiliates (p. 399)
subsidiary detriment (p. 400)
de-jobbing (p. 404)
hierarchy (p. 404)

Questions

1. Why is organizational structure an important issue for international companies?
2. What are the main strengths and weaknesses of the use of an international division as part of a company's organizational structure? Under what circumstances might such a structure be an appropriate choice for a company?
3. Compare and contrast geographic and product structures for international companies.
4. Your matrix organization isn't working; decisions are taking too long, and it seems to you that instead of best solutions, you're getting compromises. What can you, the CEO, do?
5. You are the CEO of Mancon Incorporated, and you have just acquired Pozoli, the Italian small-appliance maker (electric shavers, small household and personal care appliances). It has been in business 30 years and has manufacturing plants in Italy, Mexico, Ireland, and Spain. Its output is sold in more than 100 markets worldwide, including the United States. Your company is now organized into two product groups—shaving and personal care—along with an international division at the top level. How are you going to include Pozoli in your organization? Explain your rationale.
6. It is obvious that in formulating new strategies, management may uncover a need to change its organization. Can you describe some situations where the reverse may be true?
7. In determining whether decisions will be made by the parent company or by its subsidiaries, what are the considerations when equipment and products are standardized worldwide rather than tailored to individual national circumstances and markets?
8. a. In an IC, what are some decisions that could result in detriment for a subsidiary but greater benefit for the enterprise?

   b. In such circumstances, where will the decision be made—at IC headquarters or at the affected subsidiary?
9. What measures can be utilized to control subsidiaries that are less than 100 percent owned by the firm or joint venture partners in which the firm has no ownership?
10. Some companies use standardized organizational controls across their entire organization, in that the same control systems are used for each unit or operation worldwide. For example, companies such as Starbucks, Kentucky Fried Chicken, or McDonald's apply the same rigid quality controls throughout all aspects of their organizations, even as they expand internationally. Why would a company such as these impose rigorous corporate quality standards, regardless of the country in which it operates? What modifications in these quality standards, if any, should the company permit because of differences across nations or regions of the world? Why is the company allowing these modifications to occur?
11. Explain the argument that the world is de-jobbing.

Research Task

globalEDGE.msu.edu 

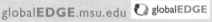

Use the globalEDGE™ site (http://globalEDGE.msu.edu) to complete the following exercises:

1. *Fortune* magazine conducts an annual survey and publishes the rankings of the "Global Most Admired Companies." Locate the most recent publicly available ranking, follow the link to the best and worst companies, and focus on the nine factors highlighted by *Fortune* magazine. On the basis of these data, prepare an executive summary of the strategic and organizational success factors of a company of your choice.
2. Your firm seeks to maximize the infrastructure of the most globalized countries so that its products and services are more accessible worldwide. A co-worker recently informed you that an A. T. Kearney report on globalization may assist in better assessing which countries may be optimal to begin worldwide operations. Locate the report, and identify the five most globalized countries. What are the measures used in the report to determine each country's level of globalization?

Electrex, Inc.—Must It Reorganize? Minicase 14.1

Electrex, Inc., manufactures electronic and electrical connectors used on such diverse products as computers, home appliances, telecommunications, and the air bag and antiskid systems of automobiles. The company has been in business since 1965. The table below provides the important financial information for the last five years.

For some time, Electrex had been exporting to Asia, where its major markets are Australia, Singapore, Malaysia, Thailand, South Korea, China, and Taiwan. When its foreign sales were confined to exports, the company functioned well with an export department whose manager reported to the company's marketing manager. In 2005, however, another American firm tried to enter the Taiwan market, and there were rumors that a Taiwanese firm from a related industry was searching for a licensor in the United States to supply it with manufacturing technology. As a result, Electrex decided to set up its first foreign plant in Taiwan. When it did, it hired financial and marketing people with Asian experience and established an international division at headquarters to oversee the Taiwan operation. The president felt that the situation would be repeated in China, Singapore, and perhaps other nations. These were all good export markets at the time, but it was reasonable to suppose that some competitor would soon set up manufacturing facilities in one or more of them, which could dramatically impact the potential for exporting to these markets. Having a small international division with some Asian expertise that is responsible for monitoring these markets would help the firm avoid being surprised by a competitor's move.

After the Taiwan Electrex plant was in production, more firms in that nation were willing to do business with the company than had been the case when it had served the market through exports. In fact, the major portion of the 2006 sales increase was due to improved sales to Taiwan. However, the new customers also brought the company into a new, higher level of competition than it had known before. Other Taiwanese competitors were bringing out new products at a considerably faster rate than Electrex was. The president wondered if horizontal linkages across functions, such as the linkages automakers have used to reduce their design time, might help his firm. Also, on his trips to Taiwan, the marketing people told him things about the market and the competitors that were not being sent to the Electrex home office.

It was obvious to the president that overseas production and growth in overseas sales demanded a reorganization of the firm. Even though the company had only one plant overseas, in Taiwan, the president was confident that other plants would soon be needed. How should the company be organized to handle the new foreign production facilities? How can Electrex reduce the time needed to bring new designs to market?

Electrex Five-Year Financial Highlight Summary ($ millions)

	2006	2005	2004	2003	2002
Net sales	$353.0	$298.2	$271.9	$257.4	$231.1
Gross profit	134.1	116.3	110.3	106.7	94.9
Selling, general, and administrative expense	70.5	61.2	55.8	51.8	45.1
Income from operations	63.6	55.1	54.5	54.9	49.8
Income taxes	23.9	20.9	20.9	21.8	20.9
Effective tax rate (%)	37.6	37.9	38.3	39.7	42.0
Net income	39.7	34.2	33.6	33.1	28.9

Competition within the International Company Minicase 14.2

Worldwide (W) is an IC with subsidiary manufacturing plants in several countries around the world. W has just won a very large contract to supply locomotives to Paraguay, which is modernizing its entire railway system with financing from the World Bank.

W's home country is the United States, and W can manufacture parts of or the complete locomotives in its U.S. plants. W subsidiary companies in Spain, Argentina, and Australia can also manufacture parts of the complete locomotives. The managers of all those subsidiaries know about the big new contract, and each is eager to get the work involved in performing it.

A meeting of the subsidiary chief executive officers (CEOs) is called at W's headquarters in New York to discuss which plant or plants will get the work. The manager of the American locomotive division is also at the meeting, and she makes a strong case that her plant needs the work. It has laid off 3,000 workers, and this big job would permit it to recall them. In addition, the American factory has all the latest technology, some of which has not been shared with the subsidiaries.

Each CEO argues that there is unemployment in his or her host country and that, as a responsible citizen, he or she must hire more local people. Doing so, moreover, would reduce hostility in the host country and give the subsidiary defenses against political attacks on foreign-owned companies. One subsidiary CEO suggests that each subsidiary and the American division enter competitive bids and let Paraguayan Railways make the decision.

You are the CEO of W and have the responsibility for allocating parts of or all the work to one or more of the plants. List and explain the considerations that will govern your decisions.

15 Assessing and Analyzing Markets

Think locally, offer value, and be patient. That last one is key: You can make an elephant dance. But it takes time to learn the right tune.

—*Om Malik on marketing to India,* Business 2.0, *July 2004*

Marketing Research

Clotaire Rapaille is a charlatan—or possibly an adviser your company simply cannot do without. Originally a psychologist treating autistic children in Europe, Rapaille now operates from a mansion in upstate New York, where top management seeks his advice on "the code" that will allow them access to the Indian, French, or Norwegian psyche. And from there, this insight should help them understand the motivations that will draw these people to buy their products.

Rapaille's earlier insights came when comparing French and American attitudes toward cheese. For the French, he says, cheese is alive, and the French would not put cheese in the refrigerator any more than one would put one's cat in the fridge. Both are "alive." But for Americans, Rapailles's insight is that cheese is "dead," so Americans seal it in a plastic "casket" and put it in a refrigerator, which is really a "morgue." Americans are more concerned about safety than taste: The French reverse these preferences. So more French than American consumers die from eating cheese: But the Americans eat a relatively sterile and tasteless product, while the French enjoy a variety of cheeses that Americans cannot fathom.

Rapaille was also influential in the development of Chrysler's PT Cruiser, the retro car that has enjoyed great success. Chrysler does acknowledge that he was involved but downplays his role in its development. Rapaille has in total 50 of the Fortune 100 firms as clients. He claims that teams under his direction have "broken the code" for "anti-Americanism," "China," "seduction," the "teen Internet," and more. A recent excursion to India led him to pronounce that the caste system was simply a "practical" way of signaling to all their places in society. "It's not a problem, it's a solution," he summarizes.

Rapaille displays a certain confidence bordering on arrogance, and he follows a research method that is unusual, to say the least. Rather than relying on focus groups or surveys, he "breaks the code" of certain countries in roughly three-hour sessions. In these sessions, paid respondents first discuss the topic of interest; then they are asked to tap into their emotional reactions; and finally Rapaille explores, as he puts it, their "reptilian brain." It is the last that he finds useful. "Never believe what people say," Rapaille says. "I want to understand why people do what they do." Ultimately, he has respondents on the floor in the fetal position, reliving childhood memories. From this process, he says, he discovers cultural archetypes, which are long-lasting, although opinions may change more readily. Former clients have scoffed at him, using "the cheese is dead" as a constant mantra, mocking his methods. Yet many of the same clients come back to him, as P&G has come back 35 times.

As managers, we may (or may not) hire Clotaire Rapaille or his company. But international managers must search constantly for methods, both new and old, that will allow them to analyze foreign markets and to understand these markets. It is to this topic that we now turn. ■

Source: Danielle Sacks, "Crack This Code," *Fast Company*, April 2006, pp. 97–101: www.pbs.org/wgbh/pages/frontline/shows/persuaders/interviews/rapaille.html (October 3, 2006); www.archetypediscoveries.com (October 4, 2006); "Pushing Your Buy Button: Neuroscience Meets Marketing," *Forbes*, 2003, www.archetypediscoveriesworldwide.com/6.pdf.; and "The Last Word: Clotaire Rapaille," *Newsweek*, international ed., www.msnbc.msn.com/id/4710897 (October 4, 2006).

CONCEPT PREVIEWS

After reading this chapter, you should be able to:

discuss environmental analysis and two types of market screening

explain market indicators and market factors

describe some statistical techniques for estimating market demand and grouping similar markets

discuss the value to businesspeople of trade missions and trade fairs

discuss some of the problems market researchers encounter in foreign markets

explain the difference between country screening and segment screening

identify the sources of information for the screening process

discuss the utility of the Internet as a source of market research data

As described above, Clotaire Rapaille's seeming skill at reducing complex motivations to understandable "sound bites" may or may not ring hollow, but we can appreciate our need as managers to understand complex foreign markets.

While noting our fascination with Rapaille's methods, many international managers might prefer a more systematic approach as outlined in this chapter. In the following pages we describe in some detail a market screening process.

market screening
A version of environmental scanning in which the firm identifies desirable markets by using the environmental forces to eliminate the less desirable markets

environmental scanning
A procedure in which a firm scans the world for changes in the environmental forces that might affect it

The first step in the market screening process is determining the basic need potential. We shall describe this process fully in the next section. **Market screening** is a modified version of environmental scanning in which the firm identifies markets by using the environmental forces to eliminate the less desirable markets.

Environmental scanning, from which market screening is derived, is a procedure in which a firm scans the world for changes in the environmental forces that might affect it.[1] For some time, environmental scanning has been used by managers during the planning process to provide information about world threats and opportunities. Those who do environmental scanning professionally may belong to such organizations as the Society of Competitive Intelligence Professionals (www.scip.org). In addition, environmental scanning services are available from a number of private firms. Examples of such service providers include Smith Brandon International (www.smithbrandon.com) and Stratfor, Inc. (www.stratfor.com).

Market screening assists two different kinds of firms. One is selling exclusively in the domestic market but believes it might increase sales by expanding into overseas markets. The other is already a multinational, but wants to avoid missing potential new markets. In both situations, managers require an ordered, relatively fast method of analyzing and assessing the nearly 200 countries (and multiple market segments within countries) to pinpoint the most suitable prospects.

Market Screening

Market screening is a method of market analysis and assessment that permits management to identify a small number of desirable markets by eliminating those judged to be less attractive. This is accomplished by subjecting the markets to a series of screenings based on the environmental forces examined in Section Three. Although these forces may be placed in any order, the arrangement suggested in Figure 15.1 is designed to progress from the least

FIGURE 15.1

Selection of Foreign Markets

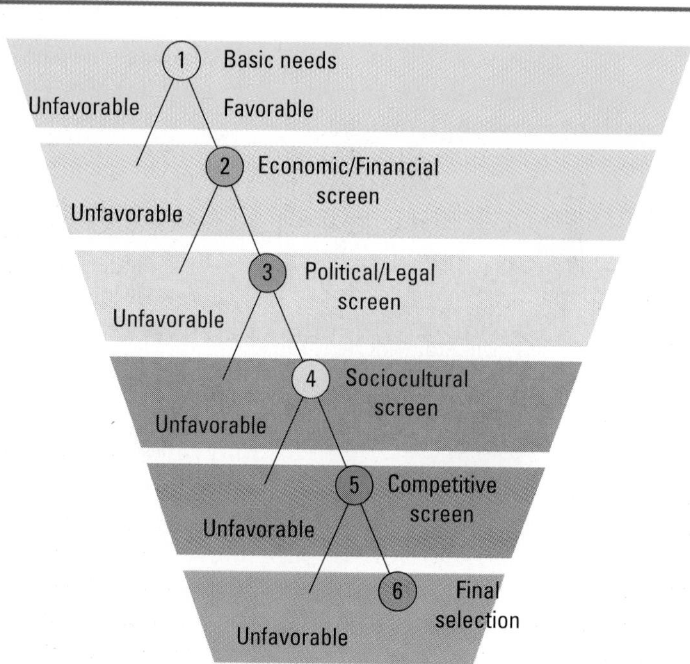

to the most difficult analysis based on the accessibility and subjectivity of the data. In this way, the smallest number of candidates is left for the final, most difficult screening.

TWO TYPES OF SCREENING

In this chapter we will look at two types of market screening procedures. The first, which could be called **country screening,** takes countries as the relevant unit of analysis. The second, which we might call **segment screening,** is based on a subnational analysis of groups of consumers.

country screening
Using countries as the basis for market selection

segment screening
Using market segments as the basis for market selection

INITIAL SCREENING

Basic Need Potential

An initial screening based on the basic need potential is a logical first step, because if the need is lacking, no reasonable expenditure of effort and money will enable the firm to market its goods or services. For example, the basic need potential of certain goods is dependent on various physical forces, such as climate, topography, and natural resources. If the firm produces air conditioners, the analyst will look for countries with warm climates. Manufacturers of large farm tractors might not consider Switzerland a likely prospect because of its mountainous terrain, and only areas known to possess gold deposits are probable markets for gold-dredging equipment.

Generally, producers of specialized industrial materials or equipment experience little difficulty in assessing their basic need potential. A builder of cement kilns, for example, can obtain the names and addresses of cement plants worldwide through the Web site of the Portland Cement Association, near Chicago. A list of firms in an industry, often on a worldwide basis, is available either from the industry association or from specialized trade journals. What about less specialized products that are widely consumed? For example, it is problematic to establish a basic need for chocolate and harder still to do so for MP3 players, consumer robots, or movies on DVD. In this case we are moving from needs to wants.

Foreign Trade

Analysts who want to know where American competitors are exporting their products can go to the Web site of the International Trade Administration (ITA), www.ita.doc.gov. The U.S. Department of Commerce also has the report *U.S. Exports of Merchandise* on the National Trade Data Bank (NTDB), which is available online for a subscription fee. This report's information is especially useful, as it includes both units and dollar values, permitting the analyst to calculate the average price of the unit exported. Commerce compiles and releases foreign trade statistics on a monthly and cumulative basis in its report *U.S. International Trade in Goods and Services,* commonly referred to as the FT900. Recently the FT900 showed, for instance, that U.S. income from royalties and licensing increased each year from 2004-2006. It is published as a press release.

For help in their search for markets, analysts can obtain from the nearest Department of Commerce office numerous studies prepared by U.S. embassies. *Annual Worldwide Industry Reviews* and *International Market Research Reports* indicate major markets for many products.

The *Country Market Surveys* indicate products for which there is a good, established market in a given country. We shall discuss these publications in greater detail in Chapter 18. Other countries publish similar data. For example, the data office of the European Community, Eurostat, publishes an annual, *External Trade,* and JETRO, the Japanese External Trade Organization, publishes a wide assortment of trade and industry data, many of which are put on its Internet site.

Imports Don't Completely Measure Market Potential

Even when a basic need is clearly indicated, experienced researchers will still investigate the trade flows to have an idea of the magnitude of present sales. Management is aware, of course, that imports alone seldom measure the full market potential. Myriad reasons are responsible, among which are poor marketing, lack of foreign exchange, and high prices (duties and markups). Nor can imports give much indication of the potential demand for a really new product.

Moreover, import data indicate only that a market has been buying certain products from abroad and are no guarantee that it will continue to do so. A competitor may decide to produce locally, which in many markets will cause imports to cease. Change in a country's political structure also may stop imports, as we saw in the case of Iran after the revolution there, where orders worth billions of dollars were suddenly canceled. Nevertheless, import data do enable the firm to know how much is currently being purchased and provide managers with a conservative estimate of the immediate market potential at the going price. If local production is being considered and calculations show that goods produced in the country could be sold at a lower price, the firm can reasonably expect to sell more than the quantity being imported.

SECOND SCREENING—FINANCIAL AND ECONOMIC FORCES

After the initial screening, the analyst will have a much smaller list of prospects. This list may be further reduced by a second screening based on the financial and economic forces. Trends in inflation, exchange, and interest rates are among the major financial points of concern. The analyst should consider other financial factors, such as credit availability, paying habits of customers, and rates of return on similar investments. It should be noted that this screening is not a complete financial analysis. That will come later if the market analysis and assessment disclose that a country has sufficient potential for capital investment.

Economic data may be employed in a number of ways, but two measures of market demand based on them are especially useful. These are *market indicators* and *market factors.* Other methods for estimating demand that depend on economic data are *trend analysis* and *cluster analysis.*

market indicators
Economic data used to measure relative market strengths of countries or geographic areas

Market Indicators

Market indicators are economic data that serve as yardsticks for measuring the relative market strengths of various geographic areas.

As an example, we developed an index of e-commerce potential for Latin America so that the countries in the region could be compared. The results appear in Table 15.1. In this methodology, we assembled data on 20 Latin American countries and then ranked the countries against each other. We wanted to include indicators of the strength and growth rate of the overall economy, as well as factors related more specifically to e-commerce or to communications that would aid the growth of e-commerce. We developed three indexes. Each indicator is given equal weight in each index.

Market size = size of urban population + electricity consumption

Market growth rate = average growth rate in commercial energy use + real growth rate in GDP

E-commerce readiness = mobile phones per 1,000 + number of PCs per 1,000 + Internet hosts per million people

The rankings on these three indexes were then utilized to form a composite ranking. We called this composite ranking "e-commerce potential." As you can see in Table 15.1, utilizing our methodology the countries with the most e-commerce potential appear to be Chile, Costa Rica, Jamaica, and Brazil, while Paraguay, Nicaragua, and Haiti appear to have the least potential.

market factors
Economic data that correlate highly with market demand for a product

Market Factors

Market factors are similar to market indicators except that they tend to correlate highly with the market demand for a given product. If the analyst of a foreign market has no factor for that market, he or she may be able to use one from the domestic market to get an approximation. Moreover, an analyst who works for a multinational firm may be able to obtain market factors developed by comparable subsidiaries. To be able to transfer these relationships to the country under study, the analyst must assume that the underlying conditions affecting demand are similar in the market.

estimation by analogy
Process of using a market factor that is successful in one market to estimate demand in a similar market

We can illustrate this process, which is called **estimation by analogy,** by using the following example: If a supplier of laptops knows that one-fifth of all laptops are replaced every year in the United Kingdom, he or she might use the same relationship to estimate demand for replacement computers in a new overseas market. If there are 3 million existing laptops in the new market, the analyst might forecast that 3 million × 0.20, or 600,000, replacement laptops will be sold annually. The constant in the country under study may be somewhat different (it usually is), but with this approach, the estimates will be in the right ballpark. Many

TABLE 15.1 E-Commerce Potential: Rankings for Latin America

Countries	Market Size	Market Growth Rate	E-Commerce Readiness	Overall E-Commerce Potential
South America				
Argentina	4	17	3	6
Bolivia	17	5	15	15
Brazil	5	12	3	4
Chile	1	5	1	1
Colombia	11	7	9	9
Ecuador	14	1	9	6
Paraguay	12	16	15	17
Peru	12	3	15	11
Uruguay	7	20	9	12
Venezuela	2	19	7	9
Caribbean				
Dominican Republic	10	9	9	9
Haiti	20	18	20	19
Jamaica	3	14	2	3
Central America				
Costa Rica	6	2	3	2
El Salvador	15	13	9	12
Guatemala	17	11	9	12
Honduras	15	4	19	15
Mexico	6	15	3	6
Nicaragua	17	10	15	17
Panama	5	6	7	4

Source: Michael S. Minor and Alexandra Brandt, "A Possible Index of E-Commerce Potential for Latin America," working paper, January 8, 2002, updated June 2006 by Adeseguno Oyedele. Reprinted with permission of the authors.

such factors exist, and generally research personnel, either at the home office or in foreign subsidiaries, are familiar with them.

Trend Analysis When the historical growth rates of either the pertinent economic variables or the imports of a product are known, future growth can be forecast by means of **trend analysis.** A time series may be constructed in a manner similar to the way a regression model is made, or the arithmetic mean of past growth rates may be applied to historical data. Caution is advised when using the second method because if the average annual growth rate is applied mechanically, in just a few years the dependent variable may reach an incredible size. For example, a 5 percent growth rate compounded annually will result in a doubling of the original value in only 15 years. Because trend analysis is based on the assumption that past conditions affecting the dependent variable will remain constant, analysts will generally modify the outcome to take into account any changes that can be foreseen. Often there are obvious constraints that will limit growth. One of these constraints is the near certainty that competitors will enter the market if large increases in demand continue for very long.

trend analysis
Statistical technique by which successive observations of a variable at regular time intervals are analyzed to establish regular patterns that are used for establishing future values

Cluster Analysis and Other Techniques As multinationals extend their presence to more markets, managers are searching for ways to group countries and geographic regions by common characteristics. **Cluster analysis** divides objects (market areas, individuals, customers, and other variables) into groups so that the variables within each group are similar. For example, all the people sitting at a table in a restaurant are a "cluster." Marketers, for example, use cluster analysis to identify a group of markets where a single promotional approach

cluster analysis
Statistical technique that divides objects into groups so that the objects within each group are similar

BUILDING YOUR GLOBAL RÉSUMÉ — Acquiring and Using Your Global Analytical Tool Kit

In any building process, the right tools are necessary to get the job completed. Listed below are a number of solid analytical tools and skills that can be applied to analyzing global markets. If you understand how to use them and apply them appropriately, you will typically generate higher-quality analytical results and then be able to make better decisions. (To find out more about any of these tools, try an Internet search or check out one of the Web sites listed below.)

- Pareto Principle (80/20 rule)
- Project management process
- Market development planning
- Feasibility study
- Boston Consulting Group Matrix
- SWOT analysis
- Porter's Five Forces Model
- PEST and PESTELI analysis
- PRO's & CON's weighted analysis
- SOSTAC Planning Model
- P&L account planning, accounting, and reporting
- ROI analysis
- Business plan–marketing plan writing
- Strategies and tactics of sales

High-quality secondary market data and economic statistics about global markets are becoming readily available with just a few keystrokes and will support your market understanding for better application of these tools. When it comes to using the results these tools will generate, here are two concepts to always keep in mind:

- *The First Law of Cybernetics states,* "The unit within the system with the most behavioral responses available to it controls the system."
- *P. T. Barnum said,* "If you can't put your idea on the back of your business card, you don't have a clear idea."

Make sure that you have enough analytical data to make a solid recommendation, and then you own the recommendation. When you present your recommendations, you will look professional if you do so in a clear, succinct, and understandable way.

World Wide Resources:

www.internationalbusinessstrategies.com
http://dir.yahoo.com/Business_and_Economy/Trade/Statistics
http://unstats.un.org/unsd/default.htm
http://unstats.un.org/unsd/methods/inter-natlinks/refs3.htm
www.marketresearch.com
www.imriresearch.com

can be employed; attorneys can use it to group nations according to similarities in certain types of laws; and so forth. In other words, cluster analysis is used to classify a "mountain" of information into meaningful "piles."

Periodic Updating If the estimates are altered appreciably in the periodic updatings that all long-term forecasts undergo, managers may change the extent of the firm's involvement to be in line with the new estimates. Fortunately, the alternative forms of participation in a market permit the firm to become progressively more involved, with corresponding increases in investment. Most companies can enter a market in stages, perhaps in this sequence: exporting, establishment of a foreign sales company, local assembly, and, finally, local manufacturing.

Even when the decision is whether to produce overseas, management may plan to assemble a combination of imported and domestically produced parts initially and then progressively to manufacture more components locally as demand rises. Automobile manufacturers have begun a number of foreign operations employing this strategy.

THIRD SCREENING—POLITICAL AND LEGAL FORCES

The elements of the political and legal forces that can eliminate a market from further consideration (or make it more attractive) are numerous.

Entry Barriers Import restrictions can be positive or negative, depending on whether managers are considering exporting (can the firm's products enter the country?) or setting up a foreign plant (will competitive imports be kept out?). If an objective is 100 percent ownership, will the nation's laws permit it, or is some local participation required? Will the government accept a minority local ownership, or must a minimum of 51 percent of the subsidiary be in the hands of nationals? Are there laws that reserve certain industries for either the government or its citizens?[2] Is the host government demanding that the foreign owner turn over technology to its proposed affiliate that it wishes to keep at the home plant? Perhaps the host government has local content restrictions that the prospective investor considers excessive. There may be a government-owned company that would compete with the proposed plant. Depending on the circumstances and how strongly management wishes to enter the market, any one of these conditions may be sufficient cause to eliminate a nation from further consideration.

Profit Remittance Barriers When there are no objectionable requisites for entry, a nation may still be excluded if there are what management believes to be undue restrictions on the repatriation of earnings. Limits linked to the amount of foreign investment or other criteria may be set, or the nation may have a history of inability to provide foreign exchange for profit remittances.

Policy Stability Another factor of importance to management in studying the possibilities of investing in a country is the stability of government policy. Is there continuity in policy when a new leader takes office, for example? What is the political climate? Is the government stable, or is there infighting among government leaders? How about the public? Is there visible unrest? Do the armed forces have a history of intervention when there are public disturbances? Business can adapt to the form of government and thrive as long as the conditions are stable. But instability creates uncertainty, and this complicates planning. An often-heard complaint is, "They've changed the rules again."

It is important to make a distinction between *political stability* and *policy stability.* Rulers may come and go, but if the policies that affect businesses don't change very much, these political changes really may not be important. In fact, if one measures political stability in terms of changes in leadership at the top, the United States is politically unstable compared to many countries!

Sources of analysis on political and policy stability are numerous. Some, such as Stratfor, have already been mentioned. In addition, Business Environment Risk Intelligence S.A. (www.beri.com) and Political Risk Services (www.prsgroup.com) publish rankings comparing countries on the issue of political risk. You may also want to review the discussion of country risk assessment in Chapter 9.

FOURTH SCREENING—SOCIOCULTURAL FORCES

A screening of the remaining candidates on the basis of sociocultural factors is arduous. First, sociocultural factors are fairly subjective. Second, data are difficult to assemble, particularly from a distance. The analyst, unless he or she is a specialist in the country, must rely on the opinions of others. It is possible to hire consultants, who typically are "old hands" with experience in the country or region. Others may have a particular methodology, such as Clotaire Rapaille mentioned at the beginning of the chapter. Also, professional organizations and universities frequently hold seminars to explain the sociocultural aspects of doing business in a particular area or country.

Reading *Overseas Business Reports* (U.S. Department of Commerce), international business publications *(Business International, Financial Times, The Economist),* and specialized books will augment the analyst's sociocultural knowledge. The use of a checklist of the principal sociocultural components, as explained in Chapter 6, will serve as a reminder of the many factors the analyst must consider in this screening.

Although there are many difficulties, it is possible that recent immigrants or students from foreign countries may be used to shed light on potential sociocultural issues.

> *One of the authors took a visiting speaker who was originally from Japan to visit a local firm. This business, which manufactured dessert items such as individual cherry pies, wanted to break into the Japanese market but had not been successful. The Japanese speaker tasted the product and told them firmly that their cherry pie was too sweet for Japanese palates. We found that this company had never actually asked a Japanese person for a reaction to its products! Although the firm needed to confirm this single opinion by using other methods, the taster nonetheless offered insight into an issue about which the firm was unaware.*

A danger, of course, is that immigrants and students have been affected by their residence abroad. Therefore, they are not necessarily reliable indicators of the reaction your product might receive from an audience "back home."

After the fourth screening, the analyst should have a list of countries for which an industry demand appears to exist. However, what management really wants to know is which of these markets seem to be the best prospects for the *firm's* products. A fifth screening based on the competitive forces will help provide this information.

FIFTH SCREENING—COMPETITIVE FORCES

In this screening, the analyst examines markets on the basis of such elements of the competitive forces as:

1. The number, size, and financial strength of the competitors.
2. Their market shares.
3. Their marketing strategies.
4. The apparent effectiveness of their promotional programs.
5. The quality levels of their product lines.
6. The source of their products—imported or locally produced.
7. Their pricing policies.
8. The levels of their after-sales service.
9. Their distribution channels.
10. Their coverage of the market. (Could market segmentation produce niches that are currently poorly served?)

Concerning item 10, it may be important to examine regional or ethnic subcultures in a particular foreign market. These subcultures may be natural or at least identifiable segments for which specific marketing programs may be successful. This is analogous to the fact that there are sufficient Hispanic, Chinese, and other subcultures in the United States to merit the importation of Chinese and Latin American products into the United States.

Perhaps other countries have significant immigrant or subcultural populations whose needs you already understand and can serve. As an example, Japan has a small but growing population of immigrants from Latin America whose parents emigrated from Japan to Latin America in earlier times. These returnees tend to preserve their Latin heritage in Japan and might provide a market niche for firms whose strength is marketing to Latin Americans rather than to the Japanese.

Countries in which management believes strong competitors make a profitable operation difficult to attain are eliminated unless management (1) is following a strategy of being present wherever its global competitors are or (2) believes entering a competitor's home market will distract the competitor's attention from its home market, a reason for foreign investment we discussed in Chapter 3.

FINAL SELECTION OF NEW MARKETS

While much can be accomplished through analysis, there is no substitute for personal visits to markets that appear to have the best potential. An executive of the firm should visit those countries that still appear to be good prospects. Before leaving, this person should review the data from the various screenings along with any new information that the researcher can supply.

On the basis of this review and experience in making similar domestic decisions, the executive should prepare a list of points on which information must be obtained on arrival. Management will want the facts uncovered by the desk study (the five screenings) to be corroborated and will expect a firsthand report on the market, including information on competitive activity and an appraisal of the suitability of the firm's present marketing mix and the availability of support services (warehousing, media agencies, credit, and so forth).

Field Trip The field trip should not be hurried; as much time should be allotted to this part of the study as would be spent on a similar domestic field trip. The point is to try to develop a "feel" for what is going on, and this can't be accomplished quickly. For example, while Japanese youths model themselves after American basketball stars by wearing Nike sneakers, it appears that they change into off-brand sneakers when they actually play basketball. As another example, it seems to be relatively common for men to shop in grocery stores in Chile, as compared to elsewhere in Latin America. And there is not much tradition in East Asia of men taking on the "do-it-yourself" projects for which Home Depot and similar brands are famous. This type of insight is not likely to develop without actual visits to the market.

trade mission
A group of businesspeople and/or government officials (state or federal) that visits a market in search of business opportunities

trade fair
A large exhibition, generally held at the same place and same time periodically, at which companies maintain booths to promote the sale of their products

Government-Sponsored Trade Missions and Trade Fairs When government trade specialists perceive an overseas market opportunity for an industry, they may organize a **trade mission.** The purpose is to send a group of executives from firms in the industry to a country or group of countries to learn firsthand about the market, meet important customers face-to-face, and make contacts with people interested in representing their products. Because of discounted airfares, hotels, and so forth, the cost to the firm may be less than it would pay if it went on its own.

Moreover, the impact of a group visit is greater than that of an individual visit. Before the mission's arrival, consulate or embassy officials will have publicized the visit and made contact with local companies they believe are interested. For example, in 2002 the prime minister of Canada led a group of Canadian businesses on a trade mission to Germany and Russia, resulting in agreements representing $584 million in business for Canadian firms.[3] State governments, trade associations, chambers of commerce, and other export-oriented organizations also organize trade missions.

Probably every nation in the world holds a **trade fair** periodically. Usually each nation has a specifically marked area (Chinese pavilion, Argentine pavilion, etc.) at the fairgrounds where its exhibitors have their own booths staffed by company sales representatives. Trade fairs are open to the public, but during certain hours (generally mornings), entrance is limited to businesspeople interested in doing business with the exhibitors.

While most fairs in developing countries are general, with displays of many kinds of products, those in Europe are specialized. A famous example is the annual CeBIT computer and telecommunications trade fair—the largest computer-related trade fair in the world—held annually in Hannover, Germany. Over 450,000 people made the trip to this show in 2006 alone to see exhibits from 6,167 exhibitors.[4]

Besides making contact with prospective buyers and agents (direct sales are often concluded), most exhibitors use these fairs to learn more about the market and gather competitive intelligence. They not only receive feedback from visitors to their exhibits but also have the opportunity to observe their competitors in action.

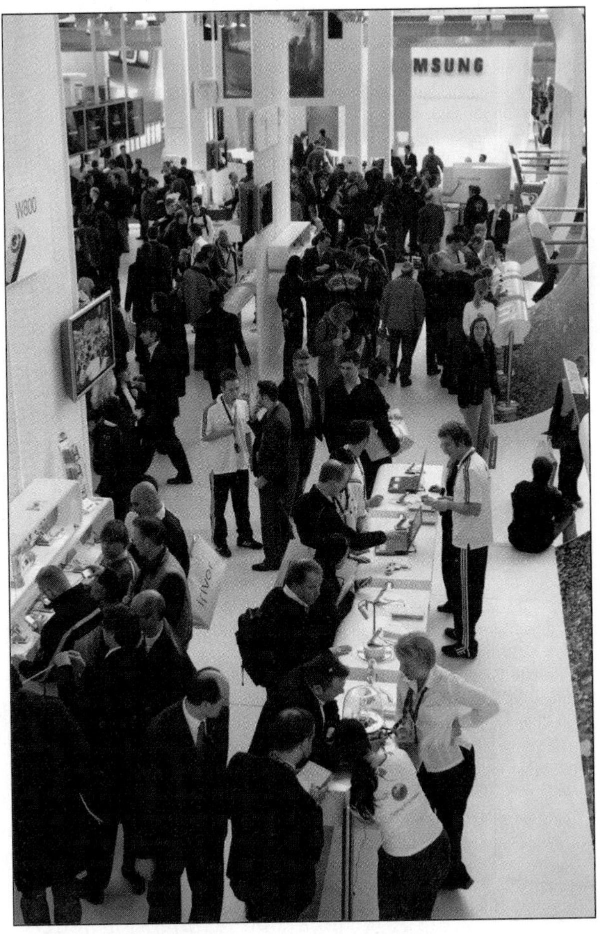

Visitors explore the exhibits at the CeBIT Technology Fair in Hannover, Germany. Besides making sales contacts, most exhibitors use these fairs to learn more about the market and gather competitive intelligence. They not only receive feedback from visitors to their exhibits but also have the opportunity to observe their competitors in action.

Sometimes Local Research Is Required For many situations, the manager's field report will be the final input to the information on which the decision is based. Occasionally, however, the proposed human and financial resource commitments are so great that management will insist on gathering data in the potential market rather than depending solely on the desk and field reports.[5] This would undoubtedly be the position of a consumer products manufacturer that envisions entering a large competitive market of an industrialized country. It might also be the recommendation of the manager making the field trip if he or she discovered that market conditions were substantially different from those to which the firm was accustomed. Often, in face-to-face interviews, information is revealed that would never be written. In these situations, research in the local market not only will supply information on market definition and projection but also will assist in the formulation of an effective marketing mix.

Research in the Local Market

When a firm's research personnel have had no experience in the country, management should probably hire a local research group to do the work. Generally, home country research techniques may be used, though they may need to be adapted to local conditions. It is imperative, therefore, that the person in charge of the project have experience either in that country or in one that is culturally similar and preferably in the same geographic area.

If secondary data are unavailable, the researchers must collect primary data, and here they face other complications caused by *cultural problems* and *technical difficulties.*

Cultural Problems If the researchers are from one culture and are working in another, they may encounter some cultural problems. When they are not proficient in the local language or dialect, the research instrument or the respondents' answers must be translated. As we learned in the chapter on sociocultural forces, a number of languages may be spoken in a country, and even in countries where only one language is used, a word's meaning may change from one region to another.

Other cultural problems plague researchers as they try to collect data. Low levels of literacy may make the use of mail questionnaires virtually impossible. If a husband is interviewed in a market where the wife usually makes the buying decisions, the data obtained from him are worthless. Nor is it always clear who should be interviewed. Respondents sometimes refuse to answer questions because of their general distrust of strangers. In other instances, the custom of politeness toward everyone will cause respondents to give answers calculated to please the interviewer; this is known as *social desirability bias.*

Often, people have practical reasons for not wanting to be interviewed. In some countries, income taxes are based on the apparent worth of individuals as measured by their tangible assets. In such countries, when asked if there is a stereo or TV in the household, the respondent may suspect the interviewer of being a tax assessor and refuse to answer. To overcome such a problem, experienced researchers often hire college students as interviewers because their manner of speech and their dress correctly identify them as what they are.

Technical Difficulties As if the cultural problems were not enough, researchers may also encounter technical difficulties. First, up-to-date maps are often unavailable. The streets chosen to be sampled may have three or four different names along their length, and the houses may not be numbered. In Japan, it is said, only cab drivers can find street addresses. Telephone surveys can be a formidable undertaking, because in some markets only the wealthy have telephones. Although China is the largest mobile phone market in the world, over three-fourths of the nation's cell phone users are in just three cities—Beijing, Shanghai, and Guangzhou.[6]

Mail surveys can be troublesome too, as mail deliveries within a city may take weeks or are sometimes not made at all. For instance, the postal service in Italy has been so slow (two weeks for a letter to go from Rome to Milan) that Italian firms have used private couriers to go to Switzerland to dispatch their foreign mail. The response to a mail survey is often low if the respondent must go to the post office to mail a letter. To increase returns, firms often offer such premiums as lottery tickets or product samples to persons who complete a mail questionnaire.

In some nations, researchers may have to obtain government permission to conduct interviews and, in some cases, submit questionnaires for prior approval. Some countries prohibit certain kinds of questions. For example, you cannot ask Egyptians about the ownership of consumer durables, and in Saudi Arabia you are not permitted to ask questions about nationality.[7]

mini MNE

>>Some Tips on Market Research

Wonder how to begin to get that elusive "feel" for a country from survey data? As we mentioned, one way is to do it yourself via surveys and personal visits. Two other methods involve the use of an outside firm. Under one scenario, you can hire an outside firm to do customized research for your firm's needs. The second involves using surveys that are administered only partially, or not at all, with your specific firm in mind.

CUSTOMIZED RESEARCH

Many firms that can do multicountry surveys on behalf of clients belong to ESOMAR (www.esomar.nl), the European Society of Opinion and Marketing Research. Originally member-firms were European, but there are now 4,000 members in over 100 countries.

Consumer products firms often utilize ethnographic research techniques, sometimes referred to as "corporate anthropology," to develop detailed understanding. A number of firms specialize in this type of research. These firms do extensive "on-the-ground" research, watching consumers actually use products, rather than relying on surveys or focus groups. An example of these specialist firms is Point Forward (www.pointforward.com). In one project the firm helped Lipton examine Japanese tea drinking, leading to new offerings designed to appeal to younger Japanese, who aren't drinking tea at the rate of their elders. Another firm is Envirosell (www.envirosell.com), which specializes in research on shopping.

GENERAL SURVEYS

General surveys are not done with a specific firm in mind. There are three types of general survey. The first is the *omnibus survey*. Omnibus surveys are regularly scheduled surveys conducted by research agencies with questions from different clients (that is, they are wholly or partially "syndicated"). Since several firms contribute questions, the cost is spread across several users and the surveys are relatively fast. However, these surveys can ask only a limited number of questions that are directly relevant to a particular client, and the sample may not be representative of a particular firm's potential target market. As an indication, the ESOMAR directory lists 12 firms in Argentina and 23 firms in Japan that do omnibus surveys.

One example of a firm involved in administering omnibus surveys is A. C. Nielsen (www.acnielsen.com). Although we may know Nielsen best from the "Nielsen ratings," its TV-watching media measurement service, the firm offers services in over 100 countries. Nielsen does an omnibus survey in China, among other countries. Another familiar firm—the Gallup Organization (www.gallup.com)—is involved in this type of research in a variety of countries.

In the second type of noncustomized general survey, market research firms do surveys of their own devising whose results they then market to a variety of firms. An example is the recent Asian Pacific Consumer Confidence Poll in 13 Asian Pacific markets, a Nielsen survey. Nielsen can even track TV-watching habits in China and India. Another firm that does industry-level surveys spanning a number of countries for general sale is Frost & Sullivan (www.frost.com). Frost & Sullivan recently published a report on the world voice-over Internet protocol (VOIP) market.

NONPROFIT SURVEYS

The third type of survey is administered by a government or nongovernment agency, generally not for profit. The Eurobarometer surveys (http://europa.eu.int/comm/public_opinion) are administered several times a year to thousands of respondents in European countries, under the auspices of the European Commission. Recent reports of Eurobarometer results with implications for consumer behavior include reports on attitudes toward vacations, food product safety, the young, and the family. Although these surveys are not specifically directed toward consumption issues, they are free and may be useful. Since 1995 a similar survey, called a *barómetro,* has been conducted in Latin America (www.latinobarometro.org).

THE INTERNET

The number of firms that do surveys on or about the Internet is increasing. Nielsen has a subsidiary devoted to research in Internet marketing called Nielsen NetRatings (www.nielsen-netratings.com). Another such firm is Forrester Research (www.forrester.com). In a recent report, Forrester forecast that European online trade, which represented less than 1 percent of total business trade in 2001, would skyrocket to 22 percent of trade by 2006. In the future, the technology of Internet surveys may offer any firm the opportunity to do its own surveys anywhere in the world. At the present, however, the penetration of the Internet is limited to well-to-do persons in some countries. It is not currently possible to rely on the Internet to provide access to members of all target markets.

Research as Practiced The existence of hindrances to marketing research does not mean it is not carried out in foreign markets. As you might surmise from the discussion of the availability of secondary data, marketing research is highly developed in many areas where markets are large and incorrect decisions are costly. Problems like the ones we have

WORLD view   

"Demon Wife," Blooks, YouTube

Take a Japanese businessman who went online to write about his domineering wife. Throw in YouTube, the do-it-yourself site where videos are up-and-downloaded by the thousands daily—and you have a rich smorgasbord of tools for looking at trends in other cultures.

One difference between Japan and the United States is seen in the popularity of blogs. Although Japan has less than half as many people, the Japanese write nearly as many blogs. More than one-fifth of the Japanese people are estimated to read blogs. With millions of blogs available, their possible insights into cultures is imposing. In late 2006 the most popular blog in the world was reputed to be that of Chinese actress Xu Jinglei.

We examined a small sample of the millions of YouTube videos: some 65,000 new videos are uploaded every day. Of a sample of 100, we found that 32 percent were from foreign sources (we had originally assumed that 10 percent or less were of foreign origin).

Although many foreign blogs and videos are obviously not in English and would require hiring a person proficient in the language, nonetheless blogs and the videos collected on YouTube represent an opportunity to view snippets of life in foreign countries that can "flesh out" the qualitative, subjective views that are so important at the later stages of the assessment process.

Source: Yukari Iwatani Kane, "How Demon Wife Became a Media Star and Other Tales of the 'Blook' in Japan," *The Wall Street Journal*, October 5, 2006, pp. B1, B6; Michael S. Mirror, "What You Tube Tells Us about Them," working paper, November 2006.

mentioned are prevalent in the developing nations, but they are well known to those who live there. It does not take long for the newcomer to become aware of them either, because long-time residents are quick to point them out.

Analysts tend to do less research and use simpler techniques in these nations because often the firm is in a seller's market, which means everything produced can be sold with a minimum of effort. Moreover, competition is frequently less intense in developing nations because (1) there are fewer competitors and (2) managements are struggling with problems other than marketing, which keep them from devoting more time to marketing issues. Even in Mexico, an important market for American firms, marketing research is less popular.[8] Although the situation is changing, the most common technique continues to be a combination of trend analysis and the querying of knowledgeable persons such as salespeople, channel members, and customers. Researchers then adjust the findings on the basis of subjective considerations.

Segment Screening

As was mentioned earlier, when a company intends to do business in several countries, managers can choose two broad market screening approaches: country segments or market segments. In the first approach, Brazil may be viewed as a target market segment. Using the second approach, while Brazil is the physical location of a large group of consumers, the important variables for segmentation are commonalities in needs and wants among consumers *across nationalities*. These consumers may reside in different countries and speak different languages, but they have similar desires for a product or service. From this perspective, age, income, and psychographics (lifestyles) are the essential means of identifying market segments. The relevant marketing question is not where consumers reside but whether they share similar wants and needs. The targeted consumers may be global teens, middle-class executives, or young families with small children: Each of these segments may share wants and needs across borders. An example comes from "phone surfers"—young Japanese who actively use their mobile phones to surf the Internet. The small phone screen and tiny keys may be a big turnoff for older computer users in the West who have frequent access to desktop or laptop PCs. But youngsters in the West have grown up with television games, Game Boys, and iPod nanos, and they readily adapt to the small screens and tiny buttons that are a part of using cell phones as an Internet device.

Because we usually organize the world mentally in terms of countries, we naturally tend to want to analyze markets as country segments. It is much more difficult to think of ourselves as market segments that extend across borders. Also, as was mentioned in the discussion of sociocultural differences, these data can be difficult to secure. Nonetheless, it is important to do this because this approach is the logical outgrowth of the marketing concept.

And the fact that certain types of data are difficult to gather doesn't mean that the data can be ignored. There is an old saying about research: "If you can count it, that ain't it." In our context, the easy-to-generate data are not necessarily the important data.

Among the criteria for these segments are that they should be:

1. *Definable:* We should be able to identify and measure segments. The more we rely not on socioeconomic indicators but on lifestyle differences, the more difficult this becomes, but the more accurate the resulting analysis is likely to be.
2. *Large:* Segments should be large enough to be worth the effort needed to serve a segment. Of course, as we get closer to flexible manufacturing, the need to find large segments is beginning to recede. Further, the segments should have the potential for growth in the future.
3. *Accessible:* If we literally cannot reach our target segment for either promotional or distribution purposes, we will be unsuccessful.
4. *Actionable:* If we cannot bring components of marketing programs (the 4 Ps of product, promotion, place, and price) to bear, we may not be successful. For example, in Mexico, the price of tortillas was formerly controlled by the government. Therefore, competition on the price variable was impossible. Foreigners could not penetrate the Mexican market for the standard tortilla by offering a lower price.
5. *Capturable:* Although we would love to discover market segments whose needs are completely unmet, in many cases these market segments are already being served. Nonetheless, we may still be able to compete. Where segments are completely "captured" by the competition, however, our task is much more difficult.[9]

TWO SCREENING METHODS, RECONSIDERED

In the final analysis, our view of the rest of the world is organized along national lines. However, it may be useful to attempt to leave that viewpoint behind when examining international markets.

With the increasing recognition of the existence of subcultures *within* nations and similarities between subcultures *across* nations, the international businessperson may wish to expand his or her horizon beyond the conventional view of the nation as the relevant "unit of analysis."

The next chapter takes up a series of related questions. Are our needs and desires becoming more and more alike, or are the differences in consumption preferences between us more relevant than the similarities?

Summary

Discuss environmental analysis and two types of market screening.

A complete market analysis and assessment as described in this chapter would be made by a firm that either is contemplating entering the foreign market for the first time or is already a multinational but wants to monitor world markets systematically to avoid overlooking marketing opportunities and threats. Many of the data requirements for a foreign decision are the same as those for a similar domestic decision, though it is likely that additional information about some of the international and foreign environmental forces will be needed. Essentially, the screening process consists of examining the various forces in succession and eliminating countries at each step. The sequence of screening based on (1) basic need potential, (2) financial and economic forces, (3) political and legal forces, (4) sociocultural forces, (5) competitive forces, and (6) personal visits is ordered so as to have a successively smaller number of prospects to consider at each of the succeedingly more difficult and expensive stages.

Explain market indicators and market factors.

Market indicators are economic data used to measure relative market strengths of countries or geographic areas. Market factors are economic data that correlate highly with the market demand for a product.

Describe some statistical techniques for estimating market demand and grouping similar markets.

Some statistical techniques for estimating market demand and grouping similar markets are trend analysis and cluster analysis.

Discuss the value to businesspeople of trade missions and trade fairs.

Trade missions and trade fairs enable businesspeople to visit a market inexpensively, make sales, obtain overseas representation, and observe competitors' activities.

Discuss some of the problems market researchers encounter in foreign markets.

Cultural problems, such as a low level of literacy and distrust of strangers, complicate the data-gathering process, as do technical difficulties, such as a lack of maps, telephone directories, and adequate mail service. These hindrances to marketing research do not prevent the work from being done. There is a tendency in some markets, however, to do less research and use simpler techniques.

Explain the difference between country screening and segment screening.

If we utilize country screening, we assume that countries are homogeneous units (that is, "everyone living in Mexico or Chad is essentially the same"). In segment screening, we focus our attention not on the nation as a homogeneous unit but on groups of people with similar wants and desires (market segments) across as well as within countries.

Identify the sources of information for the screening process.

The sources of information for the screening process are the environmental forces.

Discuss the utility of the Internet as a source of market research data.

Both the mini-MNE box and the Worldview box in this chapter offer insights into how the Internet is used—or may be used—to generate information. In some countries, however, the Internet is used only by relatively well-to-do and well-educated persons. What are the implications for our ability to do market research directly with potential consumers on the Internet?

Key Words

market screening (p.410)
environmental scanning (p. 410)
country screening (p. 411)
segment screening (p. 411)
market indicators (p. 412)
market factors (p. 412)
estimation by analogy (p. 412)
trend analysis (p. 413)
cluster analysis (p. 413)
trade mission (p. 417)
trade fair (p. 417)

Questions

1. Select a country and a product that you believe your firm can market there. Make a list of the sources of information you will use for each screening.
2. What is the basis for the order of screenings presented in the text?
3. A firm's export manager finds, by examining the UN's *International Trade Statistics Yearbook,* that the company's competitors are exporting. Is there a way the manager can learn to which countries the U.S. competitors are exporting?
4. Do a country's imports completely measure the market potential for a product? Why or why not?
5. What are some barriers related to the political and legal forces that may eliminate a country from further consideration?
6. Why should a firm's management consider going on a trade mission or exhibiting in a trade fair?
7. What are the two principal kinds of complications that researchers face when they collect primary data in a foreign market? Give examples.
8. What do the market size index and the market growth rate index tell you?
9. Consider the market segment screening method. Take a lifestyle segment—say, people who like do-it-yourself home decorating. How would the segment screening method suggest that you go about identifying potential foreign markets?
10. You are a consultant to the developers of the Spider-man computer game. You will tell the CEO where the likely overseas markets are. What do you do?
11. Assume that your academic unit (probably a college of business) wants to open a campus in a foreign country and that the dean has asked you to prepare a list of possible countries. How would you go about fulfilling the dean's requirement?

globalEDGE globalEDGE.msu.edu

Research Task

Use the globalEDGE™ site (http://globalEDGE.msu.edu) to complete the following exercises:

1. *Market Potential Indicators (MPI)* is an indexing study conducted by the Michigan State University Center for International Business Education and Research (MSU-CIBER) to compare emerging markets on a variety of dimensions. Provide a description of the indicators used for this index. Which of the indicators would have greater importance for a company that markets MP3 players? Considering the MPI rankings, which developing countries would you advise this company to enter first with such a product?
2. The National Retail Federation's *Stores* magazine lists the top 250 global retailers ranked by annual sales. This ranking provides economic, demographic, and industry insights on the global marketplace. Locate the ranking and provide a list of the top 10 companies for the latest year available. What is the percentage of Japanese companies on this list of global retailers?

The Sugar Daddy Chocolate Company Minicase 15.1

Jack Carlson started the Sugar Daddy Chocolate Company five years ago and is now selling about $1 million annually. Carlson would like to expand sales, but the U.S. market is very competitive. He has a friend with a small business who is now making 20 percent of his sales overseas. He wonders if any chocolates are exported.

To find out, he calls a friend of his who is a professor of international business at the university and tells him that he wants to find out if chocolate is being exported. He asks the professor to research the following questions:

1. Is chocolate being exported?
2. Which are the six largest importing nations?
3. Which of these are growing markets?
4. Carlson's export competition would probably come from which countries?

16 Entry Modes

Our development strategy adapts to different markets addressing local needs and requirements. We currently use three business strategies: joint ventures, licenses, and company-owned stores.

—Starbucks Corporation

EBay: An Early Entrant in International Markets

EBay, the online auction house, has been profitable since it started in 1995. In 2004 eBay sold more than $44.3 billion worth of products, which generated over $4.5 billion in revenues and over $340 million in pro forma net income for itself. It has profited from a network effect. Networks are like a snowball rolling, gathering size as they go. The more sellers eBay attracts, the more buyers turn to it, and that in turn draws more sellers. So eBay has grown by nearly 80 percent per year over the last five years.

EBay's business model has also succeeded abroad, where it already generates approximately half of all its revenues and which is predicted to produce an increasing proportion of eBay's revenues. The company has predicted that its operations in Europe alone could end up matching the size of its U.S. business, and more than half of its revenue will soon come from Web sites in 28 countries outside the United States. It aggressively buys firms abroad. An example is its 2004 acquisition of mobile.de, an online German site dedicated to buying and selling automobiles, and its 2005 acquisition of Skype, which provides Internet-based voice and video connections for users worldwide.

EBay has certainly profited from its early mover position, and no rival has been able to mount more than a feeble challenge. (Ask whether anyone in your class knows who the number-two company is in the online auction market.)

Early entrants, however, are by no means guaranteed success. As an example, first movers into China have often not succeeded. Often, early entrants may score some initial successes in a few affluent cities but be unable to repeat that success on a countrywide basis. For example, Procter & Gamble scored early successes with shampoo, but its multiple brands confused customers and local rivals undercut its prices, so its 50 percent market share in 1998 dropped to 30 percent in 2002.

Similarly, a recent book details the $418 million lost by a fund set up to invest hundreds of millions of dollars in China. At least in part, this misadventure was the result of having to deal with joint venture partners (of which more later). ■

Source: "A Survey of E-Commerce," *The Economist,* May 15, 2004, p. 12; "A Survey of Business in China," *The Economist,* March 20, 2004, p. 9; "Doing Business in China: The Perils of Pat," *The Economist,* April 24, 2004, p. 85; EBay Inc., "About the Company," http://pages.ebay.com/aboutebay/thecompany/companyoverview.html (August 3, 2006); and EBay Inc., *Annual Report 2005,* http://investor.ebay.com (August 3, 2006).

CONCEPT PREVIEWS

After reading this chapter, you should be able to:

explain the international market entry methods

discuss the debate on whether being a market pioneer or a fast follower is most useful

identify two different forms of piracy and discuss which might be helpful and harmful to firms doing international business

discuss the channel members available to companies that export indirectly or directly or manufacture overseas

Gli Affari Internazionali
nales
nales Geschäft Παγοσμιο Business
Negócios Internacionais Los Negócios Internacionais
ternacionales Affaires Internationales 國際商務 Παγοσμιο Business

In the opening example we saw that eBay, a market pioneer, has done very well as it expanded internationally but that several early entrants into China have done poorly. Not all pioneers capitalize on their potential advantages, yet some evidence does suggest that pioneers gain and maintain a competitive edge in new markets. For instance, researchers have found that surviving pioneers hold a significantly larger average market share when their industries reach maturity than do firms that were either fast followers or late entrants in the product category.

On the other hand, pioneers can certainly fail. One recent study, which took failed pioneers into account and averaged their performances with those of the more successful survivors, found that, overall, pioneers did not perform as well over the long haul as followers. Of course, what measures are used can be important here: Volume and market share are not the only dimensions by which success can be measured.

The truth is that there really is little evidence one way or the other concerning the effect of the *timing* of a firm's entry into a new market on its ultimate profitability in that market or the value generated for shareholders.

In many cases a firm entering into international markets becomes a follower by default, because a quicker competitor simply beats it by entering into the market first. But even when a company has the capability of being the first mover, there are possible advantages to letting others go first and shoulder the initial risks while the follower observes the pioneers' shortcomings and mistakes.

A pioneering firm stands the best chance for long-term success in market-share leadership and profitability when (1) the pioneering firm is insulated from the entry of competitors (high entry barriers), at least for a while, by strong patent protection, proprietary technology (such as a unique production process), or substantial investment requirements; or (2) the firm has sufficient size, resources, and competencies to take full advantage of its pioneering position and preserve it in the face of later competitive entries. Indeed, some recent evidence suggests that organizational competencies such as R&D and marketing skills not only affect a firm's success as a pioneer but also influence the company's decision about whether to be a pioneer in the first place. Firms that lack the competencies necessary to sustain a first-mover advantage may be more likely to wait for another company to take the lead and then enter the market later.

On the other hand, a follower will most likely succeed when there are few legal, technological, cultural, or financial barriers to inhibit entry (low entry barriers) and when it has sufficient resources or competencies to overwhelm the pioneer's early advantage. The most successful fast followers tend to have the resources to enter the new market on a larger scale than the pioneer. Thus, they can quickly reduce their unit costs and offer lower prices than incumbent competitors.[1]

Thus, the evidence is not clear on whether we should be first—or nearly first—into a foreign market. Even after that decision, we have other decisions to make regarding which entry mode we should use in entering the market first (or not). (See Table 16.1.)

Entering Foreign Markets

As you learned in Chapter 1, we can use a variety of names to identify large firms that operate on a multicountry scale: *global, multidomestic,* and *international* firms or companies, *multinational enterprise (MNE)* or *multinational company (MNC), international company (IC), transnational,* and even *multicultural multinational.* Long before companies become any of these, however, they are usually smaller companies with only domestic experience. In this chapter we examine the very start, that is, the entry into international operations. We first examine nonequity modes of market entry, followed by equity-based modes. We then will complete the chapter by discussing international channels of distribution and the different members involved in these channels.

NONEQUITY MODES OF ENTRY

Most firms begin their involvement in overseas business by exporting—that is, selling some of their regular production overseas. This method requires little investment and is relatively free of risks. It is an excellent means of getting a feel for international business without

TABLE 16.1 Modes of Market Entry

Nonequity-Based Modes of Entry
Export
  Indirect
  Direct
Subcontracting
Countertrade (discussed in Chapter 21)
Licensing
Franchising
Contract manufacturing
Management contract
Contract manufacturing

Equity-Based Modes of Entry
Wholly owned subsidiary
Joint venture
Strategic alliance (may also be nonequity)
Merger and acquisition (M&A)

committing a great amount of human or financial resources. If management does decide to export, it can choose between *direct* and *indirect* exporting. We can also consider the use of nonequity options such as turnkey projects, licensing, franchising, management contracts, and contract manufacturing.

indirect exporting
The exporting of goods and services through various types of home-based exporters

Indirect Exporting

Indirect exporting is simpler than direct exporting because it requires neither special expertise nor large cash outlays. Exporters based in the home country do the work. Exporters available are called a number of different things, including (1) *manufacturers' export agents,* who sell for the manufacturer, (2) *export commission agents,* who buy for their overseas customers, (3) *export merchants,* who purchase and sell for their own accounts, and (4) *international firms,* which use the goods overseas (mining, construction, and petroleum companies are examples).

Indirect exporters, however, pay a price for such service: (1) They pay a commission to the first three kinds of exporters; (2) foreign business can be lost if exporters decide to change their sources of supply; and (3) firms gain little experience from these transactions. This is why many companies that begin in this manner generally change to direct exporting.

direct exporting
The exporting of goods and services by the firm that produces them

Direct Exporting

To engage in **direct exporting,** the export business is handled by someone within the firm. The simplest arrangement is to give someone, often the sales manager, the responsibility for developing the export business. Domestic employees may handle the billing, credit, and shipping initially, and if the business expands, a separate export department may be set up. A firm that has been exporting to wholesale importers in an area and serving them with visits from either home office personnel or foreign-based sales representatives frequently finds that sales have grown to a point that will support a complete marketing organization.

sales company
A business established for the purpose of marketing goods and services, not producing them

Management may then decide to set up a **sales company** in the area. The sales company imports in its own name from the parent and invoices in local currency. It may employ the same channels of distribution, though the new organization may permit the use of a more profitable arrangement. This type of organization can grow quite large, often invoicing several millions of dollars annually. Before building a plant in Mexico, for many years Eastman Kodak imported and resold cameras and photographic supplies while doing a large business in local film developing. Many firms that began with local repair facilities later expanded to produce simple components. Gradually, they produced more of the product locally until, after a period of time, they were manufacturing all the components in the country.

Tips from Your Personal Global Mentor

Shinichi Iwamoto is president of Japan Telegaertner Ltd. (JTL), headquartered in Shibuya, Tokyo, Japan. Telegaertner Germany established JTL as a Japanese corporation in January 1995 to have a local-market sales presence for Japanese customers. The company serves customers desiring to use high-quality European optical communications products in the network environment (for Internet, broadband, fiber communication networks, FTTX, and wireless LANs) as Japanese demand increases for expansion into an advanced "next generation" communications system infrastructure. According to Shinichi, Japan Telegaertner Ltd. "provides products to comply with the specifications of the customer's requirement" beyond the range of the catalog. The company has a "Quick Response" mind-set to maintain customer satisfaction. In each country the Telegaertner distributor's goals are "cooperation and the offer of product service after the sale is done." Shinichi does business in Germany, Taiwan, China, Hong Kong, Australia, Singapore, Malaysia, Italy, and the United Kingdom and has traveled professionally to the USA, the United Kingdom, Germany, Italy, Switzerland, Taiwan, Hong Kong, China, and South Korea.

Shinichi's advice on how to get a job in international business:

- "It is difficult but important to find a good partner."

Shinichi's advice on succeeding in international business:

- "Though it is difficult, the effort to acquire a partner's knowledge [is] necessary. Don't neglect effort."
- "We must be able to gain credit so that a small company especially may succeed in the foreign country."
- "You must be able to understand and cope with the business transactions of the other country."
- "The ability to communicate in a foreign language/country and zeal are also important."

World Wide Resource:

www.telegaertner.co.jp/index-eng.html

www.telegartner.com

The Internet has made direct exporting much easier. For the beginning exporter, the possibility of making availability of your product or service known abroad is much increased. And although it is likely that a substantial international presence on the Internet will require a significant investment, the cost of trial is now very low.

Turnkey Projects

A *turnkey project* is an export of technology, management expertise, and in some cases capital equipment. The contractor agrees to design and erect a plant, supply the process technology, provide the necessary suppliers of raw materials and other production inputs, and then train the operating personnel. After a trial run, the facility is turned over to the purchaser.

The exporter of a turnkey project may be a contractor that specializes in designing and erecting plants in a particular industry, such as petroleum refining or steel production. It may also be a company in the industry that wishes to earn money from its expertise by delivering a plant ready to run rather than merely selling its technology. Another kind of supplier of a turnkey project is the producer of a factory.

One of the authors used to sell Goodyear latex to a U.S. manufacturer of paint driers. The manufacturer found it could lock in contracts to supply its products overseas by selling investors in developing countries a complete paint factory. It designed the plant, hired a contractor to erect it, trained the people to operate it, and provided ongoing technical assistance after the factory was delivered to the owners. The company also acted as a distributor for American producers of other inputs and manufacturers of paint-making machinery.

Licensing

Frequently, worldwide companies are called on to furnish technical assistance to firms that have sufficient capital and management strength. By means of a **licensing** agreement, one firm (the licensor) will grant to another firm (the licensee) the right to use any kind of expertise, such as manufacturing processes (patented or unpatented), marketing procedures, and trademarks for one or more of the licensor's products.

licensing
A contractual arrangement in which one firm grants access to its patents, trade secrets, or technology to another for a fee

The licensee generally pays a fixed sum when signing the licensing agreement and then pays a royalty of 2 to 5 percent of sales over the life of the contract (five to seven years with an option for renewal is one common way to structure such agreements). The exact amount of the royalty will depend on the amount of assistance given and the relative bargaining power of the two parties. In 2005, the total paid to American firms in royalties and license fees amounted to \$57.4 billion, versus only \$24.5 billion that U.S. firms paid out to foreign licensors.

mini MNE

>>Where Will Your Cargo End Up?

A new naval patrol ship drops anchor in front of cargo vessel in the bay of Jakarta, Indonesia, in August 2004. Thailand will join three other Southeast Asian navies in patrolling the vital Strait of Malacca shipping lane to combat piracy and terrorism, Indonesia's military chief said.

The 2003 release of the movie *Pirates of the Caribbean* pushed actor Johnny Depp's career into the stratosphere, and the arrival of the second installment in 2006 continued this ascent. Swashbuckling is back on the big screen.

But pirates are not just movie characters. The beginning exporter may find that real piracy is a threat to precious cargo. The danger of being a sailor is increasing because of piracy. The number of sailors killed on the high seas in early 2004 was nearly double the number for the same period in 2003.

Over 2,000 sailors were taken hostage in the 10 years from 1992 to 2002. Pirates today can be anyone from highly trained guerrillas to rogue military units (such as in Indonesia) to international criminal gangs or cartels. Pirates might belong to international terrorist organizations (particularly Abu Sayaf out of the Philippines, which has strong links to al Qaeda as well as Asian crime syndicates and the heroin trade), or they might simply be local down-and-out fishermen who see a rich prize steaming by and can't resist trying to capture it (poverty has driven many to piracy in the Caribbean, Nigeria, Bangladesh, and elsewhere). The main areas pirates seem to operate in are west of Indonesian waters to as far east as Taiwan and the Philippines (favoring the vital shipping lanes through the Malacca Strait and the dangerous waters of the South China Sea), as well as off the coast of Brazil, off the Somali coast of East Africa, and off West Africa. The vital Malacca Strait, in particular, is plagued by pirates, as $500 billion in goods passes through the strait annually, sometimes as many as 600 ships a day. The Strait, which in some places is less than a mile wide, is a target-rich environment for pirates and one that is not particularly well policed, although Indonesia, Malaysia, and Singapore signed an agreement in 2004 to coordinate patrols there.

Most ships are relatively defenseless: Crews are small and seldom carry weapons. They rely instead on antipiracy devices, such as carpet tacks spread on decks, fire hoses, deck patrols, dummies set at the railings at night, brilliant deck lights, and new satellite tracking devices that can help the International Maritime Bureau and local navies locate hijacked ships. But it is nearly impossible to keep determined pirates off a ship, and it is best for a crew not to resist (as in many cases pirates do not kidnap or kill). Some shipping companies that have the resources have employed more high-tech and expensive measures, such as wiring decks to administer lethal electric charges, closed-circuit TV cameras to detect someone slipping aboard a ship, and, particularly in the case of cruise ships, armed mercenaries (some cruise lines are known to use Nepalese Gurkhas).

Nor is piracy just financially motivated. According to Jonathan Pearce, "There is increasingly an *ideological slant* to modern piracy. In Indonesia, it appears that Islamic militants, like terrorists the world over, are mixing their religious fervour with the juicy temptations of crime. I am frankly surprised that there has not been more written on how easy it would be for a terrorist group to get hold of even a small-sized motor boat, fill it chockfull of explosives, sail it up the Thames, the Rhine or any other major river you can think of, and blow it up."

Source: Jonathan Pearce, "Modern Piracy on the High Seas," February 18, 2004, www.samizdata.net/blog/archives/005583.htm (July 28, 2004); "Pirates Attack LPG Tanker off Indonesia," *The Business Times*, July 28, 2004, http://business-times.asia1.com.sg/sub/shippingtimes/story/0,4574,123788,00.html (July 29, 2004); and "Review of Dangerous Waters," www.self-help-hub.com/Dangerous_Waters_Modern_Piracy_and_Terror_on_the_High_Seas_0452284139.html (July 29, 2004).

In the past, licensing was not a primary source of income for international firms. This changed in recent years, however, especially in the United States, because (1) the courts began upholding patent infringement claims more than they used to, (2) patent holders became more vigilant in suing violators, and (3) the federal government pressed foreign governments to enforce their patent laws.

This forced foreign companies to obtain licenses instead of making illegal copies. Texas Instruments (TI), for example, sued nine Japanese electronics manufacturers for using its

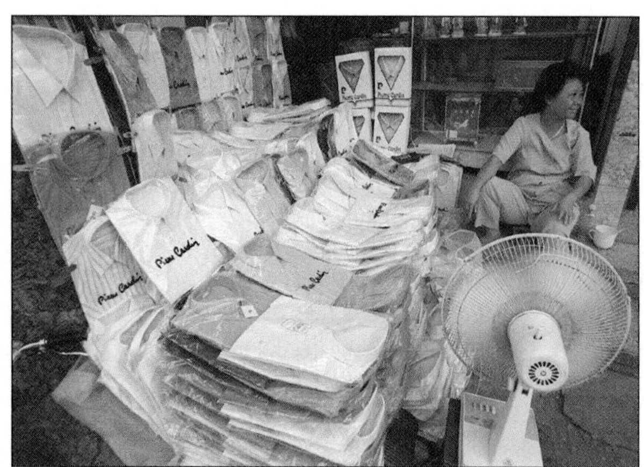

A woman sits beside her stall with Pierre Cardin shirts on a Hanoi street in June 2004. The shirts are made under French designer Pierre Cardin's firm license by a local garment factory. Each shirt sells for around 10 US dollars.

patented processes without paying licensing fees. The defendants have paid the company over $1 billion since 1986. Although the company does not publish its royalty receipts in its income statements, to give you an idea of the magnitude of the earnings from royalties associated with its 6,000 patents, TI announced 10-year agreements with both Hyundai Electronics and Samsung Electronics. Each of these agreements was projected to yield royalty payments of more than $1 billion to Texas Instruments.[2]

Technology is not the only thing that is licensed. In the fashion industry, a number of designers license the use of their names. Pierre Cardin, one of the largest such licensors, reported over 900 licenses in over 170 countries for everything from a broad range of clothing to such items as skis, frying pans, sardines, floor tiles, and silk cigarettes. These licenses have earned the company approximately $75 million annually. As Mr. Cardin himself commented, "If someone asked me to do toilet paper, I'd do it. Why not?"[3]

Are you giving Coca-Cola free advertising on your t-shirt? The company's manager for merchandise licensing expects the company to make millions from an agreement with the founder of Gloria Vanderbilt. He says the firm agreed to the arrangement because "clothes enhance our image. The money is not important."

Another industry, magazine publishing, is licensing overseas editions. For example, you can buy *Cosmopolitan* in over 100 countries, and it is printed in 32 different languages.[4] *Playboy* is available in 20 different international editions, in addition to the U.S. version.[5]

Despite the opportunity to obtain a sizable income from licensing, many firms, especially those that produce high-tech products, will not grant licenses. They fear that a licensee will become a competitor upon expiration of the agreement or that it will aggressively seek to market the products outside its territory. At one time, licensors routinely inserted a clause in the licensing agreement that prohibited exports, but most governments will not accept such a prohibition.

franchising
A form of licensing in which one firm contracts with another to operate a certain type of business under an established name according to specific rules

Franchising Firms have also gone overseas with a different kind of licensing—**franchising.** Franchising permits the franchisee to sell products or services under a highly publicized brand name and a well-proven set of procedures with a carefully developed and controlled marketing strategy. Of some 500 U.S. franchisers with approximately 50,000 outlets worldwide, fast-food operations (such as McDonald's, Kentucky Fried Chicken, Subway, and Tastee-Freeze) are the most numerous—McDonald's alone has approximately 30,000 restaurants in 120 countries outside the United States. Other types of franchisers are hotels (Hilton), business services (Muzak, The UPS Store), fitness (Curves, Jazzercise), home maintenance (ServiceMaster, Nationwide Exterminating), and automotive products (Midas).

management contract
An arrangement by which one firm provides management in all or specific areas to another firm

Management Contract The **management contract** is an arrangement under which a company provides managerial know-how in some or all functional areas to another party for a fee that typically ranges from 2 to 5 percent of sales. International companies make such contracts with (1) firms in which they have no ownership (examples: Hilton Hotel provides management for nonowned overseas hotels that use the Hilton name, and Delta provides management assistance to foreign airlines), (2) joint venture partners, and (3) wholly owned subsidiaries. The last arrangement is made solely for the purpose of allowing the parent to siphon off some of the subsidiary's profits. This becomes extremely important when, as in many foreign exchange–poor nations, the parent firm is limited in the amount of profits it can repatriate. Moreover, because the fee is an expense, the subsidiary receives a tax benefit.

contract manufacturing
An arrangement in which one firm contracts with another to produce products to its specifications but assumes responsibility for marketing

Contract Manufacturing International firms employ **contract manufacturing** in two ways. One way is as a means of entering a foreign market without investing in plant facilities. The firm contracts with a local manufacturer to produce products for it according to its specifications. The firm's sales organization markets the products under its own brand.

When Gates Rubber licensed its V belt technology to General Tire's Chilean plant, it drew up a novel licensing agreement that included contract manufacturing. General Tire was obliged to produce part of its output with the Gates label. Gates executives knew that in Chile, once General Tire began production, the government would stop the importation of all V belts, including theirs. Gates would gain in a number of ways: (1) It would earn a royalty on all belts made in Chile, (2) it would have belts made in Chile to Gates' specifications without making any investment in production facilities, and (3) competition from a dozen importers would be eliminated. There would be only one local competitor, General Tire. General Tire gained because it increased its product mix and offered another product to its present channels of distribution.

The second way is to subcontract assembly work or the production of parts to independent companies overseas. Although the international firm has no equity in the subcontractor, this practice does resemble foreign direct investment. When the international firm is the largest or only customer of the subcontractors, it has in effect created in another country a new company that generates employment and foreign exchange for the host nation. Frequently, the international firm will lend capital to the foreign contractor in the same way that a global or multinational firm will lend funds to its subsidiary. Because of these similarities, this practice is sometimes called *foreign direct investment without investment.*

EQUITY-BASED MODES OF ENTRY

When management does decide to make a foreign direct investment, it usually has several alternatives available, though not all of them may be feasible in a particular country. They are:

1. Wholly owned subsidiary
2. Joint venture
3. Strategic alliances

Wholly Owned Subsidiary

A company that wishes to own a foreign subsidiary outright may (1) start from the ground up by building a new plant (greenfield investment), (2) acquire a going concern, or (3) purchase its distributor, thus obtaining a distribution network familiar with its products. In this last case, of course, production facilities will typically have to be built.

Historically, firms making a foreign direct investment generally have preferred wholly owned subsidiaries, but they have not had a marked preference for any of the three means of obtaining them. However, this has not been the case for foreign investors in the United States, who have demonstrated a general preference for acquiring going concerns for the instant access to the market they provide. Moreover, they also have one less competitor after the purchase. Figure 16.1 shows the level of investments into the United States by foreign investors that was used for acquiring American firms versus creating new businesses. In 2005, 91 percent of the $86.8 billion that was invested was used for acquiring companies, versus only $7.6 billion that was spent to create new businesses. The average size of an acquisition in recent years has been about nine times that of an investment to create a new firm.

Of course, international companies do not use merger and acquisition (M&A) only to enter the United States. As Table 16.2 shows, cross-border M&As are a prominent characteristic of foreign direct investment across almost all nations of the world. In 2004, of total foreign direct investments of $648 billion, nearly 59 percent ($381 billion) was spent worldwide on cross-border M&As. The proportion of FDI that was accounted for by M&As is even higher in the developed countries. In 2004, over 83 percent ($316 billion) of the $380 billion in FDI inflows was associated with cross-border M&As.

Sometimes it is not possible to have a wholly owned foreign subsidiary. The host government may not permit it, the firm may lack either capital or expertise to undertake the investment alone, or there may be tax and other advantages that favor another form of investment, such as a joint venture.

joint venture
A cooperative effort among two or more organizations that share a common interest in a business enterprise or undertaking

Joint Venture

A **joint venture** may be (1) a corporate entity formed by an international company and local owners, (2) a corporate entity formed by two international companies for the purpose of doing business in a third market, (3) a corporate entity formed by a government

FIGURE 16.1

Investments into the United States for Acquisitions versus New Establishments, 1985–2005

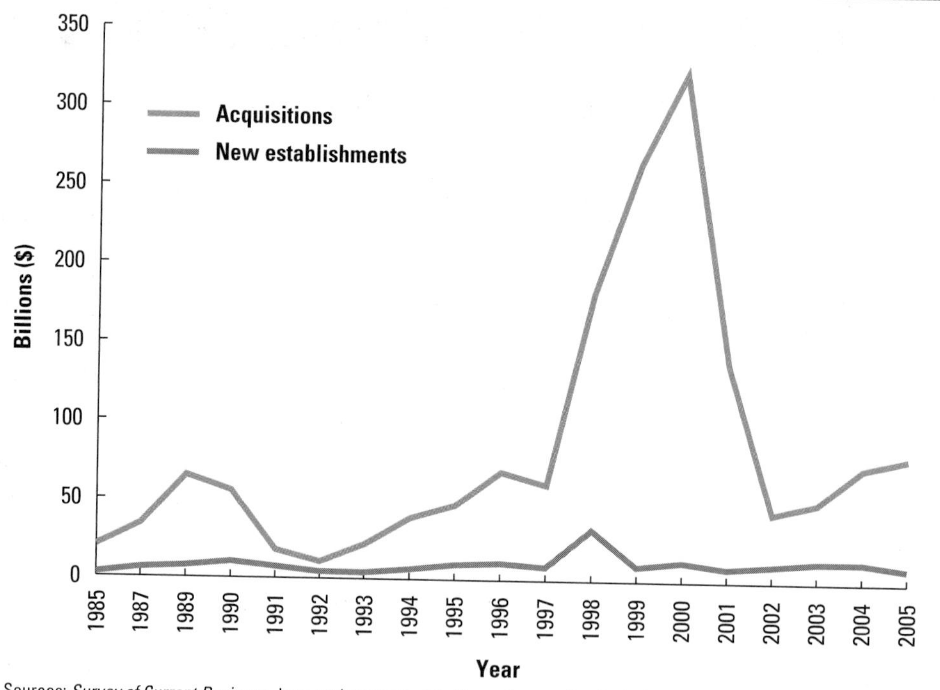

Sources: *Survey of Current Business*, June, various years, http://www.bea.gov/bea/pubs.htm (August 3, 2006).

agency (usually in the country of investment) and an international firm, or (4) a cooperative undertaking between two or more firms of a limited-duration project. Large construction jobs such as a dam or an airport are frequently handled by this last form.

Several years ago, Ford and Volkswagen formed a novel joint venture in which their operations in Argentina and Brazil were merged into a holding company, Autolatina, in an effort to eliminate the losses suffered by both. The joint venture, owned 51 percent by Volkswagen and 49 percent by Ford, assembled products based on VW and Ford designs, but both companies marketed the vehicles through their own distribution channels. Although sales subsequently reached $7.58 billion, the companies decided to terminate the operation. One industry expert says that Ford wanted to leave because Autolatina did not fit its new global strategy of having global vehicles. In a news release, the companies said the termination of the joint venture reflected "the necessity of the companies to make better use of the force and resources of their worldwide organizations."[6]

Sometimes, forming a joint venture can allow the partners to avoid making expensive and time-consuming investments of their own, while simultaneously helping to avoid a dangerous competition with another company.

When the CEO of General Mills decided to enter the European market, where a very tough rival, Kellogg, was entrenched, he knew it would be very expensive to set up manufacturing facilities and a huge marketing force. However, he knew that another food giant, Nestlé, the world's largest food company, had a famous name in Europe, a number of manufacturing plants, and a strong distribution system. It also lacked strong cereal brand names, something that General Mills, the number-two American cereal company, had. Just two weeks after the initial discussions, General Mills and Nestlé formed a joint venture: Cereal Partners Worldwide. General Mills provided the cereal technology, brand names, and cereal marketing expertise. Nestlé supplied its name, distribution channels, and production capacity. Cereal Partners Worldwide distributes cereals everywhere in the world except the United States and Canada. Within two years, the new company had already passed Quaker Oats, the longtime number two in Europe after Kellogg, and the company's profit margins have been increasing steadily. According to General Mills's vice chairman, building factories and distribution channels from scratch would have taken years: "We felt a sense of urgency." General Mills and PepsiCo won approval from the European Union to merge their European snack food businesses into what became the largest company in the European snack market.[7]

TABLE 16.2 Cross-Border Mergers and Acquisitions for Selected Countries and Regions, 1990–2005 (in billions of U.S. dollars)

	1990	1995	1996	1997	1998	1999	2000	2001	2002	2003	2004	2005
World												
Sales	151	187	227	305	532	766	1144	594	370	297	381	716
Purchases	151	187	227	305	532	766	1144	594	370	297	381	716
Developed countries												
Sales	134	164	1886	232	443	680	1056	496	308	244	316	598
Purchases	143	173	197	269	509	701	1088	534	341	257	340	626
Developing countries												
Sales	16	17	36	67	83	74	71	86	45	40	55	101
Purchases	7	13	30	35	22	63	49	56	28	31	40	83
United States												
Sales	55	53	68	82	210	252	324	185	73	70	82	106
Purchases	28	57	61	81	137	120	159	96	78	82	110	148
Canada												
Sales	6	12	11	9	16	24	77	42	16	5	20	27
Purchases	3	13	9	19	36	19	40	39	13	16	34	23
European Union												
Sales	62	75	82	115	188	357	587	213	194	126	179	429
Purchases	87	81	97	142	284	517	802	327	214	121	165	387
United Kingdom												
Sales	29	36	31	40	91	133	180	69	53	31	58	172
Purchases	26	30	36	58	95	214	382	112	69	57	47	91
France												
Sales	8	8	14	18	17	24	35	14	30	18	20	32
Purchases	22	9	15	21	31	89	159	59	34	9	15	46
Germany												
Sales	6	8	12	12	19	40	247	49	47	25	36	63
Purchases	7	19	18	13	67	86	59	57	45	20	19	42
Latin America & Caribbean												
Sales	10	9	21	41	64	42	45	36	22	12	25	31
Purchases	2	4	8	11	13	45	19	27	12	11	16	14
South, East, & South-East Asia												
Sales	4	6	10	19	16	28	21	33	17	20	24	45
Purchases	3	7	18	18	6	11	21	25	11	17	19	35
Africa												
Sales	1	1	2	4	3	3	3	16	5	6	5	11
Purchases	0	1	2	3	3	6	7	3	2	1	3	16

Note: *Sales* refers to the dollar volume of sales of companies from the specified nation to companies headquartered in other nations. *Purchases* refers to the dollar volume of purchases of foreign companies by companies headquartered in the specified nation.

Source: Various country fact sheets; *World Investment Report 2003*, United Nations Conference on Trade and Development (New York: United Nations, 2003); and *World Investment Report 2006*, United Nations Conference on Trade and Development (New York: United Nations, 2006).

When the government of a host country requires that companies have some local participation, foreign firms must engage in joint ventures with local owners to do business in that country. In some situations, however, a foreign firm will seek local partners even when there is no local requirement to do so.

Virgin, 7-Eleven, MTV, and others are all MVNOs. A Mobile Virtual Network Operator is a mobile phone operator that does not own its own network. Instead, MVNOs have arrangements with traditional mobile operators to buy minutes of use (MOU) for sale to their own customers. So Virgin Mobile USA actually uses the Sprint network: Sprint has the equipment, and Virgin adds cachet and the ability to target the youth market. America Movil of Mexico targets the Hispanic community in the United States. Big media brands such as Disney are also interested in the possibility of being MVNOs, since the ability to watch television is the next frontier in mobile phones.[8]

Strong Nationalism Strong nationalistic sentiment may cause the foreign firm to try to lose its identity by joining with local investors. Care must be taken with this strategy, however. Although a large number of people in many developing countries dislike multinationals for "exploiting" them, they still believe, often with good reason, that the products of the foreign companies are superior to those of purely national firms. One solution to this ambivalence has been to form a joint venture in which the local partners are highly visible, give it an indigenous name, and then advertise that a foreign firm (actually the partner) is supplying the technology. Even wholly owned subsidiaries have followed this strategy.

Expertise, Tax, and Other Benefits Other factors that influence companies to enter joint ventures are the ability to acquire expertise that is lacking, the special tax benefits some governments extend to companies with local partners, and the need for additional capital and experienced personnel.

Merck, one of the world's largest makers of ethical drugs, spent $313 million to acquire 50.5 percent of Banyu Pharmaceutical in Japan. Management had been dissatisfied with the performance of Merck's Japanese subsidiary in the world's second-largest ethical drug market. With this acquisition, the 600-person sales force of Merck-Japan was augmented by Banyu's 350 sales representatives. Merck's chairman said, "To bring new products effectively to market in Japan required a larger and more effective marketing organization. With a controlling interest in Banyu, I would hope for a better penetration of the Japanese market." Merck subsequently purchased the remainder of Banyu and made it a wholly owned company, increasing its ability to control and integrate its operations worldwide.

Some firms, as a matter of policy, enter joint ventures to reduce investment risk. Their strategy is to enter into a joint venture with either native partners or another worldwide company. Still others, such as Ford and Volkswagen, have joined together to achieve economies of scale. Incidentally, any division of ownership in a joint venture is possible unless there are specific legal requirements.

Disadvantages of Joint Ventures Although a joint venture arrangement offers the advantage of a smaller commitment of financial and managerial resources and thus less risk, there are some disadvantages for the foreign firm. One, obviously, is that profits must be shared. Furthermore, if the law allows the foreign investor to have no more than 49 percent participation, it may not have control. If the stock markets in these countries are small or nonexistent, it is generally impossible to distribute the shares widely enough to permit the foreign firm with its 49 percent to be the largest stockholder.

Lack of control over the joint venture is the reason why many companies resist making such arrangements. They feel that they must have tight control of their foreign subsidiaries to obtain an efficient allocation of investments and production and to maintain a coordinated marketing plan worldwide. For example, local partners might wish to export to markets that the global company serves from its own plants, or they might want to make the complete product locally when the global company's strategy is to produce only certain components there and import the rest from other subsidiaries.

In the recent past, numerous governments of developing nations passed laws requiring local majority ownership for the purpose of giving control of firms within their borders to their own citizens. Despite these laws, control with a minority ownership may still be feasible.

Control with Minority Ownership

There have been occasions when the foreign partner has ensured its control by taking 49 percent of the shares and giving 2 percent or more to its local law firm or another trusted national. Another method is to take in a local majority partner, such as a government agency, an insurance company, or a financial institution, that is content to invest merely for a return while leaving the venture's management to the foreign partner (this is called a "sleeping" partner).[9] If neither arrangement can be made, the foreign company may still control the joint venture, at least in the areas of major concern, by means of non-ownership-based control mechanisms such as a *management contract.*

Control of Joint Ventures through Management Contracts Management contracts, which were discussed earlier in this chapter under nonequity-based modes of entry, can enable the global partner to control many aspects of a joint venture even when holding only a minority position. If it supplies key personnel, such as the production and technical managers, the global company can be assured of the product quality with which its name may be associated. It may also be able to earn additional income by selling the joint venture inputs manufactured in the home plant. This is possible because the larger global company is more vertically integrated. A local paint factory, for example, might have to import certain semiprocessed pigments and driers that the foreign partner produces in its home country for domestic operations. If these can be purchased elsewhere at a lower price, the local majority could insist on other sources of supply.

This rarely happens, because the production and technical managers can argue that only inputs from their employer will produce a satisfactory product. They are the experts, and they generally have the final word.

Strategic Alliances

Faced with expanding global competition, the growing cost of research, product development, and marketing, and the need to move faster in carrying out their global strategies, many firms are forming **strategic alliances** with customers, suppliers, and competitors. In fact, consultants Ernst & Young in a 12-country study found that 65 percent of non-U.S. and 75 percent of U.S. companies are engaged in some form of strategic alliance.[10] The aim of these companies is to achieve faster market entry and start-up; gain access to new products, technologies, and markets; and share costs, resources, and risks. Alliances include various types of partnerships and may or may not include equity. Companies wanting to share technology may cross-license their technology (each will license its technology to the other). If their aim is to pool research and design resources, they may form an R&D partnership.

strategic alliances
Partnerships between competitors, customers, or suppliers that may take one or more of various forms, both equity and non equity

Intel, Motorola, and Advanced Micro Devices, three of the most prominent names in the computer chip industry, announced the formation of a not-for-profit company named EUV (Extreme Ultraviolet). Valued at $250 million, the project was the largest American commercial research partnership ever formed up to that time between industry and government. The three government laboratories will get the rights to use the resulting technologies as they wish, and the computer chip companies will have the right to use them to create faster chips. In 2005, EUV Technology's LPR1016 Reflectometer was awarded R&D Magazine's "R&D 100 Award" and heralded by the magazine's editors as "one of the 100 most technologically significant products introduced into the marketplace over the past year."[11]

Nokia, Ericsson, and Motorola (which at the time jointly accounted for over 75 percent of the world's mobile phone sales) formed a joint venture with Psion (then a major manufacturer of handheld computers). An objective of the venture was to license Psion's software and develop it into an operating system for the next generation of "smart" mobile phones that could link to the Internet and perform many of the functions of a palm-top computer. Motorola subsequently left the alliance, but Japan's Panasonic, Germany's Siemens, Korea's Samsung, and the Swedish-Japanese Sony Ericsson joint venture subsequently joined as equity partners in this alliance. The alliance is intended to enhance the competitiveness of the partners' future lines of wireless phones and other handheld devices as well as reduce their potential dependence on Microsoft and its Windows CE operating software.[12]

Alliances May Be Joint Ventures Other companies carry the cooperation further by forming joint ventures in manufacturing and marketing.

Nissan of Japan was a struggling automaker in the 1990s, with $20 billion in debt and declining market share. Renault of France decided to form an alliance with Nissan rather than merge the companies. Renault sent Carlos Ghosn to become CEO and president of Nissan. Ghosn's team developed and implemented an aggressive turnaround plan, one that has *provided benefits for both partners. They have leveraged their size and competencies to enter new markets more rapidly and with lower costs, since they do not need to build new plants. For example, Renault has used Nissan's assembly plants in Mexico, and Nissan uses Renault's Brazilian plant and distribution network. The alliance has increased sales, profitability, and market capitalization for both of the partners. In 2006, these two partners began discussing the possibility of an alliance with another ailing automaker, General Motors of the United States.*

Trading versus Pooling Alliances A useful distinction can be made between pooling and trading alliances. *Pooling alliances* are driven by similarity and integration, while *trading alliances* are driven by the logic of contributing dissimilar resources. These two types are typically different in their goals (common vs. compatible goals), optimal structures (many vs. few partners), and managerial challenges (low vs. high coordination needs).[13]

Alliances versus Mergers and Acquisitions Generally mergers and acquisitions are not considered alliances. However, both may be ways for firms to get their hands on new technology, by either acquiring or working with smaller, innovative firms.

The merger between Canadian brewer Molson and U.S. brewer Coors was analyzed as a union of two "struggling" mid-size beer companies. Sandoz, a Swiss pharmaceutical manufacturer, acquired Gerber for $3.7 billion in order to double the size of its food products division. Two years later, because of the increased global competition and the mounting cost of technology, Sandoz and Ciba Geigy, another Swiss drug company, merged to form Novartis, which then became the second-largest pharmaceutical firm in the world.

Future of Alliances Many alliances fail or are taken over by one of the partners. The existence of two or more partners, which are often competitors as well as partners and typically have differences in strategies, operating practices, and organizational cultures, often causes alliances to be difficult to manage, particularly in rapidly changing international competitive environments.[14] Alliances can also allow a partner to acquire the firm's technological or other competencies, and thereby raise important competitive concerns. The management consulting firm McKinsey & Co. surveyed 150 companies whose alliances with Japanese partners had been terminated. It found that three-quarters of the alliances had been taken over by Japanese partners.

Despite the challenges involved with forming and managing alliances successfully, there is no question that some alliances have accomplished what they set out to accomplish. CFM International, the alliance between General Electric and France's Snecma Moteurs, has been producing jet engines for more than two decades. Airbus Industrie, an alliance among British, French, German, and Spanish aircraft manufacturers, is now the world's largest commercial aircraft producer. It seems that alliances in their various forms will continue to be used as important strategic and tactical weapons, particularly given the financial, technological, political, and other challenges facing companies involved in increasingly competitive international marketplaces.

Channels of Distribution

Another entry mode decision to be made concerns channels of distribution. The channel system through which a product and its title pass from the producer to the user involves both controllable and uncontrollable variables. We shall discuss the uncontrollable aspects in this section, where we examine all the uncontrollable forces, and then return to them in Chapter 17, when we will consider them as controllable variables in the marketing mix.

How can a channel of distribution be both controllable and uncontrollable? It is controllable to the extent that the channel captain* is free to choose from the available channel members those that will enable the firm to reach its target market, perform the functions it requires at a reasonable cost, and permit it the amount of control it desires. If the company considers that the established channels are inadequate, it may assemble a different network.

*The *channel captain* is the dominant and controlling member of a channel of distribution.

For example, Coca-Cola became dissatisfied with its penetration in China and India of only large urban areas. It launched efforts to penetrate tiny villages. This required it to send dealers into farm villages to reach the tiniest retailers, including betel-nut vendors and repair shops, which sell small quantities of the diminutive (6.5-ounce, 200-milliliter) contoured glass bottles per year.[15]

International Channel-of-Distribution Members

The selection of channel-of-distribution members to link the producer with the foreign user depends, first of all, on the method of entry into the market. As was discussed earlier in this chapter, to supply a foreign market, a firm must either export to a foreign country or manufacture in it. If the decision is to export, the firm may do so *directly* or *indirectly*. Figure 16.2 shows that management has considerable latitude in forming the channels.

INDIRECT EXPORTING

For indirect exporting, a number of U.S.-based exporters (A) sell for the manufacturer, (B) buy for their overseas customers, (C) buy and sell for their own account, or (D) purchase on behalf of foreign middlemen or users. Although each type of exporter usually operates in the manner explained below, any given company may actually perform one or more of these functions.

A. Exporters That Sell for the Manufacturer

1. *Manufacturers' export agents* act as the international representatives for various noncompeting domestic manufacturers. They usually direct promotion, consummate sales, invoice, ship, and handle the financing. They commonly are paid a commission for carrying out these functions in the name of the manufacturer.
2. *Export management companies (EMCs)* act as the export department for several noncompeting manufacturers. They also transact business in the name of the manufacturer and handle the routine details of shipping and promotion. When the EMC works on a commission basis, the manufacturer invoices the customer directly and carries any financing required by the foreign buyer. However, most EMCs work on a buy-and-sell arrangement under which they pay the manufacturer, resell the product abroad, and invoice the customer directly. Depending on the arrangement, the EMC may act in the name of the firm it represents or in its own name.
3. *International trading companies* are similar to EMCs in that they also act as agents for some companies and as merchant wholesalers for others. This, however, is only part of their activities. They frequently export as well as import, own their own transportation facilities, and provide financing. W. R. Grace was at one time a major trading company that operated on the Pacific coast of South America. It owned sugar mills, large import houses, various manufacturing plants, a steamship company, and an airline. Although a number of European and American international trading companies have been in operation for centuries, certainly the most diversified and the largest are the Japanese **sogo shosha** (general trading companies).

   sogo shosha
   The largest of the Japanese general trading companies

   a. *Sogo shosha:* The general trading companies were originally established by the *zaibatsu*—centralized, family-dominated economic groups, such as Mitsui, Mitsubishi, and Sumitomo—to be the heart of their commercial operations. The general trading companies obtained export markets, raw materials, and technical assistance for other companies of the zaibatsu and also imported goods for resale. Included in the zaibatsu were not only banks and general trading companies but also transportation, insurance, and real estate companies and various manufacturing firms. Although the zaibatsu were forced to dissolve after World War II, the companies that had been their major components survived. Although unified ownership and management ceased after World War II, cross-shareholdings and collaborative relationships resulted in the close coordination of many business activities among the affiliated companies. In recent years, the level of cross-shareholdings and coordination has evidenced some decline, a development promoted by liberalization of

FIGURE 16.2

International Channels of Distribution

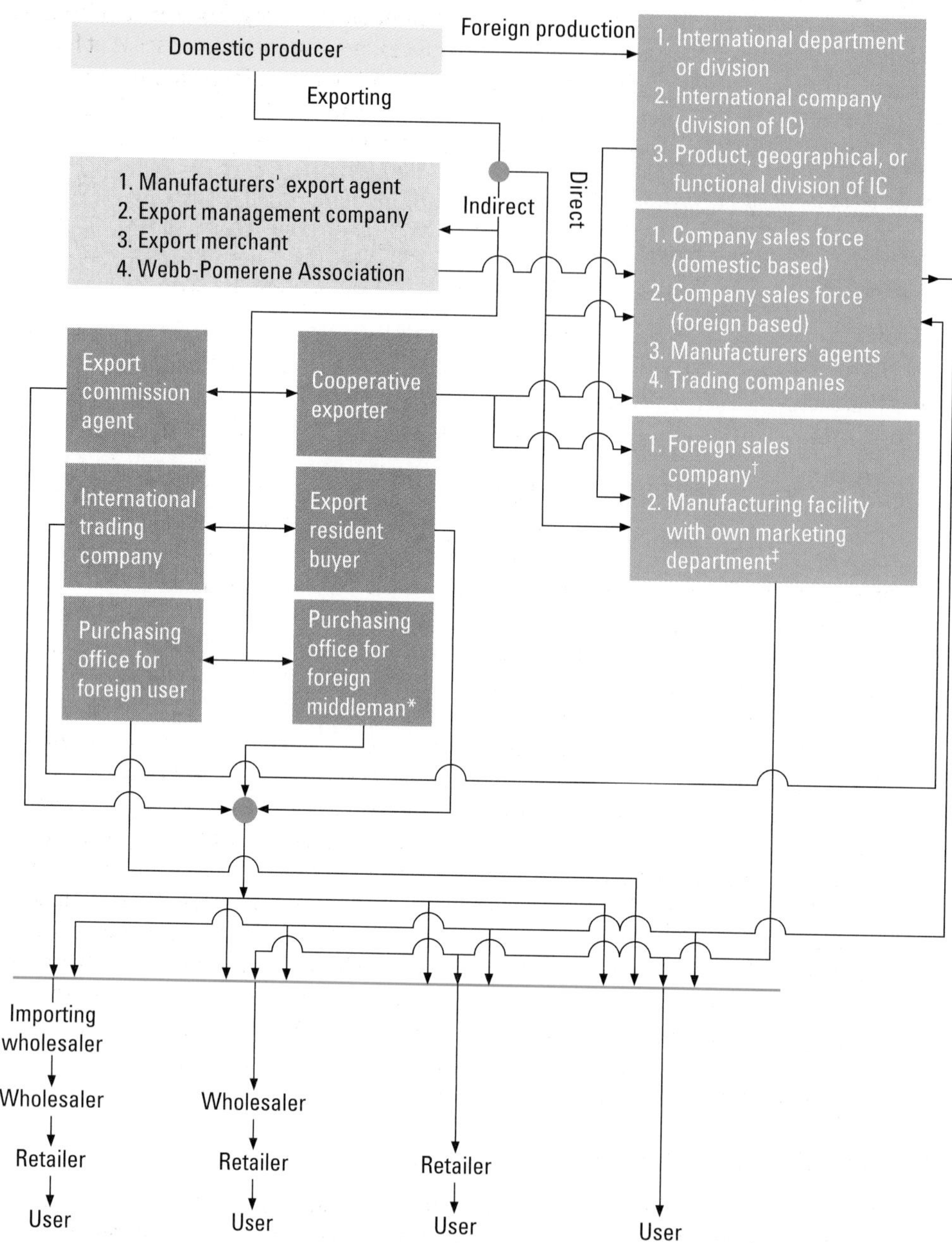

*There should be no direct connection between this category and the user. For simplification, a separate line to eliminate the user is not shown.

†Can be wholly owned or a joint venture. The foreign sales company may sell imports as well as local production from the licensee, contract manufacturer, or joint venture.

‡Can be wholly owned, a joint venture, or a licensee.

Source: From *World Development Report 1999/2000* by World Bank. Copyright by World Bank. Reproduced with permission of World Bank in the format textbook via Copyright Clearance Center.

financial markets, pressures for improved performance and corporate governance, and other factors.

In the 1980s, Japan had several thousand general trading companies. There are 20 general trading companies with more than 2,000 Japanese and overseas business locations. Their combined sales amount to over $1 trillion annually.[16] Mitsui & Co., for example, had sales of over $10.5 billion in 2006 and employed 6,089 employees in 172 offices worldwide.[17] Although Mitsui & Co. is huge, it is only one company in the Mitsui Group, which consists of several hundred companies encompassing a wide range of businesses, including steelmaking, shipbuilding, banking, insurance, paper, electronics, petroleum, warehousing, tourism, and nuclear energy. The Mitsui Group is not a legal entity but exists as an informal organization of major enterprises that have related interests and related financial structures. They cooperate in promoting the economic interests of group members. To ensure cooperation, the top executives of the major components of the former Mitsui zaibatsu meet for a weekly luncheon.

b. *Korean general trading companies:* Similar in scope to the Japanese sogo shosha, the Korean general trading companies are owned by the huge Korean diversified conglomerates called *chaebol.* They are responsible for a major part of Korea's exports and are also that country's principal importers of key raw materials.

c. *Export trading companies:* Impressed by the success of the Japanese, Taiwanese, and Korean general trading companies, the Reagan administration obtained passage of the Export Trading Company Act. This measure provided the mechanism for creating a new indirect export channel, the **export trading company (ETC).** For the first time in U.S. history, businesses were permitted to join together to export goods and services or offer export facilitating services without fear of violating antitrust legislation. Bank holding companies were also permitted to participate in ETCs. This has not only increased the ability of trading companies to finance export transactions but also given them access to the banks' extensive international information systems. Furthermore, because ETCs can import as well as export, they can engage in countertrade by selling their customers' products in other markets. Concerns raised within the World Trade Organization regarding the ETC Act led to a revocation in 2002 of many of the aspects of this act. Any potential exporter may apply to the Department of Commerce for a *certificate of review,* a legal document that provides immunity from state and federal antitrust prosecution and significant protection from certain private antitrust lawsuits. The certificate allows firms and associations to engage in joint price setting and joint bidding and gives them the freedom to divide export markets among companies and jointly own warranty, service, and training centers in various overseas markets. Note that the benefits of the ETC Act are available to *all exporters,* not just export trading companies. The Commerce Department has issued over 100 certificates covering 4,400 companies. Most companies that have received certificates are export intermediaries for two or more firms from the same industry, although now the majority of the certificates are being issued to groups of companies. For example, the National Tooling and Machining Association is a national trade association with 3,150 members. The American Film Marketing Association (170 members) is another example.

export trading company (ETC)
A firm established principally to export domestic goods and services and to help unrelated companies export their products

B. Exporters That Buy for Their Overseas Customers

1. *Export commission agents* represent overseas purchasers, such as import firms and large industrial users. They are paid a commission by the purchaser for acting as resident buyers in industrialized nations.

C. Exporters That Buy and Sell for Their Own Account

1. *Export merchants* purchase products directly from the manufacturer and then sell, invoice, and ship them in their own names so that foreign customers have no direct dealings with the manufacturer, as they do in the case of an export agent. If export merchants have an exclusive right to sell the manufacturer's products in an overseas territory, they are generally called *export distributors.* Some EMCs may actually be export distributors for a number of their clients.
2. Sometimes called *piggyback exporters,* **cooperative exporters** are established international manufacturers that sell the products of other companies in foreign markets along with their own. Carriers (exporters) may purchase and resell in their own name, or they may work on a commission basis. Carriers, like EMCs, serve as the export departments for the firms they represent. Large companies, such as General Electric and Borg-Warner, have been acting as piggyback exporters for years.

cooperative exporters
Established international manufacturers that export other manufacturers' goods as well as their own

3. *Webb-Pomerene Associations* are organizations of competing firms that have joined together for the sole purpose of export trade. At this time, there are fewer than 25 such associations. The Motion Picture Association (MPA), which is the legacy of a Webb-Pomerene Association, is the primary organization combating movie piracy around the world.

D. Exporters That Purchase for Foreign Users and Middlemen

1. Large foreign users, such as mining, petroleum, and international construction companies, buy for their own use overseas. The purchasing departments of all the worldwide companies are continually buying for their foreign affiliates, and both foreign governments and foreign firms maintain purchasing offices in industrialized countries.
2. *Export resident buyers* perform essentially the same functions as export commission agents. However, they are generally more closely associated with a foreign firm. They may be appointed as the official buying representatives and paid a retainer, or they may even be employees. This is in contrast to the export commission agent, who usually represents a number of overseas buyers and works on a transaction-by-transaction basis.

DIRECT EXPORTING

If the firm chooses to do its own exporting, it has four basic types of overseas middlemen from which to choose: (a) manufacturers' agents, (b) distributors, (c) retailers, and (d) trading companies. These may be serviced by sales personnel who either travel to the market or are based in it. If the sales volume is sufficient, a foreign sales company may be established to take the place of the wholesale importer. The manufacturing affiliates of most worldwide companies also import from home country plants or from other subsidiaries products that they themselves do not produce.

manufacturers' agents
Independent sales representatives of various noncompeting suppliers

a. **Manufacturers' agents** are residents of the country or region in which they are conducting business for the firm. They represent various noncompeting foreign suppliers, and they take orders in those firms' names. Manufacturers' agents usually work on a commission basis, pay their own expenses, and do not assume any financial responsibility. They often stock the products of some of their suppliers, thus combining the functions of agent and wholesale distributor.

distributors
Independent importers that buy for their own account for resale

b. **Distributors,** or *wholesale importers,* are independent merchants that buy for their own account. They import and stock for resale. Distributors are usually specialists in a particular field, such as farm equipment or pharmaceuticals. They may be given exclusive representation and, in return, agree not to handle competing brands. Distributors may buy through manufacturers' agents when the exporter employs them, or they may send their orders directly to the exporting firm. Instead of hiring manufacturers' agents, exporters may employ their own salespeople to cover the territory and assist the distributors. For years, worldwide companies such as Caterpillar and Goodyear have utilized field representatives in export territories.

c. *Retailers,* especially of consumer products, are frequently direct importers. Contact on behalf of the exporter is maintained either by a manufacturers' agent or by the exporter's sales representative based in the territory or traveling from the home office.

trading companies
Firms that develop international trade and serve as intermediaries between foreign buyers and domestic sellers and vice versa

d. **Trading companies** are relatively unknown in the United States but are extremely important importers in other parts of the world. In a number of African nations, trading companies not only are the principal importers of goods ranging from consumer products to capital equipment but also export such raw materials as ore, palm oil, and coffee. In addition, they operate department stores, grocery stores, and agencies for automobiles and farm machinery. Although many trading companies are large, they are in no way comparable in either size or diversification (products and functions performed) to the sogo shosha. Trading companies in Brazil, Korea, Taiwan, and Malaysia are a recent development. They are of little use to exporters to those countries inasmuch as their primary function is to promote their own country's exports. On the other hand, the English *importer/factor,* which

WORLD view   

Piracy as Product Diffusion

Ash, Pikachu, and Misty (background) in 4Kids Entertainment's animated adventure "Pokemon3," distributed by Warner Bros. Pictures.

Although we earlier discussed the threats to shipping from pirates, piracy can also contribute to the global spread of a product—sort of market entry by accident.

Japanese *anime* has global sales of $80 billion, 10 times what it was a decade ago. Japanese Prime Minister Junichiro Koizumi has called it the "savior of Japanese culture." Disney has purchased the American right to a number of anime films. The Cartoon Network shows several anime series as part of its Adult Swim programming. TOKOPOP will publish 400 volumes of translated Japanese comics for U.S. consumption.

Two decades ago there was no U.S. market for Japanese anime. The change occurred not through a concerted push from Japanese media companies but in response to American fans who pulled anime in.

Although Japanese anime was exported to the West in the early 1960s, some saw it as inappropriate for American children and by the late 1960s it was available only in Japanese overseas communities. The advent of the video tape recorder allowed dubbing and sharing, and soon anime fans were contacting both Japanese and G.I.s stationed in Japan for tapes. Fan clubs emerged as essentially lending libraries and dubbing centers. In the late 1980s and 1990s amateurs began dubbing these tapes into English: This "fansubbing" spread. In the early 1990s large-scale anime conventions brought artists and distributors from Japan, who were astonished to see this thriving content they had never marketed. They returned to Japan ready to service this market commercially. The fan clubs continued their operations, but stopped fansubbing and distributing titles as they became commercially available.

This "piracy" is now supported by the commercial industry, which in fact sponsors events where fan-made *manga*,* highly derivative of the commercial product, is sold. The media companies use these events to publicize their own releases, spot new talent, and monitor shifts in audience tastes.

The idea that some piracy actually helps to diffuse new products is not limited to Japanese anime. It has also been tested for software.

Careful analysis actually found that software piracy is not necessarily harmful to a software firm seeking to launch a new product, since it establishes initial adopters (pirates) and speeds up software diffusion: These initial adopters then influence others to buy the product. Generally speaking, however, as the product diffuses in the market, the level of protection against piracy should be increased.

**Anime* in Japan refers to an animated film, and *manga* is a printed cartoon.

Source: Henry Jenkins, "When Piracy Becomes Promotion," *MIT Technology Review*, August 10, 2004; Ernan Haruvy, Vijay Mahajan, and Ashutosh Prasad, "The Effect of Piracy on the Market Penetration of Subscription Software," *Journal of Business* 77 (April 2004), pp. S81–S108; and Ashutosh Prasad and Vijay Mahajan, "How Many Pirates Should a Software Firm Tolerate? An Analysis of Piracy Protection on the Diffusion of Software," *International Journal of Research in Marketing* 20, no. 4 (2003), pp. 337–53.

performs some of the functions of a trading company, is of value to exporters. It will, on behalf of foreign manufacturers, warehouse goods, price them for the local market, deliver anywhere in the country, and factor (buy the seller's accounts receivable). The exporter must still develop the sales, however. Another form of trading company is owned by the state. State trading companies handle exports and imports in North Korea and Cuba, and in noncommunist nations where an industry is a government monopoly, such as petroleum in Mexico, exporters or their agents must deal with these government-owned entities.

Wholesale Institutions

In developed nations, the marketer will be able to select wholesalers that take title to the goods (merchant wholesalers, rack jobbers, drop shippers, cash-and-carry wholesalers, truck jobbers) and those that do not (agents, brokers). However, just as in the United States, as retailers have become larger, they have sought to bypass wholesalers and purchase directly from local manufacturers and foreign suppliers.

Diversity of Wholesaling Structures Generally, wholesaling and retailing structures vary with the stage of economic development. In developing countries that depend on imports to supply the market, the importing wholesalers are large and few in number and the channels are long. Historically, many of the importers were trading companies formed by international companies to import the machinery and supplies required by their local operation and to export raw materials for use in the home country plants. To obtain distributor prices, they were required by their suppliers to sell to other customers as well. Some of these operations became extremely diversified, owning automobile and industrial machinery agencies, grocery stores, and department stores. They literally could and did supply a complete city and an industry with all of its requirements.

As colonies became nations, the new governments began applying pressure to convert these trading companies to local ownership. Furthermore, these countries were industrializing, which meant more goods were being produced locally and fewer goods were being imported. Many of the local manufacturers were able to take control of the channels from the import jobber. To obtain more extensive market coverage, they canceled the importing wholesaler's exclusivity and gave their product lines to new wholesalers, many of which were formed by ex-employees of the importer. As economic development continued, markets broadened, permitting greater specialization by more and smaller wholesalers.

We began the chapter with a discussion of whether being first in the market meant profitability, and discovered that the answer is, "It depends." Whether one is first, an early follower, or a late entrant, there are still chances for success.

Summary

Explain the international market entry methods.

Methods of entering foreign markets can be assessed as nonequity- or equity-based. Nonequity-based modes of entry include indirect or direct exporting, turnkey projects, licensing, franchising, management contracts, and contract manufacturing. Equity-based modes of market entry include wholly owned subsidiaries, joint ventures, and strategic alliances.

Discuss the debate on whether being a market pioneer or a fast follower is most useful.

A firm can succeed from any position, as the examples illustrate. In general, however, a follower is more likely to succeed if it has lots of resources. Smaller, less-well-financed followers are less likely to be successful.

Identify two different forms of piracy and discuss which might be helpful and harmful to firms doing international business.

Piracy on the high seas is clearly harmful to the exporter and the importer, as well as to members of the ship crews. On the other hand, piracy as a form of distribution may or may not be harmful to the parties involved.

Discuss the channel members available to companies that export indirectly or directly or manufacture overseas.

Channel members are available to those who (1) indirectly export or are exporters that sell for manufacturers, (2) buy for their overseas customers, or (3) purchase for foreign users or middlemen. Direct exporters use manufacturers' agents, distributors, retailers, and trading companies. Firms that manufacture overseas generally have the same kinds of channel members as they have in their domestic market, although their manner of operation may be different from what they are accustomed to.

Key Words

indirect exporting (p. 427)
direct exporting (p. 427)
sales company (p. 427)
licensing (p. 428)
franchising (p. 430)
management contract (p. 430)
contract manufacturing (p. 430)
joint venture (p. 431)
strategic alliances (p. 435)
sogo shosha (p. 437)
export trading company (ETC) (p. 439)
cooperative exporters (p. 439)
manufacturers' agents (p. 440)
distributors (p. 440)
trading companies (p. 440)

Questions

1. What are the methods by which a firm can enter foreign markets?
2. What two forms of piracy are discussed in the chapter? Which one is never beneficial to an exporter? Which one might be beneficial?
3. What is the difference, if any, between a joint venture and a strategic alliance?
4. Under what conditions might a company prefer a joint venture to a wholly owned subsidiary when making a foreign investment?
5. Why would the foreign partner in a joint venture wish to have a management contract with the local partner?
6. Why would a global firm or multinational require that a wholly owned foreign subsidiary sign a management contract when it already owns the subsidiary?
7. What is indirect exporting, and how does it differ from direct exporting? What are the main types of indirect exporting, and what are the primary strengths and weaknesses of each type?
8. How do sogo shosha differ from their American counterparts?
9. What entry mode do fashion designers such as Pierre Cardin, and some high-tech firms like Texas Instruments, share in common?

Research Task

globalEDGE globalEDGE.msu.edu

Use the globalEDGE™ site (http://globalEDGE.msu.edu) to complete the following exercises:

1. Your firm is a small international business (IB) consulting services provider that has thus far only had clients based in the United States. However, a recent internal initiative is encouraging the internationalization of your firm. Each IB consultant will be traveling for 50 to 75 percent of all work assignments. In developing your strategic plan for the next five years, you want to analyze future travel patterns. For this analysis, you wish to identify the 25 largest passenger airports in the world. A friend mentions to you that a Web site called *Geohive* lists this information. Find the list, and identify which countries are represented in this list. Do you see any patterns?
2. Your firm is a large conglomerate, involved in every business sector, that until now has focused exclusively on the domestic market of the United States. However, given a recent economic boom internationally, your firm has decided to assess which countries might be suitable for exporting its many products and services. Your manager recently stated that the five countries you must focus on for this preliminary analysis are Brazil, China, Russia, South Africa, and the United Arab Emirates. A colleague has indicated that a database of *Country Market Analysis* reports prepared by the WTO International Trade Centre might assist you. Assess the national import profile of each country, and include the following in your report for all five countries: (1) the highest-ranking identifiable category of products or services and (2) the top two countries from which these products or services are currently imported.

Method of Entry—The McGrew Company Minicase 16.1

The McGrew Company, a manufacturer of peanut combines, has for years sold a substantial number of machines in Brazil. However, a Brazilian firm has begun to manufacture them, and McGrew's local distributor has told Jim Allen, the president, that if McGrew expects to maintain its share of the market, it will also have to manufacture locally. Allen is in a quandary. The market is too good to lose, but McGrew has had no experience with foreign manufacturing operations. Because Brazilian sales and repairs have been handled by the distributor, no one in McGrew has had any firsthand experience in that country.

Allen has made some rough calculations that indicate the firm can make money by manufacturing in Brazil, but the firm's lack of marketing expertise in the country troubles him. He calls in Joan Beal, the export manager, and asks her to prepare a list of all the options open to McGrew, with their advantages and disadvantages. Allen also asks Beal to indicate her preference.

1. Assume you are Joan Beal. Prepare a list of all the options, and give the advantages and disadvantages of each.
2. Which of the options would you recommend?
3. Assuming that the president's calculations are correct and that a factory to produce locally the number of machines that McGrew now exports to Brazil will offer a satisfactory return on investment, what special information about Brazil will you want to gather?

17 Export and Import Practices

Containers in the shipping yard at the Port of Hamburg, Germany

The fact that trade protection hurts the economy of the country that imposes it is one of the oldest but still most startling insights economics has to offer. The idea dates back to the origin of economic science itself. Adam Smith's *The Wealth of Nations,* which gave birth to economics, already contained the argument for free trade: by specializing in production instead of producing everything, each nation would profit from free trade.

Jagdish Bagwati, professor, Columbia University,
The Concise Encyclopedia of Economics

How a Box Transformed the World

Fifty years ago, on April 26, a war-surplus oil tanker, the *Ideal-X,* left port in Newark, New Jersey, with a steel frame welded to its deck. The frame held aluminum containers that were off-loaded five days later in Houston, onto trucks. That was the beginning of a revolution in shipping that has made our world smaller. Containerization drastically reduced shipping costs and allowed manufacturers to leave the waterfronts and move, literally, offshore, to take advantage of cheap labor to produce goods that previously could not be exported profitably.

Malcolm McLean, a North Carolina farm boy turned trucker, had hauled cotton bales to Hoboken, where he had to sit around a whole day for his shipment to be unloaded. He waited, and he watched the process. It was slow, hard labor and gave rise to pilferage, as well. His idea was to detach the truck bodies and ship them on boats made to hold them.

No one understood how the box would change everything having to do with export and import, ships and ports, goods traded, trade routes, and labor unions. Marc Levinson, author of *The Box: How the Shipping Container Made the World Smaller and the World Economy Bigger,* calls containerization a monument to the most powerful law in economics, the law of unintended consequences. ■

Source: Wally Bock, "A Man Who Changed the World," *Monday Memo,* June 11, 2001, www.mondaymemo.net/010611feature.htm (August 1, 2006); Marc Levinson, *The Box: How the Shipping Container Made the World Smaller and the World Economy Bigger* (Princeton University Press, 2006); Marc Levinson, "Unforeseen Consequence: How a Box Transformed the World," *Financial Times,* April 25, 2006, p. 17.

CONCEPT PREVIEWS

After reading this chapter, you should be able to:

explain why firms export and the three challenge areas of exporting

identify the sources of export counseling and support

discuss the meaning of the various terms of sale

identify some sources of export financing

describe the activities of a foreign freight forwarder

outline the export documents required

identify import sources

explain the Harmonized Tariff Schedule of the United States (HTSUSA)

Export—Why and Why Not?

With the added, complex dimensions of doing business overseas, why do companies become involved in exporting instead of staying in the home country? There are a number of reasons, all of which are linked to the business goal to increase profits and sales or to protect them from being eroded. Here are the most common reasons companies export:

- To serve markets where the firm has no or limited production facilities. Many large multinationals, like DuPont, supply some of their foreign markets by exporting because no firm, no matter how large, can afford to manufacture a complete product line in every country where its goods are sold. Markets without local factories are supplied through exports from the home country or from a foreign affiliate. In markets of sufficient size to justify the production of some but not all of the product mix, the affiliate will supplement local production with imports. A car plant in a developing nation may produce the least expensive cars and import luxury models. Also, the more vertically integrated plants may export semifinished products that are inputs for the less integrated subsidiaries.
- To satisfy a host government's requirement that the local subsidiary have exports. Governments of developing nations often require that the local affiliate export, and some require that it earn sufficient foreign exchange to cover the cost of its imports. This is why Ford located a radio plant in Brazil that exports to Ford's European assembly plants.[1]
- To remain price-competitive in the home market. Many firms import labor-intensive components produced in their foreign affiliates, or export components for assembly in countries where labor is less expensive and import the finished product.
- To test foreign markets and foreign competition inexpensively. This is a common strategy for firms that want to test a product's acceptance before investing in local production facilities. Exports may also enable firms to test market strategies and make adjustments with reduced risk in a smaller market. If the strategy or product fails, the firm can withdraw without having a costly and sometimes damaging failure to the entire firm. There is, however, a downside to this strategy: Whatever the firm does in the foreign market may be seen by a competitor. This is especially true for large, global firms such as Unilever and Procter & Gamble (P&G). Former P&G CEO Edwin Artzt changed the company's strategy for introducing new products. Rather than postpone a global launch until the firm accumulated marketing experience in a country, P&G began to introduce products on a worldwide basis early in their development to avoid giving competitors time to react in other markets.
- To meet actual or prospective customer requests for the firm to export. This type of accidental exporting is fairly common. A foreign buyer often will search for something it cannot find locally by consulting the Internet or the *Thomas Register,* a publication listing American producers for hundreds of products.
- To offset cyclical sales in the domestic market.
- To achieve additional sales, which allow the firm to use excess production capacity to lower per-unit fixed costs.
- To extend a product's life cycle by exporting to currently unserved markets where the product will be at the introduction stage of the life cycle.
- To respond strategically to foreign competitors that are in the firm's home market by entering their home market.
- To achieve the success the firm's management has seen others achieve by exporting.
- To improve the efficiency of manufacturing equipment, which usually works better at or near full capacity.

WORLD view   

The 12 Most Common Mistakes Made by New Exporters

1. **Failure to obtain qualified export counseling and to develop a master international strategy and marketing plan before starting an export business.** To be successful, a firm must first figure out what its goals and objectives are and develop a plan for how they will be achieved. Unless the firm is fortunate enough to possess a staff with considerable export expertise, taking this crucial first step may require qualified outside guidance.
2. **Insufficient commitment by top management to overcome the initial difficulties and financial requirements of exporting.** Establishing a firm in foreign markets usually takes more time than doing so in domestic ones. Although the early delays and costs involved in exporting may seem difficult to justify compared to the situation in established domestic markets, the exporter should take a long-term view of this process and carefully monitor international marketing efforts through these early difficulties. If a good foundation is laid for export business, the benefits derived should eventually outweigh the investment.
3. **Insufficient care in selecting overseas sales representatives and distributors.** The selection of each foreign distributor is crucial. The complexity introduced by overseas communication and transportation requires that international distributors act with greater independence than do their domestic counterparts. Since a new exporter's history, trademarks, and reputation may be unknown in the foreign market, foreign customers may buy on the strength of a distributor's reputation. A firm should therefore conduct a personal evaluation of the personnel handling its account, the distributor's facilities, and the management methods employed.
4. **Chasing orders from around the world instead of establishing a basis for profitable operations and orderly growth.** If exporters expect distributors to promote their accounts actively, the distributors must be trained and assisted and their performance must be monitored continually. This may require a company executive located in the distributor's geographic region. New exporters may want to concentrate their efforts in one or two geographic areas until they have sufficient business to support a company representative. Then, while this initial core area is expanded, the exporter can move into the next targeted geographic area.
5. **Neglecting export business when the home market booms.** Often companies turn to exporting when business falls off in their home market. When domestic business starts to boom again, they neglect their export trade. Such neglect can harm the profits and motivation of a company's overseas representatives, strangle its own export trade, and leave the firm without recourse when domestic business falls off again.
6. **Failure to treat international distributors and customers on an equal basis with their domestic counterparts.** Often, companies carry out institutional advertising campaigns, special discount offers, sales incentive programs, special credit term programs, warranty offers, and so forth, in the home market but fail to make similar assistance available to their international distributors and customers. This is a mistake that can destroy the vitality of overseas marketing efforts.
7. **Assuming that a given market technique and product will automatically be successful in all countries.** What works in one market may not work in others. Each market has to be treated separately until the company has sufficient knowledge about its export markets to generalize about them.
8. **Unwillingness to modify products to meet regulations or cultural preferences of other countries.** Local safety codes and import restrictions cannot be ignored, nor can cultural preferences. If necessary modifications are not made at the factory, the distributor must make them, often at greater cost and perhaps not as well.
9. **Failure to provide service, sales, and warranty information in locally understood languages.** Although many people may speak English, assume that they will want to read instructions and product information in their own language. This holds for customers and distributors.
10. **Failure to consider the use of an export management company.** If a firm decides it cannot afford its own export department, it should consider the possibility of using an export management company (EMC).
11. **Failure to consider licensing or joint venture agreements.** Import restrictions in some countries, insufficient personnel or financial resources, or an overly limited product line can cause many companies to dismiss international marketing as unfeasible. Yet many products that compete on a national basis in a home market can be marketed successfully in many markets of the world through licensing or joint venture arrangements.
12. **Failure to provide readily available servicing for the product.** A product without the necessary service support can acquire a bad reputation in a short period, potentially preventing further sales.

Source: Adapted from *Small Business Success, Vol. 1, Pacific Bell Directory*, in cooperation with the U.S. Small Business Administration, 2006.

The two major reasons U.S. firms give for not exporting are their preoccupation with the vast American market and a reluctance to become involved in a new, unknown, and therefore risky operation. When managers of nonexporting firms are probed further on why they are not active in international markets, they generally mention the following three areas in which they lack knowledge: locating foreign markets, payment and financing procedures, and export procedures.

Considerable assistance is available from the federal and state departments of commerce, banks, the Small Business Administration, small business development centers, and private consultants, to mention a few sources. Too few managers are taking advantage of this assistance. Below we examine each of the areas that hinder managers in developing exporting capability: locating foreign markets, payment and financing procedures, and export procedures.

Locating Foreign Markets and Developing a Plan

The first step in locating foreign markets is to determine whether a market exists for the firm's products. The initial screening step described in Chapter 16 indicated a procedure to follow that will pose no problem for an experienced market analyst who is well acquainted with the available sources of information and assistance. However, newcomers to exporting, especially smaller firms, may still be at a loss as to how to begin their foreign market research. For them, a number of helpful export assistance programs are available. Once the potential exporter has established that there may be a market for the firm's products, it's time to draft the export marketing plan.

SOURCES OF EXPORT INFORMATION, COUNSELING, AND SUPPORT

Export.gov is the U.S. government's trade portal, established by the Department of Commerce. It brings together resources on exporting from a number of government agencies, including the U.S. International Trade Administration, U.S. Commercial Service, Department of Commerce, Export-Import Bank, Agency for International Development, Small Business Administration, Department of State, and Overseas Private Investment Corporation. See www.export.gov/exportcounseling.html. A good place to start is at the Trade Information Center, the first stop for information about all federal export assistance programs as well as country and regional market information. Support is available by phone or e-mail. The Trade Information Center Web site is www.ita.doc.gov/td/tic. There you will find links to government export programs, trade promotion events, and trade lead information.

For firms that already are exporting, the International Trade Administration (ITA) offers a wide range of export promotion activities that include export counseling, analysis of foreign markets, assessment of industry competitiveness, and development of market opportunities and sales representation through export promotion events. Three departments in ITA work together to provide these services:

1. *Market Access and Compliance (MAC):* MAC specialists seek to open foreign markets to American products by developing strategies to overcome obstacles faced by U.S. businesses in foreign countries and regions. They also monitor foreign country compliance with trade agreements.

2. *Trade Development:* This department promotes the trade interests of American industries and offers information on markets and trade practices worldwide. Its industry desk officers work by sector with industry representatives and associations to identify trade opportunities by product or service, industry sector, and market. They also develop export marketing plans and programs. Trade Development experts also conduct executive trade missions, trade fairs, and marketing seminars.

3. *U.S. Commercial Service (USCS):* The USCS has commercial officers working in 107 U.S. domestic locations and 150 countries who can provide background information on foreign companies and assist in finding foreign representatives, conducting market research, and identifying trade and investment opportunities for American firms. The district offices also conduct export workshops and keep businesspeople

BUILDING YOUR GLOBAL RÉSUMÉ — Consider a Job in Import–Export Management for Entry into International Business

With the growing volume of shipments between countries daily, there is demand for people to work in entry-level positions in import–export management. Managing the movement of products into and out of countries is a fundamental task in international trade, and job opportunities exist in every type of business dealing with foreign customers or suppliers and ranging in size from small businesses to Fortune 500 companies. To succeed in import–export management, you will need to know about the fundamentals of business, customer service, international business considerations, purchasing, marketing, fundamental import–export operations, documentation for licenses, bills of lading, insurance, domestic and foreign country customs laws, and international trade regulations for the countries in which the importer–exporter is dealing. Language skills are valuable. Entry-level salaries are in the range of $31,000 to $42,000, midlevel salaries are between $46,000 and $64,000, and salaries for top-level import–export managers range from $69,000 to more than $96,000, based on experience. Here are places where import–export management jobs can be found:

- Import–export houses
- International trading companies
- Manufacturers of all sizes that trade internationally
- Wholesalers importing or exporting products
- Retail chains (positions at the corporate level)
- Purchasing departments for international companies
- Customhouse brokers
- Freight forwarders
- Supply chain management organizations
- Airlines and ocean shipping firms

To advance your career and move into higher levels of import–export management, you may want to earn the U.S. Customs broker's license.

World Fact: According to the U.S. Census Bureau, the following 10 countries are the United States' largest trading partners (listed in rank order of largest to smallest in terms of import and export dollars): (1) Canada, (2) Mexico, (3) Japan, (4) China, (5) Germany, (6) United Kingdom, (7) France, (8) Republic of Korea (South Korea), (9) Taiwan, and (10) Singapore.

World Wide Resources:

www.export911.com

www.fibre2fashion.com/texterms/exim/exim_terms1.htm

importexportcoach.com

www.ita.doc.gov/

www.exporthotline.com

informed about domestic and overseas trade events that offer potential for promoting American products.

The Office of International Trade of the Small Business Administration (SBA) offers assistance through SBA district offices to current and potential small business exporters through two programs that are provided in field offices around the country, Business Development and Financial Assistance. The Office of International Trade also works through the SCORE program, in which experienced executives offer free one-on-one counseling to small firms; Small Business Development Centers (SBDCs), located in many universities and colleges, which give export counseling, especially to inexperienced newcomers; Centers for International Business and Research (CIBERs), located in 30 U.S. universities, which also assist firms with exporting; and U.S. Export Assistance Centers, which are one-stop offices ready to help small and medium-size businesses with local export assistance.

The Department of Commerce Export Assistance Program (EAP) helps potential exporters narrow down their potential markets. It has offices in over 100 U.S. cities and 80 foreign cities. After learning about the company and its products, the EAP international trade specialist might advise the potential exporter to consult the National Trade Data Bank (NTDB), a service that selects the most recent trade promotions, "how to" publications, and international trade and economic data from 15 federal agencies and puts them on one CD-ROM that is updated monthly. The NTDB provides a comprehensive guide for new exporters and a source of specific product and regional information for experienced exporters searching for new markets. It also contains the Foreign Traders Index, a list of foreign importers that includes descriptions of each and the products it wishes to import. From this list, the exporter can prepare a list of those interested in its products for contact. An individual can subscribe to the NTDB as part of the trade and economic information available at the Commerce Web site, www.stat-usa.gov.

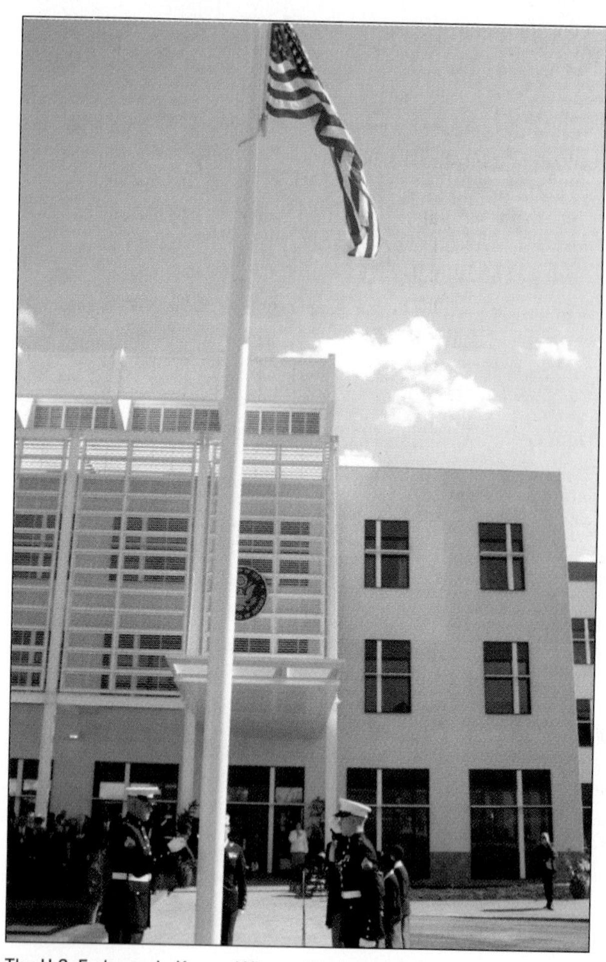

The U.S. Embassy in Kenya. When a firm is exploring exporting options, one source of information regarding potential business partners and market opportunities might be the Gold Key Service offered by many U.S. Embassies.

The trade specialist might also suggest using the Trade Opportunities Program (TOP), which provides current sales leads from overseas firms that want to buy from or represent American firms. These leads are accessible through STAT-USA free of charge at a Federal Depositary Library and as a component of the subscription service through STAT-USA. TOP leads are also published weekly in leading commercial newspapers. Another possibility is advertising in *Commercial News,* a catalog-magazine published bimonthly to promote American products and services in overseas markets.[2]

Once the existence of a potential market is established, the firm must choose between exporting indirectly through U.S.-based exporters and exporting directly using its own staff. If it opts for indirect exporting as a way to test the market, the trade specialist can provide assistance. If the firm prefers to set up its own export operation, it must then obtain overseas distribution. The exporter may use the Export.gov portal to find agents, distributors, or joint venture partners.[3] Credit reporting agencies, such as Dun & Bradstreet, the Finance, Credit, and International Business Association (FCIB), and the exporter's bank will supply credit information.

If the firm wants to make a foreign trip, Commerce offers the *Gold Key Matching Service* through many U.S. embassies. This is tailored for managers of American companies who are coming to visit the country and includes orientation briefings, market research, introductions to potential partners, and assistance in developing a marketing strategy for the particular country. The U.S. Commercial Office makes the arrangements. The Foreign Agricultural Service of the U.S. Department of Agriculture offers similar services to potential exporters of agricultural products.

The Department of Commerce also organizes trade events known as "Show and Sells" that are helpful in both locating foreign representatives and making sales. There are four kinds:

1. *U.S. pavilions:* Commerce selects about 100 global trade fairs every year for which it recruits American companies to participate at a U.S. pavilion. Preference is given to fairs in markets suitable for firms that are ready to export. Exhibitors receive extensive support from Commerce in management and overseas promotional campaigns to attract business audiences.
2. *Trade missions:* These focus on an industry sector. Participants are given detailed marketing information, advanced publicity, logistical support, and prearranged appointments with potential buyers and government officials. Generally, a mission consists of 5 to 12 business executives.
3. *Product literature center:* Commerce trade development specialists represent U.S. companies at various international trade shows, where they distribute literature. They then tell the companies who the interested visitors were so that the companies can follow up.
4. *Reverse trade missions:* The U.S. Trade Development Agency may fund visits to the United States by representatives of foreign governments so that they can meet with American industry and government representatives. The foreign officials represent purchasing authorities interested in buying U.S. equipment for specific projects.

WORLD view   

The Long and the Short of Exporting

DuPont has been able to remain a competitor in the tough chemical export market because exports have been a part of its strategic thinking since it first exported to Spain in 1805. It paid increasingly serious attention to exports in 1978, when the dollar fell sharply, making U.S. exports cheaper for foreigners to buy. There were other strategic reasons to increase the focus on exports at DuPont: "We recognized that our business was changing from national to regional or global, so you didn't have a lot of options," says P. J. Roessel, DuPont's director of international planning. "If you didn't participate in those foreign markets, your competitors would gradually get stronger and come and eat your lunch in the U.S."

DuPont's marketing strategy is to promote the sale of U.S. exports by its 165 overseas manufacturing subsidiaries. "We have plotted back for 25 years and have found that as we have invested and built abroad, exports have gone up in complete tandem," says Roessel. "Such subsidiaries are able to 'pull' products from the parent company to achieve real market synergy." A Japanese DuPont subsidiary, for example, makes engineering plastics for autos and has developed markets for polyester and acetyl products made by DuPont in the United States. In 2005, DuPont's exports from the United States amounted to $6.575 billion, making the company one of the largest U.S. exporters. It now has operational locations in 70 countries.

On the other hand, the Canadian firm Crosskeys Systems Corporation had no exports in 1992, its first year of operation, and no plans for exporting. However, the management of the information technology company changed its plans in 1995 when it realized it had earned 65 percent of its revenues from a single U.S.-based customer. In 1997, only five years after it began operations, the firm's export revenues reached C$17.3 million and then almost doubled to C$32.2 million. In just six years, sales revenues grew from C$87,000 to C$36.7 million, 420 times the first year's revenues. Because of its success, Crosskeys was an attractive target, and was taken over by the British company Orchestream, which was then, in turn, bought by the Texas-based Metasolv.

Source: "DuPont at a Glance," *About DuPont,* www.dupont.com/corp/gbl-company/overview.html (July 27, 2006); "Crosskeys Systems Corporation," *Best Practices and Exporting Successes,* Industry Canada, October 15, 2003, http://strategis.ic.gc.ca/epic/internet/intawv-uamo.nsf/en/qv01666e.html (July 31, 2004); *Dupont 2005 Data Book,* www.dupont.com/corp/news/publications/dupfinancial/databk.pdf (July 25, 2006); and "Dupont Worldwide," www1.dupont.com/NASApp/dupontglobal/corp/index.jsp?page=/content/US/en_US/overview/worldwide/index.html (July 28, 2006).

In addition to the federal government, other sources of assistance available to the exporter include state governments, all of which have export development programs and many of which have export financing programs. In the private sector, the World Trade Centers Association, a membership organization of nearly 300 centers worldwide, provides networking opportunities and an online trading system.

EXPORT MARKETING PLAN

As soon as possible, the firm needs to draft its export marketing plan. An experienced firm will already have a plan in operation, but newcomers may need to wait until they have accumulated at least some information from foreign market research. Essentially, the export marketing plan is the same as the domestic marketing plan. It should be specific about the markets to be developed, the marketing strategy for serving them, and the tactics required to carry out the strategy. Sales forecasts and budgets, pricing policies, product characteristics, promotional plans, and details on arrangements with foreign representatives are required. In other words, the export marketing plan spells out what must be done and when, who should do it, and what the costs are. An outline for an export marketing plan appears in the appendix at the end of this chapter. In Chapter 18 we focus on the marketing mix, but two aspects of the mix require some explanation here: export pricing and sales agreements for foreign representatives.

terms of sale
Conditions of a sale that stipulate the point at which all costs and risks are borne by the buyer

INCOTERMS
Universal trade terminology developed by the International Chamber of Commerce

One pricing area of concern for many firms beginning to export is the need to quote **terms of sale** that differ from those used in domestic markets. For foreign transactions, the exporter needs to be familiar with **INCOTERMS,** 13 trade terms that describe the responsibilities of the buyer and seller in international trade.[4] They were created by the International Chamber of Commerce and are revised every 10 years. For example, for domestic sales, the company may be quoting a price **FOB (free on board)** factory, which

FOB (free on board) Pricing policy in which risks pass from seller to buyer at the factory door; U.S. equivalent of Ex-Works

Ex-Works INCOTERM equivalent of FOB

means all costs and risks from that point on are borne by the buyer. The INCOTERM equivalent is **Ex-Works.** Foreign customers, however, will expect one of the following terms of sale:

1. *FAS (free alongside ship, port of call):* The seller pays all the transportation and delivery expense up to the ship's side and clears the goods for export.
2. *CIF (cost, insurance, freight, foreign port):* The price includes the cost of the goods, insurance, and all transportation and miscellaneous charges to the named port of final destination.
3. *CFR (cost and freight, foreign port):* CFR is similar to CIF except that the buyer purchases the insurance, either because it can be obtained at a lower cost or because the buyer's government, to save foreign exchange, insists on use of a local insurance company.
4. *DAF (delivered at frontier):* The term *DAF* is often used by exporters to Canada and Mexico. The price covers all costs up to the border, where the shipment is delivered to the buyer's representative. The buyer's responsibility is to arrange for receiving the goods after they are cleared for export, carry them across the border, clear them for importation, and make delivery to the buyer.

CIF and CFR terms of sale are more convenient for foreign buyers because to establish their cost, they merely have to add the import duties, landing charges, and freight from the port of arrival to their warehouse. New exporters need to remember the miscellaneous costs—wharf storage and handling charges, freight forwarder's charges, and consular fees—incurred in making a CIF shipment. Note that the domestic marketing and general administrative costs included in the domestic selling price are frequently greater than the actual cost of making a CIF export sale.

The preferred pricing method is the use of the *factory door cost* (production cost without domestic marketing and general administrative costs), to which are added the direct cost of making the export sale, a percentage of the general administrative overhead, and a profit margin. This percentage can be derived from managers' estimates of the part of their total time spent on export matters. The minimum FOB, or Ex-Works, price is the sum of these costs plus the required profit margin. If research in a market has shown either that there is little competition or that competitive prices are higher, then of course the exporter is free to match the competition in that market (price skim) or set a low price to gain market share (penetration pricing). The course of action taken will depend on the firm's sales objectives, just as in the domestic market.

The other area of major difference in exporting is the sales agreement. It should specify as simply as possible the duties of the representative and the firm. Most of what is contained in the contract for a domestic representative can be used in export also, but special attention must be paid to two points, the designation of the responsibilities for patent and trademark registration and the designation of the country and state or province whose laws will govern any contractual dispute. To be absolutely safe, the firm should register all patents and trademarks. Policing them may be left to the local representative; however, the firm should have the help of an experienced international attorney when drawing up an agreement. Exporters from any country are likely to prefer to stipulate the laws of their home country. Many nations, especially those of Latin America, follow the Calvo Doctrine, which holds that cases should be tried under local and not foreign law.

Payment and Financing Procedures

The second major hurdle for new exporters is to build an understanding of the payment and financing procedures involved in export sales. We'll review the process of export payment and the terms used, approaches to export financing, and other government incentives that have been established to support exporters in the finance area.

mini MNE

>>Experts Help Small Firms Export

David Kratka, president of MMO Music Group, a small producer of sing-along tapes for karaoke machines in Elmsford, New York, didn't have to search for foreign business; foreign customers came to him. Although this seems like an enviable situation, in reality, Kratka figures the company probably lost foreign sales in the 1980s because he was too busy attending to the domestic market. He didn't have time to answer faxes and telephone calls from Asia and Europe. A year after Kratka finally decided he could no longer handle the foreign inquiries alone, he hired an international sales director. By mid-1995 foreign sales were about 15 percent of the firm's total $8 million sales. This was up from 5 percent before the director was hired.

MMO Music is still in business (as Pocket Songs), and the company's founder, Irv Kratka, was acknowledged as the "father of karaoke" in 1995. Of course, the cassette tapes have given way to the CD and CD + G (lyrics on a screen) format.

Other companies find it easier and more economical to get exporting help from an outsider. A consulting firm, Global Resource Associates, taught exporting techniques to CoBatCo, a waffle-griddle maker in Illinois with 21 employees. Exports amounted to 13 percent of total sales in only three years.

Other small-firm managers without the time or international expertise to handle foreign sales turn to export management companies (EMCs) that typically handle everything from sales and distribution to credit and shipping, charging a fee of 10 to 15 percent of the shipment's value. The advantage of this approach is that experts handle the export function. The disadvantage is that the control of the company's export business lies in the hands of outsiders.

Source: "The History of Karaoke," www.pocketsongs.com/MainPages/karaokehistory.asp (July 29, 2006); "About Pocket Songs: The Karaoke Music Super Store," www.pocketsongs.com/MainPages/about.asp (July 29, 2006); and Global Resource Associates, www.fastrack-global.com (July 29, 2006).

EXPORT PAYMENT TERMS

Payment terms, as every marketer knows, are often a decisive factor in obtaining an order. As a sales official of an international grain exporter put it, "If you give credit to a guy who is broke, he'll pay any price for your product." This is somewhat exaggerated, but customers will often pay higher prices when terms are more lenient, especially in countries where capital is scarce and interest rates are high. Among the payment terms offered by exporters to foreign buyers are cash in advance, open account, consignment, letters of credit, and documentary drafts. We'll look at each of these in turn.

When the credit standing of the buyer is not known or is uncertain, *cash in advance* is desirable. However, very few buyers will accept these terms, because part of their working capital will be tied up until the merchandise has been received and sold. Furthermore, they have no guarantee that they will receive what they ordered. As a result, few customers will pay cash in advance unless the order is for a custom-made product.

When a sale is made on *open account,* the seller assumes all of the risk, and therefore such terms should be offered only to reliable customers. The exporter's capital is tied up until payment has been received. However, exporters that insist on less risky payment terms, such as a letter of credit, may find that they are losing business to competitors who do sell on open account. Well-known global firms such as Mercedes Benz do not accept the extra cost of obtaining letters of credit and give their business to suppliers that will offer them open account terms. To establish the buyer's credit, exporters can get credit reports and credit information on foreign firms from several agencies such as Dun & Bradstreet, Owens Online, and Asian CIS.

letter of credit (L/C)
Document issued by the buyer's bank in which the bank promises to pay the seller a specified amount under specified conditions

Consignment means that goods are shipped to the buyer and payment is not made until they have been sold. All of the risk is assumed by the seller, so such terms should not be offered without making the same extensive investigation of the buyer and country as that recommended for open account terms. Multinationals frequently sell goods to their subsidiaries on this basis.

Only cash in advance offers more protection to the seller than does an export **letter of credit (L/C).** This document is issued by the buyer's bank, which promises to pay the seller

confirmed L/C
A confirmation made by a correspondent bank in the seller's country by which it agrees to honor the issuing bank's letter of credit

irrevocable L/C
A stipulation that a letter of credit cannot be canceled

a specified amount when the bank has received certain documents stipulated in the letter of credit by a specified time. Generally, the seller will request that the letter of credit be *confirmed* and *irrevocable.* In a **confirmed L/C,** a correspondent bank in the seller's country confirms that it will honor the issuing bank's letter of credit. With an **irrevocable L/C,** once the seller has accepted the credit, the customer cannot alter or cancel it without the seller's consent. Figure 17.1 is an example of a bank's confirmation of an irrevocable letter of credit. If the letter of credit is *not* confirmed, the correspondent bank (Merchants National Bank of Mobile) has no obligation to pay the seller (Smith & Co.) when it receives the documents listed in the letter of credit. Only the issuing bank (Banco Americano in Bogotá) is responsible. If the seller (Smith & Co.) wishes to be able to collect from an American bank, it will insist that the credit be confirmed by such a bank. This confirmation is generally done by the correspondent bank, as it is in Figure 17.1. When the Merchants National Bank of Mobile confirms the credit, it undertakes an obligation to pay Smith & Co. if all the documents listed in the letter are presented on or before the stipulated date. Note that nothing is mentioned

FIGURE 17.1

Letter of Credit

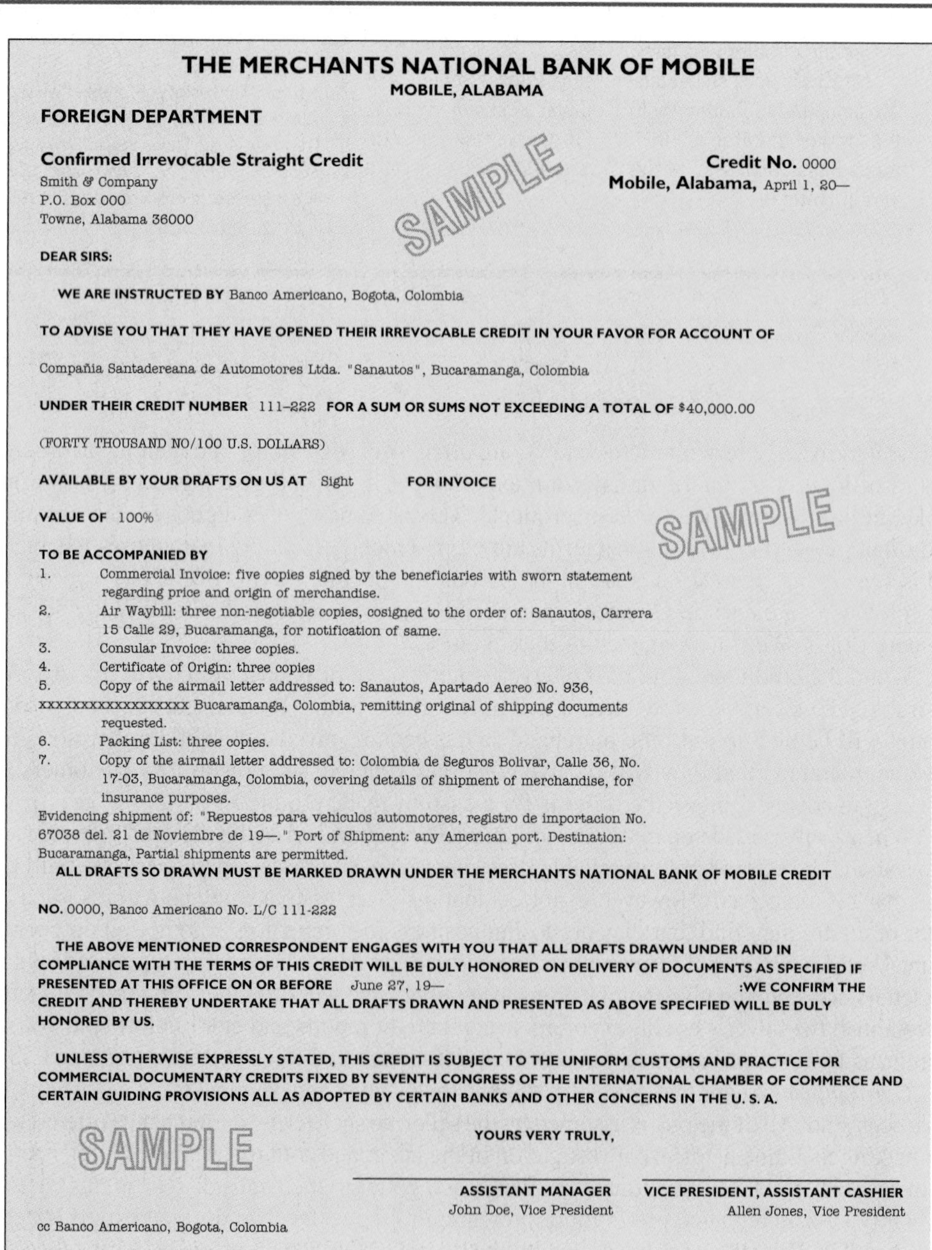

THE MERCHANTS NATIONAL BANK OF MOBILE
MOBILE, ALABAMA

FOREIGN DEPARTMENT

Confirmed Irrevocable Straight Credit — **Credit No.** 0000
Smith & Company
P.O. Box 000
Towne, Alabama 36000

Mobile, Alabama, April 1, 20—

SAMPLE

DEAR SIRS:

WE ARE INSTRUCTED BY Banco Americano, Bogota, Colombia

TO ADVISE YOU THAT THEY HAVE OPENED THEIR IRREVOCABLE CREDIT IN YOUR FAVOR FOR ACCOUNT OF

Compañia Santadereana de Automotores Ltda. "Sanautos", Bucaramanga, Colombia

UNDER THEIR CREDIT NUMBER 111-222 FOR A SUM OR SUMS NOT EXCEEDING A TOTAL OF $40,000.00

(FORTY THOUSAND NO/100 U.S. DOLLARS)

AVAILABLE BY YOUR DRAFTS ON US AT Sight FOR INVOICE

VALUE OF 100%

SAMPLE

TO BE ACCOMPANIED BY

1. Commercial Invoice: five copies signed by the beneficiaries with sworn statement regarding price and origin of merchandise.
2. Air Waybill: three non-negotiable copies, cosigned to the order of: Sanautos, Carrera 15 Calle 29, Bucaramanga, for notification of same.
3. Consular Invoice: three copies.
4. Certificate of Origin: three copies
5. Copy of the airmail letter addressed to: Sanautos, Apartado Aereo No. 936, xxxxxxxxxxxxxxxxxx Bucaramanga, Colombia, remitting original of shipping documents requested.
6. Packing List: three copies.
7. Copy of the airmail letter addressed to: Colombia de Seguros Bolivar, Calle 36, No. 17-03, Bucaramanga, Colombia, covering details of shipment of merchandise, for insurance purposes.

Evidencing shipment of: "Repuestos para vehiculos automotores, registro de importacion No. 67038 del. 21 de Noviembre de 19—." Port of Shipment: any American port. Destination: Bucaramanga, Partial shipments are permitted.

ALL DRAFTS SO DRAWN MUST BE MARKED DRAWN UNDER THE MERCHANTS NATIONAL BANK OF MOBILE CREDIT

NO. 0000, Banco Americano No. L/C 111-222

THE ABOVE MENTIONED CORRESPONDENT ENGAGES WITH YOU THAT ALL DRAFTS DRAWN UNDER AND IN COMPLIANCE WITH THE TERMS OF THIS CREDIT WILL BE DULY HONORED ON DELIVERY OF DOCUMENTS AS SPECIFIED IF PRESENTED AT THIS OFFICE ON OR BEFORE June 27, 19— :WE CONFIRM THE CREDIT AND THEREBY UNDERTAKE THAT ALL DRAFTS DRAWN AND PRESENTED AS ABOVE SPECIFIED WILL BE DULY HONORED BY US.

UNLESS OTHERWISE EXPRESSLY STATED, THIS CREDIT IS SUBJECT TO THE UNIFORM CUSTOMS AND PRACTICE FOR COMMERCIAL DOCUMENTARY CREDITS FIXED BY SEVENTH CONGRESS OF THE INTERNATIONAL CHAMBER OF COMMERCE AND CERTAIN GUIDING PROVISIONS ALL AS ADOPTED BY CERTAIN BANKS AND OTHER CONCERNS IN THE U. S. A.

SAMPLE

YOURS VERY TRULY,

ASSISTANT MANAGER
John Doe, Vice President

VICE PRESIDENT, ASSISTANT CASHIER
Allen Jones, Vice President

cc Banco Americano, Bogota, Colombia

about the goods themselves; the buyer has stipulated only that an **air waybill** issued by the carrier be presented as proof that shipment has been made. Even if bank officials know that the plane had crashed after the takeoff, they would still pay Smith & Co. Banks are concerned with documents, not merchandise.

air waybill
A bill of lading issued by an air carrier

Before opening a letter of credit, a buyer frequently requests a **pro forma invoice.** This is the exporter's formal quotation containing a description of the merchandise, price, delivery time, proposed method of shipment, ports of exit and entry, and terms of sale. It is more than a quotation, however. Generally, the bank will use it when opening a letter of credit, and in countries requiring import licenses or permits to purchase foreign exchange, government officials will insist on receiving copies.

pro forma invoice
Exporter's formal quotation containing a description of the merchandise, price, delivery time, method of shipping, terms of sale, and points of exit and entry

Figure 17.2 illustrates the routes taken by the merchandise, letter of credit, and documents in a letter-of-credit transaction between a U.S. seller and a German buyer. When the German buyer accepts the terms of sale that provide for a confirmed and irrevocable letter of credit, she goes to her bank to arrange for opening the required letter. The buyer will furnish the bank with the information contained in the pro forma invoice, specify the documents that the exporter must present to obtain payment, and set the expiration date for the credit.

The German bank then instructs its correspondent bank in the United States to confirm the credit and inform the seller that it has been established. The seller prepares the merchandise for shipment and notifies the freight forwarder, which books space on a ship, prepares the export documents, and arranges to have the merchandise delivered to the port. The documents, together with a sight or time draft drawn by the seller, are presented to the U.S. bank, which pays the seller and forwards the documents for collection to the German bank. To obtain the documents that give title to the shipment, the buyer in Germany must either pay the *sight draft* or accept a *time draft*. Having done so, the buyer receives the documents, which are then given to the customhouse broker. The customhouse broker acts as the buyer's agent in receiving the goods from the steamship line and clearing them through German customs.

If the exporter believes the political and commercial risks are not sufficient to require a letter of credit, the exporter may agree to payment on a *documentary draft basis,* which is

FIGURE 17.2

Letter of Credit Transaction

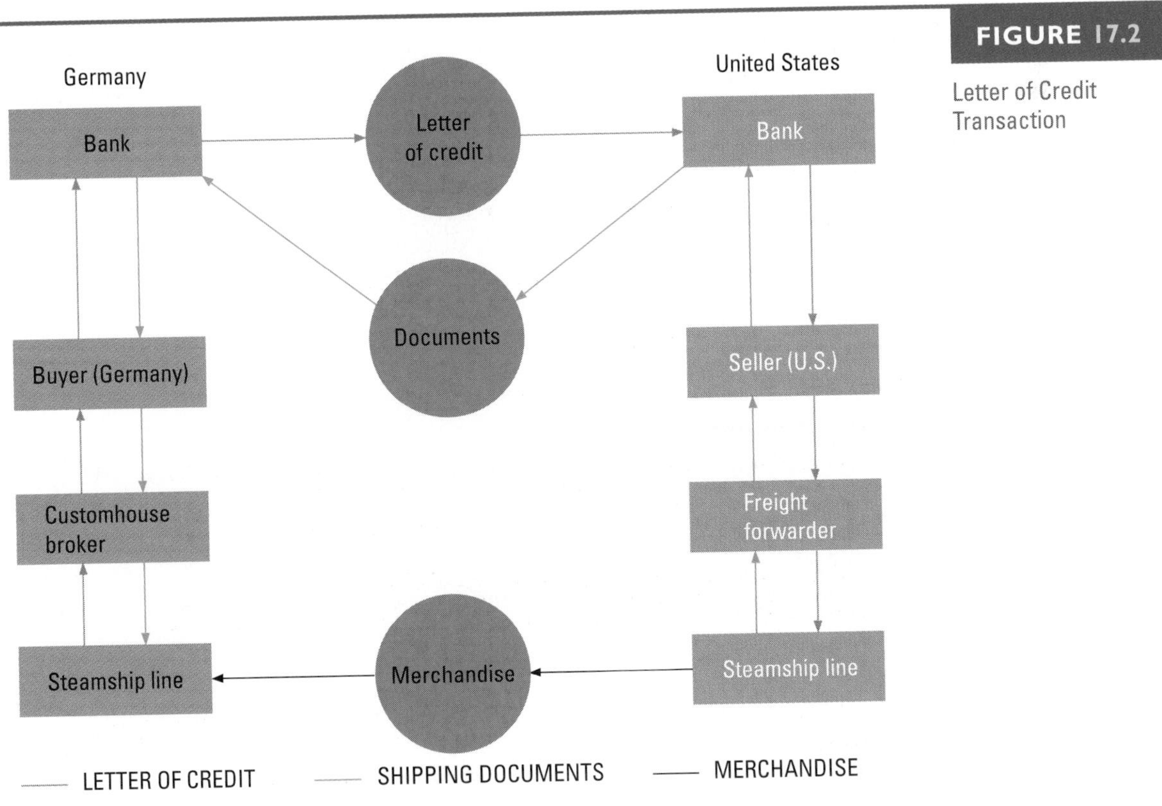

FIGURE 17.3

Sight Draft

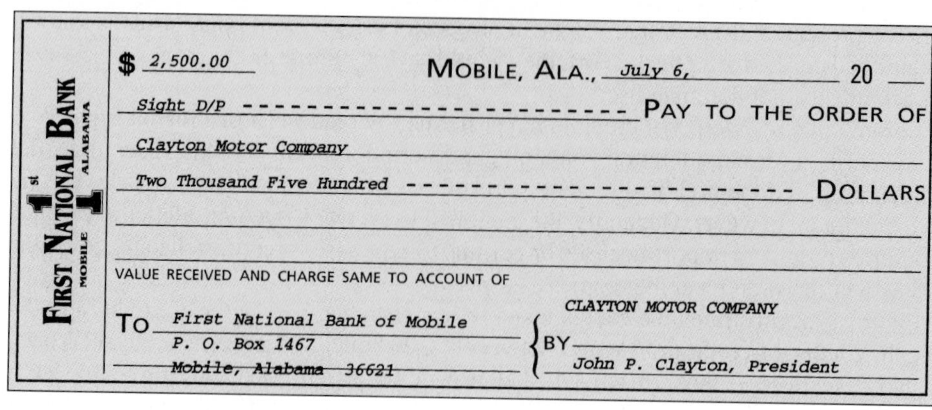
$ 2,500.00 MOBILE, ALA., July 6, 20 ___

Sight D/P ------------------------ PAY TO THE ORDER OF

Clayton Motor Company

Two Thousand Five Hundred ------------------------ DOLLARS

VALUE RECEIVED AND CHARGE SAME TO ACCOUNT OF

CLAYTON MOTOR COMPANY

TO First National Bank of Mobile
P. O. Box 1467
Mobile, Alabama 36621

BY John P. Clayton, President

export draft
An unconditional order drawn by the seller that instructs the buyer to pay the draft's amount on presentation **(sight draft)** or at an agreed future date **(time draft)** and that must be paid before the buyer receives shipping documents

less costly to the buyer. An **export draft,** shown in Figure 17.3, is an unconditional order drawn by the seller on the buyer instructing the buyer to pay the amount of the order on presentation (**sight draft**) or at an agreed future date (**time draft**). Generally, the seller will ask its bank to send the draft and documents to a bank in the buyer's country, which will proceed with the collection as described in the letter-of-credit transaction.

Although documentary draft and letter-of-credit terms are similar, there is one important difference. A confirmed letter of credit guarantees payment to the seller if the seller conforms to its requirements. There is no guarantee with a documentary draft. An unscrupulous buyer can refuse to pay the draft when presented and then attempt to bargain with the seller for a lower price. The seller must then acquiesce, try to find another buyer, pay a large freight bill to bring back the goods, or abandon them. If the seller chooses the last alternative, customs will auction off the goods, and chances are that the original buyer will be able to acquire them at a bargain price. The seller would receive nothing.

Figure 17.4 illustrates that the risks and costs vary inversely among the various export payment terms.

EXPORT FINANCING

Although exporters would prefer to sell on the almost riskless letter-of-credit terms, increased foreign competition and the universally tight money situation are forcing them to offer credit. To do so, they must be familiar with the available sources and kinds of export financing, both private and public.

Private Source

Commercial banks have always been a source of export financing through loans for working capital and the discounting of time drafts. A bank may discount an export time draft, pay the seller and keep it until maturity or, if it is the bank on which the

FIGURE 17.4

Payment Risk/Cost Trade-Off

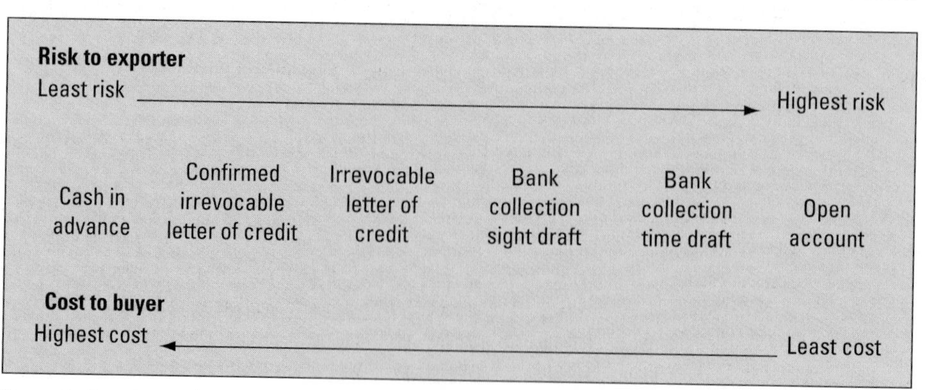

Source: *Business America* (U.S. Dept. of Commerce Publication), February 1995.

mini MNE

>>Dump the L/Cs; Pay with Plastic!

The safe and laborious way to guarantee both payment and shipment of an export or import order has been with letter-of-credit (L/C) payment terms. But there has always been a risk that conversion rate changes would result in a loss. For some situations, credit cards provide a good alternative. For example, the president of a small manufacturing company said that if his company hadn't accepted payment by credit card, it couldn't have done business in 95 countries. He's also pleased that with the immediate completion of the sale, credit card companies guarantee that payment is made directly to the seller's bank account within 72 hours at the daily U.S. dollar rate, avoiding transaction losses on the foreign exchange conversion and increasing cash flow.

For information on using credit cards to accept payments, see sites such as www.usa.visa.com/business. Come to think of it, maybe PayPal will become an alternative. With over 105 million accounts in 55 markets, PayPal is becoming a third alternative. See Paypal's site (https://www.paypal.com/cgl-bin/webscr?cmd=xpt/merchant/Index-outside) or that of Moneybookers (www.moneybookers.com/app), which is especially friendly to international transactions.

Source: www. paypal.com (July 31, 2006).

draft is drawn, "accept" it. By accepting a time draft, a bank assumes the responsibility for making payment at maturity of the draft. The accepting bank may or may not purchase (at a discount) the draft. If it does not, the exporter can sell a **banker's acceptance** readily in the open market.

banker's acceptance
A time draft with maturity of less than 270 days that has been accepted by the bank on which the draft was drawn, thus becoming the accepting bank's obligation; may be bought and sold at a discount in the financial markets like other commercial paper

In recent years, two new types of financing have been developed, factoring and forfaiting. **Factoring** permits the exporter to be more competitive by selling on open account rather than by means of the more costly letter-of-credit method. This financing technique is the sale of export accounts receivable to a third party, which assumes the credit risk. Factoring is essentially discounting without recourse. A factor may be a factoring house or a special department in a commercial bank. Under the export factoring arrangement, the seller passes its order to the factor for approval of the credit risk. Once the order has been approved, the exporter has complete protection against bad debts and political risk. The customer pays the factor, which in effect acts as the exporter's credit and collection department. The period of settlement generally does not exceed 180 days.

Forfaiting is the purchase of obligations that arise from the sale of goods and services that fall due at some date beyond the 90 to 180 days that is customary for factoring. These receivables are usually in the form of trade drafts or promissory notes with maturities ranging from six months to five years. Because forfaited debt is sold without recourse, it is nearly always accompanied by bank security in the form of a guarantee or *aval.* Whereas the guarantee is a separate document, the aval is a promise to pay that is written directly in the document. The forfaiter purchases the bill and discounts it for the entire credit period. Thus, the exporter, through forfaiting, has converted its credit-based sale into a cash transaction. Although banks have traditionally concentrated on short-term financing, they have become involved in medium- and even long-term financing because numerous government and government-assisted organizations are offering export credit guarantees and insurance against commercial and political risks.

factoring
Discounting without recourse an account receivable

forfaiting
Purchasing without recourse an account receivable whose credit terms are longer than the 90 to 180 days usual in factoring; unlike factoring, political and transfer risks are borne by the forfaiter

Public Source The U.S. Export-Import Bank (**Ex-Im Bank**) is the principal government agency responsible for aiding the financing of American exports, through a variety of loan, guarantee, and insurance programs. Ex-Im Bank's programs are available to any American export firm regardless of size. The bank provides two types of loans, direct loans to foreign buyers of American exports and intermediary loans to responsible parties, such as a foreign government lending agency that relends to foreign buyers of capital goods and related services. An example of the latter is a maintenance contract for a jet passenger plane. Both programs cover up to 85 percent of the value of the exported goods and services, with repayment terms of one year or more.

Ex-Im Bank
Principal government agency that aids American exporters by means of loans, guarantees, and insurance programs

Ex-Im Bank's *Working Capital Guarantee* helps small businesses obtain working capital to cover their export sales. It guarantees working capital loans extended by banks to eligible exporters with exportable inventory or export receivables as collateral. The guarantee provides repayment protection for private sector loans to buyers of U.S. capital equipment and related services.

Ex-Im Bank also offers *export credit insurance.* An exporter may reduce financing risks by purchasing insurance to protect against the political and commercial risks of a foreign buyer's defaulting on payment. The coverage may be comprehensive or be limited to political risk only. Since its inception in 1934, Ex-Im Bank has supported more than $400 billion in American exports, mostly to developing markets.[5]

Other Public Incentives

Other government incentives for trade, although not strictly a part of export financing, are so closely related to it that we mention them here. These are the Overseas Private Investment Corporation and the foreign trade zone.[6]

Overseas Private Investment Corporation (OPIC)
Government corporation that offers American investors in developing countries insurance against expropriation, currency inconvertibility, and damages from wars and revolutions

The **Overseas Private Investment Corporation (OPIC)** is a government corporation formed to stimulate private investment in developing countries. It offers investors insurance against expropriation, currency inconvertibility, and damages from wars or revolutions. OPIC also offers specialized insurance for American service contractors and exporters operating in foreign countries. Exports of capital equipment and semiprocessed raw materials generally follow these investments.

foreign trade zone (FTZ)
Duty-free area designed to facilitate trade by reducing the effect of customs restrictions

Foreign trade zones (FTZs) are duty-free areas designed to facilitate trade by reducing the effect of customs restrictions. These areas may be free ports, transit zones, free perimeters, export processing zones, or free trade zones. In each instance, a specific and limited area is involved, into which imported goods may be brought without the payment of import duties. There are hundreds of these areas in more than 28 countries. Of the five types, the free trade zone is the most common.

free trade zone
An area designated by the government as outside its customs territory

The **free trade zone** is an enclosed area considered to be outside the customs territory of the country in which it is located. Goods of foreign origin may be brought into the zone for eventual transshipment, reexportation, or importation into the country. While the goods are in the zone, no import duties need be paid. Examples range from the Zhuhai Free Trade Zone, near Macao in China, to Chabahar in Iran. In the United States, free trade zones have been growing in popularity, and 230 of these zones, with over 400 subzones, are now in operation.[7] Many are situated at seaports, but some are located at inland distribution points. Goods brought into the FTZ may be stored, inspected, repackaged, or combined with American components. Because of differences in the import tariff schedule, the finished product often incurs lower duty than would the disassembled parts. Bicycles have been assembled in the Kansas City FTZ for that reason. Importers of machinery and automobiles improve their cash flow by storing spare parts in an FTZ, because duty is not paid until they are withdrawn.

customs drawbacks
Rebates on customs duties

In addition to their advantages to importers, FTZs can also benefit exporters. By using FTZs, exporters may be eligible for accelerated export status in regard to excise tax rebates and **customs drawbacks.** These customs duty rebates are available for items such as tires, trucks, and tobacco products. The federal government collects the tax when the item is manufactured; when it is exported, the tax is rebated. The processing time for tax rebates can be initiated by putting the goods into FTZs because a product is considered exported as soon as it enters the FTZ. Although U.S. Customs has had the duty-drawback program in place for 200 years, many firms do not claim the money they're owed. As a result, each year up to $2 billion in customs duty refunds goes unclaimed.[8] FTZs offer another benefit to exporters: When manufacturing or assembly is done in FTZs using imported components, no duties need ever be paid when the finished product is exported.

Export Procedures

When those new to exporting are concerned about the complexity of export procedures, they are generally referring to documentation. Instead of dealing with the two documents used in domestic shipments, the freight bill and the bill of lading, export novices are suddenly confronted with five

TABLE 17.1 Official Procedures for Exporting and Importing

Region or Economy	Documents for Export (number)	Time for Export (days)	Cost to Export (US$ per container)	Documents for Import (number)	Time for Import (days)	Cost to Import (US$ per Container)
East Asia & Pacific	6.9	23.9	884.8	9.3	25.9	1,037.1
Europe & Central Asia	7.4	29.2	1,450.2	10.0	37.1	1,589.3
Latin America & Caribbean	7.3	22.2	1,067.5	9.5	27.9	1,225.5
Middle East & North Africa	7.1	27.1	923.9	10.3	35.4	1,182.8
OECD	4.8	10.5	811.0	5.9	12.2	882.6
South Asia	8.1	34.4	1,236.0	12.5	41.5	1,494.9
Sub-Saharan Africa	8.2	40.0	1,561.1	12.2	51.5	1,946.9

Source: World Bank, International Finance Corporation, http://www.doingbusiness.org/ExploreTopics/TradingAcrossBorders (Sept. 29, 2005).

to six times as many documents, depending on the country. Table 17.1 summarizes documentation requirements for major groups. Additional data on specific countries are available at the World Bank's Doing Business site, www.doingbusiness.org/ExploreTopics/TradingAcrossBorders.

"Exports move on a sea of documents" is a popular saying in the industry, and it seems an accurate description. Many firms give at least part of this work to a *foreign freight forwarder,* who acts as an agent for the exporter. Foreign freight forwarders prepare documents, book space with a carrier, and in general act as the firm's export traffic department. If asked, they will offer advice about markets, import and export regulations, the best mode of transport, and export packing. They also will supply cargo insurance. After shipment, they forward documents to the importer or to the paying bank, according to the exporter's requirements. We look now at the two basic elements of exporting, the paperwork and the actual transportation of goods. Then, in the next section, we look at import procedures, often the mirror image of export procedures.

EXPORT DOCUMENTS

Correct documentation is vital to the success of any export shipment. Interestingly enough, error rates reported for export and import documentation hover around 50 percent. Think of the impact of that—goods waiting in a container, on a dock, or in a warehouse, tying up working capital. We'll review the two sets of documents required to ship and collect goods.

"Any fruits or vegetables?"

Source: © The New Yorker Collection 1998 Mick Stevens from cartoonbank.com. All Rights Reserved.

Shipping Documents

Shipping documents are prepared by exporters or their freight forwarders so that the shipment can pass through U.S. Customs, be loaded on the carrier, and be sent to its destination. They include the domestic bill of lading, the export packing list, the shipper's export declaration, the export licenses, the export bill of lading, and the insurance certificate. The first two documents are nearly the same as those used in domestic traffic, so we'll focus here on the other four.

shipper's export declaration (SED)
U.S. Department of Commerce form used to control export shipments and record export statistics

automated export system (AES)
U.S. Customs electronic filing system

validated export license
A required document issued by the U.S. government authorizing the export of a strategic commodity or a shipment to an unfriendly country

general export license
Any export license covering export commodities for which a validated license is not required; no formal application is required

export bill of lading (B/L)
Contract of carriage between shipper and carrier: straight bill of lading is nonnegotiable; endorsed "to order" bill gives the holder claim on merchandise

The **shipper's export declaration (SED**) is required by the Department of Commerce to control exports and supply export statistics. An SED contains:

1. Names and addresses of the shipper and consignee.
2. U.S. port of exit and foreign port of unloading.
3. Description and value of the goods.
4. Export license number and bill-of-lading number.
5. Name of the carrier transporting the merchandise.

Shippers or their agents (foreign freight forwarders) deliver the SED to the carrier, which turns it in to U.S. Customs with the carrier's manifest (list of the vessel's cargo) before the carrier leaves the United States. An **automated export system (AES)** with electronic filing was introduced in 2004. The goals of this paperless reporting are to speed up export processing and reduce the 50 percent error rate on the forms.

An *export license* from the U.S. federal government is required for all exported goods except those going to U.S. possessions or, with a few exceptions, to Canada. These licenses are either validated or general. A **validated export license** is required for strategic materials and all shipments to unfriendly countries. This is a special authorization for a specific shipment and is issued by the Department of Commerce Office of Export Administration. It is required for scarce materials, strategic goods, and technology. The Department of State issues the validated license for war materials. A **general export license** is used for all products that do not require the validated license.

An **export bill of lading (B/L)** serves three purposes: It functions as a contract for carriage between the shipper and the carrier, a receipt from the carrier for the goods shipped, and a certificate of ownership. B/Ls are either *straight* or *to order*. A straight bill of lading is nonnegotiable. Only the person stipulated in it may obtain the merchandise on arrival. An order bill of lading, however, is negotiable. It can be endorsed like a check or left blank. With an order B/L, the holder is the owner of the merchandise.

The *insurance certificate* is evidence that the shipment is insured against loss or damage while in transit. Unlike domestic carriers, oceangoing steamship companies assume no responsibility for the merchandise they carry unless the loss is caused by their negligence. Marine insurance may be arranged by either the exporter or the importer, depending on the terms of sale. The laws of some countries may require that the importer buy such insurance, thus protecting the local insurance industry and saving foreign exchange. If the exporter has sold on sight draft terms, the firm carries the risk while the goods are in transit. In this case, the exporter should buy contingent interest insurance to protect it in the event that the shipment is lost or damaged and collection from the buyer is not successful. We believe that the exporter selling on CFR terms (the buyer purchases the insurance) should also buy contingent interest insurance to protect itself in case the buyer's insurance does not cover all risks.

There are three kinds of marine insurance policies: basic named perils, broad named perils, and all risks. *Basic named perils* include perils of the sea, fires, jettisons, explosions, and hurricanes. *Broad named perils* include theft, pilferage, nondelivery, breakage, and leakage in addition to the basic perils. *All risks* covers all physical loss or damage from any external cause and is more expensive than the other policies. War risks are covered under a separate contract. Premiums depend on a number of factors, such as the goods insured, the destination, the age of the ship, whether the goods are stowed on deck or under deck, the volume of business, how the goods are packed, and the number of claims the shipper has filed. Brokers will sometimes admit that in the long run it is preferable not to file numerous small claims, even if justified, because the higher premiums charged for future shipments will be greater than the money recovered.

Collection Documents

The seller is required to provide the buyer with collection documents to receive payment. These documents vary among countries and customers, but some of the most common are invoices, both commercial and consular, certificates of origin, and inspection certificates.

Export invoices are similar to domestic invoices. The commercial invoice includes additional information, such as the origin of the goods, export packing marks, and a clause stating that the goods will not be transshipped to another country. Invoices for letter-of-credit sales name the bank and the credit numbers. Some importing countries require that the commercial invoice be in their language and be visaed or endorsed by their local consul. The *consular invoice* is a special form purchased from the consul, prepared in the language of the country, and then visaed by the consul. Along with the export invoice, many governments require a *certificate of origin,* which is usually issued by the local chamber of commerce and visaed by the consul.

An *inspection certificate* is required frequently by buyers of grain, foodstuffs, and live animals. In the United States, inspection certificates are issued by the Department of Agriculture. Purchasers of machinery or products containing a specified combination of ingredients may insist that an American engineering firm or laboratory inspect the merchandise and certify that it is exactly as ordered. The EU requires the **CE (Conformite Europeene) mark** on about half of the exports it receives from the United States. This mark indicates that the merchandise conforms to European health, safety, and environmental requirements.[9] The certification process has been streamlined, and most merchandisers can self-certify that their merchandise conforms to EU regulations. Inspection by authorized testing houses is required of hazardous goods.

CE (Conformite Europeene) mark
EU mark that indicates that the merchandise conforms to European health, safety and environmental requirements

EXPORT SHIPMENTS

Most newcomers to exporting are so focused on making their sale and handling the documentation that they fail to be concerned about the actual physical movement of their goods. Innovations in material-handling techniques can help exporters reduce costs and perhaps reach markets they previously could not serve. Containerization, LASH, RO-RO, size, and air freight all offer increasingly cheaper, faster, and safer transportation solutions, shrinking our globe.

One means of drastically reducing both theft and handling costs is to use containers. *Containers* are large boxes—8 feet by 8 feet by 10, 20, or 40 feet—that the seller fills with the shipment in the firm's warehouse. Their origins are interesting, as explained in the chapter's opening section. Once packed, the containers are then sealed; they are opened when the goods arrive at their final destination. Containers are transported by truck or rail from the warehouse to shipside for loading. From the port of entry, railroads or trucks deliver them, often unopened even for customs inspection, to the buyer's warehouse. In most countries, customs officials go to the warehouse to examine the shipment. This integrated process reduces handling time and the risk of damage and theft because the buyer's own employees unload the containers.

If the importer or exporter has a warehouse on a river too shallow for ocean vessels, the firm can save time and expense by loading containers on barges. *LASH* (lighter aboard ship) vessels provide direct access to ocean freight service for exporters and importers located on shallow inland waterways. Sixty-foot-long barges ("lighters") are towed to inland locations, loaded, and towed back to deep water, where they are loaded aboard anchored LASH ships.

Another innovation in cargo handling is *RO-RO* (roll on–roll off) ships. Loaded trailers and any equipment on wheels can be driven onto these specially designed vessels. RO-RO service has brought the benefits of containerization to ports that have been unable to invest in the expensive lifting equipment required for containers.

Ship size continues to expand. Until recently, the standard largest size was "Panamax," which fit through the Panama Canal's locks with only feet to spare. "Post-Panamax" ("Suezmax," "capesize") ships are too big for the canal—nearly 44 feet too wide and over 200 feet longer than the canal can accept. Some 160 of these ships will be put in operation over the next few years, many to carry Chinese exports. So Panama must build a third set of even larger locks.

Air freight has had a profound effect on international business because it permits shipments that once required 30 days to arrive in 1 day. Huge freight planes carry payloads of 200,000 pounds, most of which goes either in containers or on pallets. Airlines guarantee overnight delivery from New York to many European airports and claim that their planes can be loaded or unloaded in 45 minutes.

Newcomers to exporting might assume that ocean freight is a better choice than air freight because ocean freight is so much cheaper. Comparison of total costs of each mode may suggest otherwise. Total cost components that may be lower for air freight include insurance rates, because of much less chance of damage during shipment; packing costs, because

WORLD view   

Shoes for People with Two Left Feet

For days, cargo thieves were watching construction crews enlarging one of Los Angeles's large container terminals. Toward the end of the work, the crews began moving the fences out to the expanded perimeter. When they ran out of heavy-security fence, they used lightweight fencing temporarily. This was the chance the thieves had been waiting for. That night, they cut the fence and drove a tractor-trailer truck up to a line of containers. After breaking into a number of them, they found one full of sports shoes that retailed for $150 a pair. They connected it to their tractor-trailer and escaped in the darkness.

But it was the importer who had the last laugh. A week later, the police found the abandoned container with its cargo intact. The thieves didn't know that the importer routinely shipped all its left shoes in one container and its right shoes in another. They had stolen a container with left shoes. Instead of buying expensive global positioning devices, the importer used cheap, low-tech methods. Ship all left shoes.

Source: "Sneaking Up on Security," www.internationalbusiness.com/feb/log297.htm (February 20, 1998).

the shipment does not need the heavier, more costly export packing, which is usually done by an outside firm; customs duties, when calculated on gross weights; replacement costs for damaged goods, again because of the reduced damage risk; and inventory costs, because the rapid delivery by air freight often eliminates the need for expensive warehouses. For example, Mercedes-Benz includes in the price of its luxury sports car Brabus SLR McLaren air freight from Bottrop, Germany, to anywhere in the world. Another cost saving is that machinery shipped by air does not require a heavy coat of grease to protect it from the elements, as does machinery sent by ship. Table 17.2 provides a sample comparison of the cost elements of ocean and air freight.

Even when the total shipping costs are higher for air freight, shipping by air may still be advantageous for several reasons:

1. *Total cost may decrease.* Getting the product to the buyer more quickly results in a more satisfied customer and faster payment, which speeds up the return on investment and improves cash flow. The firm's capital is released more quickly and can be invested

TABLE 17.2 Sea-Air Total Cost Comparison, Shipment of Spare Parts

	Ocean Freight (with warehousing)	Air Freight (no warehousing)
Warehouse administrative costs	$ 1,020	—
Warehouse rent	1,680	—
Inventory costs		
Taxes and insurance	756	$ 396
Inventory financing	288	192
Inventory obsolescence	1,800	0
Seller's warehouse and handling costs	1,810	1,140
Transportation	420	2,400
Packaging and handling	300	120
Cargo insurance	72	36
Customs duties	132	127
Total	$8,278	$4,411

in other profit-making ventures or used to repay borrowed capital, thus reducing interest payments. Production equipment may be assembled and sent by air so that it goes into production sooner, without the transit and setup delays associated with ocean shipments, a strong sales argument. These production and opportunity costs, although difficult to calculate, are part of the total cost.

2. *Either the firm or the product may be air-dependent.* Perishable food products being shipped to Europe, Japan, and the Middle East are in this category, as are live animals (newly hatched poultry and prize bulls) and fresh flowers. Without air freight, firms exporting such products would be out of business.
3. *The market may be perishable.* For goods with short life cycles, such as high-fashion products, delivery speed matters. When a fashion fad dies, its market goes with it.
4. *Competitive position may be strengthened.* The sales argument that spare parts and factory technical personnel are available within a few hours is a strong one for an exporting firm competing with overseas manufacturers.

Importing

In one sense, importers are the reverse of exporters: They sell domestically and buy in foreign markets. However, many of their concerns are similar. As in the case of exporters, there are small firms whose only business is to import, and there are global corporations for which importing components and raw materials valued at millions of dollars is just one of their functions. We will examine sources for imports, the role of customhouse brokers, and the payment of import duties here.

SOURCES FOR IMPORTS

Before importing, a firm may have difficulty determining whether the desired items exist and, if so, where to find them. How does the prospective importer identify import sources? There are a number of ways. First, similar imported products may already be in the market. By simple close examination, you can learn where they are made and often by whom. U.S. law requires that the country of origin be clearly marked on each product or on its container if product marking is not feasible (individual cigarettes, for example). The consul or embassy of the country of origin can help with names of manufacturers. One of the principal duties of all foreign government representatives is to promote exports, and they do this through newsletters, trade shows, industry shows, and collaborative events with their home country chamber of commerce group and other organizations, such as, for Japan, the Japan External Trade Organization (JETRO), which has a number of offices outside Japan. The process is the same if the product is not being imported. You simply have less information with which to begin.

Other sources of information are electronic bulletin boards such as those of the World Trade Centers. Accidental importing also occurs with some frequency. When you visit a foreign country, look for products that may have a market at home. Finding one could put you into a new business, one that makes foreign travel tax-deductible.

Now we turn to some of the technical aspects of importing, customhouse brokers and import duties.

CUSTOMHOUSE BROKERS

In every nation, there are **customhouse brokers,** whose functions parallel those of foreign freight forwarders but are on the import side of the transaction. As the agent for the importer, the customhouse broker brings the imported goods through customs, which requires that they know well the many import regulations and an extensive, complex tariff schedule. If a customs official places the import in a category requiring higher import duties than the importer had planned on, the importing firm may not be able to compete. To levy customs, evaluators everywhere generally use units shipped for products that carry specific duties and the invoice

customhouse brokers
Independent businesses that handle import shipments for compensation

price for ad valorem duties. There are some exceptions. The practice of U.S. Customs is to use the transaction price, which appears on the commercial invoice accompanying the shipment, plus any other charges not included in the transaction price. These may be royalty or license fees, packing, or any assists. *Assist* is the U.S. Customs term applied to any item that the buyer provides free or at reduced cost for use in the production or sale of merchandise for export to the United States. Examples are molds and dies sent overseas to produce a specific product, a common practice of importers who want the goods produced using their design, and components and parts that the buyer provides for incorporation in the finished article.

Customhouse brokers also provide other services, such as arranging transportation for the goods after they have left customs if the exporter has not arranged for it. They also keep track of which imports are subject to import quotas and how much of the quota has been filled at the time of the import. No matter which port the goods arrive at, U.S. Customs knows immediately the quantity that has been imported. Merchandise subject to import quotas can be on the dock of an American port awaiting clearance through customs, but if the quota fills anywhere during the wait, those goods cannot be imported for the rest of the fiscal year. The would-be importer can put them in a **bonded warehouse** or a foreign trade zone, where merchandise can be stored without paying duty, and wait for the rest of the year; abandon them; or send them to another country. Importers of high-fashion clothing have lost millions of dollars when quotas became filled and they had a shipment that had not yet cleared. They could not sell the clothing until the following year, by which time it was out of fashion.

bonded warehouse
An area authorized by customs authorities for storage of goods on which payment of import duties is deferred until the goods are removed

Customs has moved to the **Automated Commercial System (ACS)** to track, control, and process all commercial goods imported into the United States. ACS reduces the paperwork, cuts costs, and facilitates merchandise processing. Importers that use the system to file import documents can also pay the customs fees and import duties electronically all in one transaction. Like AES, ACS interfaces with other government agencies to transfer data electronically on import transactions for faster cargo release. An Automated Manifest System also speeds the flow of cargo and entry processing, with the result that cargo remains on the dock for less time before its release to the importers.[10]

Automated Commercial System (ACS)
Electronic tracking system used by U.S. Customs to track, control, and process all commercial goods imported into the United States

IMPORT DUTIES

Every importer should know how U.S. Customs calculates import duties and the importance of the product classification system, the **Harmonized Tariff Schedule of the United States (HTSUSA),** the American version of the global tariff code, the Harmonized System. The Harmonized System is a classification system for the over 200,000 commodities traded internationally, and it includes interpretive notes that help determine the classifications.

Harmonized Tariff Schedule of the United States (HTSUSA)
American version of the Harmonized System used worldwide to classify imported products

In HTSUSA each product has its own unique number. Figure 17.5 shows a page from the HTSUSA. All member-countries use the same system, and so it is possible to describe the product in any language by using the first six digits. The other four digits are for use just in the United States. The HTSUSA also shows the *reporting units,* which U.S. Customs uses in its paperwork. The last three columns have to do with the rate of duty.

Rates of duty are broken down into three levels for each item—general, special, and a third-rate level for countries not considered friends of the United States. HTSUSA is accessible on the Internet.[11]

New importers would do well to follow this advice: Disclose fully to the U.S. Customs Service all foreign and financial arrangements before passing the goods through U.S. Customs. The penalties for fraud are high. Get the advice of a customhouse broker *before* making the transaction. Frequently, a simple change in the product description can result in a much lower import duty. For example, jeans carry higher duties if the label is outside the back pocket instead of under the belt. If the words on the label are stylized, the duties are higher as well. Any clothing that is ornamented has higher duty. One importer brings in plain sports shirts and then sews on an animal figure after the products are in the United States. One last word of advice: Calculate carefully the landed price in advance. If you are unsure of the import category, ask U.S. Customs to determine the category in advance and to put it in writing, just like advanced rulings from the Internal Revenue Service. At the time of importation, customs inspectors must respect this determination.

FIGURE 17.5

Page from the HTSUSA

HARMONIZED TARIFF SCHEDULE of the UNITED STATES (1995)

Annotated for Statistical Reporting Purposes

XVI
84–62

Heading/ Subheading	Stat. Suf- fix	Article Description	Units of Quantity	Rates of Duty 1 General	1 Special	2
8461		Machine tools for planing, shaping, slotting, broaching, gear cutting, gear grinding or gear finishing, sawing, cutting-off and other machine tools working by removing metal, sintered metal carbides or cerments, not elsewhere specified or included:				
8461.10		Planing machines:				
8461.10.40		Numerically controlled	....	4.4%	Free (A,CA,E,IL,J, MX)	30%
	20	Used or rebuilt	No.			
	60	Other	No.			
8461.10.80		Other	....	4.4%	Free (A,CA,E,IL,J, MX)	30%
	20	Used or rebuilt	No.			
	40	Other, valued under $3,025 each ...	No.			
	80	Other	No.			
8461.20		Shaping or slotting machines:				
8461.20.40	00	Numerically controlled	No. ...	4.4%	Free (A,CA,E,IL,J, MX)	30%
8461.20.80		Other	....	4.4%	Free (A,CA,E,IL,J, MX)	30%
	30	Used or rebuilt	No.			
	70	Other, valued under $3,025 each ...	No.			
	90	Other	No.			
8461.30		Broaching machines:				
8461.30.40		Numerically controlled	....	4.4%	Free (A,CA,E,IL,J, MX)	30%
	20	Used or rebuilt	No.			
	60	Other	No.			
8461.30.80		Other	....	4.4%	Free (A,CA,E,IL,J, MX)	30%
	20	Used or rebuilt	No.			
	40	Other, valued under $3,025 each ..	No.			
	80	Other	No.			
8461.40		Gear cutting, gear grinding or gear finishing machines:				
8461.40.10		Gear cutting machines	....	5.8%	Free (A,CA,E,IL,J, MX)	40%
	10	Used or rebuilt	No.			
		Other:				
	20	For bevel gears	No.			
		Other:				
	30	Gear hobbers	No.			
	40	Gear shapers	No.			
	60	Other	No.			
8461.40.50		Gear grinding or finishing machines	....	4.4%	Free (A,CA,E,IL,J, MX)	30%
	20	Used or rebuilt	No.			
	40	Other, valued under $3,025 each ..	No.			
		Other:				
	50	For bevel gears	No.			
	70	Other	No.			
8461.50		Sawing or cutting-off machines:				
8461.50.40		Numerically controlled	....	4.4%	Free (A,CA,E,IL,J, MX)	30%
	10	Used or rebuilt	No.			
	50	Other	No.			
8461.50.80		Other	....	4.4%	Free (A,CA,E,IL,J, MX)	30%
	10	Used or rebuilt	No.			
	20	Other, valued under $3,025 each ..	No.			
	90	Other	No.			
8461.90		Other:				
8461.90.40		Numerically controlled	....	4.4%	Free (A,CA,E,IL,J, MX)	30%
	10	Used or rebuilt	No.			
	40	Other	No.			
8461.90.80		Other	....	4.4%	Free (A,CA,E,IL,J, MX)	30%
	10	Used or rebuilt	No.			
	20	Other, valued under $3,025 each ..	No.			
	80	Other	No.			

Source: Harmonized Tariff Schedule of the United States (Washington, DC: U.S. Government Printing Office, 1995), p. 84-62.

Summary

Explain why firms export and the three challenge areas of exporting.

Smaller firms, like larger ones, export to increase sales. Some begin to export accidentally, while others seek out foreign customers. Large multinationals export to serve markets where they have no manufacturing plants or where the local plant does not produce all of the product mix. Some host governments require an affiliate to export, and many firms export to remain competitive in the home market. Exporting is also an inexpensive way to test foreign markets. A product's life can be extended by exporting the product to markets where it is at the introduction stage of the product life cycle. The three challenge areas of exporting are (1) locating foreign markets, (2) payment and financing procedures, and (3) export procedures.

Identify the sources of export counseling and support.

The Trade Information Center, Small Business Administration, Small Business Development Centers, Department of Agriculture, state offices for export assistance, and World Trade Centers Association are some sources of export counseling. The Department of Commerce, the federal department in charge of export assistance, offers many programs covering all aspects of exporting. Commerce also assists in locating foreign representatives and making sales through trade fairs, matchmaker programs, and catalog and video shows.

Discuss the meaning of the various terms of sale.

Various terms of sale are possible in exporting. *FAS* (free alongside ship) means the seller pays all transportation expenses to the ship's side and is required to clear the goods for export. *CIF* (cost, insurance, and freight) means the seller quotes a price that includes cost of goods, insurance, and transportation to a specified destination. *CFR* (cost and freight) is like CIF except that the buyer pays the insurance costs. *DAF* (delivered at frontier) means that the seller's obligations are met when the goods have arrived at the border and been cleared for export. The buyer's responsibility is to arrange for its forwarder to pick up the goods after they are cleared for export, clear them for importation, and make delivery.

Identify some sources of export financing.

Some sources of export financing are commercial banks, factors, forfaiting, the Export-Import Bank (Ex-Im Bank), and the Small Business Administration.

Describe the activities of a foreign freight forwarder.

Foreign freight forwarders act as agents for exporters. They prepare documents, book space on carriers, and function as a firm's export traffic department.

Outline the export documents required.

Correct documentation is vital to the success of any export shipment. Shipping documents include export packing lists, export licenses, export bills of lading, shipper's export declaration, and insurance certificates. Collection documents include commercial invoices, consular invoices, certificates of origin, and inspection certificates.

Identify import sources.

Prospective importers can identify sources in a number of ways. They can examine the product label to see where the product is made and then contact the nearest embassy of that country to request the name of the manufacturer. Foreign chambers of commerce and trade organizations provide information on their countries' exporters. Electronic bulletin boards and data banks are also useful.

Explain the Harmonized Tariff Schedule of the United States (HTSUSA).

The HTSUSA is the American version of the Harmonized System used worldwide to classify imported products. A sample page from the HTSUSA is shown in Figure 17.5, and the listings can be viewed online at www.usitc.gov/tata/hts/index.htm.

Key Words

terms of sale (p. 451)
INCOTERMS (p. 451)
FOB (p. 452)
Ex-Works (p. 452)
letter of credit (L/C) (p. 453)
confirmed L/C (p. 454)
irrevocable L/C (p. 454)
air waybill (p. 455)
pro forma invoice (p. 455)
export, sight, and time drafts (p. 456)
banker's acceptance (p. 457)
factoring (p. 457)
forfaiting (p. 457)
Ex-Im Bank (p. 458)
Overseas Private Investment Corporation (OPIC) (p. 458)
foreign trade zone (FTZ) (p. 458)
free trade zone (p. 458)
customs drawbacks (p. 458)
shipper's export declaration (SED) (p. 460)

automated export system (AES) (p. 460)
validated export license (p. 460)
general export license (p. 460)
export bill of lading (B/L) (p. 460)
CE (Conformite Europeene) mark (p. 461)
customhouse broker (p. 463)
bonded warehouse (p. 464)
Automated Commercial System (ACS) (p. 464)
Harmonized Tariff Schedule of the United States (HTSUSA) (p. 464)

Questions

1. What are the common terms of sale quoted by exporters? For each, explain to what point the seller must pay transportation and delivery costs. Where does the responsibility for loss or damage pass to the buyer?
2. a. Explain the various export payment terms that are available.
   b. Which two offer the most protection to the seller?
3. What is the procedure for a letter-of-credit transaction?
4. The manager of the international department of the Cape Cod Five Bank learns on the way to work that the ship on which a local exporter shipped some goods to Spain has sunk. She has received all the documents required in the letter of credit and is ready to pay the exporter for the shipment. In view of the news about the ship, the manager now knows that the foreign customer will never receive the goods. Should the manager pay the exporter, or should she withhold payment and notify the overseas customer?
5. What is a foreign trade zone? Check with a customhouse broker or a U.S. Customs official or do some online research to determine the advantages of a foreign trade zone over a bonded warehouse.
6. What are the purposes of an export bill of lading?
7. An importer brings plain sports shirts to this country because the import duty is lower than it is for shirts with adornments. The importer then sews on a figure of a fox in this country. Should the importer do this operation in a foreign trade zone?
8. How would you find sources for a product that you want to import?
9. What does a customhouse broker do?
10. What does a freight forwarder do?

globalEDGE globalEDGE.msu.edu

Research Task

Use the globalEDGE site (http://globalEDGE.msu.edu) to complete the following exercises:

1. Your company is planning to expand its operations to Morocco. Considering each country has its own import and export regulations, prepare a report for top management of your company on Morocco's foreign trade barriers, listing current regulations and limitations on trade for both imports and exports in Morocco.
2. You own a company that specializes in fishery products. Until now, your firm has been selling to European markets (e.g., Germany, France, and the United Kingdom). Based on your experience with these companies, you are confident in your ability to engage in international business transactions appropriately. Therefore, you are convinced that it is time to expand into Asian markets. Nevertheless, the size of investment is significant, and you must have a clear picture of the current agricultural import regulations and standards for Asian countries. Using reports created by the U.S. Foreign Agriculture Service, find information on major agricultural import regulations and standards for Malaysia and Thailand.

Minicase 17.1 State Manufacturing Export Sales Price

State Manufacturing Company, a producer of farm equipment, had just received an inquiry from a large distributor in Italy. The quantity on which the distributor wanted a price was sufficiently large that Jim Mason, the sales manager, felt he had to respond. He knew the inquiry was genuine, because he had called two of the companies that the distributor said he represented, and both had assured him that the Italian firm was a serious one. It paid its bills regularly with no problems. Both companies were selling to the firm on open account terms.

Mason's problem was that he had never quoted on a sale for export before. His first impulse was to take the regular FOB factory price and add the cost of the extra-heavy export packing plus the inland freight cost to the nearest U.S. port. This price should enable the company to make money if he quoted the price FAS port of exit.

However, the terms of sale were bothering him. The traffic manager had called a foreign freight forwarder to learn about the frequency of sailings to Italy, and during the conversation she had suggested to the traffic manager that she might be able to help Mason. When Mason called her, he learned that because of competition, many firms like State Manufacturing were quoting CIF foreign port as a convenience to the importer. She asked him what payment terms he would quote, and he replied that his credit manager had suggested an irrevocable, confirmed letter of credit to be sure of receiving payment for the sale. He admitted that the distributor, however, had asked for payment against a 90-day time draft.

The foreign freight forwarder urged Mason to consider quoting CIF port of entry in Italy with payment as requested by the distributor to be more competitive. She informed him that he could get insurance to protect the company against commercial risk. To help him calculate a CIF price, she offered to give him the various charges if he would tell her the weight and value of his shipment FOB factory. He replied that the total price was $21,500 and that the gross weight, including the container, was 3,629 kilos.

Two hours later, she called to give him the following charges:

1. Containerization	$ 200.00
2. Inland freight less handling	798.00
3. Forwarding and documentation	90.00
4. Ocean freight	2,633.00
5. Commercial risk insurance	105.00
6. Marine insurance (total of items 1–5 × 1.1 = $27,858.60 at 60¢/$100)*	167.15

During that time, Mason had been thinking about the competition. Could he lower the FOB price for an export sale? He looked at the cost figures. Sales expense amounted to 20 percent of the sales price. Couldn't this be deducted on a foreign order? Research and development amounted to 10 percent. Should this be charged? Advertising and promotional expense amounted to another 10 percent. What about that? Because this was an unsolicited inquiry, there was no selling expense for this sale except for his and the secretary's time. Mason felt that it wasn't worth calculating this time.

If you were Jim Mason, how would you calculate the CIF port of entry price?

*Total coverage of marine insurance is commonly calculated on the basis of the total price plus 10 percent.

Minicase 17.2 Morgan Guaranty Trust Company Confirmation Letter

1. Who issued the letter of credit (shown on page 469)?
2. Is it irrevocable?
3. Has it been confirmed?
4. If so, by whom?
5. Who is the buyer?
6. Who is the seller?
7. What kind of draft is to be presented?
8. What documents are required?
9. What are the terms of sale?
10. When does the letter of credit expire?
11. Where does the seller go for payment?
12. Who pays the freight?
13. Who pays the marine insurance?
14. Must the steamship company attest that the merchandise has been loaded on ship?
15. What is the reason for your answer to question 14?

MORGAN GUARANTY TRUST COMPANY
OF NEW YORK
INTERNATIONAL BANKING DIVISION
23 WALL STREET, NEW YORK, N.Y. 10015

March 5, 20__

Smith Tool Co. Inc.
29 Bleecker Street
New York, N.Y. 10012

On all communications please refer to
NUMBER IC — 152647

Dear Sirs:

We are instructed to advise you of the establishment by
. Bank of South America, Puerto Cabello, Venezuela . . . .
of their IRREVOCABLE Credit No. 19845 . . . .
in your favor, for the account of John Doe, Puerto Cabello, Venezuela . . . .
for U. S. $3,000.00 (THREE THOUSAND U. S. DOLLARS) . . . .
available upon presentation to us of your drafts at sight on us, accompanied by:
Commercial Invoice in triplicate, describing the merchandise as indicated below

Consular Invoice in triplicate, all signed and stamped by the Consul of Venezuela

Negotiable Insurance Policy and/or Underwriter's Certificate, endorsed in blank, covering marine and war risks

Full set of straight ocean steamer Bills of Lading, showing consignment to the Bank of South America, Puerto Cabello, stamped by Venezuelan Consul and marked "Freight Prepaid",

evidencing shipment of UNA MAQUINA DE SELLAR LATAS, C.I.F. Puerto Cabello, from United States Port to Puerto Cabello, Venezuela

Except as otherwise expressly stated herein, this credit is subject to the Uniform Customs and Practice for Documentary Credits (1974 revision), International Chamber of Commerce Publication No. 290.

The above bank engages with you that all drafts drawn under and in compliance with the terms of this advice will be duly honored if presented to our Commercial Credits Department, 15 Broad Street, New York, N. Y. 10015, on or before March 31, 20* on which date this credit expires.

We confirm the foregoing and undertake that all drafts drawn and presented in accordance with its terms will be duly honored.

Yours very truly,

Authorized Signature

Immediately upon receipt, please examine this instrument and if its terms are not clear to you or if you need any assistance in respect to your availment of it, we would welcome your communicating with us. Documents should be presented promptly and not later than 3 P.M.

Appendix: Sample Outline for the Export Business Plan

I. Purpose—Why has the plan been written?

II. Table of contents—Include a list of any appendixes.

III. Executive summary—This is short and concise (not over two pages) and covers the principal points of the report. It is prepared after the plan has been written.

IV. Introduction—Explains why the firm will export.

V. Situation analysis.

- **A.** Description of the firm and products to be exported.
- **B.** Company resources to be used for the export business.
- **C.** Competitive situation in the industry.
  - **1.** Product comparisons.
  - **2.** Market coverage.
  - **3.** Market share.

D. Export organization—personnel and structure.

VI. Export marketing plan.

A. Long- and short-term goals.

1. Total sales in units.

2. Total sales in dollars.

3. Sales by product lines.

4. Market share.

5. Profit and loss forecasts.

B. Characteristics of ideal target markets.

1. GNP/capita.

2. GNP/capita growth rate.

3. Size of target market.

C. Identify, assess, and select target markets.

1. Market contact programs.

(a) U.S. Department of Commerce.

(b) World Trade Centers.

(c) Chamber of Commerce.

(d) Company's bank.

(e) State's export assistance program.

(f) Small Business Administration.

(g) Small Business Development Center in local university.

(h) Export hotline directory.

2. Market screening.

(a) First screening—basic need potential.

(b) Second screening—financial and economic forces.

(1) GNP/capita growth rate.

(2) Size of target market.

(3) Growth rate of target market.

(4) Exchange rate trends.

(5) Trends in inflation and interest rates.

(c) Third screening—political and legal forces.

(1) Import restrictions.

(2) Product standards.

(3) Price controls.

(4) Government and public attitude toward buying American products.

(d) Fourth screening—sociocultural forces.

(1) Attitudes and beliefs.

(2) Education.

(3) Material culture.

(4) Languages.

(e) Fifth screening—competitive forces.

(1) Size, number, and financial strength of competitors.

(2) Competitors' market shares.

(3) Effectiveness of competitors' marketing mixes.

(4) Levels of after-sales service.

(5) Competitors' market coverage—Can market segmentation produce niches that are now poorly attended?

(f) Field trips to best prospects.

(1) Department of Commerce trade mission.

(2) Trade missions organized by state or trade association.

D. Export marketing strategies.

1. Product lines to export.

2. Export pricing methods.

3. Channels of distribution.

(a) Direct exporting.

(b) Indirect exporting.

4. Promotion methods.

5. After-sales and warranty policies.

6. Buyer financing methods.

7. Methods for ongoing competitor analysis.

8. Sales forecast.

VII. Export financial plan.

- **A.** Pro forma profit and loss statement.
- **B.** Pro forma cash flow analysis.
- **C.** Break-even analysis.

VIII. Export performance evaluation.

- **A.** Frequency.
  - **1.** Markets.
  - **2.** Product lines.
  - **3.** Export personnel.
- **B.** Variables to be measured.
  - **1.** Sales by units and dollar volume in each market.
  - **2.** Sales growth rates in each market.
  - **3.** Product line profitability.
  - **4.** Market share.
  - **5.** Competitors' efforts in each market.
  - **6.** Actual results compared to budgeted results.

18 Marketing Internationally

Procter & Gamble European headquarters in Geneva, Switzerland

A global company should always go about its business in a way that's responsive to the major differences from one country to another, in terms of, for example, how retailing or distribution or payment systems work. But the core product or service should remain unchanged, . . . since that is what is "globalized."

—*Theodore Levitt, author of the landmark* Harvard Business Review *piece on standardization, "The Globalization of Markets"*

But when it comes to questions of taste and, especially, aesthetic preference, consumers do not like averages. . . . The lure of a universal product is a false allure.

—*Kenichi Ohmae*

Procter & Gamble's Path to Globalization

Procter & Gamble's global marketing efforts have brought results—Ariel, Tide, Pert, Pantene, and the Gillette-owned brands accessed by its 2005 acquisition. Today some of the 210-plus P&G brands are major brands everywhere around the world, and 21 of them are in the top-ranked billion-dollar sales category. In addition, 53 percent of P&G sales were outside the United States in 2005. China is the second-largest market by sales volume, and 4 percent of the 2006 sales originated in the Northeast Asia group. These results are remarkable given that P&G faces more pressures in many foreign markets than it does in its U.S. markets. For example, in the European markets, because the EU makes shipping across borders quite easy, competition in the household products sector is stiff. In France, P&G competes against Swedish, Danish, and Italian firms in many of its product categories. There are also unanticipated issues possibly related to nationalism that P&G repeatedly is required to address in foreign markets. In China in October 2006, P&G stopped selling its skin care products and began a massive refund effort when China's General Administration of Quality Supervision, Inspection and Quarantine said it had found trace levels of the metals chromium and neodymium in P&G products. In such situations, localization is mandated.

P&G's strategy for its international markets has evolved in an interesting way. In the 1940s, P&G's approach was to export its core products from the United States, build foreign demand, and then establish local sales companies and possibly production facilities. None of those products was launched with global distribution in mind. P&G's philosophy was to employ overseas the same policies and procedures that had worked for it in the United States. As a result, 15 years were needed for P&G to get Pampers into 70 countries. However, in the early 1990s, Edwin Artzt, then P&G's CEO, changed the firm's marketing strategy. Instead of waiting to introduce a new product worldwide until after it had accumulated marketing experience, the company would introduce products on a worldwide scale early in their development. The aim of this approach was to avoid giving competitors time to react in all other markets. As Artzt put it, "If P&G were introducing Pampers today, it would plan to get the product into world markets in five years or less." Today the present P&G CEO, A. G. Lafley, has commented that P&G can manage a worldwide rollout in less than 18 months.

At times in the past, the company has used a regional rather than a global approach, changing many of its products to suit the regional markets. Camay's smell, Crest's flavor, and Head & Shoulders' formula are some examples of products that varied from one region to another, as did the company's marketing strategy. Occasionally, P&G has recycled ad campaigns from the United States to other markets. For example, when the firm introduced Orange Crush in Peru, it used a TV spot showing a small boy who promised to save his soccer-playing brother's Orange Crush but then succumbed to temptation and drank it himself. This spot was credited with an important role in a 60 percent sales increase.

Now P&G has organized into three global business units, Beauty and Health, Household Care, and Gillette. Using this simple structure, it sells products in over 180 countries, primarily through mass merchandisers, grocery stores, membership club stores, and drugstores. P&G's global marketing officer, James Stengel, is

CONCEPT PREVIEWS

After reading this chapter, you should be able to:

explain why there are differences between domestic and international marketing

discuss why international marketing managers may wish to standardize the marketing mix

explain why it is often impossible to standardize the marketing mix worldwide

discuss the importance of distinguishing among the total product, the physical product, and the brand name

explain why consumer products generally require greater modification for international sales than do industrial products or services

discuss the product strategies that can be formed from three product alternatives and three kinds of promotional messages

explain "glocal" advertising strategies

discuss some of the effects the Internet may have on international marketing

discuss the distribution strategies of international marketers

Gli Affari Internazionali

nales Geschäft Παγοσμιο Business

Negócios Internacionais Los Negócios Internacionais

reluctant to apply the phrase "think global, act local" as P&G's marketing mantra today, because he is convinced that the relationships and interaction are more sophisticated than that. "I think P&G may be ahead in thinking through what the right balance is on global and local. My buzz word is that we must win with local consumers, day in day out. It's as simple and as difficult as that." To do so demands localization, woven seamlessly into the product mix. For example, each national or regional market has its own Internet presence. You can begin exploring P&G's global operations and markets at www.pg.com/company/who_we_are/globalops.jhtml. ■

Source: Procter & Gamble, *2006 Annual Report*, www.pg.com (October 6, 2006); "Survey: Creative Business: The World's Biggest Marketing Job: P&G," *Financial Times*, April 23, 2002; "P&G Suspends Skincare Sales in China," *Financial Times*, September 22, 2006, www.FT.com (October 7, 2006).

The opening vignette illustrates how P&G has changed its marketing strategy from using the same procedures and policies overseas that have proved successful in the United States to making global plans, adjusting them for regions, and then adapting products to satisfy local demands.

Whether a policy or technique is first designed for global use and then adapted for local market differences or, as in the case of the Orange Crush advertisement, the idea comes from the home country and then is used overseas, marketers must know where to look for possible differences between marketing domestically and marketing internationally. Sometimes the differences are great; at other times there may be few or even no differences.

Whether the differences between international and domestic marketing are great or small, marketers everywhere must know their markets, develop products or services to satisfy their customers' needs, price the products or services so that they are readily acceptable in the market, make them available to buyers, and inform potential customers, persuading them to buy.

Added Complexities of International Marketing

Although the basic functions of domestic and international marketing are the same, the international markets served often differ widely because of the great variations in the uncontrollable environmental forces—sociocultural, resource and environmental, economic and socioeconomic, legal, financial, and labor—that we examined in Section Three. Moreover, even the forces we think of as controllable vary across markets within wide limits. For example, distribution channels to which the marketer is accustomed may be unavailable. This is the case in Japan and in China. Certain aspects of the product may need to be different, for a number of reasons that range from taste and aesthetic preferences to voltage patterns and altitude issues. Then, too, the promotional mixes often must be dissimilar. Finally, distinct cost structures of specific markets may require that different prices be set.

The international marketing manager's task is complex. She or he frequently must plan and control a variety of marketing strategies, rather than a single unified and standardized one, and then coordinate and integrate those strategies into a single marketing program. Even marketing managers of global firms, such as P&G's global marketing officer, James Stengel, who may want to use a single worldwide strategy realize that doing so is impossible. They must know enough about the uncontrollable variables to be able to make quick and decisive implementation changes when necessary. P&G's recent issues in China with alleged skin care product contamination are a case in point.

Both global and multinational marketing managers, much like their domestic counterparts, have the same general challenges. They must develop marketing strategies by assessing the firm's potential foreign markets and analyzing the many alternative marketing mixes. Their aim here is to select target markets that the firm can serve at a profit and then to formulate combinations of tactics for product, price, promotion, and distribution channels that will best serve those markets. In Chapter 15, we examined the market assessment and selection process in the international domain; in this chapter, we shall study the formulation of the marketing mix for the international environment.

The Marketing Mix (What to Sell and How to Sell It)

The *marketing mix* is a set of strategy decisions made in the areas of product, promotion, pricing, and distribution in order to satisfy the needs and desires of customers in a target market. The number of variable factors included in these four marketing areas is large, making possible hundreds of combinations. Often a company's domestic operation has already established a successful marketing mix, and the temptation to follow the same strategies and tactics overseas is strong. Yet, as we have seen, important differences between the domestic and foreign environments are likely to make a wholesale transfer of the mix—its standardization—impossible, however desirable such a transfer may be from a business viewpoint. The question that the international marketing manager must resolve for each market is, "Can we standardize worldwide, should we make some changes, or should we formulate a completely different marketing mix?"

STANDARDIZE, ADAPT, OR FORMULATE ANEW?

Often top management would prefer to standardize the marketing mix globally; that is, the strategic decision makers would prefer to use the same marketing mix in all of the firm's markets because standardization can produce significant cost savings. If the product sold in the domestic market can be exported, regardless of where the product is made, there can be longer production runs, which lower manufacturing costs. In addition to these economies of scale, the longer experience curve, or learning curve, can create economies as well: The more experience we have doing something, the better we get at that activity, usually. Both of these economies, scale and experience, apply to marketing. A standardized approach can result in significant savings.

When advertising campaigns, promotional materials (catalogs, point-of-purchase displays), and sales training programs can be standardized, the expensive creative work and artwork need be done only once. A standardized corporate visual identity (CVI) (firm name, slogan, and graphics) can help project a consistent image for a multinational with publics dispersed across geographic locales.[1] Standardized pricing strategies for firms that serve markets from several different subsidiaries prevent the embarrassment of having an important customer receive two unequal price quotations for the same product. In summary, in addition to the cost benefits from standardization of the marketing mix, control and coordination are easier, and time spent preparing the marketing plan is reduced significantly.

In spite of the advantages of standardization, almost all firms find that this chapter's opening quote by Kenichi Ohmae is accurate for them: Standardization is seldom as easy as it seems. Many firms find it necessary to modify the present marketing mix or develop a new one. The extent of the changes depends on the type of product, the environmental forces, and the degree of market penetration desired. Further, given that the very concept of standardization is in a state of tension with the marketing principle, which centers on the needs of the buyer, not the seller, we probably should not be too disappointed that the economies that would come with complete standardization are almost never available to the seller, especially the seller in consumer goods.

Even Coca-Cola, the firm often portrayed as the exemplar of the standardized product, has found that its increasingly standardized strategy had run its course. According to Coca-Cola's former chair Douglas Daft: "As the [20th] century was drawing to a close, the world had changed course, and we had not. The world was demanding greater flexibility, responsiveness and local sensitivity, while we were further consolidating decision making and standardizing our practices. . . . The next big evolutionary step of 'going global' now has to be 'going local.' "[2] The tuition for Coke's learning was its loss of international market share to its competition, both global and local.

PRODUCT STRATEGIES

The product is the central focus of the marketing mix. If it fails to satisfy the needs of consumers, no amount of promotion, price cutting, or distribution will persuade people to buy. Consumers will not repurchase a detergent if the clothes do not come out as clean as commercials say they will. They will not be deceived by advertisements announcing friendly service when their own experience demonstrates otherwise.

total product

What the customer buys, including the physical product, brand name, accessories, after-sales service, warranty, instructions for use, company image, and package

In formulating product strategies, international marketing managers must remember that the product is more than a physical object. The **total product,** which is what the customer buys, includes the physical product, brand name, accessories, after-sales service, warranty, instructions for use, company image, and package (see Figure 18.1). That the total product is what the customer purchases may present the company with product adaptation opportunities that are less expensive and easier than would be the case if every adaptation had to alter the product's physical characteristics. Different package sizes and promotional messages, for example, can create a new total product for a distinct market. The relative ease of creating a new total product without changing the manufacturing process explains why there is more physical product standardization internationally than one might expect. Remember that a product can be localized by adaptation of the package, brand name, accessories, after-sales service, warranty, instructions for use, and company image.

Consider two products that Cadbury-Schweppes, the British-based food and soft-drink multinational, produces: tonic water and chocolate. Tonic water is a global product physically, but as a total product it is multidomestic because people in different markets buy it for different reasons. The French drink it straight, while the English mix it with alcohol. Chocolate is neither a global physical product nor a global total product; it is eaten as a snack in some areas, put in sandwiches in others, and eaten as a dessert elsewhere. Because of strong local preferences, it also varies greatly in taste, going from its pure, bitter taste to a quite sweet taste or a taste with some heat, depending on what is added to it. Nestlé instant coffee is produced in 200 different blends globally, all of which are sold under the brand name Nescafé, so there is brand-name globalization and physical product localization.[3]

Type of Product

The amount of change to be made in a product is affected by whether it is a consumer or industrial product or service and by the foreign environmental forces. Generally, consumer products require greater adaptation than do industrial products. If the consumer products are stylish or the result of a fad, they are especially likely to require changes. These product types form a continuum ranging from insensitive to the foreign environment to highly sensitive, as shown in Figure 18.2.

Industrial Products As Figure 18.2 suggests, many industrial products can be sold unchanged worldwide. Chips, for example, are used wherever computers are manufactured. If product changes are required, they may be cosmetic, such as converting gauges to read from

FIGURE 18.1

Components of the Total Product

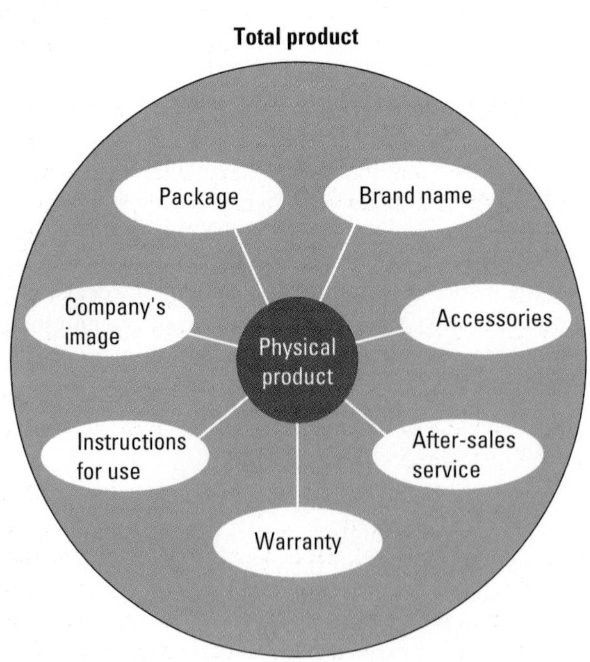

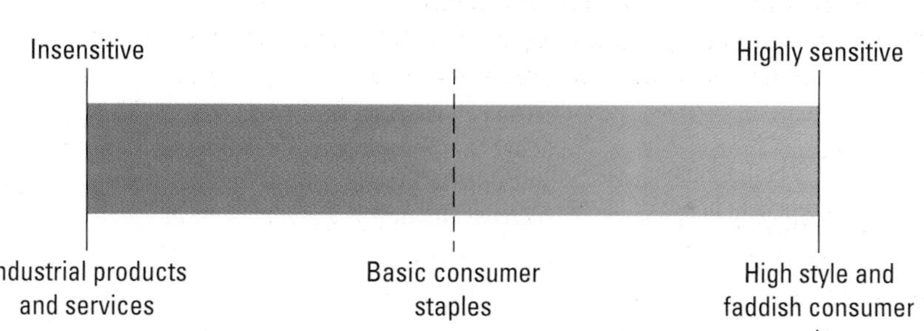

FIGURE 18.2

Continuum of Sensitivity to the Foreign Environment

the metric system to the U.S. or British Imperial system of feet and inches or printing instructions in another language. Note that the U.S. adherence to the feet and inches measurement system (the U.S. system) may limit export possibilities, since the majority of countries follow the metric system and want their machinery and parts to be on the metric scale. The United States, Liberia, and Burma are the three nations that have not switched to the metric system, also known as the *SI* or *International System of Units*.

When product adaptations are necessary, they may be relatively simple ones, such as lengthening pedals and changing seat positions to compensate for consumer preferences among markets. However, somewhat more drastic modifications in the physical product may be necessary. In developing countries, there is a tendency to both overload equipment and overlook its maintenance. To overcome these market differences, manufacturers such as Caterpillar and Allis-Chalmers established thorough training programs as a part of the total product purchase wherever their products are sold. The other alternative is to modify the equipment, perhaps using a simpler bearing system that requires little maintenance.

Occasionally adaptations are necessary to meet local legal requirements, such as those that govern noise, safety, or exhaust emissions. To avoid the need to change the product, some manufacturers design it to meet the most stringent laws even though it will be overdesigned for the rest of its markets. In some instances, governments have passed strict laws with the intent of protecting a local manufacturer from import competition. When this occurs, the company may prefer to design the product for the country with the next most stringent laws and stay out of the first market. Of course, this is what the government had in mind when it passed the law. However, a word of caution based on one of the author's experiences: The company in this situation would be advised to test the local manufacturer's product before giving up on the market. On occasion, the local product also has failed to meet the specifications. When confronted with this evidence, the government has had to change its laws.

Consumer Products Although consumer products generally require greater modification to meet local market requirements than do industrial products, some of them can be sold unchanged to certain market segments that have similar characteristics across countries. Consumer products of this kind include a number of luxury items, such as automobiles, sports equipment, and perfumes. Every country in the world contains a market segment that is more similar to the same segment in other countries with respect to economic status, buyer behavior, tastes, and preferences than it is to the rest of the segments in the same country. This market segment includes the cosmopolitan consumers: foreign-educated and well-traveled citizens and expatriates. Many products and services foreign to local tastes and preferences have been successfully introduced in a number of countries by first being marketed to these similar groups. Gradually, members of other market segments have purchased these products and services until consumption has become widespread.

While "jet-setters" may share much in common across countries, marketers tend to find greater dissimilarities in social and cultural values as they go down the economic strata in each country. It follows from this that, in general, the deeper the desired immediate market penetration is, the greater must be the product modification. Remember that this observation does not suggest that for deeper market penetration, the physical product has to be changed. Perhaps a modification of one of the other elements of the total product is sufficient—a different

WORLD view

On Global Marketing

Employees stand behind the counter of the first McDonald's fast-food restaurant in New Delhi, India. The store features Maharaja Macs and Vegetable Burgers with Cheese on its menu.

"The globalization of markets is at hand. With that, the multinational commercial world nears its end and so does the multinational corporation. Different cultural preferences, national tastes and standards, and business institutions are vestiges of the past." So said the marketing scholar Theodore Levitt, a Harvard Business School professor emeritus in 1983. Levitt cited such examples as Coca-Cola, Pepsi-Cola, McDonald's, and Revlon. Though he sensed that the world markets were changing, his conclusion was too simple.

Coca-Cola's own advertising director replied, "What looks good as a generalization sometimes doesn't follow. The world is certainly becoming more globalized, but the global village is certainly not here, nor will it ever be." At PepsiCo, overseas offices choose and reedit commercials made in the United States. Local operations also produce local products. An example is the soft drink Shani, a currant-and-blackberry soda popular in the Mideast during Ramadan, the Muslim holy month. As for McDonald's, it sells beer in Germany, the McAloo Tikki in India, pot pies in Australia, and noodles in the Philippines. "We rely on the people native to the country to develop marketing programs," says the marketing vice president.

In a 20-year retrospective on Levitt's article, Sir Martin Sorrell, chief executive of the WPP Group, noted that Levitt's perspective had ignored the power of the customer. "The customer is in control," he said. "There will continue to be substantial and enduring differences around the world in what and how consumers consume." In fact, Sorrell expressed the opinion that firms' marketing focus would become even more localized over the coming years. To sum up, the success of global marketing depends on the kind of product and on knowing when product or promotional adaptations are beneficial.

Source: Theodore Levitt, "The Globalization of Markets," *Harvard Business Review*, May–June 1983, pp. 92, 96; "Ad Fad," *The Wall Street Journal*, May 12, 1988, pp. 1, 17; WWP, http://ww2.wpp.com (October 8, 2006); and Garry Emmons, "Globalization Revisited," www.alumni.hbs.edu/bulletin/2003/september/globalization.html (June 20, 2004).

size or color of the package, a change in the brand name, or a new positioning, if the product is consumed differently. Different emphasis in after-sales service is also important.

An example illustrates the repositioning and repackaging possibilities. Mars, one of the largest privately owned and family operated companies, faced a drop in Bahrain's imports of candy when it was ready to launch M&Ms. Fortunately, its marketing research discovered that Bahrainis consider the peanut to be a health food, so Mars repositioned its peanut M&Ms as a health food. The company also was able to turn the hot Gulf climate to its advantage by emphasizing the packaging through its traditional slogan, "M&Ms melt in your mouth, not in your hand." As you will see later in this chapter, Mars followed promotional strategy number 2, same product–different message, although even part of the message (the slogan) remained the same.

Services The marketing of services, like the marketing of industrial products, is generally less complex globally than is the marketing of consumer products. The consulting firm Accenture has 110 offices in 48 countries offering the same kinds of business expertise as the firm provides in the United States.[4] However, laws and customs sometimes do mandate that providers alter their services. For example, Manpower cannot operate in some markets because in those countries, private employment agencies are against the law. Accounting laws vary substantially among nations, but the large accounting firms operate globally, making local adaptations where necessary. Ernst & Young has 114,000 professionals in 140 countries.[5] VISA, MasterCard, and American Express are examples of successful companies in the global credit card industry. They had combined billings of $1.7 trillion in 1996; nine years later, Visa alone had card sales volume of just over $4 trillion.[6]

Foreign Environmental Forces In Section Three we examined the foreign environmental forces extensively, so here we will limit our discussion to a few concrete examples of how some of these forces might affect product offerings.

Sociocultural Forces Dissimilar cultural patterns often require changes, either in the physical product or in aspects of the total product, in food and other consumer goods. The worldwide variation in consumer preferences for clothes washing is a challenge for appliance makers. The French want top-loading washing machines, and the British want front-loaders; the Germans insist on high-speed machines that remove most of the moisture in the spin-dry cycle, but the Italians prefer slower spin speeds because they let the sun do the drying. Hence, Whirlpool must produce a variety of models, although after buying the Philips appliance business in 1991 and Maytag in early 2006, it has taken huge steps toward integrating a collection of independent national companies into regional manufacturing facilities and product platforms, on the model of integration in the Whirlpool European organization that shares a few common platforms. When Whirlpool's European integration began in 1994, its CEO at the time argued that the national differences are exaggerated: "This business is the same all over the world. There is great opportunity to leverage that sameness."[7] After a painful restructuring in which Whirlpool closed a surplus Spanish plant, laid off 2,000 workers, centralized inventory control, and reduced its 36 European warehouses to 8, both European sales and operating margins improved. In fact, Whirlpool has created a "world washer," called Duet in the United States and Dreamspace in Europe, combining the U.S. preference for large-load capacity, the European preference for front-loading machines,[8] and sensor technology that selects wash time and water consumption.

While some international firms, such as Campbell's, have been extremely successful in employing the same brand name, label, and colors worldwide, other firms learn they must change names, labels, or colors because of cultural differences. Gold appears frequently on packages in Latin America because Latin Americans view it as a symbol of quality and prestige. Procter & Gamble found that a gold package has value in Europe, too, after it launched its silver-boxed Crest Tartar Control Formula in the United Kingdom, which was followed two months later by Colgate's equivalent in a gold box. P&G officials agreed that Colgate's choice of gold was better than their silver. They explained that silver was how the product was packaged in the United States.[9] The meaning that colors have for people in different cultures is also a marketing consideration. For example, in the Netherlands blue is considered warm and feminine, but the Swedes consider it masculine and cold.

Even if the colors can remain the same, instructions on labels must be translated into the language of the market. Firms selling in areas where two or more languages are spoken, such as Canada, Switzerland, Belgium, and the United States, may need to use multilingual labels. Where instructions are not required, as in the case of some consumer or industrial products whose use is well known, there is an advantage to printing the label in the language of the country best known for the product. A French label on a perfume helps strengthen the product's image in the United States.

A perfectly good brand name may have to be scrapped because of its unfavorable connotations in another language. An American product failed to survive in Sweden because its name translated to "enema." In Latin America, a product had to be taken off the market when the manufacturer found that the name meant "jackass oil." Of course, this problem occurs in both directions, as a Belgian brewery found when it tried to introduce its Delerium Tremens lager to the U.S. market. American authorities told the company the name was an incitement to drinking.[10] Sometimes a firm will not use a perfectly good name because the firm makes assumptions about the impact of the name on foreign locals and doesn't test

Pemex gasoline doesn't go.

WORLD view   

Will "Smart Mobs" Dictate Consumer Trends?

Product preferences and social trends wash across countries and continents. Evidence is clear that the speed of diffusion of these trends is increasing. And the mechanisms for even faster diffusion are already with us—technologies such as myspace, wikis, instant messaging, and cell phones. At least one thinker has dubbed what happens when technology connects people together as "smart mobs." In 2001, Philippine president Joseph Estrada was ousted after a wave of popular protests. Although this was not the first time a leader was toppled by protesters, this incident is noteworthy because the protests were organized by wireless communication—a smart mob.

Just as protesters can be assembled quickly by wireless communication, partygoers can stay in touch by phone and move from one party to another in coordinated (but largely leaderless) movements. Howard Rheingold, who may have coined the "smart mobs" term, noticed flocks of Japanese teenagers converging on public places, coordinated by text messages. Some smart mobs have even become institutionalized—for example, the Aula community in Helsinki and cyberspace is composed of Finns who use mobile media to socialize and collaborate in geographic and virtual places simultaneously. In the United States the Dodgeball service lets you contact it from a location, say, a bar, and identifies which of your friends is in the area. The practice of "bluejacking"—sending messages to other Bluetooth-enabled phones in an area—is also growing.

From a marketing standpoint, the word-of-mouth marketing capability these innovations represent is desirable. The combination of mobile communications and the Internet provides a good environment for word-of-mouth transmission of product news.

Source: Malcolm Gladwell, *The Tipping Point: How Little Things Can Make a Big Difference* (Boston: Little, Brown, 2000); Sean Carton, "It's Not about the Technology," www.clickz.com/tech/lead-edge/print.php/1443551 (August 12, 2002); Dan Gilmore, "Finland's Smart Mobs," www.siliconvalley.com/mld/siliconvalley/business/columnists/dangillmor/ejournal/3772371.htm (September 17, 2002); Howard Rheingold, *Smart Mobs: The Next Social Revolution* (Cambridge, MA: Perseus, 2002); various postings from www.aula.cc.; and Eric Bender, "Social Lives of a Cell Phone," *MIT Technology Review*, July 12, 2004.

these assumptions with locals. This is what happened with the Nova. As the story goes, Chevrolet couldn't sell Novas in (the storyteller picks a Spanish-speaking country) because Nova means *no va* ("doesn't go") in Spanish. But the two words are pronounced very differently—*Nova* has the accent on the first syllable, whereas the accent for *no va* falls on the *va*. Therefore, to someone speaking Spanish, the words have very different meanings. Native Spanish-speaking people would be likely to connect *nova* with "star," which is probably what General Motors had in mind. You may be surprised to learn that Pemex, the government-owned petroleum monopoly in Mexico, once called its regular gasoline *Nova*.

An important difference in social forces to which American marketers are not accustomed is people's preference in other nations for making daily visits to small neighborhood specialty shops and large, open markets where they can socialize while shopping. More frequent buying involves smaller packages, which is important to a shopper who has no automobile in which to carry purchases. However, this custom is changing in Europe, where consumers are demanding the kinds of assortments that only a large store can offer. Shopping frequency is also slowing as European women are finding that they have less free time than previously. The solution has been the huge combination supermarket–discount house (*hypermarché* in France) with ample parking, located in the suburbs. A similar situation has been occurring in Mexico, especially since NAFTA ended many of the country's import restrictions.

There is a parallel here to the situation that began in the 1940s in the United States. The same conditions of rising incomes, a growing middle class, and a large number of working wives have combined to put a premium on the shopper's time, and just as occurred in the United States, mass merchandising and catalog and Internet shopping have moved in to fill this need.

Legal Forces Legal forces can be a formidable constraint in the design of product strategies because if the firm fails to adhere to a country's laws governing the product, it will be unable to do business in that country. Laws concerning pollution, consumer protection, and operator safety are being enacted rapidly in many parts of the world and limit the marketer's freedom to standardize the product mix internationally. For example, American machinery manufacturers exporting to Sweden have found that Swedish operator safety requirements are stricter than those required by the Occupational Safety and Health Act (OSHA), so if they wish to market in Sweden, they must produce a special model. Of course, product standards set ostensibly to protect a nation's citizens can be effective in protecting indigenous industry from foreign competitors.

Laws prohibiting certain classes of imports are common in developing nations, as potential exporters learn when they research the world for markets. Products considered luxuries, as well as products already being manufactured, are among the first to be excluded from importation, but such laws also affect local production.

Foods and pharmaceuticals are especially influenced by laws concerning purity and labeling. Food products sold in Canada, whether imported or produced locally, are subject to strict rules that require both English and French on the labels as well as metric and inch/pound units. The law even dictates the space permitted between the number and the unit—"16 oz." is correct, but "16oz." is not. The Venezuelan government has decreed that the manufacturer or the importer must affix to the package the maximum retail price at which many products can be sold. Because of Saudi Arabians' concern about avoiding food containing pork, the label of any product containing animal fat or meat that is sold in Saudi Arabia must identify the kind of animal used or state that no swine products were used.

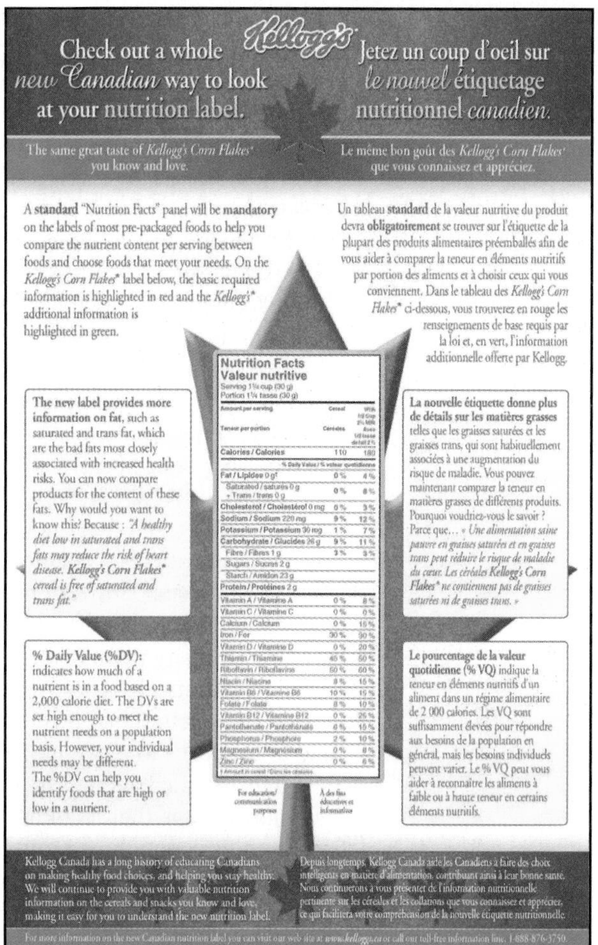

Firms planning to market their products in Canada must adhere to that country's strict labeling regulations, requiring labels to include both English and French as well as metric and inch/pound units.

Legal forces also may prevent a worldwide firm from employing its brand name in all its overseas markets. Managements accustomed to the American law, which establishes the right to a brand name by priority in use, are surprised to learn that in code law countries, a brand belongs to the person registering it first. Thus, the marketer may go into foreign markets expecting to use the company's long-established brand name only to find that someone else owns it. The name may have been registered by someone who is employing it legitimately for his or her own products, or it may have been pirated, that is, registered by someone who hopes to profit by selling the name back to the originating firm.

To avoid this predicament, the firm must register its brand names in every country where it wants to use them or where it might use them in the future. And this must be done rapidly. The Paris Convention grants a firm that has registered a name in one country only six months' priority to register it elsewhere. To be certain that it has enough names for new products, Unilever, the English-Dutch manufacturer of personal care products, has over 100,000 trademarks registered throughout the world, most of which are not in use but are kept in reserve.

The use of domain names on the Internet shows that these problems have not decreased. A study found that American Express, for example, had registered the domain name "americanexpress" in 19 countries, while in 11 others the name was registered to someone other than American Express. In a more extreme example, CBS found that it had 4 registrations but others had 46. When kanji characters became an option for registering Japanese domain names, tiny Web Japan Co. got a head start by registering some 100 domain names, including those of major corporations.[11]

Economic Forces The disparity in income throughout the world is an obstacle to worldwide product standardization. Some products are priced too high for some consumers in developing nations, and so the firm must adjust to the consumers' ability to pay. Such adjustments may include simplification or repackaging. Procter & Gamble sells shampoo for individual use in India, in addition to the regular bottle quantity. Many of the DVD players sold in India are $45 do-it-yourself assembly kits.[12] In addition, many consumers throughout the world buy cell phone air time by purchasing prepaid cards worth only a few dollars or even by renting cell phones by the call from intermediaries. As C. K. Prahalad points out in his *The Fortune at the Bottom of the Pyramid*, the 5 billion people in poverty in developing nations have $14 trillion in purchasing power.[13]

In some cases the foreign subsidiary cannot afford to produce as complete a product mix as does the parent. Most automobile manufacturers assemble the less expensive and higher-volume line locally and broaden the local product mix by importing, when permitted, the luxury cars. International firms practice this marketing technique whenever possible because a captive foreign sales organization is available to promote the sales of the home organization's exports and because the revenue derived helps pay the subsidiary's overhead. Yet GM has been successful with its Buick in China by introducing the Buick as a premium brand and then moving to mid-range and economy vehicles. Despite a late start in the market (1994), GM ranks second only to Volkswagen, which has been there for two decades. Sales for GM in China rose over 50 percent between 2003 and 2004 and hit a record in 2005. Thanks to Buick, GM has 11.2 percent of the market in China.[14]

Physical Forces Physical forces, such as climate and terrain, also militate against international product standardization. Manufacturers of clothes washers have found success in India by "hardening" their machines against heat, dirt, and power outages. The heat and high humidity in many parts of the tropics require that electrical equipment be built with extra-heavy insulation. Consumer goods that are affected by moisture must be specially packaged to resist its penetration. Thus, pills are wrapped individually in foil and baked goods are packaged in tin boxes to prevent their degradation by moisture.

High altitudes frequently require product alteration. Food manufacturers have found that they must change their cooking instructions for people who live at high altitudes because at such altitudes cooking takes longer. The thinner atmosphere requires that producers of cake mixes include less yeast as well. Gasoline and diesel motors generate less power at high altitudes, so the manufacturer must often supply a larger engine.

Mountainous terrain implies high-cost highways, and so in the poorer countries, roads may require heavy-duty capabilities. Trucks traveling poorer-quality roads need tires with thicker treads and heavy-duty suspensions. Because of the rough ride, packaging must be stronger than that used in the United States. From these examples, we can appreciate that even though an unchanged product may be culturally and economically acceptable in a market, the effect of the physical forces alone may be strong enough to require some product modification.

Environmental forces may play a major part in foreign product strategies. Their influence is pervasive in the design of the entire marketing mix. A useful guide for the marketing mix preparation is a matrix in which the marketing mix variables are tabulated against the environmental forces. Such a guide is at the end of this chapter.

PROMOTIONAL STRATEGIES

promotion
Any form of communication between a firm and its publics

Promotion, one of the basic elements of the marketing mix, is communication that secures understanding between a firm and its publics to bring about a favorable buying action and achieve long-lasting confidence in the firm and the product or service it provides. Note that this definition employs the plural *publics*, because the seller's promotional efforts must be directed to more than just the ultimate consumers, including retailers and other members of the distribution channel.

Promotion both influences and is influenced by the other marketing mix variables. Nine distinct promotion strategies are possible, by combining the three alternatives of (1) marketing the same physical product everywhere, (2) adapting the physical product for foreign markets, and (3) designing a different physical product with (*a*) the same, (*b*) adapted, or (*c*) different messages.[15] We examine below the six strategies most commonly used:

1. *Same product–same message:* When marketers find that target markets vary little with respect to product use and consumer attitudes, they can offer the same product and use the same promotional appeals in all markets. Avon, Maidenform, and A.T. Cross follow this strategy.

2. *Same product–different message:* The same product may satisfy a different need or be used differently elsewhere. This means the product may be left unchanged but a different message is required. Honda's early "You meet the nicest people on a Honda" campaign appealed to Americans who used their motorcycles as pleasure vehicles, but in Brazil Honda stressed the use of motorcycles as basic transportation. Honda has captured about 90 percent of the Brazilian motorcycle market.
3. *Product adaptation–same message:* In cases where the product serves the same function but must be adapted to different conditions, the same message is employed with a changed product. In Japan, Lever Brothers puts Lux soap in fancy boxes because much of it is sold as gifts.
4. *Product adaptation–message adaptation:* In some cases, both the product and the promotional message must be modified for foreign markets. In Latin America, Tang is especially sweetened, premixed, and ready to drink in pouches. Unlike Americans, Latin Americans do not drink it for breakfast. There it is promoted as a drink for mealtimes and for throughout the day but not for breakfast.
5. *Different product–same message:* In many markets the potential customers cannot afford the product as manufactured for developed markets. To overcome this obstacle, companies frequently produce a very distinct product for these markets. Substituting a low-cost plastic squeeze bottle for an aerosol can and a manually operated washing machine for an automated one are two examples. The promotional message, however, can be very similar to what is used in the developed markets if the product performs the same functions.
6. *Different product for the same use–different message:* Frequently, the different product requires a different message as well. Welding torches rather than automatic welding machines would be sold on the basis of low acquisition cost rather than high output per hour. The governments of developing countries faced with high unemployment would be persuaded by a message emphasizing the job-creating possibilities of labor-intensive processes rather than the labor saving of highly automated machinery.

The tools for communicating these messages—the promotional mix—are advertising, personal selling, sales promotion, public relations, and publicity. No one of these tools is inherently superior to the others, though circumstances in a given situation may dictate that one of them be emphasized more than the others. Just as in the case of the product strategies, the composition of the promotional mix will depend on the type of product, the environmental forces, and the amount of market penetration desired.

Advertising Among all the promotional mix elements, **advertising** may be the one with the greatest similarities worldwide. This is the case because much advertising is based on American practices. U.S. ad agencies have followed their corporate customers into the global realm through wholly owned subsidiaries, joint ventures, and working agreements with local agencies. The decision to go global, as Apple has with the iPod, or to go either local or regional, as Intel, P&G, and McDonald's all have, is not an easy one. One commentator observes that the trend is toward localization, at least for a while.[16]

advertising
Paid, nonpersonal presentation of ideas, goods, or services by an identified sponsor

Cultural dimensions play a major role in these decisions. Here is a summary of their influence, adapted from work by the scholar and researcher Lars Perner:[17]

Directness vs. indirectness: U.S. advertising tends to be direct. What are the product benefits? Such bluntness may be considered too pushy for Japanese consumers, where such directness is read as arrogance. How could the seller presume to know what the consumer would like?

Comparison: Comparative advertising is banned in most countries and would probably be counterproductive in Asia, seen as an insulting instance of confrontation and bragging, even if it were allowed. In the United States, comparison advertising has proved effective (although its implementation is tricky).

Humor: Although humor is a relatively universal phenomenon, what is considered funny differs greatly across cultures, so pretesting is essential.

Gender roles: A study found that women in U.S. advertising tended to be shown in more traditional roles than in Europe or Australia. Some countries are more traditional than the United States. A Japanese ad describing a camera as "so simple that even a woman can use it" was not found to be insulting.

Explicitness: Europeans tend to tolerate more explicit advertisements, often with sexual overtones, than do Americans.

Sophistication: Europeans, particularly the French, demand considerably more sophistication than Americans, who may react more favorably to emotional appeals.

Popular vs. traditional culture: U.S. ads tend to employ contemporary, popular culture, often including current music, while those in more traditional cultures tend to refer more to classical culture.

Information content vs. fluff: American ads often contain puffery, which was found to be ineffective in Eastern European countries because it resembled communist propaganda. The Eastern European consumers instead want facts.

Global and Regional Brands Manufacturers are increasingly using global or regional brands for a number of reasons:

1. Cost is most often cited. By producing one TV commercial for use across a region, a firm can save up to 50 percent of the production cost.
2. There is a better chance of obtaining one regional source to do high-quality work than of finding sources in various countries that will work to the same high standard.
3. Some marketing managers believe their companies must have a single image throughout a region.
4. Companies are establishing regionalized organizations where many functions, such as marketing, are centralized.
5. Global and regional satellite and cable television is widely available.

Economies of scale are one reason some firms emphasize the regional or global standardization of advertising. Coca-Cola, for example, once estimated that it saved over $8 million annually in the cost of thinking up new imagery by repeating the same theme everywhere.

The head of a consulting firm specializing in brands and corporate identity has a different idea. He says, "There are too many businesses out there doing the same thing. Global branding is a way of saying your company makes a difference, which moves you up the pecking order."[18] Look at the value placed on the world's most valuable brands (Table 18.1).

Global or National The debate continues among international marketers about using global, regional, or national brands. Companies that acquired successful regional or national brands on purchasing the original owner have been extremely cautious about converting them to their global brands. Nestlé is an example of a large global firm that uses both. Nestlé tries to achieve consumer familiarity and marketing efficiency by using two brands on a single product, a local brand that may be familiar and appeal only to a small group of consumers and a corporate strategic brand such as Nestlé or Nescafé. In some markets, in Asian ones, for example, product quality across many categories is suggested by a shared brand. This developed from the *keiretsu* structure as evidenced by Mitsubishi, C. Itoh, and Mitsui.

Private Brands Private brands have become serious competitors for manufacturers' brands and are responsible for a shift in power from manufacturers to retailers. Private labels have flooded Japan's large supermarket chains, capturing one-third of the British and Swiss food markets and one-fifth of the French and German markets. The trend toward private labels also has caught on in Spain and the Netherlands. The Swedish food group Axfood AB notes that it profits twice from private-label manufacturing: first when it sells the product (such as ketchup) at a lower price to its stores, and then when the profit margin is higher when selling to the ultimate consumer.[19]

TABLE 18.1 Comparing Global Brand Values, 2004–2006

Rank 2006 (2004)	Brand	Value ($ millions)
1 (1)	Coca-Cola, U.S	$67,000
2 (2)	Microsoft, U.S.	56,926
3 (3)	IBM, U.S.	56,201
4 (4)	GE, U.S.	48,907
5 (5)	Intel, U.S.	32,319
6 (6)	Nokia, Finland	30,131
7 (9)	Toyota, Japan	27,941
8 (7)	Disney, U.S.	27,848
9 (8)	McDonald's, U.S.	27,501
10 (11)	Mercedes-Benz, Germany	21,795
11 (12)	Citibank, U.S.	21,458
12 (10)	Marlboro, U.S.	21,350
13 (13)	Hewlett-Packard, U.S.	20,458
14 (14)	American Express, U.S.	19,641
15 (16)	BMW, Germany	19,617
16 (15)	Gillette, U.S.	19,579
17 (18)	Louis Vuitton, France	17,606
18 (17)	Cisco, U.S.	17,532
19 (19)	Honda, Japan	17,049
20 (20)	Samsung, Korea	16,169

Source: "The Top 100 Brands 2006," *BusinessWeek Online*, www.bwnt.com/brand/2006 (October 10, 2006).

Availability of Media Satellite TV broadcasters make possible numerous programming networks to provide service to millions of households in dozens of countries and in many languages. International print media include local, national, and regional editions. *The European*, a daily newspaper; the international edition of *The Herald Tribune;* the Asian and European editions of *The Wall Street Journal;* and the international editions of the *Manchester Guardian* and *The Financial Times* are some of the newspapers with wide circulation. Advertisers can also go to other media to reach their markets. Cinema advertising is heavily used in many parts of the world (including Norway, Austria, the United Kingdom, and Brazil), as are billboards. In a number of developing countries, automobiles equipped with loudspeakers circulate through the cities announcing products, and street signs are furnished by advertisers whose messages hang on them. Homeowners can get a free coat of paint by permitting advertisers to put ads on their walls. Busses and trains carry advertisements. Where mail delivery is reliable, direct mail is a powerful medium, as are trade fairs. Probably one of the most ingenious campaigns ever was that of a tea company that gave away thousands of printed prayers with a tea commercial on the other side to pilgrims bound for Mecca.

The point is that media of some kind are available in every market, and the local managers and ad agencies are familiar with the advantages of each kind. Media selection is extremely difficult for international advertising managers who try to standardize their media mix from the home office. The variation in media availability is a strong reason for leaving this part of the advertising program to the local organization.

Internet Advertising We mentioned the importance of the Internet as a market research tool in Chapter 15, and it is important as an advertising medium as well. Among the appealing factors of online advertising in the international sphere are the following:

1. The Internet provides an affluent, reachable audience. A high number of users in a wide variety of countries read English or other common languages well. Native-language sites are strongly preferred, though.

2. Unlike TV or newspaper ads, Internet communications are two-way. They are cheap. And they are possibly less regulated than other advertising forms. In Europe, where direct advertising of prescription drug products is banned, Internet sites are a way to provide potential consumers with product information. The disclaimer that the information is for U.S. audiences only may be ignored.
3. The possibility exists of involving customers in determining which messages and information they receive. For this reason, there is some possibility that company Web offerings will be tailor-made by the user. This customization increases the application of the marketing concept.
4. Although the Internet doesn't reach all possible groups, for some groups it may be among the best media choices. For teenagers in particular, Internet advertising can be important because teenagers spend less time watching TV than any other demographic group, preferring to spend time on the Internet or to play computer games.

Type of Product Buyers of industrial goods and luxury products usually act on the same motives the world over; thus, these products lend themselves to a standardized approach. Such standardization enables manufacturers of capital goods, such as General Electric and Caterpillar, to prepare international campaigns that require very little modification in their various markets. Certain consumer goods markets are similar, too. Another set of characteristics also permits firms to use the same appeals and sales arguments worldwide: when the product is low-priced, is consumed in the same way, and is bought for the same reasons. Examples of such products are gasoline, soft drinks, detergents, cosmetics, and airline services. Firms such as Exxon (Esso), Coca-Cola, Apple and Avon have used the international approach successfully. Generally, the changes they have made are a translation into the local language and the use of indigenous models.

Foreign Environmental Forces Like variations in media availability, foreign environmental forces act as deterrents to the international standardization of advertising, and as you would expect, among the most influential of these forces are the *sociocultural* forces, which we examined in Chapter 6.

A basic cultural decision for the marketer is whether to position the product as foreign or local. Which way to go seems to depend on the country, the product type, and the target market. In Germany, for example, consumers are not at all impressed by the carmaker that announces it has American know-how. At the same time, such purely American products as bourbon, fast-food restaurants, and blue jeans have made tremendous inroads there and in the rest of Europe.

Similarly, in Japan and elsewhere in Asia, the national identity of some consumer products enhances their image. The rage among Chinese teenagers is anything from Korea. The influence of American-style fast-food restaurants on Japanese youth was emphasized in a survey taken by the Japanese Ministry of Agriculture, which found that more than 50 percent of the country's teenagers would rather eat Western foods than the traditional dishes. U.S.-based fast-food restaurants such as McDonald's (Japan's largest restaurant business), KFC (the third largest), Dairy Queen, and Mister Donut account for half the total restaurant business. And KFC is zeroing in on an even larger Asian market—it had well over 2,000 restaurants in China at the beginning of 2006 and is expanding by over 200 units a year.[20] An indication of the significance of national identity is the Japanese *anime*-style cartoons that dominate the time slots in the after-school and Saturday morning American TV schedules.[21]

The experience of suppliers to the youth market indicates that this, too, is an international market segment, much like the market for luxury goods. A former director of MTV Europe observed that "18-year-olds in Paris have more in common with 18-year-olds in New York than with their own parents. They buy the same products, go to the same movies, listen to the same music, sip the same colas. Global advertising merely works on that premise." This similarity suggests that marketers can formulate global advertising campaigns for these consumers that will require little more than a translation into the local language, unless the product strategy goes with a foreign identity. That decision should be made with local input.

Because communication, the reason for advertising, is impossible if the language is not understood, translations must be made into the language of the consumers. Unfortunately for the advertiser, almost every language varies from one country to another. The same word may be perfectly apt in one country while connoting something completely different in another. To avoid connotation errors in translation, the experienced advertising manager will use a back translation and plenty of illustrations with short copy.

Because a nation's laws generally reflect public opinion, the cultural forces tend to be closely allied to the legal forces, which exert a strong and pervasive influence on advertising. We have seen how laws affect media availability; they also restrict the kinds of products that can be advertised and the copy employed in the advertisements.

American firms accustomed to using comparative advertising at home are surprised to find that legal restrictions on this technique exist in some markets. Since the early 1990s PepsiCo has used comparative advertising to knock Coca-Cola, and wherever possible, Coke has used the courts to stop the ads. PepsiCo launched a series of TV commercials, the Pepsi Challenge campaign, in 1995 to test the comparative advertising laws of 30 countries. The ads presented the competitor's product in a way that is specifically prohibited in some countries as unfair advertising. The marketing head of PepsiCo said that the company "intended to push the envelope on comparison advertising in markets around the world."[22] Because of the grueling legal battle between PepsiCo and Coca-Cola over the Pepsi Challenge campaign, as well as other conflicts over comparative advertising, laws in various Latin American countries were found to be inadequate. To avoid the passage of more laws, members of the advertising industry have established self-regulatory bodies in a number of these nations to settle disputes out of court.[23] In Europe, the EU Commission authorized comparative advertising subject to restrictions because some member countries permitted it while others did not. Germany's comparative advertising law is so strict that Goodyear couldn't use its multinational tire campaign stating that nylon tire cord is stronger than steel.

Advertisers in the Islamic countries face limitations, although these vary widely across the Middle East. A recent study shows that women appear about as often in Lebanese and Egyptian TV ads as in U.S. ads, although only half as often in Saudi ads. The women were just as likely to be dressed "immodestly" in Lebanese as in U.S. ads, although less often in Egyptian and never in Saudi ads.[24] In Japan, images of Western women in suggestive poses were acceptable, while similar images of Japanese women were not.

Are these teens in Japan or the United States? Japan. But, like teens in the United States, they wear Levi's and carry American skateboards.

Globalization versus Localization With so many obstacles to international standardization, what should be the approach of the international advertising manager? The opinion of some experts is that good brands and good product ideas can cross international borders but each may have to be adjusted for the local market. Let's examine this situation more closely.

A global product and a global brand, such as Apple's iPod or the Big Mac, reaches many markets unchanged or virtually unchanged. An ability to standardize both the product and the brand can lead to valuable cost savings.[25] Such products tend to be innovations. A global product with a local brand is often the result of mergers. Germany's Henkel, owner of Right Guard, Dial Soap, and other consumer products, has kept local packaging and standardized the physical product, its soap powder. Such a combination of localization of the product packaging and standardization of the contents makes manufacturing efficiencies possible. The final option, a local product with a local brand, is the most localized approach and is appropriate when, for perhaps cultural reasons, the product that sells well in one country will not transfer to another, or does so for quite a different set of purposes. Dish soaps that are adjusted for the hardness of local water and sell under local names is an example. P&G's Fairy Liquid, a dishwashing soap that is a leading brand in the United Kingdom, similar to Joy in the U.S. market, is one example of localization of the product on both brand and content. Remember, too, that, as the director of multinational accounts at McCann-Erickson claims, social classes across different countries have shared sensibilities: "A male middle executive in Italy has more in common with a male middle executive in the U.K. than with a farmer in Italy. It is those shared sensibilities that make global branding possible."[26] That is, if the marketer can identify those segments and reach them.

Such global branding approaches look for similarities across segments and countries to capitalize on them by providing promotional themes with worldwide appeal. A second approach believes that even though human nature is the same everywhere, it is also true that a Spaniard will remain a Spaniard and a Belgian a Belgian. Thus, it is preferable to develop separate appeals to take advantage of the differences among customers in different cultures and countries.

Neither Purely Global nor Purely Local You probably have already gathered from this discussion that for most firms neither a purely global nor a purely local campaign is the best way to handle international advertising. In fact, companies at either end of the global-local spectrum, with purely global campaigns or only local campaigns, tend to be moving toward the middle, with a "glocal" approach. Advertisers have followed glocalization to reduce costs. It allows them to develop a common strategy for large regions.[27] Coca-Cola says simply, "Think globally, but act locally."

Gillette's Panregional Approach Gillette has its advertising organized in the following regional and cultural clusters: pan-Latin America, pan-Middle East, pan-Africa, and pan-Atlantic. The company believes it can identify the same needs and buying motives among consumers in regions or countries linked by culture, consumers' habits, and level of market development for their products. Gillette might use the same European-style advertising for Australia and South Africa, but in Asia it would link developing economies such as the Philippines, Indonesia, Thailand, and Malaysia. It will market the Asian tigers—Singapore, Hong Kong, and Taiwan—together but will handle Japan, China, and India separately. In the summer of 2005, Gillette introduced a modified version of its Mach 3 Turbo in India using a local marketing agency. The agency parked modified trucks with shaving booths, sound systems, and female marketers outside call centers and shopping malls. Trial led many of the consumers to switch immediately to the Gillette razor, giving up the traditional double-edged razor that is still common in India.[28] With its regional-where-possible approach to marketing, Gillette is moving toward a global marketing strategy in the markets where such an approach might be appropriate, while allowing for regional and national differences.[29]

programmed-management approach
A middle-ground advertising strategy between globally standardized and entirely local programs

Programmed-Management Approach The **programmed-management approach** is another middle-ground advertising strategy in which the home office and the foreign subsidiaries agree on marketing objectives, after which each subsidiary puts together a tentative advertising campaign. This is submitted to the home office for review and suggestions. The campaign is then market-tested locally, and the results are submitted to the home office, which reviews them and offers comments. The subsidiary then submits a complete campaign to the home office for review. When the home office is satisfied, the budget is approved and the subsidiary begins implementing the campaign. The result may be a highly standardized campaign for all markets or one that has been individualized to the extent necessary to cope with local market conditions. The programmed-management approach gives the home office a chance to standardize those parts of the campaign that can be standardized but still permits flexibility in responding to different marketing conditions.

Personal Selling Along with advertising, personal selling constitutes a principal component of the promotional mix. The importance of this promotional tool compared to advertising depends to a great extent on the relative costs, the funds available, media availability, and the type of product sold.

Manufacturers of industrial products rely more on personal selling than on advertising to communicate with their overseas markets. However, producers of consumer products may also emphasize personal selling overseas, especially in the developing countries, because this may be more effective in the local environment.

Personal Selling and the Internet Evidence suggests that the Internet, when used to build trust (through consumer orientation, competence, dependability, candor, and likability[30]), can be an effective tool in personal selling. It may be enhanced by face-to-face communication as well. There are evolving approaches to trust building in a virtual environment that seem to be working, such as the eBay community and other sales and social sites.

International Standardization By and large, the organization of an overseas sales force, sales presentation, and training methods are very similar to those employed in the home country, whenever possible. Avon was following the same plan of person-to-person selling in its major markets when, without notice, China outlawed door-to-door selling in 1998. The Chinese government claimed to be concerned about consumer safety and fraudulent pyramid schemes.[31] The success of Amway in China, whose personal selling may have come close to proselytizing, may also have been a concern. Avon had begun in China in 1990 with a $40 million manufacturing base in Guangzhou, which started manufacturing in 1998. To comply with Chinese law, Avon China shifted to a retail model and in 2006 provided products through a network of 6,000 beauty boutiques and 1,000 beauty counters. In mid-2006, China approved Avon for person-to-person selling in China. It will resume the successful model, running the personal selling out of its 7,000 retail sites. Meanwhile, during the same period in Venezuela and Russia, Avon was extremely successful with the same personal selling approach it uses in the United States. It has also been successful in Mexico, but when it entered the Mexican market, local experts predicted that its plan would fail because the Mexican middle-class woman is not home during the day. She is socializing. The wall around the house would keep the Avon lady from reaching the front door, and when she rang the bell, the maid would not let her in. Other American firms had used this approach and had failed for these reasons. However, Avon made small but important changes. It mounted a massive advertising campaign to educate Mexicans as to what they could expect from the visits, which used the standardized U.S. advertising, adding some education about the selling approach. In addition, Avon recruited educated, middle-class women as representatives and trained them well. They were encouraged to visit their friends, too. In both China and Mexico, changing the essentially American plan as necessary for legal reasons and cultural differences supported Avon's successful entry.

Other firms also follow their home country approach. Missionary salespeople from pharmaceutical manufacturers such as Pfizer and Upjohn introduce their products to physicians, just as they do in the United States. Salespeople calling on channel members perform the same tasks of informing middlemen, setting up point-of-purchase displays, and fighting for shelf space as do their American counterparts.

BUILDING YOUR GLOBAL RÉSUMÉ — Consider a Career in International Marketing

In international business, the saying "Nothing happens till somebody sells something" holds critical meaning considering the significant investments of money, time, and human capital required to establish a base of sales in a foreign market. Marketing creates and drives sales in foreign as well as domestic markets. The principles of marketing apply to all markets globally, but the overriding international business concept of "think globally, act locally" requires marketing flexibility to be able to make strategic and tactical marketing decisions based on a keen understanding of local consumers and market conditions.

Here are a few tips from the U.S. Department of Labor:

Marketing career and job description: There will be special prospects in international marketing because international marketing employees are faced with a vast array of social, economic, and political conditions combined with added responsibilities due to decentralized decision making and the increased distance between offices and central offices. International planning and managerial jobs typically are offered to those who have obtained some experience in international marketing at the company's central offices. Beginning positions in international marketing at a company's central offices can include a vast array of different responsibilities, but for those with a master's degree they normally include research, planning, and coordination efforts.

International marketing career opportunities: Although a few American firms such as Colgate-Palmolive, CPC International, Eli Lilly, Gillette, and Nestlé hire for international marketing positions, most companies choose people who have shown their worth working in domestic operations. Since so many international jobs are awarded to personnel within the firm, the best way to obtain such a job is probably by beginning in a domestic sales job for an international company.

Career training and qualifications: It is helpful to be fluent in related foreign languages as well as have lived in one or more of the countries the company trades with. Potential workers should have a solid and broad foundation in marketing, based particularly on sales management and market research. The majority of firms hiring for international marketing positions will hire those with bachelor degrees or MBAs, preferring MBAs of course.

World Wide Resources:

International Marketing:
www.careers-in-marketing.com

International Market Development:
www.mba.com/mba/AssessCareersAndTheMBA/MBACareerOpportunities/ADayintheLifeProfiles/MarketingDayinLifeProfiles_related/MeganOsorioInternationalMarketDevelopmentManager.htm

International Product Management:
www.mba.com/mba/AssessCareersAndTheMBA/MBACareerOpportunities/ADayintheLifeProfiles/MarketingDayinLifeProfiles_related/CristinaBarbuProductManager.htm

International Brand Management:
www.mba.com/mba/AssessCareersAndTheMBA/MBACareerOpportunities/ADayintheLifeProfiles/MarketingDayinLifeProfiles_related/NicolasAmayaAssociateBrandManager.htm

International Advertising:
http://marketing.monster.com/articles/advertisingabroad

International Public Relations:
http://marketing.monster.com/articles/prcareersabroad

International Sports Marketing:
http://marketing.monster.com/articles/sportsabroad

International Market Research:
http://text.tns-global.com/index.htm
www.marketresearchworld.net
www.fita.org/trade_info.html

Source: Bureau of Labor Statistics, U.S. Department of Labor.

Recruitment Recruiting salespeople in foreign countries is at times more difficult than recruiting them at home because sales managers may have to cope with the stigma attached to selling that exists in some areas. There is also the need to hire salespeople who are culturally acceptable to customers and channel members. This can be difficult and costly in an already small market that is further subdivided into several distinct cultures with different customs and languages.

sales promotion
Any of various selling aids, including displays, premiums, contests, and gifts

Sales Promotion

Sales promotion provides the selling aids for the marketing function and includes activities such as the preparation of point-of-purchase displays, contests, premiums, trade show exhibits, money-off offers, and coupons.

The international standardization of the sales promotion function is not difficult, because experience has shown that what is successful in the United States generally proves effective overseas, although often at a diminished rate. Couponing is a good example. A Nielsen report surveyed consumers on cost-saving measures that would move them to increased coupon use. In the United States 46 percent of consumers stated that they would increase coupon use, while the global average was 19 percent.[32] One major difference on coupon use among markets is the method of distribution. In the United States, the freestanding insert is most frequently used, while in Europe coupons are distributed in stores, usually on the package itself. In some European countries couponing is illegal. This is because price discrimination among consumers is illegal. In other countries, the selling price of specific goods is set within a narrow range.

When marketers are considering transferring sales promotion techniques to other markets, they must consider some cultural constraints.

Sociocultural and Economic Constraints Cultural and economic constraints influence sales promotions. For example, a premium used as a sales aid for the product must be meaningful to the purchaser. A kitchen gadget might be valued by an American but will not be particularly attractive to a Latin American of similar economic status with two maids. Putting a prize inside the package is no guarantee that it will be there when the purchaser takes the package home. While living in Mexico, one of this book's authors bought a product for the plastic toy it contained. When he opened the package at home, there was no toy. Examining the package closely, he found that a small slit had been made in the top. Where labor costs and store revenues are low, the income from the sale of these premiums is an extra profit for the retailer.

Contests, raffles, and games have been extremely successful in countries where people love to play the odds. If Latin Americans or the Irish will buy a lottery ticket week after week, hoping to win the grand prize playing against odds of 500,000 to 1, why shouldn't they participate in a contest that costs them nothing to enter? Point-of-purchase displays are well accepted by retailers, though many establishments are so small that there is simply no place to put all the displays that are offered to them. Sales promotion may not be as sophisticated overseas as it is in the United States, and our experience indicates that even American subsidiaries do not make sufficient use of the ideas coming from headquarters. The marketing manager who prepares a well-planned program after studying the constraints of the local markets can expect excellent results from the time and money invested.

Public Relations

Public relations is the firm's communications and relationships with its various publics, including the governments where it operates, or as one writer has put it, "Public relations is the marketing of the firm." Although American internationals have had organized public relations programs for many years in the United States, they have paid much less attention to this important function elsewhere. Informing the local public of what they are doing has been overlooked by some U.S. corporations. For example, the Ford Foundation, a philanthropy begun in 1936 by Edsel Ford and two Ford Motor Company executives, has an international graduate fellowships program (IFP) to provide $280 million in graduate fellowships for students from Africa, the Middle East, Asia, Latin America, and Russia between 2000 and 2012.[33] Yet this information is not referenced by the overseas Ford Motor Company sites.

public relations
Various methods of communicating with the firm's publics to secure a favorable impression

Nationalism and antimultinational feeling in many countries have made it imperative that companies with international operations improve their communications to their nonbusiness publics with more effective public relations programs. International pharmaceutical manufacturers are viewed with suspicion by the public in developing nations because, although their products may alleviate suffering, they do so at a profit, made from the poor. To improve their images, major pharmaceuticals have begun programs related to disease globally. Their AIDS campaigns in Africa have received much public attention. One of the most vexing problems for firms is how to deal with critics of their operations and motives. Some try to defuse criticism by holding regularly scheduled meetings at which topics of interest are debated. Others prefer to meet with critics privately, though they may find themselves caught in a never-ending relationship in which the critics continually escalate their demands.

A strategy that has been employed successfully by some firms is to address the issue without dealing directly with the critics. Instead, the firms work with international or governmental agencies. For example, in China recently a number of foreign firms that have achieved success—among them Toshiba, Philips, and Canon—have found themselves under fire by the Chinese media. Scott Kronick of Ogilvy Public Relations Worldwide recommended that if the coverage was too unbalanced, firms should complain to the Propaganda Department. Although the department is not actually part of the government, it is a committee of the Central Committee of the Communist Party of China, whose chairperson is an alternate member of the Politburo.[34]

Another alternative is to do nothing. If the criticism receives no publicity, it may die from lack of interest. Yet sometimes a libeled company chooses to defend its reputation in court. McDonald's was the victim in London when Helen Steel and Dave Morris distributed leaflets accusing the company of starving the Third World, exploiting children in its advertising, and destroying the Central American rain forests. It was also cruel to animals, they alleged, because at times chickens were still conscious when their throats were cut. McDonald's sued Steel and Morris in 1994. It became the longest libel trial in history, ending two and a half years later. McDonald's was awarded $98,000 in damages in a case it had spent $16 million to pursue. Despite the award, which McDonald's has never collected, there is now a major anti-McDonald's Web site (www.McSpotlight.org) dedicated to protests against McDonald's, and October 16 has become established as Worldwide Anti-McDonald's Day.[35]

PRICING STRATEGIES

Pricing, the third element of the marketing mix, is an important and complex consideration in formulating the marketing strategy. Pricing decisions affect other corporate functions, directly determine the firm's gross revenue, and are a major determinant of profits. Most pricing research has been done on North Americans, and this raises serious problems for its generalizability.[36] Americans like sales, for example, while consumers in countries where goods are more scarce may attribute sales to low quality rather than to a desire to gain market share. There is some evidence that perceived price-quality relationships are quite high in Britain and Japan. Thus, discount stores have had difficulty in both these markets. In developing countries, there is less trust of outsiders in the market. Cultural differences may influence the effort a buyer puts into evaluating deals in these markets, where buy decisions rest on relationships. That consumers in some economies are usually paid weekly rather than biweekly or monthly may influence the effectiveness of framing attempts as well. "A dollar a day" is a much bigger chunk from a weekly than a monthly paycheck.

Pricing, a Controllable Variable

Effective price setting consists of more than mechanically adding a standard markup to a cost. To obtain the maximum benefits from pricing, management must regard pricing in the same manner as it does other controllable variables. Pricing is one element of the marketing mix that can be varied to achieve the marketing objectives of the firm.

For instance, if the marketer wishes to position a product as a high-quality item, setting a relatively high price will reinforce promotion that emphasizes quality. However, combining a low price with a promotional emphasis on quality could result in a contradiction that would adversely affect credibility with the consumer. Pricing can also be a determinant in the choice of middlemen, because if the firm requires a wholesaler to take title to, stock, promote, and deliver the merchandise, it must give the wholesaler a much larger trade discount than would be demanded by a broker, whose services are much more limited.

These examples illustrate one of the reasons for the complexity of price setting: the interaction of pricing with the other elements of the marketing mix. In addition, two other sets of forces influence this variable: the interaction between marketing and the other functional areas of the firm and environmental forces.

Interaction between Marketing and the Other Functional Areas

To illustrate this point, consider the following:

1. The finance people want prices that are both profitable and conducive to steady cash flow.

2. Production supervisors want prices that create large sales volumes, which permit long production runs with their associated lower cost benefits.
3. The legal department worries about possible antitrust violations when different prices are set according to type of customer. It also worries about global trademark protection and intellectual property issues.
4. The tax people are concerned with the effects of prices on tax loads.
5. The domestic sales manager wants export prices to be high enough to avoid having to compete with company products that are purchased for export and then diverted to the domestic market (one aspect of parallel importing).

The marketer must address all these concerns and also consider the impact of the legal and other environmental forces that we examined in Section Three. Table 18.2 at the end of this chapter examines this aspect of pricing in greater detail.

Standardizing Prices

Companies that pursue a policy of unified, global corporate pricing know that pricing is acted on by the same forces that militate against the international standardization of the other marketing mix components. Pricing for the overseas markets is more complex because managements must be concerned with two kinds of pricing: **foreign national pricing,** which is domestic pricing in another country, and **international pricing** for exports.

foreign national pricing
Local pricing in another country

international pricing
Setting prices of goods for export for both unrelated and related firms

Foreign National Pricing

Some foreign governments fix prices on just about everything, while others are concerned only with pricing on essential goods. In nations with laws on unfair competition, the minimum sales price may be controlled rather than the maximum. The German law is so comprehensive that under certain conditions even premiums and cents-off coupons may be prohibited because they violate the minimum price requirements.

Prices can vary because of cost differentials on opposite sides of a border. One government may levy higher import duties on imported raw materials or may subsidize public utilities, while another may not. Differences in labor legislation cause labor costs to vary. Competition among local suppliers may be intense in one market, permitting the affiliate to buy inputs at better prices than those paid by an affiliate in another market.

Competition on the selling side may be diverse also. Frequently, an affiliate in one market will face heavy local competition and be limited in the price it can charge, while in a neighboring market a lack of competitors will allow another affiliate to charge a higher price. As regional economic groupings reduce trade barriers among members, such opportunities are becoming fewer because firms must meet regional as well as local competition.

International Pricing

International pricing involves the setting of prices for goods produced in one country and sold in another. The pricing of exports to unrelated customers falls in this category and has been addressed in Chapter 17. A special kind of exporting, *intracorporate sales*, is common among large companies as they attempt to require that subsidiaries specialize in the manufacture of some products and import others. Their imports may consist of components that are assembled into the end product, such as computer chips made in one country that are mounted on boards built in another, or they may be finished products imported to complement the product mix of an affiliate. In either case, judgment is needed in setting a **transfer price.**

transfer price
Intracorporate price, or the price of a good or service sold by one affiliate to another, the home office to an affiliate, or vice versa

It is possible for the firm as a whole to gain while both the buying and the selling subsidiaries "lose," that is, receive prices that are lower than would be obtained through an outside transaction. The tendency is for transfer prices to be set at headquarters so that the company may obtain a profit from *both* the seller and the buyer or locate its profit in lower-tax environments. The selling affiliate would like to charge other subsidiaries the same price it charges all customers, but when combined with transportation costs and import duties, such a price may make it impossible for the importing subsidiary to compete in its market. If headquarters dictates that a lower-than-market transfer price be charged, the seller will be unhappy because its profit-and-loss statement suffers. This can be problematic for managers whose promotion bonuses depend on the bottom line. Figure 18.3 shows how firms can protect profits from taxation with transfer pricing.

Increasingly the Internet is redefining pricing options. It is a tremendous tool for comparing prices—already sites can scan hundreds of outlets for prices on certain goods—and so national boundaries may mean less and less. In a sense, world prices for consumers may be on the way to being achieved. The effect extends to business-to-business pricing as well.

DISTRIBUTION STRATEGIES

The development of distribution strategies is difficult in the home country and even more so internationally, where marketing managers must concern themselves with two functions rather than one: getting the products *to* foreign markets (exporting) and distributing the products *within* each foreign market.

Interdependence of Distribution Decisions

Distribution decisions are often interdependent with the other marketing mix variables. For example, if the product requires considerable after-sales servicing, the firm will want to sell through dealers with the facilities, personnel, and capital to purchase spare parts and train service people. Channel decisions are critical because they are long-term decisions; once established, they are far less easy to change than those made for price, product, and promotion. Coca-Cola recently made a major decision to change its channel system in China; at great cost it moved from using a traditional channel, where competing interests of the channel members were slowing up their connection to the market, to building relationships with its small retail sellers.[37]

Standardizing Distribution

Although management would prefer to standardize distribution patterns internationally, there are two fundamental constraints on doing so: the variation in the availability of channel members among the firm's markets and the environmental forces present in these different markets. International managers have found flexibility around an overall policy to be effective. The subsidiaries implement the distribution policy and design channel strategies to meet local conditions.

Availability of Channel Members As a starting point in their channel design, local managers have the successful distribution system used in the domestic operation. Headquarters' support for a policy of employing the same channels worldwide will be especially strong when the entire marketing mix has been built around a particular channel type, such as direct sales force or franchised operators. McDonald's is an example of a firm that relies primarily on franchise operators at home and abroad.

FIGURE 18.3

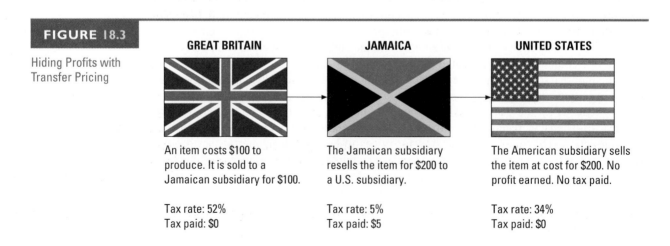

Hiding Profits with Transfer Pricing

GREAT BRITAIN	JAMAICA	UNITED STATES
An item costs $100 to produce. It is sold to a Jamaican subsidiary for $100.	The Jamaican subsidiary resells the item for $200 to a U.S. subsidiary.	The American subsidiary sells the item at cost for $200. No profit earned. No tax paid.
Tax rate: 52% Tax paid: $0	Tax rate: 5% Tax paid: $5	Tax rate: 34% Tax paid: $0

Foreign Environmental Forces Environmental differences among markets add to the difficulty in standardizing distribution channels. Basic geographic differences matter greatly in distribution, as explained in Chapter 7. Just think about Switzerland's challenges. Changes caused by the cultural forces generally occur over time, but those caused by the legal forces can be radical and quick. To illustrate, hypermarkets are changing distribution patterns everywhere, including Europe. The EU's Royer Law gives local urban commissions, often dominated by small merchants, the power to refuse construction permits for supermarkets and hypermarkets.

Japan's Large Scale Retailers Law, very similar to the Royer Law, had also slowed the opening of large retailers. However, the Japanese government scrapped the law completely in 1997. The Japanese have adopted Internet shopping, and one result is that retail stores now seem almost superfluous. When Sony launched its electronic pet *Aibo* (Japanese for "companion") in 1999, it sold out of stock in 20 minutes on SonyStyle.com; no units were shipped to stores. Sony later opened physical SonyStyle stores in addition to its existing Sony outlets.[38]

Another restriction of distribution has been tried in the EU. Manufacturers have attempted to prevent distributors from selling across national borders, but the EU Commission has prohibited them from doing so by invoking EU antitrust laws. Exclusive distributorships have been permitted, but every time the manufacturer has included a clause prohibiting the distributor from exporting to another EU country, the clause has been stricken from the contract. In effect, a firm that has two factories in the EU with different costs, and thus distinct prices, is practically powerless to prevent products from the lower-cost affiliate from competing with higher-cost products from the other affiliate.

Economic differences also make international standardization difficult, although marketers can adapt to economic changes. In Japan, women no longer have time to shop and prepare the traditional Japanese foods. They fill their needs by purchasing more convenience foods advertised on TV with home delivery or by going to the more than 50 chains of convenience stores. The largest, 7-Eleven, has about 11,000 stores, many of which are run by former small shopkeepers.

Can retailing be globalized? Retailers such as France's Carrefour, with stores in France, Spain, Brazil, Argentina, and the United States, think it can. So do Safeway, Gucci, Cartier, Benetton, and Toys 'R' Us, which have made aggressive penetration in Canada, Europe, Hong Kong, and Singapore. Kaufhof, the German retailing giant, has 100 shoe stores located in Austria, France, Switzerland, and Germany and is also the leading mail-order shoe retailer in Europe. Wal-Mart, now with operations in 14 countries, is learning that global retailing takes localization.

Disintermediation

The term *disintermediation* refers to the unraveling of traditional distribution structures and is most often the result of being able to combine the Internet with fast delivery services such as FedEx and UPS. Increasingly, these tools are shaking up traditional distribution channels and making possible rapid service with or without a distribution structure. Our increasing ability to ship products quickly may mean that the lack of dedicated channels makes less difference over time.

CHANNEL SELECTION

Direct or Indirect Marketing

The first decision that management must make is whether to use middlemen, because there is frequently the option of marketing directly to the final user. Sales to original equipment manufacturers (OEMs)* and governments are usually made directly, as are the sales of high-priced industrial products such as turbines and locomotives, because the firm is dealing with relatively few customers and transactions but with large dollar value. Even in these cases, export sales may be made by local

*Original equipment manufacturers buy components that are incorporated into the products they produce (for example, spark plugs to an automobile manufacturer).

agents if management believes this is politically expedient or if the country's laws demand it. Other types of industrial products and consumer goods are marketed indirectly. The channel members are selected on the basis of their market coverage, cost, and susceptibility to company control. They must also be able to perform the functions required by management.

Factors Influencing Channel Selection

The factors that influence the selection of market channels may be classified as the characteristics of the market, the product, the company, and the middlemen.

Market Characteristics

The obvious place to start in channel selection is at the target markets. Which among the alternatives offers the best coverage? The firm may require multiple channels for multiple target markets. Large retailers, governments, and OEMs may be handled by the company sales force or manufacturers' agents, while smaller retailers are supplied through wholesalers.

Product Characteristics A low-cost product sold in small quantities per transaction generally requires long channels, but if the goods are perishable, short channels are preferable. If the product is highly technical, it may be impossible to obtain knowledgeable middlemen, so the manufacturer is forced either to sell directly through company-owned distributors or to train independent middlemen. Caterpillar has enjoyed tremendous success by choosing the second alternative.

Company Characteristics A firm that has adequate financial and managerial resources is in a good position to employ its own sales force or agents. A financially weak company must use middlemen that take title to and pay for the goods. If management is inexperienced in selling to certain markets, it needs to employ middlemen who have that experience.

Middlemen's Characteristics Most industrial equipment, large household appliances, and automobiles require considerable after-sales servicing, and much of the firm's success in marketing depends on being able to deliver it. If the firm is not prepared to provide this service, it cannot use agents. The same is true for warehousing and promotion to the final user. If the firm is unable to perform these functions or perceives a cost advantage in not performing them, it must select middlemen that will service, warehouse, and promote its products. It may be that no channel members are available to reach the firm's target markets and perform the desired functions. If there are none, management must decide to refrain from entering the market, select other target markets, or create a new channel. For example, if a frozen-food processor finds that cold-storage facilities are nonexistent, it can either abandon the market or persuade middlemen to acquire the facilities. In a number of overseas markets, firms have purchased the necessary equipment such as warehouse freezers, refrigerated trucks, and so on, and rented, leased, or sold them on easy terms to distributors and retailers. To develop its distribution channel members in Brazil, an Italian cheese producer there supplied cold-storage equipment and set up gathering facilities for the dairy farmers. The company provided veterinarians and dairy experts to teach the dairy farmers how to maintain their herds and increase output. Nestlé has similar programs in its developing country markets.

FOREIGN ENVIRONMENTAL FORCES AND THE MARKETING MIX MATRIX

The matrix[39] in Table 18.2 summarizes many of the constraints on the internationalization of the marketing mix that have been discussed in this chapter and in Section Three. Table 18.2 can serve as a reminder of the many factors marketing managers should consider when contemplating the standardization of marketing mix elements.

TABLE 18.2 Environmental Constraints to International Standardization of Marketing Mix

Factors Limiting Standardization	Product	Price	Distribution	Personal Selling	Promotion
1. Physical forces	1. Climatic conditions—special packaging, extra insulation, mildew protection, extra cooling capacity, special lubricants, dust protection, special instructions 2. Difficult terrain—stronger parts, larger engines, stronger packing	1. Special product requirements add to costs 2. Difficult terrain—extra transportation costs, higher sales expense (car maintenance, longer travel time, more per diem expense)	1. Difficult terrain—less customer mobility, requiring more outlets, each with more stock 2. Varying climatic conditions—more stock needed when distinct products required for different climates	1. Buyers widely dispersed or concentrated—affects territory and sales force size 2. Difficult terrain—high travel expense, longer travel time, fewer daily sales calls 3. Separate cultures created by physical barriers—salespeople from each culture may be needed	1. Cultural pockets created by barriers—separate ads for languages, dialects, words, customs 2. Different climates—distinct advertising themes
2. Sociocultural forces	1. Consumer attitudes toward product 2. Colors of product and package—varying significance 3. Languages—labels, instructions 4. Religion—consumption patterns 5. Attitudes toward time—differences in acceptance of time-saving products 6. Attitudes toward change—acceptance of new products 7. Educational levels—ability to comprehend instructions, ability to use product 8. Tastes and customs—product use and consumption 9. Different buying habits—package size 10. Who is decision maker? 11. Rural-urban population mix	1. Cultural objections to product—lower prices to penetrate market 2. Lower educational level, lower income—lower prices for mass market 3. Attitudes toward bargaining—affects list prices 4. Customers' attitude toward price	1. More and perhaps specialized outlets to market to various subcultures 2. Buyers accustomed to bargaining—requires small retailers 3. Attitudes toward change—varying acceptance of new kinds of outlets 4. Different buying habits—different types of outlets	1. Separate cultures—separate salespeople 2. Varying attitudes toward work, time, achievement, and wealth among cultures—difficult to motivate and control sales force 3. Different buying behavior—different kinds of sales forces 4. Cultural stigma attached to selling?	1. Language, different or same but with words having different connotations—advertisements, labels, instructions 2. Literacy, low—simple labels, instructions, ads with plenty of graphics 3. Symbolism—responses differ 4. Colors—significances differ 5. Attitudes toward advertising 6. Buying influence—gender, committee, family 7. Cultural pockets—different promotions 8. Religion—taboos and restrictions vary 9. Attitudes toward foreign products and firms
3. Legal-political forces	1. Some products prohibited 2. Certain features required or prohibited 3. Label and packaging requirements	1. Varying retail price maintenance laws 2. Government-controlled prices or markups 3. Antitrust laws 4. Import duties 5. Tax laws	1. Some kinds of channel members outlawed 2. Markups government-controlled 3. Retail price maintenance 4. Turnover taxes	1. Laws governing discharge of salespeople 2. Laws requiring compensation on discharging salespeople	1. Use of languages 2. Legal limits to expenditures 3. Taxes on advertising 4. Prohibition of promotion for some products 5. Special legal requirements for some products (cigarettes, pharmaceuticals)

(Continued)

TABLE 18.2 Continued

Factors Limiting Standardization	Product	Price	Distribution	Personal Selling	Promotion
3. Legal-political forces (continued)	4. Varying product standards 5. Varying patent, copyright, and trademark laws 6. Varying import duties 7. Varying import restrictions 8. Local production required of all or part of product 9. Requirements to use local inputs that are different from home country inputs 10. Cultural stigma attached to brand name or artwork?	6. Transfer pricing controls	5. Only government-owned channels permitted for some products 6. Restrictions on channel members—number, lines handled, licenses for each line 7. Laws on canceling contracts of channel members	3. Laws requiring profit sharing, overtime, working conditions 4. Restrictions on channel members	6. Media availability 7. Trademark laws 8. Taxes that discriminate against some kinds of promotion 9. Controls on language or claims used in ads for some products
4. Economic forces	1. Purchasing power—package size, product sophistication, quality level 2. Wages—varying requirements for labor-saving products 3. Condition of infrastructure—heavier products, hand- instead of power-operated 4. Market size—varying width of product mix	1. Different prices 2. Price elasticity of demand	1. Availability of outlets 2. Size of inventory 3. Size of outlets 4. Dispersion of outlets 5. Extent of self-service 6. Types of outlets 7. Length of channels	1. Sales force expense 2. Availability of employees in labor market	1. Media availability 2. Funds available 3. Emphasis on saving time 4. Experience with products 5. TV, radio ownership 6. Print media readership 7. Quality of media 8. Excessive costs to reach certain market segments
5. Competitive forces	1. Rate of new product introduction 2. Rate of product improvement 3. Quality levels 4. Package size 5. Strength in market	1. Competitors' prices 2. Number of competitors 3. Importance of price in competitors' marketing mix	1. Competitors' control of channel members 2. Competitors' margins to channel members 3. Competitors' choice of channel members	1. Competitors' sales force—number and ability 2. Competitors' emphasis on personal selling in promotional mix 3. Competitors' rates and methods of compensation	1. Competitors' promotional expenditures 2. Competitors' promotional mix 3. Competitors' choice of media
6. Distributive forces	1. Product servicing requirements 2. Package size 3. Branding—dealers' brands	1. Margins required by channel members 2. Special payments required—stocking, promotional	1. Availability of channel members 2. Number of company distribution centers 3. Market coverage by channel members 4. Demands of channel members	1. Size of sales force 2. Kind and quality of sales force	1. Kinds of promotion 2. Amounts of promotion

Summary

Explain why there are differences between domestic and international marketing.

Whether a policy or a technique is designed for global use or is first used in the home market and then used overseas, marketers must know where to look for possible differences between marketing domestically and marketing internationally. Sometimes there are great differences; sometimes there are none. Although the basic functions of marketing are the same for all markets, international markets can differ greatly because of the variations in the uncontrollable environmental forces. The marketing manager must decide if the marketing program can be standardized worldwide, if some changes must be made, or if a completely different marketing mix must be prepared.

Explain why international marketing managers may wish to standardize the marketing mix.

International marketing managers prefer to standardize the marketing mix regionally or worldwide because there can be considerable cost savings from marketing the same product and using the same promotional material and the same advertising. A standardized marketing mix is easier to control, and less time is spent preparing the marketing plan.

Explain why it is often impossible to standardize the marketing mix worldwide.

A manager may not be able to standardize the marketing mix worldwide because of differences in the environmental forces. The amount of change depends considerably on the product type and the degree of market penetration desired by the manager.

Discuss the importance of distinguishing among the total product, the physical product, and the brand name.

Much of the confusion about whether a global firm can have global products arises because the discussants do not differentiate between physical and total products. A total product is easier than a physical product to standardize. A brand name or a product concept may be standardized even though the physical product varies among markets. Also, a firm may have to use a different brand name in a market because its present one has a bad connotation or because it may already be copyrighted by someone else.

Explain why consumer products generally require greater modification for international sales than do industrial products or services.

Industrial products and services generally can be marketed globally with less change than can consumer products because they are less sensitive to the foreign environment, as Figure 18.2 indicates.

Discuss the product strategies that can be formed from three product alternatives and three kinds of promotional messages.

Six commonly used promotional strategies can be formulated by combining the three alternatives of marketing the same product everywhere, adapting it, or designing a new product with the same, adapted, or different message.

Explain "glocal" advertising strategies.

International advertising agencies will design an international program for an advertiser and then make local adjustments that local managers deem necessary. The programmed-management approach is an advertising strategy for combining inputs from global advertising advocates of the home office with the opinions of local managers.

Discuss some of the effects the Internet may have on international marketing.

Among those mentioned are (1) making more pricing data available worldwide, (2) potentially making traditional channel structures less important, and (3) making the offering much more personalized and therefore more in line with the marketing concept.

Discuss the distribution strategies of international marketers.

Although an international firm might prefer to standardize its distribution patterns internationally, the facts that the same kinds of channel members are not available everywhere and that environmental forces vary among markets make standardization difficult or impossible at times.

Key Words

total product (p. 476)
promotion (p. 482)
advertising (p. 483)
programmed-management approach (p. 488)
sales promotion (p. 490)
public relations (p. 491)
foreign national pricing (p. 493)
international pricing (p. 493)
transfer price (p. 493)

Questions

1. "Consumers are not standardized globally; therefore, with global brands, you either get lowest common denominator advertising or you get advertising that's right somewhere but wrong elsewhere." This is an actual statement by a CEO of an international advertising agency. What's your opinion?
2. What future do you see for global advertising?
3. Are there any advantages to standardizing the marketing mix worldwide?
4. Why are manufacturers increasing their use of global and regional brands?
5. What is the basis for Gillette's taking its panregional approach?
6. What is a generality about similarities of social and cultural values in a country?
7. Why is food retailing changing in Europe and Japan?
8. In a question for an earlier chapter, we asked you to assume the role of consultant to the developers of the Spiderman computer game. From the standardization/adaptation perspective, what changes, if any, would you make to your game to appeal to various foreign markets?
9. On the basis of the discussion in the personal selling section about problems with Internet communication, which of the following two firms is more likely to be successful? Firm A expects to use the Internet as a tool to continue the relationships with its foreign customers that were first set up in person. Firm B expects to use the Internet to make a first sale to overseas buyers. The firm's salespeople will then make personal selling trips to those firms that have already proved they are worth a visit because they have made a first purchase over the Internet.
10. Does the Venezuelan (and Colombian) system of requiring that every product be marked with a maximum price—*precio valido al publico*, or pvp—operate to the benefit of manufacturers? Of retailers? Of end users? Why or why not?

Research Task

globalEDGE.msu.edu 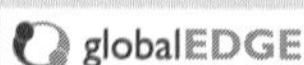

Use the globalEDGE™ site (http://globalEDGE.msu.edu) to complete the following exercises:

1. Locate and retrieve the most current ranking of *global brands*. Identify the criteria that are utilized in these rankings. Which country has considerable representation in the top 100 global brands list? Prepare a short report identifying the countries and industries that possess global brands and the potential reasons for success. Are there any specific industries in which countries represented on the list may have a specialization?
2. Thorough planning is essential to export success. In this respect, pricing for specific markets is one of the critical components for successfully planning a multinational export initiative. One aspect of determining the proper price of your firm's market offerings in a given market is determining the cost of living in each general location. According to a colleague, a simple way to do this is by locating a report on this subject by the human resource consulting firm Mercer. Considering that your company emphasizes a strategy based on price competitiveness, prepare an executive summary of how to perform an initial pricing analysis for international markets. In addition, which 10 cities worldwide have the highest cost of living?

Minicase 18.1 U.S. Pharmaceutical of Korea*

U.S. Pharmaceutical of Korea (USPK) was formed in 1969. Its one manufacturing plant is located just outside Seoul, the capital. Although the company distributes its products throughout South Korea, 40 percent of its total sales of $5 million were made in the capital last year.

There are no governmental restrictions on whom the company can sell to. The only requirement is that the wholesaler, retailer, or end user have a business license and a taxation number. Of the 400 wholesalers in the country, 130 are customers of USPK, accounting for 46 percent of the company's total sales. The company also sells directly to 2,100 of the country's 10,000 retailers; these account for 45 percent of total sales. The remaining sales are made directly to high-volume end users, such as hospitals and clinics.

Tom Sloane, marketing manager of USPK, would prefer to make about 90 percent of the company's sales directly to retailers and the remaining 10 percent directly to high-volume users. He believes, however, that this strategy is not possible because there are so many small retailers. Not only is the sales volume per retailer small, but there is also a risk involved in extending the retailers credit. USPK tends to deal directly with large urban retailers and leaves most of the nonurban retailers to the wholesalers.

However, the use of wholesalers bothers Sloane for two reasons: (1) He has to give them larger discounts than he gives retailers that buy directly from the firm, and (2) because of the intense competition (300 pharmaceutical manufacturers in Korea), his wholesalers frequently demand larger discounts as the price for remaining loyal to USPK.

This intense competition affects another aspect of USPK's operations—collecting receivables. USPK has found that many wholesalers collect quickly from retailers but delay paying USPK. Instead, they invest in ventures that offer high short-term returns. For example, lending to individuals can bring them interest rates of up to 3 percent a month. The company's receivables, meanwhile, range from 75 to 130 days. Wholesalers are also the cause of another problem. Many are understaffed and have to rely on "drug peddlers" for sales. The drug peddlers (there are perhaps 4,000 just in Seoul) make most of their money either by cutting the wholesalers' margins (selling at lower-than-recommended prices) or by bartering USPK's products for other pharmaceuticals. They do this by finding retail outlets where products are sold for less than the printed price. They exchange USPK's products at a discount for other drugs, which they sell to other retail outlets at a profit. As a result, USPK's products end up on retailers' shelves at prices lower than those that the company and its reputable wholesalers are selling them for.

The pharmaceutical industry has made some progress in persuading wholesalers and retailers to adhere to company price lists, but nonadherence is still a serious problem. One issue that manufacturers have not been able to resolve yet is the manner in which demands from hospitals and physicians for gifts should be handled.

Sloane believes the industry can do much to solve these problems, although intense competition has thus far kept the pharmaceutical manufacturers from joining together to map out a solution.

1. What should Tom Sloane and U.S. Pharmaceutical of Korea do to improve collections from wholesalers?
2. How would you handle the distribution problem?
3. Can anything be done through firms in the industry to improve the situation?
4. How would you handle the demands for gifts?

*Based on an actual situation in Korea.

An Ethical Situation* Minicase 18.2

The Swiss pharmaceutical global corporation Hoffman-La Roche has made a major breakthrough in the relief of a serious disabling disease that affects 3 percent of the world's population. Its new product Tigason is the first product that effectively controls severe cases of psoriasis and dyskeratoses, skin disorders that cause severe flaking of the skin. Sufferers from these diseases frequently retreat from society because of fear of rejection, thus losing their families and jobs. Tigason does not cure the diseases, but it causes the symptoms to disappear.

There is one potential problem. Because of the risk of damage to unborn babies, women should not take the drug for one year before conception or during pregnancy. Hoffman-La Roche is well aware of the potential for harm to the company if the product is misused. It has seen the problems of another Swiss firm, Nestlé. After much discussion, the company has decided the product is too important to keep off the market. It is, after all, the product that gives the greatest relief to sufferers.

The marketing department is asked to formulate a strategy for disseminating product information and controlling Tigason's use.

As the marketing manager, what do you recommend?

*This is an actual situation.

19 Global Operations and Supply Chain Management

Creating overseas production sites merely in order to meet local consumption looks an increasingly fragile basis for foreign investment. A much better one is the ability to make the best use of a company's competitive advantages by locating production wherever it is most efficient. Today's multinationals create widespread networks of research, component production, assembly, and distribution.

—*Martin Wolf, global business analyst*

Zara: Transforming the International Fashion Industry through Innovative Supply Chain Management

After World War II, the leading designers of women's fashions typically looked to Paris and other European fashion centers for insight into what clothing to offer to the markets. Upscale fashion houses like Chanel, Armani, and Gucci displayed their clothing lines twice a year in glamorous fashion shows, which provided the foundation for upscale boutiques to make their merchandise purchase decisions. These designs, which often cost thousands of dollars, were affordable only by the very rich. As a result, the designs were subsequently copied by mall retailers and sold to the masses at lower prices, helping to ensure that consumer trends moved in sync with the fashion industry. The limited parameters of what designs were being produced helped to simplify planning and allowed clothing companies to survive even when they took six to nine months to bring a product from design to market.

That business model is disappearing rapidly. The international women's fashion industry is currently undergoing a major transformation, toward what has been termed "fast fashion"—involving up-to-the-minute fashion, low prices, and a clear market focus. Helping to lead this revolution is a Spanish company called Zara. One of the world's most rapidly expanding retailers, with a chain of nearly 1,000 clothing stores located in leading cities across 62 countries, Zara's annual sales exceed $4.5 billion. The company is known for its fashionable and affordable clothing, offered in stores that project a modern, clean, and stylish image. Zara's competitive advantage, however, comes from its world-class supply chain management skills and its ability to reengineer the clothing supply chain.

The company's strategy of speed and flexibility has enabled Zara to shorten the fashion cycle almost to the point where it no longer exists. Store managers and roving observers use handheld devices to collect and send information regarding which designs are being well received by the buying public, which ones are not, and what will be the next hot trend. At headquarters, this information is used by its staff of over 200 in-house designers to help stay on top of fashion trends. Zara's information systems also enable the company to better manage inventory, the primary cost of goods sold for clothing manufacturers and retailers. The textile manufacturers used by the company are mostly located close to Zara's headquarters, rather than lower-cost sources in the Far East that can lengthen the cycle time to market. In those cases where it does buy fabric from more distant mills, Zara buys cloth only in four colors, enabling it to postpone dyeing and printing until the last possible moment.

Zara uses information technology and advanced supply chain management techniques to maintain tight control and integration of the various elements of the entire process, from textile mill to retail store. As a result, Zara has reduced the cycle time from initial garment design to appearance on hangers in the company's retail stores to as little as 14 days—versus a cycle time

CONCEPT PREVIEWS

After reading this chapter, you should be able to:

understand the concept of supply chain management

recognize the relationship between design and supply chain management

describe the five global sourcing arrangements

appreciate the importance of the added costs of global sourcing

understand the increasing role of electronic purchasing for global sourcing

understand the just-in-time (JIT) production system and potential problems with its implementation

understand synchronous manufacturing and mass customization

comprehend the concept of Six Sigma systems and their application

explain the potential of global standardization of production processes and procedures, and identify impediments to standardization efforts

know the two general classes of activities, productive and supportive, that must be performed in all manufacturing systems

Gli Affari Internazionali
cionales
onales Geschäft Παγοσμιο Business
Negócios Internacionais Los Negócios Internacionais
國際商務 Παγοσμιο Business

of 3 to 15 months for most of its rivals' products. Rapid turnaround times also mean the company can keep its best-selling designs well stocked, limit excess inventory of designs that do not resonate with the consumer, and add looks that were not initially in its collections. "If I tried to source my collections in Asia, I would not be able to get them quickly enough to our stores. By manufacturing close to home, I can scrap collections when they are not selling. And without this rapid response, I would not be able to extract a good relation between quality, price and fashion, which is what our customers have come to expect," said Jose Maria Castellano, the CEO of Inditex and architect of Zara's fast-fashion business model.

As a result of these innovations, Zara can design merchandise inspired by and similar in style to what appears in fashion shows of the world's most prestigious fashion brands in Paris and Milan—and can have the merchandise on sale throughout the Zara chain long before the original designer's products have reached the market. A consequence, ironically, is that consumers may perceive the original product to be a copy, rather than Zara's offerings.

The company's business strategy also focuses on continual renewal of clothing lines. It ruthlessly removes its product lines, even ones that have been selling well, every three weeks or so. This approach enables Zara to have a near-continuous stream of new merchandise, always offer fresh styles, and help its customers to never feel out of fashion. Producing a range of 11,000 different items per year, Zara's culture of reacting very quickly to new fashion trends means that each time a customer walks into a Zara store, she can get the feel of entering a new place, one with fresh styles on display. Customers have thus come to know Zara as a chain offering a steady stream of new, "gotta-have-it" merchandise, and the limited availability of its merchandise promotes impulse purchases—a "grab it while you can" mentality among shoppers. To enhance its legitimacy in the fashion world and promote the style of its offerings, Zara uses top fashion models in image ad campaigns that are placed in leading fashion magazines such as *Vogue*.

Even high-end shoppers who have traditionally been loyal to designer labels have begun to mix high fashion with the fast-fashion products pioneered by companies such as Zara. Cost, quality, and design have become lower priorities than an ability to deliver a constant stream of fashionable new merchandise. Attracted by the rapid introduction of new styles and the excitement of buying 10 inexpensive knockoff designs for less than the price of a single "authentic" jacket, even many wealthy customers have become loyal to Zara's fast-fashion approach. For example, a long pink boucle jacket similar to a current offering from the Chanel collection cost $129 at Zara, versus an original (albeit one with additional pearl buttons and a skirt) that was priced at $7,326. "Once it was embarrassing to be seen entering these stores. But now, not at all," proclaimed Franca Sozzani, the editor-in-chief of *Vogue Italia.*

Zara's revolutionary approach to the fashion industry means that it dictates industry standards on such dimensions as time to market, order fulfillment, costs, and customer satisfaction, as well as the ability to manage the linkages between these factors. The result is that high-end designers and fashion houses are being pressured to change their own operations and improve their ability to compete on speed. "What luxury brands can learn from these companies is their short time to market and constantly new merchandise. Even in the luxury business, customers want new merchandise all the time," explained Fabio Gnocchi, director of worldwide operations for the Italian fashion house Etro SpA. Building strong relationships with suppliers and improving capabilities in supply chain management seem to be requirements for other retailers hoping to respond to the fast-fashion model.

Propelled by the company's outstanding operational capabilities and execution in supply chain management, the Zara label has not only become the strongest Spanish consumer brand. It has also become a label with impressive international pull within the fashion industry and a major factor in transforming the industry globally. Fast fashion already makes up more than 12 percent of the market in the United Kingdom and 18 percent in Spain, and the U.S. fast-fashion segment is expected to increase dramatically from the 1 percent it had in 2005. Daniel Piette, fashion director for the upscale fashion house Louis Vuitton, described Zara as "possibly the most innovative and devastating retailer in the world." As Zara shows, effective supply chain management can indeed result in international competitive advantage. ■

Source: Leslie Crawford, "Inditex Sizes Up Europe in Expansion Drive," *Financial Times,* February 1, 2005, p. 18; "Zara," www.inditex.com/en/who_we_are/concepts/zara (July 17, 2006); Grupo Inditex, *2005 Annual Report,* www.inditex.com/en/shareholders_and_investors/investor_relations/annual_reports (July 17, 2006); Sarah Raper Larenaudie, "Inside the H&M Fashion Machine," *Time,* Spring 2004, pp. 48–50; "Branding Espana to the Rest of the World," *Brand Strategy,* March 2004, p. 12; Cecilie Rohwedder, "Style and Substance: Making Fashion Faster; As Knockoffs Beat Originals to Market, Designers Speed the Trip from Sketch to Store," *The Wall Street Journal,* February 24, 2004, p. B1; Teri Agins, "Pick-and-Mix Shoppers Force Fashion Industry to Abandon Old Models," *The Asian Wall Street Journal,* September 10–12, 2004, pp. A1, A10; Leonie Barrie, "Making a Mark: Some of the Issues to Watch in 2004: Fast Fashion Continues to Speed Up," *Just-Style,* January 2004, pp. 17–19; and Stephen Tierney, "New Research Proves Link between Supply Line and Bottom Line," *Frontline Solutions,* October 2003, p. 31.

As firms continue to enter global markets, global competition increases. This forces management of both international and domestic companies to search for ways to lower costs while improving their products or services in order to remain competitive. Sometimes the desired results are obtained through improvements within existing operations, such as the Six Sigma programs discussed later in this chapter. Other times, improved competitiveness is pursued by having the company open new—or transfer existing—operations abroad or find alternative outside sources for the labor, raw materials, or other inputs that it is currently sourcing from other organizations. A third option involves **outsourcing,** that is, hiring others to perform some of the noncore activities and decision making in a company's value chain, instead of continuing to do them in-house. Commonly, outsourcing firms provide key components of data processing, logistics, payroll, and accounting, although any activity in the value chain can be outsourced. It is common that managements will pursue some combination of these different options in their efforts to enhance their companies' international competitiveness. The efforts to improve the efficiency and effectiveness of a firm's international operations are often referred to as **supply chain management.** In this chapter, we will discuss the topic of global supply chain management and critical issues in the management of global operations, including global sourcing, manufacturing systems, productivity and performance of international manufacturing operations, and issues associated with the global standardization versus localization of international operations.

outsourcing
Hiring others to perform some of the noncore activities and decision making in a company's value chain, rather than having the company and its employees continue to perform those activities

supply chain management
The process of coordinating and integrating the flow of materials, information, finances, and services within and among companies in the value chain from suppliers to the ultimate consumer

Managing Global Supply Chains

Supply chain management has become an increasingly popular and strategically important topic in international business in recent years. *Supply chain* refers to the activities that are involved in producing a company's products and services and how these activities are linked together. The concept of supply chain management involves the applications of a total systems approach to managing the overall flow of materials, information, finances, and services within and among companies in the value chain—from raw materials and components suppliers through manufacturing facilities and warehouses and on to the ultimate customer.[1] Supply chains are an integral part of global quality and cost management initiatives, since a typical company's supply chain costs can represent over 50 percent of assets and over 80 percent of revenues.[2] Figure 19.1 illustrates a global supply chain for an American laptop computer company. This example broadly illustrates the activities and linkages involved in transforming initial designs into finished goods and support services delivered to the consumer, including product design, suppliers that provide the various inputs, assembly and testing activities, warehousing and distribution of finished goods, and the sales and technical support operations.

Because inventory is carried at each stage in the supply chain, and because inventory ties up money, it has been argued that the ultimate goal of effective supply chain management

FIGURE 19.1 Supply Chain Network: A Hypothetical Example of an American Laptop Computer Company

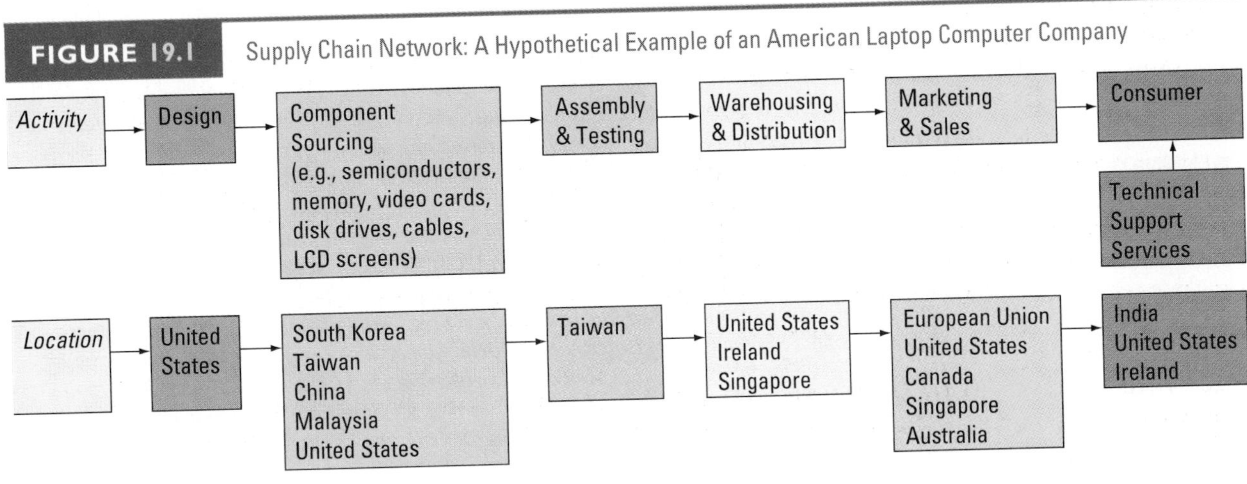

systems is to reduce inventory, consistent with the prerequisites that the company's products be available when needed and at the desired level of quality and quantity. For that reason, it is critical that the operations at each stage in the supply chain are synchronized in order to minimize the size of these buffer inventories. Shorter, less predictable product life cycles, as well as the impact of unplanned economic, political, and social events, have placed further emphasis on the achievement of effective supply chain performance.[3] New technologies, including Web-enabled tools for supply chain planning, execution, and optimization, have enhanced the availability of data and integration with suppliers and customers, helping to enhance the international competitiveness of companies that have adopted and mastered these technologies.

As highlighted in the Wal-Mart minicase at the end of Chapter 13 or the Zara example at the beginning of this chapter, global supply chain management has been receiving increasing attention because many companies have achieved significant international competitive advantage as a result of the manner in which they have configured and managed their global supply chain activities. Some organizations, such as the computer and information technology company Dell, have reconfigured their international supply chains to substantially reduce or eliminate activities such as finished goods warehousing and retail stores, thus reducing costs and increasing effectiveness.[4] Other companies, such as the Hong Kong export trading company Li and Fung, have transformed their operations to enter into new, value-adding activities in an industry's value chain.[5] Effective supply chain management can also enhance a company's ability to manage regulatory, social, and other environmental pressures, both nationally and globally.

In the McDonald's Worldwide Corporate Responsibility Report, *the company states, "Supporting responsible actions in our supply chain helps to advance important social, economic, and environmental goals and will ensure the continued supply of high-quality ingredients we need in the future. That's why social responsibility is one of our key strategic supply chain priorities." McDonald's manages performance of its global chain of suppliers in such areas as food quality and safety, rain forest protection, fisheries sustainability, reducing impacts of packaging, promoting antibiotic effectiveness, biotechnology awareness, and animal welfare.*[6]

Design of Products and Services

An important factor in the structure and management of a company's global supply chain is the issue of design. The design of a company's products and services has a fundamental relationship with the type of inputs that the company will require, including labor, materials, information, and financing. As we discussed in Chapter 13, an important consideration in design is the extent to which the international company's products and services will be standardized across nations or regions or adapted to meet the different needs of various markets. The decision on standardization versus localization of designs is impacted by a range of competitive, cultural, regulatory, and other factors and is an important strategic consideration for a company.

The multinational automaker Ford set up a pioneering assembly plant in Camacari, Brazil, that includes in-house suppliers, just-in-time parts delivery, and a "just in sequence" flexible assembly line that can produce a range of different models. However, Ford's performance in Latin America suffered due to attempts to sell "tropicalized" versions of autos designed for the United States and Europe that had only minor adaptations for the local market, such as reinforced suspensions to better handle rugged roads. In response, Ford of Brazil developed a small team of local engineers, dubbed the "Amazon group," to design a vehicle more specifically oriented toward consumer needs in Latin America. The final product, an affordable light sport-utility vehicle called the Ecosport that was well suited to the more rugged Latin American operating context, achieved such success with consumers that Ford captured 80 percent of the SUV market in Brazil. Export demand has also been brisk from nations such as Argentina, Chile, Venezuela, and Mexico. "Local design has been the key to success," said David Breedlove, Ford's product development director for South America. "We used to copy U.S. models and then we recognized the need to focus on the South American market."[7]

A traditional approach to product design has been termed the "over-the-wall" approach. This involves a sequential approach to design: an initial step in which the designers prepare the product's design, followed by sending the newly created design to the company's manufacturing engineers, who must then address the production-related problems that often result from their exclusion from the initial design activity. Of course, decisions on product and service design are seldom made in isolation, because of the problems that can arise from such an orientation.

An alternative approach to design is to promote cross-functional participation in the design stage, thereby helping to identify and avoid many of the potential sourcing, manufacturing, and other difficulties that can be associated with a particular design. Many companies also involve key customers in the design activities, to ensure that designs are consistent with the customers' needs. Using this type of concurrent engineering approach allows the proposed designs to be subjected to earlier assessments on cost, quality, and manufacturability dimensions, thereby enhancing the efficiency and effectiveness of subsequent manufacturing and supply chain management activities. Indeed, design decisions must often be integrated with assessment of the various supply chain considerations, such as whether and where the company can obtain the inputs needed for the company's operations, whether the firm will source locally or from foreign locations, and whether the company has the capability to produce and deliver the product or service in a competitively viable manner.

Nokia, the worldwide leader in wireless handsets and a leading competitor in wireless networks, has initiated a program called "Design for Environment" (DfE) as part of the company's global environmental strategy. The goal of Nokia's DfE initiative is to design products (including packaging) that have improved environmental performance, while simultaneously meeting cost, performance, quality, and other requirements. In part, the DfE program is intended to help Nokia to conform to new environmental legislation being introduced by the European Union and legislative bodies in other parts of the world, such as the United States, China, Japan, and Korea. But these efforts also reflect Nokia's attempt to be an industry leader in environmental performance and to better meet the evolving environmental needs of wireless operators and users worldwide. The DfE program ensures that Nokia's designers integrate environmental considerations associated with raw material supply, supplier activities, assembly and testing operations, product use, and end-of-life practices (i.e., reuse, recovery, recycling, and disposal) in all of their product design activities.[8]

Sourcing Globally

REASONS FOR SOURCING GLOBALLY

Although the primary reason for sourcing globally is to obtain lower prices, there are other reasons. Perhaps certain products the company requires are not available locally and must be imported. Another possibility is that the firm's foreign competitors are using components of better quality or design than those available in the home country. To be competitive, the company may have to source these components or production machinery in foreign countries. The term **offshoring** is commonly used for a company's relocating of activities to foreign locations.

offshoring
Relocating some or all of a business's activities or processes to a foreign location

When deciding to source internationally, companies can either set up their own facilities or outsource the production to other companies. Outsourcing has become an increasingly common option for companies, as they try to focus scarce resources on their core competencies and leverage the skills of other companies to reduce costs and capital investments, improve flexibility and speed of response, enhance quality, or provide other strategic benefits. The activities can be outsourced either to another company in the same country or to a company in another country (the latter would constitute "offshore outsourcing").

Global access to vendors, falling costs of interactions, and improved information technologies and communication links are providing companies with unprecedented choices regarding how to structure their businesses. Any part of the value chain can be outsourced, including product design, raw material or component supply, manufacturing or assembly, logistics, distribution, marketing, sales, service, human resources, or other activities. Done properly, including a strong link to strategy, outsourcing can deliver dramatic increases in value for companies and their customers.

Outsourcing decisions, including the decision to use global sources of supply, are extensions of the make-or-buy decisions of earlier eras. The pros and cons of these decisions usually include comparisons of costs as well as managerial control of confidential product design specifications, delivered quantity, quality, design, and delivery time and method. Other considerations include the manufacturing expertise required to make the raw material or components and the added cost of not being able to take advantage of the scale or larger volumes a vendor may have. In global purchasing, these issues are exacerbated by such factors as distance, different languages of buyers and sellers, and different national laws and regulations. Over time, many organizations have developed the ability to manage these obstacles fully or in part, thus enabling global outsourcing to become a viable option for an increasing number of firms. When possible, it is better for companies to initially outsource simple activities and gradually outsource more complex activities as both the outsourcer and the service provider gain experience.

The lure of global sourcing is the existence of suppliers with improved competitiveness in terms of cost, quality, timeliness, and other relevant dimensions. For example, certain nations may provide access to lower-cost or better-quality minerals or other important raw materials or components compared to what might be available domestically (such as bauxite in Jamaica or dynamic random-access memory chips in South Korea). In addition, the existence of industrially less developed countries with inexpensive and abundant unskilled labor may provide an attractive source of supply for labor-intensive products with low skill requirements. This helps explain why many relatively standardized and labor-intensive operations (such as the assembly of athletic shoes or men's dress shirts) have moved away from the more industrialized countries, where labor is more expensive. The international product life cycle theory, which was discussed in Chapter 3, helps to explain this migration of operations from the developed to the less developed nations of the world. As these emerging economies develop industrially, and some have developed rather rapidly, they have typically moved forward on the product and process continuum from high-labor-content products made with light, unsophisticated process equipment, such as sewing machines, to more sophisticated processes and more complex, lower-labor-content machinery, or even to skill-intensive engineering and design services.

The rate at which developing nations shift to more sophisticated processes is often more rapid than the initial emergence of these processes in a developed country. In part, this may be a result of an emerging nation's ability to transfer technology and processes previously invented and commercialized in the more developed nations, thus avoiding the cost and time of inventing these technologies on its own. There can be important implications for nations that may be losing jobs as a result of the migration of developing nations into more sophisticated, higher-value sectors. Many times, a worker put out of a high-labor-content job in a more industrially developed nation may lack the ability or training to move up the ladder to a more sophisticated job. Governments, concerned with the potential loss of jobs, may attempt to take actions to prevent or delay movement of the work to the developing country.

The ability to effectively and efficiently use global sources has been enhanced by the plummeting cost of communications, widespread use of standardized interfaces such as World Wide Web browsers, and the increasing pace at which companies are automating and digitizing data. As more of a company's operational activities are automated, it becomes easier and more economical to outsource these activities. Increasing numbers of companies have begun to compete for outsourcing business, and customers have become more accustomed to using these services.

GLOBAL SOURCING ARRANGEMENTS

As was suggested in Chapter 16, any of the following arrangements can provide a firm with foreign products:

1. *Wholly owned subsidiary:* May be established in a country with low-cost labor to supply components to the home country plant, or the subsidiary may produce a product that either is not made in the home country or is of higher quality.

BUILDING YOUR GLOBAL RÉSUMÉ

Consider a Career in Global Logistics and Supply Chain Management

In international business, just-in-time manufacturing and lean manufacturing are increasingly important strategic concerns that can critically impact the bottom line of any organization operating globally. Third-party logistics suppliers are growing in importance because they are assuming responsibility for the logistics of supply chain management of many world-class corporations. Demand is increasing for professionals trained in purchasing, inventory control, warehouse management, and inbound/outbound distribution management worldwide. Managing global operations is an emerging field, and here are a number of career opportunities, with salary information, for you to consider:

Entry Level

- Buyer/planner
- Inventory analyst
- Transportation coordinator
- Import/export clerk
- Quality assurance technician
- Salary range: mid $20s–mid $30s

Mid-level Management

- Purchasing manager
- Logistics manager
- Inventory control manager
- Director of quality assurance
- Manager of quality compliance
- International transportation manager
- Salary range: mid $40s–mid $50s+

Senior Level Management

- Director of supply chain management
- Director of import-export management
- Vice president–logistics
- Vice president–production and inventory control
- Salary range: $70,000+

World Wide Resources:

www.supplychainmanagement101.com

www.logisticsmgmt.com

www.glscs.com

2. *Overseas joint venture:* Established where labor costs are lower, or quality higher, than in the home country to supply components to the home country.
3. *In-bond plant contractor:* Home country plant sends components to be machined and assembled or only assembled by an independent contractor in an in-bond plant.
4. *Overseas independent contractor:* Common in the clothing industry, in which firms with no production facilities, such as DKNY, Nike, and Liz Claiborne, contract with foreign manufacturers to make clothing to their specifications with their labels.
5. *Independent overseas manufacturer.*

IMPORTANCE OF GLOBAL SOURCING

A strong relationship exists between global sourcing and ownership of the foreign sources. *Intrafirm trade,* which includes trade between a parent company and its foreign affiliates, accounts for 30 to 40 percent of exports of goods and 35 to 45 percent of imports in the case of the United States.[9]

In U.S. industry, the proportion of purchased materials in the overall cost of goods sold has been rising for several decades, from an average of 40 percent in 1945 to 50 percent in 1960 and 55 to 79 percent today.[10] There are several reasons for this phenomenon, including greater complexity of products and increasing pressure for firms to focus on their core business and outsource other activities in which they lack strong competitive ability.

In addition, competitive pressures and an emphasis on reduced concept-to-market cycle times in many product and service sectors have resulted in a rapid increase in the number of new products that are made available to the market. It has been estimated that at least 50 percent of products currently on the market were not available five years ago. This development has created additional pressure to locate suppliers worldwide that can provide inputs at competitive prices and quality and with quick responsiveness to market changes.

FINDING GLOBAL SOURCES

The import sources discussed in Chapter 17 are the ones a professional purchasing agent would contact to learn about independent foreign sources. Foreign consulates and embassies are especially useful in furnishing the names of national firms searching for foreign customers. Many countries have programs to promote their industries that are similar to those of the U.S. Department of Commerce. As part of their sales promotional programs, local branches of foreign banks will generally assist in locating sources in their home countries when requested. Some even have newsletters with offers from firms in the home country to sell as well as buy.

THE INCREASING USE OF ELECTRONIC PURCHASING FOR GLOBAL SOURCING

Simply entering "exporter" and the name of the product in a search engine will bring up the Web sites of dozens of exporters around the world that have online catalogs and information on how to order their products. There are also buyers, some of them from large companies, looking for products. In recent years, many firms have set up electronic procurement (e-procurement) exchanges, individually or in conjunction with other firms, to identify potential suppliers or customers and facilitate efficient and dynamic interactions among these prospective buyers and suppliers.

BAE Systems, the Boeing Company, Lockheed Martin Corporation, Rolls-Royce, and Raytheon have a combined annual procurement budget of over $80 billion, more than 37,000 suppliers, and hundreds of airline and government customers. Those five companies formed Exostar.com, a global, Web-based business-to-business (B2B) electronic marketplace for the aerospace and defense industry, with the goal of helping member companies to simplify and standardize procurement processes, streamline supply chains, reduce costs, improve productivity, and reach new markets.

John Rose, chief executive of Rolls-Royce, stated, "Exostar will allow us to reduce material and procurement costs, shorten lead times, and reduce our inventory. It will also enable us to collaborate more effectively with partners on designs for future projects. Exostar will allow design teams to hold shared, secure information, which can receive input from around the world. This will allow us to bring ideas to life in the marketplace more quickly, enabling a rapid response to customer requirements." By 2006, Exostar connected over 300 procurement systems, located in 20 different nations, and had over 16,000 registered trading partners.[11]

Other ambitious B2B e-procurement projects have been announced in automobile manufacturing (e.g., Covisint.com, an integrated auto parts supplier exchange developed by Ford, DaimlerChrysler, and General Motors), chemicals (e.g., ChemConnect.com), steel (e.g., e-steel.com), insurance, petroleum, hospital supplies, electric utilities, and a wide range of other industries. Wal-Mart conducts all of its business with suppliers via a proprietary B2B network.

In many companies, the purchasing function has been neglected for many years, often being viewed as a prime candidate for outsourcing to other firms. However, purchasing is increasingly being considered a strategic function, a trend encouraged by rapid developments in e-procurement. While direct production–oriented goods have been the focus of management attention for many years, the purchasing of goods and services that are not part of finished goods—termed *indirect procurement*—is also critical. Including such items as maintenance, repair, operating supplies, office equipment, and other services and supplies, indirect procurement can account for as much as 70 percent of the total purchasing expenditures in a company. Although many organizations have continued to rely on traditional paper-based processes for indirect procurement despite their cost and inefficiency, new technologies are quickly encouraging change in this approach, even for small and mid-size companies.

Options for Global Electronic Procurement

Among the most basic transactions that can occur over electronic purchasing exchanges are catalog purchases. Suppliers will provide a catalog of the products available, and buyers can access, review, and place orders for desired items at a listed price. The supplier can keep the catalog updated in real time, adjusting prices according to inventory levels and the need to move particular products. Electronic

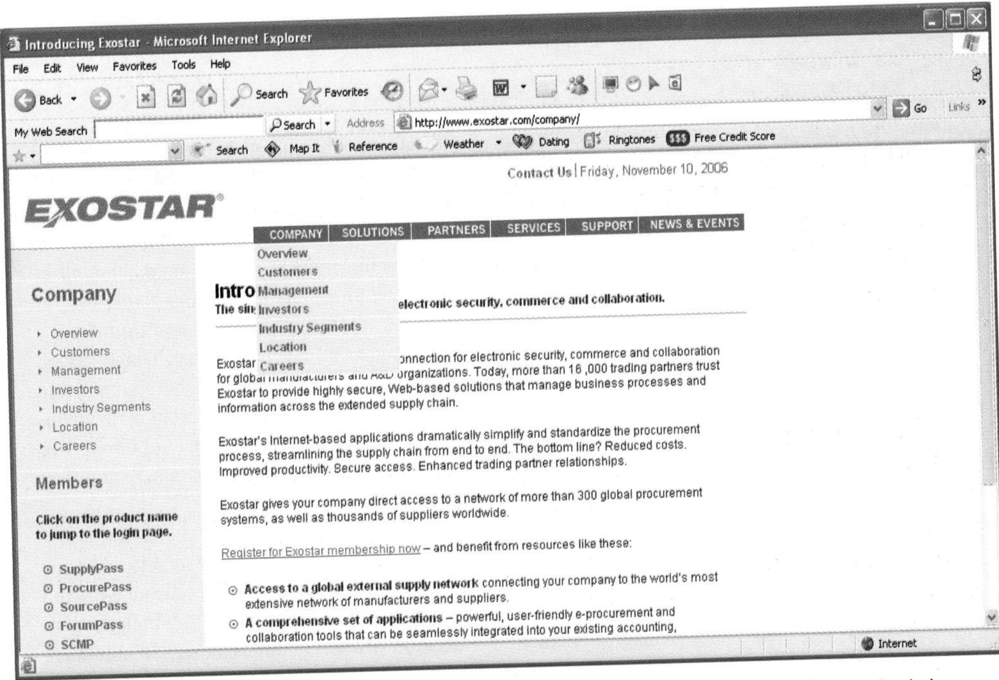

Web sites like Exostar help companies simplify and standardize procurement processes, streamline supply chains, reduce costs, improve productivity, and reach new markets.

Source: Exostar. Used by Permission.

exchanges can also permit buyers and suppliers to interact through a standard bid/quote system in which buyers can post their purchasing needs online for all prospective suppliers to view and the suppliers can then submit private quotes to the buyer. The buyer can then select among the submitted quotations on the basis of price, delivery times, or other factors. Industry-sponsored exchanges can also facilitate obtaining letters of credit, contracting for logistics and distribution, and monitoring daily prices and order flows, among other services.

Benefits of Global Electronic Procurement Systems

The benefits of electronic purchasing initiatives can be quite substantial. For example, Oracle Corporation announced that it would save $2 billion annually from companywide e-business initiatives that have allowed the company to streamline operations, cut costs, and improve productivity in supply chain management and customer response.[12] Research found that suppliers cut invoice and ordering errors by an average of 69 percent when using an e-marketplace, enhancing efficiency and reducing costs.[13]

> *Owens Corning established a goal of eliminating 80 percent of the company's paper invoices, meaning that all centralized purchasing would be done electronically (the remaining 20 percent of purchasing is decentralized). The company had four main goals when it launched its e-procurement initiative: hard-dollar cost reductions, supply chain visibility, business process integration, and a common, standardized process for all suppliers. Another major benefit of e-procurement has been a decreased need to rework invoices that are received either in incorrect formats or with incorrect information, cutting the number of reworked invoices by 70 percent. Jim Hawkins, e-sourcing project team leader, said the response by the company's suppliers has been mixed. "We've had suppliers who have jumped on . . . others really struggle or are not comfortable with the idea." While he says the transition to the company's new e-procurement system has been much easier for smaller and less technically advanced suppliers, "E does not necessarily stand for easy. Moving to electronic interchange is never as easy as you think it will be at first."*[14]

Smaller companies are also using the Internet to purchase raw materials as well as to sell their products to customers, often on a worldwide basis. Developments such as e-procurement exchanges have opened the door for many smaller suppliers, which now have to spend very little to get into the market, lowering barriers to entry to domestic and international market opportunities. As asserted by Amanda Mesler, managing director of KPMG Consulting in

mini MNE

>>Cognizant Technology Solutions: Sourcing Low-Cost Talent Internationally to Achieve Global Competitive Advantage

India has become a global center for high-technology businesses in recent years, with an estimated 800,000 information technology (IT) workers by 2006. The IT services sector has been supported by the Indian government for decades, a position enhanced by strong educational systems established by the British during colonial times. "The difference between India's universities and a school like Harvard is that an Indian university is harder to get into," said Mukesh Mehta, vice president of corporate systems for Metropolitan Life Insurance Company, which outsources IT services to an Indian supplier. Companies such as Microsoft, Oracle, and Sun have established research and development (R&D) facilities in Bangalore, Mumbai, and other Indian cities in an effort to utilize inexpensive and well-trained Indian engineers instead of expensive talent in the United States. IDC, a market research firm, estimated that by 2007, 23 percent of all IT work done for U.S.-based companies will be offshore, up from 5 percent in 2003.

One company seeking to exploit this opportunity is Cognizant Technology Solutions of Teaneck, New Jersey. With an electrical engineering degree from Cambridge and an MBA from Harvard Business School, the company's chairman and CEO, Kumar Mahadeva, was well prepared to build a technology-based business. Observing the thriving software industry that was emerging in India in the early 1990s, Mahadeva recognized an opportunity. He realized that he could achieve a strong cost advantage over other U.S. companies by employing talented entry-level programmers in India for $6,000 to $9,000 per year, compared to an average salary in the United States of about $50,000. He founded Cognizant in 1994 as a division of Dun & Bradstreet Corporation, initially focusing on large-scale full life-cycle software projects.

Providing software development and maintenance services, Cognizant competes on the basis of price, speed, and agility. The centerpiece of the company's operations is an innovative "offshore-onshore" business model. Under this model, about 30 percent of the company's more than 28,000 computer science and engineering professionals work at customer sites in the United States or other Western nations, and the remainder work at one of its 28 development centers, primarily located in India. Cognizant's hourly billable rates of $24 were substantially below comparable rates from domestic American providers, which charged upward of $70 per hour.

Once a contract has been signed, a global "virtual project team" is set up. A small portion of the team is located at the client's site, mainly Indian nationals who come for a couple of years to handle project management activities and manage client relationships on a daily basis. The remainder of the team is located in India, where software development, coding, maintenance, and other activities are completed on an around-the-clock, seven-days-a-week basis. This approach allows Cognizant's project managers to interact intensely with its clients during working hours in the West, intimately understanding the clients' strategies and needs, while prototype development, coding, and system upgrading activities are conducted overnight in a "chasing the sun" model of customer support.

To facilitate effective management of the offshore and on-site components of the multinational team, the company has set up a satellite- and fiber-optic-cable–based voice/data communications infrastructure, including e-mail and videoconferencing capabilities. To minimize misunderstandings and other problems as thoughts are translated from one culture to another, Cognizant's recruitment efforts target English-speaking students from computer science, engineering, and information technology programs at leading Indian universities. The company also provides extensive project management training programs. In addition, the company has a proprietary Project Management Tool that allows project managers to monitor the workflow of individual team members and track the status of components and various development activities.

Despite a fiercely competitive marketplace, Cognizant has achieved sustained success with its innovative business model. The company went public in 1998 on the Nasdaq, and by 2006 it had nearly 200 clients, primarily in health care, financial services, and manufacturing/retail/logistics, including a number of prominent domestic and international companies such as Nielsen Media Research, the Body Shop, GM, Sears, Levis, United Healthcare, and Northwest Airlines. Included each year from 2002 to 2006 on *BusinessWeek*'s listing of the top 100 "hot growth" companies, Cognizant has quickly soared to a market valuation of approximately $9 billion, revenues of $1 billion, and a rate of growth that is more rapid than the industry as a whole.

Source: Interviews with executives at Cognizant Technology Solutions; Cognizant Technology Solutions, *2005 Annual Report*, www.cognizant.com/html/content/casestudies/annualreport/AnnualReport05.pdf (July 17, 2006); Alex Salkever, "Recognizing Cognizant as a High-Tech Bargain," *BusinessWeek*, March 28, 2000, www.businessweek.com/bwdaily/dnflash/mar2000/sw00328.htm (September 25, 2004); Cognizant Technology Solutions, www.cognizant.com (July 17, 2006); and Larry Greenemeier, "Offshore Outsourcing Grows to Global Proportions," *Information Week*, February 11, 2002, www.informationweek.com/story/IWK20020207S0011 (September 25, 2004).

Houston, Texas, "The promise of an exchange is that it allows them [smaller companies] to leverage their size further and get into more markets, especially globally and internationally, than they ever have before."[15]

Overall, emerging industry-based B2B exchanges can help optimize the supply chain across an entire network of organizations, not merely within a single company. These exchanges can create value by aggregating the purchasing power of buyers, improving process efficiency, integrating supply chains, enhancing content dissemination, and improving overall market efficiency within and across nations.

PROBLEMS WITH GLOBAL SOURCING

Although global sourcing is a standard procedure for half the U.S. firms with sales over $10 million, it does have some disadvantages.[16] Inasmuch as lower price is the primary reason companies make foreign purchases, they may be surprised that what initially appeared to be a lower price is not really lower once all the costs connected to the purchase are considered.

> *In their rush to source from China, many companies are blindly walking into a strategic trap. The trap is thinking sourcing from China will result in lower product costs, when, in reality, the supply chain dynamics will drive up overall costs and reduce profitability—thereby creating an opening for a competitor.*[17]

For purchases of capital goods, such as manufacturing equipment, many U.S. buying organizations now use "life cycle costing" to analyze purchasing decisions through the life of the purchased item, including trade-in or future estimated salvage value. Even on components, firms increasingly are including full costing, including the use of activity-based costing systems, to ensure that all the costs associated with foreign sourcing (e.g., transportation, insurance, increased inventory levels to insulate against delays in delivery) are fully recognized when they make purchasing decisions.[18] It is essential that global sourcing decisions be closely linked to the organization's strategy and that explicit objectives for suppliers (such as delivery times and cost objectives) be defined and incorporated in contracts, ideally with incentives for meeting or exceeding them. Cross-company teams should also be developed in order to enhance the likelihood that best practices can be effectively shared between the organization and its suppliers, in order to avoid supply problems.

Added Costs

The buyer must understand the terms of sale discussed in Chapter 17 because international freight, insurance, and packing can add as much as 10 to 12 percent to the quoted price, depending on the sales term used. The following is a list of the costs of importing, with an estimate of the percentage of the quoted price that each cost adds:

1. International freight, insurance, and packing (10–12%).
2. Import duties (0–50%).
3. Customhouse broker's fees (3–5%).
4. Transit or pipeline inventory (5–15%).
5. Cost of letter of credit (1%).
6. International travel and communication costs (2–8%).
7. Company import specialists (5%).
8. Reworking of products out of specification (0–15%).

Explanation of Added Costs To be certain of the cost of freight, insurance, and packing, the prospective importer should request a quotation with sales terms of CIF port of entry and stipulate that the merchandise be packed for export unless all shipments will be sent by air freight. As discussed in Chapter 17, import duties can be extremely high if the exporting country is in column 2 of the Harmonized Tariff Schedule for the United States (HTSUSA). Unless the goods enter duty-free, the duty must be added as part of the landed cost. To estimate the import duty, the importer should ask the customhouse broker for assistance. Brokers have experience in customs classification and usually can get nonbinding opinions from the customs inspectors with whom they work. If the product will be imported regularly, the importer should ask U.S. Customs to provide a binding tariff classification. This will be made in writing and must be honored by customs officials.

Costs for inventory in the pipeline will vary according to the exporter's delivery promise. If it can ship from stock and air freight is a viable means, the importer may be able to work with only two weeks' inventory. If, however, the exporter must produce to fill the order and ship by ocean freight, it may need two months' inventory. Carrying costs include the opportunity cost of capital, the cost of storage facilities, insurance, pilferage, depreciation, taxes, and handling.

If there is considerable import activity, the importer may want to set up an import group of employees to be in charge of the operation. One other item that requires explanation is the rework expense and scrap charges. Sometimes a foreign exporter will submit a sample of the article it is quoting that is perfect in every respect, yet the actual shipment may include various pieces out of specification. If the importer has not made arrangements in the purchasing contract for rebates or replacement, the costs can escalate severely.

Other Disadvantages One disadvantage an importer should not have to face is an increase in price because the home currency has lost value as a result of exchange rate fluctuation. For example, if an American importer requires that the exporter quote dollar prices, the importer has no exchange rate risk. However, if the firm has a large volume of imports and the dollar is unstable, management may want a quotation in foreign currency. In that case, the chief financial officer of the importing company probably will protect the company from exchange rate risk by using one of the hedging techniques discussed in Chapter 21. Hedging has been used for many years by companies that operate internationally, particularly if their raw materials include one or more of the commodities traded on established commodities markets. In most cases, such hedging has been done not for speculative reasons but as a means of protecting the company from the risk of rapid price fluctuations.

The emergence of e-procurement has also been accompanied by problems. E-procurement and electronic commerce as a whole cannot be isolated from the company's overall business system. Many early efforts at developing e-procurement systems have been made in isolation and have subsequently failed to deliver on their potential. Successful electronic commerce initiatives include connections to traditional systems for fulfilling procurement and other value chain activities, as well as considerations on how to manage the transition to new, electronic approaches. The traditional functions of purchasing—supplier determination, analysis, and selection—still have to be accomplished before the actual purchasing via e-procurement. In most instances, a company may be able to use the Internet for quicker data acquisition about possible suppliers and generally from a much broader information base than was previously available in a timely manner. Ensuring that a supplier is selected that can meet all the company's conditions for its raw material in terms of quality, delivery, price, and so forth, remains a challenge, particularly in a broadscale e-procurement network involving suppliers with which the company is not familiar. Suppliers located in emerging nations may also encounter difficulty in accessing and supporting sophisticated IT infrastructures, which can impact e-procurement performance.

Security also is often a significant concern for e-procurement. For B2B electronic commerce to achieve its full potential, access to the company's internal systems from outside is critical. Companies are wary of opening up the details of their business—including pricing, inventory, or design specifications—to competitors, as well as risking the loss of brand equity and margins. In addition, exposing internal business systems to access via the Internet can expose the firm to a wide range of potential security issues, such as unauthorized entry ("hacking") and fraudulent orders. Although extensive research and development efforts have been undertaken in encryption technology and other technology and processes to ensure integrity, much progress still remains to be achieved before these systems can be considered fully secure. Different country standards are also of concern in attempting to implement international e-procurement systems. Governmental concerns with potential anticompetitive effects of collaboration among competitors may also cause problems for industrywide B2B exchanges.

Manufacturing Systems

Inasmuch as international firms maintain manufacturing facilities in countries at various levels of development—facilities utilizing factors of production that vary considerably in cost and quality from one country to another—it is understandable that manufacturing systems will also vary considerably even within the same company. Therefore, a single company may have a combination of plants that range from those with the most advanced production technology, such as plants in Japan and the United States, to those with the less advanced technology of most developing nations.* The manufacturing systems in place within and across a company's international operations can have important implications for the way in which the company's global supply chain is set up and managed.

ADVANCED PRODUCTION TECHNIQUES TO ENHANCE QUALITY AND LOWER COSTS

Growing international competition requires increasing efforts from companies to achieve efficiency and effectiveness in their international production activities. As a result, companies all over the world have pursued ways to improve their competitiveness, putting into place advanced production systems such as just-in-time supply chains or highly synchronized manufacturing systems. Others have installed computer integrated manufacturing (CIM), utilizing computers and robots to further improve productivity and quality. Although these innovations can be a major challenge to implement successfully, their impact on international companies' competitiveness can be impressive.

What did Japan have to do to achieve international competitiveness after its manufacturing infrastructure was destroyed in World War II? Japanese manufacturers realized that because of the limited size of the country's economy, they would have to export to grow. They were also aware that because of the country's lack of natural resources, they would have to earn foreign exchange from exports to pay for the importation of energy sources such as petroleum and coal, as well as raw materials. In order to meet the requirements of export markets, Japanese companies would have to provide high-quality products at low prices. But during the initial postwar years, "Made in Japan" meant poor quality and shoddy manufacture to the rest of the world. In the 1950s, the Japanese brought in various American experts on manufacturing and quality improvement techniques, such as Juran, Feigenbaum, and Deming.[19] *W. Edwards Deming, a statistician who had taught thousands of American industrial engineers how to use statistics in manufacturing during the war, helped teach Japanese manufacturers that statistics can be used to analyze what the system is doing and get it under control to produce quality products while simultaneously controlling costs.*[20]

As illustrated in the above example, when examining the components of their costs, Japanese managers realized what all firms know: Inventory costs are a major factor. Getting rid of inventory can lower labor cost by 40 percent, for example. To operate without inventory, however, Japanese manufacturers had to meet certain requirements:

1. Components, whether purchased from outside suppliers or made in the same plant, had to be defect-free, or the production line would be shut down while the workers in all successive operations waited for usable inputs.
2. Parts and components had to be delivered to each point in the production process at the time they were needed, hence the name **just-in-time (JIT).** Henry Ford incorporated elements of JIT in his moving assembly lines in the early 1900s.
3. Customers everywhere want delivery when they make the purchase, and so sellers maintain inventories of finished products. Sales often are made because one firm can supply the product from stock but a competitor cannot. How long do you want to wait for delivery of your car after you buy it? Eliminating inventories of finished goods while still responding quickly to customers' orders required the manufacturers to set up flexible production units, which necessitated rapid setup times.

just-in-time (JIT)
A balanced system in which there is little or no delay time and idle in-process and finished goods inventory

*There are always exceptions to this generalization.

4. It was also necessary to reduce process time. One way to do this is to lower the time needed to transport work in progress from one operation to the next. American and European preoccupation with economic order lots resulted in their grouping machines by function (all drill presses together, punch presses together, and so forth), but transporting the machines' output to the next functional area takes time and costs money. Japanese firms grouped machines according to the workflow of a single product (a separate production line for each product), which virtually eliminated transport cost. Also, because parts were arriving immediately from one operation to the next, when the output of the preceding operation was defective, that operation could be stopped until the cause was rectified. Since each succeeding operation acted as quality inspection, this also lowered production costs because fewer defective parts were produced.
5. Flexible manufacturing allows product changes to be made rapidly, but each change in the production line still costs money. Therefore, the manufacturers simplified product lines and designed the products to use as many of the same parts as possible. This also contributed to the company suppliers' acceptance of the JIT concept because they received fewer but larger orders, which permitted longer, less costly (fewer production changeovers) production runs.
6. For just-in-time to be successful, manufacturers had to have the cooperation of their suppliers. They could not follow the common American practice of having numerous vendors, which buyers often play against one another to get the best price. Japanese firms used fewer vendors and sought to establish close relationships with them, including calling them in during the design of the product.
7. To lower costs, improve quality, and lower production times, Japanese managements required that product designers, production managers, purchasing people, and marketers work as a team.
8. Getting these people together enabled suppliers to suggest using the lower-cost standard parts they regularly produce, manufacturing to indicate when a design change could simplify the production process, and marketing to contribute the customer's viewpoint, *all before the first product was produced.*[21]

Reducing costs has been critical in recent years as companies, especially those from developed countries, face increasing competitive threats from lower-cost nations such as India and China. The competitive challenges posed by these nations have been viewed as a major cause of the "hollowing out" of the industrial sector in nations such as Japan, the United States, and Germany as manufacturing and assembly activities have been relocated to lower-cost locations, such as China, Mexico, or Eastern Europe.

total quality management (TQM) System in which the entire organization is managed so that it excels on all dimensions of product and services that are important to the customer

quality circle (quality control circle) Small work group that meets periodically to discuss ways to improve its functional areas and the quality of the product

Improve Quality

To improve quality, everyone in the organization—from top management to workers—has to be committed to quality. **Total quality management (TQM),** a companywide management approach to ensure quality throughout the organization, was invented in the Bell Laboratories in the 1920s. Teams are necessary in the implementation of TQM, and one useful kind of team is the **quality circle,** an idea of Ishikawa, a Japanese quality expert.[22] Look at how the president of Komatsu, Caterpillar's Japanese competitor, describes the use of quality circles in his company.

The objective of the quality circle is to take part of the responsibility for the quality goal of each section: "Quality circle members are aware of the extent to which their achievement of their objectives will contribute to the results of their department, and also to the business of the company as a whole."

A small group of employees, led by a foreman who has previously received quality control education, independently undertakes quality control activities. The circle's activities are divided among subdivisions of the circle led by a person junior to the foreman. Here is an example that illustrates that quality circles are used in all functional areas, not just in manufacturing.

One day, telephone operators received complaints from outside callers regarding delays in answering telephones, so they surveyed company employees, who confirmed that the com-

WORLD view   

Chasing the Sun

"Big Ben strikes 5, and a team of engineers in London saves the latest files on a major design project and heads home to their flats. At about that time, a second team is pouring its first cups of coffee in rainy Seattle, eight time zones behind, and setting to work where the Brits left off. At the end of their eight-hour day, the Americans flip the proverbial baton over the Great Wall to a Beijing team, who will later complete the 24-hour cycle by giving way to the London team arriving for breakfast."

Sound far-fetched or futuristic? Think again, because this type of activity is occurring in a growing number of multinational corporations. Driven by increasing global competition and pressure to reduce concept-to-market cycle time, many international competitors—particularly in high-technology sectors such as information technology—have been forced to fundamentally rethink the way they structure their operations. The result is an approach termed *global, concurrent engineering,* or "chasing the sun" in more common terms.

Facilitated by rapid advances in computing and telecommunications technology and infrastructure, companies such as Hewlett-Packard (H-P), Boeing, and Cognizant Technology Solutions (discussed in the mini MNE box in this chapter) are trying to gain an advantage over their competitors by developing systems that permit around-the-clock development of new products. As stated by Mark Canepa, who is responsible for workstation systems strategy at H-P, "There's enormous pressure to make better and better products, faster than the competition, and time to market is the biggest differentiator." In rolling out its latest major initiative, the Open Enterprise Computing program, H-P is using a "virtual" team of specialists from around the world who are linked with each other—and with an array of international customers and partners—regardless of location and time.

Leveraging 24-hour global computer networks, project-focused Web sites, and teams of engineers and other technical personnel located at various offices around the globe, companies such as H-P are attempting to enable around-the-clock communication among clients and coworkers and thereby facilitate continuous real-time engineering enhancements, updating of blueprints, and related project management activities. In essence, they are attempting to revolutionize the way business is conducted. The benefits can be particularly valuable if around-the-clock systems are implemented during or before the detailed design phase of an international project, which tends to result in a significant improvement in the quality of designs through multiple reviews by different, geographically dispersed teams.

Implemented properly, these new approaches can yield valuable cross-fertilization of ideas to stimulate productivity and innovation among international teams, produce staggering reductions in lead time for new projects, and deliver a flood of new and enhanced products and services to the market ahead of competitors. The result: a powerful advantage in the demanding global competitive marketplace.

Source: Ray Bert, "Around the World in 24 Hours," *ASEE Prism*, American Society of Engineering Education, March 2000, www.asee.org/prism/march/html/feature2.html (September 25, 2004); Rossmore Group, "Chasing the Sun," www.rossmore.co.uk/pdfs-downloads/contact3.pdf (July 17, 2006); David Evans, "Chasing the Sun," *Computer Weekly*, April 27, 1995, p. 33; and James Ott, "Cargo 'Mods'; Boeing Applies Production Expertise to Its 747-400SF Conversion Program," *Aviation Week & Space Technology*, April 5, 2004, p. 56.

plaints were valid. They then studied the average time they were taking to answer a call and found that it was 7.4 seconds. They called the telephone company, which informed them that its standard was three seconds. The quality circle then discussed how to reach the three-second standard.[23]

Problems with Implementing the JIT System Many manufacturers in the United States and elsewhere rushed to Japan to study the just-in-time "miracle" and mistakenly copied only one part of it: the narrow focus on scheduling goods inventories, called by some "little JIT." They failed to realize that what is important is "big JIT," a *total system* covering the management of people, materials, and relations with suppliers (also called *lean production*).[24] Moreover, many did not understand that JIT includes TQM, of which continuous improvement is an integral part.

Taylor's scientific management system
System based on scientific measurements that prescribes a division of work whereby planning is done by managers and plan execution is left to supervisors and workers

Another difficulty was the difference in attitudes (a cultural force) between Japanese and Western managers. American managers and unions still valued highly the specialization of worker functions based on **Taylor's scientific management system.** This system contradicts the principles of quality circles: (1) participative decision making and (2) problem-solving capabilities of workers. Americans, pressured for quick results, were disappointed when quality circles did not offer immediate solutions for improvement. The practice of not guaranteeing long-term employment also made it more difficult to attain company loyalty for JIT. A further problem in implementing JIT systems was failure to train and integrate suppliers into the system.

In trying to transform their supply chains, operations management experts also realized that there could be problems with JIT itself:

1. JIT is restricted to operations that produce the same parts repeatedly because it is a *balanced* system; that is, all operations are designed to produce the same quantity of parts. Yet repetitive operations may appear only in parts of the manufacturing process. It is far less useful for job shops (firms or departments within larger firms that specialize in producing small numbers of custom-designed products)* in which there is no dominant flow of production through the processes.
2. Because JIT is a balanced system, if one operation stops, the entire production line stops—there is no inventory to keep succeeding operations working.
3. Achieving a balanced system is difficult because production capacities differ among the various classes of machines. It may require five lathes to keep one punch press busy, for example, and it takes dozens of tire-building machines to use the output of just one calender, a huge machine (similar in size to a newspaper printing press) that rubberizes the fabric used in making tires. This problem is less severe for large production units, of course.
4. JIT makes no allowances for contingencies, and so every piece must be defect-free when it is received and delivery promises must be kept. **Preventive (planned) maintenance** is crucial. A sudden machine breakdown will stop the entire production process.

preventive (planned) maintenance
Maintenance done according to plan, not when machines break down

Toyota found out how vulnerable its just-in-time system is to the failure of just one supplier to deliver a part at the planned time. A fire at one of its keiretsu members, the exclusive producer of its brake parts, shut down all of the company's auto plants in Japan, causing it to lose a week's production. Not only did the fire paralyze Toyota's manufacturing activities; it caused hundreds of other Toyota suppliers to stop the production of its parts. After the fire, Toyota's chairman acknowledged that the just-in-time inventory system needed improvement. His company had to give orders to more than one supplier to prevent further crippling stoppages caused by a lack of parts. The single supplier concept, of course, has been a key component of its kereitsu network.[25]

5. Much trial and error are required to put the system into effect.[26]

Synchronous Manufacturing The problems with JIT, especially the long time required for its installation in a manufacturing system, caused some firms to realize that something else was needed to assist them in gaining market share. Many turned to **synchronous manufacturing,** also called the *theory of constraints (TOC),* a scheduling and manufacturing control system that seeks to locate and then eliminate or minimize any constraints to greater production output, such as machines, people, tools, and facilities. The system's output is determined by and limited to the output of the slowest operation (**bottleneck**) that is working at full capacity.

synchronous manufacturing
An entire manufacturing system with unbalanced operations that emphasizes total system performance

bottleneck
Operation in a manufacturing system whose output sets the limit for the entire system's output

A computer program developed by Dr. Goldtratt, the originator of TOC, schedules work, taking into consideration bottleneck and nonbottleneck operations. This makes scheduling much faster because production schedules and simulation can be done on a computer instead of having to arrive at schedules by trial and error, as is necessary with JIT. Also, once a bottleneck is discovered, the operations manager can concentrate on increasing the production rate of that process. After resolving that, the manager can repeat the process on the next-slowest operation.[27]

Instead of attempting to achieve a balanced system like JIT, in which the capacities of all operations are equal, synchronous manufacturing aims to balance the *product flow* through the system, which leaves output levels of the various operations *unbalanced.* For example, with the bottleneck operation producing at full capacity, perhaps only 60 percent capacity is needed at another operation. Because there is no reason for this operation to produce over 60 percent of its capacity, it is stopped at that point; anything more would be unwanted

**Job shop* also refers to a production system in which departments are organized around specific operations (grinding, drilling, and so forth).

inventory. Inasmuch as work is assigned to each operation rather than to the entire system, as in JIT, there is no need for more work in process than that which is actually being worked on. Inventory may also be placed near the bottleneck to avoid any shutdown in this crucial operation, and sometimes, unlike the case with JIT, there may even be a quality control inspector to check the bottleneck operation's input.

As we mentioned previously, management's attention is focused on the bottleneck rather than on the other operations, because a production increase at the bottleneck means an increase for the entire production system; an increase in a nonbottleneck operation adds to only that machine's idle time.

Note another important difference between JIT and synchronous manufacturing: A defective part or component at any point in the production process can shut down a JIT system. But because a synchronous manufacturing system has excess capacity in all operations except at the bottleneck, any defective part produced before the bottleneck can be remade, and thus the entire system is not stopped.

Incidentally, as firms adopt new manufacturing techniques such as synchronous manufacturing, they find that traditional accounting methods are inadequate to measure the costs of overhead. Managers are turning to *activity-based costing* to allocate the overhead burden according to its components, which vary among products.

Mass Customization **Mass customization** refers to a company's use of flexible, usually computer-aided, manufacturing systems to produce and deliver customized products and services for different customers worldwide. These systems typically combine the low unit costs and rapid production speeds associated with mass-production processes with the flexibility of customization for the demands of individual customers. As an approach to manufacturing, mass customization has been around since at least World War II, when Toyota began using it. Mass customization is now applied to varying degree by a range of companies in such fields as computers (Dell), greeting cards (Hallmark), clothing (L.L.Bean), footwear (adidas), diamond rings (adiamondisforever.com), and cars (Land-Rover).

mass customization
The use of flexible, usually computer-aided, manufacturing systems to produce and deliver customized products and services for different customers worldwide

There are four basic approaches to mass customization: (1) collaborative—a company helps customers choose the required product features; (2) adaptive—the company offers a

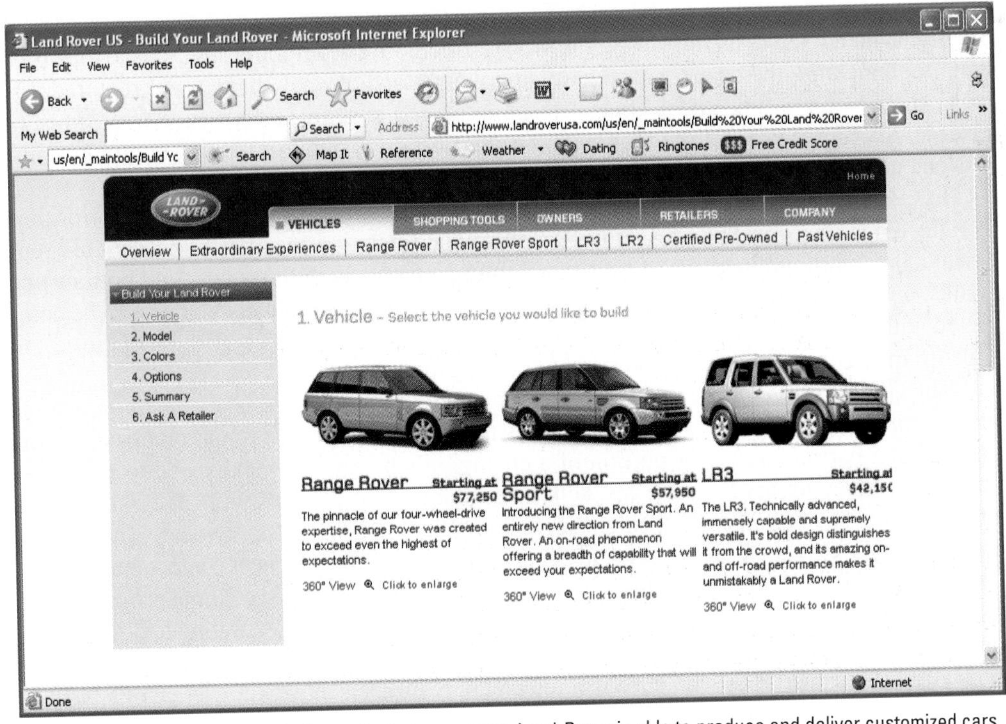

Through the use of computer-aided manufacturing systems, Land-Rover is able to produce and deliver customized cars for different customers worldwide.

Source: Land Rover US

standard product that users can modify themselves; (3) cosmetic—only the product's presentation is customized, such as packaging or color; and (4) transparent—customers are provided with individualized product or service offerings without their knowing it, such as Web site interfaces).[28]

Mass customization is usually appropriate in situations where there is the potential for delaying the task of differentiating the product for a particular customer until the last possible point in the supply network. This typically requires that the company reconceptualize the design of its product as well as the design and integration of the processes used for producing and delivering the product to customers. In practice, this means reconceptualizing and often reconfiguring the company's entire supply chain. But the benefits of such a comprehensive approach to operations are that the company will be able to function at maximum efficiency and to rapidly respond to customers' needs, while maintaining a minimum level of inventory.

Six Sigma
Business management process for reducing defects and eliminating variation

Six Sigma **Six Sigma** is a business management process that combines rigorous analytical tools with a well-defined infrastructure and leadership from the top in order to solve problems and optimize processes. It concentrates on eliminating variation and reducing defects from work processes, and as defects go down, so do costs and cycle time, while customer satisfaction goes up.

Six Sigma literally means a maximum of 3.4 defects per million occurrences, versus the Two or Three Sigma level (more than 300,000 unsatisfactory experiences per million customer contacts) at which most businesses operate. It has been estimated that up to one-third of the work done in the United States consists of redoing what was already done previously and that the cost of poor quality consumes 20 to 40 percent of the total effort.[29] Six Sigma attempts to overcome this problem.

The Six Sigma approach includes five steps: define, measure, analyze, improve, and control. It begins by defining the process, asking who the customers are and what their problems are. Key characteristics important to the customer are identified, along with the processes that support these characteristics. Next, Six Sigma focuses on measuring the process, including categorizing key characteristics, verifying measurement systems, and collecting data. The third step is analysis, converting raw data into information that provides insight into the process and identifies the fundamental and most important causes of defects or problems. Six Sigma then focuses on improving the process, including developing solutions to the problem, implementing the changes, and assessing whether additional changes are required. Finally, the process is put under control to monitor and sustain performance over time. In essence, Six Sigma is a method for creating a closed-loop system for making continuous improvements in business processes.

In selecting projects for Six Sigma, there should be a clear link with business priorities, as reflected in the organization's strategic and annual operating plans. A project should represent a breakthrough in terms of significant improvements in both process and bottom-line results, with clear, quantitative measures of success. Projects should also be able to be completed within about three to six months (or be divided into subprojects of such duration), in order to maintain progress and company interest in the project.[30]

The CEO is often the driving force for implementing Six Sigma. The *champion,* who is responsible for the project's success, provides the necessary resources and breaks down organizational barriers. A major portion of a champion's bonus is typically tied to his or her success in achieving Six Sigma goals, helping ensure that the projects will have a substantial impact on the business. Project leaders are called "Black Belts" (BBs), typically individuals with a history of accomplishment and significant experience. Project team members are called "Green Belts" (GBs), and they do not spend all their time on Six Sigma projects. Both BBs and GBs tend to be change agents, and they should be open to generating and rigorously evaluating new ideas. Master Black Belts (MBBs), who are resources for project teams, are typically experienced BBs who have worked on many projects, have knowledge of advanced tools, have received business and leadership training, and have teaching experience. The primary responsibility of MBBs is training and mentoring new BBs.[31]

A Quality Online survey found that the biggest advantage of Six Sigma among organizations using the methodology was increased cost savings (45 percent of respondents), followed by an increase in customer satisfaction (20 percent), reduction of defects (15 percent), increased company growth (10 percent), and increased quality (5 percent). As one respondent said, "It is hard to pinpoint any single advantage of Six Sigma for a company. Engaging in Six Sigma increases customer satisfaction, lowers overall cost, and decreases defects, which is a competitive advantage for any company."[32]

Credited with originally creating Six Sigma, since 1987 Motorola's Six Sigma initiatives have generated documented savings in the company of over $16 billion as well as reducing the cost of poor quality by over 84 percent per unit and increasing employee productivity by 12 percent per year.[33]

The Six Sigma methodology involves reevaluation of the value-adding status of many elements of an organization (some being modified, others being discontinued). As a result, moving from Two Sigma to Six Sigma thinking often requires that companies rethink the way they do things and that they adapt their culture, sometimes dramatically. In challenging the existing way of doing things, Six Sigma may yield conflict with the organization's system of values and ethics.

Successful culture change requires a concerted, long-term effort, particularly if the organization is multinational, with subsidiaries and offices around the world. The way organizations change is influenced by organizational and national culture, which impact such things as how companies ascribe status, recognize performance, structure reporting lines, and communicate internally. This means that culture and cultural change must be actively managed from the outset. Increased acceptance may require that the organization (1) demonstrate the need for Six Sigma, (2) shape the vision of a Six Sigma culture and associated behaviors, (3) identify and properly manage organizational resistance to Six Sigma (including technical, political, and organizational sources), and (4) change the systems and structures of the organization (including hiring, development, performance assessment, and rewards for organizational personnel).[34] It is also essential to maintain the involvement and commitment of functional groups that provide the resources, data, and expertise necessary for successful implementation of Six Sigma change initiatives, including finance, information technology, human resources, engineering, R&D, and purchasing.

Logistics

Logistics refers to managerial functions associated with the movement of materials such as raw materials, work in progress, or finished goods. The effectiveness of supply chain management efforts is strongly influenced by how a company manages the interface of logistics with sourcing and manufacturing, as well as with other activities such as design, engineering, and marketing.[35] Given the strong emphasis on minimization of inventory and handling in supply chains, especially under just-in-time systems, the way a product (or the components and materials that will go into a product) is designed can significantly influence the cost of delivering the product. For example, packaging and transportation requirements for a product can significantly influence logistics costs, and these factors should be addressed during design as well as in other steps in the value chain.

Many companies have chosen to outsource their logistics needs to outside specialists, particularly for managing international logistics activities. Companies such as Federal Express, DHL, and UPS have developed expertise in handling and tracking materials within and across nations, including sophisticated computer technology and systems for tracking shipments. For example, Federal Express's Web site (www.fedex.com) allows a company to arrange pickups and then monitor the status of each item being transported, including information on the time the shipment was picked up, when and where it has been transferred within FedEx's network, and delivery location, time, and recipient. Many of these logistics companies have developed systems whereby their customers' in-house information systems are integrated with the logistics company's shipping and tracking systems. It is also common

WORLD view   

Johnson Controls: Exploiting Design and Manufacturing Excellence for Global Advantage

Johnson Controls (JCI) was founded in 1885 to market its founder's invention, the electric room thermostat. By 2006, JCI had 136,000 employees in 1,000 locations worldwide and was generating annual revenues of nearly $28 billion, 60 percent from international markets. Its primary business is automotive parts and systems, although it has substantial activities in the building controls business as well.

In the early 1980s, JCI was known for heating controls and plastic containers, not automotive products. Until about 1985 auto manufacturers made car seats in their own factories. Then JCI and another company, Lear, conceived the idea of supplying those essential parts of a car's interior. Now JCI estimates that nearly 90 percent of the seating in American-made cars is outsourced, while in Europe the comparable proportion is 75 percent. According to JCI, demand from automakers to have only a single supplier of seating systems is expected to continue to grow "due to opportunities system integration creates for cost reduction, parts consolidation, weight reduction, quality and safety improvements, enhanced functionality, and vehicle differentiation."

Initially, JCI's auto seating business was focused on production of car seat frames, making them vulnerable to lower-priced competition. Over the past 15 years, JCI has focused on developing a broad range of assembly, integration, and R&D skills that help set it apart from competitors worldwide. JCI now designs and assembles not only seats but entire vehicle cockpits, and it conducts more customer research on interiors than any automaker.

Because of its unique capabilities, JCI has continual contact with an automaker's entire design and engineering team, beginning early and continuing throughout the vehicle planning process. As a result, JCI obtains proprietary information that yields deep insight into the automaker's needs and activities. JCI is now striving to increase its engineers' input to the design and engineering work so that it can use the results in the seats of other car manufacturers. "Three years ago, 80 percent of our development work was done on behalf of individual customers and only 20 percent was our own proprietary designs," said JCI's president. "Today the proportion is about 60:40 and our goal is to turn this to 20:80." Overall, these are capabilities that traditional parts suppliers cannot match, making JCI a supplier of choice in markets around the world, reducing bidding volatility and allowing it to plan with greater certainty. As Bill Fluharty, vice president of Industrial Design in JCI's Automotive Group, stated, "Tier One suppliers in the automotive industry earn their success primarily through being highly efficient manufacturers, producing parts and components that meet customer specifications. Intuitively, such a situation would suggest a limited role for design. But at Johnson Controls, that's not the case. Our industrial design team has established itself as a highly integrated and valued part of the organization. We have a 20-year track record of accomplishment, and we feel we're a significant influence on the success of our company."

As JCI's customers move overseas, they expect JCI to supply them from local facilities. In response, JCI is "growing globally by expanding regional capabilities as well as making the investments to follow [its] customers as they expand their global presence." Although most of JCI's 260 plants are in the United States and Europe, it has also established facilities in Eastern

for logistics companies to offer a broad range of services beyond shipping, including warehousing, distribution management, and customs and brokerage services.

Standardization and the Management of Global Operations

standards
Documented agreements containing technical specifications or other precise criteria that will be used consistently as guidelines, rules, or definitions of the characteristics of a product, process, or service

Standards are documented agreements containing technical specifications or other precise criteria that will be used consistently as guidelines, rules, or definitions of the characteristics of a product, process, or service. Standards help ensure that materials, products, processes, and services are appropriate for their purpose. Credit cards and phone cards are produced to an accepted standard, including an optimal thickness of 0.76 mm, so that these cards can be used worldwide. The same symbols for automobile controls are displayed in cars throughout the world, no matter where the vehicles are produced.

In most countries standards have been developed across product lines and for various functions. In the United States, for example, the standards developed by the American Society for the Testing of Materials (ASTM) and other organizations are used in lieu of specific detailed requirements to ensure an expected level of use and quality. In Europe, the most used standard for quality is ISO 9000. This is a set of five universal standards for a quality assurance system that has been agreed to by the International Organization for Standards (ISO), a federation of standards bodies from approximately 100 countries. The intention is that ISO 9000 standards will be applicable worldwide, avoiding technical barriers to trade attributable to the existence of nonharmonized standards between countries and thus facilitating international exchange of

Europe, India, China, Mexico, and other locations around the world in order to meet customer needs. Many are satellite plants located close to big car factories, to which seats are delivered straight to the assembly line as needed. JCI serves every major automaker, and it delivered interior components for over 35 million 2006 model-year vehicles. To manage the complexity of a global production system, JCI is creating a standardized business operating system and a single, global infrastructure, helping to eliminate variation and inefficiencies across factories.

JCI has also implemented an Internet-based database that employees worldwide can use to post and retrieve factory-tested best practices and ideas for improving performance in such areas as quality, cost, timelines, productivity, and morale of employees. Global engineering teams in JCI's technology centers in Germany, France, Japan, and the United States can collaborate in real time. A private Web site allows JCI's suppliers to provide real-time status updates, provide quotations, submit cost reduction ideas, and generate progress reports. It also helps JCI's program managers to quickly identify problems. Customers can have real-time access to key information about product launches and enhanced communication with members of product development teams. As the company states, "There are not significant differences between JCI and its competitors in the types of machinery we use, or the infrastructure investments we make, yet we have been able to separate ourselves from the competition. Our advantage, and growth, comes from our ability to continually add value. We've been successful at doing this because of the quality of our management and employees, and their commitment and ability to think of innovative solutions for customers."

Another strategy of JCI's has been to expand its role from supplying seating to supplying nonseating parts of car interiors, including doors, instrument panels, electronics, storage, roof interiors, and trim. This move to supply a "total interior" service to automakers has been successful, and today JCI is the world's largest independent supplier of automotive interior systems. As JCI's CEO said, "A key growth driver continues to be our ability to find new ways to serve customers. In our interiors business that means supplying larger modules and creating distinctive consumer features that help us garner a greater share of the vehicle interior." In pursuit of its goal, JCI has introduced Six Sigma principles throughout its facilities worldwide, including training over 2,000 people in its techniques, to facilitate the discovery of new ways of enhancing product quality and service delivery. The thousands of projects completed as part of the company's Six Sigma program have produced substantial savings in costs as well as improved performance quality. For example, the program reduced electrical installation defect rates in the United Kingdom from 21 to 3 percent by improving electrical drawings. In Germany, it reduced errors on incoming vendor invoices by 80 percent, eliminating costly reworking. In Japan, it increased productivity on a just-in-time seat production line by 70 to 75 percent. In the United States, it eliminated unnecessary tooling changes caused by incorrect or incomplete engineering drawings of automotive interiors, saving over $2 million per year for JCI and $3.5 million per year for its customers. The program is being extended beyond JCI to also include suppliers, in an effort to further enhance supply chain effectiveness for itself and its customers.

Source: Adrian Slywotzky and Richard Wise, "Three Keys to Groundbreaking Growth: A Demand Innovation Strategy, Nurturing Practices, and a Chief Growth Officer," *Strategy & Leadership* 31, no. 5 (2003), pp. 12–19; Johnson Controls, *Annual Report 2005*, www.johnsoncontrols.com/annualreports/2005/JC_05report_spreads.pdf (July 18, 2006); Adrian Slywotsky, "Go Ahead, Take a Risk," *The Wall Street Journal*, June 22, 2004, p. B2; Bill Fluharty, "A Place at the Table: Taking Design from Service to Corporate Function," *Design Management Review*, Spring 2004, pp. 17–22; Jyoti Thottam, "What Can America Make?" *Time*, January 12, 2004, p. B1; and Gary S.Vasilash, "Creating the Inviting Interior," *Automotive Design and Production*, January 2004, pp. 34–35.

goods and services. If a product or service is purchased from a company that is registered to the appropriate ISO 9000 standard, the buyer will have important assurances that the quality of what was received will be what was expected. Indeed, registered companies have reported dramatic reductions in customer complaints as well as reduced operating costs and increased demand for their products and services. The United States has adopted the ISO 9000 series verbatim as the ANSI/AQC900 series.

The most comprehensive of the standards is ISO 9001. It applies to industries involved in the design, development, manufacturing, installation, and servicing of products and services. The standards apply uniformly to companies, regardless of their size or industry. In general, companies that want to do business in Europe must have ISO 9000 registration, and many companies also require registration by their suppliers to provide further assurance of compliance. There is also an ISO 14000 series that provides a similar framework for quality assurance in the area of environmental management.

Although it has been widely adopted as a standard for quality, not all quality "experts" agree that ISO 9000 is superior to other alternatives: "The focus of the standards is to establish quality management procedures, through detailed documentation, work instructions, and record keeping. These procedures . . . say nothing about the actual quality of the product—they deal entirely with standards to be followed." Phil Crosby, a noted quality expert and the author of several practitioner quality books, states, "It is a delusion that sound management can be replaced by an information format. It is like putting a Bible in every hotel room with the thought that occupants will act according to its contents."[36]

The advantages of synchronous manufacturing and TQM are compelling reasons why numerous global and multinational corporations are installing them worldwide. Certainly, customers everywhere want quality products at low prices. Firms from industrialized nations commonly copy home country manufacturing systems when setting up and operating in their subsidiaries in other industrialized nations.

> *Intel, the worldwide leader in supplying semiconductor memory products and related computer components, introduced an approach called "Copy Exactly" for achieving standardization in its factories. "Copy Exactly solves the problem of getting production facilities up to speed quickly by duplicating everything from the development plant to the volume-manufacturing plant." Managers from high-volume facilities participate in the development plant as new process technology is created. "Everything at the development plant—the process flow, equipment set, suppliers, plumbing, manufacturing clean room, and training methodologies—is selected to meet high-volume needs, recorded, and then copied exactly to the high-volume plant. Time after time, factory yields start at higher levels, and even improve when multiple factories come online using Copy Exactly."*[37]

In addition to those just mentioned, there are other important, although perhaps less obvious, reasons for global standardization. The following sections discuss some of these reasons.

ORGANIZATION AND STAFFING

Some of the reasons for the global standardization of a firm's manufacturing systems are the effects on organization and staffing.

Simpler and Less Costly When Standardized The standardization of production processes and procedures simplifies the manufacturing organization at headquarters because their replication enables the work to be accomplished with a smaller staff of support personnel. Fewer labor hours in plant design are involved because each new plant is essentially a scaled-up or scaled-down version of an existing one. The permanent group of experts that international companies maintain to give technical assistance to overseas plants can be smaller. Extra technicians accustomed to working with the same machinery can be borrowed from the domestic operation as needed.

Worldwide uniformity or standardization in manufacturing methods also increases headquarters' effectiveness in keeping the production specifications current. Every firm has hundreds of specifications, and those specifications are constantly being changed because of new raw materials or manufacturing procedures. If all plants, domestic and foreign, possess the same equipment, notice of a change can be given with one indiscriminate notification (e.g., a mailing); there is no need for highly paid engineers to check each affiliate's list of equipment to see which ones are affected. Companies whose manufacturing processes are not unified have found that maintaining a current separate set of specifications for each of 15 or 20 affiliates is both more costly (larger staff) and more error-prone.

An Intel employee checks wafers processing in a vertical diffusion furnace, one of the many tools through which wafers must pass as they go through the hundreds of steps that make up the manufacturing process. Intel, the worldwide leader in supplying semiconductor memory products and related computer components, uses a "Copy Exactly" strategy, which solves the problem of getting production facilities up to speed quickly by duplicating production facilities.

Logistics of Supply As we discussed at the beginning of this chapter on the value of a supply chain management orientation, management has become increasingly aware that greater profits may be obtained by organizing all of its companies' production facilities into one logistical supply system that includes all the activities required to move raw materials, parts, and finished inventory from vendors, between enterprise facilities, and to customers. The standardization of processes and machinery provides a reasonable guarantee that parts manufactured in the firm's various plants will be interchangeable. This assurance of interchangeability enables management to divide the production of components among a number of subsidiaries to achieve greater economies of scale and take advantage of the lower production costs in some countries.

Rationalization **Manufacturing rationalization,** as this production strategy is called, involves a change from a subsidiary's manufacturing only for its own national market to its producing a limited number of components for use by all subsidiaries.

manufacturing rationalization
Division of production among a number of production units, thus enabling each to produce only a limited number of components for all of a firm's assembly plants

> *SKF, a major bearing manufacturer with headquarters in Sweden, was able to reduce the number of types of ball bearings produced in five major overseas subsidiaries years ago from 50,000 to 20,000. Of the 20,000 remaining types, 7,000 have been rationalized among the five plants, and the other 13,000 are produced solely by one or another subsidiary for its local customers.*[38]

For manufacturing rationalization to be possible, the product mix must first be rationalized; that is, the firm must elect to produce products that are identical worldwide or regionwide. Once this has been done, each subsidiary can be assigned to produce certain components for other foreign plants, thus attaining a higher volume with a lower production cost than would be possible if it manufactured the complete product for its national market only. Obviously, this strategy is not viable when consumers' tastes and preferences differ markedly among markets. For less differentiated products, however, manufacturing rationalization permits economies of scale in production and engineering that would otherwise be impossible.

Purchasing When foreign subsidiaries are unable to purchase raw materials and machinery locally, they generally look for assistance from the purchasing department at headquarters. Because unified processes require the same materials everywhere, buyers can handle foreign requirements by simply increasing their regular orders to their usual suppliers and passing on the volume discounts to the subsidiaries. However, when special materials are required, purchasing agents must search out new vendors and place smaller orders, often at higher prices.

CONTROL

All the advantages of global standardization cited thus far also pertain to the other functions of management. Three aspects of control—quality, production, and maintenance—merit additional discussion.

Quality Control When production equipment is similar, home office control of quality in foreign affiliates is less difficult because management can expect all plants to adhere to the same standard. The home office can compare the periodic reports that all affiliates submit and quickly spot deviations from the norm that require remedial action, such as a large number of product rejects. Separate standards for each plant because of equipment differences are unnecessary.

Production and Maintenance Control A single standard also lessens the task of maintenance and production control. The same machinery should produce at the same rate of output and have the same frequency of maintenance no matter where it is located. In practice, deviations will occur because of the human and physical factors (dust, humidity, temperature), but at least similar machinery permits the home office to establish standards by which to determine the effectiveness of local managements. Furthermore, the maintenance experience of other production units in regard to the frequency of overhauls and the stock of spare parts needed will help plants avoid costly, unforeseen stoppages from sudden breakdowns.

PLANNING

When a new plant can be built that is a duplicate of others already functioning, the planning and design will be both simpler and quicker because they are essentially a repetition of work already done:

1. Design engineers need only copy the drawings and lists of materials that they have in their files.
2. Vendors will be requested to furnish equipment that they have supplied previously.

3. The technical department can send the current manufacturing specifications without alteration.
4. Labor trainers experienced in the operation of the machinery can be sent to the new location without undergoing special training on new equipment.
5. Reasonably accurate forecasts of plant erection time and output can be based on experience with existing facilities.

In other words, the duplication of existing plants greatly reduces the engineering time required in planning and designing the new facilities and eliminates many of the start-up difficulties inherent in any new operation. To be sure, a newly designed plant causes problems when it is erected domestically, but those problems tend to be greater when the plant is located in a different environment at a great distance from headquarters. Just how important the savings from plant duplication are was emphasized in a study of the chemical and refining industries that indicated that the cost of technology transfer was lowered by 34 and 19 percent for the second and third start-ups, respectively.[39]

Since the case for global standardization of production is so strong, why do differences among plants in the same company persist?

Impediments to Standardization of Global Operations

Generally, it is easier for international corporations to standardize the concepts of total quality management and synchronous manufacturing in their overseas affiliates than it is to standardize the actual manufacturing facilities. Units of an international multiplant operation differ in size, machinery, and procedures because of the intervention of the foreign environmental forces, especially the economic, cultural, and political forces.

ENVIRONMENTAL FORCES

Let us examine the impact of the three kinds of forces just mentioned.

Economic Forces The most important element of the economic forces that impedes production standardization is the wide range of market sizes, discussed in Chapter 18.

> *A number of studies confirmed by personal experience have shown that the foremost criterion for plant design is the output desired. Once this is known, the engineering department of a multiplant operation will check to see whether a factory already has been built with a capacity similar to the output specified. If so, this facility will serve as a design standard for the new plant, though modifications may be made to eliminate any problems encountered in the original design. Many large multiplant firms actually have standard designs for large, medium, and small production outputs.*

To cope with the great variety of production requirements, the designer generally has the option of selecting either a *capital-intensive process* incorporating automated, high-semimanual-output machinery or a *labor-intensive process* employing more people and general-purpose equipment with lower productive capacity. The automated machinery is severely limited in flexibility (variety of products and range of sizes), but once set up, it will turn out in a few days what may be a year's supply for some markets.[40] For many processes, this problem may be resolved by installing one machine of the type used by the hundreds in the larger home plant. However, sometimes this option is not available; some processes use only one or two large machines, even in manufacturing facilities with large output, as we mentioned in the discussion of standardized manufacturing. Until recently, when the option was not available, plant designers had to choose between the high-output specialized machinery and the lower-output general-purpose machines mentioned earlier. The major differences are that general-purpose machines require skills that are built into a special-purpose machine. The general-purpose machine usually produces a product of lower quality and higher per-unit costs than does the special-purpose machine.

WORLD view   

Nestlé: Standardizing Processes and Systems to Exploit Global Opportunity

Nestlé is the world's largest food and beverage company, with over 500 factories around the world and over 250,000 employees. In 2005, it achieved sales of $75 billion from its portfolio of well-known brands, such as Nescafé, Taster's Choice, Arrowhead, Perrier, Carnation, Libby's, Dreyer's, PowerBar, Stouffer's, Lean Cuisine, Kit Cat, Butterfinger, Purina, and Friskies.

At the end of the 1990s, Nestlé's CEO, Peter Brabeck, confronted a difficult challenge. Although present around the world, Nestlé had traditionally operated as "a collection of independent fiefdoms," rather than as an integrated global company. As a result, although his company was achieving excellent growth, the high overhead expenses from inefficiency and duplication of efforts caused Nestlé's profit to be below the industry's average. The company's primary coffee brand, Nescafé, had over 200 formulations to suit various local tastes. Nestlé's vast, inefficient global supply chain, compounded by wasteful purchasing practices and inefficient operational and marketing efforts, was constraining performance. In the area of enterprise planning systems, Nestlé had 14 different SAP systems operating in various countries, each with different ways of formatting data and handling forms. Information technology costs were spiraling out of control. Trying to control the thousands of supply chains, dozens of demand forecasting methods, and the diverse array of methods for invoicing customers and collecting receivable was proving to be increasingly difficult.

To address this problem, Brabeck launched the Global Business Excellence (GLOBE) program in 2000, the most ambitious business process reengineering program Nestlé had ever attempted. GLOBE would develop a single, standardized system that would enable managers worldwide to forecast demand, purchase supplies, collect receivables, and promote and sell the company's 127,000 different sizes and types of products. Projected to cost approximately $2.5 billion, the GLOBE project had 3 main objectives:

- *Best practices:* GLOBE would compile a set of best practices from throughout the scattered Nestlé operations and make these business processes available to managers across all nations, products, and functions. By creating a common business process architecture, Nestlé would have a common, transparent way for addressing activities such as sales forecasting, production planning, purchasing, and customer service.
- *Data standardization:* To create a standardized set of Nestlé data, GLOBE would establish common coding for items such as raw and packaging materials, finished goods, vendors, and customers. By consolidating this information, Nestlé's managers could readily obtain a global picture of how much product the company purchased, globally, from each supplier; how much the company sold, on a product-by-product basis, to key international customers such as Wal-Mart or Carrefour; and how many units of products such as Butterfingers or Kit Kat chocolate bars had been sold through different channels, such as supermarkets or vending machines.
- *Common information systems:* To support the first two objectives, a common global information system was required. Developing this system would involve reducing the company's data centers from about 100 to only 4, standardizing computer hardware and software, and establishing global agreements with key suppliers such as SAP, Microsoft, and Dell.

Brabeck hoped that GLOBE would enable Nestlé to use information as a competitive advantage through facilitating better decision making, better management of complexity, improved speed and flexibility, and improved focus on customers. Benefits would include an improved ability to regroup elements of Nestlé's business, respond faster to global business trends, drive down operational business costs, enhance insight into customers, ensure product safety and traceability, and exploit economies of scale to further enhance the company's global competitiveness. Nestlé predicted that it could reduce the number of suppliers from 600,000 to 167,000 and simultaneously reduce costs by $750 million a year.

Implementation of the GLOBE initiative would take many years to complete, and it encountered a number of problems. Nestlé had a long-established culture of decentralization and relative autonomy at the country level. Country managers resisted the GLOBE effort, fearing that it would hurt their bottom-line performance and reduce their authority. Managers were trying to compete within a mosaic of divergent local and national markets, each with different requirements for logistics, sales, and customer service. These managers rebelled against the concept of imposing standardized methods for supply chain or customer relationship management. However, if it was mandated that a method would be standardized, then each of the managers tended to lobby for his or her own country's practice to be selected as the global template, arguing that the particular way in his or her country was "best." Trying to address these complaints and complete a radical transformation of Nestlé, and to do so within an initially projected time frame of about three and a half years, appeared foolhardy to many in the company.

Nestlé's leadership did not waver in its resolve. Ronald Hafner, the global relationship partner for Nestlé from Pricewaterhouse Coopers, said the company's executives "laid down the law: standardize everything. The plan did not allow for any deviation." A team was formed to oversee the process, beginning with efforts to obtain and screen a set of prospective best practices from throughout Nestlé's global operations, and then convert these into a standardized set of processes and information systems to apply universally. This process took over a year. The company then selected a handful of nations to serve as the initial test markets for the standardization process, with rollout expanding over time as system integrity was proved. "The biggest challenge is in the mind," said Martial Rolland, managing director of Nestlé India. "Yes, it's an equipment change. But, ultimately, it's a mind change."

Eventually the templates were developed and installed, and the implementation continued despite opposition. By June 2006, GLOBE had been rolled out to over 90,000 users, 300 factories, 350 distribution centers, and 250 sales offices. Nestlé projected that 80 percent of the company would be operating under GLOBE systems by the end of 2006. GLOBE has provided the foundation for Nestlé to operate as a truly global company. The company's leaders hope that this project will give Nestlé a sustainable advantage over its global competitors, which have not yet undertaken such a phenomenal change of systems and mind-set.

Source: Nestlé "GLOBE," www.ir.nestle.com/Nestle_Overview/Operational_Performance/Globe/GLOBE.htm (July 18, 2006); "Nestlé at a Glance," www.nestle.com/NR/rdonlyres/74F5A6ED-C072-4CD2-B701-C1AE3C5E482C/0/carte_GB.pdf (July 18, 2006); Chris Johnson, "GLOBE: Unlocking Our Potential," www.ir.nestle.com/NR/rdonlyres/3D107E55-7B6C-4E4C-9E92-2414E602F136/0/GLOBEMrChrisJohnson.pdf (July 18, 2006); Tom Steinert-Threlkeld, "Nestlé, Pieces It Together," *Baseline*, January 2006, pp. 36–52; Larry Barrett, "Roadblock: Regional Managers," *Baseline*, January 2006, p. 50; and Nestlé 2005 Financial Statements, www.investis.com/reports/ZMgj68xYd5Ot82w/report.php?type=0 (July 18, 2006).

A third alternative is available: computer-integrated manufacturing (CIM), which many international firms are using. However, its cost and high technological content generally limit its application to the industrialized nations and the more advanced developing nations. CIM systems enable a machine to make one part as easily as another in random order on an instruction from a bar code reader of the kind used in supermarkets. This reduces to one the economic batch quantity—the minimum number of a part that can be made economically by a factory—and it facilitates the potential for mass customization that we discussed earlier in this chapter. There is a limit, nevertheless, to the variety of shapes, sizes, and materials that can be accommodated.

Another economic factor that influences the designer's selection of processes is the *cost of production.* Automation tends to increase the productivity per worker because it requires less labor and results in higher output per machine. But if the desired output requires that the machines be operated only a fraction of the time, the high capital costs of automated equipment may result in excessive production costs even though labor costs are low. In situations where production costs favor semimanual equipment, the designer may be compelled to install high-capacity machines instead because of a lack of floor space. Generally, the space occupied by a few high-capacity machines is less than that required for the greater number of semimanual machines needed to produce the same output. However, because the correct type and quality of process materials are indispensable for specialized machinery, the engineers cannot recommend this equipment if such materials are unobtainable either from local sources or through importation. Occasionally, management will bypass this obstacle by means of **backward vertical integration;** that is, manufacturing capacity to produce essential inputs will be included in the plant design even though it would be preferable from an economic standpoint to purchase those materials from outside vendors. For example, a textile factory might include a facility for producing nylon fibers.

backward vertical integration
Arrangement in which facilities are established to manufacture inputs used in the production of a firm's final products

The economic forces we have described are fundamental considerations in plant design, yet elements of the cultural and political forces may be sufficiently significant to override decisions based on purely economic reasoning.

Cultural Forces

When a factory is to be built in an industrialized nation that has a sizable market and high labor costs, capital-intensive processes will undoubtedly be employed. However, such processes may also be employed in developing countries, which commonly lack skilled workers despite their abundant supply of labor. This situation favors the use of specialized machines because although a few highly skilled persons are needed for maintenance and setup, the job of *attending* these machines (starting, feeding stock) can be performed by unskilled workers after a short training period. In contrast, general-purpose machinery requires many more skilled operators.

These operators could be trained in technical schools, but the low prestige of such employment, a cultural characteristic, affects both the demand for and the supply of vocational education. Students do not demand it, and the traditional elitist attitude of the educational administrators in many developing nations causes resources to be directed to professional education instead of to the trades where they are needed.

Firms that attempt to reduce their requirements for skilled workers by installing automatic machinery are of course left vulnerable to another cultural characteristic of the developing countries: absenteeism. If the setup and maintenance crews fail to report to work, the entire production line may be shut down. Some managers resolve this problem by training a few extra people as backups. Having extra personnel is viewed as production insurance necessary to keep the plant in operation. This extra expense may be far less than the expense of handling the greater number of labor-management problems resulting from a larger work force in a nonautomated factory with a similar capacity.

These economic and cultural variables, important as they are, are not the only considerations of management; the requirements of the host government must be met if the proposed plant is to become a reality.

Political Forces

When planning a new manufacturing facility in a developing country, management is frequently confronted by an intriguing paradox. Although the country desperately needs new job creation, which favors labor-intensive processes, government officials often insist on the most modern equipment. Local pride may be the cause, or it may be that these officials, wishing to see the new firm export, believe that only a factory with advanced technology can compete in world markets. They not only may be reluctant to take chances on "inferior" or untried alternatives but also may feel that low-productivity technology will keep the country dependent on the industrialized countries. In some developing countries, this fear has been formalized by laws prohibiting the importation of used machinery.

Global automakers have announced investments of over $10 billion in factories in China. However, most of the large automakers' plants are not designed to exploit China's large pool of low-cost labor. Rather, the plants are about as capital-intensive as American auto plants. Part of the reason for this is the Chinese government's desire to lure the latest technology, a goal it has promoted by a range of incentives. Acceding to these demands of the government can also be simpler for the automakers. As Mustafa Mharatem, the senior economist at General Motors, states, "Because of the way information travels these days, people in developing countries aren't any longer willing to buy cars that are one or two generations old. And if you're going to do the current-generation car, then keeping the process as similar as processes around the world makes sense."[41]

SOME DESIGN SOLUTIONS

More often than not, after consideration of the environmental variables, the resultant plant design will be a hybrid or one using intermediate technology.

Hybrid Design

Commonly, in designing plants for developing countries, engineers will use a hybrid of capital-intensive processes when they are considered essential to ensure product quality and labor-intensive processes to take advantage of the abundance of unskilled labor. For example, they may stipulate machine welding rather than hand welding but then use semimanual equipment for the painting, packaging, and materials handling.

Intermediate Technology

In recent years, the press of a growing population and the rise in capital costs have forced the governments of developing nations to search for something less than highly automated processes. They are becoming convinced that there should be something midway between the capital- and labor-intensive processes that will create more jobs, require less capital, but still produce the desired product quality. Governments are urging investors to consider an **intermediate technology,** which, unfortunately, is not readily available in the industrialized nations. This means that international companies cannot transfer the technology with which they are familiar but must develop new and different manufacturing methods. It is also possible that the savings in reduced capital costs of the intermediate technology may be nullified by higher start-up costs and the greater expense of its transfer.

intermediate technology
Production methods between capital- and labor-intensive methods

Local Manufacturing System

BASIS FOR ORGANIZATION

Except for plants in large industrialized nations, the local manufacturing organization is commonly a scaled-down version of that found in the parent company. If the firm is organized by product companies or divisions (tires, industrial products, chemicals) in its home nation, the subsidiary will be divided into product departments. Manufacturing firms that use process organizations (departmentalized according to production processes) in the domestic operation will set up a similar structure in their foreign affiliates. In a paper-box factory, separate departments will cut the logs, produce the paper, and assemble the boxes. The only noticeable difference between the foreign and domestic operations is that in the foreign plant all these processes are more likely to be at one location because of the smaller size of each department.

HORIZONTAL AND VERTICAL INTEGRATION

The local manufacturing organization is rarely integrated either vertically or horizontally to the extent the parent is. Some vertical integration is traditional, as in the case of the paper-box factory, and some will occur if it is necessary to ensure a supply of raw materials. In this situation, the subsidiary might be more vertically integrated than the parent, which depends on outside sources for many of its inputs. However, the additional investment is a deterrent to vertical integration, as are the extra profits gained by supplying inputs to these captive customers from the home plants. Some countries prohibit vertical integration for certain industries. In Mexico, for example, severe restrictions on private investment (Mexican or foreign) in the petroleum and petrochemical industry still exist and keep producers of products that use petrochemicals from achieving backward vertical integration. In contrast, some countries require a percentage of local content in finished products. When the subsidiary cannot meet the requirement by local sourcing, it may be forced to produce components that its parent does not.

Horizontal integration is much less prevalent in foreign subsidiaries, although restaurant chains, banks, food-processing plants, and other industries characterized by small production units will, of course, integrate horizontally in the manner of the domestic company. Overseas affiliates themselves become conglomerates when the parent acquires a multinational.

DESIGN OF THE MANUFACTURING SYSTEM

A *manufacturing system* is essentially a functionally related group of activities for creating value. The design of a manufacturing system influences the flow and efficiency of activities in a plant. Although the manufacturing system as described below is basically one for producing tangible goods, nearly everything that is said applies equally to the production of services. Factors involved in the efficient operation of a manufacturing system include:

1. Plant location
2. Plant layout
3. Materials handling
4. Human element

Plant Location

Plant location is significant because of its effect on both production and distribution costs, which are frequently in conflict. The gain in government incentives and in the lower land and labor costs obtained by locating away from major cities may be offset by the increased expense of warehousing and transportation to serve those markets. Management will, after ascertaining that adequate labor, raw materials, water, and power are available, seek the least-cost location, or the one for which the sum of production and transfer costs is minimized. Management's first choice may then be modified by market requirements, the influence of competitors' locations, employee preference (climate, recreational facilities), and conditions imposed by the local authorities.

Sony shifted production of camcorders destined for the U.S. market from China to Japan. Although manufacturing costs may be higher than in China, the company justified its decision to produce these high-value-added products in Japan, stating, "By making the camcorders in Japan we can cut our lead times to half of what they are when they are made in Shanghai."[42]

Governments that are anxious to limit the congestion of large urban areas may either prohibit firms from locating in the major cities or offer them important financial inducement to locate elsewhere.

Firms that have come to a country to take advantage of low labor costs and export their production have a limited selection of plant locations. They must locate in *export processing zones,* as we discussed in Chapter 2, such as Mexico's in-bond manufacturing zones. Similar zones exist in South Korea, Taiwan, Singapore, and some 50 other nations.

Plant Layout Modern practice dictates that the arrangement of machinery, personnel, and service facilities should be made before the erection of the building. In this way, the building is accommodated to the layout that is judged most capable of obtaining a smoothly functioning production system.

The designer must attempt to obtain the maximum utility from costly building space while providing room for the future expansion of each department. Space can become critical very quickly if forecasts, especially for new products, prove to have been unduly pessimistic. Managements of plants located in developing countries may attempt to stint on space for employees' facilities, reasoning that the workers' standard of living in these countries is lower and that they will accept less just to have employment. Often, however, foreign labor laws are more demanding than those of the home country.

Materials Handling Considerable savings in production costs can be achieved by a careful planning of materials handling, which, as you have seen, is a major consideration in synchronous manufacturing. Operations managers often failed to appreciate that inefficient handling of materials could cause excessive inventories of partly finished parts to accumulate at some workstations while at others expensive machinery was idle for lack of work (bottleneck). This concerned marketers too, because poor materials handling can result in late deliveries and damaged goods, which in turn lead to order cancellation and a loss of customers. Therefore, marketers must also be included in the total quality control approach that we discussed earlier in this chapter.

Human Element The effectiveness of the manufacturing system depends on people, who are in turn affected by the system. Productivity suffers when there is extreme heat or cold, excessive noise, or faulty illumination. Colors also influence human behavior—pale colors are restful and unobtrusive, whereas bright colors attract attention. Plant designers take advantage of this fact by painting the walls of the working areas pale blue and green but marking exits with bright yellow and painting safety equipment red. This practice is accepted nearly everywhere, although, as we indicated in Chapter 6 in the discussion of cultural forces, color connotations vary among cultures.

For safety and ease of operation, controls of imported machinery must frequently be altered to accommodate smaller workers. Extra lifting devices, unnecessary in the home country, may be required. Where illiteracy is a problem, safety signs must include pictures. For example, a picture of a burning cigarette with a red line through it may substitute for a "no smoking" sign. Plants in multilingual nations and plants that employ large numbers of foreign workers require warnings in more than one language.

Because of the prohibitive cost of automobiles in many developing nations, employees ride bicycles to work, and so bicycle stands must be provided in parking lots. Special dietary kitchens are necessary when workers from more than one culture work together. These and other special conditions caused by environmental differences must be reckoned with in the design of the manufacturing system.

OPERATION OF THE MANUFACTURING SYSTEM

Once the manufacturing system has been put into operation, two general classes of activities, *productive* and *supportive,* must be performed.

Manufacturing Activities After the initial trial period, during which workers become familiar with the manufacturing processes, management will expect the system to produce at a rate sufficient to satisfy market demand. It is the function of the line organization—from operations manager to first-level supervisor—to work with labor, raw materials, and machinery to produce on time the required amount of product with the desired quality at the budgeted cost.

Although competitors such as Apple, Gateway, and IBM have closed or relocated their computer manufacturing operations to lower-cost locations such as Asia, Dell has expanded its European manufacturing facilities, which are based in Ireland. Dell's survival is due to managerial systems dedicated to sustained operational improvements that help compensate for higher European labor rates. Nicky Hartery, who runs the 3,000-employee plant, says, "We're at all times looking for better, faster ways of doing things. Our staff are aligned not just to making PCs, which I would call sustaining engineering, but there's a development engineering function—developing better tools, better techniques, improved tools, improved techniques—so that our throughput is significantly better and the quality of what we do is significantly better." A team of 50 to 80 people works full-time on identifying ways of improving processes and the plant's continuous-improvement culture has resulted in productivity gains of 3 to 4 percent per quarter. The plant's lean production approach, based on JIT procedures and strong supply chain management practices, allows it to carry only two hours of inventory, while its suppliers' inventory has simultaneously declined by 40 percent in the past year. Most components come directly from delivery truck to assembly line. "We don't just work on productivity within the four walls of the factory," said Hartery. "I don't think we'd survive doing that. We have to make sure it is the right model, end to end, from our vendor base, our sub-tier vendor base, all the way to our customer." Rather than depending on expensive high-technology equipment, he argues, the plant's performance is the result of superior application of human intelligence.[43]

Obstacles to Meeting Manufacturing Standards

Management must be prepared to deal with any obstacle to meeting the manufacturing standards. Among these obstacles are (1) low output, (2) inferior quality, and (3) excessive manufacturing costs.

Low Output Any number of factors may be responsible for the system's failure to meet the design standards for output, and these factors can be the source of managerial uncertainty.

1. Raw materials suppliers may fail to meet delivery dates or may furnish material out of specification. This is a common occurrence in the sellers' markets of developing countries, but it is also occasionally a problem in the industrialized countries. The purchasing department must attempt to educate the vendor about the importance of delivery dates and specifications, although the effectiveness of this strategy is limited when, as is often the case in developing nations, there is only one supplier. Increasing the price paid and sending technicians to assist the vendor generally improve this situation.
2. Poor coordination of production scheduling slows the delivery of finished products when, for example, completely assembled automobiles wait for bumpers. Scheduling personnel may require additional training or closer supervision. Often, scheduling personnel—or any production workers, for that matter—are unaware of the importance of their jobs because they have not been shown "the big picture." Firms find that teaching employees why they do what they do, as well as how, pays off in creating a better attitude, which results in higher productivity. This has become crucial as firms strive for participative management, which is essential to synchronous manufacturing.

Cultural forces of attitude toward authority and the great difference between educational levels, common in many countries, establish a gulf between managers and workers. In fact, this is one of the reasons Japanese affiliates have had trouble introducing their production methods in the United States, where distances between managers and workers are much smaller than they are in most developing nations. Getting the participative management necessary for JIT and synchronous manufacturing will necessitate workers making sizable cultural changes, which in our opinion will require many years to attain.

Another cultural problem is the desire to please everyone and the aversion to long-range planning. You have seen the importance of planning for the success of JIT, and you also learned that firm production schedules at least a month long may be necessary. The desire to please everyone, which is prevalent in some cultures, tends to cause neglect of the schedule while production stops to attend the latest request from a customer. Moreover, because the markets are smaller in developing countries than they are in industrialized nations, product variations will have to be pared even more and production systems will have to be even more flexible, if possible.

3. *Absenteeism,* always a problem for production managers everywhere in meeting production standards, becomes even more significant in a bottleneck operation of a synchronous manufacturing system. Imagine the problems that occur when an entire department is idled because workers are at home helping the extended family with the harvest. When poor transportation systems make getting to work difficult, companies frequently provide transportation. To counteract absences due to illness and injury, they subsidize workers' lunches—prepared by trained nutritionists—and provide special shoes and protective clothing. Of course, management has the problem of educating workers not to remove the restraining apparel that they have never used before.

Low morale conducive to high absenteeism will result if foreign managers trying to introduce the participative management necessary for synchronous manufacturing fail to assume the role of *patron* that most workers in developing countries expect. When employees have personal problems, they assume that the boss, not the personnel office, will find a solution. Personal debts, marital problems, and difficulties with the police are all part of manager-employee relations.

All too often, expatriate managers accept high absenteeism and low productivity as the norm instead of attempting to correct them. Yet those who apply all the corrective means used at home, making adjustments for the foreign environment when necessary, do achieve notable success. One corrective measure, the discharge of unsatisfactory workers, is frequently impossible to apply because of legal constraints, but a consistent, energetic program of employee training, good union and labor relations, and the use of such morale builders as employee recognition, company reunions, sponsorship of team sports, and even suggestion boxes with rewards can be as successful in a foreign location as in the domestic operation.

Inferior Product Quality Good quality is relative. What passes for good quality in the industrialized nations may actually be poor quality where a lack of maintenance and operating skills requires looser bearing fits and strong but more unwieldy parts. If the product or service satisfies the purpose for which it is purchased, the buyer considers it to be of good quality.

Product quality standards are not set arbitrarily. It is the responsibility of the marketers, after studying their target market, to choose the price-quality combination they believe is most apt to satisfy that market. On the basis of this information, the quality standards for incoming materials, in-process items, and finished products should be established.

When the headquarters of global corporations insist that all foreign subsidiaries maintain the high-quality standards of the domestic plants, a number of problems can occur. Production may have to accept inputs of poorer quality when there is no alternative source of supply and then rework them. As we have pointed out, quality tolerances are especially tight for automated machinery. Finished-product standards set by a home office concerned about maintaining its global reputation can cause a product to be too costly for the local market. Many international companies resolve this problem by permitting the subsidiary to manufacture products of lower quality under different brand names. If they want the local plant to be a part of a worldwide logistics system, they may require a special quality to be produced for export. In some areas, "export quality" still denotes a superior product. Quality control, by the way, is not left exclusively in the hands of the subsidiary. Nearly all worldwide corporations require that their foreign plants submit samples of the finished product for testing on a regular basis.

Excessive Manufacturing Costs Any manufacturing cost that exceeds the budgeted cost is excessive and naturally is of concern to the marketing and financial manager as well as to production personnel. Low output for any of the reasons we have discussed may be the cause, but the fault may also lie with the assumptions underlying the budget. Overoptimistic sales forecasts, the failure of suppliers to meet delivery dates, the failure of the government to issue import permits for essential raw materials in time, and unforeseen water or power failure are a few of the reasons output may be lower than expected.

Managers have always tried to limit inventories of raw materials, spare parts for plant machinery, and finished products, and those managers with synchronous manufacturing systems have a goal of almost complete elimination. But when there is uncertainty of supply, as in most developing nations, stocks of these items can quickly get out of control. Production tends to overstock inputs to avoid the expense of changing production schedules when a given raw material has been exhausted. Maintenance personnel lay in an excessive stock of spare parts because they worry about not having something when they need it. Marketers, fearful of the frequent delays in manufacturing, overreact by building up finished goods inventories to avoid lost sales. When sales decrease, manufacturing may continue to produce finished products rather than lay off workers because the labor laws in many countries, unlike American labor laws, make employee layoffs both difficult and costly. In countries where skilled workers are in short supply, management does not dare to lay them off even if the law permits because these people will obtain employment elsewhere. The only alternative in the short run is to keep the factory running.

Finance, the one headquarters department that would ordinarily act to limit inventory building, will not move aggressively to stop this practice in countries afflicted with hyperinflation. It knows that under this condition, sizable profits can be made by being short in cash and long in inventory.

Supportive Activities

Every manufacturing system requires staff units to provide the *supportive activities* essential to its operation. Two of these, quality control and inventory control, were examined in the previous section. Let us look now at the purchasing, maintenance, and technical functions.

Purchasing Manufacturing depends on the purchasing department to procure the raw materials, component parts, supplies, and machinery it requires to produce the finished product. The inability to obtain these materials when needed can result in costly shutdowns and lost sales. If the buyers agree to prices higher than what competitors are paying, the firm must either sell the finished product at higher prices or price competitively and earn less profit. The quality of the finished product may suffer if the quality of the purchased materials is inadequate.

For many years, some have referred to purchasing as the "management of outside manufacturing," and this was never more true than it is today with the globalization of industry. If the purchasing function is to fit in with the rest of the global operations of a firm, it must increasingly behave in the manner of a manager of manufacturing and as a key component in achieving integrated global supply chain management. In the past, the purchasing function often was responsible only for buying the cheapest possible inputs. However, as discussed in this chapter, there are many other considerations besides cost that need to be managed by the purchasing function.

Even in the industrialized countries before JIT was introduced, purchasing agents rarely could satisfy all of their companies' needs by waiting for the suppliers' representatives to come to them. They had to seek out and develop suppliers by visiting their plants and arranging for their companies' production and technical personnel to discuss material problems with the vendors' counterparts. In the developing countries, where many suppliers do not retain a sales force because they can sell everything they produce, supplier development assumes greater importance. The ability to locate vendors can easily compensate for a lack of other skills that management would require of a buyer at home.

When the firm depends heavily on imported materials, the prime criterion for hiring will be the purchasing agents' knowledge of import procedures and their connections with key government officials. The purchasing agents must constantly monitor government actions that can affect the availability of foreign exchange. They will often buy as much as possible of regularly consumed materials because they know they can always sell the excess to others, possibly at a profit.

Whether to fill the critical position of purchasing agent with a local citizen or with someone from the home office is often the subject of considerable debate at headquarters. A native has the advantage of being better acquainted with the local supply sources and government officials, but he or she might suffer from such cultural disadvantages as a tendency to favor members of the extended family or to accept as a normal business practice the giving (scarce supply) or receiving (plentiful supply) of bribes. An employee from the home office, in contrast, will be experienced in company purchasing procedures and should be free of these cultural disadvantages. Managers are not so naive as to believe that belonging to a certain culture guarantees that an individual will or will not engage in unethical activities. However, the tendency to commit these acts may be greater when there are no cultural constraints.

Maintenance A second function supporting manufacturing is the maintenance of buildings and equipment. The goal of maintenance management is to ensure an acceptable level of production, and the costs of achieving this can be substantial. One European paper company estimated, for example, that maintenance costs averaged about 30 percent of the total fixed costs of its operations in China. Several possibilities are available for accomplishing this task. As was noted several times in this chapter, JIT has caused other parts of the manufacturing function to assume greater importance, and maintenance of plant production capacity is one of these parts. Before JIT, inventory was the solution to many managerial problems by hiding the causes and effects of these problems. The removal by JIT systems of inventory as a buffer has forced industry to give greater consideration to these problem areas, one of which is the maintenance of anticipated processing capacity. This may entail the prevention of unscheduled work stoppages caused by equipment failure.

There are two primary alternatives for dealing with maintenance problems. The first option is planned maintenance or preventive maintenance. The objective here is to prevent failure before it occurs, because failure is more expensive to repair and is disruptive to production schedules. The second alternative is breakdown maintenance. That is, when a machine or another element in the production process fails, it will be repaired. Although we have all heard the saying "If it works, don't fix it," this is seldom the best maintenance alternative. There are indeed situations when companies let a process go until failure—such as lightbulbs, which we do not usually replace until they fail. However, in production activities it is often appropriate to have a redundant or backup system.

In general, companies are concerned with maintenance because unanticipated system failure and downtime are a drain on scarce productive capacity. In a global context, there may be difficulty in obtaining imported spare parts and machinery, threatening the continued productive ability of a firm. As a result, the machine shops of many maintenance departments may actually manufacture some of these items in order to keep machines operating.

It is common practice in industrialized countries to establish preventive maintenance programs in which machinery is shut down according to plan and worn parts are replaced. Such programs are especially important for a synchronous manufacturing system, as you learned earlier in this chapter. With advance notice of a shutdown, the manufacturing department can schedule around the machine, or by working the machine overtime the department can temporarily build up inventories, permitting the manufacturing process to continue during its overhaul. In other words, the company is able to maintain an acceptable level of output to service the anticipated demands of customers.

This concept is not widely accepted in developing countries, where firms seem to take a fatalistic attitude toward equipment: "If it breaks down, we'll repair it." This may be attributable to the concept that preventive maintenance in most instances requires a greater degree of skill and knowledge than does breakdown maintenance.

Furthermore, in a seller's market, maintenance personnel are pressured by production and marketing managers to keep machinery running. This short-term view allows no time for scheduled shutdowns. Subsidiaries that do practice preventive maintenance with overhaul periods based on headquarters' standards frequently find these standards inadequate because of local operating conditions (humidity, dust, and temperature) and the manner in which the operators handle the machinery. When the amount of spare parts ordered with the machinery is based on domestic experience, it is often insufficient because of differing local conditions in other nations, including the skill and training of the local machine operators and maintenance workers.

In one sense, proper maintenance is more critical than 100 percent attendance of workers. The absence of one worker from a group of six interchangeable workers usually will not halt manufacturing, but if a key machine for which there is no substitute suddenly breaks down, the entire plant can be idled.

Technical Function The function of the technical department is to provide operations management with manufacturing specifications. Usually, technical personnel are also responsible for checking the quality of inputs and the finished product. The task of the technical department in a foreign subsidiary is not simply one of maintaining a file of specifications sent by the home office, because difficulty in obtaining the same kinds and quality of raw materials as those used by the home plants may require substitutions that necessitate the complete rewriting of specifications.

The affiliate's technical manager is a key figure in the maintenance of product quality and thus is extremely influential in selecting sources of supply. Global and multidomestic companies go to great lengths in persuading host governments and joint venture partners of the need to place one of their people in this position. In this way, they are certain to keep the affiliate as a captive customer purchasing all the inputs that the more highly integrated parent manufactures.

Summary

Understand the concept of supply chain management.

Supply chain management is the process of coordinating and integrating the flow of materials, information, finances, and services within and among companies in the value chain, from suppliers to the ultimate consumer. Supply chain management is integral to the achievement of cost and quality objectives in companies and to international competitiveness.

Recognize the relationship between design and supply chain management.

The design of a company's products and services has a fundamental relationship with the types of inputs the company will require, including labor, materials, information, and financing. Concurrent engineering approaches to design allow proposed designs to be subjected to earlier assessments on cost, quality, and manufacturability dimensions, enhancing the efficiency and effectiveness of subsequent supply chain management activities.

Describe the five global sourcing arrangements.

A firm may establish a wholly owned subsidiary in a low-labor-cost country to supply components to the home country plant or to supply a product not produced in the home country. An overseas joint venture may be established in a country where labor costs are lower to supply components to the home country. The firm may send components to be machined and assembled by an independent contractor in an in-bond plant. The firm may contract with an independent contractor overseas to manufacture products to its specifications. The firm may buy from an independent overseas manufacturer.

Appreciate the importance of the added costs of global sourcing.

International freight, insurance, and packing may add 10 to 12 percent to the quoted price, depending on the sales term used. Import duties, customhouse broker's fees, cost of letter of credit, cost of inventory in the pipeline, and international travel are some of the other added costs.

Understand the increasing role of electronic purchasing for global sourcing.

The establishment of electronic purchasing systems on a company or industry basis can influence the number and type of suppliers available internationally to firms. Although there are a number of challenges to their use, electronic purchasing systems can produce significant reductions in the costs of inputs, both direct and indirect products and services. These systems can also permit the optimization of supply chains across networks of organizations, not merely within a single company.

Understand the the just-in-time (JIT) production system and potential problems with its implementation.

JIT requires coordinated management of materials, people, and suppliers. JIT's goal is to eliminate inventories, reduce process and setup times, and use participative management to ensure worker input and loyalty to the firm. JIT includes total quality management (TQM), of which continuous improvement is an integral part. JIT is restricted to repetitive operations. It is a balanced system, and so if one operation stops, the whole production line stops. But it is difficult to achieve a balanced system. In addition, JIT makes no allowances for contingencies. A sudden breakdown will stop the entire production system. Finally, putting JIT into effect is a slow process.

Understand synchronous manufacturing and mass customization.

The goal of synchronous manufacturing is unbalanced manufacturing scheduling rather than the balanced scheduling of

JIT; attention is focused on the bottleneck of the manufacturing system, and scheduling for the entire operation is controlled by the output of the bottleneck operation. Mass customization involves the use of flexible, usually computer-aided manufacturing, systems to produce and deliver customized products and services for different customers worldwide.

Comprehend the concept of Six Sigma systems and their application.

Six Sigma is a business management process that concentrates on eliminating variation and reducing defects from work processes. The five steps of the Six Sigma approach—define, measure, analyze, improve, and control—represent a method for creating a closed-loop system for making continuous improvements in business processes. The Six Sigma methodology often requires that companies rethink the way they do things and that they adapt their culture, sometimes dramatically. Successful culture change requires a concerted, long-term effort, particularly if the organization is multinational, with subsidiaries and offices around the world.

Explain the potential of global standardization of production processes and procedures, and identify impediments to standardization efforts.

Standards help to ensure that materials, products, processes, and services are appropriate for their purpose, helping companies to meet market and competitive demands. Standardization of activities helps to simplify organization and control at headquarters because replication enables the work to be accomplished with a smaller staff of support personnel and internal best practices can more readily be applied across a company's international operations. However, differences in the foreign environmental forces, especially the economic, cultural, and political forces, cause units of an international multiplant operation to differ in size, machinery, and procedures, complicating efforts to achieve standardization of processes and procedures.

Know the two general classes of activities, productive and supportive, that must be performed in all manufacturing systems.

A manufacturing system is essentially a functionally related group of activities for creating value. After the system is operable, two general classes of activities, productive and supportive, must be performed. Productive activities are all those functions that are part of the manufacturing process. Among the important supportive activities are purchasing, maintenance, and the technical function.

Key Words

outsourcing (p. 505)
supply chain management (p. 505)
offshoring (p. 507)
just-in-time (JIT) (p. 515)
total quality management (TQM) (p. 516)
quality circle (quality control circle) (p. 516)
Taylor's scientific management system (p. 517)
preventive (planned) maintenance (p. 518)
synchronous manufacturing (p. 518)
bottleneck (p. 518)
mass customization (p. 519)
Six Sigma (p. 520)
standards (p. 522)
manufacturing rationalization (p. 525)
backward vertical integration (p. 528)
intermediate technology (p. 529)

Questions

1. What recent developments have caused supply chain management to become increasingly important to international companies?
2. What are the main differences between sequential and concurrent approaches to the design of products and services?
3. Why would a company choose to source raw materials, components, or other products or services from a foreign supplier? What are the strengths and weaknesses of using foreign suppliers?
4. What are the trade-offs for a firm that uses a just-in-time production system?
5. Why does the cost of raw materials represent about 55 to 79 percent of the cost of goods sold in U.S. industry, and why has this proportion been increasing over time?
6. Who is responsible for inventory? Where does the cost of carrying inventory show up, on the balance sheet or the income statement?

7. What are the costs of carrying inventory? Is the Japanese version of the cost of carrying inventory in agreement with your calculation? (*Hint:* Start your carrying cost calculation with the opportunity cost of invested capital.)
8. What advantages does synchronous manufacturing have over JIT?
9. What difficulties do you see for global firms when they implement synchronous manufacturing in their plants located in developing countries? Are there any advantages that are more valuable to them than to plants in industrialized nations?
10. What is mass customization? What is necessary in order for a company to effectively implement a mass-customization approach to serving its customers?
11. What is the benefit to a buyer company and to a vendor company of standards such as ISO 9000?
12. What is the connection between manufacturers' insistence on receiving components with zero defects from outside suppliers and JIT?
13. What are the advantages to a worldwide firm of global standardization of its production facilities?
14. What is Six Sigma? Why are companies increasingly using Six Sigma processes in their operations? What concerns might there be regarding the implementation of Six Sigma within an international company? How might a company go about addressing these concerns?
15. Discuss the influence of the uncontrollable environmental forces in global standardization of a firm's production facilities.
16. Who should be in charge of the purchasing function of an overseas affiliate, a local person or someone from the home office? Why?
17. What is the importance of preventive maintenance? Why might it be difficult to establish a preventive program in an overseas plant? Do you know of any situations for which breakdown maintenance is a viable alternative?

Research Task

globalEDGE.msu.edu 

Use the globalEDGE site (http://globalEDGE.msu.edu) to complete the following exercises:

1. The travel of products by large transport containers has become a primary method by which goods are transported worldwide. Since your firm is involved in the U.S. supply chain industry, a report is needed concerning the 10 largest container ports outside the United States. Using a Web site called *Geohive* as your resource to provide such a list, analyze the relative volume passing through each of the 10 largest ports in your report. What is the relative difference between the container ports ranking first and tenth in your report?
2. Struggling to remain competitive in the medical devices industry, your firm has decided to begin sourcing components internationally. Though your firm's current operations are only in the United States and the Netherlands, you must assess the relative costs for manufacturing medical devices in a variety of cities worldwide. Your manager, previously a consultant with KPMG, indicates that the *Competitive Alternatives* surveys published annually by KPMG may assist you. Develop two brief reports to answer the following questions: (a) Which three cities in the survey have the lowest and highest manufacturing costs for your firm's specific industry? (b) Do you think that changing your firm's sourcing strategy will resolve the current problems?

Minicase 19.1 Penwick–El Pais

Maquinas para el Hogar Penwick is a manufacturing subsidiary of Penwick Home Appliances in Boston. It is located in El Pais, a nation with 25 million inhabitants whose GNP per capita is $1,980. The country's annual inflation rate is about 30 percent, but the local company makes a good profit, in part because it keeps large stocks of components and raw materials purchased as much as 12 months before they are needed for production. The finished products are sold at prices set as if the raw materials and components had been purchased recently; hence the high profits. Penwick's competitors use the same strategy.

Penwick–El Pais has three competitors, none of which produces as complete a product mix or as many variations in each of the product lines of refrigerators, kitchen stoves, and washing machines as does the local Penwick plant. José Garcia, the local marketing manager, is proud that Penwick–El Pais makes as many kinds of products and variations of products as the much larger home plant, and he has told the managing director of the local company that it is the wide product mix that maintains Penwick–El Pais's number-one position in sales. Manuel Cardenas, the local operations manager, and Garcia frequently have heated discussions because

Cardenas wants to make fewer product variations. Garcia accuses him of wanting to make black stoves like Henry Ford made black cars, but Cardenas claims he could double his output if he could make fewer kinds of products with fewer variations. Cardenas knows the value of long manufacturing runs and tries to get them. Garcia retorts that if Cardenas would pay attention to what he wants instead of making what Cardenas wants to make, he could sell more.

This is a sore spot with Cardenas because he tries hard to produce a new product according to Garcia's written request. If Garcia's memo says he wants a new-size refrigerator in three colors to be available with or without beverage coolers or ice cube makers, these are the models Cardenas asks the product design department to design and make production specifications for. Garcia at one time or another has asked to attend meetings with Cardenas and his staff, but Cardenas considers this a waste of time. After all, he doesn't waste the design department's time by asking to attend their meetings; why should a salesperson attend his meetings? He has enough problems with the high prices for parts that the purchasing department people give him. When he complains, they tell him that everything he orders is special manufacture for the vendors. Cardenas says that's their problem; this is what the design department specifies, and this is what he has to use to build the product.

Cardenas has more pressing problems. Headquarters has adopted a new manufacturing system, synchronous manufacturing, and now wants him to do the same. In fact, he had to send his assistant manager to Boston for a month's training. Now she and the design manager, who also went, are back, and they have brought one of the home office experts with them. They're all going to have a long meeting with him this afternoon. Cardenas has read about synchronous manufacturing in technical journals and feels it does seem to have some advantages. But all of them have been in highly industrialized nations, and there are a lot of cultural and economic differences between El Pais and those countries.

You might role-play this case. Imagine you are a member of the three-person group that has come from Boston. Even though you know the local plant has orders to convert to synchronous manufacturing, you still have to win over the local personnel.

1. What will you say?
2. Can you think of any advantages that might be even more important for the local plant than they are for the larger home plant?
3. What problems do you foresee in putting synchronous manufacturing in place?

20 Human Resource Management*

Paradoxically, in spite of the opportunities for [human resource management, or HR] to contribute to globalization in added-value ways, the HR function is not perceived in many companies as a full partner in the globalization process. Sometimes it is viewed as an obstacle, slowing down the process through bureaucratic central procedures. The ethnocentric and parochial HR systems and policies inherited from the past, focused on the parent company and projected onto the rest of the world, are all too often a barrier to the implementation of effective global organizational processes.

—*Paul Evans, Vladimir Pucik, and Jean-Louis Barsoux,* The Global Challenge, *2002*

*An earlier version of this chapter was prepared with the assistance of Jere Ramsey of California Polytechnic State University.

Becoming an Expatriate, or Expat, as They Are Sometimes Called

You are happy and proud; you can hardly wait to get back to your office to phone your family with the news. Your boss has called you in and said, "We have a problem in Asia that we need you to solve." You are doing well with the company in the home, domestic market, but now the company has discovered markets away from home, and you have not seen anything away from home since you and your college friend backpacked in the Argentine mountains to Bariloche. You have read about dining at Singapore's Raffles Hotel with the ghost of Somerset Maugham, exploring Bangkok's temples, and enjoying the helicopter and Rolls-Royce service and harbor views of Hong Kong's Peninsula Hotel.

You are about to become an **expatriate.** Your family will love it, and the foreign experience will be your passport to your company's top executive positions. Your career will be made. Right?

Maybe. You must be very careful. For too many employees who take foreign assignments, it is out of sight, out of mind, and you may find yourself well out of the loop. On the other hand, however, these assignments can be passports to the top if you take the right steps before you make the move.

If at all possible, arrange to have someone fairly high in the company hierarchy be your mentor, ideally a person who has also served in an expatriate role so that there can be a base of international experience that you can draw from. That home country mentor should keep you advised of changes and developments in the company back at home and should keep your name in consideration and not forgotten while you are on your assignment abroad. You might also consider finding a mentor in the host country, who can assist you in understanding the local culture, introduce you to valuable business contacts, and help you in interpreting situations that you encounter while in your position abroad.

Before you take the job, you should insist that your bosses tell you exactly what the company expects you to accomplish. Are you to get a plant up and running, install systems or practices that are currently in use in the home country, arrange customer financing, negotiate investment, or perhaps groom a host country replacement? Will this be an extended on-site assignment, such as two to four years in length, or will it merely involve one or several short-term assignments that are primarily intended to work on a specific problem or transfer specific knowledge?

Of course, there is the chance that despite all your efforts and precautions, your company will forget or not value you. Realizing this possibility, you should have been profiting from your foreign assignment by doing your job well; learning new markets; gaining proficiency in the language, which will permit you to better understand the culture; and networking. The networking can be done by being active in such things as local chambers of commerce, social clubs, and sports clubs.

All this will make you valuable to other companies and make them aware of you. In essence, you have received a million dollars' worth of training paid for by your company, and you and other companies can utilize it. After all, this is an important source of third country national executives. ■

CONCEPT PREVIEWS

After reading this chapter, you should be able to:

discuss the importance of creating a company "global mind-set"

explain the relationship between competitive strategies (international, multidomestic, regional, and transnational) and international human resource management approaches (ethnocentric, polycentric, regiocentric, and global)

compare home country, host country, and third country nationals as IC executives

explain the difficulties of finding qualified executives for international companies (ICs) and the importance of foreign language knowledge

explain what an expatriate is and some of the challenges and opportunities of an expat position

discuss the increasing importance of accommodating the trailing spouse of an expatriate executive

identify some of the complications of compensation packages for expatriate executives

Gli Affari Internazionali
nales
nales Geschäft Παγοσμιο Business
Negócios Internacionais Los Negócios Internacionais
ernacionales Affaires Internationales 國際商務 Παγοσμιο Business

expatriate
A person living outside his or her country of citizenship

The effectiveness of every organization depends to a great extent on the nature of its work force and how well its human resources are utilized. Their effective use depends on management's policies and practices. Management of a company's human resources is a shared responsibility. The day-to-day supervision of people on the job is the duty of the operating managers, who must integrate the human, financial, and physical resources into an efficient production system. However, the formulation of policies and procedures for (1) estimation of work force needs, (2) recruitment and selection, (3) training and development, (4) motivation, (5) compensation, (6) discipline, and (7) employment termination is generally the responsibility of personnel managers working in cooperation with executives from marketing, production, and finance as well as the firm's lawyers.

Finding the right people to manage an organization can be difficult under any circumstances, but it is especially difficult to find good managers of overseas operations. Such positions require more and different skills than do purely domestic executive jobs. The right persons need to be bicultural, with knowledge of the business practices in the home country plus an understanding of business practices and customs in the host country. And to fully understand a culture, any culture, it is usually necessary to speak the language of its people. Only with a good grasp of the language can one understand the subtleties and humor and know what is really going on in the host country. Although difficult to locate, such managers do exist, and they may be found in (1) the home country, (2) the host country, or (3) a third country.

Siemens, the German engineering and electronics conglomerate, generates almost 80 percent of its sales outside its home country, up from 45 percent in 1990. As a result, 60 percent of its employees are located outside Germany. Heinrich von Pierer, Siemens' CEO and president, says, "We need employees and managers who are close to our customers and understand their needs." Siemens relies on local managers to oversee its far-flung network of operations. In Italy, most of the managers are Italian, while in the United States, most of the managers are American. In China, he has directed his 200 managers, who are mainly expatriates from the West, to develop Chinese managers to succeed them in their posts within the next five years. Yet, despite the localization of managerial talent, the company remains German at its core. "English increasingly is becoming our company's common language, but the rules and culture in Germany are still a bit different." As a result, he emphasizes his desire to have more young foreign managers spend time working in Germany, so that they can function better within the company's culture.

global mind-set
A mind-set that combines an openness to and an awareness of diversity across markets and cultures with a propensity and ability to synthesize across this diversity

Research by Vijay Govindarajan and Anil Gupta indicates that many CEOs feel that developing a company **global mind-set** is a "prerequisite for global industry dominance."[1] Govindarajan and Gupta identify four possible mind-sets, determined by individuals' or organizations' level of knowledge differentiation and their skill in knowledge integration. They define a global mind-set as "one that combines an openness to and awareness of diversity across cultures and markets with a propensity and ability to synthesize across this diversity." Percy Barnevik, who served as the leader for the merger of Swedish Asea with Swiss Brown Boveri to create the global engineering and manufacturing giant ABB, aptly observed, "Global managers have exceptionally open minds. They respect how different countries do things, and they have the imagination to appreciate why they do them that way. But they are also incisive, they push the limits of the culture. Global managers don't passively accept it when someone says, 'You can't do that in Italy or Spain because of the unions,' or 'You can't do that in Japan because of the Ministry of Finance.' They sort through the debris of cultural excuses and find opportunities to innovate."[2]

The International Human Resource Management Approach

Chapter 13 explained that two competing forces, the pressure to achieve global integration and reduce costs and the pressure to respond to local differentiation, determine which of four alternative competitive strategies (home replication, multidomestic, global, or transnational) a company should adopt. A company's competitive strategy should, in turn, drive the organization's approach to international human resource management (IHRM).

Heenan and Perlmutter developed a model that considers these four competitive strategies to determine whether the organization's approach to IHRM should be **ethnocentric, polycentric, regiocentric,** or **geocentric.**[3] Further, along with this decision, the employees used in the organization may be classified into one of three categories: (1) **home country nationals** or **parent country nationals (PCNs),** (2) **host country nationals (HCNs),** and (3) **third country nationals (TCNs).** These relationships are illustrated in Table 20.1.

ethnocentric
As used here, related to hiring and promoting employees on the basis of the parent company's home country frame of reference

polycentric
As used here, related to hiring and promoting employees on the basis of the specific local context in which the subsidiary operates

regiocentric
As used here, related to hiring and promoting employees on the basis of the specific regional context in which the subsidiary operates

geocentric
As used here, related to hiring and promoting employees on the basis of ability and experience without considering race or citizenship

home country national
Same as parent country national

parent country national (PCNs)
Employee who is a citizen of the nation in which the parent company is headquartered; also called *home country national*

host country national (HCN)
Employee who is a citizen of the nation in which the subsidiary is operating, which is different from the parent company's home nation

Recruitment and Selection of Employees

The recruitment and selection of employees, frequently referred to as *staffing,* should be determined in a manner consistent with one of the four IHRM approaches the organization is pursuing, as discussed below.[4]

ETHNOCENTRIC STAFFING POLICY

Companies with a primarily international strategic orientation (characterized by low pressures for cost reduction and low pressures for local responsiveness) may adopt an ethnocentric staffing policy. In this approach, most decisions are made at headquarters, using the home country's frame of reference. ICs utilize citizens of their own countries, or PCNs, in key foreign management and technical positions.

At first, PCNs are usually not knowledgeable about the host country culture and language. Many such expatriates have adapted, learned the language, and become thoroughly accepted in the host country, although it is also common that such managers encounter difficulty overcoming the biases of their own cultural experience and being able to understand and perform effectively within the new operating context.

Labor negotiators and other specialists may be sent to troubleshoot such problems as product warranty, international contracts, taxes, accounting, and reporting. Teams may be sent from the home country to assist with new plant start-up, and they would probably stay until subsidiary personnel were trained to run and maintain the new facilities.

An advantage to using home country citizens abroad is to broaden their experience in preparation for becoming high-level managers at headquarters. Firms earning a large percentage of their profits from international sources require top executives who have a worldwide perspective, both business and political. It is difficult to impossible to acquire that sort of perspective without living and working abroad for a substantial period of time.

If new technology for the subsidiary is involved, the parent company will probably station at least one of its technologically qualified experts at the subsidiary until its local personnel learn the technology. In this way, the home office can be confident that someone is immediately available to explain headquarters' policies and procedures, see that they are observed, and interpret what is happening locally for the IC's management. Positions that an IC must take or demands that it must make are sometimes not popular with a host government. It can seem unpatriotic for a host country national to do such things, whereas the host government can understand, and sometimes accept, such positions or demands from a foreigner.

> *One of the authors remembers the relief expressed by the Argentinean executives of an Argentine subsidiary of an American IC because an American manager was present to press the Argentine government for what seemed to be unusually extensive payment guarantees. The contract was for a product that, while partly manufactured and assembled in Argentina, was mostly manufactured in the United States and imported into Argentina. The Argentinean executives feared that the very specific and high-level payment guarantees would antagonize government officials. The subsidiary was an Argentine company, subject to that country's laws and dependent in part on business from government departments and government-owned companies. Its managers were residents and would stay in Argentina, while the American was there only until the signing of this contract and the guarantees. After he flew away, the local people could blame him and the American parent IC, thus deflecting anger and resentment from themselves.*

TABLE 20.1 Strategic Approach, Organizational Concerns, and the International Human Resource Management Approach to Be Used

Aspects of the Enterprise	Orientation			
	Ethnocentric	**Polycentric**	**Regiocentric**	**Geocentric**
Primary strategic orientation/stage	Home Replication	Multidomestic	Regional	Transnational
Perpetuation (recruiting, staffing, development)	People of home country developed for key positions everywhere in the world	People of local nationality developed for key positions in their own country	Regional people developed for key positions anywhere in the region	Best people everywhere in the world developed for key positions every where in the world
Complexity of the organization	Complex in home country, simple in subsidiaries	Varied and independent	Highly interdependent on a regional basis	"Global web," complex, independent, worldwide alliances/network
Authority, decision making	High in headquarters	Relatively low in headquarters	High regional headquarters and/or high collaboration among subsidiaries	Collaboration of headquarters and subsidiaries around the world
Evaluation and control	Home standards applied to people and performance	Determined locally	Determined regionally	Globally integrated
Rewards	High in headquarters, low in subsidiaries	Wide variations, can be high or low rewards for subsidiary performance	Rewards for contribution to regional objectives	Rewards to international and local executives for reaching local and worldwide objectives based on global company goals
Communication, information flow	High volume of orders, commands, advice to subsidiaries	Little to and from headquarters, little among subsidiaries	Little to and from corporate headquarters, but may be high to and from regional headquarters and among countries	Horizontal, network relations
Geographic identification	Nationality of owner	Nationality of host country	Regional company	Truly global company, but identifying with national interests ("glocal")

Source: Adapted from David A. Heenan and Howard V. Perlmutter, *Multinational Organization Development* (Boston: Addison-Wesley, 1979).

WORLD view   

Executives with the Right Stuff Are in Big Demand

Demand for executives with the "right stuff" is the case everywhere, but it is particularly true in developing economies. One can look at China and Latin America for examples of what is meant by this.

Kodak's Chinese operation brought in Western managers who were excellent with the technical aspects of their jobs. Nevertheless, they failed miserably because they did not understand the culture of the country.

In an attempt to solve the problem, Kodak and other foreign companies recruit Chinese-speaking staff from Asian and other countries. But there are still cultural considerations, says Kay Kutt, managing director of Cendant Intercultural Assignment Services, Asia-Pacific division. "It's almost worse than sending a Westerner, to send someone who has the Chinese language but not Chinese values," as she puts it. Local hires are less costly than expatriates and they often have better understanding of the Chinese market and customers. Having a boss who is a local can be motivating to ambitious junior employees, and can enhance communication and morale. As Wal-Mart China executive Du Limin says about the response of her Chinese employees, "They take me as their big sister and they confide their family issues with me. That is impossible if you're an expatriate." Yet finding an adequate number and quality of local talent in China can be difficult for international companies. "Companies want to localize but the majority of people who are local mainland Chinese don't have experience with global principles," said Joy Chen, a principal at the executive search firm Heidrick & Struggles.

Hundreds of non–Latin American businesses trying to operate in that region have openings for bilingual executives. "Our objective is to find the best talent that we can for any position that is open . . . and knowing a second language does create an advantage," said Mark Bailey, director of staffing at General Mills. But merely being fluent in the language does not mean that prospective employees have the skills required for a particular position. These companies are looking for people who can operate in a dual mode, combining U.S. efficiency and business culture with the Latin way of doing things, which is more personal and requires knowledge of Spanish or Portuguese.

An example of cultural contrast is given by Ignacio Kleinman of I-Network.com. An American might try to close a deal over the phone, but the Latin style is to take a plane ride to the customer's country, have lunch, and talk about soccer and the family. "Afterward, that Latin customer is going to feel closer to you," Kleinman says. "If there is no personal chemistry, there is likely to be no business."

Source: Julian Teixeira, "More Companies Recruit Bilingual Employees," www.shrm.org/ema/EMT/articles/2004/Fall04teixeira.asp (July 25, 2006); Cui Rong, "More Firms in China Think Globally, Hire Locally," *The Wall Street Journal*, February 27, 2006, p. 29; "Leaders of the Right Stuff in Big Demand," *Financial Times*, June 7, 2000, p. 12; Jiang Yan, "Thirst for Talent," *China Business Weekly*, September 12–18, 2005, p. 4; "Latino Talent Pinch Hobbling U.S. Firms' Expansion Plans," *Los Angeles Times*, June 25, 2000, pp. C1, 5; and Amy Yee, "China's War for Talent Hots Up," *Financial Times*, February 16, 2006, p. 8.

POLYCENTRIC STAFFING POLICY

When the company's primary strategic orientation is multidomestic, with low pressures for cost reduction and high pressures for local responsiveness, a polycentric approach may be used, involving human resource policies that are created at the local level for the specific context in which the local operations operate. Companies primarily hire HCNs for subsidiaries and PCNs for headquarters' positions; movement from the local subsidiaries to headquarters' positions is uncommon.

third country national (TCN)
Employee who is a citizen of neither the parent company nation nor the host country

When HCNs are employed at the subsidiary level, there is no problem of their being unfamiliar with local customs, culture, and language. Furthermore, the first costs of employing them are generally lower (compared to the costs of employing home country nationals and paying to move them and their families to the host country), although considerable training costs are sometimes necessary. If there is a strong feeling of nationalism in the host country, having nationals as managers can make the subsidiary seem less foreign. As Fujio Mitarai, chairman and CEO of Canon, said, "If you look at capital investment strategy, marketing, research and development, those types of activities are international. But if you talk about people, humans, it is quite local in nature."[5]

The government development plans and laws of some countries demand that employment in all sectors and at all levels reflect the racial composition of the society. In other words, more skilled and managerial slots must be given to the local people. If foreign-owned firms in Indonesia fail to hire enough *pribumi* (indigenous Indonesians), those firms are likely to encounter difficulties with reentry permits for foreign employees as well as with other government licenses and permits that they need. Bribery requests have been known to increase until more pribumi were hired and promoted. Malaysia threatens to revoke the operating licenses of foreign-owned firms that fail to have a satisfactory number of *bumiputra* (indigenous Malays) in sufficiently elevated jobs.

A disadvantage of hiring local managers is that they are often unfamiliar with the home country of the IC and with its corporate culture, policies, and practices. As Liu Zhengrong, head of human resources for the German chemical group Lanxess, said of hiring local managers, "You lose something in terms of communication with the headquarters, but you get more hints about the local marketplace."[6] Differences in attitudes and values, as discussed in Chapter 6, can cause these locally hired managers to act in ways that surprise or displease headquarters. Also, local managers may create their own upward immobility if, because of strong cultural or family ties, they are reluctant to accept promotions that would require them to leave the country to work at parent headquarters or at another subsidiary.

Foreign-owned companies that hire and train local, host country people frequently experience a common, and disruptive, IHRM problem. The best of these people may be pirated away by local firms or other IC subsidiaries, as local executive recruiters are constantly on the lookout to make raids and entice the most talented employees to leave the original IC and join another firm that is seeking to overcome its own shortage of skilled personnel.

Finally, there can be a conflict of loyalty between the host country and the employer. For example, the host country national may give preference to a local supplier even though imported products may be less expensive or of better quality. Local managers may oppose headquarters' requests to set low transfer prices in order to lower taxes payable to the host government.

REGIOCENTRIC STAFFING POLICY

Companies with a regional strategic approach (with slightly higher pressures for cost reduction and slightly lower pressures for local responsiveness than the multidomestic strategy) can employ a regiocentric staffing approach. In this approach, regional employees are selected for key positions in the region, employing a variety of HCNs and TCNs.

The disadvantages often encountered when using employees from the home or host country can sometimes be avoided by sending third country nationals (TCNs) to fill management posts. A Chilean going to Argentina would have little cultural or language difficulty, but IC headquarters should be careful not to rely too heavily on similarities in language as a guide to similarities in other aspects of cultures. Mexicans, for example, would have to make considerable adjustments if they were transferred to Argentina, and they would find a move to Spain even more difficult. This is because the Mexican culture, in general, is far less European than that of either Argentina or Chile. Although the latter two cultures are certainly not identical, they do have many similarities. A fair generalization is that after an executive has adapted once to a new culture and language, a second or succeeding adaptation is easier.

An employer should not count on cost savings in using third country nationals. Although they may come from countries where salary scales are lower, in such countries as Brazil and most of the nations of northwestern Europe, salaries may be higher than American companies are paying at comparable position levels. Furthermore, many multinationals give international status* to both home country nationals and third country nationals, who then receive the same perquisites and compensation packages for the same job.

*International status is discussed later in this chapter.

GEOCENTRIC STAFFING POLICY

Companies with a transnational strategic orientation, driven simultaneously by high pressures for cost reduction and high pressures for local responsiveness, follow a geocentric staffing policy. These organizations select the best person for each job without considering national origin and can therefore capitalize on the advantages of each staffing policy. With a geocentric staffing policy, HRM strategy tends to be consistent across all subsidiaries, borrowing best practices from wherever they may be found across the company's worldwide network of operations rather than showing preference only to the practices used at headquarters within a local context.

Training and Development

Training and development involve efforts to facilitate the acquisition of job-related knowledge, behavior, and skills. The training and development of managers and other key IC employees vary somewhat, depending on whether the candidate is from the home country, the host country, or a third country.

HOME OR PARENT COUNTRY NATIONAL

Relatively few recent college graduates are hired for the express purpose of being sent overseas. Usually they spend a number of years in the domestic (parent) company, and they may get into the company's international operations by design and persistence, by luck, or by a combination of those elements. They may first be assigned to the international division at the firm's headquarters, where they handle problems submitted by foreign affiliates and meet visiting overseas personnel.

If the company feels that it probably will send PCNs abroad, it will frequently encourage them to study the language and culture of the country to which they are going. Such employees will probably be sent on short trips abroad to handle special assignments and to be exposed to foreign surroundings. Newly hired PCNs with prior overseas experience may undergo similar but shorter training periods.

Axcelis Technologies, Inc., a manufacturer of semiconductor-processing equipment based in Beverly, Massachusetts, decided to outsource some of its engineering jobs to India. Cultural differences between India and the United States were a concern for Axcelis' management: India is a "high context" society that relies heavily on moral codes and relationships, while the United States is a "low context" nation that depends on legal codes and is very direct. Worrying that some of its American workers might resent or otherwise not be able to work effectively with their new Indian co-workers, the company trained 60 employees about Indian cultural practices. The training included such topics as how to shake hands and why Indian workers might not make eye contact during meetings, as well as role-playing of Indian-U.S. interactions. Randy Longo, human resources director at Axcelis, said, "At first, I was skeptical and wondered what I'd get out of the class. But it was enlightening for me. Not everyone operates like we do in America."[7]

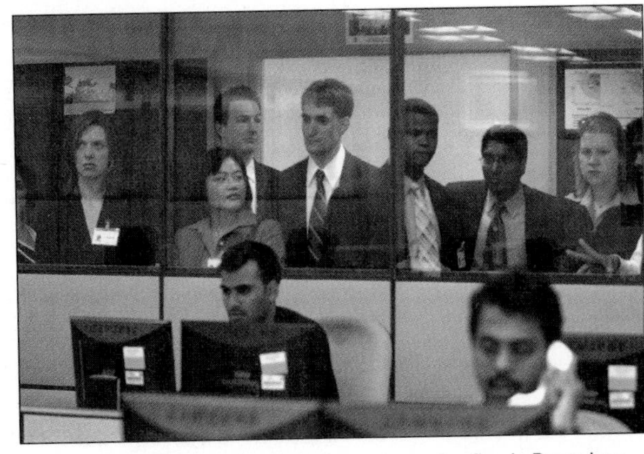

Visitors from the United States tour an outsourcing firm in Bangalore, India, in March 2004. Relatively few recent college graduates are hired for the express purpose of being sent overseas. When a company feels managers are ready for an overseas assignment, it may send them on short trips abroad to handle special assignments and to be exposed to foreign surroundings.

It is increasingly possible for American ICs to supplement their in-house training for overseas work with courses in American business schools. In recognition of the growing importance of international business, those schools are expanding the number and scope of international business courses they offer. In addition, a number of university-level business schools are now operating in other countries.

A large problem that has plagued employers is caused by the families of executives transferred overseas. Even

WORLD view   

Are Women Appropriate for International Assignments?

Although women make up about 47 percent of the work force in the United States, they represent only a relatively small fraction of the population of expatriates. Why this difference, especially with the pressing need for finding and developing competent global leaders? Adler examined three myths about women in international management:

Myth 1: Women do not want to be international managers.

Myth 2: Companies refuse to send women abroad.

Myth 3: Foreigners' prejudice against women renders them ineffective.

When Adler tested these myths empirically, neither the first nor the third was supported, but only the second one. Adler's research suggested that 70 percent of her sample of international companies were hesitant to select women for expatriate assignments. Why? Among the reasons expressed were that women in dual-career relationships would experience problems with international assignments, that gender-based prejudice would limit women's performance in many challenging countries or cultures, that women might feel lonely and isolated in an international assignment or be subjected to sexual harassment, or that the men making selection decisions regarding international assignments were themselves biased by traditional views and stereotypes regarding the appropriateness of assigning women to expatriate positions.

Is this hesitancy by companies regarding selecting women for international assignments justified? Research has shown that women are just as eager to go abroad as are men, sometimes more so. Additional research has shown that gender is unrelated to the performance ratings of expatriates, with the adjustment of expatriates to the host country context, or with the intention of expatriates to leave their ICs. Recent studies have even suggested that the skills and identity typically associated with women (e.g., attentiveness to personal aspects of business and skill in building interpersonal relationships) may actually give women an edge over men for some expatriate assignments. In addition, rather than cultural attributes serving as a barrier to the effectiveness of women expats (e.g., a women-unfriendly environment in some host country cultures), as has sometimes been argued in explaining why women could not or should not be assigned to international positions, these structural aspects may serve as an advantage for women in international roles. For example, Taylor and Napier reported on the success of female expatriates in Japan in achieving improved cross-cultural adjustment and work success due to their having higher visibility and memorability as a result of their gender and their status as foreigners. Indeed, women may be able to divert attention from gender by demonstrating individualized sources of legitimacy and power, such as functional expertise and experience, and thereby enhance their effectiveness in international assignments.

So are ICs listening and selecting more women for expatriate assignments? In 1994, the GMAC Global Relocation Services annual Global Relocation Trends Survey showed that only 8 to 10 percent of expatriates were women. Ten years later, the proportion had risen to 18 percent. By 2005, it was up another 5 percent, to 23 percent of all international assignees. Expectations are that this proportion will continue to increase in coming years, particularly as more women are moving into management positions. Apparently, myths about the appropriateness of women candidates for international assignments are beginning to be shattered, and ICs are taking advantage of this pool of talented employees for promoting the organizations' international success.

Source: Jan Selmer, "Adjustment of Western European vs. North American Expatriate Managers in China," *Personnel Review* 30, no. 1–2 (2001), pp. 6–21; Paula M. Caligiuri and Rosalie L. Tung, "Male and Female Expatriates Success in Masculine and Feminine Countries," *International Journal of Human Resource Management* 10, no. 5 (1999), pp. 763–82; Mary G. Tye and Peter Y. Chen, "Selection of Expatriates: Decision-Making Models Used by HR Professionals," *Human Resource Planning* 28, no. 4 (2005), pp. 15–20; Nancy J. Adler, "Women Do Not Want International Careers: And Other Myths about International Management," *Organizational Dynamics* 13, no. 2 (1984), pp. 66–80; "Expatriate Workforce Demographics," *HR Magazine* 51, no. 5 (May 2006), p. 16; Sully Taylor and Nancy Napier, "Working in Japan: Lessons from Women Expatriates," *Sloan Management Review* 37, no. 3 (1996), pp. 76–84; and Paula M. Caligiuri and Wayne Cascio, "Can We Send Her There? Maximizing the Success of Western Women on Global Assignments," *Journal of World Business* 33 (1998), pp. 394–417.

though the employee may adapt to and enjoy the foreign experience, the family may not, and an unhappy family may sour the employee on the job or even split up the marriage. In such cases, the company may have to ship the family back home at great expense—seldom less than $25,000. Consequently, many companies try to assess whether the executive's family can adapt to the foreign ambience before assigning the executive abroad. This is part of the subject of expatriates that is dealt with later in this chapter.

HOST COUNTRY NATIONAL

The same general criteria for selecting home country employees apply to host country nationals. Usually, however, the training and development activities undertaken for HCNs will differ from those used for home country nationals in that host country nationals are more likely to lack knowledge of advanced business techniques, particularly those that are specific to business applications and operations of the IC, and knowledge of the company as a whole.

HCNs Hired in the Home Country

Many multinationals try to solve the business technique problem by hiring host country students on their graduation from home country business schools. After being hired, these new employees are usually sent to IC headquarters to receive indoctrination in the firm's policies and procedures as well as on-the-job training in a specific function, such as finance, marketing, or production.

HCNs Hired in the Host Country

Because the number of host country citizens graduating from home country universities is limited, multinationals must also recruit locally for their management positions. To impart knowledge of business techniques, the company may do one or more things. It may set up in-house training programs in the host country subsidiary, or it may utilize business courses in the host country's universities. The IC may also send new employees to home country business schools or to parent company training programs. In addition, employees who show promise will be sent repeatedly to the parent company headquarters, divisions, and other subsidiaries to observe the various enterprise operations and meet the other executives with whom they will be communicating during their careers. Such visits are also learning experiences for the home office and the other subsidiaries.

Craig Barrett, Chairman of the semiconductor giant Intel, views the current international business environment as undergoing "probably the biggest change in the history of mankind," the opening of China, as well as Brazil, Russia and India, to the global economy. This is creating major new markets, as well as potential competitors, for his company, and one of Intel's responses is to aggressively recruit the best talent he can find, especially in host countries. More than a third of Intel's employees are now outside the United States. "We are going to go after the best international resources wherever they are. There are great engineers in China and they also happen to cost less than in the United States. China happens to be our fastest growing marketplace and having your presence there is important."[8]

THIRD COUNTRY NATIONAL

Hiring personnel who are citizens of neither the home country nor the host country is often advantageous. TCNs may accept lower wages and benefits than will employees from the home country, and they may come from a culture similar to that of the host country. In addition, they may have worked for another unit of the IC and thus be familiar with the company's policies, procedures, and people. This can simplify the training and development requirements for such recruits.

The use of TCNs has become particularly prevalent in the developing countries because of shortages of literate, not to mention skilled, locals. It can be an advantage to get someone already residing in the country who has the necessary work permits and knowledge of the local languages and customs.

Jianjiang Group, the largest hotel operator in China and also government owned, found its Shanghai home base being attacked by numerous international hotel chains. To compete it had to do something to enhance its performance on service and branding—two dimensions that have largely been lacking among Chinese firms. As a result, rather than looking for a manager in China as the company had traditionally done, it instead hired a headhunting firm specifically to recruit a Westerner from an established hotel chain. Christopher Bachran, with over 30 years of hotel industry experience including nearly 20 years in Southeast Asia, was ultimately persuaded to join Jianjiang. Part of the deal he negotiated, though, was authorization to bring in 4 to 6 senior managers from outside China, in areas such as operations, food-and-beverage operations, sales, marketing, human resources, and engineering services.[9]

Host Country Attitudes If the host government emphasizes employment of its own citizens, third country nationals will be no more welcome than will home country people. Actually, third country nationals could face an additional obstacle in obtaining necessary work permits. For example, the host government can understand that the German parent company of a subsidiary would want some German executives to look after its interest in the host country. It may be harder to convince the government that a third country native is any better for the parent than a local executive would be.

Generalizations about TCNs Are Difficult We must be careful with generalizations about third country personnel, partly because people achieve that status in different ways. They may be foreigners hired in the home country and sent to a host country subsidiary either because they have had previous experience there or because that country's culture is similar to their own. Third country nationals may have originally been home country personnel who were sent abroad and became dissatisfied with the job but not with the host country. After leaving the firm that sent them abroad, they take positions with subsidiaries of multinationals from different home countries. Another way in which third country nationals can be created is by promotion within an IC. For instance, if a Spanish executive of the Spanish subsidiary of an Italian multinational is promoted to be general manager of the Italian firm's Colombian subsidiary, the Spanish executive is then a third country national.

As multinationals increasingly take the *geocentric* view toward promoting (according to ability and not nationality), we are certain to see greater use of TCNs. This development will be accelerated as more and more executives of all nationalities gain experience outside their native lands. Another, and growing, source for third country nationals is the heterogeneous body of international agencies. As indicated in Chapter 4, these agencies deal with virtually every field of human endeavor, and all member-countries send their nationals as representatives to the headquarters and branch office cities all over the world. Many of those people become available to, or can be hired away by, international companies.

Expatriates

In Chapters 1 and 2, we discussed the fact that many of the world's leading international companies obtain 50 percent or more of both their revenues and their profits abroad, and that international markets are becoming increasingly important to success for even small and medium-size companies. To exploit these international opportunities, staffing of positions in international operations is an important strategic issue. Although many of the employees may be hired in the host country (called *inpatriates*), ICs have continued to send employees on foreign assignments. Some of the international positions, especially those that deal with addressing a specific technical problem or transferring specialized knowledge, will be staffed with home or third country employees who are on short-term assignments (called *flexpatriates*). Yet companies will continue to staff many key positions with expatriates, employees who are relocated to the host country from the home country or a third country, with the assignment lasting for an extended period of time (two to four years is a common length of time for an expatriate assignment). In fact, about 80 percent of medium- and large-size companies have employees working abroad, and 44 percent of responding companies in a recent survey said that they were increasing the use of expats.[10] The average age of expats is getting somewhat younger as well, with 54 percent now being between 20 and 39 years, versus 41 percent in 1994.[11]

Why use expatriates rather than just hire local employees? Expatriates can bring technical or managerial skills that are scarce in the host country; they can help transfer or install companywide systems or cultures; they may provide a trusted connection for facilitating oversight or control over foreign operations; or the international assignment may enable the expat to develop the skills and experiences that will allow a subsequent promotion into leadership positions of greater scope and responsibility within the IC.

The costs of using expatriates are substantial, estimated at about $50 billion annually for U.S. companies, so the performance of expatriates is an important issue for ICs.[12] Yet various studies report that failure rates for expatriate assignments—including failing to achieve performance targets for an international assignment or prematurely returning from the assignment—range from 25 to 45 percent.[13] Furthermore, approximately 20 percent of expatriates leave their companies within six months of their return from abroad, hindering the IC's ability to retain and leverage the skills and experience that the expatriate has gained from the international assignment. A major cause of expatriate performance problems is culture shock, which is discussed in the nearby Worldview entitled "Culture Shock."

To enhance expatriate performance, ICs should consider the support that they provide to the employee predeparture, while away on assignment, and upon repatriation.[14] Preassignment, the focus of support efforts should be on ensuring that the expatriate has the skills needed for successful performance in the foreign assignment, including language and cultural training, career counseling, and any needed technical or other skill development. Support during assignment includes the use of mentors (both home and host country), career counseling, and communication strategies to ensure that the expatriate remains connected to the IC's strategy, people, policies, and culture. Repatriation support, including management of the relocation to the home or other nation and reintegration into the company, is discussed later in this section. Organizational support has been shown to be a predictor of the success of expatriates' adjustment to their international postings.[15]

THE EXPATRIATE'S FAMILY

It has been suggested that as many as 9 out of 10 expatriates' failures are family-related, and 81 percent of the employees who declined relocations in 2005 cited family concerns as the basis for their decision. In contrast to immigrants, who typically commit themselves to becoming part of their new country of residence, expats usually are only living temporarily in the new nation, so they often fail to adopt the host country's culture and seldom attempt to gain citizenship in that nation. Many expatriates and their family members also experience culture shock, which can significantly impact the quality of the international experience. The cultural adaptation pressures may be particularly great for the accompanying spouses, especially since they often are unable to work in the host country and may experience more challenges with regard to their personal identity. Spouses also typically need to interact more extensively with the local host community than do their expatriate partners, for such things as shopping, schools, and the management of domestic help, and related issues exacerbate adjustment pressures.[16] The stress an overseas move places on spouses and children will ultimately affect employees no matter how dedicated they may be to the company. Unhappy spouses are the biggest reason for employees to ask to go home early, and relocation expenses for high-level executives can run into the hundreds of thousands of dollars. Even worse, the company is losing a "million-dollar corporate-training investment" in the executive. On the other hand, expatriates tend to have better satisfaction and performance when their spouses and other family members are able to adjust well to the new host country context.[17]

A family purchases train tickets in London. It has been suggested that as many as 9 out of 10 expatriates' failures are family-related.

Trailing Spouses in Two-Career Families

The number of two-career families is growing, and that can complicate matters when one spouse is offered a juicy job abroad. The implications of the international assignment for the employee's partner and the partner's career prospects is a major factor impacting expatriate adjustment and performance.[18] It is reported that 20 to 25 percent of the spouses of expatriates are unable to obtain employment in the host country, even though 60 percent of them were employed before their spouse's international assignment began.[19] In efforts to ease the problem, some companies are starting programs that

WORLD view   

Culture Shock

Culture shock refers to the anxiety people experience when they move from a culture that they are familiar with to one that is entirely different. Because familiar signs and symbols are no longer present in the new culture, a person experiencing culture shock tends to feel lack of direction, or inadequacy from not knowing what to do or how things are done in the new culture. Physical and emotional discomfort and feelings of disorientation and confusion are a common experience for people who go to other nations to work, live, or study. Many expatriates and members of their families are affected by culture shock, sometimes to a very great degree.

Researchers have identified three different dimensions associated with cross-cultural adjustment. The first is associated with the work context, such as the extent of job clarity, inherent conflict in the person's role, and amount of discretion associated with completing the job tasks. Adjustment to the general environment, the second dimension, is associated with reacting to differences in housing, food, education, health, safety, and transportation. The third dimension, interaction with local nationals, involves adjusting to differences in behavioral norms, ways of dealing with conflict, communication patterns, and other relationship issues that can produce anger or frustration. An expatriate can experience some degree of culture shock associated with any or all of these three dimensions.

Phases of culture shock

Culture shock often consists of distinct phases, although not everyone progresses through all of the phases. These phases include:

- *The honeymoon phase:* This phase begins when one first encounters the new culture. During this phase, differences between the familiar and the new culture are seen in a positive way, things seem fascinating and wonderful (e.g., the new foods, pace of life, habits of the people). New experiences tend to be filtered through the lens of one's home culture, often relying on stereotypes to interpret the host culture.
- *The distress phase:* This phase, which can occur within a few days, weeks, or months of arrival, involves increasing annoyance with the minor, and sometimes great, differences between the old and new cultures. Common feelings include impatience, anger, sadness, and discontent during the process of transitioning between one's traditional old ways and the ways of the new country. Some people never break out of this phase, and in severe cases it can trigger an expatriate or family member to return home prematurely from an overseas assignment. Some people will reject the new culture and only remember the good things of their home culture. Much of their time may be spent speaking their own language, watching videos or television shows from their home country, eating traditional foods from home, and socializing only with other expatriates from the home country (often spending much of this time complaining about the host culture).
- *The acceptance phase:* For those who survive the second phase, or skip it completely, the next phase will involve becoming accustomed to the differences associated with the new culture, without reacting positively or negatively to the differences. As you gain some understanding of the new culture, some degree of pleasure may be felt about the culture, as well as some sense of psychological balance. You are more comfortable with the host country's language and customs, although there still may be difficulties, and you can begin to compare and evaluate the old ways versus the new ones.
- *The integration phase:* In this phase, you realize that the new culture has both bad and good things to offer, and you have a more substantive sense of belonging. Your focus returns to the basic concerns of everyday living and working and to establishing goals for living.
- *Reverse culture shock:* Once a person has grown accustomed to a new culture, returning to one's home culture can produce the same experiences as described in the preceding phases. Having become accustomed to things as they are in the host culture, you may find that you no longer feel fully at ease in your home culture. Things may have changed during your time abroad, and probably you yourself have changed in many ways. As a result, it often takes a while to successfully reacclimate.

Coping with culture shock

A number of suggestions have been made regarding how to deal effectively with culture shock. Some of the more common are:

- Prepare before departure, through such things as reading about the country and its culture, so that the new place and its people will seem more familiar once you arrive and you will be better prepared to deal with differences that you encounter.
- Be open-minded about the culture that you are visiting, and try to maintain a healthy, accepting attitude toward the new culture and the experiences you are having.
- Develop patience, avoid trying too hard, and practice relaxation and stress reduction techniques, such as exercise, meditation, and a healthy sense of humor.
- Maintain contact with the new culture, including learning the language and getting involved with social activities.
- Find cultural guides or mentors who can help you to learn and understand the new culture.
- Be attentive to relationships with your family and friends and at work to reinforce your support network during stressful periods.

Although adjusting to a new culture can be a frustrating and difficult process, it can also be a vibrant, renewing time of life, stimulating you to reconsider many aspects of your life and beliefs and allowing you to grow as a person.

Source: Lalervo Oberg, "Culture Shock and the Problem of Adjustment to New Cultural Environments," www.worldwide.edu/travel_planner/culture_shock.html (July 23, 2006); Duncan Mason, "Culture Shock: A Fish Out of Water," http://international.ouc.bc.ca/cultureshock/printext.htm (July 23, 2006); Margaret A. Shaffer, David A. Harrison, and K. Matthew Gilley, "Dimensions, Determinants, and Differences in the Expatriate Adjustment Process," *Journal of International Business Studies* 30, no. 3 (1999), pp.557–81; and "Culture Shock," http://edweb.sdsu.edu/people/CGuanipa/cultshok.htm (July 23, 2006).

give trailing spouses more help in adjusting. Such help may take the form of assisting with job hunting in the host country, writing CVs, providing language and cultural training, identifying career opportunities, or giving tips on local interview techniques. If all else fails, some companies even hire a trailing spouse themselves. An added complication is that in many countries, the employee's spouse does not have the legal right to work, as work permits for foreigners may be difficult or nearly impossible to acquire.

Expatriate Children May Suffer the Most Children are an important but often overlooked consideration when planning for an international move, parti-cularly since 45 percent of expats have children between the ages of 5 and 12.[20] Although an overseas stint may be seen as critical for career advancement of a parent, it can wreak havoc upon children's lives. Children are seldom involved in the initial decision making process associated with a move abroad. This can result in the children's experiencing many feelings, such as insecurity, frustration and powerlessness, from being uprooted from friends and many of the sources of their own identity. A move does not merely involve changing schools; there are also new systems, new learning styles, new language, and so forth, that the child must contend with. Sometimes these children are referred to as *third culture kids* (or *TCKs*) because they often speak several different languages, hold passports from more than one country, and have difficulty explaining where they are from (where "home" is). As a consequence of these challenges, companies are increasing their focus on easing the disruptions faced by children. For example, the Bennett Group, a Cendant Corporation unit in Chicago, gets the children of a family about to be transferred to a foreign city in touch with expatriate children who have already settled successfully into that city. There is even a Web site, www.Ori-and-Ricki.net, specifically designed for expatriate children.

LANGUAGE TRAINING

Foreign language skill has been shown to be a critical factor influencing effective adjustment of expatriates and their family members within the host country, and American companies are taking more seriously the language abilities of their employees. But neither they nor most Australian, British, Canadian, and New Zealand firms appear to be sufficiently serious about ensuring language fluency, since few ICs ensure that adequate time and resources are devoted to language training prior to or during international assignments. The English speakers appear to be stuck in a **language trap.**

language trap
A situation in which a person doing international business can speak only his or her home language

The English language has become the *lingua franca* of the world; in effect, it is everybody's second language. In China alone, up to one-fifth of the population is learning English. This does not mean that English has taken over life in other parts of the world. For example, according to the EU, only 47 percent of Western Europeans (including the British and Irish) speak English well enough to carry on a conversation. If you want to sell shampoo or cell phones, you have to do it in Danish, Finnish, French, German, Greek, Italian, Portuguese, Spanish, Swedish, or whatever the local language or dialect may be. Even the British and U.S. media companies that stand to benefit most from the spread of English have been hedging their bets; CNN broadcasts in Spanish, and the *Financial Times* has launched a daily German-language edition.

When you are trying to sell to potential customers, it is much better to speak their language. As English speakers try to sell abroad, it is far more likely that their customers will speak English than that the English speakers will be able to speak the customers' language. Customers can then hide behind their language during negotiations.

If your career involves international business—and few can avoid at least some exposure to it—it is likely to suffer to at least some extent if you speak English only. A survey carried out on behalf of the Community of European Management highlighted the value recruiters place on multilingual ability. A large majority responded that English alone is not sufficient.[21] Chinese language skills will become more and more useful and sought after. China is the world's most populous country, and there are very large numbers of Chinese—often businesspeople—living outside China. In coming decades, perhaps Chinese will become the new "hot" language to know.

BUILDING YOUR GLOBAL RÉSUMÉ — Speak a Foreign Language

The quickest way to identify yourself as a prospective international business professional is to speak a foreign language. As an American, speaking a foreign language puts you into an extremely small group of people who are bilingual, and being bilingual is a critical asset of the international business professional. U.S. Department of Education data show that:

- Less than 1 percent of American high school students study globally important languages such as Arabic, Chinese, Japanese, Farsi, Korean, Russian, or Urdu.
- More than 200 million Chinese are studying English, but only approximately 24,000 Americans study Chinese.

You don't need to speak like a native, but to at least be able to be conversant or conversational is typically looked upon favorably and seen as a sign of commitment by your foreign counterparts. Even though English is considered the "language of business," the ability to speak a foreign language gives you an advantage in dealing internationally and professionally—it puts you in the "priority group" on the international career track.

World Fact: There are approximately 6,800 languages spoken in the world, and with dialects, this number could exceed 10,000. Mandarin Chinese is spoken by the most people (836+ million), followed by Hindi (333+ million), Spanish (332+ million), and English (322+ million).

Culture Cue: In Japan and Pacific Rim countries, your business card is a critical and mandatory business tool. Treat it seriously. The information it typically contains should be accurately translated into the language of the country you are visiting, because your foreign counterparts will most likely be able to read both sides.

World Wide Resources:

www.solvit.org.uk

www.foreignword.com

REPATRIATION—THE SHOCK OF RETURNING HOME

There is often reverse culture shock when an expatriate returns to the home company and country. The expatriate will have gained new skills and knowledge, and the company's attitudes and people will have changed. Expatriates who have become accustomed to high levels of autonomy while abroad often struggle with the more restrictive work context when they return home, as well as experiencing the common frustration of failing to be promoted or have their job expectations fulfilled after repatriation.

That is why planning for an expat's return should start well before the overseas assignment even begins. The person and the employer should discuss up front how the assignment will fit the employee's long-range career goals and how the company will handle the return. When expats come back, companies have to understand that they are going to be different and harness their new knowledge.[22] Nevertheless, only 49 percent of ICs have repatriation programs, and 68 percent of expatriates report that they do not have any guaranteed position in their IC after the end of their international assignment.[23] "We are seeing rapid globalization, and it's going to become a real problem to find people who are willing and qualified to go overseas if everyone hears about people who were not satisfied" after they are repatriated, said Lisa Johnson, the director of consulting services for Cendant Mobility.[24]

Above, we spoke of the pain that is often suffered by an expat family's children; returning home can prove even more traumatic. That is especially true for those who have spent their formative years abroad. Repatriation counseling is available, which includes distinct children's programs and begins months before the family heads home.[25]

EXPATRIATE SERVICES

Although most U.S. expatriates currently continue health coverage with their company's domestic plans, we can expect that to change in the near future as expatriate health care programs are being created to assist companies and expatriates with claims administration, language translations, currency conversions, and service standardization.[26] Banks are also developing expatriate services, allowing expatriates to sign up for services online and providing 24-hour assistance to their customers, regardless of where in the world the expatriate is working.[27] Specialized companies are being developed to provide expatriate tax services.[28]

In recognition of expatriate family issues, some companies have begun to prepare and assist these families. Assistance may take the form of realistic job previews for expatriates (and sometimes for their family members), training in the culture and language of the host country, assistance in finding suitable schools or medical specialists, or even arranging for long-distance care for elderly relatives or parents while the family is living abroad. House-hunting help may be given, and the new transplants should be taken on grocery and hardware shopping trips with locals and expats who have been in the host country for a while. Locals can teach you the social norms and where to shop and not to shop. Expats can teach you where to get things only expats want. Web sites that focus on expatriate issues and can assist you in preparing for, adjusting to, or returning from an expatriate assignment include www.ExpatExpert.com and www.branchor.com.

An example of the types of organizations that can assist expatriates and their companies is a unit of Prudential Financial, called Prudential Relocation, which has 36 years of experience in relocation services. The unit promotes itself as being "a full-service global mobility management firm dedicated to supporting the recruitment, retention, and relocation of your most important asset: your human capital. We provide comprehensive, integrated domestic and international relocation services." The unit has 1,300 employees, fluent in 35 languages, who are focused on relocation issues across 82 nations.[29]

Compensation

Establishing a compensation plan that is equitable and consistent and yet does not overcompensate the overseas executive is a challenging, complex task, especially since a "one-size-fits-all" approach does not match up well with the reality of diverse company and country assignments. Rebecca Powers of Mercer Human Resource Consulting said, "More companies are now sending employees on expatriate assignments, so there is a greater need to keep pace with the cost of living changes. Employers need to be proactive in managing their expatriate programs to ensure they receive a proper return on their investment and employees are compensated fairly."[30] If ICs are not able to compensate in a manner that is perceived to be fair and attractive, it will become ever more difficult to attract the quantity and quality of potential expatriates needed to satisfy the company's international requirements.

The method favored by the majority of American ICs has been to pay a base salary equal to that paid to a domestic counterpart and then, in the belief that no one should be worse off for accepting foreign employment, to add a variety of allowances and bonuses. Table 20.2 provides an example of some of the compensation costs for sending an American manager on a two-year assignment to Russia. Many international assignments will entail significantly higher levels of additional costs, when compared to those in the home country, than suggested by this example.

© 1997 Roger Beale. Used by permission.

SALARIES

The practice of paying home country nationals the same salaries as their domestic counterparts permits worldwide consistency for this part of the compensation package. Because of the increasing use of third country nationals, those personnel are generally treated in the same way.

Some firms take the equal-pay-for-equal-work concept one step further and pay the same base salaries to host country nationals. In countries that legislate yearly bonuses and family allowances for their citizens, a local

TABLE 20.2 Total Compensation Costs for Sending an Expatriate American Manager to Russia

The following compensation costs are illustrative of those an IC might encounter annually when sending an American manager and his or her family (spouse, two children) to Russia for a two-year assignment.

Compensation Component	Annual Cost (US$)
Base salary	$150,000
Incentive plan	15,000
Location differential (hardship premium)	5,000
Housing allowance	75,200
Cost-of-living allowance	6,200
Automobile allowance	36,500
Home leave	10,000
Educational assistance	24,000
Relocation/repatriation expenses	22,000
Total compensation before tax	**$343,900**
Tax assistance	51,200
Total compensation expense	**$395,100**
Other Expenses	
Preparation services (passports, visas, language training, etc.)	2,800
Settling-in services	3,600
Emergency leave	6,000
Total annual cost for expatriate	**$407,500**

Source: "U.S. Firms Extend Global Reach," *Workforce Management*, December 2004, p. 142.

national may receive what appears to be a higher salary than is paid the expatriate, although companies usually make extra payments to prevent expatriates from falling behind in this regard. In the United Kingdom, it is the practice to pay executives relatively lower salaries and to provide them with expensive perquisites, such as chauffeured automobiles, housing, and club memberships. A number of American companies follow British practices in compensating their executives working in Britain.

ALLOWANCES

allowances
Employee compensation payments added to base salaries because of higher expenses encountered when living abroad

Allowances are payments made to compensate expatriates for the extra costs they must incur to live as well abroad as they did in the home country. The most common allowances are for housing, cost of living, tax differentials, education, and moving.

Housing Allowances

Housing allowances are designed to permit executives to live in houses as good as those they had at home. A common rule of thumb is for the firm to pay all of the rent that is in excess of 15 percent of the executive's salary.

Cost-of-Living Allowances

Cost-of-living allowances are based on differences in the prices paid for food, utilities, transportation, entertainment, clothing, personal services, and medical expenses overseas compared to the prices paid for these items in the headquarters' city. Many ICs use the U.S. Department of State index, which is based on the cost of these items in Washington, D.C., but have found it is not altogether satisfactory. For one thing, critics claim this index is not adjusted often enough to account for either the rapid inflation in some countries or the changes in relative currency values.

TABLE 20.3 Ranking of 50 Cities from Most to Least Expensive, 2006

Rank	City	Rank	City
1	Tokyo, Japan	26	Abidjan, Ivory Coast
2	Osaka, Japan	27	Warsaw, Poland
3	London, U.K.	28	Prague, Czech Republic
4	Moscow, Russia	29	Taipei, Taiwan
5	Seoul, South Korea	30	Shanghai, China
6	Geneva, Switzerland	31	Bratislava, Slovak Republic
7	Zürich, Switzerland	32	Düsseldorf, Germany
8	Copenhagen, Denmark	33	Luxembourg
9	Hong Kong	34	Singapore
10	Oslo, Norway	34	Frankfurt, Germany
11	Milan, Italy	36	Dakar, Senegal
12	Paris, France	37	Munich, Germany
13	New York City, USA	38	Berlin, Germany
13	Dublin, Ireland	39	Tel Aviv, Israel
15	St. Petersburg, Russia	40	Glasgow, U.K.
16	Vienna, Austria	41	Athens, Greece
17	Rome, Italy	41	Brussels, Belgium
18	Stockholm, Sweden	43	Barcelona, Spain
19	Beijing, China	44	Los Angeles, USA
20	Sydney, Australia	45	White Plains, USA
20	Helsinki, Finland	46	Madrid, Spain
22	Istanbul, Turkey	47	Birmingham, U.K.
22	Douala, Cameroon	48	Zagreb, Croatia
24	Amsterdam, Netherlands	49	Hamburg, Germany
24	Budapest, Hungary	50	Hanoi, Vietnam
		50	San Francisco, USA

Source: Used with permission Mercer Human Resource Counsulting, 2006 Cost-of-Living Survey, www.mercerhr.com/pressrelease/details.jhtml/dynamic/idContent/1142150 (July 23, 2006).

Another objection is that the index does not include many cities in which the firm operates. As a result, many companies take their own surveys or use data from the United Nations, the World Bank, the International Monetary Fund, or private consulting firms. Figures and comparisons on costs of living, prices, and wages can also be found in private publications. Table 20.3 provides a ranking of 50 cities, from most to least expensive as of 2006.

Allowances for Tax Differentials ICs pay tax differentials when the host country taxes are higher than the taxes that the expatriates would pay on the same compensation and consumption at home. The objective is to ensure that expatriates will not have less after-tax take-home pay in the host country than they would at home. This can create a considerable extra financial burden on an American parent company because, among other things, the U.S. Internal Revenue Code treats tax allowances as additional taxable income. There are other tax disincentives for Americans to work abroad.*

*For more on this subject and other effects of U.S. laws on American ICs, see the taxation section in Chapter 11.

Education Allowances

Expatriates are naturally concerned that their children receive educations at least equal to those they would get in their home countries, and many want their children taught in their native language. Primary and secondary schools with teachers from most industrialized home countries are available in many cities around the world, but these are private schools and therefore charge tuition. ICs either pay the tuition or, if there are enough expatriate children, operate their own schools. For decades, petroleum companies in the Middle East and Venezuela have maintained schools for their employees' children.

Moving and Orientation Allowances

Companies generally pay the total costs of transferring their employees overseas. These costs include transporting the family, moving household effects, and maintaining the family in a hotel on a full expense account until the household effects arrive. Some firms find it less expensive to send the household effects by air rather than by ship because the reduction in hotel expenses more than compensates for the higher cost of air freight. It has also been found that moving into a house sooner raises the employee's morale.

Companies may also pay for some orientation of the employees and their families. Companies frequently pay for language instruction, and some will provide the family with guidance on the intricacies of everyday living, such as shopping, hiring domestic help, and sending children to school.

BONUSES

bonuses
Expatriate employee compensation payments in addition to base salaries and allowances because of hardship, inconvenience, or danger

Bonuses (or *premiums*), unlike allowances, are paid by firms in recognition that expatriates and their families undergo some hardships and inconveniences and make sacrifices while living abroad. Bonuses include overseas premiums, contract termination payments, and home leave reimbursement.

Overseas Premiums

Overseas premiums are additional payments to expatriates and are generally established as a percentage of the base salary. They typically range from 10 to 25 percent. If the living conditions are extremely disagreeable, the company may pay larger premiums for hardship posts. The U.S. Department of State maintains a list of hardship differential pay premiums that is often used as a reference by ICs and expats. Table 20.4 shows the hardship differentials for selected cities as of 2006.

Contract Termination Payments

These payments are made as inducements for employees to stay on their jobs and work out the periods of their overseas contracts. The payments are made at the end of the contract periods only if the employees have worked out their contracts. Such bonuses are used in the construction and petroleum industries and by other firms that have contracts requiring work abroad for a specific period of time or for a specific project. They may also be used if the foreign post is a hardship or not a particularly desirable one.

Home Leave[31]

ICs that post home country—and sometimes third country—nationals in foreign countries make it a practice to pay for periodic trips back to the home country by such employees and their families. The reasons for this are twofold. One, companies do not want employees and their families to lose touch with the home country and its culture. Two, companies want to have employees spend at least a few days at company headquarters to renew relationships with headquarters' personnel and catch up with new company policies and practices.

Some firms grant three-month home leaves after an employee has been abroad about three years, but it is a more common practice to give two to four weeks' leave each year. All

TABLE 20.4 Hardship Differential Pay Premiums for Selected Cities and Countries, 2006

City and Country	Differential Pay Premium, %
Kabul, Afghanistan	25
Bahrain	10
Sarajevo, Bosnia-Herzegovina	15
Sao Paulo, Brazil	10
Sofia, Bulgaria	20
Beijing, China	15
Bogota, Columbia	5
Cairo, Egypt	15
Athens, Greece	5
Calcutta, India	25
Jakarta, Indonesia	25
Baghdad, Iraq	25
Tel Aviv, Israel	10
Seoul, Korea	5
Mexico City, Mexico	15
Lagos, Nigeria	25
Warsaw, Poland	5
Riyadh, Saudi Arabia	20
Johannesburg, South Africa	5
Columbo, Sri Lanka	20
Bangkok, Thailand	10
Istanbul, Turkey	10
Kiev, Ukraine	20
Caracas, Venezuela	15

Source: U.S. Department of State, "Hardship Differential and Danger Pay," January 2006, www.state.gov/m/a/als/qtrpt/60845.htm (July 23, 2006).

transportation costs are paid to and from the executive's hometown, and all expenses are paid during the executive's stay at company headquarters.

COMPENSATION PACKAGES CAN BE COMPLICATED

compensation packages
For expatriate employees, packages that can incorporate many types of payments or reimbursements and must take into consideration exchange rates and inflation

One might think from the discussion to this point that **compensation packages,** while costly—the extras frequently total 50 percent or more of the base salary—are fairly straightforward in their calculation. Nothing could be further from the truth.

What Percentage?

All allowances and a percentage of the base salary are usually paid in the host country currency. What should this percentage be? In practice, it varies from 65 to 75 percent, with the remainder being banked wherever the employee wishes. One reason for such practices is to decrease the local portion of the salary, thereby lowering host country income taxes and giving the appearance to government authorities and local employees that there is less difference between the salaries of local and foreign employees than is actually the case. Another reason is that expatriate employees have various expenses that must be paid in home country currency. Such expenses may include professional society memberships, purchases during home leave, payments on outstanding debts in the employee's home country (e.g., mortgage, school loans), and tuition and other costs for children in home country universities.

What Exchange Rate? Inasmuch as most of the expatriate's compensation is usually denominated in the host country currency but established in terms of the home country currency to achieve comparable compensation throughout the enterprise, a currency exchange rate must be chosen. In countries whose currencies are freely convertible into other currencies, this presents no serious problem, although the experienced expatriate will argue that an exchange rate covers only international transactions and may not represent a true purchasing power parity between the local and home country currencies. For instance, such items as bread and milk are rarely traded internationally, and living costs and inflation rates may be much higher in the host country than in the home country. International companies attempt to compensate for such differences in the cost-of-living allowances.

More difficult problems must be solved in countries that have exchange controls and nonconvertible currencies. Without exception, those currencies are overvalued at the official rate, and if the firm uses that rate, its expatriate employees are certain to be shortchanged. Reference may be made to the free market rate for the host country currency in free currency markets in, for example, the United States or Switzerland or to the black market rate in the host country, but these do not give the final answers. In the end, all companies must pay their expatriate employees enough to enable them to live as well as others who have similar positions in other firms, regardless of how the amount is calculated.

A common compensation component at many American companies is a stock plan that gives employees opportunities to acquire the company's stock on favorable terms. Such programs are designed to increase loyalty and productivity, but they sometimes run into problems outside the United States.

Share ownership is unknown or restricted in numerous countries. PepsiCo's vice president of compensation and benefits says, "We had to develop a customized approach in every country we operate in." DuPont discovered it could not give stock options in 25 of 53 nations, primarily because those countries' laws ban or limit ownership of foreign shares.

COMPENSATION OF THIRD COUNTRY NATIONALS

Although some companies have different compensation plans for third country nationals, there is a trend toward treating them the same as home country expatriates. In either event, there are areas in which problems can arise. One of these areas is the calculation of income tax differentials when an American expatriate is compared with an expatriate from another country, a situation exacerbated by tax changes passed by the U.S. Congress in 2006.[32] This results from the unique American government practice of taxing U.S. citizens even though they live and work abroad and treating tax differential payments made to those citizens as additional taxable income. No other major country taxes its nationals in those ways.

Another possible problem area is the home leave bonus. The two purposes of home leave are to prevent expatriates from losing touch with their native cultures and to have them visit IC headquarters. A third country national must visit two countries instead of only one to achieve both purposes, and the additional costs can be substantial. Compare the cost of sending an Australian employee home from Mexico with that required to send an American from Mexico to Dallas.

Regardless of problems, the use of third country nationals is growing in popularity. As businesses race to enlarge their ranks of qualified international managers, third country nationals are in greater demand. They often win jobs because they speak several languages and know an industry or country well.

As the number of third country nationals employed as executives by ICs continues to grow, the possible combinations of nationalities and host countries are virtually limitless, further complicating compensation efforts.

INTERNATIONAL STATUS

In all of this discussion, we have been describing compensation for expatriates who have been granted **international status.** Merely being from another country does not automatically qualify an employee for all the benefits we have mentioned. A subsidiary may hire home country nationals or third country nationals and pay them the same as it pays host country employees. However, managements have found that although an American, for example, may agree initially to take a job and be paid on the local scale, sooner or later bad feeling and friction will develop as that person sees fellow Americans enjoying international status perquisites to which he or she is not entitled.

international status
Entitles the expatriate employee to all the allowances and bonuses applicable to the place of residence and employment

Sometimes firms promote host country employees to international status even without transferring them abroad. This is a means of rewarding valuable people and preventing them from leaving the company for better jobs elsewhere.

Thus, international status means being paid some or all of the allowances and bonuses we have discussed, and there can be other sorts of payments as individual circumstances and people's imaginations combine to create them. Compensation packages for expatriates and other international executives are sufficiently important and complicated to have become a specialization in the personnel management field; at one firm, the title is "international employee benefits consultant." Help is also available from outside the IC. From time to time, the large consulting firms publish pamphlets advising about the transfer of executives to specific countries.

PERKS

Perks originated in the perquisites of the medieval lords of the manor, whose workers paid parts of their profits or produce to the lords to be allowed to continue working. Today, perks are symbols of rank in the corporate hierarchy and are used to compensate executives while minimizing taxes. Among the most common perks are:

Cars, which may include chauffeurs, especially for executives higher up the organization ladder.

Private pension plan.

Retirement payment.

Life insurance.

Health insurance.

Emergency evacuation services (for medical or other reasons).

Kidnapping insurance.

Company house or apartment.

Directorship of a foreign subsidiary.

Seminar holiday travel.

Club memberships.

Hidden slush fund (such funds may be illegal, but some corporations are said to have them).

WHAT'S IMPORTANT TO YOU?

While working abroad as an executive of an American multinational, one of the authors had a colleague who was an American expatriate married to a French woman. They had raised a family in several countries where they had been assigned by the company. Together with some other cosmopolites, they devised a table of items deemed important to at least one of them in choosing a city for the location of a company facility that employs foreigners.

The list included the usual items, such as cost of living, safety of personnel, medical facilities, housing, and schools. It also included such other items as availability of good wine at reasonable prices, quality of theater and whether it was live or cinema, number and type of one-star or better *(Michelin Guide)** restaurants, type and accessibility of sports facilities for both participants and viewers, and shopping facilities for fashionable clothes.

The table of items was circulated informally throughout the firm's many locations, and many cities in its network were graded as to each item on a 1-to-10 scale. When the New York headquarters saw the table, there was much mirth and merriment; suggestions—perhaps not all of them serious—were made as to additional items about which they would like information when they visited the cities.

However, the mirth and merriment subsided as more and more executives being assigned or reassigned abroad used the table to demand better compensation packages. Some even refused transfers because of the ratings given a city.

Also important to employees may be the number of vacation days they are likely to get from country to country. As to vacation days, Europeans are well ahead of Americans and Japanese. The minimum number of legally mandated paid days of vacation for full-time workers who have worked for at least one year in a company is 10 in Japan, while in France and Sweden it is five weeks, in Germany, the Netherlands, and Ireland it is four weeks, and in Spain it is 30 days. The U.S. has no national requirement, but the average ranges from 8 days at small private companies to 10 days at medium and large-size companies.[33]

Also of importance in decisions on where to locate a business operation are considerations such as cost of living, business environment, and office rents. Table 20.3 shows cost-of-living comparisons for a number of the world's cities. The survey compares the prices of goods and services typically consumed by the families of executives being sent abroad. You will note that although Tokyo, Osaka, and London are the most expensive, many of the cities ranked in the top 50 are located in emerging countries.

Despite labor market problems and less attractive market opportunities, the quality of the business environment in West European and North American countries remains higher than that in most emerging markets because those countries possess sophisticated institutions, such as advanced financial sectors, reliable legal systems, and political stability, that companies value.

There are numerous sources of information available about living, managing, and working abroad. One is Meridian Resources Associates, which offers a range of Web-based and other resources to prepare managers for successful performance in international contexts. For example, Meridian's highly acclaimed Web-based "GlobeSmart" program is a Web tool providing business managers with quick and easy access to extensive knowledge on over 50 topics in order to help the trainee conduct business effectively with people from 40 countries around the world. Other titles available from Meridian include "Managing in China," "Working with China," "Working with Japan," "Globally Speaking," "Working with Americans," "Living in Asia," "Assignment USA," and "Information on Consulting and Training Services." Meridian can be contacted by phone at 1-800-626-2047 or 1-415-321-7900 or at www.meridianglobal.com.

*The *Michelin Guide* rates restaurants and hotels in France and neighboring countries.

Summary

Discuss the importance of creating a company "global mind-set."

Successful managers in international companies must demonstrate a combination of high knowledge differentiation and high knowledge integration.

Explain the relationship between competitive strategies (home replication, multidomestic, regional, and transnational) and international human resource management approaches (ethnocentric, polycentric, regiocentric, and global).

Recognize that competitive strategy should be a primary determinant of the IHRM policies that an IC will use.

Compare home country, host country, and third country nationals as IC executives.

Sources of IC executives may be the home country, host countries, or third countries, and their differing culture, language, ability, and experience can strengthen IC management.

Explain the difficulties of finding qualified executives for international companies (ICs) and the importance of foreign language knowledge.

Knowledge of a people's language is essential to understand its culture and to know what's going on, as every effective manager must.

Explain what an expatriate is and some of the challenges and opportunities of an expat position.

Expatriate positions allow employees to work in foreign locations, which can provide the foundation for learning and growth, both personally and professionally, and a basis for movement upward in an organization's hierarchy. Expats can also find themselves "out of sight, out of mind," with unclear performance objectives and bases for performance evaluation. The families of many expatriates find the adjustment to a foreign posting difficult to manage successfully.

Explain the increasing importance of accommodating the trailing spouse of an expatriate executive.

The growing prevalence of two-career families is complicating problems of accommodating the spouse of an executive who is being transferred to another country.

Identify some of the complications of compensation packages for expatriate executives.

Expatriate manager compensation packages can be extremely complicated. Among other sources of complications are fluctuating currency exchange rates and differing inflation rates. Basic elements of those packages are salaries, allowances, and bonuses.

Key Words

expatriate (p. 542)
global mind-set (p.542)
ethnocentric (p. 543)
polycentric (p. 543)
regiocentric (p. 543)
geocentric (p. 543)
home country national (p. 543)
parent country national (PCN) (p. 543)
host country national (HCN) (p. 543)
third country national (TCN) (p. 545)
language trap (p. 553)
allowances (p. 556)
bonuses (p. 558)
compensation packages (p. 559)
international status (p. 561)

Questions

1. Why should the international human resource management approaches used by an international company be closely linked to the competitive strategy the company is using?
2. Compare and contrast ethnocentric, polycentric, regiocentric, and geocentric staffing policies.
3. In staffing a multinational organization for service outside the IC home country, what are some advantages and disadvantages of hiring home country personnel?
4. Why has there been an increasing use of third country nationals in the foreign operations of ICs?

5. Why are problems involving the trailing spouses of expatriate executives so common? What are some companies doing to solve those problems?

6. What is the English language trap?

7. Why are expatriate employees frequently paid more than their colleagues at equivalent job levels in the home office?

8. Why are compensation packages for expatriates more complicated than those for domestic employees?

9. What are some of the quality-of-life issues executives should consider before taking their families into an expatriate experience?

10. Suppose you are the CEO of an American multinational. On your staff and in the U.S. operating divisions of your company are several bright, able, dedicated female executives. They are also ambitious, and in your company, international experience is a must before an executive can hope to get into top management. An opening comes up for the position of executive vice president in the company's Mexican subsidiary. One of the women on your staff applies for the position, and she is well qualified for the job, better than anyone else in the company. Would you give her the position? What are the arguments pro and con?

11. Using the company example in question 10, suppose another position becomes available, this one as treasurer of the Japanese subsidiary. The chief financial officer of the company's California division applies for this job. She has performed to everyone's satisfaction, and she seems thoroughly qualified to become the treasurer in Japan. In addition, she speaks and writes Japanese. She is the daughter of a Japanese mother and an American father, and they encouraged her to become fluent in both English and Japanese. Would you give her the job? Why or why not?

Research Task

globalEDGE.msu.edu 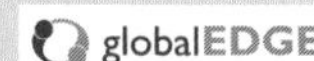

Use the globalEDGE site (http://globalEDGE.msu.edu/) to complete the following exercises:

1. Mercer HR Consulting measures the overall *Quality of Living* for many cities worldwide. Locate the report and find the cities ranking highest and lowest. Also, provide a brief explanation on what measures are included in determining a city's quality of living and how multinational corporations can use this information.

2. The text discusses the importance of establishing a good compensation plan for foreign employment. Using the *Quarterly Reports for Living Costs Abroad*, published by the U.S. Department of State, provide a report comparing the cities of Melbourne and Lima.

Minicase 20.1 Casey Miller: Should She Accept an International Assignment?

Casey Miller, a 37-year-old manager with Techtonics International, had just returned to her office early on a Thursday afternoon. During a lunchtime meeting in the company's executive lunchroom, her boss had just offered her a chance to move to Shanghai, China, where she would be in charge of establishing the company's new office for the East Asia region. As she sat at her desk looking out over the Los Angeles skyline, she was filled with a mix of excitement and trepidation. Should she accept the position she was offered? Or should she pass on this opportunity and wait for something else in the future? What factors should she consider in making this important decision?

Casey had joined Techtonics shortly after completing her bachelor's degree in business, starting as an assistant sales manager. Since then, she had been promoted several times and was now the vice president in charge of North American operations for one of Techtonics's main business areas, overseeing a work force of more than 2,100 people and sales in excess of $500 million. Identified as one of the "rising stars" in Techtonics, and mentored by one of the senior vice presidents of the company, she seemed to have no limits to her career path.

Casey had always dreamed of living and working abroad. As a student, she studied abroad for a semester in Spain and spent a month afterward traveling around Europe with several friends. After graduation, she worked on a six-month internship with AIESEC, working for a small exporting company based in Poland. Since joining Techtonics, her international experience had primarily consisted of business trips to Canada or Mexico, attending several conferences and visiting a few selected client companies in Europe and Asia, and going on two extended vacations: one to Thailand and another to the Caribbean. When her boss mentioned the possibility of going to China, she could barely contain her enthusiasm!

However, Casey also began to think about her family and how an international assignment might impact them. Her husband,

Jerry, was an accountant in the Los Angeles office of a large accounting firm. Although he had a successful career, she thought that he might be open to a change. She also had two children: Jerry, Jr., who was 8, and Susan, who was 12. How would they respond to moving to a new country? Would now be a good time for such a move, or would it be better to wait for a few years?

And what if she was to accept the offer to go to China? What issues would she need to discuss with the company regarding the implications of a move to China? Her boss said that he would like to have Casey's decision within about a week and that she would need to move to Shanghai within four to six months if she accepted the job.

As she watched the traffic begin to jam up on the freeway outside her office building, Casey thought about reaching for her cell phone and calling her good friend for advice on how to deal with the job opportunity that she had been offered.

If you were a good friend of Casey Miller, what recommendation would you give regarding whether she should accept the international assignment that has been offered to her and what issues she should focus on in making such a decision?

21 Financial Management and Accounting

Quick decisions are unsafe decisions.

—*Sophocles, 496–406 BC*

Arrange whatever pieces come your way.

—*Virginia Woolf*

Chinese IPOs Abandon New York

Just after his appointment as chairman of the U.S. Securities and Exchange Commission, Christopher Cox told a room filled with Chinese financial regulators and politicians in Beijing that their country's capitalism was in danger of meeting the same end as did the Qing dynasty. It was a bloody end that closed China's imperial age in 1911.

We have all learned to be polite to our hosts, a lesson easily forgotten when you are annoyed. The SEC chairman was annoyed with China's approach to its financial markets, as are many internationally focused financiers in the United States. And he let his annoyance show, another cultural gaffe. China has chosen to stay away from, or protect its capital markets and companies from, foreign influence. That means less business for the U.S. exchanges and banks—a lot less business, so it appears.

The China Construction Bank went to the Hong Kong market in late 2005 with an initial public offering (IPO) of $9.2 billion, the largest single offering in five years. This looks like the beginning of a trend. According to the consulting company McKinsey, the next entries into the top 100 global company lists will come from Asian emerging markets. That Asian stock exchanges could dwarf New York is a reasonable concern for Christopher Cox. In the last year alone, Chinese companies have raised more than US$14 billion through IPOs based in Hong Kong. That is larger than the total amount Chinese companies have raised in New York in the past 10 years, $12 billion.

Investment bankers explain China's preference for Hong Kong as a desire to avoid the high-cost U.S. burdens of regulation and compliance, most of which they attribute to the Sarbanes-Oxley Act, the demanding corporate reporting legislation the United States introduced in the wake of a series of financial scandals. These rules are blamed because they add costs and legal risks. The *Financial Times* reports that an Asian finance director "estimates the extra cost of employing lawyers and accountants to comply with the legislation at tens of millions of dollars a year."* In addition, the Sarbanes-Oxley rules put quoted companies at additional risk of costly, time-consuming class action suits. One of the reasons Asian companies liked to list in the United States was the prestige that came with doing so, and another was the available liquidity. But with the China Construction bank listing, it looks as if there's enough liquidity in Hong Kong to support major offerings. That offering drew in US$80 billion of demand from investors across the globe.

In markets that restrict foreign ownership of investments, such as India and Taiwan, companies have issued global depository receipts, which are traded on global markets but held by local banks, and thus, legally, they are traded as domestic shares.

The paradox, that increasing globalization of capital flows is marginalizing New York's financial market, may lead these very markets to more international involvement through mergers and acquisitions of the markets themselves.

In Chapters 5 and 11, we spoke of some of the major financial forces international managers face in their daily operations. Now we look at how managers deal with these forces. We begin with the major financial management issue, how the company's capital is structured, and then move to cash management strategies, including multilateral netting and strategies created by

CONCEPT PREVIEWS

After reading this chapter, you should be able to:

explain capital structure choices and their potential impact on the MNC

describe the process of multilateral netting and what its contribution is to cash flow management

describe the importance of leading and lagging in cash flow management

categorize foreign exchange risks into transaction exposure, translation exposure, and economic exposure

describe the basic idea of a swap transaction and its various applications

explain a currency swap contract and its usefulness to the financial manager

recognize the usefulness and dangers of using derivatives

explain the role of and approaches to sales without money

identify the major challenges faced in international accounting

describe the international accounting standards' convergence process and its importance

Gli Affari Internazionali
nales
nales Geschäft Παγοσμιο Business
Negócios Internacionais Los Negócios Internacionais
ernacionales Affaires Internationales 國際商務 Παγοσμιο Business

currency fluctuations. Other financial management issues that have direct impact on the financial management of the firm are taxation and transfer pricing. Because accounting practices and standards change across national borders, we conclude with a look at some of these differences and the move toward convergence of standards in international accounting. In our discussion, when we describe specific practices, we will do so using the U.S. MNC for the sake of simplicity, remembering that MNCs can be any nationality. ■

*Francesco Guerrera and Andrei Postelnicu, "A Not So Foreign Exchange: China Shuns the West as a Location for Its Big Corporate Share Offers," *Financial Times*, November 18, 2005, p. 13.

Capital Structure of the Firm

We have seen that firms are becoming increasingly international in their markets and their sourcing in order to exploit attractive opportunities. Such an opportunity is also available for the capital structure of the firm, and, increasingly, chief financial officers (CFO) have been tapping international financial markets, both public and private. In fact, the private equity market has been growing by leaps and bounds.[1] Because financial markets are not globally integrated, varying opportunities arise among them with varying costs. So if a CFO can raise capital in a foreign market at a lower cost than that in the home market, such an opportunity may be attractive as a way to increase shareholder value.

The firm raises capital through its retained earnings and then, externally, through either equity, the issuing of shares, or debt (leveraging). Many firms choose to issue stocks in foreign markets, in part to tap into a broader investor pool, which can raise the stock price and reduce the cost of capital. This also may have a significant marketing advantage, raising the profile of the brand name abroad. Foreign companies that have issued shares in the United States include Unilever, Fuji Film, Canadian Pacific, KLM, Sony, Toyota, and Cemex. Sometimes, foreign shares are directly traded in the American stock markets, but many times, they are traded in the form of **American depository receipts (ADRs),** the U.S. version of the global depository receipts mentioned above. These receipts represent shares that are held by the custodian, usually an American bank, in the stock's home market. They are denominated in dollars and traded on the U.S. exchange, eliminating the need to have a broker in the country of issue and the issue of currency exchange. Because there is concern about foreigners having control of domestic assets, in some countries there may be restrictions on foreign ownership of equity. These restrictions are more prevalent in developing countries. For example, in India, Mexico, and Indonesia, foreign ownership in specific sectors is limited to 49 percent. Some sectors in developed nations are also protected from foreign ownership, often through an approval process. Such is the case in the United States and in the United Kingdom. For example, in the United States in 2006, Dubai Ports World, a major United Arab Emirates–based shipping and cargo firm, withdrew its $6.8 billion acquisition bid for the British Peninsular & Oriental Steam Navigation Co. of London. The British firm had been running portions of six major U.S. ports, and the security concerns in the United States became a public issue. Rather than face almost certain rejection at the government approval stage, Dubai Ports withdrew its bid for the U.S. portion of the British business. Another example is U.S. airlines, which must be directed and operationally controlled by a U.S. citizen.[2]

American depository receipts (ADRs)
Foreign shares held by a custodian, usually a U.S. bank, in the issuer's home market and traded in dollars on the U.S. exchange

Debt markets are the other source of capital for the firm, and increasingly the tendency is to tap local markets first. That may mean that a foreign subsidiary of the Japanese firm Toyota would look first to its foreign market in the United States for funds to use in the U.S. operations. In this area, multinational corporations (MNCs) have an advantage over purely domestic companies because, in addition to obtaining funds at the corporate level, they can explore borrowing in their domestic and international debt markets, increasing the opportunities to reduce the cost of capital. They also have access to **offshore financial centers,** locations that specialize in financing by nonresidents, where the taxation levels are low and the banking regulations are slim. Switzerland, the Cayman Islands, Hong Kong, and the Bahamas are examples of offshore financial centers.

offshore financial center
Location that specializes in financing nonresidents, with low taxes and few banking regulations

Debt financing is thought to be less expensive than is equity financing, since the interest paid on the debt is usually tax-deductible, while dividends paid out to investors are not. Yet the choice of debt or equity financing is also influenced by local practice.

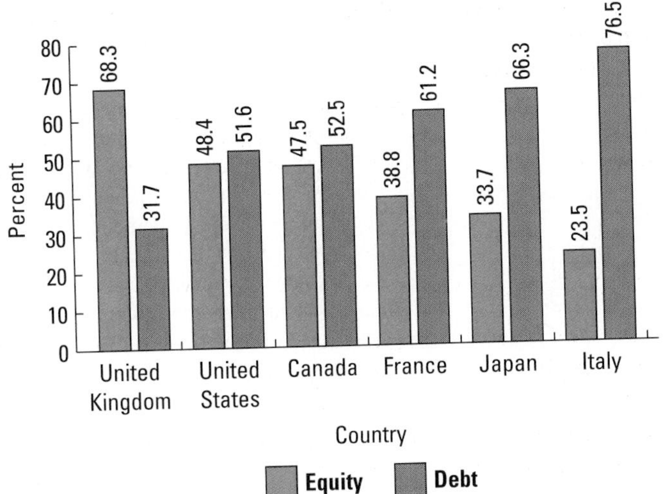

FIGURE 21.1

Capital Structure Percentages for Selected Countries

Source: Adapted from S. Besley and E. Brigham, *Essentials of Managerial Finance* (Mason, OH: Thompson South-Western, 2005), chap. 9.

Companies in the United States, the United Kingdom, and Canada tend to rely on equity more heavily than do companies in many other countries. Figure 21.1 illustrates the different equity and debt capital structures of firms in selected countries. In both Japan and Germany, banks traditionally play a more central role than do the stock markets in the financing picture. In Japan, we find the interlocking relationships of the *keiretsu*, where related companies in a larger family, such as Mitsubishi, Sumitomo, and C. Itoh, are connected with interlocking ownership of stocks and bonds, with the company bank at their center. Essentially, this structure eliminates the stakeholder conflicts between bondholders and stockholders, an appropriate characteristic for a national culture where harmony is an important cultural value.

In addition to differing tax treatments and local practices, other country-level policies may influence the firm's capital sturcture. Exchange controls may limit dividend payments to foreign equity holders, and national policies designed to encourage local reinvenstment may control the remission of dividends.

Decsions a financial manager would make in the process of raising capital are:

1. In what currency should the capital be raised, considering an estimate of its long-term strength or weakness?
2. How should the capital raised be structured between equity and debt?[3]
3. What are the sources of capital available? Should money be borrowed from a commercial bank by an ordinary loan, a bank as part of a swap, another company as part of a swap, another part of the MNC, or a public offering in one of the world's capital markets, for example, in the New York or Eurobond market?
4. If the decision is made to use one of the world's capital markets, management must then decide in which of those markets it can achieve its objectives at the lowest cost. The MNC can shop among the national markets in such diverse centers as New York, London, Paris, Zurich, Bahrain, Singapore, Tokyo, and the Cayman Islands.
5. Are there other sources of money available? For example, if the company is in a joint venture operation, the joint venture partner may be a source of money. Or perhaps there is private capital available. This source of funds is rapidly internationalizing. Or if the move is into a country or area that wants the MNC's technology or management knowledge, or the jobs that will be created, the government may be a source of low-cost funds. Under such circumstances, the company may also be able to negotiate tax reductions or holidays.

mini MNE

>>Microloans: Debt That Is Almost Always Paid in Full

With the help of PADME, an ACCION partner in the West African country of Benin, Fatouma Dijbril Issifou was able to obtain a loan and make more profit selling vegetables. She is now able to save money to fulfill her dreams and comfortably provide for her family.

You might think it would be utter folly to lend money to a developing country. What about a loan to a new small business or entrepreneur such as a vegetable stand or a tailor in a developing country?

Worldwide, development organizations are finding that some of the world's poorest entrepreneurs repay their debts at rates approaching 100 percent. To encourage grassroots private business in Latin America, Asia, and Africa, these organizations are expanding programs that already lend thousands of small entrepreneurs amounts ranging from $50 to several hundred dollars. Tiny businesses in developing countries commonly repay these "microloans" faithfully because of community pressure and the security of a favorable credit rating. Microloans rescue them from the clutches of loan sharks and let them borrow again in hard times. The money helps them start or expand their businesses—selling vegetables, sewing, repairing shoes, making furniture, and the like—and boosts their local economies.

The micro-credit concept was developed by Professor Muhammad Yunus, a U.S. trained PhD economist, through the Grameen Bank in Bangladesh, which he established to administer his program, and ACCION, a U.S. micro-credit organization. Dr. Yunus was awarded the Nobel Peace Prize in 2006.

The microloan repayment performance shines when compared with that of some sovereign nations. It also looks mighty good compared with a default rate of 5.4 percent among U.S. recipients of federally guaranteed student loans. ACCION reports a repayment rate over the life of its program of 97 percent.

ACCION International spokesperson Gabriela Romanow cites the case of Aaron Aguilar, an unemployed factory worker in Monterrey, Mexico, who borrowed $100 to buy clay and glazes for making figurines with his wife in their backyard. In six years, the couple took out and repaid five loans and built their business to 18 full-time employees.

Sometimes borrowers have to struggle against setbacks that might seem weird in a developed nation. One group of women in Cameroon received $100 from Trickle Up, another microloan agency, to start a rabbit-breeding business, but the rabbit ate her offspring, recalls Mildred Leet, Trickle Up's cofounder. Undaunted, the women switched to chickens and made enough money selling eggs to branch out into tomatoes and tailoring, ultimately opening two shops.

AVERAGE LOAN: LATIN AMERICA—$634; AFRICA—$594; UNITED STATES—$3,647

Fatouma Dijbril Issifou, a client of ACCION partner PADME in Parakou, Benin, sold vegetables as a child, along with her mother, in Benin, West Africa. Fatouma inherited the stall and was ready to live the subsistence life that had passed on to her. She knew, though, that if she could expand her business, her children could go to school. She learned about PADME from a friend. PADME saw Fatouma's drive and approved her for a loan of $130. She used it to buy bulk vegetables at lower costs. A second loan for $260 allowed for inventory expansion. She reports earnings of about $2 on a bushel of carrots and a little more for a kilo of potatoes.

This may not seem like much, but for Fatouma, the loans made a huge difference. Before the loans, she was able to save just $13 a year to invest in her tiny stand, and she struggled to support her three children. Today, two of them are in school, and the youngest is eager to follow in their footsteps. "The loans have helped me a lot," she says. "I can buy medicine and there is enough food for the children. Now, I don't worry anymore."

Critics point out, though, that one microloan is not going to pull a budding entrepreneur out of poverty, let alone a whole country. As ACCION's examples show, a series of loans is probably necessary, combined with training and support. When Tufts University received an endowment to set up a microloan program, specialists were ready to warn Tufts of the ethical aspects of microloans: Its program needs to be much more than banking.

Source: www.ACCION.org (July 8, 2006); Rashmi Dyal-Chand, "The Pitfalls of Microlending," *Boston Globe*, November 13, 2005, www.boston.com/news/globe/editorial_opinion/oped/articles/2005/11/13/the_pitfalls_of_microlending (July 7, 2006).

6. How much money does the company need and for how long? For instance, if the company is moving into a new market or product, there will probably be a period during product introduction or plant construction when the new venture will need more capital than it can generate.

Cash Flow Management

The management of cash flows is an important part of international financial management that differs from the management of cash and cash flows in a purely domestic firm, although there are some basic commonalities. For example, all firms would want to source funds in low-cost markets and place excess funds where they would get the best return. The global cash management picture is more complex than that of a domestic firm due to the number of national locations in which the firm has subsidiaries. For an MNC, operating in 25 local currencies is not uncommon. Two common cash flow management techniques used are multilateral netting and leading and lagging.

MULTILATERAL NETTING

In addition to the currencies, the types of cash flows associated with subsidiaries can vary as well, including loans from the parent to the subsidiary and increased investment in the form of equity capital. The flows from the subsidiary back to the parent might include cash from sales, dividends, royalties, and fees. One common strategy for cash management is **multilateral netting.** Multilateral netting is a centralized approach in which subsidiaries transfer their net cash flows within the company to a cash center that disperses cash to net receivers.

multilateral netting Strategy in which subsidiaries transfer net intracompany cash flows through a centralized clearing center

Why should companies consider this centralized process? First of all, the transfer of funds has a cost attached to it, called the *transaction cost,* and the funds while in transit are not working for the company. By reducing the transfer transactions, the costs are reduced and there are fewer foreign exchange transactions, as well. They too, have a cost. Netting would require each subsidiary with a net payable position to transfer its funds to a central account once a month, where the central account manager would then transfer funds to the net receivers. Compare the two approaches in Figure 21.2. Without netting, reconciling the positions would require eight transactions and $1.2 million in transit. With netting, there are four transactions, and 600,000 in transit. Plus, the foreign exchange transaction costs are reduced.

LEADING AND LAGGING

Sometimes, especially in developing economies, the government might prohibit currency conversion or the repatriation of profits or royalties. This could be caused by low foreign reserves and evidenced by a worsening trade account balance. Such host government actions leave the MNC unable to move cash assets out of the country, not a good position to be in when the reason for making the foreign investment in the first place is to provide returns to the shareholders.

FIGURE 21.2 Advantages of Multilateral Netting

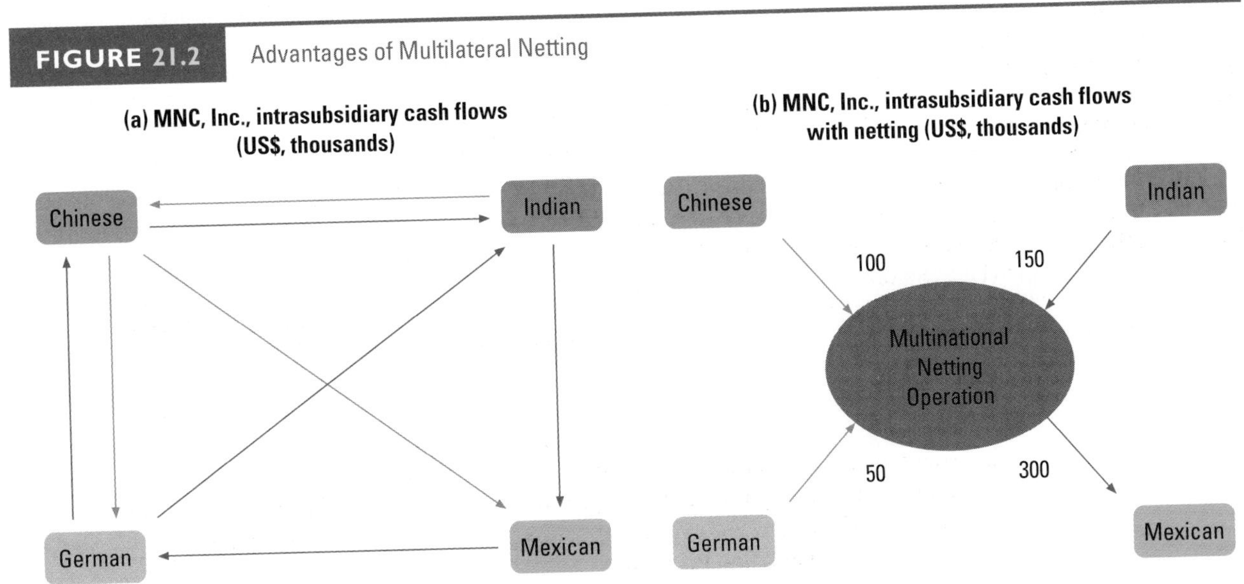

mini MNE

>>An Integrated Approach to Risk

MNEs set up centralized finance departments in the 1970s, and they have tended to look at risks in isolation. They have hedged foreign exchange and developed an interest rate strategy, for example, but they have looked at these risks separately. The next step will be to pull all the risk analysis together and centralize it. That might mean looking at commodity trends, currencies, and interest rates, as well as pension commitments, from a central, companywide perspective. Smaller companies will have an easier time of doing this, since one of the barriers to such integration is internal territoriality and company politics. For example, shifting the analysis of commodity price increase risk in an MNC from the procurement department to the corporate finance department or treasury would be a formidable challenge, as would moving the pension analysis out of the human resource department.

Source: Gillian Tett, "The Corporate View: Treasury: Living in a Time of Great Challenge," *Financial Times*, May 31, 2006, p. 5.

blocked funds
Funds whose conversion from a host currency or repatriation is not allowed by a host government

There are several ways to address the issue of **blocked funds.** One useful technique is **leading and lagging,** which involves the timing of payments. A lead approach is to collect receivables early when the foreign currency is expected to weaken and fund payables early when the foreign currency is expected to strengthen. A lag approach is to collect receivables late when the currency is expected to strengthen and fund payables late when the currency is expected to weaken. Leading and lagging can be coordinated among MNC subsidiaries to reposition funds and help to compensate for blocked funds or funds about to be blocked.

leading and lagging
Timing payments early (lead) or late (lag), depending on anticipated currency movements, so that they have the most favorable impact for company

In addition to leading and lagging, another way to deal with blocked funds includes using the blocked funds to purchase goods on the local market and then export them. Such exports might include air travel on a domestic carrier of the government blocking funds for the MNC worldwide, paying for such travel in local, blocked currency and having business meetings in the country where the funds are blocked, so that these funds are expended for corporate purposes.

Foreign Exchange Risk Management

When operating across different currencies, MNC managers regularly encounter currency exchange rate movements. These unanticipated shifts present risks to the international business because they represent unplanned-for changes in the value of assets and liabilities. These significant risks are usually categorized into three types: transaction exposure, translation exposure, and economic exposure. These exposures result in positions that are either uncovered or covered, that is, hedged.

TRANSACTION EXPOSURE

transaction exposure
Change in the value of a financial position created by foreign currency changes between the establishment and the settlement of a contract

Transaction exposure occurs when the firm has transactions denominated in a foreign currency. The exposure is due to currency exchange rate fluctuations between the time the commitment is made and the time it is payable. For example, an order for German diesel truck engines is placed by a Massachusetts company, for payment in 180 days in euros, €150,000 (US$189,000 at the then-prevailing exchange rate of $1.26 per euro). If the euro strengthens against the dollar to $1.38 when the company converts its dollars to euro, the engines' price in dollar terms would increase by $18,000 to US$207,000. In this case, there would be a cash flow effect for the importer but no effect for the exporter. Had the exporter quoted the engines' price in U.S. dollars, the situation would have been reversed.

The key issue with a transaction exposure is that the business has made a contract to pay or accept payment in another currency. An initial observation is that the company could avoid this exposure by refusing to enter into such contracts. Yet the desire to conduct business across currency borders suggests a willingness to accept this risk. One party will always have to, and doing so might be a part of the contract negotiation strategy. There are other approaches to dealing with eliminating the risk of a transaction exposure, or **hedging,** at the operations level. Remember the discussion of leading and lagging? Let's look at an example.

hedging
A process to reduce or eliminate financial risk

The U.S. company Nucor is exporting to Spain a €20 million boutique steel order, made from recycled steel, payable in euros. Nucor has accepted the foreign exchange risk as a part of its marketing strategy. It may also have factored a currency shift expectation into its euro pricing.

Here are the foreign exchange and interest data:

EU interest rate:	2.75
U.S. interest rate:	5.00
Spot rate	$1.2553
Forward rate	$1.28 (one year forward)

Nucor would like to lag its receivable, since the market indicates that the dollar may well weaken further against the euro. That suggests that Nucor will be able to buy more dollars for its receivable in the future. And the Spanish customer may well want to lag the payment as well if there is no incentive for early payment. If the customer is Euro-based, the currency's strengthening against the dollar will have no appreciable effect on its cash flows.

In another way to hedge on transaction exposure through company actions, many multinationals follow a centralized practice similar to multilateral netting: *exposure netting.* The firm will run a centralized clearing account that matches and nets out foreign exchange exposures across currencies or across currency families. Working with currency families recognizes that some currencies tend to move in lockstep with one another.

forward market hedge
Foreign currency contract sold or bought forward in order to protect against foreign currency movement

There are also ways to hedge foreign currency exposure by engaging in contracts known as *hedges* and *swaps.* A **forward market hedge** involves a quite simple transaction: The company sells forward its foreign currency receivables for its home currency, matching the time forward to the due date of the receivables. When the Spanish company pays, Nucor will deliver the amount to its bank, the partner in the forward market hedge contract. Nucor will not have been exposed to currency risk in the Spanish sale. Because the forward market hedge is a way to cover the complete exposure in a given transaction, it is the most widely used approach. Yet because the forward market hedge assumes all of the foreign exchange risk, it eliminates the chance of gaining from a currency move in the company's favor.

currency option hedge
An option to buy or sell a specific amount of foreign currency at a specific time in order to protect against foreign currency risk

An approach to hedging an exposure but not losing the opportunity to gain from a currency appreciation is a *foreign currency option.* With a **currency option hedge,** you purchase an option to buy or sell a specific amount of currency at a specific time, but the option can be exercised or not. These hedges are *calls*—or contracts with an option to buy—for foreign currency payables and *puts*—or contracts to sell—for foreign currency receivables. Since these are options, if the market works against you, you can exercise the contract. If the market works for you, you don't need to exercise the option.

money market hedge
A method to hedge foreign currency exposure by borrowing and lending in the domestic and foreign money markets

The money markets also afford an opportunity to hedge a foreign transaction. In a **money market hedge,** Nucor would borrow euros in the European money market in the amount of the receivables from the Spanish sale. The basic idea here is to match the balance sheet asset with a liability in the same currency. Here's how the money market hedge works: Nucor borrows $20 million for a period that matches the receivable's due date. Then Nucor converts the euros to dollars at the spot rate and then invests them. The euros that are received from the Spanish company will be used to close out the euro loan. Then the invested dollars plus their interest provide Nucor the dollar amount for the Spanish sale.

swap contract
A spot sale/purchase of an asset against a future purchase/sale of an equal amount in order to hedge a financial position

Swap contracts are also used to hedge foreign currency exposure. This is an agreement to exchange currencies at specified rates and on a specified date or sequence of dates. Swaps are quite flexible and may be undertaken for long periods, much longer than in the forward market. So if Nucor had a series of sales in the EU over the next 10 years, all denominated in euro, it could enter into a series of swaps so that the exchange rate or series of exchange rates would be known in advance. We discuss swaps in greater detail below.

TRANSLATION EXPOSURE

translation exposure Potential change in the value of a company's financial position due to exposure created during the consolidation process

Translation exposure occurs when subsidiary financial statements are consolidated at the corporate level for the companywide financial reports. Since the foreign subsidiaries operate in nondollar currencies, there is a need to translate subsidiary financial reports to the parent company's currency during the corporate consolidation process. Exchange rate movements can have substantial impact on the value of these financial statements, which may affect per-share earnings and stock price. Take a U.S. company that has subsidiaries in Brazil, Japan, Spain, and the United Kingdom. The subsidiary financial reports will be prepared in their own currency, so amounts in four currencies will be translated. Any changes in the exchange rates will affect the dollar values. Such changes, either gains or losses, are not reflected in cash flow; they are paper or unrealized changes.

current rate method An approach in foreign currency translation in which current assets and liabilities are valued at current spot rates and noncurrent assets and liabilities are translated at their historic exchange rates

temporal method An approach in foreign currency translation in which monetary accounts are valued at the spot rate and accounts carried at historical cost are translated at their historic exchange rates

The issue related to translation exposure is what currency exchange rate to use for the translation. There are two basic approaches, the current rate method and the temporal method. By the **current rate method,** assets and liabilities are translated at the rate in effect the day the balance sheet is produced. By the **temporal method,** monetary items such as cash, receivables, and payables are translated at the current exchange rate. Fixed assets and long-term liabilities are translated at the rates in effect the date they were acquired or incurred. In the United States, Financial Accounting Standards Board (FASB) Statement 52 establishes when use of each method is appropriate, depending on the functional currency of the subsidiary. Approaches to translation exposure differ by country.

Many organizations do not hedge translation exposure because hedging a translation exposure can actually increase transaction exposure. If the translation exposure is hedged through a matching foreign exchange liability, such as a debt, then that debt is an exposure at the transaction level. Transaction exposure is fundamental to a corporation's value. Hedging of translation exposure is discussed below in our focus on swaps.

ECONOMIC EXPOSURE

economic exposure The potential for the value of future cash flows to be affected by unanticipated exchange rate movements

Economic exposure occurs at the operations level and results from exchange rate changes on projected cash flows. Unlike transaction exposure, which addresses the individual transaction, economic exposure is firmwide and long-term. For example, when the dollar strengthens, as it did in the 1990s, U.S. export prices increased in terms of other currencies, and so sales plummeted. U.S. exported goods became less price-competitive in foreign markets. Yet when the dollar weakens, as it did in mid-2006, U.S. export prices become more attractive in foreign markets. These changes are examples of the possible effects of economic exposure. Economic exposure can affect both the dollar value of the company's foreign assets and liabilities and the company's cash flow, because it has an impact on foreign sales. Asset exposure includes the fixed assets as well as the financial assets. The exposure of cash flow to currency fluctuation is known as *operating exposure.* Operating exposure is difficult to measure. It involves both the cash flows and the larger commercial context, the competitive conditions connected to obtaining inputs and selling. For example, if a foreign supply becomes more costly in home currency terms because of a home currency weakening, the added cost might be covered through pricing or through switching the supply source. The company may be able to pass the cost increase on to the buyer or to switch into a lower-cost market for the supply. Such options contribute to the reduction of exposure and actually involve the company's competitive position and the structure of the market.[4] The management of economic exposure draws on the hedging and swap contracts we have discussed as ways to manage transaction exposure, on flexibility in sourcing, and on a portfolio approach to foreign market involvement.

Swaps and Derivatives

We mentioned swaps above as a way to protect against transaction risks. They are actually more likely to be used against translation risks and are most likely to be used to raise or transfer capital. In this section, we examine their wide range of uses separately and address the dangers of derivatives.

WORLD view   

U.S. Law Has Unintended Consequences for Overseas Funding

The U.S. American Jobs Creation Act of 2004 was an attempt by Congress to encourage U.S. MNCs to bring home their foreign cash holdings by cutting the tax paid on repatriated cash. In fact, under this repatriation provision, the corporation is allowed a deduction equal to 85 percent of the repatriated cash amount. Bank of America calculates that this is an effective tax rate of 5.25 percent on repatriated dividends instead of the usual 35 percent rate. Such an opportunity encourages managers to consider repatriation of earnings in low-tax countries and not keep earnings for reinvestment. Instead, managers look to the local debt markets for loans to cover working capital and investment needs. Thus, this opportunity created by the U.S. American Job Creation Act has motivated managers to examine their sources of funds and how they finance their subsidiaries. In the process, many companies realized that they had unused debt capacity in certain subsidiaries that offered the opportunity to raise funds locally. Most MNCs have funded from the center out and down, through equity and debt, but now capital markets in developing countries look more attractive in terms of raising capital locally, especially for local bond issues, according to Michael Corbat, head of Citigroup's global corporate bank. Foreign debt is attractive, too, because it is a way to hedge the foreign exchange risk connected to a subsidiary's earnings. Citigroup, General Electric, and auto manuffacturers have been at the forefront of these developing bond markets.

Such transfer of financial risk to the subsidiary comes at a good time, too, when several developing nations have threatened more restrictive repatriation rules or outright nationalization. Sourcing funds locally has many advantages—it offers a currency foreign exchange risk hedge at no cost, it helps to maintain good political relations with host country financiers and politicians, and because locals are involved, it may even offer protection against nationalization. For U.S. MNCs, all this began with an effort by the U.S. government to bring cash home to stimulate job growth.

Source: *CapitalEyes*, Bank of America e-newsletter, July 2005, www.bofabusinesscapital.com/resources/capeyes/a07-05-291.html?bucket=5 (accessed July 3, 2006); David Wighton, "New Trend: Subsidiary Financing: Financial Risk Takes a Local Approach," *Financial Times*, June 28, 2006, p. 3.

SWAPS

We look now at four types of swaps—spot and forward market swaps, parallel loans, bank swaps, and currency swaps—that are useful as hedges against foreign currency risk exposure. Interest rate swaps are also available on the market.

spot and forward market swaps
Use of the spot and forward markets to hedge foreign currency exposure

Spot and forward market swaps is a two-step hedging transaction that involves matching an exposure with a forward transaction. Suppose an American parent company wants to lend euros to its Italian subsidiary and avoid currency exchange risk. First, the parent company will buy euros in the spot market and lend them to the subsidiary. Then, at about the same time, the parent will buy the same amount of U.S. dollars to be paid for in euros for forward delivery at the due date of the loan. The short euro position is covered with the euros repaid by the subsidiary, and the parent receives the dollars. The cost will depend on the discount rate in the forward market compared to the spot market rate.

parallel loans
Matched loans across currencies that are made to cover risk

Parallel loans avoid the foreign market. They involve matching loans across currencies. Continuing with our example of the American parent and its Italian subsidiary, let's add an Italian parent company and its American subsidiary. Assume that each parent wants to lend to its subsidiary in the subsidiary's currency. The Italian parent lends the agreed amount in euros to the Italian subsidiary of the American parent. At the same time and with the same loan maturity, the American parent lends the same amount (at the spot EU-US$ rate) in U.S. dollars to the American subsidiary of the Italian parent. Each loan is made and repaid in one currency, thus avoiding foreign exchange risk.

Parallel loan swaps can be adapted to many circumstances and can involve more than two countries or companies. If a subsidiary in a blocked-currency country has a surplus of that currency in its local operation, perhaps the local subsidiary of another IC needs capital.[5] The other MNC would like to provide that capital but does not want to convert more of its hard currency into a soft currency. The subsidiary of the first MNC lends its surplus currency to the subsidiary of the second MNC. The parent company of the second MNC lends the parent company of the first MNC an equivalent amount in some other currency that it can use.

Interest may or may not be charged on swaps, usually depending on whether interest rates in the two countries are similar or are widely different. If the gap is large, the borrower getting the higher-cost currency might pay an equivalently higher rate of interest on repayment.

"We need two hundred million bucks by Friday—any ideas?"

Source: Cartoon Features Syndicate

You may have observed that we have not mentioned banks in our discussion of swaps. These company-to-company loans are competition for commercial banks, but some banks will facilitate negotiations or act as a broker between clients in arranging swaps. Investment banks and other money brokers sometimes facilitate or even instigate swaps as a service to clients.

bank swap
Swap made between banks to acquire temporary foreign currencies

Banks swaps also exist. They may be between banks (commercial or central) of two or more countries for the purpose of acquiring temporarily needed foreign exchange or may be with MNCs. A typical use of a bank swap is to finance the expansion of an MNC subsidiary in a developing country whose currency is soft and nonconvertible or blocked. The mechanics are simple. Assume that a Swiss MNC wishes to expand a subsidiary's plant in Indonesia and, in doing so, to minimize foreign exchange risks and avoid exchanging any more hard convertible Swiss francs (CHFs) for soft Indonesian rupiahs (IDRs). The Swiss parent company may deal either with a commercial bank in Indonesia or with the Indonesian central bank. The Swiss MNC deposits CHFs in a Swiss bank to the credit of the Indonesian bank. In turn, the Indonesian bank lends IDRs to the Indonesian subsidiary. At an agreed future date, the Indonesian bank repays the CHFs and the subsidiary repays the IDRs. In this example, the Indonesian rupiahs are lent and repaid in Indonesia and the Swiss francs are lent and repaid in Switzerland, which eliminates the need to use the foreign exchange markets. Thus, exchange market costs are avoided, and both parties obtain a foreign currency for which they have a use.

currency swap
An exchange of debt service of a loan or bond in one currency for the debt service of a loan or bond in another currency

Currency swaps help companies raise money in an environment in which they are not well known and must therefore pay a higher interest rate than would be available to a local or better-known borrower. For example, a medium-size American company may have need of Swiss francs, but even though it is a sound credit risk, it may be relatively unknown in Switzerland. If it can find, or if a bank or broker can pair it with, a Swiss company that wants U.S. dollars, the swap would work as follows: The American company would borrow U.S. dollars in the United States, where it is well known and can get a low interest rate; the Swiss company would borrow Swiss francs in Switzerland for the same reason. They would then swap the currencies and service each other's loans; that is, the Swiss company would repay the US$ loan, while the American company would repay the CHF loan.

interest rate swap
An exchange of interest rate flows in order to manage interest rate exposure

Interest rate swaps have grown on the currency swap model, and they arbitrage the fixed and floating rate markets. Two parties, usually a foreign bank and a U.S. company unknown in the foreign market, exchange interest rates on borrowing made in the foreign market, fixed for floating and floating for fixed. Interest rate swaps allow a company to alter its interest rate exposure.

HEDGES AND SWAPS AS "DERIVATIVES"

derivative
A contract whose value is tied to the performance of a financial instrument or commodity

Currency value changes are one of the risks against which international business managers use hedges and swaps. These vehicles are sometimes referred to as **derivatives,** contracts whose value changes over time based on the performance of an underlying commodity or financial instrument. The term *derivative* covers standardized, exchange-traded futures and options contracts as well as over-the-counter swaps, options, and other customized instruments.[6] These contracts can be seen to shift risk from a party that does not want to bear it to one that does, hoping for a large reward. However, if used unwisely for speculation, derivatives contracts can be as dangerous as the risks against which they are supposed to protect. Investor Warren Buffett called them "financial weapons of mass destruction."[7] One of the most notorious derivatives disasters occurred in the early 1990s when Nick Leeson, a manager in the futures trading market at Barings Bank, the oldest investment bank in the United Kingdom, made unauthorized speculative trades in his employer's account.

Leeson's trades were initially profitable, so the question of their authorization did not arise, interestingly enough. When his trading resulted in losses, he used the banks' error account to

BUILDING YOUR GLOBAL RÉSUMÉ — Earn Your MBA with a Specialization in International Business

In the 2005 AACSB international publication *Why Management Education Matters,* the authors defended the economic value of the MBA degree and stated that the average compensation for MBAs had increased from $56,000 to $387,600 over the 10-year period from 1992 to 2002. Though this included bonuses and other compensation, holding an MBA has significant economic value when compared to the $43,000 average salary for those holding a nonmanagement college degree. And for international MBAs the nonsalary valued-added benefits of paid international travel and foreign experiences clearly enhance the attractiveness of this additional level of education. So where are the top MBA programs? Here are several to consider, listed in rank order by two publications:

U.S. News & World Report

1. Thunderbird American Graduate School
2. University of South Carolina (Moore)
3. University of Pennsylvania (Wharton)
4. New York University (Stern)
5. Columbia University

Business Week

1. INSEAD (Paris)
2. Queen's University (Ontario)
3. IMD (Switzerland)
4. London Business School
5. University of Toronto
6. Western Ontario University
7. Rotterdam School of Management
8. IESE (Barcelona)
9. HEC (Paris)
10. York University (Toronto)

World Fact: The average American works 46.2 weeks per year, but the French average 40 weeks per year. In many European countries the practice is to take the entire month of July or August off for holiday in addition to other government or local culturally designated holidays.

Culture Cue: In many parts of the world, but primarily in Latin America and Asia, Americans are viewed as working too much and criticized for not spending enough time with family and friends and having little respect for elders.

World Wide Resources:

www.careerdynamo.com

www.princetonreview.com/mba/research/articles/find/internationalDifferences.asp

www.bschool.com/best_b-schools.html

hide them. By the end of 1992, the account's losses were over £2 million, which ballooned to £208 million by the end of 1994. In early January, the day before the Kobe earthquake, Leeson placed a short straddle (a type of short selling) for derivatives in the Singapore and Tokyo stock exchanges, betting that the markets would not move overnight. The Kobe earthquake, on January 17, 1995, sent Asian markets into chaos, and Leeson's investments along with them. Each attempt he made to recover his losses was a riskier bet, and his losses mounted, reaching $1.4 billion, twice the trading capital of Barings. The bank collapsed.

Derivatives are not exactly new—Japanese rice traders, for example, used futures in the 17th century. But derivatives have become much more sophisticated and widely used in recent years. Examples of the vast number of potential applications are derivatives that can be written so that they will pay out if temperatures rise above a certain figure, which could be a boon for an electric utility in the summer, or if snowfall during the winter is lower than expected, which could help a ski resort. The gross market value of global OTC derivative contracts has soared. The combined financial markets and OTC derivatives total for 2004 recorded by the Bank for international Settlements was $273 trillion. The total market for OTC derivatives recorded by the Bank for International Settlements in the fourth quarter of 2005 was $344 trillion.

Credit default swaps (CDSs), an exotic derivative less than a decade ago, have become one of the key building blocks of the bond and loan markets. CDSs appeal to bankers because they can reduce their exposure to a particular client without the client becoming aware that the loan has in effect been sold. Admitting that a loan has been syndicated to other institutions can be damaging to the client relationship. Banks are the main buyers of CDS cover, while insurers are the main sellers. As the market has developed, CDSs have become tradable securities in their own right.[8]

A logical question at this point might be, "Are derivatives safe?" The short answer is that they are risk-management tools. Used properly, they can be remarkably effective; firms and institutions of all sorts use them to take or limit risks in ways that were not possible until recently. Risk management is a tricky, three-stage process, conceptually simple but in implementation quite complex:

- Identify where the risks lie.
- Design an appropriate strategy for managing them.
- Select the right tools to execute the strategy.

The implementation of their risk strategy may become too complex for many managers. Just as it is uneconomical and dangerous for the executives of most firms to identify and solve all their legal problems, it may be that many firms need outsiders' help in devising and executing risk-management strategies. As long as the firms' managers keep control of basic decisions, it may be best to leave the execution of hedging strategy and the final choice of instruments to outside experts.

NETWORKING TO FIND PARTNERS

How do financial managers learn about potential partners for swaps, parallel loans, and other derivatives? In many cases, their international banks are the answer. In an increasing number of instances, they are finding partners at risk-management meetings such as the Risk Management Conference. These conferences are sponsored by publications such as the *Financial Times*, *Euromoney*, the *Asian Wall Street Journal*, and *Business International* and by international financial houses. At such meetings, financial executives meet their counterparts from other MNCs as well as people representing banks, other financial organizations, and international agencies such as the World Bank and regional development banks. Increasingly, such networking provides the partners they need to protect their organizations and/or profit using derivatives contracts.

Our discussion so far has assumed that money is playing a role in the exchange. There are situations in which countries do not have the foreign currency to pay for imports. In such cases, sales without money are an option.

Sales without Money

A number of countries desire goods and products for which they do not have the convertible currency to pay. That has not prevented efforts by many suppliers to sell to them anyway. Such countries are usually less developed and poor. There are two main approaches to nonmonetary trade, countertrade and industrial cooperation.

COUNTERTRADE

countertrade
The trade of goods or services for other goods or services

Countertrade is the trade of goods and services for other goods and services. In the international environment, it often involves the substitution of developing country goods for foreign exchange so that purchases from the developed country can be completed. Countertrade usually involves two basic contracts, one for the purchase of developed country products or services and one for the purchase of developing country products. Six modifications of countertrade are counterpurchase, compensation, barter, switch, offset, and clearing account arrangements. These contracts may be relatively simple, involving only two countries or companies, or quite complex, calling for a number of countries, companies, currencies, and contracts.

counterpurchase
Countertrade in which the goods supplied do not rely on the goods imported

In **counterpurchase,** the goods supplied by the developing country do not rely on the goods or products imported from the developed country. An example of counterpurchase is PepsiCo's arrangement with Russia, to which PepsiCo sells the concentrate for Pepsi-Cola, which is then bottled and sold in that country. In exchange, in lieu of money, PepsiCo has exclusive rights to export Russian vodka for sale in the West. In 1990, the two parties renewed and expanded their agreement, increasing the amounts of Pepsi-Cola and vodka to be sold and adding a new element to account for an excess of Pepsi-Cola demand in Russia over the demand for Russian vodka in the West. PepsiCo has also committed itself to buying at least 10 Russian-built freighters and tankers. PepsiCo intends to lease them on the world market through a Norwegian partner.

Counterpurchase agreements helped PepsiCo enter the Eastern European market. As a result, the company continues to grow and expand its operations in that region. For example, this PepsiCo truck is one of a fleet of 70 vehicles based in Warsaw, Poland.

In **compensation** transactions, the developing country makes payment in products produced by use of developed country equipment. These products are shipped to the developed country in payment for the equipment. Dresser Industries has a compensation agreement with Poland for tractors. Poland is paying with tractors and other machines that Dresser then markets.

Barter is an ancient form of commerce and the simplest sort of countertrade. The developing country sends products to the developed country that are equal in value to the products delivered by the developed country to the developing country.

Switch trading developed to deal with the problem of there being no market in the developed country for the developing country's goods. When a third party is brought in to dispose of these products, we have switch trading.

Offset occurs when the importing nation requires that a portion of the materials, components, or subassemblies of a product be procured in its local market. The exporter may set up a parts manufacturing and assembly facility in the importing country.

Clearing account arrangements are used to facilitate the exchange of products over a specified time period. When the period ends, any balance outstanding must be cleared by the purchase of additional goods or settled by a cash payment. The bank or broker acts as an intermediary to facilitate settlement of the clearing accounts by finding markets for counterpurchased goods or by converting goods or cash payments into products desired by the country with a surplus.

Frequently, countertrade agreements and their executions are not reported publicly. Indeed, the parties often prefer privacy and confidentiality for competitive reasons and to avoid setting precedents for future deals. Therefore, estimates of the extent of countertrade vary widely. The U.S. Commerce Department and the United Nations estimate that between 10 and 20 percent of world trade is now subject to some form of countertrade and that the proportion is growing.[9] In addition to countertrade, industrial cooperation is another approach to trade without—or with less—money.

compensation
Countertrade in which the developing country makes payment in products produced by use of developed country equipment.

barter
A direct exchange of goods or services for goods or services without the use of money

switch trading
The use of a third party to market products received in countertrade

offset
Trade arrangement that requires that a portion of the inputs be supplied by the receiving country

clearing account arrangement
A process to settle a trading account within a specified time

INDUSTRIAL COOPERATION

Industrial cooperation, which developing countries favor, requires long-term relationships, with part or all of the production being done in the developing country. A portion of the products are sold in the developing country or in other developing countries. We have identified five methods used in industrial cooperation:

1. *Joint venture:* Two or more companies or state agencies combine assets to form a new and distinct economic entity, and they share management, profits, and losses.
2. *Coproduction and specialization:* The factory in the developing country produces certain agreed-on components of a product, while a company in the developed country produces the other components. The product is then assembled at both locations for their respective markets.
3. *Subcontracting:* The developing country factory manufactures a product according to specifications of the developed country company and delivers the product to the developed country company, which then markets it.
4. *Licensing:* The developing country and developed country parties enter into a license agreement whereby the developing country enterprise uses developed country technology to manufacture a product. The developed country company is paid a license royalty fee in money or in product. The developing country usually prefers to pay in product.

industrial cooperation
An exporter's commitment to a longer-term relationship than that in a simple export sale, in which some of the production occurs in the receiving country

5. *Turnkey plants:* The developed country party is responsible for building the entire plant, starting it, training developing country personnel, and turning over the keys to the developing country party. The developing country will pay in products of the new plant.

Two threads run through countertrade and industrial cooperation. The first is that the developing country does not have enough hard, convertible currency to buy what it wants from the developed country. That leads to the second thread, which is the effort of the developing country to substitute goods for currency.

Taxation and Transfer Pricing

income tax
Direct tax levied on earnings

value-added tax (VAT)
Indirect tax collected from the parties as they add value to the product

withholding tax
Indirect tax paid by the payor, usually on passive income

In Chapter 11, we discussed taxation as a financial force and outlined three major types of taxation that governments around the world use—income tax, value-added tax, and withholding tax. **Income tax** is a direct tax levied on earnings. **Value-added tax (VAT)** is an indirect tax, in that the tax authority collects it from the person or firm that adds value during the production and marketing process, not from the owner of the item taxed. The ultimate user of the product pays the full amount of tax that is rebated to the others in the value chain. Thus, the government is collecting the tax on the value added in the process. The **withholding tax** is also an indirect tax, in that it is paid not by the person whose labor generates the income but by the business that makes the payment for the labor. Usually the withholding tax is levied on passive income such as royalties, dividends, and interest. Governments follow two approaches to the jurisdiction of their taxes, either worldwide or territorial. A worldwide approach is to tax residents of the country on their worldwide income. The United States follows a policy of worldwide taxation, and it can be argued convincingly that, despite tax treaties, such taxation put U.S. firms operating foreign subsidiaries at a disadvantage compared with their foreign domestic competitors.[10] A territorial taxation policy taxes income earned within the nation's borders. There are tax credits, based on treaties that reduce or eliminate double taxation for U.S. residents and companies, as long as the foreign tax liability is less than the U.S. equivalent would be.

branch
Legal extension of the parent company

subsidiary
Separate legal entity owned by the parent company

How the foreign operations of a company are organized is key to its U.S. tax liability on foreign earnings. If the operation is a **branch,** that is, an extension of the parent company, not a separate legal entity incorporated in the foreign country, its losses may be deducted by the parent company from its U.S. taxable income. If the foreign entity is a **subsidiary,** that is, a separate legal entity incorporated in the foreign country, its ownership by the MNC may be minority, that is, between 10 and 50 percent. Such minority company income, both active and passive, is taxed only when it is remitted to the parent company. If the foreign subsidiary is actually controlled by the parent company, with more than 50 percent ownership, it is known as a *controlled foreign corporation (CFC)* and its active income is taxed in the United States when that income is remitted to the parent company but its passive income (royalties, licensing fees, dividends, service fees) is taxed as it occurs. When deciding where to locate and how to structure a foreign operation, MNC managers would want to review the tax rates of possible locations and also consider what legal form their operations should take. Often, start-ups have several years of losses, so establishment of a branch rather than a subsidiary might generate valuable losses, from a tax point of view, for the parent company.

transfer price
The cost of intracompany sales of goods or services

Transfer pricing is another way for MNCs to reduce their tax liability. The **transfer price** is the bookkeeping cost of goods transferred from one unit of a business (subsidiary or division) to another in another country or tax jurisdiction. For example, a high transfer price on goods coming to the parent from a foreign subsidiary will move profits from the parent to the subsidiary side of the MNC. This result may be used to shift the impact of tax rates from the parent company's home country to that of the subsidiary. This sort of move makes sense if the tax rate in the home country is higher than that in the subsidiary's country. Conversely, the tax impact could be shifted to the home country from the subsidiary. One caveat is that the transfer price can never be lower than the cost of the transferred product's inputs. If this were to happen, the MNC would be open to charges of dumping. Transfer pricing has many uses because it allows an MNC to adjust the amount of profit its individual businesses are showing.

International Accounting

The purpose of accounting in all countries is to provide managers with financial data for use in their decision making and to provide external constituencies (investors, governments, lenders, suppliers, etc.) the quantitative information they seek to inform their decisions. Also, it provides data governments need to levy taxes. The idea of what constitutes useful data, separate from their reliability, varies from country to country. For example, in Germany, the primary users of financial information historically have been creditors, so accounting focuses on the balance sheet, which contains information about the company's assets. By contrast, in the United States, investors are major users of financial information, and they look to the income statement as a sign of the company's future.[11] An international company has to address transactions in foreign currencies, a situation that has an obvious impact on the practice of accounting. But the differences do not end there. Different needs of varying constituencies in different countries have led to large variations in financial statements across the globe. That is to say, culture plays a significant role in the practice of accounting. Sidney Gray has applied Geert Hofstede's work on cultural dimensions, explained in Chapter 6, to the practice of accounting. In this section, we examine both transactions in foreign currencies and the role of culture in accounting, and then we go on to look at possible convergence among these various approaches.

ACCOUNTING AND FOREIGN CURRENCY

There are two points at which operating in a foreign currency raises issues from an accounting perspective: when transactions are made in foreign currencies and when branches and subsidiaries operate in foreign currencies and their results need to be made a part of the parent company's financial reports. We look first at transactions and then at translation and consolidation, the two processes involved in merging subsidiary financial results with those of the parent company.

When the U.S.-based company has foreign currency–based transactions such as sales, purchases, and loans (made and taken), they need to be recorded as revenues, expenses, assets, or liabilities. Suppose the transaction is a purchase of Swiss watches in Geneva for 25,000 Swiss francs (CHFs). How is this handled when the company books are prepared in U.S. dollars? The transaction is entered in dollars at the exchange rate at purchase. Let's say it's \$1.224/CHF. The purchase entry would be \$30,600. Accounts payable would also be \$30,600, and the exchange rate notation "CHF 25,000 @ \$1.224" would be made. Now, if the payment is immediate or stipulated in US\$, that would be fine. But if the transaction is stipulated in CHF and if there is a time lag and the exchange rate moves, the underlying dollar value of the purchase would change. Let's say the exchange rate moves to \$1.26/CHF at the 60-day point, when the payable is due. Now the U.S. company has to pay \$31,500. The \$900 difference constitutes a foreign exchange loss. In this case, the journal entries would remain the same, and the loss (or gain) would be recorded in the income statement. This process is described by FASB 52, which requires that companies record foreign currency–based transactions at the spot rate at the time of the transaction. Any gains or losses from changes in exchange rates for items carried as payables or receivables are posted in the income statement.

Now to our second concern about foreign currencies in accounting operations. When a U.S. MNC's foreign subsidiary reports results, these results need to be translated into the parent company's operating currency, dollars, and made to conform to U.S. GAAP. Then these various results are aggregated into one financial report. This process is called **consolidation.** The two basic approaches to translation, the current rate method and the temporal method, were described above in our discussion of foreign currency translation risk. The objective of these two methods is to accurately reflect business results.

consolidation
The process of translating subsidiary results and aggregating them into one financial report

Choice of translation method depends on the **functional currency** of the foreign operation. The functional currency is the primary currency of the operation, the currency in which cash flows, pricing, expenses, and financing are denominated. If the functional currency is the local one, the current rate method must be used. If the functional currency is that of the parent company, the temporal method must be used. The current rate method translates assets at the spot rate on the day the balance sheet is prepared. The income statement is translated at an average exchange rate for the reporting period. Owner's equity is translated at the rates in

functional currency
The primary currency of a business

effect when the stock was issued and when retained earnings were posted. With the temporal method, monetary assets are translated at the spot rate. Fixed assets are translated at their acquisition exchange rates. The income statement items are translated at the average rate for the period, except that cost of goods sold and depreciation are translated at their historic rates.

In inflationary economies, you can imagine that translation presents special problems. If the local currency is the functional currency, fixed assets could disappear if the current rate method were used for translation. This phenomenon has been called the "disappearing plant." To address the translation issues presented by inflationary economies, FASB 52 mandates that the translation be performed as if the functional currency were the reporting currency, using the temporal method. That way, fixed assets and other large, important accounts will not lose value compared to their book value.

ACCOUNTING AND CULTURE

We know that accounting follows different patterns in different parts of the world. Gray suggests that differences in accounting measurement and disclosure practices, that is, how companies value assets and what information companies provide, are influenced by culture. His study classified countries on two dimensions, secrecy-transparency and optimism-conservatism. Figure 21.3 summarizes this classification.[12]

The dimension of secrecy-transparency measures the degree to which companies disclose information to the public. As Figure 21.3 suggests, Germany, Japan, and Switzerland tend to value secrecy or privacy over transparency. In the United Kingdom and the United States, there is more disclosure and less privacy. The dimension of optimism-conservatism measures the degree to which a company is cautious in its valuing of assets and measuring of income. Accounting reports in countries with more conservative asset-valuing approaches tend to understate assets and income, while those in countries whose asset-valuing approach is more optimistic tend toward overstatement. In France, Germany, and Japan, public companies' capital structure tends to depend more on debt rather than equity, with banks being a major source of the debt. Banks are concerned with liquidity. A conservative statement of profits may reduce tax exposure and dividend payouts, contributing to cash reserves that can be

FIGURE 21.3

Cultural Differences in Measurement and Disclosure for Accounting Systems

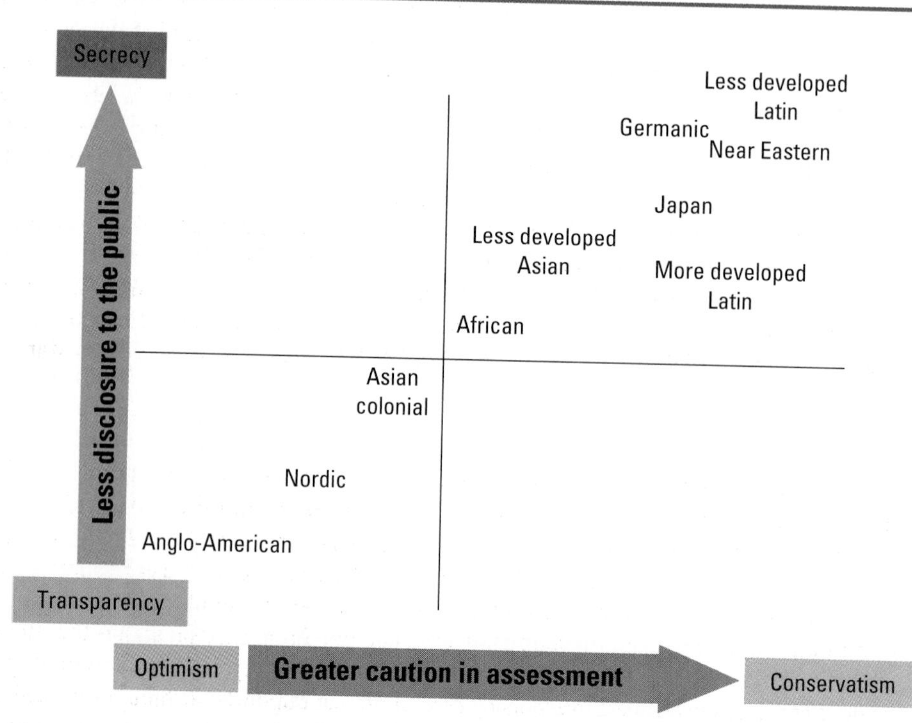

Source: Adapted from Lee Radebaugh and Sidney J. Gray, *Accounting and Multinational Enterprises*, 5th Edition (New York: John Wiley & Sons, 2002).

tapped for debt service. On the optimism measure, U.S. and, in a more restrained way, U.K. companies want to show impressive earnings that will attract investors.

Until 2005, there were considerable differences in reporting standards across selected countries. With the income statement, called the *profit and loss account (P&L)* in the United Kingdom, the basic understanding of what constituted income varied considerably. For example, how to measure inventory differed, as did the treatment of goodwill and depreciation methods for property and equipment. In Germany, income was declared only when a contract was completed, while in the United Kingdom and Japan, a percentage completion method was used, as in the United States.

CONVERGENCE OF ACCOUNTING STANDARDS

Largely due to globalization and MNCs' desires to list stock in foreign markets to tap into their potential as a source of shareholders, a process known as *cross-listing,* there is a growing movement toward convergence of accounting standards. Such harmonization requires long and careful negotiation. The body that establishes accounting standards in the United States is a private organization, the Financial Accounting Standards Board (FASB). The more international body is the International Accounting Standards Board (IASB), whose predecessor organization was founded in 1973 by a multilateral effort among accounting bodies in Australia, Canada, France, Germany, Japan, Mexico, the Netherlands, the United Kingdom, Ireland, and the United States. In 2002, both FASB and IASB agreed in principle on harmonization of standards and convergence. The FASB's standards are the U.S. Generally Accepted Accounting Principles (U.S.GAAP), while the IASB's standards are the International Financial Reporting Standards (IFRS). Significant progress has been made on this commitment by a negotiating group, with a target date of 2009. With so many important and heavily detailed aspects of specific standards to be reconciled, the progress toward convergence is impressive.

In the meantime, the EU Parliament and the Council of Europe decided to require IASB standards for financial reporting as of June 15, 2005, for public businesses unless they have a small business exemption, and as of December 15, 2005, for small businesses. Australia and New Zealand have joined the EU in this step forward. The transition seems to have gone smoothly. Presently there are over 75 countries that require public companies to list using IFRS. That represents a broad-based negotiation process by many countries in the world and creates pressure for FASB to converge. The Security and Exchange Commission has indicated that when it is satisfied that IASB standards are reliable, it will follow them. So there is an increasing tilt toward IASB. Deloitte and Touche partner D. J. Gannon has called the U.S. acceptance of IFRS "inevitable."[13] The U.S. market is the only major market that follows U.S. GAAP at this point.[14] With convergence, financial markets around the world will become more integrated because the statements will be comparable.

In 2002, the U.S. Congress passed the Sarbanes-Oxley Act, largely as a result of a series of corporate scandals in which accounting practices were at the center. Sarbanes-Oxley also provides motivation for the private FASB to harmonize with IASB. It allocated the Security and Exchange Commission responsibility for recognizing the standard setter.[15] Table 21.1 summarizes the progress IFRS has made in its move toward becoming the world standard.

TRIPLE-BOTTOM-LINE ACCOUNTING

Increasingly, companies have made efforts to report on their environmental, social, and financial results. Such a reporting framework has been termed **triple bottom line (3BL),** a term credited to John Elkington in his 1997 book, *Cannibals with Forks: The Triple Bottom Line of 21st Century Business.*[16] The book's argument is that capitalism can become civilized; capitalists can be taught to eat with forks, due to consumer pressure and other social forces. Corporate capitalism can become sustainable capitalism. Elkington argues that there are seven drivers of this transformation: markets, values, transparency, life-cycle technology, partnerships, time, and corporate governance. This approach supports sustainability, which we discussed in Chapter 7, and corporate social reform (CSR). As we have seen in our earlier discussion of sustainability, it is a systems concept that has three major aspects: the

triple bottom line (3BL)
A results or impact report on the environmental, social, and financial impacts of the business

TABLE 21.1 Use of International Financial Reporting Standards

	Europe/Central Asia	Americas	Asia-Pacific	Africa/Middle East
Required IFRS	Armenia Austria Bangladesh Belgium Bulgaria Croatia Cyprus Czech Republic Denmark Estonia Finland France Georgia Germany Greece Hungary Ireland Italy Kyrgystan Latvia Lithuania Luxembourg Macedonia Malta Netherlands Norway Poland Portugal Romania Russia Slovakia Slovenia Spain Sweden Switzerland Tajikistan Ukraine United Kingdom	Bahamas Barbados Costa Rica Dominican Republic Ecuador Guyana Haiti Honduras Jamaica Panama Papua New Guinea Peru Trinidad & Tobago	Australia Brunei Nepal Singapore Taiwan	Egypt Jordan Kenya Kuwait Malawi Mauritius Oman Tunesia
Converging with IFRS	Moldova Uzbekistan	Argentina Brazil Canada Cayman Islands Chile Guatemala Mexico United States Uruguay Venezuela	New Zealand China/Hong Kong India Indonesia Japan Malaysia Philippines South Korea Thailand	Iran Israel Pakistan South Africa Zimbabwe

environmental or ecological, the social, and the economic. Presently we measure at the economic level, and where required by government or social pressure, we measure at the environmental level, as with emission controls and hazardous waste, and at the social level, as with the Equal Employment Opportunity Commission's enforcement of the federal civil rights laws. Yet even in the environmental and social areas, we tend to know more about the problems—what is reported in the media—than about the company-level thinking on these important issues. Companies should measure and make public the environmental and social effects of their decisions. That is, in summary, the major argument for 3BL.

The major argument against 3BL is neither a substantive disagreement with the desirability of ecologically responsible business practices that support sustainability nor a disagreement with the idea of business being socially responsible; rather, it is the claim that measurement will not get us closer to the desired state. Wayne Norman and Chris MacDonald argue that social performance and environmental impact cannot be objectively measured in ways that are comparable to our economic measurements of a firm's activities.[17] They point out that the rhetoric may be appealing but no widely implementable framework exists for measuring a company's performance in environmental and social areas, although there are high levels of consulting in these areas. In fact, they suggest that a focus on the measurement of these activities may well detract from efforts to figure out ways to combine sustainability and social responsibility with positive economic results, which is a more difficult challenge. There is a parallel with codes of ethics: What matters is what a

WORLD view   

Sarbanes-Oxley Not a Good Export

Harvey Pitt, former chairman of the SEC (2001–2003), has lashed out at the U.S. Congress for its required export of a hastily written and poorly conceptualized law, the Sarbanes-Oxley Act (SOX), enacted in the wake of the corporate scandals of 2001. Its "one size-fits-all" approach to regulation stifles innovation, creativity, risk taking, and competitiveness. Worse, Pitt says, "Congress's exportation of SOX's standards has created huge difficulties for multinational companies and produced scorn for U.S. standards." He suggests that the scorn is justified, that there are better standards out there. What he characterizes as "American geocentrism" has resulted in the loss of foreign listings on U.S. exchanges and the movement of IPOs to non-U.S. sites.

Faced with evidence that they are increasingly irrelevant in the global economy, U.S. stock exchanges have been out on the market, trying to buy foreign exchanges. This means that the SOX requirements, in addition to applying to any company with a U.S. listing, will apply to companies listed on U.S.-owned foreign exchanges. For example, if Euronext, a European stock exchange with subsidiaries in Belgium, France, Netherlands, Portugal and the United Kingdom, is U.S.-owned, SOX will impose U.S. regulatory standards across all these subsidiary exchanges. Harvey Pitt argues that this would not be a step in the right direction.

Source: Harvey Pitt, "Sarbanes-Oxley Is an Unhealthy Export," *Financial Times*, June 21, 2006, p. 15.

company actually does, not whether a code of ethics is hanging on the wall of every office. The poster is rhetoric. Posting it is not ethical action. Decisions in the field that have to do with implementation are what matter, as well as how the organization's members understand the company's values and what those values say about their duties to stakeholders.

International Finance Center

The increasing complexity of global financing, combined with increasing global competition, has encouraged MNCs to pay more attention to financial management, as mentioned earlier in "An Integrated Approach to Risk." International financial management has become increasingly different from domestic financial management, and in several MNCs the centralized finance operation has become a profit center and is no longer merely a service. Some of the new developments are (1) floating exchange rates, whose fluctuations are sometimes volatile, (2) growth in the number of capital and foreign exchange markets where an MNC can shop for lower interest costs and better currency rates, (3) different and changing inflation rates from country to country, (4) advances in electronic cash management systems, (5) realization by financial managers that through innovative management of temporarily idle cash balances of the MNC units, they can increase yields and the enterprise's profit, and (6) the explosive growth of the use of derivatives to protect against commodity, currency, interest rate, and other risks. As a result, many MNCs have established international finance centers. Such operations can balance and hedge currency exposures, tap capital markets, manage inflation rate risk, manage cash management technological innovation, manage derivatives use, handle internal and external invoicing, help a weak-currency affiliate, and strengthen affiliate evaluation and reporting systems.

Summary

Explain capital structure choices and their potential impact on the MNC.

The firm raises capital through its retained earnings, and then, externally, through either equity, the issuing of shares, or debt (leveraging). Firms may choose to issue stocks in foreign markets, in part to tap into a broader investor pool, which can raise the stock price and reduce the cost of capital. Such local issues also may have a significant marketing advantage. Debt markets are the other source of capital for the firm, and increasingly the tendency is to tap local markets first. Offshore financial centers, where taxation is low and banking regulations are slim, are also a source of debt financing. Debt financing is thought to be less expensive that equity financing, but local practices and taxation are some of the factors that are considered in making decisions about the capital structure of the firm.

Describe the process of multilateral netting and what its contribution is to cash flow management.

Multilateral netting is a centralized approach through which subsidiaries transfer their net cash flows within the company to a cash center that disperses cash to net receivers. It leads to cost savings.

Describe the importance of leading and lagging in cash flow management.

Leading and lagging involve the timing of payments. A lead approach is to collect receivables early when the foreign currency is expected to weaken, and fund payables early when the foreign currency is expected to strengthen. A lag approach is to collect receivables late when the currency is expected to strengthen, and fund payables late when the currency is expected to weaken. It is a helpful technique when there are expectations that host governments may block fund transfers.

Categorize foreign exchange risks into transaction exposure, translation exposure, and economic exposure.

Transaction exposure occurs when the firm has transactions denominated in a foreign currency. The exposure is due to currency exchange rate fluctuations between the time the commitment is made and when it is payable.

Translation exposure occurs when subsidiary financial statements are consolidated at the corporate level for the companywide financial reports. Since the foreign subsidiaries operate in nondollar currencies, there is a need to translate subsidiary financial reports to the parent company's currency during the corporate consolidation process.

Economic exposure is at the operations level and results from exchange rate changes on projected cash flows. Unlike transaction exposure, which addresses the individual transaction, economic exposure is firmwide and long-term.

Describe the basic idea of a swap transaction and its various applications.

Swaps invlove matching an exposure with a forward transaction. Spot swaps are at the spot exchange rate at a stipulated time in the future, and forward market swaps are at a forward market rate. Many financial instruments may be matched in these swaps, including parallel loans, bank swaps, and currency swaps.

Explain a currency swap contract and its usefulness to the financial manager.

A currency swap is used to raise money in an environment in which the company raising the funds is not well known. The company finds a local partner, and then each company borrows in its home market at preferred rates. They then swap the loans. This is done to reduce interest rate costs.

Recognize the usefulness and dangers of using derivatives.

Derivatives are contracts whose value changes over time based on the performance of an underlying commodity or financial instrument. The term *derivative* covers standardized, exchange-traded futures and options contracts as well as over-the-counter swaps, options, and other customized instruments.[18] These contracts can be seen to shift risk from a party that does not want to bear it to one that does, hoping for a large reward. Used unwisely for speculation, derivatives contracts can be as dangerous as the risks against which they are supposed to protect.

Explain the role of and approaches to sales without money.

Non-monetary trade may be a way for countries that don't have hard currency to import goods. There are two main approaches to non-monetary trade, countertrade and industrial cooperation. Countertrade usually involves two basic contracts, one for the purchase of developed country products or services and one for the purchase of developing country products. Industrial cooperation involves long-term relationships, including local production, with part or all of the output sold in the host country.

Identify the major challenges faced in international accounting.

International accounting has to address transactions in foreign currencies, In addition, different needs by varying constituencies in different countries have led to large variations in financial statements across the globe. These cultural differences also have to be bridged in international accounting.

Describe the international accounting standards' convergence process and its importance.

The body that establishes accounting standards in the U.S. is the private organization, the Financial Accounting Standards Board (FASB). The more international body is the International Accounting Standards Board (IASB). The FASB's standards are the U.S. Generally Accepted Accounting Principles (U.S. GAAP), while the IASB's standards are the International Financial Reporting Standards (IFRS). Significant progress has been made towards convergence by a negotiating group, with a target date of 2009. Convergence is important for further integration of global markets.

Key Words

American depository receipt (ADR) (p. 568)
offshore financial center (p. 568)
multilateral netting (p. 571)
blocked funds (p. 572)
leading and lagging (p. 572
transaction exposure (p. 572)
hedging (p. 573)
forward market hedge (p. 573)
currency option hedge (p. 573)
money market hedge (p. 573)
swap contract (p. 573)
translation exposure (p. 574)
current rate method (p. 574)
temporal method (p. 574)
economic exposure (p. 574)
spot and forward market swaps (p. 575)
parallel loans (p. 575)

bank swap (p. 576)
currency swap (p. 576)
interest rate swap (p. 576)
derivative (p. 576)
countertrade (p. 578)
counterpurchase (p. 578)
compensation (p. 579)
barter (p. 579)
switch trading (p. 579)
offset (p. 579)
clearing account arrangement (p. 579)
industrial cooperation (p. 579)
income tax (p.580)
value-added tax (VAT) (p. 580)
withholding tax (p. 580)
branch (p. 580)
subsidiary (p. 580)
transfer price (p. 580)
consolidation (p. 581)
functional currency (p. 581)
triple bottom line (3BL) (p. 583)

Questions

1. You are establishing your first overseas subsidiary. As you consider how to capitalize your business, what are your concerns about using the local and home country debt and equity markets?
2. A local exporter has signed a sales contract that specifies payment of $3 million in Saudi riyals in six months. Discuss the hedge options you would advise the exporter to consider.
3. Why would an MNC set up a centralized cash management operation?
4. What are the dangers associated with derivatives contracts?
5. What are the differences between transaction and translation exposure? Can you hedge for both simultaneously?
6. You want to sell into a high-inflation economy that has a strong agricultural sector. What types of countertrade arrangements might you explore?
7. The cultural analysis of accounting Gray presents suggests that transparency is the result of a cultural characteristic of some countries and secrecy of others. Could the same attributes be explained by the hypothesis that transparent cultures are less trusting and need the transparency to satisfy their cultural distrust? What do you think?
8. How might Sarbanes-Oxley influence the progress of the convergence of international accounting standards?
9. How might triple-bottom-line accounting improve the social and environmental behavior of companies?
10. What is your assessment of the movement pushing for 3BL? Explain your thinking.

globalEDGE globalEDGE.msu.edu

Research Task

Use the globalEDGE site (http://globalEDGE.msu.edu/) to complete the following exercises:

1. The globalEDGE site offers a Country Comparison tool through its Country Insights section that allows for comparing countries based on statistical indicators. Utilize this tool to identify in which of the following countries the accounting historic cost principle cannot provide accurate results: Argentina, Bulgaria, Ecuador, Indonesia, Latvia, Malaysia, Mexico, Romania, Russia, and Senegal. Utilize the "rank countries" tool to identify other countries in which the historic cost principle would not provide valid results.
2. Deloitte Touche Tohmatsu hosts an *International Accounting Standards* (IAS) Web page that provides information and guidelines regarding accounting guidelines approved by IASC. Locate the Web site, go to the section on standards, and prepare a short description of the international accounting standards for recording inventory levels.

Dealing with Transaction Risk in a Yuan Contract — Minicase 21.1

You are the finance manager of an American multinational that has sold US$6 million of your high-tech product to a Chinese importer. Because of stiff competition for the contract against other American and European companies, you agreed that the negotiators could accept payment in yuan. This concession may have won your company the contract.

The sales contract calls for the Chinese importer to make three equal payments at 6, 12 and 18 months from the date of delivery. Your plan is to translate the yuan to dollars on their receipt; your company has no operations in China and no need for the currency. How could you cover your transaction exposure?

Chapter 1 Video Case Cirque du Soleil

In 1984, Guy Laliberté left his home in Canada to make his way across Europe as a circus performer. There he and other artists performed in the street. The troupe was called Cirque du Soleil—"circus of the sun." It started with a simple dream: a group of young artists getting together to entertain audiences, see the world, and have fun doing it.[1] Laliberté and company quickly found that their entertainment form without words—stilt-walking, juggling, music, and fire breathing—transcended all barriers of language and culture. Though he understood that an entertainer could bring the exotic to every corner of the world, Laliberté did not envision the scope to which his Cirque du Soleil would succeed. Today Cirque performs nine permanent shows, such as *Algeria,* which is touring Japan, and *Mystere, O,* and *ZUMANITY,* all with permanent homes at the MGM Mirage resorts in Las Vegas. In 20 years of live performances, 44 million people have seen a Cirque show.[2] Despite a long-term decline in the circus industry, Cirque has increased revenue 22-fold over the last 10 years.[3]

Cirque du Soleil is a family of more than 600 individuals from 40 different countries. Each of Cirque's 3,000 employees is encouraged to make contributions to the group. This input has resulted in rich, deep performances and expansion into alternative media outlets such as music, books, television, Web sites, and merchandising. The company's diversity ensures that every show reflects many different cultural influences. Many different markets will have an exotic experience at a Cirque show, regardless of which show is playing where. Cirque does target specific markets with products designed to engage a particular audience. Yet Cirque has little need to adapt its product to new markets; the product is already a blend of global influences. The result is a presentation of acrobatic arts and traditional, live circus with an almost indescribable freshness and beauty.

Cirque du Soleil's commitment to excellence and innovation transcends cultural differences and the limits of many modern media. Its intense popularity has made Cirque both the global standard of live entertainment and the place for talented individuals from around the world to perfect their talents. The extent of the diversity, however, does pose a host of unique challenges. Every employee must be well versed in various forms and styles. To foster cultural enrichment, Cirque purchases and shares a large collection of art with employees and gives them tickets to different events and shows.

The performers work in the most grueling and intimate situations, with their lives depending on one another. The astounding spectacles they create on stage result from hours of planning, practice, and painstaking attention to detail among artists from diverse cultures who speak 25 different languages. Sensitivity, compromise, and hunger for new experiences are prerequisites for success at Cirque. The organization has learned the art of sensitivity and compromise in its recruiting. Cirque du Soleil has had a presence in the Olympics for a decade. It works closely with coaches and teams to help athletes consider a career with Cirque *after* their competitive years are over, rather than luring talent away from countries that have made huge investments in athletes. This practice has given Cirque a huge advantage in the athletic community, a source of great talent from all over the world.

Guy Laliberté has not forgotten his own humble beginnings as a Canadian street performer. Now that Cirque du Soleil has achieved an international presence and incredible success—the group expects to be doing $1 billion in annual gross revenue by 2007—it has chosen to help at-risk youth, especially street kids. Cirque allocates 1 percent of its revenues to outreach programs targeting youth in difficulty, regardless of location in the world.[4] Guy understands that to be successful in a world market, one must be a committed and sensitive neighbor. Cirque's headquarters in Montreal is the center of an urban revitalization project sponsored by Cirque. Community participation and outreach bring the company international goodwill and help Cirque du Soleil transcend many of the difficulties global brands often face when spanning cultures.

Questions for Discussion

1. Why is Cirque du Soleil successful throughout the world? How does the product transcend culture differences between countries?
2. How have the five major drivers of globalization influenced Cirque du Soleil?
3. Why is it important for Cirque du Soleil to be a good corporate citizen? How does the organization strive to fulfill this role?

Sources

1. "Founder's Message," www.cirquedusoleil.com.
2. Mario D'Amico, and Vincent Gagné, "Big Top Television," *Marketing* 109, no. 26 (August 9–August 16, 2004), p. 20.
3. Chan Kim and Renee Mauborgne, "Blue Ocean Strategy," *Harvard Business Review,* October 2004, p. 77.
4. "Social Action," www.cirquedusoleil.com.

Chapter 2 Video Case China Syndrome, China Brands

In April 2006 when President Hu Jintao of China visited the United States on a four-day business mission, his first stop was Seattle, home to Microsoft, Boeing, and Starbucks. Although these firms rolled out the red carpet for Jintao, his trip was not without controversy. From Capitol Hill to the floor of U.S. factories, many are charging that when it comes to trade, China isn't playing fair.

With 1.3 billion people, China has the largest population in the world. Its economy is exploding with 10 percent economic growth annually. Oil consumption in China is surging, helping to drive up the price on the world market. China now produces more steel than the United States, Japan, and Europe combined, in mills subsidized by interest-free loans, an undervalued currency, and export tax breaks.[1]

As China's economy has grown, so have Western concerns about its undervalued currency; rampant piracy of movies, music, and software; and generous subsidies to attract businesses. U.S. politicians argue that as a result of such practices, Chinese firms are producing goods much cheaper than American companies are, a situation contributing to a $200 million trade imbalance. Chinese officials spurn these accusations, arguing that banks are chasing firms in China to lend them money.[2]

Evidence points to the contrary. Zachary Mottl owns a manufacturing business in Chicago. His revenues have declined 50 percent in the last six years. Competing with the Chinese on price has hurt profits. A bracket Mottl's company makes, for example, sells for $1.10, while the price in China is 41 cents—a price the Chicago firm simply cannot meet. Many experts believe that a significant revaluation of its currency by China would have some impact on the large price discrepancy between China and the United States.

Another contentious issue is piracy. Problems with piracy in China still remain severe and widespread, according to a senior U.S. commerce official.[3] Though laws against piracy exist, China has not been able to enforce them at the local level. As a result, the United States is raising red flags over illegal Chinese copies of software, music, and movies. For instance, 90 percent of the DVDs in China are thought to be illegal; the piracy is costing U.S. producers $2 billion a year. According to Dan Glickman, president of the Motion Picture Association of America, some films are on the street in China at the same time as, or in some cases before, their worldwide release.

Asia expert Derek Mitchell says that going after China on economic grounds is risky, because the country is so important to the U.S. economy. China has long provided the inexpensive labor to produce much of the world's goods. Now it offers foreign sellers the world's largest consumer market. China is a big buyer of all things American. From Wal-Mart to GM to Reebok, U.S. firms have a strong presence there. American exports to China have grown 160 percent in five years.

China is playing another vital role in the U.S. economy as an increasing number of Chinese-branded products make their way to stores abroad. In the past decade, a number of prominent Chinese brands have emerged in China. Many Chinese manufacturers are looking to take their brands global after successfully marketing to more than 1 billion domestic consumers.[4] If they can expand these products to foreign markets, Chinese companies could end up producing the world's most popular brands. Chinese firms have been manufacturing products for well-known firms like Sony and Xerox, but now the Chinese firms are taking their manufacturing expertise and selling products with their own brand names.

Many Chinese brands have arrived in America. Leading Chinese appliance manufacturer Haier has accelerated its push into U.S. markets. Haier already has products in the top 10 U.S. retail chains and more than 240 subsidiaries worldwide, with manufacturing facilities in the United States.[5] Lenovo, the number-one selling PC in China, is also known throughout Asia. In 2006, Lenovo took its first steps toward making a name for itself in the United States when it unveiled a series of notebooks and desktops under the Lenovo brand.[6] Television manufacturer SVA is another Chinese brand looking for American customers with its competitively priced flat-screen TVs at Target and Office Depot. Tsingtao is the number-two Asian beer in the United States, after Japan's Sapporo.[7] Finally, Chinese automobile manufacturer Chery may be heading to America. Chery's best-selling export is a four-door compact priced between $7,000 and $8,000. In 2008 the company hopes to compete globally and export 300,000 to 400,000 cars.[8] Chinese brands are proving they can compete globally.

Questions for Discussion

1. Is China cheating when it comes to international trade? How big a problem is piracy?
2. How dependent is the U.S. economy on China? How far should the United States push China on matters such as currency, piracy, and subsidies?
3. What impact could Chinese brands have on international trade? Do you think brands from China will become as popular as brands from Japan?

Sources

1. Pete Engardio and Catherine Yang, "The Runaway Giant," *BusinessWeek,* April 24, 2006, p. 30.
2. Andrew Browne, "Rapid Economic Growth at Home Adds to Heat on Hu to Adjust Yuan," *The Wall Street Journal,* April 20, 2006, p. A1.
3. Andrew Yeh, "China's Piracy Problems Remain Severe," *FT.com,* September 14, 2005, p. 1.
4. Gordon Orr, "Building Chinese Brands beyond China," *FT.com,* August 25, 2005, p. 1.
5. Laura Heller, "Manufacturers Long for Brand Equity," *Retailing Today,* August 7, 2006, pp. 1–2.
6. Edward F. Moltzen, "Lenovo Takes Off," *CRN,* February 27, 2006, p. 14.
7. Leslie P. Norton, "Let's Lift a Glass to Tsingtao," *Baron's,* June 12, 2006, p. M6.
8. Gordon Fairclough, "China Auto Exports May Roil Rivals," *The Wall Street Journal,* February 16, 2006, p. A2.

Chapter 3 Video Case Wal-Mart in China

Chinese cities have been making the dramatic leap from communism to capitalism in the past few decades. A striking example is Shanghai, where one can ride on the world's fastest train and stay in the world's tallest hotel. The "dragonhead" of an industrial boom in the Yangtze River delta, Shanghai transformed its Pudong section in less than 15 years from an economically stagnant semi-rural area to a futuristic financial capital.[1] The state-owned industries that have dominated the city's economy since 1949 are giving way to private enterprises, both local and foreign-owned.

Among the new businesses Shanghai's Pudong area boasts is a Wal-Mart Supercenter, one of 15 stores the retailer opened in China in 2005. Locating in large urban centers, Wal-Mart has enticed throngs of Chinese consumers with its large, clean stores, wide selection, helpful employees, and low, low prices.

Wal-Mart has been operating stores in China since the early 1990s. Its efforts to establish outlets in China were slowed by government regulations that limited foreign retail companies to operating in only a few large cities and required them to offer at least 35 percent of each store to local business partners.[2] In December 2004, the government in Beijing started to allow foreign retailers to invest independently in any Chinese city. Wal-Mart has not rushed to take advantage of the changes in laws governing foreign direct investment, however, and has continued to develop stores with joint venture partners.[3] By mid-2006, Wal-Mart operated 56 stores in China that employed 30,000 people, and it planned to open 20 more stores by year-end and add 150,000 employees over the next five years.

Opening stores in China poses several challenges. In many Chinese cities, the best real estate is controlled by the local government, which may give preference to state-owned retailers. Each supercenter requires hiring and training 500 employees. Wal-Mart has been pressured by the All-China Federation of Trade Unions (ACFTU), a powerful organization closely tied to the Chinese government that wants to establish unions in foreign companies in China. Wal-Mart, which has no unionized stores in the United States, has said that it would work with ACFTU to start grass-roots unions in each of its stores throughout China.[4]

The biggest challenge, according to Wal-Mart's Asia CEO Joe Hatfield, is finding qualified managers.[5] Like most multinational firms today, Wal-Mart looks for local talent to fill management positions. In the mid-1990s, almost all foreign firms' management positions in China were filled by foreigners; now one consulting firm in Beijing says that Chinese workers hold about 70 percent of foreign companies' top positions. Executives at foreign companies in China find that local employees cost less to employ than managers from Western countries and that they have a better understanding of the Chinese market.[6]

In China Wal-Mart has replicated its corporate culture, with its Five Commitments of Merchandising, red shirts for employees, and store pep rallies and cheering. It *has* altered the store offerings to cater to Chinese consumers, who mostly walk to stores and buy small quantities of food every day or two. While offering a broad mixture of food and general merchandise as usual, supercenters in China devote a large portion of floor space to food, especially perishable products. Shoppers can select from a vast array of produce and live grass fish, turtles, lobsters, and bullfrogs. The favorite item in most supercenters is the freshly prepared lunch of two meats, two vegetables, rice, and a cup of hot soup—all for less than $1.[7]

The stores carry many U.S. brands, such as Crest toothpaste, Clairol shampoo, Oreos, and Gatorade, but almost all the merchandise is made in China. China-based suppliers each year provide $18 billion of merchandise, mostly toys, footwear, Christmas decorations, and sporting equipment. Wal-Mart accounts for 3 percent of China's total exports; if it were a country, it would be China's sixth-largest export market.[8]

Wal-Mart executives have long seen China, with its population of 1.3 billion, as the best prospect for long-term global growth. One executive said China is the one place in the world where Wal-Mart could replicate the success it has achieved in the United States.[9] Wal-Mart operates more than 2,000 stores outside the United States, and international sales amount to 20 percent of the company's overall sales of $285 billion from roughly 5,700 stores. While the company's China stores now amount to less than 2 percent of its international sales, analysts have predicted that Wal-Mart could gain $20 billion in sales a year by gaining just 3 percent of the Chinese retail market.[10] It faces competition in China from French retailer Carrefour SA, which operates 61 hypermarkets and eight supermarkets there. China's largest foreign retailer, Carrefour arrived in China a year later than Wal-Mart but expanded more quickly, often avoiding central government restrictions by making alliances with local governments. Carrefour executives view local retailers as having the advantage in a large economy like China's, but they say they will match Wal-Mart's expansion in China store for store.[11]

Questions for Discussion

1. What were some of the reasons behind Wal-Mart's entry into the Chinese retail market?
2. What advantages has Wal-Mart gained by forming joint partnerships with Chinese developers?
3. Why do you think Wal-Mart sees China as its best bet for repeating the success it has achieved in America?

Sources

1. "Dragonhead Dreams," *The Economist,* January 7, 2006, p. 56.
2. Clay Chandler, "The Great Wal-Mart of China," *Fortune,* July 25, 2005, p. 104.
3. Mike Troy, "Can Presence in China Really Double by 2006?" *DSN Retailing Today,* August 8, 2005, p. 22.
4. Mei Fong, "Wal-Mart Meets with Officials from China Union," *The Wall Street Journal,* August 10, 2006, p. A2.
5. Chandler, "The Great wal-Mart."
6. "Firms in China Think Globally, Hire Locally," *The Wall Street Journal,* February 27, 2006, p. B1.
7. Chandler, "The Great wal-Mart."
8. Ibid.
9. Ibid.
10. "Wal-Mart Stores Inc.: Retailer Plans to Nearly Double Stores in China by End of 2006," *The Wall Street Journal,* July 26, 2005, p. D7.
11. Chandler, "The Great wal-Mart."

Chapter 4 Video Case U.S. Farmers and CAFTA

In the summer of 2005, Congress passed the Central America Free Trade Agreement (CAFTA), one of the most controversial trade pacts in U.S. history.[1] The agreement to open trade between the United States and Costa Rica, the Dominican Republic, El Salvador, Guatemala, Honduras, and Nicaragua continues to be a hot topic in rural America. Proponents of CAFTA argue that the pact will benefit U.S. consumers and businesses as well as improve economic conditions in Central America; critics claim the agreement will result in losses of jobs and production in America.[2]

What farmers think of CAFTA depends on what they produce. Duane Alberts, a fifth-generation corn and dairy farmer in southeastern Minnesota, runs a high-tech operation. He thinks that America produces the best agricultural products in the world and they should be exported as much as possible. That's why he is a strong supporter of liberalizing trade with the Dominican Republic and the five Central American nations. According to Alberts, CAFTA creates the opportunity to have another 44 million consumers of American-produced agricultural goods, whether pork, beef, corn, or others.

Hog farmers, for example, could have a much larger market. Before CAFTA, pork entering Central American countries was subject to import duties as high as 47 percent. Hence, not much pork was exported to the region. Larry Liepold, president of the Minnesota Pork Producers Association, believes that under CAFTA farmers will export a lot more pork. He points out how the pork industry has benefited in the past from other free trade agreements. After the North American Free Trade Agreement (NAFTA) was passed, the number of pigs exported to Mexico rose greatly. The pork industry also benefited from free trade agreements involving Korea, Taiwan, and Australia—a prime example, Leopold says, that free trade agreements are working.

Most American agricultural groups endorsed CAFTA, with the belief that it will allow farmers to sell more of their products outside the United States. One group of farmers, however, has been very vocal in its opposition to CAFTA. Sugar producers are not directly subsidized by the U.S. government as are farmers of most other commodities. Instead, the government sharply limits the import of sugar, which means American farmers don't face competition from abroad and thus can charge higher prices. Some sugar producers think that if import limits are lifted, countries will be able to dump sugar on the American market at far below cost. Sugar beet farmer Mark Olson notes that every other country subsidizes the production of sugar. When a country produces more than it needs, the excess supply gets dumped on the world market below production cost. Olson believes that as efficient as American sugar production is, it can't compete with foreign governments.

Sugar producers see CAFTA as the end of the U.S. sugar industry, which employs 140,000 people. Ninety percent of the sugar processed in America is done in farmer-owned co-ops like the Southern Minnesota Beet Sugar Cooperative. Co-op president John Richmond thinks CAFTA will result in less sugar production and less profit and will eventually cause U.S. producers to discontinue production. The Bush administration maintains that sugar farmers are exaggerating the impact of CAFTA, which would allow less than 2 percent more sugar from Central America into the United States.

Free trade advocates like Russell Roberts of George Mason University say it's time to stop protecting the sugar industry. He thinks the price of sugar in the United States is about double what it would be in a free market. This cost translates into higher profits for sugar farmers and higher prices for U.S. consumers for many products that contain sugar—such as ketchup and many others. The sugar industry put up a valiant fight. Sugar accounts for just 1 percent of all agricultural goods, but the industry is a large donor to political campaigns and has many allies in Washington, such as Republican Gil Gutknecht from Minnesota. He is not convinced that CAFTA will lead to greater exports, and he says that NAFTA did not help most American farmers.

The Bush administration defends NAFTA, saying it led to 30 percent economic growth in the United States, Canada, and Mexico. The verdict on CAFTA is still out, but as the agreement is coming to fruition, investment is picking up in the Central America region. The largest announcement has come from the International Textile Group's Core Denim Business, which plans to build a $100 million mill in Nicaragua employing about 750 workers.[3] As more nations implement the agreement—all but Costa Rica are expected to do so with certainty—export-oriented businesses and infrastructure projects are expected to benefit immediately.[4]

Questions for Discussion

1. What is the purpose of CAFTA?
2. What are the arguments in favor of CAFTA? What are the arguments against CAFTA?
3. Do you think history suggests that CAFTA will be successful? Explain your answer.

Sources

1. Lara L. Sowinski, "What Can DR-CAFTA Do for You?" *World Trade,* March 2006, pp. 68–69.
2. Glenn Hubbard, "CAFTA: A Win-Win Case," *BusinessWeek,* July 4, 2005, p. 102.
3. Kathleen DesMarteau, "CAFTA-DR Investment Increases," *Apparel,* June 2006, p. 33.
4. "Honduras Economy: Growth Remains Robust," *EIU ViewsWire,* July 19, 2006.

Chapter 5 Video Case — International Monetary Fund: Economic Aid in South Korea and Uganda

The International Monetary Fund (IMF) was established in 1944 in the midst of World War II, in an atmosphere of intense protectionism and nationalism. Since then, it has grown into a major international coalition of 184 members, including all of the world's major industrial countries, and become a leading force in the global economic system.

The IMF describes its main goals as providing stability in the international financial system and contributing in the fight against poverty worldwide. The international group uses a three-pronged strategy to promote global financial stability. It lends money to nations in financial crisis, it examines member-countries' economies and the general world economic outlook, and it helps financially troubled members set up sound fiscal practices.

The IMF is probably most well known as a lender to countries in financial crisis. When Asian financial markets collapsed in the late 1990s, South Korea borrowed $21 billion from the IMF to keep its banks from failing. Korean companies had borrowed excessive amounts of money, much of it in dollars rather than Korean won. When the value of the won fell on foreign exchange markets, Korean companies had to earn more profits to service their debt and many went bankrupt. Large South Korean corporations had borrowed huge amounts of money from banks and other institutions that they themselves controlled; when the companies encountered financial problems, so did the banks.

To obtain IMF loans, a country must agree to policies designed to stabilize the crisis, often by controlling inflation and currency exchange rates. Governments also must address underlying problems in their financial structure, budgets, banking practices, or corporate policies. In South Korea's case, the IMF required that the country restructure its banking and other corporate sectors.

The IMF's role in reducing world poverty is illustrated in Uganda, where since 1989 it has provided expertise and funds to combat economic decline from decades of political instability and ineffective financial policies. To qualify for a new IMF program, Uganda had to devise a plan to reduce poverty and spur economic growth. With the World Bank, the IMF helped the nation obtain $1 billion in debt relief, savings Uganda has put into education and health care. IMF officials say that such debt reduction initiatives, for which 26 countries qualified in mid-2003, work because a nation's government has ownership of the program.

Each IMF member contributes funds and holds voting power according to a quota based on the size of its economy compared to the world economy. Critics have argued that the major industrial nations, such as the United States, Germany, and Japan, dominate policy. IMF officials counter that because decisions require a 70 or 85 percent majority, a coalition of developing nations could veto a decision since together they comprise 37 percent of the total voting power. Officials also point out that members with the largest quotas do not always share the same opinion.

Another criticism is that the prospect of IMF intervention leads to the problem of "moral hazard," a situation in which people make reckless decisions because they know they will be rescued if things go wrong. Critics claim that because both parties think little risk is involved, governments borrow more than they can afford from foreign investors who otherwise would not make such questionable loans. IMF officials say that a country would never risk a debilitating financial crisis simply to get bailed out by the IMF, and they explain that investors assuming too much risk have indeed lost money, for example, in Russia in 1998, when the IMF did not lend money to cover the country's debt load. Because countries are required to repay IMF loans, officials explain, there is no such thing as an IMF bailout.

Questions for Discussion

1. Evaluate the IMF's quota system, which determines the contributions and voting share of members. Is it equitable? Is there a better way to determine members' financial responsibility or decision-making power?
2. What safeguards does the IMF have in place so that it does not encourage moral hazard?
3. Horst Kohler, the IMF's managing director, says that reducing poverty in low-income countries is as important as maintaining financial stability. Do you think this goal is appropriate for an international organization? Why or why not?

Chapter 6 Video Case The Peace Corps

Since 1960, Americans by the thousands have answered the call to service and have given more than two years of their lives as Peace Corps volunteers. Far from home and its comforts, they have lived and worked under unfamiliar and often extreme conditions, in countries such as Belize, Armenia, Ghana, Poland, China, Latvia, and Malawi, to name only a few. They have dug ditches, taught high school chemistry, set up computer centers, educated people about AIDS, counseled teens, and conducted a myriad of other activities.

The Peace Corps' overall goal is improving the development of infrastructure in impoverished areas of the world. In working toward that goal, the nonprofit organization must recognize cultural differences on a scale beyond what many global business organizations must do in their operations. In each unique location and for each project, the Peace Corps not only factors in cultural differences but makes bridging these differences its mission.

The Peace Corps traces its roots and mission to 1960, when John F. Kennedy, then a U.S. senator, challenged college students to serve their country by living and working in developing countries. In 1961 Congress authorized the Peace Corps as a federal agency with the purpose of promoting world peace and friendship by the United States. The organization was established to target three international needs: (1) to help interested countries meet their needs for trained workers; (2) to promote a better understanding of Americans; and (3) to promote a better understanding of other peoples on the part of Americans. Since the first group of volunteers—5,000 of them—the Peace Corps has placed more than 170,000 Americans in 136 host countries.

The talented volunteers provide skills in fields ranging from information technology to agriculture to medicine within communities that desperately need those skills. To facilitate the Peace Corps' mission, the workers must take a crash course on local culture to ensure sensitivity to the differences between American culture and that of the host country. Communication is a vital ingredient. Speaking a foreign language is not a necessity for volunteers, but most of them become at least passably fluent in the local tongue. Perhaps more significant than spoken language is mastering unspoken language and adopting local customs and mores so that a Peace Corps volunteer becomes part of the community. To blend in and fit comfortably, the Americans must make most of the concessions in cultural relationships; they are the ones who are serving, after all. Indeed, the volunteers ask a great deal of a community simply by bringing unfamiliar technology and methodology to a place with its own traditions.

Some of the most sensitive cultural differences are religious. While the Peace Corps is a secular organization—one not based on religious belief—many of its volunteers are motivated by personal religious convictions to provide service to others. Religion often plays an important role in how the group achieves its mission. Peace Corps volunteers are taught to be sensitive to the religions of the local communities where they serve, so that they may practice their own beliefs as much as possible without unintentionally challenging the local people's beliefs.

Information technology is a significant novelty that the Peace Corps brings to impoverished communities. In many locations, the volunteers are the first to expose a community to the Internet. Volunteers apply the methods of instant communication and on-demand access to obtain information in areas like ecology, agriculture, and meteorology. With this wealth of information and well-placed volunteers, the Peace Corps can fill a community's educational gaps caused by poverty or the loss of skilled, local members to more profitable, urban markets.

Peace Corps volunteers become like family to the communities they serve, even though they often are of a different race or economic background. Strong ties result from long, painstaking study of the culture and a patient program of personal compromise and diplomacy that earns the community's respect. Successes in the areas of medicine, agriculture, and business development play an important role in the Peace Corps mission, of course, but such successes could not be achieved without the personal relationship between the volunteers and those they serve.

While Peace Corps members volunteer their time and expertise, they receive benefits other than pay. The organization provides transportation costs, complete medical and dental care, and a living allowance that enables them to live in a manner similar to the local people. After completing their 27 months of service, volunteers receive about $6,000 to use as they prefer—to travel, continue their education, make a move, or obtain housing.

Questions for Discussion

1. Why is religion one of the most important and sensitive cultural factors for Peace Corps volunteers?
2. How does the Peace Corps use technology in its international mission? Which cultural aspects of technology must it consider?
3. What language issues present challenges for Peace Corps volunteers? How does the organization meet those challenges?

Chapter 7 Video Case Clearing the Air

The argument surrounding global warming has centered on how best to reduce emissions of carbon dioxide and other greenhouse gases that are causing the world's climate to change. While a solution is sought, the costs are already being felt by businesses and cities around the world. Consider the following:

- Because icy roads are melting, Canadian diamond miners must airlift equipment rather than trucking it in, at a large increase in cost.
- Oil companies must build stronger rigs and cities stronger seawalls because of the severity of storms and rising seas.
- Since the rainy season is now too short for rice and the dry season too hot for potatoes, agriculture is

threatened in Mali, Africa.

- Later winters in British Columbia have let beetles spread, killing 22 million acres of pine forests.
- Villages in Alaska may be forced to relocate because of the loss of permafrost and protective sea ice.
- A surge in parasites associated with higher water temperature is threatening the Yukon River fishing industry.[1]

Now the global-warming debate is heating up in cities across the United States. Instead of waiting for federal mandates, several of the nation's municipalities are taking their own measures to curb greenhouse gases. Seattle is a good example. As the cruise ship *Diamond Princess* arrives at the port of Seattle, it discharges exhaust from its huge diesel engine. Under an agreement with the city, the engine is shut down while the ship docks. As the ship loads and unloads passengers, power is supplied from an electrical connection on shore. This method keeps nearly 200 tons of sulfur dioxide emissions from entering Seattle air over the summer.

Most ships keep the diesel engine running while in port. But Seattle mayor Greg Nickels has a plan for Seattle to meet the terms of the Kyoto Agreement, which calls for the United States to reduce greenhouse gas emissions 7 percent below 1990 levels by the year 2012. President George W. Bush pulled the United States out of the treaty in 2001, saying the science about global warming was unclear: "The Kyoto Protocol was fatally flawed in fundamental ways. No one can say with any certainty what constitutes a dangerous level of warming, and therefore, what level must be avoided."

Mayor Nickels disagrees that global warming isn't a proven problem. He cites an unusually warm winter in the Pacific Northwest that closed ski resorts and threatened the city's water supply. He thinks that mild winter, along with hurricanes in Florida, heavy rains and mudslides in Southern California, and the heat wave in Europe, constitutes a clear trend. When the Kyoto Protocol took effect in 141 countries in 2005, but not in the United States, Nickels put forth the U.S. Mayors' Climate Protection Agreement at a U.S. Conference of Mayors meeting. The initiative would reduce dependence on fossil fuels by promoting wind and solar energy and more efficient vehicles and biofuels. In unanimous support, 168 mayors in 37 states—both blue and red—committed their cities to the Kyoto Agreement. By April 2006, 218 mayors in 39 states representing nearly 44 million Americans have signed on.[2] The cities constitute a diverse group ranging from liberal to conservative, Vermont to California. The common denominator is concern for what global warming is doing to these cities.

The concern is not unfounded. In the Pacific Northwest, National Park Service geologist John Riedel says global warming could create a water shortage. He says carbon dioxide in the atmosphere is higher than at any time since records have been kept. The average temperature in the Northwest has risen almost 2 degrees in the last century. About 40 percent of the ice cover in the mountains, where most of the region gets its water supply, has been lost over the last 150 years. Riedel thinks global warming is without a doubt the cause. To try to solve this problem, Seattle is offering developers incentives to build energy-efficient buildings. The city has also converted many of its vehicles to biodiesel fuel.

President Bush has maintained throughout his presidency that actions to reduce greenhouse gases are too costly. He thinks abiding by the Kyoto Treaty would harm the economy and cost Americans 5 million jobs. The mayors argue there are business opportunities in reducing greenhouse emissions. For instance, John Plaza founded Seattle Biofuels to manufacture biodiesel fuel, which is a low-polluting fuel made from soybean oil. The company is profitable, with revenues between $8 million and $10 million. Companies such as Aventive, a producer and marketer of ethanol, and VeraSun, the second-largest ethanol producer in the United States behind Archer Daniels Midland, have successfully gone public and have brought in more than $800 million in their initial offerings.[3]

The new technology has problems, such as the cost of converting to the new fuels. Even the mayors who support curbing emissions are concerned whether a city-by-city approach will work. Even though Seattle has reduced its own emissions by 60 percent since 1990, greenhouse gases from all sources in the Puget Sound area are expected to increase 20 percent above the 1990 level within a few years. In Portland, Oregon, greenhouse emissions have fallen 13 percent on a per capita basis; with population growth, however, the total emissions in the region have barely dropped below 1990 levels. There are limits to what a city can do by itself. Mayor Nickels remains optimistic that cities will eventually make it impossible for the federal government to say no. In the meantime, President Bush is advocating that industries take voluntary steps to reduce emissions.

Questions for Discussion

1. Do you think it is critical for the United States to develop a strategy to halt the trend toward global warming? Why or why not?
2. At which level should greenhouse emissions be attacked—city, state, or federal? Do you support the Kyoto Treaty, or do you agree with the Bush administration's stance?
3. What are some of the environmental and economic consequences of failing to reverse the trend toward global warming? What can we learn from cities such as Seattle and Portland?

Sources

1. John Carey, "Business on a Warmer Planet," *BusinessWeek,* July 17, 2006, p. 26.

2. Margot Roosevelt, "Saving One City at a Time," *Time,* April 3, 2006, p. 48.

3. Joseph Chang, "Biofuels Cash In on Field of Dreams," *Chemical Market Reporter,* July 17–July 23, 2006, p. 14.

Chapter 8 Video Case Three Billion New Capitalists

If you want to see where the world's economy is heading, look to the East. That's the message in *Three Billion New Capitalists: The Great Shift of Wealth and Power,* by Clyde Prestowitz, an expert on Asia who began his career as a trade negotiator in the Reagan administration. Prestowitz believes that India and China are on a course to become global leaders and that, without taking dramatic steps, the United States will fall behind.[1] The factory workers in China and the outsourced jobs in India that we hear about signal the beginning of a shift in economic power, a shift that Westerners will need to accept.

Prestowitz maintains that America is seeing the middle of a two-part revolution. First are the 3 billion people from China, India, and the former Soviet bloc entering the global economy at the same time. These 3 billion people represent a population at least as large as that of the United States, and larger than that of Japan or of any country in Europe. This population is highly skilled and can perform any type of work "every bit as good" as can workers in the United States, Japan, or any of the other developed countries, and it can do so for 10 cents, maybe 25 to 30 cents, on the dollar. By "every bit as good," Prestowitz means as good as or better than the output of top U.S. doctors, professors, business leaders, entrepreneurs, and so on. Educated in our best universities, trained in our best hospitals, or with start-up experience in the Silicon Valley, these individuals are returning home to China and India, where there are great opportunities waiting for them.

China leads the pack as a center for global outsourcing, thanks to its large population of nearly 1.5 billion people. Within the last decade, outsourcing has begun to move into service areas, such as human resources, call centers, and finance and accounting functions.[2] India alone had revenues of $22 million last year from answering customer phone calls, managing computer networks, and writing software for firms all over the world; Russia has followed India's lead into the software industry.[3]

The second revolution, according to Prestowitz, is that the Internet and transportation companies like Federal Express have eliminated time and distance. Any task done on the Internet is only seconds away from anyplace in the world. Even manufacturing firms with products to deliver can reach virtually anywhere in the world in 36 hours. Effectively, people throughout the world are sitting together at the same table.

In order to compete in this connected environment, the United States must be more competitive. First, better education and more training for workers are required. But training and education will not be enough, and a new approach to international economics is needed. The U.S. semiconductor industry offers a good example. Prestowitz argues that the United States is the best place in the world to make these products, yet two-thirds of the plants being built today are in Asia. The economic development leaders of many Asian countries use tax incentives and capital to make it very lucrative for U.S. firms to manufacture semiconductors in their countries. The decision to locate a plant in Asia has little to do with market forces or free trade. Yet neither Democratic nor Republican administrations in the United States have responded to what Prestowitz thinks is, in effect, bribery.

Some argue that concerns about China and India are similar to the fear America had about Japan 15 to 20 years ago. Many believed that Japan was becoming a world power and that, without a national competitive industrial policy, America would be left behind. Of course, this scenario never really materialized, and the U.S. economy has done fairly well in the last two decades. But, Prestowitz thinks, the current challenge is different from the one posed by Japan in the 1980s. In response to Japan, the U.S. government established an organization to promote development of the U.S. semiconductor equipment industry. Agreements were negotiated with Japan to stop the dumping of chips on U.S. markets and to open Japanese markets to more foreign products. Success in the 1990s is due at least in part to these government actions. What is occurring now in China and India is quite similar to the situation with Japan in the 1980s, but the population is much larger, more countries are involved, and China is a much tougher player than Japan.

Some analysts maintain that the U.S. economy continues to grow faster than the economies of Japan or Europe. Prestowitz is concerned that this growth is fueled by debt. The United States has moved from being the world's largest net creditor to the largest net debtor, with a $3 trillion debt, growing at $700 million annually. The country is using 80 percent of its global savings, and if it reaches 100 percent, the economic outlook isn't good. Paul Volcker, former undersecretary of the U.S. Department of the Treasury and chairman of the Federal Reserve, has warned of a major financial crisis in the next five years; he puts the probability at 75 percent.

While the emergence of China and India poses serious competition for the United States, these countries face major challenges themselves. The United States has stable institutions, the best graduate schools, the best infrastructure, and an entrepreneurial culture that encourages innovation. India and China, on the other hand, face obstacles of energy availability, energy cost, water availability, and pollution.[4] As these nations become large energy users, with no other source of oil, they will be more dependent on the Middle East than is the United States. The aging population is becoming an issue in China, especially given its policy of one child per family, and pension and health care issues will be difficult to address. India has favorable demographics, with half the population under the age of 25. For India, already the fourth-largest economy in the world, a competitive business environment, a thriving service sector, and an increase in foreign investment point to a bright future.[5]

Prestowitz maintains that the United States should want both India and China to succeed, since a failed China and India would not help the United States. He calls for a complementary economic relationship that lets all parties succeed. What is needed is a strategy enabling the United States to take the steps necessary to compete and meet the challenges that lie ahead.

Questions for Discussion

1. What economic and socioeconomic factors explain the optimistic economic outlook for China and India?
2. What role does the cost of labor play in the rise of China and India? How can U.S. firms compete in this environment?
3. Should the U.S. government take actions in response to incentives used by Asian countries to attract American firms? If so, what actions would you suggest?

Sources

1. Hardy Green, "Paperback Picnic," *BusinessWeek,* June 26, 2006, p. 108.
2. "The Global Outsourcing 100," *Fortune,* April 3, 2006, pp. A1–A8.
3. Andy Reinhardt, Manjeet Kripalani, Geri Smith, and Jason Bush, "Angling to Be the Next Bangalore," *BusinessWeek,* January 30, 2006, p. 62.
4. Colum Murphy, "Interview," *Far Eastern Economic Review,* April 2006, pp. 58–59.
5. Joseph Luna, "A Matter of Time: India's Emerging Economic Prowess," *Harvard International Review,* Winter 2006, pp. 36–39.

Chapter 9 Video Case Controversy over U.S. Port Security

In early 2006, it came to the attention of Congress and the American people that a company from the United Arab Emirates would soon manage six major U.S. ports, including New York–New Jersey. When Dubai Ports World (DPW) arranged in November 2005 to buy British-based Peninsula & Oriental Steam Navigation Co. (P&O) for $6.9 billion, the management of the six U.S. ports was part of the deal.

In the huge controversy that ensued, opponents claimed an Arab company presented too many possible security risks to have authority over U.S. trade entry points vulnerable to terrorism. Less than five years after 9/11, fearing more terrorist attacks, many Americans were baffled and angered at the idea of an Arab-based company in charge of U.S. ports. Congress considered passing special legislation to prevent an Arab-owned company from operating U.S. port terminals. Even Republican members did not align with President George W. Bush, a supporter of free trade who backed the deal and threatened to veto any congressional action to stop it. The controversy ended when DPW, in order to "preserve its strong relationship with the United States," announced it would find an American company to take over management of the six ports.

The port controversy showed that Americans and their leaders lacked knowledge of U.S. port management and security. Dubai Ports World would not have been the first foreign operator of a U.S. port—far from it. More than 60 percent of the container terminals at the country's 10 busiest ports are managed to some degree by foreign operators, some of which are controlled by foreign governments.[1] The DPW deal erupted into a public controversy for political reasons. A Miami firm, Continental Stevedoring & Terminals, Inc., had been wrestling with the British-owned P&O over divisions of port operations in Miami. When the DPW purchase of P&O was announced, this gave Continental a chance to take its turf battle from the courts to the political arena, where fear of terrorism was a top issue. Continental used a Washington lobbyist to build congressional opposition to the deal on the grounds of national security.[2]

Port security is a vital matter, with 90 percent of the world's cargo shipped by container and 46 percent of all U.S. imports arriving by oceangoing cargo containers.[3] Terminal operators, however, do not inspect containers unloaded at ports. Most port authorities act as landlords who lease waterfronts to ocean carriers and stevedoring firms.[4] Federal agencies, including U.S. Customs and Border Protection, part of the Department of Homeland Security, are responsible for U.S. port security.

Federal agents inspect about 5.5 percent of the 9 million containers entering the United States each year. After the DPW furor, some members of Congress proposed that all containers be scanned. Nearly everyone in the maritime industry agrees that even if federal agencies had the resources, inspecting all containers is not the answer to security concerns. It would take weeks to move cargo containers through a port if each had to be opened and inspected. Such delays would kill just-in-time manufacturing—since many U.S. companies now keep only a day's supply of parts—and cause slowdowns and shutdowns. Instead of supporting impractical screening requirements, some industry analysts recommend steps such as a national portwide identification system for cargo containers, background checks on all port employees, and certification programs ensuring that foreign firms have security standards in place to prevent the inclusion of contraband in cargo containers.[5]

The maritime industry has argued for years that U.S. harbors need more federal funding, not only to enhance security but also to manage growing trade. The American Association of Port Authorities has said that the United States needs to invest more than $17 billion to upgrade and modernize port facilities to handle the growth in trade and $3 billion to meet proposed federal requirements for cargo screening.[6]

In May 2006 Congress passed the Security and Accountability for Every (SAFE) Port Act, which authorized $5.5 billion for port security and required that the government finish installing radiation screening equipment at major U.S. ports by the end of 2007. The bill allows the United States to deny entry to cargo from countries that refuse to cooperate with increased security checks abroad.[7] Some observers expect Congress to enact a law requiring that foreign companies file information about proposed acquisitions in the United States, particularly those giving control over infrastructure, and granting itself the power to approve or disapprove foreign acquisitions that might affect national security.[8]

Questions for Discussion

1. What political forces are illustrated in the DPW port controversy?
2. Should Congress have the power to restrict foreign investment and ownership in the United States? Why or why not?
3. Why was the prospect of U.S. ports being controlled by a Dubai-owned company so alarming to Americans, when other foreign companies already managed U.S. ports? Should any foreign-owned companies be allowed to manage U.S. infrastructure?

Sources

1. James Aaron Cooke, "The DP World Controversy Could Help Our Seaports," *Logistics Management,* April 2006, p. 80.
2. Neil Shister, "Dubai Ports Controversy Misses the Big Picture," *World Trade,* April 2006, p. 6.
3. Jeffrey L. Holmes, "The Container Security Initiative," *Fleet Equipment,* August 2004, p. 15.
4. Cooke, "The DP world Controversy."
5. Robert J. Verdisco and Morrison G. Cain, "Safe Ports, Secure Economy," *Retail Merchandiser,* February 2002, p. 9.
6. Cooke, "The DP world Controversy."
7. R. G. Edmonson, "House Passes Safe Ports Bill," *Journal of Commerce,* May 4, 2006, p. 1.
8. "Stricter Exon-Florio Process Expected after Ports Flap," *Mergers and Acquisitions,* April 2006, p. 12.

Chapter 10 Video Case The Challenge of Illegal Immigration

Every day, border patrol guards along the Rio Grande seize illegal immigrants sneaking into the United States. Many get through, knowing where they can cross the border from Mexico. It is along the Mexican border that issues of immigration are keenly understood and that anxiety and disagreement abound over what to do about undocumented workers, a majority of whom are Hispanic. According to Diana Palacious, city manager of Crystal City, Texas, "The face of this country is changing, and some people want to find any way possible to keep that from happening." Crystal City is a town of migrant workers in which Latinos make up the majority of the population and now hold political offices. The immigration debate in Crystal City is passionate nonetheless. Residents think some illegal immigrants come to work the system, while others like Judge Joe Luna say they come out of necessity and should be paid a fair wage.

The Latino town of Maywood, California, took the debate to a new level. City leaders vowed to defy any crackdown on illegal immigrants. Mayor Felipe Aguirre made it clear that the city of Maywood would not have its police officers act as immigration agents. "We would not have the city employees ask anybody who comes into city hall whether they have legal documents or not," Aguirre said.

The impact of illegal immigration, once felt most severely in Texas, California, and Arizona, is now felt far and wide in the United States. Besides those three states, Florida, New York, Illinois, New Jersey, and North Carolina account for two-thirds of the undocumented population. In a growing number of cities across the country, illegal workers are lining up on street corners for jobs. An estimated 12 million illegal immigrants live in the United States, and the federal government and many corporations are being pressured to reduce the number of illegals.[1]

For years federal agents conducted job site raids and arrested undocumented workers; employers were generally fined. Then the Department of Homeland Security, in its efforts to curb illegal immigration, began using laws traditionally directed against drug smugglers and organized crime. In one case, immigration and custom agents arrested dozens of illegals in raids of more than 40 plants nationwide owned by the global firm IFCO Systems, supplier of shipping containers and pallets to large retailers. The investigation mainly targeted seven current and former executives thought to have directly aided in the employment and harboring of illegal aliens. Advocates of tougher enforcement say this approach is long overdue.

Some are taking matters into their own hand. Four current and former workers at carpet maker Mohawk Industries in the town of Calhoun, Georgia, brought a class action against the company; their suit claims Mohawk conspired to depress their wages by hiring illegal immigrants.[2] The U.S. Supreme Court chose to hear the case; observers noted that a rejection of Mohawk's defense would imply that companies hiring illegals would basically have to become the border patrol.

Politicians, both Republicans and Democrats, are responding to public concern about the huge numbers of illegal immigrants living in the United States. In late 2005 the U.S. House of Representatives passed legislation making it a felony for businesses to hire illegal workers. Companies that incorrectly fill out certain paperwork on employees could be fined $25,000. "It doesn't take too many of those (fines) to drive a small business out of business," says John Gay of the National Restaurant Association.[3] The U.S. Senate favored a guest-worker program that would allow foreigners to take jobs Americans do not fill. Polls show that most Americans want to curb illegal immigration but also support some form of the temporary guest-worker program supported by President George W. Bush and approved by the U.S. Senate.[4] Illegals would have to pay back taxes and go to the end of the citizenship line. Despite these requirements, restrictionists called the Senate bill "amnesty."[5] A compromise between the two houses is likely to require that companies confirm the legal status of all current and prospective employees. Angelo Amador, the immigration policy director for the U.S. Chamber of Commerce, calls that plan a bureaucratic nightmare that would cost employers at least $12 billion in compliance.[6]

Immigration is a huge issue for many U.S. businesses, which rely on foreign workers for their labor needs. In March 2006 Bill Gates told congressional leaders that immigration is Microsoft's number-one issue in Washington. "If we hope to maintain our economic and intellectual leadership in the United States, we must renew this commitment [to immigration]," he said in a letter to lawmakers. "Unless there is reform, American competitiveness will suffer as other countries benefit from the international talent that U.S. employers cannot hire or retain."[7]

While America's illegal immigrants have become the target of mostly negative national attention, the buying power of 12 million consumers has attracted the interest of U.S. companies. Immigrants, documented or not, are seen by many as a potential source of growth, with more than 700,000 new consumers added to the economy each year.[8] In the spring of 2006, more than 1 million immigrants in cities from Los Angeles to New York stayed away from work and school and took to the streets to protest calls for sealing borders and to demonstrate the extent of their economic power. This sea of humanity vowed to push for immigration reform so that they can continue to call America home.

Questions for Discussion

1. What are the pros and cons of illegal immigrants' obtaining jobs in America?
2. What legal forces are most relevant to illegal immigration? Why is it difficult to enforce U.S. immigration laws?
3. Is it realistic to think that the vast numbers of illegal immigrants can be returned to their native lands? If not, what impact might the presence of so many illegals have on the legal environment?

Sources

1. Richard S. Dunham, "Immigration Reform: Why Business Could Get Burned," *BusinessWeek,* April 10, 2006, p. 41.
2. Brian Grow, "A Body Blow to Illegal Labor?" *BusinessWeek,* March 27, 2006, p. 86.
3. Dunham, "Immigration Reform."
4. "Illegal Immigration: Better Nothing at All than Congress's Draconian Bill," *Financial Times,* July 19, 2006, p. 18.
5. "An Immigration Compromise?" *The Wall Street Journal,* August 7, 2006, p. A12.
6. Dunham, "Immigration Reform."
7. Ibid.
8. Brian Grow, Adrienne Carter, Roger O. Crockett, and Geri Smith, "Embracing Illegals," *BusinessWeek,* July 18, 2005, p. 56.

Chapter 11 Video Case China: Changing the Yuan/Dollar

On July 21, 2005, after months of political pressure from the United States, the Chinese government revalued the yuan by raising it 2.1 percent higher against the U.S. dollar.[1] For over a decade the yuan had been pegged—or fixed—to the U.S. dollar at a rate of 8.28 yuan for every dollar. Critics of China's currency policy, including U.S. Treasury secretary John Snow, maintained that the yuan was undervalued, a situation that allowed Chinese exporters to undercut competitors worldwide. Talk on Capital Hill centered on the United States' large trade deficit with China and possible trade sanctions. How much effect China's revaluation will have on the global economy is uncertain.

The revaluation of the yuan may take the United States a step toward getting what it wants, though a small one, says Nariman Behravesh, chief economist at the economic forecasting firm Global Insight. The meager 2.1 percent increase amounts to little or nothing, and much depends on what China does next. If the Chinese continue raising the value of the yuan through a series of steps, Behravesh believes this could make a difference. Peter Morici, business professor at the University of Maryland and former chief economist at the International Trade Commission, agrees that the revaluation is a very small step toward the goal of the United States. By some estimates, the yuan is undervalued by as much as 40 percent, he says. With a 2 percent increase, Chinese exporters can make up the price changes by slightly improving their productivity. Even if the yuan is allowed to float consistently, it will take a long time to reduce China's comparative advantage in manufacturing labor costs.[2]

Slightly increasing the yuan's value when it is so undervalued is part of China's development strategy to increase exports, since the undervaluation provides a large subsidy to exporters. To maintain this favorable situation, China has to purchase dollars in amounts equal to about one-third the value of its exports. This purchase translates into a 33 percent subsidy on Chinese exports. In other words, China has an export-driven industrial policy.

The revaluation may or may not have a heavy impact on China's imports, depending on the extent of the revaluation. While Behravesh agrees the 2 percent will do little in terms of raising the price of imports, further changes in the value of the yuan will reduce the competitiveness of Chinese exports and increase the competitiveness of U.S. exports. The initial 2 percent, however, is simply nowhere close to making a difference.

According to Morici, the slight revaluation is much more a political move on China's part than an economic one. President George W. Bush and Secretary Snow have been very accommodating to the Chinese, pressuring them only to the extent that there was congressional pressure to do so. The revaluation enables Snow to say he delivered something, though it isn't much. Behravesh agrees that politics played an important role, but adds that China also revalued the yuan for other reasons. China has been receiving large sums of speculative money to finance investments. Raising the exchange rate even a small amount reduces the inflow of money as China looks to cool down its economy.

Will a revalued yuan allow Chinese workers to earn more and producers to see a better payday? Assuming the yuan continues to increase, Behravesh thinks the purchasing power of the average Chinese worker will rise, as will the standard of living. If the yuan stays as it is, the slight change will have little impact. The current policy of maintaining an undervalued yuan keeps prices low, but it also keeps individuals poor and profits thin. Unless the Chinese government does more to alter its policy on its currency, Behravesh expects leaders to come under continual pressure to increase the value of the yuan. Nonetheless, at the one-year anniversary of the yuan's revaluation, a similar move had not occurred.[3]

Questions for Discussion

1. Explain why an undervalued currency is a benefit to Chinese exporters. What is the major advantage of this policy?
2. Why is the United States pressuring China to revalue the yuan? What has been the effect of the 2.1 percent increase?
3. What could motivate China to increase the value of the yuan further? Are there any drawbacks to maintaining an undervalued yuan?

Sources

1. "Yuan Shift Appears Unlikely Soon," *The Wall Street Journal*, August 29, 2005, p. C3.
2. Carl Weinberg, "The Yuan Revaluation: A Bad Deal for Everyone," *Baron's*, July 25, 2005, p. 23.
3. Isabelle Lindenmayer, "Dollar Falls against Yen and Euro as Investors Ponder Next Fed Move," *The Wall Street Journal*, July 22, 2006, p. B6.

Chapter 12 Video Case Outsourcing

What seems to many like a smart business strategy has become the central focus in the debate about ethics in corporate America. *Outsourcing,* in its simplest form, is using an outside vendor to do work that is normally performed in-house.[1] Now the term generally refers to sending jobs outside the United States to foreign workers to realize cost savings. Offshore outsourcing began with manufacturing jobs leaving the United States in the late 1970s. In the late 1980s and early 1990s, software development was being outsourced to other countries; since the late1990s, with Internet bandwidth more affordable to transmit graphs, images, audio, and video, U.S. companies are outsourcing information technology (IT) services, such as tax return processing and financial and insurance services.

Today outsourcing is a strategy so widespread that almost any company of any size engages in the practice to take advantage of cheaper labor and production overseas. Outsourcing manufacturing jobs to China is so prevalent that many believe it is a major cause of the United States' $200 billion trade deficit with that country.[2] More than 70 percent of the Fortune 2000 companies say outsourcing is an important part of their overall growth strategy; India remains the leading offshore destination.[3]

Moving jobs offshore has taken center stage in the controversy surrounding American job loss. Proponents of outsourcing argue that it saves money and makes U.S. firms more competitive. In most cases the objective of outsourcing is a 20 percent savings in cost.[4] The city of Chicago, for instance, saved approximately $10 million over a three-year period by outsourcing its information technology systems, and the time it took to deliver services to citizens was reduced by 35 percent.[5]

Countless firms have reaped the cost-saving benefit of outsourcing, but many people in the United States decry the loss of jobs for Americans. The Manufacturers Alliance, a business and public policy research group, says that from 1999 to 2002, U.S. manufacturing plants declined by 20,000, while U.S. companies opened 246 facilities in foreign countries. Now thousands of white-collar jobs are moving overseas each year. One research firm estimates that at least 3.3 million jobs in service industries, accounting for $136 billion in wages, will leave the United States by 2015 for countries where workers earn less.[6]

Some point out that savings accrued through outsourcing allows firms to create new, higher-paying jobs domestically. By the year 2008, according to a recent study, 317,367 jobs will be created in the United States across many industries, a result of companies in several sectors saving $20.9 billion by outsourcing just their computer operations. This prospect is little consolation for the 276,954 workers who hold the computer-related jobs this same study predicts will be moving offshore by 2010.

Herein lies the crux of the debate over outsourcing. Is it good business that benefits everyone, or is it an insensitive and unethical practice that is consuming the livelihood of American workers? According to Jack Welch, the renowned former CFO of General Electric, if a firm cannot remain competitive, it can't pay the employees. Outsourcing is necessary for U.S. firms to compete globally. Others argue that Welch is missing the bigger picture. In the long run, businesses that say no to outsourcing and keep jobs in the United States will foster greater trust and goodwill among workers, unions, and consumers.

Some industry watchers contend that for American workers to survive outsourcing, they must learn new skills, which will also enhance the competitiveness of U.S. firms in the global marketplace. Companies are often reluctant to train older workers in new skills, and workers who are left without jobs often don't have the means to learn these skills on their own.[7] For workers whose jobs are eliminated because of outsourcing, training programs are essential to provide skills needed for the new jobs being created. When North Carolina started losing numerous jobs overseas, the state revamped its education system with the goal of creating a globally competitive workforce. Besides making the curriculum more rigorous from preschool through eighth grade, North Carolina plans to redesign high schools to give every student the chance to earn two years of college by the time they graduate, as well as to create new, small career-themed schools that emphasize engineering, science, or business.[8] If there is one point of agreement in the debate about outsourcing, it is that the best jobs will go to those with the greatest skills.

Questions for Discussion

1. Does outsourcing violate the trust between management and labor?
2. What are the arguments in support of outsourcing? The arguments against?
3. Where do you stand on the debate? Is it ethical or unethical? Support your stance.

Sources

1. Sunita S. Ahlawat and Sucheta Ahlawat, "Competing in the Global Economy: Implications for Business Education," *Journal of the American Academy of Business,* March 2006, pp. 101–5.
2. "Learning to Live with Offshoring," *BusinessWeek,* January 30, 2006, p. 122.
3. Stephanie Overby, "2006 Global Outsourcing Guide," *CIO*, July 15, 2006, p. 1.
4. George C. Elliott, "International Outsourcing: Values vs. Economics," *Quality Progress,* August 2006, pp. 20–25.
5. "The Global Outsourcing 100," *Fortune,* April 3, 2006, pp. A1–A8.
6. Ahlawat and Ahlawat, "Competing."
7. Catherine L. Mann, "How to Ease the Pain of Globalization," *CIO*, February 1, 2006, p. 1.
8. Barbara Kantrowitz, "The Future Is in Their Hands," *Newsweek,* June 12, 2006, p. 46.

Chapter 13 Video Case GM Global Research Network

With only about 12 percent of the world's population of 6 billion owning cars or trucks, the auto industry today is a growth industry with lots of room for expansion. There is potential for global annual sales of 65 to 70 million vehicles for 2010, with much of the expansion in China, India, Russia, and Brazil.[1] GM plans to take advantage of this potential with a strategy of alliance and technology networks. The auto giant is laying the groundwork for a new generation of cars and trucks with a new business model that partners with other auto companies and uses an extensive network of the world's brightest researchers and engineers.

GM is the world's largest automaker, with manufacturing operations in 32 countries and sales in 200 countries. Its approach to globalization has included forming an alliance network that includes General Motors, Opel/Vauxhall/Holden, Saab, Fiat Auto, Isuzu, Subaru, and Suzuki. Together, these companies sell more than 13 million vehicles a year.[2] Alliances with some of these companies, which produce cars that are smaller and lower-priced than the usual entry-level vehicles in the United States, will allow GM to build a presence in Asian markets more quickly.

Global competition has forced auto companies to increase their focus on innovation. Years before the design of a vehicle begins, research and development specialists are at work seeking the next level of innovation. Emission and safety regulations, along with competition from Europe and Asia, prompted GM to redirect its technology priorities. GM has changed its business model to reflect the technology revolution and the expanding technical leverage capabilities around the world, according to Alan Taub, executive director of GM Global Research and Development. Relying on technology requires a network of research minds not only in the United States but throughout the world. GM has recruited engineers and scientists from North and South America, Europe, the Middle East, China, Taiwan, India, and Korea.

"It became very clear to me that a research model based on bringing the best minds to Michigan just isn't going to work any more," says Larry Burns, head of GM's research and development since 1998. "There's too much talent all over the world."[3] Today, for every two researchers and engineers working inside GM labs, there is one external partner. The change requires a work force that is global, mobile, and comfortable working with many different cultures.

GM has formed research partnerships with other manufacturers, suppliers, universities, and governmental agencies. Research projects include internal combustion engine development, fuel cell technology, advanced chassis systems, electronics and communications systems, and many others.[4] The GM research model is evident at the GM Sweden Science Office at Saab headquarters in Trollhattan, Sweden. This new venture is developing centers of expertise and coordinating GM research and development activities. A $26 million agreement with the Swedish government supports automotive research in Sweden and extends for at least three years. GM hopes to build up its Saab division and to support efforts elsewhere by using Saab's core expertise—innovation of interiors, safety, and turbo engines. The Sweden Science Office is part of a strategy to leverage the company's global engineering resources, relationships, skills, and knowledge to increase the quality of research.

GM uses a two-pronged approach to technology research. In its innovation program, engineers can approach R&D management and be funded to take an idea from the drawing board to production. An example is improving driver interfaces. GM engineers are working on devices that let drivers watch the road while using navigation systems, climate control, mobile phones, or sound systems.[5] The second part is the company's strategic technologies program, which calls for a panel of GM experts to determine the 10 areas fundamental to the future of the company and of the entire auto industry.

Three areas key to GM's future research are powertrain control, electronic control and software, and hydrogen and fuel cells. The fuel cell and hydrogen technologies, R&D chief Burns says, provide an opportunity to relieve our 98 percent dependence on petroleum as an energy source for vehicles.[6] He envisions that a fuel cell engine, with one-tenth of the moving parts of an internal combustion engine, will provide enormous design opportunities. Combined with research on advanced materials, fuel cell development could make the car of the future safer, friendlier to the environment, and more affordable—an advantage in reaching new global markets.

Questions for Discussion

1. How is technology influencing strategy at GM? What factors should managers at GM consider when developing an international strategy?
2. Does GM have a competitive advantage? If so, what is it? If not, what does the firm need to do to establish one?
3. How can GM's global research network assist in the global strategic planning process?

Sources

1. Larry J. Howell and Jamie C. Hsu, "Globalization within the Auto Industry," *Research Technology Management,* July–August 2002, pp. 43–49.
2. Ibid.
3. "Interview—Larry Burns: Global Search," *The Engineer,* September 19, 2005, p. 30.
4. Howell and Hsu, "Globalization."
5. "Interview."
6. Ibid.

Chapter 14 Video Case DHL Global Delivery Service

The express delivery business has become a multibillion-dollar industry. Companies such as UPS, FedEx, DHL, TNT, and the United States Postal Service (USPS) have developed vast transportation and service networks to deliver millions of packages daily around the world, many overnight. FedEx, for instance, processes 1.4 million items on a typical night through its Memphis hub, where they are scanned, routed, sorted, and shipped to arrive at their destination by the next morning. UPS processes 1 million packages each day through its world port in Louisville, Kentucky; it delivers 230 packages every second during the holidays. Growing worldwide demand for express delivery has led to intense competition and has forced firms to improve efficiency and performance. Through mergers and acquisitions, new technology, and improved service, firms continue to battle for a share of this lucrative market. A case in point is DHL.

DHL was founded in San Francisco in 1969 by Adrian Dalsey, Larry Hillblom, and Robert Lynn; the initials of the last names formed the company name.[1] Major competitors include FedEx, UPS, and the U.S. Postal Service. Today, DHL is an $18.6 billion company, making it the market leader in international express delivery. DHL did not gain this position overnight; for years it expanded throughout the world until it developed a complete global network, refined to the point where it could serve customers worldwide, including Fortune 500 companies. As a result, DHL is the largest express carrier in both Europe and Asia, with a 40 percent share of each market.[2]

While DHL is a hugely successful company, it is dominated in the U.S. market by FedEx and UPS, which together have a 78 percent share of the domestic market, compared to DHL's 7 percent share.[3] By acquiring Airborne Express in 2003, DHL bolstered its express shipping infrastructure on the domestic level. The integration of the two companies was difficult, since each had different business models, different customers, and different geographic considerations.[4] By taking the best of both companies and making them work together, the new DHL is the number-one international delivery service. The company carries more than 1 billion shipments a year in more than 200 countries and territories worldwide. Serving more than 4.2 million customers, DHL generates revenues in excess of $50 billion a year.

To meet customer expectations of speed and reliability, DHL must maintain efficient operations at each point of the sorting and delivery process. The delivery process originates with the customer, who contacts DHL and advises that a package is ready and indicates where it is going. A courier picks up the package within 15 minutes of the time requested, whether prescheduled for large customers or ad hoc for small customers. Scanning activities, including the names of the sender and the receiver, weight, contents, and address for delivery, are performed at the customer's site. The package is then transported to a service center for shipment. Bar codes allow both DHL and the customer to track the package while en route. Known as "track and trace," the system has the fundamental purpose of giving customers peace of mind. While tracking was historically done through the DHL customer service department, customers now can have shipping-process equipment in their offices or can track packages on the Internet.

Packages are shipped from the local service office to the hub for sorting. Once sorted, packages are shipped to a regional sorting facility. Sometimes the sorting facility is a gateway where all international shipments must go to clear customs before leaving the United States. DHL employs a regional hub system. The U.S. hub is located in Cincinnati, while gateways are located in Miami, New York (JFK), Dallas, Los Angeles, and San Francisco. All packages are fed through the hub system. A package shipped from Orlando to Miami, for instance, would first go to Cincinnati and then to Miami. Hubs primarily service gateways, and a gateway is usually a port that services local pickup and delivery centers as well as exports to foreign destinations. For instance, the Miami gateway also services all of Latin America.

Gateways generally operate from Tuesday through Saturday. A morning shift handles planes coming in from hubs such as Cincinnati. An evening shift is mainly an outbound operation, sending packages that have arrived during the day from service centers out to the hubs. Couriers pick up from and deliver directly to the customer. International delivery requires some extra steps to clear packages through customs, which is located on site at the gateways.

DHL continues to expand its distribution facilities and build on Airborne's domestic network. With more than 700 daily flights in the United States, DHL hopes to challenge market leaders FedEx and UPS through its service to customers—better, quicker, and to more parts of the world. Express delivery groups such as these are taking an increasing role in the global economy as companies seek greater speed and reliability in their supply chains.[5]

Questions for Discussion

1. How do express delivery companies help customers improve efficiency? What types of organizational designs are most effective in this environment?
2. Why is it important for DHL to achieve superior performance? How does the company improve efficiency?
3. What role do express delivery companies play in the global economy? What techniques discussed in this chapter could DHL use to establish controls?

Sources

1. http://en.wikipedia.org/wiki/DHL.
2. Mark Ritson, "DHL Is Struggling to Deliver in the U.S.," *Marketing,* April 5, 2006, p. 21.
3. Jack Ewing, Dean Foust, and Michael Eidam, "DHL's American Adventure," *BusinessWeek,* November 29, 2004, p. 126.
4. Rick Whiting, "Best of Two Worlds," *InformationWeek,* June 26, 2006, pp. 48–49.
5. Andrew Ward, "FedEx Delivers Strong Results on Solid Growth," *Financial Times,* June 22, 2006, p. 27.

Chapter 17 Video Case Cretors & Co.

Chicago-based Cretors & Co. is the world's oldest and largest manufacturer of machines for popping and flavoring popcorn. Other products include machines for roasting and flavoring nuts, spinning cotton candy, and making other concession items. In business since 1885, Cretors began exporting its machines as early as 1897 and now ships equipment throughout the world. Exports were about 36 percent of its sales in 2002.

This small, family-run business, valued at around $10 million, dominates the world market for commercial machines for movie theaters. While Canada, Mexico, and Western European countries are its largest international customers, Cretors sells throughout Europe, North and South America, and Asia. The firm sells internationally through distributors, who often learn of Cretors' products through trade shows, word of mouth, and its Internet Web site and then contact the company and request to sell its equipment. Personal relationships with distributors are essential elements in building an export business, says Charlie Cretors, the great-grandson of the company's founder and its current CEO. Distributors link Cretors to customers not only for initial sales but also for after-sales service and support.

Flexibility has enabled Cretors to meet several challenges of international sales. Its various financing methods include open accounts (for smaller orders and established customers) and deposits or full payment (for large or unique orders and new customers). The company modifies machines for specific markets to meet different voltage, safety, and operating requirements. Cretors works with customers to reduce their costs. The manufacturer has altered equipment so that its resulting classification minimizes import duties. When shipping, Cretors packs its machines into containers and adds other suppliers' products that a distributor might want from the United States. This practice of combining shipments fosters goodwill for Cretors and strengthens its international partnerships.

Questions for Discussion

1. Exporters face the problem of locating foreign markets. How does Cretors deal with this problem?
2. What are the benefits of using distributors to sell in foreign countries? What are the possible drawbacks? Why might foreign distributors see Cretors as a desirable business partner?
3. How does Cretors meet the challenges of financing international sales?

Chapter 18 Video Case Domino's Pizza in Mexico

Domino's Pizza learned the hard way that moving into foreign markets without local input can be challenging. According to Tim McIntyre, vice president of communications for Domino's, the firm expected foreign cultures to adapt to Domino's offerings. After a few years, millions of dollars, and several attempts to penetrate foreign markets, the pizza company executives realized they would be more successful if Domino's abandoned its one-size-fits-all approach and adapted to the cultures of foreign countries. Patrick Doyle, executive president of Domino's international division, explains: "Local operators can act quickly to make changes in promotional and pricing strategies. If we were trying to do all of that from here in Ann Arbor, we would have a big struggle."[1]

One example of the problems Domino's encountered took place when it attempted to use its U.S. slogan "One Call Does It All" in England. What the firm failed to realize was that a call in England meant a personal visit. Customers couldn't understand why Domino's was celebrating the fact that all you had to do was come to the store and pick up your pizza.

Domino's venture outside the United States began in 1983 in Winnipeg, Canada. Since Domino's made the decision to focus more on local markets, overseas business has steadily increased. By 1995, Domino's had 1,000 stores outside the United States, 1,500 by 1997, and 3,000 in 2006. Today, Domino's has a presence in more than 50 markets and plans to go into more countries in the future. Domino's goal in all markets is to be the leader in the *delivery* pizza business. According to Michael Lawton, vice president of international operations, Domino's has succeeded in every market it has entered.

Domino's operates consistently throughout the world. Storefronts are similar at all Domino's outlets worldwide. The internal operation of the stores is also very similar. This has led to some interesting situations. In 1985, Domino's discovered there was no Japanese word for pepperoni, the most popular topping in the world. Japanese consumers thought it was some kind of small pepper and returned pizzas when they discovered it was a meat product. Today, it is the number-one topping in Japan, and the Japanese word for pepperoni is *pepperoni.*

Domino's has made several additions to its standard menu to adapt to local preferences. Examples include squid in Japan, tuna and sweet corn in England, lamb and pickled ginger in India, and barbecued chicken in the Bahamas, to name a few. Adjustments have also been made to accommodate different cultures. In India, pepperoni was replaced with spicy chicken in respect to the Hindu reverence for cows. Site selection in the Philippines is based on *feng shui,* the belief that prosperity is a function of building design and the arrangement of equipment inside. Special street maps were created in the United Arab Emirates because streets have three different names used interchangeably.

Mexico is the largest international market for Domino's, whose presence there is greater than that of McDonald's and Burger King combined.[2] Since entering the Mexican market in 1990, Domino's has grown to more than 500 stores. This growth can be attributed to several factors. The North American Free Trade Agreement (NAFTA), signed in 1993 and put into effect the following year, opened the door for restaurant investment; Mexico's trade with the United States and Canada has tripled since NAFTA was implemented.[3] Alberto Torrado, an innovative franchisee, has encouraged Domino's growth by bringing a new understanding of food and franchising to Mexico. When he started, there were no Domino's franchises. Torrado had to educate people about the franchise concept, the types of support Domino's provides, and the royalties it requires. This was no easy task. But by nurturing stores and providing training and services such as accounting and marketing support, Torrado helped Domino's grow into a powerhouse in Mexico.

Domino's has repositioned since it first entered Mexico at the high end of the market, targeting upper-middle-class consumers. Domino's pizzas were expensive, and that strategy was effective until the Mexican economy collapsed. Domino's shifted its target market by lowering prices and advertising that pizza is a great meal for the entire family. The company became much more profitable with this approach, another factor contributing to Domino's rise to being the number-one restaurant chain in Mexico.

Questions for Discussion

1. What problems did Domino's encounter when trying to standardize its product throughout the world? Why was local input beneficial?
2. How did the pizza giant adapt to different markets and cultures?
3. What factors have contributed to Domino's success in Mexico?

Sources

1. Amy Garber, "Operators across Globe Hungry for Slice of Domino's Pie," *Nation's Restaurant News,* January 19, 2004, p. 4.
2. Julia Boorstin, "Delivering at Domino's Pizza," *Fortune,* February 7, 2005, p. 28.
3. Ron Ruggless, "Crossing the Border," *Nation's Restaurant News,* December 8, 2003, p. 29.

Chapter 19 Video Case: Starbucks: Building Relationships with Coffee Growers

Starbucks, the world's largest supplier of premium coffee, works hard to guarantee a steady supply of quality coffee beans. An international giant, the company has nearly 6,000 outlets in 30 countries and sales of over $3.5 billion. Starbucks relies on the coffee bean for its success and faces the challenge of maintaining quality standards during a time of expansion and a global coffee crisis.

Coffee is produced in 70 tropical nations, and the quality varies tremendously. Starbucks buys a grade of coffee that is grown at high altitudes and that possesses a density or compaction of flavors as a result. For five years the supply of this specialty coffee exceeded demand and prices dropped below production costs for many growers. The situation drove many growers out of business. Those who remained were forced to cut back on crop maintenance, which resulted in lower quality. To continue to expand globally, Starbucks must ensure a steady supply of specialty coffee in the years ahead. When the supply of quality beans drops, Starbucks and other buyers must spend more time searching for specialty coffee.

One strategy Starbucks is using to face this challenge is to build long-term relationships with suppliers. The company purchases beans primarily from smaller farmers, invests in their operations, and teaches them how to produce specialty coffee. The firm also pays more for coffee—often above market price—which helps suppliers survive during a period of price volatility. In an effort to stabilize prices, Starbucks offers long-term contracts at set prices. Growers are assured future sales at established prices, and Starbucks is guaranteed a predictable supply of quality coffee. Another benefit to both parties is that farmers can use the profit to invest in their business and ensure supply in the years to come. Starbucks' risk is reduced as the company continues to grow and needs more beans.

Starbucks also has established other relationships as part of its global efforts. It partnered with two nonprofit organizations, Ecological Enterprise Ventures and Conservation International, to offer affordable credit to Latin American coffee growers. The credit works like bridge loans to ecologically friendly farmers in need of money to hold them over until the crop is harvested and to pay pickers. The loans help farmers survive so that they can be a constant source of coffee in the future. Starbucks also has partnered with Conservation International to encourage environmentally friendly growing practices. In Mexico, for example, trees had been cut down so that coffee trees could be planted in the sun. Trees are no longer cut down, and the result is the popular Shade Grown Mexico, a smooth, mellow coffee grown in shade.

Starbucks has also begun selling Fair Trade Coffee in its stores. Many workers in the coffee industry face terrible working conditions, and many growers are paid such low prices that they face poverty or debt. To be Fair Trade–certified, coffee producers must belong to democratically run cooperatives or associations and must implement crop management and environmental protection plans. Producers are guaranteed a fair price, long-term relationships with importers, and credit.

Questions for Discussion

1. Why is it important for Starbucks to guarantee a steady supply of coffee beans? How does the available supply of specialty coffee influence Starbucks' global expansion efforts?
2. Why are relationships with suppliers critical to Starbucks' success? What strategies are used by Starbucks to develop long-term relationships with suppliers?
3. How does Starbucks benefit from its relationships with Ecological Enterprise Ventures and Conservation International? Do you agree with Starbucks' decision to sell Fair Trade Coffee? Explain.

Chapter 20 Video Case: Johnson & Johnson: Creating a Global Learning Organization

Headquartered on a small campus in New Jersey, Johnson & Johnson (J&J) is one of the most globalized companies in the world. The organization is made up of over 230 companies operating primarily in the health care and personal care industries. Johnson & Johnson has manufacturing facilities in more than 60 countries and sells products in virtually every country in the world. Known for its customer-based values, the highly decentralized organization faces a major challenge managing many diverse companies.

The foundation of the Johnson & Johnson culture for all its companies is its Credo, a set of value statements that provides guidelines for employees. For nearly 70 years, the Credo has created the cultural ties that bind the organization, although—by design—the (J&J) family of companies is anything but tied together. Johnson & Johnson began to decentralize long before decentralization became fashionable in corporate America. Each of its companies is encouraged to act independently, deciding whom to hire and what products to produce. Decentralization has become so ingrained in the organization that each business is able to operate as a separate entity, which is part of Johnson & Johnson's strength: It is a very large organization with the flexibility of a smaller one.

The organization gains competitive advantage by letting the diverse companies create their own identities and pursue their own markets. In this environment, knowledge management injects life into the organization and translates into profits. Every year each company invests millions of dollars in education and training for its work force, consistent with the Credo values. With the core competencies of most jobs today changing rapidly, organizations like Johnson & Johnson face the challenge of reacting quickly to meet the learning needs of employees. Traditional methodologies limit a company's ability to react quickly and efficiently.

To maintain a decentralized structure, provide development for all employees, and deliver knowledge and skills rapidly, Johnson & Johnson created eUniversity in 2002. It's an electronic platform that offers a searchable resource for learning and development opportunities for J&J employees around the world.[1] With so many companies and more than 100,000 employees spread across the globe, eUniversity consolidates disparate learning technologies into a single system and allows J&J to control quality and costs.[2] It connects learning units as opposed to simply implementing a new technology.

The principle of eUniversity is to tap into the independence of each Johnson & Johnson group and capture the diversity of thought. This complex principle requires making use of both Web-based education and the classroom. The time together is spent in application and real-life problem solving instead of simply learning basic concepts. More than 75 Johnson & Johnson companies have offered training programs to other J&J companies through eUniversity. This cross-fertilization of knowledge has given employees not only an opportunity to learn but also a career competitive advantage. Participation has grown, and now a new user registers every 1.3 minutes; over three years, J&J employees completed 900,000 courses.[3]

Johnson & Johnson has realized several benefits from eUniversity. First, employees have learned much more from peers in similar situations than management thought they would. Second, smaller companies have gained access to the best learning experiences of the other companies, which was not possible before. Third, Johnson & Johnson has leveraged vendor-produced content across its courses and saved costs. Classroom training for sales representatives has been reduced by 30 to 40 percent, travel costs have dropped 20 percent, and the number of actual selling days for qualified sales reps has increased.[4]

Questions for Discussion

1. Why is eUniversity a valuable human resource tool for the Johnson & Johnson organization?
2. How does eUniversity manage to operate effectively in a decentralized environment?
3. What are the benefits of eUniversity to individual employees and to the organization?

Sources

1. www.jnj.com.
2. Kee Meng Yeo, "Johnson & Johnson: A New Paradigm for Learning Systems Management," *Chief Learning Officer Magazine,* March 2006, www.CLOmedia.com/content/anmviewer.as?a=1282&print=yes.
3. Ibid.
4. Ibid.

Endnotes

CHAPTER 1

1. For example, see Cornelis A. de Kluyver and John A. Pearce, II, *Strategy: A View from the Top*, 2nd ed. (Upper Saddle River, NJ: Pearson Prentice Hall, 2006), p. 38; InvestorDictionary.com, "Multinational Corporation: What's the Definition?" http://investordictionary.com/definition/multinational+corporation.aspx (July 6, 2006); and "Multinational Corporation," http://en.wikipedia.org/wiki/Multinational_corporation (July 6, 2006).

2. UNCTAD, "Transnational Corporations Statistics," www.unctad.org/templates/Page.asp?intItemID=3159&lang=1 (July 6, 2006).

3. Anne-Wil Harzing, "An Empirical Analysis and Extension of the Bartlett and Goshal Typology of Multinational Corporations," *Journal of International Business Studies,* First Quarter 2000, pp. 101–19; and C. A. Bartlett and S. Goshal, *Managing across Borders: The Transnational Solution* (Boston: Harvard Business School Press, 1989).

4. "The Black Death," www.insecta-inspecta.com/fleas/bdeath/bdeath.html (July 2, 2006); and Robbie Robertson, "Globalization Is Not Made in the West," www.globalpolicy.org/globaliz/define/2005/0413notmadeinthewest.htm (July 5, 2006).

5. "A Quick Guide to the World History of Globalization," www.sas.upenn.edu/~dludden/global1.htm (July 2, 2006); "Dutch East India Company," http://en.wikipedia.org/wiki/Dutch_East_India_Company#History (July 3, 2006); BBC News, "Globalization: What on Earth Is It About?" http://news.bbc.co.uk/1/hi/special_report/1999/02/99/e-cyclopedia/711906.stm (July 2, 2006); and "The Growth of Global Industry," *The Wheel Extended,* no. 4 (1989), p. 11.

6. "Multinationals Come into Their Own," *Financial Times,* December 6, 2000, p. 16.

7. Bayer, "History," www.bayer.com/bayer-group/history/page701.htm (July 3, 2006).

8. Alfred D. Chandler, Jr., and Bruce Mazlish (eds.), *Leviathans: Multinational Corporations and the New Global History* (New York: Cambridge University Press, 2005), pp. 66, 88–89.

9. Fred W. Riggs, "Globalization Is a Fuzzy Term but It May Convey Special Meanings," *The Theme of the IPSA World Congress 2000,* July 1999, www2.hawaii.edu/~fredr/ipsaglo.htm (July 29, 2000); and "Globalization," http://en.wikipedia.org/wiki/Globalization (July 2, 2006).

10. Theodore Levitt, "The Globalization of Markets," Harvard Business Review 61, no. 3 (May–June 1983), pp. 92–93.

11. Daniel Yergin, "The Word of the Week," *Daily Davos Home Views,* February 3, 1999, www.dailydavos.com/nw-srv/printed/special/davos/vw; and Daniel Yergin, "The Word of the Week," *Newsweek.com,* www.daily-davos.com/nw-srv/printed/special/davos/vw/vw0199tu_1.htm.

12. www.globality.org.uk (July 3, 2006).

13. "Running a Global Company Well Poses Major Operational Challenges," http://knowledge.wharton.upenn.edu (July 4, 2006), p. 2.

14. World Trade Organization, *International Trade Statistics 2005,* (Geneva: World Trade Organization, 2005).

15. "Foreign Direct Investment Flows," UNCTAD GlobStat database, http://globstat.unctad.org/html/index.html (July 4, 2006); "Foreign Affiliates in Host Economies," UNCTAD GlobStat database, http://globstat.unctad.org/html/index.html (July 4, 2006); "International Trade in Merchandise and Services," UNCTAD GlobStat database, http://globstat.unctad.org/html/index.html (July 4, 2006); World Trade Organization, *International Trade Statistics 2005;* and UNCTAD, *World Investment Report 2005* (New York:.United Nations, 2005).

16. UNCTAD, *World Investment Report 1997* (New York: United Nations, 1997), p. XV.

CHAPTER 2

1. The International Monetary Fund's Programme on Transnational Corporations uses the stock of foreign direct investment as a measure of the productive capacity of international corporations in foreign countries.

2. T. Callen and W. J. McKibben, "Policies and Prospects in Japan and the Implications for the Asia-Pacific Region," IMF Working Paper WP/01/131, International Monetary Fund, September 2001, p. 13.

3. Internet URLs are as follows:

a. Office of Trade and Economic Analysis, www.ita.doc.gov/td/industry/otea.
b. *U.S. Foreign Trade Highlights,* www.ita.doc.gov/industry/otea/usfth.
c. *U.S. Commodity Trade with Top 80 Trading Partners,* www.ita.doc.gov/td/ industry/otea/usfth/top80cty/top80cty.html.
d. *U.S. Industry and Trade Outlook 2002,* www.ita.doc.gov/td/industry/otea/outlook/index.html.

4. Bureau of Economic Analysis, "U.S. International Investment Position, 2005," June 29, 2006, www.bea.gov/bea/newsrelarchive/2006/intinv05.htm (July 15, 2006).

5. Russell B. Scholl, "The International Investment Position of the United States at Year-End 1999," *Survey of Current Business,* July 2000, pp. 46–56, www.bea.doc.gov/bea/pubs.htm; and Bureau of Economic Analysis, "U.S. International Investment Position, 2005."

6. Japan External Trade Organization, "Foreign Direct Investment in Japan Rises over 60% in April–September 2003 ," January 15, 2004, www.jetro.go.jp/en/market/trend/topic/2004_01_fdi.html (July 15, 2006);*Outward Direct Investment by Country and Region* (Tokyo: Ministry of Finance, June 1, 2000), www.mof.go.jp/english/fdi/e1c008h2.htm (November 13, 2000); and JETRO, *White Paper on Foreign Direct Investment 2000,* www.jetro.go.jp/it/e/pub/whitepaper/invest2002.pdf (August 24, 2002).

7. "Technical Notes," *World Development Report 2001* (Washington, DC: World Bank, 2001), p. 231.

8. Ibid., p. 232.

9. "Economic Performance," *Human Development Report 2005,* pp. 266–69, www.sd.undp.org/HDR/HDR05e.pdf (July 11, 2006).

10. "Incentives and State Aids Granted to the Enterprises in Turkey," www.turkisheconomy.org.uk/investment/incentives.htm (July 11, 2006).

11. "International Performance Outshines Domestic Results," *Business International,* September 29, 1986, p. 305.

12. "The 100 Largest U.S. Multinationals," *Forbes,* July 18, 1994, pp. 276–79.

13. Jon E. Hilsenrath, "U.S. Multinationals Reap Overseas Bounty," *The Wall Street Journal,* April 4, 2005, p. A2.

14. William C. Gruben and Sherry L. Kiser, "NAFTA and Maquiladoras: Is the Growth Connected?" www.maquilaportal.com/public/navegar/nav48.htm (June 30, 2002).

15. "Maquila Overview," www.maquilaportal.com/Visitors_Site/nav21.htm (July 12, 2006).

16. Takashi Kozu, Ko Nakayama, Aiko Mineshima, and Yumi Saita, "Changes in Japan's Export and Import Structures," *Bank of Japan Monthly Bulletin,* May 2002.

17. "U.S. Companies See 1992 as a Opportunity," *San Jose Mercury News,* March 26, 1989, p. 1.

CHAPTER 3

1. Government administrators involved in project evaluation are increasingly applying socioeconomic rather than purely financial criteria. For example, social rates of discount and opportunity costs are considered rather than the pure costs of borrowing money. Although marketing managers do not have to be development economists any more than they need to be specialists in marketing research, they should have knowledge of the basic concepts.

2. "Fortress of Mercantilism," *Insight,* July 18, 1988, pp. 15–17.

3. Brian Bremner, "Don't Let 'Mr. Dollar' Get Away with It; Japan's Zembei Mizoguchi Is Driving Down the Yen; He Ought to Be Stopped," *BusinessWeek,* March 22, 2004, p. 76; and Sebastian Moffett and Jason Sapsford, "As the Yen Surges, Tokyo Remains on the Sidelines," *The Wall Street Journal,* November 26, 2004, p. A2.

4. David Ricardo, "The Principles of Political Economy and Taxation," in *International Trade Theory: Hume to Ohlin,* ed. William R. Allen (New York: Random House, 1965), pp. 62–67.

5. The idea that only hours of labor determine production costs is known as the *labor theory of value.* In fairness to Ricardo, we must admit that he included the cost of capital as "embodied labor" in his labor costs. Actually, the theory of comparative advantage can be explained by the cost of all factors of production.

6. Eli F. Heckscher, "The Effect of Foreign Trade on the Distribution of Income," *Economisk Tidskrift* 21 (1919), pp. 497–512; and Bertil Ohlin, *Interregional and International Trade* (Cambridge, MA: Harvard University Press, 1933).

7. The economist Bela Belassa, in his *Stages Approach to Comparative Advantage,* published by the World Bank in 1977, found in a study of 26 developed and developing nations that "the intercountry differences in the structure of exports are in a large part explained by differences in physical and human capital endowments."

8. J. Sachs and H. Shatz, "Trade and Jobs in U.S. Manufacturing," cited in *The Economist,* October 1, 1994, p. 19.

9. Dennis R. Appleyard, Alfred J. Field, Jr., and Steven L. Cobb, *International Economics,* 5th ed. (Burr Ridge, IL: McGraw-Hill Irwin, 2006), pp. 151–55, provide a substantial review of different explanations for the Leontief paradox, including citations to a number of empirical studies that have tested these alternative explanations.

10. Appleyard, Field, and Cobb, *International Economics,* pp. 174–77.

11. R. Vernon, "International Investment and International Trade in the Product Cycle," *Quarterly Journal of Economics* 80 (1966), pp. 190–207.

12. Many new products come not from the manufacturer's laboratories but from its suppliers of machinery and raw materials.

13. Belassa, *Stages Approach to Comparative Advantage,* pp. 26–27.

14. Akira Takeishi and Takahiro Fujimoto, "Modularization in the Auto Industry: Interlinked Multiple Hierarchies of Product, Production, and Supplier Systems," Working Paper 01-02, Institute of Innovation Research, Hitotsubashi University, Tokyo, February 2001; Larry Weiss, "Automakers Test Labor-Cutting Strategy in Brazil," *Labor Report on the Americas,* March–April 1999, www.labournet.de/branchen/auto/vw/modular.html (July 7, 2006); Ronaldo Couto Parente, *Strategic Modularization in the Brazilian Automotive Industry: An Empirical Analysis of Its Antecedents and Performance Implications,* Ph.D. thesis, Temple University, Philadelphia, August 2003, http://baru.ibict.br/tede-ibict/tde_arquivos/1/TDE-2004-11-08T12:48:34Z-48/Publico/RonaldoParente.pdf (July 7, 2006); and Gregory L. White, "Chrysler Makes Manufacturing Inroads at Plant in Brazil," *The Wall Street Journal,* August 13, 1998.

15. Richard B. Chase, F. Robert Jacobs, and Nicholas J. Aquilano, *Operations Management for Competitive Advantage,* 11th ed. (Burr Ridge, IL: McGraw-Hill Irwin, 2005).

16. Paul R. Krugman, "Increasing Returns, Monopolistic Competition and International Trade," *Journal of International Economics* 9, no. 4 (1979), pp. 469–79; and Paul R. Krugman, "Scale Economies, Product Differentiation and the Pattern of Trade," *American Economic Review* 70, no. 4 (1980), pp. 950–59.

17. Gerard Tellis and Peter Golder, "First to Market, First to Fail? Real Causes of Enduring Marketing Leadership," *Sloan Management Review* 37, no. 2, cited in "Why First May Not Last," *The Economist,* March 16, 1996, p. 65.

18. Alfred Marshall, *Principles of Economics,* 8th ed. (London: Macmillan, 1920).

19. Michael E. Porter, *The Competitive Advantage of Nations* (New York: Free Press, 1990).

20. For example, see Christophe Lecuyer, *Making Silicon Valley: Innovation and the Growth of High Tech, 1930–1970,* (Cambridge, MA: MIT Press, 2005).

21. John H. Dunning, "The Competitive Advantage of Countries and the Activities of Transnational Corporations," *Transnational Corporations,* February 1992, pp. 135–68.

22. John H. Dunning, *The Globalization of Business* (London: Routledge, 1993), p. 106.

23. "Footwear Industry Tells Congress 'Shoe Gap' Threatens U.S. Defense," *The Wall Street Journal,* August 24, 1984, p. 21; and Thomas A. Pugel, *International Economics,* 13th ed. (New York: McGraw-Hill Irwin, 2007), pp. 197–98.

24. See Hossein Askari, John Forrer, Jiawen Yang, and Tarek Hachem, "Measuring Vulnerability to U.S. Foreign Economic Sanctions," *Business Economics* 40, no. 2 (April 2005), pp. 41–55.

25. Lance Davis and Stanley Engerman, "History Lessons: Sanctions: Neither War nor Peace," *Journal of Economic Perspectives* 17, no. 2 (Spring 2003), p. 187.

26. Gary C. Hufbauer, "Economic Sanctions: America's Folly," in *Economic Casualties: How U.S. Foreign Policy Undermines Trade, Growth, and Liberty,* ed. S. Singleton and D. T. Griswold (Washington, DC: Cato Institute, 1999), pp. 91–99; and Askari et al, "Measuring Vulnerability."

27. Hendrik Van den Berg, *International Economics* (New York: McGraw-Hill Irwin, 2004), p. 240.

28. Larry Elliott, "Two Countries, One Booming, One Struggling: Which One Followed the Free-Trade Route?: A Look at Vietnam and Mexico Exposes the Myth of Market Liberalisation," *The Guardian,* December 12, 2005, p. 23.

29. Dexter Robers and Paul Magnusson, "China's Trade Boss: Vice-Premier Wu Li Has an Iron Will; She'll Need It When She Comes to Washington to Lead Talks," *BusinessWeek,* April 12, 2004, p. 16; Chris Cziborr, "Chipmakers Watch as U.S., China Fight over Chip Tax," *Orange County Business Journal,* March 29–April 4, 2004, p. 6; Dai Yan, "Agreement Ends First Complaint at WTO," *China Daily,* July 15, 2004, p. 2; and Office of the Foreign Trade Representative, *2004 National Trade Estimate Report on Foreign Trade Barriers* (Washington, DC: United States Trade Representative, 2004), p. 60.

30. "How to Lower Price of Ethanol; Kill the Tariff, Help Consumers," *Rocky Mountain News,* May 14, 2006, p. 5E; Alan Beattie, "Brake on Biofuels as Obstacles Clog the Road," *Financial Times,* May 9, 2006, p. 6; and "Holman W. Jenkins, Jr., "What's Wrong with Free Trade in Biofuels," *The Wall Street Journal,* February 22, 2006, p. A15.

31. "Brie and Hormones," *The Economist,* January 7, 1989, pp. 21–22; "Europe's Burden," *The Economist,* May 22, 1999, p. 84; and Office of the Foreign Trade Representative, *2006 National Trade Estimate Report on Foreign Trade Barriers,* March 2006, www.ustr.gov/Document_Library/Reports_Publications/2006/2006_NTE_Report/Section_Index.html (July 9, 2006), p.242.

32. Andrew Bounds, "Sino-EU Trade Relations Wane over Footwear Tariffs Dispute," *Financial Times,* July 5, 2006, p. 4; David Rennie, "Mandelson Child Shoe Levy 'Will Hit the Poor," *The Daily Telegraph,* July 5, 2006, p. 2; Tobias Buck, "How EU Textile Quotas Became a Chinese Puzzle," *Financial Times,* August 24, 2005, p. 2; Alexandra Harney, "Limits

Force Chinese Clothing Makers to Tighten Their Belts," *Financial Times,* August 24, 2005, p. 2; and "EU to Decide Shoe Dumping Action," http://news.bbc.co.uk/2/hi/business/4789346.stm (July 8, 2006).

33. Hugo Gurdon, "The U.S. Should Unsign Kyoto," *The Wall Street Journal Europe,* October 11, 2002, p. A6: and Alistair Ulph and Laura Valentini, "Is Environmental Dumping Greater When Plants Are Footloose?" *Scandinavian Journal of Economics* 103, no. 4 (December 2001), p. 673.

34. Robert Anderson, "Slovakia's 'Soviet' Skills Set to Create Car World-Beater," *Financial Times,* April 20, 2006, p. 4; John Gapper, "It Is Time for the Big Three to Shut Up," *Financial Times,* October 20, 2005, p. 19; "The New Rules of Trade," National Review, April 18, 1994, pp. 40–44; and Marc Champion and Adam Z. Horvath, "EU Expansion Fuels Debate on Taxes," *The Wall Street Journal,* May 3, 2004, p. A18.

35. "Agriculture: Support Estimates, 2004," *OECD in Figures—2005 Edition* (Paris: OECD, 2005), http://dx.doi.org/10.1787/758034618756 (July 31, 2006).

36. Paul Wolfowitz, "Doha's Last Chance," *The Wall Street Journal,* July 1, 2006, p. A10; Scott Miller, "France Digs In for Subsidy Fight," *The Wall Street Journal Europe,* May 16, 2006, p. 1; Juliane von Reppert-Bismarck, "EU to Take Up Disclosing Who Gets Farm Aid; Publishing Subsidy Lists Could Fuel Global Pressure to End Agricultural Support," *The Wall Street Journal,* November 7, 2005, p. A18; and "Agriculture: Support Estimates, 2004," *OECD in Figures—2005 Edition* (Paris: OECD, 2005).

37. "The Fruits of Free Trade: Protection's Price," *2002 Annual Report—Federal Reserve Bank of Dallas,* Federal Reserve Bank of Dallas, www.dallasfed.org/fed/annual/2002/ar02f.html (June 30, 2004).

38. "Non-Tariff Barriers: A Rising Trend in World Trade," *World Economic Situation and Prospects 2006* (New York: United Nations, 2006).

39. Council of the European Union, "Council Regulation (EC) No 1964/2006 of 29 November 2005 on the Tariff Rates for bananas," http://europa.eu.int/eur-ex/lex/LexUriServ/site/en/oj/2005/l_316/l/31620051202en00010002.pdf (July 9, 2006); and Scott Miller, "Trading Partners Meet New EU," *The Wall Street Journal,* May 4, 2004, p. A17.

40. "A Summary of the Final Act of the Uruguay Round," www.fas.usda.gov/itp/ policy/gatt/sum_fact.html#cAgreement (December 18, 2000).

41. World Trade Organization, *Annual Report 2003* (Lausanne, Switzerland: WTO, 2003); OECD, *Farm Household Income, Issues and Policy Responses* (Paris: OECD, 2003).

42. *Report on United States Barriers to Trade and Investment* (Brussels: European Commission, December 2003).

43. Office of the Foreign Trade Representative, *2006 National Trade Estimate Report on Foreign Trade Barriers.*

44. Ibid.

45. Ibid.

46. G. Thomas Sims, "Uncommon Market: Corn Flakes Class Shows the Glitches in European Union," *The Wall Street Journal,* November 1, 2005, p. A1.

47. Office of the Foreign Trade Representative, *2006 National Trade Estimate Report on Foreign Trade Barriers,* pp. 238–41; Doris de Guzman, "EU Biotech Labeling Laws Frustrate Ag Industry," *Chemical Market Reporter,* July 14, 2003, p. 14; and "Moment of Truth over GM as U.S. Files WTO Complaint," Friends of the Earth, Belgium, May 13, 2003, www.foeeurope.org/ press/2003 /AW_13_May_moment.htm (April 15, 2004).

48. The OECD publishes *Costs and Benefits of Protection,* which evaluates a wide range of studies on import restrictions of manufactured goods in OECD countries. Patrick A. Messerlin, *Measuring the Costs of Protection in Europe: European Commercial Policy in the 2000s* (Washington, DC: International Institute for Economics, 2001), examined costs in 22 highly protected industries in the EU. The 2002 annual report of the Federal Reserve Bank of Dallas, www.dallasfed.org/fed/annual/2002/ar02f.html (July 9, 2006), provides a listing of the jobs saved and total costs of protecting these jobs for 20 selected industries.

49. World Trade Organization, *Annual Report 2003.*

50. Kofi A. Annan, "Help the Third World Help Itself," *The Wall Street Journal,* November 29, 1999, p. A19. Copyright 1999 by Dow Jones & Co. Inc. Reproduced with permission of Dow Jones & Co. Inc. in the format textbook via Copyright Clearance Center.

51. Charles Kindleberger, *American Business Abroad* (New Haven, CT: Yale University Press, 1969), pp. 43–44.

52. See, for example, J. H. Dunning, *Multinational Enterprises and the Global Economy* (Addison-Wesley, 1992); and F. T. Knickerbocker, *Oligopolistic Reaction and Multinational Enterprise* (Boston: Harvard Business School, 1973).

53. Stephen Hymer, *The International Operations of International Firms: A Study in Direct Investment* (Cambridge, MA: MIT Press, 1976).

54. Ricard Caves, "International Corporations: The Industrial Economics of Foreign Investment," *Economica,* February 1971, pp. 5–6.

55. R. Z. Aliber, "A Theory of Direct Investment," *The International Corporation* (Cambridge, MA: MIT Press, 1970), pp. 17–34.

56. A. Rugman, *International Diversification and the Multinational Enterprise* (Lexington, MA: Lexington Books, 1979).

57. F. T. Knickerbocker, *Oligopolistic Reaction and Multinational Enterprise.*

58. E. M. Graham, "Transatlantic Investments by Multinational Firms: A Rivalistic Phenomenon," *Journal of Post-Keynesian Economics, Fall* 1978, pp. 82–99.

59. P. Buckley and M. Casson, *The Future of Multinational Enterprise* (New York: Macmillan, 1976).

60. John H. Dunning, *International Production and the Multinational Enterprise* (London: George Allen & Unwin, 1981), pp. 109–10.

CHAPTER 4

1. Martin Wolfe, "Why Washington and Beijing Need Strong Global Institutions," *Financial Times,* April 19, 2006, p. 13.

2. See www.un.org/partners/business/other pages/factsheets/fs3.htm (accessed May 19, 2006).

3. United Nations, www.un.org.

4. See www.global-challenges.org/000why-and-how.html (accessed May 20, 2006).

5. Michael D. Kennedy, "The Cultural Politics of Energy Security," University of Michigan, September 23, 2005; www.witbd.org/articles/nato.html (accessed May 11, 2006).

6. See NATO treaty, Article 5, www.nato.int.

7. "NATO, Russia Agree to Partnership," *The Wall Street Journal,* May 15, 2002, p. A14.

8. See www.aseansec.org/64.htm (accessed May 19, 2006).

9. See www.wto.org/english/news_e/pres 98_e/pr88_e.htm (accessed May 12, 2006).

10. See www.wto.org/English/thewto _e/whatis_e/tif_e/fact4_e.htm (accessed May 11, 2006).

11. "GATT Comes Right," *The Economist,* December 18, 1993, pp. 13–14.

12. See www.wto.org (accessed May 12, 2006).

13. Elizabeth Becker, "Delegates from Poorer Nations Walk Out of World Trade Talks," *New York Times,* September 15, 2003, p. 1.

14. Scott Miller, "French Resistance to Trade Accord Has Cultural Roots," *The Wall Street Journal,* May 16, 2006, p. 1.

15. The Australian government issues helpful WTO Doha bulletins that are posted at www.dfat.gov.au/trade/negotiations/wto_bulletin (accessed May 12, 2006).

16. See http://trade.businessroundtable.org/trade_2006/wto/success.html (accessed May 12, 2006).

17. Jagdish Bhagwati, "How to Resolve the Deadlock Holding Back World Trade Talks," *Financial Times,* November 15, 2005, p. 15.

18. Guy de Jonquières, "WTO Urged to Act on Regional Pacts," *Financial Times,* February 6, 1997, p. 10.

19. "EU Slips Up over Banana Imports," *Financial Times,* July 18, 2000, p. 7.

20. Perez Alfonze, "The Organization of Petroleum Exporting Countries," *Monthly Bulletin* (Caracas), no. 2 (1966).

21. *International Petroleum Encyclopedia* (Tulsa, OK: Pennwell Publishing, 1979), pp. 194–95, table 6.

22. Luis Vallenilla, *Oil: The Making of a New Economic Order* (New York: McGraw-Hill, 1975).

23. James Cook, "Comeuppance," *Forbes,* May 9, 1983, pp. 55–56.

24. "The Impact of Lower Oil Prices," *IMF World Economic Outlook,* May 1994, pp. 20–21.

25. The G8 Research Centre at the University of Toronto, an independent education and research body, is accessible at www.g7.utoronto.ca.

26. UNDP, *Human Development Report 2005,* www.undp.org

27. To view a short film that summarizes the criticism of a 2005 G8 meeting, see www.camcorderguerillas.net/FILMS/G8.

28. Ambassador Rob Portman was the U.S. trade representative as of April 2005. He was appointed by President Bush to be director of the Office of Management and Budget (OMB) in April 2006. Susan Schwab was nominated as U.S. trade representative. She had been deputy trade representative. See www.ustr.gov/Document_Library/Press_Releases/2006/March/Joint_Statement_from_the_Meeting_of_the_NAFTA_Free_Trade_Commission.html.

29. See www.ustr.gov, under "trade facts."

30. See the Canadian Broadcasting Corporation's summary at www.cbc.ca/news/background/softwood_lumber.

31. See www.cocef.org and www.nadb.org.

32. See www.era.anthropology.ac.uk/Era_Resources/Era/Peasants/theory12.htm.

33. "The Paper Chase," *The Economist,* March 16, 2006. See www.economist.com/displaystory.cfm?story_id=5636381 (accessed May 18, 2006).

34. "The Diminishing of Brazil," The Economist, May 11, 2006. See www.economist.com/displaystory.cfm?story_id=6919442 (accessed May 18, 2006).

35. See www.export.gov/fta/complete/CAFTA (accessed May 18, 2006).

36. "Venezuela Quits Andean Trade Block," BBC News, April 20, 2006, http://news.bbc.co.uk/1/hi/business/4925056.stm (accessed May 23, 2006).

37. See www.oas.org/main/main.asp?sLang=E&sLink=http://www.oas.org/36ag/english (accessed May 18, 2006).

38. Derek Urwin, *The Community of Europe: A History of European Integration since 1945* (New York: Longman, 1991), p. 8.

39. World Trade Organization, www.wto.org/English/news_e/pres05_e/pr401_e.htm, (accessed May 13, 2006).

40. See the EU Web site for further information on accession: http://ec.europa.eu/comm/enlargement/towards_EU_membership/index_en.htm (accessed May 13, 2006).

41. *The Wall Street Journal,* June 23, 2004, p. C16.

42. "Charlemagne," *The Economist,* May 11, 2006. See www.economist.com (accessed May 19, 2006).

43. See http://europa.eu/abc/history/index_en.htm (accessed May 13, 2006).

44. BBC News report, May 11, 2006, http://news.bbc.co.uk/1/hi/world/europe/4762495.stm (accessed May 13, 2006).

45. See http://europa.eu/abc/panorama/howorganised (accessed May 15, 2006).

46. This is as of the end of 2004 and will change when new countries join the EU. See www.consilium.europa.eu/cms3_fo/showPage.asp?id=242&lang=EN&mode=g (accessed May 14, 2006).

47. "Bringing New Practices to Europe's Top Table," *Financial Times,* July 3, 2002, p. 9.

48. See http://ec.europa.eu/budget/budget_glance/where_from_en.htm (accessed May 14, 2006).

49. Wendell H. McCulloch, Jr., "United States of Europe?" *Backgrounder,* Heritage Foundation, no. 706, May 5, 1989.

50. Simon Wilson, "The Shocking Fraud at the Heart of the EU," *Money Week,* November 18, 2005, www.moneyweek.com/file/4567/eu-fraud-2411.html/ (accessed May 20, 2006).

51. Raphael Minder, "Turnout Low among New Member States," *Financial Times,* June14, 2004, p. 2.

52. "Increasingly, Rules of Global Economy Are Set in Brussels," *The Wall Street Journal,* April 23, 2002, p. A1.

53. See http://europa.eu.int/scadplus/leg/en/lvb/l21210.htm (accessed May 17, 2006).

54. See http://mkaccdb.eu.int/cgi-bin/stb/mkstb.pl (accessed May 17, 2006).

55. See http://ec.europa.eu/comm/external_relations/japan/intro/eco_trade_relat.htm (accessed May 17, 2006).

56. See http://ec.europa.eu/comm/trade/issues/bilateral/countries/usa/index_en.htm (accessed August 20, 2006).

CHAPTER 5

1. Financial Action Task Force, "Annual and Overall Review of Noncooperative Countries or Territories, 2005." See www.fatf-gafi.org/document/4/0,2340,en_32250379_32236992_33916420_1_1_1_1,00.html (accessed June 1, 2006).

2. Patrick M. Jost and Harjit Singh Sandhu, "The Hawala Alternative Remittance System and Its Role in Money Laundering," Interpol, 2000. See www.interpol.int/Public/Financial-Crime/MoneyLaundering/hawala/default.asp? (accessed June 1, 2006).

3. Cheol S. Eun and Bruce G. Resnick, *International Financial Management* (Burr Ridge, IL: McGraw-Hill Irwin), p. 25.

4. Charles N. Henning, William Pigott, and Robert Haney Scott, *International Financial Management* (New York: McGraw-Hill, 1978), p. 149.

5. Albert C. Whitaker, *Foreign Exchange,* 2nd ed. (New York: Appleton-Century-Crofts, 1933), p. 157.

6. Davie Hume, *Of the Jealousy of Trade,* 1758, http://cepa.newschool.edu/het/profiles/hume.htm (accessed May 26, 2006).

7. Paul Krugman, "The Gold Bug Variations," November 1996, www.pkarchive.org/cranks/goldbug.html (accessed May 26, 2006).

8. Ibid.

9. Jacques Rueff, *La réforme du système monétaire international* (Paris: Plon, 1973).

10. Quoted by Gareth Smyth, "Iranians' Scramble to Buy Gold Highlights Tensions," *Financial Times,* April 20, 2006, p. 6.

11. A. Acheson et al., *Bretton Woods Revisited* (Toronto: University of Toronto Press, 1972).

12. IMF, "Articles of Agreement,". www.imf.org/external/pubs/ft/aa/aa01.htm (accessed May 26, 2006).

13. *Federal Reserve Bulletin,* September 1969 and January 1974.

14. *Federal Reserve Bulletin,* December 1971 and January 1974.

15. The Triffin paradox was pointed out by Yale economist Robert Triffin.

16. "The IMF at a Glance: Factsheet," April 2006. See www.imf.org/external/np/exr/facts/glance.htm (accessed May 30, 2006).

17. IMF, April 2006. See www.imf.org/external/np/exr/facts/finfac.htm (accessed May 25, 2006).

18. As of April 2006. See www.imf.org/external/np/exr/facts/quotas.htm (accessedMay 26, 2006).

19. Chris Giles and Krishna Guha, "Shake-up Agreed on IMF World Trade Role," *Financial Times,* April 24, 2006, p. 1.

20. Jeffrey Sachs, "How the Fund Can Regain Global Legitimacy," *Financial Times,* April 20, 2006, p. 13.

21. Andrew Balls, "IMF Dilemma as New Loans Start to Decline," *Financial Times,* December 28, 2005, p. 4.

22. The World Bank Group, www.worldbank.org.

23. See www.bis.org (accessed May 27, 2006).

24. www.imf.org. These are 2005 data.

25. Bank for International Settlements, "Central Bank Survey of Foreign Exchange and Derivatives Market Activity in 2004," March 17, 2005, http://www.bis.org/press/p050316.htm? (accessed May 28, 2006).

26. "World Market," *Financial Times,* June 1, 2002, p. 26.

27. Federal Reserve Bank of New York, "Foreign Exchange Rates." See www.ny.frb.org/markets/fxrates/historical/fx.cfm (accessed May 28, 2006).

28. Herbert Stein, "Balance of Payments," in *The Concise Encyclopedia of Economics,* David R. Hendersen, ed., 1993, www.econlib.org/library/Enc/BalanceofPayments.html (accessed May 29, 2006).

29. Ibid.

30. Bureau of Economic Analysis, U.S. Department of Commerce, U.S. International Transactions, Fourth Quarter and Year 2005, March 14, 2006. See http://www.bea.gov/bea/newsrel/transnewsrelease.htm (accessed May 3, 2006).

31. Stein, "Balance of Payments."

32. Ibid.

33. Ibid.

34. "Some Facts about the SDR," *IMF Survey,* April 1, 1996.

35. IMF, "Articles of Agreement."

CHAPTER 6

1. "How to Win Friends and Influence Clients," *The European,* January 21–27, 1994, p. 11.

2. I. Brady and B. Isaac, *A Reader in Cultural Change,* vol. 1 (Cambridge, MA: Schenkman Publishing, 1975), p. x.

3. Hy Mariampolski, *Ethnography for Marketers: A Guide to Consumer Immersion* (Thousand Oaks, CA: Sage Publications), p. 123.

4. "Cultural Traits," *Future Culture,* www.wepworld.com/future/tcoc.htm (January 2, 1998).

5. Vern Terpstra and Kenneth David, *The Cultural Environment of International Business* (Cincinnati: South-Western, 1985), p. 7.

6. E. T. Hall, *Beyond Culture* (Garden City, NY: Doubleday, 1977), p. 54.

7. "Make It Simple," *BusinessWeek,* September 9, 1996, pp. 96–104; "P&G Viewed China as a National Market and Is Conquering It," *The Wall Street Journal,* September 12, 1995, p. A1; "P&G Rewrites the Marketing Rules," *Fortune,* November 6, 1989, pp. 34–46; and "After Early Stumbles, P&G Is Making Inroads Overseas," *The Wall Street Journal,* February 6, 1989, p. B1.

8. "P&G's Joy Makes an Unlikely Splash in Japan," *The Wall Street Journal,* December12, 1997, p. B1.

9. Yung-Cheng Shen and Ting-Chen Chen, "When East Meets West: The Effect of Cultural Tone Congruity in Ad Music and Message on Consumer Ad Memory and Attitudes," *International Journal of Advertising* 25, no. 1 (2006), pp. 51–70.

10. One of the writers installed new production equipment in a Spanish factory to replace old but still serviceable machinery. Before leaving for a week's work in Madrid, he tested the equipment, trained some workers to use it, and advised the supervisor that it was ready. On his return, he was surprised to find that the new equipment was not being used. The supervisor explained that the old machinery was working well and he didn't want to "disrupt production." Actually, the new equipment was easier to use and would greatly increase output. Realizing that drastic action was called for, the writer grabbed a sledgehammer and made a token effort to destroy the old equipment. Only then did the supervisor get the message. The action was unorthodox, but it did bring immediate results.

11. "Mouse Trap," *The Wall Street Journal,* March 10, 1994, p. A12.

12. This classification depends in part on M. J. Herskovits, *Man and His Works* (New York: Alfred A. Knopf, 1952), p. 634. It was embellished by anthropologists at the University of South Alabama.

13. "Nike Recalls Shoes Bearing Logo That Muslims Found Offensive," *The Oregonian,* June 25, 1997, p. A18: Marc Champion, "Muslim Outrage Mounts over Cartoons in EU," *The Wall Street Journal,* February 3, 2006, p. A6.

14. Minda Zetlin, "Feng Shui: Smart Business or Superstition?" *Management Review,* August 1995, pp. 26–27.

15. Anita Snow, "Ad Featuring 'Che' Guevara Sparks Furor," *The Monitor,* August10, 2000, p. 8a.

16. Herskovits, *Man and His Works,* p. 414.

17. "The Middle East Mirage," *International Management,* April 1989, p. 21.

18. Sanjyot P. Dunung, *Doing Business in Asia: The Complete Guide* (New York: Lexington Books, 1995).

19. "Middle East Mirage," p. 23.

20. "Revolution in Mexico City: The One-Hour Lunch," *International Herald Tribune,* October 20, 1999, p. 14.

21. "Boom Times Erode Spain's Siesta Time," *The Oregonian,* December 26, 1999, p. A24.

22. Thomas E. Maher and Yim Yu Wong, "The Impact of Cultural Differences on the Growing Tensions between Japan and the United States," *SAM Advanced Management Journal,* Winter 1994, p. 45.

23. "German View: You Americans Work Too Hard—and for What?" *The Wall Street Journal,* July 14, 1994, p. B1.

24. "Average Annual Hours in Manufacturing, 12 Countries, 1950–1996," *Foreign Labor Statistics,* http://stats.bls.gov/news.release/prod4.t06.htm (January 7, 1998); "Working Hours per Full Working Week," *Japan 1997* (Tokyo: Keizai Koho Center, 1997), p. 97; and "Hours of Actual Work per Month, 1983–2001," Japan Ministry of Labor, http://jin.jcic.or.jp/stat/stats/09LAB41.html (August 9, 2002).

25. It is difficult to translate adequately the connotations of the two words. No one proudly says he is an *obrero* even if he earns more than an *empleado* who is a file clerk.

26. "How the Japanese Are Changing," *Fortune,* Pacific Rim, 1990, pp. 15–22.

27. Samia Nakhoul, "Born to Be Untouchable," *Financial Times,* July 22–23, 2000, pp. i, iii.

28. Pravin K. Shah, "Religions of India," *Jain BBS Email Bulletin,* August 1994, http://SunSITE.sut.ac.jp.pub/academic/rel . . . dia/jain/world_religions (June 6, 1997); and "History and Practices," *Sikhism in Brief,* www.sikhs.org/summary.htm (March 16, 2001).

29. "Taoism and the Taoist Arts," www.taoistsarts.net (August 15, 2002).

30. "Children of the Islamic Revolution: A Survey of Iran," *The Economist,* January 18, 1997, pp. 1–15.

31. "The Internet Economy Indicators," www.internetindicators.com/keyfindings.html (August 15, 2002).

32. Joseph Coleman, "Liquor Stores Phasing Out Beer Vending Machines," *The McAllen Monitor,* June 2, 2000, p. 6A.

33. "English Is Still on the March," *The Economist,* February 24, 2001, pp. 50–51.

34. Judy Dempsey, "Brussels Faces a Real Tongue Twister," *Financial Times,* January27/28, 2002, p. 2.

35. "Why Speaking English Is No Longer Enough," *International Management,* November 1986, p. 42.

36. An incident happened to one of the writers, newly arrived in Brazil, that went all over the country. The ad manager, a Brazilian, brought him a campaign emphasizing that car

owners should maintain 24 pounds per square inch in their tires to get maximum wear. To get the point across, life-size figures of a tire company salesman were made up, with the name of the company and a large "24" printed across his chest. Dealers were to set them up on a "D day." The writer, proud of the unusually good coordination of the campaign, began receiving calls from competitors. The message was that 24 in Brazilian Portuguese refers to gay men.

37. "French Watchdogs Seek to Limit English Web Sites," *The Mexico City News,* January 8, 1997, p. 32; and "French Lobby Loses Case," *Financial Times,* June 10, 1997, p. 2.

38. "Multilingual Website Widens the Way to a New Online World," *Financial Times,* February 7, 2001, p. 1.

39. "McDonald's: Burger and Fries a la Francaise," *The Economist,* April 17, 2004, pp. 60, 61.

40. "A Little Bad English Goes a Long Way in Japan's Boutiques," *The Wall Street Journal,* May 5, 1993, p. A1.

41. Among several sources are Nancy Armstrong and Melissa Wagner, *Field Guide to Gestures: How to Identify and Interpret Virtually Every Gesture Known to Man* (Quirk Books, 2003).

42. Gillian Tett, "Mori Gaffe May Hit Ruling Party's Poll Hopes," *Financial Times,* June 9, 2000, p. 16.

43. E. T. Hall, *The Hidden Dimension* (Garden City, NY: Doubleday, 1969), pp. 134–35.

44. Terri Morrison and Wayne A. Conaway, "Global Business Basics: The Problem of Proxemics," www.getcustoms.com/2004GTC/Articles/iw0100.html (July 26, 2004); "The Body Language of Proxemics," http://members.aol.com/Katydidit/bodylang.htm (July 19, 2006).

45. "A Global Guide to Gift Giving," *Los Angeles Times,* December 1, 1993, p. D4: Roger Axtell, *Do's and Taboos around the World* (New York: Wiley, 1990), pp. 113–47; and country-by-country gift-giving advice at www.giftelan.com/international_gift_giving.htm (July 26, 2004).

46. Neil H. Jacoby, Peter Nehemkis, and Richard Eells, *Bribery and Extortion in World Business* (New York: Macmillan, 1977), pp. 174–75.

47. "TI's Vision, Mission, Values Approach and Strategy," www.transparency.org/about_ti/mission.html#mission (July 26, 2004).

48. Herskovits, *Man and His Works,* p. 303.

49. Geert Hofstede, "Cultural Dimensions in Management and Planning," *Asia Pacific Journal of Management,* January 1984, p. 83; communication with Hofstede, October 27, 2004.

50. Hofstede, "Cultural Dimensions," p. 83.

51. Lisa Hoecklin, *Managing Cultural Differences* (Workingham, England: Addison-Wesley, 1995), pp. 28–30.

52. Ibid., p. 31.

53. Rose Knotts and Sheryann Tomlin, "A Comparison of TQM Practices in U.S. and Mexican Companies," *Production and Inventory Management Journal,* First Quarter 1994, p. 54.

54. Hoecklin, *Managing Cultural Differences,* pp. 31–32.

55. Hofstede, "Cultural Dimensions," pp. 81 and 84.

CHAPTER 7

1. M. E. Porter, *The Competitive Advantage of Nations* (New York: Free Press, 1990).

2. U.S. Department of State, Bureau of European and Eurasian Affairs, "Background Note on Austria," February 2006, www.state.gov/r/pa/ei/bgn/3165.htm, (accessed June 6, 2006).

3. *CIA Factbook,* June 1, 2006, www.cia.gov/cia/publications/factbook/geos/us.html (accessed June 6, 2006).

4. U.S. Department of Agriculture, Economic Research Service. See a.gov/Briefing/FruitandTreeNuts/Trade.htm (accessed June 6, 2006).

5. Federal Research Division, Library of Congress, "Afghanistan," Country Studies/Area Handbook Series, http://countrystudies.us/afghanistan/32.htm (accessed June 6, 2006).

6. World Facts, "Facts about Afghanistan," http://worldfacts.us/Afghanistan.htm (accessed June 6, 2006).

7. "Spain's Regions," *The Economist,* November 16, 1996, pp. 55–56.

8. BBC, "ETA Permanent Ceasefire Begins," March 24, 2006, http://news.bbc.co.uk/2/hi/europe/4839554.stm (accessed June 6, 2006).

9. Encyclopaedia Britannica, "Canadian Shield," www.britannica.com/eb/article-43264 (accessed June6, 2006).

10. United Nations, "The World Population Prospects, the 2004 Revision," February 24, 2005, www.un.org/esa/population/publications/WPP2004/wpp2004.htm (accessed July 6, 2006).

11. EUR Activ, EU News and Policy Positions, "EU Action Plan Seeks to Shift Freight to Rivers," January 18, 2006, updated May 29, 2006, www.euractiv.com/en/transport/eu-action-plan-seeks-shift-freight-rivers/article-151643 (accessed June 6, 2006).

12. BBC News Online, "Three Gorges Dam Wall Completed," May 20, 2006, http://news.bbc.co.uk/2/hi/asia-pacific/5000092.stm (accessed June 6, 2006).

13. International Rivers Network is an organization whose goal is to foster environmentally responsible river use. It is usually opposed to major dams because of the environmental degradation and violation of human rights these massive projects often involve. See www.irn.org.

14. One of the writers, representing a Chilean subsidiary of an American multinational, called on a large government-owned mine in Bolivia to sell Chilean-made products. The purchasing agent asked how anyone could expect her, a Bolivian, to buy goods made in Chile. Although appreciating that the parent company was American, she said, "The products are still made in Chile."

15. Rhoads Murphey, *The Scope of Geography,* 2nd ed. (Skokie, IL: Rand McNally, 1973), pp. 188–89.

16. Jared Diamond, *Guns, Germs, and Steel: The Fates of Human Societies* (New York: W.W. Norton 1997).

17. Andrew M. Karmack, *The Tropics and Economic Development* (Washington, DC: World Bank, 1976), p. 5.

18. There are many current ideas about the banning of DDT that do not take into account the science or actual history of DDT. Dr. Alan Lymbery, a parisotologist at Murdoch University, Australia, summarizes the current situation well. "The manufacture and use of DDT was banned in the US in 1972, on the advice of the US Environmental Protection Agency. The use of DDT has since been banned in most other developed nations, but it is not banned for public health use in most areas of the world where malaria is endemic. Indeed, DDT was recently exempted from a proposed worldwide ban on organophosphate chemicals.

"DDT usage for malaria control involves spraying the walls and backs of furniture, so as to kill and repel adult mosquitoes that may carry the malaria parasite. Other chemicals are available for this purpose, but DDT is cheap and persistent and is often a very effective indoor insecticide which is still used in many parts of the world.

"DDT is not used for outdoor mosquito control, partly because scientific studies have demonstrated toxicity to wildlife, but mainly because its persistence in the environment rapidly leads to the development of resistance to the insecticide in mosquito populations. There are now much more effective and acceptable insecticides, such as Bacillus thuringiensis, to kill larval mosquitoes outdoors. . . . Malaria is a major, ongoing disease problem in much of the developing world. Increases in the incidence of the disease have occurred for complex reasons. Reduced insecticide usage is one, but others include the resistance to treatment in both the parasite and the mosquito vectors, changes in land use that have provided new mosquito habitat, and the movement of people into new, high-risk areas.

"Most nations where malaria is a problem, and most health professionals working in the field of malaria control, support the targeted use of DDT, as part of the tool kit for malaria control. Most also agree that more cost-effective, less environmentally persistent alternatives are needed. There are some effective alternative chemicals for the control of adult mosquitoes, but preventing their further development is lack of investment by industry, because malaria is largely a disease of the poor." Feb. 2, 2004, *The Australian.* Quoted by Professor Ken Miles MBBS, FRCR, MSc (Nuclear Medicine), MD.

19. Joseph Kahn, "A Sea of Sand Is Threatening China's Heart," *New York Times,* June 8, 2006, p. 1.

20. Kenneth Deffeyes, *Hubbert's Peak: The Impending World Oil Shortage* (Princeton, NJ: Princeton University Press, 2001), p. 146.

21. "Third 'Major' Oil Discovery Is Made at El Nar in Sudan," *The Wall Street Journal,* January 21, 1997, p. B5; "Treasure under the Sea," *Financial Times,* May 1, 1997, p. 11; and "Pulling Oil from Davy Jones' Locker," *BusinessWeek,* October 30, 1995, pp. 74–76.

22. Association for the Study of Peak Oil and Gas, www.peakoil.net (accessed June 7, 2006).

23. Energy Information Administration, "Annual Energy Outlook 2005," www.eia.doe.gov/oiaf/aeo (accessed June 7, 2006).

24. Adam Porter, "'Peak Oil' Enters Mainstream Debate," *BBC News: UK edition,* June 10, 2005, http://news.bbc.co.uk/1/hi/business/4077802.stm co.uk/1/hi/sci/tech/3623549.stm (accessed June 6, 2006).

25. Canadian Association of Petroleum Producers, "Oil Sands Resources, Production and Projects," May 2006, www.capp.ca/default.asp?V_DOC_ID=1162 (accessed June 7, 2006).

26. Russell Gold, "As Prices Surge, Oil Giants Turn Sludge into Gold," *The Wall Street Journal,* March 27, 2006, p. 1.

27. Office of Deputy Assistant Secretary for Petroleum Reserves and Office of Naval Petroleum and Oil Shale Reserves, *Strategic Significance of America's Oil Shale Resource,* Vol. II: *Oil Shale Resources, Technology and Economics* (Washington, DC: U.S. Department of Energy, March 2004).

28. Greenpeace Australia Pacific, www.greenpeace.org.au/climate/causes/criminals/shaleoil/overview.html (accessed June 7, 2006).

29. Sasol, "Sasol Oil-from-Coal Process," www.sasol.com/sasol_internet/downloads/CTL_Brochure_1125921891488.pdf (accessed August 24, 2006).

30. On April 25, 1986, the world's worst nuclear power accident so far occurred at Chernobyl in Ukraine. The Chernobyl nuclear power plant, 80 miles north of Kiev, had four reactors, and while testing reactor number 4, personnel disregarded safety procedures. At 1:23 a.m. the chain reaction in the reactor became out of control, creating explosions and a fireball that blew off the reactor's heavy steel and concrete lid. See www.chernobyl.co.uk (accessed June 7, 2006).

31. Tim Flannery, "Nuclear: Back on the Horizon," *The Melbourne Age,* September 26, 2005 (accessed June 8, 2006).

32. Jeffrey Ball, "With a Big Nuclear Push, France Transforms Its Energy Equation," *The Wall Street Journal,* March 28, 2006, p. 1.

33. U.S. Energy Information Administration, "International Energy Outlook 2005," June 2005,. www.eia.doe.gov/oiaf/ieo/coal.html (accessed June 11, 2006).

34. U.S. Energy Information Administration, "International Energy Outlook 2004,", www.eia.doe.gov (accessed July 2, 2004).

35. Simon Romro, "Will Coal Be the Fuel of the 21st Century?" *New York Times,* May 31, 2006, www.iht.com/articles/2006/05/29/business/coal.php (accessed through ITH site June 8, 2006).

36. Keith Bradsher and David Barboza, "Clouds from Chinese Coal Cast a Long Shadow," *New York Times,* June 11, 2006, p. 1.

37. International Energy Agency, "Natural Gas," *Key World Energy Statistics 2005,* www.iea.org (accessed June 8, 2006).

38. American Wind Energy Association, "Global Wind Energy Market Report,", www.awea.org (accessed June 9, 2006).

39. American Wind Energy Association, "Record Year for Wind Energy," February 17, 2006, www.awea.org (accessed June 8, 2006).

40. Canadian Renewable Fuels Association, "Fuel Change," September 22, 2005, www.greenfuels.org/fuelchange/index.htm (accessed June 13, 2006).

41. www.fuelcells.org (accessed June 9, 2006).

42. Phillip Sutton, "Sustainability, What Does It Mean?" Green Innovations homepage, August 28, 2000, www.green-innovations.asn.au/sustblty.htm (accessed June 10, 2006).

43. Ibid.

44. Paul Hawken, *The Ecology of Commerce,* (New York: HarperCollins, 1994), p. 139.

45. Brundtland Commission, *Our Common Future: From One Earth to One World,* World Commission on Environment and Development (Oxford: Oxford University Press, 1987).

46. Economics Network, UK Higher Education Academy, "Development Survey on Definitions: Sustainable," www.economicsnetwork.ac.uk (accessed June 10, 2006).

47. Dino Mahtani, "Nigerian Oil Industry Helpless as Militants Declare War on Obasanjo," *Financial Times,* February 21, 2006.

48. Francesco Guerrera and Richard Waters, "IBM Chief Wants End to Colonial Companies," *Financial Times,* June 12, 2006, p. 1; Samuel Palmisano, "Multinationals Have Been Superseded," *Financial Times,* June 12, 2006, p. 15.

49. R. Edward Freeman, *Strategic Management: A Stakeholder Approach* (Boston: Pitman, 1984).

50. R. Edward Freeman, Andrew C. Wicks, and Bidhan Pamar, "'Stakeholder Theory' and the Corporate Objective Revisited," *Organizational Science* 15, no. 3 (May–June 2004), pp. 364–69.

51. F. R. Kluckhohn and F. L. Strodtbeck *Variations in Value Orientations* (Evanston, IL: Row Petersen, 1961).

52. "Sustainable Development Society Hosts Patagonia CEO Michael Crooke," *The Harbus Online,* Harvard Business School, May 10, 2004, www.harbus.org/news/2002/03/11News/Sustainable.Development.Society.Hosts.Patagonia.Ceo.Michael.Crooke-207418.shtml (accessed July 4, 2004).

53. Y. Chouinard, *Patagonia: The Next Hundred Years* (1995), p. 8, www.svn.org/initiativesfall2002/PDF_PatagoniaNext100Yrs.pdf (accessed September 17, 2004).

CHAPTER 8

1. Many of these factors also affect domestic firms, but multinational firms are generally more vulnerable and usually must act more quickly.

2. If management is interested in a country as a possible site for investment, it will require the same detailed information as it does for an area where the firm is already doing business.

3. *International Bibliography, Information, Documentation (IBID),* an excellent bibliography, is published quarterly by UNIPUB. It includes abstracts of publications and studies containing economic and demographic data.

4. "Country Classification," http://web.worldbank.org/WBSITE/EXTERNAL/DATASTATISTICS/0,,contentMDK:20420458~menuPK:64133156~pagePK:64133150~piPK:64133175~theSitePK:239419,00.html (October 7, 2006).

5. *2006 World Development Indicators,* table 1.6, http://devdata.worldbank.org (October 7, 2006). GNI is explained in *World Development Indicators 2001* (Washington, DC: World Bank, 2002), p. 15.

6. Friedrich Schneider and Dominik Enste, *Hiding in the Shadows: The Growth of the Underground Economy* (Washington, DC: International Monetary Fund, 2002), table 2, www.imf.org/external/pubs/ft/issues/issues30/index.htm (June 30, 2004); and Friedrich Schneider and Robert Klinglmair, "Shadow Economies around the World: What do We Know?" March 2004, http://papers.ssrn.com/so13/papers.cfm?abstract_id=518526 (October 8, 2006).

7. World Bank, "Structure of Consumption in PPP Terms," *2000 World Development Indicators* (Washington, DC: World Bank, 2000), p. 224.

8. Joseph Khan, "Youth and His Hopes Die in Front of China Train," *San Antonio Express-News,* August 1, 2004, p. 21A.

9. "The Swoosh Index for Emerging Markets," *BusinessWeek,* May 5, 1997, p. 8; "Pangs of Conscience," *BusinessWeek,* July 29, 1996, pp. 46–47; "Nike, Inc.," *The Wall Street Journal,* September 23, 1997, p. B12; "Where Asia Goes from Here," *Fortune,* November 24, 1997, p. 104; and Matthew Forney, "How Nike Figured Out China," *Time Online Edition,* November 2004, www. time.com/time/globalbusiness/article/0,9171, 1101041025-725113,00.html (November 10, 2004).

10. "Debt Sustainability," *World Development Indicators 1997,* p. 225.

11. International Telecommunication Union, www.itu.int/ITU-D/icteye/Indicators/Indicators.aspx# (October 6, 2006).

12. *Human Development Report 2005* (New York: United Nations Development Program, 2005), pp. 232–34.

13. "Strictly Speaking, Wal-Mart May Need Lessons in French," *The Wall Street Journal,* April 13, 1994, p. B7; and "Wal-Mart Again Runs into Language-Law Trouble," *The Wall Street Journal,* June 24, 1994, p. A4.

CHAPTER 9

1. Ian Brownlie, *Principles of Public International Law* (Oxford, England: Oxford University Press, 1966), pp. 435–36.

2. "Why Planned Economies Fail," *The Economist,* June 25, 1988, p. 67. See also "Wounded Pride: Why Communism Fell," *The Economist,* May 25, 1991, pp. 98–99.

3. Jack Lowenstein, "Ready to Join the Big League?" *Euromoney,* October 1990, pp. 66–73.

4. Robert Graham, "Rightwing Coalition Confident of French Poll Win," *Financial Times,* June 8–9, 2002, p. 2.

5. *The Right Guide,* 4th ed. (Ann Arbor, MI: Economics America, 2000); and *The Left Guide,* 3rd ed. (Ann Arbor, MI: Economics America, 2001).

6. Richard L. Holman, "EC Widens Business Control," *The Wall Street Journal,* July 25, 1991, p. A10.

7. "Thatcher's Sales," *BusinessWeek,* December 10, 1990, p. 26.

8. Jill Leovy, "Lockheed Looks to Expand Its Airport Business," *Los Angeles Times,* May 31, 1994, pp. D1, 6.

9. Hilary Clarke, "Europe Flies Its Airport Revolution to the World," *The European,* May 22–28, 1997, p. 15.

10. Martin Dickson, "America's Sale of the Century," *Financial Times,* June 1, 1992, p. 12.

11. Roger Matthews, "Mozambique Brings In the British," *Financial Times,* June 17, 1997, p. 9.

12. Kathy Chen, "Cracking Open the Door," *The Asian Wall Street Journal,* April 14, 1997, p. 5.

13. "Privatization in Practice: Fourth Pan African Investment Summit," *Financial Times,* October 16, 2000, p. 14.

14. Gerhard Pohl, Robert Anderson, Stijn Claessens, and Simeon Djankov, "Privatisation and Restructuring in Central and Eastern Europe," World Bank Technical Paper No. 386 (Washington, DC: World Bank, June 1997); and Kevin Done, "Europe's Privatisation Fast Track," *Financial Times,* July 4, 1997, p. 10.

15. Gekko, "Random Walk: Wall Street," *National Review,* June 27, 1994, p. 26.

16. Virginia Marsh and Shawn Dorman, "Church Groups Catch the Privatization Spirit," *Financial Times,* January 8–9, 2000, p. 3.

17. "Water Industry: Frozen Taps," *The Economist,* May 31, 2003, p. 56. © 2003 The Economist Newspaper Group, Inc. Reprinted with permission. Further reproduction prohibited. Also, Colin Robinson, "Reviving the Scottish Water Industry," www.policyinstitute.info/AllPDFs/Robinson-Mar05.pdf (August 1, 2006).

18. John Lancaster, "U.S. Arms Sales in Gulf Risk Being Eroded by China and Others," *International Herald Tribune,* July 17, 1997, p. 6.

19. James Phillips and James H. Anderson, "International Terrorism: Containing and Defeating Terrorist Threats," *Issues 2000,* Heritage Foundation, Washington, DC, August 2000.

20. "The Price of Paying Ransoms," *The Economist,* September 2, 2000, p. 17.

21. Sarah Butcher, "No Hostages to Fortune," *Financial Times,* March 4, 2002, p. 10.

22. Butcher, "No Hostages to Fortune."

23. Sue Zesiger, "Freeze," *Fortune,* April 28, 1997, pp. 417–20.

24. Michael Bond, "Europe Alert over Threat of Nuclear Terrorism," *The European,* March 10–24, 1994, pp. 1, 2.

25. David Wessel, "Flow of Capital to Developing Nations Surges Even as Aid to Poorest Shrinks," *The Wall Street Journal,* March 24, 1997, p. A5.

26. www.duke/edu/~charvey/ Country_risk/pol .htm; and http://www.polrisk. com/products.htm. (July 21, 2002).

CHAPTER 10

1. "Shanghai Sees Law as Key to Being Commercial Hub," *Financial Times,* July 1, 2002, p. vi.

2. Mark A. Goldstein, "The UN Sales Convention," *Business America,* November 21, 1988, pp. 12–13.

3. A. H. Herman, "Growth in International Trade Law," *Financial Times,* March 30, 1989, p. 10.

4. Frances Williams, "GATT Joins Battle for Right to Protect," *Financial Times,* July 7, 1994, p. 7.

5. Jack Kemp, "Greenspan Is Right: Abolish Capital Gains Taxes," *The Wall Street Journal,* February 24, 1997, p. A22.

6. Madelaine Drohan, "The Fine Art of Avoiding Bewildering Italian Taxes," *The Globe and Mail,* September 28, 1996, p. D4.

7. Jonathan Schwarz, "Stimuli for Freer Trade," *Financial Times,* May 20, 1994, p. II.

8. "The Disappearing Taxpayer," *The Economist,* May 31, 1997, p. 15; and "Disappearing Taxes," *The Economist,* May 31, 1997, pp. 21–23.

9. "When We Wear the Black Hats," *The Wall Street Journal,* March 22, 1990, p. A16.

10. Richard L. Holman, "EC Antitrust Efforts Boosted," *The Wall Street Journal,* March 20, 1991, p. A17; and "EC Court Reinforces Commission's Antitrust Clout," *Eurecom,* April 1991, p. 1.

11. The Lex Column, *Financial Times* (London), June 16–17, 2001, p. 24.

12. Pierre Verkhhovsky and Clifford Chance, "Advising Japanese Clients on EU Competition Law" *International Journal of Competition Policy and Regulation,* www.globalcompetitionreview.com/apar/jap_eu.cfm (July 30, 2004).

13. *The Economist,* June 9, 1979, pp. 91–92.

14. For example, see *Continental Ore Co. v. Union Carbide & Carbon Corp.*, 370 U.S. 690 (1962); *Timberline Lumber Co. v. Bank of America*, 549 F.2d 597 (9th Cir. 1976); and *United States v. Aluminum Co. of America*, 148 F.2d 416 (2d Cir. 1945).

15. "Brussels Clears AOL–Time Warner Merger," *Financial Times,* October 12, 2000, p. 24; and Mary Jacoby, "EU Hits Microsoft with $358.3 Million Penalty," *The Wall Street Journal* (July 13, 2006), p. A3.

16. John R. Wilke, "U.S. Court Rules Antitrust Laws Apply to Foreigners," *The Wall Street Journal,* March 19, 1997, p. B6.

17. "Japan's Fair Trade Commission, Pussycat," *The Economist,* October 23, 1993, pp. 85–86.

18. "Caught in a Web of Jurisdiction," *Financial Times,* May 15, 2002, p. 13.

19. "U.S. Endorses a Global Approach to Antitrust," *The Wall Street Journal,* September 15, 2000, p. A15; and "Call to Align Global Policy on Competition," *Financial Times,* September 15, 2000, p. 6.

20. "Plan for Global Insolvency Accord," *Financial Times,* October 26, 2000, p. 4.

21. Thomas G. Donlan, "Not So Free Trade: U.S. Preaches What It Doesn't Always Practice," *Barron's,* June 27, 1988, pp. 70–71.

22. Carolyn Lochhead, "Strict Liability Causing Firms to Give Up on Promising Ideas," *Washington Times,* August 22, 1988, p. B5.

23. Sandra N. Hurd and Frances E. Zollers, "Desperately Seeking Harmony: The European Community's Search for Uniformity in Product Liability Law," *American Business Law Journal* 30 (1992), pp. 35–68.

24. Ibid.

25. "Product Liability," *The Economist,* May 25, 1996, p. 67; and Katherine Dowling, "Wide-Ranging Suits against Manufacturers May Keep Lifesaving Medical Devices on the Shelf and out of Reach," *The Wall Street Journal,* August 19, 1997, p. A4.

26. Barbara Crutchfield George and Linda McCallister, "The Effect of Cultural Attitudes on Product Liability Laws," *Southwestern Association of Administrative Disciplines,* March 4, 1993; and Craig P. Wagnild, "Civil Law Discovery in Japan: A Comparison of Japanese and US Methods of Evidence Collection in Civil Litigation," Asia-Pacific Law and Policy Journal 3, no. 1 (Winter 2002), www.hawaii.edu/aplpj/pdfs/v3-01-Wagnild.pdf (July 20, 2006)..

27. Barbara Crutchfield George, "The U.S. Foreign Corrupt Practices Act: The Price Business Is Paying for the Unilateral Criminalization of Bribery," *International Journal of Management,* September 1987, pp. 391–402; and "Some Guidelines on Dealing with Graft," *Business International,* February 25, 1983, p. 62.

CHAPTER 11

1. Ronald McKinnon, "The Euro versus the Dollar," www.stanford.edu/~mckinnon/briefs/salvatoreJEPMKenen.pdf (accessed August 5, 2004).

2. Paul Solomon and the international economist Fred Bergson discussed the market psychology involved in the dollar's decline in a WGBH segment called "Dollar's Decline," on May 27, 2003. You can watch the video or read the interview at www.pbs.org/newshour/bb/economy/jan-june03/dollar_05-27.html (accessed June 23, 2006).

3. Bank for International Settlements, "Triennial Central Bank Survey of Foreign Exchange and Derivatives Market Activity, 2005," March 2005, www.bis.org/publ/rpfx05.htm (accessed-June 21, 2006).

4. "U.S. Probes Whether Big Banks Stifle Rival in Currency Trading," *The Wall Street Journal,* May 15, 2002, p. A1.

5. Cheol S. Eun and Bruce G. Resnick, *International Financial Management,* 4th ed. (Burr Ridge, IL: McGraw Hill Irwin, 2007), pp. 147–48. The technical explanations here are clearly described and well illustrated.

6. Ibid., p. 149.

7. Ibid., p. 151.

8. Cheol Eun and Sanjiv Sabherwal, "Forecasting Exchange Rates: *Do* the Banks Know Better?" *Global Finance Journal* (2002), pp. 195–215.

9. Richard Levich, "Evaluating the Performance of the Forecasters," in *The Management of Foreign Exchange Risk,* 2nd ed. (New York: Euromoney Publication), pp. 121–34.

10. Eun and Resnick, *International Financial Management,* p. 499.

11. *OECD Factbook 2006,* http://puck.sourceoecd.org/vl=14933899/cl=14/nw=1/rpsv/factbook/03-01-03.htm (accessed June 24, 2006).

CHAPTER 12

1. U.S. Census Bureau, International, "Midyear Population, by Age and Sex," www.census.gov/cgi-bin/ipc/idbagg (July 27, 2006).

2. Ibid.

3. *Global Employment Trends Brief* (Geneva: International Labour Office, January 2006).

4. U.S. Census Bureau, International, "Midyear Population, by Age and Sex."

5. UNCTAD, *Developing Countries in International Trade 2005* (New York: United Nations, 2005).

6. *Global Employment Trends Brief.*

7. "Standardised Unemployment Rates: Men," *OECD Factbook,* http://dx.doi.org/10.1787/814540438321 (July 27, 2006); and "Standardized Unemployement Rates: Women," *OECD Factbook,* http://dx.doi.org/10.1787/122757651858 (July 27, 2006).

8. *Facts on Labour Migration* (Geneva: International Labour Organization, 2006).

9. *Costs and Benefits of International Migration* (New York: Council on Foreign Relations, September 2005).

10. Mohamad Yusop bin Awang Damit, Tin Maung Maung Than, Anthony L Smith, Russell Heng et al., *Regional Outlook: Southeast Asia,* 2003–2004, p. 10.

11. For example, see *World Migration 2005: Costs and Benefits of International Migration* (New York: Council on Foreign Relations, September 2005), www.cfr.org/publication/8987/world_migration_2005.html (July 28, 2006).

12. *Facts on Labour Migration.*

13. Stefan Wagstyl, "Comment and Analysis," *Financial Times,* February 9, 2004, p. 11.

14. Leslie Crawford, "Immigrants Help Sustain Spain's Long Building Boom," *Financial Times,* April 19, 2006, p. 8.

15. *Costs and Benefits of International Migration.*

16. Steven A. Camarota, *Immigrants at Mid-Decade: A Snapshot of America's Foreign-Born Population in 2005* (Washington, DC: Center for Immigration Studies, December 2005), www.cis.org/articles/2005/back1405.html (July 29, 2006).

17. U.S. Census Bureau, "Percent of People Who Are Foreign Born: 2004," http://factfinder.census.gov/servlet/GRTTable?_bm=y&-_box_head_nbr=R0501&-ds_name=ACS_2004_EST_G00_&-mt_name=ACS_2004_EST_G00_R0501_US30&-format=US-30 (July 28, 2006).

18. The most recent immigration data from the U.S. Census Bureau can be accessed at www.census.gov/population.

19. *Facts on Labour Migration.*

20. *Facts on Child Labor*—2006 (Geneva: International Labour Organization, 2006).

21. Emily Wax, "In Rural Ethiopia, Child Labor Can Mean Survival," *The Tribune* (San Luis Obispo, CA), January 4, 2006, p. A11; and "Brutal Ethiopian Nature and Politics Compound Child Labor Situation," *The Tribune* (San Luis Obispo, CA), January 4, 2006, p. A11.

22. Edward Luce, "Ikea's Grown-Up Plan to Tackle Child Labour," *Financial Times,* September 15, 2004, p. 7.

23. *The End of Child Labour—Within Reach* (Geneva: International Labour Organization, 2006), www.ilo.org/public/english/standards/relm/ilc/ilc95/pdf/rep-i-b.pdf (July 29, 2006).

24. Raphael Minder, "Child Labour on Decline, Says ILO," *Financial Times,* May 5, 2006, p. 7.

25. "Forced Labor," www.anti-slaverysociety.addr.com/forcedlabor.htm (July 28, 2006).

26. Matthias Busse and Sebastian Braun, *International Labor Review* 142, no. 1 (2003), p. 49.

27. OECD, "Trends in International Migration Reflect Increasing Labour-Related Immigration and Persistent Integration Problems," 2004, www. oecd.org. (August 2, 2004).

28. "Africa Economy: EU Foreign Ministers Bid to Stop Africa's Brain-Drain," *EIU ViewsWire* (New York), March 30, 2006.

29. *Science and Engineering Indicators 2002,* www.nsf.gov/sbe/srs/seind02/c3/fig03-21.htm (July 14, 2002, and August 12, 2002), and "UNDP Oldthink," *Foreign Policy,* October 2001, p. 15.

30. Alan M. Webber, "Reverse Brain Drain Threatens U.S. Economy," *USA Today,* February 23, 2004, www.USAtoday.com (February 24, 2004).

31. http://rbd.nstda.or.th/rbdweb/about_rbd/index.php (July 28, 2006).

32. "Exploitation and Abuse of Migrant Workers in Saudi Arabia," *Human Rights Watch,* http://hrw.org/mideast/saudi/labor/ (July 30, 2006).

33. Neil Heathcote, "Saudi Women Break into Business," *BBC News,* February 27, 2006, http://news.bbc.co.uk/1/hi/world/middle_east/4754430.stm (July 30, 2006).

34. Jillian Talbot, *Dominion Post,* February 25, 2004. p. C.1.

35. "Women and Girls: Education, Not Discrimination," *OECD Observer* (electronic edition), November 3, 2000.

36. N. Boyacigiller, S. Beechler, S. Taylor, and O. Levy, "The Crucial yet Illusive Global Mindset," in *The Blackwell Handbook of Global Management: A Guide to Managing Complexity,* ed. H. W. Lane, M. Maznevski, M. Mendenhall, and J. McNett (Oxford, UK, and Malden, MA: Blackwell, 2004).

37. European Trade Union Confederation, "Our Members," www.etuc.org/r/13 (July 28, 2006).

CHAPTER 13

1. For a discussion of strategy, see Michael E. Porter, "What Is Strategy?" *Harvard Business Review,* November–December 1996, pp. 61–78.

2. Jay B. Barney, "Looking Inside for Competitive Advantage," *Academy of Management Executive,* no. 9 (1995), pp. 49–61. Copyright 1995 by Academy of Management. Reproduced with permission of Academy of Management in the format textbook via Copyright Clearance Center.

3. "An Executive Take on the Top Business Trends: A McKinsey Global Survey," *The McKinsey Quarterly,* April 2006, www.mckinseyquarterly.com/article_print.aspx?L2=21&L3=114&ar=1754 (April 27, 2006).

4. Bain & Company, "About the Survey," www.bain.com/management_tools/about_overview.asp?groupCode=1 (June 12, 2006).

5. Jeffrey R. Immelt, chairman and CEO, GE, "Letter to Stakeholders," *General Electric 2003 Annual Report,* www.ge.com/ar2003/chairman/letter_1.jsp (August 3, 2004).

6. "Case Study: Keeping Proprietary Technology in Japan," 2003 JETRO White Paper on International Trade and Foreign Direct Investment (Tokyo: Japan External Trade Organization), p. 44; and Michiyo Nakamoto, "Japan Goes after Industrial Spies," *Financial Times,* February 9, 2004, p. 8.

7. DuPont, "Sustainable Growth," www2.dupont.com/Our_Company/en_US/glance/sus_growth/sus_growth.html (June 12, 2006).

8. Kathryn Kranhold, "China's Price for Market Entry: Give Us Your Technology, Too," *The Wall Street Journal,* February 26, 2004, pp. A1, A6.

9. Reggie Van Lee, Lisa Fabish, and Nancy McGaw, "The Value of Corporate Values," *Strategy + Business,* www.strategy-business.com/article/05206?gko=7869b-1876-9176155&tid=230&pg=all (June 12, 2006).

10. "J&J Mission," www.naukri.com/jg/johnson/global.htm (June 12, 2006).

11. Unilever, "Our Mission," www.unilever.co.za/company_mission.asp (June 12, 2006).

12. "General," *Amazon.com 2005 Annual Report,* http://library.corporate-ir.net/library/97/976/97664/items/193688/AMZN2005AnnualReport.pdf (June 12, 2006).

13. "Vision Statement," www1.dupont.com/NASApp/dupontglobal/corp/index.jsp?page=/content/US/en_US/overview/glance/vision/index.html (August 5, 2004).

14. Sumitomo Corporation, "SC Values," www.sumitomocorp.co.jp/english/company_e/scvalues/index.shtml (June 12, 2006).

15. "About McDonald's," www.mcdonalds.com/corporate/corp.html (September 15, 2002).

16. "Intel's Mission Statement, Values, and Objectives," www.intel.com/intel/company/corp1.htm (June 12, 2006).

17. BP, "Structure and Management: Overview," www.bp.com/sectiongenericarticle.do?categoryId=2010726&contentId=2015515 (August 5, 2004); and BP, "How We Run the Business: Our Objectives," www.bp.com/sectiongenericarticle.do?categoryId=26&contentId=2000563 (June 12, 2006).

18. "About 3M: Frequently Asked Questions," www.corporateir.net/ireye/ir_site.zhtml?ticker_MMM&script_1800 (December 12, 2000).

19. Goodyear Tire & Rubber, *2005 Annual Report,* p. 10, www.goodyear.com/investor/pdf/2005_annual_report.pdf (June 12, 2006).

20. Liu Baijia, "Schneider to Localize in China," *China Daily,* July 12, 2004, p. 10; and Schneider Electric, "Local Operations," www.schneiderelectric.com/wps/myportal/!ut/p/.cmd/cs/.ce/7_0_A/.s/7_0_PJ/_s.7_0_A/7_0_PJ?toservice=WIBPB_1042_CORP&wibCountryDB=CORP&idContent=4d94ff2c0e40af49c1256e7f00468ff4&fromservice=AUTON_0017_CORP (June 13, 2006).

21. Ginny Parker, "Going Global Can Hit Snags, Vodafone Finds," *The Wall Street Journal,* June 16, 2004, p. B1; David Pringle and Taska Manzaroli, "Vodafone Seeks to Buy Out Its Japanese Units," *The Wall Street Journal,* May 26, 2004, p. B2; Robert Budden and Tim Burt, "Brand Is a Big Issue; When People Think Mobile Products and Services, We Want Them to Go to Vodafone," *Financial Times,* December 22, 2003, p. 9; and "Vodafone's Global Ambitions Got Hung Up in Japan," *The Wall Street Journal,* March 18–19, 2006, p. 1.

22. Cornelis A. de Kluyver and John A. Pearce, II, *Strategy: A View from the Top,* 2nd ed. (Upper Saddle River, NJ: Pearson Prentice Hall, 2006), p. 9.

23. Erik Berkman, "How to Use the Balanced Scorecard," *CIO Magazine,* May 15, 2002, www.cio.com/archive/051502/scorecard.html (June 13, 2006).

24. 3M, "To Our Shareholders," *3M Annual Report 2003,* p. 4.

25. Gary Hamel, "Strategy as Revolution," *Harvard Business Review,* July–August 1996, p. 70.

26. Eric D. Beinhocker and Sarah Kaplan, "Tired of Strategic Planning?" *The McKinsey Quarterly,* 2002 (special edition on risk and resilience), www.mckinseyquarterly.com/article_print.aspx?L2=21&L3=37&ar=1191 (April 13, 2006).

27. Alan Murray, "The CEO as Global Corporate Ambassador," *The Wall Street Journal,* March 20, 2006, p. 2.

28. "The New Breed of Strategic Planner," *BusinessWeek,* September 19, 1984, p. 64.

29. Ibid., p. 66.

30. Alfred Chan, "As in Chess, Strategic Planning Is a Good Move," *Enterprise 50,* http://biztimes.asia1.com/bizcentre/ Enterprise50/plan9701.html (March 19, 1998).

31. Andrew Campbell and Marcus Alexander, "What's Wrong with Strategy?" *Harvard Business Review,* November–December 1997, p. 46.

32. "Introduction to Shell Global Scenarios to 2025 by Jeroen van der Veer Chief Executive," www.shell.com/home/Framework?siteId=royal-en&FC2=/royal-en/html/iwgen/our_strategy/scenarios/introduction_to_global_scenarios/zzz_lhn.html&FC3=/royal-en/html/iwgen/our_strategy/scenarios/introduction_to_global_scenarios/intro_jvdv_scenarios_28022005.html (June 12, 2006); "20-20 Vision," Global Scenarios, www.shell.com/b/b2_03.html (March 15, 1998); and P. W. Beck, "Corporate Planning for an Uncertain Certain Future," *Long-Range Planning,* August 1982, p. 14.

33. Jeffrey R. Immelt, *General Electric 2003 Annual Report,* www.ge.com/ar2003/strategy/index_fla.jsp (August 3, 2004).

34. Frederick W. Gluck, "A Fresh Look at Strategic Management," *Journal of Business Strategy,* Fall 1985, p. 6.

35. "Corporate Spies Feel a Sting," *BusinessWeek,* July 14, 1997, pp. 75–77; and "For Pills, Not Projectiles," *The Economist,* July 12, 1997, p. 22.

36. Richard Isaacs, "A Field Day for Spies: While a Deal Advances," *Mergers and Acquisitions,* January 2004, pp. 30–35.

37. Ibid.

38. Bill Fiora, "Forward-Looking Intelligence," *Pharmaceutical Executive* 26, no. 2 (February 2006), pp. S22–26; and Outward In-

sights LLC, "Ostriches and Eagles: Competitive Intelligence Usage and Understanding in U.S. Companies," February 2005, www.outwardinsights.com (June 13, 2006).

39. A. M. Ahmed, M. Zairi, and K. S. Almarri, "SWOT Analysis for Air China Performance and Its Experience with Quality," *Benchmarking: An International Journal* 13, no. 1–2 (2006), pp. 160–173; and "What Ronald McDonald, Mickey Mouse Taught Nissan," *Business International*, February 22, 1993, pp. 57–58.

CHAPTER 14

1. Nitin Nohria, *Note on Organization Structure* (Boston: Harvard Business School, 1991).

2. Met-Pro Corporation, "International Division," www.met-pro.com/html/sales.htm (June 21, 2006); Met-Pro Corporation, "Form 10-K for Met Pro Corp," April 13, 2006, www.met-pro.com/html/news.htm (June 21, 2006); and Met-Pro Corporation, "Met-Pro Corporation Divisions and Subsidiaries," www.met-pro.com/html/subdiv.htm (June 21, 2006).

3. Wal-Mart Stores, Inc., *2006 Annual Report*, www.walmartfacts.com/docs/1779_2006annualreport_1547171566.pdf (June 21, 2006); and "International Overview," walmartstores.com/GlobalWMStoresWeb/navigate.do?catg=369 (June 21, 2006).

4. John M. Stopford and Louis T. Wells, *Strategy and Structure of the Multinational Enterprise* (New York: Basic Books, 1972).

5. Deutsche Post World Net, "The Group at a Glance," http://investors.dpwn.com/en/investoren/der_konzern_im_ueberblick/uebersichtsgrafik/index.htm (June 21, 2006); Deutsche Post World Net, *Annual Report 2005*, www3.financialreports.dpwn.com/2005/ar/en/servicepages/welcome?SESSID=8cf2ec8d7a14bedd6844b213736d6753e47a7d67 (June 21, 2006); and "Organization Chart," www.dpwn.de/dpwn?tab=1&skin=hi&check=yes&lang=de_EN&xmlFile=2002753 (June 21, 2006).

6. ExxonMobil, *2005 Annual Report*, http://exxonmobil.com/corporate/files/corporate/sar_2005.pdf (July 31, 2006); and "To Our Shareholders," *ExxonMobil 1999 Annual Report*, www.exxonmobil.com/shareholder_publications/c_annual_99/c_shareholder.html (December 12, 2000).

7. Mittal Steel, "Structure," www.mittalsteel.com/Company/Structure.htm (June 21, 2006); "Mittal Steel Company N.V.," http://finance.google.com/finance?q=mittal+steel&btnG=Search (June 21, 2006); and Mittal Steel, "Profile," www.mittalsteel.com/Company/Profile.htm (June 21, 2006).

8. Sarah Ellison, "Kimberly-Clark to Reorganize; High-Ranking Official to Retire," *The Wall Street Journal*, January 20, 2004, p. A3; *Kimberly-Clark 10-K*, 2003, www. kimberly-clark.com (July 24, 2004); Kimberly-Clark, "Kimberly-Clark Announces Organizational and Senior Management Changes to Further Its Global Business Plan," http://investor.kimberly-clark.com/news/20040119-126799.cfm?t=n (June 20, 2006); and Kimberly-Clark, *2005 Annual Report*, www.rkconline.net/AR/KimberlyClark05/PDF/AR05.pdf (June 20, 2006).

9. Genentech, "Corporate Brochure," www.gene.com/gene/news/kits/corporate/pdf/corporate-brochure.pdf (June 21, 2006); and Genentech, Inc., *Form 10-K*, www.gene.com/gene/ir/downloadDoc.do?id=2801 (June 21, 2006).

10. Deborah Ball, "Unilever Shakes Up Its Management to Spur Growth," *The Wall Street Journal*, February 11, 2005, p. A2; Unilever, "Company Structure," www.unilever.com/ourcompany/aboutunilever/companystructure/default.asp (June 21, 2006); and Unilever, *2005 Annual Report*, www.unilever.com/Images/2005_Annual_Report_English%20amended_tcm13-35722.pdf (June 21, 2006).

11. Nokia Corporation, *Form 20-F*, www.nokia.com/NOKIA_COM_1/About_Nokia/Financials/nokia_form_20f_2005.pdf (June 21, 2006).

12. BP, "How BP Works," www.bp.com/sectiongenericarticle.do?categoryId=25&contentId=2014279 (June 21, 2006); and BP, "Organized for Growth," www.bp.com/genericarticle.do?categoryId=25&contentId=2006395 (June 21, 2006).

13. Michelin, "Organization," www.michelin.com/corporate/front/templates/affich.jsp?codeRubrique=11&lang=EN (June 21, 2006).

14. Caterpillar Inc., *2005 Annual Report*, www.cat.com/cda/files/329216/7/yecx0018_2005_annual_report.pdf (July 31, 2006).

15. Shell Chemicals, "Glossary & Trademarks," www.shellchemicals.com/glossary/1,1098,1159,00.html#P (June 21, 2006).

16. BP, "Organized for Growth."

17. Cassell Bryan-Low, "Vodafone Reorganizes, Names Morrow Head of Europe Group," *The Wall Street Journal*, April 7, 2006, p. B7; and Vodafone, "New Organisational Structure at Vodafone," April 6, 2006, www.vodafone.com/assets/files/en/vod1245gmprl.pdf (June 21, 2006).

18. Coca-Cola Company, "International Operations," January 17, 2006, www2.coca-cola.com/presscenter/nr_20060117_corporate_kent.html (June 21, 2006).

19. Lowell L. Bryan and Claudia Joyce, "The 21st-Century Organization," *The McKinsey Quarterly*, no. 3 (2005), www.mckinseyquarterly.com/article_print.aspx?L2=18&L3=30&ar=1628 (April 27, 2006).

20. Remo Häcki and Julian Lighton, "The Future of the Networked Company," *The McKinsey Quarterly*, no. 3 (2001), pp. 26–39.

21. Glenn R. Simpson, "Wearing of the Green: Irish Subsidiary Lets Microsoft Slash Taxes in U.S. and Europe; Tech and Drug Firms Move Key Intellectual Property to Low-Levy Island Haven; Center of Windows Licensing," *The Wall Street Journal*, November 7, 2005, p. A1.

22. "Microsoft Unit in Ireland Tops List; Top Profit Makers in Ireland Are Units of U.S. Companies," *The Wall Street Journal*, December 20, 2005, p. A1; "Plan Would End Use of Tax Havens for Patents," *The Wall Street Journal*, February 8, 2006, p. A1; Simpson, "Wearing of the Green"; Glenn R. Simpson, "U.S. Companies Might Overstate Irish Earnings for Tax Benefits," *The Wall Street Journal*, March 28, 2006, p. A6; and Jesse Drucker, "Symantec Is in $1 Billion IRS Dispute," *The Wall Street Journal*, June 20, 2006, p. A2.

23. William Bridges, "The End of the Job," *Fortune*, September 19, 1994, pp. 62–74. © 1994 Time Inc. Reprinted with permission.

CHAPTER 15

1. A good introduction to scanning the environment is Chun Wei Choo, "Environmental Scanning as Information Seeking and Organizational Knowing," *Prima Vera*, Working Paper Series 2002-01, http://primavera.fee.uva.nl/PDFdocs/2002-01.pdf (January 2002). Also see Ian Wylie, "There Is No Alternative to . . . ," *Fast Company*, www. fastcompany.com/online/60/tina.html (July 2002).

2. Virtually all governments have barriers to foreign direct investment and at the same time offer a variety of incentives to potential foreign investors. For example, Mexico currently restricts foreign investment in the petroleum industry. See, e.g.,UNCTAD, "Prospects for FDI Flows, Transnational Corporation Strategies and Promotion Policies: 2004–2007," www.unctad.org/sections/dite_dir/docs/survey_FDI.pdf (August 1, 2004).

3. "Team Canada 2002," www.tcm-mec.gc.ca/tc2002/menu-en.asp (August 1, 2004).

4. "CeBIT," www.cebit.de/homepage_e?x=1 (August 1, 2004); "Trade Show Statistics: Review 2006," www.cebit.de/7588?x=1 (October 5, 2006).

5. Secondary data and sometimes primary data will be gathered on a field trip, but the visitor rarely has the time or ability to conduct a complete field study.

6. Yuezhi Zhao, "The 'People's Phone' on Hold," *Foreign Policy*, July–August 2002, pp. 83–85.

7. "Third World Research Is Difficult, but It's Possible," *Marketing News*, August 26, 1997, p. 51.

8. For a sophisticated example in Mexico, see www.pearson-research.com/flash.shtml (August 1, 2004).

9. This approach was inspired by Masaaki Kotabe and Kristiaan Helsen, *Global Marketing Management* (New York: Wiley, 2003), p. 219.

CHAPTER 16

1. This discussion owes a great deal to Orville C. Walker, Jr., Harper W. Boyd, Jr., John Mullins, and Jean-Claude Larreche, *Marketing Strategy: A Decision-Focused Approach* (Burr Ridge, IL: Irwin/McGraw-Hill, 2003).

2. "Cross-License Agreement Expected to Bring More than $1 Billion to TI over Next 10 Years," press release, May 23, 1999, www.ti.com/corp/docs/press/company/1999/c99024.shtml (November 20, 2000).

3. Thayne Forbes, "Set the Right Royalty Rate," www.intangiblebusiness.com/Content/796 (August 3, 2006).

4. "Cosmopolitan," www.hearst.com/magazines/property/mag_prop_cosmo.html (August 3, 2006).

5. "Is *Playboy* Available outside North America?" www.playboy.com/worldofplayboy/faq/subscribing.html#4 (August 3, 2006).

6. "Bruised in Brazil: Ford Slips as Market Booms," *The Wall Street Journal,* December 13, 1996, p. A10; and "Ford and VW Split Up Venture in Latin America," *The Wall Street Journal,* December 2, 1994, p. A8.

7. Ian Friendly, "Cereal Partners Worldwide: A World of Opportunity," www.ir.nestle.com/NR/rdonlyres/4DC2CE3F-E882-4DE3-A023-987826A64416/0/cpw.pdf (August 2, 2006); and "Café au Lait, a Croissant—and Trix," *BusinessWeek,* August 24, 1992, p. 50.

8. "Mobile Telecoms: The Virtues of Being Virtual," *The Economist,* July 10, 2004, pp. 56–57; and "What Is an MVNO?" www.mobilein.com/what_is_a_mvno. htm (August 16, 2004).

9. Peter J. Buckley, Jeremy Clegg, and Hui Tan, "Knowledge Transfer to China: Policy Lessons from Foreign Affiliates," *Transnational Corporations* 13, no. 1 (April 2004), pp. 31–72.

10. Frank Tian Xie and Wesley J. Johnston, "Strategic Alliances: Incorporating the Impact of E-Business Technological Innovations," *Journal of Business and Industrial Marketing* 19, no. 3 (2004), pp. 208–22.

11. "About EUV Technology," http://euvl.com/about.php (August 3, 2006); and "Chip Makers Unite in Project to Raise Computer Power to New Levels," *International Herald Tribune,* September 12, 1997, p. 15.

12. Symbian, "Fast Facts," www.symbian.com/about/fastfacts/fastfacts.html (August 3, 2006); and "Symbian Cellphone Alliance Faces Growing Threat from Microsoft," *The Wall Street Journal,* November 6, 2000, pp. B1, B4.

13. Edward J. Zajac, "Creating an Academic Framework for Strategic Alliances," www.kellogg.northwestern.edu/kwo/sum02/indepth/theory.htm (August 8, 2004).

14. For discussion of challenges in managing international joint ventures and alliances, see Colette A. Frayne and J. Michael Geringer, "Challenges Facing General Managers of International Joint Ventures," in *Readings and Cases in International Human Resource Management,* 2nd ed., ed. M. Mendenhall and G. Oddou (Cincinnati, OH: South-Western, 1995), pp. 85–97; J. Michael Geringer and C. Patrick Woodcock, "Agency Costs and the Structure and Performance of International Joint Ventures," *Group Decision and Negotiation* 4, no. 5 (1995), pp. 453–67; and Colette A. Frayne and J. Michael Geringer, "Joint Venture General Managers: Key Issues in Research and Training," in *Research in Personnel and Human Resources Management,* ed. K. M. Rowland, B. Shaw, and P. Kirkbride (Greenwich, CT: JAI Press, 1993), supplement 3, pp. 301–21.

15. Leslie Chang, Chad Terhune, and Betsy McKay, "Coke's Big Gamble in Asia: Digging Deeper in China, India," *The Wall Street Journal,* August 11, 2004, pp. A1, A6.

16. "What Is Sogo Shosha?" www.fjt.co.jp/_jftc_sogo.htm (February 9, 1998).

17. Mitsui and Co., Ltd., "Corporate Info," www.mitsui.co.jp/en/company/index.html (August 3, 2006).

CHAPTER 17

1. Telephone conversation with Ford International representative.

2. *Commercial News USA,* U.S. Commercial Service, www.thinkglobal.us (July 29, 2006).

3. Export.gov, www.export.gov/partners.html#intlpartners (July 27, 2006).

4. "INCOTERMS 2000," www.iccwbo.org (July 30, 2006). These terms are copyrighted by the International Chamber of Commerce.

5. Export Import Bank, "Mission," www.exim.gov/about/mission.html (July 29, 2006).

6. A third support for exporters, the Foreign Sales Corporation (FSC), offered tax breaks for U.S.-owned foreign subsidiaries meeting specific criteria. This amounted to an export subsidy, claimed the EU. The claim was upheld by the WTO. Congress enacted legislation to end the FSC in May 2006.

7. Foreign Trade Corporation, "Foreign Trade Zone Resource Center," www.foreign-trade-zone.com/history.htm. (July 29, 2006).

8. See http://alliancechb.com (July 31, 2006).

9. Export.gov, Trade Information Center, "European CE Mark Requirements," http://web.ita.doc.gov/ticwebsite/FAQs.nsf/6683DCE2E5871DF9852565BC00785DDF/ED3167DEE3B48B03852569B400586FFB?OpenDocument (July 31, 2006).

10. "Automated Commercial System," U.S. Customs and Border Protection, www.cbp.gov/xp/cgov/import/ operations_support/automated_systems/acs (August 2, 2006).

11. The HTSUSA is available at www.usitc.gov/tata/hts/index.htm I (August 3, 2006).

CHAPTER 18

1. T. C. Melewar and John Saunders, "International Corporate Visual Identity: Standardization or Localization?" *Journal of International Business Studies,* Third Quarter 1999, pp. 583–98; and Adesegun Oyedele, Osama J. Butt, and Michael S. Minor, "The Extent of Global Visual Identity as Expressed in Web Sites: An Empirical Assessment," working paper, 2004.

2. Douglas Daft, "Back to Classic Coke," *Financial Times,* March 27, 2000, p. 16.

3. "Multinational, Not Global," *The Economist,* December 24, 1988, p. 99; and "Nestlé Shows How to Gobble Markets," *Fortune,* January 16, 1989, p. 75.

4. "About Accenture," www.accenture.com (October 8, 2006).

5. "About Ernst & Young," www.ey.com/global/content.nsf/International/About_EY (October 10, 2006).

6. *2005 Annual Report,* www.visa.com (October 8, 2006).

7. "Call It Worldpool," *BusinessWeek,* November 29, 1994, pp. 98–99.

8. Peter Marsh, "The World's Wash Day," *Financial Times,* April 29, 2002, p. 6; http://duet.whirlpool.com (May 31, 2004); and "Whirlpool Corporation Announces Changes at Several Manufacturing Facilities in North America," October 3, 2006, www.whirlpoolcorp.com (October 8, 2006).

9. "A Global Comeback," *Advertising Age,* August 20, 1987, p. 146.

10. "Belgium's Strong Drinks," *International Management,* June 1992, p. 65.

11. http://currents.net/newstoday/00/03/07/news4.html (December 1, 2000); and http://globalarchive.ft.com/globalarchive/article.html?id_001205001403 (December 5, 2000).

12. Om Malik, "The New Land of Opportunity," *Business 2.0,* July 2004, p. 78.

13. C. K. Prahalad, *The Fortune at the Bottom of the Pyramid: Eradicating Poverty through Profits* (Upper Saddle River, NJ: Wharton School Publishing, 2005).

14. GM Worldwide site, www.gm.com/company/corp_info/global_operations/asia_pacific/chin.html (October 10, 2006).

15. Warren J. Keegan, "Multinational Product Planning Strategic Alternatives," *Journal of Marketing,* January 1969, pp. 56–62, combines these strategies to formulate five product and promotional strategies.

16. Geoffrey Fowler, "Intel's Game: Play It Local but Make It Global," *The Wall Street Journal,* September 30, 2005.

17. Lars Perner, University of Southern California, www.ConsumerPsychologist.com (October 14, 2006).

18. "Shimmering Symbols of the Modern Age," *Financial Times,* October 17, 1997, p. 12.

19. "About Axfood: Strategic Matters," www.axfood.se/showdoc.asp?docId=3&channelId=103&folderid=22&objectname=Strategi&selectedchannelId=103&priority=2&startfolderid=22&setlanguageid=4 (August 2, 2004).

20. "KFC and McDonald's: A Model of Blended Culture," *China Daily,* June 1, 2004, www.chinadaily.com.cn/english/doc/2004-06/01/content_335488.htm (October 10, 2006); and Yum Brands, *Annual Report, 2006,* www.yum.com (October 10, 2006).

21. Douglas McCray, "Japan's Gross National Cool," *Foreign Policy,* May–June 2002, pp. 44–54.

22. "PepsiCo's New Campaign to Knock Rival Coca-Cola," *Financial Times,* January 19, 1995, p. 12.

23. "Mexico Unleashes Watchdog to Avoid Legal Ad Disputes," *Advertising Age,* September 18, 1995, p. 16.

24. Morris Kalliny, Grace Dagher, and Michael S. Minor, "The Impact of Cultural Differences and Religion on Television Advertising: A Content Analysis of the U.S. and the Arab World," presented at the American Marketing Association annual conference, August 2004.

25. "Brands That Stop at the Border," *Financial Times,* October 6, 2006, p. 10.

26. "Ad Agencies Take On the World," *International Management,* April 1994, pp. 50–52.

27. "World Brands," *Advertising Age,* February 2, 1992, p. 33.

28. Eric Pfanner, "On Advertising: A Race to Connect in India," *International Herald Tribune,* November 27, 2005, www.iht.com/articles/2005/11/27/business/ad28.php (October 12, 2006).

29. Advertising Age International, http://www.producto.com.ve/191/notas/ multinacionales.html (August 2, 2004).

30. Stephen X. Doyle and George Thomas Roth, "Selling and Sales Management in Action: The Use of Insight and Coaching to Improve Relationship Selling," *Journal of Personal Selling & Sales Management,* Winter 1992, p. 62.

31. Melissa Campanelli, "Avon's Calling in China," *DM News,* March 10, 2006. www.dmnews.com/cms/dm-news/international/36010.html (October 12, 2006).

32. "Our Social Lives and Personal Image the First to Suffer When the Going Gets Tough," ACNielsen, April 25, 2006, www2.acnielsen.com/news/20060425.shtml (October 13, 2006).

33. "Ford Foundation International Fellowships Program," www.fordfound.org (October 12, 2004).

34. "Agencies Responsible for Censorship in China," U.S. Congressional Executive Commission on China, www.cecc.gov/pages/virtualAcad/exp/expcensors.php (October 13, 2006).

35. "McDonald's Wins Its Libel Case against Two Activists in the UK," *The Wall Street Journal,* June 20, 1997, p. B2; and www. mcspotlight.org/case/index.html (May 31, 2004).

36. Lars Perner, "International Marketing," www.consumerpsychologist.com/international-_continued.htm (October 14, 2006). These introductory observations draw closely on his work.

37. "Coke Ends Year on the Better Side of Earnings," *Financial Times,* December 31, 2005, www.ft.com (October 14, 2006).

38. Alexandra Nusbaum and Naoko Nakamae, "Store Wars in Cyberspace," *Financial Times,* February 8, 2000, p. 18; www.stonystyle.com (October 14, 2006).

39. The idea for this matrix, a checklist to help those working on the standardization of an element of the marketing mix to remember the impact of the uncontrollable forces, was developed by one of the authors who wishes, when he was an international marketing manager, that he had such a tool.

CHAPTER 19

1. Donald J. Bowersox, David J. Closs, and M. Bixby Cooper, *Supply Chain Logistics Management,* 2nd ed. (Burr Ridge, IL: McGraw-Hill Irwin, 2007), pp. 2–18.

2. Robert D'Avanzo, "The Reward of Supply-Chain Excellence," *Optimize,* December 2003, p. 68.

3. David Demers and Priya Sathyanarayanan, "Charting the Supply Chain DNA," *Supply Chain Management Review,* November–December 2003, pp. 48–58.

4. Joan Magretta, "The Power of Virtual Integration: An Interview with Dell Computer's Michael Dell," *Harvard Business Review,* March–April 1998, pp. 73–84.

5. Joan Magretta, "Fast, Global, and Entrepreneurial: Supply Chain Management, Hong Kong Style—An Interview with Victor Fung," *Harvard Business Review,* September–October 1998, pp. 3–14.

6. McDonald's Corporation, *McDonald's Worldwide Corporate Responsibility Report 2004,* www.mcdonalds.com/corp/values/socialrespons/sr_report.html (July 17, 2006), p. 12. Used with permission of McDonald's Corporation.

7. Geraldo Samor, "Ford Discovers Future Ideas in Brazilian Unit," *Pittsburgh Post-Gazette,* www.post-gazette.com/pg/06191/704782-185.stm (July 17, 2006); and Raymond Colitt, "Brazil Engineers Turnaround for Ford," *Financial Times,* September 28, 2004, p. 20.

8. Nokia, "Design for Environment," www.nokia.com/NOKIA_COM_1/About_Nokia/Environment/Publications/enviroinbrief.pdf (July 16, 2006).

9. William J. Zeile, "U.S. Affiliates of Foreign Companies: Operations in 2000," *Survey of Current Business,* August 2002, p. 161.

10. L. J. Krajewski and L. P. Ritzman, *Operations Management,* 5th ed. (Boston: Addison-Wesley, 1999), p. 456; J. Heizer and B. Render, *Principles of Operations Management,* 4th ed. (Upper Saddle River, NJ: Prentice Hall, 2001), p. 436, table 11.2; and Bowersox, Closs, and Bixby Cooper, *Supply Chain Logistics Management,* p. 81.

11. "The Founding Investors on Exostar," http://exostar.com/company/investors.asp (July 17, 2006); and "The Exostar Vision: Creating a Global Supply Network for the Aerospace and Defense Industry," http://exostar.com/company/overview/ (July 17, 2006).

12. Sam Jaffe, "Oracle: A B2B Rebirth That Few Foretold," *BusinessWeek,* April 6, 2000, www.businessweek.com (November 24, 2000).

13. Sam Fortescue, "Companies Warm to Doing Deals on e-Marketplaces," *Supply Management,* June 10, 2004, p. 10.

14. David Hannon, "Owens Corning Plans to Go 80% Paperless by End-2004," *Purchasing,* January 15, 2004, pp. 16–17.

15. Ibid.

16. Richard B. Chase, F. Robert Jacobs, and Nicholas J. Aquilano, *Operations Management for Competitive Advantage,* 11th ed. (Burr Ridge, IL: McGraw-Hill Irwin, 2006), chap. 10.

17. George Stalk, Jr., quoted in Paul B. Brown, "What's Offline," *New York Times,* June 10, 2006, p. B5.

18. Ronald C. Ritter and Robert A. Sternfels, "When Offshore Manufacturing Doesn't Make Sense," *The McKinsey Quarterly,* no. 4, 2004, www.mckinseyquarterly.com/article_print.aspx?L2=1&L3=106&ar=1510 (April 13, 2006).

19. J. M. Juran, "A History of Managing for Quality in the United States," *Quality Digest,* December 1995, pp. 34–45; and Lloyd Dobyns

and Clare Crawford-Mason, *Quality or Else* (Boston: Houghton Mifflin, 1991), p. 18.

20. Chase, Jacobs, and Aquilano, *Operations Management for Competitive Advantage,* pp. 320–21.

21. "Innovation," *BusinessWeek,* Special Issue, June 1989, p. 107.

22. Peter Kolesar, "Juran's Message to Japanese Executives in 1954: Some Lessons for Us in 2004," July 2004, www2.gsb.columbia.edu/divisions/dro/working_papers/2004/DRO2004-06.pdf (July 16, 2006).

23. "Motivation Systems for Small-Group Quality Control Activities," *Japan Economic Journal,* June 28, 1988, pp. 33–35.

24. Chase, Jacobs, and Aquilano, *Operations Management for Competitive Advantage,* chap. 12.

25. "Toyota to Recalibrate 'Just-in-Time,'" *International Herald Tribune,* February 8–9, 1997, p. 9; and "Brakes on a Toyota," *Financial Times,* February 7, 1997, p. 8.

26. Chase, Jacobs, and Aquilano, *Operations Management for Competitive Advantage,* chap. 12.

27. "Bottlenecks," http://members.aol.com/williamfla/bottle.htm (September 26, 2004); and Chase, Jacobs, and Aquilano, *Operations Management for Competitive Advantage,* chap. 18.

28. Bain and Company, "Mass Customization," www.bain.com/management_tools/tools_mass_customization.asp?groupCode=2 (July 17, 2006).

29. Joseph M. Juran and A. Blanton Godfrey, *Juran's Quality Handbook,* 5th ed. (New York: McGraw-Hill, 1999).

30. Ronald D. Snee, "Dealing with the Achilles' Heel of Six Sigma Initiatives," *Quality Progress* 34, no. 3 (March 2001), pp. 66–72.

31. James M. Lucas, "The Essential Six Sigma," *Quality Progress* 35, no. 1 (January 2002), pp. 27–31.

32. "Six Sigma Gets Its Day," *Quality* 41, no. 1 (January 2002), p. 48.

33. Dennis Sester, "Motorola: A Tradition of Quality," *Quality* 40, no. 10 (October 2001), pp. 30–34; and "Experience," www.motorola.com/content/0,,2403-5008,00.html (August 5, 2004).

34. George Eckes, "Making Six Sigma Last (and Work)," *Ivey Business Journal* 66, no. 3 (January–February 2002), pp. 77–81.

35. Chase, Jacobs, and Aquilano, *Operations Management for Competitive Advantage,* pp. 413–14.

36. Heizer and Render, *Principles of Operations Management,* p. 173.

37. Intel, "Copy Exactly, Factory Strategy," www.intel.com/pressroom/kits/manufacturing/copy_exactly_bkgrnd.htm (July 17, 2006).

38. Conversation with SKF executive.

39. D. J. Teece, "Technology Transfer by Multinational Firms," reprinted in M. Casson (ed.), *The International Library of Critical Writings in Economics I* (London, England: Edward Elgar, 1990), pp. 185–204.

40. A highly automated machine may make only one or two sizes or types of a product, whereas a general-purpose machine may be capable of producing not only all sizes of a product but other products as well. Its output, however, may be as little as 1 percent of that of a specialized machine.

41. David Wessel, "China Rewrites Rules for Building Wealth," *The Wall Street Journal,* January 29, 2004, p. A2.

42. Michiyo Nakamoto, "Sony Moves Camcorder Output," *Financial Times,* July 24, 2002, p. 19.

43. Dell, "Locations," www1.euro.dell.com/content/topics/topic.aspx/global/hybrid/careers/content/ebe52809-2b75-4be2-816a-489d9a58d7ef?c=ie&l=en&s=corp (July 18, 2006); and John Murray Brown, "How Dell Keeps Going in Europe," *Financial Times,* June 1, 2004, p. 6.

CHAPTER 20

1. Vijay Govindarajan and Anil Gupta, *The Quest for Global Dominance: Transforming Global Presence into Global Competitive Advantage* (San Francisco: Jossey-Bass, 2001), p. 106.

2. Ibid., p. 111.

3. David A. Heenan and Howard V. Perlmutter, *Multinational Organization Development* (Boston: Addison-Wesley, 1979).

4. Consistency between mind-set and IHRM practices was reported in Linda K. Stroh and Paula M. Caligiuri, "Strategic Human Resources: A New Source for Competitive Advantage in the Global Arena," *International Journal of Human Resource Management* 9, no. 1 (1998), pp. 1–17.

5. David Pilling and Francesco Guerrera, "We Are a Mixture: Western Style in Management but with an Eastern Touch," *Financial Times,* September 26, 2003, p. 13.

6. Geoff Dyer, "A Tale of Two Corporate Cultures," *Financial Times,* May 23, 2006, p. 8.

7. Pui-Wing Tam, "Cultural Training Smooths Outsourcing Issues," *The Wall Street Journal,* Midwestern Edition, May 25, 2004, p. A11. Copyright 2004 by Dow Jones & Co. Inc. Reproduced with permission of Dow Jones & Co. Inc. via Copyright Clearance Center.

8. Richard Waters and Tom Foremski, "Intel Insider Looks to Asia," *Financial Times,* September 22, 2003, p. 8.

9. Ben Dolven, "China Recruits Foreign Talent," *The Wall Street Journal,* Midwestern Edition, April 15, 2004, p. A13. Copyright 2004 by Dow Jones & Co. Inc. Reproduced with permission of Dow Jones & Co. Inc. via Copyright Clearance Center.

10. GMAC Global Relocation Services, *Global Relocation Trends 2003/2004 Survey Report,* www.gmacglobalrelocation.com/2003survey (July 24, 2006); and Mary G. Tye and Peter Y. Chen, "Selection of Expatriates: Decision-Making Models Used by HR Professionals," *Human Resource Planning* 28, no. 4 (2005), pp. 15–20.

11. "Expatriate Workforce Demographics," *HR Magazine* 51, no. 5 (May 2006), p. 16.

12. John C. Beck, "Globalization: Don't Go There . . . ," www.accenture.com/Global/Research_and_Insights/ (July 24, 2006).

13. Juan I. Sanchez, Paul E. Spector, and Cary L. Cooper, "Adapting to a Boundaryless World: A Developmental Expatriate Model," *Academy of Management Executive* 14, no. 2 (May 2000), pp. 96–106.

14. Deirdre McCaughey and Nealia S. Bruning, "Enhancing Opportunities for Expatriate Job Satisfaction: HR Strategies for Foreign Assignment Success," *Human Resource Planning* 28, no. 4 (2005), pp. 21–29.

15. Margaret A. Shaffer, David A. Harrison, and K. Matthew Gilley, "Dimensions, Determinants, and Differences in the Expatriate Adjustment Process," *Journal of International Business Studies* 30, no. 3 (1999), pp. 557–81.

16. Margaret A. Shaffer and David A. Harrison, "Forgotten Partners of International Assignments: Development and Test of a Model of Spouse Adjustment," *Journal of Applied Psychology* 86, no. 2 (2001), pp. 238–54.

17. Riki Takeuchi, Seokhwa Yun, and Paul E Tesluk, "An Examination of Crossover and Spillover Effects of Spousal and Expatriate Cross-Cultural Adjustment on Expatriate Outcomes," Journal of Applied Psychology 87, no. 4 (August 2002), p. 655.

18. GMAC Global Relocation Services, *Global Relocation Trends 2003/2004 Survey Report.*

19. Michael Harvey, "Dual-Career Expatriates: Expectations, Adjustment and Satisfaction with International Relocation," *Journal of International Business Studies* 28, no. 3 (1997), pp. 627–58; and Perri Capell, "What 'Trailing Spouses' Can Do," *The Wall Street Journal,* May 2, 2006, p. B6.

20. Expatica, "Helping Families Meet the Challenge of Moving Abroad," www.expatica.com/source/site_article.asp?subchannel_id=157&story_id=10453 (July 23, 2006); and Expatica, "How Children View Moving Abroad," www.consultus.net/pressroom/Cold_Feet_Expatriate.pdf (July 23, 2006).

21. Linda Anderson, "Language Skills Highly Ranked," *Financial Times,* April 23, 2001, p. 18.

22. Annette Haddad and Scott Doggett, "Road Home Hard after Working Overseas," *Los Angeles Times,* March 13, 2000, p. C2.

23. GMAC Global Relocation Services, *Global Relocation Trends 2003/2004 Survey Report*; and Kathryn Tyler, "Retaining Repatriates," *HR Magazine* 51, no. 3 (March 2006), pp. 97–102.

24. Tyler, "Retaining Repatriates."

25. Lublin, "To Smooth a Transfer Abroad, a New Focus on Kids," *The Wall Street Journal*, January 26, 1999, pp. B1, 14.

26. Joanne Wojcik and Sarah Veysey, "Expatriate Health Coverage Often Hard to Coordinate," *Crain Communications*, 2004, p. 10.

27. "The New Frontier of Banking," *Lafferty Publications Limited*, August 23, 2002, p. 10.

28. "Taxing Situations for Expatriates," *Crain Communications*, June 1, 2003, p. 100.

29. Prudential Financial, "About Us," www.prudential.com/HTMLEmbed/0,1469,intPageID%253D10006%2526bInPrinter-Friendly%253D0,00.html (July 22, 2006).

30. "Worldwide Cost of Living Survey 2006—City Rankings," www.mercerhr.com/pressrelease/details.jhtml/dynamic/idContent/1142150 (July 23, 2006).

31. Some writers regard paid home leave as an allowance, but our experience convinces us that it is a bonus, because ICs consistently give more frequent or longer home leaves to employees working in less desirable assignments.

32. Tom Herman, "Americans Working Overseas May See Big Jump in Tax Bill," *The Wall Street Journal*, May 20, 2006, p. B4.

33. "Vacation Time. How Much Is the Norm?" www.ilr.cornell.edu/library/research/QuestionOfTheMonth/archive/vacationtime.html (July 23, 2006).

CHAPTER 21

1. Peter Smith and James Politi, "Against the Flow: How 'Private Equity's Google' Is Profiting from Contrarianism," *Financial Times*, July 3, 2006, p. 1.

2. James Oberstar, House Transportation and Infrastructure Committee testimony before the U.S. Senate Committee on Commerce, Science and Transportation, May 9, 2006, www.house.gov/transportation_democrats/SenForeignOwnershipHearing (accessed July 15, 2006).

3. When equity securities (stock) are issued, part of the ownership is being sold. No money is being borrowed that must be repaid, as is the case when debt securities (bonds) are issued.

4. Cheol S. Eun and Bruce G. Resnick, *International Financial Management*, 4th ed. (Burr Ridge, IL: McGraw-Hill Irwin, 2007), pp. 228–34.

5. A blocked-currency situation arises either because there is no satisfactory market for the currency or because of a country's laws.

6. "Derivatives," *Financial Times Survey*, June 27, 1997, pp. i–viii.

7. "Risk: Living Dangerously," *The Economist*, January 22, 2004, www.economist.com/displaystory.cfm?story_id=2347805 (accessed July 6, 2006).

8. Charles Batchelor, "Credit Default Swaps Join Booming Derivatives Line-Up," *Financial Times*, February 11, 2004, p. 26.

9. Prema Nakra, "Countertrade and International Marketing: Take a Proactive Approach," December 27, 2005, www.i-b-t.net/anm/templates/trade_article.asp?articleid=206&zoneid=3 (accessed July 7, 2006).

10. Daniel Mitchell, "Job Creation and the Taxation of Foreign Earned Income," Executive Memorandum 911, The Heritage Foundation, 2004.

11. John Daniels, Lee Radebaugh, and Daniel Sullivan, *International Business: Environments and Operations*, 11th ed. (Upper Saddle River, NJ: Pearson, 2007), p. 639.

12. Sidney J. Gray, "Towards a Theory of Cultural Influence on the Development of Accounting Systems Internationally," *Abacus* 24, no. 1 (1998), pp. 1–15.

13. D. J. Gannon, "International Financial Reporting Standards: Of Growing Importance for U.S. Companies," Deloitte and Touche, 2003, www.iasplus.com/dttpubs/usifrs (accessed July 4, 2006).

14. "Use of IFRSs for Reporting by Domestic Companies," Deloitte, March 2006, www.iasplus.com/country/useias.htm#*? (accessed July 2, 2006).

15. "IFRS and US GAAP: A Pocket Comparison," Deloitte, 2005, www.deloitte.com/dtt/cda/doc/content/dtt_audit_2005ifrsusgaap_01_05_06.pdf (accessed July 2, 2006).

16. John Elkington, *Cannibals with Forks: The Triple Bottom Line of 21st Century Business*, (Gabriola Island, BC, Canada: New Society Publishers, 1997).

17. Wayne Norman and Chris MacDonald, "Getting to the Bottom of 'Triple Bottom Line,'" *Business Ethics Quarterly*, April 2004, www.businessethics.ca (accessed July 4, 2006).

18. "Derivatives," *Financial Times Survey*, June 27, 1997, pp. I–VIII.

Glossary

A

absolute advantage Theory that a nation has absolute advantage when it can produce a larger amount of a good or service for the same amount of inputs as can another country or when it can produce the same amount of a good or service using fewer inputs than could another country

ad valorem duty An import duty levied as a percentage of the invoice value of imported goods

advertising Paid, nonpersonal presentation of ideas, goods, or services by an identified sponsor

aesthetics A culture's sense of beauty and good taste

affiliates A term sometimes used interchangeably with subsidiaries, but more forms exist than just stock ownership

air waybill A bill of lading issued by an air carrier

allowances Employee compensation payments added to base salaries because of higher expenses encountered when living abroad

American depository receipts (ADRs) Foreign shares held by a custodian, usually a U.S. bank, in the issuer's home market and traded in dollars on the U.S. exchange

Andean Community (CAN) South American five-nation trading bloc

antitrust laws Laws to prevent price fixing, market sharing, and business monopolies

appropriate technology The technology (advanced, intermediate, or primitive) that most closely fits the society using it

arbitrage The process of buying and selling instantaneously to make profit with no risk

arbitration A process, agreed to by parties to a dispute in lieu of going to court, by which a neutral person or body makes a binding decision

Asian religions Primary ones: Hinduism, Buddhism, Jainism, and Sikhism (India); Confucianism and Taoism (China); and Shintoism (Japan)

ask price Sales price

Association of Southeast Asian Nations (ASEAN) Ten-member body formed to promote peace and cooperation in the Southeast Asian region

associations Social units based on age, gender, or common interest, not on kinship

Automated Commercial System (ACS) Electronic tracking system used by U.S. Customs to track, control, and process all commercial goods imported into the United States

automated export system (AES) U.S. Customs electronic filing system

B

backward vertical integration Arrangement in which facilities are established to manufacture inputs used in the production of a firm's final products

balance of payments (BOP) Record of a country's transactions with the rest of the world

banker's acceptance A time draft with maturity of less than 270 days that has been accepted by the bank on which the draft was drawn, thus becoming the accepting bank's obligation; may be bought and sold at a discount in the financial markets like other commercial paper

Bank for International Settlements Institution for central bankers; operates as their bank

bank swap Swap made between banks to acquire temporary foreign currencies

barter A direct exchange of goods or services for goods or services without the use of money

benchmarking A technique for measuring a firm's performance against the performance of others that may be in the same or a completely different industry

bid price Price offered to buy

biomass A category of fuels whose energy source is photosynthesis, through which plants transform the sun's energy into chemical energy; sources include corn, sugarcane, wheat

blocked funds Funds whose conversion from a host currency or repatriation is not allowed by a host government

bonded warehouse An area authorized by customs authorities for storage of goods on which payment of import duties is deferred until the goods are removed

bonuses Expatriate employee compensation payments in addition to base salaries and allowances because of hardship, inconvenience, or danger

boomerang effect Situation in which technology sold to companies in another nation is used to produce goods to compete with those of the seller of the technology.

bottleneck Operation in a manufacturing system whose output sets the limit for the entire system's output

bottom-up planning Planning process that begins at the lowest level in the organization and continues upward

brain drain The loss by a country of its most intelligent and best-educated people.

branch Legal extension of the parent company

Bretton Woods The New Hampshire town where treasury and central bank representatives met near the end of World War II; they established the IMF, the World Bank, and the gold exchange standard

bribes Gifts or payments to induce the receiver to do something illegal for the giver

C

Canadian Shield A massive area of bedrock covering one-half of Canada's landmass

capital account Record of the net changes in a nation's international financial assets and liabilities

capitalism An economic system in which the means of production and distribution are for the most part privately owned and operated for private profit

caste The group to which people belong in a system under which people's place or level in a multilevel society is established at birth as being the same level as that of their parents

caste system An aspect of Hinduism by which the entire society is divided into four groups (plus the outcasts) and each is assigned a certain class of work

CE (Conformite Europeene) mark EU mark that indicates that the merchandise conforms to European health, safety and environmental requirements

Central American Free Trade Agreement (CAFTA) FTA among the United States and several Central American nations

central reserve asset Asset, usually currency, held by a government's central bank

child labor The labor of children below 16 years of age who are forced to work in production and usually are given little or no formal education

clearing account arrangement A process to settle a trading account within a specified time

climate Meteorological conditions, including temperature, precipitation, and wind, that prevail in a region

cluster analysis Statistical technique that divides objects into groups so that the objects within each group are similar

collective bargaining The process in which a union represents the interests of a bargaining unit (which sometimes includes both union members and nonmembers) in negotiations with management

Collective Security Treaty Organization (CSTO) Security alliance of six members of the Commonwealth of Independent States (former Union of Soviet Socialist Republics)

Common Market Customs union that includes mobility of services, people, and capital within the union

communism Marx's theory of a classless society, developed by his successors into control of society by the Communist Party and the attempted worldwide spread of communism

comparative advantage Theory that a nation having absolute disadvantages in the production of two goods with respect to another nation has a comparative or relative advantage in the production of the good in which its absolute disadvantage is less

compensation Countertrade in which the developing country makes payment in products produced by use of developed country equipment.

compensation packages For expatriate employees, packages that can incorporate many types of payments or reimbursements and must take into consideration exchange rates and inflation

competition policy The European Union equivalent of antitrust laws

competitive advantage The ability of a company to have higher rates of profits than its competitors

competitive strategies Action plans to enable organizations to reach their objectives

competitor analysis Process in which principal competitors are identified and their objectives, strengths, weaknesses, and product lines are assessed

competitor intelligence system (CIS) Procedure for gathering, analyzing, and disseminating information about a firm's competitors

complete economic integration Integration on both economic and political levels

compound duty A combination of specific and ad valorem duties

confirmed L/C A confirmation made by a correspondent bank in the seller's country by which it agrees to honor the issuing bank's letter of credit

confiscation Government seizure of the property within its borders owned by foreigners without payment to them

Confucian work ethic Drive toward hard work and thrift; similar to Protestant work ethic

conservative A person, group, or party that wishes to minimize government activities and maximize private ownership and business

consolidation The process of translating subsidiary results and aggregating them into one financial report

contingency plans Plans for the best- or worst-case scenarios or for critical events that could have a severe impact on the firm

contract manufacturing An arrangement in which one firm contracts with another to produce products to its specifications but assumes responsibility for marketing

controllable forces Internal forces that management administers to adapt to changes in the uncontrollable forces

cooperative exporters Established international manufacturers that export other manufacturers' goods as well as their own

Council of the European Union Group that is the EU's primary policy-setting institution

counterpurchase Countertrade in which the goods supplied do not rely on the goods imported

countertrade The trade of goods or services for other goods or services

countervailing duties Additional import taxes levied on imports that have benefited from export subsidies

country risk assessment (CRA) An evaluation, conducted by a bank or business having an asset in or payable from a foreign country or considering a loan or an investment there, that assesses the country's economic situation and policies and its politics to determine how much risk exists of losing the asset or not being paid

country screening Using countries as the basis for market selection

cross investment Foreign direct investment by oligopolistic firms in each other's home countries as a defense measure

cross rates Currency exchange rates for trading directly between non-US$ currencies

culture Sum total of beliefs, rules, techniques, institutions, and artifacts that characterize human populations

currency devaluation The lowering of a currency's price in terms of other currencies

currency option hedge An option to buy or sell a specific amount of foreign currency at a specific time in order to protect against foreign currency risk

currency swap An exchange of debt service of a loan or bond in one currency for the debt service of a loan or bond in another currency

current account Record of a country's exports and imports in goods and services

current rate method An approach in foreign currency translation in which current assets and liabilities are valued at current spot rates and noncurrent assets and liabilities are translated at their historic exchange rates

customhouse brokers Independent businesses that handle import shipments for compensation

customs drawbacks Rebates on customs duties

Customs Union Collaboration that adds common external tariffs to an FTA

D

de-jobbing Replacing fixed jobs with tasks performed by evolving teams

demonstration effect Result of having seen others with desirable goods

derivative A contract whose value is tied to the performance of a financial instrument or commodity

developed A classification for all industrialized nations, which are the most technically developed

developing A classification for the world's lower-income nations, which are less technically developed

direct exporting The exporting of goods and services by the firm that produces them

direct investment The purchase of sufficient stock in a firm to obtain significant management control

direct investments Investments located in one country that are effectively controlled by residents of another country

discretionary income The amount of income left after paying taxes and making essential purchases

distributors Independent importers that buy for their own account for resale

Doha Development Agenda WTO extended conference on trade; also called *Doha Round*

domestic environment All the uncontrollable forces originating in the home country that surround and influence the firm's life and development

dumping Selling a product abroad for less than the cost of production, the price in the home market, or the price to third countries

dynamic capability Theory that for a firm to successfully invest overseas, it must have not only ownership of unique knowledge or resources but the ability to dynamically create and exploit these capabilities over time

E

eclectic theory of international production Theory that for a firm to invest overseas, it must have three kinds of advantages: ownership-specific, internalization, and location-specific

Economic and Social Council (ECOSOC) UN body concerned with economic and social issues such as trade, development, education, and human rights

economic exposure The potential for the value of future cash flows to be affected by unanticipated exchange rate movements

efficient market approach Assumption that current market prices fully reflect all available relevant information

environment All the forces surrounding and influencing the life and development of the firm

environmental scanning A procedure in which a firm scans the world for changes in the environmental forces that might affect it

environmental sustainability Economic state in which the demands placed upon the environment by people and commerce can be met without reducing the capacity of the environment to provide for future generations

estimation by analogy Process of using a market factor that is successful in one market to estimate demand in a similar market

ethnocentric As used here, related to hiring and promoting employees on the basis of the parent company's home country frame of reference

ethnocentricity Belief in the superiority of one's own ethnic group (see the *self-reference criterion* in Chapter 1)

Euro (€) Currency of the European Monetary Union

European Central Bank (ECB) Institution that sets and implements EU monetary policy

European Commission Institution that runs the EU's day-to-day operations

European Court of Justice (ECJ) Court that rules on issues related to EU policies

European Free Trade Agreement (EFTA) Four-nation non-EU FTA in Europe

European Monetary Union (EMU) Group that established use of euro (€) in the 12-country euro zone

European Parliament EU legislative body whose members are popularly elected from member-nations

European Union (EU) A body of 25 European countries dedicated to economic and political integration

exchange rate The price of one currency stated in terms of another currency

Ex-Im Bank Principal government agency that aids American exporters by means of loans, guarantees, and insurance programs

expatriate A person living outside his or her country of citizenship

export bill of lading (B/L) Contract of carriage between shipper and carrier: straight bill of lading is nonnegotiable; endorsed "to order" bill gives the holder claim on merchandise

export draft An unconditional order drawn by the seller that instructs the buyer to pay the draft's amount on presentation (sight draft) or at an agreed future date (time draft) and that must be paid before the buyer receives shipping documents

exporting The transportation of any domestic good or service to a destination outside a country or region; the opposite of importing, which is the transportation of any good or service into a country or region, from a foreign origination point

export processing zone A government-designated zone in which workers are permitted to import parts and materials without paying import duties, as long as these imported items are then exported once they have been processed or assembled

export trading company (ETC) A firm established principally to export domestic goods and services and to help unrelated companies export their products

expropriation Government seizure of the property within its borders owned by foreigners, followed by prompt, adequate, and effective compensation paid to the former owners

extended family Family that includes blood relatives and relatives by marriage

extortion Demand for payment to keep the receiver from causing harm to the payer

extraterritorial application of laws A country's attempt to apply its laws to foreigners or nonresidents and to acts and activities that take place outside its borders

Ex-Works INCOTERM equivalent of FOB

F

factor conditions Attributes that a country inherits, such as climate and natural resources, and those a country can mold, such as the labor force and infrastructure

factor endowment Heckscher-Ohlin theory that countries export products requiring large amounts of their abundant production factors and import products requiring large amounts of their scarce production factors

factoring Discounting without recourse an account receivable

fiscal policies Policies that address the collecting and spending of money by the government

Fisher effect The relationship between real and nominal interest rates: The real interest rate will be the nominal interest rate minus the expected rate of inflation

fixed currency exchange rates Rates that governments agree on and undertake to maintain

floating currency exchange rates Rates that are allowed to float against other currencies and are determined by market forces

FOB (free on board) Pricing policy in which risks pass from seller to buyer at the factory door; U.S. equivalent of Ex-Works

Foreign Corrupt Practices Act (FCPA) U.S. law against making payments to foreign government officials for special treatment

foreign direct investment Direct investments in equipment, structures, and organizations in a foreign country at a level that is sufficient to obtain significant management control; does not include mere foreign investment in stock markets

foreign environment All the uncontrollable forces originating outside the home country that surround and influence the firm

foreign national pricing Local pricing in another country

foreign sourcing The overseas procurement of raw materials, components, and products

foreign tax credits Allowances by which U.S. taxpayers who reside and pay income taxes in another country can credit those taxes against U.S. income tax

foreign trade zone (FTZ) Duty-free area designed to facilitate trade by reducing the effect of customs restrictions

forfaiting Purchasing without recourse an account receivable whose credit terms are longer than the 90 to 180 days usual in factoring; unlike factoring, political and transfer risks are borne by the forfaiter

forward currency market Trading market for currency contracts deliverable 30, 60, 90, or 180 days in the future

forward market hedge Foreign currency contract sold or bought forward in order to protect against foreign currency movement

forward rate The exchange rate between two currencies for delivery in the future, usually 30, 60, 90, or 180 days

franchising A form of licensing in which one firm contracts with another to operate a certain type of business under an established name according to specific rules

free trade area (FTA) Area in which tariffs among members have been eliminated, but members keep their external tariffs

free trade zone An area designated by the government as outside its customs territory

functional currency The primary currency of a business

fundamental approach Exchange rate prediction based on econometric models that attempt to capture the variables and their correct relationships

G

General Agreement on Tariffs and Trade (GATT) International agreement that functioned to encourage trade liberalization from 1947 to 1995

General Assembly Deliberative body of the UN made up of all member-nations, each with one vote regardless of size, wealth, or power

general export license Any export license covering export commodities for which a validated license is not required; no formal application is required

geocentric As used here, related to hiring and promoting employees on the basis of ability and experience without considering race or citizenship

global company (GC) An organization that attempts to standardize and integrate operations worldwide in all functional areas

global mind-set A mind-set that combines an openness to and an awareness of diversity across markets and cultures with a propensity and ability to synthesize across this diversity

gold standard The use of gold at an established number of units per currency

goods or merchandise account Record of tangible exports and imports

gross national income (GNI) The total value of all income generated by a nation's residents from international and domestic activity

Group of Eight (G8) Group of government leaders from industrialized nations that meets regularly to discuss issues of concern

guest workers People who go to a foreign country legally to perform certain types of jobs

H

Harmonized Tariff Schedule of the United States (HTSUSA) American version of the Harmonized System used worldwide to classify imported products

hedging A process to reduce or eliminate financial risk

hierarchy A body of persons organized or classified according to rank or authority

home country national Same as parent country national

horizontal corporation A form of organization characterized by lateral decision processes, horizontal networks, and a strong corporatewide business philosophy

host country national (HCN) Employee who is a citizen of the nation in which the subsidiary is operating, which is different from the parent company's home nation

human-needs approach View that defines economic development as a reduction of poverty and unemployment as well as an increase in income

hybrid organization Structure organized by more than one dimension at the top level

I

import substitution The local production of goods to replace imports

in-bond plants (maquiladoras) Production facilities in Mexico that temporarily import raw materials, components, or parts duty-free to be manufactured, processed, or assembled with less expensive local labor, after which the finished or semifinished product is exported

income distribution A measure of how a nation's income is apportioned among its people, commonly reported as the percentage of income received by population quintiles

income tax Direct tax levied on earnings

INCOTERMS Universal trade terminology developed by the International Chamber of Commerce

indirect exporting The exporting of goods and services through various types of home-based exporters

industrial cooperation An exporter's commitment to a longer-term relationship than that in a simple export sale, in which some of the production occurs in the receiving country

industrial espionage Act of spying on a competitor to learn secrets about its strategy and operations

inland waterways Waterways that provide access to interior regions

instability Characteristic of a government that cannot maintain itself in power or that makes sudden, unpredictable, or radical policy changes

intellectual property Patents, trademarks, trade names, copyrights, and trade secrets, all of which result from the exercise of someone's intellect

interest rate swap An exchange of interest rate flows in order to manage interest rate exposure

intermediate technology Production methods between capital- and labor-intensive methods

internalization theory An extension of the market imperfection theory: the concept that to obtain a higher return on its investment, a firm will transfer its superior knowledge to a foreign subsidiary rather than sell it in the open market

international company (IC) Either a global or a multidomestic company

International Court of Justice (ICJ) UN body that renders legal decisions involving disputes between national governments

international division A division in the organization that is at the same level as the domestic division and is responsible for all non-home country activities

international environment Interaction between domestic and foreign environmental forces or between sets of foreign environmental forces

international Fisher effect Concept that the interest rate differentials for any two currencies will reflect the expected change in their exchange rates

International Monetary Fund (IMF) Institution that coordinates multilateral monetary rules and their enforcement

international pricing Setting prices of goods for export for both unrelated and related firms

international product life cycle (IPLC) A theory explaining why a product that begins as a nation's export eventually becomes its import

international status Entitles the expatriate employee to all the allowances and bonuses applicable to the place of residence and employment

international strategy The way firms make choices about acquiring and using scarce resources in order to achieve their international objectives

intervention currency A currency used by a country to intervene in the foreign currency exchange markets, often to buy (strengthen) its own currency

irrevocable L/C A stipulation that a letter of credit cannot be canceled

iterative planning Repetition of the bottom-up or top-down planning process until all differences are reconciled

J

Jamaica Agreement The 1976 IMF agreement that allows flexible exchange rates among members

joint venture A cooperative effort among two or more organizations that share a common interest in a business enterprise or undertaking

just-in-time (JIT) A balanced system in which there is little or no delay time and idle in-process and finished goods inventory

K

Kyoto Protocol United Nations Framework Convention on Climate Change, which calls for nations to reduce global warming by reducing their emissions of the gasses that contribute to it

L

labor market The pool of available potential employees with the necessary skills within commuting distance from an employer

labor mobility The movement of people from country to country or area to area to get jobs

labor quality The skills, education, and attitudes of available employees

labor quantity The number of available employees with the skills required to meet an employer's business needs

labor unions Organizations of workers

language trap A situation in which a person doing international business can speak only his or her home language

law of one price Concept that in an efficient market, like products will have like prices

leading and lagging Timing payments early (lead) or late (lag), depending on anticipated currency movements, so that they have the most favorable impact for company

left wing A more extreme liberal position

letter of credit (L/C) Document issued by the buyer's bank in which the bank promises to pay the seller a specified amount under specified conditions

liberal In the contemporary United States, a person, group, or party that urges greater government involvement in business and other aspects of human activities

licensing A contractual arrangement in which one firm grants access to its patents, trade secrets, or technology to another for a fee

lingua franca A foreign language used to communicate among a nation's diverse cultures that have diverse languages

M

management contract An arrangement by which one firm provides management in all or specific areas to another firm

manufacturers' agents Independent sales representatives of various noncompeting suppliers

manufacturing rationalization Division of production among a number of production units, thus enabling each to produce only a limited number of components for all of a firm's assembly plants

market factors Economic data that correlate highly with market demand for a product

market indicators Economic data used to measure relative market strengths of countries or geographic areas

market screening A version of environmental scanning in which the firm identifies desirable markets by using the environmental forces to eliminate the less desirable markets

mass customization The use of flexible, usually computer-aided, manufacturing systems to produce and deliver customized products and services for different customers worldwide

material culture All human-made objects; concerned with *how* people make things (technology) and *who* makes *what* and *why* (economics)

matrix organization An organizational structure composed of one or more superimposed organizational structures in an attempt to mesh product, regional, functional, and other expertise

matrix overlay An organization in which top-level divisions are required to heed input from a staff composed of experts of another organizational dimension in an attempt to avoid the double-reporting difficulty of a matrix organization but still mesh two or more dimensions

mercantilism An economic philosophy based on the belief that (1) a nation's wealth depends on accumulated treasure, usually gold, and (2) to increase wealth, government policies should promote exports and discourage imports

Mercosur (Mercosul) Economic free trade area in South America modeled on the EU

minorities A relatively smaller number of people identified by race, religion, or national origin who live among a larger majority

mission statement A broad statement that defines the organization's purpose and scope

monetary policies Government policies that control the amount of money in circulation and its growth rate

money market hedge A method to hedge foreign currency exposure by borrowing and lending in the domestic and foreign money markets

monopolistic advantage theory Theory that foreign direct investment is made by firms in oligopolistic industries possessing technical and other advantages over indigenous firms

most favored nation (MFN) clause Agreement that GATT member-nations would treat all members equally in trade matters

multidomestic company (MDC) An organization with multicountry affiliates, each of which formulates its own business strategy based on perceived market differences

multilateral netting Strategy in which subsidiaries transfer net intracompany cash flows through a centralized clearing center

N

national competitiveness A nation's relative ability to design, produce, distribute, or service products within an international trading context while earning increasing returns on its resources

national tax jurisdiction A tax system for expatriate citizens of a country whereby the country taxes them on the basis of nationality even though they live and work abroad

natural resources Anything supplied by nature on which people depend

newly industrialized economies (NIEs) The fast-growing upper-middle-income and high-income economies of South Korea, Taiwan, Hong Kong, and Singapore

newly industrializing countries (NICs) The four Asian tigers and the middle-income economies such as Brazil, Mexico, Malaysia, Chile, and Thailand

nonrevenue tax purposes Purposes such as redistributing income, discouraging consumption of products such as tobacco and alcohol, and encouraging purchase of domestic rather than imported products

nontariff barriers (NTBs) All forms of discrimination against imports other than import duties

North American Free Trade Agreement (NAFTA) Agreement creating a free trade area among Canada, Mexico, and the United States

North American Treaty Organization (NATO) Security alliance of 26 North American and European nations

official reserves account Record of the assets held by the government, gold, foreign currencies, and accounts in foreign banks; a balance of the country's foreign currency

offset Trade arrangement that requires that a portion of the inputs be supplied by the receiving country

offshore financial center Location that specializes in financing nonresidents, with low taxes and few banking regulations

offshoring Relocating some or all of a business's activities or processes to a foreign location

orderly marketing arrangements Formal agreements between exporting and importing countries that stipulate the import or export quotas each nation will have for a good

Organisation for Economic Cooperation and Development (OECD) Group of developed countries dedicated to promoting economic expansion in its member-nations

Organization of Petroleum Exporting Countries (OPEC) Cartel of 11 petroleum-exporting countries

organizational structure The way that an organization formally arranges its domestic and international units and activities, and the relationships among these various organizational components

outsourcing Hiring others to perform some of the noncore activities and decision making in a company's value chain, rather than having the company and its employees continue to perform those activities

Overseas Private Investment Corporation (OPIC) Government corporation that offers American investors in developing countries insurance against expropriation, currency inconvertibility, and damages from wars and revolutions

P

parallel loans Matched loans across currencies that are made to cover risk

parent country national (PCNs) Employee who is a citizen of the nation in which the parent company is headquartered; also called home country national

par value Stated value

passive processing The finishing or refining in Eastern European countries of semifinished goods from the West, which are then returned to the West after finishing; similar to Mexican maquiladora operations

polycentric As used here, related to hiring and promoting employees on the basis of the specific local context in which the subsidiary operates

population density A measure of the number of inhabitants per area unit (inhabitants per square kilometer or square mile)

population distribution A measure of how the inhabitants are distributed over a nation's area

portfolio investment The purchase of stocks and bonds to obtain a return on the funds invested

portfolio investments Long-term investments that do not give the investors control over the investment

preferential trading arrangement An agreement by a small group of nations to establish free trade among themselves while maintaining trade restrictions with all other nations

preventive (planned) maintenance Maintenance done according to plan, not when machines break down

private international law Laws governing transactions of individuals and companies that cross international borders

privatization The transfer of public sector assets to the private sector, the transfer of management of state activities through contracts and leases, and the contracting out of activities previously conducted by the state

product liability Standard that holds a company and its officers and directors liable and possibly subject to fines or imprisonment when their product causes death, injury, or damage

pro forma invoice Exporter's formal quotation containing a description of the merchandise, price, delivery time, method of shipping, terms of sale, and points of exit and entry

programmed-management approach A middle-ground advertising strategy between globally standardized and entirely local programs

promotion Any form of communication between a firm and its publics

promotional mix A blend of the promotional methods a firm uses to sell its products

Protestant work ethic Duty to glorify God by hard work and the practice of thrift

public international law Legal relations between governments

public relations Various methods of communicating with the firm's publics to secure a favorable impression

purchasing power parity (PPP) The number of units of a currency required to buy the same amounts of goods and services in the domestic market that one dollar would buy in the United States; the theory that predicts that currency exchange rates between two countries should equal the ratio of the price levels of their commodity baskets

Q

quality circle (quality control circle) Small work group that meets periodically to discuss ways to improve its functional areas and the quality of the product

questionable or dubious payments Bribes paid to government officials by companies seeking purchase contracts from those governments

quotas Numerical limits placed on specific classes of imports

R

random walk hypothesis Assumption that the unpredictability of factors suggests that the best predictor of tomorrow's prices is today's prices

regiocentric As used here, related to hiring and promoting employees on the basis of the specific regional context in which the subsidiary operates

Rhine waterway A system of rivers and canals that is the main transportation artery of Europe

right wing A more extreme conservative position

rural-to-urban shift The movement of a nation's population from rural areas to cities

S

sales company A business established for the purpose of marketing goods and services, not producing them

sales promotion Any of various selling aids, including displays, premiums, contests, and gifts

scenarios Multiple, plausible stories about the future

Secretariat The staff of the UN, headed by the secretary-general

Security Council Main policy-setting body of the UN, composed of 15 members including 5 permanent members

segment screening Using market segments as the basis for market selection

self-reference criterion Unconscious reference to one's own cultural values when judging behaviors of others in a new and different environment

services account Record of intangibles that are exchanged internationally

shale A fissile rock (capable of being split) composed of laminated layers of claylike, fine-grained sediment

shipper's export declaration (SED) U.S. Department of Commerce form used to control export shipments and record export statistics

short-term capital flows Changes in international assets and liabilities with an original maturity of one year or less

Six Sigma Business management process for reducing defects and eliminating variation

socialism Public, collective ownership of the basic means of production and distribution, operating for use rather than profit

sogo shosha The largest of the Japanese general trading companies

special drawing right (SDR) An international reserve asset established by the IMF; the unit of account for the IMF and other international organizations

specific duty A fixed sum levied on a physical unit of an imported good

spot and forward market swaps Use of the spot and forward markets to hedge foreign currency exposure

spot rate The exchange rate between two currencies for delivery within two business days

stability Characteristic of a government that maintains itself in power and whose fiscal, monetary, and political policies are predictable and not subject to sudden, radical changes

stakeholder theory An understanding of how business operates that takes into account all identifiable interest holders

standards Documented agreements containing technical specifications or other precise criteria that will be used consistently as guidelines, rules, or definitions of the characteristics of a product, process, or service

strategic alliances Partnerships between competitors, customers, or suppliers that may take one or more of various forms

strategic business unit (SBU) Business entity with a clearly defined market, specific competitors, the ability to carry out its business mission, and a size appropriate for control by a single manager

strict liability Standard that holds the designer/manufacturer liable for damages caused by a product without the need for a plaintiff to prove negligence in the product's design or manufacture

subsidiaries Companies controlled by other companies through ownership of enough voting stock to elect board-of-directors majorities

subsidiary Separate legal entity owned by the parent company

subsidiary detriment Situation in which a small loss for a subsidiary results in a greater gain for the total IC

subsidies Financial contributions, provided directly or indirectly by a government, which confer a benefit; include grants, preferential tax treatment, and government assumption of normal business expenses

supply chain management The process of coordinating and integrating the flow of materials, information, finances, and services within and among companies in the value chain from suppliers to the ultimate consumer

swap contract A spot sale/purchase of an asset against a future purchase/sale of an equal amount in order to hedge a financial position

switch trading The use of a third party to market products received in countertrade

synchronous manufacturing An entire manufacturing system with unbalanced operations that emphasizes total system performance

T

tariffs Taxes on imported goods for the purpose of raising their price to reduce competition for local producers or stimulate local production

tax treaties Treaties between countries that bind the governments to share information about taxpayers and cooperate in tax law enforcement; often called tax conventions

Taylor's scientific management system System based on scientific measurements that prescribes a division of work whereby planning is done by managers and plan execution is left to supervisors and workers

technical analysis An approach that analyzes data for trends and then projects these trends forward

technological dualism The side-by-side presence of technologically advanced and technologically primitive production systems

temporal method An approach in foreign currency translation in which monetary accounts are valued at the spot rate and accounts carried at historical cost are translated at their historic exchange rates

terms of sale Conditions of a sale that stipulate the point at which all costs and risks are borne by the buyer

territorial tax jurisdiction A tax system in which expatriate citizens who neither live nor work in the country— and therefore receive none of the services for which taxes pay—are exempt from the country's taxes

terrorism Unlawful acts of violence committed for a wide variety of reasons, including for ransom, to overthrow a government, to gain release of imprisoned colleagues, to exact revenge for real or imagined wrongs, and to punish nonbelievers of the terrorists' religion

third country national (TCN) Employee who is a citizen of neither the parent company nation nor the host country

top-down planning Planning process that begins at the highest level in the organization and continues downward

topography The surface features of a region

total product What the customer buys, including the physical product, brand name, accessories, after-sales service, warranty, instructions for use, company image, and package

total quality management (TQM) System in which the entire organization is managed so that it excels on all dimensions of product and services that are important to the customer

trade balance The balance on the merchandise account

trade fair A large exhibition, generally held at the same place and same time periodically, at which companies maintain booths to promote the sale of their products

trade mission A group of businesspeople and/or government officials (state or federal) that visits a market in search of business opportunities

trade-related intellectual property rights (TRIPS) the acronym TRIPS refers to the WTO agreement that protects copyrights, trademarks, trade secrets, and other intellectual property matters

trading at a discount Situation in which a currency's forward rate quotes are weaker than spot

trading at a premium Situation in which a currency's forward rate quotes are stronger than spot

trading companies Firms that develop international trade and serve as intermediaries between foreign buyers and domestic sellers and vice versa

traditional hostilities Long-standing enmities between tribes, races, religions, ideologies, or countries

traditional societies Tribal peoples before they turn to organized agriculture or industry; traditional customs may linger after the economy changes

transaction exposure Change in the value of a financial position created by foreign currency changes between the establishment and the settlement of a contract

transfer price Intracorporate price, or the price of a good or service sold by one affiliate to another, the home office to an affiliate, or vice versa

transfer price The cost of intracompany sales of goods or services

translation exposure Potential change in the value of a company's financial position due to exposure created during the consolidation process

treaties Agreements between countries, which may be bilateral (between two countries) or multilateral (involving more than two countries); also called conventions, covenants, compacts, or protocols

trend analysis Statistical technique by which successive observations of a variable at regular time intervals are analyzed to establish regular patterns that are used for establishing future values

Triffin paradox The concept that a national currency that is also a reserve currency will eventually run a deficit, which eventually inspires a lack of confidence in the reserve currency and leads to a financial crisis

triple bottom line (3BL) A results or impact report on the environmental, social, and financial impacts of the business

U

uncontrollable forces External forces over which management has no direct control, although it can exert an influence

underground economy The part of a nation's income that, because of unreporting or underreporting, is not measured by official statistics

unilateral transfer A transfer with no matched return flow, no reciprocity

United Nations (UN) International organization of 191 member-nations dedicated to the promotion of peace and global stability; has many functions related to business

unit labor costs Total direct labor costs divided by units produced

unspoken language Nonverbal communication, such as gestures and body language

Uruguay Round The last extended conference of GATT negotiations

V

validated export license A required document issued by the U.S. government authorizing the export of a strategic commodity or a shipment to an unfriendly country.

value-added tax (VAT) Indirect tax collected from the parties as they add value to the product

values statement A clear and concise description of the fundamental values, beliefs, and priorities of the organization's members.

variable levy An import duty set at the difference between world market prices and local government-supported prices

vehicle currency A currency used as a vehicle for international trade or investment

vertically integrated Descriptive term for a firm that produces inputs for its subsequent manufacturing processes

virtual corporation An organization that coordinates economic activity to deliver value to customers using resources outside the traditional boundaries of the organization

vision statement A description of the company's desired future position if it can acquire the necessary competencies and successfully implement its strategy

voluntary export restraints (VERs) Export quotas imposed by the exporting nation

W

withholding tax Indirect tax paid by the payor, usually on passive income

World Bank Institution that focuses on funding of development projects

World Trade Organization (WTO) A multinational body of 149 members that deals with rules of trade between nations

Photo Credits

Figure number	Credit	Page number
1-1	Digital Vision / Getty Images	4
1-2	Getty Images	7
1-3	PhotoDisc / Getty Images	8
1-4	© Gabe Palmer / Corbis	15
1-5	Daniel Sheehan / Getty Images	18
2-1	Royalty Free / Getty Images	30
2-2	AP / Wide World Photo	50
3-1	Digital Vision / Getty Image	62
3-2	AP Wide World Photo	70
3-3	AP Wide World Photo	86
4-1	Tim Graham / Getty Images	102
4-2	AP Wide World Photos	106
4-3	WTO / Jay Louvion (Studio Casagrande) © WTO	111
4-4	Courtesy of Lin (Jimmy) Chiang	116
4-5	© Royalty-Free / Corbis	122
4-6	European Commission Audiovisual Library	130
5-1	Robert Clare / Getty Images	138
5-2	AFP / Getty Images	141
5-3	iStockphoto	145
5-4	www.bis.org © Bank for International Settlements	146
6-1	© Randy Faris / Corbis	158
6-2	Yoshikazu Tsuno / AFP / Getty Images	162
6-3	Courtesy of Kelty McRae	165
6-5	Richard Passmore / Getty Images	172
6-7	© Charles Gupton / StockBoston	180
7-1	Royalty-Free / Corbis	190
7-2	Hans Wolf	207
7-3	© Royalty-Free / Corbis	212
7-4	Drs. Lianne Ball and Paul Doherty	214
7-5	© Reuters / Corbis	218
8-1	Frederic N. Brown / AFP / Getty Images	226
8-2	Courtesy of Tim Taddei	230
8-3	Sena Vidanagama / AFP / Getty Images	238
9-1	© Sean Gallup / Getty Images	254
9-2	Steven Weinberg/ Getty Images	257
9-3	© DPA / The Image Works	271
10-1	Courtesy International Court of Justice, Photo Van der Plas & Van den Eeden	278

Photo Credits Continued

Figure number	Credit	Page number
10-2	© Wolfgang Kaehler / Corbis	284
10-3	AP Wide World Photo	296
11-1	© Bridgeman Art Library, London / Superstock	302
11-2	Ryan McVay / Getty Images	305
11-3	Shawkat Khan / AFP / Getty Images	312
12-1	© Fujifotos / The Image Works	322
12-2	MedioImages / Getty Images	326
12-3	© Marilyn Humphries/ The Image Works	331
13-1	© Steve Chenn / Corbis	350
13-2	Tim Boyle / Getty Images	355
13-3	Courtesy of Katherine McCormick	359
14-1	eStock Photo	384
14-2	Courtesy of Michelle Teteak	389
14-3	© Royalty-Free / Corbis	398
15-1	Taxi / Getty Images	408
15-2	Getty Images	417
16-1	Getty Images	424
16-2	AP / Wide World Photo	429
16-3	Hoang Dinh Namal / AFP / Getty Images	430
16-4	Warner Bros. Pictures / Getty Images	441
17-1	The Image Works	444
17-2	AP / Wide World Photo	450
17-3	© Michael Newman / Photo Edit	466
18-1	AP Wide World	476
18-2	AFP / Douglas E. Curran / Getty Images	482
18-3	Victoria Ball	483
18-4	Kellogg Company	485
18-5	Catherine Karnow / Woodfin Camp	491
19-1	Photo courtesy of Inditex	502
19-4	Photo courtesy of Intel Corporation	524
20-1	Royalty Free / Getty Images	540
20-2	AP / Wide World Photo	547
20-3	The Image Bank / Getty Images	551
21-1	Antony Edwards / Getty Images	566
21-2	Rohanna Mertens for ACCION International	570
21-3	Pepsi-Cola Company	579

Name Index

Page numbers followed by n indicate notes.

Company Index

S

T

U

V

W

X

Z

Subject Index

Page numbers followed by n indicate notes.

B

C

D

H

I

M

N

O

P

T

U

V